The Top 6000 Companies in South East England

Companies with assets exceeding £20,000,000

John D Blackburn
Editor

dp

First Edition

Spring 2019

ISBN-13: 978-1-912736-22-5

ISBN-10: 1-912736-22-5

Printed in 8pt Nimbus Sans L

Designed by URW++ Design and Development GmbH

Dellam Publishing Limited

2 Heath Drive, Sutton, Surrey, SM2 5RP

Fax: 020 8770 7478 email: enquiries@dellam.com

SAN: 0177881 EAN/GLN: 5030670177882

Table of Contents

1 Acknowledgements iv

2 Map of regions v

3 Map of regions showing counties vi

4 Introduction vii

5 Total Assets League Table 1

- As a measure of size, total assets is preferable to turnover which is influenced by profit margins and whether companies are capital or labour intensive.

6 Age of Companies 47

- Each company is ranked by its date of incorporation. Newcomers are defined as those registered since 2017.

7 Company Profiles 79

- Full company name, date incorporated, net worth, total assets, registered office, activities, shareholders and parent company, directors (with date of birth, nationality and occupation) and number of employees (if available).

8 Standard Industrial Classification 653

- These codes are used to classify businesses by the type of economic activity in which they are engaged.

9 *finis* 697

Acknowledgements

This is a long and detailed publication containing thousands of facts and figures. It is only to be expected, despite continuous and repeated editing and checking, that errors may occur. In such cases, once we are aware of any, we publish a correction on our website.

Readers are encouraged to check regularly at www.dellam.com/books for any corrections and updates.

Although we take extreme care to ensure accuracy and being up-to-date, we cannot accept responsibility for any errors or omissions.

We appreciate your interest in our publications, and your comments and suggestions are always welcome. Please contact us at enquiries@dellam.com.

Scotland
Northern Ireland
North East (England)
North West (England)
Yorkshire and The Humber
East Midlands (England)
West Midlands (England)
Wales
East of England
See London Inset
South East (England)
South West (England)

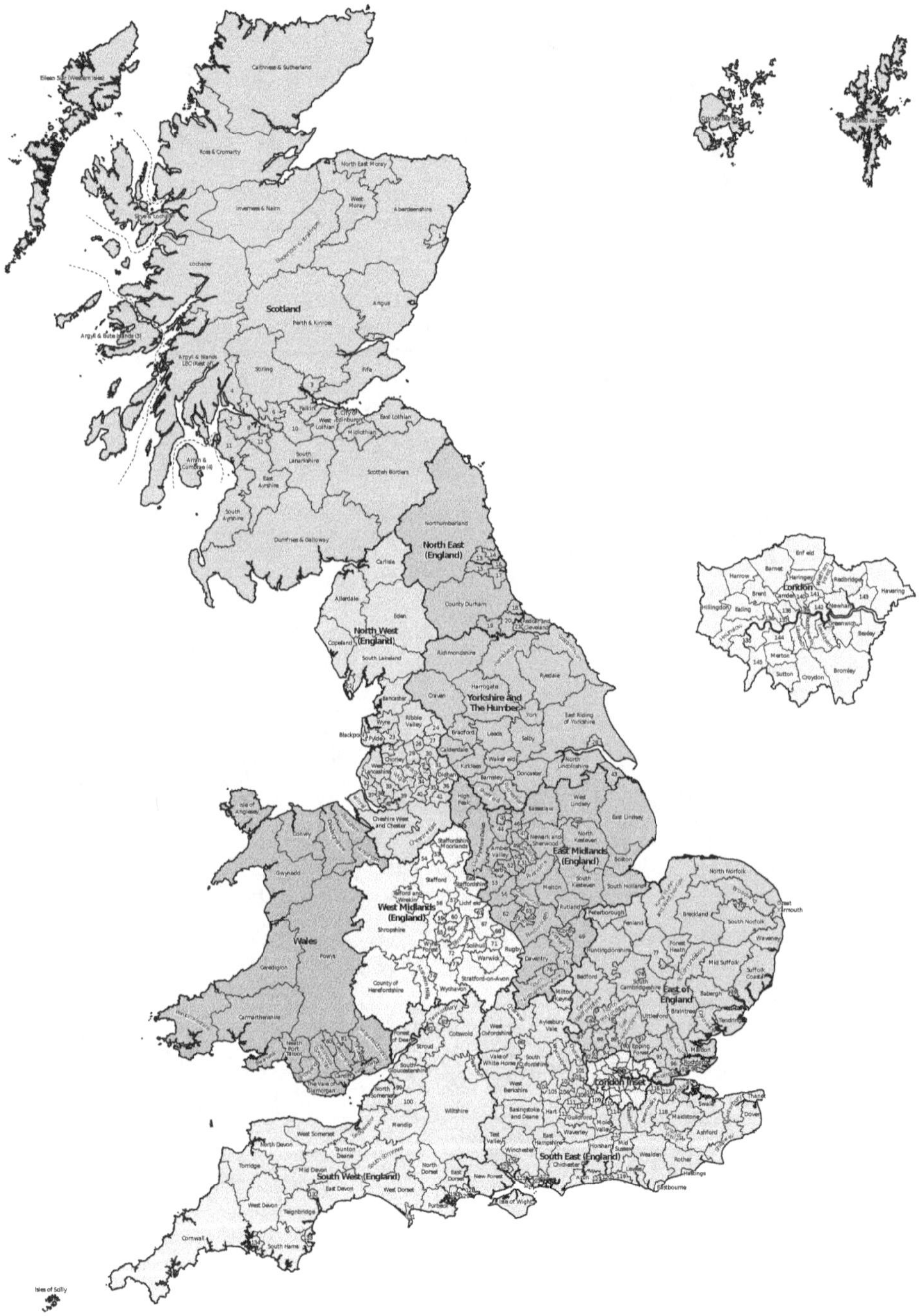
Scotland
North East (England)
North West (England)
Yorkshire and The Humber
East Midlands (England)
West Midlands (England)
Wales
East of England
London
South East (England)
South West (England)

Introduction

This study looks at all companies registered in South East England and where their total assets are more than £20,000,000.

South East England (excluding London) is the most populous region with a population of 9.1 million in 2017 (UK 66 million).

The region comprises the counties of Berkshire, Buckinghamshire, East Sussex, Hampshire, the Isle of Wight, Kent, Oxfordshire, Surrey and West Sussex. The main cities are Brighton, Canterbury, Chichester, Oxford, Portsmouth, Southampton and Winchester.

The aim of this study is to provide an overview of the key movers and shakers in South East England's corporate sector. Only key data has been isolated, particularly the company's net worth and total assets, but also its full name, date incorporated, registered office, activities, shareholders, directors (with date of birth, occupation and nationality) and number of employees.

Two indicators of size are used: net worth and total assets. These are preferable to turnover which is influenced by profit margins and whether the companies are capital or labour intensive.

A short summary of the corporate sector in South East England:

Total regional output (GVA), in 2016, was £259 billion (UK £1,748 billion) with total output (GVA) per head, in 2016, being £28,683 (UK being £26,621).

Employment level, May-July 2018, was 4,540,000 (UK 32,397,000) with an employment rate of 78.1% (UK 75.5%).

There were 431,000 manufacturing jobs in the South East and London in 2018, accounting for 4.0% of the region's total workforce, the lowest of any region.

The South East and London accounted for just under a quarter (24.8%) of all UK manufactured exports in 2017, the largest of any region.

The South East and London is the most productive region in the UK with London's productivity at 127.8% of the UK average and the South East's at 104.3%.

London and the South East have considerably more businesses than any other region. At the start of 2018: London (1.1 million) and the South East (874,000) had the most private sector businesses, accounting for 35% of the UK business population.

In 2017, here were 299,000 manufacturing jobs in the region (6% of all jobs).

In 2017, there were 51,965 new businesses (up 12%) and 48,295 businesses ceased trading (up 11%).

Standard cataloguing guidelines for company names in the profile section have been used, but there will be occurrences when the name may not be strictly alphabetical. A certain licence was adopted where it was felt that strictly alphabetical could lead to improper cataloguing. Some company names have been shortened in the league tables for aesthetic reasons.

John D Blackburn
Editor

This page is intentionally left blank

Total Assets League Table

Company	Value
DS (Holdings) 3 Limited	£700,200,189,952
EDU UK Management Services Limited	£435,426,000,896
Vodafone 2.	£258,799,370,240
Vodafone Holdings Luxembourg Limited	£177,893,588,992
BP International Limited	£160,948,404,224
Vodafone Group Public Limited Company	£145,610,997,760
Vodafone International Operations Limited	£142,090,059,776
GlaxoSmithKline Finance PLC	£135,010,271,232
Vodafone Intermediate Enterprises Limited	£127,809,896,448
Vodaphone Limited	£120,346,157,056
Vodafone Benelux Limited	£117,624,102,912
Vodafone Americas 4	£113,643,651,072
The Edward James Foundation Limited	£90,996,490,240
Houserate Limited	£89,736,880,128
Vodafone Finance UK Limited	£86,096,789,504
Vodata Limited	£82,321,711,104
Vodafone International Holdings Limited	£78,708,416,512
Vodafone European Investments	£62,744,809,472
GlaxoSmithKline Holdings Limited	£60,131,000,320
GlaxoSmithKline PLC	£56,381,001,728
Vodafone Euro Hedging Limited	£52,929,667,072
BP Holdings North America Limited	£51,804,418,048
BP America Limited	£51,778,732,032
Reckitt Benckiser Investments Limited	£49,974,116,352
Reckitt Benckiser PLC	£49,818,198,016
BP Exploration Operating Company Limited	£49,403,691,008
Hanson Quarry Products Europe Limited	£48,023,728,128
Vodafone Finance Limited	£47,205,191,680
Reckitt Benckiser Treasury Services PLC	£46,614,740,992
BP Capital Markets P.L.C.	£44,762,333,184
Vodafone Worldwide Holdings Limited	£43,352,322,048
ROC Transformation (Corporate) Limited	£39,823,577,088
Allergan Holdco UK Limited	£39,011,266,560
Hanson Holdings (1) Limited	£38,641,995,776
Hanson Overseas Holdings Limited	£37,201,846,272
Reckitt Benckiser Group PLC	£37,013,000,192
Setfirst Limited	£35,656,830,976
Vodafone 6 UK	£31,920,627,712
FIL Life Insurance Limited	£29,620,381,696
Hanson Finance (2003) Limited	£28,796,837,888
Reckitt & Colman Holdings Limited	£26,165,360,640
Old Mutual Wealth Life & Pensions Limited	£25,837,291,520
Vodafone Marketing UK	£24,650,733,568
Effem Holdings Limited	£24,567,478,272
Royal & Sun Alliance Insurance PLC	£24,476,000,256
Just Group PLC	£24,164,900,864
GlaxoSmithKline Consumer Healthcare Holdings	£20,771,000,320
Centrica PLC	£20,668,000,256
Vodafone Mobile Enterprises Limited	£18,664,331,264
ExxonMobil Holding Company Limited	£18,504,316,928
Heathrow Airport Holdings Limited	£18,395,000,832
Sky UK Limited	£18,364,999,680
HeidelbergCement UK Holding Limited	£18,321,776,640
FGP Topco Limited	£18,304,000,000
Kemble Water Finance Limited	£18,115,999,744
Thames Water Utilities Limited	£18,003,200,000
Sky Limited	£18,001,999,872
Vodafone Finance Sweden	£17,986,588,672
Hanson Limited	£17,968,152,576
Hanson Building Materials Limited	£17,815,826,432
Virgin Media Limited	£17,811,765,248
Kemble Water Holdings Limited	£17,783,500,800
Linde UK Holdings Limited	£17,694,590,976
Heathrow Airport Limited	£17,422,000,128
Bottling Holdings Europe Limited	£16,759,967,744
British Airways PLC	£16,677,999,616
Vodafone Mobile Network Limited	£16,567,668,736
BAE Systems (Holdings) Limited	£16,538,336,256
Virgin Media Finance PLC	£16,046,799,872
Coca-Cola European Partners PLC	£15,913,583,616
Vodafone 5 Limited	£15,891,663,872
Old Mutual Wealth Life Assurance Limited	£15,659,899,904

Company	Value
HeidelbergCement UK Holding II Limited	£15,646,927,872
Heathrow Finance PLC	£15,616,000,000
Sun Life Assurance Co of Canada (U.K.) Ltd	£15,375,290,368
Heathrow (SP) Limited	£15,258,000,384
Volkswagen Financial Services (UK) Limited	£14,847,398,912
Just Retirement Limited	£14,798,900,224
INEOS Holdings Limited	£14,607,802,368
Sony Global Treasury Services PLC	£14,148,797,440
Chromium Acquisitions Limited	£13,984,549,888
BP Global Investments Limited	£13,726,040,064
Centrica Holdings Limited	£13,557,688,320
Cadbury Seven LLP	£13,519,614,976
Akzo Nobel ICI Holdings	£13,498,999,808
GB Gas Holdings Limited	£13,443,493,888
Lehigh UK Limited	£13,437,815,808
MJ UK Holdings Limited	£12,750,233,600
Compass Group PLC	£12,266,000,384
Virgin Media Communications Limited	£12,160,775,168
BP Russian Investments Limited	£11,975,698,432
Heathrow Holdco Limited	£11,914,999,808
Compass Overseas Holdings No.2 Limited	£11,884,215,296
Glaxo Group Limited	£11,776,435,200
Virgin Media Investment Holdings Limited	£11,721,251,840
LHR Airports Limited	£11,187,999,744
Carnival PLC	£11,003,194,368
General Cable Limited	£10,960,166,912
BMW Financial Services (GB) Limited	£10,893,739,008
Vodafone Limited	£10,822,800,384
Virgin Media Finco Limited	£10,793,962,496
CSL Behring Holdings Limited	£10,703,140,864
Chubb Group Limited	£10,658,702,336
GlaxoSmithKline Capital PLC	£10,646,939,648
Hospitality Holdings Limited	£10,528,145,408
Kraft Foods Investment Holdings UK Limited	£10,462,016,512
Chubb Limited	£10,439,570,432
Aldermore Group PLC	£10,432,700,416
Six Continents Limited	£10,364,999,680
Cadbury Limited	£10,277,645,312
Telefonica Germany Holdings Limited	£9,999,205,376
Direct Line Insurance Group PLC	£9,948,199,936
Telefonica Europe PLC	£9,905,000,448
Sky Operational Finance Limited	£9,861,266,432
Vantas International Limited	£9,697,094,656
Mallinckrodt UK Ltd	£9,481,590,784
Invesco Pensions Limited	£9,309,619,200
Compass Group Holdings PLC	£8,942,300,160
BAE Systems (Operations) Limited	£8,915,000,320
British Gas Trading Limited	£8,864,199,680
CCEP Holdings UK Limited	£8,796,600,320
The BOC Group Limited	£8,620,199,936
Onesavings Bank PLC	£8,589,100,032
Verizon UK Holding Limited	£8,376,727,552
Sky International Operations Limited	£8,306,297,344
O2 Holdings Limited	£8,264,999,936
Heathrow (AH) Limited	£8,156,000,256
Wolseley Limited	£8,133,097,984
Wolseley Overseas Limited	£8,078,825,472
BL Bottling Holdings UK Limited	£7,980,585,984
BP Exploration (Angola) Limited	£7,970,078,720
Entco Situla Holding Ltd	£7,968,043,008
Cadbury Schweppes Overseas Limited	£7,902,595,072
Verizon UK Financing Limited	£7,794,118,144
Imperial Chemical Industries Limited	£7,784,000,000
Wolseley Group Holdings Limited	£7,776,714,240
INEOS Industries Limited	£7,721,331,712
Xerox Overseas Holdings Limited	£7,706,999,808
Atlantica Yield PLC	£7,616,390,144
Hutchison 3G UK Limited	£7,568,008,192
Mercedes-Benz Financial Services UK Limited	£7,566,894,080
Santander Consumer (UK) PLC	£7,537,210,880
GlaxoSmithKline Intellectual Property Mngmnt	£7,432,076,800
ITW Holdings I Limited	£7,397,315,072

Company	Value
ITW Holdings VI Limited	£7,397,127,680
Scotia Gas Networks Limited	£7,328,300,032
Southern Water Services Limited	£7,258,299,904
Hanson Finance Limited	£7,145,700,864
Reckitt Benckiser Luxembourg (No.2) Limited	£7,142,112,256
Arqiva Financing No 1 Limited	£7,116,100,096
ITW Holdings III Limited	£7,103,780,352
ViiV Healthcare Limited	£7,080,999,936
BP Exploration (Caspian Sea) Limited	£7,042,281,472
ViiV Healthcare UK Limited	£7,015,779,840
Asahi Breweries Europe Ltd	£6,961,224,704
INEOS Oxide Limited	£6,927,117,824
Chromium Assets Limited	£6,845,971,968
Shapedirect Limited	£6,791,440,896
Equitable Life Assurance Society,(The)	£6,791,000,064
IHS Global Limited	£6,688,296,448
GlaxoSmithKline Intellectual Property Limited	£6,631,912,960
Voda Limited	£6,620,496,896
Ergon Investments UK Limited	£6,546,396,160
GlaxoSmithKline Investment Holdings Limited	£6,483,027,968
BP Asia Pacific Holdings Limited	£6,405,887,488
AA Senior Co Limited	£6,400,699,904
INEOS Finance Company 3 Limited	£6,386,802,688
Mondi PLC	£6,383,600,640
Allianz Holdings PLC	£6,253,300,224
Virgin Media Senior Investments Limited	£6,231,620,096
BP Australia Swaps Management Limited	£6,225,776,640
O2 (Europe) Limited	£6,179,268,096
CNOOC UK Limited	£6,177,024,512
Hutchison 3G UK Holdings Limited	£6,136,456,192
Toyota Financial Services (UK) PLC	£6,119,365,120
Virgin Media Investments Limited	£6,021,791,744
Reckitt Benckiser Luxembourg (No.4) Limited	£5,987,720,192
IHS Group Holdings Limited	£5,985,950,208
Rentokil Initial 1927 PLC	£5,959,199,744
Six Continents Hotels International Limited	£5,887,932,928
Vodafone UK Limited	£5,884,290,048
BP Exploration (Azerbaijan) Limited	£5,863,719,424
Subsea 7 Treasury (UK) Limited	£5,851,809,280
Telefonica UK Limited	£5,821,000,192
B & Q PLC	£5,801,800,192
Vodafone Overseas Holdings Limited	£5,756,371,456
BP Exploration (Delta) Limited	£5,733,650,944
ADI Finance 2 Limited	£5,717,000,192
Allianz Insurance PLC	£5,635,100,160
Urenco Limited	£5,607,186,432
RCI Financial Services Limited	£5,533,118,976
Vodafone Yen Finance Limited	£5,450,707,968
BP Corporate Holdings Limited	£5,420,483,584
SSE Energy Supply Limited	£5,415,799,808
Reckitt & Sons Limited	£5,362,917,888
Ergon Investments International Limited	£5,332,260,864
Heathrow (DSH) Limited	£5,270,000,128
ADI Finance 1 Limited	£5,231,000,064
Virgin Media Secured Finance PLC	£5,158,961,152
IHS International Holdings Limited	£5,145,225,216
Reckitt Benckiser (Grosvenor) Holdings Limited	£5,141,645,824
Hitachi Capital (UK) PLC	£5,090,800,128
Arqiva Financing No 2 Limited	£5,072,812,032
Arqiva Broadcast Intermediate Limited	£5,069,043,200
TBC Bank Group PLC	£5,045,101,056
Pladis Foods Limited	£5,041,800,192
Citrix Global Holdings UK Limited	£5,016,166,400
Arqiva Group Intermediate Limited	£5,007,191,040
Taylor Wimpey PLC	£4,966,099,968
Southern Gas Networks PLC	£4,954,399,744
HSBC Invoice Finance (UK) Limited	£4,932,506,112
Reckitt Benckiser Finance (2010) Limited	£4,880,451,072
ITW Holdings II Limited	£4,805,328,896
Mondelez UK Holdings & Services Limited	£4,785,999,872
The Berkeley Group Holdings PLC	£4,776,500,224
Green,Young & Company Limited	£4,764,143,104
BP Gas Marketing Limited	£4,760,592,896
Millennium & Copthorne Hotels PLC	£4,714,999,808
Mallinckrodt Pharmaceuticals Limited	£4,702,202,368
Autodesk UK Holdings Limited	£4,648,249,344
GlaxoSmithKline Mercury Limited	£4,645,296,128
Honda Motor Europe Limited	£4,639,191,040
SSE Generation Limited	£4,567,900,160
Linde Investments No.1 Limited	£4,556,568,064
Berkeley Group PLC (The)	£4,548,788,224
BP Holdings Canada Limited	£4,533,431,808
Arqiva Financing No 3 PLC	£4,508,499,968
Reckitt Benckiser Holdings (Luxembourg) Limited	£4,508,191,232
Royal International Insurance Holdings Limited	£4,481,500,160
Chromium Suchex LLP	£4,466,366,976
Vodafone Mobile Communications Limited	£4,438,440,448
AA Mid Co Limited	£4,417,800,192
Arqiva Group Limited	£4,387,800,064
GlaxoSmithKline Intellectual Property Holdings Ltd	£4,385,067,008
Taylor Wimpey UK Limited	£4,373,367,808
Thames Water Utilities Holdings Limited	£4,369,299,968
Arqiva Broadcast Parent Limited	£4,343,699,968
ViiV Healthcare UK (No.3) Limited	£4,336,324,096
Arqiva Group Parent Limited	£4,329,399,808
Reckitt Colman Chiswick (OTC) Limited	£4,301,777,920
Xerox UK Holdings Limited	£4,295,000,064
Forester Life Limited	£4,291,504,128
Hanson America Holdings (1) Limited	£4,283,414,016
Esso Exploration and Production UK Limited	£4,283,000,064
Bottling Great Britain Limited	£4,272,129,280
Cargill Global Funding PLC	£4,270,958,336
Subsea 7 Senior Holdings (UK) Limited	£4,240,687,360
Kemble Water Eurobond PLC	£4,233,299,968
BOC Helex	£4,186,635,264
Vodafone Overseas Finance Limited	£4,182,124,800
GlaxoSmithKline IHC Limited	£4,119,490,048
Royal Insurance Holdings Limited	£4,096,000,000
BE Aerospace Global Holdings Limited	£4,060,818,176
Micro Focus Group Limited	£4,043,976,448
Telewest Communications Networks Limited	£3,997,603,072
Food Manufacturers (G.B. Company)	£3,976,732,928
IBM United Kingdom Limited	£3,942,799,872
Schlumberger Oilfield UK PLC	£3,935,472,128
Reckitt Benckiser Healthcare (UK) Limited	£3,929,607,936
Dimension Data Holdings PLC	£3,889,280,768
Convatec Group PLC	£3,800,900,096
Telewest Limited	£3,798,996,992
Nestle UK Ltd.	£3,759,622,912
The Globe Insurance Company Limited	£3,723,699,968
B O C Holdings	£3,713,143,040
Reckitt Benckiser Luxembourg (No.3) Limited	£3,680,079,872
Virgin Media SFA Finance Limited	£3,649,946,112
Micro Focus International PLC	£3,605,430,016
Vodafone Investment UK	£3,570,189,824
INEOS Styrolution Holding Limited	£3,566,881,792
United Biscuits (UK) Limited	£3,558,799,872
Volkswagen Group United Kingdom Limited	£3,532,100,096
Hanson Holdings Limited	£3,476,107,008
BP (Abu Dhabi) Limited	£3,456,190,976
ExxonMobil Finance Company Limited	£3,412,931,840
Autodesk Holdings LLP	£3,392,922,368
Arqiva Limited	£3,381,100,032
Invesco Holding Company Limited	£3,377,114,624
Xerox Limited	£3,376,000,000
T-Mobile Holdings Limited	£3,339,591,936
BP Exploration (Alpha) Limited	£3,334,274,304
Mondi Investments Limited	£3,314,483,712
ViiV Healthcare Trading Services UK Limited	£3,306,328,064
Reckitt Benckiser (USA) Limited	£3,289,890,048
BAE Systems (Funding Two) Limited	£3,247,131,136
Berkeley Homes Public Limited Company	£3,215,473,920
PSA Finance UK Limited	£3,208,998,912
Virgin Media Wholesale Limited	£3,200,429,056

Company	Value
Southern Electric Power Distribution PLC	£3,194,299,904
Gatwick Airport Limited	£3,185,499,904
Ageas Insurance Limited	£3,175,699,968
Rentokil Initial Holdings Limited	£3,124,499,968
Rentokil Initial PLC	£3,107,699,968
Nestle Holdings (U.K.) PLC	£3,106,449,920
Entserv UK Limited	£3,104,868,096
HeidelbergCement Canada Holding Limited	£3,086,672,896
Linde North America Holdings Limited	£3,083,053,568
Hilton International IP Holding Limited	£3,080,324,096
Centrica Overseas Holdings Limited	£3,077,502,976
TD United Kingdom Acquisition Limited	£3,072,709,376
Arqiva Telecoms Investment Limited	£3,043,326,976
Mash Holdings Limited	£3,041,364,992
Esso UK Limited	£3,028,000,000
Mortar Investments International Limited	£3,025,893,120
Asia Pacific Holdings Limited	£3,019,723,008
Igroup 8 Limited	£3,009,617,920
Thames Water Utilities Finance PLC	£2,981,100,032
INEOS Finance PLC	£2,968,974,592
Hilton Worldwide Holding LLP	£2,958,253,056
Lafarge Building Materials Limited	£2,930,156,032
Unum Limited	£2,928,732,928
Mondelez UK Limited	£2,928,550,912
Taylor Wimpey Developments Limited	£2,906,313,984
AA Intermediate Co Limited	£2,905,999,872
Argos Limited	£2,905,533,952
Galliford Try PLC	£2,893,299,968
Compass Group North America Investments Ltd	£2,889,749,248
WIH UK Limited	£2,882,777,856
VMFH Limited	£2,880,235,008
Vodafone Cellular Limited	£2,859,026,688
NTL Rectangle Limited	£2,827,026,944
BP Exploration (Epsilon) Limited	£2,825,721,856
Mondelez UK Biscuit Financing Limited	£2,820,495,616
Hastings Group Holdings PLC	£2,817,499,904
Cucina Finance (UK) Limited	£2,813,700,096
Akzo Nobel Finance Limited	£2,809,158,912
Nomad Foods Europe Midco Limited	£2,808,313,600
Home Retail Group (UK) Limited	£2,790,338,048
Channel Tunnel Group Limited (The)	£2,782,522,880
AA Corporation Limited	£2,780,499,968
UMV Global Foods Holding Company Ltd.	£2,754,500,096
ITW Limited	£2,745,051,904
INEOS Finance Company 2	£2,743,992,320
INEOS Finance Company 1	£2,742,068,480
Thames Water Limited	£2,712,900,096
Vodafone Europe UK	£2,704,178,432
Esso Petroleum Company,Limited	£2,680,000,000
George Wimpey Limited	£2,676,461,056
Brambles Holdings Unlimited	£2,660,660,480
IBM United Kingdom Financial Services Limited	£2,659,856,896
Cucina Acquisition (UK) Limited	£2,655,300,096
Saga PLC	£2,643,800,064
GlaxoSmithKline Services Unlimited	£2,630,000,128
Nomad Foods Europe Limited	£2,627,912,960
BAE Systems Enterprises Limited	£2,627,752,960
Belron Finance Limited	£2,611,092,992
Reckitt & Colman (UK) Limited	£2,600,382,976
Arqiva Group Holdings Limited	£2,599,322,880
ITW Holdings IV Limited	£2,594,297,088
Subsea 7 Interim UK Holdings Limited	£2,577,399,296
Hilton Worldwide Manage Limited	£2,571,142,144
GR Bottling Holdings UK Limited	£2,541,998,592
CSC Computer Sciences International Operations	£2,539,431,936
Travelport Global Limited	£2,526,378,240
Hilton International IP Holding 2 Limited	£2,523,724,800
RSA Finance	£2,506,701,056
BE Aerospace International Holdings Limited	£2,500,399,360
SmithKline Beecham Limited	£2,496,000,000
Cadbury Eight LLP	£2,478,514,176
Travelport Operations Limited	£2,469,649,408
Reckitt Benckiser Corporate Services Limited	£2,469,594,880
Subsea 7 Offshore Resources (UK) Limited	£2,468,395,520
Home Retail Group Limited	£2,453,499,904
Arqiva Holdings Limited	£2,441,600,000
Cucina Lux Investments Limited	£2,434,200,064
Greensands Senior Finance Limited	£2,423,399,936
Reckitt Benckiser Treasury (2007) Limited	£2,421,181,952
Glaxochem (UK) Unlimited	£2,420,489,984
Micro Focus CHC Limited	£2,416,492,288
Motor Insurers' Bureau	£2,400,355,072
ITW Holdings VII Limited	£2,399,663,360
Hilton Worldwide Holding 2 Limited	£2,394,284,288
Micro Focus Midco Limited	£2,345,740,288
Siemens Public Limited Company	£2,339,685,888
Alphabet (GB) Limited	£2,327,781,888
SNC-Lavalin (GB) Holdings Limited	£2,316,271,872
Suntory UK Holdings Limited	£2,312,583,424
Rentokil Limited	£2,290,642,944
ViiV Healthcare Finance Limited	£2,271,303,936
Brambles Finance PLC	£2,266,366,976
Intercontinental Hotels Group PLC	£2,262,524,160
SNC-Lavalin (GB) Limited	£2,262,006,272
Sanofi-Aventis UK Holdings Limited	£2,259,814,912
BCA Marketplace PLC	£2,256,100,096
ExxonMobil Financial Investment Company Ltd	£2,254,188,544
Leaseplan UK Limited	£2,253,332,992
Reckitt Benckiser (UK) Limited	£2,247,467,008
Brambles Investment Ltd.	£2,233,382,144
NTL (B) Limited	£2,226,475,008
Automobile Association Developments Limited	£2,218,899,968
Mondi Finance PLC	£2,212,484,352
GlaxoSmithKline Holdings (Ireland) Limited	£2,196,562,944
Verizon European Holdings Limited	£2,187,184,640
Reckitt Benckiser Holdings (USA) Limited	£2,186,580,992
Six Continents Overseas Holdings Limited	£2,185,080,064
Rentokil Initial (1896) Limited	£2,180,212,992
UPS (UK) Limited	£2,179,633,664
Asahi Europe Ltd	£2,172,581,120
INEOS European Holdings Limited	£2,171,935,744
Hyundai Capital UK Limited	£2,166,573,056
BMW (UK) Limited	£2,145,181,952
UPS Global Treasury PLC	£2,141,116,800
CB Equity LLP	£2,114,128,512
Greensands (UK) Limited	£2,113,400,064
Greensands Junior Finance Limited	£2,109,699,968
United Biscuits Bidco Limited	£2,108,099,968
Saga Mid Co Limited	£2,102,734,976
Vodafone Investments Limited	£2,096,534,656
UMV Global Foods Company Ltd.	£2,077,799,936
Capital Home Loans Limited	£2,068,568,960
Argos Holdings Limited	£2,064,024,064
BAE Systems Surface Ships Limited	£2,058,785,024
INEOS Industries Holdings Limited	£2,057,548,160
I C I Finance Limited	£2,040,600,064
Kimberly-Clark International Holding Limited	£2,039,592,448
Cilva Holdings Limited	£2,019,148,032
Greensands Europe Limited	£2,003,299,968
Cross London Trains Limited	£1,989,815,040
Cross London Trains Holdco 2 Limited	£1,989,815,040
Tech Data UK Finance Limited	£1,983,862,272
Schlumberger UK Limited	£1,978,862,976
Telewest Communications Holdings Limited	£1,969,148,032
Lafarge International Holdings Limited	£1,965,474,048
BMW (UK) Holdings Limited	£1,965,374,976
Taylor Wimpey Holdings Limited	£1,941,644,032
Arqiva Services Limited	£1,941,600,000
Thales UK Limited	£1,930,288,000
Siemens Holdings PLC	£1,918,364,032
Invesco Finance PLC	£1,909,806,464
NATS Holdings Limited	£1,901,400,064
Datatec PLC	£1,896,177,664
Novar Limited	£1,890,841,984

Company	Value	Company	Value
Suffolk Finance Company Limited	£1,889,229,952	Anno 2017 Joint Holding (UK) Limited	£1,611,495,936
Thales Holdings UK PLC	£1,888,355,968	SSE EPM Limited	£1,608,700,032
Pfizer Limited	£1,879,758,976	British Gas Services Limited	£1,603,451,008
Schlumberger Public Limited Company	£1,876,827,008	Bovis Homes Limited	£1,602,083,968
Intercontinental (PB) 1	£1,874,495,616	Linden Limited	£1,588,732,032
GlaxoSmithKline International Limited	£1,866,791,040	Nomad Foods Europe Finco Limited	£1,585,529,856
Cable & Wireless UK Holdings Limited	£1,863,223,040	Brake Bros Holding I Limited	£1,585,500,032
Spirit Norway Limited	£1,857,423,872	Kellogg Brown & Root Holdings Limited	£1,585,053,056
GlaxoSmithKline Consumer Healthcare (Overseas)	£1,856,691,968	Bovis Homes Group PLC	£1,584,376,960
Avis Europe Holdings Limited	£1,850,199,040	Friends Life Holdings PLC	£1,580,999,936
Cadbury Nine LLP	£1,845,740,032	Radian Group Limited	£1,578,747,008
Wellcome Limited	£1,843,000,064	Siemens Financial Services Limited	£1,578,504,960
RMIS (RTW) Limited	£1,841,937,024	GlaxoSmithKline Intellectual Property Development	£1,572,909,056
RB Holdings (Nottingham) Limited	£1,840,948,992	M & C Singapore Holdings (UK) Limited	£1,568,007,424
Syneos Health Holdings UK Limited	£1,840,349,952	Hilton HHC Limited	£1,552,382,464
Brake Bros Limited	£1,835,500,032	Mizzen Mezzco Limited	£1,551,892,992
Parkview Treasury Services (UK) Limited	£1,834,680,960	Edwardian Group Limited	£1,551,187,968
Cable & Wireless Worldwide Limited	£1,833,421,952	GE Money Home Lending Holdings Limited	£1,547,659,136
Sky CP Limited	£1,830,000,000	Biffa Waste Services Limited	£1,547,399,936
AA PLC	£1,827,000,064	SCIH Branston 3	£1,545,536,000
South East Water Limited	£1,808,726,016	Spirit Energy Production UK Limited	£1,535,412,992
Aryzta UK Holdings I Limited	£1,806,012,928	Premium Credit Limited	£1,533,364,992
Spectris PLC	£1,798,899,968	BNP Paribas Leasing Solutions Limited	£1,529,538,944
GlaxoSmithKline Consumer Healthcare Finance	£1,798,552,960	CF 2016 LLP	£1,520,000,128
Signet Group Limited	£1,798,029,184	CNOOC Petroleum Europe Limited	£1,519,397,376
Avis Europe Investments Limited	£1,796,929,024	IBM United Kingdom Holdings Limited	£1,514,599,936
Old Mutual Wealth Holdings Limited	£1,792,427,008	Serco Group PLC	£1,512,800,000
Kellogg Brown & Root Limited	£1,787,815,936	BP Oil UK Limited	£1,510,000,000
CSC Computer Sciences International Holdings	£1,782,630,016	Procter & Gamble Overseas Limited	£1,509,418,752
BP Finance P.L.C	£1,781,024,000	Firebolt RB Holdings Limited	£1,503,451,136
Syngenta Holdings Limited	£1,777,755,136	NBS Trade and Investment Limited	£1,501,340,416
Invesco UK Limited	£1,746,840,064	Enterprise Rent-a-Car European Holdings Ltd	£1,499,531,008
Spectris Group Holdings Limited	£1,745,929,984	John Crane Group Limited	£1,496,412,032
CSC Computer Sciences International Limited	£1,736,317,056	BAE Systems Surface Ships (Holdings) Limited	£1,490,412,032
Centrica Lake Limited	£1,735,707,008	Hilton International Hotels (UK) Limited	£1,487,772,288
Virgin Atlantic Two Limited	£1,724,800,000	Covea Insurance PLC	£1,487,491,968
Virgin Atlantic Limited	£1,723,800,064	Dairy Crest Limited	£1,479,000,064
Micro Focus (US) Holdings	£1,722,185,344	Crest Nicholson Holdings PLC	£1,477,900,032
Travelport Travel Commerce Platform Limited	£1,721,926,528	J D Wetherspoon PLC	£1,476,313,984
GlaxoSmithKline Research & Development Ltd	£1,721,917,952	Capital Hospitals Ltd.	£1,476,226,944
De Lage Landen Leasing Limited	£1,721,616,000	Capital Hospitals (Holdings) Ltd.	£1,476,226,944
Coca-Cola European Partners Hldgs Great Britain	£1,720,679,040	Procter & Gamble Finance (UK) Limited	£1,474,711,936
Esure Insurance Limited	£1,716,000,000	Enterprise Rent-a-Car UK Limited	£1,472,199,040
Centrica Beta Holdings Limited	£1,715,495,040	De La Rue Holdings Limited	£1,468,836,992
Interserve PLC	£1,715,399,936	SAB Australia Beverage Holdings LLP	£1,468,508,544
Honeywell Group Holding UK II	£1,700,272,000	ExxonMobil Chemical Investment Company Limited	£1,466,121,984
RMAC Securities No. 1 PLC	£1,693,400,064	Bourne Leisure Holdings Limited	£1,465,027,968
Smiths Medical Group Limited	£1,690,849,024	Procter & Gamble Holdings (UK) Limited	£1,450,305,536
Exploration & Production Services (Holdings) Ltd	£1,684,684,544	Serco Holdings Limited	£1,446,995,968
FCA Automotive Services UK Ltd	£1,684,007,936	Halma Public Limited Company	£1,446,855,936
BP Shipping Limited	£1,682,076,032	Capital Hospitals (Issuer) PLC	£1,446,487,040
Tech Data Holding Limited	£1,680,162,304	Sky Telecommunications Services Limited	£1,444,999,936
GlaxoSmithKline Intellectual Property (No.2) Ltd	£1,679,232,000	Coats Group Finance Company Limited	£1,441,565,824
Hilton Finance (UK) Limited	£1,676,255,104	Kimberly-Clark Holding Limited	£1,439,970,944
Greensands Investments Limited	£1,675,299,968	United Biscuits Holdco Limited	£1,439,299,968
National House-Building Council	£1,674,989,952	Britvic Soft Drinks Limited	£1,437,943,040
Unilever UK Limited	£1,671,614,976	Procter & Gamble Investment Company (UK) Ltd	£1,430,648,704
Compass Overseas Holdings Limited	£1,667,874,048	Ardonagh Finco PLC	£1,424,423,040
Britvic PLC	£1,664,099,968	DPG Holdings Limited	£1,423,794,944
United Biscuits Holdco 2 Limited	£1,658,300,032	Mercedes-Benz Cars UK Limited	£1,414,178,048
John Wiley & Sons UK LLP	£1,657,449,984	Bristow Aviation Holdings Limited	£1,409,321,984
Fidelity China Special Situations PLC	£1,654,736,000	Cineworld Group PLC	£1,407,200,000
Virgin Atlantic Airways Limited	£1,653,299,968	Belron Lending UK Limited	£1,406,666,624
NATS (En Route) Public Limited Company	£1,652,800,000	Lucozade Ribena Suntory Limited	£1,394,434,944
Centrica Energy Limited	£1,649,904,000	Symantec (UK) Holding Limited	£1,390,139,136
Kraft Foods UK IP & Production Holdings Limited	£1,648,612,992	Merck Holding Ltd.	£1,389,846,400
Investec Asset Finance PLC	£1,644,205,056	NTL (CWC) Limited	£1,388,226,048
HDF (UK) Holdings Limited	£1,642,569,984	ITW Holdings V Limited	£1,387,344,768
Cabot Credit Management Limited	£1,640,199,936	Gallaher Limited	£1,385,600,000
CSC Computer Sciences Limited	£1,639,655,040	Vodafone Group Services Limited	£1,385,153,280
F.M. Insurance Company Limited	£1,635,216,000	Ikea Properties Investments Limited	£1,384,669,056
Limecay Limited	£1,621,892,992	Centrica Finance (Canada) Limited	£1,383,364,992

Company	Value
TBG (3) 2009 Limited	£1,382,528,000
Hewlett - Packard Limited	£1,377,300,992
Saga Group Limited	£1,377,177,984
Birchwood Omnia Limited	£1,374,844,032
Vodafone Oceania Limited	£1,372,180,096
LGC Science Group Holdings Limited	£1,370,514,944
Elwy 2 Limited	£1,370,514,944
Elwy 3 Limited	£1,370,514,944
Intercontinental (PB) 3 Limited	£1,369,897,600
Big Yellow Group PLC	£1,369,840,000
Exel Limited	£1,368,381,056
UB Overseas Limited	£1,367,154,048
INEOS Canada Limited	£1,360,560,896
Cornerstone Telecommunications Infrastructure	£1,359,960,960
Ceesail Limited	£1,354,002,944
Aventis Pharma Holdings Limited	£1,350,290,048
Nomad Foods Europe Holdco Limited	£1,348,299,264
BFIM Limited	£1,344,396,032
Astellas Pharma Europe Ltd.	£1,343,135,104
McLaren Group Limited	£1,340,724,992
Crest Nicholson PLC	£1,339,200,000
Hilton UK Hotels Limited	£1,338,172,928
Michael Page International Recruitment Limited	£1,333,287,936
Black & Decker Europe	£1,330,647,040
Towergate Insurance Limited	£1,327,869,056
Glaxo Operations UK Limited	£1,324,759,040
Hamol Limited	£1,322,630,016
Sun Alliance and London Insurance Limited	£1,322,238,976
AA Brand Management Limited	£1,322,200,064
Chubb Group (International) Limited	£1,315,275,008
Abbott Asia Investments Limited	£1,312,792,064
RAK Petroleum PLC	£1,310,131,840
Crest Nicholson Operations Limited	£1,309,500,032
Travelport Group Investments Limited	£1,307,796,480
Avios Group (AGL) Limited	£1,307,650,048
MES Interco	£1,299,442,944
Coca-Cola European Partners Great Britain Ltd	£1,293,049,984
PizzaExpress Financing 2 PLC	£1,280,556,032
SSE Services PLC	£1,278,000,000
Essentra Finance Limited	£1,269,492,992
Honeywell Group Ltd	£1,268,519,040
Greater Gabbard Offshore Winds Limited	£1,267,900,032
Centrica Energy Marketing Limited	£1,262,000,000
Paratus AMC Limited	£1,259,399,936
Qinetiq Limited	£1,258,800,000
JTI (UK) Management Ltd	£1,257,982,976
Alliance Healthcare (Distribution) Limited	£1,248,999,936
PNC Financial Services UK Ltd	£1,246,605,440
Berendsen Limited	£1,246,099,968
Rentokil Overseas Holdings Limited	£1,240,717,056
Essentra PLC	£1,239,699,968
TJX UK	£1,234,300,032
PizzaExpress Group Holdings Limited	£1,233,755,008
PizzaExpress Financing 1 PLC	£1,233,755,008
Cabot Financial (UK) Limited	£1,231,095,040
AERL Holding Limited	£1,227,772,672
BAE Systems Marine Limited	£1,226,480,000
Vodafone Sales & Services Limited	£1,225,272,320
Galliford Try Construction & Investments Holdings	£1,224,300,032
DHL Supply Chain Limited	£1,214,093,056
Cable & Wireless Europe Holdings Limited	£1,209,196,032
Eli Lilly and Company Limited	£1,206,620,032
CSC Computer Sciences Financing LLP	£1,206,585,984
PizzaExpress Operations Limited	£1,203,827,968
Signet Holdings Limited	£1,202,115,712
Southern Water Limited	£1,201,699,968
Biffa Group Limited	£1,201,200,000
CG EU NSC Limited	£1,200,497,536
Qinetiq Group PLC	£1,198,000,000
Sky Group Finance PLC	£1,193,028,992
Abbott Asia Holdings Limited	£1,189,374,976
NTL Cablecomms Holdings No.1 Limited	£1,166,099,968
Meslink Limited	£1,159,083,008
Cirrus Logic UK International Holding Co. Ltd.	£1,157,642,240
Safestore Holdings PLC	£1,156,600,064
Belron Finance Issuer Limited	£1,153,383,552
Subsea 7 Investments (UK) Limited	£1,149,899,776
Compass Group Finance No.2 Limited	£1,143,321,984
Mallinckrodt UK Finance LLP	£1,142,992,384
Subsea 7 Limited	£1,134,483,968
Centrica Finance (US) Limited	£1,127,905,024
Cadbury Four LLP	£1,124,563,968
BOC Limited	£1,123,000,064
LGC (Holdings) Limited	£1,122,893,056
Honda Finance Europe PLC	£1,122,119,936
Samsung Electronics (UK) Limited	£1,121,426,048
AA Acquisition Co Limited	£1,118,599,936
Honeywell Acquisitions Limited	£1,118,036,992
PizzaExpress Group Limited	£1,113,291,008
Black & Decker International	£1,113,223,040
Restaurant Holdings Limited	£1,111,698,944
CAF Bank Limited	£1,106,256,000
St George PLC	£1,104,471,040
Sony Europe Limited	£1,102,010,112
Centrica Gamma Holdings Limited	£1,098,353,024
BP Pipelines (SCP) Limited	£1,095,581,312
Diamond Cable Communications Limited	£1,095,374,976
INEOS Styrolution Financing Limited	£1,095,338,112
Ringmerit Limited	£1,093,650,048
CSC Computer Sciences UK Holdings Limited	£1,090,516,992
Equiniti Holdings Limited	£1,089,864,960
Indivior PLC	£1,087,758,976
Kesa Holdings Limited	£1,087,058,432
MC Treasury Limited	£1,086,730,624
Kidde International Limited	£1,084,392,960
Ultra Electronics Holdings PLC	£1,083,816,960
BP Chemicals East China Investments Limited	£1,083,757,312
Canal & River Trust	£1,082,000,000
Interserve Finance Limited	£1,079,881,984
AE Consolidation Limited	£1,076,919,040
Erac UK Finance Limited	£1,076,040,960
Avis Budget EMEA Limited	£1,071,400,000
BAE Systems Electronics Limited	£1,068,348,032
Johnson & Johnson Management Limited	£1,066,600,000
Lafarge Minerals Limited	£1,065,000,000
INEOS Investments International Limited	£1,063,833,536
Tesco Underwriting Limited	£1,061,100,032
BCA Central Limited	£1,060,424,000
Perpetual Income and Growth Investment Trust	£1,056,697,024
MJN International Holdings (UK), Ltd.	£1,054,898,432
Biffa PLC	£1,054,300,032
Suez Recycling and Recovery Holdings UK Ltd	£1,050,508,032
Mitsubishi Electric Finance Europe PLC	£1,049,174,016
Tech Data Limited	£1,047,009,024
Goodrich Inertial Limited	£1,042,073,024
Cargill Financial Markets Limited	£1,041,751,616
Fidelity European Values PLC	£1,038,979,968
Cidron Healthcare - It 3 Limited	£1,036,360,960
Yazaki Europe Limited	£1,034,148,224
ISS UK Limited	£1,033,267,008
Abbott Equity Holdings Unlimited	£1,032,654,016
Shilton Bidco Limited	£1,029,436,992
Six Continents Holdings Limited	£1,028,201,984
Atkins Limited	£1,027,699,968
London Airports 1992 Limited	£1,026,076,032
P & O Ferries Division Holdings Limited	£1,023,758,976
Senior Engineering Investments Limited	£1,019,582,976
Castle Bidco PLC	£1,019,200,000
Procter & Gamble UK Parent Company Limited	£1,013,041,408
Honeywell Acquisitions II Limited	£1,012,302,016
British Gas Energy Procurement Limited	£1,006,400,000
Sky Television Limited	£1,006,201,024
Avis Finance Company Limited	£1,004,884,544
Coats Group PLC	£1,002,335,232

Company	Value
Oracle Corporation UK Limited	£1,001,036,992
Aramark Investments Limited	£997,553,984
Microsoft Limited	£997,073,024
Crown Agents Bank Limited	£993,044,992
Zebra Diamond Holdings Limited	£989,404,224
Robert Bosch UK Holdings Limited	£988,782,016
Cognita BondCo Parent Limited	£988,616,000
Galaxy Acquisition Co 1 Ltd	£988,417,216
Galaxy Acquisition Co 2 Ltd	£988,417,216
3M Asia Pacific UK Holding Ltd	£988,356,800
UCB (Investments) Limited	£987,009,984
Hilton Worldwide FS Treasury Limited	£986,574,848
RB Luxembourg (2016) Limited	£985,870,976
PizzaExpress (Restaurants) Limited	£983,900,032
Capgemini UK PLC	£980,796,992
IHS Global Investments Limited	£980,758,912
Societe Generale Equipment Finance Limited	£977,971,968
LKQ Euro Limited	£977,774,976
Philips U.K. Limited	£977,500,032
3M United Kingdom Public Limited Company	£973,875,968
Interbay ML, Ltd	£972,910,016
British Gas Insurance Limited	£972,748,032
Logicalis Group Limited	£970,493,824
CALA Group (Holdings) Limited	£968,812,032
Northgate Information Solutions Holdings Ltd	£965,958,016
Allianz (UK) Limited	£965,641,984
Arqiva PP Financing PLC	£964,030,016
ExxonMobil Investment Company Limited	£964,005,312
Pharmacia Limited	£963,942,016
Honeywell Safety Products International Ltd.	£961,805,568
SCJ UK Finco Ltd	£960,801,024
Spirit Energy North Sea Limited	£956,955,008
MacDermid Continental Investments Limited	£951,390,016
Senior PLC	£950,800,000
Rank Nemo (Twenty-Five) Limited	£950,800,000
Britannia Soft Drinks Limited	£950,691,968
Michael Page Holdings Limited	£948,027,008
Reed Business Information Limited	£946,572,992
RCL Cruises Ltd	£945,661,312
Old Mutual Wealth UK Holding Limited	£945,518,976
SGL No.1 Limited	£944,232,000
Kimberly-Clark Finance Limited	£938,726,976
Zebra Technologies Europe Limited	£935,570,560
GE Healthcare Limited	£932,070,016
Hewlett-Packard (Bracknell) Holdings Limited	£931,268,992
Morgan Advanced Materials PLC	£929,699,968
Equiniti Group PLC	£927,600,000
Garrett Thermal Systems UK Limited	£925,329,984
McLaren Automotive Limited	£920,251,008
Brambles U.K. Limited	£920,161,024
Fluor Limited	£914,633,024
BMW (UK) Manufacturing Limited	£914,313,984
Sailtown Limited	£908,083,584
Kofax London Holdings Limited	£907,213,824
Cognita Holdings Limited	£907,203,008
Cognita UK Holdings Limited	£907,203,008
Cygnet Health UK Limited	£906,067,968
Interserve Group Holdings Limited	£905,601,984
Reckitt Benckiser Holdings (TFFC) Limited	£902,689,024
Arqiva Financing PLC	£900,854,976
ADT Finance Limited	£900,652,992
Verizon UK Limited	£899,713,024
INEOS Grangemouth PLC	£899,344,000
Coats Limited	£896,296,000
Costco Wholesale UK Limited	£895,956,992
CSC Computer Sciences International Services	£895,566,976
Travelport International Operations Limited	£894,539,392
Costco UK Holdings Limited	£893,710,016
Perform Group Limited	£892,328,000
UK Acquisitions No. 6 Limited	£892,033,984
Skanska UK PLC	£891,872,000
Brambles Holdings (UK) Limited	£888,199,168
Air Bidco Limited	£887,954,432
Pioneer International Group Holdings Limited	£887,662,976
Reckitt Benckiser (Brands) Limited	£887,260,992
BE Aerospace (UK) Europe Holdings Limited	£886,728,960
Halma International Limited	£884,907,008
ExxonMobil UK Limited	£882,305,984
Sir Robert McAlpine (Holdings) Limited	£880,270,976
Reckitt Benckiser Luxembourg (2010) Limited	£880,072,000
Hexagon Manufacturing Intelligence Management	£874,900,928
HeidelbergCement Euro II Limited	£869,166,080
Honeywell Group Holding UK	£865,548,992
ViiV Healthcare Finance 2 Limited	£861,767,552
Stada UK Holdings Ltd.	£861,665,920
Sky Subscribers Services Limited	£858,601,024
Rank Leisure Holdings Limited	£841,622,976
Towers Watson Global 2 Limited	£840,491,712
Daimler UK Limited	£836,051,968
Air Products Group Limited	£834,520,000
Barloworld Holdings Limited	£833,827,968
Sir Robert McAlpine Limited	£833,086,016
Capital Safety Acquisitions Limited	£831,978,816
Southern Water Services Group Limited	£828,700,032
Bidcorp Foodservice (Europe) Limited	£825,315,968
PizzaExpress Limited	£824,732,032
Harsco Infrastructure Group Limited	£824,603,200
Southern Electric Gas Limited	£823,200,000
Intercontinental Hotels Limited	£820,990,976
Haven Leisure Limited	£818,675,968
Halma Overseas Funding Limited	£817,015,616
Premier Lotteries Capital UK Limited	£815,200,000
Premier Lotteries UK Limited	£814,899,968
Serco Limited	£814,600,000
Micro Focus MHC Limited	£812,556,288
Castrol Limited	£811,875,008
De La Rue International Limited.	£811,558,016
Xerox Capital (Europe) Limited	£807,499,008
Akzo Nobel UK Ltd	£807,200,000
SSL International PLC	£806,897,984
Expro Holdings UK 3 Limited	£804,689,088
Wiley Europe Limited	£803,859,008
BP Biofuels Brazil Investments Limited	£800,981,376
Sabroe Limited	£799,350,976
Mars Wrigley Confectionery UK Limited	£797,521,984
Onix Investments UK Ltd	£795,908,160
Arqiva UK Broadcast Holdings Limited	£793,025,024
Northgate UK Holdings 4 Limited	£790,800,000
Genus PLC	£789,200,000
INEOS Investment Holdings (Germany) Limited	£788,634,560
Laing O'Rourke PLC.	£788,600,000
Home Retail Group Card Services Limited	£788,092,992
LGC Science Investments Limited	£787,196,032
Park Holidays UK Limited	£786,558,976
Compass Hotels Chertsey	£783,217,024
GlaxoSmithKline Consumer Trading Services Ltd	£781,051,008
Newarthill Limited	£781,009,984
Air Products Public Limited Company	£778,465,984
LRC Products Limited	£776,812,032
Ocean Partners Holdings Limited	£775,645,184
Skanska Construction UK Limited	£774,459,008
Catalina Worthing Insurance Limited	£773,193,024
Fisons Limited	£771,542,016
Host Europe Group Limited	£771,225,024
Towers Watson Limited	£770,336,000
Citrix Systems UK Limited	£770,060,864
Gallaher Group Limited	£769,382,976
United Technologies Holdings Limited	£768,590,016
IQVIA Ltd.	£768,030,016
Nissan Motor (GB) Limited	£767,649,024
ESPUG Finance Limited	£765,907,968
P & O Ferries Holdings Limited	£765,254,976
CP Holdings Limited	£762,854,976
ADT Fire and Security PLC	£761,942,016

Company	Value
Kidde UK	£761,939,968
CooperVision (UK) Holdings Limited	£759,608,320
Compass Group North America Investments No.2	£754,867,776
Superdrug Stores PLC	£753,222,016
WP Midco3 Limited	£752,249,984
Novar Europe Limited	£750,708,992
nVent International (UK) Ltd	£749,903,168
GE Healthcare UK Limited	£748,172,032
TIM Intermediateco Limited	£747,200,000
St James Group Limited	£744,556,992
Britannic Trading Limited	£742,389,248
Hexagon Corporate Management Limited	£742,117,184
Chubb International Holdings Limited	£740,940,032
Lafarge UK Holdings Limited	£737,894,976
Nuffield Health	£737,299,968
Telewest Communications Midlands & North West	£737,171,008
Air Products (BR) Limited	£736,190,016
Fidelity Special Values PLC	£733,105,024
Mott MacDonald Limited	£732,182,016
Seqirus Limited	£731,576,512
Halma Financing Limited	£729,502,336
Grafton Group (UK) Public Limited Company	£728,055,616
Sky Finance Europe Limited	£727,587,968
Iris Group Limited	£727,154,688
HeidelbergCement Euro III Limited	£725,532,800
GlaxoSmithKline UK Limited	£723,723,008
Belron International Limited	£723,329,984
Alent Limited	£722,862,976
HPI Holding Limited	£722,752,000
Kentucky Fried Chicken (Great Britain) Limited	£722,492,992
Toyota (G.B.) PLC	£721,769,024
Ageas (UK) Limited	£721,718,016
The Rank Group PLC	£720,300,032
Wimpey Overseas Holdings Limited	£719,470,976
Yanfeng UK Automotive Interior Systems Co., Ltd	£718,915,136
CDK Global Holdings (UK) Limited	£717,516,032
Genus Investments Limited	£716,008,000
Acco Brands Europe Limited	£715,107,456
Rentokil Initial (1993) Limited	£712,499,968
Mott MacDonald Group Limited	£712,019,968
Chemring Group PLC	£711,600,000
Aliaxis Holdings UK Limited	£711,140,992
Safetykleen Group Services Limited	£710,739,008
Hurricane Energy PLC	£706,626,752
Cineworld Cinemas Limited	£706,400,000
Laing O'Rourke Services Limited	£704,140,992
Wates Group Limited	£702,764,032
BP Senegal Investments Limited	£701,984,000
Automatic Data Processing Limited	£701,867,008
Welcome Break Group Limited	£701,206,016
Johnson Controls-Hitachi Air Conditioning Hldg UK	£701,055,232
IQVIA RDS UK Holdings Ltd.	£699,758,016
Wiley Europe Investment Holdings Limited	£698,851,968
Doosan Babcock Limited	£697,980,032
GE Medical Systems Limited	£695,057,984
Colorcon European Holdings (No.5) Limited	£695,000,000
ISS Facility Services Limited	£694,902,016
AB InBev Harmony Limited	£693,750,656
Scania (Great Britain) Limited	£692,945,984
Hitachi Europe Limited	£692,308,992
VS International Holdings Limited	£690,030,784
Sky In-Home Service Limited	£689,548,032
Invesco Fund Managers Limited	£689,425,024
RB UK Commercial Limited	£689,331,008
NIS Acquisitions Limited	£687,932,032
Software (Holdco 4) Limited	£687,751,296
Virgin Mobile Telecoms Limited	£686,273,024
GlaxoSmithKline Consumer Healthcare UK Trading	£685,875,968
Software (Holdco2) Limited	£684,937,984
DL Insurance Services Limited	£684,000,000
Tata Global Beverages Group Limited	£683,667,008
BP Exploration Beta Limited	£683,506,112
B & Q Properties Limited	£680,160,000
Franklin UK Bidco Limited	£680,102,464
Afton Chemical UK LLP	£678,587,008
GHH Holdings Limited	£676,824,896
W.S. Atkins International Limited	£676,515,008
Cargill PLC	£676,387,008
GH Equity UK Limited	£675,421,248
Evonik UK Holdings Limited	£674,511,296
The Rothschild Foundation	£673,321,664
YH Limited	£672,841,024
Akzo Nobel Finance (2) Limited	£672,532,992
Augustus 2 Limited	£671,014,016
Chloride Group Limited	£670,611,008
Xerox (UK) Limited	£667,699,968
UPS Limited	£664,441,984
Havas Holdings Limited	£664,367,680
Reckitt Benckiser Service Bureau Limited	£664,321,984
INEOS Chemicals Grangemouth Limited	£664,244,992
Costain Group PLC	£661,100,032
BNP Paribas Commercial Finance Limited	£659,718,720
Dell Corporation Limited	£659,374,976
Hanson Packed Products Limited	£657,454,016
Reckitt Benckiser USA Finance (No.1) Limited	£656,515,968
AWE Management Limited	£656,380,992
Eaton Limited	£656,057,024
Honeywell International UK Limited	£654,585,024
Avis Europe Investment Holdings Limited	£653,451,008
Kellogg Brown & Root Overseas Projects Limited	£653,177,088
Camelot UK Lotteries Limited	£651,699,968
Wimpey Dormant Investments Limited	£651,478,976
RB Luxembourg Holdings (TFFC) Limited	£651,155,008
Dulux Limited	£651,012,992
Kimberly-Clark Europe Limited	£649,741,632
Siemens Industrial Turbomachinery Limited	£649,585,984
Equiniti Limited	£648,099,968
Sky Ventures Limited	£647,968,000
Sopra Steria Limited	£646,472,000
BFS Group Limited	£645,164,032
Tokyo Electron Europe Limited	£644,873,792
TJX Europe Limited	£643,612,992
Reckitt Benckiser Healthcare (CIS) Limited	£643,354,176
DF Group Limited	£642,947,648
Syngenta Limited	£640,000,000
Arora Hotels Limited	£635,217,024
AWE PLC	£635,142,016
Seqirus Holdings UK Limited	£634,094,336
Dairy Crest Group PLC	£628,200,000
NTL Cambridge Limited	£627,492,992
.Big Yellow Self Storage Company Limited	£626,955,008
Dawsongroup PLC	£625,916,032
INEOS Commercial Services UK Limited	£625,029,824
Bluefield SIF Investments Limited	£624,281,664
Cineworld Holdings Limited	£623,516,032
Biffa Holdings Limited	£622,896,000
Nomad Foods BondCo PLC	£621,933,056
Halma Investment Holdings Limited	£621,440,256
Havas UK Limited	£620,940,992
WSH Hospitality Limited	£620,857,024
Renewable Energy Systems Holdings Limited	£620,592,000
The Hospital Company (Southmead) Limited	£620,545,984
Hospital Company (Southmead) Holdings Ltd	£620,545,984
Compass Group Finance No. 3 Limited	£619,163,008
Intralot Finance UK Limited	£618,260,544
Azlan Group Limited	£617,600,000
CC 1 (2011) Limited	£617,559,616
BAE Systems Properties Limited	£616,368,000
Beazer Limited	£615,137,024
Arqiva Broadcast Finance PLC	£614,636,992
Vodafone Enterprise U.K.	£613,563,008
NSK Europe Limited	£612,325,184
WS Atkins Limited	£611,299,968
Trellis Acquisitions Limited	£610,833,984

Company	Value	Company	Value
Edwardian Hotel Finance Ltd	£610,369,024	Tiger Topco 1 Limited	£541,753,024
Expro Holdings UK 4 Limited	£609,754,688	Vodafone Financial Operations	£539,256,640
Menzies Aviation PLC	£609,699,968	Kerry Foods Limited	£538,807,168
Chubb Group Security Limited	£606,934,976	Riverstone Holdings Limited	£538,518,976
Bourne Leisure Limited	£606,860,032	BP Pipelines Tap Limited	£537,848,320
Sabre Insurance Group PLC	£605,953,024	John Dewar and Sons Limited	£537,265,024
Arqiva Senior Finance Limited	£603,500,992	P & O Short Sea Ferries Limited	£536,428,992
Iris Capital Limited	£603,346,944	ADT Group Limited	£535,039,008
London International Group Limited	£603,320,000	IHG Hotels Limited	£534,344,992
Ocean Partners UK Limited	£602,769,920	Ricardo Investments Limited	£533,633,984
Associated International Cement Limited	£602,089,984	Riverstone Insurance Limited	£532,907,008
Berendsen Finance Limited	£601,037,824	CGS Holdings Ltd.	£531,456,992
Honeywell North Atlantic Holdings Limited	£600,358,016	Tata Global Beverages Services Limited	£529,515,008
United Biscuits Vlnco Limited	£600,000,000	Wyevale Garden Centres Limited	£528,996,000
INEOS Derivatives France Limited	£599,658,752	Watson Wyatt (UK) Acquisitions 1 Limited	£528,770,624
Proudreed Limited	£599,505,024	Rhombi Holdings Limited	£528,601,536
Coats Finance Co. Limited	£598,715,840	Jacobs U.K. Limited	£528,472,992
HCL EAS Ltd	£596,680,640	Dun & Bradstreet Finance Limited	£528,404,000
Perform Sports Media Limited	£595,744,000	BOC Investment Holdings Limited	£527,736,000
Suez UK Group Holdings Ltd	£592,094,016	Black & Decker	£527,616,992
Wates Construction Limited	£591,993,024	TBG (4) Limited	£525,227,008
Watson Wyatt (UK) Acquisitions 2 Limited	£590,958,976	IGE Energy Services (UK) Limited	£523,944,000
Tiger Topco Limited	£590,934,976	Sun Alliance Insurance Overseas Limited	£523,000,000
Thames Water (Kemble) Finance PLC	£590,460,032	BP Exploration (Shah Deniz) Limited	£522,955,648
Ikea Limited	£589,835,008	Hewlett-Packard Holdings Limited	£522,928,992
Beecham Group P L C	£588,897,024	Britax Group Limited	£522,811,552
Tech Data UK Finance Partner Limited	£588,056,768	Mercedes-Benz Retail Group UK Limited	£519,217,984
Xchanging UK Limited	£585,593,024	TWG Europe Limited	£519,175,008
Zurich UK General Services Limited	£584,336,704	Hogg Robinson Limited	£519,100,000
The Ambassador Theatre Group Limited	£581,097,024	Westcoast (Holdings) Limited	£517,742,016
Kellogg Brown & Root International Group Limited	£578,924,608	Broadcast Relay Service (Overseas) Limited	£516,967,008
Just Retirement Group Holdings Limited	£576,958,976	Linde Canada Holdings Limited	£514,917,760
Camellia Public Limited Company	£576,499,968	St George Blackfriars Limited	£514,294,368
Galliford Try Building Limited	£576,496,000	Elekta Limited	£514,169,984
Safestore Acquisition Limited	£576,177,024	HIC Treasury Limited	£514,079,584
Elysium Healthcare Holdings 2 Limited	£575,473,024	Laing O'Rourke Construction Limited	£513,598,016
Costain Limited	£574,165,312	Metropole Hotels (Holdings) Limited	£512,972,992
Beam Suntory UK Limited	£573,376,000	Parker Hannifin Manufacturing Limited	£512,844,000
Kimberly-Clark European Services Limited	£572,953,024	Kellogg Brown & Root Holdings (U.K.) Limited	£512,745,984
KP Snacks Limited	£571,792,000	Oil Spill Response Limited	£512,464,000
Runecorp Limited	£571,641,024	BP Pipelines (BTC) Limited	£509,718,560
Senior Five Limited	£570,557,504	FT North America Limited	£508,661,312
GlaxoSmithKline Investment Services Limited	£570,209,984	Suez Recycling and Recovery UK Group Holdings	£508,148,992
Blackberry UK Limited	£568,162,496	Hotel Intercontinental London (Holdings) Limited	£508,111,008
Sopra Steria Holdings Limited	£567,552,000	TBG (1) 2009 Limited	£507,999,008
Renewi European Holdings Limited	£567,320,000	CTS Metropark Limited	£507,940,992
Hyundai Motor UK Limited	£566,403,968	Cognita Midco Limited	£507,576,992
AVX Limited	£566,296,512	Capital Safety Global Holdings Limited	£507,398,592
Biffa Corporate Holdings Limited	£565,246,016	D.E Holding UK Limited	£507,120,000
Dairy Crest UK Limited	£565,105,984	M & C Asia Holdings (UK) Limited	£506,616,576
Riverstone Insurance (UK) Limited	£564,441,920	Scentrics Information Security Technologies Limited	£505,965,952
HeidelbergCement Euro I Limited	£561,074,496	INEOS Chemicals France Holdings Limited	£505,849,088
EDU UK Topco Limited	£560,800,000	Hogg Robinson Group Limited	£505,300,000
CHG Overseas Ltd	£560,188,992	Reckitt Benckiser Holdings (Overseas) Limited	£504,535,008
EDU UK Intermediate Limited	£559,800,000	Acco Europe Limited	£503,971,008
Cargill UK Holdings Limited	£556,501,952	Christ's Hospital	£503,764,000
Vinci PLC	£556,436,992	Mapil Topco Limited	£503,628,000
Black & Decker Finance	£555,758,656	ExxonMobil Chemical Limited	£502,000,000
SWM UK Wind One Limited	£555,629,632	The Body Shop International Limited	£502,000,000
CSL UK Holdings Limited	£555,302,016	Rhodia Holdings Limited	£501,308,992
McLaren Finance PLC	£550,508,992	DLR (No.1) Limited	£500,100,000
London May Fair Hotel Limited	£550,019,968	Pagegroup PLC	£499,812,000
Innotech Advisers Limited	£549,925,120	Hanson Retail Limited	£499,681,984
Edwards Limited	£549,156,992	BP Exploration (Algeria) Limited	£499,201,024
Stock Spirits Group PLC	£548,683,712	HIC Racing (Chiswick) Limited	£499,137,952
Biffa Group Holdings (UK) Limited	£547,592,576	Eaton Electric Limited	£498,177,984
Kimberly - Clark Limited	£547,524,992	Renewi Holdings Limited	£497,993,984
Chubb Fire & Security Limited	£546,145,024	Mars Petcare UK	£497,560,000
Vinci Construction UK Limited	£546,112,000	London Square Developments (Holdings) Limited	£496,519,008
MGT Teesside Limited	£544,942,976	Tato Holdings Limited	£495,609,632
Royal & Sun Alliance Reinsurance Limited	£544,027,008	SmithKline Beecham (Investments) Limited	£495,331,008
Safestore Group Limited	£543,182,976	Towergate Underwriting Group Limited	£494,864,992

Company	Value
Chemring North America Unlimited	£493,990,016
Blue Minerva Limited	£492,627,136
PRA Group (UK) Limited	£492,511,008
Greeneden UK Acquisition Company Limited	£492,469,984
Autonomy Systems Limited	£492,281,472
Harsco (UK) Group Limited	£491,493,920
Waterlogic Group Holdings Limited	£490,826,240
Waterlogic Holdings Limited	£490,823,968
Honeywell Control Systems Limited	£490,540,992
WSH UK & Ireland Limited	£489,639,008
BAM Construct UK Limited	£489,200,000
Iris Software Group Limited	£489,140,992
Spirit Energy Resources Limited	£488,572,992
Dairy Crest France Holdings 1 Limited	£487,660,000
DHL Exel Supply Chain Limited	£487,226,624
First Rate Exchange Services Limited	£486,819,008
First Rate Exchange Services Holdings Limited	£484,660,992
ISS UK Holding Limited	£483,235,008
Hoechst Marion Roussel Limited	£480,816,000
Audiotonix Group Limited	£479,676,288
Kia Motors (UK) Limited	£478,931,008
Essentra International Limited	£478,504,000
Alvis Limited	£476,745,984
Xchanging Holdings Limited	£475,608,000
Smiths Interconnect Group Limited	£474,943,008
Akzo Nobel Coatings (BLD) Limited	£473,483,008
London Square Developments (Ventures) Limited	£473,415,008
Cabot Financial Debt Recovery Services Limited	£473,355,008
London General Insurance Company Limited	£472,912,000
CEB Holdings UK 2 Limited	£472,727,008
BCA Osprey I Limited	£472,600,000
Consort Medical PLC	£472,100,000
Beam Suntory UK Holdings Limited	£470,887,008
Akzo Nobel Limited	£469,012,000
WSH Investments Limited	£468,308,000
Walkers Snack Foods Limited	£467,982,016
Cine-UK Limited	£467,367,008
RB Reigate (UK) Limited	£467,292,000
DS (Holdings) 2 Limited	£467,195,776
McKay Securities P L C	£467,108,000
Welcome Break No. 1 Limited	£466,100,000
Bristow Helicopter Group Limited	£465,792,928
Harris Federation	£465,664,992
Perform Investment Limited	£464,953,984
Smith Kline & French Laboratories Limited	£464,873,984
Solvecorp Limited	£464,835,008
Johnson Controls Investments (UK) Limited	£463,808,288
Civil and Marine Limited	£463,433,984
London Square Limited	£460,803,008
Barloworld UK Limited	£460,524,000
UnumProvident Finance Company Limited	£457,712,992
Wellcome Foundation Limited (The)	£457,700,992
Yattendon Group PLC	£457,383,008
Wyevale Garden Centres Holdings Limited	£455,476,992
Spectris US Holdings Limited	£455,179,008
Virgin Atlantic International Limited	£454,659,008
Hastings Insurance Services Limited	£453,897,984
Hoover Ferguson Group Holdings Limited	£453,896,800
Vodafone (New Zealand) Hedging Limited	£453,859,808
Hoover Ferguson Group Limited	£453,673,824
CSC Computer Sciences EMEA Finance Limited	£452,943,168
Wilhelmsen Lines Car Carriers Ltd.	£452,423,040
Berendsen UK Limited	£451,841,984
O.C.S. Group Limited	£451,606,016
Ipsen Developments Limited	£451,131,008
Appia Europe Limited	£450,569,984
SSCP Spring Topco Limited	£450,452,992
P & O Ferries Limited	£449,163,008
Pinewood Group Limited	£448,764,000
HFG Finance Limited	£448,454,976
Safestore Limited	£447,948,000
Pegasus Life Limited	£447,932,000
Ultra Electronics Limited	£447,919,008
GlaxoSmithKline Export Limited	£447,628,000
Sabre Insurance Company Limited	£447,563,008
BCMV Limited	£446,764,992
AECOM Infrastructure & Environment UK Limited	£446,300,000
HFG Investments Limited	£446,067,808
Tanjong Public Limited Company	£444,819,264
Kimberly-Clark U.K. Operations Limited	£444,174,080
Westcoast Limited	£443,567,008
Vodafone Global Enterprise Limited	£441,131,488
Gallaher Overseas (Holdings) Limited	£440,740,000
Regentrealm Limited	£439,400,000
Shilton Holdco Limited	£439,038,016
NTL Communications Services Limited	£437,619,008
Automobile Association Insurance Services Limited	£436,600,000
Kuehne + Nagel Limited	£436,123,008
Siemens Gamesa Renewable Energy Limited	£435,076,992
Bio Products Laboratory Holdings Limited	£434,364,000
Bacardi U.K. Limited	£433,732,000
Cognita Financing PLC	£433,271,008
Procter & Gamble Product Supply (U.K.) Limited	£432,592,992
M & C New York Finance (UK) Limited	£431,978,080
SAP (UK) Limited	£431,924,000
Northgate Public Services (UK) Limited	£431,332,000
CooperVision Manufacturing Limited	£431,320,000
Saga Services Limited	£430,273,984
Cabot Credit Management Group Limited	£430,044,000
Sovereign Housing Capital PLC	£429,559,008
WDFG UK Holdings Limited	£429,328,000
Abbott Laboratories Limited	£428,572,000
Siemens Pension Funding Limited	£427,636,928
Philips Electronics UK Limited	£427,000,000
WorleyParsons UK Finance Sub Limited	£426,903,008
BAE Systems Land Systems (Finance) Limited	£426,222,016
BAE Systems Global Combat Systems Munitions Ltd	£426,000,000
Oil Spill Response (Capping) Limited	£424,874,656
Qinetiq Group Holdings Limited	£424,500,000
Glory Global Solutions Ltd	£423,939,168
Coventry and Rugby Hospital Company PLC	£423,859,008
Coventry and Rugby Hospital Company Holdings Ltd	£423,775,008
Johnson Controls International Holdings Ltd	£423,506,048
Welcome Break Limited	£423,462,016
Wyevale Garden Centres Capital Limited	£422,868,000
Trellis Investments Limited	£422,860,992
Trellis Finance Limited	£422,680,000
Mars Petcare UK Holdings Limited	£421,537,984
Benson & Hedges Limited	£420,400,000
Kew Green Group Limited	£420,263,904
Syneos Health International Limited	£419,843,520
Future Electronics Limited	£418,320,000
Tiger Midco 2 Limited	£417,625,984
EMC Computer Systems (U.K.) Limited	£417,184,992
Healthcare Support (North Staffs) Limited	£417,032,000
Healthcare Support (North Staffs) Holdings Limited	£417,032,000
Castle Cement Limited	£416,790,016
Vodafone Euro Hedging Two	£416,108,576
Elster Solutions Limited	£415,911,008
Peterborough (Progress Health) Holdings Limited	£415,440,992
Peterborough (Progress Health) PLC	£415,440,992
Janssen-Cilag Limited	£415,416,992
BCA Remarketing Group Limited	£413,350,016
Ericsson Limited	£413,096,992
SLF of Canada UK Limited	£412,174,016
Promon-Logicalis Latin America Limited	£411,554,528
Edwardian Finance Ltd	£411,384,992
Procter & Gamble (Health & Beauty Care) Limited	£411,360,000
Lockheed Martin UK Holdings Limited	£410,401,984
M.P. Evans Group PLC	£409,914,112
Naga UK Topco Limited	£409,176,992
Celltech Group Limited	£409,132,000
Kodak International Finance Limited	£408,733,472
HEL Bidco Ltd	£408,340,000

Company	Amount
Lubricants UK Limited	£408,201,984
BOC Netherlands Holdings Limited	£406,809,984
Franklin UK Midco Limited	£406,509,920
Derby Healthcare PLC	£405,967,008
Derby Healthcare (Holdings) Limited	£405,956,992
Healthcare Support (North Staffs) Finance PLC	£405,620,992
Mapil Midco 1 Limited	£404,497,984
AGCO Finance Limited	£404,260,000
O2 Networks Limited	£403,140,992
WorleyParsons Europe Limited	£401,252,992
O'Rourke Investments Holdings (UK) Limited	£400,808,000
ATG London Limited	£400,655,008
IMO Car Wash Group Limited	£400,265,984
CC 4 (2011) Limited	£400,104,896
Kellogg Brown & Root DH Limited	£399,282,432
HellermannTyton Holdings Limited	£399,104,352
AbbVie Ltd	£398,508,992
Hanson (ER - No 5) Limited	£397,152,000
Prysmian Cables & Systems Limited	£396,783,008
Consort Healthcare (Mid Yorkshire) Limited	£395,601,984
Consort Healthcare (Mid Yorkshire) Holdings Ltd	£395,601,984
A6 Audio Bidco Limited	£395,585,984
Nomad Foods Europe Holdings Limited	£394,835,936
Towers Watson Global 3 Limited	£394,667,456
McCormick International Holdings	£394,406,016
WSH International Investments Limited	£393,848,992
John Wyeth & Brother Limited	£393,776,992
IHC May Fair (Holdings) Limited	£392,679,008
ExxonMobil Gas Marketing Europe Limited	£392,000,000
Central Nottinghamshire Hospitals (Holdings) Ltd	£391,337,984
Central Nottinghamshire Hospitals PLC	£391,337,984
Howard Lloyd & Company,Limited	£390,136,000
Galaxy Group Bidco Limited	£390,119,008
BAE Systems (Overseas Holdings) Limited	£390,096,000
Spirent Communications PLC	£389,905,824
Mobile Broadband Network Limited	£389,560,000
Sanden International (Europe) Limited	£389,180,896
Rentokil Initial UK Ltd	£389,139,008
Schweppes Limited	£389,079,008
NTL Cablecomms Group Limited	£389,001,984
BAE Systems Global Combat Systems Limited	£389,000,000
123-Reg Limited	£388,724,000
First Technology Limited	£388,662,016
Marlin Intermediate Holdings PLC	£388,655,008
Garmin (Europe) Limited	£387,989,344
Consort Healthcare (Mid Yorkshire) Funding PLC	£386,988,992
Preziosa Cruise Limited	£386,967,136
Boing Acquisitions Limited	£386,828,000
Chubb Fire Limited	£385,910,016
Deep Sea Stavanger (UK) Ltd	£385,603,104
Fiat Chrysler Automobiles UK Ltd	£385,438,016
BE Aerospace Thermal and Power Mgmnt Hldgs UK	£385,366,464
Moneybarn No.1 Limited	£384,886,016
Farnborough Limited	£383,839,872
Red Funnel Limited	£383,686,016
Rose Midco Limited	£383,684,992
Brighthouse Limited	£383,449,984
Kerry Holdings (U.K.) Limited	£382,593,792
Forth Health Holdings Limited	£382,000,992
Forth Health Limited	£381,987,008
GlaxoSmithKline Consumer Healthcare (UK) IP Ltd	£381,208,000
Healthcare Support (Newcastle) Limited	£381,011,008
Healthcare Support (Newcastle) Holdings Limited	£381,011,008
Domino's Pizza Group PLC	£380,900,000
Healthcare Support (Newcastle) Finance PLC	£380,844,992
FRC Star Group Holdings Limited	£380,794,272
Johnson Controls Enterprises Ltd	£380,654,016
Rank Group Finance PLC	£379,888,000
Reckitt Benckiser Finance (2005) Limited	£379,395,008
UOP Limited	£379,372,992
Elysium Healthcare Holdings 3 Limited	£377,808,992
John Wiley & Sons Limited	£377,636,992
Mentmore Limited	£376,945,984
Zoom Gas Pipelines Limited	£376,759,008
Deep Sea Atlantic (UK) Ltd	£376,590,624
Endon Europe Power 3 Limited	£376,488,992
Zoom Infrastructure Limited	£375,833,984
Zoom Holding Limited	£375,684,992
BP Mauritania Investments Limited	£374,844,672
Aventis Pharma Limited	£373,788,000
Robinsons Soft Drinks Limited	£371,625,984
Tata Global Beverages Investments Limited	£371,004,000
FIL Investment Services (UK) Limited	£370,270,016
London Square Developments Limited	£370,248,000
Synamedia Limited	£369,984,768
Perform Media Channels Ltd	£369,636,992
Signet Trading Limited	£369,443,008
Expro International Group Limited	£368,718,848
IBM United Kingdom Asset Leasing Limited	£367,753,984
PEAC (UK) Limited	£367,700,000
South East Water (Holdings) Limited	£367,340,000
British Agricultural Services Limited	£367,166,016
Kellogg Brown & Root Group Limited	£366,753,312
Cygnet Health Care Limited	£366,398,016
MNA Finance Limited	£366,308,992
Bandhart Overseas	£364,975,008
Pegasuslife Development Limited	£364,956,992
Naga UK Bidco Limited	£364,713,984
TT Electronics PLC	£364,600,000
Manzana Bidco Limited	£363,640,000
F5 Networks Limited	£363,392,096
Sorbon Homes Limited	£362,632,832
Hitachi Vantara Limited	£362,460,000
Hibu Group Limited	£362,200,000
Kodak Alaris Holdings Limited	£361,712,192
Edwardian Hotel Investments Ltd	£361,648,000
Galliford Try Partnerships Limited	£361,056,000
Perform Media Services Ltd	£360,615,008
BAE Systems (Oman) Limited	£360,497,984
Axios Bidco Limited	£360,417,984
NTL Midlands Limited	£360,168,992
Micro Focus IP Development Limited	£359,788,928
GE Money Servicing Limited	£359,737,984
Carat UK Midco Limited	£359,652,992
Sutton and East Surrey Water PLC	£358,622,016
Tiger Midco 1 Limited	£358,198,016
3M UK Holdings Limited	£358,096,992
Bristow (UK) LLP	£357,026,464
Hurricane GLA Limited	£356,287,296
Becton, Dickinson U.K. Limited	£355,676,000
Newhospitals (St Helens & Knowsley) Finance PLC	£355,201,984
Siemens Mobility Limited	£354,891,008
Alent Finance Limited	£354,185,984
SSE Renewables Walney (UK) Limited	£354,000,000
British Car Auctions Limited	£353,433,984
Fluor International Limited	£353,100,992
BAM Construction Limited	£351,600,000
Archer Daniels Midland (UK) Limited	£351,168,640
FRC Star Group Bidco Limited	£351,048,448
Bayer Public Limited Company	£350,952,992
MMA Holdings UK PLC	£350,336,000
NTL Glasgow Holdings Limited	£350,199,008
Teddington 2 Limited	£350,064,000
Transaction Services Group Limited	£350,052,128
CEB Holdings UK 1 Limited	£349,908,000
Archer Assets UK Limited	£349,323,712
Novartis Grimsby Limited	£348,511,008
Novartis UK Limited	£347,400,000
Suez Recycling and Recovery UK Ltd	£346,992,000
Host Europe Investments Limited	£346,960,000
NPS (Holdings) Limited	£346,600,000
Argon NPS Limited	£346,600,000
BA Cityflyer Limited	£346,233,984
LGC Science Holdings Limited	£345,708,992

Company	Value
Burnt Tree Group Limited	£345,360,000
Deutsche Leasing (UK) Limited	£345,053,664
Ericsson (Holdings) Limited	£344,708,000
Cardif Pinnacle Insurance Holdings PLC	£344,260,000
FCA Dealer Services UK Ltd	£343,659,008
De La Rue Finance Limited	£343,049,984
Fifthgrange Limited	£342,580,992
Welcome Break Holdings Limited	£342,236,992
IHC Overseas (U.K.) Limited	£341,574,016
Mapil Midco 2 Limited	£341,451,008
Toyota Material Handling UK Limited	£340,287,008
WDFG UK Limited	£340,180,000
Theseus No. 1 Limited	£339,864,000
HellermannTyton Group PLC	£339,853,056
Ricardo PLC	£339,700,000
Theseus No. 2 Limited	£339,665,984
Huawei Technologies (UK) Co., Ltd.	£339,543,008
Volvo Car UK Limited	£339,385,984
Xchanging Limited	£339,188,000
Kellogg Brown & Root London Limited	£339,168,064
M & C (CD) Limited	£339,152,800
M & C (CB) Limited	£339,152,800
Welcome Break No. 2 Limited	£339,100,992
Canon (UK) Limited	£337,932,992
Honeywell UK Limited	£337,739,008
Ingersoll-Rand UK Limited	£337,224,000
RWS (Overseas) Limited	£337,112,352
Renewable Energy Systems Limited	£336,766,016
LGC Limited	£336,591,008
Britvic Overseas Limited	£336,556,992
Sally UK Holdings Limited	£334,478,560
Shepherd Neame Limited	£334,227,008
SF Funding Limited	£334,044,992
Harsco Investment Limited	£333,897,984
Fat Face Limited	£333,780,000
Day Lewis PLC	£333,744,992
Accolade Wines Limited	£333,712,000
Caversham Finance Limited	£333,688,000
Nampak Holdings (UK) Limited	£333,298,176
Verint Technology UK Limited	£333,026,240
HP Inc UK Limited	£332,872,000
Smiths Medical International Limited	£332,592,000
Pinnacle Insurance PLC	£332,326,016
Just Retirement (Holdings) Limited	£332,139,008
JCHAC UK Holdco Limited	£331,825,984
United Biscuits BondCo Limited	£331,800,000
Sonet Scholl Overseas Investments Limited	£331,776,000
Reckitt Benckiser USA Finance (No.2) Limited	£330,468,000
RWS Group Limited	£330,401,344
WorleyParsons UK Finance Sub No. 2 Ltd	£330,134,528
Mondelez UK Finance Company Limited	£329,451,520
De La Rue PLC	£328,600,000
Newhospitals (St Helens and Knowsley) Limited	£327,828,992
Newhospitals (St Helens and Knowsley) Holdings Ltd	£327,828,992
Volution Group PLC	£326,948,992
Old ML Limited	£325,898,144
Richard Costain Limited	£325,867,616
Pinewood-Shepperton Studios Limited	£325,759,008
Augustus 1 Limited	£325,528,992
Inter Pipeline Europe Limited	£325,313,984
Atkins Investments UK Limited	£325,300,000
Thales Electronics Limited	£325,000,000
Highway Management M80 Investment Limited	£324,671,008
INEOS FPS Limited	£324,302,016
BAM Nuttall Limited	£324,135,008
Anduff Car Wash Limited	£324,005,056
Merseyside Energy Recovery Holdings Ltd	£323,318,016
Merseyside Energy Recovery Ltd	£323,318,016
Iris Software Limited	£323,285,568
GDC Holding Limited	£322,968,000
Reckitt & Colman (Overseas) Limited	£322,519,008
Rolls-Royce Motor Cars Limited	£322,323,008
Scholl Limited	£322,296,992
BP Exploration Angola (Kwanza Benguela) Limited	£321,866,336
Avis Budget UK Limited	£321,808,000
Highway Management (Scotland) Limited	£321,515,008
Highway Management (Scotland) Holding Limited	£321,515,008
Welcome Break Holdings (1) Limited	£321,244,992
Westbury Street Limited	£320,564,000
Ferrybridge MFE Limited	£320,400,000
J Wiley Limited	£320,128,000
NATS Limited	£320,100,000
LG Electronics U.K. Ltd	£319,664,992
Nice Systems US Finance Limited	£319,611,296
Toshiba of Europe Limited	£318,844,928
Cabot Financial Limited	£317,705,984
ACI Worldwide (EMEA) Limited	£316,646,016
Harman Automotive UK Limited	£316,307,360
CF Corporate Finance Limited	£316,279,008
Audley Group Limited	£315,832,992
Nexen Petroleum U.K. Holdings Limited	£315,630,880
Travelopia Holdings Limited	£315,241,472
Millipore UK Holdings LLP	£314,942,016
Skanska Construction Holdings UK Limited	£314,691,008
Tesla Motors Limited	£314,548,416
Marchwood Power Limited	£314,396,000
Cullum Capital Ventures Limited	£314,381,312
Superlift UK Limited	£314,275,200
Oracle Corporation UK Holdings Limited	£313,872,992
DHL International (UK) Limited	£313,620,992
Gannett International Finance LLP	£313,151,264
Lake Bridge International PLC	£312,154,112
Urenco Enrichment Company Limited	£312,150,784
Vale of Aylesbury Housing Trust Limited	£310,596,000
Laing O'Rourke Holdings Limited	£310,592,000
Envision Pharma Group Limited	£310,448,224
Discoverie Group PLC	£310,400,000
WP Safety-Kleen Limited	£310,040,000
McCormick Europe Limited	£309,884,000
CEB Global Holdings Limited	£309,841,984
Xerox Finance Limited	£309,790,016
Lenovo Technology (United Kingdom) Limited	£309,658,880
Chiltern International Holdings Limited	£308,764,000
Virgin Media Business Limited	£308,745,984
LexisNexis Risk Solutions UK Limited	£308,595,072
Procter & Gamble Limited	£307,380,992
Travelport Finance Limited	£307,008,992
Signet UK Finance PLC	£306,881,696
BP Chemicals Investments Limited	£306,761,504
Kofax Holdings International Limited	£306,429,856
Micron Europe Limited	£306,213,344
Whatman Limited	£305,492,992
DSTI Holdings Limited	£305,128,992
ESNT International Limited	£304,440,000
Westbury Street Holdings Limited	£304,436,000
Walkers Snacks Limited	£304,375,008
BTC Pipeline Holding Company Limited	£304,127,968
Novartis Pharmaceuticals UK Limited	£303,975,008
Barloworld Equipment UK Limited	£303,657,440
Galaxy Holdco 1 Ltd	£303,035,488
Galaxy Holdco 2 Ltd	£303,035,488
Optivo Finance PLC	£302,900,000
Bio Products Laboratory Limited	£302,643,008
Dawsongroup Truck and Trailer Limited	£302,532,992
Big Yellow Self Storage Company A Limited	£301,947,008
Killinchy Aerospace Holdings Limited	£301,856,000
Host Europe Limited	£301,600,992
Reckitt Benckiser Healthcare International Limited	£301,283,008
Endon Europe Power 1 Limited	£301,216,992
Renault U.K. Limited	£300,583,008
Cargill Investments	£300,479,424
Spirit Energy Southern North Sea Limited	£300,243,456
DLR (No.2) Limited	£300,004,992
Restore PLC	£300,000,000

Company	Value	Company	Value
ST & H Limited	£299,948,000	Merial Limited	£272,727,264
Inland Homes PLC	£299,600,000	Virgin Holidays Limited	£272,508,000
Keystone Investment Trust PLC	£299,432,992	Spirit Europe Limited	£271,979,104
Chichester Diocesan Fund and Board of Finance	£299,036,992	Silver Acquisition Co Limited	£271,498,624
Prysmian UK Group Limited	£298,881,984	ESP Utilities Group Limited	£271,476,000
Pic Fyfield Limited	£298,352,000	Lockheed Martin UK Limited	£271,347,008
Claas Financial Services Limited	£298,054,016	Six Continents Investments Limited	£271,191,008
Kew Green Hotels Limited	£297,879,168	NATS (Services) Limited	£270,900,000
Martin-Brower UK Ltd	£297,467,008	DHL Global Forwarding (UK) Limited	£270,824,000
New Terex Holdings UK Limited	£296,780,000	Henkel Limited	£270,438,016
Johnson Controls China Investment (UK) Limited	£295,674,848	Evonik Speciality Organics Limited	£270,403,136
Robinsons (Finance) No.2 Limited	£295,481,984	BNK (UK) Limited	£269,637,024
Northgate Information Solutions Limited	£295,300,000	St William Homes LLP	£269,284,000
Softcat PLC	£294,235,008	Parker Hannifin 2007 LLP	£268,478,016
Audley Court Limited	£292,196,992	Goodwood Estate Company Limited (The)	£268,383,264
Bristol-Myers Squibb Holdings 2002 Limited	£291,864,992	International Car Wash Group Financing PLC	£268,332,992
GDC Group Limited	£291,771,008	Dairy Crest (Services) Limited	£268,000,992
Orthofix Limited	£291,487,008	WP Midco2 Limited	£267,900,000
Fidelity Asian Values PLC	£291,380,992	Big Yellow Self Storage Company M Limited	£267,835,008
INEOS Silicas Holdings Limited	£290,558,016	Annes Gate Property PLC	£267,806,000
Verus Petroleum (UKCS) Limited	£290,048,992	AGP Holdings (1) Limited	£267,806,000
Yell Limited	£290,008,992	The Innovation Group Limited	£267,650,000
The Vitec Group PLC.	£289,700,000	General Cable Programming Limited	£267,413,440
The Pirbright Institute	£289,688,000	Eaton Holding Limited	£267,275,008
BCA Trading Limited	£289,598,016	Bluecastle Enterprises Limited	£267,046,032
Alent New Finance (UK) Limited	£289,468,992	Bellerbys Educational Services Limited	£266,564,000
Bristow Helicopters Limited	£289,103,136	Parker Hannifin (GB) Limited	£266,548,992
Fatface Group Borrowings Limited	£289,091,008	Alligent Biopharm Consulting (Europe) Limited	£266,205,456
Glory Global Solutions (International) Limited	£288,607,232	Invesco International Holdings Limited	£265,755,008
Johnson Controls Holding UK Ltd	£288,126,272	Store Property Investments Limited	£265,173,728
Syneos Health IVH UK Limited	£287,761,664	ICI Chemicals & Polymers Limited	£265,000,000
DHL Air Limited	£287,357,024	Fizzy Enterprises LLP	£264,131,008
Sorbon Investments Limited	£287,305,344	Filtrona Limited	£263,876,000
Phivco UK II Limited	£287,228,992	Seqirus Vaccines Limited	£263,800,000
Johnson Controls Air Conditioning (UK) Limited	£287,173,056	Dairy Crest France Holdings 2 Limited	£262,887,008
BCA Osprey II Limited	£286,600,000	Newsquest Media Group Limited	£262,886,000
State Oil Limited	£286,220,000	Otsuka Pharmaceutical Europe Ltd.	£262,469,072
Avis Budget Services Limited	£286,212,992	GE Money Home Finance Limited	£262,042,608
Sopra Steria Services Limited	£286,088,000	Johnson Controls Air Conditioning Investments UK	£261,494,864
Inter Terminals Limited	£285,651,008	Alere as Holdings Limited	£261,367,008
Newbury Investments (UK) Limited	£285,363,008	Secure Meters (UK) Limited	£260,913,168
DSTI Group LLP	£284,953,984	Qinetiq Holdings Limited	£260,900,000
Gym Offshore One Limited	£284,949,696	MMO2 Limited	£260,700,000
Fatface Group Parent Limited	£284,577,984	Vitec Investments Limited	£260,059,008
SDL PLC	£283,600,000	Cape Intermediate Holdings Limited	£260,000,000
Hertz (U.K.) Limited	£282,980,992	Select Plant Hire Company Limited	£259,896,992
Store Property Holdings Limited	£281,789,408	HCL Technologies UK Limited	£259,556,000
HRG Debtco Limited	£281,552,192	RPR (US) Limited	£258,583,008
British Gas New Heating Limited	£281,048,992	Mapil Bidco Limited	£258,519,008
WP Midco1 Limited	£280,068,992	Genesis Specialist Care UK Limited	£257,914,624
Advanced Computer Software Group Limited	£279,764,000	Verint WS Holdings Limited	£257,842,000
The Kemnal Academies Trust	£279,572,992	Haymarket Media Group Ltd.	£256,752,000
St James Holdings Limited	£279,559,008	BAE Systems (Property Investments) Limited	£256,627,008
Amersham Biosciences	£278,908,224	ViiV Healthcare UK (No.4) Limited	£256,428,992
Esure Finance Limited	£278,740,992	Pfizer Consumer Healthcare Limited	£256,190,000
Hystead Limited	£278,608,736	Cornwall Energy Recovery Ltd	£255,950,000
Syneos Health UK Limited	£278,504,672	Cornwall Energy Recovery Holdings Ltd	£255,950,000
Birds Eye Limited	£278,430,016	BCA Group Europe Limited	£255,940,000
Bristol-Myers Squibb Pharmaceuticals Limited	£276,734,016	F M Conway Limited	£255,916,480
Mothercare PLC.	£276,700,000	Flight Centre (UK) Limited	£255,576,992
S.H.B. Hire Limited	£276,442,112	Kodak Limited	£255,500,000
Piramal Critical Care Limited	£276,387,680	Brighthouse Holdings Limited	£254,842,000
Almus Pharmaceuticals Limited	£275,978,528	British American Tobacco UK Limited	£254,247,008
Riposte Limited	£275,720,992	Spirent Investment Limited	£254,237,296
BCA Holdings Limited	£275,256,992	Medispeed	£253,904,288
Whatman International Limited	£274,862,016	Air BP Limited	£252,219,584
CC 2 (2011) Limited	£274,811,712	Majestic Wine PLC	£251,967,008
SSE Contracting Limited	£274,200,000	Procter & Gamble UK Group Holdings Limited	£251,772,000
Ocean Overseas Holdings Limited	£273,966,016	William Grant & Sons Brands Limited	£251,652,000
McLaren Services Limited	£273,292,000	Saipem Limited	£251,528,448
M.P.Evans & Co Limited	£273,184,192	Storm UK Holdco Limited	£251,430,000
Rose Holdco Limited	£273,116,992	Pinewood Finco PLC	£250,472,000

Company	Value
Abbott (UK) Holdings Limited	£250,420,000
Pulsant Group Holdings Limited	£250,235,008
Specsavers UK Holdings Limited	£249,955,008
Seqirus UK Limited	£249,937,088
Coty Brands Group Limited	£249,650,000
Linden Germany B Limited	£249,152,752
Leumi ABL Limited	£248,936,992
Copthorne Hotel Holdings Limited	£248,588,000
Shimtech Industries Holdco2 Limited	£248,446,000
PandoraExpress 2 Limited	£248,162,000
Ingram Micro (UK) Limited	£247,646,000
GPG (UK) Holdings Limited	£247,484,992
Subsea 7 International Contracting Limited	£247,003,392
Novar ED & S Limited	£246,922,000
Stena Line Ports Limited	£246,896,000
PandoraExpress 4 Limited	£246,580,000
PGA European Tour	£246,515,536
Gyron Internet Limited	£246,318,000
JCDecaux UK Limited	£246,292,000
Aesica Pharmaceuticals Limited	£246,000,000
CALA 1 Limited	£245,650,768
Esure Group PLC	£245,200,000
Honeywell Analytics Limited	£244,958,000
Portsmouth Water Limited	£244,846,000
PandoraExpress 3 Limited	£244,707,008
Convergence Pharmaceuticals Limited	£244,148,848
JRL Group Holdings Limited	£244,142,128
BP Exploration Libya Limited	£244,057,344
Q Squared Solutions Holdings Limited	£243,836,000
Storeshield Limited	£243,415,008
Xafinity Consulting (Reading) Limited	£243,382,000
Tech Data as UK Limited	£243,294,000
Black & Decker International Finance (UK) Limited	£243,247,456
Cordant Group PLC	£242,836,992
Croudace Homes Group Limited	£242,700,992
CooperSurgical Holdings Limited	£242,641,264
PKA WLWF Holding (UK) Limited	£242,544,000
BP Aromatics Limited	£242,243,344
CFCPP LLP	£241,430,592
Tata Global Beverages GB Limited	£241,331,008
Akzo Nobel Holdings Limited	£240,726,000
Allergan Holdings Limited	£239,548,000
Gist Limited	£239,378,000
UPS (UK Holding) Limited	£239,067,920
Photo - Me International P L C	£238,908,992
Edwardian New Finance Limited	£238,123,008
Hamsard 3352 Limited	£237,866,800
United Technologies Finance (U.K.) Limited	£237,822,000
West London Energy Recovery Holdings Ltd	£237,766,000
West London Energy Recovery Ltd	£237,766,000
Invesco Asia Trust PLC	£237,240,000
Esure Holdings Limited	£237,040,992
Rackspace Limited	£236,999,472
Reed Exhibitions Limited	£236,997,920
Pulsant Parent Limited	£236,727,008
Invesco Asset Management Limited	£235,982,000
Kronos Worldwide Limited	£235,976,384
BAE Systems Marine (Holdings) Limited	£235,434,000
Hovis Limited	£234,578,000
Procter & Gamble Technical Centres Limited	£234,520,000
Aura Finance Limited	£234,196,032
Southern Water Capital Limited	£233,700,000
Brighthouse Group Limited	£233,292,000
Givaudan UK Limited	£233,268,000
Longsand Limited	£233,113,728
Northgate UK Holdings 2 Limited	£232,900,000
Afton Chemical Limited	£232,878,000
People Against Dirty Holdings Limited	£232,747,920
Makita International Europe Limited	£232,562,000
Computer Associates Holding Limited	£232,235,008
Mizzen Midco Limited	£232,080,992
Baxterstorey Limited	£232,078,000
Northgate UK Holdings 3 Limited	£232,000,000
Northgate UK Holdings 1 Limited	£232,000,000
Wiggle Limited	£231,918,000
Johnson Controls Metal Components Birmingham Ltd	£231,720,992
RWS Holdings PLC	£231,544,000
Millennium & Copthorne (Jersey Holdings) Limited	£231,444,992
Avis Europe Overseas Limited	£231,382,000
Mothercare UK Limited	£231,000,000
Tim Bidco 1 Limited	£230,316,992
BAE Systems (Dynamics) Limited	£230,008,992
Tim Holdco Limited	£229,859,008
Amoco (Fiddich) Limited	£229,542,288
JRL Group Limited	£229,338,288
Charles River Laboratories Holdings Limited	£229,232,992
Mondays (Topco) Limited	£228,910,000
Radian Capital PLC	£228,728,992
Currie Motors Limited	£228,563,008
Arca Shipping Limited	£228,000,000
Sinclair Gardens Investments (Kensington) Limited	£227,857,984
Tim Midco Limited	£227,807,008
Virgin Media Mobile Finance Limited	£227,052,000
Adda Hotels	£226,913,728
Novar (Stelrad) Limited	£226,738,000
Stiefel Consumer Healthcare (UK) Limited	£226,192,000
Fatface Group Limited	£224,748,992
Saxon Weald Capital PLC	£224,572,000
Fidelity Japan Trust PLC	£224,475,008
UOP International Holdings Limited	£224,458,000
WL One Holdco Limited	£224,458,000
WP SK Limited	£224,239,008
Noon Products Limited	£224,222,848
Paragon Treasury PLC	£224,140,000
Chep UK Limited	£223,976,000
The British Car Auction Group Limited	£223,723,008
Safestore Properties Limited	£223,668,992
LGC Science Group Limited	£223,668,992
Arqiva Smart Metering Limited	£223,186,000
HH Global Group Limited	£223,102,000
E.S. Pipelines Limited	£223,075,008
Tubifoam Limited	£222,840,992
TT Electronics Group Holdings Limited	£222,830,000
Steria UK Corporate Limited	£222,722,000
Wednesdays (Bidco) Limited	£222,330,000
Accolade Wines Holdings Europe Limited	£222,027,008
Linden Germany A Limited	£221,846,352
Biocompatibles UK Limited	£221,192,992
Citysprint (UK) Holdings Limited	£220,903,552
Hovis Holdings Limited	£220,691,008
W.E.Black Limited	£220,541,120
Suzuki GB PLC	£220,314,000
Manpower UK Limited	£220,271,008
Porsche Cars Great Britain Limited	£220,220,992
Mabey Holdings Limited	£219,060,992
Newsquest Capital Limited	£219,000,000
Nice Systems UK Finance Limited	£218,074,064
QA Limited	£217,856,032
Alent Investments Limited	£217,808,000
Dnata Aviation Services Limited	£217,536,000
Tradebe Environmental Services Limited	£217,479,008
Krispy Kreme Holding UK Ltd	£217,436,000
Millennium Hotels London Limited	£217,300,000
Glory Global Solutions (Holdings) Limited	£217,207,456
St Mary's Football Group Limited	£216,800,000
McGraw-Hill Global Education UK Holdco Limited	£216,799,120
Stock Spirits (UK) Limited	£216,776,992
SK Hynix UK Limited	£216,451,216
MK International Limited	£216,360,000
Sonet Investments Limited	£216,330,000
Apogee Group Limited	£216,275,008
BP Alternative Energy Investments Limited	£216,051,520
Helsinki Bidco Limited	£215,931,008
International Paint Limited	£215,400,000

Company	Turnover
Zenimax Europe Limited	£215,146,592
Pulsant Acquisitions Limited	£215,129,360
Macmillan Publishers International Limited	£215,110,000
Atkins International Holdings Limited	£214,945,408
McGrove Developments Limited	£214,795,008
Atlantic 2/3 UK Holdings Limited	£214,789,936
Towry Finance Company Limited	£214,524,992
Kenwood Limited	£213,496,000
Shanly Homes Limited	£213,357,648
D & B Group Holdings (UK)	£213,040,992
British Airways Holidays Limited	£212,999,008
Cabot Financial (Europe) Limited	£212,895,008
Medtronic Limited	£212,692,992
Iris Holdings Limited	£212,590,912
Hotel Inter-Continental London Limited	£212,570,000
Continental U.K. Group Holdings Limited	£212,311,008
Rhodia Limited	£211,896,000
First Technology (2002) Limited	£211,855,392
Windsor Television Limited	£211,638,000
Glory Global Solutions (Topco) Limited	£211,610,576
P & O North Sea Ferries Limited	£211,534,000
Porthaven Properties Limited	£211,394,768
McNeil Healthcare (UK) Limited	£210,890,000
Hexagon Positioning Intelligence Limited	£210,702,000
Honeywell Normalair-Garrett (Holdings) Limited	£210,480,000
Grenke Leasing Limited	£209,893,136
Cygnet Propco Limited	£209,755,008
MDL Marinas Group Limited	£209,352,992
Britair Holdings Limited	£209,104,992
Global Draw Limited	£208,888,000
Roche Diagnostics Limited	£208,670,000
Kone Public Limited Company	£208,575,008
Corus Hotels Limited	£208,328,000
Croudace Homes Limited	£207,668,000
QA-IQ Group Limited	£207,454,352
Bristow Helicopters (International) Limited	£207,360,112
Solvay Solutions UK Limited	£207,010,000
Finance Ireland Limited	£206,919,440
Tech Data UK Resources Limited	£206,429,984
Interserve Finance (Switzerland) Holdings Limited	£205,938,000
Treasury Wine Estates EMEA Limited	£205,760,000
Perform Group Financing PLC	£205,448,000
Petco Trading (UK) Limited	£205,126,992
Costco Limited	£205,079,008
Sanofi-Synthelabo UK Limited	£204,998,000
Edwardian Pastoria Hotels Ltd	£204,695,008
Atlas Copco UK Holdings Limited	£204,647,008
Worthing Homes Limited	£204,392,992
Cargill UK Finance Limited	£204,367,008
Johnson & Johnson Limited	£204,111,008
Sondex Limited	£203,868,000
BPHA Finance PLC	£203,838,336
Armatire Limited	£203,647,488
HTC Europe Co. Ltd	£203,483,888
INEOS Sales (UK) Limited	£203,429,552
Menzies Group Holdings Limited	£203,200,000
Cineworld Cinemas Holdings Limited	£202,770,000
Skanska Rashleigh Weatherfoil Limited	£202,738,000
BSH Home Appliances Limited	£202,705,984
Linde Holdings Limited	£202,627,008
DHL Aviation (UK) Limited	£202,607,008
Sharp Electronics (Europe) Limited	£202,510,208
Apogee Corporation Limited	£202,495,008
South Downs Capital Limited	£202,456,992
Avis Investment Services Limited	£202,434,000
GlaxoSmithKline Holdings (One) Limited	£202,339,008
University of Winchester	£202,306,000
Nextpharma UK Topco Limited	£202,245,184
CGG Services (UK) Limited	£202,191,760
Sound Energy PLC	£202,152,000
Lockheed Martin Helicopter Company Ltd	£202,123,808
Eskaylab Limited	£201,900,000
Nestle Purina Petcare (U.K.) Limited	£201,740,000
The Tower, One St George Wharf Limited	£201,730,000
McGraw-Hill Global Education UK Holdco II Limited	£201,636,832
Bottomline Technologies Limited	£201,402,720
Ricardo UK Limited	£201,140,992
Britax Childcare Holdings Limited	£201,032,992
Glasgow Learning Quarter Limited	£200,922,960
Feilo Sylvania Europe Limited	£200,551,376
Volution Ventilation Group Limited	£200,487,008
Home Retail Group (Finance) LLP	£200,362,000
Axon Group Limited	£199,728,000
Game Digital PLC	£199,400,000
Gym Renewables One Limited	£199,106,000
Bristow Technical Services Limited	£199,003,488
ISS Mediclean Limited	£198,944,992
KBR (U.K.) Investments Limited	£198,719,136
I.P. Clarke & Co. Limited	£198,687,008
UK Waste Management Limited	£198,639,008
Connacht SPV 1 Limited	£198,085,408
Zellis UK Limited	£198,071,008
WJH Holdings Limited	£198,068,720
XPS Pensions Group PLC	£198,036,992
Glasgow Learning Quarter (Holdings) Limited	£198,024,576
Specsavers Optical Superstores Limited	£197,983,008
Allianz Management Services Limited	£197,943,008
Reckitt Benckiser Healthcare Central & Eastern Europe	£197,468,992
Black & Decker International Finance Holdings UK Ltd	£197,285,120
Avis Finance Company (No.2) Limited	£197,228,000
Hyster-Yale UK Limited	£197,120,784
Canterbury Christ Church University	£197,060,992
Leigh Academies Trust	£196,876,000
Delta Limited	£196,550,000
BH (City Forum) Limited	£196,340,000
RATP DEV UK Ltd	£195,572,992
Accesso Technology Group PLC	£195,532,960
Audio UK 2 Limited	£195,316,000
Audio UK 3 Limited	£195,316,000
CH & Co Catering Group (Holdings) Limited	£195,026,000
CH & Co Catering Group Limited	£195,007,008
Shurgard UK Limited	£194,987,392
Linde Material Handling (UK) Limited	£194,840,992
Shimtech Industries Group Limited	£194,229,792
Harwoods Limited	£194,096,800
JEG Acquisition Company Limited	£193,891,008
Zennor Petroleum Limited	£193,829,936
Bidcorp (UK) Limited	£193,600,000
Ascension Healthcare PLC	£193,266,000
A J Walter Aviation Limited	£192,894,608
Hendy Automotive Limited	£192,752,992
British Gas Finance Limited	£192,504,000
CAS Healthcare Properties Limited	£192,394,000
Afton Chemical UK Holdings Limited	£192,381,968
AB InBev International Brands Limited	£192,296,464
Citysprint (UK) Bidco Limited	£192,281,952
Abbott (UK) Finance Limited	£192,264,000
Nuvias Group Limited	£191,974,000
Egger (UK) Limited	£191,336,000
INS-Sure Services Limited	£191,274,000
Allianz Properties Limited	£191,128,000
BAE Systems (MEH) Limited	£191,100,624
Tailwind Mistral Ltd	£190,924,192
Intervet UK Limited	£190,439,008
Aura Holdings (Newcastle) Limited	£190,340,992
Celgene Limited	£190,243,632
Grosvenor Casinos (GC) Limited	£190,210,000
Gym Offshore Two Limited	£190,189,776
Servier IP UK Limited	£189,847,904
GL Education Group Limited	£189,812,000
Sir Robert McAlpine Enterprises Limited	£189,664,992
Grosvenor Casinos Limited	£189,588,992
Envision Pharma Finco Limited	£189,551,776
Tata Global Beverages Holdings Limited	£189,515,008

Company	Value
Siemens Transmission and Distribution Limited	£189,503,008
Dun & Bradstreet Limited	£189,356,992
Trellis Holdco Limited	£189,350,000
CCV Risk Solutions Limited	£189,132,992
JCHAC India Holdco Limited	£189,077,968
Pyxis Investment Strategies LLP	£188,715,376
Western United Investment Company Limited	£188,700,000
Trifast PLC	£188,656,000
Giffgaff Limited	£188,624,000
Expro Benelux Limited	£188,439,776
Sanofi Pasteur Holding Limited	£188,395,008
Marina Developments Limited	£188,224,992
GLF Schools	£188,108,000
Prax Petroleum Limited	£188,040,848
INEOS Treasury (UK) Limited	£187,967,920
Ascot Authority (Holdings) Limited	£187,751,008
TP-Link UK Limited	£187,512,992
Eurovia UK Limited	£187,143,040
Galliford Try Homes Limited	£186,766,000
Sogea Holdings (UK) Limited	£186,660,992
Transform Schools (Knowsley) Holdings Limited	£186,576,992
Transform Schools (Knowsley) Limited	£186,576,992
Haltermann Carless UK Limited	£186,391,008
Espalier Ventures Limited	£186,300,000
Transform Schools (North Lanarkshire) Limited	£185,952,992
Transform Schools (North Lanarkshire) Holdings Ltd	£185,952,992
NTL Manchester Cablevision Holding Company	£185,863,008
Tuskerdirect Limited	£185,849,040
BRF Invicta Limited	£185,527,008
Novell UK Software Limited	£185,444,000
Helsinki Topco Limited	£185,426,000
VM Transfers (No 5) Limited	£185,422,000
Infinity SDC Limited	£185,052,992
Southampton Football Club Limited	£184,922,000
Silicon Storage Technology Ltd	£184,910,112
The National Museum of The Royal Navy	£184,765,936
Brighton & Hove Albion Holdings Limited	£184,711,760
G4S Secure Solutions (UK) Limited	£184,500,992
Genesis Specialist Care Holding UK Limited	£184,424,096
H Young Holdings Public Limited Company	£184,108,000
Lakefield Holdings Limited	£184,108,000
Britvic Brands LLP	£184,016,000
Premier Marinas Holdings Limited	£183,960,992
Galvani Bioelectronics Limited	£183,852,000
Q Squared Solutions Limited	£183,684,000
The Gym Group PLC	£183,447,008
Tradebe Management Limited	£183,418,000
Expro North Sea Limited	£183,028,976
Senior Finance Four Limited	£183,024,992
Anixter Limited	£182,810,000
Sir Robert McAlpine Capital Ventures Limited	£182,715,392
Edwardian Investments Ltd	£182,242,000
Bourne Holidays Limited	£181,990,000
Invesco Perpetual UK Smaller Co's Investment Trust	£181,842,000
Kellogg Brown & Root Overseas Operations Ltd	£181,719,616
Megger Group Limited	£181,630,432
Mallinckrodt Enterprises UK Limited	£181,503,984
Mushi UK Holdings Limited	£181,503,984
Eastbury Park Limited	£181,107,008
Eastbury Park (Holdings) Limited	£181,107,008
Invesco Income Growth Trust PLC	£180,864,000
Utilita Group Limited	£180,798,000
Johnson & Johnson UK Treasury Company Limited	£180,791,296
Lake International Ltd	£180,703,904
NTL Victoria Limited	£180,482,000
The Marine Insurance Company Limited	£180,386,000
Morgan Finance Management Limited	£180,232,992
LSQ Holdco 3 Limited	£179,984,000
WL One Bidco Limited	£179,403,008
TCFG Holdings Limited	£179,362,000
Elysium Healthcare No. 2 Limited	£179,348,992
Beko PLC	£179,327,008

Company	Value
DHL Services Limited	£179,232,000
Invesco Pacific Group Limited	£179,208,816
Reckitt Benckiser Finance Company Limited	£179,144,000
Ageas Retail Limited	£178,812,000
SQIB Limited	£178,522,848
Novar Systems Limited	£178,494,000
Resource Recovery Solutions (Derbyshire) Ltd	£177,975,008
Sun Valley Foods Limited	£177,972,000
LPSO Limited	£177,784,000
Keltbray Group (Holdings) Limited	£177,407,840
The Bidvest Group (UK) Limited	£176,969,360
First Central Insurance Management Limited	£176,763,008
Bandhart	£176,762,000
BP Exploration North Africa Limited	£176,713,184
Cubic Transportation Systems Limited	£176,706,000
Keltbray Group Limited	£176,649,984
Suez Recycling and Recovery Suffolk Ltd	£176,440,992
Hargreaves Property Holdings Limited	£176,436,976
WP SK Midco Limited	£176,288,992
Southern Water (NR) Holdings Limited	£176,100,000
Virgin Travel Group Limited	£176,088,992
ESNT Holdings (No.1) Limited	£175,962,000
Sorbon Estates Limited	£175,584,336
Sovereign Advances Limited	£175,556,992
CPRT LLP	£175,546,000
Transform Schools (North Lanarkshire) Funding PLC	£175,468,992
Everyday Lending Limited	£175,402,000
Mizzen Bidco Limited	£175,308,992
A A Homes and Housing Ltd	£175,096,832
Berkeley (SQP) Limited	£174,989,664
Berkeley Homes (Southall) Limited	£174,928,992
Porthaven Properties No 2 Limited	£174,895,712
Cognita Funding 1 Limited	£174,806,000
Motorline Holdings Limited	£174,670,896
Idox PLC	£174,570,000
Hastings Water (UK) Limited	£173,603,008
Wilson Connolly Holdings Limited	£173,555,008
IQVIA RDS Holdings	£173,538,000
Micheldever Tyre Services Limited	£173,140,000
The Compleat Food Group Limited	£173,102,000
Bidvest Services Group (UK) Limited	£172,964,608
Accolade Wines Europe No. 2 Limited	£172,960,000
Westerngeco Limited	£172,503,008
Inesa UK Limited	£172,465,488
Connacht SPV 3 Limited	£172,441,104
Connacht SPV 2 Limited	£172,406,080
Aramark Japan Holdings Limited	£172,375,296
Housing Solutions Capital PLC	£172,371,008
Platinum Topco Limited	£171,971,168
Axiom Education (Edinburgh) Limited	£171,948,992
Wightlink Limited	£171,871,008
Tiger Group Limited	£171,698,000
By Chelmer (Holdings) Limited	£171,388,992
By Chelmer PLC	£171,388,992
Blackstown Holdings Limited	£170,688,736
Hudson Energy Supply UK Limited	£170,670,000
IG Design Group PLC	£170,628,000
Britvic International Investments Limited	£170,228,000
Alere UK Holdings Limited	£170,150,000
Invesco Perpetual Select Trust PLC	£170,064,000
Ichnaea UK Bidco Limited	£170,022,000
Interserve Investments Limited	£170,008,992
Logoplaste UK Parent Limited	£169,986,128
Stena Line (UK) Limited	£169,800,000
Trend Control Systems Limited	£169,760,000
G4S Cash Solutions (UK) Limited	£169,738,000
Givaudan Holdings UK Limited	£169,695,008
Marlin Portfolio Holdings Limited	£169,674,000
Envision Pharma Bidco Limited	£169,534,848
Inland Limited	£169,394,176
Arora T5 Holdings Limited	£169,359,520
Gilead Sciences Europe Ltd.	£169,275,008

Company	Value
Watford Association Football Club Limited (The)	£168,852,896
Vestey Holdings Limited	£168,658,000
Butlins Skyline Limited	£168,567,008
Jungheinrich Lift Truck Finance Limited	£168,527,008
Manpower Public Limited Company	£168,376,000
Anesco Acquisitionco Limited	£168,339,216
Honeywell Limited	£168,220,000
SC Leisure Group Limited	£168,168,992
Del Monte Foods International Limited	£167,848,000
Advanced Business Software and Solutions Limited	£167,384,992
The Leaders Romans Midco 2 Limited	£167,336,256
TSG Holdings (UK) Limited	£166,970,592
TAG Farnborough (Holdings) Limited	£166,773,168
J.T.D. Investments Limited	£166,517,840
Bewley Homes PLC	£166,478,960
The Leaders Romans Group Limited	£166,117,984
Kidde Products Limited	£166,066,000
Advanced Elastomer Systems Limited	£165,834,000
Hydac Limited	£165,738,576
Financial Administration Services Limited	£165,559,008
Fulham Football Leisure Limited	£165,480,000
Cougar Holdco London Limited	£165,476,992
Mizzen Mezzco 2 Limited	£165,444,000
RIF Holdings Limited	£165,064,064
JCHAC Europe Finco Limited	£164,991,344
Chiltern International Limited	£164,932,992
The Walsall Hospital Company (Holdings) Limited	£164,771,008
The Walsall Hospital Company PLC	£164,771,008
LGC Investments Limited	£164,500,992
Safety-Kleen U.K. Limited	£164,420,000
Keysight Technologies UK Limited	£164,348,992
Vitec Production Solutions Limited	£164,204,000
Emperor 3 Limited	£163,971,008
The Gym Group Midco1 Limited	£163,891,104
The Gym Group Midco2 Limited	£163,884,160
ADT (UK) Limited	£163,707,008
Cyxtera Technology UK Limited	£163,550,000
Graham Care (YB) Limited	£163,476,544
Endeavour SCH Holdings Limited	£163,332,000
Endeavour SCH PLC	£163,332,000
The Ambassador Entertainment Group Limited	£163,067,008
Game Retail Limited	£162,883,008
Darty Limited	£162,811,552
LGC Whirlwind Limited	£162,715,008
Gym Renewables Limited	£162,695,008
Hand Picked Hotels Limited	£162,676,064
IHS Markit Global Funding Limited	£162,559,296
Dun & Bradstreet Investments Limited	£162,498,000
Tata Global Beverages Capital Limited	£162,334,000
Vitec Group Holdings Limited	£162,190,000
NHS Professionals Limited	£162,048,992
Burroughs Wellcome International Limited	£162,024,000
Martin-Baker Aircraft Company Limited	£161,972,992
On Semiconductor Limited	£161,569,296
Mars Food UK Limited	£161,460,000
First Technology Overseas Limited	£161,383,008
Del Monte Europe Limited	£161,174,000
NSK Bearings Europe Limited	£160,969,344
Future Electronics Management Services Limited	£160,879,008
The W1 London Limited	£160,808,032
BP Middle East Limited	£160,749,520
ESNT Holdings (No.2) Limited	£160,740,000
Caravan Club Limited (The)	£160,706,000
McLaren Racing Limited	£160,582,000
Centrica Renewable Energy Limited	£160,564,992
DPSK Limited	£160,401,344
Wyatt Company Holdings Limited (The)	£160,240,992
Cucina Fresh Finance Limited	£160,200,000
Retirement Villages Group Limited	£160,166,000
Haulfryn Group Limited	£160,151,008
Lego Company Limited	£160,032,000
BAE Systems Applied Intelligence Limited	£159,803,008
Old Mutual Wealth Business Services Limited	£159,424,000
Mars Investments	£159,407,008
Rydon Group Limited	£159,254,000
Vernon Wholesale Investments Company Limited	£159,151,008
Leasys UK Ltd	£158,987,008
The Charity Bank Limited	£158,610,000
Economydrive Cars Limited	£158,582,000
British Midland Airways Limited	£158,500,000
Group 1 Automotive UK Limited	£158,474,000
GCP Applied Technologies (UK) Limited	£158,232,992
Winterbotham,Darby & Co.Limited	£158,110,000
Hendy Group Limited	£157,952,000
Landmark Mortgages Limited	£157,900,000
GE Bio-Sciences Investments Limited	£157,712,000
Kidde Finance Limited	£157,560,000
Boehringer Ingelheim Limited	£157,427,008
Kuwait Petroleum International Aviation Co UK Ltd	£157,263,424
May & Baker Limited	£157,120,992
DHL Parcel UK Limited	£157,003,008
The Gym Limited	£156,844,000
The Leaders Romans Midco Limited	£156,313,616
Inhealth Group Limited	£156,195,008
Pall European Holdings Limited	£156,093,536
SGN Commercial Services Limited	£156,082,000
Stanley Black & Decker UK Limited	£155,943,008
Black Tip Capital Holdings Limited	£155,918,000
Huyck.Wangner UK Limited	£155,884,000
Utilita Energy Limited	£155,603,008
Continental Tyre Group Ltd.	£155,530,000
Bespak Europe Limited	£155,496,992
BBGI Holding Limited	£155,398,144
NTL Cablecomms Cheshire	£155,074,000
TTG Investments Limited	£155,038,000
Neusentis Limited	£155,036,992
Waterlogic Finance Limited	£155,011,568
Renewi Financial Management Limited	£154,980,992
SMR Automotive Mirror Parts and Holdings UK Ltd	£154,942,096
Holtzbrinck Investment Limited	£154,875,008
Falcon Acquisitions Limited	£154,747,008
Edwardian International Hotels Ltd	£154,612,000
All Metal Services Limited	£154,515,056
TEG Holdings Limited	£154,504,000
Kofax US Holdings Limited	£154,452,960
Fresh Direct Group Limited	£154,200,000
Suez Recycling and Recovery Surrey Ltd	£154,164,000
The Spicers-Officeteam Group Limited	£153,911,008
Hollywood Bowl Group PLC	£153,584,000
International Car Wash Group Ltd.	£153,356,000
Axiom Education (Perth & Kinross) Limited	£153,326,000
Moat Homes Finance PLC	£153,255,008
Aviva Management Services UK Limited	£153,170,000
Cognita Schools Limited	£152,970,000
RWS UK Holding Co Limited	£152,845,552
Care Management Group Limited	£152,823,120
EUSA Pharma (UK) Limited	£152,351,008
Sun Life Financial of Canada UK Overseas Invest	£152,328,992
ExxonMobil Marine Limited	£152,302,000
Monier (UK) Holdings Limited	£152,170,000
Inhealth Group Holdings PLC	£152,156,992
OCS Group UK Limited	£152,020,000
Menzies Aviation Holdings Limited	£151,800,000
Pegasystems Limited	£151,736,368
BP Marine Limited	£151,731,200
MCG (Holdings) Ltd	£151,723,344
M C Group Limited	£151,719,440
Towers Watson Software Limited	£151,673,472
Juniper Networks (UK) Limited	£151,603,760
Dimension Data Network Services Limited	£151,504,000
Coty UK & I Ltd	£151,286,000
Exploration Service Company Limited	£151,240,768
Adelie Foods Bidco Limited	£150,892,992
Midland Quarry Products Limited	£150,768,992

Company	Value
Helsinki Midco Limited	£150,652,000
Shared Services Connected Ltd	£150,602,000
Next Generation Data Infrastructure 1 Limited	£150,591,008
Martin Grant (Holdings) Limited	£150,571,200
Allianz Equity Investments Limited	£150,502,000
Console Bidco Limited	£150,419,008
John Guest Holdings Limited	£150,349,984
Weight Watchers UK Holdings Ltd	£150,088,176
Bowers & Wilkins Holding Ltd	£150,051,536
Aptos Solutions UK Limited	£150,008,000
Safestore Investments Limited	£150,000,000
Pulsant Bidco Limited	£149,950,752
Akzo Nobel Packaging Coatings Limited	£149,916,992
Platinum Acquisition Limited	£149,896,496
Beckman Holdings Limited	£149,832,992
Senior UK Limited	£149,584,000
ExxonMobil International Limited	£149,532,000
Reckitt Benckiser USA Finance (No.3) Limited	£149,368,000
Inhealth UK Holdings Limited	£149,200,992
Costain Engineering & Construction Limited	£148,963,776
BCA Vehicle Finance Limited	£148,940,992
Paydens Limited	£148,709,936
The Community Stadium Limited	£148,667,888
ABJ Trading LLP	£148,512,000
Optionis Limited	£148,430,544
SSCP Spring Midco 2 Limited	£148,200,992
Bespak Holdings Limited	£148,196,992
Mavenir Global Limited	£147,948,336
Amphenol Limited	£147,920,000
Mustard Global Limited	£147,909,088
Allocate Topco Limited	£147,862,000
Court Cavendish Limited	£147,824,000
How Group Limited	£147,767,008
Makita (UK) Limited	£147,726,000
The Little Group Limited	£147,676,880
BNP Paribas Lease Group PLC	£147,532,992
Spectris UK Holdings Limited	£146,976,992
Knoll UK Investments Unlimited	£146,950,176
Sports Information Services Limited	£146,928,992
Forextra Developments Limited	£146,904,336
Telewest Communications (London South) Limited	£146,903,008
Koala Bidco Limited	£146,696,000
William Grant & Sons UK Limited	£146,531,008
Burnfield Limited	£146,500,000
Honeywell Europe Finance Limited	£146,272,000
Equiniti Services Limited	£146,148,992
Wolters Kluwer Holdings (UK) PLC	£146,081,552
WW GBR Limited	£145,891,008
Cabot Financial Holdings Group Limited	£145,784,000
Inhealth Limited	£145,763,008
Kerridge Commercial Systems Group Limited	£145,532,000
Buckingham Group Contracting Limited	£145,475,792
Milton Keynes Parks Trust Limited	£145,340,992
Galileo Global Technologies Ltd	£145,212,464
Galileo Holdco 1 Limited	£145,208,784
Parexel International Holding UK Limited	£145,184,992
Pulsant Group Limited	£145,164,000
Ruby Topco Limited	£145,100,000
ESSCI Limited	£145,068,992
Harvest Midco Limited	£145,030,000
Travelport International Limited	£144,884,000
Guildford Diocesan Board of Finance (The)	£144,804,000
Lonza Biologics PLC	£144,699,008
3M Products Limited	£144,572,000
Bewley Group Limited	£144,282,224
Redwing Holdings 2 Limited	£144,091,856
Seqirus Vaccines Holdings Limited	£143,595,008
WL One Midco 1 Limited	£143,346,000
Fat Face Holdings Limited	£143,342,000
London Vista Hotel Limited	£143,279,008
WL One Midco 2 Limited	£143,188,000
Red Bull Technology Limited	£143,099,008
Parker Hannifin Limited	£143,076,000
TAG Farnborough Airport Limited	£142,810,128
Gattaca PLC	£142,774,000
Geodis FF United Kingdom Ltd.	£142,608,992
Sports Information Services (Holdings) Limited	£142,440,000
Durkan Holdings Limited	£142,434,064
Defence Investments Limited	£142,263,008
Allocate Midco Limited	£142,212,992
BP Oil International Limited	£142,143,008
Tuesdays (Midco) Limited	£141,940,000
H & T Group PLC	£141,936,000
Kellogg Brown & Root (U.K.) Limited	£141,891,008
Plaza on Hyde Park Limited	£141,871,712
Druid Group Limited	£141,682,000
Harman International Industries Limited	£141,404,992
Whistl UK Limited	£141,404,000
Johnson Controls Building Efficiency UK Limited	£141,308,992
Charles Wells,Limited	£141,250,000
UCB Pharma Limited	£141,030,000
Portchester Equity Limited	£140,914,000
Copart UK Limited	£140,756,000
Alder Hey (Special Purpose Vehicle) Limited	£140,735,008
Alder Hey Holdco 3 Limited	£140,735,008
Winchester Diocesan Board of Finance (The)	£140,656,000
Vestel UK Limited	£140,486,176
The Gym Group Operations Limited	£140,251,776
Onkar International Limited	£140,223,632
GVS Prepaid Limited	£139,968,496
General Mills UK Limited	£139,491,008
Teledyne Limited	£139,464,992
Glory Global Solutions (Midco) Limited	£139,370,000
Autolink Concessionaires (M6) PLC	£139,007,008
Stantec Europe Limited	£138,834,000
Majestic Wine Warehouses Limited	£138,679,008
RHP Finance PLC	£138,651,008
PMP Recruitment Limited	£138,570,784
GL Assessment Limited	£138,482,000
Consort Healthcare (Blackburn) Limited	£138,435,008
Consort Healthcare (Blackburn) Holdings Limited	£138,435,008
Envision Pharma Midco Limited	£138,337,456
Universal Salvage Limited	£138,166,000
Harvey & Thompson Limited	£137,972,992
Direct Wines Holdings Limited	£137,971,008
Allport Group Limited	£137,777,280
Sungard Availability Services (UK) Limited	£137,739,008
Student Castle Limited	£137,570,592
Elysium Healthcare LC Limited	£137,518,000
Premier Marinas Limited	£137,364,000
Sonepar UK Limited	£137,339,008
John Guest International Limited	£137,306,512
Dimension Data (UK) Investments Limited	£137,254,880
Southampton International Airport Limited	£137,055,008
Stena Line Limited	£137,000,000
James Walker Group Limited	£136,724,992
Hampden Holdings Limited	£136,648,496
Bourne Education Trust	£136,623,536
O & M-Movianto UK Holdings Ltd.	£136,410,000
The University of Law Limited	£136,400,000
Rank Group Gaming Division Limited	£136,159,008
Vodafone Property Investments Limited	£136,118,000
Colas Limited	£136,019,008
Centrica KPS Limited	£135,938,000
Keltbray Limited	£135,913,392
Thrive Homes Finance PLC	£135,878,000
Macro 4 Limited	£135,856,992
Workdry International Limited	£135,715,008
Affinion International Limited	£135,672,000
Empresaria Group PLC	£135,500,000
Parexel International Limited	£135,332,992
KBC Process Technology Limited	£134,964,000
Porcelanosa U.K. Limited	£134,772,000
Wyevale Acquisitions Borrower Limited	£134,244,992

Company	Value
Kimberly-Clark Intercontinental Holding Limited	£134,222,144
Copart Europe Limited	£134,063,000
Pall Manufacturing UK Limited	£134,012,000
Costa Express Limited	£133,937,000
Trans Ocean Bulk Logistics Limited	£133,872,640
Huhtamaki Finance Limited	£133,624,000
Merkur Casino UK Ltd	£133,593,000
Biffa Municipal Limited	£133,547,000
Morgan North America Holding Limited	£133,511,000
Kellogg Brown & Root International Group Holdings	£133,496,968
Ichnaea UK Holdings Limited	£133,437,016
Linton Park Public Limited Company	£133,432,264
Astellas Pharma Ltd.	£133,302,000
Lantmannen Unibake UK Limited	£133,280,000
Link Asset Services (Holdings) Limited	£133,232,328
GGI Holdings Limited	£133,229,000
Towers Perrin Europe Limited	£133,222,000
Pentair UK Holdings Limited	£133,198,552
Zennor CNS Limited	£132,967,536
Kuehne + Nagel (UK) Limited	£132,956,480
United Living Group Limited	£132,833,000
Consort Medical Finance Limited	£132,617,608
Taylor Woodrow Construction	£132,612,000
B & CE Holdings Limited	£132,603,000
H Young (Operations) Limited	£132,413,000
Dnata World Travel Limited	£132,321,000
Exel Overseas Limited	£132,299,920
BOC Investments No.1 Limited	£132,230,000
Avalon Cellars Two Limited	£132,179,000
Brake Bros Foodservice Limited	£132,150,000
Iris Business Software Limited	£132,089,384
Micro Focus (IP) Ltd	£132,065,032
Old Mutual Wealth Limited	£132,054,000
Morgan Holdings Limited	£131,916,000
James Latham Public Limited Company	£131,763,000
Link Market Services Limited	£131,760,304
Aibel Group Limited	£131,695,928
Dealcyber Limited	£131,680,000
Pinewood Studios Limited	£131,588,000
ViiV Healthcare Overseas Limited	£131,581,000
Study Group UK Limited	£131,459,000
PB Topco Limited	£131,370,000
MDL Development Company Number 2 Limited	£131,226,000
Aprite (GB) Limited	£131,193,000
Hogg Robinson (Travel) Limited	£131,091,992
CMG Holdco Limited	£131,002,000
Senior Finance Six Limited	£130,925,520
Imagination Technologies Group Limited	£130,912,000
St Mary's University, Twickenham	£130,741,000
Marlin Senior Holdings Limited	£130,649,000
Cognita Limited	£130,597,000
Kaysail Limited	£130,549,824
Bynorth Limited	£130,389,000
Bynorth (Holdings) Limited	£130,389,000
Ali UK Limited	£130,357,000
Vector Aerospace International Limited	£130,261,000
Petroleum Geo-Services (UK) Limited	£130,185,000
Dormole Limited	£130,002,000
ME III Limited	£129,792,000
Hastoe Capital PLC	£129,685,000
Millipore (U.K.) Limited	£129,667,000
Overture Bidco Limited	£129,579,000
Reliance Vanco Group Limited	£129,491,488
Colt Investments Limited	£129,119,000
Colt Group Limited	£129,117,000
DST Process Solutions Limited	£129,104,000
CNOOC Ettrick U.K. Limited	£129,054,616
Paydens Holdings Limited	£128,977,896
Telefonica Digital Limited	£128,938,000
SAS Software Limited	£128,887,496
DG Partners Services Limited	£128,885,464
Bohunt Education Trust	£128,827,440
Systagenix Wound Management, Limited	£128,827,000
NPL Management Limited	£128,708,000
Haymarket UK2 Limited	£128,682,680
Thursdays (UK) Limited	£128,667,000
Oki Europe Limited	£128,627,400
Terrassen Holdings Limited	£128,616,000
Rydon Holdings Limited	£128,395,000
Autolink Concessionaires (A19) Limited	£128,286,992
Stackhouse Poland Group Limited	£128,186,000
Medivet Group Limited	£128,100,616
Ingram Micro Holdings Limited	£128,053,000
Reckitt Benckiser (RUMEA) Limited	£127,924,000
Holiday Extras Investments Limited	£127,729,000
Cramlington Renewable Energy Developments Hold	£127,721,000
Intercontinental Hotels Group Services Company	£127,499,000
KCI UK Holdings Limited	£127,373,000
Linde Cryogenics Limited	£127,236,976
Colorado Holdco Limited	£127,216,000
Draper Tool Group Limited (The)	£127,199,304
Intersurgical Limited	£127,195,864
RMS Holdco Limited	£127,123,000
Autolink Holdings (M6) Ltd	£127,078,000
Hanson Aggregates Marine Limited	£126,924,000
Pioneer Concrete Holdings Limited	£126,924,000
Foray 989 Limited	£126,810,000
WD-40 Company Limited	£126,676,000
Northgate Public Services Limited	£126,600,000
Australian Pacific Touring (U.K.) Limited	£126,385,120
GBF Capital Limited	£126,329,784
Pandrol International Limited	£126,180,000
Procter & Gamble (L & CP) Limited	£125,951,000
Chemetall Limited	£125,886,000
Lathams Limited	£125,868,000
Anesco Bidco 1 Limited	£125,741,584
Paydens Group Holdings Limited	£125,737,032
Thorntons Limited	£125,707,000
Costain Civil Engineering Limited	£125,581,720
Granitte Investments (UK) Limited	£125,554,400
Into University Partnerships Limited	£125,447,000
HellermannTyton Limited	£125,222,000
Elu Power Tools Ltd	£125,080,000
Platinum Newco II Limited	£125,000,000
Avtrade Holdings Limited	£124,874,360
Acco-Rexel Group Services Limited	£124,768,000
MB Group Limited	£124,661,000
Varian Medical Systems UK Limited	£124,600,352
Allocate Bidco Limited	£124,390,000
GD UK Holdings, Ltd	£124,193,000
The Howard Partnership Trust	£124,044,000
NEP UK Film II Limited	£123,991,000
Newincco 1270 Limited	£123,700,328
Kellogg Brown & Root (Greenford) Limited	£123,680,904
Honda Trading Europe Limited	£123,634,000
BPS Offshore Services Limited	£123,600,000
Evonik Chemicals Limited	£123,518,000
Sodexo Motivation Solutions U.K. Limited	£123,465,000
Boing Midco Limited	£123,128,000
D & B Europe Limited	£123,076,000
AbbVie Investments Limited	£123,065,248
The Ambassador Theatre Group (Venues) Limited	£123,034,000
Overture Topco Limited	£122,598,000
Apperly Estates Limited	£122,557,816
Kion Financial Services Limited	£122,484,896
Guide Dogs for the Blind Association (The)	£122,400,000
Open Text UK Limited	£122,314,392
Allegis Group Limited	£122,184,840
Jungheinrich UK Limited	£122,148,000
Citysprint (UK) Midco Limited	£121,963,880
Arkarius Bidco Limited	£121,735,624
Aesica BC Limited	£121,700,000
Gama Aviation PLC	£121,511,072
Matchtech Group (UK) Limited	£121,491,000

VA Tech (UK) Limited	£121,481,000
TF1 Limited	£121,257,000
Overseas Air Travel Limited	£121,246,000
Gartner U.K. Limited	£121,190,000
CDL Hotels (U.K.) Limited	£121,185,000
3D European Holdings Limited	£121,134,000
Willoughby (880) Limited	£120,908,000
Atlas Copco Limited	£120,718,000
Whistl Group Holdings Limited	£120,346,000
Cygnet Behavioural Health Limited	£120,235,000
MacDermid (UK) Limited	£120,187,000
BP Technology Ventures Limited	£120,078,968
K Capital Investment Ltd	£120,054,952
Cochlear Europe Limited	£120,014,048
Quaker Holdings (UK) Limited	£119,866,592
CEB Global Limited	£119,790,000
John Crane UK Limited	£119,741,000
Taylor Wimpey Property Company Limited	£119,677,000
Mabey Engineering (Holdings) Limited	£119,507,480
BA and AA Holdings Limited	£119,417,072
Ferrero UK Limited	£119,285,000
Mattel U.K. Limited	£119,275,000
ACS International Schools Limited	£119,153,392
Early Learning Centre Limited	£119,100,000
Caridon Holdings LLP	£118,772,880
Taylor Wimpey 2007 Limited	£118,685,000
Geo Underwriting Services Limited	£118,682,344
Travel Republic Ltd	£118,592,000
Intervet UK Production Limited	£118,581,000
Chaptre Investments Limited	£118,546,072
Corona Energy Retail 4 Limited	£118,481,440
Holiday Extras Limited	£118,374,000
PizzaExpress Merchandising Limited	£118,259,000
Barcrest Group Limited	£118,188,000
Pulsant Midco 2 Limited	£118,125,360
Pulsant Midco 1 Limited	£118,125,360
Friends Life FPL Limited	£118,098,000
Johnson Controls China Holding (UK) Limited	£118,094,360
Siemens Financial Services Holdings Limited	£118,007,000
Centrica Services Limited	£117,945,000
Biogen Idec Limited	£117,888,000
Volex PLC	£117,791,552
ADT South Africa Holding Limited	£117,785,000
MVV Environment Ridham Limited	£117,564,096
Trevellyan Developments Limited	£117,325,632
Triumph Aerospace Operations UK, Ltd.	£117,256,144
Eco Animal Health Group PLC	£117,185,000
Upperton Holdings Limited	£117,124,000
Colorado Bidco Limited	£117,112,000
Meridian Hospital Company PLC	£116,998,000
Meridian Hospital Company (Holdings) Limited	£116,998,000
Quality Spirits International Limited	£116,992,000
Family Capital Limited	£116,953,088
Activision Blizzard UK Ltd	£116,756,000
Osborne Group Holdings Ltd	£116,717,000
John Guest Limited	£116,658,504
Sharp International Finance (U.K.) PLC	£116,652,608
Martin Grant Homes Limited	£116,623,960
Berendsen Finance (Euro) Limited	£116,564,496
Graduation Topco Limited	£116,431,000
Taylor Wimpey SH Capital Limited	£116,364,000
EUSA Pharma Holdco 1 (UK) Limited	£116,354,376
EUSA Pharma Holdco 2 (UK) Limited	£116,352,608
Stearn Electric Company Limited	£116,069,000
BAE Systems (Defence Systems) Limited	£115,937,000
Cohort PLC	£115,573,000
Gardners Books Limited	£115,263,656
Oscar Mayer Limited	£115,167,984
PB Bidco Limited	£115,077,000
Direct Wines Limited	£115,033,000
Nice Systems UK Limited	£114,989,504
Legolas Debt Holdco Limited	£114,980,712

Jungheinrich Financial Services Limited	£114,947,000
Visiontrend Limited	£114,855,480
Grand Union Group Funding PLC	£114,800,000
Verizon International Limited	£114,782,008
Numatic International Limited	£114,768,000
Vostochnaya Technica UK Limited	£114,761,320
Western Wines Holdings Limited	£114,755,000
Casebia Therapeutics Limited Liability Partnership	£114,720,544
Crop Demetra Limited	£114,708,304
Bacardi-Martini Limited	£114,699,000
CHB P H R Limited	£114,672,000
The Baron Homes Corporation Limited	£114,662,304
Perform Media Sales Ltd	£114,639,000
Talkmobile Limited	£114,482,000
Unum European Holding Company Limited	£114,407,000
Rhone-Poulenc Rorer Limited	£114,358,000
INS-Sure Holdings Limited	£114,317,000
Paymaster (1836) Limited	£114,300,000
PB Holdco Limited	£114,291,000
PB Midco Limited	£114,290,000
United Living (South) Limited	£114,285,000
Tillotson Commercial Motors Limited	£114,266,000
Hanson America Holdings (4) Limited	£114,262,000
Johnson Wax Limited	£114,221,000
Ambassador Theatre Group Overseas Holdings Ltd	£114,213,856
Lenovo Global Technology UK Limited	£114,094,632
Stadium MK Group Limited	£113,836,768
Furniture Village Limited	£113,785,000
Avon Capital Estates 1 LLP	£113,694,992
Pall Europe Limited	£113,301,000
Lantmannen UK Holding Limited	£113,233,000
Fulham Stadium Limited	£113,179,000
O'Halloran & O'Brien Limited	£113,127,728
Care Management Group (Acquisition) Limited	£113,076,000
Study Group Holdings UK Limited	£113,022,976
Fujifilm Speciality Ink Systems Limited	£113,018,000
Geoffrey Osborne Limited	£112,879,000
Belton Associates Limited	£112,876,000
Intrum UK Finance Limited	£112,716,000
Cross London Trains Finance Company Limited	£112,677,000
Graduation Holdco Limited	£112,513,000
Fresca Group Limited	£112,336,000
Inula Holding UK Limited	£112,326,000
M.A.T. Davies Holdings Limited	£112,299,000
J.T. Davies & Sons Holdings Limited	£112,299,000
Motorway Services Limited	£112,291,000
Wakefield Waste PFI Limited	£112,236,000
Wakefield Waste Holdings Limited	£112,236,000
Cygnet Aspirations Developments Limited	£112,173,000
Hotel Management International (Holdings) Limited	£112,061,000
Bharat Forge International Limited	£112,049,960
Exel Investments Limited	£111,956,000
Crossknowledge Group Limited	£111,920,072
Chandlers Garage Holdings Limited	£111,831,472
Thales Transport and Security Limited	£111,779,000
ELWA Limited	£111,730,000
ELWA Holdings Limited	£111,730,000
Rockwell Automation Limited	£111,699,000
Cargill Holdings	£111,631,192
Ocobase Limited	£111,565,152
Honeywell Avionics Systems Limited	£111,527,000
Compass Group Finance No.4 Limited	£111,322,264
The Edward Gostling Foundation	£111,282,168
Newship Limited	£111,119,000
Alliance Healthcare (IT Services) Limited	£111,040,000
OTC Direct Limited	£111,000,000
Exel Logistics Property Limited	£110,964,000
Pandrol Finance Limited	£110,940,000
BP Greece Limited	£110,869,536
Asset Advantage Group Limited	£110,817,408
Harvest Energy Limited	£110,559,824
Praesepe Holdings Limited	£110,447,000

Company	Turnover	Company	Turnover
Pura Foods Limited	£110,393,752	BOC Korea Holdings Limited	£105,864,000
BMT Group Limited	£110,380,000	Corona Gas Management Limited	£105,769,296
G4S Security Services (UK) Limited	£110,271,000	Volga-Dnepr UK Ltd.	£105,627,016
Fujifilm UK Limited	£110,252,000	Altair Filter Technology Ltd	£105,344,000
Northumberland Energy Recovery Ltd	£110,215,000	Brentwick Limited	£105,310,128
Northumberland Energy Recovery Holdings Ltd	£110,215,000	Sixt Rent A Car Limited	£105,307,000
CFBT Schools Trust	£110,212,000	Motus Group (UK) Limited	£105,122,000
CPL Bidco Limited	£110,157,000	BP Chemicals (Korea) Limited	£105,049,000
Choice Care Group Holdings Limited	£110,112,240	Choice Care Group 3 Limited	£105,048,928
PEAC Holdings (UK) Limited	£110,077,000	Officeteam Limited	£104,854,000
Enstar Acquisitions Limited	£109,924,864	Mitsubishi Heavy Industries Air-Conditioning Europe	£104,789,312
PCL Bidco Limited	£109,900,000	Citysprint (UK) Limited	£104,778,560
Capital Safety Limited	£109,877,000	United Helicopters Limited	£104,754,048
Johnson Controls UAE Holding Ltd.	£109,775,080	Aston Carter International Limited	£104,563,664
INC Research Europe Holdings Limited	£109,755,960	Der Touristik UK Limited	£104,552,000
Lockheed Martin UK Ampthill Limited	£109,705,000	CPI Mortars Limited	£104,528,416
Purelake Properties Limited	£109,685,592	Stratton House Leasing Limited	£104,199,000
Asahi UK Ltd	£109,625,000	Edwardian Hampshire Hotels Ltd	£104,171,000
Goshawk Insurance Holdings Limited	£109,595,184	Ascot Racecourse Limited	£104,145,000
Just Develop It Limited	£109,557,768	Marlin Midway Limited	£104,075,000
Friends Life FPG Limited	£109,520,000	Hanson Quarry Products Ventures Limited	£104,040,000
Kew Green (LRG1) Limited	£109,454,512	Belton Associates (Group Holdings) Limited	£103,847,000
Allport Cargo Services Limited	£109,364,136	PFC Property Ltd	£103,663,744
Newship Group Limited	£109,240,000	B & W Acquisition Ltd	£103,570,624
Consort Healthcare (Blackburn) Funding PLC	£109,179,000	VS Alliance Limited	£103,512,560
Tradeteam Limited	£108,880,000	Brighton College	£103,459,160
Affiperf Limited	£108,874,000	Alestra Limited	£103,388,792
B & M Care Group Limited	£108,836,704	GCH Corporation Limited	£103,256,360
Morrisroe Group Limited	£108,799,408	Club Company (Group) Limited	£103,128,000
CAE STS Limited	£108,605,000	BIMM Topco Limited	£103,096,376
J.T.D. Finance Limited	£108,458,464	Grove HR Limited	£103,054,368
Shimtech Industries Holdco Limited	£108,458,000	Snows Business Holdings Limited	£102,906,976
Eli Lilly Group Limited	£108,451,000	BP Amoco Exploration (Faroes) Limited	£102,787,704
GT NEPS (Holdings) Limited	£108,400,856	Caledonian Helicopters Limited	£102,763,312
GT NEPS Limited	£108,400,856	Harsco Metals Group Limited	£102,759,000
Keadby Wind Farm Limited	£108,400,000	Hotelplan (U.K. Group) Limited	£102,723,000
Aura (Newcastle) Project Company Limited	£108,321,000	Perceptive Eclinical Limited	£102,702,000
Sabre Global Technologies Limited	£108,301,144	April Topco Limited	£102,693,000
RB Mexico Investments Limited	£108,184,080	The Potanin Foundation	£102,669,944
Melesey Limited	£108,172,000	Hogg Robinson Money Matters Limited	£102,499,792
Panavision Europe Limited	£108,122,000	GS Acquisitions Limited	£102,444,000
Asset Advantage Limited	£107,989,792	GCP Cardale PFI Ltd	£102,363,056
Coty Manufacturing UK Limited	£107,977,000	Thales Properties Limited	£102,333,000
University of Brighton Academies Trust	£107,894,000	Proudreed Real Estate Limited	£102,313,000
Vivid Imaginations Limited	£107,855,000	Aviva Administration Limited	£102,208,000
RCL (UK) Ltd.	£107,839,368	Harsco Mole Valley Limited	£102,038,728
Hampshire Aviation LLP	£107,838,992	Saga Cruises Limited	£101,972,000
Edwardian Exclusive Hotels Ltd	£107,778,000	Harsco Leatherhead Limited	£101,955,128
Georgica Limited	£107,615,000	Sorbon Finance Limited	£101,949,224
LR (UK) Limited	£107,567,520	BP Chemicals Limited	£101,846,000
The University of Chichester	£107,533,000	Golden Leaves Limited	£101,814,112
Avesco Holdings Limited	£107,448,000	Capital Safety Row Limited	£101,773,368
Sunny Topco Limited	£107,375,296	Arqiva No 2 Limited	£101,764,000
Sunny Bidco Limited	£107,374,400	Cadbury Schweppes Finance Limited	£101,588,000
Mapleco1 Ltd	£107,351,000	Ferholding UK Ltd	£101,576,000
NTL Kirklees Holdings Limited	£107,295,000	Expeditors International (UK) Limited	£101,461,000
MC Rental Limited	£107,021,840	MacDermid Europe Limited	£101,278,000
W.H. Brakspear & Sons Limited	£106,872,000	Rightmove Group Limited	£101,245,000
Blackwell Science (Overseas Holdings) Limited	£106,719,000	OCS Group International Limited	£101,186,000
Kew Green (LRG2) Limited	£106,638,624	SLR Management Limited	£101,139,400
Emcor Group (UK) PLC	£106,556,000	Yattendon Estates Limited	£101,130,000
USF International Limited	£106,498,208	The Royal Navy and Royal Marines Charity	£101,062,496
Novo Nordisk Limited	£106,459,000	The Clancy Group PLC	£101,001,464
Marlin Financial Group Limited	£106,453,000	SMC Pneumatics (U.K.) Limited	£100,994,928
Mecca Bingo Limited	£106,409,000	Faithful+Gould Limited	£100,931,000
Michael Page International Southern Europe Ltd	£106,235,000	Maple Topco Limited	£100,901,000
Mazda Motors UK Limited	£106,210,000	The Disabilities Trust	£100,786,000
HFC Prestige Products Limited	£106,194,000	Allegis Group (UK) Holdings II Limited	£100,687,336
Premier Asset Management Group PLC	£106,012,000	Rentokil Initial Finance Limited	£100,583,544
UK Highways M40 (Holdings) Limited	£105,969,000	The Original Bowling Company Limited	£100,523,000
UK Highways M40 Limited	£105,964,000	Samsung SDS Europe Limited	£100,519,000
CSG Systems UK Limited	£105,900,000	Millgate Developments Limited	£100,427,000

Company	Amount
Becton Dickinson Infusion Therapy UK	£100,424,000
Beck & Pollitzer Limited	£100,397,808
Bishops U.K. Limited	£100,348,200
Zotefoams PLC	£100,264,000
Glen House Estates Limited	£100,152,992
MF UK FC Limited	£100,144,592
Hurricane Holdings Limited	£100,015,376
Colgate Holdings	£100,000,000
INEOS Upstream Limited	£99,983,000
Belton Associates Holdings Limited	£99,935,000
Arris Solutions UK Ltd.	£99,819,824
Park Lane Limited	£99,669,000
Walker Greenbank PLC.	£99,653,000
De La Rue Investments Limited	£99,511,000
Action for Children	£99,481,000
Norebo Europe Limited	£99,121,456
Moove Lubricants Limited	£99,059,000
Guangdong Investments Limited	£98,892,904
Pearl River Delta Investments Limited	£98,754,248
Elite Hotels (Rotherwick) Limited	£98,636,800
Hawk Incentives Limited	£98,199,000
Allergan Limited	£98,128,000
NEOS Networks Limited	£98,100,000
Edwardian Grafton Hotel Ltd	£98,025,000
Selwood Ltd	£98,014,000
M & C Finance (1) Limited	£98,009,000
The Northview Group Limited	£97,998,000
BAM Group (UK) Limited	£97,996,000
B & W Group Ltd	£97,936,264
Watchstone Group PLC	£97,914,000
BAE Systems (Military Air) Overseas Limited	£97,717,000
Kerridge Commercial Systems (Bidco) Limited	£97,526,000
Allegis Group (UK) Holdings Limited	£97,518,888
Berkeley Two Hundred and Three Limited	£97,515,000
Glasgow Square Limited	£97,492,000
ISG Retail Limited	£97,351,000
Skanska J.V. Projects Ltd	£97,344,000
Pizza Hut (U.K.) Limited	£97,308,000
Matchtech Group (Holdings) Limited	£97,148,904
Pet Plan Limited	£97,120,000
Wolters Kluwer (UK) Limited	£97,016,512
Synchro Clutch Company Limited	£96,960,448
Michelmersh Brick Holdings PLC	£96,935,000
Grigny (UK) Limited	£96,418,048
Masternaut Group Holdings Limited	£96,400,536
Sonardyne Group Limited	£96,389,896
Johnson & Johnson Consumer Services EAME Ltd	£96,342,808
RB (China Trading) Limited	£96,318,000
AON Consulting Limited	£96,285,000
Trident Acquisition Limited	£96,172,688
GCP Rooftop Solar Finance PLC	£96,093,096
Edwards High Vacuum International Limited	£96,081,000
O2 Cedar Limited	£96,001,392
Vestey Group Limited	£95,996,000
Selwood Holdings Limited	£95,950,000
Leo Laboratories Limited	£95,717,000
Transform Schools (Rotherham) Limited	£95,697,000
Synventive Acquisition UK Limited	£95,638,120
Wates Developments Limited	£95,624,000
Kodak Alaris Limited	£95,606,152
Hephaestus II Limited	£95,577,264
J.P.McDougall & Co.Limited	£95,502,000
Parthenon Entertainment Limited	£95,502,000
Stockford Limited	£95,469,000
Peter Waddell Holdco Limited	£95,383,856
Next Generation Data Ltd	£95,246,000
Spicers Limited	£95,105,000
PGS Exploration (UK) Limited	£94,821,744
EMC Europe Limited	£94,817,000
Gym Offshore Three Limited	£94,800,064
Essentra Components Limited	£94,762,000
Abbott Capital India Limited	£94,710,000
Eden Automotive Investments Limited	£94,694,248
The Manor House Hotel (Castle Combe) Limited	£94,559,960
Sondex Wireline Limited	£94,505,000
Geo Specialty Group Holdings Limited	£94,402,144
Edwardian Mercer Street Ltd	£94,290,000
Dreams Topco Limited	£94,250,000
Dreams Limited	£94,250,000
Mars Melton UK Holdings Limited	£94,197,000
Riverstone Corporate Capital Limited	£94,180,000
Uranit UK Limited	£94,147,704
Edwardian Bloomsbury Street Limited	£94,130,000
Renesas Electronics Europe Limited	£93,864,256
Step Academy Trust	£93,763,000
S.S.S.Gears Limited	£93,697,616
IMCD UK Limited	£93,651,000
Kidde Limited	£93,275,000
Avtrade Limited	£93,260,144
Mermaid UK Holdco Limited	£93,189,656
Centrica LNG Company Limited	£93,177,400
Johnson & Johnson Finance Limited	£93,168,000
Mars Slough UK Holdings Limited	£93,096,000
Hamsard 3353 Limited	£93,007,432
Colgate-Palmolive (U.K.) Limited	£92,973,000
TRAD Hire & Sales Limited	£92,950,464
Southall Travel Limited	£92,942,480
Treasury Wine Estates UK Brands Limited	£92,878,672
Surrey Satellite Technology Limited	£92,824,000
Cabot Financial (Marlin) Limited	£92,738,000
Luxury Travel Holdings Limited	£92,718,000
CTDI Repair Services Limited	£92,669,624
Colorado Midco Limited	£92,638,000
Colorado Newco Limited	£92,636,000
Active Assistance Finance Limited	£92,591,960
St. Patrick's International College Limited	£92,561,656
Swale Academies Trust	£92,538,136
Wartsila Voyage Holding Limited	£92,429,616
Schindler Ltd.	£92,323,000
HH Global Limited	£92,304,000
Michael Lonsdale Limited	£92,284,232
Movianto UK Limited	£92,244,000
UK Highways A55 Limited	£92,167,000
UK Highways A55 (Holdings) Limited	£92,167,000
Biffa GS UK Holdings Limited	£92,156,000
SNA Solutions UK Limited	£92,079,976
M & C Hotels Holdings Limited	£92,073,000
Wiley Heyden Limited	£92,049,000
Cadbury South Africa (Holdings)	£91,930,488
Alestra Group Holdings Limited	£91,926,704
Tenva TS Holdings Limited	£91,926,000
Renhe Sports Management Co Limited	£91,875,864
John Parker & Son Limited	£91,812,000
Heronswood Holdings Limited	£91,766,264
Ringway Infrastructure Services Limited	£91,745,000
Spire Automotive Limited	£91,670,752
Stantec UK Limited	£91,520,000
Skanska Infrastructure Investment UK Limited	£91,503,000
SLS Holding Company Limited	£91,498,000
Surrey Lighting Services Limited	£91,498,000
Verint Systems UK Limited	£91,495,000
SC Walmgate Limited	£91,441,480
Day Group Limited	£91,422,856
Balton CP Limited	£91,419,928
Greenshaw Learning Trust	£91,406,000
Ty Danjuma Family Office Limited	£91,351,000
Dunlop International Group Limited	£91,293,000
Caffyns Public Limited Company	£91,267,000
The Thinking Schools Academy Trust	£91,073,000
Takeda UK Limited	£91,023,712
ADM Pura Limited	£90,900,880
AGF Holdings (UK) Limited	£90,864,000
Snap-On Business Solutions Limited	£90,818,536
Cucina French Holdings Limited	£90,817,704

Company	Amount
Novar Electrical Holdings Limited	£90,798,000
Galliford Try Services Limited	£90,749,000
Aurasma Limited	£90,695,504
Swindon Pressings Limited	£90,676,000
IAG GBS Limited	£90,665,000
Countyroute Limited	£90,498,000
Countyroute (A130) PLC.	£90,498,000
Batt Cables Public Limited Company	£90,481,880
Qinetiq Overseas Holdings Limited	£90,387,000
Platinum Midco Limited	£90,332,704
Platinum Midco 2 Limited	£90,332,704
GCP Programme Funding 1 Limited	£90,294,408
Kenwood Appliances Limited	£90,281,000
Michael J. Lonsdale Limited	£90,222,120
RIHL Limited	£90,090,000
Cygnet NW Limited	£90,059,000
Rank Digital Holdings Limited	£90,059,000
Giles W. Pritchard-Gordon & Co. Limited	£90,024,160
The Regard Partnership Limited	£89,982,000
Colleycare Limited	£89,918,456
Counties Home Loan Management Limited	£89,916,704
Micheldever Group Limited	£89,859,000
CPL Topco Limited	£89,850,000
MacDermid Performance Solutions UK Limited	£89,792,000
ISDC Developments (No2) Limited	£89,764,000
Ability Hotels (III) Finance Limited	£89,742,664
Maxxia Finance Limited	£89,681,024
Eastern Quarry Limited	£89,669,000
Ultra-Centrifuge Nederland Limited	£89,521,248
Sun Insurance Office Limited	£89,500,000
CHG-Meridian UK Limited	£89,425,000
Bard Limited	£89,395,000
Canterbury Diocesan Board of Finance	£89,341,000
Exclusive Networks Limited	£89,261,792
Furniture Village Holdings Limited	£89,110,000
SITA Information Networking Computing UK Limited	£89,077,264
Biffa Waste Management Limited	£88,983,000
The Rosedale Hewens Academy Trust	£88,925,000
J C C Lighting Holdings Limited	£88,785,000
Sally Salon Services Limited	£88,778,000
A.G. Thames Holdings Limited	£88,771,000
Avaya UK	£88,728,768
Lawrie Group Public Limited Company	£88,532,648
Coldunell Limited	£88,482,592
Tax Systems PLC	£88,376,000
Canon Europe Limited	£88,300,000
DX (Group) PLC	£88,200,000
Boeing UK Training and Flight Services Limited	£88,160,776
Liberty Leasing Limited	£87,941,120
Lindt & Sprungli (U.K.) Limited	£87,928,000
Glynwed Pipe Systems Limited	£87,824,000
Guildford Education Partnership	£87,772,000
Skanska TAM Limited	£87,536,000
Halma Euro Trading Limited	£87,525,712
PHH 1 Limited	£87,468,000
Pritchard-Gordon Tankers Limited	£87,383,320
Gibb Holdings Ltd	£87,326,000
FT Finance Limited	£87,207,000
Millennium Hotels Limited	£87,177,000
Kew Green Intermediate One Limited	£87,110,312
Croydon and Lewisham Lighting Services (Holdings)	£87,063,000
Croydon and Lewisham Lighting Services Limited	£87,063,000
Blue Auto Holdings Limited	£87,038,000
DX Network Services Limited	£87,000,000
Akaal Group PLC	£86,872,256
Aria Petroleum (UK) Ltd.	£86,859,600
Signet Direct Diamond Sourcing Limited	£86,724,216
Bycentral Holdings Limited	£86,624,000
Bycentral Limited	£86,624,000
NSK UK Limited	£86,559,160
H+S Aviation Limited	£86,544,000
BP Exploration Indonesia Limited	£86,533,776
Davidson Kempner European Partners, LLP	£86,433,064
Draper Tools Limited	£86,430,976
F.C. Stark Limited	£86,386,232
Garreg Lwyd Energy Limited	£86,383,000
London Britannia Hotel Limited	£86,241,000
Remy Cointreau UK Limited	£86,171,200
Russell & Bromley Limited	£86,099,560
Total Aircraft Product Support (Holdings) Limited	£86,094,720
Siemens Industry Software Computational Dynamics	£86,061,000
Pandrol Group Limited	£85,962,000
Linden Homes (Sherford) LLP	£85,858,000
Consolidated Timber Holdings Limited	£85,816,000
Offshore Containers Holdings Limited	£85,758,864
Adelie Foods Limited	£85,728,000
Pandrol Holdings Limited	£85,686,000
LGC Genomics Limited	£85,633,000
Techtronic Industries (UK) Ltd	£85,589,400
Greenham Trust Ltd	£85,569,000
Mariner International (UK) Limited	£85,543,000
Pentagon Holdings Limited	£85,540,848
TIG Acquisition Holdings	£85,517,904
Caversham Trading Limited	£85,510,000
Southern Communications Group Limited	£85,502,248
Andrew Page 1917 Limited	£85,414,000
Purelake Investments Limited	£85,338,672
Away Resorts Limited	£85,240,272
Aston Carter Group Limited	£85,211,240
Think One Limited	£85,175,616
J. Reddington Ltd	£85,098,440
Genesis Specialist Care UK No 2 Limited	£85,048,792
Cygnet Inter-Holdings Limited	£85,000,000
Ringway Jacobs Limited	£84,995,408
Rydon Construction Limited	£84,980,216
Unit4 Business Software Limited	£84,972,000
Safety-Kleen UK (Europe) Limited	£84,911,000
IHC UK (Holdings) Limited	£84,874,000
IUP 2 LLP	£84,851,000
Prospect Healthcare (Hairmyres) Limited	£84,789,000
Jato Dynamics Limited	£84,783,872
Bristow Southeast Asia Limited	£84,767,504
Indoor Bowling Equity Limited	£84,709,000
Black & Veatch Limited	£84,677,000
BP Car Fleet Limited	£84,655,000
Mavenir Systems Limited	£84,625,000
Transform Schools (Bassetlaw) Limited	£84,582,000
Prysmian Powerlink Services Limited	£84,558,600
Tyco Fire Products Manufacturing Limited	£84,488,000
Forester Holdings (Europe) Limited	£84,484,000
Kent Education Partnership (Holdings) Limited	£84,467,000
Kent Education Partnership Limited	£84,467,000
Expanded Limited	£84,460,000
Imagination Technologies Limited	£84,409,000
Leeu London Limited	£84,405,816
Emperor 2 Limited	£84,367,000
Prospect Healthcare (Hairmyres) Group Limited	£84,352,000
Cosan Lubes Investments Limited	£84,226,000
Blue Light Partnership (ASP) Newco Limited	£84,159,000
Eco Animal Health Ltd.	£84,152,288
ESP Connections Limited	£84,047,000
Ferdinand Bilstein UK Limited	£84,026,000
Clinphone Limited	£83,951,000
Geneva Investment Group Limited	£83,916,720
Yoplait UK Limited	£83,861,000
Edgewell Personal Care Holdings UK Ltd.	£83,820,000
Siemens Industry Software Limited	£83,811,000
Aerotron Limited	£83,719,184
Services Support (Manchester) Holdings Limited	£83,626,000
Services Support (Manchester) Limited	£83,626,000
PandoraExpress 7 Limited	£83,505,000
A.J. Morrisroe & Sons Limited	£83,417,040
Rochester Diocesan Society and Board of Finance	£83,379,000
Drew Marine UK Holdings Ltd	£83,342,152

Galileo Holdco 2 Limited	£82,833,048
Overture Midco Limited	£82,830,000
Overture Midco II Limited	£82,830,000
Rubicon Drinks Limited	£82,823,000
LRH Care Homes Limited	£82,756,456
Shoosmiths LLP	£82,722,000
Limay Drilling Rigs Limited	£82,636,072
BIMM 1 Limited	£82,605,400
PizzaExpress (Wholesale) Limited	£82,605,000
Agility Logistics Limited	£82,599,000
Pinewood PSB Limited	£82,596,000
Walgreens Boots Alliance Services Limited	£82,593,000
Aramark Limited	£82,579,000
Computer Associates UK Limited	£82,549,000
Ann Summers Ltd.	£82,357,000
SAS Holdings Limited	£82,320,000
SSE Hornsea Limited	£82,300,000
The Entertainer (Amersham) Limited	£82,294,000
Heathrow Enterprises Limited	£82,188,000
Fyffes Group Limited	£82,186,000
Hotel Management International Limited	£82,119,000
Console Midco Limited	£82,102,016
Perkinelmer (UK) Holdings Limited	£82,093,000
Shepperton Studios Limited	£82,082,000
Radlett Limited	£82,074,680
Napsbury Limited	£82,074,680
Lotus Leisure Ltd	£82,010,008
BP Africa Limited	£81,949,376
International Group Limited	£81,943,000
Travel Technology Investments Limited	£81,911,000
H+H UK Limited	£81,904,000
Gold Group International Limited	£81,888,840
Huhtamaki (UK) Limited	£81,866,000
Blue Light Partnership (ASP) Limited	£81,816,000
Blue Light Partnership (ASP) Holdings Limited	£81,816,000
Crown House Technologies Limited	£81,762,000
Intrum UK Holdings Limited	£81,738,000
Colorcon Limited	£81,699,008
Wescot Acquisitions Limited	£81,687,000
April Bidco Limited	£81,668,000
Raymarine UK Limited	£81,630,000
Emery Oleochemicals UK Limited	£81,512,520
Copthorne Hotels Limited	£81,507,000
Durkan Limited	£81,418,736
East Surrey Holdings Limited	£81,411,136
Cross London Trains Holdco Limited	£81,268,000
Walon Limited	£81,161,000
Gerald Palmer Eling Trust Company	£81,057,744
Reckitt Benckiser Asia Pacific Limited	£80,899,000
Opal (Silvertown) LLP	£80,879,000
Aura (Newcastle) Project Company Phase 2 Ltd	£80,853,000
Shorefield Holidays Limited	£80,820,976
Westfalia Fruit International Limited	£80,812,896
Graduation Bidco Limited	£80,784,000
Walkers Snacks (Distribution) Limited	£80,737,000
GCP Social Housing 1 Limited	£80,671,512
BVG Group Limited	£80,657,672
ADM Arkady Limited	£80,653,456
Jupiter Midco 1 Limited	£80,529,784
Wood Group Industrial Services Limited	£80,461,000
Ability Hotels (Cambridge) Limited	£80,440,672
Transform Schools (Birmingham) Limited	£80,415,000
Transform Schools (Birmingham) Holdings Limited	£80,415,000
Alan Firmin Limited	£80,383,344
NTL Cablecomms East Lancashire	£80,380,000
Mott MacDonald International Limited	£80,366,896
SAS International Limited	£80,366,000
Scottish Borders Education Partnership (Holdings) Ltd	£80,360,000
Scottish Borders Education Partnership Limited	£80,360,000
H+H UK Holdings Limited	£80,273,000
ND1T Limited	£80,257,536
CDK Global (UK) Limited	£80,191,000
UK Assistance Accident Repair Centres Limited	£80,181,000
Haymarket Group Limited	£80,116,000
John Menzies Finance Limited	£80,100,000
Ramac Holdings (Trading) Limited	£80,006,272
Synventive Acquisition Unlimited	£79,989,104
Micro Focus Limited	£79,895,000
Apollo Submarine Cable System Limited	£79,821,776
Covance Clinical and Periapproval Services Limited	£79,749,000
Monier Redland Limited	£79,748,000
Local Car and Van Rental Limited	£79,721,456
S & B Herba Foods Limited	£79,704,000
Salaft Properties Limited	£79,544,768
Horlicks Limited	£79,499,000
Cordant People Limited	£79,454,632
Euro Alloys Limited	£79,417,480
Kendallco Limited	£79,369,000
Key Equipment Finance Europe Limited	£79,268,224
QSC 1209 Limited	£79,262,000
Dawsongroup Bus and Coach Limited	£79,261,000
QA-IQ Investments Limited	£79,243,000
De Lage Landen Limited	£79,230,000
Ralph Lauren UK Limited	£79,218,344
St. Nicholas Court Farms Limited	£79,154,632
Everyday Loans Holdings Limited	£79,091,000
Barretts of Canterbury Limited	£78,996,000
Masterson Holdings Limited	£78,976,696
Henry Schein UK Finance Limited	£78,904,512
Benecol Limited	£78,854,000
SSL Group (UK) Limited	£78,824,912
Inspiral Oldham Holding Company Limited	£78,819,000
Inspiral Oldham Limited	£78,819,000
Surface Treatments Limited	£78,754,000
Regenter Myatts Field North Holding Co Ltd	£78,731,000
Regenter Myatts Field North Limited	£78,731,000
Biocompatibles International Limited	£78,690,000
Xylem Water Solutions UK Holdings Limited	£78,650,000
Luxury Travel Acquisitions Limited	£78,649,000
Grove Court Properties (Holdings) Limited	£78,637,632
Bowland Resources Limited	£78,598,000
Shires Holdings Limited	£78,567,000
RES UK & Ireland Limited	£78,506,000
Gucci Limited	£78,492,000
EWDB Limited	£78,486,000
Ergo Tec LLP	£78,431,184
FIL Pensions Management	£78,394,000
Stryker UK Limited	£78,394,000
Blue Chip Customer Engineering Limited	£78,379,000
Britax Childcare Group Limited	£78,327,000
IHC Hotel Limited	£78,290,000
Serco-IAL Limited	£78,222,000
Aibel Finance Limited	£78,209,768
Fevore Limited	£78,099,904
CDK U.K. Limited	£78,097,000
Dyno-Rod Limited	£78,029,000
London Residential Healthcare Limited	£78,004,168
Alpha Assembly Solutions UK Limited	£77,988,000
Sir Robert McAlpine Road Holdings Limited	£77,887,336
ND2F Limited	£77,814,816
Cargill Financial Services Europe Limited	£77,807,256
ND3M Limited	£77,729,696
Powerscreen International Limited	£77,711,000
Zurich Management Services Limited	£77,650,216
Toll Investments (NA) Ltd	£77,613,328
Enterprise Services Information Security UK Limited	£77,596,000
Rhone Products (UK) Limited	£77,570,408
Southern Communications Investments Limited	£77,560,800
ViiV Healthcare UK (No.5) Limited	£77,537,000
Services Support (SEL) Limited	£77,453,000
Services Support (SEL) Holdings Limited	£77,453,000
Gus UK Management Limited	£77,451,648
Constantine Group Limited	£77,407,000
John Menzies (108) Limited	£77,400,000

Company	Turnover	Company	Turnover
Eurovia Infrastructure Limited	£77,383,840	Shimtech Industries Limited	£74,196,240
Jupiter Topco Limited	£77,377,568	Edif Group Limited	£74,147,000
Church & Dwight UK Limited	£77,353,000	Quantel Holdings (2010) Limited	£74,137,000
April Midco Limited	£77,321,000	Strongdraw Limited	£74,018,000
Cable & Wireless Global Telecommunication Services	£77,265,000	Change, Grow, Live	£74,011,000
Lavazza Professional UK Limited	£77,259,000	Photo-Me Limited	£73,950,312
Orange Business Holdings UK Limited	£77,253,000	RB Sport & Leisure Holdings PLC	£73,947,648
Aspen Pumps Limited	£77,242,000	B & P Buyco Limited	£73,912,480
Barons Automotive Limited	£77,181,096	Bell Microsystems Limited	£73,883,896
South Downs Limited	£77,171,000	Onecom Group Limited	£73,876,784
Stackhouse Poland Holdings Ltd	£77,162,000	Natures Way Foods Limited	£73,873,112
Britannia Refined Metals Limited	£77,058,000	SHL Group Limited	£73,779,000
Elster Water Metering Holdings Limited	£77,008,000	Britannia Security Group Limited	£73,758,000
Softbox (Topco) Limited	£76,984,640	Glyndebourne Productions Limited	£73,737,816
Travelport (UK) Services Limited	£76,916,552	Chemring Countermeasures Limited	£73,729,000
Puzzler Media Limited	£76,868,808	Panini UK Limited	£73,684,416
Cygnet 2002 Limited	£76,754,000	Tranche 5 Limited	£73,683,544
HCL Great Britain Limited	£76,664,000	Everyday Loans Limited	£73,633,000
Consolidated Timber Holdings Group Limited	£76,628,080	Wilkinson Sword Limited	£73,601,000
Acco UK Limited	£76,585,000	Trapoc Limited	£73,593,000
Anixter International Limited	£76,498,000	Girls' Learning Trust	£73,564,000
SC Johnson Ltd	£76,456,000	Sun Mark Limited	£73,485,520
Tax Systems Holdings Limited	£76,449,880	TWG Services Limited	£73,476,000
Heathrow Express Operating Company Limited	£76,440,000	Interserve PFI Holdings 2014 Limited	£73,430,000
Brentford FC Limited	£76,384,984	Del Monte (UK) Limited	£73,371,000
Nuffield Health Pension Trustees Limited	£76,287,696	Bristow Aircraft Leasing Limited	£73,353,976
Electrium Sales Limited	£76,279,000	Innisfree Schools (F2C) Limited	£73,336,000
Hodgson Automotive Limited	£76,274,912	Anesco Limited	£73,320,472
Inter Terminals UK Limited	£76,242,000	Jacobs Field Services Limited	£73,293,000
Comland Group Limited	£76,224,000	P & O European Ferries (Irish Sea) Limited	£73,217,000
VWS (UK) Ltd	£76,190,000	Clancy Docwra Limited	£73,155,760
Next Generation Data Infrastructure 2 Limited	£76,170,000	CFCEPS LLP	£73,140,096
Boskalis Subsea Limited	£76,115,000	Sunsail Worldwide Sailing Limited	£72,913,000
Innisfree Schools (Secondary) Limited	£76,075,000	Subsea 7 Engineering Limited	£72,891,000
Harsco Metals Holdings Limited	£76,063,008	Armstrong World Industries Limited	£72,850,000
Ichnaea UK Limited	£76,056,432	Bytes Software Services Limited	£72,827,568
Intec Telecom Systems Limited	£76,050,000	Langbourn Properties Limited	£72,824,720
Solventis Ltd.	£76,020,016	Icon Clinical Research (U.K.) Limited	£72,754,968
QlikTech UK Limited	£75,926,000	Data Select Limited	£72,733,216
Southampton IoW and S England Royal Mail	£75,901,000	Crosswater Limited	£72,733,000
Toucan Gen Co Limited	£75,889,176	KBC Advanced Technologies Limited	£72,729,000
Xtrac Transmissions (Holdings) Limited	£75,838,000	B & C E Insurance Limited	£72,691,000
Havas Shared Services Limited	£75,835,000	Grove Developments Limited	£72,611,760
New Blue Chip Limited	£75,807,000	Complete Cover Group Limited	£72,565,000
CooperVision Lens Care Limited	£75,802,000	Stena Line Irish Sea Ferries Limited	£72,438,000
Kuwait Petroleum (U.K. Holdings) Limited	£75,475,000	Puzzler Media Holdings Limited	£72,380,280
London United Busways Limited	£75,454,000	Medivet Partnership LLP	£72,368,000
London Tara Hotel Limited	£75,439,000	Chubb Group Properties Limited	£72,308,000
Hargreaves Properties Limited	£75,347,512	Niftylift Limited	£72,273,000
Tenpin Limited	£75,270,000	The Cloud Networks Limited	£72,240,000
Suez Recycling and Recovery Lancashire Ltd	£75,249,000	RWS Translations Limited	£72,210,096
OMC Investments Limited	£75,202,016	Every Child, Every Day Academy Trust	£72,198,816
Harris Defence Limited	£75,183,000	Steris UK Holding Limited	£72,182,376
Haig Housing Trust	£75,164,000	Kazakh Projects Joint Venture Limited	£72,145,216
FBL Holdings Limited	£75,101,000	Mallinckrodt Chemical Limited	£72,142,376
Stackhouse Poland Bidco Limited	£75,007,000	Durkan Estates Limited	£72,139,800
NIS Receivables No.1 Limited	£75,000,000	Nestle Waters UK Limited	£72,126,000
Hanson (SH) Limited	£74,940,000	Perkinelmer Life Sciences International Holdings	£72,018,000
H. K. S. Holdings Limited	£74,859,520	The Deltic Group Holdings Limited	£72,011,000
Cauta Capital Limited	£74,775,320	Ten Entertainment Group PLC	£72,000,000
FBG Holdings (UK) Limited	£74,748,000	Exagon Industries Limited	£71,939,616
Gravity Media Group Holdings Limited	£74,647,000	Glaxo Wellcome UK Limited	£71,871,000
55VS No 2 Limited	£74,521,776	GFM Education	£71,837,496
T G Products Limited	£74,453,000	Rightmove PLC	£71,813,000
Kent Catholic Schools' Partnership	£74,448,000	BCA Europe Limited	£71,803,000
The Joseph Rank Trust	£74,443,000	Kebbell Holdings Limited	£71,795,368
Hertz Europe Limited	£74,385,000	The Conair Group Limited	£71,789,208
Adare International Holdings Limited	£74,368,000	SSG Logistic Solutions Limited	£71,774,000
Azlan Limited	£74,256,976	Ensign Highways Limited	£71,576,144
Portsmouth Diocesan Board of Finance (The)	£74,232,064	Constantine Wind Energy Limited	£71,529,256
Fast Training Services Limited	£74,227,000	Onecom Limited	£71,520,112
Fast Holdings Limited	£74,227,000	Dawsongroup UK Limited	£71,413,000

Company	Value
Cellnex UK Midco Limited	£71,397,336
Community Homes of Intensive Care and Education	£71,376,296
Alphalarch Limited	£71,274,000
Sir Robert McAlpine (A19) Limited	£71,256,816
Mars Chocolate UK Holdings Limited	£71,160,024
Formaplex Limited	£71,160,000
Midgard Ltd	£71,057,872
Kuehne + Nagel Drinkflow Logistics Limited	£70,906,000
Kuehne + Nagel Drinkflow Logistics Holdings Limited	£70,906,000
3SE (Barnsley, Doncaster & Rotherham) Limited	£70,899,000
Covea Life Limited	£70,879,000
Edgewell Personal Care UK Limited	£70,825,568
Fresh Direct (UK) Limited	£70,722,000
Kebbell Development Limited	£70,591,016
Park Avenue Estates Limited	£70,582,160
Rambler Metals and Mining PLC	£70,515,392
Lenta Properties Limited	£70,508,912
Toucan Solar Assets 2 Holdco Limited	£70,416,288
Horder Healthcare	£70,395,000
Readypower Rail Services Group Limited	£70,379,944
Jacobs E & C Limited	£70,363,000
Flight Centre Robin Limited	£70,343,792
Ability Developments Limited	£70,342,472
Allocate Software Limited	£70,327,000
Halamar (Chancery Lane) Limited	£70,298,448
The Deltic Group Limited	£70,244,000
Officeteam Group Limited	£70,184,000
Vanderbilt Homes Limited	£70,113,000
MYA Property Limited	£70,069,704
Stoke Park Limited	£70,058,000
Mothercare Group Limited (The)	£70,013,000
Towry Group Limited	£70,007,000
NetApp UK Ltd	£69,980,512
Celgene Europe Limited	£69,875,936
Vanderbilt Topco Ltd	£69,853,000
Acquaspen Limited	£69,832,000
Medequip Group Limited	£69,806,000
CooperVision Limited	£69,786,000
MFS Portfolio Limited	£69,784,000
Suez Recycling and Recovery Tees Valley Ltd	£69,767,000
Linden/Downland Graylingwell LLP	£69,750,000
Logicalis UK Limited	£69,739,000
Heathrow Edwardian Hotel Ltd	£69,716,000
Greensands Limited	£69,715,000
Asteral Holdings Limited	£69,706,888
Quantum Funding Limited	£69,678,000
WWF-UK	£69,625,000
Travel Republic Holdings Ltd.	£69,617,000
SmithKline Beecham (H) Limited	£69,504,000
Ascenti Health Limited	£69,405,472
Game Digital Holdings Limited	£69,404,000
Bristol Laboratories Limited	£69,361,760
Beam Global Finance UK Limited	£69,350,016
Hotelplan Limited	£69,209,000
Boeing UK Training and Flight Services Holding Ltd	£69,204,344
Sesame Limited	£69,173,000
Ferguson Group Services Limited	£69,112,000
Lafarge Nigeria (UK) Limited	£69,032,000
Formaplex Group Limited	£68,950,000
HiFX Europe Limited	£68,876,000
PCL Holdco Limited	£68,861,000
Bridge Leisure Topco Limited	£68,786,960
Snows Motor Group Limited	£68,783,856
Arun Estate Agencies Limited	£68,745,000
Kidsprog Limited	£68,727,000
City Technology Limited	£68,656,000
Schenker Limited	£68,653,000
Brown and Mason Holdings Limited	£68,638,608
Flexera Software Holdings Limited	£68,637,000
Crystalate Electronics Limited	£68,620,000
Alcon Eye Care UK Limited	£68,618,000
TW Metals Limited	£68,520,000
Porter and Haylett Limited	£68,469,000
Bathroom Brands Group Limited	£68,454,000
Independent Technology Systems Limited	£68,386,000
Ability Hotels (Liverpool) Limited	£68,349,192
Computer Software Group Limited	£68,262,000
Smiths Industries Industrial Group Limited	£68,211,000
Yacht Havens Group Limited	£68,203,976
Edwardian Free Trade Hall Ltd	£68,085,000
JLW Excellent Homes for Life Holding Co Ltd	£67,991,000
JLW Excellent Homes for Life Limited	£67,991,000
Southampton Row Trust Limited	£67,766,000
LSG/Sky Chefs Europe Holdings Limited	£67,589,000
Edwardian Ltd	£67,572,000
Bristol-Myers Squibb Business Services Limited	£67,446,000
Fossil (UK) Limited	£67,411,000
Clean Viking Holdings Limited	£67,360,176
The Penspen Group Limited	£67,325,000
The Park Federation Academy Trust	£67,274,000
Elysium Healthcare No. 3 Limited	£67,242,000
Suez UK Environment Ltd	£67,233,000
Parametric Holdings (UK) Limited	£67,224,880
A24 Group Limited	£67,204,384
Esure Services Limited	£67,200,000
SGB Infrastructure Middle East Limited	£67,144,000
Sunny Midco Limited	£67,133,896
Solarsoft Acquisition Limited	£67,079,472
NTL Cablecomms Surrey	£67,074,000
Centrica Brigg Limited	£67,073,000
Cranleigh School	£67,034,000
Blake Morgan Group LLP	£67,034,000
Cognita International Holdings Limited	£66,981,000
Exel Holdings Limited	£66,979,000
Masternaut Bidco Limited	£66,977,796
Kerridge Commercial Systems (Midco) Limited	£66,974,000
Isoft Group (UK) Limited	£66,950,000
Kingston Technology Europe Co LLP	£66,927,244
UCC Coffee UK Limited	£66,925,424
Safety-Kleen Europe Limited	£66,915,000
B & P Acquisitionco Limited	£66,913,632
BIMM Limited	£66,888,728
Summerleaze Limited	£66,876,152
Technical Staffing Resources Limited	£66,808,688
The Gap Partnership Group Limited	£66,720,896
Vanderbilt Thames Valley Limited	£66,667,000
Jawaby Property Investment Limited	£66,645,216
Abaris Holdings Limited	£66,599,000
Rico Logistics Ltd	£66,564,000
SCJ EurAFNE Ltd	£66,510,000
IHS Markit Global Limited	£66,482,440
Rackspace UK Leasing Limited	£66,431,580
Britvic Finance Partnership LLP	£66,350,000
Hilbre Holdings Limited	£66,326,000
Gate Gourmet London Limited	£66,306,000
Syneos Health Clinical Development Services Limited	£66,266,880
The Last Mile Company Limited	£66,203,000
S D C (Holdings) Limited	£66,188,496
Independent Growth Finance Limited	£66,175,492
Newbury Racecourse PLC	£66,164,000
Brown and Mason Limited	£66,133,708
Eden Automotive Limited	£66,124,600
M.& W.Mack Limited	£66,083,000
Wyevale Garden Centres Acquisitions Limited	£66,081,000
Renewi Cumbria Limited	£66,065,000
Elliott Baxter & Company Limited	£66,061,000
Wyevale Garden Centres G & L Limited	£66,015,000
Premier Portfolio Managers Limited	£65,943,000
Avon Capital Estates (Australia) Limited	£65,941,440
Citysprint (UK) Group Limited	£65,913,632
Bandai Namco Holdings UK Limited	£65,900,000
Millennium Hotels (West London) Limited	£65,847,000
Markerstudy Insurance Services Limited	£65,741,000
Skillbond Limited	£65,711,776

Curtis Holt Limited	£65,687,000	Millbrook Industries Limited	£63,308,000
Crown Golf Group Limited	£65,677,000	Sensient Flavors Limited	£63,280,836
Edwardian Exclusive Ltd	£65,669,000	Air Partner PLC	£63,254,000
Sekisui Diagnostics (UK) Limited	£65,660,568	Wireless Logic Limited	£63,225,000
Dolphin Drilling Operations Limited	£65,631,372	NEP Visions Limited	£63,179,220
Vodafone Global Content Services Limited	£65,571,856	3663 Transport Limited	£63,074,000
Arcus Investment Limited	£65,508,132	Carefusion U.K. 306 Limited	£63,054,944
Lotus Flower Holdings Limited	£65,505,608	SES (Engineering Services) Limited	£62,982,000
Cucina Fresh Investments Limited	£65,500,000	JRL Plant and Logistics Limited	£62,889,348
Ashcourt Rowan Limited	£65,455,000	Bathroom Brands Limited	£62,771,000
Street Family Group of Companies (Holdings) Ltd	£65,420,112	Crown Golf Property Limited	£62,770,000
Milton Keynes Development Partnership LLP	£65,392,000	T A Fisher (Holdings) Limited	£62,766,680
Inter Terminals Immingham Limited	£65,324,000	Ellenbrook Developments PLC	£62,760,000
University of Chichester (Multi) Academy Trust	£65,304,000	Ellenbrook Holdings Limited	£62,760,000
PizzaExpress International Holdings Limited	£65,241,000	Electrical Contractors Association Limited (The)	£62,661,440
Slough Heat & Power Limited	£65,200,000	Carestream Health UK, Limited	£62,592,000
J.T.Davies & Sons Limited	£65,178,176	Ability Housing Association	£62,583,428
Fortis Lease UK Ltd	£65,173,000	South Downs Real Estate Limited	£62,515,272
Creabilis Holdings Limited	£65,159,316	GlaxoSmithKline Consumer Healthcare Finance No.2	£62,455,720
Retirement Villages Limited	£65,107,568	Dawsongroup Vans Limited	£62,420,000
Grandir UK Limited	£65,098,000	Johnston Sweepers Limited	£62,408,000
KIMS Property Company Limited	£65,092,936	Veeam Software UK Limited	£62,334,832
Charles Wells Brewery Limited	£65,067,000	Sesame Bankhall Group Limited	£62,323,000
CHG Overseas Investments Limited	£64,954,000	Suez Recycling and Recovery Packington Ltd	£62,237,000
Technetix Group Limited	£64,900,000	Axon Solutions Limited	£62,234,000
Flexera Software Limited	£64,877,000	Boehringer Ingelheim Animal Health UK Limited	£62,210,000
Kingswood Learning and Leisure Group Limited	£64,845,000	The HMS Victory Preservation Company	£62,190,632
Hy-Ten Group Limited	£64,761,272	Mattel UK Holdings Limited	£62,164,000
Benugo Limited	£64,754,000	Trade Sale Ltd	£62,124,796
Eastern Leasing Company Limited (The)	£64,699,000	Suez Recycling and Recovery Kirklees Ltd	£62,060,000
Kallo Foods Limited	£64,671,028	Elster Metering Holdings Limited	£62,041,000
CHG-Meridian Computer Leasing UK Limited	£64,564,000	Direct Wines Finance Limited	£62,039,000
Ferring Laboratories Limited	£64,455,896	Cater Link Limited	£62,036,000
Weydon Multi Academy Trust	£64,445,260	Aqualisa Holdings (International) Limited	£61,965,000
Veetee Rice Limited	£64,440,648	FIL Investments International	£61,927,000
Glynwed Overseas Holdings Limited	£64,416,000	Dawsongroup Temperature Control Solutions Ltd	£61,924,000
Hayes & Jarvis (Travel) Limited	£64,323,000	Ergomed PLC	£61,913,000
Alimera Sciences Limited	£64,319,340	Thorn Security Limited	£61,857,000
Milton Keynes Community Foundation Limited	£64,318,392	U K Land Ltd.	£61,847,744
Natures Way Foods Europe Limited	£64,314,088	Lamp Group Limited	£61,794,000
Tech 21 UK Limited	£64,286,460	NPS (UK2) Limited	£61,786,000
Beckman Coulter United Kingdom Limited	£64,166,000	ACM Group Limited	£61,776,344
Hill of Towie Limited	£64,152,000	South East Surrey Schools Education Trust	£61,745,000
Biwater International Limited	£64,142,000	Romans 3 Limited	£61,690,316
SPI Lasers UK Limited	£64,137,000	Ability Hotels (III) Group Limited	£61,687,668
Crown Blue Line Limited	£64,114,824	Acer U.K. Limited	£61,678,000
Ceres Power Intermediate Holdings Limited	£64,097,984	McNeil Products Limited	£61,570,000
Inter Bay Financial II Limited	£64,080,000	Bridge Leisure Bidco Limited	£61,511,060
Readypower Rail Services Group Holdings Limited	£64,078,876	Equiniti Financial Services Limited	£61,500,000
Advanced Health and Care Limited	£64,043,000	IAG Cargo Limited	£61,458,000
Landmark Space Limited	£63,933,000	Diebold Nixdorf (UK) Limited	£61,346,000
Oxford International Education 1 Limited	£63,895,920	First Title Insurance PLC	£61,340,000
Signature Senior Lifestyle Finance Limited	£63,823,416	Eastbourne College (Incorporated)	£61,311,000
Subsea 7 Crewing Limited	£63,792,680	Discoverie Nordic Holdings Limited	£61,300,076
The Principal London Limited	£63,768,000	Warborough Investments Limited	£61,271,024
Data Solutions 2016 Limited	£63,767,000	Gardeners' Royal Benevolent Society	£61,241,000
Beck MBI Limited	£63,762,080	Mutual Services (Portsmouth) Limited	£61,233,104
Xchanging Global Insurance Solutions Limited	£63,728,000	Parker Hannifin Manufacturing (UK) Limited	£61,215,000
ITT Industries Limited	£63,721,000	C.L.C. Contractors Limited	£61,154,000
Millbrook Proving Ground Limited	£63,680,000	Allocate Holdco Limited	£61,137,000
Renewi UK Services Limited	£63,642,000	Samsung Semiconductor Europe Limited	£61,102,300
Erith Holdings Limited	£63,617,000	Gemalto UK Limited	£61,101,000
Belron UK Limited	£63,566,000	Six Continents Restaurants Limited	£61,100,000
Millennium Hotels Europe Holdings Limited	£63,557,728	GCP Biomass 1 Ltd	£61,095,576
Aunt Bessie's Limited	£63,495,000	Antler Homes PLC	£61,077,000
Eastern Airways (UK) Limited	£63,488,000	Altair (UK) Ltd	£61,074,296
PFU (EMEA) Limited	£63,459,240	Glenchamber Wind Energy Limited	£61,071,000
ENRA Group Limited	£63,454,864	Girls' Education Company,Limited	£61,070,000
Gillette U.K. Limited	£63,434,000	Marylebone Finco Limited	£61,022,936
Education Support (Swindon) Limited	£63,428,000	Berkeley Homes (PCL) Limited	£61,021,000
Education Support (Swindon) Holdings Limited	£63,428,000	Faber Prest Limited	£61,003,836
Penspen Limited	£63,387,000	NFAG Limited	£60,975,000

NEP UK Film I Limited	£60,956,000
Wates Living Space (Maintenance) Limited	£60,934,000
A W James Limited	£60,900,548
Minster Care Management Limited	£60,828,656
Modern Schools (Exeter) Limited	£60,781,000
Matrix SCM Limited	£60,740,224
Kedleston Group Limited	£60,707,804
Howitzer Acquisition Limited	£60,699,324
Thakeham Homes Limited	£60,685,088
Amphora Acquisitions Limited	£60,684,000
Symantec Security (UK) Limited	£60,658,000
TWE Finance (UK) Limited	£60,580,812
Camelot Global Lottery Solutions Limited	£60,554,000
Clean Viking Acquisition Co Limited	£60,533,956
Clackmannanshire Schools Education Partnership Hldgs	£60,522,000
Clackmannanshire Schools Education Partnership Ltd	£60,522,000
ILB Investments Limited	£60,520,232
Autumnpaper Limited	£60,438,316
Air Charter Service Group Limited	£60,419,000
Shukco Ltd	£60,371,000
Maiden Erlegh Trust	£60,368,000
Premier Asset Management Holdings Ltd.	£60,348,000
Fisher & Paykel Appliances Limited	£60,322,000
Sega Europe Limited	£60,303,000
Interserve Service Futures Limited	£60,264,276
Cathay Investments Limited	£60,255,724
Gojo Industries - Europe Limited	£60,227,816
CSL Behring UK Limited	£60,219,000
Covidien UK Limited	£60,209,000
Emac Limited	£60,206,000
Carisbrooke Shipping Holdings Limited	£60,198,048
CLC Group Limited	£60,182,000
Genesis Cancer Care UK Limited	£60,160,416
NTL Cablecomms Greater Manchester	£60,159,000
Kingston Bidco Limited	£60,137,024
Merck Serono Limited	£60,114,000
Tritoria UK Ltd	£60,103,044
Perkinelmer Limited	£60,081,000
Cape Claims Services Limited	£60,072,000
Aluminium Services (UK) Limited	£60,000,024
Nampak Plastics Europe Limited	£59,979,000
KAC Alarm Company Limited	£59,923,000
Laleham Health and Beauty Limited	£59,888,000
Eden Springs UK Limited	£59,880,000
Hamsard 3414 Limited	£59,844,420
Grass Valley Limited	£59,821,000
Laing O'Rourke Infrastructure Limited	£59,629,000
Xylem Water Holdings Limited	£59,614,000
Bamboo Topco Limited	£59,525,744
CPI Mortars (North) Limited	£59,518,592
Flir Systems Limited	£59,498,000
Cineworld Estates Limited	£59,493,000
Ability Hotels (III) UK Limited	£59,399,856
NHS Shared Business Services Limited	£59,393,000
Dreachmhor Wind Farm Limited	£59,372,000
Morgan Europe Holding Limited	£59,364,000
Essentra Packaging & Security Limited	£59,358,000
Advanced Legal Solutions Limited	£59,226,000
Heidelberg Graphic Equipment Limited	£59,182,000
London Arena Investments Limited	£59,096,132
Autodesk Limited	£59,085,504
Valley Invicta Academies Trust	£59,020,000
Britannia Pharmaceuticals Limited	£59,009,000
L-J Finco Limited	£58,988,000
Epilepsy Society	£58,977,000
Alexander Fraser Holdings Limited	£58,880,576
Baldwin House Limited	£58,877,656
Rockwell Collins UK Limited	£58,850,000
Valour Bidco Limited	£58,793,560
Vendcrown Limited	£58,671,000
Hendy Holdings Limited	£58,627,000
Raisio UK Limited	£58,564,000
BP Properties Limited	£58,560,000
Civil and Marine (Holdings) Limited	£58,560,000
Rentokil Initial Investments South Africa	£58,533,316
Vinci UK Developments Limited	£58,511,000
GCP Rooftop Solar 6 PLC	£58,499,368
IG Design Group UK Limited	£58,422,000
ACAL Electronics Holdings Limited	£58,418,000
Sharnbrook Academy Federation	£58,341,944
Bose Limited	£58,338,000
Anthony Nicholas (UK) Limited	£58,186,260
Harlequin FC Holdings Limited	£58,163,112
Nastor Investments Limited	£58,098,000
Fitesa Limited	£58,042,936
Teletrac Navman (UK) Ltd	£58,012,000
Norbain Holdings Limited	£58,005,000
Oxford International Education 3 Limited	£58,002,268
SF Ground Rents Limited	£57,922,540
Althea UK and Ireland Limited	£57,900,000
CT Automotive Group Limited	£57,863,064
Hy-Ten Limited	£57,861,488
Clinimed (Holdings) Limited	£57,811,084
Dnata Limited	£57,703,000
Spincrest Limited	£57,678,024
Zodiac Europe Limited	£57,647,000
The Whiteley Homes Trust	£57,607,644
Industrial and Financial Systems, IFS UK Ltd	£57,601,820
Avante Care and Support Limited	£57,550,196
Omex Agricultural Holdings Ltd.	£57,546,420
Neilcott Construction Limited	£57,488,768
TT Electronics IoT Solutions Limited	£57,442,000
Southern Co-operative Funerals Limited	£57,423,404
Leaders Limited	£57,419,616
Horsted Estates Limited	£57,372,200
Rayner Surgical Group Limited	£57,308,000
Regenter B3 Holdco Limited	£57,194,000
Regenter B3 Limited	£57,194,000
Digico UK Limited	£57,102,000
Driveline Limited	£57,100,272
International Marine Transportation Limited	£57,075,828
Essentra Packaging Limited	£57,013,000
Armadillo Storage Holding Company Limited	£57,007,000
Biwater Holdings Limited	£57,000,000
Evolution (Shinfield) LLP	£56,992,000
HCP Packaging UK Limited	£56,988,204
Leaders The Rental Agents Limited	£56,956,028
QSC 1208 Limited	£56,909,872
BP Pension Trustees Limited	£56,905,000
Genus Breeding Limited	£56,904,000
BP Investment Management Limited	£56,856,624
Aesica Queenborough Limited	£56,800,000
Boskalis Westminster (Holdings) Limited	£56,750,000
Bywest (Holdings) Limited	£56,724,000
Bywest Limited	£56,723,000
Geo. Kingsbury Holdings Limited	£56,679,628
Yourcash Limited	£56,644,000
Nature Delivered Limited	£56,597,200
Yum! Restaurant Holdings	£56,545,000
Premier Global Infrastructure Trust PLC	£56,489,000
SmithKline Beecham Overseas Limited	£56,486,000
European Investments (Cornwall) Limited	£56,410,928
Marlin Europe II Limited	£56,401,000
Renaissance Retirement Limited	£56,394,280
Wartsila UK Limited	£56,391,000
Bartholomews (Holdings) Limited	£56,337,804
Edgewell Personal Care Investments UK Ltd.	£56,288,000
The Gap Partnership Bidco Limited	£56,270,084
Xtralis (UK) Limited	£56,254,000
NCL Holdings Limited	£56,203,348
Apollo Fire Detectors Limited	£56,143,184
Group Fabricom Limited	£56,141,000
Sandown Surrey and Hampshire Limited	£56,138,000
Rhodia International Holdings Limited	£55,991,000

Company	Value	Company	Value
Idox Software Ltd	£55,990,396	Alfa Laval Limited	£54,131,000
Creative Technology Group Limited	£55,965,000	Cerestar UK Ltd	£54,078,356
Centrica (Lincs) Wind Farm Limited	£55,846,000	TP Group PLC	£54,024,000
Kuwait Petroleum International Aviation Co Ltd	£55,840,000	Sungard Availability Services (DR) Limited	£54,004,000
Wealmoor Limited	£55,834,576	Saywell International Limited	£53,995,216
Seiko U.K. Limited	£55,748,000	Rebus Group Limited	£53,963,000
L. Lynch (Plant Hire & Haulage) Limited	£55,744,604	Inspiring Learning (Holdings) Limited	£53,890,000
Hamilton Palace Limited	£55,743,392	Anglo Suisse Investments Limited	£53,741,056
Ability Hotels (IV) Finance Limited	£55,695,048	Safran Helicopter Engines UK Limited	£53,722,556
We Buy Any Car Limited	£55,664,000	Optegra International Limited	£53,722,528
Softwareone UK Limited	£55,639,360	Apex Car Rental PLC	£53,663,936
Discoverie Management Services Limited	£55,553,000	Dewhurst PLC	£53,657,000
Xchanging Holdco No.3 Limited	£55,539,000	Glendola Leisure (Holdings) Limited	£53,577,000
BOC Investments No.5	£55,538,000	Safe Haven London	£53,576,304
Clean Linen Services Limited	£55,512,176	Bytes Technology Group Limited	£53,560,000
Kingsbridge Estates Limited	£55,506,396	Symrise Holding Limited	£53,461,332
Xtrac Limited	£55,453,000	Pulsant Topco Limited	£53,450,548
SC Osney Lane Limited	£55,449,400	Angmering Park Farms LLP	£53,428,416
Siemens Healthcare Diagnostics Ltd	£55,420,000	Vestey Foods UK Limited	£53,420,000
Coastal Academies Trust	£55,416,044	Buyagift PLC	£53,391,976
H.E. Group Ltd	£55,409,788	Nesstra Services (UK) Limited	£53,372,868
Choice Care Group 2 Limited	£55,314,620	Thames Properties Ltd.	£53,337,912
Fort Pitt Thomas Aveling Academies	£55,282,144	Xpanse Limited	£53,329,000
ANSYS UK Limited	£55,263,000	Gruma Europe Limited	£53,273,000
Intelliflo Holdings 2013 Limited	£55,258,876	Spaces Personal Storage Limited	£53,262,000
Intelliflo Midco Limited	£55,258,872	Hinds Ltd	£53,229,980
Hornby Hobbies Limited	£55,248,000	Detica Group Limited	£53,208,000
Elster Metering Limited	£55,227,000	Invesco Far East Limited	£53,202,932
United Living (South) Group Limited	£55,203,000	Twickenham Experience Ltd	£53,160,000
Home Grown Hotels Limited	£55,176,340	Parkside Capital Limited	£53,131,352
United Healthcare (South Buckinghamshire) Group	£55,167,000	Luxury Travel Financing Limited	£53,064,000
Toucan Solar Assets 1 Holdco Limited	£55,142,260	UK Electric Limited	£53,052,000
TJX Europe Buying Limited	£55,088,000	BCA Fleet Solutions Limited	£53,041,000
Sumika Polymer Compounds (Europe) Ltd	£55,065,000	Rebus Holdings Limited	£53,017,000
Mission Aviation Fellowship International	£55,045,568	Monster Energy Europe Limited	£53,013,208
Salutem LD Bidco Limited	£54,990,000	Boral (UK) Limited	£53,009,000
Bullitt Group Limited	£54,975,732	Crest Nicholson Developments (Chertsey) Limited	£53,000,000
Essentra Filter Products International Limited	£54,970,000	ADM Milling Limited	£52,998,376
Optum UK Solutions Group Limited	£54,957,288	Gallaher Overseas Limited	£52,846,000
Focusrite PLC	£54,926,000	Bradenstoke Solar Park Limited	£52,818,064
BNP Paribas Rental Solutions Limited	£54,920,000	UK Broadband Limited	£52,781,064
Maxxia (UK) Limited	£54,919,792	Education Development Trust	£52,733,000
Cluff Oil Limited	£54,890,000	Bullitt Mobile Limited	£52,680,028
APCOA Parking Holdings (UK) Limited	£54,863,068	O.S.T.C. Limited	£52,668,920
Borelli Tea Holdings Limited	£54,827,008	Binder Holdco Limited	£52,662,424
The Schelwood Trust	£54,801,880	Nespresso UK Ltd	£52,598,000
Arqiva No 3 Limited	£54,786,000	B & P Holdings II Limited	£52,587,844
The Milton Group Limited	£54,775,520	Carewatch Bidco Limited	£52,561,000
One GE Healthcare UK	£54,736,000	Euro Food Brands Limited	£52,531,304
FWPJV Limited	£54,723,048	Chas.A.Blatchford & Sons,Limited	£52,506,000
KPJV Limited	£54,723,048	Alliance BMP Limited	£52,475,000
The Challenger Multi Academy Trust	£54,674,760	Vertiv Infrastructure Ltd	£52,474,000
Aquila Air Traffic Management Services Limited	£54,671,000	M New Holdings Limited	£52,452,424
Radnor House School (Holdings) Limited	£54,664,096	Brighton I-360 Limited	£52,412,804
Genesys Telecommunications Laboratories - Europe	£54,656,000	Cementation Skanska Limited	£52,347,000
JBS Global (UK) Limited	£54,645,752	EWOS Limited	£52,320,000
MacDermid G.B. Holdings Limited	£54,642,000	Miles 33 Group Limited	£52,316,000
S.D.C. Builders Limited	£54,579,932	Burhill Group Limited	£52,311,364
The National Fostering Agency Limited	£54,551,000	Capital Professional Limited	£52,286,144
Holroyd Howe Limited	£54,516,000	Rank Hovis Milling Limited	£52,255,000
Pandrol Limited	£54,439,000	PTP Software Limited	£52,246,808
Trifast Overseas Holdings Limited	£54,421,000	Hyster-Yale Group Limited	£52,241,564
ICS Group Holdings Limited	£54,369,556	Essentra Filter Products Limited	£52,233,000
Stowe School,Limited	£54,321,720	Optoma Europe Ltd	£52,228,000
Imagine Cruising Limited	£54,304,696	Millmead Properties Limited	£52,219,892
Decco Limited	£54,295,000	INC Research Holding Limited	£52,150,108
CNM Estates (Tolworth Tower MB) Limited	£54,246,356	A.C. Lighting (Holdings) Limited	£52,121,268
Chaptre Finance PLC	£54,245,000	Barfoot Holdings Limited	£51,999,560
Boorley Green LLP	£54,241,000	Wasp Management Software Limited	£51,981,000
Oceanic Finance Limited	£54,238,528	Enterprise Rent-a-Car UK Holdings Limited	£51,979,000
Ericsson Television Limited	£54,179,000	Countrywide Principal Services Limited	£51,941,000
Marlin Capital Europe Limited	£54,163,000	P & O Ferries Pride of Hull Limited	£51,845,000

Company	Amount
British Airways Associated Companies Limited	£51,810,000
Blake Morgan LLP	£51,801,000
Valour Holdco Limited	£51,776,156
Search Consultancy Topco Limited	£51,752,000
Crane Payment Innovations International Ltd	£51,723,000
Airspan Communications Limited	£51,686,728
Arora Management Services Limited	£51,631,480
Brasserie Bar Co Limited	£51,583,560
J C C Lighting Products Limited	£51,580,672
Acenden Limited	£51,547,000
Bloc Hotel Group Limited	£51,517,192
Kedleston Schools Limited	£51,455,176
CAE Training & Services UK Ltd	£51,444,000
Gravesend and District Real Estate Company Ltd	£51,402,836
Lactalis Nestle Chilled Dairy Company Limited	£51,369,000
Tricomm Housing (Portsmouth) Limited	£51,347,824
Three Rivers Property Investments Limited	£51,317,440
Elysium Healthcare (Lighthouse) Limited	£51,317,000
Luton Hoo Park Limited	£51,297,848
Oyezstraker Group Limited	£51,260,000
Thales Ground Transportation Systems UK Limited	£51,224,000
Trant Holding Company Limited	£51,177,000
Snell Corporation Limited	£51,167,000
Miles 33 Limited	£51,152,000
Heart Internet Limited	£51,146,000
Daikin Airconditioning UK Limited	£51,144,000
Tata Global Beverages Overseas Holdings Limited	£51,138,000
Cleansing Service Group Limited	£51,061,864
Symmetry Logistics Holdings Limited	£51,057,244
Folkestone Harbour Holdings Limited	£51,049,840
Smith International (North Sea) Limited	£51,043,000
Allergy Therapeutics PLC	£51,016,000
Spirit Resources (Armada) Limited	£50,855,000
The Reading Football Club Limited	£50,809,012
Tropicana United Kingdom Limited	£50,739,000
Malta Topco Limited	£50,732,000
Prater Limited	£50,723,148
Southern Co-operative Properties Limited	£50,647,000
The Willow Learning Trust	£50,639,000
Venson Automotive Solutions Limited	£50,620,388
Stonefield Estates, Limited	£50,552,612
Devine Holdings Limited	£50,540,040
Sabre Retail Fashion Limited	£50,532,000
Doosan Power Systems Overseas Investments Ltd	£50,513,000
Acheson Industries (Europe) Limited	£50,488,000
ABHL Digital Limited	£50,468,000
Advanced 365 Limited	£50,449,000
Cromwell Holdings Limited	£50,442,000
Impact Oil & Gas Limited	£50,431,184
Tates of Sussex Limited	£50,424,912
Groupe SEB UK Limited	£50,423,000
Intelliflo Bidco Limited	£50,401,736
CSL Communications Group Limited	£50,398,536
York Engineered Systems Limited	£50,356,000
Trenchard Aviation Limited	£50,345,828
Needspace? Limited	£50,340,344
Vanderbilt Development Finance Ltd	£50,253,000
Barfoots of Botley Limited	£50,230,328
Medina Holdings Limited	£50,164,084
Metropolis Group Holdings Limited	£50,160,608
Lord Wandsworth College	£50,147,784
Vines Limited	£50,147,448
Guildford Portfolios Limited	£50,147,448
PSI - Pay Ltd	£50,119,196
Project Ventures Rail Investments I Limited	£50,100,000
Fridays Limited	£50,088,196
First Hampshire & Dorset Limited	£50,083,000
The Meller Educational Trust	£50,062,852
Hampton School	£50,031,768
Hanover Displays Limited	£49,961,548
Tombstone Limited	£49,950,428
NPS (UK5) Limited	£49,887,000
TTNG Investments Limited	£49,877,500
Floplast Limited	£49,819,096
Hireco (TL) Limited	£49,794,180
MTWOM B Limited	£49,793,000
Suez Advanced Solutions Holding UK Limited	£49,707,000
Indoor Bowling Acquisitions Limited	£49,701,000
Southern Water Investments Limited	£49,700,000
Environments for Learning Sandwell PFI Holdco	£49,700,000
Environments for Learning Sandwell PFI One Limited	£49,700,000
Surfcontrol Limited	£49,694,708
St George's Weybridge	£49,638,200
Bathroom Brands Holdings UK Limited	£49,631,000
The Romans Group (UK) Limited	£49,610,972
Personal Group Holdings PLC	£49,568,000
Ability Hotels (Syon Park) Limited	£49,532,904
D.J.Squire & Co.,Limited	£49,522,000
UK Software Holdings Limited	£49,512,000
No.7 Limited	£49,497,208
Sonardyne International Limited	£49,461,796
Clinisys Solutions Limited	£49,438,000
Kent EHFA Projectco Limited	£49,430,544
Blackwell Science Limited	£49,430,000
Combined Counties Properties Limited	£49,416,748
Sword Soft Limited	£49,414,896
Commvault Systems Limited	£49,356,848
Albain Bidco UK Limited	£49,298,092
W.J.King (Garages) Limited	£49,264,216
Informatica Software Limited	£49,263,856
Delice de France Limited	£49,231,404
Jain International Foods Limited	£49,184,888
TY Properties (UK) Limited	£49,173,000
The Williamson Trust	£49,124,800
Rayner Intraocular Lenses Limited	£49,124,000
Mastek (UK) Ltd.	£49,106,184
NIS Receivables No. 2 Limited	£49,100,000
Dell Emerging Markets (EMEA) Limited	£49,076,000
Dominvs Project Company 9 Limited	£49,072,352
Sparshatts Holdings Limited	£49,030,188
Dawsongroup Material Handling Limited	£49,025,000
Daler-Rowney Limited	£49,018,000
United Kenning Rental Group Limited	£49,009,000
Cashino Gaming Limited	£48,951,000
Micromuse Limited	£48,949,308
Scott Health & Safety Limited	£48,938,000
Chemidex Pharma Limited	£48,929,356
Alex Brands Rocket Holdings Limited	£48,893,388
Windsor Learning Partnership	£48,872,824
Rohm Electronics Europe Limited	£48,865,000
Siemens Healthcare Diagnostics Products Ltd	£48,849,000
EDL (UK) LFG Generation Limited	£48,837,960
The Luxury Travel Group Limited	£48,829,000
Cooper Estates Limited	£48,811,544
KIMS Kent Holdings Limited	£48,789,120
E & J Capital Partners Limited	£48,787,560
Kingston Topco Limited	£48,750,108
The Innovation Group (EMEA) Limited	£48,730,000
Regulus Bidco Limited	£48,721,544
Thesis Unit Trust Management Limited	£48,684,904
Marlin Financial Intermediate II Limited	£48,680,000
System C Healthcare Limited	£48,630,304
Interbay Funding, Ltd.	£48,629,000
Wates Group Services Limited	£48,559,000
Smiths Detection-Watford Limited	£48,547,000
Kewsaw Limited	£48,544,000
OTV Birwelco Limited	£48,530,000
Strollmoor Limited	£48,476,724
Pinnacle Schools (Gateshead) Limited	£48,456,844
Robinson Webster (Holdings) Limited	£48,406,000
Soka Gakkai International - UK	£48,387,364
Tesla Engineering Limited	£48,323,000
White Rock Land LLP	£48,318,000
European Investments (Cornwall) Holdings Limited	£48,295,900

Company	Amount	Company	Amount
Becton Dickinson Infusion Therapy Holdings UK Ltd	£48,294,000	Trafalgar Insurance Public Limited Company	£46,897,000
Kent EHFA Holdco Limited	£48,288,048	Greencell Limited	£46,811,000
Porsche Retail Group Limited	£48,279,000	William Reed Holdings Limited	£46,802,000
Chartwell Properties Limited	£48,270,424	Amscan International Limited	£46,771,000
Ellis & Sons Amalgamated Properties Limited	£48,258,832	Sedgemoor Limited	£46,707,000
Mitac Technology UK Ltd.	£48,232,568	ST & H Group Limited	£46,685,000
British Fittings Group Limited	£48,164,000	Blue Sky Intermodal (UK) Ltd.	£46,668,008
Ella's Kitchen (Brands) Limited	£48,126,140	Allegis Global Solutions Limited	£46,655,436
Canal & River Trading CIC	£48,124,308	Experis Group Limited	£46,643,000
Exel UK Limited	£48,120,000	Buxted Construction Limited	£46,615,080
Graduation Midco Limited	£48,116,000	Exela Technologies Limited	£46,578,000
Bel UK Limited	£48,115,000	Beardow Adams Holdings Ltd	£46,559,456
Krispy Kreme U.K. Limited	£48,113,000	Park Garage Group PLC	£46,549,408
Imperial Car Supermarkets Limited	£48,101,000	Kingston Digital Europe Co LLP	£46,547,424
CBI International Parent Limited	£48,096,888	Mapeley Steps Contractor Limited	£46,538,000
MCF Commercial Limited	£48,084,928	Speyside Renewable Energy Finance PLC	£46,536,000
W & R Buxton Holdings Limited	£48,058,900	Europa Road Limited	£46,527,488
PDC Brands UK Limited	£48,029,652	Sericol Ink Limited	£46,495,000
CAS St Paul's Limited	£48,020,000	Benenden School (Kent) Limited	£46,487,000
Sevenoaks School	£48,017,000	Collins 2017 Limited	£46,422,452
E.H. Nicholls Holdings Limited	£47,994,392	Blackwell Publishing (Holdings) Limited	£46,408,000
Harvey & Son (Lewes) Limited	£47,975,480	Honeywell Holdings Limited	£46,383,000
Bio Energy (UK) Limited	£47,917,588	Farnborough Finance (2007) Limited	£46,380,404
Crescent Pharmaceuticals Limited	£47,916,996	London Tower Crane Hire & Sales Limited	£46,363,016
Premier Fleet Management and Contract Hire Ltd	£47,869,992	Beck Interiors Limited	£46,355,192
Hatch, Mansfield Agencies Limited	£47,861,024	Tamar Energy Limited	£46,351,000
Beadles Group Limited	£47,849,796	B & P Midco 1 Limited	£46,345,424
Churchill Insurance Company Limited	£47,799,000	Jacobs Process Limited	£46,337,000
Longview Holding Parent UK Limited	£47,795,592	Richstone Properties Limited	£46,332,496
Beck & Pollitzer Engineering Limited	£47,730,452	TCR UK Limited	£46,323,968
Arrow Business Communications Holdings Limited	£47,714,532	Websense SC Holdings Limited	£46,323,700
Clearswift Holding Limited	£47,657,000	Archer Daniels Midland Erith Limited	£46,321,200
Cargill Cotton Limited	£47,646,000	SWS Group Holdings Limited	£46,300,000
Panalpina World Transport Limited	£47,638,000	SWS Holdings Limited	£46,300,000
Wadlow Energy Limited	£47,619,000	Caligor Opco UK, Ltd	£46,252,908
Deta Electrical Company Limited	£47,605,000	The Car Finance Company (2007) Ltd	£46,217,000
JCA Charitable Foundation	£47,593,000	Vink UK Limited	£46,216,000
Elite Homes (North West) Limited	£47,590,000	Plexus Holdings PLC	£46,154,000
Citrix R & D Limited	£47,513,728	Just Retirement Management Services Limited	£46,142,000
Wilsons Automobiles and Coachworks Limited	£47,490,304	Cheshunt Lakeside Developments Limited	£46,140,764
Voluntary Service Overseas	£47,489,000	Hurricane (Whirlwind) Limited	£46,050,448
James Villa Holidays Limited	£47,470,552	Argos Business Solutions Limited	£46,026,000
Spritestore Limited	£47,458,560	WP SK Holdings Limited	£46,000,000
RGCM Limited	£47,456,760	Pennyhill Park Limited	£45,962,144
Zennor Pathway Limited	£47,456,000	BMC Software Limited	£45,955,104
Electronic Arts Limited	£47,419,000	United Healthcare (South Buckinghamshire) Ltd	£45,954,000
Berthon Boat Company Limited (The)	£47,408,296	Bike Alert PLC	£45,941,720
Renoir Bidco Limited	£47,338,000	Servomex Group Limited	£45,937,000
Porsche Financial Services Great Britain Limited	£47,314,604	Siva Holdings Limited	£45,913,316
Sandoz Limited	£47,303,000	Romans 2 Limited	£45,899,672
Octagon Group Limited	£47,297,000	Towers Watson UK Limited	£45,887,000
Boskalis Westminster Limited	£47,290,000	Lousada PLC	£45,876,936
Brand Energy & Infrastructure Services UK, Ltd.	£47,269,000	Westec Holding Company Limited	£45,861,412
Crescent Pharma Limited	£47,265,104	Invesco Software Holdings Limited	£45,828,160
CP Regents Park Two Limited	£47,227,640	Premier Medical Holdings Limited	£45,809,084
Sky SNI Limited	£47,161,000	Lime Wood Group Limited	£45,776,488
Grouse Topco Limited	£47,114,000	Digico Global Limited	£45,657,132
Allos Holdings Limited	£47,086,120	Storrington Equityco Limited	£45,589,000
Gurit Material Systems (UK) Limited	£47,085,000	SLR Consulting Limited	£45,580,956
Custodes Midco Limited	£47,083,628	Firmenich UK Limited	£45,554,000
Erith Contractors Limited	£47,079,216	O2 International Holdings Limited	£45,546,000
Whistler Acquisitions Limited	£47,073,000	Ben-Motor and Allied Trades Benevolent Fund	£45,529,000
Lea Redway Limited	£47,061,912	Howard Humphreys & Partners Limited	£45,467,092
St Barnabas Hospices (Sussex) Ltd	£47,057,000	Tyrolese (751) Limited	£45,411,928
HSH Hotels (2017) Limited	£47,056,040	Waremoss Limited	£45,366,268
Yacht Havens Limited	£47,021,132	Yum! Franchise II LLP	£45,353,404
Novar International Limited	£47,010,000	Thorney Lane LLP	£45,342,036
APCOA Parking (UK) Limited	£46,994,404	Inland Property Limited	£45,341,128
JDA Software UK Limited	£46,949,000	CeleritiFinTech Limited	£45,320,000
Allianz Engineering Inspection Services Limited	£46,903,448	Woodcote Estates Limited	£45,316,128
Taylor Made Golf Limited	£46,902,000	Share PLC	£45,286,000
Pye Properties Limited	£46,900,996	BP Oil Vietnam Limited	£45,285,296

The Civil Service Benevolent Fund	£45,249,000
Transform Housing & Support	£45,192,000
Cross Stone Securities Limited	£45,185,536
Lighthouse Healthcare Group Limited	£45,142,000
Premier Fruit & Nut Limited	£45,135,876
CBI UK Topco Limited	£45,131,328
Bellevue Education International Limited	£45,101,192
Wipac Limited	£45,089,432
ZG Lighting (UK) Limited	£45,073,000
1509 Group	£45,072,384
Europa Worldwide Group Limited	£45,062,596
Five Arrows Limited	£45,047,000
BI Worldwide Limited	£45,043,664
Green Hill Energy Limited	£45,007,000
Oakfield (Foods) Limited	£44,994,880
Swan Mill (Holdings) Limited	£44,979,000
UPS SCS (UK) Limited	£44,975,000
Netcall PLC	£44,958,000
Bapchild Motoring World (Kent) Limited	£44,938,208
Charity for St Joseph's Missionary Society (Generalate)	£44,919,296
Thornton Park (London) Limited	£44,908,752
Centre for Health and Disability Assessments Ltd	£44,858,720
Chilton Home Farms Ltd	£44,841,792
Partridge of Hampshire Holdings Limited	£44,750,732
Rocco Homes Limited	£44,745,772
Elliott Brothers (Builders Merchants) Limited	£44,719,000
Fasttrax Holdings Limited	£44,718,000
Fasttrax Limited	£44,712,000
Purelake New Homes Limited	£44,710,352
The Romsey School	£44,674,568
Sinclair Knight Merz (Europe) Limited	£44,633,000
Octagon Developments Limited	£44,604,000
United Reformed Church (Wessex) Trust Limited	£44,573,088
David Cover and Son Limited	£44,571,616
Brioche Pasquier U.K. Limited	£44,564,856
The Royal Air Force Central Fund	£44,561,656
BP Investments Asia Limited	£44,532,652
West Raynham Solar Limited	£44,512,368
Vectis Property Co. Limited	£44,387,352
B & P Midco 2 Limited	£44,345,424
Brisko Scaffolding Limited	£44,339,620
Tonbridge School	£44,337,820
Aurora Academies Trust	£44,305,000
Windmill Organics Limited	£44,271,744
Fourfront Holdings Limited	£44,251,040
F.Hinds Limited	£44,240,396
Stanmore Contractors Limited	£44,200,124
Coats Industrial Thread Limited	£44,122,168
Sparshatts of Kent Limited	£44,086,932
Rydon Maintenance Limited	£44,077,060
Teddington School	£44,062,220
Street Property (Holdings) Limited	£44,051,604
Hawk Incentives Holdings Limited	£44,010,000
MSV Group Limited	£43,991,000
Sensient Holdings UK	£43,981,096
Stats UK Holdco Limited	£43,975,316
Medequip Assistive Technology Limited	£43,960,000
Brentford Phase II LLP	£43,948,000
Hurstpierpoint College Limited	£43,918,000
Transserv UK Limited	£43,903,200
Secom PLC	£43,885,000
Elysium Healthcare (Ultimate Care) Limited	£43,884,684
Fire Support (SSFR) Holdings Limited	£43,880,000
Fire Support (SSFR) Limited	£43,880,000
ESP Electricity Limited	£43,873,000
DHM Plastics Limited	£43,846,000
TGS Geophysical Company (UK) Limited	£43,833,228
Propane Company Limited (The)	£43,813,068
Montgomery Property Group Limited	£43,807,376
Marlin Europe I Limited	£43,782,000
Hertswood Academy	£43,777,864
Chobham Manor LLP	£43,774,000
Flight Centre Travel Group (European Holdings) Ltd	£43,769,828
John Street & Company (Surrey) Limited	£43,769,624
Swan Group	£43,723,000
The Ordnance Building Limited	£43,701,624
NSSLGlobal Limited	£43,698,000
CSL (Dualcom) Limited	£43,686,032
Henry Construction Projects Limited	£43,675,720
Kuehne + Nagel Drinks Logistics Limited	£43,669,000
Coombe Academy Trust	£43,633,000
Africa Express Line Limited	£43,632,960
Tanita International Ltd.	£43,626,796
IMCD UK Acquisitions Limited	£43,591,000
Dai Europe Ltd	£43,542,000
Toshiba Tec U.K. Imaging Systems Limited	£43,535,000
Costain Oil, Gas & Process Limited	£43,493,608
Optum Solutions UK Holdings Limited	£43,473,144
Technetix Limited	£43,462,000
City Link (Cardiff) Limited	£43,447,000
Watson Wyatt Holdings (Europe) Limited	£43,446,796
Linde Creighton Limited	£43,411,000
The Langley Academy Trust	£43,376,212
Inter Terminals Seal Sands Limited	£43,375,000
JCDecaux United Limited	£43,353,000
Celltech R & D Limited	£43,325,000
Sumitomo Electric Europe Limited	£43,287,000
A.A.Fisher (Properties) Limited	£43,273,648
Laing Limited	£43,262,000
Direct Wines International Limited	£43,203,088
Denmaur Independent Papers Limited	£43,184,064
Edwardian Canary Wharf Hotel Limited	£43,167,000
Zanlia Limited	£43,096,324
Scott Dunn Limited	£43,091,000
ICS Cool Energy Limited	£43,085,904
Evolution (Woking) Limited	£43,064,000
PHF Investments Limited	£43,045,832
BRE Trust	£43,026,000
In-Sync Group Limited	£43,021,132
Serena Software Europe Limited	£42,992,000
Audatex (UK) Limited	£42,971,800
Reading Transport Limited	£42,945,000
Old Thorns Golf Hotel and Country Estate Limited	£42,910,688
Pioneer Educational Trust	£42,896,000
British Airways Maintenance Cardiff Limited	£42,889,000
Pentland Homes (Holdings) Limited	£42,882,248
Kenneth Green Associates Limited	£42,828,352
Doncaster School Solutions Limited	£42,817,000
Doncaster School Solutions (Holdings) Limited	£42,817,000
Chemidex Generics Limited	£42,801,256
Abriand Limited	£42,796,000
Camden Ventures Limited	£42,794,000
Old Thorns Golf Hotel and Country Estate Holdings	£42,793,096
Adelie Foods Group Limited	£42,783,000
Southwick Solar Farm Limited	£42,722,420
Gama Aviation (Engineering) Limited	£42,697,000
Wintel Petrochemicals Limited	£42,683,424
Murex Biotech Limited	£42,680,000
Abbott Healthcare Products Ltd	£42,670,000
Motus Holdings (UK) Limited	£42,667,856
Cleanland Limited	£42,653,320
Maisonparc Ltd	£42,652,240
United Living (North) Holdings Limited	£42,618,000
STI Enterprises Limited	£42,614,000
8x8 UK Investments Limited	£42,604,680
Pentland Homes Limited	£42,573,540
Interserve PFI Holdings Limited	£42,556,000
Thursdays (Holdings) Limited	£42,550,000
Chingford Fruit Limited	£42,549,000
Microsoft Properties UK Limited	£42,548,000
IHC May Fair Hotel Limited	£42,486,000
Huntswood CTC Limited	£42,464,440
RB Hotels Limited	£42,454,992
Global Invacom Holdings Limited	£42,454,956

Security Monitoring Centres Limited	£42,449,000	Reigate Grammar School	£41,145,264
Hartford Care Group Limited	£42,423,672	Avicenna Holdings Ltd	£41,143,000
Warrant Investments PLC	£42,415,112	Bollore Logistics UK Ltd	£41,135,144
ADA PD UK Limited	£42,404,728	Maxell Europe Limited	£41,125,600
Merritts Properties Limited	£42,388,588	Linden Wates (Royston) LLP	£41,105,000
Zionstone Limited	£42,309,000	Linden (Northstowe) LLP	£41,094,000
J.& H.Robinson (Ilford Farms) Limited	£42,295,364	Services Sound and Vision Corporation (The)	£41,036,000
Water Process Limited	£42,276,000	Unipath Limited	£41,001,000
Vivid Topco Ltd	£42,276,000	Wyboston Lakes Limited	£40,988,432
PIG Improvement Company UK Limited	£42,245,000	Alfa Laval Holdings Limited	£40,983,000
Langley Park Learning Trust	£42,240,000	Westmoreland Developments Limited	£40,961,376
Watson Wyatt European Region Limited	£42,237,204	Welborne Energy LLP	£40,948,368
ESRI Holdings Limited	£42,185,500	MessageLabs Limited	£40,946,000
Medica Group PLC	£42,163,000	SDH Holdco Limited	£40,905,444
Wryde Croft Wind Farm Limited	£42,107,000	Wilky Group Limited (The)	£40,837,968
CHEP Pallecon Solutions Limited	£42,080,944	Synbra UK Limited	£40,757,260
Microchip Limited	£42,055,428	Medreich PLC	£40,756,208
Kordal Limited	£42,047,696	Descram Holdings Limited	£40,742,104
Edif Group Finance Limited	£42,035,000	Octagon Group Holdings Limited	£40,730,000
Aliunde Limited	£42,024,648	Suez Advanced Solutions UK Limited	£40,718,000
Shukco 327 Ltd	£42,015,000	Invesco UK Holdings Limited	£40,707,000
Akzo Nobel Powder Coatings Limited	£41,981,000	Howarth Homes PLC	£40,702,896
Incomm Europe Limited	£41,967,016	Rockwell European Holdings Limited	£40,651,000
Bio-Rad Laboratories Limited	£41,961,000	Ambec Limited	£40,640,376
Mizen Properties Limited	£41,955,016	Elster Water Metering Limited	£40,624,000
Birmingham Schools Partnership Limited	£41,926,000	W.T. Lamb Holdings Limited	£40,614,824
Premier Asset Management Midco Ltd.	£41,920,000	ChildrenSalon Limited	£40,552,280
Selwood Group Limited	£41,918,000	Invesco GT Asset Management Limited	£40,548,968
JTL	£41,899,648	Metropolis International Group Ltd	£40,544,320
Acambis Research Limited	£41,899,000	Interquest Group (UK) Limited	£40,527,684
Harepath Estates LLP	£41,831,352	MDH (Group) Limited	£40,517,000
Berkhamsted Schools Group	£41,814,000	Gurit (UK) Limited	£40,502,000
The University of Southampton Science Park Limited	£41,792,820	Treloar Trust	£40,499,000
Wescot Topco Limited	£41,748,000	Milton Keynes Education Trust	£40,484,816
Epson (U.K.) Limited	£41,722,000	Kentstone Properties Limited	£40,457,036
Honeywell Specialty Wax & Additives Limited	£41,700,000	Xafinity Consulting Limited	£40,452,000
International Society for Krishna Consciousness Ltd	£41,681,696	Watts Gallery	£40,436,452
Norma UK Limited	£41,667,864	Partridge of Hampshire Limited	£40,427,520
St. Catherine's School, Bramley	£41,666,404	INEOS Capital Limited	£40,427,176
Econocom Limited	£41,658,000	Emerald Topco Limited	£40,401,000
Bottomline Technologies Europe Limited	£41,644,104	ABL Capital Investments Ltd	£40,394,560
Creative Foods Europe Limited	£41,642,936	MFG Parentco Limited	£40,391,000
LDFA Limited	£41,633,020	ATP Media Operations Limited	£40,368,924
Riverstone Management Limited	£41,604,000	The Alec Reed Academy	£40,347,000
Porthaven Management Limited	£41,589,348	Basinghall Estate Company Limited	£40,333,468
Queens' School (Bushey)	£41,587,780	Burhill Golf and Leisure Limited	£40,325,740
L-J Bidco Limited	£41,577,000	COL Newco Limited	£40,321,000
Epsom College	£41,569,000	DX (VCP) Limited	£40,300,000
Harlequin Estates (Twickenham) Limited	£41,536,592	Mitchellson Formwork & Civil Engineering Limited	£40,298,424
Merant Holdings	£41,525,000	Ramac Holdings Limited	£40,258,468
European Glass Group Limited	£41,500,052	Kingston Midco Limited	£40,253,276
Marley Plastics Limited	£41,500,000	BECAP Spicers (UK) Limited	£40,249,000
Tensator Limited	£41,491,000	Iris Payroll Solutions Limited	£40,244,940
Claydon Estate LLP	£41,473,832	NTL Wirral Telephone and Cable TV Company	£40,243,000
Explore Manufacturing Limited	£41,435,000	The Vernon Educational Trust Limited	£40,220,160
Columbus Bidco Limited	£41,429,000	Veritas Technologies (UK) Limited	£40,190,000
Sirigen II Limited	£41,425,020	Amazon Spring Waters Investment Limited	£40,174,640
Blue Auto Finance Limited	£41,382,000	The Protection Specialist Limited	£40,166,728
Natural Sante Limited	£41,377,484	Project Farm Topco Limited	£40,158,924
Atlantis Holdings Limited	£41,366,652	SRM (Redcar & Cleveland) Limited	£40,153,800
Sloggett Group Limited	£41,359,968	Hala Limited	£40,136,568
K2M UK Limited	£41,350,028	AVMI Group Limited	£40,075,000
Milton Property Investments Limited	£41,349,264	Expro Eurasia Limited	£40,054,172
Delaquest Limited	£41,333,924	Networkers International (UK) Limited	£40,041,000
Beacon Community College Academy Trust	£41,323,052	Klober Limited	£40,028,992
Thomas Homes Limited	£41,321,548	Massey Group Limited	£39,990,436
Cargill Investments Holdings Limited	£41,304,000	Siva Plastics Limited	£39,980,168
Meritas Group Holdings Limited	£41,288,968	Newschools (Merton) Limited	£39,979,000
Wilton Park Developments Limited	£41,221,760	Linden (Enfield) LLP	£39,953,000
Aesica M2 Limited	£41,200,000	St Bede's School Trust Sussex	£39,939,000
Aesica M1 Limited	£41,200,000	Prowting Investments PLC	£39,889,556
ABC Drug Stores Limited	£41,183,192	Heathrow Airport Fuel Company Limited	£39,882,000

Binder Bidco Limited	£39,872,776	Premier Research International Us Limited	£38,697,000
Envision Pharma Holdco Limited	£39,868,740	Prime Care Solutions (Kingston) Limited	£38,657,000
Services Support (Gravesend) Limited	£39,864,000	Prime Care Solutions (Kingston) Holdings Limited	£38,657,000
Services Support (Gravesend) Holdings Limited	£39,864,000	Russell Finex Limited	£38,615,720
Pentagon Freight Services PLC	£39,823,044	Sevita (UK) Limited	£38,614,000
CAE Technology Services Limited	£39,802,160	Trenchard Aviation Group Limited	£38,609,824
Menzies Aviation (ASIG) Limited	£39,800,000	Medway Power Limited	£38,600,000
ROC Transformation (Holdings) Limited	£39,766,988	Picturehouse Cinemas Limited	£38,594,624
Biogen (UK) Limited	£39,763,000	Stackhouse Poland Midco Limited	£38,579,000
Brevan Howard Asset Management LLP	£39,723,056	Civil Service Motoring Association,Limited (The)	£38,575,348
Domantis Limited	£39,719,000	Hyperformance Limited	£38,561,000
Stansted Park Foundation	£39,718,180	Canon Medical Systems Limited	£38,547,000
Centrica Distributed Generation Limited	£39,710,000	Dual Energy Direct Limited	£38,538,564
Agria Pet Insurance Limited	£39,673,584	Motoring & Leisure Services Limited	£38,537,088
Foreman Homes Group Limited	£39,662,984	Vanderbilt Hotels Limited	£38,533,000
RBMR Topco Limited	£39,638,328	Choice Holdings Limited	£38,518,132
The Lady Eleanor Holles School	£39,625,652	Bolzoni Capital UK Limited	£38,513,380
Menzies Aviation (UK) Limited	£39,600,000	Gruffalo Bidco Limited	£38,508,872
Wind Farm Holdings Limited	£39,600,000	W.J.Daniel & Company Limited	£38,507,464
Quantel Group Limited	£39,590,000	Intelliflo Intermediate Holdings Limited	£38,501,876
William Willett Learning Trust	£39,579,000	Tonroe Group Limited	£38,496,136
TechnoGym U.K. Limited	£39,574,148	Ardo UK Limited	£38,470,160
National Adhesives Holding Ltd.	£39,540,000	Liz Earle Beauty Co. Limited	£38,463,136
Centerprise Intl Holdings Limited	£39,533,076	Tengo (Holdings) Limited	£38,451,932
Fleetwood Developments Limited	£39,505,720	ASIG Holdings Limited	£38,400,000
Portsmouth Aviation Holdings Limited	£39,500,888	Business Lending Residential Funding Limited	£38,371,984
Kensington Mortgage Company Limited	£39,478,000	FMP Global Holdings Limited	£38,236,000
Biogen Holdings Limited	£39,454,000	Patrolmake Limited	£38,229,480
McLaren Applied Technologies Limited	£39,447,000	KLM Cityhopper UK Limited	£38,219,000
D4T4 Solutions PLC	£39,416,000	Cognita UK Brazil Holdings Limited	£38,215,000
E.F.B. Group Limited	£39,415,512	The Share Centre Limited	£38,213,000
Mavenir Systems UK Limited	£39,400,000	Enghouse Holdings (UK) Limited	£38,208,060
Sega Publishing Europe Limited	£39,371,000	Fynecast Limited	£38,197,432
GEA Group Holdings (UK) Limited	£39,334,848	Hambridge Limited	£38,155,672
MessageLabs Group Limited	£39,319,000	Manco South Limited	£38,147,944
Frontier Software PLC	£39,306,400	Standard Commercial Tobacco Company (UK) Limited	£38,134,232
Lovering Foods Limited	£39,301,000	Motorline Limited	£38,117,216
Terrestrial Developments Ltd	£39,288,088	S A Designer Parfums Limited	£38,092,696
Faithdean PLC	£39,278,256	Aitch Care Homes (London) Limited	£38,078,000
Wessex Petroleum Limited	£39,265,928	Canon Holdings (UK) Limited	£38,061,752
Swiss Post Solutions Ltd	£39,237,000	Surface Technology International Limited	£38,027,000
St.Swithuns School (Winchester)	£39,225,996	Pricketts Limited	£38,022,408
CML Reporting Limited	£39,176,156	King Edward VI School Southampton	£38,006,304
Trenchard Aviation Holdings 1 Limited	£39,133,680	Brand Reputation Compliance Limited	£37,995,408
Imperial Cars of Swanwick Limited	£39,128,000	BP Subsea Well Response Limited	£37,991,692
Sirhowy Enterprise Way Limited	£39,123,000	GCP Rooftop Solar 4 Limited	£37,965,640
Sirhowy Enterprise Way (Holdings) Limited	£39,123,000	Prospects Group 2011 Limited	£37,933,000
Millwood Designer Homes Limited	£39,120,000	Stackhouse Poland Limited	£37,922,000
Serena Holdings	£39,090,080	Gantrade Europe Limited	£37,915,792
Havas Canada Holdings Limited	£39,053,000	Riverdale Developments Limited	£37,863,328
Routeco Limited	£39,037,000	Downe House School	£37,853,000
A.N.A. Aviation Group Holdings Ltd	£39,029,508	London Square (Streatham) Limited	£37,852,000
Capula Investment Management LLP	£39,008,164	Swan Mill Paper Company Limited	£37,843,000
Femcare Limited	£38,999,036	Sunspot Tours Limited	£37,841,624
York Cee Holdings Limited	£38,987,000	DST Global Solutions (Realty) Limited	£37,835,000
Trant Engineering Limited	£38,926,000	Axiom Education (Edinburgh) Holdings Limited	£37,823,000
Tensator Holdings Ltd	£38,924,000	Winchester Holdings Limited	£37,813,092
Synaptic Trust	£38,895,000	E & J Ground Rents No6 LLP	£37,761,040
Carte Blanche Greetings Limited	£38,886,304	Bartholomews Agri Food Limited	£37,759,328
Bedfordia Group Limited	£38,883,044	Weald of Kent Grammar School Academy Trust	£37,756,752
TBE (Southern) Limited	£38,875,668	Petrofac Engineering Limited	£37,749,000
Impact Multi Academy Trust	£38,875,000	CHMC Limited	£37,741,000
Carefusion U.K. 235 Limited	£38,864,256	E & J Ground Rents No3 LLP	£37,740,560
DYRMS - An Academy with Military Traditions	£38,813,724	Tearfund	£37,725,000
Key Bidco Limited	£38,796,000	GE Energy (UK) Limited	£37,720,000
Staples UK Limited	£38,789,000	Ipreo UK Holdings Ltd	£37,693,000
Vision Engineering Limited	£38,766,024	Tandridge Learning Trust	£37,693,000
Elbrook (Cash & Carry) Limited	£38,748,460	Ginger Bidco Limited	£37,686,736
Andreas Stihl Limited	£38,716,048	Progress Software Limited	£37,678,000
Surrey Blue Limited	£38,712,928	Adeptus Limited	£37,675,484
Drift Bridge Garage Limited	£38,710,368	Berendsen Finance (DKK) Limited	£37,665,180
ATP Media Holdings Limited	£38,699,312	Hewlett-Packard CDS Limited	£37,663,000

Company	Amount	Company	Amount
GlaxoSmithKline Caribbean Limited	£37,655,000	Onyx Information Technology Holdings Limited	£36,589,256
Red Bull Racing Limited	£37,651,000	Kellogg Brown & Root (Services) Limited	£36,539,200
Aqualisa Products Limited	£37,650,000	Bargate Homes Limited	£36,531,596
National Film and Television School (The)	£37,639,464	Church Communities UK	£36,531,324
Seagreen Wind Energy Limited	£37,613,000	W.N. Developments Limited	£36,522,976
Reliance Communications (U.K.) Limited	£37,609,052	NPS (UK4) Limited	£36,500,000
ACG Rented Properties PLC	£37,607,384	TJX Germany Ltd.	£36,500,000
Montgomery Property Investments Limited	£37,592,876	Bandt Holdings Limited	£36,493,000
Worldwide Flight Services Limited	£37,583,808	Ludgate 329 Limited	£36,485,988
Sysmex UK Limited	£37,554,648	Cordant Security Limited	£36,478,744
Eagle Estates Limited	£37,552,272	Tradebe Fawley Limited	£36,464,000
Fulham Football Club Limited	£37,528,000	Perform Sporting News Limited	£36,441,864
Papa John's (GB) Limited	£37,525,000	Kelvion Limited	£36,426,000
BI Worldwide Holdings Limited	£37,491,824	Zurich Holdings (UK) Limited	£36,410,000
Trans Global Limited	£37,490,000	Chem Aviation LLP	£36,394,536
Towergate Risk Solutions Limited	£37,428,432	John Reilly (Civil Engineering) Limited	£36,394,180
Marsh Wall Limited	£37,376,164	SEM Limited	£36,391,328
Panalux Limited	£37,341,000	Reach Holdings Limited	£36,387,000
Ubisoft Limited	£37,321,000	Calverton Finance Limited	£36,386,992
W K Webster & Co Ltd	£37,320,556	Healthcare Providers (Gloucester) Limited	£36,378,000
Renatus Property Management Limited	£37,320,448	Gloucester Healthcare Partnership Limited	£36,378,000
Thales Training & Simulation (Ace) Limited	£37,320,000	The Grand Central Hotel Glasgow Limited	£36,370,000
Dage Precision Industries Limited	£37,294,408	Key Midco Limited	£36,345,000
Trans Global Freight Management Limited	£37,289,880	Smartspace Software PLC	£36,344,000
Ability Hotels (Luton) Limited	£37,286,244	Wootton Academy Trust	£36,341,524
Tindle Press Holdings Limited	£37,237,612	Iris Payroll Software Limited	£36,310,344
Charles River U.K. Limited	£37,237,000	Harwood Properties Limited	£36,295,164
Toshiba Information Systems (UK) Limited	£37,230,544	Hilton UK Manage Limited	£36,292,152
Travelport Holdings (UK) Limited	£37,226,724	Nike Land Securities Limited	£36,287,336
TAG Aviation (UK) Limited	£37,214,180	Foss Holdings Limited	£36,265,248
Verizon Connect UK Limited	£37,205,376	Anchorage Capital Europe, LLP	£36,264,800
Skillcrown Holdings Limited	£37,200,196	Waters Limited	£36,251,000
Schoolsworks Academy Trust	£37,177,000	Ruddy Joinery Limited	£36,239,128
CSC Life Sciences Limited	£37,162,304	Emerald Midco 1 Limited	£36,238,000
British Kidney Patient Association (The)	£37,131,252	Emerald Midco 2 Limited	£36,219,000
Marlin Financial Intermediate Limited	£37,119,000	Siemens Healthcare Diagnostics Manufacturing Ltd	£36,215,000
Prospects Services	£37,111,000	Richard Hochfeld Management Limited	£36,207,264
Grigg Investments Limited	£37,086,944	Independent Inspections Limited	£36,191,000
WLHC Projectco Limited	£37,067,272	Radnor House School (Property) Limited	£36,183,008
Project Farm Bidco Limited	£37,061,456	Van Oord UK Limited	£36,153,704
Bidvest Freight UK Limited	£37,057,792	Britten Properties LLP	£36,153,532
EMC Consulting (UK) Limited	£37,052,000	103-105 Bath Road Limited	£36,119,000
Millbrook Healthcare Ltd	£37,048,000	The Richmond West Schools Trust	£36,118,740
Green Network UK PLC	£37,046,680	Syneos Health International Holdings Limited	£36,101,752
Cadbury Ten LLP	£37,031,568	Kyocera Document Solutions (U.K.) Limited	£36,096,192
Foundation Developments Limited	£36,966,392	Ash Properties Limited	£36,090,872
Keltbray Plant Limited	£36,962,956	Choice Support	£36,087,000
E & J Ground Rents No4 LLP	£36,952,304	Premier Asset Management Limited	£36,079,000
Veritas UK Holding Limited	£36,946,128	GCP Green Energy 1 Limited	£36,076,976
Lenster Investments Limited	£36,915,084	Pall Technology UK Limited	£36,075,900
Gruffalo Topco Limited	£36,903,484	Chobham School Academy (Stratford)	£36,049,000
Gama Aviation (UK) Limited	£36,897,000	Rentokil Initial Americas Limited	£36,043,000
Schueco UK Limited	£36,897,000	Portals Group Limited	£36,036,000
B & P Midco Limited	£36,868,316	Nutfield Holdings Limited	£36,018,000
ACP Europe Limited	£36,865,424	Coinford Holdings Limited	£36,017,072
R.Swain & Sons Limited	£36,858,296	Centrica LNG UK Limited	£36,017,000
SD Worx UK Limited	£36,830,000	Saga Cruises IV Limited	£36,016,000
Victorygame Limited	£36,794,544	Vestas Technology UK Limited	£36,010,000
By Design (UK) Limited	£36,768,708	Evolution (Saffron Walden) LLP	£36,010,000
Apatech Limited	£36,755,124	Brendoncare Foundation (The)	£36,009,000
Education for The 21st Century	£36,751,264	Transform Schools (Stoke) Holdings Limited	£36,008,000
Nikon UK Limited	£36,741,208	Transform Schools (Stoke) Limited	£36,008,000
B & C E Financial Services Limited	£36,739,000	Honeywell Security UK Limited	£36,002,000
Johnson & Johnson Innovation Limited	£36,677,000	Selits Limited	£35,990,508
Glinwell Public Limited Company	£36,657,000	St Bartholomew's School	£35,965,372
White Horse Caravan Company Limited	£36,647,516	Kedleston Wings Holdco Ltd	£35,954,744
Ricardo-AEA Limited	£36,639,000	The Principal Manchester Limited	£35,954,000
Cadence Design Systems Limited	£36,614,000	The Pegasus Academy Trust	£35,930,000
Handsale Limited	£36,610,476	Hornby PLC	£35,923,000
Beck & Pollitzer Holdings Limited	£36,608,288	Magma Global Limited	£35,912,080
RAL Limited	£36,601,640	Rectory Homes Limited	£35,903,320
Oxford International Education 2 Limited	£36,600,000	BAM Properties Limited	£35,893,000

Company	Amount
Blue Diamond UK Limited	£35,891,000
Johnson Controls Systems Development Limited	£35,871,348
Garth Enterprises Partnership LLP	£35,852,572
British and Foreign Wharf Company Limited (The)	£35,837,532
Claude Fenton (Holdings) Limited	£35,812,000
National Foundation for Educational Research in E&W	£35,798,000
P.H Jones Group Limited	£35,797,000
Marco Island Developments Limited	£35,785,968
FMP Global Bidco Limited	£35,779,000
Tenterden Schools Trust	£35,766,656
Columbus Topco Limited	£35,765,000
Oxford Aviation Academy (Oxford) Limited	£35,762,000
Jardines (U.K.) Limited	£35,723,272
KCI Medical Limited	£35,710,000
Continua Limited	£35,705,000
Greenclose Holdings Limited	£35,686,280
T.S.L. Finance Limited	£35,641,412
Bard Holdings Limited	£35,572,000
Kuwait Petroleum International Limited	£35,566,000
Wycombe High School Academies Trust	£35,518,004
Heathrow Truck Centre Limited	£35,505,696
Kohler Uninterruptible Power Limited	£35,500,504
NCMT Limited	£35,459,000
Kelly Services (UK) Limited	£35,458,000
Patek Philippe Salon Limited	£35,443,052
Danu II Holdings Limited	£35,410,976
Bedales School	£35,399,896
TUV SUD (UK) Limited	£35,398,000
Vanguard Holdings Limited	£35,381,472
A Gomez Limited	£35,375,696
Science, Engineering and Mfg Technologies Alliance	£35,358,000
Unity Schools Trust	£35,321,000
Quantel Limited	£35,309,000
Camelot Business Solutions Limited	£35,300,000
T.R. Fastenings Limited	£35,298,000
Bic U.K. Limited	£35,294,000
Sky Comedy Limited	£35,250,000
The University of Kent Academies Trust	£35,228,000
Pallant House Gallery	£35,225,600
Advantedge Commercial Finance Limited	£35,207,200
Croudace Trading Group Limited	£35,197,768
Logoplaste UK Limited	£35,195,872
Zipcar International Finance Company Limited	£35,139,432
Tyco Building Services Products (UK) Limited	£35,127,000
Domnick Hunter Group Limited	£35,116,000
Net Pay (EUR) Limited	£35,109,772
Dennis & Robinson Limited	£35,107,000
United Living (North) Limited	£35,102,000
Brymore Investments Limited	£35,100,756
MacIntyre Care	£35,098,000
London Pharma & Chemicals Holdings Ltd	£35,091,484
Harwood Wealth Management Group PLC	£35,091,000
Covea Insurance Services Limited	£35,075,000
PPP Capital Limited	£35,069,812
Ontex Retail UK Limited	£35,052,964
Softbox (Bidco) Limited	£35,043,948
Neilson Active Holidays (Holdings) Limited	£35,042,000
Fairfax Acquisitions Limited	£35,041,592
Travel Up Limited	£35,034,504
Northumberland Waste Management Limited	£35,024,000
Building Research Establishment Limited	£35,017,000
Kronos Systems Limited	£35,007,464
CSSC Properties Limited	£34,992,000
Centrica Business Solutions UK Limited	£34,959,000
Fogarty Group Limited	£34,951,916
Castacrete Limited	£34,940,376
DHL Distribution Holdings (UK) Limited	£34,931,000
Eckoh PLC	£34,918,000
Carefusion U.K. 305 Limited	£34,892,040
MC Truck & Bus Limited	£34,889,420
Hertz Holdings III UK Limited	£34,875,000
Pathways Care Group Limited	£34,873,000
Meridian Residential Developments Limited	£34,862,720
Steris CH Limited	£34,842,332
Beadles Sidcup Limited	£34,839,892
Lionel Road Developments Ltd	£34,820,496
KWay Holdings Limited	£34,809,120
St Mary's School Ascot	£34,791,000
Furniture Village Group Limited	£34,781,000
British Airways 777 Leasing Limited	£34,769,000
Foreign Currency Direct PLC	£34,767,336
Flight Centre (UK) Wholesale Limited	£34,764,000
Trenchard Aviation Holdings Limited	£34,763,996
The Kite Academy Trust	£34,758,720
Runnymede Investments Limited	£34,758,336
Sky Home Communications Limited	£34,752,000
Berry Gardens Limited	£34,746,000
Alexion Pharma UK Limited	£34,744,548
B.I.B. Underwriters Limited	£34,731,716
CPRT European Investments Limited	£34,716,916
Leaderboard Golf Holdings Limited	£34,707,660
The Learning Alliance Academy Trust	£34,703,016
Claremont Fan Court Foundation Limited (The)	£34,701,552
Valour Midco I Limited	£34,694,064
Valour Midco II Limited	£34,694,064
Arrow Business Communications Group Limited	£34,658,904
Gemini Rail Services UK Ltd	£34,624,000
Dynamic Procurement Holdings Limited	£34,603,140
CTV Outside Broadcasts Limited	£34,603,000
The Club Company Acquisitions (Holdings) Limited	£34,596,000
BPDM Group Ltd	£34,548,844
Blue Lizard Consulting Limited	£34,547,744
Zeltiq Limited	£34,529,580
Travel Up Group PLC	£34,515,496
SDL Tridion Limited	£34,494,056
CH & Co Catering Limited	£34,451,988
Clancy Plant Limited	£34,449,128
Chapman Freeborn Airchartering Limited	£34,439,348
Tindle Newspapers Limited	£34,429,744
Sourcecode UK Limited	£34,420,536
ARRK Product Development Group Limited	£34,413,000
Interserve Engineering Limited	£34,379,000
Sussex Learning Trust	£34,353,000
Paymentshield Services Limited	£34,345,000
Costain Alcaidesa Limited	£34,306,008
Michelmersh Brick UK Limited	£34,294,000
Jelmac Properties	£34,260,152
Avtrade Leasing Limited	£34,252,116
Corona Energy Retail 1 Limited	£34,249,204
Ginger Topco Limited	£34,242,800
NTL Kirklees	£34,230,000
Console Lowco Limited	£34,227,728
Collins Construction Ltd	£34,222,440
Lyndendown Limited	£34,180,372
Virgin Media Payments Ltd	£34,173,000
Optiva Solutions (UK) Limited	£34,161,892
Achieving for Children Community Interest Company	£34,152,000
Vent-Axia Group Limited	£34,130,000
Egdon Resources PLC	£34,125,396
Atkins ATK Investments Limited	£34,102,000
Hotchkiss Group Ltd	£34,096,000
Slough and East Berkshire C of E Multi Academy	£34,066,424
Fibercore Limited	£34,064,536
The Police Rehabilitation Centre	£34,054,292
Countrystyle Recycling Limited	£34,037,104
Countrystyle Group Limited	£34,037,104
Esure Property Limited	£34,014,000
Reilly JDM Holdings Limited	£34,004,840
Focusrite Audio Engineering Limited	£34,002,000
Nicholas James Care Homes Ltd	£33,972,356
BBC Studioworks Limited	£33,958,312
NCMT Holdings Limited	£33,940,000
Brambles Enterprises Limited	£33,937,000
Ousedale School	£33,919,824

Company	Amount	Company	Amount
Tangmere Airfield Nurseries Ltd	£33,911,460	MTS Systems Limited	£32,938,512
Aspen Marketing Group Limited	£33,899,000	ARRI (GB) Limited	£32,916,000
Sumika Polymer Compounds (UK) Ltd	£33,891,000	Greenstone Oxford Limited	£32,909,552
TSL Limited	£33,886,424	Waingels Academies Trust	£32,906,436
Foundocean Group Limited	£33,864,664	Phoenix Software Limited	£32,899,000
Haynes Brothers,Limited	£33,857,296	Pinnacle Schools (Fife) Limited	£32,899,000
ILI Limited	£33,845,880	London Square (Putney) Limited	£32,865,840
MSK Holdings Limited	£33,842,548	Alder Hey Holdco 2 Limited	£32,808,000
Linden (Brampton) LLP	£33,835,000	Alder Hey Holdco 1 Limited	£32,808,000
The Portsmouth Grammar School	£33,812,544	Peter Brett Associates LLP	£32,766,530
Rapport Housing and Care	£33,806,760	JCB Medway Limited	£32,758,146
Secureworks Europe Limited	£33,757,000	Ferring Asset Management Limited	£32,750,000
Tilhill Forestry Limited	£33,755,000	Beaconsfield High School	£32,735,524
Lunar 101 Limited	£33,739,000	Magal Engineering Limited	£32,734,108
Lancer Property Holdings Limited	£33,733,008	British Gas Social Housing Limited	£32,715,000
The Organised Group Limited	£33,676,676	Wozair Limited	£32,712,796
Police Care UK	£33,646,736	Nurse Plus and Carer Plus (UK) Limited	£32,708,020
Mary Rose Trust (The)	£33,645,604	Maintenance Management Limited	£32,688,378
Heythrop Park Limited	£33,644,216	Linden (Avery Hill) LLP	£32,658,000
CAS Aspirations Properties Limited	£33,638,000	Gazelli Art House Limited	£32,650,528
Runtime Collective Limited	£33,625,744	Danshell Healthcare Limited	£32,604,000
Clive Barford Limited	£33,610,000	SSE Production Services Limited	£32,600,000
CPRT (Europe) Limited	£33,583,692	E & J Ground Rents No5 LLP	£32,581,266
5 Dimensions Trust	£33,572,072	Annodata Limited	£32,548,760
Worth Abbey	£33,568,976	Redsky IT Holdings Limited	£32,542,000
Ensono Limited	£33,558,000	Yorkshire Transformations Limited	£32,537,000
INEOS U.K. Finance Company Limited	£33,548,200	Hurtwood House School LLP	£32,536,492
Kedleston (Wings Education) Limited	£33,542,588	Hawk-Eye Innovations Limited	£32,507,000
Perceptive Informatics UK Limited	£33,534,000	Jas Forwarding (UK) Limited	£32,490,200
Synventive Holding Limited	£33,511,908	Dwellcourt Limited	£32,484,010
Readypower Rail Services Finance Limited	£33,509,584	Puzzler Media Group Limited	£32,481,222
Baltray No. 1 Limited	£33,492,000	The Hazeley Academy	£32,471,284
Bowland Resources (No.2) Limited	£33,491,000	Bovis Peer LLP	£32,452,554
F.G. Barnes & Sons Limited	£33,478,740	Chapman Freeborn International Limited	£32,425,978
McCormick Kutas Food Service Limited	£33,466,626	Key Properties Limited	£32,403,564
Williams Trade Supplies Limited	£33,458,266	BIMM Holdings Limited	£32,390,748
Hurstlane Limited	£33,431,456	Croudace Finance Limited	£32,381,100
Grove Court Properties (Beaconsfield) Limited	£33,413,948	Moog Reading Limited	£32,379,382
Carewatch Holdings Limited	£33,405,000	Aspire Pharma Holdings Limited	£32,370,296
CSB Holdings Limited	£33,398,270	Leven Wharf Limited	£32,341,948
Bonne Bouche Catering Limited	£33,374,368	Trafalgar Entertainment Group Limited	£32,341,000
Pyramid Schools (Sheffield) Limited	£33,368,000	H.K.S. Motors Limited	£32,315,680
TLC (Southern) Limited	£33,350,280	Affinity (Reading) Limited	£32,271,964
Viavi Solutions UK Limited	£33,317,000	Ginger Midco Limited	£32,271,278
Roos Energy Limited	£33,296,000	Bloc Gatwick Limited	£32,269,984
Ashcourt Holdings Limited	£33,249,000	Caterham School Limited	£32,258,000
SMR Automotive Mirrors UK Limited	£33,245,724	Carte Blanche Group Limited	£32,247,094
Akzo Nobel Decorative Coatings Limited	£33,237,000	Barrow Hepburn International Limited	£32,246,000
BP Exploration China Limited	£33,227,468	Nikon X-Tek Systems Limited	£32,208,000
TIGI International Limited	£33,217,912	Brymore Holdings Limited	£32,207,900
Readypower Rail Services Limited	£33,216,620	Mova Property Limited	£32,178,886
Skanska Cementation International Limited	£33,210,000	Merck Consumer Healthcare Limited	£32,178,000
Attewell Limited	£33,207,000	V1 Limited	£32,158,000
Altonwood Holdings Limited	£33,185,860	Four Coal Shipping Limited	£32,154,102
Xchanging US Funding Limited	£33,180,498	The National Fostering Agency (Scotland) Limited	£32,132,000
RB Lease Company Ltd	£33,154,304	Tate Bros. Limited	£32,126,454
BOC Gases Limited	£33,151,000	Amsric Holdings Limited	£32,116,938
Intex (Radiographic) Limited	£33,150,932	FTR Holdings Ltd	£32,104,168
Carewatch Care Services Limited	£33,150,000	Ranbaxy Holdings (UK) Limited	£32,096,450
Evergreen Finance Limited	£33,140,000	Verifone (U.K.) Limited	£32,080,000
T A Fisher & Sons Limited	£33,119,560	Record PLC	£32,076,000
Tasmar Limited	£33,117,756	T & E Ferris Limited	£32,046,104
Sugarich Limited	£33,083,772	Suez Recycling and Recovery South East Ltd	£32,036,000
Elliott Brothers Limited	£33,038,584	Selecta Refreshments Limited	£32,032,000
Lockheed Martin UK Ampthill Group Limited	£33,037,000	Interserve Developments No.2 Limited	£32,005,000
Navitas Life Sciences Holdings Limited	£32,995,410	Dynama Solutions Ltd	£31,952,000
Ultima Business Solutions Ltd.	£32,987,508	JAE Europe, Limited	£31,950,444
OGF Bidco Limited	£32,987,248	Bordure Limited	£31,912,990
Inspiring Learning Services Limited	£32,987,000	Expro Resources Limited	£31,907,536
Rebound Technology Group Holdings Limited	£32,978,704	Viridor Resource Management Limited	£31,902,000
Johnson Controls Batteries Limited	£32,965,000	Gluco RX Limited	£31,867,320
Campmoss Property Company Limited	£32,951,648	Defence Support (St Athan) Limited	£31,851,000

Company	Amount
Defence Support (St Athan) Holdings Limited	£31,851,000
Interserve Working Futures Limited	£31,849,514
Airinmar Limited	£31,844,340
Beardow and Adams (Adhesives) Limited	£31,820,200
Kinetrol Limited	£31,818,934
Gracewell Healthcare Limited	£31,813,000
The Collegiate Trust	£31,812,864
Sanlam Private Investments (UK) Holdings Ltd	£31,809,000
Area Sq. Limited	£31,770,456
G4S Cash Centres (UK) Limited	£31,722,000
Orleans Park School	£31,701,936
Terex Cranes UK Limited	£31,691,000
Hill of The Hermitage Limited	£31,672,452
IQVIA Ies European Holdings	£31,657,000
Premier Research Group Limited	£31,621,000
HRT UK Limited	£31,611,000
Coast2coast Technologies Limited	£31,605,100
Adams Morey Holdings Limited	£31,598,216
Scancem Recovery Limited	£31,595,000
Exodus Travels Limited	£31,576,000
ICS Incorporation Limited	£31,552,244
Ladham Properties Limited	£31,546,912
Upham Group Limited	£31,542,000
Sunrise UK Holdco Limited	£31,534,000
Lousada Investments Limited	£31,533,344
Medica Reporting Finance Limited	£31,527,144
Lancing College Limited	£31,526,408
Havenhill Limited	£31,515,382
Pittway Systems Technology Group Europe Limited	£31,514,000
Kerridge Commercial Systems Limited	£31,511,000
Danfoss Limited	£31,494,000
Collaborative Services Support (NE) Holdings Ltd	£31,484,000
Collaborative Services Support NE Limited	£31,484,000
Tridonic UK Limited	£31,482,000
The Children's Trust	£31,475,000
Yavneh College Academy Trust	£31,446,916
Tudor Holdings (UK) Limited	£31,437,104
The DHL UK Foundation	£31,435,420
County Catering & Leisure Limited	£31,412,516
Barrow Hepburn Group Limited	£31,397,000
Fujifilm Ink Solutions Limited	£31,393,956
Bugler Group Limited	£31,377,884
Schlumberger Cambridge Research Limited	£31,375,000
Cyberfort Group Limited	£31,373,432
Symrise Limited	£31,371,000
The Jankel Group Limited	£31,346,048
D Hales Limited	£31,339,000
Jankel Armouring Limited	£31,338,052
Pourshins Limited	£31,332,000
Consort Medical Finance 2010 Limited	£31,327,000
Southwater Property Promotion Limited	£31,320,696
Venture Life Group PLC	£31,309,000
Ensco 1212 Limited	£31,291,344
LSQ (Crimscott Street) Holdings Limited	£31,261,704
Egdon Resources U.K. Limited	£31,255,816
V.B. Investments Limited	£31,251,000
Chichester Festival Theatre	£31,163,476
Dresser-Rand (U.K.) Limited	£31,100,000
DX Holdings Limited	£31,100,000
Mission Foods UK Limited	£31,083,000
Esher Mail Order Limited	£31,067,310
APG Cash Drawer UK, Ltd	£31,027,776
Specialist Holidays (Travel) Limited	£31,027,000
Donamount Limited	£31,020,032
T A Fisher Developments Limited	£31,012,510
Ensco 1214 Limited	£31,000,000
Chatham & Clarendon Grammar School	£30,997,382
Dominvs Project Company Limited	£30,983,056
Quayside Homes Holdings Limited	£30,958,776
Motorsport Vision Limited	£30,917,884
Foundation and Friends of The Royal Botanic Gardens	£30,912,000
Richard Hochfeld Limited	£30,856,096
Continental Trade and Commodity Services Limited	£30,833,654
Lyndon Scaffolding PLC	£30,829,792
Arinso People Services Limited	£30,823,936
Leo Energy Limited	£30,804,952
CDB (U.K.) Limited	£30,763,000
Lonepiper Limited	£30,743,972
Andrew Weir & Company Limited	£30,743,000
Leica Geosystems Limited	£30,730,000
Bridge Leisure Finco Limited	£30,725,428
Pelham Capital Real Estate Limited	£30,717,572
Wilfred T Fry Limited	£30,712,948
Bridge Leisure Midco Limited	£30,684,620
BL Wind Limited	£30,665,000
S Elvin Limited	£30,662,140
Allen Diesels Limited	£30,627,280
Arjun Infrastructure Partners II Limited	£30,621,192
St Mary's Training Ground Limited	£30,587,804
Matsim Properties Limited	£30,573,182
ESRI (UK) Limited	£30,528,396
AMG Healthcare Limited	£30,528,000
MacIntyre Hudson LLP	£30,524,516
Royale Parks Limited	£30,513,246
Nippon Express (U.K.) Limited	£30,495,964
Avery Dennison U.K. Limited	£30,487,000
Echostar UK Holdings Limited	£30,446,216
Suez Recycling and Recovery South Gloucestershire	£30,445,000
GXS Limited	£30,418,454
East Sussex Energy Infrastructure and Development	£30,404,000
Costain Building & Civil Engineering Limited	£30,403,146
FKA Brands Limited	£30,401,890
Crown Lift Trucks Limited	£30,334,000
Amer Sports UK Limited	£30,313,356
Bostall Estates Limited	£30,305,232
Capital Investment and Finance Ltd	£30,284,442
Bugler Developments Limited	£30,251,396
Opal Ventures Limited	£30,214,660
World Vision UK	£30,207,000
Wessanen Great Britain Holdings Limited	£30,207,000
BBGI (NI) Limited	£30,183,276
WEL Solar Park 2 Limited	£30,179,792
Dynatrace Limited	£30,178,560
SCCI Group Limited	£30,145,584
QED (Clacton) Limited	£30,126,000
Brobot Petroleum Limited	£30,122,572
Software of Excellence UK Holdings Limited	£30,106,948
Marshall Amplification PLC	£30,101,176
IZH Holdings Ltd	£30,100,012
DX Services Limited	£30,100,000
Edge UK Holdings Limited	£30,089,006
Hospira UK Limited	£30,085,000
County Catering & Leisure Properties Limited	£30,071,024
AHL Holdings (Manchester) Limited	£30,064,000
Amey Highways Lighting (Manchester) Limited	£30,064,000
Elysium Healthcare Property 2 Limited	£30,056,000
Michael Wenman Limited	£30,052,412
Saga Personal Finance Limited	£30,046,000
Exagris Limited	£30,044,408
Lampton School Academy Trust	£30,033,000
Boustead International Heaters Limited	£30,013,080
Lenham Storage Company Limited	£30,010,920
Ellucian Global Limited	£30,010,564
AS & Sons Ltd	£29,992,296
Home Retail Group Insurance Services Limited	£29,932,000
Hanwha Techwin Europe Limited	£29,918,000
Techaid Facilities Limited	£29,912,552
Elliott TurboMachinery Limited	£29,906,000
West's Group International Limited	£29,904,000
Prospect Healthcare (Reading) Limited	£29,903,000
MHI Vestas Offshore Wind Blades UK Ltd	£29,897,000
The East Malling Trust	£29,881,836
Epicor Software (UK) Limited	£29,879,666
GCP Asset Finance 1 Limited	£29,873,892

Company	Value
Software of Excellence United Kingdom Limited	£29,869,568
Nutrix Capital Limited	£29,850,992
The Harry Levy Group Limited	£29,850,702
Beamish Investments Limited	£29,806,586
Liberata UK Limited	£29,794,000
Hillier Nurseries Limited	£29,756,622
DP Group Developments Limited	£29,724,000
Cullum Family Trust	£29,719,796
Cellarmaster Wines Holdings (UK) Limited	£29,715,000
Perpetual Limited	£29,713,284
East Sussex Press Limited	£29,706,208
Agricultural Central Trading Limited	£29,703,392
The Mountbatten School	£29,701,510
Brighton & Hove Seaside Community Homes Limited	£29,680,164
Academy Services (Waltham Forest) Limited	£29,670,000
Capital (Hair and Beauty) Limited	£29,652,584
Hewlett-Packard Cain Holdings Limited	£29,650,000
Guild Resources Limited	£29,632,140
Portsmouth Surgical Holdings Limited	£29,631,684
Landlink Estates Limited	£29,623,802
Ardingly College Limited	£29,621,472
Allergy Therapeutics (UK) Limited	£29,611,000
Network Aviation Group Ltd	£29,602,844
Blackmoor Estate Limited (The)	£29,596,446
Bellevue Education Group Limited	£29,585,864
Walnut Investments Limited	£29,585,306
Childbase Partnership Limited	£29,576,340
Roke Manor Research Limited	£29,575,000
Manitowoc Crane Group (UK) Limited	£29,569,000
M R Stephenson Limited	£29,563,524
TH UK & Ireland Limited	£29,562,736
Collard Group Limited	£29,551,774
Erith School	£29,549,000
Camden Motors (Holdings) Limited	£29,539,000
William Reed Business Media Ltd	£29,530,000
Humphrey Farms Limited	£29,519,000
Sangers (Maidstone) Limited	£29,492,576
Brookworth Group Limited	£29,489,940
Gearhouse Broadcast Limited	£29,481,000
Ennogen Healthcare Ltd	£29,465,110
Evolution Morpeth LLP	£29,457,000
Aqualisa Holdings Limited	£29,442,000
Woodgavil Properties Limited	£29,440,504
Target Media Limited	£29,422,000
Channel Commercials PLC	£29,378,040
William Reed Group Ltd	£29,375,000
Defaqto Group Limited	£29,360,876
Fire Fighters Charity	£29,345,296
RMET	£29,340,000
Home and Legacy Insurance Services Limited	£29,334,260
Universe Group PLC	£29,281,000
SESW Holding Company Limited.	£29,278,068
Palmier Ltd	£29,273,812
Commercial Freeholds & Investments Ltd	£29,262,552
Modern Schools (Barnsley) Limited	£29,249,000
Royal British Legion Poppy Factory Limited (The)	£29,247,398
The Langley Park School for Boys Academy Trust	£29,243,000
Websense SC Operations Limited	£29,237,138
Visual Impact (UK) Limited	£29,229,290
G.E.W. (EC) Limited	£29,227,032
JRL Property Holdings Limited	£29,217,624
Newincco 1222 Limited	£29,213,034
Changeregard Limited	£29,188,286
Viva Eyewear UK Limited	£29,155,000
INEOS Manufacturing (Hull) Limited	£29,148,000
IBRC Asset Finance Limited	£29,145,804
Hall Farm Wind Farm Ltd	£29,138,000
Grant & Stone Limited	£29,137,628
Mersen UK Portslade Limited	£29,133,362
London Square (Fulham) Limited	£29,057,560
Urbis Schreder Ltd	£29,056,368
Wilton House Limited	£29,044,988
Compressor Products Holdings Limited	£29,029,686
Karium Ltd	£29,025,880
LSI Logic Europe Limited	£29,006,364
Emerald Bidco Limited	£29,002,000
Explorer Holdings UK Limited	£29,000,000
Linde Sterling Limited	£28,998,000
Tradebe Solvent Recycling Limited	£28,998,000
Alandale Logistics Limited	£28,983,552
Compatriot Holdings Limited	£28,924,362
City Hotel (London) Limited	£28,924,362
Teoco UK Limited	£28,921,400
Hobbs Brook Limited	£28,919,000
E.L.Head Limited	£28,908,524
The Book People Limited	£28,901,036
Tchibo Coffee International Limited	£28,856,822
The Borrow Foundation	£28,828,684
Jupiter Midco 2 Limited	£28,821,590
LGC (Teddington) Limited	£28,820,978
Wedge Property Company Limited (The)	£28,819,740
Newmarket Promotions Limited	£28,809,550
Westgate Properties Limited	£28,806,000
Meritas Group Limited	£28,790,814
Nucleus Financial Group PLC	£28,785,000
St Edward Homes Limited	£28,772,000
Flamepro Limited	£28,763,098
Air Menzies International Limited	£28,753,000
Saba Infra Holdings UK Limited	£28,750,320
Burt Boulton Holdings Limited	£28,742,776
West London YMCA	£28,731,302
Country Estates Holdings Limited	£28,713,440
Akari Therapeutics, PLC	£28,707,494
Sunlight Clinical Solutions Limited	£28,688,580
Whistl Limited	£28,680,000
Croudace Investment Group Limited	£28,663,196
Stock Finance (Koruna) Limited	£28,645,654
Amber Solar Parks Limited	£28,640,000
Yourcash Europe Limited	£28,639,000
Healthcare Facilities Management Services Limited	£28,629,000
Lambert Pressland Limited	£28,628,188
Danu Holding Limited	£28,618,104
Whistl Group Limited	£28,609,000
Direct Line Group Limited	£28,597,000
Mast-Jaegermeister UK Limited	£28,586,000
Lamberts Healthcare Limited	£28,585,000
Sowmac Investments Limited	£28,576,408
Elekta Holdings Limited	£28,552,000
Global Invacom Limited	£28,541,746
Amber Solar Parks (Holdings) Limited	£28,532,000
Hasbro U.K. Limited	£28,522,000
The Denbigh Alliance	£28,515,304
Espalier Finance Limited	£28,500,980
Forum Products Holdings Limited	£28,498,912
Broadway Malyan Employee Ownership Trustees Ltd	£28,492,000
Tristmire Limited	£28,489,294
Fizzy Canning Town LLP	£28,485,000
Smith Bradbeer & Company Limited	£28,469,072
Orthopaedic Research UK	£28,451,824
Chrysalis (Stanhope) Limited	£28,434,720
Flexibon Limited	£28,428,516
E & J Ground Rents No2 LLP	£28,417,428
Cablefile Limited	£28,416,222
Exclaimer Group Limited	£28,390,980
Williams Trade Supplies Holdings Limited	£28,389,528
Vodafone Panafon UK	£28,383,658
Cygnet Surrey Limited	£28,382,000
Wood Hall Land & Properties Limited	£28,376,944
ACI Global Limited	£28,367,000
Ranbaxy (U.K.) Limited	£28,360,372
Robert Cort Properties Limited	£28,351,874
Factory Services UK Limited	£28,332,676
Spirent Holdings Limited	£28,315,000
Cyberfort Bidco Limited	£28,312,204

Company	Turnover
Thomas Sanderson Limited	£28,285,000
Harefield Academy Trust	£28,260,000
Teneo Group Limited	£28,246,322
DP Realty Limited	£28,234,000
Neilson Active Holidays Limited	£28,216,000
The Petersham Hotel Limited	£28,215,508
CNM Estates Holdings Limited	£28,212,946
Fawley Waterside Limited	£28,181,000
QED (Leeds) Limited	£28,176,000
EMAP Publishing Limited	£28,163,124
Brookton 2000 Limited	£28,104,794
Trafficinvest Limited	£28,090,748
Kingston Grammar School	£28,075,000
J & E Hall Limited	£28,074,000
Deltec International Courier Limited	£28,045,200
Cardiff Property Public Limited Company (The)	£28,043,000
Nicholas King Developments PLC	£28,041,000
Community Reinsurance Corporation Limited	£28,039,992
SITA Advanced Travel Solutions Limited	£28,013,746
Steamer Properties Limited	£28,001,416
Dunmoore (West London) Limited	£27,999,956
Channel Commercials Kent Ltd	£27,989,204
Harsco Metals 385 Limited	£27,980,780
Bookcash Trading Limited	£27,975,000
AA Underwriting Limited	£27,975,000
Aeromobile Communications Limited	£27,962,126
Bosch Automotive Service Solutions Ltd	£27,956,000
ITAB UK Ltd	£27,955,988
Tektronix U.K.Limited	£27,947,000
Broadway Malyan Holdings Limited	£27,942,000
SPI Lasers PLC	£27,936,000
Pinewood MBS Lighting Limited	£27,935,808
Woldingham School	£27,910,932
Lesser & Pavey Ltd.	£27,842,092
Milton Keynes Academy Trust	£27,840,644
Althea (Leicester 2) Limited	£27,822,708
Newhall Projects Limited	£27,813,504
Lutob Investment Ltd	£27,806,644
Stantec Treatment Group Limited	£27,792,000
Roffey Homes Limited	£27,778,732
Simon Elvin Holdings Limited	£27,777,356
Hall Hunter Partnership (Farming)	£27,772,376
The Creative Assembly Limited	£27,756,866
Fizzy Stepney Green LLP	£27,755,000
Durrington Multi Academy Trust	£27,752,384
Peterborough (Progress Health) Nominee Limited	£27,749,000
Try Homes Limited	£27,716,000
Jeppesen U.K. Limited	£27,710,200
Eagle Racing Limited	£27,694,472
L. Lynch (Holdings) Limited	£27,694,116
Campact Limited	£27,693,000
Andigestion Limited	£27,692,776
Grouse Bidco Limited	£27,680,528
Nestec York Ltd.	£27,667,000
Sauvello Limited	£27,625,672
Newmafruit Farms Limited	£27,622,816
DDD Investments Limited	£27,611,426
Venn Partners LLP	£27,595,680
Biffa Environmental Municipal Services Limited	£27,585,000
Royal British Legion Industries Ltd.	£27,579,000
Hanson Marine Limited	£27,563,000
Veetee Foods Limited	£27,535,366
London Square (Holdings) Limited	£27,528,478
The Dover Federation for The Arts	£27,527,534
Organised Computer Systems Limited	£27,522,672
Home and Comforts Limited	£27,512,000
Creative Technology Limited	£27,494,000
ID Medical Group Limited	£27,489,010
Global Consortium Limited	£27,480,968
Minster Care Group Limited	£27,477,660
Ability Hotels (Manchester) Limited	£27,470,850
P.C. Harrington Holdings Limited	£27,437,000

Company	Turnover
RL Retail Services Limited	£27,429,290
PSN Holdco Limited	£27,428,000
XP Power PLC	£27,426,000
Sopheon PLC	£27,403,028
George Hammond PLC	£27,396,552
James Walker & Co. Limited	£27,391,000
Prior's Court Foundation	£27,385,808
Optegra UK Limited	£27,385,258
European Toughened Glass (UK) Limited	£27,384,222
Future Schools Trust	£27,373,000
Larger London Land Company Limited	£27,365,056
Doctors Chambers (UK) Limited	£27,341,378
Cash Processing Solutions Limited	£27,331,000
Associated Fisheries Limited	£27,329,548
Terex Pegson Limited	£27,317,000
Creative Video Productions Limited	£27,303,416
Garbuio Limited	£27,267,000
Jeensbannet Investments Limited	£27,257,904
Sea Corner Group Limited	£27,253,186
Glenside Care Group Limited	£27,236,110
Arlaform Limited	£27,226,648
GCP Biomass 4 Limited	£27,220,052
Spectrum Franchising Limited	£27,182,000
Russell School Trust	£27,174,608
E & J Ground Rents LLP	£27,156,218
Masternaut Holdings Limited	£27,153,000
Jessops (Group) Limited	£27,151,020
Xeretec Group Limited	£27,142,838
D.D.D. Limited	£27,138,234
3D Systems Europe Limited	£27,130,000
Newlands Girls' School	£27,103,622
Samsung C & T U.K. Limited	£27,098,000
Bandai Namco Amusement Europe Limited	£27,074,000
John E.Fells & Sons Limited	£27,073,200
The Taunton Linac Company Limited	£27,053,000
Grouse Midco Limited	£27,037,648
Regulus Topco Limited	£27,001,328
Regulus Midco Limited	£26,996,276
CDL Hotels (Chelsea) Limited	£26,996,000
Luff Investments Limited	£26,994,260
M.J. Allen Holdings Limited	£26,987,284
Crawley Down Holdings Ltd	£26,978,964
Transeur Properties Limited	£26,975,800
INEOS U.S. Finance Company Limited	£26,975,174
DHL GBS (UK) Limited	£26,954,060
Centrica PB Limited	£26,945,000
Archaylen Property Limited	£26,938,988
Appleby Group Limited	£26,936,000
CNM Estates (Tolworth Tower SBP) Limited	£26,901,492
Icopal Limited	£26,900,000
Royale Park Home Estates Limited	£26,897,790
CNM Estates (Tolworth Tower MBP) Limited	£26,888,992
Evolving Systems Holdings Limited	£26,885,484
Suez Recycling and Recovery North East Ltd	£26,868,000
Cygnet Learning Disabilities Limited	£26,862,000
Crown Products (Kent) Limited	£26,850,324
Help/Systems International Limited	£26,824,632
Boston Limited	£26,768,804
Construction Industry Solutions Limited	£26,744,806
Atlantic Foods Limited	£26,738,164
Euroforest Limited	£26,732,000
Big Yellow (Battersea) Limited	£26,725,000
Nuneham Estate Limited	£26,720,908
Toshiba Global Commerce Solutions (U.K.) Limited	£26,720,284
Albright International Limited	£26,699,772
Liberty Property Trust UK Limited	£26,697,092
Heiton Holdings UK Limited	£26,697,000
MTS Cleansing Services Limited	£26,693,916
Ian Allan Group Limited	£26,685,968
Huhtamaki Limited	£26,664,000
Chloride Supplies Limited	£26,645,000
PJ Care Limited	£26,641,616

Company	Amount
Compagnie Fruitiere UK Limited	£26,638,000
TVH Fizzy Holdings Limited	£26,628,000
The Horse Trust	£26,617,376
Linde Jewsbury's Limited	£26,605,000
Honey Monster Foods Limited	£26,594,000
Lymington Precision Engineering (LPE) Limited	£26,579,000
The Knowledge Academy Holdings Limited	£26,543,516
The Salterns Academy Trust	£26,521,170
Jayar Components Limited	£26,519,804
TRL Limited	£26,507,000
Resurgam Holdings Limited	£26,494,532
SAI Global CIS UK Limited	£26,484,280
Heartstone Inns Limited	£26,479,900
Wildern Academy Trust	£26,464,192
WSH Events Limited	£26,454,000
Ability Hotels (Luton Inn) Limited	£26,448,556
Paradigm Commercial PLC	£26,445,000
H.I.G. Europe - Fibercore Bidco Limited	£26,438,722
NewVoiceMedia Limited	£26,424,108
Link Market Services Trustees Limited	£26,423,796
Herne Bay High School	£26,422,436
Longacres Garden Centre Limited	£26,421,984
SSE Seabank Investments Limited	£26,400,000
Careprogress Limited	£26,391,724
London Care Partnership Limited	£26,390,636
Overton Grange School	£26,386,000
Melton House Investments Limited	£26,362,588
Therakos (UK), Ltd	£26,275,732
Perkinelmer LAS (UK) Limited	£26,261,000
Advanced Lighting Technologies Europe Limited	£26,249,848
VFS Legal Limited	£26,235,670
New Era Cap Company Limited	£26,233,362
Kirkmore Capital Limited	£26,217,256
Gould Publication Papers UK Limited	£26,193,992
Orange Business UK Limited	£26,168,826
AKA London Limited	£26,163,468
Elmwey Learning Trust	£26,149,000
Transport Research Foundation	£26,137,000
Shearwater Geoservices Limited	£26,130,916
Universal Meats (UK) Limited	£26,120,000
Fujifilm Sericol Overseas Holdings Limited	£26,115,000
Grange Renewable Energy Limited	£26,079,000
Tavistock Investments PLC	£26,071,000
Trochair Limited	£26,068,000
Attwood Academies	£26,065,816
Abertis Motorways UK Limited	£26,056,128
Harsco Rail Limited	£26,048,890
Greenshields JCB Holdings Limited	£26,032,000
Chemring Technology Solutions Limited	£26,001,000
Biomerieux UK Limited	£25,999,608
Moretons Investments Limited	£25,986,796
Red Circle Security Services Limited	£25,980,226
R & M Electrical Group Limited	£25,978,636
The Victoria Foundation	£25,976,000
Longview Holding UK 2 Limited	£25,975,620
Lufthansa Technik Landing Gear Services UK Limited	£25,961,000
CAE (UK) PLC	£25,928,000
Porthaven Finance Limited	£25,910,068
Cordek Limited	£25,904,564
Coca-Cola European Partners Services Europe Ltd	£25,873,000
Charles Darwin Academy Trust	£25,857,472
Keystone Holdco Limited	£25,853,262
Watson Wyatt European Investment Holdings Limited	£25,851,184
Clearwater Technology Bidco Limited	£25,850,644
SmithKline Beecham Research Limited	£25,847,000
BP Turkey Refining Limited	£25,843,286
Oldercare (Haslemere) Limited	£25,825,426
EHGT Limited	£25,817,214
George Farmiloe & Sons Limited	£25,801,146
Convergence Pharmaceuticals Holdings Limited	£25,782,080
Clearwater Technology Holdco Limited	£25,777,080
Noble Energy (Oilex) Limited	£25,766,688
New Topco 1 Limited	£25,749,740
CSPH Limited	£25,739,364
Wessex Children's Hospice Trust	£25,720,740
Celsis International Limited	£25,719,000
Columbus Midco Limited	£25,698,000
Axis Group Integrated Services Limited	£25,680,000
Redring Xpelair Group Ltd	£25,661,000
D-R Holdings (UK) Ltd	£25,660,000
Geos Group Limited	£25,651,604
Rockley Sands (Estates) Limited	£25,649,000
Paula Hawkins Limited	£25,613,192
Cathay Investments 2 Limited	£25,577,716
Axiom Education (Perth & Kinross) Holdings Limited	£25,549,000
Grafton UK Leasing Company Limited	£25,542,216
Sentinel Health Care Limited	£25,525,984
Kaye Enterprises Limited	£25,524,538
Greenshields JCB Limited	£25,500,000
Cable & Wireless Global Holding Limited	£25,460,000
UK Cables Limited	£25,421,000
Fresenius Kabi Oncology PLC	£25,414,000
Bourne Leisure Group Limited	£25,413,000
M & J Seafood Limited	£25,411,000
Esselte Holdings Limited	£25,404,000
Optionis Group Limited	£25,394,012
Admiral House Property Trading Limited	£25,393,188
BDML Connect Limited	£25,389,648
Mersham Hatch Estate LLP	£25,387,036
Charters School	£25,386,304
Fishdance Limited	£25,374,212
AVM Impact Ltd	£25,368,000
Feltham Group Limited	£25,350,444
MCPA Limited	£25,347,940
Cleartone Group Limited	£25,346,826
Dolphin Two Limited	£25,342,000
Rydon Homes Limited	£25,341,240
KN Network Services (Northern Ireland) Limited	£25,332,280
Humberside International Airport Limited	£25,315,000
Exemplar Properties Limited	£25,309,252
BAE Systems (Land and Sea Systems) Limited	£25,294,000
Jenoptik Traffic Solutions UK Ltd	£25,291,334
Trek Bicycle Corporation Limited	£25,287,584
Volt Europe Limited	£25,277,672
Ansa UK Limited	£25,275,000
Rush Hair Group Limited	£25,265,000
Thornton Properties Limited	£25,253,648
Chinatool UK Limited	£25,247,000
ProAV Holdings Limited	£25,243,768
Thanet Earth Limited	£25,242,000
Buy 2 Let Cars Ltd	£25,240,802
Royalton Group Holdings Limited	£25,218,560
X P PLC	£25,207,000
Kamkorp Limited	£25,202,976
Gruffalo Midco Limited	£25,202,548
Clinisys Group Limited	£25,175,000
Lodge Bros. (Funerals) Limited	£25,171,020
W Lamb Limited	£25,146,604
Thanet Earth Holdings Limited	£25,128,000
European Laminate Glass Limited	£25,121,528
Johnson Controls Auto India Ltd	£25,117,000
SDH Bidco Limited	£25,114,396
Scandinavian Tobacco Group United Kingdom Limited	£25,105,782
NTT Security (UK) Limited	£25,090,184
Green Flag Holdings Limited	£25,087,408
Collingwood College	£25,084,264
Kimal Holdings Limited	£25,082,000
Newcourt Residential (Wadhurst) Limited	£25,080,012
Strand Court Properties Limited	£25,068,000
Chislehurst and Sidcup Grammar School	£25,066,720
Skills for Life Trust	£25,064,252
Laing Construction Limited	£25,064,000
Stanley Electric Holding Europe Co., Limited	£25,063,614
O2 Unify Limited	£25,054,000

Company	Amount
Purecircle (UK) Limited	£25,042,014
Winterhalter Ltd	£25,037,508
Inspiring Learning Limited	£25,036,000
Raymond Brown Minerals & Recycling Ltd	£25,027,376
GFZ Properties Limited	£25,026,456
Odyssey Trust for Education	£25,015,000
Jacobs UK Holdings Limited	£25,014,000
Cook Trading Limited	£24,970,496
Woodgavil Limited	£24,964,550
Connor Investments (UK) LLP	£24,963,888
Dermalogica (UK) Limited	£24,956,168
HR Gardens Limited	£24,943,000
Hazelwick School	£24,914,216
Harvey Water Softeners Limited	£24,909,988
Saftdwin Limited	£24,902,216
L.E. Pritchitt & Company Limited	£24,888,000
The New Victoria Hospital Limited	£24,828,000
INEOS Paraform Holdings Limited	£24,824,630
BCA Vehicle Services Limited	£24,821,000
T S S Group PLC	£24,804,046
Comland Commercial Limited	£24,775,468
Cuffe Holdings Limited	£24,774,800
Project Tristar Limited	£24,763,000
Inprint Systems Limited	£24,744,000
Sky IQ Limited	£24,724,000
Ability Hotels (Liverpool Plaza) Limited	£24,713,962
The Oratory Schools Association	£24,704,566
Wolters Kluwer Health (Medical Research) Limited	£24,669,000
York International (Holdings) Limited	£24,669,000
Pilgrims Hospices in East Kent	£24,661,000
Aitch Care Homes Holdco Limited	£24,653,000
Sesame Services Limited	£24,636,000
Mood Media Limited	£24,609,000
The Waldegrave Trust	£24,606,262
United Healthcare (South Buckinghamshire) Holdings	£24,603,000
Remy's Limited	£24,588,120
Pureprint Group Limited	£24,576,468
Birchwood Garages Limited	£24,533,000
Mobil Trading and Supply Limited	£24,515,328
Premier Rugby Limited	£24,510,050
UK Mail Group Limited	£24,509,000
World Mission Agency - Winners Chapel International	£24,500,488
Northamber PLC	£24,484,000
Cox Green School	£24,483,796
Tensator Group Limited	£24,480,000
Holly Lodge (Kingswood) Limited	£24,475,440
Cygnet Learning Disabilities Midlands Limited	£24,475,000
Peter Press Limited	£24,468,000
Endeavour Holdings Limited	£24,464,952
J.B.Howard Properties Limited	£24,461,964
The Offer Group Ltd	£24,458,782
Henry Streeter (Sand & Ballast) Limited	£24,456,736
Uxbridge High School Academy Trust	£24,446,592
Ww.co.uk Online Limited	£24,441,000
Dolphin Head Group Holdings PLC	£24,436,050
Aspentech Ltd.	£24,436,000
Simon Elvin Limited	£24,422,124
Investsave Limited	£24,400,630
Sands Heritage Ltd	£24,397,516
Wy (Nutfield Priory) Limited	£24,383,960
1948 Group Limited	£24,381,192
Labcorp Neon Ltd.	£24,357,550
Navy,Army and Air Force Institutes,(The)	£24,351,000
Francotyp-Postalia Limited	£24,351,000
MDL Developments Limited	£24,347,000
MIQ Logistics Limited	£24,334,236
MEMS Power Generation Limited	£24,310,780
Lapid Developments Limited	£24,292,516
Celsis Group Limited	£24,290,000
Omega (After Alpha) Limited	£24,258,556
Royalton RS Limited	£24,254,922
Conway Aecom Limited	£24,222,362
Idemitsu International (Europe) Limited	£24,216,754
County & District Properties Limited	£24,201,854
AGB Properties (Woking) Limited	£24,187,820
The Wisley Golf Club PLC	£24,183,180
Reckitt Benckiser Luxembourg (No. 1) Limited	£24,171,000
South Darenth Farms and Cold Store Co Ltd	£24,169,964
Furze Platt Senior School	£24,165,856
S A Printing Group Limited	£24,165,000
Sime Darby London Limited	£24,157,000
PJ Care Group Limited	£24,134,532
Frimley Topco Limited	£24,121,000
Lilac Limited	£24,119,000
Watson Wyatt Holdings Limited	£24,110,628
Blanc Brasseries Limited	£24,101,238
Health Management Limited	£24,074,084
Rockwell Commercial Holdings Limited	£24,071,000
Axis Electronics Limited	£24,063,894
Education Support (Enfield 2) Holdings Limited	£24,059,000
Education Support (Enfield 2) Limited	£24,059,000
Nextonline Limited	£24,053,180
Ability Hotels (Dunblane) Limited	£24,052,766
Dolphin Head Group Limited	£24,050,550
Geting Capital Limited	£24,031,000
Humiseal Europe Limited	£24,029,398
IDE Group Limited	£24,001,432
Leeds Castle Foundation	£23,998,000
RSA Accident Repairs Limited	£23,996,000
Towers Perrin UK Holdings Limited	£23,994,000
Cranbury Investment Company Limited	£23,982,832
Alexander McQueen Trading Limited	£23,968,636
Lanxess Limited	£23,961,000
Carscreugh Renewable Energy Park Limited	£23,955,000
Yourway Transport Limited	£23,926,840
GMK Limited	£23,926,818
Citizen Watch United Kingdom, Ltd	£23,924,448
Johnson Controls Facilities Limited	£23,898,000
The Childcare Corporation Limited	£23,892,000
PT UK Holding Limited	£23,870,848
Chatham Street Technologies Limited	£23,870,846
Prinhold Limited	£23,869,468
Arnold Wills and Company Limited	£23,868,674
Alenco (Holdings) Limited	£23,867,000
Tesla Limited	£23,846,000
Braeforge Investment Limited	£23,845,288
Cordant Cleaning Limited	£23,836,580
Cogeco Peer 1 (UK) Ltd.	£23,828,568
REG Holdings Limited	£23,815,574
GCP RIW Holdings Limited	£23,800,000
Chaucer Management Services Limited	£23,751,280
Chemigraphic Limited	£23,734,952
Tamar Energy Operating Company (One) Limited	£23,734,000
HPC Public Limited Company	£23,685,000
Kennet School Academies Trust	£23,676,000
Clearswift Limited	£23,649,000
Clean Viking Bidco Limited	£23,648,950
SNC-Lavalin Co. Ltd.	£23,647,700
Carshalton Boys Sports College	£23,633,000
Ski Bound Limited	£23,616,000
Search Consultancy Group Limited	£23,594,000
Associated Cold Stores & Transport Limited	£23,587,624
Rohde & Schwarz U.K. Limited	£23,586,832
Harvestore Systems (Holdings) Limited	£23,573,078
Bowsprit Property Development Limited	£23,566,000
Telegenic Limited	£23,560,308
Shoppertrak Limited	£23,559,000
BAP Pharma Group Limited	£23,531,140
P A Crocker Limited	£23,519,248
Medway Fundco Limited	£23,485,214
Godrej UK Limited	£23,470,900
Wadlow Energy Holdings Limited	£23,460,000
Paradigm (UK) Holding Limited	£23,453,904
Acquisition U.K. Limited	£23,452,524

Company	Value
Motorola Mobility UK Ltd	£23,442,000
Homesun Limited	£23,434,332
Doctors Chambers Group Limited	£23,411,548
Prospect Healthcare (Hinchingbrooke) Limited	£23,405,000
Interdist Alliances Limited	£23,395,220
St. Margaret's School Bushey	£23,384,684
Antler New Homes Limited	£23,356,000
E & J Ground Rents No 15 Limited	£23,351,914
Compass Group Procurement Limited	£23,340,000
Empire Bespoke Foods Limited	£23,339,932
Nilvip Holdings Limited	£23,335,044
Infotech Trade Services Ltd	£23,333,800
Motorline (Kent) Limited	£23,309,046
Hemel Snowcentre Limited	£23,288,000
Snowcentres Limited	£23,279,000
Cams Hill School	£23,264,864
Grangette Ltd	£23,261,768
Cargobull Finance Limited	£23,251,000
Moorepay Limited	£23,245,000
Autosport Media UK Ltd	£23,229,918
Safenet UK Limited	£23,215,000
Monier (China) Holdings Limited	£23,212,000
Necessity Supplies Limited	£23,210,598
Loesche Energy Systems Limited	£23,197,602
Dynniq UK Ltd	£23,196,000
Amtech Group Limited	£23,194,000
AA Financial Services Limited	£23,192,000
Berendsen Finance (Euro 2) Limited	£23,157,344
Trescal Limited	£23,153,244
GCP Rooftop Solar 5 Ltd	£23,152,332
Linden (Biddenham) LLP	£23,149,000
Colgate-Palmolive Finance (UK) PLC	£23,144,536
Wilson Connolly Limited	£23,140,000
Yehudi Menuhin School Limited (The)	£23,135,464
Jacobs Engineering UK Limited	£23,131,000
Radiosite Limited	£23,128,140
BAE Systems Applied Intelligence (International) Ltd	£23,119,000
Brooklime Limited	£23,115,240
Central G H Trust	£23,115,232
Yourcash Solutions Limited	£23,115,000
MIQ Logistics EU Limited	£23,101,756
Storrington Industries Limited	£23,087,000
Grays of Cambridge (International) Limited	£23,080,968
Parallel Learning Trust	£23,066,000
TFX Group Limited	£23,063,000
Comland Holdings Limited	£23,055,412
Clinphone Development Limited	£23,050,000
Wisdom Properties Limited	£23,045,208
Kent Auto Panels Limited	£23,043,332
NSL (Holdings) Limited	£23,043,112
Davison & Co. (Barford) Limited	£23,040,450
St James Homes (Grosvenor Dock) Limited	£23,036,194
Costain Integrated Services Limited	£23,020,318
BAP Pharma Limited	£23,013,438
Nibgreen	£22,979,872
Milkwood Care Ltd	£22,975,510
Langmead Farms Limited	£22,975,116
Crest A2D (Walton Court) LLP	£22,975,000
Zion Care Limited	£22,973,620
Sanlam Private Investments (UK) Ltd	£22,966,000
NMRN Operations	£22,942,300
PCL Transport 24/7 Limited	£22,939,000
The Woodland Academy Trust	£22,939,000
Karelia Tobacco Company (UK) Limited	£22,936,140
Leighton Park Trust	£22,935,076
Arlacross Limited	£22,897,600
IMCD Holding UK Ltd	£22,885,000
The Automated Technology Group Limited	£22,882,000
MTI Technology Group Limited	£22,870,972
SG Equipment Finance (December) Limited	£22,868,920
TRAD Scaffolding Co.Limited	£22,854,960
Salisbury Holdings Limited	£22,835,000
RWF Health and Community Developers (Tranche 1)	£22,827,822
Skanska Major Projects Limited	£22,816,000
G & O Securities Limited	£22,798,464
Heathrow Hydrant Operating Company Limited	£22,793,000
Somerhill Charitable Trust Limited	£22,766,304
Avamore Limited	£22,756,118
Medina Dairy Limited	£22,723,420
Record Currency Management Limited	£22,723,000
Flexibox International Limited	£22,659,000
Wood Group Kenny Limited	£22,648,000
Vestey Foods Limited	£22,644,000
Bidvest Outsourced Services Limited	£22,606,430
Personal Group Limited	£22,585,000
ESSCI Technical Services Limited	£22,552,000
Derrin Brothers Properties Limited	£22,542,756
Icrossing Europe Limited	£22,533,716
Henley Camland Ebbsfleet 801H Limited	£22,518,494
Thompsons (UK) Holdings Limited	£22,517,220
Search Consultancy Acquisition Limited	£22,515,000
John Ingham & Sons Limited	£22,497,804
Contemplation Holdings Limited	£22,461,094
Staten Investments Limited	£22,459,124
Gould International UK Limited	£22,452,140
Partnerships in Children's Services Limited	£22,451,042
Bridgwater Bros.Holdings Limited	£22,437,940
Networkers International Limited	£22,432,000
Riemser Pharma UK Limited	£22,431,392
Somerset Equipment Finance (UK) Ltd	£22,412,556
Hastings (Holdings) Limited	£22,412,000
The Nuance Group (UK) Limited	£22,405,000
Tigers Logistics Group Limited	£22,401,420
Linden St Albans LLP	£22,389,000
York International Investments	£22,362,000
Canterbury Pharmacies Limited	£22,360,948
Barons Autostar Limited	£22,359,580
ADM Trading (UK) Limited	£22,346,016
International Property Finance (Spain) Limited	£22,340,606
Skanska Infrastructure Development UK Limited	£22,338,000
Essentra Services Limited	£22,337,610
Edif Group Management Limited	£22,334,000
The Gordon Foundation	£22,324,208
Grafise Holdings Limited	£22,282,996
Marwell Wildlife	£22,280,718
Oakview Estates Limited	£22,275,000
Walthamstow Hall	£22,273,568
Biwater Overseas Limited	£22,241,000
Parker Hannifin (Holdings) Limited	£22,234,000
R. Hunt (Agricultural Engineers) Limited	£22,229,770
Castle Marinas Limited	£22,207,032
Aquilant Limited	£22,197,580
Canadian & Arcadia Limited	£22,179,252
Falck UK Limited	£22,175,792
Canterbury Pharmacies Holdings Limited	£22,170,330
Falcon Coffees Limited	£22,163,182
QH Estates Ltd	£22,161,596
Leaders Lettings Limited	£22,161,460
Sea Cloud 1 Limited	£22,157,740
Thames Water Products Limited	£22,153,000
Towry Holdings Limited	£22,134,000
Barfoot Farms Limited	£22,110,768
Corona Energy Limited	£22,062,484
The Regard ACH Holdco Limited	£22,046,000
Manitowoc Crane Group (UK) Subco Limited	£22,040,852
Quayside Homes Limited	£22,026,744
A A Homes and Housing (Exchange Court) Limited	£22,000,000
Kallar Investments Limited	£21,993,636
Polycom (United Kingdom) Ltd.	£21,985,260
Optasense Limited	£21,964,000
Dinnages Garages Limited	£21,957,000
Bourne Leisure (Hopton) Limited	£21,937,000
Saab Seaeye Limited	£21,932,248
Holophane Europe Limited	£21,915,646

Old Thorns Luxury Apartments Limited	£21,905,572
Wurth UK Limited	£21,901,000
SPX Flow Technology Crawley Limited	£21,873,000
Clarenco LLP	£21,870,000
Thames Hospice	£21,862,000
HTEC Limited	£21,851,000
Jessops Europe Limited	£21,845,692
WCR Group Limited	£21,838,092
FNH UK Limited	£21,828,000
J.W. Spear & Sons Limited	£21,794,000
Natco Foods Limited	£21,791,392
The Southern Motor Group Limited	£21,786,532
The Piggott Church of England School	£21,781,780
Atkins Properties Limited	£21,766,000
Initial Medical Services Limited	£21,761,000
Sir William Ramsay School Academy Trust	£21,760,852
Contact Technologies UK Limited	£21,736,164
The Stowe House Preservation Trust	£21,734,460
Citizen Machinery UK Ltd	£21,732,640
Andrew Colin Investments Limited	£21,710,406
Egger (UK) Holdings Limited	£21,704,000
Volution Holdings Limited	£21,703,000
Axial Systems Ltd.	£21,692,472
Sopra Steria Recruitment Limited	£21,681,000
Acre 1176 Limited	£21,609,390
J.L.G.Investments Limited	£21,596,648
The HMS Trincomalee Trust	£21,589,668
Ridge Hill Trading Limited	£21,589,348
Agfa Healthcare UK Limited	£21,589,000
Exclaimer Group (Holdings) Limited	£21,588,340
WNDirect Limited	£21,585,420
Paultons Park Limited	£21,573,410
Serocor Holdings Limited	£21,570,000
Talacrest 2000 A.D. Limited	£21,567,384
Salisbury Workplace Services Limited	£21,566,000
Majestic Securities Limited	£21,535,766
Woburn Enterprises Limited	£21,520,904
Filemaker International	£21,506,580
Harding Holdings U.K. Limited	£21,506,000
Britannia Holdings (UK) Limited	£21,503,176
Stanley Electric (U.K.) Company Limited	£21,499,160
Crown Golf Operations Limited	£21,491,000
Rolta UK Limited	£21,473,340
Jacobs Douwe Egberts R & D GB Ltd	£21,470,000
John Laing Construction Limited	£21,434,000
Ixcellerate Limited	£21,431,840
Broadleaf Park LLP	£21,410,000
World Duty Free Limited	£21,408,000
RS Furbs Limited	£21,404,464
Red Tree (2004) LLP	£21,403,640
T.J.D. Trade Limited	£21,399,280
Endon Europe Power 6 Limited	£21,397,000
Trek Investco Limited	£21,376,324
Femcare Group Limited	£21,354,664
Bedford Education Partnership Holdings Limited	£21,329,000
Bedford Education Partnership Limited	£21,329,000
London Irish Holdings Limited	£21,320,320
Portrait Software Limited	£21,307,000
Newbury & Thatcham Hospital Building Trust	£21,267,470
Affinion International Travel Limited	£21,244,000
Ercol (Holdings) Limited	£21,239,000
Topps Europe Limited	£21,238,248
Relta Limited	£21,222,828
George House Developments Limited	£21,215,624
Courier and Passenger Transport Holdings Limited	£21,211,452
Click Entertainment Limited	£21,210,268
Chemigraphic Mid-Co Limited	£21,209,288
Sealion Shipping Limited	£21,199,110
Impact Africa Limited	£21,193,022
The Principal Edinburgh George Street Limited	£21,181,000
Atkins Holdings Limited	£21,170,000
Olive Business Solutions Limited	£21,160,996
Blackfen School for Girls	£21,128,000
R. J. and D. E. Billings Limited	£21,091,332
Richard Cook Limited	£21,089,582
Sun Hotel Limited	£21,087,584
Sopress Investments Limited	£21,077,000
Kenwood International Limited	£21,045,000
Britax Excelsior Limited	£21,002,000
Jembir Estates Limited	£20,992,208
Walker Logistics (Holdings) Ltd	£20,948,136
Isleworth and Syon School for Boys	£20,925,000
Prospect School, Reading	£20,911,444
Endace Europe Limited	£20,908,974
Cross Stone Properties Limited	£20,908,094
Blenheim House Construction Limited	£20,895,484
Chatham Historic Dockyard Trust (The)	£20,885,736
Walbrook Investments Limited	£20,875,936
Jakks Pacific (UK) Ltd	£20,872,778
Zest Living Limited	£20,862,288
TASIS The American School in England	£20,860,680
TASIS UK Limited	£20,860,670
Steelstock UK Limited	£20,816,836
Scape Opportunities Dublin Limited	£20,804,240
Facelift (GB) Limited	£20,800,388
Core Property Developments Limited	£20,796,380
Robert May's School	£20,780,596
Gate Gourmet Holdings U.K. Limited	£20,761,000
Deneep Limited	£20,740,986
Doctorlink Limited	£20,735,152
T Clark & Son Limited	£20,720,190
Continental Investment Limited	£20,695,000
Kinedexe UK Limited	£20,690,110
John Guest Speedfit Limited	£20,689,954
Pangbourne Developments Limited	£20,678,000
Energy Developments (UK) Limited	£20,661,088
LQAL UK Limited	£20,657,178
Stoneham Park Developments LLP	£20,646,572
Thames Water Investments Limited	£20,643,620
RFC Prop Co Limited	£20,640,716
J Clubb Limited	£20,621,548
SHOO 802AA Limited	£20,611,000
Crown Golf St Mellion Limited	£20,599,000
Evonik Goldschmidt UK Limited	£20,582,184
Andrew Jacobs LLP	£20,581,454
Whitehill & Bordon Development Company Phase 1A	£20,580,000
Historic House Hotels Limited	£20,545,322
The Manor Trust	£20,544,000
Tallentire Energy Limited	£20,532,000
Berkeley Seventy-Six Limited	£20,493,448
Sandy Balls Estate Limited	£20,488,504
Arinso UK Limited	£20,461,006
Forum Health Products Ltd.	£20,454,704
Kimal PLC	£20,453,000
ESNT Filter Products Limited	£20,452,492
Goodman Property Investments (Hove) Limited	£20,450,708
ACAL BFI Central Procurement UK Limited	£20,447,750
Famous Brands UK Limited	£20,426,000
H & D Support Services (Holdings) Limited	£20,426,000
H & D Support Services Limited	£20,426,000
EDL Holdings (UK) Limited	£20,424,804
Linde Severnside Limited	£20,420,000
Guernsey Home Loans Limited	£20,400,000
Brentford School for Girls	£20,395,524
Combat Stress	£20,353,000
Strides Pharma Global (UK) Ltd	£20,348,244
Vanguard Learning Trust	£20,323,000
The Abbey School, Reading	£20,318,562
Specialized (UK) Ltd	£20,316,866
Zene Finance Limited	£20,308,716
The Cowplain School	£20,306,770
IMBOLC Limited	£20,299,934
3T Bros Limited	£20,283,026
Bullers Wood Multi Academy Trust	£20,273,000

Company	Value
Fulston Manor Academies Trust	£20,265,348
Moss Electrical Holdings Limited	£20,248,884
Capital Safety Group (Northern Europe) Limited	£20,231,000
Bellman Property Group Limited	£20,216,372
Laing O'Rourke Manufacturing Limited	£20,212,000
Oval (2284) Limited	£20,198,324
Renand Properties Limited	£20,191,398
GCP Onshore Wind 3 Limited	£20,183,832
Baylis Court Trust	£20,176,332
Bishopshalt School	£20,159,984
Premiere Employment Group Limited	£20,152,888
Education Support (Newham) Limited	£20,119,000
Education Support (Newham) Holdings Limited	£20,119,000
Goulden Properties Limited	£20,116,018
Marbank Construction Limited	£20,111,000
Meantime Brewing Company Limited	£20,091,000
CSM Motor Group Limited	£20,085,642
Britvic EMEA Limited	£20,076,000
Shadowgrade Developments Limited	£20,069,988
Rye Academy Trust	£20,069,100
Mallinckrodt Medical Holdings (UK) Limited	£20,057,250
Perbury (Developments) Limited	£20,030,540
Brook Learning Trust	£20,025,016
Elysium Healthcare No. 4 Limited	£20,008,000
Oairo Alliance Limited	£20,000,100

This page is intentionally left blank

Age of Companies

1800s [53]

Akzo Nobel Packaging Coatings Ltd
BAE Systems Electronics Ltd
BOC Group Limited
Berthon Boat Co Ltd
Burt Boulton Holdings Limited
W.H. Brakspear & Sons Limited
Brighton College
Britannia Soft Drinks Limited
Cadbury Schweppes Overseas Ltd
Camellia PLC
Cape Intermediate Holdings Ltd
Cardiff Property PLC
Chloride Group Limited
Chubb International Holdings Ltd
Coca-Cola European Partners GB Ltd
De La Rue Holdings Limited
Delta Limited
Entserv UK Limited
Equitable Life Assurance Society,(The)
Esso Petroleum Co Ltd
Faber Prest Limited
George Farmiloe & Sons Ltd
Fisons Limited
Five Arrows Limited
Girls' Education Co Ltd
Gordon Foundation
Halma PLC
Hanson Packed Products Limited
Haynes Brothers,Limited
Hendy Holdings Limited
I C I Finance Limited
International Paint Limited
JCA Charitable Foundation
Kentstone Properties Limited
Kodak Limited
Marine Insurance Co Ltd
Mondelez UK Holdings & Services Ltd
Nestle UK Ltd.
Pic Fyfield Limited
RB Lease Co Ltd
Reading Football Club Limited
Rentokil Initial (1896) Ltd
Rhodia International Holdings Ltd
Siemens Mobility Limited
Smith Bradbeer & Co Ltd
Smith Kline & French Laboratories
Solvay Solutions UK Limited
Southampton Football Club Ltd
Southampton Isle of Wight and South of England Royal Mail Steam Packet Co
Walker Greenbank PLC.
West's Group International Ltd
Wilkinson Sword Limited
Wolseley Limited

1900-1909 [36]

Air Products PLC
Allianz Insurance PLC
British Car Auction Group Ltd
British and Foreign Wharf Co Ltd
Caffyns PLC
Chemring Group PLC
I.P. Clarke & Co. Limited
Clean Linen Services Limited
Coats Group PLC
Robert Cort Properties Ltd
Early Learning Centre Limited
Elliott Brothers (Builders Merchants)
Elster Metering Holdings Ltd
Eskaylab Limited
Evonik Chemicals Limited
Exel Limited
Fyffes Group Limited
Havas Shared Services Limited
Hilton UK Hotels Limited
Honeywell International UK Ltd
Interserve Investments Limited
Interserve PLC
Larger London Land Co Ltd
James Latham PLC
Lubricants UK Limited
Newbury Racecourse PLC
Procter & Gamble Limited
Renault U.K. Limited
Royal & Sun Alliance Insurance PLC
Royal & Sun Alliance Reinsurance Ltd
SPX Flow Technology Crawley Ltd
Sun Alliance Insurance Overseas Ltd
TT Electronics PLC
Trafalgar Insurance PLC
Vestey Holdings Limited
Watford Association Football Club

1910-1919 [51]

Abbey School, Reading
Accolade Wines Limited
Agility Logistics Limited
Akzo Nobel Decorative Coatings Ltd
Akzo Nobel UK Ltd
Apperly Estates Limited
Archer Daniels Midland Erith Ltd
Atlas Copco Limited
BP Shipping Limited
Barloworld UK Limited
Benson & Hedges Limited
Chas.A.Blatchford & Sons,Limited
Canterbury Diocesan Board of Finance
Castrol Limited
Chichester Diocesan Fund and Board of Finance (Incorporated)
Chubb Fire Limited
D.D.D. Limited
J.T.Davies & Sons Limited
Dewhurst PLC
Dun & Bradstreet Limited
Eastbourne College (Incorporated)
Eaton Limited
Electrical Contractors Association
GE Energy (UK) Limited
GPG (UK) Holdings Limited
Grays of Cambridge (International)
F.Hinds Limited
Honeywell Specialty Wax & Additives
Howard Lloyd & Co Ltd
IBM United Kingdom Holdings Ltd
Nespresso UK Ltd
Nestle Purina Petcare (U.K.) Ltd
Novartis Pharmaceuticals UK Ltd
Pfizer Consumer Healthcare Ltd
Rayner Surgical Group Limited
Reed Business Information Ltd
Rochester Diocesan Society and Board of Finance
Royal British Legion Industries Ltd.
Royal International Insurance Holdings
S & B Herba Foods Limited
SEM Limited
Scandinavian Tobacco Group United Kingdom
Selecta Refreshments Limited
Shepherd Neame Limited
St.Swithuns School (Winchester)
Volex PLC
Charles Wells,Limited
Western United Investment Co Ltd
Whatman International Limited
Winchester Diocesan Board of Finance
John Wyeth & Brother Limited

1920-1929 [86]

3M UK Holdings Limited
Acco UK Limited
Alfa Laval Limited
Alpha Assembly Solutions UK Ltd
Armstrong World Industries Ltd
Associated Fisheries Limited
B O C Holdings
BAE Systems (Defence Systems) Ltd
BAE Systems Marine Limited
BFS Group Limited
BP Chemicals Limited
BP Greece Limited
BP Pension Trustees Limited
Barrow Hepburn Group Limited
Basinghall Estate Co Ltd
Beecham Group P L C
Benenden School (Kent) Limited
Berendsen UK Limited
Bidvest Freight UK Limited
Black & Decker International
Blackmoor Estate Limited
Bollore Logistics UK Ltd
Chemring Countermeasures Ltd
Chep UK Limited
Colgate-Palmolive (U.K.) Ltd
Corus Hotels Limited
John Crane UK Limited
DHL Distribution Holdings (UK) Ltd
Daler-Rowney Limited
Del Monte Europe Limited
Endeavour Holdings Limited
Esso Exploration and Production UK
John E.Fells & Sons Limited
Fiat Chrysler Automobiles UK Ltd
Wilfred T Fry Limited
GlaxoSmithKline Finance PLC
Glynwed Overseas Holdings Ltd
Guildford Diocesan Board of Finance
Harsco Infrastructure Group Ltd
Harvey & Son (Lewes) Limited
Hendy Group Limited
Henkel Limited
Honeywell Control Systems Ltd
Horlicks Limited
Imperial Chemical Industries Ltd
Inter Terminals Immingham Ltd
Johnson & Johnson Management Ltd
Johnson Wax Limited
Johnston Sweepers Limited
John Laing Construction Ltd
Leighton Park Trust
MacDermid Europe Limited
Mondelez UK Limited
Mothercare Group Limited
Navy,Army and Air Force Institutes,(The)
Novar ED & S Limited
Novartis Grimsby Limited
P & O Ferries Limited
Porsche Retail Group Limited
Portals Group Limited
Portsmouth Diocesan Board of Finance
William Reed Holdings Limited
Rentokil Initial 1927 PLC
Rentokil Limited

Rhodia Limited
Ricardo PLC
Royal British Legion Poppy Factory
Serco Limited
Skanska Construction UK Ltd
Slough Heat & Power Limited
SmithKline Beecham Research Ltd
Stearn Electric Co Ltd
Stowe School,Limited
Suffolk Finance Co Ltd
Sun Insurance Office Limited
TT Electronics IoT Solutions Ltd
Tanjong PLC
Thorntons Limited
Tillotson Commercial Motors Ltd
UCB Pharma Limited
United Technologies Finance (U.K.)
Vitec Group PLC.
James Walker Group Limited
Wellcome Foundation Limited
Westgate Properties Limited
H Young Holdings PLC

1930-1939 [97]

Abbott Laboratories Limited
Ageas Insurance Limited
Anixter Limited
BAM Nuttall Limited
BOC Limited
BP Chemicals Investments Ltd
BP Exploration Operating Co Ltd
BP Global Investments Limited
BP Investment Management Ltd
BP Oil International Limited
Bacardi-Martini Limited
F.G. Barnes & Sons Limited
Barretts of Canterbury Limited
Bedales School
Birds Eye Limited
Black & Decker
Blackwell Science Limited
Boskalis Westminster (Holdings) Ltd
Bovis Homes Group PLC
Britannia Refined Metals Ltd
Britax Excelsior Limited
Chemetall Limited
Chloride Supplies Limited
Civil Service Motoring Association,Limited
T Clark & Son Limited
Coats Industrial Thread Ltd
Combat Stress
Continental Tyre Group Ltd.
Cooper Estates Limited
Richard Costain Limited
Coty UK & I Ltd
Covidien UK Limited
W.J.Daniel & Co Ltd
Dinnages Garages Limited
Ellis & Sons Amalgamated Properties
Essentra Filter Products Ltd
G4S Cash Solutions (UK) Ltd
GE Medical Systems Limited
Gillette U.K. Limited
Glaxo Group Limited
Glyndebourne Productions Ltd
Gould International UK Limited
Gravesend and District Real Estate Co
Guide Dogs for the Blind Association
H+H UK Limited
Hanson Quarry Products Europe Ltd
Haulfryn Group Limited
Haymarket Media Group Ltd.
Richard Hochfeld Limited
Honeywell Limited
Honeywell UK Limited
Horse Trust
Hotelplan Limited
John Ingham & Sons Limited
Invesco Holding Co Ltd
Kimberly - Clark Limited
Eli Lilly and Co Ltd
Linde Material Handling (UK) Ltd
Lindt & Sprungli (U.K.) Ltd
J.P.McDougall & Co.Limited
Mentmore Limited
Morgan Advanced Materials PLC
National House-Building Council
Novar Systems Limited
Oratory Schools Association
P & O European Ferries (Irish Sea)
Panalpina World Transport Ltd
Propane Co Ltd
Reckitt & Colman (UK) Limited
Reckitt Benckiser Healthcare (UK)
Redring Xpelair Group Ltd
Rentokil Initial UK Ltd
Roke Manor Research Limited
Russell Finex Limited
Security Monitoring Centres Ltd
Sedgemoor Limited
Senior PLC
SmithKline Beecham (Investments) Ltd
J.W. Spear & Sons Limited
D.J.Squire & Co.,Limited
F.C. Stark Limited
Stena Line Irish Sea Ferries Ltd
Stonefield Estates, Limited
Suez Recycling and Recovery South East
Swan Mill (Holdings) Limited
TT Electronics Group Holdings Ltd
Taylor Wimpey PLC
Terex Pegson Limited
Trochair Limited
Unilever UK Limited
VWS (UK) Ltd
Wates Group Services Limited
Wilson Connolly Limited
Wilsons Automobiles and Coachworks
Xerox (UK) Limited
Xerox Finance Limited
Yattendon Group PLC

1940-1949 [98]

3663 Transport Limited
Acheson Industries (Europe) Ltd
Associated International Cement Ltd
B & CE Holdings Limited
BAE Systems Global Combat Systems
BP Exploration (Caspian Sea) Ltd
BP Oil UK Limited
Bacardi U.K. Limited
Barrow Hepburn International Ltd
Bartholomews Agri Food Limited
Beadles Sidcup Limited
Bic U.K. Limited
W.E.Black Limited
Bovis Homes Limited
Brentwick Limited
British Agricultural Services Ltd
British Car Auctions Limited
British Midland Airways Ltd
Broadcast Relay Service (Overseas)
Cadbury Schweppes Finance Ltd
Church & Dwight UK Limited
Church Communities UK
Clancy Docwra Limited
J Clubb Limited
Consort Medical PLC
Coty Manufacturing UK Limited
David Cover and Son Limited
Dairy Crest (Services) Limited
Dawsongroup UK Limited
Day Group Limited
Decco Limited
Dennis & Robinson Limited
Der Touristik UK Limited
Elliott Baxter & Co Ltd
Ericsson (Holdings) Limited
Essentra Filter Products International
M.P.Evans & Co Limited
Claude Fenton (Holdings) Ltd
Flexibox International Limited
John Guest Holdings Limited
H+S Aviation Limited
Haltermann Carless UK Limited
Harwoods Limited
Honeywell Analytics Limited
Honeywell Normalair-Garrett (Holdings)
Hotchkiss Group Ltd
Hotelplan (U.K. Group) Limited
ICI Chemicals & Polymers Ltd
ISS UK Limited
Inter Terminals Seal Sands Ltd
J.L.G.Investments Limited
Jacobs Process Limited
Jembir Estates Limited
W.T. Lamb Holdings Limited
W Lamb Limited
Lea Redway Limited
Lego Co Ltd
Lenham Storage Co Ltd
M.& W.Mack Limited
McKay Securities P L C
Mercedes-Benz Retail Group UK Ltd
Metropole Hotels (Holdings) Ltd
Millmead Properties Limited
Monier Redland Limited
Motor Insurers' Bureau
Nampak Plastics Europe Limited
Nestle Holdings (U.K.) PLC
Novartis UK Limited
Pandrol International Limited
Parker Hannifin (GB) Limited
Philips Electronics UK Limited
Pinewood Studios Limited
Pricketts Limited
Procter & Gamble (Health & Beauty Care)
Rhone Products (UK) Limited
J.& H.Robinson (Ilford Farms) Ltd
SSL International PLC
Schenker Limited
Scott Health & Safety Limited
Serco-IAL Limited
Services Sound and Vision Corporation
Sixt Rent A Car Limited
Skanska Cementation International
Smiths Medical International Ltd
Southern Co-operative Funerals Ltd
Specialist Holidays (Travel) Ltd
Spicers Limited
Spirent Communications PLC
Strand Court Properties Ltd
John Street & Company (Surrey) Ltd
R.Swain & Sons Limited
Taylor Wimpey Holdings Limited
Unipath Limited

Wates Developments Limited
Andrew Weir & Co Ltd
Arnold Wills and Co Ltd
Wolters Kluwer (UK) Limited
York Engineered Systems Ltd

1950-1959 [156]

Acco-Rexel Group Services Ltd
Alenco (Holdings) Limited
Appleby Group Limited
Associated Cold Stores & Transport
BP Exploration (Angola) Ltd
BP International Limited
BP Middle East Limited
BP Oil Vietnam Limited
BP Turkey Refining Limited
Sandy Balls Estate Limited
Bandhart Overseas
Bartholomews (Holdings) Ltd
Beckman Coulter United Kingdom Ltd
Becton Dickinson Infusion Therapy UK
Bedfordia Group Limited
Belron UK Limited
Berkhamsted Schools Group
Bristow Helicopters (International)
Bristow Helicopters Limited
Bristow Technical Services Ltd
British Airways Associated Companies
British Airways Holidays Ltd
Britvic Soft Drinks Limited
Burroughs Wellcome International Ltd
CP Holdings Limited
Capital (Hair and Beauty) Ltd
Caravan Club Limited
Charity for St Joseph's Missionary Society (Generalate)
Chubb Fire & Security Limited
Chubb Group Limited
Cleansing Service Group Ltd
Coldunell Limited
Collins Construction Ltd
Continental U.K. Group Holdings Ltd
Copthorne Hotel Holdings Ltd
Costain Limited
Covea Insurance PLC
Curtis Holt Limited
DHL Supply Chain Limited
DHM Plastics Limited
Davison & Co. (Barford) Ltd
Derrin Brothers Properties Ltd
Deta Electrical Co Ltd
John Dewar and Sons Limited
Draper Tools Limited
Epilepsy Society
Essentra Components Limited
Alan Firmin Limited
Alexander Fraser Holdings Ltd
GCP Applied Technologies (UK) Ltd
GE Money Home Finance Limited
Geodis FF United Kingdom Ltd.
Gist Limited
Glaxo Wellcome UK Limited
GlaxoSmithKline Caribbean Ltd
Goodman Property Investments (Hove)
Goodwood Estate Co Ltd
Grove Court Properties (Holdings)
HPC PLC
Hamol Limited
Hanson (ER - No 5) Limited
Hanson Aggregates Marine Ltd
Hanson Building Materials Ltd
Hanson Marine Limited
Harsco Metals Holdings Limited
Hayes & Jarvis (Travel) Ltd
E.L.Head Limited
Hertz (U.K.) Limited
Hogg Robinson Money Matters Ltd
J.B.Howard Properties Limited
Howard Humphreys & Partners Ltd
Hy-Ten Limited
ITW Limited
Intercontinental Hotels Group Services Company
International Marine Transportation
Johnson & Johnson Consumer Services EAME
Kebbell Development Limited
Kellogg Brown & Root Limited
Keystone Investment Trust PLC
Kimberly-Clark Finance Limited
Kinetrol Limited
Geo. Kingsbury Holdings Ltd
Lafarge International Holdings Ltd
Leumi ABL Limited
Linton Park PLC
Lockheed Martin UK Ampthill Ltd
London International Group Ltd
Lyndendown Limited
Manpower PLC
Sir Robert McAlpine Limited
Mobil Trading and Supply Ltd
Mood Media Limited
Moog Reading Limited
Mothercare UK Limited
Motorway Services Limited
Newmafruit Farms Limited
Novar Europe Limited
Nuffield Health
Ocean Overseas Holdings Ltd
P & O Ferries Pride of Hull Ltd
Pandrol Limited
Paydens Limited
Penspen Limited
Pfizer Limited
Pharmacia Limited
Pirbright Institute
Porter and Haylett Limited
Portsmouth Aviation Holdings Ltd
RMIS (RTW) Limited
Rayner Intraocular Lenses Ltd
Reckitt & Colman (Overseas) Ltd
Reckitt & Sons Limited
Reckitt Benckiser PLC
Reckitt Colman Chiswick (OTC) Ltd
Rentokil Initial Investments South Africa
Rentokil Overseas Holdings Ltd
Roche Diagnostics Limited
Rockley Sands (Estates) Ltd
Rockwell Collins UK Limited
Rohde & Schwarz U.K. Limited
Russell & Bromley Limited
S.S.S.Gears Limited
Saga Group Limited
Salaft Properties Limited
Saywell International Limited
Schlumberger Cambridge Research Ltd
Schweppes Limited
Selits Limited
Selwood Ltd
Shorefield Holidays Limited
Siemens Transmission and Distribution
Signet Group Limited
Smiths Detection-Watford Ltd
Store Property Investments Ltd
Henry Streeter (Sand & Ballast) Ltd
Sun Alliance and London Insurance
Tate Bros. Limited
Taylor Wimpey Developments Ltd
Tektronix U.K.Limited
Thales Electronics Limited
UOP Limited
United Helicopters Limited
United Living (North) Limited
Varian Medical Systems UK Ltd
Vectis Property Co. Limited
Vision Engineering Limited
Volkswagen Group United Kingdom Ltd
Watson Wyatt Holdings Limited
Wedge Property Co Ltd
Whatman Limited
John Wiley & Sons Limited
Wimpey Dormant Investments Ltd
Woodgavil Properties Limited
Xchanging Global Insurance Solutions
Xerox Limited
Yattendon Estates Limited

1960-1969 [253]

AA Financial Services Limited
ACAL BFI Central Procurement UK Ltd
ACS International Schools Ltd
ADM Arkady Limited
ADM Pura Limited
ADM Trading (UK) Limited
AECOM Infrastructure & Environment UK
Abbott Healthcare Products Ltd
Adda Hotels
Adeptus Limited
Agricultural Central Trading Ltd
Alcon Eye Care UK Limited
Ian Allan Group Limited
M.J. Allen Holdings Limited
Allport Cargo Services Limited
Altair Filter Technology Ltd
Alvis Limited
Amphenol Limited
Astellas Pharma Ltd.
Atkins Limited
Atkins Properties Limited
Attewell Limited
Automatic Data Processing Ltd
Avery Dennison U.K. Limited
Avis Budget UK Limited
B & W Group Ltd
BAE Systems Enterprises Ltd
BNP Paribas Leasing Solutions Ltd
BOC Helex
BP (Abu Dhabi) Limited
BP Amoco Exploration (Faroes) Ltd
BP Car Fleet Limited
BP Exploration Beta Limited
BP Gas Marketing Limited
BP Properties Limited
Baldwin House Limited
Bard Limited
Barons Autostar Limited
Bayer PLC
Beazer Limited
Becton, Dickinson U.K. Limited
Bel UK Limited
Biffa Environmental Municipal Services
Biffa Waste Services Limited
Biwater Holdings Limited
Boehringer Ingelheim Limited
Bonne Bouche Catering Limited
Bordure Limited

Bosch Automotive Service Solutions Ltd
Boskalis Westminster Limited
Bourne Leisure Group Limited
Brake Bros Foodservice Limited
Bridgwater Bros.Holdings Ltd
Britannic Trading Limited
British Fittings Group Limited
Brown and Mason Limited
CAE (UK) PLC
CSC Computer Sciences Limited
Capgemini UK PLC
Castacrete Limited
Caversham Finance Limited
Cellarmaster Wines Holdings (UK) Ltd
Cementation Skanska Limited
Charles River U.K. Limited
Clancy Plant Limited
Colt Group Limited
Compagnie Fruitiere UK Limited
Constantine Group Limited
F M Conway Limited
Richard Cook Limited
Copart UK Limited
Copthorne Hotels Limited
Costain Oil, Gas & Process Ltd
County & District Properties Ltd
Covea Life Limited
Cranbury Investment Co Ltd
Croudace Homes Limited
Crown Blue Line Limited
Crystalate Electronics Limited
DHL Parcel UK Limited
De La Rue International Limited.
Doosan Babcock Limited
Dresser-Rand (U.K.) Limited
Drift Bridge Garage Limited
Dun & Bradstreet Finance Ltd
Education Development Trust
Elster Metering Limited
Emcor Group (UK) PLC
Equiniti Services Limited
Ericsson Limited
Exel UK Limited
ExxonMobil Chemical Limited
F.M. Insurance Co Ltd
Ferguson Group Services Ltd
Ferrero UK Limited
T A Fisher (Holdings) Limited
A.A.Fisher (Properties) Ltd
Fynecast Limited
Galliford Try PLC
Galliford Try Partnerships Ltd
Givaudan UK Limited
Glaxo Operations UK Limited
GlaxoSmithKline Research & Development
Glen House Estates Limited
Gold Group International Ltd
Green,Young & Co Ltd
Grosvenor Casinos Limited
Grove Court Properties (Beaconsfield)
Gucci Limited
John Guest Speedfit Limited
HFC Prestige Products Limited
HR Gardens Limited
HSBC Invoice Finance (UK) Ltd
Hambridge Limited
George Hammond PLC
Hargreaves Properties Limited
Hargreaves Property Holdings Ltd
Harsco Metals Group Limited
Hewlett - Packard Limited
Hilton International Hotels (UK) Ltd
Holophane Europe Limited
Honda Motor Europe Limited
Huhtamaki (UK) Limited
Hy-Ten Group Limited
IBM United Kingdom Limited
IHS Global Limited
ISS Facility Services Limited
ITT Industries Limited
International Society for Krishna Consciousness
Intervet UK Limited
Intex (Radiographic) Limited
Invesco Asset Management Ltd
Invesco Fund Managers Limited
Invesco GT Asset Management Ltd
JCDecaux United Limited
Jeensbannet Investments Ltd
Jungheinrich UK Limited
Kebbell Holdings Limited
Kellogg Brown & Root (Greenford) Ltd
Kent Auto Panels Limited
Kentucky Fried Chicken (Great Britain)
Kenwood Limited
Key Properties Limited
Killinchy Aerospace Holdings Ltd
Kimal PLC
W.J.King (Garages) Limited
LRC Products Limited
Lafarge UK Holdings Limited
Lathams Limited
Leica Geosystems Limited
Leo Laboratories Limited
Linde Holdings Limited
Lodge Bros. (Funerals) Limited
London Britannia Hotel Limited
Lousada PLC
Lyndon Scaffolding PLC
MacIntyre Care
Macro 4 Limited
Marshall Amplification PLC
Martin-Baker Aircraft Co Ltd
Menzies Group Holdings Limited
Merritts Properties Limited
Mersen UK Portslade Limited
Millbrook Healthcare Ltd
Moorepay Limited
Motus Group (UK) Limited
NCMT Limited
Natco Foods Limited
National Foundation for Educational Research in England and Wales
Noble Energy (Oilex) Limited
Northgate Public Services (UK) Ltd
Novar Electrical Holdings Ltd
Numatic International Limited
Geoffrey Osborne Limited
P & O North Sea Ferries Ltd
PIG Improvement Company UK Ltd
Pall Manufacturing UK Limited
John Parker & Son Limited
Perbury (Developments) Limited
Photo - Me International P L C
Pioneer Concrete Holdings Ltd
Porsche Cars Great Britain Ltd
Prysmian Cables & Systems Ltd
RSA Accident Repairs Limited
Ramac Holdings Limited
Rapport Housing and Care
Reed Exhibitions Limited
Rockwell Automation Limited
Roffey Homes Limited
SC Leisure Group Limited
SES (Engineering Services) Ltd
ST & H Group Limited
Saga Services Limited
Sanofi-Synthelabo UK Limited
Scania (Great Britain) Limited
Schindler Ltd.
Senior Engineering Investments Ltd
Siemens Financial Services Ltd
Siemens PLC
Sinclair Gardens Investments (Kensington)
Six Continents Hotels International
Six Continents Investments Ltd
Six Continents Limited
Six Continents Restaurants Ltd
Skanska Rashleigh Weatherfoil Ltd
Skanska UK PLC
Smiths Industries Industrial Group
South Darenth Farms and Cold Store Co
Southern Motor Group Limited
Sowmac Investments Limited
St Barnabas Hospices (Sussex) Ltd
Strongdraw Limited
Sun Life Assurance Company of Canada (U.K.)
Sun Valley Foods Limited
Superdrug Stores PLC
Surface Treatments Limited
Suzuki GB PLC
Symrise Limited
TW Metals Limited
Taylor Wimpey Property Co Ltd
Tchibo Coffee International Ltd
Thales UK Limited
Thorn Security Limited
Tindle Newspapers Limited
Toshiba Information Systems (UK) Ltd
Toyota (G.B.) PLC
Toyota Material Handling UK Ltd
Trans Global Limited
Trant Engineering Limited
Tridonic UK Limited
Triumph Aerospace Operations UK, Ltd.
Tubifoam Limited
United Living (South) Limited
United Technologies Holdings Ltd
Vanguard Holdings Limited
Vertiv Infrastructure Ltd
Viavi Solutions UK Limited
Vinci PLC
Vinci UK Developments Limited
Vodafone Cellular Limited
Voluntary Service Overseas
A J Walter Aviation Limited
Warborough Investments Limited
Wilson Connolly Holdings Ltd
Winterbotham,Darby & Co.Limited
Wipac Limited
Woburn Enterprises Limited
Wolseley Overseas Limited
Wyatt Company Holdings Limited
Wyevale Garden Centres Limited
Yacht Havens Limited
Yehudi Menuhin School Limited
H Young (Operations) Limited

1970-1979 [351]

3M Products Limited
3M United Kingdom PLC
A.G. Thames Holdings Limited
ADT Fire and Security PLC
AGF Holdings (UK) Limited
AVX Limited

Abaris Holdings Limited
Ability Housing Association
Aerotron Limited
Affinion International Limited
Afton Chemical Limited
Ageas (UK) Limited
Ageas Retail Limited
Air BP Limited
Air Partner PLC
Albright International Limited
All Metal Services Limited
Allergan Limited
Ambassador Theatre Group (Venues)
Amoco (Fiddich) Limited
Amscan International Limited
Anduff Car Wash Limited
Antler Homes PLC
Aqualisa Products Limited
Aramark Limited
Archer Daniels Midland (UK) Ltd
Ardo UK Limited
Argos Limited
W.S. Atkins International Ltd
Atlas Copco UK Holdings Ltd
Aviva Management Services UK Ltd
B & Q PLC
BAE Systems Applied Intelligence Ltd
BAM Group (UK) Limited
BI Worldwide Limited
BMW (UK) Holdings Limited
BMW (UK) Limited
BMW Financial Services (GB) Ltd
BP Africa Limited
BP Asia Pacific Holdings Ltd
BP Capital Markets P.L.C.
BP Exploration (Algeria) Ltd
BP Exploration (Alpha) Limited
BP Exploration (Delta) Limited
BP Exploration (Epsilon) Ltd
BP Exploration Indonesia Ltd
BP Marine Limited
BPDM Group Ltd
Balton CP Limited
Batt Cables PLC
Beardow and Adams (Adhesives) Ltd
Berkeley Group PLC
Biffa Holdings Limited
Biffa Waste Management Limited
Biomerieux UK Limited
Biwater International Limited
Black & Decker Finance
Body Shop International Ltd
Boral (UK) Limited
Borelli Tea Holdings Limited
Bose Limited
Bourne Leisure (Hopton) Ltd
Britannia Security Group Ltd
British Gas Social Housing Ltd
British Kidney Patient Association
Brobot Petroleum Limited
Brymore Investments Limited
C.L.C. Contractors Limited
CDK Global (UK) Limited
CHG-Meridian Computer Leasing UK Ltd
CHG-Meridian UK Limited
CNOOC Petroleum Europe Limited
Caledonian Helicopters Limited
Canon (UK) Limited
Canon Medical Systems Limited
Carefusion U.K. 235 Limited
Cargill Holdings
Cargill PLC
Cashino Gaming Limited
Chapman Freeborn Airchartering Ltd
Chapman Freeborn International Ltd
Chemigraphic Limited
Citizen Machinery UK Ltd
City Technology Limited
Claremont Fan Court Foundation Ltd
Cluff Oil Limited
Colorcon Limited
Combined Counties Properties Ltd
Community Reinsurance Corporation
Conair Group Limited
Continental Trade and Commodity Services
CooperVision Lens Care Limited
Cordek Limited
Costain Building & Civil Engineering
Costain Group PLC
Crest Nicholson Operations Ltd
Crest Nicholson PLC
Cubic Transportation Systems Ltd
Currie Motors Limited
DHL International (UK) Limited
Daimler UK Limited
Day Lewis PLC
Direct Wines Limited
Dormole Limited
Draper Tool Group Limited
Durkan Holdings Limited
Durkan Limited
Dyno-Rod Limited
EMC Europe Limited
ESRI (UK) Limited
Edwardian Group Limited
Edwards High Vacuum International
Simon Elvin Limited
Epson (U.K.) Limited
Erith Contractors Limited
Esher Mail Order Limited
Esselte Holdings Limited
Essentra International Limited
Essentra Services Limited
Euroforest Limited
Europa Road Limited
Evonik Goldschmidt UK Limited
Exel Logistics Property Ltd
Exela Technologies Limited
Exodus Travels Limited
Exploration and Production Services (Holdings)
Expro North Sea Limited
FIL Investments International
Faithdean PLC
Fevore Limited
First Title Insurance PLC
Flir Systems Limited
Fluor International Limited
Fluor Limited
Fogarty Group Limited
Food Manufacturers (G.B. Company)
Fridays Limited
Fujifilm UK Limited
G4S Secure Solutions (UK) Ltd
GDC Group Limited
GE Healthcare Limited
GXS Limited
Galliford Try Services Limited
Gemalto UK Limited
Genus Breeding Limited
George House Developments Ltd
GlaxoSmithKline Services Unlimited
Glinwell PLC
Martin Grant (Holdings) Ltd
Martin Grant Homes Limited
Grass Valley Limited
Grigny (UK) Limited
Groupe SEB UK Limited
John Guest Limited
Gurit (UK) Limited
Halma International Limited
Hanson Finance (2003) Limited
Harlequin Estates (Twickenham) Ltd
Harsco Rail Limited
Harvestore Systems (Holdings) Ltd
Harvey Water Softeners Limited
Heidelberg Graphic Equipment Ltd
Hertz Europe Limited
Hillier Nurseries Limited
Historic House Hotels Limited
Hogg Robinson (Travel) Limited
Honeywell Security UK Limited
Hotel Inter-Continental London Ltd
Hotel Management International Ltd
R. Hunt (Agricultural Engineers)
Hyster-Yale Group Limited
IBM United Kingdom Asset Leasing Ltd
IBM United Kingdom Financial Services
IG Design Group PLC
Imagination Technologies Ltd
International Group Limited
Interserve Engineering Limited
Jacobs Field Services Limited
Janssen-Cilag Limited
Jayar Components Limited
Jeppesen U.K. Limited
Johnson & Johnson Finance Ltd
Johnson Controls Batteries Ltd
KAC Alarm Co Ltd
KBC Advanced Technologies Ltd
KCI Medical Limited
Kellogg Brown & Root (Services) Ltd
Keltbray Limited
Kone PLC
Kuehne + Nagel (UK) Limited
Laleham Health and Beauty Ltd
Lapid Developments Limited
Lawrie Group PLC
Leaseplan UK Limited
Leeds Castle Foundation
Lesser & Pavey Ltd.
Liberata UK Limited
Eli Lilly Group Limited
Linden Limited
London Tara Hotel Limited
Lovering Foods Limited
Luff Investments Limited
MC Truck & Bus Limited
MTS Systems Limited
MacDermid Performance Solutions UK
Makita (UK) Limited
Marina Developments Limited
Marwell Wildlife
Mary Rose Trust
Massey Group Limited
Oscar Mayer Limited
Sir Robert McAlpine Enterprises Ltd
Medtronic Limited
Merck Consumer Healthcare Ltd
Merck Serono Limited
Monier (China) Holdings Ltd
A.J. Morrisroe & Sons Limited
Mott MacDonald Group Limited
Mott MacDonald Limited
Movianto UK Limited
NSK Bearings Europe Limited

National Film and Television School
Neilcott Construction Limited
Newarthill Limited
Newship Group Limited
Niftylift Limited
Nike Land Securities Limited
Nikon UK Limited
Novo Nordisk Limited
Nuance Group (UK) Limited
O'Halloran & O'Brien Limited
O.C.S. Group Limited
OMC Investments Limited
Ocobase Limited
Octagon Developments Limited
Old Mutual Wealth Life Assurance Ltd
Omex Agricultural Holdings Ltd.
PSA Finance UK Limited
Panini UK Limited
Penspen Group Limited
Pentagon Freight Services PLC
Pentland Homes Limited
Perpetual Limited
Pet Plan Limited
Peter Press Limited
Pinnacle Insurance PLC
Pizza Hut (U.K.) Limited
PizzaExpress Limited
Powerscreen International Ltd
Premier Portfolio Managers Ltd
Giles W. Pritchard-Gordon & Co. Ltd
Puzzler Media Limited
Quantel Limited
RWS (Overseas) Limited
RWS Translations Limited
Riverstone Insurance (UK) Ltd
Riverstone Management Limited
Robinson Webster (Holdings) Ltd
Routeco Limited
Ruddy Joinery Limited
Russell School Trust
Rydon Construction Limited
S.D.C. Builders Limited
S.H.B. Hire Limited
SAS Software Limited
SHL Group Limited
SITA Advanced Travel Solutions Ltd
SMC Pneumatics (U.K.) Limited
Safety-Kleen U.K. Limited
Safran Helicopter Engines UK Ltd
Saftdwin Limited
Sally Salon Services Limited
Samsung C & T U.K. Limited
Sanden International (Europe) Ltd
Sangers (Maidstone) Limited
Schlumberger PLC
Sea Corner Group Limited
Sealion Shipping Limited
Seiko U.K. Limited
Sensient Holdings UK
Serena Software Europe Limited
Sime Darby London Limited
Siva Holdings Limited
Skanska Major Projects Limited
Skillbond Limited
Snap-On Business Solutions Ltd
Snows Motor Group Limited
Sonardyne International Ltd
Sopra Steria Recruitment Ltd
Sopress Investments Limited
Sorbon Estates Limited
Sparshatts of Kent Limited
Spectris Group Holdings Ltd
Spincrest Limited
St Bede's School Trust Sussex
Stackhouse Poland Limited
Standard Commercial Tobacco Company (UK)
Stantec UK Limited
Stena Line Limited
Steria UK Corporate Limited
Andreas Stihl Limited
Store Property Holdings Ltd
Storeshield Limited
Strollmoor Limited
Subsea 7 Crewing Limited
Subsea 7 Treasury (UK) Limited
Suez Recycling and Recovery Packington
Suez UK Environment Ltd
Ann Summers Ltd.
Sunspot Tours Limited
Synchro Clutch Co Ltd
T.R. Fastenings Limited
TRAD Scaffolding Co.Limited
Taylor Made Golf Limited
Taylor Wimpey UK Limited
Tearfund
Techaid Facilities Limited
Terrassen Holdings Limited
Thales Properties Limited
Trans Global Freight Management Ltd
Transform Housing & Support
Travelport International Ltd
UCB (Investments) Limited
UK Waste Management Limited
Universal Salvage Limited
Unum Limited
Urbis Schreder Ltd
Urenco Limited
Vantas International Limited
Vent-Axia Group Limited
Vernon Educational Trust Ltd
Vink UK Limited
WW GBR Limited
Walon Limited
Waremoss Limited
Wartsila UK Limited
Wates Living Space (Maintenance) Ltd
Wealmoor Limited
W K Webster & Co Ltd
Michael Wenman Limited
Wessex Petroleum Limited
Westerngeco Limited
Whistl Group Limited
Wightlink Limited
Wilky Group Limited
George Wimpey Limited
Winterhalter Ltd
Wolters Kluwer Holdings (UK) PLC
Wood Group Kenny Limited
Wurth UK Limited
Wyboston Lakes Limited

1980-1989 [659]

ACAL Electronics Holdings Ltd
ACG Rented Properties PLC
ACI Worldwide (EMEA) Limited
ADM Milling Limited
ADT (UK) Limited
ADT Finance Limited
ADT South Africa Holding Ltd
ARRI (GB) Limited
ARRK Product Development Group Ltd
Ability Hotels (Syon Park) Ltd
Acco Europe Limited
Acer U.K. Limited
Activision Blizzard UK Ltd
Advanced 365 Limited
Advanced Legal Solutions Ltd
Akzo Nobel Holdings Limited
Akzo Nobel Powder Coatings Ltd
Allergan Holdings Limited
Allianz (UK) Limited
Allianz Equity Investments Ltd
Allianz Properties Limited
Andigestion Limited
Anixter International Limited
Annodata Limited
Apex Car Rental PLC
Apollo Fire Detectors Limited
Aquilant Limited
Aspentech Ltd.
Atkins Holdings Limited
WS Atkins Limited
Audatex (UK) Limited
Australian Pacific Touring (U.K.)
Autodesk Limited
Automobile Association Developments
Automobile Association Insurance Services
Aventis Pharma Limited
Avios Group (AGL) Limited
Avis Budget Services Limited
Avis Europe Holdings Limited
Avis Finance Company (No.2) Ltd
Avis Finance Co Ltd
Avis Investment Services Ltd
Avon Capital Estates (Australia) Ltd
Avtrade Limited
Axial Systems Ltd.
Azlan Limited
B & C E Financial Services Ltd
B & M Care Group Limited
B.I.B. Underwriters Limited
BAE Systems (Operations) Ltd
BAE Systems Global Combat Systems Munitions
BAE Systems Marine (Holdings) Ltd
BAM Construction Limited
BCA Trading Limited
BMC Software Limited
BMT Group Limited
BNP Paribas Lease Group PLC
BOC Korea Holdings Limited
BP Chemicals (Korea) Limited
BP Exploration (Azerbaijan) Ltd
BP Technology Ventures Limited
BPS Offshore Services Limited
BSH Home Appliances Limited
Bandhart
Bard Holdings Limited
Barfoots of Botley Limited
Clive Barford Limited
Barloworld Holdings Limited
Barons Automotive Limited
Baxterstorey Limited
Beadles Group Limited
Beckman Holdings Limited
Beko PLC
Bellerbys Educational Services Ltd
Belron International Limited
Ben-Motor and Allied Trades Benevolent Fund
Berendsen Limited
Berry Gardens Limited
Bidvest Outsourced Services Ltd
Bike Alert PLC
R. J. and D. E. Billings Ltd

Ferdinand Bilstein UK Limited
Biogen Idec Limited
Black & Decker Europe
Blue Chip Customer Engineering Ltd
Blue Diamond UK Limited
Boehringer Ingelheim Animal Health UK
Book People Limited
Bourne Holidays Limited
Bowsprit Property Development Ltd
Brake Bros Limited
Brambles Enterprises Limited
Brambles U.K. Limited
Brendoncare Foundation
Bristol-Myers Squibb Business Services
Britannia Pharmaceuticals Ltd
British Airways Maintenance Cardiff
British Airways PLC
British American Tobacco UK Ltd
Britvic EMEA Limited
Britvic International Investments
Brown and Mason Holdings Ltd
Buckingham Group Contracting Ltd
Bugler Developments Limited
Burhill Golf and Leisure Ltd
Burnfield Limited
Burnt Tree Group Limited
Bytes Software Services Ltd
CAF Bank Limited
CDB (U.K.) Limited
CDK U.K. Limited
CLC Group Limited
CSB Holdings Limited
CSC Life Sciences Limited
CSL Behring UK Limited
Campact Limited
Campmoss Property Co Ltd
Capital Home Loans Limited
Capital Safety Group (Northern Europe)
Carte Blanche Greetings Ltd
Castle Cement Limited
Celltech Group Limited
Celltech R & D Limited
Centrica Brigg Limited
Centrica Business Solutions UK Ltd
Cerestar UK Ltd
Channel Commercials PLC
Channel Tunnel Group Limited
Chatham Historic Dockyard Trust
Chatham Street Technologies Ltd
Chemidex Pharma Limited
Chemring Technology Solutions Ltd
Childbase Partnership Limited
Children's Trust
Chiltern International Limited
Chilton Home Farms Ltd
Chubb Group (International) Ltd
Chubb Group Properties Limited
Churchill Insurance Co Ltd
Cilva Holdings Limited
Cineworld Cinemas Holdings Ltd
Cineworld Cinemas Limited
Civil and Marine Limited
Cognita Schools Limited
Colleycare Limited
Compass Group Holdings PLC
Consolidated Timber Holdings Ltd
Construction Industry Solutions Ltd
Continental Investment Limited
Cordant Cleaning Limited
Costain Alcaidesa Limited
Costain Engineering & Construction
Costain Integrated Services Ltd
Coty Brands Group Limited
Counties Home Loan Management Ltd
Country Estates Holdings Ltd
Countrywide Principal Services Ltd
Covance Clinical and Periapproval Services
Creative Technology Group Ltd
Creative Technology Limited
Creative Video Productions Ltd
Cromwell Holdings Limited
Cross Stone Properties Limited
Crown Agents Bank Limited
Crown Lift Trucks Limited
Crown Products (Kent) Limited
Cygnet Health Care Limited
Cygnet Learning Disabilities Ltd
D & B Europe Limited
D.E Holding UK Limited
D4T4 Solutions PLC
DHL Air Limited
DHL Aviation (UK) Limited
DHL Exel Supply Chain Limited
DHL GBS (UK) Limited
DHL UK Foundation
Dai Europe Ltd
Dairy Crest Limited
Dawsongroup Bus and Coach Ltd
Dawsongroup PLC
Dawsongroup Temperature Control Solutions
De Lage Landen Leasing Limited
Del Monte (UK) Limited
Del Monte Foods International Ltd
Delice de France Limited
Dell Corporation Limited
Deltec International Courier Ltd
Denmaur Independent Papers Ltd
Dermalogica (UK) Limited
Descram Holdings Limited
Dimension Data Network Services Ltd
Direct Line Insurance Group PLC
Disabilities Trust
Discoverie Group PLC
Discoverie Management Services Ltd
Dolphin Head Group Holdings PLC
Dulux Limited
Durkan Estates Limited
Dwellcourt Limited
Dynatrace Limited
Dynniq UK Ltd
EMC Computer Systems (U.K.) Ltd
ESNT International Limited
EWDB Limited
EWOS Limited
Eagle Racing Limited
Eastern Leasing Co Ltd
Eco Animal Health Group PLC
Egger (UK) Holdings Limited
Elbrook (Cash & Carry) Limited
Electrium Sales Limited
Electronic Arts Limited
Elite Homes (North West) Ltd
Elite Hotels (Rotherwick) Ltd
Elliott TurboMachinery Limited
Elu Power Tools Ltd
Entertainer (Amersham) Limited
Epicor Software (UK) Limited
Ercol (Holdings) Limited
Ergon Investments International Ltd
Ergon Investments UK Limited
Esso UK Limited
Esure Services Limited
M.P. Evans Group PLC
Exel Holdings Limited
Exel Investments Limited
Expeditors International (UK) Ltd
FBG Holdings (UK) Limited
FIL Investment Services (UK) Ltd
FIL Pensions Management
FNH UK Limited
Facelift (GB) Limited
Faithful+Gould Limited
Femcare Limited
Ferring Laboratories Limited
Financial Administration Services
First Hampshire & Dorset Ltd
First Technology Limited
Fleetwood Developments Limited
Focusrite Audio Engineering Ltd
Forextra Developments Limited
Fortis Lease UK Ltd
Forum Health Products Ltd.
Francotyp-Postalia Limited
Fujifilm Ink Solutions Limited
Fulham Football Club Limited
Furniture Village Limited
Future Electronics Limited
G4S Cash Centres (UK) Limited
G4S Security Services (UK) Ltd
GL Assessment Limited
Gallaher Limited
Gallaher Overseas Limited
Gama Aviation (UK) Limited
Gantrade Europe Limited
Garbuio Limited
Gardners Books Limited
Gartner U.K. Limited
Gate Gourmet Holdings U.K. Ltd
Gatwick Airport Limited
Genus Investments Limited
Gibb Holdings Ltd
GlaxoSmithKline Capital PLC
GlaxoSmithKline Export Limited
GlaxoSmithKline International Ltd
Global Invacom Limited
Glynwed Pipe Systems Limited
A Gomez Limited
William Grant & Sons UK Ltd
Grant & Stone Limited
Group Fabricom Limited
H.E. Group Ltd
HIC Racing (Chiswick) Limited
HIC Treasury Limited
HTEC Limited
Handsale Limited
Hanover Displays Limited
Hanson Holdings (1) Limited
Hanson Quarry Products Ventures Ltd
Hanson Retail Limited
Harman International Industries Ltd
Harsco Metals 385 Limited
Hasbro U.K. Limited
Haven Leisure Limited
Hawk Incentives Holdings Ltd
Heathrow Airport Limited
Heathrow Truck Centre Limited
Hitachi Capital (UK) PLC
Hitachi Europe Limited
Hitachi Vantara Limited
Hogg Robinson Limited
Holiday Extras Limited
Honeywell Avionics Systems Ltd
Hornby Hobbies Limited
Hornby PLC
Hospira UK Limited
How Group Limited

Howarth Homes PLC
Huhtamaki Limited
Humberside International Airport Ltd
Humiseal Europe Limited
Domnick Hunter Group Limited
IG Design Group UK Limited
IHC Hotel Limited
IHC May Fair (Holdings) Ltd
IHC May Fair Hotel Limited
IHC Overseas (U.K.) Limited
IHC UK (Holdings) Limited
IHS Group Holdings Limited
IMCD UK Limited
ISS Mediclean Limited
Idemitsu International (Europe) Ltd
Ikea Limited
Ingram Micro (UK) Limited
Ingram Micro Holdings Limited
Innotech Advisers Limited
Interserve Working Futures Ltd
Intersurgical Limited
Invesco International Holdings Ltd
Invesco Perpetual UK Smaller Companies Investment Trust
Invesco UK Holdings Limited
Investec Asset Finance PLC
Iris Business Software Limited
Iris Payroll Solutions Limited
JCDecaux UK Limited
JDA Software UK Limited
Jankel Armouring Limited
Jardines (U.K.) Limited
Jas Forwarding (UK) Limited
Jato Dynamics Limited
Jawaby Property Investment Ltd
Johnson & Johnson Limited
KBC Process Technology Limited
Kaye Enterprises Limited
Kellogg Brown & Root (U.K.) Ltd
Kellogg Brown & Root DH Ltd
Kellogg Brown & Root Holdings (U.K.)
Kellogg Brown & Root Overseas Operations
Kellogg Brown & Root Overseas Projects
Keltbray Plant Limited
Kenwood Appliances Limited
Kenwood International Limited
Kerry Holdings (U.K.) Limited
Kimberly-Clark Holding Limited
Klober Limited
Kodak International Finance Ltd
Kuehne + Nagel Limited
Kuwait Petroleum (U.K. Holdings) Ltd
Kuwait Petroleum International Aviation Company (U.K.)
Kuwait Petroleum International Aviation Co
Kuwait Petroleum International Ltd
Kyocera Document Solutions (U.K.)
LG Electronics U.K. Ltd
LHR Airports Limited
LSI Logic Europe Limited
Leaders Limited
Leigh Academies Trust
Lenster Investments Limited
Lenta Properties Limited
Lockheed Martin UK Limited
London General Insurance Co Ltd
London United Busways Limited
Michael J. Lonsdale Limited
M C Group Limited
MB Group Limited
MC Rental Limited
MDL Developments Limited
MDL Marinas Group Limited
MEMS Power Generation Limited
MTS Cleansing Services Limited
Mabey Engineering (Holdings) Ltd
Mabey Holdings Limited
Macmillan Publishers International
Majestic Wine PLC
Majestic Wine Warehouses Ltd
Mallinckrodt Chemical Limited
Mallinckrodt UK Ltd
Manitowoc Crane Group (UK) Ltd
Manor House Hotel (Castle Combe) Ltd
Markerstudy Insurance Services Ltd
Martin-Brower UK Ltd
Matrix SCM Limited
Mattel U.K. Limited
Maxell Europe Limited
May & Baker Limited
McLaren Applied Technologies Ltd
McLaren Automotive Limited
McLaren Racing Limited
McLaren Services Limited
Mecca Bingo Limited
Menzies Aviation (ASIG) Ltd
Merant Holdings
Mercedes-Benz Cars UK Limited
Micheldever Tyre Services Ltd
Micro Focus Limited
Microchip Limited
Micromuse Limited
Micron Europe Limited
Microsoft Limited
Millbrook Proving Ground Ltd
Millgate Developments Limited
Milton Keynes Community Foundation
Mitchellson Formwork & Civil Engineering
Mizen Properties Limited
Moove Lubricants Limited
Morgan Holdings Limited
Mothercare PLC.
Motorline Limited
Mott MacDonald International Ltd
NPS (UK4) Limited
NSK Europe Limited
NSK UK Limited
NTL Cablecomms Cheshire
NTL Cablecomms East Lancashire
NTL Cablecomms Greater Manchester
NTL Cambridge Limited
NTL Manchester Cablevision Holding Company
NTL Midlands Limited
Necessity Supplies Limited
Nesstra Services (UK) Limited
Nestec York Ltd.
Nestle Waters UK Limited
Netcall PLC
Newmarket Promotions Limited
Newsquest Media Group Limited
Nikon X-Tek Systems Limited
Nippon Express (U.K.) Limited
Noon Products Limited
Norma UK Limited
Northamber PLC
Novar (Stelrad) Limited
Novar Limited
OTV Birwelco Limited
Oakfield (Foods) Limited
Offer Group Ltd
Oil Spill Response Limited
Oki Europe Limited
Old Mutual Wealth Business Services
Old Mutual Wealth Holdings Ltd
Old Mutual Wealth Limited
Old Mutual Wealth UK Holding Ltd
Old Thorns Golf Hotel and Country Estate
Omega (After Alpha) Limited
Onkar International Limited
Ontex Retail UK Limited
Oracle Corporation UK Limited
PFU (EMEA) Limited
PGA European Tour
Michael Page Holdings Limited
Parexel International Limited
Park Holidays UK Limited
Park Lane Limited
Paultons Park Limited
Pennyhill Park Limited
Petersham Hotel Limited
Philips U.K. Limited
Picturehouse Cinemas Limited
Pilgrims Hospices in East Kent
Pittway Systems Technology Group Europe
Pourshins Limited
Prater Limited
Premier Fruit & Nut Limited
Premium Credit Limited
L.E. Pritchitt & Co Ltd
Progress Software Limited
Proudreed Limited
Prowting Investments PLC
Pura Foods Limited
Pureprint Group Limited
QA Limited
Quality Spirits International Ltd
Quantel Group Limited
R & M Electrical Group Limited
RAL Limited
RWS Group Limited
Rank Group Finance PLC
Rank Leisure Holdings Limited
Reading Transport Limited
Record Currency Management Ltd
Record PLC
Red Circle Security Services Ltd
John Reilly (Civil Engineering) Ltd
Remy's Limited
Renewable Energy Systems Ltd
Renewi UK Services Limited
Rhone-Poulenc Rorer Limited
Ricardo Investments Limited
Rockwell European Holdings Ltd
Romans Group (UK) Limited
Royal Insurance Holdings Ltd
Rubicon Drinks Limited
Rydon Group Limited
Rydon Maintenance Limited
S D C (Holdings) Limited
SAP (UK) Limited
SAS Holdings Limited
SG Equipment Finance (December) Ltd
SSE Contracting Limited
SSE Generation Limited
SSE Services PLC
ST & H Limited
Saab Seaeye Limited
Sabre Insurance Co Ltd
Sabroe Limited
Safenet UK Limited
Sandoz Limited
Sanlam Private Investments (UK) Ltd
Santander Consumer (UK) PLC
Scholl Limited
Science, Engineering and Manufacturing

Technologies Alliance
Scott Dunn Limited
Secure Meters (UK) Limited
Sega Europe Limited
Select Plant Hire Co Ltd
Senior UK Limited
Sensient Flavors Limited
Serco Group PLC
Servomex Group Limited
Sesame Services Limited
Setfirst Limited
Shadowgrade Developments Ltd
Shoppertrak Limited
Shukco Ltd
Siemens Healthcare Diagnostics Manufacturing
Siemens Healthcare Diagnostics Products
Siemens Industry Software Computational Dynamics
Siva Plastics Limited
Ski Bound Limited
Sky In-Home Service Limited
Sky Limited
Sky Subscribers Services Ltd
Sky Television Limited
Sloggett Group Limited
SmithKline Beecham Limited
Snows Business Holdings Ltd
Softcat PLC
Somerhill Charitable Trust Ltd
Sonardyne Group Limited
Sony Europe Limited
Southall Travel Limited
Southampton International Airport
Southern Water Limited
Southern Water Services Ltd
Sparshatts Holdings Limited
Specialized (UK) Ltd
Specsavers Optical Superstores Ltd
Spectris PLC
Spectrum Franchising Limited
Sports Information Services (Holdings)
St Mary's School Ascot
Stantec Europe Limited
Stena Line (UK) Limited
Stena Line Ports Limited
Stockford Limited
Stratton House Leasing Limited
Suez Recycling and Recovery North East
Suez Recycling and Recovery UK Ltd
Suez UK Group Holdings Ltd
Summerleaze Limited
Sungard Availability Services (UK)
Sunsail Worldwide Sailing Ltd
Surface Technology International Ltd
Surfcontrol Limited
Surrey Satellite Technology Ltd
Sutton and East Surrey Water PLC
Swan Group
Swan Mill Paper Co Ltd
Syneos Health Clinical Development Services
Syneos Health IVH UK Limited
System C Healthcare Limited
TASIS The American School in England
TASIS UK Limited
TBE (Southern) Limited
TTG Investments Limited
TWG Services Limited
Tangmere Airfield Nurseries Ltd
Tech Data Limited
Telefonica UK Limited
Telegenic Limited
Teletrac Navman (UK) Ltd
Telewest Communications (London South)
Thames Properties Ltd.
Thames Water Limited
Thames Water Products Limited
Thames Water Utilities Finance PLC
Thames Water Utilities Limited
Three Rivers Property Investments
Thursdays (Holdings) Limited
Tombstone Limited
Toyota Financial Services (UK) PLC
Treasury Wine Estates EMEA Ltd
Trek Bicycle Corporation Ltd
Trend Control Systems Limited
Trevellyan Developments Ltd
Trifast PLC
Tyco Fire Products Manufacturing Ltd
UB Overseas Limited
UCC Coffee UK Limited
UPS (UK) Limited
UPS Global Treasury PLC
UPS Limited
Ubisoft Limited
Unit4 Business Software Ltd
United Reformed Church (Wessex) Trust
Universal Meats (UK) Limited
University of Southampton Science Park
V1 Limited
Van Oord UK Limited
Veetee Rice Limited
Verifone (U.K.) Limited
Victoria Foundation
Victorygame Limited
Vinci Construction UK Limited
Vines Limited
Virgin Atlantic Airways Ltd
Virgin Holidays Limited
Virgin Media Business Limited
Virgin Travel Group Limited
Visual Impact (UK) Limited
Vitec Production Solutions Ltd
Voda Limited
Vodafone Enterprise U.K.
Vodafone Finance Sweden
Vodafone Group PLC
Vodafone Investments Limited
Vodafone Limited
Vodafone UK Limited
Vodaphone Limited
Volt Europe Limited
Volvo Car UK Limited
W.N. Developments Limited
WD-40 Co Ltd
James Walker & Co. Limited
Walkers Snack Foods Limited
Wates Construction Limited
Wates Group Limited
Welcome Break Limited
Wellcome Limited
Westcoast Limited
J D Wetherspoon PLC
White Horse Caravan Co Ltd
Wiley Europe Limited
Wiley Heyden Limited
Williams Trade Supplies Ltd
Wilton House Limited
Windsor Television Limited
Wisley Golf Club PLC
Wolters Kluwer Health (Medical Research)
World Vision UK
Wyevale Garden Centres Holdings Ltd
X P PLC
Xtrac Limited
Xtralis (UK) Limited
Yacht Havens Group Limited
Yazaki Europe Limited
Zellis UK Limited
Zest Living Limited
Zionstone Limited
Zurich Holdings (UK) Limited

1990-1994 [438]

3D European Holdings Limited
A A Homes and Housing Ltd
ABC Drug Stores Limited
ADT Group Limited
AGCO Finance Limited
APCOA Parking (UK) Limited
AVM Impact Ltd
AWE PLC
AbbVie Investments Limited
Acambis Research Limited
Accolade Wines Europe No. 2 Ltd
Advanced Elastomer Systems Ltd
Advanced Health and Care Ltd
Air Menzies International Ltd
Air Products (BR) Limited
Allegis Group Limited
Allocate Software Limited
Ambassador Theatre Group Ltd
Amer Sports UK Limited
Amsric Holdings Limited
Apogee Corporation Limited
Aramark Investments Limited
Arqiva Limited
Arqiva No 3 Limited
Arun Estate Agencies Limited
Asset Advantage Group Limited
Astellas Pharma Europe Ltd.
Avante Care and Support Ltd
Avicenna Holdings Ltd
Axis Electronics Limited
Axon Solutions Limited
Azlan Group Limited
BA Cityflyer Limited
BAE Systems (Dynamics) Limited
BAE Systems (Land and Sea Systems)
BAE Systems (Military Air) Overseas
BAE Systems (Overseas Holdings) Ltd
BAE Systems Land Systems (Finance)
BAE Systems Properties Limited
BDML Connect Limited
BNP Paribas Commercial Finance Ltd
BOC Gases Limited
BOC Netherlands Holdings Ltd
BP Russian Investments Limited
Bandai Namco Holdings UK Ltd
Barloworld Equipment UK Ltd
Baron Homes Corporation Ltd
Beck & Pollitzer Engineering Ltd
Bewley Homes PLC
Biocompatibles International Ltd
Biwater Overseas Limited
Bookcash Trading Limited
Boston Limited
Brighton & Hove Albion Holdings Ltd
Bristol-Myers Squibb Pharmaceuticals
Bristow Helicopter Group Ltd
Brookton 2000 Limited
Buxted Construction Limited
CAE Technology Services Ltd
CDL Hotels (Chelsea) Limited
CDL Hotels (U.K.) Limited

CGS Holdings Ltd.
CH & Co Catering Limited
CHB P H R Limited
CHG Overseas Ltd
CPI Mortars (North) Limited
Cadence Design Systems Limited
Camelot UK Lotteries Limited
Canon Holdings (UK) Limited
Canterbury Pharmacies Limited
Cardif Pinnacle Insurance Holdings PLC
Care Management Group Limited
Carefusion U.K. 305 Limited
Carewatch Care Services Ltd
Cargill Financial Markets Ltd
Cargill Global Funding PLC
Celsis International Limited
Centrica Energy Limited
Chubb Group Security Limited
Cineworld Estates Limited
Citrix Systems UK Limited
Civil and Marine (Holdings) Ltd
Cleanland Limited
Clinimed (Holdings) Limited
Coats Finance Co. Limited
Colas Limited
Colgate-Palmolive Finance (UK) PLC
Colt Investments Limited
Community Homes of Intensive Care and Education
Compass Overseas Holdings Ltd
Continua Limited
CooperVision Manufacturing Ltd
Cordant People Limited
Corona Energy Retail 4 Limited
Corona Gas Management Limited
Costain Civil Engineering Ltd
Costco Limited
Costco Wholesale UK Limited
County Catering & Leisure Ltd
County Catering & Leisure Properties
Covea Insurance Services Ltd
Crown Golf Operations Limited
Cygnet Learning Disabilities Midlands
DL Insurance Services Limited
DP Realty Limited
Dage Precision Industries Ltd
Danfoss Limited
Dawsongroup Material Handling Ltd
De La Rue Investments Limited
De Lage Landen Limited
Delaquest Limited
Diamond Cable Communications Ltd
Direct Line Group Limited
Direct Wines International Ltd
Downe House School
Druid Group Limited
ELWA Limited
EMC Consulting (UK) Limited
ESP Utilities Group Limited
ESRI Holdings Limited
East Surrey Holdings Limited
East Sussex Press Limited
Eco Animal Health Ltd.
Edwardian Exclusive Hotels Ltd
Edwardian International Hotels Ltd
Edwardian Ltd
Egger (UK) Limited
Elekta Holdings Limited
Elliott Brothers Limited
Elysium Healthcare No. 3 Ltd
Enghouse Holdings (UK) Limited
Enterprise Rent-a-Car UK Holdings
Enterprise Rent-a-Car UK Ltd
Enterprise Services Information Security UK
Erac UK Finance Limited
Erith Holdings Limited
Euro Alloys Limited
Euro Food Brands Limited
European Toughened Glass (UK) Ltd
Eurovia UK Limited
Evergreen Finance Limited
Evonik Speciality Organics Ltd
Evonik UK Holdings Limited
Exclusive Networks Limited
Exel Overseas Limited
Expro International Group Ltd
ExxonMobil Gas Marketing Europe Ltd
FCA Automotive Services UK Ltd
FT Finance Limited
Fat Face Limited
Feilo Sylvania Europe Limited
Fibercore Limited
Fidelity European Values PLC
Fidelity Japan Trust PLC
Fidelity Special Values PLC
Firmenich UK Limited
T A Fisher & Sons Limited
T A Fisher Developments Ltd
Flight Centre (UK) Limited
Floplast Limited
Forester Life Limited
Foundation Developments Ltd
Foundation and Friends of The Royal Botanic Gardens, Kew
Frontier Software PLC
G & O Securities Limited
G.E.W. (EC) Limited
GE Bio-Sciences Investments Ltd
GEA Group Holdings (UK) Ltd
GL Education Group Limited
Galliford Try Building Limited
Garmin (Europe) Limited
Gearhouse Broadcast Limited
Genesys Telecommunications Laboratories - Europe
Genus PLC
Globe Insurance Co Ltd
Gojo Industries - Europe Ltd
Golden Leaves Limited
Goshawk Insurance Holdings Ltd
Goulden Properties Limited
Grafton Group (UK) PLC
Kenneth Green Associates Ltd
Guildford Portfolios Limited
HMS Trincomalee Trust
Hamilton Palace Limited
Harding Holdings U.K. Limited
P.C. Harrington Holdings Ltd
Harris Defence Limited
Harvest Energy Limited
Harvey & Thompson Limited
Hatch, Mansfield Agencies Ltd
Havas UK Limited
Haymarket Group Limited
Heathrow Enterprises Limited
Heathrow Hydrant Operating Co Ltd
Hoechst Marion Roussel Limited
Holly Lodge (Kingswood) Ltd
Honda Trading Europe Limited
Hydac Limited
Hyster-Yale UK Limited
IQVIA RDS Holdings
ISG Retail Limited
Icon Clinical Research (U.K.) Ltd
Icopal Limited
Idox Software Ltd
Imagination Technologies Group Ltd
Independent Inspections Ltd
Invesco Pacific Group Limited
Invesco UK Limited
Investsave Limited
Jacobs Engineering UK Limited
Jacobs U.K. Limited
Johnson Controls Facilities Ltd
Kallo Foods Limited
Kamkorp Limited
Karium Ltd
Kelly Services (UK) Limited
Keltbray Group (Holdings) Ltd
Kerry Foods Limited
Kidsprog Limited
Kronos Systems Limited
LGC Limited
Lafarge Minerals Limited
Landlink Estates Limited
Langbourn Properties Limited
Ralph Lauren UK Limited
Linde Creighton Limited
Linde Jewsbury's Limited
Linde Sterling Limited
Linden Germany A Limited
Linden Germany B Limited
Link Market Services Limited
Link Market Services Trustees Ltd
London Airports 1992 Limited
Lonza Biologics PLC
L. Lynch (Holdings) Limited
L. Lynch (Plant Hire & Haulage) Ltd
M.A.T. Davies Holdings Limited
MIQ Logistics Limited
MK International Limited
Mallinckrodt Medical Holdings (UK)
Marbank Construction Limited
Mariner International (UK) Ltd
Mastek (UK) Ltd.
Mavenir Systems Limited
Sir Robert McAlpine (Holdings) Ltd
McNeil Healthcare (UK) Limited
McNeil Products Limited
Medina Dairy Limited
Medway Power Limited
Megger Group Limited
John Menzies (108) Limited
Menzies Aviation PLC
Mercedes-Benz Financial Services UK
Metropolis International Group Ltd
Michelmersh Brick UK Limited
Microsoft Properties UK Ltd
Miles 33 Group Limited
Miles 33 Limited
Millennium & Copthorne Hotels PLC
Millwood Designer Homes Ltd
Milton Keynes Parks Trust Ltd
Mission Foods UK Limited
Mitsubishi Electric Finance Europe PLC
Montgomery Property Investments Ltd
Morgan Europe Holding Limited
Mortar Investments International Ltd
Motoring & Leisure Services Ltd
Murex Biotech Limited
NPL Management Limited
NTL (B) Limited
NTL Cablecomms Surrey
NTL Kirklees
NTL Wirral Telephone and Cable TV Company

Nampak Holdings (UK) Limited
Natures Way Foods Limited
Neilson Active Holidays Ltd
NetApp UK Ltd
New Terex Holdings UK Limited
Newbury Investments (UK) Ltd
Nissan Motor (GB) Limited
Northgate Information Solutions Holdings
Northumberland Waste Management Ltd
Novar International Limited
O2 Holdings Limited
O2 Networks Limited
OCS Group International Ltd
Orange Business UK Limited
Organised Computer Systems Ltd
Orthofix Limited
PGS Exploration (UK) Limited
Panavision Europe Limited
Papa John's (GB) Limited
Paradigm Commercial PLC
Pegasystems Limited
Petrofac Engineering Limited
Petroleum Geo-Services (UK) Ltd
Phoenix Software Limited
Pinewood-Shepperton Studios Ltd
Pioneer International Group Holdings
PizzaExpress (Restaurants) Ltd
PizzaExpress (Wholesale) Ltd
Portsmouth Water Limited
Premier Marinas Limited
Pritchard-Gordon Tankers Ltd
Procter & Gamble UK Group Holdings
Purelake New Homes Limited
Purelake Properties Limited
REG Holdings Limited
RGCM Limited
RWS Holdings PLC
Ranbaxy (U.K.) Limited
Readypower Rail Services Ltd
Rebus Holdings Limited
Reckitt Benckiser Healthcare International
Rectory Homes Limited
William Reed Business Media Ltd
Reliance Vanco Group Limited
Rentokil Initial (1993) Ltd
Rentokil Initial Holdings Ltd
Ricardo UK Limited
Rico Logistics Ltd
Ringway Infrastructure Services Ltd
Riverstone Holdings Limited
Riverstone Insurance Limited
Robinsons Soft Drinks Limited
Runnymede Investments Limited
SAS International Limited
SDL PLC
SSE Production Services Ltd
SSE Seabank Investments Ltd
Saba Infra Holdings UK Limited
Sanofi Pasteur Holding Limited
Secom PLC
Selwood Group Limited
Sentinel Health Care Limited
Sesame Limited
Shanly Homes Limited
Share Centre Limited
Share PLC
Sharp International Finance (U.K.) PLC
Shepperton Studios Limited
Siemens Holdings PLC
Six Continents Overseas Holdings Ltd
Sky Operational Finance Ltd
Sky Telecommunications Services Ltd
Sky UK Limited
Smith International (North Sea) Ltd
SmithKline Beecham Overseas Ltd
Sodexo Motivation Solutions U.K. Ltd
Software of Excellence United Kingdom
Sopra Steria Services Limited
South East Water Limited
Southern Electric Gas Limited
Spirit Energy Resources Ltd
St George PLC
St George's Weybridge
Stanmore Contractors Limited
Staples UK Limited
Stoke Park Limited
Suez Recycling and Recovery Lancashire
Suez Recycling and Recovery Tees Valley
Sumika Polymer Compounds (Europe) Ltd
Sumika Polymer Compounds (UK) Ltd
Sungard Availability Services (DR)
Syneos Health International Holdings
Syngenta Limited
Sysmex UK Limited
T G Products Limited
T S S Group PLC
TFX Group Limited
TLC (Southern) Limited
Technetix Limited
TechnoGym U.K. Limited
Techtronic Industries (UK) Ltd
Telewest Communications (Midlands and North West)
Telewest Communications Holdings Ltd
Terex Cranes UK Limited
Tesla Engineering Limited
Thames Water Investments Ltd
Theseus No. 1 Limited
Theseus No. 2 Limited
Tokyo Electron Europe Limited
Topps Europe Limited
Tradebe Fawley Limited
Trifast Overseas Holdings Ltd
Tropicana United Kingdom Ltd
Try Homes Limited
Tyco Building Services Products (UK)
U K Land Ltd.
UK Assistance Accident Repair Centres
UK Cables Limited
UK Electric Limited
UK Highways M40 (Holdings) Ltd
UK Mail Group Limited
UPS SCS (UK) Limited
Ultima Business Solutions Ltd.
Ultra Electronics Holdings PLC
Ultra Electronics Limited
Ultra-Centrifuge Nederland Ltd
United Biscuits (UK) Limited
United Kenning Rental Group Ltd
Universe Group PLC
Unum European Holding Co Ltd
Uranit UK Limited
VM Transfers (No 5) Limited
Vanderbilt Hotels Limited
Venson Automotive Solutions Ltd
Verint Systems UK Limited
Veritas Technologies (UK) Ltd
Verizon UK Limited
Vernon Wholesale Investments Co Ltd
Verus Petroleum (UKCS) Limited
Vestas Technology UK Limited
Vestey Foods Limited
Virgin Media Limited
Virgin Media Wholesale Limited
Vivid Imaginations Limited
Vodafone Global Enterprise Ltd
Vodafone International Holdings Ltd
Vodafone International Operations
Vodafone Overseas Holdings Ltd
Vodata Limited
Volkswagen Financial Services (UK)
WDFG UK Limited
Warrant Investments PLC
Waters Limited
Watson Wyatt Holdings (Europe) Ltd
Wessex Children's Hospice Trust
Westfalia Fruit International Ltd
Wiggle Limited
Xafinity Consulting Limited
Yoplait UK Limited
York International (Holdings) Ltd
York International Investments
ZG Lighting (UK) Limited
Zebra Technologies Europe Ltd
Zotefoams PLC
Zurich Management Services Ltd

1995 [121]

AON Consulting Limited
Abertis Motorways UK Limited
Advanced Lighting Technologies Europe
Air Products Group Limited
Airinmar Limited
Automated Technology Group Ltd
Autonomy Systems Limited
Avaya UK
Avis Europe Investment Holdings Ltd
B & C E Insurance Limited
BAE Systems (Oman) Limited
BCA Group Europe Limited
BCA Holdings Limited
BCMV Limited
Bandt Holdings Limited
Beck Interiors Limited
Bell Microsystems Limited
Bio-Rad Laboratories Limited
British Gas Services Limited
British Gas Trading Limited
CSL Behring Holdings Limited
Cargill Investments
Centrica PLC
Cine-UK Limited
Colgate Holdings
Compass Overseas Holdings No.2 Ltd
Dawsongroup Truck and Trailer Ltd
Dnata Limited
Dunlop International Group Ltd
Eagle Estates Limited
Liz Earle Beauty Co. Limited
European Laminate Glass Ltd
Forester Holdings (Europe) Ltd
Fossil (UK) Limited
Fresh Direct (UK) Limited
Graham Care (YB) Limited
Hala Limited
J & E Hall Limited
Hampden Holdings Limited
Hanson America Holdings (1) Ltd
Hanson America Holdings (4) Ltd
Harwood Properties Limited
Hastings Insurance Services Ltd
Hewlett-Packard CDS Limited
Home and Legacy Insurance Services
Horder Healthcare
Houserate Limited
IBRC Asset Finance Limited

IHG Hotels Limited
IQVIA Ltd.
Ikea Properties Investments Ltd
Inula Holding UK Limited
Invesco Asia Trust PLC
Invesco Income Growth Trust PLC
J C C Lighting Products Ltd
Kensington Mortgage Co Ltd
Kofax London Holdings Limited
LGC (Holdings) Limited
Laing Construction Limited
Lotus Leisure Ltd
Makita International Europe Ltd
Matsim Properties Limited
Sir Robert McAlpine Capital Ventures
McCormick Europe Limited
Medreich PLC
Millennium Hotels Limited
NTL Cablecomms Group Limited
National Fostering Agency Ltd
Newhall Projects Limited
Newsquest Capital Limited
Northview Group Limited
OCS Group UK Limited
OTC Direct Limited
Orange Business Holdings UK Ltd
Overseas Air Travel Limited
PEAC (UK) Limited
Porcelanosa U.K. Limited
Premier Asset Management Ltd
Premier Rugby Limited
Procter & Gamble Product Supply (U.K.)
Prospects Services
Ranbaxy Holdings (UK) Limited
Rank Group PLC
Rebus Group Limited
Red Bull Racing Limited
Rhodia Holdings Limited
SD Worx UK Limited
SK Hynix UK Limited
Sabre Global Technologies Ltd
Saga Personal Finance Limited
Samsung Electronics (UK) Ltd
Sandown Surrey and Hampshire Ltd
Siemens Healthcare Diagnostics Ltd
Skanska Infrastructure Development UK
Sky Comedy Limited
Sky Ventures Limited
Sonet Investments Limited
Spirit Energy Production UK Ltd
Study Group UK Limited
Subsea 7 International Contracting
Sun Mark Limited
Synamedia Limited
TJX Europe Limited
TJX UK
TRL Limited
Tata Global Beverages GB Ltd
Tata Global Beverages Overseas Holdings
Tata Global Beverages Services Ltd
Tech Data as UK Limited
Telewest Communications Networks Ltd
Tesla Limited
Thales Training & Simulation (Ace)
Thales Transport and Security Ltd
Tradeteam Limited
Transport Research Foundation
Tristmire Limited
UK Highways M40 Limited
Viva Eyewear UK Limited
Vodafone Finance Limited
Wozair Limited
Xerox Capital (Europe) Limited

1996 [136]

A24 Group Limited
AA Underwriting Limited
Ability Developments Limited
Advanced Business Software and Solutions
Alandale Logistics Limited
Alphabet (GB) Limited
Aprite (GB) Limited
Argos Business Solutions Ltd
Arqiva Holdings Limited
Arqiva Services Limited
Ascenti Health Limited
Autolink Concessionaires (M6) PLC
Avis Europe Investments Ltd
Avis Europe Overseas Limited
BAM Properties Limited
BOC Investment Holdings Ltd
BOC Investments No.1 Limited
BP Exploration (Shah Deniz) Ltd
BRE Trust
Beam Global Finance UK Limited
Berendsen Finance Limited
Birchwood Garages Limited
Black & Veatch Limited
Blackwell Publishing (Holdings) Ltd
Blackwell Science (Overseas Holdings)
Blenheim House Construction Ltd
Brisko Scaffolding Limited
Bristow Aviation Holdings Ltd
CPI Mortars Limited
CSL (Dualcom) Limited
Camden Motors (Holdings) Ltd
Centrica Renewable Energy Ltd
Chandlers Garage Holdings Ltd
Changeregard Limited
Chiltern International Holdings Ltd
Coca-Cola European Partners Holdings Great Britain
Coca-Cola European Partners Services Europe
Compass Group Finance No.2 Ltd
Cordant Security Limited
Corona Energy Limited
Corona Energy Retail 1 Limited
Costa Express Limited
P A Crocker Limited
Dairy Crest France Holdings 1 Ltd
Dairy Crest Group PLC
Dell Emerging Markets (EMEA) Ltd
Doosan Power Systems Overseas Investments
ESP Connections Limited
Elekta Limited
Elysium Healthcare No. 4 Ltd
Emac Limited
Energy Developments (UK) Ltd
Ensono Limited
Fidelity Asian Values PLC
Foray 989 Limited
GB Gas Holdings Limited
Galliford Try Homes Limited
Greenshields JCB Limited
D Hales Limited
Hanson Overseas Holdings Ltd
Heathrow Airport Fuel Co Ltd
Heathrow Express Operating Co Ltd
Honda Finance Europe PLC
IQVIA Ies European Holdings
Independent Technology Systems Ltd
Industrial and Financial Systems, IFS UK
Ingersoll-Rand UK Limited
Initial Medical Services Ltd
Innovation Group Limited
Intervet UK Production Limited
Ipsen Developments Limited
Iris Group Limited
Iris Software Limited
JAE Europe, Limited
Kofax Holdings International Ltd
Landmark Mortgages Limited
Little Group Limited
Lockheed Martin UK Holdings Ltd
McCormick Kutas Food Service Ltd
Midland Quarry Products Ltd
Mission Aviation Fellowship International
Monier (UK) Holdings Limited
Montgomery Property Group Ltd
NATS Limited
NTL (CWC) Limited
Oldercare (Haslemere) Limited
Open Text UK Limited
Oyezstraker Group Limited
P & O Short Sea Ferries Ltd
PTP Software Limited
Park Avenue Estates Limited
Patrolmake Limited
Paymaster (1836) Limited
Perceptive Eclinical Limited
Perpetual Income and Growth Investment Trust
Personal Group Holdings PLC
PizzaExpress Merchandising Ltd
Procter & Gamble (L & CP) Ltd
Procter & Gamble Technical Centres
RPR (US) Limited
Rank Group Gaming Division Ltd
J. Reddington Ltd
Regard Partnership Limited
Renaissance Retirement Limited
SPI Lasers UK Limited
Safestore Properties Limited
Saga Cruises Limited
Sanofi-Aventis UK Holdings Ltd
Shukco 327 Ltd
Six Continents Holdings Ltd
SmithKline Beecham (H) Limited
Sopheon PLC
St James Group Limited
St. Margaret's School Bushey
Suez Recycling and Recovery Surrey Ltd
Sumitomo Electric Europe Ltd
Synbra UK Limited
TIGI International Limited
TP Group PLC
TUV SUD (UK) Limited
Tata Global Beverages Holdings Ltd
Tato Holdings Limited
Taylor Woodrow Construction
Telewest Limited
Tilhill Forestry Limited
Vendcrown Limited
Virgin Media Investment Holdings Ltd
Vodafone Worldwide Holdings Ltd
WDFG UK Holdings Limited
Walbrook Investments Limited
Walthamstow Hall
Welcome Break Group Limited
Welcome Break Holdings Limited
West London YMCA
Xerox Overseas Holdings Ltd
York Cee Holdings Limited

1997 [115]

3T Bros Limited
Alliance Healthcare (Distribution)
Alphalarch Limited
Amersham Biosciences
Autolink Holdings (M6) Ltd
Avis Budget EMEA Limited
Aviva Administration Limited
Axon Group Limited
BAM Construct UK Limited
BVG Group Limited
Bio Energy (UK) Limited
Borrow Foundation
Boustead International Heaters Ltd
Bristol Laboratories Limited
Building Research Establishment Ltd
CSC Computer Sciences EMEA Finance
Cabot Financial (Europe) Ltd
Clancy Group PLC
Clearswift Limited
Clinisys Solutions Limited
Comland Commercial Limited
Cordant Group PLC
Creative Assembly Limited
DHL Services Limited
DP Group Developments Limited
Dairy Crest France Holdings 2 Ltd
Detica Group Limited
EDL Holdings (UK) Limited
EHGT Limited
ESNT Holdings (No.1) Limited
ESNT Holdings (No.2) Limited
Eastern Airways (UK) Limited
Eaton Holding Limited
Eckoh PLC
Egdon Resources U.K. Limited
Empire Bespoke Foods Limited
FIL Life Insurance Limited
Fulham Football Leisure Ltd
Fulham Stadium Limited
GE Healthcare UK Limited
Gallaher Group Limited
Garrett Thermal Systems UK Ltd
Gate Gourmet London Limited
Greenham Trust Ltd
HCL Great Britain Limited
Holroyd Howe Limited
Honeywell Group Ltd
ITAB UK Ltd
Informatica Software Limited
Invesco Far East Limited
Johnson Controls Metal Components Birmingham
KCI UK Holdings Limited
Kingswood Learning and Leisure Group
Lafarge Building Materials Ltd
Lantmannen Unibake UK Limited
Leasys UK Ltd
Linde Cryogenics Limited
Linde Severnside Limited
London Irish Holdings Limited
London Residential Healthcare Ltd
London Vista Hotel Limited
Lufthansa Technik Landing Gear Services UK
Marley Plastics Limited
Medivet Group Limited
Merial Limited
Meridian Hospital Company (Holdings)
Meridian Hospital Company PLC
Michelmersh Brick Holdings PLC
Motorsport Vision Limited
NEOS Networks Limited
NTL Communications Services Ltd
NTT Security (UK) Limited
Neusentis Limited
Newbury & Thatcham Hospital Building Trust
Nice Systems UK Limited
Optoma Europe Ltd
Otsuka Pharmaceutical Europe Ltd.
PMP Recruitment Limited
Pagegroup PLC
Pathways Care Group Limited
Perform Media Services Ltd
Plaza on Hyde Park Limited
Plexus Holdings PLC
Portrait Software Limited
Portsmouth Grammar School
RCI Financial Services Limited
Radian Group Limited
Reckitt Benckiser Healthcare (CIS)
Reckitt Benckiser Healthcare (Central & Eastern Europe)
Renand Properties Limited
Resurgam Holdings Limited
Samsung Semiconductor Europe Ltd
Shapedirect Limited
Siemens Industry Software Ltd
Sinclair Knight Merz (Europe) Ltd
Sogea Holdings (UK) Limited
Solventis Ltd.
Spirent Holdings Limited
Spritestore Limited
Steelstock UK Limited
Stowe House Preservation Trust
Suez Recycling and Recovery Holdings UK
TAG Farnborough Airport Ltd
Takeda UK Limited
Tanita International Ltd.
Toshiba of Europe Limited
Towers Watson Software Limited
Trade Sale Ltd
United Healthcare (South Buckinghamshire) Holdings
United Healthcare (South Buckinghamshire)
Walkers Snacks Limited
Westcoast (Holdings) Limited
World Duty Free Limited
Wyevale Garden Centres G & L Ltd
Yum! Restaurant Holdings

1998 [126]

ABHL Digital Limited
ACI Global Limited
ATP Media Operations Limited
AWE Management Limited
Airspan Communications Limited
Akzo Nobel Limited
Ali UK Limited
Allegis Global Solutions Ltd
Allergy Therapeutics (UK) Ltd
Altonwood Holdings Limited
Ansa UK Limited
Arcus Investment Limited
Arinso UK Limited
Avtrade Leasing Limited
BAE Systems (Property Investments)
BBC Studioworks Limited
Barcrest Group Limited
Becton Dickinson Infusion Therapy Holdings UK
Benugo Limited
Bespak Europe Limited
Big Yellow Group PLC
Bostall Estates Limited
Brentford FC Limited
Britair Holdings Limited
Raymond Brown Minerals & Recycling Ltd
Bytes Technology Group Limited
CAE Training & Services UK Ltd
Calverton Finance Limited
Capital Safety Limited
Cargill Investments Holdings Ltd
City Link (Cardiff) Limited
Complete Cover Group Limited
Computer Associates Holding Ltd
CooperVision Limited
Countyroute Limited
Cranleigh School
Crosswater Limited
DF Group Limited
Data Select Limited
Dealcyber Limited
Econocom Limited
Effem Holdings Limited
Endeavour SCH Holdings Limited
Endeavour SCH PLC
Endon Europe Power 1 Limited
Endon Europe Power 3 Limited
Endon Europe Power 6 Limited
European Glass Group Limited
Experis Group Limited
Fasttrax Limited
Filemaker International
Flamepro Limited
Fresenius Kabi Oncology PLC
Global Draw Limited
The Edward Gostling Foundation
Green Flag Holdings Limited
Havenhill Limited
Heiton Holdings UK Limited
HiFX Europe Limited
Hireco (TL) Limited
Hodgson Automotive Limited
Honeywell Holdings Limited
IGE Energy Services (UK) Ltd
INEOS Oxide Limited
Inprint Systems Limited
Inter Terminals UK Limited
Invesco Pensions Limited
JCB Medway Limited
James Villa Holidays Limited
Jenoptik Traffic Solutions UK Ltd
LSG/Sky Chefs Europe Holdings Ltd
Laing Limited
Lanxess Limited
Luton Hoo Park Limited
MacDermid (UK) Limited
Millbrook Industries Limited
Milton Group Limited
Minster Care Management Ltd
NPS (UK5) Limited
NewVoiceMedia Limited
Organised Group Limited
Paratus AMC Limited
Park Garage Group PLC
Parker Hannifin Manufacturing (UK)
Perceptive Informatics UK Ltd
Prior's Court Foundation
Prospect Healthcare (Hairmyres) Ltd
Purelake Investments Limited
Reckitt & Colman Holdings Ltd
Reckitt Benckiser Service Bureau Ltd
Redsky IT Holdings Limited
Riverstone Corporate Capital Ltd
Rolls-Royce Motor Cars Limited

Safety-Kleen Europe Limited
Safety-Kleen UK (Europe) Ltd
Scancem Recovery Limited
Henry Schein UK Finance Ltd
Services Support (SEL) Limited
Sesame Bankhall Group Limited
Skanska J.V. Projects Ltd
Societe Generale Equipment Finance
Sondex Wireline Limited
Sonet Scholl Overseas Investments
Sorbon Homes Limited
Sorbon Investments Limited
Spaces Personal Storage Ltd
St. Catherine's School, Bramley
Stryker UK Limited
Suez Recycling and Recovery Kirklees Ltd
TAG Aviation (UK) Limited
TAG Farnborough (Holdings) Ltd
TRAD Hire & Sales Limited
Tenva TS Holdings Limited
Thesis Unit Trust Management Ltd
UK Highways A55 (Holdings) Ltd
UK Highways A55 Limited
VA Tech (UK) Limited
Virgin Atlantic Two Limited
Virgin Media Communications Ltd
Viridor Resource Management Ltd
Vitec Investments Limited
Walkers Snacks (Distribution) Ltd
Windmill Organics Limited
Worthing Homes Limited
Xchanging UK Limited
Xerox UK Holdings Limited

1999 [145]

1948 Group Limited
AA Corporation Limited
Abbott (UK) Holdings Limited
Ardingly College Limited
Area Sq. Limited
Arqiva Telecoms Investment Ltd
Aventis Pharma Holdings Ltd
B & Q Properties Limited
BA and AA Holdings Limited
Belron Finance Limited
Bidcorp (UK) Limited
Birmingham Schools Partnership Ltd
Boeing UK Training and Flight Services Holding
Boeing UK Training and Flight Services
Bottomline Technologies Europe Ltd
Buyagift PLC
CSSC Properties Limited
Cable & Wireless Global Holding Ltd
Cable & Wireless UK Holdings Ltd
Cabot Financial (UK) Limited
Careprogress Limited
Carisbrooke Shipping Holdings Ltd
Cater Link Limited
Change, Grow, Live
Charles River Laboratories Holdings
Chartwell Properties Limited
Chemidex Generics Limited
Chingford Fruit Limited
Cochlear Europe Limited
Computer Associates UK Limited
Countyroute (A130) PLC.
Cyxtera Technology UK Limited
De La Rue PLC
Diebold Nixdorf (UK) Limited
Dimension Data Holdings PLC
Domino's Pizza Group PLC
Donamount Limited
E.S. Pipelines Limited
Echostar UK Holdings Limited
Empresaria Group PLC
Ericsson Television Limited
Esure Holdings Limited
Esure Insurance Limited
ExxonMobil International Ltd
ExxonMobil Marine Limited
ExxonMobil UK Limited
F5 Networks Limited
GE Money Servicing Limited
Glasgow Square Limited
GlaxoSmithKline PLC
Gruma Europe Limited
John Guest International Ltd
Hand Picked Hotels Limited
Heythrop Park Limited
Hilton Finance (UK) Limited
Honeywell Group Holding UK
Honeywell Group Holding UK II
Hurstpierpoint College Limited
Hutchison 3G UK Limited
Huyck.Wangner UK Limited
Hyperformance Limited
ICS Incorporation Limited
ID Medical Group Limited
INEOS Capital Limited
Igroup 8 Limited
Inter Terminals Limited
Isoft Group (UK) Limited
A W James Limited
Johnson Controls Enterprises Ltd
Juniper Networks (UK) Limited
Kellogg Brown & Root Holdings Ltd
Keysight Technologies UK Ltd
Kingston Grammar School
LPSO Limited
Lambert Pressland Limited
Lancing College Limited
Langmead Farms Limited
Last Mile Co Ltd
Lime Wood Group Limited
Logicalis UK Limited
Logoplaste UK Limited
M & C (CB) Limited
M & C (CD) Limited
MES Interco
MMA Holdings UK PLC
Manpower UK Limited
Meantime Brewing Co Ltd
Meslink Limited
MessageLabs Group Limited
MessageLabs Limited
Milkwood Care Ltd
Millennium Hotels London Ltd
NSSLGlobal Limited
NTL Cablecomms Holdings No.1 Ltd
Oakview Estates Limited
On Semiconductor Limited
Pandrol Finance Limited
Pandrol Group Limited
Pandrol Holdings Limited
Parametric Holdings (UK) Ltd
Parkside Capital Limited
Perkinelmer (UK) Holdings Ltd
Perkinelmer LAS (UK) Limited
Perkinelmer Limited
Pinewood Group Limited
Polycom (United Kingdom) Ltd.
Porsche Financial Services Great Britain
Prospect Healthcare (Reading) Ltd
Qinetiq Limited
RL Retail Services Limited
Rackspace Limited
Regentrealm Limited
Renewi Holdings Limited
Retirement Villages Limited
Runecorp Limited
Runtime Collective Limited
SDL Tridion Limited
SLR Consulting Limited
SSE Energy Supply Limited
Signet Holdings Limited
Signet Trading Limited
Solvecorp Limited
Southampton Row Trust Limited
St. Patrick's International College
T-Mobile Holdings Limited
Talacrest 2000 A.D. Limited
Tata Global Beverages Group Ltd
Teledyne Limited
Tradebe Environmental Services Ltd
Tradebe Solvent Recycling Ltd
Trek Investco Limited
Tuskerdirect Limited
Upperton Holdings Limited
Virgin Mobile Telecoms Limited
Vitec Group Holdings Limited
Vodafone Group Services Ltd
Vodafone Intermediate Enterprises
Volga-Dnepr UK Ltd.
Weight Watchers UK Holdings Ltd
Westec Holding Co Ltd
Wireless Logic Limited
Worldwide Flight Services Ltd
Wy (Nutfield Priory) Limited
Zanlia Limited
Zurich UK General Services Ltd

2000 [189]

1509 Group
ANSYS UK Limited
ATG London Limited
Abbott (UK) Finance Limited
Accesso Technology Group PLC
Air Charter Service Group Ltd
Alfa Laval Holdings Limited
Aliaxis Holdings UK Limited
Alliance Healthcare (IT Services)
Allianz Management Services Ltd
Arqiva No 2 Limited
Asia Pacific Holdings Limited
Atlantic 2/3 UK Holdings Ltd
Aunt Bessie's Limited
Autolink Concessionaires (A19) Ltd
Autumnpaper Limited
BCA Europe Limited
BCA Vehicle Services Limited
BMW (UK) Manufacturing Limited
BP Corporate Holdings Limited
Berkeley Homes PLC
Bespak Holdings Limited
Biffa Group Holdings (UK) Ltd
Birchwood Omnia Limited
Blackberry UK Limited
Bluecastle Enterprises Limited
Bourne Leisure Holdings Ltd
Bourne Leisure Limited
Brioche Pasquier U.K. Limited
Butlins Skyline Limited
Bywest (Holdings) Limited
Bywest Limited
CAS St Paul's Limited

CNOOC Ettrick U.K. Limited
Cable & Wireless Global Telecommunication Services
Cabot Financial Debt Recovery Services
Cabot Financial Holdings Group Ltd
Canon Europe Limited
Cargobull Finance Limited
Carnival PLC
Centrica Finance (Canada) Ltd
Centrica Overseas Holdings Ltd
Childcare Corporation Limited
Chubb Limited
Citizen Watch United Kingdom, Ltd
Comland Holdings Limited
Commvault Systems Limited
Compass Group PLC
Computer Software Group Ltd
Costco UK Holdings Limited
Coventry and Rugby Hospital Company (Holdings)
Cygnet Behavioural Health Ltd
Cygnet NW Limited
DHL Global Forwarding (UK) Ltd
Devine Holdings Limited
Domantis Limited
Eastern Quarry Limited
Eden Springs UK Limited
Edgewell Personal Care Holdings UK Ltd.
Epsom College
Ergomed PLC
Esure Property Limited
Exploration Service Co Ltd
Explore Manufacturing Limited
Farnborough Limited
Fast Training Services Limited
Fat Face Holdings Limited
Fifthgrange Limited
Fisher & Paykel Appliances Ltd
Friends Life FPL Limited
GDC Holding Limited
Gallaher Overseas (Holdings) Ltd
Geneva Investment Group Ltd
Geo Underwriting Services Ltd
Georgica Limited
Greencell Limited
H+H UK Holdings Limited
Harsco Investment Limited
Hogg Robinson Group Limited
Home Retail Group Card Services Ltd
Home Retail Group Insurance Services
Hospitality Holdings Limited
Huntswood CTC Limited
Hurstlane Limited
Hutchison 3G UK Holdings Ltd
INEOS Investment Holdings (Germany)
INEOS Investments International Ltd
INEOS Silicas Holdings Limited
INEOS Treasury (UK) Limited
INEOS U.K. Finance Co Ltd
INEOS U.S. Finance Co Ltd
INS-Sure Services Limited
Idox PLC
Intec Telecom Systems Limited
Interquest Group (UK) Limited
Iris Holdings Limited
JTL
Johnson & Johnson Innovation Ltd
Johnson Controls Investments (UK)
KWay Holdings Limited
Kelvion Limited
Kew Green Hotels Limited
Kidde Finance Limited
Kidde International Limited
Kidde Limited
Kimberly-Clark Europe Limited
Kimberly-Clark European Services Ltd
LGC (Teddington) Limited
Lehigh UK Limited
Logicalis Group Limited
Mapeley Steps Contractor Ltd
Mattel UK Holdings Limited
McCormick International Holdings
Melesey Limited
Menzies Aviation (UK) Limited
Menzies Aviation Holdings Ltd
Millipore (U.K.) Limited
NATS (En Route) PLC
NATS (Services) Limited
NCL Holdings Limited
Networkers International (UK) Ltd
Networkers International Ltd
Nextonline Limited
E.H. Nicholls Holdings Ltd
Nilvip Holdings Limited
Old ML Limited
Onecom Limited
PJ Care Limited
Michael Page International Recruitment
Michael Page International Southern Europe
Parker Hannifin (Holdings) Ltd
Pentagon Holdings Limited
Pinnacle Schools (Fife) Ltd
Pyramid Schools (Sheffield) Ltd
Quantel Holdings (2010) Ltd
Reckitt Benckiser (UK) Limited
Reckitt Benckiser Corporate Services
Reigate Grammar School
Rightmove Group Limited
Ringmerit Limited
Rohm Electronics Europe Ltd
SITA Information Networking Computing UK
SMR Automotive Mirror Parts and Holdings UK
SMR Automotive Mirrors UK Ltd
Samsung SDS Europe Limited
Search Consultancy Group Ltd
Seqirus Vaccines Limited
Serco Holdings Limited
Services Support (Gravesend) Holdings
Services Support (Gravesend) Ltd
Services Support (SEL) Holdings Ltd
Skanska Construction Holdings UK Ltd
Sony Global Treasury Services PLC
Sopra Steria Limited
Southern Electric Power Distribution PLC
Spirent Investment Limited
St James Homes (Grosvenor Dock) Ltd
Stanley Electric (U.K.) Co Ltd
State Oil Limited
Steamer Properties Limited
Suez Recycling and Recovery South Gloucestershire
Sun Life Financial of Canada (U.K.) Overseas Investments
Swindon Pressings Limited
Syngenta Holdings Limited
T.S.L. Finance Limited
Tensator Limited
Thales Holdings UK PLC
Toshiba Tec U.K. Imaging Systems Ltd
Towergate Underwriting Group Ltd
Transform Schools (Stoke) Holdings
Transform Schools (Stoke) Ltd
Twickenham Experience Ltd
Vestey Foods UK Limited
Vodafone 2.
Vodafone Euro Hedging Limited
Vodafone Euro Hedging Two
Vodafone European Investments
Vodafone Finance UK Limited
Vodafone Financial Operations
Vodafone Global Content Services Ltd
Vodafone Mobile Communications Ltd
Vodafone Mobile Enterprises Ltd
Vodafone Mobile Network Ltd
Vodafone Oceania Limited
Vodafone Property Investments Ltd
WWF-UK
Welcome Break Holdings (1) Ltd
XP Power PLC
Yourcash Limited

2001 [153]

3D Systems Europe Limited
AGP Holdings (1) Limited
Abbott Asia Holdings Limited
Abbott Capital India Limited
Abbott Equity Holdings Unlimited
Adelie Foods Limited
Advantedge Commercial Finance Ltd
Africa Express Line Limited
Agria Pet Insurance Limited
Alere UK Holdings Limited
Althea UK and Ireland Limited
Annes Gate Property PLC
Apatech Limited
Arlacross Limited
Arlaform Limited
Ascot Authority (Holdings) Ltd
Ascot Racecourse Limited
Asset Advantage Limited
Avtrade Holdings Limited
BAE Systems (Funding Two) Ltd
BAE Systems (MEH) Limited
BH (City Forum) Limited
BI Worldwide Holdings Limited
BOC Investments No.5
BP Chemicals East China Investments
BP Finance P.L.C
BP Pipelines (BTC) Limited
Barfoot Farms Limited
Barfoot Holdings Limited
Biffa Municipal Limited
Biocompatibles UK Limited
Blue Lizard Consulting Limited
Brambles Holdings (UK) Limited
Bugler Group Limited
Capital Investment and Finance Ltd
Centrica Finance (US) Limited
Centrica PB Limited
Charity Bank Limited
Chichester Festival Theatre
Choice Holdings Limited
Citysprint (UK) Limited
Clinisys Group Limited
Compass Hotels Chertsey
Court Cavendish Limited
Cross Stone Securities Limited
Darty Limited
Digico UK Limited
Ellenbrook Developments PLC
Ellenbrook Holdings Limited
Enterprise Rent-a-Car European Holdings
Fast Holdings Limited
Fasttrax Holdings Limited
First Rate Exchange Services Holdings

First Rate Exchange Services Ltd
First Technology Overseas Ltd
Formaplex Limited
Furniture Village Group Ltd
GHH Holdings Limited
Giffgaff Limited
GlaxoSmithKline Holdings (One) Ltd
GlaxoSmithKline UK Limited
Glaxochem (UK) Unlimited
Glendola Leisure (Holdings) Ltd
Gloucester Healthcare Partnership
Grafise Holdings Limited
Gyron Internet Limited
Hall Hunter Partnership (Farming)
Hanwha Techwin Europe Limited
Hawk Incentives Limited
Hawk-Eye Innovations Limited
Healthcare Providers (Gloucester)
Help/Systems International Ltd
Hewlett-Packard Cain Holdings Ltd
Hewlett-Packard Holdings Ltd
Hotel Management International (Holdings)
Huawei Technologies (UK) Co., Ltd.
INEOS Holdings Limited
INS-Sure Holdings Limited
Innovation Group (EMEA) Ltd
Intrum UK Finance Limited
Intrum UK Holdings Limited
JBS Global (UK) Limited
Nicholas James Care Homes Ltd
Jankel Group Limited
Kesa Holdings Limited
Kidde UK
King Edward VI School Southampton
Kingsbridge Estates Limited
Laing O'Rourke Construction Ltd
Laing O'Rourke Holdings Ltd
Laing O'Rourke Infrastructure Ltd
Laing O'Rourke PLC.
Lakefield Holdings Limited
Liberty Leasing Limited
Lockheed Martin UK Ampthill Group
MMO2 Limited
Maintenance Management Limited
Marchwood Power Limited
Masternaut Holdings Limited
Masterson Holdings Limited
Mazda Motors UK Limited
Medequip Assistive Technology Ltd
Milton Property Investments Ltd
NATS Holdings Limited
NTL Glasgow Holdings Limited
NTL Kirklees Holdings Limited
NTL Rectangle Limited
Newship Limited
No.7 Limited
O2 (Europe) Limited
O2 International Holdings Ltd
Octagon Group Limited
Old Mutual Wealth Life & Pensions
PRA Group (UK) Limited
Panalux Limited
Qinetiq Holdings Limited
Quaker Holdings (UK) Limited
Quayside Homes Holdings Ltd
Ramac Holdings (Trading) Ltd
Royale Park Home Estates Ltd
S A Designer Parfums Limited
SC Johnson Ltd
SCJ EurAFNE Ltd
SESW Holding Co Ltd.
SWS Group Holdings Limited
SWS Holdings Limited
Schlumberger Oilfield UK PLC
Services Support (Manchester) Holdings
Services Support (Manchester) Ltd
Siemens Financial Services Holdings
Sopra Steria Holdings Limited
South Downs Capital Limited
South Downs Limited
Spirit Resources (Armada) Ltd
Sports Information Services Ltd
Stackhouse Poland Holdings Ltd
Subsea 7 Limited
TCR UK Limited
Talkmobile Limited
Tensator Group Limited
United Healthcare (South Buckinghamshire) Group
Vodafone (New Zealand) Hedging Ltd
Vodafone Benelux Limited
Vodafone Holdings Luxembourg Ltd
Vodafone Overseas Finance Ltd
Westmoreland Developments Ltd
Whistl Limited
Wiley Europe Investment Holdings Ltd
Wimpey Overseas Holdings Ltd
WorleyParsons Europe Limited
Xpanse Limited
YH Limited
Yell Limited

2002 [146]

A.C. Lighting (Holdings) Ltd
AGB Properties (Woking) Ltd
Acquisition U.K. Limited
Alestra Limited
Ashcourt Holdings Limited
Aston Carter International Ltd
Atkins ATK Investments Limited
Avon Capital Estates 1 LLP
BP Pipelines (SCP) Limited
Bewley Group Limited
Bio Products Laboratory Holdings Ltd
Blue Sky Intermodal (UK) Ltd.
Bottling Great Britain Limited
Brake Bros Holding I Limited
Brambles Finance PLC
Brevan Howard Asset Management LLP
Bristol-Myers Squibb Holdings 2002
CSL UK Holdings Limited
Cabot Financial (Marlin) Ltd
Celgene Europe Limited
Coats Limited
Community Stadium Limited
Consort Healthcare (Blackburn) Funding
Consort Healthcare (Blackburn) Holdings
Consort Healthcare (Blackburn) Ltd
Cook Trading Limited
Coventry and Rugby Hospital Company PLC
Croudace Homes Group Limited
Crown Golf Group Limited
Cuffe Holdings Limited
Cygnet 2002 Limited
Cygnet Surrey Limited
D & B Group Holdings (UK)
DG Partners Services Limited
Daikin Airconditioning UK Ltd
Defence Support (St Athan) Holdings
Defence Support (St Athan) Ltd
Eaton Electric Limited
Education Support (Enfield 2) Holdings
Education Support (Enfield 2) Ltd
Education Support (Newham) Holdings
Education Support (Newham) Ltd
FCA Dealer Services UK Ltd
FKA Brands Limited
Famous Brands UK Limited
Fire Fighters Charity
First Technology (2002) Ltd
Foreman Homes Group Limited
Fujifilm Speciality Ink Systems Ltd
Galliford Try Construction & Investments Holdings
Gattaca PLC
Gould Publication Papers UK Ltd
Grenke Leasing Limited
Guangdong Investments Limited
Guernsey Home Loans Limited
Gurit Material Systems (UK) Ltd
H.K.S. Motors Limited
Hanson Limited
Health Management Limited
Healthcare Support (Newcastle) Holdings
Healthcare Support (Newcastle) Ltd
Hinds Ltd
Inhealth Group Limited
Intercontinental Hotels Ltd
Interserve PFI Holdings Ltd
Jacobs UK Holdings Limited
KLM Cityhopper UK Limited
Karelia Tobacco Company (UK) Ltd
Kia Motors (UK) Limited
Kidde Products Limited
Kimberly-Clark U.K. Operations Ltd
Krispy Kreme U.K. Limited
Laing O'Rourke Services Ltd
Lamberts Healthcare Limited
Longsand Limited
M & C Hotels Holdings Limited
Magal Engineering Limited
Marlin Capital Europe Limited
Matchtech Group (UK) Limited
Mavenir Systems UK Limited
Alexander McQueen Trading Ltd
Moneybarn No.1 Limited
New Era Cap Co Ltd
Newschools (Merton) Limited
Parthenon Entertainment Ltd
Pearl River Delta Investments Ltd
Perkinelmer Life Sciences International Holdings
Prax Petroleum Limited
Promon-Logicalis Latin America Ltd
Puzzler Media Group Limited
Qinetiq Group PLC
Qinetiq Overseas Holdings Ltd
RB Holdings (Nottingham) Ltd
RB Sport & Leisure Holdings PLC
RCL (UK) Ltd.
Rank Nemo (Twenty-Five) Ltd
The Joseph Rank Trust
Raymarine UK Limited
Reckitt Benckiser Holdings (Overseas)
The Alec Reed Academy
Regenter B3 Holdco Limited
Regenter B3 Limited
Reliance Communications (U.K.) Ltd
Relta Limited
Renesas Electronics Europe Ltd
Rolta UK Limited
SCIH Branston 3
SSE Hornsea Limited
SSG Logistic Solutions Limited
Sericol Ink Limited
Skanska Infrastructure Investment UK

Sondex Limited
Southern Water Capital Limited
Southern Water Services Group Ltd
Spectris UK Holdings Limited
Spectris US Holdings Limited
Spirit Energy North Sea Ltd
M R Stephenson Limited
Swiss Post Solutions Ltd
Symrise Holding Limited
Syneos Health UK Limited
TD United Kingdom Acquisition Ltd
TSL Limited
Tailwind Mistral Ltd
Tesla Motors Limited
Tonroe Group Limited
Tower, One St George Wharf Ltd
Towers Perrin Europe Limited
Towers Perrin UK Holdings Ltd
Tradebe Management Limited
Transeur Properties Limited
Treloar Trust
Verizon European Holdings Ltd
Vestey Group Limited
Vodafone Yen Finance Limited
Volution Holdings Limited
Volution Ventilation Group Ltd
Water Process Limited
Watson Wyatt European Region Ltd
Western Wines Holdings Limited
Whistl UK Limited
Wisdom Properties Limited
Worth Abbey
Ww.co.uk Online Limited
Xylem Water Solutions UK Holdings
Zene Finance Limited

2003 [157]

AHL Holdings (Manchester) Ltd
Academy Services (Waltham Forest)
Action for Children
Adams Morey Holdings Limited
Affinity (Reading) Limited
Aibel Group Limited
Akzo Nobel Coatings (BLD) Ltd
Amey Highways Lighting (Manchester)
Arinso People Services Limited
BNP Paribas Rental Solutions Ltd
BTC Pipeline Holding Co Ltd
Bapchild Motoring World (Kent) Ltd
Bedford Education Partnership Holdings
Bedford Education Partnership Ltd
Bellevue Education Group Ltd
Biffa GS UK Holdings Limited
Bishops U.K. Limited
Blanc Brasseries Limited
Britax Childcare Group Limited
British Airways 777 Leasing Ltd
W & R Buxton Holdings Limited
Bycentral Holdings Limited
Bycentral Limited
CEB Global Limited
CSM Motor Group Limited
Cable & Wireless Europe Holdings Ltd
Cabot Credit Management Group Ltd
Canterbury Christ Church University
Cathay Investments Limited
Ceesail Limited
Centrica Beta Holdings Limited
Centrica Distributed Generation Ltd
Centrica Gamma Holdings Ltd
ChildrenSalon Limited
Cleartone Group Limited
Clinphone Development Limited
Coast2coast Technologies Ltd
Contemplation Holdings Limited
Crescent Pharma Limited
Crest Nicholson Developments (Chertsey)
Derby Healthcare (Holdings) Ltd
Derby Healthcare PLC
Deutsche Leasing (UK) Limited
Driveline Limited
ESP Electricity Limited
Edgewell Personal Care Investments UK Ltd.
Endace Europe Limited
Feltham Group Limited
Fujifilm Sericol Overseas Holdings
General Cable Limited
General Mills UK Limited
Gerald Palmer Eling Trust Company
Greater Gabbard Offshore Winds Ltd
Grigg Investments Limited
HH Global Limited
HRT UK Limited
HTC Europe Co. Ltd
Hanson Finance Limited
Harwood Wealth Management Group PLC
Hastings Water (UK) Limited
Heart Internet Limited
JRL Plant and Logistics Ltd
Jacobs E & C Limited
Just Retirement Management Services
KN Network Services (Northern Ireland)
Kallar Investments Limited
Kedleston (Wings Education) Ltd
LGC Investments Limited
Lamp Group Limited
Lenovo Technology (United Kingdom)
London May Fair Hotel Limited
London Tower Crane Hire & Sales Ltd
Ludgate 329 Limited
MSV Group Limited
Medina Holdings Limited
Moss Electrical Holdings Ltd
Motorline (Kent) Limited
O2 Cedar Limited
Olive Business Solutions Ltd
PandoraExpress 2 Limited
PandoraExpress 3 Limited
PandoraExpress 4 Limited
PandoraExpress 7 Limited
Parker Hannifin Manufacturing Ltd
PizzaExpress Operations Ltd
Premier Global Infrastructure Trust PLC
Premier Research Group Limited
Premiere Employment Group Ltd
Prime Care Solutions (Kingston) Holdings
Prime Care Solutions (Kingston) Ltd
Principal London Limited
Principal Manchester Limited
Prospect Healthcare (Hairmyres) Group
Prospect Healthcare (Hinchingbrooke)
QED (Clacton) Limited
QED (Leeds) Limited
Quayside Homes Limited
RES UK & Ireland Limited
RS Furbs Limited
Rebound Technology Group Holdings
Reckitt Benckiser Finance Co Ltd
Reckitt Benckiser Holdings (USA) Ltd
Reckitt Benckiser Investments Ltd
Reckitt Benckiser USA Finance (No.1)
Reckitt Benckiser USA Finance (No.2)
Reckitt Benckiser USA Finance (No.3)
Renewable Energy Systems Holdings
Riposte Limited
Rydon Homes Limited
Safestore Acquisition Limited
Safestore Group Limited
Safestore Holdings PLC
Thomas Sanderson Limited
Scotia Gas Networks Limited
Seqirus Vaccines Holdings Ltd
Sevenoaks School
Shurgard UK Limited
Siemens Industrial Turbomachinery
Sirhowy Enterprise Way (Holdings)
Sirhowy Enterprise Way Limited
Sourcecode UK Limited
South East Water (Holdings) Ltd
Southern Water (NR) Holdings Ltd
Southern Water Investments Ltd
Stansted Park Foundation
Stantec Treatment Group Ltd
Steris CH Limited
Synventive Holding Limited
T.J.D. Trade Limited
Tax Systems PLC
Tenpin Limited
Thomas Homes Limited
Tigers Logistics Group Limited
Tindle Press Holdings Limited
Tonbridge School
Towry Holdings Limited
Transform Schools (Rotherham) Ltd
Travel Republic Ltd
UK Broadband Limited
UPS (UK Holding) Limited
University of Chichester
UnumProvident Finance Co Ltd
Urenco Enrichment Co Ltd
Utilita Energy Limited
Utilita Group Limited
V.B. Investments Limited
Verint WS Holdings Limited
Verizon International Limited
Vestel UK Limited
Walnut Investments Limited
Wessanen Great Britain Holdings Ltd
Whiteley Homes Trust
Wind Farm Holdings Limited
Woodcote Estates Limited
Yorkshire Transformations Ltd
Yum! Franchise II LLP
Zodiac Europe Limited

2004 [176]

.Big Yellow Self Storage Co Ltd
123-Reg Limited
AA Acquisition Co Limited
AA Intermediate Co Limited
AA Mid Co Limited
AA PLC
ACM Group Limited
AMG Healthcare Limited
APCOA Parking Holdings (UK) Ltd
Accolade Wines Holdings Europe Ltd
Aesica Pharmaceuticals Limited
Aitch Care Homes (London) Ltd
Akari Therapeutics, PLC
Allergy Therapeutics PLC
Allianz Holdings PLC
Allport Group Limited
Almus Pharmaceuticals Limited
Apollo Submarine Cable System Ltd
Arqiva Financing No 3 PLC
Arqiva Group Limited

Arqiva UK Broadcast Holdings Ltd
Asahi UK Ltd
Aspen Marketing Group Limited
Atkins Investments UK Limited
Audley Court Limited
Augustus 1 Limited
Augustus 2 Limited
BAE Systems (Holdings) Limited
Beck & Pollitzer Holdings Ltd
Berkeley Group Holdings PLC
Berkeley Homes (PCL) Limited
Berkeley Seventy-Six Limited
Bidcorp Foodservice (Europe) Ltd
Blue Minerva Limited
CP Regents Park Two Limited
Cablefile Limited
Carte Blanche Group Limited
Centrica KPS Limited
Chinatool UK Limited
Cineworld Group PLC
Cineworld Holdings Limited
Clinphone Limited
Cloud Networks Limited
Club Company Acquisitions (Holdings)
Cognita Holdings Limited
Cognita Limited
Compass Group Finance No.4 Ltd
Countrystyle Recycling Limited
John Crane Group Limited
Crown Golf Property Limited
Crown Golf St Mellion Limited
Crown House Technologies Ltd
D-R Holdings (UK) Ltd
DDD Investments Limited
DSTI Group LLP
DSTI Holdings Limited
DX Network Services Limited
DX Services Limited
Davidson Kempner European Partners, LLP
Education Support (Swindon) Holdings
Education Support (Swindon) Ltd
Ella's Kitchen (Brands) Ltd
Ensign Highways Limited
Evolving Systems Holdings Ltd
Expanded Limited
Expro Eurasia Limited
ExxonMobil Finance Co Ltd
ExxonMobil Investment Co Ltd
FT North America Limited
Fairfax Acquisitions Limited
Femcare Group Limited
Finance Ireland Limited
Folkestone Harbour Holdings Ltd
Foreign Currency Direct PLC
Fresca Group Limited
Future Electronics Management Services
GE Money Home Lending Holdings Ltd
General Cable Programming Ltd
Geos Group Limited
Grafton UK Leasing Co Ltd
H & D Support Services (Holdings)
H & D Support Services Limited
H & T Group PLC
Halma Financing Limited
Halma Investment Holdings Ltd
Hanson Holdings Limited
Harefield Academy Trust
Healthcare Support (Newcastle) Finance
Healthcare Support (North Staffs) Finance
Healthcare Support (North Staffs) Holdings
Healthcare Support (North Staffs)
Hobbs Brook Limited

Richard Hochfeld Management Ltd
Honeywell Acquisitions Limited
Hurricane Energy PLC
INEOS European Holdings Ltd
INEOS Paraform Holdings Ltd
Incomm Europe Limited
Inhealth Limited
Intercontinental Hotels Group PLC
International Property Finance (Spain)
Just Retirement (Holdings) Ltd
Just Retirement Limited
Kaysail Limited
Knoll UK Investments Unlimited
Lilac Limited
Michael Lonsdale Limited
MIQ Logistics EU Limited
Mars Investments
Medway Fundco Limited
Micro Focus (IP) Ltd
Micro Focus International PLC
Modern Schools (Barnsley) Ltd
Modern Schools (Exeter) Ltd
Mondi Investments Limited
NEP Visions Limited
NHS Shared Business Services Ltd
Net Pay (EUR) Limited
Nexen Petroleum U.K. Holdings Ltd
O'Rourke Investments Holdings (UK)
O.S.T.C. Limited
Ocean Partners Holdings Ltd
Ocean Partners UK Limited
Officeteam Group Limited
Officeteam Limited
Original Bowling Co Ltd
Pallant House Gallery
Perform Media Sales Ltd
Piramal Critical Care Limited
Procter & Gamble Finance (UK) Ltd
Procter & Gamble Holdings (UK) Ltd
Procter & Gamble Investment Company (UK)
Procter & Gamble Overseas Ltd
Pyxis Investment Strategies LLP
QA-IQ Group Limited
QlikTech UK Limited
RWF Health and Community Developers (Tranche 1)
Radiosite Limited
Rambler Metals and Mining PLC
Reckitt Benckiser Asia Pacific Ltd
Reckitt Benckiser Holdings (Luxembourg)
Red Bull Technology Limited
Red Tree (2004) LLP
Rentokil Initial Finance Ltd
Restore PLC
Riverdale Developments Limited
Sailtown Limited
Serena Holdings
Sky Home Communications Ltd
Smiths Medical Group Limited
Soka Gakkai International - UK
Southern Co-operative Properties Ltd
Southern Gas Networks PLC
Spirit Europe Limited
Sun Hotel Limited
Sunlight Clinical Solutions Ltd
Tasmar Limited
Tavistock Investments PLC
Technetix Group Limited
Telefonica Europe PLC
Teneo Group Limited
Thames Hospice
Travel Up Limited

Travelport (UK) Services Ltd
UOP International Holdings Ltd
Vanderbilt Homes Limited
Verizon Connect UK Limited
Virgin Media Finance PLC
Vostochnaya Technica UK Ltd
WP SK Holdings Limited
WP SK Limited
Wilhelmsen Lines Car Carriers Ltd.
Wood Group Industrial Services Ltd
Wryde Croft Wind Farm Limited
Xchanging Holdco No.3 Limited
Yourway Transport Limited

2005 [183]

AA Senior Co Limited
AB InBev International Brands Ltd
ACP Europe Limited
AS & Sons Ltd
Abbott Asia Investments Ltd
Ability Hotels (Luton Inn) Ltd
Acco Brands Europe Limited
Acenden Limited
Aliunde Limited
Allianz Engineering Inspection Services
Anglo Suisse Investments Ltd
Arca Shipping Limited
Arora Hotels Limited
Arora Management Services Ltd
Ashcourt Rowan Limited
Atlantic Foods Limited
Avesco Holdings Limited
Axiom Education (Perth & Kinross) Holdings
Axiom Education (Perth & Kinross)
BCA Fleet Solutions Limited
BP Exploration Libya Limited
BP Exploration North Africa Ltd
BP Investments Asia Limited
Bargate Homes Limited
Beam Suntory UK Holdings Ltd
Beam Suntory UK Limited
Berkeley (SQP) Limited
Biffa Corporate Holdings Ltd
Biogen (UK) Limited
Brighton I-360 Limited
Britannia Holdings (UK) Ltd
Britax Childcare Holdings Ltd
Britvic PLC
Broadway Malyan Holdings Ltd
By Chelmer (Holdings) Limited
By Chelmer PLC
CF Corporate Finance Limited
CTV Outside Broadcasts Limited
Camden Ventures Limited
Cape Claims Services Limited
Capital Hospitals (Holdings) Ltd.
Capital Hospitals (Issuer) PLC
Capital Hospitals Ltd.
Capula Investment Management LLP
Carefusion U.K. 306 Limited
Cargill Cotton Limited
Caterham School Limited
Caversham Trading Limited
Celgene Limited
Central Nottinghamshire Hospitals (Holdings)
Central Nottinghamshire Hospitals PLC
Centrica Holdings Limited
Compass Group North America Investments
Compass Group North America Investments No.2
Compleat Food Group Limited
Crossknowledge Group Limited

Cullum Capital Ventures Ltd
DLR (No.1) Limited
Defaqto Group Limited
E.F.B. Group Limited
Elster Water Metering Holdings Ltd
Elysium Healthcare Property 2 Ltd
Emery Oleochemicals UK Limited
Essentra Finance Limited
Essentra PLC
Everyday Loans Limited
Factory Services UK Limited
GBF Capital Limited
Geo Specialty Group Holdings Ltd
Gilead Sciences Europe Ltd.
GlaxoSmithKline Holdings Ltd
Godrej UK Limited
Greensands Limited
Gym Limited
H. K. S. Holdings Limited
HCP Packaging UK Limited
HDF (UK) Holdings Limited
Hanson (SH) Limited
Havas Holdings Limited
HellermannTyton Limited
Hertz Holdings III UK Limited
Hewlett-Packard (Bracknell) Holdings
Humphrey Farms Limited
Hyundai Motor UK Limited
ICS Cool Energy Limited
ICS Group Holdings Limited
ILI Limited
IMCD Holding UK Ltd
ISS UK Holding Limited
Infinity SDC Limited
Inhealth Group Holdings PLC
Inland Homes PLC
Inland Limited
Inter Pipeline Europe Limited
Interbay Funding, Ltd.
Into University Partnerships Ltd
Kent Education Partnership (Holdings)
Kent Education Partnership Ltd
Lafarge Nigeria (UK) Limited
Landmark Space Limited
Langley Academy Trust
Liberty Property Trust UK Ltd
Link Asset Services (Holdings) Ltd
MDL Development Company Number 2 Ltd
MFS Portfolio Limited
MacDermid G.B. Holdings Ltd
MacIntyre Hudson LLP
Micheldever Group Limited
Motorline Holdings Limited
Motus Holdings (UK) Limited
National Fostering Agency (Scotland)
Needspace? Limited
Newhospitals (St Helens and Knowsley) Finance
Newhospitals (St Helens and Knowsley) Holdings
Newhospitals (St Helens and Knowsley)
Nucleus Financial Group PLC
Nurse Plus and Carer Plus (UK) Ltd
Nutfield Holdings Limited
Oracle Corporation UK Holdings Ltd
Orthopaedic Research UK
Patek Philippe Salon Limited
Perform Media Channels Ltd
Pinnacle Schools (Gateshead) Ltd
Potanin Foundation
Premier Marinas Holdings Ltd
Principal Edinburgh George Street
Proudreed Real Estate Limited
Puzzler Media Holdings Limited
Pye Properties Limited
Quantum Funding Limited
RMAC Securities No. 1 PLC
Reckitt Benckiser (USA) Ltd
Reckitt Benckiser Finance (2005) Ltd
Reckitt Benckiser Luxembourg (No. 1)
Reckitt Benckiser Luxembourg (No.2)
Reckitt Benckiser Luxembourg (No.3)
Reckitt Benckiser Luxembourg (No.4)
Renewi Financial Management Ltd
Rentokil Initial PLC
Retirement Villages Group Ltd
Ringway Jacobs Limited
Rydon Holdings Limited
SPI Lasers PLC
Safe Haven London
Safestore Limited
Sega Publishing Europe Limited
Signature Senior Lifestyle Finance
Sky Group Finance PLC
Smartspace Software PLC
Sound Energy PLC
South Downs Real Estate Ltd
St George Blackfriars Limited
Storrington Industries Limited
Synventive Acquisition UK Ltd
Synventive Acquisition Unlimited
Target Media Limited
Taunton Linac Co Ltd
Tech 21 UK Limited
Total Aircraft Product Support (Holdings)
Towers Watson Limited
Transform Schools (Bassetlaw) Ltd
Transform Schools (Birmingham) Holdings
Transform Schools (Birmingham) Ltd
Transform Schools (North Lanarkshire) Funding
Transform Schools (North Lanarkshire) Holdings
Transform Schools (North Lanarkshire)
Tricomm Housing (Portsmouth) Ltd
United Living (North) Holdings Ltd
Vale of Aylesbury Housing Trust Ltd
Veetee Foods Limited
Venture Life Group PLC
Visiontrend Limited
WP SK Midco Limited
Walker Logistics (Holdings) Ltd
Watchstone Group PLC
Watson Wyatt (UK) Acquisitions 1 Ltd
Watson Wyatt (UK) Acquisitions 2 Ltd
Watson Wyatt European Investment Holdings
Wescot Acquisitions Limited
Wescot Topco Limited
Wintel Petrochemicals Limited
Wolseley Group Holdings Ltd
Zion Care Limited

2006 [182]

ADI Finance 1 Limited
ADI Finance 2 Limited
Advanced Computer Software Group Ltd
Aibel Finance Limited
Akaal Group PLC
Alexion Pharma UK Limited
Althea (Leicester 2) Limited
Amtech Group Limited
Argos Holdings Limited
Atlantis Holdings Limited
Aura Holdings (Newcastle) Ltd
Avamore Limited
Axiom Education (Edinburgh) Holdings
Axiom Education (Edinburgh) Ltd
BFIM Limited
BP Alternative Energy Investments
BP Holdings North America Ltd
Baltray No. 1 Limited
Bandai Namco Amusement Europe Ltd
Berkeley Homes (Southall) Ltd
Black Tip Capital Holdings Ltd
Brambles Holdings Unlimited
Brambles Investment Ltd.
Brasserie Bar Co Limited
By Design (UK) Limited
CAE STS Limited
CCV Risk Solutions Limited
CHG Overseas Investments Ltd
Cabot Credit Management Ltd
Cabot Financial Limited
Care Management Group (Acquisition)
Carestream Health UK, Limited
Carscreugh Renewable Energy Park Ltd
Castle Bidco PLC
Castle Marinas Limited
Catalina Worthing Insurance Ltd
Channel Commercials Kent Ltd
Chrysalis (Stanhope) Limited
Claas Financial Services Ltd
Clackmannanshire Schools Education Partnership (Holdings)
Clackmannanshire Schools Education Partnership
Cohort PLC
Consort Healthcare (Mid Yorkshire) Funding
Consort Healthcare (Mid Yorkshire) Holdings
Consort Healthcare (Mid Yorkshire)
Contact Technologies UK Ltd
Cornwall Energy Recovery Holdings Ltd
Cornwall Energy Recovery Ltd
Countrystyle Group Limited
Crane Payment Innovations International
Cullum Family Trust
DPG Holdings Limited
DS (Holdings) 2 Limited
DX Holdings Limited
J.T. Davies & Sons Holdings Ltd
Doncaster School Solutions (Holdings)
Doncaster School Solutions Ltd
EDL (UK) LFG Generation Ltd
Eastbury Park (Holdings) Ltd
Eastbury Park Limited
Edwardian Hampshire Hotels Ltd
Edwardian Pastoria Hotels Ltd
Elysium Healthcare (Lighthouse) Ltd
Elysium Healthcare (Ultimate Care)
Everyday Lending Limited
Everyday Loans Holdings Ltd
Explorer Holdings UK Limited
FGP Topco Limited
Forth Health Holdings Limited
Forth Health Limited
Genesis Cancer Care UK Limited
HRG Debtco Limited
Harepath Estates LLP
Havas Canada Holdings Limited
Heathrow Airport Holdings Ltd
Hilton HHC Limited
Home Retail Group (UK) Limited
Home Retail Group Limited
Honey Monster Foods Limited
Honeywell Acquisitions II Ltd
Honeywell Europe Finance Ltd

Honeywell North Atlantic Holdings
Howitzer Acquisition Limited
Icrossing Europe Limited
Imperial Cars of Swanwick Ltd
Interbay ML, Ltd
Invesco Perpetual Select Trust PLC
Iris Payroll Software Limited
J.T.D. Finance Limited
J.T.D. Investments Limited
JTI (UK) Management Ltd
Jungheinrich Financial Services Ltd
Jungheinrich Lift Truck Finance Ltd
Kedleston Schools Limited
Kemble Water Eurobond PLC
Kemble Water Finance Limited
Kemble Water Holdings Limited
Kuehne + Nagel Drinkflow Logistics Holdings
Kuehne + Nagel Drinkflow Logistics
Kuehne + Nagel Drinks Logistics Ltd
Lactalis Nestle Chilled Dairy Co Ltd
Lancer Property Holdings Ltd
Limecay Limited
Lionel Road Developments Ltd
Local Car and Van Rental Ltd
Loesche Energy Systems Limited
Lonepiper Limited
MSK Holdings Limited
MYA Property Limited
Marlin Europe I Limited
Midgard Ltd
Millennium & Copthorne (Jersey Holdings)
Mondi Finance PLC
Morrisroe Group Limited
Mutual Services (Portsmouth) Ltd
NFAG Limited
NTL Victoria Limited
New Victoria Hospital Limited
Nomad Foods Europe Finco Ltd
Nomad Foods Europe Holdco Ltd
Nomad Foods Europe Holdings Ltd
Nomad Foods Europe Limited
Nomad Foods Europe Midco Ltd
Northumberland Energy Recovery Holdings
Northumberland Energy Recovery Ltd
Old Thorns Golf Hotel and Country Estate (Holdings)
Optegra UK Limited
P & O Ferries Division Holdings Ltd
P & O Ferries Holdings Limited
PSI - Pay Ltd
Premier Fleet Management and Contract Hire
QSC 1208 Limited
QSC 1209 Limited
RB Reigate (UK) Limited
Reckitt Benckiser (Grosvenor) Holdings
Reckitt Benckiser Treasury Services PLC
Restaurant Holdings Limited
SGN Commercial Services Ltd
Safestore Investments Limited
Sally UK Holdings Limited
Scottish Borders Education Partnership (Holdings)
Scottish Borders Education Partnership
Servier IP UK Limited
Spire Automotive Limited
Spirit Energy Southern North Sea Ltd
Spirit Norway Limited
St Edward Homes Limited
St Mary's University, Twickenham
Stanley Electric Holding Europe Co.,
Staten Investments Limited
Study Group Holdings UK Ltd
Subsea 7 Engineering Limited
Suez Advanced Solutions UK Ltd
Suez Recycling and Recovery UK Group Holdings
Superlift UK Limited
TGS Geophysical Company (UK) Ltd
TIG Acquisition Holdings
Tata Global Beverages Capital Ltd
Tata Global Beverages Investments
Thales Ground Transportation Systems UK
Thursdays (UK) Limited
Towry Finance Co Ltd
Trans Ocean Bulk Logistics Ltd
Travelopia Holdings Limited
UK Software Holdings Limited
United Biscuits Bidco Limited
United Biscuits BondCo Limited
United Biscuits Holdco 2 Ltd
United Biscuits Holdco Limited
United Biscuits VInco Limited
University of Winchester
Virgin Media Payments Ltd
Vodafone Europe UK
Vodafone Investment UK
We Buy Any Car Limited
Charles Wells Brewery Limited
Xchanging Holdings Limited
Xchanging Limited
Zennor CNS Limited
Zoom Gas Pipelines Limited
Zoom Holding Limited
Zoom Infrastructure Limited

2007 [182]

Ability Hotels (Cambridge) Ltd
Ability Hotels (Dunblane) Ltd
Ability Hotels (Liverpool) Ltd
Acquaspen Limited
Aesica Queenborough Limited
Agfa Healthcare UK Limited
Alliance BMP Limited
Aluminium Services (UK) Ltd
Apogee Group Limited
Archer Assets UK Limited
Arqiva Financing No 1 Limited
Arqiva Financing No 2 Limited
Aston Carter Group Limited
Atkins International Holdings Ltd
Aura (Newcastle) Project Co Ltd
Avalon Cellars Two Limited
Away Resorts Limited
B & P Acquisitionco Limited
B & P Holdings II Limited
B & P Midco Limited
BAE Systems Surface Ships (Holdings)
BAE Systems Surface Ships Ltd
BIMM Limited
BP Aromatics Limited
Beck MBI Limited
Biffa Group Limited
Brighthouse Group Limited
Brighthouse Holdings Limited
Brighthouse Limited
Bristow Southeast Asia Limited
Brooklime Limited
Bynorth (Holdings) Limited
Bynorth Limited
CML Reporting Limited
Car Finance Company (2007) Ltd
Cargill Financial Services Europe
Centrica LNG Co Ltd
Christ's Hospital
Cognita International Holdings Ltd
Comland Group Limited
Compass Group Procurement Ltd
Compressor Products Holdings Ltd
Connor Investments (UK) LLP
Copart Europe Limited
Courier and Passenger Transport Holdings
Cucina Acquisition (UK) Ltd
Cucina Finance (UK) Limited
Cucina Lux Investments Limited
Cygnet Propco Limited
DS (Holdings) 3 Limited
Danu Holding Limited
Eden Automotive Investments Ltd
Eden Automotive Limited
Edwards Limited
Egdon Resources PLC
Elysium Healthcare No. 2 Ltd
Equiniti Financial Services Ltd
Equiniti Holdings Limited
Equiniti Limited
Europa Worldwide Group Limited
Exagris Limited
Expro Holdings UK 4 Limited
Falcon Acquisitions Limited
Farnborough Finance (2007) Ltd
Fatface Group Limited
Formaplex Group Limited
Foss Holdings Limited
Furniture Village Holdings Ltd
Future Schools Trust
GGI Holdings Limited
Givaudan Holdings UK Limited
Greensands (UK) Limited
Greensands Europe Limited
Greensands Investments Limited
Greensands Junior Finance Ltd
Greensands Senior Finance Ltd
Group 1 Automotive UK Limited
Hampshire Aviation LLP
Hampton School
Harris Federation
Harsco (UK) Group Limited
Harsco Leatherhead Limited
Harsco Mole Valley Limited
Heathrow (AH) Limited
Heathrow (DSH) Limited
Heathrow (SP) Limited
Heathrow Finance PLC
Heathrow Holdco Limited
HeidelbergCement UK Holding II Ltd
HeidelbergCement UK Holding Ltd
Hemel Snowcentre Limited
Hilton UK Manage Limited
Hotel Intercontinental London (Holdings)
Inspiring Learning (Holdings) Ltd
Inspiring Learning Limited
Interserve Group Holdings Ltd
Intralot Finance UK Limited
Iris Capital Limited
Iris Software Group Limited
Key Equipment Finance Europe Ltd
LR (UK) Limited
Linde UK Holdings Limited
Linden/Downland Graylingwell LLP
London Care Partnership Ltd
MC Treasury Limited
MCF Commercial Limited
MacDermid Continental Investments
Marlin Europe II Limited
Marsh Wall Limited

Medispeed
John Menzies Finance Limited
Milton Keynes Academy Trust
Mobile Broadband Network Ltd
Mondi PLC
Monster Energy Europe Limited
NCMT Holdings Limited
NIS Acquisitions Limited
NIS Receivables No. 2 Limited
Nature Delivered Limited
Next Generation Data Ltd
Anthony Nicholas (UK) Limited
Norbain Holdings Limited
Norebo Europe Limited
Northgate Information Solutions Ltd
Octagon Group Holdings Limited
Optum UK Solutions Group Ltd
Oxford Aviation Academy (Oxford) Ltd
Parker Hannifin 2007 LLP
Parkview Treasury Services (UK) Ltd
Pentland Homes (Holdings) Ltd
Perform Group Limited
Peterborough (Progress Health) Holdings
Peterborough (Progress Health) Nominee
Peterborough (Progress Health) PLC
Pinewood PSB Limited
Premier Asset Management Group PLC
Premier Asset Management Holdings Ltd.
Premier Asset Management Midco Ltd.
Project Tristar Limited
QA-IQ Investments Limited
Reach Holdings Limited
Reckitt Benckiser Group PLC
Reckitt Benckiser Treasury (2007)
Redwing Holdings 2 Limited
Rightmove PLC
Rocco Homes Limited
Royal Navy and Royal Marines Charity
SCCI Group Limited
SGB Infrastructure Middle East Ltd
SGL No.1 Limited
SNA Solutions UK Limited
SRM (Redcar & Cleveland) Ltd
Selwood Holdings Limited
Serocor Holdings Limited
Shires Holdings Limited
Snowcentres Limited
Software (Holdco2) Limited
St James Holdings Limited
Stadium MK Group Limited
Stock Spirits (UK) Limited
Sword Soft Limited
Taylor Wimpey 2007 Limited
Thames Water Utilities Holdings Ltd
Thanet Earth Holdings Limited
Thanet Earth Limited
Towergate Risk Solutions Ltd
Transform Schools (Knowsley) Holdings
Transform Schools (Knowsley) Ltd
Trapoc Limited
Travel Republic Holdings Ltd.
Vector Aerospace International Ltd
Vodafone Americas 4
Vodafone Panafon UK
Walsall Hospital Company (Holdings)
Walsall Hospital Company PLC
Watts Gallery
Websense SC Holdings Limited
Websense SC Operations Limited
Westbury Street Limited
Wyevale Acquisitions Borrower Ltd
Zenimax Europe Limited
Zennor Pathway Limited

2008 [132]

ASIG Holdings Limited
Ability Hotels (Luton) Limited
Affinion International Travel Ltd
Akzo Nobel ICI Holdings
Aldermore Group PLC
Appia Europe Limited
BE Aerospace (UK) Europe Holdings
BNK (UK) Limited
Bowland Resources (No.2) Ltd
Peter Brett Associates LLP
Bristow (UK) LLP
British Gas Insurance Limited
British Gas New Heating Ltd
CAS Aspirations Properties Ltd
CSPH Limited
Cadbury Limited
Carewatch Bidco Limited
Carewatch Holdings Limited
Cellnex UK Midco Limited
Central G H Trust
Chemring North America Unlimited
Cognita UK Holdings Limited
Collard Group Limited
Cygnet Health UK Limited
Cygnet Inter-Holdings Limited
DLR (No.2) Limited
Dairy Crest UK Limited
Danu II Holdings Limited
De La Rue Finance Limited
Direct Wines Holdings Limited
Dolphin Head Group Limited
Dual Energy Direct Limited
Edwardian Bloomsbury Street Ltd
Edwardian New Finance Limited
Enstar Acquisitions Limited
Expro Benelux Limited
Expro Holdings UK 3 Limited
Expro Resources Limited
FBL Holdings Limited
Falck UK Limited
First Central Insurance Management
Flexera Software Limited
Forum Products Holdings Ltd
Global Invacom Holdings Ltd
Glory Global Solutions (Holdings)
Glory Global Solutions (International)
Glory Global Solutions (Midco) Ltd
Glory Global Solutions (Topco) Ltd
HCL EAS Ltd
HPI Holding Limited
Haig Housing Trust
Halma Overseas Funding Limited
Haymarket UK2 Limited
Healthcare Facilities Management Services
Highway Management (Scotland) Holding
Highway Management (Scotland) Ltd
Host Europe Limited
Hurtwood House School LLP
IHS International Holdings Ltd
ILB Investments Limited
INEOS Derivatives France Ltd
INEOS Manufacturing (Hull) Ltd
ISDC Developments (No2) Ltd
Inspiring Learning Services Ltd
Inter Bay Financial II Limited
Intercontinental (PB) 1
Interdist Alliances Limited
Interserve Finance Limited
JEG Acquisition Co Ltd
JRL Group Limited
Jakks Pacific (UK) Ltd
The Edward James Foundation Ltd
Jelmac Properties
P.H Jones Group Limited
Just Develop It Limited
Kazakh Projects Joint Venture Ltd
Kedleston Wings Holdco Ltd
Nicholas King Developments PLC
Kofax US Holdings Limited
Kohler Uninterruptible Power Ltd
Laing O'Rourke Manufacturing Ltd
Lavazza Professional UK Ltd
Linden St Albans LLP
Luxury Travel Group Limited
MGT Teesside Limited
Magma Global Limited
Mars Chocolate UK Holdings Ltd
Mars Food UK Limited
Mars Melton UK Holdings Ltd
Mars Petcare UK
Mars Petcare UK Holdings Ltd
Mars Slough UK Holdings Ltd
Mars Wrigley Confectionery UK Ltd
NHS Professionals Limited
NIS Receivables No.1 Limited
NPS (UK2) Limited
National Adhesives Holding Ltd.
National Museum of The Royal Navy
Offshore Containers Holdings Ltd
Optasense Limited
Optiva Solutions (UK) Limited
PHF Investments Limited
Parexel International Holding UK Ltd
Petco Trading (UK) Limited
Portsmouth Surgical Holdings Ltd
Premier Research International Us
SLF of Canada UK Limited
SLR Management Limited
Safetykleen Group Services Ltd
Sanlam Private Investments (UK) Holdings
Scentrics Information Security Technologies
Sevita (UK) Limited
Smiths Interconnect Group Ltd
Snell Corporation Limited
Software of Excellence UK Holdings
Softwareone UK Limited
Solarsoft Acquisition Limited
St. Nicholas Court Farms Ltd
Symantec (UK) Holding Limited
Systagenix Wound Management, Ltd
Tensator Holdings Ltd
Thorney Lane LLP
Trescal Limited
Veeam Software UK Limited
Vodafone 5 Limited
WCR Group Limited
WP Midco1 Limited
WP Midco2 Limited
WP Midco3 Limited
WP Safety-Kleen Limited
Woldingham School
WorleyParsons UK Finance Sub Ltd

2009 [159]

Allen Diesels Limited
Amazon Spring Waters Investment Ltd
Ambassador Entertainment Group Ltd
Anchorage Capital Europe, LLP
Angmering Park Farms LLP
Antler New Homes Limited
Ash Properties Limited

Aura (Newcastle) Project Company Phase 2
BAE Systems Applied Intelligence (International)
BCA Central Limited
BCA Osprey I Limited
BCA Osprey II Limited
BCA Remarketing Group Limited
Bathroom Brands Holdings UK Ltd
Black & Decker International Finance (UK)
Black & Decker International Finance Holdings (UK)
Bovis Peer LLP
Bowland Resources Limited
Brighton & Hove Seaside Community Homes
British Gas Finance Limited
Brymore Holdings Limited
Bullitt Group Limited
Bullitt Mobile Limited
CGG Services (UK) Limited
CHMC Limited
CSC Computer Sciences Financing LLP
CSC Computer Sciences International Holdings
CSC Computer Sciences International
CSC Computer Sciences International Operations
CSC Computer Sciences International Services
CSC Computer Sciences UK Holdings
Cable & Wireless Worldwide Ltd
Cadbury South Africa (Holdings)
Centrica (Lincs) Wind Farm Ltd
Chobham School Academy (Stratford)
Chromium Acquisitions Limited
Chromium Assets Limited
Chromium Suchex LLP
Clarenco LLP
Click Entertainment Limited
Cogeco Peer 1 (UK) Ltd.
Cognita Funding 1 Limited
Coinford Holdings Limited
Collaborative Services Support (NE) Holdings
Collaborative Services Support NE
Crest Nicholson Holdings PLC
Cygnet Aspirations Developments Ltd
Direct Wines Finance Limited
E & J Capital Partners Limited
E & J Ground Rents LLP
E & J Ground Rents No2 LLP
ESNT Filter Products Limited
Economydrive Cars Limited
Environments for Learning Sandwell PFI Holdco One
Environments for Learning Sandwell PFI One
Equiniti Group PLC
Esure Finance Limited
Esure Group PLC
T & E Ferris Limited
Fire Support (SSFR) Holdings Ltd
Fire Support (SSFR) Limited
Fitesa Limited
Flexibon Limited
Flight Centre (UK) Wholesale Ltd
Friends Life FPG Limited
Friends Life Holdings PLC
GlaxoSmithKline Investment Holdings
GlaxoSmithKline Investment Services
GlaxoSmithKline Mercury Ltd
Goodrich Inertial Limited
Grand Central Hotel Glasgow Ltd
Green Hill Energy Limited
Hall Farm Wind Farm Ltd
Halma Euro Trading Limited
Heartstone Inns Limited
HeidelbergCement Canada Holding Ltd
Hill of Towie Limited
Hospital Company (Southmead) Holdings
Hospital Company (Southmead) Ltd
IMO Car Wash Group Limited
INC Research Holding Limited
INEOS Chemicals Grangemouth Ltd
INEOS Finance PLC
INEOS Industries Holdings Ltd
INEOS Industries Limited
IQVIA RDS UK Holdings Ltd.
Imagine Cruising Limited
Inhealth UK Holdings Limited
Intercontinental (PB) 3 Ltd
Interserve Service Futures Ltd
JRL Group Holdings Limited
Jain International Foods Ltd
Just Retirement Group Holdings Ltd
K2M UK Limited
Keadby Wind Farm Limited
Kellogg Brown & Root Group Ltd
Kellogg Brown & Root International Group Holdings LLP
Kellogg Brown & Root International Group
Kerridge Commercial Systems Ltd
Kewsaw Limited
LGC Science Group Limited
LGC Science Investments Ltd
Lady Eleanor Holles School
Leaders Lettings Limited
London Pharma & Chemicals Holdings Ltd
M & C Finance (1) Limited
MCG (Holdings) Ltd
Mash Holdings Limited
Masternaut Group Holdings Ltd
Medivet Partnership LLP
Meller Educational Trust
Millipore UK Holdings LLP
Motorola Mobility UK Ltd
Nastor Investments Limited
Natures Way Foods Europe Ltd
Optum Solutions UK Holdings Ltd
PCL Transport 24/7 Limited
Phivco UK II Limited
Protection Specialist Limited
RSA Finance
Renewi Cumbria Limited
Resource Recovery Solutions (Derbyshire)
Rockwell Commercial Holdings Ltd
Rose Holdco Limited
Rose Midco Limited
SLS Holding Co Ltd
SWM UK Wind One Limited
Schueco UK Limited
Seagreen Wind Energy Limited
Senior Finance Four Limited
Sovereign Advances Limited
Sovereign Housing Capital PLC
St Mary's Football Group Ltd
St Mary's Training Ground Ltd
Stanley Black & Decker UK Ltd
Sugarich Limited
Surrey Lighting Services Ltd
TBG (1) 2009 Limited
TBG (3) 2009 Limited
TWG Europe Limited
Teddington 2 Limited
Tesco Underwriting Limited
Thornton Properties Limited
Towers Watson UK Limited
Towry Group Limited
Ty Danjuma Family Office Ltd
Venn Partners LLP
ViiV Healthcare Limited
ViiV Healthcare Overseas Ltd
ViiV Healthcare Trading Services UK
ViiV Healthcare UK Limited
Virgin Media Investments Ltd
Virgin Media Secured Finance PLC
Vodafone Marketing UK
Vodafone Sales & Services Ltd
WLHC Projectco Limited
Walgreens Boots Alliance Services
Woodgavil Limited
World Mission Agency - Winners Chapel International

January-June 2010 [71]

Aeromobile Communications Ltd
Afton Chemical UK Holdings Ltd
BIMM Holdings Limited
Boskalis Subsea Limited
CB Equity LLP
Canterbury Pharmacies Holdings Ltd
Cargill UK Holdings Limited
Civil Service Benevolent Fund
Consort Medical Finance 2010 Ltd
Crawley Down Holdings Ltd
Crescent Pharmaceuticals Ltd
DST Global Solutions (Realty) Ltd
DST Process Solutions Limited
DYRMS - An Academy with Military Traditions
Dnata Aviation Services Ltd
EDU UK Intermediate Limited
EDU UK Management Services Ltd
EDU UK Topco Limited
East Malling Trust
Ergo Tec LLP
Essentra Packaging & Security Ltd
Fidelity China Special Situations PLC
GCH Corporation Limited
GS Acquisitions Limited
Gama Aviation PLC
GlaxoSmithKline IHC Limited
Gym Offshore One Limited
Gym Offshore Three Limited
Gym Offshore Two Limited
Gym Renewables Limited
Gym Renewables One Limited
Hastings (Holdings) Limited
Henry Construction Projects Ltd
Impact Africa Limited
Inspiral Oldham Holding Co Ltd
Inspiral Oldham Limited
Ixcellerate Limited
Andrew Jacobs LLP
LGC Science Holdings Limited
London Square (Holdings) Ltd
London Square Developments Ltd
ME III Limited
Marlin Financial Group Limited
Marlin Financial Intermediate Ltd
Micro Focus (US) Holdings
Micro Focus IP Development Ltd
Opal Ventures Limited
Pall Europe Limited
Paydens Group Holdings Limited
Paydens Holdings Limited
Portchester Equity Limited
Premier Lotteries Capital UK Ltd
Premier Lotteries UK Limited

Pulsant Bidco Limited
Qinetiq Group Holdings Limited
RATP DEV UK Ltd
Raisio UK Limited
Saipem Limited
Sky IQ Limited
Student Castle Limited
Suez Advanced Solutions Holding UK
Surrey Blue Limited
TP-Link UK Limited
TY Properties (UK) Limited
Thakeham Homes Limited
Toll Investments (NA) Ltd
Travel Technology Investments Ltd
United Living (South) Group Ltd
University of Brighton Academies Trust
University of Kent Academies Trust
Virgin Media SFA Finance Ltd

July-December 2010 [86]

103-105 Bath Road Limited
A.N.A. Aviation Group Holdings Ltd
Anesco Limited
BAP Pharma Limited
BE Aerospace Thermal and Power Management Holdings (UK)
Beamish Investments Limited
Bharat Forge International Ltd
Bio Products Laboratory Ltd
Bloc Hotel Group Limited
Robert Bosch UK Holdings Ltd
Britax Group Limited
Britvic Overseas Limited
Brook Learning Trust
Burhill Group Limited
CC 1 (2011) Limited
CC 2 (2011) Limited
CC 4 (2011) Limited
CFBT Schools Trust
CSG Systems UK Limited
Cadbury Four LLP
Cathay Investments 2 Limited
Celsis Group Limited
Centerprise Intl Holdings Ltd
Chatham & Clarendon Grammar School
Chemigraphic Mid-Co Limited
Citysprint (UK) Group Limited
Dawsongroup Vans Limited
Dun & Bradstreet Investments Ltd
E & J Ground Rents No3 LLP
ELWA Holdings Limited
Erith School
Eurovia Infrastructure Limited
FWPJV Limited
Fort Pitt Thomas Aveling Academies
Fulston Manor Academies Trust
Gazelli Art House Limited
Gracewell Healthcare Limited
Grove Developments Limited
H.I.G. Europe - Fibercore Bidco Ltd
HEL Bidco Ltd
Highway Management M80 Investment
Hilton Worldwide Manage Ltd
Homesun Limited
IMCD UK Acquisitions Limited
INC Research Europe Holdings Ltd
INEOS Commercial Services UK Ltd
INEOS Sales (UK) Limited
JLW Excellent Homes for Life Holding Co
JLW Excellent Homes for Life Ltd
KPJV Limited
Kellogg Brown & Root London Ltd
Kemnal Academies Trust
Lampton School Academy Trust
LexisNexis Risk Solutions UK Ltd
Linde Canada Holdings Limited
Navitas Life Sciences Holdings Ltd
Nice Systems UK Finance Ltd
Nice Systems US Finance Ltd
One GE Healthcare UK
Onesavings Bank PLC
PNC Financial Services UK Ltd
Pioneer Educational Trust
Pulsant Midco 1 Limited
Pulsant Midco 2 Limited
Pulsant Topco Limited
RCL Cruises Ltd
Radnor House School (Holdings) Ltd
Radnor House School (Property) Ltd
Reckitt Benckiser Finance (2010) Ltd
Reckitt Benckiser Luxembourg (2010)
Robinsons (Finance) No.2 Ltd
Rothschild Foundation
SAI Global CIS UK Limited
Saga Cruises IV Limited
Schlumberger UK Limited
Sekisui Diagnostics (UK) Ltd
Shearwater Geoservices Limited
Suez Recycling and Recovery Suffolk Ltd
Swale Academies Trust
TBG (4) Limited
TCFG Holdings Limited
Thinking Schools Academy Trust
Towergate Insurance Limited
Travelport Finance Limited
Wadlow Energy Limited
Weald of Kent Grammar School Academy Trust

January-June 2011 [117]

5 Dimensions Trust
AE Consolidation Limited
Allegis Group (UK) Holdings II Ltd
Allegis Group (UK) Holdings Ltd
Ambec Limited
Amphora Acquisitions Limited
BECAP Spicers (UK) Limited
BP Biofuels Brazil Investments Ltd
BP Exploration Angola (Kwanza Benguela)
Baylis Court Trust
Bellman Property Group Limited
Bohunt Education Trust
Britvic Finance Partnership LLP
Bullers Wood Multi Academy Trust
Buy 2 Let Cars Ltd
Camelot Business Solutions Ltd
Camelot Global Lottery Solutions Ltd
Capital Professional Limited
Carshalton Boys Sports College
Chislehurst and Sidcup Grammar School
Coastal Academies Trust
Collingwood College
Compatriot Holdings Limited
Constantine Wind Energy Ltd
Convergence Pharmaceuticals Holdings
Croydon and Lewisham Lighting Services (Holdings)
Croydon and Lewisham Lighting Services
Charles Darwin Academy Trust
Defence Investments Limited
Denbigh Alliance
Doctors Chambers (UK) Limited
Doctors Chambers Group Limited
Dolphin Drilling Operations Ltd
Dynamic Procurement Holdings Ltd
East Sussex Energy Infrastructure and Development
Edif Group Finance Limited
Edif Group Limited
Edif Group Management Limited
Education for The 21st Century
GLF Schools
Girls' Learning Trust
Glenside Care Group Limited
Gluco RX Limited
Grange Renewable Energy Ltd
Greenshaw Learning Trust
Guildford Education Partnership
Hazeley Academy
Hazelwick School
Herne Bay High School
Holiday Extras Investments Ltd
Home Grown Hotels Limited
Home Retail Group (Finance) LLP
Howard Partnership Trust
Hudson Energy Supply UK Ltd
Impact Multi Academy Trust
Impact Oil & Gas Limited
Invesco Finance PLC
KBR (U.K.) Investments Limited
KIMS Property Co Ltd
Kennet School Academies Trust
Keystone Holdco Limited
Kraft Foods Investment Holdings UK
Kraft Foods UK IP & Production Holdings
LGC Genomics Limited
LGC Whirlwind Limited
Ladham Properties Limited
Langley Park School for Boys Academy Trust
London Square (Putney) Limited
Lymington Precision Engineering (LPE)
Maiden Erlegh Trust
Melton House Investments Ltd
Milton Keynes Education Trust
Mountbatten School
Ousedale School
Overton Grange School
Parker Hannifin Limited
Pegasus Academy Trust
Piggott Church of England School
Porthaven Finance Limited
Procter & Gamble UK Parent Co Ltd
Prospect School, Reading
Prysmian Powerlink Services Ltd
QH Estates Ltd
Queens' School (Bushey)
RMET
Regenter Myatts Field North Holding Co
Regenter Myatts Field North Ltd
Renoir Bidco Limited
Rentokil Initial Americas Ltd
Rhombi Holdings Limited
Roos Energy Limited
Rosedale Hewens Academy Trust
SSE Renewables Walney (UK) Ltd
STI Enterprises Limited
Sharnbrook Academy Federation
Shimtech Industries Limited
Signet Direct Diamond Sourcing Ltd
Step Academy Trust
Synaptic Trust
TJX Europe Buying Limited
TWE Finance (UK) Limited
Technical Staffing Resources Ltd
Thames Water (Kemble) Finance PLC
Treasury Wine Estates UK Brands Ltd

Uxbridge High School Academy Trust
Valley Invicta Academies Trust
Wadlow Energy Holdings Limited
Westbury Street Holdings Ltd
Weydon Multi Academy Trust
Wildern Academy Trust
John Wiley & Sons UK LLP
William Willett Learning Trust
Williamson Trust
Willow Learning Trust
Wycombe High School Academies Trust
Xylem Water Holdings Limited
Yavneh College Academy Trust

July-December 2011 [122]

3SE (Barnsley, Doncaster & Rotherham)
Abriand Limited
Active Assistance Finance Ltd
Aesica BC Limited
Aesica M1 Limited
Aesica M2 Limited
Alere as Holdings Limited
Archaylen Property Limited
Aurasma Limited
BBGI Holding Limited
Belton Associates (Group Holdings)
Belton Associates Holdings Ltd
Belton Associates Limited
Bishopshalt School
Bloc Gatwick Limited
Bourne Education Trust
Britvic Brands LLP
Brookworth Group Limited
CSL Communications Group Ltd
Cadbury Eight LLP
Cadbury Nine LLP
Cadbury Seven LLP
Cadbury Ten LLP
Cams Hill School
Canal & River Trust
Capital Safety Row Limited
Claydon Estate LLP
Clearswift Holding Limited
Cox Green School
Cross London Trains Holdco 2 Ltd
Cross London Trains Limited
Datatec PLC
Deltic Group Holdings Limited
Deltic Group Limited
Digico Global Limited
Dnata World Travel Limited
Dolphin Two Limited
E & J Ground Rents No4 LLP
EMAP Publishing Limited
Edwardian Canary Wharf Hotel Ltd
Edwardian Free Trade Hall Ltd
Edwardian Mercer Street Ltd
Ellucian Global Limited
Ennogen Healthcare Ltd
Exemplar Properties Limited
Ferrybridge MFE Limited
Frimley Topco Limited
Furze Platt Senior School
GFM Education
Gama Aviation (Engineering) Ltd
Game Digital Holdings Limited
Game Retail Limited
GlaxoSmithKline Intellectual Property Management
Greeneden UK Acquisition Co Ltd
Home and Comforts Limited
IDE Group Limited
In-Sync Group Limited
Ipreo UK Holdings Ltd
Key Bidco Limited
Key Midco Limited
Kion Financial Services Ltd
LKQ Euro Limited
Langley Park Learning Trust
Lantmannen UK Holding Limited
Leaderboard Golf Holdings Ltd
Learning Alliance Academy Trust
London Square (Fulham) Limited
London Square Developments (Ventures)
London Square Limited
Longacres Garden Centre Ltd
Lord Wandsworth College
MTWOM B Limited
Manor Trust
Mapil Bidco Limited
Mapil Midco 1 Limited
Mapil Midco 2 Limited
Mapil Topco Limited
Matchtech Group (Holdings) Ltd
Robert May's School
Micro Focus Group Limited
Moat Homes Finance PLC
Odyssey Trust for Education
Onyx Information Technology Holdings
Pangbourne Developments Ltd
Porthaven Management Limited
Porthaven Properties Limited
Praesepe Holdings Limited
Prinhold Limited
Prospects Group 2011 Limited
Purecircle (UK) Limited
RB Hotels Limited
RIHL Limited
Radian Capital PLC
Sir William Ramsay School Academy Trust
Renatus Property Management Ltd
Romsey School
SAB Australia Beverage Holdings LLP
Senior Finance Six Limited
Senior Five Limited
Slough and East Berkshire C of E Multi Academy Trust
Software (Holdco 4) Limited
Somerset Equipment Finance (UK) Ltd
St Bartholomew's School
Subsea 7 Interim UK Holdings Ltd
Subsea 7 Offshore Resources (UK) Ltd
Subsea 7 Senior Holdings (UK) Ltd
Sussex Learning Trust
Tamar Energy Limited
Telefonica Digital Limited
Tenterden Schools Trust
Trellis Acquisitions Limited
Unity Schools Trust
Upham Group Limited
VFS Legal Limited
Vanguard Learning Trust
Verint Technology UK Limited
WNDirect Limited
Wasp Management Software Ltd
Woodland Academy Trust
Wootton Academy Trust
Xchanging US Funding Limited
Zeltiq Limited

January-March 2012 [45]

AVMI Group Limited
AbbVie Ltd
Adelie Foods Group Limited
BP Exploration China Limited
BP Subsea Well Response Ltd
Beacon Community College Academy Trust
Big Yellow Self Storage Company A
Blackfen School for Girls
Braeforge Investment Limited
COL Newco Limited
Capital Safety Acquisitions Ltd
City Hotel (London) Limited
Coombe Academy Trust
Cowplain School
Fizzy Enterprises LLP
Glory Global Solutions Ltd
HMS Victory Preservation Company
Hastoe Capital PLC
Hertswood Academy
Huhtamaki Finance Limited
Hyundai Capital UK Limited
Isleworth and Syon School for Boys
Kimal Holdings Limited
L-J Bidco Limited
L-J Finco Limited
MVV Environment Ridham Limited
Merseyside Energy Recovery Holdings Ltd
O2 Unify Limited
Oil Spill Response (Capping) Ltd
Optivo Finance PLC
Police Rehabilitation Centre
SDH Bidco Limited
SDH Holdco Limited
Sabre Retail Fashion Limited
Salisbury Workplace Services Ltd
Schelwood Trust
Schoolsworks Academy Trust
Skills for Life Trust
TVH Fizzy Holdings Limited
Tallentire Energy Limited
Trellis Finance Limited
Trellis Holdco Limited
Trellis Investments Limited
University of Law Limited
Wyevale Garden Centres Capital Ltd

April-June 2012 [43]

Alimera Sciences Limited
Amber Solar Parks (Holdings) Ltd
Amber Solar Parks Limited
Arqiva Broadcast Intermediate Ltd
Arqiva Broadcast Parent Ltd
Arqiva Group Parent Limited
Aryzta UK Holdings I Limited
Aurora Academies Trust
Bellevue Education International Ltd
Biogen Holdings Limited
Bottomline Technologies Ltd
Canal & River Trading CIC
Chobham Manor LLP
Cognita UK Brazil Holdings Ltd
Collegiate Trust
Cornerstone Telecommunications Infrastructure
Cosan Lubes Investments Ltd
Cross London Trains Finance Co Ltd
Cross London Trains Holdco Ltd
Dover Federation for The Arts
Drew Marine UK Holdings Ltd
S Elvin Limited
European Investments (Cornwall) Ltd
Fizzy Canning Town LLP
GlaxoSmithKline Consumer Trading Services
Grove HR Limited
IAG Cargo Limited

IUP 2 LLP
Kronos Worldwide Limited
Linde North America Holdings Ltd
MF UK FC Limited
Merseyside Energy Recovery Ltd
Mersham Hatch Estate LLP
Onecom Group Limited
Paradigm (UK) Holding Limited
Prysmian UK Group Limited
SC Walmgate Limited
Saxon Weald Capital PLC
Sharp Electronics (Europe) Ltd
Shoosmiths LLP
Sky International Operations Ltd
Virgin Media Finco Limited
Zebra Diamond Holdings Limited

July-September 2012 [55]

ABJ Trading LLP
Alent Finance Limited
Alent Investments Limited
Alent Limited
Aria Petroleum (UK) Ltd.
Arqiva Group Holdings Limited
Arqiva Group Intermediate Ltd
Arqiva Senior Finance Limited
Blue Light Partnership (ASP) Holdings
Blue Light Partnership (ASP) Ltd
CEB Holdings UK 1 Limited
CEB Holdings UK 2 Limited
CPRT (Europe) Limited
Charters School
Columbus Bidco Limited
Columbus Midco Limited
Columbus Topco Limited
Connacht SPV 1 Limited
Connacht SPV 2 Limited
Connacht SPV 3 Limited
Crop Demetra Limited
E & J Ground Rents No5 LLP
Espalier Finance Limited
Espalier Ventures Limited
Essentra Packaging Limited
Every Child, Every Day Academy Trust
Granitte Investments (UK) Ltd
Housing Solutions Capital PLC
Kedleston Group Limited
Kent Catholic Schools' Partnership
Marlin Portfolio Holdings Ltd
Marlin Senior Holdings Limited
Merkur Casino UK Ltd
Mizzen Bidco Limited
Mizzen Mezzco 2 Limited
Mizzen Mezzco Limited
O & M-Movianto UK Holdings Ltd.
Orleans Park School
Park Federation Academy Trust
Partnerships in Children's Services
Pegasus Life Limited
Porthaven Properties No 2 Ltd
Reckitt Benckiser (Brands) Ltd
Remy Cointreau UK Limited
Ricardo-AEA Limited
Rye Academy Trust
Siemens Pension Funding Ltd
Sirigen II Limited
Teddington School
Telefonica Germany Holdings Ltd
Toshiba Global Commerce Solutions (U.K.)
VS Alliance Limited
Wakefield Waste PFI Limited
Waldegrave Trust
Wood Hall Land & Properties Ltd

October-December 2012 [62]

AB InBev Harmony Limited
Alent New Finance (UK) Limited
Aqualisa Holdings Limited
Arqiva Broadcast Finance PLC
Arqiva Financing PLC
Arris Solutions UK Ltd.
Aspen Pumps Limited
Aura Finance Limited
BP Australia Swaps Management Ltd
BP Holdings Canada Limited
Berendsen Finance (DKK) Ltd
Berendsen Finance (Euro 2) Ltd
Berendsen Finance (Euro) Ltd
Brentford School for Girls
Business Lending Residential Funding
CHEP Pallecon Solutions Ltd
Colorcon European Holdings (No.5)
Conway Aecom Limited
Flight Centre Robin Limited
GCP Rooftop Solar 4 Limited
Garreg Lwyd Energy Limited
GlaxoSmithKline Intellectual Property (No.2)
GlaxoSmithKline Intellectual Property Development
GlaxoSmithKline Intellectual Property Holdings
GlaxoSmithKline Intellectual Property
Green Network UK PLC
Greenclose Holdings Limited
Grosvenor Casinos (GC) Limited
Harman Automotive UK Limited
Helsinki Bidco Limited
Helsinki Midco Limited
Helsinki Topco Limited
Ichnaea UK Limited
Johnson Controls Auto India Ltd
KP Snacks Limited
London Arena Investments Ltd
Majestic Securities Limited
Marlin Intermediate Holdings PLC
Marlin Midway Limited
Meridian Residential Developments
Milton Keynes Development Partnership LLP
Moretons Investments Limited
ND1T Limited
ND2F Limited
ND3M Limited
Network Aviation Group Ltd
PCL Bidco Limited
PCL Holdco Limited
PHH 1 Limited
Partridge of Hampshire Limited
Project Ventures Rail Investments I
Street Family Group of Companies (Holdings)
Street Property (Holdings) Ltd
Tandridge Learning Trust
Therakos (UK), Ltd
Travelport Holdings (UK) Ltd
Tyrolese (751) Limited
ViiV Healthcare UK (No.3) Ltd
Welcome Break No. 1 Limited
Welcome Break No. 2 Limited
XPS Pensions Group PLC
Xafinity Consulting (Reading) Ltd

January-March 2013 [50]

Admiral House Property Trading Ltd
Alder Hey (Special Purpose Vehicle)
Alder Hey Holdco 1 Limited
Alder Hey Holdco 2 Limited
Alder Hey Holdco 3 Limited
Ambassador Theatre Group Overseas Holdings
CALA 1 Limited
CALA Group (Holdings) Limited
CFCEPS LLP
CFCPP LLP
CNOOC UK Limited
Dominvs Project Co Ltd
Dreams Limited
Dreams Topco Limited
E & J Ground Rents No6 LLP
Filtrona Limited
GCP Biomass 1 Ltd
GFZ Properties Limited
GMK Limited
Glasgow Learning Quarter (Holdings)
Glasgow Learning Quarter Ltd
HellermannTyton Group PLC
HellermannTyton Holdings Ltd
Innisfree Schools (F2C) Ltd
Innisfree Schools (Secondary) Ltd
Interserve Developments No.2 Ltd
Jessops (Group) Limited
Jessops Europe Limited
M & C Asia Holdings (UK) Ltd
M & C Singapore Holdings (UK) Ltd
MCPA Limited
Marlin Financial Intermediate II Ltd
Maxxia (UK) Limited
Maxxia Finance Limited
McGraw-Hill Global Education UK Holdco II
McGraw-Hill Global Education UK Holdco
Mitsubishi Heavy Industries Air-Conditioning Europe, Ltd.
Natural Sante Limited
Newincco 1222 Limited
Perform Sporting News Limited
Police Care UK
Shared Services Connected Ltd
Skanska TAM Limited
Sky SNI Limited
Southwick Solar Farm Limited
Taylor Wimpey SH Capital Ltd
Think One Limited
Towers Watson Global 2 Limited
Yourcash Europe Limited
Yourcash Solutions Limited

April-June 2013 [48]

Akzo Nobel Finance Limited
Arqiva PP Financing PLC
BL Wind Limited
Bluefield SIF Investments Ltd
Britten Properties LLP
Carat UK Midco Limited
Cargill UK Finance Limited
Andrew Colin Investments Ltd
Creabilis Holdings Limited
Creative Foods Europe Limited
Danshell Healthcare Limited
Dreachmhor Wind Farm Limited
Elster Solutions Limited
Envision Pharma Holdco Limited
ExxonMobil Holding Co Ltd
GCP Asset Finance 1 Limited
GCP Onshore Wind 3 Limited
Gym Group Midco1 Limited
Gym Group Midco2 Limited

Gym Group Operations Limited
Gym Group PLC
Host Europe Group Limited
Invesco Software Holdings Ltd
Just Group PLC
Kingston Digital Europe Co LLP
Kingston Technology Europe Co LLP
Kodak Alaris Holdings Limited
Kodak Alaris Limited
Linden Homes (Sherford) LLP
London Square (Streatham) Ltd
Medica Group PLC
Medica Reporting Finance Ltd
Merck Holding Ltd.
Metropolis Group Holdings Ltd
NBS Trade and Investment Ltd
Naga UK Bidco Limited
Naga UK Topco Limited
RAK Petroleum PLC
Reckitt Benckiser (RUMEA) Ltd
Royal Air Force Central Fund
SQIB Limited
Symmetry Logistics Holdings Ltd
Tiger Group Limited
Towers Watson Global 3 Limited
West London Energy Recovery Holdings Ltd
West London Energy Recovery Ltd
West Raynham Solar Limited
Wyevale Garden Centres Acquisitions

July-September 2013 [52]

AA Brand Management Limited
Albain Bidco UK Limited
Arqiva Smart Metering Limited
Ascension Healthcare PLC
Beaconsfield High School
CMG Holdco Limited
Choice Care Group 2 Limited
Choice Care Group 3 Limited
Choice Care Group Holdings Ltd
Cougar Holdco London Limited
DX (Group) PLC
Edwardian Grafton Hotel Ltd
Edwardian Hotel Finance Ltd
Edwardian Hotel Investments Ltd
Elster Water Metering Limited
Evolution (Woking) Limited
Fizzy Stepney Green LLP
Gemini Rail Services UK Ltd
HCL Technologies UK Limited
Paula Hawkins Limited
Heathrow Edwardian Hotel Ltd
Hexagon Corporate Management Ltd
Host Europe Investments Ltd
INEOS Chemicals France Holdings Ltd
INEOS Grangemouth PLC
Infotech Trade Services Ltd
Intelliflo Bidco Limited
Intelliflo Holdings 2013 Ltd
Intelliflo Intermediate Holdings Ltd
Intelliflo Midco Limited
Knowledge Academy Holdings Ltd
Leaders The Rental Agents Ltd
Lucozade Ribena Suntory Ltd
Mast-Jaegermeister UK Limited
Millennium Hotels (West London) Ltd
Neilson Active Holidays (Holdings)
PB Bidco Limited
PB Holdco Limited
PB Midco Limited
PB Topco Limited
Parallel Learning Trust
Reckitt Benckiser Holdings (TFFC)
Romans 2 Limited
Romans 3 Limited
S A Printing Group Limited
Stada UK Holdings Ltd.
Stock Spirits Group PLC
TJX Germany Ltd.
University of Chichester (Multi) Academy Trust
Vanderbilt Development Finance Ltd
Vanderbilt Thames Valley Ltd
White Rock Land LLP

October-December 2013 [64]

55VS No 2 Limited
8x8 UK Investments Limited
Aitch Care Homes Holdco Ltd
Alestra Group Holdings Limited
Altair (UK) Ltd
Atlantica Yield PLC
BBGI (NI) Limited
BCA Vehicle Finance Limited
Big Yellow Self Storage Company M
Brand Energy & Infrastructure Services UK, Ltd.
British Gas Energy Procurement Ltd
CG EU NSC Limited
CPRT LLP
Centrica Energy Marketing Ltd
Chaucer Management Services Ltd
Core Property Developments Ltd
ENRA Group Limited
Edwardian Exclusive Ltd
Edwardian Finance Ltd
Edwardian Investments Ltd
Fishdance Limited
Gardeners' Royal Benevolent Society
Grand Union Group Funding PLC
Gus UK Management Limited
Harlequin FC Holdings Limited
Hexagon Positioning Intelligence Ltd
Hibu Group Limited
Honeywell Safety Products International Ltd.
Horsted Estates Limited
INEOS Finance Company 1
INEOS Finance Company 2
Interserve Finance (Switzerland) Holdings
J C C Lighting Holdings Ltd
Johnson Controls Systems Development
Kent EHFA Holdco Limited
Kent EHFA Projectco Limited
Kingston Bidco Limited
Kingston Midco Limited
Kingston Topco Limited
Linde Investments No.1 Limited
Lotus Flower Holdings Limited
Mondelez UK Biscuit Financing Ltd
Morgan North America Holding Ltd
Newincco 1270 Limited
Pall European Holdings Limited
Pall Technology UK Limited
RB UK Commercial Limited
SNC-Lavalin Co Ltd
Saga Mid Co Limited
Saga PLC
Skillcrown Holdings Limited
Stock Finance (Koruna) Limited
Teoco UK Limited
Tranche 5 Limited
Transserv UK Limited
Trant Holding Co Ltd
Tudor Holdings (UK) Limited
Vodafone 6 UK
WEL Solar Park 2 Limited
WSH Hospitality Limited
WSH International Investments Ltd
WSH UK & Ireland Limited
J Wiley Limited
Zennor Petroleum Limited

January-March 2014 [39]

Achieving for Children CIC
Armadillo Storage Holding Co Ltd
BP America Limited
BPHA Finance PLC
Blake Morgan Group LLP
Blake Morgan LLP
Capital Safety Global Holdings Ltd
Ceres Power Intermediate Holdings
Chem Aviation LLP
DPSK Limited
DX (VCP) Limited
Durrington Multi Academy Trust
Fatface Group Borrowings Ltd
William Grant & Sons Brands Ltd
Hilton Worldwide FS Treasury Ltd
Hilton Worldwide Holding 2 Ltd
Hovis Holdings Limited
Hovis Limited
Interserve PFI Holdings 2014 Ltd
Kimberly-Clark International Holding
Lighthouse Healthcare Group Ltd
Marco Island Developments Ltd
Millennium Hotels Europe Holdings
NSL (Holdings) Limited
Oceanic Finance Limited
Oxford International Education 1 Ltd
Oxford International Education 2 Ltd
Oxford International Education 3 Ltd
Pentair UK Holdings Limited
ProAV Holdings Limited
Pulsant Acquisitions Limited
RB Luxembourg Holdings (TFFC) Ltd
Salisbury Holdings Limited
Salterns Academy Trust
Steris UK Holding Limited
Tengo (Holdings) Limited
Thrive Homes Finance PLC
Virgin Atlantic Limited
Welborne Energy LLP

April-June 2014 [80]

Affiperf Limited
Allocate Bidco Limited
Allocate Holdco Limited
Allocate Midco Limited
Allocate Topco Limited
Asteral Holdings Limited
BCA Marketplace PLC
Benecol Limited
Boing Acquisitions Limited
Boing Midco Limited
Bridge Leisure Finco Limited
Bridge Leisure Midco Limited
Bridge Leisure Topco Limited
Centre for Health and Disability Assessments
Choice Support
Console Bidco Limited
Console Midco Limited
CooperVision (UK) Holdings Ltd
Discoverie Nordic Holdings Ltd
Emerald Bidco Limited
Emerald Midco 1 Limited

Emerald Midco 2 Limited
Emerald Topco Limited
Emperor 2 Limited
Emperor 3 Limited
Falcon Coffees Limited
Fatface Group Parent Limited
Ferring Asset Management Ltd
Foundocean Group Limited
Four Coal Shipping Limited
GCP Biomass 4 Limited
GCP Rooftop Solar 5 Ltd
Game Digital PLC
GlaxoSmithKline Consumer Healthcare Holdings
Glenchamber Wind Energy Ltd
Hilton Worldwide Holding LLP
Holtzbrinck Investment Limited
International Car Wash Group Financing
International Car Wash Group Ltd.
Johnson Controls Building Efficiency UK
Kew Green (LRG1) Limited
Kew Green Group Limited
Kew Green Intermediate One Ltd
LSQ Holdco 3 Limited
Limay Drilling Rigs Limited
London Square Developments (Holdings)
Longview Holding UK 2 Limited
M & C New York Finance (UK) Ltd
MDH (Group) Limited
Mallinckrodt Enterprises UK Ltd
Masternaut Bidco Limited
McGrove Developments Limited
Mizzen Midco Limited
Mushi UK Holdings Limited
Nomad Foods BondCo PLC
Pulsant Group Holdings Limited
Pulsant Group Limited
Pulsant Parent Limited
Richstone Properties Limited
Royalton Group Holdings Ltd
Ruby Topco Limited
SF Funding Limited
SF Ground Rents Limited
SNC-Lavalin (GB) Limited
Sands Heritage Ltd
Signet UK Finance PLC
Softbox (Bidco) Limited
Softbox (Topco) Limited
Speyside Renewable Energy Finance PLC
Spicers-Officeteam Group Ltd
Storrington Equityco Limited
Tamar Energy Operating Company (One)
Travelport Global Limited
Travelport Operations Limited
Travelport Travel Commerce Platform
Vanderbilt Topco Ltd
Virgin Media Mobile Finance Ltd
Volution Group PLC
W1 London Limited
Wilton Park Developments Ltd

July-September 2014 [46]

A A Homes and Housing (Exchange Court)
Acre 1176 Limited
Attwood Academies
Blue Auto Finance Limited
Blue Auto Holdings Limited
Bridge Leisure Bidco Limited
Centrica Lake Limited
Cirrus Logic UK International Holding Co
Console Lowco Limited
GVS Prepaid Limited
GlaxoSmithKline Consumer Healthcare (Overseas)
GlaxoSmithKline Consumer Healthcare (UK) IP
GlaxoSmithKline Consumer Healthcare (UK) Trading
GlaxoSmithKline Holdings (Ireland)
Hephaestus II Limited
IAG GBS Limited
INEOS Upstream Limited
Ichnaea UK Holdings Limited
Indivior PLC
Kendallco Limited
Kew Green (LRG2) Limited
Kinedexe UK Limited
Koala Bidco Limited
Lousada Investments Limited
MHI Vestas Offshore Wind Blades UK Ltd
Mavenir Global Limited
Mitac Technology UK Ltd.
Optionis Group Limited
Optionis Limited
Pinewood MBS Lighting Limited
PizzaExpress Financing 1 PLC
PizzaExpress Financing 2 PLC
PizzaExpress Group Holdings Ltd
PizzaExpress Group Limited
Reilly JDM Holdings Limited
Renewi European Holdings Ltd
SC Osney Lane Limited
Sonepar UK Limited
Subsea 7 Investments (UK) Ltd
Sunrise UK Holdco Limited
Travel Up Group PLC
UK Acquisitions No. 6 Limited
United Living Group Limited
WSH Events Limited
Workdry International Limited
Yanfeng UK Automotive Interior Systems Co.,

October-December 2014 [88]

Ability Hotels (III) Finance Ltd
Ability Hotels (III) Group Ltd
Ability Hotels (III) UK Ltd
Ability Hotels (IV) Finance Ltd
Ability Hotels (Liverpool Plaza) Ltd
Ability Hotels (Manchester) Ltd
Afton Chemical UK LLP
Air Bidco Limited
Anesco Bidco 1 Limited
Aquila Air Traffic Management Services
Argon NPS Limited
Aspire Pharma Holdings Limited
Berkeley Two Hundred and Three Ltd
Big Yellow (Battersea) Limited
Blue Light Partnership (ASP) Newco
Bradenstoke Solar Park Limited
CAS Healthcare Properties Ltd
CDK Global Holdings (UK) Ltd
Challenger Multi Academy Trust
Clean Viking Bidco Limited
Clean Viking Holdings Limited
Colorado Bidco Limited
Colorado Holdco Limited
Colorado Midco Limited
Colorado Newco Limited
Consort Medical Finance Ltd
Cucina Fresh Finance Limited
EUSA Pharma (UK) Limited
Fawley Waterside Limited
Focusrite PLC
Fresh Direct Group Limited
GCP Green Energy 1 Limited
GCP Social Housing 1 Limited
GT NEPS (Holdings) Limited
GT NEPS Limited
GlaxoSmithKline Consumer Healthcare Finance
Hamsard 3352 Limited
Hamsard 3353 Limited
Hartford Care Group Limited
HeidelbergCement Euro I Ltd
HeidelbergCement Euro II Ltd
INEOS Finance Company 3 Ltd
Indoor Bowling Acquisitions Ltd
Kerridge Commercial Systems (Bidco)
Kerridge Commercial Systems Group
Labcorp Neon Ltd.
Longview Holding Parent UK Ltd
Luxury Travel Acquisitions Ltd
Luxury Travel Financing Ltd
Luxury Travel Holdings Limited
M & J Seafood Limited
Mondays (Topco) Limited
NPS (Holdings) Limited
Northgate Public Services Ltd
Novell UK Software Limited
Opal (Silvertown) LLP
Oval (2284) Limited
Paragon Treasury PLC
Pegasuslife Development Ltd
Pladis Foods Limited
RFC Prop Co Limited
RHP Finance PLC
Rank Hovis Milling Limited
Royale Parks Limited
SSCP Spring Topco Limited
Shimtech Industries Group Ltd
Shimtech Industries Holdco Ltd
Shimtech Industries Holdco2 Ltd
Silver Acquisition Co Limited
Southwater Property Promotion Ltd
St William Homes LLP
Stackhouse Poland Bidco Ltd
Stackhouse Poland Group Ltd
Stackhouse Poland Midco Ltd
Terrestrial Developments Ltd
Trident Acquisition Limited
Tuesdays (Midco) Limited
UMV Global Foods Co Ltd.
UMV Global Foods Holding Co Ltd.
VMFH Limited
Valour Bidco Limited
Valour Holdco Limited
Valour Midco I Limited
Valour Midco II Limited
Waterlogic Group Holdings Ltd
Waterlogic Holdings Limited
Wednesdays (Bidco) Limited
Xtrac Transmissions (Holdings) Ltd

January 2015 [18]

Blackstown Holdings Limited
Clearwater Technology Holdco Ltd
Club Company (Group) Limited
Commercial Freeholds & Investments Ltd
Convergence Pharmaceuticals Ltd
Cucina Fresh Investments Ltd
EUSA Pharma Holdco 1 (UK) Ltd
EUSA Pharma Holdco 2 (UK) Ltd
HP Inc UK Limited
Jacobs Douwe Egberts R & D GB Ltd
Kerridge Commercial Systems (Midco)
Personal Group Limited

SSL Group (UK) Limited
WL One Bidco Limited
WL One Holdco Limited
WL One Midco 1 Limited
WL One Midco 2 Limited
Windsor Learning Partnership

February 2015 [15]

Adelie Foods Bidco Limited
Ardonagh Finco PLC
Arjun Infrastructure Partners II Ltd
BIMM 1 Limited
Clearwater Technology Bidco Ltd
Custodes Midco Limited
GCP Rooftop Solar 6 PLC
Harvest Midco Limited
HeidelbergCement Euro III Ltd
Johnson Controls International Holdings
Manco South Limited
SCJ UK Finco Ltd
SSE EPM Limited
Sky Finance Europe Limited
Stiefel Consumer Healthcare (UK) Ltd

March 2015 [27]

AERL Holding Limited
Alex Brands Rocket Holdings Ltd
April Bidco Limited
April Midco Limited
April Topco Limited
BRF Invicta Limited
CH & Co Catering Group (Holdings)
CH & Co Catering Group Limited
Hilbre Holdings Limited
IZH Holdings Ltd
Inland Property Limited
Johnson Controls Holding UK Ltd
Johnson Controls-Hitachi Air Conditioning Holding (UK)
Lake Bridge International PLC
Lake International Ltd
Leo Energy Limited
PSN Holdco Limited
PizzaExpress International Holdings
Regulus Bidco Limited
Regulus Midco Limited
Regulus Topco Limited
SSCP Spring Midco 2 Limited
Sky CP Limited
Symantec Security (UK) Limited
Travelport Group Investments Ltd
Williams Trade Supplies Holdings Ltd
Willoughby (880) Limited

April 2015 [14]

Caridon Holdings LLP
Cauta Capital Limited
E & J Ground Rents No 15 Ltd
Evolution (Shinfield) LLP
Genesis Specialist Care UK Ltd
Genesis Specialist Care UK No 2 Ltd
JCHAC Europe Finco Limited
JCHAC India Holdco Limited
JCHAC UK Holdco Limited
Medequip Group Limited
Newcourt Residential (Wadhurst) Ltd
Secureworks Europe Limited
Stats UK Holdco Limited
Virgin Atlantic International Ltd

May 2015 [8]

Edgewell Personal Care UK Ltd
GCP Cardale PFI Ltd
Genesis Specialist Care Holding UK
Indoor Bowling Equity Limited
Leven Wharf Limited
Seqirus Holdings UK Limited
Seqirus Limited
Seqirus UK Limited

June 2015 [13]

Cramlington Renewable Energy Developments Hold Co
Elmwey Learning Trust
Evolution Morpeth LLP
Ferholding UK Ltd
Halamar (Chancery Lane) Ltd
Hastings Group Holdings PLC
Imperial Car Supermarkets Ltd
Linden (Biddenham) LLP
Sir Robert McAlpine (A19) Ltd
Sir Robert McAlpine Road Holdings
Q Squared Solutions Holdings Ltd
Q Squared Solutions Limited
Waingels Academies Trust

July 2015 [22]

ADA PD UK Limited
APG Cash Drawer UK, Ltd
Beardow Adams Holdings Ltd
Boorley Green LLP
CBI International Parent Ltd
CBI UK Topco Limited
CTS Metropark Limited
CeleritiFinTech Limited
Citrix R & D Limited
Cognita BondCo Parent Limited
Cognita Financing PLC
Cognita Midco Limited
Cucina French Holdings Limited
Heronswood Holdings Limited
Johnson Controls Air Conditioning (UK)
Johnson Controls Air Conditioning Investments (UK)
Newlands Girls' School
Perform Group Financing PLC
Perform Investment Limited
Perform Sports Media Limited
Royalton RS Limited
Strides Pharma Global (UK) Ltd

August 2015 [11]

Axios Bidco Limited
BAP Pharma Group Limited
Coca-Cola European Partners PLC
ESSCI Limited
ESSCI Technical Services Ltd
Thompsons (UK) Holdings Ltd
Tiger Midco 1 Limited
Tiger Midco 2 Limited
Tiger Topco Limited
Travelport International Operations
nVent International (UK) Ltd

September 2015 [21]

Aqualisa Holdings (International)
Axis Group Integrated Services Ltd
CEB Global Holdings Limited
CNM Estates (Tolworth Tower MB) Ltd
CNM Estates (Tolworth Tower MBP) Ltd
CNM Estates (Tolworth Tower SBP) Ltd
CNM Estates Holdings Limited
Cheshunt Lakeside Developments Ltd
Flexera Software Holdings Ltd
Kite Academy Trust
Mallinckrodt Pharmaceuticals Ltd
Mallinckrodt UK Finance LLP
Nuvias Group Limited
PEAC Holdings (UK) Limited
Project Farm Bidco Limited
Project Farm Topco Limited
Rackspace UK Leasing Limited
Sorbon Finance Limited
TSG Holdings (UK) Limited
Transaction Services Group Ltd
Whistl Group Holdings Limited

October 2015 [14]

AKA London Limited
Flight Centre Travel Group (European Holdings)
Galileo Global Technologies Ltd
Keltbray Group Limited
Lockheed Martin Helicopter Co Ltd
Mustard Global Limited
RWS UK Holding Co Limited
Scape Opportunities Dublin Ltd
Thornton Park (London) Limited
Trenchard Aviation Group Ltd
Trenchard Aviation Holdings 1 Ltd
Trenchard Aviation Holdings Ltd
Trenchard Aviation Limited
ViiV Healthcare Finance 2 Ltd

November 2015 [16]

Akzo Nobel Finance (2) Limited
CooperSurgical Holdings Ltd
Croudace Finance Limited
Croudace Investment Group Ltd
Croudace Trading Group Limited
Franklin UK Bidco Limited
Franklin UK Midco Limited
Garth Enterprises Partnership LLP
Guild Resources Limited
Hendy Automotive Limited
Hill of The Hermitage Limited
ITW Holdings I Limited
Kordal Limited
People Against Dirty Holdings Ltd
Riemser Pharma UK Limited
TTNG Investments Limited

December 2015 [31]

3M Asia Pacific UK Holding Ltd
Audley Group Limited
Centrica LNG UK Limited
Chaptre Finance PLC
Chaptre Investments Limited
Clean Viking Acquisition Co Ltd
Edge UK Holdings Limited
Elwy 2 Limited
Elwy 3 Limited
Hexagon Manufacturing Intelligence Management
Hystead Limited
INEOS Styrolution Financing Ltd
INEOS Styrolution Holding Ltd
ITW Holdings II Limited
ITW Holdings III Limited
ITW Holdings IV Limited
ITW Holdings V Limited

Inesa UK Limited
Johnson & Johnson UK Treasury Co Ltd
KIMS Kent Holdings Limited
LGC Science Group Holdings Ltd
The Harry Levy Group Limited
Micro Focus MHC Limited
RB (China Trading) Limited
Syneos Health International Ltd
USF International Limited
Veritas UK Holding Limited
ViiV Healthcare UK (No.4) Ltd
Wakefield Waste Holdings Ltd
Waterlogic Finance Limited
Winchester Holdings Limited

January 2016 [19]

Armatire Limited
BP Senegal Investments Limited
CTDI Repair Services Limited
Caligor Opco UK, Ltd
Canadian & Arcadia Limited
Crest A2D (Walton Court) LLP
Data Solutions 2016 Limited
Leaders Romans Group Limited
Leaders Romans Midco 2 Limited
Leaders Romans Midco Limited
Micro Focus CHC Limited
Micro Focus Midco Limited
OGF Bidco Limited
Premier Medical Holdings Ltd
RBMR Topco Limited
ViiV Healthcare Finance Ltd
ViiV Healthcare UK (No.5) Ltd
WJH Holdings Limited
Zipcar International Finance Co Ltd

February 2016 [26]

Allos Holdings Limited
BP Pipelines Tap Limited
Casebia Therapeutics Limited Liability Partnership
Citysprint (UK) Bidco Limited
Citysprint (UK) Holdings Ltd
Citysprint (UK) Midco Limited
FMP Global Bidco Limited
FMP Global Holdings Limited
Galaxy Acquisition Co 1 Ltd
Galaxy Acquisition Co 2 Ltd
Galaxy Holdco 1 Ltd
Galaxy Holdco 2 Ltd
Galvani Bioelectronics Limited
Gannett International Finance LLP
IHS Global Investments Limited
Marylebone Finco Limited
NMRN Operations
Northgate UK Holdings 1 Ltd
Northgate UK Holdings 2 Ltd
Northgate UK Holdings 3 Ltd
Northgate UK Holdings 4 Ltd
Nuffield Health Pension Trustees Ltd
PPP Capital Limited
RIF Holdings Limited
TBC Bank Group PLC
Tritoria UK Ltd

March 2016 [15]

Bolzoni Capital UK Limited
Cash Processing Solutions Ltd
Cidron Healthcare - It 3 Ltd
Exagon Industries Limited
FTR Holdings Ltd
Fourfront Holdings Limited
Independent Growth Finance Ltd
LDFA Limited
Logoplaste UK Parent Limited
Lunar 101 Limited
PDC Brands UK Limited
Richmond West Schools Trust
Ridge Hill Trading Limited
Southern Communications Group Ltd
Southern Communications Investments

April 2016 [28]

Alligent Biopharm Consulting (Europe)
B & W Acquisition Ltd
BL Bottling Holdings UK Ltd
Bowers & Wilkins Holding Ltd
Brentford Phase II LLP
Compass Group Finance No. 3 Ltd
Envision Pharma Bidco Limited
Envision Pharma Finco Limited
Envision Pharma Group Limited
Envision Pharma Midco Limited
GR Bottling Holdings UK Ltd
Galileo Holdco 1 Limited
Galileo Holdco 2 Limited
Gap Partnership Bidco Limited
Gap Partnership Group Limited
Grangette Ltd
Kimberly-Clark Intercontinental Holding
Maisonparc Ltd
Mondelez UK Finance Co Ltd
New Topco 1 Limited
Next Generation Data Infrastructure 1
Next Generation Data Infrastructure 2
Palmier Ltd
Paymentshield Services Limited
RB Mexico Investments Limited
Sea Cloud 1 Limited
WIH UK Limited
Whistler Acquisitions Limited

May 2016 [8]

Binder Bidco Limited
Binder Holdco Limited
Bottling Holdings Europe Ltd
CCEP Holdings UK Limited
Gravity Media Group Holdings Ltd
Nutrix Capital Limited
Toucan Solar Assets 1 Holdco Ltd
Trafficinvest Limited

June 2016 [19]

Aptos Solutions UK Limited
Arrow Business Communications Group
Arrow Business Communications Holdings
Bathroom Brands Group Limited
Dunmoore (West London) Limited
Simon Elvin Holdings Limited
Graduation Bidco Limited
Hamsard 3414 Limited
Hollywood Bowl Group PLC
Ichnaea UK Bidco Limited
Jupiter Midco 2 Limited
Jupiter Topco Limited
Lenovo Global Technology UK Ltd
Napsbury Limited
Old Thorns Luxury Apartments Ltd
Optegra International Limited
PJ Care Group Limited
Radlett Limited
Siemens Gamesa Renewable Energy Ltd

July 2016 [19]

Arora T5 Holdings Limited
BIMM Topco Limited
Bristow Aircraft Leasing Ltd
CPRT European Investments Ltd
Evolution (Saffron Walden) LLP
Exclaimer Group (Holdings) Ltd
Exclaimer Group Limited
GCP Programme Funding 1 Ltd
Hilton International IP Holding Ltd
IMBOLC Limited
Jupiter Midco 1 Limited
Linden (Brampton) LLP
Linden (Enfield) LLP
Linden (Northstowe) LLP
New Blue Chip Limited
PT UK Holding Limited
TF1 Limited
TH UK & Ireland Limited
Xeretec Group Limited

August 2016 [30]

Allergan Holdco UK Limited
Asahi Europe Ltd
Autosport Media UK Ltd
B & P Buyco Limited
Biffa PLC
Doctorlink Limited
GlaxoSmithKline Consumer Healthcare Finance No. 2
Global Consortium Limited
Graduation Holdco Limited
Graduation Midco Limited
Graduation Topco Limited
IHS Markit Global Funding Ltd
IHS Markit Global Limited
Johnson Controls UAE Holding Ltd.
Linden (Avery Hill) LLP
MFG Parentco Limited
Manzana Bidco Limited
Pelham Capital Real Estate Ltd
Photo-Me Limited
Platinum Acquisition Limited
Platinum Midco Limited
Platinum Newco II Limited
Platinum Topco Limited
Regard ACH Holdco Limited
Sunny Bidco Limited
Sunny Midco Limited
Sunny Topco Limited
Suntory UK Holdings Limited
Verizon UK Financing Limited
Verizon UK Holding Limited

September 2016 [24]

Aramark Japan Holdings Limited
Autodesk Holdings LLP
B & P Midco 1 Limited
B & P Midco 2 Limited
Beck & Pollitzer Limited
Broadway Malyan Employee Ownership Trustees
CF 2016 LLP
Citrix Global Holdings UK Ltd
Convatec Group PLC
Firebolt RB Holdings Limited
HFG Finance Limited
HFG Investments Limited
Hoover Ferguson Group Holdings Ltd
Hoover Ferguson Group Limited
Johnson Controls China Holding (UK)

Kirkmore Capital Limited
Lutob Investment Ltd
Andrew Page 1917 Limited
Peter Waddell Holdco Limited
Platinum Midco 2 Limited
Storm UK Holdco Limited
Toucan Solar Assets 2 Holdco Ltd
Virgin Media Senior Investments Ltd
Wartsila Voyage Holding Ltd

October 2016 [19]

Autodesk UK Holdings Limited
BE Aerospace Global Holdings Ltd
BE Aerospace International Holdings
CT Automotive Group Limited
Elysium Healthcare Holdings 2 Ltd
Elysium Healthcare Holdings 3 Ltd
ExxonMobil Chemical Investment Co Ltd
Grouse Bidco Limited
Grouse Midco Limited
Grouse Topco Limited
Krispy Kreme Holding UK Ltd
MNA Finance Limited
Morgan Finance Management Ltd
Overture Bidco Limited
Overture Midco II Limited
Overture Midco Limited
Overture Topco Limited
Rush Hair Group Limited
Trafalgar Entertainment Group Ltd

November 2016 [26]

Brand Reputation Compliance Ltd
Coats Group Finance Co Ltd
Dimension Data (UK) Investments Ltd
Dynama Solutions Ltd
Elysium Healthcare LC Limited
Family Capital Limited
Gruffalo Bidco Limited
Gruffalo Midco Limited
Gruffalo Topco Limited
ITW Holdings VI Limited
ITW Holdings VII Limited
LRH Care Homes Limited
NEP UK Film I Limited
NEP UK Film II Limited
RB Luxembourg (2016) Limited
Readypower Rail Services Finance Ltd
Readypower Rail Services Group Holdings
Readypower Rail Services Group Ltd
Renhe Sports Management Co Ltd
Sauvello Limited
South East Surrey Schools Education Trust
Syneos Health Holdings UK Ltd
Tiger Topco 1 Limited
Toucan Gen Co Limited
VS International Holdings Ltd
WSH Investments Limited

December 2016 [21]

Arkarius Bidco Limited
BP Mauritania Investments Ltd
Bamboo Topco Limited
Ensco 1212 Limited
ExxonMobil Financial Investment Co Ltd
Grandir UK Limited
Greenstone Oxford Limited
Hilton International IP Holding 2
INEOS Canada Limited
K Capital Investment Ltd
MTI Technology Group Limited
Malta Topco Limited
Meritas Group Limited
Mova Property Limited
Nuneham Estate Limited
Oairo Alliance Limited
Ordnance Building Limited
Preziosa Cruise Limited
Tech Data UK Finance Limited
Tech Data UK Resources Limited
WorleyParsons UK Finance Sub No. 2 Ltd

January 2017 [11]

A6 Audio Bidco Limited
ABL Capital Investments Ltd
Centrica Services Limited
Collins 2017 Limited
Deep Sea Atlantic (UK) Ltd
Deep Sea Stavanger (UK) Ltd
Dominvs Project Company 9 Ltd
Ensco 1214 Limited
Entco Situla Holding Ltd
Geting Capital Limited
Meritas Group Holdings Limited

February 2017 [23]

Asahi Breweries Europe Ltd
Audio UK 2 Limited
Audio UK 3 Limited
Audiotonix Group Limited
Consolidated Timber Holdings Group
Deneep Limited
GCP RIW Holdings Limited
GD UK Holdings, Ltd
Greenshields JCB Holdings Ltd
JRL Property Holdings Limited
M New Holdings Limited
Maple Topco Limited
Mapleco1 Ltd
Mermaid UK Holdco Limited
RMS Holdco Limited
Salutem LD Bidco Limited
TEG Holdings Limited
TIM Intermediateco Limited
Tech Data Holding Limited
Tech Data UK Finance Partner Ltd
Tim Bidco 1 Limited
Tim Holdco Limited
Tim Midco Limited

March 2017 [15]

HSH Hotels (2017) Limited
Hurricane (Whirlwind) Limited
Hurricane GLA Limited
Hurricane Holdings Limited
INEOS FPS Limited
LSQ (Crimscott Street) Holdings Ltd
Leeu London Limited
Legolas Debt Holdco Limited
MJ UK Holdings Limited
Partridge of Hampshire Holdings Ltd
Rank Digital Holdings Limited
William Reed Group Ltd
Ten Entertainment Group PLC
Vivid Topco Ltd
Whitehill & Bordon Development Company Phase 1A

April 2017 [16]

Anesco Acquisitionco Limited
CPL Bidco Limited
CPL Topco Limited
Cyberfort Bidco Limited
European Investments (Cornwall) Holdings
Johnson Controls China Investment (UK)
McLaren Group Limited
Minster Care Group Limited
Nibgreen
SHOO 802AA Limited
SNC-Lavalin (GB) Holdings Ltd
Search Consultancy Acquisition Ltd
Search Consultancy Topco Ltd
Shilton Bidco Limited
Shilton Holdco Limited
Silicon Storage Technology Ltd

May 2017

Cyberfort Group Limited
Linden Wates (Royston) LLP
MJN International Holdings (UK), Ltd.

June 2017 [13]

Adare International Holdings Ltd
Anno 2017 Joint Holding (UK) Ltd
GCP Rooftop Solar Finance PLC
GH Equity UK Limited
Henley Camland Ebbsfleet 801H Ltd
LQAL UK Limited
Manitowoc Crane Group (UK) Subco Ltd
McLaren Finance PLC
Nextpharma UK Topco Limited
PKA WLWF Holding (UK) Limited
Red Funnel Limited
Specsavers UK Holdings Limited
Tax Systems Holdings Limited

July 2017 [6]

ATP Media Holdings Limited
Bidvest Group (UK) Limited
Bidvest Services Group (UK) Ltd
Broadleaf Park LLP
HH Global Group Limited
Stoneham Park Developments LLP

August 2017

ESPUG Finance Limited
Onix Investments UK Ltd
PFC Property Ltd

September 2017 [5]

FRC Star Group Bidco Limited
FRC Star Group Holdings Ltd
ROC Transformation (Corporate) Ltd
ROC Transformation (Holdings) Ltd
Sabre Insurance Group PLC

October 2017

Bathroom Brands Limited
Belron Finance Issuer Limited
Belron Lending UK Limited
Tates of Sussex Limited

November 2017

Osborne Group Holdings Ltd
Pinewood Finco PLC

December 2017

Galaxy Group Bidco Limited
Ginger Bidco Limited
Ginger Midco Limited
Ginger Topco Limited

This page is intentionally left blank

Company Profiles

.Big Yellow Self Storage Company Limited
Incorporated: 30 June 2004 *Employees:* 335
Net Worth: £431,592,992 *Total Assets:* £626,955,008
Registered Office: 2 The Deans, Bridge Road, Bagshot, Surrey, GU19 5AT
Activities: Activities of real estate investment trusts
Parent: Big Yellow Group PLC
Officers: Shauna Louise Beavis, Secretary; James Ernest Gibson [1960] Director; Adrian Charles Jonathan Lee [1965] Director; John Richard Trotman [1977] Director/Chartered Accountant; Nicholas John Vetch [1961] Director

103-105 Bath Road Limited
Incorporated: 21 October 2010
Net Worth: £15,067,000 *Total Assets:* £36,119,000
Registered Office: 103-105 Bath Road, Slough, Berks, SL1 3UH
Activities: Non-trading company
Parent: Reckitt Benckiser PLC
Officers: Christine Anne-Marie Logan, Secretary; Richard Mark Greensmith [1973] Group Tax Director; Jonathan Timmis [1975] Finance Director

123-Reg Limited
Incorporated: 7 December 2004 *Employees:* 200
Previous: Webfusion Limited
Net Worth: £340,713,984 *Total Assets:* £388,724,000
Registered Office: 5th Floor, The Shipping Building, Old Vinyl Factory, 252-254 Blyth Road, Hayes, Middlesex, UB3 1HA
Activities: Data processing, hosting and related activities
Parent: Host Europe Limited
Officers: Richard Anthony Winslow [1979] Director; Jonathan Ying Kit Wong [1976] Director

1509 Group
Incorporated: 8 November 2000 *Employees:* 183
Previous: The Royal Grammar School, Guildford
Net Worth: £36,633,680 *Total Assets:* £45,072,384
Registered Office: Royal Grammar School, High Street, Guildford, Surrey, GU1 3BB
Activities: Primary education
Officers: Robert Anthony Ukiah, Secretary; Clive Durac Barnett [1949] Director/Educational Consultant; Robert Lloyd Cotton [1958] Director/Minister of Religion; Sarah Kathleen Creedy [1963] Director; Christopher Allan Critchlow [1951] Director/Circuit Judge; Patrick William Fell [1957] Director/Accountant; Simon George Stanford George Gimson [1961] Director/Consultant; Michael George Finnimore Parsons [1946] Director/Mayor; Dr Henry James Pearson [1955] Director; Peter Graham Peel [1948] Director/Chartered Accountant

1948 Group Limited
Incorporated: 12 February 1999 *Employees:* 174
Net Worth: £10,529,983 *Total Assets:* £24,381,192
Registered Office: Henwood House, Henwood, Ashford, Kent, TN24 8DH
Activities: Other business support service activities n.e.c.
Shareholders: Leslie John Ray; Lorraine Winifred Ray
Officers: Leslie John Ray, Secretary/Director; Leslie John Ray [1948] Director; Lorraine Winifred Ray [1951] Director/Secretary; Spencer Ray [1974] Director; Wesley Ray [1977] Director

3663 Transport Limited
Incorporated: 30 June 1948 *Employees:* 1,349
Net Worth: £29,763,000 *Total Assets:* £63,074,000
Registered Office: 814 Leigh Road, Slough, SL1 4BD
Activities: Other transportation support activities
Parent: Bid Corporation Limited
Officers: Thamer Hamandi, Secretary; Andrew Mark Selley [1965] Director; Norman James Wemyss [1960] Director

3D European Holdings Limited
Incorporated: 18 September 1990
Net Worth: £90,965,000 *Total Assets:* £121,134,000
Registered Office: Mark House, Mark Road, Hemel Hempstead, Herts, HP2 7UA
Activities: Activities of head offices
Parent: 3D Systems Corporation
Officers: David James Langfield, Secretary; Andrew Johnson [1974] Director/Legal [American]; David James Langfield [1974] Finance Director

3D Systems Europe Limited
Incorporated: 2 April 2001 *Employees:* 119
Net Worth: £17,942,000 *Total Assets:* £27,130,000
Registered Office: Mark House, Mark Road, Hemel Hempstead, Herts, HP2 7UA
Activities: Wholesale of other machinery and equipment
Officers: David James Langfield, Secretary; Andrew Johnson [1974] Director/Legal [American]; David James Langfield [1974] Finance Director

3M Asia Pacific UK Holding Ltd
Incorporated: 8 December 2015
Net Worth: £987,586,176 *Total Assets:* £988,356,800
Registered Office: 3M Centre, Cain Road, Bracknell, Berks, RG12 8HT
Activities: Activities of other holding companies n.e.c.
Parent: 3M Intermediate Acquisitions B.V.
Officers: Ian Richard Brown, Secretary; Sarah Mary Grauze [1966] Director/Treasurer and Vice-President, Finance [American]; Jed Larkin [1970] Director/Vice President, Tax and Real Estate [American]; Mohammad Irfan Malik [1965] Director [Pakistani]; Simla Semerciyan [1973] Director/Finance Manager [Turkish]

3M Products Limited
Incorporated: 18 July 1973
Net Worth: £123,478,000 *Total Assets:* £144,572,000
Registered Office: 3M Centre, Cain Road, Bracknell, Berks, RG12 8HT
Activities: Activities of other holding companies n.e.c.
Parent: 3M UK Holdings Limited
Officers: Ian Richard Brown, Secretary; David James Ashley [1968] Director/General Counsel; David John Pawson [1962] Director/Human Resource Leader [Canadian]; Simla Semerciyan [1973] Director/Finance Manager [Turkish]

3M UK Holdings Limited
Incorporated: 23 August 1929
Net Worth: £332,238,016 *Total Assets:* £358,096,992
Registered Office: 3M Centre, Cain Road, Bracknell, Berks, RG12 8HT
Activities: Activities of other holding companies n.e.c.
Officers: Ian Richard Brown, Secretary; David James Ashley [1968] Director/General Counsel; James Raymond Grigg [1964] Director/Manufacturing Operations Leader; Mohammad Irfan Malik [1965] Director [Pakistani]; David John Pawson [1962] Director/Human Resource Leader [Canadian]; Simla Semerciyan [1973] Director/Finance Manager [Turkish]

3M United Kingdom Public Limited Company
Incorporated: 17 July 1973 *Employees:* 2,427
Net Worth: £399,304,000 *Total Assets:* £973,875,968
Registered Office: 3M Centre, Cain Road, Bracknell, Berks, RG12 8HT
Activities: Manufacture of paints, varnishes and similar coatings, mastics and sealants
Parent: 3M Products Limited
Officers: Ian Richard Brown, Secretary; James Raymond Grigg [1964] Director/Manufacturing Operations Leader; Mohammad Irfan Malik [1965] Director [Pakistani]; David John Pawson [1962] Director/Human Resource Leader [Canadian]; Simla Semerciyan [1973] Director/Finance Manager [Turkish]

3SE (Barnsley, Doncaster & Rotherham) Limited
Incorporated: 24 October 2011
Net Worth Deficit: £9,094,000 *Total Assets:* £70,899,000
Registered Office: Dunedin House, Auckland Park, Mount Farm, Milton Keynes, Bucks, MK1 1BU
Activities: Other service activities n.e.c.
Parent: 3SE (Barnsley, Doncaster & Rotherham) Holdings Limited
Officers: Philip Bernard Griffin-Smith, Secretary; Alistair Daniel Brookes [1976] Director; Ashley Comerford [1978] Director [Irish]; Adam Nathaniel Richford [1976] Director; Jonathan James Sime [1979] Director

3T Bros Limited
Incorporated: 20 November 1997
Net Worth: £20,281,226 *Total Assets:* £20,283,026
Registered Office: Aspen House, 13 Highpoint Business Village, Henwood, Ashford, Kent, TN24 8DH
Activities: Activities of other holding companies n.e.c.
Parent: WCR Group Limited
Officers: Kevin David Saunby, Secretary; Anthony Record [1939] Director; William Jon Record [1966] Director

5 Dimensions Trust
Incorporated: 7 April 2011 *Employees:* 206
Previous: Shenley Brook End School
Net Worth: £30,176,012 *Total Assets:* £33,572,072
Registered Office: Shenley Brook End School, Walbank Grove, Shenley Brook End, Milton Keynes, Bucks, MK5 7ZT
Activities: General secondary education
Officers: Ian Peter Clarkson [1954] Director/Chairman; Malcolm Hugh Dobell [1951] Director; Nicholas John Dredge [1959] Director; Peter John Gibson Horrocks [1959] Director/Consultant; Rebecca Jayne Howell [1974] Director/Senior Education Consultant; Dr Huw Christopher Humphreys [1959] Director/Educational Researcher; Roger Stuart Malpass [1960] Director/Training and Development; Glen David Martin [1961] Director/Principal; Jean Marion Nicholas [1944] Director/Retired Accountant; Dr John Graham Arthur Pembery [1958] Director; Darren Mark Thomas [1970] Director/Financial Analyst; Dr Margaret Elizabeth Wyke [1953] Director/Retired

55VS No 2 Limited
Incorporated: 13 November 2013
Net Worth: £8,366,763 *Total Assets:* £74,521,776
Registered Office: Markerstudy House, 45 Westerham Road, Bessels Green, Sevenoaks, Kent, TN13 2QB
Activities: Other business support service activities n.e.c.
Parent: 55VS No1 Limited
Officers: Christopher James Payne, Secretary; Keith John Barber [1974] Director; Gary Humphreys [1965] Director; Kevin Ronald Spencer [1965] Director

8x8 UK Investments Limited
Incorporated: 6 November 2013
Net Worth: £42,589,416 *Total Assets:* £42,604,680
Registered Office: Oxford House, Bell Business Park, Aylesbury, Bucks, HP19 8JR
Activities: Activities of other holding companies n.e.c.
Parent: 8x8, Inc
Officers: Edward Alec Kemp, Secretary; Mary Ellen Genovese [1959] Director/Chief Financial Officer [American]; Bryan R Martin [1967] Director/Chief Technology Officer [American]; Vikram Verma [1964] Director/Chief Executive Officer [American]

A A Homes and Housing (Exchange Court) Limited
Incorporated: 15 August 2014
Net Worth: £12,000,000 *Total Assets:* £22,000,000
Registered Office: The Lodge, Coombe Road, Croydon, Surrey, CR0 5RD
Activities: Development of building projects
Officers: Dr Anwar Rauf Ansari [1957] Director

A A Homes and Housing Ltd
Incorporated: 13 May 1994 *Employees:* 1
Net Worth: £112,040,520 *Total Assets:* £175,096,832
Registered Office: The Lodge, Coombe Road, Croydon, Surrey, CR0 5RD
Activities: Other letting and operating of own or leased real estate
Officers: Sabeen Ansari, Secretary; Dr Anwar Rauf Ansari [1957] Director/Doctor

A.C. Lighting (Holdings) Limited
Incorporated: 16 August 2002 *Employees:* 280
Net Worth: £32,245,020 *Total Assets:* £52,121,268
Registered Office: Centauri House, Hillbottom Road, Sands Industrial Estate, High Wycombe, Bucks, HP12 4HQ
Activities: Activities of head offices
Major Shareholder: David Arthur Leggett
Officers: Phillip Robert Capstick, Secretary; David Arthur Leggett [1953] Director

A.G. Thames Holdings Limited
Incorporated: 19 August 1970 *Employees:* 462
Net Worth: £37,722,000 *Total Assets:* £88,771,000
Registered Office: Thames House, Thames Road, Crayford, Kent, DA1 4QP
Activities: Wholesale of fruit and vegetables
Major Shareholder: Leon Aichen
Officers: Christopher Oakley, Secretary; David Alex Aichen [1969] Director; Gwendolyn Ethel Aichen [1927] Director; Leon Aichen [1941] Director; Gary Raymond Linsell [1970] Managing Director; Christopher Richard Oakley [1963] Finance Director; John Walter Sutcliffe [1950] Director

A.N.A. Aviation Group Holdings Ltd
Incorporated: 2 September 2010 *Employees:* 168
Net Worth: £15,596,706 *Total Assets:* £39,029,508
Registered Office: First Floor, Unit A2 Windsor Place, Faraday Road, Crawley, W Sussex, RH10 9TF
Activities: Other transportation support activities
Parent: Network Aviation Group Ltd
Officers: Andrew Michael Ballard, Secretary; Andrew Michael Ballard [1983] Director; Andrew Jeremy King [1953] Director; Andrew Graham Leslie [1952] Director

A24 Group Limited
Incorporated: 11 October 1996 *Employees:* 355
Net Worth: £50,737,968 *Total Assets:* £67,204,384
Registered Office: 92-96 Lind Road, Sutton, Surrey, SM1 4PL
Activities: Temporary employment agency activities
Major Shareholder: Penelope Marion Streeter
Officers: Nishma Patel, Secretary; Charles Louis Rees [1960] Director/Chartered Accountant; Penelope Marion Streeter [1967] Director

A6 Audio Bidco Limited
Incorporated: 19 January 2017 *Employees:* 6
Net Worth: £166,402,000 *Total Assets:* £395,585,984
Registered Office: Unit 10 Silverglade Business Park, Leatherhead Road, Chessington, Surrey, KT9 2QL
Activities: Activities of other holding companies n.e.c.
Parent: Audio UK 3 Limited
Officers: Francois de Mitry, Secretary; James Barton [1970] Director; Michael Beetz [1982] Investor, Associate Director [German]; Helen Mary Culleton [1964] Director; Francois de Mitry [1966] Director/Investor, Partner [Luxembourger]; Stephane Epin [1978] Director/Investor, Partner [French]; James David Gordon [1972] Director

AA Acquisition Co Limited
Incorporated: 19 January 2004
Net Worth: £885,200,000 *Total Assets:* £1,118,599,936
Registered Office: Fanum House, Basing View, Basingstoke, Hants, RG21 4EA
Activities: Activities of head offices
Parent: AA Intermediate Co Limited
Officers: Nadia Hoosen, Secretary; Dr Martin Andrew Clarke [1955] Executive Director; Gillian Pritchard [1975] Director/Head of Finance; Mark William Strickland [1962] Finance Director

AA Brand Management Limited
Incorporated: 10 July 2013
Net Worth: £596,000,000 *Total Assets:* £1,322,200,064
Registered Office: Fanum House, Basing View, Basingstoke, Hants, RG21 4EA
Activities: Activities of patent and copyright agents; other legal activities n.e.c.
Parent: Automobile Association Developments Limited
Officers: Nadia Hoosen, Secretary; Dr Martin Andrew Clarke [1955] Executive Director; Gillian Pritchard [1975] Director/Head of Finance; Mark William Strickland [1962] Finance Director

AA Corporation Limited
Incorporated: 24 June 1999
Net Worth: £1,643,000,064 *Total Assets:* £2,780,499,968
Registered Office: Fanum House, Basing View, Basingstoke, Hants, RG21 4EA
Activities: Activities of head offices
Parent: AA Senior Co Limited
Officers: Nadia Hoosen, Secretary; Simon John Breakwell [1965] Director; Dr Martin Andrew Clarke [1955] Executive Director; Gillian Pritchard [1975] Director/Head of Finance

AA Financial Services Limited
Incorporated: 2 August 1967
Net Worth: £21,469,000 *Total Assets:* £23,192,000
Registered Office: Fanum House, Basing View, Basingstoke, Hants, RG21 4EA
Activities: Financial intermediation not elsewhere classified
Parent: Automobile Association Insurance Services Holdings Limited
Officers: Nadia Hoosen, Secretary; Lewis David Miles [1981] Director/Head of Finance Financial Services; David Searle [1979] Director

AA Intermediate Co Limited
Incorporated: 9 June 2004 *Employees:* 7,177
Net Worth Deficit: £643,000,000 *Total Assets:* £2,905,999,872
Registered Office: Fanum House, Basing View, Basingstoke, Hants, RG21 4EA
Activities: Activities of head offices
Parent: AA Mid Co Limited
Officers: Nadia Hoosen, Secretary; Dr Martin Andrew Clarke [1955] Executive Director; Gillian Pritchard [1975] Director/Head of Finance; Mark William Strickland [1962] Finance Director

AA Mid Co Limited
Incorporated: 30 March 2004
Net Worth: £1,435,200,000 *Total Assets:* £4,417,800,192
Registered Office: Fanum House, Basing View, Basingstoke, Hants, RG21 4EA
Activities: Activities of head offices
Parent: AA PLC
Officers: Nadia Hoosen, Secretary; Dr Martin Andrew Clarke [1955] Executive Director; Gillian Pritchard [1975] Director/Head of Finance; Mark William Strickland [1962] Finance Director

AA PLC
Incorporated: 9 June 2004 *Employees:* 7,221
Net Worth Deficit: £1,755,000,064 *Total Assets:* £1,827,000,064
Registered Office: Fanum House, Basing View, Basingstoke, Hants, RG21 4EA
Activities: Activities of other holding companies n.e.c.
Officers: Nadia Hoosen, Secretary; Stephen David Barber [1952] Director/Chartered Accountant; Andrew Mark Blowers [1960] Director; Simon John Breakwell [1965] Director/Chief Executive Officer; Mark David Brooker [1971] Director; Dr Martin Andrew Clarke [1955] Executive Director; John Leslie Leach [1948] Director; Cathryn Elizabeth Riley [1962] Director; Cathryn Elizabeth Riley [1962] Director; Suzanne Dorothy Williams [1967] Director

AA Senior Co Limited
Incorporated: 29 December 2005
Net Worth: £410,000,000 *Total Assets:* £6,400,699,904
Registered Office: Fanum House, Basing View, Basingstoke, Hants, RG21 4EA
Activities: Activities of head offices
Parent: AA Acquisition Co Limited
Officers: Nadia Hoosen, Secretary; Dr Martin Andrew Clarke [1955] Executive Director; Gillian Pritchard [1975] Director/Head of Finance; Mark William Strickland [1962] Finance Director

AA Underwriting Limited
Incorporated: 8 August 1996
Net Worth: £27,956,000 *Total Assets:* £27,975,000
Registered Office: Fanum House, Basing View, Basingstoke, Hants, RG21 4EA
Activities: Non-life insurance
Parent: Automobile Association Holdings Limited
Officers: Nadia Hoosen, Secretary; Jay Stewart [1980] Director/Actuary; Robert Warner [1976] Director/Actuary

AB InBev Harmony Limited
Incorporated: 16 November 2012
Previous: Sabmiller Harmony Limited
Net Worth: £691,126,720 *Total Assets:* £693,750,656
Registered Office: Ab InBev House, Church Street West, Woking, Surrey, GU21 6HT
Activities: Activities of other holding companies n.e.c.
Parent: AB InBev Harmony Holdings Limited
Officers: Joanne Elizabeth Dobbie [1971] Legal Director; Michelle Kocaoglu [1976] Tax Director; Mehmet Hursit Zorlu [1959] Director [Turkish]

AB InBev International Brands Limited
Incorporated: 18 July 2005
Previous: Sabmiller International Brands Limited
Net Worth: £188,827,824 *Total Assets:* £192,296,464
Registered Office: Ab InBev House, Church Street West, Woking, Surrey, GU21 6HT
Activities: Other business support service activities n.e.c.
Parent: AB InBev Holdings Limited
Officers: Kevin Jean-Frederic Douws [1982] Director [Belgian]; Sibil Jiang [1990] Director [Australian]; Stephen John Turner [1966] Director/Accountant

Abaris Holdings Limited
Incorporated: 19 April 1974 *Employees:* 565
Net Worth: £30,998,000 *Total Assets:* £66,599,000
Registered Office: Chalfont House, Oxford Road, Denham, Bucks, UB9 4DX
Activities: Activities of head offices
Parent: Walker Greenbank PLC
Officers: Caroline Geary, Secretary; Michael David Gant [1969] Director; Christopher Charles Bevan Rogers [1960] Director; Terry George Stannard [1950] Director/Consultant

The Abbey School, Reading
Incorporated: 31 January 1914 *Employees:* 343
Net Worth: £15,148,256 *Total Assets:* £20,318,562
Registered Office: 17 Kendrick Road, Reading, Berks, RG1 5DZ
Activities: General secondary education
Officers: Juliet Anderson [1967] Director/Head of CPD; Sanya Elizabeth Burgess [1991] Director/Newspaper Editor; Susan Lesley Colebrook [1947] Director/Retired; Julie Lydon Cornell [1956] Director/Volunteer; Simon Mark Dimmick [1952] Director/Lawyer; Michael Emmanuel [1967] Director/Restaurateur; Elizabeth Ann Harrison [1949] Director/Civil Service; Dr Ian Charles Kemp [1948] Director/General Practitioner; Dr Carole Frances Print [1946] Director/Lecturer; Jeremy Richard Sheehan [1964] Director/Telecoms Executive; Colin Geoffrey Singer [1955] Director/Actuary; Paramjit Singh Uppal [1967] Director/Entrepreneur; Elizabeth Hynd West [1961] Director/Solicitor; David Nigel Williams [1960] Director/Retired Headteacher

Abbott (UK) Finance Limited
Incorporated: 17 March 2000
Net Worth: £192,260,992 *Total Assets:* £192,264,000
Registered Office: Abbott House, Vanwall Business Park, Vanwall Road, Maidenhead, Berks, SL6 4XE
Activities: Activities of financial services holding companies
Parent: Abbott UK Holdings Ltd
Officers: Kevan Gogay, Secretary; Neil Harris [1974] Director/General Manager; Georgios Mountrichas [1977] Director/General Manager [Greek]; Brian Yoor [1969] Director/Business Executive [American]

Abbott (UK) Holdings Limited
Incorporated: 23 March 1999
Net Worth Deficit: £1,294,000 *Total Assets:* £250,420,000
Registered Office: Abbott House, Vanwall Business Park, Vanwall Road, Maidenhead, Berks, SL6 4XE
Activities: Activities of other holding companies n.e.c.
Parent: Abbott Equity Holdings Unlimited
Officers: Kevan Gogay, Secretary; Neil Harris [1974] Director/General Manager; Georgios Mountrichas [1977] Director/General Manager [Greek]; Brian Yoor [1969] Director/Business Executive [American]

Abbott Asia Holdings Limited
Incorporated: 22 February 2001
Net Worth: £1,128,425,984 *Total Assets:* £1,189,374,976
Registered Office: Abbott House, Vanwall Business Park, Vanwall Road, Maidenhead, Berks, SL6 4XE
Activities: Activities of other holding companies n.e.c.
Parent: Abbott Asia Investments Ltd
Officers: Kevan Gogay, Secretary; Neil Harris [1974] Director/General Manager; Georgios Mountrichas [1977] Director/General Manager [Greek]; Brian Yoor [1969] Director/Business Executive [American]

Abbott Asia Investments Limited
Incorporated: 7 September 2005
Net Worth: £1,312,792,064 *Total Assets:* £1,312,792,064
Registered Office: Abbott House, Vanwall Business Park, Vanwall Road, Maidenhead, Berks, SL6 4XE
Activities: Activities of other holding companies n.e.c.
Shareholders: Abbott Laboratories; Abbott Laboratories Inc.
Officers: Kevan Gogay, Secretary; Neil Harris [1974] Director/General Manager; Georgios Mountrichas [1977] Director/General Manager [Greek]; Brian Yoor [1969] Director/Business Executive [American]

Abbott Capital India Limited
Incorporated: 22 February 2001
Net Worth: £77,011,000 *Total Assets:* £94,710,000
Registered Office: Abbott House, Vanwall Business Park, Vanwall Road, Maidenhead, Berks, SL6 4XE
Activities: Activities of other holding companies n.e.c.
Parent: Abbott Asia Investments Ltd
Officers: Kevan Gogay, Secretary; Neil Harris [1974] Director/General Manager; Georgios Mountrichas [1977] Director/General Manager [Greek]; Brian Yoor [1969] Director/Business Executive [American]

Abbott Equity Holdings Unlimited
Incorporated: 15 February 2001
Net Worth: £109,871,000 *Total Assets:* £1,032,654,016
Registered Office: Abbott House, Vanwall Business Park, Vanwall Road, Maidenhead, Berks, SL6 4XE
Activities: Activities of other holding companies n.e.c.
Shareholders: Abbott Laboratories; Abbott Laboratories Inc.
Officers: Kevan Gogay, Secretary; Neil Harris [1974] Director/General Manager; Georgios Mountrichas [1977] Director/General Manager [Greek]; Brian Yoor [1969] Director/Business Executive [American]

Abbott Healthcare Products Ltd
Incorporated: 5 March 1969 *Employees:* 18
Net Worth: £40,318,000 *Total Assets:* £42,670,000
Registered Office: Abbott House, Vanwall Business Park, Vanwall Road, Maidenhead, Berks, SL6 4XE
Activities: Wholesale of pharmaceutical goods
Shareholders: Abbott Laboratories Inc.; Abbott Laboratories
Officers: Kevan Gogay, Secretary; Neil Harris [1974] Director/General Manager; Georgios Mountrichas [1977] Director/General Manager [Greek]; Brian Yoor [1969] Director/Business Executive [American]

Abbott Laboratories Limited
Incorporated: 23 June 1937 *Employees:* 516
Net Worth: £224,132,000 *Total Assets:* £428,572,000
Registered Office: Abbott House, Vanwall Business Park, Vanwall Road, Maidenhead, Berks, SL6 4XE
Activities: Wholesale of pharmaceutical goods
Parent: Abbott UK Holdings Limited
Officers: Kevan Gogay, Secretary; Neil Harris [1974] Director/General Manager; Georgios Mountrichas [1977] Director/General Manager [Greek]; Brian Yoor [1969] Director/Business Executive [American]

AbbVie Investments Limited
Incorporated: 17 October 1994
Net Worth: £122,921,104 *Total Assets:* £123,065,248
Registered Office: AbbVie House, Vanwall Business Park, Vanwall Road, Maidenhead, Berks, SL6 4UB
Activities: Activities of other holding companies n.e.c.
Parent: AbbVie Inc.
Officers: Kyle Poots, Secretary; Jerome Stephane Bouyer [1969] Director/Business Executive [French]; William Joseph Chase [1967] Director/Chief Financial Officer [American]; Gwenan Mair White [1969] UK Director of Communications

AbbVie Ltd
Incorporated: 23 March 2012 *Employees:* 647
Net Worth: £287,118,016 *Total Assets:* £398,508,992
Registered Office: AbbVie House, Vanwall Business Park, Vanwall Road, Maidenhead, Berks, SL6 4UB
Activities: Wholesale of pharmaceutical goods
Parent: AbbVie Inc.
Officers: Kyle Alexander Poots, Secretary; Jerome Stephane Bouyer [1969] Director/Business Executive [French]; William Joseph Chase [1967] Director [American]; Gwenan Mair White [1969] Director of Communications

ABC Drug Stores Limited
Incorporated: 10 June 1993 *Employees:* 185
Net Worth Deficit: £1,440,215 *Total Assets:* £41,183,192
Registered Office: 2 Peterwood Way, Croydon, Surrey, CR0 4UQ
Activities: Dispensing chemist in specialised stores
Parent: Healthcare Drugstores Limited
Officers: Ameetkumar Patel, Secretary; Dr Caroline Parkhurst [1965] Director/Pharmacist; Heena Patel [1963] Finance Director; Jayanti Chimanbhai Patel Junior [1984] Director

Abertis Motorways UK Limited
Incorporated: 13 April 1995
Net Worth: £18,298,856 *Total Assets:* £26,056,128
Registered Office: Moorcrofts LLP, Thames House, Mere Park, Dedmere Road, Marlow, Bucks, SL7 1PB
Activities: Other business support service activities n.e.c.
Parent: Abertis Infraestructuras S.A
Officers: Virginia Navarro Virgos, Secretary; Francisco Jose Aljaro Navarro [1961] Director/Chief Financial Officer [Spanish]; Victor Ensenat Coe [1974] Director/Planning Manager Abertis [Spanish]; Javier Carol Vilarasau [1962] Director [Spanish]; Virginia Navarro Virgos [1982] Director/Lawyer [Spanish]

ABHL Digital Limited
Incorporated: 1 April 1998
Net Worth: £49,830,000 *Total Assets:* £50,468,000
Registered Office: Crawley Court, Winchester, Hants, SO21 2QA
Activities: Activities of head offices
Parent: Arqiva UK Broadcast Holdings Limited
Officers: Jeremy Mavor, Secretary; Elizabeth Jane Aikman [1965] Director; Simon Piers Beresford-Wylie [1958] Director; Paul Graham Stratton [1959] Director/Accountant

Ability Developments Limited
Incorporated: 19 November 1996 *Employees:* 9
Net Worth: £62,655,208 *Total Assets:* £70,342,472
Registered Office: Hilton London, Syon Park, London Road, Brentford, Middlesex, TW8 8JF
Activities: Development of building projects
Officers: Juin Yong Chin, Secretary; Andreas Costas Panayiotou [1966] Director

Ability Hotels (Cambridge) Limited
Incorporated: 5 November 2007 *Employees:* 83
Net Worth: £31,175,140 *Total Assets:* £80,440,672
Registered Office: Hilton London, Syon Park, London Road, Brentford, Middlesex, TW8 8JF
Activities: Hotels and similar accommodation
Parent: Ability Hotels (Luton) Limited
Officers: Juin Yong Chin, Secretary; Andreas Costas Panayiotou [1966] Director

Ability Hotels (Dunblane) Limited
Incorporated: 5 November 2007 *Employees:* 201
Net Worth Deficit: £12,345,912 *Total Assets:* £24,052,766
Registered Office: Hilton London, Syon Park, London Road, Brentford, Middlesex, TW8 8JF
Activities: Hotels and similar accommodation
Parent: Ability Hotels (III) Finance Limited
Officers: Juin Yong Chin, Secretary; Andreas Costas Panayiotou [1966] Director

Ability Hotels (III) Finance Limited
Incorporated: 24 November 2014
Net Worth Deficit: £422,095 *Total Assets:* £89,742,664
Registered Office: Hilton London, Syon Park, London Road, Brentford, Middlesex, TW8 8JF
Activities: Activities of other holding companies n.e.c.
Parent: Ability Hotels (III) UK Limited
Officers: Juin Yong Chin, Secretary; Andreas Costas Panayiotou [1966] Director

Ability Hotels (III) Group Limited
Incorporated: 24 November 2014
Net Worth: £3,043,469 *Total Assets:* £61,687,668
Registered Office: Hilton London, Syon Park, London Road, Brentford, Middlesex, TW8 8JF
Activities: Activities of other holding companies n.e.c.
Officers: Juin Yong Chin, Secretary; Andreas Costas Panayiotou [1966] Director

Ability Hotels (III) UK Limited
Incorporated: 24 November 2014
Net Worth: £2,905,710 *Total Assets:* £59,399,856
Registered Office: Hilton London, Syon Park, London Road, Brentford, Middlesex, TW8 8JF
Activities: Activities of other holding companies n.e.c.
Parent: Ability Hotels (III) Holdings Limited
Officers: Juin Yong Chin, Secretary; Andreas Costas Panayiotou [1966] Director

Ability Hotels (IV) Finance Limited
Incorporated: 1 December 2014
Net Worth Deficit: £748,245 *Total Assets:* £55,695,048
Registered Office: Hilton London, Syon Park, London Road, Brentford, Middlesex, TW8 8JF
Activities: Activities of other holding companies n.e.c.
Parent: Ability Hotels (IV) UK Limited
Officers: Juin Yong Chin, Secretary; Andreas Costas Panayiotou [1966] Director

Ability Hotels (Liverpool Plaza) Limited
Incorporated: 18 December 2014
Net Worth: £7,841,540 *Total Assets:* £24,713,962
Registered Office: Hilton London, Syon Park, London Road, Brentford, Middlesex, TW8 8JF
Activities: Other letting and operating of own or leased real estate
Parent: Ability Hotels (IV) Finance Limited
Officers: Juin Yong Chin, Secretary; Andreas Costas Panayiotou [1966] Director/Property Developer

Ability Hotels (Liverpool) Limited
Incorporated: 25 June 2007 *Employees:* 192
Net Worth: £9,165,320 *Total Assets:* £68,349,192
Registered Office: Hilton London, Syon Park, London Road, Brentford, Middlesex, TW8 8JF
Activities: Hotels and similar accommodation
Parent: Ability Hotels (III) Finance Limited
Officers: Juin Yong Chin, Secretary; Andreas Costas Panayiotou [1966] Director

Ability Hotels (Luton Inn) Limited
Incorporated: 26 January 2005 *Employees:* 32
Net Worth: £9,631,122 *Total Assets:* £26,448,556
Registered Office: Hilton London, Syon Park, London Road, Brentford, Middlesex, TW8 8JF
Activities: Development of building projects
Parent: Ability Hotels (Luton) Limited
Officers: Juin Yong Chin, Secretary; Andreas Costas Panayiotou [1966] Director

Ability Hotels (Luton) Limited
Incorporated: 9 May 2008
Net Worth Deficit: £6,667,929 *Total Assets:* £37,286,244
Registered Office: Hilton London, Syon Park, London Road, Brentford, Middlesex, TW8 8JF
Activities: Activities of other holding companies n.e.c.
Parent: Ability Hotels (Luton) Holdings Limited
Officers: Juin Yong Chin, Secretary; Andreas Costas Panayiotou [1966] Director

Ability Hotels (Manchester) Limited
Incorporated: 4 November 2014
Net Worth: £5,176,168 *Total Assets:* £27,470,850
Registered Office: Hilton London, Syon Park, London Road, Brentford, Middlesex, TW8 8JF
Activities: Other letting and operating of own or leased real estate
Parent: Ability Hotels (Manchester) Holdings Limited
Officers: Juin Yong Chin, Secretary; Andreas Costas Panayiotou [1966] Director/Property Developer

Ability Hotels (Syon Park) Limited
Incorporated: 5 December 1985 *Employees:* 124
Net Worth: £1,728,268 *Total Assets:* £49,532,904
Registered Office: Hilton London, Syon Park, London Road, Brentford, Middlesex, TW8 8JF
Activities: Hotels and similar accommodation
Parent: Ability Hotels (Syon) Limited
Officers: Juin Yong Chin, Secretary; Andreas Costas Panayiotou [1966] Director

Ability Housing Association
Incorporated: 3 June 1976 *Employees:* 158
Net Worth: £16,961,960 *Total Assets:* £62,583,428
Registered Office: The Coach House, Gresham Road, Staines upon Thames, Middlesex, TW18 2AE
Activities: Renting and operating of Housing Association real estate
Officers: Peter Stuart Gardiner, Secretary; Jane Mary Harrison [1962] Director; Karen Hillhouse [1963] Director/Development Manager; Ian Lines [1965] Director/Asset Investment Manager; James MacIntyre [1970] Director; Vince John Mewett [1962] Director; Maureen Osborne [1967] Director; Nicola Philp [1968] Director/HR Specialist; Sally Jane Reay [1958] Finance Director; Gina Small [1963] Social Housing Director; Dominic Wallace [1964] Director/Chief Risk Officer

ABJ Trading LLP
Incorporated: 15 August 2012
Net Worth: £18,599,000 *Total Assets:* £148,512,000
Registered Office: 1st Floor, Midas House, 2 Knoll Rise, Orpington, Kent, BR6 0EL

ABL Capital Investments Ltd
Incorporated: 11 January 2017 *Employees:* 31
Net Worth: £17,582,272 *Total Assets:* £40,394,560
Registered Office: Unit 1 Station Industrial Park, Duncan Road, Park Gate, Fareham, Hants, SO31 1BX
Activities: Activities of construction holding companies
Shareholder: Brian Harry Prebble
Officers: Karen Spake, Secretary; Alan John Foreman [1945] Director/Builder; Graham Foreman [1971] Director/Property Developer; Lynda Joan Foreman [1950] Director/Property Manager; Nicholas Hardcastle [1979] Director/Management Accountant; Brian Harry Prebble [1947] Director/Car Dealer; Gary Prebble [1971] Director/Estate; Karen Spake [1974] Director/Property Manager

Abriand Limited
Incorporated: 1 July 2011 *Employees:* 1,099
Net Worth Deficit: £32,419,000 *Total Assets:* £42,796,000
Registered Office: Wizard House, 2a Cambridge Road, Teddington, Middlesex, TW11 8DR
Activities: Activities of head offices
Parent: Core GP II LLP
Officers: Christopher Patrick Edward Guy, Secretary; Raymond Rene Alfred Blanc [1949] Director/Chef Patron [French]; Mark Derry [1960] Director/Chief Executive Officer; Stephen Peter Edwards [1964] Director; Christopher Patrick Edward Guy [1981] Finance Director; Helen Louise Melvin [1968] Director

Academy Services (Waltham Forest) Limited
Incorporated: 5 November 2003
Net Worth Deficit: £5,514,000 *Total Assets:* £29,670,000
Registered Office: 8 White Oak Square, London Road, Swanley, Kent, BR8 7AG
Activities: Combined facilities support activities
Parent: Academy Services (Waltham Forest) (Holdings) Limited
Officers: Christopher James [1968] Investment Director; Alastair James Watson [1974] Investment Director

ACAL BFI Central Procurement UK Limited
Incorporated: 26 November 1969
Net Worth: £6,778,113 *Total Assets:* £20,447,750
Registered Office: 3 The Business Centre, Molly Millars Lane, Wokingham, Berks, RG41 2EY
Activities: Other business support service activities n.e.c.
Parent: ACAL Electronics Holdings Limited
Officers: Joanna Alwen Harkus Madge, Secretary; Susan Catley [1982] Finance Director; Simon Mark Gibbins [1966] Director/Chartered Accountant; Darren Louis Gray [1971] Logistics Director; Ian Russell Greatorex [1962] Director/Chartered Accountant; Ian James Munro [1956] Director/Chartered Accountant; Paul Graham Webster [1954] Director

ACAL Electronics Holdings Limited
Incorporated: 1 March 1982
Net Worth: £1,672,000 *Total Assets:* £58,418,000
Registered Office: 2 Chancellor Court, Occam Road, Surrey Research Park, Guildford, Surrey, GU2 7AH
Activities: Activities of head offices
Shareholders: ACAL PLC; Discoverie Group PLC
Officers: Joanna Alwen Harkus Madge, Secretary; Simon Mark Gibbins [1966] Director/Chartered Accountant; Nicholas John Jefferies [1966] Director; Jeremy James Morcom [1964] Director; Paul Howard Neville [1967] Director; Martin Franz Eckhard Pangels [1967] Director [German]; Paul Graham Webster [1954] Director

Acambis Research Limited
Incorporated: 18 December 1992 *Employees:* 2
Net Worth: £33,329,000 *Total Assets:* £41,899,000
Registered Office: One Onslow Street, Guildford, Surrey, GU1 4YS
Activities: Other research and experimental development on natural sciences and engineering
Parent: Sanofi
Officers: Francois-Xavier Duhalde [1965] Director/Chief Financial Officer [French]; Hugo Rupert Alexander Fry [1970] Director/UK Country Chair

Accesso Technology Group PLC
Incorporated: 29 March 2000 *Employees:* 881
Net Worth: £132,038,416 *Total Assets:* £195,532,960
Registered Office: Unit 5 The Pavilions, Ruscombe Park, Twyford, Berks, RG10 9NN
Activities: Other business support service activities n.e.c.
Officers: Martha Blanche Waymark Bruce, Secretary; John Alder [1968] Director/Chartered Accountant; Thomas James Wardlaw Burnet [1967] Director; David Ranken Gammon [1961] Director; Andrew Malpass [1962] Director; Royce Paul Noland Jr [1959] Director/CEO Accesso Technology Group [American]; William Vernon Russell [1952] Director [American]; Karen Slatford [1956] Director

Acco Brands Europe Limited
Incorporated: 10 August 2005
Net Worth: £393,598,592 *Total Assets:* £715,107,456
Registered Office: Oxford House, Oxford Road, Aylesbury, Bucks, HP21 8SZ
Activities: Activities of head offices
Officers: Richard Mark Geddie, Secretary; Neal Vernon Fenwick [1961] Director; Christopher Neil Hopkinson [1969] Director; Dr. Walter Joe Thomas [1966] Director/Solicitor

Acco Europe Limited
Incorporated: 23 June 1987
Net Worth: £214,523,008 *Total Assets:* £503,971,008
Registered Office: Oxford House, Oxford Road, Aylesbury, Bucks, HP21 8SZ
Activities: Activities of head offices
Officers: Richard Mark Geddie, Secretary; Neal Vernon Fenwick [1961] Director; Christopher Neil Hopkinson [1969] Director; Pamela Rolnick Schneider [1959] Director/Legal Counsel [American]; Dr. Walter Joe Thomas [1966] Director/Solicitor

Acco UK Limited
Incorporated: 6 May 1924 *Employees:* 332
Net Worth: £12,903,000 *Total Assets:* £76,585,000
Registered Office: Oxford House, Oxford Road, Aylesbury, Bucks, HP21 8SZ
Activities: Manufacture of paper stationery
Officers: Richard Mark Geddie, Secretary; George Lee Foot [1972] Director; Christopher Neil Hopkinson [1969] Director; Michael Howard O'Connell Stranders [1975] Director/VP, EMEA Marketing; Marc Alphons Temmerman [1966] Director/VP Operations and Logistics [Belgian]; Dr. Walter Joe Thomas [1966] Director/Solicitor; Mark George Wilkinson [1972] Director/Marketing and Business Development Manager

Acco-Rexel Group Services Limited
Incorporated: 11 March 1950
Net Worth: £124,767,000 *Total Assets:* £124,768,000
Registered Office: Oxford House, Oxford Road, Aylesbury, Bucks, HP21 8SZ
Activities: Activities of head offices
Officers: Richard Mark Geddie, Secretary; Richard Mark Geddie [1970] Director/Accountant; Christopher Neil Hopkinson [1969] Director; Dr. Walter Joe Thomas [1966] Director/Solicitor

Accolade Wines Europe No. 2 Limited
Incorporated: 15 May 1992
Net Worth: £27,039,000 *Total Assets:* £172,960,000
Registered Office: Thomas Hardy House, 2 Heath Road, Weybridge, Surrey, KT13 8TB
Activities: Non-trading company
Parent: Accolade Wines Holdings Europe Limited
Officers: Anthony Graham Wood, Secretary; Adrian Francis McKeon [1963] Regional Managing Director, UKIR; Andrew Peter Smith [1974] Director/Accountant; Anthony Graham Wood [1975] Director/Financial Controller [Australian]

Accolade Wines Holdings Europe Limited
Incorporated: 21 July 2004 *Employees:* 676
Net Worth: £107,025,000 *Total Assets:* £222,027,008
Registered Office: Thomas Hardy House, 2 Heath Road, Weybridge, Surrey, KT13 8TB
Activities: Activities of head offices
Parent: Amphora Finance Limited
Officers: Adrian Francis McKeon [1963] Regional Managing Director, UKIR; Andrew Peter Smith [1974] Director/Accountant; Anthony Graham Wood [1975] Director/Financial Controller [Australian]

Accolade Wines Limited
Incorporated: 13 August 1914 *Employees:* 587
Net Worth: £158,856,000 *Total Assets:* £333,712,000
Registered Office: Thomas Hardy House, 2 Heath Road, Weybridge, Surrey, KT13 8TB
Activities: Manufacture of wine from grape
Parent: Accolade Brands Europe Limited
Officers: Anthony Graham Wood, Secretary; Adrian Francis McKeon [1963] Regional Managing Director, UKIR; Andrew Peter Smith [1974] Director/Accountant; Anthony Graham Wood [1975] Director/Financial Controller [Australian]

Acenden Limited
Incorporated: 3 March 2005 *Employees:* 9
Net Worth: £22,447,000 *Total Assets:* £51,547,000
Registered Office: Ascot House, Maidenhead Office Park, Maidenhead, Berks, SL6 3QQ
Activities: Financial intermediation not elsewhere classified
Parent: Elevate Bidco Limited
Officers: Rajesh Gupta [1969] Director; Olive Generaldine Joyce [1962] Director [Irish]; Diana Susan Miller [1950] Director; Mark Jeffrey Preston [1960] Director

Acer U.K. Limited
Incorporated: 9 May 1988 *Employees:* 51
Net Worth: £28,186,000 *Total Assets:* £61,678,000
Registered Office: Acer House, Heathrow Boulevard 3, 282 Bath Road, West Drayton, Middlesex, UB7 0DQ
Activities: Wholesale of computers, computer peripheral equipment and software
Parent: Acer Europe B.V
Officers: Adam Gallop, Secretary; Emmanuel Pierre Marie Fromont [1967] Director [French]; Tai-Chi Shih [1965] Director [Taiwanese]

ACG Rented Properties PLC
Incorporated: 3 November 1989
Net Worth: £37,457,384 *Total Assets:* £37,607,384
Registered Office: 61 Thames Street, Windsor, Berks, SL4 1QW
Activities: Buying and selling of own real estate
Parent: The ACT Foundation
Officers: James Michael Kerr, Secretary; Derek Maurice Joseph [1949] Director/Housing Consultant; James Michael Kerr [1968] Director/Accountant; Denis Newman Taylor [1953] Director/Chartered Surveyor

Acheson Industries (Europe) Limited
Incorporated: 26 June 1947
Net Worth: £32,774,000 *Total Assets:* £50,488,000
Registered Office: Henkel Limited, Wood Lane End, Hemel Hempstead, Herts, HP2 4RQ
Activities: Non-trading company
Parent: Henkel of America Inc.
Officers: Sutinder Bhandal, Secretary; Sutinder Singh Bhandal [1968] Director/Legal Counsel; Peter David Budden [1963] Director/Accountant; Eamonn Gallagher [1960] Director

Achieving for Children Community Interest Company
Incorporated: 5 February 2014 *Employees:* 961
Net Worth Deficit: £39,189,000 *Total Assets:* £34,152,000
Registered Office: Gifford House, 67c St Helier Avenue, Morden, Surrey, SM4 6HY
Activities: General public administration activities
Shareholders: The London Borough of Richmond upon Thames; The Royal Borough of Kingston upon Thames
Officers: Ian Matthew Dodds, Secretary; David Cameron Archibald [1952] Director/Consultant; Elizabeth Ann Bruce [1957] Director of Adult Social Services; Nicola Charlotte Craig [1973] Director/Head of Human Resources; Ian Matthew Dodds [1970] Director/Deputy Chief Executive; Nina Hingorani-Crain [1973] Director/Chief Operating Officer; Sarah Jane Ireland [1966] Director/Local Government Officer; Catherine Ann Jervis [1965] Director/Chartered Accountant; Kevin Paul McDaniel [1967] Director of Children's Services; Jane Spencer [1958] Director/Magistrate; Christopher Charles Symons [1969] Director; Sian Elizabeth Wicks [1966] Director/Executive Nurse

ACI Global Limited
Incorporated: 11 September 1998 *Employees:* 193
Net Worth: £27,120,000 *Total Assets:* £28,367,000
Registered Office: 55-57 Clarendon Road, Watford, Herts, WD17 1FQ
Activities: Business and domestic software development
Parent: ACI Worldwide (EMEA) Limited
Officers: Dennis P. Byrnes, Secretary; Scott William Behrens [1971] Director/Accountant [American]; Dennis P. Byrnes [1963] Director/Attorney [American]; David Graham King [1966] Director/Businessman; Simon Paul Stokes [1965] Director/Corporate Executive

ACI Worldwide (EMEA) Limited
Incorporated: 28 October 1988 *Employees:* 340
Net Worth: £267,070,000 *Total Assets:* £316,646,016
Registered Office: 55-57 Clarendon Road, Watford, Herts, WD17 1FQ
Activities: Information technology consultancy activities
Parent: Applied Communications Inc. U.K. Holding Limited
Officers: Bryan Peterson, Secretary; Scott William Behrens [1971] Director/Accountant [American]; David Graham King [1966] Director/Businessman; Bryan Anthony Peterson [1962] Director/Certified Public Accountant [American]; Simon Paul Stokes [1965] Director/Corporate Executive

ACM Group Limited
Incorporated: 3 August 2004 *Employees:* 65
Previous: ACM Group PLC
Net Worth: £6,186,387 *Total Assets:* £61,776,344
Registered Office: Amelia House, Crescent Road, Worthing, W Sussex, BN11 1QR
Activities: Financial intermediation not elsewhere classified
Major Shareholder: Tony Afram
Officers: Tony Afram [1962] Director [Lebanese]; Derek Andrew Grech [1968] Director, Sales & Marketing; Roger Ian Hambury [1968] Director; Kurt Hoeksema [1976] Director [American]; Muhammad Rasoul [1973] Director [American]; Scott Raymond Sandat [1977] Director

ACP Europe Limited
Incorporated: 15 April 2005 *Employees:* 21
Net Worth: £8,895,905 *Total Assets:* £36,865,424
Registered Office: Mazars LLP, The Pinnacle, 160 Midsummer Boulevard, Milton Keynes, Bucks, MK9 1FF
Activities: Activities auxiliary to financial intermediation n.e.c.
Major Shareholder: Kevin Michael Ulrich
Officers: Thibault Gournay [1978] Director/Portfolio Manager [French]

Acquaspen Limited
Incorporated: 21 February 2007
Net Worth: £28,206,000 *Total Assets:* £69,832,000
Registered Office: Apex Way, Hailsham, E Sussex, BN27 3WA
Activities: Other business support service activities n.e.c.
Parent: The Pump Group Limited
Officers: Nicholas James Redman, Secretary; Hamish David William Middleton [1971] Director; Adrian William Thompson [1967] Director

Acquisition U.K. Limited
Incorporated: 17 December 2002
Net Worth Deficit: £10,768,836 *Total Assets:* £23,452,524
Registered Office: 420 Thames Valley Park Drive, Reading, Berks, RG6 1PT
Activities: Activities of head offices
Parent: GXS UK Holding Limited
Officers: Gordon Allan Davies [1962] Director/Chief Legal Officer & Corporate Development [Canadian]; Oliver Jon Gallienne [1973] Director/VP, Worldwide Professional Services; Madhu Ranganathan [1964] Director/EVP & Chief Financial Officer [American]; Christian Waida [1966] Director/VP, General Counsel Worldwide Field Operations [German]

Acre 1176 Limited
Incorporated: 9 September 2014 *Employees:* 7
Net Worth: £1,007,563 *Total Assets:* £21,609,390
Registered Office: Vista Centre, 50 Salisbury Road, Hounslow, Middlesex, TW4 6JQ
Activities: Other letting and operating of own or leased real estate
Shareholder: Sanjeet Singh Babbar
Officers: Waryam Singh Kakol [1970] Director [Dutch]; Gurmeet Singh Sethi [1983] Director

ACS International Schools Limited
Incorporated: 5 July 1967 *Employees:* 1,019
Net Worth: £73,784,008 *Total Assets:* £119,153,392
Registered Office: Heywood, Portsmouth Road, Cobham, Surrey, KT11 1BL
Activities: General secondary education
Major Shareholder: David Terence Thomas
Officers: Gavin Charles, Secretary; Stefan Beurier [1973] Director/Divisional Chief Financial Officer [French]; Nicholas Edward Bobay [1963] Director/Consultant [American]; Jason Stuart Elsom [1974] Director/Consultant; Clare Joanna Elizabeth Ferguson [1970] Director/Consultant; Nicole Louis [1967] Director/Chief Marketing Officer; Robert Magnus MacNaughton [1963] Director/Chairman; Pamela Mundy [1959] Director; Russell Charles Prior [1964] Director/Head of Philanthropy and Social Investment; Jake Brangwyn Sheridan Swallow [1949] Director/Consultant; Corry Justina Wille [1960] Director/Consultant [Belgian]

Action for Children
Incorporated: 14 May 2003 *Employees:* 3,283
Net Worth: £78,775,000 *Total Assets:* £99,481,000
Registered Office: 3 The Boulevard, Ascot Road, Watford, Herts, WD18 8AG
Activities: Child day-care activities
Officers: Richard Hood, Secretary; Sheryl Milanda Anderson [1953] Director/Methodist Minister; Richard Anthony Cryer [1947] Director/Retired; Gillian Ellis [1958] Director/Retired; Evelyn Patricia Gordon [1956] Charity Director and Non-Executive Director; Tracy Ann Griffin [1962] Director; Kate Guthrie [1963] HR Director; Josephine Audrey Larbie [1956] Director/Management Consultant & Executive Coach; Deborah Jayne Morgan [1961] Director/Retired; Daleep Satyanand Mukarji [1946] Retired Director of Christian Aid; Sarika Bijendra Patel [1965] Director; Markus Hardy Ruetimann [1958] Director [British/Swiss]; Fiona Talitha Flora Thorne [1969] Director/Communications Advisor

Active Assistance Finance Limited
Incorporated: 14 July 2011
Net Worth Deficit: £7,736,439 *Total Assets:* £92,591,960
Registered Office: 1 Suffolk Way, Sevenoaks, Kent, TN13 1YL
Activities: Other human health activities
Parent: Active Assistance (UK) Group Limited
Officers: David Petrie [1969] Director; Matthew Russell Tillett [1968] Director/Chief Financial Officer; Christina Anne Walsh [1967] Director/Chief Operating Officer

Activision Blizzard UK Ltd
Incorporated: 25 March 1983 *Employees:* 133
Net Worth: £19,623,000 *Total Assets:* £116,756,000
Registered Office: Ditton Park, Riding Court Road, Datchet, Slough, Berks, SL3 9LL
Activities: Ready-made interactive leisure and entertainment software development
Parent: Activision Europe Limited
Officers: Paul Nicholas Bland [1971] Finance Director; Ian Dennis Mattingly [1969] Director/Lawyer

ADA PD UK Limited
Incorporated: 27 July 2015
Net Worth: £23,369,712 *Total Assets:* £42,404,728
Registered Office: Trinity Gardens, 9-11 Bromham Road, Bedford, MK40 2BP
Activities: Non-trading company
Officers: Karen Ruth Abel [1981] Director/Chartered Accountant; Sylvia Anne Jensch [1971] Director [German]; Wilhelm Konning [1958] Director [German]

Adams Morey Holdings Limited
Incorporated: 2 January 2003 *Employees:* 346
Net Worth: £11,376,915 *Total Assets:* £31,598,216
Registered Office: Stag Gates House, 63-64 The Avenue, Southampton, SO17 1XS
Activities: Other letting and operating of own or leased real estate
Shareholders: Michael Charles Adams; Elizabeth Ann Adams
Officers: Michael Charles Adams, Secretary; Elizabeth Ann Adams [1946] Director; Michael Charles Adams [1948] Managing Director

Adare International Holdings Limited
Incorporated: 20 June 2017 *Employees:* 549
Net Worth Deficit: £24,223,000 *Total Assets:* £74,368,000
Registered Office: Lilly House, Priestley Road, Basingstoke, Hants, RG24 9LZ
Activities: Activities of other holding companies n.e.c.
Parent: Endless LLP
Officers: Raymond Phillip Berry [1977] Director; Andrew Mark Dutton [1971] Director/Chief Executive Officer; Aidan Paul Robson [1978] Director/Private Equity Partner

Adda Hotels
Incorporated: 17 May 1966
Net Worth Deficit: £73,370,872 *Total Assets:* £226,913,728
Registered Office: Maple Court, Central Park, Reeds Crescent, Watford, Herts, WD24 4QQ
Activities: Hotels and similar accommodation
Parent: Hilton Worldwide Limited
Officers: Stuart Beasley [1971] Director/Financial Controller; Richard Geoffrey Beeston [1982] Director/Chartered Accountant; Stephen Patrick Cassidy [1968] Director/SVP Operations UK & Ireland; Michelle Momdjian [1976] Director/Attorney; George Christopher Ogle [1974] Director/Attorney; James Owen Percival [1968] Director/Accountant; Brian McKay Wilson [1962] Director/Company Secretary

Adelie Foods Bidco Limited
Incorporated: 23 February 2015 *Employees:* 11
Net Worth: £49,878,000 *Total Assets:* £150,892,992
Registered Office: 2 The Square, Southall Lane, Heathrow, Southall, Middlesex, UB2 5NH
Activities: Activities of head offices
Parent: Harvest Midco Limited
Officers: Martin Johnson [1973] Director; Mark David Stott [1966] Director

Adelie Foods Group Limited
Incorporated: 24 February 2012 *Employees:* 2
Net Worth: £10,097,000 *Total Assets:* £42,783,000
Registered Office: 2 The Square, Southall Lane, Heathrow, Southall, Middlesex, UB2 5NH
Activities: Activities of other holding companies n.e.c.
Parent: Adelie Investco UK Limited
Officers: Martin Johnson [1973] Director; Mark David Stott [1966] Director

Adelie Foods Limited
Incorporated: 17 August 2001 *Employees:* 2,413
Previous: Buckingham Foods Limited
Net Worth: £4,008,000 *Total Assets:* £85,728,000
Registered Office: 2 The Square, Southall Lane, Heathrow, Southall, Middlesex, UB2 5NH
Activities: Manufacture of other food products n.e.c.
Parent: Adelie Foods Group Limited
Officers: Martin Johnson [1973] Director; Mark David Stott [1966] Director

Adeptus Limited
Incorporated: 20 May 1960
Net Worth: £18,624,108 *Total Assets:* £37,675,484
Registered Office: E3 The Premier Centre, Premier Way, Abbey Park, Romsey, Hants, SO51 9DG
Activities: Buying and selling of own real estate
Major Shareholder: Priscilla Graham
Officers: Michael Chee Keong See, Secretary; Priscilla Sarah Graham [1946] Director

ADI Finance 1 Limited
Incorporated: 28 February 2006
Net Worth: £2,486,000,128 *Total Assets:* £5,231,000,064
Registered Office: The Compass Centre, Nelson Road, Hounslow, Middlesex, TW6 2GW
Activities: Activities of head offices
Parent: FGP Topco Limited
Officers: Ahmed Ali Al-Hammadi [1981] Director [Qatari]; Stuart Harvey Baldwin [1969] Director/Investment Manager; Christopher William Beale [1947] Director [American]; Jinhong Chen [1990] Director [Chinese]; Samuel Coxe [1975] Alternate Director [American]; Olivier Georges Xavier Fortin [1974] Director [French]; Jorge Gil Villen [1972] Director/Lawyer/Economist [Spanish]; Mr Deven Arvind Karnik [1967] Alternate Director; Tom Kelly [1989] Director [Irish]; Alexander Leonard [1985] Director; Inigo Meiras [1963] Alternate Director [Spanish]; Michael James Powell [1972] Director; David Jinlin Xie [1978] Alternate Director [American]

ADI Finance 2 Limited
Incorporated: 28 February 2006
Net Worth: £5,624,000,000 *Total Assets:* £5,717,000,192
Registered Office: The Compass Centre, Nelson Road, Hounslow, Middlesex, TW6 2GW
Activities: Activities of head offices
Parent: ADI Finance 1 Limited
Officers: Ahmed Ali Al-Hammadi [1981] Director [Qatari]; Stuart Harvey Baldwin [1969] Director/Investment Manager; Christopher William Beale [1947] Director [American]; Jinhong Chen [1990] Director [Chinese]; Samuel Coxe [1975] Alternate Director [American]; Olivier Georges Xavier Fortin [1974] Director [French]; Jorge Gil Villen [1972] Director/Lawyer/Economist [Spanish]; Mr Deven Arvind Karnik [1967] Alternate Director; Tom Kelly [1989] Director [Irish]; Alexander Leonard [1985] Director; Inigo Meiras [1963] Alternate Director [Spanish]; Michael James Powell [1972] Director; David Jinlin Xie [1978] Alternate Director [American]

ADM Arkady Limited
Incorporated: 1 May 1967 *Employees:* 24
Net Worth: £48,857,644 *Total Assets:* £80,653,456
Registered Office: 5 Hercules Way, Leavesden Park, Watford, Herts, WD25 7GS
Activities: Wholesale of grain, unmanufactured tobacco, seeds and animal feeds
Parent: Archer Daniels Midland Company
Officers: Paul William Briggs, Secretary; Graham Lawrence Atkinson [1960] Director/Commodity Trader; Paul William Briggs [1958] Director

ADM Milling Limited
Incorporated: 21 November 1989 *Employees:* 440
Net Worth: £30,101,084 *Total Assets:* £52,998,376
Registered Office: ADM International Limited, Church Manorway, Erith, Kent, DA8 1DL
Activities: Grain milling
Parent: Archer Daniels Midland (UK) Limited
Officers: Timothy James Cook [1957] Managing Director; Mark Lee Kolkhorst [1964] Director/President [American]; Orla Margaret Muldoon [1969] Managing Director [Irish]; Fabian James Dunbar Somerville-Cotton [1964] Managing Director

ADM Pura Limited
Incorporated: 19 May 1965
Net Worth: £88,303,544 *Total Assets:* £90,900,880
Registered Office: ADM International Offices, Church Manorway, Erith, Kent, DA8 1DL
Activities: Activities of production holding companies
Parent: Archer Daniels Midland (UK) Limited
Officers: Helen Louise McLelland [1975] Director/Financial Controller; Lance Thomas Rogers [1973] Director/Financial Controller

ADM Trading (UK) Limited
Incorporated: 9 September 1964 *Employees:* 28
Net Worth: £13,876,150 *Total Assets:* £22,346,016
Registered Office: Church Manorway, Erith, Kent, DA8 1DL
Activities: Wholesale of dairy products, eggs and edible oils and fats
Parent: Archer Daniels Midland (UK) Limited
Officers: Marcus Degen [1966] Director/General Manager [Dutch]; Martin Paul Farrow [1956] Director/General Manager; Phillipa Girard [1980] Director/UK Oilseeds Country Controller; Dr Martin Kropp [1965] Director/Vice President [German]; Orla Margaret Muldoon [1969] Managing Director [Irish]; Lance Thomas Rogers [1973] Director/Financial Controller

Admiral House Property Trading Limited
Incorporated: 4 February 2013 *Employees:* 1
Net Worth: £5,509,584 *Total Assets:* £25,393,188
Registered Office: First Floor, Unit 1b St Georges Business Centre, St Georges Square, Portsmouth, PO1 3EY
Activities: Buying and selling of own real estate
Shareholders: Simon Christopher Brock; Graham Nicholas Hazell
Officers: Simon Christopher Brock [1964] Director

ADT (UK) Limited
Incorporated: 6 August 1984
Net Worth Deficit: £709,883,008 *Total Assets:* £163,707,008
Registered Office: Security House, The Summit, Hanworth Road, Sunbury on Thames, Middlesex, TW16 5DB
Activities: Activities of head offices
Parent: ADT Group Limited
Officers: Mark Ayre [1963] Finance Director; Peter Schieser [1967] Director [German]

ADT Finance Limited
Incorporated: 8 August 1985
Previous: ADT Finance Public Limited Company
Net Worth: £159,860,000 *Total Assets:* £900,652,992
Registered Office: Security House, The Summit, Hanworth Road, Sunbury on Thames, Middlesex, TW16 5DB
Activities: Financial intermediation not elsewhere classified
Parent: ADT (UK) Limited
Officers: Mark Ayre [1963] Finance Director; Peter Schieser [1967] Director [German]

ADT Fire and Security PLC
Incorporated: 22 February 1974 *Employees:* 3,270
Net Worth: £578,139,008 *Total Assets:* £761,942,016
Registered Office: Security House, The Summit, Hanworth Road, Sunbury on Thames, Middlesex, TW16 5DB
Activities: Other service activities n.e.c.
Parent: Tyco Holdings (UK) Limited
Officers: Mark Ayre, Secretary; James Paul Earnshaw [1976] Finance Director; Andrew John Ellis [1961] Director; Richard Hilton Jones [1964] Director; Moosa Farook Meah [1965] Director

ADT Group Limited
Incorporated: 1 March 1990
Previous: ADT Group Public Limited Company
Net Worth: £511,744,000 *Total Assets:* £535,039,008
Registered Office: Security House, The Summit, Hanworth Road, Sunbury on Thames, Middlesex, TW16 5DB
Activities: Activities of head offices
Parent: ADT (UK) Holdings Limited
Officers: Mark Ayre [1963] Finance Director; Peter Schieser [1967] Director [German]

ADT South Africa Holding Limited
Incorporated: 16 October 1984
Net Worth: £117,390,000 *Total Assets:* £117,785,000
Registered Office: Security House, The Summit, Hanworth Road, Sunbury on Thames, Middlesex, TW16 5DB
Activities: Non-trading company
Parent: Tyco Holdings (UK) Limited
Officers: Mark Ayre [1963] Finance Director; Peter Schieser [1967] Director [German]

Advanced 365 Limited
Incorporated: 21 April 1987 *Employees:* 314
Net Worth: £19,422,000 *Total Assets:* £50,449,000
Registered Office: Ditton Park, Riding Court Road, Datchet, Berks, SL3 9LL
Activities: Other information technology service activities
Parent: Business Systems Group Holdings Limited
Officers: Natalie Amanda Shaw, Secretary; Andrew William Hicks [1975] Director/Chief Financial Officer; Gordon James Wilson [1960] Director

Advanced Business Software and Solutions Limited
Incorporated: 20 June 1996 *Employees:* 794
Net Worth: £52,489,000 *Total Assets:* £167,384,992
Registered Office: Ditton Park, Riding Court Road, Datchet, Berks, SL3 9LL
Activities: Information technology consultancy activities
Parent: Redac Limited
Officers: Natalie Amanda Shaw, Secretary; Andrew William Hicks [1975] Director/Chief Financial Officer; Gordon James Wilson [1960] Director

Advanced Computer Software Group Limited
Incorporated: 12 October 2006
Previous: Advanced Computer Software Group PLC
Net Worth: £167,844,000 *Total Assets:* £279,764,000
Registered Office: Ditton Park, Riding Court Road, Datchet, Berks, SL3 9LL
Activities: Activities of head offices
Parent: Air Bidco Limited
Officers: Natalie Amanda Shaw, Secretary; Adrian Roberto Alonso [1984] Director [American]; Bret Richard Bolin [1968] Director [American]; Andrew William Hicks [1975] Director/Chief Financial Officer; Maneet Singh Saroya [1979] Director [American]; Brian Niranjan Sheth [1975] Director/President, Private Equity Firm [American]; Robert Frederick Smith [1962] Director/Chairman and CEO [American]; Martin Andrew Taylor [1969] Director/Operating Principal [American]; Gordon James Wilson [1960] Director

Advanced Elastomer Systems Limited
Incorporated: 15 June 1990 *Employees:* 85
Net Worth: £149,600,000 *Total Assets:* £165,834,000
Registered Office: Ermyn House, Ermyn Way, Leatherhead, Surrey, KT22 8UX
Activities: Manufacture of plastics in primary forms
Parent: ExxonMobil Chemical Investment Company Limited
Officers: Fiona Harness, Secretary; Richard Robert Henderson [1966] Director/Oil Company Executive; Tom Van Nuland [1974] Director/Oil Company Executive [Belgian]

Advanced Health and Care Limited
Incorporated: 15 June 1994 *Employees:* 218
Net Worth: £43,146,000 *Total Assets:* £64,043,000
Registered Office: Ditton Park, Riding Court Road, Datchet, Berks, SL3 9LL
Activities: Information technology consultancy activities
Parent: Advanced Computer Software Group Limited
Officers: Natalie Amanda Shaw, Secretary; Andrew William Hicks [1975] Director/Chief Financial Officer; Gordon James Wilson [1960] Director; Dr Francis Alexander Yeates [1959] Medical Director

Advanced Legal Solutions Limited
Incorporated: 11 July 1983 *Employees:* 171
Net Worth: £17,762,000 *Total Assets:* £59,226,000
Registered Office: Ditton Park, Riding Court Road, Datchet, Berks, SL3 9LL
Activities: Information technology consultancy activities
Parent: Alphalaw Limited
Officers: Natalie Amanda Shaw, Secretary; Andrew William Hicks [1975] Director/Chief Financial Officer; Gordon James Wilson [1960] Director

Advanced Lighting Technologies Europe Limited
Incorporated: 20 June 1995 *Employees:* 61
Net Worth: £7,515,482 *Total Assets:* £26,249,848
Registered Office: c/o Venture Lighting Europe Ltd, Trinity Court, Batchworth Island, Church Street, Rickmansworth, Herts, WD3 1RT
Activities: Activities of head offices
Officers: Philip Colin Croker [1978] Managing Director; Sabu Krishnan [1958] Director/Engineer [American]; Richard John Morris [1963] Managing Director

Advantedge Commercial Finance Limited
Incorporated: 26 April 2001 *Employees:* 38
Previous: Factor 21 Limited
Net Worth: £8,954,271 *Total Assets:* £35,207,200
Registered Office: 1 London Street, Reading, Berks, RG1 4PN
Activities: Factoring
Parent: Hamsard 3415 Limited
Officers: Darren John Cottenden [1968] Director; Neal Errington [1956] Director/Factor; Jonathan David Leigh Gregory [1961] Director; David James Tilling [1961] Managing Director

AE Consolidation Limited
Incorporated: 10 June 2011
Net Worth: £102,099,432 *Total Assets:* £1,076,919,040
Registered Office: Avis Budget House, Park Road, Bracknell, Berks, RG12 2EW
Activities: Activities of head offices
Parent: AE Holdco Limited
Officers: Inderpal Lall, Secretary; Paul Leslie Ford [1970] Director/Accountant; Rochelle Miriam Tarlowe [1970] Director/Treasurer [American]

AECOM Infrastructure & Environment UK Limited
Incorporated: 27 May 1966 *Employees:* 3,069
Previous: URS Infrastructure & Environment UK Limited
Net Worth: £28,514,000 *Total Assets:* £446,300,000
Registered Office: Midpoint, Alencon Link, Basingstoke, Hants, RG21 7PP
Activities: Environmental consulting activities
Parent: AECOM International Holdings UK Limited
Officers: Bolaji Moruf Taiwo, Secretary; David Charles Webb Barwell [1965] Director; Andrew Noel Jones [1965] Director; Cheryl Rosalind McCall [1974] Director/Accountant; William Jan Charles Quarterman [1962] Director/Chief Operating Officer, UK and Ireland

AERL Holding Limited
Incorporated: 10 March 2015
Net Worth: £801,287,744 *Total Assets:* £1,227,772,672
Registered Office: Waterside, Harmondsworth, West Drayton, Middlesex, UB7 0GB
Activities: Activities of head offices
Parent: International Consolidated Airlines Group S.A.
Officers: Enrique Dupuy de Lome Chavarr [1957] Director/Chief Financial Officer [Spanish]; Christopher Mark Haynes [1970] Director/General Counsel; Marcia Yor Ing Lin [1971] Director

Aeromobile Communications Limited
Incorporated: 19 January 2010 *Employees:* 18
Net Worth: £20,242,276 *Total Assets:* £27,962,126
Registered Office: Three Pegasus Place, Gatwick Road, Crawley, W Sussex, RH10 9AY
Activities: Wireless telecommunications activities
Officers: Ann-Marie Mullan, Secretary; Mark Alan Jennings [1964] Director/Chief Operating Officer; Julie Christine Lichty [1974] Senior Director [American]; Jeff Sare [1962] Director/Vice President [American]; Seigo Tada [1961] Director [Japanese]

Aerotron Limited
Incorporated: 16 August 1973 *Employees:* 53
Net Worth: £45,484,112 *Total Assets:* £83,719,184
Registered Office: Westley House, Fleming Way, Crawley, W Sussex, RH10 9GA
Activities: Operation of warehousing and storage facilities for air transport activities
Parent: Total Aircraft Product Support (Holdings) Limited
Officers: Jacqueline Westley, Company Secretary; Kevin Goodall [1956] Director; Gene Whitford Mashlan [1944] Director/Aviation Consultant [New Zealander]; Anthony Maurice Westley [1946] Director/Chairman; Jacqueline Westley [1946] Director/Company Secretary; Mark Peter Westley [1975] Managing Director; Neil Anthony Westley [1970] Director; Robert John Wilson [1942] Director/Chartered Accountant

Aesica BC Limited
Incorporated: 15 July 2011
Net Worth Deficit: £8,300,000 *Total Assets:* £121,700,000
Registered Office: Suite B Breakspear Park, Breakspear Way, Hemel Hempstead, Herts, HP2 4TZ
Activities: Manufacture of basic pharmaceutical products
Parent: Aesica M2 Limited
Officers: Andrew Leonard Jackson, Secretary; Jonathan Martin Glenn [1968] Director; Paul Andrew Hayes [1966] Director

Aesica M1 Limited
Incorporated: 10 August 2011
Net Worth: £2,300,000 *Total Assets:* £41,200,000
Registered Office: Suite B Breakspear Park, Breakspear Way, Hemel Hempstead, Herts, HP2 4TZ
Activities: Manufacture of basic pharmaceutical products
Parent: Aesica Holdco Limited
Officers: Andrew Leonard Jackson, Secretary; Jonathan Martin Glenn [1968] Director; Paul Andrew Hayes [1966] Director

Aesica M2 Limited
Incorporated: 10 August 2011
Net Worth: £10,400,000 *Total Assets:* £41,200,000
Registered Office: Suite B Breakspear Park, Breakspear Way, Hemel Hempstead, Herts, HP2 4TZ
Activities: Manufacture of basic pharmaceutical products
Parent: Aesica M1 Limited
Officers: Andrew Leonard Jackson, Secretary; Jonathan Martin Glenn [1968] Director; Paul Andrew Hayes [1966] Director

Aesica Pharmaceuticals Limited
Incorporated: 23 July 2004 *Employees:* 191
Net Worth: £133,800,000 *Total Assets:* £246,000,000
Registered Office: Suite B Breakspear Park, Breakspear Way, Hemel Hempstead, Herts, HP2 4TZ
Activities: Manufacture of basic pharmaceutical products
Parent: Aesica BC Limited
Officers: Andrew Leonard Jackson, Secretary; Dr Manja Hermina Elisabeth Maria Boerman [1966] Director [Dutch]; Jonathan Martin Glenn [1968] Director; Paul Andrew Hayes [1966] Director

Aesica Queenborough Limited
Incorporated: 22 August 2007 *Employees:* 457
Net Worth: £9,200,000 *Total Assets:* £56,800,000
Registered Office: Suite B Breakspear Park, Breakspear Way, Hemel Hempstead, Herts, HP2 4TZ
Activities: Manufacture of basic pharmaceutical products
Parent: Aesica Pharmaceuticals Limited
Officers: Andrew Leonard Jackson, Secretary; Dr Manja Hermina Elisabeth Maria Boerman [1966] Director [Dutch]; Jonathan Martin Glenn [1968] Director; Paul Andrew Hayes [1966] Director

Affinion International Limited
Incorporated: 22 April 1971 *Employees:* 408
Net Worth: £32,683,000 *Total Assets:* £135,672,000
Registered Office: Charter Court, 50 Windsor Road, Slough, Berks, SL1 2EJ
Activities: Other business support service activities n.e.c.
Parent: Affinion International Holdings Limited
Officers: Iphigenie Fossati-Kotz, Secretary; Michele Conforti [1967] Managing Director & CFO - Affinion International [Italian]; Karen Rachel Wheeler [1972] Director

Affinion International Travel Limited
Incorporated: 1 July 2008 *Employees:* 109
Net Worth: £2,356,000 *Total Assets:* £21,244,000
Registered Office: Charter Court, 50 Windsor Road, Slough, Berks, SL1 2EJ
Activities: Other business support service activities n.e.c.
Parent: Affinion International Travel Holdco Limited
Officers: Iphigenie Fossati-Kotz, Secretary; Michele Conforti [1967] Director [Italian]; Karen Rachel Wheeler [1972] Director

Affinity (Reading) Limited
Incorporated: 30 July 2003
Net Worth: £4,911,562 *Total Assets:* £32,271,964
Registered Office: 8 White Oak Square, London Road, Swanley, Kent, BR8 7AG
Activities: Combined facilities support activities
Shareholders: Affinity (Reading) Holdings Limited; Affinity (Reading) Holdings Limited
Officers: Susanne Coleman [1965] Director/Regional Operations Manager; Malcolm Robert Lambert [1977] Director/Accountant; Christopher James Neil [1985] Director/Financial Controller; Josephine Ruth Roberts [1971] Director/Head of Specialist Housing

Affiperf Limited
Incorporated: 4 June 2014 *Employees:* 45
Net Worth: £22,493,000 *Total Assets:* £108,874,000
Registered Office: Havas House, Hermitage Court, Hermitage Lane, Maidstone, Kent, ME16 9NT
Activities: Advertising agencies
Parent: Havas UK Limited
Officers: Allan John Ross, Secretary; Jorge Irizar Alonso [1968] Director [Spanish]; Darren Todhunter [1968] Director/Accountant; Paul Francis Woodhouse [1955] Director/Accountant

Africa Express Line Limited
Incorporated: 1 October 2001 *Employees:* 21
Net Worth: £17,515,836 *Total Assets:* £43,632,960
Registered Office: 22 Mount Ephraim, Tunbridge Wells, Kent, TN4 8AS
Activities: Sea and coastal freight water transport
Major Shareholder: Robert Fabre
Officers: Frederick Jean Philippe Fabre [1960] Director/Logistics Manager [French]; Armando Alfonso Larragan Acuna [1958] Director/Agronomist [Costa Rican]; David Marcelin Gabriel Moreau [1969] Director/General Manager [French]; Mathew Shed [1967] Technical Director; Jan Baptist Van Opstal [1951] Managing Director [French]

Afton Chemical Limited
Incorporated: 19 May 1975 *Employees:* 256
Net Worth: £134,758,000 *Total Assets:* £232,878,000
Registered Office: London Road, Bracknell, Berks, RG12 2UW
Activities: Other manufacturing n.e.c.
Parent: Afton Chemical UK Holdings Limited
Officers: David Richard Ellis [1964] Technical Director; Catherine Charlotte Martin [1976] Marketing Director; Andrew David Walker [1970] Finance Director

Afton Chemical UK Holdings Limited
Incorporated: 8 January 2010
Net Worth: £95,249,016 *Total Assets:* £192,381,968
Registered Office: London Road, Bracknell, Berks, RG12 2UW
Activities: Activities of head offices
Parent: Afton Chemical UK LLP
Officers: David Richard Ellis [1964] Technical Director; Catherine Charlotte Martin [1976] Marketing Director; Andrew David Walker [1970] Finance Director

Afton Chemical UK LLP
Incorporated: 11 December 2014
Net Worth: £678,565,440 *Total Assets:* £678,587,008
Registered Office: London Road, Bracknell, Berks, RG12 2UW

AGB Properties (Woking) Limited
Incorporated: 26 November 2002 *Employees:* 4
Net Worth: £13,388,694 *Total Assets:* £24,187,820
Registered Office: Maria House, 35 Millers Road, Brighton, BN1 5NP
Activities: Other letting and operating of own or leased real estate
Major Shareholder: Anthony Grant Bloom
Officers: Ronald Bloom, Secretary; Anthony Grant Bloom [1970] Director; Ronald Bloom [1935] Director; Adam Stephen Franks [1971] Director; Lee Peter Pattenden [1958] Director

AGCO Finance Limited
Incorporated: 11 July 1990 *Employees:* 35
Net Worth: £30,421,000 *Total Assets:* £404,260,000
Registered Office: Building 7, Croxley Park, Hatters Lane, Watford, Herts, WD18 8YN
Activities: Financial intermediation not elsewhere classified
Shareholders: De Lage Landen Leasing Limited; AGCO International Limited
Officers: Julia Laura Kortz, Secretary; Mark Albert Casement [1965] Director; Duncan John Hullis [1963] Director; Saul Brendan Jones [1974] Director

Ageas (UK) Limited
Incorporated: 30 January 1973 *Employees:* 128
Net Worth: £670,412,992 *Total Assets:* £721,718,016
Registered Office: Ageas House, Hampshire Corporate Park, Templars Way, Eastleigh, Hants, SO53 3YA
Activities: Activities of financial services holding companies
Parent: Ageas SA/NV
Officers: Rosemary Anne Smith, Secretary; Gregor Frank Ball [1963] Director; Antonio Cano [1963] Director [Dutch]; Jozef Germain de Mey [1943] Director [Belgian]; Malcolm Graham McCaig [1955] Director; Lionel Perl [1948] Director [Belgian]; Andrew Stuart Watson [1962] Director; Mark Winlow [1962] Director

Ageas Insurance Limited
Incorporated: 1 July 1939 *Employees:* 2,060
Net Worth: £440,000,000 *Total Assets:* £3,175,699,968
Registered Office: Ageas House, Hampshire Corporate Park, Templars Way, Eastleigh, Hants, SO53 3YA
Activities: Non-life insurance
Parent: Ageas (UK) Limited
Officers: Rosemary Anne Smith, Secretary; Gregor Frank Ball [1963] Director; Antonio Cano [1963] Director [Dutch]; Jozef Germain de Mey [1943] Director [Belgian]; Malcolm Graham McCaig [1955] Director; Andrew Stuart Watson [1962] Director/Chief Executive; Mark Winlow [1962] Director

Ageas Retail Limited
Incorporated: 10 August 1977 *Employees:* 1,375
Net Worth: £15,575,000 *Total Assets:* £178,812,000
Registered Office: Ageas House, Hampshire Corporate Park, Templars Way, Eastleigh, Hants, SO53 3YA
Activities: Activities of insurance agents and brokers
Parent: Ageas (UK) Limited
Officers: Rosemary Anne Smith, Secretary; Gregor Frank Ball [1963] Director; Antonio Cano [1963] Director [Dutch]; Malcolm Graham McCaig [1955] Director; Anthony Edward Middle [1970] Director; Lionel Perl [1948] Director [Belgian]; Andrew Stuart Watson [1962] Managing Director Retail; Mark Winlow [1962] Director

AGF Holdings (UK) Limited
Incorporated: 25 October 1973
Net Worth: £87,406,000 *Total Assets:* £90,864,000
Registered Office: 57 Ladymead, Guildford, Surrey, GU1 1DB
Activities: Activities of head offices
Parent: Allianz SE
Officers: Robin Christian Jack-Kee, Secretary; Jonathan Mark Dye [1966] Director/Chief Executive; Fernley Keith Dyson [1965] Director/Chief Financial Officer; Graham Arthur Gibson [1967] Director

Agfa Healthcare UK Limited
Incorporated: 18 July 2007 *Employees:* 96
Net Worth: £13,545,000 *Total Assets:* £21,589,000
Registered Office: 6-9 The Square, Stockley Park, Uxbridge, Middlesex, UB11 1FW
Activities: Other information technology service activities
Parent: Agfa Healthcare NV
Officers: Iskandar Emile Accaoui [1961] Director/General Manager - Imaging [French]; Peter Maria Victor Gielen [1960] Sales Director and Support Manager [Belgian]

Agility Logistics Limited
Incorporated: 29 October 1910 *Employees:* 352
Net Worth: £23,693,000 *Total Assets:* £82,599,000
Registered Office: Unit 6 North Radius Park, Faggs Road, Feltham, Middlesex, TW14 0NG
Activities: Other transportation support activities
Parent: Agility Logistics Holdings Limited
Officers: Colm Patrick McAlinden [1968] Director/Forwarder; Sait Mohammed Esa Oomer [1972] Director [Indian]; Hitesh Nathwani [1970] Director/Accountant; Paul Terence O'Keefe [1960] Director; Steven John Ryan [1972] Director/Accountant

AGP Holdings (1) Limited
Incorporated: 1 February 2001
Net Worth: £18,345,000 *Total Assets:* £267,806,000
Registered Office: 8 White Oak Square, London Road, Swanley, Kent, BR8 7AG
Activities: Buying and selling of own real estate
Parent: Infrastructure Investments Holdings Limited
Officers: David John Carr [1969] Finance Director; Glynn Newby [1966] Director/Business Management; Natalia Poupard [1977] Director/Asset Manager; Mark Christopher Wayment [1958] Director

Agria Pet Insurance Limited
Incorporated: 25 July 2001 *Employees:* 103
Net Worth: £11,683,386 *Total Assets:* £39,673,584
Registered Office: First Floor, Blue Leanie, Walton Street, Aylesbury, Bucks, HP21 7QW
Activities: Financial intermediation not elsewhere classified
Officers: Stuart Clarke [1973] Finance Director; Monica Dreijer [1961] Director/Deputy CEO Agria Forsakringsaktiebolaget [Swedish]; Agnes Fabricius [1972] Director/Chief Executive Officer [Swedish]; Baharan Hellstrom [1979] Director/BA Manager Europe at Agria [Swedish]; Simon Wheeler [1960] Managing Director

Agricultural Central Trading Limited
Incorporated: 24 January 1962 *Employees:* 97
Net Worth: £14,101,143 *Total Assets:* £29,703,392
Registered Office: 90 The Broadway, Chesham, Bucks, HP5 1EG
Activities: Agents selling agricultural raw materials, livestock, textile raw materials and semi-finished goods
Officers: Helen Mary Isabel Fellows, Secretary; Andrew John Sidney Beaty [1970] Director/Farmer; Malcolm George Corfield [1953] Director/Farmer; Ian Richard Davey [1965] Director/Farmer; John Dursley Hamilton [1954] Director/Chief Executive; John Lewis Rowlands [1949] Director/Accountant

AHL Holdings (Manchester) Limited
Incorporated: 17 April 2003
Net Worth Deficit: £2,425,000 *Total Assets:* £30,064,000
Registered Office: 8 White Oak Square, London Road, Swanley, Kent, BR8 7AG
Activities: Construction of commercial buildings
Shareholders: Amey Ventures Investments Limited; JLIF (GP) Limited
Officers: Neeti Mukundrai Anand [1984] Director; Carl Harvey Dix [1966] Operations Director; Asif Ghafoor [1970] Director; Katherine Pearman [1961] Director/Chartered Accountant; Carlos Vela Lazaga [1989] Director/Junior Valuation Analyst [Spanish]

Aibel Finance Limited
Incorporated: 31 October 2006
Net Worth Deficit: £44,370,928 *Total Assets:* £78,209,768
Registered Office: Station House, 50 North Street, Havant, Hants, PO9 1QU
Activities: Activities of other holding companies n.e.c.
Parent: Aibel Ltd
Officers: Simen Heyerdahl-Larsen Ausland, Secretary; Simen Heyerdahl-Larsen Ausland [1978] Director/Lawyer [Norwegian]; Jon Aksel Svensson [1972] Director/Group Controller [Norwegian]

Aibel Group Limited
Incorporated: 15 May 2003
Net Worth: £131,689,792 *Total Assets:* £131,695,928
Registered Office: Station House, 50 North Street, Havant, Hants, PO9 1QU
Activities: Activities of other holding companies n.e.c.
Parent: Aibel Finance Limited
Officers: Simen Heyerdahl-Larsen Ausland, Secretary; Simen Heyerdahl-Larsen Ausland [1978] Director/Lawyer [Norwegian]; Jon Aksel Svensson [1972] Director/Group Controller [Norwegian]

Air Bidco Limited
Incorporated: 20 November 2014
Net Worth Deficit: £289,756,960 *Total Assets:* £887,954,432
Registered Office: Ditton Park, Riding Court Road, Datchet, Berks, SL3 9LL
Activities: Activities of other holding companies n.e.c.
Officers: Natalie Amanda Shaw, Secretary; Adrian Roberto Alonso [1984] Director [American]; Maneet Singh Saroya [1979] Director [American]

Air BP Limited
Incorporated: 11 December 1973
Net Worth: £64,494,364 *Total Assets:* £252,219,584
Registered Office: Chertsey Road, Sunbury on Thames, Middlesex, TW16 7BP
Activities: Wholesale of other fuels and related products
Parent: BP Global Investments Limited
Officers: Matthew Howard Elliott [1972] Director/Oil Company Executive [New Zealander]; Jonathan Peter Platt [1967] Director/Oil Company Executive; Jonathan William Winston Wood [1962] Director/Oil Company Executive

Air Charter Service Group Limited
Incorporated: 6 July 2000 *Employees:* 386
Previous: Air Charter Service Group PLC
Net Worth: £11,982,000 *Total Assets:* £60,419,000
Registered Office: Millbank House, 171-185 Ewell Road, Surbiton, Surrey, KT6 6AP
Activities: Non-scheduled passenger air transport
Parent: Mountfitchet Group Limited
Officers: Omar Saeed, Secretary; Justin Christopher Bowman [1972] Director/Executive; William Andrew Christie [1976] Director; Ruan Patrick Courtney [1972] Director/Executive; Justin James Lancaster [1977] Director/Sales Executive; Christopher Denis Stephen Leach [1949] Director/Executive; Stewart Pitt [1972] Finance Director

Air Menzies International Limited
Incorporated: 23 February 1994 *Employees:* 155
Net Worth: £2,566,000 *Total Assets:* £28,753,000
Registered Office: 2 World Business Centre Heathrow, Newall Road, London Heathrow Airport, Hounslow, Middlesex, TW6 2SF
Activities: Other service activities n.e.c.
Parent: Menzies Aviation PLC
Officers: Mark Edward Lawrence [1959] Director/Accountant; Mark Rhynes [1981] Director/Accountant; Sharon Wright [1957] Director

Air Partner PLC
Incorporated: 28 May 1970 *Employees:* 267
Net Worth: £11,523,000 *Total Assets:* £63,254,000
Registered Office: 2 City Place, Beehive Ring Road, Gatwick, W Sussex, RH6 0PA
Activities: Non-scheduled passenger air transport
Officers: Judith Banks, Secretary; Mark Andrew Briffa [1964] Director/Chief Executive Officer; Joanne Elizabeth Estell [1971] Director/Accountant; Richard Trevor Relton Jackson [1952] Director/Executive; Shaun Michael Smith [1961] Finance Director; Amanda Elizabeth Wills [1962] Director

Air Products (BR) Limited
Incorporated: 17 August 1990
Net Worth: £70,965,000 *Total Assets:* £736,190,016
Registered Office: Hersham Place Technology Park, Molesey Road, Walton on Thames, Surrey, KT12 4RZ
Activities: Manufacture of industrial gases
Officers: Mark Jamie Sambrook, Secretary; Richard John Boocock [1961] Director/President, Industrial Gases-Middle East, India; Charles George Stinner [1963] Director/Vice President, Taxes [American]; Gregory Earl Weigard [1954] Director/Vice President and Corporate Treasurer [American]

Air Products Group Limited
Incorporated: 13 September 1995
Net Worth: £566,960,000 *Total Assets:* £834,520,000
Registered Office: Hersham Place Technology Park, Molesey Road, Hersham, Walton on Thames, Surrey, KT12 4RZ
Activities: Activities of head offices
Officers: Mark Jamie Sambrook, Secretary; Richard John Boocock [1961] Director/President, Industrial Gases-Middle East, India; Charles George Stinner [1963] Director/Vice President, Taxes [American]; Gregory Earl Weigard [1954] Director/Vice President and Corporate Treasurer [American]

Air Products Public Limited Company
Incorporated: 5 July 1909 *Employees:* 1,378
Net Worth: £421,652,000 *Total Assets:* £778,465,984
Registered Office: Hersham Place Technology Park, Molesey Road, Walton on Thames, Surrey, KT12 4RZ
Activities: Manufacture of industrial gases
Parent: Air Products Group Limited
Officers: Mark Jamie Sambrook, Secretary; Richard John Boocock [1961] Director/President, Industrial Gases-Middle East, India; David Leney [1967] Director/Financial Controller; Charles George Stinner [1963] Director/Vice President, Taxes [American]; Gregory Earl Weigard [1954] Director/Vice President and Corporate Treasurer [American]

Airinmar Limited
Incorporated: 14 November 1995 *Employees:* 136
Net Worth: £30,623,618 *Total Assets:* £31,844,340
Registered Office: 1 Ivanhoe Road, Hogwood Industrial Estate, Finchampstead, Berks, RG40 4QQ
Activities: Other business support service activities n.e.c.
Parent: AAR International, Inc.
Officers: Robert Regan, Secretary; John Holmes [1976] Director/Business Executive [American]; Eric Pachapa [1973] Director/Business Executive [American]; Robert John Regan [1957] Director/Vice President General Counsel & Secretary [American]

Airspan Communications Limited
Incorporated: 26 January 1998 *Employees:* 496
Net Worth Deficit: £155,847,584 *Total Assets:* £51,686,728
Registered Office: Capital Point, 33 Bath Road, Slough, Berks, SL1 3UF
Activities: Wireless telecommunications activities
Officers: Raymond Francis Flaherty, Secretary; David Mark Elias Brant [1963] Director/Accountant; Paul Nicholas Senior [1964] Director/Manager; Eric Donald Stonestrom [1961] Director/Engineer [American]

Aitch Care Homes (London) Limited
Incorporated: 15 January 2004 *Employees:* 629
Net Worth: £17,983,000 *Total Assets:* £38,078,000
Registered Office: Unit 6 & 7 Princeton Mews, 167-169 London Road, Kingston upon Thames, Surrey, KT2 6PT
Activities: Other business support service activities n.e.c.
Parent: Aitch Care Homes Holdco Limited
Officers: Nicola Hopkins, Secretary; Nicola Rosemary Lucy Hopkins [1968] Director/Chartered Accountant

Aitch Care Homes Holdco Limited
Incorporated: 26 November 2013
Previous: Montreux Almayer Limited
Net Worth Deficit: £8,602,000 *Total Assets:* £24,653,000
Registered Office: Unit 6 & 7 Princeton Mews, 167-169 London Road, Kingston upon Thames, Surrey, KT2 6PT
Activities: Residential care activities for the elderly and disabled
Parent: Aitch Care Homes Topco Limited
Officers: Nicola Hopkins, Secretary; Nicola Rosemary Lucy Hopkins [1968] Director/Chartered Accountant

AKA London Limited
Incorporated: 29 October 2015
Net Worth Deficit: £442,005 *Total Assets:* £26,163,468
Registered Office: Morton House, Coombe Park, Kingston upon Thames, Surrey, KT2 7JB
Activities: Buying and selling of own real estate
Major Shareholder: Aibibula Nuermaimaiti
Officers: Aibibula Nuermaimaiti [1989] Director [Chinese]; Aibibula Paliwanmuhaimaiti [1991] Director [Chinese]

Akaal Group PLC
Incorporated: 5 October 2006 *Employees:* 288
Net Worth: £66,641,928 *Total Assets:* £86,872,256
Registered Office: 3 Roberts Mews, Orpington, Kent, BR6 0JP
Activities: Activities of head offices
Major Shareholder: Rajbir Singh Manak
Officers: Tanya Maria Barrett, Secretary; Harbhajan Kaur Manak [1940] Director [Indian]; Rajbir Singh Manak [1966] Managing Director [Indian]

Akari Therapeutics, PLC
Incorporated: 7 October 2004 *Employees:* 21
Previous: Celsus Therapeutics PLC
Net Worth: £23,538,988 *Total Assets:* £28,707,494
Registered Office: Elder House, St Georges Business Park, 207 Brooklands Road, Weybridge, Surrey, KT13 0TS
Activities: Other business support service activities n.e.c.
Officers: Dov Elefant, Secretary; David Anthony Byrne [1959] Director; Peter Feldschreiber [1943] Director; Michael Grissinger [1953] Director [American]; Dr James Ferguson Hill [1945] Director/Retired; Raymond Richard Prudo-Chlebosz [1944] Director/Doctor [Canadian]; Clive Stuart Richardson [1965] Director; Stuart Charles Ungar [1943] Director; Donald Allen Williams [1958] Director [American]

Akzo Nobel Coatings (BLD) Limited
Incorporated: 18 December 2003
Net Worth: £470,431,008 *Total Assets:* £473,483,008
Registered Office: The Akzonobel Building, Wexham Road, Slough, Berks, SL2 5DS
Activities: Activities of head offices
Parent: Akzo Nobel N.V.
Officers: Stephen Bruce Ray [1962] Director/Pensions Accounting Manager; Michael Smalley [1958] Director

Akzo Nobel Decorative Coatings Limited
Incorporated: 9 April 1915 *Employees:* 3
Net Worth: £10,648,000 *Total Assets:* £33,237,000
Registered Office: The Akzonobel Building, Wexham Road, Slough, Berks, SL2 5DS
Activities: Activities of head offices
Parent: Akzo Nobel Coatings (BLD) Limited
Officers: Michael Smalley [1958] Director; Matthew Welham Trueblood [1962] Director

Akzo Nobel Finance (2) Limited
Incorporated: 25 November 2015
Net Worth: £669,241,792 *Total Assets:* £672,532,992
Registered Office: The Akzonobel Building, Wexham Road, Slough, Berks, SL2 5DS
Activities: Non-trading company
Parent: Akzo Nobel Finance Limited
Officers: James Laurence Keane [1963] Director; Stephen Bruce Ray [1962] Director; Michael Smalley [1958] Director; David Allan Turner [1971] Director

Akzo Nobel Finance Limited
Incorporated: 8 April 2013 *Employees:* 3
Net Worth: £1,655,381,376 *Total Assets:* £2,809,158,912
Registered Office: The Akzonobel Building, Wexham Road, Slough, Berks, SL2 5DS
Activities: Financial intermediation not elsewhere classified
Parent: Akzo Nobel N.V.
Officers: James Laurence Keane [1963] Director; Stephen Bruce Ray [1962] Director; Michael Smaley [1958] Director; David Allan Turner [1971] Director

Akzo Nobel Holdings Limited
Incorporated: 13 June 1983
Net Worth: £238,240,992 *Total Assets:* £240,726,000
Registered Office: The Akzonobel Building, Wexham Road, Slough, Berks, SL2 5DS
Activities: Activities of head offices
Parent: Akzo Nobel Limited
Officers: Louise Margaret Dinnage [1970] Director; Michael Smalley [1958] Director

Akzo Nobel ICI Holdings
Incorporated: 14 March 2008
Net Worth: £413,000,000 *Total Assets:* £13,498,999,808
Registered Office: The Akzonobel Building, Wexham Road, Slough, Berks, SL2 5DS
Activities: Financial intermediation not elsewhere classified
Parent: Akzo Nobel N.V.
Officers: Stephen Bruce Ray [1962] Director/Pensions Accounting Manager; Michael Smalley [1958] Director; David Allan Turner [1971] Director

Akzo Nobel Limited
Incorporated: 25 February 1998
Net Worth Deficit: £318,185,984 *Total Assets:* £469,012,000
Registered Office: The Akzonobel Building, Wexham Road, Slough, Berks, SL2 5DS
Activities: Activities of head offices
Parent: Akzo Nobel N.V.
Officers: Michael Smalley [1958] Director; Matthew Welham Trueblood [1962] Director

Akzo Nobel Packaging Coatings Limited
Incorporated: 8 December 1898 *Employees:* 230
Net Worth: £46,767,000 *Total Assets:* £149,916,992
Registered Office: The Akzonobel Building, Wexham Road, Slough, Berks, SL2 5DS
Activities: Manufacture of paints, varnishes and similar coatings, mastics and sealants
Parent: Dulux Limited
Officers: David John James [1964] Director; Michael Smalley [1958] Director

Akzo Nobel Powder Coatings Limited
Incorporated: 20 May 1983 *Employees:* 160
Net Worth Deficit: £7,281,000 *Total Assets:* £41,981,000
Registered Office: The Akzonobel Building, Wexham Road, Slough, Berks, SL2 5DS
Activities: Manufacture of paints, varnishes and similar coatings, mastics and sealants
Parent: Akzo Nobel Coatings (BLD) Limited
Officers: Arthur Moseley [1958] Director/Marketing Manager; Michael Smalley [1958] Director; Simon Marc Timmins [1976] Director; Judith Claire Toolan [1973] Director; David Allan Turner [1971] Director

Akzo Nobel UK Ltd
Incorporated: 3 April 1913 *Employees:* 15
Net Worth: £688,300,032 *Total Assets:* £807,200,000
Registered Office: The Akzonobel Building, Wexham Road, Slough, Berks, SL2 5DS
Activities: Activities of head offices
Parent: Akzo Nobel Limited
Officers: Michael Smalley [1958] Director; Matthew Welham Trueblood [1962] Director; David Allan Turner [1971] Director

Alandale Logistics Limited
Incorporated: 18 November 1996 *Employees:* 158
Net Worth: £5,698,987 *Total Assets:* £28,983,552
Registered Office: 1 Brook Court, Blakeney Road, Beckenham, Kent, BR3 1HG
Activities: Other specialised construction activities n.e.c.
Officers: David Trevor Bulman [1969] Director/Health & Safety; Michael John Stocker-Harris [1965] Financial Director

Albain Bidco UK Limited
Incorporated: 25 September 2013
Net Worth: £48,576,400 *Total Assets:* £49,298,092
Registered Office: Velocity V1, Brooklands Drive, Weybridge, Surrey, KT13 0SL
Activities: Activities of other holding companies n.e.c.
Officers: Dena Michelle L O'Bue, Secretary; Stephen James Hamilton [1969] Director/Country Tax Manager, UK & Ireland; Holly Caroline Webster [1974] Director/Lawyer

Albright International Limited
Incorporated: 24 September 1976 *Employees:* 191
Net Worth: £17,916,732 *Total Assets:* £26,699,772
Registered Office: Unit E, Evingar Trading Estate, Ardglen Road, Whitchurch, Hants, RG28 7BB
Activities: Manufacture of electronic components
Parent: Lea Redway Limited
Officers: Richard Hunt, Secretary/Finance Manager; Maria Adaway [1965] Director; Luke Edward Victor Bedggood [1974] Director/Sales and Technical; Nigel Edward Lawrence Bedggood [1941] Director/Engineer; Kevin John Holland [1958] Operations Director; Richard Hunt [1958] Director/CIMA

Alcon Eye Care UK Limited
Incorporated: 16 June 1964 *Employees:* 190
Net Worth: £25,339,000 *Total Assets:* £68,618,000
Registered Office: Frimley Business Park, Frimley, Camberley, Surrey, GU16 7SR
Activities: Other business support service activities n.e.c.
Parent: Alcon Inc.
Officers: Cheryl Tsu Lynn Khoo, Secretary; Haseeb Ahmad [1976] Director; Ian Howard Bell [1970] Director/Region President, EMEA; Oriane Fanny Lacaze [1979] Director/Country Chief Financial Officer [French]

Alder Hey (Special Purpose Vehicle) Limited
Incorporated: 6 February 2013
Net Worth: £611,000 *Total Assets:* £140,735,008
Registered Office: 8 White Oak Square, London Road, Swanley, Kent, BR8 7AG
Activities: Construction of commercial buildings
Parent: Alder Hey Holdco 1 Limited
Officers: Robert James Marsden [1955] Director; Tristan James Meredith [1980] Bid Director; Andrew Stephen Pearson [1964] Managing Director; Alan Travis [1971] Director

Alder Hey Holdco 1 Limited
Incorporated: 5 February 2013
Net Worth: £30,000 *Total Assets:* £32,808,000
Registered Office: 8 White Oak Square, London Road, Swanley, Kent, BR8 7AG
Activities: Activities of head offices
Parent: Alder Hey Holdco 2 Limited
Officers: Robert James Marsden [1955] Director; Tristan James Meredith [1980] Bid Director; Andrew Stephen Pearson [1964] Managing Director; Alan Travis [1971] Director

Alder Hey Holdco 2 Limited
Incorporated: 4 February 2013
Net Worth: £30,000 *Total Assets:* £32,808,000
Registered Office: 8 White Oak Square, London Road, Swanley, Kent, BR8 7AG
Activities: Activities of head offices
Parent: Alder Hey Holdco 3 Limited
Officers: Robert James Marsden [1955] Director; Tristan James Meredith [1980] Bid Director; Andrew Stephen Pearson [1964] Managing Director; Alan Travis [1971] Director

Alder Hey Holdco 3 Limited
Incorporated: 20 February 2013
Net Worth: £611,000 *Total Assets:* £140,735,008
Registered Office: 8 White Oak Square, London Road, Swanley, Kent, BR8 7AG
Activities: Activities of head offices
Shareholders: John Laing Investments Limited; Laing O'Rourke PLC
Officers: Robert James Marsden [1955] Director; Tristan James Meredith [1980] Bid Director; Andrew Stephen Pearson [1964] Managing Director; Alan Travis [1971] Director

Aldermore Group PLC
Incorporated: 3 December 2008 *Employees:* 936
Net Worth: £758,000,000 *Total Assets:* £10,432,700,416
Registered Office: 4th Floor, Block D, Apex Plaza, Forbury Road, Reading, Berks, RG1 1AX
Activities: Activities of financial services holding companies
Officers: Marius Van Niekerk, Secretary; Patrick Noel Butler [1960] Director [Irish]; Danuta Gray [1958] Director; John Charles Fortescue Hitchins [1955] Director; Hetash Surendrakumar Kellan [1971] Director [South African]; Christopher James Mack [1971] Director; David Phillip Monks [1960] Director; Christine Joan Palmer [1966] Director/Chief Risk Officer; Alan Patrick Pullinger [1965] Director [South African]; Peter Anderson Shaw [1959] Director; Christopher Paul Stamper [1955] Director; Catherine Lucy Turner [1963] Director

Alenco (Holdings) Limited
Incorporated: 30 June 1950
Net Worth: £18,488,000 *Total Assets:* £23,867,000
Registered Office: Parker House, 55 Maylands Avenue, Hemel Hempstead Industrial Estate, Hemel Hempstead, Herts, HP2 4SJ
Activities: Non-trading company
Parent: Parker Hannifin (Holdings) Limited
Officers: Graham Mark Ellinor, Secretary; Graham Mark Ellinor [1964] Director/Accountant; James Alan David Elsey [1970] HR Director

Alent Finance Limited
Incorporated: 27 September 2012
Net Worth Deficit: £13,456,000 *Total Assets:* £354,185,984
Registered Office: Unit 2 Genesis Business Park, Albert Drive, Sheerwater, Woking, Surrey, GU21 5RW
Activities: Non-trading company
Parent: Alent Investments Limited
Officers: Paul Antony Ashworth [1964] Director/Accountant; John Patrick Connolly [1966] Director/Chief Financial Officer [American]

Alent Investments Limited
Incorporated: 15 August 2012
Net Worth: £200,355,008 *Total Assets:* £217,808,000
Registered Office: Unit 2 Genesis Business Park, Albert Drive, Sheerwater, Woking, Surrey, GU21 5RW
Activities: Activities of head offices
Parent: Alent Limited
Officers: Paul Antony Ashworth [1964] Director/Accountant; John Patrick Connolly [1966] Director/Chief Financial Officer [American]

Alent Limited
Incorporated: 31 August 2012
Previous: Alent PLC
Net Worth: £634,800,000 *Total Assets:* £722,862,976
Registered Office: Unit 2 Genesis Business Park, Albert Drive, Sheerwater, Woking, Surrey, GU21 5RW
Activities: Activities of head offices
Officers: John Edward Capps, Secretary; Paul Antony Ashworth [1964] Director/Accountant; Scot Robert Benson [1961] Director/President of Performance Applications [American]; Paul Andrew Bray [1969] Managing Director; John Edward Capps [1964] Director [American]; Terence Joseph Clarke [1957] Marketing and R&D Director; John Patrick Connolly [1966] Director/Chief Financial Officer [American]

Alent New Finance (UK) Limited
Incorporated: 8 October 2012
Net Worth: £43,197,000 *Total Assets:* £289,468,992
Registered Office: Unit 2 Genesis Business Park, Albert Drive, Sheerwater, Woking, Surrey, GU21 5RW
Activities: Non-trading company
Parent: Alent Finance Limited
Officers: Paul Antony Ashworth [1964] Director/Accountant; John Patrick Connolly [1966] Director/Chief Financial Officer [American]

Alere as Holdings Limited
Incorporated: 26 July 2011
Net Worth: £184,520,000 *Total Assets:* £261,367,008
Registered Office: Clearblue Innovation Centre, Priory Business Park, Stannard Way, Bedford, MK44 3UP
Activities: Activities of head offices
Parent: Alere International Limited
Officers: David Andrew Bond [1971] Director/Chartered Accountant; Benjamin Edward Oosterbaan [1963] Director/Assistant Treasurer [American]

Alere UK Holdings Limited
Incorporated: 9 August 2001
Net Worth Deficit: £28,013,000 *Total Assets:* £170,150,000
Registered Office: Clearblue Innovation Centre, Priory Business Park, Stannard Way, Bedford, MK44 3UP
Activities: Activities of head offices
Parent: Alere Switzerland GmbH
Officers: David Andrew Bond [1971] Director/Chartered Accountant; Benjamin Edward Oosterbaan [1963] Director/Assistant Treasurer [American]; Brian Gregory Shoup [1969] Director [American]

Alestra Group Holdings Limited
Incorporated: 9 December 2013 *Employees:* 445
Net Worth: £36,892,584 *Total Assets:* £91,926,704
Registered Office: 1 Princeton Mews, 167-169 London Road, Kingston upon Thames, Surrey, KT2 6PT
Activities: Other business support service activities n.e.c.
Officers: Monika Anna Marie Carlsson [1974] Director [American]; Manuela Dina Maria Eleuteri [1952] Director; Erik Staffan Encrantz [1951] Director [Swedish]; Donata Van Der Veen [1954] Director/Administrator [Italian]

Alestra Limited
Incorporated: 19 November 2002 *Employees:* 3
Net Worth: £101,180,712 *Total Assets:* £103,388,792
Registered Office: 1 Princeton Mews, 167-169 London Road, Kingston upon Thames, Surrey, KT2 6PT
Activities: Non-trading company
Parent: Alestra Group Holdings Limited
Officers: Monika Anna Marie Carlsson [1974] Director [American]; Manuela Dina Maria Eleuteri [1952] Director/Corporate Consultant; Staffan Encrantz [1951] Director [Swedish]; Donata Van Der Veen [1954] Director/Administrator [Italian]

Alex Brands Rocket Holdings Limited
Incorporated: 20 March 2015
Net Worth: £40,770,104 *Total Assets:* £48,893,388
Registered Office: 22 Wycombe End, Beaconsfield, Bucks, HP9 1NB
Activities: Retail sale of games and toys in specialised stores
Parent: Poof-Alex Holdings LLC
Officers: Kenneth Dunaj [1966] Director/President and COO [American]

Alexion Pharma UK Limited
Incorporated: 17 October 2006 *Employees:* 74
Net Worth: £3,460,531 *Total Assets:* £34,744,548
Registered Office: 3 Furzeground Way, Stockley Park, Uxbridge, Middlesex, UB11 1EZ
Activities: Other business support service activities n.e.c.
Parent: Alexion Pharmaceuticals, Inc.
Officers: Philippe Dufaux, Secretary; Michael Ira Kenneth Elloian [1972] Director/VP, Chief of Tax, Finance [American]; Vivien Ruth Greer [1976] Director Finance [Irish]; Sean Richardson [1970] Director/General Manager - Pharmaceuticals

Alfa Laval Holdings Limited
Incorporated: 7 September 2000 *Employees:* 3
Net Worth: £32,537,000 *Total Assets:* £40,983,000
Registered Office: 7 Doman Road, Camberley, Surrey, GU15 3DN
Activities: Activities of head offices
Parent: Alfa Laval Iberia S.A.
Officers: Lawrence Fox, Secretary; Lawrence Fox [1977] Director/Accountant [British/French]; Mikael Hellborg [1961] Managing Director [Swedish]; Nainesh Mahendra Patel [1962] Director/Executive Vice President

Alfa Laval Limited
Incorporated: 22 January 1923 *Employees:* 206
Net Worth Deficit: £21,012,000 *Total Assets:* £54,131,000
Registered Office: 7 Doman Road, Camberley, Surrey, GU15 3DN
Activities: Manufacture of other general-purpose machinery n.e.c.
Parent: Alfa Laval Holdings Limited
Officers: Lawrence Fox, Secretary; Lawrence Fox [1977] Director/Accountant [British/French]; Mikael Hellborg [1961] Managing Director [Swedish]; Nainesh Mahendra Patel [1962] Director/Executive Vice President

Ali UK Limited
Incorporated: 20 February 1998 *Employees:* 3
Net Worth: £81,506,000 *Total Assets:* £130,357,000
Registered Office: 60 Barwell Business Park, Leatherhead Road, Chessington, Surrey, KT9 2NY
Activities: Other food services
Major Shareholder: Filippo Berti
Officers: Michael Hans May, Secretary; Maurizio Anastasia [1970] Director [Italian]; Michael Hans May [1951] Director; Angelo Speranza [1962] Director

Aliaxis Holdings UK Limited
Incorporated: 30 November 2000 *Employees:* 10
Net Worth: £503,084,000 *Total Assets:* £711,140,992
Registered Office: Dickley Lane, Lenham, Maidstone, Kent, ME17 2DE
Activities: Activities of production holding companies
Officers: Ian Charles McNair, Secretary; Ian Charles McNair [1960] Director/Accountant; Koen Jozef Sticker [1976] Director [Belgian]

Alimera Sciences Limited
Incorporated: 3 April 2012 *Employees:* 30
Net Worth: £2,410,611 *Total Assets:* £64,319,340
Registered Office: Royal Pavilion, Wellesley Road, Aldershot, Hants, GU11 1PZ
Activities: Other business support service activities n.e.c.
Parent: Alimera Sciences, Inc.
Officers: Philip John Ashman [1965] Managing Director; Richard S. Eiswirth Jr [1969] Director/President and CFO of Alimera Sciences, Inc [American]; Charles Daniel Myers Jr [1954] Director/CEO of Alimera Sciences, Inc [American]

Aliunde Limited
Incorporated: 29 July 2005 *Employees:* 1
Net Worth: £1,453,004 *Total Assets:* £42,024,648
Registered Office: 12 Hatherley Road, Sidcup, Kent, DA14 4DT
Activities: Security and commodity contracts dealing activities
Major Shareholder: Bertrand Velge
Officers: Bertrand Roger Velge [1959] Director

All Metal Services Limited
Incorporated: 8 February 1974 *Employees:* 305
Net Worth: £90,441,312 *Total Assets:* £154,515,056
Registered Office: Unit 6 Horton Industrial Park, Horton Road, West Drayton, Middlesex, UB7 8JD
Activities: Agents involved in the sale of machinery, industrial equipment, ships and aircraft
Officers: Karla Renee Lewis [1965] Director/Chief Financial Officer [American]; Gregg James Mollins [1954] Director [American]; David Leslie Potts [1946] Director; William Sales [1957] Director [American]; Sara Williams [1967] Financial Director

Ian Allan Group Limited
Incorporated: 1 November 1962 *Employees:* 159
Net Worth: £19,248,860 *Total Assets:* £26,685,968
Registered Office: Terminal House, Station Approach, Shepperton, Surrey, TW17 8AS
Activities: Activities of head offices
Officers: Derek Arthur Hart, Secretary; David Ian Allan [1954] Executive Director; Edwin Paul Allan [1957] Executive Director; Gillian Susan Allan [1957] Director; Michael Andrew Smith [1960] Director/Chartered Accountant; Anthony Douglas Watkins [1944] Director/Chartered Accountant

Allegis Global Solutions Limited
Incorporated: 22 April 1998 *Employees:* 222
Net Worth: £16,082,875 *Total Assets:* £46,655,436
Registered Office: Maxis 2, Western Road, Bracknell, Berks, RG12 1RT
Activities: Computer facilities management activities
Shareholders: Randall Dean Sones; Richard Alan Butler; Fred Ridley
Officers: Gregory Alan Barber [1967] Director; John Nicholas Glenn [1972] Director

Allegis Group (UK) Holdings II Limited
Incorporated: 10 January 2011
Net Worth: £100,590,048 *Total Assets:* £100,687,336
Registered Office: Maxis 2, Western Road, Bracknell, Berks, RG12 1RT
Activities: Computer facilities management activities
Shareholders: Randall Dean Sones; Richard Alan Butler; Fred S. Ridley
Officers: Paul Joseph Bowie [1967] Director/Business Executive [American]; Christopher Lee Hartman [1968] Director/Business Executive [American]; Sean Hendrick Zimdahl [1968] Director [German]

Allegis Group (UK) Holdings Limited
Incorporated: 7 January 2011
Net Worth: £78,653,792 *Total Assets:* £97,518,888
Registered Office: Maxis 2, Western Road, Bracknell, Berks, RG12 1RT
Activities: Computer facilities management activities
Shareholders: Randall Dean Soanes; Richard Alan Butler
Officers: Paul Joseph Bowie [1967] Director/Business Executive [American]; Christopher Lee Hartman [1968] Director/Business Executive [American]

Allegis Group Limited
Incorporated: 25 November 1993 *Employees:* 637
Net Worth: £86,983,048 *Total Assets:* £122,184,840
Registered Office: Maxis 2, Western Road, Bracknell, Berks, RG12 1RT
Activities: Computer facilities management activities
Shareholders: Randall Dean Sones; Richard Alan Butler; Fred Ridley
Officers: Andrew David Williams [1981] Director; Sean Hendrick Zimdahl [1968] Director [German]

Allen Diesels Limited
Incorporated: 18 August 2009 *Employees:* 28
Net Worth: £27,709,290 *Total Assets:* £30,627,280
Registered Office: Sandland Court, Pilgrim Centre, Brickhill Drive, Bedford, MK41 7PZ
Activities: Manufacture of engines and turbines, except aircraft, vehicle and cycle engines
Officers: Roger John Smyth, Secretary; Paul Martin Knight [1964] Director

M.J. Allen Holdings Limited
Incorporated: 26 July 1961 *Employees:* 245
Net Worth: £16,242,066 *Total Assets:* £26,987,284
Registered Office: Cobbs Wood Industrial Estate, Hilton Road, Ashford, Kent, TN23 1EW
Activities: Activities of head offices
Shareholders: Michael John Allen; Jackie Jean Allen
Officers: Alan Charles Gibson, Secretary/Director; Ben Allen [1991] Director; Jacqueline Jean Allen [1938] Director; Michael Nicholas Allen [1966] Director; Michael John Allen [1936] Director; Timothy John Allen [1960] Director; Alan Charles Gibson [1954] Director

Allergan Holdco UK Limited
Incorporated: 2 August 2016
Net Worth: £38,933,528,576 *Total Assets:* £39,011,266,560
Registered Office: 1st Floor, Marlow International, Parkway, Marlow, Bucks, SL7 1YL
Activities: Activities of head offices
Parent: Allergan PLC
Officers: Patricia Maria Haran, Secretary; Glen Curran [1973] Director [Australian]; Nick Hudson [1975] Director; Paul Johnson [1972] Director; Duncan James Reeves [1978] Director

Allergan Holdings Limited
Incorporated: 10 October 1988 *Employees:* 139
Net Worth: £185,138,000 *Total Assets:* £239,548,000
Registered Office: 1st Floor, Marlow International, The Parkway, Marlow, Bucks, SL7 1YL
Activities: Activities of head offices
Parent: Allergan Holdco UK Limited
Officers: Patricia Maria Haran, Secretary; Judith Tomkins, Secretary; Kevin Asher [1978] Director; Paul Johnson [1972] Director

Allergan Limited
Incorporated: 13 April 1972 *Employees:* 283
Net Worth: £35,379,000 *Total Assets:* £98,128,000
Registered Office: 1st Floor, Marlow International, The Parkway, Marlow, Bucks, SL7 1YL
Activities: Wholesale of pharmaceutical goods
Parent: Allergan Holdings Limited
Officers: Patricia Maria Haran, Secretary; Judith Tomkins, Secretary; Kevin Asher [1978] Director; Paul Johnson [1972] Director; Nicholas Barry Spicer [1978] Director

Allergy Therapeutics (UK) Limited
Incorporated: 7 January 1998 *Employees:* 250
Net Worth Deficit: £87,187,000 *Total Assets:* £29,611,000
Registered Office: Dominion Way, Worthing, W Sussex, BN14 8SA
Activities: Manufacture of pharmaceutical preparations
Parent: Allergy Therapeuatics Holdings Limited
Officers: Sara Louise Goldsbrough, Secretary; Manuel Llobet [1964] Director [Spanish]; Nicolas Alexander Ulrich Wykeman [1964] Director

Allergy Therapeutics PLC
Incorporated: 1 June 2004 *Employees:* 499
Net Worth: £23,034,000 *Total Assets:* £51,016,000
Registered Office: Dominion Way, Worthing, W Sussex, BN14 8SA
Activities: Manufacture of pharmaceutical preparations
Shareholder: Abbott Laboratories
Officers: Sara Louise Goldsbrough, Secretary; Peter Sinclair Jensen [1950] Director; Scott Michael Leinenweber [1971] Director [American]; Manuel Llobet [1965] Director/Chief Executive Officer; Dr Babatunde Adekunle Otulana [1956] Director/Physician [American/Nigerian]; Stephen Rushworth Smith [1953] Director; Nicolas Alexander Ulrich Wykeman [1964] Director

Alliance BMP Limited
Incorporated: 17 January 2007 *Employees:* 1
Net Worth: £36,571,000 *Total Assets:* £52,475,000
Registered Office: 2 The Heights, Brooklands, Weybridge, Surrey, KT13 0NY
Activities: Other business support service activities n.e.c.
Parent: WBA Group Limited
Officers: Frank Standish, Secretary [Irish]; Mattia D'Alessandro [1975] Director [Italian]; Alexandro Depau [1970] Director [American]; John Kallend [1959] Director

Alliance Healthcare (Distribution) Limited
Incorporated: 7 October 1997
Net Worth: £258,000,000 *Total Assets:* £1,248,999,936
Registered Office: 43 Cox Lane, Chessington, Surrey, KT9 1SN
Activities: Wholesale of pharmaceutical goods
Parent: Alliance Boots Holdings Limited
Officers: Lucie Charlotte Massart, Secretary; Alexandro Depau [1970] Director [American]; Julian David Mount [1965] Director; Pablo Cortes Rivas [1972] Director [Spanish]

Alliance Healthcare (IT Services) Limited
Incorporated: 13 March 2000
Net Worth: £9,290,000 *Total Assets:* £111,040,000
Registered Office: 2 The Heights, Brooklands, Weybridge, Surrey, KT13 0NY
Activities: Other information technology service activities
Parent: Alliance Boots Holdings Limited
Officers: Frank Standish, Secretary [Irish]; Mark Francis Muller [1964] Director; Steven Rempel [1961] Director [American]; Anthony Charles Roberts [1962] Director

Allianz (UK) Limited
Incorporated: 13 February 1986
Net Worth: £910,550,976 *Total Assets:* £965,641,984
Registered Office: 57 Ladymead, Guildford, Surrey, GU1 1DB
Activities: Other business support service activities n.e.c.
Shareholders: Allianz Europe Limited; Allianz SE
Officers: Steven James Hutchings, Secretary; Christian Wilhelm Tore Dinesen [1961] Director [Danish]; Jonathan Mark Dye [1966] Director/Chief Executive; Richard Owen Hudson [1952] Director; Denise Janet Larnder [1960] Director; Rosanne Mary Murison [1960] Director; Niranjan Christopher Peiris [1961] Director/Member of The Board of Management of Allianz SE [Australian]; David Andrew Torrance [1953] Director

Allianz Engineering Inspection Services Limited
Incorporated: 3 May 2005
Net Worth: £10,466,302 *Total Assets:* £46,903,448
Registered Office: 57 Ladymead, Guildford, Surrey, GU1 1DB
Activities: Other engineering activities
Parent: Allianz Holdings PLC
Officers: Robin Christian Jack-Kee, Secretary; Philip Gennoy [1958] Director HR; Christopher Martyn Little [1969] Managing Director; Simon Cavendish McGinn [1970] Director/General Manager Commercial & Personal

Allianz Equity Investments Limited
Incorporated: 16 September 1987
Net Worth: £150,430,000 *Total Assets:* £150,502,000
Registered Office: 57 Ladymead, Guildford, Surrey, GU1 1DB
Activities: Financial intermediation not elsewhere classified
Parent: Allianz Insurance PLC
Officers: Robin Christian Jack-Kee, Secretary; Jonathan Mark Dye [1966] Director/Chief Executive; Fernley Keith Dyson [1965] Director/Chief Financial Officer; Stuart John Robertson [1960] Director/Accountant

Allianz Holdings PLC
Incorporated: 21 May 2004 *Employees:* 4,466
Net Worth: £1,875,699,968 *Total Assets:* £6,253,300,224
Registered Office: 57 Ladymead, Guildford, Surrey, GU1 1DB
Activities: Activities of head offices
Parent: Allianz (UK) Limited
Officers: Steven James Hutchings, Secretary; Christian Wilhelm Tore Dinesen [1961] Director [Danish]; Jonathan Mark Dye [1966] Director/Chief Executive; Richard Owen Hudson [1952] Director; Denise Janet Larnder [1960] Director; Rosanne Mary Murison [1960] Director; Niranjan Christopher Peiris [1961] Director/Member of The Board of Management of Allianz SE [Australian]; David Andrew Torrance [1953] Director

Allianz Insurance PLC
Incorporated: 18 May 1905
Net Worth: £1,201,500,032 *Total Assets:* £5,635,100,160
Registered Office: 57 Ladymead, Guildford, Surrey, GU1 1DB
Activities: Non-life insurance
Parent: Allianz Holdings PLC
Officers: Steven James Hutchings, Secretary; Christian Wilhelm Tore Dinesen [1961] Director [Danish]; Jonathan Mark Dye [1966] Director/Chief Executive; Richard Owen Hudson [1952] Director; Denise Janet Larnder [1960] Director; Rosanne Mary Murison [1960] Director; Niranjan Christopher Peiris [1961] Director/Member of The Board of Management of Allianz SE [Australian]; David Andrew Torrance [1953] Director

Allianz Management Services Limited
Incorporated: 14 March 2000 *Employees:* 4,376
Net Worth Deficit: £171,240,000 *Total Assets:* £197,943,008
Registered Office: 57 Ladymead, Guildford, Surrey, GU1 1DB
Activities: Other business support service activities n.e.c.
Parent: Allianz Holdings PLC
Officers: Robin Christian Jack-Kee, Secretary; Jonathan Mark Dye [1966] Director/Chief Executive; Fernley Keith Dyson [1965] Director/Chief Financial Officer; Philip Gennoy [1958] Director/HR Executive

Allianz Properties Limited
Incorporated: 6 November 1986
Net Worth: £185,806,000 *Total Assets:* £191,128,000
Registered Office: 57 Ladymead, Guildford, Surrey, GU1 1DB
Activities: Other business support service activities n.e.c.
Parent: Allianz Insurance PLC
Officers: Robin Christian Jack-Kee, Secretary; Jonathan Mark Dye [1966] Director/Chief Executive; Fernley Keith Dyson [1965] Director/Chief Financial Officer; Stuart John Robertson [1960] Director/Chief Accountant

Alligent Biopharm Consulting (Europe) Limited
Incorporated: 21 April 2016 *Employees:* 14
Net Worth: £243,588,864 *Total Assets:* £266,205,456
Registered Office: Envision House, 5 North Street, Horsham, W Sussex, RH12 1XQ
Activities: Other professional, scientific and technical activities n.e.c.
Parent: Envision Pharma Bidco Limited
Officers: John David Gillie [1970] Finance Director; Bruno Serge Leon Ladriere [1961] Managing Director (Private Equity) [French]; Daniel Jacques Joseph Alexandre Setton [1983] Director [French]; Benjamin Maurice Frederick Witcher [1987] Director/Investment Professional

Allocate Bidco Limited
Incorporated: 1 May 2014 *Employees:* 5
Net Worth Deficit: £24,430,000 *Total Assets:* £124,390,000
Registered Office: 2nd Floor, 1 Church Road, Richmond, Surrey, TW9 2QE
Activities: Information technology consultancy activities
Parent: Allocate Midco Limited
Officers: Ryan Friedman Atlas [1984] Director [American]; Nicholas Stephen Wilson [1971] Director/Chief Executive Officer

Allocate Holdco Limited
Incorporated: 1 May 2014
Net Worth Deficit: £821,000 *Total Assets:* £61,137,000
Registered Office: 2nd Floor, 1 Church Road, Richmond, Surrey, TW9 2QE
Activities: Information technology consultancy activities
Parent: Allocate Topco Limited
Officers: Ryan Friedman Atlas [1984] Director [American]; Nicholas Stephen Wilson [1971] Director/Chief Executive Officer

Allocate Midco Limited
Incorporated: 1 May 2014 *Employees:* 408
Net Worth Deficit: £27,971,000 *Total Assets:* £142,212,992
Registered Office: 2nd Floor, 1 Church Road, Richmond, Surrey, TW9 2QE
Activities: Information technology consultancy activities
Parent: Allocate Holdco Limited
Officers: Ryan Friedman Atlas [1984] Director [American]; Nicholas Stephen Wilson [1971] Director/Chief Executive Officer

Allocate Software Limited
Incorporated: 5 May 1993 *Employees:* 378
Previous: Allocate Software PLC
Net Worth: £20,600,000 *Total Assets:* £70,327,000
Registered Office: 2nd Floor, 1 Church Road, Richmond, Surrey, TW9 2QE
Activities: Information technology consultancy activities
Parent: Allocate Bidco Limited
Officers: Ryan Friedman Atlas [1984] Director [American]; Jonathan James Harston [1976] Director/Chief Financial Officer; Nicholas Stephen Wilson [1971] Director/Chief Executive Officer

Allocate Topco Limited
Incorporated: 1 May 2014 *Employees:* 413
Net Worth Deficit: £29,458,000 *Total Assets:* £147,862,000
Registered Office: 2nd Floor, 1 Church Road, Richmond, Surrey, TW9 2QE
Activities: Information technology consultancy activities
Parent: Antidote Bidco Limited
Officers: Ryan Friedman Atlas [1984] Director [American]; Nicholas Stephen Wilson [1971] Director/Chief Executive Officer

Allos Holdings Limited
Incorporated: 24 February 2016 *Employees:* 111
Previous: LHEO Holding Co. Ltd
Net Worth: £43,244,232 *Total Assets:* £47,086,120
Registered Office: 5 The Links, Ascot, Berks, SL5 7TN
Activities: Manufacture of other food products n.e.c.
Shareholder: Alison Mackie Barnes
Officers: Alison Mackie Barnes [1951] Director/Chartered Accountant; Alastair Lionel Hitchen [1953] Director; Peter Thomas Hitchen [1955] Director

Allport Cargo Services Limited
Incorporated: 3 September 1963 *Employees:* 649
Net Worth: £21,362,684 *Total Assets:* £109,364,136
Registered Office: Allport House, 1 Cowley Business Park, High Street, Cowley, Middlesex, UB8 2AD
Activities: Other transportation support activities
Parent: Allport Group Limited
Officers: Jeremy Martin Gray [1957] Director; Shek Yau John Lau [1947] Director [Chinese]; Charles McGurin [1965] Director; David James Thomas [1962] Director; William Alfred John Toye [1942] Freight Forwarder Director; Heath Brian Zarin [1975] Director/Finance [Kittitian]

Allport Group Limited
Incorporated: 15 January 2004 *Employees:* 915
Net Worth: £35,517,076 *Total Assets:* £137,777,280
Registered Office: Allport House, 1 Cowley Business Park, High Street, Cowley, Middlesex, UB8 2AD
Activities: Activities of head offices
Major Shareholder: Heath Brian Zarin
Officers: Mark Davis, Secretary; Clyde Buntrock [1972] Director; Jeremy Martin Gray [1957] Director; Shek Yau John Lau [1947] Director [Chinese]; Charles McGurin [1965] Director; Simon Richard Pearson [1967] Director; David James Thomas [1962] Director; William Alfred John Toye [1942] Freight Forwarder-Director; Steve John Williams [1972] Director; Heath Brian Zarin [1975] Director/Finance [American]

Almus Pharmaceuticals Limited
Incorporated: 6 February 2004 *Employees:* 13
Net Worth: £274,858,464 *Total Assets:* £275,978,528
Registered Office: 2 The Heights, Brooklands, Weybridge, Surrey, KT13 0NY
Activities: Other business support service activities n.e.c.
Parent: Alliance Boots Holdings Limited
Officers: Frank Standish, Company Secretary [Irish]; Alexandro Depau [1970] Director [American]; Richard Joseph Anthony Gorsuch [1970] Director/Chartered Accountant; Careen Elizabeth Snadden [1967] Director

Alpha Assembly Solutions UK Limited
Incorporated: 1 September 1925 *Employees:* 65
Previous: Alpha Fry Limited
Net Worth: £64,018,000 *Total Assets:* £77,988,000
Registered Office: Unit 2 Genesis Business Park, Albert Drive, Sheerwater, Woking, Surrey, GU21 5RW
Activities: Manufacture of other chemical products n.e.c.
Parent: Alent Investments Limited
Officers: John Edward Capps [1964] Director [American]; Thaddeus Scott Ericson [1976] Director/VP Finance [American]; Michael Jerome Siegmund [1960] Director [American]; Valentijn Van Velthoven [1971] Director [Belgian]

Alphabet (GB) Limited
Incorporated: 21 November 1996 *Employees:* 440
Net Worth: £216,363,008 *Total Assets:* £2,327,781,888
Registered Office: Alphabet House, Summit Avenue, Farnborough, Hants, GU14 0FB
Activities: Financial leasing
Parent: BMW (UK) Holdings Limited
Officers: William Edwin Johnson, Secretary; Nicholas John Brownrigg [1960] Director; John Chuhan [1973] Director/Accountant; Stefan Oswald [1967] Director/Chief Financial Officer [Swiss/German]

Alphalarch Limited
Incorporated: 22 July 1997
Net Worth: £20,005,000 *Total Assets:* £71,274,000
Registered Office: 161 Chertsey Road, Twickenham, Middlesex, TW1 1ER
Activities: Other letting and operating of own or leased real estate
Parent: Curfin (Netherlands Antilles) B.V.
Officers: Joseph Michael Jaffe [1955] Director/Business Executive; Derek Jonathan Murray [1960] Director/Company Executive; Glenn Robert Bruce Pitzer [1968] Director/Company Executive

Altair (UK) Ltd
Incorporated: 13 November 2013 *Employees:* 95
Net Worth: £53,878,824 *Total Assets:* £61,074,296
Registered Office: Parker House, 55 Maylands Avenue, Hemel Hempstead Industrial Estate, Hemel Hempstead, Herts, HP2 4SJ
Activities: Manufacture of other special-purpose machinery n.e.c.
Parent: Parker Hannifin Corporation
Officers: Graham Mark Ellinor [1964] Finance Director; James Alan David Elsey [1970] Human Resources Director; Javaid Riaz [1967] Director/Division Operations Manager

Altair Filter Technology Ltd
Incorporated: 26 May 1966
Net Worth: £105,317,000 *Total Assets:* £105,344,000
Registered Office: The Arena, Downshire Way, Bracknell, Berks, RG12 1PU
Activities: Activities of other holding companies n.e.c.
Parent: GE Energy Services (UK) Limited
Officers: James Edward Dennison [1972] Tax Director

Althea (Leicester 2) Limited
Incorporated: 4 May 2006
Previous: Asteral (Leicester 2) Limited
Net Worth: £7,160,224 *Total Assets:* £27,822,708
Registered Office: Unit 4 Ely Road, Theale, Reading, Berks, RG7 4BQ
Activities: Renting and leasing of other machinery, equipment and tangible goods n.e.c.
Parent: Althea UK and Ireland Limited
Officers: Jason Richard Long [1968] New Business Director; David Anthony Rolfe [1972] Director; Stephen James Tuddenham [1980] Commercial Director

Althea UK and Ireland Limited
Incorporated: 26 November 2001 *Employees:* 644
Previous: Asteral Limited
Net Worth: £17,538,000 *Total Assets:* £57,900,000
Registered Office: Unit 4 Ely Road, Theale, Reading, Berks, RG7 4BQ
Activities: Other professional, scientific and technical activities n.e.c.
Parent: Asteral Holdings Limited
Officers: Jason Richard Long [1968] New Business Director; David Anthony Rolfe [1972] Director; Stephen James Tuddenham [1980] Commercial Director

Altonwood Holdings Limited
Incorporated: 8 July 1998 *Employees:* 224
Net Worth: £24,518,858 *Total Assets:* £33,185,860
Registered Office: Streete Court, Rooks Nest Park, Godstone, Surrey, RH9 8BY
Activities: Activities of head offices
Major Shareholder: Novello Lesley Nugee
Officers: Peter Geoffrey Bevis [1956] Director; Ian Christian Granne [1971] Director/Investment Trader; Simon Hodsdon [1965] Managing Director; Christopher Godfrey Honeywill [1951] Director/Chartered Surveyor; Justine Clare Noades [1966] Director; Kelly-Jane Noades [1979] Director; Ryan Oliver Noades [1987] Director; Novello Lesley Nugee [1957] Director

Aluminium Services (UK) Limited
Incorporated: 2 March 2007
Net Worth: £26,703,060 *Total Assets:* £60,000,024
Registered Office: Unit 6 Horton Industrial Park, Horton Road, West Drayton, Middlesex, UB7 8JD
Activities: Activities of head offices
Parent: Reliance Steel and Aluminum
Officers: Karla Renee Lewis [1965] Director/Chief Financial Officer [American]; Gregg James Mollins [1954] Director [American]; David Leslie Potts [1946] Director; William Sales [1957] Director [American]; Sara Williams [1967] Financial Director

Alvis Limited
Incorporated: 30 July 1962 *Employees:* 3
Net Worth: £240,274,000 *Total Assets:* £476,745,984
Registered Office: P O Box 87, Warwick House, Farnborough Aerospace Centre, Farnborough, Hants, GU14 6YU
Activities: Activities of other holding companies n.e.c.
Parent: BAE Systems (Holdings) Limited
Officers: David Stanley Parkes, Secretary; Adam Robert Collins [1980] Finance Director; Jennifer Blair Osbaldestin [1973] Director

Amazon Spring Waters Investment Limited
Incorporated: 2 September 2009
Net Worth: £39,686,940 *Total Assets:* £40,174,640
Registered Office: 19 London End, Beaconsfield, Bucks, HP9 2HN
Activities: Other professional, scientific and technical activities n.e.c.
Major Shareholder: Lawrence Phillips
Officers: Michael Baines, Secretary; Lawrence Phillips [1971] Director/Businessman [New Zealander]; Timothy Ashley Sparks [1956] Director

The Ambassador Entertainment Group Limited
Incorporated: 16 October 2009
Net Worth: £109,175,000 *Total Assets:* £163,067,008
Registered Office: 2nd Floor, Alexander House, Church Path, Woking, Surrey, GU21 6EJ
Activities: Operation of arts facilities
Parent: International Entertainment Investments Ltd
Officers: Mark Ralph Delano Cornell [1966] Director; Adam Lee Kenwright [1972] Commercial Director; Ralf Kokemueller [1962] Director/CEO - BB Group [German]; Michael Cowper Lynas [1957] Director; Nicholas Graham Potter [1968] Managing Director; Shanmae Teo [1976] Director

The Ambassador Theatre Group (Venues) Limited
Incorporated: 17 August 1979 *Employees:* 1,214
Net Worth: £24,671,000 *Total Assets:* £123,034,000
Registered Office: 2nd Floor, Alexander House, Church Path, Woking, Surrey, GU21 6EJ
Activities: Operation of arts facilities
Parent: The Ambassador Theatre Group Limited
Officers: Mark Cornell [1966] Director; Adam Lee Kenwright [1972] Commercial Director; Michael Cowper Lynas [1957] Executive Director; Nicholas Graham Potter [1968] Managing Director; Shanmae Teo [1976] Director

The Ambassador Theatre Group Limited
Incorporated: 13 December 1991 *Employees:* 136
Net Worth: £97,081,000 *Total Assets:* £581,097,024
Registered Office: 2nd Floor, Alexander House, Church Path, Woking, Surrey, GU21 6EJ
Activities: Operation of arts facilities
Parent: The Ambassador Entertainment Group Ltd
Officers: Mark Cornell [1966] Director; Adam Lee Kenwright [1972] Commercial Director; Michael Cowper Lynas [1957] Executive Director; Nicholas Graham Potter [1968] Managing Director; Shanmae Teo [1976] Director

The Ambassador Theatre Group Overseas Holdings Limited
Incorporated: 22 March 2013
Net Worth: £80,660,576 *Total Assets:* £114,213,856
Registered Office: 2nd Floor, Alexander House, Church Path, Woking, Surrey, GU21 6EJ
Activities: Operation of arts facilities
Parent: The Ambassador Theatre Group Limited
Officers: Mark Ralph Delano Cornell [1966] Director; Adam Lee Kenwright [1972] Commercial Director; Michael Cowper Lynas [1957] Executive Director; Shanmae Teo [1976] Director

Ambec Limited
Incorporated: 6 May 2011 *Employees:* 3
Net Worth: £28,691,102 *Total Assets:* £40,640,376
Registered Office: 20 Church Road, Tunbridge Wells, Kent, TN1 1JP
Activities: Buying and selling of own real estate
Major Shareholder: Andrew Michael Brooks
Officers: John Anthony Burke, Secretary; Andrew Michael Brooks [1985] Director/Property Manager; Charlotte Brooks [1985] Director; Helen Amy Partridge [1989] Director/Property Manager

Amber Solar Parks (Holdings) Limited
Incorporated: 25 May 2012
Net Worth: £9,689,000 *Total Assets:* £28,532,000
Registered Office: 8 White Oak Square, London Road, Swanley, Kent, BR8 7AG
Activities: Production of electricity
Parent: John Laing Environmental Assets Group (UK) Limited
Officers: Giuseppe La Loggia [1975] Director/Entrepreneur [Italian]; Joseph Mark Linney [1958] Director/Chartered Quantity Surveyor; Christopher James Tanner [1972] Investment Director

Amber Solar Parks Limited
Incorporated: 25 May 2012
Net Worth: £9,783,000 *Total Assets:* £28,640,000
Registered Office: 8 White Oak Square, London Road, Swanley, Kent, BR8 7AG
Activities: Production of electricity
Parent: Amber Solar Parks (Holdings) Limited
Officers: Giuseppe La Loggia [1975] Director/Entrepreneur [Italian]; Joseph Mark Linney [1958] Director/Chartered Quantity Surveyor; Christopher James Tanner [1972] Investment Director

Amer Sports UK Limited
Incorporated: 20 October 1992 *Employees:* 131
Net Worth: £3,389,228 *Total Assets:* £30,313,356
Registered Office: Theta, Lyon Way, Frimley, Camberley, Surrey, GU16 7ER
Activities: Manufacture of sports goods
Parent: Amer Sports UK Services Limited
Officers: Lauri Petteri Hiltunen [1984] Director, Business Development [Finnish]; Jussi Pekka Kaarlo Siitonen [1969] Director/Chief Financial Officer [Finnish]; Domenico John Speciale [1969] Director; Tero Tapani Tynkkynen [1969] Director/Zone Manager [Finnish]

Amersham Biosciences
Incorporated: 10 June 1997
Net Worth: £254,633,136 *Total Assets:* £278,908,224
Registered Office: Pollards Wood, Nightingales Lane, Chalfont St Giles, Bucks, HP8 4SP
Activities: Activities of head offices
Parent: Amersham NMP China Limited
Officers: Julia Elizabeth Casey [1980] Managing Director, Business Development; Katherine Ann Jones [1976] Director/Financial Controller

Amey Highways Lighting (Manchester) Limited
Incorporated: 17 April 2003
Net Worth Deficit: £2,425,000 *Total Assets:* £30,064,000
Registered Office: 8 White Oak Square, London Road, Swanley, Kent, BR8 7AG
Activities: Construction of commercial buildings
Parent: AHL Holdings (Manchester) Limited
Officers: Neeti Mukundrai Anand [1984] Director; Carl Harvey Dix [1966] Operations Director; Asif Ghafoor [1970] Director; Katherine Pearman [1961] Director/Chartered Accountant; Carlos Vela Lazaga [1989] Director/Junior Valuation Analyst [Spanish]

AMG Healthcare Limited
Incorporated: 5 March 2004 *Employees:* 165
Net Worth: £16,082,000 *Total Assets:* £30,528,000
Registered Office: 1st Floor, Selsdon House, 212-220 Addington Road, South Croydon, Surrey, CR2 8LD
Activities: Dispensing chemist in specialised stores
Parent: Avicenna Holdings Ltd
Officers: Shiraz Kassam Hirji [1947] Director; Salim Kassamali Esmail Jetha [1953] Director/Pharmacist; Jayanti Chimanbhai Patel Junior [1984] Director

Amoco (Fiddich) Limited
Incorporated: 19 March 1971
Net Worth: £82,234,152 *Total Assets:* £229,542,288
Registered Office: Chertsey Road, Sunbury on Thames, Middlesex, TW16 7BP
Activities: Extraction of crude petroleum
Parent: Britoil Limited
Officers: Karen MacLennan [1971] Director/Oil Company Executive; Sandra Jean MacRae [1963] Director/Oil Company Executive

Amphenol Limited
Incorporated: 11 December 1963 *Employees:* 244
Net Worth: £40,683,000 *Total Assets:* £147,920,000
Registered Office: Thanet Way, Tankerton, Whitstable, Kent, CT5 3JF
Activities: Manufacture of electronic components
Parent: Amphenol-Borg Limited
Officers: Lance Edward D'Amico, Secretary; Craig Anthony Lampo [1969] Director/Business Executive [American]; Richard Adam Norwitt [1969] Director/Business Executive [American]; Luc Walter [1958] Director/Business Executive [American]

Amphora Acquisitions Limited
Incorporated: 21 June 2011 *Employees:* 3
Net Worth: £25,553,000 *Total Assets:* £60,684,000
Registered Office: One London Road, Staines upon Thames, Middlesex, TW18 4EX
Activities: Information technology consultancy activities
Parent: Ensono Opco Holdings Limited
Officers: Peter John Bazil [1972] Director/General Counsel [American]; Norman Smagley [1958] Director/Chief Financial Officer [American]

Amscan International Limited
Incorporated: 7 August 1973 *Employees:* 140
Net Worth: £13,494,000 *Total Assets:* £46,771,000
Registered Office: Brudenell Drive, Brinklow, Milton Keynes, Bucks, MK10 0DA
Activities: Non-specialised wholesale trade
Officers: Joseph Francis Hennigan [1983] Director/Chartered Accountant

Amsric Holdings Limited
Incorporated: 7 December 1992 *Employees:* 1,053
Net Worth: £6,644,873 *Total Assets:* £32,116,938
Registered Office: 21-25 Church Street West, Woking, Surrey, GU21 6DJ
Activities: Activities of head offices
Officers: Dina Patel, Secretary; Dina Patel [1962] Director; Ragin Patel [1960] Director

Amtech Group Limited
Incorporated: 2 May 2006 *Employees:* 93
Net Worth: £17,670,000 *Total Assets:* £23,194,000
Registered Office: Bank House, 171 Midsummer Boulevard, Central Milton Keynes, Bucks, MK9 1EB
Activities: Other software publishing
Parent: Trimble Europe B.V.
Officers: James Anthony Kirkland, Secretary; John Henry Gale Heelas [1963] Director/Accountant; James Anthony Kirkland [1959] Director/VP Assistant Secretary and General Counsel [Amerlcan]; Robbert Hendrik Herman Reeder [1970] European Director of Finance [Dutch]

Anchorage Capital Europe, LLP
Incorporated: 17 February 2009 *Employees:* 21
Net Worth: £26,047,352 *Total Assets:* £36,264,800
Registered Office: Mazars LLP, The Pinnacle, 160 Midsummer Boulevard, Milton Keynes, Bucks, MK9 1FF
Officers: Thibault Gournay [1978] Member; James Frost [1977] LLP Member; Arun Nagwaney [1971] LLP Member

Andigestion Limited
Incorporated: 12 September 1984 *Employees:* 40
Net Worth: £3,912,873 *Total Assets:* £27,692,776
Registered Office: 7 Summerleaze Road, Maidenhead, Berks, SL6 8SP
Activities: Manufacture of fertilizers and nitrogen compounds
Parent: Summerleaze Limited
Officers: Jeremy Paul Malkinson, Secretary; Michael Andrew Lowe [1963] Director; Jeremy Paul Malkinson [1959] Finance Director; Peter Herbert Prior [1943] Managing Director

Anduff Car Wash Limited
Incorporated: 17 March 1970 *Employees:* 56
Net Worth: £280,204,128 *Total Assets:* £324,005,056
Registered Office: 35-37 Amersham Hill, High Wycombe, Bucks, HP13 6NU
Activities: Other service activities n.e.c.
Officers: Peter James Davies [1978] Director; Stewart Malcolm Greenhalgh [1949] Technical Director; Nazim Ilyas [1982] Finance Director; Tim Neil Walton [1973] Managing Director

Anesco Acquisitionco Limited
Incorporated: 12 April 2017 *Employees:* 172
Net Worth Deficit: £9,191,287 *Total Assets:* £168,339,216
Registered Office: Unit 9 The Green, Easter Park, Benyon Road, Reading, Berks, RG7 2PQ
Activities: Other business support service activities n.e.c.
Officers: Kevin Clifford Mouatt [1961] Director; Christopher George Mutter [1960] Director; Stephen Frank Shine [1957] Director; Charles Henry Oliver St John [1963] Director; Natalia Tsitoura [1983] Director/Investment Professional [Greek]; Alex Arthur Walker [1981] Director/Solicitor

Anesco Bidco 1 Limited
Incorporated: 31 October 2014
Net Worth Deficit: £27,363,444 *Total Assets:* £125,741,584
Registered Office: The Green, Easter Park, Benyon Road, Reading, Berks, RG7 2PQ
Activities: Other business support service activities n.e.c.
Parent: Anesco Midco Limited
Officers: Kevin Clifford Mouatt [1961] Director; Christopher George Mutter [1960] Director; Stephen Frank Shine [1957] Director; Natalia Tsitoura [1983] Director/Investment Professional [Greek]; Alex Arthur Walker [1981] Director/Solicitor

Anesco Limited
Incorporated: 17 November 2010 *Employees:* 172
Net Worth: £47,624,108 *Total Assets:* £73,320,472
Registered Office: The Green, Easter Park, Benyon Road, Reading, Berks, RG7 2PQ
Activities: Other specialised construction activities n.e.c.
Parent: Anesco Bidco 1 Limited
Officers: Kevin Clifford Mouatt [1961] Director; Christopher George Mutter [1960] Director; Stephen Frank Shine [1957] Director/Chairman; Natalia Tsitorua [1983] Director/Investment Professional; Alex Arthur Walker [1981] Director

Anglo Suisse Investments Limited
Incorporated: 28 February 2005 *Employees:* 5
Net Worth: £20,918,286 *Total Assets:* £53,741,056
Registered Office: B E Roberts & Co, 3 Kirkleas Road, Surbiton, Surrey, KT6 6QJ
Activities: Activities of venture and development capital companies
Shareholder: Geoffrey John de Jager
Officers: Benjamin Thomas Geoffrey de Jager, Secretary; Jonathan Geoffrey de Jager, Secretary; Benjamin Thomas Geoffrey de Jager [1996] Director; Caroline Mary de Jager [1961] Director; Geoffrey John de Jager [1950] Director; Jonathan Geoffrey de Jager [1977] Director

Angmering Park Farms LLP
Incorporated: 20 July 2009
Net Worth: £51,642,460 *Total Assets:* £53,428,416
Registered Office: The Estate Office, Upper Broomhurst Farm, Crossbush Lane, Arundel, W Sussex, BN18 9PQ
Officers: Nigel Gordon Helm Draffan [1950] Member; William Walter Raleigh Kerr [1950] Member; Andrew Herbert Lane [1957] Member; Philip Esme Lord Howard of Penrith [1945] Member; Giles Herchard Mounsey Heysham [1948] Member

Anixter International Limited
Incorporated: 7 June 1988
Net Worth: £74,783,000 *Total Assets:* £76,498,000
Registered Office: Inspired, Easthampstead Road, Bracknell, Berks, RG12 1YQ
Activities: Non-trading company
Parent: Anixter International Inc
Officers: Theodore Dosch [1959] Director/Senior Vice President [American]; Colin Paul Smith [1970] Director/Vice President of Human Resources; Philippe Jean Rene Walpot [1967] EMEA Director of Tax & Statutory Reporting [Belgian]

Anixter Limited
Incorporated: 21 June 1930 *Employees:* 557
Net Worth: £57,280,000 *Total Assets:* £182,810,000
Registered Office: Inspired, Easthampstead Road, Bracknell, Berks, RG12 1YQ
Activities: Non-specialised wholesale trade
Parent: Anixter International Inc
Officers: Theodore Dosch [1959] Director/Senior Vice President [American]; Vitaliy Skovorodko [1984] Director of Finance EMEA [Ukrainian]; Colin Paul Smith [1970] Director/Vice President of Human Resource; Philippe Jean Rene Walpot [1967] EMEA Director of Tax & Statutory Reporting [Belgian]

Annes Gate Property PLC
Incorporated: 31 January 2001
Net Worth: £18,345,000 *Total Assets:* £267,806,000
Registered Office: 8 White Oak Square, London Road, Swanley, Kent, BR8 7AG
Activities: Other business support service activities n.e.c.
Parent: AGP Holdings (1) Limited
Officers: David John Carr [1969] Director/Chartered Accountant; Glynn Newby [1966] Director/Business Management; Natalia Poupard [1977] Director/Asset Manager; Mark Christopher Wayment [1958] Director

Anno 2017 Joint Holding (UK) Limited
Incorporated: 20 June 2017
Net Worth: £244,512,000 *Total Assets:* £1,611,495,936
Registered Office: 8 White Oak Square, London Road, Swanley, Kent, BR8 7AG
Activities: Activities of other holding companies n.e.c.
Shareholders: PFA Neptune Holding (UK) Limited; PKA WLWF Holding (UK) Limited
Officers: James Edward Burbidge [1975] Director/Chartered Accountant; Mark Alan Cade [1972] Director/Chartered Engineer; Christian Krogsgaard [1974] Director [Danish]; Domenico Tripodi [1984] Director [Italian]

Annodata Limited
Incorporated: 20 April 1988 *Employees:* 291
Net Worth: £11,171,027 *Total Assets:* £32,548,760
Registered Office: The Maylands Building, Maylands Avenue, Hemel Hempstead Industrial Estate, Hemel Hempstead, Herts, HP2 7TG
Activities: Other information technology service activities
Parent: Kyocera Document Solutions Inc
Officers: Richard McClure, Secretary; Graham Cox [1959] Director; Norihiko Ina [1963] Director [Japanese]; Hironao Katsukura [1965] Director [Japanese]; Takuya Marubayashi [1967] Director [Japanese]; Rod Tonna-Barthet [1968] Sales Director

Ansa UK Limited
Incorporated: 14 April 1998 *Employees:* 12
Net Worth: £3,996,000 *Total Assets:* £25,275,000
Registered Office: 2 AC Court, High Street, Thames Ditton, Surrey, KT7 0SR
Activities: Other specialised construction activities n.e.c.
Parent: IGUK Support Services Limited
Officers: Alan Albert Horton [1963] Director; Stuart Pace [1962] Director

ANSYS UK Limited
Incorporated: 27 January 2000 *Employees:* 161
Net Worth: £39,124,000 *Total Assets:* £55,263,000
Registered Office: 47 Castle Street, Reading, Berks, RG1 7SR
Activities: Activities of other holding companies n.e.c.
Parent: ANSYS Luxembourg Holding Company S.A.R.L
Officers: Philippe Antonio [1978] Director [French]; Richard Alan Belcher [1970] Director/Chartered Accountant

Antler Homes PLC
Incorporated: 15 September 1972 *Employees:* 15
Net Worth: £46,576,000 *Total Assets:* £61,077,000
Registered Office: Portland House, Park Street, Bagshot, Surrey, GU19 5AQ
Activities: Construction of domestic buildings
Parent: Antler New Homes Limited
Officers: David Ian Wilcock, Secretary; Dane Wilson Houlahan [1979] Director [Australian]; Andrew James Rinaldi [1968] Director; David Ian Wilcock [1969] Finance Director

Antler New Homes Limited
Incorporated: 28 May 2009 *Employees:* 15
Net Worth: £7,097,000 *Total Assets:* £23,356,000
Registered Office: Portland House, Park Street, Bagshot, Surrey, GU19 5AQ
Activities: Activities of head offices
Parent: Rottnest Bidco Limited
Officers: David Ian Wilcock, Secretary; Dane Wilson Houlahan [1979] Director [Australian]; Andrew James Rinaldi [1968] Director; David Ian Wilcock [1969] Finance Director

AON Consulting Limited
Incorporated: 16 November 1995
Net Worth: £77,094,000 *Total Assets:* £96,285,000
Registered Office: Briarcliff House, Kingsmead, Farnborough, Hants, GU14 7TE
Activities: Management consultancy activities other than financial management
Parent: AON Benfield Limited
Officers: David Charles Battle [1960] Director; Pelagia Katsaouni-Dodd [1979] Director/Chartered Accountant [Greek]; Julie Anne Page [1967] Director/Chief Executive

Apatech Limited
Incorporated: 1 March 2001 *Employees:* 65
Net Worth: £34,201,144 *Total Assets:* £36,755,124
Registered Office: 370 Centennial Avenue, Centennial Park, Elstree, Herts, WD6 3TJ
Activities: Manufacture of other chemical products n.e.c.
Parent: Baxter Holding BV
Officers: Andrew Neil Goldney [1968] Director/General Manager; Brian Keith Morgan [1969] Director/Business Executive [American]

APCOA Parking (UK) Limited
Incorporated: 11 January 1991 *Employees:* 1,821
Net Worth: £333,820 *Total Assets:* £46,994,404
Registered Office: Wellington House, 4-10 Cowley Road, Uxbridge, Middlesex, UB8 2XW
Activities: Other business support service activities n.e.c.
Parent: APCOA Parking Holdings (UK) Limited
Officers: David Ian Carruthers, Secretary; David Ian Carruthers [1959] Director/Solicitor; Kamini Challis [1970] Director; John Peter Goodwin [1976] Director

APCOA Parking Holdings (UK) Limited
Incorporated: 25 June 2004
Net Worth: £18,171,076 *Total Assets:* £54,863,068
Registered Office: Wellington House, 4-10 Cowley Road, Uxbridge, Middlesex, UB8 2XW
Activities: Other business support service activities n.e.c.
Parent: APCOA Parking Holdings GmbH
Officers: David Ian Carruthers, Secretary; David Ian Carruthers [1959] Director/Solicitor; Kamini Challis [1970] Director; John Peter Goodwin [1976] Director

Apex Car Rental PLC
Incorporated: 21 December 1987 *Employees:* 31
Net Worth: £47,211,120 *Total Assets:* £53,663,936
Registered Office: 61 Cavendish Place, Eastbourne, E Sussex, BN21 3RL
Activities: Renting and leasing of cars and light motor vehicles
Major Shareholder: Roland Barrie Standley
Officers: Deana Grondona, Secretary; Deana Grondona [1968] Director/Administrator; Roland Barrie Standley [1969] Director/Car Hire Specialist

APG Cash Drawer UK, Ltd
Incorporated: 1 July 2015 *Employees:* 169
Net Worth: £10,388,794 *Total Assets:* £31,027,776
Registered Office: 4 The Drove, Newhaven, E Sussex, BN9 0LA
Activities: Manufacture of other fabricated metal products n.e.c.
Officers: Michael Timothy Davies [1966] Director [American]; Mark Olson [1955] Director [American]; Todd Polzin [1967] Director [American]; Brian Smith [1959] Director [American]

Apogee Corporation Limited
Incorporated: 15 September 1993 *Employees:* 824
Net Worth: £76,589,000 *Total Assets:* £202,495,008
Registered Office: Nimbus House, Liphook Way, 20-20 Business Park, Maidstone, Kent, ME16 0FZ
Activities: Other information technology service activities
Parent: Apogee Group Limited
Officers: Alan Pierpoint, Secretary; James Alexander Clark [1979] Finance Director; Jason Patrick Collins [1970] Director; Gary Arthur Downey [1967] Director; Martin Keith Randall [1959] Director/Chartered Accountant; Robin James Stanton-Gleaves [1968] Director; Graham Thomas [1960] Director

Apogee Group Limited
Incorporated: 5 December 2007 *Employees:* 1,125
Net Worth: £76,064,000 *Total Assets:* £216,275,008
Registered Office: Nimbus House, Liphook Way, 20/20 Business Park, Maidstone, Kent, ME16 0FZ
Activities: Activities of other holding companies n.e.c.
Parent: Manzana Bidco Limited
Officers: Alan Pierpoint, Secretary; James Alexander Clark [1979] Finance Director; Jason Patrick Collins [1970] Director; Gary Arthur Downey [1967] Director; Martin Keith Randall [1959] Director/Chartered Accountant; Robin James Stanton-Gleaves [1968] Director; Graham Thomas [1960] Director

Apollo Fire Detectors Limited
Incorporated: 5 March 1980 *Employees:* 410
Net Worth: £25,944,440 *Total Assets:* £56,143,184
Registered Office: 36 Brookside Road, Havant, Hants, PO9 1JR
Activities: Manufacture of other electrical equipment
Parent: Halma PLC
Officers: Steven Malcolm Brown [1966] Director/Sector Vice President; Edward Browning [1967] Sales Director; Charles Lombard [1970] Managing Director [French]; Jennifer Lynn Rudder [1973] Finance Director [American]; Paul Simmons [1967] Director/Sector President; Karl Stephen Westhead [1971] Technical Director

Apollo Submarine Cable System Limited
Incorporated: 22 March 2004
Net Worth: £44,823,744 *Total Assets:* £79,821,776
Registered Office: Vodafone House, The Connection, Newbury, Berks, RG14 2FN
Activities: Other telecommunications activities
Parent: The Eastern Leasing Company Limited
Officers: Alexander Henricus Lentink [1966] Director/Company Secretary [Dutch]; Richard Charles Perry [1954] Director

Apperly Estates Limited
Incorporated: 25 July 1919
Net Worth: £88,995,448 *Total Assets:* £122,557,816
Registered Office: Bourbon Court, Nightingales Corner, Little Chalfont, Bucks, HP7 9QS
Activities: Other letting and operating of own or leased real estate
Officers: Rachel Claire Azcona, Secretary; David Robert Apperly [1956] Director/Chartered Surveyor; Rachel Claire Azcona [1966] Director/Commercial Strategy Consultant; Jonathan Charles Bennett Houlton [1961] Finance Director; Richard Henry Faber Merriam [1957] Director/Chartered Surveyor; Arthur Peter MacLean Mullineux [1981] Director/Investment Manager; Jonathan Vivian Richard Stevenson [1981] Director/Head of Acquisitions & Development; Alison Charlotte Winkfield [1962] Director/Travel Consultant

Appia Europe Limited
Incorporated: 31 January 2008
Net Worth: £72,311,000 *Total Assets:* £450,569,984
Registered Office: 2 Vantage Court, Tickford Street, Newport Pagnell, Bucks, MK16 9EZ
Activities: Activities of other holding companies n.e.c.
Officers: Joseph James Barrett [1966] Director [Irish]; John Diviney [1979] Director/Chief Executive Officer [Irish]; Niall Dolan [1973] Director/Financial Controller [Irish]; Charles John Gore Hazelwood [1963] Director/Accountant; Surinder Singh Toor [1972] Director/Accountant

Appleby Group Limited
Incorporated: 20 September 1951
Net Worth: £26,936,000 *Total Assets:* £26,936,000
Registered Office: Hanson House, 14 Castle Hill, Maidenhead, Berks, SL6 4JJ
Activities: Activities of other holding companies n.e.c.
Parent: Civil and Marine (Holdings) Limited
Officers: Wendy Fiona Rogers, Secretary; Nicholas Arthur Dawe Benning-Prince [1974] Director/Chartered Accountant; Robert Charles Dowley [1972] Director/Chartered Accountant; Edward Alexander Gretton [1970] Director; Dr Carsten Matthias Wendt [1976] Director [German]; Simon Lloyd Willis [1965] Director/Chief Executive, Hanson UK

April Bidco Limited
Incorporated: 11 March 2015 *Employees:* 8
Net Worth Deficit: £13,814,000 *Total Assets:* £81,668,000
Registered Office: Camino Park, James Watt Way, Crawley, W Sussex, RH10 9TZ
Activities: Activities of other holding companies n.e.c.
Officers: William Andrew Wardrop [1963] Director

April Midco Limited
Incorporated: 9 March 2015
Net Worth: £52,423,000 *Total Assets:* £77,321,000
Registered Office: Camino Park, James Watt Way, Crawley, W Sussex, RH10 9TZ
Activities: Activities of other holding companies n.e.c.
Officers: William Andrew Wardrop [1963] Director

April Topco Limited
Incorporated: 11 March 2015 *Employees:* 1,265
Net Worth: £9,112,000 *Total Assets:* £102,693,000
Registered Office: Camino Park, James Watt Way, Crawley, W Sussex, RH10 9TZ
Activities: Activities of other holding companies n.e.c.
Officers: George Thomas Edward Moss [1979] Director/Investment Manager; William Andrew Wardrop [1963] Director

Aprite (GB) Limited
Incorporated: 10 October 1996 *Employees:* 586
Net Worth: £13,363,000 *Total Assets:* £131,193,000
Registered Office: The Rivers Office Park, Denham Way, Rickmansworth, Herts, WD3 9YS
Activities: Sale of new cars and light motor vehicles
Parent: Nissan Motor (GB) Limited
Officers: Steven Neil Tiffin, Secretary; Laurent Frank Christian David [1971] Director [French]; Gareth John Main [1967] Director/General Manager; Jordi Vila Onses [1963] Director/Vice President Sales [Spanish]

Aptos Solutions UK Limited
Incorporated: 17 June 2016 *Employees:* 157
Net Worth: £61,880,000 *Total Assets:* £150,008,000
Registered Office: Marlow International, Parkway, Marlow, Bucks, SL7 1YL
Activities: Information technology consultancy activities
Parent: Aptos UK Holding No. 2 Limited
Officers: David Baum [1967] Director/In-House Lawyer [Canadian]; Jeffrey Monroe Laborde [1972] Director [American]; Steven Mark Towe [1971] Director/Chief Operating Officer

Aqualisa Holdings (International) Limited
Incorporated: 7 September 2015 *Employees:* 304
Net Worth Deficit: £2,670,000 *Total Assets:* £61,965,000
Registered Office: Westerham Trade Centre, The Flyers Way, Westerham, Kent, TN16 1DE
Activities: Activities of production holding companies
Shareholders: LDC Equity IV LP; LDC IV LP
Officers: Stephen John Spencer Lee [1966] Director; Ian Richard Plummer [1953] Director; Robin Clive Powell [1965] Director; Adam Christian Rhodes [1961] Sales Director; Benjamin George Snow [1981] Investment Director; Colin James Sykes [1960] Director/Chief Operating Officer

Aqualisa Holdings Limited
Incorporated: 4 December 2012 *Employees:* 2
Net Worth: £5,124,000 *Total Assets:* £29,442,000
Registered Office: Westerham Trade Centre, The Flyers Way, Westerham, Kent, TN16 1DE
Activities: Activities of production holding companies
Parent: Aqualisa Holdings (International) Limited
Officers: Andrew Hawksley [1977] Director/Accountant; Colin James Sykes [1960] Director

Aqualisa Products Limited
Incorporated: 14 October 1976 *Employees:* 304
Net Worth: £26,914,000 *Total Assets:* £37,650,000
Registered Office: The Flyer's Way, Westerham, Kent, TN16 1DE
Activities: Manufacture of taps and valves
Parent: Aqualisa Finance Ltd
Officers: Andrew Hawksley [1977] Director/Accountant; Adam Christian Rhodes [1961] Director; Colin James Sykes [1960] Director/Chartered Accountant

Aquila Air Traffic Management Services Limited
Incorporated: 9 October 2014 *Employees:* 241
Net Worth: £4,109,000 *Total Assets:* £54,671,000
Registered Office: 350 Longwater Avenue, Green Park, Reading, Berks, RG2 6GF
Activities: Other transportation support activities
Shareholders: NATS (Services) Limited; Thales UK Limited
Officers: Michael William Peter Seabrook, Secretary; Guy Anthony Adams [1968] Director; Stuart Michael Boulton [1963] Director; Alexander Colin Kynaston Cresswell [1963] Director/Professional Engineer; Martin John Rolfe [1972] Director; Michael Paul Stoller [1966] Director

Aquilant Limited
Incorporated: 19 January 1987 *Employees:* 102
Net Worth Deficit: £532,872 *Total Assets:* £22,197,580
Registered Office: Aquilant House, Unit B1-B2 Bond Close, Kingsland Business Park, Basingstoke, Hants, RG24 8PZ
Activities: Non-specialised wholesale trade
Parent: Healthcare Acquisition Limited
Officers: Richard Dew [1980] Director; David Charles Frederick [1966] Director; PJ Owens [1975] Finance Director [Irish]

Aramark Investments Limited
Incorporated: 13 April 1993 *Employees:* 5
Net Worth: £626,444,032 *Total Assets:* £997,553,984
Registered Office: 2nd Floor, 250 Fowler Avenue, Farnborough Business Park, Farnborough, Hants, GU14 7JP
Activities: Other business support service activities n.e.c.
Parent: Aramark
Officers: Mary-Ann Deasy, Secretary; Monica Andrea Aravena Baez [1973] Director [Chilean]; Matthew William Carroll [1976] Director/Financial Controller; Rajat Chawla [1980] Finance Director; John Clive Cooper [1966] Director/Vice President European Supply Chain; Frank Michael Gleeson [1966] Director/Chief Executive [Irish]; Jane Elizabeth Stephenson-Smith [1981] Director of Taxation

Aramark Japan Holdings Limited
Incorporated: 22 September 2016
Net Worth: £172,375,296 *Total Assets:* £172,375,296
Registered Office: 2nd Floor, 250 Fowler Avenue, Farnborough Business Park, Farnborough, Hants, GU14 7JP
Activities: Other business support service activities n.e.c.
Parent: Aramark
Officers: Mary-Ann Deasy, Secretary; Matthew William Carroll [1976] Director/Financial Controller; John Clive Cooper [1966] Director/Vice President European Supply Chain; Paul Joseph Sizer [1981] Director/VP Finance [American]

Aramark Limited
Incorporated: 7 July 1970 *Employees:* 6,500
Net Worth: £52,220,000 *Total Assets:* £82,579,000
Registered Office: 2nd Floor, 250 Fowler Avenue, Farnborough Business Park, Farnborough, Hants, GU14 7JP
Activities: Other food services
Parent: Aramark Investments Limited
Officers: Mary Ann Deasy, Secretary; Monica Andrea Aravena Baez [1973] Director [Chilean]; Matthew William Carroll [1976] Director/Financial Controller; Rajat Chawla [1980] Finance Director; Frank Michael Gleeson [1966] Director/Chief Operations Officer [Irish]; Lawrence Reza Shirazian [1974] Managing Director; Neil Shroeder [1971] Managing Director; Andrew MacLeod Thomson [1970] Managing Director

Arca Shipping Limited
Incorporated: 14 June 2005
Previous: MEIF Shipping Limited
Net Worth Deficit: £103,399,000 *Total Assets:* £228,000,000
Registered Office: Gunwharf Terminal, Gunwharf Road, Portsmouth, PO1 2LA
Activities: Activities of head offices
Parent: Arca Bidco Limited
Officers: Jonathan Pascoe, Secretary; Robert John Gregor [1969] Director/Managing Partner Investment Adviser [Australian]; Holt William John Hanna [1977] Director/Vice President Investment Office; Steven Lowry [1972] Director/Partner Investment Adviser; Jonathan Mark Pascoe [1967] Director/Chartered Accountant

Archaylen Property Limited
Incorporated: 14 September 2011 *Employees:* 2
Net Worth: £6,832,227 *Total Assets:* £26,938,988
Registered Office: Beeches Farm, Icknield Way, Tring, Herts, HP23 4LA
Activities: Development of building projects
Shareholders: Peter Donald Dean; Andrew Frederick Screech; Susan Jane Dean; Sarah Lois Dean; Stephen Douglas John Marshall; Gubblecote Properties Limited
Officers: Andrew Frederick Screech, Secretary; Peter Donald Dean [1944] Director; Sarah Lois Dean [1971] Director; Stephen Douglas John Marshall [1955] Director; Andrew Frederick Screech [1975] Director/Property Manager

Archer Assets UK Limited
Incorporated: 13 September 2007
Net Worth: £46,705,972 *Total Assets:* £349,323,712
Registered Office: New Kings Court, Tollgate, Chandler's Ford, Eastleigh, Hants, SO53 3LG
Activities: Activities of head offices
Officers: Espen Joranger [1977] Director/Group Controller [Norwegian]; John Michael Lechner [1962] Director/Chief Executive Officer [American]; Adam Mark Alexander Todd [1977] Director/Lawyer [Canadian]

Archer Daniels Midland (UK) Limited
Incorporated: 15 January 1973 *Employees:* 69
Net Worth: £304,771,360 *Total Assets:* £351,168,640
Registered Office: Church Manorway, Erith, Kent, DA8 1DL
Activities: Wholesale of grain, unmanufactured tobacco, seeds and animal feeds
Parent: Archer Daniels Midland Company
Officers: Gary Thomas McGuigan [1971] Director [Irish]; Orla Margaret Muldoon [1969] Managing Director [Irish]; John Patrick Stott [1967] Director/Accountant

Archer Daniels Midland Erith Limited
Incorporated: 10 October 1919 *Employees:* 110
Net Worth: £34,342,700 *Total Assets:* £46,321,200
Registered Office: Erith Oil Works, Church Manorway, Erith, Kent, DA8 1DL
Activities: Other processing and preserving of fruit and vegetables
Parent: Archer Daniels Midland (UK) Limited
Officers: Martin Paul Farrow [1956] Director/General Manager; Dr Martin Kropp [1965] Director/Vice President [German]

Arcus Investment Limited
Incorporated: 11 June 1998 *Employees:* 16
Net Worth: £53,075,240 *Total Assets:* £65,508,132
Registered Office: Elder House, St Georges Business Park, 207 Brooklands Road, Weybridge, Surrey, KT13 0TS
Activities: Security and commodity contracts dealing activities
Shareholder: Peter Tasker
Officers: Mark Anthony Pearson [1960] Director; Steven Wheeler [1960] Director/Chief Operating Officer

Ardingly College Limited
Incorporated: 28 May 1999 *Employees:* 411
Net Worth: £15,672,216 *Total Assets:* £29,621,472
Registered Office: Ardingly College, College Road, Ardingly, Haywards Heath, W Sussex, RH17 6SQ
Activities: Primary education
Parent: The Woodard Corporation
Officers: Jane Armstrong [1958] Director Head of Business Development; Robert Haynes Brown [1959] Managing Director; Peter Bryan [1960] Director of Corporate Resources & Deputy Master; Sian Louise Champkin [1980] Director/Solicitor; Guy Dixon [1977] Director/Governor; Elizabeth Mary Hewer [1977] Director/Headmistress; Mary Ireland [1956] Director/Headteacher; Douglas Howard Johnson-Poensgen [1969] Director; Dr Simon Kay [1961] Director/International Operations & Governance Manager; Louise Lindsay [1968] Director/Governor; James Fergus Sloane [1954] Director/Management Consultant; Helen Elizabeth Smith [1957] Director/Medical Academic; Kate Sweeney [1975] Director/Partner; Graham Neil Turner [1946] Director

Ardo UK Limited
Incorporated: 10 March 1970 *Employees:* 133
Net Worth: £25,623,872 *Total Assets:* £38,470,160
Registered Office: Ashford Road, Charing, Ashford, Kent, TN27 0DF
Activities: Other processing and preserving of fruit and vegetables
Parent: Ardo Holding NV
Officers: Simon Rowland Hurran, Secretary; Bernard Haspeslagh [1959] Director [Belgian]; Ignace Cyriel Marie Haspeslagh [1957] Director [Belgian]; Jan Jozef Maria Haspeslagh [1961] Director [Belgian]; Simon Rowland Hurran [1966] Finance Director; Roger Maes [1954] Director [Belgian]

Ardonagh Finco PLC
Incorporated: 5 February 2015
Previous: Kirs Finco PLC
Net Worth: £532,979,008 *Total Assets:* £1,424,423,040
Registered Office: Towergate House, Eclipse Park, Sittingbourne Road, Maidstone, Kent, ME14 3EN
Activities: Activities of financial services holding companies
Parent: Ardonagh Midco 3 PLC
Officers: Dean Clarke, Secretary; Clive Bouch [1961] Director; Matthieu Yann Arnaud Boulanger [1975] Director/Investment Manager; Patrick Noel Butler [1960] Director [Irish]; Diane Cougill [1963] Director/Chief Finance Officer; Aurelio Cusaro [1985] Director; Christine Elaine Dandridge [1956] Director; Vahe Alex Dombalagian [1973] Director/Private Equity [American]; Scot French [1970] Director [American]; Feilim Mackle [1967] Director [Irish]; Matthew William Raino [1978] Director [American]; David Christopher Ross [1969] Director [Irish]; John Ivan Tiner [1957] Director

Area Sq. Limited
Incorporated: 5 November 1999 *Employees:* 263
Net Worth: £4,352,085 *Total Assets:* £31,770,456
Registered Office: The Old Post Office, 33 Station Road, Egham, Surrey, TW20 9LA
Activities: Other specialised construction activities n.e.c.
Parent: Fourfront Group Ltd
Officers: Paul Ames [1964] Contracts Director; Steven Vincent Baldock [1956] Managing Director; Justin Marc Bass [1968] Managing Director; Gary James Chandler [1969] Managing Director; James Elwin Cornwell [1964] Director; Sion Davies [1976] Managing Director; Lee Richard Marple [1968] Operations Director; Simon Pearson [1969] Contracts Director; Colin Christopher Pye [1964] Director; Mark Joseph Scott [1968] Director/Chief Financial Officer; Aki Stamatis [1960] Director; Christopher Stewart [1973] Divisional Director

Argon NPS Limited
Incorporated: 3 December 2014 *Employees:* 7
Net Worth: £48,000,000 *Total Assets:* £346,600,000
Registered Office: Peoplebuilding 2, Peoplebuilding Estate, Maylands Avenue, Hemel Hempstead Industrial Estate, Hemel Hempstead, Herts, HP2 4NW
Activities: Other information technology service activities
Parent: Argon NPS (Holdings) Limited
Officers: Stephen James Callaghan [1960] Director; Alan George O'Reilly [1961] Director [Irish]

Argos Business Solutions Limited
Incorporated: 6 August 1996 *Employees:* 74
Net Worth: £32,841,000 *Total Assets:* £46,026,000
Registered Office: 489-499 Avebury Boulevard, Milton Keynes, Bucks, MK9 2NW
Activities: Activities of financial services holding companies
Parent: Argos Limited
Officers: Timothy Fallowfield, Secretary; Claire Louise Catlin [1980] Director

Argos Holdings Limited
Incorporated: 28 June 2006 *Employees:* 2
Net Worth: £1,262,541,056 *Total Assets:* £2,064,024,064
Registered Office: 489-499 Avebury Boulevard, Milton Keynes, Bucks, MK9 2NW
Activities: Activities of head offices
Parent: Home Retail Group (UK) Limited
Officers: Timothy Fallowfield, Secretary; Claire Louise Catlin [1980] Director

Argos Limited
Incorporated: 13 November 1972 *Employees:* 26,611
Net Worth: £571,054,976 *Total Assets:* £2,905,533,952
Registered Office: 489-499 Avebury Boulevard, Milton Keynes, Bucks, MK9 2NW
Activities: Other retail sale in non-specialised stores
Parent: Argos Holdings Limited
Officers: Timothy Fallowfield, Secretary; Claire Louise Catlin [1980] Director; Patrick Dunne [1968] Director; John Terence Rogers [1968] Director

Aria Petroleum (UK) Ltd.
Incorporated: 5 September 2012 *Employees:* 47
Net Worth: £80,017,952 *Total Assets:* £86,859,600
Registered Office: 80 Sidney Street, Folkestone, Kent, CT19 6HQ
Activities: Extraction of crude petroleum
Parent: Aria Petroleum (Cy) Limited
Officers: Dermot Aidan Hassett [1958] Director/Manager [Irish]; Oleg Paska [1965] Director/Manager [Ukrainian]

Arinso People Services Limited
Incorporated: 3 July 2003
Net Worth: £30,823,936 *Total Assets:* £30,823,936
Registered Office: Peoplebuilding 2, Peoplebuilding Estate, Maylands Avenue, Hemel Hempstead Industrial Estate, Hemel Hempstead, Herts, HP2 4NW
Activities: Information technology consultancy activities
Parent: Northgate Information Solutions Holdings Limited
Officers: Malcolm Robert Bennett, Secretary; Steven James Chalker [1974] Chief Financial Director; Andrew Phillip Monshaw [1962] Director [American]

Arinso UK Limited
Incorporated: 2 January 1998
Net Worth: £20,461,006 *Total Assets:* £20,461,006
Registered Office: Peoplebuilding 2, Peoplebuilding Estate, Maylands Avenue, Hemel Hempstead Industrial Estate, Hemel Hempstead, Herts, HP2 4NW
Activities: Other information technology service activities
Parent: Northgate Information Solutions Holdings Limited
Officers: Malcolm Robert Bennett, Secretary; Steven James Chalker [1974] Chief Financial Director; Andrew Phillip Monshaw [1962] Director [American]

Arjun Infrastructure Partners II Limited
Incorporated: 9 February 2015
Net Worth Deficit: £131,851 *Total Assets:* £30,621,192
Registered Office: Loddon Reach, Reading Road, Arborfield, Reading, Berks, RG2 9HU
Activities: Fund management activities
Parent: AIP Infrastructure LP
Officers: Charles John Gore Hazelwood [1963] Director; Surinder Singh Toor [1972] Director

Arkarius Bidco Limited
Incorporated: 19 December 2016 *Employees:* 4
Net Worth Deficit: £7,953,684 *Total Assets:* £121,735,624
Registered Office: KD Tower, Cotterells, Hemel Hempstead, Herts, HP1 1FW
Activities: Activities of head offices
Parent: Arkarius Midco Limited
Officers: Kevin John Budge [1961] Director; Derek Andrew Kelly [1972] Director; Jeremy Steven Newman [1959] Director

Arlacross Limited
Incorporated: 24 April 2001 *Employees:* 148
Net Worth Deficit: £13,992,132 *Total Assets:* £22,897,600
Registered Office: E3 The Premier Centre, Abbey Park, Romsey, Hants, SO51 9DG
Activities: Other business support service activities n.e.c.
Officers: Renold Lee on Tang, Secretary/Accountant; Sofia Mohd Ja'afar [1972] Director [Bruneian]; Renold Lee on Tang [1956] Director/Accountant

Arlaform Limited
Incorporated: 24 April 2001
Net Worth Deficit: £6,003,442 *Total Assets:* £27,226,648
Registered Office: E3 The Premier Centre, Abbey Park, Romsey, Hants, SO51 9DG
Activities: Other business support service activities n.e.c.
Officers: Renold Lee on Tang, Secretary/Accountant; Sofia Mohd Ja'afar [1972] Director [Bruneian]; Renold Lee on Tang [1956] Director/Accountant

Armadillo Storage Holding Company Limited
Incorporated: 3 March 2014 *Employees:* 46
Net Worth: £27,288,000 *Total Assets:* £57,007,000
Registered Office: 2 The Deans, Bridge Road, Bagshot, Surrey, GU19 5AT
Activities: Activities of head offices
Officers: Shauna Beavis, Secretary; James Ernest Gibson [1960] Director; Robert Gerard Gregg [1962] Director/Corporate Advisor [Australian]; Adrian Charles Jonathan Lee [1963] Operations Director; Jon Perrins [1961] Director/Founder/Executive Chairman of Steel Storage [Australian]; John Richard Trotman [1977] Director/Chartered Accountant

Armatire Limited
Incorporated: 7 January 2016 *Employees:* 198
Net Worth Deficit: £200,529 *Total Assets:* £203,647,488
Registered Office: 45 Westerham Road, Bessels Green, Sevenoaks, Kent, TN13 2QB
Activities: Other business support service activities n.e.c.
Shareholders: Amanda Jane Spencer; Kevin Ronald Spencer
Officers: Christopher James Payne, Secretary; Kevin Ronald Spencer [1965] Director

Armstrong World Industries Limited
Incorporated: 7 August 1925 *Employees:* 179
Net Worth: £57,900,000 *Total Assets:* £72,850,000
Registered Office: 2nd Floor, Harman House, 1 George Street, Uxbridge, Middlesex, UB8 1QQ
Activities: Manufacture of other non-metallic mineral products n.e.c.
Parent: Armstrong (U.K.) Investments
Officers: Michael James Bignell, Secretary; Sara Joanne Carter [1976] HR Director; Lee Alan Davidson [1973] Director/Chartered Accountant; Mark Alan Laikin [1968] Finance Director; Stephen Francis McNamara [1966] Director/Controller [American]; Willem Antonius Middel [1967] VP and Managing Director EMEA [Dutch]; Yang Ming Tham [1982] Director [American]; William Mark Willis Jones [1957] Director/Barrister

Arora Hotels Limited
Incorporated: 29 July 2005 *Employees:* 1,467
Previous: Arora Staff Houses Limited
Net Worth: £293,436,992 *Total Assets:* £635,217,024
Registered Office: World Business Centre, 3 Newall Road, London Heathrow Airport, Hounslow, Middlesex, TW6 2TA
Activities: Activities of other holding companies n.e.c.
Parent: Grove Acquisitions Limited
Officers: Athos George Yiannis, Secretary; Sunita Arora [1964] Director; Surinder Arora [1958] Director; Carlton Jeffrey Brown [1972] Director/Chartered Accountant; Athos George Yiannis [1963] Director/Chartered Accountant

Arora Management Services Limited
Incorporated: 27 November 2005 *Employees:* 62
Net Worth: £20,519,416 *Total Assets:* £51,631,480
Registered Office: World Business Centre, 3 Newall Road, London Heathrow Airport, Hounslow, Middlesex, TW6 2TA
Activities: Activities of head offices
Parent: Grove Acquisitions Limited
Officers: Athos George Yiannis, Secretary; Sanjay Arora [1989] Director; Sunita Arora [1964] Director; Surinder Arora [1958] Director; Carlton Jeffrey Brown [1972] Director/Chartered Accountant; Athos George Yiannis [1963] Director/Chartered Accountant

Arora T5 Holdings Limited
Incorporated: 13 July 2016
Net Worth: £128,193,832 *Total Assets:* £169,359,520
Registered Office: World Business Centre, 3 Newall Road, London Heathrow Airport, Hounslow, Middlesex, TW6 2TA
Activities: Activities of head offices
Parent: Arora Hotels Limited
Officers: Athos George Yiannis, Secretary; Carlton Jeffrey Brown [1972] Director/Chartered Accountant; Athos George Yiannis [1963] Director/Chartered Accountant

Arqiva Broadcast Finance PLC
Incorporated: 19 December 2012
Net Worth: £228,000 *Total Assets:* £614,636,992
Registered Office: Crawley Court, Winchester, Hants, SO21 2QA
Activities: Activities of head offices
Parent: Arqiva Broadcast Parent Limited
Officers: Jeremy Mavor, Secretary; Peter Charles Adams [1982] Director/Investment Management [Canadian]; Mark William Braithwaite [1965] Director; Franck Emmanuel Dangeard [1958] Director [French]; Michael William Darcey [1965] Director; Sally Margaret Davis [1953] Director; Paul Michael Donovan [1958] Director; Maximilian Jacob Fieguth [1986] Director/Vice President; Martin Robert Healey [1973] Managing Director [Canadian]; Neil Edmund King [1963] Managing Director - Finance; Nathan Andrew Luckey [1979] Director/Investment Manager; Michael William John Parton [1954] Director; Christian Seymour [1964] Director/Investment Manager

Arqiva Broadcast Intermediate Limited
Incorporated: 28 May 2012
Net Worth: £3,493,252,096 *Total Assets:* £5,069,043,200
Registered Office: Crawley Court, Winchester, Hants, SO21 2QA
Activities: Activities of head offices
Parent: Arqiva Financing No 2 Limited
Officers: Jeremy Mavor, Secretary; Peter Charles Adams [1982] Director/Investment Management [Canadian]; Mark William Braithwaite [1965] Director; Franck Emmanuel Dangeard [1958] Director [French]; Michael William Darcey [1965] Director; Sally Margaret Davis [1953] Director; Paul Michael Donovan [1958] Director; Maximilian Jacob Fieguth [1986] Director/Vice President; Martin Robert Healey [1973] Managing Director [Canadian]; Neil Edmund King [1963] Managing Director - Finance; Nathan Andrew Luckey [1979] Director/Investment Manager; Michael William John Parton [1954] Director; Christian Seymour [1964] Director/Investment Manager

Arqiva Broadcast Parent Limited
Incorporated: 28 May 2012 *Employees:* 2,088
Net Worth Deficit: £1,508,400,000 *Total Assets:* £4,343,699,968
Registered Office: Crawley Court, Winchester, Hants, SO21 2QA
Activities: Activities of head offices
Parent: Arqiva Financing No 3 PLC
Officers: Jeremy Mavor, Secretary; Peter Charles Adams [1982] Director/Investment Management [Canadian]; Mark William Braithwaite [1965] Director; Franck Emmanuel Dangeard [1958] Director [French]; Michael William Darcey [1965] Director; Sally Margaret Davis [1953] Director; Paul Michael Donovan [1958] Director; Maximilian Jacob Fieguth [1986] Director/Vice President; Martin Robert Healey [1973] Managing Director [Canadian]; Neil Edmund King [1963] Managing Director - Finance; Nathan Andrew Luckey [1979] Director/Investment Manager; Michael William John Parton [1954] Director; Christian Seymour [1964] Director/Investment Manager

Arqiva Financing No 1 Limited
Incorporated: 5 March 2007
Net Worth Deficit: £1,109,299,968 *Total Assets:* £7,116,100,096
Registered Office: Crawley Court, Winchester, Hants, SO21 2QA
Activities: Activities of head offices
Parent: Arqiva Group Intermediate Limited
Officers: Jeremy Mavor, Secretary; Peter Charles Adams [1982] Director/Investment Management [Canadian]; Simon Piers Beresford-Wylie [1958] Director; Mark William Braithwaite [1965] Director; Franck Emmanuel Dangeard [1958] Director [French]; Michael William Darcey [1965] Director; Sally Margaret Davis [1953] Director; Paul Michael Donovan [1958] Director; Maximilian Jacob Fieguth [1986] Director/Vice President; Martin Robert Healey [1973] Managing Director [Canadian]; Neil Edmund King [1963] Managing Director - Finance; Nathan Andrew Luckey [1979] Director/Investment Manager; Michael William John Parton [1954] Director; Christian Seymour [1964] Director/Investment Manager

Arqiva Financing No 2 Limited
Incorporated: 5 March 2007
Net Worth: £3,350,876,928 *Total Assets:* £5,072,812,032
Registered Office: Crawley Court, Winchester, Hants, SO21 2QA
Activities: Activities of head offices
Parent: Arqiva Broadcast Parent Limited
Officers: Jeremy Mavor, Secretary; Peter Charles Adams [1982] Director/Investment Management [Canadian]; Mark William Braithwaite [1965] Director; Franck Emmanuel Dangeard [1958] Director [French]; Michael William Darcey [1965] Director; Sally Margaret Davis [1953] Director; Paul Michael Donovan [1958] Director; Maximilian Jacob Fieguth [1986] Director/Vice President; Martin Robert Healey [1973] Managing Director [Canadian]; Neil Edmund King [1963] Managing Director - Finance; Nathan Andrew Luckey [1979] Director/Investment Manager; Michael William John Parton [1954] Director; Christian Seymour [1964] Director/Investment Manager

Arqiva Financing No 3 PLC
Incorporated: 8 October 2004
Net Worth: £1,466,099,968 *Total Assets:* £4,508,499,968
Registered Office: Crawley Court, Winchester, Hants, SO21 2QA
Activities: Activities of head offices
Parent: Arqiva Broadcast Holdings Limited
Officers: Jeremy Mavor, Secretary; Peter Charles Adams [1982] Director/Investment Management [Canadian]; Mark William Braithwaite [1965] Director; Franck Emmanuel Dangeard [1958] Director [French]; Michael William Darcey [1965] Director; Sally Margaret Davis [1953] Director; Paul Michael Donovan [1958] Director; Maximilian Jacob Fieguth [1986] Director/Vice President; Martin Robert Healey [1973] Managing Director [Canadian]; Neil Edmund King [1963] Managing Director - Finance; Nathan Andrew Luckey [1979] Director/Investment Manager; Michael William John Parton [1954] Director; Christian Seymour [1964] Director/Investment Manager

Arqiva Financing PLC
Incorporated: 19 December 2012
Net Worth: £71,000 *Total Assets:* £900,854,976
Registered Office: Crawley Court, Winchester, Hants, SO21 2QA
Activities: Activities of head offices
Parent: Arqiva Group Intermediate Limited
Officers: Jeremy Mavor, Secretary; Peter Charles Adams [1982] Director/Investment Management [Canadian]; Simon Piers Beresford-Wylie [1958] Director; Mark William Braithwaite [1965] Director; Franck Emmanuel Dangeard [1958] Director [French]; Michael William Darcey [1965] Director; Sally Margaret Davis [1953] Director; Paul Michael Donovan [1958] Director; Maximilian Jacob Fieguth [1986] Director/Vice President; Martin Robert Healey [1973] Managing Director [Canadian]; Neil Edmund King [1963] Managing Director - Finance; Nathan Andrew Luckey [1979] Director/Investment Manager; Michael William John Parton [1954] Director; Christian Seymour [1964] Director/Investment Manager; Helena Paivi Whitaker [1963] Director [Finnish]

Arqiva Group Holdings Limited
Incorporated: 19 September 2012
Net Worth: £2,599,302,912 *Total Assets:* £2,599,322,880
Registered Office: Crawley Court, Winchester, Hants, SO21 2QA
Activities: Activities of head offices
Parent: Arqiva Financing No 1 Limited
Officers: Jeremy Mavor, Secretary; Peter Charles Adams [1982] Director/Investment Management [Canadian]; Elizabeth Jane Aikman [1965] Director; Simon Piers Beresford-Wylie [1958] Director; Mark William Braithwaite [1965] Director; Franck Emmanuel Dangeard [1958] Director [French]; Michael William Darcey [1965] Director; Sally Margaret Davis [1953] Director; Paul Michael Donovan [1958] Director; Maximilian Jacob Fieguth [1986] Director/Vice President; Martin Robert Healey [1973] Managing Director [Canadian]; Neil Edmund King [1963] Managing Director - Finance; Nathan Andrew Luckey [1979] Director/Investment Manager; Michael William John Parton [1954] Director; Christian Seymour [1964] Director/Investment Manager

Arqiva Group Intermediate Limited
Incorporated: 2 July 2012
Net Worth: £3,431,377,920 *Total Assets:* £5,007,191,040
Registered Office: Crawley Court, Winchester, Hants, SO21 2QA
Activities: Activities of head offices
Parent: Arqiva Group Parent Limited
Officers: Jeremy Mavor, Secretary; Peter Charles Adams [1982] Director/Investment Management [Canadian]; Simon Piers Beresford-Wylie [1958] Director; Mark William Braithwaite [1965] Director; Franck Emmanuel Dangeard [1958] Director [French]; Michael William Darcey [1965] Director; Sally Margaret Davis [1953] Director; Paul Michael Donovan [1958] Director; Maximilian Jacob Fieguth [1986] Director/Vice President; Martin Robert Healey [1973] Managing Director [Canadian]; Neil Edmund King [1963] Managing Director - Finance; Nathan Andrew Luckey [1979] Director/Investment Manager; Michael William John Parton [1954] Director; Christian Seymour [1964] Director/Investment Manager

Arqiva Group Limited
Incorporated: 8 October 2004 *Employees:* 2,088
Previous: Arqiva Broadcast Holdings Limited
Net Worth Deficit: £3,375,899,904 *Total Assets:* £4,387,800,064
Registered Office: Crawley Court, Winchester, Hants, SO21 2QA
Activities: Activities of head offices
Shareholder: Macquarie Infrastructure and Real Assets (Europe) Limited
Officers: Jeremy Mavor, Secretary; Peter Charles Adams [1982] Director/Investment Management [Canadian]; Mark William Braithwaite [1965] Director; Franck Emmanuel Dangeard [1958] Director [French]; Michael William Darcey [1965] Director; Sally Margaret Davis [1953] Director; Paul Michael Donovan [1958] Director; Maximilian Jacob Fieguth [1986] Director/Vice President; Martin Robert Healey [1973] Managing Director [Canadian]; Neil Edmund King [1963] Managing Director - Finance; Nathan Andrew Luckey [1979] Director/Investment Manager; Michael William John Parton [1954] Director; Christian Seymour [1964] Director/Investment Manager

Arqiva Group Parent Limited
Incorporated: 28 May 2012 *Employees:* 2,088
Net Worth Deficit: £1,366,400,000 *Total Assets:* £4,329,399,808
Registered Office: Crawley Court, Winchester, Hants, SO21 2QA
Activities: Activities of head offices
Parent: Arqiva Broadcast Intermediate Limited
Officers: Jeremy Mavor, Secretary; Peter Charles Adams [1982] Director/Investment Management [Canadian]; Simon Piers Beresford-Wylie [1958] Director; Mark William Braithwaite [1965] Director; Franck Emmanuel Dangeard [1958] Director [French]; Michael William Darcey [1965] Director; Sally Margaret Davis [1953] Director; Paul Michael Donovan [1958] Director; Maximilian Jacob Fieguth [1986] Director/Vice President; Martin Robert Healey [1973] Managing Director [Canadian]; Daniel Marc Richard Jaffe [1975] Director; Neil Edmund King [1963] Managing Director - Finance; Nathan Andrew Luckey [1979] Director/Investment Manager; Michael William John Parton [1954] Director; Christian Seymour [1964] Director/Investment Manager

Arqiva Holdings Limited
Incorporated: 27 August 1996
Net Worth: £1,494,599,936 *Total Assets:* £2,441,600,000
Registered Office: Crawley Court, Winchester, Hants, SO21 2QA
Activities: Activities of head offices
Parent: Arqiva Telecoms Investment Limited
Officers: Jeremy Mavor, Secretary; Peter Charles Adams [1982] Director/Investment Management [Canadian]; Elizabeth Jane Aikman [1965] Director; Simon Piers Beresford-Wylie [1958] Director; Mark William Braithwaite [1965] Director; Franck Emmanuel Dangeard [1958] Director [French]; Michael William Darcey [1965] Director; Sally Margaret Davis [1953] Director; Paul Michael Donovan [1958] Director; Maximilian Jacob Fieguth [1986] Director/Vice President; Martin Robert Healey [1973] Managing Director [Canadian]; Neil Edmund King [1963] Managing Director - Finance; Nathan Andrew Luckey [1979] Director/Investment Manager; Michael William John Parton [1954] Director; Christian Seymour [1964] Director/Investment Manager

Arqiva Limited
Incorporated: 2 April 1990 *Employees:* 2,071
Net Worth: £1,936,600,064 *Total Assets:* £3,381,100,032
Registered Office: Crawley Court, Winchester, Hants, SO21 2QA
Activities: Television programme production activities
Parent: Arqiva Holdings Limited
Officers: Jeremy Mavor, Secretary; Peter Charles Adams [1982] Director/Investment Management [Canadian]; Elizabeth Jane Aikman [1965] Director; Simon Piers Beresford-Wylie [1958] Director; Mark William Braithwaite [1965] Director; Franck Emmanuel Dangeard [1958] Director [French]; Michael William Darcey [1965] Director; Sally Margaret Davis [1953] Director; Paul Michael Donovan [1958] Director; Maximilian Jacob Fieguth [1986] Director/Vice President; Martin Robert Healey [1973] Managing Director [Canadian]; Neil Edmund King [1963] Managing Director - Finance; Nathan Andrew Luckey [1979] Director/Investment Manager; Michael William John Parton [1954] Director; Christian Seymour [1964] Director/Investment Manager

Arqiva No 2 Limited
Incorporated: 10 February 2000
Net Worth: £49,364,000 *Total Assets:* £101,764,000
Registered Office: Crawley Court, Winchester, Hants, SO21 2QA
Activities: Other telecommunications activities
Parent: Arqiva Services Limited
Officers: Jeremy Mavor, Secretary; Simon Piers Beresford-Wylie [1958] Director; Paul Graham Stratton [1959] Director/Accountant

Arqiva No 3 Limited
Incorporated: 6 October 1994
Net Worth: £20,474,000 *Total Assets:* £54,786,000
Registered Office: Crawley Court, Winchester, Hants, SO21 2QA
Activities: Other business support service activities n.e.c.
Parent: Arqiva No. 2 Limited
Officers: Jeremy Mavor, Secretary; Simon Piers Beresford-Wylie [1958] Director; Paul Graham Stratton [1959] Director/Accountant

Arqiva PP Financing PLC
Incorporated: 4 June 2013
Net Worth: £70,000 *Total Assets:* £964,030,016
Registered Office: Crawley Court, Winchester, Hants, SO21 2QA
Activities: Activities of head offices
Parent: Arqiva Financing No 1 Limited
Officers: Jeremy Mavor, Secretary; Peter Charles Adams [1982] Director/Investment Management [Canadian]; Simon Piers Beresford-Wylie [1958] Director; Mark William Braithwaite [1965] Director; Franck Emmanuel Dangeard [1958] Director [French]; Michael William Darcey [1965] Director; Sally Margaret Davis [1953] Director; Paul Michael Donovan [1958] Director; Maximilian Jacob Fieguth [1986] Director/Vice President; Martin Robert Healey [1973] Managing Director [Canadian]; Neil Edmund King [1963] Managing Director - Finance; Nathan Andrew Luckey [1979] Director/Investment Manager; Michael William John Parton [1954] Director; Christian Seymour [1964] Director/Investment Manager; Helena Paivi Whitaker [1963] Director [Finnish]

Arqiva Senior Finance Limited
Incorporated: 3 July 2012
Net Worth: £398,404,992 *Total Assets:* £603,500,992
Registered Office: Crawley Court, Winchester, Hants, SO21 2QA
Activities: Activities of head offices
Parent: Arqiva Group Intermediate Limited
Officers: Jeremy Mavor, Secretary; Peter Charles Adams [1982] Director/Investment Management [Canadian]; Simon Piers Beresford-Wylie [1958] Director; Mark William Braithwaite [1965] Director; Franck Emmanuel Dangeard [1958] Director [French]; Michael William Darcey [1965] Director; Sally Margaret Davis [1953] Director; Paul Michael Donovan [1958] Director; Maximilian Jacob Fieguth [1986] Director/Vice President; Martin Robert Healey [1973] Managing Director [Canadian]; Neil Edmund King [1963] Managing Director - Finance; Nathan Andrew Luckey [1979] Director/Investment Manager; Michael William John Parton [1954] Director; Christian Seymour [1964] Director/Investment Manager

Arqiva Services Limited
Incorporated: 9 May 1996
Net Worth: £1,256,499,968 *Total Assets:* £1,941,600,000
Registered Office: Crawley Court, Winchester, Hants, SO21 2QA
Activities: Other business support service activities n.e.c.
Parent: Arqiva Holdings Limited
Officers: Jeremy Mavor, Secretary; Peter Charles Adams [1982] Director/Investment Management [Canadian]; Elizabeth Jane Aikman [1965] Director; Simon Piers Beresford-Wylie [1958] Director; Mark William Braithwaite [1965] Director; Franck Emmanuel Dangeard [1958] Director [French]; Michael William Darcey [1965] Director; Sally Margaret Davis [1953] Director; Paul Michael Donovan [1958] Director; Maximilian Jacob Fieguth [1986] Director/Vice President; Martin Robert Healey [1973] Managing Director [Canadian]; Neil Edmund King [1963] Managing Director - Finance; Nathan Andrew Luckey [1979] Director/Investment Manager; Michael William John Parton [1954] Director; Christian Seymour [1964] Director/Investment Manager

Arqiva Smart Metering Limited
Incorporated: 9 September 2013
Net Worth Deficit: £1,121,000 *Total Assets:* £223,186,000
Registered Office: Crawley Court, Winchester, Hants, SO21 2QA
Activities: Other telecommunications activities
Parent: Arqiva Smart Parent Limited
Officers: Jeremy Mavor, Secretary; Peter Charles Adams [1982] Director/Investment Management [Canadian]; Mark William Braithwaite [1965] Director; Franck Emmanuel Dangeard [1958] Director [French]; Michael William Darcey [1965] Director; Sally Margaret Davis [1953] Director; Paul Michael Donovan [1958] Director; Maximilian Jacob Fieguth [1986] Director/Vice President; Martin Robert Healey [1973] Managing Director [Canadian]; Neil Edmund King [1963] Managing Director - Finance; Nathan Andrew Luckey [1979] Director/Investment Manager; Michael William John Parton [1954] Director; Christian Seymour [1964] Director/Investment Manager

Arqiva Telecoms Investment Limited
Incorporated: 18 January 1999
Net Worth Deficit: £1,204,909,952 *Total Assets:* £3,043,326,976
Registered Office: Crawley Court, Winchester, Hants, SO21 2QA
Activities: Other telecommunications activities
Parent: Arqiva Group Holdings Limited
Officers: Jeremy Mavor, Secretary; Peter Charles Adams [1982] Director/Investment Management [Canadian]; Elizabeth Jane Aikman [1965] Director; Simon Piers Beresford-Wylie [1958] Director; Mark William Braithwaite [1965] Director; Franck Emmanuel Dangeard [1958] Director [French]; Michael William Darcey [1965] Director; Sally Margaret Davis [1953] Director; Paul Michael Donovan [1958] Director; Maximilian Jacob Fieguth [1986] Director/Vice President; Martin Robert Healey [1973] Managing Director [Canadian]; Neil Edmund King [1963] Managing Director - Finance; Nathan Andrew Luckey [1979] Director/Investment Manager; Michael William John Parton [1954] Director; Christian Seymour [1964] Director/Investment Manager

Arqiva UK Broadcast Holdings Limited
Incorporated: 8 October 2004
Net Worth: £736,513,984 *Total Assets:* £793,025,024
Registered Office: Crawley Court, Winchester, Hants, SO21 2QA
Activities: Activities of head offices
Parent: Arqiva Group Holdings Limited
Officers: Jeremy Mavor, Secretary; Peter Charles Adams [1982] Director/Investment Management [Canadian]; Elizabeth Jane Aikman [1965] Director; Simon Piers Beresford-Wylie [1958] Director; Mark William Braithwaite [1965] Director; Franck Emmanuel Dangeard [1958] Director [French]; Michael William Darcey [1965] Director; Sally Margaret Davis [1953] Director; Paul Michael Donovan [1958] Director; Maximilian Jacob Fieguth [1986] Director/Vice President; Martin Robert Healey [1973] Managing Director [Canadian]; Neil Edmund King [1963] Managing Director - Finance; Nathan Andrew Luckey [1979] Director/Investment Manager; Michael William John Parton [1954] Director; Christian Seymour [1964] Director/Investment Manager

ARRI (GB) Limited
Incorporated: 23 December 1982 *Employees:* 82
Net Worth: £18,619,000 *Total Assets:* £32,916,000
Registered Office: 2 Highbridge, Oxford Road, Uxbridge, Middlesex, UB8 1LX
Activities: Wholesale of household goods (other than musical instruments) n.e.c
Shareholders: Christoph Stahl; Carolin Stahl; Florian Stahl
Officers: Dawn Melanie Oatley [1963] Finance Director; Dr. Jorg Pohlman [1963] Managing Director [German]

Arris Solutions UK Ltd.
Incorporated: 1 November 2012 *Employees:* 102
Previous: General Instrument UK Ltd.
Net Worth: £95,451,968 *Total Assets:* £99,819,824
Registered Office: 710 Wharfedale Road, Winnersh, Wokingham, Berks, RG41 5TP
Activities: Other information service activities n.e.c.
Parent: Arris International PLC
Officers: Stephen John McCaffery [1966] Director/Business Executive; David Bernard Potts [1957] Director/Businessman [American]; Anthony Emilien Zuyderhoff [1971] Director [American]

ARRK Product Development Group Limited
Incorporated: 18 October 1988 *Employees:* 7
Net Worth: £23,241,000 *Total Assets:* £34,413,000
Registered Office: PTC Technical Centre, The Hyde, Langrish, Petersfield, Hants, GU32 1RL
Activities: Activities of other holding companies n.e.c.
Parent: ARRK Corporation
Officers: Simon Holmes, Secretary; Antony Stephen Hunter Lowe [1964] Managing Director; Yasuki Shiraishi [1965] Director/Corporate Executive [Japanese]

Arrow Business Communications Group Limited
Incorporated: 15 June 2016 *Employees:* 6
Net Worth: £2,156,556 *Total Assets:* £34,658,904
Registered Office: The Wharf, Abbey Mill Business Park, Lower Eashing, Godalming, Surrey, GU7 2QN
Activities: Other telecommunications activities
Parent: Arrow Business Communications Holdings Limited
Officers: Michael James Blake [1968] Director; Richard Edward Burke [1979] Director; Paul Joseph Gibbons [1968] Finance Director; John Duncan Harber [1971] Director; Christopher John Russell [1971] Director; Richard Shaw [1981] Director; Tracey Dawn Tribe [1974] Marketing Director

Arrow Business Communications Holdings Limited
Incorporated: 15 June 2016 *Employees:* 154
Net Worth Deficit: £3,663,535 *Total Assets:* £47,714,532
Registered Office: The Wharf, Abbey Mill Business Park, Lower Eashing, Godalming, Surrey, GU7 2QN
Activities: Other telecommunications activities
Shareholder: GCP IV GP LLP
Officers: Michael James Blake [1968] Director; Richard Edward Burke [1979] Director; Paul Joseph Gibbons [1968] Finance Director; John Duncan Harber [1971] Director; Christopher John Russell [1971] Director; Richard Shaw [1981] Director; Tracey Dawn Tribe [1974] Marketing Director

Arun Estate Agencies Limited
Incorporated: 4 April 1991 *Employees:* 1,006
Net Worth: £59,830,000 *Total Assets:* £68,745,000
Registered Office: St Leonards House, North Street, Horsham, W Sussex, RH12 1RJ
Activities: Other business support service activities n.e.c.
Officers: Christopher Andrew Coxon, Secretary/Chartered Accountant; Christopher Andrew Coxon [1957] Director/Chartered Accountant; David James Lench [1958] Marketing Director; Paul Anthony Rooney [1947] Director

Aryzta UK Holdings I Limited
Incorporated: 12 April 2012
Net Worth: £1,805,984,768 *Total Assets:* £1,806,012,928
Registered Office: Delice House, 149 Brent Road, Southall, Middlesex, UB2 5LJ
Activities: Activities of head offices
Officers: Sean Timothy Murphy, Secretary; Thierry Cacaly [1971] Director/Head of Aryzta Food Solutions UK [French]; John McNiff [1976] Director [Irish]; Sean Timothy Murphy [1969] Director/Accountant [Irish]

AS & Sons Ltd
Incorporated: 1 July 2005
Net Worth: £8,312,372 *Total Assets:* £29,992,296
Registered Office: 2 Lake End Court, Taplow Road, Taplow, Maidenhead, Berks, SL6 0JQ
Activities: Management of real estate on a fee or contract basis
Major Shareholder: Abdul Sattar
Officers: Ali Raza Sattar, Secretary; Abdul Sattar [1961] Managing Director

Asahi Breweries Europe Ltd
Incorporated: 8 February 2017 *Employees:* 21
Net Worth: £6,608,400,384 *Total Assets:* £6,961,224,704
Registered Office: Front Suite, Ground Floor, Goldvale House, Church Street West, Woking, Surrey, GU21 6DH
Activities: Activities of head offices
Parent: Asahi Group Holdings, Ltd.
Officers: Andrew Bailey [1968] Director; Ryoichi Kitagawa [1963] Director [Japanese]; Paolo Alberto Francesco Lanzarotti [1966] Director; Satoshi Mori [1970] Director [Japanese]; Hikaru Sato [1970] Director [Japanese]

Asahi Europe Ltd
Incorporated: 16 August 2016 *Employees:* 40
Net Worth: £2,134,615,808 *Total Assets:* £2,172,581,120
Registered Office: One Forge End, Woking, Surrey, GU21 6DB
Activities: Activities of head offices
Parent: Asahi Group Holdings, Ltd.
Officers: Edward Perks, Secretary; Rohan Cummings [1975] Director; Hector Gorosabel [1960] Managing Director [Canadian]; Ryoichi Kitagawa [1963] Director [Japanese]; Satoshi Mori [1970] Director [Japanese]; Yusuke Naritsuka [1972] Director [Japanese]

Asahi UK Ltd
Incorporated: 23 December 2004 *Employees:* 188
Previous: Miller Brands (UK) Limited
Net Worth: £28,456,000 *Total Assets:* £109,625,000
Registered Office: One Forge End, Woking, Surrey, GU21 6DB
Activities: Wholesale of wine, beer, spirits and other alcoholic beverages
Parent: Asahi Europe Limited
Officers: Edward William Perks, Secretary; Timothy James Clay [1966] Managing Director; Rohan Cummings [1975] Director/Chief Financial Officer; Hector Gorosabel [1960] Managing Director Western Europe [Canadian]; Yusuke Naritsuka [1972] Director [Japanese]; Michael Richard Randles [1975] Director/Chartered Accountant

Ascension Healthcare PLC
Incorporated: 25 September 2013 *Employees:* 31
Previous: Pro Bono Bio PLC
Net Worth Deficit: £42,862,000 *Total Assets:* £193,266,000
Registered Office: 4th Floor, Reading Bridge House, George Street, Reading, Berks, RG1 8LS
Activities: Activities of other holding companies n.e.c.
Parent: Russian Federation Duly Represented By The Federal Agency for State Property Management, Ministry of Economic Development
Officers: Jonathan Robert Aisbitt [1957] Director; Ali Jalal Baruni [1947] Director/Consultant; Oleg Vladimirovich Kiselev [1953] Director [Russian]; David Paul Quint [1950] Director [British/American]; Irina Rapoport [1968] Director [Russian]; Biresh Roy [1962] Director/Chief Executive Officer; Dmitrii Volokhov [1984] Director/Investment Advisor [Russian]; Dr Richard Wolf-Garraway [1966] Director

Ascenti Health Limited
Incorporated: 17 July 1996 *Employees:* 782
Previous: The Integrated Care Clinics Limited
Net Worth: £34,468,072 *Total Assets:* £69,405,472
Registered Office: Carnac House, Carnac Court, Cams Hall Estate, Fareham, Hants, PO16 8UZ
Activities: General medical practice activities
Parent: Ascenti Holdings Limited
Officers: Stephanie Elizabeth Squire Dobrikova [1985] Director of Business Services; Kevin Doyle [1980] Director/Physiotherapist [Irish]; Christopher Ian Jessop [1953] Director; Bernard Vince Rowe [1951] Director/Solicitor

Ascot Authority (Holdings) Limited
Incorporated: 21 August 2001 *Employees:* 157
Net Worth: £52,128,000 *Total Assets:* £187,751,008
Registered Office: Ascot Racecourse, Ascot, Berks, SL5 7JX
Activities: Operation of sports facilities
Shareholders: Harry Michael Charles Morley; Jonathan Roger Weatherby; Francis George Windham Brooke
Officers: Sir Francis George Windham Brooke [1963] Director [Irish]; Guy Bryce Davison [1957] Director/Investment Manager; Guy Henderson [1958] Director/Chief Executive; Ian Donald McGregor [1962] Director/Chartered Accountant; Harry Michael Charles Morley [1965] Director; Juliet Mary Slot [1968] Commercial Director; Alastair James McGregor Warwick [1972] Director/General Manager; Johnny Roger Weatherby [1959] Director/Chairman

Ascot Racecourse Limited
Incorporated: 12 November 2001 *Employees:* 157
Net Worth: £3,921,000 *Total Assets:* £104,145,000
Registered Office: Ascot Racecourse, Ascot, Berks, SL5 7JX
Activities: Operation of sports facilities
Parent: Ascot Authority Holdings Limited
Officers: Guy Henderson [1958] Director/Chief Executive; Ian Donald McGregor [1962] Director/Chartered Accountant; Jonathan Robert Parker [1968] Director/Caterer; Juliet Mary Slot [1968] Commercial Director; Nicholas Kester Smith [1972] Director; Alastair James McGregor Warwick [1972] Operations Director

Ash Properties Limited
Incorporated: 20 March 2009 *Employees:* 2
Net Worth: £14,399,855 *Total Assets:* £36,090,872
Registered Office: 38 The Drive, Ickenham, Middlesex, UB10 8AG
Activities: Residents property management
Shareholders: Sital Kaur; Kuldeep Singh
Officers: Sital Kaur, Secretary; Kuldeep Singh [1967] Director/Businessman

Ashcourt Holdings Limited
Incorporated: 30 July 2002
Net Worth: £9,298,000 *Total Assets:* £33,249,000
Registered Office: The Observatory, Western Road, Bracknell, Berks, RG12 1TL
Activities: Activities of financial services holding companies
Parent: Ashcourt Rowan Limited
Officers: Rehana Hasan, Secretary; Andrew Martin Baddeley [1964] Director; Donald William Sherret Reid [1959] Director/Chief Operating Officer; Christopher Woodhouse [1961] Director/Chief Executive Officer

Ashcourt Rowan Limited
Incorporated: 30 March 2005
Previous: Ashcourt Rowan PLC
Net Worth: £38,551,000 *Total Assets:* £65,455,000
Registered Office: The Observatory, Western Road, Bracknell, Berks, RG12 1TL
Activities: Activities of financial services holding companies
Parent: Towry Finance Company Limited
Officers: Rehana Hasan, Secretary; Andrew Martin Baddeley [1964] Director; Donald William Sherret Reid [1959] Director/Chief Operating Officer; Christopher Woodhouse [1961] Director/Chief Executive Officer

Asia Pacific Holdings Limited
Incorporated: 7 March 2000
Net Worth: £2,143,913,984 *Total Assets:* £3,019,723,008
Registered Office: Broadwater Park, Denham, Bucks, UB9 5HR
Activities: Other business support service activities n.e.c.
Parent: Six Continents Limited
Officers: Fiona Cuttell, Secretary; Michael Jon Cockcroft [1974] Director/Accountant; Michael Todd Glover [1971] Director/Financial Controller [American]; Nicolette Henfrey [1969] Director

ASIG Holdings Limited
Incorporated: 20 March 2008
Net Worth: £37,600,000 *Total Assets:* £38,400,000
Registered Office: 2 World Business Centre Heathrow, Newall Road, London Heathrow Airport, Hounslow, Middlesex, TW6 2SF
Activities: Scheduled passenger air transport
Parent: BBA Holdings Limited
Officers: John Francis Alexander Geddes, Secretary; Deon Van Niekerk [1972] Director/Accountant [South African]; Laura Relf [1982] Director/Accountant

Aspen Marketing Group Limited
Incorporated: 12 October 2004 *Employees:* 1
Net Worth: £7,055,000 *Total Assets:* £33,899,000
Registered Office: Ground Floor, Block A, Dukes Court, Duke Street, Woking, Surrey, GU21 5BH
Activities: Non-trading company
Parent: Reach Holdings Limited
Officers: Charlene Emma Friend, Secretary; Charlene Emma Friend [1984] Director/Accountant; Todd Johnson [1965] Director [American]; Justine Maxwell [1978] Director/Chartered Accountant

Aspen Pumps Limited
Incorporated: 13 November 2012 *Employees:* 106
Net Worth: £22,597,000 *Total Assets:* £77,242,000
Registered Office: Apex Way, Hailsham, E Sussex, BN27 3WA
Activities: Other manufacturing n.e.c.
Parent: Acquaspen Limited
Officers: Nicholas James Redman, Secretary; Serge Guillaume Becker [1977] Sales Director [Dutch]; Kevin Christopher Bergin [1959] Commercial Director; Kelly John Frederick Butler [1968] Marketing Director; Christopher John Gee [1958] Technical Director; Robert Edward Kienlen [1973] Finance Director; Hamish David William Middleton [1971] Director; Adrian William Thompson [1967] Director; Andrew Shaun Wakelin [1961] Commercial Director

Aspentech Ltd.
Incorporated: 2 March 1983 *Employees:* 125
Net Worth: £18,624,000 *Total Assets:* £24,436,000
Registered Office: C2 Reading International Business Park, Basingstoke Road, Reading, Berks, RG2 6DT
Activities: Information technology consultancy activities
Parent: Aspen Technology, Inc.
Officers: Richard David Claye, Secretary; Frederic George Hammond [1959] Director/Attorney [American]; Karl Eric Johnsen [1968] Director [American]; Antonio Jose Pietri [1965] Director [American]

Aspire Pharma Holdings Limited
Incorporated: 11 November 2014 *Employees:* 32
Net Worth: £5,940,265 *Total Assets:* £32,370,296
Registered Office: 102 High Street, Godalming, Surrey, GU7 1DS
Activities: Wholesale of pharmaceutical goods
Shareholders: Graham Julian Fraser-Pye; Juno Pharmaceuticals Luxembourg S.A.R.L
Officers: Jacqueline Elizabeth Fraser-Pye, Secretary; Debra Joy Roberts, Secretary; Graham Julian Fraser-Pye [1968] Director; Ian Jacobson [1960] Director/Chief Executive [Canadian]; Debra Joy Roberts [1962] Financial Director; Mark Derek Roberts [1967] Director

Asset Advantage Group Limited
Incorporated: 13 November 1992 *Employees:* 46
Net Worth: £19,201,690 *Total Assets:* £110,817,408
Registered Office: Matrix House, Basing View, Basingstoke, Hants, RG21 4DZ
Activities: Financial intermediation not elsewhere classified
Major Shareholder: Jonathan Charles Grenville Eddy
Officers: Jonathan Charles Grenville Eddy [1968] Director; Philip James Knight [1964] Director; Michael Pelham Morris Olive [1956] Director/Company Executive; Alastair James Ramsay [1970] Director

Asset Advantage Limited
Incorporated: 20 April 2001
Net Worth: £10,233,369 *Total Assets:* £107,989,792
Registered Office: Matrix House, Basing View, Basingstoke, Hants, RG21 4DZ
Activities: Financial intermediation not elsewhere classified
Officers: Jonathan Charles Grenville Eddy [1968] Director; Philip James Knight [1964] Director; Michael Pelham Morris Olive [1956] Director/Company Executive; Alastair James Ramsay [1970] Director

Associated Cold Stores & Transport Limited
Incorporated: 11 August 1955 *Employees:* 202
Net Worth: £17,571,460 *Total Assets:* £23,587,624
Registered Office: Linton Park, Linton, Maidstone, Kent, ME17 4AB
Activities: Operation of warehousing and storage facilities for land transport activities
Parent: Associated Fisheries Limited
Officers: Amarpal Takk, Secretary; Thomas Kenric Franks [1963] Director; Malcolm Johnstone [1956] Director; Katrina Ann LEA [1967] Director; Steven Tomlinson [1968] Director

Associated Fisheries Limited
Incorporated: 28 February 1929
Net Worth: £4,625,698 *Total Assets:* £27,329,548
Registered Office: Linton Park, Linton, Maidstone, Kent, ME17 4AB
Activities: Activities of head offices
Parent: Bordure Limited
Officers: Amarpal Takk, Secretary; Thomas Kenric Franks [1963] Director; Susan Ann Walker [1967] Director

Associated International Cement Limited
Incorporated: 28 June 1949
Net Worth: £601,616,000 *Total Assets:* £602,089,984
Registered Office: Park Lodge, London Road, Dorking, Surrey, RH4 1TH
Activities: Activities of head offices
Parent: Blue Circle International Holdings BV
Officers: Howard Bruce Moller, Secretary; Simon Gregory Crossley [1973] Director; Laurent Jaques [1976] Director/Holding Management [Swiss]; Howard Bruce Moller [1962] Director/Finance Manager

Astellas Pharma Europe Ltd.
Incorporated: 29 March 1990 *Employees:* 399
Net Worth: £870,882,368 *Total Assets:* £1,343,135,104
Registered Office: 2000 Hillswood Drive, Chertsey, Surrey, KT16 0RS
Activities: Wholesale of pharmaceutical goods
Parent: Astellas Pharma Inc.
Officers: Sally Anne Hinchliffe, Secretary; Jochen Norbert Bohner [1971] Director/SVP Finance, Procurement & IS EMEA [German]; Masaaki Hirano [1967] Director/Businessman [Japanese]; Dr Dirk Armin Kosche [1963] Director/President EMEA Operations [German]; Daniel Benjamin Matthias Schulze [1975] Director/Vice President and General Counsel [German]; Toru Yoshimitsu [1963] Director [Japanese]

Astellas Pharma Ltd.
Incorporated: 10 January 1964 *Employees:* 195
Net Worth: £49,799,000 *Total Assets:* £133,302,000
Registered Office: 2000 Hillswood Drive, Chertsey, Surrey, KT16 0RS
Activities: Wholesale of pharmaceutical goods
Parent: Astellas Pharma Inc.
Officers: Ian Michael Hall [1966] Director/Chartered Accountant; Dr Jose Maria Sanz [1972] Director/General Manager

Asteral Holdings Limited
Incorporated: 3 June 2014
Net Worth: £22,361,440 *Total Assets:* £69,706,888
Registered Office: Unit 4 Theale Commercial Estate, Ely Road, Theale, Berks, RG7 4BQ
Activities: Activities of other holding companies n.e.c.
Shareholders: Althea Group S.P.A; Althea Group Limited
Officers: Stephen James Tuddenham [1980] Director

Aston Carter Group Limited
Incorporated: 23 April 2007
Net Worth: £60,326,088 *Total Assets:* £85,211,240
Registered Office: Maxis 2, Western Road, Bracknell, Berks, RG12 1RT
Activities: Activities of head offices
Shareholders: Randall Dean Sones; Richard Alan Butler; Fred Ridley
Officers: Andrew David Williams [1981] Director; Sean Hendrick Zimdahl [1968] Director [German]

Aston Carter International Limited
Incorporated: 29 October 2002 *Employees:* 38
Net Worth: £89,739,712 *Total Assets:* £104,563,664
Registered Office: Maxis 2, Western Road, Bracknell, Berks, RG12 1RT
Activities: Other activities of employment placement agencies
Shareholders: Randall Dean Sones; Richard Alan Butler; Fred S. Ridley
Officers: Andrew David Williams [1981] Director; Sean Hendrick Zimdahl [1968] Director [German]

ATG London Limited
Incorporated: 5 January 2000 *Employees:* 396
Net Worth: £8,624,000 *Total Assets:* £400,655,008
Registered Office: 2nd Floor, Alexander House, Church Path, Woking, Surrey, GU21 6EJ
Activities: Operation of arts facilities
Parent: The Ambassador Theatre Group Ltd
Officers: Mark Ralph Delano Cornell [1966] Director; Adam Lee Kenwright [1972] Commercial Director; Michael Cowper Lynas [1957] Programming Director; Nicholas Graham Potter [1968] Managing Director; Shanmae Teo [1976] Director

Atkins ATK Investments Limited
Incorporated: 26 March 2002
Previous: Atkins Investments UK Limited
Net Worth: £33,122,000 *Total Assets:* £34,102,000
Registered Office: Woodcote Grove, Ashley Road, Epsom, Surrey, KT18 5BW
Activities: Other business support service activities n.e.c.
Parent: WS Atkins Limited
Officers: Louise Mary McAllister, Secretary; Elliot Michael Nobelen, Secretary; Mark Stephen Anderson [1965] Director/Accountant; Simon Glenister Cole [1965] Director/Accountant; Alan James Cullens [1963] Group HR Director

Atkins Holdings Limited
Incorporated: 6 March 1985 *Employees:* 9
Net Worth: £18,409,000 *Total Assets:* £21,170,000
Registered Office: Cedars Cottage, 16 Church Street, Epsom, Surrey, KT17 4QB
Activities: Activities of head offices
Shareholders: William Stewart Gregg; Bruce Meredith Caporn
Officers: Charles Elliott Marr, Secretary; Catherine Clare Butler [1962] Director; Bruce Meredith Caporn [1934] Director/Solicitor; William Stewart Gregg [1949] Director/Chartered Accountant; Charles Elliott Marr [1958] Director/Chartered Accountant; Christopher Charles Micklethwaite [1958] Director; Reverend Peter William Micklethwaite [1962] Director/Minister of Religion; Nicholas Robert Worthington [1960] Director

Atkins International Holdings Limited
Incorporated: 22 November 2007
Previous: Atkins Gamma Limited
Net Worth: £72,040,000 *Total Assets:* £214,945,408
Registered Office: Woodcote Grove, Ashley Road, Epsom, Surrey, KT18 5BW
Activities: Other business support service activities n.e.c.
Parent: WS Atkins Limited
Officers: Louise Mary McAllister, Secretary; Elliot Michael Nobelen, Secretary; Mark Stephen Anderson [1965] Director/Accountant; Simon Glenister Cole [1965] Director/Accountant; Alan James Cullens [1963] Group HR Director

W.S. Atkins International Limited
Incorporated: 23 January 1973 *Employees:* 13
Net Worth: £240,802,000 *Total Assets:* £676,515,008
Registered Office: Woodcote Grove, Ashley Road, Epsom, Surrey, KT18 5BW
Activities: Other business support service activities n.e.c.
Parent: Atkins International Holdings Limited
Officers: Louise Mary McAllister, Secretary; Elliot Michael Nobelen, Secretary; Mark Stephen Anderson [1965] Director/Accountant; Christopher Ball [1973] Director; Christopher Laine Birdsong [1952] Director/Project Manager [American]; Martin Alexander Chalmers [1964] Director/Manager; Simon Glenister Cole [1965] Director/Accountant; Alan James Cullens [1963] Group HR Director; Martin MacDonald Grant [1958] Director/Mechanical Engineer; Philip David Hoare [1970] Director/Chartered Civil Engineer; Michael McNicholas [1961] Director/Civil Engineer; Nicholas John Roberts [1968] Director/Chartered Geologist; Neil James Corfield Thomas [1962] Director/Chartered Engineer

Atkins Investments UK Limited
Incorporated: 14 December 2004
Previous: Atkins Beta Limited
Net Worth: £120,300,000 *Total Assets:* £325,300,000
Registered Office: Woodcote Grove, Ashley Road, Epsom, Surrey, KT18 5BW
Activities: Other business support service activities n.e.c.
Parent: WS Atkins Limited
Officers: Louise Mary McAllister, Secretary; Elliot Michael Nobelen, Secretary; Mark Stephen Anderson [1965] Director/Accountant; Simon Glenister Cole [1965] Director/Accountant; Alan James Cullens [1963] Group HR Director

Atkins Limited
Incorporated: 30 March 1961 *Employees:* 7,144
Net Worth: £298,900,000 *Total Assets:* £1,027,699,968
Registered Office: Woodcote Grove, Ashley Road, Epsom, Surrey, KT18 5BW
Activities: Management consultancy activities other than financial management
Parent: Atkins Investments UK Limited
Officers: Louise Mary McAllister, Secretary; Elliot Michael Nobelen, Secretary; Mark Stephen Anderson [1965] Director/Accountant; Christopher Ball [1973] Director; Martin Alexander Chalmers [1964] Director/Manager; Simon Glenister Cole [1965] Director/Accountant; Alan James Cullens [1963] Group HR Director; Martin MacDonald Grant [1958] Director/Mechanical Engineer; Philip David Hoare [1970] Director/Chartered Civil Engineer; Michael McNicholas [1961] Director/Civil Engineer; Nicholas John Roberts [1968] Director/Chartered Geologist; Neil James Corfield Thomas [1962] Director/Chartered Engineer

WS Atkins Limited
Incorporated: 13 February 1985
Previous: WS Atkins PLC
Net Worth: £235,300,000 *Total Assets:* £611,299,968
Registered Office: Woodcote Grove, Ashley Road, Epsom, Surrey, KT18 5BW
Activities: Activities of head offices
Parent: SNC-Lavalin (GB) Holdings Limited
Officers: Louise Mary McAllister, Secretary; Elliot Michael Nobelen, Secretary; Mark Stephen Anderson [1965] Director/Accountant; Christopher Ball [1973] Director; Simon Glenister Cole [1965] Director/Accountant; James Richard Compston [1965] Director/Executive; Alan James Cullens [1963] Group HR Director; Martin MacDonald Grant [1958] Director/Mechanical Engineer

Atkins Properties Limited
Incorporated: 7 March 1961 *Employees:* 9
Net Worth: £20,011,000 *Total Assets:* £21,766,000
Registered Office: Cedars Cottage, 16 Church Street, Epsom, Surrey, KT17 4QB
Activities: Other letting and operating of own or leased real estate
Parent: Atkins Holdings Limited
Officers: Charles Elliott Marr, Secretary; Charles Elliott Marr [1958] Director/Chartered Accountant; Christopher Charles Micklethwaite [1958] Director; Roderick Stephen Milne [1959] Director/Chartered Surveyor

Atlantic 2/3 UK Holdings Limited
Incorporated: 20 September 2000
Net Worth: £214,780,416 *Total Assets:* £214,789,936
Registered Office: Chertsey Road, Sunbury on Thames, Middlesex, TW16 7BP
Activities: Non-trading company
Parent: BP Exploration Operating Company Limited
Officers: David Alan Rider [1964] Director/Oil Company Executive; Katherine Anne Thomson [1968] Director/Oil Company Executive

Atlantic Foods Limited
Incorporated: 18 January 2005 *Employees:* 33
Net Worth: £18,896,830 *Total Assets:* £26,738,164
Registered Office: 10 Watchmoor Park, Riverside Way, Camberley, Surrey, GU15 3YL
Activities: Production of meat and poultry meat products
Parent: Atlantic Foods Group Limited
Officers: Russell Alexander Powis Maddock, Secretary; Kevin Lawrence Cahill [1970] Director [Irish]; William Blair Coulten [1981] Finance Director; Sherry Anne Demeulenaere [1958] Director [American]; Russell Alexander Powis Maddock [1965] Director; David Gerard McDonald [1964] Director [American]; Kevin Richard Scott [1959] Director [American]

Atlantica Yield PLC
Incorporated: 17 December 2013 *Employees:* 181
Previous: Abengoa Yield PLC
Net Worth: £1,276,755,200 *Total Assets:* £7,616,390,144
Registered Office: Great West House, (GW1), Great West Road, Brentford, Middlesex, TW8 9DF
Activities: Production of electricity
Shareholder: ACIL Luxco 1 S.A.
Officers: Irene Maria Hernandez Martin de Arriva, Secretary; Andrea Brentan [1949] Director [Italian]; Christopher Kenneth Jarratt [1958] Director [Canadian]; Francisco Jose Martinez [1958] Director [Spanish]; Ian Edward Robertson [1959] Director [Canadian]; Jackson Robinson [1942] Director [American]; Santiago Seage [1969] Director/Chief Executive Officer [Spanish]; Daniel Villalba [1947] Director [Spanish]

Atlantis Holdings Limited
Incorporated: 7 April 2006 *Employees:* 4
Net Worth: £10,765,239 *Total Assets:* £41,366,652
Registered Office: First Floor, 23-24 Market Place, Reading, Berks, RG1 2DE
Activities: Other letting and operating of own or leased real estate
Officers: Andrew James Strong [1981] Director; John Jac Sykes [1971] Director/Chairman

Atlas Copco Limited
Incorporated: 21 October 1919 *Employees:* 532
Net Worth: £34,502,000 *Total Assets:* £120,718,000
Registered Office: Swallowdale Lane, Hemel Hempstead, Herts, HP2 7EA
Activities: Other business support service activities n.e.c.
Parent: Atlas Copco UK Holdings Limited
Officers: Alex Christiaan Jan Bongaerts, Secretary; Alex Christiaan Jan Bongaerts [1960] Director/Holding Manager [Belgian]; Geert Henri Follens [1959] Director [Belgian]; Kevin George Prince [1961] Director; Andrew Walker [1961] Director [Irish]

Atlas Copco UK Holdings Limited
Incorporated: 23 December 1974 *Employees:* 22
Net Worth: £165,663,008 *Total Assets:* £204,647,008
Registered Office: Swallowdale Lane, Hemel Hempstead, Herts, HP2 7EA
Activities: Activities of head offices
Parent: Atlas Copco Airpower N.V.
Officers: Alex Christiaan Jan Bongaerts, Secretary; Alex Christiaan Jan Bongaerts [1960] Director/Holding Manager [Belgian]; Geert Henri Follens [1959] Director [Belgian]

ATP Media Holdings Limited
Incorporated: 18 July 2017 *Employees:* 32
Net Worth: £4,933,332 *Total Assets:* £38,699,312
Registered Office: Thames House, Portsmouth Road, Esher, Surrey, KT10 9AD
Activities: Activities of other holding companies n.e.c.
Officers: Tom Bullock, Secretary; Andrea Gaudenzi [1973] Director/Entrepreneur [Italian]; Stuart James Watts [1965] Director/Chief Operating Officer; Mark Andrew Webster [1962] Director/Chief Executive Officer; Mark Vernon Young [1958] Director/Sports Executive [American]; Gavin Ziv [1975] Director/Vice President, Tennis Canada [Canadian]

ATP Media Operations Limited
Incorporated: 15 October 1998 *Employees:* 32
Previous: Tennis Properties Limited
Net Worth: £4,963,838 *Total Assets:* £40,368,924
Registered Office: Thames House, Portsmouth Road, Esher, Surrey, KT10 9AD
Activities: Television programme production activities
Officers: Thomas Bullock, Secretary; Andrea Gaudenzi [1973] Director/Entrepreneur [Italian]; Stuart James Watts [1965] Director/Chief Operating Officer; Mark Andrew Webster [1962] Director/Chief Executive Officer; Mark Vernon Young [1958] Director/Attorney/Business Executive [American]; Gavin Ziv [1975] Director/Vice President Tennis Canada [Canadian]

Attewell Limited
Incorporated: 11 December 1962 *Employees:* 102
Net Worth: £23,432,000 *Total Assets:* £33,207,000
Registered Office: 7 A/B, Millington Road, Hayes, Middlesex, UB3 4AZ
Activities: Other manufacturing n.e.c.
Parent: Shimtech Industries Limited
Officers: Heath Denis Batwell [1983] Director/Accountant [Irish]; Alastair Scott Fanning [1967] Director/Chartered Accountant; Matthew Giggle [1967] Director; Christopher Eric Smith [1971] Director

Attwood Academies
Incorporated: 25 July 2014 *Employees:* 128
Net Worth: £24,745,914 *Total Assets:* £26,065,816
Registered Office: Manor House, Slip Mill Road, Hawkhurst, Cranbrook, Kent, TN18 5AE
Activities: General secondary education
Officers: Susan Foley, Secretary; Sara Moira Attwood [1954] Director/Magistrate; Thomas Roger Attwood [1952] Director/Retired; Stephen Christopher Gough [1979] Director/Accountant; Alban Francis Xavier Green [1950] Director/Retired; Catherine Heidi Sale [1958] Director/Headteacher; Jonathan Peter Sale [1965] Educational Business Director

Audatex (UK) Limited
Incorporated: 25 September 1986 *Employees:* 200
Net Worth: £14,264,269 *Total Assets:* £42,971,800
Registered Office: The Forum, Station Road, Theale, Reading, Berks, RG7 4RA
Activities: Other information technology service activities
Parent: Audatex (Schweiz) GmbH
Officers: Tony Aquila [1964] Director/Chairman [American]; Jason Michael Brady [1968] Director/Senior VP, General Counsel and Secretary [American]; Renato Carlo Giger [1960] Director [Swiss]; Franciscus Johanes Carolus Overtoom [1966] Director/Regional Finance Officer [Dutch]; David John Shepherd [1953] Regional Managing Director

Audio UK 2 Limited
Incorporated: 23 February 2017
Net Worth: £167,315,008 *Total Assets:* £195,316,000
Registered Office: Unit 10 Silverglade Business Park, Leatherhead Road, Chessington, Surrey, KT9 2QL
Activities: Activities of other holding companies n.e.c.
Parent: Audiotonix Group Limited
Officers: Francois de Mitry, Secretary; James Barton [1970] Director; Michael Beetz [1982] Investor, Associate Director [German]; Helen Mary Culleton [1964] Director; Francois de Mitry [1966] Director/Investor, Partner [Luxembourger]; Stephane Epin [1978] Director/Investor, Partner [French]; James David Gordon [1972] Director

Audio UK 3 Limited
Incorporated: 23 February 2017
Net Worth: £167,315,008 *Total Assets:* £195,316,000
Registered Office: Unit 10 Silverglade Business Park, Leatherhead Road, Chessington, Surrey, KT9 2QL
Activities: Activities of other holding companies n.e.c.
Parent: Audio UK 2 Limited
Officers: Francois de Mitry, Secretary; James Barton [1970] Director; Michael Beetz [1982] Investor, Associate Director [German]; Helen Mary Culleton [1964] Director; Francois de Mitry [1966] Director/Investor, Partner [Luxembourger]; Stephane Epin [1978] Director/Investor, Partner [French]; James David Gordon [1972] Director

Audiotonix Group Limited
Incorporated: 23 February 2017
Net Worth: £7,373,979 *Total Assets:* £479,676,288
Registered Office: Unit 10 Silverglade Business Park, Leatherhead Road, Chessington, Surrey, KT9 2QL
Activities: Activities of other holding companies n.e.c.
Officers: Francois de Mitry, Secretary; James Barton [1970] Director; Michael Beetz [1982] Investor, Associate Director [German]; Helen Mary Culleton [1964] Director; Francois de Mitry [1966] Director/Investor, Partner [Luxembourger]; Stephane Epin [1978] Director/Investor, Partner [French]; James David Gordon [1972] Director

Audley Court Limited
Incorporated: 22 June 2004 *Employees:* 373
Net Worth: £145,519,008 *Total Assets:* £292,196,992
Registered Office: 65 High Street, Egham, Surrey, TW20 9EY
Activities: Buying and selling of own real estate
Parent: Audley Group Limited
Officers: Jonathan Martin Austen [1956] Director/Chief Financial Officer; Nicholas William John Edwards [1973] Finance Director; Marc Edward Charles Gilbard [1962] Director/CEO of Private Equity Real Estate Fund Manager; Paul David Morgan [1969] Operations Director; John William Nettleton [1970] Director/Chartered Surveyor; Katherine Elizabeth Rose [1964] Director; Malcolm Nicholas Sanderson [1959] Director/Property Developer; Kevin Anthony Shaw [1977] Sales and Development Director

Audley Group Limited
Incorporated: 8 December 2015 *Employees:* 375
Net Worth: £239,752,000 *Total Assets:* £315,832,992
Registered Office: 65 High Street, Egham, Surrey, TW20 9EY
Activities: Activities of other holding companies n.e.c.
Parent: Maref Topco Limited
Officers: Jonathan Martin Austen [1956] Director/Chief Financial Officer; Michael Bruhn [1959] Director [Danish]; Nicholas William John Edwards [1973] Director; Marc Edward Charles Gilbard [1962] Director; Paul David Morgan [1969] Director; Malcolm Nicholas Sanderson [1959] Director; Kevin Anthony Shaw [1977] Director

Augustus 1 Limited
Incorporated: 23 August 2004
Net Worth: £30,824,000 *Total Assets:* £325,528,992
Registered Office: 8th Floor, Vantage London, Great West Road, Brentford, Middlesex, TW8 9AG
Activities: Activities of other holding companies n.e.c.
Parent: Crown UK Holdco Limited
Officers: Fiona Elizabeth Smith, Secretary; Nisan Cohen [1972] Director [Israeli]; Israel Greidinger [1961] Director/Cinema Proprietor [Israeli]; Shaun Alan Jones [1970] Director; Nir Lion [1981] Director [Israeli]

Augustus 2 Limited
Incorporated: 26 August 2004
Net Worth: £108,211,000 *Total Assets:* £671,014,016
Registered Office: 8th Floor, Vantage London, Great West Road, Brentford, Middlesex, TW8 9AG
Activities: Activities of other holding companies n.e.c.
Parent: Augustus 1 Limited
Officers: Fiona Elizabeth Smith, Secretary; Nisan Cohen [1972] Director [Israeli]; Israel Greidinger [1961] Director/Cinema Proprietor [Israeli]; Shaun Alan Jones [1970] Director; Nir Lion [1981] Director [Israeli]

Aunt Bessie's Limited
Incorporated: 12 April 2000 *Employees:* 393
Net Worth: £36,243,000 *Total Assets:* £63,495,000
Registered Office: 1 New Square, Feltham, Middlesex, TW14 8HA
Activities: Manufacture of other food products n.e.c.
Parent: Nomad Foods Europe Limited
Officers: Edward John Heaton Marriott, Secretary; Wayne Brian Hudson [1964] Director; Sarah Pollard [1974] Finance Director

Aura (Newcastle) Project Company Limited
Incorporated: 24 January 2007
Net Worth Deficit: £12,812,000 *Total Assets:* £108,321,000
Registered Office: Eaton Court, Maylands Avenue, Hemel Hempstead Industrial Estate, Hemel Hempstead, Herts, HP2 7TR
Activities: Construction of commercial buildings
Parent: Aura (Newcastle) Holding Company Limited
Officers: Kevin John Pearson, Secretary; John Stephen Gordon [1962] Director; Peter Kenneth Johnstone [1965] Finance Director; John McDonagh [1969] Director; Kirsty Jane Thirwell [1971] Director

Aura (Newcastle) Project Company Phase 2 Ltd
Incorporated: 29 September 2009
Net Worth Deficit: £7,797,000 *Total Assets:* £80,853,000
Registered Office: Eaton Court, Maylands Avenue, Hemel Hempstead Industrial Estate, Hemel Hempstead, Herts, HP2 7TR
Activities: Activities of head offices
Parent: Aura (Newcastle) Holding Company Phase 2 Limited
Officers: Kevin John Pearson, Secretary; John Stephen Gordon [1962] Director; Peter Kenneth Johnstone [1965] Finance Director; John McDonagh [1969] Director; Kirsty Jane Thirlwell [1971] Director

Aura Finance Limited
Incorporated: 11 December 2012 *Employees:* 4
Net Worth: £29,113,396 *Total Assets:* £234,196,032
Registered Office: 3rd Floor, Premiere House, Elstree Way, Borehamwood, Herts, WD6 1JH
Activities: Other business support service activities n.e.c.
Parent: Aura Finance (Holdco) Limited
Officers: Emily Henrietta Gestetner [1967] Director; David Stewart [1965] Director; Stephen Bryan Wasserman [1984] Director; Danny Stephen Waters [1984] Director

Aura Holdings (Newcastle) Limited
Incorporated: 20 December 2006
Net Worth Deficit: £20,514,000 *Total Assets:* £190,340,992
Registered Office: Eaton Court, Maylands Avenue, Hemel Hempstead Industrial Estate, Hemel Hempstead, Herts, HP2 7TR
Activities: Activities of head offices
Shareholders: Dalmore Capital (Aura) Limited; Elgin BSF Limited
Officers: Kevin John Pearson, Secretary; John Stephen Gordon [1962] Director; Peter Kenneth Johnstone [1965] Finance Director; Robert John William Wotherspoon [1967] Director/Accountant

Aurasma Limited
Incorporated: 7 December 2011
Net Worth: £75,730,064 *Total Assets:* £90,695,504
Registered Office: Amen Corner, Cain Road, Bracknell, Berks, RG12 1HN
Activities: Other information technology service activities
Officers: Caroline Morin [1971] Finance Director [French]; Peter Yennadhiou [1963] Director

Aurora Academies Trust
Incorporated: 15 June 2012 *Employees:* 284
Net Worth: £41,384,000 *Total Assets:* £44,305,000
Registered Office: Glenleigh Park Academy, Gunters Lane, Bexhill on Sea, E Sussex, TN39 4ED
Activities: Other education n.e.c.
Officers: Martha Jane Ireland Burnige, Secretary; Christine Ann Bayliss [1958] Director Education Consultancy Company; Anthony Nathaniel Blaker [1969] Director/Police Officer; Mark Quentin Brunet [1954] Director/Education Officer; Martha Jane Ireland Burnige [1978] Director/Solicitor; Stephen Mark Dawson [1981] Director/Church Elder; Jonathan Hodson [1983] Director/Commercial Manager; Ronald Jay Packard [1963] Director [American]; Maria Andrea Ursula Szalay [1966] Director/Executive [American]; David Wootton [1956] Director/Education and Leadership Consultant

Australian Pacific Touring (U.K.) Limited
Incorporated: 7 September 1982 *Employees:* 25
Net Worth: £104,260,104 *Total Assets:* £126,385,120
Registered Office: 1st Floor, Chalfont Court, 5 Hill Avenue, Amersham, Bucks, HP6 5BD
Activities: Travel agency activities
Shareholder: Geoffrey William McGeary
Officers: Ross Kemp, Secretary; Christopher Phillips Hall [1967] Director [Australian]; Ross Malcolm Kemp [1964] Finance Director [Australian]; Robert Howard McGeary [1968] Director [Australian]

Autodesk Holdings LLP
Incorporated: 13 September 2016 *Employees:* 2
Net Worth: £3,341,511,680 *Total Assets:* £3,392,922,368
Registered Office: One Discovery Place, Columbus Drive, Farnborough, Hants, GU14 0NZ

Autodesk Limited
Incorporated: 8 August 1984 *Employees:* 614
Net Worth: £34,291,344 *Total Assets:* £59,085,504
Registered Office: One Discovery Place, Columbus Drive, Farnborough, Hants, GU14 0NZ
Activities: Business and domestic software development
Parent: Autodesk UK Holdings Limited
Officers: Victoria Grace Getty, Secretary; Walter Dopplmair [1969] Director [Austrian]; Stephen William Hope [1967] Director [American]; Lucia Margarita Salazar Lecaro [1975] Director [American]

Autodesk UK Holdings Limited
Incorporated: 14 October 2016 *Employees:* 3
Net Worth: £4,643,141,120 *Total Assets:* £4,648,249,344
Registered Office: One Discovery Place, Columbus Drive, Farnborough, Hants, GU14 0NZ
Activities: Activities of other holding companies n.e.c.
Parent: Autodesk, Inc.
Officers: Laurence Francis Berry [1973] Director/Business Executive; Stephen William Hope [1967] Director/Vice President, Corporate Controller [American]; Kirsten Marie Nordlof [1973] Director/Business Executive [American]

Autolink Concessionaires (A19) Limited
Incorporated: 23 June 2000
Net Worth: £14,450,725 *Total Assets:* £128,286,992
Registered Office: Eaton Court, Maylands Avenue, Hemel Hempstead Industrial Estate, Hemel Hempstead, Herts, HP2 7TR
Activities: Construction of roads and motorways
Parent: Autolink Holdings (A19) Limited
Officers: Kevin John Pearson, Secretary; Antony Richard Gates [1967] Managing Director; Robert John William Wotherspoon [1967] Director/Accountant

Autolink Concessionaires (M6) PLC
Incorporated: 21 May 1996
Net Worth: £2,122,000 *Total Assets:* £139,007,008
Registered Office: Eaton Court, Maylands Avenue, Hemel Hempstead Industrial Estate, Hemel Hempstead, Herts, HP2 7TR
Activities: Construction of commercial buildings
Parent: Autolink Holdings (M6) Limited
Officers: Kevin John Pearson, Secretary; David Richard Bradbury [1969] Director/Senior Investment Manager; Benjamin Christopher Jacob Dean [1979] Investment Director; Antony Richard Gates [1967] Managing Director; David Honeyman [1967] Director/Financial Controller; Christopher James [1968] Investment Director; Robert John William Wotherspoon [1967] Director/Accountant

Autolink Holdings (M6) Ltd
Incorporated: 17 February 1997
Net Worth: £3,820,000 *Total Assets:* £127,078,000
Registered Office: Eaton Court, Maylands Avenue, Hemel Hempstead, Herts, HP2 7TR
Activities: Construction of roads and motorways
Parent: Innisfree Nominees Limited (Acting in its Capacity as Nominee of Innisfree M & G PPP LP)
Officers: Kevin John Pearson, Secretary; David Richard Bradbury [1969] Director/Senior Investment Manager; Benjamin Christopher Jacob Dean [1979] Investment Director; Antony Richard Gates [1967] Managing Director; Christopher James [1968] Investment Director; Robert John William Wotherspoon [1967] Director/Accountant

The Automated Technology Group Limited
Incorporated: 3 October 1995 *Employees:* 261
Net Worth: £10,866,000 *Total Assets:* £22,882,000
Registered Office: Compass Point, Kingston Road, Staines upon Thames, Middlesex, TW18 1DT
Activities: Manufacture of electricity distribution and control apparatus
Parent: Automated Technology Group Holdings Limited
Officers: Iain Angus Jones, Secretary; Darren Ashford [1966] Installations Director; Nigel Brookes [1962] Sales Director; Ian Paul Farmer [1969] Technical Director; Leslie John Hinder [1956] Director; Simon Litchfield [1967] Operations Director; Andrew Robinson [1968] Director

Automatic Data Processing Limited
Incorporated: 11 March 1969 *Employees:* 651
Net Worth: £13,556,000 *Total Assets:* £701,867,008
Registered Office: Syward Place, Pyrcroft Road, Chertsey, Surrey, KT16 9JT
Activities: Other information technology service activities
Parent: ADP Network Services Limited
Officers: Peter Hadley [1972] Director; Jeffrey Lewis Phipps [1968] Managing Director; Lorna Wake [1976] Director/Accountant

Automobile Association Developments Limited
Incorporated: 18 January 1985 *Employees:* 7,177
Net Worth: £1,286,200,064 *Total Assets:* £2,218,899,968
Registered Office: Fanum House, Basing View, Basingstoke, Hants, RG21 4EA
Activities: Other business support service activities n.e.c.
Parent: AA Corporation Limited
Officers: Nadia Hoosen, Secretary; Simon John Breakwell [1965] Director; Dr Martin Andrew Clarke [1955] Executive Director; Gareth Robert Kirkwood [1963] Director/Chief Customer Operations Officer; Mark William Strickland [1962] Finance Director

Automobile Association Insurance Services Limited
Incorporated: 17 August 1989
Net Worth: £302,100,000 *Total Assets:* £436,600,000
Registered Office: Fanum House, Basing View, Basingstoke, Hants, RG21 4EA
Activities: Activities of insurance agents and brokers
Parent: AA Corporation Limited
Officers: Nadia Hoosen, Secretary; Janet Connor [1964] Managing Director; Dr Timothy Victor Holliday [1970] Director; Gareth Robert Kirkwood [1963] Director/Chief Customer Operations Officer; Jonathan Caldwell Roe [1955] Director; David William Smith [1959] Director

Autonomy Systems Limited
Incorporated: 31 May 1995 *Employees:* 92
Net Worth: £209,392,624 *Total Assets:* £492,281,472
Registered Office: Cain Road, Amen Corner, Bracknell, Berks, RG12 1HN
Activities: Other information technology service activities
Parent: Micro Focus International PLC
Officers: Barry Gareth Cashman [1966] Sales Director; Christopher Henry Yelland [1967] Director/Accountant

Autosport Media UK Ltd
Incorporated: 9 August 2016 *Employees:* 103
Net Worth Deficit: £3,019,014 *Total Assets:* £23,229,918
Registered Office: 1 Eton Street, Richmond, Surrey, TW9 1EF
Activities: Publishing of consumer and business journals and periodicals
Parent: Autosport.Com, LLC
Officers: Timothy Keith Chadwick, Secretary; Yura V Barabash [1974] Director [American]

Autumnpaper Limited
Incorporated: 31 October 2000 *Employees:* 200
Net Worth: £5,927,161 *Total Assets:* £60,438,316
Registered Office: 5th Floor, Rear Suite, Oakfield House, 35 Perrymount Road, Haywards Heath, W Sussex, RH16 3BW
Activities: Other business support service activities n.e.c.
Parent: Birdswan Solutions Limited
Officers: Emmanuel Andre Gintzburger [1974] Director/Chief Executive Officer of Alexander McQueen [French]; Eric Sandrin [1964] Director/Group General Counsel [French]

Avalon Cellars Two Limited
Incorporated: 10 January 2007
Net Worth: £38,473,000 *Total Assets:* £132,179,000
Registered Office: Thomas Hardy House, 2 Heath Road, Weybridge, Surrey, KT13 8TB
Activities: Activities of head offices
Parent: Accolade Wines Europe No. 2 Limited
Officers: Anthony Graham Wood, Secretary; Adrian Francis McKeon [1963] Regional Managing Director, UKIR; Andrew Peter Smith [1974] Director/Accountant; Anthony Graham Wood [1975] Director/Financial Controller [Australian]

Avamore Limited
Incorporated: 13 September 2006 *Employees:* 10
Net Worth: £4,734,240 *Total Assets:* £22,756,118
Registered Office: 1st Floor, 44-50 The Broadway, Southall, Middlesex, UB1 1QB
Activities: Buying and selling of own real estate
Major Shareholder: Sant Ram Ghai
Officers: Sant Ram Ghai [1966] Director/Businessman

Avante Care and Support Limited
Incorporated: 4 December 1990 *Employees:* 1,248
Net Worth: £36,644,584 *Total Assets:* £57,550,196
Registered Office: De Gelsey House, 1 Jubilee Way, Faversham, Kent, ME13 8GD
Activities: Residential care activities for the elderly and disabled
Officers: Deborah Jane Pert, Secretary; Jacqueline Churchward-Cardiff [1959] Director; Michelle Nicole Gardener [1962] Director/Business Consultant; Gillian Anne Gibb [1966] Director; Sandra Michelle Hendry [1962] Director/Retired; Peter Richard Horn [1955] Director/Retired; Mark John Hosea [1974] Project Director; Andrew Patrick Ireland [1956] Director/Social Care Consultant; Finbarr Murray [1971] Director of Estates & Facilities; Robert Merrony Perkins [1939] Director/Retired; Peter William Smallridge [1943] Director/Retired

Avaya UK
Incorporated: 26 April 1995 *Employees:* 412
Net Worth: £43,697,584 *Total Assets:* £88,728,768
Registered Office: 1000 Cathedral Square, Cathedral Hill, Guildford, Surrey, GU2 7YL
Activities: Other telecommunications activities
Parent: Avaya UK Holdings Limited
Officers: Lee Hastings, Secretary; Ena Jennifer Hunter, Secretary; Lee Hastings [1975] Director/Accountant; Ena Jennifer Hunter [1976] Director/Solicitor/Corporate Counsel; Ioan Griffith MacRae [1973] Managing Director; Stephen John Wright [1974] Finance Director

Aventis Pharma Holdings Limited
Incorporated: 3 September 1999
Net Worth: £3,308,000 *Total Assets:* £1,350,290,048
Registered Office: One Onslow Street, Guildford, Surrey, GU1 4YS
Activities: Activities of other holding companies n.e.c.
Parent: Sanofi
Officers: Francois-Xavier Duhalde [1965] Director/Chief Financial Officer [French]; Hugo Rupert Alexander Fry [1970] Director/UK Country Chair

Aventis Pharma Limited
Incorporated: 18 December 1980 *Employees:* 685
Net Worth: £106,780,000 *Total Assets:* £373,788,000
Registered Office: One Onslow Street, Guildford, Surrey, GU1 4YS
Activities: Wholesale of pharmaceutical goods
Parent: Sanofi-Aventis UK Holdings Limited
Officers: Francois-Xavier Duhalde [1965] Director/Chief Financial Officer [French]; Hugo Rupert Alexander Fry [1970] Director/UK Country Chair

Avery Dennison U.K. Limited
Incorporated: 12 November 1963 *Employees:* 25
Net Worth: £9,448,000 *Total Assets:* £30,487,000
Registered Office: 1 Thomas Road, Wooburn Industrial Park, Wooburn Green, High Wycombe, Bucks, HP10 0PE
Activities: Manufacture of other articles of paper and paperboard n.e.c.
Parent: Avery Dennison Holding Limited
Officers: Michael Collins [1967] Director European Finance Shared Services [Irish]; Huibert Nicolaas Van Gijn [1962] Finance Director [Dutch]; Christopher Russell Johnson [1975] Director [American]

Avesco Holdings Limited
Incorporated: 7 April 2005
Previous: Creative Technology Group Limited
Net Worth: £94,982,000 *Total Assets:* £107,448,000
Registered Office: Unit E2, Sussex Manor Business Park, Gatwick Road, Crawley, W Sussex, RH10 9NH
Activities: Activities of head offices
Parent: Creative Technology Group Limited
Officers: David Leadbetter, Secretary; David Andrew Crump [1961] Director; Generald Delon [1970] Director [American]; Mark Andrew Wilson [1975] Director/Chartered Accountant

Avicenna Holdings Ltd
Incorporated: 24 August 1994 *Employees:* 198
Previous: Avicenna Holdings PLC
Net Worth: £25,888,000 *Total Assets:* £41,143,000
Registered Office: Selsdon House, 212-220 Addington Road, South Croydon, Surrey, CR2 8LD
Activities: Dispensing chemist in specialised stores
Officers: Anita Larsen, Secretary; Ian Archie Gray [1953] Director; Shiraz Kassam Hirji [1947] Director; Salim Kassamali Esmail Jetha [1953] Director/Pharmacist

Avios Group (AGL) Limited
Incorporated: 19 May 1988 *Employees:* 547
Net Worth Deficit: £243,399,008 *Total Assets:* £1,307,650,048
Registered Office: Astral Towers, Betts Way, London Road, Crawley, W Sussex, RH10 9XY
Activities: Other business support service activities n.e.c.
Parent: British Airways PLC
Officers: Luke Alexander Michael Straver, Secretary; Jose Antonio Barrionuevo Urgel [1972] Director [Spanish]; Robert Boyle [1964] Director/Airline Manager; Andrew George Crawley [1966] Director/Airline Executive; Robert Leonard French [1970] Director/Accountant; Stephen William Lawrence Gunning [1967] Director/Chief Financial Officer; Christopher Mark Haynes [1970] Director/Solicitor; Maria Jesus Lopez Solas [1979] Director [Spanish]; Carolina Sandra Martinoli [1969] Director/Business Manager [Argentinian]; Karen Anne Williams [1975] Director

Avis Budget EMEA Limited
Incorporated: 28 January 1997 *Employees:* 2
Net Worth: £1,055,200,000 *Total Assets:* £1,071,400,000
Registered Office: Avis Budget House, Park Road, Bracknell, Berks, RG12 2EW
Activities: Activities of head offices
Parent: AE Consolidation Ltd
Officers: Inderpal Lall, Secretary; Paul Leslie Ford [1970] Director/Chartered Accountant; Mark Jeffrey Servodidio [1965] Director [American]

Avis Budget Services Limited
Incorporated: 19 December 1985 *Employees:* 412
Net Worth: £222,080,992 *Total Assets:* £286,212,992
Registered Office: Avis Budget House, Park Road, Bracknell, Berks, RG12 2EW
Activities: Other business support service activities n.e.c.
Parent: Avis Finance Company (No. 2) Limited
Officers: Inderpal Lall, Secretary; Paul Leslie Ford [1970] Director/Chartered Accountant; Paul Edward Rollason [1979] Director/Accountant

Avis Budget UK Limited
Incorporated: 24 April 1964 *Employees:* 961
Net Worth: £85,000 *Total Assets:* £321,808,000
Registered Office: Avis Budget House, Park Road, Bracknell, Berks, RG12 2EW
Activities: Other service activities n.e.c.
Parent: Avis Europe Overseas Ltd
Officers: Inderpal Lall, Secretary; Thomas Matthew Mannion, Secretary; Nina Anne Bell [1969] Managing Director; Paul Leslie Ford [1970] Director/Chartered Accountant; Mark John Kightley [1970] Director/Accountant

Avis Europe Holdings Limited
Incorporated: 4 March 1986
Net Worth: £505,931,008 *Total Assets:* £1,850,199,040
Registered Office: Avis Budget House, Park Road, Bracknell, Berks, RG12 2EW
Activities: Activities of head offices
Parent: Cilva Holdings Limited
Officers: Inderpal Lall, Secretary; Paul Leslie Ford [1970] Director/Chartered Accountant; Paul Edward Rollason [1979] Director/Accountant

Avis Europe Investment Holdings Limited
Incorporated: 15 May 1995 *Employees:* 2
Net Worth: £653,012,992 *Total Assets:* £653,451,008
Registered Office: Avis Budget House, Park Road, Bracknell, Berks, RG12 2EW
Activities: Activities of head offices
Parent: Avis Budget EMEA Ltd
Officers: Inderpal Lall, Secretary; Paul Leslie Ford [1970] Director/Chartered Accountant; Paul Edward Rollason [1979] Director/Accountant

Avis Europe Investments Limited
Incorporated: 16 September 1996 *Employees:* 2
Net Worth: £25,086,000 *Total Assets:* £1,796,929,024
Registered Office: Avis Budget House, Park Road, Bracknell, Berks, RG12 2EW
Activities: Activities of head offices
Parent: Avis Europe Investment Holdings Ltd
Officers: Inderpal Lall, Secretary; Paul Leslie Ford [1970] Director/Chartered Accountant; Paul Edward Rollason [1979] Director/Accountant

Avis Europe Overseas Limited
Incorporated: 16 September 1996
Net Worth Deficit: £68,957,000 *Total Assets:* £231,382,000
Registered Office: Avis Budget House, Park Road, Bracknell, Berks, RG12 2EW
Activities: Activities of head offices
Parent: Avis Europe Holdings Ltd
Officers: Inderpal Lall, Secretary; Paul Leslie Ford [1970] Director/Chartered Accountant; Paul Edward Rollason [1979] Director/Accountant

Avis Finance Company (No.2) Limited
Incorporated: 26 August 1987
Net Worth: £197,228,000 *Total Assets:* £197,228,000
Registered Office: Avis Budget House, Park Road, Bracknell, Berks, RG12 2EW
Activities: Activities of head offices
Parent: Avis Europe Holdings Limited
Officers: Inderpal Lall, Secretary; Paul Leslie Ford [1970] Director/Chartered Accountant; Paul Edward Rollason [1979] Director/Accountant

Avis Finance Company Limited
Incorporated: 16 April 1987 *Employees:* 5
Net Worth: £342,007,104 *Total Assets:* £1,004,884,544
Registered Office: Avis Budget House, Park Road, Bracknell, Berks, RG12 2EW
Activities: Other business support service activities n.e.c.
Parent: Avis Europe Holdings Ltd
Officers: Inderpal Lall, Secretary; Paul Leslie Ford [1970] Director/Chartered Accountant; Paul Edward Rollason [1979] Director/Accountant

Avis Investment Services Limited
Incorporated: 7 November 1986
Net Worth: £202,434,000 *Total Assets:* £202,434,000
Registered Office: Avis Budget House, Park Road, Bracknell, Berks, RG12 2EW
Activities: Activities of head offices
Parent: Avis Europe Holdings Limited
Officers: Inderpal Lall, Secretary; Paul Leslie Ford [1970] Director/Chartered Accountant; Paul Edward Rollason [1979] Director/Accountant

Aviva Administration Limited
Incorporated: 26 August 1997
Previous: Friends Life Services Limited
Net Worth: £62,563,000 *Total Assets:* £102,208,000
Registered Office: Pixham End, Dorking, Surrey, RH4 1QA
Activities: Other business support service activities n.e.c.
Parent: Friends Life FPL Limited
Officers: Andrew David Briggs [1966] Director; Jason Michael Windsor [1972] Director

Aviva Management Services UK Limited
Incorporated: 30 June 1970
Previous: Friends Life Management Services Limited
Net Worth: £38,242,000 *Total Assets:* £153,170,000
Registered Office: Pixham End, Dorking, Surrey, RH4 1QA
Activities: Other business support service activities n.e.c.
Parent: Friends Life FPL Limited
Officers: Julian Charles Baddeley [1981] Director/Solicitor; Karina Jane Bye [1972] Director/Company Secretary; Mary Harper [1977] Director; Andrew Muir Jenkins [1962] Director

AVM Impact Ltd
Incorporated: 8 February 1990 *Employees:* 382
Net Worth: £5,075,000 *Total Assets:* £25,368,000
Registered Office: Europe House, 170 Windmill Road, Sunbury on Thames, Middlesex, TW16 7HB
Activities: Other professional, scientific and technical activities n.e.c.
Parent: AVM Limited
Officers: John Allen, Secretary; John Allen [1961] Director; Edward Charles Peregrine Phelps Cook [1967] Director

AVMI Group Limited
Incorporated: 20 March 2012 *Employees:* 414
Net Worth Deficit: £11,375,000 *Total Assets:* £40,075,000
Registered Office: Europe House, Windmill Road, Sunbury on Thames, Middlesex, TW16 7HB
Activities: Activities of head offices
Officers: John Allen [1961] Director; Edward Charles Peregrine Phelps Cook [1967] Director; Adrian Paul Lurie [1973] Director/Investment Management; Nick Richard Motum Seaman [1981] Director/Investment Professional

Avon Capital Estates (Australia) Limited
Incorporated: 20 July 1981 *Employees:* 2
Net Worth: £52,646,300 *Total Assets:* £65,941,440
Registered Office: Lower Wield House, Lower Wield, Alresford, Hants, SO24 9RX
Activities: Development of building projects
Shareholders: Lucy Pepita Whittome; Ashley Abinger Whittome
Officers: Ashley Abinger Whittome, Secretary/Director; Vincent Anthony Acalinovich [1946] Director [Australian]; Ashley Abinger Whittome [1963] Director; Lucy Pepita Whittome [1967] Director

Avon Capital Estates 1 LLP
Incorporated: 13 June 2002
Net Worth: £75,556,648 *Total Assets:* £113,694,992
Registered Office: Lower Wield House, Lower Wield, Alresford, Hants, SO24 9RX
Officers: Linda Maria Bates [1965] Member; Francis Robert Brake [1933] Member; Wanda Brake [1938] Member; Adam Vere Balfour Broke [1941] Member; Sarah Penelope Broke [1941] Member; James David Forbes Calder [1968] Member; Joanna Calder [1969] Member; Charlotte Sarah Douglas [1973] Member; Georgina Clare Farran [1968] Member; Mary Cecilia Farran [1935] Member; Sean Patrick Fernback [1963] Member; Arthur William Brownlow Fforde [1956] Member; Georgina Catherine Fowle [1969] Member; Michelle Louise Gardner [1960] Member; Fiona Mary Hancock [1944] Member; Jonathan Harper [1962] Member; Penny Harvey-Samuel [1974] Member; Louise Hayling [1957] Member; Debrina Lloyd-Davies [1963] Member; James Andrew Lloyd-Davies [1962] Member; Sarah Louise Platnauer [1972] Member; Jacqueline Anne Thomson [1964] Member; Julian George Tregoning [1946] Member; Tessa Jane Tregoning [1948] Member; Deborah Carol Turner-Fernback [1966] Member; Jeremy Geoffrey Vernon-Evans [1962] Member; Sally Jane Vernon-Evans [1968] Member; Peter Vivian Walford [1953] Member; Ashley Abinger Whittome [1963] Member; Lucy Pepita Whittome [1967] Member

Avtrade Holdings Limited
Incorporated: 15 March 2001 *Employees:* 249
Net Worth: £78,922,512 *Total Assets:* £124,874,360
Registered Office: Avtrade Global Headquarters, Sayers Common, W Sussex, BN6 9JQ
Activities: Other business support service activities n.e.c.
Shareholders: Graeme Frank Brooks; Yvonne Catherine Brooks
Officers: Graeme Frank Brooks, Secretary/Director; Graeme Frank Brooks [1954] Director; Yvonne Catherine Brooks [1955] Director

Avtrade Leasing Limited
Incorporated: 9 June 1998
Net Worth: £16,904,964 *Total Assets:* £34,252,116
Registered Office: Avtrade Global Headquarters, Sayers Common, W Sussex, BN6 9JQ
Activities: Other letting and operating of own or leased real estate
Shareholders: Graeme Frank Brooks; Yvonne Catherine Brooks
Officers: Graeme Frank Brooks, Secretary/Director; Graeme Frank Brooks [1954] Director; Yvonne Catherine Brooks [1955] Director

Avtrade Limited
Incorporated: 29 May 1985 *Employees:* 249
Net Worth: £65,101,216 *Total Assets:* £93,260,144
Registered Office: Avtrade Global Headquarters, Sayers Common, W Sussex, BN6 9JQ
Activities: Other retail sale in non-specialised stores
Shareholders: Graeme Frank Brooks; Yvonne Catherine Brooks
Officers: Graeme Frank Brooks, Secretary; Graeme Frank Brooks [1954] Director; Yvonne Catherine Brooks [1955] Director

AVX Limited
Incorporated: 28 November 1975 *Employees:* 336
Net Worth: £381,291,712 *Total Assets:* £566,296,512
Registered Office: Prospect House, 6 Archipelago, Lyon Way, Frimley, Camberley, Surrey, GU16 7ER
Activities: Manufacture of electronic components
Parent: AVX Corporation
Officers: Nicholas Rodger Birkett, Secretary; Michael Hufnagel [1953] Director/Vice President, CFO & Treasurer [American]; Martin Joseph McGuigan [1956] Director/Divisional Vice President; Alexander Schenkel [1974] Director/General Manager European Sales [German]; Evan Meyer Slavitt [1957] Director/Vice President for Business & Legal Affairs [American]

Away Resorts Limited
Incorporated: 21 December 2007 *Employees:* 32
Net Worth Deficit: £20,601,112 *Total Assets:* £85,240,272
Registered Office: IMEX, 575-599 Maxted Road, Hemel Hempstead, Herts, HP2 7DX
Activities: Holiday centres and villages
Parent: Away Resorts Holdings Ltd
Officers: Neill Timothy Ryder, Secretary; Carl Anthony Castledine [1969] Director; Greg Lashley [1964] Director; Neill Timothy Ryder [1976] Director

AWE Management Limited
Incorporated: 10 November 1998 *Employees:* 5,033
Net Worth: £18,753,000 *Total Assets:* £656,380,992
Registered Office: Room 20, Building F161.2, Atomic Weapons Establishment, Aldermaston, Reading, Berks, RG7 4PR
Activities: Defence activities
Parent: Lockheed Martin UK Strategic Systems Limited
Officers: Jonathan David Smith, Secretary; Thomas Irwin Bradley [1959] Director [American]; Iain Michael Coucher [1961] Director/Chief Executive; Kevin David Craven [1961] Director; Terence Hagen [1964] Director [American]; Scott Keller [1963] Director/Vice President and General Manager [American]; Peter Robert Lutwyche [1962] Director/Vice President; Peter George Morton [1970] Director/CFO, AWE PLC; Colin William Reynell [1969] Director; Dr Jerry Stephen Rottler [1958] Director/Retired Executive [American]; Ian Paul Tyler [1960] Director

AWE PLC
Incorporated: 6 November 1992 *Employees:* 5,033
Net Worth: £10,975,000 *Total Assets:* £635,142,016
Registered Office: Room 20, Building F161.2, Atomic Weapons Establishment, Aldermaston, Reading, Berks, RG7 4PR
Activities: Other manufacturing n.e.c.
Parent: AWE Management Limited
Officers: Jonathan David Smith, Secretary; Gary John Butler [1962] Director; Haydn Clulow [1965] Director; Iain Michael Coucher [1961] Director; Peter George Morton [1970] Director/CFO, AWE PLC

Axial Systems Ltd.
Incorporated: 6 June 1988 *Employees:* 57
Net Worth: £15,386,107 *Total Assets:* £21,692,472
Registered Office: Tectonic Place, Holyport Road, Maidenhead, Berks, SL6 2YE
Activities: Other information technology service activities
Officers: Timothy Charles Jones, Secretary; Guy Steven Blackman [1964] Director; Antony Ian English [1968] Director; Timothy Charles Jones [1967] Finance Director; Peter Anthony Lloyd [1955] Director; Paul Russell Spencer [1958] Managing Director

Axiom Education (Edinburgh) Holdings Limited
Incorporated: 15 September 2006
Net Worth: £27,617,000 *Total Assets:* £37,823,000
Registered Office: c/o Galliford Try PLC, Cowley Business Park, Cowley, Uxbridge, Middlesex, UB8 2AL
Activities: Activities of other holding companies n.e.c.
Parent: Zealburg Holdings Limited
Officers: Mark Geoffrey David Holden [1957] Director; Geoffrey Alan Quaife [1955] Director

Axiom Education (Edinburgh) Limited
Incorporated: 28 November 2006
Net Worth Deficit: £53,286,000 *Total Assets:* £171,948,992
Registered Office: Cowley Business Park, Cowley, Uxbridge, Middlesex, UB8 2AL
Activities: Management of real estate on a fee or contract basis
Parent: Axiom Education (Edinburgh) Holdings Limited
Officers: Mark Geoffrey David Holden [1957] Director; Geoffrey Alan Quaife [1955] Director

Axiom Education (Perth & Kinross) Holdings Limited
Incorporated: 28 July 2005
Net Worth: £16,860,000 *Total Assets:* £25,549,000
Registered Office: Cowley Business Park, Cowley, Uxbridge, Middlesex, UB8 2AL
Activities: Activities of other holding companies n.e.c.
Parent: Yorker Holdings PKR Limited
Officers: Mark Geoffrey David Holden [1957] Director; Geoffrey Alan Quaife [1955] Director

Axiom Education (Perth & Kinross) Limited
Incorporated: 4 August 2005
Net Worth Deficit: £84,243,000 *Total Assets:* £153,326,000
Registered Office: c/o Galliford Try PLC, Cowley Business Park, Cowley, Uxbridge, Middlesex, UB8 2AL
Activities: Management of real estate on a fee or contract basis
Parent: Axiom Education (Perth & Kinross) Holdings Limited
Officers: Mark Geoffrey David Holden [1957] Director; Geoffrey Alan Quaife [1955] Director

Axios Bidco Limited
Incorporated: 26 August 2015
Net Worth Deficit: £312,577,984 *Total Assets:* £360,417,984
Registered Office: Yarmouth House, 1300 Parkway, Solent Business Park, Whiteley, Fareham, Hants, PO15 7AE
Activities: Activities of other holding companies n.e.c.
Parent: Tiger Midco 2 Limited
Officers: Timothy Philip Griffiths [1960] Director/Chief Executive; Gerard Christopher Loftus [1960] Director; Alasdair Marnoch [1963] Director

Axis Electronics Limited
Incorporated: 26 October 1994 *Employees:* 177
Net Worth: £16,890,822 *Total Assets:* £24,063,894
Registered Office: Silbury Court, 420 Silbury Boulevard, Central Milton Keynes, Bucks, MK9 2AF
Activities: Manufacture of electronic components
Shareholders: Philip John Inness; Axis EMS Group Ltd
Officers: Paul Chaplin [1970] Purchasing Director; Sarah Clough [1966] Director; Philip John Inness [1961] Director; Paul Jackson [1968] Director; Christian William Jukes [1966] QA Director; Matthew James Turner [1968] Engineering Director

Axis Group Integrated Services Limited
Incorporated: 24 September 2015 *Employees:* 2,683
Net Worth: £5,431,000 *Total Assets:* £25,680,000
Registered Office: Ground Floor Suite, River House, Maidstone Road, Sidcup, Kent, DA14 5RH
Activities: Other business support service activities n.e.c.
Shareholder: Jonathan Stephen Levine
Officers: Roger Leonard Burdett [1950] Director; Simon Kenneth Giles [1974] Finance Director; Jonathan Stephen Levine [1952] Director/Chief Executive Officer; David John Mundell [1957] Director

Axon Group Limited
Incorporated: 14 August 1997 *Employees:* 5
Net Worth: £199,672,000 *Total Assets:* £199,728,000
Registered Office: Axoncentre, Church Road, Egham, Surrey, TW20 9QB
Activities: Activities of head offices
Parent: HCL EAS Ltd
Officers: Manish Anand [1968] Director [Indian]; Prahlad Rai Bansal [1957] Director/Service [Indian]; Ajit Krishnan Kutty Kumar [1964] Director [Indian]; Rahul Singh [1963] Director [Indian]; Shiv Kumar Walia [1969] Director [Australian]

Axon Solutions Limited
Incorporated: 7 October 1994 *Employees:* 497
Net Worth: £36,359,000 *Total Assets:* £62,234,000
Registered Office: Axon Centre, Church Road, Egham, Surrey, TW20 9QB
Activities: Information technology consultancy activities
Parent: Axon Group Limited
Officers: Manish Anand [1968] Director [Indian]; Subramanian Gopalakrishnan [1967] Director [Indian]; Ajit Krishnan Kutty Kumar [1964] Director [Indian]; Rahul Singh [1963] Director [Indian]; Shiv Kumar Walia [1969] Director [Australian]

Azlan Group Limited
Incorporated: 25 November 1992
Net Worth: £551,100,032 *Total Assets:* £617,600,000
Registered Office: Redwood 2, Crockford Lane, Chineham Business Park, Chineham, Basingstoke, Hants, RG24 8WQ
Activities: Activities of head offices
Parent: TD United Kingdom Acquisition Ltd
Officers: Philip James Auld, Secretary; Andrew Gass [1964] Director; Howard Tuffnail [1964] Director [Canadian]

Azlan Limited
Incorporated: 10 February 1986
Net Worth: £28,740,558 *Total Assets:* £74,256,976
Registered Office: Redwood 2, Crockford Lane, Chineham, Basingstoke, Hants, RG24 8WQ
Activities: Activities of head offices
Parent: Maneboard Ltd
Officers: Andrew Gass [1964] Director; Howard Tuffnail [1964] Director [Canadian]

B & C E Financial Services Limited
Incorporated: 21 December 1987
Net Worth: £25,450,000 *Total Assets:* £36,739,000
Registered Office: Manor Royal, Crawley, W Sussex, RH10 9QP
Activities: Financial intermediation not elsewhere classified
Parent: People's Financial Services Limited
Officers: Lydia Florinette Gabrielle Harratt, Secretary; John Allott [1962] Director/Trade Union Officer; Patricia Marusia Billingham [1952] Director; John MacAulay Cullen [1956] Director/Pension Scheme Manager; Patrick Iain Heath-Lay [1968] Director/Chief Executive Officer; John William Hough [1953] Director; Jamshaid Islam [1975] Director; James Frederick McKinnon [1953] Director; Chandrasekhar Ramamurthy [1956] Director/Retired; John Ashurst Southworth [1947] Director; Stephen Terrell [1954] Director

B & C E Insurance Limited
Incorporated: 16 August 1995
Net Worth: £61,773,000 *Total Assets:* £72,691,000
Registered Office: Manor Royal, Crawley, W Sussex, RH10 9QP
Activities: Life insurance
Parent: People's Financial Services Limited
Officers: Lydia Florinette Gabrielle Harratt, Secretary; John Allott [1962] Director/Trade Union Officer; Patricia Marusia Billingham [1952] Director; John MacAulay Cullen [1956] Director/Pension Scheme Manager; Patrick Iain Heath-Lay [1968] Director/Chief Executive Officer; John William Hough [1953] Director; Jamshaid Islam [1975] Director; James Frederick McKinnon [1953] Director; Chandrasekhar Ramamurthy [1956] Director/Retired; John Ashurst Southworth [1947] Director/Consultant; Stephen Terrell [1954] Director

B & CE Holdings Limited
Incorporated: 21 November 1942 *Employees:* 458
Previous: Building & Civil Engineering Holidays Scheme Management Limited
Net Worth: £108,439,000 *Total Assets:* £132,603,000
Registered Office: Manor Royal, Crawley, W Sussex, RH10 9QP
Activities: Financial intermediation not elsewhere classified
Officers: Lydia Florinette Gabrielle Harratt, Secretary; John Allott [1962] Director/Trade Union Officer; Robert John Blackman [1950] Director/Retired Trade Union Official; David Booth [1953] Director/Management Accountant; Henry Frew [1950] Director/Trade Union Secretary; James McGlinchey Gilmour [1951] Managing Director; Keir William Henry Greenaway [1985] Director/Trade Union; James Martin O'Callaghan [1950] Director [Irish]; Chandrasekhar Ramamurthy [1956] Director; David Smith [1939] Director/Retired Training Manager; Jeremy Paul Swain [1958] Director; Stephen Terrell [1954] Director

B & M Care Group Limited
Incorporated: 23 April 1986 *Employees:* 1,348
Net Worth: £67,901,384 *Total Assets:* £108,836,704
Registered Office: Old Town Court, 70 Queensway, Hemel Hempstead, Herts, HP2 5HD
Activities: Activities of head offices
Major Shareholder: William John Hughes
Officers: Trinna Ann Bruton, Secretary; Trinna Ann Bruton [1967] Director; William John Hughes [1941] Director [Irish]; Rachel Ann Rodgers [1964] Director; Ian Sloan [1959] Director/Quantity Surveyor; Dr Colleen Mary Wood [1977] Director/Clinical Advisor

B & P Acquisitionco Limited
Incorporated: 19 September 2007 *Employees:* 3
Net Worth Deficit: £19,906,980 *Total Assets:* £66,913,632
Registered Office: Burnham Road, Dartford, Kent, DA1 5BD
Activities: Activities of other holding companies n.e.c.
Parent: B & P Midco Limited
Officers: Ivo Vesselinov, Secretary; Andrew Hodgson [1965] Director; Romain Jean Patrick Prouvost [1979] Director [French]; Ivo Vesselinov [1976] Financial Director

B & P Buyco Limited
Incorporated: 16 August 2016 *Employees:* 3
Net Worth: £475,817 *Total Assets:* £73,912,480
Registered Office: Burnham Road, Sandpit Road, Dartford, Kent, DA1 5BD
Activities: Activities of venture and development capital companies
Parent: Graphite Capital Management LLP
Officers: Andrew Hodgson [1965] Director; Romain Jean Patrick Prouvost [1979] Director [French]; Ivo Vesselinov [1976] Finance Director

B & P Holdings II Limited
Incorporated: 15 August 2007 *Employees:* 4
Previous: Beck & Pollitzer Limited
Net Worth: £481,003 *Total Assets:* £52,587,844
Registered Office: Burnham Road, Dartford, Kent, DA1 5BD
Activities: Activities of other holding companies n.e.c.
Parent: Burgundy Buyco Limited
Officers: Ivo Vesselinov, Secretary; Andrew Hodgson [1965] Director; Janusz Lach [1963] Director [Polish]; Romain Jean Patrick Prouvost [1979] Director [French]; Ivo Vesselinov [1976] Finance Director

B & P Midco 1 Limited
Incorporated: 2 September 2016 *Employees:* 3
Net Worth Deficit: £1,491,461 *Total Assets:* £46,345,424
Registered Office: Burnham Road, Sandpit Road, Dartford, Kent, DA1 5BD
Activities: Activities of venture and development capital companies
Parent: Graphite Capital Management LLP
Officers: Andrew Hodgson [1965] Director; Romain Jean Patrick Prouvost [1979] Director [French]; Ivo Vesselinov [1976] Finance Director

B & P Midco 2 Limited
Incorporated: 2 September 2016
Net Worth: £1,869,913 *Total Assets:* £44,345,424
Registered Office: Burnham Road, Sandpit Road, Dartford, Kent, DA1 5BD
Activities: Activities of venture and development capital companies
Parent: Graphite Capital Management LLP
Officers: Andrew Hodgson [1965] Director; Romain Jean Patrick Prouvost [1979] Director [French]; Ivo Vesselinov [1976] Finance Director

B & P Midco Limited
Incorporated: 15 August 2007 *Employees:* 3
Net Worth: £657,280 *Total Assets:* £36,868,316
Registered Office: Burnham Road, Dartford, Kent, DA1 5BD
Activities: Activities of other holding companies n.e.c.
Officers: Ivo Vesselinov, Secretary; Andrew Hodgson [1965] Director; Romain Jean Patrick Prouvost [1979] Director [French]; Ivo Vesselinov [1976] Finance Director

B & Q PLC
Incorporated: 26 February 1970 *Employees:* 25,490
Net Worth: £4,754,800,128 *Total Assets:* £5,801,800,192
Registered Office: B & Q House, Chestnut Avenue, Chandler's Ford, Eastleigh, Hants, SO53 3LE
Activities: Other retail sale in non-specialised stores
Officers: Paul Moore, Secretary; Graham Robert Bell [1963] Director; Catherine Burge [1964] Director; Paul Grahame Crisp [1967] Director; Dr Sandra Dembeck [1974] Director [German]; Martin Brian Lee [1967] Director/Supply Chain Manager; Andrew David Moat [1971] Director; Paul Lewis White [1976] Director

B & Q Properties Limited
Incorporated: 29 November 1999
Net Worth: £614,782,016 *Total Assets:* £680,160,000
Registered Office: B & Q House, Chestnut Avenue, Chandler's Ford, Eastleigh, Hants, SO53 3LE
Activities: Buying and selling of own real estate
Parent: Sheldon Holdings Limited
Officers: Graham Robert Bell [1963] Director; Paul Grahame Crisp [1967] Director

B & W Acquisition Ltd
Incorporated: 28 April 2016
Net Worth: £82,344,256 *Total Assets:* £103,570,624
Registered Office: B & W Group Ltd, Dale Road, Worthing, W Sussex, BN11 2BH
Activities: Activities of production holding companies
Parent: Eva Automation Inc
Officers: Jung Il Kim [1973] Director/Chief Financial Officer [American]; David Liu [1972] Director/Business Executive [American]; Gideon Yu [1971] Director [American]

B & W Group Ltd
Incorporated: 1 June 1966 *Employees:* 860
Net Worth: £29,699,476 *Total Assets:* £97,936,264
Registered Office: Dale Road, Worthing, W Sussex, BN11 2BH
Activities: Manufacture of consumer electronics
Parent: Eva Automation Inc
Officers: Jung Il Kim [1973] Director/Chief Financial Officer [American]; David Liu [1972] Director/Business Executive [American]; Gideon Yu [1971] Director [American]

B O C Holdings
Incorporated: 3 April 1926
Net Worth: £3,386,297,088 *Total Assets:* £3,713,143,040
Registered Office: The Priestley Centre, 10 Priestley Road, The Surrey Research Park, Guildford, Surrey, GU2 7XY
Activities: Activities of head offices
Parent: The BOC Group Limited
Officers: Susan Kathleen Kelly, Secretary; Julian Michael Bland [1967] Director/Head of Accounting; Benjamin Patterson [1962] Director/Solicitor; Sally Ann Williams [1970] Director/Accountant

B.I.B. Underwriters Limited
Incorporated: 25 November 1988 *Employees:* 55
Net Worth: £16,698,191 *Total Assets:* £34,731,716
Registered Office: Tower Gate House, Eclipse Park, Sittingbourne Road, Maidstone, Kent, ME14 3EN
Activities: Non-life insurance
Parent: B.I.B.U Acquisitions Limited
Officers: Dean Clarke, Secretary; Paul John Dilley [1970] Director; Antonios Erotocritou [1971] Director/Deputy CFO [Cypriot]; Christopher John Kent [1983] Finance Director

BA and AA Holdings Limited
Incorporated: 13 September 1999
Net Worth: £119,286,808 *Total Assets:* £119,417,072
Registered Office: British Airways PLC, P O Box 365, Waterside, Harmondsworth, West Drayton, Middlesex, UB7 0GB
Activities: Activities of head offices
Parent: British Airways PLC
Officers: Luke Alexander Michael Straver, Secretary; Andrew Ian Fleming [1979] Director/Company Secretary; Simon Philcox [1979] Director/Accountant

BA Cityflyer Limited
Incorporated: 2 January 1991 *Employees:* 538
Net Worth: £61,009,000 *Total Assets:* £346,233,984
Registered Office: P O Box 365, Waterside, Harmondsworth, West Drayton, Middlesex, UB7 0GB
Activities: Scheduled passenger air transport
Parent: British Airways PLC
Officers: Katie Louise Bishop, Secretary; Neil Alan Chernoff [1973] Director [American]; Colm Leo Lacy [1970] Director/Airline Executive [Irish]; Rebecca Louise Napier [1980] Director/Accountant; Thomas David Stoddart [1979] Director/Airline Manager

Bacardi U.K. Limited
Incorporated: 26 April 1941 *Employees:* 4
Net Worth: £34,005,000 *Total Assets:* £433,732,000
Registered Office: Bacardi Brown-Forman House, Kings Worthy, Winchester, Hants, SO23 7TW
Activities: Activities of head offices
Officers: Amanda Claire Almond [1972] Managing Director; Ross Tomas Bilsland [1980] Finance Director; Francis Debeuckelaere [1964] Managing Director [Belgian]; Robert Arnoldus Johannes Poll [1969] Director [Dutch]

Bacardi-Martini Limited
Incorporated: 12 October 1935 *Employees:* 232
Net Worth: £48,721,000 *Total Assets:* £114,699,000
Registered Office: Bacardi Brown-Forman House, Kings Worthy, Winchester, Hants, SO23 7TW
Activities: Wholesale of wine, beer, spirits and other alcoholic beverages
Parent: Bacardi U.K. Limited
Officers: Amanda Claire Almond [1972] Managing Director; Ross Tomas Bilsland [1980] Finance Director

BAE Systems (Defence Systems) Limited
Incorporated: 19 January 1929
Net Worth: £58,030,000 *Total Assets:* £115,937,000
Registered Office: P O Box 87, Warwick House, Farnborough Aerospace Centre, Farnborough, Hants, GU14 6YU
Activities: Defence activities
Parent: BAE Systems (Holdings) Limited
Officers: David Stanley Parkes, Secretary; Richard Checkley [1971] Director; Anthony Peter Varney [1961] Director/Accountant

BAE Systems (Dynamics) Limited
Incorporated: 1 May 1991
Net Worth: £179,392,992 *Total Assets:* £230,008,992
Registered Office: P O Box 87, Warwick House, Farnborough Aerospace Centre, Farnborough, Hants, GU14 6YU
Activities: Other business support service activities n.e.c.
Parent: BAE Systems (Holdings) Limited
Officers: David Stanley Parkes, Secretary; David Alexander Green [1964] Finance Director; Ann-Louise Holding [1961] Director/Chartered Secretary; David Stanley Parkes [1963] Director/Company Secretary; Mark Andrew Reason [1959] Commercial Director

BAE Systems (Funding Two) Limited
Incorporated: 3 December 2001
Net Worth: £2,998,896,896 *Total Assets:* £3,247,131,136
Registered Office: Warwick House, Farnborough Areospace Centre, Farnborough, Hants, GU14 6YU
Activities: Other business support service activities n.e.c.
Parent: BAE Systems (Holdings) Limited
Officers: David Stanley Parkes, Company Secretary; Brian Chapman [1963] Director/Tax Manager; Rajdeep Patara [1972] Director/Treasurer

BAE Systems (Holdings) Limited
Incorporated: 20 October 2004
Net Worth: £10,788,758,528 *Total Assets:* £16,538,336,256
Registered Office: P O Box 87, Warwick House, Farnborough Aerospace Centre, Farnborough, Hants, GU14 6YU
Activities: Activities of other holding companies n.e.c.
Parent: BAE Systems PLC
Officers: Ann-Louise Holding, Secretary; Peter John Lynas [1958] Financial Director; Charles Nicholas Woodburn [1971] Director

BAE Systems (Land and Sea Systems) Limited
Incorporated: 5 September 1990 *Employees:* 2
Net Worth Deficit: £13,894,000 *Total Assets:* £25,294,000
Registered Office: P O Box 87, Warwick House, Farnborough Aerospace Centre, Farnborough, Hants, GU14 6YU
Activities: Defence activities
Parent: BAE Systems (Holdings) Limited
Officers: Ann-Louise Holding, Secretary; Ann-Louise Holding [1961] Director/Chartered Secretary; David Stanley Parkes [1963] Director/Company Secretary

BAE Systems (MEH) Limited
Incorporated: 31 October 2001 *Employees:* 2
Net Worth: £130,623,312 *Total Assets:* £191,100,624
Registered Office: P O Box 87, Warwick House, Farnborough Aerospace Centre, Farnborough, Hants, GU14 6YU
Activities: Activities of other holding companies n.e.c.
Parent: BAE Systems (Holdings) Limited
Officers: David Stanley Parkes, Secretary; Brian William Ierland [1965] Finance Director; Peter Declan Murphy [1967] Director

BAE Systems (Military Air) Overseas Limited
Incorporated: 30 November 1990 *Employees:* 46
Net Worth: £36,295,000 *Total Assets:* £97,717,000
Registered Office: P O Box 87, Warwick House, Farnborough Aerospace Centre, Farnborough, Hants, GU14 6YU
Activities: Defence activities
Parent: BAE Systems (Holdings) Limited
Officers: David Stanley Parkes, Company Secretary; David Iain Armstrong [1963] Director; Simon Daniel Wood [1975] Finance Director

BAE Systems (Oman) Limited
Incorporated: 7 December 1995 *Employees:* 141
Net Worth: £95,214,000 *Total Assets:* £360,497,984
Registered Office: Warwick House, Farnborough Aerospace Centre, Farnborough, Hants, GU14 6YU
Activities: Defence activities
Parent: BAE Systems (Holdings) Limited
Officers: David Stanley Parkes, Secretary; Anthony Kevin Gilchrist [1967] Director; Brian William Ierland [1965] Finance Director; Simon Daniel Wood [1975] Finance Director

BAE Systems (Operations) Limited
Incorporated: 6 March 1986 *Employees:* 19,065
Net Worth: £1,583,000,064 *Total Assets:* £8,915,000,320
Registered Office: P O Box 87, Warwick House, Farnborough Aerospace Centre, Farnborough, Hants, GU14 6YU
Activities: Manufacture of air and spacecraft and related machinery
Parent: BAE Systems Enterprises Limited
Officers: David Stanley Parkes, Secretary; Christopher George Boardman [1961] Managing Director; Peter Robert Earl [1960] Finance Director; Brian William Ierland [1965] Finance Director; Peter John Lynas [1958] Financial Director

BAE Systems (Overseas Holdings) Limited
Incorporated: 4 January 1993
Net Worth: £60,359,000 *Total Assets:* £390,096,000
Registered Office: Warwick House, Farnborough Aerospace Centre, Farnborough, Hants, GU14 6YU
Activities: Activities of head offices
Parent: BAE Systems (Holdings) Limited
Officers: Linda Susan Goodge, Secretary; Ann-Louise Holding [1961] Director/Chartered Secretary; David Stanley Parkes [1963] Director/Company Secretary

BAE Systems (Property Investments) Limited
Incorporated: 21 October 1998
Net Worth: £188,004,000 *Total Assets:* £256,627,008
Registered Office: P O Box 87, Warwick House, Farnborough Aerospace Centre, Farnborough, Hants, GU14 6YU
Activities: Other letting and operating of own or leased real estate
Parent: BAE Systems (Holdings) Limited
Officers: Linda Susan Goodge, Secretary; Ann Louise Holding, Secretary; David Alexander Green [1964] Finance Director; Ann-Louise Holding [1961] Director/Chartered Secretary; David Stanley Parkes [1963] Director/Company Secretary; Mark Andrew Reason [1959] Commercial Director

BAE Systems Applied Intelligence (International) Limited
Incorporated: 10 February 2009 *Employees:* 54
Net Worth: £2,151,000 *Total Assets:* £23,119,000
Registered Office: Priestley Road, Surrey Research Park, Guildford, Surrey, GU2 7YP
Activities: Information technology consultancy activities
Parent: Detica Group Limited
Officers: David Stanley Parkes, Secretary; Anthony Graham Jordan [1980] Director/Chartered Accountant; Michael Stuart Watson [1963] Director/Chartered Accountant

BAE Systems Applied Intelligence Limited
Incorporated: 4 November 1977 *Employees:* 2,986
Net Worth Deficit: £138,206,000 *Total Assets:* £159,803,008
Registered Office: Surrey Research Park, Guildford, Surrey, GU2 7YP
Activities: Information technology consultancy activities
Parent: Detica Group Limited
Officers: David Stanley Parkes, Secretary; Julian Frederick Charles Cracknell [1971] Managing Director; Anthony Graham Jordan [1980] Director/Chartered Accountant; Michael Stuart Watson [1963] Director/Chartered Accountant

BAE Systems Electronics Limited
Incorporated: 20 July 1897 *Employees:* 3
Net Worth: £42,565,000 *Total Assets:* £1,068,348,032
Registered Office: P O Box 87, Warwick House, Farnborough Aerospace Centre, Farnborough, Hants, GU14 6YU
Activities: Defence activities
Parent: Meslink Limited
Officers: Ann-Louise Holding, Secretary; David Iain Armstrong [1963] Director; Brian William Ierland [1965] Finance Director

BAE Systems Enterprises Limited
Incorporated: 2 December 1963 *Employees:* 2
Net Worth: £1,179,037,056 *Total Assets:* £2,627,752,960
Registered Office: P O Box 87, Warwick House, Farnborough Aerospace Centre, Farnborough, Hants, GU14 6YU
Activities: Other business support service activities n.e.c.
Parent: BAE Systems (Holdings) Limited
Officers: Linda Susan Goodge, Secretary; Ann-Louise Holding [1961] Director/Chartered Secretary; David Stanley Parkes [1963] Director/Company Secretary

BAE Systems Global Combat Systems Limited
Incorporated: 12 July 1946 *Employees:* 653
Net Worth: £103,000,000 *Total Assets:* £389,000,000
Registered Office: P O Box 87, Warwick House, Farnborough Aerospace Centre, Farnborough, Hants, GU14 6YU
Activities: Manufacture of motor vehicles
Parent: BAE Systems Land Systems (Finance) Limited
Officers: David Stanley Parkes, Company Secretary; Adam Robert Collins [1980] Finance Director; Jennifer Blair Osbaldestin [1973] Director; Joseph Thomas Senftle [1954] Director/Vice President [American]

BAE Systems Global Combat Systems Munitions Limited
Incorporated: 20 August 1984 *Employees:* 1,109
Net Worth: £83,000,000 *Total Assets:* £426,000,000
Registered Office: P O Box 87, Warwick House, Farnborough Aerospace Centre, Farnborough, Hants, GU14 6YU
Activities: Manufacture of weapons and ammunition
Parent: BAE Systems (Holdings) Limited
Officers: David Stanley Parkes, Secretary; Adam Robert Collins [1980] Finance Director; Jennifer Blair Osbaldestin [1973] Director

BAE Systems Land Systems (Finance) Limited
Incorporated: 21 August 1991
Net Worth: £139,354,000 *Total Assets:* £426,222,016
Registered Office: P O Box 87, Warwick House, Farnborough Aerospace Centre, Farnborough, Hants, GU14 6YU
Activities: Activities of other holding companies n.e.c.
Parent: Alvis Limited
Officers: David Stanley Parkes, Company Secretary; Adam Robert Collins [1980] Finance Director; Jennifer Blair Osbaldestin [1973] Director

BAE Systems Marine (Holdings) Limited
Incorporated: 12 November 1985 *Employees:* 3
Net Worth: £86,093,000 *Total Assets:* £235,434,000
Registered Office: P O Box 87, Warwick House, Farnborough Aerospace Centre, Farnborough, Hants, GU14 6YU
Activities: Activities of other holding companies n.e.c.
Parent: Meslink Limited
Officers: David Stanley Parkes, Secretary; Jamie MacRae Collard [1970] Director; Clifford Mark Robson [1959] Managing Director

BAE Systems Marine Limited
Incorporated: 18 April 1928 *Employees:* 7,472
Net Worth Deficit: £217,083,008 *Total Assets:* £1,226,480,000
Registered Office: P O Box 87, Warwick House, Farnborough Aerospace Centre, Farnborough, Hants, GU14 6YU
Activities: Building of ships and floating structures
Parent: BAE Systems Marine (Holdings) Limited
Officers: David Stanley Parkes, Secretary; Jamie MacRae Collard [1970] Director; Clifford Mark Robson [1959] Managing Director

BAE Systems Properties Limited
Incorporated: 19 October 1993 *Employees:* 134
Net Worth Deficit: £57,843,000 *Total Assets:* £616,368,000
Registered Office: P O Box 87, Warwick House, Farnborough Aerospace Centre, Farnborough, Hants, GU14 6YU
Activities: Management of real estate on a fee or contract basis
Parent: BAE Systems (Property Investments) Limited
Officers: David Stanley Parkes, Company Secretary; David Alexander Green [1964] Finance Director; Ann-Louise Holding [1961] Director/Chartered Secretary; David Stanley Parkes [1963] Director/Company Secretary; Mark Andrew Reason [1959] Commercial Director

BAE Systems Surface Ships (Holdings) Limited
Incorporated: 2 March 2007 *Employees:* 5
Net Worth: £81,070,000 *Total Assets:* £1,490,412,032
Registered Office: Warwick House, Farnborough Aerospace Centre, Farnborough, Hants, GU14 6YU
Activities: Activities of other holding companies n.e.c.
Parent: BAE Systems (Holdings) Limited
Officers: David Stanley Parkes, Company Secretary; David Edward Bristow [1966] Director/Accountant; Sunil Kumar Chaddah [1973] Director; David John Mitchard [1965] Director; Stephen Edward Timms [1965] Managing Director

BAE Systems Surface Ships Limited
Incorporated: 14 March 2007 *Employees:* 6,543
Net Worth: £520,995,008 *Total Assets:* £2,058,785,024
Registered Office: P O Box 87, Warwick House, Farnborough Aerospace Centre, Farnborough, Hants, GU14 6YU
Activities: Building of ships and floating structures
Parent: BAE Systems Surface Ships (Holdings) Limited
Officers: Ann-Louise Holding, Secretary; David Edward Bristow [1966] Director/Accountant; Sunil Kumar Chaddah [1973] Director; David John Mitchard [1965] Director; Stephen Edward Timms [1965] Managing Director

Baldwin House Limited
Incorporated: 9 May 1961
Net Worth: £23,902,838 *Total Assets:* £58,877,656
Registered Office: 20 Greyfriars Road, Reading, Berks, RG1 1NL
Activities: Other letting and operating of own or leased real estate
Parent: McKay Securities PLC
Officers: Joanne Sarah McKeown, Secretary; Thomas Charles Elliott [1975] Director/Chartered Surveyor; Simon Christopher Perkins [1965] Director/Chartered Surveyor; Giles Pollock Salmon [1966] Director/Chartered Accountant

Sandy Balls Estate Limited
Incorporated: 1 July 1959 *Employees:* 205
Net Worth: £18,011,456 *Total Assets:* £20,488,504
Registered Office: IMEX, 575-599 Maxted Road, Hemel Hempstead Industrial Estate, Hemel Hempstead, Herts, HP2 7DX
Activities: Holiday centres and villages
Parent: Away Resorts Ltd
Officers: Carl Anthony Castledine [1969] Director; Greg Lashley [1964] Director; Neill Timothy Ryder [1976] Director

Balton CP Limited
Incorporated: 22 December 1976 *Employees:* 1,209
Net Worth: £21,451,602 *Total Assets:* £91,419,928
Registered Office: CP House, Otterspool Way, Watford, Herts, WD25 8HU
Activities: Non-specialised wholesale trade
Parent: Premier Telecommunication International Limited
Officers: Eric Lewis, Secretary; Andrew Joseph Baker [1965] Director/Chief Executive Officer; Paul Andrew Filer [1957] Director/Chartered Accountant; Alexei James Schreier [1976] Director; Kevin Edgar Torlage [1964] Director/Chief Finance Officer

Baltray No. 1 Limited
Incorporated: 10 April 2006
Net Worth: £6,128,000 *Total Assets:* £33,492,000
Registered Office: c/o Pinewood Studios, Pinewood Road, Iver Heath, Bucks, SL0 0NH
Activities: Motion picture production activities
Parent: Pinewood-Shepperton Studios Limited
Officers: Bridget Sheldon-Hill, Secretary; Paul William Martin Golding [1965] Director/Partner; Chris John Naisby [1972] Director; Andrew Mark Smith [1962] Director

BAM Construct UK Limited
Incorporated: 3 February 1997 *Employees:* 2,297
Net Worth: £155,400,000 *Total Assets:* £489,200,000
Registered Office: Breakspear Park, Breakspear Way, Hemel Hempstead, Herts, HP2 4FL
Activities: Construction of commercial buildings
Parent: BAM Group (UK) Limited
Officers: Frazer Hamilton Wardhaugh, Secretary; Douglas Walker Keillor [1969] Director; James William Robert Wimpenny [1964] Executive Director

BAM Construction Limited
Incorporated: 4 May 1989
Net Worth: £69,400,000 *Total Assets:* £351,600,000
Registered Office: Breakspear Park, Breakspear Way, Hemel Hempstead, Herts, HP2 4FL
Activities: Construction of commercial buildings
Parent: BAM Construct UK Limited
Officers: Frazer Hamilton Wardhaugh, Secretary; Timothy George Chell [1968] Director; David Bruce Dickson [1966] Director; David Richard Ellis [1961] Director; Ian Edward Fleming [1961] Director; Adam Charles Harding [1972] Director; Douglas Walker Keillor [1969] Regional Director; John Eric Phillips [1961] Director; Roderic Stiles [1963] Regional Director; James William Robert Wimpenny [1964] Regional Director

BAM Group (UK) Limited
Incorporated: 26 September 1978
Net Worth: £26,581,000 *Total Assets:* £97,996,000
Registered Office: St James House, Knoll Road, Camberley, Surrey, GU15 3XW
Activities: Activities of construction holding companies
Parent: Koninklijke BAM Groep N.V.
Officers: Michelle Jane Davey, Secretary; Leendert Frans Den Houter [1974] Director/Chief Financial Officer [Dutch]; Geoffrey Mark Renshaw [1956] Director

BAM Nuttall Limited
Incorporated: 20 September 1935 *Employees:* 2,843
Net Worth: £113,813,000 *Total Assets:* £324,135,008
Registered Office: St James House, Knoll Road, Camberley, Surrey, GU15 3XW
Activities: Construction of roads and motorways
Parent: BAM Group (UK) Ltd
Officers: Michelle Jane Davey, Secretary; Stephen Charles Fox [1962] Director/Civil Engineer; Geoffrey Mark Renshaw [1956] Director

BAM Properties Limited
Incorporated: 19 November 1996
Net Worth: £27,883,000 *Total Assets:* £35,893,000
Registered Office: Breakspear Park, Breakspear Way, Hemel Hempstead, Herts, HP2 4FL
Activities: Buying and selling of own real estate
Officers: Euan Miller, Secretary; Douglas Peters [1967] Director/Accountant; James William Robert Wimpenny [1964] Director

Bamboo Topco Limited
Incorporated: 8 December 2016 *Employees:* 70
Net Worth: £4,858,556 *Total Assets:* £59,525,744
Registered Office: 1st Floor, Grenville House, Nelson Gate, Southampton, SO15 1GX
Activities: Credit granting by non-deposit taking finance houses and other specialist consumer credit grantors
Officers: Nicholas Aspinall, Secretary; Nicholas Aspinall [1964] Director/Lawyer; Scott Christopher Jones [1960] Director/Investment Professional [American]

Bandai Namco Amusement Europe Limited
Incorporated: 27 October 2006 *Employees:* 117
Net Worth: £14,950,000 *Total Assets:* £27,074,000
Registered Office: 37-39 Kew Foot Road, Richmond, Surrey, TW9 2SS
Activities: Other business support service activities n.e.c.
Parent: Bandai Namco Holdings UK Ltd.
Officers: Raymond Bradley, Secretary; Raymond Bradley [1965] Finance Director; Iwanaga Kato [1967] Director [Japanese]; John McKenzie [1965] Director

Bandai Namco Holdings UK Limited
Incorporated: 5 November 1991 *Employees:* 7
Net Worth: £64,654,000 *Total Assets:* £65,900,000
Registered Office: 37-39 Kew Foot Road, Richmond, Surrey, TW9 2SS
Activities: Non-specialised wholesale trade
Parent: Bandai Namco Holdings Inc.
Officers: Raymond Bradley, Secretary; Raymond Bradley [1965] Finance Director; Masaaki Tsuji [1953] Director [Japanese]

Bandhart
Incorporated: 23 September 1980
Net Worth: £176,756,000 *Total Assets:* £176,762,000
Registered Office: 210 Bath Road, Slough, Berks, SL1 3YD
Activities: Activities of head offices
Parent: Emhart International Limited
Officers: Steven John Costello [1980] Director/Chartered Accountant; Mark Richard Smiley [1977] Director/General Manager UK & ROI; Amit Kumar Sood [1978] Director/Accountant

Bandhart Overseas
Incorporated: 13 February 1950
Net Worth: £324,780,992 *Total Assets:* £364,975,008
Registered Office: 210 Bath Road, Slough, Berks, SL1 3YD
Activities: Activities of head offices
Parent: Black & Decker
Officers: Steven John Costello [1980] Director/Chartered Accountant; Mark Richard Smiley [1977] Director/General Manager UK & ROI; Amit Kumar Sood [1978] Director/Accountant

Bandt Holdings Limited
Incorporated: 31 May 1995 *Employees:* 2
Net Worth: £5,576,000 *Total Assets:* £36,493,000
Registered Office: Interserve House, Ruscombe Park, Twyford, Reading, Berks, RG10 9JU
Activities: Activities of other holding companies n.e.c.
Parent: Bandt Limited
Officers: Andrew John McDonald, Secretary; Andrew John McDonald [1974] Director/Company Secretary; Anthony Kenneth Smythe [1965] Director/Accountant

BAP Pharma Group Limited
Incorporated: 13 August 2015 *Employees:* 15
Net Worth: £10,529,731 *Total Assets:* £23,531,140
Registered Office: 103 Buckingham Avenue, Slough, Berks, SL1 4PF
Activities: Other business support service activities n.e.c.
Shareholders: Bashir Ahmed Parkar; Nafisa Parkar
Officers: Dr Bashir Ahmed Parkar [1959] Commercial Director; Nafisa Parkar [1962] Director

BAP Pharma Limited
Incorporated: 13 October 2010 *Employees:* 13
Net Worth: £10,783,829 *Total Assets:* £23,013,438
Registered Office: 103 Buckingham Avenue, Slough, Berks, SL1 4PF
Activities: Other human health activities
Parent: Bappharma Group Limited
Officers: Dr Bashir Ahmed Parkar [1959] Director/Pharmacists; Nafisa Parkar [1962] Director

Bapchild Motoring World (Kent) Limited
Incorporated: 23 April 2003 *Employees:* 195
Net Worth: £16,702,141 *Total Assets:* £44,938,208
Registered Office: The Showroom, Lakeside Services, Sturry Road, Canterbury, Kent, CT1 1DS
Activities: Sale of used cars and light motor vehicles
Parent: Peter Waddell Holdco Limited
Officers: Jemima Ferguson, Secretary; Peter Jackson Waddell [1966] Director/Chief Executive; Michael John Watts [1973] Director

Barcrest Group Limited
Incorporated: 22 January 1998 *Employees:* 176
Net Worth: £56,411,000 *Total Assets:* £118,188,000
Registered Office: SG House, 1 Dukes Green Avenue, Feltham, Middlesex, TW14 0LR
Activities: Gambling and betting activities
Parent: Scientific Games International Holdings Limited
Officers: Phillip Douglas Horne [1961] Managing Director; Paul Phillips [1978] Finance Director

Bard Holdings Limited
Incorporated: 24 July 1987
Net Worth: £35,559,000 *Total Assets:* £35,572,000
Registered Office: Forest House, Brighton Road, Crawley, W Sussex, RH11 9BP
Activities: Activities of head offices
Parent: Bard International Holdings BV
Officers: Kevin Edward Pratt, Secretary; Kevin Edward Pratt [1965] Director/Accountant; David Wheal [1971] Director/Chartered Accountant

Bard Limited
Incorporated: 30 September 1968 *Employees:* 277
Net Worth: £64,241,000 *Total Assets:* £89,395,000
Registered Office: Forest House, Brighton Road, Crawley, W Sussex, RH11 9BP
Activities: Non-specialised wholesale trade
Parent: Bard Holdings Limited
Officers: Kevin Edward Pratt, Secretary; Herman Victor Cueto [1974] Director/Executive [American]; Helen Hardwick [1976] Business Director; Nathan John Royds-Jones [1977] Director/Chartered Accountant

Barfoot Farms Limited
Incorporated: 28 September 2001 *Employees:* 168
Net Worth: £8,578,458 *Total Assets:* £22,110,768
Registered Office: Sefter Farm, Pagham Road, Bognor Regis, W Sussex, PO21 3PX
Activities: Growing of cereals (except rice), leguminous crops and oil seeds
Parent: Posbrook Holdings Limited
Officers: Peter Charles Barfoot [1950] Director; Nathan John Dellicott [1966] Farming Director; Dr Henry Kinloch [1937] Director/Chairman; Nicholas James Lake [1971] Finance Director; Julian David Marks [1967] Director

Barfoot Holdings Limited
Incorporated: 20 September 2001 *Employees:* 323
Net Worth: £34,554,032 *Total Assets:* £51,999,560
Registered Office: Sefter Farm, Pagham Road, Bognor Regis, W Sussex, PO21 3PX
Activities: Dormant company
Parent: Posbrook Holdings Limited
Officers: Nicholas James Lake, Secretary/Accountant; Peter Charles Barfoot [1950] Director; Dr Henry Kinloch [1937] Director/Acting Chairman

Barfoots of Botley Limited
Incorporated: 15 May 1989 *Employees:* 314
Net Worth: £34,638,500 *Total Assets:* £50,230,328
Registered Office: Sefter Farm, Pagham Road, Bognor Regis, W Sussex, PO21 3PX
Activities: Wholesale of fruit and vegetables
Parent: Posbrook Holdings Limited
Officers: Peter Charles Barfoot [1950] Director; Ryan Ross Beszant [1979] Commercial Director; Nathan John Dellicott [1966] Director/Farm Manager; Dr Henry Kinloch [1937] Director/Chairman; Nicholas James Lake [1971] Finance Director; Julian David Marks [1967] Managing Director; Christopher Paul White [1964] Director; Keston Williams [1973] Director

Clive Barford Limited
Incorporated: 3 July 1986 *Employees:* 160
Net Worth: £10,577,000 *Total Assets:* £33,610,000
Registered Office: Dumpers Drove, Horton Heath, Eastleigh, Hants, SO50 7DP
Activities: Renting and leasing of construction and civil engineering machinery and equipment
Shareholder: Charlotte Gay Male
Officers: David Stephen Butler, Secretary/Finance Manager; Camilla June Appleyard [1969] Director; Lucy Maria Atherton [1966] Director; James Edward Clive Barford [1972] Director/Consultant; Nicholas George Glossop [1971] Director; Peter George Glossop [1932] Director; Alexandra Merrie Griffin [1969] Director/Artist; William Thomas Jackson Griffin [1928] Director; Georgemma Sarah Lewis [1963] Director/Paediatric Health Care Assistant; Charlotte Gay Male [1967] Director/Strategic Planning Manager

Bargate Homes Limited
Incorporated: 17 November 2005 *Employees:* 54
Net Worth: £12,476,535 *Total Assets:* £36,531,596
Registered Office: The New Barn, Winchester Road, Fair Oak, Eastleigh, Hants, SO50 7HD
Activities: Construction of domestic buildings
Shareholders: Gerard Colquhoun Price; Prowting Investments PLC
Officers: Susan Price, Secretary; Jeremy Neal William Trezise, Secretary/Accountant; Barry Peter Amos-Yeo [1980] Director; Steven Charles Birch [1963] Land Director; Rachel Davies [1971] Technical Director; Andrew Kirkpatrick [1964] Construction Director; Robert Lambie [1959] Director; Gerard Colqhoun Price [1964] Director/Builder; Jeremy Neal William Trezise [1966] Director/Accountant; Wendy Jane Trott [1966] Director; Mark White [1970] Commercial Director

Barloworld Equipment UK Limited
Incorporated: 8 December 1994 *Employees:* 8
Net Worth: £173,250,464 *Total Assets:* £303,657,440
Registered Office: First Floor, Aurora Vanwall Business Park, Vanwall Road, Maidenhead, Berks, SL6 4UB
Activities: Renting and leasing of trucks and other heavy vehicles
Parent: Barloworld UK Limited
Officers: Stephen Patrick Burroughs, Secretary; Paolo Fellin [1954] Director/Manager [Italian]; Anton Leonidovich Globus [1979] Finance Director [South African]; Emmanuel Leeka [1969] Director/CEO Equipment Southern Africa [South African]; Trevor Quinton McGeer [1964] Director [South African]; Dominic Malentsha Sewela [1965] Director/CEO Barloworld Limited [South African]

Barloworld Holdings Limited
Incorporated: 20 January 1984 *Employees:* 2,439
Previous: Barloworld Holdings PLC
Net Worth: £506,075,008 *Total Assets:* £833,827,968
Registered Office: First Floor, Aurora Vanwall Business Park, Vanwall Road, Maidenhead, Berks, SL6 4UB
Activities: Activities of head offices
Parent: Barloworld Limited
Officers: Peter John Blackbeard [1957] Director; Anton Leonidovich Globus [1979] Finance Director [South African]; Michael David Lynch-Bell [1953] Director; Trevor Quinton McGeer [1964] Director [South African]; Dominic Malentsha Sewela [1965] Director/Chief Executive Officer [South African]; Eugene Luke Smith [1961] Director; Donald Gert Wilson [1957] Director/Chartered Accountant [South African]

Barloworld UK Limited
Incorporated: 12 August 1914 *Employees:* 4
Net Worth: £334,121,984 *Total Assets:* £460,524,000
Registered Office: First Floor, Aurora Vanwall Business Park, Vanwall Road, Maidenhead, Berks, SL6 4UB
Activities: Activities of head offices
Parent: Barloworld Holdings Limited
Officers: Anton Leonidovich Globus [1979] Finance Director [South African]; Trevor Quinton McGeer [1964] Director [South African]; Donald Gert Wilson [1957] Finance Director [South African]

F.G. Barnes & Sons Limited
Incorporated: 16 November 1936 *Employees:* 213
Net Worth: £10,717,686 *Total Assets:* £33,478,740
Registered Office: c/o F G Barnes, Slyfield Green, Woking Road, Guildford, Surrey, GU1 1RT
Activities: Sale of new cars and light motor vehicles
Major Shareholder: Douglas Graham Barnes
Officers: Derrick Roger Marshall, Secretary; Douglas Graham Barnes [1944] Director; Bala Waran [1958] Operations Director

The Baron Homes Corporation Limited
Incorporated: 18 May 1994 *Employees:* 16
Net Worth: £43,704,664 *Total Assets:* £114,662,304
Registered Office: 10 Prince Albert Street, Brighton, BN1 1HE
Activities: Development of building projects
Officers: Martin Blencowe [1986] Director; Michael Anthony Richard Blencowe [1983] Director/Property Developer; Montgomery Blencowe [1993] Director; Nazila Karimi Blencowe [1963] Director

Barons Automotive Limited
Incorporated: 31 January 1983 *Employees:* 280
Previous: Elms Automotive Limited
Net Worth: £4,832,829 *Total Assets:* £77,181,096
Registered Office: Chandlers, Victoria Road, Portslade, Brighton, BN41 1YH
Activities: Sale of new cars and light motor vehicles
Officers: Darryl Burman, Secretary; Darryl Michael Burman [1958] Director/VP and General Counsel [American]; Darren Guiver [1968] Director; Earl Julius Hesterberg [1953] Director [American]; Daniel James McHenry [1974] Finance Director; John Rickel [1961] Director [American]

Barons Autostar Limited
Incorporated: 13 November 1964 *Employees:* 277
Previous: Robinson's Autostar Garage Limited
Net Worth: £7,372,606 *Total Assets:* £22,359,580
Registered Office: Chandlers BMW, Victoria Road, Portslade, Brighton, BN41 1YH
Activities: Sale of new cars and light motor vehicles
Shareholders: Group One Automotive UK Limited; R.Robinson & Co.(Motor Services) Limited
Officers: Darryl Burman, Secretary; Darryl Michael Burman [1958] Director/General Counsel [American]; Darren Guiver [1968] Director; Earl Julius Hesterberg [1953] Director [American]; Daniel James McHenry [1974] Director; John Rickel [1961] Director [American]

Barretts of Canterbury Limited
Incorporated: 1 February 1939 *Employees:* 420
Net Worth: £23,822,000 *Total Assets:* £78,996,000
Registered Office: 28-30 St Peters Street, Canterbury, Kent, CT1 2BL
Activities: Sale of new cars and light motor vehicles
Shareholder: Paul Jonathan Barrett
Officers: Gillian Elizabeth Barrett [1960] Director; Patricia Barrett [1965] Director; Paul Jonathan Barrett [1960] Director; Shaun Robert Barrett [1962] Director

Barrow Hepburn Group Limited
Incorporated: 24 September 1920
Net Worth: £26,188,000 *Total Assets:* £31,397,000
Registered Office: 3M Centre, Cain Road, Bracknell, Berks, RG12 8HT
Activities: Activities of head offices
Parent: Capital Safety Limited
Officers: Ian Richard Brown, Secretary; David James Ashley [1968] Director/General Counsel; Simla Semerciyan [1973] Director/Finance Manager [Turkish]

Barrow Hepburn International Limited
Incorporated: 27 January 1943
Net Worth: £32,246,000 *Total Assets:* £32,246,000
Registered Office: 3M Centre, Cain Road, Bracknell, Berks, RG12 8HT
Activities: Activities of head offices
Parent: Barrow Hepburn Group Limited
Officers: Ian Richard Brown, Secretary; David James Ashley [1968] Director/General Counsel; Simla Semerciyan [1973] Director/Finance Manager [Turkish]

Bartholomews (Holdings) Limited
Incorporated: 26 January 1955 *Employees:* 197
Net Worth: £13,868,469 *Total Assets:* £56,337,804
Registered Office: Portfield, Chichester, W Sussex, PO19 7TT
Activities: Activities of head offices
Officers: Timothy Andrew Gleeson, Secretary; John Martin Bartholomew [1954] Director/Agronomist; Karel Lydia Bartholomew [1936] Director; Richard Samuel Churchill Bartholomew [1972] Director; Gary Scott Herman [1961] Director; Barry William Smith [1958] Group Financial Director

Bartholomews Agri Food Limited
Incorporated: 17 June 1944 *Employees:* 89
Net Worth: £5,727,641 *Total Assets:* £37,759,328
Registered Office: Portfield, Chichester, W Sussex, PO19 7TT
Activities: Support activities for crop production
Parent: Bartholomews (Holdings) Limited
Officers: Timothy Andrew Gleeson, Secretary; John Martin Bartholomew [1954] Director/Agronomist; Richard Samuel Churchill Bartholomew [1972] Director; Gary Scott Herman [1961] Managing Director

Basinghall Estate Company Limited
Incorporated: 2 March 1928 *Employees:* 5
Net Worth: £35,384,656 *Total Assets:* £40,333,468
Registered Office: Camburgh House, 27 New Dover Road, Canterbury, Kent, CT1 3DN
Activities: Other letting and operating of own or leased real estate
Officers: Simon Peter John Howell, Secretary/Solicitor; Dr Julia Catherine Weir Aglionby [1969] Director/Chartered Surveyor & Agricultural Valuer; Jonathan Michael Edward Allsebrook Hazel [1963] Director/Government Servant; Simon Peter John Howell [1948] Director/Solicitor; Henry Julian Aglionby Stanford [1965] Director/Partner of Albion Ventures LLP

Bathroom Brands Group Limited
Incorporated: 20 June 2016
Net Worth: £34,000,000 *Total Assets:* £68,454,000
Registered Office: Lake View House, Rennie Drive, Dartford, Kent, DA1 5FU
Activities: Activities of other holding companies n.e.c.
Officers: Vikram Kant, Secretary; David John Anning [1966] Director; Clive Aubrey Charles Chaplin [1951] Director/Lawyer; Vikram Kant [1984] Director [Indian]

Bathroom Brands Holdings UK Limited
Incorporated: 11 May 2009 *Employees:* 12
Previous: Crosswater Holdings UK Limited
Net Worth: £10,485,000 *Total Assets:* £49,631,000
Registered Office: Lake View House, Rennie Drive, Dartford, Kent, DA1 5FU
Activities: Wholesale of hardware, plumbing and heating equipment and supplies
Parent: Bathroom Brands Group Limited
Officers: Vikram Kant, Secretary; David Richard Hance [1965] Director/Group Chairman; Vikram Kant [1984] Director [Indian]

Bathroom Brands Limited
Incorporated: 11 October 2017 *Employees:* 285
Net Worth: £26,859,000 *Total Assets:* £62,771,000
Registered Office: Lake View House, Rennie Drive, Dartford, Kent, DA1 5FU
Activities: Activities of other holding companies n.e.c.
Officers: Vikram Kant, Secretary; David John Anning [1966] Director; Jeremy Guy Nicholas Bird [1961] Director; Clive Aubrey Charles Chaplin [1951] Director/Lawyer; Philip Roger Cooper [1948] Director/Consultant; Tanis Lee Crosby [1983] Group Director [South African]; Nico Albert de Beer [1960] Group Director; David Richard Hance [1965] Group Director; Vikram Kant [1984] Director [Indian]; Timothy Martin Powell [1972] Director [Australian]; Derek Patrick Riley [1961] Executive Director [Irish]

Batt Cables Public Limited Company
Incorporated: 17 February 1978 *Employees:* 299
Net Worth: £54,032,940 *Total Assets:* £90,481,880
Registered Office: The Belfry, Fraser Road, Erith, Kent, DA8 1QH
Activities: Wholesale of other intermediate products
Major Shareholder: Peter John Holm
Officers: Stephen Martin Brown, Secretary; Stephen Martin Brown [1968] Financial Director; Peter John Holm [1958] Director; Robert Waddington [1955] Sales Director

Baxterstorey Limited
Incorporated: 21 November 1985 *Employees:* 8,561
Net Worth: £116,365,000 *Total Assets:* £232,078,000
Registered Office: TVP2, 300 Thames Valley Park Drive, Reading, Berks, RG6 1PT
Activities: Other food services
Parent: Westbury Street Limited
Officers: Marc Bradley, Secretary; John David Bennett [1963] Director; Marc Bradley [1975] Director/Chartered Accountant; Simon Paul Esner [1962] Director/Sales & Marketing; Simon Toby Fennell [1976] Director; David James Hawkes [1971] Director; Christopher Noel Mahony [1966] Director [Irish]; Sarah Jane Miller [1966] Director; Alastair Dunbar Storey [1953] Director; Gifford Jeremy Wood [1963] Director

Bayer Public Limited Company
Incorporated: 8 July 1968 *Employees:* 739
Net Worth: £57,264,000 *Total Assets:* £350,952,992
Registered Office: 400 South Oak Way, Reading, Berks, RG2 6AD
Activities: Wholesale of pharmaceutical goods
Parent: Bayer Global Investments B.V.
Officers: Colin Andrew Barker, Secretary; Lars Friedrich Bruening [1963] Director [German]; Vera Hahn [1967] Director/Manager [Austrian]; Sreeparna Arun Kurdikar [1969] Director/Chief Financial Officer [American]

Baylis Court Trust
Incorporated: 8 June 2011 *Employees:* 175
Previous: Baylis Court School
Net Worth: £16,436,142 *Total Assets:* £20,176,332
Registered Office: Gloucester Avenue, Slough, Berks, SL1 3AH
Activities: General secondary education
Officers: Patrick Henry Spence, Secretary; Deborah Ajose [1964] Director/Headteacher; Robert John Kenwrick [1955] Director/Retired; Veronica Patricia Mayer [1942] Director; Rachel Beatrice Helen O'Brien [1967] Managing Director; Deborah Jane Parsons [1962] Director/HR Consultant; Carol Pearce [1949] Director/Professional Leader in Education; Simon Douglas Ian Pickett [1968] Director/Self Employed; Jonathan McNaughton Reekie [1940] Director; John Frederick Thomas [1943] Director/Retired

BBC Studioworks Limited
Incorporated: 1 July 1998 *Employees:* 94
Previous: BBC Studios and Post Production Limited
Net Worth: £24,250,308 *Total Assets:* £33,958,312
Registered Office: Room N101, Neptune House, BBC Elstree Centre, Eldon Avenue, Borehamwood, Herts, WD6 1NL
Activities: Television programme production activities
Parent: BBC Commercial Holdings Limited
Officers: Peter John Ranyard, Secretary; David Conway [1976] Managing Director; Robert Glyn Isherwood [1968] Group Finance and Operations Director

BBGI (NI) Limited
Incorporated: 6 December 2013
Net Worth: £7,307,708 *Total Assets:* £30,183,276
Registered Office: 1 Grenfell Road, Maidenhead, Berks, SL6 1HN
Activities: Activities of head offices
Parent: BBGI Sicav S.A.
Officers: Ian Tayler, Secretary; Peter Duncan Ball [1965] Director [Canadian]; Michael Denny [1977] Finance Director [Irish]; Frank Manfred Schramm [1968] Director [German]; Ian Tayler [1976] Director/Chartered Accountant

BBGI Holding Limited
Incorporated: 8 August 2011 *Employees:* 1
Net Worth: £121,536,008 *Total Assets:* £155,398,144
Registered Office: 1 Grenfell Road, Maidenhead, Berks, SL6 1HN
Activities: Activities of head offices
Parent: BBGI Sicav S.A.
Officers: Ian Tayler, Secretary; Martin Stuart Pugh [1963] Director; Frank Manfred Schramm [1968] Director [German]; Ian Tayler [1976] Director/Chartered Accountant

BCA Central Limited
Incorporated: 30 October 2009 *Employees:* 17
Previous: BCA Central Ltd
Net Worth: £529,680,992 *Total Assets:* £1,060,424,000
Registered Office: Headway House, Crosby Way, Farnham, Surrey, GU9 7XG
Activities: Activities of head offices
Parent: BCA Remarketing Group Limited
Officers: Martin Richard Letza, Secretary; Timothy Giles Lampert [1970] Director; Avril Palmer-Baunack [1964] Director

BCA Europe Limited
Incorporated: 3 February 2000 *Employees:* 20
Net Worth: £66,107,000 *Total Assets:* £71,803,000
Registered Office: Headway House, Crosby Way, Farnham, Surrey, GU9 7XG
Activities: Activities of head offices
Parent: BCA Group Europe Limited
Officers: Martin Richard Letza, Secretary; Timothy Giles Lampert [1970] Director; Avril Palmer-Baunack [1964] Director

BCA Fleet Solutions Limited
Incorporated: 28 February 2005 *Employees:* 456
Previous: Paragon Automotive Limited
Net Worth: £3,378,000 *Total Assets:* £53,041,000
Registered Office: Headway House, Crosby Way, Farnham, Surrey, GU9 7XG
Activities: Maintenance and repair of motor vehicles
Parent: TF1 Ltd
Officers: Martin Richard Letza, Secretary; David Francis Harris [1971] Director/Accountant; Timothy Giles Lampert [1970] Director; David John Seabridge [1969] Director

BCA Group Europe Limited
Incorporated: 22 September 1995
Net Worth: £254,940,000 *Total Assets:* £255,940,000
Registered Office: Headway House, Crosby Way, Farnham, Surrey, GU9 7XG
Activities: Activities of head offices
Parent: BCA Holdings Limited
Officers: Martin Richard Letza, Secretary; Timothy Giles Lampert [1970] Director; Avril Palmer-Baunack [1964] Director

BCA Holdings Limited
Incorporated: 12 October 1995
Net Worth: £153,434,000 *Total Assets:* £275,256,992
Registered Office: Headway House, Crosby Way, Farnham, Surrey, GU9 7XG
Activities: Activities of head offices
Parent: BCA Central Limited
Officers: Martin Richard Letza, Secretary; Timothy Giles Lampert [1970] Director; Avril Palmer-Baunack [1964] Director

BCA Marketplace PLC
Incorporated: 30 April 2014 *Employees:* 7,205
Net Worth: £1,156,600,064 *Total Assets:* £2,256,100,096
Registered Office: Haversham House, Coronation Business Park, Kiln Road, Kempston, Hardwick, Bedford, MK43 9PR
Activities: Activities of head offices
Officers: Martin Richard Letza, Secretary; Petrus Antonius Johannes Coelewij [1960] Director; Stephen Gutteridge [1954] Director; Jonathan Damian Kamaluddin [1973] Director/Chartered Accountant; Timothy Giles Lampert [1970] Director; David George Lis [1950] Director; Avril Palmer-Baunack [1964] Director

BCA Osprey I Limited
Incorporated: 1 December 2009
Net Worth: £472,600,000 *Total Assets:* £472,600,000
Registered Office: Headway House, Crosby Way, Farnham, Surrey, GU9 7XG
Activities: Activities of head offices
Parent: BCA Marketplace PLC
Officers: Martin Richard Letza, Secretary; Timothy Giles Lampert [1970] Director; Avril Palmer-Baunack [1964] Director

BCA Osprey II Limited
Incorporated: 17 November 2009
Net Worth: £286,600,000 *Total Assets:* £286,600,000
Registered Office: Headway House, Crosby Way, Farnham, Surrey, GU9 7XG
Activities: Activities of head offices
Parent: BCA Osprey I Limited
Officers: Martin Richard Letza, Secretary; Timothy Giles Lampert [1970] Director; Avril Palmer-Baunack [1964] Director

BCA Remarketing Group Limited
Incorporated: 23 November 2009
Net Worth: £413,350,016 *Total Assets:* £413,350,016
Registered Office: Headway House, Crosby Way, Farnham, Surrey, GU9 7XG
Activities: Activities of head offices
Parent: BCA Osprey II Limited
Officers: Martin Richard Letza, Secretary; Timothy Giles Lampert [1970] Director; Avril Palmer-Baunack [1964] Director

BCA Trading Limited
Incorporated: 27 January 1989
Net Worth: £227,132,000 *Total Assets:* £289,598,016
Registered Office: Headway House, Crosby Way, Farnham, Surrey, GU9 7XG
Activities: Activities of head offices
Parent: The British Car Auction Group Limited
Officers: Martin Richard Letza, Secretary; Timothy Giles Lampert [1970] Director; Avril Palmer-Baunack [1964] Director

BCA Vehicle Finance Limited
Incorporated: 1 October 2013 *Employees:* 58
Net Worth: £17,948,000 *Total Assets:* £148,940,992
Registered Office: Headway House, Crosby Way, Farnham, Surrey, GU9 7XG
Activities: Other credit granting n.e.c.
Parent: BCA Trading Limited
Officers: Martin Richard Letza, Secretary; Andrew Hodgson [1971] Director; Timothy Giles Lampert [1970] Director; Malcolm David Thompson [1958] Director

BCA Vehicle Services Limited
Incorporated: 11 July 2000 *Employees:* 415
Previous: Paragon Vehicle Services Limited
Net Worth: £8,404,000 *Total Assets:* £24,821,000
Registered Office: Headway House, Crosby Way, Farnham, Surrey, GU9 7XG
Activities: Maintenance and repair of motor vehicles
Parent: BCA Fleet Solutions Limited
Officers: Martin Richard Letza, Secretary; David Francis Harris [1971] Director/Accountant; Timothy Giles Lampert [1970] Director; Steven Richard Tallon [1972] Director

BCMV Limited
Incorporated: 30 June 1995
Net Worth Deficit: £496,185,984 *Total Assets:* £446,764,992
Registered Office: Media House, Bartley Wood Business Park, Hook, Hants, RG27 9UP
Activities: Other business support service activities n.e.c.
Parent: General Cable Limited
Officers: Gillian Elizabeth James, Secretary; Robert Dominic Dunn [1966] Director/Chief Financial Officer; Mine Ozkan Hifzi [1966] Director/Solicitor

BDML Connect Limited
Incorporated: 1 February 1993 *Employees:* 131
Net Worth: £1,715,853 *Total Assets:* £25,389,648
Registered Office: 45 Westerham Road, Sevenoaks, Kent, TN13 2QB
Activities: Non-life insurance
Major Shareholder: Kevin Ronald Spencer
Officers: Christopher James Payne, Secretary; Keith John Barber [1974] Director; Ross Leslie Barrington [1980] Managing Director; Michael Richard Brittain [1975] Director/Financial Controller; Christopher Thomas Collings [1955] Director; Gary Humphreys [1965] Director; John David Jackson [1953] Director; Kevin Ronald Spencer [1965] Commercial Director

BE Aerospace (UK) Europe Holdings Limited
Incorporated: 10 January 2008
Net Worth: £652,098,368 *Total Assets:* £886,728,960
Registered Office: c/o Rockwell Collins, 730 Wharfedale Road, Winnersh, Wokingham, Berks, RG41 5TP
Activities: Activities of head offices
Parent: BE Aerospace International Holdings Limited
Officers: Steven Jon Buesing [1974] Director/Vice President & Controller [American]; Daniel John Middleton [1979] Director/Solicitor; Peter Ross [1964] Director, Accounting & Controls, Actuation

BE Aerospace Global Holdings Limited
Incorporated: 6 October 2016
Net Worth: £3,212,818,176 *Total Assets:* £4,060,818,176
Registered Office: c/o Rockwell Collins, 730 Wharfedale Road, Winnersh, Wokingham, Berks, RG41 5TP
Activities: Other service activities n.e.c.
Officers: Steven Jon Buesing [1974] Director/Vice President & Controller [American]; Daniel John Middleton [1979] Director/Solicitor; Peter Ross [1964] Director, Accounting & Controls, Actuation

BE Aerospace International Holdings Limited
Incorporated: 7 October 2016
Net Worth: £2,052,925,056 *Total Assets:* £2,500,399,360
Registered Office: c/o Rockwell Collins, 730 Wharfedale Road, Winnersh, Wokingham, Berks, RG41 5TP
Activities: Other service activities n.e.c.
Parent: BE Aerospace Global Holdings Limited
Officers: Steven Jon Buesing [1974] Director/Vice President & Controller [American]; Daniel John Middleton [1979] Director/Solicitor; Peter Ross [1964] Director, Accounting & Controls, Actuation

BE Aerospace Thermal and Power Management Holdings (UK) Limited
Incorporated: 16 December 2010
Net Worth: £200,976,272 *Total Assets:* £385,366,464
Registered Office: c/o Rockwell Collins, 730 Wharfedale Road, Winnersh, Wokingham, Berks, RG41 5TP
Activities: Activities of head offices
Parent: United Technologies Corporation
Officers: Steven Jon Buesing [1974] Director/Vice President & Controller [American]; Daniel John Middleton [1979] Director/Solicitor; Peter Ross [1964] Director, Accounting & Controls, Actuation

Beacon Community College Academy Trust
Incorporated: 22 February 2012 *Employees:* 199
Net Worth: £39,910,204 *Total Assets:* £41,323,052
Registered Office: Beacon Community College Academy Trust, North Beeches Road, Crowborough, E Sussex, TN6 2AS
Activities: General secondary education
Officers: Chris Courtney [1985] Director/Teacher; Mark Francis Creamer [1957] Director/Retired; Viral Dinkerrai Desai [1969] Director/Certified Chartered Accountant; Nigel Timothy Gourlay [1955] Director/Business Consultant; Christopher Michael Hinton [1952] Director/Educational Consultant & Author; John Robert Maddison [1973] Director/IT Consultant; Alan David George Powell [1954] Director/Retired; Anna Ruth Louise Robinson [1973] Director/Headteacher; Lorna Simm [1973] Director/Retailer; Margaret Elizabeth Stebbing [1960] Director/Teacher; Peter Anthony Weston [1950] Director/Self Employed Consultant; Gwen Young [1955] Director/Retired

Beaconsfield High School
Incorporated: 5 September 2013 *Employees:* 107
Net Worth: £30,235,520 *Total Assets:* £32,735,524
Registered Office: Beaconsfield High School, Wattleton Road, Beaconsfield, Bucks, HP9 1RR
Activities: General secondary education
Officers: Zoe Arabella Barrows [1966] Director/Teacher; Dr Lorraine Diane Couves [1964] Director; Gemma Davies [1993] Director/Teacher; Sara Louise Davies [1969] Director/Architect; Janet Mary Dixon [1959] Director/Teacher; Christopher Thomas Edmonds [1969] Director; Michael James Edwards [1970] Director/Management Consultant; Sanjiv Bhimji Gohil [1973] Director/Police Officer; Gaby Clare Heppner-Logan [1969] Communications Director; Alison Mary Hood [1965] Director/Solicitor; Kate Joanna Ing [1968] Director/School Administration Manager [British/German]; Clare Louise Lewis [1966] Director/Housewife; James Nicholas Robert Morton [1981] Director/Head of Strategy; Bhupendra Manibhai Patel [1955] Director/Executive Coach & Strategy Consultant; Charles Richard Pybus [1965] Director/Chartered Accountant; Rachel Ann Smith [1964] Director/Headteacher; Deborah Maria Starrs [1966] Director/Teaching Assistant

Beadles Group Limited
Incorporated: 15 January 1987 *Employees:* 7
Net Worth: £26,024,552 *Total Assets:* £47,849,796
Registered Office: Chandlers BMW, Victoria Road, Portslade, Brighton, BN41 1YH
Activities: Sale of new cars and light motor vehicles
Parent: Group 1 Automotive UK Limited
Officers: Darryl Burman, Secretary; Darryl Michael Burman [1958] Director/General Counsel [American]; Darren Guiver [1968] Managing Director; Earl Julius Hesterberg [1953] Director [American]; Daniel James McHenry [1974] Director; John Rickel [1961] Director [American]

Beadles Sidcup Limited
Incorporated: 14 June 1948 *Employees:* 162
Net Worth: £3,099,758 *Total Assets:* £34,839,892
Registered Office: Chandlers BMW, Victoria Road, Portslade, Brighton, BN41 1YH
Activities: Sale of new cars and light motor vehicles
Parent: Beadles Group Ltd
Officers: Darryl Burman, Secretary; Darryl Michael Burman [1958] Director/General Counsel [American]; Darren Guiver [1968] Managing Director; Earl Julius Hesterberg [1953] Director [American]; Daniel James McHenry [1974] Director; John Rickel [1961] Director [American]

Beam Global Finance UK Limited
Incorporated: 13 August 1996
Net Worth: £9,475,752 *Total Assets:* £69,350,016
Registered Office: 2 Longwalk Road, Stockley Park, Uxbridge, Middlesex, UB11 1BA
Activities: Other service activities n.e.c.
Officers: Aoife Clarke [1980] Public Affairs Director - International [Irish]; Richard Dalton [1962] Director/General Manager - Cooley Distillery [Irish]; William Lindquist [1977] Director [Irish]; Leonard John Mathews [1975] Director/Financial Controller [Irish]

Beam Suntory UK Holdings Limited
Incorporated: 1 November 2005
Previous: Beam Inc UK Holdings Limited
Net Worth: £464,076,992 *Total Assets:* £470,887,008
Registered Office: 2 Longwalk Road, Stockley Park, Uxbridge, Middlesex, UB11 1BA
Activities: Activities of other holding companies n.e.c.
Officers: Nadim Assi [1967] Director/CFO International [Canadian]; Madame Del Pino Bermudez de La Puente Sanchez-Aguilera [1974] Director/Associate General Counsel [Spanish]

Beam Suntory UK Limited
Incorporated: 13 October 2005 *Employees:* 186
Previous: Beam Inc UK Limited
Net Worth: £474,952,000 *Total Assets:* £573,376,000
Registered Office: 2 Longwalk Road, Stockley Park, Uxbridge, Middlesex, UB11 1BA
Activities: Distilling, rectifying and blending of spirits
Parent: Beam Suntory UK Holdings Limited
Officers: Nadim Assi [1967] Director/CFO International [Canadian]; Madame Del Pino Bermudez de La Puente Sanchez-Aguilera [1974] Director/Associate General Counsel [Spanish]; Pryce William David Greenow [1970] Director/President International; Jose Padilla Munoz [1959] Senior Director International Supply Chain Finance [Spanish]; David William James Wilson [1964] Director/MD Global Travel Retail

Beamish Investments Limited
Incorporated: 21 October 2010 *Employees:* 2
Net Worth: £3,035,636 *Total Assets:* £29,806,586
Registered Office: Hill View House, The Hill, Cranbrook, Kent, TN17 3AD
Activities: Fund management activities
Shareholders: Nicola Jane Johnson; Christopher Guy Johnson
Officers: Stephen Thomas Clews [1967] Director; Christopher Guy Johnson [1964] Director

Beardow Adams Holdings Ltd
Incorporated: 13 July 2015 *Employees:* 245
Net Worth: £15,845,612 *Total Assets:* £46,559,456
Registered Office: 32 Blundells Road, Bradville, Milton Keynes, Bucks, MK13 7HF
Activities: Activities of production holding companies
Shareholders: Robert Edward Adams; Kim Neo Beardow; Nicholas James Beardow
Officers: Nicholas James Beardow, Secretary; Robert Edward Adams [1950] Director/Research Chemist; Nicolas James Beardow [1960] Sales Director; Adrian James Day [1977] Finance Director

Beardow and Adams (Adhesives) Limited
Incorporated: 16 July 1976 *Employees:* 106
Net Worth: £16,872,476 *Total Assets:* £31,820,200
Registered Office: 32 Blundells Road, Bradville, Milton Keynes, Bucks, MK13 7HF
Activities: Manufacture of glues
Parent: Beardow Adams Holdings Limited
Officers: Nicholas James Beardow, Secretary; Robert Edward Adams [1950] Director/Research Chemist; Nicholas James Beardow [1960] Sales Director; Adrian James Day [1977] Director/Accountant; Graeme Edward Nutting [1956] Director/UK Sales; Lesley Elizabeth Sheldon [1961] Product Development & Technical Services Director

Beazer Limited
Incorporated: 7 June 1968
Net Worth: £7,125,000 *Total Assets:* £615,137,024
Registered Office: Hanson House, 14 Castle Hill, Maidenhead, Berks, SL6 4JJ
Activities: Activities of other holding companies n.e.c.
Parent: Hanson Overseas Holdings Limited
Officers: Wendy Fiona Rogers, Secretary; Nicholas Arthur Dawe Benning-Prince [1974] Director/Chartered Accountant; Robert Charles Dowley [1972] Director/Chartered Accountant; Edward Alexander Gretton [1970] Director; Dr Carsten Matthias Wendt [1976] Director [German]

BECAP Spicers (UK) Limited
Incorporated: 7 April 2011
Net Worth Deficit: £1,659,000 *Total Assets:* £40,249,000
Registered Office: c/o OfficeTeam, Unit 4, 500 Purley Way, Croydon, Surrey, CR0 4NZ
Activities: Activities of head offices
Major Shareholder: Jonathan Paul Moulton
Officers: Philippa Anne Maynard, Secretary; Andrew Graham Mobbs [1978] Director

Beck & Pollitzer Engineering Limited
Incorporated: 22 November 1993 *Employees:* 144
Net Worth: £32,209,252 *Total Assets:* £47,730,452
Registered Office: Burnham Road, Dartford, Kent, DA1 5BD
Activities: Installation of industrial machinery and equipment
Parent: Beck & Pollitzer Engineering Holdings Ltd
Officers: Ivo Vesselinov, Secretary; Andrew Hodgson [1965] Director; Romain Jean Patrick Prouvost [1979] Director [French]; Ivo Vesselinov [1976] Finance Director

Beck & Pollitzer Holdings Limited
Incorporated: 25 October 2004 *Employees:* 3
Net Worth: £26,480,580 *Total Assets:* £36,608,288
Registered Office: Burnham Road, Dartford, Kent, DA1 5BD
Activities: Activities of other holding companies n.e.c.
Parent: B & P Acquisitionco Limited
Officers: Ivo Vesselinov, Secretary; Andrew Hodgson [1965] Director; Romain Jean Patrick Prouvost [1979] Director [French]; Ivo Vesselinov [1976] Finance Director

Beck & Pollitzer Limited
Incorporated: 1 September 2016 *Employees:* 860
Net Worth Deficit: £1,611,941 *Total Assets:* £100,397,808
Registered Office: Burnham Road, Sandpit Road, Dartford, Kent, DA1 5BD
Activities: Activities of venture and development capital companies
Parent: Graphite Capital Management LLP
Officers: Andrew Hodgson [1965] Director; Charles Lewis Matthews [1953] Director; Romain Jean Patrick Prouvost [1979] Director [French]; Ivo Vesselinov [1976] Finance Director

Beck Interiors Limited
Incorporated: 21 February 1995 *Employees:* 194
Net Worth: £21,243,542 *Total Assets:* £46,355,192
Registered Office: Victory House, Cox Lane, Chessington, Surrey, KT9 1SG
Activities: Joinery installation
Parent: Beck MBI Ltd
Officers: Edward Corrigan, Secretary; Mark Andrew Banham [1971] Director; Robert Andrew Bishop [1954] Commercial Director; Shaun Carvalho [1964] Director; Dalbir Chana [1979] Board Director; Jonathan Embling Dart [1959] Director; Christopher Sinclair Galloway [1972] Operations Director; Brian Paul Hutchison [1964] Director; Edward Kent [1976] Board Director

Beck MBI Limited
Incorporated: 23 October 2007 *Employees:* 258
Net Worth: £34,185,200 *Total Assets:* £63,762,080
Registered Office: Victory House, Cox Lane, Chessington, Surrey, KT9 1SG
Activities: Other specialised construction activities n.e.c.
Parent: Beck MBI2 Ltd
Officers: Jonathan Dart, Secretary; Mark Andrew Banham [1971] Director; Jonathan Embling Dart [1959] Financial Director; Christopher Sinclair Galloway [1972] Director; Robert Horvath [1956] Director/Chairman

Beckman Coulter United Kingdom Limited
Incorporated: 2 November 1959 *Employees:* 197
Net Worth: £34,242,000 *Total Assets:* £64,166,000
Registered Office: Oakley Court, Kingsmead Business Park, London Road, High Wycombe, Bucks, HP11 1JU
Activities: Non-specialised wholesale trade
Parent: VJ Holdco UK Limited
Officers: Jan Pospisil [1959] Director/VP Commercial Operations Europe [Czech]; Keith Graham Ward [1953] Director; Robert Todd Young [1972] Director

Beckman Holdings Limited
Incorporated: 10 October 1988
Net Worth: £101,891,000 *Total Assets:* £149,832,992
Registered Office: Oakley Court, Kingsmead Business Park, London Road, High Wycombe, Bucks, HP11 1JU
Activities: Non-trading company
Parent: Launchchange Limited
Officers: Jan Pospisil [1959] Director/VP Commercial Operations Europe [Czech]; Keith Graham Ward [1953] Director; Robert Todd Young [1972] Director

Becton Dickinson Infusion Therapy Holdings UK Limited
Incorporated: 27 March 1998
Net Worth: £46,545,000 *Total Assets:* £48,294,000
Registered Office: 1030 Eskdale Road, Winnersh Triangle, Wokingham, Berks, RG41 5TS
Activities: Other business support service activities n.e.c.
Parent: Becton, Dickinson U.K. Limited
Officers: Michael John Fairbourn [1959] Director/Vice President, General Manager; Edward Daniel Hopkin [1973] Director/International Counsel; John Konrad Neat [1967] Finance Director

Becton Dickinson Infusion Therapy UK
Incorporated: 26 July 1954 *Employees:* 316
Net Worth: £40,230,000 *Total Assets:* £100,424,000
Registered Office: 1030 Eskdale Road, Winnersh Triangle, Wokingham, Berks, RG41 5TS
Activities: Manufacture of medical and dental instruments and supplies
Officers: Michael John Fairbourn [1959] Director/Vice President & General Manager; Edward Daniel Hopkin [1973] Director/International Counsel; John Konrad Neat [1967] Finance Director

Becton, Dickinson U.K. Limited
Incorporated: 25 June 1965 *Employees:* 906
Net Worth: £255,384,992 *Total Assets:* £355,676,000
Registered Office: 1030 Eskdale Road, Winnersh Triangle, Wokingham, Berks, RG41 5TS
Activities: Manufacture of medical and dental instruments and supplies
Parent: Becton Dickinson and Company
Officers: Michael John Fairbourn [1959] Director/Vice President & General Manager; Edward Daniel Hopkin [1973] Director/International Counsel; John Konrad Neat [1967] Finance Director

Bedales School
Incorporated: 12 June 1933 *Employees:* 252
Net Worth: £19,178,632 *Total Assets:* £35,399,896
Registered Office: Bedales School, Petersfield, Hants, GU32 2DG
Activities: General secondary education
Officers: Richard Douglas Longfield Lushington, Secretary; Clare Louise Bradbury [1972] Director/Headteacher; Felix Grey [1988] Director/Postgraduate Student; Avril Florence Hardie [1949] Director; Joanna Pamela Michele Johnson [1961] Director; Owen Richard Jonathan [1952] Director; Dr Anna Julia Keay [1974] Director of The Landmark Trust; Richard John Lippiett [1949] Director/Chief Executive Mary Rose Trust; Stephen Anthony Nokes [1952] Director/Education Consultant; Matthew Frederick William Rice [1962] Director/Designer; Professor Geoffrey Christopher Ward [1954] Director/Principal, Homerton College Cambridge; Charles Basil Lucas Watson [1962] Director; Timothy Peter Wise [1961] Director/Banking

Bedford Education Partnership Holdings Limited
Incorporated: 6 March 2003
Net Worth Deficit: £3,758,000 *Total Assets:* £21,329,000
Registered Office: Part First Floor, 1 Grenfell Road, Maidenhead, Berks, SL6 1HN
Activities: Financial intermediation not elsewhere classified
Parent: BBGI Sicav S.A.
Officers: Emeka Ikechi Ehenulo, Secretary; Albert Hendrik Naafs [1965] Director [Dutch]; Ian Tayler [1976] Director/General Manager

Bedford Education Partnership Limited
Incorporated: 6 March 2003
Net Worth Deficit: £3,758,000 *Total Assets:* £21,329,000
Registered Office: Part First Floor, 1 Grenfell Road, Maidenhead, Berks, SL6 1HN
Activities: Financial intermediation not elsewhere classified
Parent: Bedford Education Partnership Holdings Limited
Officers: Emeka Ikechi Ehenulo, Secretary; Albert Hendrik Naafs [1965] Director [Dutch]; Ian Tayler [1976] Director/General Manager

Bedfordia Group Limited
Incorporated: 11 September 1959 *Employees:* 42
Previous: Bedfordia Group PLC
Net Worth: £30,029,236 *Total Assets:* £38,883,044
Registered Office: Milton Parc, Milton Ernest, Beds, MK44 1YU
Activities: Activities of head offices
Officers: Terry Wilding, Secretary; David Alistair Gray [1955] Director/Chartered Accountant; John Charles Ibbett [1962] Director; Yolanda Alexandra Ibbett [1969] Director

Beecham Group P L C
Incorporated: 23 January 1928
Net Worth: £587,270,016 *Total Assets:* £588,897,024
Registered Office: 980 Great West Road, Brentford, Middlesex, TW8 9GS
Activities: Other business support service activities n.e.c.
Parent: SmithKline & French Laboratories Limited
Officers: Victoria Anne Whyte, Secretary; Adam Walker [1967] Director

Beko PLC
Incorporated: 22 August 1989 *Employees:* 238
Net Worth: £30,350,000 *Total Assets:* £179,327,008
Registered Office: Beko House, 1 Greenhill Crescent, Watford, Herts, WD18 8QU
Activities: Manufacture of electric domestic appliances
Parent: Arcelik A.S.
Officers: Gul Arslanoglu, Secretary; Mehmet Ragip Balcioglu [1967] Director; Hakan Hamdi Bulgurlu [1972] Director/Mechanical Engineer [Turkish]; Levent Cakiroglu [1967] Director [Turkish]; Fatih Kemal Ebiclioglu [1967] Director [Turkish]; Mustafa Rahmi Koc [1930] Director [Turkish]; Sir David Norman Reddaway [1953] Director; Polat SEN [1976] Director [Turkish]

Bel UK Limited
Incorporated: 1 September 1966 *Employees:* 52
Net Worth: £28,592,000 *Total Assets:* £48,115,000
Registered Office: Suite 1, Floor 2, 160 London Road, Sevenoaks, Kent, TN13 2JA
Activities: Wholesale of dairy products, eggs and edible oils and fats
Parent: La Societe Industrielle Commerciale et de Participation
Officers: Aubry Marc Degroote, Secretary; Rodolphe Bernard Boivin [1970] Director/CFO for Europe [French]

Bell Microsystems Limited
Incorporated: 15 September 1995 *Employees:* 328
Net Worth: £1,244,368 *Total Assets:* £73,883,896
Registered Office: New Hampshire Court, St Pauls Road, Southsea, Hants, PO5 4AQ
Activities: Other information technology service activities
Shareholder: Alastair Matthew Bell
Officers: Alastair Matthew Bell, Secretary/Director; Alastair Matthew Bell [1961] Director; Manpreet Kaur Gill [1979] Finance Director; Nicholas William Petheram [1965] Director

Bellerbys Educational Services Limited
Incorporated: 6 December 1988 *Employees:* 1,064
Net Worth: £53,863,000 *Total Assets:* £266,564,000
Registered Office: Brighton Study Centre, 1 Billinton Way, Brighton, BN1 4LF
Activities: General secondary education
Parent: Study Group UK Limited
Officers: Gordon Anthony Bull, Secretary; Gordon Anthony Bull [1975] Director/Solicitor; Michael John Everett [1966] Director/Chief Operating Officer; Robert Wayne Morgan [1959] Director/Global Chief Operating Officer [American]; James Henry Pitman [1961] Managing Director

Bellevue Education Group Limited
Incorporated: 7 October 2003
Net Worth: £17,023,974 *Total Assets:* £29,585,864
Registered Office: 1 Wolsey Road, East Molesey, Surrey, KT8 9EL
Activities: Educational support services
Parent: Bellevue Education International Limited
Officers: Nicholas Edward Holt [1980] Director; Mark William Malley [1974] Director; Jay Sunny Varkey [1984] Director [Indian]

Bellevue Education International Limited
Incorporated: 12 April 2012 *Employees:* 607
Net Worth: £11,269,233 *Total Assets:* £45,101,192
Registered Office: Ground Floor, 1 Wolsey Road, East Molesey, Surrey, KT8 9EL
Activities: Pre-primary education
Parent: Project Beta Limited
Officers: Nicholas Edward Holt [1980] Director; Mark William Malley [1974] Director; Jay Sunny Varkey [1984] Director [Indian]

Bellman Property Group Limited
Incorporated: 10 February 2011 *Employees:* 2
Net Worth: £8,559,297 *Total Assets:* £20,216,372
Registered Office: Ground Floor, Unit 501 Centennial Park, Centennial Avenue, Elstree, Borehamwood, Herts, WD6 3FG
Activities: Other service activities n.e.c.
Shareholder: Laurence Alan Bellman
Officers: Sarah Jane Bellman, Secretary; Laurence Alan Bellman [1956] Director, Surveyor and Property Manager; Neil Andrew Evans [1954] Director/Solicitor

Belron Finance Issuer Limited
Incorporated: 20 October 2017
Net Worth: £105,792 *Total Assets:* £1,153,383,552
Registered Office: Milton Park, Stroude Road, Egham, Surrey, TW20 9EL
Activities: Management consultancy activities other than financial management
Parent: Belron Finance Limited
Officers: Claire Dakin, Secretary; Rebecca Scudamore, Secretary; Gary Lubner [1959] Director/Business Executive; David Brian Meller [1966] Finance Director

Belron Finance Limited
Incorporated: 21 September 1999
Net Worth: £1,234,381,440 *Total Assets:* £2,611,092,992
Registered Office: Milton Park, Stroude Road, Egham, Surrey, TW20 9EL
Activities: Management consultancy activities other than financial management
Parent: Belron Lending UK Limited
Officers: Robert Bass, Secretary; Gary Lubner [1959] Director; David Brian Meller [1966] Finance Director

Belron International Limited
Incorporated: 13 November 1989 *Employees:* 184
Net Worth: £680,422,976 *Total Assets:* £723,329,984
Registered Office: Milton Park, Stroude Road, Egham, Surrey, TW20 9EL
Activities: Activities of head offices
Parent: Belron Finance Limited
Officers: Robert Bass, Secretary; Gary Lubner [1959] Director/Business Executive; David Brian Meller [1966] Finance Director; Richard Robert Tyler [1971] Group Operations & Supply Chain Director

Belron Lending UK Limited
Incorporated: 20 October 2017
Net Worth: £1,406,666,624 *Total Assets:* £1,406,666,624
Registered Office: Milton Park, Stroude Road, Egham, Surrey, TW20 9EL
Activities: Management consultancy activities other than financial management
Parent: S.A. D'Ieteren N.V.
Officers: Claire Elizabeth Dakin, Secretary; Rebecca Scudamore, Secretary; Gary Lubner [1959] Director/Business Executive; David Brian Meller [1966] Finance Director

Belron UK Limited
Incorporated: 23 April 1951 *Employees:* 2,448
Net Worth: £8,231,000 *Total Assets:* £63,566,000
Registered Office: 1 Priory Business Park, Cardington, Bedford, MK44 3US
Activities: Maintenance and repair of motor vehicles
Parent: Belron International Limited
Officers: Neil Andrew Fraser Morgan, Secretary; Nigel Jeremy Doggett [1965] Managing Director; Taxiarchis Konstantopoulos [1970] Managing Director [Greek]; David Brian Meller [1966] Finance Director

Belton Associates (Group Holdings) Limited
Incorporated: 8 December 2011 *Employees:* 3
Net Worth Deficit: £1,131,000 *Total Assets:* £103,847,000
Registered Office: Frays Court, 71 Cowley Road, Uxbridge, Middlesex, UB8 2AE
Activities: Other social work activities without accommodation n.e.c.
Parent: SSCP Spring Bidco Limited
Officers: Helen Elizabeth Lecky, Secretary; Antony Vincent Holt [1959] Director/Chartered Accountant; Jean-Luc Emmanuel Janet [1970] Director [French]; David Jon Leatherbarrow [1969] Director/Group Chief Executive Officer

Belton Associates Holdings Limited
Incorporated: 9 December 2011 *Employees:* 3
Net Worth Deficit: £3,912,000 *Total Assets:* £99,935,000
Registered Office: Frays Court, 71 Cowley Road, Uxbridge, Middlesex, UB8 2AE
Activities: Other social work activities without accommodation n.e.c.
Parent: Belton Associates Group Limited
Officers: Helen Elizabeth Lecky, Secretary; Antony Vincent Holt [1959] Director/Chartered Accountant; Jean-Luc Emmanuel Janet [1970] Director [French]; David Jon Leatherbarrow [1969] Director/Group Chief Executive Officer

Belton Associates Limited
Incorporated: 12 December 2011 *Employees:* 8
Net Worth: £26,806,000 *Total Assets:* £112,876,000
Registered Office: Frays Court, 71 Cowley Road, Uxbridge, Middlesex, UB8 2AE
Activities: Other social work activities without accommodation n.e.c.
Parent: Belton Associates Holdings Limited
Officers: Helen Elizabeth Lecky, Secretary; Antony Vincent Holt [1959] Director/Chartered Accountant; Jean-Luc Emmanuel Janet [1970] Director/Chief Financial Officer [French]; David Jon Leatherbarrow [1969] Director/Group Chief Executive Officer

Ben-Motor and Allied Trades Benevolent Fund
Incorporated: 14 September 1987 *Employees:* 398
Net Worth: £42,274,000 *Total Assets:* £45,529,000
Registered Office: Lynwood Court, Lynwood Village, Rise Road, Ascot, Berks, SL5 0FG
Activities: Other accommodation
Officers: David James Ellis, Secretary; Sharon Ashcroft [1965] Human Resources Director; Brian Philip Back [1947] Director/Chairman; Daksh Gupta [1970] Director/Chief Executive Officer; Jeremy Christopher Hicks [1962] Managing Director; Richard Anthony Jeffcoat [1958] Business Services Director; Michael Judge [1940] Director/Retired; Generald Ernest Lee [1952] Director/Chief Executive; Steven Gerry Nash [1955] Director/Chief Executive; Mark Robert Canning Outhwaite [1957] Director/Management Consultant; Graeme John Potts [1957] Managing Director; Robin Shaw [1965] Managing Director; Christopher David Thomas [1964] Finance Director; Robin Arthur John Woolcock [1947] Director/Special Advisor

Benecol Limited
Incorporated: 29 May 2014 *Employees:* 15
Net Worth: £56,775,000 *Total Assets:* £78,854,000
Registered Office: The Mille, 1000 Great West Road, Brentford, Middlesex, TW8 9DW
Activities: Manufacture of other food products n.e.c.
Parent: Raisio UK Limited
Officers: Merja Sisko Lumme [1961] Director/VP Human Resources [Finnish]; Iiro Tapio Wester [1963] Director/Chief Commercial Officer [Finnish]

Benenden School (Kent) Limited
Incorporated: 13 March 1924 *Employees:* 377
Net Worth: £36,553,000 *Total Assets:* £46,487,000
Registered Office: Benenden School, Benenden, Cranbrook, Kent, TN17 4AA
Activities: General secondary education
Officers: Martin Christopher Lander, Secretary; Joanna Sarah Birkett [1960] Director/Solicitor; Wendy Margaret Carey [1946] Director; Alison Jane Clarke [1960] Director/Public Relations Consultant; Dr Fiona Elizabeth Cornish [1960] Director/Doctor; Dr Rupert William Evenett [1963] Charity Director; Laurette Gallagher [1965] Director/Quantity Surveyor; Anne Elizabeth McNab [1958] Director/Chartered Accountant; John Anthony Augustine McParland [1953] Director/Headmaster [Irish]; Christopher George Nicolle [1958] Director/Financial Adviser; Jonathan Peter Pearce [1957] Director/Retired; Giles St Aubyn Pugh [1958] Director; Paul Anthony Simpkin [1968] Director/Banking; Simon Sean Smart [1947] Director/Retired; Professor Liba Chaia Taub [1954] Museum Director [British/American]

Benson & Hedges Limited
Incorporated: 24 December 1910 *Employees:* 7
Net Worth: £420,400,000 *Total Assets:* £420,400,000
Registered Office: Members Hill, Brooklands Road, Weybridge, Surrey, KT13 0QU
Activities: Activities of head offices
Parent: Gallaher Overseas (Holdings) Limited
Officers: Nicholas Charles David Craig, Secretary; Andrew Chamberlain [1965] Director/Accountant; Charles Ashley Cunningham-Reid [1968] Director; Alison Maria Hawkett [1968] Director/Accountant; Paul Bernard Hennessy [1980] Director [Irish]; Jeroen Rusbach [1977] Director/Accountant [Dutch]; Daniel Sciamma [1970] Director [French]

Benugo Limited
Incorporated: 5 February 1998 *Employees:* 1,238
Net Worth: £29,236,000 *Total Assets:* £64,754,000
Registered Office: TVP2, 300 Thames Valley Park Drive, Reading, Berks, RG6 1PT
Activities: Licenced restaurants
Parent: Westbury Street Limited
Officers: Marc Bradley, Secretary; Paul Robert Bowley [1970] Director; Marc Bradley [1975] Director; Alastair Dunbar Storey [1953] Director; Benedict Warner [1964] Director/Catering

Berendsen Finance (DKK) Limited
Incorporated: 6 December 2012
Net Worth: £4,697,809 *Total Assets:* £37,665,180
Registered Office: Intec 3, Wade Road, Basingstoke, Hants, RG24 8NE
Activities: Non-trading company
Parent: Berendsen Limited
Officers: Mark Leslie Franklin [1969] Director/Workwear Representative; Mark South [1963] Finance Director

Berendsen Finance (Euro 2) Limited
Incorporated: 7 December 2012
Net Worth: £22,370,440 *Total Assets:* £23,157,344
Registered Office: Intec 3, Wade Road, Basingstoke, Hants, RG24 8NE
Activities: Non-trading company
Parent: Berendsen Finance (Euro) Limited
Officers: Mark Leslie Franklin [1969] Director/Workwear Representative; Mark South [1963] Finance Director

Berendsen Finance (Euro) Limited
Incorporated: 6 December 2012
Net Worth: £14,268,315 *Total Assets:* £116,564,496
Registered Office: Intec 3, Wade Road, Basingstoke, Hants, RG24 8NE
Activities: Non-trading company
Parent: Berendsen Limited
Officers: Mark Leslie Franklin [1969] Director/Workwear Representative; Mark South [1963] Finance Director

Berendsen Finance Limited
Incorporated: 15 July 1996
Net Worth: £433,330,656 *Total Assets:* £601,037,824
Registered Office: Intec 3, Wade Road, Basingstoke, Hants, RG24 8NE
Activities: Non-trading company
Parent: Berendsen Limited
Officers: Mark Leslie Franklin [1969] Director/Workwear Representative; Didier Lachaud [1959] Director [French]; Mark South [1963] Finance Director

Berendsen Limited
Incorporated: 18 February 1980 *Employees:* 65
Previous: Berendsen PLC
Net Worth: £524,800,000 *Total Assets:* £1,246,099,968
Registered Office: Intec 3, Wade Road, Basingstoke, Hants, RG24 8NE
Activities: Activities of other holding companies n.e.c.
Parent: Elis SA
Officers: Mark Leslie Franklin [1969] Director/Manager; Xavier Jean-Francois Martire [1971] Director [French]

Berendsen UK Limited
Incorporated: 6 March 1928 *Employees:* 7,310
Net Worth: £91,794,000 *Total Assets:* £451,841,984
Registered Office: Intec 3, Wade Road, Basingstoke, Hants, RG24 8NE
Activities: Renting and leasing of other personal and household goods
Parent: Berendsen Limited
Officers: Mark Leslie Franklin [1969] Director/Manager; Richard O'Brien [1963] Director/Manager; Mark South [1963] Director

Berkeley (SQP) Limited
Incorporated: 4 March 2005
Previous: Berkeley Eighty-Eight Limited
Net Worth: £79,180,176 *Total Assets:* £174,989,664
Registered Office: Berkeley House, 19 Portsmouth Road, Cobham, Surrey, KT11 1JG
Activities: Non-trading company
Parent: Berkeley Homes (Capital) PLC
Officers: Jared Stephen Philip Cranney, Secretary; Antony Ball [1975] Director; Peter John Davidson [1982] Director; James Matthew Davies [1975] Finance Director; David Anthony Fox [1967] Finance Director; Sean James Gavin [1971] Director [Irish]; David Hall [1970] Director; Harry James Hulton Lewis [1975] Director; Edward Patrick McKenna [1970] Director [Irish]; David Michael Mullin [1981] Director; Robert Charles Grenville Perrins [1965] Director; Anthony William Pidgley [1947] Director; Richard James Stearn [1968] Director; Justin Tibaldi [1970] Director

The Berkeley Group Holdings PLC
Incorporated: 7 July 2004 *Employees:* 2,617
Net Worth: £2,620,000,000 *Total Assets:* £4,776,500,224
Registered Office: Berkeley House, 19 Portsmouth Road, Cobham, Surrey, KT11 1JG
Activities: Activities of head offices
Officers: Jared Stephen Philip Cranney, Secretary; Sir John Alexander Armitt [1946] Director; Glyn Barker [1953] Director; Diana Sarah Brightmore-Armour [1954] Director; Rachel Sara Downey [1969] Director; Sean Ellis [1968] Director; Adrian Man-Kiu Li [1973] Director; Andrew William Myers [1964] Director; Alison Nimmo [1964] Director; Robert Charles Grenville Perrins [1965] Director; Anthony William Pidgley [1947] Director; Richard James Stearn [1968] Director; Justin Tibaldi [1970] Director; Paul Mark Vallone [1964] Director; Peter Sean Vernon [1959] Director; Veronica Judith Colleton Wadley [1952] Director; Karl Whiteman [1965] Director

Berkeley Group PLC (The)
Incorporated: 15 October 1979
Net Worth: £2,001,586,048 *Total Assets:* £4,548,788,224
Registered Office: Berkeley House, 19 Portsmouth Road, Cobham, Surrey, KT11 1JG
Activities: Activities of head offices
Parent: The Berkeley Group Holdings PLC
Officers: Jared Stephen Philip Cranney, Secretary; Sean Ellis [1968] Director; Robert Charles Grenville Perrins [1965] Director; Anthony William Pidgley [1947] Director; Richard James Stearn [1968] Director; Justin Tibaldi [1970] Director; Paul Mark Vallone [1964] Director; Karl Whiteman [1965] Director

Berkeley Homes (PCL) Limited
Incorporated: 15 September 2004
Net Worth: £56,945,000 *Total Assets:* £61,021,000
Registered Office: Berkeley House, 19 Portsmouth Road, Cobham, Surrey, KT11 1JG
Activities: Non-trading company
Parent: Berkeley Homes (Central London) Limited
Officers: Jared Stephen Philip Cranney, Secretary; Simon Piers Howard [1974] Director; Allen Edmond Michaels [1981] Director; Angus James Michie [1966] Director; Robert Charles Grenville Perrins [1965] Director; Anthony William Pidgley [1947] Director; Richard James Stearn [1968] Director; Paul Mark Vallone [1964] Director; Karl Whiteman [1965] Director; Dexter Whiting [1978] Director

Berkeley Homes (Southall) Limited
Incorporated: 29 November 2006 *Employees:* 62
Previous: St James West London Limited
Net Worth Deficit: £9,345,000 *Total Assets:* £174,928,992
Registered Office: Berkeley House, 19 Portsmouth Road, Cobham, Surrey, KT11 1JG
Activities: Development of building projects
Parent: Berkeley Homes Public Limited Company
Officers: Jared Stephen Philip Cranney, Secretary; Nigel Graham Davis [1968] Finance Director; Alison Jane Dowsett [1966] Director; Sean Ellis [1968] Director; Peter Kemkers [1971] Director; Damian Joseph Leydon [1967] Director; Robert Charles Grenville Perrins [1965] Director; Anthony William Pidgley [1947] Director; Richard James Stearn [1968] Director; Karl Whiteman [1965] Director

Berkeley Homes Public Limited Company
Incorporated: 6 October 2000 *Employees:* 1,529
Net Worth: £1,831,058,944 *Total Assets:* £3,215,473,920
Registered Office: 19 Portsmouth Road, Cobham, Surrey, KT11 1JG
Activities: Activities of head offices
Parent: TBG (3) 2009 Limited
Officers: Jared Stephen Philip Cranney, Secretary; Christopher Lee Gilbert [1971] Director; Angus James Michie [1966] Development Director; Robert Charles Grenville Perrins [1965] Director; Anthony William Pidgley [1947] Director; Andrew Michael Saunders-Davies [1958] Director; Peter James Smith [1971] Director; Richard James Stearn [1968] Director; Justin Tibaldi [1970] Director; Paul Mark Vallone [1964] Director; Karl Whiteman [1965] Director

Berkeley Seventy-Six Limited
Incorporated: 16 September 2004
Net Worth: £20,252,492 *Total Assets:* £20,493,448
Registered Office: Berkeley House, 19 Portsmouth Road, Cobham, Surrey, KT11 1JG
Activities: Non-trading company
Shareholders: Berkeley Homes Public Limited Company; St James Group Limited
Officers: Jared Stephen Philip Cranney, Secretary; David Martin Lowry [1981] Director; Robert Charles Grenville Perrins [1965] Director; Anthony William Pidgley [1947] Director; Richard James Stearn [1968] Director

Berkeley Two Hundred and Three Limited
Incorporated: 23 October 2014
Net Worth: £1,851,499 *Total Assets:* £97,515,000
Registered Office: Berkeley House, 19 Portsmouth Road, Cobham, Surrey, KT11 1JG
Activities: Other business support service activities n.e.c.
Parent: The Berkeley Group PLC
Officers: Jared Stephen Philip Cranney, Secretary; Alison Jane Dowsett [1966] Director; Sean Ellis [1968] Director; Peter Kemkers [1971] Director; Robert Charles Grenville Perrins [1965] Director; Anthony William Pidgley [1947] Director; Richard James Stearn [1968] Director

Berkhamsted Schools Group
Incorporated: 5 March 1959 *Employees:* 317
Net Worth: £34,173,000 *Total Assets:* £41,814,000
Registered Office: 6 Chesham Road, Berkhamsted, Herts, HP4 3AA
Activities: Pre-primary education
Officers: Stephen Robert Elliff, Secretary; David John Atkins [1966] Director/Chartered Surveyor; Professor Sarah-Jayne Blakemore [1974] Director/Neuroscientist; Anne Kathleen Fahy [1960] Director/Chief Financial Officer [Irish]; Dr Mark Alexander Fenton [1965] Director/Headmaster; Andrew Russell Hart [1962] Director/Solicitor; Gavin Crawford Laws [1957] Director; Kerry Musgrave [1968] Director/Legal Trainer; Christopher Nicholls [1954] Director/Retired; Stuart Stacy Rolland [1964] Managing Director; Sarah Ann Shields [1973] Director/VP and General Manager; Samantha Jeanne Tidey [1965] Director; Sandra Turner [1952] Director; Andrew John Wilcock [1955] Director/Headmaster; Jonathan David Williams [1966] Director/Partner

Berry Gardens Limited
Incorporated: 3 May 1983 *Employees:* 385
Net Worth: £9,841,000 *Total Assets:* £34,746,000
Registered Office: Tatlingbury Oast, Five Oak Green, Tonbridge, Kent, TN12 6RG
Activities: Wholesale of fruit and vegetables
Parent: Berry Gardens Growers Limited
Officers: Nicholas Allen, Secretary; Nicholas Allen [1971] Finance Director; Alastair Brooks [1961] Director/Farmer; Michael Allan Gibbon [1984] Sales Director; Jacqui Green [1973] Sales and Procurement Director; Graham Keniston-Cooper [1958] Director; Charles Richard Kidson [1975] Director/Farmer; David Stuart Northcroft [1977] Technical and Development Director; Robert Keith Pascall [1955] Director/Farmer; Marion Frances Regan [1960] Director/Farmer; Robin Peter Walker [1954] Director/Business Consultant

Berthon Boat Company Limited (The)
Incorporated: 26 October 1877 *Employees:* 127
Net Worth: £33,800,340 *Total Assets:* £47,408,296
Registered Office: The Shipyard, Lymington, Hants, SO41 3YL
Activities: Repair and maintenance of ships and boats
Officers: Karen Marie Light, Secretary; Brian Oliver John May [1961] Director; Dominic Oliver May [1963] Director

Bespak Europe Limited
Incorporated: 24 February 1998 *Employees:* 734
Net Worth: £107,336,000 *Total Assets:* £155,496,992
Registered Office: Suite B Breakspear Park, Breakspear Way, Hemel Hempstead, Herts, HP2 4TZ
Activities: Manufacture of basic pharmaceutical products
Parent: Consort Medical PLC
Officers: Andrew Leonard Jackson, Secretary; Dr Keyvan Djamarani [1961] Director; Jonathan Martin Glenn [1968] Company Director; Paul Andrew Hayes [1966] Director

Bespak Holdings Limited
Incorporated: 14 April 2000
Net Worth: £108,031,000 *Total Assets:* £148,196,992
Registered Office: Suite B Breakspear Park, Breakspear Way, Hemel Hempstead, Herts, HP2 4TZ
Activities: Activities of head offices
Parent: Consort Medical PLC
Officers: Andrew Leonard Jackson, Secretary; Jonathan Martin Glenn [1968] Director; Paul Andrew Hayes [1966] Director

Bewley Group Limited
Incorporated: 26 November 2002 *Employees:* 136
Net Worth: £43,760,340 *Total Assets:* £144,282,224
Registered Office: Inhurst House, Brimpton Road, Baughurst, Hants, RG26 5JJ
Activities: Construction of domestic buildings
Officers: Terence Richard Bacon, Secretary; Terence Richard Bacon [1967] Director; Andrew John Brooks [1971] Director; John Michael Hudson [1968] Director; Gregson Horace Locke [1956] Director

Bewley Homes PLC
Incorporated: 25 February 1991 *Employees:* 112
Net Worth: £72,832,744 *Total Assets:* £166,478,960
Registered Office: Inhurst House, Brimpton Road, Baughurst, Hants, RG26 5JJ
Activities: Construction of domestic buildings
Parent: Bewley Group Limited
Officers: Terence Richard Bacon, Secretary; Terence Richard Bacon [1967] Director; Andrew John Brooks [1971] Director; Peter Anthony Carpinelli [1965] Development Director; Gregson Horace Locke [1956] Director; Andrew John Morris [1961] Director; Elaine Stratford [1963] Sales Director; Simon Roger Taphouse [1971] Director

BFIM Limited
Incorporated: 11 October 2006
Net Worth: £902,698,944 *Total Assets:* £1,344,396,032
Registered Office: 2nd Floor, 400 Dashwood Lang Road, Bourne Business Park, Addlestone, Surrey, KT15 2HJ
Activities: Activities of other holding companies n.e.c.
Parent: Brambles Investment Ltd.
Officers: Peter Jonathon Caisley Bruford [1964] Director/Accountant; Pascal Huart [1963] Director/Regional Treasurer [Belgian]; Rafe Anthony Warren [1959] Director/Accountant

BFS Group Limited
Incorporated: 22 May 1929 *Employees:* 5,001
Net Worth: £183,226,000 *Total Assets:* £645,164,032
Registered Office: 814 Leigh Road, Slough, SL1 4BD
Activities: Non-specialised wholesale of food, beverages and tobacco
Officers: Thamer Hamandi, Secretary/Solicitor; Stephen David Bender [1964] Director/Accountant; Alison Brogan [1973] Finance Director; David Edward Cleasby [1962] Director/Accountant [South African]; Grant Leslie Cox [1967] Director [South African]; Andrew Robert Kemp [1954] Sales Director; Andrew Mark Selley [1965] Director; Norman James Wemyss [1960] Director

BH (City Forum) Limited
Incorporated: 22 February 2001
Net Worth Deficit: £2,642,000 *Total Assets:* £196,340,000
Registered Office: Berkeley House, 19 Portsmouth Road, Cobham, Surrey, KT11 1JG
Activities: Construction of domestic buildings
Parent: Berkeley Homes (Capital) PLC
Officers: Jared Stephen Philip Cranney, Secretary; Christopher Abel [1974] Director; Louis Charles Aldred [1984] Director; Brian Benfield [1958] Director; James Matthew Davies [1975] Finance Director; David Anthony Fox [1967] Finance Director; Harry James Hulton Lewis [1975] Director; Brian Keith McKenzie [1976] Director; Robert Charles Grenville Perrins [1965] Director; Anthony William Pidgley [1947] Director; Blake Sanders [1984] Director; John Paul Sanders [1971] Director; Richard James Stearn [1968] Director; Justin Tibaldi [1970] Director; Mark David Tomlinson [1962] Director

Bharat Forge International Limited
Incorporated: 3 December 2010 *Employees:* 13
Net Worth: £9,000,902 *Total Assets:* £112,049,960
Registered Office: Boston House, Business Center, 69-75 Boston Manor Road, Brentford, Middlesex, TW8 9JJ
Activities: Wholesale trade of motor vehicle parts and accessories
Officers: Kedar Prakash Dixit [1976] Director [Indian]; Sanjeev Gajanan Joglekar [1957] Director [Indian]; Amit Babasaheb Kalyani [1975] Director [Indian]; Babasaheb Neelkanth Kalyani [1949] Director [Indian]

BI Worldwide Holdings Limited
Incorporated: 6 June 2001 *Employees:* 246
Net Worth: £5,872,739 *Total Assets:* £37,491,824
Registered Office: 1 Vantage Court, Tickford Street, Newport Pagnell, Bucks, MK16 9EZ
Activities: Activities of head offices
Shareholder: Lawrence Guy Schoenecker
Officers: Jeffrey Brian Beegle [1951] Director/Vice President [American]; Michael Leslie Davies [1968] Director; Dale Patrick Kunz [1949] Director [American]; Lawrence Guy Schoenecker [1954] Director [American]; Nicola Urquhart [1970] Director/Chief Financial Officer

BI Worldwide Limited
Incorporated: 28 August 1979 *Employees:* 246
Net Worth: £13,452,707 *Total Assets:* £45,043,664
Registered Office: 1 Vantage Court, Tickford Street, Newport Pagnell, Bucks, MK16 9EZ
Activities: Travel agency activities
Shareholder: Lawrence Guy Schoenecker
Officers: Jeffrey Brian Beegle [1951] Director/Vice President [American]; Michael Leslie Davies [1968] Managing Director; Dale Patrick Kunz [1949] Director [American]; Lawrence Guy Schoenecker [1954] Director [American]; Nicola Urquhart [1970] Director/Chief Financial Officer

Bic U.K. Limited
Incorporated: 4 August 1944 *Employees:* 37
Net Worth: £13,859,000 *Total Assets:* £35,294,000
Registered Office: Bic UK Limited, Chaplin House, Widewater Place, Moorhall Road, Harefield, Middlesex, UB9 6NS
Activities: Wholesale of household goods (other than musical instruments) n.e.c
Parent: Societe Bic SA
Officers: Andrea Serafini, Secretary; Gonzalve Marie Leon Bich [1979] Director/General Manager [American]; Benoit Arnaud Marotte [1966] Director/General Manager [French]; Henri Claude Nicolau-Guillaumet [1969] Director/General Manager [French]

Bidcorp (UK) Limited
Incorporated: 17 March 1999 *Employees:* 5
Previous: Bidvest (UK) Limited
Net Worth: £44,911,000 *Total Assets:* £193,600,000
Registered Office: 814 Leigh Road, Slough, SL1 4BD
Activities: Non-specialised wholesale of food, beverages and tobacco
Parent: Bid Corporation Limited
Officers: Stephen David Bender, Secretary; Stephen David Bender [1964] Director/Accountant; David Edward Cleasby [1962] Director/Accountant [South African]; Andrew Mark Selley [1965] Managing Director

Bidcorp Foodservice (Europe) Limited
Incorporated: 25 February 2004
Previous: Bidvest Foodservice (Europe) Limited
Net Worth: £378,372,992 *Total Assets:* £825,315,968
Registered Office: 814 Leigh Road, Slough, SL1 4BD
Activities: Non-specialised wholesale of food, beverages and tobacco
Parent: Bid Corporation Limited
Officers: Stephen David Bender, Secretary/Accountant; Stephen David Bender [1964] Director/Accountant; David Edward Cleasby [1962] Director/Accountant [South African]; Andrew Mark Selley [1965] Director

Bidvest Freight UK Limited
Incorporated: 27 June 1928 *Employees:* 2
Previous: Bidcorp Limited
Net Worth: £2,838,179 *Total Assets:* £37,057,792
Registered Office: Unit 2 Langley Park, Waterside Drive, Langley, Slough, SL3 6AD
Activities: Activities of head offices
Parent: BID Services Division (UK) Limited
Officers: Paul Clement Scott, Secretary/Accountant; Anthony William Dawe [1965] Director/Accountant; Paul Clement Scott [1958] Director/Accountant; Mark John Steyn [1970] Director/Accountant

The Bidvest Group (UK) Limited
Incorporated: 7 July 2017
Net Worth: £12,418 *Total Assets:* £176,969,360
Registered Office: Unit 2 Langley Park, Waterside Drive, Langley, Slough, SL3 6AD
Activities: Activities of other holding companies n.e.c.
Officers: Paul Clement Scott, Secretary; Alan Fainman [1963] Director [South African]; Lindsay Peter Ralphs [1955] Director/Chief Executive Officer [South African]; Paul Clement Scott [1958] Director/Accountant; Trevor Graham Scruse [1960] Director [South African]; Mark John Steyn [1970] Director/Accountant; Alexandria Varley [1975] Director/Accountant

Bidvest Outsourced Services Limited
Incorporated: 7 March 1986 *Employees:* 2
Previous: Bidcorp Outsourced Services Limited
Net Worth: £22,541,812 *Total Assets:* £22,606,430
Registered Office: Unit 2 Langley Park, Waterside Drive, Langley, Slough, SL3 6AD
Activities: Activities of head offices
Parent: Bidvest Freight UK Limited
Officers: Paul Clement Scott, Secretary; Paul Clement Scott [1958] Director/Company Secretary; Alexandria Varley [1975] Director/Accountant

Bidvest Services Group (UK) Limited
Incorporated: 7 July 2017
Net Worth Deficit: £5,292 *Total Assets:* £172,964,608
Registered Office: Unit 2 Langley Park, Waterside Drive, Langley, Slough, SL3 6AD
Activities: Activities of other holding companies n.e.c.
Parent: The Bidvest Group (UK) Limited
Officers: Paul Clement Scott, Secretary; Alan Fainman [1963] Director [South African]; Lindsay Peter Ralphs [1955] Director/Chief Executive Officer [South African]; Paul Clement Scott [1958] Director/Accountant; Trevor Graham Scruse [1960] Director [South African]; Mark John Steyn [1970] Director/Accountant; Alexandria Varley [1975] Director/Accountant

Biffa Corporate Holdings Limited
Incorporated: 16 December 2005
Net Worth Deficit: £704,572,032 *Total Assets:* £565,246,016
Registered Office: Coronation Road, Cressex, High Wycombe, Bucks, HP12 3TZ
Activities: Collection of non-hazardous waste
Parent: Biffa Group Holdings (UK) Ltd
Officers: Richard Neil Pike [1969] Director/Chief Financial Officer; Michael Robert Mason Topham [1972] Director/Chief Executive Officer

Biffa Environmental Municipal Services Limited
Incorporated: 10 May 1967 *Employees:* 717
Previous: Cory Environmental Municipal Services Limited
Net Worth: £7,868,000 *Total Assets:* £27,585,000
Registered Office: Coronation Road, Cressex Business Park, High Wycombe, Bucks, HP12 3TZ
Activities: Collection of non-hazardous waste
Parent: Biffa Waste Services Limited
Officers: Rachael Hambrook, Secretary; Richard Neil Pike [1969] Director/Chief Financial Officer; Michael Robert Mason Topham [1972] Director/Chief Executive Officer

Biffa Group Holdings (UK) Limited
Incorporated: 2 October 2000
Previous: Biffa Limited
Net Worth: £511,986,304 *Total Assets:* £547,592,576
Registered Office: Coronation Road, Cressex, High Wycombe, Bucks, HP12 3TZ
Activities: Activities of head offices
Parent: Biffa Group Limited
Officers: Richard Neil Pike [1969] Director/Chief Financial Officer; Michael Robert Mason Topham [1972] Director/Chief Executive Officer

Biffa Group Limited
Incorporated: 25 October 2007
Net Worth: £859,400,000 *Total Assets:* £1,201,200,000
Registered Office: Coronation Road, Cressex, High Wycombe, Bucks, HP12 3TZ
Activities: Activities of head offices
Parent: Biffa Group Holdings Ltd
Officers: Rachael Hambrook, Secretary; Richard Neil Pike [1969] Director/Chief Financial Officer; Michael Robert Mason Topham [1972] Director/Chief Executive Officer

Biffa GS UK Holdings Limited
Incorporated: 9 January 2003
Previous: Greenstar UK Holdings Limited
Net Worth: £10,497,000 *Total Assets:* £92,156,000
Registered Office: Coronation Road, Cressex, High Wycombe, Bucks, HP12 3TZ
Activities: Collection of non-hazardous waste
Parent: Biffa GS Holdings Limited
Officers: Richard Neil Pike [1969] Director/Chief Financial Officer; Michael Robert Mason Topham [1972] Director/Chief Executive Officer

Biffa Holdings Limited
Incorporated: 22 November 1971
Net Worth: £378,456,992 *Total Assets:* £622,896,000
Registered Office: Coronation Road, Cressex, High Wycombe, Bucks, HP12 3TZ
Activities: Collection of non-hazardous waste
Parent: Reclamation & Disposal Ltd
Officers: Richard Neil Pike [1969] Director/Chief Financial Officer; Michael Robert Mason Topham [1972] Director/Chief Executive Officer

Biffa Municipal Limited
Incorporated: 12 November 2001 *Employees:* 2,314
Net Worth: £58,177,000 *Total Assets:* £133,547,000
Registered Office: Coronation Road, Cressex, High Wycombe, Bucks, HP12 3TZ
Activities: Collection of non-hazardous waste
Parent: Biffa GS UK Holdings Limited
Officers: Rachael Hambrook, Secretary; Stephen Cole [1972] Finance Director; Simon Crook [1961] Business Director; Peter Barnaby Dickson [1973] Development Director; Roger John Edwards [1969] Managing Director; David Simon Maidman [1963] Operation Director; Michael Robert Mason Topham [1972] Director/Chief Executive Officer

Biffa PLC
Incorporated: 18 August 2016 *Employees:* 7,773
Net Worth: £341,200,000 *Total Assets:* £1,054,300,032
Registered Office: Coronation Road, Cressex, High Wycombe, Bucks, HP12 3TZ
Activities: Activities of other holding companies n.e.c.
Officers: Rachael Hambrook, Secretary; Michael Charles Edward Averill [1951] Director; Gab Saturnio Barbaro [1971] Managing Director [Italian/Australian]; Carol Tredway Chesney [1962] Director [American]; Kenneth Lever [1953] Director; David Robert Martin [1951] Director; Richard Neil Pike [1969] Director/Chief Financial Officer; Michael Robert Mason Topham [1972] Director/Chief Financial Officer

Biffa Waste Management Limited
Incorporated: 4 October 1973
Net Worth: £60,486,000 *Total Assets:* £88,983,000
Registered Office: Coronation Road, Cressex, High Wycombe, Bucks, HP12 3TZ
Activities: Collection of non-hazardous waste
Parent: UK Waste Management Holdings Limited
Officers: Richard Neil Pike [1969] Director/Chief Financial Officer; Michael Robert Mason Topham [1972] Director/Chief Executive Officer

Biffa Waste Services Limited
Incorporated: 16 January 1969 *Employees:* 4,469
Net Worth: £427,800,000 *Total Assets:* £1,547,399,936
Registered Office: Coronation Road, Cressex, High Wycombe, Bucks, HP12 3TZ
Activities: Collection of non-hazardous waste
Parent: Biffa Holdings Ltd
Officers: Rachael Hambrook, Secretary; Richard Neil Pike [1969] Director/Chief Financial Officer; Michael Robert Mason Topham [1972] Director/Chief Executive Officer

Big Yellow (Battersea) Limited
Incorporated: 1 December 2014
Net Worth: £4,834,000 *Total Assets:* £26,725,000
Registered Office: 2 The Deans, Bridge Road, Bagshot, Surrey, GU19 5AT
Activities: Other letting and operating of own or leased real estate
Parent: Big Yellow Group PLC
Officers: Shauna Beavis, Secretary; James Ernest Gibson [1960] Director; Adrian Charles Jonathan Lee [1965] Director; John Richard Trotman [1977] Director; Nicholas John Vetch [1961] Director

Big Yellow Group PLC
Incorporated: 26 August 1998 *Employees:* 335
Net Worth: £981,148,032 *Total Assets:* £1,369,840,000
Registered Office: Unit 2 The Deans, Bridge Road, Bagshot, Surrey, GU19 5AT
Activities: Activities of head offices
Officers: Shauna Louise Beavis, Secretary; Timothy Nicholas Clark [1951] Director/Company Adviser; Richard Robert Cotton [1956] Director; James Ernest Gibson [1960] Director; Georgina Harvey [1964] Director; Stephen Richard Johnson [1963] Director/Retail Consultant; Adrian Charles Jonathan Lee [1965] Director; James Vincent Niblett [1958] Director; John Richard Trotman [1977] Director/Chartered Accountant; Nicholas John Vetch [1961] Director/Property Developer

Big Yellow Self Storage Company A Limited
Incorporated: 25 January 2012
Net Worth: £107,873,000 *Total Assets:* £301,947,008
Registered Office: Unit 2 The Deans, Bridge Road, Bagshot, Surrey, GU19 5AT
Activities: Other letting and operating of own or leased real estate
Parent: Big Yellow Group PLC
Officers: Shauna Louise Beavis, Secretary; James Ernest Gibson [1960] Director; Adrian Charles Jonathan Lee [1965] Director; John Richard Trotman [1977] Director/Chartered Accountant; Nicholas John Vetch [1961] Director/Property Developer

Big Yellow Self Storage Company M Limited
Incorporated: 4 December 2013
Net Worth: £71,254,000 *Total Assets:* £267,835,008
Registered Office: Unit 2 The Deans, Bridge Road, Bagshot, Surrey, GU19 5AT
Activities: Other letting and operating of own or leased real estate
Parent: Big Yellow Group PLC
Officers: Shauna Louise Beavis, Secretary; James Ernest Gibson [1960] Director; Adrian Charles Jonathan Lee [1965] Director; John Richard Trotman [1977] Director/Chartered Accountant

Bike Alert PLC
Incorporated: 21 December 1989 *Employees:* 36
Net Worth: £40,452,492 *Total Assets:* £45,941,720
Registered Office: 30 Optima Park, Thames Road, Crayford, Dartford, Kent, DA1 4QX
Activities: Sale, maintenance and repair of motorcycles and related parts and accessories
Major Shareholder: Chris Boyiantzeas
Officers: Susan Olive Marsh, Secretary; Chris Boyiantzeas [1955] Director/Import/Export Manager [Greek]; Christophoros Constantinou [1975] Director/Accountant [Cypriot]; Susan Olive Marsh [1957] Director/Import/Export Manager

R. J. and D. E. Billings Limited
Incorporated: 13 May 1986 *Employees:* 7
Net Worth: £4,824,991 *Total Assets:* £21,091,332
Registered Office: Gay Dawn Offices, Pennis Lane, Fawkham, Longfield, Kent, DA3 8LY
Activities: Hotels and similar accommodation
Officers: Stephen John Billings, Secretary; Andrew John Billings [1964] Director; Clive John Billings [1955] Director; Ronald John Billings [1960] Director/Manager; Stephen John Billings [1961] Director

Ferdinand Bilstein UK Limited
Incorporated: 16 March 1988 *Employees:* 247
Previous: Automotive Distributors Limited
Net Worth: £39,514,000 *Total Assets:* £84,026,000
Registered Office: 9 Wheelbarrow Park, Pattenden Lane, Marden, Kent, TN12 9QJ
Activities: Wholesale trade of motor vehicle parts and accessories
Parent: Bilstein Beteiligungs GmbH
Officers: Christopher John Dickinson, Secretary; Paul Philip Dodgson [1978] Operations Director; Martin Gorton [1965] Sales Director; Karsten Schuessler-Bilstein [1971] Director/Chairman [German]; Jan Tobias Siekermann [1979] Director [German]

BIMM 1 Limited
Incorporated: 18 February 2015 *Employees:* 1
Net Worth: £13,812,425 *Total Assets:* £82,605,400
Registered Office: 38-42 Brunswick Street West, Hove, E Sussex, BN3 1EL
Activities: First-degree level higher education
Parent: BIMM Topco Limited
Officers: Adam Peter Carswell, Secretary; Adam Peter Carswell [1968] Director/Chartered Accountant; David Jones-Owen [1980] Director; Antony Ronald Wadsworth [1956] Music Consultant and Director

BIMM Holdings Limited
Incorporated: 1 March 2010
Net Worth: £19,527,066 *Total Assets:* £32,390,748
Registered Office: 38-42 Brunswick Street West, Hove, E Sussex, BN3 1EL
Activities: First-degree level higher education
Parent: BIMM 1 Limited
Officers: Adam Peter Carswell, Secretary; Adam Peter Carswell [1968] Director/Chartered Accountant; David Jones-Owen [1980] Director

BIMM Limited
Incorporated: 20 August 2007 *Employees:* 278
Net Worth Deficit: £32,090,816 *Total Assets:* £66,888,728
Registered Office: 38-42 Brunswick Street West, Hove, E Sussex, BN3 1EL
Activities: First-degree level higher education
Parent: BIMM Group Limited
Officers: Adam Peter Carswell, Secretary; Adam Peter Carswell [1968] Director/Chartered Accountant; Vaseema Hamilton [1960] Director/College Principal; David Jones-Owen [1980] Director

BIMM Topco Limited
Incorporated: 7 July 2016 *Employees:* 423
Net Worth Deficit: £5,872,661 *Total Assets:* £103,096,376
Registered Office: 38-42 Brunswick Street West, Hove, E Sussex, BN3 1EL
Activities: Other business support service activities n.e.c.
Shareholders: BB Shelf 4 LLP; Sovereign Capital IV Limited Partnership
Officers: David Jones-Owen, Secretary; Adam Peter Carswell [1968] Director/Chartered Accountant; Alistair Cox [1961] Director; Dr Jeremy John Frampton [1965] Director; Mark Andrew Hunt [1960] Director; David Jones-Owen [1980] Director; Antony Ronald Wadsworth [1956] Director

Binder Bidco Limited
Incorporated: 26 May 2016
Net Worth Deficit: £2,995,554 *Total Assets:* £39,872,776
Registered Office: A1 Omega Enterprise Park, Electron Way, Chandler's Ford, Eastleigh, Hants, SO53 4SE
Activities: Financial management
Parent: Binder Holdco Ltd
Officers: James Ross Ancell [1953] Director; Edward James Timothy Brett [1967] Director/Investment Manager; Stephen Charles Clasby [1965] Director; Donald William Coates [1960] Director; James Alan Cunningham [1964] Director/Investment Manager; Wayne Roberts [1972] Director/Accountant [New Zealander]

Binder Holdco Limited
Incorporated: 26 May 2016 *Employees:* 223
Net Worth Deficit: £5,839,205 *Total Assets:* £52,662,424
Registered Office: A1 Omega Enterprise Park, Electron Way, Chandler's Ford, Eastleigh, Hants, SO53 4SE
Activities: Activities of other holding companies n.e.c.
Parent: Elysian Capital II LP
Officers: James Ross Ancell [1953] Director; Edward James Timothy Brett [1967] Director/Investment Manager; Stephen Charles Clasby [1965] Director; Donald William Coates [1960] Director; James Alan Cunningham [1964] Director/Investment Manager; Wayne Roberts [1972] Director/Accountant [New Zealander]

Bio Energy (UK) Limited
Incorporated: 25 March 1997
Net Worth: £4,148,361 *Total Assets:* £47,917,588
Registered Office: Chancery House, 199 Silbury Boulevard, Milton Keynes, Bucks, MK9 1JL
Activities: Activities of other holding companies n.e.c.
Parent: EDL Holdings (UK) Limited
Officers: James Christopher Harman [1968] Director [Australian]; David Truelove [1975] Director

Bio Products Laboratory Holdings Limited
Incorporated: 16 October 2002 *Employees:* 2,893
Net Worth: £149,928,000 *Total Assets:* £434,364,000
Registered Office: Bio Products Laboratory, Dagger Lane, Elstree, Herts, WD6 3BX
Activities: Other human health activities
Shareholders: Naga UK Bidco Limited; Naga UK Bidco Limited
Officers: Kieu Hoang [1944] Director [American]; Kevin Lane [1961] Director/President [American]; Xu Wu [1967] Director [Chinese]

Bio Products Laboratory Limited
Incorporated: 11 August 2010
Net Worth: £74,935,000 *Total Assets:* £302,643,008
Registered Office: c/o Bio Products Laboratory, Dagger Lane, Elstree, Herts, WD6 3BX
Activities: Other business support service activities n.e.c.
Parent: Bio Products Laboratory Holdings Limited
Officers: Kieu Hoang [1944] Director [American]; Kevin Lane [1961] Director/President [American]; Xu Wu [1967] Director [Chinese]

Bio-Rad Laboratories Limited
Incorporated: 11 April 1995 *Employees:* 146
Net Worth: £21,641,000 *Total Assets:* £41,961,000
Registered Office: 3rd and 4th Floor, The Junction, Station Road, Watford, Herts, WD17 1ET
Activities: Non-specialised wholesale trade
Parent: Bio-Metrics (U.K.) Limited
Officers: Philip Howard [1957] Director/Regional Sales Manager; Norman David Schwartz [1950] Director/C.E.O. & President [American]

Biocompatibles International Limited
Incorporated: 3 April 1992
Net Worth: £76,370,000 *Total Assets:* £78,690,000
Registered Office: Chapman House, Farnham Business Park, Farnham, Surrey, GU9 8QL
Activities: Other business support service activities n.e.c.
Parent: BTG PLC
Officers: Elaine Maureen Johnston, Secretary; Elaine Maureen Johnston [1976] Director/Lawyer [Irish]; Timothy John Martel [1975] Director/Accountant; Peter William Stratford [1963] Director/Scientist; John Richard Sylvester [1964] Director

Biocompatibles UK Limited
Incorporated: 16 October 2001 *Employees:* 299
Net Worth: £21,356,000 *Total Assets:* £221,192,992
Registered Office: Chapman House, Farnham Business Park, Weydon Lane, Farnham, Surrey, GU9 8QL
Activities: Other manufacturing n.e.c.
Parent: BTG International (Holdings) Limited
Officers: Elaine Maureen Johnston, Secretary; Elaine Maureen Johnston [1976] Director/Lawyer [Irish]; Timothy John Martel [1975] Director/Accountant; Peter William Stratford [1963] Director/Scientist; John Richard Sylvester [1964] Director

Biogen (UK) Limited
Incorporated: 8 November 2005 *Employees:* 94
Net Worth Deficit: £5,872,000 *Total Assets:* £39,763,000
Registered Office: Milton Parc, Milton Ernest, Beds, MK44 1YU
Activities: Production of electricity
Parent: Biogen Holdings Limited
Officers: Adam Feneley [1980] Finance Director; Cathryn Lister [1982] Compliance Director; Simon Musther [1958] Commercial Director; Graeme Kenneth Charles Vincent [1965] Operations Director

Biogen Holdings Limited
Incorporated: 22 June 2012 *Employees:* 94
Net Worth: £21,873,000 *Total Assets:* £39,454,000
Registered Office: Milton Parc, Milton Ernest, Bedford, MK44 1YU
Activities: Activities of extraterritorial organisations and bodies
Parent: Ancala Bioenergy Limited
Officers: Adam Feneley [1980] Finance Director; Cathryn Lister [1982] Compliance Director; Simon Musther [1958] Commercial Director; Graeme Kenneth Charles Vincent [1965] Operations Director

Biogen Idec Limited
Incorporated: 19 May 1980 *Employees:* 234
Net Worth: £50,516,000 *Total Assets:* £117,888,000
Registered Office: Innovation House, 70 Norden Road, Maidenhead, Berks, SL6 4AY
Activities: Agents specialised in the sale of other particular products
Parent: Biogen Inc.
Officers: Lorraine Deborah Barr [1966] Director; Simon Charlton Beck [1958] Director; Johanna Friedl-Naderer [1968] Director [Austrian]; Steven John Green [1977] Finance Director; Trevor Anthony Mill [1971] Director/Pharmacist; Terry Milton O'Regan [1966] Director; Jonathan Mark Randell [1971] Director; Neil Raymond Sisak [1971] Senior Director, Head of Finance Europe [American]

Biomerieux UK Limited
Incorporated: 19 July 1972 *Employees:* 108
Net Worth: £8,694,751 *Total Assets:* £25,999,608
Registered Office: Grafton House, Unit H, Grafton Way, Basingstoke, Hants, RG22 6HY
Activities: Other manufacturing n.e.c.
Parent: Biomerieux SA
Officers: Ivan Chemarin, Secretary; Ivan Chemarin [1967] Finance Director [French]; Veronique Audrey Comte [1978] Finance Director [French]; Jean-Louis Tissier [1960] Managing Director [French]

Birchwood Garages Limited
Incorporated: 18 March 1996 *Employees:* 163
Net Worth: £2,632,000 *Total Assets:* £24,533,000
Registered Office: Lottbridge Drove, Eastbourne, E Sussex, BN23 6PX
Activities: Activities of head offices
Major Shareholder: Michael John Hunt
Officers: Simon Derek Rebbetts, Secretary; Chester John Hunt [1969] Director; Ian Kenneth Sexton [1956] Director/Motor Trader

Birchwood Omnia Limited
Incorporated: 23 June 2000
Net Worth: £1,374,770,944 *Total Assets:* £1,374,844,032
Registered Office: Hanson House, 14 Castle Hill, Maidenhead, Berks, SL6 4JJ
Activities: Activities of construction holding companies
Parent: HeidelbergCement UK Holding Limited
Officers: Wendy Fiona Rogers, Secretary; Nicholas Arthur Dawe Benning-Prince [1974] Director/Chartered Accountant; Robert Charles Dowley [1972] Director/Chartered Accountant; Edward Alexander Gretton [1970] Director; Dr Carsten Matthias Wendt [1976] Director [German]

Birds Eye Limited
Incorporated: 18 August 1938 *Employees:* 578
Net Worth: £194,418,000 *Total Assets:* £278,430,016
Registered Office: 1 New Square, Bedfont Lakes Business Park, Feltham, Middlesex, TW14 8HA
Activities: Manufacture of other food products n.e.c.
Parent: Nomad Foods Europe Limited
Officers: Edward John Heaton Marriott, Secretary; Craig Hamilton [1971] Director/Factory General Manager; Wayne Brian Hudson [1964] Managing Director; Sarah Ann Pollard [1974] Finance Director

Birmingham Schools Partnership Limited
Incorporated: 14 October 1999
Net Worth Deficit: £1,576,000 *Total Assets:* £41,926,000
Registered Office: 8 White Oak Square, London Road, Swanley, Kent, BR8 7AG
Activities: Development of building projects
Parent: Birmingham Schools Partnership (Holdings) Limited
Officers: Gaynor Birley Smith [1966] Investment Director; Richard Keith Sheehan [1975] Investment Director

Bishops U.K. Limited
Incorporated: 23 December 2003
Net Worth: £7,068,616 *Total Assets:* £100,348,200
Registered Office: 45 Westerham Road, Sevenoaks, Kent, TN13 2QB
Activities: Buying and selling of own real estate
Parent: SQIB Limited
Officers: Christopher James Payne, Secretary; Keith John Barber [1974] Finance Director; Gary Humphreys [1965] Underwriting Director; Kevin Ronald Spencer [1965] Director

Bishopshalt School
Incorporated: 6 October 2011 *Employees:* 165
Net Worth: £17,860,696 *Total Assets:* £20,159,984
Registered Office: Royal Lane, Hillingdon, Uxbridge, Middlesex, UB8 3RF
Activities: General secondary education
Officers: Irene Denise Warnock, Secretary; Abdi Abby [1964] Director; Tahira Naheed Ansari [1970] Director; Gail Bond [1957] Director; Lyndon Bray [1969] Director/Police Officer; Andrew Brown [1950] Director/Teacher; Michelle Brown [1969] Director/School Administrator; Peter Charles Coombs [1955] Director/Teacher; Michael John Deighton [1962] Director/Teacher; Lydia Mary Holland [1952] Director/Retired; Professor William Leahy [1959] Director/Academic; Nancy Kirsten Rawlings [1967] Director; Kim David Rowe [1961] Director/Headteacher; Julie Ann Spikings [1967] Director/Deputy Headteacher; Nicola St Paul [1980] Director/International Marketing Manager; Peter Charles William Underwood [1937] Director/Retired; Stephen White [1989] Director/Student Welfare Officer

Biwater Holdings Limited
Incorporated: 28 March 1968 *Employees:* 384
Net Worth: £14,300,000 *Total Assets:* £57,000,000
Registered Office: Biwater House, Station Approach, Dorking, Surrey, RH4 1TZ
Activities: Activities of head offices
Shareholders: David Frederick Wigram White; Lady Gillian Denise White; Lars Alexander Haussmann; Markus Stutz
Officers: Jonathan Stuart Lamb, Secretary; John Justin Jones [1966] Director; Jonathan Stuart Lamb [1967] Director/Solicitor; Paul Barry Stevens [1966] Finance Director; Adrian Edwin White [1942] Director/Engineer; Alastair Graham White [1984] Business Development Director; Richard Barrington White [1984] Director

Biwater International Limited
Incorporated: 3 April 1970 *Employees:* 167
Net Worth: £44,509,000 *Total Assets:* £64,142,000
Registered Office: Biwater House, Station Approach, Dorking, Surrey, RH4 1TZ
Activities: Water collection, treatment and supply
Parent: Biwater Holdings Ltd
Officers: Felicity Mary Monro, Secretary; Justine Margaret Edwards [1957] Director/Accountant; Giles Henry Jackson [1956] Director; Mark Benedict Robinson [1977] Finance Director; Richard Farley Smith [1958] Director; Paul Barry Stevens [1966] Director/Chief Financial Officer; Adrian Edwin White [1942] Director/Engineer; Alastair Graham White [1984] Business Development Director

Biwater Overseas Limited
Incorporated: 5 June 1991
Net Worth Deficit: £705,858 *Total Assets:* £22,241,000
Registered Office: Biwater House, Station Approach, Dorking, Surrey, RH4 1TZ
Activities: Activities of head offices
Parent: Biwater Holdings Ltd
Officers: Jonathan Stuart Lamb, Secretary; Jonathan Stuart Lamb [1967] Director/Solicitor; Adrian Edwin White [1942] Director

BL Bottling Holdings UK Limited
Incorporated: 21 April 2016
Net Worth: £6,767,248,384 *Total Assets:* £7,980,585,984
Registered Office: Pemberton House, Bakers Road, Uxbridge, Middlesex, UB8 1EZ
Activities: Activities of other holding companies n.e.c.
Parent: Bottling Holdings Europe Limited
Officers: Paul Van Reesch, Secretary; Frank Govaerts [1961] Director [Belgian]; Joyce Marie King-Lavinder [1959] Director [American]; Paul Van Reesch [1976] Director; Edward Owen Walker [1967] Director

BL Wind Limited
Incorporated: 9 May 2013
Net Worth Deficit: £5,939,000 *Total Assets:* £30,665,000
Registered Office: 8 White Oak Square, London Road, Swanley, Kent, BR8 7AG
Activities: Production of electricity
Parent: JLEAG Wind Limited
Officers: Christopher Holmes [1976] Investment Adviser/Director; Joseph Mark Linney [1958] Director/Chartered Quantity Surveyor

Black & Decker
Incorporated: 25 August 1934 *Employees:* 51
Net Worth: £168,666,000 *Total Assets:* £527,616,992
Registered Office: 210 Bath Road, Slough, Berks, SL1 3YD
Activities: Manufacture of electric domestic appliances
Parent: Black & Decker Europe
Officers: Erica Lynn Brennan [1974] Director/Chief Financial Officer [Canadian]; Mark Richard Smiley [1977] Director/General Manager UK & ROI

Black & Decker Europe
Incorporated: 21 August 1984 *Employees:* 172
Net Worth: £674,678,976 *Total Assets:* £1,330,647,040
Registered Office: 210 Bath Road, Slough, Berks, SL1 3YD
Activities: Activities of head offices
Parent: Black & Decker International
Officers: Erica Lynn Brennan [1974] Director/Chief Financial Officer [Canadian]; Mark Richard Smiley [1977] Director/General Manager UK & ROI

Black & Decker Finance
Incorporated: 10 May 1973
Net Worth: £400,071,296 *Total Assets:* £555,758,656
Registered Office: 210 Bath Road, Slough, Berks, SL1 3YD
Activities: Activities of head offices
Parent: Stanley Black & Decker Inc.
Officers: Steven John Costello [1980] Director/Chartered Accountant; Mark Richard Smiley [1977] Director/General Manager UK & ROI; Amit Kumar Sood [1978] Director/Accountant; Catherine S Torello [1966] Director/Assistant Treasurer [American]

Black & Decker International
Incorporated: 20 November 1925
Net Worth: £649,417,024 *Total Assets:* £1,113,223,040
Registered Office: 210 Bath Road, Slough, Berks, SL1 3YD
Activities: Manufacture of power-driven hand tools
Parent: Stanley Black & Decker UK Group Ltd
Officers: Steven John Costello [1980] Director/Chartered Accountant; Mark Richard Smiley [1977] Director/General Manager UK & ROI; Amit Kumar Sood [1978] Director/Accountant; Catherine S Torello [1966] Director/Assistant Treasurer [American]

Black & Decker International Finance (UK) Limited
Incorporated: 28 October 2009
Net Worth: £206,433,904 *Total Assets:* £243,247,456
Registered Office: 210 Bath Road, Slough, Berks, SL1 3YD
Activities: Other professional, scientific and technical activities n.e.c.
Parent: Black & Decker International Finance Holdings (UK) Limited
Officers: Steven John Costello [1980] Director/Chartered Accountant; Mark Richard Smiley [1977] Director/General Manager UK & ROI; Amit Kumar Sood [1978] Director/Accountant

Black & Decker International Finance Holdings (UK) Limited
Incorporated: 1 December 2009
Net Worth: £16,356,309 *Total Assets:* £197,285,120
Registered Office: 210 Bath Road, Slough, Berks, SL1 3YD
Activities: Activities of head offices
Parent: Stanley Black & Decker Inc.
Officers: Steven John Costello [1980] Director/Chartered Accountant; Mark Richard Smiley [1977] Director/General Manager UK & ROI; Amit Kumar Sood [1978] Director/Accountant

Black & Veatch Limited
Incorporated: 23 February 1996 *Employees:* 597
Net Worth: £20,756,000 *Total Assets:* £84,677,000
Registered Office: 60 High Street, Redhill, Surrey, RH1 1SH
Activities: Construction of water projects
Officers: Francis Declan Finbar Tempany McCormack, Secretary; David Scott MacDonald Aitken [1966] Director/Civil Engineer; Dr Hoe Wai Cheong [1956] Director [Malaysian]; Robert Allan Joyce [1976] Director/Accountant; Ian Michael Robinson [1965] Director/Accountant; Christopher William Timpson Scott [1962] Director/Chartered Civil Engineer; Cindy Lynn Wallis-Lage [1962] Director [American]

W.E.Black Limited
Incorporated: 7 December 1946 *Employees:* 23
Net Worth: £208,373,440 *Total Assets:* £220,541,120
Registered Office: Hawridge Place, Hawridge Common, Hawridge, Chesham, Bucks, HP5 2ZD
Activities: Construction of domestic buildings
Major Shareholder: Eric John Spencer Gadsden
Officers: Judith Long, Secretary; Eric John Spencer Gadsden [1944] Director; Sarah Louise Gadsden [1985] Planning Director; Judith Elizabeth Long [1955] Finance Director; James Ian Lyons [1963] Construction Director

Black Tip Capital Holdings Limited
Incorporated: 7 September 2006
Net Worth: £87,059,000 *Total Assets:* £155,918,000
Registered Office: Marlin House, 16-22 Grafton Road, Worthing, W Sussex, BN11 1QP
Activities: Activities of head offices
Officers: Charlotte Taggart, Secretary; Craig Anthony Buick [1969] Finance Director [British/Australian]; Peter Charles Richardson [1959] Director; Kenneth John Stannard [1966] Director

Blackberry UK Limited
Incorporated: 22 June 2000 *Employees:* 253
Net Worth: £307,551,264 *Total Assets:* £568,162,496
Registered Office: Ground Floor, The Pearce Building, West Street, Maidenhead, Berks, SL6 1RL
Activities: Wireless telecommunications activities
Parent: Blackberry Limited
Officers: Gregory Best, Secretary; Steven Capelli [1957] Director/Business Person [American]; Satwinder Rai [1969] Director/Business Person [Canadian]

Blackfen School for Girls
Incorporated: 2 March 2012 *Employees:* 157
Net Worth: £19,230,000 *Total Assets:* £21,128,000
Registered Office: Blackfen School for Girls, Blackfen Road, Sidcup, Kent, DA15 9NU
Activities: General secondary education
Officers: Jane Andrews [1954] Director; Launa Joy Ashdown [1960] Director/Delivery Driver; Kim Brewer [1973] Director/Teacher; Matthew Francis William Brown [1964] Director/Teacher; Anita Dhorajiwala [1972] Director/Regulatory Manager; Stuart James Fitz Generald [1950] Director/Lecturer; Danielle Moore [1972] Director/Local Government Employee - School Improvement; Trevor Victor Perrin [1947] Director/Semi Retired; Janet Mary Phelps [1950] Director/Casual Clerk - Bexley Clerkship Practice; Robert Joseph Shaw [1980] Director/Teacher; William Anthony Stone [1959] Director; Lee Christopher Thomas [1971] Director; Carol Susan Townsend [1954] Director/Housewife; Louise Clare Twiner [1973] Director/Relationship Support Manager

Blackmoor Estate Limited (The)
Incorporated: 30 October 1924 *Employees:* 40
Net Worth: £22,520,840 *Total Assets:* £29,596,446
Registered Office: Estate Office, Blackmoor, Liss, Hants, GU33 6BS
Activities: Growing of cereals (except rice), leguminous crops and oil seeds
Officers: Victoria Emma Baum, Secretary; Victoria Emma Baum [1971] Director/Lawyer; Paul David Cherry [1961] Director/Farmer; The Hon Timothy John Palmer [1953] Director/Farmer; Viscount William Lewis Palmer Wolmer [1971] Managing Director

Blackstown Holdings Limited
Incorporated: 8 January 2015 *Employees:* 701
Previous: Graham Care Group Limited
Net Worth: £101,012,120 *Total Assets:* £170,688,736
Registered Office: 20 Cranley Road, Hersham, Walton on Thames, Surrey, KT12 5BP
Activities: Activities of other holding companies n.e.c.
Shareholders: William Ernest Graham; Karen Elizabeth Graham
Officers: Dr Karen Elizabeth Graham [1962] Director/Medical Doctor; William Ernest Graham [1961] Director

Blackwell Publishing (Holdings) Limited
Incorporated: 22 February 1996
Net Worth: £46,408,000 *Total Assets:* £46,408,000
Registered Office: The Atrium, Southern Gate, Chichester, W Sussex, PO19 8SQ
Activities: Other service activities n.e.c.
Parent: Wiley Europe Ltd
Officers: Caroline Jane McPhee, Secretary; Ursula D'Arcy [1970] Financial Director [Irish]; Rosamund Claire Johnson [1961] Director; Philip Jeffrey Mac Kisray [1960] Director; John Anthony Kritzmacher [1960] Director [American]

Blackwell Science (Overseas Holdings) Limited
Incorporated: 22 February 1996
Net Worth: £106,321,000 *Total Assets:* £106,719,000
Registered Office: The Atrium, Southern Gate, Chichester, W Sussex, PO19 8SQ
Activities: Other service activities n.e.c.
Parent: Blackwell Science Ltd
Officers: Caroline Jane McPhee, Secretary; Ursula D'Arcy [1970] Financial Director [Irish]; Rosamund Claire Johnson [1961] Director; Philip Jeffrey Mac Kisray [1960] Director; John Anthony Kritzmacher [1960] Director [American]

Blackwell Science Limited
Incorporated: 15 February 1939
Net Worth: £48,692,000 *Total Assets:* £49,430,000
Registered Office: The Atrium, Southern Gate, Chichester, W Sussex, PO19 8SQ
Activities: Publishing of consumer and business journals and periodicals
Parent: Blackwell Publishing (Holdings) Ltd
Officers: Caroline Jane McPhee, Secretary; Ursula D'Arcy [1970] Financial Director [Irish]; Rosamund Claire Johnson [1961] Director; Philip Jeffrey Mac Kisray [1960] Director; John Anthony Kritzmacher [1960] Director [American]

Blake Morgan Group LLP
Incorporated: 21 March 2014 *Employees:* 881
Net Worth: £36,782,000 *Total Assets:* £67,034,000
Registered Office: Harbour Court, Compass Road, North Harbour, Portsmouth, PO6 4ST
Officers: Niall Patrick Brook [1956] Member; Elizabeth Anne Carr [1960] Member; Bruce John Potter [1958] Member; Simon Grant Treherne [1961] Member; Michael Vernon Wilson [1961] Member; Bradley Albuery [1963] LLP Member; Stephen Thomas Archibald [1971] LLP Member; Jill Bainbridge [1970] LLP Member; James Robert Harrison Bessey [1968] LLP Member; Helen Elizabeth Bunker [1973] LLP Member; Simon Nicholas Burge [1960] LLP Member; Ronald Langdon Burgess [1968] LLP Member; Paul Matthew Caldicott [1970] LLP Member; Deborah Jane Castle [1957] LLP Member; Robert Paul Cherry [1967] LLP Member; Steven William Cole [1971] LLP Member; Guy Stanford Page Constant [1967] LLP Member; Anthony Gerard Coyne [1962] LLP Member; Daniel Jamie Curtis [1980] LLP Member; Prashant Dave [1973] LLP Member; Joanne Frances Davies [1964] LLP Member; Dr John Stewart Deech [1943] LLP Member; Penri Desscan [1965] LLP Member; Philip David Diamond [1952] LLP Member; Christopher Patrick Dolan [1961] LLP Member; William James Linfield Downing [1970] LLP Member; Susan Jane Dryden [1961] LLP Member; James Fraser Richard Egan [1975] LLP Member; Stojan Paul Essex [1975] LLP Member; Andrew Farmery [1974] LLP Member; Lee Andrew Fisher [1973] LLP Member; Timothy John Forer [1962] LLP Member; Rupert Michael Graham-Evans [1967] LLP Member; James Ernan Fairchild Greig [1967] LLP Member; Nigel Thomas Griffiths [1960] LLP Member; Flora Allegra Grossman [1968] LLP Member; Rachel Clarke Gwilliam [1976] LLP Member; John Hamilton [1971] LLP Member; Sara Virginia Hanrahan [1967] LLP Member; Alan John Harlow [1960] LLP Member; Michael Robin Havard [1957] LLP Member; James Edward Hawkeswood [1974] LLP Member; Mark Bowden Hepworth [1953] LLP Member; Mark Stuart Hiley [1960] LLP Member; Louise Howells [1976] LLP Member; Richard Edwin Humphreys [1963] LLP Member; Kathryn Elizabeth James [1979] LLP Member; Meera Jansen [1971] LLP Member; Philip Jeffrey Jardine [1961] LLP Member; Sian Denise Jones [1966] LLP Member; Rajiv Joshi [1976] LLP Member; Paula Marie Kathrens [1973] LLP Member; Martin Colin Kay [1956] LLP Member; Claire Lamkin [1974] LLP Member; Nicholas John Leale [1974] LLP Member; Tomos Emyr Lewis [1957] LLP Member; Rebecca Jane McCabe-North [1981] LLP Member; Simon Paul McCann [1969] LLP Member; Alison Jane McClure [1962] LLP Member; Guthrie Ewing McGruer [1955] LLP Member; Edward Nicholas McMullen [1975] LLP Member; Sadak Miah [1969] LLP Member; Graham John Miles [1956] LLP Member; Andrew Ian Farquharson Miscampbell [1959] LLP Member; David Alexander Mortimer [1956] LLP Member; Lorna Elizabeth Munro [1961] LLP Member; Sean Gavin Palka [1966] LLP Member; Alison Bridget Patten-Hall [1965] LLP Member; Sarah Vivien Peacock [1958] LLP Member; Lawrence Stephen Phillips [1956] LLP Member; Eve Maria Piffaretti [1969] LLP Member; Christine Ann Plews [1963] LLP Member; Richard Alan Portlock [1963] LLP Member; Christopher David Charles Potts [1962] LLP Member; Kimberley Anne Provan [1972] LLP Member; Claire Leanne Rawle [1966] LLP Member; Geoffrey Bennett Reed [1958] LLP Member; Joanna Rees [1969] LLP Member; Sarah Caroline Rees [1966] LLP Member; Penny Rinta-Suksi [1970] LLP Member; Daniel John Scognamigilo [1972] LLP Member; Kathryn Jane Shimmin [1964] LLP Member; Kate Beth Silverman [1969] LLP Member; Arshdeep Kaur Singh [1970] LLP Member; Douglas James Smith [1964] LLP Member; Matthew James Tyndall Smith [1969] LLP Member; William Oliver Hugo Sowton [1968] LLP Member; Mark David Spash [1958] LLP Member; Neil Jonathan Stafford [1968] LLP Member; Simon Jonathan Staples [1969] LLP Member; Simon Jeremy Stokes [1963] LLP Member; Manoj Styche-Patel [1971] LLP Member; Jamie Piers Sutton [1953] LLP Member; Jeremy Forsythe Taylor [1961] LLP Member; Jessica Anne Rose Tresham [1977] LLP Member; Richard Samuel Marlar Wade [1968] LLP Member; David Stephen Thomas Wadsworth [1969] LLP Member; Stephanie Anne Evelyn Walls [1960] LLP Member; Michael Philip Ward [1970] LLP Member

Blake Morgan LLP
Incorporated: 21 March 2014 *Employees:* 660
Net Worth: £24,801,000 *Total Assets:* £51,801,000
Registered Office: Harbour Court, Compass Road, North Harbour, Portsmouth, PO6 4ST
Officers: Niall Patrick Brook [1956] Member; Elizabeth Anne Carr [1960] Member; Bruce John Potter [1958] Member; Simon Grant Treherne [1961] Member; Michael Vernon Wilson [1961] Member; Bradley Albuery [1963] LLP Member; Stephen Thomas Archibald [1971] LLP Member; Jill Bainbridge [1970] LLP Member; James Robert Harrison Bessey [1968] LLP Member; Helen Elizabeth Bunker [1973] LLP Member; Simon Nicholas Burge [1960] LLP Member; Ronald Langdon Burgess [1968] LLP Member; Paul Matthew Caldicott [1970] LLP Member; Deborah Jane Castle [1957] LLP Member; Robert Paul Cherry [1967] LLP Member; Steven William Cole [1971] LLP Member; Guy Stanford Page Constant [1967] LLP Member; Anthony Gerard Coyne [1962] LLP Member; Daniel Jamie Curtis [1980] LLP Member; Prashant Dave [1973] LLP Member; Joanne Frances Davies [1964] LLP Member; Dr John Stewart Deech [1943] LLP Member; Penri Desscan [1965] LLP Member; Philip David Diamond [1952] LLP Member; Christopher Patrick Dolan [1961] LLP Member; William James Linfield Downing [1970] LLP Member; Susan Jane Dryden [1961] LLP Member; James Fraser Richard Egan [1975] LLP Member; Stojan Paul Essex [1975] LLP Member; Andrew Farmery [1974] LLP Member; Lee Andrew Fisher [1973] LLP Member; Timothy John Forer [1962] LLP Member; Rupert Michael Graham-Evans [1967] LLP Member; James Ernan Fairchild Greig [1967] LLP Member; Nigel Thomas Griffiths [1960] LLP Member; Flora Allegra Grossman [1968] LLP Member; Rachel Clarke Gwilliam [1976] LLP Member; John Hamilton [1971] LLP Member; Sara Virginia Hanrahan [1967] LLP Member; Alan John Harlow [1960] LLP Member; Robin Havard [1957] LLP Member; James Edward Hawkeswood [1974] LLP Member; Mark Bowden Hepworth [1953] LLP Member; Mark Stuart Hiley [1960] LLP Member; Louise Howells [1976] LLP Member; Richard Edwin Humphreys [1963] LLP Member; Kathryn Elizabeth James [1979] LLP Member; Meera Jansen [1971] LLP Member; Philip Jeffrey Jardine [1961] LLP Member; Sian Denise Jones [1966] LLP Member; Rajiv Joshi [1976] LLP Member; Paula Marie Kathrens [1973] LLP Member; Martin Colin Kay [1956] LLP Member; Claire Lamkin [1974] LLP Member; Nicholas John Leale [1974] LLP Member; Tomos Emyr Lewis [1957] LLP Member; Rebecca Jane McCabe-North [1981] LLP Member; Simon Paul McCann [1969] LLP Member; Alison Jane McClure [1962] LLP Member; Guthrie Ewing McGruer [1955] LLP Member; Edward Nicholas McMullen [1975] LLP Member; Sadak Miah [1969] LLP Member; Graham John Miles [1956] LLP Member; Andrew Ian Farquharson Miscampbell [1959] LLP Member; David Alexander Mortimer [1956] LLP Member; Lorna Elizabeth Munro [1961] LLP Member; Sean Gavin Palka [1966] LLP Member; Alison Bridget Patten-Hall [1965] LLP Member; Sarah Vivien Peacock [1958] LLP Member; Lawrence Stephen Phillips [1956] LLP Member; Eve Maria Piffaretti [1969] LLP Member; Christine Ann Plews [1963] LLP Member; Richard Alan Portlock [1963] LLP Member; Christopher David Charles Potts [1962] LLP Member; Kimberley Anne Provan [1972] LLP Member; Claire Leanne Rawle [1966] LLP Member; Geoffrey Bennett Reed [1958] LLP Member; Joanna Rees [1969] LLP Member; Sarah Caroline Rees [1966] LLP Member; Penny Rinta-Suksi [1970] LLP Member; Daniel John Scognamigilo [1972] LLP Member; Kathryn Jane Shimmin [1964] LLP Member; Kate Beth Silverman [1969] LLP Member; Arshdeep Kaur Singh [1970] LLP Member; Douglas James Smith [1964] LLP Member; Matthew James Tyndall Smith [1969] LLP Member; William Oliver Hugo Sowton [1968] LLP Member; Mark David Spash [1958] LLP Member; Neil Jonathan Stafford [1968] LLP Member; Simon Jonathan Staples [1969] LLP Member; Simon Jeremy Stokes [1963] LLP Member; Manoj Styche-Patel [1971] LLP Member; Jamie Piers Sutton [1953] LLP Member; Jeremy Forsythe Taylor [1961] LLP Member; Jessica Anne Rose Tresham [1977] LLP Member; Richard Samuel Marlar Wade [1968] LLP Member; David Stephen Thomas Wadsworth [1969] LLP Member; Stephanie Anne Evelyn Walls [1960] LLP Member; Michael Philip Ward [1970] LLP Member

Blanc Brasseries Limited
Incorporated: 30 May 2003 *Employees:* 604
Net Worth Deficit: £22,155,240 *Total Assets:* £24,101,238
Registered Office: Wizard House, 2a Cambridge Road, Teddington, Middlesex, TW11 8DR
Activities: Licenced restaurants
Parent: Brasserie Bar Co Limited
Officers: Raymond Rene Alfred Blanc [1949] Director/Chef Patron [French]; Jeremy Brown [1966] Director; Kathryn Coury [1964] Director; Mark Derry [1960] Restaurant Group Managing Director; Clive Andrew Fretwell [1961] Director/Executive Chef; Christopher Patrick Edward Guy [1981] Finance Director; Helen Louise Melvin [1968] Director/Accountant

Chas.A.Blatchford & Sons,Limited
Incorporated: 24 December 1919 *Employees:* 818
Net Worth: £13,812,000 *Total Assets:* £52,506,000
Registered Office: Lister Road, Basingstoke, Hants, RG22 4AH
Activities: Other manufacturing n.e.c.
Parent: Evolution Bidco Limited
Officers: Stephen David Downey [1961] Operations Director; Adrian Stenson [1963] Clinical Services Director; Zoe Annette Stephens-Truman [1969] HR Director; Professor Mir Saeed Zahedi [1957] Technical Director

Blenheim House Construction Limited
Incorporated: 4 October 1996 *Employees:* 76
Net Worth: £3,620,501 *Total Assets:* £20,895,484
Registered Office: The Old Bank House, 11-13 London Street, Chertsey, Surrey, KT16 8AP
Activities: Construction of commercial buildings
Shareholders: David Huw Pearce; Anne Pearce; Michael Curtis
Officers: Michael Curtis, Secretary; Ian Roland Bosley [1970] Director/Quantity Surveyor; Anthony Peter Francis Brewester [1971] Director/Quantity Surveyor; Michael Curtis [1965] Commercial Director; Richard David Jones [1962] Director/Civil Engineer; Marc Matthews [1969] Director/Quantity Surveyor; David Huw Pearce [1955] Managing Director; Richard Henderson Taylor [1966] Director/Civil Engineer

Bloc Gatwick Limited
Incorporated: 30 November 2011
Net Worth: £7,055,859 *Total Assets:* £32,269,984
Registered Office: Bloc Hotels, South Terminal, London Gatwick Airport, Gatwick, W Sussex, RH6 0NN
Activities: Hotels and similar accommodation
Parent: Bloc Hotel Group Limited
Officers: Rebecca Jane Elizabeth Morgan [1966] Director; Robert Llewelyn Morgan [1966] Director; Christopher Paul Salter [1964] Director

Bloc Hotel Group Limited
Incorporated: 2 November 2010 *Employees:* 39
Net Worth: £24,962,650 *Total Assets:* £51,517,192
Registered Office: Bloc Hotels, Gatwick South Terminal, London Gatwick Airport, Gatwick, W Sussex, RH6 0NN
Activities: Hotels and similar accommodation
Major Shareholder: Robert Llewelyn Morgan
Officers: Andrew Tadeusz Jurenko [1950] Director/Chartered Accountant; Rebecca Jane Elizabeth Morgan [1966] Director; Robert Llewelyn Morgan [1966] Director; Daniel Quai [1974] Senior Managing Director [Italian]; Thomas Bernhard Reckers [1981] Director; Christopher Paul Salter [1964] Director

Blue Auto Finance Limited
Incorporated: 4 August 2014
Net Worth Deficit: £619,000 *Total Assets:* £41,382,000
Registered Office: Darenth House, 84 Main Road, Sundridge, Sevenoaks, Kent, TN14 6ER
Activities: Activities of financial services holding companies
Parent: Blue Auto Holdings Limited
Officers: Samuel Robert Jones [1942] Director; Tikendra Patel [1965] Director; Tarun Sharma [1978] Director

Blue Auto Holdings Limited
Incorporated: 1 August 2014 *Employees:* 135
Net Worth: £6,696,000 *Total Assets:* £87,038,000
Registered Office: Darenth House, 84 Main Road, Sundridge, Sevenoaks, Kent, TN14 6ER
Activities: Activities of financial services holding companies
Officers: Samuel Robert Jones [1942] Director/Secretary; Tikendra Patel [1965] Director; Tarun Sharma [1978] Director

Blue Chip Customer Engineering Limited
Incorporated: 13 July 1987 *Employees:* 242
Net Worth: £40,522,000 *Total Assets:* £78,379,000
Registered Office: Franklin Court, Priory Business Park, Bedford, MK44 3JZ
Activities: Other software publishing
Shareholder: Brian Meredith
Officers: Andy Rounding, Secretary; Lee John Bailey [1976] Director; Eddy Conway [1960] Director; Brian Meredith [1950] Director; Sadie Vanessa Nesbitt [1967] Director; Andrew James Rounding [1972] Director/Accountant; Tim Stringer [1976] Director; Derek Waterman [1972] Director

Blue Diamond UK Limited
Incorporated: 12 September 1989 *Employees:* 1,359
Net Worth: £6,190,000 *Total Assets:* £35,891,000
Registered Office: Brambridge Park Garden Centre, Kiln Lane, Brambridge, Eastleigh, Hants, SO50 6HT
Activities: Other retail sale of new goods in specialised stores (not commercial art galleries and opticians)
Officers: Richard James Hemans [1973] Director/Chartered Accountant; Alan Roper [1961] Director

Blue Light Partnership (ASP) Holdings Limited
Incorporated: 26 July 2012
Net Worth: £523,000 *Total Assets:* £81,816,000
Registered Office: Part First Floor, 1 Grenfell Road, Maidenhead, Berks, SL6 1HN
Activities: Financial intermediation not elsewhere classified
Parent: Blue Light Partnership (ASP) Newco Limited
Officers: Emeka Ikechi Ehenulo, Secretary; Albert Hendrik Naafs [1965] Director [Dutch]; Frank Manfred Schramm [1968] Director [German]; Ian Tayler [1976] Director/General Manager

Blue Light Partnership (ASP) Limited
Incorporated: 17 July 2012
Net Worth: £523,000 *Total Assets:* £81,816,000
Registered Office: Part First Floor, 1 Grenfell Road, Maidenhead, Berks, SL6 1HN
Activities: Financial intermediation not elsewhere classified
Parent: Blue Light Partnership (ASP) Holdings Limited
Officers: Emeka Ikechi Ehenulo, Secretary; Albert Hendrik Naafs [1965] Director [Dutch]; Frank Manfred Schramm [1968] Director [German]; Ian Tayler [1976] Director/General Manager

Blue Light Partnership (ASP) Newco Limited
Incorporated: 14 November 2014
Net Worth: £2,916,000 *Total Assets:* £84,159,000
Registered Office: 1 Grenfell Road, Maidenhead, Berks, SL6 1HN
Activities: Activities of head offices
Parent: BBGI Sicav S.A.
Officers: Michael Denny [1977] Finance Director [Irish]; Frank Manfred Schramm [1968] Director [German]; Ian Tayler [1976] Director

Blue Lizard Consulting Limited
Incorporated: 23 May 2001 *Employees:* 13
Net Worth: £1,374,723 *Total Assets:* £34,547,744
Registered Office: Maria House, 35 Millers Road, Brighton, BN1 5NP
Activities: Buying and selling of own real estate
Major Shareholder: Anthony Grant Bloom
Officers: Adam Stephen Franks, Secretary; Anthony Grant Bloom [1970] Director; Ronald Bloom [1935] Director; Adam Stephen Franks [1971] Director; Lee Peter Pattenden [1958] Director; Marc Louis Sugarman [1972] Director

Blue Minerva Limited
Incorporated: 21 May 2004 *Employees:* 2
Net Worth Deficit: £93,413,520 *Total Assets:* £492,627,136
Registered Office: Riding Court House, Datchet, Berks, SL3 9JT
Activities: Activities of head offices
Parent: Iris Capital Limited
Officers: Michael David Cox [1983] Director; Kevin Peter Dady [1964] Director; Elona Mortimer-Zhika [1979] Director

Blue Sky Intermodal (UK) Ltd.
Incorporated: 27 November 2002 *Employees:* 27
Net Worth: £7,518,534 *Total Assets:* £46,668,008
Registered Office: 1st Floor, Anglers Court, 34-44 Spittal Street, Marlow, Bucks, SL7 1DB
Activities: Non-specialised wholesale trade
Shareholders: Geoffrey James Mornard; P & R Equipment & Finance Corp
Officers: Suzanne Claire Hewlett-Lankshear, Secretary; Keith James Hotston [1970] Director/Business Admin and IT; Beat Leisibach [1981] Director/Manager [Swiss]; Geoffrey James Mornard [1959] Director/Marketing Manager; Nigel John Stribley [1953] Director/Marine Container Leasing

Bluecastle Enterprises Limited
Incorporated: 20 December 2000
Net Worth Deficit: £29,417,268 *Total Assets:* £267,046,032
Registered Office: Suite No 2, First Floor, Kenwood House, 77a Shenley Road, Borehamwood, Herts, WD6 1AG
Activities: Tax consultancy
Major Shareholder: Vadim Giner
Officers: Jennifer Elizabeth Westmoreland [1967] Director/Financial Controller

Bluefield SIF Investments Limited
Incorporated: 20 June 2013 *Employees:* 5
Net Worth: £131,357,112 *Total Assets:* £624,281,664
Registered Office: 2nd Floor, 2 City Place, Beehive Ring Road, Gatwick, W Sussex, RH6 0PA
Activities: Other business support service activities n.e.c.
Parent: Bluefield Solar Income Fund Limited
Officers: James Robert Armstrong [1972] Investment Director; Michael Antony Rand [1978] Director/Partner; John Leonard Rennocks [1945] Director; John Philip Henry Schomberg Scott [1952] Director; Neil Anthony Wood [1980] Director/Accountant

BMC Software Limited
Incorporated: 2 July 1985 *Employees:* 312
Net Worth: £30,487,964 *Total Assets:* £45,955,104
Registered Office: E2 Eskdale Road, Winnersh, Wokingham, Berks, RG41 5TS
Activities: Information technology consultancy activities
Officers: Ted Cory Bleuer [1970] Director/SVP, Controller & Chief Accounting Officer [American]; Jonathan Rendle [1972] Director/VP, Customer Support; Arno Jan Ter Avest [1968] Director Accounting and Controller [Dutch]

BMT Group Limited
Incorporated: 18 February 1985 *Employees:* 1,450
Net Worth: £31,667,000 *Total Assets:* £110,380,000
Registered Office: Third Floor, 1 Park Road, Teddington, Middlesex, TW11 0AP
Activities: Management consultancy activities other than financial management
Officers: Trudy Michelle Grey, Secretary; Wendy Jacqueline Barnes [1957] Director; Sir John Antony Hood [1952] Chairman & Director [New Zealander]; Sarah Louise Kenny [1973] Director; David Keith McSweeney [1958] Director; Charles Max Packshaw [1952] Director; Minoo Homi Patel [1949] Director/Professor of Mechanical Engineering; Douglas Russell Webb [1961] Director

BMW (UK) Holdings Limited
Incorporated: 20 May 1975 *Employees:* 6
Net Worth: £1,321,676,032 *Total Assets:* £1,965,374,976
Registered Office: Summit One, Summit Avenue, Farnborough, Hants, GU14 0FB
Activities: Activities of head offices
Parent: Bayerische Motoren Werke AG
Officers: William Edwin Johnson, Secretary; Karen Rosemarie Delvai [1970] Director [German]; Michael Charles Dennett [1967] Director/Chartered Accountant; Dr Andreas Liepe [1973] Director/Lawyer [German]; Neil Charles Wharton [1967] Director/Accountant

BMW (UK) Limited
Incorporated: 11 July 1978 *Employees:* 407
Net Worth: £257,790,000 *Total Assets:* £2,145,181,952
Registered Office: Summit One, Summit Avenue, Farnborough, Hants, GU14 0FB
Activities: Sale of new cars and light motor vehicles
Parent: BMW (UK) Holdings Limited
Officers: William Edwin Johnson, Secretary; Graeme Charles Grieve [1961] Managing Director; Michael Kreeft [1960] Director [Dutch]; Jean-Phillipe Parain [1962] Director [French]

BMW (UK) Manufacturing Limited
Incorporated: 14 March 2000 *Employees:* 4,398
Net Worth: £531,655,008 *Total Assets:* £914,313,984
Registered Office: Summit One, Summit Avenue, Farnborough, Hants, GU14 0FB
Activities: Manufacture of motor vehicles
Parent: BMW (UK) Holdings Limited
Officers: William Edwin Johnson, Secretary; Frank Juergen Bachmann [1961] Director [Swiss]; Jeremy Patrick Stoyle [1971] Finance Director

BMW Financial Services (GB) Limited
Incorporated: 30 November 1976 *Employees:* 386
Net Worth: £793,769,024 *Total Assets:* £10,893,739,008
Registered Office: Summit One, Summit Avenue, Farnborough, Hants, GU14 0FB
Activities: Credit granting by non-deposit taking finance houses and other specialist consumer credit grantors
Parent: BMW (UK) Holdings Ltd
Officers: William Edwin Johnson, Secretary; Michael Dennett [1969] Director; Tobias Ambros Essig [1970] Director [German]; Philip Kerry [1970] Director/Accountant; Tracey June Leith [1969] Director/Chief Operations Officer [South African]

BNK (UK) Limited
Incorporated: 7 March 2008 *Employees:* 15
Net Worth: £6,603,691 *Total Assets:* £269,637,024
Registered Office: Salatin House, 19 Cedar Road, Sutton, Surrey, SM2 5DA
Activities: Wholesale of other fuels and related products
Officers: Andrei Dashutin [1957] Director [Belarusian]

BNP Paribas Commercial Finance Limited
Incorporated: 5 May 1992 *Employees:* 37
Net Worth: £21,471,262 *Total Assets:* £659,718,720
Registered Office: Brockbourne House, 77 Mount Ephraim, Tunbridge Wells, Kent, TN4 8BS
Activities: Factoring
Parent: BNP Paribas Fortis Factor NV
Officers: Nirmala Doobay, Secretary; Patrick Pierre Marie Galouzeau de Villepin [1958] Director [French]; Simon Barnaby Gates [1975] Director/Investment Banker; Christopher Derek Hart [1965] Director; Luc Marinus [1968] Director [Belgian]; David John Morris [1962] Director; Christophe John Roger Moyroud [1975] Director [French]

BNP Paribas Lease Group PLC
Incorporated: 1 February 1989
Net Worth: £147,532,992 *Total Assets:* £147,532,992
Registered Office: Northern Cross, Basing View, Basingstoke, Hants, RG21 4HL
Activities: Financial leasing
Parent: BNP Paribas SA
Officers: Nicholas David James, Secretary; Jean-Michel Robert Boyer [1963] Director/CEO - Country Manager [French]; Nicholas David James [1960] Director/Chartered Accountant

BNP Paribas Leasing Solutions Limited
Incorporated: 17 March 1967 *Employees:* 428
Net Worth: £140,219,008 *Total Assets:* £1,529,538,944
Registered Office: Northern Cross, Basing View, Basingstoke, Hants, RG21 4HL
Activities: Financial leasing
Parent: BNP Paribas Lease Group PLC
Officers: Nicholas David James, Secretary; Jean-Michel Robert Boyer [1963] Director/CEO - Country Manager [French]; Simon Barnaby Gates [1975] Director/Banker; Nicholas David James [1960] Director/Chartered Accountant; Pascal Layan [1965] Director/Head of International Business Lines [French]; Michael John Quinn [1967] Risk Director; Thierry Bernard Veillet Lavallee [1957] Director [French]; Morgan Erwan Alexandre Vessier [1974] Director/Head of Risk [French]

BNP Paribas Rental Solutions Limited
Incorporated: 12 November 2003
Previous: Artegy Limited
Net Worth: £4,308,000 *Total Assets:* £54,920,000
Registered Office: Northern Cross, Basing View, Basingstoke, Hants, RG21 4HL
Activities: Renting and leasing of trucks and other heavy vehicles
Parent: BNP Paribas SA
Officers: Nicholas David James, Secretary; Jean-Michel Robert Boyer [1963] Director/CEO - Country Manager [French]; Nicholas David James [1960] Director/Chartered Accountant

BOC Gases Limited
Incorporated: 28 February 1991
Net Worth: £30,847,000 *Total Assets:* £33,151,000
Registered Office: The Priestley Centre, 10 Priestley Road, The Surrey Research Park, Guildford, Surrey, GU2 7XY
Activities: Activities of head offices
Parent: The BOC Group Limited
Officers: Susan Kathleen Kelly, Secretary; Julian Michael Bland [1967] Director/Head of Accounting; Benjamin Patterson [1962] Director/Solicitor; Sally Ann Williams [1970] Director/Accountant

The BOC Group Limited
Incorporated: 26 January 1886 *Employees:* 149
Net Worth: £7,473,200,128 *Total Assets:* £8,620,199,936
Registered Office: The Priestley Centre, 10 Priestley Road, The Surrey Research Park, Guildford, Surrey, GU2 7XY
Activities: Activities of head offices
Shareholders: Linde UK Holdings Limited; Medispeed
Officers: Susan Kathleen Kelly, Secretary; Julian Michael Bland [1967] Director/Head of Accounting; Christopher James Cossins [1966] Director/Tax Manager; Benjamin Patterson [1962] Director/Solicitor; Oliver Christian Pfann [1968] Director/Regional Business Unit Head UK/Ireland/Africa [German]; Sally Ann Williams [1970] Director/Accountant

BOC Helex
Incorporated: 13 December 1966 *Employees:* 2
Net Worth: £4,042,863,360 *Total Assets:* £4,186,635,264
Registered Office: The Priestley Centre, 10 Priestley Road, The Surrey Research Park, Guildford, Surrey, GU2 7XY
Activities: Activities of head offices
Parent: Linde Investments No.1 Limited
Officers: Susan Kathleen Kelly, Secretary; Julian Michael Bland [1967] Director/Business Accounting Manager; Christopher James Cossins [1966] Director/Tax Manager; Benjamin Patterson [1962] Director/Solicitor; Sally Ann Williams [1970] Director/Accountant

BOC Investment Holdings Limited
Incorporated: 28 March 1996
Net Worth: £527,366,016 *Total Assets:* £527,736,000
Registered Office: The Priestley Centre, 10 Priestley Road, The Surrey Research Park, Guildford, Surrey, GU2 7XY
Activities: Activities of head offices
Parent: BOC Holdings
Officers: Susan Kathleen Kelly, Secretary; Julian Michael Bland [1967] Director/Head of Accounting; Benjamin Patterson [1962] Director/Solicitor; Sally Ann Williams [1970] Director/Accountant

BOC Investments No.1 Limited
Incorporated: 28 March 1996
Net Worth: £132,056,000 *Total Assets:* £132,230,000
Registered Office: The Priestley Centre, 10 Priestley Road, The Surrey Research Park, Guildford, Surrey, GU2 7XY
Activities: Activities of head offices
Parent: BOC Holdings
Officers: Susan Kathleen Kelly, Secretary; Julian Michael Bland [1967] Director/Head of Accounting; Benjamin Patterson [1962] Director/Solicitor; Sally Ann Williams [1970] Director/Accountant

BOC Investments No.5
Incorporated: 26 September 2001
Net Worth: £55,115,000 *Total Assets:* £55,538,000
Registered Office: The Priestley Centre, 10 Priestley Road, The Surrey Research Park, Guildford, Surrey, GU2 7XY
Activities: Activities of head offices
Parent: Linde Cryogenics Limited
Officers: Susan Kathleen Kelly, Secretary; Julian Michael Bland [1967] Director/Head of Accounting; Benjamin Patterson [1962] Director/Solicitor; Sally Ann Williams [1970] Director/Accountant

BOC Korea Holdings Limited
Incorporated: 25 April 1989
Net Worth: £90,489,000 *Total Assets:* £105,864,000
Registered Office: The Priestley Centre, 10 Priestley Road, The Surrey Research Park, Guildford, Surrey, GU2 7XY
Activities: Activities of head offices
Parent: The BOC Group Limited
Officers: Susan Kathleen Kelly, Secretary; Julian Michael Bland [1967] Director/Head of Accounting; Benjamin Patterson [1962] Director/Solicitor; Sally Ann Williams [1970] Director/Accountant

BOC Limited
Incorporated: 8 March 1938 *Employees:* 2,839
Net Worth: £611,600,000 *Total Assets:* £1,123,000,064
Registered Office: The Priestley Centre, 10 Priestley Road, The Surrey Research Park, Guildford, Surrey, GU2 7XY
Activities: Manufacture of industrial gases
Parent: BOC Netherlands Holdings Limited
Officers: Susan Kathleen Kelly, Secretary; Julian Michael Bland [1967] Director/Head of Accounting; Christopher James Cossins [1966] Director/Tax Manager; Andrew John Harvey [1962] Director/Head of EMEA Healthcare RBU; Benjamin Patterson [1962] Director/Solicitor; Oliver Christian Pfann [1968] Director/Regional Business Unit Head UK/Ireland/Africa [German]; Sally Ann Williams [1970] Director/Accountant

BOC Netherlands Holdings Limited
Incorporated: 18 July 1990
Net Worth: £281,614,016 *Total Assets:* £406,809,984
Registered Office: The Priestley Centre, 10 Priestley Road, The Surrey Research Park, Guildford, Surrey, GU2 7XY
Activities: Activities of head offices
Parent: The BOC Group Limited
Officers: Susan Kathleen Kelly, Secretary; Julian Michael Bland [1967] Director/Head of Accounting; Benjamin Patterson [1962] Director/Solicitor; Sally Ann Williams [1970] Director/Accountant

The Body Shop International Limited
Incorporated: 1 November 1976 *Employees:* 5,870
Previous: The Body Shop International PLC
Net Worth: £272,000,000 *Total Assets:* £502,000,000
Registered Office: Watersmead, Littlehampton, W Sussex, BN17 6LS
Activities: Wholesale of perfume and cosmetics
Officers: Peter O'Byrne, Secretary; Robert Claus Chatwin [1970] Director/Executive/Chartered Accountant; Itamar Gaino Filho [1976] Director/Attorney [Brazilian]

Boehringer Ingelheim Animal Health UK Limited
Incorporated: 20 November 1985 *Employees:* 183
Previous: Merial Animal Health Limited
Net Worth: £15,859,000 *Total Assets:* £62,210,000
Registered Office: c/o Boehringer Ingelheim Limited, Ellesfield Avenue, Bracknell, Berks, RG12 8YS
Activities: Manufacture of basic pharmaceutical products
Officers: Uday Kumar Bose [1975] Director; Richard James Butson [1965] Director; Benjamin James Moynihan [1972] Director

Boehringer Ingelheim Limited
Incorporated: 1 January 1962 *Employees:* 530
Net Worth: £45,469,000 *Total Assets:* £157,427,008
Registered Office: Ellesfield Avenue, Bracknell, Berks, RG12 8YS
Activities: Manufacture of basic pharmaceutical products
Officers: Uday Kumar Bose [1975] Director; Benjamin James Moynihan [1972] Director/Accountant

Boeing UK Training and Flight Services Holding Limited
Incorporated: 12 July 1999 *Employees:* 5
Net Worth: £54,539,308 *Total Assets:* £69,204,344
Registered Office: Boeing House, Crawley Business Quarter, Manor Royal, Crawley, W Sussex, RH10 9AD
Activities: Activities of head offices
Parent: The Boeing Company
Officers: Simon Howard Jones, Secretary; Sir Michael Anthony Arthur [1950] Director/Businessman; Angela Jane Golder [1964] Director/Campus Manager; Martyn Anthony Townsend Smith [1957] Director/Head of Training; Thomas Ronald Fletcher Watson [1953] Director/Chartered Accountant; Christopher James Wolter [1965] Director [American]

Boeing UK Training and Flight Services Limited
Incorporated: 7 July 1999 *Employees:* 77
Net Worth: £74,484,576 *Total Assets:* £88,160,776
Registered Office: Boeing House, Crawley Business Quarter, Manor Royal, Crawley, W Sussex, RH10 9AD
Activities: Service activities incidental to air transportation
Parent: Boeing UK Training and Flight Services Holdings Limited
Officers: Simon Howard Jones, Secretary; Sir Michael Anthony Arthur [1950] Director/Businessman; Angela Jane Golder [1964] Director/Campus Manager; Martyn Anthony Townsend Smith [1957] Director/Head of Training; Thomas Ronald Fletcher Watson [1953] Director/Chartered Accountant; Christopher James Wolter [1965] Director [American]

Bohunt Education Trust
Incorporated: 18 February 2011 *Employees:* 622
Net Worth: £122,794,776 *Total Assets:* £128,827,440
Registered Office: Longmoor Road, Liphook, Hants, GU30 7NY
Activities: General secondary education
Officers: Raine Ryland, Secretary; Julie Butler [1959] Director/Purchase Ledger Administrator; Steven Peter Corkerton [1961] HR Director; David Jonathan Glaser [1957] Director; David Alistair Halliday [1959] Director/Retired Naval Officer; Robert Brookes Kearsley [1982] Operations Director; Dr Raymond Joseph Morton [1947] Director/Chemical Engineer; Dr Graham Duncan Parr [1953] Director/Pharmaceutical Consultant; Jean Margaret Sanderson [1965] Director/Financial Consultant; Neil David Strowger [1973] Director/Headteacher; James Peter Winfield [1981] Director/Solicitor; Professor Steven Michael Wood [1976] Director/University Professor

Boing Acquisitions Limited
Incorporated: 9 June 2014
Net Worth: £63,425,000 *Total Assets:* £386,828,000
Registered Office: 35-37 Amersham Hill, High Wycombe, Bucks, HP13 6NU
Activities: Other retail sale in non-specialised stores
Parent: Boing Midco Limited
Officers: Jonathan Samuel Booth [1961] Director; Thomas Bruce Mangas [1967] Director/Chief Executive Officer [American]; Nilesh Kundanlal Pandya [1971] Director; Michael Andrew James Smith [1962] Director

Boing Midco Limited
Incorporated: 9 June 2014 *Employees:* 4
Net Worth: £116,122,000 *Total Assets:* £123,128,000
Registered Office: 35-37 Amersham Hill, High Wycombe, Bucks, HP13 6NU
Activities: Other retail sale in non-specialised stores
Parent: Boing Topco Limited
Officers: Jonathan Samuel Booth [1961] Director; Thomas Bruce Mangas [1967] Director/Chief Executive Officer [American]; Nilesh Kundanlal Pandya [1971] Director; Michael Andrew James Smith [1962] Director

Bollore Logistics UK Ltd
Incorporated: 17 August 1928 *Employees:* 438
Previous: SDV Ltd
Net Worth: £9,248,027 *Total Assets:* £41,135,144
Registered Office: Unit 1 Skyline, Great South West Road, Heathrow, Feltham, Middlesex, TW14 8NT
Activities: Other transportation support activities
Parent: Bollore
Officers: John David Gavin Love, Secretary; Thierry Joseph Ehrenbogen [1960] Director/CEO Europe [French]; Henri Antoine Le Gouis [1967] Director/CEO Western Europe [French]; David Smith [1965] Director

Bolzoni Capital UK Limited
Incorporated: 30 March 2016
Net Worth Deficit: £606,456 *Total Assets:* £38,513,380
Registered Office: Centennial House, Building 4.5, Frimley Business Park, Frimley, Camberley, Surrey, GU16 7SG
Activities: Manufacture of other fabricated metal products n.e.c.
Parent: Hyster-Yale Materials Handling, Inc.
Officers: Claire Mair, Secretary; Claire Mair [1975] Director of Taxes, EMEA; Kenneth Schilling [1959] Director/Chief Financial Officer [American]; Suzanne Schulze Taylor [1962] Director/VP Deputy General Counsel and Assistant Secretary [American]; Roger Toby Stoodley Tyler [1974] Director/Associate General Counsel, EMEA; Colin Wilson [1954] Director/Chief Executive Officer [American]

Bonne Bouche Catering Limited
Incorporated: 29 July 1965 *Employees:* 49
Net Worth: £22,410,320 *Total Assets:* £33,374,368
Registered Office: Unit 23 Fleetway Business Park, 14-16 Wadsworth Road, Perivale, Middlesex, UB6 7JD
Activities: Manufacture of bread; manufacture of fresh pastry goods and cakes
Major Shareholder: Rolf Ferdinand Biller
Officers: Marcia Biller, Secretary; Marcia Biller [1946] Director; Rolf Ferdinand Biller [1942] Director [German]

The Book People Limited
Incorporated: 26 August 1988 *Employees:* 345
Net Worth Deficit: £6,020,660 *Total Assets:* £28,901,036
Registered Office: Salisbury House, Weyside Park, Catteshall Lane, Godalming, Surrey, GU7 1XE
Activities: Retail sale via stalls and markets of other goods
Officers: Ajay Patel, Secretary; Simon Christopher Mason [1976] Director; William Mark Oldroyd [1959] Logistics Director; Ajay Patel [1964] Director; Scott Scott [1974] Director; William Valerian Wellesley [1966] Director

Bookcash Trading Limited
Incorporated: 4 January 1994 *Employees:* 71
Net Worth: £12,771,000 *Total Assets:* £27,975,000
Registered Office: Hunton House, Highbridge Estate, Oxford Road, Uxbridge, Middlesex, UB8 1LX
Activities: Licenced restaurants
Parent: PizzaExpress (Restaurants) Limited
Officers: Andrew David Pellington, Secretary; Andrew David Pellington [1964] Director; Jinlong Wang [1957] Director [American]

Boorley Green LLP
Incorporated: 20 July 2015
Net Worth Deficit: £126,000 *Total Assets:* £54,241,000
Registered Office: Cowley Business Park, Cowley, Uxbridge, Middlesex, UB8 2AL

Boral (UK) Limited
Incorporated: 19 March 1971 *Employees:* 2
Net Worth: £51,861,000 *Total Assets:* £53,009,000
Registered Office: Wayside, Rushmere Lane, Orchard Leigh, Chesham, Bucks, HP5 3QY
Activities: Other specialised construction activities n.e.c.
Officers: Alice Sophie Stoker, Secretary; Graham Charles Froebel [1955] Director/Accountant [Australian]; Stephen John Morrison [1962] Managing Director

Bordure Limited
Incorporated: 29 May 1963
Net Worth: £3,816,895 *Total Assets:* £31,912,990
Registered Office: Linton Park, Linton, Maidstone, Kent, ME17 4AB
Activities: Activities of head offices
Parent: Eastern Produce Investments Limited
Officers: Amarpal Takk, Secretary; Graham Harold McLean [1969] Managing Director; Susan Ann Walker [1967] Director

Borelli Tea Holdings Limited
Incorporated: 19 March 1976
Net Worth: £39,460,080 *Total Assets:* £54,827,008
Registered Office: Woodlands, 79 High Street, Greenhithe, Kent, DA9 9RD
Activities: Activities of agricultural holding companies
Parent: McLeod Russel India Limited
Officers: Dilsher SEN, Secretary/Solicitor; Kamal Kishore Baheti [1963] Director/Company Executive [Indian]; Aditya Khaitan [1968] Director/Industrialist [Indian]; Stephen Knight [1960] Director; Barry John Ruck [1959] Director; Dilsher SEN [1968] Director/Solicitor

The Borrow Foundation
Incorporated: 17 January 1997 *Employees:* 10
Net Worth: £26,207,720 *Total Assets:* £28,828,684
Registered Office: Padnell Grange, Cowplain, Portsmouth, PO8 8ED
Activities: Other professional, scientific and technical activities n.e.c.
Officers: Nigel Frederick Borrow [1963] Director; John Trefor Price Roberts [1944] Director/Solicitor; Professor Andrew John Rugg Gunn [1939] Director/Retired; Professor Ulla Maria Christina Stecksen-Blicks [1949] Director/Professor [Swedish]; Dr Nigel Martin Thomas [1948] Director/Dental Surgeon

Bosch Automotive Service Solutions Ltd
Incorporated: 25 May 1966 *Employees:* 201
Net Worth: £17,895,000 *Total Assets:* £27,956,000
Registered Office: Robert Bosch Ltd, Broadwater Park, North Orbital Road, Denham, Uxbridge, Middlesex, UB9 5HJ
Activities: Non-specialised wholesale trade
Parent: Robert Bosch UK Holdings Limited
Officers: Jonathan David Burton, Secretary; David Roy Butterworth [1969] Managing Director; Robert Josef Hilbert [1965] Director/Manager [German]; Dr Steffen Tobias Hoffmann [1965] Director [German]; Fedra Ribeiro [1972] Director/Vice President Global [Portuguese]

Robert Bosch UK Holdings Limited
Incorporated: 1 October 2010 *Employees:* 53
Net Worth: £613,361,024 *Total Assets:* £988,782,016
Registered Office: Broadwater Park, North Orbital Road, Denham, Uxbridge, Middlesex, UB9 5HJ
Activities: Activities of head offices
Parent: Robert Bosch Investment Nederland BV
Officers: Jonathan Burton, Secretary; Andrew Ralph Castle [1957] Director; Dr Steffen Tobias Hoffmann [1965] Director [German]

Bose Limited
Incorporated: 17 October 1974 *Employees:* 209
Net Worth: £41,130,000 *Total Assets:* £58,338,000
Registered Office: Bose House, Quayside, Chatham Maritime, Chatham, Kent, ME4 4QZ
Activities: Wholesale of audio tapes, records, CDs and video tapes and the equipment on which these are played
Shareholders: Herbert Batchelder; Robert Maresca; Ursula Bose
Officers: Sheila Colette Burke [1969] Director [Irish]; Veronique Thoelen [1971] Director of Finance [Belgian]

Boskalis Subsea Limited
Incorporated: 20 January 2010 *Employees:* 20
Previous: VBMS (UK) Limited
Net Worth: £7,149,000 *Total Assets:* £76,115,000
Registered Office: Westminster House, Crompton Way, Segensworth West, Fareham, Hants, PO15 5SS
Activities: Construction of commercial buildings
Parent: Koninklijke Boskalis Westminster N.V.
Officers: Raymond Victor Richards, Secretary; Stuart Ian Cameron [1974] Managing Director; Jan Jakob Johannes Mulder [1964] Finance Director [Dutch]; Arnoldus Martinus Josephus Van Poppel [1965] Director [Dutch]

Boskalis Westminster (Holdings) Limited
Incorporated: 2 December 1933 *Employees:* 103
Net Worth: £20,221,000 *Total Assets:* £56,750,000
Registered Office: Westminster House, Crompton Way, Fareham, Hants, PO15 5SS
Activities: Other specialised construction activities n.e.c.
Parent: Boskalis Westminster International B.V.
Officers: Raymond Victor Richards, Secretary; Paul Maurice de Jong [1964] Managing Director [Dutch]; Raymond Victor Richards [1958] Director/Head of Finance

Boskalis Westminster Limited
Incorporated: 27 December 1962 *Employees:* 76
Net Worth: £20,602,000 *Total Assets:* £47,290,000
Registered Office: Westminster House, Crompton Way, Segensworth West, Fareham, Hants, PO15 5SS
Activities: Other specialised construction activities n.e.c.
Parent: Boskalis Westminster (Holdings) Limited
Officers: Raymond Victor Richards, Secretary; Paul Maurice de Jong [1964] Managing Director [Dutch]; Raymond Victor Richards [1958] Director/Head of Finance

Bostall Estates Limited
Incorporated: 15 June 1998 *Employees:* 3
Net Worth: £16,322,744 *Total Assets:* £30,305,232
Registered Office: 3 Montpelier Avenue, Bexley, Kent, DA5 3AP
Activities: Development of building projects
Major Shareholder: Manjit Singh Heer
Officers: Manjit Singh Heer [1968] Director/Businessman

Boston Limited
Incorporated: 8 December 1992 *Employees:* 154
Net Worth: £4,792,572 *Total Assets:* £26,768,804
Registered Office: 5 Theobald Court, Theobald Street, Elstree, Herts, WD6 4RN
Activities: Other information technology service activities
Officers: Ashok Uttamlal Chauhan, Secretary; Manojkumar Nayee [1963] Director/Computer Sales

Bottling Great Britain Limited
Incorporated: 11 September 2002
Net Worth: £2,462,513,408 *Total Assets:* £4,272,129,280
Registered Office: Pemberton House, Bakers Road, Uxbridge, Middlesex, UB8 1EZ
Activities: Activities of head offices
Officers: Huma Allana, Secretary; Huma Allana [1975] Company Secretary/Director; Michael Clark [1970] Director; Leendert Pieter Den Hollander [1969] Director/Vice President & General Manager CCE Ltd [Dutch]; Frank Govaerts [1961] Director [Belgian]; Angela Corina Sabadus [1979] Director [French]; Florian Tornow [1974] Director [German]; Kathleen Veirman [1965] Director [Belgian]; Ed Owen Walker [1967] Director

Bottling Holdings Europe Limited
Incorporated: 25 May 2016
Net Worth: £15,390,483,456 *Total Assets:* £16,759,967,744
Registered Office: Pemberton House, Bakers Road, Uxbridge, Middlesex, UB8 1EZ
Activities: Activities of other holding companies n.e.c.
Shareholders: CCEP Holdings UK Limited; Coca-Cola European Partners PLC
Officers: Paul Van Reesch, Secretary; Frank Govaerts [1961] Director [Belgian]; Paul Van Reesch [1976] Director; Edward Owen Walker [1967] Director

Bottomline Technologies Europe Limited
Incorporated: 11 January 1999 *Employees:* 3
Net Worth: £9,039,984 *Total Assets:* £41,644,104
Registered Office: 115 Chatham Street, Reading, Berks, RG1 7JX
Activities: Activities of financial services holding companies
Parent: Bottomline Technologies Incorporated
Officers: Richard Douglas Booth [1969] Director/Chief Executive [American]; Harpaul Dharwar [1973] Finance Director; Robert Eberle [1960] Director [American]; Nigel Kevin Savory [1966] Director

Bottomline Technologies Limited
Incorporated: 8 June 2012 *Employees:* 382
Net Worth: £69,120,032 *Total Assets:* £201,402,720
Registered Office: 115 Chatham Street, Reading, Berks, RG1 7JX
Activities: Data processing, hosting and related activities
Parent: Bottomline Technologies Incorporated
Officers: Richard Douglas Booth [1969] Director/Chief Executive [American]; Harpaul Dharwar [1973] Director; Robert Eberle [1960] Director [American]; Nigel Kevin Savory [1966] Director

Burt Boulton Holdings Limited
Incorporated: 3 August 1898
Net Worth: £28,255,790 *Total Assets:* £28,742,776
Registered Office: Sheridan House, 40-43 Jewry Street, Winchester, Hants, SO23 8RY
Activities: Other letting and operating of own or leased real estate
Parent: Thomas Roberts Estates Limited
Officers: Gillian Hemmings, Secretary; Jonathan Roger Coninx [1955] Director/Chartered Accountant; Craig Neil Collier Lowrey [1960] Director; James Roberts [1953] Director

Bourne Education Trust
Incorporated: 9 September 2011 *Employees:* 841
Net Worth: £123,260,240 *Total Assets:* £136,623,536
Registered Office: Epsom and Ewell High School, Ruxley Lane, Epsom, Surrey, KT19 9JW
Activities: Primary education
Officers: Kathrine Sanders, Secretary; Peter Charles Deane [1956] Director; Stephen Dennison [1953] Director/Retired; Susan Mary Gibbin [1963] Director/Management Consultant; Sara Elizabeth Anne Lipscombe-Nott [1966] Communications Director; Chris Marston [1964] Director/Commercial Manager; Christopher Ross Munro [1960] Director/Business Development Manager; Sarah Louise Pittam [1968] Director/Education Consultant; Alex Russell [1962] Director/Headteacher; Audrey Wade [1971] Director/Chartered Accountant

Bourne Holidays Limited
Incorporated: 12 October 1984 *Employees:* 2,573
Net Worth: £55,252,000 *Total Assets:* £181,990,000
Registered Office: No 1 Park Lane, Hemel Hempstead, Herts, HP2 4YL
Activities: Development of building projects
Parent: Bourne Leisure Limited
Officers: Jane Elizabeth Bentall [1970] Director/Accountant; Paul Charles Flaum [1970] Director; Iain Stuart Macmillan [1976] Director; Simon Thompson [1971] Director

Bourne Leisure (Hopton) Limited
Incorporated: 19 January 1973 *Employees:* 185
Net Worth: £8,971,000 *Total Assets:* £21,937,000
Registered Office: 1 Park Lane, Hemel Hempstead, Herts, HP2 4YL
Activities: Recreational vehicle parks, trailer parks and camping grounds
Parent: Bourne Leisure Group Limited
Officers: Jane Elizabeth Bentall [1970] Director/Accountant; Paul Charles Flaum [1970] Director; Iain Stuart Macmillan [1976] Director

Bourne Leisure Group Limited
Incorporated: 13 June 1969
Net Worth: £54,000 *Total Assets:* £25,413,000
Registered Office: 1 Park Lane, Hemel Hempstead, Herts, HP2 4YL
Activities: Recreational vehicle parks, trailer parks and camping grounds
Parent: Colaingrove Limited
Officers: Jane Elizabeth Bentall [1970] Director/Accountant; Paul Charles Flaum [1970] Director; Iain Stuart Macmillan [1976] Director

Bourne Leisure Holdings Limited
Incorporated: 9 June 2000 *Employees:* 13,721
Net Worth: £437,088,992 *Total Assets:* £1,465,027,968
Registered Office: No 1 Park Lane, Hemel Hempstead, Herts, HP2 4YL
Activities: Recreational vehicle parks, trailer parks and camping grounds
Officers: Colin David Russell Allen [1960] Director; Jane Elizabeth Bentall [1970] Director/Accountant; Richard John Cook [1972] Director; Geoffrey Ian Cooper [1954] Director; Roisin Jane Catherine Donnelly [1961] Director; Paul Charles Flaum [1970] Director; Paul Edward Woodstock Harris [1969] Director; Iain Stuart Macmillan [1976] Director; Simon Thompson [1971] Director

Bourne Leisure Limited
Incorporated: 9 June 2000 *Employees:* 3
Net Worth: £6,439,000 *Total Assets:* £606,860,032
Registered Office: No 1 Park Lane, Hemel Hempstead, Herts, HP2 4YL
Activities: Recreational vehicle parks, trailer parks and camping grounds
Parent: Foray 989 Limited
Officers: Jane Elizabeth Bentall [1970] Director/Accountant; Paul Charles Flaum [1970] Director; Iain Stuart Macmillan [1976] Director

Boustead International Heaters Limited
Incorporated: 22 April 1997 *Employees:* 44
Net Worth: £19,064,952 *Total Assets:* £30,013,080
Registered Office: Europa House, Woodlands Court, Albert Drive, Burgess Hill, W Sussex, RH15 9TN
Activities: Other engineering activities
Parent: BIH Holdings PTE Ltd
Officers: Susan Elizabeth Hoffman, Secretary; Shiok Faun Chan [1962] Director/Group Senior Vice President - Finance [Singaporean]; Stuart James Cummings [1974] Director/Chief Executive; Peter John Halstead [1978] Finance Director; Kai Keong Loh [1953] Director/Group Chief Financial Officer [Singaporean]; Fong Fui Wong [1943] Director/Group Chairman [Singaporean]; Yu Loon Wong [1974] Group Investment Director [Singaporean]

Bovis Homes Group PLC
Incorporated: 4 November 1935 *Employees:* 1,297
Net Worth: £1,056,576,000 *Total Assets:* £1,584,376,960
Registered Office: 11 Tower View, Kings Hill, West Malling, Kent, ME19 4UY
Activities: Buying and selling of own real estate
Officers: Martin Trevor Digby Palmer, Chartered Secretary; Margaret Christine Browne [1960] Director/Chief Operating Officer, Tui Aviation; Ralph Graham Findlay [1961] Director/Chief Executive Officer; Gregory Paul FitzGenerald [1964] Director; Katherine Christina Mary Innes Ker [1960] Director; Nigel John Keen [1961] Property and Development Director; Earl Sibley [1972] Director/Chartered Accountant; Michael John Stansfield [1956] Director; Ian Paul Tyler [1960] Director

Bovis Homes Limited
Incorporated: 8 August 1945 *Employees:* 1,297
Net Worth: £573,107,968 *Total Assets:* £1,602,083,968
Registered Office: 11 Tower View, Kings Hill, West Malling, Kent, ME19 4UY
Activities: Buying and selling of own real estate
Parent: Bovis Homes Group PLC
Officers: Martin Trevor Digby Palmer, Chartered Secretary; Keith Bryan Carnegie [1969] Director/Solicitor; Gregory Paul FitzGenerald [1964] Director; Earl Sibley [1972] Director/Chartered Accountant; Anthony James Watson [1972] Managing Director; Darrell Phillip White [1971] Director

Bovis Peer LLP
Incorporated: 18 December 2009
Net Worth: £12,050,503 *Total Assets:* £32,452,554
Registered Office: 11 Tower View, Kings Hill, West Malling, Kent, ME19 4UY

Bowers & Wilkins Holding Ltd
Incorporated: 28 April 2016 *Employees:* 850
Net Worth: £54,764,808 *Total Assets:* £150,051,536
Registered Office: B & W Group Ltd, Dale Road, Worthing, W Sussex, BN11 2BH
Activities: Activities of production holding companies
Parent: Eva Automation Inc
Officers: Jung Il Kim [1973] Director/Chief Financial Officer [American]; David Liu [1972] Director/Business Executive [American]; Gideon Yu [1971] Director [American]

Bowland Resources (No.2) Limited
Incorporated: 25 April 2008
Net Worth Deficit: £3,565,000 *Total Assets:* £33,491,000
Registered Office: 1st Floor, 20 Kingston Road, Staines upon Thames, Middlesex, TW18 4LG
Activities: Support activities for petroleum and natural gas mining
Officers: Nicola MacLeod, Secretary; Generald Martin Harrison [1954] Director; Andrew Daryl Le Poidevin [1958] Director; Nicola Jane MacLeod [1974] Director/General Counsel

Bowland Resources Limited
Incorporated: 5 February 2009
Net Worth: £4,636,000 *Total Assets:* £78,598,000
Registered Office: 1st Floor, 20 Kingston Road, Staines upon Thames, Middlesex, TW18 4LG
Activities: Support activities for petroleum and natural gas mining
Parent: Spirit North Sea Gas Limited
Officers: Nicola MacLeod, Secretary; Generald Martin Harrison [1954] Director; Andrew Daryl Le Poidevin [1958] Director; Nicola Jane MacLeod [1974] Director/General Counsel

Bowsprit Property Development Limited
Incorporated: 9 March 1989
Net Worth: £9,574,000 *Total Assets:* £23,566,000
Registered Office: Southern House, Yeoman Road, Worthing, W Sussex, BN13 3NX
Activities: Development of building projects
Parent: Bowsprit Holdings Limited
Officers: Joanne Statton, Secretary; Ian James McAulay [1965] Director; Joanne Statton [1969] Director/Solicitor

BP (Abu Dhabi) Limited
Incorporated: 18 September 1962
Net Worth: £662,224,192 *Total Assets:* £3,456,190,976
Registered Office: Chertsey Road, Sunbury on Thames, Middlesex, TW16 7BP
Activities: Support activities for petroleum and natural gas mining
Parent: BP Exploration Company Limited
Officers: Andrew James Alexander McAuslan [1961] Director/Oil Company Executive; John Myers [1967] Director/Oil Company Executive

BP Africa Limited
Incorporated: 10 November 1971
Net Worth: £40,856,280 *Total Assets:* £81,949,376
Registered Office: Chertsey Road, Sunbury on Thames, Middlesex, TW16 7BP
Activities: Activities of head offices
Parent: BP PLC.
Officers: Guy Jan Julia Moeyens [1965] Director/Oil Company Executive [Belgian]; Thierry Jose Henri Rondeau [1959] Director/Oil Company Executive [French]

BP Alternative Energy Investments Limited
Incorporated: 14 November 2006
Previous: BP Biofuels UK Limited
Net Worth: £161,085,632 *Total Assets:* £216,051,520
Registered Office: Chertsey Road, Sunbury on Thames, Middlesex, TW16 7BP
Activities: Activities of head offices
Parent: BP International Limited
Officers: David Thomas Anderson [1964] Director/Oil Company Executive; Mario Lindenhayn [1964] Director/Oil Company Executive [Brazilian/German]; Nicholas James Wayth [1973] Director/Oil Company Executive

BP America Limited
Incorporated: 13 January 2014
Net Worth: £51,778,691,072 *Total Assets:* £51,778,732,032
Registered Office: Chertsey Road, Sunbury on Thames, Middlesex, TW16 7BP
Activities: Activities of head offices
Parent: BP Holdings North America Limited
Officers: Jens Bertelsen [1959] Director/Deputy Secretary; Jan Clayton Lyons [1965] Director/Oil Company Executive [American]; Peter James Mather [1960] Director/Oil Company Executive

BP Amoco Exploration (Faroes) Limited
Incorporated: 10 August 1965
Net Worth: £69,042,400 *Total Assets:* £102,787,704
Registered Office: Chertsey Road, Sunbury on Thames, Middlesex, TW16 7BP
Activities: Extraction of crude petroleum
Parent: BP Exploration Operating Company Limited
Officers: Ariel David Flores [1977] Director/Oil Company Executive [American]

BP Aromatics Limited
Incorporated: 25 April 2007 *Employees:* 20
Net Worth: £143,959,152 *Total Assets:* £242,243,344
Registered Office: Chertsey Road, Sunbury on Thames, Middlesex, TW16 7BP
Activities: Manufacture of other inorganic basic chemicals
Parent: BP Aromatics Holdings Limited
Officers: Alessia Alberoni [1977] Director/Oil Company Executive [Italian]; Graham Michael Knights [1969] Director/Oil Company Executive; David Jozef Vermylen [1972] Director/Oil Company Executive [Belgian]

BP Asia Pacific Holdings Limited
Incorporated: 5 February 1973
Net Worth: £3,637,187,840 *Total Assets:* £6,405,887,488
Registered Office: Chertsey Road, Sunbury on Thames, Middlesex, TW16 7BP
Activities: Activities of head offices
Parent: BP Global Investments Limited
Officers: David Alan Rider [1964] Director/Oil Company Executive; Katherine Anne Thomson [1968] Director/Oil Company Executive

BP Australia Swaps Management Limited
Incorporated: 19 November 2012
Net Worth: £4,722,393,088 *Total Assets:* £6,225,776,640
Registered Office: Chertsey Road, Sunbury on Thames, Middlesex, TW16 7BP
Activities: Financial intermediation not elsewhere classified
Parent: BP International Limited
Officers: Kathryn Mary Berry [1967] Director/Oil Company Executive; Jan Clayton Lyons [1965] Director/Oil Company Executive [American]

BP Biofuels Brazil Investments Limited
Incorporated: 23 February 2011
Net Worth: £800,981,376 *Total Assets:* £800,981,376
Registered Office: Chertsey Road, Sunbury on Thames, Middlesex, TW16 7BP
Activities: Activities of head offices
Parent: BP Asia Pacific Holdings Limited
Officers: David Thomas Anderson [1964] Director/Oil Company Executive; Mario Lindenhayn [1964] Director/Oil Company Executive [Brazilian/German]; Nicholas James Wayth [1973] Director/Oil Company Executive

BP Capital Markets P.L.C.
Incorporated: 14 December 1976
Net Worth: £562,711,872 *Total Assets:* £44,762,333,184
Registered Office: Chertsey Road, Sunbury on Thames, Middlesex, TW16 7BP
Activities: Financial intermediation not elsewhere classified
Parent: BP International Limited
Officers: Dr Brian Gilvary [1962] Director; Jayne Angela Hodgson [1969] Director/Oil Company Executive; Katherine Anne Thomson [1968] Director/Oil Company Executive

BP Car Fleet Limited
Incorporated: 8 March 1960
Previous: BP Car Finance Limited
Net Worth: £84,639,000 *Total Assets:* £84,655,000
Registered Office: Chertsey Road, Sunbury on Thames, Middlesex, TW16 7BP
Activities: Financial leasing
Parent: BP PLC.
Officers: Dr Brian Gilvary [1962] Director; Katherine Anne Thomson [1968] Director/Oil Company Executive

BP Chemicals (Korea) Limited
Incorporated: 11 November 1988
Net Worth: £104,169,000 *Total Assets:* £105,049,000
Registered Office: Chertsey Road, Sunbury on Thames, Middlesex, TW16 7BP
Activities: Activities of head offices
Shareholder: BP Chemicals Limited
Officers: Nigel Clifford Dunn [1967] Director/Oil Company Executive; Catherine Ann McCann [1966] Director/Oil Company Executive; Terence Michael Thornton [1963] Director/Oil Company Executive

BP Chemicals East China Investments Limited
Incorporated: 2 February 2001
Net Worth: £1,083,322,880 *Total Assets:* £1,083,757,312
Registered Office: Chertsey Road, Sunbury on Thames, Middlesex, TW16 7BP
Activities: Activities of head offices
Parent: BP Global Investments Limited
Officers: Nicholas John Charles Evans [1969] Director/Oil Company Executive; Rita Elizabeth Griffin [1963] Director/Oil Company Executive [American]; Terence Michael Thornton [1963] Director/Oil Company Executive

BP Chemicals Investments Limited
Incorporated: 2 September 1935
Net Worth: £245,367,824 *Total Assets:* £306,761,504
Registered Office: Chertsey Road, Sunbury on Thames, Middlesex, TW16 7BP
Activities: Activities of head offices
Parent: BP International Limited
Officers: Rita Elizabeth Griffin [1963] Director/Oil Company Executive [American]; Catherine Ann McCann [1966] Director/Oil Company Executive; Terence Michael Thornton [1963] Director/Oil Company Executive

BP Chemicals Limited
Incorporated: 9 January 1924 *Employees:* 439
Net Worth: £95,729,000 *Total Assets:* £101,846,000
Registered Office: Chertsey Road, Sunbury on Thames, Middlesex, TW16 7BP
Activities: Manufacture of other inorganic basic chemicals
Parent: BP Chemicals Investments Limited
Officers: Nigel Clifford Dunn [1967] Director/Oil Company Executive; Catherine Ann McCann [1966] Director/Oil Company Executive; Terence Michael Thornton [1963] Director/Oil Company Executive

BP Corporate Holdings Limited
Incorporated: 23 November 2000
Net Worth: £5,403,174,400 *Total Assets:* £5,420,483,584
Registered Office: Chertsey Road, Sunbury on Thames, Middlesex, TW16 7BP
Activities: Activities of head offices
Parent: BP International Limited
Officers: Dr Brian Gilvary [1962] Director; Jayne Angela Hodgson [1969] Director/Oil Company Executive; Katherine Anne Thomson [1968] Director/Oil Company Executive

BP Exploration (Algeria) Limited
Incorporated: 19 February 1970 *Employees:* 6
Net Worth: £499,087,200 *Total Assets:* £499,201,024
Registered Office: Chertsey Road, Sunbury on Thames, Middlesex, TW16 7BP
Activities: Extraction of crude petroleum
Parent: BP Exploration Operating Company Limited
Officers: Amna Bon [1980] Director [Australian]; Timothy King [1978] Director/Oil Company Executive [Irish]; Wissam Al Monthiry [1980] Director/Oil Company Executive [Canadian]

BP Exploration (Alpha) Limited
Incorporated: 16 August 1971 *Employees:* 43
Net Worth: £2,852,660,480 *Total Assets:* £3,334,274,304
Registered Office: Chertsey Road, Sunbury on Thames, Middlesex, TW16 7BP
Activities: Extraction of crude petroleum
Parent: BP Exploration Operating Company Limited
Officers: Ariel David Flores [1977] Director/Oil Company Executive [American]; Sandra Jean MacRae [1963] Director/Oil Company Executive; Sashi Kumar Mukundan [1957] Director/Oil Company Executive [American]; David Alan Rider [1964] Director/Oil Company Executive; Dr Bryan David Ritchie [1975] Director/Oil Company Executive

BP Exploration (Angola) Limited
Incorporated: 24 November 1958
Net Worth: £6,367,930,880 *Total Assets:* £7,970,078,720
Registered Office: Chertsey Road, Sunbury on Thames, Middlesex, TW16 7BP
Activities: Extraction of crude petroleum
Parent: BP Exploration Operating Company Limited
Officers: Sandra Jean MacRae [1963] Director/Oil Company Executive; David Alan Rider [1964] Director/Oil Company Executive; Stephen Willis [1962] Director/Oil Company Executive

BP Exploration (Azerbaijan) Limited
Incorporated: 2 September 1987
Net Worth: £5,288,811,008 *Total Assets:* £5,863,719,424
Registered Office: Chertsey Road, Sunbury on Thames, Middlesex, TW16 7BP
Activities: Extraction of crude petroleum
Parent: BP Exploration Operating Company Limited
Officers: Jaqui Freeman [1968] Director/Oil Company Executive; Robert Gary Jones [1960] Director/Oil Company Executive

BP Exploration (Caspian Sea) Limited
Incorporated: 11 February 1946 *Employees:* 3,226
Net Worth: £4,594,371,584 *Total Assets:* £7,042,281,472
Registered Office: Chertsey Road, Sunbury on Thames, Middlesex, TW16 7BP
Activities: Extraction of crude petroleum
Parent: BP Exploration Operating Company Limited
Officers: Jaqui Freeman [1968] Director/Oil Company Executive; Robert Gary Jones [1960] Director/Oil Company Executive

BP Exploration (Delta) Limited
Incorporated: 6 July 1970
Net Worth: £4,603,390,464 *Total Assets:* £5,733,650,944
Registered Office: Chertsey Road, Sunbury on Thames, Middlesex, TW16 7BP
Activities: Extraction of crude petroleum
Parent: BP Exploration Operating Company Limited
Officers: Hesham Saad Mekawi [1960] Director/Oil Company Executive [Egyptian]; John Myers [1967] Director/Oil Company Executive; Karim Mohamed Alaaeldin Abdelhakim Youssef [1981] Director/Oil Company Executive [Egyptian]

BP Exploration (Epsilon) Limited
Incorporated: 17 March 1971 *Employees:* 388
Net Worth: £2,364,617,728 *Total Assets:* £2,825,721,856
Registered Office: Chertsey Road, Sunbury on Thames, Middlesex, TW16 7BP
Activities: Extraction of crude petroleum
Parent: BP Exploration Operating Company Limited
Officers: Andrew James Alexander McAuslan [1961] Director/Oil Company Executive; Yousuf Mohamed Salim Al Ojaili [1963] Director/Oil Company Executive [Omani]; Michael Andrew Wenham [1959] Director/Oil Company Executive

BP Exploration (Shah Deniz) Limited
Incorporated: 3 July 1996
Net Worth: £2 *Total Assets:* £522,955,648
Registered Office: Chertsey Road, Sunbury on Thames, Middlesex, TW16 7BP
Activities: Extraction of crude petroleum
Parent: BP Exploration Operating Company Limited
Officers: Jaqui Freeman [1968] Director/Oil Company Executive; Robert Gary Jones [1960] Director/Oil Company Executive

BP Exploration Angola (Kwanza Benguela) Limited
Incorporated: 8 February 2011
Net Worth: £300,309,120 *Total Assets:* £321,866,336
Registered Office: Chertsey Road, Sunbury on Thames, Middlesex, TW16 7BP
Activities: Test drilling and boring
Parent: BP Exploration Operating Company Limited
Officers: Howard Leach [1962] Director/Oil Company Executive; David Alan Rider [1964] Director/Oil Company Executive; Stephen Willis [1962] Director/Oil Company Executive

BP Exploration Beta Limited
Incorporated: 12 January 1967
Net Worth: £521,550,272 *Total Assets:* £683,506,112
Registered Office: Chertsey Road, Sunbury on Thames, Middlesex, TW16 7BP
Activities: Extraction of crude petroleum
Parent: BP Exploration Operating Company Limited
Officers: Ariel David Flores [1977] Director/Oil Company Executive [American]; Howard Leach [1962] Director/Oil Company Executive; Sandra Jean MacRae [1963] Director/Oil Company Executive; David Alan Rider [1964] Director/Oil Company Executive; Stephen Willis [1962] Director/Oil Company Executive

BP Exploration China Limited
Incorporated: 2 March 2012
Net Worth Deficit: £2,959,859 *Total Assets:* £33,227,468
Registered Office: Chertsey Road, Sunbury on Thames, Middlesex, TW16 7BP
Activities: Support activities for petroleum and natural gas mining
Parent: BP Exploration Operating Company Limited
Officers: Edward Gallatin Bryant [1960] Director/Oil Company Executive [American]; Sandra Jean MacRae [1963] Director/Oil Company Executive; Dr Lorna Taryn Malcolm [1972] Director/Oil Company Executive

BP Exploration Indonesia Limited
Incorporated: 3 May 1971
Net Worth: £19,343,708 *Total Assets:* £86,533,776
Registered Office: Chertsey Road, Sunbury on Thames, Middlesex, TW16 7BP
Activities: Extraction of crude petroleum
Parent: BP Exploration Operating Company Limited
Officers: Sandra Jean MacRae [1963] Director/Oil Company Executive; Alan Philip Martin [1971] Director/Oil Company Executive; Svetlana Pereverzeva [1972] Director/Oil Company Executive; Alison Sheila Young [1965] Director/Oil Company Executive; Nader Zaki [1973] Director/Oil Company Executive [Egyptian]

BP Exploration Libya Limited
Incorporated: 18 January 2005 *Employees:* 1
Net Worth: £175,523,264 *Total Assets:* £244,057,344
Registered Office: Chertsey Road, Sunbury on Thames, Middlesex, TW16 7BP
Activities: Extraction of crude petroleum
Parent: BP Exploration Operating Company Limited
Officers: Andrew James Alexander McAuslan [1961] Director/Oil Company Executive; Jasper Adrianus Marinus Matthaeus Peijs [1969] Director/Oil Company Executive [Dutch]; Karim Mohamed Alaaeldin Abdelhakim Youssef [1981] Director/Oil Company Executive [Egyptian]

BP Exploration North Africa Limited
Incorporated: 18 January 2005
Net Worth: £174,196,880 *Total Assets:* £176,713,184
Registered Office: Chertsey Road, Sunbury on Thames, Middlesex, TW16 7BP
Activities: Extraction of crude petroleum
Parent: BP Exploration Operating Company Limited
Officers: Hesham Saad Mekawi [1960] Director/Oil Company Executive [Egyptian]; John Myers [1967] Director/Oil Company Executive; Karim Mohamed Alaaeldin Abdelhakim Youssef [1981] Director/Oil Company Executive [Egyptian]

BP Exploration Operating Company Limited
Incorporated: 12 October 1935 *Employees:* 3,625
Net Worth: £43,361,202,176 *Total Assets:* £49,403,691,008
Registered Office: Chertsey Road, Sunbury on Thames, Middlesex, TW16 7BP
Activities: Extraction of crude petroleum
Parent: BP Exploration Company Limited
Officers: Emma Louise Delaney-Mc Knight [1973] Director/Oil Company Executive [Irish]; Ariel David Flores [1977] Director/Oil Company Executive [American]; Dr Andrew Beaton Johnston [1959] Director/Oil Company Executive; Karen MacLennan [1971] Director/Oil Company Executive; Sandra Jean MacRae [1963] Director/Oil Company Executive; Peter James Mather [1960] Director/Oil Company Executive; Peter William Anderson Miller [1968] Director/Oil Company Executive; Doris Friederike Reiter [1970] Director/Oil Company Executive [Austrian/American]

BP Finance P.L.C
Incorporated: 22 January 2001
Net Worth: £1,780,986,624 *Total Assets:* £1,781,024,000
Registered Office: Chertsey Road, Sunbury on Thames, Middlesex, TW16 7BP
Activities: Financial intermediation not elsewhere classified
Parent: BP International Limited
Officers: Martin Francis Giles [1961] Director/Oil Company Executive; Dr Brian Gilvary [1962] Director; Richard Alastair Hubbard [1963] Director/Oil Company Executive; Katherine Anne Thomson [1968] Director/Oil Company Executive

BP Gas Marketing Limited
Incorporated: 22 June 1967
Net Worth: £1,105,419,008 *Total Assets:* £4,760,592,896
Registered Office: Chertsey Road, Sunbury on Thames, Middlesex, TW16 7BP
Activities: Support activities for petroleum and natural gas mining
Parent: BP Exploration Operating Company Limited
Officers: Robert John Harrison [1964] Director/Oil Company Executive; David William Knipe [1974] Director/Oil Company Executive; Robert Stephen Lawson [1970] Director/Oil Company Executive

BP Global Investments Limited
Incorporated: 24 March 1932
Net Worth: £9,464,045,568 *Total Assets:* £13,726,040,064
Registered Office: Chertsey Road, Sunbury on Thames, Middlesex, TW16 7BP
Activities: Activities of head offices
Parent: BP PLC.
Officers: David James Bucknall [1968] Director/Oil Company Executive; Dr Brian Gilvary [1962] Director; Jayne Angela Hodgson [1969] Director/Oil Company Executive; Jan Clayton Lyons [1965] Director/Oil Company Executive [American]; Michael John O'Sullivan [1964] Director/Oil Company Executive; Katherine Anne Thomson [1968] Director/Oil Company Executive

BP Greece Limited
Incorporated: 7 September 1921
Net Worth: £108,807,912 *Total Assets:* £110,869,536
Registered Office: Chertsey Road, Sunbury on Thames, Middlesex, TW16 7BP
Activities: Activities of head offices
Parent: BP Global Investments Limited
Officers: Nicholas John Charles Evans [1969] Director/Oil Company Executive; David Alan Rider [1964] Director/Oil Company Executive; Terence Michael Thornton [1963] Director/Oil Company Executive

BP Holdings Canada Limited
Incorporated: 30 October 2012
Net Worth: £4,533,431,808 *Total Assets:* £4,533,431,808
Registered Office: Chertsey Road, Sunbury on Thames, Middlesex, TW16 7BP
Activities: Activities of head offices
Parent: BP PLC.
Officers: Martin Francis Giles [1961] Director/Oil Company Executive; Jan Clayton Lyons [1965] Director/Oil Company Executive [American]; Katherine Anne Thomson [1968] Director/Oil Company Executive

BP Holdings North America Limited
Incorporated: 20 December 2006
Net Worth: £51,804,327,936 *Total Assets:* £51,804,418,048
Registered Office: Chertsey Road, Sunbury on Thames, Middlesex, TW16 7BP
Activities: Activities of head offices
Parent: BP P L C
Officers: Dr Brian Gilvary [1962] Director; Jayne Angela Hodgson [1969] Director/Oil Company Executive; Katherine Anne Thomson [1968] Director/Oil Company Executive

BP International Limited
Incorporated: 29 December 1954
Net Worth: £43,699,302,400 *Total Assets:* £160,948,404,224
Registered Office: Chertsey Road, Sunbury on Thames, Middlesex, TW16 7BP
Activities: Wholesale of other fuels and related products
Parent: BP PLC.
Officers: David James Bucknall [1968] Director/Group Treasurer; Dr Brian Gilvary [1962] Director; Jayne Angela Hodgson [1969] Director/Oil Company Executive; Jan Clayton Lyons [1965] Director/Oil Company Executive [American]; Michael John O'Sullivan [1964] Director/Oil Company Executive; Katherine Anne Thomson [1968] Director/Oil Company Executive

BP Investment Management Limited
Incorporated: 7 December 1936
Net Worth: £52,308,912 *Total Assets:* £56,856,624
Registered Office: Chertsey Road, Sunbury on Thames, Middlesex, TW16 7BP
Activities: Other business support service activities n.e.c.
Parent: BP Pension Trustees Limited
Officers: Diana Patricia Legge, Secretary; Douglas Roderick MacLeod [1953] Director/Oil Company Executive; Paul Jonathan Reed [1956] Director; Shane Michael Roche [1976] Director/Oil Company Executive [Irish]; Mark Edward Stageman [1953] Managing Director - GIR Limited

BP Investments Asia Limited
Incorporated: 29 November 2005
Net Worth: £44,532,648 *Total Assets:* £44,532,652
Registered Office: Chertsey Road, Sunbury on Thames, Middlesex, TW16 7BP
Activities: Activities of head offices
Parent: BP Global Investments Limited
Officers: Jonathan Peter Platt [1967] Director/Oil Company Executive; Clive Colin Gerard Sinnott [1963] Director/Oil Company Executive

BP Marine Limited
Incorporated: 29 May 1975
Net Worth: £116,557,536 *Total Assets:* £151,731,200
Registered Office: Chertsey Road, Sunbury on Thames, Middlesex, TW16 7BP
Activities: Wholesale of other fuels and related products
Parent: BP International Limited
Officers: Jens Jacob Andersen [1970] Director/Oil Company Executive [Danish]; Robert David Mutchell [1974] Director/Oil Company Executive; Kamuran Yazganoglu [1976] Director/Oil Company Executive [Turkish]

BP Mauritania Investments Limited
Incorporated: 9 December 2016
Net Worth: £321,781,760 *Total Assets:* £374,844,672
Registered Office: c/o BP Exploration (West Africa) Limited, Chertsey Road, Sunbury on Thames, Middlesex, TW16 7BP
Activities: Activities of other holding companies n.e.c.
Parent: BP Exploration Operating Company Limited
Officers: Emma Louise Delaney-McKnight [1973] Director/Oil Company Executive [Irish]; Andrew Charles Lane [1963] Director/Oil Company Executive; Russell Irving Smith [1960] Director/Oil Company Executive

BP Middle East Limited
Incorporated: 30 September 1957
Net Worth: £25,116,584 *Total Assets:* £160,749,520
Registered Office: Chertsey Road, Sunbury on Thames, Middlesex, TW16 7BP
Activities: Wholesale of other fuels and related products
Parent: BP PLC.
Officers: Jens Bertelsen [1959] Director/Deputy Secretary; Nicholas John Charles Evans [1969] Director/Oil Company Executive; Terence Michael Thornton [1963] Director/Oil Company Executive

BP Oil International Limited
Incorporated: 28 December 1936
Net Worth: £142,143,008 *Total Assets:* £142,143,008
Registered Office: Chertsey Road, Sunbury on Thames, Middlesex, TW16 7BP
Activities: Wholesale of other fuels and related products
Parent: BP International Limited
Officers: Alan Henry Haywood [1966] Director; Carol-Lee Howle [1972] Director/Oil Company Executive; Robert Stephen Lawson [1970] Director/Oil Company Executive; Brian Michael Puffer [1969] Director/Oil Company Executive [British/American]; Geir Patrick Robinson [1968] Director/Oil Company Executive

BP Oil UK Limited
Incorporated: 20 December 1947 *Employees:* 341
Net Worth: £816,000,000 *Total Assets:* £1,510,000,000
Registered Office: Chertsey Road, Sunbury on Thames, Middlesex, TW16 7BP
Activities: Mineral oil refining
Parent: BP International Limited
Officers: Neil Emmett [1970] Director/Oil Company Executive; Nicola Louise Grady-Smith [1973] Director/Oil Company Executive; William George Warren Harland [1975] Director/Oil Company Executive; Peter James Mather [1960] Director/Oil Company Executive

BP Oil Vietnam Limited
Incorporated: 8 June 1956
Net Worth: £45,285,296 *Total Assets:* £45,285,296
Registered Office: Chertsey Road, Sunbury on Thames, Middlesex, TW16 7BP
Activities: Wholesale of other fuels and related products
Parent: BP Asia Pacific Holdings Limited
Officers: Sandra Jean MacRae [1963] Director/Oil Company Executive

BP Pension Trustees Limited
Incorporated: 25 May 1928
Net Worth: £52,000,000 *Total Assets:* £56,905,000
Registered Office: Chertsey Road, Sunbury on Thames, Middlesex, TW16 7BP
Activities: Pension funding
Parent: BP PLC.
Officers: Diana Legge, Secretary; Grahame Paul Cook [1963] Director; Emma Louise Delaney-McKnight [1973] Director/Oil Company Executive [Irish]; Catherine Sarah Gillam [1979] Director/Oil Company Executive; David John Jackson [1953] Director/Solicitor; Jan Clayton Lyons [1965] Director/Oil Company Executive [American]; Peter James Mather [1960] Director/Oil Company Executive; Sir Ian Maurice Gray Prosser [1943] Director; Mark Edward Stageman [1953] Director; Angus James Walker [1963] Director

BP Pipelines (BTC) Limited
Incorporated: 5 November 2001
Net Worth: £475,656,736 *Total Assets:* £509,718,560
Registered Office: Chertsey Road, Sunbury on Thames, Middlesex, TW16 7BP
Activities: Activities of head offices
Parent: BTC Pipeline Holding Company Limited
Officers: Jaqui Freeman [1968] Director/Oil Company Executive; Robert Gary Jones [1960] Director/Oil Company Executive

BP Pipelines (SCP) Limited
Incorporated: 23 May 2002
Net Worth: £1,095,581,312 *Total Assets:* £1,095,581,312
Registered Office: Chertsey Road, Sunbury on Thames, Middlesex, TW16 7BP
Activities: Activities of head offices
Parent: BP Global Investments Limited
Officers: Jaqui Freeman [1968] Director/Oil Company Executive; Robert Gary Jones [1960] Director/Oil Company Executive

BP Pipelines Tap Limited
Incorporated: 25 February 2016
Net Worth: £338,963,616 *Total Assets:* £537,848,320
Registered Office: Chertsey Road, Sunbury on Thames, Middlesex, TW16 7BP
Activities: Activities of head offices
Parent: BP Exploration Operating Company Limited
Officers: Jaqui Freeman [1968] Director/Oil Company Executive; Robert Gary Jones [1960] Director/Oil Company Executive

BP Properties Limited
Incorporated: 27 July 1961
Net Worth: £56,512,000 *Total Assets:* £58,560,000
Registered Office: Chertsey Road, Sunbury on Thames, Middlesex, TW16 7BP
Activities: Buying and selling of own real estate
Parent: BP PLC
Officers: Juliet Nadine Filose [1960] Director/Oil Company Executive; David Alan Rider [1964] Director/Oil Company Executive; Katherine Anne Thomson [1968] Director/Oil Company Executive

BP Russian Investments Limited
Incorporated: 5 December 1990
Net Worth: £11,790,125,056 *Total Assets:* £11,975,698,432
Registered Office: Chertsey Road, Sunbury on Thames, Middlesex, TW16 7BP
Activities: Activities of head offices
Parent: BP International Limited
Officers: Joanne Elizabeth Cross [1965] Director/Oil Company Lawyer; Sandra Jean MacRae [1963] Director/Oil Company Executive; David Alan Rider [1964] Director/Oil Company Executive; Lord George Islay MacNeill Robertson [1946] Director

BP Senegal Investments Limited
Incorporated: 29 January 2016 *Employees:* 1
Net Worth: £640,183,808 *Total Assets:* £701,984,000
Registered Office: Chertsey Road, Sunbury on Thames, Middlesex, TW16 7BP
Activities: Support activities for petroleum and natural gas mining
Parent: BP Exploration Operating Company Limited
Officers: Emma Louise Delaney-Mc Knight [1973] Director/Oil Company Executive [Irish]; Andrew Charles Lane [1963] Director/Oil Company Executive; Russell Irving Smith [1960] Director/Oil Company Executive

BP Shipping Limited
Incorporated: 30 April 1915
Net Worth: £1,602,840,704 *Total Assets:* £1,682,076,032
Registered Office: Chertsey Road, Sunbury on Thames, Middlesex, TW16 7BP
Activities: Sea and coastal freight water transport
Parent: BP International Limited
Officers: Carol-Lee Howle [1972] Director/Oil Company Executive; Roderick Guy Mason [1964] Director/Oil Company Executive; Aleida Garza Rios [1968] Director/Oil Company Executive [American]; Katherine Anne Thomson [1968] Director/Oil Company Executive; Chunming Zhao [1966] Director/Oil Company Executive [Chinese]

BP Subsea Well Response Limited
Incorporated: 2 March 2012
Net Worth: £35,110,936 *Total Assets:* £37,991,692
Registered Office: Chertsey Road, Sunbury on Thames, Middlesex, TW16 7BP
Activities: Other business support service activities n.e.c.
Parent: BP Exploration Operating Company Limited
Officers: Gordon Young Birrell [1963] Director/Oil Company Executive; Jaqui Freeman [1968] Director/Oil Company Executive; Timothy Robert Schofield [1963] Director/Oil Company Executive

BP Technology Ventures Limited
Incorporated: 27 March 1981
Previous: BP Alternative Energy International Limited
Net Worth: £68,475,040 *Total Assets:* £120,078,968
Registered Office: Chertsey Road, Sunbury on Thames, Middlesex, TW16 7BP
Activities: Activities of head offices
Parent: BP International Limited
Officers: David Geoffrey Philip Eyton [1961] Director/Oil Company Executive; Anna Marie Floyer-LEA [1976] Director/Oil Company Executive; David Ian Gilmour [1960] Sales & Marketing Director

BP Turkey Refining Limited
Incorporated: 15 August 1958
Net Worth: £16,496,006 *Total Assets:* £25,843,286
Registered Office: Chertsey Road, Sunbury on Thames, Middlesex, TW16 7BP
Activities: Mineral oil refining
Parent: BP PLC.
Officers: Nicholas John Charles Evans [1969] Director/Oil Company Executive; Richard James Lord [1980] Director/Oil Company Executive; Terence Michael Thornton [1963] Director/Oil Company Executive

BPDM Group Ltd
Incorporated: 31 January 1972 *Employees:* 2
Previous: B.P. Direct Mail Company Limited
Net Worth: £34,107,092 *Total Assets:* £34,548,844
Registered Office: Castle House, Castle Hill Avenue, Folkestone, Kent, CT20 2TQ
Activities: Other letting and operating of own or leased real estate
Shareholders: Diana Pauline Burford; Ronald Albert Burford
Officers: Diana Pauline Burford, Secretary; Diana Pauline Burford [1947] Director/Secretary; Ronald Albert Burford [1946] Director/Accounts Manager

BPHA Finance PLC
Incorporated: 6 March 2014
Net Worth: £12,500 *Total Assets:* £203,838,336
Registered Office: Bedford Heights, Manton Lane, Bedford, MK41 7BJ
Activities: Security dealing on own account
Officers: Philippa Spratley, Secretary; Kevin Ronald Bolt [1957] Director/Management Consultant; Paul Lawrence Gray [1961] Director/Chartered Accountant; Malgorzata Motler [1973] Director/Head of Corporate Finance

BPS Offshore Services Limited
Incorporated: 19 November 1981
Net Worth: £115,455,000 *Total Assets:* £123,600,000
Registered Office: Riverbank, Meadows Business Park, Blackwater, Camberley, Surrey, GU17 9AB
Activities: Non-trading company
Parent: Rentokil Limited
Officers: Catherine Stead, Secretary; Daragh Patrick Feltrim Fagan [1969] Director/Solicitor; Catherine Jane Stead [1978] Director/Company Secretary

Bradenstoke Solar Park Limited
Incorporated: 5 November 2014
Net Worth Deficit: £15,324,218 *Total Assets:* £52,818,064
Registered Office: 40 Brighton Road, Sutton, Surrey, SM2 5BN
Activities: Production of electricity
Officers: Charles Bondi [1972] Director/Accountant; Kenneth Reid Ross [1968] Director

Braeforge Investment Limited
Incorporated: 5 March 2012 *Employees:* 308
Net Worth: £4,368,894 *Total Assets:* £23,845,288
Registered Office: Empress House, 129-155 Empress Road, Southampton, SO14 0JW
Activities: Activities of production holding companies
Parent: BWP (Cambridge) Limited
Officers: Gideon James Bishop [1970] Director; Mark David Langslow [1970] Director; Timothy Daniel Lowth [1968] Finance Director; Michael John Mitchell [1962] Director/Business Consultant; Dave Roy Terry [1968] Operations Director

Brake Bros Foodservice Limited
Incorporated: 30 October 1961 *Employees:* 129
Net Worth: £132,150,000 *Total Assets:* £132,150,000
Registered Office: Enterprise House, Eureka Business Park, Ashford, Kent, TN25 4AG
Activities: Non-specialised wholesale of food, beverages and tobacco
Parent: Brake Bros Limited
Officers: Sarah Leanne Whibley, Secretary; Michael David Ball [1967] Director/Group Chief Financial Officer; Ajoy Hari Karna [1966] Director/Senior Vice President [American]; Sarah Leanne Whibley [1976] Director/Group Secretary & General Counsel

Brake Bros Holding I Limited
Incorporated: 19 June 2002
Net Worth: £1,585,500,032 *Total Assets:* £1,585,500,032
Registered Office: Enterprise House, Eureka Business Park, Ashford, Kent, TN25 4AG
Activities: Activities of head offices
Parent: Cucina Acquisition (UK) Limited
Officers: Sarah Leanne Whibley, Secretary; Michael David Ball [1967] Director/Group Chief Financial Officer; Ajoy Hari Karna [1966] Director/Senior Vice President [American]; Sarah Leanne Whibley [1976] Director/Group Secretary & General Counsel

Brake Bros Limited
Incorporated: 8 July 1986 *Employees:* 14,770
Net Worth: £703,000,000 *Total Assets:* £1,835,500,032
Registered Office: Enterprise House, Eureka Business Park, Ashford, Kent, TN25 4AG
Activities: Non-specialised wholesale of food, beverages and tobacco
Parent: Brake Bros Holding I Limited
Officers: Sarah Leanne Whibley, Secretary; Michael David Ball [1967] Director/Group Chief Financial Officer; Ajoy Hari Karna [1966] Director/Senior Vice President [American]; Sarah Leanne Whibley [1976] Director/Group Secretary & General Counsel

W.H. Brakspear & Sons Limited
Incorporated: 28 January 1896 *Employees:* 25
Net Worth: £59,174,000 *Total Assets:* £106,872,000
Registered Office: Bull Courtyard, Bell Street, Henley on Thames, Oxon, RG9 2BA
Activities: Wholesale of wine, beer, spirits and other alcoholic beverages
Parent: J.T.D. Investments Limited
Officers: David Generald Nathan, Secretary; Michael Anthony Trehearne Davies [1953] Director; Thomas Anthony Trehearne Davies [1980] Director; David Generald Nathan [1970] Director

Brambles Enterprises Limited
Incorporated: 21 December 1988 *Employees:* 80
Net Worth: £8,135,000 *Total Assets:* £33,937,000
Registered Office: 2nd Floor, 400 Dashwood Lang Road, Bourne Business Park, Addlestone, Surrey, KT15 2HJ
Activities: Activities of head offices
Parent: Cyan Logistics Limited
Officers: Daniel Robert Berry [1973] Director/Lawyer; Michael Bruce Pooley [1967] Director/President, CHEP Europe

Brambles Finance PLC
Incorporated: 31 October 2002
Net Worth: £120,559,008 *Total Assets:* £2,266,366,976
Registered Office: 2nd Floor, 400 Dashwood Lang Road, Bourne Business Park, Addlestone, Surrey, KT15 2HJ
Activities: Financial intermediation not elsewhere classified
Parent: Brambles Holdings Unlimited
Officers: Peter Jonathon Caisley Bruford [1964] Director/Accountant; Pascal Huart [1963] Director/Treasurer [Belgian]; Rafe Anthony Warren [1959] Director/Accountant

Brambles Holdings (UK) Limited
Incorporated: 23 February 2001 *Employees:* 130
Net Worth: £845,748,032 *Total Assets:* £888,199,168
Registered Office: 2nd Floor, 400 Dashwood Lang Road, Bourne Business Park, Addlestone, Surrey, KT15 2HJ
Activities: Activities of head offices
Parent: Brambles U.K. Limited
Officers: Peter Jonathon Caisley Bruford [1964] Director/Accountant; Pascal Huart [1963] Director/Treasurer [Belgian]; Rafe Anthony Warren [1959] Director/Accountant

Brambles Holdings Unlimited
Incorporated: 10 October 2006
Net Worth: £2,419,762,688 *Total Assets:* £2,660,660,480
Registered Office: 2nd Floor, 400 Dashwood Lang Road, Bourne Business Park, Addlestone, Surrey, KT15 2HJ
Activities: Activities of other holding companies n.e.c.
Officers: Peter Jonathon Caisley Bruford [1964] Director/Accountant; Pascal Huart [1963] Director/Regional Treasurer [Belgian]; Rafe Anthony Warren [1959] Director/Accountant

Brambles Investment Ltd.
Incorporated: 11 October 2006
Net Worth: £1,455,966,848 *Total Assets:* £2,233,382,144
Registered Office: 2nd Floor, 400 Dashwood Lang Road, Bourne Business Park, Addlestone, Surrey, KT15 2HJ
Activities: Activities of other holding companies n.e.c.
Parent: Brambles Holdings Unlimited
Officers: Peter Jonathon Caisley Bruford [1964] Director/Accountant; Pascal Huart [1963] Director/Regional Treasurer [Belgian]; Rafe Anthony Warren [1959] Director/Accountant

Brambles U.K. Limited
Incorporated: 3 December 1980
Net Worth: £786,406,016 *Total Assets:* £920,161,024
Registered Office: 2nd Floor, 400 Dashwood Lang Road, Bourne Business Park, Addlestone, Surrey, KT15 2HJ
Activities: Activities of other holding companies n.e.c.
Parent: BFIM Limited
Officers: Peter Jonathon Caisley Bruford [1964] Director/Accountant; Pascal Huart [1963] Director/Treasurer [Belgian]; Rafe Anthony Warren [1959] Director/Accountant

Brand Energy & Infrastructure Services UK, Ltd.
Incorporated: 11 October 2013 *Employees:* 1,043
Net Worth: £11,948,000 *Total Assets:* £47,269,000
Registered Office: Regent Park, 299 Kingston Road, Leatherhead, Surrey, KT22 7SG
Activities: Other service activities n.e.c.
Major Shareholder: Donald J. Gogel
Officers: Michael Edward Herke [1964] Director [Irish]; James David Maskell [1972] Director; Christopher McGalpine [1962] Director/VP Engineering, Asset and Project Management; Benjamin Stevenson Read [1974] Director/Chartered Accountant

Brand Reputation Compliance Limited
Incorporated: 21 November 2016 *Employees:* 35
Net Worth Deficit: £5,397,430 *Total Assets:* £37,995,408
Registered Office: LGC, Queens Road, Teddington, Middlesex, TW11 0LY
Activities: Other professional, scientific and technical activities n.e.c.
Shareholders: LGC (Holdings) Limited; LGC (Holdings) Limited
Officers: Navneet Kaur Ogle, Secretary; Helen Dickinson [1966] Director; Steven Esom [1960] Director; Tessa Leueen Anne Kelly [1953] Director; Euan Ralph Herbert O'Sullivan [1979] Managing Director; Manish Patel [1971] Director; Mark Christopher Proctor [1960] Director; Edward Smyth [1973] Director/Accountant

Brasserie Bar Co Limited
Incorporated: 6 February 2006 *Employees:* 35
Net Worth Deficit: £3,022,373 *Total Assets:* £51,583,560
Registered Office: Wizard House, 2a Cambridge Road, Teddington, Middlesex, TW11 8DR
Activities: Licenced restaurants
Parent: Abriand Ltd
Officers: Jeremy Brown [1966] Director; Kathryn Coury [1964] Director; Mark Derry [1960] Director; Stephen Peter Edwards [1964] Director/Venture Capitalist; Clive Andrew Fretwell [1961] Director; Christopher Patrick Edward Guy [1981] Finance Director; Helen Louise Melvin [1968] Director/Accountant

BRE Trust
Incorporated: 22 November 1996 *Employees:* 638
Net Worth Deficit: £17,176,000 *Total Assets:* £43,026,000
Registered Office: Bucknalls Lane, Garston, Watford, Herts, WD25 9XX
Activities: Other research and experimental development on natural sciences and engineering
Officers: Anthony Richard Tanner, Secretary; June Mary Barnes [1954] Non-Executive Director of Urban and Civic PLC; Julia Bernadette Barrett [1966] Director of Sustainability; Francesca Anne Howard Berriman [1964] Director/Chief Executive; Professor Nicholas Robert Jennings [1966] Director/Academic; Peter William MacDonald Lobban [1947] Director/Chief Executive; James Garwood Michael Wates [1960] Director; Philip George Wilbraham [1960] Expansion Programme Director; Gary Wingrove [1960] Projects and Construction Director

Brendoncare Foundation (The)
Incorporated: 14 February 1984 *Employees:* 667
Net Worth: £19,678,000 *Total Assets:* £36,009,000
Registered Office: The Old Malthouse, Victoria Road, Winchester, Hants, SO23 7DU
Activities: Residential care activities for the elderly and disabled
Officers: Rachel Jane McIlroy, Secretary; Dr Jacqueline Mary Bridges [1966] Director/Academic; Nick Cardale Capon [1951] Director/Lecturer; Fay Gillott [1955] Director; Dr Sarah Lindsay Hobhouse [1966] Director/Doctor; Ian David Jacobs [1962] Director; Lynne Carol Lockyer [1950] Director/Consultant; Joseph Patrick MacHale [1951] Director; David John Parfitt [1950] Director/Retired; Jonathan Mark Pullen [1951] Director; Dr Helen Roberts [1961] Director/Professor; Dr David Paul Stern [1959] Director/Management Consultant

Brentford FC Limited
Incorporated: 1 October 1998 *Employees:* 132
Net Worth: £2,600,290 *Total Assets:* £76,384,984
Registered Office: Griffin Park, Braemar Road, Brentford, Middlesex, TW8 0NT
Activities: Activities of sport clubs
Major Shareholder: Matthew Alexander Benham
Officers: Lisa Jane Skelhorn, Secretary; Rasmus Ankersen [1983] Sporting Director, Club Director [Danish]; Monique Choudhuri [1961] Director/Personal Development Consultant; Clifford Crown [1956] Finance Director; Philip Robert Giles [1979] Sporting Director, Club Director; Donald Gilbert Kerr [1952] Director/Marketing Consultant; David Leigh Merritt [1973] Director/Accountant; Michael John Power [1947] Director/Retired Business Executive; Nityajit Saidev Raj [1973] Director/Lawyer

Brentford Phase II LLP
Incorporated: 21 April 2016
Net Worth: £16,574,000 *Total Assets:* £43,948,000
Registered Office: First Floor, North Station House, 500 Elder Gate, Milton Keynes, Bucks, MK9 1BB

Brentford School for Girls
Incorporated: 8 November 2012 *Employees:* 103
Net Worth: £16,604,538 *Total Assets:* £20,395,524
Registered Office: Brentford School for Girls, 5 Boston Manor Road, Brentford, Middlesex, TW8 0PG
Activities: General secondary education
Officers: Caren Benn, Secretary; Shamiala Amin [1989] Director/Teacher; Marie Elizabeth Anderson [1977] Director/Marketing Consultant; Dr Katia Babbar [1978] Director/Banker; Renu Badiani [1978] Director/Solicitor; Paul Chambers [1974] Director/Procurement Manager; Simon French [1981] Director/Economist; Terri George [1965] Director/Teacher; Nicola Faye Gouldstone [1962] Director/Branding Consultant; Rosemary Ann Griffiths [1976] Director/Housewife; Nancy Horsnell [1954] Director/School Administrator; Sameem Malek [1970] Director/Teacher; Anna Moore [1979] Director/Solicitor; Sari-Maries Nesbeth [1970] Director/Headteacher; Julie Woodward [1976] Director/Programme Manager; Alison Wren [1980] Director/Housewife

Brentwick Limited
Incorporated: 28 February 1940
Net Worth: £105,310,128 *Total Assets:* £105,310,128
Registered Office: Cadbury House, Sanderson Road, Uxbridge, Middlesex, UB8 1DH
Activities: Other business support service activities n.e.c.
Parent: Kraft Foods Investment Holdings UK Limited
Officers: Adrian John Paul Arrighi [1978] Tax Director; Michael Brendan Foye [1965] Treasury Director; John Michael Hladusz [1972] Director/Chartered Accountant; Carole Noelle Keene [1966] Director

Peter Brett Associates LLP
Incorporated: 28 January 2008 *Employees:* 640
Net Worth: £15,772,019 *Total Assets:* £32,766,530
Registered Office: Buckingham Court, Kingsmead Business Park, London Road, High Wycombe, Bucks, HP11 1JU

Brevan Howard Asset Management LLP
Incorporated: 16 July 2002
Net Worth: £33,480,604 *Total Assets:* £39,723,056
Registered Office: 4th Floor, Reading Bridge House, George Street, Reading, Berks, RG1 8LS
Officers: Craig Richard Adams [1971] Member; Jonathan Paul Hughes [1982] Member; Ryan Edward Taylor [1975] Member; Jeremy Frederick Benjamin [1971] LLP Member; Daniel Bernheim [1970] LLP Member; Stuart Bygrave [1967] LLP Member; Andrea French [1972] LLP Member; Alan Eldad Howard [1963] LLP Member; Vivienne Jack [1969] LLP Member; Nagi Robert Kawkabani [1957] LLP Member; Aron Landy [1962] LLP Member; Trifon Alkiviades Natsis [1959] LLP Member; Miriam Porat [1975] LLP Member

BRF Invicta Limited
Incorporated: 12 March 2015 *Employees:* 148
Net Worth: £35,111,000 *Total Assets:* £185,527,008
Registered Office: 130 Eureka Park, Upper Pemberton, Boughton Aluph, Ashford, Kent, TN25 4AZ
Activities: Activities of distribution holding companies
Shareholders: Colin James Norton; BRF S.A.
Officers: Rubens Fernandes Pereira [1972] Director [Brazilian]; Daniel Paulo Hamada [1983] Director [Brazilian]; Elcio Mitsuhiro Ito [1975] Director/Business Administrator [Brazilian]; Colin James Norton [1968] Director

Bridge Leisure Bidco Limited
Incorporated: 3 July 2014 *Employees:* 3
Net Worth Deficit: £8,610,928 *Total Assets:* £61,511,060
Registered Office: 31 & 32 Shenley Pavilions, Chalkdell Drive, Shenley Wood, Milton Keynes, Bucks, MK5 6LB
Activities: Activities of head offices
Parent: Bridge Leisure Midco Ltd
Officers: Simon John Elliott [1969] Director/Investment Professional; Andrew Stephen Howe [1968] Director/Investment Professional; Simon Jamie Williams [1972] Director/Investment Professional

Bridge Leisure Finco Limited
Incorporated: 24 June 2014 *Employees:* 3
Net Worth Deficit: £9,412,108 *Total Assets:* £30,725,428
Registered Office: 31 & 32 Shenley Pavilions, Chalkdell Drive, Shenley Wood, Milton Keynes, Bucks, MK5 6LB
Activities: Activities of head offices
Parent: Bridge Leisure Topco Limited
Officers: Simon John Elliott [1969] Director/Investment Professional; Andrew Stephen Howe [1968] Director/Investment Professionals; Simon Williams [1972] Director

Bridge Leisure Midco Limited
Incorporated: 24 June 2014 *Employees:* 3
Net Worth: £75,465 *Total Assets:* £30,684,620
Registered Office: 31 & 32 Shenley Pavilions, Chalkdell Drive, Shenley Wood, Milton Keynes, Bucks, MK5 6LB
Activities: Activities of head offices
Parent: Bridge Leisure Finco Limited
Officers: Simon John Elliott [1969] Director/Investment Professional; Andrew Stephen Howe [1968] Director/Investment Professional; Simon Jamie Williams [1972] Director/Investment Professional

Bridge Leisure Topco Limited
Incorporated: 12 June 2014 *Employees:* 369
Net Worth Deficit: £13,813,769 *Total Assets:* £68,786,960
Registered Office: 31 & 32 Shenley Pavilions, Chalkdell Drive, Shenley Wood, Milton Keynes, Bucks, MK5 6LB
Activities: Activities of head offices
Officers: Simon John Elliott [1969] Director/Investment Professional; Andrew Stephen Howe [1968] Director/Investment Professional; Richard Andrew Hunt [1961] Director/Investment Professional; Alastair William Muirhead [1953] Director; William Skinner [1984] Director/Investment Professional; Simon Williams [1972] Director/Investment Professional

Bridgwater Bros.Holdings Limited
Incorporated: 9 December 1966 *Employees:* 196
Net Worth: £19,495,880 *Total Assets:* £22,437,940
Registered Office: Hamilton House, 39 Kings Road, Haslemere, Surrey, GU27 2QA
Activities: Other letting and operating of own or leased real estate
Officers: Duncan John Reynolds [1974] Director; George Christopher Reynolds [1972] Director

Brighthouse Group Limited
Incorporated: 16 May 2007 *Employees:* 2,526
Previous: Brighthouse Group PLC
Net Worth: £71,324,000 *Total Assets:* £233,292,000
Registered Office: 5 Hercules Way, Leavesden, Watford, Herts, WD25 7GS
Activities: Retail sale of audio and video equipment in specialised stores
Officers: David John Harwood, Secretary; Graeme James Campbell [1972] Finance Director; Hamish Stewart Paton [1976] Director

Brighthouse Holdings Limited
Incorporated: 17 May 2007
Net Worth: £196,879,008 *Total Assets:* £254,842,000
Registered Office: 5 Hercules Way, Leavesden, Watford, Herts, WD25 7GS
Activities: Retail sale of audio and video equipment in specialised stores
Parent: Brighthouse Group PLC
Officers: David John Harwood, Secretary; Graeme James Campbell [1972] Finance Director; Hamish Stewart Paton [1976] Director

Brighthouse Limited
Incorporated: 30 January 2007 *Employees:* 2,526
Net Worth: £222,264,000 *Total Assets:* £383,449,984
Registered Office: 5 Hercules Way, Leavesden, Watford, Herts, WD25 7GS
Activities: Retail sale of electrical household appliances in specialised stores
Parent: Brighthouse Holdings Ltd
Officers: David John Harwood, Secretary; Graeme James Campbell [1972] Finance Director; Hamish Stewart Paton [1976] Director

Brighton & Hove Albion Holdings Limited
Incorporated: 31 August 1993 *Employees:* 288
Net Worth Deficit: £42,329,760 *Total Assets:* £184,711,760
Registered Office: American Express, Community Stadium, Village Way, Brighton, BN1 9BL
Activities: Activities of head offices
Major Shareholder: Anthony Grant Bloom
Officers: Robert Francis Comer, Secretary; Paul Barber [1967] Director; Anthony Grant Bloom [1970] Director; Raymond Alexander Bloom [1946] Director; Derek Leonard Chapman [1957] Director; Robert Francis Comer [1956] Director; Adam Stephen Franks [1971] Director; Peter Winston Patrick Godfrey [1948] Director; David Andrew Jones [1960] Director; Martin John Perry [1947] Director; Marc Louis Sugarman [1972] Director; Michelle Jane Walder [1974] Director

Brighton & Hove Seaside Community Homes Limited
Incorporated: 27 March 2009 *Employees:* 5
Net Worth Deficit: £4,884,388 *Total Assets:* £29,680,164
Registered Office: Unit F, Hove Technology Centre, St Josephs Close, Hove, E Sussex, BN3 7ES
Activities: Other accommodation
Officers: Kevin Witterick Allen [1944] Director/Councillor; Christopher James Carlisle [1947] Director/Retired; David Stuart Gibson [1959] Director/Tenant Involvement Officer; Mary Bridget Mears [1947] Director/Councillor; Christopher Moquet [1948] Director/Retired; Baboucarr Mbye Sohna [1949] Director/Retired [Gambian]; Philip Stephen Woodgate [1963] Director/Accountant

Brighton College
Incorporated: 18 September 1873 *Employees:* 665
Net Worth: £82,793,544 *Total Assets:* £103,459,160
Registered Office: Brighton College, Eastern Road, Brighton, BN2 0AL
Activities: Pre-primary education
Officers: Paul Trevor Westbrook, Secretary; Neville Victor Abraham [1937] Director; Martina Asmar [1962] Director/Lawyer; Andrew Cayley [1964] Director/Barrister; Joel Edward Cohen [1980] Director/Solicitor; Joan Miner Deslandes [1958] Director/Headmistress; Robert James Hannington [1955] Chartered Surveyor, Non-Executive Director; William Henry Peter Jackson [1965] Director/Finance; Nicola Leach JP [1961] Director/Management Consultant; Christina Jane Maude [1957] Director/Architect; Francis Anthony Aylmer Maude [1953] Director/Member of Parliament; Geoffrey Ruscoe Miller [1938] Director/Retired Bank Executive; Lord John Frederick Mogg [1943] Director/Chairman; Adam Sven Pettitt [1966] Director/Headmaster; Nicholas Alexander Pink [1968] Director; Richard Thomas Ricci [1962] Director/Retired [American]; Andrew John Symonds [1941] Director/Chartered Quantity Surveyor; Miles Templeman [1947] Director/Chairman; Philip Charles Ward [1960] Director/Headmaster; Elizabeth Louise Weeks [1978] Director/Solicitor; Robert John Stuart Weir [1948] Director/Chartered Accountant

Brighton I-360 Limited
Incorporated: 4 August 2005 *Employees:* 74
Net Worth Deficit: £3,661,981 *Total Assets:* £52,412,804
Registered Office: Brighton I360, Lower Kings Road Arches, Brighton, BN1 2LN
Activities: Other amusement and recreation activities n.e.c.
Parent: Brighton I-360 Holdings Limited
Officers: Julia Barbara Barfield [1952] Director/Architect; Benjamin Jesse Barfield Marks [1986] Director; Eleanor Jean Harris [1971] Director/Management Consultant; Dr John Maxwell Roberts [1948] Director/Consulting Engineer; Richard Andrew Russell [1942] Director/Legal Consultant

Brioche Pasquier U.K. Limited
Incorporated: 24 July 2000 *Employees:* 101
Net Worth: £7,618,810 *Total Assets:* £44,564,856
Registered Office: 8 Garamonde Drive, Wymbush, Milton Keynes, Bucks, MK8 8DF
Activities: Manufacture of bread; manufacture of fresh pastry goods and cakes
Officers: Pascal Pasquier [1957] Director [French]; Fabrice Sciumbata [1968] Director [French]

Brisko Scaffolding Limited
Incorporated: 24 October 1996 *Employees:* 43
Net Worth: £2,472,482 *Total Assets:* £44,339,620
Registered Office: Unit 16 Kingsmill Business Park, Chapel Mill Lane, Kingston upon Thames, Surrey, KT1 3GZ
Activities: Other specialised construction activities n.e.c.
Officers: Shanmuganathan Subramaniam, Secretary; Lalit Premchandani [1974] Director; Anil Munish Kumar Arjan Taurani [1968] Director/Business Person [Indian]; Arjan Taurani [1936] Director/Business Person [Indian]; Lalit Arjan Taurani [1974] Director/Business Person [Indian]

Bristol Laboratories Limited
Incorporated: 27 June 1997 *Employees:* 335
Net Worth: £44,480,316 *Total Assets:* £69,361,760
Registered Office: Unit 3 Canalside, North Bridge Road, Berkhamsted, Herts, HP4 1EG
Activities: Wholesale of pharmaceutical goods
Parent: Bristol Laboratories Group Limited
Officers: Sreekumar Nair Kodupurath, Secretary; Sanjay Shrikishan Pashine [1975] Director; Raju Puthenvilayil Mathaikutty [1956] Director; Priti Ramachandran [1982] Director; Thembalath Ramachandran [1949] Director

Bristol-Myers Squibb Business Services Limited
Incorporated: 29 September 1986 *Employees:* 324
Net Worth Deficit: £5,028,000 *Total Assets:* £67,446,000
Registered Office: Uxbridge Business Park, Sanderson Road, Uxbridge, Middlesex, UB8 1DH
Activities: Other business support service activities n.e.c.
Parent: Bristol-Myers Squibb Holdings 2002 Limited
Officers: Bruno Marie Pierre Lauras [1961] Director/Head of Business and Finance Services, Europe [French]; Joanne Elizabeth Rishworth [1977] Director

Bristol-Myers Squibb Holdings 2002 Limited
Incorporated: 31 October 2002 *Employees:* 3
Net Worth: £291,720,992 *Total Assets:* £291,864,992
Registered Office: Uxbridge Business Park, Sanderson Road, Uxbridge, Middlesex, UB8 1DH
Activities: Activities of head offices
Officers: Bertrand Pierre Marie Grosjean [1969] Finance Director [French]; Katherine Reynolds Kelly [1976] Director/Vice President & Assistant General Counsel [American]; Veronique Maguin EP Walsh [1961] Director/General Manager (UK & Ireland) [French]

Bristol-Myers Squibb Pharmaceuticals Limited
Incorporated: 2 April 1990 *Employees:* 414
Net Worth: £165,060,992 *Total Assets:* £276,734,016
Registered Office: Uxbridge Business Park, Sanderson Road, Uxbridge, Middlesex, UB8 1DH
Activities: Manufacture of basic pharmaceutical products
Parent: Bristol-Myers Squibb Holdings 2002 Limited
Officers: Bertrand Pierre Marie Grosjean [1969] Finance Director [French]; Veronique Maguin EP Walsh [1961] Director/General Manager (UK & Ireland) [French]

Bristow (UK) LLP
Incorporated: 22 August 2008
Net Worth: £357,026,464 *Total Assets:* £357,026,464
Registered Office: Redhill Aerodrome, Kings Mill Lane, Redhill, Surrey, RH1 5JZ

Bristow Aircraft Leasing Limited
Incorporated: 21 July 2016
Net Worth: £487,072 *Total Assets:* £73,353,976
Registered Office: Redhill Aerodrome, Kings Mill Lane, Redhill, Surrey, RH1 5JZ
Activities: Renting and leasing of air passenger transport equipment
Parent: Bristow Helicopter Group Limited
Officers: James Lort Howell-Richardson, Secretary; Alan William George Corbett [1957] Director; James Lort Howell-Richardson [1980] Director

Bristow Aviation Holdings Limited
Incorporated: 6 August 1996 *Employees:* 3,753
Net Worth Deficit: £1,108,569,984 *Total Assets:* £1,409,321,984
Registered Office: Redhill Aerodrome, Kings Mill Lane, Redhill, Surrey, RH1 5JZ
Activities: Non-scheduled passenger air transport
Shareholders: Caledonia Investments PLC; Bristow Group Inc.
Officers: James Lort Howell-Richardson, Secretary; Alan William George Corbett [1957] Director; James Lort Howell-Richardson [1980] Director/Legal Counsel; Mr Stephen Anthony King [1960] Director; Lloyd Donelson Miller [1962] Director/Executive Officer [American]

Bristow Helicopter Group Limited
Incorporated: 29 August 1991 *Employees:* 1
Net Worth: £92,359,072 *Total Assets:* £465,792,928
Registered Office: Redhill Aerodrome, Redhill, Surrey, RH1 5JZ
Activities: Non-scheduled passenger air transport
Parent: Bristow Aviation Holdings Limited
Officers: James Lort Howell-Richardson, Secretary; Alan William George Corbett [1957] Director; James Lort Howell-Richardson [1980] Director/Legal Counsel; Richard James Lake [1961] Director; Michael Peter Nicol [1985] Director; Timothy John Rolfe [1968] Director, Aviation Safety

Bristow Helicopters (International) Limited
Incorporated: 12 May 1958 *Employees:* 7
Net Worth: £6,475,221 *Total Assets:* £207,360,112
Registered Office: Redhill Aerodome, Kings Mill Lane, Redhill, Surrey, RH1 5JZ
Activities: Non-scheduled passenger air transport
Parent: United Helicopters Limited
Officers: James Lort Howell-Richardson, Secretary; Alan William George Corbett [1957] Director; Michael Peter Nicol [1985] Director; Oladapo Akinloye Oyeleke [1962] Director [Nigerian]; Timothy John Rolfe [1968] Director, Aviation Safety

Bristow Helicopters Limited
Incorporated: 24 June 1955 *Employees:* 1,036
Net Worth Deficit: £43,402,072 *Total Assets:* £289,103,136
Registered Office: Redhill Aerodrome, Kings Mill Lane, Redhill, Surrey, RH1 5JZ
Activities: Non-scheduled passenger air transport
Parent: United Helicopters Limited
Officers: James Lort Howell-Richardson, Secretary; Alan William George Corbett [1957] Director; Russell James Gould [1971] Director; Michael Peter Nicol [1985] Director; Captain Matthew Rhodes [1975] Director/Area Manager and Commercial Pilot; Timothy John Rolfe [1968] Director, Aviation Safety; Russell John Torbet [1959] Director

Bristow Southeast Asia Limited
Incorporated: 16 October 2007 *Employees:* 2
Net Worth: £9,852,723 *Total Assets:* £84,767,504
Registered Office: Redhill Aerodrome, Redhill, Surrey, RH1 5JZ
Activities: Renting and leasing of air passenger transport equipment
Parent: Caledonian Helicopters Limited
Officers: James Lort Howell-Richardson, Secretary; James Lort Howell-Richardson [1980] Director/Legal Counsel; Oladapo Akinloye Oyeleke [1962] Director [Nigerian]

Bristow Technical Services Limited
Incorporated: 6 June 1953
Net Worth: £88,178,304 *Total Assets:* £199,003,488
Registered Office: Redhill Aerodrome, Kings Mill Lane, Redhill, Surrey, RH1 5JZ
Activities: Service activities incidental to air transportation
Parent: Bristow Helicopters Limited
Officers: James Lort Howell-Richardson, Secretary; Alan William George Corbett [1957] Director; Russell James Gould [1971] Director; Michael Peter Nicol [1985] Director; Timothy John Rolfe [1968] Director, Aviation Safety

Britair Holdings Limited
Incorporated: 25 March 1998
Net Worth: £112,907,000 *Total Assets:* £209,104,992
Registered Office: P O Box 365, Waterside, Harmondsworth, Middlesex, UB7 0GB
Activities: Activities of head offices
Parent: British Airways PLC
Officers: Luke Alexander Michael Straver, Secretary; Andrew Ian Fleming [1979] Director/Company Secretary; Simon Philcox [1979] Director/Accountant

Britannia Holdings (UK) Limited
Incorporated: 29 March 2005 *Employees:* 130
Net Worth: £13,821,066 *Total Assets:* £21,503,176
Registered Office: 30-34 North Street, Hailsham, E Sussex, BN27 1DW
Activities: Activities of head offices
Major Shareholder: Colin Kenneth Manser
Officers: Gillian Manser, Secretary; Colin Kenneth Manser [1956] Director/Sweet Manufacturer; Martin James Manser [1985] Director; Stephen Kenneth Manser [1986] Director

Britannia Pharmaceuticals Limited
Incorporated: 21 April 1981 *Employees:* 80
Net Worth: £40,942,000 *Total Assets:* £59,009,000
Registered Office: 200 Longwater Avenue, Green Park, Reading, Berks, RG2 6GP
Activities: Wholesale of pharmaceutical goods
Parent: Genus Pharmaceuticals Holdings Limited
Officers: Elizabeth Robinson, Secretary; Christoph Dengler [1969] Director [German]; Robert Kenneth Wood [1976] Managing Director

Britannia Refined Metals Limited
Incorporated: 4 December 1930 *Employees:* 161
Net Worth: £48,243,000 *Total Assets:* £77,058,000
Registered Office: Botany Road, Northfleet, Kent, DA11 9BG
Activities: Precious metals production
Parent: Xstrata Limited
Officers: Howard Stephen Gilroy, Secretary; Anna Carson [1970] Director/Fluorspar Manager; Carole Anne Constant [1961] Director/IT Superintendent; Howard Stephen Gilroy [1955] Director/Accountant; Jeffrey William Henderson [1961] Director/Compliance Manager; Carlos Navalpotro [1985] Director/Asset Manager [Spanish]; Florian Jurgen Bogislaw Von Steinkeller [1979] Director/Economist [German]

Britannia Security Group Limited
Incorporated: 11 September 1978
Net Worth: £42,066,000 *Total Assets:* £73,758,000
Registered Office: Security House, The Summit, Hanworth Road, Sunbury on Thames, Middlesex, TW16 5DB
Activities: Activities of head offices
Parent: ADT Group Limited
Officers: Mark Ayre [1963] Finance Director; Peter Schieser [1967] Director [German]

Britannia Soft Drinks Limited
Incorporated: 5 March 1896
Net Worth: £163,152,000 *Total Assets:* £950,691,968
Registered Office: Breakspear Park, Breakspear Way, Hemel Hempstead, Herts, HP2 4TZ
Activities: Manufacture of soft drinks; production of mineral waters and other bottled waters
Parent: Britvic PLC
Officers: Judith Moore, Secretary; Mathew James Dunn [1974] Director/Chief Financial Officer; Peter Simon Litherland [1964] Director/Chief Executive; Alexandra Clare Thomas [1974] Director/General Counsel and Company Secretary

Britannic Trading Limited
Incorporated: 21 February 1966
Net Worth: £421,945,568 *Total Assets:* £742,389,248
Registered Office: Chertsey Road, Sunbury on Thames, Middlesex, TW16 7BP
Activities: Other business support service activities n.e.c.
Parent: BP International Limited
Officers: Alan Henry Haywood [1966] Director; Carol-Lee Howle [1972] Director/Oil Company Executive; Robert Stephen Lawson [1970] Director/Oil Company Executive; Brian Michael Puffer [1969] Director/Oil Company Executive [British/American]; Geir Patrick Robinson [1968] Director/Oil Company Executive

Britax Childcare Group Limited
Incorporated: 22 October 2003 *Employees:* 27
Net Worth: £72,293,000 *Total Assets:* £78,327,000
Registered Office: Building A, Riverside Way, Watchmoor Park, Camberley, Surrey, GU15 3YL
Activities: Activities of head offices
Parent: Britax Childcare Holdings Limited
Officers: Alexander Lacik [1965] Director [Swedish]; Markus Nagel [1967] Director [German]

Britax Childcare Holdings Limited
Incorporated: 24 August 2005
Net Worth: £199,460,000 *Total Assets:* £201,032,992
Registered Office: Building A, Riverside Way, Watchmoor Park, Camberley, Surrey, GU15 3YL
Activities: Activities of head offices
Parent: CC 4 (2011) Limited
Officers: Alexander Lacik [1965] Director [Swedish]; Markus Nagel [1967] Director [German]

Britax Excelsior Limited
Incorporated: 30 November 1934 *Employees:* 126
Net Worth: £10,929,000 *Total Assets:* £21,002,000
Registered Office: Building A, Riverside Way, Watchmoor Park, Camberley, Surrey, GU15 3YL
Activities: Other manufacturing n.e.c.
Parent: Britax Childcare Investments Limited
Officers: Alexander Lacik [1965] Director [Swedish]; Markus Nagel [1967] Director [German]; Erwin Sander Wieffering [1972] Director [Dutch]

Britax Group Limited
Incorporated: 13 December 2010 *Employees:* 1,112
Net Worth: £198,390,720 *Total Assets:* £522,811,552
Registered Office: Building A, Riverside Way, Watchmoor Park, Camberley, Surrey, GU15 3YL
Activities: Activities of head offices
Parent: CC 2 (2011) Limited
Officers: Mr Olof Bertil Faxander [1970] Director [Swedish]; Nils-Olof Robert Campbell Furuhjelm [1969] Director [Finnish]; Tiemo Grimm [1978] Director/Investment Professional [German]; Alexander Lacik [1965] Director [Swedish]; Markus Nagel [1967] Director [German]

British Agricultural Services Limited
Incorporated: 8 August 1946
Net Worth: £358,921,984 *Total Assets:* £367,166,016
Registered Office: Hanson House, 14 Castle Hill, Maidenhead, Berks, SL6 4JJ
Activities: Other letting and operating of own or leased real estate
Parent: Hanson Overseas Holdings Limited
Officers: Wendy Fiona Rogers, Secretary; Jeremy Lees Dawes [1966] Director/Accountant; Edward Alexander Gretton [1970] Director; Dr Carsten Matthias Wendt [1976] Director [German]; James Stuart Whitelaw [1972] Managing Director

British Airways 777 Leasing Limited
Incorporated: 5 November 2003
Net Worth Deficit: £12,705,000 *Total Assets:* £34,769,000
Registered Office: P O Box 365, Waterside, Harmondsworth, Middlesex, UB7 0GB
Activities: Financial leasing
Parent: British Airways PLC
Officers: Luke Alexander Michael Straver, Secretary; Andrew Ian Fleming [1979] Director/Company Secretary; Simon Philcox [1979] Director/Accountant

British Airways Associated Companies Limited
Incorporated: 6 September 1957
Net Worth: £51,727,000 *Total Assets:* £51,810,000
Registered Office: P O Box 365, Waterside, Harmondsworth, Middlesex, UB7 0GB
Activities: Activities of head offices
Parent: British Airways PLC
Officers: Luke Alexander Michael Straver, Secretary; Andrew Ian Fleming [1979] Director/Company Secretary; Simon Philcox [1979] Director/Accountant

British Airways Holidays Limited
Incorporated: 6 September 1955 *Employees:* 260
Net Worth: £43,694,000 *Total Assets:* £212,999,008
Registered Office: P O Box 365, Waterside HBB3, Harmondsworth, West Drayton, Middlesex, UB7 0GB
Activities: Scheduled passenger air transport
Parent: British Airways PLC
Officers: Katie Louise Bishop, Secretary; Claire Marie Elizabeth Bentley [1968] Director/Airline Executive; Andrew Peter David Brem [1968] Director [Swiss]; Colm Leo Lacy [1970] Director/Airline Executive [Irish]; Sarah Elizabeth Mussenden [1965] Director; Duncan Alexander John Roberts [1973] Commercial Director; Jack Robert Smith [1977] Director

British Airways Maintenance Cardiff Limited
Incorporated: 10 December 1987 *Employees:* 625
Net Worth: £36,436,000 *Total Assets:* £42,889,000
Registered Office: P O Box 365, Waterside, Harmondsworth, Middlesex, UB7 0GB
Activities: Repair and maintenance of aircraft and spacecraft
Parent: British Airways PLC
Officers: Carole Hibbs, Secretary; William Armstrong [1971] Director/Manager; Robert Llewellyn Crew [1964] Director/Engineer; Sian Louise Davies [1973] Director/Accountant; Melanie Jane Grant-Stevens [1962] Director/Human Resources Advisor; Jason Patrick Mahoney [1971] Director/Engineer [Irish]; Louise Anne Street [1974] Director/Manager

British Airways PLC
Incorporated: 13 December 1983 *Employees:* 43,125
Net Worth: £5,774,000,128 *Total Assets:* £16,677,999,616
Registered Office: P O Box 365, Waterside, Harmondsworth, Middlesex, UB7 0GB
Activities: Scheduled passenger air transport
Shareholders: LDC (NCS) Limited; International Consolidated Airlines Group S.A
Officers: Andrew Ian Fleming, Secretary; Alejandro Cruz de Llano [1966] Director/Chairman and CEO [Spanish]; Lynne Louise Embleton [1969] Director/Airline Executive; Stephen William Lawrence Gunning [1967] Director/Chief Financial Officer; Gavin Echlin Patterson [1967] Director; Alison Clare Reed [1956] Director/Accountant; Julia Elizabeth Simpson [1958] Director

British American Tobacco UK Limited
Incorporated: 13 February 1989 *Employees:* 198
Net Worth: £36,803,000 *Total Assets:* £254,247,008
Registered Office: One Eton Street, Richmond upon Thames, London, TW9 1EF
Activities: Wholesale of tobacco products
Parent: Weston Investment Company Limited
Officers: Jessica Munday, Secretary; Christopher Mathew John Barraclough [1982] Director/Head of HR; Nigel Graeme Hardy [1968] Director/General Manager; William Richard Darvell Hill [1977] Director/Head of Legal & External Affairs, UK&I; Dimitri Alexandros Tounis [1980] Director/Head of Finance; Gemma Bridget Webb [1963] Director/Business Manager [Irish]

British and Foreign Wharf Company Limited (The)
Incorporated: 8 March 1907 *Employees:* 41
Net Worth: £31,251,888 *Total Assets:* £35,837,532
Registered Office: 43 Ormside Way, Holmethorpe Industrial Estate, Redhill, Surrey, RH1 2LG
Activities: Buying and selling of own real estate
Shareholder: George Stanhope Pitt
Officers: David James Dring, Secretary; David James Dring [1972] Director; Jeremy Baxter Leathers [1946] Managing Director; Tara Charlotte Leathers [1972] Director/Executive; George Stanhope Pitt [1946] Director/Chartered Accountant; Nicola Naomi Pitt [1977] Director/Physiotherapist

The British Car Auction Group Limited
Incorporated: 23 January 1902
Net Worth: £222,220,992 *Total Assets:* £223,723,008
Registered Office: Headway House, Crosby Way, Farnham, Surrey, GU9 7XG
Activities: Activities of head offices
Parent: BCA Group Europe Limited
Officers: Martin Richard Letza, Secretary; Timothy Giles Lampert [1970] Director; Avril Palmer-Baunack [1964] Director

British Car Auctions Limited
Incorporated: 14 July 1947 *Employees:* 2,021
Net Worth: £106,674,000 *Total Assets:* £353,433,984
Registered Office: Headway House, Crosby Way, Farnham, Surrey, GU9 7XG
Activities: Other business support service activities n.e.c.
Parent: BCA Trading Limited
Officers: Martin Richard Letza, Secretary; Timothy Giles Lampert [1970] Director; Avril Palmer-Baunack [1964] Director; Stuart John Pearson [1971] Managing Director; Craig Stuart Purvey [1971] Director/Chief Commercial Officer; Nikheel Shah [1981] Director/Accountant

British Fittings Group Limited
Incorporated: 4 September 1964
Net Worth: £31,609,000 *Total Assets:* £48,164,000
Registered Office: 1020 Eskdale Road, Winnersh Triangle, Wokingham, Berks, RG41 5TS
Activities: Activities of head offices
Officers: Graham Middlemiss, Secretary; Simon Gray [1967] Director/Accountant

British Gas Energy Procurement Limited
Incorporated: 11 December 2013
Net Worth: £92,700,000 *Total Assets:* £1,006,400,000
Registered Office: Millstream, Maidenhead Road, Windsor, Berks, SL4 5GD
Activities: Trade of electricity
Parent: British Gas Trading Limited
Officers: Gab Saturnio Barbaro [1971] Director [Italian/Australian]; Mark Steven Hodges [1965] Director; Ivan Edward Ronald [1972] Director; Dr Rajarshi Roy [1975] Director; Sarwjit Sambhi [1969] Director

British Gas Finance Limited
Incorporated: 20 January 2009
Net Worth: £48,480,000 *Total Assets:* £192,504,000
Registered Office: Millstream, Maidenhead Road, Windsor, Berks, SL4 5GD
Activities: Other business support service activities n.e.c.
Parent: GB Gas Holdings Limited
Officers: Ivan Edward Ronald [1972] Director; Peter Michael Simon [1975] Director [Irish]

British Gas Insurance Limited
Incorporated: 2 June 2008
Net Worth: £138,942,000 *Total Assets:* £972,748,032
Registered Office: Millstream, Maidenhead Road, Windsor, Berks, SL4 5GD
Activities: Non-life insurance
Parent: GB Gas Holdings Limited
Officers: Amanda Helen Bowe [1968] Director; John Castagno [1958] Director/Insurance Professional [Italian]; Elizabeth Margaret Catchpole [1965] Director; David John Hindley [1960] Director; David Alan Johnson [1965] Director of Underwriting and Actuarial; Stephen John O'Dwyer [1969] Director; Robin Ashley Phipps [1950] Director; Sarwjit Sambhi [1969] Director; Stuart Robert Vann [1971] Director

British Gas New Heating Limited
Incorporated: 14 October 2008 *Employees:* 1,849
Net Worth: £162,864,000 *Total Assets:* £281,048,992
Registered Office: Millstream, Maidenhead Road, Windsor, Berks, SL4 5GD
Activities: Electrical installation
Parent: GB Gas Holdings Limited
Officers: Emma Ariadne Henrietta Connell [1972] Director/Accountant; Steven James Hughes [1975] Business Services Director; Andrew Mark Reaney [1967] Director; Dr Rajarshi Roy [1975] Director

British Gas Services Limited
Incorporated: 22 December 1995 *Employees:* 9,951
Net Worth: £769,267,008 *Total Assets:* £1,603,451,008
Registered Office: Millstream, Maidenhead Road, Windsor, Berks, SL4 5GD
Activities: Other service activities n.e.c.
Parent: GB Gas Holdings Limited
Officers: Matthew James Bateman [1968] Director; Amanda Helen Bowe [1968] Director; John Castagno [1958] Director/Insurance Professional [Italian]; Elizabeth Margaret Catchpole [1965] Director; David John Hindley [1960] Director; Charles Lee McLeod [1972] Finance Director; Robin Ashley Phipps [1950] Director; Ivan Edward Ronald [1972] Director; Sarwjit Sambhi [1969] Director; Stuart Robert Vann [1971] Director

British Gas Social Housing Limited
Incorporated: 1 October 1971 *Employees:* 462
Net Worth: £8,133,000 *Total Assets:* £32,715,000
Registered Office: Millstream, Maidenhead Road, Windsor, Berks, SL4 5GD
Activities: Electrical installation
Parent: P.H. Jones Group Limited
Officers: Mark Steven Hodges [1965] Director; Ivan Edward Ronald [1972] Director; Dr Rajarshi Roy [1975] Director

British Gas Trading Limited
Incorporated: 6 July 1995 *Employees:* 12,924
Net Worth: £4,440,099,840 *Total Assets:* £8,864,199,680
Registered Office: Millstream, Maidenhead Road, Windsor, Berks, SL4 5GD
Activities: Distribution of electricity
Parent: GB Gas Holdings Limited
Officers: Gab Saturnio Barbaro [1971] Director [Italian/Australian]; Mark Steven Hodges [1965] Director; Claire Miles [1972] Managing Director; Ivan Edward Ronald [1972] Director; Dr Rajarshi Roy [1975] Director; Sarwjit Sambhi [1969] Managing Director, E&P

British Kidney Patient Association (The)
Incorporated: 29 September 1975 *Employees:* 22
Net Worth: £35,684,672 *Total Assets:* £37,131,252
Registered Office: 3 The Windmills, St Mary's Close, Turk Street, Alton, Hants, GU34 1EF
Activities: Other social work activities without accommodation n.e.c.
Officers: Alison Jane Burnapp [1964] Director/Nurse; Andrew Chapman [1952] Director/Retired; Marcelle Elizabeth de Sousa [1950] Director/Retired Nurse Specialist; Patricia Gooden [1959] Director/Chair of Arbitration; Angela May Griffiths [1956] Director/Business Development Consultant; Ingrid Rachelle Gubbay [1955] Director/Solicitor [Australian/British]; Sarah Harriet Hillary [1965] Director/Chartered Accountant; Sir Jonathan Michael [1945] Director/Retired; Ofrah Muflahi [1973] Director/Nurse; Professor Donal Joseph O'Donoghue [1956] Director/Consultant Nephrologist; Dr Lesley Rees [1951] Director/Doctor of Medicine; Christopher Derek Rolfe [1955] Director/Retired Chartered Accountant

British Midland Airways Limited
Incorporated: 16 February 1949
Net Worth: £47,900,000 *Total Assets:* £158,500,000
Registered Office: P O Box 365, Waterside, Speedbird Way, Harmondsworth, Middlesex, UB7 0GB
Activities: Renting and leasing of air passenger transport equipment
Parent: British Midland Limited
Officers: Andrew Ian Fleming, Secretary; Sian Louise Davies [1973] Director/Accountant; Simon Philcox [1979] Director/Accountant

Britten Properties LLP
Incorporated: 25 April 2013
Net Worth: £31,388,452 *Total Assets:* £36,153,532
Registered Office: Gracious Pond Farm, Gracious Pond Road, Chobham, Woking, Surrey, GU24 8HL
Officers: Diana Marilyn Britten [1945] Member; Graham Leonard Chambers [1946] Member; Ann Marie Cole [1970] Member; Sophie Simone Biggs [1972] LLP Member; Fleur Leonie Britten [1974] LLP Member; Chloe Augusta Stirling [1974] LLP Member

Britvic Brands LLP
Incorporated: 27 October 2011
Net Worth: £183,176,000 *Total Assets:* £184,016,000
Registered Office: Breakspear Park, Breakspear Way, Hemel Hempstead, Herts, HP2 4TZ
Officers: Mathew James Dunn [1974] LLP Member; Alexandra Clare Thomas [1974] LLP Member

Britvic EMEA Limited
Incorporated: 13 October 1986 *Employees:* 42
Net Worth Deficit: £52,337,000 *Total Assets:* £20,076,000
Registered Office: Breakspear Park, Breakspear Way, Hemel Hempstead, Herts, HP2 4TZ
Activities: Manufacture of soft drinks; production of mineral waters and other bottled waters
Parent: Britannia Soft Drinks Limited
Officers: Judith Moore, Secretary; Christophe Garcia [1975] Director [French]; Hessel Douwe de Jong [1969] International Managing Director [Dutch]; Stephen Andrew Smith [1972] Director

Britvic Finance Partnership LLP
Incorporated: 22 February 2011
Net Worth: £66,307,000 *Total Assets:* £66,350,000
Registered Office: Breakspear Park, Breakspear Way, Hemel Hempstead, Herts, HP2 4TZ

Britvic International Investments Limited
Incorporated: 13 October 1986
Net Worth: £169,670,000 *Total Assets:* £170,228,000
Registered Office: Breakspear Park, Breakspear Way, Hemel Hempstead, Herts, HP2 4TZ
Activities: Manufacture of soft drinks; production of mineral waters and other bottled waters
Parent: Britannia Soft Drinks Limited
Officers: Judith Moore, Secretary; Mathew James Dunn [1974] Director/Chief Financial Officer; Peter Simon Litherland [1964] Director/Chief Executive; Alexandra Clare Thomas [1974] Director/General Counsel and Company Secretary

Britvic Overseas Limited
Incorporated: 17 August 2010
Net Worth: £74,459,000 *Total Assets:* £336,556,992
Registered Office: Breakspear Park, Breakspear Way, Hemel Hempstead, Herts, HP2 4TZ
Activities: Manufacture of soft drinks; production of mineral waters and other bottled waters
Parent: Britannia Soft Drinks Limited
Officers: Judith Moore, Secretary; Mathew James Dunn [1974] Director/Chief Financial Officer; Peter Simon Litherland [1964] Director/Chief Executive; Alexandra Clare Thomas [1974] Director/General Counsel and Company Secretary

Britvic PLC
Incorporated: 27 October 2005 *Employees:* 4,781
Net Worth: £377,300,000 *Total Assets:* £1,664,099,968
Registered Office: Breakspear Park, Breakspear Way, Hemel Hempstead, Herts, HP2 4TZ
Activities: Manufacture of soft drinks; production of mineral waters and other bottled waters
Officers: Jonathan Mark Adelman, Secretary; Suniti Kiransinh Chauhan [1974] Director/Finance [American]; Susan Michelle Clark [1964] Director; John Patrick Daly [1956] Director [Irish]; Mathew James Dunn [1974] Director/Chief Financial Officer; Christopher William Eccleshare [1955] Director; Peter Simon Litherland [1964] Director/Chief Executive; Ian Philip McHoul [1960] Director/Chief Financial Officer; Euan Angus Sutherland [1969] Director

Britvic Soft Drinks Limited
Incorporated: 16 March 1953 *Employees:* 1,903
Net Worth: £768,606,016 *Total Assets:* £1,437,943,040
Registered Office: Breakspear Park, Breakspear Way, Hemel Hempstead, Herts, HP2 4TZ
Activities: Manufacture of soft drinks; production of mineral waters and other bottled waters
Parent: Britannia Soft Drinks Limited
Officers: Alexandra Clare Thomas, Secretary; Matthew Robert Barwell [1966] Strategic Marketing & Innovation Director; Mathew James Dunn [1974] Director/Chief Financial Officer; Richard Paul Graham [1968] Director/General Manager; Clive Alastair Hooper [1964] Director; Peter Simon Litherland [1964] Director/Chief Executive

Broadcast Relay Service (Overseas) Limited
Incorporated: 11 January 1947
Net Worth: £54,470,000 *Total Assets:* £516,967,008
Registered Office: Riverbank, Meadows Business Park, Blackwater, Camberley, Surrey, GU17 9AB
Activities: Dormant company
Parent: Rentokil Initial (1993) Limited
Officers: Catherine Stead, Secretary; Daragh Patrick Feltrim Fagan [1969] Director/Solicitor; Christopher Brian Terrence Filby [1961] Director; Jonathan Ellis Hauck [1973] Director/Accountant

Broadleaf Park LLP
Incorporated: 10 July 2017
Net Worth: £8,029,000 *Total Assets:* £21,410,000
Registered Office: Gate House, Turnpike Road, High Wycombe, Bucks, HP12 3NR

Broadway Malyan Employee Ownership Trustees Limited
Incorporated: 2 September 2016 *Employees:* 495
Net Worth: £3,459,000 *Total Assets:* £28,492,000
Registered Office: Unit 3 Weybridge Business Park, Addlestone Road, Weybridge, Surrey, KT15 2BW
Activities: Other business support service activities n.e.c.
Officers: Francesca Yeomans, Secretary; Antonio Miguel Condeco de Sousa [1978] Director/Architect [Portuguese]; Peter Anthony Crossley [1957] Director/Architect; David Campbell McDonald [1976] Director; James Edward Tanswell Rayner [1963] Director/Architect; Kate Stone [1968] Director/UK Bid Leader; Philip Peter Stone [1972] Director/Technician; Daniela Viloria [1984] Director/Architect [Spanish]

Broadway Malyan Holdings Limited
Incorporated: 8 April 2005 *Employees:* 495
Net Worth: £11,354,000 *Total Assets:* £27,942,000
Registered Office: 3 Weybridge Business Park, Addlestone Road, Weybridge, Surrey, KT15 2BW
Activities: Activities of head offices
Parent: Broadway Malyan Employee Ownership Trustees Limited
Officers: Francesca Yeomans, Secretary; David Hugh Anderson [1962] Director/Architect; Ian Apsley [1973] Director/Architect; Edward Luke Baker [1973] Director/Urban Designer; Martin Bates [1974] Director/Architect; Margarida de Ordaz Caldeira [1962] Director/Architect [Portuguese]; Peter Anthony Crossley [1957] Director/Architect; Anne Kathryn Howard [1969] Finance Director; John Charles Oliver [1955] Director/Accountant; Jorge Eduardo Ponce Dawson Petrocelli [1963] Director/Architect [Spanish]; James Edward Tanswell Rayner [1963] Director/Masterplanner; Stuart Rough [1960] Director; Jeremy John Salmon [1968] Director/Architect; Ian Andrew Simpson [1966] Director/Architect; Peter Anthony Vaughan [1960] Director/Architect; Gary Whittle [1959] Director/Architect

Brobot Petroleum Limited
Incorporated: 23 January 1978 *Employees:* 275
Net Worth: £20,887,252 *Total Assets:* £30,122,572
Registered Office: Prax House, Horizon Business Village, 1 Brooklands Road, Weybridge, Surrey, KT13 0TJ
Activities: Retail sale of automotive fuel in specialised stores
Parent: Brobot Group Limited
Officers: Arani Soosaipillai, Secretary; Don Camillo Emilio Borneo [1957] Director; Winston Sanjeevkumar Soosaipillai [1973] Director

Brook Learning Trust
Incorporated: 7 September 2010 *Employees:* 194
Net Worth: £14,931,034 *Total Assets:* £20,025,016
Registered Office: The Hayesbrook School, Brook Street, Tonbridge, Kent, TN9 2PH
Activities: General secondary education
Officers: Louise Elizabeth Burgess, Secretary; Jeanette Batten [1970] Director of Estates and Facilities Management; Natalina Bertoli [1966] Director/Mergers and Acquisitions Consultant; Ian Martin Daker [1950] Director/Property Management Consultant; Martin Charles Garner [1958] Director/Bank Manager; Linda Carolyn Garratt [1964] Director/IT Technician; Myles Stephen McIntosh [1969] Director/Solicitor; Carol Moretta Morris [1966] Director/Teacher; Bruce Geoffrey Walsh [1967] Director/Accountant

Brooklime Limited
Incorporated: 5 July 2007
Net Worth: £83,159 *Total Assets:* £23,115,240
Registered Office: Suite 576, 2nd Floor, Elder House, Elder Gate, Milton Keynes, Bucks, MK9 1LR
Activities: Financial intermediation not elsewhere classified
Officers: Lindsay Treasure, Secretary; Jonathan Paul Silver [1956] Director

Brookton 2000 Limited
Incorporated: 5 February 1990 *Employees:* 4
Net Worth: £22,544,978 *Total Assets:* £28,104,794
Registered Office: Ashton House, 12 The Precinct, Winchester Road, Chandler's Ford, Hants, SO53 2GB
Activities: Management of real estate on a fee or contract basis
Officers: Daniel Andrew Kaye [1967] Director/Chartered Surveyor; Nigel James Lapage [1957] Director; Richard Misselbrook Stevens [1939] Director; Jacqueline Tracey Weston [1962] Director/Interim HR Consultant

Brookworth Group Limited
Incorporated: 19 August 2011
Net Worth: £1 *Total Assets:* £29,489,940
Registered Office: Brookworth House, 99 Bell Street, Reigate, Surrey, RH2 7AN
Activities: Activities of construction holding companies
Parent: Surrey Blue Limited
Officers: Justin Douglas William Barnes [1965] Director

Brown and Mason Holdings Limited
Incorporated: 17 January 1984 *Employees:* 425
Net Worth: £11,462,295 *Total Assets:* £68,638,608
Registered Office: Anson House, Schooner Court, Crossways Business Park, Dartford, Kent, DA2 6QQ
Activities: Other business support service activities n.e.c.
Officers: Laura Ann Hadden, Secretary; Nicholas Terry Brown [1974] Director; Terry Alfred Brown [1944] Director/Demolition Contractor

Brown and Mason Limited
Incorporated: 14 March 1961 *Employees:* 425
Net Worth: £10,865,878 *Total Assets:* £66,133,708
Registered Office: Anson House, Schooner Court, Crossways Business Park, Dartford, Kent, DA2 6QQ
Activities: Demolition
Parent: Brown and Mason Holdings Limited
Officers: Laura Ann Hadden, Secretary; Lee Fredrick Alfred Brown [1978] Director; Nicholas Terry Brown [1974] Director; Richard William Brown [1976] Director; Terry Alfred Brown [1944] Director/Demolition Contractor; Charles Ernest Buckingham [1954] Director; Alex Hadden [1967] Safety Director; Laura Ann Hadden [1980] Director; Miles Hamilton Jacob [1961] Director; John Anthony Payton [1954] Director/Contracts Manager

Raymond Brown Minerals & Recycling Ltd
Incorporated: 21 July 1998 *Employees:* 162
Net Worth: £5,914,244 *Total Assets:* £25,027,376
Registered Office: A1 Omega Enterprise Park, Electron Way, Chandler's Ford, Eastleigh, Hants, SO53 4SE
Activities: Operation of gravel and sand pits; mining of clays and kaolin
Parent: RBMR Topco Ltd
Officers: Wayne William Roberts, Secretary; Stephen Charles Clasby [1965] Director; Donald William Coates [1960] Director; Wayne Roberts [1972] Director/Accountant [New Zealander]

Brymore Holdings Limited
Incorporated: 24 September 2009
Net Worth: £23,788,044 *Total Assets:* £32,207,900
Registered Office: 8 Tavistock Court, Tavistock Road, Croydon, Surrey, CR9 2ED
Activities: Activities of head offices
Parent: Brymore Organisation Ltd
Officers: Lucinda Jane Lewis, Secretary; Leonard Sidney Lewis [1956] Director; Miles Jason Webber [1969] Director

Brymore Investments Limited
Incorporated: 28 February 1973
Net Worth: £28,959,942 *Total Assets:* £35,100,756
Registered Office: 8 Tavistock Court, Tavistock Road, Croydon, Surrey, CR9 2ED
Activities: Renting and operating of Housing Association real estate
Parent: Brymore Holdings Limited
Officers: Lucinda Jane Lewis, Secretary; Leonard Sidney Lewis [1956] Director; Miles Jason Webber [1969] Non-Executive Director

BSH Home Appliances Limited
Incorporated: 28 August 1984 *Employees:* 1,196
Net Worth: £59,053,536 *Total Assets:* £202,705,984
Registered Office: Grand Union House, Old Wolverton Road, Wolverton, Milton Keynes, Bucks, MK12 5PT
Activities: Wholesale of radio, television goods & electrical household appliances (other than records, tapes, CDs)
Parent: BSH Finance & Holding GmbH
Officers: Kevin John Athow, Secretary; Thomas Baader [1965] Director [German]; Dr Andreas Meier [1968] Director/Chief Executive [German]; Ting Mensing [1972] Director/Chief Financial Officer [German]; Christian Gerhard Walter Prenzel [1967] Director/Head of Region Europe - Business Administration [German]

BTC Pipeline Holding Company Limited
Incorporated: 3 November 2003
Net Worth: £304,127,968 *Total Assets:* £304,127,968
Registered Office: Chertsey Road, Sunbury on Thames, Middlesex, TW16 7BP
Activities: Activities of head offices
Parent: BP Global Investments Limited
Officers: Jaqui Freeman [1968] Director/Oil Company Executive; Robert Gary Jones [1960] Director/Oil Company Executive; Katherine Anne Thomson [1968] Director/Oil Company Executive

Buckingham Group Contracting Limited
Incorporated: 21 October 1987 *Employees:* 477
Net Worth: £31,725,242 *Total Assets:* £145,475,792
Registered Office: Blackpit Farm, Stowe, Buckingham, MK18 5LJ
Activities: Construction of commercial buildings
Officers: Patricia Jane Wheeler, Secretary; Timothy John Brown [1955] Commercial Director; Michael Thomas Kempley [1961] Director; Andrew Stuart Kerr [1965] Director; Ian McKinley McSeveney [1967] Civil Engineer and Director; Kevin Underwood [1955] Director; Simon David Walkley [1963] Civil Engineer and Director; Paul Watson Wheeler [1954] Director/Company Manager

Bugler Developments Limited
Incorporated: 30 July 1981 *Employees:* 66
Net Worth: £10,335,437 *Total Assets:* £30,251,396
Registered Office: Bugler House, 25 High Street, Rickmansworth, Herts, WD3 1ET
Activities: Development of building projects
Parent: Bugler Group Limited
Officers: Andrew Philip Hawkins, Secretary; Andrew Thomas Bugler [1968] Director/Solicitor; Denis Patrick Bugler [1961] Director/Builder; Kieran Thomas Bugler [1963] Director; Jeremy Graham [1969] Construction Director; Steven James Tough [1973] Surveying Director

Bugler Group Limited
Incorporated: 22 March 2001 *Employees:* 66
Previous: Bugler Holdings Limited
Net Worth: £11,384,305 *Total Assets:* £31,377,884
Registered Office: Bugler House, 25 High Street, Rickmansworth, Herts, WD3 1ET
Activities: Development of building projects
Shareholders: Andrew Thomas Bugler; Denis Patrick Bugler; Kieran Thomas Bugler
Officers: Andrew Philip Hawkins, Secretary; Andrew Thomas Bugler [1968] Director/Solicitor; Denis Patrick Bugler [1961] Director/Builder; Kieran Thomas Bugler [1963] Director/Builder; Steven James Tough [1973] Commercial Director

Building Research Establishment Limited
Incorporated: 17 February 1997 *Employees:* 339
Net Worth Deficit: £29,692,000 *Total Assets:* £35,017,000
Registered Office: Bucknalls Lane, Garston, Watford, Herts, WD25 9XX
Activities: Other research and experimental development on natural sciences and engineering
Parent: BRE Group Ltd
Officers: Anthony Richard Tanner, Secretary; Nicholas Brian Farrimond [1965] Director/Chief Finance Officer; Niall Gerard Trafford [1962] Director/Chief Operating Officer

Bullers Wood Multi Academy Trust
Incorporated: 1 April 2011
Previous: Bullers Wood School
Net Worth: £18,206,000 *Total Assets:* £20,273,000
Registered Office: Bullers Wood School, St Nicholas Lane, Logs Hill, Chislehurst, Kent, BR7 5LJ
Activities: General secondary education
Officers: Isobel Sophia Cattermole [1949] Director/Consultant Education and Social Care; Ben Greene [1970] Director/Headteacher; Katharine Howell [1988] Director/Special Adviser (Currently on Maternity Leave); Susan Simons [1952] Director; Jeffrey Simon Ward [1960] Director/Chartered Accountant; Leonard John Webb [1953] Director/Retired (Part-Time Consultant)

Bullitt Group Limited
Incorporated: 4 June 2009 *Employees:* 120
Net Worth: £3,225,783 *Total Assets:* £54,975,732
Registered Office: One Valpy, Valpy Street, Reading, Berks, RG1 1AR
Activities: Other business support service activities n.e.c.
Parent: Bullitt Bidco Limited
Officers: Kurt Demeuleneere [1968] Director [Belgian]; Peter Warren Stephens [1966] Managing Director [American]

Bullitt Mobile Limited
Incorporated: 26 June 2009 *Employees:* 85
Net Worth Deficit: £2,892,017 *Total Assets:* £52,680,028
Registered Office: One Valpy, Valpy Street, Reading, Berks, RG1 1AR
Activities: Non-specialised wholesale trade
Parent: Bullitt Group Limited
Officers: Kurt Demeuleneere [1968] Director [Belgian]; Peter Warren Stephens [1966] Managing Director [American]

Burhill Golf and Leisure Limited
Incorporated: 19 May 1980 *Employees:* 530
Net Worth: £24,871,794 *Total Assets:* £40,325,740
Registered Office: Burhill, Walton on Thames, Surrey, KT12 4BX
Activities: Operation of sports facilities
Parent: Burhill Group Limited
Officers: James Conlan, Secretary/Chartered Accountant/Director; James Conlan [1956] Chartered Accountant & Director; Colin Michael Mayes [1955] Director/Chief Executive

Burhill Group Limited
Incorporated: 22 November 2010 *Employees:* 679
Net Worth: £38,474,208 *Total Assets:* £52,311,364
Registered Office: Burhill, Burwood Road, Walton on Thames, Surrey, KT12 4BX
Activities: Activities of head offices
Officers: James Conlan, Secretary; Edward George Clive [1968] Director; James Conlan [1956] Chartered Accountant & Director; Georgia Honor Fanshawe [1966] Director; Arthur Edward Rory Guinness [1969] Director [Irish]; Robin Ivan Howard [1955] Director; Colin Michael Mayes [1955] Director/Chief Executive; Lady Honor Victoria Montagu [1979] Director; Simon O'Donnell [1952] Director

Burnfield Limited
Incorporated: 16 October 1980
Net Worth: £145,872,000 *Total Assets:* £146,500,000
Registered Office: Heritage House, Church Road, Egham, Surrey, TW20 9QD
Activities: Other business support service activities n.e.c.
Parent: Spectris US Holdings Limited
Officers: Rebecca Louise Dunn, Secretary; Anthony William Dumpleton [1969] Director/Accountant; Clive Graeme Watson [1958] Director

Burnt Tree Group Limited
Incorporated: 15 May 1989
Net Worth: £37,238,000 *Total Assets:* £345,360,000
Registered Office: Enterprise House, Vicarage Road, Egham, Surrey, TW20 9FB
Activities: Renting and leasing of cars and light motor vehicles
Parent: Enterprise Rent-a-Car UK Limited
Officers: Teresa Anne Holderer, Secretary; Ricky Allan Short [1958] Director [American]

Burroughs Wellcome International Limited
Incorporated: 26 January 1955
Net Worth: £161,970,000 *Total Assets:* £162,024,000
Registered Office: 980 Great West Road, Brentford, Middlesex, TW8 9GS
Activities: Activities of head offices
Parent: Wellcome Consumer Healthcare Limited
Officers: James Borger [1963] Director/VP, Group Financial Planning and Analysis [American]; Alan George Burns [1975] Director

Business Lending Residential Funding Limited
Incorporated: 1 November 2012
Net Worth: £1,871,429 *Total Assets:* £38,371,984
Registered Office: Crown House, 1 Crown Square, Woking, Surrey, GU21 6HR
Activities: Financial intermediation not elsewhere classified
Parent: Business Lending Development Funding Limited
Officers: Cecile Anne Louise Parfitt, Secretary; Michael Terence Baker [1961] Director/Accountant; Stuart Howard Parfitt [1966] Director; Jonathan Winston Rose [1973] Director; Ian Jonathan Shaw [1968] Director; William Peter Wade [1955] Director

Butlins Skyline Limited
Incorporated: 9 June 2000 *Employees:* 3,843
Net Worth: £53,970,000 *Total Assets:* £168,567,008
Registered Office: No 1 Park Lane, Hemel Hempstead, Herts, HP2 4YL
Activities: Recreational vehicle parks, trailer parks and camping grounds
Parent: Bourne Leisure Limited
Officers: Jane Elizabeth Bentall [1970] Director/Accountant; Paul Charles Flaum [1970] Director; Iain Stuart Macmillan [1976] Director

Buxted Construction Limited
Incorporated: 15 February 1994 *Employees:* 103
Net Worth: £13,264,568 *Total Assets:* £46,615,080
Registered Office: Lower Lowlands Farm, Buxted, Uckfield, E Sussex, TN22 4PX
Activities: Construction of domestic buildings
Major Shareholder: Robert MacKay Ruthven
Officers: Judith Sarah Ruthven, Secretary; Paul Richard Dennison [1966] Commercial Director; James Noel Hanifin [1979] Surveying Director; James Paul Hanifin [1950] Construction Director; Mario Marco Paparozzi [1975] Director/Quantity Surveyor [Italian]; Robert MacKay Ruthven [1953] Managing Director

W & R Buxton Holdings Limited
Incorporated: 19 June 2003
Net Worth: £21,465,126 *Total Assets:* £48,058,900
Registered Office: 8 Gleneagles Court, Brighton Road, Crawley, W Sussex, RH10 6AD
Activities: Other letting and operating of own or leased real estate
Shareholders: Steven Wavel Buxton; Madeline Buxton; Gillian Sue Buxton
Officers: David William Buxton [1944] Director; Steven Wavel Buxton [1970] Director; Graham John Davies [1951] Director

Buy 2 Let Cars Ltd
Incorporated: 12 May 2011
Net Worth: £1,607,406 *Total Assets:* £25,240,802
Registered Office: 1 Bell Parade, Glebe Way, West Wickham, Kent, BR4 0RH
Activities: Renting and leasing of cars and light motor vehicles
Parent: Raedex Consortium Limited
Officers: Reginald Larry-Cole [1970] Director/Car Salesman; Scott Andrew Martin [1978] Director/Car Salesman

Buyagift PLC
Incorporated: 25 November 1999 *Employees:* 125
Net Worth: £7,119,070 *Total Assets:* £53,391,976
Registered Office: 4 Imperial Place, Maxwell Road, Borehamwood, Herts, WD6 1JN
Activities: Retail sale via mail order houses or via Internet
Major Shareholder: Pierre-Edouard Robert Raymond Marie-Joseph Sterin
Officers: Daniel Jeremy Mountain, Secretary; Syed Kashif Abbas [1979] Director [Pakistani]; Pierre Charles Boccon-Liaudet [1969] Director [French]; Daniel Jeremy Mountain [1974] Managing Director; John Richard Perkins [1964] Director

BVG Group Limited
Incorporated: 27 June 1997 *Employees:* 924
Previous: The BVG Airflo Group Limited
Net Worth: £20,395,008 *Total Assets:* £80,657,672
Registered Office: 3rd Floor, Cumberland House, 15-17 Cumberland Place, Southampton, SO15 2BG
Activities: Activities of head offices
Shareholder: Iain Burgess
Officers: Iain Burgess, Secretary; Iain Burgess [1972] Director; David James Cox [1960] Director; Paul Leslie Oldham [1964] Director; Daniel Russell Price [1972] Director; Gary John Michael Rees [1964] Finance Director

By Chelmer (Holdings) Limited
Incorporated: 29 June 2005
Net Worth Deficit: £14,769,000 *Total Assets:* £171,388,992
Registered Office: 8 White Oak Square, London Road, Swanley, Kent, BR8 7AG
Activities: Activities of head offices
Parent: Infrared Infrastructure Yield Holdings Limited
Officers: James Christopher Heath [1975] Director; Mark Geoffrey David Holden [1957] Director; Mark Christopher Wayment [1958] Director; Elena Giorgiana Wegener [1975] Director/Investment Executive

By Chelmer PLC
Incorporated: 21 July 2005
Net Worth Deficit: £14,769,000 *Total Assets:* £171,388,992
Registered Office: 8 White Oak Square, London Road, Swanley, Kent, BR8 7AG
Activities: Non-trading company
Parent: By Chelmer (Holdings) Limited
Officers: Anthony Robert Faulkner [1973] Director/Chartered Accountant; James Christopher Heath [1975] Director; Mark Geoffrey David Holden [1957] Director; Mark Christopher Wayment [1958] Director; Elena Giorgiana Wegener [1975] Director/Investment Executive

By Design (UK) Limited
Incorporated: 5 December 2006 *Employees:* 2
Net Worth: £36,720,496 *Total Assets:* £36,768,708
Registered Office: 44 Grand Parade, Brighton, BN2 9QA
Activities: Other business support service activities n.e.c.
Officers: Brent Shawzin Hoberman [1968] Director/Entrepreneur [Portuguese]; Thomas Alfred Teichman [1947] Director

Bycentral Holdings Limited
Incorporated: 10 March 2003
Net Worth Deficit: £43,957,000 *Total Assets:* £86,624,000
Registered Office: 8 White Oak Square, London Road, Swanley, Kent, BR8 7AG
Activities: Activities of head offices
Parent: Infrastructure Investments Holdings Limited
Officers: David John Carr [1969] Finance Director; Sarah Louise Gledhill [1975] Director; Mark Geoffrey David Holden [1957] Director; Stephen Howard McDonald [1968] Director

Bycentral Limited
Incorporated: 10 March 2003
Net Worth Deficit: £43,957,000 *Total Assets:* £86,624,000
Registered Office: 8 White Oak Square, London Road, Swanley, Kent, BR8 7AG
Activities: Other service activities n.e.c.
Parent: Bycentral Holdings Limited
Officers: David John Carr [1969] Finance Director; Sarah Louise Gledhill [1975] Director; Mark Geoffrey David Holden [1957] Director; Stephen Howard McDonald [1968] Director

Bynorth (Holdings) Limited
Incorporated: 3 May 2007
Net Worth Deficit: £65,396,000 *Total Assets:* £130,389,000
Registered Office: 8 White Oak Square, London Road, Swanley, Kent, BR8 7AG
Activities: Activities of head offices
Parent: Infrared Infrastructure Yield Holdings Limited
Officers: Anthony Robert Faulkner [1973] Director; Mark Christopher Wayment [1958] Director; Elena Giorgiana Wegener [1975] Director/Investment Executive

Bynorth Limited
Incorporated: 3 May 2007
Net Worth Deficit: £65,396,000 *Total Assets:* £130,389,000
Registered Office: 8 White Oak Square, London Road, Swanley, Kent, BR8 7AG
Activities: Construction of commercial buildings
Parent: Bynorth (Holdings) Limited
Officers: Anthony Robert Faulkner [1973] Director; Mark Christopher Wayment [1958] Director; Elena Giorgiana Wegener [1975] Director/Investment Executive

Bytes Software Services Limited
Incorporated: 25 February 1982 *Employees:* 266
Net Worth: £17,470,788 *Total Assets:* £72,827,568
Registered Office: Bytes House, Randalls Way, Leatherhead, Surrey, KT22 7TW
Activities: Other information technology service activities
Officers: Tina Elizabeth Sexton, Secretary; Neil Robert Murphy [1964] Sales Director; Amanda Jane Nicholson [1967] Director; Keith Alan Richardson [1959] Finance Director; Robert Eben Venter [1960] Director [South African]

Bytes Technology Group Limited
Incorporated: 28 September 1998 *Employees:* 6
Net Worth: £14,625,000 *Total Assets:* £53,560,000
Registered Office: Bytes House, Randalls Way, Leatherhead, Surrey, KT22 7TW
Activities: Information technology consultancy activities
Officers: Tina Elizabeth Sexton, Secretary; Andrew Holden [1967] Director [South African]; David Nicholas Maw [1950] Director/Accountant; Neil Robert Murphy [1964] Managing Director; Mteto Nyati [1964] Director [South African]; Keith Alan Richardson [1959] Director; Robert Eben Venter [1960] Director/Chief Executive [South African]

Bywest (Holdings) Limited
Incorporated: 22 September 2000
Net Worth Deficit: £9,712,000 *Total Assets:* £56,724,000
Registered Office: 8 White Oak Square, London Road, Swanley, Kent, BR8 7AG
Activities: Activities of head offices
Parent: Infrastructure Investments Holdings Limited
Officers: Sarah Louise Gledhill [1975] Director; Mark John Griffiths [1967] Operations Director; Mark Geoffrey David Holden [1957] Director; Glynn Newby [1966] Director; Rachel Louise Turnbull [1978] Director

Bywest Limited
Incorporated: 25 September 2000
Net Worth Deficit: £7,083,000 *Total Assets:* £56,723,000
Registered Office: 8 White Oak Square, London Road, Swanley, Kent, BR8 7AG
Activities: Other service activities n.e.c.
Parent: Bywest (Holdings) Limited
Officers: Sarah Louise Gledhill [1975] Director; Mark John Griffiths [1967] Operations Director; Mark Geoffrey David Holden [1957] Director; Glynn Newby [1966] Director; Rachel Louise Turnbull [1978] Director

C.L.C. Contractors Limited
Incorporated: 20 October 1975 *Employees:* 939
Net Worth: £38,347,000 *Total Assets:* £61,154,000
Registered Office: Unit 2 Northbrook Industrial Estate, Vincent Avenue, Southampton, SO16 6PB
Activities: Electrical installation
Parent: CLC Group Limited
Officers: Philip Iain Armitage [1970] IT Director; Paul Beattie [1959] Divisional Director; Robert Boal [1963] Director; Lee Elliott [1973] Director; Matthew Simon Hilton [1986] Director; Nicholas Andrew Hilton [1961] Sales Director; Timothy Marris [1960] Branch Director; Adrian John McDonald [1964] Director; Christopher Paul Pritchard [1965] Branch Director; Simon Reeve [1966] Director; John Ryder [1961] Director; Michael James Triner [1965] Director

Cable & Wireless Europe Holdings Limited
Incorporated: 7 February 2003
Net Worth: £1,062,540,992 *Total Assets:* £1,209,196,032
Registered Office: Vodafone House, The Connection, Newbury, Berks, RG14 2FN
Activities: Activities of head offices
Parent: Cable & Wireless UK Holdings Limited
Officers: Alexander Henricus Lentink [1966] Director/Company Secretary [Dutch]; Neil Andrew Wright [1970] Director/Finance Executive

Cable & Wireless Global Holding Limited
Incorporated: 22 March 1999
Net Worth: £25,458,000 *Total Assets:* £25,460,000
Registered Office: Vodafone House, The Connection, Newbury, Berks, RG14 2FN
Activities: Other telecommunications activities
Parent: The Eastern Leasing Company Limited
Officers: Gregory Mook [1961] Director; Neil Andrew Wright [1970] Director/Finance Executive

Cable & Wireless Global Telecommunication Services Limited
Incorporated: 3 August 2000
Net Worth Deficit: £1,648,000 *Total Assets:* £77,265,000
Registered Office: Vodafone House, The Connection, Newbury, Berks, RG14 2FN
Activities: Other business support service activities n.e.c.
Shareholders: The Eastern Leasing Company Limited; The Eastern Leasing Company Limited
Officers: Marcus Glover [1970] Director; Alexander Henricus Lentink [1966] Director/Company Secretary [Dutch]; Alan Mark Milton [1978] Director

Cable & Wireless UK Holdings Limited
Incorporated: 14 September 1999
Net Worth: £701,358,016 *Total Assets:* £1,863,223,040
Registered Office: Vodafone House, The Connection, Newbury, Berks, RG14 2FN
Activities: Activities of head offices
Parent: Cable & Wireless Worldwide PLC
Officers: Gregory Mook [1961] Director; Neil Andrew Wright [1970] Director/Finance Executive

Cable & Wireless Worldwide Limited
Incorporated: 24 September 2009
Previous: Cable & Wireless Worldwide PLC
Net Worth: £1,540,712,960 *Total Assets:* £1,833,421,952
Registered Office: Vodafone House, The Connection, Newbury, Berks, RG14 2FN
Activities: Other telecommunications activities
Parent: Vodafone International Operations Limited
Officers: Paul George Stephenson [1966] Director/Accountant; Neil Andrew Wright [1970] Director/Finance Executive

Cablefile Limited
Incorporated: 26 April 2004 *Employees:* 2
Net Worth: £18,171,862 *Total Assets:* £28,416,222
Registered Office: Oceanic House, Cracknore Hard, Marchwood, Southampton, SO40 4ZD
Activities: Other letting and operating of own or leased real estate
Shareholders: Southampton Power Boat Centre Limited; Cracknore Power Limited
Officers: Harry John Hutchinson, Secretary/Surveyor; Philip John Hutchinson [1949] Director; Lawrence Edward Smith [1956] Director/Professional Sailor

Cabot Credit Management Group Limited
Incorporated: 16 October 2003
Previous: Cabot Financial Holdings Group Limited
Net Worth Deficit: £8,694,000 *Total Assets:* £430,044,000
Registered Office: 1 Kings Hill Avenue, Kings Hill, West Malling, Kent, ME19 4UA
Activities: Activities of head offices
Parent: Cabot Financial Limited
Officers: Charlotte Taggart, Secretary; Craig Anthony Buick [1969] Finance Director [British/Australian]; Brendan Edward Gilligan [1956] Director [Irish]; Ashish Masih [1965] Director [American]; Kenneth John Stannard [1966] Director/Chief Executive Officer

Cabot Credit Management Limited
Incorporated: 24 March 2006 *Employees:* 1,859
Previous: Cabot Credit Management PLC
Net Worth: £188,800,000 *Total Assets:* £1,640,199,936
Registered Office: 1 Kings Hill Avenue, Kings Hill, West Malling, Kent, ME19 4UA
Activities: Activities of financial services holding companies
Parent: Cabot UK Holdco Limited
Officers: Charlotte Taggart, Secretary; Craig Anthony Buick [1969] Finance Director [British/Australian]; Kenneth John Stannard [1966] Director/Chief Executive Officer

Cabot Financial (Europe) Limited
Incorporated: 19 September 1997 *Employees:* 614
Net Worth: £1,004,000 *Total Assets:* £212,895,008
Registered Office: 1 Kings Hill Avenue, Kings Hill, West Malling, Kent, ME19 4UA
Activities: Financial intermediation not elsewhere classified
Officers: Charlotte Taggart, Secretary; Craig Anthony Buick [1969] Finance Director [British/Australian]; Kenneth John Stannard [1966] Director/Chief Executive Officer; Charlotte Taggart [1973] Director/Lawyer

Cabot Financial (Marlin) Limited
Incorporated: 16 December 2002 *Employees:* 59
Previous: Marlin Financial Services Limited
Net Worth: £1,354,000 *Total Assets:* £92,738,000
Registered Office: Marlin House, 16-22 Grafton Road, Worthing, W Sussex, BN11 1QP
Activities: Other business support service activities n.e.c.
Parent: Marlin Senior Holdings Limited
Officers: Charlotte Taggart, Secretary; Craig Anthony Buick [1969] Finance Director [British/Australian]; Peter Charles Richardson [1959] Director; Kenneth John Stannard [1966] Director

Cabot Financial (UK) Limited
Incorporated: 21 April 1999
Net Worth: £13,524,000 *Total Assets:* £1,231,095,040
Registered Office: 1 Kings Hill Avenue, Kings Hill, West Malling, Kent, ME19 4UA
Activities: Financial intermediation not elsewhere classified
Parent: Cabot Financial Debt Recovery Services Limited
Officers: Charlotte Taggart, Secretary; Craig Anthony Buick [1969] Finance Director [British/Australian]; Kenneth John Stannard [1966] Director/Chief Executive Officer; Charlotte Taggart [1973] Director/Solicitor

Cabot Financial Debt Recovery Services Limited
Incorporated: 29 February 2000
Net Worth Deficit: £58,378,000 *Total Assets:* £473,355,008
Registered Office: 1 Kings Hill Avenue, Kings Hill, West Malling, Kent, ME19 4UA
Activities: Activities of financial services holding companies
Parent: Cabot Financial Holdings Group Limited
Officers: Charlotte Taggart, Secretary; Craig Anthony Buick [1969] Finance Director [British/Australian]; Kenneth John Stannard [1966] Director/Chief Executive Officer; Charotte Taggart [1973] Director/General Counsel

Cabot Financial Holdings Group Limited
Incorporated: 14 September 2000
Previous: Cabot Credit Management Group Limited
Net Worth: £834,000 *Total Assets:* £145,784,000
Registered Office: 1 Kings Hill Avenue, Kings Hill, West Malling, Kent, ME19 4UA
Activities: Financial intermediation not elsewhere classified
Officers: Charlotte Taggart, Secretary; Craig Anthony Buick [1969] Finance Director [British/Australian]; Kenneth John Stannard [1966] Director/Chief Executive Officer; Charlotte Taggart [1973] Director/Lawyer

Cabot Financial Limited
Incorporated: 20 February 2006
Net Worth: £283,204,000 *Total Assets:* £317,705,984
Registered Office: 1 Kings Hill Avenue, Kings Hill, West Malling, Kent, ME19 4UA
Activities: Activities of financial services holding companies
Parent: Cabot Credit Management Limited
Officers: Charlotte Taggart, Secretary; Craig Anthony Buick [1969] Finance Director [British/Australian]; Kenneth John Stannard [1966] Director/Chief Executive Officer; Charlotte Taggart [1973] Director/Solicitor

Cadbury Eight LLP
Incorporated: 18 August 2011
Net Worth: £2,478,514,176 *Total Assets:* £2,478,514,176
Registered Office: Cadbury House, Sanderson Road, Uxbridge, Middlesex, UB8 1DH

Cadbury Four LLP
Incorporated: 5 November 2010
Net Worth: £1,124,563,968 *Total Assets:* £1,124,563,968
Registered Office: Cadbury House, Sanderson Road, Uxbridge, Middlesex, UB8 1DH

Cadbury Limited
Incorporated: 7 February 2008
Net Worth: £10,277,645,312 *Total Assets:* £10,277,645,312
Registered Office: Cadbury House, Sanderson Road, Uxbridge, Middlesex, UB8 1DH
Activities: Activities of head offices
Parent: Chromium Acquisitions Limited
Officers: Adrian John Paul Arrighi [1978] Tax Director; Michael Brendan Foye [1965] Treasury Director; John Michael Hladusz [1972] Director/Chartered Accountant; Carole Noelle Keene [1966] Director

Cadbury Nine LLP
Incorporated: 9 August 2011
Net Worth: £1,845,699,968 *Total Assets:* £1,845,740,032
Registered Office: Cadbury House, Sanderson Road, Uxbridge, Middlesex, UB8 1DH

Cadbury Schweppes Finance Limited
Incorporated: 24 February 1949
Net Worth: £83,496,000 *Total Assets:* £101,588,000
Registered Office: Cadbury House, Sanderson Road, Uxbridge, Middlesex, UB8 1DH
Activities: Activities of head offices
Parent: Mondelez UK Holdings & Services Limited
Officers: Adrian John Paul Arrighi [1978] Tax Director; Michael Brendan Foye [1965] Treasury Director; John Michael Hladusz [1972] Director/Chartered Accountant; Carole Noelle Keene [1966] Director

Cadbury Schweppes Overseas Limited
Incorporated: 13 June 1899
Net Worth: £7,902,566,912 *Total Assets:* £7,902,595,072
Registered Office: Cadbury House, Sanderson Road, Uxbridge, Middlesex, UB8 1DH
Activities: Activities of head offices
Parent: Chromium Assets Limited
Officers: Adrian John Paul Arrighi [1978] Tax Director; Michael Brendan Foye [1965] Treasury Director; John Michael Hladusz [1972] Director/Chartered Accountant; Carole Noelle Keene [1966] Director

Cadbury Seven LLP
Incorporated: 19 December 2011
Net Worth: £13,519,614,976 *Total Assets:* £13,519,614,976
Registered Office: Cadbury House, Sanderson Road, Uxbridge, Middlesex, UB8 1DH

Cadbury South Africa (Holdings)
Incorporated: 16 December 2009
Net Worth: £91,929,080 *Total Assets:* £91,930,488
Registered Office: Cadbury House, Sanderson Road, Uxbridge, Middlesex, UB8 1DH
Activities: Activities of head offices
Parent: Cadbury Schweppes Overseas Limited
Officers: David John Groves [1963] Director/Finance Controller [South African]; Karol Leszek Jozwicki [1980] Director/Financial Controller [Polish]

Cadbury Ten LLP
Incorporated: 19 December 2011
Net Worth: £36,659,304 *Total Assets:* £37,031,568
Registered Office: Cadbury House, Sanderson Road, Uxbridge, Middlesex, UB8 1DH

Cadence Design Systems Limited
Incorporated: 9 January 1990 *Employees:* 187
Net Worth: £16,784,000 *Total Assets:* £36,614,000
Registered Office: Maxis, 1 Western Road, Bracknell, Berks, RG12 1RT
Activities: Specialised design activities
Parent: Cadence Design Systems, Inc.
Officers: James Judson Cowie [1964] Director/Lawyer [American]; Amanda Jane Elliffe [1976] Director/Senior Finance Manager [Irish]; John Michael Wall [1970] Director/Accountant [Irish]

CAE (UK) PLC
Incorporated: 2 November 1967 *Employees:* 88
Net Worth: £13,463,000 *Total Assets:* £25,928,000
Registered Office: Innovation Drive, Burgess Hill, W Sussex, RH15 9TW
Activities: Other education n.e.c.
Officers: James Anthony Boyle, Secretary; Pietro D'Ulisse [1960] Director/Engineer [Canadian]; Hasnain Mohsin [1978] Director/Accountant; Andrew Naismith [1962] Director

CAE STS Limited
Incorporated: 6 December 2006 *Employees:* 136
Net Worth: £65,442,000 *Total Assets:* £108,605,000
Registered Office: CAE, Innovation Drive, York Road, Burgess Hill, W Sussex, RH15 9TW
Activities: Other transportation support activities
Officers: William Richard Balicki, Secretary; Sonya Branco [1975] Director/Vice President Finance and Chief Financial Officer [Canadian]; Hasnain Mohsin [1978] Director of Finance; Andrew Naismith [1962] Director/General Manager

CAE Technology Services Limited
Incorporated: 7 February 1992 *Employees:* 242
Net Worth: £9,711,106 *Total Assets:* £39,802,160
Registered Office: CAE House, Colonial Way, Watford, Herts, WD24 4PT
Activities: Other information technology service activities
Parent: Seckloe 194 Limited
Officers: Richard Behan [1978] Director; Umesh Chauhan [1965] Finance Director; Justin Matthew Harling [1973] Managing Director

CAE Training & Services UK Ltd
Incorporated: 2 July 1998 *Employees:* 73
Net Worth: £5,712,000 *Total Assets:* £51,444,000
Registered Office: Fleming Way, Crawley, W Sussex, RH10 9UH
Activities: Other transportation support activities
Officers: William Richard Balicki, Secretary; Hasnain Mohsin [1978] Director of Finance; Onno Rijsdijk [1965] Legal Director [Dutch]; Johannes Hendrik Van Engelen [1967] Director [Dutch]

CAF Bank Limited
Incorporated: 2 August 1984 *Employees:* 96
Net Worth: £41,350,000 *Total Assets:* £1,106,256,000
Registered Office: 25 Kings Hill Avenue, Kings Hill, West Malling, Kent, ME19 4JQ
Activities: Banks
Officers: Kate Louise Mayor, Secretary; Martyn Joseph Beauchamp [1972] Director; Sheragh Mary Beirne [1970] Director/Banker [Irish]; Kees Diepstraten [1967] Director [Dutch]; John William Grout [1962] Director; Malcolm Himsworth [1955] Director; Mairi Margaret Johnstone [1961] Director; Sir John Menzies Low [1953] Director; Carole Machell [1962] Executive Director; Janet Edna Pope [1960] Executive Director; Alistair Graham Ray [1974] Director/Investment Manager; Graham Philip Toy [1956] Director

Caffyns Public Limited Company
Incorporated: 30 October 1909 *Employees:* 413
Net Worth: £27,123,000 *Total Assets:* £91,267,000
Registered Office: Meads Road, Eastbourne, E Sussex, BN20 7DR
Activities: Sale of new cars and light motor vehicles
Officers: Sarah Jane Caffyn, Secretary; Sarah Jane Caffyn [1968] Director & Company Secretary; Simon Graham Morris Caffyn [1960] Director/Chief Executive; Nigel Timothy Gourlay [1955] Director/Accountant; Nicholas William Hollingworth [1952] Director/Chief Executive; Michael Warren [1964] Finance Director; Richard Crossley Wright [1945] Director

CALA 1 Limited
Incorporated: 4 March 2013 *Employees:* 7
Net Worth: £17,284,766 *Total Assets:* £245,650,768
Registered Office: Cala House, 54 The Causeway, Staines upon Thames, Surrey, TW18 3AX
Activities: Construction of domestic buildings
Parent: CALA Group (Holdings) Limited
Officers: Jasan Fitzpatrick, Secretary; Matteo Charles Colombo [1980] Director/Investment Professional; Neil John Stoddart [1969] Finance Director; Geoffrey Julian Timms [1960] Director/Solicitor; Kevin Whitaker [1969] Director

CALA Group (Holdings) Limited
Incorporated: 4 March 2013 *Employees:* 873
Net Worth: £338,294,016 *Total Assets:* £968,812,032
Registered Office: Cala House, 54 The Causeway, Staines upon Thames, Surrey, TW18 3AX
Activities: Construction of domestic buildings
Parent: Haut Investments 2 Limited
Officers: Jasan Fitzpatrick, Secretary; Matteo Charles Colombo [1980] Director/Investment Professional; Emma Hardaker-Jones [1973] Director; Kerrigan William Procter [1969] Director; Neil John Stoddart [1969] Finance Director; Geoffrey Julian Timms [1960] Director/Solicitor; Kevin Whitaker [1969] Director

Caledonian Helicopters Limited
Incorporated: 21 July 1970 *Employees:* 2
Net Worth: £86,040,856 *Total Assets:* £102,763,312
Registered Office: Redhill Aerodrome, Redhill, Surrey, RH1 5JZ
Activities: Renting and leasing of air passenger transport equipment
Parent: United Helicopters Limited
Officers: James Lort Howell-Richardson, Secretary; Alan William George Corbett [1957] Director; James Lort Howell-Richardson [1980] Director/Legal Counsel

Caligor Opco UK, Ltd
Incorporated: 7 January 2016
Net Worth: £13,782,084 *Total Assets:* £46,252,908
Registered Office: Caligor Opco UK Ltd, Unit 8 Masthead, Capstan Court, Crossways Business Park, Dartford, Kent, DA2 6QG
Activities: Other service activities n.e.c.
Officers: Kevin Daekyung Ma [1985] Director/Investor [American]; Ron Nayot [1978] Director/Finance [Canadian]

Calverton Finance Limited
Incorporated: 10 August 1998 *Employees:* 45
Net Worth: £3,947,118 *Total Assets:* £36,386,992
Registered Office: Calverton House, 1 Keller Close, Kiln Farm, Milton Keynes, Bucks, MK11 3LL
Activities: Factoring
Parent: Calverton Group Limited
Officers: Samantha Etherington, Secretary; Mark Gerard Byrne [1960] Factoring Director; Carol Anne Cordrey [1951] Director; Peter Graham Cordrey [1947] Director/Banker; David Hogg [1949] Director; Gregory David Hussey [1971] Operations Director; Sharon Simpson [1973] Sales Director

Camden Motors (Holdings) Limited
Incorporated: 18 September 1996 *Employees:* 2
Net Worth: £25,774,000 *Total Assets:* £29,539,000
Registered Office: 11 Osier Way, Olney Office Park, Olney, Bucks, MK46 5FP
Activities: Other letting and operating of own or leased real estate
Major Shareholder: Paul John Dunkley
Officers: David William Hammond, Secretary; Paul John Dunkley [1958] Director; David William Hammond [1963] Director

Camden Ventures Limited
Incorporated: 13 June 2005 *Employees:* 5
Net Worth: £34,455,000 *Total Assets:* £42,794,000
Registered Office: 11 Osier Way, Olney Office Park, Olney, Bucks, MK46 5FP
Activities: Other letting and operating of own or leased real estate
Major Shareholder: Paul John Dunkley
Officers: David William Hammond, Secretary; Paul John Dunkley [1958] Director; David William Hammond [1963] Director

Camellia Public Limited Company
Incorporated: 15 August 1889 *Employees:* 80,275
Net Worth: £368,400,000 *Total Assets:* £576,499,968
Registered Office: Linton Park, Linton, Maidstone, Kent, ME17 4AB
Activities: Activities of head offices
Officers: Amarpal Takk, Secretary; Gautam Shashichandra Dalal [1955] Director/Accountant; Thomas Kenric Franks [1963] Director; The Honourable William Knatchbull Gibson [1951] Director; Graham Harold McLean [1969] Director; Malcolm Courtney Perkins [1945] Director/Chartered Accountant; Christopher John Relleen [1948] Director; Frederic Vuilleumier [1967] Director/Lawyer [Swiss]; Susan Ann Walker [1967] Director

Camelot Business Solutions Limited
Incorporated: 7 March 2011 *Employees:* 87
Net Worth: £2,900,000 *Total Assets:* £35,300,000
Registered Office: Magdalen House, Tolpits Lane, Watford, Herts, WD18 9RN
Activities: Gambling and betting activities
Parent: Premier Lotteries UK Limited
Officers: John Edward Michael Dillon, Secretary; John Edward Michael Dillon [1963] Legal Director and Company Secretary; Ilya Kachko [1979] Director/Portfolio Manager [Canadian]; Andrew Jonathan Mark Taylor [1961] Director/Private Equity Investor

Camelot Global Lottery Solutions Limited
Incorporated: 7 March 2011 *Employees:* 209
Previous: Camelot Strategic Solutions Limited
Net Worth Deficit: £11,544,000 *Total Assets:* £60,554,000
Registered Office: Magdalen House, Tolpits Lane, Watford, Herts, WD18 9RN
Activities: Gambling and betting activities
Parent: Premier Lotteries UK Limited
Officers: John Edward Michael Dillon, Secretary; Bogdan Cenanovic [1976] Director/Vice President, Technology, Media & Telecom [Canadian]; Ilya Kachko [1979] Director/Portfolio Manager [Canadian]; Dr David Thomas Kelly [1963] Non-Executive Director; Michael Charles Lightman [1963] Director [American]; John Henderson McNeil [1968] Director [American]; Wayne Lawrence Pickup [1976] Director/Chief Executive [New Zealander]; Jane Sarah Rowe [1959] Director/Senior Vice President [Canadian]; Robert Oscar Rowley [1949] Director

Camelot UK Lotteries Limited
Incorporated: 27 May 1993 *Employees:* 667
Net Worth: £33,600,000 *Total Assets:* £651,699,968
Registered Office: Tolpits Lane, Watford, Herts, WD18 9RN
Activities: Gambling and betting activities
Parent: Premier Lotteries UK Limited
Officers: John Edward Michael Dillon, Secretary; Ilya Kachko [1979] Director/Portfolio Manager [Canadian]; David Thomas Kelly [1963] Non-Executive Director; Nigel Railton [1967] Director/Chief Executive; Sir Hugh Michael Robertson [1962] Director/Chairman; Sarah Jane Rowe [1959] Director/Senior Vice President [Canadian]; Robert Oscar Rowley [1949] Director; Andrew Jonathan Mark Taylor [1961] Regional Managing Director; Jennelle Lisa Tilling [1969] Director [Australian/British]; Robert Malcolm Walker [1945] Director/Deputy Chairman

Campact Limited
Incorporated: 13 May 1988 *Employees:* 31
Net Worth: £6,195,000 *Total Assets:* £27,693,000
Registered Office: 21-25 Church Street West, Woking, Surrey, GU21 6DJ
Activities: Manufacture of plastics in primary forms
Parent: Egger (UK) Holdings Limited
Officers: Bernd Steinlechner, Secretary; Elfriede Bretterklieber-Taye [1979] Director [Austrian]; Michael Robert Livesey [1959] Director; Martin Steinhagen [1979] Technical Director (Resin Plants) [German]; Bernd Steinlechner [1971] Finance Director [Austrian]

Campmoss Property Company Limited
Incorporated: 16 January 1987 *Employees:* 1
Net Worth: £16,956,708 *Total Assets:* £32,951,648
Registered Office: 56 Station Road, Egham, Surrey, TW20 9LF
Activities: Buying and selling of own real estate
Shareholder: Christabel Scott-Balls
Officers: Karen Louise Chandler, Secretary; Edward Richard Goodwin [1939] Director; John Richard Wollenberg [1948] Director

Cams Hill School
Incorporated: 24 August 2011 *Employees:* 160
Net Worth: £21,650,544 *Total Assets:* £23,264,864
Registered Office: Cams Hill School, Shearwater Avenue, Fareham, Hants, PO16 8AH
Activities: General secondary education
Officers: Jorden Anderson [1987] Director/Teacher; Joanna Bowles [1969] Director; Sara Brooker [1972] Director; Richard Cheatle [1966] Director/Health, Safety, Facilities and Environment Manager; Gwennan Harrison-Jones [1974] Director/Headteacher; Andrew David Kaye [1977] Director/Teacher; Nicola Rawlings [1973] Director; Sonya Read [1972] Director; Chris Reilly [1992] Director/Teacher; Nicola Trend [1979] Director/Yoga Instructor; Ann Williams [1972] Director; Emma Louise Woollard [1965] Director of Finance

Canadian & Arcadia Limited
Incorporated: 8 January 2016 *Employees:* 2
Net Worth Deficit: £3,622,659 *Total Assets:* £22,179,252
Registered Office: 8-10 South Street, Epsom, Surrey, KT18 7PF
Activities: Buying and selling of own real estate
Parent: Canadian & Portland Estates (Holdings) Limited
Officers: Samantha Clark, Secretary; Emma Tiptaft, Secretary; Samantha Clark [1968] Director/Surveyor; John Paul Miles [1953] Director/Surveyor

Canal & River Trading CIC
Incorporated: 15 May 2012
Net Worth: £38,067,180 *Total Assets:* £48,124,308
Registered Office: First Floor, North Station House, 500 Elder Gate, Milton Keynes, Bucks, MK9 1BB
Activities: Development of building projects
Parent: Canal & River Trust
Officers: Yetunde Salami, Secretary; Thomas James Deards [1976] Director/Solicitor; Sandra Claire Kelly [1960] Director/Chartered Accountant; Stuart Christopher Mills [1967] Property Director; Quentin Patrick Pickford [1961] Director/Chartered Management Accountant; Steven Pullinger [1959] Director/Accountant

Canal & River Trust
Incorporated: 12 October 2011 *Employees:* 1,698
Net Worth: £791,200,000 *Total Assets:* £1,082,000,000
Registered Office: First Floor, North Station House, 500 Elder Gate, Milton Keynes, Bucks, MK9 1BB
Activities: Water collection, treatment and supply
Officers: Thomas James Deards, Secretary; Dame Jennifer Gita Abramsky [1946] Director; Nigel Charles Annett [1958] Director; Joseph Benjamin Gordon [1959] Director; Janet Hogben [1957] Director/Chief People Officer; Sir Christopher William Kelly [1946] Director; Allan Leslie Leighton [1953] Director/Trustees; Tim Reeve [1973] Director/Trustee; Susan Linda Wilkinson [1956] Director

Canon (UK) Limited
Incorporated: 21 June 1976 *Employees:* 1,786
Net Worth Deficit: £209,720,992 *Total Assets:* £337,932,992
Registered Office: Woodhatch, Reigate, Surrey, RH2 8BF
Activities: Other business support service activities n.e.c.
Parent: Canon Holdings (UK) Limited
Officers: Zoe Eshelby, Secretary; Peter John Anthem [1962] Finance Director; Yusuke Mizoguchi [1960] Managing Director [Japanese]

Canon Europe Limited
Incorporated: 20 October 2000 *Employees:* 797
Net Worth: £60,299,000 *Total Assets:* £88,300,000
Registered Office: 3 The Square, Stockley Park, Uxbridge, Middlesex, UB11 1ET
Activities: Manufacture of other electrical equipment
Parent: Canon Inc
Officers: David John Bateson, Secretary/Director; Jeppe Frandsen [1960] Director [Danish]; Yuichi Ishizuka [1955] Director [Japanese]; Takanobu Nakamasu [1958] Director [Japanese]; Alessandro Stanzani [1962] Director [Italian]; Aitake Wakiya [1955] Director [Japanese]; Stefano Zenti [1961] Director [Italian]

Canon Holdings (UK) Limited
Incorporated: 20 October 1993
Net Worth: £38,056,684 *Total Assets:* £38,061,752
Registered Office: Woodhatch, Cockshot Hill, Reigate, Surrey, RH2 8BF
Activities: Manufacture of other electrical equipment
Parent: Canon Inc
Officers: David John Bateson, Secretary; Peter John Anthem [1962] Finance Director

Canon Medical Systems Limited
Incorporated: 2 July 1970 *Employees:* 138
Previous: Toshiba Medical Systems Limited
Net Worth: £5,636,000 *Total Assets:* £38,547,000
Registered Office: Boundary Court, Gatwick Road, Crawley, W Sussex, RH10 9AX
Activities: Manufacture of irradiation, electromedical and electrotherapeutic equipment
Parent: Canon Medical Systems Europe BV
Officers: Mark Holmshaw, Secretary; Nobuyuki Hatakeyama [1965] Director/Business Executive [Japanese]; Jonathan Mark Hitchman [1960] Business Director; Mark Holmshaw [1960] Director/Business Executive

Canterbury Christ Church University
Incorporated: 10 June 2003 *Employees:* 1,585
Net Worth: £95,228,000 *Total Assets:* £197,060,992
Registered Office: Rochester House, St Georges Place, Canterbury, Kent, CT1 1UT
Activities: First-degree level higher education
Officers: Alison Clare Sear, Secretary; Nadra Khanum Ahmed [1958] Director; Susan Elizabeth Appleby [1948] Director; Judith Jane Armitt [1953] Director/Retired Public Sector Professional; Staynton Brown [1982] Director; Dr Alison Christine Eyden [1970] Director/University Professional; Julian Philip Faber [1965] Director/IT Professional; Philip John Fletcher [1946] Director; Judith Anne Sally Harding [1963] Project Director; Sir William Ian Ridley Johnston [1945] Director/Security Industry Regulator; Pamela Christine Jones [1954] Director; Philip Kloppenborg [1993] Director/Student; Frank Martin [1952] Director/Retired Chief Executive - Hornby PLC; Concepta Bernadette Nolan [1958] Director/Senior University Lecturer; Meradin Peachey [1957] Public Health Director Local Authority; Quentin Leonard Roper [1969] Director of Education Diocese of Canterbury; Reverend Robert Stevenson [1952] Director/Planning Consultant; Professor Rama Shankaran Thirunamachandran [1966] Director/University Vice Chancellor; Trevor Willmott [1950] Director/Clerk in Holy Orders

Canterbury Diocesan Board of Finance
Incorporated: 29 December 1916 *Employees:* 197
Net Worth: £82,680,000 *Total Assets:* £89,341,000
Registered Office: Diocesan House, Lady Woottons Green, Canterbury, Kent, CT1 1NQ
Activities: Other business support service activities n.e.c.
Officers: Julian James Hills, Secretary/Diocesan Secretary; Aimee Hester Joan Babbs [1987] Director/Admin Assistant; Amanda Arianwen Cecilia Cottrell [1941] Director; Miranda Daphne Ford [1949] Retired Director; The Venerable Joanne Kelly-Moore [1968] Director/The Archdeacon of Canterbury; Reverend Estella Ruth Last [1976] Director/Priest; Nigel Stephen Mansley [1957] Non-Executive Director of East Kent Hospitals; The Venerable Darren Noel Miller [1967] Director/Archdeacon of Ashford; Lieutenant Colonel Retired John Peter Morrison [1950] Director/Retired Army Officer; Dr John Pedder Moss [1957] Director/Retired; Reverend Shiela Porter [1950] Director/Vicar; Reverend Michael Johann Resch [1963] Director/Clerk in Holy Orders; Revd Canon Andrew William Sewell [1961] Director/Priest; Philip Frederick Sibbald [1975] Director/Senior Business Analyst; Reverend Carol Smith [1955] Director/Priest; Stephen Ronald Taylor [1955] Director/Archdeacon of Maidstone; Justin Portal Welby [1956] Director/Archbishop of Canterbury; Robert Andrew Willis [1947] Director/Dean of Canterbury; Trevor Willmott [1950] Director/Bishop of Dover

Canterbury Pharmacies Holdings Limited
Incorporated: 24 March 2010 *Employees:* 331
Net Worth: £3,353,751 *Total Assets:* £22,170,330
Registered Office: c/o Paydens Limited, Parkwood, Sutton Road, Maidstone, Kent, ME15 9NE
Activities: Dispensing chemist in specialised stores
Parent: Paydens Group Holdings Limited
Officers: John Patrick McConville [1959] Director; Alexander George Pay [1984] Managing Director; Dennis Charles Pay [1942] Director/Pharmacist

Canterbury Pharmacies Limited
Incorporated: 13 January 1994 *Employees:* 331
Net Worth: £13,743,334 *Total Assets:* £22,360,948
Registered Office: c/o Paydens Limited, Parkwood, Sutton Road, Maidstone, Kent, ME15 9NE
Activities: Dispensing chemist in specialised stores
Parent: Canterbury Pharmacies Holdings Limited
Officers: John Patrick McConville [1959] Director; Alexander George Pay [1984] Managing Director; Dennis Charles Pay [1942] Director/Pharmacist

Cape Claims Services Limited
Incorporated: 6 May 2005 *Employees:* 3
Net Worth: £8,119,000 *Total Assets:* £60,072,000
Registered Office: First Floor, Office 1, 2 The Future Works, Brunel Way, Slough, SL1 1FQ
Activities: Banks
Parent: Cape Intermediate Holdings Limited
Officers: Richard Friend Allan [1964] Director; Lord Meghnad Jagdishchandra Desai [1940] Director; Christopher Richard Pond [1952] Director/Charity Chief Executive

Cape Intermediate Holdings Limited
Incorporated: 28 December 1893
Net Worth: £162,600,000 *Total Assets:* £260,000,000
Registered Office: First Floor, Office 1, 2 The Future Works, Brunel Way, Slough, SL1 1FQ
Activities: Activities of head offices
Parent: Cape Holdco Limited
Officers: Ran Oren [1978] Director [French]

Capgemini UK PLC
Incorporated: 10 December 1968 *Employees:* 7,838
Net Worth: £2,812,000 *Total Assets:* £980,796,992
Registered Office: 1 Forge End, Woking, Surrey, GU21 6DB
Activities: Information technology consultancy activities
Parent: CGS Holdings Limited
Officers: Julie Mangan, Secretary; Aiman Ezzat [1961] Director/Chief Financial Officer of Capgemini Group [French]; Carole Gabriella Ferrand [1970] Director/Group Chief Financial Officer [French]; Clive David Hart [1973] Finance Director; Christine Mary Hodgson [1964] Director/CEO Technology Services North West; Paul Arthur Margetts [1966] Managing Director; Rosemary Joy Stark [1963] Director/Vice President

Capital (Hair and Beauty) Limited
Incorporated: 11 March 1954 *Employees:* 430
Net Worth: £22,084,154 *Total Assets:* £29,652,584
Registered Office: Capital (Hair & Beauty) Ltd, Crowhurst Corner, Crowhurst Road, Brighton, BN1 8AP
Activities: Wholesale of perfume and cosmetics
Shareholder: Peter Ross Vans Agnew
Officers: Peter Ross Vans Agnew, Secretary; David John Harrison [1963] Director; Harry Anthony Sleet [1968] Director/Chartered Accountant; Hamish Michael Vans Agnew [1958] Director; Peter Ross Vans Agnew [1960] Managing Director; Rachel Generaldine Vans Agnew [1966] Director; Sally Jane Vans Agnew [1966] Director

Capital Home Loans Limited
Incorporated: 6 October 1987 *Employees:* 117
Net Worth: £187,160,992 *Total Assets:* £2,068,568,960
Registered Office: Admiral House, Harlington Way, Fleet, Hants, GU51 4YA
Activities: Activities of mortgage finance companies
Parent: Promontoria (Lansdowne) Limited
Officers: Hilary Susanna Young, Secretary; David Robert Clinton [1954] Director; Michiel Jozef Alexander Heijmeijer [1959] Managing Director [Dutch]; Charlotte Marie Insinger [1965] Director/Management and Business Advisory [Dutch]; Lee James Kelly [1970] Director/Chartered Accountant; Hiteshkumar Rameshchandra Patel [1961] Director

Capital Hospitals (Holdings) Ltd.
Incorporated: 25 May 2005
Net Worth: £14,919,000 *Total Assets:* £1,476,226,944
Registered Office: 8 White Oak Square, London Road, Swanley, Kent, BR8 7AG
Activities: Combined facilities support activities
Parent: Innisfree Nominees Ltd
Officers: Paul Alan Bannister [1959] Director; Gaynor Birley Smith [1966] Investment Director; Louis Javier Falero [1977] Director; Jennifer Kathryn Fegan [1973] Director/Lawyer; Martine Caroline Gagnon [1963] Portfolio Director [French]; Nils Ulf Henrik Norehn [1955] Director [Swedish]; Timothy Richard Pearson [1962] Director; Sabrina Sidhu [1979] Investment Director

Capital Hospitals (Issuer) PLC
Incorporated: 25 May 2005
Net Worth: £50,000 *Total Assets:* £1,446,487,040
Registered Office: 8 White Oak Square, London Road, Swanley, Kent, BR8 7AG
Activities: Other credit granting n.e.c.
Parent: Capital Hospitals (Holdings) Ltd
Officers: Paul Alan Bannister [1959] Director; Gaynor Birley Smith [1966] Investment Director; Louis Javier Falero [1977] Director; Jennifer Kathryn Fegan [1973] Director/Lawyer; Nils Ulf Henrik Norehn [1955] Director [Swedish]; Timothy Richard Pearson [1962] Director; Sabrina Sidhu [1979] Investment Director

Capital Hospitals Ltd.
Incorporated: 25 May 2005
Net Worth: £14,869,000 *Total Assets:* £1,476,226,944
Registered Office: 8 White Oak Square, London Road, Swanley, Kent, BR8 7AG
Activities: Combined facilities support activities
Parent: Capital Hospitals (Holdings) Ltd
Officers: Paul Alan Bannister [1959] Director; Gaynor Birley Smith [1966] Investment Director; Louis Javier Falero [1977] Director; Jennifer Kathryn Fegan [1973] Director/Lawyer; Nils Ulf Henrik Norehn [1955] Director [Swedish]; Timothy Richard Pearson [1962] Director; Sabrina Sidhu [1979] Investment Director

Capital Investment and Finance Ltd
Incorporated: 6 July 2001
Net Worth: £169,972 *Total Assets:* £30,284,442
Registered Office: 52a Spring Grove Road, Hounslow, Middlesex, TW3 4BN
Activities: Buying and selling of own real estate
Major Shareholder: Sivarajah Manivannan
Officers: Manivannan Meenadharshani, Secretary; Sivarajah Manivannan [1960] Director

Capital Professional Limited
Incorporated: 30 March 2011 *Employees:* 172
Net Worth: £40,571,584 *Total Assets:* £52,286,144
Registered Office: 6th Floor, Reading Bridge, George Street, Reading, Berks, RG1 8LS
Activities: Financial management
Parent: CPL Bidco
Officers: Matthew Charles Moore [1971] Director; Nigel Stockton [1966] Director

Capital Safety Acquisitions Limited
Incorporated: 11 January 2012
Net Worth: £794,866,240 *Total Assets:* £831,978,816
Registered Office: 3M Centre, Cain Road, Bracknell, Berks, RG12 8HT
Activities: Activities of head offices
Parent: Capital Safety Global Holdings Limited
Officers: Ian Richard Brown, Secretary; David James Ashley [1968] Director/General Counsel; Donald Gray [1968] Director/Finance Manager; Simla Semerciyan [1973] Director/Finance Manager [Turkish]

Capital Safety Global Holdings Limited
Incorporated: 13 March 2014
Net Worth: £507,384,032 *Total Assets:* £507,398,592
Registered Office: 3M Centre, Cain Road, Bracknell, Berks, RG12 8HT
Activities: Activities of head offices
Officers: Ian Richard Brown, Secretary; David James Ashley [1968] Director/General Counsel; Donald Gray [1964] Director/Finance Manager - Europe; Simla Semerciyan [1973] Director/Finance Manager [Turkish]

Capital Safety Group (Northern Europe) Limited
Incorporated: 4 June 1985 *Employees:* 37
Net Worth: £8,388,000 *Total Assets:* £20,231,000
Registered Office: 3M Centre, Cain Road, Bracknell, Berks, RG12 8HT
Activities: Other manufacturing n.e.c.
Parent: Barrow Hepburn Group Limited
Officers: Ian Richard Brown, Secretary; David James Ashley [1968] Director/General Counsel; Simla Semerciyan [1973] Director/Finance Manager [Turkish]

Capital Safety Limited
Incorporated: 11 March 1998
Net Worth: £80,722,000 *Total Assets:* £109,877,000
Registered Office: 3M Centre, Cain Road, Bracknell, Berks, RG12 8HT
Activities: Activities of head offices
Officers: Ian Richard Brown, Secretary; David James Ashley [1968] Director/General Counsel; Simla Semerciyan [1973] Director/Finance Manager [Turkish]

Capital Safety Row Limited
Incorporated: 22 December 2011
Net Worth: £99,835,160 *Total Assets:* £101,773,368
Registered Office: 3M Centre, Cain Road, Bracknell, Berks, RG12 8HT
Activities: Activities of head offices
Parent: Capital Safety Acquisitions Limited
Officers: Ian Richard Brown, Secretary; David James Ashley [1968] Director/General Counsel; Donald Gray [1964] Finance Director; Simla Semerciyan [1973] Director/Finance Manager [Turkish]

Capula Investment Management LLP
Incorporated: 24 May 2005
Net Worth: £38,604,544 *Total Assets:* £39,008,164
Registered Office: 4th Floor, Reading Bridge House, George Street, Reading, Berks, RG1 8LS
Officers: Masao Asai [1966] Member; Yan Huo [1968] Member; Sam Lowe [1965] Member; Neil McCallum [1961] Member; Mark Barnett [1972] LLP Member; Piyush Bharti [1976] LLP Member; Jonathan Simon Bloom [1967] LLP Member; Jean-Marc Botazzi [1968] LLP Member; David Dymov [1982] LLP Member; Fredrik Gentzel [1974] LLP Member; Taku Iida [1981] LLP Member; Ryan Lucas Letchworth [1982] LLP Member; Taisuke Nakamura [1972] LLP Member; Ali Saiedabadi [1970] LLP Member; Angel Serrat [1967] LLP Member; David Sobotka [1956] LLP Member; Bing-Le Wu [1962] LLP Member; Xin Yeung [1981] LLP Member

The Car Finance Company (2007) Ltd
Incorporated: 22 January 2007 *Employees:* 147
Net Worth Deficit: £68,738,000 *Total Assets:* £46,217,000
Registered Office: 47-51 Kingston Crescent, Portsmouth, PO2 8AA
Activities: Credit granting by non-deposit taking finance houses and other specialist consumer credit grantors
Parent: The Car Finance Company (2015) Limited
Officers: Nigel Timothy John Clibbens [1959] Director; Dr Andreas Driver [1973] Director/Attorney at Law [German]; William David Cleaton Jenkins [1971] Director/Accountant; Christoph Stralek [1975] Director/Lawyer [German]

Carat UK Midco Limited
Incorporated: 4 April 2013
Net Worth: £85,000 *Total Assets:* £359,652,992
Registered Office: 1 Kings Hill Avenue, Kings Hill, West Malling, Kent, ME19 4UA
Activities: Activities of financial services holding companies
Parent: Carat UK Holdco Limited
Officers: Charlotte Taggart, Secretary; Craig Anthony Buick [1969] Director/Chief Financial Officer [British/Australian]

Caravan Club Limited (The)
Incorporated: 31 December 1959 *Employees:* 961
Net Worth: £135,634,000 *Total Assets:* £160,706,000
Registered Office: East Grinstead House, East Grinstead, W Sussex, RH19 1UA
Activities: Activities of other membership organisations n.e.c.
Officers: Nicholas David John Lomas, Secretary; Glynn Malcolm Ball [1956] Director/Defence Consultant (Marine Engineering); Edward Baxter [1949] Director/Accountant; Grenville James Chamberlain [1950] Director/General Manager; Dr John Peter Gass [1955] Director/Retired Senior Lecturer; Malcolm Groves [1947] Director/Consultant; Peter Johnson [1939] Director; Rodney Norwood Paul Lambert [1944] Director/Retired; John Francis Lefley [1948] Director/Retired; Christopher John MacGowan [1947] Director/Chief Executive; Janet Irene Moore [1945] Director/Administrator; Barry John Sharratt [1949] Managing Director (Retired); Gordon Fordyce Smart [1950] Director/Retired Airline Manager; Hamish Edward Stuart [1950] Director/Retired; David Charles Turner [1954] Director/Retired; Alison Clare Woodhams [1956] Finance Director

Cardif Pinnacle Insurance Holdings PLC
Incorporated: 5 May 1992 *Employees:* 245
Net Worth: £142,234,000 *Total Assets:* £344,260,000
Registered Office: Pinnacle House, A1 Barnet Way, Borehamwood, Herts, WD6 2XX
Activities: Life insurance
Parent: BNP Paribas Cardif
Officers: Matthew Justin Lorimer, Secretary; Gerard Binet [1953] Development and Strategy Director [French]; Peter John Box [1952] Director; Stanislas Louis Paul Francois Chevalet [1961] Director [French]; Marie Haderer [1979] Director/Actuary [French]; Matthew Justin Lorimer [1967] Director/Solicitor; Nicholas Dutfield Rochez [1954] Director; Andrew Miles Wigg [1972] Director

Cardiff Property Public Limited Company (The)
Incorporated: 31 May 1886 *Employees:* 6
Net Worth: £27,290,000 *Total Assets:* £28,043,000
Registered Office: 56 Station Road, Egham, Surrey, TW20 9LF
Activities: Buying and selling of own real estate
Shareholder: John Richard Wollenberg
Officers: Karen Louise Chandler, Secretary; Karen Louise Chandler [1972] Finance Director; Nigel Dare Jamieson [1950] Director/Chartered Surveyor; John Richard Wollenberg [1948] Director

Care Management Group (Acquisition) Limited
Incorporated: 5 July 2006 *Employees:* 3
Net Worth: £14,076,000 *Total Assets:* £113,076,000
Registered Office: Ground Floor, Q1 The Square, Randalls Way, Leatherhead, Surrey, KT22 7TW
Activities: Activities of head offices
Parent: CMG Holdco Limited
Officers: Garry John Fitton, Secretary; Garry John Fitton [1972] Director/Chartered Accountant; Peter Kinsey [1964] Director; David Andrew Spruzen [1967] Director

Care Management Group Limited
Incorporated: 22 November 1994 *Employees:* 2,241
Net Worth: £67,697,648 *Total Assets:* £152,823,120
Registered Office: Ground Floor, Q1 The Square, Randalls Way, Leatherhead, Surrey, KT22 7TW
Activities: Residential care activities for learning difficulties, mental health and substance abuse
Parent: CMG Holdco Limited
Officers: Garry John Fitton, Secretary; Garry John Fitton [1972] Director/Chartered Accountant; Peter Kinsey [1964] Director; David Andrew Spruzen [1967] Director

Carefusion U.K. 235 Limited
Incorporated: 24 May 1978
Net Worth: £38,699,816 *Total Assets:* £38,864,256
Registered Office: Chineham Gate, Chineham Business Park, Crockford Lane, Basingstoke, Hants, RG24 8NA
Activities: Other human health activities
Shareholders: Andrew Guille; Jacqueline Mary Le Maitre Ward; Simon Cresswell
Officers: Kevin Mark Klemz [1961] Director

Carefusion U.K. 305 Limited
Incorporated: 3 October 1994 *Employees:* 180
Net Worth: £18,086,020 *Total Assets:* £34,892,040
Registered Office: The Crescent, Jays Close, Basingstoke, Hants, RG22 4BS
Activities: Manufacture of medical and dental instruments and supplies
Parent: Becton, Dickinson and Company
Officers: Michael John Fairbourn [1959] Director/VP International Marketing; Edward Daniel Hopkin [1973] Director/Senior Counsel; John Konrad Neat [1967] Director/Finance Controller

Carefusion U.K. 306 Limited
Incorporated: 8 June 2005 *Employees:* 174
Net Worth: £13,285,835 *Total Assets:* £63,054,944
Registered Office: 1030 Eskdale Road, Winnersh Triangle, Wokingham, Berks, RG41 5TS
Activities: Manufacture of medical and dental instruments and supplies
Parent: Becton, Dickinson U.K. Limited
Officers: Michael John Fairbourn [1959] Director/VP International Marketing; Edward Daniel Hopkin [1973] Director/Senior Counsel; John Konrad Neat [1967] Director/Finance Controller

Careprogress Limited
Incorporated: 26 October 1999 *Employees:* 207
Net Worth: £13,218,546 *Total Assets:* £26,391,724
Registered Office: c/o Elysium Healthcare, 2 Imperial Place, Maxwell Road, Borehamwood, Herts, WD6 1JN
Activities: Residential care activities for the elderly and disabled
Parent: Elysium Healthcare Holdings 3 Limited
Officers: Sarah Juliette Livingston, Secretary; Lesley Joy Chamberlain [1963] Director/Group Chief Executive; Dr Quazi Shams Mahfooz Haque [1968] Executive Medical Director; Steven John Woolgar [1955] Director of Policy and Regulation

Carestream Health UK, Limited
Incorporated: 21 September 2006 *Employees:* 114
Net Worth: £44,108,000 *Total Assets:* £62,592,000
Registered Office: One Park Lane, Hemel Hempstead, Herts, HP2 4YJ
Activities: Manufacture of medical and dental instruments and supplies
Parent: Carestream Health Netherlands BV
Officers: Orsolya Corr, Secretary; Charles McCaffrey [1964] Director; Jane Victoria Moverley [1973] Director/Chartered Accountant; Mandy Diane Parsons [1966] Director/HR Manager

Carewatch Bidco Limited
Incorporated: 4 August 2008
Net Worth: £34,142,000 *Total Assets:* £52,561,000
Registered Office: Libra House, Sunrise Parkway, Linford Wood, Milton Keynes, Bucks, MK14 6PH
Activities: Activities of head offices
Parent: Carewatch Holdings Limited
Officers: Alistair McKenzie Miller [1969] Director/Chartered Accountant; Mark Rogerson [1964] Director/Chairman

Carewatch Care Services Limited
Incorporated: 18 July 1994 *Employees:* 4,705
Net Worth: £5,862,000 *Total Assets:* £33,150,000
Registered Office: Libra House, Sunrise Parkway, Linford Wood, Milton Keynes, Bucks, MK14 6PH
Activities: Social work activities without accommodation for the elderly and disabled
Parent: Carewatch Acquisitions Limited
Officers: Mark Rogerson [1964] Director/Chairman

Carewatch Holdings Limited
Incorporated: 13 August 2008 *Employees:* 4,705
Net Worth Deficit: £6,043,000 *Total Assets:* £33,405,000
Registered Office: Libra House, Sunrise Parkway, Linford Wood, Milton Keynes, Bucks, MK14 6PH
Activities: Activities of head offices
Parent: Lyceum Capital (GP2) Limited
Officers: Alistair McKenzie Miller [1969] Director/Chartered Accountant; Mark Rogerson [1964] Director/Chairman

Cargill Cotton Limited
Incorporated: 15 September 2005 *Employees:* 13
Net Worth: £6,322,000 *Total Assets:* £47,646,000
Registered Office: Velocity V1, Brooklands Drive, Weybridge, Surrey, KT13 0SL
Activities: Growing of fibre crops
Parent: Cargill PLC
Officers: Dena Michelle L O'Bue, Secretary; Stephen James Hamilton [1969] Director/Country Tax Manager UK & Ireland; Carl Patrick Peltzer [1966] Director/UK Cotton Commercial Manager

Cargill Financial Markets Limited
Incorporated: 26 April 1990
Net Worth: £447,032,256 *Total Assets:* £1,041,751,616
Registered Office: Velocity V1, Brooklands Drive, Weybridge, Surrey, KT13 0SL
Activities: Financial intermediation not elsewhere classified
Parent: Cargill Holdings
Officers: Dena Michelle L O'Bue, Secretary; Paul Justin Robert Bothamley [1965] Director, EMEA Tax; Clifford Andrew Bottomley [1970] Director, Treasury Europe

Cargill Financial Services Europe Limited
Incorporated: 30 May 2007
Net Worth: £16,537,606 *Total Assets:* £77,807,256
Registered Office: Velocity V1, Brooklands Drive, Weybridge, Surrey, KT13 0SL
Activities: Activities auxiliary to financial intermediation n.e.c.
Officers: Dena Michelle L O'Bue, Secretary; Keith Livingston Milne [1964] Director/Marketing Manager, EMEA Cargill Risk Management; Federico Urquidi Negron [1965] Director/UK & Ireland Country Controller [Spanish]; Raymond Geoffrey Ward [1964] Director/Derivatives Compliance Senior Adviser

Cargill Global Funding PLC
Incorporated: 24 September 1993 *Employees:* 51
Net Worth: £196,052,288 *Total Assets:* £4,270,958,336
Registered Office: Velocity V1, Brooklands Drive, Weybridge, Surrey, KT13 0SL
Activities: Financial intermediation not elsewhere classified
Parent: Cargill Holdings
Officers: Dena Michelle L O'Bue, Secretary; Judith Helen Mawhood [1959] Director/Accountant; Alison Mulholland [1970] Director/EMEA Regional Lead, Treasury Services Group; Jayme Donald Olson [1956] Director/Financial Manager [American]

Cargill Holdings
Incorporated: 10 August 1970
Net Worth: £55,574,784 *Total Assets:* £111,631,192
Registered Office: Velocity V1, Brooklands Drive, Weybridge, Surrey, KT13 0SL
Activities: Non-trading company
Officers: Dena Michelle L O'Bue, Secretary; Stephen James Hamilton [1969] Director/Country Tax Manager UK & Ireland; Michael James Timewell [1974] Director/Solicitor

Cargill Investments
Incorporated: 7 February 1995 *Employees:* 2
Net Worth: £237,169,728 *Total Assets:* £300,479,424
Registered Office: Velocity V1, Brooklands Drive, Weybridge, Surrey, KT13 0SL
Activities: Financial intermediation not elsewhere classified
Parent: Cargill Investments Holdings Limited
Officers: Dena Michelle L O'Bue, Secretary; Paul Justin Robert Bothamley [1965] Director; Clifford Andrew Bottomley [1970] Director, Treasury Europe

Cargill Investments Holdings Limited
Incorporated: 2 June 1998
Net Worth: £41,296,000 *Total Assets:* £41,304,000
Registered Office: Velocity V1, Brooklands Drive, Weybridge, Surrey, KT13 0SL
Activities: Non-trading company
Parent: Cargill Holdings
Officers: Dena Michelle L O'Bue, Secretary; Paul Justin Robert Bothamley [1965] Director; Clifford Andrew Bottomley [1970] Director, Treasury Europe

Cargill PLC
Incorporated: 6 September 1978 *Employees:* 599
Net Worth: £356,444,000 *Total Assets:* £676,387,008
Registered Office: Velocity V1, Brooklands Drive, Weybridge, Surrey, KT13 0SL
Activities: Wholesale of other intermediate products
Parent: Cargill UK Holdings Limited
Officers: Dena Michelle L O'Bue, Secretary; Peter de Braal [1959] Director/Accountant [Dutch]; Paul Jonathan Kingston [1970] Director/Chemical Engineer; Samina Kosar [1970] Director/Global Head, Cargill Risk Operations and Execution; Melanie Ann Pollard [1970] Director/General Manager, Cargill Grain and Oilseeds UK; Michael James Timewell [1974] Director/Solicitor

Cargill UK Finance Limited
Incorporated: 23 May 2013
Net Worth: £203,440,992 *Total Assets:* £204,367,008
Registered Office: Velocity V1, Brooklands Drive, Weybridge, Surrey, KT13 0SL
Activities: Financial intermediation not elsewhere classified
Officers: Dena Michelle L O'Bue, Secretary; Paul Justin Robert Bothamley [1965] Director, EMEA Tax; Clifford Andrew Bottomley [1970] Director, Treasury Europe

Cargill UK Holdings Limited
Incorporated: 25 March 2010
Net Worth: £314,753,664 *Total Assets:* £556,501,952
Registered Office: Velocity V1, Brooklands Drive, Weybridge, Surrey, KT13 0SL
Activities: Non-trading company
Officers: Dena Michelle L O'Bue, Secretary; Stephen James Hamilton [1969] Director/Country Tax Manager UK & Ireland; Michael James Timewell [1974] Director/Solicitor

Cargobull Finance Limited
Incorporated: 11 December 2000 *Employees:* 1
Net Worth: £9,228,000 *Total Assets:* £23,251,000
Registered Office: Building 7, Croxley Park, Hatters Lane, Watford, Herts, WD18 8YN
Activities: Renting and leasing of cars and light motor vehicles
Officers: Thies Johannes Philipp Engering [1974] Director [German]; Duncan John Hullis [1963] Director/General Manager; Simon John Trudgeon [1968] Director/Credit Risk Officer

Caridon Holdings LLP
Incorporated: 1 April 2015
Net Worth: £25,965,504 *Total Assets:* £118,772,880
Registered Office: Wrencote House, 123 High Street, Croydon, Surrey, CR0 0XJ
Officers: Abbas Alidina [1979] Member; Mario Joseph Carrozzo [1972] Member; Roy Andrew Ledgister [1973] LLP Member

Carisbrooke Shipping Holdings Limited
Incorporated: 2 June 1999 *Employees:* 60
Net Worth: £26,090,586 *Total Assets:* £60,198,048
Registered Office: Bridge House, 38 Medina Road, Cowes, Isle of Wight, PO31 7DA
Activities: Sea and coastal freight water transport
Officers: Paul Charles Over [1956] Director/Management Consultant; Helen Tveitan-De Jong [1967] Director/Financial Consultant [Dutch]; Willem Wester [1944] Director; Christopher Lloyd Williams [1966] Commercial Director

Carnival PLC
Incorporated: 19 July 2000
Net Worth: £6,419,860,480 *Total Assets:* £11,003,194,368
Registered Office: Carnival House, 100 Harbour Parade, Southampton, SO15 1ST
Activities: Sea and coastal freight water transport
Officers: Arnaldo Perez, Secretary/Executive & Attorney [American]; Michael Meir Arison [1949] Director/Executive [American]; Sir Jonathon Band [1950] Director; Jason Glen Cahilly [1970] Director [American]; Helen Deeble CBE [1961] Director; Arnold Wayne Donald [1954] Director/Executive [American]; Richard Glasier [1945] Director [American]; Debra Jo Kelly-Ennis [1957] Director [American]; Kathleen Lahey [1950] Director/Executive Chairman [Australian]; Sir Thomas John Parker [1942] Director; Stuart Subotnick [1942] Director [American]; Laura Weil [1957] Director [American]; Randall John Weisenburger [1958] Director [American]

Carscreugh Renewable Energy Park Limited
Incorporated: 27 October 2006
Net Worth Deficit: £3,211,000 *Total Assets:* £23,955,000
Registered Office: Edgeborough House, Upper Edgeborough Road, Guildford, Surrey, GU1 2BJ
Activities: Other business support service activities n.e.c.
Parent: JLEAG Wind Limited
Officers: Joseph Mark Linney [1958] Director/Chartered Quantity Surveyor; Christopher James Tanner [1972] Investment Director

Carshalton Boys Sports College
Incorporated: 16 May 2011 *Employees:* 141
Net Worth: £21,205,000 *Total Assets:* £23,633,000
Registered Office: Carshalton Boys Sport College, Winchcombe Road, Carshalton, Surrey, SM5 1RW
Activities: General secondary education
Officers: Jenny Gaylor, Secretary; Daniel Olumide Ayeni [1976] Director/Team Manager (Education), Cognus Limited; Simon Barber [1957] Director/Principal; David Baron [1959] Director/Retail Management; Stephen Bosdet [1979] Director/Teacher; Joanne Damianou [1971] Director/SHC & Procurement Co-ordinator; Catherine Suzanne Fontinelle [1969] Director/Biomedical Scientist; Alan Forder [1955] Director/Education; Jenny Gaylor [1971] Director/Vice Principal; Jean Carole Knight [1939] Director; Andrew Lee [1970] Project Director Construction; Deborah Anne Martin [1964] Director/School Business Manager; Nicholas Maybanks [1985] Director/Teacher; Rebecca McGowan [1978] Director/Pension Consultant; Susan Eleanor O'Neill [1948] Director; Chris O'Sullivan [1968] Director/Senior Network Support Engineer; Valerie Verona Roberts [1966] Director/Senior Curriculum Support Officer; Edwina Rozek [1964] Director/Administrative Manager; Graham Skipp [1962] Director/Operations Manager; Mark William Twigg [1975] Executive Director of Cicero Group; Oliver Wilson-Hughes [1984] Director/English Teacher; Hayley Margaret Anne Wood [1964] Director/Lab Technician Manager

Carte Blanche Greetings Limited
Incorporated: 7 June 1988
Net Worth: £30,546,666 *Total Assets:* £38,886,304
Registered Office: Unit 3 Chichester Business Park, Tangmere, Chichester, W Sussex, PO20 2FT
Activities: Other publishing activities
Parent: Carte Blanche Group Limited
Officers: Stephen William Haines [1962] Director/Chairman; Alister Robert Marchant [1966] Sales Director; Robert John Poerscout-Edgerton [1978] Finance Director; Duncan Spence [1943] Director

Carte Blanche Group Limited
Incorporated: 25 November 2004 *Employees:* 179
Net Worth: £24,857,876 *Total Assets:* £32,247,094
Registered Office: 3 Unit Chichester Business Park, Tangmere, Chichester, W Sussex, PO20 2FT
Activities: Activities of head offices
Major Shareholder: Stephen William Haines
Officers: William Douglass Dodd [1946] Director/Chartered Accountant; Stephen William Haines [1962] Director/Chairman; Alister Robert Marchant [1966] Sales Director; Robert John Poerscout-Edgerton [1978] Finance Director; Duncan Spence [1943] Director

CAS Aspirations Properties Limited
Incorporated: 7 August 2008
Previous: Care Aspirations Properties Limited
Net Worth: £2,367,000 *Total Assets:* £33,638,000
Registered Office: Nepicar House, London Road, Wrotham Heath, Sevenoaks, Kent, TN15 7RS
Activities: Activities of other holding companies n.e.c.
Parent: Cygnet Learning Disabilities Limited
Officers: Anthony James Coleman, Secretary; Mark George Ground [1970] Director; Laurence Lee Harrod [1956] Director [American]; Michael James McQuaid [1958] Director; Antonio Romero [1971] Director [Spanish]

CAS Healthcare Properties Limited
Incorporated: 17 December 2014
Previous: Cambian Healthcare Properties Limited
Net Worth: £157,512,992 *Total Assets:* £192,394,000
Registered Office: Nepicar House, London Road, Wrotham Heath, Sevenoaks, Kent, TN15 7RS
Activities: Activities of head offices
Parent: Cygnet Behavioural Health Limited
Officers: Anthony James Coleman, Secretary; Mark Ground [1970] Director; Laurence Lee Harrod [1958] Director [American]; Michael James McQuaid [1958] Director; Dr Antonio Romero [1971] Director [Spanish]

CAS St Paul's Limited
Incorporated: 3 February 2000
Previous: Cambian St Paul's Limited
Net Worth: £47,461,000 *Total Assets:* £48,020,000
Registered Office: Nepicar House, London Road, Wrotham Heath, Sevenoaks, Kent, TN15 7RS
Activities: Hospital activities
Parent: CAS Aspirations Properties Limited
Officers: Anthony James Coleman, Secretary; Mark George Ground [1970] Director; Laurence Lee Harrod [1956] Director [American]; Michael James McQuaid [1958] Director; Dr Antonio Romero [1971] Director [Spanish]

Casebia Therapeutics Limited Liability Partnership
Incorporated: 12 February 2016 *Employees:* 29
Net Worth: £105,716,888 *Total Assets:* £114,720,544
Registered Office: c/o Jacksons-Accountants, The Old Bakehouse, Course Road, Ascot, Berks, SL5 7HL

Cash Processing Solutions Limited
Incorporated: 17 March 2016 *Employees:* 73
Net Worth: £14,885,000 *Total Assets:* £27,331,000
Registered Office: 4th Floor, Matrix House, Basing View, Basingstoke, Hants, RG21 4DZ
Activities: Activities of other holding companies n.e.c.
Parent: CPS Topco Limited
Officers: Andrew Julian Crawshaw [1966] Director/Chief Financial Officer; Christopher Rajendran Hyman [1963] Director; Stephen Charles Keating [1966] Director/Investor; Adam Troy Lawrence [1971] Director/Chief Executive Officer; Vardhan Ashok Rajkumar [1967] Director

Cashino Gaming Limited
Incorporated: 14 January 1972 *Employees:* 904
Net Worth Deficit: £5,865,000 *Total Assets:* £48,951,000
Registered Office: Seebeck House, 1a Seebeck Place, Knowlhill, Milton Keynes, Bucks, MK5 8FR
Activities: Gambling and betting activities
Parent: Praesepe Holdings Limited
Officers: Stefan Bruns [1971] Director/Chief Executive Officer [German]; Borris Lungen [1962] Director/Chief Financial Officer [German]; Mark Stefan Schertle [1977] Director [German]

Castacrete Limited
Incorporated: 28 March 1966 *Employees:* 114
Net Worth: £20,596,172 *Total Assets:* £34,940,376
Registered Office: Stone House, Dean Street, East Farleigh, Maidstone, Kent, ME15 0PW
Activities: Manufacture of concrete products for construction purposes
Major Shareholder: Terence Arnold Smallman
Officers: Simon John King, Secretary; Rosemary Melina Smallman [1952] Director/Secretary; Terence Arnold Smallman [1945] Director

Castle Bidco PLC
Incorporated: 3 November 2006
Previous: Castle Bidco Limited
Net Worth: £512,000,000 *Total Assets:* £1,019,200,000
Registered Office: Crest House, Pyrcroft Road, Chertsey, Surrey, KT16 9GN
Activities: Activities of head offices
Parent: Crest Nicholson Holdings PLC
Officers: Kevin Maguire, Secretary; Patrick Joseph Bergin [1966] Director/Group Financial Controller; Robin Patrick Hoyles [1954] Group Land & Planning Director; Stephen Stone [1954] Managing Director; Nigel Christopher Tinker [1960] Urban Land Director

Castle Cement Limited
Incorporated: 23 October 1987 *Employees:* 746
Net Worth: £286,403,008 *Total Assets:* £416,790,016
Registered Office: Hanson House, 14 Castle Hill, Maidenhead, Berks, SL6 4JJ
Activities: Manufacture of cement
Parent: HeidelbergCement UK Limited
Officers: Wendy Fiona Rogers, Secretary; Matthew David Barlow [1979] Supply Chain Director; James Alexander Claydon [1960] Director; John Godbert [1962] Director/Accountant; Edward Alexander Gretton [1970] Director; Dr Lorenz Nager [1960] Director/CFO Heidelbergcement AG [German]; Dr Bernd Scheifele [1958] Director/CEO Heidelbergcement AG [German]; Dr Ralph Dominik Von Achten [1965] Director [German]; Dr Carsten Matthias Wendt [1976] Director [German]; Simon Lloyd Willis [1965] Director/Chief Executive, Hanson UK

Castle Marinas Limited
Incorporated: 24 January 2006 *Employees:* 3
Net Worth Deficit: £7,968,722 *Total Assets:* £22,207,032
Registered Office: Birdham Pool Marina, Birdham, Chichester, W Sussex, PO20 7BG
Activities: Other letting and operating of own or leased real estate
Officers: Richard James Smith, Secretary; Michael Allen Braidley [1961] Operations Director; Richard James Smith [1967] Director/Accountant; John Sebastian Whateley [1981] Director; John Grahame Whateley [1943] Director

Castrol Limited
Incorporated: 23 January 1918
Net Worth: £623,900,032 *Total Assets:* £811,875,008
Registered Office: Technology Centre, Whitchurch Hill, Pangbourne, Reading, Berks, RG8 7QR
Activities: Activities of head offices
Parent: Burmah Castrol PLC
Officers: Robert David Mutchell [1974] Director/Oil Company Executive; Daniel Chukumah Odogwu [1966] Director/Oil Company Executive; Ramchander Avanavadi Subramaniam [1962] Director/Oil Company Executive [Indian]; Paul Ian Winton Turner [1963] Director/Oil Company Executive

Catalina Worthing Insurance Limited
Incorporated: 13 October 2006
Previous: Hartford Financial Products International Limited
Net Worth: £182,388,000 *Total Assets:* £773,193,024
Registered Office: DLM House, Downlands Business Park, Lyons Way, Worthing, W Sussex, BN14 9RX
Activities: Non-life insurance
Parent: Catalina Holdings UK Limited
Officers: Roland Philip Jackson, Secretary; Timothy Michael Cox [1947] Director/Insurance Executive; Christopher John Fleming [1973] Director/Executive; Generald Sidney Haase [1976] Director/Insurance Executive [American]; Philip Michael Hernon [1958] Director/Executive; Roland Philip Jackson [1963] Director/Solicitor; Graeme John McAndrew [1968] Director/Chief Financial Officer [Australian]; David O'Connor [1957] Director/Executive [Irish]

Cater Link Limited
Incorporated: 12 March 1999 *Employees:* 3,534
Net Worth: £28,672,000 *Total Assets:* £62,036,000
Registered Office: TVP 2, 300 Thames Valley Park Drive, Reading, Berks, RG6 1PT
Activities: Other food services
Parent: Westbury Street Limited
Officers: Marc Bradley, Secretary; John David Bennett [1963] Director; Marc Bradley [1975] Director/Chartered Accountant; Stephen Charles Cox [1980] Finance Director; Richard Anthony Flynn [1966] Director; Neil Fuller [1971] Director; Alastair Dunbar Storey [1953] Director

Caterham School Limited
Incorporated: 1 April 2005 *Employees:* 335
Net Worth: £18,623,000 *Total Assets:* £32,258,000
Registered Office: Caterham School, Harestone Valley Road, Caterham, Surrey, CR3 6YA
Activities: Pre-primary education
Officers: Angela Denise Higgs, Secretary; David Philip Charlesworth [1947] Director; Dr Stephen Richard Critchley [1951] Director; Ian Robert Michael Edwards [1954] Director; Tracey Frances Eldridge-Hinmers [1962] Director/Solicitor; Anne Margaret Fletcher [1955] Director; Revd Nicola Jayne Furley-Smith [1961] Director/Minister of Religion; Jeremy Joiner [1955] Director/Solicitor; Monisha Amrit Shah [1969] Director; John Edward Kitson Smith [1954] Director/Chartered Accountant; Mark Haskett Peplow Smith [1981] Director; Ewan Paul Russell Turney [1980] Director; Mary Lavinia Whenman [1969] Director; Suzi Mary Whittle [1954] Director/Accountant; Anthony Peter Wilson [1966] Director/Clerk to The Skinners Company

Cathay Investments 2 Limited
Incorporated: 21 December 2010 *Employees:* 262
Net Worth: £6,533,323 *Total Assets:* £25,577,716
Registered Office: A2 Yeoman Gate, Yeoman Way, Worthing, W Sussex, BN13 3QZ
Activities: Activities of head offices
Shareholders: Maria Yee Sui Chaing; Simon Denbond Chaing; Benjamin Ka Ping Chaing
Officers: Benjamin Ka Ping Chaing [1952] Director; Maria Yee Sui Chaing [1958] Director; Simon Denbond Chaing [1990] Director; Kevin Andrew Johnson [1969] Director/Accountant; David John Nicholas [1981] Director/Chartered Accountant; Gregory Mark Thwaites [1973] Director/Solicitor

Cathay Investments Limited
Incorporated: 19 March 2003 *Employees:* 277
Net Worth: £9,609,013 *Total Assets:* £60,255,724
Registered Office: A2 Yeoman Gate, Yeoman Way, Worthing, W Sussex, BN13 3QZ
Activities: Activities of head offices
Major Shareholder: Benjamin Ka Ping Chaing
Officers: Maria Yee Sui Chaing, Secretary; Benjamin Ka Ping Chaing [1952] Director; Kevin Andrew Johnson [1969] Director/Accountant

Cauta Capital Limited
Incorporated: 10 April 2015 *Employees:* 2
Net Worth: £69,405,632 *Total Assets:* £74,775,320
Registered Office: 61-63 Crockhamwell Road, Woodley, Reading, Berks, RG5 3JP
Activities: Activities of other holding companies n.e.c.
Major Shareholder: William Abundes
Officers: William Abundes [1954] Director [American]

Caversham Finance Limited
Incorporated: 24 December 1963 *Employees:* 1,868
Net Worth: £134,201,000 *Total Assets:* £333,688,000
Registered Office: 5 Hercules Way, Leavesden, Watford, Herts, WD25 7GS
Activities: Retail sale of electrical household appliances in specialised stores
Parent: Brighthouse Limited
Officers: David John Harwood, Secretary; Brian Edward Brodie [1965] Director; Graeme James Campbell [1972] Director; Stuart John Deane [1965] Director; Lysa Maria Hardy [1970] Director; Hugh John Harvey [1959] Director; Ian David Larkin [1968] Director [Irish]; Lars Magnus Mattsson [1973] Director [Swedish]; Hamish Stewart Paton [1976] Commercial Director; David Anthony Poole [1969] Director

Caversham Trading Limited
Incorporated: 17 March 2005 *Employees:* 658
Net Worth: £73,485,000 *Total Assets:* £85,510,000
Registered Office: 5 Hercules Way, Leavesden, Watford, Herts, WD25 7GS
Activities: Retail sale of electrical household appliances in specialised stores
Parent: Caversham Finance Ltd
Officers: David John Harwood, Secretary; Graeme James Campbell [1972] Finance Director; Hamish Stewart Paton [1976] Director

CB Equity LLP
Incorporated: 5 January 2010
Net Worth: £2,114,017,408 *Total Assets:* £2,114,128,512
Registered Office: 1 Princeton Mews, 167-169 London Road, Kingston upon Thames, Surrey, KT2 6PT

CBI International Parent Limited
Incorporated: 30 July 2015
Net Worth: £12,287,512 *Total Assets:* £48,096,888
Registered Office: Belmont House, Station Way, Crawley, W Sussex, RH10 1JA
Activities: Other human health activities
Officers: Yvonne Emma Hignell [1980] Managing Director; Stephen James Hogan [1964] Director [American]; David Wolmer [1976] Director/Attorney [American]

CBI UK Topco Limited
Incorporated: 29 July 2015 *Employees:* 303
Net Worth: £14,881,581 *Total Assets:* £45,131,328
Registered Office: Belmont House, Station Way, Crawley, W Sussex, RH10 1JA
Activities: Other human health activities
Officers: Yvonne Emma Hignell [1980] Managing Director; Stephen James Hogan [1964] Director [American]; David Wolmer [1976] Director/Attorney [American]

CC 1 (2011) Limited
Incorporated: 13 December 2010 *Employees:* 1,832
Net Worth Deficit: £69,818,000 *Total Assets:* £617,559,616
Registered Office: Building A, Riverside Way, Watchmoor Park, Camberley, Surrey, GU15 3YL
Activities: Activities of head offices
Officers: Mr Olof Bertil Faxander [1970] Director [Swedish]; Nils-Olof Robert Campbell Furuhjelm [1969] Director [Finnish]; Tiemo Grimm [1978] Director/Investment Professional [German]; Alexander Lacik [1965] Director [Swedish]; Markus Nagel [1967] Director [German]; Lihong Xu [1970] Director [Chinese]

CC 2 (2011) Limited
Incorporated: 13 December 2010
Net Worth Deficit: £323,860,512 *Total Assets:* £274,811,712
Registered Office: Building A, Riverside Way, Watchmoor Park, Camberley, Surrey, GU15 3YL
Activities: Activities of head offices
Parent: CC 1 (2011) Limited
Officers: Alexander Lacik [1965] Director [Swedish]; Markus Nagel [1967] Director [German]

CC 4 (2011) Limited
Incorporated: 10 November 2010
Net Worth: £362,784,640 *Total Assets:* £400,104,896
Registered Office: Building A, Riverside Way, Watchmoor Park, Camberley, Surrey, GU15 3YL
Activities: Activities of head offices
Parent: Britax Group Limited
Officers: Alexander Lacik [1965] Director [Swedish]; Markus Nagel [1967] Director [German]

CCEP Holdings UK Limited
Incorporated: 13 May 2016
Net Worth: £8,683,429,888 *Total Assets:* £8,796,600,320
Registered Office: Pemberton House, Bakers Road, Uxbridge, Middlesex, UB8 1EZ
Activities: Activities of other holding companies n.e.c.
Parent: Coca-Cola European Partners PLC
Officers: Paul Van Reesch, Secretary; Frank Govaerts [1961] Director [Belgian]; Paul Van Reesch [1976] Director; Edward Owen Walker [1967] Director

CCV Risk Solutions Limited
Incorporated: 18 July 2006 *Employees:* 197
Net Worth: £89,239,000 *Total Assets:* £189,132,992
Registered Office: Tower Gate House, Eclipse Park, Sittingbourne Road, Maidstone, Kent, ME14 3EN
Activities: Non-life insurance
Parent: Cullum Capital Ventures Limited
Officers: Dean Clarke, Secretary; Antonios Erotocritou [1971] Director/Deputy CFO [Cypriot]; David Christopher Ross [1969] Director [Irish]; Robert Laurance Worrell [1968] Director/Chartered Insurance Broker

CDB (U.K.) Limited
Incorporated: 8 December 1983
Net Worth: £29,797,000 *Total Assets:* £30,763,000
Registered Office: c/o Hold Store Limited, Unit 33a Enterprise House, 44-46 Terrace Road, Walton on Thames, Surrey, KT12 2SD
Activities: Activities of financial services holding companies
Parent: Irish Government (Minister for Finance)
Officers: James Ednie Brydie [1959] Director/Banker; Robert Dix [1953] Director [Irish]

CDK Global (UK) Limited
Incorporated: 14 October 1976 *Employees:* 733
Net Worth: £33,869,000 *Total Assets:* £80,191,000
Registered Office: Cygnet Way, Charnham Park, Hungerford, Berks, RG17 0YL
Activities: Other information technology service activities
Parent: CDK Global Holdings (UK) Limited
Officers: Lee James Brunz [1969] Director/Lawyer [American]; Neil Packham [1970] Director/President; Andrew James Edward Thomson [1970] Director/Chief Financial Officer

CDK Global Holdings (UK) Limited
Incorporated: 9 December 2014 *Employees:* 61
Net Worth: £507,703,008 *Total Assets:* £717,516,032
Registered Office: Cygnet Way, Charnham Park, Hungerford, Berks, RG17 0YL
Activities: Other information technology service activities
Parent: CDK Global, Inc
Officers: Russell Wyn John Alexander [1967] Director/Solicitor; Lee James Brunz [1969] Director/Lawyer [American]; Neil Packham [1970] Director/President; Andrew James Edward Thomson [1970] Director

CDK U.K. Limited
Incorporated: 5 August 1988
Net Worth: £77,989,000 *Total Assets:* £78,097,000
Registered Office: Building 9, Croxley Park, Hatters Lane, Watford, Herts, WD18 8WW
Activities: Activities of head offices
Officers: Joanne Pascucci, Secretary; Oliver Ellis [1972] Sales & Marketing Director; Mark Justin Elsey [1967] Finance Director; Jacqueline Fielding [1964] Vice President (Director)

CDL Hotels (Chelsea) Limited
Incorporated: 16 August 1993 *Employees:* 138
Net Worth: £21,409,000 *Total Assets:* £26,996,000
Registered Office: Victoria House, Victoria Road, Horley, Surrey, RH6 7AF
Activities: Hotels and similar accommodation
Parent: Millennium Hotels London Limited
Officers: Jonathon MacKenzie Grech [1977] Director/Senior VP Group Legal Counsel; Leng Beng Kwek [1941] Director [Singaporean]

CDL Hotels (U.K.) Limited
Incorporated: 8 July 1992 *Employees:* 365
Net Worth: £85,524,000 *Total Assets:* £121,185,000
Registered Office: Victoria House, Victoria Road, Horley, Surrey, RH6 7AF
Activities: Hotels and similar accommodation
Parent: Millennium Hotels London Limited
Officers: Jonathon MacKenzie Grech [1977] Director/Senior VP Group Legal Counsel; Leng Beng Kwek [1941] Director [Singaporean]

CEB Global Holdings Limited
Incorporated: 8 September 2015
Net Worth: £309,825,984 *Total Assets:* £309,841,984
Registered Office: Tamesis, The Glanty, Egham, Surrey, TW20 9AH
Activities: Activities of other holding companies n.e.c.
Parent: CEB Holdings UK 1 Limited
Officers: William Joseph Dorgan [1967] Director/GVP Legal Operations [American]; Craig Safian [1969] Director [American]

CEB Global Limited
Incorporated: 1 October 2003 *Employees:* 371
Previous: The Corporate Executive Board Company (UK) Ltd.
Net Worth: £6,544,000 *Total Assets:* £119,790,000
Registered Office: Tamesis, The Glanty, Egham, Surrey, TW20 9AH
Activities: Other information service activities n.e.c.
Parent: Gartner U.K. Limited
Officers: William Joseph Dorgan [1967] Director/Group Vice President of Legal Operations [American]; Craig Warren Safian [1969] Director/CFO, Chief Operations [American]

CEB Holdings UK 1 Limited
Incorporated: 26 July 2012
Net Worth: £61,109,000 *Total Assets:* £349,908,000
Registered Office: Tamesis, The Glanty, Egham, Surrey, TW20 9AH
Activities: Management consultancy activities other than financial management
Parent: CEB Inc.
Officers: William Joseph Dorgan [1967] Director/Group Vice President of Legal Operations [American]; Craig Warren Safian [1969] Director/CFO, Financial Operations [American]

CEB Holdings UK 2 Limited
Incorporated: 27 July 2012
Net Worth: £472,687,008 *Total Assets:* £472,727,008
Registered Office: Tamesis, The Glanty, Egham, Surrey, TW20 9AH
Activities: Management consultancy activities other than financial management
Parent: CEB Global Holdings Limited
Officers: William Joseph Dorgan [1967] Director/Global Vice President of Legal Operations [American]; Craig Warren Safian [1969] Director/CFO Financial Operations [American]

Ceesail Limited
Incorporated: 22 January 2003
Net Worth: £1,345,713,024 *Total Assets:* £1,354,002,944
Registered Office: 1st Floor, Ash House, Littleton Road, Ashford, Middlesex, TW15 1TZ
Activities: Activities of head offices
Parent: Beesail Limited
Officers: Lynne Banis, Secretary; Christian Bruno Jean Idczak [1963] Director/Business Executive [French]; James Terence George Laurence [1964] Financial Director; Patricia Catherine Moran [1964] Finance Director [American]; Louise Kay Thompson [1983] Director/Chartered Management Accountant

CeleritiFinTech Limited
Incorporated: 8 July 2015
Net Worth: £36,475,000 *Total Assets:* £45,320,000
Registered Office: Axon Centre, Church Road, Egham, Surrey, TW20 9QB
Activities: Information technology consultancy activities
Shareholders: Computer Sciences Corporation; HCL Technologies UK Limited
Officers: Prateek Aggarwal [1967] Director [Indian]; Joanne Mason [1967] Director/Service; Sunil Sharma [1966] Director; Rahul Singh [1963] Director [Indian]; Shiv Kumar Walia [1969] Director/Service [Australian]

Celgene Europe Limited
Incorporated: 13 February 2002 *Employees:* 102
Net Worth: £57,526,308 *Total Assets:* £69,875,936
Registered Office: 1 Longwalk Road, Stockley Park, Uxbridge, Middlesex, UB11 1DB
Activities: Other research and experimental development on natural sciences and engineering
Parent: Celgene Corporation
Officers: Jonathan Prim Biller [1963] Director [American]; Jurg Oehen [1966] Director [Swiss]; Tuomo Tapani Patsi [1964] Director [Finnish]; Anne Patricia Janine Pellier [1956] Director [French]; Nakisa Serry [1965] Director [American]

Celgene Limited
Incorporated: 2 June 2005 *Employees:* 152
Net Worth: £83,576,944 *Total Assets:* £190,243,632
Registered Office: 1 Longwalk Road, Stockley Park, Uxbridge, Middlesex, UB11 1DB
Activities: Wholesale of pharmaceutical goods
Parent: Celgene UK Manufacturing (II) Limited
Officers: Jonathan Prim Biller [1963] Director [American]; Remo Gujer [1973] Director [Swiss]; Jurg Oehen [1966] Director [Swiss]; Tuomo Tapani Patsi [1964] Director [Finnish]; Nakisa Serry [1965] Director [American]

Cellarmaster Wines Holdings (UK) Limited
Incorporated: 29 January 1968
Net Worth: £29,715,000 *Total Assets:* £29,715,000
Registered Office: 9th Floor, Regal House, 70 London Road, Twickenham, Middlesex, TW1 3QS
Activities: Manufacture of wine from grape
Officers: Michelle Elizabeth Brampton [1972] Finance Director; Richard John Renwick [1969] Director/Chief Financial Officer Europe

Cellnex UK Midco Limited
Incorporated: 29 March 2008
Previous: Shere Midco Limited
Net Worth: £66,666,400 *Total Assets:* £71,397,336
Registered Office: 2 River Court, Albert Drive, Woking, Surrey, GU21 5RP
Activities: Activities of head offices
Parent: Cellnex UK Limited
Officers: Peter Charles Collins [1956] Director; Mary Annabel Gatehouse [1973] Director/Lawyer; Alexandre Mestre Molins [1964] Director/Manager [Spanish]; Alexander James Woodward [1963] Director/Chartered Accountant

Celltech Group Limited
Incorporated: 28 August 1987
Net Worth: £365,734,016 *Total Assets:* £409,132,000
Registered Office: 208 Bath Road, Slough, Berks, SL1 3WE
Activities: Activities of head offices
Parent: UCB (Investments) Limited
Officers: Mark Glyn Hardy, Secretary; Dan Coombes [1975] Area Head, British & Irish Isles (Managing Director); Mark Glyn Hardy [1953] Director/Solicitor; Yogesh Khatri [1965] Director/Head of Finance and Administration

Celltech R & D Limited
Incorporated: 11 January 1980 *Employees:* 486
Net Worth: £37,863,000 *Total Assets:* £43,325,000
Registered Office: 208 Bath Road, Slough, Berks, SL1 3WE
Activities: Human resources provision and management of human resources functions
Parent: Celltech Group Limited
Officers: Mark Glyn Hardy, Secretary; Dan Coombes [1975] Area Head, British & Irish Isles (Managing Director); Mark Glyn Hardy [1953] Director/Solicitor; Yogesh Khatri [1965] Director/Head of Finance and Administration

Celsis Group Limited
Incorporated: 27 October 2010
Net Worth: £24,290,000 *Total Assets:* £24,290,000
Registered Office: Charles River Laboratories, Manston Road, Margate, Kent, CT9 4LT
Activities: Manufacture of other chemical products n.e.c.
Parent: Charles River Laboratories Holdings Limited
Officers: Sarah Margaret Price, Secretary; Foster Timmons Jordan [1967] Director/Corporate Senior Vice President [American]; Dr John Gary Montana [1963] Director/Scientist; David Ross Smith [1965] Director/Corporate Senior Vice President

Celsis International Limited
Incorporated: 16 June 1993
Net Worth: £25,335,000 *Total Assets:* £25,719,000
Registered Office: Charles River Laboratories, Manston Road, Margate, Kent, CT9 4LT
Activities: Manufacture of other chemical products n.e.c.
Parent: Nastor Investments Limited
Officers: Sarah Margaret Price, Secretary; Foster Timmons Jordan [1967] Director/Corporate Senior Vice President [American]; Dr John Gary Montana [1963] Director/Scientist; David Ross Smith [1965] Director/Corporate Senior Vice President

Cementation Skanska Limited
Incorporated: 21 August 1968 *Employees:* 378
Net Worth: £25,968,000 *Total Assets:* £52,347,000
Registered Office: Maple Cross House, Denham Way, Maple Cross, Rickmansworth, Herts, WD3 9SW
Activities: Construction of commercial buildings
Parent: Skanska Construction UK Limited
Officers: Steven Leven, Secretary; James Maxwell Dunbar [1964] Director; Dr Jonathan David Morris [1973] Director

Centerprise Intl Holdings Limited
Incorporated: 3 August 2010 *Employees:* 162
Net Worth: £26,749,884 *Total Assets:* £39,533,076
Registered Office: Hampshire International Business Park, Lime Tree Way, Chineham, Basingstoke, Hants, RG24 8GQ
Activities: Manufacture of computers and peripheral equipment
Major Shareholder: Rafi Arif Abdul Razzak
Officers: Jeremy Shane Nash [1969] Director/Chief Executive Officer; Adam Laith Razzak [1984] Director; Rafi Arif Abdul Razzak [1949] Director; Ramsey Arif Razzak [1988] Director; Rebecca Razzak [1946] Director

Central G H Trust
Incorporated: 25 July 2008
Net Worth: £22,558,140 *Total Assets:* £23,115,232
Registered Office: Noble House, Eaton Road, Hemel Hempstead Industrial Estate, Hemel Hempstead, Herts, HP2 7UB
Activities: Other business support service activities n.e.c.
Officers: Christopher Edward Stedman, Secretary; Colin Paul Barnes [1971] Director/Partner; Philip James Hutchinson [1945] Director/Manager; Laurie Roy Pollard [1979] Director; Oliver Muckle Whiley [1955] Director

Central Nottinghamshire Hospitals (Holdings) Limited
Incorporated: 19 May 2005
Net Worth Deficit: £129,000 *Total Assets:* £391,337,984
Registered Office: 8 White Oak Square, London Road, Swanley, Kent, BR8 7AG
Activities: Activities of other holding companies n.e.c.
Shareholders: Innisfree Secondary Partners 1 LLP; Innisfree Secondary Partners 2 LLP
Officers: Gaynor Birley Smith [1966] Investment Director; Sabrina Sidhu [1979] Investment Director; Benjamin Michael Watson [1985] Director/Portfolio Manager

Central Nottinghamshire Hospitals PLC
Incorporated: 25 May 2005
Net Worth Deficit: £129,000 *Total Assets:* £391,337,984
Registered Office: 8 White Oak Square, London Road, Swanley, Kent, BR8 7AG
Activities: Hospital activities
Parent: Central Nottinghamshire Hospitals (Holdings) Limited
Officers: Gaynor Birley Smith [1966] Investment Director; Michael Davis [1946] Director; Sabrina Sidhu [1979] Investment Director; Benjamin Michael Watson [1985] Director/Portfolio Manager

The Centre for Health and Disability Assessments Limited
Incorporated: 5 June 2014 *Employees:* 2,254
Net Worth: £19,720,802 *Total Assets:* £44,858,720
Registered Office: Ash House, The Broyle, Ringmer, Lewes, E Sussex, BN8 5NN
Activities: Other human health activities
Parent: Maximus Companies Ltd
Officers: Michael Batty [1972] Director; James Farren [1967] Director; Dr Paul Anthony Williams [1963] Managing Director

Centrica (Lincs) Wind Farm Limited
Incorporated: 7 December 2009
Net Worth: £54,222,000 *Total Assets:* £55,846,000
Registered Office: Millstream, Maidenhead Road, Windsor, Berks, SL4 5GD
Activities: Activities of head offices
Parent: Centrica Renewable Energy Limited
Officers: Mark Ramsey Futyan [1978] Operations Director; Robert William Marsden [1974] Director/Accountant; Richard Matthew McCord [1973] Director/Accountant

Centrica Beta Holdings Limited
Incorporated: 25 March 2003
Net Worth: £150,256,000 *Total Assets:* £1,715,495,040
Registered Office: Millstream, Maidenhead Road, Windsor, Berks, SL4 5GD
Activities: Other business support service activities n.e.c.
Parent: Centrica PLC
Officers: Ian Grant Dawson [1959] Director; Charlotte Redcliffe [1964] Director/Chartered Accountant; Alistair Mark Todd [1975] Finance Director

Centrica Brigg Limited
Incorporated: 24 February 1989 *Employees:* 9
Net Worth: £26,021,000 *Total Assets:* £67,073,000
Registered Office: Millstream, Maidenhead Road, Windsor, Berks, SL4 5GD
Activities: Production of electricity
Parent: GB Gas Holdings Limited
Officers: Mark Ramsey Futyan [1978] Operations Director; Richard Matthew McCord [1973] Director/Accountant

Centrica Business Solutions UK Limited
Incorporated: 31 December 1984 *Employees:* 201
Previous: Ener-G Combined Power Limited
Net Worth: £5,569,000 *Total Assets:* £34,959,000
Registered Office: Millstream, Maidenhead Road, Windsor, Berks, SL4 5GD
Activities: Manufacture of electrical and electronic equipment for motor vehicles and their engines
Parent: Ener-G Power2 Limited
Officers: Alan Kenneth Barlow [1964] Director/Engineer [Irish]; Colin Spencer Dixon [1962] Director; Ian Anthony Hopkins [1972] Director; Peter Law [1970] Director/Engineer; Richard McCord [1973] Director; Christopher Richard Pike [1980] Director; Dr Jorge Pablo Pikunic [1976] Director; David Winstanley [1975] Director/Chartered Accountant

Centrica Distributed Generation Limited
Incorporated: 27 March 2003
Previous: Centrica RPS Limited
Net Worth: £27,940,000 *Total Assets:* £39,710,000
Registered Office: Millstream, Maidenhead Road, Windsor, Berks, SL4 5GD
Activities: Production of electricity
Parent: GB Gas Holdings Limited
Officers: Mark Ramsey Futyan [1978] Operations Director; Richard Matthew McCord [1973] Director/Accountant

Centrica Energy Limited
Incorporated: 2 December 1993 *Employees:* 26
Net Worth: £125,319,000 *Total Assets:* £1,649,904,000
Registered Office: Millstream, Maidenhead Road, Windsor, Berks, SL4 5GD
Activities: Wholesale of other fuels and related products
Parent: GB Gas Holdings Limited
Officers: Cassim Managerah [1968] Director; Jonathan Damian Westby [1972] Director/Global Head of LNG; Peter John Worby [1956] Finance Director

Centrica Energy Marketing Limited
Incorporated: 9 December 2013
Net Worth: £426,700,000 *Total Assets:* £1,262,000,000
Registered Office: Millstream, Maidenhead Road, Windsor, Berks, SL4 5GD
Activities: Trade of electricity
Parent: GB Gas Holdings Limited
Officers: David Andrew Isenegger [1964] Director/General Counsel; Cassim Managerah [1968] Director; Peter John Worby [1956] Finance Director

Centrica Finance (Canada) Limited
Incorporated: 14 August 2000
Net Worth: £882,862,016 *Total Assets:* £1,383,364,992
Registered Office: Millstream, Maidenhead Road, Windsor, Berks, SL4 5GD
Activities: Other business support service activities n.e.c.
Parent: Centrica Gamma Holdings Limited
Officers: Ian Grant Dawson [1959] Director; Charlotte Redcliffe [1964] Director/Chartered Accountant; Alistair Mark Todd [1975] Finance Director

Centrica Finance (US) Limited
Incorporated: 15 January 2001
Net Worth: £798,465,024 *Total Assets:* £1,127,905,024
Registered Office: Millstream, Maidenhead Road, Windsor, Berks, SL4 5GD
Activities: Other business support service activities n.e.c.
Parent: Centrica Beta Holdings Limited
Officers: Ian Grant Dawson [1959] Director; Charlotte Redcliffe [1964] Director/Chartered Accountant; Alistair Mark Todd [1975] Finance Director

Centrica Gamma Holdings Limited
Incorporated: 25 March 2003
Net Worth: £1,098,353,024 *Total Assets:* £1,098,353,024
Registered Office: Millstream, Maidenhead Road, Windsor, Berks, SL4 5GD
Activities: Other business support service activities n.e.c.
Parent: Centrica Overseas Holdings Limited
Officers: Ian Grant Dawson [1959] Director; Charlotte Redcliffe [1964] Director/Chartered Accountant; Alistair Mark Todd [1975] Finance Director

Centrica Holdings Limited
Incorporated: 16 November 2005
Net Worth: £1,991,101,952 *Total Assets:* £13,557,688,320
Registered Office: Millstream, Maidenhead Road, Windsor, Berks, SL4 5GD
Activities: Activities of head offices
Parent: Centrica PLC
Officers: Ian Grant Dawson [1959] Director; Christopher Michael O'Shea [1973] Director

Centrica KPS Limited
Incorporated: 5 January 2004
Net Worth Deficit: £8,187,000 *Total Assets:* £135,938,000
Registered Office: Millstream, Maidenhead Road, Windsor, Berks, SL4 5GD
Activities: Production of electricity
Parent: GB Gas Holdings Limited
Officers: Mark Ramsey Futyan [1978] Operations Director; Richard Matthew McCord [1973] Director/Accountant

Centrica Lake Limited
Incorporated: 17 September 2014
Net Worth: £1,734,851,968 *Total Assets:* £1,735,707,008
Registered Office: Millstream, Maidenhead Road, Windsor, Berks, SL4 5GD
Activities: Activities of other holding companies n.e.c.
Parent: GB Gas Holdings Limited
Officers: Matthew Blake [1976] Director/Accountant; Christopher Michael O'Shea [1973] Director; Alistair Mark Todd [1975] Finance Director

Centrica LNG Company Limited
Incorporated: 11 September 2007
Net Worth: £31,651,976 *Total Assets:* £93,177,400
Registered Office: Millstream, Maidenhead Road, Windsor, Berks, SL4 5GD
Activities: Support activities for petroleum and natural gas mining
Parent: GB Gas Holdings Limited
Officers: David Lee Dunlavy [1956] Director/Head of Business Development LNG [American]; Arturo Faustino Gallego Diaz [1973] Director [Spanish]; Cassim Managerah [1968] Director; Jonathan Damian Westby [1972] Director/Global Head of LNG; Peter John Worby [1956] Finance Director

Centrica LNG UK Limited
Incorporated: 17 December 2015
Net Worth Deficit: £18,384,000 *Total Assets:* £36,017,000
Registered Office: Millstream, Maidenhead Road, Windsor, Berks, SL4 5GD
Activities: Support activities for petroleum and natural gas mining
Parent: GB Gas Holdings Limited
Officers: David Lee Dunlavy [1956] Director/Head of Business Development LNG [American]; Arturo Faustino Gallego Diaz [1973] Director [Spanish]; Cassim Managerah [1968] Director; Jonathan Damian Westby [1972] Director/Global Head of LNG; Peter John Worby [1956] Finance Director

Centrica Overseas Holdings Limited
Incorporated: 4 February 2000
Net Worth: £544,030,976 *Total Assets:* £3,077,502,976
Registered Office: Millstream, Maidenhead Road, Windsor, Berks, SL4 5GD
Activities: Other business support service activities n.e.c.
Parent: GB Gas Holdings Limited
Officers: Ian Grant Dawson [1959] Director; Charlotte Redcliffe [1964] Director/Chartered Accountant; Alistair Mark Todd [1975] Finance Director

Centrica PB Limited
Incorporated: 31 July 2001 *Employees:* 18
Net Worth: £10,854,000 *Total Assets:* £26,945,000
Registered Office: Millstream, Maidenhead Road, Windsor, Berks, SL4 5GD
Activities: Production of electricity
Parent: GB Gas Holdings Limited
Officers: Mark Ramsey Futyan [1978] Operations Director; Richard Matthew McCord [1973] Director/Accountant

Centrica PLC
Incorporated: 16 March 1995 *Employees:* 34,901
Net Worth: £2,699,000,064 *Total Assets:* £20,668,000,256
Registered Office: Millstream, Maidenhead Road, Windsor, Berks, SL4 5GD
Activities: Production of electricity
Officers: Ian Grant Dawson, Secretary; Charles Andrew Berry [1952] Director; Iain Cameron Conn [1962] Director; Margherita Della Valle [1965] Director [Italian/British]; Joan Hogan Gillman [1963] Director [American]; Stephen Alan Michael Hester [1960] Director; Mark Steven Hodges [1965] Director; Richard Hookway [1961] Director; Manveen Kaur [1964] Director [Indian]; Christopher Michael O'Shea [1973] Director; Carlos Enrique Pascual [1958] Director [American]; Stephen Charles Pusey [1961] Director; Jonathan Scott Wheway [1966] Director

Centrica Renewable Energy Limited
Incorporated: 4 November 1996
Net Worth: £160,155,008 *Total Assets:* £160,564,992
Registered Office: Millstream, Maidenhead Road, Windsor, Berks, SL4 5GD
Activities: Activities of head offices
Parent: GB Gas Holdings Limited
Officers: Mark Ramsey Futyan [1978] Operations Director; Richard Matthew McCord [1973] Director/Accountant

Centrica Services Limited
Incorporated: 9 January 2017 *Employees:* 2,198
Net Worth: £12,291,000 *Total Assets:* £117,945,000
Registered Office: Millstream, Maidenhead Road, Windsor, Berks, SL4 5GD
Activities: Activities of head offices
Parent: GB Gas Holdings Limited
Officers: Ian Grant Dawson [1959] Director; Alistair Mark Todd [1975] Finance Director

Ceres Power Intermediate Holdings Limited
Incorporated: 11 February 2014
Net Worth: £64,093,984 *Total Assets:* £64,097,984
Registered Office: Viking House, Foundry Lane, Horsham, W Sussex, RH13 5PX
Activities: Other research and experimental development on natural sciences and engineering
Parent: Ceres Power Holdings PLC
Officers: Caroline Buchan, Secretary; Alan John Aubrey [1961] Director; Philip Joseph Caldwell [1970] Director; Stephen James Callaghan [1960] Director; Richard Timothy Preston [1969] Director

Cerestar UK Ltd
Incorporated: 22 June 1987
Net Worth: £53,920,024 *Total Assets:* £54,078,356
Registered Office: Velocity V1, Brooklands Drive, Weybridge, Surrey, KT13 0SL
Activities: Non-trading company
Officers: Dena Michelle L O'Bue, Secretary; Stephen James Hamilton [1969] Director/Country Tax Manager UK & Ireland; Michael James Timewell [1974] Director/Solicitor

CF 2016 LLP
Incorporated: 19 September 2016
Net Worth: £1,520,000,128 *Total Assets:* £1,520,000,128
Registered Office: Millstream, Maidenhead Road, Windsor, Berks, SL4 5GD

CF Corporate Finance Limited
Incorporated: 5 April 2005
Net Worth: £15,079,000 *Total Assets:* £316,279,008
Registered Office: Reading International Business Park, Reading, Berks, RG2 6AA
Activities: Financial leasing
Parent: Investec Bank PLC
Officers: Connie Mei Ling Law, Secretary; James Stephen Collins [1985] Director/Head of Finance; Michael Richard Francis [1966] Director/Chartered Accountant; Andrew Stuart Hart [1974] Managing Director; Ian Robert Wohlman [1954] Director

CFBT Schools Trust
Incorporated: 13 December 2010 *Employees:* 1,079
Net Worth: £95,575,000 *Total Assets:* £110,212,000
Registered Office: Highbridge House, 16-18 Duke Street, Reading, Berks, RG1 4RU
Activities: Pre-primary education
Officers: Sheila Patricia McKenzie, Secretary; Heather Dawson [1947] Director/Management Consultant [Canadian]; Dr Angela Elizabeth McFarlane [1957] Director/Consultant; Duncan Roger Parkes [1964] Director/Management Consultant; Sally Elizabeth Wilson [1965] Director; Philip Kenneth Wood [1955] Director

CFCEPS LLP
Incorporated: 8 March 2013
Net Worth: £73,139,104 *Total Assets:* £73,140,096
Registered Office: Millstream, Maidenhead Road, Windsor, Berks, SL4 5GD

CFCPP LLP
Incorporated: 8 March 2013
Net Worth: £241,430,592 *Total Assets:* £241,430,592
Registered Office: Millstream, Maidenhead Road, Windsor, Berks, SL4 5GD

CG EU NSC Limited
Incorporated: 11 December 2013
Net Worth: £1,196,654,848 *Total Assets:* £1,200,497,536
Registered Office: 240 Bath Road, Slough, SL1 4DX
Activities: Activities of head offices
Shareholders: CNI CV; Fiat Chrysler Automobiles N.V.
Officers: Daniel Wayne Devine [1964] Director/Vice President, Tax [American]; Jon Kurt Nelson [1974] Director/Company Executive [American]

CGG Services (UK) Limited
Incorporated: 3 June 2009 *Employees:* 737
Net Worth: £50,074,564 *Total Assets:* £202,191,760
Registered Office: CGG, Crompton Way, Manor Royal Estate, Crawley, W Sussex, RH10 9QN
Activities: Other professional, scientific and technical activities n.e.c.
Parent: CGG SA
Officers: Samantha Boast, Secretary; Samantha Boast [1968] Director/Solicitor; Clementine Maveyraud [1985] Finance Director [French]; Mark John Richards [1959] Director/Senior Vice President; Peter Mark Whiting [1963] Director/SVP SI EAME [Australian]

CGS Holdings Ltd.
Incorporated: 10 March 1993
Net Worth: £531,456,992 *Total Assets:* £531,456,992
Registered Office: 1 Forge End, Woking, Surrey, GU21 6DB
Activities: Activities of head offices
Parent: Capgemini S.E.
Officers: Julie Mangan, Secretary; Carole Gabriella Ferrand [1970] Director/Group Chief Financial Officer [French]; Paul Hermelin [1952] Director/CEO Capgemini Group [French]; Christine Mary Hodgson [1964] Director/CEO Technology Services North West; Paul Arthur Margetts [1966] Managing Director

CH & Co Catering Group (Holdings) Limited
Incorporated: 23 March 2015 *Employees:* 6,372
Net Worth Deficit: £2,353,000 *Total Assets:* £195,026,000
Registered Office: Second Floor, 550 Thames Valley Park, Reading, Berks, RG6 1PT
Activities: Activities of head offices
Shareholder: MML Capital Partners Fund VI GP Limited
Officers: Nicholas Edward Heale Thomas, Secretary; Simon James Hodson [1956] Director/Solicitor; Timothy John Jones [1959] Director; Richard Daniel Mayers [1975] Director/Chartered Accountant; Elizabeth McMeikan [1962] Director; Madeleine Suzanne Musselwhite [1976] Director; Nicholas Edward Heale Thomas [1962] Director; William James Toner [1958] Director; Terry Waldron [1969] Group Relationship Director [Irish]; Ian Scott Wallis [1970] Director/Private Equity Investor

CH & Co Catering Group Limited
Incorporated: 23 March 2015 *Employees:* 6,372
Net Worth Deficit: £3,263,000 *Total Assets:* £195,007,008
Registered Office: Second Floor, 550 Thames Valley Park, Reading, Berks, RG6 1PT
Activities: Activities of head offices
Parent: CH & Co Catering Group (Holdings) Limited
Officers: Nicholas Edward Heale Thomas, Secretary; Timothy John Jones [1959] Director; Richard Daniel Mayers [1975] Director/Chartered Accountant; Madeleine Suzanne Musselwhite [1976] Director; Nicholas Edward Heale Thomas [1962] Director; William James Toner [1958] Director; Terry Waldron [1969] Group Relationship Director [Irish]; Ian Scott Wallis [1970] Director/Private Equity Investor

CH & Co Catering Limited
Incorporated: 23 May 1991 *Employees:* 2,571
Net Worth: £10,722,127 *Total Assets:* £34,451,988
Registered Office: Second Floor, 550 Thames Valley Park, Reading, Berks, RG6 1PT
Activities: Licenced restaurants
Parent: CH & Co Catering Group Limited
Officers: Nicholas Edward Heale Thomas, Secretary; Timothy John Jones [1959] Director/Chartered Accountant; Madeleine Suzanne Musselwhite [1976] Director; Nicholas Edward Heale Thomas [1962] Director; William James Toner [1958] Director

The Challenger Multi Academy Trust
Incorporated: 17 October 2014 *Employees:* 548
Net Worth: £46,060,028 *Total Assets:* £54,674,760
Registered Office: Kempston Challenger Academy, Hill Rise, Kempston, Bedford, MK42 7EB
Activities: Other business support service activities n.e.c.
Officers: Stephen Martyn Chamberlain [1965] Director/Chief Executive Officer; Sally Ann Sheila Dicketts [1955] Director/Chief Executive; Alban Francis Xavier Green [1950] Director; Peter James Knell [1973] Business Director

Chandlers Garage Holdings Limited
Incorporated: 12 June 1996 *Employees:* 7
Net Worth: £50,932,104 *Total Assets:* £111,831,472
Registered Office: Chandlers, Victoria Road, Portslade, Brighton, BN41 1YH
Activities: Activities of head offices
Shareholders: Group 1 Automotive UK Limited; Group 1 Automotive UK Limited
Officers: Darryl Michael Burman, Secretary/General Counsel [American]; Darryl Michael Burman [1958] Director/General Counsel [American]; Darren Guiver [1968] Director; Earl Julius Hesterberg [1953] Director [American]; Daniel James McHenry [1974] Finance Director; John Rickel [1961] Director [American]

Change, Grow, Live
Incorporated: 19 October 1999 *Employees:* 3,614
Previous: Crime Reduction Initiatives
Net Worth: £27,226,000 *Total Assets:* £74,011,000
Registered Office: 3rd Floor, North West Suite, Tower Point, 44 North Road, Brighton, BN1 1YR
Activities: Other social work activities without accommodation n.e.c.
Officers: Mark Moody, Secretary; Sheena Nadine Marie Asthana [1964] Director/University Professor; Rachel Atkinson [1972] Director/Civil Servant; Wilfred John Bardsley [1958] Nurse and Director; Nicholas Ernest Burstin [1957] Director/Advertising Consultant; Jean Margaret Daintith [1953] Director; John Howard Harris [1956] Director/Management Consultant; Stuart Russell McMinnies [1968] Director/Managing Partner; Gillian Parker [1954] Director/Retired; Michael Alexander Leary Pringle [1950] Director/University Professor; Dr Andreas Raffel [1958] Non-Executive Director and Advisor [German]

Changeregard Limited
Incorporated: 2 August 1996 *Employees:* 111
Net Worth: £21,664,078 *Total Assets:* £29,188,286
Registered Office: 97 Leigh Road, Eastleigh, Hants, SO50 9DR
Activities: Construction of commercial buildings
Major Shareholder: Seamus Cleary
Officers: Seamus Cleary [1959] Director/Civil Engineer [Irish]

Channel Commercials Kent Ltd
Incorporated: 20 November 2006 *Employees:* 210
Net Worth: £5,276,818 *Total Assets:* £27,989,204
Registered Office: Brunswick Road, Cobbs Wood Estate, Ashford, Kent, TN23 1EH
Activities: Activities of head offices
Shareholders: Anthony Richard Chudleigh; Ronald Sydney Stupple
Officers: Michael Ronald MacIntyre, Secretary; Russell John Ades [1970] Sales Director; Clive Ayears [1959] Parts Director; Paul Reynolds Elliott [1960] General Director; Michael Ronald MacIntyre [1963] Managing Director; John Anthony Stupple [1972] Service Director; Paul Taylor [1969] Sales Director

Channel Commercials PLC
Incorporated: 30 June 1987 *Employees:* 210
Net Worth: £5,586,921 *Total Assets:* £29,378,040
Registered Office: Brunswick Road, Cobbs Wood Industrial Estate, Ashford, Kent, TN23 1EH
Activities: Sale of other motor vehicles
Parent: Channel Commercials Holdings Ltd
Officers: Michael Ronald MacIntyre, Secretary; Russell John Ades [1970] Director/Sales Manager; Clive Ayears [1959] Director/Parts Manager; Paul Reynolds Elliott [1960] Director/General Manager; Michael Ronald MacIntyre [1963] Director/Accountant; John Anthony Stupple [1972] Director/Service Manager; Paul Taylor [1969] Director/Sales Manager

Channel Tunnel Group Limited (The)
Incorporated: 26 April 1984
Net Worth: £174,896,992 *Total Assets:* £2,782,522,880
Registered Office: UK Terminal, Ashford Road, Folkestone, Kent, CT18 8XX
Activities: Other passenger land transport
Parent: Eurotunnel Holding SAS
Officers: Francois Gauthey [1962] Director [French]; Jacques Gounon [1953] Director [French]

Chapman Freeborn Airchartering Limited
Incorporated: 9 May 1972 *Employees:* 74
Net Worth: £19,412,344 *Total Assets:* £34,439,348
Registered Office: 3 City Place, Beehive Ring Road, Gatwick, W Sussex, RH6 0PA
Activities: Non-scheduled passenger air transport
Parent: Chapman Freeborn International Ltd
Officers: Peter Joarder, Secretary; Russi Batliwala [1964] Director [German]; Peter Joarder [1969] Finance Director; Shahe Ouzounian [1970] Managing Director

Chapman Freeborn International Limited
Incorporated: 1 May 1973 *Employees:* 3
Net Worth: £21,470,364 *Total Assets:* £32,425,978
Registered Office: 3 City Place, Beehive Ring Road, Gatwick, W Sussex, RH6 0PA
Activities: Freight air transport
Parent: Chapman Freeborn Holdings Limited
Officers: Peter Joarder, Secretary; Russi Batliwala [1964] Director [German]; Peter Joarder [1969] Finance Director; Shahe Ouzounian [1970] Director

Chaptre Finance PLC
Incorporated: 23 December 2015
Net Worth: £50,000 *Total Assets:* £54,245,000
Registered Office: 8 White Oak Square, London Road, Swanley, Kent, BR8 7AG
Activities: Financial intermediation not elsewhere classified
Parent: Chaptre Holdings Limited
Officers: Matthew James Spencer Booth [1971] Director/Investment Banker; Jens Christian Clausen [1948] Director/Consultant [Danish]; Kasper Hansen [1978] Director [Danish]; Andrew Horsley Clifford Hartley [1958] Director; David Jensen [1974] Director/Senior Asset Manager [Danish]

Chaptre Investments Limited
Incorporated: 9 December 2015
Net Worth: £26,230,500 *Total Assets:* £118,546,072
Registered Office: 8 White Oak Square, London Road, Swanley, Kent, BR8 7AG
Activities: Financial intermediation not elsewhere classified
Parent: Chaptre Greenco Limited
Officers: Matthew John Edgar [1985] Director/Senior Vice President [Australian]; Andrew Horsley Clifford Hartley [1958] Managing Director; Adam Cade Nancarrow [1975] Director [Australian]

The Charity Bank Limited
Incorporated: 28 November 2001 *Employees:* 63
Net Worth: £20,368,000 *Total Assets:* £158,610,000
Registered Office: Fosse House, 182 High Street, Tonbridge, Kent, TN9 1BE
Activities: Financial intermediation not elsewhere classified
Parent: Big Society Capital Limited
Officers: Jenny Edwards, Secretary; George Patrick Blunden [1952] Director; Robin Francis Budenberg [1959] Director; Michael Curtis Crabb [1957] Director; Malcolm Christopher Elliott [1966] Director/Bank Employee; David Warren Godfrey [1950] Director/Civil Servant; Sara Llewellin [1956] Director; Sir John Menzies Low [1953] Director/Chief Executive; Catherine Lois Sayer [1956] Director/Consultant; Anna Lindsay Shiel [1979] Director; Edward Siegel [1962] Director [American/British]; Toby Jonathan Walter [1972] Director/Banker

Charity for St Joseph's Missionary Society (Generalate)
Incorporated: 20 October 1950 *Employees:* 3
Net Worth: £43,773,764 *Total Assets:* £44,919,296
Registered Office: P O Box 3608, St Joseph's Parish Centre, Cookham Road, Maidenhead, Berks, SL6 7EG
Activities: Non-trading company
Officers: Edmund Richard Cotter, Secretary; Jos Boerkamp [1952] Director [Dutch]; Rev Michael Gerard Corcoran [1960] Director/Priest [Irish]; Rev Jimmy Adolacion Lindero [1975] Director/Roman Catholic Missionary Priest [Filipino]; Rev Desmond McGillicuddy [1949] Director/Priest [Irish]; Rev Andrew Mukulu [1968] Director/Roman Catholic Missionary Priest [Ugandan]

Charles River Laboratories Holdings Limited
Incorporated: 10 December 1999
Net Worth: £51,488,000 *Total Assets:* £229,232,992
Registered Office: Manston Road, Margate, Kent, CT9 4LT
Activities: Non-trading company
Officers: Gary Andrews, Secretary; Colin Dunn [1967] Director; David P Johst [1961] Director/Corporate Executive Vice President [American]; David Ross Smith [1965] Financial Director

Charles River U.K. Limited
Incorporated: 18 March 1969 *Employees:* 113
Net Worth: £33,108,000 *Total Assets:* £37,237,000
Registered Office: Manston Road, Margate, Kent, CT9 4LT
Activities: Research and experimental development on biotechnology
Officers: Gary Andrews, Secretary; Colin Dunn [1967] Director; David P Johst [1961] Director/Corporate Executive Vice President [American]; David Ross Smith [1965] Director

Charters School
Incorporated: 10 September 2012 *Employees:* 214
Net Worth: £20,990,036 *Total Assets:* £25,386,304
Registered Office: Charters School, Charters Road, Sunningdale, Ascot, Berks, SL5 9QY
Activities: General secondary education
Officers: Julie Adams, Secretary; Gareth Huw Davies [1963] Director; Richard Lee Evans [1971] Director/Head of School Improvement; Mark John Holdaway [1965] Director; Adam Robert Jezard [1964] Director/Journalist; Nicola Claire Morgan [1988] Director/Teacher; Richard John Pilgrim [1961] Director/Headteacher; Fareeda Qasim [1968] Director; Denis Simon Raymond [1973] Director; Gureshwar Singh Jhajj [1978] Director; Richard Robert Tyler [1971] Director; Elaine Margaret Wallace [1969] Managing Director

Chartwell Properties Limited
Incorporated: 10 August 1999
Net Worth: £41,141,080 *Total Assets:* £48,270,424
Registered Office: Kingswick House, Kingswick Drive, Ascot, Berks, SL5 7BH
Activities: Other letting and operating of own or leased real estate
Major Shareholder: Mark Lee
Officers: Vikash Tanna, Secretary; Victoria Lucy James [1981] Director; Mark Lee [1955] Director/Land Investor

Chatham & Clarendon Grammar School
Incorporated: 30 November 2010 *Employees:* 175
Net Worth: £28,296,580 *Total Assets:* £30,997,382
Registered Office: Chatham & Clarendon Grammar School, Chatham Street, Ramsgate, Kent, CT11 7PS
Activities: General secondary education
Officers: Chris Freeman, Secretary; Richard Anthony Bath [1951] Director/Retired Headteacher; Lorraine Nicole Duffy [1972] Director/Senior Lecturer; David Douglas Harris [1964] Director/Consultant; Rosemary Helen Hewett [1962] Director/Cover Manager/School Administrator; Mark Christian Hutchings [1969] Director/Teacher; Joanne King [1969] Director/Office Manager/Teacher; Debra Jayne Liddicoat [1963] Director/Teacher; Alistair Joseph Milne [1978] Director; Claire Louise Tonkin Jukes [1971] Director/Teacher; Rosie Travers [1963] Director/Psychologist; John William Waker [1957] Director/Retired; Stephen John Wren [1966] Director/Accountant

Chatham Historic Dockyard Trust (The)
Incorporated: 28 March 1984 *Employees:* 142
Net Worth: £19,048,366 *Total Assets:* £20,885,736
Registered Office: The Fitted Rigging House, The Historic Dockyard, Chatham, Kent, ME4 4TZ
Activities: Other letting and operating of own or leased real estate
Officers: Andrew Patrick Lionel Fermor, Secretary; Sir Ian Charles Franklin Andrews [1953] Director/Chairman; Rodney Brian Chambers [1943] Director/Councillor; William Anthony Corbett [1948] Director/Retired Marine Consultant; Murray Hallam [1946] Director/Solicitor; Paul David Hudson [1947] Director/Examining Inspector-National Infrastructure; Sandra Marie Matthews-Marsh [1964] Director/Chief Executive, Visit Kent; Laura Cicely Alison Nesfield [1981] Director/Chartered Surveyor; Sarah Elizabeth Roots [1969] Director/Attractions Specialist; Pommy Prodaman Kumar Sarwal [1951] Director/Corporate Finance; Sir Trevor Alan Soar [1957] Director

Chatham Street Technologies Limited
Incorporated: 8 May 1985
Net Worth: £12,588,633 *Total Assets:* £23,870,846
Registered Office: 115 Chatham Street, Reading, Berks, RG1 7JX
Activities: Data processing, hosting and related activities
Parent: Bottomline Technologies Incorporated
Officers: Richard Douglas Booth [1969] Director/Chief Executive [American]; Harpaul Dharwar [1973] Financial Director; Robert Eberle [1960] Director [American]; Paul Fannon [1968] Director; Christopher Wilson Peck [1965] Sales Director; Nigel Kevin Savory [1966] Director

Chaucer Management Services Limited
Incorporated: 16 December 2013 *Employees:* 2
Net Worth Deficit: £6,480,001 *Total Assets:* £23,751,280
Registered Office: 3 Jubilee Way, Faversham, Kent, ME13 8GD
Activities: Financial management
Parent: Chaucer Management Holdings Limited
Officers: Julie Ann Freeman, Secretary; Christopher Charles Laslett [1969] Director; Martin John Wassell [1971] Director

CHB P H R Limited
Incorporated: 12 December 1991
Net Worth: £14,667,000 *Total Assets:* £114,672,000
Registered Office: Hanson House, 14 Castle Hill, Maidenhead, Berks, SL6 4JJ
Activities: Activities of other holding companies n.e.c.
Parent: CHB Group Limited
Officers: Wendy Fiona Rogers, Secretary; Nicholas Arthur Dawe Benning-Prince [1974] Director/Chartered Accountant; Robert Charles Dowley [1972] Director/Chartered Accountant; Edward Alexander Gretton [1970] Director; Dr Carsten Matthias Wendt [1976] Director [German]

Chem Aviation LLP
Incorporated: 23 January 2014
Net Worth: £32,886,658 *Total Assets:* £36,394,536
Registered Office: Hawkslease, Chapel Lane, Lyndhurst, Hants, SO43 7FG
Officers: Andrew Christopher Currie [1955] Member; James Arthur Ratcliffe [1952] Member; John Reece [1957] Member

Chemetall Limited
Incorporated: 19 December 1930 *Employees:* 62
Net Worth: £108,570,000 *Total Assets:* £125,886,000
Registered Office: 65 Denbigh Road, Bletchley, Milton Keynes, Bucks, MK1 1PB
Activities: Wholesale of chemical products
Parent: Chemetall GmbH
Officers: Wayne Brown, Secretary; Wolfram Alfred Antonius Boegner [1965] Director/Lawyer [German]; Herr Giorgio Cortellaro [1964] Director/Vice President, General Manager [German]; Christopher Hans-Walter Hoffmann [1960] Managing Director [German]

Chemidex Generics Limited
Incorporated: 23 July 1999 *Employees:* 1
Net Worth: £41,655,200 *Total Assets:* £42,801,256
Registered Office: Chemidex House, Unit 7 Egham Business Village, Crabtree Road, Egham, Surrey, TW20 8RB
Activities: Wholesale of pharmaceutical goods
Shareholders: Navinchandra Jamnadas; Varsha Navinchandas Engineer
Officers: Nikesh Engineer [1985] Director/Doctor

Chemidex Pharma Limited
Incorporated: 8 November 1982 *Employees:* 20
Net Worth: £29,905,596 *Total Assets:* £48,929,356
Registered Office: Chemidex House, Unit 7 Egham Business Village, Crabtree Road, Egham, Surrey, TW20 8RB
Activities: Manufacture of basic pharmaceutical products
Shareholders: Navinchandra Jamnadas; Varsha Navinchandra
Officers: Nikesh Engineer [1985] Director/Doctor

Chemigraphic Limited
Incorporated: 13 March 1972 *Employees:* 137
Net Worth: £17,693,648 *Total Assets:* £23,734,952
Registered Office: Unit A2, The Fleming Centre, Flemingway, Crawley, W Sussex, RH10 9NF
Activities: Manufacture of electricity distribution and control apparatus
Officers: Alexander Francis Erickson, Secretary; Alexander Francis Erickson [1982] Finance Director; Dominic Riley [1961] Director/Chairman; Christopher Wootton [1963] Director

Chemigraphic Mid-Co Limited
Incorporated: 13 December 2010
Net Worth Deficit: £15,386,437 *Total Assets:* £21,209,288
Registered Office: Unit A2, The Fleming Centre, Flemingway, Crawley, W Sussex, RH10 9NF
Activities: Activities of other holding companies n.e.c.
Officers: Alexander Francis Erickson, Secretary; Richard Charles Austin Caston [1967] Director; Alexander Francis Erickson [1982] Finance Director; Dominic Riley [1961] Director/Chairman; Christopher Wootton [1963] Director

Chemring Countermeasures Limited
Incorporated: 16 December 1926 *Employees:* 393
Net Worth: £27,854,000 *Total Assets:* £73,729,000
Registered Office: Roke Manor, Old Salisbury Lane, Romsey, Hants, SO51 0ZN
Activities: Manufacture of explosives
Parent: Chemring Group PLC
Officers: Sarah Louise Ellard, Secretary; Sarah Louise Ellard [1970] Group Legal Director; Sarah Louise Ellard [1970] Group Legal Director; Andrew Lade Hogben [1969] Director; Andrew Gregory Lewis [1971] Director; Michael Ord [1967] Director; Julia Caroline Whalvin [1970] Director

Chemring Group PLC
Incorporated: 30 November 1905 *Employees:* 2,510
Net Worth: £410,800,000 *Total Assets:* £711,600,000
Registered Office: Roke Manor, Old Salisbury Lane, Romsey, Hants, SO51 0ZN
Activities: Activities of head offices
Officers: Sarah Louise Ellard, Secretary; Andrew Oswell Bede Davies [1963] Director; Sarah Louise Ellard [1970] Group Legal Director; Carl-Peter Edmund Moriz Forster [1954] Director [German]; Mr Stephen Anthony King [1960] Director; Andrew Gregory Lewis [1971] Director; Michael Ord [1967] Director; Nigel Robert Young [1953] Director

Chemring North America Unlimited
Incorporated: 26 March 2008 *Employees:* 3
Net Worth: £455,353,984 *Total Assets:* £493,990,016
Registered Office: Roke Manor, Old Salisbury Lane, Romsey, Hants, SO51 0ZN
Activities: Activities of head offices
Parent: Chemring North America Group, Inc.
Officers: Sarah Louise Ellard, Secretary; Sarah Louise Ellard [1970] Group Legal Director; Andrew Gregory Lewis [1971] Director; Michael Ord [1967] Director

Chemring Technology Solutions Limited
Incorporated: 17 November 1980 *Employees:* 73
Previous: Chemring EOD Limited
Net Worth: £10,321,000 *Total Assets:* £26,001,000
Registered Office: Roke Manor, Old Salisbury Lane, Romsey, Hants, SO51 0ZN
Activities: Defence activities
Parent: Chemring Energetics Limited
Officers: Sarah Louise Ellard, Secretary; Paul John Davidson [1978] Director; Sarah Louise Ellard [1970] Group Legal Director; Andrew Gregory Lewis [1971] Director; David Alexander McDonald [1963] Director; Michael Ord [1967] Director

CHEP Pallecon Solutions Limited
Incorporated: 4 December 2012 *Employees:* 119
Net Worth: £2,991,387 *Total Assets:* £42,080,944
Registered Office: 2nd Floor, 400 Dashwood Lang Road, Bourne Business Park, Addlestone, Surrey, KT15 2HJ
Activities: Other transportation support activities
Parent: Brambls Holdings (UK) Ltd
Officers: Daniel Robert Berry [1973] Director/Lawyer; Steven John McGhee [1971] Senior Director, Sales and Marketing; Craig Patrick Willmott [1973] Director/Finance Professional [Australian]

Chep UK Limited
Incorporated: 8 May 1924 *Employees:* 906
Net Worth: £87,173,000 *Total Assets:* £223,976,000
Registered Office: 2nd Floor, 400 Dashwood Lang Road, Bourne Business Park, Addlestone, Surrey, KT15 2HJ
Activities: Renting and leasing of other machinery, equipment and tangible goods n.e.c.
Parent: Cyan Logistics Limited
Officers: Maureen Barwell [1968] Human Resources Director; Daniel Robert Berry [1973] Director/Lawyer; Carla Mae Brocklehurst [1975] Finance Director; Helen Victoria Lane [1981] Director/VP Northern Europe

Cheshunt Lakeside Developments Limited
Incorporated: 25 September 2015 *Employees:* 4
Net Worth: £252,634 *Total Assets:* £46,140,764
Registered Office: Decimal Place, Chiltern Avenue, Amersham, Bucks, HP6 5FG
Activities: Development of building projects
Shareholder: Inland Homes PLC
Officers: Andrew John Chrysostomou [1984] Director; Benjamin George Anker David [1977] Director; Nishith Malde [1958] Director; Gary John Skinner [1968] Managing Director

CHG Overseas Investments Limited
Incorporated: 20 March 2006 *Employees:* 3
Net Worth: £51,275,000 *Total Assets:* £64,954,000
Registered Office: Roke Manor, Old Salisbury Lane, Romsey, Hants, SO51 0ZN
Activities: Non-trading company
Parent: Chemring Group PLC
Officers: Sarah Louise Ellard, Secretary; Sarah Louise Ellard [1970] Group Legal Director; Andrew Gregory Lewis [1971] Director

CHG Overseas Ltd
Incorporated: 16 July 1992 *Employees:* 3
Net Worth: £47,949,000 *Total Assets:* £560,188,992
Registered Office: Roke Manor, Old Salisbury Lane, Romsey, Hants, SO51 0ZN
Activities: Activities of head offices
Parent: Chemring Group PLC
Officers: Sarah Louise Ellard, Secretary; Sarah Louise Ellard [1970] Group Legal Director; Andrew Gregory Lewis [1971] Director; Michael Ord [1967] Director

CHG-Meridian Computer Leasing UK Limited
Incorporated: 6 September 1976
Net Worth: £973,000 *Total Assets:* £64,564,000
Registered Office: Barons Court, 22 The Avenue, Egham, Surrey, TW20 9AB
Activities: Financial leasing
Officers: Declan Martin McGlone [1965] Director [Irish]; Dr Mathias Wagner [1971] Director/Chief Sales Officer International [German]; Simon Young [1976] Sales Director

CHG-Meridian UK Limited
Incorporated: 3 September 1971 *Employees:* 47
Net Worth: £37,885,000 *Total Assets:* £89,425,000
Registered Office: Barons Court, 22 The Avenue, Egham, Surrey, TW20 9AB
Activities: Financial leasing
Officers: Declan Martin McGlone [1965] Director [Irish]; Dr Mathias Wagner [1971] Director/Chief Sales Officer International [German]; Simon Young [1976] Sales Director

The Chichester Diocesan Fund and Board of Finance (Incorporated)
Incorporated: 26 January 1914 *Employees:* 57
Net Worth: £289,708,992 *Total Assets:* £299,036,992
Registered Office: Diocesan Church House, 211 New Church Road, Hove, E Sussex, BN3 4ED
Activities: Activities of religious organisations
Officers: Gabrielle Higgins, Secretary; John David Sebastian Booth [1958] Director/Investment Banker; Philip Gray Bowden [1953] Director/Pensions Consultant; Valerie Lynda Burgess [1947] Director/Home Maker; The Reverend Philip James Coekin [1964] Director/Incumbent; Martin Anthony Cruttenden [1933] Director/Retired; Robert Edward MacKenzie Dowler [1967] Director/Archdeacon; Philip Mark Gilbert [1962] Director/Priest; Janine Michelle Patricia Hobbs [1957] Director/Retired Civil Servant; The Reverend James William Hollingsworth [1969] Director/Incumbent; Richard Charles Jackson [1961] Director/Bishop; The Reverend Martin Peter James King [1973] Director/Incumbent; Martin Clifford Lloyd Williams [1965] Director/Archdeacon; Lesley Lynn [1956] Director/Retired Banker; Alison Ruth Marchant [1944] Director/Retired; Amelia Dawn Zenobia Murphy [1960] Director/Senior Finance Officer; Julia Kathleen Peaty [1953] Director/Rural Dean; Bradley Francis Smith [1983] Director/Bookshop Manager; The Right Reverend Mark Crispin Rake Sowerby [1963] Director/Clerk in Holy Orders Suffragan Bishop; Sara Jane Stonor [1948] Director/Teacher and Designer of Embroidery; The Reverend David Alan Twinley [1966] Director/Incumbent; Jacob Peter Vince [1960] Director/Chief Executive; Stephen John Waine [1959] Director/Dean; The Revd Canon Ann Elizabeth Waizeneker [1956] Director/Vicar; The Right Reverend Dr Martin Clive Warner [1958] Director/Bishop of Chichester; Lesley Margaret Webster [1949] Director/Tribunal Judge; The Venerable Julie Fiona Windsor [1959] Director/Archdeacon

Chichester Festival Theatre
Incorporated: 2 May 2001 *Employees:* 161
Net Worth: £24,654,656 *Total Assets:* £31,163,476
Registered Office: Oaklands Park, Chichester, W Sussex, PO19 6AP
Activities: Performing arts
Officers: Simon Kenneth Parsonage, Secretary; Nicholas Paul Backhouse [1963] Director; Alan Brodie [1955] Director/Literary Agent; Sir William Martin Castell [1947] Director; Jill Rosemary Green [1959] Director/Film Producer; Odile Lesley Griffith [1954] Director/Property Development and Refurbishment; Shelagh Jane Legrave [1958] Director/Principal of Chichester College; Richard John Lippiett [1949] Director/Consultant; Harry Nsamba Matovu [1963] Director/Lawyer; Michael John McCart [1948] Director; Denise Lesley Anne Patterson [1955] Director; Sonalini Stephanie Street Sylvestre [1977] Director/Actress and Playwright; Patricia Mary Tull [1946] Director/Councillor; Christina Webster [1955] Director/Solicitor; Susan Jane Wells [1959] Director

Childbase Partnership Limited
Incorporated: 31 August 1989 *Employees:* 1,691
Net Worth Deficit: £2,860,626 *Total Assets:* £29,576,340
Registered Office: Kingston House, Northampton Road, Newport Pagnell, Bucks, MK16 8NJ
Activities: Pre-primary education
Parent: Childbase Employee Ownership Trustee Limited
Officers: Michael Anthony Norcott Thompson, Secretary; Kate Alicia Broadhurst [1977] Director/Retail Specialist; Sarah Louise Hill [1973] Operations Director; Virginia Mead-Herbert [1960] Marketing Director; Emma Paula Rooney [1981] Director; Michael Anthony Norcott Thompson [1962] Director; Paul Simon Thompson [1969] Finance Director

The Childcare Corporation Limited
Incorporated: 11 December 2000 *Employees:* 659
Previous: The Childcare Corporation PLC
Net Worth: £15,028,000 *Total Assets:* £23,892,000
Registered Office: Tuscany House, White Hart Lane, Basingstoke, Hants, RG21 4AF
Activities: Other social work activities without accommodation n.e.c.
Shareholder: Jean-Emmanuel Rodocanachi
Officers: Colin James Lawson [1966] Director/Accountant; Adrian Richard Moore [1964] Director

The Children's Trust
Incorporated: 30 September 1983 *Employees:* 505
Net Worth: £28,932,000 *Total Assets:* £31,475,000
Registered Office: Tadworth Court, Tadworth, Surrey, KT20 5RU
Activities: Primary education
Officers: Colin Kerr, Secretary; Elizabeth Sarah Baker [1959] Director/Healthcare Consultant; Tim John Davies [1955] Director/Retired; Michael David Gercke [1952] Director/Chartered Accountant; Duncan George Ingram [1955] Former FTSE100 Director; Denise Elizabeth Matthams [1958] Director/Independent Governing Body Board Nurse; Toby Jonathan Mullins [1961] Director/Executive Headteacher; Nigel Keith Lethbridge Scott [1952] Director/Charity Consultant; Katherine Anne Walker [1959] Director/Consultant

ChildrenSalon Limited
Incorporated: 17 December 2003 *Employees:* 6
Net Worth: £28,060,972 *Total Assets:* £40,552,280
Registered Office: 9 High Street, Tunbridge Wells, Kent, TN1 1UL
Activities: Retail sale of clothing in specialised stores
Parent: ChildrenSalon Group Ltd
Officers: John Frederick Brudenell-Leech, Secretary/Accountant; John Frederick Brudenell-Leech [1966] Director/Accountant; Ian Davidson [1952] Group Director of Technology; Michele Mary Beatrice Harriman Smith [1952] Managing Director; Sorcha Harriman-Smith [1987] Director; Melissa NG [1982] Director; Afsaneh Scott-Read [1985] Director; George Frederick Smith [1947] Director

Chiltern International Holdings Limited
Incorporated: 12 January 1996 *Employees:* 2
Net Worth: £231,438,000 *Total Assets:* £308,764,000
Registered Office: Osprey House, Westacott Way, Maidenhead, Berks, SL6 3QH
Activities: Activities of head offices
Parent: Chiltern International Group Limited
Officers: Floyd Samuel Eberts III, Secretary; Floyd Samuel Eberts III [1959] Director/Chief Legal Officer [American]; Glenn Andrew Eisenberg [1961] Director/Chief Financial Officer [American]; Robert Pringle [1964] Director

Chiltern International Limited
Incorporated: 19 May 1982 *Employees:* 477
Net Worth: £55,901,000 *Total Assets:* £164,932,992
Registered Office: Osprey House, Westacott Way, Maidenhead, Berks, SL6 3QH
Activities: Other professional, scientific and technical activities n.e.c.
Parent: Chiltern International Holdings Limited
Officers: Floyd Samuel Eberts III, Secretary; Floyd Samuel Eberts III [1959] Director/Chief Legal Officer [American]; Glenn Andrew Eisenberg [1961] Director/Chief Financial Officer [American]; Robert Pringle [1964] Director

Chilton Home Farms Ltd
Incorporated: 10 October 1980 *Employees:* 89
Net Worth: £39,325,256 *Total Assets:* £44,841,792
Registered Office: Estate Office, Dorton Road, Chilton, Aylesbury, Bucks, HP18 9NA
Activities: Growing of cereals (except rice), leguminous crops and oil seeds
Officers: Lady Sara Roberta Aubrey-Fletcher, Secretary; Sir Henry Egerton Aubrey Fletcher [1945] Director/Farmer; Harry Buchanan Aubrey-Fletcher [1982] Director/Property Promotion & Development; Lady Sara Roberta Aubrey-Fletcher [1950] Director

Chinatool UK Limited
Incorporated: 19 May 2004 *Employees:* 36
Net Worth: £3,474,000 *Total Assets:* £25,247,000
Registered Office: 3000a Parkway, Whiteley, Hants, PO15 7FX
Activities: Wholesale trade of motor vehicle parts and accessories
Major Shareholder: Simon Phillips
Officers: Victoria Louise Thomas, Secretary; Victoria Louise Thomas [1964] Finance Director; Mr David Paul Wilkinson [1981] Finance Director

Chingford Fruit Limited
Incorporated: 20 September 1999 *Employees:* 263
Net Worth: £27,328,000 *Total Assets:* £42,549,000
Registered Office: Thames House, Thames Road, Crayford, Kent, DA1 4QP
Activities: Wholesale of fruit and vegetables
Parent: AG Thames Holdings Limited
Officers: Christopher Oakley, Secretary; David Alex Aichen [1969] Director; Leon Aichen [1941] Director; Gary Raymond Linsell [1970] Managing Director; Christopher Richard Oakley [1963] Finance Director

Chislehurst and Sidcup Grammar School
Incorporated: 1 June 2011 *Employees:* 123
Net Worth: £23,947,378 *Total Assets:* £25,066,720
Registered Office: Hurst Road, Sidcup, Kent, DA15 9AG
Activities: General secondary education
Officers: June Rose Ben Rabah [1958] Director; Dawn Burton [1966] Director/Primary School Teacher; Helen Everett [1964] Director/Teacher; Jason Gardiner [1963] Director/Compliance Consultant; Jane Elizabeth Gritt [1963] Director/Human Resources Manager; Joe Henry [1970] Director/Management Consultant; Janice Power [1958] Director/Administrator; Michael Sradling [1974] Director/Barrister; Lindsey Stewart [1969] Director/Doctoral Researcher; Amanda Lisa Sutton [1965] Director; Nigel Austin Walker [1966] Director/Headteacher; Richard Anthony Wallbridge [1969] Director; Susan Margaret Watson [1955] Director

Chloride Group Limited
Incorporated: 12 December 1891 *Employees:* 32
Net Worth: £649,960,000 *Total Assets:* £670,611,008
Registered Office: c/o Vertiv, Tor, Saint-Cloud Way, Maidenhead, Berks, SL6 8BN
Activities: Other professional, scientific and technical activities n.e.c.
Parent: Vertiv Holdings II Limited
Officers: Eamon John Rowan, Secretary; Stephen Paul Wood, Secretary; Giordano Albertazzi [1966] Director [Italian]; Colin Flannery [1965] Director/Vice President and General Counsel [Australian]; Eamon John Rowan [1959] Director/Vice President Finance [Irish]

Chloride Supplies Limited
Incorporated: 6 April 1933
Net Worth: £2,929,000 *Total Assets:* £26,645,000
Registered Office: c/o Vertiv, Tor, Saint-Cloud Way, Maidenhead, Berks, SL6 8BN
Activities: Other professional, scientific and technical activities n.e.c.
Parent: Chloride Group Limited
Officers: Stephen Paul Wood, Secretary; Michael Anthony O'Keeffe [1964] Director; Eamon John Rowan [1959] Director/Vice President Finance [Irish]

CHMC Limited
Incorporated: 6 May 2009 *Employees:* 51
Net Worth: £20,564,000 *Total Assets:* £37,741,000
Registered Office: Enbrook Park, Sandgate, Folkestone, Kent, CT20 3SE
Activities: Financial intermediation not elsewhere classified
Parent: CHMC Holdings Limited
Officers: Victoria Haynes, Secretary; Lance Henry Lowe Bachelor [1964] Director/Group Chief Executive; Caroline Alexandra Finnis [1969] Operations Director; Chris Nelson [1969] Director; James Quin [1969] Director

Chobham Manor LLP
Incorporated: 13 June 2012
Net Worth: £35,502,000 *Total Assets:* £43,774,000
Registered Office: Gate House, Turnpike Road, High Wycombe, Bucks, HP12 3NR

Chobham School Academy (Stratford)
Incorporated: 13 March 2009 *Employees:* 185
Net Worth: £31,975,000 *Total Assets:* £36,049,000
Registered Office: 4th Floor, Norfolk House, Wellesley Road, Croydon, Surrey, CR0 1LH
Activities: General secondary education
Officers: Alan John Bates [1970] Project Director; Angela Marie Forbes [1979] Commercial Director; Jeremy Stuart Fraser [1958] Director/Vicar; Duncan Cowan Gray [1983] Director/Strategy Consultant; William Nigel Hugill [1958] Director/Consultant

Choice Care Group 2 Limited
Incorporated: 11 July 2013
Previous: Caledonia Choice 2 Limited
Net Worth: £50,686,148 *Total Assets:* £55,314,620
Registered Office: Linden House, Lime Walk, Bagshot Road, Bracknell, Berks, RG12 9DY
Activities: Residential care activities for learning difficulties, mental health and substance abuse
Parent: Choice Care Group Holdings Limited
Officers: Edwina Jane Johnston, Secretary; Jonathan Green [1974] Director/Chief Operating Officer; Edwina Jane Johnston [1961] Director; Gareth David Williams [1978] Finance Director

Choice Care Group 3 Limited
Incorporated: 19 July 2013
Previous: Caledonia Choice 3 Limited
Net Worth: £60,279,036 *Total Assets:* £105,048,928
Registered Office: Linden House, Lime Walk, Bagshot Road, Bracknell, Berks, RG12 9DY
Activities: Residential care activities for learning difficulties, mental health and substance abuse
Parent: Choice Care Group 2 Limited
Officers: Edwina Jane Johnston, Secretary; Jonathan Green [1974] Director/Chief Operating Officer; Edwina Jane Johnston [1961] Director; Gareth David Williams [1978] Finance Director

Choice Care Group Holdings Limited
Incorporated: 10 July 2013 *Employees:* 1,849
Previous: Caledonia Choice Limited
Net Worth: £58,282,948 *Total Assets:* £110,112,240
Registered Office: Linden House, Lime Walk, Bagshot Road, Bracknell, Berks, RG12 9DY
Activities: Residential care activities for learning difficulties, mental health and substance abuse
Parent: Ichoice Health 3 Limited
Officers: Edwina Jane Johnston, Secretary; Jonathan Green [1974] Director/Chief Operating Officer; Edwina Jane Johnston [1961] Director; Gareth David Williams [1978] Finance Director

Choice Holdings Limited
Incorporated: 23 November 2001
Net Worth: £10,418,519 *Total Assets:* £38,518,132
Registered Office: Linden House, Lime Walk, Bagshot Road, Bracknell, Berks, RG12 9DY
Activities: Residential care activities for learning difficulties, mental health and substance abuse
Parent: Choice Care Group 3 Limited
Officers: Edwina Jane Johnston, Secretary; Jonathan Green [1974] Director/Chief Operating Officer; Edwina Jane Johnston [1961] Director; Gareth David Williams [1978] Finance Director

Choice Support
Incorporated: 1 April 2014 *Employees:* 1,217
Previous: MCCH
Net Worth: £29,994,000 *Total Assets:* £36,087,000
Registered Office: One Hermitage Court, Hermitage Lane, Maidstone, Kent, ME16 9NT
Activities: Residential care activities for learning difficulties, mental health and substance abuse
Parent: Partnership Support Group
Officers: Mark Richard Ferry, Secretary; Ian Bell [1962] Director/IT Consultant; Chris Dorey [1953] Director/Retired; Lynda Frampton [1949] Director/Retired; Peter Vincence Hasler [1958] Director; Philippa Jane Holroyd [1960] Director/Retired; Sharon Landa [1958] Director/Retired; Paul McGee [1944] Director/Consultant; Colin George Mills [1954] Director/Accountant; Oliver Arthur Seymour Mills [1951] Director/Retired; Maurice Edward Rumbold [1948] Trustee Director; Kate Victoria Wood [1970] Director

Christ's Hospital
Incorporated: 1 May 2007 *Employees:* 550
Previous: Christ's Hospital School
Net Worth: £436,816,000 *Total Assets:* £503,764,000
Registered Office: Christ's Hospital, The Avenue, Horsham, W Sussex, RH13 0LJ
Activities: General secondary education
Officers: Nicholas John Tesseyman, Secretary; Nicholas James Atkinson [1974] Director/Audit Partner; Nicholas Michael Bensted-Smith [1963] Director/Retired Investment Manager; Jan Tadeusz de Walden [1954] Director; Marianne Bernadette Fredericks [1965] Director/Common Councilman City of London; Dominic Lawrence Charleworth Fry [1959] Communications Director Marks & Spencer; Diana Anjoli Garnham [1954] Director/Portfolio Career Consultant; Thomas Garnier [1968] Director/Headteacher; Andrew Edward Gordon [1953] Director/Chartered Accountant; Robert William Judson [1962] Director; James Alexander MacLean [1969] Managing Director Contracting Engineering; Professor Michael Raymond Mainelli [1958] Professor and Director [Irish]; Delva Frances Patman [1946] Director/Chartered Surveyor; Guido Perricone [1962] Director/Chief Executive [Italian]; Christopher John Steane [1956] Director/Global Head

Chromium Acquisitions Limited
Incorporated: 5 October 2009
Net Worth: £9,493,148,672 *Total Assets:* £13,984,549,888
Registered Office: Cadbury House, Sanderson Road, Uxbridge, Middlesex, UB8 1DH
Activities: Activities of other holding companies n.e.c.
Parent: Mondelez International, Inc
Officers: Adrian John Paul Arrighi [1978] Tax Director; Michael Brendan Foye [1965] Treasury Director; John Michael Hladusz [1972] Director/Chartered Accountant; Carole Noelle Keene [1966] Director

Chromium Assets Limited
Incorporated: 5 October 2009
Net Worth: £6,845,971,968 *Total Assets:* £6,845,971,968
Registered Office: Cadbury House, Sanderson Road, Uxbridge, Middlesex, UB8 1DH
Activities: Activities of head offices
Parent: Kraft Foods Investment Holdings UK Limited
Officers: Adrian John Paul Arrighi [1978] Tax Director; Michael Brendan Foye [1965] Treasury Director; John Michael Hladusz [1972] Director/Chartered Accountant; Carole Noelle Keene [1966] Director

Chromium Suchex LLP
Incorporated: 27 October 2009
Net Worth: £4,466,366,976 *Total Assets:* £4,466,366,976
Registered Office: Cadbury House, Sanderson Road, Uxbridge, Middlesex, UB8 1DH

Chrysalis (Stanhope) Limited
Incorporated: 16 October 2006
Net Worth: £67,176 *Total Assets:* £28,434,720
Registered Office: 8 White Oak Square, London Road, Swanley, Kent, BR8 7AG
Activities: Other business support service activities n.e.c.
Parent: Chrysalis (Stanhope) Holdings Limited
Officers: Neeti Mukundrai Anand [1984] Director; Stewart Chalmers Grant [1951] Director; Angela Louise Roshier [1975] Director/Asset Management

Chubb Fire & Security Limited
Incorporated: 9 October 1953 *Employees:* 1,853
Net Worth: £166,360,000 *Total Assets:* £546,145,024
Registered Office: Littleton Road, Ashford, Middlesex, TW15 1TZ
Activities: Activities of head offices
Parent: Chubb Group Security Limited
Officers: Robert John Sloss, Secretary; Laura Jayne Wilcock, Secretary; Anthony Brennan [1966] Finance Director [Irish]; Craig Alexander Forbes [1963] Director

Chubb Fire Limited
Incorporated: 25 February 1914 *Employees:* 109
Net Worth: £356,032,992 *Total Assets:* £385,910,016
Registered Office: Littleton Road, Ashford, Middlesex, TW15 1TZ
Activities: Fire service activities
Shareholders: United Technologies Holdings Limited; Chubb Group Security Limited
Officers: Robert John Sloss, Secretary/Solicitor; Anthony Brennan [1966] Finance Director [Irish]; Craig Alexander Forbes [1963] Finance Director

Chubb Group (International) Limited
Incorporated: 25 August 1988
Net Worth: £170,246,000 *Total Assets:* £1,315,275,008
Registered Office: 1st Floor, Ash House, Littleton Road, Ashford, Middlesex, TW15 1TZ
Activities: Activities of head offices
Parent: Chubb Group Limited
Officers: Robert Sloss, Secretary; Laura Wilcock, Secretary; Neil Andrew Vincent Gregor MacGregor [1955] Director/Accounting and Controls Manager; Robert John Sloss [1967] Director/Solicitor

Chubb Group Limited
Incorporated: 18 June 1957 *Employees:* 4
Net Worth: £2,884,808,960 *Total Assets:* £10,658,702,336
Registered Office: 1st Floor, Ash House, Littleton Road, Ashford, Middlesex, TW15 1TZ
Activities: Activities of head offices
Parent: Chubb Limited
Officers: Robert Sloss, Secretary; Laura Wilcock, Secretary; Neil Andrew Vincent Gregor MacGregor [1955] Director/Accounting and Controls Manager; Robert John Sloss [1967] Director/Solicitor

Chubb Group Properties Limited
Incorporated: 21 April 1987
Net Worth: £30,906,000 *Total Assets:* £72,308,000
Registered Office: 1st Floor, Ash House, Littleton Road, Ashford, Middlesex, TW15 1TZ
Activities: Activities of head offices
Parent: Chubb Group Limited
Officers: Robert Sloss, Secretary; Laura Wilcock, Secretary; Neil Andrew Vincent Gregor MacGregor [1955] Director/Accounting and Controls Manager; Robert John Sloss [1967] Director/Solicitor

Chubb Group Security Limited
Incorporated: 1 November 1994 *Employees:* 54
Net Worth: £593,108,992 *Total Assets:* £606,934,976
Registered Office: Littleton Road, Ashford, Middlesex, TW15 1TZ
Activities: Activities of head offices
Parent: Goodrich Aftermarket Services Limited
Officers: Laura Wilcock, Secretary; Anthony Brennan [1966] Finance Director [Irish]; Robert John Sloss [1967] Director/Senior Counsel

Chubb International Holdings Limited
Incorporated: 14 December 1882
Net Worth: £687,595,008 *Total Assets:* £740,940,032
Registered Office: 1st Floor, Ash House, Littleton Road, Ashford, Middlesex, TW15 1TZ
Activities: Activities of head offices
Parent: Chubb Limited
Officers: Robert Sloss, Secretary; Laura Wilcock, Secretary; Neil Andrew Vincent Gregor MacGregor [1955] Director/Accounting and Controls Manager; Robert John Sloss [1967] Director/Solicitor

Chubb Limited
Incorporated: 17 July 2000
Net Worth: £388,857,984 *Total Assets:* £10,439,570,432
Registered Office: 1st Floor, Ash House, Littleton Road, Ashford, Middlesex, TW15 1TZ
Activities: Activities of head offices
Parent: Goodrich Inertial Limited
Officers: Robert Sloss, Secretary; Laura Wilcock, Secretary; Neil Andrew Vincent Gregor MacGregor [1955] Director/Accounting and Controls Manager; Robert John Sloss [1967] Director/Solicitor

Church & Dwight UK Limited
Incorporated: 27 August 1942 *Employees:* 272
Net Worth: £52,386,000 *Total Assets:* £77,353,000
Registered Office: Wear Bay Road, Folkestone, Kent, CT19 6PG
Activities: Manufacture of basic pharmaceutical products
Parent: Church & Dwight Co. Inc.
Officers: Paul Fair, Secretary; David James Upton, Secretary; Steven Paul Cugine [1962] Director [American]; Robert David Dancy [1962] Director; Michael Robinsohn [1968] Director [French]; David James Upton [1977] Finance Director

Church Communities UK
Incorporated: 11 June 1948
Net Worth: £34,893,544 *Total Assets:* £36,531,324
Registered Office: Darvell, Robertsbridge, E Sussex, TN32 5DR
Activities: Book publishing
Officers: Gregory John Winter, Secretary; Bernard Denman Hibbs [1981] Director/Member of Religious Order; Joseph Enoch Hine [1974] Director/Member of Religious Order [British/American]; Sarah Louise Kang [1981] Director/Member of Religious Order; Lael Andre Page [1976] Director/Member of Religious Order; Gregory John Winter [1977] Director/Member of Religious Order

Churchill Insurance Company Limited
Incorporated: 17 May 1988
Net Worth: £12,780,000 *Total Assets:* £47,799,000
Registered Office: Churchill Court, Westmoreland Road, Bromley, Kent, BR1 1DP
Activities: Non-life insurance
Parent: U K Insurance Limited
Officers: Roger Cheston Clifton, Secretary; Michael Nicholas Biggs [1952] Director/Chartered Accountant; Paul Robert Geddes [1969] Director/Bank Official; Danuta Gray [1958] Director; Mark Julian Gregory [1963] Director; Jane Carolyn Hanson [1967] Director; Michael Anthony Holliday-Williams [1970] Director; Penelope Jane James [1969] Director; Sebastian Richard Edward Cuthbert James [1966] Director/Group CEO; Fiona Catherine McBain [1961] Director; Gregor Ninian Stewart [1964] Director; Clare Eleanor Thompson [1954] Director; Doctor Richard Churchill Ward [1957] Director

Cidron Healthcare - It 3 Limited
Incorporated: 18 March 2016
Net Worth: £1,036,359,296 *Total Assets:* £1,036,360,960
Registered Office: Forum 3, Solent Business Park, Parkway South, Whiteley, Fareham, Hants, PO15 7FH
Activities: Other professional, scientific and technical activities n.e.c.
Officers: Christopher Russell Lodge [1982] Director/Investment Professional; Raj Rashmikant Shah [1968] Director/Investment Professional

Cilva Holdings Limited
Incorporated: 1 February 1989
Net Worth: £2,019,148,032 *Total Assets:* £2,019,148,032
Registered Office: Avis Budget House, Park Road, Bracknell, Berks, RG12 2EW
Activities: Activities of head offices
Parent: Avis Europe Investments Limited
Officers: Inderpal Lall, Secretary; Paul Leslie Ford [1970] Director/Chartered Accountant; Paul Edward Rollason [1979] Director/Accountant

Cine-UK Limited
Incorporated: 4 January 1995 *Employees:* 2,877
Net Worth: £66,303,000 *Total Assets:* £467,367,008
Registered Office: 8th Floor, Vantage London, Great West Road, Brentford, Middlesex, TW8 9AG
Activities: Motion picture distribution activities
Parent: Cineworld Holdings Limited
Officers: Fiona Smith, Secretary; Israel Greidinger [1961] Director/Cinema Proprietor [Israeli]; Mr Moshe Joseph Greidinger [1952] Director/Cinema Proprietor [Israeli]; Shaun Alan Jones [1970] Director; Nir Lion [1981] Director [Israeli]

Cineworld Cinemas Holdings Limited
Incorporated: 16 April 1986
Net Worth: £56,227,000 *Total Assets:* £202,770,000
Registered Office: 8th Floor, Vantage London, Great West Road, Brentford, Middlesex, TW8 9AG
Activities: Activities of head offices
Parent: Cineworld Holdings Limited
Officers: Fiona Elizabeth Smith, Secretary; Nisan Cohen [1972] Director [Israeli]; Israel Greidinger [1961] Director/Cinema Proprietor [Israeli]; Mr Moshe Joseph Greidinger [1952] Director/Cinema Proprietor [Israeli]; Shaun Alan Jones [1970] Director; Nir Lion [1981] Finance Director [Israeli]

Cineworld Cinemas Limited
Incorporated: 22 May 1985 *Employees:* 2,418
Net Worth: £66,213,000 *Total Assets:* £706,400,000
Registered Office: 8th Floor, Vantage London, Great West Road, Brentford, Middlesex, TW8 9AG
Activities: Motion picture distribution activities
Parent: Cineworld Cinemas Holdings Limited
Officers: Fiona Smith, Secretary; Israel Greidinger [1961] Director/Cinema Proprietor [Israeli]; Mr Moshe Joseph Greidinger [1952] Director/Cinema Proprietor [Israeli]; Shaun Alan Jones [1970] Director; Nir Lion [1981] Director [Israeli]

Cineworld Estates Limited
Incorporated: 23 March 1990
Net Worth: £59,475,000 *Total Assets:* £59,493,000
Registered Office: 8th Floor, Vantage London, Great West Road, Brentford, Middlesex, TW8 9AG
Activities: Other business support service activities n.e.c.
Parent: Cineworld Cinemas Limited
Officers: Fiona Elizabeth Smith, Secretary; Shaun Alan Jones [1970] Director; Nir Lion [1981] Director [Israeli]

Cineworld Group PLC
Incorporated: 23 August 2004 *Employees:* 10,232
Net Worth: £778,600,000 *Total Assets:* £1,407,200,000
Registered Office: 8th Floor, Vantage London, Great West Road, Brentford, Middlesex, TW8 9AG
Activities: Activities of other holding companies n.e.c.
Officers: Fiona Smith, Secretary; Anthony Herbert Bloom [1939] Director; Nisan Cohen [1972] Director [Israeli]; Camela Galano [1957] Director [American]; Israel Greidinger [1961] Director/Cinema Proprietor [Israeli]; Mr Moshe Joseph Greidinger [1952] Director/Cinema Proprietor [Israeli]; Alicja Kornasiewicz [1951] Director [Polish]; Dean Roderick Moore [1957] Director; Scott S. Rosenblum [1949] Director/Attorney at Law [American]; Arni Samuelsson [1942] Director/Cinema Proprietor [Icelander]; Eric Hartley Senat [1949] Director; Julie Helen Southern [1959] Director; Renana Teperberg [1977] Director [Israeli]

Cineworld Holdings Limited
Incorporated: 23 August 2004
Net Worth: £290,352,000 *Total Assets:* £623,516,032
Registered Office: 8th Floor, Vantage London, Great West Road, Brentford, Middlesex, TW8 9AG
Activities: Activities of head offices
Parent: Augustus 2 Limited
Officers: Fiona Elizabeth Smith, Secretary; Nisan Cohen [1972] Director [Israeli]; Israel Greidinger [1961] Director/Cinema Proprietor [Israeli]; Shaun Alan Jones [1970] Director; Nir Lion [1981] Director [Israeli]

Cirrus Logic UK International Holding Co. Ltd.
Incorporated: 8 August 2014
Net Worth: £1,157,641,472 *Total Assets:* £1,157,642,240
Registered Office: 3 The Sector, Newbury Business Park, London Road, Newbury, Berks, RG14 2PZ
Activities: Activities of other holding companies n.e.c.
Parent: Cirrus Logic, Inc.
Officers: Gregory Scott Thomas, Secretary; Pedro Andrade [1979] Director [American]; Thurman Klay Case [1956] Director/Vice President [American]; Allan William Hughes [1960] Director

Citizen Machinery UK Ltd
Incorporated: 24 June 1974 *Employees:* 48
Net Worth: £10,542,794 *Total Assets:* £21,732,640
Registered Office: 1 Park Avenue, Bushey, Herts, WD23 2DA
Activities: Agents involved in the sale of machinery, industrial equipment, ships and aircraft
Parent: Citizen Machinery Co., Ltd.
Officers: Jonathan Matthew Hart [1979] Director; Edward Harry James [1969] Managing Director; Hiromitsu Kamata [1963] Director/Financial Manager [Japanese]; Toshiyuki Nagasawa [1957] Director/General Manager [Japanese]; Darren Michael John Wilkins [1965] Deputy Managing Director

Citizen Watch United Kingdom, Ltd
Incorporated: 8 November 2000 *Employees:* 55
Net Worth: £16,200,105 *Total Assets:* £23,924,448
Registered Office: Citizen House, 7 Ashville Way, Wokingham, Berks, RG41 2PL
Activities: Manufacture of jewellery and related articles
Parent: Citizen Watch Company of America Inc
Officers: Brian Paul Gillingham, Secretary; Toshiyuki Furukawa [1963] Director [Japanese]; Norio Takeuchi [1958] Director [Japanese]; Takashi Tsukamoto [1975] Director [Japanese]

Citrix Global Holdings UK Limited
Incorporated: 28 September 2016
Net Worth: £4,687,946,752 *Total Assets:* £5,016,166,400
Registered Office: Building 3, Chalfont Park, Chalfont St Peter, Gerrards Cross, Bucks, SL9 0BG
Activities: Activities of other holding companies n.e.c.
Parent: Citrix Systems Inc.
Officers: David Dunn, Secretary; Caoimhe NI Ghiosain [1968] Director/International Controller [Irish]; Brian Lee Shytle [1973] Director/Vice President, Tax and Treasury, Finance & Administration [American]

Citrix R & D Limited
Incorporated: 31 July 2015 *Employees:* 241
Net Worth: £10,955,678 *Total Assets:* £47,513,728
Registered Office: Building 3, Chalfont Park, Chalfont St Peter, Gerrards Cross, Bucks, SL9 0BG
Activities: Business and domestic software development
Officers: David Dunn, Secretary; Caoimhe NI Ghiosain [1968] Director/International Controller - EMEA [Irish]; Brian Lee Shytle [1973] Director/VP, Tax and Treasury [American]

Citrix Systems UK Limited
Incorporated: 9 June 1994 *Employees:* 232
Net Worth: £79,558,768 *Total Assets:* £770,060,864
Registered Office: Building 3, Chalfont Park, Chalfont St Peter, Gerrards Cross, Bucks, SL9 0BG
Activities: Business and domestic software development
Officers: David Johnathan Dunn, Secretary; Caoimhe NI Ghiosain [1968] Director/International Controller - EMEA [Irish]; Brian Lee Shytle [1973] Director [American]

City Hotel (London) Limited
Incorporated: 6 January 2012 *Employees:* 50
Net Worth: £12,140,746 *Total Assets:* £28,924,362
Registered Office: 1 London Street, Reading, Berks, RG1 4PN
Activities: Hotels and similar accommodation
Parent: Compatriot Holdings Limited
Officers: Arpana Jaymalsinh Mangrola [1964] Director; Anthony Edward Michael Simler [1971] Director; Pritpal Singh Ahluwalia [1990] Director; Sukhpal Singh Ahluwalia [1958] Director

City Link (Cardiff) Limited
Incorporated: 22 April 1998
Net Worth Deficit: £104,000 *Total Assets:* £43,447,000
Registered Office: Astral House, Imperial Way, Watford, Herts, WD24 4WW
Activities: Activities of head offices
Parent: City Link (Cardiff) Holdings Limited
Officers: Ian David Hudson [1964] Director/Chartered Accountant; Rory John Murphy [1969] Director/Chartered Surveyor

City Technology Limited
Incorporated: 22 August 1977 *Employees:* 182
Net Worth: £66,523,000 *Total Assets:* £68,656,000
Registered Office: Honeywell House, Skimped Hill Lane, Bracknell, Berks, RG12 1EB
Activities: Other manufacturing n.e.c.
Parent: Comstack Limited
Officers: Hicham Khellafi [1979] Director [French]; John J Tus [1958] Director [American]

Citysprint (UK) Bidco Limited
Incorporated: 4 February 2016 *Employees:* 3
Net Worth Deficit: £13,633,294 *Total Assets:* £192,281,952
Registered Office: Red Central, 60 High Street, Redhill, Surrey, RH1 1SH
Activities: Activities of distribution holding companies
Parent: Citysprint (UK) Midco Limited
Officers: David Robert John Burtenshaw [1952] Director; Patrick Gallagher [1967] Director; Jessica Grace Hardy [1988] Director; Gerard Anthony Keenan [1968] Director; Andrew Steven Lyndon [1969] Director

Citysprint (UK) Group Limited
Incorporated: 26 October 2010
Net Worth Deficit: £12,285,207 *Total Assets:* £65,913,632
Registered Office: Red Central, 60 High Street, Redhill, Surrey, RH1 1SH
Activities: Dormant company
Parent: Citysprint (UK) Holdings Limited
Officers: Gerard Keenan, Secretary; Patrick Gallagher [1967] Director/Senior Executive; Gerard Anthony Keenan [1968] Director/Accountant

Citysprint (UK) Holdings Limited
Incorporated: 4 February 2016 *Employees:* 906
Net Worth: £18,866,044 *Total Assets:* £220,903,552
Registered Office: Red Central, 60 High Street, Redhill, Surrey, RH1 1SH
Activities: Activities of distribution holding companies
Shareholder: LDC V LP
Officers: David Robert John Burtenshaw [1952] Director; Patrick Gallagher [1967] Director; Jessica Grace Hardy [1988] Director; Gerard Anthony Keenan [1968] Director; Andrew Steven Lyndon [1969] Director

Citysprint (UK) Limited
Incorporated: 23 November 2001 *Employees:* 903
Net Worth: £42,261,208 *Total Assets:* £104,778,560
Registered Office: Ground Floor, Red Central, 60 High Street, Redhill, Surrey, RH1 1SH
Activities: Unlicensed carriers
Parent: The Courier and Passenger Transport Group Limited
Officers: Gerard Keenan, Secretary; Patrick Gallagher [1967] Director/Senior Executive; Gerard Keenan [1968] Director/Accountant

Citysprint (UK) Midco Limited
Incorporated: 4 February 2016
Net Worth: £1 *Total Assets:* £121,963,880
Registered Office: Red Central, 60 High Street, Redhill, Surrey, RH1 1SH
Activities: Activities of distribution holding companies
Parent: Citysprint (UK) Holdings Limited
Officers: David Robert John Burtenshaw [1952] Director; Patrick Gallagher [1967] Director; Jessica Grace Hardy [1988] Director; Gerard Anthony Keenan [1968] Director; Andrew Steven Lyndon [1969] Director

Civil and Marine (Holdings) Limited
Incorporated: 17 September 1993
Net Worth: £58,560,000 *Total Assets:* £58,560,000
Registered Office: Hanson House, 14 Castle Hill, Maidenhead, Berks, SL6 4JJ
Activities: Activities of construction holding companies
Parent: Civil and Marine Limited
Officers: Wendy Fiona Rogers, Secretary; Nicholas Arthur Dawe Benning-Prince [1974] Director/Chartered Accountant; Robert Charles Dowley [1972] Director/Chartered Accountant; Edward Alexander Gretton [1970] Director; Dr Carsten Matthias Wendt [1976] Director [German]

Civil and Marine Limited
Incorporated: 30 September 1988 *Employees:* 76
Net Worth: £359,699,008 *Total Assets:* £463,433,984
Registered Office: Hanson House, 14 Castle Hill, Maidenhead, Berks, SL6 4JJ
Activities: Manufacture of cement
Parent: Hanson Holdings Limited
Officers: Wendy Fiona Rogers, Secretary; James Alexander Claydon [1960] Director; John Godbert [1962] Director/Accountant; Edward Alexander Gretton [1970] Director/Head of Legal; Dr Carsten Matthias Wendt [1976] Director [German]; Simon Lloyd Willis [1965] Director/Chief Executive, Hanson UK

The Civil Service Benevolent Fund
Incorporated: 16 June 2010
Net Worth: £42,772,000 *Total Assets:* £45,249,000
Registered Office: 5 Anne Boleyns Walk, Cheam, Sutton, Surrey, SM3 8DY
Activities: Other business support service activities n.e.c.
Officers: Elizabeth Lucy Dymond, Secretary; Mark Eric Addison [1951] Director/Retired; Janet Mary Aiston [1965] Director of Personal Tax; Selvin Brown [1971] Director/Civil Servant; Barry Thomas Burton [1958] Director/Civil Servant; Ross Stuart Campbell [1968] Director; Vivienne Margaret Dews [1952] Director/Civil Servant; Deborah Jane Loudon [1955] Director/Recruitment Consultant; Susan Jane Owen [1955] Director/Permanent Secretary; Wendy Sara Coltman Proctor [1954] Director/Civil Servant; Jonathan Michael Russell [1963] Director/Civil Servant; Kevin Ian Sadler [1962] Director/Civil Servant; Mal Singh [1961] Director/Civil Servant

Civil Service Motoring Association,Limited (The)
Incorporated: 13 December 1930 *Employees:* 240
Net Worth: £32,932,624 *Total Assets:* £38,575,348
Registered Office: Britannia House, 21 Station Street, Brighton, BN1 4DE
Activities: Activities of other membership organisations n.e.c.
Officers: Colin John Slinn, Secretary; Carl Fillery [1966] Director/Group Chief Executive; Heather Glanville [1949] Director/Club Leader; Madeleine Grubb [1951] Director; Thomas John Howe [1954] Director; Martin George Hunter [1952] Director; Colin John Slinn [1967] Director/Accountant; Glenn Bradley Steward [1957] Director; Alan Charles Thurbon [1949] Director/Company Treasurer

Claas Financial Services Limited
Incorporated: 22 June 2006 *Employees:* 12
Net Worth: £28,452,000 *Total Assets:* £298,054,016
Registered Office: Northern Cross, Basing View, Basingstoke, Hants, RG21 4HL
Activities: Financial leasing
Shareholders: BNP Paribas Leasing Solutions Limited; Claas UK Limited
Officers: Nicholas David James, Secretary; Jean-Michel Robert Boyer [1963] Director [French]; Nicholas David James [1960] Finance & Operations Director; Carole Perrot [1967] Director/Business Manager [French]; Anthony Richard Taylor [1964] Director/Financial Services; Nicholas William Alexander Taylor [1974] Managing Director; Arthur Trevor Tyrrell [1967] Director

Clackmannanshire Schools Education Partnership (Holdings) Limited
Incorporated: 6 October 2006
Net Worth Deficit: £18,432,000 *Total Assets:* £60,522,000
Registered Office: Part First Floor, 1 Grenfell Road, Maidenhead, Berks, SL6 1HN
Activities: Financial intermediation not elsewhere classified
Parent: BBGI Sicav S.A.
Officers: Emeka Ikechi Ehenulo, Secretary; Albert Hendrik Naafs [1965] Director [Dutch]; Frank Manfred Schramm [1968] Director [German]

Clackmannanshire Schools Education Partnership Limited
Incorporated: 6 October 2006
Net Worth Deficit: £18,432,000 *Total Assets:* £60,522,000
Registered Office: Part First Floor, 1 Grenfell Road, Maidenhead, Berks, SL6 1HN
Activities: Financial intermediation not elsewhere classified
Parent: Clackmannanshire Schools Education Partnership (Holdings) Limited
Officers: Emeka Ikechi Ehenulo, Secretary; Albert Hendrik Naafs [1965] Director [Dutch]; Frank Manfred Schramm [1968] Director [German]

Clancy Docwra Limited
Incorporated: 31 March 1947 *Employees:* 2,195
Net Worth: £14,777,747 *Total Assets:* £73,155,760
Registered Office: Coppermill Lane, Harefield, Middlesex, UB9 6HZ
Activities: Construction of water projects
Parent: The Clancy Group PLC
Officers: David Pegg, Secretary; Matthew Bailey [1970] Director; Nicholas John Blaber [1968] Director/Chief Financial Officer; Matthew Stephen Canon [1979] Director/Chief Executive Officer; Dermot Michael Clancy [1951] Joint Managing Director; Kevin Thomas Clancy [1950] Contracts Director [Irish]; James Bernard Davey [1964] Director; James Seamus Augustine Keogh [1961] Director [Irish]; Jonathan Loveday [1969] Director/Chief Commercial Officer

The Clancy Group PLC
Incorporated: 25 March 1997 *Employees:* 2,314
Net Worth: £29,175,624 *Total Assets:* £101,001,464
Registered Office: Clare House, Coppermill Lane, Harefield, Middlesex, UB9 6HZ
Activities: Activities of construction holding companies
Shareholders: Kevin Thomas Clancy; Dermot Michael Clancy
Officers: David Pegg, Secretary; Nicholas John Blaber [1968] Director/Chief Financial Officer; Matthew Stephen Canon [1979] Director/Chief Executive; Dermot Michael Clancy [1951] Director/Civil Engineer; Kathleen Philomena Clancy [1925] Director/Housewife [Irish]; Kevin Thomas Clancy [1950] Director/Civil Engineer [Irish]; Mary Philomena Clancy [1948] Director/Administrator; Ian Archie Gray [1953] Director; James Seamus Augustine Keogh [1961] Director [Irish]; Jonathan Loveday [1969] Director; David Pegg [1961] Director

Clancy Plant Limited
Incorporated: 21 February 1962 *Employees:* 230
Previous: Clancy Plant Hire Limited
Net Worth: £8,433,524 *Total Assets:* £34,449,128
Registered Office: Coppermill Lane, Harefield, Middlesex, UB9 6HZ
Activities: Renting and leasing of construction and civil engineering machinery and equipment
Shareholders: Kevin Thomas Clancy; Dermot Michael Clancy; Mary Philomena Clancy
Officers: David Pegg, Secretary; Matthew Stephen Canon [1979] Director/Chief Executive Officer; Dermot Michael Clancy [1951] Joint Managing Director; Kevin Thomas Clancy [1950] Contracts Director [Irish]; Mary Philomena Clancy [1948] Director/Secretary; Bernard John Stack [1958] Director

Claremont Fan Court Foundation Limited (The)
Incorporated: 10 June 1976 *Employees:* 201
Net Worth: £31,804,604 *Total Assets:* £34,701,552
Registered Office: Claremont Fan Court School, Claremont Drive, Esher, Surrey, KT10 9LY
Activities: Pre-primary education
Officers: Jane Mary Jenkins, Secretary; Jeremy David Alton Bachelor [1948] Director/Retired; Nigel Beavor [1950] Director/Voluntary Worker; Angela Christine Bishop [1960] Director/Voluntary Work; Stephen Charles Eggins [1950] Director/Business Executive; David Alan Ford [1949] Director/Retired Teacher [American]; Julian John Gall [1955] Director/Project Manager; Gordon Frederick Hunt [1945] Director/Retired; Catherine Lindsay Jackson [1964] Director/Management Consultant; Jennifer Frances Long [1977] Director/Senior Bank Executive; Patricia Ann Rickard [1959] Director/Retired; Dr Generald Smart [1943] Director/Retired; John Andrew Sutherland [1947] Director/Educationalist and Teacher

Clarenco LLP
Incorporated: 5 February 2009 *Employees:* 188
Net Worth: £20,796,000 *Total Assets:* £21,870,000
Registered Office: Unit 6 Lancaster Court, Coronation Road, Cressex Business Park, High Wycombe, Bucks, HP12 3TD
Officers: Carol Ann Clare [1958] Member; Michael George Clare [1955] Member

T Clark & Son Limited
Incorporated: 22 April 1931 *Employees:* 5
Net Worth: £15,802,865 *Total Assets:* £20,720,190
Registered Office: Midanbury House, Woodmill Lane, Midanbury, Southampton, SO18 2NN
Activities: Other letting and operating of own or leased real estate
Parent: T Clark and Son Remuneration Trust
Officers: John George Upfield Clark, Secretary; Donald James Buckle [1938] Director/Retired; John George Upfield Clark [1936] Director/Builder; Richard Babington Clark [1974] Director/Manager

I.P. Clarke & Co. Limited
Incorporated: 17 May 1907
Total Assets: £198,687,008
Registered Office: 1 The Square, Stockley Park, Uxbridge, Middlesex, UB11 1TD
Activities: Activities of head offices
Parent: Coats Holdings Ltd
Officers: Richard Charles Reade [1973] Director; Claire Thompson [1984] Director/Solicitor

Claydon Estate LLP
Incorporated: 22 July 2011 *Employees:* 23
Net Worth: £39,862,464 *Total Assets:* £41,473,832
Registered Office: The Claydon Estate, Estate Office, Claydon Park, Middle Claydon, Bucks, MK18 2EX
Officers: Stuart John Richmond-Watson [1951] Member; Sir Edmund Ralph Verney [1950] Member; Nicholas Edmund Verney [1983] Member; Thomas Michael Wheelwright [1946] Member

CLC Group Limited
Incorporated: 5 March 1985 *Employees:* 939
Net Worth: £36,224,000 *Total Assets:* £60,182,000
Registered Office: Unit 2 Northbrook Industrial Estate, Vincent Avenue, Southampton, SO16 6PB
Activities: Activities of head offices
Parent: Hilbre Holdings Limited
Officers: Peter Benjamin Thomas Armitage [1946] Non-Executive Director Chairman; Philip Iain Armitage [1970] IT Director; Nicholas Andrew Hilton [1961] Sales Director; Simon Reeve [1966] Director

Clean Linen Services Limited
Incorporated: 9 March 1906 *Employees:* 1,391
Net Worth: £13,912,095 *Total Assets:* £55,512,176
Registered Office: Clean House, Grove Business Park, Waltham Road, White Waltham, Maidenhead, Berks, SL6 3TN
Activities: Washing and (dry-)cleaning of textile and fur products
Parent: Clean Viking Acquisition Co Limited
Officers: James Dean Kearns [1963] Director/Business Management [American]; Jason Clyde Miller [1969] Director/General Manager; Robert Cowie Steiner [1950] Director/Business Management [American]

Clean Viking Acquisition Co Limited
Incorporated: 14 December 2015 *Employees:* 3
Net Worth Deficit: £8,560,143 *Total Assets:* £60,533,956
Registered Office: Clean House, Grove Business Park, Waltham Road, White Waltham, Maidenhead, Berks, SL6 3TN
Activities: Washing and (dry-)cleaning of textile and fur products
Parent: Clean Viking Bidco Limited
Officers: James Dean Kearns [1963] Director/Business Management [American]; Jason Miller [1969] Director; Robert Cowie Steiner [1950] Director/Business Management [American]

Clean Viking Bidco Limited
Incorporated: 25 November 2014
Net Worth Deficit: £840,531 *Total Assets:* £23,648,950
Registered Office: Clean House, Grove Business Park, Waltham Road, White Waltham, Maidenhead, Berks, SL6 3TN
Activities: Washing and (dry-)cleaning of textile and fur products
Parent: Clean Viking Holdings Limited
Officers: James Dean Kearns [1963] Director/Business Management [American]; Jason Clyde Miller [1969] Director/General Manager; Robert Cowie Steiner [1950] Director/Business Management [American]

Clean Viking Holdings Limited
Incorporated: 24 November 2014 *Employees:* 1,398
Net Worth Deficit: £24,745,620 *Total Assets:* £67,360,176
Registered Office: Clean House, Grove Business Park, Waltham Road, White Waltham, Maidenhead, Berks, SL6 3TN
Activities: Washing and (dry-)cleaning of textile and fur products
Parent: Alsco Linen Services Limited
Officers: James Dean Kearns [1963] Director/Business Management [American]; Jason Clyde Miller [1969] Director/General Manager; Robert Cowie Steiner [1950] Director/Business Management [American]

Cleanland Limited
Incorporated: 1 March 1991
Net Worth: £42,399,896 *Total Assets:* £42,653,320
Registered Office: 35-37 Amersham Hill, High Wycombe, Bucks, HP13 6NU
Activities: Buying and selling of own real estate
Officers: Peter James Davies [1978] Director; Nazim Ilyas [1982] Finance Director; Tim Neil Walton [1973] Managing Director

Cleansing Service Group Limited
Incorporated: 17 March 1954 *Employees:* 495
Net Worth: £33,851,276 *Total Assets:* £51,061,864
Registered Office: Chartwell House, 5 Barnes Wallis Road, Segensworth East, Fareham, Hants, PO15 5TT
Activities: Activities of head offices
Shareholders: Heatehr Margaret Trewman Gould; Janet Hilary Hart
Officers: Brian Dollen, Secretary; Jennifer Carella Cartmell [1976] Treatment Director; Brian Dollen [1967] Director/Accountant; Heather Margaret Trewman Gould [1941] Director; Stephen Hicks [1971] HR Director; Janet Anne Mulholland [1969] Director; Neil Richards [1956] Director; Anthony Paul John Wilkinson [1946] Director/Consultant

Clearswift Holding Limited
Incorporated: 18 July 2011 *Employees:* 141
Previous: Newincco 1120 Limited
Net Worth Deficit: £8,091,000 *Total Assets:* £47,657,000
Registered Office: 1310 Waterside, Arlington Business Park, Theale, Reading, Berks, RG7 4SA
Activities: Other information technology service activities
Officers: Urs Breitmeier [1963] Director [Swiss]; Heath John Davies [1966] Director; Urs Kiener [1965] Director [Swiss]; Joseph Edward Roffey [1979] Director

Clearswift Limited
Incorporated: 9 May 1997 *Employees:* 121
Net Worth: £2,009,000 *Total Assets:* £23,649,000
Registered Office: 1310 Waterside, Arlington Business Park, Theale, Reading, Berks, RG7 4SA
Activities: Other information technology service activities
Officers: Guy Barry Bunker [1964] Director; Heath John Davies [1966] Director; Julie Anne Gordon [1974] Director; Ciaran Brendan Rafferty [1971] Sales Director; Joseph Edward Roffey [1979] Director; Maksym Schipka [1977] IT Director; Dat Thrower [1968] Director

Cleartone Group Limited
Incorporated: 4 February 2003 *Employees:* 1
Net Worth: £23,639,766 *Total Assets:* £25,346,826
Registered Office: County House, 17 Friar Street, Reading, Berks, RG1 1DB
Activities: Other telecommunications activities
Major Shareholder: Richard Charles Hill
Officers: Hannah Louise Allen, Secretary; Edward Anthony Robertson Balding [1946] Director; Oliver Charles Richard Hill [1989] Director; Richard Charles Hill [1953] Director/Engineer Consultant

Clearwater Technology Bidco Limited
Incorporated: 4 February 2015 *Employees:* 476
Net Worth Deficit: £9,633,144 *Total Assets:* £25,850,644
Registered Office: Ground Floor, Building 1, Archipelago, Lyon Way, Frimley, Camberley, Surrey, GU16 7ER
Activities: Other service activities n.e.c.
Parent: Clearwater Technology Midco Limited
Officers: David John Barrass [1951] Director; James Oliver Benfield [1974] Director; Spencer Michael Davis [1964] Director; Gary Nigel Howse [1960] Director; Andrew Perry [1973] Director/Accountant; Karl David Wharton [1961] Director

Clearwater Technology Holdco Limited
Incorporated: 8 January 2015
Net Worth Deficit: £12,080,152 *Total Assets:* £25,777,080
Registered Office: Ground Floor, Building 1, Archipelago, Lyon Way, Frimley, Camberley, Surrey, GU16 7ER
Activities: Other service activities n.e.c.
Shareholder: BCPE II General Partner LLP
Officers: David John Barrass [1951] Director; James Oliver Benfield [1974] Director; Spencer Michael Davis [1964] Director; Gary Nigel Howse [1960] Director; Andrew Perry [1973] Director/Accountant; Karl David Wharton [1961] Director

Click Entertainment Limited
Incorporated: 9 March 2009 *Employees:* 32
Net Worth: £5,100,896 *Total Assets:* £21,210,268
Registered Office: Unit 5 ZK Park, 23 Commerce Way, Croydon, Surrey, CR0 4ZS
Activities: Wholesale of electronic and telecommunications equipment and parts
Shareholder: Jake Wright
Officers: Anders Aagaard Andresen [1961] Director [Danish]; Karsten Vagn Olsen [1971] Director/Chief Operational Officer [Danish]; Jake Wright [1986] Director

Clinimed (Holdings) Limited
Incorporated: 23 August 1991 *Employees:* 643
Net Worth: £38,254,960 *Total Assets:* £57,811,084
Registered Office: Cavell House, Knaves Beech Way, Loudwater, High Wycombe, Bucks, HP10 9QY
Activities: Activities of head offices
Shareholders: Nigel Denis Piercey; Julian Mark Piercey; Daniel Jared Piercey
Officers: Suzanne Bryden, Secretary; Dr Daniel Jared Piercey [1963] Director; Julian Mark Piercey [1959] Managing Director; Nigel Denis Piercey [1954] Managing Director

Clinisys Group Limited
Incorporated: 18 December 2001 *Employees:* 3
Net Worth: £652,000 *Total Assets:* £25,175,000
Registered Office: Two Bridges, Guildford Street, Chertsey, Surrey, KT16 9AU
Activities: Business and domestic software development
Parent: QSC 1209 Limited
Officers: Jason Phillip Conley [1975] Finance Director [American]; Robert Christopher Crisci [1975] Finance Director [American]; Robin Tarquinn Morris-Weston [1970] Director; John Kenneth Stipancich [1968] Director/Vice President, General Counsel and Secretary [American]

Clinisys Solutions Limited
Incorporated: 8 December 1997 *Employees:* 120
Net Worth: £19,643,000 *Total Assets:* £49,438,000
Registered Office: Two Bridges, Guildford Street, Chertsey, Surrey, KT16 9AU
Activities: Business and domestic software development
Officers: Jason Phillip Conley [1975] Finance Director [American]; Robert Christopher Crisci [1975] Finance Director [American]; Robin Tarquinn Morris-Weston [1970] Director; John Kenneth Stipancich [1968] Director/Vice President, General Counsel and Secretary [American]

Clinphone Development Limited
Incorporated: 9 October 2003 *Employees:* 458
Net Worth Deficit: £12,744,000 *Total Assets:* £23,050,000
Registered Office: Hart House, Priestley Road, Basingstoke, Hants, RG24 9PU
Activities: Information technology consultancy activities
Parent: Perceptive Informatics UK Limited
Officers: Michael Francis Crowley III, Secretary; Michael Francis Crowley III [1969] Director/Business Executive [American]; Duncan Jamie MacDonald [1968] Director/Chief Executive Officer [British/American]

Clinphone Limited
Incorporated: 12 August 2004
Net Worth: £80,814,000 *Total Assets:* £83,951,000
Registered Office: Hart House, Priestley Road, Basingstoke, Hants, RG24 9PU
Activities: Data processing, hosting and related activities
Parent: PI UK Acquisition Company Limited
Officers: Michael Francis Crowley III, Secretary; Michael Francis Crowley III [1969] Director/Business Executive [American]; Duncan Jamie MacDonald [1968] Director/Chief Executive Officer [British/American]

The Cloud Networks Limited
Incorporated: 28 May 2004 *Employees:* 61
Net Worth: £47,020,000 *Total Assets:* £72,240,000
Registered Office: Grant Way, Isleworth, Middlesex, TW7 5QD
Activities: Other telecommunications activities
Parent: Sky UK Limited
Officers: Christopher Jon Taylor, Secretary; David Nicholas Rey [1970] Managing Director; Colin Smith [1973] Finance Director

Club Company (Group) Limited
Incorporated: 8 January 2015 *Employees:* 1,064
Net Worth: £26,399,000 *Total Assets:* £103,128,000
Registered Office: c/o Castle Royle Golf & Country Club, Bath Road, Knowl Hill, Reading, Berks, RG10 9AL
Activities: Activities of other holding companies n.e.c.
Parent: Eldrickco Limited
Officers: Paul Scott Stephens, Secretary; Thierry Delsol [1964] Director [French]; Paul Scott Stephens [1969] Director/Chartered Accountant

The Club Company Acquisitions (Holdings) Limited
Incorporated: 17 March 2004 *Employees:* 840
Net Worth: £25,683,000 *Total Assets:* £34,596,000
Registered Office: c/o Castle Royle Golf & Country Club, Bath Road, Knowl Hill, Reading, Berks, RG10 9AL
Activities: Activities of head offices
Parent: Club Company (Group) Limited
Officers: Martin Ewart Hemmings, Secretary; Thierry Delsol [1964] Director/Accountant [French]; Paul Scott Stephens [1969] Director/Chartered Accountant

J Clubb Limited
Incorporated: 30 September 1947 *Employees:* 62
Net Worth: £14,981,999 *Total Assets:* £20,621,548
Registered Office: Church Hill, Wilmington, Dartford, Kent, DA2 7DZ
Activities: Operation of gravel and sand pits; mining of clays and kaolin
Parent: Deneep Limited
Officers: Simon William Clubb [1960] Managing Director, F.C.C.A; Colin Dring [1957] Works Director; Jonathan James Lovett [1955] Commercial Director

Cluff Oil Limited
Incorporated: 18 December 1972
Net Worth: £54,890,000 *Total Assets:* £54,890,000
Registered Office: 4th Floor, Communications House, South Street, Staines upon Thames, Surrey, TW18 4PR
Activities: Activities of head offices
Officers: Kevin Patrick Ernest Davies, Secretary; Kevin Patrick Ernest Davies [1957] Director/Transitional Manager

CMG Holdco Limited
Incorporated: 19 September 2013 *Employees:* 2,242
Net Worth: £39,477,000 *Total Assets:* £131,002,000
Registered Office: Ground Floor, Q1 The Square, Randalls Way, Leatherhead, Surrey, KT22 7TW
Activities: Residential care activities for learning difficulties, mental health and substance abuse
Parent: Galaxy Group Bidco Limited
Officers: Garry Fitton, Secretary; Ruben Kumar Bhagobati [1971] Director/Partner; Malcolm Brown [1967] Director/Senior Principal; Garry John Fitton [1972] Director/Chartered Accountant; Peter Kinsey [1964] Director; Adam Ringer [1980] Investment Director; David Andrew Spruzen [1967] Director

CML Reporting Limited
Incorporated: 31 October 2007
Previous: Capita Medical Limited
Net Worth: £34,299,444 *Total Assets:* £39,176,156
Registered Office: 4th Floor, Park Gate, 161-163 Preston Road, Brighton, BN1 6AF
Activities: Other service activities n.e.c.
Parent: Premier Medical Holdings Limited
Officers: Dr Henry Otto Brunjes [1954] Director/Doctor; Dr Robert Colin Goodall [1955] Medical Director

CNM Estates (Tolworth Tower MB) Limited
Incorporated: 8 September 2015
Net Worth: £13,510,236 *Total Assets:* £54,246,356
Registered Office: Aissela, 46 High Street, Esher, Surrey, KT10 9QY
Activities: Development of building projects
Parent: CNM Estates (Tolworth Tower MBP) Limited
Officers: Wahid Samady [1961] Director/Consultant

CNM Estates (Tolworth Tower MBP) Limited
Incorporated: 7 September 2015
Net Worth: £13,506,661 *Total Assets:* £26,888,992
Registered Office: Aissela, 46 High Street, Esher, Surrey, KT10 9QY
Activities: Development of building projects
Parent: CNM Estates Holdings Limited
Officers: Wahid Samady [1961] Director/Consultant

CNM Estates (Tolworth Tower SBP) Limited
Incorporated: 7 September 2015
Net Worth: £13,516,786 *Total Assets:* £26,901,492
Registered Office: Aissela, 46 High Street, Esher, Surrey, KT10 9QY
Activities: Development of building projects
Parent: CNM Estates (Tolworth Tower MB) Limited
Officers: Wahid Samady [1961] Director/Consultant

CNM Estates Holdings Limited
Incorporated: 7 September 2015
Net Worth: £13,408,390 *Total Assets:* £28,212,946
Registered Office: Aissela, 46 High Street, Esher, Surrey, KT10 9QY
Activities: Development of building projects
Major Shareholder: Wahid Samady
Officers: Wahid Samady [1961] Director/Consultant

CNOOC Ettrick U.K. Limited
Incorporated: 13 April 2000
Previous: CNOOC Ettrick U.K Limited
Net Worth: £108,092,656 *Total Assets:* £129,054,616
Registered Office: Prospect House, 97 Oxford Road, Uxbridge, Middlesex, UB8 1LU
Activities: Extraction of crude petroleum
Parent: Nexen Petroleum U.K. Limited
Officers: Jamie David Doyle, Secretary; Jamie David Doyle [1975] Director; Zhi Fang [1962] Director [Chinese]; Ray Christopher John Riddoch [1961] Managing Director; Ian Michael Smale [1960] Director; Brent Christian Tilford [1978] Finance Director

CNOOC Petroleum Europe Limited
Incorporated: 24 April 1972 *Employees:* 590
Previous: Nexen Petroleum U.K. Limited
Net Worth: £235,028,256 *Total Assets:* £1,519,397,376
Registered Office: Prospect House, 97 Oxford Road, Uxbridge, Middlesex, UB8 1LU
Activities: Extraction of crude petroleum
Parent: CNOOC UK Limited
Officers: Jamie David Doyle, Secretary; Jamie David Doyle [1975] Director; Zhi Fang [1962] Director [Chinese]; Ray Christopher John Riddoch [1961] Managing Director; Ian Michael Smale [1960] Director; Brent Christian Tilford [1978] Finance Director

CNOOC UK Limited
Incorporated: 6 February 2013
Net Worth: £5,234,651,648 *Total Assets:* £6,177,024,512
Registered Office: Prospect House, 97 Oxford Road, Uxbridge, Middlesex, UB8 1LU
Activities: Other business support service activities n.e.c.
Parent: CNOOC Limited
Officers: Jamie David Doyle, Secretary; Jamie David Doyle [1975] Director; Zhi Fang [1962] Director [Chinese]; Ray Christopher John Riddoch [1961] Managing Director; Brent Christian Tilford [1978] Finance Director

Coast2coast Technologies Limited
Incorporated: 5 November 2003 *Employees:* 1
Net Worth: £17,251,286 *Total Assets:* £31,605,100
Registered Office: Ground Floor, 1-7 Station Road, Crawley, W Sussex, RH10 1HT
Activities: Activities of other holding companies n.e.c.
Shareholders: James Robert Bareham; Alison Callister
Officers: Jennifer Doris Petch [1982] Director

Coastal Academies Trust
Incorporated: 4 March 2011 *Employees:* 528
Net Worth: £47,747,944 *Total Assets:* £55,416,044
Registered Office: King Ethelbert School, Canterbury Road, Birchington, Kent, CT7 9BL
Activities: General secondary education
Officers: Judy Brace, Secretary; Christopher Lee Argent [1949] Director/Chartered Accountant; Robin Henry Curtis [1947] Director/Retired; Paul Jeremy Luxmoore [1960] Director/Headteacher; Claudine Ann Murray [1970] Director/HR Business Partner; Professor Carl Parsons [1948] Director/Professor; Dave Roberts [1951] Director/Retired from The Civil Service; Neil Anthony Smith [1949] Director

Coats Finance Co. Limited
Incorporated: 13 March 1991
Net Worth: £162,464,816 *Total Assets:* £598,715,840
Registered Office: 1 The Square, Stockley Park, Uxbridge, Middlesex, UB11 1TD
Activities: Other business support service activities n.e.c.
Parent: Coats Holdings Ltd
Officers: Nicholas James Kidd [1977] Director; Andrew James Stockwell [1966] Director

Coats Group Finance Company Limited
Incorporated: 7 November 2016 *Employees:* 3
Net Worth: £1,156,718,208 *Total Assets:* £1,441,565,824
Registered Office: 1 The Square, Stockley Park, Uxbridge, Middlesex, UB11 1TD
Activities: Activities of financial services holding companies
Parent: Coats PLC
Officers: Stuart John Morgan, Secretary; Simon Boddie [1960] Director; Rajiv Sharma [1966] Director [Singaporean]; Andrew James Stockwell [1966] Director

Coats Group PLC
Incorporated: 17 June 1909 *Employees:* 19,085
Previous: Guinness Peat Group PLC
Net Worth: £215,216,576 *Total Assets:* £1,002,335,232
Registered Office: 1 The Square, Stockley Park, Uxbridge, Middlesex, UB11 1TD
Activities: Activities of head offices
Officers: Stuart John Morgan, Secretary; Michael Nicholas Allen [1959] Director [New Zealander]; Simon Boddie [1960] Director; Nicholas James Douglas Bull [1952] Director; Michael Clasper [1953] Director; Anne Kathleen Fahy [1960] Director [Irish]; David Peter Gosnell [1957] Director; Hongyan Echo Lu [1974] Director [Chinese]; Frances Paxson Philip [1958] Director [American]; Richard Alan Rosling [1962] Director; Rajiv Sharma [1966] Director [Singaporean]

Coats Industrial Thread Limited
Incorporated: 13 October 1937
Net Worth: £39,971,380 *Total Assets:* £44,122,168
Registered Office: 1 The Square, Stockley Park, Uxbridge, Middlesex, UB11 1TD
Activities: Activities of head offices
Parent: Coats Group Finance Company Limited
Officers: Wai Kuen Chiang [1968] Director [Singaporean]; Richard Charles Reade [1973] Director

Coats Limited
Incorporated: 18 December 2002 *Employees:* 2
Previous: Coats PLC
Net Worth: £815,443,968 *Total Assets:* £896,296,000
Registered Office: 1 The Square, Stockley Park, Uxbridge, Middlesex, UB11 1TD
Activities: Activities of head offices
Parent: Coats Group PLC
Officers: Stuart John Morgan, Secretary; Simon Boddie [1960] Director; Rajiv Sharma [1966] Director [Singaporean]

Coca-Cola European Partners Great Britain Limited
Incorporated: 24 July 1888 *Employees:* 3,440
Previous: Coca-Cola Enterprises Limited
Net Worth: £739,393,024 *Total Assets:* £1,293,049,984
Registered Office: Pemberton House, Bakers Road, Uxbridge, Middlesex, UB8 1EZ
Activities: Manufacture of soft drinks; production of mineral waters and other bottled waters
Parent: Coca-Cola European Partners Holdings Great Britain Limited
Officers: Huma Allana, Secretary; Huma Allana [1975] Company Secretary/Director; Michael Clark [1970] Director; Leendert Pieter Den Hollander [1969] Director/Vice President & General Manager CCE Ltd [Dutch]; Frank Govaerts [1961] Director/European General Counsel [Belgian]; Ed Owen Walker [1967] Director

Coca-Cola European Partners Holdings Great Britain Limited
Incorporated: 15 March 1996
Previous: Coca-Cola Enterprises Great Britain Limited
Net Worth: £1,429,897,984 *Total Assets:* £1,720,679,040
Registered Office: Pemberton House, Bakers Road, Uxbridge, Middlesex, UB8 1EZ
Activities: Activities of head offices
Parent: Bottling Great Britain Limited
Officers: Huma Allana, Secretary; Huma Allana [1975] Company Secretary/Director; Michael Clark [1970] Director; Leendert Pieter Den Hollander [1969] Director/Vice President & General Manager CCE Ltd [Dutch]; Frank Govaerts [1961] Director/European General Counsel [Belgian]; Ed Owen Walker [1967] Director

Coca-Cola European Partners PLC
Incorporated: 4 August 2015 *Employees:* 24
Net Worth: £5,847,109,120 *Total Assets:* £15,913,583,616
Registered Office: Pemberton House, Bakers Road, Uxbridge, Middlesex, UB8 1EZ
Activities: Manufacture of soft drinks; production of mineral waters and other bottled waters
Officers: Clare Wardle, Secretary; Jan Bennink [1956] Director [Dutch]; Francisco Javier Crespo Benitez [1965] Director [American]; Christine Cross [1951] Director; Sol Daurella [1966] Director/Chairperson; Javier Ferran [1956] Director; Irial Finan [1957] Director/Executive Vice President [Irish]; Damian Paul Gammell [1970] Director [Irish]; Nathalie Laurence Gaveau [1975] Director [French]; Alvaro Gomez-Trenor Aguilar [1952] Director [Spanish]; Philip Humann [1945] Director [American]; Orrin Henry Ingram II [1960] Director [American]; Thomas Johnson [1949] Director [American]; Alfonso Libano Daurella [1954] Director [Spanish]; Mario Rotllant Sola [1951] Director [Spanish]; Jose Ignacio Comenge Sanchez Real [1951] Director [Spanish]; Garry Watts [1956] Director/Chairman of BTG PLC; Curtis Welling [1949] Director [American]

Coca-Cola European Partners Services Europe Limited
Incorporated: 19 July 1996 *Employees:* 326
Previous: Coca-Cola Enterprises Europe Limited
Net Worth: £10,440,000 *Total Assets:* £25,873,000
Registered Office: Pemberton House, Bakers Road, Uxbridge, Middlesex, UB8 1EZ
Activities: Activities of head offices
Parent: Coca-Cola European Partners Holdings Great Britain Limited
Officers: Huma Allana, Secretary; Huma Allana [1975] Company Secretary/Director; Michael Clark [1970] Director; Frank Govaerts [1961] Director/European General Counsel [Belgian]; Stephen James Lusk [1970] Director; Ed Owen Walker [1967] Director

Cochlear Europe Limited
Incorporated: 10 November 1999 *Employees:* 127
Net Worth: £77,203,344 *Total Assets:* £120,014,048
Registered Office: 6 Dashwood Lang Road, Bourne Business Park, Addlestone, Surrey, KT15 2HJ
Activities: Other human health activities
Officers: David Thomas Mark Ashton, Secretary; David Thomas Mark Ashton [1959] Director/Vice President Business Operations; Richard John Brook [1963] Director/President Europe Middle East; Brent Andrew Cubis [1964] Director [Australian]; Christian Paul Zuscak [1975] Director/Finance Manager [Australian]

Cogeco Peer 1 (UK) Ltd.
Incorporated: 21 March 2009 *Employees:* 125
Previous: Peer 1 (UK) Ltd.
Net Worth: £7,872,733 *Total Assets:* £23,828,568
Registered Office: 30-31 Town Quay, Southampton, SO14 2AQ
Activities: Other information technology service activities
Officers: Susan Bowen [1974] Director/Vice President & General Manager EMEA; Philippe Jette [1963] Director/Engineer [Canadian]

Cognita BondCo Parent Limited
Incorporated: 3 July 2015 *Employees:* 7,098
Net Worth Deficit: £5,505,000 *Total Assets:* £988,616,000
Registered Office: EMW, Seebeck House, 1 Seebeck Place, Knowlhill, Milton Keynes, Bucks, MK5 8FR
Activities: Activities of other holding companies n.e.c.
Parent: Cognita Midco Limited
Officers: Christopher Trevor Peter Jansen [1970] Director; Jayne Pinchbeck [1980] Legal Director; Michael Uzielli [1970] Finance Director

Cognita Financing PLC
Incorporated: 3 July 2015
Net Worth: £1,174,000 *Total Assets:* £433,271,008
Registered Office: EMW, Seebeck House, 1 Seebeck Place, Knowlhill, Milton Keynes, Bucks, MK5 8FR
Activities: Activities of other holding companies n.e.c.
Parent: Cognita BondCo Parent Limited
Officers: Christopher Trevor Peter Jansen [1970] Director; Jayne Pinchbeck [1980] Legal Director; Michael Uzielli [1970] Finance Director

Cognita Funding 1 Limited
Incorporated: 21 January 2009
Net Worth: £174,791,008 *Total Assets:* £174,806,000
Registered Office: Seebeck House, 1 Seebeck Place, Knowlhill, Milton Keynes, Bucks, MK5 8FR
Activities: Activities of other holding companies n.e.c.
Parent: Cognita Holdings Limited
Officers: Christopher Trevor Peter Jansen [1970] Director; Jayne Pinchbeck [1980] Legal Director; Michael Uzielli [1970] Finance Director

Cognita Holdings Limited
Incorporated: 9 November 2004 *Employees:* 6,475
Net Worth: £39,434,000 *Total Assets:* £907,203,008
Registered Office: Seebeck House, One Seebeck Place, Knowlhill, Milton Keynes, Bucks, MK5 8FR
Activities: Activities of other holding companies n.e.c.
Parent: Cognita BondCo Parent Limited
Officers: Christopher Trevor Peter Jansen [1970] Director; Jayne Pinchbeck [1980] Legal Director; Michael Uzielli [1970] Finance Director

Cognita International Holdings Limited
Incorporated: 10 May 2007
Net Worth: £35,597,000 *Total Assets:* £66,981,000
Registered Office: Seebeck House, One Seebeck Place, Knowlhill, Milton Keynes, Bucks, MK5 8FR
Activities: Activities of other holding companies n.e.c.
Parent: Cognita Limited
Officers: Christopher Trevor Peter Jansen [1970] Director; Jayne Pinchbeck [1980] Legal Director; Michael Uzielli [1970] Finance Director

Cognita Limited
Incorporated: 9 November 2004 *Employees:* 7
Net Worth Deficit: £88,138,000 *Total Assets:* £130,597,000
Registered Office: Seebeck House, One Seebeck Place, Knowlhill, Milton Keynes, Bucks, MK5 8FR
Activities: Activities of other holding companies n.e.c.
Parent: Cognita UK Holdings Limited
Officers: Christopher Trevor Peter Jansen [1970] Director; Jayne Pinchbeck [1980] Legal Director; Michael Uzielli [1970] Finance Director

Cognita Midco Limited
Incorporated: 3 July 2015
Net Worth: £507,576,992 *Total Assets:* £507,576,992
Registered Office: EMW, Seebeck House, 1 Seebeck Place, Knowlhill, Milton Keynes, Bucks, MK5 8FR
Activities: Activities of other holding companies n.e.c.
Officers: Christopher Trevor Peter Jansen [1970] Director; Jayne Pinchbeck [1980] Legal Director; Michael Uzielli [1970] Finance Director

Cognita Schools Limited
Incorporated: 4 November 1988 *Employees:* 2,424
Net Worth: £67,497,000 *Total Assets:* £152,970,000
Registered Office: Seebeck House, One Seebeck Place, Knowlhill, Milton Keynes, Bucks, MK5 8FR
Activities: Pre-primary education
Parent: Cognita Limited
Officers: Christopher Trevor Peter Jansen [1970] Director; Jayne Pinchbeck [1980] Legal Director; Stuart Stacy Rolland [1964] Director; Michael Uzielli [1970] Finance Director

Cognita UK Brazil Holdings Limited
Incorporated: 12 June 2012
Net Worth: £38,215,000 *Total Assets:* £38,215,000
Registered Office: Seebeck House, 1 Seebeck Place, Knowlhill, Milton Keynes, Bucks, MK5 8FR
Activities: Activities of other holding companies n.e.c.
Parent: Cognita Funding 1 Limited
Officers: Christopher Trevor Peter Jansen [1970] Director; Jayne Pinchbeck [1980] Legal Director; Michael Uzielli [1970] Finance Director

Cognita UK Holdings Limited
Incorporated: 23 September 2008 *Employees:* 6,475
Net Worth: £39,434,000 *Total Assets:* £907,203,008
Registered Office: Seebeck House, One Seebeck Place, Knowlhill, Milton Keynes, Bucks, MK5 8FR
Activities: Activities of other holding companies n.e.c.
Parent: Cognita Holdings Limited
Officers: Christopher Trevor Peter Jansen [1970] Director; Jayne Pinchbeck [1980] Legal Director; Michael Uzielli [1970] Finance Director

Cohort PLC
Incorporated: 23 January 2006 *Employees:* 795
Net Worth: £73,089,000 *Total Assets:* £115,573,000
Registered Office: 1 Waterside Drive, Arlington Business Park, Theale, Reading, Berks, RG7 4SW
Activities: Activities of head offices
Officers: Simon Robert Walther, Finance Director; Albert Edward Stanley Carter [1942] Director; Jeffrey Lawrence Perrin [1951] Director; Nicholas Martin Prest [1953] Director; Andrew Stephen Thomis [1964] Director; Sir Robert Walmsley [1941] Director; Simon Robert Walther [1967] Director

Coinford Holdings Limited
Incorporated: 22 April 2009 *Employees:* 125
Net Worth: £10,534,641 *Total Assets:* £36,017,072
Registered Office: Redeham Hall, 137 Redehall Road, Burstow, Surrey, RH6 9RJ
Activities: Activities of construction holding companies
Shareholders: James Gerard Hickey; Michael Anthony Hickey
Officers: James Gerard Hickey [1962] Director [Irish]; Paul David Timlin [1979] Director [Irish]

COL Newco Limited
Incorporated: 2 February 2012
Net Worth: £40,293,000 *Total Assets:* £40,321,000
Registered Office: Braboeuf Manor, St Catherines, Guildford, Surrey, GU3 1HA
Activities: Post-graduate level higher education
Parent: L-J Bidco Limited
Officers: Arkady Etingen [1979] Director

Colas Limited
Incorporated: 11 September 1991 *Employees:* 1,102
Net Worth: £35,859,000 *Total Assets:* £136,019,008
Registered Office: Wallage Lane, Rowfant, Crawley, W Sussex, RH10 4NF
Activities: Construction of roads and motorways
Parent: Colas S.A.
Officers: Graham Derek Stanton, Secretary; David Pennington Craik [1956] Director; Carl James Fergusson [1963] Director; Frederic Jean Pierre Gardes [1971] Deputy Managing Director [Swedish]; Simon Andrew Higginson [1962] Commercial Director; Donna Elizabeth Hitchcock [1971] Executive Director; Sean Francis Jeffery [1966] Executive Director; Laurent Le Boulc'h [1965] Deputy Managing Director [French]; Raphael Llobregat [1974] Regional Director BIMEA [French]; Mark David Overton [1968] Finance Director; Stewart Leishman Struthers [1958] Director

Coldunell Limited
Incorporated: 8 January 1959
Net Worth: £52,519,100 *Total Assets:* £88,482,592
Registered Office: Dawes Court House, Dawes Court, High Street, Esher, Surrey, KT10 9QD
Activities: Other letting and operating of own or leased real estate
Shareholder: David Henry Dunsdon
Officers: John Aoun, Secretary; Rita Vivienne O'Rourke, Secretary; David Henry Dunsdon [1982] Director; Rita Vivienne O'Rourke [1928] Director

Colgate Holdings
Incorporated: 8 August 1995
Net Worth: £100,000,000 *Total Assets:* £100,000,000
Registered Office: Guildford Business Park, Middleton Road, Guildford, Surrey, GU2 8JZ
Activities: Other business support service activities n.e.c.
Parent: Colgate-Palmolive Comany
Officers: Christopher Robert Burniston [1980] Associate Legal Director; Philip Durocher [1964] Director [Canadian/American]; Charalabos Klados [1967] Director/Division General Counsel [German]; Dean Pratt [1965] Finance Director

Colgate-Palmolive (U.K.) Limited
Incorporated: 7 January 1922
Net Worth: £32,711,000 *Total Assets:* £92,973,000
Registered Office: Guildford Business Park, Middleton Road, Guildford, Surrey, GU2 8JZ
Activities: Wholesale of perfume and cosmetics
Parent: Colgate-Palmolive Company
Officers: Christopher Robert Burniston [1980] Associate Legal Director; Philip Durocher [1964] Managing Director [Canadian/American]; Charalabos Klados [1967] Director/Division General Counsel [German]; Dean Pratt [1965] Finance Director

Colgate-Palmolive Finance (UK) PLC
Incorporated: 23 March 1993
Net Worth: £23,118,928 *Total Assets:* £23,144,536
Registered Office: Unit 1b Guildford Business Park, Guildford, Surrey, GU2 8JZ
Activities: Financial intermediation not elsewhere classified
Parent: Colgate Palmolive Company
Officers: Christopher Robert Burniston, Secretary; Christopher Robert Burniston [1980] Associate Legal Director; Philip Durocher [1964] Director [Canadian/American]; Charalabos Klados [1967] Director/Division General Counsel [German]; Dean Pratt [1965] Finance Director

Andrew Colin Investments Limited
Incorporated: 17 April 2013 *Employees:* 1
Net Worth: £2,834,341 *Total Assets:* £21,710,406
Registered Office: One Gloucester Place, Brighton, BN1 4AA
Activities: Activities of head offices
Major Shareholder: Andrew Jeremy Colin
Officers: Timothy Slater [1972] Director/Accountant

Collaborative Services Support (NE) Holdings Limited
Incorporated: 16 February 2009
Net Worth Deficit: £6,785,000 *Total Assets:* £31,484,000
Registered Office: 8 White Oak Square, London Road, Swanley, Kent, BR8 7AG
Activities: Activities of head offices
Parent: Palio (No 14) Limited
Officers: Keerthana Sivanathan [1988] Director/Senior Management Accountant; Neil Woodburn [1979] Director/Chartered Building Surveyor

Collaborative Services Support NE Limited
Incorporated: 5 March 2009
Net Worth Deficit: £6,785,000 *Total Assets:* £31,484,000
Registered Office: 8 White Oak Square, London Road, Swanley, Kent, BR8 7AG
Activities: Construction of commercial buildings
Parent: Collaborative Services Support (NE) Holdings Limited
Officers: Keerthana Sivanathan [1988] Director/Senior Management Accountant; Neil Woodburn [1979] Director/Chartered Building Surveyor

Collard Group Limited
Incorporated: 19 December 2008 *Employees:* 211
Net Worth: £17,548,986 *Total Assets:* £29,551,774
Registered Office: Victoria House, Victoria Road, Farnborough, Hants, GU14 7PG
Activities: Activities of head offices
Major Shareholder: Robert John Collard
Officers: John Christopher White, Secretary; Robert John Collard [1968] Director

The Collegiate Trust
Incorporated: 4 May 2012 *Employees:* 258
Previous: Riddlesdown Collegiate Academy Trust
Net Worth: £27,989,108 *Total Assets:* £31,812,864
Registered Office: Riddlesdown Collegiate, Honister Heights, Purley, Surrey, CR8 1EX
Activities: General secondary education
Officers: David Clarke, Secretary; Keith Charles Beattie [1974] Director/Management Consultant; Philip Richard Hogan [1959] Director/Retired; Fiona Margaret McSorley [1953] Director/Retired; Sylvia Doreen Moys [1959] Director/Chartered Secretary; Alastair Roseweir [1975] Director/IT; Gordon Hodge Smith [1966] Director/Headteacher

Colleycare Limited
Incorporated: 16 March 1988 *Employees:* 867
Net Worth: £58,875,964 *Total Assets:* £89,918,456
Registered Office: Old Town Court, 70 Queensway, Hemel Hempstead, Herts, HP2 5HD
Activities: Residential nursing care facilities
Parent: B & M Care Group Limited
Officers: Trinna Ann Bruton, Secretary; Trinna Ann Bruton [1967] Director; William John Hughes [1941] Director [Irish]; Rachel Ann Rodgers [1964] Director; Ian Sloan [1959] Director/Quantity Surveyor; Dr Colleen Mary Wood [1977] Director/Clinical Advisor

Collingwood College
Incorporated: 3 June 2011 *Employees:* 172
Net Worth: £21,227,100 *Total Assets:* £25,084,264
Registered Office: Collingwood College, Kingston Road, Camberley, Surrey, GU15 4AE
Activities: General secondary education
Officers: Susan Mary Rutherford, Secretary; Paul Mark Andrews [1983] Director/Teacher; Christopher Michael Bailey [1975] Director/Senior Adviser; Steven William Barker [1958] Director/Educational Governance Consultant; Quita Barnett [1963] Director/National Accounts Development Manager; Edwina Bridle [1950] Director/Horticulturist; Hugh McKerrow Cowan [1949] Director; Alison Feldman [1969] HR Director; Shaun Francis Garrett [1969] Director/Sales Manager; Vivienne Anne Garven [1971] Director/Senior Trade Mark Paralegal; Karen Jane Griffiths [1956] Director/Teacher; Samuel Edward Kay [1986] Director/Chartered Accountant; Lisa Diane Marsden [1966] Director/Accountant; Andrew Robert Mead [1969] Director/Telecommunications Architect; Marian Raine [1952] Director/In Education; Dr Lara Syneve Rachel Silverstein [1968] Director/Manager; Eden Martin Tanner [1957] Director/Teacher; Dr John William Richard Welch [1974] Director/IT; Lisa Carla Wiles [1976] Director/Teacher; David Arthur Wykes [1952] Director/Retired; Mark Zymela [1962] Director/Manager

Collins 2017 Limited
Incorporated: 30 January 2017 *Employees:* 124
Net Worth: £9,313,874 *Total Assets:* £46,422,452
Registered Office: No 1 Croydon, 12-16 Addiscombe Road, Croydon, Surrey, CR0 0XT
Activities: Development of building projects
Shareholders: Christopher David Bartram; Hannah Frances Bartram
Officers: Michael Maximillian Barrett [1970] Director/Contracts Manager; Christopher David Bartram [1967] Director/Surveyor; Hannah Frances Bartram [1968] Director/Housewife; Mary Louise Brooks [1971] Director/Chartered Accountant; Stephen Davies [1971] Director; Mark Joseph Dockery [1967] Director; Stuart James Johnson [1972] Director; Colin Payne [1969] Director; Jason Mark Warren [1968] Director

Collins Construction Ltd
Incorporated: 25 January 1956 *Employees:* 124
Previous: Collins Construction PLC
Net Worth: £7,337,646 *Total Assets:* £34,222,440
Registered Office: No 1 Croydon, 12-16 Addiscombe Road, Croydon, Surrey, CR0 0XT
Activities: Other specialised construction activities n.e.c.
Parent: Collins 2017 Limited
Officers: Christopher David Bartram, Secretary; Michael Maximillian Barrett [1970] Director/Contracts Manager; Christopher David Bartram [1967] Director/Surveyor; Hannah Frances Bartram [1968] Director/Housewife; Mary Louise Brooks [1971] Director/Chartered Accountant; Stephen Davies [1971] Director; Mark Joseph Dockery [1967] Director; Stuart James Johnson [1972] Director; Colin Payne [1969] Director; Jason Mark Warren [1968] Director

Colorado Bidco Limited
Incorporated: 10 November 2014 *Employees:* 6
Net Worth Deficit: £31,349,000 *Total Assets:* £117,112,000
Registered Office: Aspen Buildings, Apex Way, Hailsham, E Sussex, BN27 3WA
Activities: Activities of head offices
Parent: Colorado Newco Limited
Officers: Nicholas James Redman, Secretary; Hamish David William Middleton [1971] Director; Adrian William Thompson [1967] Director

Colorado Holdco Limited
Incorporated: 10 November 2014 *Employees:* 177
Net Worth Deficit: £31,884,000 *Total Assets:* £127,216,000
Registered Office: Aspen Building, Apex Way, Hailsham, E Sussex, BN27 3WA
Activities: Activities of head offices
Shareholder: 3i PE 2013-16c LP
Officers: Richard Andrew Connell [1955] Director; Jonathan Stephen Crane [1977] Director; Hamish David William Middleton [1971] Director; Adrian William Thompson [1967] Director; Peter John Wilson [1981] Director/Partner

Colorado Midco Limited
Incorporated: 10 November 2014
Net Worth: £461,000 *Total Assets:* £92,638,000
Registered Office: Aspen Building, Apex Way, Hailsham, E Sussex, BN27 3WA
Activities: Activities of head offices
Parent: Colorado Holdco Limited
Officers: Nicholas James Redman, Secretary; Hamish David William Middleton [1971] Director; Adrian William Thompson [1967] Director

Colorado Newco Limited
Incorporated: 10 November 2014
Net Worth: £1,364,000 *Total Assets:* £92,636,000
Registered Office: Aspen Buildings, Apex Way, Hailsham, E Sussex, BN27 3WA
Activities: Activities of head offices
Parent: Colorado Midco Limited
Officers: Nicholas James Redman, Secretary; Hamish David William Middleton [1971] Director; Adrian William Thompson [1967] Director

Colorcon European Holdings (No.5) Limited
Incorporated: 2 November 2012
Net Worth: £642,689,152 *Total Assets:* £695,000,000
Registered Office: Flagship House, Victory Way, Crossways, Dartford, Kent, DA2 6QD
Activities: Activities of other holding companies n.e.c.
Parent: Colorcon European Holdings (No.4) Limited
Officers: Stephen John Bachelor, Secretary; David Francis Bain [1971] Managing Director - EMEA; Stephen John Bachelor [1967] Director; Martti Tapani Hedman [1958] Director/Chief Executive Officer [Finnish]

Colorcon Limited
Incorporated: 7 January 1971 *Employees:* 252
Net Worth: £35,843,076 *Total Assets:* £81,699,008
Registered Office: Flagship House, Victory Way, Crossways, Dartford, Kent, DA2 6QD
Activities: Manufacture of basic pharmaceutical products
Parent: Colorcon European Holdings (No.5) Limited
Officers: Stephen John Bachelor, Secretary; David Francis Bain [1971] Managing Director - EMEA; Stephen John Bachelor [1967] Finance Director; Martti Tapani Hedman [1958] Director/Chief Executive Officer [Finnish]

Colt Group Limited
Incorporated: 12 May 1967 *Employees:* 1,064
Net Worth: £46,937,000 *Total Assets:* £129,117,000
Registered Office: Unit 12 The Briars, Waterberry Drive, Waterlooville, Hants, PO7 7YH
Activities: Activities of head offices
Parent: Colt Investments Limited
Officers: James Anderson Liddiard, Secretary; Andrew Jack Leitch [1967] Director/Chief Financial Officer; James Anderson Liddiard [1969] Group Legal & Commercial Director; Kenneth William Miller [1939] Director; Mark Stephen Oliver [1962] Director/Chief Executive Officer; Lindsay Poston [1953] Director; Lukas Verlage [1965] Director [German]

Colt Investments Limited
Incorporated: 19 September 1991 *Employees:* 1,060
Net Worth: £46,939,000 *Total Assets:* £129,119,000
Registered Office: Unit 12 The Briars, Waterberry Drive, Waterlooville, Hants, PO7 7YH
Activities: Activities of head offices
Officers: James Anderson Liddiard, Secretary; Jane Anne Corbisiero [1959] Director; Christina Mary Fitzsimons [1960] Director; Clare Mary Gilchrist [1961] Director; Juliette Mary Leach [1964] Director/Physiotherapist; Patricia Lebus [1942] Director; Peter O'Hea [1964] Director/Environmental Scientist; Simon O'Hea [1961] Director; Alan Ohea [1927] Director; Jerome Ohea [1933] Director; Paul Jerome Ohea [1958] Director

Columbus Bidco Limited
Incorporated: 16 August 2012
Net Worth Deficit: £6,606,000 *Total Assets:* £41,429,000
Registered Office: 74 North Street, Guildford, Surrey, GU1 4AW
Activities: Other education n.e.c.
Parent: Columbus Midco Limited
Officers: Lucy Jane Everard, Secretary; Lisa Marie Haycox [1981] Operations Director; Alan Kelsey [1949] Director/Chairman; Craig Jonathan Light [1979] Finance Director; William Stabb Mills [1966] Director; Catriona Jane Scott [1982] People Director

Columbus Midco Limited
Incorporated: 15 August 2012 *Employees:* 5
Net Worth Deficit: £11,744,000 *Total Assets:* £25,698,000
Registered Office: 74 North Street, Guildford, Surrey, GU1 4AW
Activities: Other education n.e.c.
Parent: Columbus Topco Limited
Officers: Lucy Jane Everard, Secretary; Lisa Marie Haycox [1981] Operations Director; Robert Cerdic William Hicks [1966] Director; Alan Kelsey [1949] Director/Chairman; Craig Jonathan Light [1979] Finance Director; William Stabb Mills [1966] Director; Catriona Jane Scott [1982] People Director

Columbus Topco Limited
Incorporated: 15 August 2012 *Employees:* 2,987
Net Worth Deficit: £23,499,000 *Total Assets:* £35,765,000
Registered Office: 74 North Street, Guildford, Surrey, GU1 4AW
Activities: Other education n.e.c.
Parent: Graphite Capital General Partner VII LLP
Officers: Lucy Jane Everard, Secretary; Lisa Marie Haycox [1981] Operations Director; Alan Kelsey [1949] Director/Chairman; Craig Jonathan Light [1979] Finance Director; William Stabb Mills [1966] Director; Catriona Jane Scott [1982] People Director

Combat Stress
Incorporated: 11 May 1931 *Employees:* 312
Previous: Ex-Services Mental Welfare Society
Net Worth: £19,510,000 *Total Assets:* £20,353,000
Registered Office: Tyrwhitt House, Oaklawn Road, Leatherhead, Surrey, KT22 0BX
Activities: Specialists medical practice activities
Officers: Jeffrey Malcolm Harrison, Secretary; Peter Allen [1946] Director; Sally Goldthorpe [1961] Director/HR Business Partner; Lieutenant General Andrew John Noble Graham [1956] Director; Mark Andrew Izatt [1969] Director/Communications; Calvin Cheuk Lun Manager [1973] Director/Consultant; Christian Kenneth Bowring Melville [1965] Director/Lawyer; Mary Molesworth-St.Aubyn [1942] Director/Chairman NHS Trust; Michael Peter Morrissey [1959] Director/Head of Distribution; Jan Janusz Sobieraj [1957] Director/Head of Leadership; Dr Suzy Nicola Walton [1963] Director; Professor Sir Simon Charles Wessely [1956] Director/Doctor

Combined Counties Properties Limited
Incorporated: 22 March 1978 *Employees:* 10
Net Worth: £45,769,784 *Total Assets:* £49,416,748
Registered Office: Coldunell House, Dawes Court, Esher, Surrey, KT10 9QD
Activities: Buying and selling of own real estate
Officers: John Aoun, Secretary; Rita Vivienne O'Rourke, Secretary; David Henry Dunsdon [1982] Director; Sarah Hildred Gay Dunsdon [1949] Director

Comland Commercial Limited
Incorporated: 4 November 1997 *Employees:* 10
Net Worth: £20,337,672 *Total Assets:* £24,775,468
Registered Office: Lunar House, Mercury Park, Wooburn Green, High Wycombe, Bucks, HP10 0HH
Activities: Management of real estate on a fee or contract basis
Parent: MCF Commercial Limited
Officers: Christopher Giles Martin, Secretary/Chartered Accountant; Christopher Robert Ayres [1982] Director; Stuart James Crossley [1944] Director; Christopher Giles Martin [1968] Director/Chartered Accountant

Comland Group Limited
Incorporated: 13 June 2007 *Employees:* 55
Previous: Comland Group PLC
Net Worth: £64,596,000 *Total Assets:* £76,224,000
Registered Office: Lunar House, Wooburn Green, High Wycombe, Bucks, HP10 0HH
Activities: Activities of head offices
Shareholders: Stuart James Crossley; Christopher Giles Martin
Officers: Christopher Giles Martin, Secretary/Director; Christopher Robert Ayres [1982] Director; Stuart James Crossley [1944] Director; Christopher Giles Martin [1968] Director

Comland Holdings Limited
Incorporated: 10 August 2000 *Employees:* 3
Net Worth: £12,862,180 *Total Assets:* £23,055,412
Registered Office: Lunar House, Mercury Park, Wooburn Green, High Wycombe, Bucks, HP10 0HH
Activities: Non-trading company
Parent: Comland Commercial Limited
Officers: Christopher Giles Martin, Secretary/Chartered Accountant; Christopher Robert Ayres [1982] Director; Stuart James Crossley [1944] Director; Christopher Giles Martin [1968] Director/Chartered Accountant

Commercial Freeholds & Investments Ltd
Incorporated: 12 January 2015 *Employees:* 5
Net Worth: £1,743,297 *Total Assets:* £29,262,552
Registered Office: 5 Elstree Gate, Elstree Way, Borehamwood, Herts, WD6 1JD
Activities: Development of building projects
Major Shareholder: Christopher Richard Cradock
Officers: Samantha Bolton [1972] Director; Christopher Richard Cradock [1942] Director; Francis Christoper Richard Cradock [1962] Director; Susan Margret Drake Cradock [1942] Director; Tracy Margaret Jeannie MacDonald [1964] Director

Community Homes of Intensive Care and Education Limited
Incorporated: 8 April 1992 *Employees:* 1,846
Net Worth: £9,342,403 *Total Assets:* £71,376,296
Registered Office: Linden House, Lime Walk, Bagshot Road, Bracknell, Berks, RG12 9DY
Activities: Residential care activities for the elderly and disabled
Parent: Choice Holdings Limited
Officers: Edwina Jane Johnston, Secretary; Jonathan Green [1974] Director/Chief Operating Officer; Edwina Jane Johnston [1961] Director/Chief Executive; Gareth David Williams [1978] Finance Director

Community Reinsurance Corporation Limited
Incorporated: 15 November 1972 *Employees:* 5
Net Worth: £4,638,412 *Total Assets:* £28,039,992
Registered Office: Hampden House, Great Hampden, Great Missenden, Bucks, HP16 9RD
Activities: Non-life insurance
Parent: Hampden Insurance Group Limited
Officers: Charles Guy Camroux-Oliver [1970] Director/Solicitor; Stephen Leonard Carter [1955] Director/Solicitor; Francis William Johnston [1952] Director/Chartered Accountant; Christopher John Ridgwell [1945] Executive Director; Heather Susan Russell [1961] Director/Reinsurance Manager

The Community Stadium Limited
Incorporated: 9 December 2002 *Employees:* 10
Net Worth Deficit: £11,428,026 *Total Assets:* £148,667,888
Registered Office: American Express, Community Stadium, Village Way, Brighton, BN1 9BL
Activities: Operation of sports facilities
Parent: Brighton & Hove Albion Holdings Limited
Officers: Robert Francis Comer, Secretary; Paul Barber [1967] Director; Anthony Grant Bloom [1970] Director; Raymond Alexander Bloom [1946] Director; Derek Leonard Chapman [1957] Director; Robert Francis Comer [1956] Director; Adam Stephen Franks [1971] Director; Peter Winston Patrick Godfrey [1948] Director; David Andrew Jones [1960] Director; Martin John Perry [1947] Director; Marc Louis Sugarman [1972] Director; Michelle Jane Walder [1974] Director

Commvault Systems Limited
Incorporated: 4 September 2000 *Employees:* 266
Net Worth: £18,368,376 *Total Assets:* £49,356,848
Registered Office: 3rd Floor, Apex Plaza, Forbury Road, Reading, Berks, RG1 1AX
Activities: Information technology consultancy activities
Parent: Commvault Systems International B.V
Officers: Ronald Jan Daniel Kapelle, Secretary; Brian Michael Carolan [1970] Director [American]; Neil Robert Hammer [1942] Director [American]; Warren Henry Mondschein [1969] Director [American]

Compagnie Fruitiere UK Limited
Incorporated: 30 December 1969 *Employees:* 113
Net Worth: £18,376,000 *Total Assets:* £26,638,000
Registered Office: 12 Newtons Court, Galleon Boulevard, Crossways Business Park, Dartford, Kent, DA2 6QL
Activities: Wholesale of fruit and vegetables
Major Shareholder: Robert Elie Gabriel Fabre
Officers: Jerome Ferdinand Laurent Pierre Fabre [1978] Director [French]; William Francis Feeney [1942] Director [French/American]; Gautier Christian Philippe Fischel [1982] Director/Vice President Distribution and Marketing [French]; Keith Ernest Sadler [1958] Director; Jan Baptist Van Opstal [1951] Director [French]

Compass Group Finance No. 3 Limited
Incorporated: 21 April 2016
Net Worth: £615,609,984 *Total Assets:* £619,163,008
Registered Office: Compass House, Guildford Street, Chertsey, Surrey, KT16 9BQ
Activities: Activities of head offices
Shareholders: Compass Overseas Holdings Limited; Compass Overseas Holdings No.2 Limited
Officers: Sarah Jane Sergeant [1973] Director/Accountant; Alison Rebecca Yapp [1965] Director/Solicitor

Compass Group Finance No.2 Limited
Incorporated: 28 February 1996
Net Worth: £392,780,992 *Total Assets:* £1,143,321,984
Registered Office: Compass House, Guildford Street, Chertsey, Surrey, KT16 9BQ
Activities: Activities of head offices
Parent: Compass Group PLC
Officers: Sarah Jane Sergeant [1973] Director/Accountant; Alison Rebecca Yapp [1965] Director/Solicitor

Compass Group Finance No.4 Limited
Incorporated: 25 February 2004
Net Worth: £104,034,168 *Total Assets:* £111,322,264
Registered Office: Compass House, Guildford Street, Chertsey, Surrey, KT16 9BQ
Activities: Non-trading company
Shareholders: Compass Group PLC; Compass Group Finance No.5 Limited; Walbrook Asset Management Limited
Officers: Sarah Jane Sergeant [1973] Director/Accountant; Alison Rebecca Yapp [1965] Director/Solicitor

Compass Group Holdings Public Limited Company
Incorporated: 16 January 1987
Net Worth: £3,901,499,904 *Total Assets:* £8,942,300,160
Registered Office: Compass House, Guildford Street, Chertsey, Surrey, KT16 9BQ
Activities: Event catering activities
Parent: Hospitality Holdings Limited
Officers: Alison Rebecca Yapp, Secretary; Dominic William Blakemore [1969] Director; Charles Palmer Brown [1971] Director/Accountant and Lawyer [American]; Alison Rebecca Yapp [1965] Director/Solicitor

Compass Group North America Investments Limited
Incorporated: 8 September 2005
Net Worth: £2,650,300,672 *Total Assets:* £2,889,749,248
Registered Office: Compass House, Guildford Street, Chertsey, Surrey, KT16 9BQ
Activities: Non-trading company
Parent: Compass Overseas Holdings No.2 Limited
Officers: Sarah Jane Sergeant [1973] Director/Accountant; Alison Rebecca Yapp [1965] Director/Solicitor

Compass Group North America Investments No.2
Incorporated: 16 February 2005
Net Worth: £1,572,128 *Total Assets:* £754,867,776
Registered Office: Compass House, Guildford Street, Chertsey, Surrey, KT16 9BA
Activities: Non-trading company
Parent: Compass Group Holdings PLC
Officers: Sarah Jane Sergeant [1973] Director/Accountant

Compass Group PLC
Incorporated: 29 September 2000 *Employees:* 595,841
Net Worth: £2,615,000,064 *Total Assets:* £12,266,000,384
Registered Office: Compass House, Guildford Street, Chertsey, Surrey, KT16 9BQ
Activities: Activities of head offices
Officers: Alison Rebecca Yapp, Secretary; Carol Ann Arrowsmith [1954] Director/Partner, Deloitte; John George Bason [1957] Director; Dominic William Blakemore [1969] Director; Stefan Bomhard [1967] Director [German]; John Anthony Bryant [1965] Director [American]; Gary Richard Green [1957] Director; Anne-Francoise Nesmes [1971] Director [French]; Nelson Luiz Costa Silva [1955] Director [Brazilian]; Ireena Vittal [1968] Director [Indian]; Paul Steven Walsh [1955] Director

Compass Group Procurement Limited
Incorporated: 21 February 2007
Net Worth: £9,469,000 *Total Assets:* £23,340,000
Registered Office: Compass House, Guildford Street, Chertsey, Surrey, KT16 9BQ
Activities: Event catering activities
Parent: Compass Group Holdings PLC
Officers: Paul Martin Baker [1969] Director; Sarah Jane Sergeant [1973] Director/Accountant; Venkatesh Shantaram [1972] Managing Director

Compass Hotels Chertsey
Incorporated: 4 July 2001
Net Worth: £773,878,016 *Total Assets:* £783,217,024
Registered Office: Compass House, Guildford Street, Chertsey, Surrey, KT16 9BQ
Activities: Non-trading company
Parent: Compass Overseas Holdings No.2 Limited
Officers: Sarah Jane Sergeant [1973] Director/Accountant

Compass Overseas Holdings Limited
Incorporated: 11 May 1992
Net Worth: £1,488,889,984 *Total Assets:* £1,667,874,048
Registered Office: Compass House, Guildford Street, Chertsey, Surrey, KT16 9BQ
Activities: Activities of head offices
Parent: Compass Overseas Holdings No.2 Limited
Officers: Sarah Jane Sergeant [1973] Director/Accountant; Alison Rebecca Yapp [1965] Director/Solicitor

Compass Overseas Holdings No.2 Limited
Incorporated: 11 July 1995
Net Worth: £7,930,598,912 *Total Assets:* £11,884,215,296
Registered Office: Compass House, Guildford Street, Chertsey, Surrey, KT16 9BQ
Activities: Activities of head offices
Parent: Compass Group Holdings PLC
Officers: Sarah Jane Sergeant [1973] Director/Accountant; Alison Rebecca Yapp [1965] Director/Solicitor

Compatriot Holdings Limited
Incorporated: 18 April 2011 *Employees:* 50
Net Worth: £12,140,746 *Total Assets:* £28,924,362
Registered Office: 1 London Street, Reading, Berks, RG1 4PN
Activities: Activities of other holding companies n.e.c.
Parent: Dominvs Project Company 14 Limited
Officers: Arpana Jaymalsinh Mangrola [1964] Director; Anthony Edward Michael Simler [1971] Director; Pritpal Singh Ahluwalia [1990] Director; Sukhpal Singh Aluwalia [1958] Director

The Compleat Food Group Limited
Incorporated: 21 July 2005 *Employees:* 78
Net Worth: £8,991,000 *Total Assets:* £173,102,000
Registered Office: Granville House, Gatton Park Business Centre, Wells Place, Redhill, Surrey, RH1 3AS
Activities: Combined office administrative service activities
Parent: TCFG Holdings Limited
Officers: David Jonathan Kimber, Secretary; Steven James Higginson [1960] Director; David Houghton [1972] Director/Technical Manager; Mark John Lane [1970] Director; Damian Johnson Shaw [1971] Director

Complete Cover Group Limited
Incorporated: 9 June 1998 *Employees:* 267
Previous: The A & A Group Limited
Net Worth: £14,609,000 *Total Assets:* £72,565,000
Registered Office: Elmbrook House, 18-19 Station Road, Sunbury on Thames, Surrey, TW16 6SU
Activities: Non-life insurance
Parent: Key Bidco Limited
Officers: Angela Margaret Darling [1959] Compliance Director; Shaun Ian Hooper [1972] Director/Chief Executive; Tim Paul Wills [1972] Finance Director

Compressor Products Holdings Limited
Incorporated: 23 July 2007 *Employees:* 3
Net Worth: £28,619,936 *Total Assets:* £29,029,686
Registered Office: Unit 5 Smitham Bridge Road, Hungerford, Berks, RG17 0QP
Activities: Other business support service activities n.e.c.
Parent: Enpro Industries, Inc
Officers: Julie Fogg, Secretary; Robert Savage McLean, Secretary; Christopher Drake [1970] Director/Attorney [American]; William Favenesi [1963] Director/CPI Division President [American]; Robert Savage McLean [1964] Director [American]

Computer Associates Holding Limited
Incorporated: 17 August 1998 *Employees:* 67
Net Worth: £176,902,000 *Total Assets:* £232,235,008
Registered Office: Ditton Park, Riding Court Road, Datchet, Slough, SL3 9LL
Activities: Activities of head offices
Parent: CA, Inc.
Officers: Narinder Singh Phull [1970] UKI Director FP&A; Deborah Lynn Streeter [1967] Director/VP Human Resources [American]

Computer Associates UK Limited
Incorporated: 15 January 1999 *Employees:* 171
Net Worth: £40,985,000 *Total Assets:* £82,549,000
Registered Office: Ditton Park, Riding Court Road, Datchet, Slough, SL3 9LL
Activities: Information technology consultancy activities
Parent: CA Limited
Officers: Narinder Singh Phull [1970] UKI Director FP&A; Deborah Lynn Streeter [1967] Director/VP Human Resources [American]

Computer Software Group Limited
Incorporated: 23 June 2000 *Employees:* 54
Net Worth: £43,291,000 *Total Assets:* £68,262,000
Registered Office: Ditton Park, Riding Court Road, Datchet, Berks, SL3 9LL
Activities: Other information technology service activities
Parent: Computer Software Holdings Limited
Officers: Natalie Amanda Shaw, Secretary; Andrew William Hicks [1975] Director/Chief Financial Officer; Gordon James Wilson [1960] Director

The Conair Group Limited
Incorporated: 17 September 1973 *Employees:* 99
Net Worth: £42,036,496 *Total Assets:* £71,789,208
Registered Office: Prospect Court, 3 Waterfront Business Park, Fleet, Hants, GU51 3TW
Activities: Wholesale of radio, television goods & electrical household appliances (other than records, tapes, CDs)
Parent: Babyliss SARL
Officers: Christine Marie Chessell, Secretary; Christine Marie Chessell [1965] Finance Director; Ian Christopher Nuttall [1964] Director; Anthony Verde [1959] Director of Internal Audit [American]

Connacht SPV 1 Limited
Incorporated: 7 August 2012 *Employees:* 3
Previous: Exponent (Connacht) SPV 1 Limited
Net Worth: £105,090,760 *Total Assets:* £198,085,408
Registered Office: 47-49 London Road, Redhill, Surrey, RH1 1LU
Activities: Activities of other holding companies n.e.c.
Parent: Franklin UK Bidco Ltd
Officers: Conor Flanagan, Secretary; Patrick Generald Francis Faherty [1963] Commercial Director [Irish]; Marc Frappier [1973] Director [French]; Patrick Gerard Waldron [1962] Director/Chief Executive [Irish]

Connacht SPV 2 Limited
Incorporated: 7 August 2012 *Employees:* 2
Previous: Exponent (Connacht) SPV 2 Limited
Net Worth: £156,046,288 *Total Assets:* £172,406,080
Registered Office: 47-49 London Road, Redhill, Surrey, RH1 1LU
Activities: Activities of other holding companies n.e.c.
Parent: Connacht SPV 1 Ltd
Officers: Patrick Generald Francis Faherty [1963] Director [Irish]; Patrick Gerard Waldron [1962] Director [Irish]

Connacht SPV 3 Limited
Incorporated: 7 August 2012 *Employees:* 2
Previous: Exponent (Connacht) SPV 3 Limited
Net Worth: £163,011,504 *Total Assets:* £172,441,104
Registered Office: 47-49 London Road, Redhill, Surrey, RH1 1LU
Activities: Activities of other holding companies n.e.c.
Parent: Conancht SPV 2 Ltd
Officers: Patrick Generald Francis Faherty [1963] Director [Irish]; Patrick Gerard Waldron [1962] Director [Irish]

Connor Investments (UK) LLP
Incorporated: 9 May 2007
Net Worth: £11,333,085 *Total Assets:* £24,963,888
Registered Office: 28 Wilton Road, Bexhill on Sea, E Sussex, TN40 1EZ
Officers: David Charles Connor [1959] Member; Louise Connor [1963] Member; Ellie Louise Connor [1994] LLP Member; Freddie Charles Connor [1992] LLP Member

Console Bidco Limited
Incorporated: 13 June 2014
Net Worth Deficit: £22,771,000 *Total Assets:* £150,419,008
Registered Office: Unit 10 Silverglade Business Park, Leatherhead Road, Chessington, Surrey, KT9 2QL
Activities: Management consultancy activities other than financial management
Parent: Console Lowco Limited
Officers: Helen Mary Culleton, Secretary; Helen Mary Culleton [1964] Director; James David Gordon [1972] Managing Director

Console Lowco Limited
Incorporated: 10 July 2014
Net Worth: £1 *Total Assets:* £34,227,728
Registered Office: Unit 10 Silverglade Business Park, Leatherhead Road, Chessington, Surrey, KT9 2QL
Activities: Dormant company
Parent: Console Midco Limited
Officers: Helen Mary Culleton [1964] Director; James David Gordon [1972] Managing Director

Console Midco Limited
Incorporated: 13 June 2014
Net Worth Deficit: £24,255,224 *Total Assets:* £82,102,016
Registered Office: Unit 10 Silverglade Business Park, Leatherhead Road, Chessington, Surrey, KT9 2QL
Activities: Activities of other holding companies n.e.c.
Parent: Audiotonix Limited
Officers: Helen Mary Culleton [1964] Director; James David Gordon [1972] Managing Director

Consolidated Timber Holdings Group Limited
Incorporated: 8 February 2017 *Employees:* 210
Net Worth: £9,983,359 *Total Assets:* £76,628,080
Registered Office: Clock House, Station Approach, Shepperton, Surrey, TW17 8AN
Activities: Activities of head offices
Officers: David John Colman [1962] Director; Jonathan David Leigh Gregory [1961] Director/Chartered Accountant; Simon David Holdsworth [1956] Director/Chartered Accountant; Michael James Laughlin [1961] Director; Montague John Meyer [1944] Director; Stephen Peter Sabine [1963] Director; Andrew Peter Smith [1959] Director; Andrew James Tilbury [1959] Director

Consolidated Timber Holdings Limited
Incorporated: 12 September 1988 *Employees:* 210
Net Worth: £26,268,436 *Total Assets:* £85,816,000
Registered Office: Clock House, Station Approach, Shepperton, Surrey, TW17 8AN
Activities: Activities of head offices
Parent: Consolidated Timber Holdings Group Limited
Officers: David John Colman [1962] Director/Chartered Accountant; Jonathan David Leigh Gregory [1961] Director/Chartered Accountant; Simon David Holdsworth [1956] Director/Chartered Accountant; Michael James Laughlin [1961] Director; Stephen Peter Sabine [1963] Director/Sales Executive; Andrew Peter Smith [1959] Director; Andrew James Tilbury [1959] Director/Sales Executive

Consort Healthcare (Blackburn) Funding PLC
Incorporated: 26 September 2002
Net Worth: £57,000 *Total Assets:* £109,179,000
Registered Office: 8 White Oak Square, Swanley, Kent, BR8 7AG
Activities: Other business support service activities n.e.c.
Parent: Consort Healthcare (Blackburn) Holdings Limited
Officers: James Christopher Heath [1975] Director; Mark Geoffrey David Holden [1957] Director/Asset Manager; Elena Giorgiana Wegener [1975] Director [Romanian]

Consort Healthcare (Blackburn) Holdings Limited
Incorporated: 26 September 2002
Net Worth: £4,223,000 *Total Assets:* £138,435,008
Registered Office: 8 White Oak Square, Swanley, Kent, BR8 7AG
Activities: Activities of head offices
Parent: Infrastructure Investments Holdings Limited
Officers: James Christopher Heath [1975] Director; Mark Geoffrey David Holden [1957] Director/Asset Manager; Elena Giorgiana Wegener [1975] Director [Romanian]

Consort Healthcare (Blackburn) Limited
Incorporated: 26 September 2002
Net Worth: £4,173,000 *Total Assets:* £138,435,008
Registered Office: Unit 8 White Oak Square, Swanley, Kent, BR8 7AG
Activities: Other business support service activities n.e.c.
Parent: Consort Healthcare (Blackburn) Holdings Limited
Officers: James Christopher Heath [1975] Director; Mark Geoffrey David Holden [1957] Director/Asset Manager; Elena Giorgiana Wegener [1975] Director [Romanian]

Consort Healthcare (Mid Yorkshire) Funding PLC
Incorporated: 21 November 2006
Net Worth: £50,000 *Total Assets:* £386,988,992
Registered Office: 8 White Oak Square, London Road, Swanley, Kent, BR8 7AG
Activities: Hospital activities
Parent: Consort Healthcare (Mid Yorkshire) Holdings Limited
Officers: Richard Martin Goulder [1971] Director; Mark Geoffrey David Holden [1957] Investment Director, Infrastructure

Consort Healthcare (Mid Yorkshire) Holdings Limited
Incorporated: 12 December 2006
Net Worth: £1,638,000 *Total Assets:* £395,601,984
Registered Office: 8 White Oak Square, London Road, Swanley, Kent, BR8 7AG
Activities: Hospital activities
Parent: Infrastructure Investments Holdings Limited
Officers: Richard Martin Goulder [1971] Director; Mark Geoffrey David Holden [1957] Investment Director, Infrastructure

Consort Healthcare (Mid Yorkshire) Limited
Incorporated: 21 November 2006
Net Worth: £1,588,000 *Total Assets:* £395,601,984
Registered Office: 8 White Oak Square, London Road, Swanley, Kent, BR8 7AG
Activities: Hospital activities
Parent: Consort Healthcare (Mid Yorkshire) Holdings Limited
Officers: Richard Martin Goulder [1971] Director; Mark Geoffrey David Holden [1957] Investment Director, Infrastructure

Consort Medical Finance 2010 Limited
Incorporated: 1 April 2010
Net Worth Deficit: £6,570,000 *Total Assets:* £31,327,000
Registered Office: Suite B Breakspear Park, Breakspear Way, Hemel Hempstead, Herts, HP2 4TZ
Activities: Financial intermediation not elsewhere classified
Parent: Consort Medical PLC
Officers: Andrew Leonard Jackson, Secretary; Jonathan Martin Glenn [1968] Director; Paul Andrew Hayes [1966] Director

Consort Medical Finance Limited
Incorporated: 23 December 2014
Net Worth: £23,422,132 *Total Assets:* £132,617,608
Registered Office: Suite B Breakspear Park, Breakspear Way, Hemel Hempstead, Herts, HP2 4TZ
Activities: Financial intermediation not elsewhere classified
Parent: Bespak Holdings Limited
Officers: Andrew Leonard Jackson, Secretary; Jonathan Martin Glenn [1968] Director; Paul Andrew Hayes [1966] Director

Consort Medical PLC
Incorporated: 22 March 1946 *Employees:* 2,018
Net Worth: £246,300,000 *Total Assets:* £472,100,000
Registered Office: Suite B Breakspear Park, Breakspear Way, Hemel Hempstead, Herts, HP2 4TZ
Activities: Manufacture of medical and dental instruments and supplies
Officers: Andrew Leonard Jackson, Secretary; Christopher David Brinsmead [1959] Director; Stephen Paul Crummett [1965] Director; Dr Peter John Fellner [1943] Director; Maria Charlotta Ginman [1965] Director [Finnish]; Jonathan Martin Glenn [1968] Director/Chief Executive Officer; Paul Andrew Hayes [1966] Director; Dr Andrew Joseph Hosty [1965] Director; Dr William John Jenkins [1947] Director; Ian James Nicholson [1960] Director

Constantine Group Limited
Incorporated: 12 February 1960 *Employees:* 225
Net Worth: £50,158,000 *Total Assets:* £77,407,000
Registered Office: First Floor, River Court, The Old Mill Office Park, Mill Lane, Godalming, Surrey, GU7 1EZ
Activities: Activities of head offices
Shareholder: George Vernon
Officers: Dominic Lovett Akers-Douglas [1979] Director; Kathleen Child-Villiers [1965] Director/Banker [American]; Rossanna Mary Anderson Harrison [1976] Director; Alastair John Vernon Prescot [1960] Director; Nigel Kenrick Grosvenor Prescot [1962] Director

Constantine Wind Energy Limited
Incorporated: 8 June 2011 *Employees:* 32
Net Worth: £1,438,951 *Total Assets:* £71,529,256
Registered Office: First Floor, River Court, The Old Mill Office Park, Mill Lane, Godalming, Surrey, GU7 1EZ
Activities: Other business support service activities n.e.c.
Shareholder: Constantine Energy Limited
Officers: Dominic Lovett Akers-Douglas [1979] Director; Jonathan Charles Stuart Chenevix Trench [1961] Director/Business Manager; Anthony Leigh de Normann [1961] Director/Business Manager; Bruce John Alexander Hutt [1965] Director; Nigel Kenrick Grosvenor Prescot [1962] Director

Construction Industry Solutions Limited
Incorporated: 21 July 1986 *Employees:* 192
Net Worth: £11,979,670 *Total Assets:* £26,744,806
Registered Office: Coins Building, 11 St Laurence Way, Slough, Berks, SL1 2EA
Activities: Business and domestic software development
Parent: CSB Holdings
Officers: Adrian Halls, Secretary; Timothy Peter Armitage [1965] Director; Nigel Leslie Cope [1957] Director; Joanne Franklin [1966] Commercial Director; Michael Timothy James [1961] Sales Director; Derek Leaver [1952] Director; Lawrence John Sullivan [1953] Director

Contact Technologies UK Limited
Incorporated: 17 November 2006
Net Worth: £15,817,375 *Total Assets:* £21,736,164
Registered Office: c/o APEM Components Ltd, Drakes Drive, Long Crendon, Bucks, HP18 9BA
Activities: Activities of head offices
Officers: Joel Rene Gerard Becquet [1957] Director/Chief Financial Officer [French]; James Peter Minton Cooper [1975] Managing Director; Marc Francois Jean-Marie Enjalbert [1962] Director/President [French]

Contemplation Holdings Limited
Incorporated: 9 September 2003 *Employees:* 392
Net Worth: £10,679,037 *Total Assets:* £22,461,094
Registered Office: 19a Picton House, Hussar Court, Waterlooville, Hants, PO7 7SQ
Activities: Activities of head offices
Shareholder: Peter John Whotton
Officers: Nigel Stuart Craig [1956] Director/Solicitor; David Kingsley Glover [1940] Director/Retired; Clare Louise Norris [1970] Director; Peter John Whotton [1948] Director/Accountant

Continental Investment Limited
Incorporated: 14 April 1989
Net Worth: £20,687,000 *Total Assets:* £20,695,000
Registered Office: Continental House, 191 High Street, Yiewsley, West Drayton, Middlesex, UB7 7XW
Activities: Non-trading company
Parent: Continental U.K. Group Holdings Limited
Officers: Matthew Owen, Secretary; David Thomas Smith [1965] Finance Director; Johannes Suttmeyer [1959] Director/Lawyer [German]

Continental Trade and Commodity Services Limited
Incorporated: 2 June 1977 *Employees:* 54
Net Worth: £2,577,242 *Total Assets:* £30,833,654
Registered Office: Alexander House, 31-39 London Road, Sevenoaks, Kent, TN13 1AR
Activities: Non-specialised wholesale of food, beverages and tobacco
Officers: Teunis Snoek [1948] Director [Dutch]

Continental Tyre Group Ltd.
Incorporated: 28 January 1935 *Employees:* 160
Net Worth: £50,891,000 *Total Assets:* £155,530,000
Registered Office: Continental House, 191 High Street, Yiewsley, West Drayton, Middlesex, UB7 7XW
Activities: Wholesale trade of motor vehicle parts and accessories
Parent: Continental Tyres Limited
Officers: Matthew Owen, Secretary; Arthur Jordan Gregg [1962] Sales & Marketing Director; David Thomas Smith [1965] Managing Director

Continental U.K. Group Holdings Limited
Incorporated: 15 May 1956
Net Worth: £51,527,000 *Total Assets:* £212,311,008
Registered Office: 191-195 High Street, Yiewsley, West Drayton, Middlesex, UB7 7XW
Activities: Activities of head offices
Parent: Continental Aktiengesellschaft
Officers: Matthew Owen, Secretary; Gerd Bartels [1967] Director/Business Executive [German]; David Thomas Smith [1965] Managing Director; Johannes Suttmeyer [1959] Director/Lawyer [German]

Continua Limited
Incorporated: 14 November 1994 *Employees:* 15
Net Worth: £33,536,000 *Total Assets:* £35,705,000
Registered Office: Riverview, Oxford Road, Uxbridge, Middlesex, UB8 1HS
Activities: Other business support service activities n.e.c.
Parent: Xerox Limited
Officers: Mark Christopher Canons [1963] Managing Director; Stephen Charles Dillon [1944] Director/Solicitor; David Brian Dyas [1963] Director/President, UK & Ireland, Eurasia, India, MEA; Rodney Noonoo [1962] Director/CFO, UK & Ireland, Eurasia, India, MEA [American]

Convatec Group PLC
Incorporated: 6 September 2016 *Employees:* 9,541
Net Worth: £1,523,800,064 *Total Assets:* £3,800,900,096
Registered Office: 3 Forbury Place, 23 Forbury Road, Reading, Berks, RG1 3JH
Activities: Other service activities n.e.c.
Officers: Clare Jane Bates, Secretary; Rick Dale Anderson [1960] Director [American]; Dr Regina Benjamin [1956] Director/Doctor [American]; Margaret Ewing [1955] Director/Chartered Accountant; Sir Christopher Charles Gent [1948] Director; Steven John Holliday [1956] Director; Jens Jesper Ovesen [1959] Director [Danish]; Dr Rosalind Catherine Rivaz [1955] Director; Sten Scheibye [1951] Director [Danish]; Frank Schulkes [1961] Director/Chief Financial Officer [Dutch]

Convergence Pharmaceuticals Holdings Limited
Incorporated: 7 April 2011
Net Worth: £25,691,120 *Total Assets:* £25,782,080
Registered Office: 70 Norden Road, Maidenhead, Berks, SL6 4AY
Activities: Research and experimental development on biotechnology
Parent: Silver Acquisition Co Limited
Officers: Steven John Green [1977] Director; Trevor Anthony Mill [1971] Director/Vice President, Regulatory Affairs

Convergence Pharmaceuticals Limited
Incorporated: 6 January 2015 *Employees:* 11
Net Worth Deficit: £20,244,908 *Total Assets:* £244,148,848
Registered Office: 70 Norden Road, Maidenhead, Berks, SL6 4AY
Activities: Research and experimental development on biotechnology
Parent: Biogen Inc.
Officers: Steven John Green [1977] Finance Director; Trevor Anthony Mill [1971] Director/Vice President, Regulatory Affairs

Conway Aecom Limited
Incorporated: 27 November 2012 *Employees:* 143
Net Worth: £1,277,084 *Total Assets:* £24,222,362
Registered Office: Conway House, Vestry Road, Sevenoaks, Kent, TN14 5EL
Activities: Construction of roads and motorways
Shareholders: F M Conway Ltd; AECOM Ltd
Officers: David Ian Bennett [1966] Director; Michael Joseph Conway [1955] Director; David Thomas Donnelly [1953] Director; Andrew Stephen Hansen [1967] Director; Rory Ian Poole [1969] Director

F M Conway Limited
Incorporated: 25 October 1961 *Employees:* 1,469
Net Worth: £80,021,264 *Total Assets:* £255,916,480
Registered Office: Conway House, Vestry Road, Sevenoaks, Kent, TN14 5EL
Activities: Construction of roads and motorways
Major Shareholder: Michael Joseph Conway
Officers: Kim Conway [1957] Director/Secretary; Michael Joseph Conway [1955] Director/Public Works Contractor; David Thomas Donnelly [1953] Director; John William Forecast [1952] Director; Joanne Garwood [1981] Director; Andrew Stephen Hansen [1967] Director; Christopher Webster [1958] Director; Ronald John Woodland [1947] Director/Lawyer

Richard Cook Limited
Incorporated: 27 May 1964 *Employees:* 5
Net Worth: £20,034,740 *Total Assets:* £21,089,582
Registered Office: 26 Windsor Street, Chertsey, Surrey, KT16 8AS
Activities: Buying and selling of own real estate
Shareholders: Richard Cook; Henry Richard Cook; Chania Victoria Cook
Officers: Henry Richard Cook, Secretary; Chania Victoria Cook [1982] Marketing Director; Henry Richard Cook [1973] Director/Property Dealer; Richard Cook [1943] Director; Susan Camilla Cook [1946] Director/Business Executive

Cook Trading Limited
Incorporated: 6 December 2002 *Employees:* 886
Net Worth: £9,252,467 *Total Assets:* £24,970,496
Registered Office: The Cook Kitchen, Eurolink Way, Sittingbourne, Kent, ME10 3HH
Activities: Manufacture of other food products n.e.c.
Officers: Quintin John Neil Martin Hogg, Secretary; Rosalie Anne Brown [1975] Director/Chief Operating Officer; Nicholas John Candler [1963] Director/Chairman; Andrew Elliot Perry [1945] Director; Edward Andrew Perry [1971] Director/Retailer; James Elliot Perry [1972] Director

Coombe Academy Trust
Incorporated: 11 January 2012 *Employees:* 311
Previous: The Coombe Secondary Schools Academy Trust
Net Worth: £39,844,000 *Total Assets:* £43,633,000
Registered Office: c/o Coombe Boys School, College Gardens, Blakes Lane, New Malden, Surrey, KT3 6NU
Activities: General secondary education
Officers: Diana Mary Brotherston [1955] Director/Retired; Alan David Burbridge [1944] Director/Consultant; Judith Catherine Davies [1945] Director/Retired; Janet Elizabeth Galloway [1966] Director/Solicitor; Margaret Hunnaball [1960] Director/Retired; Derek James Morgan [1953] Director/Businessman; Naomi Vijeyarani Sellayah [1960] Director/Accountant; Emma Katherine Thomas [1979] Deputy Director of Finance; Deborah Ann Walls [1964] Director/Headteacher; Marion Webb [1950] Director/Retired

Cooper Estates Limited
Incorporated: 14 December 1933 *Employees:* 13
Net Worth: £39,523,572 *Total Assets:* £48,811,544
Registered Office: Claremont House, 65c Main Road, Longfield, Kent, DA3 7QT
Activities: Development of building projects
Officers: Wendy Caroline Parker, Secretary; David Gough Cooper [1975] Director/Surveyor; George Ian Gough Cooper [1948] Director/Builder; Henry William Gough-Cooper [1950] Director/Farmer; James Henry Gough-Cooper [1968] Director/Accountant; Jennifer Gough-Cooper [1942] Director/Exhibition Organiser; Malcolm Keith Honey [1946] Director/Chartered Surveyor; David Howard Scotton [1955] Director/Architect

CooperSurgical Holdings Limited
Incorporated: 18 November 2015
Net Worth: £124,282,112 *Total Assets:* £242,641,264
Registered Office: Delta Park, 8 Concorde Way, Segensworth North, Fareham, Hants, PO15 5RL
Activities: Activities of other holding companies n.e.c.
Parent: The Cooper Companies, Inc.
Officers: Brian George Andrews [1978] Director/Corporate Executive [American]; Kerry Lee Blair [1957] Director/Corporate Executive [American]; Randal Louis Golden [1961] Director/Corporate Executive [American]; Agostino Ricupati [1967] Director/Corporate Executive [American]; Alan Thompson Tucker [1963] Director/Chief Financial Officer [American]

CooperVision (UK) Holdings Limited
Incorporated: 13 May 2014
Net Worth: £530,695,200 *Total Assets:* £759,608,320
Registered Office: Delta Park, Concorde Way, Segensworth North, Fareham, Hants, PO15 5RL
Activities: Other business support service activities n.e.c.
Parent: CooperVision International Holding Company, L.P.
Officers: Brian George Andrews [1978] Director/Corporate Executive [American]; Richard Michael Cheshire [1969] Finance Director; Randal Louis Golden [1961] Director/Corporate Executive [American]; Mark Stephen Harty [1962] Director/President Europe; Agostino Ricupati [1967] Director/Corporate Executive [American]

CooperVision Lens Care Limited
Incorporated: 11 September 1972
Previous: Sauflon Pharmaceuticals Limited
Net Worth: £69,024,000 *Total Assets:* £75,802,000
Registered Office: Delta Park, Concorde Way, Segensworth North, Fareham, Hants, PO15 5RL
Activities: Wholesale of pharmaceutical goods
Parent: CooperVision (UK) Holdings Limited
Officers: Brian George Andrews [1978] Director/Corporate Executive [American]; Kevin Paul Barrett [1959] Director; Richard Michael Cheshire [1969] Finance Director; Randal Louis Golden [1961] Director/Corporate Executive [American]; Mark Stephen Harty [1962] Director/President, Europe; Stephen Mathieson [1967] Managing Director; Agostino Ricupati [1967] Director/Corporate Executive [American]; Michael Francis Wilkinson [1962] Director/General Manager - Ace Region

CooperVision Limited
Incorporated: 17 December 1998 *Employees:* 12
Net Worth: £39,830,000 *Total Assets:* £69,786,000
Registered Office: Delta Park, Concorde Way, Segensworth North, Fareham, Hants, PO15 5RL
Activities: Manufacture of medical and dental instruments and supplies
Parent: CooperVision (UK) Holdings Limted
Officers: Brian George Andrews [1978] Director/Corporate Executive [American]; Richard Michael Cheshire [1969] Finance Director; Randal Louis Golden [1961] Director/Corporate Executive [American]; Mark Stephen Harty [1962] Director/President, Europe; Agostino Ricupati [1967] Director/Corporate Executive [American]; Michael Francis Wilkinson [1962] Director/Regional President and VP of Marketing, EMEA

CooperVision Manufacturing Limited
Incorporated: 5 August 1992 *Employees:* 2,613
Net Worth: £291,244,000 *Total Assets:* £431,320,000
Registered Office: Delta Park, Concorde Way, Segensworth North, Fareham, Hants, PO15 5RL
Activities: Manufacture of medical and dental instruments and supplies
Parent: CooperVision (UK) Holdings Limited
Officers: Brian George Andrews [1978] Director/Corporate Executive [American]; Kevin Paul Barrett [1959] Director; Richard Michael Cheshire [1969] Finance Director; Randal Louis Golden [1961] Director/Corporate Executive [American]; Mark Stephen Harty [1962] Director/President, Europe; Stephen Mathieson [1967] Managing Director; Agostino Ricupati [1967] Director/Corporate Executive [American]

Copart Europe Limited
Incorporated: 3 April 2007
Net Worth Deficit: £9,433,000 *Total Assets:* £134,063,000
Registered Office: Acrey Fields, Woburn Road, Wootton, Beds, MK43 9EJ
Activities: Activities of other holding companies n.e.c.
Parent: CPRT LLP
Officers: Aaron Jayson Adair [1969] Director/Chief Executive Officer [American]; Jonathan David Canning [1972] Director/General Counsel; Gregory Depasquale [1968] Director/SVP, General Counsel and Secretary of Copart, Inc [American]; William Easley Franklin [1956] Director/Chief Financial Officer [American]; Nigel James Paget [1966] Managing Director

Copart UK Limited
Incorporated: 28 March 1968 *Employees:* 765
Net Worth: £81,679,000 *Total Assets:* £140,756,000
Registered Office: Acrey Fields, Woburn Road, Wootton, Beds, MK43 9EJ
Activities: Sale of used cars and light motor vehicles
Parent: Universal Salvage Limited
Officers: Aaron Jayson Adair [1969] Director/Chief Executive Officer [American]; Jonathan David Canning [1972] Director/General Counsel; Gregory Depasquale [1968] Director/SVP, General Counsel and Secretary of Copart, Inc [American]; William Easley Franklin [1956] Director/Chief Financial Officer [American]; Nigel James Paget [1966] Managing Director; Simon Sheldon-Wilson [1969] Director; Paul Anthony Styer [1956] Director/General Counsel [American]

Copthorne Hotel Holdings Limited
Incorporated: 29 April 1959
Net Worth: £210,080,992 *Total Assets:* £248,588,000
Registered Office: Victoria House, Victoria Road, Horley, Surrey, RH6 7AF
Activities: Activities of head offices
Parent: Millennium & Copthorne Hotels PLC
Officers: Jonathon MacKenzie Grech [1977] Director/Senior VP Group Legal Counsel

Copthorne Hotels Limited
Incorporated: 2 May 1963 *Employees:* 63
Net Worth: £52,610,000 *Total Assets:* £81,507,000
Registered Office: Victoria House, Victoria Road, Horley, Surrey, RH6 7AF
Activities: Activities of head offices
Parent: Copthorne Hotel Holdings Limited
Officers: Jonathon MacKenzie Grech [1977] Director/Senior VP Group Legal Counsel; Clive Anthony Harrington [1967] Director/Chief Commercial Officer

Cordant Cleaning Limited
Incorporated: 23 June 1981 *Employees:* 2,649
Previous: Dynamiq Cleaning Limited
Net Worth: £5,075,506 *Total Assets:* £23,836,580
Registered Office: Chevron House, 346 Long Lane, Hillingdon, Middlesex, UB10 9PF
Activities: General cleaning of buildings
Parent: Cordant Security Limited
Officers: Alan Connor, Secretary; Chris Martin Kenneally [1960] Director; Jack Rainer Ullmann [1928] Director; Phillip Lionel Ullmann [1964] Director

Cordant Group PLC
Incorporated: 12 June 1997 *Employees:* 39,513
Net Worth: £19,937,000 *Total Assets:* £242,836,992
Registered Office: Chevron House, 346 Long Lane, Hillingdon, Middlesex, UB10 9PF
Activities: Other service activities n.e.c.
Shareholders: Jack Ullmann; Marianne Flora Ullmann; Phillip Ullmann
Officers: Alan Connor, Secretary; Alan Connor [1976] Director; Richard Mark Gerver [1969] Director; Chris Martin Kenneally [1960] Director; Daniel Liebert [1964] Director; Ken Steers [1969] Director; Deborah Miriam Ullman [1968] Director; Harry Ullmann [1931] Director; Jack Rainer Ullmann [1928] Director; Phillip Lionel Ullmann [1964] Director; Uri Ullmann [1976] Director

Cordant People Limited
Incorporated: 9 August 1991 *Employees:* 4,921
Previous: Prime Time Recruitment Limited
Net Worth: £9,203,971 *Total Assets:* £79,454,632
Registered Office: Chevron House, 346 Long Lane, Hillingdon, Middlesex, UB10 9PF
Activities: Temporary employment agency activities
Parent: Cordant Group PLC
Officers: Alan Connor, Secretary; Chris Martin Kenneally [1960] Director; Jack Rainer Ullmann [1928] Director; Phillip Lionel Ullmann [1964] Director

Cordant Security Limited
Incorporated: 31 January 1996 *Employees:* 4,123
Previous: Advance Security UK Limited
Net Worth: £12,959,835 *Total Assets:* £36,478,744
Registered Office: Chevron House, Long Lane, Hillingdon, Uxbridge, Middlesex, UB10 9PF
Activities: Other service activities n.e.c.
Parent: Cordant Group PLC
Officers: Alan Connor, Secretary/Director; Chris Martin Kenneally [1960] Director; Jack Rainer Ullmann [1928] Director; Phillip Lionel Ullmann [1964] Director

Cordek Limited
Incorporated: 27 November 1973 *Employees:* 71
Net Worth: £21,027,178 *Total Assets:* £25,904,564
Registered Office: Spring Copse Business Park, Stane Street, Slinfold, Horsham, W Sussex, RH13 0SZ
Activities: Manufacture of builders ware of plastic
Officers: Grant Naris, Secretary; Patrick Henry Fane [1949] Director; Stephen Hearn [1964] Director; Grant Naris [1962] Director/Accountant; William Robert Oliver [1944] Director/Civil Engineer; Christopher Nigel Poland [1972] Operations Director; Alastair Charles Seaton [1958] Director; John Rodney White [1942] Director/Chairman; Rosemary Ann White [1952] Director

Core Property Developments Limited
Incorporated: 19 December 2013
Net Worth: £10,994,914 *Total Assets:* £20,796,380
Registered Office: 35 Ruddlesway, Windsor, Berks, SL4 5SF
Activities: Development of building projects
Shareholders: Kulwinder Singh Dhaliwal; Darbara Singh Dhanoa
Officers: Kulwinder Singh Dhaliwal [1962] Director; Darbara Singh Dhanoa [1961] Managing Director

Cornerstone Telecommunications Infrastructure Limited
Incorporated: 29 May 2012 *Employees:* 124
Net Worth: £518,113,984 *Total Assets:* £1,359,960,960
Registered Office: Hive 2, 1530 Arlington Business Park, Theale, Reading, Berks, RG7 4SA
Activities: Other telecommunications activities
Shareholders: Vodafone Mobile Network Limited; 02 Networks Limited
Officers: Belinda Ann Fawcett, Secretary; Laura Patricia Fernandez [1972] Finance Director [Italian]; Derek McManus [1965] Director; Brendan O'Reilly [1978] Director/Chief Network Officer; Scott James Petty [1968] Director [Australian]; Emanuele Tournon [1960] Finance Director [Italian]; David Michael Wormald [1968] Director/Head of Commercial Finance - Technology

Cornwall Energy Recovery Holdings Ltd
Incorporated: 15 February 2006
Previous: SITA Cornwall Holdings Limited
Net Worth: £9,368,000 *Total Assets:* £255,950,000
Registered Office: Suez House, Grenfell Road, Maidenhead, Berks, SL6 1ES
Activities: Activities of head offices
Shareholders: Suez Recycling and Recovery UK Ltd; I-Environment Investments Limited; PIP Infrastructure Investments (No 5) Limited
Officers: Nicholas Tommy Cole [1978] Investment Director; Florent Thierry Antoine Duval [1976] Director/Chief Finance Officer [French]; Rahul Dipinkumar Kadiwar [1984] Director/Head of Business Development; Belinda Faith Knox [1972] Investment Director; Graham Arthur McKenna-Mayes [1968] Director/Public Sector Commercial Manager; Ian Anthony Sexton [1956] Director/Chairman; Yuji Suzuki [1970] Managing Director [Japanese]

Cornwall Energy Recovery Ltd
Incorporated: 2 February 2006
Previous: SITA Cornwall Limited
Net Worth: £9,368,000 *Total Assets:* £255,950,000
Registered Office: Suez House, Grenfell Road, Maidenhead, Berks, SL6 1ES
Activities: Collection of non-hazardous waste
Parent: Cornwall Energy Recovery Holdings Ltd
Officers: Nicholas Tommy Cole [1978] Investment Director; Florent Thierry Antoine Duval [1976] Director/Chief Finance Officer [French]; Rahul Dipinkumar Kadiwar [1984] Director/Head of Business Development; Belinda Faith Knox [1972] Investment Director; Graham Arthur McKenna-Mayes [1968] Director/Chief Operating Officer; Ian Anthony Sexton [1956] Director/Chairman; Yuji Suzuki [1970] Managing Director [Japanese]

Corona Energy Limited
Incorporated: 22 August 1996
Net Worth: £15,665,727 *Total Assets:* £22,062,484
Registered Office: Building 2, Level 2, Croxley Park, Watford, Herts, WD18 8YA
Activities: Activities of head offices
Parent: Macquarie Corona Energy Holdings Limited
Officers: Shaheda Begum Thomas, Secretary; Neil Trevor Mitchell [1974] Commercial Director; Philip Morton [1968] Finance Director; Paul Christian Plewman [1972] Director/Banker [Irish]

Corona Energy Retail 1 Limited
Incorporated: 22 August 1996 *Employees:* 212
Net Worth: £11,361,115 *Total Assets:* £34,249,204
Registered Office: Building 2, Level 2, Croxley Park, Watford, Herts, WD18 8YA
Activities: Trade of gas through mains
Parent: Corona Energy Limited
Officers: Shaheda Begum Thomas, Secretary; Neil Trevor Mitchell [1974] Commercial Director; Philip Morton [1968] Finance Director; Paul Christian Plewman [1972] Director/Banker [Irish]

Corona Energy Retail 4 Limited
Incorporated: 11 March 1993
Net Worth: £7,582,111 *Total Assets:* £118,481,440
Registered Office: Building 2, Level 2, Croxley Park, Watford, Herts, WD18 8YA
Activities: Trade of electricity
Parent: Corona Energy Limited
Officers: Shaheda Begum Thomas, Secretary; Neil Trevor Mitchell [1974] Commercial Director; Philip Morton [1968] Finance Director; Paul Christian Plewman [1972] Director/Banker [Irish]

Corona Gas Management Limited
Incorporated: 10 December 1993
Net Worth: £1,048,717 *Total Assets:* £105,769,296
Registered Office: Building 2, Level 2, Croxley Park, Watford, Herts, WD18 8YA
Activities: Wholesale of other fuels and related products
Parent: Corona Energy Retail 1 Limited
Officers: Shaheda Begum Thomas, Secretary; Neil Trevor Mitchell [1974] Commercial Director; Philip Morton [1968] Finance Director; Paul Christian Plewman [1972] Director/Banker [Irish]

Robert Cort Properties Limited
Incorporated: 11 May 1908 *Employees:* 8
Previous: Robert Cort and Son (Properties) Limited
Net Worth: £27,302,580 *Total Assets:* £28,351,874
Registered Office: 34 Britten Road, Elgar Road South, Reading, Berks, RG2 0AU
Activities: Other letting and operating of own or leased real estate
Major Shareholder: Athena Mary Zographos
Officers: Stella Scouller [1921] Director; Jonathan Edward Skull [1987] Director/Property Manager; John Martin Willmott [1948] Director/Chartered Accountant; Athena Mary Zographos [1949] Director/Retired

Corus Hotels Limited
Incorporated: 4 November 1920 *Employees:* 605
Net Worth: £106,107,000 *Total Assets:* £208,328,000
Registered Office: Corus House, 1 Auckland Park, Milton Keynes, Bucks, MK1 1BU
Activities: Hotels and similar accommodation
Parent: Malayan United Industries
Officers: Khurram Mohmand, Secretary; Andrew Khoo [1972] Director [Australian]; Kay Peng Khoo [1938] Director [Malaysian]; Kim Li Kwa [1956] Director [Singaporean]; Yet King Loy [1946] Director [Canadian]; Nyen Faat Wong [1957] Director [Malaysian]

Cosan Lubes Investments Limited
Incorporated: 3 April 2012
Net Worth: £13,893,000 *Total Assets:* £84,226,000
Registered Office: Moove, Dering Way, Gravesend, Kent, DA12 2QX
Activities: Activities of head offices
Parent: Cosan Limited
Officers: Gary Michael Sands, Secretary; Michael Winston Bewsey [1965] Director; Marcelo de Souza Scarcela Portela [1961] Director [Brazilian]; Renato Aparecido Fontalva [1967] Director/Business Administration [Brazilian]; Nelson Roseira Gomes Neto [1971] Director [Brazilian]; Marcos Marinho Lutz [1969] Director [Brazilian]; Marcelo Eduardo Martins [1966] Director [Brazilian]; Rubens Ometto Silveira Mello [1950] Director [Brazilian]; Gary Michael Sands [1961] Director

Costa Express Limited
Incorporated: 11 January 1996
Previous: Coffee Nation Limited
Net Worth: £115,413,000 *Total Assets:* £133,937,000
Registered Office: 3 Knaves Beech, Loudwater, High Wycombe, Bucks, HP10 9QR
Activities: Other business support service activities n.e.c.
Parent: Costa Express Holdings Limited
Officers: Russell William Fairhurst, Secretary; Sarah Louise Highfield [1978] Finance Director; Scott Martin [1969] Managing Director; Nicholas Clive Orrin [1966] Director

Costain Alcaidesa Limited
Incorporated: 30 July 1986
Net Worth: £3,488,435 *Total Assets:* £34,306,008
Registered Office: Costain House, Vanwall Business Park, Maidenhead, Berks, SL6 4UB
Activities: Activities of head offices
Parent: Costain Engineering & Construction Limited
Officers: Tracey Alison Wood, Secretary; Anthony Oliver Bickerstaff [1964] Director/Accountant FCCA; Lucy Jane Fleming [1976] Director/Chartered Surveyor; Andrew Wyllie [1962] Director/Chartered Engineer

Costain Building & Civil Engineering Limited
Incorporated: 12 May 1972
Net Worth: £22,735,918 *Total Assets:* £30,403,146
Registered Office: Costain House, Vanwall Business Park, Maidenhead, Berks, SL6 4UB
Activities: Construction of roads and motorways
Parent: Costain Engineering & Construction Limited
Officers: Tracey Alison Wood, Secretary; Anthony Oliver Bickerstaff [1964] Director/Accountant FCCA; Martin David Hunter [1959] Director/Chartered Accountant; Tracey Alison Wood [1969] Director/Solicitor; Andrew Wyllie [1962] Director/Chartered Engineer

Costain Civil Engineering Limited
Incorporated: 22 October 1992
Net Worth: £4,228,905 *Total Assets:* £125,581,720
Registered Office: Costain House, Vanwall Business Park, Maidenhead, Berks, SL6 4UB
Activities: Activities of head offices
Parent: Costain Group PLC
Officers: Tracey Alison Wood, Secretary; Martin David Hunter [1959] Director/Chartered Accountant; Tracey Alison Wood [1969] Director/Solicitor; Andrew Wyllie [1962] Director/Chartered Engineer

Costain Engineering & Construction Limited
Incorporated: 7 November 1989 *Employees:* 3,246
Net Worth: £83,524,040 *Total Assets:* £148,963,776
Registered Office: Costain House, Vanwall Business Park, Maidenhead, Berks, SL6 4UB
Activities: Construction of roads and motorways
Parent: Costain Group PLC
Officers: Tracey Alison Wood, Secretary; Anthony Oliver Bickerstaff [1964] Director/Accountant FCCA; Martin David Hunter [1959] Director/Chartered Accountant; Tracey Alison Wood [1969] Director/Solicitor; Andrew Wyllie [1962] Director/Chartered Engineer

Costain Group PLC
Incorporated: 12 October 1978 *Employees:* 4,118
Net Worth: £154,000,000 *Total Assets:* £661,100,032
Registered Office: Costain House, Vanwall Business Park, Maidenhead, Berks, SL6 4UB
Activities: Construction of roads and motorways
Officers: Tracey Alison Wood, Secretary; Anthony Oliver Bickerstaff [1964] Director/Accountant FCCA; Jacqueline de Rojas CBE [1962] Non-Executive Director, Advisor & Business Mentor; Dr Paul Golby [1951] Director/Chairman; Jane Lodge [1955] Director; David McManus [1953] Director; Alison Jane Wood [1963] Portfolio Non-Executive Director; Andrew Wyllie [1962] Director/Chartered Engineer

Costain Integrated Services Limited
Incorporated: 26 February 1985 *Employees:* 150
Previous: Rhead Group Limited
Net Worth: £13,907,067 *Total Assets:* £23,020,318
Registered Office: Costain House, Vanwall Business Park, Maidenhead, Berks, SL6 4UB
Activities: Other engineering activities
Parent: Costain Limited
Officers: Tracey Alison Wood, Secretary; Alexander John Vaughan [1969] Director; Tracey Alison Wood [1969] Director/Solicitor

Costain Limited
Incorporated: 25 August 1958 *Employees:* 3,516
Net Worth: £108,224,960 *Total Assets:* £574,165,312
Registered Office: Costain House, Vanwall Business Park, Maidenhead, Berks, SL6 4UB
Activities: Construction of roads and motorways
Parent: Costain Civil Engineering Limited
Officers: Tracey Alison Wood, Secretary; Sally Margaret Austin [1976] HR Director; Anthony Oliver Bickerstaff [1964] Director/Accountant FCCA; Martin David Hunter [1959] Director/Chartered Accountant; Darren Glyn James [1967] Director/Chartered Civil Engineer; Dr Maxine Eleanor Mayhew [1973] Director; David Roy Taylor [1964] Group Commercial Director; Alexander John Vaughan [1969] Director/Chartered Surveyor; Tracey Alison Wood [1969] Director/Solicitor; Andrew Wyllie [1962] Director/Chartered Engineer

Richard Costain Limited
Incorporated: 29 March 1933
Net Worth: £16,407,576 *Total Assets:* £325,867,616
Registered Office: Costain House, Vanwall Business Park, Maidenhead, Berks, SL6 4UB
Activities: Other engineering activities
Parent: Costain Group PLC
Officers: Tracey Alison Wood, Secretary; Anthony Oliver Bickerstaff [1964] Director/Accountant FCCA; Martin David Hunter [1959] Director/Chartered Accountant; Andrew Wyllie [1962] Director/Chartered Engineer

Costain Oil, Gas & Process Limited
Incorporated: 1 January 1964 *Employees:* 200
Net Worth: £26,467,604 *Total Assets:* £43,493,608
Registered Office: Costain House, Vanwall Business Park, Maidenhead, Berks, SL6 4UB
Activities: Construction of other civil engineering projects n.e.c.
Parent: Costain Engineering & Construction Limited
Officers: Tracey Alison Wood, Secretary; Anthony Oliver Bickerstaff [1964] Director/Accountant FCCA; Martin David Hunter [1959] Director/Chartered Accountant; Darren Glyn James [1967] Director; Alexander John Vaughan [1969] Director; Andrew Wyllie [1962] Director/Chartered Engineer

Costco Limited
Incorporated: 23 December 1992
Net Worth: £203,444,000 *Total Assets:* £205,079,008
Registered Office: Hartspring Lane, Watford, Herts, WD25 8JS
Activities: Other letting and operating of own or leased real estate
Parent: Costco Wholesale UK Limited
Officers: Magan Khushalbhai Chauhan, Secretary; Magan Khushalbhai Chauhan [1951] Director; James Patrick Murphy [1952] Managing Director [American]; Stephen Michael Pappas [1954] Director [American]

Costco UK Holdings Limited
Incorporated: 28 February 2000 *Employees:* 6,628
Net Worth: £590,630,976 *Total Assets:* £893,710,016
Registered Office: UK Home Office, Hartspring Lane, Watford, Herts, WD25 8JS
Activities: Non-specialised wholesale trade
Parent: Costco Wholesale Corporation
Officers: Magan Khushalbhai Chauhan, Secretary; Richard Galanti [1956] Director/Chief Financial Officer [American]; James Patrick Murphy [1952] Director/Senior Vice President - Europe [American]

Costco Wholesale UK Limited
Incorporated: 6 August 1991 *Employees:* 6,556
Net Worth: £595,078,016 *Total Assets:* £895,956,992
Registered Office: UK Home Office, 213 Hartspring Lane, Watford, Herts, WD25 8JS
Activities: Non-specialised wholesale trade
Parent: Costco UK Holdings Limited
Officers: Magan Khushalbhai Chauhan, Secretary; Walter Craig Jelinek [1952] Director [American]; James Patrick Murphy [1952] Director [American]; Stephen Michael Pappas [1954] Director [American]

Coty Brands Group Limited
Incorporated: 9 May 1988
Net Worth: £211,074,000 *Total Assets:* £249,650,000
Registered Office: Eureka Park, Ashford, Kent, TN25 4AQ
Activities: Activities of other holding companies n.e.c.
Officers: Emma Walters, Secretary; Vengadan Swaminathan [1977] Director; Emma Morag Dorothy Walters [1974] Director/Financial Controller

Coty Manufacturing UK Limited
Incorporated: 23 January 1947 *Employees:* 306
Net Worth: £24,224,000 *Total Assets:* £107,977,000
Registered Office: Eureka Park, Ashford, Kent, TN25 4AQ
Activities: Manufacture of perfumes and toilet preparations
Parent: Coty Inc
Officers: Emma Walters, Secretary; Alberto Meloni [1976] Director [Italian]; Vengadan Swaminathan [1977] Director; Emma Morag Dorothy Walters [1974] Director/Financial Controller

Coty UK & I Ltd
Incorporated: 19 December 1932
Previous: Wella (U.K.) Limited
Net Worth: £119,647,000 *Total Assets:* £151,286,000
Registered Office: Coty UK & I Ltd, Eureka Park, Ashford, Kent, TN25 4AQ
Activities: Retail sale of cosmetic and toilet articles in specialised stores
Officers: Emma Walters, Secretary; Vengadan Swaminathan [1977] Director; Emma Morag Dorothy Walters [1974] Director/Financial Controller

Cougar Holdco London Limited
Incorporated: 8 July 2013 *Employees:* 270
Net Worth Deficit: £9,800,000 *Total Assets:* £165,476,992
Registered Office: The Training Ground, Motspur Park, New Malden, Surrey, KT3 6PT
Activities: Other sports activities
Shareholders: The Shahid Rafiq Khan Family Trust A; The Shahid Rafiq Khan Family Trust B
Officers: Neville Darren Preston, Secretary; Shahid Rafiq Khan [1950] Director/Executive [American]; Mark Lamping [1958] Director/President Jacksonville Jaguars [American]

Counties Home Loan Management Limited
Incorporated: 26 October 1989
Net Worth: £194,008 *Total Assets:* £89,916,704
Registered Office: 30 Church Street, Epsom, Surrey, KT17 4NL
Activities: Banks
Parent: National Counties Building Society
Officers: Andrew David Barnard [1971] Finance Director; Christopher Rendell Croft [1951] Solicitor and Director; Rodger Grant Hughes [1948] Director

Country Estates Holdings Limited
Incorporated: 4 December 1986 *Employees:* 32
Previous: Country Estates Holdings PLC
Net Worth: £21,531,520 *Total Assets:* £28,713,440
Registered Office: Kingfisher House, 17 Albury Close, Loverock Road, Reading, Berks, RG30 1BD
Activities: Activities of construction holding companies
Major Shareholder: Gary Paul Smith
Officers: Carol Annette Richey, Secretary; William James Annan [1953] Director/Solicitor; Graham John Denton [1957] Director; Gary Paul Smith [1943] Director

Countrystyle Group Limited
Incorporated: 13 January 2006 *Employees:* 288
Net Worth: £13,024,114 *Total Assets:* £34,037,104
Registered Office: Head Office, Countrystyle Group, Ashford Road, Lenham, Maidstone, Kent, ME17 2DL
Activities: Treatment and disposal of non-hazardous waste
Major Shareholder: Trevor Lewis Heathcote
Officers: Stuart Butler-Gallie, Secretary; June Dorothy Heathcote [1935] Director; Trevor Lewis Heathcote [1965] Director

Countrystyle Recycling Limited
Incorporated: 16 April 2004 *Employees:* 288
Net Worth: £13,024,114 *Total Assets:* £34,037,104
Registered Office: Head Office, Countrystyle Group, Ashford Road, Lenham, Maidstone, Kent, ME17 2DL
Activities: Treatment and disposal of non-hazardous waste
Major Shareholder: Trevor Lewis Heathcote
Officers: Stuart Butler-Gallie, Secretary; Trevor Lewis Heathcote [1965] Director

Countrywide Principal Services Limited
Incorporated: 17 March 1983 *Employees:* 755
Net Worth: £37,456,000 *Total Assets:* £51,941,000
Registered Office: Countrywide House, 6 Caldecotte Lake Business Park, Caldecotte Lake Drive, Caldecotte, Milton Keynes, Bucks, MK7 8JT
Activities: Financial intermediation not elsewhere classified
Parent: Balanus Limited
Officers: Gareth Rhys Williams, Secretary; Natalie Anna Ceeney [1971] Director; Paul Lewis Creffield [1954] Director; Peter Curran [1966] Director

County & District Properties Limited
Incorporated: 18 November 1960
Net Worth: £23,918,176 *Total Assets:* £24,201,854
Registered Office: Costain House, Vanwell Business Park, Maidenhead, Berks, SL6 4UB
Activities: Buying and selling of own real estate
Parent: Costain Group PLC
Officers: Tracey Alison Wood, Secretary; Anthony Oliver Bickerstaff [1964] Director/Accountant FCCA; Andrew Wyllie [1962] Director/Chartered Engineer

County Catering & Leisure Limited
Incorporated: 6 June 1990 *Employees:* 1
Net Worth: £14,713,635 *Total Assets:* £31,412,516
Registered Office: Albury Mill, Mill Lane, Chilworth, Guildford, Surrey, GU4 8RU
Activities: Other letting and operating of own or leased real estate
Major Shareholder: Peter David Prestidge
Officers: John Duguid Laird, Secretary; Peter David Prestidge [1951] Director

County Catering & Leisure Properties Limited
Incorporated: 12 March 1992 *Employees:* 1
Net Worth: £10,871,791 *Total Assets:* £30,071,024
Registered Office: Albury Mill, Mill Lane, Chilworth, Guildford, Surrey, GU4 8RU
Activities: Other letting and operating of own or leased real estate
Major Shareholder: Peter David Prestidge
Officers: John Duguid Laird, Secretary; Peter David Prestidge [1951] Director

Countyroute (A130) PLC.
Incorporated: 28 September 1999
Net Worth Deficit: £24,508,000 *Total Assets:* £90,498,000
Registered Office: 8 White Oak Square, London Road, Swanley, Kent, BR8 7AG
Activities: Construction of roads and motorways
Parent: Countyroute Limited
Officers: Alexander David Gates [1973] Director/Investment Manager; Andrew Stephen Pearson [1964] Managing Director

Countyroute Limited
Incorporated: 8 December 1998
Net Worth Deficit: £24,508,000 *Total Assets:* £90,498,000
Registered Office: 8 White Oak Square, London Road, Swanley, Kent, BR8 7AG
Activities: Construction of roads and motorways
Parent: John Laing Infrastructure Limited
Officers: Alexander David Gates [1973] Director/Investment Manager; Andrew Stephen Pearson [1964] Managing Director

Courier and Passenger Transport Holdings Limited
Incorporated: 13 June 2007
Net Worth Deficit: £21,392,128 *Total Assets:* £21,211,452
Registered Office: Ground Floor, Red Central, 60 High Street, Redhill, Surrey, RH1 1NY
Activities: Activities of distribution holding companies
Parent: Citysprint (UK) Group Limited
Officers: Gerard Anthony Keenan, Secretary; Patrick Gallagher [1967] Director/Senior Executive; Gerard Anthony Keenan [1968] Director/Accountant

Court Cavendish Limited
Incorporated: 20 September 2001 *Employees:* 2,269
Net Worth: £40,159,000 *Total Assets:* £147,824,000
Registered Office: River Bridge House, Guildford Road, Leatherhead, Surrey, KT22 9AD
Activities: Management consultancy activities other than financial management
Major Shareholder: Chaitanya Bhupendra Patel
Officers: Catherine Assunta Valenti, Secretary; Chaitanya Bhupendra Patel [1954] Director; Katharine Anne Patel [1963] Director; Catherine Assunta Valenti [1961] Director/Chartered Accountant

Covance Clinical and Periapproval Services Limited
Incorporated: 23 May 1986 *Employees:* 1,447
Net Worth: £44,665,000 *Total Assets:* £79,749,000
Registered Office: Osprey House, Maidenhead Office Park, Westacott Way, Maidenhead, Berks, SL6 3QH
Activities: Other research and experimental development on natural sciences and engineering
Parent: Covance Limited
Officers: Floyd Samuel Eberts III [1959] Director/Chief Legal Officer [American]; Glenn Andrew Eisenberg [1961] Director [American]; Robert Stewart Pringle [1964] Director

Covea Insurance PLC
Incorporated: 20 October 1958
Net Worth: £315,689,984 *Total Assets:* £1,487,491,968
Registered Office: Norman Place, Reading, Berks, RG1 8DA
Activities: Non-life insurance
Parent: MMA Holdings UK PLC
Officers: Annabel Felicity Wilson, Secretary; Nicholas Michael Caplan [1959] Independent Non-Executive Director; Stephen Andrew Clarke [1954] Director; Simon Joseph Cooter [1964] Insurance Director; Jane Elizabeth Dale [1960] Director; Carol Evans [1967] Director; Adrian Charles Furness [1966] Director; Bertrand Lefebvre [1963] Director [French]; Pierre Albert Jean Michel [1968] Director [French]; Karl Peter Murphy [1969] Independent Non-Executive Director [Irish]; Edgardo Paunlagui Penollar [1966] Finance Director; James William Reader [1970] Director/Chief Executive Officer; Dominique Salvy [1957] Director [French]

Covea Insurance Services Limited
Incorporated: 5 September 1994 *Employees:* 1,576
Previous: Sterling Insurance Group Limited
Net Worth: £2,118,000 *Total Assets:* £35,075,000
Registered Office: 2 Norman Place, Reading, Berks, RG1 8DA
Activities: Other activities auxiliary to insurance and pension funding
Parent: MMA Holdings UK PLC
Officers: Annabel Felicity Wilson, Secretary; Francois Xavier Michel Josse [1972] Insurance Director [French]; Bertrand Lefebvre [1963] Director [French]; Pierre Albert Jean Michel [1968] Director [French]; Edgardo Paunlagui Penollar [1966] Finance Director; James William Reader [1970] Director/Chief Executive Officer; Dominique Salvy [1957] Director [French]

Covea Life Limited
Incorporated: 21 July 1967
Previous: Covea Life Limited
Net Worth: £21,693,000 *Total Assets:* £70,879,000
Registered Office: 2 Norman Place, Reading, Berks, RG1 8DA
Activities: Life insurance
Parent: Covea Insurance Services Limited
Officers: Annabel Felicity Wilson, Secretary; Nicholas Michael Caplan [1959] Independent Non-Executive Director; Stephen Andrew Clarke [1954] Director/Accountant; Jane Elizabeth Dale [1960] Director; Bertrand Lefebvre [1963] Director [French]; Pierre Albert Jean Michel [1968] Director [French]; Karl Peter Murphy [1969] Independent Non-Executive Director [Irish]; Edgardo Paunlagui Penollar [1966] Finance Director; James William Reader [1970] Director/Chief Executive Officer; Dominique Salvy [1957] Director [French]

The Coventry and Rugby Hospital Company (Holdings) Limited
Incorporated: 22 December 2000
Net Worth Deficit: £48,684,000 *Total Assets:* £423,775,008
Registered Office: 8 White Oak Square, London Road, Swanley, Kent, BR8 7AG
Activities: Activities of financial services holding companies
Parent: Innisfree Continuation Partners LLP
Officers: Sheila Jamieson Clark [1973] Director; Nicholas John Edward Crowther [1960] Investment Director; Benjamin Christopher Jacob Dean [1979] Director/Investment Manager

The Coventry and Rugby Hospital Company PLC
Incorporated: 12 August 2002
Net Worth Deficit: £48,601,000 *Total Assets:* £423,859,008
Registered Office: 8 White Oak Square, London Road, Swanley, Kent, BR8 7AG
Activities: Combined facilities support activities
Parent: The Coventry and Rugby Hospital Company (Holdings) Limited
Officers: Sheila Jamieson Clark [1973] Director; Nicholas John Edward Crowther [1960] Investment Director; Benjamin Christopher Jacob Dean [1979] Director/Investment Manager; Michael Edward Fry [1958] Director

David Cover and Son Limited
Incorporated: 6 July 1945 *Employees:* 434
Net Worth: £33,276,188 *Total Assets:* £44,571,616
Registered Office: Sussex House, Quarry Lane, Chichester, W Sussex, PO19 8PE
Activities: Sawmilling and planing of wood
Shareholders: JH & FW Green Limited; JH and FW Green Limited
Officers: Rupert John Henry Green, Secretary/Director; Nigel John Bewley Atkinson [1953] Director; Edward Richard Green [1988] Director/Chartered Surveyor; Henry Charles Edward Green [1971] Director; Patrick William Green [1946] Director; Rupert John Henry Green [1959] Director; Jeremy Robin Lear [1945] Director; Nicholas Brian Walker [1956] Director; Steven John Weston [1969] Director/Builders Merchant

Covidien UK Limited
Incorporated: 29 January 1937
Net Worth: £2,376,000 *Total Assets:* £60,209,000
Registered Office: Building 9, Croxley Park, Hatters Lane, Watford, Herts, WD18 8WW
Activities: Manufacture of knitted and crocheted hosiery
Parent: CDK U.K. Limited
Officers: Joanne Pascucci, Senior Corporate Secretary; Mark Justin Elsey [1967] Finance Director; Jacqueline Fielding [1964] Vice President (Director)

The Cowplain School
Incorporated: 17 February 2012 *Employees:* 119
Previous: Cowplain Community School
Net Worth: £18,767,020 *Total Assets:* £20,306,770
Registered Office: The Cowplain School, Hart Plain Avenue, Cowplain, Waterlooville, Hants, PO8 8RY
Activities: General secondary education
Officers: Deborah Pidgeon, Secretary; Lee Berrecloth [1971] Director/Teacher; Dean Cox [1963] Director/Systems Engineer; Ian Richard Gates [1970] Director/Headmaster; Lorraine Vanessa Harbour [1958] Director/Administrator; Stephen Robert Head [1951] Director/Electronic Engineer; Michael John Holding [1958] Director; Christopher William Scott [1939] Director/Finance Manager; Glenn Jonathan Taylor [1969] Director/Risk Manager; Bhanumattee Tewari [1964] Director [American]; Susan Lesley Young [1967] Director/Sales and Service Manager

Cox Green School
Incorporated: 1 November 2011 *Employees:* 103
Net Worth: £21,812,300 *Total Assets:* £24,483,796
Registered Office: Cox Green School, Highfield Lane, Maidenhead, Berks, SL6 3AX
Activities: General secondary education
Officers: Gill Newman, Secretary; Tarah Al-Jibouri [1987] Director/Mentor; Simon Ward Armstrong [1966] Director/Technical Liaison Officer; Matthew Foster [1971] Director/Teacher; Sophie Franks [1978] Director/Finance and Operations Co-ordinator; Helen Hannam [1970] Director/Deputy Headteacher; Jacqueline Haywood [1977] Director; Graham Jons [1965] Director/Data Manager; Lara Lester [1969] Director/HR Manager; Paul Louden [1947] Director/Retired; Wen-Lan Richard [1973] Director/Systems Analyst; Laura Claire Simmonds [1982] Improvement Director; Peter Thorn [1947] Director/Retired; Frances Siena Walsh [1965] Director/Headteacher

CP Holdings Limited
Incorporated: 22 March 1957 *Employees:* 7,059
Net Worth: £395,296,000 *Total Assets:* £762,854,976
Registered Office: CP House, Otterspool Way, Watford, Herts, WD25 8JJ
Activities: Activities of head offices
Shareholders: Lady Lilly Schreier; Iris Gibbor; Mark Gibbor; Robert Glatter; Michael Montague Wreschner; Alexei James Schreier
Officers: Eric Lewis, Secretary; Paul Andrew Filer [1957] Director/Chartered Accountant; Iris Gibbor [1951] Director; Mark Gibbor [1988] Director; Robert Glatter [1937] Director; Mark Hennebry [1966] Director [Irish]; Michael Barry Hirst OBE [1943] Director; Philip Hoffbrand [1967] Director/Solicitor; Eric Lewis [1927] Director/Solicitor; Alexei James Schreier [1976] Director/Executive; Lady Lilly Schreier [1924] Director; John Ernest Smith [1949] Director

CP Regents Park Two Limited
Incorporated: 8 December 2004 *Employees:* 124
Net Worth: £1,011,530 *Total Assets:* £47,227,640
Registered Office: CP House, Otterspool Way, Watford, Herts, WD25 8JJ
Activities: Hotels and similar accommodation
Parent: CP Holdings Limited
Officers: Eric Lewis, Secretary; Paul Andrew Filer [1957] Director/Chartered Accountant; Iris Gibbor [1951] Director; Mark Gibbor [1988] Director; Mark Hennebry [1966] Director [Irish]; Eric Lewis [1927] Director/Solicitor; Alexei James Schreier [1976] Director

CPI Mortars (North) Limited
Incorporated: 14 June 1993
Net Worth: £50,520,976 *Total Assets:* £59,518,592
Registered Office: Oak Green House, 250-256 High Street, Dorking, Surrey, RH4 1QT
Activities: Manufacture of mortars
Parent: Grafton Group (UK) PLC
Officers: Brian O'Hara [1967] Director/Accountant [Irish]; Garrett Wilkinson [1979] Director/Accountant [Irish]

CPI Mortars Limited
Incorporated: 12 December 1996 *Employees:* 159
Net Worth: £8,083,345 *Total Assets:* £104,528,416
Registered Office: Oak Green House, 250-256 High Street, Dorking, Surrey, RH4 1QT
Activities: Manufacture of mortars
Parent: Grafton Group (UK) PLC
Officers: David Llewelyn Arnold [1966] Finance Director; Lawrence Dale [1961] Director; Brian O'Hara [1967] Director/Accountant [Irish]; Gavin Slark [1965] Director; Garrett Wilkinson [1979] Director/Accountant [Irish]

CPL Bidco Limited
Incorporated: 19 April 2017
Net Worth: £60,246,000 *Total Assets:* £110,157,000
Registered Office: 6th Floor, Reading Bridge House, George Street, Reading, Berks, RG1 8LS
Activities: Activities of other holding companies n.e.c.
Parent: CPL Midco Limited
Officers: Matthew Charles Moore [1971] Director; Nigel Stockton [1966] Director

CPL Topco Limited
Incorporated: 19 April 2017 *Employees:* 349
Net Worth: £33,450,000 *Total Assets:* £89,850,000
Registered Office: 6th Floor, Reading Bridge House, George Street, Reading, Berks, RG1 8LS
Activities: Activities of other holding companies n.e.c.
Officers: Felice Rea, Secretary; Delmade Federico Alvarez [1981] Director [Argentinian]; Wai-Fong Au [1956] Director; Beverley Michael Covell [1954] Director; Alison Endemano [1970] Director/HR; Matthew Charles Moore [1971] Director; Nigel Stockton [1966] Director

CPRT (Europe) Limited
Incorporated: 19 September 2012
Net Worth: £32,841,488 *Total Assets:* £33,583,692
Registered Office: Acrey Fields, Woburn Road, Wootton, Beds, MK43 9EJ
Activities: Sale of other motor vehicles
Parent: Universal Salvage Limited
Officers: Aaron Jayson Adair [1969] Director/Chief Executive Officer [American]; Jonathan David Canning [1972] Director/General Counsel; Gregory Depasquale [1968] Director/SVP, General Counsel and Secretary of Copart, Inc [American]; William Easley Franklin [1956] Director/Chief Financial Officer [American]; Nigel James Paget [1966] Managing Director

CPRT European Investments Limited
Incorporated: 22 July 2016
Net Worth: £34,715,160 *Total Assets:* £34,716,916
Registered Office: Acrey Fields, Woburn Road, Wootton, Beds, MK43 9EJ
Activities: Financial management
Parent: Universal Salvage Limited
Officers: Aaron Jayson Adair [1969] Director/Chief Executive Officer [American]; Jonathan David Canning [1972] Director/General Counsel; Gregory Depasquale [1968] Director/SVP, General Counsel and Secretary of Copart, Inc [American]; William Easley Franklin [1956] Director/Executive Vice President of Copart, Inc [American]; Nigel James Paget [1966] Managing Director

CPRT LLP
Incorporated: 27 November 2013
Net Worth: £175,546,000 *Total Assets:* £175,546,000
Registered Office: Acrey Fields, Woburn Road, Wootton, Beds, MK43 9EJ

Cramlington Renewable Energy Developments Hold Co Limited
Incorporated: 4 June 2015
Net Worth Deficit: £7,284,000 *Total Assets:* £127,721,000
Registered Office: 8 White Oak Square, London Road, Swanley, Kent, BR8 7AG
Activities: Activities of other holding companies n.e.c.
Shareholders: Equitix ESI CHP 2 Limited; John Laing Investments Limited
Officers: Maxwell Francis Aitken [1977] Director; David Richard Bradbury [1969] Director/Senior Investment Manager; Benjamin Matthew Cashin [1972] Director; Paul John Ireland [1979] Director; David Adam Whitehurst [1971] Director/Investment Professional

Cranbury Investment Company Limited
Incorporated: 14 March 1963 *Employees:* 6
Net Worth: £21,960,940 *Total Assets:* £23,982,832
Registered Office: Cranbury Park, Winchester, Hants, SO21 2HL
Activities: Development of building projects
Parent: Cranbury (Holdings) Limited
Officers: Timothy James Piper, Secretary; Penelope Mary Alexandra Tankerville Chamberlayne-Macdonald [1936] Director; Diana Mary Countess of Lindsay [1961] Director; James Thomas Wingfield Hewitt [1979] Director/Investment Manager; The Viscount Edward James Wingfield Lifford [1949] Director/Fund Manager; Timothy James Piper [1970] Director/Chartered Surveyor; Geoffrey William Richards [1948] Director/Solicitor

John Crane Group Limited
Incorporated: 26 May 2004
Net Worth: £328,399,008 *Total Assets:* £1,496,412,032
Registered Office: Buckingham House, 361-366 Buckingham Avenue, Slough, Berks, SL1 4LU
Activities: Activities of head offices
Parent: Smiths Group International Holdings
Officers: Christopher David Hughes, Secretary; Ruben Raul Alvarez Sancho [1971] Director/Vice President, Global First Fit and Projects [Spanish]; John Frank Donatiello [1953] Director/Vice President [American]; Adam David Powell [1981] Director/EMEA Regional Controller

Crane Payment Innovations International Ltd
Incorporated: 31 March 2006 *Employees:* 78
Previous: MEI UK International, Ltd
Net Worth: £33,247,000 *Total Assets:* £51,723,000
Registered Office: Unit 51-52 Suttons Business Park, Suttons Park Avenue, Reading, Berks, RG6 1AZ
Activities: Other business support service activities n.e.c.
Parent: Crane Payment Innovations Inc
Officers: Richard Wilkinson, Secretary; Kurt Franklin Gallo [1965] Director/President [American]; Richard Gibson [1964] Director; Richard Andrew Maue [1970] Director/Business Executive [American]; Max Homer Mitchell [1963] Director/Business Executive [American]; Ray Sherwood [1968] Director [American]; Richard Wilkinson [1967] Director

John Crane UK Limited
Incorporated: 25 August 1923 *Employees:* 383
Net Worth: £90,881,000 *Total Assets:* £119,741,000
Registered Office: 361-366 Buckingham Avenue, Slough, Berks, SL1 4LU
Activities: Machining
Shareholder: John Crane Group Limited
Officers: Christopher David Hughes, Secretary; John Frank Donatiello [1953] Director/Vice President [American]; John George Long [1971] John Crane First Fit Europe Managing Director; Adam David Powell [1981] Director/EMEA Regional Controller

Cranleigh School
Incorporated: 9 July 1998 *Employees:* 321
Net Worth: £38,271,000 *Total Assets:* £67,034,000
Registered Office: Horseshoe Lane, Cranleigh, Surrey, GU6 8QQ
Activities: Primary education
Officers: Patrick Temple Roberts, Secretary/Bursar; Sarah Elizabeth Bayliss [1963] Director/Voluntary Sector; Jenny Anne Brown [1969] Director/Headmistress; Dr Michael Peter Cathcart [1979] Director/Senior Teaching Fellow University of Surrey; Dr Rosalind Margaret Chesser [1969] Director/Medical Doctor; Mary Monica Sophia Fisher [1954] Director; Mark Foster [1959] Board Director; Patrick Simon Parker Going [1965] Director/Chartered Surveyor; Sanjaya Gunapala [1977] Director/Chartered Accountant; Richard Lawrence Johnson [1972] Director/Pilot; Jonathan Arnold Manley Knight [1956] Design Director; Adrian James Lajtha [1957] Director/Management Consultant; Alison Jennie Lye [1974] Director/Solicitor; Elizabeth Stanton [1954] Director/Chartered Accountant; Nicholas David Leslie Sweet [1957] Director/Designer; Sam James Watkinson [1968] Director/Venture Capitalist; Oliver Alexander Radford Weiss [1950] Director/Solicitor; Peter Maltus Wells [1957] Director/Retired IAPS Headmaster; David Guy Westcott [1957] Director/Barrister; Simon John Whitehouse [1960] Director/Management Consultant; Professor Robert James Wilkins [1968] Director/University Lecturer; David Anthony Ellis Williams [1953] Director/Retired; Melanie Jane Williamson [1966] Director/Publicity Consultant

Crawley Down Holdings Ltd
Incorporated: 12 January 2010 *Employees:* 271
Net Worth: £11,441,160 *Total Assets:* £26,978,964
Registered Office: Brockbourne House, 77 Mount Ephraim, Tunbridge Wells, Kent, TN4 8BS
Activities: Activities of head offices
Officers: Nicola Suzanne Izard, Secretary; Nicholas John Caunter [1958] Managing Director; Sarah Louise Caunter [1964] Director; Rev Timothy David Giles [1946] Director/Clergyman; Nicola Suzanne Izard [1962] Operations Director; Bertam George Voller [1936] Director/Chairman; Christopher Bertram Voller [1968] Commercial Director; John William Voller [1945] Director

Creabilis Holdings Limited
Incorporated: 7 June 2013
Previous: Creabilis Holdings PLC
Net Worth: £65,159,316 *Total Assets:* £65,159,316
Registered Office: Camburgh House, 27 New Dover Road, Canterbury, Kent, CT1 3DN
Activities: Research and experimental development on biotechnology
Parent: Sienna Biopharmaceuticals, Inc.
Officers: Timothy Kirk Andrews [1978] Director/Attorney [American]; John William Smither [1953] Director [American]

The Creative Assembly Limited
Incorporated: 28 August 1997 *Employees:* 372
Net Worth: £19,971,728 *Total Assets:* £27,756,866
Registered Office: 27 Great West Road, Brentford, Middlesex, TW8 9BW
Activities: Ready-made interactive leisure and entertainment software development
Parent: Sega Sammy Holdings Inc
Officers: Nicola Ormrod, Secretary; Gary Robert Dale [1961] Director/Chief Operating Officer; Tatsuyuki Miyazaki [1967] Director [Japanese]; David Jonathon Ward [1965] Director/Chief Financial Officer

Creative Foods Europe Limited
Incorporated: 17 April 2013
Previous: Flagship Europe Ltd
Net Worth: £8,213,663 *Total Assets:* £41,642,936
Registered Office: 10 Watchmoor Park, Riverside Way, Camberley, Surrey, GU15 3YL
Activities: Manufacture of other food products n.e.c.
Parent: Gands (U.K.)
Officers: Russell Alexander Powis Maddock, Secretary; Kevin Lawrence Cahill [1970] Director [Irish]; William Blair Coulten [1981] Finance Director; Sherry Anne Demeulenaere [1958] Director [American]; Russell Alexander Powis Maddock [1965] Director; David Gerard McDonald [1964] Director [American]; Kevin Richard Scott [1959] Director [American]

Creative Technology Group Limited
Incorporated: 2 February 1984
Previous: Avesco Group Limited
Net Worth: £51,959,000 *Total Assets:* £55,965,000
Registered Office: Unit E2, Sussex Manor Business Park, Gatwick Road, Crawley, W Sussex, RH10 9NH
Activities: Activities of head offices
Parent: NEP UK Film II Limited
Officers: David Mark Leadbetter, Secretary; David Andrew Crump [1961] Director; Generald Delon [1970] Director [American]; Mark Andrew Wilson [1975] Director/Chartered Accountant

Creative Technology Limited
Incorporated: 21 July 1986 *Employees:* 148
Net Worth: £11,191,000 *Total Assets:* £27,494,000
Registered Office: Unit E2, Sussex Manor Business Park, Gatwick Road, Crawley, W Sussex, RH10 9NH
Activities: Renting and leasing of media entertainment equipment
Parent: Avesco Holdings Limited
Officers: David Mark Leadbetter, Secretary; David Andrew Crump [1961] Director; Generald Delon [1970] Director [American]; Mark Stephen Elliott [1961] Director; Mark Andrew Wilson [1975] Director/Chartered Accountant

Creative Video Productions Limited
Incorporated: 2 June 1989 *Employees:* 120
Net Worth: £13,791,374 *Total Assets:* £27,303,416
Registered Office: 23 Shield Drive, West Cross Industrial Estate, Brentford, Middlesex, TW8 9EX
Activities: Motion picture production activities
Parent: Infinity Media Group Limited
Officers: Mark Andrew Forth [1969] Director; Jon Fry [1973] Director; Mansukh Kerai [1971] Director; Darren Simpson [1974] Director; Yevgeny Subbotin [1974] Director

Crescent Pharma Limited
Incorporated: 1 May 2003 *Employees:* 42
Net Worth: £17,988,892 *Total Assets:* £47,265,104
Registered Office: Units 3-4 Quidhampton Business Units, Polhampton Lane, Overton, Basingstoke, Hants, RG25 3ED
Activities: Manufacture of basic pharmaceutical products
Officers: Mohammed Al-Doori [1965] Director/Engineer

Crescent Pharmaceuticals Limited
Incorporated: 6 January 2010 *Employees:* 42
Net Worth: £18,417,192 *Total Assets:* £47,916,996
Registered Office: Units 3-4 Quidhampton Business Units, Polhampton Lane, Overton, Basingstoke, Hants, RG25 3ED
Activities: Activities of other holding companies n.e.c.
Major Shareholder: Mohammed Khalid Aldoori
Officers: Mohammed Al-Doori [1965] Managing Director

Crest A2D (Walton Court) LLP
Incorporated: 22 January 2016
Net Worth: £1,461,000 *Total Assets:* £22,975,000
Registered Office: Crest House, Pyrcroft Road, Chertsey, Surrey, KT16 9GN

Crest Nicholson Developments (Chertsey) Limited
Incorporated: 23 March 2003
Net Worth: £13,700,000 *Total Assets:* £53,000,000
Registered Office: Crest House, Pyrcroft Road, Chertsey, Surrey, KT16 9GN
Activities: Non-trading company
Parent: Crest Nicholson PLC
Officers: Kevin Maguire, Secretary; Patrick Joseph Bergin [1966] Director/Group Financial Controller; Anil Bungar [1972] Director; Stephen Stone [1954] Managing Director; Nigel Christopher Tinker [1960] Urban Land Director

Crest Nicholson Holdings PLC
Incorporated: 23 January 2009 *Employees:* 905
Net Worth: £817,800,000 *Total Assets:* £1,477,900,032
Registered Office: Crest House, Pyrcroft Road, Chertsey, Surrey, KT16 9GN
Activities: Activities of head offices
Officers: Kevin Maguire, Secretary; Lucinda Margaret Bell [1964] Director; Patrick Joseph Bergin [1966] Director/Group Financial Controller; Sharon Emma Flood [1965] Director; Louise Jane Hardy [1966] Director; Octavia Kate Morley [1968] Director; Stephen Stone [1954] Managing Director; Nigel Christopher Tinker [1960] Urban Land Director; Philippe Leslie Van de Walle [1956] Director/Deputy Chairman [French]

Crest Nicholson Operations Limited
Incorporated: 26 April 1974 *Employees:* 895
Net Worth: £503,200,000 *Total Assets:* £1,309,500,032
Registered Office: Crest House, Pyrcroft Road, Chertsey, Surrey, KT16 9GN
Activities: Development of building projects
Parent: Crest Nicholson PLC
Officers: Kevin Maguire, Secretary; Patrick Joseph Bergin [1966] Director/Group Financial Controller; Robin Patrick Hoyles [1954] Group Land & Planning Director; Stephen Stone [1954] Managing Director; Nigel Christopher Tinker [1960] Urban Land Director

Crest Nicholson PLC
Incorporated: 31 January 1972 *Employees:* 905
Net Worth: £742,800,000 *Total Assets:* £1,339,200,000
Registered Office: Crest House, Pyrcroft Road, Chertsey, Surrey, KT16 9GN
Activities: Activities of head offices
Parent: Castle Bidco Limited
Officers: Kevin Maguire, Secretary; Patrick Joseph Bergin [1966] Director/Group Financial Controller; Robin Patrick Hoyles [1954] Group Land & Planning Director; Stephen Stone [1954] Managing Director; Nigel Christopher Tinker [1960] Urban Land Director

P A Crocker Limited
Incorporated: 18 December 1996 *Employees:* 1,799
Previous: PA Crocker Limited
Net Worth: £4,472,872 *Total Assets:* £23,519,248
Registered Office: 95-97 High Street, Margate, Kent, CT9 1JT
Activities: Unlicenced restaurants and cafes
Major Shareholder: Paul Crocker
Officers: Kim Isabelle Crocker, Secretary; Paul Crocker [1959] Director/McDonalds Owner Operator

Cromwell Holdings Limited
Incorporated: 21 March 1983 *Employees:* 14
Net Worth: £36,299,000 *Total Assets:* £50,442,000
Registered Office: Park Place House, 24 Church Street, Epsom, Surrey, KT17 4QB
Activities: Activities of head offices
Major Shareholder: James Perry Hallam
Officers: Alison Hedges, Secretary; Darren Colin Bradley [1969] Director/Chartered Surveyor; James Perry Hallam [1978] Director; Michael Stuart Hastings [1942] Director/Certified Accountant; Albert Richard Perry [1924] Director

Crop Demetra Limited
Incorporated: 3 September 2012 *Employees:* 92
Net Worth: £43,844,136 *Total Assets:* £114,708,304
Registered Office: Highlands House, Basingstoke Road, Spencers Wood, Reading, Berks, RG7 1NT
Activities: Activities of agricultural holding companies
Officers: Olivier Alain Roger Deneufbourg [1963] Director [French]; Juli Jessen [1961] Director/Chief Executive Officer [American]; Dr Dominic Joseph Lamb [1960] Director

Cross London Trains Finance Company Limited
Incorporated: 19 June 2012
Net Worth Deficit: £63,000 *Total Assets:* £112,677,000
Registered Office: 8 White Oak Square, London Road, Swanley, Kent, BR8 7AG
Activities: Financial leasing
Parent: Cross London Trains Holdco Limited
Officers: Graham Maurice Beazley-Long [1960] Director/Investment Manager; John Ivor Cavill [1972] Director; Timothy John Kashem [1970] Director/Fund Manager; Scott Bruce Michael Moseley [1978] Director/Partner; Andrew Christopher Pitt [1959] Director; Petra Regge [1973] Director/Investment Manager [German]; Basil Justin Bromley Wetters [1967] Director

Cross London Trains Holdco 2 Limited
Incorporated: 17 October 2011 *Employees:* 2
Net Worth Deficit: £236,660,000 *Total Assets:* £1,989,815,040
Registered Office: 8 White Oak Square, London Road, Swanley, Kent, BR8 7AG
Activities: Financial leasing
Shareholders: 3i Infrastructure PLC; Project Ventures Rail Investments I Limited; Innisfree Secondary Partners 2 LLP
Officers: Graham Maurice Beazley-Long [1960] Director/Investment Manager; John Ivor Cavill [1972] Director; Timothy John Kashem [1970] Director/Fund Manager; Scott Bruce Michael Moseley [1978] Director/Partner; Andrew Christopher Pitt [1959] Director; Petra Regge [1973] Director/Investment Manager [German]; Basil Justin Bromley Wetters [1967] Director

Cross London Trains Holdco Limited
Incorporated: 19 June 2012
Net Worth: £30,392,000 *Total Assets:* £81,268,000
Registered Office: 8 White Oak Square, London Road, Swanley, Kent, BR8 7AG
Activities: Financial leasing
Parent: Cross London Trains Holdco 2 Limited
Officers: Graham Maurice Beazley-Long [1960] Director/Investment Manager; John Ivor Cavill [1972] Director; Timothy John Kashem [1970] Director/Fund Manager; Scott Bruce Michael Moseley [1978] Director/Partner; Andrew Christopher Pitt [1959] Director; Petra Regge [1973] Director/Investment Manager [German]; Basil Justin Bromley Wetters [1967] Director

Cross London Trains Limited
Incorporated: 17 October 2011 *Employees:* 2
Net Worth Deficit: £236,596,992 *Total Assets:* £1,989,815,040
Registered Office: 8 White Oak Square, London Road, Swanley, Kent, BR8 7AG
Activities: Financial leasing
Parent: Cross London Trains Holdco Limited
Officers: Graham Maurice Beazley-Long [1960] Director/Investment Manager; John Ivor Cavill [1972] Director; Timothy John Kashem [1970] Director/Fund Manager; Scott Bruce Michael Moseley [1978] Director/Partner; Andrew Christopher Pitt [1959] Director; Petra Regge [1973] Director/Investment Manager [German]; Basil Justin Bromley Wetters [1967] Director

Cross Stone Properties Limited
Incorporated: 20 November 1985 *Employees:* 2
Net Worth: £20,905,100 *Total Assets:* £20,908,094
Registered Office: The Old Mill, The Warren, Crowborough, E Sussex, TN6 1UB
Activities: Development of building projects
Shareholder: Hilary Anne Barbour
Officers: Robert Kenneth Reilly, Secretary; Alexander Ross Barbour [1994] Director/Surveyor; Charles Ross Fraser Barbour [1960] Director/Architect & Property Developer; James Fraser Barbour [1992] Director/Solicitor; Terence Kenny [1953] Trust Director

Cross Stone Securities Limited
Incorporated: 29 May 2001 *Employees:* 2
Net Worth: £12,891,800 *Total Assets:* £45,185,536
Registered Office: The Old Mill, The Warren, Crowborough, E Sussex, TN6 1UB
Activities: Development of building projects
Shareholder: Hilary Anne Barbour
Officers: Robert Kenneth Reilly, Secretary; Alexander Ross Barbour [1994] Director/Surveyor; Charles Ross Fraser Barbour [1960] Director/Architect & Property Developer; James Fraser Barbour [1992] Director/Solicitor; Terence Kenny [1953] Trust Director

Crossknowledge Group Limited
Incorporated: 18 May 2005 *Employees:* 26
Net Worth: £93,846,360 *Total Assets:* £111,920,072
Registered Office: The Atrium, Southern Gate, Chichester, W Sussex, PO19 8SQ
Activities: Technical and vocational secondary education
Parent: J Wiley Ltd
Officers: Caroline Jane McPhee, Secretary; Ursula Leonie D'Arcy [1970] Director [Irish]; Rosamund Claire Johnson [1961] Director; John Anthony Kritzmacher [1960] Director [American]

Crosswater Limited
Incorporated: 20 August 1998 *Employees:* 203
Net Worth: £20,590,000 *Total Assets:* £72,733,000
Registered Office: Lake View House, Rennie Drive, Dartford, Kent, DA1 5FU
Activities: Wholesale of hardware, plumbing and heating equipment and supplies
Parent: Bathroom Brands Holdings UK Limited
Officers: Vikram Kant, Secretary; David John Anning [1966] Director; David Michael Button [1966] Director; David Richard Hance [1965] Director/Group Chairman; Vikram Kant [1984] Director [Indian]

Croudace Finance Limited
Incorporated: 12 November 2015
Net Worth: £20,879,748 *Total Assets:* £32,381,100
Registered Office: Temple House, 25 High Street, Lewes, E Sussex, BN7 2LU
Activities: Credit granting by non-deposit taking finance houses and other specialist consumer credit grantors
Parent: Croudace Trading Group Ltd
Officers: David Beard, Secretary; Anthony Brotherton-Ratcliffe [1950] Director; John George Cook [1955] Director; Neil David Scott [1959] Director/Chartered Surveyor

Croudace Homes Group Limited
Incorporated: 13 February 2002 *Employees:* 274
Net Worth: £143,644,992 *Total Assets:* £242,700,992
Registered Office: Croudace House, Tupwood Lane, Caterham, Surrey, CR3 6XQ
Activities: Construction of domestic buildings
Officers: Caroline Jane Bailey Boakes, Secretary; Anthony Brotherton-Ratcliffe [1950] Director; Allan Robert Carey [1956] Director/Chartered Accountant; Russell Kane Denness [1959] Director; Richard John Holmans [1959] Director; Steven Michael Thomas [1975] Finance Director

Croudace Homes Limited
Incorporated: 22 July 1964 *Employees:* 274
Net Worth: £134,716,992 *Total Assets:* £207,668,000
Registered Office: Croudace House, Caterham, Surrey, CR3 6XQ
Activities: Construction of domestic buildings
Parent: Croudace Homes Group Limited
Officers: Caroline Jane Bailey Boakes, Secretary; Simon John Boakes [1966] Director; Ian John Burgess [1977] Director; Allan Robert Carey [1956] Director/Chartered Accountant; Jason Alexander Cross [1976] Director; Russell Kane Denness [1959] Director; Stuart Alan Elvidge [1968] Director; Richard John Holmans [1959] Director; Matthew Robert Houson [1970] Director; Matthew Adam Norris [1975] Director; Steven Michael Thomas [1975] Finance Director; Benjamin William Yallop [1976] Director

Croudace Investment Group Limited
Incorporated: 12 November 2015
Net Worth: £20,733,196 *Total Assets:* £28,663,196
Registered Office: Temple House, 25 High Street, Lewes, E Sussex, BN7 2LU
Activities: Activities of other holding companies n.e.c.
Shareholders: Julia Mary Brotherton; David Charles Brotherton-Ratcliffe; Anthony Brotherton-Ratcliffe
Officers: David Beard, Secretary; Anthony Brotherton-Ratcliffe [1950] Director; John George Cook [1955] Director; Neil David Scott [1959] Director/Chartered Surveyor

Croudace Trading Group Limited
Incorporated: 12 November 2015
Net Worth: £35,197,768 *Total Assets:* £35,197,768
Registered Office: Temple House, 25 High Street, Lewes, E Sussex, BN7 2LU
Activities: Activities of other holding companies n.e.c.
Shareholders: Julia Mary Brotherton; David Charles Brotherton-Ratcliffe; Anthony Brotherton-Ratcliffe
Officers: David Beard, Secretary; Anthony Brotherton-Ratcliffe [1950] Director; John George Cook [1955] Director; Neil David Scott [1959] Director/Chartered Surveyor

Crown Agents Bank Limited
Incorporated: 12 January 1989 *Employees:* 118
Net Worth: £57,664,000 *Total Assets:* £993,044,992
Registered Office: Quadrant House, The Quadrant, Sutton, Surrey, SM2 5AS
Activities: Financial intermediation not elsewhere classified
Parent: Cabim Limited
Officers: Nicholas Charles Beecroft [1960] Director/Financial Consultant; Rajesh Bhatia [1963] Director/Banker; Susanne Chishti [1971] Director [Austrian]; Arnold Onyekwere Ekpe [1953] Director; Richard Charles Hallett [1966] Director/Accountant; Albert Cornelis Maasland [1960] Director [Dutch]; Carole Machell [1962] Director/Chartered Accountant; Douglas Davidson MacLennan [1964] Director; Derek Neil McMenamin [1955] Director; Jeremy Parrish [1955] Director; Simon Hilliard Poole [1966] Director

Crown Blue Line Limited
Incorporated: 21 January 1969 *Employees:* 188
Net Worth: £61,027,744 *Total Assets:* £64,114,824
Registered Office: Origin One, 108 High Street, Crawley, W Sussex, RH10 1BD
Activities: Other service activities n.e.c.
Parent: First Choice Leisure Limited
Officers: Janet Northey, Secretary; Cheryl Frances Brown [1969] Director; Trevor Fahy [1979] Director/Accountant

Crown Golf Group Limited
Incorporated: 19 November 2002 *Employees:* 932
Previous: Bennelong Golf Limited
Net Worth: £5,893,000 *Total Assets:* £65,677,000
Registered Office: Pine Ridge Golf Club, Old Bisley Road, Frimley, Camberley, Surrey, GU16 9NX
Activities: Other sports activities
Officers: Jeffrey Robert Chapman [1948] Director [Australian]; Daniel George Fulcher [1987] Finance Director; Stephen Towers [1970] Director/Chief Executive Officer [Irish]

Crown Golf Operations Limited
Incorporated: 12 July 1993 *Employees:* 900
Previous: Bennelong Golf Partners Subsidiary Limited
Net Worth Deficit: £52,549,000 *Total Assets:* £21,491,000
Registered Office: Pine Ridge Golf Club, Old Bisley Road, Frimley, Camberley, Surrey, GU16 9NX
Activities: Other sports activities
Parent: Crown Golf Property Limited
Officers: Daniel George Fulcher [1987] Finance Director; Stephen Towers [1970] Director/Chief Executive Officer [Irish]

Crown Golf Property Limited
Incorporated: 9 November 2004
Previous: Bennelong Golf Partners Limited
Net Worth: £17,272,000 *Total Assets:* £62,770,000
Registered Office: Pine Ridge Golf Club, Old Bisley Road, Frimley, Camberley, Surrey, GU16 9NX
Activities: Other letting and operating of own or leased real estate
Parent: Crown Golf Group Limited
Officers: Daniel George Fulcher [1987] Finance Director; Stephen Towers [1970] Director/Chief Executive Officer [Irish]

Crown Golf St Mellion Limited
Incorporated: 29 November 2004
Previous: Bennelong Golf (St Mellion) Limited
Net Worth: £2,743,000 *Total Assets:* £20,599,000
Registered Office: Pine Ridge Golf Club, Old Bisley Road, Frimley, Camberley, Surrey, GU16 9NX
Activities: Other letting and operating of own or leased real estate
Parent: Crown Golf Property Limited
Officers: Daniel George Fulcher [1987] Finance Director; Stephen Towers [1970] Director/Chief Executive Officer [Irish]

Crown House Technologies Limited
Incorporated: 24 March 2004
Net Worth: £49,503,000 *Total Assets:* £81,762,000
Registered Office: Bridge Place, Anchor Boulevard, Admirals Park, Dartford, Kent, DA2 6SN
Activities: Construction of commercial buildings
Parent: Laing O'Rourke Holdings Limited
Officers: Robert Edward Turner, Secretary; Stephen John Harley [1951] Director; Alexander Stewart McIntyre [1956] Director; Hubert Desmond O'Rourke [1949] Director/Structural Engineer [Irish]

Crown Lift Trucks Limited
Incorporated: 18 November 1988 *Employees:* 250
Net Worth Deficit: £6,834,000 *Total Assets:* £30,334,000
Registered Office: Rutherford Road, Basingstoke, Hants, RG24 8PD
Activities: Wholesale of other machinery and equipment
Major Shareholder: James F Dicke II
Officers: Sarah Victoria Talbot, Secretary; Simon Barkworth [1973] Managing Director; James Frederick Dicke III [1971] Director/Chairman [American]; Kenneth James Dufford [1964] Director [American]; John Elton Tate [1955] Director [American]

Crown Products (Kent) Limited
Incorporated: 17 March 1986 *Employees:* 269
Net Worth: £20,113,938 *Total Assets:* £26,850,324
Registered Office: Eddington Works, Eddington Lane, Herne Bay, Kent, CT6 5TR
Activities: Manufacture of kitchen furniture
Officers: Vadakke Vayante Valappil Zaheer, Secretary; Richard Taylor Evans [1969] Director; Barry John Head [1968] Director; Michael John Head [1943] Director; Anthony Gerard McCarthy [1960] Director

Croydon and Lewisham Lighting Services (Holdings) Limited
Incorporated: 8 February 2011
Net Worth Deficit: £19,106,000 *Total Assets:* £87,063,000
Registered Office: 8 White Oak Square, London Road, Swanley, Kent, BR8 7AG
Activities: Activities of head offices
Shareholders: JLIF Holdings (Croydon and Lewisham Street Lighting) Limited; Skanska TAM Limited
Officers: Paul Alan Bannister [1959] Director/Accountant; David Richard Bradbury [1969] Director/Senior Investment Manager; Jennifer Kathryn Fegan [1973] Director/Lawyer; Katherine Mary Rae [1980] Director/Legal Advisor; Paul Sydney Shadbolt [1957] Asset Management Director; Keerthana Sivanathan [1988] Director/Senior Management Accountant

Croydon and Lewisham Lighting Services Limited
Incorporated: 9 February 2011
Net Worth Deficit: £19,106,000 *Total Assets:* £87,063,000
Registered Office: 8 White Oak Square, London Road, Swanley, Kent, BR8 7AG
Activities: Other business support service activities n.e.c.
Parent: Croydon and Lewisham Lighting Services (Holdings) Limited
Officers: Paul Alan Bannister [1959] Director/Accountant; David Richard Bradbury [1969] Director/Senior Investment Manager; Jennifer Kathryn Fegan [1973] Director/Lawyer; Katherine Mary Rae [1980] Director/Legal Advisor; Paul Sydney Shadbolt [1957] Asset Management Director; Keerthana Sivanathan [1988] Director/Senior Management Accountant

Crystalate Electronics Limited
Incorporated: 4 May 1961
Net Worth: £63,876,000 *Total Assets:* £68,620,000
Registered Office: Fourth Floor, St Andrews House, West Street, Woking, Surrey, GU21 6EB
Activities: Activities of head offices
Parent: TT Electronics Group Holdings Limited
Officers: Lynton David Boardman, Secretary; Lynton David Boardman [1967] Director/Solicitor; Stephen Giles Harrow [1972] Director/Accountant; Christopher Adrian Jewell [1964] Director

CSB Holdings Limited
Incorporated: 22 June 1989 *Employees:* 353
Previous: CSB Holdings PLC
Net Worth: £12,426,241 *Total Assets:* £33,398,270
Registered Office: The Coins Building, 11 St Laurence Way, Slough, Berks, SL1 2EA
Activities: Other information technology service activities
Major Shareholder: Lawrence John Sullivan
Officers: Adrian Halls, Secretary; Timothy Peter Armitage [1965] Director; Nigel Leslie Cope [1957] Director; Michael Timothy James [1961] Director; Derek Leaver [1952] Director; Lawrence John Sullivan [1953] Director; Richard Louis Werner [1938] Director/Executive [American]

CSC Computer Sciences EMEA Finance Limited
Incorporated: 11 August 1997
Net Worth: £262,115,456 *Total Assets:* £452,943,168
Registered Office: Royal Pavilion, Wellesley Road, Aldershot, Hants, GU11 1PZ
Activities: Financial management
Parent: CSC Computer Sciences International Operations Limited
Officers: Sara Ann de La Harpe [1969] Tax Director; Tina Anne Gough [1962] Finance Director; Michael Charles Woodfine [1971] Director/Solicitor

CSC Computer Sciences Financing LLP
Incorporated: 14 December 2009
Net Worth: £1,206,166,016 *Total Assets:* £1,206,585,984
Registered Office: Royal Pavilion, Wellesley Road, Aldershot, Hants, GU11 1PZ

CSC Computer Sciences International Holdings Limited
Incorporated: 11 November 2009
Net Worth: £1,115,699,968 *Total Assets:* £1,782,630,016
Registered Office: Royal Pavilion, Wellesley Road, Aldershot, Hants, GU11 1PZ
Activities: Activities of other holding companies n.e.c.
Parent: Computer Sciences Corporation
Officers: Sara Ann de La Harpe [1969] Tax Director; Tina Anne Gough [1962] Finance Director; Michael Charles Woodfine [1971] Director/Solicitor

CSC Computer Sciences International Limited
Incorporated: 11 November 2009 *Employees:* 79
Net Worth: £860,795,008 *Total Assets:* £1,736,317,056
Registered Office: Royal Pavilion, Wellesley Road, Aldershot, Hants, GU11 1PZ
Activities: Other information technology service activities
Parent: CSC Computer Sciences International Services Limited
Officers: Sara Ann de La Harpe [1969] Director; Tina Anne Gough [1962] Finance Director; Michael Charles Woodfine [1971] Director/Solicitor

CSC Computer Sciences International Operations Limited
Incorporated: 11 November 2009
Net Worth: £1,758,754,048 *Total Assets:* £2,539,431,936
Registered Office: Royal Pavilion, Wellesley Road, Aldershot, Hants, GU11 1PZ
Activities: Activities of other holding companies n.e.c.
Parent: CSC Computer Sciences International Limited
Officers: Sara Ann de La Harpe [1969] Tax Director; Tina Anne Gough [1962] Finance Director; Michael Charles Woodfine [1971] Director/Solicitor

CSC Computer Sciences International Services Limited
Incorporated: 11 November 2009
Net Worth: £895,276,992 *Total Assets:* £895,566,976
Registered Office: Royal Pavilion, Wellesley Road, Aldershot, Hants, GU11 1PZ
Activities: Activities of other holding companies n.e.c.
Parent: CSC Computer Sciences International Holdings Limited
Officers: Sara Ann de La Harpe [1969] Tax Director; Tina Anne Gough [1962] Finance Director; Michael Charles Woodfine [1971] Director/Solicitor

CSC Computer Sciences Limited
Incorporated: 9 October 1969 *Employees:* 3,562
Net Worth: £457,767,008 *Total Assets:* £1,639,655,040
Registered Office: Royal Pavilion, Wellesley Road, Aldershot, Hants, GU11 1PZ
Activities: Information technology consultancy activities
Parent: CSC Computer Sciences UK Holdings Limited
Officers: Michael Charles Woodfine, Secretary; Tina Anne Gough [1962] Director; Maruf Ahmad Majed [1955] Director [American]; Michael Charles Woodfine [1971] Director/Solicitor

CSC Computer Sciences UK Holdings Limited
Incorporated: 11 November 2009
Net Worth: £841,422,016 *Total Assets:* £1,090,516,992
Registered Office: Royal Pavilion, Wellesley Road, Aldershot, Hants, GU11 1PZ
Activities: Activities of other holding companies n.e.c.
Parent: CSC Computer Sciences International Operations Limited
Officers: Sara Ann de La Harpe [1969] Tax Director; Tina Anne Gough [1962] Finance Director; Michael Charles Woodfine [1971] Director/Solicitor

CSC Life Sciences Limited
Incorporated: 30 November 1987
Net Worth: £36,783,464 *Total Assets:* £37,162,304
Registered Office: Royal Pavilion, Wellesley Road, Aldershot, Hants, GU11 1PZ
Activities: Other human health activities
Parent: Computer Sciences Corporation
Officers: Michael Charles Woodfine, Secretary; Tina Anne Gough [1962] Director; Maruf Ahmad Majed [1955] Director [American]; Michael Charles Woodfine [1971] Director/Solicitor

CSG Systems UK Limited
Incorporated: 21 September 2010
Net Worth: £89,288,000 *Total Assets:* £105,900,000
Registered Office: Wells Court, Albert Drive, Woking, Surrey, GU21 5UB
Activities: Other business support service activities n.e.c.
Parent: CSG Systems International Inc
Officers: Fiona Mary O'Connor [1970] Director/Business Executive [Irish]; David Neil Schaaf [1969] Director/Senior VP, Business Finance & Treasury [American]

CSL (Dualcom) Limited
Incorporated: 6 February 1996 *Employees:* 96
Net Worth: £23,684,504 *Total Assets:* £43,686,032
Registered Office: Salamander Quay West, Park Lane, Harefield, Middlesex, UB9 6NZ
Activities: Other manufacturing n.e.c.
Parent: Dualcom Holdings Limited
Officers: Simon James Banks [1967] Director; Santosh Satish Chandorkar [1974] Director; Robert John Evans [1968] Director; Edward Heale [1973] Director; Philip Hollett [1961] Director; Thomas William Elliott Leigh [1971] Director; Anthony Edward Mann [1970] Director; Jon Shipp [1967] Director

CSL Behring Holdings Limited
Incorporated: 25 May 1995
Net Worth: £10,702,278,656 *Total Assets:* £10,703,140,864
Registered Office: 4 Milton Road, Haywards Heath, W Sussex, RH16 1AH
Activities: Wholesale of pharmaceutical goods
Officers: Paul Richard Fellingham, Secretary; Dr Lutz Guenter Bonacker [1965] Director/Vice President and General Manager, Western Europe [German]; John Andrew Goodman Levy [1959] Director/Group Financial Controller [Australian]; Edward Owens [1956] Director/General Manager; Val Gene Romberg [1958] Director/Chemist [American]

CSL Behring UK Limited
Incorporated: 16 March 1982 *Employees:* 41
Net Worth: £40,338,000 *Total Assets:* £60,219,000
Registered Office: 4 Milton Road, Haywards Heath, W Sussex, RH16 1AH
Activities: Wholesale of pharmaceutical goods
Officers: Paul Richard Fellingham, Secretary; Dr Lutz Guenter Bonacker [1965] Director/Vice President and General Manager, Western Europe [German]; John Andrew Goodman Levy [1959] Director/Group Financial Controller [Australian]; Edward Owens [1956] Director/General Manager

CSL Communications Group Limited
Incorporated: 2 December 2011
Net Worth Deficit: £19,988,428 *Total Assets:* £50,398,536
Registered Office: Salamander Quay West, Park Lane, Harefield, Middlesex, UB9 6NZ
Activities: Activities of head offices
Parent: Sunny Bidco Limited
Officers: Simon James Banks [1967] Director; Paraag Dave [1975] Director; Edward Heale [1973] Director; Philip Hollett [1961] Director; Thomas William Elliott Leigh [1971] Director

CSL UK Holdings Limited
Incorporated: 12 March 2002
Net Worth: £1,289,000 *Total Assets:* £555,302,016
Registered Office: 4 Milton Road, Haywards Heath, W Sussex, RH16 1AH
Activities: Activities of head offices
Officers: Paul Richard Fellingham, Secretary; John Andrew Goodman Levy [1959] Director/Accountant [Australian]; Antje Michel [1966] Director/In House Counsel Assistant General Counsel & Head [German]

CSM Motor Group Limited
Incorporated: 24 February 2003 *Employees:* 198
Net Worth: £4,056,998 *Total Assets:* £20,085,642
Registered Office: J Davy Basingstoke, West Ham, Basingstoke, Hants, RG22 6PL
Activities: Activities of head offices
Officers: David James Sear Mayes, Secretary; Christopher Clarkson [1952] Director/Executive; David James Sear Mayes [1961] Director/Executive

CSPH Limited
Incorporated: 7 March 2008 *Employees:* 82
Net Worth: £1,772,423 *Total Assets:* £25,739,364
Registered Office: Duffy House, 1 Mount Road, Feltham, Middlesex, TW13 6AR
Activities: Activities of head offices
Major Shareholder: Jonathan Bernard Duffy
Officers: Joanna Margaret Duffy, Secretary; Donal Corbett [1959] Director/Quantity Surveyor [Irish]; Jonathan Bernard Duffy [1978] Director; Stephen Peter Vincett [1980] Director/Accountant

CSSC Properties Limited
Incorporated: 7 December 1999
Net Worth: £33,419,000 *Total Assets:* £34,992,000
Registered Office: Compton Court, 20-24 Temple End, High Wycombe, Bucks, HP13 5DR
Activities: Buying and selling of own real estate
Officers: Simon Norris Lee, Secretary; Wendy Eley [1976] Director; Raymond John Peter Haskell [1960] Director/Estate Manager; Marian Holmes [1952] Director/Civil Servant; Simon Norris Lee [1961] Director/Chief Executive

CT Automotive Group Limited
Incorporated: 28 October 2016 *Employees:* 2,361
Net Worth Deficit: £3,404,336 *Total Assets:* £57,863,064
Registered Office: 1000 Lakeside North Harbour, Western Road, Portsmouth, PO6 3EN
Activities: Manufacture of other parts and accessories for motor vehicles
Major Shareholder: Simon Phillips
Officers: Mr David Paul Wilkinson [1981] Director

CTDI Repair Services Limited
Incorporated: 27 January 2016
Net Worth: £92,146,536 *Total Assets:* £92,669,624
Registered Office: CTDI Repair Services Limited, Featherstone Road, Wolverton Mill, Milton Keynes, Bucks, MK12 5TH
Activities: Repair of other equipment
Parent: CTDI Holdings Limited
Officers: Matthew James Bull [1975] Managing Director; Dieter Hollenbach [1964] Director [German]; Brian Christopher Parsons [1979] Director/Vice President [American]; Generald Joseph Parsons [1952] Director/Chairman [American]; Leo David Parsons [1960] Director/President [American]; Monika Rueth [1968] Director [German]

CTS Metropark Limited
Incorporated: 29 July 2015 *Employees:* 2,285
Net Worth: £2,438,000 *Total Assets:* £507,940,992
Registered Office: 1 Towers Place, Eton Street, Richmond, Surrey, TW9 1EG
Activities: Hotels and similar accommodation
Parent: China National Travel Service Group Corporation
Officers: Rong Chen [1966] Director [Chinese]; Weihong Feng [1970] Director [Chinese]; Peng Huang [1967] Director/General Manager [Chinese]; Yan Huang [1967] Director [Chinese]; Jamie Andrew Lamb [1972] Director/Chartered Accountant; Alex Edward Pritchard [1976] Director/Chief Operating Officer; Yiyin Sun [1962] Director [Chinese]

CTV Outside Broadcasts Limited
Incorporated: 23 March 2005 *Employees:* 142
Net Worth: £16,621,000 *Total Assets:* £34,603,000
Registered Office: Unit 3 The Merlin Centre, Lancaster Road, Cressex Business Park, High Wycombe, Bucks, HP12 3QL
Activities: Television programme production activities
Officers: Andrew David Maries, Secretary; Hamish Francis Alexander Greig [1957] Director/Engineer; Barry Gibson Johnstone [1945] Managing Director [New Zealander]; Andrew David Maries [1965] Director/Accountant

Cubic Transportation Systems Limited
Incorporated: 2 August 1978 *Employees:* 984
Net Worth: £73,701,000 *Total Assets:* £176,706,000
Registered Office: AFC House, Honeycrock Lane, Salfords, Redhill, Surrey, RH1 5LA
Activities: Manufacture of other electrical equipment
Parent: Cubic Surface Transportation Systems Limited
Officers: James Richard Edwards, Secretary; Anshooman Aga [1975] Director/Executive [American]; Matthew Cole [1979] Director/President; James Richard Edwards [1951] Director/VP Senior Counsel & Corporate Secretary [American]; Laurent Albert Eskenazi [1962] Managing Director [French]; David Alan Wear [1967] Director/Vice President and Regional CFO

Cucina Acquisition (UK) Limited
Incorporated: 14 June 2007
Net Worth: £2,428,199,936 *Total Assets:* £2,655,300,096
Registered Office: Enterprise House, Eureka Business Park, Ashford, Kent, TN25 4AG
Activities: Activities of head offices
Parent: Cucina Finance (UK) Limited
Officers: Sarah Leanne Whibley, Secretary; Michael David Ball [1967] Director/Group Chief Financial Officer; Ajoy Hari Karna [1966] Director/Senior Vice President [American]; Sarah Leanne Whibley [1976] Director/Group Secretary & General Counsel

Cucina Finance (UK) Limited
Incorporated: 6 July 2007
Net Worth: £2,764,999,936 *Total Assets:* £2,813,700,096
Registered Office: Enterprise House, Eureka Business Park, Ashford, Kent, TN25 4AG
Activities: Activities of head offices
Parent: Cucina Lux Investments Limited
Officers: Sarah Leanne Whibley, Secretary; Michael David Ball [1967] Director/Group Chief Financial Officer; Ajoy Hari Karna [1966] Director/Senior Vice President [American]

Cucina French Holdings Limited
Incorporated: 3 July 2015
Net Worth: £90,730,064 *Total Assets:* £90,817,704
Registered Office: Enterprise House, Eureka Business Park, Ashford, Kent, TN25 4AG
Activities: Activities of other holding companies n.e.c.
Parent: Brake Bros Limited
Officers: Sarah Whibley, Secretary; Michael David Ball [1967] Director/Group Chief Financial Officer; Ajoy Hari Karna [1966] Director/Senior Vice President [American]; Sarah Leanne Whibley [1976] Director/Solicitor

Cucina Fresh Finance Limited
Incorporated: 7 November 2014
Net Worth: £109,500,000 *Total Assets:* £160,200,000
Registered Office: Enterprise House, Eureka Business Park, Ashford, Kent, TN25 4AG
Activities: Activities of head offices
Shareholders: Cucina Acquisition (UK) Limited; Cucina Fresh Investments Limited
Officers: Sarah Whibley, Secretary; Michael David Ball [1967] Director/Group Chief Financial Officer; Joel Todd Grade [1970] Director/Executive VP & CFO [American]; Ajoy Hari Karna [1966] Director/Senior Vice President [American]

Cucina Fresh Investments Limited
Incorporated: 28 January 2015
Net Worth: £65,500,000 *Total Assets:* £65,500,000
Registered Office: Enterprise House, Eureka Business Park, Ashford, Kent, TN25 4AG
Activities: Activities of head offices
Shareholders: M & J Seafood Holdings Limited; Brake Bros Limited
Officers: Sarah Whibley, Secretary; Michael David Ball [1967] Director/Group Chief Financial Officer; Sarah Leanne Whibley [1976] Director/Solicitor

Cucina Lux Investments Limited
Incorporated: 6 July 2007
Net Worth: £1,145,600,000 *Total Assets:* £2,434,200,064
Registered Office: Enterprise House, Eureka Business Park, Ashford, Kent, TN25 4AG
Activities: Activities of head offices
Officers: Sarah Whibley, Secretary; Joel Todd Grade [1970] Director/Executive VP & CFO [American]; Ajoy Hari Karna [1966] Director/Senior Vice President [American]; Russell Thomas Libby [1996] Director/Executive VP [American]

Cuffe Holdings Limited
Incorporated: 22 March 2002 *Employees:* 37
Net Worth: £16,714,759 *Total Assets:* £24,774,800
Registered Office: 19 Penrhyn Road, Kingston upon Thames, Surrey, KT1 2BZ
Activities: Other letting and operating of own or leased real estate
Major Shareholder: Arthur Charles Cowdery
Officers: Ian Maxwell Dodd, Secretary; Arthur Charles Cowdery [1953] Director

Cullum Capital Ventures Limited
Incorporated: 10 October 2005
Net Worth: £82,101,848 *Total Assets:* £314,381,312
Registered Office: Tower Gate House, Eclipse Park Sittingbourne Road, Maidstone, Kent, ME14 3EN
Activities: Non-life insurance
Parent: Towergate Insurance Limited
Officers: Dean Clarke, Secretary; Antonios Erotocritou [1971] Director/Deputy CFO [Cypriot]; David Christopher Ross [1969] Director [Irish]

Cullum Family Trust
Incorporated: 20 November 2006 *Employees:* 3
Net Worth: £29,607,154 *Total Assets:* £29,719,796
Registered Office: Wealden Hall, Parkfield, Sevenoaks, Kent, TN15 0HX
Activities: Non-trading company
Officers: Peter Geoffrey Cullum, Secretary/Executive Chairman; Ann Cullum [1960] Director/Executive PA; Claire Louise Cullum [1981] Director/Sales Executive; Peter Geoffrey Cullum [1950] Director/Executive Chairman; Simon Cullum [1977] Director/E-Trading Executive

Currie Motors Limited
Incorporated: 13 July 1979 *Employees:* 614
Net Worth: £123,356,000 *Total Assets:* £228,563,008
Registered Office: 161 Chertsey Road, Twickenham, Middlesex, TW1 1ER
Activities: Other letting and operating of own or leased real estate
Parent: Curfin (Netherlands Antilles) B.V.
Officers: Joseph Michael Jaffe [1955] Director/Business Executive; Derek Jonathan Murray [1960] Director/Company Executive; Glenn Robert Bruce Pitzer [1968] Director/Company Executive

Curtis Holt Limited
Incorporated: 5 March 1954 *Employees:* 532
Net Worth: £50,736,000 *Total Assets:* £65,687,000
Registered Office: Long Reach, Galleon Boulevard, Crossways Business Park, Dartford, Kent, DA2 6QE
Activities: Non-specialised wholesale trade
Parent: Dormole Ltd
Officers: Robert David Rowe, Secretary; Andrew James Thomas Strong [1955] Director; Timothy John Strong [1958] Director; John Randall Charles Twallin [1933] Director

Custodes Midco Limited
Incorporated: 16 February 2015 *Employees:* 1,300
Net Worth: £21,658,990 *Total Assets:* £47,083,628
Registered Office: River House, Maidstone Road, Sidcup, Kent, DA14 5RH
Activities: Residential nursing care facilities
Parent: Custodes Pikco Limited
Officers: Nils Ian Stoesser [1974] Managing Director [German]; Colin Leslie Stokes [1975] Director; Nicholas John Yarrow [1967] Director

Cyberfort Bidco Limited
Incorporated: 27 April 2017 *Employees:* 6
Net Worth Deficit: £1,022,909 *Total Assets:* £28,312,204
Registered Office: Venture West, Greenham Business Park, Greenham, Thatcham, Berks, RG19 6HX
Activities: Activities of head offices
Parent: Cyberfort Group Limited
Officers: Philip Neil Bindley [1969] Director; Anthony John Dickin [1970] Director; Andrew Denzil Maurice Hague [1970] Director; Alan Miles Howarth [1945] Director; David Edward Jay [1958] Director; Andrew James Strickland [1982] Director

Cyberfort Group Limited
Incorporated: 31 May 2017 *Employees:* 70
Net Worth Deficit: £1,271,403 *Total Assets:* £31,373,432
Registered Office: Venture West, Greenham Business Park, Greenham, Thatcham, Berks, RG19 6HX
Activities: Activities of head offices
Parent: Palatine Private Equity Fund III LP
Officers: Philip Neil Bindley [1969] Director; Anthony John Dickin [1970] Director; Andrew Denzil Maurice Hague [1970] Director; Alan Miles Howarth [1945] Director; David Edward Jay [1958] Finance Director; Andrew James Strickland [1982] Director

Cygnet 2002 Limited
Incorporated: 23 July 2002 *Employees:* 6
Net Worth Deficit: £10,135,000 *Total Assets:* £76,754,000
Registered Office: Nepicar House, London Road, Wrotham Heath, Sevenoaks, Kent, TN15 7RS
Activities: Hospital activities
Parent: Cygnet Inter-Holdings Ltd
Officers: Anthony James Coleman, Secretary; Mark George Ground [1970] Finance Director; Laurence Harrod [1956] Director/Finance [American]; Dr Antonio Romero [1971] Director [Spanish]

Cygnet Aspirations Developments Limited
Incorporated: 16 October 2009
Previous: CAS Aspirations Developments Limited
Net Worth: £56,207,000 *Total Assets:* £112,173,000
Registered Office: Nepicar House, London Road, Wrotham Heath, Sevenoaks, Kent, TN15 7RS
Activities: Hospital activities
Parent: Cygnet Health Care Limited
Officers: Anthony James Coleman, Secretary; Mark George Ground [1970] Director; Laurence Lee Harrod [1956] Director [American]; Michael James McQuaid [1958] Director; Dr Antonio Romero [1971] Director/Doctor [Spanish]

Cygnet Behavioural Health Limited
Incorporated: 20 April 2000 *Employees:* 1,227
Previous: CAS Behavioural Health Limited
Net Worth: £1,885,000 *Total Assets:* £120,235,000
Registered Office: Nepicar House, London Road, Wrotham Heath, Sevenoaks, Kent, TN15 7RS
Activities: Hospital activities
Parent: Cygnet Health Care Limited
Officers: Anthony James Coleman, Secretary; Mark George Ground [1970] Director; Laurence Lee Harrod [1956] Director [American]; Michael James McQuaid [1958] Director; Dr Antonio Romero [1971] Director/Doctor [Spanish]

Cygnet Health Care Limited
Incorporated: 18 June 1987 *Employees:* 1,956
Net Worth: £172,720,992 *Total Assets:* £366,398,016
Registered Office: Nepicar House, London Road, Wrotham Heath, Sevenoaks, Kent, TN15 7RS
Activities: Hospital activities
Parent: Cygnet 2002 Limited
Officers: Anthony James Coleman, Secretary; Mark George Ground [1970] Finance Director; Laurence Harrod [1956] Director/Finance [American]; Michael James McQuaid [1958] Director; Dr Antonio Romero [1971] Director [Spanish]

Cygnet Health UK Limited
Incorporated: 4 January 2008 *Employees:* 6,268
Previous: Cygnet 2008 Limited
Net Worth: £828,275,968 *Total Assets:* £906,067,968
Registered Office: Nepicar House, London Road, Wrotham Heath, Sevenoaks, Kent, TN15 7RS
Activities: Hospital activities
Parent: UK Acquisitions No. 6 Limited
Officers: Mark George Ground, Secretary; Mark George Ground [1970] Director; Laurence Harrod [1956] Director/Finance [American]; Michael James McQuaid [1958] Director; Dr Antonio Romero [1971] Director [Spanish]

Cygnet Inter-Holdings Limited
Incorporated: 4 January 2008
Net Worth Deficit: £169,370,000 *Total Assets:* £85,000,000
Registered Office: Nepicar House, London Road, Wrotham Heath, Sevenoaks, Kent, TN15 7RS
Activities: Hospital activities
Parent: Cygnet Health UK Limited
Officers: Anthony James Coleman, Secretary; Mark George Ground [1970] Finance Director; Laurence Harrod [1956] Director/Finance [American]; Dr Antonio Romero [1971] Director [Spanish]

Cygnet Learning Disabilities Limited
Incorporated: 18 March 1987 *Employees:* 221
Previous: CAS Learning Disabilities Limited
Net Worth: £13,884,000 *Total Assets:* £26,862,000
Registered Office: Nepicar House, London Road, Wrotham Heath, Sevenoaks, Kent, TN15 7RS
Activities: Residential care activities for learning difficulties, mental health and substance abuse
Parent: Cygnet Aspirations Developments Limited
Officers: Anthony James Coleman, Secretary; Mark George Ground [1970] Director; Laurence Lee Harrod [1956] Director [American]; Michael James McQuaid [1958] Director; Dr Antonio Romero [1971] Director [Spanish]

Cygnet Learning Disabilities Midlands Limited
Incorporated: 3 July 1991 *Employees:* 593
Previous: CAS Learning Disabilities Midlands Limited
Net Worth: £9,579,000 *Total Assets:* £24,475,000
Registered Office: Nepicar House, London Road, Wrotham Heath, Sevenoaks, Kent, TN15 7RS
Activities: Residential care activities for learning difficulties, mental health and substance abuse
Parent: Cygnet Aspirations Developments Limited
Officers: Anthony James Coleman, Secretary; Mark George Ground [1970] Director; Laurence Lee Harrod [1956] Director [American]; Michael James McQuaid [1958] Director; Dr Antonio Romero [1971] Director [Spanish]

Cygnet NW Limited
Incorporated: 25 August 2000 *Employees:* 730
Previous: Alpha Hospitals (NW) Limited
Net Worth: £85,213,000 *Total Assets:* £90,059,000
Registered Office: Nepicar House, London Road, Wrotham Heath, Sevenoaks, Kent, TN15 7RS
Activities: Other human health activities
Parent: Cygnet Surrey Limited
Officers: Anthony James Coleman, Secretary; Mark George Ground [1970] Director; Laurence Harrod [1956] Director/Finance [American]; Dr Antonio Romero [1971] Director [Spanish]

Cygnet Propco Limited
Incorporated: 30 October 2007
Net Worth: £17,592,000 *Total Assets:* £209,755,008
Registered Office: Nepicar House, London Road, Wrotham Heath, Sevenoaks, Kent, TN15 7RS
Activities: Hospital activities
Parent: Cygnet Propco Holdco Limited
Officers: Anthony James Coleman, Secretary; Mark George Ground [1970] Finance Director; Laurence Harrod [1956] Director/Finance [American]; Dr Antonio Romero [1971] Director [Spanish]

Cygnet Surrey Limited
Incorporated: 14 November 2002 *Employees:* 214
Previous: Alpha Hospitals Limited
Net Worth Deficit: £14,948,000 *Total Assets:* £28,382,000
Registered Office: Nepicar House, London Road, Wrotham Heath, Sevenoaks, Kent, TN15 7RS
Activities: Hospital activities
Parent: Cygnet Hospitals Holdings Limited
Officers: Anthony James Coleman, Secretary; Mark George Ground [1970] Director; Laurence Harrod [1956] Director/Finance [American]; Dr Antonio Romero [1971] Director [Spanish]

Cyxtera Technology UK Limited
Incorporated: 26 July 1999 *Employees:* 67
Previous: CenturyLink Technology UK Limited
Net Worth: £106,582,000 *Total Assets:* £163,550,000
Registered Office: Eskdale Road, Winnersh Triangle, Wokingham, Berks, RG41 5TS
Activities: Other telecommunications activities
Officers: Michael Paul Bennett [1966] Director; Rene Rodriguez [1976] Director/Chief Financial Officer [American]; Victor Semah [1981] Director/Attorney [American]

D & B Europe Limited
Incorporated: 5 August 1988 *Employees:* 88
Net Worth: £114,389,000 *Total Assets:* £123,076,000
Registered Office: Marlow International, Parkway, Marlow, Bucks, SL7 1AJ
Activities: Activities of head offices
Parent: D & B Group Holdings (UK)
Officers: Paramdeep Sidhu, Secretary; Rosemarie Jane Ellis [1968] Director; Jorge Humberto Forton Palomino [1962] Director [Peruvian]; Piers Dominic Gilchrist Woolston [1960] Director

D & B Group Holdings (UK)
Incorporated: 5 June 2002
Net Worth: £73,965,000 *Total Assets:* £213,040,992
Registered Office: Marlow International, Parkway, Marlow, Bucks, SL7 1AJ
Activities: Non-trading company
Officers: Emma Kimberley Morris, Secretary; Rosemarie Jane Ellis [1968] Director; Jorge Humberto Forton Palomino [1962] Director [Peruvian]; Piers Dominic Gilchrist Woolston [1960] Director

D-R Holdings (UK) Ltd
Incorporated: 18 October 2004
Net Worth: £6,557,000 *Total Assets:* £25,660,000
Registered Office: Faraday House, Sir William Siemens Square, Frimley, Camberley, Surrey, GU16 8QD
Activities: Activities of head offices
Parent: Siemens Aktiengesellschaft
Officers: Simone Eufemia Agatha Davina, Secretary; Lee Dawson [1978] Director/Accountant; Daniel Mann [1976] Director/Business Executive

D.D.D. Limited
Incorporated: 16 May 1912 *Employees:* 304
Net Worth: £4,715,009 *Total Assets:* £27,138,234
Registered Office: 94 Rickmansworth Road, Watford, Herts, WD18 7JJ
Activities: Manufacture of basic pharmaceutical products
Parent: DDD Investments Limited
Officers: Carl Atkinson [1974] Director; Hanna Joy Coonagh [1972] Director; Digby Lawrence Spence Halsby [1976] Non Executive Director; Roger Harrison [1969] Managing Director; Simon Morris [1973] HR Director; Charles Philip Wadsworth [1962] Finance Director

D.E Holding UK Limited
Incorporated: 28 April 1981
Net Worth: £432,563,008 *Total Assets:* £507,120,000
Registered Office: Horizon, Honey Lane, Hurley, Maidenhead, Berks, SL6 6RJ
Activities: Activities of head offices
Officers: Sophy Pashley, Secretary; Justin Richard Cook [1967] Director/General Manager Retail UK & Ireland; David Peter Gwynne Jones [1972] Finance Director

D4T4 Solutions PLC
Incorporated: 6 March 1985 *Employees:* 122
Previous: I S Solutions PLC
Net Worth: £20,985,000 *Total Assets:* £39,416,000
Registered Office: Windmill House, 91-93 Windmill Road, Sunbury upon Thames, Middlesex, TW16 7EF
Activities: Other information technology service activities
Officers: James Henry Thorne, Secretary; Mark Geoffrey Boxall [1963] Operations Director; James Lloyd Dodkins [1956] Director; Peter John Kear [1955] Sales Director; John Lythall [1948] Director; Roger Steven McDowell [1955] Director; Peter Anthony Simmonds [1958] Director/Accountant; Mathew Tod [1964] Director; Carmel Elizabeth Warren [1964] Finance Director; Peter Frederick Whiting [1966] Director

Dage Precision Industries Limited
Incorporated: 27 February 1992 *Employees:* 138
Net Worth: £26,065,836 *Total Assets:* £37,294,408
Registered Office: 25 Faraday Road, Rabans Lane Industrial Estate, Aylesbury, Bucks, HP19 8RY
Activities: Other manufacturing n.e.c.
Officers: Gina Anne Beredo [1974] Director/Laywer [American]; Liaqat Ali Sadiq [1961] Finance Director; Philip Vere [1956] Director/President

Dai Europe Ltd
Incorporated: 26 October 1984 *Employees:* 156
Net Worth: £4,299,000 *Total Assets:* £43,542,000
Registered Office: 3rd Floor, Block C, Westside, London Road, Apsley, Hemel Hempstead, Herts, HP3 9TD
Activities: Management consultancy activities other than financial management
Parent: DAI Global LLC
Officers: Erin Cerpa, Secretary; James John Boomgard [1954] Director [American]; Michael James Jakobowski [1960] Director [American]; Christopher Lockett [1963] Managing Director

Daikin Airconditioning UK Limited
Incorporated: 13 December 2002 *Employees:* 261
Net Worth: £18,119,000 *Total Assets:* £51,144,000
Registered Office: The Heights, Brooklands, Weybridge, Surrey, KT13 0NY
Activities: Steam and air conditioning supply
Parent: Daikin Europe N.V.
Officers: Hendrik Jan Van Den Berg, Secretary; Wim de Schacht [1968] Director/Manager [Belgian]; Mark Dyer [1972] Director/Sales Management; Hiroyasu Ishikawa [1977] Director [Japanese]; Angela McGinlay [1963] Managing Director; Toshitaka Tsubouchi [1958] Director/Manager [Japanese]; Junji Umamoto [1961] Director [Japanese]

Daimler UK Limited
Incorporated: 22 October 1973
Net Worth: £723,057,984 *Total Assets:* £836,051,968
Registered Office: Mercedes-Benz Cars UK Limited, Delaware Drive, Tongwell, Milton Keynes, Bucks, MK15 8BA
Activities: Activities of head offices
Parent: Daimler AG (HRB 19360)
Officers: Jonathan Philip Rueben Lipman, Secretary; Harald Henn [1964] Director/Economist [German]; Gary Mark Savage [1961] Director

Dairy Crest (Services) Limited
Incorporated: 31 March 1943
Net Worth: £257,376,992 *Total Assets:* £268,000,992
Registered Office: Claygate House, Littleworth Road, Esher, Surrey, KT10 9PN
Activities: Non-trading company
Parent: Dairy Crest France Holdings 1
Officers: Isobel Jean Hinton, Secretary; Mark Allen [1959] Managing Director; Thomas Alexander Atherton [1970] Director/Chartered Accountant

Dairy Crest France Holdings 1 Limited
Incorporated: 21 June 1996
Net Worth: £337,920,000 *Total Assets:* £487,660,000
Registered Office: Claygate House, Littleworth Road, Esher, Surrey, KT10 9PN
Activities: Other business support service activities n.e.c.
Parent: Dairy Crest Limited
Officers: Isobel Jean Hinton, Secretary; Mark Allen [1959] Managing Director; Thomas Alexander Atherton [1970] Director/Chartered Accountant; Robert Thomas Arthur Willock [1966] Director

Dairy Crest France Holdings 2 Limited
Incorporated: 24 November 1997
Net Worth: £115,949,000 *Total Assets:* £262,887,008
Registered Office: Claygate House, Littleworth Road, Esher, Surrey, KT10 9PN
Activities: Liquid milk and cream production
Parent: Dairy Crest France Holdings 1 Limited
Officers: Isobel Jean Hinton, Secretary; Mark Allen [1959] Managing Director; Thomas Alexander Atherton [1970] Director/Chartered Accountant

Dairy Crest Group PLC
Incorporated: 22 February 1996 *Employees:* 1,097
Net Worth: £243,700,000 *Total Assets:* £628,200,000
Registered Office: Claygate House, Littleworth Road, Esher, Surrey, KT10 9PN
Activities: Manufacture of margarine and similar edible fats
Officers: Roger James Robotham, Secretary; Stephen Harold Alexander [1955] Director; Mark Allen [1959] Director; Thomas Alexander Atherton [1970] Director/Chartered Accountant; Adam Braithwaite [1975] Director; Susan Jane Farr [1956] Director; John Michael Gibney [1960] Director; Richard Auld MacDonald [1954] Director/Consultant; Sheikh Mansurah Tal-At Mannings [1963] Director

Dairy Crest Limited
Incorporated: 23 December 1986 *Employees:* 1,047
Net Worth: £176,100,000 *Total Assets:* £1,479,000,064
Registered Office: Claygate House, Littleworth Road, Esher, Surrey, KT10 9PN
Activities: Manufacture of margarine and similar edible fats
Parent: Dairy Crest UK Limited
Officers: Roger James Robotham, Secretary; Mark Allen [1959] Director/MD Cheese; Thomas Alexander Atherton [1970] Director/Chartered Accountant; Richard Steven Jones [1969] Procurement Director; Robert Thomas Arthur Willock [1966] Director

Dairy Crest UK Limited
Incorporated: 22 August 2008
Net Worth: £235,256,000 *Total Assets:* £565,105,984
Registered Office: Claygate House, Littleworth Road, Esher, Surrey, KT10 9PN
Activities: Other business support service activities n.e.c.
Parent: Dairy Crest Group
Officers: Isobel Jean Hinton, Secretary; Thomas Alexander Atherton [1970] Director/Chartered Accountant; Richard Steven Jones [1969] Procurement Director

Daler-Rowney Limited
Incorporated: 19 December 1923 *Employees:* 231
Net Worth: £11,653,000 *Total Assets:* £49,018,000
Registered Office: Daler Rowney House, Southern Industrial Area, Bracknell, Berks, RG12 8SS
Activities: Other manufacturing n.e.c.
Parent: Renoir Bidco Limited
Officers: Stefano de Rosa, Secretary; Massimo Candela [1965] Director [Italian]; Stefano de Rosa [1968] Finance Director [Italian]; Dominique Willy Michel Ghislain Paradis [1966] Director [Belgian]

Danfoss Limited
Incorporated: 29 April 1991 *Employees:* 227
Net Worth: £16,437,000 *Total Assets:* £31,494,000
Registered Office: 22 Wycombe End, Beaconsfield, Bucks, HP9 1NB
Activities: Other manufacturing n.e.c.
Officers: Torben Christensen [1966] Director [Danish]; Jens Garde Gad [1964] Director [Danish]; Marcus Postings [1962] Director; Anders Stahlschmidt [1967] Director/Lawyer [Danish]; Nick Andrew Wanless [1968] Director/Accountant

W.J.Daniel & Company Limited
Incorporated: 26 October 1931 *Employees:* 141
Net Worth: £25,501,860 *Total Assets:* £38,507,464
Registered Office: 120-125 Peascod Street, Windsor, Berks, SL4 1DP
Activities: Other retail sale in non-specialised stores
Officers: William John Daniel, Secretary; Aaran Anthony Daniel [1964] Director/Developer; Peter William Daniel [1937] Director/Draper; Stephen Michael Daniel [1966] Director/Retail Manager; William John Daniel [1962] Director/Accountant; Anthony John Durkin [1959] Director/Manager; Trudy Nicola Durkin [1963] Director/Manager; Heidi Joanne Marion [1975] Director/Food Retailer

Danshell Healthcare Limited
Incorporated: 14 May 2013 *Employees:* 829
Net Worth Deficit: £8,049,000 *Total Assets:* £32,604,000
Registered Office: Nepicar House, London Road, Wrotham Heath, Sevenoaks, Kent, TN15 7RS
Activities: Residential nursing care facilities
Parent: Cygnet Health Care Limited
Officers: Anthony Coleman, Secretary; Generald Thomas Corbett [1963] Director/Finance [American]; Mark George Ground [1970] Director; Clynton John Hall [1977] Finance Director; Laurence Harrod [1956] Director/Finance [American]; Michael James McQuaid [1958] Director; Antonio Romero [1971] Director [Spanish]

Danu Holding Limited
Incorporated: 7 December 2007
Net Worth Deficit: £8,204,993 *Total Assets:* £28,618,104
Registered Office: Munro House, Portsmouth Road, Cobham, Surrey, KT11 1PP
Activities: Other business support service activities n.e.c.
Parent: Gravis Onshore Wind 1 Limited
Officers: Stephen Campbell Joseph Ellis [1959] Director; Rollo Andrew Johnstone Wright [1976] Director; Philip William Kent [1984] Director; Ronan Niall Kierans [1978] Director [Irish]; Nicholas Simon Parker [1969] Director

Danu II Holdings Limited
Incorporated: 17 December 2008 *Employees:* 5
Net Worth Deficit: £11,944,455 *Total Assets:* £35,410,976
Registered Office: Munro House, Portsmouth Road, Cobham, Surrey, KT11 1PP
Activities: Other business support service activities n.e.c.
Parent: Gravis Onshore Wind 2 Limited
Officers: Stephen Campbell Joseph Ellis [1959] Director; Rollo Andrew Johnstone Wright [1976] Director; Philip William Kent [1984] Director; Ronan Niall Kierans [1978] Director [Irish]; Nicholas Simon Parker [1969] Director

Darty Limited
Incorporated: 11 June 2001
Previous: Darty PLC
Net Worth: £145,418,688 *Total Assets:* £162,811,552
Registered Office: 4th Floor, Reading Bridge House, George Street, Reading, Berks, RG1 8LS
Activities: Activities of head offices
Parent: FNAC Darty SA
Officers: Frederique Giavarini [1972] Director [French]; Vincent Henri Bernard Gufflet [1973] Commercial Director of Products and Services [French]; Jean-Brieuc-Pierre-Marie Le Tinier [1971] Director/Chief Financial Officer and Financial Manager [French]

Charles Darwin Academy Trust
Incorporated: 7 March 2011 *Employees:* 268
Net Worth: £23,673,216 *Total Assets:* £25,857,472
Registered Office: Charles Darwin School, Jail Lane, Biggin Hill, Westerham, Kent, TN16 3AU
Activities: General secondary education
Officers: Julia Ann Hodgkinson, Secretary; Anoop Singh Bamrah [1982] Commercial Director; Julian Wybergh Benington [1939] Director/Local Councillor; Sunil Chotai [1959] Director/Headteacher; David Dilling [1949] Director; Helen Claire Hartley [1971] Director/Secretary; Mervin Peter Sharp [1943] Director/Consultant; Paul Generald Woolfenden [1953] Director/Business Consultant

Data Select Limited
Incorporated: 5 November 1998 *Employees:* 139
Net Worth: £15,225,905 *Total Assets:* £72,733,216
Registered Office: Network House, Third Avenue, Globe Park, Marlow, Bucks, SL7 1EY
Activities: Other telecommunications activities
Shareholders: Data Select Group Limited; Peter David Jones
Officers: James Edward Peter Holdgate, Secretary; Fergal Andrew Donovan [1972] Director/Senior Vice President [Irish]; Peter David Jones [1966] Director; Nicholas David Willcox [1970] Director/Group CFO

Data Solutions 2016 Limited
Incorporated: 26 January 2016 *Employees:* 444
Net Worth Deficit: £2,578,000 *Total Assets:* £63,767,000
Registered Office: The Databank, Unit 5 Redhill Distribution Centre, Salbrook Road, Redhill, Surrey, RH1 5DY
Activities: Other business support service activities n.e.c.
Parent: Restore PLC
Officers: Sarah Lesley Waudby, Secretary; Adam Thomas Councell [1978] Director; Charles Antony Lawrence Skinner [1960] Director

Datatec PLC
Incorporated: 20 October 2011
Net Worth: £443,304,960 *Total Assets:* £1,896,177,664
Registered Office: 110 Buckingham Avenue, Slough, SL1 4PF
Activities: Activities of head offices
Parent: Datatec Limited
Officers: Simon Morris, Secretary; Stephen James Davidson [1955] Independent Non-Executive Director; Ivan Philip Dittrich [1972] Director/Chief Financial Officer [South African]; Jens Peter Montanana [1960] Director/Chief Executive Officer

Davidson Kempner European Partners, LLP
Incorporated: 20 May 2004 *Employees:* 56
Net Worth: £53,763,424 *Total Assets:* £86,433,064
Registered Office: 4th Floor, Reading Bridge House, George Street, Reading, Berks, RG1 8LS
Officers: Michael Herzog [1971] Member; Jogeesvaran Chris Krishanthan [1973] Member; Zachary Gozali [1974] LLP Member; Risto Oskari Koivula [1975] LLP Member; Jeremy Clement Lowe [1974] LLP Member; Brian Ratner [1966] LLP Member

J.T. Davies & Sons Holdings Limited
Incorporated: 1 November 2006 *Employees:* 221
Net Worth: £59,057,000 *Total Assets:* £112,299,000
Registered Office: The Bull Courtyard, Bell Street, Henley on Thames, Oxon, RG9 2BA
Activities: Activities of head offices
Parent: M.A.T. Davies Holdings Limited
Officers: David Generald Nathan, Secretary; Michael Anthony Trehearne Davies [1953] Director/Chairman; Thomas Anthony Trehearne Davies [1980] Director; Timothy Alfred Davies [1938] Director; Peter Furness-Smith [1953] Director; David Generald Nathan [1970] Director; Edward James Turner [1967] Director

J.T.Davies & Sons Limited
Incorporated: 7 September 1911 *Employees:* 7
Net Worth: £64,428,696 *Total Assets:* £65,178,176
Registered Office: The Bull Courtyard, Bell Street, Henley on Thames, Oxon, RG9 2BA
Activities: Public houses and bars
Parent: J.T.D. Investments Limited
Officers: David Generald Nathan, Secretary; Michael Anthony Trehearne Davies [1953] Director/Chairman; Thomas Anthony Trehearne Davies [1980] Director; Timothy Alfred Davies [1938] Director; David Generald Nathan [1970] Director

Davison & Co. (Barford) Limited
Incorporated: 7 July 1959 *Employees:* 29
Net Worth: £15,163,640 *Total Assets:* £23,040,450
Registered Office: College Farm, Great Barford, Beds, MK44 3JJ
Activities: Mixed farming
Shareholders: Duncan & Toplis Trustees Limited; Phillippa Brenda Davison; Edward Frank Davison
Officers: Gary Mark Davison, Secretary; Anthony Edward Davison [1961] Director; Charles Johnathan Davison [1961] Director/Farmer; Edward James Davison [1970] Director; Edward Frank Davison [1932] Director/Farmer; Gary Mark Davison [1960] Director/Farmer

Dawsongroup Bus and Coach Limited
Incorporated: 20 October 1989 *Employees:* 56
Previous: Dawsonrentals Bus and Coach Limited
Net Worth: £22,201,000 *Total Assets:* £79,261,000
Registered Office: c/o Dawsongroup PLC, Delaware Drive, Tongwell, Milton Keynes, Bucks, MK15 8JH
Activities: Renting and leasing of other machinery, equipment and tangible goods n.e.c.
Parent: Dawsongroup UK Limited
Officers: Lucinda Anne Kent, Secretary; Stephen David Callahan [1963] Director; Anthony Coleman [1973] Finance Director; Fraser John Innes [1966] Director/Sales Manager; Stephen James Miller [1965] Group Managing Director; Adrian Joseph Peter O'Reilly [1964] Director; Paul David Sainthouse [1967] Director

Dawsongroup Material Handling Limited
Incorporated: 8 October 1991 *Employees:* 103
Previous: Dawsonrentals Materials Handling Equipment Limited
Net Worth: £22,287,000 *Total Assets:* £49,025,000
Registered Office: Delaware Drive, Tongwell, Milton Keynes, Bucks, MK15 8JH
Activities: Renting and leasing of other machinery, equipment and tangible goods n.e.c.
Parent: Dawsongroup UK Limited
Officers: Lucinda Anne Kent, Secretary; Stephen David Callahan [1963] Director; Anthony Coleman [1973] Finance Director; Stephen James Miller [1965] Group Managing Director; Adrian Joseph Peter O'Reilly [1964] Director; Timothy Paul Shires [1960] Director

Dawsongroup PLC
Incorporated: 3 April 1985 *Employees:* 797
Net Worth: £245,322,000 *Total Assets:* £625,916,032
Registered Office: Delaware Drive, Tongwell, Milton Keynes, Bucks, MK15 8JH
Activities: Activities of head offices
Parent: Bryan Cave Leighton Paisner LLP
Officers: Lucinda Anne Kent, Secretary; Anthony Coleman [1973] Director; Freya Olivia Dawson [1987] Director; Peter Michael Dawson [1938] Director/Executive Chairman; Ian Jones [1954] Director; Stephen James Miller [1965] Director

Dawsongroup Temperature Control Solutions Limited
Incorporated: 18 February 1982 *Employees:* 111
Previous: Dawsonrentals Temperature Control Solutions Limited
Net Worth: £35,580,000 *Total Assets:* £61,924,000
Registered Office: Delaware Drive, Tongwell, Milton Keynes, Bucks, MK15 8JH
Activities: Renting and leasing of other machinery, equipment and tangible goods n.e.c.
Parent: Dawsongroup UK Limited
Officers: Lucinda Anne Kent, Secretary; Roderick Peter Benham [1958] Director; Stephen David Callahan [1963] Director; Anthony Coleman [1973] Finance Director; Jonathan David McKie [1978] Operations Director; Stephen James Miller [1965] Group Managing Director; Adrian Joseph Peter O'Reilly [1964] Director; David John Quinn [1961] Director; Gary Smith [1961] Director

Dawsongroup Truck and Trailer Limited
Incorporated: 17 July 1995 *Employees:* 198
Previous: Dawsonrentals Truck and Trailer Limited
Net Worth: £59,980,000 *Total Assets:* £302,532,992
Registered Office: Delaware Drive, Tongwell, Milton Keynes, Bucks, MK15 8JH
Activities: Renting and leasing of trucks and other heavy vehicles
Parent: Dawsongroup UK Limited
Officers: Lucinda Anne Kent, Secretary; Stephen David Calllahan [1963] Director; Anthony Coleman [1973] Finance Director; Peter Michael Dawson [1938] Director/Chairman; John Fletcher [1966] Director; Stephen James Miller [1965] Director; Adrian Joseph Peter O'Reilly [1964] Director; Peter Stuart Smith [1966] Sales Director; Peter Snowden [1963] Director

Dawsongroup UK Limited
Incorporated: 3 May 1948 *Employees:* 3
Previous: Dawsonrentals Limited
Net Worth: £71,413,000 *Total Assets:* £71,413,000
Registered Office: Delaware Drive, Tongwell, Milton Keynes, Bucks, MK15 8JH
Activities: Non-trading company
Parent: Dawsongroup PLC
Officers: Lucinda Anne Kent, Secretary; Anthony Coleman [1973] Finance Director; Peter Michael Dawson [1938] Director; Stephen James Miller [1965] Group Managing Director

Dawsongroup Vans Limited
Incorporated: 25 October 2010 *Employees:* 145
Previous: Dawsonrentals Vans Limited
Net Worth: £11,540,000 *Total Assets:* £62,420,000
Registered Office: Delaware Drive, Tongwell, Milton Keynes, Bucks, MK15 8JH
Activities: Renting and leasing of cars and light motor vehicles
Parent: Dawsongroup UK Limited
Officers: Lucinda Anne Kent, Secretary; Stephen David Callahan [1963] Director; Anthony Coleman [1973] Finance Director; Charles Piers Leighton Dawson [1990] Director; Stephen James Miller [1965] Managing Director; Adrian Joseph Peter O'Reilly [1964] Accounting Director; David Simon Ridley [1967] Director

Day Group Limited
Incorporated: 2 April 1947 *Employees:* 466
Net Worth: £33,562,568 *Total Assets:* £91,422,856
Registered Office: Day Group House, Transport Avenue, Brentford, Middlesex, TW8 9HF
Activities: Manufacture of other non-metallic mineral products n.e.c.
Officers: David Spencer Churchill, Secretary; Adam Michael Day [1968] Contracting Director; Alan John Day [1941] Director/Chairman; Dominic Peter Day [1973] Director; James Alan Day [1965] Managing Director; Jonathan Matthew Day [1967] Director

Day Lewis PLC
Incorporated: 7 March 1975 *Employees:* 2,501
Net Worth: £91,534,000 *Total Assets:* £333,744,992
Registered Office: 2 Peterwood Way, Croydon, Surrey, CR0 4UQ
Activities: Dispensing chemist in specialised stores
Shareholders: Naliniben Kiritkumar Patel; Rupa Patel; Jayanti Chimanbhai Patel Jnr; Kirit Chimanbhai Tulsibhai Patel Jnr
Officers: Ameetkumar Ramananbhai Patel, Secretary; Jayantibhai Chimanbhai Patel, Secretary; Carey Charles Edwards [1955] Director; Peter James Glover [1947] Director; Heena Patel [1963] Finance Director; Jayanti Chimanbhai Patel Junior [1984] Director; Kirit Chimanbhai Patel Junior [1980] Director

DDD Investments Limited
Incorporated: 1 June 2004 *Employees:* 304
Net Worth: £5,322,656 *Total Assets:* £27,611,426
Registered Office: 94 Rickmansworth Road, Watford, Herts, WD18 7JJ
Activities: Activities of head offices
Officers: Carl Atkinson [1974] Director; Hanna Joy Coonagh [1972] Director; Digby Lawrence Spence Halsby [1976] Director; Roger Harrison [1969] Managing Director; Simon Morris [1973] HR Director; Charles Philip Wadsworth [1962] Finance Director

De La Rue Finance Limited
Incorporated: 7 January 2008
Net Worth: £343,049,984 *Total Assets:* £343,049,984
Registered Office: De La Rue House, Jays Close, Viables, Basingstoke, Hants, RG22 4BS
Activities: Other business support service activities n.e.c.
Parent: De La Rue Holdings Limited
Officers: Jean Francois Hermans, Secretary; Jean-Francois Hermans [1958] Director/Chartered Secretary; Edward Hugh Davidson Peppiatt [1967] Director/Lawyer; Lesley Sharon Roche [1967] Director/Accountant - Group Financial Controller

De La Rue Holdings Limited
Incorporated: 1 July 1898 *Employees:* 47
Previous: De La Rue Holdings PLC
Net Worth: £424,220,992 *Total Assets:* £1,468,836,992
Registered Office: De La Rue House, Jays Close, Viables, Basingstoke, Hants, RG22 4BS
Activities: Activities of other holding companies n.e.c.
Parent: DLR (No.1) Limited
Officers: Jean-Francois Hermans, Secretary; Jean-Francois Hermans [1958] Director/Chartered Secretary; Edward Hugh Davidson Peppiatt [1967] Director/Lawyer; Lesley Sharon Roche [1967] Director/Accountant - Group Financial Controller; Helen Margaret Willis [1964] Director/Chief Financial Officer

De La Rue International Limited.
Incorporated: 2 April 1962 *Employees:* 2,028
Net Worth: £379,216,000 *Total Assets:* £811,558,016
Registered Office: De La Rue House, Jays Close, Basingstoke, Hants, RG22 4BS
Activities: Printing n.e.c.
Parent: De La Rue Holdings Limited
Officers: Jean-Francois Hermans, Secretary; Jean-Francois Hermans [1958] Director/Chartered Secretary; Edward Hugh Davidson Peppiatt [1967] Director/Lawyer; Lesley Sharon Roche [1967] Director/Accountant - Group Financial Controller; Helen Margaret Willis [1964] Director/Chief Financial Officer

De La Rue Investments Limited
Incorporated: 2 August 1990
Net Worth: £99,511,000 *Total Assets:* £99,511,000
Registered Office: De La Rue House, Jays Close, Basingstoke, Hants, RG22 4BS
Activities: Activities of other holding companies n.e.c.
Parent: De La Rue Holdings Limited
Officers: Jean-Francois Hermans, Secretary; Edward Hugh Davidson Peppiatt [1967] Director/Lawyer; Lesley Sharon Roche [1967] Director/Accountant - Group Financial Controller

De La Rue PLC
Incorporated: 31 August 1999 *Employees:* 3,188
Net Worth Deficit: £29,600,000 *Total Assets:* £328,600,000
Registered Office: De La Rue House, Jays Close, Viables, Basingstoke, Hants, RG22 4BS
Activities: Printing n.e.c.
Officers: Jean-Francois Hermans, Secretary; Edward Hugh Davidson Peppiatt, Secretary; Nicholas Paul Seaton Bray [1965] Director/Chief Financial Officer; Dr Sabri Challah [1954] Director; Maria Juana Da Cunha Da Silva [1963] Solicitor and Director [Spanish]; Philip Graham Rogerson [1945] Director; Andrew John Stevens [1956] Director/Retired CEO; Martin Conrad Sutherland [1968] Director/Chief Executive Officer; Helen Margaret Willis [1964] Director/Chief Financial Officer

De Lage Landen Leasing Limited
Incorporated: 4 May 1989 *Employees:* 176
Net Worth: £153,748,992 *Total Assets:* £1,721,616,000
Registered Office: Building 7, Croxley Park, Hatters Lane, Watford, Herts, WD18 8YN
Activities: Financial leasing
Parent: De Lage Landen Limited
Officers: Duncan John Hullis [1963] Director/General Manager; Vijay Chandulal Shah [1969] Director/Country Finance Manager; Simon John Trudgeon [1968] Director/Credit Risk Officer

De Lage Landen Limited
Incorporated: 17 December 1992
Net Worth: £78,956,000 *Total Assets:* £79,230,000
Registered Office: Building 7, Croxley Park, Hatters Lane, Watford, Herts, WD18 8YN
Activities: Activities of head offices
Parent: De Lage Landen International B.V.
Officers: Duncan John Hullis [1963] Director/General Manager; Simon John Trudgeon [1968] Director/Credit Risk Officer; Bas Van Asseldonk [1977] Director/Executive Vice President [Dutch]

Dealcyber Limited
Incorporated: 7 April 1998
Net Worth: £77,538,000 *Total Assets:* £131,680,000
Registered Office: 980 Great West Road, Brentford, Middlesex, TW8 9GS
Activities: Other business support service activities n.e.c.
Parent: SmithKline Beecham Limited
Officers: Adam Walker [1967] Director

Decco Limited
Incorporated: 12 August 1946 *Employees:* 315
Net Worth: £38,510,000 *Total Assets:* £54,295,000
Registered Office: Votec House, Hambridge Lane, Newbury, Berks, RG14 5TN
Activities: Wholesale of wood, construction materials and sanitary equipment
Parent: Newbury Investments (UK) Ltd
Officers: Leo Yu, Secretary; Nigel John Palmer [1956] Director/Chairman; Steven Westbrook [1956] Director/Chief Executive; Leo Yu [1984] Director

Deep Sea Atlantic (UK) Ltd
Incorporated: 30 January 2017
Net Worth: £6,910,227 *Total Assets:* £376,590,624
Registered Office: Harbour Court, Compass Road, North Harbour, Portsmouth, PO6 4ST
Activities: Support activities for petroleum and natural gas mining
Parent: Odfjell Drilling Ltd
Officers: Simen Lieungh [1960] Director/Chief Executive Officer [Norwegian]; Thomas Marsoner [1960] Director/Banker [Austrian]; Helene Odfjell [1965] Director/Board Member [Norwegian]

Deep Sea Stavanger (UK) Ltd
Incorporated: 30 January 2017
Net Worth: £10,381,094 *Total Assets:* £385,603,104
Registered Office: Harbour Court, Compass Road, North Harbour, Portsmouth, PO6 4ST
Activities: Support activities for petroleum and natural gas mining
Parent: Odfjell Drilling Ltd
Officers: Simen Lieungh [1960] Director/Chief Executive Officer [Norwegian]; Thomas Marsoner [1960] Director/Banker [Austrian]; Helene Odfjell [1965] Director/Board Member [Norwegian]

Defaqto Group Limited
Incorporated: 4 May 2005 *Employees:* 3
Net Worth: £26,865,056 *Total Assets:* £29,360,876
Registered Office: Financial Research Centre, Haddenham Business Park, Pegasus Way, Haddenham, Aylesbury, Bucks, HP17 8LJ
Activities: Activities of head offices
Parent: Regulus Bidco Limited
Officers: Remko Peter Bijtjes [1971] Director/Sales Executive [Dutch]; Syed Zahid Hussain Bilgrami [1971] Director/Executive; Alastair Colin Gillies Brown [1974] Director/Accountant

Defence Investments Limited
Incorporated: 3 May 2011
Net Worth: £50,474,000 *Total Assets:* £142,263,008
Registered Office: 1010 Eskdale, Eskdale Road, Winnersh, Wokingham, Berks, RG41 5TS
Activities: Other business support service activities n.e.c.
Parent: Exelis Luxembourg SARL
Officers: Keith Nicholas Norton [1958] Director/Business Manager

Defence Support (St Athan) Holdings Limited
Incorporated: 19 April 2002
Net Worth Deficit: £920,000 *Total Assets:* £31,851,000
Registered Office: 8 White Oak Square, London Road, Swanley, Kent, BR8 7AG
Activities: Activities of head offices
Parent: John Laing Social Infrastructure Limited
Officers: Guy Frederick Walker [1984] Director/Accountant

Defence Support (St Athan) Limited
Incorporated: 19 April 2002
Net Worth Deficit: £920,000 *Total Assets:* £31,851,000
Registered Office: 8 White Oak Square, London Road, Swanley, Kent, BR8 7AG
Activities: Construction of commercial buildings
Parent: Defence Support (St Athan) Holdings Limited
Officers: Guy Frederick Walker [1984] Director/Accountant

Del Monte (UK) Limited
Incorporated: 23 August 1989 *Employees:* 172
Net Worth: £59,015,000 *Total Assets:* £73,371,000
Registered Office: 240 London Road, Staines upon Thames, Middlesex, TW18 4JD
Activities: Wholesale of fruit and vegetables
Parent: Del Monte Fresh Produce SARL
Officers: Cecelia Dempsey, Secretary; Richard Contreras [1950] Director/Businessman [American]; Martin John Selley [1961] Director; Youssef Zakharia [1961] Director/VP [Lebanese]

Del Monte Europe Limited
Incorporated: 28 December 1926 *Employees:* 5
Net Worth: £51,574,000 *Total Assets:* £161,174,000
Registered Office: 240 London Road, Staines upon Thames, Middlesex, TW18 4JD
Activities: Other processing and preserving of fruit and vegetables
Parent: Del Monte Foods International Ltd
Officers: Cecelia Dempsey, Secretary; Richard Contreras [1950] Director/Businessman [American]; Gianpaolo Renino [1968] Director/VP Europe and Africa [Italian]; Youssef Zakharia [1961] Director/VP [Lebanese]

Del Monte Foods International Limited
Incorporated: 27 December 1989
Net Worth: £223,000 *Total Assets:* £167,848,000
Registered Office: 240 London Road, Staines upon Thames, Middlesex, TW18 4JD
Activities: Wholesale of fruit and vegetables
Parent: Del Monte Fresh Produce SARL
Officers: Cecelia Dempsey, Secretary; Gianpaolo Renino [1968] Director/VP Europe and Africa [Italian]; Youssef Zakharia [1961] Director/VP [Lebanese]

Delaquest Limited
Incorporated: 29 November 1993 *Employees:* 215
Net Worth: £14,107,833 *Total Assets:* £41,333,924
Registered Office: Corus House, 1 Auckland Park, Milton Keynes, Bucks, MK1 1BU
Activities: Hotels and similar accommodation
Parent: Corus Hotels Limited
Officers: Khurram Mohmand, Secretary; Andrew Khoo [1972] Director [Australian]; Yet King Loy [1946] Director [Canadian]; Khurram Mohmand [1972] Director/Accountant

Delice de France Limited
Incorporated: 20 July 1987 *Employees:* 382
Net Worth: £19,953,060 *Total Assets:* £49,231,404
Registered Office: 149 Brent Road, Southall, Middlesex, UB2 5LJ
Activities: Non-specialised wholesale of food, beverages and tobacco
Officers: Thierry Cacaly, Secretary; Thierry Cacaly [1971] Director/Head of Aryzta Food Solutions UK [French]; Sean Timothy Murphy [1969] Director/Accountant [Irish]; James Anthony Proctor [1972] Director [Irish]

Dell Corporation Limited
Incorporated: 8 December 1986 *Employees:* 1,369
Net Worth: £130,498,000 *Total Assets:* £659,374,976
Registered Office: Dell House, The Boulevard, Cain Road, Bracknell, Berks, RG12 1LF
Activities: Information technology consultancy activities
Parent: Dell Technologies Inc.
Officers: Fiona Margaret Dibley, Secretary; Janet Merritt Bawcom [1964] Director/Lawyer [American]; Edward James Cattermole [1974] Director; Claire Susan Vyvyan [1965] Director/General Management

Dell Emerging Markets (EMEA) Limited
Incorporated: 22 October 1996 *Employees:* 69
Net Worth: £45,029,000 *Total Assets:* £49,076,000
Registered Office: Dell House, The Boulevard, Cain Road, Bracknell, Berks, RG12 1LF
Activities: Wholesale of computers, computer peripheral equipment and software
Parent: Dell Technologies, Inc
Officers: Fiona Margaret Dibley, Secretary; Janet Merritt Bawcom [1964] Director/Lawyer [American]; Gary Fox [1965] Finance Director [Irish]; Anna Anja Monrad [1966] Director [Danish]; Mohammed Amin Salem [1963] Director [Canadian]

Delta Limited
Incorporated: 12 March 1888
Net Worth: £55,339,000 *Total Assets:* £196,550,000
Registered Office: Elder House, St Georges Business Park, Brooklands Road, Weybridge, Surrey, KT13 0TS
Activities: Activities of head offices
Parent: Valmont Industries, Inc.
Officers: Timothy Perry Francis [1976] Director/VP Corporate Controller [American]; Mark Charles Jaksich [1957] Director/Corporate Controller [American]; Gary Steven Lebens [1963] Director/Corporate Finance [American]; Roger Andrew Massey [1969] Director/Corporate Attorney [American]; Karen Colleen Potts [1980] Director/Corporate Attorney [American]; Jamie Austin Taylor [1971] Financial Director

Deltec International Courier Limited
Incorporated: 24 June 1985 *Employees:* 231
Net Worth: £18,172,252 *Total Assets:* £28,045,200
Registered Office: Skynet House, 18-21 Pulborough Way, Hounslow, Middlesex, TW4 6DE
Activities: Unlicensed carriers
Shareholders: John Barry Ellis; Dianne Joy Ellis
Officers: Dianne Joy Ellis, Secretary; John Barry Ellis [1939] Director/General Manager

The Deltic Group Holdings Limited
Incorporated: 5 December 2011 *Employees:* 1,345
Previous: Ranimul 1 Limited
Net Worth: £9,789,000 *Total Assets:* £72,011,000
Registered Office: Aurora House, Deltic Avenue, Rooksley, Milton Keynes, Bucks, MK13 8LW
Activities: Activities of other holding companies n.e.c.
Shareholder: Paul John Evans
Officers: Steven Lindsay Cloran [1964] Director/Company Executive; Paul John Evans [1947] Director; Alan James Fall [1965] Director/Company Executive; Peter Jack Marks [1960] Director/Chief Executive; Lawrence Edward McGreal [1960] Director/Accountant

The Deltic Group Limited
Incorporated: 5 December 2011 *Employees:* 1,345
Previous: The Luminar Group Limited
Net Worth: £9,656,000 *Total Assets:* £70,244,000
Registered Office: Aurora House, Deltic Avenue, Rooksley, Milton Keynes, Bucks, MK13 8LW
Activities: Licenced clubs
Parent: The Deltic Group Holdings Limited
Officers: Kelly Anne Young, Secretary; Robert Brannan [1956] Director; Steven Lindsay Cloran [1964] Director/Company Executive; Paul John Evans [1947] Director; Alan James Fall [1965] Director/Company Executive; Peter Jack Marks [1960] Director/Chief Executive; Lawrence Edward McGreal [1960] Director/Accountant; Alex Millington [1978] Finance Director

The Denbigh Alliance
Incorporated: 11 February 2011 *Employees:* 200
Previous: Denbigh School
Net Worth: £24,997,048 *Total Assets:* £28,515,304
Registered Office: Burchard Crescent, Shenley Church End, Milton Keynes, Bucks, MK5 6EX
Activities: General secondary education
Officers: William Gibson Butler [1953] Director/Management Consultant; John Robert Cove [1958] Director; Andrew Peter Dransfield [1947] Director; Bruce Hawthorne [1965] Director; Aleck Edward Hornshaw [1968] Director; John Stewart Howe [1950] Director/Retired; Roger Charles Lane-Nott [1945] Director/Retired; Sharon McGuire [1960] Director; Thornton George Naylor [1955] Director/Retired; Maureen O'Brien [1962] Director [Irish]; Deborah Plumb [1961] Director/Pharmacist; Colin Jonathan Solloway [1960] Director/School; Deborah Jane Sporn [1973] Director/PR Manager; Amdrew Squires [1970] Director/Headteacher

Deneep Limited
Incorporated: 24 February 2017 *Employees:* 62
Net Worth: £14,803,929 *Total Assets:* £20,740,986
Registered Office: Church Hill, Wilmington, Dartford, Kent, DA2 7DZ
Activities: Activities of construction holding companies
Shareholder: Simon William Clubb
Officers: James Spencer Clubb [1954] Director; Simon William Clubb [1960] Director; Colin Dring [1957] Director; Alexandra Mary Fernyhough [1959] Director; Sarah Jane Gillan [1961] Director; Jonathan James Lovett [1955] Director; Iris Nash [1935] Director; Caroline Ann Reynolds [1963] Director

Denmaur Independent Papers Limited
Incorporated: 17 March 1983 *Employees:* 111
Net Worth: £5,512,814 *Total Assets:* £43,184,064
Registered Office: Paper Mews, Bourncrete House, Bonham Drive, Sittingbourne, Kent, ME10 3RY
Activities: Wholesale of other intermediate products
Shareholder: Michael Noble Gee
Officers: Kelly Farewell, Secretary; Andrew John Buxton [1959] Sales Director; Andrew Faithful [1971] Sales Director; Kelly Farewell [1971] Director/Accountant; Michael Noble Gee [1953] Director/Trader; Nicholas Malcolm Gee [1961] Director/Trader; Ricky Cecil Hirshfield [1967] Director/Paper Merchant; Douglas Alan Jessop [1966] Director; John Stephen Mason [1946] Director; Julian Paul Townsend [1963] Sales Director

Dennis & Robinson Limited
Incorporated: 8 November 1948 *Employees:* 270
Net Worth: £11,322,000 *Total Assets:* £35,107,000
Registered Office: Paula Rosa Manhattan, Blenheim Road, Lancing Business Park, Lancing, W Sussex, BN15 8UH
Activities: Manufacture of kitchen furniture
Parent: Southdown Kitchen Furniture Limited
Officers: Andrew James Lord, Secretary; Magnus Arne Hegdal [1967] Director [Swedish]; Andrew James Lord [1966] Finance Director; Eric Andrew Prescott [1957] Managing Director; Johan Anders Wassberg [1965] Director/Chief Executive Officer [Swedish]

Der Touristik UK Limited
Incorporated: 25 May 1945 *Employees:* 747
Previous: Kuoni Travel Limited
Net Worth: £9,714,000 *Total Assets:* £104,552,000
Registered Office: Touristik House, One Dorking Office Park, Dorking, Surrey, RH4 1HJ
Activities: Tour operator activities
Officers: Matthew John Quinlisk, Secretary; Derek Jones [1963] Managing Director; Boris Schnabel [1970] Director [German]; Francis Torrilla [1960] Director; Leif Vase Larsen [1963] Director [Danish]

Derby Healthcare (Holdings) Limited
Incorporated: 11 February 2003
Net Worth Deficit: £35,439,000 *Total Assets:* £405,956,992
Registered Office: 8 White Oak Square, London Road, Swanley, Kent, BR8 7AG
Activities: Combined facilities support activities
Parent: Innisfree Nominees Limited (as Nominee for Innisfree PFI Continuation Fund)
Officers: Gaynor Birley Smith [1966] Investment Director; Richard Keith Sheehan [1975] Investment Director

Derby Healthcare PLC
Incorporated: 17 February 2003
Net Worth Deficit: £35,429,000 *Total Assets:* £405,967,008
Registered Office: 8 White Oak Square, London Road, Swanley, Kent, BR8 7AG
Activities: Development of building projects
Parent: Derby Healthcare (Holdings) Limited
Officers: Gaynor Birley Smith [1966] Investment Director; Michael Davis [1946] Director; Richard Keith Sheehan [1975] Investment Director

Dermalogica (UK) Limited
Incorporated: 1 June 1988 *Employees:* 342
Net Worth: £19,056,980 *Total Assets:* £24,956,168
Registered Office: The Manser Building, Thorncroft Manor, Thorncroft Drive, Dorking Road, Leatherhead, Surrey, KT22 8JB
Activities: Wholesale of perfume and cosmetics
Parent: Unilever Overseas Holdings Limited
Officers: James Oliver Earley, Secretary; Richard Clive Hazell, Secretary; Pamela Dickson [1968] Finance Director; Stuart Colin Parkinson Hill [1979] Director/CFO Dermalogica; Glenn Derrick Poy [1957] Director/General Manager [Canadian]; Anthony Colin Rudd [1975] Finance Director

Derrin Brothers Properties Limited
Incorporated: 19 May 1959 *Employees:* 3
Net Worth Deficit: £6,142,571 *Total Assets:* £22,542,756
Registered Office: 1 Princeton Mews, 167-169 London Road, Kingston upon Thames, Surrey, KT2 6PT
Activities: Non-trading company
Major Shareholder: Willy Schaperkotter
Officers: Winny Borgas [1938] Director [Belgian]; John Donnelly [1973] Director/Chartered Accountant [Irish]; Carine Martinez [1961] Director/Accountant [Swiss]

Descram Holdings Limited
Incorporated: 23 November 1988 *Employees:* 193
Net Worth: £35,068,336 *Total Assets:* £40,742,104
Registered Office: 1 Halton Brook Business Park, Weston Road, Aston Clinton, Aylesbury, Bucks, HP22 5WF
Activities: Activities of head offices
Shareholder: Charles Robert Desoutter
Officers: Clare Dovey, Secretary; Charles Robert Desoutter [1954] Director/Engineer; George Charles Desoutter [1978] Director/Engineer; Maximillian Roger Desoutter [1980] Director; Roger Charles Desoutter [1923] Director; William Paul Desoutter [1982] Director; Alexandra Rose Wansbrough [1977] Director

Deta Electrical Company Limited
Incorporated: 10 October 1958 *Employees:* 128
Net Worth: £23,894,000 *Total Assets:* £47,605,000
Registered Office: Votec House, Hambridge Lane, Newbury, Berks, RG14 5TN
Activities: Wholesale of radio, television goods & electrical household appliances (other than records, tapes, CDs)
Parent: Newbury Investments (UK) Ltd
Officers: Leo Yu, Secretary; Nigel John Palmer [1956] Director/Chairman; Steven Westbrook [1956] Director/Chief Executive; Leo Yu [1984] Director

Detica Group Limited
Incorporated: 5 March 1997
Net Worth: £51,943,000 *Total Assets:* £53,208,000
Registered Office: P O Box 87, Warwick House, Farnborough Aerospace Centre, Farnborough, Hants, GU14 6YU
Activities: Activities of other holding companies n.e.c.
Parent: BAE Systems (Holdings) Limited
Officers: David Stanley Parkes, Secretary; Julian Frederick Charles Cracknell [1971] Managing Director; Anthony Graham Jordan [1980] Director/Chartered Accountant; Michael Stuart Watson [1963] Director/Chartered Accountant

Deutsche Leasing (UK) Limited
Incorporated: 11 April 2003 *Employees:* 34
Net Worth: £20,101,992 *Total Assets:* £345,053,664
Registered Office: 1st Floor, West Wing, The Omnibus Building, Lesbourne Road, Reigate, Surrey, RH2 7LD
Activities: Financial leasing
Parent: Deutsche Sparkassen Leasing AG & Co. KG
Officers: Neil Douglas, Secretary; Neil Douglas [1960] Director/FCMA; Simon Timothy Dufton [1962] Director; Kai Ostermann [1968] Director/Economist [German]; Bernd Willi Schroeck [1958] Director [German]

Devine Holdings Limited
Incorporated: 22 March 2000 *Employees:* 51
Net Worth: £29,658,414 *Total Assets:* £50,540,040
Registered Office: 133 Church Hill Road, Sutton, Surrey, SM3 8NE
Activities: Activities of head offices
Major Shareholder: James Timothy Devine
Officers: Brian Philip Beckett, Secretary; James Timothy Devine [1949] Managing Director [Irish]

John Dewar and Sons Limited
Incorporated: 24 October 1958 *Employees:* 356
Net Worth: £188,070,000 *Total Assets:* £537,265,024
Registered Office: c/o Bacardi-Martini Limited, Bacardi Brown-Forman House, Kings Worthy, Winchester, Hants, SO23 7TW
Activities: Distilling, rectifying and blending of spirits
Parent: Bacardi U.K. Limited
Officers: Jean Marc Lambert [1965] Director, Supply Chain and Manufacturing [French]; Iain MacGregor Lochhead [1962] Director/Executive; Ian Stuart Lowthian [1959] Chairman/Global Technical Director; Matthew James Phillips [1983] Finance Director; Paolo Camillo Tucci [1963] Finance Director

Dewhurst PLC
Incorporated: 5 November 1919 *Employees:* 395
Net Worth: £35,951,000 *Total Assets:* £53,657,000
Registered Office: Unit 9 Hampton Business Park, Hampton Road West, Feltham, Middlesex, TW13 6DB
Activities: Manufacture of other electrical equipment
Officers: Jared Conan Sinclair, Secretary; John Robert Bailey [1970] Director; David Dewhurst [1961] Director/Export Sales Manager; Richard Melbourne Dewhurst [1956] Director/Accountant; Jared Conan Sinclair [1970] Director/Accountant; Peter Alfred Tett [1939] Director; Alan Michael Warren [1957] Director; Richard John Young [1956] Director/Engineer

DF Group Limited
Incorporated: 3 June 1998
Net Worth: £610,102,464 *Total Assets:* £642,947,648
Registered Office: 417 Bridport Road, Greenford, Middlesex, UB6 8UA
Activities: Other business support service activities n.e.c.
Parent: Ultra Electronics Holdings PLC
Officers: Anant Prakash, Secretary; Mark Richard Nelson [1966] Director Group Finance; Simon Charles Conrad Pryce [1961] Director; Amitabh Sharma [1967] Finance Director

DG Partners Services Limited
Incorporated: 26 June 2002 *Employees:* 17
Previous: London Diversified Fund Management (UK) Limited
Net Worth: £14,755,444 *Total Assets:* £128,885,464
Registered Office: 4th Floor, Reading Bridge House, George Street, Reading, Berks, RG1 8LS
Activities: Other business support service activities n.e.c.
Officers: David Michael Gorton [1963] Director/Investment Manager; Robert Charles Standing [1960] Director/Investment Manager

DHL Air Limited
Incorporated: 11 October 1982 *Employees:* 381
Net Worth: £37,547,956 *Total Assets:* £287,357,024
Registered Office: Southern Hub, Unit 1 Horton Road, Colnbrook, Berks, SL3 0BB
Activities: Non-scheduled passenger air transport
Officers: Olivier Alexandroff [1968] Director; Roy Hughes [1968] Director; Geoffrey Kehr [1960] Director/Aviation Manager; Thomas Mackle [1963] Managing Director

DHL Aviation (UK) Limited
Incorporated: 4 February 1987 *Employees:* 1,928
Net Worth: £15,327,000 *Total Assets:* £202,607,008
Registered Office: Southern Hub, Unit 1 Horton Road, Colnbrook, Berks, SL3 0BB
Activities: Non-scheduled passenger air transport
Officers: Neil Ivie Lamont Ferguson [1952] Director/Manager; Annette Marian Meijer [1964] Director/Regulatory Affairs Manager [Dutch]; Daniel Bruno Pedri [1957] Director/General Manager

DHL Distribution Holdings (UK) Limited
Incorporated: 19 September 1923
Net Worth: £34,931,000 *Total Assets:* £34,931,000
Registered Office: Southern Hub, Unit 1 Horton Road, Colnbrook, Berks, SL3 0BB
Activities: Other business support service activities n.e.c.
Officers: Keith James Austin [1962] Director/Lawyer; David Archibald Duncan [1958] Director/Chief Financial Officer

DHL Exel Supply Chain Limited
Incorporated: 29 December 1987
Net Worth: £253,195,584 *Total Assets:* £487,226,624
Registered Office: Ocean House, The Ring, Bracknell, Berks, RG12 1AN
Activities: Activities of head offices
Parent: Exel Limited
Officers: Steven Fink [1975] Director/Vice President,Commercial and Company Law; Thorsten Kuhl [1974] Director [German]; Michael James Trimm [1968] Director/Accountant

DHL GBS (UK) Limited
Incorporated: 18 November 1981 *Employees:* 257
Net Worth: £16,784,344 *Total Assets:* £26,954,060
Registered Office: Ocean House, The Ring, Bracknell, Berks, RG12 1AN
Activities: Other business support service activities n.e.c.
Officers: Keith James Austin [1962] Director/Solicitor; Bridget Deborah Baxter [1968] Director/Head of HR; Alexander Howard Bridgeman [1963] Director/VP Risk & Insurance; Peter Gerrard Flanagan [1964] Director; Graeme Hugh Galloway [1971] Director/Head of IT; Eelain Ong [1973] Director/Chartered Accountant; Kevin Paul Sey [1964] Director/Chartered Surveyor; Michael James Trimm [1968] Director/Accountant; Jane Wiltshire [1963] Director/Head of Procurement

DHL Global Forwarding (UK) Limited
Incorporated: 15 August 2000 *Employees:* 944
Net Worth: £104,168,000 *Total Assets:* £270,824,000
Registered Office: Eastworth House, Eastworth Road, Chertsey, Surrey, KT16 8SH
Activities: Other transportation support activities
Officers: Vari Isabel Cameron [1961] Finance Director; Remco Pieter Van Oerle [1966] Director [Dutch]; Michael Paul Young [1972] Director

DHL International (UK) Limited
Incorporated: 24 September 1974
Net Worth: £88,386,000 *Total Assets:* £313,620,992
Registered Office: Southern Hub, Unit 1 Horton Road, Colnbrook, Berks, SL3 0BB
Activities: Other service activities n.e.c.
Officers: David Archibald Duncan [1958] Director/Chief Financial Officer; Ian David Wilson [1966] Managing Director

DHL Parcel UK Limited
Incorporated: 10 November 1969 *Employees:* 2,758
Previous: UK Mail Limited
Net Worth: £53,259,000 *Total Assets:* £157,003,008
Registered Office: 120 Buckingham Avenue, Slough, SL1 4LZ
Activities: Licensed carriers
Parent: Deutsche Post AG
Officers: Peter Stanley Fuller [1964] Director/Chief Executive; Peter Michael Krohn [1957] Finance Director [Danish]; Scott Laird [1982] Director/Vice President - Operations; Albert Christopher Mangham [1964] Director/Chief Operating Officer - Mail and IT

DHL Services Limited
Incorporated: 26 February 1997 *Employees:* 39,767
Net Worth Deficit: £213,874,000 *Total Assets:* £179,232,000
Registered Office: 251 Midsummer Boulevard, Milton Keynes, Bucks, MK9 1EQ
Activities: Other business support service activities n.e.c.
Parent: DHL Supply Chain Limited
Officers: Lindsay Elizabeth Bridges [1969] Director [Irish]; Karen Brown [1965] Director/Solicitor; Ian David Clough [1967] Director; Peter Gerrard Flanagan [1964] Director; James Andrew Hartshorne [1976] Director; Thorsten Kuhl [1974] Director [German]; Gavin John Murdoch [1967] Director; Jose Fernando Nava [1963] Director [American]; David Julian Pierpoint [1968] Director; Paul Robin Richardson [1963] Director; Philip William Roe [1966] Director; Timothy John Slater [1968] Managing Director; Martin James Willmor [1980] Managing Director; Marcus Wurker [1977] Director [German]

DHL Supply Chain Limited
Incorporated: 4 February 1954
Net Worth: £442,270,016 *Total Assets:* £1,214,093,056
Registered Office: 251 Midsummer Boulevard, Milton Keynes, Bucks, MK9 1EQ
Activities: Freight transport by road
Parent: Exel Investments Limited
Officers: Lindsay Elizabeth Bridges [1969] Director [Irish]; Ian David Clough [1967] Director; James Andrew Hartshorne [1976] Director; Thorsten Kuhl [1974] Director [German]; Jose Fernando Nava [1963] Director [American]; David Julian Pierpoint [1968] Director; Paul Robin Richardson [1963] Director; Philip William Roe [1966] Director/Transport Manager; Timothy John Slater [1968] Managing Director; Martin James Willmor [1980] Managing Director; Marcus Wurker [1977] Director [German]

The DHL UK Foundation
Incorporated: 22 February 1988 *Employees:* 7
Net Worth: £30,917,176 *Total Assets:* £31,435,420
Registered Office: Ocean House, The Ring, Bracknell, Berks, RG12 1AN
Activities: Other business support service activities n.e.c.
Officers: Ralf Durrwang [1961] Director/Vice President Corporate Citizenship [German]; John Martin Nestor [1962] Director; Timothy John Slater [1968] Divisional Managing Director; Barbara Storch [1966] Charity Director [German]; Perry Frederick Watts [1959] Director/Retired; Ian David Wilson [1966] Director

DHM Plastics Limited
Incorporated: 14 April 1955 *Employees:* 541
Net Worth: £16,078,000 *Total Assets:* £43,846,000
Registered Office: Dickley Lane, Lenham, Maidstone, Kent, ME17 2DE
Activities: Manufacture of other plastic products
Parent: Marley Plastics Limited
Officers: Ian Charles McNair, Secretary; Fabien Gauthier-Lafaye [1975] Director [French]; Stanley Carl James [1962] Director; Warwick Denis Mitton [1969] Director/Accountant; Frankie Bernard Eugene Thielen [1974] Director [Luxembourger]

Diamond Cable Communications Limited
Incorporated: 31 August 1994
Net Worth: £623,160,000 *Total Assets:* £1,095,374,976
Registered Office: Media House, Bartley Wood Business Park, Hook, Hants, RG27 9UP
Activities: Other telecommunications activities
Parent: Virgin Media Senior Investments Limited
Officers: Gillian Elizabeth James, Secretary; Robert Dominic Dunn [1966] Director/Chief Financial Officer; Mine Ozkan Hifzi [1966] Director/Solicitor

Diebold Nixdorf (UK) Limited
Incorporated: 15 September 1999 *Employees:* 547
Previous: Wincor Nixdorf Ltd
Net Worth: £19,654,000 *Total Assets:* £61,346,000
Registered Office: One The Boulevard, Cain Road, Bracknell, Berks, RG12 1WP
Activities: Manufacture of other electrical equipment
Parent: Diebold Nixdorf, Incorporated
Officers: John Michael Ennis [1960] Director; Ben Major Gale [1970] Director; Paul George Young [1975] Finance Director

Digico Global Limited
Incorporated: 23 September 2011
Net Worth: £14,845,678 *Total Assets:* £45,657,132
Registered Office: Unit 10 Silverglade Business Park, Leatherhead Road, Chessington, Surrey, KT9 2QL
Activities: Dormant company
Parent: Console Bidco Limited
Officers: Helen Mary Culleton [1964] Director; James David Gordon [1972] Managing Director; John Robert Stadius [1956] Technical Director

Digico UK Limited
Incorporated: 7 December 2001 *Employees:* 103
Net Worth: £47,599,000 *Total Assets:* £57,102,000
Registered Office: Unit 10 Silverglade Business Park, Chessington, Surrey, KT9 2QL
Activities: Manufacture of other electrical equipment
Parent: Digico Europe Limited
Officers: Helen Mary Culleton, Secretary/Director; Helen Mary Culleton [1964] Director; James David Gordon [1972] Managing Director; John Robert Stadius [1956] Director

Dimension Data (UK) Investments Limited
Incorporated: 15 November 2016
Net Worth: £72,254,728 *Total Assets:* £137,254,880
Registered Office: Dimension Data House, Waterfront Business Park, Fleet Road, Fleet, Hants, GU51 3QT
Activities: Activities of head offices
Parent: Dimension Data Holdings PLC
Officers: Judith Margaret Duck, Secretary; Gareth Richard Mortimer [1981] Financial Director [South African]; David Brian Sheriffs [1963] Director [South African]

Dimension Data Holdings PLC
Incorporated: 28 January 1999 *Employees:* 21,219
Net Worth: £654,821,760 *Total Assets:* £3,889,280,768
Registered Office: Dimension Data House, Building 2, Waterfront Business Park, Fleet Road, Fleet, Hants, GU51 3QT
Activities: Activities of other holding companies n.e.c.
Parent: Nippon Telegraph and Telephone Corporation
Officers: Susan Ponting, Secretary; Jason Matthew Goodall [1967] Director/Chief Executive Officer [South African]; Akitoshi Hattori [1970] Director [Japanese]; Stephen Michael Joubert [1958] Director [South African]; Hideki Kurihara [1965] Director [Japanese]; John Ernest Newbury [1942] Director/Businessman [South African]; Moses Modidima Ngoasheng [1957] Director [South African]; Tsunehisa Okuno [1960] Director [Japanese]; Jeremy John Ord [1957] Director [South African]; Patrick Keith Quarmby [1954] Director [South African]; Roderick Michael Scott [1954] Director/Accountant; David Brian Sheriffs [1963] Director [South African]

Dimension Data Network Services Limited
Incorporated: 30 June 1980 *Employees:* 598
Net Worth: £48,731,000 *Total Assets:* £151,504,000
Registered Office: Dimension Data House, Building 2, Waterfront Business Park, Fleet Road, Fleet, Hants, GU51 3QT
Activities: Other information technology service activities
Parent: Dimension Data (UK) Investments Limited
Officers: Judith Margaret Duck, Secretary; Paul Francis Cooper [1974] Director/Chief Operating Officer [Australian]; Sir Peter Robert Harrison [1937] Director; David Geoffrey Wilcox [1966] Director/Chief Operating Officer [Australian]

Dinnages Garages Limited
Incorporated: 24 January 1935 *Employees:* 141
Net Worth: £3,552,000 *Total Assets:* £21,957,000
Registered Office: 22 Wivelsfield Road, Haywards Heath, W Sussex, RH16 4EQ
Activities: Sale of new cars and light motor vehicles
Officers: Adam Edmond Broyd, Secretary; Adam Edmond Broyd [1964] Financial Director; Daniel James Broyd [1961] Managing Director; Joseph Colin William Broyd [1966] Director/Administration Manager; Josephine Maughan Broyd [1936] Director; Michael Edmond Broyd [1930] Director

Direct Line Group Limited
Incorporated: 21 April 1993
Net Worth: £28,588,000 *Total Assets:* £28,597,000
Registered Office: Churchill Court, Westmoreland Road, Bromley, Kent, BR1 1DP
Activities: Activities of head offices
Parent: Direct Line Insurance Group PLC
Officers: Roger Cheston Clifton, Secretary; Roger Cheston Clifton [1964] Director/Secretary; Helen Clare O'Murchu [1967] Director; Humphrey Michael Tomlinson [1962] Director/General Counsel & Company Secretary

Direct Line Insurance Group PLC
Incorporated: 26 July 1988 *Employees:* 10,949
Net Worth: £3,061,600,000 *Total Assets:* £9,948,199,936
Registered Office: Churchill Court, Westmoreland Road, Bromley, Kent, BR1 1DP
Activities: Activities of head offices
Officers: Roger Cheston Clifton, Secretary; Michael Nicholas Biggs [1952] Director/Chartered Accountant; Paul Robert Geddes [1969] Director/Bank Official; Danuta Gray [1958] Director; Mark Julian Gregory [1963] Director; Jane Carolyn Hanson [1967] Director; Michael Anthony Holliday-Williams [1970] Director; Penelope Jane James [1969] Director; Sebastian Richard Edward Cuthbert James [1966] Director/Group CEO; Fiona Catherine McBain [1961] Director; Gregor Ninian Stewart [1964] Director; Clare Eleanor Thompson [1954] Director; Doctor Richard Churchill Ward [1957] Director

Direct Wines Finance Limited
Incorporated: 12 June 2009
Net Worth Deficit: £5,371,000 *Total Assets:* £62,039,000
Registered Office: One Waterside Drive, Arlington Business Park, Theale, Berks, RG7 4SW
Activities: Financial intermediation not elsewhere classified
Parent: Direct Wines Holdings Limited
Officers: Barbara Anne Laithwaite [1946] Director; Dr Angus James Porter [1957] Director; David Andrew Thatcher [1962] Managing Director; James William Hartland Weir [1965] Director

Direct Wines Holdings Limited
Incorporated: 23 April 2008 *Employees:* 863
Net Worth: £72,726,000 *Total Assets:* £137,971,008
Registered Office: One Waterside Drive, Arlington Business Park, Theale, Berks, RG7 4SW
Activities: Non-trading company
Parent: BTL Family Company Limited
Officers: Alison Jane Clifford-King [1966] Director/Consultant; Barbara Anne Laithwaite [1946] Director/Wine Merchant; Henry John Hugh Laithwaite [1980] Director; Thomas Anthony Eric Laithwaite [1983] Director; William Wilson Laithwaite [1982] Director; Dr Angus James Porter [1957] Director; David Andrew Thatcher [1962] Managing Director; James William Hartland Weir [1965] Director

Direct Wines International Limited
Incorporated: 4 November 1994
Net Worth Deficit: £1,835,856 *Total Assets:* £43,203,088
Registered Office: One Waterside Drive, Arlington Business Park, Theale, Berks, RG7 4SW
Activities: Activities of head offices
Parent: Direct Wines Holdings Limited
Officers: Barbara Anne Laithwaite [1946] Director/Wine Merchant; Dr Angus James Porter [1957] Director; David Andrew Thatcher [1962] Managing Director; James William Hartland Weir [1965] Director

Direct Wines Limited
Incorporated: 8 February 1973 *Employees:* 630
Net Worth: £70,620,000 *Total Assets:* £115,033,000
Registered Office: One Waterside Drive, Arlington Business Park, Theale, Berks, RG7 4SW
Activities: Retail sale via mail order houses or via Internet
Parent: Direct Wines Holdings Limited
Officers: Alison Jane Clifford-King [1966] Director/Consultant; Barbara Anne Laithwaite [1946] Director and Wine Merchant; Dr Angus James Porter [1957] Director; David Andrew Thatcher [1962] Managing Director; James William Hartland Weir [1965] Director

The Disabilities Trust
Incorporated: 12 January 1989 *Employees:* 1,719
Net Worth: £92,650,000 *Total Assets:* £100,786,000
Registered Office: 1st Floor, 32 Market Place, The Martlets, Burgess Hill, W Sussex, RH15 9NP
Activities: Residential care activities for the elderly and disabled
Officers: Dr Caroline Susan Drugan [1965] Director/Retired Dentist; Michael Green [1959] Director/Property Consultant Partner; Stephen William Howell [1955] Director; Roger Anthony Hoyle [1952] Director; Eileen Christina Jackman [1948] Director; Themis Sara Livadeas [1964] Trustee Director; Christopher Edwin Philipsborn [1965] Trustee Director; Mark Keith Rowe [1960] Director/Financial Services; Christine Margaret Yorath [1950] Director

Discoverie Group PLC
Incorporated: 9 April 1986 *Employees:* 3,986
Previous: ACAL PLC
Net Worth: £129,300,000 *Total Assets:* £310,400,000
Registered Office: 2 Chancellor Court, Occam Road, Surrey Research Park, Guildford, Surrey, GU2 7AH
Activities: Activities of head offices
Officers: Joanna Alwen Harkus Madge, Secretary; Richard John Brooman [1955] Independent Non-Executive Director; Malcolm McDonald Diamond [1948] Director; Simon Mark Gibbins [1966] Director/Chartered Accountant; Tracey Graham [1965] Director; Nicholas John Jefferies [1966] Director; Henrietta Elizabeth Marsh [1959] Director; Bruce McKenzie Thompson [1955] Director

Discoverie Management Services Limited
Incorporated: 11 July 1986 *Employees:* 37
Previous: ACAL Management Services Limited
Net Worth: £6,585,000 *Total Assets:* £55,553,000
Registered Office: 2 Chancellor Court, Occam Road, Surrey Research Park, Guildford, Surrey, GU2 7AH
Activities: Activities of head offices
Parent: ACAL PLC
Officers: Joanna Alwen Harkus Madge, Secretary; Simon Mark Gibbins [1966] Director/Chartered Accountant; Nicholas John Jefferies [1966] Director

Discoverie Nordic Holdings Limited
Incorporated: 27 May 2014
Previous: ACAL Nordic Holdings Limited
Net Worth: £51,763,384 *Total Assets:* £61,300,076
Registered Office: 2 Chancellor Court, Occam Road, Surrey Research Park, Guildford, Surrey, GU2 7AH
Activities: Activities of head offices
Parent: ACAL PLC
Officers: Joanna Alwen Harkus Madge, Secretary; Simon Mark Gibbins [1966] Director/Chartered Accountant; Nicholas John Jefferies [1966] Director; Paul Howard Neville [1967] Director

DL Insurance Services Limited
Incorporated: 15 December 1994 *Employees:* 10,949
Net Worth: £449,400,000 *Total Assets:* £684,000,000
Registered Office: Churchill Court, Westmoreland Road, Bromley, Kent, BR1 1DP
Activities: Non-life insurance
Parent: Direct Line Insurance Group PLC
Officers: Roger Cheston Clifton, Secretary; Paul Robert Geddes [1969] Director/Bank Official; Jonathan Paul Greenwood [1968] Director/Bank Official; Penelope Jane James [1969] Director; Steven Maddock [1968] Director/Bank Official; Neil Manser [1974] Director/Accountant; Humphrey Michael Tomlinson [1962] Director/General Counsel & Company Secretary

DLR (No.1) Limited
Incorporated: 31 May 2005
Net Worth: £23,014,000 *Total Assets:* £500,100,000
Registered Office: De La Rue House, Jays Close Viables, Basingstoke, Hants, RG22 4BS
Activities: Activities of other holding companies n.e.c.
Parent: DLR (No. 2) Limited
Officers: Jean-Francois Hermans, Company Secretary; Jean-Francois Hermans [1958] Director/Chartered Secretary; Edward Hugh Davidson Peppiatt [1967] Director/Lawyer; Lesley Sharon Roche [1967] Director/Accountant - Group Financial Controller

DLR (No.2) Limited
Incorporated: 3 April 2008
Net Worth: £16,334,000 *Total Assets:* £300,004,992
Registered Office: De La Rue House, Jays Close, Viables, Basingstoke, Hants, RG22 4BS
Activities: Activities of other holding companies n.e.c.
Parent: De La Rue PLC
Officers: Jean Francois Hermans, Secretary; Jean-Francois Hermans [1958] Director/Chartered Secretary; Edward Hugh Davidson Peppiatt [1967] Director/Lawyer; Lesley Sharon Roche [1967] Director/Accountant - Group Financial Controller

Dnata Aviation Services Limited
Incorporated: 14 January 2010 *Employees:* 4
Net Worth: £141,756,000 *Total Assets:* £217,536,000
Registered Office: Dakota House, Poyle Road, Colnbrook, Berks, SL3 0QX
Activities: Activities of head offices
Officers: Robert Stewart Angus [1965] Director; Christopher Chandy [1980] Director [Indian]; Ruth Claire Rhea [1984] Director

Dnata Limited
Incorporated: 14 August 1995 *Employees:* 2,169
Net Worth: £5,300,000 *Total Assets:* £57,703,000
Registered Office: Dakota House, Poyle Road, Colnbrook, Berks, SL3 0QX
Activities: Operation of warehousing and storage facilities for air transport activities
Parent: Dnata Aviation Services Limited
Officers: Robert Stewart Angus [1965] Director; Rosario Selli Marino [1966] Director; Gary Ian Morgan [1959] Director/Chief Executive Officer

Dnata World Travel Limited
Incorporated: 1 December 2011
Net Worth Deficit: £3,890,000 *Total Assets:* £132,321,000
Registered Office: Clarendon House, 147 London Road, Kingston upon Thames, Surrey, KT2 6NH
Activities: Activities of head offices
Officers: Iain Andrew [1965] Director; Asif Hamza Parkar [1974] Director/Finance Manager

Doctorlink Limited
Incorporated: 19 August 2016 *Employees:* 14
Previous: Medvivo Digital Limited
Net Worth Deficit: £1,072,162 *Total Assets:* £20,735,152
Registered Office: Oakhill House, 130 Tonbridge Road, Hildenborough, Kent, TN11 9DZ
Activities: Other human health activities
Officers: Mariano Gustavo Albera [1977] Director/Technology Executive [Italian]; John Bernard Behrendt [1961] Director; Andrew Philip Gardner [1957] Director/Executive Chairman

Doctors Chambers (UK) Limited
Incorporated: 7 January 2011 *Employees:* 112
Net Worth: £8,862,003 *Total Assets:* £27,341,378
Registered Office: Crown House, William Street, Windsor, Berks, SL4 1AT
Activities: Other human health activities
Parent: Doctors Chambers Group Limited
Officers: Janet Johnston [1961] Director; Bippon Chander Vinayak [1961] Director/Consultant Surgeon

Doctors Chambers Group Limited
Incorporated: 7 January 2011 *Employees:* 112
Net Worth: £5,120,998 *Total Assets:* £23,411,548
Registered Office: Crown House, William Street, Windsor, Berks, SL4 1AT
Activities: Activities of head offices
Major Shareholder: Bippon Chander Vinayak
Officers: Janet Johnston [1961] Director; Bippon Chander Vinayak [1961] Director/Consultant Surgeon

Dolphin Drilling Operations Limited
Incorporated: 19 May 2011
Net Worth: £65,631,372 *Total Assets:* £65,631,372
Registered Office: New Kings Court, Tollgate, Chandler's Ford, Eastleigh, Hants, SO53 3LG
Activities: Support activities for petroleum and natural gas mining
Parent: Fred Olsen Energy ASA
Officers: James David Lomax, Secretary; James Douglas Graham [1975] Director; Jorn Johansen [1970] Director [Norwegian]; James David Lomax [1955] Director/Contracts Manager

Dolphin Head Group Holdings PLC
Incorporated: 9 March 1987 *Employees:* 10
Net Worth: £12,368,994 *Total Assets:* £24,436,050
Registered Office: 103 Frimley Road, Camberley, Surrey, GU15 2PP
Activities: Development of building projects
Parent: Dolphin Head Group Limited
Officers: Gavin Alexander Price, Secretary/Director; Gavin Alexander Price [1964] Working Director; Warren Lindsey Price [1978] Director

Dolphin Head Group Limited
Incorporated: 14 August 2008 *Employees:* 10
Net Worth: £11,698,865 *Total Assets:* £24,050,550
Registered Office: Dolphin House, 103 Frimley Road, Camberley, Surrey, GU15 2PP
Activities: Buying and selling of own real estate
Officers: Angela Price, Secretary; Angela Price [1948] Director; Russell Price [1946] Director

Dolphin Two Limited
Incorporated: 28 November 2011
Net Worth: £11,982,000 *Total Assets:* £25,342,000
Registered Office: Costain House, Vanwall Business Park, Maidenhead, Berks, SL6 4UB
Activities: Other education n.e.c.
Parent: Costain Pension Scheme Trustees Limited
Officers: Tracey Wood, Secretary; Alistair John Handford [1951] Director/Civil Engineer; Gary William Mills [1956] Director/Chartered Civil Engineer

Domantis Limited
Incorporated: 17 January 2000
Net Worth: £39,675,000 *Total Assets:* £39,719,000
Registered Office: 980 Great West Road, Brentford, Middlesex, TW8 9GS
Activities: Other research and experimental development on natural sciences and engineering
Parent: Glaxo Group Limited
Officers: Victoria Anne Whyte, Secretary; James Borger [1963] Director/VP, Group Financial Planning and Analysis [American]; Alan George Burns [1975] Director

Domino's Pizza Group PLC
Incorporated: 5 October 1999 *Employees:* 1,749
Net Worth: £43,800,000 *Total Assets:* £380,900,000
Registered Office: 1 Thornbury, West Ashland, Milton Keynes, Bucks, MK6 4BB
Activities: Licenced restaurants
Officers: Adrian John Bushnell, Secretary; Stephen David Barber [1952] Director; David Gregory Bauernfeind [1968] Director/Accountant; Colin Halpern [1937] Director [American]; Stephen Glen Hemsley [1957] Director/Chartered Accountant; Kevin Paul Higgins [1963] Director [Irish]; Ebbe Pelle Jacobsen [1949] Director [Danish]; Helen Margaret Keays [1964] Director; David James Wild [1955] Director

Dominvs Project Company 9 Limited
Incorporated: 30 January 2017
Net Worth Deficit: £1,263 *Total Assets:* £49,072,352
Registered Office: 1 London Street, Reading, Berks, RG1 4QW
Activities: Development of building projects
Officers: Pritpal Singh Ahluwalia [1990] Director; Sukhpal Singh Ahluwalia [1963] Director; Aran Handa [1955] Director; Arpana Jaymalsinh Mangrola [1964] Director Administration; Anthony Edward Michael Simler [1971] Director

Dominvs Project Company Limited
Incorporated: 19 March 2013 *Employees:* 84
Net Worth: £6,032,266 *Total Assets:* £30,983,056
Registered Office: 1 London Street, Reading, Berks, RG1 4QW
Activities: Development of building projects
Officers: Husnell Singh Ahluwalia [1985] Director; Pritpal Singh Ahluwalia [1990] Director; Sukhpal Singh Ahluwalia [1958] Director; Arpana Jaymalsinh Mangrola [1964] Director Administration; Anthony Edward Michael Simler [1971] Director

Donamount Limited
Incorporated: 30 September 1999
Net Worth Deficit: £20,872,466 *Total Assets:* £31,020,032
Registered Office: NJHco, Suite 1, The Sanctuary, 23 Oak Hill Grove, Surbiton, Surrey, KT6 6DU
Activities: Activities of other holding companies n.e.c.
Major Shareholder: Klaas Johannes Zwart
Officers: Paul Emmanuel O'Neill [1978] Director [Irish]; Adrian Relph [1967] Director; Stuart William Wilson [1967] Director

Doncaster School Solutions (Holdings) Limited
Incorporated: 28 November 2006
Net Worth Deficit: £11,247,000 *Total Assets:* £42,817,000
Registered Office: Astral House, Imperial Way, Watford, Herts, WD24 4WW
Activities: Activities of head offices
Parent: Vinci Pensions Limited
Officers: Ian David Hudson [1964] Director/Chartered Accountant; Rory John Murphy [1969] Director/Chartered Surveyor

Doncaster School Solutions Limited
Incorporated: 28 November 2006
Net Worth Deficit: £11,247,000 *Total Assets:* £42,817,000
Registered Office: Astral House, Imperial Way, Watford, Herts, WD24 4WW
Activities: Development of building projects
Parent: Doncaster School Solutions (Holdings) Limited
Officers: Ian David Hudson [1964] Director/Chartered Accountant; Rory John Murphy [1969] Director/Chartered Surveyor

Doosan Babcock Limited
Incorporated: 1 March 1965 *Employees:* 2,972
Net Worth: £403,920,992 *Total Assets:* £697,980,032
Registered Office: Doosan House, Crawley Business Quarter, Manor Royal, Crawley, W Sussex, RH10 9AD
Activities: Manufacture of other special-purpose machinery n.e.c.
Officers: Mark Sunley, Secretary; Andrew Adam Colquhoun [1968] Director; Suk Joo Kang [1968] Director [South Korean]; Byoung Man Kim [1970] Director [South Korean]; Jinwon Mok [1970] Director [South Korean]

Doosan Power Systems Overseas Investments Limited
Incorporated: 19 April 1996
Net Worth Deficit: £11,706,000 *Total Assets:* £50,513,000
Registered Office: Doosan House, Crawley Business Quarter, Manor Royal, Crawley, W Sussex, RH10 9AD
Activities: Manufacture of other special-purpose machinery n.e.c.
Parent: Doosan Babcock Limited
Officers: Mark Sunley, Secretary; Andrew Adam Colquhoun [1968] Director; Suk Joo Kang [1968] Director [South Korean]; Byoung Man Kim [1970] Director [South Korean]

Dormole Limited
Incorporated: 10 January 1974 *Employees:* 934
Net Worth: £94,078,000 *Total Assets:* £130,002,000
Registered Office: Long Reach, Galleon Boulevard, Crossways Business Park, Dartford, Kent, DA2 6QE
Activities: Activities of head offices
Officers: Robert David Rowe, Secretary; Barry Gordon Karl Brice [1948] Director/Solicitor; John Nicholas Christie [1942] Director/Chartered Accountant; Stephen John Clemson [1951] Director; Andrew James Thomas Strong [1955] Director; Timothy John Strong [1958] Director; John Randall Charles Twallin [1933] Director

The Dover Federation for The Arts
Incorporated: 20 April 2012 *Employees:* 237
Net Worth: £21,890,408 *Total Assets:* £27,527,534
Registered Office: Astor College, Astor Avenue, Dover, Kent, CT17 0AS
Activities: Pre-primary education
Officers: Rebecca Sarah Tolhurst, Secretary; Helen Katrina Baacke [1970] Director of Student and Parent Support; Angela Billing [1970] Director/Housewife; Carol Anne Boxall [1959] Director/District School Nurse; Neil Peter Castle [1969] Director/Senior Lecturer; Carol Donovan [1946] Director/Retired; John William Horne [1958] Director/Artist; Una Mills [1952] Director/Local Authority Officer; Simon Paul Paget [1968] Director/Assistant Principal; Barry James Williams [1955] Director/Independent Financial Advisor

Downe House School
Incorporated: 12 September 1991 *Employees:* 285
Net Worth: £26,772,000 *Total Assets:* £37,853,000
Registered Office: The Bursary, Downe House School, Cold Ash, Newbury, Berks, RG18 9JJ
Activities: General secondary education
Officers: Colin Bernard Kauntze-Cockburn, Secretary; Elizabeth Jane Clarke [1968] Director/Marketing Consultant; Simon Charles Creedy-Smith [1959] Director/Accountant; Caroline Ann Cunningham [1962] Director/Dermatologist; Joanna Margaret Grant Peterkin [1949] Director/Education Consultant; Anne Frances Hazlitt [1963] Director; Fiona Mary Holmes [1963] Director; Nicholas Michael Hornby [1967] Director/Stockbroker; Matthew John Lushintgon Kirk [1960] Director; Christopher O'Kane [1960] Director/Research Fellow; Christopher Graham Radford [1957] Director; Dr Clare Iona Ratnage [1983] Director/Doctor; Veryan Jane Richards [1973] Director/Solicitor; Mark Keoki Ridley [1970] Director/Chartered Surveyor; Joseph Smith [1972] Director/Headmaster; Mark Alexander Wippell [1958] Director/Solicitor

DP Group Developments Limited
Incorporated: 13 August 1997
Net Worth Deficit: £2,056,000 *Total Assets:* £29,724,000
Registered Office: 1 Thornbury, West Ashland, Milton Keynes, Bucks, MK6 4BB
Activities: Development of building projects
Parent: Domino's Pizza Group PLC
Officers: Adrian John Bushnell, Secretary; David Gregory Bauernfeind [1968] Director/Accountant; Adrian John Bushnell [1964] Director/Chartered Secretary; Robin Keith Nigel Caley [1960] Director; David James Wild [1955] Director

DP Realty Limited
Incorporated: 15 December 1993 *Employees:* 4
Net Worth: £3,709,000 *Total Assets:* £28,234,000
Registered Office: 1 Thornbury, West Ashland, Milton Keynes, Bucks, MK6 4BB
Activities: Development of building projects
Parent: Domino's Pizza Group PLC
Officers: Adrian John Bushnell, Secretary; David Gregory Bauernfeind [1968] Director/Accountant; Adrian John Bushnell [1964] Director/Chartered Secretary; Robin Keith Nigel Caley [1960] Director; David James Wild [1955] Director

DPG Holdings Limited
Incorporated: 28 June 2006
Net Worth: £1,337,788,032 *Total Assets:* £1,423,794,944
Registered Office: 1 Thornbury, West Ashland, Milton Keynes, Bucks, MK6 4BB
Activities: Activities of head offices
Parent: Domino's Pizza Group PLC
Officers: Adrian John Bushnell, Secretary; David Gregory Bauernfeind [1968] Director/Accountant; Adrian John Bushnell [1964] Director/Chartered Secretary; Stephen Glen Hemsley [1957] Director; David James Wild [1955] Director

DPSK Limited
Incorporated: 28 March 2014 *Employees:* 97
Net Worth: £106,917,944 *Total Assets:* £160,401,344
Registered Office: Fortune House, Crabtree Office Village, Eversley Way, Egham, Surrey, TW20 8RY
Activities: Other food services
Officers: Gurprit Dhaliwal [1982] Director; Surinderjit Singh Kandola [1965] Director

Draper Tool Group Limited (The)
Incorporated: 16 May 1978 *Employees:* 348
Net Worth: £117,883,072 *Total Assets:* £127,199,304
Registered Office: Hursley Road, Chandler's Ford, Eastleigh, Hants, SO53 1YF
Activities: Activities of head offices
Officers: John Norman Draper, Secretary; John Norman Draper [1950] Director; Terence Francis McGowan [1947] Director

Draper Tools Limited
Incorporated: 23 August 1956 *Employees:* 340
Net Worth: £78,343,088 *Total Assets:* £86,430,976
Registered Office: Draper Tools Limited, Hursley Road, Chandler's Ford, Eastleigh, Hants, SO53 1YF
Activities: Wholesale of machine tools
Parent: The Draper Tool Group Limited
Officers: John Norman Draper, Secretary; Andrew Cole [1962] Director; Peter John Denney [1965] Director; John Norman Draper [1950] Director; Joseph Daniel Draper [1987] Director; Thomas Edward Draper [1984] Director; Terence Francis McGowan [1947] Director; Clive Vincent Anthony Richardson [1956] Director; Philip William Rowley [1966] Sales Director; Graham John Wade [1964] Director

Dreachmhor Wind Farm Limited
Incorporated: 17 April 2013
Net Worth Deficit: £4,872,000 *Total Assets:* £59,372,000
Registered Office: Edgeborough House, Upper Edgeborough Road, Guildford, Surrey, GU1 2BJ
Activities: Production of electricity
Parent: JLEAG Wind Limited
Officers: Joseph Mark Linney [1958] Director/Chartered Quantity Surveyor; Muxin Ma [1975] Director/Chartered Financial Analyst [Chinese]; Yit Ho Tang [1974] Director/Investment Manager [Singaporean]; Simon Owen Vince [1963] Construction & Operations Director

Dreams Limited
Incorporated: 4 March 2013 *Employees:* 1,837
Net Worth: £33,143,000 *Total Assets:* £94,250,000
Registered Office: Knaves Beech Business Centre, 14 Davies Way, Loudwater, High Wycombe, Bucks, HP10 9YU
Activities: Retail of furniture, lighting, and similar (not musical instruments or scores) in specialised store
Parent: Dreams Holdco Limited
Officers: Kim Suhail Zaheer, Secretary; Michael Francis Logue [1972] Director/Chief Executive Officer; Kim Suhail Zaheer [1971] Director

Dreams Topco Limited
Incorporated: 4 March 2013 *Employees:* 1,837
Net Worth: £32,043,000 *Total Assets:* £94,250,000
Registered Office: 14 Knaves Beech Business Centre, Davies Way, Loudwater, High Wycombe, Bucks, HP10 9YU
Activities: Activities of other holding companies n.e.c.
Officers: Paul David Daccus [1972] Managing Director

Dresser-Rand (U.K.) Limited
Incorporated: 6 May 1963 *Employees:* 74
Net Worth: £19,778,000 *Total Assets:* £31,100,000
Registered Office: Faraday House, Sir William Siemens Square, Frimley, Camberley, Surrey, GU16 8QD
Activities: Repair of machinery
Parent: D-R Holdings (UK) Ltd
Officers: Simone Eufemia Agatha Davina, Secretary; Lee Dawson [1978] Director/Accountant; Daniel Mann [1976] Director/Business Executive

Drew Marine UK Holdings Ltd
Incorporated: 22 May 2012 *Employees:* 196
Net Worth: £8,273,740 *Total Assets:* £83,342,152
Registered Office: Westbourne Suite, Building 6000, Langstone Technology Park, Langstone Road, Havant, Hants, PO9 1SA
Activities: Activities of other holding companies n.e.c.
Officers: Thomas Cessario [1954] Director/Senior Vice President Global Manufacturing, HR [American]; Francis Quinn [1957] Director of Treasury [American]

Drift Bridge Garage Limited
Incorporated: 15 August 1961 *Employees:* 308
Net Worth: £6,134,811 *Total Assets:* £38,710,368
Registered Office: Drift Bridge Garage, Reigate Road, Epsom, Surrey, KT17 3LA
Activities: Sale of new cars and light motor vehicles
Parent: Drift Bridge Group Holdings Limited
Officers: Edwin John Frost [1939] Director/Garage Proprietor; Michael Vernon Frost [1939] Director/Garage Proprietor

Driveline Limited
Incorporated: 2 January 2003 *Employees:* 322
Net Worth Deficit: £748,990 *Total Assets:* £57,100,272
Registered Office: Motorline House, Shalloak Road, Broad Oak, Canterbury, Kent, CT2 0PR
Activities: Other business support service activities n.e.c.
Parent: Motorline Holdings Limited
Officers: Glen Richard Obee, Secretary; Paul Alex Betts [1954] Director/Chartered Accountant; Gary Myles Obee [1961] Director/Motor Dealer; Glen Richard Obee [1963] Director/Motor Dealer; Thomas Giles Obee [1968] Director/Motor Dealer

Druid Group Limited
Incorporated: 27 October 1993
Net Worth: £123,891,000 *Total Assets:* £141,682,000
Registered Office: Three Cherry Trees Lane, Hemel Hempstead, Herts, HP2 7AH
Activities: Activities of head offices
Parent: Sopra Steria Holdings Limited
Officers: Peter Atherton Cashmore, Secretary; Davinder Singh Ahluwalia [1952] Director; John Powell Torrie [1954] Director

DS (Holdings) 2 Limited
Incorporated: 28 September 2006
Previous: Office Depot (Holdings) 2 Limited
Net Worth Deficit: £236,439,968 *Total Assets:* £467,195,776
Registered Office: Allen House, 1 Westmead Road, Sutton, Surrey, SM1 4LA
Activities: Activities of head offices
Major Shareholder: Chi Wai Tammy Lam
Officers: Stewart Roland Hussey [1958] Director

DS (Holdings) 3 Limited
Incorporated: 20 December 2007
Previous: Office Depot (Holdings) 3 Limited
Net Worth: £700,200,189,952 *Total Assets:* £700,200,189,952
Registered Office: Allem House, 1 Westmead Road, Sutton, Surrey, SM1 4LA
Activities: Activities of head offices
Parent: Office Depot (Holdings) 2 Limited
Officers: Stewart Roland Hussey [1958] Director

DST Global Solutions (Realty) Limited
Incorporated: 24 May 2010 *Employees:* 1
Net Worth: £36,528,000 *Total Assets:* £37,835,000
Registered Office: DST House, St Marks Hill, Surbiton, Surrey, KT6 4QD
Activities: Buying and selling of own real estate
Parent: DST Process Solutions Limited
Officers: Patrick John Louis Pedonti [1951] Director [American]

DST Process Solutions Limited
Incorporated: 1 June 2010 *Employees:* 35
Net Worth: £109,323,000 *Total Assets:* £129,104,000
Registered Office: DST House, St Mark's Hill, Surbiton, Surrey, KT6 4QD
Activities: Information technology consultancy activities
Parent: DSTI Holdings Limited
Officers: Patrick John Louis Pedonti [1951] Director [American]

DSTI Group LLP
Incorporated: 11 August 2004
Net Worth: £277,791,008 *Total Assets:* £284,953,984
Registered Office: DST House, St Marks Hill, Surbiton, Surrey, KT6 4QD

DSTI Holdings Limited
Incorporated: 23 August 2004 *Employees:* 116
Net Worth: £174,487,008 *Total Assets:* £305,128,992
Registered Office: DST House, St Marks Hill, Surbiton, Surrey, KT6 4QD
Activities: Activities of head offices
Officers: Patrick John Louis Pedonti [1961] Director [American]; William Slattery [1955] Director [Irish]

Dual Energy Direct Limited
Incorporated: 10 January 2008 *Employees:* 78
Net Worth: £113,264 *Total Assets:* £38,538,564
Registered Office: Premium House, The Esplanade, Worthing, W Sussex, BN11 2BJ
Activities: Trade of electricity
Parent: Dual Energy Limited
Officers: Kieran William Murphy, Secretary; Richard David Bartlett [1979] Director; Benjamin Neil Giddings [1973] Director; Anna Martin [1961] Director; Kieran William Murphy [1967] Finance Director; Graham Michael Thornley [1952] Director; Arthur Wingrove [1948] Director/Entrepreneur

Dulux Limited
Incorporated: 20 August 1986
Net Worth: £647,297,024 *Total Assets:* £651,012,992
Registered Office: The Akzonobel Building, Wexham Road, Slough, Berks, SL2 5DS
Activities: Activities of head offices
Parent: Ergon Investments UK Limited
Officers: Stephen Bruce Ray [1962] Director/Pensions Accounting Manager; Michael Smalley [1958] Director

Dun & Bradstreet Finance Limited
Incorporated: 2 April 1965
Net Worth: £49,012,000 *Total Assets:* £528,404,000
Registered Office: Marlow International, Parkway, Marlow, Bucks, SL7 1AJ
Activities: Other business support service activities n.e.c.
Parent: Dun & Bradstreet Limited
Officers: Emma Kimberley Morris, Secretary; Susan Beriont [1958] Director [American]; Rosemarie Jane Ellis [1968] Director; Kathleen Guinnessey [1960] Director/Treasurer [American]; Piers Dominic Gilchrist Woolston [1960] Director

Dun & Bradstreet Investments Limited
Incorporated: 16 August 2010
Net Worth: £162,472,000 *Total Assets:* £162,498,000
Registered Office: Marlow International, Parkway, Marlow, Bucks, SL7 1AJ
Activities: Activities of head offices
Parent: Dun & Bradstreet Finance Limited
Officers: Emma Kimberley Morris, Secretary; Susan Beriont [1958] Director/Vice President [American]; Rosemarie Jane Ellis [1968] Director (Tax); Kathleen Guinnessey [1960] Director/Treasurer [American]; Piers Dominic Gilchrist Woolston [1960] Director (Strategy)

Dun & Bradstreet Limited
Incorporated: 28 October 1919 *Employees:* 328
Net Worth: £112,305,000 *Total Assets:* £189,356,992
Registered Office: Marlow International, Parkway, Marlow, Bucks, SL7 1AJ
Activities: Other business support service activities n.e.c.
Parent: D & B Europe Limited
Officers: Paramdeep Sidhu, Secretary; Greg Battisson [1978] Director/UK Finance Leader; Rosemarie Jane Ellis [1968] Director; Sabine Leferink [1970] Director/Worldwide Network Leader [Dutch]; Julian Nicholas Nigel Prower [1966] Director/Senior Company Officer; Edward Charles John Thorne [1980] Managing Director

Dunlop International Group Limited
Incorporated: 4 September 1995 *Employees:* 4
Previous: Dunlop Slazenger Group Limited
Net Worth: £24,784,000 *Total Assets:* £91,293,000
Registered Office: Thorncroft Manor, Thorncroft Drive, Dorking Road, Leatherhead, Surrey, KT22 8JB
Activities: Non-trading company
Parent: Dunlop International Group Holdings Limited
Officers: Tetsuo Shimizu, Secretary; Masahiro Asahino [1963] Director/Chief Executive Officer [Japanese]; Takuya Inabetsu [1967] Director/General Manager [Japanese]; Hidekazu Nishiguchi [1960] Director [Japanese]; Yasuo Watanabe [1962] Director/General Manager [Japanese]

Dunmoore (West London) Limited
Incorporated: 24 June 2016
Net Worth: £4,535,392 *Total Assets:* £27,999,956
Registered Office: Brightwalton House, Brightwalton, Newbury, Berks, RG20 7BZ
Activities: Other letting and operating of own or leased real estate
Parent: Dunmoore Ventures Limited
Officers: Jeffrey Robert Hobby [1968] Director; Tomas Souto [1988] Director

Durkan Estates Limited
Incorporated: 19 May 1987 *Employees:* 9
Net Worth: £12,984,717 *Total Assets:* £72,139,800
Registered Office: 4 Elstree Gate, Elstree Way, Borehamwood, Herts, WD6 1JD
Activities: Development of building projects
Officers: Ronan Patrick Murphy, Secretary; Daniel Gerard Durkan [1964] Director - Sales [Irish]; Ronan Patrick Murphy [1969] Director/Chartered Accountant [Irish]

Durkan Holdings Limited
Incorporated: 9 June 1977 *Employees:* 175
Net Worth: £58,871,960 *Total Assets:* £142,434,064
Registered Office: 4 Elstree Gate, Elstree Way, Borehamwood, Herts, WD6 1JD
Activities: Development of building projects
Officers: Ronan Patrick Murphy, Secretary; Daniel Gerard Durkan [1964] Director/Chief Executive [Irish]; Ronan Patrick Murphy [1969] Director/Chartered Accountant [Irish]

Durkan Limited
Incorporated: 15 December 1970 *Employees:* 171
Net Worth: £37,842,612 *Total Assets:* £81,418,736
Registered Office: 4 Elstree Gate, Elstree Way, Borehamwood, Herts, WD6 1JD
Activities: Development of building projects
Officers: Ronan Patrick Murphy, Secretary; James Philip Briggs [1960] Managing Director; Ian Philip Cresswell [1965] Health & Safety Director; Daniel Gerard Durkan [1964] Director/Chief Executive [Irish]; Dean Martin [1968] Construction Director; Ronan Patrick Murphy [1969] Director/Chartered Accountant [Irish]; Shane Rooney [1965] Commercial Director [Irish]

Durrington Multi Academy Trust
Incorporated: 14 February 2014 *Employees:* 224
Net Worth: £25,470,636 *Total Assets:* £27,752,384
Registered Office: Durrington High Academy, The Boulevard, Worthing, W Sussex, BN13 1JX
Activities: General secondary education
Officers: Nickolas John Roberts, Secretary; Lianne Allison [1970] Director; John Richard Digby [1957] Director; Sue Marooney [1963] Director/Headteacher; Paul Noakes [1970] Director/Accountant; Nicola Jane Thomas [1964] Director/Education Consultant; Emma Rosemary Watkins [1973] Director/Physical Education Consultant

Dwellcourt Limited
Incorporated: 17 August 1984 *Employees:* 188
Net Worth: £21,016,544 *Total Assets:* £32,484,010
Registered Office: Downs Farm, Reigate Road, Ewell, Surrey, KT17 3BY
Activities: Activities of head offices
Major Shareholder: Thomas Albert Hilliard
Officers: Jeffrey Thomas Hilliard, Secretary; James Michael Bowry [1987] Finance Director; Jeffrey Thomas Hilliard [1964] Development Director; Douglas William McClelland [1949] Director; Terry Kirk Sims [1971] Director; Steven John Turnbull [1976] Director

DX (Group) PLC
Incorporated: 19 September 2013 *Employees:* 3,264
Net Worth: £24,900,000 *Total Assets:* £88,200,000
Registered Office: Ditton Park, Riding Court Road, Datchet, Slough, SL3 9GL
Activities: Activities of head offices
Officers: David Kevin Mulligan, Secretary; David Russell Black [1939] Director; Lloyd John Charles Dunn [1958] Director/Chief Executive Officer; Paul Andrew Goodson [1963] Director; Ian Archie Gray [1953] Director/Chartered Accountant; David Kevin Mulligan [1969] Director/Chief Finance Officer; Ronald Charles Series [1951] Director/Chairman

DX (VCP) Limited
Incorporated: 10 February 2014
Net Worth Deficit: £185,600,000 *Total Assets:* £40,300,000
Registered Office: Ditton Park, Riding Court Road, Datchet, Slough, SL3 9GL
Activities: Activities of other holding companies n.e.c.
Parent: DX (Group) PLC
Officers: David Kevin Mulligan [1969] Director/Chief Finance Officer; Ronald Charles Series [1951] Director/Chairman

DX Holdings Limited
Incorporated: 13 June 2006
Net Worth Deficit: £66,500,000 *Total Assets:* £31,100,000
Registered Office: Ditton Park, Riding Court Road, Datchet, Slough, SL3 9GL
Activities: Activities of head offices
Parent: DX (VCP) Limited
Officers: David Kevin Mulligan [1969] Director/Chief Finance Officer; Ronald Charles Series [1951] Director/Chairman

DX Network Services Limited
Incorporated: 27 January 2004 *Employees:* 3,222
Net Worth: £20,000,000 *Total Assets:* £87,000,000
Registered Office: Ditton Park, Riding Court Road, Datchet, Slough, SL3 9GL
Activities: Licensed carriers
Parent: DX Services Limited
Officers: Lloyd John Charles Dunn [1958] Director/Chief Executive Officer; Paul John Ibbetson [1971] Managing Director; Martin Illidge [1973] Director; Kerensa Leatherland [1969] Director; David Kevin Mulligan [1969] Director/Chief Finance Officer; Michael John Sherry [1970] IT Director

DX Services Limited
Incorporated: 4 June 2004
Net Worth Deficit: £21,400,000 *Total Assets:* £30,100,000
Registered Office: Ditton Park, Riding Court Road, Datchet, Slough, SL3 9GL
Activities: Activities of head offices
Parent: DX Holdings Limited
Officers: David Kevin Mulligan [1969] Director/Chief Finance Officer; Ronald Charles Series [1951] Director/Chairman

Dynama Solutions Ltd
Incorporated: 1 November 2016 *Employees:* 31
Net Worth: £830,000 *Total Assets:* £31,952,000
Registered Office: 2nd Floor, 1 Church Road, Richmond, Surrey, TW9 2QE
Activities: Other business support service activities n.e.c.
Parent: Allocate Bidco Limited
Officers: Jonathan James Harston [1976] Director/Chief Financial Officer; Charles George Munro [1975] Director/Accountant; Nicholas Stephen Wilson [1971] Director/Chief Executive Officer

Dynamic Procurement Holdings Limited
Incorporated: 15 June 2011 *Employees:* 57
Net Worth: £13,188,588 *Total Assets:* £34,603,140
Registered Office: 249 Midsummer Boulevard, Milton Keynes, Bucks, MK9 1EA
Activities: Activities of other holding companies n.e.c.
Shareholders: Julian John Lindsay Young; Ian Reiner Wolter
Officers: Graham John Anthony Dolan, Secretary; Paul Santo Martin [1971] Director; Ian Reiner Wolter [1966] Director; Julian John Lindsay Young [1966] Director

Dynatrace Limited
Incorporated: 15 October 1980 *Employees:* 99
Previous: Compuware Limited
Net Worth: £10,115,792 *Total Assets:* £30,178,560
Registered Office: Quantum, 60 Norden Road, Maidenhead, Berks, SL6 4AY
Activities: Other information technology service activities
Parent: Dynatrace LLC
Officers: Francesca Jones, Secretary; Richard Edward Bowers [1973] Finance Director; Craig Newfield [1959] Director/General Counsel [American]

Dynniq UK Ltd
Incorporated: 11 April 1980 *Employees:* 478
Previous: Imtech Traffic & Infra UK Limited
Net Worth: £8,208,000 *Total Assets:* £23,196,000
Registered Office: Hazelwood House, Lime Tree Way, Chineham Business Park, Basingstoke, Hants, RG24 8WZ
Activities: Manufacture of other electrical equipment
Parent: Dynniq Group BV
Officers: Stephen Dines [1977] Finance Director; Anthony O'Brien [1964] Managing Director [Irish]

Dyno-Rod Limited
Incorporated: 21 March 1972 *Employees:* 107
Net Worth: £70,069,000 *Total Assets:* £78,029,000
Registered Office: Millstream, Maidenhead Road, Windsor, Berks, SL4 5GD
Activities: Other service activities n.e.c.
Parent: British Gas Services Limited
Officers: Mark Steven Hodges [1965] Director; Ivan Edward Ronald [1972] Director; Dr Rajarshi Roy [1975] Director

DYRMS - An Academy with Military Traditions
Incorporated: 30 March 2010 *Employees:* 164
Net Worth: £31,687,978 *Total Assets:* £38,813,724
Registered Office: Duke of York's Royal Military School, Dover, Kent, CT15 5EQ
Activities: General secondary education
Officers: Adam James Kent, Secretary; Jeffrey Applegate [1957] Director/Chartered Accountant; James Baxter [1946] Director/Retired; Brigadier Matthew Bazeley [1968] Director/Civil Servant; Russell Graham Collier [1968] Director/Civil Servant; Alexander Lorie Foreman [1975] Director/Principal; Stuart Graham [1970] Director/Civil Servant; Jenny Lycett [1962] Director/Retired; Georgina Martin [1971] Director/Marketing and PR Manager; Andrew Nunn [1950] Director/Retired; Leyland Bradshaw Ridings [1937] Director/Honorary Alderman; Colonel Andy Thorne [1971] Director/Civil Servant; Tyrone Urch [1965] Director/Commander Home Command; Daniela Steluta Vandepeer [1960] Director/Teacher; Christopher Blake Wacher [1951] Director/Solicitor

E & J Capital Partners Limited
Incorporated: 2 April 2009 *Employees:* 9
Net Worth: £18,843,232 *Total Assets:* £48,787,560
Registered Office: Prospect Place, Moorside Road, Winchester, Hants, SO23 7RX
Activities: Financial intermediation not elsewhere classified
Parent: E & J Holdings Ltd
Officers: Christopher Russell Jarvis, Secretary; James Edward Tuttiett [1963] Director

E & J Ground Rents LLP
Incorporated: 3 April 2009
Net Worth: £7,270,307 *Total Assets:* £27,156,218
Registered Office: Prospect Place, Moorside Road, Winchester, Hants, SO23 7RX

E & J Ground Rents No 15 Limited
Incorporated: 30 April 2015 *Employees:* 1
Net Worth: £6,498,320 *Total Assets:* £23,351,914
Registered Office: Prospect Place, Moorside Road, Winchester, Hants, SO23 7RX
Activities: Buying and selling of own real estate
Parent: SF Ground Rents Ltd
Officers: James Edward Tuttiett [1963] Director

E & J Ground Rents No2 LLP
Incorporated: 18 December 2009
Net Worth: £7,417,736 *Total Assets:* £28,417,428
Registered Office: Prospect Place, Moorside Road, Winchester, Hants, SO23 7RX

E & J Ground Rents No3 LLP
Incorporated: 8 December 2010
Net Worth: £7,597,254 *Total Assets:* £37,740,560
Registered Office: Prospect Place, Moorside Road, Winchester, Hants, SO23 7RX

E & J Ground Rents No4 LLP
Incorporated: 3 November 2011
Net Worth: £8,988,648 *Total Assets:* £36,952,304
Registered Office: Prospect Place, Moorside Road, Winchester, Hants, SO23 7RX

E & J Ground Rents No5 LLP
Incorporated: 28 August 2012
Net Worth: £6,074,683 *Total Assets:* £32,581,266
Registered Office: Prospect Place, Moorside Road, Winchester, Hants, SO23 7RX

E & J Ground Rents No6 LLP
Incorporated: 13 March 2013
Net Worth: £6,357,427 *Total Assets:* £37,761,040
Registered Office: Prospect Place, Moorside Road, Winchester, Hants, SO23 7RX

E.F.B. Group Limited
Incorporated: 20 May 2005 *Employees:* 112
Net Worth: £13,711,032 *Total Assets:* £39,415,512
Registered Office: The Pinnacle, 170 Midsummer Boulevard, Milton Keynes, Bucks, MK9 1FE
Activities: Activities of head offices
Shareholders: E.F.B. Trustees Limited; Stephen Charles Barlow
Officers: Michael Adams [1956] Director; Stephen Charles Barlow [1956] Director/Chief Executive Officer; Peter John Butler [1966] Managing Director; Phil Gotch [1976] Financial Director; Brandon William Ransley [1965] Director/Solicitor

E.S. Pipelines Limited
Incorporated: 10 August 1999 *Employees:* 55
Net Worth: £71,257,000 *Total Assets:* £223,075,008
Registered Office: 1st Floor, Bluebird House, Mole Business Park, Leatherhead, Surrey, KT22 7BA
Activities: Transport via pipeline
Parent: ESPUG Finance Limited
Officers: Thomas William Butler [1959] Finance Director [Irish]; Nicholas John Clark [1960] Director; Anna Louise Dellis [1973] Director/Investment Executive; Paul Miles [1971] Director/Chief Financial Officer; Kevin O'Connor [1976] Director/Chief Executive Officer; Sebastian Schwengber [1979] Director/Investment Professional [German]; Victoria Caroline Spiers [1969] Director/Manager; Stuart Peter Williams [1965] Operations Director

Eagle Estates Limited
Incorporated: 4 October 1995 *Employees:* 5
Net Worth: £17,593,408 *Total Assets:* £37,552,272
Registered Office: 99 Western Road, Hove, E Sussex, BN3 1FA
Activities: Buying and selling of own real estate
Shareholder: Farzin Sobhanpanah
Officers: Ghanim Hamza, Secretary/Director; Farzin Sobhanpanah, Secretary/Director; Ghanim Hamza [1957] Director; Farzin Sobhanpanah [1957] Director

Eagle Racing Limited
Incorporated: 5 December 1988 *Employees:* 2
Net Worth: £16,190,943 *Total Assets:* £27,694,472
Registered Office: 150 High Street, Sevenoaks, Kent, TN13 1XE
Activities: Sale of used cars and light motor vehicles
Major Shareholder: Henry James Pearman
Officers: Karen Joy Ibberson, Secretary; Karen Ibberson [1963] Director; Henry James Pearman [1963] Director/Car Restorer

Liz Earle Beauty Co. Limited
Incorporated: 20 June 1995 *Employees:* 923
Net Worth: £27,686,640 *Total Assets:* £38,463,136
Registered Office: The Green House, Nicholson Road, Ryde, Isle of Wight, PO33 1BD
Activities: Manufacture of perfumes and toilet preparations
Parent: Alliance Boots Holdings Limited
Officers: Andrew Richard Thompson, Secretary; Rosemary Frances Counsell [1963] Director/Chief Financial Officer - Global Brands; Anne Louise Murphy [1967] Director; David Waller [1980] Director

Early Learning Centre Limited
Incorporated: 25 March 1909 *Employees:* 24
Net Worth Deficit: £114,600,000 *Total Assets:* £119,100,000
Registered Office: Cherry Tree Road, Watford, Herts, WD24 6SH
Activities: Other retail sale of new goods in specialised stores (not commercial art galleries and opticians)
Parent: Early Learning Holdings Limited
Officers: Lynne Samatha Medini, Secretary; Kirsty Rowena Homer [1974] HR Director; William Glyn Lawrence Hughes [1976] Director/Chief Financial Officer; Mark Newton-Jones [1967] Director; Kevin Jonathan Rusling [1977] Managing Director, International

The East Malling Trust
Incorporated: 24 February 2010 *Employees:* 19
Net Worth: £28,830,044 *Total Assets:* £29,881,836
Registered Office: Bradbourne House, East Malling, Kent, ME19 6DZ
Activities: Buying and selling of own real estate
Officers: Karyn Margaret Hood, Secretary; Kevin Dennis Attwood [1959] Director/Farmer; Allis Beasley [1965] Director/Solicitor; Karen Christina Blackiston [1981] Director/Accountant; Dr Oliver Peter Doubleday [1952] Director/Farmer; Dr Jonathan David Knight [1959] Director; Professor John David Mumford [1953] Director/Academic

East Surrey Holdings Limited
Incorporated: 5 November 1991
Net Worth: £79,670,392 *Total Assets:* £81,411,136
Registered Office: 66-74 London Road, Redhill, Surrey, RH1 1LJ
Activities: Activities of other holding companies n.e.c.
Parent: Sumisho Osaka Gas Water UK Limited
Officers: Anthony John David Ferrar [1957] Director; Graham David Holman [1966] Director/Solicitor; Paul Kerr [1973] Finance and Regulation Director; Akira Masuo [1969] Director [Japanese]; Ryuichi Nishida [1965] Managing Director [Japanese]; Jeremy David Pelczer [1957] Director

East Sussex Energy Infrastructure and Development Limited
Incorporated: 12 May 2011 *Employees:* 15
Net Worth Deficit: £1,119,000 *Total Assets:* £30,404,000
Registered Office: Innovation Centre, Highfield Drive, St Leonards, E Sussex, TN38 9UH
Activities: Development of building projects
Officers: Lord David Ampthill [1947] Director/Retired/District Councillor; Sonia Jane Blizzard [1971] Managing Director; Professor Julian Moray Crampton [1952] Director/Vice Chancellor; Kim Forward [1958] Director/Councillor, Independent Living Support Assistant; Gareth Peter Jones [1966] Managing Director; Steven John Manwaring [1961] Managing Director; Susan Mary McHugh [1961] Director/Chief Operating Officer; Councillor Rupert Alexandre James Simmons [1953] Director/Publisher

East Sussex Press Limited
Incorporated: 17 November 1993 *Employees:* 431
Net Worth Deficit: £1,110,303 *Total Assets:* £29,706,208
Registered Office: Beacon House, Brambleside, Uckfield, E Sussex, TN22 1PL
Activities: Printing n.e.c.
Shareholders: Mark William Handford; BGF GP Limited
Officers: Bridget Mary Tucker, Secretary; Ian Brown [1955] Finance Director; Mark Gunnar Bryant [1962] Director/Investment Manager; David John Bullivant [1968] Director; Mark William Handford [1965] Director/Printer; Andrew John Nash [1957] Director; Richard Osborne [1962] Managing Director; Bridget Mary Tucker [1967] Director/Secretary

Eastbourne College (Incorporated)
Incorporated: 22 April 1911 *Employees:* 412
Net Worth: £47,591,000 *Total Assets:* £61,311,000
Registered Office: Marlborough House, Old Wish Road, Eastbourne, E Sussex, BN21 4JY
Activities: Pre-primary education
Officers: Christopher Mark Bentley-Mawer, Secretary; Philip Arthur John Broadley [1961] Finance Director; Alexander James Gore Brown [1967] Director/Surveyor; Charles Martin Peter Bush [1952] Director/Retired; Jeremy Richard Ernest Compton [1964] Director/Senior VP Research & Development; Amanda Claire Coxen [1970] Director; Richard Vivian Davidson-Houston [1972] Director/General Manager; Colin Michael Davies [1953] Director/Chartered Surveyor; Nicola Lindsey Eckert [1958] Director; Nicholas James Philip Elliott [1973] Director/Marketing Consultant; Professor Keith Gull [1948] Director/University Professor; Victoria Jane Henley [1959] Director/P R Consultant; Claire Phillippa Locher [1962] Director/Recruitment Consultant; George Marsh [1943] Director/Retired Headmaster; Dr Robert Andrew McNeilly [1961] Director/Medical Practitioner; James William Steuart Piper [1976] Director/Headmaster; Cherine Radwan [1968] Director/Solicitor; Thomas Shepherd Richardson [1958] Director/Chartered Surveyor; Andrew Mark Robinson [1961] Director/Chartered Accountant; John Hamilton Ryley [1961] Director/Head of Sky News; Helen Jane Toole [1965] Director; Jonathan Peter Watmough [1968] Director/Solicitor; Julie Ann Wheeldon [1980] Director/Chartered Accountant

Eastbury Park (Holdings) Limited
Incorporated: 7 June 2006
Net Worth Deficit: £36,378,000 *Total Assets:* £181,107,008
Registered Office: 8 White Oak Square, London Road, Swanley, Kent, BR8 7AG
Activities: Activities of head offices
Shareholders: Infrared Infrastructure Yield Holdings Limited; Infrastructure Investments Holdings Limited
Officers: Ross William Driver [1981] Director; Mark Christopher Wayment [1958] Director/Investment Banker

Eastbury Park Limited
Incorporated: 7 June 2006
Net Worth Deficit: £36,378,000 *Total Assets:* £181,107,008
Registered Office: 8 White Oak Square, London Road, Swanley, Kent, BR8 7AG
Activities: Defence activities
Parent: Eastbury Park (Holdings) Limited
Officers: Ross William Driver [1981] Director; Mark Christopher Wayment [1958] Director/Investment Banker

Eastern Airways (UK) Limited
Incorporated: 19 November 1997 *Employees:* 341
Net Worth: £4,197,000 *Total Assets:* £63,488,000
Registered Office: Redhill Aerodrome, Kings Mill Lane, Redhill, Surrey, RH1 5JZ
Activities: Scheduled passenger air transport
Parent: Eastern Airways (Europe) Limited
Officers: James Lort Howell-Richardson, Secretary; Alan William George Corbett [1957] Director; James Lort Howell-Richardson [1980] Director/Legal Counsel; Richard James Lake [1961] Managing Director; Michael Peter Nicol [1985] Director

Eastern Leasing Company Limited (The)
Incorporated: 20 October 1982
Net Worth: £45,976,000 *Total Assets:* £64,699,000
Registered Office: Vodafone House, The Connection, Newbury, Berks, RG14 2FN
Activities: Other business support service activities n.e.c.
Parent: Cable & Wireless UK Holdings Limited
Officers: Gregory Mook [1961] Director; Neil Andrew Wright [1970] Director/Finance Executive

Eastern Quarry Limited
Incorporated: 8 November 2000
Previous: LS Eastern Quarry Limited
Net Worth: £29,041,000 *Total Assets:* £89,669,000
Registered Office: 1 Christchurch Way, Woking, Surrey, GU21 6JG
Activities: Non-trading company
Parent: Henley Camland Ebbsfleet 801 Limited
Officers: Andrew James Brandon [1969] Director/Accountant; Peter Nelson [1961] Director; Ian Rickwood [1967] Director

Eaton Electric Limited
Incorporated: 13 December 2002 *Employees:* 269
Net Worth: £135,120,992 *Total Assets:* £498,177,984
Registered Office: 554 Abbey Park, Southampton Road, Titchfield, Fareham, Hants, PO14 4QA
Activities: Manufacture of other electrical equipment
Parent: Eaton Limited
Officers: Paul Warren Hartley [1970] Director; Jorma Mannerkoski [1965] Director [Finnish]; Keith Ramsay Miller [1957] Director; Martin Gerard Mullin [1966] Director; Ian Patrick Russell Thompson [1965] Director

Eaton Holding Limited
Incorporated: 11 February 1997
Net Worth Deficit: £56,203,000 *Total Assets:* £267,275,008
Registered Office: P O Box 554, Abbey Park, Southampton Road, Titchfield, Hants, PO14 4QA
Activities: Non-trading company
Parent: Eaton Holding LLC
Officers: Ian Bruce Yule [1968] Director/Accountant

Eaton Limited
Incorporated: 30 May 1919 *Employees:* 2,099
Net Worth: £90,144,000 *Total Assets:* £656,057,024
Registered Office: 554 Abbey Park, Southampton Road, Titchfield, Fareham, Hants, PO14 4QA
Activities: Machining
Parent: Eaton Holding Limited
Officers: Leo Michael Hayes [1961] Director; Jorma Mannerkoski [1965] Director [Finnish]; Martin Gerard Mullin [1966] Director

Echostar UK Holdings Limited
Incorporated: 6 August 1999
Net Worth: £21,644,560 *Total Assets:* £30,446,216
Registered Office: Hughes House, Rockingham Drive, Linford Wood, Milton Keynes, Bucks, MK14 6PD
Activities: Activities of head offices
Parent: Echostar Corporation
Officers: Michael Talmon Dugan [1949] Director [American]; Charles William Ergen [1953] Director [American]; Dr Dean Alfred Manson [1967] Director/Lawyer [American]

Eckoh PLC
Incorporated: 12 September 1997 *Employees:* 214
Net Worth: £21,809,000 *Total Assets:* £34,918,000
Registered Office: Telford House, Corner Hall, Hemel Hempstead, Herts, HP3 9HN
Activities: Other telecommunications activities
Officers: Christine Gillian Herbert, Secretary; David John Coghlan [1954] Director [British/Australian]; Christine Gillian Herbert [1970] Director; Christopher John Humphrey [1957] Director; Guy Leighton Millward [1965] Director; Nicholas Barnaby Philpot [1964] Director/Chief Executive Officer

Eco Animal Health Group PLC
Incorporated: 22 May 1984 *Employees:* 207
Net Worth: £99,690,000 *Total Assets:* £117,185,000
Registered Office: 78 Coombe Road, New Malden, Surrey, KT3 4QS
Activities: Wholesale of pharmaceutical goods
Officers: Julia Trouse, Secretary; Brett Timothy Clemo [1962] Global Operations Director; Dr Andrew Alfred Jones [1960] Director/Management Consultant; Peter Anthony Lawrence [1948] Director; Marc Denham Loomes [1961] Director; Anthony Paul Rawlinson [1957] Director/Chartered Accountant; Kevin Anthony Stockdale [1965] Finance Director; Julia Trouse [1966] Director

Eco Animal Health Ltd.
Incorporated: 22 November 1991 *Employees:* 51
Net Worth: £26,555,696 *Total Assets:* £84,152,288
Registered Office: 78 Coombe Road, New Malden, Surrey, KT3 4QS
Activities: Manufacture of basic pharmaceutical products
Officers: Julia Trouse, Secretary; Andrew Buglass [1972] Global Sales Director; Brett Timothy Clemo [1962] Director; Peter Anthony Lawrence [1948] Director; Marc Denham Loomes [1961] Managing Director; Kevin Anthony Stockdale [1965] Finance Director

Econocom Limited
Incorporated: 25 February 1998 *Employees:* 34
Net Worth: £7,533,000 *Total Assets:* £41,658,000
Registered Office: Eton House, 18-24 Paradise Road, Richmond upon Thames, Surrey, TW9 1SE
Activities: Renting and leasing of office machinery and equipment (including computers)
Parent: Econocom Group SE
Officers: Laurent Olivier Caparros [1966] Managing Director [French]; Chris Labrey [1969] Director; Nicolas Noquet [1980] Financial Director [French]; Galliane Edmee Anne Colette Touze [1972] Director [French]

Economydrive Cars Limited
Incorporated: 8 June 2009
Net Worth Deficit: £2,629,000 *Total Assets:* £158,582,000
Registered Office: 61 London Road, Redhill, Surrey, RH1 1QA
Activities: Activities of financial services holding companies
Parent: Banque PSA Finance
Officers: Kathleen Fiona Conroy, Secretary; Cruciano Infosino [1964] Director/Chief Executive [Belgian]; Nigel John Willetts [1972] Director/Chartered Accountant

Eden Automotive Investments Limited
Incorporated: 23 May 2007 *Employees:* 673
Net Worth: £17,563,378 *Total Assets:* £94,694,248
Registered Office: 38-40 Portman Road, Reading, Berks, RG30 1JG
Activities: Management consultancy activities other than financial management
Major Shareholder: Graeme John Potts
Officers: Nicola Hadley, Secretary; Nicola Hadley [1961] Finance Director; Graeme John Potts [1957] Director

Eden Automotive Limited
Incorporated: 23 May 2007 *Employees:* 522
Previous: Eden 2018 Limited
Net Worth: £16,555,174 *Total Assets:* £66,124,600
Registered Office: 38-40 Portman Road, Reading, Berks, RG30 1JG
Activities: Sale of new cars and light motor vehicles
Parent: Eden Automotive Investments Limited
Officers: Nicola Hadley, Secretary; Nicola Hadley [1961] Finance Director; Graeme John Potts [1957] Director

Eden Springs UK Limited
Incorporated: 1 September 2000 *Employees:* 380
Net Worth: £15,251,000 *Total Assets:* £59,880,000
Registered Office: Unit D, Fleming Centre, Fleming Way, Crawley, W Sussex, RH10 9NN
Activities: Manufacture of soft drinks; production of mineral waters and other bottled waters
Parent: Cott Corporation
Officers: Ron Zev Frieman [1955] Director [American]; Brian Richard Macpherson [1971] Deputy Managing Director; Shane Perkey [1976] Director [American]

Edge UK Holdings Limited
Incorporated: 4 December 2015
Net Worth: £2,329,340 *Total Assets:* £30,089,006
Registered Office: Priory House, Pilgrims Court, Sydenham Road, Guildford, Surrey, GU1 3RX
Activities: Activities of other holding companies n.e.c.
Parent: Village Roadshow Digital Pty Ltd
Officers: Raffaela Cosentino, Secretary; Caroline Margaret Aubrey [1964] Director; Patrick Francis Garner [1946] Director; Simon Phillipson [1962] Director [Australian]

Edgewell Personal Care Holdings UK Ltd.
Incorporated: 25 February 2000 *Employees:* 5
Previous: Energizer Holdings UK Company Limited
Net Worth: £47,179,000 *Total Assets:* £83,820,000
Registered Office: Sword House, Totteridge Road, High Wycombe, Bucks, HP13 6DG
Activities: Non-trading company
Parent: Edgewell Personal Care Investments UK Ltd
Officers: David Paul Hatfield [1960] Director/Executive Officer [American]; Colin Anthony Hutchison [1958] Director/Chief Operating Officer; Rod Ryan Little [1969] Director/Chief Financial Officer [American]

Edgewell Personal Care Investments UK Ltd.
Incorporated: 14 March 2003
Previous: Energizer Investments UK Limited
Net Worth: £56,288,000 *Total Assets:* £56,288,000
Registered Office: Sword House, Totteridge Road, High Wycombe, Bucks, HP13 6DG
Activities: Non-trading company
Parent: Edgewell Personal Care Company
Officers: David Paul Hatfield [1960] Director/Executive Officer [American]; Colin Anthony Hutchison [1958] Director/Chief Operating Officer; Rod Ryan Little [1969] Director/Chief Financial Officer [American]

Edgewell Personal Care UK Limited
Incorporated: 13 May 2015
Net Worth: £59,372,320 *Total Assets:* £70,825,568
Registered Office: Sword House, Totteridge Road, High Wycombe, Bucks, HP13 6DG
Activities: Non-trading company
Parent: Wilkinson Sword Limited
Officers: David Paul Hatfield [1960] Director/Executive [American]; Colin Anthony Hutchison [1958] Director/Chief Operating Officer; Rod Ryan Little [1969] Director/Chief Financial Officer [American]

Edif Group Finance Limited
Incorporated: 19 January 2011
Net Worth: £7,492,000 *Total Assets:* £42,035,000
Registered Office: Era Building, Cleeve Road, Leatherhead, Surrey, KT22 7SA
Activities: Activities of head offices
Parent: Edif Group Limited
Officers: Roberto Cavanna [1961] Director [Italian]; Annelie Du Plessis [1972] Director/Financial Controller

Edif Group Limited
Incorporated: 19 January 2011
Net Worth: £74,147,000 *Total Assets:* £74,147,000
Registered Office: Era Building, Cleeve Road, Leatherhead, Surrey, KT22 7SA
Activities: Engineering related scientific and technical consulting activities
Officers: Roberto Cavanna [1961] Director [Italian]; Annelie Du Plessis [1972] Director/Financial Controller

Edif Group Management Limited
Incorporated: 19 January 2011 *Employees:* 2
Net Worth Deficit: £51,472,000 *Total Assets:* £22,334,000
Registered Office: Era Building, Cleeve Road, Leatherhead, Surrey, KT22 7SA
Activities: Activities of head offices
Parent: Edif Group Finance Limited
Officers: Roberto Cavanna [1961] Director [Italian]; Annelie Du Plessis [1972] Director/Financial Controller

EDL (UK) LFG Generation Limited
Incorporated: 25 August 2006
Net Worth: £15,578,526 *Total Assets:* £48,837,960
Registered Office: Chancery House, 199 Silbury Boulevard, Milton Keynes, Bucks, MK9 1JL
Activities: Production of electricity
Parent: Bio Energy (UK) Limited
Officers: James Christopher Harman [1968] Director [Australian]; David Truelove [1975] Director

EDL Holdings (UK) Limited
Incorporated: 25 March 1997
Net Worth: £7,500,373 *Total Assets:* £20,424,804
Registered Office: Chancery House, 199 Silbury Boulevard, Milton Keynes, Bucks, MK9 1JL
Activities: Activities of other holding companies n.e.c.
Parent: CK William UK Holdings Limited
Officers: James Christopher Harman [1968] Director [Australian]; David Truelove [1975] Director

EDU UK Intermediate Limited
Incorporated: 15 June 2010 *Employees:* 3,245
Net Worth: £34,800,000 *Total Assets:* £559,800,000
Registered Office: Brighton Study Centre, 1 Billinton Way, Brighton, BN1 4LF
Activities: Activities of head offices
Parent: EDU UK Topco Limited
Officers: Emma Voirrey Lancaster [1969] Director/Chief Executive Officer; David Bernard Leigh [1971] Director/Chairman; Arvid Charles Petersen [1951] Director [Australian]; Dany Rammal [1974] Managing Director [French]; Peter Osgood Wilde Jr [1968] Director [American]

EDU UK Management Services Limited
Incorporated: 15 June 2010 *Employees:* 3
Previous: EDU UK Bidco Limited
Net Worth: £175,348,006,912 *Total Assets:* £435,426,000,896
Registered Office: Brighton Study Centre, 1 Billinton Way, Brighton, BN1 4LF
Activities: Activities of head offices
Parent: EDU UK Intermediate Limited
Officers: Emma Voirrey Lancaster [1969] Director/Chief Executive Officer; David Bernard Leigh [1971] Director/Chairman; Arvid Charles Petersen [1951] Director [Australian]; Dany Rammal [1974] Managing Director [French]; Peter Osgood Wilde Jr [1968] Managing Director [American]

EDU UK Topco Limited
Incorporated: 15 June 2010 *Employees:* 3,245
Net Worth Deficit: £158,600,000 *Total Assets:* £560,800,000
Registered Office: Brighton Study Centre, 1 Billinton Way, Brighton, BN1 4LF
Activities: Activities of head offices
Officers: Sir Keith Burnett [1953] Director/University Teacher and Administrator; Sir John Anthony Hood [1952] Director/Chairman [New Zealander]; Emma Voirrey Lancaster [1969] Director/Chief Executive Officer; David Bernard Leigh [1971] Director/Chairman; Arvid Charles Petersen [1951] Director [Australian]; Dany Rammal [1974] Managing Director [French]; Peter Osgood Wilde Jr [1968] Director [American]; Nicholas Williams [1970] Director/Chief Financial Officer

Education Development Trust
Incorporated: 31 December 1965 *Employees:* 1,039
Previous: CFBT Education Trust
Net Worth: £28,553,000 *Total Assets:* £52,733,000
Registered Office: Highbridge House, 16-18 Duke Street, Reading, Berks, RG1 4RU
Activities: General secondary education
Officers: Robert Gerard Miles, Secretary; Christine Bridget Gilbert [1949] Director; Julia Catherine Grant [1960] Director; Yetunde Yewande Hofmann [1963] Director; Ilse Robin Charis Howling [1965] Director/Chairman; Robert Griffith Humphreys [1957] Director; Dr Angela Elizabeth McFarlane [1957] Director; Dr Peter Rawlinson [1954] Director

Education for The 21st Century
Incorporated: 10 March 2011 *Employees:* 349
Net Worth: £33,393,884 *Total Assets:* £36,751,264
Registered Office: The Ravensbourne School, Hayes Lane, Bromley, Kent, BR2 9EH
Activities: General secondary education
Officers: Mark Benjamin Anderson [1960] Director/Retired Solicitor; Michael Atkinson [1972] Director/Accountant; Richard Defriend [1949] Director/Retired; Ann Patricia Dempsey [1955] Director/Retired; Paul Featherstone [1967] Director of IT and Digital Transformation; David John McKivett [1957] Director/Consultant; Mark Whitby [1964] Director/Education Consultant

Education Support (Enfield 2) Holdings Limited
Incorporated: 22 March 2002
Net Worth Deficit: £2,086,000 *Total Assets:* £24,059,000
Registered Office: 8 White Oak Square, London Road, Swanley, Kent, BR8 7AG
Activities: Construction of commercial buildings
Parent: Palio (No 17) Limited
Officers: Gresa Daullxhi [1986] Director/Chartered Accountant (ACA); Neil Woodburn [1979] Director/Chartered Building Surveyor

Education Support (Enfield 2) Limited
Incorporated: 19 April 2002
Net Worth Deficit: £2,086,000 *Total Assets:* £24,059,000
Registered Office: 8 White Oak Square, London Road, Swanley, Kent, BR8 7AG
Activities: Construction of commercial buildings
Parent: Education Support (Enfield 2) Holdings Limited
Officers: Gresa Daullxhi [1986] Director/Chartered Accountant (ACA); Neil Woodburn [1979] Director/Chartered Building Surveyor

Education Support (Newham) Holdings Limited
Incorporated: 19 April 2002
Net Worth Deficit: £2,001,000 *Total Assets:* £20,119,000
Registered Office: 8 White Oak Square, London Road, Swanley, Kent, BR8 7AG
Activities: Construction of commercial buildings
Parent: Palio (No 18) Limited
Officers: Gresa Daullxhi [1986] Director/Chartered Accountant; Neil Woodburn [1979] Director/Chartered Building Surveyor

Education Support (Newham) Limited
Incorporated: 19 April 2002
Net Worth Deficit: £2,001,000 *Total Assets:* £20,119,000
Registered Office: 8 White Oak Square, London Road, Swanley, Kent, BR8 7AG
Activities: Construction of commercial buildings
Parent: Education Support (Newham) Holdings Limited
Officers: Gresa Daullxhi [1986] Director/Chartered Accountant (ACA); Neil Woodburn [1979] Director/Chartered Building Surveyor

Education Support (Swindon) Holdings Limited
Incorporated: 6 July 2004
Net Worth Deficit: £8,330,000 *Total Assets:* £63,428,000
Registered Office: 8 White Oak Square, London Road, Swanley, Kent, BR8 7AG
Activities: Activities of head offices
Parent: Palio (No 16) Limited
Officers: Carl Harvey Dix [1966] Operations Director; Vikki Louise Everett [1971] Director/Project Manager

Education Support (Swindon) Limited
Incorporated: 6 July 2004
Net Worth Deficit: £8,330,000 *Total Assets:* £63,428,000
Registered Office: 8 White Oak Square, London Road, Swanley, Kent, BR8 7AG
Activities: Construction of commercial buildings
Parent: Education Support (Swindon) Holdings Limited
Officers: Carl Harvey Dix [1966] Operations Director; Vikki Louise Everett [1971] Director/Project Manager

Edwardian Bloomsbury Street Limited
Incorporated: 18 February 2008 *Employees:* 129
Net Worth: £52,511,000 *Total Assets:* £94,130,000
Registered Office: 140 Bath Road, Hayes, Middlesex, UB3 5AW
Activities: Hotels and similar accommodation
Parent: Edwardian Hotel Investments Ltd
Officers: Vijay Wason, Secretary; John Robert Morley [1945] Director/Financial Consultant; Jasminder Singh [1951] Director/Hotelier

Edwardian Canary Wharf Hotel Limited
Incorporated: 28 September 2011 *Employees:* 132
Net Worth: £27,377,000 *Total Assets:* £43,167,000
Registered Office: Radisson Edwardian Heathrow, 140 Bath Road, Hayes, Middlesex, UB3 5AW
Activities: Hotels and similar accommodation
Parent: Edwardian Hotel Investments Ltd
Officers: Vijay Wason, Secretary; John Robert Morley [1945] Director/Financial Consultant; Jasminder Singh [1951] Director/Hotelier

Edwardian Exclusive Hotels Ltd
Incorporated: 8 April 1993 *Employees:* 91
Net Worth: £65,220,000 *Total Assets:* £107,778,000
Registered Office: 140 Bath Road, Hayes, Middlesex, UB3 5AW
Activities: Hotels and similar accommodation
Parent: Edwardian Exclusive Ltd
Officers: Vijay Wason, Secretary; John Robert Morley [1945] Director/Financial Consultant; Shashi Merag Shah [1945] Director; Jasminder Singh [1951] Director/Hotelier; Vijay Wason [1948] Director/Company Secretary

Edwardian Exclusive Ltd
Incorporated: 16 October 2013
Net Worth: £28,123,000 *Total Assets:* £65,669,000
Registered Office: 140 Bath Road, Hayes, Middlesex, UB3 5AW
Activities: Activities of other holding companies n.e.c.
Parent: Edwardian Group Limited
Officers: Vijay Wason, Secretary; John Robert Morley [1945] Director/Financial Consultant; Jasminder Singh [1951] Director/Hotelier

Edwardian Finance Ltd
Incorporated: 16 October 2013
Net Worth: £262,532,992 *Total Assets:* £411,384,992
Registered Office: 140 Bath Road, Hayes, Middlesex, UB3 5AW
Activities: Activities of other holding companies n.e.c.
Parent: Edwardian Group Limited
Officers: Vijay Wason, Secretary; John Robert Morley [1945] Director/Financial Consultant; Jasminder Singh [1951] Director/Hotelier

Edwardian Free Trade Hall Ltd
Incorporated: 27 September 2011 *Employees:* 229
Net Worth: £51,466,000 *Total Assets:* £68,085,000
Registered Office: Radisson Edwardian Heathrow, 140 Bath Road, Hayes, Middlesex, UB3 5AW
Activities: Hotels and similar accommodation
Parent: Edwardian Hotel Finance Ltd
Officers: Vijay Wason, Secretary; John Robert Morley [1945] Director/Financial Consultant; Jasminder Singh [1951] Director/Hotelier

Edwardian Grafton Hotel Ltd
Incorporated: 27 August 2013 *Employees:* 174
Net Worth: £46,032,000 *Total Assets:* £98,025,000
Registered Office: 140 Bath Road, Hayes, Middlesex, UB3 5AW
Activities: Hotels and similar accommodation
Parent: Edwardian Hotel Investments Ltd
Officers: Vijay Wason, Secretary; John Robert Morley [1945] Director/Financial Consultant; Jasminder Singh [1951] Director/Hotelier

Edwardian Group Limited
Incorporated: 2 June 1977 *Employees:* 2,349
Net Worth: £945,161,984 *Total Assets:* £1,551,187,968
Registered Office: 140 Bath Road, Hayes, Middlesex, UB3 5AW
Activities: Activities of other holding companies n.e.c.
Major Shareholder: George Robinson Machan
Officers: Vijay Wason, Secretary; Andrew Hart [1947] Director/Solicitor Consultant; John Robert Morley [1945] Director/Financial Consultant; Shashi Merag Shah [1945] Director; Amrit Singh [1959] Director; Inderneel Singh [1984] Managing Director; Jasminder Singh [1951] Director/Hotelier

Edwardian Hampshire Hotels Ltd
Incorporated: 2 November 2006 *Employees:* 156
Net Worth: £52,712,000 *Total Assets:* £104,171,000
Registered Office: 140 Bath Road, Hayes, Middlesex, UB3 5AW
Activities: Hotels and similar accommodation
Parent: Edwardian New Finance Limited
Officers: Vijay Wason, Secretary; John Robert Morley [1945] Director/Financial Consultant; Jasminder Singh [1951] Director/Hotelier

Edwardian Hotel Finance Ltd
Incorporated: 27 August 2013
Net Worth: £262,551,008 *Total Assets:* £610,369,024
Registered Office: 140 Bath Road, Hayes, Middlesex, UB3 5AW
Activities: Activities of other holding companies n.e.c.
Parent: Edwardian Finance Ltd
Officers: Vijay Wason, Secretary; John Robert Morley [1945] Director/Financial Consultant; Shashi Merag Shah [1945] Director; Jasminder Singh [1951] Director/Hotelier; Vijay Wason [1948] Director/Company Secretary

Edwardian Hotel Investments Ltd
Incorporated: 27 August 2013
Net Worth: £126,940,000 *Total Assets:* £361,648,000
Registered Office: 140 Bath Road, Hayes, Middlesex, UB3 5AW
Activities: Activities of other holding companies n.e.c.
Parent: Edwardian Investments Ltd
Officers: Vijay Wason, Secretary; John Robert Morley [1945] Director/Financial Consultant; Shashi Merag Shah [1945] Director; Jasminder Singh [1951] Director/Hotelier; Vijay Wason [1948] Director/Company Secretary

Edwardian International Hotels Ltd
Incorporated: 8 April 1993 *Employees:* 73
Net Worth: £152,712,992 *Total Assets:* £154,612,000
Registered Office: 140 Bath Road, Hayes, Middlesex, UB3 5AW
Activities: Hotels and similar accommodation
Parent: Edwardian Group Limited
Officers: Vijay Wason, Secretary; John Robert Morley [1945] Director/Financial Consultant; Jasminder Singh [1951] Director/Hotelier

Edwardian Investments Ltd
Incorporated: 16 October 2013
Net Worth: £126,919,000 *Total Assets:* £182,242,000
Registered Office: 140 Bath Road, Hayes, Middlesex, UB3 5AW
Activities: Activities of other holding companies n.e.c.
Parent: Edwardian Group Limited
Officers: Vijay Wason, Secretary; John Robert Morley [1945] Director/Financial Consultant; Jasminder Singh [1951] Director/Hotelier

Edwardian Ltd
Incorporated: 8 April 1993 *Employees:* 111
Net Worth: £40,780,000 *Total Assets:* £67,572,000
Registered Office: 140 Bath Road, Hayes, Middlesex, UB3 5AW
Activities: Hotels and similar accommodation
Parent: Edwardian Hotel Investments Ltd
Officers: Vijay Wason, Secretary; John Robert Morley [1945] Director/Financial Consultant; Jasminder Singh [1951] Director/Hotelier

Edwardian Mercer Street Ltd
Incorporated: 27 September 2011 *Employees:* 128
Net Worth: £45,835,000 *Total Assets:* £94,290,000
Registered Office: Radisson Edwardian Heathrow, 140 Bath Road, Hayes, Middlesex, UB3 5AW
Activities: Hotels and similar accommodation
Parent: Edwardian Hotel Investments Ltd
Officers: Vijay Wason, Secretary; John Robert Morley [1945] Director/Financial Consultant; Jasminder Singh [1951] Director/Hotelier

Edwardian New Finance Limited
Incorporated: 26 March 2008
Net Worth: £87,109,000 *Total Assets:* £238,123,008
Registered Office: 140 Bath Road, Hayes, Middlesex, UB3 5AW
Activities: Activities of other holding companies n.e.c.
Parent: Edwardian Group Limited
Officers: Vijay Wason, Secretary; John Robert Morley [1945] Director/Financial Consultant; Shashi Merag Shah [1945] Director; Jasminder Singh [1951] Director/Hotelier; Vijay Wason [1948] Director/Company Secretary

Edwardian Pastoria Hotels Ltd
Incorporated: 2 November 2006
Net Worth: £3,384,000 *Total Assets:* £204,695,008
Registered Office: 140 Bath Road, Hayes, Middlesex, UB3 5AW
Activities: Hotels and similar accommodation
Parent: Edwardian New Finance Limited
Officers: Vijay Wason, Secretary; John Robert Morley [1945] Director/Financial Consultant; Jasminder Singh [1951] Director/Hotelier

Edwards High Vacuum International Limited
Incorporated: 30 November 1973 *Employees:* 270
Net Worth: £73,579,000 *Total Assets:* £96,081,000
Registered Office: Innovation Drive, Burgess Hill, W Sussex, RH15 9TW
Activities: Manufacture of pumps
Parent: Edwards Limited
Officers: Caroline Amanda Peace, Secretary; Alex Christiaan Jan Bongaerts [1960] Director [Belgian]; Gareth Valentine Harte [1966] Director/Chartered Accountant [Irish]; Martin Ernst Tollner [1973] Director/President, High Vacuum Division, Atlas Copco Group [British/South African]

Edwards Limited
Incorporated: 22 February 2007 *Employees:* 434
Net Worth: £459,615,008 *Total Assets:* £549,156,992
Registered Office: Innovation Drive, Burgess Hill, W Sussex, RH15 9TW
Activities: Manufacture of pumps
Parent: Atlas Copco UK Holdings Limited
Officers: Caroline Amanda Peace, Secretary; Alex Jan Christiaan Bongaerts [1960] Director [Belgian]; Geert Henri Follens [1959] Director/President Vacuum Solutions Division [Belgian]; Gareth Valentine Harte [1966] Director/Chartered Accountant [Irish]

Effem Holdings Limited
Incorporated: 24 December 1998
Net Worth: £24,389,394,432 *Total Assets:* £24,567,478,272
Registered Office: 3D Dundee Road, Slough, Berks, SL1 4LG
Activities: Activities of head offices
Officers: Gillian Mary Enevoldsen [1962] Director; David James Haines [1969] Director; Ian James Langer [1965] Director; Andrew Richard Parton [1968] Director

Egdon Resources PLC
Incorporated: 25 October 2007 *Employees:* 12
Net Worth: £30,726,696 *Total Assets:* £34,125,396
Registered Office: The Wheat House, 98 High Street, Odiham, Hook, Hants, RG29 1LP
Activities: Extraction of crude petroleum
Shareholder: Petrichor Holdings Cooperatief, U.A.
Officers: Walter Rookehurst Roberts, Secretary; Mark Anthony William Abbott [1961] Director/Chief Executive Officer; Martin John Durham [1957] Director/Geologist; Andrew Geoffrey Lodge [1956] Director/Principal Oil Industry Advisor; Kenneth Maurice Ratcliff [1950] Director/Accountant; Walter Rookehurst Roberts [1951] Director/Lawyer; Philip Henry Peter Stephens [1942] Director

Egdon Resources U.K. Limited
Incorporated: 26 August 1997 *Employees:* 6
Net Worth: £2,932,667 *Total Assets:* £31,255,816
Registered Office: The Wheat House, 98 High Street, Odiham, Hook, Hants, RG29 1LP
Activities: Extraction of crude petroleum
Parent: Egdon Resources PLC
Officers: Walter Rookehurst Roberts, Secretary; Mark Anthony William Abbott [1961] Director/Chief Executive Officer; Martin John Durham [1957] Director/Geologist; James Paul Starr Elston [1968] Commercial Director; Walter Rookehurst Roberts [1951] Director/Lawyer; Philip Henry Peter Stephens [1942] Director

Egger (UK) Holdings Limited
Incorporated: 23 April 1981
Net Worth Deficit: £872,000 *Total Assets:* £21,704,000
Registered Office: 21-25 Church Street West, Woking, Surrey, GU21 6DJ
Activities: Other business support service activities n.e.c.
Officers: Bernd Steinlechner, Secretary; Michael Robert Livesey [1959] Managing Director; Bernd Steinlechner [1971] Finance Director [Austrian]

Egger (UK) Limited
Incorporated: 22 April 1993 *Employees:* 716
Net Worth: £85,413,000 *Total Assets:* £191,336,000
Registered Office: 21-25 Church Street West, Woking, Surrey, GU21 6DJ
Activities: Manufacture of veneer sheets and wood-based panels
Officers: Bernd Steinlechner, Secretary; Heiko Lichtblau [1979] Production & Technical Director (Barony Plant) [German]; Michael Robert Livesey [1959] Director; Bernd Steinlechner [1971] Finance Director [Austrian]; Tobias Zimmermann [1971] Production & Technical Director [German]

EHGT Limited
Incorporated: 10 November 1997
Net Worth: £25,813,604 *Total Assets:* £25,817,214
Registered Office: Wyevale Garden Centres, Syon Park, London Road, Brentford, Middlesex, TW8 8JF
Activities: Activities of head offices
Parent: Wyevale Garden Centres Limited
Officers: Laura Harradine-Greene, Secretary; Anthony Generald Jones [1973] Director; Richard MacLachlan [1976] Director

Elbrook (Cash & Carry) Limited
Incorporated: 9 August 1984 *Employees:* 63
Net Worth: £22,717,016 *Total Assets:* £38,748,460
Registered Office: 105 Bond Road, Mitcham, Surrey, CR4 3HG
Activities: Retail sale in non-specialised stores with food, beverages or tobacco predominating
Shareholder: Fukhera Khalid
Officers: Amjad Khalid [1983] Director; Fukhera Khalid [1968] Managing Director

Electrical Contractors Association Limited (The)
Incorporated: 19 April 1916 *Employees:* 7
Net Worth: £53,958,332 *Total Assets:* £62,661,440
Registered Office: Eca Court, 24-26 South Park, Sevenoaks, Kent, TN13 1DU
Activities: Activities of business and employers membership organisations
Officers: Terence David Foreman, Secretary; Martin Richard Bailey [1959] Director; Stephen John Bratt [1964] Director; Martyn James Burnley [1953] Director; Jonathan Stuart Dunwell [1974] Director; David John Kieft [1963] Director; Paul Campbell McNaughton [1958] Director; David Salter [1956] Director; Sean Tracy Smyth [1955] Director

Electrium Sales Limited
Incorporated: 2 March 1988 *Employees:* 368
Net Worth: £42,998,000 *Total Assets:* £76,279,000
Registered Office: Faraday House, Sir William Siemens Square, Frimley, Camberley, Surrey, GU16 8QD
Activities: Manufacture of electricity distribution and control apparatus
Parent: Siemens Holdings PLC
Officers: Simone Eufemia Agatha Davina, Secretary; Paul Henry Fisher [1955] Director/Country Division Lead; Robert James Peters [1966] Director/Accountant

Electronic Arts Limited
Incorporated: 23 September 1986 *Employees:* 287
Net Worth: £29,412,000 *Total Assets:* £47,419,000
Registered Office: Onslow House, Onslow Street, Guildford, Surrey, GU1 4TN
Activities: Other software publishing
Parent: Electronic Arts, Inc.
Officers: Shaun David Campbell [1963] Director/General Manager [Australian]; Derek Wai Seng Chan [1979] Financial Director [Canadian]; Keith Alan Kallweit [1962] Director [American]; Jacob Joseph Schatz [1968] Director/General Counsel [American]; Matthew Wisbey [1966] Director/Solicitor

Elekta Holdings Limited
Incorporated: 20 March 1992
Net Worth: £27,856,000 *Total Assets:* £28,552,000
Registered Office: Linac House, Fleming Way, Crawley, W Sussex, RH10 9RR
Activities: Activities of head offices
Parent: Elekta AB
Officers: Samantha Cookman, Secretary; Andrew Stuart Ainsworth [1975] Director/Finance Manager; Steven Mark Wort [1963] Director/Senior VP Operations

Elekta Limited
Incorporated: 2 September 1996 *Employees:* 660
Net Worth: £129,945,000 *Total Assets:* £514,169,984
Registered Office: Linac House, Fleming Way, Crawley, W Sussex, RH10 9RR
Activities: Manufacture of medical and dental instruments and supplies
Parent: Elekta Holdings Limited
Officers: Samantha Cookman, Secretary; Andrew Stuart Ainsworth [1975] Director/Finance Manager; Thomas Tetley Beazley [1961] Director/VP Strategy Development; Richard Hausmann [1960] Director/Physicist [German]; John Lapre [1964] Director/Chief Technology Officer [Dutch]; Ioannis Panagiotelis [1972] Director [Greek]; Maurits Wolleswinkel [1971] Director/Chief Strategy Officer [Dutch]; Steven Mark Wort [1963] Director/Senior VP Operations

Elite Homes (North West) Limited
Incorporated: 20 September 1988
Net Worth: £19,720,000 *Total Assets:* £47,590,000
Registered Office: 11 Tower View, Kings Hill, West Malling, Kent, ME19 4UY
Activities: Buying and selling of own real estate
Parent: Elite Homes Group Limited
Officers: Martin Trevor Digby Palmer, Chartered Secretary; Keith Bryan Carnegie [1969] Director/Solicitor; Earl Sibley [1972] Director/Chartered Accountant

Elite Hotels (Rotherwick) Limited
Incorporated: 26 March 1985 *Employees:* 1,055
Net Worth Deficit: £5,729,535 *Total Assets:* £98,636,800
Registered Office: Ashdown Park, Wych Cross, Forest Row, E Sussex, RH18 5JR
Activities: Hotels and similar accommodation
Officers: Ronan Sean Callaghan, Secretary; Graeme Carl Bateman [1961] Managing Director; Ronan Sean Callaghan [1983] Finance Director; Andrew Henry Warde Dixon [1947] Director; Stephen Lightfoot [1961] Director; Simon Jeremy Willis [1968] Director of Operations

Ella's Kitchen (Brands) Limited
Incorporated: 19 July 2004 *Employees:* 68
Net Worth: £26,065,994 *Total Assets:* £48,126,140
Registered Office: Ella's Barn, 22 Greys Green Farm, Rotherfield Greys, Henley on Thames, Oxon, RG9 4QG
Activities: Manufacture of other food products n.e.c.
Parent: Ella's Kitchen Group Limited
Officers: Nicholas Keen, Secretary; Mark Nicholas John Cuddigan [1973] Managing Director; Denise Menikheim Faltischek [1973] Director/Attorney [American]; James Michael Langrock [1965] Director [American]; Mark Lawrence Schiller [1961] Director [American]

Ellenbrook Developments PLC
Incorporated: 7 November 2001
Net Worth: £1,918,000 *Total Assets:* £62,760,000
Registered Office: 8 White Oak Square, Swanley, Kent, BR8 7AG
Activities: Other business support service activities n.e.c.
Parent: Ellenbrook Holdings Limited
Officers: Neeti Mukundrai Anand [1984] Director; Angela Louise Roshier [1975] Director/Finance

Ellenbrook Holdings Limited
Incorporated: 7 November 2001
Net Worth: £1,918,000 *Total Assets:* £62,760,000
Registered Office: 8 White Oak Square, Swanley, Kent, BR8 7AG
Activities: Activities of other holding companies n.e.c.
Parent: DIF Infra Yield 1 UK Limited
Officers: Neeti Mukundrai Anand [1984] Director; Angela Louise Roshier [1975] Director/Finance

Elliott Baxter & Company Limited
Incorporated: 4 January 1949 *Employees:* 291
Net Worth: £51,917,000 *Total Assets:* £66,061,000
Registered Office: Nexus Park, Lysons Avenue, Ash Vale, Farnborough, Hants, GU12 5QE
Activities: Wholesale of other intermediate products
Shareholders: Timothy Elliott; Jeremy Elliott
Officers: Andrew David Edwards, Secretary; Rodney Victor Benwell [1966] Commercial Director; Andrew David Edwards [1968] Finance Director; Matthew James Elliott [1982] Managing Director; Timothy Elliott [1953] Director/Chairman; Christopher James Sandwell [1968] Sales Director; David MacDonald Tennent [1965] Director

Elliott Brothers (Builders Merchants) Limited
Incorporated: 25 June 1901 *Employees:* 300
Net Worth: £21,494,000 *Total Assets:* £44,719,000
Registered Office: Millbank Wharf, Northam, Southampton, SO14 5AG
Activities: Agents involved in the sale of timber and building materials
Officers: Paul Chadwick, Secretary; Nicholas John Chase [1949] Director/Chartered Accountant; Stuart Graham Mason-Elliott [1951] Director; Thomas Edward Mason-Elliott [1984] Finance Director; David John Platt [1940] Director/Accountant; Dr Caroline Ann Williams [1954] Director/Solicitor

Elliott Brothers Limited
Incorporated: 12 June 1990 *Employees:* 269
Net Worth: £16,056,506 *Total Assets:* £33,038,584
Registered Office: Millbank Wharf, Northam, Southampton, SO14 5AG
Activities: Agents involved in the sale of timber and building materials
Parent: Elliott Brothers (Builders Merchants) Ltd
Officers: Paul William Chadwick [1979] Director/Accountant; Paul Cleary [1959] Sales Director; Lauren Haines [1954] Director Builders Merchants; Stuart Graham Mason-Elliott [1951] Director; Thomas Edward Mason-Elliott [1984] Managing Director

Elliott TurboMachinery Limited
Incorporated: 18 May 1987 *Employees:* 125
Net Worth: £17,452,000 *Total Assets:* £29,906,000
Registered Office: Unit 11 Easter Park, Benyon Road, Silchester, Berks, RG7 2PQ
Activities: Repair of other equipment
Parent: Elliott Company Co Inc
Officers: Ronald Frye [1956] Director/Vice President Global Service [American]; Shugo Hosoda [1966] Director/Vice President, Engineered Products [Japanese]; Peter Norman Laud [1967] Director/Service Centre Manager; Matthew Rhodes [1971] Repair Operations Director

Ellis & Sons Amalgamated Properties Limited
Incorporated: 19 June 1939 *Employees:* 4
Net Worth: £43,119,648 *Total Assets:* £48,258,832
Registered Office: Shalden Park, Steading, Shalden, Alton, Hants, GU34 4DS
Activities: Buying and selling of own real estate
Shareholders: Ellis & Sons Amalgamated Investments Ltd; Ellis & Sons (Southern) Property Investments Ltd
Officers: Linda Frances Campbell, Secretary; Jamie Loudoun Craven Campbell [1970] Director; Linda Frances Campbell [1941] Director; Michael David Colin Craven Campbell [1942] Director; Laura Grace Montgomery [1977] Director

Ellucian Global Limited
Incorporated: 18 November 2011 *Employees:* 37
Net Worth: £18,402,772 *Total Assets:* £30,010,564
Registered Office: Floors 2 & 3, Baird House, Seebeck Place, Knowlhill, Milton Keynes, Bucks, MK5 8FR
Activities: Information technology consultancy activities
Parent: Ellucian UK Limited
Officers: James Dever Bennett [1960] Director/Business Executive [American]; Harshan Bhangdia [1965] Director/Chief Financial Officer [Indian]; Richard James Forrest [1974] Director/VP Global Product Strategy; John Tom Georges [1971] Director/VP Tax and Treasury [American]

Elmwey Learning Trust
Incorporated: 5 June 2015 *Employees:* 132
Net Worth: £23,871,000 *Total Assets:* £26,149,000
Registered Office: Heathside School, Brooklands Lane, Weybridge, Surrey, KT13 8UZ
Activities: General secondary education
Officers: Rebecca Harris, Secretary; Maria Cicero-Scott [1963] Director/Head of HR & Recruitment; Helen France Cooper [1983] Director/Actuary; Anne Louise Cullum [1962] Director/Principal; Francis Michael Nicholas [1972] Commercial Director; Nathan George Roberts [1972] Director/IT Consultant [American]; Guy Jonathan Solway [1964] Director/Chartered Quantity Surveyor; Dr Robert Alan Wright [1949] Director

Elster Metering Holdings Limited
Incorporated: 24 December 1907
Net Worth: £10,280,000 *Total Assets:* £62,041,000
Registered Office: Honeywell House, Skimped Hill Lane, Bracknell, Berks, RG12 1EB
Activities: Activities of head offices
Parent: Honeywell International Inc.
Officers: Gary Mark Vincent [1971] Director

Elster Metering Limited
Incorporated: 14 March 1966 *Employees:* 128
Net Worth: £28,386,000 *Total Assets:* £55,227,000
Registered Office: Honeywell House, Skimped Hill Lane, Bracknell, Berks, RG12 1EB
Activities: Manufacture of non-electronic measuring, testing etc. equipment, not for industrial process control
Parent: Elster Metering Holdings Limited
Officers: Paul Melville [1966] Director/Site Lead; Gary Mark Vincent [1971] Director

Elster Solutions Limited
Incorporated: 13 June 2013
Net Worth: £367,825,984 *Total Assets:* £415,911,008
Registered Office: Honeywell House, Skimped Hill Lane, Bracknell, Berks, RG12 1EB
Activities: Activities of head offices
Parent: Honeywell International Inc.
Officers: Mark Barrow [1960] Director; Paschal Christopher Morris [1966] Director

Elster Water Metering Holdings Limited
Incorporated: 22 July 2005
Net Worth: £62,940,000 *Total Assets:* £77,008,000
Registered Office: Honeywell House, Skimped Hill Lane, Bracknell, Berks, RG12 1EB
Activities: Activities of head offices
Parent: Honeywell International Inc.
Officers: Gary Mark Vincent [1971] Director

Elster Water Metering Limited
Incorporated: 25 July 2013 *Employees:* 202
Net Worth Deficit: £7,616,000 *Total Assets:* £40,624,000
Registered Office: Honeywell House, Skimped Hill Lane, Bracknell, Berks, RG12 1EB
Activities: Manufacture of non-electronic measuring, testing etc. equipment, not for industrial process control
Parent: Elster Water Metering Holdings Limited
Officers: Mark Barrow [1960] Director; Gary Mark Vincent [1971] Managing Director

Elu Power Tools Ltd
Incorporated: 15 July 1983
Net Worth: £125,080,000 *Total Assets:* £125,080,000
Registered Office: 210 Bath Road, Slough, Berks, SL1 3YD
Activities: Manufacture of electric motors, generators and transformers
Parent: Stanley Black & Decker Inc.
Officers: Steven John Costello [1980] Director/Chartered Accountant; Mark Richard Smiley [1977] Director/General Manager UK & ROI; Amit Kumar Sood [1978] Director/Accountant

Simon Elvin Holdings Limited
Incorporated: 1 June 2016 *Employees:* 172
Net Worth: £24,467,816 *Total Assets:* £27,777,356
Registered Office: c/o Simon Elvin Limited, Thomas Road, Wooburn Industrial Park, Wooburn Green, High Wycombe, Bucks, HP10 0PE
Activities: Activities of head offices
Shareholder: Simon Peel Elvin
Officers: Janet Elizabeth Elvin [1940] Director; Jonathan Charles Elvin [1971] Director/Property Developer; Julian Peel Elvin [1968] Director/Advertising Manager; Simon Peel Elvin [1941] Director

S Elvin Limited
Incorporated: 13 June 2012 *Employees:* 5
Previous: Simon Elvin Holdings Limited
Net Worth: £21,728,240 *Total Assets:* £30,662,140
Registered Office: c/o Simon Elvin Ltd, Thomas Road, Woodburn Industrial Park, Woodburn Green, Bucks, HP10 0PE
Activities: Activities of head offices
Officers: Mark Stuart Blundell, Secretary; Janet Elizabeth Elvin [1940] Director; Jonathan Charles Elvin [1971] Director; Julian Peel Elvin [1968] Director; Simon Peel Elvin [1941] Director; Stuart McKay [1946] Director

Simon Elvin Limited
Incorporated: 16 August 1977 *Employees:* 69
Net Worth: £23,718,536 *Total Assets:* £24,422,124
Registered Office: Wooburn Industrial Park, Wooburn Green, Bucks, HP10 0PE
Activities: Other publishing activities
Officers: Mark Stuart Blundell, Secretary; Janet Elizabeth Elvin [1940] Director; Jonathan Charles Elvin [1971] Director/Property Developer; Julian Peel Elvin [1968] Director/Advertising Manager; Simon Peel Elvin [1941] Director; Ian Kenneth Alexander Jackson [1959] Director; Stuart McKay [1946] Director; David Malcolm Orr [1950] Operations Director

ELWA Holdings Limited
Incorporated: 28 September 2010
Net Worth: £15,159,000 *Total Assets:* £111,730,000
Registered Office: Dunedin House, Auckland Park, Mount Farm, Milton Keynes, Bucks, MK1 1BU
Activities: Non-trading company
Parent: John Laing Environmental Assets Group (UK) Limited
Officers: Philip Bernard Griffin-Smith, Secretary; Alistair Daniel Brookes [1976] Director; Johannes Petrus Heemelaar [1956] Director [Dutch]; Joseph Mark Linney [1958] Director; Adam Nathaniel Richford [1976] Director

ELWA Limited
Incorporated: 25 March 1992
Net Worth: £15,159,000 *Total Assets:* £111,730,000
Registered Office: Dunedin House, Auckland Park, Mount Farm, Milton Keynes, Bucks, MK1 1BU
Activities: Other service activities n.e.c.
Parent: ELWA Holdings Limited
Officers: Philip Bernard Griffin-Smith, Secretary; Dorothy Abena Akwaboah [1963] Director; Alistair Daniel Brookes [1976] Director; Johannes Petrus Heemelaar [1956] Asset Director [Dutch]; Joseph Mark Linney [1958] Director; Adam Nathaniel Richford [1976] Director

Elwy 2 Limited
Incorporated: 7 December 2015 *Employees:* 2,626
Net Worth Deficit: £181,108,992 *Total Assets:* £1,370,514,944
Registered Office: Queens Road, Teddington, Middlesex, TW11 0LY
Activities: Other business support service activities n.e.c.
Parent: Elwy 1 Limited
Officers: Navneet Kaur Ogle, Secretary; Mark Simon Danzey [1979] Director, KKR Capital Markets; Edouard Jean Charles Pillot [1977] Director [French]

Elwy 3 Limited
Incorporated: 7 December 2015 *Employees:* 2,626
Net Worth: £494,812,992 *Total Assets:* £1,370,514,944
Registered Office: LGC, Queens Road, Teddington, Middlesex, TW11 0LY
Activities: Other business support service activities n.e.c.
Parent: Elwy 2 Limited
Officers: Navneet Kaur Ogle, Secretary; Edouard Jean Charles Pillot [1977] Director [French]

Elysium Healthcare (Lighthouse) Limited
Incorporated: 18 May 2006 *Employees:* 15
Previous: Lighthouse Healthcare Limited
Net Worth: £48,078,000 *Total Assets:* £51,317,000
Registered Office: 2 Imperial Place, Maxwell Road, Borehamwood, Herts, WD6 1JN
Activities: Activities of head offices
Parent: Lighthouse Healthcare Group Limited
Officers: Sarah Juliette Livingston, Secretary; Lesley Joy Chamberlain [1963] Director/Group Chief Executive; Dr Quazi Shams Mahfooz Haque [1968] Executive Medical Director; Steven John Woolgar [1955] Director of Policy and Regulation

Elysium Healthcare (Ultimate Care) Limited
Incorporated: 20 February 2006 *Employees:* 654
Previous: St George Ultimate Care Limited
Net Worth: £4,425,032 *Total Assets:* £43,884,684
Registered Office: c/o Elysium Healthcare, 2 Imperial Place, Maxwell Road, Borehamwood, Herts, WD6 1JN
Activities: Other human health activities
Parent: Elysium Healthcare Holdings 3 Limited
Officers: Sarah Juliette Livingston, Secretary; Lesley Joy Chamberlain [1963] Director/Group Chief Executive; Dr Quazi Shams Mahfooz Haque [1968] Executive Medical Director; Steven John Woolgar [1955] Director of Policy and Regulation

Elysium Healthcare Holdings 2 Limited
Incorporated: 10 October 2016 *Employees:* 3,290
Net Worth: £63,930,000 *Total Assets:* £575,473,024
Registered Office: 2 Imperial Place, Maxwell Road, Borehamwood, Herts, WD6 1JN
Activities: Non-trading company
Parent: Elysium Healthcare Holdings 1 Limited
Officers: Sarah Juliette Livingston, Secretary; Lesley Joy Chamberlain [1963] Director/Chief Executive Officer; Dr Quazi Shams Mahfooz Haque [1968] Executive Medical Director; Steven John Woolgar [1955] Director of Policy and Regulation

Elysium Healthcare Holdings 3 Limited
Incorporated: 10 October 2016 *Employees:* 11
Net Worth: £54,745,000 *Total Assets:* £377,808,992
Registered Office: 2 Imperial Place, Maxwell Road, Borehamwood, Herts, WD6 1JN
Activities: Non-trading company
Parent: Elysium Healthcare Holdings 2 Limited
Officers: Sarah Juliette Livingston, Secretary; Lesley Joy Chamberlain [1963] Director/Chief Executive Officer; Dr Quazi Shams Mahfooz Haque [1968] Executive Medical Director; Steven John Woolgar [1955] Director of Policy and Regulation

Elysium Healthcare LC Limited
Incorporated: 22 November 2016
Net Worth: £134,075,000 *Total Assets:* £137,518,000
Registered Office: 2 Imperial Place, Maxwell Road, Borehamwood, Herts, WD6 1JN
Activities: Non-trading company
Parent: Elysium Healthcare Holdings 3 Limited
Officers: Sarah Juliette Livingston, Secretary; Lesley Joy Chamberlain [1963] Director/Chief Executive Officer; Dr Quazi Shams Mahfooz Haque [1968] Executive Medical Director

Elysium Healthcare No. 2 Limited
Incorporated: 11 May 2007 *Employees:* 1,356
Previous: Priory Secure Services Limited
Net Worth: £23,858,000 *Total Assets:* £179,348,992
Registered Office: 2 Imperial Place, Maxwell Road, Borehamwood, Herts, WD6 1JN
Activities: Hospital activities
Parent: Elysium Healthcare Holdings 3 Limited
Officers: Sarah Juliette Livingston, Secretary; Lesley Joy Chamberlain [1963] Director/Chief Executive Officer; Dr Quazi Shams Mahfooz Haque [1968] Executive Medical Director; Steven John Woolgar [1955] Director of Policy and Regulation

Elysium Healthcare No. 3 Limited
Incorporated: 14 November 1994 *Employees:* 176
Previous: Craegmoor Hospitals Limited
Net Worth: £24,619,000 *Total Assets:* £67,242,000
Registered Office: 2 Imperial Place, Maxwell Road, Borehamwood, Herts, WD6 1JN
Activities: Other human health activities
Parent: Elysium Healthcare Holdings 3 Limited
Officers: Sarah Juliette Livingston, Secretary; Lesley Joy Chamberlain [1963] Director/Chief Executive Officer; Dr Quazi Shams Mahfooz Haque [1968] Executive Medical Director; Steven John Woolgar [1955] Director of Policy and Regulation

Elysium Healthcare No. 4 Limited
Incorporated: 26 September 1996 *Employees:* 107
Previous: Speciality Care (Care Homes) Limited
Net Worth: £7,037,000 *Total Assets:* £20,008,000
Registered Office: 2 Imperial Place, Maxwell Road, Borehamwood, Herts, WD6 1JN
Activities: Other human health activities
Parent: Elysium Healthcare No. 3 Limited
Officers: Sarah Juliette Livingston, Secretary; Lesley Joy Chamberlain [1963] Director/Chief Executive Officer; Dr Quazi Shams Mahfooz Haque [1968] Executive Medical Director; Steven John Woolgar [1955] Director of Policy and Regulation

Elysium Healthcare Property 2 Limited
Incorporated: 29 March 2005
Previous: Partnerships in Care Property 13 Limited
Net Worth: £9,098,000 *Total Assets:* £30,056,000
Registered Office: 2 Imperial Place, Maxwell Road, Borehamwood, Herts, WD6 1JN
Activities: Hospital activities
Parent: Elysium Healthcare Limited
Officers: Sarah Juliette Livingston, Secretary; Lesley Joy Chamberlain [1963] Director/Chartered Accountant; Dr Quazi Shams Mahfooz Haque [1968] Group Medical Director

Emac Limited
Incorporated: 8 February 1996 *Employees:* 95
Net Worth: £21,469,000 *Total Assets:* £60,206,000
Registered Office: 1300 Parkway, Whiteley, Fareham, Hants, PO15 7AE
Activities: Other service activities n.e.c.
Parent: Ingleby (1879) Limited
Officers: Magdalena Baugh [1980] Director/FD, Chartered Accountant [Polish]; Alasdair Marnoch [1963] Director; Christopher Timothy Miles Toulson-Clarke [1964] Director/Chief Executive

EMAP Publishing Limited
Incorporated: 14 December 2011 *Employees:* 217
Net Worth: £20,133,616 *Total Assets:* £28,163,124
Registered Office: 7th Floor, Vantage London, Great West Road, Brentford, Middlesex, TW8 9AG
Activities: Other publishing activities
Parent: Metropolis Group Holdings Limited
Officers: Richard Hutchinson, Secretary; Richard Hutchinson [1966] Director; Robert Andrew Marr [1965] Director/Chief Executive Officer

EMC Computer Systems (U.K.) Limited
Incorporated: 1 September 1986 *Employees:* 729
Net Worth: £76,230,000 *Total Assets:* £417,184,992
Registered Office: Dell EMC Tower, Great West Road, Brentford, Middlesex, TW8 9AN
Activities: Other information technology service activities
Parent: Dell Technologies Inc
Officers: Fiona Margaret Dibley, Secretary; Janet Merritt Bawcom [1964] Director/Vice President & Assistant Secretary [American]; Richard William Rawcliffe [1964] Director/VP - Sales

EMC Consulting (UK) Limited
Incorporated: 8 April 1991 *Employees:* 29
Net Worth: £8,053,000 *Total Assets:* £37,052,000
Registered Office: Dell EMC Tower, Great West Road, Brentford, Middlesex, TW8 9AN
Activities: Information technology consultancy activities
Parent: Dell Technologies Inc.
Officers: Fiona Margaret Dibley, Secretary; Janet Merritt Bawcom [1964] Director/Vice President and Assistant Secretary [American]; Richard William Rawcliffe [1964] Director/VP - Sales

EMC Europe Limited
Incorporated: 2 October 1970 *Employees:* 520
Net Worth: £74,017,000 *Total Assets:* £94,817,000
Registered Office: Dell EMC Tower, Great West Road, Brentford, Middlesex, TW8 9AN
Activities: Information technology consultancy activities
Parent: Dell Technologies Inc
Officers: Fiona Margaret Dibley, Secretary; Janet Merritt Bawcom [1964] Director/Vice President & Assistant Secretary [American]; Richard William Rawcliffe [1964] Director/VP - Sales

Emcor Group (UK) PLC
Incorporated: 27 May 1964 *Employees:* 3,870
Net Worth: £3,513,000 *Total Assets:* £106,556,000
Registered Office: 1 The Crescent, Surbiton, Surrey, KT6 4BN
Activities: Electrical installation
Officers: Michael Lawrence Walker, Secretary; Keith Chanter [1958] Director; Christopher John Howse [1961] Director/Business Executive; Christopher Kehoe [1972] Director/Executive; David John Parker [1967] Director/Executive

Emerald Bidco Limited
Incorporated: 12 June 2014
Net Worth: £10,352,000 *Total Assets:* £29,002,000
Registered Office: Mandeville House, 62 The Broadway, Amersham, Bucks, HP7 0HJ
Activities: Activities of head offices
Parent: Emerald Midco 2 Limited
Officers: Richard James Riegel [1963] Director [American]; Karen Jane Roy [1966] Director; Jacqueline Susan Veness [1960] Director/Chartered Accountant

Emerald Midco 1 Limited
Incorporated: 30 April 2014
Net Worth: £33,235,000 *Total Assets:* £36,238,000
Registered Office: Mandeville House, 62 The Broadway, Amersham, Bucks, HP7 0HJ
Activities: Activities of head offices
Parent: Overture Topco Limited
Officers: Richard James Riegel [1963] Director [American]; Karen Jane Roy [1966] Director; Jacqueline Susan Veness [1960] Director/Chartered Accountant

Emerald Midco 2 Limited
Incorporated: 30 April 2014
Net Worth: £27,668,000 *Total Assets:* £36,219,000
Registered Office: Mandeville House, 62 The Broadway, Amersham, Bucks, HP7 0HJ
Activities: Activities of head offices
Parent: Emerald Midco 1 Limited
Officers: Richard James Riegel [1963] Director [American]; Karen Jane Roy [1966] Director; Jacqueline Susan Veness [1960] Director/Chartered Accountant

Emerald Topco Limited
Incorporated: 30 April 2014 *Employees:* 3
Net Worth: £36,191,000 *Total Assets:* £40,401,000
Registered Office: Mandeville House, 62 The Broadway, Amersham, Bucks, HP7 0HJ
Activities: Activities of head offices
Parent: Overture Bidco Limited
Officers: Richard James Riegel [1963] Director [American]; Karen Jane Roy [1966] Director; Jacqueline Susan Veness [1960] Director/Chartered Accountant

Emery Oleochemicals UK Limited
Incorporated: 6 July 2005 *Employees:* 6
Net Worth: £40,148,688 *Total Assets:* £81,512,520
Registered Office: New Kings Court, Tollgate, Chandler's Ford, Eastleigh, Hants, SO53 3LG
Activities: Other business support service activities n.e.c.
Officers: Anthony Swee Loong Cheong [1967] Director/Deputy Chief Financial Officer [Malaysian]; Joern Ellerbrake [1965] Director [German]; Jens Axel Kaehler [1946] Director/Economist [German]; Rameshweren Kanagalingam [1964] Group Chief Financial Director [Australian]; Stefan Niggemeyer [1967] Director/Finance Manager [German]

Emperor 2 Limited
Incorporated: 16 May 2014 *Employees:* 5
Net Worth Deficit: £50,365,000 *Total Assets:* £84,367,000
Registered Office: Unit 5 Priors Way, Maidenhead, Berks, SL6 2HP
Activities: Other information service activities n.e.c.
Parent: Emperor 1 Limited
Officers: Anthony Aquila [1964] Director/Chairman [American]; Jason Michael Brady [1968] Director/General Counsel [American]; Renato Carlo Giger [1960] Director [Swiss]; Franciscus Johannes Carolus Overtoom [1966] Director/Regional CFO [Dutch]; Roderick John Williams [1971] Director

Emperor 3 Limited
Incorporated: 16 May 2014 *Employees:* 5
Net Worth Deficit: £67,525,000 *Total Assets:* £163,971,008
Registered Office: Unit 5 Priors Way, Maidenhead, Berks, SL6 2HP
Activities: Other information service activities n.e.c.
Parent: Emperor 2 (Midco) Limited
Officers: Anthony Aquila [1964] Director/Chairman [American]; Jason Michael Brady [1968] Director/General Counsel [American]; Renato Carlo Giger [1960] Director [Swiss]; Franciscus Johannes Carolus Overtoom [1966] Director/Regional CFO [Dutch]; Roderick John Williams [1971] Director

Empire Bespoke Foods Limited
Incorporated: 11 August 1997 *Employees:* 63
Net Worth: £12,313,349 *Total Assets:* £23,339,932
Registered Office: 45 Rowdell Road, Europa House, Northolt, Middlesex, UB5 6AG
Activities: Wholesale of sugar and chocolate and sugar confectionery
Shareholder: Jitendra Maganbhai Patel
Officers: Anil Gunvantbhai Patel, Secretary/Director; Anil Gunvantbhai Patel [1954] Director; Chandresh Patel [1958] Director; Jitendrakumar Maganbhai Patel [1952] Director

Empresaria Group PLC
Incorporated: 25 March 1999 *Employees:* 1,367
Net Worth: £42,100,000 *Total Assets:* £135,500,000
Registered Office: Old Church House, Sandy Lane, Crawley Down, Crawley, W Sussex, RH10 4HS
Activities: Activities of head offices
Shareholder: Anthony Victor Martin
Officers: James Chapman, Secretary; Timothy David Anderson [1977] Director; Rhona Driggs [1965] Director [American]; Penelope Anne Freer [1960] Director; Anthony Victor Martin [1939] Director; Charles Kenneth Zachary Miles [1949] Director; Spencer James Wreford [1971] Director

Endace Europe Limited
Incorporated: 16 July 2003 *Employees:* 11
Net Worth: £2,940,797 *Total Assets:* £20,908,974
Registered Office: Squires House, 205a High Street, West Wickham, Kent, BR4 0PH
Activities: Other information technology service activities
Officers: Andrew Dean Harsant [1973] Director/Accountant [New Zealander]; Stuart Timothy Wilson [1959] Director/Engineer [Australian]

Endeavour Holdings Limited
Incorporated: 28 April 1920 *Employees:* 61
Net Worth: £14,435,949 *Total Assets:* £24,464,952
Registered Office: Rivervale House, 50 Victoria Road, Portslade, Brighton, BN41 1XB
Activities: Other letting and operating of own or leased real estate
Major Shareholder: Thomas Edward Brodie Sopwith
Officers: Neil Spencer Chapman, Finance Director; Neil Spencer Chapman [1955] Managing Director; Georgina Melissa Sopwith [1946] Director; Thomas Edward Brodie Sopwith [1932] Director

Endeavour SCH Holdings Limited
Incorporated: 23 November 1998
Net Worth: £11,021,000 *Total Assets:* £163,332,000
Registered Office: 8 White Oak Square, London Road, Swanley, Kent, BR8 7AG
Activities: Activities of other holding companies n.e.c.
Shareholders: Innisfree M & G PPP LLP; Semperian PPP Investment Partners No.2 Limited
Officers: David John Brooking [1967] Investment Director; Neil Rae [1971] Director; Mr Terrence Ryan [1957] Director; Alastair James Watson [1974] Investment Director

Endeavour SCH PLC
Incorporated: 23 November 1998
Net Worth: £11,021,000 *Total Assets:* £163,332,000
Registered Office: 8 White Oak Square, London Road, Swanley, Kent, BR8 7AG
Activities: Hospital activities
Parent: Endeavour SCH Holdings Limited
Officers: David John Brooking [1967] Investment Director; Neil Rae [1971] Director; Mr Terrence Ryan [1957] Director; Alastair James Watson [1974] Investment Director

Endon Europe Power 1 Limited
Incorporated: 5 June 1998 *Employees:* 2
Net Worth Deficit: £93,074,000 *Total Assets:* £301,216,992
Registered Office: Velocity V1, Brooklands Drive, Weybridge, Surrey, KT13 0SL
Activities: Non-trading company
Parent: Endon Europe Power 3 Limited
Officers: Dena Michelle L O'Bue, Secretary; Asim Iftikhar Chohan [1973] Director of Operations; Michael James Timewell [1974] Director/Solicitor

Endon Europe Power 3 Limited
Incorporated: 19 August 1998 *Employees:* 2
Net Worth Deficit: £150,242,000 *Total Assets:* £376,488,992
Registered Office: Velocity V1, Brooklands Drive, Weybridge, Surrey, KT13 0SL
Activities: Non-trading company
Shareholders: Endon Europe Power 4 Limited; Endon Europe Power 6 Limited
Officers: Dena Michelle L O'Bue, Secretary; Asim Iftikhar Chohan [1973] Director of Operations; Michael James Timewell [1974] Director/Solicitor

Endon Europe Power 6 Limited
Incorporated: 24 December 1998 *Employees:* 2
Net Worth Deficit: £20,997,000 *Total Assets:* £21,397,000
Registered Office: Velocity V1, Brooklands Drive, Weybridge, Surrey, KT13 0SL
Activities: Non-trading company
Parent: Endon Europe Power 5 Limited
Officers: Dena Michelle L O'Bue, Secretary; Asim Iftikhar Chohan [1973] Director of Operations; Michael James Timewell [1974] Director/Solicitor

Energy Developments (UK) Limited
Incorporated: 21 March 1996 *Employees:* 52
Net Worth: £7,646,070 *Total Assets:* £20,661,088
Registered Office: Chancery House, 199 Silbury Boulevard, Milton Keynes, Bucks, MK9 1JL
Activities: Production of electricity
Parent: EDL Holdings (UK) Limited
Officers: James Christopher Harman [1968] Director [Australian]; David Truelove [1975] Director

Enghouse Holdings (UK) Limited
Incorporated: 6 January 1992 *Employees:* 1
Net Worth: £33,812,168 *Total Assets:* £38,208,060
Registered Office: 337 Bath Road, Slough, Berks, SL1 5PR
Activities: Other information technology service activities
Parent: Enghouse Interactive (UK) Limited
Officers: Douglas Craig Bryson, Secretary; Stephen Sadler [1951] Director [Canadian]

Ennogen Healthcare Ltd
Incorporated: 14 October 2011 *Employees:* 10
Net Worth: £21,729,260 *Total Assets:* £29,465,110
Registered Office: Unit G4, Riverside Way, Dartford, Kent, DA1 5BS
Activities: Manufacture of basic pharmaceutical products
Major Shareholder: Gurdev Singh Rurai
Officers: Gurdev Singh Ruprai [1960] Director/Pharmacist

ENRA Group Limited
Incorporated: 13 November 2013 *Employees:* 2
Previous: ENRA Group Ltd
Net Worth Deficit: £358,797 *Total Assets:* £63,454,864
Registered Office: 3rd Floor, Premiere House, Elstree Way, Borehamwood, Herts, WD6 1JH
Activities: Other business support service activities n.e.c.
Parent: Newincco 1270 Limited
Officers: Emily Henrietta Gestetner [1967] Director; Harry Leon Landy [1978] Director; Danny Stephen Waters [1984] Director

Ensco 1212 Limited
Incorporated: 28 December 2016 *Employees:* 2
Net Worth Deficit: £450,709 *Total Assets:* £31,291,344
Registered Office: c/o Otto Bock Healthcare PLC, 32 Parsonage Road, Englefield Green, Egham, Surrey, TW20 0LD
Activities: Non-trading company
Parent: Ensco 1214 Limited
Officers: Gregor John Bates [1969] Director; Philip Anthony Yates [1963] Director

Ensco 1214 Limited
Incorporated: 12 January 2017 *Employees:* 2
Net Worth: £31,000,000 *Total Assets:* £31,000,000
Registered Office: c/o Otto Bock Healthcare PLC, 32 Parsonage Road, Englefield Green, Egham, Surrey, TW20 0LD
Activities: Non-trading company
Major Shareholder: Hans Georg Nader
Officers: Gregor John Bates [1969] Director; Philip Anthony Yates [1963] Director

Ensign Highways Limited
Incorporated: 20 May 2004 *Employees:* 7
Net Worth: £4,190,682 *Total Assets:* £71,576,144
Registered Office: Wallage Lane, Rowfant, Crawley, W Sussex, RH10 4NF
Activities: Construction of roads and motorways
Parent: Ensign Highways Holdings Limited
Officers: Graham Derek Stanton, Secretary; Francois Bernard Bidard [1966] Financial Director [French]; Eric Brangier [1962] Managing Director [French]; Raphael Llobregat [1974] Director/Chief Financial Officer [French]

Ensono Limited
Incorporated: 12 November 1996 *Employees:* 304
Previous: Attenda Limited
Net Worth: £12,769,000 *Total Assets:* £33,558,000
Registered Office: One London Road, Staines upon Thames, Middlesex, TW18 4EX
Activities: Information technology consultancy activities
Parent: Amphora Acquisitions Ltd
Officers: Peter John Bazil [1972] Director/General Counsel [American]; Norman Smagley [1958] Director/Chief Financial Officer [American]

Enstar Acquisitions Limited
Incorporated: 13 June 2008
Net Worth: £323,545 *Total Assets:* £109,924,864
Registered Office: 3 Guildford Business Park, Guildford, Surrey, GU2 8XG
Activities: Activities of head offices
Parent: Enstar Group Limited
Officers: Siobhan Mary Hextall, Secretary/Accountant [Irish]; Siobhan Mary Hextall [1968] Director/Accountant [Irish]; Derek Robert Douglas Reid [1965] Legal Director; Clive Paul Thomas [1962] Director/Accountant

Entco Situla Holding Ltd
Incorporated: 5 January 2017 *Employees:* 7,954
Net Worth: £7,084,384,256 *Total Assets:* £7,968,043,008
Registered Office: Cain Road, Amen Corner, Bracknell, Berks, RG12 1HN
Activities: Other information technology service activities
Parent: Micro Focus International PLC
Officers: Christopher Henry Yelland [1967] Finance Director

Enterprise Rent-a-Car European Holdings Limited
Incorporated: 2 July 2001 *Employees:* 4,955
Net Worth: £198,180,000 *Total Assets:* £1,499,531,008
Registered Office: Enterprise House, Vicarage Road, Egham, Surrey, TW20 9FB
Activities: Activities of head offices
Officers: Teresa Anne Holderer, Secretary; Ricky Allan Short [1958] Director [American]

Enterprise Rent-a-Car UK Holdings Limited
Incorporated: 21 June 1994
Net Worth: £48,041,000 *Total Assets:* £51,979,000
Registered Office: Enterprise House, Vicarage Road, Egham, Surrey, TW20 9FB
Activities: Activities of head offices
Parent: Enterprise Rent-a-Car European Holdings Limited
Officers: Teresa Anne Holderer, Secretary; Ricky Allan Short [1958] Director [American]

Enterprise Rent-a-Car UK Limited
Incorporated: 4 July 1994 *Employees:* 4,951
Net Worth: £202,119,008 *Total Assets:* £1,472,199,040
Registered Office: Enterprise House, Vicarage Road, Egham, Surrey, TW20 9FB
Activities: Renting and leasing of cars and light motor vehicles
Parent: Enterprise Rent-a-Car UK Holdings Limited
Officers: Teresa Anne Holderer, Secretary; Ricky Allan Short [1958] Director [American]

Enterprise Services Information Security UK Limited
Incorporated: 12 November 1990 *Employees:* 437
Previous: Hewlett Packard Enterprise Information Security UK Limited
Net Worth: £29,600,000 *Total Assets:* £77,596,000
Registered Office: Royal Pavilion, Wellesley Road, Aldershot, Hants, GU11 1PZ
Activities: Other information technology service activities
Parent: DXC Technology Company
Officers: Tina Anne Gough [1962] Finance Director; Maruf Ahmad Majed [1955] Director [American]; Michael Charles Woodfine [1971] Director/Solicitor

The Entertainer (Amersham) Limited
Incorporated: 24 September 1986 *Employees:* 1,704
Net Worth: £32,360,000 *Total Assets:* £82,294,000
Registered Office: Boughton Business Park, Bell Lane, Little Chalfont, Bucks, HP6 6GL
Activities: Retail sale of games and toys in specialised stores
Major Shareholder: Gary Peter Grant
Officers: Catherine Ann Grant, Secretary; Mark James Campbell [1974] Director; Catherine Ann Grant [1954] Director/Secretary; Duncan Peter Grant [1982] Director; Gary Peter Grant [1958] Director/Toy Retailer; Stuart James Grant [1984] Director

Entserv UK Limited
Incorporated: 21 July 1897 *Employees:* 4,780
Previous: Hewlett Packard Enterprise Services UK Limited
Net Worth: £2,137,931,008 *Total Assets:* £3,104,868,096
Registered Office: Royal Pavilion, Wellesley Road, Aldershot, Hants, GU11 1PZ
Activities: Information technology consultancy activities
Parent: DXC Technology Company
Officers: Tina Anne Gough [1962] Finance Director; Maruf Ahmad Majed [1955] Director [American]; Michael Charles Woodfine [1971] Director/Solicitor

Environments for Learning Sandwell PFI Holdco One Limited
Incorporated: 18 June 2009 *Employees:* 5
Net Worth Deficit: £5,688,000 *Total Assets:* £49,700,000
Registered Office: Interserve House, Ruscombe Park, Twyford, Reading, Berks, RG10 9JU
Activities: Activities of other holding companies n.e.c.
Parent: Environments for Learning Limited
Officers: Christopher Richard Field [1955] Director; John Stephen Gordon [1962] Director; Peter Kenneth Johnstone [1965] Director; David John Stevens [1963] Director of Adult Social Care and Health; Matthew Templeton [1973] Director

Environments for Learning Sandwell PFI One Limited
Incorporated: 18 June 2009 *Employees:* 5
Net Worth Deficit: £5,688,000 *Total Assets:* £49,700,000
Registered Office: Interserve House, Ruscombe Park, Twyford, Reading, Berks, RG10 9JU
Activities: Other business support service activities n.e.c.
Parent: Environments for Learning Sandwell PFI Holdco One Limited
Officers: Christopher Richard Field [1955] Director; John Stephen Gordon [1962] Director; Peter Kenneth Johnstone [1965] Director; David John Stevens [1963] Director of Adult Social Care and Health; Matthew Templeton [1973] Director

Envision Pharma Bidco Limited
Incorporated: 11 April 2016
Net Worth: £123,291,680 *Total Assets:* £169,534,848
Registered Office: Envision House, 5 North Street, Horsham, W Sussex, RH12 1XQ
Activities: Non-trading company
Parent: Envision Pharma Midco Limited
Officers: John David Gillie [1970] Finance Director; Bruno Serge Leon Ladriere [1961] Managing Director (Private Equity) [French]; Daniel Jacques Joseph Alexandre Setton [1983] Director [French]; Benjamin Maurice Frederick Witcher [1987] Director/Investment Professional

Envision Pharma Finco Limited
Incorporated: 11 April 2016
Net Worth: £146,693,344 *Total Assets:* £189,551,776
Registered Office: Envision House, 5 North Street, Horsham, W Sussex, RH12 1XQ
Activities: Non-trading company
Parent: Envision Pharma Group Limited
Officers: John David Gillie [1970] Finance Director; Bruno Serge Leon Ladriere [1961] Managing Director (Private Equity) [French]; Daniel Jacques Joseph Alexandre Setton [1983] Director [French]; Benjamin Maurice Frederick Witcher [1987] Director/Investment Professional

Envision Pharma Group Limited
Incorporated: 11 April 2016 *Employees:* 570
Net Worth Deficit: £39,227,120 *Total Assets:* £310,448,224
Registered Office: Envision House, 5 North Street, Horsham, W Sussex, RH12 1XQ
Activities: Non-trading company
Officers: Joseph Christopher Brown [1967] Director [American]; Gregory Spencer Caswill [1951] Director/Chartered Accountant; John David Gillie [1970] Finance Director; Brian Alexander Hepburn [1960] Marketing Director; Bruno Serge Leon Ladriere [1961] Managing Director (Private Equity) [French]; Mike Mortimer [1960] Director [American]; Daniel Jacques Joseph Alexandre Setton [1983] Director [French]; Benjamin Maurice Frederick Witcher [1987] Director/Investment Professional

Envision Pharma Holdco Limited
Incorporated: 4 June 2013 *Employees:* 4
Net Worth Deficit: £18,935,268 *Total Assets:* £39,868,740
Registered Office: Envision House, 5 North Street, Horsham, W Sussex, RH12 1XQ
Activities: Non-trading company
Parent: Alligent Biopharm Consulting (Europe) Limited
Officers: John David Gillie, Secretary; Joseph Christopher Brown [1967] Managing Director [American]; Gregory Spencer Caswill [1961] Director/Chartered Accountant; John David Gillie [1970] Director/Accountant; Brian Alexander Hepburn [1960] Marketing Director

Envision Pharma Midco Limited
Incorporated: 11 April 2016
Net Worth: £127,605,744 *Total Assets:* £138,337,456
Registered Office: Envision House, 5 North Street, Horsham, W Sussex, RH12 1XQ
Activities: Non-trading company
Parent: Envision Pharma Finco Limited
Officers: John David Gillie [1970] Finance Director; Bruno Serge Leon Ladriere [1961] Managing Director (Private Equity) [French]; Daniel Jacques Joseph Alexandre Setton [1983] Director [French]; Benjamin Maurice Frederick Witcher [1987] Director/Investment Professional

Epicor Software (UK) Limited
Incorporated: 24 January 1989 *Employees:* 236
Net Worth: £12,576,754 *Total Assets:* £29,879,666
Registered Office: No 1 The Arena, Downshire Way, Bracknell, Berks, RG12 1PU
Activities: Information technology consultancy activities
Officers: John David Ireland, Secretary/General Counsel [American]; Dawn Murray, Secretary; Richard John Clark [1964] Director/Accountant; Timothy Bernard Harrington [1955] Director/Finance VP [Irish]; John David Ireland [1962] Director/General Counsel [American]

Epilepsy Society
Incorporated: 15 March 1951 *Employees:* 334
Net Worth: £44,968,000 *Total Assets:* £58,977,000
Registered Office: Epilepsy Society, Chesham Lane, Chalfont St Peter, Bucks, SL9 0RJ
Activities: Other human health activities
Officers: Catherine Nina Alcock [1957] Director/Estate Owner; Christopher Joseph Blue [1966] Managing Director; Andrew Farrell [1955] Director/Chief Finance Officer; Professor Andrew John Timothy George [1963] Director/Deputy Vice Chancellor; Peter James Goodfellow [1979] Director/Chief Financial Officer; James Joseph Hagan [1951] Director/Scientist; Michael Stone [1957] Director/Global Corporate Fundraiser; Adrian Joseph Waddingham [1950] Director/Actuary; Deborah Wheeler [1962] Deputy Director of Nursing; Peter Anthony Worthington [1952] Chairman, Director, Consultant

Epsom College
Incorporated: 6 June 2000 *Employees:* 422
Net Worth: £22,995,000 *Total Assets:* £41,569,000
Registered Office: Epsom College, College Road, Epsom, Surrey, KT17 4JQ
Activities: General secondary education
Officers: Sarah Elizabeth Teasdale, Secretary; Dr Jeremy Shaw Bolton [1943] Director/Medical Practitioner; Tania Alison Louise Botting [1965] Director/Headmistress; Fiona Jane Boulton [1964] Director/Headmistress; Doctor Hywel Henry Bowen Perkins [1952] Director/GP; Edward James Chandler [1954] Director/Financial Consultant; Belinda Jane Dolbear [1965] Director/Solicitor; The Very Reverend Dianna Lynn Gwilliams [1957] Director/Dean of Guildford; John Hay [1948] PR Director; Dr Suzannah Rebecca Gabriella Lipscomb [1978] Director/Historian and Senior Lecturer; Ayodeji Christopher Renner Mahoney [1963] Director/Legal Consultant; Andrew John Pianca [1951] Director/Accountant; George Pincus [1942] Director/Recruitment Consultant; Alexander Murray Russell [1962] Director; Paul Andrew Stanford [1967] Managing Director; Karen Elizabeth Thomas [1958] Director/Consultant Surgeon; Clive Royston Watson [1961] Director; Dr Alastair James Wells [1960] Director/General Medical Practitioner

Epson (U.K.) Limited
Incorporated: 16 November 1979 *Employees:* 139
Net Worth Deficit: £3,378,000 *Total Assets:* £41,722,000
Registered Office: Westside, London Road, Hemel Hempstead, Herts, HP3 9TD
Activities: Wholesale of computers, computer peripheral equipment and software
Parent: Seiko Epson Corporation
Officers: Sian Faru Eva Wilkie Nath, Secretary; Andrew Duncan Campbell-Ferguson [1968] Managing Director; Hideki Kitamura [1960] Director [Japanese]; Kazuyoshi Yamamoto [1960] Director/President, Epson Europe B.V [Japanese]

Equiniti Financial Services Limited
Incorporated: 11 April 2007 *Employees:* 246
Net Worth: £28,622,000 *Total Assets:* £61,500,000
Registered Office: Aspect House, Spencer Road, Lancing, W Sussex, BN99 6DA
Activities: Activities of financial services holding companies
Parent: Equiniti Holdings Limited
Officers: Katherine Cong, Secretary; Adam Charles Green [1978] Director/Chief Risk Officer; Mark Joseph Lund [1957] Director; Jonathan Millam [1973] Director/Accountant; Timothy John Miller [1957] Director; Richard James Pearson [1966] Director; Thera Roeline Prins [1973] Director [Dutch]; Guy Richard Wakeley [1970] Director

Equiniti Group PLC
Incorporated: 30 November 2009 *Employees:* 4,578
Previous: Equiniti Group Limited
Net Worth: £491,000,000 *Total Assets:* £927,600,000
Registered Office: Sutherland House, Russell Way, Crawley, W Sussex, RH10 1UH
Activities: Activities of head offices
Officers: Katherine Cong, Secretary; Mark David Brooker [1971] Director; Alison Sarah Burns [1963] Independent Non-Executive Director; Sally-Ann Hibberd [1959] Director; Timothy John Miller [1957] Director; Cheryl Joanne Millington [1966] Director; Darren Scott Pope [1965] Director; John Stier [1966] Director/Chief Financial Officer; Guy Richard Wakeley [1970] Director; Philip Edward Yea [1954] Director

Equiniti Holdings Limited
Incorporated: 23 April 2007 *Employees:* 16
Net Worth: £104,386,000 *Total Assets:* £1,089,864,960
Registered Office: Elder House, St Georges Business Park, Brooklands Road, Weybridge, Surrey, KT13 0TS
Activities: Activities of head offices
Parent: Equiniti Group PLC
Officers: Katherine Cong, Secretary; John Stier [1966] Director/Chief Financial Officer; Guy Richard Wakeley [1970] Director

Equiniti Limited
Incorporated: 25 April 2007 *Employees:* 1,158
Net Worth: £586,400,000 *Total Assets:* £648,099,968
Registered Office: Aspect House, Spencer Road, Lancing, W Sussex, BN99 6DA
Activities: Other business support service activities n.e.c.
Parent: Equiniti Holdings Limited
Officers: Katherine Cong, Secretary; Philip Michael Ainsley [1957] Director; Stuart John Ellen [1962] Director; Steven Robert Johnson [1978] Director/Chartered Accountant; Paul Charles Matthews [1961] Director; John Stier [1966] Director/Chief Financial Officer; Guy Richard Wakeley [1970] Director

Equiniti Services Limited
Incorporated: 5 April 1963 *Employees:* 528
Net Worth: £42,038,000 *Total Assets:* £146,148,992
Registered Office: Elder House, St Georges Business Park, Brooklands Road, Weybridge, Surrey, KT13 0TS
Activities: Activities of other holding companies n.e.c.
Parent: Equiniti Limited
Officers: Katherine Cong, Secretary; Robert David Bloor [1968] Director/Accountant; John Stier [1966] Director/Chief Financial Officer; Guy Richard Wakeley [1970] Director

Equitable Life Assurance Society,(The)
Incorporated: 18 August 1892 *Employees:* 237
Total Assets: £6,791,000,064
Registered Office: The Equitable Life Assurance Society, Walton Street, Aylesbury, Bucks, HP21 7QW
Activities: Life insurance
Officers: Jean Florence Fleet, Secretary; Penelope Jane Avis [1968] Director; Ian Brimecome [1953] Director/Investment Banker; Lord Daniel William Finkelstein [1962] Director/Journalist; Ian Andrew Gibson [1949] Director; Keith Nicholson [1949] Director; Cathryn Elizabeth Riley [1962] Director; Martin Wayne Sinkinson [1967] Director/Actuary; Simon Antony Small [1961] Director

Erac UK Finance Limited
Incorporated: 18 July 1994
Net Worth: £16,000 *Total Assets:* £1,076,040,960
Registered Office: Enterprise House, Vicarage Road, Egham, Surrey, TW20 9FB
Activities: Financial management
Parent: Enterprise Rent-a-Car UK Holdings Limited
Officers: Teresa Anne Holderer, Secretary; Ricky Allan Short [1958] Director [American]

Ercol (Holdings) Limited
Incorporated: 1 December 1983 *Employees:* 164
Net Worth: £18,102,000 *Total Assets:* £21,239,000
Registered Office: Summerleys Road, Prince Risborough, Bucks, HP27 9PX
Activities: Activities of head offices
Major Shareholder: Edward Randolph Tadros
Officers: Edward Randolph Tadros, Secretary; Sophie Mirman [1956] Director [British/French]; Edward William Tadros [1980] Director; Edward Randolph Tadros [1949] Chairman/Director

Ergo Tec LLP
Incorporated: 23 March 2010
Net Worth: £30,618,192 *Total Assets:* £78,431,184
Registered Office: North House, 198 High Street, Tonbridge, Kent, TN9 1BE
Officers: Jurgis Lapienis [1989] Member; Simas Lapienis [1971] Member

Ergomed PLC
Incorporated: 29 September 2000 *Employees:* 560
Net Worth: £34,843,000 *Total Assets:* £61,913,000
Registered Office: 1 Occam Court, Surrey Research Park, Guildford, Surrey, GU2 7HJ
Activities: Other professional, scientific and technical activities n.e.c.
Shareholder: Miroslav Reljanovic
Officers: Sanja Juric, Secretary; Christopher Irvin Collins [1950] Director [South African]; Peter George [1961] Director; Stuart Robert Jackson [1960] Director; Jan Petracek [1975] Director [Czech]; Miroslav Reljanovic [1958] Director [Croatian]; Michael Spiteri [1961] Director

Ergon Investments International Limited
Incorporated: 17 November 1986
Net Worth: £5,279,419,904 *Total Assets:* £5,332,260,864
Registered Office: The Akzonobel Building, Wexham Road, Slough, Berks, SL2 5DS
Activities: Activities of head offices
Parent: Ergon Investments UK Limited
Officers: Stephen Bruce Ray [1962] Director/Pensions Accounting Manager; Michael Smalley [1958] Director; Michael Smalley [1958] Director; David Allan Turner [1971] Director

Ergon Investments UK Limited
Incorporated: 17 November 1986
Net Worth: £883,948,992 *Total Assets:* £6,546,396,160
Registered Office: The Akzonobel Building, Wexham Road, Slough, Berks, SL2 5DS
Activities: Activities of head offices
Parent: Imperial Chemical Industries Limited
Officers: Stephen Bruce Ray [1962] Director/Pensions Accounting Manager; Michael Smalley [1958] Director; David Allan Turner [1971] Director

Ericsson (Holdings) Limited
Incorporated: 8 August 1946
Net Worth: £155,064,000 *Total Assets:* £344,708,000
Registered Office: 14th Floor, Thames Tower, Station Road, Reading, Berks, RG1 1LX
Activities: Wireless telecommunications activities
Parent: Telefonaktiebolaget L. M. Ericsson
Officers: Craig Alexander Young, Secretary; Marielle Christina Lindgren [1975] Managing Director [Swedish]; Liam Kieran O'Brien [1973] Director/Accountant [Irish]; Roger James Peacock [1967] Director/Head of HR (UK and I)

Ericsson Limited
Incorporated: 12 November 1968 *Employees:* 1,788
Net Worth: £117,283,000 *Total Assets:* £413,096,992
Registered Office: 14th Floor, Thames Tower, Station Road, Reading, Berks, RG1 1LX
Activities: Wireless telecommunications activities
Parent: Ericsson (Holdings) Limited
Officers: Craig Alexander Young, Secretary; Marielle Christina Lindgren [1975] Managing Director [Swedish]; Liam Kieran O'Brien [1973] Director/Accountant [Irish]; Roger James Peacock [1967] Director/Head of Human Resources

Ericsson Television Limited
Incorporated: 14 January 1999 *Employees:* 338
Net Worth: £20,584,000 *Total Assets:* £54,179,000
Registered Office: Unit 2 Strategic Park, Comines Way, Hedge End, Southampton, SO30 4DA
Activities: Other telecommunications activities
Parent: Ericsson (Holdings) Limited
Officers: Ashley Vernon Spencer, Secretary; Liam Kieran O'Brien [1973] Director [Irish]; Thomas Oliver Walshe [1959] Operations Director [Irish]

Erith Contractors Limited
Incorporated: 15 March 1973 *Employees:* 421
Net Worth: £12,801,829 *Total Assets:* £47,079,216
Registered Office: Erith House, 7 Queen Street, Erith, Kent, DA8 1RP
Activities: Treatment and disposal of hazardous waste
Parent: Erith Holdings Limited
Officers: Steven Thomas Darsey, Secretary; David John Darsey [1969] Director; Tony Darsey [1961] Director; Steven May [1985] Director; Barry Menzies [1957] Director/Chartered Quantity Surveyor; Victoria Stokes [1974] Finance Director

Erith Holdings Limited
Incorporated: 27 February 1991 *Employees:* 626
Net Worth: £16,877,000 *Total Assets:* £63,617,000
Registered Office: Erith House, 7 Queen Street, Erith, Kent, DA8 1RP
Activities: Activities of head offices
Parent: Erith Holdings Trustee Limited
Officers: Steven Thomas Darsey, Secretary; David John Darsey [1969] Director; Steven Thomas Darsey [1958] Director; Tony Darsey [1961] Contract Director; Victoria Stokes [1974] Finance Director

Erith School
Incorporated: 10 September 2010 *Employees:* 220
Net Worth: £25,767,000 *Total Assets:* £29,549,000
Registered Office: Erith School, Avenue Road, Erith, Kent, DA8 3BN
Activities: General secondary education
Officers: Stephanie Allen [1964] Director/Headteacher; Monica Cane [1953] Director/Retired; Peter Francis Thomas Carter [1955] Director/Retired; Yvonne Enoe [1959] Director/Lecturer; Wendy Lynne Maietta-Turner [1967] Director/Community Nursery Nurse; Maria Fatima Frazao Freitas Melder [1965] Director/HR Administrator; Ann Janet Nuckley [1947] Director/Retired; Adeola Olatokunbo Apeke Olojo [1957] Director/Senior Business Manager CPS

Esher Mail Order Limited
Incorporated: 10 June 1970 *Employees:* 269
Net Worth: £14,031,608 *Total Assets:* £31,067,310
Registered Office: 3rd Floor, Cumberland House, 15-17 Cumberland Place, Southampton, SO15 2BG
Activities: Retail sale via mail order houses or via Internet
Parent: BVG Group Limited
Officers: Iain Burgess, Secretary/Director; Iain Burgess [1972] Director; Simon John Locke [1970] Director

Eskaylab Limited
Incorporated: 29 July 1908
Net Worth: £201,868,992 *Total Assets:* £201,900,000
Registered Office: 980 Great West Road, Brentford, Middlesex, TW8 9GS
Activities: Other business support service activities n.e.c.
Parent: SmithKline Beecham Limited
Officers: James Borger [1963] Director/VP, Group Financial Planning and Analysis [American]; Alan George Burns [1975] Director

ESNT Filter Products Limited
Incorporated: 29 October 2009
Net Worth: £20,447,696 *Total Assets:* £20,452,492
Registered Office: Avebury House, 201-249 Avebury Boulevard, Milton Keynes, Bucks, MK9 1AU
Activities: Non-trading company
Parent: Essentra International Limited
Officers: Tay Swee Choon George, Secretary; Tay Swee Choon George [1975] Director [Singaporean]; Robert William Pye [1964] Director [Australian]

ESNT Holdings (No.1) Limited
Incorporated: 3 July 1997
Net Worth: £175,956,000 *Total Assets:* £175,962,000
Registered Office: Avebury House, 201-249 Avebury Boulevard, Milton Keynes, Bucks, MK9 1AU
Activities: Activities of head offices
Parent: Essentra International Limited
Officers: Patricia Kendall, Secretary; Jon Michael Green [1962] Director/Company Secretary & General Counsel; Lili Liu [1972] Director

ESNT Holdings (No.2) Limited
Incorporated: 3 July 1997
Net Worth: £160,688,992 *Total Assets:* £160,740,000
Registered Office: Avebury House, 201-249 Avebury Boulevard, Milton Keynes, Bucks, MK9 1AU
Activities: Activities of head offices
Shareholders: ESNT Holdings (No.1) Limited; ESNT Holdings (No.1) Limited
Officers: Jon Michael Green, Secretary; Jon Michael Green [1962] Director/Company Secretary & General Counsel; Lili Liu [1972] Director

ESNT International Limited
Incorporated: 1 August 1985
Net Worth Deficit: £10,809,000 *Total Assets:* £304,440,000
Registered Office: Avebury House, 201-249 Avebury Boulevard, Milton Keynes, Bucks, MK9 1AU
Activities: Non-trading company
Parent: Essentra International Limited
Officers: Patricia Kendall, Secretary; Jon Michael Green [1962] Director/Company Secretary & General Counsel; Lili Liu [1972] Director

ESP Connections Limited
Incorporated: 1 August 1996
Net Worth: £18,321,000 *Total Assets:* £84,047,000
Registered Office: 1st Floor, Bluebird House, Mole Business Park, Leatherhead, Surrey, KT22 7BA
Activities: Other business support service activities n.e.c.
Parent: E.S. Pipelines Limited
Officers: Thomas William Butler [1959] Finance Director [Irish]; Nicholas John Clark [1960] Director; Paul Miles [1971] Director/Chief Financial Officer; Kevin O'Connor [1976] Director/Chief Executive Officer; Victoria Caroline Spiers [1969] Director/Manager; Stuart Peter Williams [1965] Operations Director

ESP Electricity Limited
Incorporated: 1 April 2003 *Employees:* 19
Net Worth: £9,511,000 *Total Assets:* £43,873,000
Registered Office: 1st Floor, Bluebird House, Mole Business Park, Leatherhead, Surrey, KT22 7BA
Activities: Distribution of electricity
Parent: ESPUG Finance Limited
Officers: Thomas William Butler [1959] Finance Director [Irish]; Nicholas John Clark [1960] Director; Paul Miles [1971] Director/Chief Financial Officer; Kevin O'Connor [1976] Director/Chief Executive Officer; Victoria Caroline Spiers [1969] Director/Manager; Stuart Peter Williams [1965] Operations Director

ESP Utilities Group Limited
Incorporated: 17 May 1991 *Employees:* 74
Net Worth Deficit: £14,482,000 *Total Assets:* £271,476,000
Registered Office: 1st Floor, Bluebird House, Mole Business Park, Leatherhead, Surrey, KT22 7BA
Activities: Activities of head offices
Parent: Zoom Gas Pipelines Limited
Officers: Thomas William Butler [1959] Finance Director [Irish]; Nicholas John Clark [1960] Director; Anna Louise Dellis [1973] Director; Nicholas Wenham Horler [1959] Director/Chairman; Paul Miles [1971] Director/Chief Financial Officer; Kevin O'Connor [1976] Director/Chief Executive Officer; Sebastian Schwengber [1979] Director/Investment Professional [German]; Bernardo de SA Braamcamp Sobral Sottomayor [1973] Director [Portuguese]; Victoria Caroline Spiers [1969] Director/Manager; Stuart Peter Williams [1965] Operations Director

Espalier Finance Limited
Incorporated: 2 July 2012 *Employees:* 1
Net Worth: £28,454,698 *Total Assets:* £28,500,980
Registered Office: One Gloucester Place, Brighton, BN1 4AA
Activities: Educational support services
Major Shareholder: Andrew Jeremy Colin
Officers: Timothy Slater [1972] Director/Accountant

Espalier Ventures Limited
Incorporated: 2 July 2012 *Employees:* 676
Previous: Espalier Credit Limited
Net Worth: £48,121,000 *Total Assets:* £186,300,000
Registered Office: One Gloucester Place, Brighton, BN1 4AA
Activities: Educational support services
Major Shareholder: Andrew Jeremy Colin
Officers: Andrew Jeremy Colin [1959] Director; Timothy Slater [1972] Director/Accountant; Steven George Smale [1969] Sales & Marketing Director; John Buchanan Sykes [1963] Director/Chartered Accountant

ESPUG Finance Limited
Incorporated: 25 August 2017
Net Worth: £512,523,008 *Total Assets:* £765,907,968
Registered Office: 1st Floor, Bluebird House, Mole Business Park, Leatherhead, Surrey, KT22 7BA
Activities: Activities of other holding companies n.e.c.
Parent: ESP Utilities Group Limited
Officers: Thomas William Butler [1959] Finance Director [Irish]; Nicholas John Clark [1960] Development Director; Anna Louise Dellis [1973] Director/Accountant; Paul Miles [1971] Director/Chief Financial Officer; Kevin O'Connor [1976] Director/Chief Executive Officer; Sebastian Schwengber [1979] Director/Investment Professional [German]; Bernardo de SA Braamcamp Sobral Sottomayor [1973] Director [Portuguese]; Victoria Caroline Spiers [1969] Director/Manager; Stuart Peter Williams [1965] Operations Director

ESRI (UK) Limited
Incorporated: 29 November 1976 *Employees:* 263
Net Worth: £5,359,947 *Total Assets:* £30,528,396
Registered Office: Millennium House, 65 Walton Street, Aylesbury, Bucks, HP21 7QG
Activities: Business and domestic software development
Parent: ESRI Holdings Limited
Officers: Stuart Richard Bonthrone [1965] Sales Director; Gareth Huw Davies [1967] Director/Chartered Accountant; Charles Joseph Kennelly [1965] Director/Chief Technology Officer; Timothy Luke Welch [1965] Sales Director

ESRI Holdings Limited
Incorporated: 7 May 1991 *Employees:* 368
Net Worth: £13,732,945 *Total Assets:* £42,185,500
Registered Office: Millennium House, 65 Walton Street, Aylesbury, Bucks, HP21 7QG
Activities: Other business support service activities n.e.c.
Shareholders: IMBOLC Limited; Laura Catherine Dangermond; Paul Jacob Dangermond
Officers: Stuart Richard Bonthrone [1965] Director; Charles Joseph Kennelly [1965] Director

ESSCI Limited
Incorporated: 27 August 2015 *Employees:* 2,170
Net Worth Deficit: £1,796,000 *Total Assets:* £145,068,992
Registered Office: Twenty, Kingston Road, Staines upon Thames, Middlesex, TW18 4LG
Activities: Electrical installation
Parent: EDF Energy Services Limited
Officers: Michael Andrew Booth [1974] Director/Chief Financial Officer; Michael Edward Harris [1962] Director; Gautier Jacob [1974] Director [French]; Paul John Patrick Paul Kavanagh [1957] Director/Chief Executive [Irish]; John Joseph Kelly [1969] Commercial Director; Michael Kennedy [1956] Director/Chief Operations Officer [Irish]; William Alexander Sloan [1957] HR Director

ESSCI Technical Services Limited
Incorporated: 27 August 2015 *Employees:* 24
Net Worth Deficit: £2,349,000 *Total Assets:* £22,552,000
Registered Office: Twenty, Kingston Road, Staines upon Thames, Middlesex, TW18 4LG
Activities: Electrical installation
Parent: ESSCI Limited
Officers: Michael Andrew Booth [1974] Finance Director; Paul John Patrick Paul Kavanagh [1957] Director/Chief Executive [Irish]

Esselte Holdings Limited
Incorporated: 13 November 1978
Net Worth: £25,404,000 *Total Assets:* £25,404,000
Registered Office: Oxford House, Oxford Road, Aylesbury, Bucks, HP21 8SZ
Activities: Activities of head offices
Officers: Robert Michael Grimes, Secretary; Robert Michael Grimes [1980] Director/Barrister [Irish]; Katherine Alexandra Spence [1982] Director/Company Secretary

Essentra Components Limited
Incorporated: 6 April 1955 *Employees:* 350
Net Worth: £74,999,000 *Total Assets:* £94,762,000
Registered Office: Avebury House, 201-249 Avebury Boulevard, Milton Keynes, Bucks, MK9 1AU
Activities: Manufacture of other plastic products
Parent: Essentra International Limited
Officers: Jon Michael Green, Secretary; Scott Morgan Taylor Fawcett [1971] Director; Aamir Mohiuddin [1980] Director

Essentra Filter Products International Limited
Incorporated: 17 February 1945
Net Worth: £26,564,000 *Total Assets:* £54,970,000
Registered Office: Avebury House, 201-249 Avebury Boulevard, Milton Keynes, Bucks, MK9 1AU
Activities: Activities of head offices
Parent: ESNT Filter Products Limited
Officers: Tay Swee Choon George, Secretary; Tay Swee Choon George [1975] Director [Singaporean]; Robert William Pye [1964] Director [Australian]

Essentra Filter Products Limited
Incorporated: 1 October 1931 *Employees:* 23
Net Worth: £50,860,000 *Total Assets:* £52,233,000
Registered Office: Avebury House, 201-249 Avebury Boulevard, Milton Keynes, Bucks, MK9 1AU
Activities: Dormant company
Parent: Essentra Filter Products International Limited
Officers: Tay Swee Choon George, Secretary; Tay Swee Choon George [1975] Director [Singaporean]; Robert William Pye [1964] Director [Australian]

Essentra Finance Limited
Incorporated: 27 January 2005
Net Worth: £193,628,992 *Total Assets:* £1,269,492,992
Registered Office: Avebury House, 201-249 Avebury Boulevard, Milton Keynes, Bucks, MK9 1AU
Activities: Other business support service activities n.e.c.
Parent: Essentra International Limited
Officers: Patricia Kendall, Secretary; Jon Michael Green [1962] Director/Company Secretary & General Counsel; Lili Liu [1972] Director

Essentra International Limited
Incorporated: 5 June 1974 *Employees:* 72
Net Worth: £294,852,992 *Total Assets:* £478,504,000
Registered Office: Avebury House, 201-249 Avebury Boulevard, Milton Keynes, Bucks, MK9 1AU
Activities: Activities of head offices
Parent: Essentra PLC
Officers: Patricia Kendall, Secretary; Jon Michael Green [1962] Director/Solicitor; Lili Liu [1972] Director

Essentra Packaging & Security Limited
Incorporated: 2 June 2010 *Employees:* 462
Net Worth Deficit: £38,674,000 *Total Assets:* £59,358,000
Registered Office: Avebury House, 201-249 Avebury Boulevard, Milton Keynes, Bucks, MK9 1AU
Activities: Manufacture of plastic packing goods
Parent: ESNT Packaging & Securing Solutions Limited
Officers: Jon Michael Green, Secretary; Bradley Aaron Schechtman [1981] Director [American]; Robert Sykes [1970] Director; Timothy Kenneth Wilson [1960] Director [American]

Essentra Packaging Limited
Incorporated: 24 September 2012 *Employees:* 413
Net Worth: £48,198,000 *Total Assets:* £57,013,000
Registered Office: Avebury House, 201-249 Avebury Boulevard, Milton Keynes, Bucks, MK9 1AU
Activities: Manufacture of other plastic products
Parent: ESNT International Limited
Officers: Jon Michael Green, Secretary; Iain Philip Percival [1967] Director; Andrew Colin Riley [1967] Director

Essentra PLC
Incorporated: 5 May 2005 *Employees:* 8
Net Worth: £612,300,032 *Total Assets:* £1,239,699,968
Registered Office: Avebury House, 201-249 Avebury Boulevard, Milton Keynes, Bucks, MK9 1AU
Activities: Activities of head offices
Officers: Jon Michael Green, Secretary; Thomas Benedict Breen [1959] Director [Irish]; Paul Anthony Foreman [1965] Director/Chief Executive Officer; Paul John Lester [1949] Director; Lili Liu [1972] Director; Mary Reilly [1953] Director; Margaret Lorraine Trainer [1952] Director; Ralf Klaus Wunderlich [1966] Director/Senior Adviser [German]

Essentra Services Limited
Incorporated: 1 December 1976
Net Worth Deficit: £91,627,552 *Total Assets:* £22,337,610
Registered Office: Avebury House, 201-249 Avebury Boulevard, Milton Keynes, Bucks, MK9 1AU
Activities: Non-trading company
Parent: Essentra International Limited
Officers: Patricia Kendall, Secretary; Jon Michael Green [1962] Director/Company Secretary & General Counsel; Lili Liu [1972] Director

Esso Exploration and Production UK Limited
Incorporated: 22 July 1925
Net Worth: £880,000,000 *Total Assets:* £4,283,000,064
Registered Office: Ermyn House, Ermyn Way, Leatherhead, Surrey, KT22 8UX
Activities: Extraction of crude petroleum
Parent: Esso UK Limited
Officers: Fiona Harness, Secretary; Robert Michael Cooper [1961] Director/Oil Company Executive; Jay Loren Jackson [1962] Director/Oil Company Executive [American]

Esso Petroleum Company,Limited
Incorporated: 27 April 1888 *Employees:* 1,291
Net Worth: £1,264,000,000 *Total Assets:* £2,680,000,000
Registered Office: Ermyn House, Ermyn Way, Leatherhead, Surrey, KT22 8UX
Activities: Extraction of crude petroleum
Parent: ExxonMobil UK Limited
Officers: Fiona Harness, Secretary; Robert Michael Cooper [1961] Director/Oil Company Executive; Simon Peter Downing [1964] Director/Oil Company Executive

Esso UK Limited
Incorporated: 6 October 1981
Net Worth: £1,744,000,000 *Total Assets:* £3,028,000,000
Registered Office: Ermyn House, Ermyn Way, Leatherhead, Surrey, KT22 8UX
Activities: Extraction of crude petroleum
Parent: Exxon Mobil Corporation
Officers: Fiona Harness, Secretary; Robert Michael Cooper [1961] Director/Oil Company Executive; Simon Peter Downing [1964] Director/Oil Company Executive; Jay Loren Jackson [1962] Director/Oil Company Executive [American]

Esure Finance Limited
Incorporated: 3 November 2009
Net Worth: £276,559,008 *Total Assets:* £278,740,992
Registered Office: The Observatory, Castlefield Road, Reigate, Surrey, RH2 0SG
Activities: Other business support service activities n.e.c.
Parent: Esure Group PLC
Officers: Alice Rivers, Secretary; Darren Ogden [1967] Director/Interim Chief Executive Officer; David Francis Pitt [1968] Director; Peter John Wood [1946] Director/Company Chairman

Esure Group PLC
Incorporated: 3 November 2009
Net Worth: £96,500,000 *Total Assets:* £245,200,000
Registered Office: The Observatory, Castlefield Road, Reigate, Surrey, RH2 0SG
Activities: Activities of head offices
Officers: Alice Rivers, Secretary; Luca Bassi [1970] Director/Investment Professional [Italian]; Matthew George Alfred Bryant [1983] Director/Investment Professional; Shirley Jill Garrood [1957] Director; Stephen Anthony Long [1985] Director/Interim Chief Finance Officer; Philip Loughlin [1967] Managing Director [American]; Robin Marshall [1970] Managing Director; Darren Ogden [1967] Director/Interim Chief Executive Officer; Alan Martin Rubenstein [1956] Director; Peter Anderson Shaw [1959] Director; Peter John Wood [1946] Director/Company Chairman

Esure Holdings Limited
Incorporated: 9 March 1999
Net Worth: £237,027,008 *Total Assets:* £237,040,992
Registered Office: The Observatory, Reigate, Surrey, RH2 0SG
Activities: Activities of head offices
Parent: Esure Finance Limited
Officers: Alice Rivers, Secretary; Darren Ogden [1967] Director/Interim Chief Executive Officer; David Francis Pitt [1968] Director; Peter John Wood [1946] Director/Company Chairman

Esure Insurance Limited
Incorporated: 29 November 1999
Net Worth: £418,800,000 *Total Assets:* £1,716,000,000
Registered Office: The Observatory, Reigate, Surrey, RH2 0SG
Activities: Non-life insurance
Parent: Esure Holdings Limited
Officers: Alice Rivers, Secretary; Matthew George Alfred Bryant [1983] Director/Investment Professional; Shirley Jill Garrood [1957] Director; Stephen Anthony Long [1985] Director/Interim Chief Finance Officer; Darren Ogden [1967] Director/Interim Chief Executive Officer; David Francis Pitt [1968] Director; Alan Martin Rubenstein [1956] Director; Peter Anderson Shaw [1959] Director; Peter John Wood [1946] Director/Company Chairman

Esure Property Limited
Incorporated: 10 April 2000
Net Worth: £32,000,000 *Total Assets:* £34,014,000
Registered Office: The Observatory, Reigate, Surrey, RH2 0SG
Activities: Buying and selling of own real estate
Parent: Esure Insurance Limited
Officers: Alice Rivers, Secretary; Stephen Anthony Long [1985] Director/Interim Chief Finance Officer; Darren Ogden [1967] Director/Interim Chief Executive Officer

Esure Services Limited
Incorporated: 29 May 1987 *Employees:* 1,689
Net Worth: £22,200,000 *Total Assets:* £67,200,000
Registered Office: The Observatory, Reigate, Surrey, RH2 0SG
Activities: Financial intermediation not elsewhere classified
Shareholders: Esure Holdings Limited; Esure Holdings Limited
Officers: Alice Rivers, Secretary; Matthew George Alfred Bryant [1983] Director/Investment Professional; Stephen Anthony Long [1985] Director/Interim Chief Finance Officer; Darren Ogden [1967] Director/Interim Chief Executive Officer; David Francis Pitt [1968] Director; Peter John Wood [1946] Director/Company Chairman

Euro Alloys Limited
Incorporated: 26 February 1990 *Employees:* 14
Net Worth: £12,266,735 *Total Assets:* £79,417,480
Registered Office: 9th Floor, One Croydon, 12-16 Addiscombe Road, Croydon, Surrey, CR0 0XT
Activities: Wholesale of metals and metal ores
Major Shareholder: Alfredo Riviere
Officers: Stuart Reginald Brothers, Secretary; David Charles Hogan [1948] Director/Accountant; Kevin John Rhodes [1965] Director; Alfredo Luis Riviere Rodriguez [1969] Director [Italian]

Euro Food Brands Limited
Incorporated: 11 January 1991 *Employees:* 113
Net Worth: £18,186,880 *Total Assets:* £52,531,304
Registered Office: The Pinnacle, 170 Midsummer Boulevard, Milton Keynes, Bucks, MK9 1FE
Activities: Non-specialised wholesale of food, beverages and tobacco
Parent: E.F.B. Group Limited
Officers: Michael Adams [1956] Director; Stephen Charles Barlow [1956] Director/Chief Executive Officer; Peter John Butler [1966] Managing Director; Phil Gotch [1976] Financial Director; Brandon William Ransley [1965] Director/Solicitor

Euroforest Limited
Incorporated: 20 December 1973 *Employees:* 81
Net Worth: £9,993,000 *Total Assets:* £26,732,000
Registered Office: Mead House, Bentley, Farnham, Surrey, GU10 5HY
Activities: Support services to forestry
Shareholder: Allan Wilson Jenkinson
Officers: James Stuart Tollitt, Secretary; Richard Campbell Palmer [1959] Commercial Director; Graeme Andrew Ralph [1963] Director/Forester; Douglas Cameron Smith [1965] Director/Forester; David Symons [1961] Managing Director and Forester; James Stuart Tollitt [1971] Director/Accountant; Karl Fredrik Vendel Turzik [1971] Director/CEO Miller Graphics [Swedish]; Patricia Elsie Watson [1959] Director/Accountant; Ashley Williams [1958] Director/Forester

Europa Road Limited
Incorporated: 17 November 1975 *Employees:* 598
Previous: Europa Worldwide Logistics Ltd
Net Worth: £7,760,865 *Total Assets:* £46,527,488
Registered Office: Littlebrook DC1, Shield Road, Dartford, Kent, DA1 5UR
Activities: Freight transport by road
Parent: Europa Worldwide Group Limited
Officers: Robert William Gilbert Ross, Secretary; Andrew Neville Baxter [1975] Managing Director; Daniel Paul Cook [1974] Director; Dionne Redpath [1973] Director; Robert William Gilbert Ross [1982] Finance Director

Europa Worldwide Group Limited
Incorporated: 18 January 2007 *Employees:* 600
Previous: EWG Limited
Net Worth: £6,814,644 *Total Assets:* £45,062,596
Registered Office: Littlebrook DC1, Shield Road, Dartford, Kent, DA1 5UR
Activities: Activities of head offices
Major Shareholder: Andrew Neville Baxter
Officers: Robert William Gilbert Ross, Secretary; Andrew Neville Baxter [1975] Managing Director; Richard Stephen Litchfield [1976] IT Director; Carl John Potter [1959] HR and Facilities Director; Robert William Gilbert Ross [1982] Finance Director

European Glass Group Limited
Incorporated: 12 November 1998 *Employees:* 170
Net Worth: £26,233,812 *Total Assets:* £41,500,052
Registered Office: 168 Church Road, Hove, E Sussex, BN3 2DL
Activities: Other business support service activities n.e.c.
Shareholders: Farzana Johal; Manjit Singh Johal
Officers: Farzana Johal, Secretary; Farzana Johal [1951] Director; Manjit Singh Johal [1951] Director

European Investments (Cornwall) Holdings Limited
Incorporated: 7 April 2017
Net Worth Deficit: £6,142,855 *Total Assets:* £48,295,900
Registered Office: Beaufort Court, Egg Farm Lane, off Station Road, Kings Langley, Herts, WD4 8LR
Activities: Financial intermediation not elsewhere classified
Parent: The Renewables Infrastructure Group (UK) Investments Limited
Officers: Dominic James Hearth, Secretary; Steven William Hughes [1972] Global Support Services Director, UK&I - Commercial; Mitesh Raj Patel [1982] Director/Chartered Accountant; Tracy Jane Scott [1976] Director/Delivery Project Manager; Mark Christopher Wayment [1958] Director

European Investments (Cornwall) Limited
Incorporated: 13 April 2012
Net Worth: £2,565,519 *Total Assets:* £56,410,928
Registered Office: Beaufort Court, Egg Farm Lane, off Station Road, Kings Langley, Herts, WD4 8LR
Activities: Other business support service activities n.e.c.
Parent: European Investments (SCEL) Limited
Officers: Dominic Hearth, Secretary; Steven William Hughes [1972] Global Support Services Director, UK&I - Commercial; Mitesh Raj Patel [1982] Director/Chartered Accountant; Tracy Jane Scott [1976] Director/Delivery Project Manager; Mark Christopher Wayment [1958] Director

European Laminate Glass Limited
Incorporated: 12 April 1995
Net Worth: £9,379,434 *Total Assets:* £25,121,528
Registered Office: 168 Church Road, Hove, E Sussex, BN3 2DL
Activities: Non-specialised wholesale trade
Shareholders: Farzana Johal; Majit Singh Johal
Officers: Farzana Johal, Secretary; Manjit Singh Johal [1951] Director/Executive

European Toughened Glass (UK) Limited
Incorporated: 6 April 1994 *Employees:* 105
Net Worth: £21,601,008 *Total Assets:* £27,384,222
Registered Office: 168 Church Road, Hove, E Sussex, BN3 2DL
Activities: Non-specialised wholesale trade
Shareholders: Farzana Johal; Manjit Singh Johal
Officers: Farzana Johal, Secretary; Manjit Singh Johal [1951] Director

Eurovia Infrastructure Limited
Incorporated: 27 September 2010 *Employees:* 517
Net Worth: £41,622,944 *Total Assets:* £77,383,840
Registered Office: Albion House, Springfield Road, Horsham, W Sussex, RH12 2RW
Activities: Construction of roads and motorways
Parent: Eurovia UK Limited
Officers: Susan Mary Lysionek, Secretary; Christophe Gaetan Louis Ferrer [1983] Financial Director [French]; Paul Anthony Goosey [1973] Regional Director; John Patrick Riley [1967] Director; Philippe George Skegg [1981] Director; Scott Alexander Wardrop [1966] Director

Eurovia UK Limited
Incorporated: 4 January 1994 *Employees:* 2,636
Net Worth: £34,699,584 *Total Assets:* £187,143,040
Registered Office: Albion House, Springfield Road, Horsham, W Sussex, RH12 2RW
Activities: Construction of roads and motorways
Parent: Eurovia SAS
Officers: Susan Mary Lysionek, Secretary; Pierre Anjolras [1966] Director [French]; Ludovic Guy Lucien Demierre [1971] HR Director [French]; Patrick Jutier [1961] Director [French]; Patrick Octave Achille Sulliot [1959] Director/Executive Vice President [French]; Scott Alexander Wardrop [1966] Director

EUSA Pharma (UK) Limited
Incorporated: 26 November 2014 *Employees:* 51
Net Worth: £103,497,744 *Total Assets:* £152,351,008
Registered Office: Breakspear Park, Breakspear Way, Hemel Hempstead, Herts, HP2 4TZ
Activities: Wholesale of pharmaceutical goods
Parent: EUSA Pharma Holdco 2 (UK) Limited
Officers: Emma Jane Johnson [1981] Director; Dr. Dev Kumar [1974] Director/Head of Legal and Compliance; Lee Scot Morley [1970] Director; Bryan Geoffrey Morton [1955] Director

EUSA Pharma Holdco 1 (UK) Limited
Incorporated: 28 January 2015
Net Worth: £90,787,216 *Total Assets:* £116,354,376
Registered Office: Ground Floor, Breakspear Park, Breakspear Way, Hemel Hempstead, Herts, HP2 4TZ
Activities: Management consultancy activities other than financial management
Officers: Evis Hursever [1975] Director/Principal; Emma Jane Johnson [1981] Director; Lee Scot Morley [1970] Director; Petri Tapani Vainio [1959] Managing Director [Finnish]

EUSA Pharma Holdco 2 (UK) Limited
Incorporated: 29 January 2015
Net Worth: £116,352,608 *Total Assets:* £116,352,608
Registered Office: Ground Floor, Breakspear Park, Breakspear Way, Hemel Hempstead, Herts, HP2 4TZ
Activities: Management consultancy activities other than financial management
Officers: Emma Jane Johnson [1981] Director; Lee Scot Morley [1970] Director

M.P.Evans & Co Limited
Incorporated: 26 November 1941
Net Worth: £199,260,256 *Total Assets:* £273,184,192
Registered Office: 3 Clanricarde Gardens, Tunbridge Wells, Kent, TN1 1HQ
Activities: Activities of head offices
Parent: M.P. Evans Group PLC
Officers: Katya Baptista Irene Merrick, Secretary; Matthew Harrison Coulson [1973] Director/Accountant; Peter Edwin Hadsley-Chaplin [1957] Director; Tristan Robert Julian Price [1966] Director/Economist & Finance Professional

M.P. Evans Group PLC
Incorporated: 6 April 1981 *Employees:* 4,792
Net Worth: £289,264,032 *Total Assets:* £409,914,112
Registered Office: 3 Clanricarde Gardens, Tunbridge Wells, Kent, TN1 1HQ
Activities: Other business support service activities n.e.c.
Officers: Katya Baptista Irene Merrick, Secretary; Matthew Harrison Coulson [1973] Finance Director; Philip Anthony Fletcher [1950] Director/Chartered Accountant; John McDonald Green-Armytage [1945] Director; Peter Edwin Hadsley-Chaplin [1957] Director; Tristan Robert Julian Price [1966] Director/Economist & Finance Professional; Richard Michael Robinow [1945] Director; Bruce Christian Tozer [1959] Director

Evergreen Finance Limited
Incorporated: 8 March 1991 *Employees:* 7
Net Worth: £32,159,000 *Total Assets:* £33,140,000
Registered Office: No 1 Park Lane, Hemel Hempstead, Herts, HP2 4YL
Activities: Financial intermediation not elsewhere classified
Parent: Colaingrove Limited
Officers: Jane Elizabeth Bentall [1970] Director/Accountant; Paul Charles Flaum [1970] Director; Iain Stuart Macmillan [1976] Director

Every Child, Every Day Academy Trust
Incorporated: 20 August 2012 *Employees:* 385
Previous: Grey Court School
Net Worth: £67,949,216 *Total Assets:* £72,198,816
Registered Office: Grey Court School, Ham Street, Ham, Richmond upon Thames, Surrey, TW10 7HN
Activities: General secondary education
Officers: Neil Knox-Hall, Secretary; Robert Alexander [1959] Director/Accountant; Margaret Mary Michel Bernadette Bailey [1960] Director/Headteacher; David Bealing [1964] Commercial Director; Elaine England [1954] Director/Education Advisor; Donald Henry Farquharson [1954] Director; Dr Lorna Jillian Goodwin [1961] Academic Director; Anthony Francis Cloudsley Kitson [1958] Director/Civil Servant; Penny St Martin [1972] Director/HR Manager; Bill Watkin [1958] Director

Everyday Lending Limited
Incorporated: 19 June 2006
Net Worth: £46,343,000 *Total Assets:* £175,402,000
Registered Office: Secure Trust House, Boston Drive, Bourne End, Bucks, SL8 5YS
Activities: Activities of financial services holding companies
Parent: Everyday Loans Limited
Officers: Reena Patel, Secretary; Miles Marius Cresswell-Turner [1962] Director; Paul Gill [1971] Director/Chief Risk Officer; Marc Richard Howells [1965] Director; Peter Forbes Michael Reynolds [1966] Non Executive Director; Nicholas John Teunon [1966] Director; Steven Douglas White [1968] Director/Chief Financial Officer; Jon Wiggins [1967] Director

Everyday Loans Holdings Limited
Incorporated: 23 February 2006
Net Worth: £79,091,000 *Total Assets:* £79,091,000
Registered Office: Secure Trust House, Boston Drive, Bourne End, Bucks, SL8 5YS
Activities: Activities of head offices
Parent: Non-Standard Finance Subsidiary III Limited
Officers: Reena Patel, Secretary; Miles Marius Cresswell-Turner [1962] Director; Paul Gill [1971] Director/Chief Risk Officer; Marc Richard Howells [1965] Director; Peter Forbes Michael Reynolds [1966] Director; Nicholas John Teunon [1966] Director; Steven Douglas White [1968] Director/Chief Financial Officer; Jon Wiggins [1967] Director

Everyday Loans Limited
Incorporated: 15 August 2005 *Employees:* 299
Net Worth: £64,548,000 *Total Assets:* £73,633,000
Registered Office: Secure Trust House, Boston Drive, Bourne End, Bucks, SL8 5YS
Activities: Other business support service activities n.e.c.
Parent: Everyday Loans Holdings Limited
Officers: Reena Patel, Secretary; Miles Marius Cresswell-Turner [1962] Director; Paul Gill [1971] Director/Chief Risk Officer; Marc Richard Howells [1965] Director; Peter Forbes Michael Reynolds [1966] Director; Nicholas John Teunon [1966] Director; Steven Douglas White [1968] Director/Chief Financial Officer; Jon Wiggins [1967] Director

Evolution (Saffron Walden) LLP
Incorporated: 4 July 2016
Net Worth: £1,071,000 *Total Assets:* £36,010,000
Registered Office: Cowley Business Park, Cowley, Uxbridge, Middlesex, UB8 2AL

Evolution (Shinfield) LLP
Incorporated: 20 April 2015
Net Worth: £1,637,000 *Total Assets:* £56,992,000
Registered Office: Cowley Business Park, Cowley, Uxbridge, Middlesex, UB8 2AL

Evolution (Woking) Limited
Incorporated: 25 September 2013
Net Worth Deficit: £8,894,000 *Total Assets:* £43,064,000
Registered Office: Premier House, 52 London Road, Twickenham, Middlesex, TW1 3RP
Activities: Construction of domestic buildings
Parent: Evolution (Woking) Holdings Limited
Officers: Peter Nicholas Bowden [1968] Director; Howard Peter Dawson [1970] Housing Director; Stephen Noel King [1964] Finance Director; Karen Sheedy [1961] Director/Head of Treasury

Evolution Morpeth LLP
Incorporated: 11 June 2015
Net Worth: £699,000 *Total Assets:* £29,457,000
Registered Office: Cowley Business Park, Cowley, Uxbridge, Middlesex, UB8 2AL

Evolving Systems Holdings Limited
Incorporated: 28 October 2004 *Employees:* 2
Net Worth: £23,213,212 *Total Assets:* £26,885,484
Registered Office: 2nd Floor, 31 Chertsey Street, Guildford, Surrey, GU1 4HD
Activities: Activities of head offices
Parent: Evolving Systems, Inc.
Officers: Mark Paul Szynkowski, Secretary; Matthew Stecker [1968] Director [American]; Mark Paul Szynkowski [1968] Director/Chief Financial Officer [American]

Evonik Chemicals Limited
Incorporated: 13 February 1907 *Employees:* 64
Previous: Air Products (Chemicals) Limited
Net Worth: £90,934,000 *Total Assets:* £123,518,000
Registered Office: Tego House, Chippenham Drive, Kingston, Milton Keynes, Bucks, MK10 0AF
Activities: Manufacture of other organic basic chemicals
Parent: Evonik UK Holdings Limited
Officers: Geneva Angela Stapleton, Secretary; Anh TU Luu [1979] Director/Solicitor; Howard James Lynn [1968] Director/European Operations Manager; Dr Martina Pfirmann [1962] Director/Chemist [German]; Dr Dirk Reichel [1965] Director/Chemist [German]

Evonik Goldschmidt UK Limited
Incorporated: 5 October 1972 *Employees:* 14
Net Worth: £19,500,316 *Total Assets:* £20,582,184
Registered Office: Tego House, Chippenham Drive, Kingston, Milton Keynes, Bucks, MK10 0AF
Activities: Manufacture of soap and detergents
Parent: Evonik UK Holdings Limited
Officers: Geneva Angela Stapleton, Secretary; Clive Martin Gould [1956] Director/General Manager; Anh Luu [1979] Director/Legal Counsel

Evonik Speciality Organics Limited
Incorporated: 24 April 1992 *Employees:* 1
Net Worth: £270,348,288 *Total Assets:* £270,403,136
Registered Office: Tego House, Chippenham Drive, Kingston, Milton Keynes, Bucks, MK10 0AF
Activities: Activities of head offices
Parent: Evonik UK Holdings Limited
Officers: Geneva Angela Stapleton, Secretary; Matthias Kittler [1971] Director/Legal Counsel [German]; Anh TU Luu [1979] Director/Solicitor; Vera Iris Wruck [1969] Director/HR Partner [German]

Evonik UK Holdings Limited
Incorporated: 3 March 1992 *Employees:* 7
Previous: Evonik Degussa UK Holdings Limited
Net Worth: £665,363,712 *Total Assets:* £674,511,296
Registered Office: Tego House, Chippenham Drive, Kingston, Milton Keynes, Bucks, MK10 0AF
Activities: Activities of head offices
Parent: Evonik Industries AG
Officers: Geneva Angela Stapleton, Secretary; Julio Diniz Pereira de Almeida [1968] Director/Accountant [Brazilian]; Matthias Josef Peter Hau [1963] Director [German]; Anh TU Luu [1979] Director/Solicitor

EWDB Limited
Incorporated: 2 September 1987
Net Worth: £76,228,000 *Total Assets:* £78,486,000
Registered Office: Havas House, Hermitage Court, Hermitage Lane, Maidstone, Kent, ME16 9NT
Activities: Activities of head offices
Parent: Havas UK Limited
Officers: Allan John Ross, Secretary; Alan Ralston Adamson [1966] Director/Chief Financial Officer; Paul Francis Woodhouse [1955] Director/Accountant

EWOS Limited
Incorporated: 17 May 1982 *Employees:* 76
Net Worth: £36,955,000 *Total Assets:* £52,320,000
Registered Office: Velocity V1, Brooklands Drive, Weybridge, Surrey, KT13 0SL
Activities: Support activities for animal production (other than farm animal boarding)
Parent: Albain Bidco UK Limited
Officers: Dena Michelle L O'Bue, Secretary; David Morrice [1970] Country Director; Federico Urquidi Negron [1965] Director/UK & Ireland Country Controller [Spanish]

Exagon Industries Limited
Incorporated: 3 March 2016 *Employees:* 1
Net Worth: £1,299,392 *Total Assets:* £71,939,616
Registered Office: Charles Lake House, Claire Causeway, Crossways Business Park, Dartford, Kent, DA2 6QA
Activities: Research and experimental development on biotechnology
Major Shareholder: Fabrizio Tonna
Officers: Fabrizio Tonna [1964] Director [Italian]

Exagris Limited
Incorporated: 25 June 2007 *Employees:* 473
Net Worth Deficit: £30,325,998 *Total Assets:* £30,044,408
Registered Office: Amersham Court, 154 Station Road, Amersham, Bucks, HP6 5DW
Activities: Growing of cereals (except rice), leguminous crops and oil seeds
Major Shareholder: Carolyn Sian Lilley
Officers: Timothy John Deborde, Secretary; Timothy John de Borde [1966] Director/Accountant; Dr Carolyn Sian Lilley [1967] Director/Housewife; David George Plumer Lilley [1966] Director/Investment Manager

Exclaimer Group (Holdings) Limited
Incorporated: 29 July 2016 *Employees:* 6
Net Worth Deficit: £3,405,290 *Total Assets:* £21,588,340
Registered Office: Alpha House, 9-11 Alexandra Road, Farnborough, Hants, GU14 6BU
Activities: Dormant company
Parent: Exclaimer Group Limited
Officers: Robert David Ferguson [1960] Director; John Eric Hawkins [1953] Director; Simon Hollingsworth [1983] Director [Irish]; Duncan Neil Love [1969] Director; Daniel William Richardson [1969] Director; Amy Louise Yateman-Smith [1984] Director

Exclaimer Group Limited
Incorporated: 29 July 2016 *Employees:* 62
Net Worth Deficit: £3,152,820 *Total Assets:* £28,390,980
Registered Office: Alpha House, 9-11 Alexandra Road, Farnborough, Hants, GU14 6BU
Activities: Dormant company
Shareholder: Livingbridge GP LP
Officers: Robert David Ferguson [1960] Director; John Eric Hawkins [1953] Director; Simon Hollingsworth [1983] Director [Irish]; Duncan Neil Love [1969] Director; Andrew Deryck Millington [1963] Director/Sales Manager; Daniel William Richardson [1969] Director; Amy Louise Yateman-Smith [1984] Director

Exclusive Networks Limited
Incorporated: 22 February 1994 *Employees:* 157
Net Worth: £23,037,840 *Total Assets:* £89,261,792
Registered Office: Alresford House, Mill Lane, Alton, Hants, GU34 2QJ
Activities: Wholesale of computers, computer peripheral equipment and software
Parent: Exclusive Networks SAS
Officers: Graham Aynsley [1965] Director; Graham Paul Jones [1958] Director

Exel Holdings Limited
Incorporated: 30 June 1980
Net Worth: £66,122,000 *Total Assets:* £66,979,000
Registered Office: Ocean House, The Ring, Bracknell, Berks, RG12 1AN
Activities: Activities of head offices
Parent: Exel Investments Limited
Officers: Steven Fink [1975] Director; Thorsten Kuhl [1974] Director/Accountant [German]; Michael James Trimm [1968] Director; Dermot Francis Wooliscroft [1960] Director/Head of UK Tax

Exel Investments Limited
Incorporated: 27 November 1981
Net Worth: £96,200,000 *Total Assets:* £111,956,000
Registered Office: Ocean House, The Ring, Bracknell, Berks, RG12 1AN
Activities: Activities of head offices
Parent: Exel Limited
Officers: Thorsten Kuhl [1974] Director [German]; Kevin Paul Sey [1964] Director/Chartered Surveyor; Michael James Trimm [1968] Director/Accountant

Exel Limited
Incorporated: 6 June 1902
Net Worth: £497,331,008 *Total Assets:* £1,368,381,056
Registered Office: Ocean House, The Ring, Bracknell, Berks, RG12 1AN
Activities: Activities of head offices
Officers: Steven Fink [1975] Director/Lawyer; Henrik Hanche [1958] Director [German]; Thorsten Kuhl [1974] Director [German]; Jose Fernando Nava [1963] Director [American]; Jason David Smith [1967] Director/Financial Controller; Michael James Trimm [1968] Director/Accountant

Exel Logistics Property Limited
Incorporated: 24 October 1973
Net Worth: £109,495,000 *Total Assets:* £110,964,000
Registered Office: Ocean House, The Ring, Bracknell, Berks, RG12 1AN
Activities: Non-trading company
Officers: Kevin Paul Sey [1964] Director/Chartered Surveyor; Michael James Trimm [1968] Director/Accountant

Exel Overseas Limited
Incorporated: 15 July 1991
Net Worth: £132,048,520 *Total Assets:* £132,299,920
Registered Office: Ocean House, The Ring, Bracknell, Berks, RG12 1AN
Activities: Freight transport by road
Officers: Steven Fink [1975] Director/Solicitor; Thorsten Kuhl [1974] Director [German]; Michael James Trimm [1968] Director/Accountant

Exel UK Limited
Incorporated: 20 March 1963
Net Worth: £30,883,000 *Total Assets:* £48,120,000
Registered Office: Ocean House, The Ring, Bracknell, Berks, RG12 1AN
Activities: Freight transport by road
Parent: DHL Supply Chain Limited
Officers: Thorsten Kuhl [1974] Director [German]; Jose Fernando Nava [1963] Director [American]

Exela Technologies Limited
Incorporated: 27 October 1976 *Employees:* 536
Previous: BancTec Limited
Net Worth: £6,136,000 *Total Assets:* £46,578,000
Registered Office: Baronsmede, The Avenue, Egham, Surrey, TW20 9AB
Activities: Business and domestic software development
Parent: BTC International Holdings Inc
Officers: Jaymin Chhaya, Secretary; Jaymin Chhaya [1966] Director/Chartered Accountant; Stephen John Downey [1963] Managing Director

Exemplar Properties Limited
Incorporated: 11 July 2011 *Employees:* 9
Net Worth: £20,383,602 *Total Assets:* £25,309,252
Registered Office: c/o Lewis Brownlee, Appledram Barns, Birdham Road, Chichester, W Sussex, PO20 7EQ
Activities: Management of real estate on a fee or contract basis
Shareholders: Arbor Developments Ltd; Arbor Developments Ltd
Officers: Clive Dennis Bush [1969] Director/Surveyor

Exodus Travels Limited
Incorporated: 7 December 1973 *Employees:* 138
Net Worth: £10,085,000 *Total Assets:* £31,576,000
Registered Office: Origin One, 108 High Street, Crawley, W Sussex, RH10 1BD
Activities: Travel agency activities
Parent: Trek Investco Limited
Officers: Richard William Isaacs [1975] Director/Accountant; Samuel Michael Seward [1979] Managing Director

Expanded Limited
Incorporated: 4 May 2004
Net Worth: £35,632,000 *Total Assets:* £84,460,000
Registered Office: Bridge Place, Anchor Boulevard, Admirals Park, Crossways, Dartford, Kent, DA2 6SN
Activities: Activities of head offices
Parent: Laing O'Rourke Holdings Limited
Officers: Robert Edward Turner, Secretary; Matthew Clement Hugh Gill [1971] Director/Group Financial Controller; Declan James McGeeney [1978] Director/General Manager [Irish]; Alexander Stewart McIntyre [1956] Director; Hubert Desmond O'Rourke [1949] Director/Structural Engineer [Irish]

Expeditors International (UK) Limited
Incorporated: 18 December 1984 *Employees:* 550
Net Worth: £12,036,000 *Total Assets:* £101,461,000
Registered Office: 1 Ascot Road, Bedfont, Middlesex, TW14 8QH
Activities: Other transportation support activities
Parent: Expeditors International of Washington Inc
Officers: John Joseph Hayes, Secretary; Tim Barber [1959] Director/Business Executive [American]; Philip Michael Coughlin [1960] Director [American]; Jeffrey Scott Musser [1966] Managing Director [American]

Experis Group Limited
Incorporated: 28 September 1998 *Employees:* 5
Net Worth: £33,855,000 *Total Assets:* £46,643,000
Registered Office: Capital Court, Windsor Street, Uxbridge, Middlesex, UB8 1AB
Activities: Other information technology service activities
Parent: Manpower Public Limited Company
Officers: Mark Anthony Cahill [1958] Commercial Director; Mark Joseph Donnelly [1968] Finance Director; Stefano Scabbio [1964] Director [Italian]; Damian Paul Whitham [1967] Commercial Director

Exploration and Production Services (Holdings) Limited
Incorporated: 13 November 1979
Net Worth: £433,376,512 *Total Assets:* £1,684,684,544
Registered Office: Third Floor, 14-16 Cross Street, Reading, Berks, RG1 1SN
Activities: Activities of head offices
Parent: Expro International Group Limited
Officers: Clare O'Connell, Secretary; Gordon Michael Bentham [1962] Director; Lewis John Woodburn McAlister [1966] Director

Exploration Service Company Limited
Incorporated: 9 March 2000
Net Worth: £151,140,352 *Total Assets:* £151,240,768
Registered Office: Chertsey Road, Sunbury on Thames, Middlesex, TW16 7BP
Activities: Activities of head offices
Parent: BP Global Investments Limited
Officers: Terence Michael Thornton [1963] Director/Oil Company Executive; David Jozef Vermylen [1972] Director/Oil Company Executive [Belgian]

Explore Manufacturing Limited
Incorporated: 26 July 2000
Net Worth Deficit: £22,223,000 *Total Assets:* £41,435,000
Registered Office: Bridge Place, Anchor Boulevard, Admirals Park, Crossways, Dartford, Kent, DA2 6SN
Activities: Construction of commercial buildings
Parent: R O'Rourke & Son Limited
Officers: Robert Edward Turner, Secretary; Stephen John Harley [1951] Director; Alexander Stewart McIntyre [1956] Director; Paul William McNerney [1977] Director/Business Unit Leader

Explorer Holdings UK Limited
Incorporated: 7 December 2006
Net Worth: £27,000,000 *Total Assets:* £29,000,000
Registered Office: Breakspear Park, Breakspear Way, Hemel Hempstead, Herts, HP2 4TZ
Activities: Other information technology service activities
Parent: JDM Technology Group Limited
Officers: James Douglas McFarlane [1950] Director [Canadian]

Expro Benelux Limited
Incorporated: 11 March 2008
Net Worth: £188,439,776 *Total Assets:* £188,439,776
Registered Office: Third Floor, 14-16 Cross Street, Reading, Berks, RG1 1SN
Activities: Activities of head offices
Parent: Exploration and Production Services (Holdings) Limited
Officers: Clare O'Connell, Secretary; Gordon Michael Bentham [1962] Director; Lewis John Woodburn McAlister [1966] Director

Expro Eurasia Limited
Incorporated: 13 February 2004 *Employees:* 146
Net Worth: £36,202,400 *Total Assets:* £40,054,172
Registered Office: Third Floor, 14-16 Cross Street, Reading, Berks, RG1 1SN
Activities: Support activities for petroleum and natural gas mining
Parent: Exploration and Production Services (Holdings) Limited
Officers: Clare O'Connell, Secretary; Gordon Michael Bentham [1962] Director; Lewis John Woodburn McAlister [1966] Director; Neil Ronald Sims [1965] Director

Expro Holdings UK 3 Limited
Incorporated: 4 February 2008
Net Worth: £802,823,744 *Total Assets:* £804,689,088
Registered Office: Third Floor, 14-16 Cross Street, Reading, Berks, RG1 1SN
Activities: Activities of head offices
Parent: Expro Holdings UK 2 Limited
Officers: Lewis John Woodburn McAlister, Secretary; Gordon Michael Bentham [1962] Director; Michael David Jardon [1969] Director [American]; Lewis John Woodburn McAlister [1966] Director

Expro Holdings UK 4 Limited
Incorporated: 5 November 2007
Net Worth: £235,241,120 *Total Assets:* £609,754,688
Registered Office: Third Floor, 14-16 Cross Street, Reading, Berks, RG1 1SN
Activities: Activities of head offices
Parent: Expro Holdings UK 3 Limited
Officers: Clare O'Connell, Secretary; Gordon Michael Bentham [1962] Director; Lewis John Woodburn McAlister [1966] Director

Expro International Group Limited
Incorporated: 19 February 1992
Net Worth: £368,718,848 *Total Assets:* £368,718,848
Registered Office: Third Floor, 14-16 Cross Street, Reading, Berks, RG1 1SN
Activities: Activities of head offices
Parent: Expro Holdings UK 4 Limited
Officers: Clare O'Connell, Secretary; Gordon Michael Bentham [1962] Director; Lewis John Woodburn McAlister [1966] Director

Expro North Sea Limited
Incorporated: 12 April 1973 *Employees:* 943
Net Worth: £89,594,096 *Total Assets:* £183,028,976
Registered Office: Third Floor, 14-16 Cross Street, Reading, Berks, RG1 1SN
Activities: Support activities for petroleum and natural gas mining
Parent: Exploration and Production Services (Holdings) Limited
Officers: Clare O'Connell, Secretary; Alistair George Sinclair Geddes [1962] Director; Lewis John Woodburn McAlister [1966] Director; Ian James Robb [1959] Director; Neil Ronald Sims [1965] Director

Expro Resources Limited
Incorporated: 7 April 2008
Net Worth: £15,617,573 *Total Assets:* £31,907,536
Registered Office: Third Floor, 14-16 Cross Street, Reading, Berks, RG1 1SN
Activities: Renting and leasing of other machinery, equipment and tangible goods n.e.c.
Parent: Exploration and Production Services (Holdings) Limited
Officers: Clare O'Connell, Secretary; Gordon Michael Bentham [1962] Director; Lewis John Woodburn McAlister [1966] Director

ExxonMobil Chemical Investment Company Limited
Incorporated: 7 October 2016
Net Worth: £860,182,976 *Total Assets:* £1,466,121,984
Registered Office: Ermyn House, Ermyn Way, Leatherhead, Surrey, KT22 8UX
Activities: Other business support service activities n.e.c.
Parent: Esso Exploration and Production UK Limited
Officers: Fiona Henderson Harness, Secretary; Robert Michael Cooper [1961] Director/Oil Company Executive; Andrew Mark Johnson [1976] Director/Oil Company Executive; Steven Adam Oldfield [1972] Director/Oil Company Executive

ExxonMobil Chemical Limited
Incorporated: 21 December 1965 *Employees:* 512
Net Worth: £366,000,000 *Total Assets:* £502,000,000
Registered Office: Ermyn House, Ermyn Way, Leatherhead, Surrey, KT22 8UX
Activities: Manufacture of other organic basic chemicals
Parent: ExxonMobil Chemical Investment Company Limited
Officers: Fiona Harness, Secretary; Richard Robert Henderson [1966] Director/Oil Company Executive; Larry Jacob McAlister [1978] Director/Oil Company Executive [American]

ExxonMobil Finance Company Limited
Incorporated: 26 November 2004
Net Worth: £182,122,480 *Total Assets:* £3,412,931,840
Registered Office: Ermyn House, Ermyn Way, Leatherhead, Surrey, KT22 8UX
Activities: Other business support service activities n.e.c.
Parent: ExxonMobil Investment Company Limited
Officers: Fiona Harness, Secretary; Robert Michael Cooper [1961] Director/Oil Company Executive; Andrew Mark Johnson [1976] Director/Oil Company Executive; Steven Adam Oldfield [1972] Director/Oil Company Executive

ExxonMobil Financial Investment Company Limited
Incorporated: 7 December 2016
Net Worth: £226,104,976 *Total Assets:* £2,254,188,544
Registered Office: Ermyn House, Ermyn Way, Leatherhead, Surrey, KT22 8UX
Activities: Other business support service activities n.e.c.
Parent: ExxonMobil Finance Company Limited
Officers: Fiona Henderson Harness, Secretary; Robert Michael Cooper [1961] Director/Oil Company Executive; Andrew Mark Johnson [1976] Director/Oil Company Executive; Steven Adam Oldfield [1972] Director/Oil Company Executive

ExxonMobil Gas Marketing Europe Limited
Incorporated: 1 July 1990
Net Worth: £182,000,000 *Total Assets:* £392,000,000
Registered Office: Ermyn House, Ermyn Way, Leatherhead, Surrey, KT22 8UX
Activities: Wholesale of other fuels and related products
Parent: ExxonMobil UK Limited
Officers: Fiona Henderson Harness, Secretary; Stefan Ihnen [1966] Director/Oil Company Executive [German]; Alex Volkov [1972] Director/Oil Company Executive [American]

ExxonMobil Holding Company Limited
Incorporated: 6 June 2013
Net Worth: £16,606,653,440 *Total Assets:* £18,504,316,928
Registered Office: Ermyn House, Ermyn Way, Leatherhead, Surrey, KT22 8UX
Activities: Other business support service activities n.e.c.
Shareholder: Exxon Mobil Corporation
Officers: Fiona Henderson Harness, Secretary; Robert Michael Cooper [1961] Director/Oil Company Executive; Andrew Mark Johnson [1976] Director/Oil Company Executive; Steven Adam Oldfield [1972] Director/Oil Company Executive

ExxonMobil International Limited
Incorporated: 1 September 1999 *Employees:* 252
Net Worth: £138,574,000 *Total Assets:* £149,532,000
Registered Office: Ermyn House, Ermyn Way, Leatherhead, Surrey, KT22 8UX
Activities: Extraction of crude petroleum
Parent: Esso UK Limited
Officers: Fiona Harness, Secretary; Robert Michael Cooper [1961] Director/Oil Company Executive; Jay Loren Jackson [1962] Director/Oil Company Executive [American]

ExxonMobil Investment Company Limited
Incorporated: 26 November 2004
Net Worth: £493,449,216 *Total Assets:* £964,005,312
Registered Office: Ermyn House, Ermyn Way, Leatherhead, Surrey, KT22 8UX
Activities: Other business support service activities n.e.c.
Parent: Exxon Mobil Corporation
Officers: Fiona Harness, Secretary; Robert Michael Cooper [1961] Director/Oil Company Executive; Andrew Mark Johnson [1976] Director/Oil Company Executive; Steven Adam Oldfield [1972] Director/Oil Company Executive

ExxonMobil Marine Limited
Incorporated: 20 December 1999 *Employees:* 4
Net Worth: £2,204,000 *Total Assets:* £152,302,000
Registered Office: Ermyn House, Ermyn Way, Leatherhead, Surrey, KT22 8UX
Activities: Mineral oil refining
Parent: ExxonMobil UK Limited
Officers: Fiona Harness, Secretary; Frans Bert Horjus [1967] Director/Oil Company Executive [Dutch]; Andrew Mark Johnson [1976] Director/Oil Company Executive; Luca Volta [1969] Director/Oil Company Executive [Italian]; Iain White [1962] Director/Oil Company Executive

ExxonMobil UK Limited
Incorporated: 15 December 1999
Net Worth: £881,830,976 *Total Assets:* £882,305,984
Registered Office: Ermyn House, Ermyn Way, Leatherhead, Surrey, KT22 8UX
Activities: Other business support service activities n.e.c.
Parent: Esso UK Limited
Officers: Fiona Harness, Secretary; Robert Michael Cooper [1961] Director/Oil Company Executive; Andrew Mark Johnson [1976] Director/Oil Company Executive; Steven Adam Oldfield [1972] Director/Oil Company Executive

F.M. Insurance Company Limited
Incorporated: 29 March 1963 *Employees:* 702
Net Worth: £626,254,976 *Total Assets:* £1,635,216,000
Registered Office: 1 Windsor Dials, Arthur Road, Windsor, Berks, SL4 1RS
Activities: Non-life insurance
Officers: Amy Kelly, Secretary; Rachel Cope [1973] Finance Director; Jonathan William Hall [1957] Director/Executive Vice President [American]; Omar Farooq Hameed [1968] Director/Corporate Counsel; Kevin Scott Ingram [1962] Director [American]; Christopher Johnson [1956] Director/Insurance Company Executive; Philip Johnson [1965] Director/Insurance Executive; Thomas Stephen Keevil [1960] Director/General Counsel and Company Secretary; Thomas Alan Lawson [1956] Director/Executive Vice President [American]; Natalie Spotswood [1985] Legal Director; Stefano Tranquillo [1957] Director/Business Executive; Peter Charles Wilson [1946] Director/Management Consultant

F5 Networks Limited
Incorporated: 26 July 1999 *Employees:* 383
Net Worth: £112,087,384 *Total Assets:* £363,392,096
Registered Office: Chertsey Gate West, 43-47 London Street, Chertsey, Surrey, KT16 8AP
Activities: Other information technology service activities
Parent: F5 Networks, Inc.
Officers: Steven Irving Grieger [1963] Director [American]; Scot Frazier Rogers [1967] Director/Executive Vice President, General Counsel [American]; Kunwarjit Suri [1966] Director/EMEA Corporate Controller; Chad Michael Whalen [1971] Director [American]

Faber Prest Limited
Incorporated: 29 July 1892
Net Worth: £43,625,916 *Total Assets:* £61,003,836
Registered Office: Harsco House, Regent Park, 299 Kingston Road, Leatherhead, Surrey, KT22 7SG
Activities: Activities of head offices
Parent: Harsco Metals Group Limited
Officers: Christopher Claude Lashmer Whistler, Secretary; Stephen Richard Cooper [1966] Director/Accountant; Christopher Claude Lashmer Whistler [1958] Director/Accountant

Facelift (GB) Limited
Incorporated: 15 September 1986 *Employees:* 134
Net Worth: £4,114,967 *Total Assets:* £20,800,388
Registered Office: Westside, London Road, Hickstead, W Sussex, RH17 5LZ
Activities: Renting and leasing of construction and civil engineering machinery and equipment
Major Shareholder: Gordon Charles Leicester
Officers: Michael Francis Edwards [1950] Director; Paul Standing [1981] Operations Director

Factory Services UK Limited
Incorporated: 4 March 2005 *Employees:* 154
Net Worth: £14,136,343 *Total Assets:* £28,332,676
Registered Office: Unit 8 Minster Court, Tuscam Way, Camberley, Surrey, GU15 3YY
Activities: Manufacture of prepared feeds for farm animals
Parent: Sugarich Limited
Officers: Christopher John Houghton, Secretary; Paul Richard Bright [1976] Director; Paul Anthony Featherstone [1965] Director; Nicholas Alexander Keogh [1979] Commercial Director; John Stephen Knight [1957] Director; Andrew Charles Newton [1969] Director

Fairfax Acquisitions Limited
Incorporated: 30 December 2004 *Employees:* 3
Net Worth Deficit: £5,449,505 *Total Assets:* £35,041,592
Registered Office: Buncton Barn, Buncton Lane, Bolney, Haywards Heath, W Sussex, RH17 5RE
Activities: Construction of domestic buildings
Parent: Fairfax Classical Properties Limited
Officers: Jon Peter Ball [1973] Director/Builder; James Benbow [1980] Director; Derek Evan Jacobson [1979] Director [Canadian]

Faithdean PLC
Incorporated: 15 September 1978 *Employees:* 144
Net Worth: £15,670,669 *Total Assets:* £39,278,256
Registered Office: Unit 12 The Oaks, Revenge Road, Lordswood, Chatham, Kent, ME5 8LF
Activities: Floor and wall covering
Major Shareholder: David Malcolm South
Officers: Stephen John Hocking, Secretary; Robert Spencer Davie [1965] Director; Andrew Robert Fraser [1971] Director; Anthony Steven Groves [1972] Director; Stephen Hodges [1968] Director; Christopher David South [1979] Director; David Malcolm South [1950] Director

Faithful+Gould Limited
Incorporated: 28 March 1988 *Employees:* 1,286
Net Worth: £62,140,000 *Total Assets:* £100,931,000
Registered Office: Woodcote Grove, Ashley Road, Epsom, Surrey, KT18 5BW
Activities: Management consultancy activities other than financial management
Parent: Faithful+Gould (Holdings) Limited
Officers: Louise Mary McAllister, Secretary; Elliot Michael Nobelen, Secretary; Mark Stephen Anderson [1965] Director/Accountant; Adam Brooks [1965] Director/Chartered Surveyor; Neil William Clemson [1962] Director/Project Manager; Simon Glenister Cole [1965] Director/Accountant; Andrew Stephen Constable [1957] Director/Chartered Quantity Surveyor; Alan James Cullens [1963] Group HR Director; Nicholas Kenneth Gray [1966] Director/Chartered Quantity Surveyor; Andrew Clifford Green [1959] Director/Surveyor; Jonathan Mark Sealy [1966] Director/Chartered Surveyor; John Wood [1957] Director/Quantity Surveyor

Falck UK Limited
Incorporated: 23 January 2008
Net Worth: £17,251,576 *Total Assets:* £22,175,792
Registered Office: Walker House, George Street, Aylesbury, Bucks, HP20 2HU
Activities: Other human health activities
Parent: Falck Holding A/S
Officers: Jesper Aunbol [1970] Director [Danish]; Jakob Just Bomholt [1974] Director [Danish]; Stig Tiedemann [1959] Director [Danish]

Falcon Acquisitions Limited
Incorporated: 4 May 2007
Net Worth: £256,000 *Total Assets:* £154,747,008
Registered Office: 12 Bugle Street, Southampton, SO14 2JY
Activities: Non-trading company
Parent: Red Funnel Limited
Officers: Michael Francis Campbell [1956] Director [Canadian]; Frances Charlotte Collins [1977] Director/Chief Executive Officer; Kevin Alan George [1956] Director/Chief Executive; Charles John Gore Hazelwood [1963] Director; Edward Arthur Wilson [1965] Director; Paul Richard Winter [1963] Director/Accountant

Falcon Coffees Limited
Incorporated: 9 May 2014 *Employees:* 24
Net Worth: £6,252,904 *Total Assets:* £22,163,182
Registered Office: 25 High Street, Lewes, E Sussex, BN7 2LU
Activities: Wholesale of coffee, tea, cocoa and spices
Shareholder: Scott Thomas Ford
Officers: Konrad Edward Brits [1969] Director/Chief Executive Officer; Scott Thomas Ford [1962] Director [American]; Helen Marshall [1983] Director/Accountant; Thomas Christopher Pledger [1973] Director/Attorney [American]; Matthew Cole Smith [1981] Director/Coffee Trader [American]

Family Capital Limited
Incorporated: 1 November 2016
Net Worth: £46,848,484 *Total Assets:* £116,953,088
Registered Office: Sussex House, North Street, Horsham, W Sussex, RH12 1RQ
Activities: Activities auxiliary to financial intermediation n.e.c.
Major Shareholder: Ian Robert Cooke
Officers: Ian Robert Cooke [1968] Director

Famous Brands UK Limited
Incorporated: 30 March 2002
Net Worth: £3,720,000 *Total Assets:* £20,426,000
Registered Office: 2 The Listons, Liston Road, Marlow, Bucks, SL7 1FD
Activities: Activities of head offices
Parent: Venus Solutions Limited
Officers: Adele Susanne Conradie, Secretary; Darren Paul Hele [1971] Director; Kelebogile Ntlha [1982] Finance Director [South African]

George Farmiloe & Sons Limited
Incorporated: 18 November 1897 *Employees:* 3
Net Worth: £25,299,358 *Total Assets:* £25,801,146
Registered Office: 12a Fleet Business Park, Sandy Lane, Church Crookham, Fleet, Hants, GU52 8BF
Activities: Other letting and operating of own or leased real estate
Parent: George Farmiloe & Sons Holdings Ltd
Officers: Roy Alastair Meakin Farmiloe [1923] Director; Timothy Leslie Charles Farmiloe [1959] Director; Maike Heining [1974] Development Director [German]

Farnborough Finance (2007) Limited
Incorporated: 4 December 2007
Net Worth: £46,380,404 *Total Assets:* £46,380,404
Registered Office: Spectrum Point, 279 Farnborough Road, Farnborough, Hants, GU14 7NJ
Activities: Activities of head offices
Shareholders: Hogg Robinson Switzerland Limited; HRG Debtco Limited
Officers: Aymeric Gibon [1980] Director/Vice President [French]

Farnborough Limited
Incorporated: 17 April 2000
Net Worth: £62,751,808 *Total Assets:* £383,839,872
Registered Office: Spectrum Point, 279 Farnborough Road, Farnborough, Hants, GU14 7NJ
Activities: Activities of head offices
Parent: HRG Debtco Limited
Officers: Aymeric Gibon [1980] Director/Vice President [French]; Sheena Varma [1980] Director/Senior Counsel, EMEA

Fast Holdings Limited
Incorporated: 25 June 2001
Net Worth Deficit: £9,628,000 *Total Assets:* £74,227,000
Registered Office: P O Box 87, Warwick House, Farnborough Aerospace Centre, Farnborough, Hants, GU14 6YU
Activities: Activities of other holding companies n.e.c.
Shareholders: BAE Systems Surface Ships (Holdings) Limited; L3 Mapps Limited
Officers: Ann-Louise Holding, Secretary; Roger Clive Baker [1957] Director; Leslie Ian Gregory [1957] Director; Rangesh Kasturi [1961] Director [Canadian]; Nicholas Newman Scroggie [1970] Director; James Neil Stewart [1963] Director; Matthew Steven Weingast [1965] Director [American]

Fast Training Services Limited
Incorporated: 24 January 2000
Net Worth Deficit: £9,736,000 *Total Assets:* £74,227,000
Registered Office: P O Box 87, Warwick House, Farnborough Aerospace Centre, Farnborough, Hants, GU14 6YU
Activities: Other education n.e.c.
Parent: Fast Holdings Limited
Officers: Ann-Louise Holding, Secretary; Leslie Ian Gregory [1957] Director; Rangesh Kasturi [1961] Director [Canadian]

Fasttrax Holdings Limited
Incorporated: 30 November 2001 *Employees:* 4
Net Worth: £8,827,000 *Total Assets:* £44,718,000
Registered Office: Hill Park Court, Springfield Drive, Leatherhead, Surrey, KT22 7NL
Activities: Activities of other holding companies n.e.c.
Parent: Kellogg Brown & Root Limited
Officers: Larry Jay Henry, Secretary/Director [American]; Richard Sean Card [1961] Project Director; John Ivor Cavill [1972] Director; Larry Jay Henry [1953] Director [American]; Peter John Sheldrake [1959] Director

Fasttrax Limited
Incorporated: 12 May 1998 *Employees:* 4
Net Worth: £8,821,000 *Total Assets:* £44,712,000
Registered Office: Hill Park Court, Springfield Drive, Leatherhead, Surrey, KT22 7NL
Activities: Manufacture of bodies (coachwork) for motor vehicles (except caravans)
Parent: Fasttrax Holdings Limited
Officers: Larry Jay Henry, Secretary/Director [American]; Richard Sean Card [1961] Project Director; John Ivor Cavill [1972] Director; Larry Jay Henry [1953] Director [American]; Peter John Sheldrake [1959] Director

Fat Face Holdings Limited
Incorporated: 13 January 2000
Net Worth: £142,807,008 *Total Assets:* £143,342,000
Registered Office: Unit 3 Ridgway, Havant, Hants, PO9 1QJ
Activities: Activities of head offices
Parent: Fatface Group Borrowings Limited
Officers: William John Milton Crumbie [1979] Finance Director

Fat Face Limited
Incorporated: 2 August 1994 *Employees:* 2,656
Net Worth: £156,564,992 *Total Assets:* £333,780,000
Registered Office: Unit 3 Ridgway, Havant, Hants, PO9 1QJ
Activities: Retail sale of clothing in specialised stores
Parent: Fat Face Holdings Limited
Officers: William John Milton Crumbie [1979] Finance Director

Fatface Group Borrowings Limited
Incorporated: 3 February 2014
Net Worth Deficit: £102,916,000 *Total Assets:* £289,091,008
Registered Office: Unit 3 Ridgway, Havant, Hants, PO9 1QJ
Activities: Activities of head offices
Parent: Fatface Group Parent Limited
Officers: William John Milton Crumbie [1979] Finance Director

Fatface Group Limited
Incorporated: 9 March 2007 *Employees:* 2,705
Net Worth Deficit: £14,266,000 *Total Assets:* £224,748,992
Registered Office: Unit 3 Ridgway, Havant, Hants, PO9 1QJ
Activities: Activities of head offices
Parent: Bridgepoint Europe III (GP) Limited
Officers: Benoit Nicolas Andre Alteirac [1978] Director/Venture Capitalist [French]; William John Milton Crumbie [1979] Finance Director; Patrick Adam Charles Fox [1958] Director; Simon John Greene [1961] Director; Sir Lord Rose [1949] Director; Mark Nigel Seager [1972] HR Director

Fatface Group Parent Limited
Incorporated: 12 June 2014
Net Worth: £284,577,984 *Total Assets:* £284,577,984
Registered Office: Unit 3 Ridgway, Havant, Hants, PO9 1QJ
Activities: Activities of head offices
Parent: Fatface Group Limited
Officers: William John Milton Crumbie [1979] Finance Director

Fawley Waterside Limited
Incorporated: 10 December 2014
Net Worth Deficit: £7,992,000 *Total Assets:* £28,181,000
Registered Office: The Estate Office, Stanswood Farm, Stanswood Road, Fawley, Southampton, SO45 1AB
Activities: Development of building projects
Officers: Honourable William Waldorf Astor [1979] Director; Aldred Robert Alexander Drummond [1978] Director; Timothy Piers Bennett Phillips [1969] Director/Chartered Accountant

FBG Holdings (UK) Limited
Incorporated: 16 July 1986
Net Worth: £74,747,000 *Total Assets:* £74,748,000
Registered Office: Ab InBev House, Church Street West, Woking, Surrey, GU21 6HT
Activities: Activities of head offices
Parent: Carlton and United Breweries Holdings (UK) Limited
Officers: Kevin Jean-Frederic Douws [1982] Director [Belgian]; Sibil Jiang [1990] Director [Australian]; Stephen John Turner [1966] Director/Accountant

FBL Holdings Limited
Incorporated: 20 June 2008
Net Worth Deficit: £30,647,000 *Total Assets:* £75,101,000
Registered Office: 9th Floor, Regal House, 70 London Road, Twickenham, Middlesex, TW1 3QS
Activities: Manufacture of wine from grape
Parent: Treasury Wine Estates EMEA Limited
Officers: Michelle Elizabeth Brampton [1972] Finance Director; Richard John Renwick [1969] Director/Chief Financial Officer Europe

FCA Automotive Services UK Ltd
Incorporated: 14 August 1992 *Employees:* 117
Previous: FGA Capital UK Ltd
Net Worth: £273,592,992 *Total Assets:* £1,684,007,936
Registered Office: Fiat House, 240 Bath Road, Slough, Berks, SL1 4DX
Activities: Financial leasing
Shareholders: Credit Agricole SA; Fiat Chrysler Automobiles N.V.
Officers: Peter John Farley, Secretary/Lawyer; Giacomo Carelli [1972] Director [Italian]; Anne Marie Guirchoux [1966] Director [French]; Alexander Paul Hughes [1976] Director; Sriram Krishnamoorthy [1970] Director/Motor Executive; Raffaella Papa [1969] Director/Motor Executive [Italian]

FCA Dealer Services UK Ltd
Incorporated: 22 October 2002 *Employees:* 8
Previous: FGA Wholesale UK Ltd
Net Worth: £50,251,000 *Total Assets:* £343,659,008
Registered Office: Fiat House, 240 Bath Road, Slough, Berks, SL1 4DX
Activities: Financial leasing
Shareholders: Credit Agricole SA; Fiat Chrysler Automobiles N.V.
Officers: Peter John Farley, Secretary; Christopher Thomas Duckworth [1960] Director; Alexander Paul Hughes [1976] Director; Alain Juan [1960] Director/Motor Executive [French]; Andrea Pertica [1971] Director/Motor Executive [Italian]

Feilo Sylvania Europe Limited
Incorporated: 9 June 1992 *Employees:* 117
Previous: Havells Sylvania Europe Ltd
Net Worth: £23,259,816 *Total Assets:* £200,551,376
Registered Office: Avis Way, Newhaven, E Sussex, BN9 0ED
Activities: Manufacture of electric lighting equipment
Officers: Bridget Helen Anderson [1958] Director; Matthew Carpenter [1967] SBU Director; Christopher John Harrild [1967] Director; Richard James Turner [1969] Director; Xintao Yin [1980] Director [Chinese]

John E.Fells & Sons Limited
Incorporated: 1 May 1920 *Employees:* 50
Net Worth: £10,591,224 *Total Assets:* £27,073,200
Registered Office: Fells House, Station Road, Kings Langley, Herts, WD4 8LH
Activities: Wholesale of wine, beer, spirits and other alcoholic beverages
Parent: Atlantis Wine Holdings Ltd
Officers: Louise Catherine Rimes, Secretary; Alan Robert Campbell [1962] Sales Director; Nicholas John Gurney [1970] Director/Certified Chartered Accountant; Robert Wyndham Hill-Smith [1951] Managing Director [Australian]; Stephen Antony Moody [1960] Managing Director; John Andrew Douglas Symington [1960] Director/Port Producer; Paul Douglas Symington [1953] Director/Port Producer; Edward Jared MacLeod Thornton [1965] Development Director; Simon William Michael Thorpe [1966] Commercial Director; Miguel Torres Maczassek [1974] Director [Spanish]

Feltham Group Limited
Incorporated: 10 July 2003 *Employees:* 107
Net Worth: £8,614,006 *Total Assets:* £25,350,444
Registered Office: Feltham House, 42 London Road, Newbury, Berks, RG14 1LA
Activities: Activities of head offices
Shareholders: David Stuart Yates; Andrew Barrie Brown
Officers: David Stuart Yates, Secretary; Andrew Barrie Brown [1966] Director/Chartered Builder; Leigh James Cameron [1958] Construction Director; Richard John Collins [1972] Director/Surveyor; Christopher Iain Herman [1974] Director/Surveyor; Simon Cormell Lampard [1967] Construction Director; Peter Stephen Malone [1974] Director/Surveyor; David Stuart Yates [1966] Director/Surveyor

Femcare Group Limited
Incorporated: 8 June 2004
Net Worth: £727,642 *Total Assets:* £21,354,664
Registered Office: Femcare UK, 32 Premier Way, Romsey, Hants, SO51 9DQ
Activities: Activities of head offices
Parent: Utah Medical Products, Inc.
Officers: Kevin Leighton Cornwell [1946] Director [American]; Brian Lee Koopman [1970] Director [American]

Femcare Limited
Incorporated: 3 October 1988 *Employees:* 14
Previous: Femcare - Nikomed Limited
Net Worth: £28,686,804 *Total Assets:* £38,999,036
Registered Office: Femcare UK, 32 Premier Way, Romsey, Hants, SO51 9DQ
Activities: Manufacture of medical and dental instruments and supplies
Shareholders: Femcare Group Limited; Utah Medical Products, Inc.
Officers: Kevin Leighton Cornwell [1946] Director [American]; Paul Michael Hill [1962] Director/Logistics Manager; Brian Lee Koopman [1970] Director [American]

Claude Fenton (Holdings) Limited
Incorporated: 20 October 1949 *Employees:* 93
Net Worth: £20,667,000 *Total Assets:* £35,812,000
Registered Office: Unit 1 Kennet Weir Business Park, Arrowhead Road, Theale, Reading, Berks, RG7 4AE
Activities: Other specialised construction activities n.e.c.
Officers: Matthew Robert Paul Fenton, Secretary; Matthew Robert Paul Fenton [1978] Director; Paul Robert Fenton [1941] Director/Civil Engineer; David Burnett Gammer [1934] Director/Solicitor; Douglas Allan Gray [1955] Director/Accountant; Anthony John Harper [1956] Director/Marketing Manager

Ferguson Group Services Limited
Incorporated: 27 May 1966 *Employees:* 96
Previous: Wolseley (Group Services) Limited
Net Worth: £39,646,000 *Total Assets:* £69,112,000
Registered Office: 1020 Eskdale Road, Winnersh Triangle, Wokingham, Berks, RG41 5TS
Activities: Other business support service activities n.e.c.
Parent: Wolseley Group Holdings Limited
Officers: Katherine Mary McCormick, Secretary; Mark John Fearon [1970] Director of Corporate Communications and Investor; Paul Simon Fox [1978] Director; Simon Gray [1967] Director/Accountant; Julia Amanda Mattison [1982] Director/Accountant; Simon Nicholas Oakland [1969] Director; Michael Andrew Powell [1967] Director; Philip Andrew Scott [1978] Director/Group Treasurer

Ferholding UK Ltd
Incorporated: 12 June 2015
Net Worth Deficit: £10,635,000 *Total Assets:* £101,576,000
Registered Office: 889 Greenford Road, Greenford, Middlesex, UB6 0HE
Activities: Activities of other holding companies n.e.c.
Officers: Tim John Shirley, Secretary; Salvatore Castelli [1971] Finance Director [Italian]; Pieraldo Oldano [1965] Managing Director [Italian]; Marco Pescarolo [1957] Director/Global Treasurer [Italian]

Ferrero UK Limited
Incorporated: 4 April 1966 *Employees:* 203
Net Worth Deficit: £26,873,000 *Total Assets:* £119,285,000
Registered Office: 889 Greenford Road, Greenford, Middlesex, UB6 0HE
Activities: Manufacture of cocoa and chocolate confectionery
Officers: Tim John Shirley, Secretary; Salvatore Castelli [1971] Director [Italian]; Pieraldo Oldano [1965] Director/Business Manager [Italian]; Marco Pescarolo [1957] Director [Italian]

Ferring Asset Management Limited
Incorporated: 10 June 2014 *Employees:* 1
Net Worth: £32,533,996 *Total Assets:* £32,750,000
Registered Office: Drayton Hall, Church Road, West Drayton, Middlesex, UB7 7PS
Activities: Non-trading company
Parent: Ferring Laboratories Limited
Officers: Raphael Cretegny, Secretary; Frank Christoph Lindenmann [1959] Director/Tax Lawyer [Swiss]

Ferring Laboratories Limited
Incorporated: 18 July 1980 *Employees:* 192
Net Worth Deficit: £17,292,892 *Total Assets:* £64,455,896
Registered Office: Drayton Hall, Church Road, West Drayton, Middlesex, UB7 7PS
Activities: Activities of head offices
Officers: Raphael Cretegny, Secretary; Jean Marie Duvall [1961] Director [American]; Dr Peter Wilden [1957] Director [German]

T & E Ferris Limited
Incorporated: 23 June 2009 *Employees:* 372
Net Worth: £20,061,182 *Total Assets:* £32,046,104
Registered Office: 17-19 Station Road West, Oxted, Surrey, RH8 9EE
Activities: Other retail sale of new goods in specialised stores (not commercial art galleries and opticians)
Parent: Winchester Holdings Limited
Officers: Edward William Ferris [1980] Director; Thomas James Ferris [1981] Director; William Robert Ferris [1944] Director

Ferrybridge MFE Limited
Incorporated: 20 July 2011 *Employees:* 47
Net Worth: £53,000,000 *Total Assets:* £320,400,000
Registered Office: No 1 Forbury Place, 43 Forbury Road, Reading, Berks, RG1 3JH
Activities: Production of electricity
Parent: Multifuel Energy Limited
Officers: Tarryn Bastianelli, Secretary; Mark Richard Hayward [1963] Director/Manager; Alexander Hughes Honeyman [1960] Director/Head of Project Development; Michael Francis O'Friel [1960] Director/Solicitor [American]; William Brendt Roberts [1960] Director/Senior Vice President, Operations [American]

Fevore Limited
Incorporated: 12 January 1977 *Employees:* 190
Net Worth: £15,848,670 *Total Assets:* £78,099,904
Registered Office: Denbigh House, Denbigh Road, Bletchley, Milton Keynes, Bucks, MK1 1DF
Activities: Activities of head offices
Shareholders: George Roger Oscroft; Anne Lesley Oscroft
Officers: Clive Gear, Secretary; Andrew Francis Dick [1954] Finance Director; Richard John Foreman [1955] Director; Clive Gear [1950] Director/Financial Consultant; Anne Lesley Oscroft [1945] Director; George Roger Oscroft [1947] Director; Jennifer Vivienne Mary Oscroft [1981] Director/Barrister

FGP Topco Limited
Incorporated: 28 February 2006 *Employees:* 6,740
Net Worth: £922,000,000 *Total Assets:* £18,304,000,000
Registered Office: The Compass Centre, Nelson Road, Hounslow, Middlesex, TW6 2GW
Activities: Activities of head offices
Officers: Ahmed Ali Al-Hammadi [1981] Director [Qatari]; Stuart Harvey Baldwin [1969] Director/Investment Manager; Christopher William Beale [1947] Director [American]; Jinhong Chen [1990] Director [Chinese]; Samuel Coxe [1975] Alternate Director [American]; Olivier Georges Xavier Fortin [1974] Director [French]; Jorge Gil Villen [1972] Director/Lawyer/Economist [Spanish]; Mr Deven Arvind Karnik [1967] Alternate Director; Tom Kelly [1989] Director [Irish]; Alexander Leonard [1985] Director; Inigo Meiras [1963] Alternate Director [Spanish]; Michael James Powell [1972] Director; David Jinlin Xie [1978] Alternate Director [American]

Fiat Chrysler Automobiles UK Ltd
Incorporated: 6 November 1924 *Employees:* 214
Previous: Fiat Group Automobiles UK Ltd
Net Worth: £21,408,000 *Total Assets:* £385,438,016
Registered Office: Fiat House, 240 Bath Road, Slough, Berks, SL1 4DX
Activities: Sale of new cars and light motor vehicles
Parent: Fiat Chrysler Automobiles N.V.
Officers: Peter John Farley, Secretary; Marco Rocco Cane [1978] Director/Motor Executive [Italian]; Giuliano Gerhard Davoli [1973] Director/Motor Executive [Italian/Austrian]; Riccardo Gini [1971] Director/Motor Executive [Italian]; Pietro Gorlier [1962] Director/Motor Executive [Italian]; Alexander Paul Hughes [1976] Director; Arnaud Yannick Louis Leclerc [1974] Director/Motor Executive [French]; Andrew Thomas Weller [1963] Director/Motor Executive

Fibercore Limited
Incorporated: 25 February 1993 *Employees:* 40
Net Worth: £31,434,404 *Total Assets:* £34,064,536
Registered Office: Fibercore House, University Parkway, Science Park, Southampton, SO16 7QQ
Activities: Other manufacturing n.e.c.
Parent: H.I.G. Europe-Fibercore Bidco 2 Limited
Officers: Christopher Emslie [1961] Director/Industrial Manager; James Patrick Habel [1974] Finance Director [American]; Christopher O'Connor [1963] Director/President & CEO [American]

Fidelity Asian Values PLC
Incorporated: 2 April 1996
Net Worth: £287,974,016 *Total Assets:* £291,380,992
Registered Office: Beech Gate, Millfield Lane, Lower Kingswood, Tadworth, Surrey, KT20 6RB
Activities: Activities of investment trusts
Officers: Katherine Blanche Mary Bolsover [1958] Director/Retired; Timothy Scholefield [1963] Director; Philip David Smiley [1951] Director; Grahame Stott [1954] Director/Actuary; Michael Sturrock Warren [1961] Director/Investment Professional

Fidelity China Special Situations PLC
Incorporated: 22 January 2010
Net Worth: £1,502,866,048 *Total Assets:* £1,654,736,000
Registered Office: Beech Gate, Millfield Lane, Lower Kingswood, Tadworth, Surrey, KT20 6RP
Activities: Activities of investment trusts
Officers: Michael Warren Balfour [1960] Director; Nicholas James Douglas Bull [1952] Director; David John Causer [1950] Director; The Hon Peter John Pleydell-Bouverie [1958] Director; Elisabeth Charlotte Scott [1962] Director

Fidelity European Values PLC
Incorporated: 16 August 1991
Net Worth: £1,030,048,000 *Total Assets:* £1,038,979,968
Registered Office: Beech Gate, Millfield Lane, Lower Kingswood, Tadworth, Surrey, KT20 6RB
Activities: Activities of investment trusts
Officers: Vivian Paul Bazalgette [1951] Director; Fleur Meijs [1971] Director [Dutch]; Robin Christian Howard Niblett [1961] Director; Marion Jane Sears [1962] Director; Paul Tennant Yates [1957] Director

Fidelity Japan Trust PLC
Incorporated: 7 January 1994
Previous: Fidelity Japanese Values PLC
Net Worth: £222,527,008 *Total Assets:* £224,475,008
Registered Office: Beech Gate, Millfield Lane, Lower Kingswood, Tadworth, Surrey, KT20 6RB
Activities: Activities of investment trusts
Officers: David Rowley Graham [1955] Director; Philip Bruce Kay [1955] Director; Sarah Juliet MacAulay [1962] Director; Sir Laurence Henry Philip Magnus [1955] Director and Charity Trustee; David Anthony Robins [1949] Director; Dominic Martin Matthew Ziegler [1961] Director

Fidelity Special Values PLC
Incorporated: 27 September 1994
Net Worth: £724,969,984 *Total Assets:* £733,105,024
Registered Office: Beech Gate, Millfield Lane, Lower Kingswood, Tadworth, Surrey, KT20 6RP
Activities: Activities of investment trusts
Officers: Sharon Mary Brown [1968] Director; Dean Robert Buckley [1960] Director; Nigel Foster [1952] Director; Andrew Robertson Irvine [1951] Director; Nicola Joanne McCabe [1969] Executive Director

Fifthgrange Limited
Incorporated: 14 September 2000 *Employees:* 2
Net Worth: £342,580,992 *Total Assets:* £342,580,992
Registered Office: Witan Gate House, 500-600 Witan Gate, Milton Keynes, Bucks, MK9 1BA
Activities: Activities of head offices
Parent: Homebase Group Limited
Officers: Simone Tudor, Secretary; Andrew Charles Coleman [1974] Director/General Manager, Finance & IT; Damian Garry McGloughlin [1969] Acting Managing Director

FIL Investment Services (UK) Limited
Incorporated: 2 May 1986
Net Worth: £108,307,000 *Total Assets:* £370,270,016
Registered Office: Oakhill House, 130 Tonbridge Road, Hildenborough, Tonbridge, Kent, TN11 9DZ
Activities: Security and commodity contracts dealing activities
Officers: John Clougherty [1966] Director; Peter John Horrell [1968] Director; Anthony Stephen Lanser [1968] Director; Stephen John Reedy [1965] Director; Stuart Paul Welch [1965] Director

FIL Investments International
Incorporated: 13 September 1979 *Employees:* 23
Net Worth: £49,608,000 *Total Assets:* £61,927,000
Registered Office: Oakhill House, 130 Tonbridge Road, Hildenborough, Tonbridge, Kent, TN11 9DZ
Activities: Security and commodity contracts dealing activities
Officers: Nicholas Birchall [1973] Director; Neil Kenneth Cable [1965] Director; Dominic Michael Joseph Rossi [1963] Director; Riju Sathyan [1971] Director

FIL Life Insurance Limited
Incorporated: 22 July 1997 *Employees:* 6
Net Worth: £43,703,000 *Total Assets:* £29,620,381,696
Registered Office: Oakhill House, 130 Tonbridge Road, Hildenborough, Kent, TN11 9DZ
Activities: Life insurance
Officers: David Charles Huntley [1961] Director; Kristina Isherwood [1968] Director; Marianne Jaekel [1975] Director/Lawyer [Irish]; Anthony Stephen Lanser [1968] Director/Chief Operating Officer; Stephen Peter Maher [1976] Director/Accountant; Wendy Madeline Mayall [1957] Director; Julian Roy Webb [1962] Director

FIL Pensions Management
Incorporated: 29 April 1986
Net Worth: £38,478,000 *Total Assets:* £78,394,000
Registered Office: Oakhill House, 130 Tonbridge Road, Hildenborough, Tonbridge, Kent, TN11 9DZ
Activities: Financial intermediation not elsewhere classified
Officers: Nicholas Birchall [1973] Director; John Clougherty [1966] Director; Steven Lance Edgley [1968] Director; Peter John Horrell [1968] Director

Filemaker International
Incorporated: 24 April 1998 *Employees:* 17
Net Worth: £7,884,902 *Total Assets:* £21,506,580
Registered Office: 2 Furzeground Way, Stockley Park, Uxbridge, Middlesex, UB11 1BB
Activities: Other software publishing
Officers: Sophia Crystal Yungen, Secretary; William Young Epling [1959] Director/Business Executive [American]; Roger Andrew Hale [1966] Director/Businessman; Sophia Crystal Yungen [1987] Director/Businesswoman [American]

Filtrona Limited
Incorporated: 5 March 2013
Net Worth: £21,320,000 *Total Assets:* £263,876,000
Registered Office: Avebury House, 201-249 Avebury Boulevard, Milton Keynes, Bucks, MK9 1AU
Activities: Dormant company
Parent: Essentra Finance Limited
Officers: Patricia Kendall, Secretary; Jon Michael Green [1962] Director; Lili Liu [1972] Director

Finance Ireland Limited
Incorporated: 3 June 2004 *Employees:* 99
Net Worth: £70,072,600 *Total Assets:* £206,919,440
Registered Office: The Registry, Beckenham Road, Beckenham, Kent, BR3 4TU
Activities: Activities of head offices
Shareholders: National Treasury Management Agency; Allianz SE
Officers: Lily MacKenna, Secretary; Joshua Michael Anderson [1972] Managing Director [American]; Daniel Ballen [1982] Director/Private Equity Investor [American]; Ian Alexander Black [1963] Director [Irish]; Frank Donnellan [1958] Director [Irish]; John Humphrey Gunn [1942] Director; James Hickey [1968] Director [Irish]; William Kane [1955] Director [Irish]; Kristofer Kraus [1970] Director/Investment Manager [American]; Fergal McAleavey [1970] Director [Irish]

Financial Administration Services Limited
Incorporated: 19 April 1982
Net Worth: £133,973,000 *Total Assets:* £165,559,008
Registered Office: Oakhill House, 130 Tonbridge Road, Hildenborough, Tonbridge, Kent, TN11 9DZ
Activities: Activities auxiliary to financial intermediation n.e.c.
Officers: Peter John Horrell [1968] Director; Kristina Maria Isherwood [1968] Director; Anthony Stephen Lanser [1968] Director/Chief Operating Officer; Stuart Paul Welch [1965] Director

Fire Fighters Charity
Incorporated: 8 July 2002 *Employees:* 136
Net Worth: £28,724,066 *Total Assets:* £29,345,296
Registered Office: Belvedere, Basing View, Basingstoke, Hants, RG21 4HG
Activities: Other service activities n.e.c.
Officers: Christine Bridget Goonan, Secretary; John Baines [1970] Director/Assistant Chief Fire Officer; Andrew Best [1947] Director/Retired Chief Fire Officer; David Stuart Brown [1962] Director/Publisher; Peter John Davies [1953] Director; Paul Maurice Fuller [1960] Director/Chief Fire Officer; Neil Gibbins [1959] Director/Fire Risk Advisor; Harvey Ralph Grenville [1963] Director/Civil Servant; Robert Andrew Hickmott [1969] Director/Chief Fire Officer; Dr Rowena Hill [1981] Director/Principal Lecturer; Andrew Fraser Lynch [1971] Director/Journalist; Jane Lesley Nicklin [1958] Director/Independent Allied Health Professions Advisor; Simon Routh-Jones [1950] Director/HM Chief Inspector for Scottish F&RS; Christopher Lewis Wilson [1965] Director/Fire Officer; George Howat Wood [1957] Director/Chartered Accountant

Fire Support (SSFR) Holdings Limited
Incorporated: 11 September 2009
Net Worth Deficit: £9,718,000 *Total Assets:* £43,880,000
Registered Office: Part First Floor, 1 Grenfell Road, Maidenhead, Berks, SL6 1HN
Activities: Financial intermediation not elsewhere classified
Parent: BBGI Sicav S.A.
Officers: Emeka Ikechi Ehenulo, Secretary; Sean Cook [1968] Director/Banker; Albert Hendrik Naafs [1965] Director [Dutch]; Frank Manfred Schramm [1968] Director [German]

Fire Support (SSFR) Limited
Incorporated: 13 September 2009
Net Worth Deficit: £9,718,000 *Total Assets:* £43,880,000
Registered Office: Part First Floor, 1 Grenfell Road, Maidenhead, Berks, SL6 1HN
Activities: Financial intermediation not elsewhere classified
Parent: Fire Support (SSFR) Holdings Limited
Officers: Emeka Ikechi Ehenulo, Secretary; Sean Cook [1968] Director/Banker; Albert Hendrik Naafs [1965] Director [Dutch]; Frank Manfred Schramm [1968] Director [German]

Firebolt RB Holdings Limited
Incorporated: 19 September 2016
Net Worth: £232,766,976 *Total Assets:* £1,503,451,136
Registered Office: 8 White Oak Square, London Road, Swanley, Kent, BR8 7AG
Activities: Activities of other holding companies n.e.c.
Officers: Erin Kate Eisenberg [1978] Director [American]; Charles John Gore Hazelwood [1963] Director; Philip William Kent [1984] Director; Christoph Friedrich Mertens [1969] Director [German]; David Paul Tilstone [1969] Director; Koji Wakabayashi [1973] Director [Japanese]

Firmenich UK Limited
Incorporated: 18 May 1990 *Employees:* 166
Net Worth: £25,586,000 *Total Assets:* £45,554,000
Registered Office: Hayes Road, Southall, Middlesex, UB2 5NN
Activities: Manufacture of perfumes and toilet preparations
Officers: Elodie Josiane Bouchard [1972] Senior Director Finance Europe [French]; Gary Charles Nelson [1961] Director; Paulo Sergio Menoita Nogueira [1966] Director [Brazilian/Portuguese]; Laetitia Christabel Pictet [1970] Director/Legal Counsel [Swiss]; Dominique Florence Zundel [1963] Director/VP Europe, Perfumery BHC [French]

Alan Firmin Limited
Incorporated: 25 February 1957 *Employees:* 220
Net Worth: £55,324,496 *Total Assets:* £80,383,344
Registered Office: Wares Farm, Linton, Maidstone, Kent, ME17 4BB
Activities: Freight transport by road
Shareholders: Michael Paul Firmin; Christopher Kaj Gunnar Eriksson-Lee; Paul Alan Firmin; Ian Maurice Firmin
Officers: Michael Paul Firmin, Secretary; Paul Keith Denyer [1974] Director/Transport/Property; Ian Maurice Firmin [1947] Director/Transport/Property; Michael Paul Firmin [1970] Director/Transport/Property; Paul Alan Firmin [1944] Director/Transport/Property

First Central Insurance Management Limited
Incorporated: 31 January 2008 *Employees:* 602
Net Worth: £10,643,000 *Total Assets:* £176,763,008
Registered Office: Central House, 25-27 Perrymount Road, Haywards Heath, W Sussex, RH16 3TP
Activities: Activities of insurance agents and brokers
Officers: Suzanne Debaes, Secretary; Jonathan Simon Guy [1973] Claims Director; Andrew Neil James [1967] Group Marketing Director; John Kennedy [1965] Finance Director; Michael James Leonard [1969] Director; Shaun Adrian Meadows [1963] Director; Roy Leonard Sampson [1955] Director

First Hampshire & Dorset Limited
Incorporated: 12 March 1986 *Employees:* 770
Net Worth: £2,042,000 *Total Assets:* £50,083,000
Registered Office: Bus Depot, Empress Road, Southampton, SO14 0JW
Activities: Other urban, suburban or metropolitan passenger land transport (not underground, metro or similar)
Parent: Southampton Citybus Limited
Officers: Michael Hampson, Secretary; David Brian Alexander [1965] Regional Managing Director; Simon Ian Goff [1983] Director/Transport Manager; Dean John Knight [1966] Employee Director; Marc Christopher Reddy [1971] Director/Transport Manager; Gary Warren Weaver [1974] Director/Engineer

First Rate Exchange Services Holdings Limited
Incorporated: 14 September 2001 *Employees:* 282
Net Worth: £132,922,000 *Total Assets:* £484,660,992
Registered Office: Great West House, Great West Road, Brentford, Middlesex, TW8 9DF
Activities: Banks
Shareholders: Bank of Ireland (UK) PLC; Post Office Limited
Officers: Jane Elizabeth MacLeod, Secretary; Amy Burke [1975] HR Director [Irish]; Desmond Edward Crowley [1959] Director/Banker [Irish]; Gary Fitton [1968] Director/Chief Executive Officer; Neil Anthony Fuller [1966] Director; Roger William Gale [1957] Director; Andrew James MacGregor Hardie [1967] Director; Deborah Kay Smith [1965] Director/Chief Executive; John Tudor [1969] Director; Henk Van Hulle [1971] Director, Post Office Money [Belgian]; The Reverend Paula Anne Vennells [1959] Director; Owen Pearson Woodley [1967] Managing Director, Post Office Money

First Rate Exchange Services Limited
Incorporated: 14 September 2001 *Employees:* 282
Net Worth: £135,082,000 *Total Assets:* £486,819,008
Registered Office: Great West House, Great West Road, Brentford, Middlesex, TW8 9DF
Activities: Banks
Parent: First Rate Exchange Services Holdings Limited
Officers: Jane Elizabeth MacLeod, Secretary; Amy Burke [1975] HR Director [Irish]; Desmond Edward Crowley [1959] Director/Banker [Irish]; Gary Fitton [1968] Director/Chief Executive Officer; Neil Anthony Fuller [1966] Director; Roger William Gale [1957] Director; Andrew James MacGregor Hardie [1967] Director; Deborah Kay Smith [1965] Director/Chief Executive; John Tudor [1969] Director; Henk Van Hulle [1971] Director, Post Office Money [Belgian]; The Reverend Paula Anne Vennells [1959] Director; Owen Pearson Woodley [1967] Managing Director, Post Office Money

First Technology (2002) Limited
Incorporated: 23 December 2002
Net Worth: £208,851,008 *Total Assets:* £211,855,392
Registered Office: Honeywell House, Skimped Hill Lane, Bracknell, Berks, RG12 1EB
Activities: Non-trading company
Parent: First Technology Overseas Limited
Officers: Asad Ali [1984] Director; John J Tus [1958] Director [American]

First Technology Limited
Incorporated: 4 February 1985
Net Worth: £49,759,000 *Total Assets:* £388,662,016
Registered Office: Honeywell House, Skimped Hill Lane, Bracknell, Berks, RG12 1EB
Activities: Activities of head offices
Parent: Honeywell Acquisitions II Limited
Officers: Asad Ali [1984] Director; Hicham Khellafi [1979] Director [French]; John J Tus [1958] Director [American]

First Technology Overseas Limited
Incorporated: 10 October 2001
Net Worth: £46,884,000 *Total Assets:* £161,383,008
Registered Office: Honeywell House, Skimped Hill Lane, Bracknell, Berks, RG12 1EB
Activities: Activities of head offices
Parent: First Technology International Limited
Officers: Asad Ali [1984] Director; John J Tus [1958] Director [American]

First Title Insurance PLC
Incorporated: 8 May 1973 *Employees:* 2
Net Worth: £27,181,000 *Total Assets:* £61,340,000
Registered Office: Eca Court, 24-26 South Park, Sevenoaks, Kent, TN13 1DU
Activities: Non-life insurance
Parent: First American Financial Corporation
Officers: Paul Barker, Secretary; Ian John Borders [1964] Underwriting & Operations Director; Kenneth David de Giorgio [1971] Director [American]; Kevin James Dick [1967] Director/General Counsel; Lance John Gibbins [1964] Director; William Henry John Maidens [1960] Financial Director; Justin Samuel Jackson McChesney [1973] Director; Andrew Neil McIntyre McMahon [1968] Director; Ian Michael Turner [1961] Director

Fishdance Limited
Incorporated: 9 October 2013
Net Worth: £4,843,392 *Total Assets:* £25,374,212
Registered Office: 2 Castle Business Village, Station Road, Hampton, Surrey, TW12 2BX
Activities: Raising of horses and other equines
Shareholders: David Fish; Linda Fish
Officers: Dr David John Fish [1948] Director; Linda Pamela Fish [1953] Director/Housewife

Fisher & Paykel Appliances Limited
Incorporated: 28 March 2000 *Employees:* 49
Net Worth: £55,439,000 *Total Assets:* £60,322,000
Registered Office: Turing House, Ortensia Drive, Milton Keynes, Bucks, MK17 8LX
Activities: Wholesale of radio, television goods & electrical household appliances (other than records, tapes, CDs)
Officers: Alan Kenneth Frost, Secretary/Chartered Accountant; Stuart Broadhurst [1966] Director/Chief Executive Officer [New Zealander]; Graham Raymond Judge [1951] Director/Accountant [New Zealander]; Laurence Andrew Mawhinney [1969] Director/VP Sales and Customer Experience [New Zealander]

T A Fisher & Sons Limited
Incorporated: 13 February 1991 *Employees:* 73
Net Worth: £19,032,436 *Total Assets:* £33,119,560
Registered Office: Theale Court, 11-13 High Street, Theale, Reading, Berks, RG7 5AH
Activities: Construction of commercial buildings
Parent: T A Fisher (Holdings) Limited
Officers: John Hubert Fisher, Secretary; John Hubert Fisher [1957] Director; Keith Hubert Fisher [1924] Director; Duncan Paul Mayes [1971] Director/Accountant; Robert Edward Price [1956] Director/Chartered Surveyor

T A Fisher (Holdings) Limited
Incorporated: 28 June 1963 *Employees:* 73
Net Worth: £46,508,740 *Total Assets:* £62,766,680
Registered Office: Theale Court, 11-13 High Street, Theale, Reading, Berks, RG7 5AH
Activities: Other letting and operating of own or leased real estate
Officers: John Hubert Fisher, Secretary; John Hubert Fisher [1957] Director/Builder; Keith Hubert Fisher [1924] Director/Builder; Duncan Paul Mayes [1971] Director/Accountant; Robert Edward Price [1956] Director/Chartered Surveyor

A.A.Fisher (Properties) Limited
Incorporated: 20 March 1962 *Employees:* 2
Net Worth: £31,120,048 *Total Assets:* £43,273,648
Registered Office: Unit 3 Fisher's Industrial Estate, Wiggenhall Road, Watford, Herts, WD18 0FE
Activities: Renting and operating of Housing Association real estate
Parent: A A Fisher Limited
Officers: Pamela Ann Saunders, Secretary; William Moorton Fisher [1951] Director; Pamela Jill Ryman [1954] Director

T A Fisher Developments Limited
Incorporated: 23 February 1994
Net Worth: £9,517,104 *Total Assets:* £31,012,510
Registered Office: Theale Court, 11-13 High Street, Theale, Reading, Berks, RG7 5AH
Activities: Buying and selling of own real estate
Parent: T A Fisher (Holdings) Limited
Officers: John Hubert Fisher, Secretary; John Hubert Fisher [1957] Director/Building Developer; Keith Hubert Fisher [1924] Director/Building Developer; Robert Edward Price [1956] Director/Chartered Surveyor; Peter James Webb [1955] Director/Chartered Surveyor

Fisons Limited
Incorporated: 23 July 1895 *Employees:* 431
Net Worth: £597,932,032 *Total Assets:* £771,542,016
Registered Office: One Onslow Street, Guildford, Surrey, GU1 4YS
Activities: Manufacture of pharmaceutical preparations
Parent: Sanofi-Aventis UK Holdings Limited
Officers: Francois-Xavier Duhalde [1965] Director/Chief Financial Officer [French]; Hugo Rupert Alexander Fry [1970] Director

Fitesa Limited
Incorporated: 4 June 2009
Net Worth: £56,201,080 *Total Assets:* £58,042,936
Registered Office: The Cottage, Knowl Hill Common, Reading, Berks, RG10 9YD
Activities: Non-trading company
Parent: Fitesa Sweden A.B.
Officers: Silverio Luis Americo Baranzano Brutti [1963] Director [Brazilian]; Lavinia Fraga Leite [1973] Director/Legal Counsel [Brazilian]; Fred Hal Singley Jr [1969] Director [American]

Five Arrows Limited
Incorporated: 17 July 1899
Net Worth: £25,342,000 *Total Assets:* £45,047,000
Registered Office: Windmill Hill, Silk Street, Waddesdon, Aylesbury, Bucks, HP18 0JZ
Activities: Other professional, scientific and technical activities n.e.c.
Shareholder: Nathaniel Charles Jacob Rothschild
Officers: Craig Christian Armstrong [1971] Director/Investment Manager; Magnus James Goodlad [1972] Director; The Hon Hannah Mary Rothschild [1962] Director; Lord Nathaniel Charles Jacob Rothschild [1936] Director

Fizzy Canning Town LLP
Incorporated: 26 June 2012
Net Worth: £19,617,000 *Total Assets:* £28,485,000
Registered Office: Premier House, 52 London Road, Twickenham, Middlesex, TW1 3RP

Fizzy Enterprises LLP
Incorporated: 22 March 2012
Net Worth: £215,772,000 *Total Assets:* £264,131,008
Registered Office: Premier House, 52 London Road, Twickenham, Middlesex, TW1 3RP
Officers: Henry Charles Rupert Downes [1955] LLP Member

Fizzy Stepney Green LLP
Incorporated: 20 September 2013
Net Worth: £18,201,000 *Total Assets:* £27,755,000
Registered Office: Premier House, 52 London Road, Twickenham, Middlesex, TW1 3RP

FKA Brands Limited
Incorporated: 16 January 2002 *Employees:* 52
Previous: Homedics Group Limited
Net Worth: £6,765,348 *Total Assets:* £30,401,890
Registered Office: Homedics House, Somerhill Business Park, Five Oak Green Road, Tonbridge, Kent, TN11 0GP
Activities: Agents involved in the sale of furniture, household goods, hardware and ironmongery
Parent: Salter Group Limited
Officers: Swarup Banerjee, Secretary; Simon Jonathan Bluring [1956] Managing Director EMEA; Alon David Kaufman [1962] Director/Businessman [American]; Sabyasachi SEN [1962] Director/Chief Financial Officer [American]

Flamepro Limited
Incorporated: 14 December 1998 *Employees:* 47
Net Worth: £10,891,353 *Total Assets:* £28,763,098
Registered Office: Corus House, 1 Auckland Park, Milton Keynes, Bucks, MK1 1BU
Activities: Hotels and similar accommodation
Parent: Corus Hotels Limited
Officers: Khurram Mohmand, Secretary; Andrew Khoo [1972] Director [Australian]; Yet King Loy [1946] Director [Canadian]; Khurram Mohmand [1972] Director/Accountant

Fleetwood Developments Limited
Incorporated: 18 May 1983 *Employees:* 3
Net Worth: £16,317,953 *Total Assets:* £39,505,720
Registered Office: 2 AC Court, High Street, Thames Ditton, Surrey, KT7 0SR
Activities: Other letting and operating of own or leased real estate
Major Shareholder: Roger Kilby
Officers: Maureen Elizabeth Stopher, Secretary; Roger Frederick Kilby [1946] Director/Property Development/Investment

Flexera Software Holdings Limited
Incorporated: 4 September 2015 *Employees:* 221
Net Worth: £421,000 *Total Assets:* £68,637,000
Registered Office: Flexera Software Holdings Limited, 14-18 Bell Street, Maidenhead, Berks, SL6 1BR
Activities: Activities of other holding companies n.e.c.
Officers: Joseph William Freda [1959] Director/Chief Financial Officer [American]; James Patrick Ryan [1967] Director/Chief Executive Officer [American]; Kraig Stephen Washburn [1971] Director/General Counsel [American]

Flexera Software Limited
Incorporated: 5 March 2008 *Employees:* 152
Net Worth: £9,169,000 *Total Assets:* £64,877,000
Registered Office: Malvern House, 14-18 Bell Street, Maidenhead, Berks, SL6 1BR
Activities: Business and domestic software development
Parent: Flexera Software Holdings Limited
Officers: James Patrick Ryan, Secretary/SVP and General Manager [American]; Joseph William Freda [1959] Director/Chief Financial Officer [American]; James Patrick Ryan [1967] Director/Chief Executive Officer [American]; Kraig Stephen Washburn [1971] Director/General Counsel [American]

Flexibon Limited
Incorporated: 30 January 2009
Net Worth: £832,558 *Total Assets:* £28,428,516
Registered Office: 8-10 South Street, Epsom, Surrey, KT18 7PF
Activities: Activities of venture and development capital companies
Major Shareholder: Jonathan Philip Feuer
Officers: Jonathan Philip Feuer [1962] Director

Flexibox International Limited
Incorporated: 13 April 1945
Net Worth: £22,659,000 *Total Assets:* £22,659,000
Registered Office: Buckingham House, 361-366 Buckingham Avenue, Slough, Berks, SL1 4LU
Activities: Machining
Parent: John Crane Group Ltd
Officers: Christopher David Hughes, Secretary; Ruben Raul Alvarez Sancho [1971] Director/Vice President, Global First Fit and Projects [Spanish]; Adam David Powell [1981] Director/EMEA Regional Controller; Alistair Michael Rogers [1965] Senior Director of Operations

Flight Centre (UK) Limited
Incorporated: 9 June 1994 *Employees:* 1,813
Net Worth: £105,521,000 *Total Assets:* £255,576,992
Registered Office: Level 6, CI Tower, St Georges Square, High Street, New Malden, Surrey, KT3 4TE
Activities: Travel agency activities
Officers: Adam Murray, Secretary; Chris Adrian Galanty [1974] Director/Executive GM; Graham Francis Turner [1949] Director/Travel Agent [Australian]

Flight Centre (UK) Wholesale Limited
Incorporated: 2 April 2009
Net Worth: £2,000 *Total Assets:* £34,764,000
Registered Office: Level 6, CI Tower, St Georges Square, High Street, New Malden, Surrey, KT3 4TE
Activities: Travel agency activities
Parent: Flight Centre (UK) Limited
Officers: Adam Murray, Secretary; Chris Adrian Galanty [1974] Director/Executive GM; Graham Francis Turner [1949] Director/Travel Agent [Australian]

Flight Centre Robin Limited
Incorporated: 7 December 2012
Net Worth: £70,013,456 *Total Assets:* £70,343,792
Registered Office: Level 6, CI Tower, St Georges Square, High Street, New Malden, Surrey, KT3 4TE
Activities: Other credit granting n.e.c.
Officers: Adam Murray, Secretary; Chris Adrian Galanty [1974] Director/Executive General Manager; Adam Murray [1973] Director/Chief Financial Officer; Graham Francis Turner [1949] Director/Travel Agent [Australian]

Flight Centre Travel Group (European Holdings) Ltd
Incorporated: 28 October 2015
Net Worth: £41,705,128 *Total Assets:* £43,769,828
Registered Office: Level 6, CI Tower, St Georges Square, High Street, New Malden, Surrey, KT3 4TE
Activities: Activities of other holding companies n.e.c.
Officers: Adam Murray, Secretary; Chris Adrian Galanty [1974] Managing Director; Adam Murray [1973] Director

Flir Systems Limited
Incorporated: 6 July 1977 *Employees:* 53
Net Worth: £38,334,000 *Total Assets:* £59,498,000
Registered Office: 2 Kings Hill Avenue, Kings Hill, West Malling, Kent, ME19 4AQ
Activities: Manufacture of optical precision instruments
Parent: FLIR Government Systems Inc
Officers: Craig John Cooper, Secretary; Heather Fiona Christiansen [1971] Director/Manager and Secretary [American]; Craig John Cooper [1969] Director/Accountant

Floplast Limited
Incorporated: 3 June 1991 *Employees:* 215
Net Worth: £40,479,528 *Total Assets:* £49,819,096
Registered Office: Castle Road, Eurolink Business Park, Sittingbourne, Kent, ME10 3FP
Activities: Manufacture of other plastic products
Shareholder: Patrick O'Brien
Officers: Bryan Featherstone Lynch, Secretary/Accountant [Irish]; Bryan Featherstone Lynch [1954] Director [Irish]; Stewart John Norris [1963] Managing Director; Timothy Augustine O'Brien [1941] Director [Irish]

Fluor International Limited
Incorporated: 9 June 1978
Net Worth: £33,777,000 *Total Assets:* £353,100,992
Registered Office: Fluor Centre, 140 Pinehurst Road, Farnborough, Hants, GU14 7BF
Activities: Other business support service activities n.e.c.
Parent: Fluor Enterprises Inc
Officers: Maurice Johannes Kuitems, Secretary/Senior Legal Counsel [Dutch]; Maurice Johannes Kuitems [1960] Director/General Counsel [Dutch]; Graham Melville Mason [1972] Director; Ashley Graham Rees [1965] Director/General Manager Vice President; Keri Elizabeth White [1970] Director/Financial Controller

Fluor Limited
Incorporated: 26 August 1976 *Employees:* 742
Net Worth: £356,144,000 *Total Assets:* £914,633,024
Registered Office: Fluor Centre, 140 Pinehurst Road, Farnborough, Hants, GU14 7BF
Activities: Other specialised construction activities n.e.c.
Parent: Fluor International Limited
Officers: Maurice Johannes Kuitems, Secretary [Dutch]; Robin Krishnan Chopra [1964] Director/Finance Executive; Mark Alan Landry [1964] Director/EVP, Chief Human Resources Officer [American]; Graham Melville Mason [1972] Director; Stephen George Mogose [1956] Director/Manager Process Technology; Ashley Graham Rees [1965] Managing Director; Keri Elizabeth White [1970] Director

FMP Global Bidco Limited
Incorporated: 24 February 2016 *Employees:* 3
Net Worth Deficit: £966,000 *Total Assets:* £35,779,000
Registered Office: Downlands House, Drayton Lane, Merston, Chichester, W Sussex, PO20 1EL
Activities: Activities of other holding companies n.e.c.
Parent: FMP Global Midco Limited
Officers: Justin Andrew Cottrell [1975] Director; Nicolas Dennis Cottrell [1987] Director; James Joseph Michael Faulds [1952] Director; Christian Sean Hamilton [1979] Director; Milan Kellner [1988] Director

FMP Global Holdings Limited
Incorporated: 24 February 2016 *Employees:* 136
Net Worth Deficit: £4,591,000 *Total Assets:* £38,236,000
Registered Office: Downlands House, Drayton Lane, Merston, Chichester, W Sussex, PO20 1EL
Activities: Activities of other holding companies n.e.c.
Parent: Tenzing Private Equity LLP
Officers: Justin Andrew Cottrell [1975] Director; James Joseph Michael Faulds [1952] Director; Christian Sean Hamilton [1979] Director; Milan Kellner [1988] Director

FNH UK Limited
Incorporated: 26 January 1987 *Employees:* 89
Previous: Manroy Engineering Limited
Net Worth: £5,081,000 *Total Assets:* £21,828,000
Registered Office: 6 Lakeside Business Park, Swan Lane, Sandhurst, Berks, GU47 9DN
Activities: Manufacture of weapons and ammunition
Parent: FNH UK Holdings Limited
Officers: Damon Marc Batstone [1974] Director/Chief Operating Officer; Glyn Paul Bottomley [1958] Director; Stephen Thomas Lee [1985] Director/Chief Financial Officer; Vincent Verleye [1966] Director/Vice President Industry and Technology [Belgian]; Patrick Vogne [1954] Director/Chief Financial Officer [Belgian]

Focusrite Audio Engineering Limited
Incorporated: 10 March 1989 *Employees:* 145
Net Worth: £23,693,000 *Total Assets:* £34,002,000
Registered Office: Windsor House, Turnpike Road, High Wycombe, Bucks, HP12 3FX
Activities: Manufacture of consumer electronics
Shareholders: Phillip Dudderidge; Jennifer Anne Dudderidge; Focusrite PLC
Officers: Katie Charlotte Bettison, Secretary; Timothy Paul Carroll [1962] Director [American]; Timothy John Dingley [1981] Operations Director; Philip Stephen Dudderidge [1949] Director; Damian Robert Hawley [1971] Sales Director; Simon Holt [1977] Director; Giles Richard Orford [1977] Director/Marketing; Jeremy Michael Charles Wilson [1966] Finance Director

Focusrite PLC
Incorporated: 14 November 2014 *Employees:* 209
Net Worth: £43,447,000 *Total Assets:* £54,926,000
Registered Office: Windsor House, Turnpike Road, High Wycombe, Bucks, HP12 3FX
Activities: Manufacture of other electrical equipment
Shareholders: Jennifer Anne Dudderidge; Philip Stephen Dudderidge
Officers: Francine Godrich, Secretary; David Charles Bezem [1960] Director; Timothy Paul Carroll [1962] Director [American]; Naomi Wendy Climer [1964] Director; Paul David Dean [1961] Director; Philip Stephen Dudderidge [1949] Director; Jeremy Michael Charles Wilson [1966] Finance Director

Fogarty Group Limited
Incorporated: 22 December 1977 *Employees:* 383
Net Worth: £20,643,742 *Total Assets:* £34,951,916
Registered Office: 1 Alpha Road, North Lane, Aldershot, Hants, GU12 4RG
Activities: Other business support service activities n.e.c.
Major Shareholder: Frank Fogarty
Officers: Francis John Patrick Fogarty, Secretary/Director [Irish]; Caroline Fogarty [1965] Director/Marketing Manager; Francis John Patrick Fogarty [1964] Director; Michael Joseph Fogerty [1967] Director/Site Manager [Irish]

Folkestone Harbour Holdings Limited
Incorporated: 11 May 2004
Net Worth Deficit: £8,579,899 *Total Assets:* £51,049,840
Registered Office: Strand House, Pilgrims Way, Monks Horton, Ashford, Kent, TN25 6DR
Activities: Activities of head offices
Major Shareholder: Roger Michael de Haan
Officers: Richard John Fraser, Secretary; Sir Roger Michael de Haan [1948] Director

Food Manufacturers (G.B. Company)
Incorporated: 27 November 1974 *Employees:* 8
Net Worth: £3,037,139,968 *Total Assets:* £3,976,732,928
Registered Office: 3D Dundee Road, Slough, Berks, SL1 4LG
Activities: Activities of head offices
Parent: Effem Holdings Limited
Officers: Gillian Mary Enevoldsen [1962] Director; David James Haines [1969] Director; Ian James Langer [1965] Director; David Arnaud Manzini [1972] Director [French]; Andrew Richard Parton [1968] Director; Craig Andrew Sargeant [1968] Director [Australian]; Deri Llewellyn Watkins [1973] Director

Foray 989 Limited
Incorporated: 31 December 1996 *Employees:* 3
Net Worth: £65,892,000 *Total Assets:* £126,810,000
Registered Office: 1 Park Lane, Hemel Hempstead, Herts, HP2 4YL
Activities: Activities of head offices
Parent: Bourne Leisure Holdings Limited
Officers: Jane Elizabeth Bentall [1970] Director/Accountant; Paul Charles Flaum [1970] Director; Iain Stuart Macmillan [1976] Director

Foreign Currency Direct PLC
Incorporated: 24 March 2004 *Employees:* 34
Net Worth: £2,696,681 *Total Assets:* £34,767,336
Registered Office: Currencies Mews, Badminton Court, Old Amersham, Bucks, HP7 0DD
Activities: Financial intermediation not elsewhere classified
Parent: Currency Holdings Limited
Officers: Phillipa Jane Sherman, Secretary; Martin John Bennett [1969] Director/Chairman; Tracy Anne Bownes [1977] Director; David Robert Dawson [1983] Director; Michael James Peter England [1981] Director; Thomas Richard Higham [1982] Director/Currency Broker; Phillipa Jane Sherman [1964] Finance Director

Foreman Homes Group Limited
Incorporated: 18 April 2002 *Employees:* 29
Net Worth: £11,040,752 *Total Assets:* £39,662,984
Registered Office: Unit 1 Station Industrial Park, Duncan Road, Park Gate, Southampton, SO31 1BX
Activities: Activities of head offices
Parent: ABL Capital Investments Ltd
Officers: Karen Spake, Secretary/Property Services Manager; Michael John Avery [1956] Construction Director; Stephen Paul Carrington [1970] Director/Planner; Spencer James Drake [1965] Sales Director; Graham Foreman [1971] Director/Builder; Nicholas Hardcastle [1979] Director/Accountant; Karen Spake [1974] Director/Property Services Manager

Forester Holdings (Europe) Limited
Incorporated: 23 January 1995
Net Worth: £70,213,000 *Total Assets:* £84,484,000
Registered Office: 2 Cromwell Avenue, Bromley, Kent, BR2 9BF
Activities: Activities of head offices
Parent: The Independent Order of Foresters
Officers: Jason Christopher Rose, Secretary; Euan Thomas Allison [1958] Director/Chief Executive Officer; Michael Christophers [1942] Director/Consultant; Robert Edward Lamoureux [1947] Director [Canadian]; John Todd Young [1957] Director/Retired Solicitor

Forester Life Limited
Incorporated: 2 December 1994 *Employees:* 162
Net Worth: £121,211,000 *Total Assets:* £4,291,504,128
Registered Office: 2 Cromwell Avenue, Bromley, Kent, BR2 9BF
Activities: Life insurance
Parent: Forester Holdings (Europe) Limited
Officers: Jason Christopher Rose, Secretary; Euan Thomas Allison [1958] Director/Chief Executive Officer; Michael Christophers [1942] Director/Consultant; Robert Edward Lamoureux [1947] Director [Canadian]; John Todd Young [1957] Director/Retired Solicitor

Forextra Developments Limited
Incorporated: 22 July 1986 *Employees:* 6
Net Worth: £80,567,624 *Total Assets:* £146,904,336
Registered Office: 8 Highbridge Close, Radlett, Herts, WD7 7GW
Activities: Other letting and operating of own or leased real estate
Parent: Frelene Limited
Officers: Freddy Salem [1941] Director/Buying Agent; Philip Joseph Salem [1981] Director

Formaplex Group Limited
Incorporated: 29 October 2007 *Employees:* 444
Net Worth: £4,220,000 *Total Assets:* £68,950,000
Registered Office: Access Point, Northarbour Road, Cosham, Portsmouth, PO6 3TE
Activities: Activities of head offices
Shareholder: Dunedin Buyout Fund II LP
Officers: Andrew David Bone [1963] Sales Director; Michael Thomas Bryant [1962] Operations Director; Ross Marshall [1958] Director; Charles Lewis Matthews [1953] Director; Ian Wilson [1965] Director/Sales Engineer

Formaplex Limited
Incorporated: 10 January 2001 *Employees:* 438
Net Worth: £22,347,000 *Total Assets:* £71,160,000
Registered Office: Access Point, Northarbour Road, Cosham, Portsmouth, PO6 3TE
Activities: Other manufacturing n.e.c.
Parent: Formaplex Holdings Ltd
Officers: Andrew David Bone [1963] Sales Director; Michael Thomas Bryant [1962] Operations Director; Ian Wilson [1965] Director

Fort Pitt Thomas Aveling Academies
Incorporated: 8 October 2010 *Employees:* 384
Previous: Fort Pitt Grammar School Academy Trust
Net Worth: £44,250,104 *Total Assets:* £55,282,144
Registered Office: Fort Pitt Grammar School, Fort Pitt Hill, Chatham, Kent, ME4 6TJ
Activities: General secondary education
Officers: Roger Brown [1947] Director; Kirstie Joy Cuthbert [1981] Director/HR Consultant; Patricia Daniels [1948] Director/Retired; Denise Marie Ford [1971] Director/Chartered Surveyor; Rosalind Frances Holden [1986] Director/Head of Wellbeing London South Bank University; Veenod Kumar Rama [1952] Director; Darren John Small [1972] Director/Financial Advisor; Roselyn Chinyere Unegbu [1971] Director/Head of Capital Delivery

Forth Health Holdings Limited
Incorporated: 2 November 2006
Net Worth Deficit: £114,618,000 *Total Assets:* £382,000,992
Registered Office: 8 White Oak Square, London Road, Swanley, Kent, BR8 7AG
Activities: Construction of commercial buildings
Parent: Palio (No 11) Limited
Officers: Carl Harvey Dix [1966] Operations Director; Jamie Pritchard [1971] Director/Investment Manager

Forth Health Limited
Incorporated: 2 November 2006
Net Worth Deficit: £114,619,000 *Total Assets:* £381,987,008
Registered Office: 8 White Oak Square, London Road, Swanley, Kent, BR8 7AG
Activities: Construction of commercial buildings
Parent: Forth Health Holdings Limited
Officers: Carl Harvey Dix [1966] Operations Director; Jamie Pritchard [1971] Director/Investment Manager

Fortis Lease UK Ltd
Incorporated: 28 January 1985
Net Worth: £10,547,000 *Total Assets:* £65,173,000
Registered Office: Northern Cross, Basing View, Basingstoke, Hants, RG21 4HL
Activities: Financial leasing
Parent: BNP Paribas SA
Officers: Nicholas David James, Secretary; Jean-Michel Robert Boyer [1963] Director/CEO - Country Manager [French]; Nicholas David James [1960] Finance & Operations Director

Forum Health Products Ltd.
Incorporated: 19 October 1981 *Employees:* 3
Net Worth: £2,284,257 *Total Assets:* £20,454,704
Registered Office: 2-8 Gloucester Road, Redhill, Surrey, RH1 1FH
Activities: Agents specialised in the sale of other particular products
Parent: Forum Products Holdings Limited
Officers: Neill Copp, Secretary; Joseph Marie Theodoor Wilhelmus Van Der Linden [1957] Director/Chief Financial Officer [Dutch]; Hidde Van Der Wal [1960] Director [Dutch]

Forum Products Holdings Limited
Incorporated: 15 April 2008 *Employees:* 42
Net Worth: £4,668,156 *Total Assets:* £28,498,912
Registered Office: 2-8 Gloucester Road, Redhill, Surrey, RH1 1FH
Activities: Agents specialised in the sale of other particular products
Parent: Barentz International B.V.
Officers: Neill Copp, Secretary; Joseph Marie Theodoor Wilhelmus Van Der Linden [1957] Director/Chief Financial Officer [Dutch]; Hidde Van Der Wal [1960] Director [Dutch]

Foss Holdings Limited
Incorporated: 13 December 2007 *Employees:* 90
Net Worth: £32,705,660 *Total Assets:* £36,265,248
Registered Office: 26 Reigate Road, Hookwood, Horley, Surrey, RH6 0HJ
Activities: Activities of head offices
Shareholder: Raymond Foss
Officers: Lesley Kay Foss, Secretary; Chris Adam Foss [1981] Director; Lesley Kay Foss [1961] Director; Raymond David Foss [1971] Director; Raymond Foss [1951] Director; Richard Colin Foss [1976] Director; Rachelle Ann Rowe [1973] Director

Fossil (UK) Limited
Incorporated: 30 May 1995 *Employees:* 463
Net Worth: £18,053,000 *Total Assets:* £67,411,000
Registered Office: Featherstone House, Featherstone Road, Wolverton Mill, Milton Keynes, Bucks, MK12 5TH
Activities: Wholesale of watches and jewellery
Parent: Fossil (UK) Holdings Ltd
Officers: Daniel Charles McAllister, Secretary; Richard Collins [1973] Managing Director; Antonio Nigro [1978] Director/VP Europe North [Italian]

The Foundation and Friends of The Royal Botanic Gardens, Kew
Incorporated: 3 May 1990 *Employees:* 47
Net Worth: £27,490,000 *Total Assets:* £30,912,000
Registered Office: 47 Kew Green, Kew, Richmond, Surrey, TW9 3AB
Activities: Activities of other membership organisations n.e.c.
Officers: Marcus Ambrose Paul Agius [1946] Director; Ian Karet [1963] Director/Solicitor; Kristina Louise Kenworthy [1958] Director/Solicitor; Jan Stephen Pethick [1947] Director/Chair, Troy Asset Management; Charles Nigel Cross Sherwood [1959] Director/Private Equity

Foundation Developments Limited
Incorporated: 2 October 1990 *Employees:* 37
Net Worth: £7,588,021 *Total Assets:* £36,966,392
Registered Office: Foundation House, Clarendon Road, Wallington, Surrey, SM6 8QX
Activities: Other specialised construction activities n.e.c.
Parent: Hickey Group Limited
Officers: Anne Hickey, Secretary/Director [Irish]; Stewart Paul Adcock [1965] Pre Construction Director; Anne Hickey [1951] Director [Irish]; Patrick Hickey [1954] Director/Building Contractor [Irish]; Trina Anne Hickey [1981] Finance & HR Director [Irish]; Martin Joseph McDonagh [1967] Director/Quantity Surveyor [Irish]; Shane Nicholson [1975] Construction Director [Irish]

Foundocean Group Limited
Incorporated: 10 June 2014 *Employees:* 72
Net Worth: £7,135,920 *Total Assets:* £33,864,664
Registered Office: Suite 2, Regency House, Dedmere Road, Marlow, Bucks, SL7 1FJ
Activities: Other specialised construction activities n.e.c.
Officers: Giancarlo Beraudo [1979] Director/Investment Professional [Italian]; Rolando Polli [1940] Director/Investment Professional [Italian]

Four Coal Shipping Limited
Incorporated: 20 June 2014
Net Worth: £7,319,425 *Total Assets:* £32,154,102
Registered Office: Four House, Copthorne Common Road, Copthorne, W Sussex, RH10 3LF
Activities: Sea and coastal freight water transport
Parent: KKR & Co. L.P.
Officers: Jens Martin Jensen [1964] Director [Danish]; Roberto Rondelli [1980] Director [Italian]

Fourfront Holdings Limited
Incorporated: 22 March 2016 *Employees:* 301
Net Worth: £5,255,836 *Total Assets:* £44,251,040
Registered Office: The Old Post Office, 33 Station Road, Egham, Surrey, TW20 9LA
Activities: Activities of other holding companies n.e.c.
Officers: Gary James Chandler [1969] Director/Chief Executive; James Elwin Cornwell [1967] Director; Mark Joseph Scott [1968] Director; Aki Stamatis [1960] Director

Francotyp-Postalia Limited
Incorporated: 22 November 1989 *Employees:* 101
Net Worth: £7,356,000 *Total Assets:* £24,351,000
Registered Office: 74 Questor, Powder Mill Lane, Dartford, Kent, DA1 1EF
Activities: Other business support service activities n.e.c.
Parent: Francotyp-Postalia International GmbH
Officers: Adam Joseph Branch [1968] Sales Director; Leonard James Fletcher [1949] Managing Director; Leanne Tyrrell [1971] Marketing Director; Nicola Jane Walford [1971] Operations Director

Franklin UK Bidco Limited
Incorporated: 10 November 2015 *Employees:* 11
Net Worth: £344,475,872 *Total Assets:* £680,102,464
Registered Office: 47-49 London Road, Redhill, Surrey, RH1 1LU
Activities: Activities of financial services holding companies
Parent: Franklin UK Midco Limited
Officers: Marc Frappier [1973] Director [French]; Edouard Guigou [1980] Deputy Director [French]; Jamie Anthony Keir [1981] Director; Patrick Gerard Waldron [1962] Director [Irish]

Franklin UK Midco Limited
Incorporated: 16 November 2015 *Employees:* 9
Net Worth: £373,620,128 *Total Assets:* £406,509,920
Registered Office: 47-49 London Road, Redhill, Surrey, RH1 1LU
Activities: Activities of financial services holding companies
Parent: Eurazeo S.E.
Officers: Edoardo Fracchia [1985] Director [Italian]; Marc Frappier [1973] Director [French]; Pascale Guerin-Laffineur [1964] Risk Management Director [French]; Edouard Guigou [1980] Deputy Director [French]; Jamie Anthony Keir [1981] Director; Francesco Orsi [1979] Executive Director [Italian]; Charles Petruccelli [1951] Director/Consultant [French]; David Valentine James Sear [1964] Director; Patrick Gerard Waldron [1962] Director [Irish]

Alexander Fraser Holdings Limited
Incorporated: 11 December 1959 *Employees:* 314
Net Worth: £47,080,652 *Total Assets:* £58,880,576
Registered Office: Foxhills, Stonehills Road, Ottershaw, Surrey, KT16 0EL
Activities: Activities of head offices
Major Shareholder: Pamela Lillian Hayton
Officers: Pamela Lillian Hayton, Secretary [Australian]; Marc Alexander Hayton [1964] Director/Marketing; Pamela Lillian Hayton [1939] Director [Australian]

FRC Star Group Bidco Limited
Incorporated: 27 September 2017
Net Worth: £119,694,832 *Total Assets:* £351,048,448
Registered Office: 1 High Street, Windsor, Berks, SL4 1LD
Activities: Activities of other holding companies n.e.c.
Parent: FRC Star Group Parent Limited
Officers: Sean Kime, Secretary; Ashminder Singh [1982] Director/Investment Professional [American]; John Storey [1968] Director; Claude Zinngrabe [1946] Director/Real Estate Private Equity Investment [American]

FRC Star Group Holdings Limited
Incorporated: 26 September 2017 *Employees:* 996
Net Worth: £118,582,312 *Total Assets:* £380,794,272
Registered Office: 1 High Street, Windsor, Berks, SL4 1LD
Activities: Activities of other holding companies n.e.c.
Officers: Sean Kime, Secretary; Danish Hameed [1991] Director/Investment Professional [American]; John Moore [1961] Director [American]; Ashminder Singh [1982] Director/Investment Professional [American]; John Storey [1968] Director; Claude Zinngrabe [1946] Director/Real Estate Private Equity Investment [American]

Fresca Group Limited
Incorporated: 8 December 2004 *Employees:* 888
Net Worth: £57,946,000 *Total Assets:* £112,336,000
Registered Office: The Fresh Produce Centre, Transfesa Road, Paddock Wood, Kent, TN12 6UT
Activities: Activities of head offices
Shareholder: The Fresca Esop Limited
Officers: Veronica Warner, Secretary; Ian Alexander Craig [1957] Director; Simon James Hodson [1956] Director/Solicitor; Christopher Peter Mack [1955] Director; Elizabeth McMeikan [1962] Director; Brett Geoffrey Sumner [1973] Finance Director; Nigel John Trood [1965] Director

Fresenius Kabi Oncology PLC
Incorporated: 10 December 1998 *Employees:* 47
Net Worth Deficit: £2,692,000 *Total Assets:* £25,414,000
Registered Office: Lion Court, Farnham Road, Bordon, Hants, GU35 0NF
Activities: Manufacture of basic pharmaceutical products
Parent: Fresenius SE & Co KGaA
Officers: Tanja Greve [1972] Director/Executive Vice President - CFO [German]; Michael James Newson [1963] Director [French]

Fresh Direct (UK) Limited
Incorporated: 5 May 1995 *Employees:* 1,191
Net Worth: £1,823,000 *Total Assets:* £70,722,000
Registered Office: Enterprise House, Eureka Business Park, Ashford, Kent, TN25 4AG
Activities: Wholesale of fruit and vegetables
Parent: Fresh Holdings Limited
Officers: Sarah Leanne Whibley, Secretary; Rajesh Vishwanath Tugnait [1969] Director/Chief Executive Officer; Sarah Leanne Whibley [1976] Director/Solicitor

Fresh Direct Group Limited
Incorporated: 7 November 2014
Net Worth: £104,700,000 *Total Assets:* £154,200,000
Registered Office: Enterprise House, Eureka Business Park, Ashford, Kent, TN25 4AG
Activities: Activities of head offices
Parent: Cucina Fresh Finance Limited
Officers: Sarah Whibley, Secretary; Michael David Ball [1967] Director/Group Chief Financial Officer; Joel Todd Grade [1970] Director/Executive VP & CFO [American]; Ajoy Hari Karna [1966] Director/Senior Vice President [American]

Fridays Limited
Incorporated: 23 March 1971 *Employees:* 278
Net Worth: £45,940,280 *Total Assets:* £50,088,196
Registered Office: Chequer Tree Farm, Benenden Road, Cranbrook, Kent, TN17 3PN
Activities: Wholesale of dairy products, eggs and edible oils and fats
Shareholders: Malcolm Roland Friday; Andrew David Friday
Officers: Andrew David Friday, Secretary; Yvonne Daphne Barclay [1961] Director; Andrew David Friday [1957] Director/Farmer; Kathleen Mary Friday [1952] Director/Farmer; Malcolm Roland Friday [1951] Director/Farmer; Andrew Collier Watts [1949] Director/Production Manager

Friends Life FPG Limited
Incorporated: 27 March 2009
Net Worth: £109,520,000 *Total Assets:* £109,520,000
Registered Office: Pixham End, Dorking, Surrey, RH4 1QA
Activities: Activities of financial services holding companies
Parent: Aviva Life Holdings UK Limited
Officers: Andrew David Briggs [1966] Director; Jason Michael Windsor [1972] Director

Friends Life FPL Limited
Incorporated: 23 November 2000
Net Worth: £107,993,000 *Total Assets:* £118,098,000
Registered Office: Pixham End, Dorking, Surrey, RH4 1QA
Activities: Activities of financial services holding companies
Parent: Friends Life FPG Limited
Officers: Andrew David Briggs [1966] Director; Jason Michael Windsor [1972] Director

Friends Life Holdings PLC
Incorporated: 10 August 2009
Net Worth: £363,000,000 *Total Assets:* £1,580,999,936
Registered Office: Pixham End, Dorking, Surrey, RH4 1QA
Activities: Activities of financial services holding companies
Parent: Aviva Group Holdings Limited
Officers: Julian Charles Baddeley, Secretary; Shamira Mohammed [1968] Director; Thomas Dawson Stoddard [1966] Director [American]; Susan Sharrock Yates [1958] Director/Treasurer

Frimley Topco Limited
Incorporated: 4 August 2011
Net Worth Deficit: £4,441,000 *Total Assets:* £24,121,000
Registered Office: Unit 4 Albany Park, Frimley Road, Camberley, Surrey, GU16 7PQ
Activities: Retail sale of bread, cakes, flour confectionery and sugar confectionery in specialised stores
Parent: Krispy Kreme Holding UK Limited
Officers: Joshua Alan Charlesworth [1974] Director/Chief Financial Officer [Canadian/British]; Niren Chaudhary [1963] Director/President and COO; Richard Cheshire [1968] Director; Timothy James Hennessy [1961] Director/Chief Financial Officer [American]; Margareta Caroline Elisabet Wullrich [1973] Director/Chief Financial Officer [Swedish]

Frontier Software PLC
Incorporated: 18 June 1990 *Employees:* 591
Net Worth: £16,709,134 *Total Assets:* £39,306,400
Registered Office: Frontier House, 63 Guildford Road, Lightwater, Surrey, GU18 5SA
Activities: Business and domestic software development
Officers: Jane Linda Howard, Secretary/Director; Jane Linda Howard [1948] Administrative Director; Michael Howard [1948] Managing Director; Stephen William Pritchet [1957] Director/Chartered Accountant

Wilfred T Fry Limited
Incorporated: 1 April 1926 *Employees:* 116
Net Worth: £9,638,923 *Total Assets:* £30,712,948
Registered Office: Crescent House, Crescent Road, Worthing, W Sussex, BN11 1RN
Activities: Other activities auxiliary to insurance and pension funding
Parent: Fry Wealth Limited
Officers: Richard Duncan Lloyd Butler, Secretary; Aidan Patrick Bailey [1971] Director/Financial Consultant; Richard Duncan Lloyd Butler [1956] Finance Director; Jeremy James Thomas Woodley [1970] Director/Financial Consultant

FT Finance Limited
Incorporated: 21 May 1990
Net Worth: £61,886,000 *Total Assets:* £87,207,000
Registered Office: Honeywell House, Skimped Hill Lane, Bracknell, Berks, RG12 1EB
Activities: Activities of head offices
Parent: First Technology Limited
Officers: Asad Ali [1984] Director; John J Tus [1958] Director [American]

FT North America Limited
Incorporated: 24 February 2004 *Employees:* 2
Net Worth: £467,737,696 *Total Assets:* £508,661,312
Registered Office: Honeywell House, Skimped Hill Lane, Bracknell, Berks, RG12 1EB
Activities: Activities of head offices
Parent: FT Finance Limited
Officers: Asad Ali [1984] Director; John J Tus [1958] Director [American]

FTR Holdings Ltd
Incorporated: 18 March 2016
Net Worth: £99,674 *Total Assets:* £32,104,168
Registered Office: 2nd Floor, Partis House, Knowlhill, Milton Keynes, Bucks, MK5 8HJ
Activities: Activities of other holding companies n.e.c.
Shareholders: Barry Andrew Moseley; Mark Anthony Pepper; Barry Andrew Moseley; Mark Anthony Pepper
Officers: Barry Andrew Moseley [1965] Managing Director; Mark Anthony Pepper [1972] Director

Fujifilm Ink Solutions Limited
Incorporated: 11 February 1983
Previous: Fujifilm Sericol International Limited
Net Worth Deficit: £4,624,924 *Total Assets:* £31,393,956
Registered Office: Patricia Way, Pysons Road Industrial Estate, Broadstairs, Kent, CT10 2LE
Activities: Activities of production holding companies
Parent: Fujifilm Sericol Overseas Holdings Limited
Officers: Neil Llewellyn Denham, Secretary; Aiichiro Hiruma [1959] Director [Japanese]; Martin Wilhelm Schoeppler [1955] Director/Chief Executive Officer [American/German]; Tatsuo Suzuki [1964] Director/General Manager [Japanese]; Ian David Wilkinson [1964] Director/Chief Operating Officer

Fujifilm Sericol Overseas Holdings Limited
Incorporated: 16 January 2003
Net Worth: £18,449,000 *Total Assets:* £26,115,000
Registered Office: Patricia Way, Pysons Road Industrial Estate, Broadstairs, Kent, CT10 2LE
Activities: Other manufacturing n.e.c.
Parent: Fujifilm Holdings Corporation
Officers: Neil Llewellyn Denham, Secretary; Aiichiro Hiruma [1959] Director [Japanese]; Martin Wilhelm Schoeppler [1955] Director/Chief Executive Officer [American/German]; Tatsuo Suzuki [1964] Director/General Manager [Japanese]; Ian David Wilkinson [1964] Director/Chief Operating Officer; Masato Yamamoto [1963] Director [Japanese]

Fujifilm Speciality Ink Systems Limited
Incorporated: 26 September 2002 *Employees:* 308
Net Worth: £61,552,000 *Total Assets:* £113,018,000
Registered Office: Unit 21 & 22 Patricia Way, Pysons Road Industrial Estate, Broadstairs, Kent, CT10 2LE
Activities: Other manufacturing n.e.c.
Parent: Fujifilm Ink Solutions Limited
Officers: Neil Llewellyn Denham, Secretary; Aiichiro Hiruma [1959] Director [Japanese]; Shinichiro Kuwabara [1963] Director/Manager [Japanese]; Robert Charles Platts [1975] Director/Chartered Accountant; Martin Wilhelm Schoeppler [1955] Director/Chief Executive Officer [American/German]; Tatsuo Suzuki [1964] Director/General Manager [Japanese]; Ian David Wilkinson [1964] Director/Chief Operating Officer; Masato Yamamoto [1963] Director [Japanese]

Fujifilm UK Limited
Incorporated: 22 June 1976 *Employees:* 324
Net Worth: £75,588,000 *Total Assets:* £110,252,000
Registered Office: St Martins Business Centre, St Martins Way, Bedford, MK42 0LF
Activities: Wholesale of radio, television goods & electrical household appliances (other than records, tapes, CDs)
Parent: Fujifilm Holdings Corporation
Officers: Neil Llewellyn Denham, Secretary; Yoshitaka Nakamura [1967] Director [Japanese]; Masato Yamamoto [1963] Director [Japanese]

Fulham Football Club Limited
Incorporated: 24 March 1987 *Employees:* 270
Net Worth Deficit: £49,657,000 *Total Assets:* £37,528,000
Registered Office: Fulham Football Club, Training Ground, Motspur Park, New Malden, Surrey, KT3 6PT
Activities: Activities of sport clubs
Shareholders: Shahid Rafiq Khan Family Trust A; Shahid Rafiq Khan Family Trust B
Officers: Neville Darren Preston, Secretary; David John Daly [1959] Director; Antony Rafiq Khan [1982] Director [American]; Shahid Rafiq Khan [1950] Director/Executive [American]; Mark Lamping [1958] Director/President, Jacksonville Jaguars [American]; Alistair Julian Mackintosh [1970] Director/Chief Executive Officer

Fulham Football Leisure Limited
Incorporated: 21 May 1997 *Employees:* 270
Net Worth: £76,984,000 *Total Assets:* £165,480,000
Registered Office: Fulham Football Club, Training Ground, Motspur Park, New Malden, Surrey, KT3 6PT
Activities: Activities of sport clubs
Shareholders: Shahid Rafiq Khan Family Trust A; Shahid Rafiq Khan Family Trust B
Officers: Neville Darren Preston, Secretary; Shahid Rafiq Khan [1950] Director/Executive [American]; Mark Lamping [1958] Director/President, Jacksonville Jaguars [American]; Alistair Julian Mackintosh [1970] Director/Chief Executive Officer

Fulham Stadium Limited
Incorporated: 23 May 1997
Net Worth: £104,166,000 *Total Assets:* £113,179,000
Registered Office: Fulham Football Club, Training Ground, Motspur Park, New Malden, Surrey, KT3 6PT
Activities: Operation of sports facilities
Shareholders: Shahid Rafiq Khan Family Trust A; Shahid Rafiq Khan Family Trust B
Officers: Neville Darren Preston, Secretary; Shahid Rafiq Khan [1950] Director/Executive [American]; Mark Lamping [1958] Director/President, Jacksonville Jaguars [American]; Alistair Julian Mackintosh [1970] Director/Chief Executive Officer

Fulston Manor Academies Trust
Incorporated: 12 August 2010 *Employees:* 296
Net Worth: £16,262,458 *Total Assets:* £20,265,348
Registered Office: Fulston Manor School, Brenchley Road, Sittingbourne, Kent, ME10 4EG
Activities: General secondary education
Officers: Alan Geoffrey Brookes [1953] Director/Headteacher; Peter Crouch [1957] Director; Samantha Fenn [1969] Director/Headteacher; Louise O'Sullivan [1967] Director; David Robinson [1953] Director/Chair Fulston Manor School LGB; Andrew Raymond Watton [1970] Director

Furniture Village Group Limited
Incorporated: 6 November 2001
Net Worth: £3,281,000 *Total Assets:* £34,781,000
Registered Office: 258 Bath Road, Slough, Berks, SL1 4DX
Activities: Activities of head offices
Parent: Furniture Village Holdings Limited
Officers: Claire Elizabeth Shiels, Secretary; Peter John Harrison [1946] Director; James Clifford Hodkinson [1944] Director; Stephen Anthony McPartland [1976] Director/Member of Parliament; Claire Elizabeth Shiels [1974] Director/Accountant

Furniture Village Holdings Limited
Incorporated: 27 April 2007 *Employees:* 993
Net Worth: £2,595,000 *Total Assets:* £89,110,000
Registered Office: 258 Bath Road, Slough, Berks, SL1 4DX
Activities: Activities of head offices
Major Shareholder: Peter John Harrison
Officers: Claire Elizabeth Shiels, Secretary; Peter John Harrison [1946] Director; James Clifford Hodkinson [1944] Director; Stephen Anthony McPartland [1976] Director/Member of Parliament; Claire Elizabeth Shiels [1974] Director/Accountant; Jane Elizabeth Vinson [1971] Director/Investor

Furniture Village Limited
Incorporated: 20 October 1988 *Employees:* 993
Net Worth: £15,341,000 *Total Assets:* £113,785,000
Registered Office: 258 Bath Road, Slough, Berks, SL1 4DX
Activities: Retail of furniture, lighting, and similar (not musical instruments or scores) in specialised store
Parent: Furniture Village Group Limited
Officers: Claire Elizabeth Shiels, Secretary; Peter John Harrison [1946] Director; James Clifford Hodkinson [1944] Director; Stephen Anthony McPartland [1976] Director/Member of Parliament; Claire Elizabeth Shiels [1974] Director/Accountant

Furze Platt Senior School
Incorporated: 3 November 2011 *Employees:* 157
Net Worth: £20,814,184 *Total Assets:* £24,165,856
Registered Office: Furze Platt Senior School, Furze Platt Road, Maidenhead, Berks, SL6 7NQ
Activities: General secondary education
Shareholders: Gavin Olaf William Tisshaw; Hugh James Boulter
Officers: Lynne Moore, Secretary; Hugh James Boulter [1952] Director/Aviation Consultant; Michael Andrew Clayton [1961] Director/IT; Katharine Jane Donnison [1973] Director/Senior Sales & Marketing Manager; David Dunning [1966] Director; Dr Jacqueline Ann Edwards [1965] Director; Diane Flood [1963] Director/Librarian; Laraine Holdsworth [1959] Director/Healthcare Marketing and Communications Consultant; David Leslie Holloway [1965] Director/Asbestos Surveyor; Susan Patricia Le Page [1953] Director; Dr Andrew Morrison [1973] Director/Headteacher; Dr Michelle Scott [1964] Director/Teacher; Roger Michael Smith [1965] Director/Consultant; Hugh Jerome Steed [1971] Director [Irish]; Gavin Olaf William Tisshaw [1961] Director/Chartered Financial Planner

Future Electronics Limited
Incorporated: 9 January 1987 *Employees:* 341
Net Worth: £190,015,008 *Total Assets:* £418,320,000
Registered Office: Future House, The Glanty, Egham, Surrey, TW20 9AH
Activities: Wholesale of electronic and telecommunications equipment and parts
Officers: Keith Carton, Secretary; Gary Bruce Oliver [1965] Director; Ann Shepherd [1970] Director/HR & Business Operations

Future Electronics Management Services Limited
Incorporated: 22 December 2004 *Employees:* 3
Net Worth: £148,179,008 *Total Assets:* £160,879,008
Registered Office: Future House, The Glanty, Egham, Surrey, TW20 9AH
Activities: Activities of head offices
Officers: Keith Carton, Secretary; Gary Bruce Oliver [1965] Director; Ann Shepherd [1970] HR Business Director

Future Schools Trust
Incorporated: 7 June 2007 *Employees:* 346
Net Worth: £20,197,000 *Total Assets:* £27,373,000
Registered Office: Cornwallis Academy, Hubbards Lane, Boughton Monchelsea, Maidstone, Kent, ME17 4HX
Activities: Pre-primary education
Officers: Linda Evelyn Cann [1949] Director/Retired; Michael Geoffrey Shaun Farrell [1950] Director/Retired; Marilyn Lesley Hodges [1951] Director; Mark Kirby [1976] Director/Area Sales Manager; Isabelle Noelle Helene Linney-Drouet [1971] Director/Principal [French]; Graham Niblock [1957] Director/Consultant - RBS Bank

FWPJV Limited
Incorporated: 18 November 2010 *Employees:* 12
Net Worth: £4,096,661 *Total Assets:* £54,723,048
Registered Office: Fluor Centre, 140 Pinehurst Road, Farnborough, Hants, GU14 7BF
Activities: Other business support service activities n.e.c.
Shareholders: Fluor Holdings Inc.; WorleyParsons EA Holdings
Officers: Ian Brennen [1964] Director/Office Operations Manager; Alan Stewart Gordon [1964] Regional Director Europe Central Asia; Ashley Graham Rees [1965] Director/General Manager; Christopher Gordan Stanley Wynterbee-Robey [1958] Contract Services Director

Fyffes Group Limited
Incorporated: 9 May 1901 *Employees:* 479
Net Worth Deficit: £5,552,000 *Total Assets:* £82,186,000
Registered Office: Houndmills Road, Houndmills Industrial Estate, Basingstoke, Hants, RG21 6XL
Activities: Wholesale of fruit and vegetables
Parent: FII Investments
Officers: Brian Breathnach, Secretary; Paul Alexander James Armstrong [1966] Commercial Director; Joanne Blake [1975] Director; Andrew Hugh Denham Smith [1963] Director/General Manager; Richard John Enright [1980] Finance Director [Irish]; John Hopkins [1973] Director/General Manager; Andrew James Joyce [1970] UK Operations Director; Thomas Gerard Murphy [1960] Director/Chartered Accountant [Irish]

Fynecast Limited
Incorporated: 29 October 1963 *Employees:* 5
Net Worth: £25,758,288 *Total Assets:* £38,197,432
Registered Office: 6 Spring Meadows Business Centre, Highfield Farm, Wargrave, Reading, Berks, RG10 8PZ
Activities: Development of building projects
Major Shareholder: Dale Russell Norton
Officers: Barry Russell Norton, Secretary; Barry Russell Norton [1942] Director/Chartered Surveyor; Dale Russell Norton [1967] Director/Estate Agent

G & O Securities Limited
Incorporated: 18 August 1994 *Employees:* 2
Net Worth: £10,497,599 *Total Assets:* £22,798,464
Registered Office: 60 Kingston Road, New Malden, Surrey, KT3 3JG
Activities: Buying and selling of own real estate
Parent: G & O Group Limited
Officers: Christopher John O'Dell, Secretary/Consultant; Ferdous Sultana Gossain [1962] Director; Christopher John O'Dell [1952] Director/Consultant

G.E.W. (EC) Limited
Incorporated: 8 March 1991 *Employees:* 121
Net Worth: £10,275,951 *Total Assets:* £29,227,032
Registered Office: 3rd Floor, Portland Building, 25 High Street, Crawley, W Sussex, RH10 1BG
Activities: Manufacture of other special-purpose machinery n.e.c.
Shareholders: Malcolm Charles Rae; Gillian Rae
Officers: Gillian Ella Rae, Company Secretary; Gillian Ella Rae [1956] Director/Company Secretary; Malcolm Charles Rae [1954] Director

G4S Cash Centres (UK) Limited
Incorporated: 13 March 1980 *Employees:* 1,297
Net Worth: £20,705,000 *Total Assets:* £31,722,000
Registered Office: Sutton Park House, 15 Carshalton Road, Sutton, Surrey, SM1 4LD
Activities: Private security activities
Parent: G4S UK Holdings Limited
Officers: Vaishali Jagdish Patel, Secretary; John Michael Joseph Campbell [1967] Managing Director [Irish]; Jodie Louise France [1977] Finance Director; John William Lennox [1960] Operations Director

G4S Cash Solutions (UK) Limited
Incorporated: 10 July 1939 *Employees:* 3,305
Net Worth: £108,017,000 *Total Assets:* £169,738,000
Registered Office: Sutton Park House, 15 Carshalton Road, Sutton, Surrey, SM1 4LD
Activities: Private security activities
Shareholders: G4S UK Holdings Limited; G4S UK Holdings Limited
Officers: Vaishali Jagdish Patel, Secretary; John Michael Joseph Campbell [1967] Managing Director [Irish]; Jodie Louise France [1977] Finance Director; John William Lennox [1960] Director

G4S Secure Solutions (UK) Limited
Incorporated: 14 March 1972 *Employees:* 13,555
Net Worth: £37,315,000 *Total Assets:* £184,500,992
Registered Office: Sutton Park House, 15 Carshalton Road, Sutton, Surrey, SM1 4LD
Activities: Private security activities
Parent: G4S Regional Management (UK & I) Limited
Officers: Vaishali Jagdish Patel, Secretary; Douglas Charles Hewitson [1963] Director; Graham Austen Levinsohn [1962] Director; David Paul Lobley [1965] Finance Director

G4S Security Services (UK) Limited
Incorporated: 8 May 1989 *Employees:* 4,209
Net Worth: £69,080,000 *Total Assets:* £110,271,000
Registered Office: Sutton Park House, 15 Carshalton Road, Sutton, Surrey, SM1 4LD
Activities: Private security activities
Parent: G4S Secure Solutions (UK) Limited
Officers: Vaishali Jagdish Patel, Secretary; Douglas Charles Hewitson [1963] Managing Director; Graham Austen Levinsohn [1962] Director; David Paul Lobley [1965] Finance Director

Galaxy Acquisition Co 1 Ltd
Incorporated: 11 February 2016
Net Worth: £295,055,072 *Total Assets:* £988,417,216
Registered Office: The Forum, Station Road, Theale, Reading, Berks, RG7 4RA
Activities: Activities of head offices
Parent: Galaxy Holdco 1 Ltd
Officers: Jason Michael Brady [1968] Director/Senior Vice President General Counsel and Secretary [American]; Renato Carlo Giger [1960] Director/Chief Financial Officer [Swiss]

Galaxy Acquisition Co 2 Ltd
Incorporated: 11 February 2016
Net Worth: £295,055,072 *Total Assets:* £988,417,216
Registered Office: The Forum, Station Road, Theale, Reading, Berks, RG7 4RA
Activities: Activities of head offices
Parent: Galaxy Holdco 2 Ltd
Officers: Jason Michael Brady [1968] Director/Senior Vice President General Counsel and Secretary [American]; Renato Carlo Giger [1960] Director/Chief Financial Officer [Swiss]

Galaxy Group Bidco Limited
Incorporated: 14 December 2017 *Employees:* 2,538
Net Worth: £89,760,000 *Total Assets:* £390,119,008
Registered Office: Units 6 & 7 Princeton Mews, 167-169 London Road, Kingston upon Thames, Surrey, KT2 6PT
Activities: Activities of other holding companies n.e.c.
Parent: Galaxy Group Midco Limited
Officers: Nicola Hopkins, Secretary; Ruben Kumar Bhagobati [1971] Director/Principal; Malcolm Brown [1967] Director/Head of Asset Management Europe; Garry John Fitton [1972] Finance Director; Nicola Rosemary Lucy Hopkins [1968] Director/Chartered Accountant; Peter Kinsey [1964] Director; Julie-Anne Marie Mizzi [1969] Director [Australian]; Adam Ringer [1980] Investment Director; David Andrew Spruzen [1967] Director

Galaxy Holdco 1 Ltd
Incorporated: 11 February 2016
Net Worth: £303,035,488 *Total Assets:* £303,035,488
Registered Office: The Forum, Station Road, Theale, Reading, Berks, RG7 4RA
Activities: Activities of head offices
Parent: Solera LLC
Officers: Jason Michael Brady [1968] Director/Senior Vice President General Counsel and Secretary [American]; Renato Carlo Giger [1960] Director/Chief Financial Officer [Swiss]

Galaxy Holdco 2 Ltd
Incorporated: 11 February 2016
Net Worth: £303,035,488 *Total Assets:* £303,035,488
Registered Office: The Forum, Station Road, Theale, Reading, Berks, RG7 4RA
Activities: Activities of head offices
Parent: Solera LLC
Officers: Jason Michael Brady [1968] Director/Senior Vice President General Counsel and Secretary [American]; Renato Carlo Giger [1960] Director/Chief Financial Officer [Swiss]

Galileo Global Technologies Ltd
Incorporated: 9 October 2015 *Employees:* 345
Net Worth: £46,526,992 *Total Assets:* £145,212,464
Registered Office: c/o Aztec Financial Services (UK) Limited, Forum 3, Solent Business Park, Whiteley, Fareham, Hants, PO15 7FH
Activities: Support activities for petroleum and natural gas mining
Parent: Galileo Holdco 2 Limited
Officers: Ulises de La Orden [1945] Director/Engineer [Argentinian]; Osvaldo Claudio Del Campo [1964] Director/Entrepreneur [Argentinian]; Salil Oberoi [1983] Director [Argentinian]; Thomas Joseph Sikorski [1961] Director/Partner [American]

Galileo Holdco 1 Limited
Incorporated: 20 April 2016 *Employees:* 345
Net Worth Deficit: £23,190,956 *Total Assets:* £145,208,784
Registered Office: Aztec Financial Services (UK) Limited, Forum 3, Solent Business Park, Whiteley, Fareham, Hants, PO15 7FH
Activities: Support activities for petroleum and natural gas mining
Officers: Ulises de La Orden [1945] Director/Engineer [Argentinian]; Osvaldo Claudio Del Campo [1964] Director/Entrepreneur [Argentinian]; Salil Oberoi [1983] Director [Argentinian]; Thomas Joseph Sikorski [1961] Director/Partner [American]

Galileo Holdco 2 Limited
Incorporated: 21 April 2016
Net Worth Deficit: £22,776,346 *Total Assets:* £82,833,048
Registered Office: Aztec Financial Services (UK) Limited, Parkway, Solent Business Park, Whiteley, Fareham, Hants, PO15 7FH
Activities: Support activities for petroleum and natural gas mining
Parent: Galileo Holdco 1 Limited
Officers: Ulises de La Orden [1945] Director/Engineer [Argentinian]; Osvaldo Claudio Del Campo [1964] Director/Entrepreneur [Argentinian]; Salil Oberoi [1983] Director [Argentinian]; Thomas Sikorski [1961] Director/Partner [American]

Gallaher Group Limited
Incorporated: 2 January 1997 *Employees:* 5
Net Worth: £724,998,976 *Total Assets:* £769,382,976
Registered Office: Members Hill, Brooklands Road, Weybridge, Surrey, KT13 0QU
Activities: Activities of head offices
Parent: JTI (UK) Management Ltd
Officers: Nicholas Charles David Craig, Secretary; Charles Ashley Cunningham-Reid [1968] Director; Paul Bernard Hennessy [1980] Director [Irish]; Jeroen Rusbach [1977] Director/Accountant [Dutch]; Daniel Sciamma [1970] Director [French]

Gallaher Limited
Incorporated: 12 June 1980 *Employees:* 651
Net Worth: £303,400,000 *Total Assets:* £1,385,600,000
Registered Office: Members Hill, Brooklands Road, Weybridge, Surrey, KT13 0QU
Activities: Manufacture of tobacco products
Parent: Benson & Hedges Limited
Officers: Nicholas Charles David Craig, Secretary; Stephane Berset [1975] Director [Swiss]; Charles Ashley Cunningham-Reid [1968] Director; Paul Bernard Hennessy [1980] Director [Irish]; Ross Michael Hennessy [1981] Director [Irish]; Jason Robert Melling [1971] HR Director; Daniel Sciamma [1970] Director [French]

Gallaher Overseas (Holdings) Limited
Incorporated: 10 May 2000
Net Worth: £440,740,000 *Total Assets:* £440,740,000
Registered Office: Members Hill, Brooklands Road, Weybridge, Surrey, KT13 0QU
Activities: Activities of head offices
Parent: Gallaher Group Limited
Officers: Nicholas Charles David Craig, Secretary; Charles Ashley Cunningham-Reid [1968] Director; Paul Bernard Hennessy [1980] Director [Irish]; Jeroen Rusbach [1977] Director/Accountant [Dutch]; Daniel Sciamma [1970] Director [French]

Gallaher Overseas Limited
Incorporated: 17 August 1988 *Employees:* 6
Net Worth: £37,150,000 *Total Assets:* £52,846,000
Registered Office: Members Hill, Brooklands Road, Weybridge, Surrey, KT13 0QU
Activities: Activities of head offices
Parent: Gallaher Overseas (Holdings) Limited
Officers: Nicholas Charles David Craig, Secretary; Mohammed Junab Ali [1981] Director/Accountant; Andrew Chamberlain [1965] Director/Accountant; Alison Maria Hawkett [1968] Director/Accountant; Paul Bernard Hennessy [1980] Director [Irish]; Jeroen Rusbach [1977] Director/Accountant [Dutch]; Daniel Sciamma [1970] Director [French]

Galliford Try Building Limited
Incorporated: 20 February 1990 *Employees:* 1,682
Net Worth: £57,387,000 *Total Assets:* £576,496,000
Registered Office: Cowley Business Park, Cowley, Uxbridge, Middlesex, UB8 2AL
Activities: Construction of commercial buildings
Parent: Galliford Try Construction & Investments Holdings Limited
Officers: Mark Baxter [1972] Director/Finance Manager; Michael Charles Bruce [1969] Director; Simon Burton [1963] Regional Managing Director; Neil David Cocker [1966] Director; Martin Cooper [1971] Director/Chartered Accountant; Bill Hocking [1963] Director; Ian Thomas Jubb [1964] Director/Senior Management; Michael Laws [1970] Director; Jonathan Frank Marston [1970] Director/Quantity Surveyor; Donald James McLachlan [1961] Director; James Robert Parker [1959] Director/Quantity Surveyor; Matthew Malcolm Pool [1965] Director/Chartered Surveyor; Edward James Robertson [1961] Director; Stephen Paul Scard [1966] Construction Director; Christopher Mark Slidel [1962] Director/Quantity Surveyor; Graham William West [1970] Director/Commercial Manager; Clifford James Wheatley [1977] Director/Quantity Surveyor

Galliford Try Construction & Investments Holdings Limited
Incorporated: 10 September 2002 *Employees:* 3,079
Net Worth: £113,200,000 *Total Assets:* £1,224,300,032
Registered Office: Cowley Business Park, High Street, Cowley, Uxbridge, Middlesex, UB8 2AL
Activities: Activities of head offices
Parent: Galliford Try PLC
Officers: Mark Baxter [1972] Director/Finance Manager; Martin Cooper [1971] Director/Chartered Accountant; Kevin Allan Corbett [1960] Director/Solicitor; Bill Hocking [1963] Director; Ian Thomas Jubb [1964] Director/Senior Management; Michael Laws [1970] Director; Nicholas James Salt [1970] Director

Galliford Try Homes Limited
Incorporated: 14 February 1996
Net Worth: £4,078,000 *Total Assets:* £186,766,000
Registered Office: Cowley Business Park, Cowley, Uxbridge, Middlesex, UB8 2AL
Activities: Construction of commercial buildings
Parent: Galliford Try PLC
Officers: Andrew James Duxbury [1975] Director/Accountant; Mark Robert Farnham [1965] Director/Accountant; Andrew Richard Hammond [1970] Director; Tom Marshall Nicholson [1965] Director; Stephen John Teagle [1959] Director; Peter Martin Truscott [1962] Director

Galliford Try Partnerships Limited
Incorporated: 10 April 1964 *Employees:* 746
Net Worth: £39,368,000 *Total Assets:* £361,056,000
Registered Office: Cowley Business Park, Cowley, Uxbridge, Middlesex, UB8 2AL
Activities: Construction of commercial buildings
Parent: Galliford Try Homes Limited
Officers: Clare Helen Crawford [1977] Director; Mark Robert Farnham [1965] Director/Accountant; Stephen John Teagle [1959] Director; Peter Martin Truscott [1962] Director

Galliford Try PLC
Incorporated: 3 February 1965 *Employees:* 5,485
Net Worth: £776,499,968 *Total Assets:* £2,893,299,968
Registered Office: Cowley Business Park, Cowley, Uxbridge, Middlesex, UB8 2AL
Activities: Construction of commercial buildings
Officers: Kevin Allan Corbett, Secretary; Maria Luisa Cassoni [1951] Director/Accountant; Therese Lynn Miller [1951] Director; Graham Prothero [1961] Director/Chartered Accountant; Gavin Slark [1965] Director; Jeremy Charles Douglas Townsend [1964] Director; Peter Martin Truscott [1962] Director; Peter John Ventress [1960] Director

Galliford Try Services Limited
Incorporated: 5 April 1977 *Employees:* 312
Net Worth: £30,742,000 *Total Assets:* £90,749,000
Registered Office: Cowley Business Park, Cowley, Uxbridge, Middlesex, UB8 2AL
Activities: Development of building projects
Parent: Galliford Try PLC
Officers: Kevin Allan Corbett [1960] Director/Solicitor; Graham Prothero [1961] Director; Stuart Alexander Waldman [1968] Finance Director

Galvani Bioelectronics Limited
Incorporated: 3 February 2016 *Employees:* 26
Net Worth: £162,342,000 *Total Assets:* £183,852,000
Registered Office: 980 Great West Road, Brentford, Middlesex, TW8 9GS
Activities: Other research and experimental development on natural sciences and engineering
Shareholders: Alphabet Inc.; Setfirst Limited
Officers: Dr Andrew Jason Conrad [1963] Director/President & CEO, Verily Life Sciences LLC [American]; Dr Christopher Corsico [1962] Director [American]; Dr Kaigham Jacob Gabriel [1955] Director/President & CEO, Draper [American]; Dr Brian Partick Otis [1977] Director/Chief Technology Officer, Verily Life Sciences [American]; Dr Jordi Parramon [1971] Director of Medical Devices [Spanish/American]; Dr Mohamed Moncef Slaoui [1959] Director/Chairman Global Vaccines [Belgian]; Subesh Ronald Williams [1962] Director/SVP, Global Corporate Development

Gama Aviation (Engineering) Limited
Incorporated: 10 November 2011 *Employees:* 164
Net Worth: £10,097,000 *Total Assets:* £42,697,000
Registered Office: Business Aviation Centre, Farnborough Airport, Farnborough, Hants, GU14 6XA
Activities: Repair and maintenance of aircraft and spacecraft
Parent: Gama Group Limited
Officers: Mine Taylor, Secretary; Marwan Abdel-Khalek [1960] Managing Director; Paul Ewart Bristow [1961] Director; Neil Stephen Medley [1975] Director

Gama Aviation (UK) Limited
Incorporated: 25 October 1983 *Employees:* 145
Previous: Gama Aviation Limited
Net Worth: £631,000 *Total Assets:* £36,897,000
Registered Office: Business Aviation Centre, Farnborough Airport, Farnborough, Hants, GU14 6XA
Activities: Non-scheduled passenger air transport
Parent: Gama Group Limited
Officers: Mine Taylor, Secretary; Marwan Abdel-Khalek [1960] Director; Mark Graham Gascoigne [1978] Director/Manager; Neil Stephen Medley [1975] Director; Stephen Peter Wright [1957] Director

Gama Aviation PLC
Incorporated: 25 May 2010 *Employees:* 666
Previous: Hangar 8 PLC
Net Worth: £46,278,836 *Total Assets:* £121,511,072
Registered Office: Business Aviation Centre, Farnborough Airport, Farnborough, Hants, GU14 6XA
Activities: Non-scheduled passenger air transport
Officers: Mine Taylor, Secretary; Marwan Abdel-Khalek [1960] Director/Chief Executive; Peter Richard Brown [1952] Director; Neil Stephen Medley [1975] Director; Dr Michael John Peagram [1943] Director; Sir Ralph Robins [1932] Director/Chairman; David George Stickland [1969] Director; Simon Chi Keung To [1951] Director; Stephen Peter Wright [1957] Director

Game Digital Holdings Limited
Incorporated: 29 December 2011
Previous: Capitex Holdings Limited
Net Worth: £37,085,000 *Total Assets:* £69,404,000
Registered Office: Unity House, Telford Road, Basingstoke, Hants, RG21 6YJ
Activities: Activities of other holding companies n.e.c.
Parent: Game Digital PLC
Officers: Ruth Cartwright, Secretary; Martyn Ian Gibbs [1970] Director; Raymond Gerard Kavanagh [1968] Director/Chief Financial Officer [Irish]

Game Digital PLC
Incorporated: 14 May 2014 *Employees:* 4,810
Net Worth: £98,500,000 *Total Assets:* £199,400,000
Registered Office: Unity House, Telford Road, Basingstoke, Hants, RG21 6YJ
Activities: Activities of head offices
Officers: Ruth Cartwright, Secretary; Martyn Ian Gibbs [1970] Director; Dimitri John Goulandris [1966] Director/Entrepreneur and Investor; John Ellis Jackson [1947] Director; Raymond Gerard Kavanagh [1968] Director/Chief Financial Officer [Irish]; Clare Elizabeth Urmston [1977] Director/Chief Financial Officer

Game Retail Limited
Incorporated: 7 November 2011 *Employees:* 3,941
Net Worth: £96,958,000 *Total Assets:* £162,883,008
Registered Office: Unity House, Telford Road, Basingstoke, Hants, RG21 6YJ
Activities: Retail sale of electrical household appliances in specialised stores
Parent: Game Digital Holdings Limited
Officers: Ruth Amy Cartwright, Secretary; Martyn Ian Gibbs [1970] Director; Raymond Gerard Kavanagh [1968] Director/Chief Financial Officer [Irish]

Gannett International Finance LLP
Incorporated: 29 February 2016
Net Worth: £313,151,264 *Total Assets:* £313,151,264
Registered Office: Loudwater Mill, Station Road, High Wycombe, Bucks, HP10 9TY

Gantrade Europe Limited
Incorporated: 5 April 1983 *Employees:* 15
Net Worth: £11,656,942 *Total Assets:* £37,915,792
Registered Office: 3rd Floor, Birch House, Fairfield Avenue, Staines upon Thames, Middlesex, TW18 4AB
Activities: Wholesale of chemical products
Major Shareholder: Mahendra Parekh
Officers: Jaikumar Moorthy [1962] Director [American]; Hemal Aaron Parekh [1969] Director [American]; Nayan Gregory Parekh [1968] Director/Executive [American]

The Gap Partnership Bidco Limited
Incorporated: 27 April 2016 *Employees:* 4
Net Worth Deficit: £3,845,890 *Total Assets:* £56,270,084
Registered Office: Ashlyns Hall, Chesham Road, Berkhamsted, Herts, HP4 2ST
Activities: Activities of head offices
Parent: The Gap Partnership Group Limited
Officers: Kirsten Anne Gates, Secretary; Graham Botwright [1968] Director/Management Consultant; Stephen Walter Gates [1960] Director/Training Manager; Roger Greenfield [1970] Director/Management Consultant; Nigel Ellis Wolfin [1969] Director

The Gap Partnership Group Limited
Incorporated: 27 April 2016 *Employees:* 195
Net Worth Deficit: £9,398,283 *Total Assets:* £66,720,896
Registered Office: Ashlyns Hall, Chesham Road, Berkhamsted, Herts, HP4 2ST
Activities: Activities of head offices
Officers: Kirsten Anne Gates, Secretary; Graham Botwright [1968] Director/Management Consultant; Donald John Campbell [1963] Director; Stephen Walter Gates [1960] Director/Training Manager; Roger Greenfield [1970] Director/Management Consultant; Paul Price [1955] Director [American]; Nigel Ellis Wolfin [1969] Director

Garbuio Limited
Incorporated: 1 April 1980 *Employees:* 64
Previous: Dickinson Legg Limited
Net Worth: £19,930,000 *Total Assets:* £27,267,000
Registered Office: Moorside Road, Winnal Trading Estate, Winchester, Hants, SO23 7SS
Activities: Manufacture of machinery for food, beverage and tobacco processing
Officers: Gary Szentesi, Secretary; Russell Greenwood [1976] Director

Gardeners' Royal Benevolent Society
Incorporated: 31 December 2013 *Employees:* 41
Net Worth: £60,854,000 *Total Assets:* £61,241,000
Registered Office: 115-117 Kingston Road, Leatherhead, Surrey, KT22 7SU
Activities: Other letting and operating of own or leased real estate
Officers: Peter John Newman, Secretary; Heather Anne Barrett-Mold [1948] Director/Consultant; Carole Mary Baxter [1957] Director/Horticulturist; Thomas Alan Cole [1966] Director/Horticultural Lecturer; Maureen Hart [1953] Director/Retired; Mark Lane [1959] Director/Gardens Manager; Cynthia Isabel Margaret Leslie [1951] Director/Solicitor; Steven Mark Palmer [1960] Finance Director; Carol Paris [1966] Director/Chief Executive; Dougal Ramsay George Philip [1953] Director/Retailer; James Portland Robinson [1947] Director/Retired; Neville John Stein [1960] Director/Business Consultant; Emma Natalie Tinker [1975] Director/Investment Management

Gardners Books Limited
Incorporated: 15 April 1986 *Employees:* 865
Net Worth: £59,960,376 *Total Assets:* £115,263,656
Registered Office: 1 Whittle Drive, Eastbourne, E Sussex, BN23 6QH
Activities: Non-specialised wholesale trade
Parent: The Little Group Limited
Officers: Andrew Thomas Little [1960] Director; Jonathan James Little [1965] Managing Director; Yvette Jane Stafford [1961] Director

Garmin (Europe) Limited
Incorporated: 19 June 1992 *Employees:* 309
Net Worth: £173,268,160 *Total Assets:* £387,989,344
Registered Office: Liberty House, Hounsdown Business Park, Southampton, SO40 9LR
Activities: Wholesale of electronic and telecommunications equipment and parts
Parent: Garmin Ltd
Officers: Andrew Russell Etkind, Secretary; Danny Jo Bartel [1949] Director/Marketing Executive [American]; Sean Michael Biddlecombe [1964] Director; Douglas Gerard Boessen [1962] Director [American]; Clifton Albert Pemble [1965] Director/Company Executive [American]

Garreg Lwyd Energy Limited
Incorporated: 23 October 2012
Net Worth Deficit: £3,186,000 *Total Assets:* £86,383,000
Registered Office: Beaufort Court, Egg Farm Lane, Kings Langley, Herts, WD4 8LR
Activities: Other business support service activities n.e.c.
Parent: European Wind Investments Group Limited
Officers: Dominic James Hearth, Secretary; Steven William Hughes [1972] Global Support Services Director, UK&I - Commercial; Fraser Stephen Merry [1968] Director/Chartered Surveyor; Mitesh Raj Patel [1982] Director/Group Financial Controller

Garrett Thermal Systems UK Limited
Incorporated: 5 March 1997
Net Worth: £925,329,984 *Total Assets:* £925,329,984
Registered Office: Honeywell House, Skimped Hill Lane, Bracknell, Berks, RG12 1EB
Activities: Activities of other holding companies n.e.c.
Parent: Honeywell Group Ltd
Officers: Dagmar Klimentova [1980] Director [Czech]; Sharon Treanor [1974] Director

Garth Enterprises Partnership LLP
Incorporated: 5 November 2015
Net Worth: £16,689,624 *Total Assets:* £35,852,572
Registered Office: Whiteladies Park, Prince Albert Drive, Ascot, Berks, SL5 8AQ
Officers: Arran Kay Yentob [1982] Member; Josh Yentob [1988] LLP Member; Mireille Zilkha [1947] LLP Member

Gartner U.K. Limited
Incorporated: 9 June 1988 *Employees:* 1,198
Net Worth: £11,656,000 *Total Assets:* £121,190,000
Registered Office: Tamesis, The Glanty, Egham, Surrey, TW20 9AH
Activities: Data processing, hosting and related activities
Parent: Gartner Inc
Officers: Patrick Busby [1966] Director; William Joseph Dorgan [1967] Director/Lawyer [American]; Michael Lithgow [1958] Director; Craig Warren Safian [1969] Director/Senior VP and CFO, Gartner Inc [American]

Gate Gourmet Holdings U.K. Limited
Incorporated: 22 August 1986
Net Worth: £5,914,000 *Total Assets:* £20,761,000
Registered Office: Building 1071, Heathrow West, Southampton Road, Heathrow Airport, Hounslow, Middlesex, TW6 3AQ
Activities: Activities of other holding companies n.e.c.
Officers: Sreekumar Nair, Secretary; Stephen Philip Corr [1960] Managing Director; Thomas William Fountain [1969] Director/Chartered Accountant; Willem Hendrik Human [1982] Finance Director [British/South African]

Gate Gourmet London Limited
Incorporated: 20 October 1997 *Employees:* 1,882
Net Worth: £30,185,000 *Total Assets:* £66,306,000
Registered Office: Heathrow West, Building 1071, Southampton Road, Heathrow Airport, Hounslow, Middlesex, TW6 3AQ
Activities: Event catering activities
Officers: Sreekumar Nair, Secretary; Stephen Philip Corr [1960] Managing Director; Thomas William Fountain [1969] Director/Chartered Accountant; Willem Hendrik Human [1982] Finance Director [British/South African]

Gattaca PLC
Incorporated: 29 April 2002 *Employees:* 860
Previous: Matchtech Group PLC
Net Worth: £47,019,000 *Total Assets:* £142,774,000
Registered Office: 1450 Parkway, Solent Business Park, Whiteley, Fareham, Hants, PO15 7AF
Activities: Activities of other holding companies n.e.c.
Officers: Katie Mary Selves, Secretary; Richard James Bradford [1963] Director; Salar Farzad [1965] Director/Chief Financial Officer; Kevin Freeguard [1960] Director; Samuel David Lawther [1957] Director/Advisor; Keith John Lewis [1966] Managing Director; George Douglas Peter Materna [1953] Director; Patrick Shanley [1954] Director/Accountant

Gatwick Airport Limited
Incorporated: 19 February 1986 *Employees:* 3,035
Net Worth: £371,200,000 *Total Assets:* £3,185,499,904
Registered Office: 5th Floor, Destinations Place, Gatwick Airport, Gatwick, W Sussex, RH6 0NP
Activities: Other transportation support activities
Parent: Ivy Holdco Limited
Officers: Robert David Herga, Secretary; Nicholas James Dunn [1966] Director/Chief Financial Officer; Andrew Harvey Gillespie-Smith [1967] Director; Justin Paul Ginnivan [1977] Director/Investment Manager [Australian]; Sir David Hartmann Higgins [1954] Director/Chairman; Andrew Tadeusz Jurenko [1950] Director/Senior Advisor; John Benedict McCarthy [1958] Director/Global Head of Infrastructure [Australian]; Michael John McGhee [1956] Director; David Loch McMillan [1954] Director; James Dougal Adrianus Van Hoften [1944] Director/Senior Advisor [American]; Stewart Wingate [1971] Director/Chief Executive Officer; William Alan Woodburn [1951] Director [American]

Gazelli Art House Limited
Incorporated: 20 July 2010 *Employees:* 4
Net Worth Deficit: £6,644,469 *Total Assets:* £32,650,528
Registered Office: 52 New Town, Uckfield, E Sussex, TN22 5DE
Activities: Other business support service activities n.e.c.
Major Shareholder: Malahat Askarova
Officers: Malahat Askarova [1987] Director [Azerbaijani]

GB Gas Holdings Limited
Incorporated: 15 April 1996
Net Worth: £3,550,639,104 *Total Assets:* £13,443,493,888
Registered Office: Millstream, Maidenhead Road, Windsor, Berks, SL4 5GD
Activities: Activities of head offices
Parent: Centrica Holdings Limited
Officers: Ian Grant Dawson [1959] Director; Christopher Michael O'Shea [1973] Director; Alistair Mark Todd [1975] Finance Director

GBF Capital Limited
Incorporated: 16 March 2005
Net Worth: £55,585 *Total Assets:* £126,329,784
Registered Office: 3rd Floor, Hanover House, 118 Queens Road, Brighton, BN1 3XG
Activities: Other business support service activities n.e.c.
Major Shareholder: John Downton Croft
Officers: John Downton Croft [1938] Director/Accountant

GCH Corporation Limited
Incorporated: 23 March 2010 *Employees:* 837
Previous: GCH Capital Limited
Net Worth: £64,205,408 *Total Assets:* £103,256,360
Registered Office: 2 Castle Business Village, Station Road, Hampton, Surrey, TW12 2BX
Activities: Activities of other holding companies n.e.c.
Major Shareholder: Gregory Frederick Hutchings
Officers: Cassie Hutchings, Secretary; Cassie Olivia Hutchings [1983] Director; Gregory Frederick Hutchings [1947] Director/Businessman

GCP Applied Technologies (UK) Limited
Incorporated: 13 November 1958 *Employees:* 93
Previous: Grace Construction Products Limited
Net Worth: £113,783,000 *Total Assets:* £158,232,992
Registered Office: 580-581 Ipswich Road, Slough, Berks, SL1 4EQ
Activities: Manufacture of other chemical products n.e.c.
Parent: GCP Products (UK) Limited
Officers: Andrew Julian Kelly [1964] Sales Director; Christian Koetting [1968] Director/Business Executive [German]; Alexander Holger Emil Nielsen [1966] Director/Legal Counsel [German]; Upkar Ricky Singh Tatla [1976] Director/Business Executive

GCP Asset Finance 1 Limited
Incorporated: 17 June 2013 *Employees:* 3
Net Worth Deficit: £2,002,282 *Total Assets:* £29,873,892
Registered Office: Munro House, Portsmouth Road, Cobham, Surrey, KT11 1PP
Activities: Other business support service activities n.e.c.
Parent: GCP Intermediary Holdings Limited
Officers: Stephen Campbell Joseph Ellis [1959] Director; Nicholas Simon Parker [1969] Director; Rollo Andrew Johnstone Wright [1976] Director

GCP Biomass 1 Ltd
Incorporated: 23 January 2013 *Employees:* 3
Net Worth Deficit: £9,091,509 *Total Assets:* £61,095,576
Registered Office: Munro House, Portsmouth Road, Cobham, Surrey, KT11 1PP
Activities: Other business support service activities n.e.c.
Parent: GCP Intermediary Holdings Limited
Officers: Stephen Campbell Joseph Ellis [1959] Director; Ronan Niall Kierans [1978] Director [Irish]; Rollo Andrew Johnstone Wright [1976] Director

GCP Biomass 4 Limited
Incorporated: 13 May 2014 *Employees:* 3
Net Worth: £162,600 *Total Assets:* £27,220,052
Registered Office: Munro House, Portsmouth Road, Cobham, Surrey, KT11 1PP
Activities: Other business support service activities n.e.c.
Parent: GCP Intermediary Holdings Limited
Officers: Stephen Campbell Joseph Ellis [1959] Director; Ronan Niall Kierans [1978] Director/Chartered Accountant [Irish]; Rollo Andrew Johnstone Wright [1976] Director

GCP Cardale PFI Ltd
Incorporated: 27 May 2015 *Employees:* 4
Net Worth Deficit: £1,058,115 *Total Assets:* £102,363,056
Registered Office: Munro House, Portsmouth Road, Cobham, Surrey, KT11 1PP
Activities: Other business support service activities n.e.c.
Parent: GCP Intermediary Holdings Limited
Officers: Stephen Campbell Joseph Ellis [1959] Director; Ronan Niall Kierans [1978] Director [Irish]; Nicholas Simon Parker [1969] Director; Rollo Andrew Johnstone Wright [1976] Director

GCP Green Energy 1 Limited
Incorporated: 7 October 2014 *Employees:* 4
Net Worth: £59,751 *Total Assets:* £36,076,976
Registered Office: Munro House, Portsmouth Road, Cobham, Surrey, KT11 1PP
Activities: Other business support service activities n.e.c.
Parent: GCP Intermediary Holdings Limited
Officers: Stephen Campbell Joseph Ellis [1959] Director; Ronan Niall Kierans [1978] Director/Chartered Accountant [Irish]; Nicholas Simon Parker [1969] Director; Rollo Andrew Johnstone Wright [1976] Director

GCP Onshore Wind 3 Limited
Incorporated: 10 June 2013 *Employees:* 3
Net Worth: £16,538 *Total Assets:* £20,183,832
Registered Office: Munro House, Portsmouth Road, Cobham, Surrey, KT11 1PP
Activities: Other business support service activities n.e.c.
Parent: GCP Intermediary Holdings Limited
Officers: Stephen Campbell Joseph Ellis [1959] Director; Nicholas Simon Parker [1969] Director; Rollo Andrew Johnstone Wright [1976] Director

GCP Programme Funding 1 Limited
Incorporated: 19 July 2016 *Employees:* 4
Net Worth: £45,500 *Total Assets:* £90,294,408
Registered Office: Munro House, Portsmouth Road, Cobham, Surrey, KT11 1PP
Activities: Other business support service activities n.e.c.
Parent: GCP Intermediary Holdings Limited
Officers: Stephen Campbell Joseph Ellis [1959] Director; Ronan Niall Kierans [1978] Director [Irish]; Nicholas Simon Parker [1969] Director; Rollo Andrew Johnstone Wright [1976] Director

GCP RIW Holdings Limited
Incorporated: 17 February 2017
Net Worth: £23,800,000 *Total Assets:* £23,800,000
Registered Office: 580-581 Ipswich Road, Slough, Berks, SL1 4EQ
Activities: Wholesale of chemical products
Parent: GCP Applied Technologies (UK) Limited
Officers: Andrew Julian Kelly [1964] Commercial Director Europe; Alexander Holger Emil Nielsen [1966] Director/Associate General Counsel-Corporate [German]; Upkar Ricky Singh Tatla [1976] Finance Director

GCP Rooftop Solar 4 Limited
Incorporated: 2 October 2012 *Employees:* 3
Net Worth Deficit: £5,430 *Total Assets:* £37,965,640
Registered Office: Munro House, Portsmouth Road, Cobham, Surrey, KT11 1PP
Activities: Other business support service activities n.e.c.
Parent: GCP Intermediary Holdings Limited
Officers: Stephen Campbell Joseph Ellis [1959] Director; Nicholas Simon Parker [1969] Director; Rollo Andrew Johnstone Wright [1976] Director

GCP Rooftop Solar 5 Ltd
Incorporated: 8 April 2014 *Employees:* 3
Net Worth: £4,272 *Total Assets:* £23,152,332
Registered Office: Munro House, Portsmouth Road, Cobham, Surrey, KT11 1PP
Activities: Other business support service activities n.e.c.
Parent: GCP Intermediary Holdings Limited
Officers: Stephen Campbell Joseph Ellis [1959] Director; Nicholas Simon Parker [1969] Director; Rollo Andrew Johnstone Wright [1976] Director

GCP Rooftop Solar 6 PLC
Incorporated: 27 February 2015 *Employees:* 4
Net Worth Deficit: £2,742,624 *Total Assets:* £58,499,368
Registered Office: Munro House, Portsmouth Road, Cobham, Surrey, KT11 1PP
Activities: Other business support service activities n.e.c.
Parent: GCP Intermediary Holdings Limited
Officers: David George Conlon, Secretary; Stephen Campbell Joseph Ellis [1959] Director; Ronan Niall Kierans [1978] Director/Chartered Accountant [Irish]; Nicholas Simon Parker [1969] Director; Rollo Andrew Johnstone Wright [1976] Director

GCP Rooftop Solar Finance PLC
Incorporated: 8 June 2017 *Employees:* 4
Net Worth Deficit: £1,332,193 *Total Assets:* £96,093,096
Registered Office: Munro House, Portsmouth Road, Cobham, Surrey, KT11 1PP
Activities: Other business support service activities n.e.c.
Parent: GCP Solar Finance Holdings Limited
Officers: David George Conlon, Secretary; Stephen Campbell Joseph Ellis [1959] Director; Ronan Niall Kierans [1978] Director/Chartered Accountant [Irish]; Nicholas Simon Parker [1969] Director; Rollo Andrew Johnstone Wright [1976] Director

GCP Social Housing 1 Limited
Incorporated: 2 December 2014 *Employees:* 4
Net Worth Deficit: £314,322 *Total Assets:* £80,671,512
Registered Office: Munro House, Portsmouth Road, Cobham, Surrey, KT11 1PP
Activities: Other business support service activities n.e.c.
Parent: GCP Intermediary Holdings Limited
Officers: Stephen Campbell Joseph Ellis [1959] Director; Ronan Niall Kierans [1978] Director/Chartered Accountant [Irish]; Nicholas Simon Parker [1969] Director; Rollo Andrew Johnstone Wright [1976] Director

GD UK Holdings, Ltd
Incorporated: 17 February 2017
Net Worth: £124,193,000 *Total Assets:* £124,193,000
Registered Office: 5th Floor, The Shipping Building, Old Vinyl Factory, 252-254 Blyth Road, Hayes, Middlesex, UB3 1HA
Activities: Other information technology service activities
Shareholders: Godaddy Inc.; Go Daddy Operating Company, LLC
Officers: Richard Anthony Winslow [1979] Director; Jonathan Ying Kit Wong [1976] Group Director Finance

GDC Group Limited
Incorporated: 6 May 1977 *Employees:* 639
Net Worth: £65,894,000 *Total Assets:* £291,771,008
Registered Office: Millbrook House, Grange Drive, Hedge End, Southampton, SO30 2DF
Activities: Manufacture of electric domestic appliances
Officers: Vanessa King, Secretary; Donal Francis Flynn [1973] Director/Chartered Accountant [Irish]; Stuart MacKenzie [1950] Sales & Marketing Director; Fergal John Naughton [1975] Director [Irish]; Martin Lawrence Naughton [1939] Director/Group Chairman [Irish]; Neil Stewart [1965] Managing Director

GDC Holding Limited
Incorporated: 30 November 2000 *Employees:* 3
Net Worth: £16,224,000 *Total Assets:* £322,968,000
Registered Office: Dickley Lane, Lenham, Maidstone, Kent, ME17 2DE
Activities: Activities of production holding companies
Parent: Aliaixs Holdings UK Limited
Officers: Ian Charles McNair, Secretary; Ian Charles McNair [1960] Director/Accountant; Koen Jozef Sticker [1976] Director [Belgian]

GE Bio-Sciences Investments Limited
Incorporated: 21 May 1992
Net Worth: £44,561,000 *Total Assets:* £157,712,000
Registered Office: Pollards Wood, Nightingales Lane, Chalfont St Giles, Bucks, HP8 4SP
Activities: Activities of head offices
Parent: General Electric Company
Officers: Katherine Ann Jones [1976] Director/Financial Controller; Anna Lena Walsh [1976] Director/Accountant [Irish]

GE Energy (UK) Limited
Incorporated: 1 August 1912 *Employees:* 64
Net Worth: £5,939,000 *Total Assets:* £37,720,000
Registered Office: The Arena, Downshire Way, Bracknell, Berks, RG12 1PU
Activities: Installation of industrial machinery and equipment
Parent: GE Inspection and Repair Services Limited
Officers: Richard Paul Huxley [1964] Sales Director; Andrew James Steeples [1963] Director/Finance Manager; Jason Paul Welch [1975] Service Director

GE Healthcare Limited
Incorporated: 16 February 1971 *Employees:* 851
Net Worth: £736,966,976 *Total Assets:* £932,070,016
Registered Office: Amersham Place, Little Chalfont, Bucks, HP7 9NA
Activities: Manufacture of basic pharmaceutical products
Parent: GE Industrial Consolidation Limited
Officers: William Henry Bushill-Matthews, Secretary; Tricia Ann Clark [1976] Director/Executive EHS, GE Healthcare [American]; Ian Alistair Dale [1963] Director/General Manager; Michael Joseph Murphy [1965] Director/General Manager [Irish]; Kevin Michael O'Neill [1968] Director/Accountant

GE Healthcare UK Limited
Incorporated: 17 March 1997 *Employees:* 270
Net Worth: £430,340,000 *Total Assets:* £748,172,032
Registered Office: Amersham Place, Little Chalfont, Bucks, HP7 9NA
Activities: Manufacture of basic pharmaceutical products
Parent: GE Medical Systems Limited
Officers: Judit Kalman, Secretary; Maria de Los Angeles Khoury Gonzalo [1970] Director/Financial Management [American]; Emmanuel Francois Joel Ligner [1970] Director/Management Executive [French]; Kevin Michael O'Neill [1968] Director/Accountant

GE Medical Systems Limited
Incorporated: 8 December 1930 *Employees:* 676
Net Worth: £477,595,008 *Total Assets:* £695,057,984
Registered Office: Amersham Place, Little Chalfont, Bucks, HP7 9NA
Activities: Non-specialised wholesale trade
Parent: GE UK Holdings
Officers: Jane Alison Beastall [1971] Director/Accountant; Karl Gregory William Blight [1963] Director/General Manager

GE Money Home Finance Limited
Incorporated: 4 November 1957
Net Worth: £242,772,912 *Total Assets:* £262,042,608
Registered Office: P O Box 2497, Building 4, Hatters Lane, Watford, Herts, WD18 1YY
Activities: Financial intermediation not elsewhere classified
Parent: GE Money Home Lending Finance Limited
Officers: Samantha Jones [1981] Director; Jonathan Edward Taylor [1980] Director/Risk and Compliance Leader

GE Money Home Lending Holdings Limited
Incorporated: 14 May 2004
Net Worth: £1,547,659,136 *Total Assets:* £1,547,659,136
Registered Office: P O Box 2497, Building 4, Hatters Lane, Watford, Herts, WD18 1YY
Activities: Activities of head offices
Shareholders: GE Capital International 2 Limited; GE Capital International 6 Limited; GE Capital International Holdings Limited
Officers: Paul Kilrain Goudie [1964] Director [American]; Samantha Jones [1981] Director; Jonathan Edward Taylor [1980] Director/Risk and Compliance Leader

GE Money Servicing Limited
Incorporated: 11 October 1999 *Employees:* 95
Net Worth: £265,084,000 *Total Assets:* £359,737,984
Registered Office: P O Box 2497, Building 4, Hatters Lane, Watford, Herts, WD18 1YY
Activities: Other business support service activities n.e.c.
Parent: Igroup8 Limited
Officers: Samantha Jones [1981] Director; Jonathan Edward Taylor [1980] Director/Risk and Compliance Leader

GEA Group Holdings (UK) Limited
Incorporated: 27 April 1994 *Employees:* 3
Net Worth: £2,628,028 *Total Assets:* £39,334,848
Registered Office: Chandler's Ford Industrial Estate, School Lane, Chandler's Ford, Eastleigh, Hants, SO53 4DG
Activities: Activities of head offices
Officers: Ilija Aprcovic [1966] Managing Director; Timothy John Donbavand [1967] Finance Director; Tracey Ann O'Neill [1968] HR Director

Gearhouse Broadcast Limited
Incorporated: 29 September 1993 *Employees:* 99
Net Worth: £18,893,000 *Total Assets:* £29,481,000
Registered Office: 32-34 Greenhill Crescent, Watford, Herts, WD18 8JU
Activities: Television programming and broadcasting activities
Parent: Gravity Media Group UK Holdings Limited
Officers: Nikki Petken, Secretary; Eamonn MacArten Dowdall [1963] Director; Elliot Saul Kaye [1971] Director; Kevin Moorhouse [1958] Director; John Richard Newton [1963] Director/Chief Executive; Nicholas Peter Newton [1962] Commercial Director

Gemalto UK Limited
Incorporated: 22 September 1976 *Employees:* 329
Net Worth: £24,769,000 *Total Assets:* £61,101,000
Registered Office: Concorde Way, Segensworth North, Fareham, Hants, PO15 5RX
Activities: Manufacture of electronic components
Parent: Gemalto N.V.
Officers: Cherry Ruegg, Secretary; Lloyd Spencer Smith, Secretary/Accountant; Howard Berg [1961] Region Director; Susan Jane Francis [1961] HR Director; Cherry Ruegg [1983] Director/Lawyer; Lloyd Spencer Smith [1968] Director/Accountant

Gemini Rail Services UK Ltd
Incorporated: 19 August 2013 *Employees:* 375
Previous: Knorr-Bremse Railservices (UK) Limited
Net Worth Deficit: £30,693,000 *Total Assets:* £34,624,000
Registered Office: Wolverton Works, Stratford Road, Wolverton, Milton Keynes, Bucks, MK12 5NT
Activities: Repair and maintenance of other transport equipment n.e.c.
Parent: Mutares Holding-25 AG
Officers: Lee Watkins, Secretary; Nicholas Fitzwater [1970] Managing Director; Christian Klingler [1975] Director [Austrian]; Lee Watkins [1967] Finance Director

General Cable Limited
Incorporated: 8 October 2003
Previous: Telewest UK Limited
Net Worth: £6,293,176,832 *Total Assets:* £10,960,166,912
Registered Office: Media House, Bartley Wood Business Park, Hook, Hants, RG27 9UP
Activities: Dormant company
Parent: Virgin Media Senior Investments Limited
Officers: Gillian Elizabeth James, Secretary; Robert Dominic Dunn [1966] Director/Chief Financial Officer; Mine Ozkan Hifzi [1966] Director/Solicitor

General Cable Programming Limited
Incorporated: 15 December 2004
Previous: NTL Irish Holdings Limited
Net Worth: £267,413,440 *Total Assets:* £267,413,440
Registered Office: Media House, Bartley Wood Business Park, Hook, Hants, RG27 9UP
Activities: Activities of other holding companies n.e.c.
Parent: Virgin Media Senior Investments Limited
Officers: Gillian Elizabeth James, Secretary; Robert Dominic Dunn [1966] Director/Chief Financial Officer; Mine Ozkan Hifzi [1966] Director/Solicitor

General Mills UK Limited
Incorporated: 10 January 2003 *Employees:* 254
Net Worth: £10,185,000 *Total Assets:* £139,491,008
Registered Office: Harman House, 1 George Street, Uxbridge, Middlesex, UB8 1QQ
Activities: Agents involved in the sale of food, beverages and tobacco
Parent: General Mills, Inc
Officers: Jana Gaffaney, Secretary; Jana Marie-Rose Gaffaney [1980] Legal Director [American]; Natasha Laul [1978] Finance Director [American]; Benjamin John Pearman [1972] Vice President, Managing Director

Genesis Cancer Care UK Limited
Incorporated: 26 April 2006 *Employees:* 215
Previous: CancerPartnersUK Limited
Net Worth: £27,780,264 *Total Assets:* £60,160,416
Registered Office: Wilson House, Waterberry Drive, Waterlooville, Hants, PO7 7XX
Activities: Hospital activities
Parent: Genesis Specialist Care Holding UK Limited
Officers: Christopher James Gill, Secretary; Aaron Pickett, Secretary; Michael John Allen [1963] Director; Neil Christopher Budden [1981] Finance Director; Dan Jacob Collins [1974] Director [Australian]; Dr Vincent Khoo [1962] Director/Medical Practitioner [Australian]; Aldo Rolfo [1961] Director [Australian]; John Craig Uttermare White [1962] Director [Australian]

Genesis Specialist Care Holding UK Limited
Incorporated: 22 May 2015
Net Worth: £170,396,288 *Total Assets:* £184,424,096
Registered Office: Wilson House, Waterberry Drive, Waterlooville, Hants, PO7 7XX
Activities: Hospital activities
Parent: Genesis Specialist Care UK Limited
Officers: Christopher James Gill, Secretary; Aaron Pickett, Secretary; Michael John Allen [1963] Director; Neil Christopher Budden [1981] Finance Director; Dan Jacob Collins [1974] Director [Australian]; Aldo Rolfo [1961] Director [Australian]; John Craig Uttermare White [1962] Director [Australian]

Genesis Specialist Care UK Limited
Incorporated: 14 April 2015
Net Worth: £125,352,992 *Total Assets:* £257,914,624
Registered Office: Wilson House, Waterberry Drive, Waterlooville, Hants, PO7 7XX
Activities: Activities of other holding companies n.e.c.
Parent: The State Council of China
Officers: Christopher James Gill, Secretary; Aaron Pickett, Secretary; Michael John Allen [1963] Director; Neil Christopher Budden [1981] Finance Director; Dan Jacob Collins [1974] Director/Health Care Management [Australian]; Aldo Rolfo [1961] Director [Australian]; John Craig Uttermare White [1962] Director [Australian]

Genesis Specialist Care UK No 2 Limited
Incorporated: 14 April 2015
Net Worth: £62,330,944 *Total Assets:* £85,048,792
Registered Office: Wilson House, Waterberry Drive, Waterlooville, Hants, PO7 7XX
Activities: Activities of other holding companies n.e.c.
Parent: Genesis Specialist Care Holding UK Limited
Officers: Christopher James Gill, Secretary; Aaron Pickett, Secretary; Michael John Allen [1963] Director; Neil Christopher Budden [1981] Finance Director; Dan Jacob Collins [1974] Director/Health Care Management [Australian]; Aldo Rolfo [1961] Director [Australian]; John Craig Uttermare White [1962] Director [Australian]

Genesys Telecommunications Laboratories - Europe Limited
Incorporated: 18 October 1994 *Employees:* 229
Net Worth: £21,247,000 *Total Assets:* £54,656,000
Registered Office: Genesys House, Frimley Business Park, Frimley, Camberley, Surrey, GU16 7SG
Activities: Other information technology service activities
Parent: Greeneden Topco SCA
Officers: Mark Rosine, Secretary; Mark William Alloy [1955] Director [American]

Geneva Investment Group Limited
Incorporated: 22 September 2000 *Employees:* 8
Net Worth: £52,853,976 *Total Assets:* £83,916,720
Registered Office: Geneva House, 77a Rutland Road, Hove, E Sussex, BN3 5FE
Activities: Buying and selling of own real estate
Shareholders: Matthew Jacob Sorokin; Ivor Malcolm Sorokin
Officers: Matthew Jacob Sorokin, Secretary; Ivor Malcolm Sorokin [1934] Director; Matthew Jacob Sorokin [1972] Director; Wendy Thomas [1963] Director/Office Manager

Genus Breeding Limited
Incorporated: 29 November 1974 *Employees:* 616
Net Worth: £18,473,000 *Total Assets:* £56,904,000
Registered Office: Matrix House, Basing View, Basingstoke, Hants, RG21 4DZ
Activities: Technical testing and analysis
Parent: Genus PLC
Officers: Cara Crichton, Secretary; Karim Bitar [1965] Director [American]; Janet Ann Duane [1972] Director/Financial Controller [Irish]; Denis Mary Noonan [1966] Director/Accountant [Irish]; Andrew Robert Thompson [1976] Regional Director; Stephen David Wilson [1959] Finance Director

Genus Investments Limited
Incorporated: 16 June 1986
Net Worth: £270,417,984 *Total Assets:* £716,008,000
Registered Office: Matrix House, Basing View, Basingstoke, Hants, RG21 4DZ
Activities: Activities of head offices
Parent: Genus PLC
Officers: Cara Crichton, Secretary; Karim Bitar [1965] Director [American]; Denis Mary Noonan [1966] Director/Group Head of Tax & Treasury [Irish]; Stephen David Wilson [1959] Finance Director

Genus PLC
Incorporated: 26 September 1994 *Employees:* 2,642
Net Worth: £416,600,000 *Total Assets:* £789,200,000
Registered Office: Matrix House, Basing View, Basingstoke, Hants, RG21 4DZ
Activities: Support activities for animal production (other than farm animal boarding)
Officers: Daniel William David Hartley, Secretary; Karim Bitar [1965] Director/Chief Executive [American]; Ian Charles [1957] Director; Lysanne Mary Gray [1964] Director/Accountant; Lesley Knox [1953] Director; Robert Arthur Lawson [1944] Director; Lykele Jurrit Van Der Broek [1954] Director [Dutch]; Stephen David Wilson [1959] Director

Geo Specialty Group Holdings Limited
Incorporated: 7 September 2005
Previous: Fusion Insurance Holdings Limited
Net Worth: £45,059,224 *Total Assets:* £94,402,144
Registered Office: Towergate House, Eclipse Park, Sittingbourne Road, Maidstone, Kent, ME14 3EN
Activities: Activities of financial services holding companies
Parent: Towergate Insurance Limited
Officers: Dean Clarke, Secretary; Diane Cougill [1963] Director/Chief Finance Officer; Christine Elaine Dandridge [1956] Director; Paul John Dilley [1970] Director; Christopher John Kent [1983] Finance Director; Nicholas George Kirk [1961] Director

Geo Underwriting Services Limited
Incorporated: 13 September 2000 *Employees:* 129
Previous: Fusion Insurance Services Limited
Net Worth: £83,684,464 *Total Assets:* £118,682,344
Registered Office: Towergate House, Eclipse Park, Sittingbourne Road, Maidstone, Kent, ME14 3EN
Activities: Non-life insurance
Parent: Fusion Insurance Holdings Limited
Officers: Dean Clarke, Secretary; Antonios Erotocritou [1971] Director/Deputy CFO [Cypriot]; David Christopher Ross [1969] Director [Irish]

Geodis FF United Kingdom Ltd.
Incorporated: 23 February 1959 *Employees:* 368
Previous: Geodis Wilson UK Limited
Net Worth Deficit: £20,755,000 *Total Assets:* £142,608,992
Registered Office: LHRL, 145 Faggs Road, Feltham, Middlesex, TW14 0LZ
Activities: Freight transport by road
Parent: Geodis International SA
Officers: Gareth Adrian Harries, Secretary; Gareth Adrian Harries [1976] Finance Director; Thomas Walter Kraus [1966] Director [German]; Yann Robert Noyon [1972] Director [French]; Christopher John Packwood [1975] Managing Director

George House Developments Limited
Incorporated: 8 November 1978
Net Worth: £15,381,585 *Total Assets:* £21,215,624
Registered Office: Longdene House, Hedgehog Lane, Haslemere, Surrey, GU27 2PH
Activities: Other letting and operating of own or leased real estate
Major Shareholder: John Douglas Leigh Barratt
Officers: Alexander Barratt [1976] Director/Manager; John Douglas Leigh Barratt [1939] Director; Rebecca Morrey Barratt [1949] Director/Administrator

Georgica Limited
Incorporated: 24 July 2000
Net Worth: £106,605,000 *Total Assets:* £107,615,000
Registered Office: Aragon House, Cranfield Technology Park, Cranfield, Bedford, MK43 0EQ
Activities: Other amusement and recreation activities n.e.c.
Parent: Essenden Limited
Officers: George Jason Sheppard, Secretary; Nicholas Andrew Basing [1962] Director; Graham Edwin Blackwell [1969] Commercial Director; Alan Michael Hand [1968] Operations Director [Irish]; George Jason Sheppard [1981] Director/Chartered Accountant; Mark Simon Willis [1976] Director

Geos Group Limited
Incorporated: 9 November 2004 *Employees:* 18
Net Worth: £5,940,030 *Total Assets:* £25,651,604
Registered Office: Chiltern House, 45 Station Road, Henley on Thames, Oxon, RG9 1AT
Activities: Non-trading company
Major Shareholder: Barry John Newton
Officers: Stuart Wheatley, Secretary; Barry John Newton [1968] Managing Director; Victoria Newton [1969] Marketing Director

Gerald Palmer Eling Trust Company
Incorporated: 17 April 2003 *Employees:* 4
Net Worth: £79,841,632 *Total Assets:* £81,057,744
Registered Office: Eling Estate Office, Wellhouse Lane, Hermitage, Thatcham, Berks, RG18 9UF
Activities: Other letting and operating of own or leased real estate
Officers: David Hill, Secretary; Robin Shedden Broadhurst [1946] Director/Chartered Surveyor; Angela Cropley [1952] Director/Lecturer; James William Gardiner [1965] Director/Management Consultant; Desmond Roger Wingate Harrison [1933] Director; Kenneth Robert McDiarmid [1947] Director/Land Agent

Geting Capital Limited
Incorporated: 27 January 2017 *Employees:* 62
Net Worth Deficit: £1,934,000 *Total Assets:* £24,031,000
Registered Office: Armoury House, Ordnance Business Park, Midhurst Road, Liphook, Hants, GU30 7ZA
Activities: Activities of other holding companies n.e.c.
Officers: Mark Stephen Wright Beilby [1960] Director; Nigel Derek Hammond [1964] Director/Business Owner; Sir Nigel Graham Knowles [1956] Director; Khidhr Shafiq [1987] Director; Rahul Jagmohan Shah [1969] Director; Richard Scott Taylor [1971] Director

GFM Education
Incorporated: 3 November 2011 *Employees:* 544
Previous: Bay House School
Net Worth: £66,408,264 *Total Assets:* £71,837,496
Registered Office: Bay House School, Gomer Lane, Gosport, Hants, PO12 2QF
Activities: Primary education
Officers: Jennifer Anne Bonsor [1959] Director/Consultant; Adrian Cojocaru [1964] Director/Consultant [Romanian]; Maxwell Kenneth Corkill [1990] Director/Finance Business Partner; Christopher Francis Donovan [1961] Director/Retired; Paul Joseph Robert Lane [1945] Director/Retired; Jean Carol Morgan [1955] Director; Ian Potter [1964] Director/Headteacher; Kirsty Robertson [1980] Director/Manager

GFZ Properties Limited
Incorporated: 17 January 2013
Net Worth: £3,365,661 *Total Assets:* £25,026,456
Registered Office: 2 St Andrews Place, Southover Road, Lewes, E Sussex, BN7 1UP
Activities: Development of building projects
Parent: Mizmo Investments Limited
Officers: Joseph Noel Leonard [1963] Director [Irish]; Andrew John Melrose [1954] Director; Aharon Benjamin Missri [1967] Director/Property Developer [Israeli]; Yehudah Arieh Missri [1972] Director/Lawyer [Israeli]

GGI Holdings Limited
Incorporated: 28 September 2007 *Employees:* 1,388
Net Worth: £81,992,000 *Total Assets:* £133,229,000
Registered Office: Gold Group House, Godstone Road, Whyteleafe, Surrey, CR3 0GG
Activities: Activities of head offices
Major Shareholder: David Gold
Officers: David Gold [1936] Director; Jacqueline Gold [1960] Director; Vanessa Gold [1967] Director

GH Equity UK Limited
Incorporated: 13 June 2017 *Employees:* 1
Net Worth: £60,275,984 *Total Assets:* £675,421,248
Registered Office: Third Floor, One London Square, Cross Lanes, Guildford, Surrey, GU1 1UN
Activities: Activities of other holding companies n.e.c.
Officers: Hamad Abdulla Al-Mulla [1972] Director [Qatari]; Ashley Leslie John Fernandes [1968] Director [Indian]; Kamal Rhazali [1979] Director [French]

GHH Holdings Limited
Incorporated: 15 May 2001 *Employees:* 1
Previous: Sahara Grovenor House Hospitality Limited
Net Worth: £135,079,152 *Total Assets:* £676,824,896
Registered Office: Third Floor, One London Square, Cross Lanes, Guildford, Surrey, GU1 1UN
Activities: Hotels and similar accommodation
Parent: GH Equity UK Limited
Officers: Hamad Abdulla Al-Mulla [1972] Director [Qatari]; Ashley Leslie John Fernandes [1968] Director [Indian]; Kamal Rhazali [1979] Director [French]

Gibb Holdings Ltd
Incorporated: 22 May 1989
Net Worth: £69,404,000 *Total Assets:* £87,326,000
Registered Office: 1180 Eskdale Road, Winnersh, Wokingham, Berks, RG41 5TU
Activities: Activities of head offices
Parent: Jacobs UK Limited
Officers: Tejender Singh Chaudhary, Secretary; David Ellis [1972] Director; Jonathan Ross Shattock [1964] Director/Solicitor

Giffgaff Limited
Incorporated: 9 April 2001 *Employees:* 112
Net Worth: £22,184,000 *Total Assets:* £188,624,000
Registered Office: 260 Bath Road, Slough, Berks, SL1 4DX
Activities: Other telecommunications activities
Parent: Telefonica UK Limited
Officers: Patricia Cobian [1975] Director [Spanish]; Mark Evans [1969] Director/Accountant; Ashley Paul Schofield [1970] Director

Gilead Sciences Europe Ltd.
Incorporated: 15 July 2005 *Employees:* 287
Net Worth: £79,709,000 *Total Assets:* £169,275,008
Registered Office: 2 Roundwood Avenue, Stockley Park, Uxbridge, Middlesex, UB11 1AF
Activities: Other business support service activities n.e.c.
Parent: Gilead Sciences, Inc.
Officers: Johanna Henry, Secretary; Rudolf Ertl [1960] Director [German]; Brett Pletcher [1968] Director [American]; Robin Washington [1962] Director [American]

Gillette U.K. Limited
Incorporated: 17 March 1931 *Employees:* 168
Net Worth: £29,559,000 *Total Assets:* £63,434,000
Registered Office: The Heights, Brooklands, Weybridge, Surrey, KT13 0XP
Activities: Manufacture of perfumes and toilet preparations
Parent: Gilette Industries Limited
Officers: Anthony Joseph Appleton, Secretary; Anthony Joseph Appleton [1962] Director/Solicitor; Alexander George Buckthorp [1973] Finance Director; Vijay Indroo Sitlani [1975] Finance Director [Singaporean]; Husnu Yilmaz [1971] Director/Plant Manager [Turkish]; Christopher John Young [1974] HR Director

Ginger Bidco Limited
Incorporated: 13 December 2017 *Employees:* 4
Net Worth Deficit: £811,867 *Total Assets:* £37,686,736
Registered Office: Third Floor, One London Square, Cross Lanes, Guildford, Surrey, GU1 1UN
Activities: Other business support service activities n.e.c.
Parent: Ginger Midco Limited
Officers: Nicholas Roy Baily [1969] Director/Graphics Operator; Andrew Stephen Holness [1972] Financial Director; Andrew Dafyd Mainwaring [1971] Director/Investment Management; Richard Wootton [1987] Director

Ginger Midco Limited
Incorporated: 12 December 2017 *Employees:* 4
Net Worth Deficit: £81,170 *Total Assets:* £32,271,278
Registered Office: Third Floor, One London Square, Cross Lanes, Guildford, Surrey, GU1 1UN
Activities: Other business support service activities n.e.c.
Parent: Ginger Topco Limited
Officers: Nicholas Roy Baily [1969] Director/Graphics Operator; Andrew Stephen Holness [1972] Financial Director; Andrew Dafyd Mainwaring [1971] Director/Investment Management; Richard Wootton [1987] Director

Ginger Topco Limited
Incorporated: 12 December 2017 *Employees:* 126
Net Worth Deficit: £1,472,489 *Total Assets:* £34,242,800
Registered Office: Third Floor, One London Square, Cross Lanes, Guildford, Surrey, GU1 1UN
Activities: Other business support service activities n.e.c.
Officers: Nicholas Roy Baily [1969] Director/Graphics Operator; Andrew Stephen Holness [1972] Financial Director; Andrew Dafyd Mainwaring [1971] Director/Investment Management; Andrew Derek Vaughan [1960] Director; Richard Wootton [1987] Director

Girls' Education Company,Limited
Incorporated: 21 February 1896 *Employees:* 303
Net Worth: £49,932,000 *Total Assets:* £61,070,000
Registered Office: Wycombe Abbey School, High Wycombe, Bucks, HP11 1PE
Activities: General secondary education
Officers: Niall Thomas Campbell, Secretary; Richard Harrington Ashby [1949] Director & Chartered Surveyor; Jeremy William Bailey [1955] Director/Investment Banker; Sue Carr [1964] Director/Barrister QC; Dr Louise L'estrange Fawcett Posada [1955] Director/Fellow, University Lecturer; Dr Carolyn Jane Godlee [1956] Director/General Practitioner; Simon Charles Henderson [1975] Director/Headmaster; John Patrick Lewis [1965] Director/Retailer; David Peter Lillycrop [1956] Director; Dr Margaret Jane MacDougall [1958] Director/Consultant Gynaecologist; Diana Rose [1955] Director/Headteacher; Lady Sarah Caroline Ray Sassoon [1955] Director/Textile Manufacturer & Consultant; Patrick Philip Sherrington [1951] Director/Solicitor; Alan Thomas Lawrence Wilson [1955] Director/Bishop; Richard Thomas George Winter [1963] Director/Chartered Accountant

Girls' Learning Trust
Incorporated: 10 May 2011 *Employees:* 400
Previous: Nonsuch and Wallington Education Trust
Net Worth: £65,023,000 *Total Assets:* £73,564,000
Registered Office: Nonsuch High School for Girls, Ewell Road, Cheam, Sutton, Surrey, SM3 8AB
Activities: General secondary education
Officers: Caroline Helen Latham, Secretary; Jane Victoria Burton [1965] Director/Executive Headteacher; Alexander Philip Clark [1966] Director/Executive Headteacher; Sandra Anne Gillett [1951] Director/Independent HR Consultant; Marie Josephine Grant [1951] Director/Self Employed [Irish]; Antony Robert Hyams-Parish [1965] Director/Solicitor; Malcolm Bruce Munro [1965] Director/Senior Project Manager; Nigel Sandon Pepper [1970] Director/Financial Consultant; Philip Julian Taylor [1965] Director/Sales Manager

Gist Limited
Incorporated: 22 December 1951 *Employees:* 4,661
Net Worth: £139,211,008 *Total Assets:* £239,378,000
Registered Office: The Priestley Centre, 10 Priestley Road, The Surrey Research Park, Guildford, Surrey, GU2 7XY
Activities: Freight transport by road
Parent: Storeshield Limited
Officers: Susan Kathleen Kelly, Secretary; Michael Ian Chambers [1967] Logistics Director; Michael Kevin Flynn [1961] Business Solutions Director [American]; Martin Alistair Gwynn [1964] Managing Director; Mark Sweeney [1957] Finance Director

Givaudan Holdings UK Limited
Incorporated: 8 January 2007
Net Worth: £104,930,000 *Total Assets:* £169,695,008
Registered Office: Givaudan, Kennington Road, Ashford, Kent, TN24 0LT
Activities: Financial intermediation not elsewhere classified
Officers: Caroline Jane Stiffell, Secretary; Roberto Garavagno [1965] Director/Lawyer [Swiss]; Pradeep Parmar [1958] Director/Financial Accountant

Givaudan UK Limited
Incorporated: 2 May 1961 *Employees:* 365
Net Worth: £123,494,000 *Total Assets:* £233,268,000
Registered Office: Finance Building, Kennington Road, Ashford, Kent, TN24 0LT
Activities: Other manufacturing n.e.c.
Parent: Givaudan Holdings UK Limited
Officers: Caroline Jane Stiffell, Secretary; Ian James Messenger [1968] Director/Company Manager UK; Pradeep Parmar [1958] Director/Financial Accountant

GL Assessment Limited
Incorporated: 31 October 1980 *Employees:* 100
Net Worth: £72,068,000 *Total Assets:* £138,482,000
Registered Office: 1st Floor, Vantage London, Great West Road, Brentford, Middlesex, TW8 9AG
Activities: Other publishing activities
Parent: GL Education Group Limited
Officers: Robert Dargue [1975] Director/Chartered Accountant; Gregor Stanley Watson [1965] Director

GL Education Group Limited
Incorporated: 19 April 1991 *Employees:* 77
Net Worth Deficit: £932,000 *Total Assets:* £189,812,000
Registered Office: 1st Floor, Vantage London, Great West Road, Brentford, Middlesex, TW8 9AG
Activities: Other publishing activities
Parent: Assessments Bidco Limited
Officers: Robert Dargue [1975] Director/Chartered Accountant; Gregor Stanley Watson [1965] Director

Glasgow Learning Quarter (Holdings) Limited
Incorporated: 21 February 2013
Net Worth Deficit: £20,316,298 *Total Assets:* £198,024,576
Registered Office: 8 White Oak Square, London Road, Swanley, Kent, BR8 7AG
Activities: Activities of head offices
Shareholders: FES Resources Limited; Robert McAlpine Capital Ventures Limited
Officers: Dylan Fletcher [1971] Director; David Honeyman [1967] Director/Accountant; David Niall Smith [1971] Director; Robert John William Wotherspoon [1967] Director/Accountant

Glasgow Learning Quarter Limited
Incorporated: 21 February 2013
Net Worth Deficit: £20,316,296 *Total Assets:* £200,922,960
Registered Office: 8 White Oak Square, London Road, Swanley, Kent, BR8 7AG
Activities: Other business support service activities n.e.c.
Parent: Glasgow Learning Quarter (Holdings) Limited
Officers: Dylan Fletcher [1971] Director; David Honeyman [1967] Director/Accountant; David MacDonald [1961] National Programme Director; David Niall Smith [1971] Director; Robert John William Wotherspoon [1967] Director/Accountant

Glasgow Square Limited
Incorporated: 7 October 1999 *Employees:* 2
Net Worth: £97,408,000 *Total Assets:* £97,492,000
Registered Office: 103-105 Bath Road, Slough, Berks, SL1 3UH
Activities: Activities of financial services holding companies
Parent: Reckitt & Colman Holdings Limited
Officers: Christine Anne-Marie Logan, Secretary; Richard Mark Greensmith [1973] Group Tax Director; Jonathan Timmis [1975] Finance Director

Glaxo Group Limited
Incorporated: 14 October 1935
Net Worth: £11,255,962,624 *Total Assets:* £11,776,435,200
Registered Office: 980 Great West Road, Brentford, Middlesex, TW8 9GS
Activities: Activities of head offices
Parent: GlaxoSmithKline Finance PLC
Officers: Victoria Anne Whyte, Secretary; Simon Paul Dingemans [1963] Director; Adam Walker [1967] Director

Glaxo Operations UK Limited
Incorporated: 1 January 1962 *Employees:* 4,160
Net Worth: £858,684,032 *Total Assets:* £1,324,759,040
Registered Office: 980 Great West Road, Brentford, Middlesex, TW8 9GS
Activities: Manufacture of pharmaceutical preparations
Parent: Glaxo Group Limited
Officers: Victoria Anne Whyte, Secretary; Alan George Burns [1975] Director; Freek Jongen [1980] Director [Dutch]; Regis Jean-Pierre Simard [1965] Director/Head of Supply Chain [French]

Glaxo Wellcome UK Limited
Incorporated: 25 March 1950
Net Worth: £69,164,000 *Total Assets:* £71,871,000
Registered Office: 980 Great West Road, Brentford, Middlesex, TW8 9GS
Activities: Wholesale of pharmaceutical goods
Parent: Glaxo Group Limited
Officers: Victoria Anne Whyte, Secretary; James Borger [1963] Director/VP, Group Financial Planning and Analysis [American]; Alan George Burns [1975] Director

Glaxochem (UK) Unlimited
Incorporated: 4 October 2001
Net Worth: £2,418,490,880 *Total Assets:* £2,420,489,984
Registered Office: 980 Great West Road, Brentford, Middlesex, TW8 9GS
Activities: Financial intermediation not elsewhere classified
Shareholders: GlaxoSmithKline SL LP; Setfirst Limited
Officers: Simon Paul Dingemans [1963] Director

GlaxoSmithKline Capital PLC
Incorporated: 16 May 1988
Net Worth: £37,635,000 *Total Assets:* £10,646,939,648
Registered Office: 980 Great West Road, Brentford, Middlesex, TW8 9GS
Activities: Financial intermediation not elsewhere classified
Officers: Victoria Anne Whyte, Secretary; Simon Paul Dingemans [1963] Director

GlaxoSmithKline Caribbean Limited
Incorporated: 28 July 1953 *Employees:* 49
Net Worth: £34,652,000 *Total Assets:* £37,655,000
Registered Office: 980 Great West Road, Brentford, Middlesex, TW8 9GS
Activities: Wholesale of pharmaceutical goods
Parent: SmithKline Beecham Limited
Officers: Adam Walker [1967] Director

GlaxoSmithKline Consumer Healthcare (Overseas) Limited
Incorporated: 26 September 2014 *Employees:* 53
Net Worth: £1,200,146,048 *Total Assets:* £1,856,691,968
Registered Office: 980 Great West Road, Brentford, Middlesex, TW8 9GS
Activities: Activities of other holding companies n.e.c.
Parent: GlaxoSmithKline Consumer Healthcare Holdings Limited
Officers: Richard Green [1974] Director/Head of Reporting; Tobias Hestler [1972] Director [German/Swiss]

GlaxoSmithKline Consumer Healthcare (UK) IP Limited
Incorporated: 26 September 2014
Net Worth: £260,424,000 *Total Assets:* £381,208,000
Registered Office: 980 Great West Road, Brentford, Middlesex, TW8 9GS
Activities: Activities of other holding companies n.e.c.
Parent: GlaxoSmithKline Consumer Healthcare Holdings Limited
Officers: Richard Green [1974] Director; Tobias Hestler [1972] Director [German/Swiss]

GlaxoSmithKline Consumer Healthcare (UK) Trading Limited
Incorporated: 26 September 2014 *Employees:* 1,379
Net Worth: £201,250,000 *Total Assets:* £685,875,968
Registered Office: 980 Great West Road, Brentford, Middlesex, TW8 9GS
Activities: Manufacture of pharmaceutical preparations
Parent: GlaxoSmithKline Consumer Healthcare Holdings Limited
Officers: Richard Green [1974] Director; Terence O'Neill [1965] Finance Director; Eugene Prokopchuk [1981] Finance Director [Ukrainian]

GlaxoSmithKline Consumer Healthcare Finance Limited
Incorporated: 6 November 2014
Net Worth: £231,710,000 *Total Assets:* £1,798,552,960
Registered Office: 980 Great West Road, Brentford, Middlesex, TW8 9GS
Activities: Financial intermediation not elsewhere classified
Parent: GlaxoSmithKline Consumer Healthcare Holdings Limited
Officers: Richard Green [1974] Director; Tobias Hestler [1972] Director [German/Swiss]

GlaxoSmithKline Consumer Healthcare Finance No. 2 Limited
Incorporated: 4 August 2016
Net Worth: £47,269,888 *Total Assets:* £62,455,720
Registered Office: 980 Great West Road, Brentford, Middlesex, TW8 9GS
Activities: Financial intermediation not elsewhere classified
Parent: GlaxoSmithKline Consumer Healthcare (Overseas) Limited
Officers: Richard Green [1974] Director; Tobias Hestler [1972] Director [German/Swiss]

GlaxoSmithKline Consumer Healthcare Holdings Limited
Incorporated: 15 April 2014
Net Worth: £20,770,000,896 *Total Assets:* £20,771,000,320
Registered Office: 980 Great West Road, Brentford, Middlesex, TW8 9GS
Activities: Activities of head offices
Parent: Setfirst Limited
Officers: Simon Paul Dingemans [1963] Director; Tobias Hestler [1972] Director/Chief Financial Officer [German/Swiss]; Brian McNamara [1966] Director/Head of Americas and Europe [American]; David Simon Redfern [1966] Director

GlaxoSmithKline Consumer Trading Services Limited
Incorporated: 21 June 2012
Net Worth: £19,491,000 *Total Assets:* £781,051,008
Registered Office: 980 Great West Road, Brentford, Middlesex, TW8 9GS
Activities: Wholesale of pharmaceutical goods
Parent: GlaxoSmithKline Consumer Healthcare Holdings Limited
Officers: Victoria Anne Whyte, Secretary; Richard Green [1974] Director; Tobias Hestler [1972] Director [German/Swiss]; Neil O'Hara [1973] Director

GlaxoSmithKline Export Limited
Incorporated: 18 October 1989 *Employees:* 1,214
Net Worth: £94,567,000 *Total Assets:* £447,628,000
Registered Office: 980 Great West Road, Brentford, Middlesex, TW8 9GS
Activities: Wholesale of pharmaceutical goods
Parent: Glaxo Group Limited
Officers: Victoria Anne Whyte, Secretary; Alan George Burns [1975] Director; Dylan Jackson [1972] Director/General Manager; Adam Walker [1967] Director; Jane Mary Whitmore [1968] Finance Director

GlaxoSmithKline Finance PLC
Incorporated: 2 October 1929
Net Worth: £61,286,526,976 *Total Assets:* £135,010,271,232
Registered Office: 980 Great West Road, Brentford, Middlesex, TW8 9GS
Activities: Financial intermediation not elsewhere classified
Parent: GlaxoSmithKline Holdings Limited
Officers: Victoria Anne Whyte, Secretary; Simon Paul Dingemans [1963] Director; Adam Walker [1967] Director

GlaxoSmithKline Holdings (Ireland) Limited
Incorporated: 5 August 2014
Net Worth: £2,183,034,880 *Total Assets:* £2,196,562,944
Registered Office: 980 Great West Road, Brentford, Middlesex, TW8 9GS
Activities: Financial management
Parent: Setfirst Limited
Officers: Alan George Burns [1975] Director; Adam Walker [1967] Director

GlaxoSmithKline Holdings (One) Limited
Incorporated: 7 June 2001
Net Worth: £55,996,000 *Total Assets:* £202,339,008
Registered Office: 980 Great West Road, Brentford, Middlesex, TW8 9GS
Activities: Activities of head offices
Parent: GlaxoSmithKline PLC
Officers: Victoria Anne Whyte, Secretary; Adam Walker [1967] Director

GlaxoSmithKline Holdings Limited
Incorporated: 7 December 2005
Net Worth: £15,292,999,680 *Total Assets:* £60,131,000,320
Registered Office: 980 Great West Road, Brentford, Middlesex, TW8 9GS
Activities: Activities of head offices
Parent: GlaxoSmithKline PLC
Officers: Simon Paul Dingemans [1963] Director

GlaxoSmithKline IHC Limited
Incorporated: 18 May 2010
Net Worth: £174,892,000 *Total Assets:* £4,119,490,048
Registered Office: 980 Great West Road, Brentford, Middlesex, TW8 9GS
Activities: Financial intermediation not elsewhere classified
Parent: GlaxoSmithKline Finance PLC
Officers: Victoria Anne Whyte, Secretary; James Borger [1963] Director/VP, Group Financial Planning and Analysis [American]; Alan George Burns [1975] Director; Adam Walker [1967] Director

GlaxoSmithKline Intellectual Property (No.2) Limited
Incorporated: 6 November 2012
Net Worth: £1,487,657,984 *Total Assets:* £1,679,232,000
Registered Office: 980 Great West Road, Brentford, Middlesex, TW8 9GS
Activities: Activities of other holding companies n.e.c.
Parent: GlaxoSmithKline Intellectual Property Holdings Limited
Officers: Jerome Charles Maurice Andries [1969] Director [French]; Simon Paul Dingemans [1963] Director; Kate Sophie Priestman [1973] Director/Strategy Professional; Adam Walker [1967] Director/Accountant

GlaxoSmithKline Intellectual Property Development Limited
Incorporated: 6 November 2012
Net Worth Deficit: £8,606,166,016 *Total Assets:* £1,572,909,056
Registered Office: 980 Great West Road, Brentford, Middlesex, TW8 9GS
Activities: Activities of other holding companies n.e.c.
Parent: GlaxoSmithKline Intellectual Property Mangement Limited
Officers: Jerome Charles Maurice Andries [1969] Director [French]; Simon Paul Dingemans [1963] Director; Kate Sophie Priestman [1973] Director/Strategy Professional; Adam Walker [1967] Director/Accountant

GlaxoSmithKline Intellectual Property Holdings Limited
Incorporated: 6 November 2012
Net Worth: £4,383,954,944 *Total Assets:* £4,385,067,008
Registered Office: 980 Great West Road, Brentford, Middlesex, TW8 9GS
Activities: Activities of other holding companies n.e.c.
Shareholders: Glaxo Group Limited; GlaxoSmithKline Finance PLC
Officers: Jerome Charles Maurice Andries [1969] Director [French]; Simon Paul Dingemans [1963] Director; Kate Sophie Priestman [1973] Director/Strategy Professional; Adam Walker [1967] Director/Accountant

GlaxoSmithKline Intellectual Property Limited
Incorporated: 6 November 2012
Net Worth: £6,002,445,824 *Total Assets:* £6,631,912,960
Registered Office: 980 Great West Road, Brentford, Middlesex, TW8 9GS
Activities: Activities of other holding companies n.e.c.
Parent: Glaxo Group Limited
Officers: Jerome Charles Maurice Andries [1969] Director [French]; Simon Paul Dingemans [1963] Director; Kate Sophie Priestman [1973] Director/Strategy Professional; Adam Walker [1967] Director/Accountant

GlaxoSmithKline Intellectual Property Management Limited
Incorporated: 12 August 2011
Net Worth: £7,026,833,920 *Total Assets:* £7,432,076,800
Registered Office: 980 Great West Road, Brentford, Middlesex, TW8 9GS
Activities: Other business support service activities n.e.c.
Parent: GlaxoSmithKline Intellectual Property Holdings Limited
Officers: Jerome Charles Maurice Andries [1969] Director [French]; Simon Paul Dingemans [1963] Director/Chief Financial Officer; Kate Sophie Priestman [1973] Director/Strategy Professional; Adam Walker [1967] Director/Accountant (Senior Vice President - Finance)

GlaxoSmithKline International Limited
Incorporated: 21 September 1988
Net Worth: £1,419,955,968 *Total Assets:* £1,866,791,040
Registered Office: 980 Great West Road, Brentford, Middlesex, TW8 9GS
Activities: Other business support service activities n.e.c.
Parent: Setfirst Limited
Officers: James Borger [1963] Director/VP, Group Financial Planning and Analysis [American]; Alan George Burns [1975] Director

GlaxoSmithKline Investment Holdings Limited
Incorporated: 27 November 2009
Net Worth: £6,467,611,136 *Total Assets:* £6,483,027,968
Registered Office: 980 Great West Road, Brentford, Middlesex, TW8 9GS
Activities: Activities of head offices
Parent: Setfirst
Officers: Adam Walker [1967] Director

GlaxoSmithKline Investment Services Limited
Incorporated: 21 July 2009
Net Worth: £552,454,016 *Total Assets:* £570,209,984
Registered Office: 980 Great West Road, Brentford, Middlesex, TW8 9GS
Activities: Other business support service activities n.e.c.
Parent: Setfirst Limited
Officers: Adam Walker [1967] Director

GlaxoSmithKline Mercury Limited
Incorporated: 28 August 2009
Net Worth: £4,642,886,144 *Total Assets:* £4,645,296,128
Registered Office: 980 Great West Road, Brentford, Middlesex, TW8 9GS
Activities: Activities of head offices
Parent: GlaxoSmithKline PLC
Officers: Victoria Anne Whyte, Secretary; James Borger [1963] Director/VP, Group Financial Planning and Analysis [American]; Alan George Burns [1975] Director

GlaxoSmithKline PLC
Incorporated: 6 December 1999 *Employees:* 99,349
Net Worth Deficit: £68,000,000 *Total Assets:* £56,381,001,728
Registered Office: 980 Great West Road, Brentford, Middlesex, TW8 9GS
Activities: Activities of head offices
Officers: Victoria Anne Whyte, Secretary; Manvinder Singh Banga [1954] Director [Indian]; Dr Hal Barron [1962] Director [American]; Dr Vivienne Cox [1959] Director/Businesswoman; Simon Paul Dingemans [1963] Director/Chief Financial Officer; Lynn Laverty Elsenhans [1956] Director [American]; Dr Laurie Glimcher [1951] Director [American]; Dr Jesse Goodman [1951] Director/Physician/Scientist [American]; Sir Philip Roy Hampton [1953] Director; Judith Carol Lewent [1949] Director [American]; Iain James MacKay [1961] Director; Urs Rohner [1959] Director [Swiss]; Emma Natasha Walmsley [1969] Director

GlaxoSmithKline Research & Development Limited
Incorporated: 22 January 1965 *Employees:* 3,831
Net Worth: £1,145,257,984 *Total Assets:* £1,721,917,952
Registered Office: 980 Great West Road, Brentford, Middlesex, TW8 9GS
Activities: Other research and experimental development on natural sciences and engineering
Parent: Glaxo Group Limited
Officers: Victoria Whyte, Secretary; David George Allen [1959] Director/SVP Respiratory Therapy Area; Jerome Andries [1969] Director [French]

GlaxoSmithKline Services Unlimited
Incorporated: 23 March 1972 *Employees:* 14,424
Net Worth: £1,592,000,000 *Total Assets:* £2,630,000,128
Registered Office: 980 Great West Road, Brentford, Middlesex, TW8 9GS
Activities: Activities of head offices
Parent: GlaxoSmithKline PLC
Officers: Victoria Anne Whyte, Secretary; Simon Paul Dingemans [1963] Director

GlaxoSmithKline UK Limited
Incorporated: 24 October 2001 *Employees:* 499
Net Worth: £617,320,000 *Total Assets:* £723,723,008
Registered Office: 980 Great West Road, Brentford, Middlesex, TW8 9GS
Activities: Wholesale of pharmaceutical goods
Parent: Glaxo Group Limited
Officers: Simon Paul Dingemans [1963] Director; Ville Kullervo Maukonen [1978] Finance Director [Finnish]

Glen House Estates Limited
Incorporated: 2 July 1962 *Employees:* 11
Net Worth: £49,623,096 *Total Assets:* £100,152,992
Registered Office: Glen House, Glen Road, Grayshott, Hindhead, Surrey, GU26 6NF
Activities: Buying and selling of own real estate
Shareholder: Graham Frederick Charles Mellstrom
Officers: Wendy Munday, Secretary; Bruce Robert Mellstrom [1964] Director/Solicitor; Graham Frederick Charles Mellstrom [1931] Director; Stephen Charles Mellstrom [1969] Director/Chartered Surveyor

Glenchamber Wind Energy Limited
Incorporated: 8 April 2014
Net Worth Deficit: £10,402,000 *Total Assets:* £61,071,000
Registered Office: Beaufort Court, Egg Farm Lane, Kings Langley, Herts, WD4 8LR
Activities: Production of electricity
Parent: Boreas Energy Limited
Officers: Dominic James Heath, Secretary; Peter Edward Dias [1981] Director; Christopher Peter Gaydon [1978] Director [Hungarian]; Paul Stephen Latham [1956] Director; Thomas James Rosser [1985] Director

Glendola Leisure (Holdings) Limited
Incorporated: 16 November 2001 *Employees:* 601
Net Worth: £24,574,000 *Total Assets:* £53,577,000
Registered Office: 364 High Street, Harlington, Heathrow, Hayes, Middlesex, UB3 5LF
Activities: Activities of head offices
Major Shareholder: Peter Nicholas Salussolia
Officers: Graeme John Ramsay, Secretary; Graeme John Ramsay [1967] Director/Chartered Accountant; Alexander Salussolia [1968] Director; Christina Salussolia [1950] Director/Executive Secretary; Peter Nicholas Salussolia [1968] Director

Glenside Care Group Limited
Incorporated: 25 January 2011
Net Worth: £736,110 *Total Assets:* £27,236,110
Registered Office: Hollanden Park, Coldharbour Lane, Hildenborough, Kent, TN11 9LE
Activities: Hospital activities
Parent: The Raphael Hospital Development Limited
Officers: Pradeep Lasitha Dissanayake [1964] Director/Chartered Accountant; Elizabeth Anne Florschutz [1944] Director; Gerhard Ulrich Florschutz [1944] Director

GLF Schools
Incorporated: 4 March 2011 *Employees:* 217
Previous: The Glyn Learning Foundation
Net Worth: £166,894,000 *Total Assets:* £188,108,000
Registered Office: Claygate House, Littleworth Road, Esher, Surrey, KT10 9PN
Activities: Primary education
Officers: Sarah Lynagh, Secretary; Jacqueline Elizabeth Adams [1963] Director/Human Resources Manager; Adam Braithwaite [1975] Executive Director; Martin Joseph Burke [1952] Director/Retired; Paul Duncan Carpenter [1958] Director/Solicitor; Jonathan Michael Chaloner [1969] Director/Headteacher; Colin David Charles [1959] Director/Accountant; Bruce Alan Ray Ely-Johnston [1975] Financial Director; Helen Elizabeth Mannion [1980] Director/Head of Business Intelligence; Lynne Hazel O'Reilly [1962] Director/Retired

Glinwell Public Limited Company
Incorporated: 18 March 1977 *Employees:* 287
Net Worth: £19,269,000 *Total Assets:* £36,657,000
Registered Office: c/o Mazars LLP, The Pinnacle, 160 Midsummer Boulevard, Milton Keynes, Bucks, MK9 1FF
Activities: Growing of vegetables and melons, roots and tubers
Shareholder: Felicia Cannatella
Officers: Giuseppe Colletti, Secretary; Salvatore Cannatella [1974] Director; Giuseppe Colletti [1975] Packhouse Director

Global Consortium Limited
Incorporated: 16 August 2016
Net Worth: £27,382,692 *Total Assets:* £27,480,968
Registered Office: Charwood House, Oakhurst Business Park, Southwater, W Sussex, RH13 9RT
Activities: Non-trading company
Officers: John Mark Andrews [1960] Director; Charles Allan Campbell [1965] Director

Global Draw Limited
Incorporated: 12 May 1998 *Employees:* 343
Net Worth: £52,396,000 *Total Assets:* £208,888,000
Registered Office: SG House, 1 Dukes Green Avenue, Feltham, Middlesex, TW14 0LR
Activities: Ready-made interactive leisure and entertainment software development
Parent: Scientific Games International Holdings Limited
Officers: Phillip Douglas Horne [1961] Managing Director; Paul Phillips [1978] Finance Director

Global Invacom Holdings Limited
Incorporated: 7 November 2008 *Employees:* 374
Net Worth: £10,668,558 *Total Assets:* £42,454,956
Registered Office: First Floor, Freeman House, John Roberts Business, Pean Hill, Whitstable, Kent, CT5 3BJ
Activities: Activities of head offices
Parent: Global Invacom Group Limited
Officers: Malcolm John Burrell [1959] Director; David Jonathan Wren Fugeman [1965] Director; John Stephen Parfitt [1959] Director; Anthony Brian Taylor [1962] Director

Global Invacom Limited
Incorporated: 18 November 1988 *Employees:* 54
Net Worth: £14,755,808 *Total Assets:* £28,541,746
Registered Office: 1st Floor, Freeman House, John Roberts Business Park, Pean Hill, Whitstable, Kent, CT5 3BJ
Activities: Installation of industrial machinery and equipment
Parent: Global Invacom Holdings Limited
Officers: Malcolm John Burrell [1959] Technical Director; David Jonathan Wren Fugeman [1965] Sales Director; John Stephen Parfitt [1959] Operations Director; Anthony Brian Taylor [1962] Managing Director

The Globe Insurance Company Limited
Incorporated: 26 March 1993
Net Worth: £3,082,299,904 *Total Assets:* £3,723,699,968
Registered Office: St Mark's Court, Chart Way, Horsham, W Sussex, RH12 1XL
Activities: Activities of financial services holding companies
Parent: Royal International Insurance Holdings Limited
Officers: Ian Adam Craston [1966] Director; Simon de Baat [1980] Director/Actuary; Martin David Postles [1959] Director/Group Manager, International Legacy Businesses

Glory Global Solutions (Holdings) Limited
Incorporated: 17 April 2008
Net Worth: £165,350,912 *Total Assets:* £217,207,456
Registered Office: Infinity View, 1 Hazelwood, Lime Tree Way, Chineham, Basingstoke, Hants, RG24 8WZ
Activities: Manufacture of other special-purpose machinery n.e.c.
Officers: Martin Rose, Secretary; Michael Bielamowicz [1964] Director/Executive Vice President [American]; Tomoko Fujita [1962] Director, Corporate Development [Japanese]; Akihiro Harada [1963] Director/Executive Officer of Glory Ltd [Japanese]; Martin Rose [1975] Director/Lawyer; Michael Jeffery Williams [1969] Director/Chief Financial Officer

Glory Global Solutions (International) Limited
Incorporated: 17 April 2008 *Employees:* 326
Net Worth: £117,177,152 *Total Assets:* £288,607,232
Registered Office: Infinity View, 1 Hazelwood, Lime Tree Way, Chineham, Basingstoke, Hants, RG24 8WZ
Activities: Manufacture of other special-purpose machinery n.e.c.
Officers: Martin Rose, Secretary; Tomoko Fujita [1962] Director, Corporate Development [Japanese]; Akihiro Harada [1963] Director [Japanese]; Martin Rose [1975] Director/Lawyer; Michael Jeffery Williams [1969] Director/Chief Financial Officer

Glory Global Solutions (Midco) Limited
Incorporated: 17 April 2008
Net Worth: £134,640,000 *Total Assets:* £139,370,000
Registered Office: Infinity View, 1 Hazelwood, Lime Tree Way, Chineham, Basingstoke, Hants, RG24 8WZ
Activities: Manufacture of other special-purpose machinery n.e.c.
Officers: Martin Rose, Secretary; Michael Bielamowicz [1964] Director/Executive Vice President [American]; Tomoko Fujita [1962] Director, Corporate Development [Japanese]; Akihiro Harada [1963] Director/Executive Officer of Glory Ltd [Japanese]; Martin Rose [1975] Director/Lawyer; Michael Jeffery Williams [1969] Director/Chief Financial Officer

Glory Global Solutions (Topco) Limited
Incorporated: 17 April 2008
Net Worth: £211,275,504 *Total Assets:* £211,610,576
Registered Office: Infinity View, 1 Hazelwood, Lime Tree Way, Chineham, Basingstoke, Hants, RG24 8WZ
Activities: Manufacture of other special-purpose machinery n.e.c.
Officers: Martin Rose, Secretary; Michael Bielamowicz [1964] Director/Executive Vice President [American]; Tomoko Fujita [1962] Director, Corporate Development [Japanese]; Akihiro Harada [1963] Director/Executive Officer of Glory Ltd [Japanese]; Martin Rose [1975] Director/Lawyer; Michael Jeffery Williams [1969] Director/Chief Financial Officer

Glory Global Solutions Ltd
Incorporated: 10 February 2012
Net Worth: £365,401,728 *Total Assets:* £423,939,168
Registered Office: Infinity View, 1 Hazelwood, Lime Tree Way, Chineham, Basingstoke, Hants, RG24 8WZ
Activities: Manufacture of plastics and rubber machinery
Officers: Martin Rose, Secretary; Michael Bielamowicz [1964] Director/Executive Vice President [American]; Tomoko Fujita [1962] Director, Corporate Development [Japanese]; Akihiro Harada [1963] Director/Executive Officer of Glory Ltd [Japanese]; Ian Robin Jordan [1958] Director; Kaname Kotani [1959] Director [Japanese]; Motozumi Miwa [1954] Director of Glory Ltd [Japanese]; Michael Jeffery Williams [1969] Director/Chief Financial Officer

Gloucester Healthcare Partnership Limited
Incorporated: 17 December 2001
Net Worth Deficit: £1,188,000 *Total Assets:* £36,378,000
Registered Office: Part First Floor, 1 Grenfell Road, Maidenhead, Berks, SL6 1HN
Activities: Financial intermediation not elsewhere classified
Parent: Healthcare Providers (Gloucester) Limited
Officers: Emeka Ikechi Ehenulo, Secretary; Richard Little [1979] Investment Director; Albert Hendrik Naafs [1965] Director [Dutch]; Neil Rae [1971] Director; Ian Tayler [1976] Director/General Manager

Gluco RX Limited
Incorporated: 2 February 2011 *Employees:* 60
Net Worth: £27,929,304 *Total Assets:* £31,867,320
Registered Office: 1c Henley Business Park, Pirbright Road, Guildford, Surrey, GU3 2DX
Activities: Manufacture of medical and dental instruments and supplies
Officers: Chris Chapman [1982] Sales & Marketing Director; Parag Khiroya [1963] Managing Director; Varsha Khiroya [1964] Director/Optician; Nilesh Nathwani [1961] Director/Pharmacist; Panna Nathwani [1964] Director

Glyndebourne Productions Limited
Incorporated: 16 December 1939 *Employees:* 323
Net Worth: £61,650,792 *Total Assets:* £73,737,816
Registered Office: Glyndebourne, Lewes, E Sussex, BN8 5UU
Activities: Performing arts
Officers: Abbey Gough, Secretary; Jolyon Ronald Thomas Barker [1967] Director/Partner (Consulting), Deloitte; John Chester Botts [1941] Director [American]; Lord Evan Mervyn Davies [1952] Director; Louise Flind [1966] Director/Freelance Journalist; Hamish Forsyth [1969] Director; Alina Kessel [1966] Director/Advertising Executive [American]; Franck Petitgas [1961] Director/Investment Banker [French]

Glynwed Overseas Holdings Limited
Incorporated: 21 March 1929 *Employees:* 3
Net Worth: £64,400,000 *Total Assets:* £64,416,000
Registered Office: Dickley Lane, Lenham, Maidstone, Kent, ME17 2DE
Activities: Activities of head offices
Parent: Aliaxis Holdings UK Limited
Officers: Ian Charles McNair, Secretary; Ian Charles McNair [1960] Director/Accountant; Koen Jozef Sticker [1976] Director [Belgian]

Glynwed Pipe Systems Limited
Incorporated: 9 February 1983 *Employees:* 212
Net Worth: £56,858,000 *Total Assets:* £87,824,000
Registered Office: Dickley Lane, Lenham, Maidstone, Kent, ME17 2DE
Activities: Manufacture of other plastic products
Parent: Aliaxis Holdings UK Limited
Officers: Ian Charles McNair, Secretary; Fausto Alberto Bejarano Castillo [1960] Director [Costa Rican]; Klaas Daniel Decuypere [1968] Director [Belgian]; Stanley Carl James [1962] Director

GMK Limited
Incorporated: 26 February 2013 *Employees:* 68
Net Worth: £12,698,562 *Total Assets:* £23,926,818
Registered Office: Bear House, Concorde Way, Fareham, Hants, PO15 5RL
Activities: Activities of head offices
Officers: Nils Bjorn Oskar Waktare, Secretary; Franco Gussalli Beretta [1964] Managing Director [Italian]; Nicola Perniola [1965] Managing Director [Italian]; Jorg Prediger [1965] Managing Director [German]; Dr Johan Esbjorn Patrick Waktare [1965] Director/Doctor [Swedish]; Karl Styrbjorn Waktare [1967] Director [Swedish]; Nils Bjorn Oskar Waktare [1970] Managing Director; Anna Eva Viktoria Williams [1971] Director

Godrej UK Limited
Incorporated: 24 October 2005
Net Worth: £23,470,900 *Total Assets:* £23,470,900
Registered Office: Falcon House, 115-123 Staines Road, Hounslow, Middlesex, TW3 3LL
Activities: Non-trading company
Parent: Godrej Netherlands BV
Officers: Thomas Dawes [1982] Director; Dorab Erach Mistry [1953] Director/Business Executive; Anand Rangaswamy [1971] Director [Indian]

Gojo Industries - Europe Limited
Incorporated: 22 February 1990 *Employees:* 385
Net Worth: £8,726,525 *Total Assets:* £60,227,816
Registered Office: Unit 5 & 6 Stratus Park, Brinklow, Milton Keynes, Bucks, MK10 0DA
Activities: Wholesale of perfume and cosmetics
Officers: Mark Steven Lerner, Secretary [American]; Timothy Dye [1965] Commercial Director [American]; Joseph Samuel Kanfer [1947] Director/President [American]; Mark Steven Lerner [1949] Director/Secretary & Treasurer [American]; Scott Levin [1952] Director [American]

Gold Group International Limited
Incorporated: 5 August 1965 *Employees:* 10
Net Worth: £26,546,364 *Total Assets:* £81,888,840
Registered Office: Gold Group House, Godstone Road, Whyteleafe, Surrey, CR3 0GG
Activities: Activities of head offices
Major Shareholder: David Gold
Officers: David Gold [1936] Director; Jacqueline Gold [1960] Director; Vanessa Gold [1967] Acting Managing Director

Golden Leaves Limited
Incorporated: 3 June 1994 *Employees:* 27
Net Worth: £19,686,596 *Total Assets:* £101,814,112
Registered Office: 5 Robin Hood Lane, Sutton, Surrey, SM1 2SW
Activities: Funeral and related activities
Major Shareholder: Stephen Neil Anthony Rowland
Officers: Stephen Neil Anthony Rowland, Secretary/Director; Barry William Floyd [1967] Director/Head of Operations and Marketing; Anthony Brian Arthur Rowland [1938] Funeral Director; Stephen Neil Anthony Rowland [1965] Director/Funeral Director

A Gomez Limited
Incorporated: 27 November 1989 *Employees:* 730
Net Worth: £15,835,128 *Total Assets:* £35,375,696
Registered Office: Coldharbour Lane Bridge, Canterbury, Kent, CT4 5HL
Activities: Wholesale of fruit and vegetables
Officers: Simon John Gretton, Secretary; Gerardo Gomez Yelo [1968] Director [Spanish]; Juan Hernandez [1961] Director [Spanish]; Trevor James Parmenter [1958] Director/Fruit Distributor

Goodman Property Investments (Hove) Limited
Incorporated: 22 December 1953 *Employees:* 2
Net Worth: £16,996,472 *Total Assets:* £20,450,708
Registered Office: Cornelius House, 178-180 Church Road, Hove, E Sussex, BN3 2DJ
Activities: Other letting and operating of own or leased real estate
Shareholders: Gary John Epstein; Brian Philip Peters
Officers: Brian Philip Peters, Secretary; Gary John Epstein [1954] Director/Chartered Accountant; Brian Philip Peters [1945] Director/Chartered Accountant

Goodrich Inertial Limited
Incorporated: 9 December 2009
Net Worth: £151,528,000 *Total Assets:* £1,042,073,024
Registered Office: 1st Floor, Ash House, Littleton Road, Ashford, Middlesex, TW15 1TZ
Activities: Non-trading company
Parent: United Technologies Corporation
Officers: Christian Bruno Jean Idczak [1963] Director/Business Executive [French]; Patricia Catherine Moran [1964] Finance Director [American]; Peter Ross [1964] Finance Director; Louise Kay Thompson [1983] Director/Chartered Management Accountant

Goodwood Estate Company Limited (The)
Incorporated: 18 August 1955 *Employees:* 888
Net Worth: £194,904,272 *Total Assets:* £268,383,264
Registered Office: Goodwood, Chichester, W Sussex, PO18 0PX
Activities: Mixed farming
Shareholders: Earl of March and Kinrara Charles Henry Gordon-Lennox; Richard Philip Taylor; Andrew John Taylor
Officers: Katharine Anne Palka, Secretary; Professor Brian George Allison [1933] Director/Consultant; Ian Edward Barlow [1951] Director; Jane Margaret Cole [1963] Director/Chairman Media Agency; Janet Elizabeth Gordon Lennox [1961] Director/Psychotherapist; Tracey Greaves [1966] Director/Sales & Marketing; Terence David O'Rourke [1942] Director/Architect/Town Planner; Jeremy Robert Arthur Richardson [1970] Director; Adrian Paul Sargent [1976] Director; Christopher Paul Sullivan [1957] Director/Business Consultant; Ian Christopher West [1964] Director; Christopher Edward James Woodgate [1977] Director/Accountant

The Gordon Foundation
Incorporated: 14 August 1888 *Employees:* 203
Net Worth: £16,037,737 *Total Assets:* £22,324,208
Registered Office: Gordon's School, West End, Woking, Surrey, GU24 9PT
Activities: Educational support services
Officers: Susan Margaret Meikle, Secretary; Lynn Bannister [1959] Director/Information Security Manager; Martin David Barnes [1964] Director; Attilia Gabriella de Turris [1964] Director; William Duncan Eason [1950] Investment Director; Thomas Oliver Gordon [1972] Director/Contracts Specialist; Dr John Harnden Higgs [1962] Director/Charity Administrator; Pamela Anne LEA [1953] Director/Architect; Sir Lord Lingfield [1942] Director/Conservative Peer - Education; Christopher Nicholas Lomas [1973] Director/Company Secretary; Alison MacLennan [1972] Director/Solicitor; Alan McClafferty [1963] Director; Major General Peter John Russell-Jones [1948] Director/Army Adviser BAE Systems; Anne Stephens [1966] Director [South African]; Jay Edward Tamsitt [1952] Director/Wealth Manager; Jane Valner [1954] Director/Retired; Peter Anthony Wall [1955] Director/Engineer; Charles Henry Whiffin [1955] Director/Retired Chartered Accountant; Peter Francis Wynter Bee [1955] Director/Solicitor

Goshawk Insurance Holdings Limited
Incorporated: 2 July 1990
Net Worth: £109,595,184 *Total Assets:* £109,595,184
Registered Office: 3 Guildford Business Park, Guildford, Surrey, GU2 8XG
Activities: Activities of head offices
Parent: Enstar Group Limited
Officers: Siobhan Mary Hextall, Secretary [Irish]; Siobhan Mary Hextall [1968] Director/Accountant [Irish]; Derek Robert Douglas Reid [1965] Legal Director; Clive Paul Thomas [1962] Director/Accountant

The Edward Gostling Foundation
Incorporated: 27 February 1998 *Employees:* 39
Previous: The Act Foundation
Net Worth: £98,565,912 *Total Assets:* £111,282,168
Registered Office: 61 Thames Street, Windsor, Berks, SL4 1QW
Activities: Financial intermediation not elsewhere classified
Officers: James Michael Kerr, Secretary; Colin John Clarkson [1950] Property Director; Christine Margaret Erwood [1956] Director/Tax Specialist; Russell Peter Meadows [1956] Director/Chartered Surveyor; Stephen Charles O'Sullivan [1961] Director/Lawyer [Irish]; John Joseph Osullivan [1945] Director/Fire Protection Manager; Andrew Campbell Ross [1946] Director/Retired Charity Chief Executive; Michael Anthony Street [1947] Director/Airline Executive; Denis Newman Taylor [1953] Director/Chartered Surveyor; Robert Frederick White [1948] Director/Architect

Gould International UK Limited
Incorporated: 29 August 1934 *Employees:* 43
Net Worth: £12,832,384 *Total Assets:* £22,452,140
Registered Office: Brunswick House, Regent Park, 299 Kingston Road, Leatherhead, Surrey, KT22 7LU
Activities: Wholesale of other intermediate products
Officers: Josephine Morley, Secretary; David Hillel Berkowitz [1946] Director/Chief Executive [American]; Nicholas Christopher Henry [1969] Managing Director; Edward Lawrence Silver [1969] Director/Chief Financial Officer [American]; Michael David Trachtenberg [1965] Director [American]; Darren James Wheeler [1971] Director

Gould Publication Papers UK Limited
Incorporated: 2 October 2002 *Employees:* 26
Net Worth: £8,813,394 *Total Assets:* £26,193,992
Registered Office: Brunswick House, Regent Park, 299 Kingston Road, Leatherhead, Surrey, KT22 7LU
Activities: Wholesale of other intermediate products
Parent: Gould International UK Limited
Officers: Josephine Morley, Secretary; David Hillel Berkowitz [1946] Director/Chief Executive [American]; Dominic Karl Kristian Blakey [1968] Sales Director; Edward Lawrence Silver [1969] Director/Chief Financial Officer [American]; Michael David Trachtenberg [1965] Director [American]; Darren James Wheeler [1971] Director

Goulden Properties Limited
Incorporated: 12 January 1990 *Employees:* 8
Net Worth: £18,094,560 *Total Assets:* £20,116,018
Registered Office: The Barn Lake Court, Hursley, Winchester, Hants, SO21 2LD
Activities: Buying and selling of own real estate
Officers: John Simon Goulden, Secretary; Amanda Jane Dodd [1963] Director/Administrator; John Simon Goulden [1944] Director/Builder; Maximillian Peter Goulden [1981] Director; Nicholas John Goulden [1969] Director/Property Manager; Roger Derek Woolley [1957] Director/Solicitor

GPG (UK) Holdings Limited
Incorporated: 25 October 1919
Previous: GPG (UK) Holdings PLC
Net Worth: £5,077,000 *Total Assets:* £247,484,992
Registered Office: 1 The Square, Stockley Park, Uxbridge, Middlesex, UB11 1TD
Activities: Activities of head offices
Parent: Coats Group PLC
Officers: John Sinclair Lovell [1967] Group Pensions Director

GR Bottling Holdings UK Limited
Incorporated: 21 April 2016
Net Worth: £2,541,987,328 *Total Assets:* £2,541,998,592
Registered Office: Pemberton House, Bakers Road, Uxbridge, Middlesex, UB8 1EZ
Activities: Activities of other holding companies n.e.c.
Parent: Coca-Cola European Partners PLC
Officers: Paul Van Reesch, Secretary; Frank Govaerts [1961] Director [Belgian]; Paul Van Reesch [1976] Director; Edward Owen Walker [1967] Director

Gracewell Healthcare Limited
Incorporated: 24 August 2010
Net Worth: £18,540,000 *Total Assets:* £31,813,000
Registered Office: Sunrise House, Post Office Lane, Beaconsfield, Bucks, HP9 1FN
Activities: Other human health activities
Officers: Antony Nigel Brister [1972] Director; Jerry Liang [1984] Finance Director [American]

Graduation Bidco Limited
Incorporated: 6 June 2016 *Employees:* 4
Net Worth: £27,430,000 *Total Assets:* £80,784,000
Registered Office: 2nd Floor, 1 Jubilee Street, Brighton, BN1 1GE
Activities: Activities of head offices
Parent: Graduation Holdco Limited
Officers: Timothy James Gibson [1968] Director [New Zealander]; Charles Robert William McLean [1969] Director; Martin Anthony Robinson [1962] Director

Graduation Holdco Limited
Incorporated: 24 August 2016 *Employees:* 902
Net Worth: £20,053,000 *Total Assets:* £112,513,000
Registered Office: 2nd Floor, 1 Jubilee Street, Brighton, BN1 1GE
Activities: Activities of other holding companies n.e.c.
Parent: Graduation Interco Limited
Officers: Timothy James Gibson [1968] Director [New Zealander]; Charles Robert William McLean [1969] Director; Martin Anthony Robinson [1962] Director

Graduation Midco Limited
Incorporated: 24 August 2016
Net Worth: £37,636,000 *Total Assets:* £48,116,000
Registered Office: 2nd Floor, 1 Jubilee Street, Brighton, BN1 1GE
Activities: Activities of other holding companies n.e.c.
Parent: Graduation Topco Limited
Officers: Timothy James Gibson [1968] Director [New Zealander]; Charles Robert William McLean [1969] Director; Martin Anthony Robinson [1962] Director

Graduation Topco Limited
Incorporated: 24 August 2016 *Employees:* 902
Net Worth: £23,513,000 *Total Assets:* £116,431,000
Registered Office: 2nd Floor, 1 Jubilee Street, Brighton, BN1 1GE
Activities: Activities of other holding companies n.e.c.
Parent: BDC II (SGP) Limited
Officers: Timothy James Gibson [1968] Director [New Zealander]; Robin Arthur Jordan Lawson [1975] Director; Charles Robert William McLean [1969] Director; Alan Douglas Payne [1968] Director; Martin Anthony Robinson [1962] Director

Grafise Holdings Limited
Incorporated: 6 November 2001 *Employees:* 203
Net Worth: £2,988,502 *Total Assets:* £22,282,996
Registered Office: Sterling House, 177-181 Farnham Road, Slough, Berks, SL1 4XP
Activities: Activities of head offices
Parent: CS Astra Limited
Officers: Charles Arthur Slaughter, Secretary/Director; Peter Nott [1963] Director; Charles Arthur Slaughter [1958] Director

Grafton Group (UK) Public Limited Company
Incorporated: 11 January 1994 *Employees:* 12
Net Worth: £116,454,656 *Total Assets:* £728,055,616
Registered Office: Oak Green House, 250-256 High Street, Dorking, Surrey, RH4 1QT
Activities: Activities of head offices
Officers: David Llewelyn Arnold [1966] Finance Director; Gavin Slark [1965] Director; Jonathon Paul Sowton [1962] Director; Bruce Andrew Van Der Waag [1966] Director [Dutch]

Grafton UK Leasing Company Limited
Incorporated: 13 August 2004
Net Worth: £25,260,694 *Total Assets:* £25,542,216
Registered Office: Oak Green House, 250-256 High Street, Dorking, Surrey, RH4 1QT
Activities: Financial leasing
Parent: Grafton Group (UK) PLC
Officers: Brian O'Hara [1967] Director/Accountant [Irish]; Jonathon Paul Sowton [1962] Director

Graham Care (YB) Limited
Incorporated: 4 October 1995 *Employees:* 565
Previous: Graham Care Limited
Net Worth: £84,549,256 *Total Assets:* £163,476,544
Registered Office: 20 Cranley Road, Hersham, Walton on Thames, Surrey, KT12 5BP
Activities: Residential nursing care facilities
Parent: Graham Care Group Limited
Officers: William Ernest Graham, Secretary/Business Manager; Dr Karen Elizabeth Graham [1962] Director/Medical Doctor; William Ernest Graham [1961] Director/Business Manager

The Grand Central Hotel Glasgow Limited
Incorporated: 9 April 2009 *Employees:* 280
Previous: Troy Management Services (Glasgow) Limited
Net Worth: £15,074,000 *Total Assets:* £36,370,000
Registered Office: Broadwater Park, Denham, Bucks, UB9 5HR
Activities: Hotels and similar accommodation
Parent: IHC May Fair Hotel Limited
Officers: Catherine Elizabeth Lindsay, Secretary; Michael Todd Glover [1971] Director [American]; Nicolette Henfrey [1969] Director; Geoffrey Howard Lee [1955] Director [Australian]; Daisy Eleanor Loveday Caroline Llewellyn [1971] Director; David James Taylor [1976] Director; Matthew Woollard [1985] Director

Grand Union Group Funding PLC
Incorporated: 1 November 2013
Net Worth: £50,000 *Total Assets:* £114,800,000
Registered Office: Derwent House, University Way, Cranfield Technology Park, Cranfield, Bedford, MK43 0AZ
Activities: Financial intermediation not elsewhere classified
Officers: Chris Bellamy, Secretary; Philip John Edwards [1955] Director/Semi Retired Consultant; Aileen Christine Evans [1960] Director/Chief Executive; Nicola Ewen [1974] Director/Accountant; Peter Anthony Fielder [1952] Director/Retired Banker; Mona Shah [1968] Finance Director

Grandir UK Limited
Incorporated: 12 December 2016 *Employees:* 1,109
Net Worth: £29,528,000 *Total Assets:* £65,098,000
Registered Office: Tuscany House, White Hart Lane, Basingstoke, Hants, RG21 4AF
Activities: Pre-primary education
Major Shareholder: Jean-Emmanuel Rodocanachi
Officers: Colin James Lawson [1966] Director/Accountant; Gregoire Le Sourd [1978] Director [French]; Adrian Richard Moore [1964] Director; Jean-Emmanuel Rodocanachi [1969] Director [French]

Grange Renewable Energy Limited
Incorporated: 18 May 2011
Net Worth Deficit: £4,550,000 *Total Assets:* £26,079,000
Registered Office: Beaufort Court, Egg Farm Lane, Kings Langley, Herts, WD4 8LR
Activities: Production of electricity
Parent: Trafalgar Wind Holdings Limited
Officers: Dominic James Hearth, Secretary; Steven William Hughes [1972] Generation & Asset Management Director; Fraser Stephen Merry [1968] Director/Chartered Surveyor; Mitesh Raj Patel [1982] Director/Group Financial Controller

Grangette Ltd
Incorporated: 13 April 2016
Net Worth Deficit: £723,208 *Total Assets:* £23,261,768
Registered Office: Greenstedes, Marden Paddock, Brockenhurst, Hants, SO42 7SU
Activities: Fund management activities
Officers: Margaret Jane Gosman, Secretary; Allen David Gosman [1940] Director/Professor Emeritus [Canadian]; Margaret Jane Gosman [1941] Director/Retired; Laurence Meakin [1946] Director/Administrator

Granitte Investments (UK) Limited
Incorporated: 30 July 2012
Net Worth: £125,548,904 *Total Assets:* £125,554,400
Registered Office: Ground Floor, Unit 501 Centennial Park, Centennial Avenue, Elstree, Borehamwood, Herts, WD6 3FG
Activities: Activities of other holding companies n.e.c.
Officers: Ying-Chou Yang [1955] Director [Taiwanese]

William Grant & Sons Brands Limited
Incorporated: 31 January 2014 *Employees:* 115
Net Worth: £100,693,000 *Total Assets:* £251,652,000
Registered Office: Independence House, 84 Lower Mortlake Road, Richmond, Surrey, TW9 2HS
Activities: Wholesale of wine, beer, spirits and other alcoholic beverages
Parent: William Grant & Sons Limited
Officers: Gregory Justin Bargeton, Secretary; Douglas John Bagley [1967] Director [Australian]; Gregory Justin Bargeton [1973] Director/Global Head of Legal; Gary William Brewer [1961] Director; Philip Andrew Gladman [1970] Marketing Director; Rita Marie Greenwood [1968] Director; Ewan John Henderson [1968] Director; Simon John Hunt [1971] Director [Australian/British]; Michael Lamont [1960] Director/Accountant; Christopher Wesley Mason [1953] Director; Paul Henry Rochford [1963] Director/Accountant; Jonathan Mark Yusen [1970] Director [American]

William Grant & Sons UK Limited
Incorporated: 19 August 1988 *Employees:* 143
Net Worth: £821,000 *Total Assets:* £146,531,008
Registered Office: Form 1 Bartley Wood Business Park, Bartley Way, Hook, Hants, RG27 9XA
Activities: Wholesale of wine, beer, spirits and other alcoholic beverages
Parent: William Grant & Sons Investments Limited
Officers: Karen Louise Forbes, Secretary; Neil Peter Barker [1963] Managing Director [British/Australian]; Rita Marie Greenwood [1968] Director; Ewan John Henderson [1968] Director/Group Tax and Company Secretary; Christopher Wesley Mason [1953] Managing Director; Paul Henry Rochford [1963] Director; Iain David Short [1981] Director/Chartered Accountant

Grant & Stone Limited
Incorporated: 10 February 1986 *Employees:* 276
Net Worth: £16,524,640 *Total Assets:* £29,137,628
Registered Office: Unit 2 Mill End Road, High Wycombe, Bucks, HP12 4AX
Activities: Agents involved in the sale of timber and building materials
Officers: Graham Philip Akers, Secretary; Graham Philip Akers [1960] Finance Director; Matthew Bland [1976] Director; Peter Allan Cudd [1966] Commercial Director; Peter Alan Gourd [1948] Director/Accountant; Andrew David Grant [1977] Director; Robert David Grant [1947] Director/Chairman; Susan Margaret Grant [1949] Director; Nicolas Arthur House [1957] Director/Chief Executive; Matthew Miller [1975] Director; Richard Joseph Stone [1948] Director; Susan Stone [1951] Director

Martin Grant (Holdings) Limited
Incorporated: 9 April 1974 *Employees:* 84
Net Worth: £75,976,712 *Total Assets:* £150,571,200
Registered Office: Grant House, Felday Road, Abinger Hammer, Dorking, Surrey, RH5 6QP
Activities: Other specialised construction activities n.e.c.
Major Shareholder: Catherine Grant
Officers: Catherine Grant, Secretary; John Peter Malovany, Secretary; Catherine Grant [1929] Director; Laurence Noel Grant [1953] Managing Director; Chris Andrew Hamilton [1968] Commercial Director; John Peter Malovany [1951] Director/Accountant; Andrew George Wilson [1950] Director/Chartered Surveyor

Martin Grant Homes Limited
Incorporated: 18 April 1978 *Employees:* 83
Net Worth: £33,193,332 *Total Assets:* £116,623,960
Registered Office: Grant House, Felday Road, Abinger Hammer, Dorking, Surrey, RH5 6QP
Activities: Other specialised construction activities n.e.c.
Major Shareholder: Catherine Grant
Officers: John Peter Malovany, Secretary; Andrew John Chairman [1965] Director; Laurence Noel Grant [1953] Director; Chris Andrew Hamilton [1968] Commercial Director; John Peter Malovany [1951] Director/Accountant; Dean Paul Markall [1962] Director; John Anthony Matuszewski [1955] Director; Andrew Paul Threader [1967] Production Director

Grass Valley Limited
Incorporated: 13 February 1974 *Employees:* 329
Previous: Snell Advanced Media Limited
Net Worth Deficit: £5,347,000 *Total Assets:* £59,821,000
Registered Office: 31 Turnpike Road, Newbury, Berks, RG14 2NX
Activities: Business and domestic software development
Parent: Snell Corporation Limited
Officers: Brian Edward Anderson [1974] Director/Attorney - General Counsel [American]; Timothy Banks [1973] Director; Alec Thomas Lappe [1981] Director/VP Tax [American]; Anne La Belle Malyszko [1980] Director/VP of Corporate Finance [American]

Gravesend and District Real Estate Company Limited (The)
Incorporated: 19 September 1930
Net Worth: £33,172,356 *Total Assets:* £51,402,836
Registered Office: 49 & 50 Windmill Street, Gravesend, Kent, DA12 1BG
Activities: Development of building projects
Officers: Neil Wilson Chatterton, Secretary; Alexander Guy Chambers [1968] Director; Peter Guy Chambers [1943] Director; Neil Wilson Chatterton [1963] Director/Chartered Surveyor; Brian Frederick Cradick [1949] Director/Chartered Surveyor; William John Bullen Meakin [1945] Director; Philip Stephen Rothwell [1953] Director/Solicitor

Gravity Media Group Holdings Limited
Incorporated: 19 May 2016 *Employees:* 308
Net Worth Deficit: £8,771,000 *Total Assets:* £74,647,000
Registered Office: 32-34 Greenhill Crescent, Watford, Herts, WD18 8JU
Activities: Activities of head offices
Major Shareholder: John Richard Newton
Officers: Nikki Petken, Secretary; David Wayne Checketts [1955] Director/Executive Investor [American]; Paul John Greensmith [1967] Director/Chief Financial Officer; Gordon Andrew Holmes [1969] Managing Director [Irish]; Peter Joseph Lewis [1964] Director [Australian]; Kevin Moorhouse [1958] Director; John Richard Newton [1963] Director

Grays of Cambridge (International) Limited
Incorporated: 18 October 1917 *Employees:* 136
Net Worth: £11,187,192 *Total Assets:* £23,080,968
Registered Office: Grays of Cambridge (International) Limited, Station Road, Robertsbridge, E Sussex, TN32 5DH
Activities: Manufacture of sports goods
Shareholders: Paul Douglas Gray; Richard William Gray
Officers: Paul Douglas Gray, Secretary/Director; Jason Charles Gray [1964] Director; Neil Douglas James Gray [1960] Director; Nicholas John Gray [1957] Director; Paul Douglas Gray [1961] Director; Richard William Gray [1965] Director; David Michael Noyes [1962] Director/Chairman

Greater Gabbard Offshore Winds Limited
Incorporated: 5 December 2003
Net Worth: £997,200,000 *Total Assets:* £1,267,900,032
Registered Office: No 1 Forbury Place, 43 Forbury Road, Reading, Berks, RG1 3JH
Activities: Production of electricity
Shareholders: Innogy Renewables UK Limited; SSE Renewables Holdings (UK) Limited
Officers: Alice Margaret Leggat, Secretary; Martin McEwen, Secretary; Paul Leslie Cowling [1960] Director; Richard Peter Escott [1965] Director; Richard Jennings Sandford [1971] Director/Head of Offshore Business Management; Jeremy Williamson [1966] Director

Kenneth Green Associates Limited
Incorporated: 30 September 1992 *Employees:* 310
Net Worth: £26,602,820 *Total Assets:* £42,828,352
Registered Office: Hill House, Monument Hill, Weybridge, Surrey, KT13 8RX
Activities: Wholesale of perfume and cosmetics
Shareholders: Susan Esther Green; Kenneth Charles Green
Officers: Philip John Stokes, Secretary; Kenneth Charles Green [1945] Director/Business Consultant; Brian John Stanton [1978] Managing Director [New Zealander]; Philip John Stokes [1956] Finance Director

Green Flag Holdings Limited
Incorporated: 8 June 1998
Net Worth: £25,084,020 *Total Assets:* £25,087,408
Registered Office: Churchill Court, Westmoreland Road, Bromley, Kent, BR1 1DP
Activities: Activities of other holding companies n.e.c.
Parent: Direct Line Group Limited
Officers: Roger Cheston Clifton, Secretary; Roger Cheston Clifton [1964] Director/Secretary; Helen Clare O'Murchu [1967] Director/Bank Official; Humphrey Michael Tomlinson [1962] Director/General Counsel & Company Secretary

Green Hill Energy Limited
Incorporated: 6 July 2009
Net Worth Deficit: £1,998,000 *Total Assets:* £45,007,000
Registered Office: Beaufort Court, Egg Farm Lane, Kings Langley, Herts, WD4 8LR
Activities: Other business support service activities n.e.c.
Parent: Trafalgar Wind Holdings Limited
Officers: Dominic James Hearth, Secretary; Steven William Hughes [1972] Generation & Asset Management Director; Fraser Stephen Merry [1968] Director/Chartered Surveyor; Mitesh Raj Patel [1982] Director/Group Financial Controller

Green Network UK PLC
Incorporated: 5 October 2012 *Employees:* 14
Previous: Green Network Trading UK PLC
Net Worth: £1,565,440 *Total Assets:* £37,046,680
Registered Office: New Kings Court, Tollgate, Chandler's Ford, Eastleigh, Hants, SO53 3LG
Activities: Trade of electricity
Officers: Jamie Nicholas Bradshaw [1976] Director/Consultant; Sabrina Corbo [1973] Director/Chief Executive [Italian]; David Spencer Tuomey [1970] Director/Consultant [Irish]

Green,Young & Company Limited
Incorporated: 1 January 1963
Net Worth: £4,764,143,104 *Total Assets:* £4,764,143,104
Registered Office: 103-105 Bath Road, Slough, Berks, SL1 3UH
Activities: Non-trading company
Parent: Reckitt Benckiser Investments Limited
Officers: Christine Anne-Marie Logan, Secretary; Richard Mark Greensmith [1973] Group Tax Director; Simon Andrew Neville [1957] Group Treasury Director; Jonathan Timmis [1975] Finance Director

Greencell Limited
Incorporated: 16 March 2000 *Employees:* 185
Net Worth: £12,660,000 *Total Assets:* £46,811,000
Registered Office: 42 Kings Hill Avenue, Kings Hill, West Malling, Kent, ME19 4AJ
Activities: Wholesale of fruit and vegetables
Parent: Westfalia Fruit International Limited
Officers: Chantelle Grobler, Secretary; Rian Johannes Du Toit [1971] Director [South African]; Claus Burkhard Lippert [1963] Director [German]; Graham Alexander Young [1957] Director

Greenclose Holdings Limited
Incorporated: 16 October 2012 *Employees:* 349
Net Worth: £16,716,882 *Total Assets:* £35,686,280
Registered Office: Pennington House, Ridgeway Lane, Lymington, Hants, SO41 8AA
Activities: Hotels and similar accommodation
Shareholders: John Alexander Chapman Leach; Patricia Ann Leach
Officers: Patricia Ann Leach, Secretary; Ian Richard Fry [1967] Finance Director; Catherine Rebecca Gibson [1973] Director; Richard John Haycocks [1949] Director; James Richard Hiley-Jones [1972] Managing Director; John Alexander Chapman Leach [1946] Director; Patricia Ann Leach [1944] Director; Robert Alexander Chapman Leach [1975] Director

Greeneden UK Acquisition Company Limited
Incorporated: 6 October 2011 *Employees:* 2
Net Worth: £394,084,256 *Total Assets:* £492,469,984
Registered Office: Genesys House, Frimley Business Park, Frimley, Camberley, Surrey, GU16 7SG
Activities: Activities of head offices
Parent: Greeneden Topco SCA
Officers: Mark Rosine, Secretary; Mark William Alloy [1955] Director [American]

Greenham Trust Ltd
Incorporated: 20 March 1997 *Employees:* 22
Previous: Greenham Common Community Trust Limited
Net Worth: £76,556,896 *Total Assets:* £85,569,000
Registered Office: Liberty House, The Enterprise Centre, Greenham Business Park, Greenham, Thatcham, Newbury, Berks, RG19 6HW
Activities: Other letting and operating of own or leased real estate
Officers: Oonagh Thomasina Dockley, Secretary; David John Bailey [1949] Director/Consultant; Zoe Lavinia Beatrice Benyon [1970] Director/Jeweller; Charles David Brims [1950] Director; Dr Paul Edgar Bryant [1938] Director/District Councillor; Charles Julian Cazalet [1947] Director; Victoria Jane Fishburn [1956] Director/Biographer; Biddy Hayward [1953] Director; Graham Christopher Spencer Mather [1954] Director/Solicitor; Sir Peter Colin Michael [1938] Director; Malcolm Vincent Morris [1941] Director/Accountant; Fiona Spencer-Jones [1969] Director/Chartered Surveyor; Robert Barclay Woods [1946] Director/Business Executive

Greensands (UK) Limited
Incorporated: 10 September 2007
Net Worth Deficit: £1,900,000 *Total Assets:* £2,113,400,064
Registered Office: Southern House, Yeoman Road, Worthing, W Sussex, BN13 3NX
Activities: Activities of head offices
Parent: Greensands Europe Limited
Officers: Joanne Statton, Secretary; Andrew Emerson Gilbert [1970] Director [American]; Brian Michael Goodwin [1969] Director/Investment Adviser [American]; Paul Ian Hedley [1969] Director; Susan Deborah Howard [1962] Director; Bronte Louise Somes [1972] Director/Infrastructure Investment Executive; Robert Boyd Pierre Wall [1979] Director/Investment Manager

Greensands Europe Limited
Incorporated: 10 September 2007
Net Worth Deficit: £177,200,000 *Total Assets:* £2,003,299,968
Registered Office: Southern House, Yeoman Road, Worthing, W Sussex, BN13 3NX
Activities: Activities of head offices
Officers: Joanne Statton, Secretary; Andrew Emerson Gilbert [1970] Director [American]; Brian Michael Goodwin [1969] Director/Investment Adviser [American]; Paul Ian Hedley [1969] Director; Susan Deborah Howard [1962] Director; Bronte Louise Somes [1972] Director/Infrastructure Investment Executive; Robert Boyd Pierre Wall [1979] Director/Investment Manager

Greensands Investments Limited
Incorporated: 4 July 2007
Net Worth Deficit: £817,100,032 *Total Assets:* £1,675,299,968
Registered Office: Southern House, Yeoman Road, Worthing, W Sussex, BN13 3NX
Activities: Activities of head offices
Parent: Greensands Senior Finance Limited
Officers: Joanne Statton, Secretary; Andrew Emerson Gilbert [1970] Director [American]; Brian Michael Goodwin [1969] Director/Investment Adviser [American]; Paul Ian Hedley [1969] Director; Susan Deborah Howard [1962] Director; Bronte Louise Somes [1972] Director/Infrastructure Investment Executive; Robert Boyd Pierre Wall [1979] Director/Investment Manager

Greensands Junior Finance Limited
Incorporated: 7 August 2007
Net Worth Deficit: £1,300,000 *Total Assets:* £2,109,699,968
Registered Office: Southern House, Yeoman Road, Worthing, W Sussex, BN13 3NX
Activities: Activities of head offices
Parent: Greensands (UK) Limited
Officers: Joanne Statton, Secretary; Andrew Emerson Gilbert [1970] Director [American]; Brian Michael Goodwin [1969] Director/Investment Adviser [American]; Paul Ian Hedley [1969] Director; Susan Deborah Howard [1962] Director; Bronte Louise Somes [1972] Director/Infrastructure Investment Executive; Robert Boyd Pierre Wall [1979] Director/Investment Manager

Greensands Limited
Incorporated: 17 March 2005
Net Worth: £6,763,000 *Total Assets:* £69,715,000
Registered Office: c/o Castle Royle Golf & Country Club, Bath Road, Knowl Hill, Reading, Berks, RG10 9AL
Activities: Other letting and operating of own or leased real estate
Parent: Club Company (Group) Limited
Officers: Martin Ewart Hemmings, Secretary; Thierry Delsol [1964] Director/Accountant [French]; Paul Scott Stephens [1969] Director/Accountant

Greensands Senior Finance Limited
Incorporated: 7 August 2007
Total Assets: £2,423,399,936
Registered Office: Southern House, Yeoman Road, Worthing, W Sussex, BN13 3NX
Activities: Activities of head offices
Parent: Greensands Junior Finance Limited
Officers: Joanne Statton, Secretary; Andrew Emerson Gilbert [1970] Director [American]; Brian Michael Goodwin [1969] Director/Investment Adviser [American]; Paul Ian Hedley [1969] Director; Susan Deborah Howard [1962] Director; Bronte Louise Somes [1972] Director/Infrastructure Investment Executive; Robert Boyd Pierre Wall [1979] Director/Investment Manager

Greenshaw Learning Trust
Incorporated: 13 May 2011 *Employees:* 148
Net Worth: £69,028,000 *Total Assets:* £91,406,000
Registered Office: Greenshaw Learning Trust, Grennell Road, Sutton, Surrey, SM1 3DY
Activities: General secondary education
Officers: Julie Adams, Secretary; Diana Coman [1958] Director/Consultant; Michael Cooper [1960] Director/Management Consultant; Gary Martin Miles [1955] Former Director of Management Institute; Roger Charles Mills [1956] Director/Publisher/Consultant; Ingrid Percy [1965] Director/Strategic Workforce Planner; Professor Darren Reynolds [1968] Director/University Professor; Karen Lesley Roche [1956] Director/Ofsted Inspector; William George Stewart Smith [1969] Director/Headteacher

Greenshields JCB Holdings Limited
Incorporated: 15 February 2017 *Employees:* 149
Net Worth: £1,712,000 *Total Assets:* £26,032,000
Registered Office: Alice Holt, Gravel Hill Road, Holt Pound, Farnham, Surrey, GU10 4LG
Activities: Other business support service activities n.e.c.
Major Shareholder: James Owen Willans Richardson
Officers: Ian Peter Durrant, Secretary; James Owen Willans Richardson [1981] Director

Greenshields JCB Limited
Incorporated: 7 August 1996 *Employees:* 147
Net Worth: £9,942,000 *Total Assets:* £25,500,000
Registered Office: Alice Holt, Gravel Hill Road, Holt Pound, Farnham, Surrey, GU10 4LG
Activities: Repair of machinery
Parent: Greenshields JCB Holdings Limited
Officers: Ian Peter Durrant, Secretary; Ian Peter Durrant [1971] Director; George Greenshields [1950] Director; Thomas James Greenshields [1975] Director; Robert Guest [1959] Director; James Owen Willans Richardson [1981] Director

Greenstone Oxford Limited
Incorporated: 6 December 2016 *Employees:* 2
Net Worth: £68,572 *Total Assets:* £32,909,552
Registered Office: c/o Hillier Hopkins LLP, First Floor, Radius House, 51 Clarendon Road, Watford, Herts, WD17 1HP
Activities: Other letting and operating of own or leased real estate
Parent: Greenstone Property Holdings Limited
Officers: Stephen Barrow [1956] Director; Simon Richard Hope [1964] Director

Grenke Leasing Limited
Incorporated: 19 September 2002 *Employees:* 51
Net Worth: £23,297,296 *Total Assets:* £209,893,136
Registered Office: 5th Floor, Saxon House, 3 Onslow Street, Guildford, Surrey, GU1 4SY
Activities: Financial leasing
Parent: Grenke AG
Officers: David Horton-Knights [1966] Sales Director; Robin Spurr [1959] Director; Laurent Wittmann [1975] Director [French]

Grigg Investments Limited
Incorporated: 7 September 2003 *Employees:* 3
Net Worth: £24,995,780 *Total Assets:* £37,086,944
Registered Office: Globe House, Eclipse Park, Sittingbourne Road, Maidstone, Kent, ME14 3EN
Activities: Activities of open-ended investment companies
Shareholders: Christopher Michael Brake; Francis Robert Brake; Penelope Ann Lang; Paul Reginald Brake; Michael John Trigg; Michelle Louise Leveridge; Philip Riches Wilson
Officers: Paul Reginald Brake, Secretary; Christopher Michael Brake [1956] Director; Paul Reginald Brake [1947] Director

Grigny (UK) Limited
Incorporated: 1 December 1977 *Employees:* 2
Net Worth: £840,275 *Total Assets:* £96,418,048
Registered Office: The Rivers Office Park, Denham Way, Maple Cross, Herts, WD3 9YS
Activities: Other professional, scientific and technical activities n.e.c.
Shareholders: Renault SA; Renault SA
Officers: James Alexander Blendis, Secretary; Cyril Francois Roger Abiteboul [1977] Managing Director [French]; El-Hassan Aitsaid [1964] Finance Director [Belgian]

Grosvenor Casinos (GC) Limited
Incorporated: 23 November 2012 *Employees:* 1,853
Net Worth: £152,228,992 *Total Assets:* £190,210,000
Registered Office: Tor, Saint-Cloud Way, Maidenhead, Berks, SL6 8BN
Activities: Gambling and betting activities
Parent: Rank Gaming Group Limited
Officers: Luisa Ann Wright, Secretary; William James Spencer Floydd [1969] Director; Alan Morgan [1977] Director; John Patrick O'Reilly [1960] Director

Grosvenor Casinos Limited
Incorporated: 18 April 1966 *Employees:* 3,920
Net Worth: £128,848,000 *Total Assets:* £189,588,992
Registered Office: Tor, Saint-Cloud Way, Maidenhead, Berks, SL6 8BN
Activities: Gambling and betting activities
Parent: Rank Gaming Group Limited
Officers: Luisa Ann Wright, Secretary; William James Spencer Floydd [1969] Director; Alan Morgan [1977] Director; John Patrick O'Reilly [1960] Director

Group 1 Automotive UK Limited
Incorporated: 13 February 2007
Net Worth: £36,643,000 *Total Assets:* £158,474,000
Registered Office: Chandlers BMW, Victoria Road, Portslade, Brighton, BN41 1YH
Activities: Activities of head offices
Officers: Darryl Burman, Secretary [American]; Darren Guiver [1968] Director; Earl Hesterberg [1953] Director [American]; Daniel James McHenry [1974] Finance Director; John Rickel [1961] Director [American]

Group Fabricom Limited
Incorporated: 11 November 1982
Net Worth: £56,141,000 *Total Assets:* £56,141,000
Registered Office: Suez House, Grenfell Road, Maidenhead, Berks, SL6 1ES
Activities: Activities of head offices
Parent: Suez Recycling and Recovery Holdings UK Ltd
Officers: Joan Knight, Secretary; Florent Thierry Antoine Duval [1976] Director/Chief Finance Officer [French]; David Courtenay Palmer-Jones [1963] Director/Chief Executive Officer

Groupe SEB UK Limited
Incorporated: 24 September 1979 *Employees:* 154
Net Worth: £19,414,000 *Total Assets:* £50,423,000
Registered Office: Riverside House, Riverside Walk, Windsor, Berks, SL4 1NA
Activities: Wholesale of household goods (other than musical instruments) n.e.c
Parent: SEB S.A.
Officers: Andrew Chatfield, Secretary; Andrew Chatfield [1971] Finance Director; Richard Luis Joaristi [1972] Director/General Manager UK and Ireland [Spanish]; Iris Lia Maria Jurus-Seijsener [1966] Director/Vice President Controlling Continent Europe [Dutch]; Olivier Naccache [1962] Director/Senior VP Western Europe [French]

Grouse Bidco Limited
Incorporated: 18 October 2016 *Employees:* 2
Net Worth: £2,073,010 *Total Assets:* £27,680,528
Registered Office: The Barn, Philpots Close, West Drayton, Middlesex, UB7 7RY
Activities: Activities of other holding companies n.e.c.
Parent: Grouse Midco Limited
Officers: Stephen Gallucci [1969] Director; Patrick Finbarr Keenan [1967] Director/Accountant [Irish]

Grouse Midco Limited
Incorporated: 18 October 2016 *Employees:* 2
Net Worth Deficit: £2,475,063 *Total Assets:* £27,037,648
Registered Office: The Barn, Philpots Close, West Drayton, Middlesex, UB7 7RY
Activities: Activities of other holding companies n.e.c.
Parent: Grouse Topco Limited
Officers: Stephen Gallucci [1969] Director; Patrick Finbarr Keenan [1967] Director/Accountant [Irish]

Grouse Topco Limited
Incorporated: 18 October 2016 *Employees:* 140
Net Worth Deficit: £545,000 *Total Assets:* £47,114,000
Registered Office: The Barn, Philpots Close, West Drayton, Middlesex, UB7 7RY
Activities: Activities of other holding companies n.e.c.
Parent: Growth Capital Partners Nominees Limited
Officers: Stephen Gallucci [1969] Director; Nicholas Horler [1959] Director; Patrick Finbarr Keenan [1967] Director/Accountant [Irish]; John Edward Marsh [1979] Director

Grove Court Properties (Beaconsfield) Limited
Incorporated: 6 January 1961 *Employees:* 4
Net Worth: £22,213,708 *Total Assets:* £33,413,948
Registered Office: 58 Oak End Way, Gerrards Cross, Bucks, SL9 8BR
Activities: Other letting and operating of own or leased real estate
Parent: Grove Court Properties (Holdings) Limited
Officers: Jill Hughes [1932] Director; Geoffrey Roger Williams [1962] Director

Grove Court Properties (Holdings) Limited
Incorporated: 12 May 1955 *Employees:* 321
Previous: Hughes of Beaconsfield (Holdings) Limited
Net Worth: £37,875,544 *Total Assets:* £78,637,632
Registered Office: 58 Oak End Way, Gerrards Cross, Bucks, SL9 8BR
Activities: Activities of head offices
Shareholders: Ian Fred Ledger; Nicholas Simon Harley
Officers: Jill Hughes [1932] Director; Richard John Michael Hughes [1957] Director/Accountant; Robin Anthony Hughes [1962] Director; Dominique Julie Chantal Pilling [1971] Director/Secretary; Stephanie Jill Tidswell-Norrish [1959] Director/Housewife; Geoffrey Roger Williams [1962] Managing Director

Grove Developments Limited
Incorporated: 3 December 2010 *Employees:* 38
Net Worth: £34,245,664 *Total Assets:* £72,611,760
Registered Office: World Business Centre, 3 Newall Road, London Heathrow Airport, Hounslow, Middlesex, TW6 2TA
Activities: Development of building projects
Parent: Grove Acquisitions Limited
Officers: Athos George Yiannis, Secretary; Surinder Arora [1958] Director; Carlton Jeffrey Brown [1972] Director/Chartered Accountant; Sinead Hughes [1965] Director [Irish]; Athos George Yiannis [1963] Director/Chartered Accountant

Grove HR Limited
Incorporated: 28 June 2012 *Employees:* 742
Net Worth: £49,777,560 *Total Assets:* £103,054,368
Registered Office: World Business Centre, 3 Newall Road, London Heathrow Airport, Hounslow, Middlesex, TW6 2TA
Activities: Hotels and similar accommodation
Parent: Arora Hotels Limited
Officers: Athos George Yiannis, Secretary; Sanjay Arora [1989] Director; Surinder Arora [1958] Director; Carlton Jeffrey Brown [1972] Director/Chartered Accountant; Athos George Yiannis [1963] Director/Chartered Accountant

Gruffalo Bidco Limited
Incorporated: 7 November 2016 *Employees:* 6
Net Worth: £175,679 *Total Assets:* £38,508,872
Registered Office: c/o Coffin Mew, 3rd Floor, Cumberland House, 15-17 Cumberland Place, Southampton, SO15 2BG
Activities: Retail sale of books in specialised stores
Parent: Gruffalo Midco Limited
Officers: Graham Richard Bell [1974] Director/Chief Financial and Operating Officer; Stephen Philip Boobyer [1962] Director; Simon Downes [1978] IT Director; James Lewis Hurrell [1985] Director; Martin John Nye [1964] Director; Oliver Quentin James Wyncoll [1969] Director/Investment Manager

Gruffalo Midco Limited
Incorporated: 7 November 2016
Net Worth Deficit: £2,214 *Total Assets:* £25,202,548
Registered Office: c/o Coffin Mew LLP, 3rd Floor, Cumberland House, 15-17 Cumberland Place, Southampton, SO15 2BG
Activities: Retail sale of books in specialised stores
Parent: Gruffalo Topco Limited
Officers: Graham Richard Bell [1974] Director/Chief Financial and Operating Officer; Stephen Philip Boobyer [1962] Director; Simon Downes [1978] IT Director; James Lewis Hurrell [1985] Director; Martin John Nye [1964] Director; Oliver Quentin James Wyncoll [1969] Director/Investment Manager

Gruffalo Topco Limited
Incorporated: 7 November 2016 *Employees:* 595
Net Worth Deficit: £5,830,137 *Total Assets:* £36,903,484
Registered Office: c/o Coffin Mew LLP, 3rd Floor, Cumberland House, 15-17 Cumberland Place, Southampton, SO15 2BG
Activities: Retail sale of books in specialised stores
Parent: Bridges Community Ventures Nominees Limited
Officers: Graham Richard Bell [1974] Director/Chief Financial and Operating Officer; Kenneth Charles Blair [1957] Director/Executive Chairman; Stephen Philip Boobyer [1962] Director; Simon Downes [1978] IT Director; James Lewis Hurrell [1985] Director; Arthur Maxfield [1956] Director; Martin John Nye [1964] Director; Oliver Quentin James Wyncoll [1969] Director/Investment Manager

Gruma Europe Limited
Incorporated: 9 August 1999 *Employees:* 367
Net Worth: £45,401,000 *Total Assets:* £53,273,000
Registered Office: Second Floor, Heathrow Boulevard 4, 282 Bath Road, Sipson, West Drayton, Middlesex, UB7 0DQ
Activities: Manufacture of bread; manufacture of fresh pastry goods and cakes
Shareholders: Graciela Silvia Gonzalez Moreno; Mayra Adela Gonzalez Moreno; Juan Antonio de Jesus Gonzalez Moreno
Officers: Amy Lucy Ashman, Secretary; Dannie Lee Burke [1969] Director/Treasurer [American]; Simon Mark Colaco [1975] Procurement Director; Peter Hall Ellis [1965] Managing Director; Rodolfo Maldonado [1953] Director/Chief Executive Officer [American]; Mohammed Saeed [1969] HR Director

GS Acquisitions Limited
Incorporated: 17 May 2010
Net Worth Deficit: £248,520,000 *Total Assets:* £102,444,000
Registered Office: Coronation Road, Cressex, High Wycombe, Bucks, HP12 3TZ
Activities: Activities of head offices
Parent: Biffa Group Limited
Officers: Richard Neil Pike [1969] Director/Chief Financial Officer; Michael Robert Mason Topham [1972] Director/Chief Executive Officer

GT NEPS (Holdings) Limited
Incorporated: 10 November 2014
Net Worth: £1,176,652 *Total Assets:* £108,400,856
Registered Office: Cowley Business Park, Cowley, Uxbridge, Middlesex, UB8 2AL
Activities: Construction of commercial buildings
Parent: Infrastructure Investments Holdings Limited
Officers: Jayesh Gajendra Doshi [1968] Director/Head of Portfolio Management; Joanna Lisette Fox [1970] Director; Mark Geoffrey David Holden [1957] Director; Elena Giorgiana Wegener [1975] Director

GT NEPS Limited
Incorporated: 11 November 2014
Net Worth: £1,176,652 *Total Assets:* £108,400,856
Registered Office: Cowley Business Park, Cowley, Uxbridge, Middlesex, UB8 2AL
Activities: Construction of commercial buildings
Parent: GT NEPS (Holdings) Limited
Officers: Jayesh Gajendra Doshi [1968] Director/Head of Portfolio Management; Joanna Lisette Fox [1970] Director; Mark Geoffrey David Holden [1957] Director; Elena Giorgiana Wegener [1975] Director

Guangdong Investments Limited
Incorporated: 20 December 2002
Net Worth: £98,089,368 *Total Assets:* £98,892,904
Registered Office: Chertsey Road, Sunbury on Thames, Middlesex, TW16 7BP
Activities: Activities of head offices
Parent: BP Global Investments Limited
Officers: David William Knipe [1974] Director/Oil Company Executive

Gucci Limited
Incorporated: 14 December 1961 *Employees:* 325
Net Worth: £22,272,000 *Total Assets:* £78,492,000
Registered Office: 5th Floor, Rear Suite, Oakfield House, 35 Perrymount Road, Haywards Heath, W Sussex, RH16 3BW
Activities: Retail sale of clothing in specialised stores
Parent: Kering SA
Officers: Giovanni Baldi [1969] Director/Manager [Italian]; Martina Tommasin [1978] Director/Employee [Italian]; Alberto Valente [1972] Director/Manager [Italian]

Guernsey Home Loans Limited
Incorporated: 9 August 2002
Net Worth: £2,798,000 *Total Assets:* £20,400,000
Registered Office: Reliance House, Sun Pier, Chatham, Kent, ME4 4ET
Activities: Banks
Parent: OneSavings Bank PLC
Officers: Jason Stanley Elphick, Secretary; Andrew John Golding [1969] Director; April Carolyn Talintyre [1965] Finance Director

John Guest Holdings Limited
Incorporated: 29 June 1943 *Employees:* 1,299
Net Worth: £109,191,368 *Total Assets:* £150,349,984
Registered Office: Head Office, Horton Road, West Drayton, Middlesex, UB7 8JL
Activities: Activities of production holding companies
Officers: Robert Gerard Bollman [1968] Director [American]; Jonathan Blayr Munz [1961] Director [Australian]; Heath Graham Sharp [1968] Director [Australian]

John Guest International Limited
Incorporated: 16 November 1999 *Employees:* 1,289
Net Worth: £96,891,888 *Total Assets:* £137,306,512
Registered Office: John Guest Ltd, Horton Road, West Drayton, Middlesex, UB7 8JL
Activities: Activities of production holding companies
Officers: Pernille Fabricius [1966] Director/Chief Financial Officer [Danish]; Jonathan Blayr Munz [1961] Director [Australian]; Heath Graham Sharp [1968] Director [Australian]

John Guest Limited
Incorporated: 9 August 1979 *Employees:* 908
Net Worth: £89,210,688 *Total Assets:* £116,658,504
Registered Office: Horton Road, West Drayton, Middlesex, UB7 8JL
Activities: Manufacture of other plastic products
Officers: Pernille Fabricius [1966] Director/Chief Financial Officer [Danish]; Jonathan Blayr Munz [1961] Director [Australian]; Heath Graham Sharp [1968] Director [Australian]

John Guest Speedfit Limited
Incorporated: 8 October 1962 *Employees:* 59
Net Worth: £5,705,472 *Total Assets:* £20,689,954
Registered Office: Horton Road, West Drayton, Middlesex, UB7 8JL
Activities: Agents specialised in the sale of other particular products
Officers: Pernille Fabricius [1966] Director/Chief Financial Officer [Danish]; Jonathan Blayr Munz [1961] Director [Australian]; Heath Graham Sharp [1968] Director [Australian]

Guide Dogs for the Blind Association (The)
Incorporated: 30 August 1934 *Employees:* 1,382
Net Worth: £113,500,000 *Total Assets:* £122,400,000
Registered Office: Hillfields, Reading Road, Burghfield Common, Reading, Berks, RG7 3YG
Activities: Other service activities n.e.c.
Officers: Phillippa Tracey Walther-Caine, Secretary; David Bruce Anderson [1955] Director/Retired; Amanda Helen Ariss [1963] Director/Charity Chief Executive; David John Bagley [1956] Director; Clare Elizabeth Black [1969] Director/Journalist; Catherine Mary Crofts [1975] Director/Local Government Officer; Robert Michael Deakin [1978] Director/Partner in Financial Services Consultancy; James Daryl Hambro [1949] Director/Banker; Michael Leslie Nussbaum [1946] Director/Retired; Polly Anne Shute [1967] Fundraising Director; Dr Ranjit Sondhi [1950] Director/Governance and Regulation; Patricia Mary Stafford [1961] Director; Polly Ann Williams [1965] Director/Chartered Accountant; John Derek Wrighthouse [1964] HR Director

Guild Resources Limited
Incorporated: 6 November 2015 *Employees:* 3
Net Worth: £21,015 *Total Assets:* £29,632,140
Registered Office: The Square, Basing View, Basingstoke, Hants, RG21 4EB
Activities: Human resources provision and management of human resources functions
Major Shareholder: Derek Reynolds
Officers: Derek Reynolds [1959] Director

Guildford Diocesan Board of Finance (The)
Incorporated: 27 October 1927 *Employees:* 81
Net Worth: £134,044,000 *Total Assets:* £144,804,000
Registered Office: Church House Guildford, 20 Alan Turing Road, Surrey Research Park, Guildford, Surrey, GU2 7YF
Activities: Activities of religious organisations
Officers: Peter David Coles, Secretary; John Oliver Alpass [1945] Director/Retired; Christopher Bevis [1967] Director/Lay Reader; The Revd Catherine Blair [1962] Director/Clergy; Canon Peter Nigel Edward Bruinvels [1950] Director/Management Consultant; Paul Donald Bryer [1958] Director/Clerk in Holy Orders; The Venerable Richard Paul Davies [1973] Director/Priest; Sarah Gillies [1966] Director/Lay Deanery Synod Member; Dianna Lynn Gwilliams [1957] Director/Dean of Guildford; Peter James Harwood [1964] Director/Clergy; Nigel Andrew Lewis [1956] Director/Consultant; Keith Robert Malcouronne [1959] Director/Chartered Accountant; Stephen Peter Roberts [1957] Director/Management Consultant; Adrian Vincent [1970] Director/Head of Policy for Remuneration; The Reverend Jane Elizabeth Vlach [1964] Director/Priest; The Right Reverend Andrew John Watson [1961] Director/The Bishop of Guildford; The Right Reverend Joanne Caladine Bailey Wells [1965] Director/Clergy

Guildford Education Partnership
Incorporated: 26 May 2011 *Employees:* 809
Net Worth: £76,782,000 *Total Assets:* £87,772,000
Registered Office: George Abbot School, Woodruff Avenue, Burpham, Guildford, Surrey, GU1 1XX
Activities: Primary education
Officers: Dr Jonathan Mark Cox [1966] Director/Headmaster; Christopher William Holyoak [1949] Director/Retired; Professor Jane Hilary Powell [1961] Director/Vice-Provost; Fergal Roche [1961] Director/Chief Executive; Anne Elizabeth Turner [1956] Director/Education Consultant; Christa Wijnja [1966] Director/School Business Manager [Dutch]; Linda Wilding [1959] Director; Dr Geoffrey Wyss [1954] Director/Consulting Manager; John Mark Yeomans [1957] Director/Angel Investor

Guildford Portfolios Limited
Incorporated: 4 November 1994 *Employees:* 337
Net Worth: £12,106,585 *Total Assets:* £50,147,448
Registered Office: Vines House, Slyfield Road, Guildford, Surrey, GU1 1RD
Activities: Activities of head offices
Parent: A L Shelly Marital Trust #2
Officers: Sean Patrick Kelly, Secretary; Sean Patrick Kelly [1968] Director; Brendan Gael Moynahan [1948] Director/Consultant [American]; Lesley Shelly [1948] Director/Executive [American]

Gurit (UK) Limited
Incorporated: 16 May 1978 *Employees:* 221
Net Worth: £32,842,000 *Total Assets:* £40,502,000
Registered Office: St Cross Business Park, Newport, Isle of Wight, PO30 5WU
Activities: Other manufacturing n.e.c.
Parent: Gurit Material Systems (UK) Limited
Officers: Stefan Gautschi, Secretary; Stefan Gautschi [1968] Director [Swiss]; Rudolf Hadorn [1963] Director/CEO Gurit [Swiss]

Gurit Material Systems (UK) Limited
Incorporated: 12 July 2002
Net Worth: £31,280,000 *Total Assets:* £47,085,000
Registered Office: St Cross Business Park, Newport, Isle of Wight, PO30 5WU
Activities: Other manufacturing n.e.c.
Parent: Gurit Holding AG
Officers: Angelo Roberto Quabba, Secretary; Stefan Gautschi [1968] Director/General Manager [Swiss]; Angelo Roberto Quabba [1965] Director/Chief Finance Officer [Swiss]

Gus UK Management Limited
Incorporated: 3 December 2013
Previous: GUS BV Limited
Net Worth Deficit: £614,477 *Total Assets:* £77,451,648
Registered Office: Irwin Mitchell LLP, Station Way, Crawley, W Sussex, RH10 1JA
Activities: Educational support services
Major Shareholder: Arkady Etingen
Officers: Arkady Etingen [1979] Director/Accountant

GVS Prepaid Limited
Incorporated: 29 August 2014 *Employees:* 2
Net Worth: £2,265,174 *Total Assets:* £139,968,496
Registered Office: Westside, London Road, Hemel Hempstead, Herts, HP3 9TD
Activities: Non-specialised wholesale trade
Parent: Minister for Communications Climate Action and Environment
Officers: Michelle Josephine Wainhouse, Secretary; Declan Byrne [1961] Director/Business Executive [Irish]

GXS Limited
Incorporated: 7 September 1978 *Employees:* 146
Net Worth: £11,127,795 *Total Assets:* £30,418,454
Registered Office: 420 Thames Valley Park Drive, Reading, Berks, RG6 1PT
Activities: Other information technology service activities
Parent: Acquisition U.K. Limited
Officers: Gordon Allan Davies [1962] Director/Chief Legal Officer & Corporate Development [Canadian]; Oliver Jon Gallienne [1973] Director/SVP, Worldwide Professional Services; Madhu Ranganathan [1964] Director/EVP & Chief Financial Officer [American]; Christian Waida [1966] Director/VP, General Counsel Worldwide Field Operations [German]

The Gym Group Midco1 Limited
Incorporated: 15 May 2013
Net Worth: £156,360,320 *Total Assets:* £163,891,104
Registered Office: Fifth Floor, No 1 Croydon, 12-16 Addiscombe Road, Croydon, Surrey, CR0 0XT
Activities: Activities of other holding companies n.e.c.
Parent: The Gym Group PLC
Officers: Richard James Darwin [1967] Director; Mark Alexander George [1974] Director/Chief Financial Officer

The Gym Group Midco2 Limited
Incorporated: 15 May 2013
Net Worth: £156,244,608 *Total Assets:* £163,884,160
Registered Office: Fifth Floor, No 1 Croydon, 12-16 Addiscombe Road, Croydon, Surrey, CR0 0XT
Activities: Activities of other holding companies n.e.c.
Parent: The Gym Group Midco 1 Limited
Officers: Richard James Darwin [1967] Director; Mark Alexander George [1974] Director/Chief Financial Officer

The Gym Group Operations Limited
Incorporated: 15 May 2013 *Employees:* 10
Previous: The Gym Group Limited
Net Worth: £132,308,544 *Total Assets:* £140,251,776
Registered Office: Fifth Floor, No 1 Croydon, 12-16 Addiscombe Road, Croydon, Surrey, CR0 0XT
Activities: Activities of head offices
Parent: The Gym Group Midco2 Limited
Officers: Richard James Darwin [1967] Director; Mark Alexander George [1974] Director/Chief Financial Officer

The Gym Group PLC
Incorporated: 14 May 2013
Previous: The Gym Group Limited
Net Worth: £141,846,000 *Total Assets:* £183,447,008
Registered Office: Fifth Floor, No 1 Croydon, 12-16 Addiscombe Road, Croydon, Surrey, CR0 0XT
Activities: Activities of other holding companies n.e.c.
Officers: Richard Darwin, Secretary; Richard James Darwin [1967] Director; Mark Alexander George [1974] Director/Chief Financial Officer; Paul John Thomas Gilbert [1962] Director; Penelope Lesley Hughes [1959] Director; Dr David Thomas Kelly [1963] Director; John Robert Treharne [1954] Director; Emma Margaret Woods [1968] Group Marketing and Digital Director

The Gym Limited
Incorporated: 21 December 2005 *Employees:* 272
Net Worth: £97,775,000 *Total Assets:* £156,844,000
Registered Office: Fifth Floor, No 1 Croydon, 12-16 Addiscombe Road, Croydon, Surrey, CR0 0XT
Activities: Fitness facilities
Parent: The Gym Group Operations Limited
Officers: Richard James Darwin [1967] Director; Mark Alexander George [1974] Director/Chief Financial Officer; Nicholas Charles Henwood [1968] Operations Director; Jasper Angus McIntosh [1973] Director/Chief Information Officer; Jonathan Guy Spaven [1958] Director/Chartered Surveyor

Gym Offshore One Limited
Incorporated: 23 April 2010
Net Worth: £252,600,336 *Total Assets:* £284,949,696
Registered Office: Suite 8, Pantiles Chambers, 85 High Street, Tunbridge Wells, Kent, TN1 1XP
Activities: Production of electricity
Parent: SWM UK Wind One Limited
Officers: Agnieszka Cieplinska [1972] Director/Project Manager [Polish/German]; Generald Martin Harrison [1954] Director; Christian Moldan [1974] Director/Project Manager [German]; Elaine Lynne Pavis [1968] Director/Chartered Accountant

Gym Offshore Three Limited
Incorporated: 13 May 2010
Net Worth: £84,016,944 *Total Assets:* £94,800,064
Registered Office: Suite 8, Pantiles Chambers, 85 High Street, Tunbridge Wells, Kent, TN1 1XP
Activities: Production of electricity
Parent: SWM UK Wind One Limited
Officers: Agnieszka Cieplinska [1972] Director/Project Manager [Polish/German]; Generald Martin Harrison [1954] Director; Christian Moldan [1974] Director/Project Manager [German]; Elaine Lynne Pavis [1968] Director/Chartered Accountant

Gym Offshore Two Limited
Incorporated: 29 March 2010
Net Worth: £168,623,536 *Total Assets:* £190,189,776
Registered Office: Suite 8, Pantiles Chambers, 85 High Street, Tunbridge Wells, Kent, TN1 1XP
Activities: Production of electricity
Parent: SWM UK Wind One Limited
Officers: Agnieszka Cieplinska [1972] Director/Project Manager [Polish/German]; Generald Martin Harrison [1954] Director; Christian Moldan [1974] Director/Project Manager [German]; Elaine Lynne Pavis [1968] Director/Chartered Accountant

Gym Renewables Limited
Incorporated: 17 June 2010
Net Worth: £162,680,992 *Total Assets:* £162,695,008
Registered Office: Faraday House, Sir William Siemens Square, Frimley, Camberley, Surrey, GU16 8QD
Activities: Non-trading company
Parent: Siemens Aktiengesellschaft
Officers: Simone Eufemia Agatha Davina, Secretary; Andrew John Bown [1979] Investment Director; Martin James Heath [1964] Director/Solicitor; Jamie Sue Schlueter Pietzsch [1969] Director/Head of Business Administration [American]

Gym Renewables One Limited
Incorporated: 23 April 2010
Net Worth: £172,287,008 *Total Assets:* £199,106,000
Registered Office: Faraday House, Sir William Siemens Square, Frimley, Camberley, Surrey, GU16 8QD
Activities: Other business support service activities n.e.c.
Parent: Gym Renewables Limited
Officers: Simone Eufemia Agatha Davina, Secretary; Andrew John Bown [1979] Investment Director; Martin James Heath [1964] Director/Solicitor; Jamie Sue Schlueter Pietzsch [1969] Director/Head of Business Administration [American]

Gyron Internet Limited
Incorporated: 22 June 2001 *Employees:* 116
Net Worth: £118,587,000 *Total Assets:* £246,318,000
Registered Office: 3 Centro, Boundary Way, Hemel Hempstead, Herts, HP2 7SU
Activities: Data processing, hosting and related activities
Parent: NTT Communications Corporation
Officers: Clive Hamilton [1967] Managing Director; Kiyoshi Maeda [1956] Director/Vice President [Japanese]; Ryuichi Matsuo [1963] Director/Vice President [Japanese]; Rupprecht Felix Rittweger [1970] Director/Chief Executive Officer [German]

H & D Support Services (Holdings) Limited
Incorporated: 8 January 2004
Net Worth Deficit: £5,424,000 *Total Assets:* £20,426,000
Registered Office: Astral House, Imperial Way, Watford, Herts, WD24 4WW
Activities: Activities of head offices
Parent: Infrastructure Investments Holdings Limited
Officers: Ian Hudson, Secretary; David Wyn Davies [1968] Director/Accountant; Hannah Holman [1980] Director

H & D Support Services Limited
Incorporated: 8 January 2004
Net Worth Deficit: £5,424,000 *Total Assets:* £20,426,000
Registered Office: Astral House, Imperial Way, Watford, Herts, WD24 4WW
Activities: Combined facilities support activities
Parent: H & D Support Services (Holdings) Limited
Officers: Ian Hudson, Secretary; David Wyn Davies [1968] Director/Accountant; Hannah Holman [1980] Director

H & T Group PLC
Incorporated: 23 July 2004 *Employees:* 1,102
Net Worth: £107,622,000 *Total Assets:* £141,936,000
Registered Office: Harvey & Thompson Ltd, Times House, Throwley Way, Sutton, Surrey, SM1 4AF
Activities: Activities of financial services holding companies
Officers: Stephen Anthony Fenerty, Secretary; Elaine Frances Draper [1963] Director; Stephen Anthony Fenerty [1973] Commercial Director; Peter Denis McNamara [1951] Director/Finance; John Graham Nichols [1950] Director; Mark Smith [1958] Director; James FitzGenerald Thornton [1957] Director/Chartered Accountant

H+H UK Holdings Limited
Incorporated: 22 November 2000
Net Worth: £80,273,000 *Total Assets:* £80,273,000
Registered Office: Celcon House, Ightham, Sevenoaks, Kent, TN15 9HZ
Activities: Other business support service activities n.e.c.
Parent: KWay Holdings Limited
Officers: Neil Julian Peter Griffiths, Secretary; Michael Troensegaard Andersen [1961] Director [Danish]; Calum James Forsyth [1966] Managing Director; Ian LEA Perkins [1965] Finance Director

H+H UK Limited
Incorporated: 26 April 1930 *Employees:* 252
Net Worth: £40,364,000 *Total Assets:* £81,904,000
Registered Office: Celcon House, Ightham, Sevenoaks, Kent, TN15 9HZ
Activities: Manufacture of concrete products for construction purposes
Officers: Neil Julian Peter Griffiths, Secretary; Michael Troensegaard Andersen [1961] Director [Danish]; Matthew John Carter [1968] Sales Director; Calum James Forsyth [1966] Managing Director; Clifford Alan Fudge [1957] Director/Chartered Structural Engineer; Neil Julian Peter Griffiths [1970] HR Director; Kelly Hunter [1976] Director/Commercial Manager; Peter James Lidstone [1964] Director/Chief Operating Officer; Spencer Nye [1968] Finance Director; Ian LEA Perkins [1965] Director

H+S Aviation Limited
Incorporated: 23 October 1946 *Employees:* 266
Net Worth: £62,982,000 *Total Assets:* £86,544,000
Registered Office: Airport Service Road, Portsmouth, PO3 5PJ
Activities: Service activities incidental to air transportation
Parent: BBA Aviation PLC
Officers: William James Bonder [1964] Managing Director [American]; Matthew Robert Jeram [1977] Director/Accountant; Philip Arthur Jupp [1977] Site Director; Hugh McElroy [1954] Director [American]; Mark Stubbs [1970] Director [American]

H. K. S. Holdings Limited
Incorporated: 26 May 2005 *Employees:* 573
Net Worth: £21,978,640 *Total Assets:* £74,859,520
Registered Office: Prax House, Horizon Business Village, 1 Brooklands Road, Weybridge, Surrey, KT13 0TJ
Activities: Other service activities n.e.c.
Parent: Harvest Energy Retail Limited
Officers: Arani Soosaipillai, Secretary; Don Camillo Emilio Borneo [1957] Director; Winston Sanjeevkumar Soosaipillai [1973] Director

H.E. Group Ltd
Incorporated: 2 December 1986 *Employees:* 180
Net Worth: £17,020,460 *Total Assets:* £55,409,788
Registered Office: Whitewall Road, Strood, Rochester, Kent, ME2 4DZ
Activities: Activities of head offices
Major Shareholder: Ion-Dan Edeleanu
Officers: Clare Jane Luscombe, Secretary; Peter Alfred Durey [1960] Operations Director; Hugh Robert Edeleanu [1955] Director/Engineer; Clare Jane Luscombe [1979] Financial Director

H.I.G. Europe - Fibercore Bidco Limited
Incorporated: 30 September 2010 *Employees:* 40
Net Worth: £23,785,036 *Total Assets:* £26,438,722
Registered Office: Fibercore House, University Parkway, Southampton, SO16 7QQ
Activities: Activities of head offices
Parent: Rouse Acquisitionco Limited
Officers: Christopher Emslie [1961] Director; Christopher O'Connor [1963] Director/President & CEO [American]

H.K.S. Motors Limited
Incorporated: 27 May 2002 *Employees:* 3
Net Worth: £16,252,962 *Total Assets:* £32,315,680
Registered Office: Prax House, Horizon Business Village, 1 Brooklands Road, Weybridge, Surrey, KT13 0TJ
Activities: Other service activities n.e.c.
Parent: H.K.S. Holdings Limited
Officers: Arani Soosaipillai, Secretary; Don Camillo Emilio Borneo [1957] Director; Winston Sanjeevkumar Soosaipillai [1973] Director

Haig Housing Trust
Incorporated: 14 May 2008 *Employees:* 41
Net Worth: £70,334,000 *Total Assets:* £75,164,000
Registered Office: Alban Dobson House, Green Lane, Morden, Surrey, SM4 5NS
Activities: Other letting and operating of own or leased real estate
Officers: Rakesh Gulati, Secretary; Stephen Michael Elliott [1973] Director; Fiona Marie Gordon [1968] Director/Civil Servant and Army Reservist; Cathy Lester-Walker [1953] Director; Luise Margaret Stirling Locke [1955] Director/Advocate; John Douglas Stokoe [1947] Director/Retired; Ian Alexander Vere Nicoll [1952] Director; Andrew Bruce Weir [1961] Communications Strategy Director; Dr Mark James Stewart Weir [1965] Director/Medical Practitioner; Neil Graham White [1952] Director; David Gareth Williams [1960] Director

Hala Limited
Incorporated: 15 June 1995 *Employees:* 2,139
Net Worth: £11,021,048 *Total Assets:* £40,136,568
Registered Office: First Floor, York House, 18 York Road, Maidenhead, Berks, SL6 1SF
Activities: Take-away food shops and mobile food stands
Officers: Lena Alani, Secretary; Ahmed Alani [1990] Director/Legal Counsel; Haitham Alani [1956] Director/Engineer; Lena Alani [1958] Director/Engineer; Saif Alani [1980] Operations Director

Halamar (Chancery Lane) Limited
Incorporated: 26 June 2015
Net Worth Deficit: £8,827,984 *Total Assets:* £70,298,448
Registered Office: 85-87 Holtspur Lane, Wooburn Green, Bucks, HP10 0AU
Activities: Other building completion and finishing
Shareholders: Amarpreet Singh Randhawa; New End Developments Limited
Officers: Lord Patrick James Earl of Clanwilliam [1960] Director/Business Consultant; Galina Gurinova [1970] Director [Cypriot]; Amarpreet Singh Randhawa [1982] Director

D Hales Limited
Incorporated: 18 October 1996 *Employees:* 59
Net Worth: £14,125,000 *Total Assets:* £31,339,000
Registered Office: Acrey Fields, Woburn Road, Wootton, Beds, MK43 9EJ
Activities: Sale of used cars and light motor vehicles
Parent: Copart UK Limited
Officers: Aaron Jayson Adair [1969] Director/Chief Executive Officer [American]; Jonathan David Canning [1972] Director/General Counsel; Gregory Depasquale [1968] Director/SVP, General Counsel and Secretary of Copart, Inc [American]; William Easley Franklin [1956] Director/Chief Financial Officer [American]; Nigel James Paget [1966] Managing Director; Simon Sheldon-Wilson [1969] Director; Paul Anthony Styer [1956] Director/General Counsel [American]

Hall Farm Wind Farm Ltd
Incorporated: 11 February 2009
Net Worth Deficit: £3,701,000 *Total Assets:* £29,138,000
Registered Office: Edgeborough House, Upper Edgeborough Road, Guildford, Surrey, GU1 2BJ
Activities: Production of electricity
Parent: JLEAG Wind Limted
Officers: Joseph Mark Linney [1958] Director/Chartered Quantity Surveyor; Christopher James Tanner [1972] Investment Director; Simon Owen Vince [1963] Construction & Operations Director

Hall Hunter Partnership (Farming)
Incorporated: 27 September 2001
Previous: Hall Hunter Partnership (Farming) Limited
Net Worth: £12,058,502 *Total Assets:* £27,772,376
Registered Office: Heathlands Farm, Honey Hill, Wokingham, Berks, RG40 3BG
Activities: Growing of other non-perennial crops
Major Shareholder: Harry Mark Hall
Officers: Siva Kumar Krishnan, Secretary; Harry Mark Hall [1970] Director; Mark Andrew Hall [1943] Director; Mary Alice Hall [1944] Director; David Iain Kay [1966] Managing Director; Siva Kumar Krishnan [1959] Finance Director

J & E Hall Limited
Incorporated: 1 November 1995 *Employees:* 266
Net Worth Deficit: £18,020,000 *Total Assets:* £28,074,000
Registered Office: Questor House, 191 Hawley Road, Dartford, Kent, DA1 1PU
Activities: Manufacture of non-domestic cooling and ventilation equipment
Parent: AAF McQuay UK Ltd
Officers: Ian Phillip Creasey, Secretary; Andrew Bowden [1971] Managing Director; Voon Ping Chen [1965] Director/Corporate Controller [Malaysian]; Ian Phillip Creasey [1961] Director/Accountant; Benny Woon Khin Liow [1957] Director [Malaysian]; Alan Dale Proffitt [1972] Director/Corporate Controller [American]

Halma Euro Trading Limited
Incorporated: 13 August 2009 *Employees:* 2
Net Worth Deficit: £432,014 *Total Assets:* £87,525,712
Registered Office: Misbourne Court, Rectory Way, Amersham, Bucks, HP7 0DE
Activities: Activities of head offices
Parent: Halma PLC
Officers: Mark Alun Jenkins, Secretary; Marc Arthur Ronchetti [1976] Director/Chartered Accountant; Andrew John Williams [1967] Director

Halma Financing Limited
Incorporated: 26 April 2004 *Employees:* 2
Net Worth: £729,477,184 *Total Assets:* £729,502,336
Registered Office: Misbourne Court, Rectory Way, Amersham, Bucks, HP7 0DE
Activities: Activities of head offices
Parent: Halma Overseas Funding Limited
Officers: Mark Alun Jenkins, Secretary; Marc Arthur Ronchetti [1976] Director/Chartered Accountant; Andrew John Williams [1967] Director

Halma International Limited
Incorporated: 8 April 1975 *Employees:* 67
Net Worth: £236,912,992 *Total Assets:* £884,907,008
Registered Office: Misbourne Court, Rectory Way, Amersham, Bucks, HP7 0DE
Activities: Activities of head offices
Shareholders: Halma PLC; Halma Euro Trading Limited
Officers: Mark Alun Jenkins, Secretary; Marc Arthur Ronchetti [1976] Director/Chartered Accountant; Andrew John Williams [1967] Director

Halma Investment Holdings Limited
Incorporated: 6 May 2004 *Employees:* 2
Net Worth: £608,011,648 *Total Assets:* £621,440,256
Registered Office: Misbourne Court, Rectory Way, Amersham, Bucks, HP7 0DE
Activities: Activities of head offices
Parent: Halma Financing Limited
Officers: Mark Alun Jenkins, Secretary; Marc Arthur Ronchetti [1976] Director/Chartered Accountant; Andrew John Williams [1967] Director

Halma Overseas Funding Limited
Incorporated: 14 February 2008 *Employees:* 2
Net Worth: £773,910,976 *Total Assets:* £817,015,616
Registered Office: Misbourne Court, Rectory Way, Amersham, Bucks, HP7 0DE
Activities: Activities of head offices
Parent: Halma International Limited
Officers: Mark Alun Jenkins, Secretary; Marc Arthur Ronchetti [1976] Director/Chartered Accountant; Andrew John Williams [1967] Director/Chief Executive

Halma Public Limited Company
Incorporated: 13 April 1894 *Employees:* 6,113
Net Worth: £829,024,000 *Total Assets:* £1,446,855,936
Registered Office: Misbourne Court, Rectory Way, Amersham, Bucks, HP7 0DE
Activities: Activities of head offices
Officers: Mark Alun Jenkins, Secretary; Daniela Barone Soares [1970] Director [Brazilian/British]; Carole Cran [1970] Director/Accountant; Jo Nell Harlow [1962] Director [American]; Adam Jay Meyers [1961] Director [American]; William Anthony Rice [1952] Director/Management Accountant; Marc Arthur Ronchetti [1976] Director/Chartered Accountant; Roy Michael Twite [1967] Director; Paul Ashton Walker [1957] Director; Jennifer Suzanne Ward [1973] Director [American]; Andrew John Williams [1967] Director

Haltermann Carless UK Limited
Incorporated: 8 February 1947 *Employees:* 192
Previous: Petrochem Carless Limited
Net Worth: £108,173,000 *Total Assets:* £186,391,008
Registered Office: Grove House, Guildford Road, Leatherhead, Surrey, KT22 9DF
Activities: Manufacture of other chemical products n.e.c.
Parent: PCL Bidco Limited
Officers: Christopher Michael Higgs, Secretary; Christopher Michael Higgs [1956] Finance Director; Duncan Paul Stonehouse [1970] Operations Director

Hambridge Limited
Incorporated: 19 April 1966 *Employees:* 14
Net Worth: £22,493,560 *Total Assets:* £38,155,672
Registered Office: Barley Row, 90-98 High Street, Odiham, Hook, Hants, RG29 1LP
Activities: Construction of commercial buildings
Parent: Hambridge Investment Holdings Ltd
Officers: Jeremy Robin Sanders, Secretary; Jeremy Robin Sanders [1971] Director Company Secretary

Hamilton Palace Limited
Incorporated: 12 May 1992
Net Worth: £53,243,280 *Total Assets:* £55,743,392
Registered Office: Hamilton House, 14 The Drive, Hove, E Sussex, BN3 3JA
Activities: Non-trading company
Officers: Britannia Eugenie Hamilton, Secretary; Alexander Sethi Hamilton [1988] Director/Financier; Britannia Eugenie Hamilton [1990] Director; Maximilian Rhett Hamilton [1985] Director/Financier; Richmond Louis Hamilton [1991] Director

George Hammond PLC
Incorporated: 27 April 1961 *Employees:* 128
Net Worth: £23,365,252 *Total Assets:* £27,396,552
Registered Office: Dover South Services, Limekiln Street, Dover, Kent, CT17 9EF
Activities: Retail sale in non-specialised stores with food, beverages or tobacco predominating
Shareholders: David Charles Ryeland; Christopher Blake Wacher; Robert Scruton
Officers: Paul John Lee, Secretary; Paul John Lee [1978] Director/Chartered Accountant; James Gregory Ryeland [1963] Shipping Director/Shipbroker; John Philip David Ryeland [1967] Director Petrol Retailing; Robert Scruton [1952] Director

Hamol Limited
Incorporated: 16 April 1953
Net Worth: £1,322,612,992 *Total Assets:* £1,322,630,016
Registered Office: 103-105 Bath Road, Slough, Berks, SL1 3UH
Activities: Non-trading company
Parent: Reckitt & Colman Holdings Limited
Officers: Christine Anne-Marie Logan, Secretary; Richard Mark Greensmith [1973] Group Tax Director; Jonathan Timmis [1975] Finance Director

Hampden Holdings Limited
Incorporated: 13 July 1995 *Employees:* 206
Net Worth: £66,706,440 *Total Assets:* £136,648,496
Registered Office: Hampden House, Great Hampden, Great Missenden, Bucks, HP16 9RD
Activities: Activities of head offices
Shareholders: Alexa Kate Louise Camroux Pearmund; Timothy Patrick Camroux Oliver; James Richard Camroux-Oliver; Charles Guy Camroux-Oliver
Officers: Charles Guy Camroux-Oliver [1970] Director/Solicitor; James Richard Camroux-Oliver [1967] Director; Stephen James Harris [1970] Director/Company Secretary; Timothy Patrick Camroux Oliver [1944] Director/Chairman

Hampshire Aviation LLP
Incorporated: 28 August 2007
Net Worth: £15,944,188 *Total Assets:* £107,838,992
Registered Office: Hawkslease, Chapel Lane, Lyndhurst, Hants, SO43 7FG
Officers: Andrew Christopher Currie [1955] Member; James Arthur Ratcliffe [1952] Member; John Reece [1957] Member

Hampton School
Incorporated: 31 May 2007 *Employees:* 376
Net Worth: £35,174,604 *Total Assets:* £50,031,768
Registered Office: Hampton School, Hanworth Road, Hampton, Surrey, TW12 3HD
Activities: Pre-primary education
Officers: Michael Alan King, Secretary; Stuart Alan Bull [1953] Director/Retired; Mona Choueiri [1962] Marketing Director; Marie-Louise Ellis [1953] Director/Self Employed; Laurence Richard Llewellyn [1948] Director/Strategic Consultant; Revd Ben Robert Lovell [1982] Director/Vicar; Helen Anne Lowe [1960] Director/Headmistress; Christine Ruth Mercer [1962] Director/Headmistress; Andrew Hugh Munday [1950] Director/Barrister; John Sinclair Perry [1953] Director/Solicitor; Anthony John Roberts [1944] Director; Nigel John Spooner [1950] Director/Retired; Robert Malcolm Walker [1945] Director; Richard James Keith Washington [1974] Director/Banking; Leslie Hunter Welch [1950] Director/Retired; Alice Victoria Yandle [1989] Director/Solicitor

Hamsard 3352 Limited
Incorporated: 9 October 2014 *Employees:* 177
Net Worth Deficit: £21,065,030 *Total Assets:* £237,866,800
Registered Office: Building 4, Hatters Lane, Croxley Green Business Park, Watford, Herts, WD18 8YF
Activities: Renting and leasing of cars and light motor vehicles
Officers: Laura Catherine Elizabeth Alexander [1979] Director/Chief Financial Officer; Clive Andrew Whistler Baker [1974] Director [British/South African]; Paul Gilshan [1975] Director; David Hosking [1963] Managing Director; Paul Dominic Ian McCreadie [1979] Director; Richard John Prosser [1957] Director/Chairman

Hamsard 3353 Limited
Incorporated: 9 October 2014 *Employees:* 5
Net Worth Deficit: £27,635,996 *Total Assets:* £93,007,432
Registered Office: Building 4, Hatters Lane, Croxley Green Business Park, Watford, Herts, WD18 8YF
Activities: Renting and leasing of cars and light motor vehicles
Parent: Hamsard 3352 Limited
Officers: Laura Catherine Elizabeth Alexander [1979] Director/Chief Financial Officer; Paul Gilshan [1975] Director; Paul Dominic Ian McCreadie [1979] Director

Hamsard 3414 Limited
Incorporated: 20 June 2016 *Employees:* 72
Net Worth: £5,972,705 *Total Assets:* £59,844,420
Registered Office: 1 London Street, Reading, Berks, RG1 4PN
Activities: Activities of financial services holding companies
Parent: Mobeus Equity Partners LLP
Officers: Darren John Cottenden [1968] Director; Neal Errington [1956] Director; Jonathan David Leigh Gregory [1961] Director/Investment Manager; David Albert Robertson [1946] Director; David James Tilling [1961] Director

Hand Picked Hotels Limited
Incorporated: 28 April 1999 *Employees:* 1,065
Net Worth: £28,355,944 *Total Assets:* £162,676,064
Registered Office: The Old Library, The Drive, Sevenoaks, Kent, TN13 3AB
Activities: Hotels and similar accommodation
Major Shareholder: Guy Hands
Officers: Kenneth Arkley [1954] Asset Management Director; Stewart John Fairs [1966] Finance Director; Douglas Ross Waddell [1964] Operations Director

Handsale Limited
Incorporated: 7 July 1987 *Employees:* 583
Net Worth: £12,977,782 *Total Assets:* £36,610,476
Registered Office: Zone G, Salamander Quay West, Park Lane, Harefield, Middlesex, UB9 6NZ
Activities: Buying and selling of own real estate
Shareholders: Bharat Chunilal Sodha; Bindu Sodha
Officers: Bindu Sodha, Secretary; Bharat Chunilal Sodha [1959] Director; Bindu Sodha [1961] Director/Secretary; Rishi Sodha [1989] Director

Hanover Displays Limited
Incorporated: 11 January 1985 *Employees:* 261
Net Worth: £38,001,840 *Total Assets:* £49,961,548
Registered Office: Southerham House, Southerham Lane, Lewes, E Sussex, BN8 6JN
Activities: Manufacture of other electrical equipment
Major Shareholder: David Gavin Williams
Officers: Richard Lyons Colquhoun, Secretary; Stephen Charles Aplin [1956] Director; Steven Alexander Colquhoun [1969] Director; Timothy Simon Mark [1959] Director; Craig William Stewart [1970] Director; Andrew James Williams [1969] Director; David Anthony Williams [1969] Director; David Gavin Williams [1942] Director

Hanson (ER - No 5) Limited
Incorporated: 20 March 1956
Net Worth: £397,152,000 *Total Assets:* £397,152,000
Registered Office: Hanson House, 14 Castle Hill, Maidenhead, Berks, SL6 4JJ
Activities: Activities of other holding companies n.e.c.
Parent: Shapedirect Limited
Officers: Wendy Fiona Rogers, Secretary; Nicholas Arthur Dawe Benning-Prince [1974] Director/Chartered Accountant; Robert Charles Dowley [1972] Director/Chartered Accountant; Edward Alexander Gretton [1970] Director; Dr Carsten Matthias Wendt [1976] Director [German]

Hanson (SH) Limited
Incorporated: 15 March 2005
Previous: Structherm Holdings Limited
Net Worth: £71,969,000 *Total Assets:* £74,940,000
Registered Office: Hanson House, 14 Castle Hill, Maidenhead, Berks, SL6 4JJ
Activities: Activities of other holding companies n.e.c.
Parent: Hanson Packed Products Limited
Officers: Wendy Fiona Rogers, Secretary; Nicholas Arthur Dawe Benning-Prince [1974] Director/Chartered Accountant; Robert Charles Dowley [1972] Director/Chartered Accountant; Edward Alexander Gretton [1970] Director; Dr Carsten Matthias Wendt [1976] Director [German]

Hanson Aggregates Marine Limited
Incorporated: 25 August 1950 *Employees:* 20
Net Worth: £119,045,000 *Total Assets:* £126,924,000
Registered Office: Hanson House, 14 Castle Hill, Maidenhead, Berks, SL6 4JJ
Activities: Other mining and quarrying n.e.c.
Parent: Hanson Building Products (2003) Limited
Officers: Wendy Fiona Rogers, Secretary; Jeremy Lees Dawes [1966] Director/Accountant; Edward Alexander Gretton [1970] Director; Rodolphe Lafargue [1983] Marine Director, Hanson UK [French]; Dr Carsten Matthias Wendt [1976] Director [German]; James Stuart Whitelaw [1972] Managing Director; Simon Lloyd Willis [1965] Director/Chief Executive, Hanson UK

Hanson America Holdings (1) Limited
Incorporated: 1 August 1995
Net Worth: £1,901,593,984 *Total Assets:* £4,283,414,016
Registered Office: Hanson House, 14 Castle Hill, Maidenhead, Berks, SL6 4JJ
Activities: Activities of head offices
Parent: Hanson Overseas Holdings Limited
Officers: Wendy Fiona Rogers, Secretary; Nicholas Arthur Dawe Benning-Prince [1974] Director/Chartered Accountant; Robert Charles Dowley [1972] Director/Chartered Accountant; Edward Alexander Gretton [1970] Director; Dr Carsten Matthias Wendt [1976] Director [German]

Hanson America Holdings (4) Limited
Incorporated: 7 August 1995
Net Worth: £114,262,000 *Total Assets:* £114,262,000
Registered Office: Hanson House, 14 Castle Hill, Maidenhead, Berks, SL6 4JJ
Activities: Activities of head offices
Parent: Hanson Overseas Holdings Limited
Officers: Wendy Fiona Rogers, Secretary; Nicholas Arthur Dawe Benning-Prince [1974] Director/Chartered Accountant; Robert Charles Dowley [1972] Director/Chartered Accountant; Edward Alexander Gretton [1970] Director; Dr Carsten Matthias Wendt [1976] Director [German]

Hanson Building Materials Limited
Incorporated: 8 November 1950
Net Worth: £3,184,617,984 *Total Assets:* £17,815,826,432
Registered Office: Hanson House, 14 Castle Hill, Maidenhead, Berks, SL6 4JJ
Activities: Activities of other holding companies n.e.c.
Parent: Hanson Holdings Limited
Officers: Wendy Fiona Rogers, Secretary; Nicholas Arthur Dawe Benning-Prince [1974] Director/Chartered Accountant; Robert Charles Dowley [1972] Director/Chartered Accountant; Edward Alexander Gretton [1970] Director; Dr Carsten Matthias Wendt [1976] Director [German]

Hanson Finance (2003) Limited
Incorporated: 28 March 1973
Net Worth: £484,033,984 *Total Assets:* £28,796,837,888
Registered Office: Hanson House, 14 Castle Hill, Maidenhead, Berks, SL6 4JJ
Activities: Activities of other holding companies n.e.c.
Parent: Hanson Financial Services Limited
Officers: Wendy Fiona Rogers, Secretary; Nicholas Arthur Dawe Benning-Prince [1974] Director/Chartered Accountant; Robert Charles Dowley [1972] Director/Chartered Accountant; Edward Alexander Gretton [1970] Director; Dr Carsten Matthias Wendt [1976] Director [German]

Hanson Finance Limited
Incorporated: 23 June 2003
Net Worth: £672,651,008 *Total Assets:* £7,145,700,864
Registered Office: Hanson House, 14 Castle Hill, Maidenhead, Berks, SL6 4JJ
Activities: Activities of other holding companies n.e.c.
Parent: Hanson Holdings Limited
Officers: Wendy Fiona Rogers, Secretary; Nicholas Arthur Dawe Benning-Prince [1974] Director/Chartered Accountant; Robert Charles Dowley [1972] Director/Chartered Accountant; Edward Alexander Gretton [1970] Director; Dr Carsten Matthias Wendt [1976] Director [German]

Hanson Holdings (1) Limited
Incorporated: 16 March 1989
Net Worth: £38,011,334,656 *Total Assets:* £38,641,995,776
Registered Office: Hanson House, 14 Castle Hill, Maidenhead, Berks, SL6 4JJ
Activities: Activities of other holding companies n.e.c.
Parent: Houserate Limited
Officers: Wendy Fiona Rogers, Secretary; Nicholas Arthur Dawe Benning-Prince [1974] Director/Chartered Accountant; Robert Charles Dowley [1972] Director/Chartered Accountant; Edward Alexander Gretton [1970] Director; Dr Carsten Matthias Wendt [1976] Director [German]

Hanson Holdings Limited
Incorporated: 8 January 2004 *Employees:* 4
Net Worth: £2,206,444,032 *Total Assets:* £3,476,107,008
Registered Office: Hanson House, 14 Castle Hill, Maidenhead, Berks, SL6 4JJ
Activities: Activities of other holding companies n.e.c.
Parent: Hanson Limited
Officers: Wendy Fiona Rogers, Secretary; Nicholas Arthur Dawe Benning-Prince [1974] Director/Chartered Accountant; Robert Charles Dowley [1972] Director/Chartered Accountant; Edward Alexander Gretton [1970] Director; Dr Carsten Matthias Wendt [1976] Director [German]

Hanson Limited
Incorporated: 31 December 2002 *Employees:* 2
Net Worth: £6,364,731,904 *Total Assets:* £17,968,152,576
Registered Office: Hanson House, 14 Castle Hill, Maidenhead, Berks, SL6 4JJ
Activities: Activities of construction holding companies
Parent: Lehigh UK Limited
Officers: Wendy Fiona Rogers, Secretary; Nicholas Arthur Dawe Benning-Prince [1974] Director/Chartered Accountant; Robert Charles Dowley [1972] Director/Chartered Accountant; Edward Alexander Gretton [1970] Director; Dr Lorenz Nager [1960] Director/CFO Heidelbergcement AG [German]; Dr Bernd Scheifele [1958] Director/CEO Heidelbergcement AG [German]; Dr Carsten Matthias Wendt [1976] Director [German]; Simon Lloyd Willis [1965] Director/Chief Executive, Hanson UK

Hanson Marine Limited
Incorporated: 2 March 1955 *Employees:* 2
Net Worth: £27,018,000 *Total Assets:* £27,563,000
Registered Office: Hanson House, 14 Castle Hill, Maidenhead, Berks, SL6 4JJ
Activities: Other mining and quarrying n.e.c.
Parent: Hanson Marine Holdings Limited
Officers: Wendy Fiona Rogers, Secretary; Jeremy Lees Dawes [1966] Director/Accountant; Edward Alexander Gretton [1970] Director; Rodolphe Lafargue [1983] Marine Director, Hanson UK [French]; Dr Carsten Matthias Wendt [1976] Director [German]; James Stuart Whitelaw [1972] Managing Director; Simon Lloyd Willis [1965] Director/Chief Executive, Hanson UK

Hanson Overseas Holdings Limited
Incorporated: 20 August 1996
Net Worth: £17,875,881,984 *Total Assets:* £37,201,846,272
Registered Office: Hanson House, 14 Castle Hill, Maidenhead, Berks, SL6 4JJ
Activities: Activities of other holding companies n.e.c.
Parent: Hanson Holdings (1) Limited
Officers: Wendy Fiona Rogers, Secretary; Nicholas Arthur Dawe Benning-Prince [1974] Director/Chartered Accountant; Robert Charles Dowley [1972] Director/Chartered Accountant; Edward Alexander Gretton [1970] Director; Dr Carsten Matthias Wendt [1976] Director [German]

Hanson Packed Products Limited
Incorporated: 10 April 1888 *Employees:* 78
Net Worth: £267,352,992 *Total Assets:* £657,454,016
Registered Office: Hanson House, 14 Castle Hill, Maidenhead, Berks, SL6 4JJ
Activities: Manufacture of other articles of concrete, plaster and cement
Shareholders: Hanson (ER-No 10) Limited; Houserate Limited
Officers: Wendy Fiona Rogers, Secretary; James Alexander Claydon [1960] Director; John Godbert [1962] Director/Accountant; Edward Alexander Gretton [1970] Director; Dr Carsten Matthias Wendt [1976] Director [German]; Simon Lloyd Willis [1965] Director/Chief Executive, Hanson UK

Hanson Quarry Products Europe Limited
Incorporated: 23 April 1935 *Employees:* 2,195
Net Worth: £39,987,322,880 *Total Assets:* £48,023,728,128
Registered Office: Hanson House, 14 Castle Hill, Maidenhead, Berks, SL6 4JJ
Activities: Quarrying of ornamental and building stone, limestone, gypsum, chalk and slate
Parent: UDS (No 10)
Officers: Wendy Fiona Rogers, Secretary; Matthew David Barlow [1979] Supply Chain Director; Brian Charleton [1968] Director; James Alexander Claydon [1960] Director; Gareth Day [1977] Managing Director; Edward Alexander Gretton [1970] Director; Dr Ralph Dominik Von Achten [1965] Director [German]; Dr Carsten Matthias Wendt [1976] Director [German]; James Stuart Whitelaw [1972] Director/Area General Manager, Hanson Aggregates; Simon Lloyd Willis [1965] Director/Chief Executive, Hanson UK

Hanson Quarry Products Ventures Limited
Incorporated: 4 December 1989
Net Worth: £47,039,000 *Total Assets:* £104,040,000
Registered Office: Hanson House, 14 Castle Hill, Maidenhead, Berks, SL6 4JJ
Activities: Activities of other holding companies n.e.c.
Parent: Hanson Building Materials Europe Limited
Officers: Wendy Fiona Rogers, Secretary; Nicholas Arthur Dawe Benning-Prince [1974] Director/Chartered Accountant; Robert Charles Dowley [1972] Director/Chartered Accountant; Edward Alexander Gretton [1970] Director; Dr Carsten Matthias Wendt [1976] Director [German]

Hanson Retail Limited
Incorporated: 15 March 1989
Net Worth: £391,488,992 *Total Assets:* £499,681,984
Registered Office: Hanson House, 14 Castle Hill, Maidenhead, Berks, SL6 4JJ
Activities: Activities of other holding companies n.e.c.
Parent: Hanson International Holdings Limited
Officers: Wendy Fiona Rogers, Secretary; Nicholas Arthur Dawe Benning-Prince [1974] Director/Chartered Accountant; Robert Charles Dowley [1972] Director/Chartered Accountant; Edward Alexander Gretton [1970] Director; Dr Carsten Matthias Wendt [1976] Director [German]

Hanwha Techwin Europe Limited
Incorporated: 20 December 2001 *Employees:* 102
Previous: Samsung Techwin Europe Limited
Net Worth: £16,677,000 *Total Assets:* £29,918,000
Registered Office: Heriot House, Heriot Road, Chertsey, Surrey, KT16 9DT
Activities: Wholesale of electronic and telecommunications equipment and parts
Parent: Hanwha Techwin Company Limited
Officers: Chang Baek Lee, Secretary; Ho Yon Hwang [1961] Managing Director [South Korean]; Chang Baek Lee [1976] Director/Chief Financial Officer [South Korean]

Harding Holdings U.K. Limited
Incorporated: 4 June 1991 *Employees:* 6
Net Worth: £9,690,944 *Total Assets:* £21,506,000
Registered Office: Drivers Wharf, Northam Road, Southampton, SO14 0PF
Activities: Development of building projects
Parent: Harding Consolidated Property Holdings Limited
Officers: Brian Graham Harding, Secretary; Alan George Harding [1958] Director; Brian Graham Harding [1963] Director; George Edward Harding [1934] Director; Jennifer Dorothy Harding [1936] Director; Peter Generald Harding [1959] Director

Harefield Academy Trust
Incorporated: 20 February 2004 *Employees:* 93
Net Worth: £25,604,000 *Total Assets:* £28,260,000
Registered Office: The Harefield Academy, Northwood Way, Harefield, Uxbridge, Middlesex, UB9 6ET
Activities: General secondary education
Officers: Peter James Wastall, Secretary; Jonathan Michael Green [1960] Director/Fund Manager; Haig Bertrand Oundjian [1949] Director; Michael Sidney Sherwood [1965] Director/Investment Banker

Harepath Estates LLP
Incorporated: 19 January 2006 *Employees:* 3
Net Worth: £14,490,184 *Total Assets:* £41,831,352
Registered Office: 8-10 South Street, Epsom, Surrey, KT18 7PF
Officers: Christopher Paul Ackley [1962] Member; Charlotte Iskjaer-Ackley [1961] Member; Patricia Hazel Whiteway [1961] Member; Peter James Whiteway [1958] Member

Hargreaves Properties Limited
Incorporated: 6 March 1964 *Employees:* 3
Net Worth: £2,872,238 *Total Assets:* £75,347,512
Registered Office: Kingston Manor, Kingston Gorse, East Preston, Littlehampton, W Sussex, BN16 1RR
Activities: Development of building projects
Parent: Hargreaves Group Holdings Limited
Officers: Patrick Lawrie Hamilton, Secretary; Richard Russell Andrew [1970] Director/Chartered Surveyor; Ruth Andrew [1946] Director; John Hazelwood [1946] Director/Chartered Management Accountant

Hargreaves Property Holdings Limited
Incorporated: 9 November 1967 *Employees:* 42
Net Worth: £29,862,460 *Total Assets:* £176,436,976
Registered Office: Kingston Manor, Kingston Gorse, East Preston, Littlehampton, W Sussex, BN16 1RR
Activities: Activities of other holding companies n.e.c.
Major Shareholder: Richard Russell Andrew
Officers: Patrick Lawrie Hamilton, Secretary; Richard Russell Andrew [1970] Director/Chartered Surveyor; Ruth Andrew [1946] Director; John Hazelwood [1946] Director/Chartered Management Accountant

Harlequin Estates (Twickenham) Limited
Incorporated: 22 February 1971
Net Worth: £19,624,588 *Total Assets:* £41,536,592
Registered Office: Twickenham Stoop Stadium, Langhorn Drive, Twickenham, Middlesex, TW2 7SX
Activities: Other letting and operating of own or leased real estate
Shareholders: Duncan Paul Saville; Charles David Owen Jillings; Alasdair Relph Younie
Officers: Nicholas Mark Butterworth, Secretary; Jeremy Graham Paul Campling [1969] Director/Chartered Surveyor; David Armstrong Ellis [1975] Director/Chief Executive; David John Morgan [1957] Director; Sandra Jane Pope [1963] Director/Accountant

Harlequin FC Holdings Limited
Incorporated: 20 December 2013 *Employees:* 286
Previous: Harlequin RFC Holdings Limited
Net Worth: £8,210,094 *Total Assets:* £58,163,112
Registered Office: Twickenham Stoop Stadium, Langhorn Drive, Twickenham, Middlesex, TW2 7SX
Activities: Activities of other holding companies n.e.c.
Shareholders: Duncan Paul Saville; Charles David Owen Jillings; Alasdair Relph Younie
Officers: Nicholas Mark Butterworth, Secretary; Charles David Owen Jillings [1955] Director/Fund Manager; Sandra Jane Pope [1963] Director/Accountant; Duncan Paul Saville [1957] Director/Chartered Accountant

Harman Automotive UK Limited
Incorporated: 16 October 2012 *Employees:* 37
Net Worth: £118,480,720 *Total Assets:* £316,307,360
Registered Office: Ground Floor, Westside Two, London Road, Apsley, Hemel Hempstead, Herts, HP3 9TD
Activities: Manufacture of electrical and electronic equipment for motor vehicles and their engines
Parent: Harman International Industries Limited
Officers: Marcus Allen [1973] Director; Roderick Burns [1966] Director; Frank Georg Donald Groth [1961] Director [German]; John Stacey [1965] Director [American]

Harman International Industries Limited
Incorporated: 14 March 1980 *Employees:* 83
Net Worth: £74,333,000 *Total Assets:* £141,404,992
Registered Office: Ground Floor, Westside Two, London Road, Apsley, Hemel Hempstead, Herts, HP3 9TD
Activities: Manufacture of other electrical equipment
Parent: Harman International Industries Incorporated
Officers: Marcus Allen [1973] Director; Roderick Burns [1966] Finance Director; Frank Georg Donald Groth [1961] Director [German]; John Stacey [1965] Director [Canadian]

P.C. Harrington Holdings Limited
Incorporated: 21 October 1991 *Employees:* 126
Net Worth: £9,495,000 *Total Assets:* £27,437,000
Registered Office: Harrington House, 7 Dean Way, Great Western Industrial Park, Southall, Middlesex, UB2 4SB
Activities: Activities of construction holding companies
Major Shareholder: Patrick Christopher Harrington
Officers: Eileen Harrington, Secretary; Patrick Christopher Harrington [1937] Director/Contractor [Irish]; Anne Marie McGann [1966] Director

Harris Defence Limited
Incorporated: 24 March 1993 *Employees:* 75
Previous: Exelis Defence Limited
Net Worth: £61,449,000 *Total Assets:* £75,183,000
Registered Office: 1010 Eskdale Road, Winnersh, Wokingham, Berks, RG41 5TS
Activities: Other manufacturing n.e.c.
Officers: Paul Spencer Freeman, Secretary; Keith Nicholas Norton [1958] Director/Business Executive

Harris Federation
Incorporated: 26 April 2007 *Employees:* 3,228
Net Worth: £395,575,008 *Total Assets:* £465,664,992
Registered Office: 4th Floor, Norfolk House, Wellesley Road, Croydon, Surrey, CR0 1LH
Activities: Other education n.e.c.
Officers: Mike Antoniou, Secretary; Robin Keith Alcock [1946] Director/Management Consultant; Anthony Peter Bayon [1948] Director/Retired; Dorothy Elliott [1959] Project Director; Lord Philip Charles Harris of Peckham [1942] Director; Karl James Hoods [1973] Director/Civil Servant; Paul Jacobs [1968] Director; Angela Lewina Pamela Kail [1981] Director/Management Consultant; Timothy David Moore [1965] Director/Marketing Consultant; Daniel Moynihan [1960] Director/Teacher; Dr Nigel David Rata [1973] Director/IT Manager; Philip John Saunders [1955] Director; Rosalyn Susan Wilton [1952] Director

Harsco (UK) Group Limited
Incorporated: 12 September 2007 *Employees:* 3
Net Worth: £108,478,232 *Total Assets:* £491,493,920
Registered Office: Harsco House, Regent Park, 299 Kingston Road, Leatherhead, Surrey, KT22 7SG
Activities: Activities of head offices
Officers: Graham Richard Smith, Secretary; Stephen Richard Cooper [1966] Director/Accountant; John Joseph Sweeney [1952] International Tax Director; Christopher Claude Lashmer Whistler [1958] Director/Vice President and Controller

Harsco Infrastructure Group Limited
Incorporated: 18 February 1920 *Employees:* 3
Net Worth: £173,612,752 *Total Assets:* £824,603,200
Registered Office: Harsco House, Regent Park, 299 Kingston Road, Leatherhead, Surrey, KT22 7SG
Activities: Activities of head offices
Parent: Harsco Investment Limited
Officers: Graham Richard Smith, Secretary; Stephen Richard Cooper [1966] Director/Accountant; John Joseph Sweeney [1952] International Tax Director; Christopher Claude Lashmer Whistler [1958] Director/Accountant

Harsco Investment Limited
Incorporated: 4 May 2000 *Employees:* 6
Net Worth: £212,752,000 *Total Assets:* £333,897,984
Registered Office: Harsco House, Regent Park, 299 Kingston Road, Leatherhead, Surrey, KT22 7SG
Activities: Activities of head offices
Parent: Harsco Holdings, Inc.
Officers: Graham Richard Smith, Secretary; Stephen Richard Cooper [1966] Director/Accountant; William Ian Mullen [1966] Director; John Joseph Sweeney [1952] International Tax Director

Harsco Leatherhead Limited
Incorporated: 5 October 2007 *Employees:* 4
Net Worth: £4,118,092 *Total Assets:* £101,955,128
Registered Office: Harsco House, Regent Park, 299 Kingston Road, Leatherhead, Surrey, KT22 7SG
Activities: Activities of head offices
Officers: Graham Richard Smith, Secretary; Stephen Richard Cooper [1966] Director/Accountant; William Ian Mullen [1966] Director; John Joseph Sweeney [1952] International Tax Director; Christopher Claude Lashmer Whistler [1958] Director/Vice President and Controller

Harsco Metals 385 Limited
Incorporated: 2 June 1988 *Employees:* 2
Net Worth: £27,912,736 *Total Assets:* £27,980,780
Registered Office: Harsco House, Regent Park, 299 Kingston Road, Leatherhead, Surrey, KT22 7SG
Activities: Activities of head offices
Officers: Graham Richard Smith, Secretary; Stephen Richard Cooper [1966] Director/Accountant; Christopher Claude Lashmer Whistler [1958] Director/Accountant

Harsco Metals Group Limited
Incorporated: 8 September 1961 *Employees:* 928
Net Worth: £52,229,000 *Total Assets:* £102,759,000
Registered Office: Harsco House, Regent Park, 299 Kingston Road, Leatherhead, Surrey, KT22 7SG
Activities: Activities of head offices
Officers: Stephen Richard Cooper [1966] Director/Accountant; Mauro Curi [1970] Director [Italian]; Albert Russell Mitchell [1966] Director [American]; William Ian Mullen [1966] Director; Christophe Nicolas Reitemeier [1965] Director [French]; John Joseph Sweeney [1952] International Tax Director; Christopher Claude Lashmer Whistler [1958] Director/Accountant

Harsco Metals Holdings Limited
Incorporated: 2 August 1956 *Employees:* 5
Net Worth: £72,286,552 *Total Assets:* £76,063,008
Registered Office: Harsco House, Regent Park, 299 Kingston Road, Leatherhead, Surrey, KT22 7SG
Activities: Activities of head offices
Officers: Stephen Richard Cooper [1966] Director/Accountant; William Ian Mullen [1966] Director; John Joseph Sweeney [1952] International Tax Director; Christopher Claude Lashmer Whistler [1958] Director/Accountant

Harsco Mole Valley Limited
Incorporated: 10 October 2007 *Employees:* 2
Net Worth: £99,986,448 *Total Assets:* £102,038,728
Registered Office: Harsco House, Regent Park, 299 Kingston Road, Leatherhead, Surrey, KT22 7SG
Activities: Activities of head offices
Officers: Graham Richard Smith, Secretary; Stephen Richard Cooper [1966] Director/Accountant; Christopher Claude Lashmer Whistler [1958] Director/Vice President and Controller

Harsco Rail Limited
Incorporated: 14 April 1970 *Employees:* 200
Net Worth: £15,485,124 *Total Assets:* £26,048,890
Registered Office: Harsco House, Regent Park, 299 Kingston Road, Leatherhead, Surrey, KT22 7SG
Activities: Manufacture of other general-purpose machinery n.e.c.
Parent: Ballagio S.A.R.L.
Officers: Matthew James Flint, Secretary; Matthew James Flint [1973] Director/Chartered Accountant; David Raymond Geering [1955] Director; David Charles Marsh [1969] Director; Hugo Van Audenaerde [1963] Director [Belgian]

Hartford Care Group Limited
Incorporated: 14 October 2014 *Employees:* 300
Net Worth: £21,967,320 *Total Assets:* £42,423,672
Registered Office: 2nd Floor, Clifton House, Bunnian Place, Basingstoke, Hants, RG21 7JE
Activities: Activities of head offices
Shareholder: Lindsay Caroline Levin
Officers: Sean Francis Gavin [1962] Director/Chief Executive Officer; Lindsay Caroline Levin [1963] Director; Irene Mary Pearman [1961] Director; David Anthony Steele [1959] Director

Harvest Energy Limited
Incorporated: 7 December 1994
Net Worth: £12,105,732 *Total Assets:* £110,559,824
Registered Office: Prax House, Horizon Business Village, 1 Brooklands Road, Weybridge, Surrey, KT13 0TJ
Activities: Wholesale of petroleum and petroleum products
Officers: Arani Soosaipillai, Secretary; Don Camillo Emilio Borneo [1957] Director/Oil Trader; Winston Sanjeev Kumar Soosaipillai [1973] Director

Harvest Midco Limited
Incorporated: 23 February 2015 *Employees:* 2,422
Net Worth: £55,818,000 *Total Assets:* £145,030,000
Registered Office: 2 The Square, Southall Lane, Southall, Middlesex, UB2 5NH
Activities: Activities of head offices
Parent: New Midco Limited
Officers: Martin Johnson [1973] Director; Mark Stott [1966] Director

Harvestore Systems (Holdings) Limited
Incorporated: 15 January 1974 *Employees:* 11
Net Worth: £19,123,376 *Total Assets:* £23,573,078
Registered Office: Newnham Court, Bearsted Road, Weavering, Maidstone, Kent, ME14 5LH
Activities: Other letting and operating of own or leased real estate
Major Shareholder: Brian Fredrick Pantony
Officers: Sarah Elisabeth Fern, Secretary; Brian Fredrick Pantony [1941] Director/Farmer; Douglas William Brian Pantony [1970] Director/Estate Maintenance/New Project

Harvey & Son (Lewes) Limited
Incorporated: 24 November 1928 *Employees:* 228
Net Worth: £42,178,352 *Total Assets:* £47,975,480
Registered Office: 6 Cliffe High Street, Lewes, E Sussex, BN7 2AH
Activities: Manufacture of beer
Officers: Hamish Carlyon Rundle Elder [1959] Director; Miles Anthony Jenner [1952] Director/Head Brewer; Julia Margaret Harvey Prescott [1957] Director; Adele MacKenzie Smith [1970] Director

Harvey & Thompson Limited
Incorporated: 9 August 1991 *Employees:* 1,102
Net Worth: £103,989,000 *Total Assets:* £137,972,992
Registered Office: Times House, Throwley Way, Sutton, Surrey, SM1 4AF
Activities: Financial intermediation not elsewhere classified
Officers: Stephen Anthony Fenerty, Secretary; Elaine Frances Draper [1963] Director; Stephen Anthony Fenerty [1973] Commercial Director; Mark Peter Harrold [1976] Operations Director; Peter Denis McNamara [1951] Director; John Graham Nichols [1950] Managing Director; Mark Joseph Smith [1958] Director; James FitzGenerald Thornton [1957] Director/Chartered Accountant

Harvey Water Softeners Limited
Incorporated: 12 April 1978 *Employees:* 156
Net Worth: £15,758,908 *Total Assets:* £24,909,988
Registered Office: Hipley Street, Old Woking, Surrey, GU22 9LQ
Activities: Manufacture of other special-purpose machinery n.e.c.
Parent: HWS Holdings Limited
Officers: Laurence Bower [1968] Director/Vice President; Ramune Maria Cibas-Siniakovas [1959] Director [American]; Martin Neil Hurworth [1973] Technical Director; David Patterson [1981] Finance Director; Pierpaulo Stumpo [1973] Director [Italian]

Harwood Properties Limited
Incorporated: 15 March 1995 *Employees:* 7
Net Worth: £8,979,051 *Total Assets:* £36,295,164
Registered Office: 99 Western Road, Hove, E Sussex, BN3 1FA
Activities: Other letting and operating of own or leased real estate
Officers: Ghanim Hamza, Secretary/Director; Farzin Sobhanpanah, Secretary/Director; Ann Celina Hamza [1961] Director; Ghanim Hamza [1957] Director; Catherine Mary Sobhanpanah [1960] Director; Farzin Sobhanpanah [1957] Director

Harwood Wealth Management Group PLC
Incorporated: 8 December 2003 *Employees:* 113
Previous: Compass Wealth Management Group PLC
Net Worth: £26,760,000 *Total Assets:* £35,091,000
Registered Office: 5 Lancer House, Hussar Court, Westside View, Waterlooville, Hants, PO7 7SE
Activities: Activities of financial services holding companies
Shareholder: Harwood Capital Management Limited
Officers: Nicholas Charles Osborne Bravery, Secretary; Matthew Hills, Secretary; Gillian Davies [1967] Director; Neil Dunkley [1973] Director; Alan Richard Durrant [1972] Director; Mark Philip Howard [1972] Director; Peter Mann [1958] Director; Christopher Harwood Bernard Mills [1952] Director; Paul Adam Edward Tuson [1966] Director

Harwoods Limited
Incorporated: 21 August 1941 *Employees:* 869
Net Worth: £58,365,784 *Total Assets:* £194,096,800
Registered Office: 1 Liverpool Gardens, Worthing, W Sussex, BN11 1TF
Activities: Sale of new cars and light motor vehicles
Parent: WJH Holdings Limited
Officers: Paul David Suter, Secretary/Financial Director; Eamon Bradley [1948] Director; Archie Guy Harwood [1990] Director; Guy Harwood [1939] Director; Scott Sydney Paddock [1972] Director; Amanda Jill Perrett [1969] Director; Paul David Suter [1958] Financial Director

Hasbro U.K. Limited
Incorporated: 23 January 1986 *Employees:* 218
Net Worth: £20,521,000 *Total Assets:* £28,522,000
Registered Office: 4 The Square, Stockley Park, Uxbridge, Middlesex, UB11 1ET
Activities: Operation of warehousing and storage facilities for land transport activities
Officers: Julia Rachel Runnacles, Secretary; Kay Jackie Green [1969] Director/Business Executive; Nigel George Hutton [1952] Director/Senior VP Legal Counsel

Hastings (Holdings) Limited
Incorporated: 18 February 2010
Net Worth: £1,644,000 *Total Assets:* £22,412,000
Registered Office: Conquest House, Collington Avenue, Bexhill on Sea, E Sussex, TN39 3LW
Activities: Activities of insurance agents and brokers
Officers: Anthony Stephen Leppard, Secretary; Richard Hoskins [1964] Director; Tobias Adriaan Van Der Meer [1977] Director [Dutch]

Hastings Group Holdings PLC
Incorporated: 11 June 2015 *Employees:* 2,585
Net Worth: £612,899,968 *Total Assets:* £2,817,499,904
Registered Office: Conquest House, 32-34 Collington Avenue, Bexhill on Sea, E Sussex, TN39 3LW
Activities: Activities of head offices
Officers: Anthony Stephen Leppard, Secretary; Hermanus Lambertus Bosman [1968] Director [South African]; Alison Sarah Burns [1963] Director; Elizabeth Grace Chambers [1962] Director [American]; Thomas Colraine [1958] Director; Ian Donald Cormack [1947] Director; Gary Andrew Hoffman [1960] Director; Richard Hoskins [1964] Director; Pierre Paul Joseph Leon Marie Ghislain Lefevre [1956] Director [Belgian]; Sumit Rajpal [1975] Director [American]; Dr Teresa Robson-Capps [1955] Director; Selina Shanti Sagayam [1972] Director/Solicitor [Malaysian]; Tobias Adriaan Van Der Meer [1977] Director [Dutch]

Hastings Insurance Services Limited
Incorporated: 20 October 1995 *Employees:* 2,548
Net Worth: £94,860,000 *Total Assets:* £453,897,984
Registered Office: Conquest House, Collington Avenue, Bexhill on Sea, E Sussex, TN39 3LW
Activities: Activities of insurance agents and brokers
Parent: Hastings (UK) Limited
Officers: Anthony Stephen Leppard, Secretary; Susan Anne Amies-King [1963] Managing Director; Peter William Blanc [1970] Director/Insurance Executive; Valerie Michelle Dias [1959] Director; Timothy John Money [1967] Director; Selina Shanti Sagayam [1972] Director/Solicitor [Malaysian]; Tobias Van Der Meer [1977] Managing Director [Dutch]

Hastings Water (UK) Limited
Incorporated: 14 August 2003
Net Worth: £117,952,000 *Total Assets:* £173,603,008
Registered Office: South East Water Limited, Rocroft Road, Snodland, Kent, ME6 5AH
Activities: Activities of head offices
Officers: Nicolas Truillet, Secretary; Stephen Francis Jordan [1980] Director/Portfolio Manager; Oliver Jan Schubert [1972] Executive Director [Austrian]

Hastoe Capital PLC
Incorporated: 6 March 2012
Net Worth: £50,000 *Total Assets:* £129,685,000
Registered Office: Marina House, 17 Marina Place, Hampton Wick, Kingston upon Thames, Surrey, KT1 4BH
Activities: Financial intermediation not elsewhere classified
Parent: Hastoe Housing Association
Officers: William Roberts, Secretary; Andrew Potter [1971] Director/Chief Executive; William Jeremy Roberts [1970] Finance Director; Robert Rutledge [1954] Director/Retired

Hatch, Mansfield Agencies Limited
Incorporated: 8 February 1994 *Employees:* 45
Net Worth: £8,346,666 *Total Assets:* £47,861,024
Registered Office: New Bank House, 1 Brockenhurst Road, Ascot, Berks, SL5 9DJ
Activities: Agents involved in the sale of food, beverages and tobacco
Shareholders: Maison Louis Jadot; Vina Errazuriz S.A.
Officers: Paul Andrew Hughes-D'aeth, Secretary; Mark Russell Calver [1962] Director/Wine Merchant; Eduardo Alejandro Chadwick [1959] Director/Wine Producer [Chilean]; Robert Timothey Deroose [1959] Director [American]; Pierre Henry Gagey [1955] Director/Wine Producer [French]; Paul Andrew Hughes-D'aeth [1962] Director; Benedict Anthony Knollys [1971] Sales Director; Patrick William McGrath [1960] Director/Wine Merchant

Haulfryn Group Limited
Incorporated: 6 December 1935 *Employees:* 365
Net Worth: £95,413,000 *Total Assets:* £160,151,008
Registered Office: Clarion House, Norreys Drive, Maidenhead, Berks, SL6 4FL
Activities: Other holiday and other collective accommodation
Officers: Jeremy Philip Gorman, Secretary; Matthew Victor Britton [1971] Director/Chief Financial Officer; Jonathan Paul Fenton Hurst [1959] Director; Robert John McGhee [1959] Director/Chief Executive; Adrian Nicholas Patten [1967] Director; Fiona Annette Statham [1957] Director; Michael Edward Tye [1953] Director; Georgina Mary Vestbirk [1969] Director/Accountant

Havas Canada Holdings Limited
Incorporated: 4 December 2006
Net Worth: £39,053,000 *Total Assets:* £39,053,000
Registered Office: Havas House, Hermitage Court, Hermitage Lane, Maidstone, Kent, ME16 9NT
Activities: Activities of head offices
Parent: Vivendi S.A.
Officers: Allan John Ross, Secretary; Ian Edward Moffatt [1963] Director/Global Finance Controller; Allan John Ross [1961] Director/Accountant; Paul Francis Woodhouse [1955] Director/Accountant

Havas Holdings Limited
Incorporated: 15 December 2005
Net Worth: £506,880,096 *Total Assets:* £664,367,680
Registered Office: Havas House, Hermitage Court, Hermitage Lane, Maidstone, Kent, ME16 9NT
Activities: Activities of head offices
Parent: Havas UK Limited
Officers: Allan John Ross, Secretary; Alan Ralston Adamson [1966] Director/Chief Financial Officer; Paul Francis Woodhouse [1955] Director/Accountant

Havas Shared Services Limited
Incorporated: 30 August 1901 *Employees:* 72
Net Worth: £40,255,000 *Total Assets:* £75,835,000
Registered Office: Havas House, Hermitage Court, Hermitage Lane, Maidstone, Kent, ME16 9NT
Activities: Activities of head offices
Parent: Havas UK Limited
Officers: Allan John Ross, Secretary; Alan Ralston Adamson [1966] Director/Chief Financial Officer; Francois Marie Jean Charles Laroze [1963] Director/Chief Financial Officer [French]; Paul Francis Woodhouse [1955] Director/Accountant

Havas UK Limited
Incorporated: 25 May 1993 *Employees:* 22
Net Worth: £536,486,016 *Total Assets:* £620,940,992
Registered Office: Havas House, Hermitage Court, Hermitage Lane, Maidstone, Kent, ME16 9NT
Activities: Activities of head offices
Parent: Vivendi S.A.
Officers: Allan John Ross, Secretary/Accountant; Alan Ralston Adamson [1966] Director/Chief Financial Officer; Myriam Edith Guillotin [1962] Director/Head of Consolidation [French]; Francois Marie Jean Charles Laroze [1963] Director/Chief Financial Officer [French]; Paul Francis Woodhouse [1955] Director/Accountant

Haven Leisure Limited
Incorporated: 4 December 1985 *Employees:* 6,123
Net Worth: £227,772,992 *Total Assets:* £818,675,968
Registered Office: No 1 Park Lane, Hemel Hempstead, Herts, HP2 4YL
Activities: Recreational vehicle parks, trailer parks and camping grounds
Parent: Bourne Leisure Limited
Officers: Jane Elizabeth Bentall [1970] Director/Accountant; Paul Charles Flaum [1970] Director; Iain Stuart Macmillan [1976] Director

Havenhill Limited
Incorporated: 23 March 1998
Previous: Cheema Limited
Net Worth: £24,093,480 *Total Assets:* £31,515,382
Registered Office: New Marlborough House, Arnolde Close, Rochester, Kent, ME2 4QW
Activities: Activities of head offices
Officers: Pamilla Kaur Cheema, Secretary; Surjit Singh Cheema [1962] Director/Builder

Hawk Incentives Holdings Limited
Incorporated: 17 May 1983 *Employees:* 20
Previous: The Grass Roots Group Holdings Limited
Net Worth: £10,289,000 *Total Assets:* £44,010,000
Registered Office: Westside, London Road, Hemel Hempstead, Herts, HP3 9TD
Activities: Other business support service activities n.e.c.
Parent: Blackhawk Network Holdings, Inc.
Officers: Michelle Josephine Wainhouse, Secretary; Patrick Philip Gurney [1970] Director/Accountant; Matthew David Howe [1971] Managing Director; Kirsten Ellen Richesson [1969] Director/General Counsel and Secretary [American]

Hawk Incentives Limited
Incorporated: 7 February 2001 *Employees:* 353
Previous: The Grass Roots Group UK Limited
Net Worth: £19,076,000 *Total Assets:* £98,199,000
Registered Office: Westside, London Road, Hemel Hempstead, Herts, HP3 9TD
Activities: Other business support service activities n.e.c.
Parent: Hawk Incentives Holdings Limited
Officers: Michelle Josephine Wainhouse, Secretary; Patrick Philip Gurney [1970] Director/Accountant; Matthew David Howe [1971] Managing Director; Kirsten Ellen Richesson [1969] Director/General Counsel and Secretary [American]

Hawk-Eye Innovations Limited
Incorporated: 17 July 2001 *Employees:* 224
Net Worth: £21,256,000 *Total Assets:* £32,507,000
Registered Office: Legal Department, The Heights, Brooklands, Weybridge, Surrey, KT13 0XW
Activities: Ready-made interactive leisure and entertainment software development
Parent: Sony Europe Limited
Officers: Richard James Waite, Secretary; Stephen James Carter [1979] Managing Director; Adam Charles Fry [1964] Director/Businessman; Romona Liddiard [1971] Finance Director; David McIntosh [1962] Finance Director

Paula Hawkins Limited
Incorporated: 18 July 2013 *Employees:* 1
Net Worth: £21,973,516 *Total Assets:* £25,613,192
Registered Office: c/o Alderwick James & Co, 4 The Sanctuary, 23 Oakhill Grove, Surbiton, Surrey, KT6 6DU
Activities: Book publishing
Major Shareholder: Paula Bawden Hawkins
Officers: Paula Bawden Hawkins [1972] Director

Hayes & Jarvis (Travel) Limited
Incorporated: 8 July 1952 *Employees:* 275
Net Worth Deficit: £441,000 *Total Assets:* £64,323,000
Registered Office: Origin One, 108 High Street, Crawley, W Sussex, RH10 1BD
Activities: Travel agency activities
Parent: Travelopia Holdings Limited
Officers: Janet Northey, Secretary; Sally Ann Cowdry [1968] Director; Samuel Allan McCloskey [1985] Director/Accountant

Haymarket Group Limited
Incorporated: 14 April 1993 *Employees:* 1,440
Net Worth: £19,210,000 *Total Assets:* £80,116,000
Registered Office: Bridge House, 69 London Road, Twickenham, Middlesex, TW1 3SP
Activities: Activities of head offices
Major Shareholder: Michael Ray Dibdin Heseltine
Officers: Kevin Costello [1964] Director; David Baird Fraser [1939] Director/Chartered Accountant; Brian John Freeman [1954] Director/Accountant; Mark Gibson [1953] Director/Chief Executive Charity; Lord Michael Ray Dibdin Heseltine [1933] Director/Publisher; Hon Rupert Heseltine [1967] Director/Publisher; Lord Peter Keith Levene [1941] Director

Haymarket Media Group Ltd.
Incorporated: 22 July 1932 *Employees:* 782
Net Worth: £95,681,000 *Total Assets:* £256,752,000
Registered Office: Bridge House, 69 London Road, Twickenham, Middlesex, TW1 3SP
Activities: Publishing of consumer and business journals and periodicals
Parent: Haymarket Group Limited
Officers: Kevin Costello [1964] Publishing Director; Brian John Freeman [1964] Director/Accountant; Lord Michael Ray Dibdin Heseltine [1933] Director/Publisher; Hon Rupert Heseltine [1967] Director/Publisher

Haymarket UK2 Limited
Incorporated: 2 July 2008
Net Worth: £128,164,784 *Total Assets:* £128,682,680
Registered Office: Bridge House, 69 London Road, Twickenham, Middlesex, TW1 3SP
Activities: Other business support service activities n.e.c.
Parent: Haymarket Media Group Limited
Officers: Philip Stanley Goodman, Secretary; Brian John Freeman [1964] Director/Accountant

Haynes Brothers,Limited
Incorporated: 26 June 1896 *Employees:* 265
Net Worth: £12,024,720 *Total Assets:* £33,857,296
Registered Office: 23 Ashford Road, Maidstone, Kent, ME14 5DQ
Activities: Sale of new cars and light motor vehicles
Major Shareholder: Andrew David Stirling Haynes
Officers: Trevor John Pickard, Secretary; Andrew David Stirling Haynes [1966] Director; Lesley Haynes [1942] Director/Charity Co-ordinator; Stephen Hyde [1956] Director

The Hazeley Academy
Incorporated: 20 April 2011 *Employees:* 184
Net Worth: £29,815,416 *Total Assets:* £32,471,284
Registered Office: The Hazeley Academy, Emperor Drive, Milton Keynes, Bucks, MK8 0PT
Activities: General secondary education
Officers: Jasmine Marie Ampaw-Farr [1970] Director; Matthew James Bonnett [1989] Director/Teacher; Mohammed Shaffiq Bostan [1968] Director/Computer Engineer; Ian Peter Clarkson [1954] Director; Malcolm Hugh Dobell [1951] Director; Rebecca Jayne Howell [1974] Director/Education Consultant; Taskeen Naqvi [1977] Director/Teacher; Anthony Richard Nelson [1971] Director/Headmaster; Jane Chinedu Osayimwen [1973] Director/Project Manager; Sarah Thompson [1976] Director/Apprenticeship Manager; Dr Margaret Elizabeth Wyke [1953] Director/Retired

Hazelwick School
Incorporated: 29 June 2011 *Employees:* 169
Net Worth: £23,293,696 *Total Assets:* £24,914,216
Registered Office: Hazelwick School, Hazelwick School Close, Three Bridges, Crawley, W Sussex, RH10 1SX
Activities: General secondary education
Officers: Sarah Sparrowhawk, Secretary; Vinod Bhavani [1973] Director/Chartered Engineer; Rachel Bowron [1973] Director/Veterinary Surgeon; Lewis Clarke [1957] Director/Senior Investigation Officer HMRC; Devanathan Devanayagam [1975] Director/Financial Protection Advisor; Ann Frances Fearon [1962] Director/Headteacher; Lesley Humphrey [1959] Director/Pupil Premium Mentor; Julia Jellicoe [1971] Director/Chartered Accountant; Hannah Jones [1981] Director/School Teacher; Ian Larkham [1969] Director/Accountant; Katharine Milcoy [1955] Director/University; Suzanne Stass [1959] Director/Consultant in Business; Satinder Kaur Tamber [1978] Director/Solicitor

HCL EAS Ltd
Incorporated: 11 September 2008
Net Worth: £118,785,144 *Total Assets:* £596,680,640
Registered Office: Axoncentre, Church Road, Egham, Surrey, TW20 9QB
Activities: Activities of head offices
Major Shareholder: Sivaprasad Sivasubramaniam Nadar
Officers: Manish Anand [1968] Director [Indian]; Subramanian Gopalakrishnan [1967] Director [Indian]; Ajit Krishnan Kutty Kumar [1964] Director [Indian]; Rahul Singh [1963] Director [Indian]; Shiv Kumar Walia [1969] Director [Australian]

HCL Great Britain Limited
Incorporated: 7 January 1997 *Employees:* 607
Net Worth: £31,126,000 *Total Assets:* £76,664,000
Registered Office: Axon Centre, Church Road, Egham, Surrey, TW20 9QB
Activities: Information technology consultancy activities
Parent: HCL Technologies UK Limited
Officers: Prateek Aggarwal [1967] Director [Indian]; Prahlad Rai Bansal [1957] Director [Indian]; Ajit Krishnan Kutty Kumar [1964] Director [Indian]; Rahul Singh [1963] Director [Indian]; Shiv Kumar Walia [1969] Director [Australian]

HCL Technologies UK Limited
Incorporated: 20 August 2013 *Employees:* 1,068
Net Worth: £48,883,000 *Total Assets:* £259,556,000
Registered Office: Axon Centre, Church Road, Egham, Surrey, TW20 9QB
Activities: Activities of head offices
Major Shareholder: Sivaprasad Sivasubramaniam Nadar
Officers: Manish Anand [1968] Director [Indian]; Ajit Krishnan Kutty Kumar [1964] Director [Indian]; Rahul Singh [1963] Director [Indian]; Shiv Kumar Walia [1969] Director [Australian]

HCP Packaging UK Limited
Incorporated: 23 February 2005 *Employees:* 14
Net Worth: £19,744,584 *Total Assets:* £56,988,204
Registered Office: 1 High Street, Guildford, Surrey, GU2 4HP
Activities: Other service activities n.e.c.
Major Shareholder: Jean Eric Salata Rothleder
Officers: Carlos Miguel Aquino [1962] Director [American]; Dar Cin Chen [1966] Director [American]; Alex Lee [1979] Director [Chinese]; Derek Richard Mantle [1955] Director/Engineer; Jacqueline Clare Mantle [1965] Director/Marketing Consultant; Gordon Sun Kan Shaw [1965] Director [American]; Ming Kei Wu [1966] Director

HDF (UK) Holdings Limited
Incorporated: 25 May 2005 *Employees:* 975
Net Worth: £108,722,000 *Total Assets:* £1,642,569,984
Registered Office: South East Water Limited, Rocfort Road, Snodland, Kent, ME6 5AH
Activities: Other business support service activities n.e.c.
Officers: Nicolas Alexandre Desire Truillet, Secretary; Rachel Amelia Drew [1976] Investment Director [Irish/New Zealander]; Stephen Francis Jordan [1980] Director/Portfolio Manager; Anne-Noelle Noelle Le Gal [1983] Director [French]; Oliver Jan Schubert [1972] Executive Director [Austrian]

E.L.Head Limited
Incorporated: 15 July 1954 *Employees:* 5
Net Worth: £28,468,036 *Total Assets:* £28,908,524
Registered Office: Eddington Works, Eddington Lane, Herne Bay, Kent, CT6 5TR
Activities: Manufacture of kitchen furniture
Officers: Barry John Head, Secretary; Barry John Head [1968] Director; Michael John Head [1943] Director

Health Management Limited
Incorporated: 8 February 2002 *Employees:* 697
Net Worth: £8,401,667 *Total Assets:* £24,074,084
Registered Office: Ash House, The Broyle, Ringmer, E Sussex, BN8 5NN
Activities: Other business support service activities n.e.c.
Parent: Maximus HHS Limited
Officers: David Francis, Secretary; Michael Batty [1972] Director; Dr Paul Anthony Williams [1963] Director; Matthew James Wood [1972] Director

Healthcare Facilities Management Services Limited
Incorporated: 28 July 2008
Net Worth: £12,916,000 *Total Assets:* £28,629,000
Registered Office: Princes House, 73a London Road, Reading, Berks, RG1 5UZ
Activities: Other letting and operating of own or leased real estate
Parent: Royal Berkshire NHS Foundation Trust
Officers: Caroline Lynch, Secretary; Michael Glenn Clements [1977] Deputy Director of Finance; Don Watson Fairley [1964] Director of Workforce; Tracey Ann Middleton [1966] Director

Healthcare Providers (Gloucester) Limited
Incorporated: 17 December 2001
Net Worth Deficit: £1,188,000 *Total Assets:* £36,378,000
Registered Office: Part First Floor, 1 Grenfell Road, Maidenhead, Berks, SL6 1HN
Activities: Financial intermediation not elsewhere classified
Shareholders: BBGI Sicav S.A.; Semperian PPP Investment Partners No.2 Limited
Officers: Emeka Ikechi Ehenulo, Secretary; Richard Little [1979] Investment Director; Albert Hendrik Naafs [1965] Director [Dutch]; Neil Rae [1971] Director; Ian Tayler [1976] Director/General Manager

Healthcare Support (Newcastle) Finance PLC
Incorporated: 15 December 2004
Net Worth: £429,000 *Total Assets:* £380,844,992
Registered Office: 8 White Oak Square, London Road, Swanley, Kent, BR8 7AG
Activities: Financial intermediation not elsewhere classified
Parent: Healthcare Support (Newcastle) Holdings Limited
Officers: Gaynor Birley-Smith [1966] Investment Director; David Richard Bradbury [1969] Asset Director; Robert James Marsden [1955] Projects Director; Hannah O'Gorman [1971] Director; Alastair James Watson [1974] Investment Director

Healthcare Support (Newcastle) Holdings Limited
Incorporated: 19 April 2002
Net Worth: £4,060,000 *Total Assets:* £381,011,008
Registered Office: 8 White Oak Square, London Road, Swanley, Kent, BR8 7AG
Activities: Construction of commercial buildings
Parent: Equion Health (Newcastle) Limited
Officers: Gaynor Birley-Smith [1966] Investment Director; David Richard Bradbury [1969] Asset Director; Robert James Marsden [1955] Projects Director; Hannah O'Gorman [1971] Director; Alistair James Watson [1974] Investment Director

Healthcare Support (Newcastle) Limited
Incorporated: 22 March 2002
Net Worth: £3,631,000 *Total Assets:* £381,011,008
Registered Office: 8 White Oak Square, London Road, Swanley, Kent, BR8 7AG
Activities: Construction of commercial buildings
Parent: Healthcare Support (Newcastle) Holdings Limited
Officers: Gaynor Birley-Smith [1966] Investment Director; David Richard Bradbury [1969] Asset Director; Robert James Marsden [1955] Projects Director; Hannah O'Gorman [1971] Director; Alastair James Watson [1974] Investment Director

Healthcare Support (North Staffs) Finance PLC
Incorporated: 10 December 2004
Net Worth: £733,000 *Total Assets:* £405,620,992
Registered Office: 8 White Oak Square, London Road, Swanley, Kent, BR8 7AG
Activities: Banks
Parent: Healthcare Support (North Staffs) Holdings Limited
Officers: Stuart Anthony Carter [1965] Project Director; Jonathan Nigel Edward Cowdell [1966] Director/Chartered Accountant; Jamie Pritchard [1971] Director/Investment Manager; Neil Woodburn [1979] Director/Chartered Building Surveyor

Healthcare Support (North Staffs) Holdings Limited
Incorporated: 10 December 2004
Net Worth: £7,466,000 *Total Assets:* £417,032,000
Registered Office: 8 White Oak Square, London Road, Swanley, Kent, BR8 7AG
Activities: Activities of head offices
Parent: JLIF Investments Limited
Officers: Stuart Anthony Carter [1965] Project Director; Jonathan Nigel Edward Cowdell [1966] Director/Chartered Accountant; Jamie Pritchard [1971] Director/Investment Manager; Neil Woodburn [1979] Director/Chartered Building Surveyor

Healthcare Support (North Staffs) Limited
Incorporated: 9 December 2004
Net Worth: £6,733,000 *Total Assets:* £417,032,000
Registered Office: 8 White Oak Square, London Road, Swanley, Kent, BR8 7AG
Activities: Construction of commercial buildings
Parent: Healthcare Support (North Staffs) Holdings Limited
Officers: Stuart Anthony Carter [1965] Project Director; Jonathan Nigel Edward Cowdell [1966] Director/Chartered Accountant; Jamie Pritchard [1971] Director/Investment Manager; Neil Woodburn [1979] Director/Chartered Building Surveyor

Heart Internet Limited
Incorporated: 14 August 2003 *Employees:* 78
Net Worth: £44,174,000 *Total Assets:* £51,146,000
Registered Office: 5th Floor, The Shipping Building, Old Vinyl Factory, 252-254 Blyth Road, Hayes, Middlesex, UB3 1HA
Activities: Data processing, hosting and related activities
Parent: HEL Bidco Ltd
Officers: Sara Silveira Da Costa Da Cunha Rego [1973] Director [Portuguese]; Jonathan Ying Kit Wong [1976] Director

Heartstone Inns Limited
Incorporated: 17 June 2009 *Employees:* 172
Net Worth: £17,536,892 *Total Assets:* £26,479,900
Registered Office: 1 London Street, Reading, Berks, RG1 4QW
Activities: Public houses and bars
Officers: Edward John Beale [1960] Director; James David Alexander Birch [1967] Director; Robin Kennedy Black [1958] Director; Andrew Haining [1959] Director

Heathrow (AH) Limited
Incorporated: 20 December 2007
Net Worth: £8,156,000,256 *Total Assets:* £8,156,000,256
Registered Office: The Compass Centre, Nelson Road, Hounslow, Middlesex, TW6 2GW
Activities: Activities of head offices
Parent: Heathrow (SP) Limited
Officers: Yuanyuan Ding [1979] Director; Javier Echave Espot [1980] Director [Spanish]; Nicholas Francis Golding [1963] Director

Heathrow (DSH) Limited
Incorporated: 20 December 2007
Net Worth: £4,674,999,808 *Total Assets:* £5,270,000,128
Registered Office: The Compass Centre, Nelson Road, Hounslow, Middlesex, TW6 2GW
Activities: Activities of head offices
Parent: LHR Airports Limited
Officers: Yuanyuan Ding [1979] Director; Javier Echave Espot [1980] Director [Spanish]; Nicholas Francis Golding [1963] Director

Heathrow (SP) Limited
Incorporated: 20 December 2007 *Employees:* 6,605
Net Worth Deficit: £2,635,000,064 *Total Assets:* £15,258,000,384
Registered Office: The Compass Centre, Nelson Road, Hounslow, Middlesex, TW6 2GW
Activities: Activities of head offices
Parent: Heathrow Finance PLC
Officers: Yuanyuan Ding [1979] Director; Javier Echave Espot [1980] Director [Spanish]; Charlotte Emma Tiffany Gilthorpe [1970] Director/Employed Barrister; Nicholas Francis Golding [1963] Director

Heathrow Airport Fuel Company Limited
Incorporated: 23 April 1996
Net Worth: £13,615,000 *Total Assets:* £39,882,000
Registered Office: Building 1204, Sandringham Road, Heathrow Airport, Hounslow, Middlesex, TW6 3SH
Activities: Non-trading company
Officers: Victoria Guy [1971] Director/General Manager; Mark Stephen Hayward [1979] Director/Manager; Mary Marshall Henderson [1959] Director/Oil Company Executive; Rupert Leland Agnar Hone [1966] Director/Oil Company Executive; Stephen Jonathan Newton [1961] Director; Calum James Stacey [1986] Director/Solicitor; Andrew Charles Francis Taylor [1965] Director/Oil Company Executive; Paul William Vowell [1971] Director/Manager [New Zealander]

Heathrow Airport Holdings Limited
Incorporated: 27 March 2006 *Employees:* 6,740
Net Worth: £703,000,000 *Total Assets:* £18,395,000,832
Registered Office: The Compass Centre, Nelson Road, Hounslow, Middlesex, TW6 2GW
Activities: Activities of head offices
Parent: ADI Finance 2 Limited
Officers: Carol Hui, Secretary; Akbar Abbas Al Baker [1960] Director/Chief Executive Officer [Qatari]; Ahmed Ali Al-Hammadi [1981] Director [Qatari]; Stuart Harvey Baldwin [1969] Director/Investment Manager; Christopher William Beale [1947] Director [American]; David Andrew Begg [1956] Director; Ali Bouzarif [1978] Director [Belgian]; Maria Cristina Casero Borges [1960] Director [Spanish]; Jinhong Chen [1990] Director [Chinese]; Samuel Coxe [1975] Alternate Director [American]; Lord Paul Clive Deighton [1956] Director/Company Chairman; Javier Echave Espot [1980] Director [Spanish]; Olivier Georges Xavier Fortin [1974] Director [French]; Ignacio Aitor Garcia Bilbao [1970] Alternate Director [Spanish]; Jorge Gil Villen [1972] Director/Lawyer/Economist [Spanish]; John William Holland-Kaye [1965] Director/Chief Executive Officer; Mr Deven Arvind Karnik [1967] Alternate Director; Tom Kelly [1989] Director [Irish]; Alexander Leonard [1985] Director; Rachel Janis Lomax [1945] Director; Ernesto Lopez [1964] Director/Chief Financial Officer; Inigo Meiras [1963] Alternate Director [Spanish]; Michael James Powell [1972] Director; David Jinlin Xie [1978] Alternate Director [American]; Gonzalo Velasco Zabalza [1979] Alternate Director [Spanish]

Heathrow Airport Limited
Incorporated: 19 February 1986
Net Worth: £2,430,000,128 *Total Assets:* £17,422,000,128
Registered Office: The Compass Centre, Nelson Road, Hounslow, Middlesex, TW6 2GW
Activities: Scheduled passenger air transport
Parent: Heathrow (AH) Limited
Officers: Ross Findlay Scott Baker [1974] Director; William Stuart Birrell [1964] Director/Chief Information Officer; Javier Echave Espot [1980] Director [Spanish]; Christopher Charles Garton [1961] Director; Charlotte Emma Tiffany Gilthorpe [1970] Director/Employed Barrister; John William Holland Kaye [1965] Director/Chief Executive Officer; Carol Hui [1956] Director/Lawyer; Andrew Hugh Macmillan [1975] Director; Paula Stannett [1965] HR Director

Heathrow Edwardian Hotel Ltd
Incorporated: 27 August 2013 *Employees:* 329
Net Worth: £56,853,000 *Total Assets:* £69,716,000
Registered Office: 140 Bath Road, Hayes, Middlesex, UB3 5AW
Activities: Hotels and similar accommodation
Parent: Edwardian Hotel Finance Ltd
Officers: Vijay Wason, Secretary; John Robert Morley [1945] Director/Financial Consultant; Jasminder Singh [1951] Director/Hotelier

Heathrow Enterprises Limited
Incorporated: 24 November 1992 *Employees:* 22
Net Worth: £68,422,000 *Total Assets:* £82,188,000
Registered Office: The Compass Centre, Nelson Road, Hounslow, Middlesex, TW6 2GW
Activities: Activities of head offices
Parent: LHR Airports Limited
Officers: Ross Findlay Scott Baker [1974] Director; Yuanyuan Ding [1979] Director; Javier Echave Espot [1980] Director [Spanish]

Heathrow Express Operating Company Limited
Incorporated: 11 January 1996 *Employees:* 460
Net Worth: £69,501,000 *Total Assets:* £76,440,000
Registered Office: The Compass Centre, Nelson Road, Hounslow, Middlesex, TW6 2GW
Activities: Passenger rail transport, interurban
Parent: Heathrow Airport Limited
Officers: Ross Findlay Scott Baker [1974] Director; Phillip Alan Bearpark [1966] Director; Anthony Joseph Caccavone [1972] Director; Stephen Paul Chambers [1971] Director; Leslie Freer [1966] Director; Michael Peter Hodson [1951] Director; Andrew Hugh Macmillan [1975] Director

Heathrow Finance PLC
Incorporated: 20 December 2007
Net Worth Deficit: £1,070,000,000 *Total Assets:* £15,616,000,000
Registered Office: The Compass Centre, Nelson Road, Hounslow, Middlesex, TW6 2GW
Activities: Activities of head offices
Parent: Heathrow (DSH) Limited
Officers: Patrick Dawe-Lane, Secretary; Yuanyuan Ding [1979] Director; Javier Echave Espot [1980] Director [Spanish]; Nicholas Francis Golding [1963] Director

Heathrow Holdco Limited
Incorporated: 24 October 2007
Net Worth: £3,782,000,128 *Total Assets:* £11,914,999,808
Registered Office: The Compass Centre, Nelson Road, Hounslow, Middlesex, TW6 2GW
Activities: Activities of head offices
Parent: Heathrow Airport Holdings Limited
Officers: Yuanyuan Ding [1979] Director; Javier Echave Espot [1980] Director [Spanish]; John William Holland-Kaye [1965] Commercial Director

Heathrow Hydrant Operating Company Limited
Incorporated: 21 June 1993 *Employees:* 28
Net Worth: £18,177,000 *Total Assets:* £22,793,000
Registered Office: Building 1204, Sandringham Road, Heathrow Airport, Hounslow, Middlesex, TW6 3SH
Activities: Other service activities n.e.c.
Officers: Victoria Guy [1971] Director/General Manager; Mark Stephen Hayward [1979] Director/Manager; Mary Marshall Henderson [1959] Director/Oil Company Executive; Rupert Leland Agnar Hone [1966] Director/Oil Company Executive; Malachy Joseph Murphy [1963] Director/Company Executive; Stephen Jonathan Newton [1961] Director; Calum James Stacey [1986] Director/Solicitor; Andrew Charles Francis Taylor [1965] Director/Oil Company Executive; Paul William Vowell [1971] Director/Manager [New Zealander]

Heathrow Truck Centre Limited
Incorporated: 27 October 1986 *Employees:* 300
Net Worth: £9,444,425 *Total Assets:* £35,505,696
Registered Office: Lakeside Industrial Estate, Colnbrook, Berks, SL3 0ED
Activities: Sale of other motor vehicles
Parent: Ballyvesey Holdings Limited
Officers: Harold Hugh Montgomery, Secretary; David Nigel Birkmyre [1952] Director; Peter Gibbons [1961] Director; Paul Anthony Irving [1961] Director; Harold Hugh Montgomery [1948] Director

Heidelberg Graphic Equipment Limited
Incorporated: 12 July 1974 *Employees:* 246
Net Worth: £22,763,000 *Total Assets:* £59,182,000
Registered Office: 69-76 High Street, Brentford, Middlesex, TW8 0AA
Activities: Installation of industrial machinery and equipment
Officers: Simon Richard Gamble [1967] Finance Director; Axel Lammer [1963] Director/Chairman [German]; James Robert Todd [1956] Director; Ian Terence Wilcock [1963] Service Director

HeidelbergCement Canada Holding Limited
Incorporated: 4 December 2009
Net Worth: £3,086,672,896 *Total Assets:* £3,086,672,896
Registered Office: Hanson House, 14 Castle Hill, Maidenhead, Berks, SL6 4JJ
Activities: Activities of other holding companies n.e.c.
Parent: HeidelbergCement UK Holding II Limited
Officers: Wendy Fiona Rogers, Secretary; Nicholas Arthur Dawe Benning-Prince [1974] Director/Chartered Accountant; David Blackley [1961] Director/Chartered Accountant [Canadian/British]; Robert Charles Dowley [1972] Director/Chartered Accountant; Edward Alexander Gretton [1970] Director; Jonathan Morrish [1970] Director; Dr Lorenz Nager [1960] Director/CFO, Heidelbergcement AG [German]; Christopher James Ward [1972] Director/President, Lehigh Hanson Materials Limited [American]; Dr Carsten Matthias Wendt [1976] Director [German]; Simon Lloyd Willis [1965] Director/Chief Executive, Hanson UK

HeidelbergCement Euro I Limited
Incorporated: 17 November 2014
Net Worth: £561,074,496 *Total Assets:* £561,074,496
Registered Office: Hanson House, 14 Castle Hill, Maidenhead, Berks, SL6 4JJ
Activities: Activities of head offices
Parent: Birchwood Omnia Limited
Officers: Wendy Fiona Rogers, Secretary; Nicholas Arthur Dawe Benning-Prince [1974] Director/Chartered Accountant; Robert Charles Dowley [1972] Director/Chartered Accountant; Edward Alexander Gretton [1970] Director; Dr Carsten Matthias Wendt [1976] Director [German]

HeidelbergCement Euro II Limited
Incorporated: 17 November 2014
Net Worth: £869,166,080 *Total Assets:* £869,166,080
Registered Office: Hanson House, 14 Castle Hill, Maidenhead, Berks, SL6 4JJ
Activities: Activities of head offices
Parent: HeidelbergCement UK Holding II Limited
Officers: Wendy Fiona Rogers, Secretary; Nicholas Arthur Dawe Benning-Prince [1974] Director/Chartered Accountant; Robert Charles Dowley [1972] Director/Chartered Accountant; Edward Alexander Gretton [1970] Director; Dr Carsten Matthias Wendt [1976] Director [German]

HeidelbergCement Euro III Limited
Incorporated: 12 February 2015
Net Worth: £725,532,800 *Total Assets:* £725,532,800
Registered Office: Hanson House, 14 Castle Hill, Maidenhead, Berks, SL6 4JJ
Activities: Activities of head offices
Parent: Hanson Finance Limited
Officers: Wendy Fiona Rogers, Secretary; Nicholas Arthur Dawe Benning-Prince [1974] Director/Chartered Accountant; Robert Charles Dowley [1972] Director/Chartered Accountant; Edward Alexander Gretton [1970] Director; Dr Carsten Matthias Wendt [1976] Director [German]

HeidelbergCement UK Holding II Limited
Incorporated: 28 June 2007
Net Worth: £15,646,895,104 *Total Assets:* £15,646,927,872
Registered Office: Hanson House, 14 Castle Hill, Maidenhead, Berks, SL6 4JJ
Activities: Activities of other holding companies n.e.c.
Parent: Hanson Limited
Officers: Wendy Fiona Rogers, Secretary; Nicholas Arthur Dawe Benning-Prince [1974] Director/Chartered Accountant; Henner Bottcher [1975] Director/Senior Vice President & CFO [German]; Robert Charles Dowley [1972] Director/Chartered Accountant; Edward Alexander Gretton [1970] Director; Jonathan Morrish [1970] Director; Dr Lorenz Nager [1960] Director/CFO Heidelbergcement AG [German]; Dr Carsten Matthias Wendt [1976] Director [German]; Simon Lloyd Willis [1965] Director/Chief Executive, Hanson UK

HeidelbergCement UK Holding Limited
Incorporated: 27 June 2007
Net Worth: £10,112,835,584 *Total Assets:* £18,321,776,640
Registered Office: Hanson House, 14 Castle Hill, Maidenhead, Berks, SL6 4JJ
Activities: Activities of other holding companies n.e.c.
Parent: HeidelbergCement AG
Officers: Wendy Fiona Rogers, Secretary; Nicholas Arthur Dawe Benning-Prince [1974] Director/Chartered Accountant; Robert Charles Dowley [1972] Director/Chartered Accountant; Edward Alexander Gretton [1970] Director; Dr Lorenz Nager [1960] Director/CFO Heidelbergcement AG [German]; Dr Ralph Dominik Von Achten [1965] Director [German]; Dr Carsten Matthias Wendt [1976] Director [German]; Simon Lloyd Willis [1965] Director/Chief Executive, Hanson UK

Heiton Holdings UK Limited
Incorporated: 22 July 1998
Net Worth Deficit: £28,001,000 *Total Assets:* £26,697,000
Registered Office: Oak Green House, 250-256 High Street, Dorking, Surrey, RH4 1QT
Activities: Dormant company
Parent: Grafton Group (UK) PLC
Officers: Brian O'Hara [1967] Director/Accountant [Irish]; Charles Anthony Rinn [1960] Director/Company Secretary [Irish]

HEL Bidco Ltd
Incorporated: 13 July 2010
Net Worth: £393,815,008 *Total Assets:* £408,340,000
Registered Office: 5th Floor, The Shipping Building, Old Vinyl Factory, 252-254 Blyth Road, Hayes, Middlesex, UB3 1HA
Activities: Activities of head offices
Parent: Host Europe Group Limited
Officers: Richard Anthony Winslow [1979] Director; Jonathan Ying Kit Wong [1976] Director

HellermannTyton Group PLC
Incorporated: 19 February 2013
Net Worth: £216,608,064 *Total Assets:* £339,853,056
Registered Office: Griffin House, 135 High Street, Crawley, W Sussex, RH10 1DQ
Activities: Manufacture of other plastic products
Parent: Aptiv PLC
Officers: Hayley Ria Whitehead, Secretary; Timothy Christopher Jones [1959] Director/Chief Financial Officer; Christian Herbert Niemann [1953] Director/Chief Executive [German]

HellermannTyton Holdings Limited
Incorporated: 6 March 2013
Net Worth: £381,490,048 *Total Assets:* £399,104,352
Registered Office: Griffin House, 135 High Street, Crawley, W Sussex, RH10 1DQ
Activities: Activities of head offices
Parent: HellermannTyton Group PLC
Officers: Hayley Ria Whitehead, Secretary; Sean Patrick Corcoran [1958] Director/Attorney [American]; David Matthew Sherbin [1959] Director/General Counsel [American]

HellermannTyton Limited
Incorporated: 12 December 2005 *Employees:* 666
Net Worth: £60,126,000 *Total Assets:* £125,222,000
Registered Office: Griffin House, 135 High Street, Crawley, W Sussex, RH10 1DQ
Activities: Manufacture of other plastic products
Parent: HellermannTyton Holdings Limited
Officers: Hayley Ria Whitehead, Secretary; Timothy Christopher Jones [1959] Director/Chief Financial Officer; Hans-Christian Herbert Niemann [1953] Director/Chief Executive [German]

Help/Systems International Limited
Incorporated: 5 March 2001 *Employees:* 43
Net Worth: £324,814 *Total Assets:* £26,824,632
Registered Office: Sentinel House, Building B, Harvest Crescent, Fleet, Hants, GU51 2UZ
Activities: Information technology consultancy activities
Parent: Help/Systems International Group Limited
Officers: Wesley Fredenburg, Secretary; Chris David Heim [1964] Director [American]; Dan Robert Mayleben [1961] Director [American]

Helsinki Bidco Limited
Incorporated: 5 October 2012 *Employees:* 3
Net Worth: £6,877,000 *Total Assets:* £215,931,008
Registered Office: Granville House, Gatton Park Business Centre, Redhill, Surrey, RH1 3AS
Activities: Other business support service activities n.e.c.
Parent: Helsinki Midco Ltd
Officers: Steven James Higginson [1960] Director; Mark John Lane [1970] Director; Damian Johnson Shaw [1971] Director

Helsinki Midco Limited
Incorporated: 5 October 2012 *Employees:* 3
Net Worth: £10,911,000 *Total Assets:* £150,652,000
Registered Office: Granville House, Gatton Park Business Centre, Redhill, Surrey, RH1 3AS
Activities: Other business support service activities n.e.c.
Parent: Helsinki Topco Ltd
Officers: Steven James Higginson [1960] Director; Mark John Lane [1970] Director; Damian Johnson Shaw [1971] Director

Helsinki Topco Limited
Incorporated: 5 October 2012 *Employees:* 411
Net Worth Deficit: £11,390,000 *Total Assets:* £185,426,000
Registered Office: Granville House, Gatton Park Business Centre, Redhill, Surrey, RH1 3AS
Activities: Other business support service activities n.e.c.
Shareholder: Equistone Partners Europe Ltd
Officers: Christopher Martin Coulton [1979] Director; Paul Robert Harper [1979] Director; Steven James Higginson [1960] Director; Mark John Lane [1970] Director; Paul John Monk [1957] Director/Chairman; Damian Johnson Shaw [1971] Director

Hemel Snowcentre Limited
Incorporated: 1 August 2007 *Employees:* 232
Net Worth: £13,929,000 *Total Assets:* £23,288,000
Registered Office: The Snow Centre, St Albans Hill, Hemel Hempstead, Herts, HP3 9NH
Activities: Other service activities n.e.c.
Officers: David Ian Brown [1967] Managing Director; Richard John Cook [1972] Director; Thomas Woodstock Harris [1963] Director/Engineer

Hendy Automotive Limited
Incorporated: 19 November 2015 *Employees:* 1,040
Net Worth: £17,798,000 *Total Assets:* £192,752,992
Registered Office: Hendy Group, School Lane, Chandler's Ford Industrial Estate, Eastleigh, Hants, SO53 4DG
Activities: Activities of head offices
Major Shareholder: John Bailey
Officers: Colin Moir, Secretary; Simon Bottomley [1968] Director/Chief Operating Officer; Simon James Gulliford [1958] Director; Paul Anthony Hendy [1967] Director; Jonathan Michael Moritz [1967] Finance Director; Andy Stevenson [1951] Director

Hendy Group Limited
Incorporated: 4 October 1923 *Employees:* 1,032
Net Worth: £17,386,000 *Total Assets:* £157,952,000
Registered Office: Hendy Group, School Lane, Chandler's Ford Industrial Estate, Eastleigh, Hants, SO53 4DG
Activities: Sale of new cars and light motor vehicles
Parent: Hendy Holdings Limited
Officers: Colin Moir, Secretary; Simon Bottomley [1968] Director/Chief Operating Officer; Paul Anthony Hendy [1967] Managing Director; Jonathan Michael Moritz [1967] Finance Director; Andy Stevenson [1951] Director

Hendy Holdings Limited
Incorporated: 19 April 1898 *Employees:* 8
Net Worth: £10,810,000 *Total Assets:* £58,627,000
Registered Office: Hendy Group, School Lane, Chandler's Ford Industrial Estate, Eastleigh, Hants, SO53 4DG
Activities: Activities of head offices
Parent: Hendy Automotive Limited
Officers: Colin Moir, Finance Director; Simon Bottomley [1968] Director/Chief Operating Officer; Simon James Gulliford [1958] Director/Marketing Consultant; Paul Anthony Hendy [1967] Managing Director; Jonathan Michael Moritz [1967] Finance Director; Andy Stevenson [1951] Director

Henkel Limited
Incorporated: 5 August 1926 *Employees:* 407
Net Worth: £149,992,992 *Total Assets:* £270,438,016
Registered Office: Henkel Limited, Wood Lane End, Hemel Hempstead, Herts, HP2 4RQ
Activities: Manufacture of other chemical products n.e.c.
Parent: Henkel AG & Co. KGaA
Officers: Sutinder Singh Bhandal, Secretary; Sutinder Singh Bhandal [1968] Director/Legal Counsel; Peter David Budden [1963] Director/Accountant; Mark Crane [1958] Director; Eamonn Gallagher [1960] Director/Product Development; Carsten Knobel [1969] Director/Economist [German]

Henley Camland Ebbsfleet 801H Limited
Incorporated: 9 June 2017
Net Worth Deficit: £537 *Total Assets:* £22,518,494
Registered Office: 1 Christchurch Way, Woking, Surrey, GU21 6JG
Activities: Management of real estate on a fee or contract basis
Officers: Andrew James Brandon, Secretary; Andrew James Brandon [1969] Director/Accountant; Peter Nelson [1961] Director; Ian Rickwood [1967] Director/Property Investor and Developer

Henry Construction Projects Limited
Incorporated: 14 June 2010 *Employees:* 12
Net Worth: £9,247,834 *Total Assets:* £43,675,720
Registered Office: Parkway Farm, Church Road, Cranford, Hounslow, Middlesex, TW5 9RY
Activities: Construction of commercial buildings
Parent: Henry Group Holdings Limited
Officers: Elizabeth Mary Henry, Secretary; Mark James Henry [1978] Director [Irish]; William Anthony Henry [1945] Director [Irish]; John Noone [1971] Director [Irish]

Hephaestus II Limited
Incorporated: 2 July 2014
Net Worth: £9,710,480 *Total Assets:* £95,577,264
Registered Office: Unit 1 Fishponds Road, Wokingham, Berks, RG41 2QJ
Activities: Activities of other holding companies n.e.c.
Parent: Hephaestus III BV
Officers: Robert Roy Sims [1966] Director; Christopher John Wright [1967] Director

Herne Bay High School
Incorporated: 19 January 2011 *Employees:* 233
Net Worth: £22,779,556 *Total Assets:* £26,422,436
Registered Office: Herne Bay High School, Bullockstone Road, Herne Bay, Kent, CT6 7NS
Activities: General secondary education
Officers: Alison Clifton, Secretary; Amy Elizabeth Ansell [1979] Director/Administration Manager; Mark Blesky [1959] Director/Ofsted Inspector/Social Worker; Jon David Boyes [1967] Director/Principal; Stephen Philip Eames [1952] Director/Financial Advisor; Victoria Emma Farbrace [1982] Director/Self Employed PAT Tester; Philip Gallantree [1962] Director/Teacher; Samantha Godden [1972] Director/Staff Development Manager; Michael Hills [1946] Director/Magistrate; Jennifer Anne Homer [1969] Director/Chemical Engineer; Michael O'Reilly [1961] Director/Self Employed [Irish]; Linzi Josephine Payne [1959] Director/Teacher; Tracy Shaw [1963] Director/Teaching Assistant

Heronswood Holdings Limited
Incorporated: 23 July 2015 *Employees:* 530
Net Worth: £78,974,016 *Total Assets:* £91,766,264
Registered Office: Highfield Court, Tollgate, Chandler's Ford, Eastleigh, Hants, SO53 3TY
Activities: Activities of other holding companies n.e.c.
Shareholders: Richard William Mancey; Sara Jane Mancey
Officers: Richard William Mancey [1960] Director/Leisure Park Proprietor; Sara Jane Mancey [1961] Director/Leisure Park Proprietor

Hertswood Academy
Incorporated: 15 March 2012 *Employees:* 154
Net Worth: £39,391,384 *Total Assets:* £43,777,864
Registered Office: Cowley Hill, Borehamwood, Herts, WD6 5LG
Activities: General secondary education
Officers: Joy Linda Wells Cox [1957] Director; Martin Wolfgang Doe [1966] Director/Computer Programmer; Peter Gillett [1970] Director; Fiona Helen Gubb Blackwood [1974] Director/Children's Centre Manager; Ann Muriel Harrison [1946] Director; Richard Arthur Kirk [1942] Director; Elizabeth Longworth [1968] Director/Teacher; Julie Dawn Smith [1966] Director/Sales Programme Support Manager; Christine Wainright [1954] Director/KS3 Co-ordinator

Hertz (U.K.) Limited
Incorporated: 28 January 1958 *Employees:* 413
Net Worth: £16,640,000 *Total Assets:* £282,980,992
Registered Office: Hertz House, 11 Vine Street, Uxbridge, Middlesex, UB8 1QE
Activities: Renting and leasing of cars and light motor vehicles
Parent: Hertz Holdings III UK Limited
Officers: John Christopher Finch, Secretary; Bhaven Ashok Taylor [1980] Finance Director

Hertz Europe Limited
Incorporated: 22 April 1971 *Employees:* 204
Net Worth: £33,627,000 *Total Assets:* £74,385,000
Registered Office: Hertz House, 11 Vine Street, Uxbridge, Middlesex, UB8 1QE
Activities: Other service activities n.e.c.
Parent: Hertz (U.K.) Limited
Officers: John Christopher Finch, Secretary; John Christopher Finch [1965] Director; Tracy Ann Gehlan [1968] Director; Michel Maurice Taride [1956] Director/Executive [French]

Hertz Holdings III UK Limited
Incorporated: 6 December 2005
Net Worth: £34,875,000 *Total Assets:* £34,875,000
Registered Office: Hertz House, 11 Vine Street, Uxbridge, Middlesex, UB8 1QE
Activities: Other business support service activities n.e.c.
Officers: John Christopher Finch, Secretary; Michel Maurice Taride [1956] Director/Executive [French]

Hewlett - Packard Limited
Incorporated: 24 April 1961 *Employees:* 2,871
Net Worth: £622,267,008 *Total Assets:* £1,377,300,992
Registered Office: Amen Corner, Cain Road, Bracknell, Berks, RG12 1HN
Activities: Other information technology service activities
Parent: Hewlett-Packard (Bracknell) Holdings Limited
Officers: Philippa Anne Oram [1966] Finance Director; Marc Edward Waters [1976] Managing Director

Hewlett-Packard (Bracknell) Holdings Limited
Incorporated: 8 September 2005
Net Worth: £94,908,000 *Total Assets:* £931,268,992
Registered Office: Amen Corner, Cain Road, Bracknell, Berks, RG12 1HN
Activities: Activities of head offices
Parent: Hewlett-Packard Holdings Limited
Officers: Miral Hamani-Samaan [1980] Director/Lawyer [French]; Juzer Shaikhali [1966] Director/Chartered Accountant

Hewlett-Packard Cain Holdings Limited
Incorporated: 24 October 2001
Net Worth: £29,597,000 *Total Assets:* £29,650,000
Registered Office: Amen Corner, Cain Road, Bracknell, Berks, RG12 1HN
Activities: Activities of head offices
Parent: Hewlett Packard Holdings Limited
Officers: Miral Hamani-Samaan [1980] Director/Lawyer [French]; Bas Van Der Goorbergh [1973] Tax Director [Dutch]

Hewlett-Packard CDS Limited
Incorporated: 14 March 1995 *Employees:* 521
Net Worth: £31,199,000 *Total Assets:* £37,663,000
Registered Office: c/o Hewlett Packard Limited, Amen Corner, Cain Road, Bracknell, Berks, RG12 1HN
Activities: Other information technology service activities
Parent: Hewlett Packard Enterprise Company
Officers: Philippa Anne Oram [1966] Finance Director; Marc Edward Waters [1976] Managing Director

Hewlett-Packard Holdings Limited
Incorporated: 24 October 2001
Net Worth: £504,312,000 *Total Assets:* £522,928,992
Registered Office: Hewlett Packard Ltd, Cain Road, Bracknell, Berks, RG12 1HN
Activities: Activities of head offices
Parent: Hewlett Packard Enterprise Company
Officers: Miral Hamani-Samaan [1980] Director/Lawyer [French]; Juzer Shaikhali [1966] Director/Tax Manager

Hexagon Corporate Management Limited
Incorporated: 12 September 2013
Net Worth: £738,456,704 *Total Assets:* £742,117,184
Registered Office: Cedar House, 78 Portsmouth Road, Cobham, Surrey, KT11 1AN
Activities: Financial management
Parent: Hexagon Metrology Services Ltd
Officers: Helen Elizabeth Peall, Secretary; David Anthony Mills [1972] Director/CFO, Hexagon Metrology

Hexagon Manufacturing Intelligence Management Limited
Incorporated: 22 December 2015
Net Worth: £871,914,560 *Total Assets:* £874,900,928
Registered Office: 78 Cedar House, Portsmouth Road, Cobham, Surrey, KT11 1AN
Activities: Financial management
Shareholders: Hexagon Metrology Services Ltd; Hexagon AB
Officers: Helen Elizabeth Peall, Secretary; David Anthony Mills [1972] Director/CFO Hexagon Metrology

Hexagon Positioning Intelligence Limited
Incorporated: 17 October 2013
Net Worth: £119,576,000 *Total Assets:* £210,702,000
Registered Office: Cedar House, 78 Portsmouth Road, Cobham, Surrey, KT11 1AN
Activities: Activities of head offices
Parent: Hexagon AB
Officers: Helen Elizabeth Peall, Secretary; David Anthony Mills [1972] Director

Heythrop Park Limited
Incorporated: 10 December 1999 *Employees:* 137
Previous: Firoka (Heythrop Park) Limited
Net Worth: £2,442,063 *Total Assets:* £33,644,216
Registered Office: 1 Park Lane, Hemel Hempstead, Herts, HP2 4YL
Activities: Hotels and similar accommodation
Parent: Bourne Leisure Holdings Limited
Officers: Jane Elizabeth Bentall [1970] Director/Accountant; Paul Charles Flaum [1970] Director; Iain Stuart Macmillan [1976] Director; Simon Thompson [1971] Director

HFC Prestige Products Limited
Incorporated: 24 November 1967 *Employees:* 307
Previous: P & G Prestige Products Limited
Net Worth: £33,084,000 *Total Assets:* £106,194,000
Registered Office: Bradfield Road, Eureka Science Park, Ashford, Kent, TN25 4AQ
Activities: Wholesale of perfume and cosmetics
Officers: Emma Walters, Secretary; Vengadan Swaminathan [1977] Director; Emma Morag Dorothy Walters [1974] Director/Financial Controller

HFG Finance Limited
Incorporated: 21 September 2016
Net Worth: £321,763,456 *Total Assets:* £448,454,976
Registered Office: New Kings Court, Tollgate, Chandler's Ford, Eastleigh, Hants, SO53 3LG
Activities: Activities of other holding companies n.e.c.
Parent: Hoover Ferguson Group Limited
Officers: William Russell Brown [1981] Director/Investor [American]; Cornelius Dupre II [1952] Director/Attorney [American]; Timothy James Probert [1951] Director/Senior Advisor [British/American]; Neil Alan Wizel [1977] Managing Director [American]; Donald Win Young [1973] Director [American]

HFG Investments Limited
Incorporated: 21 September 2016
Net Worth: £446,067,808 *Total Assets:* £446,067,808
Registered Office: New Kings Court, Tollgate, Chandler's Ford, Eastleigh, Hants, SO53 3LG
Activities: Activities of other holding companies n.e.c.
Parent: HFG Finance Limited
Officers: William Russell Brown [1981] Director/Investor [American]; Cornelius Dupre II [1952] Director/Attorney [American]; Timothy James Probert [1951] Director/Senior Advisor [British/American]; Neil Alan Wizel [1977] Managing Director [American]; Donald Win Young [1973] Director [American]

HH Global Group Limited
Incorporated: 26 July 2017 *Employees:* 866
Net Worth: £96,801,000 *Total Assets:* £223,102,000
Registered Office: Grove House, Guildford Road, Fetcham, Leatherhead, Surrey, KT22 9DF
Activities: Activities of other holding companies n.e.c.
Major Shareholder: Robert John Fergus Macmillan
Officers: Reinhard Schu, Secretary; Justin Glenn Barton [1963] Director; Robert John Fergus Macmillan [1972] Director; Edward James Parsons [1967] Director

HH Global Limited
Incorporated: 27 February 2003 *Employees:* 877
Net Worth: £855,000 *Total Assets:* £92,304,000
Registered Office: Grove House, Guildford Road, Fetcham, Leatherhead, Surrey, KT22 9DF
Activities: Activities of other holding companies n.e.c.
Parent: HH Global Group Limited
Officers: Reinhard Schu, Secretary; Justin Glenn Barton [1963] Director; Nicholas William Dixon [1961] Director; Kevin Dunckley [1966] Technical Director; Lee Graham Humphreys [1976] Director; Robert John Fergus Macmillan [1972] Director; Stephen Christopher Charles Nunn [1963] Director CEO - EMEA; Edward James Parsons [1967] Financial Director; Michael Edward Perez [1973] Director [American]; Andrew John Price [1963] Director [Australian]

Hibu Group Limited
Incorporated: 13 December 2013 *Employees:* 3,493
Previous: Hibu Group 2013 Limited
Net Worth Deficit: £192,800,000 *Total Assets:* £362,200,000
Registered Office: 3 Forbury Place, Forbury Road, Reading, Berks, RG1 3YL
Activities: Other publishing activities
Officers: Christian Henry Wells, Secretary; David John Lane Freer Anderson [1956] Director/Banker; Atish Banerjea [1965] Director [American]; John W Brantl [1983] Director/Investment Analyst [American]; Robert Kenneth Hall [1975] Director; Alfred Thomas Mockett [1949] Director/Executive [American]; Christopher Stewart Ripley [1976] Director [Canadian]; Parminder Singh Sandhu [1968] Director; David William Henry Sharman [1963] Director

HIC Racing (Chiswick) Limited
Incorporated: 25 November 1981
Net Worth: £499,114,144 *Total Assets:* £499,137,952
Registered Office: Maple Court, Central Park, Reeds Crescent, Watford, Herts, WD24 4QQ
Activities: Non-trading company
Parent: Hilton Worldwide Holdings, Inc
Officers: Stuart Beasley [1971] Director/Financial Controller; Richard Geoffrey Beeston [1982] Director/Chartered Accountant; Michelle Momdjian [1976] Director/Attorney; George Christopher Ogle [1974] Director/Attorney; James Owen Percival [1968] Director/Accountant

HIC Treasury Limited
Incorporated: 29 June 1982
Net Worth: £512,404,288 *Total Assets:* £514,079,584
Registered Office: Maple Court, Central Park, Reeds Crescent, Watford, Herts, WD24 4QQ
Activities: Non-trading company
Parent: Hilton Finance (UK) Limited
Officers: Stuart Beasley [1971] Director/Financial Controller; Richard Geoffrey Beeston [1982] Director/Chartered Accountant; Michelle Momdjian [1976] Director/Attorney; George Christopher Ogle [1974] Director/Attorney; James Owen Percival [1968] Director/Accountant

HiFX Europe Limited
Incorporated: 26 February 1998 *Employees:* 184
Net Worth: £17,316,000 *Total Assets:* £68,876,000
Registered Office: Maxis, 1 Western Road, Bracknell, Berks, RG12 1RT
Activities: Financial intermediation not elsewhere classified
Parent: Euronet (London) UK Holdings Limited
Officers: Juan Cristobal Bianchi [1971] Managing Director [Chilean]; Marcela Del Socorro Gonzalez [1969] Managing Director; Richard Innes Hodgson [1971] Finance Director; Alison Ingrid Sparks [1971] Legal Director

Highway Management (Scotland) Holding Limited
Incorporated: 27 August 2008
Net Worth Deficit: £43,315,000 *Total Assets:* £321,515,008
Registered Office: Part First Floor, 1 Grenfell Road, Maidenhead, Berks, SL6 1HN
Activities: Financial intermediation not elsewhere classified
Parent: Highway Management M80 Investment Limited
Officers: Emeka Ikechi Ehenulo, Secretary; David Alexander John Foot [1968] Director, Infrastructure; Carlos Abuin Garcia [1985] Director/Investment Executive [Spanish]; Albert Hendrik Naafs [1965] Director [Dutch]; Frank Manfred Schramm [1968] Director [German]

Highway Management (Scotland) Limited
Incorporated: 27 August 2008
Net Worth Deficit: £43,315,000 *Total Assets:* £321,515,008
Registered Office: Part First Floor, 1 Grenfell Road, Maidenhead, Berks, SL6 1HN
Activities: Financial intermediation not elsewhere classified
Parent: Highway Management (Scotland) Holding Limited
Officers: Emeka Ikechi Ehenulo, Secretary; David Alexander John Foot [1968] Director, Infrastructure; Carlos Abuin Garcia [1985] Director/Investment Executive [Spanish]; Albert Hendrik Naafs [1965] Director [Dutch]; Frank Manfred Schramm [1968] Director [German]

Highway Management M80 Investment Limited
Incorporated: 29 September 2010
Net Worth Deficit: £47,395,000 *Total Assets:* £324,671,008
Registered Office: Part First Floor, 1 Grenfell Road, Maidenhead, Berks, SL6 1HN
Activities: Financial intermediation not elsewhere classified
Shareholders: Infrastructure Investments Holdings Limited; Highway Management M80 Topco Limited
Officers: Emeka Ikechi Ehenulo, Secretary; David Alexander John Foot [1968] Director, Infrastructure; Carlos Abuin Garcia [1985] Director/Investment Executive [Spanish]; Albert Hendrik Naafs [1965] Director [Dutch]; Frank Manfred Schramm [1968] Director [German]

Hilbre Holdings Limited
Incorporated: 5 March 2015 *Employees:* 939
Net Worth: £25,434,000 *Total Assets:* £66,326,000
Registered Office: Unit 2 Northbrook Industrial Estate, Vincent Avenue, Southampton, SO16 6PB
Activities: Activities of head offices
Officers: Peter Benjamin Thomas Armitage [1946] Non-Executive Director Chairman; Philip Iain Armitage [1970] Director; Richard Simon Armitage [1973] Director/Chartered Accountant; Nicholas Andrew Hilton [1961] Managing Director; Simon Reeve [1966] Director

Hill of The Hermitage Limited
Incorporated: 17 November 2015
Net Worth: £31,650,730 *Total Assets:* £31,672,452
Registered Office: The Old Casino, 28 Fourth Avenue, Hove, E Sussex, BN3 2PJ
Activities: Fund management activities
Major Shareholder: Andrew James Dixon
Officers: Andrew James Dixon [1968] Director/Angel Investor

Hill of Towie Limited
Incorporated: 6 July 2009
Net Worth Deficit: £16,366,000 *Total Assets:* £64,152,000
Registered Office: Beaufort Court, Egg Farm Lane, Kings Langley, Herts, WD4 8LR
Activities: Other business support service activities n.e.c.
Parent: Trafalgar Wind Holdings Limited
Officers: Dominic James Hearth, Secretary; Steven William Hughes [1972] Generation & Asset Management Director; Fraser Stephen Merry [1968] Director/Chartered Surveyor; Mitesh Raj Patel [1982] Director/Group Financial Controller

Hillier Nurseries Limited
Incorporated: 26 May 1976 *Employees:* 514
Net Worth: £13,919,592 *Total Assets:* £29,756,622
Registered Office: Ampfield House, Ampfield, Romsey, Hants, SO51 9PA
Activities: Wholesale of flowers and plants
Shareholders: Robert Trant Hillier; John Gifford Hillier
Officers: Hossein Arshadi [1954] Director; Christopher Francis [1964] Garden Centre Director; George Adam Matthew Hillier [1973] Director of Property; Martin John Hillier [1968] Director; Robert Trant Hillier [1943] Director; David Neil Holligon [1972] Director/Consultant; Gavin Joseph Marsh [1966] Finance Director

Hilton Finance (UK) Limited
Incorporated: 18 November 1999
Net Worth: £1,663,046,016 *Total Assets:* £1,676,255,104
Registered Office: Maple Court, Central Park, Reeds Crescent, Watford, Herts, WD24 4QQ
Activities: Other business support service activities n.e.c.
Parent: Hilton UK Hotels Limited
Officers: Stuart Beasley [1971] Director/Financial Controller; Richard Geoffrey Beeston [1982] Director/Chartered Accountant; Michelle Momdjian [1976] Director/Attorney; George Christopher Ogle [1974] Director/Attorney; James Owen Percival [1968] Director/Accountant

Hilton HHC Limited
Incorporated: 19 January 2006
Net Worth: £1,552,382,464 *Total Assets:* £1,552,382,464
Registered Office: Maple Court, Central Park, Reeds Crescent, Watford, Herts, WD24 4QQ
Activities: Activities of head offices
Parent: Hilton HIH Limited
Officers: Stuart Beasley [1971] Director/Financial Controller; Richard Geoffrey Beeston [1982] Director/Chartered Accountant; Michelle Momdjian [1976] Director/Attorney; George Christopher Ogle [1974] Director/Attorney; Brian McKay Wilson [1962] Director/Company Secretary

Hilton International Hotels (UK) Limited
Incorporated: 12 June 1961
Net Worth: £666,311,040 *Total Assets:* £1,487,772,288
Registered Office: Maple Court, Central Park, Reeds Crescent, Watford, Herts, WD24 4QQ
Activities: Hotels and similar accommodation
Parent: Hilton International IP Holding Limited
Officers: Stuart Beasley [1971] Director/Financial Controller; Richard Geoffrey Beeston [1982] Director/Chartered Accountant; Stephen Patrick Cassidy [1968] Director/SVP Operations UK & Ireland; Michelle Momdjian [1976] Director/Attorney; George Christopher Ogle [1974] Director/Attorney; James Owen Percival [1968] Director/Accountant; Simon Robert Vincent [1963] Director; Brian McKay Wilson [1962] Director/Company Secretary

Hilton International IP Holding 2 Limited
Incorporated: 6 December 2016
Net Worth: £2,394,365,184 *Total Assets:* £2,523,724,800
Registered Office: Maple Court, Central Park, Reeds Crescent, Watford, Herts, WD24 4QQ
Activities: Hotels and similar accommodation
Parent: Hilton International Master Holding Limited
Officers: Stuart Beasley [1971] Director/Financial Controller; Richard Geoffrey Beeston [1982] Director/Chartered Accountant; Stephen Patrick Cassidy [1968] Director/Senior Vice President Operations; Michelle Momdjian [1976] Director/Attorney; George Christopher Ogle [1974] Director/Attorney; James Owen Percival [1968] Director/Accountant; Brian McKay Wilson [1962] Director/Company Secretary

Hilton International IP Holding Limited
Incorporated: 8 July 2016
Net Worth: £2,694,447,104 *Total Assets:* £3,080,324,096
Registered Office: Maple Court, Central Park, Reeds Crescent, Watford, Herts, WD24 4QQ
Activities: Hotels and similar accommodation
Parent: Hilton International IP Holding 2 Limited
Officers: Stuart Beasley [1971] Director/Financial Controller; Richard Geoffrey Beeston [1982] Director/Chartered Accountant; Stephen Patrick Cassidy [1968] Director/Senior Vice President Operations; Michelle Momdjian [1976] Director/Attorney; George Christopher Ogle [1974] Director/Attorney; James Owen Percival [1968] Director/Accountant; Brian McKay Wilson [1962] Director/Company Secretary

Hilton UK Hotels Limited
Incorporated: 18 May 1904
Net Worth: £1,272,785,152 *Total Assets:* £1,338,172,928
Registered Office: Maple Court, Central Park, Reeds Crescent, Watford, Herts, WD24 4QQ
Activities: Hotels and similar accommodation
Parent: Hilton Worldwide Holding 2 Limited
Officers: Stuart Beasley [1971] Director/Financial Controller; Richard Geoffrey Beeston [1982] Director/Chartered Accountant; Stephen Patrick Cassidy [1968] Senior Vice President and Managing Director; Michelle Momdjian [1976] Director/Attorney; George Christopher Ogle [1974] Director/Attorney; James Owen Percival [1968] Director/Accountant; Simon Robert Vincent [1963] Director; Brian McKay Wilson [1962] Director/Company Secretary

Hilton UK Manage Limited
Incorporated: 15 October 2007
Net Worth: £28,088,258 *Total Assets:* £36,292,152
Registered Office: Maple Court, Central Park, Reeds Crescent, Watford, Herts, WD24 4QQ
Activities: Hotels and similar accommodation
Parent: Hilton Worldwide Limited
Officers: Stuart Beasley [1971] Director/Financial Controller; Richard Geoffrey Beeston [1982] Director/Chartered Accountant; Michelle Momdjian [1976] Director/Attorney; George Christopher Ogle [1974] Director/Attorney; James Owen Percival [1968] Director/Accountant; Simon Robert Vincent [1963] Director; Brian McKay Wilson [1962] Director/Company Secretary

Hilton Worldwide FS Treasury Limited
Incorporated: 18 February 2014
Net Worth: £9,563,753 *Total Assets:* £986,574,848
Registered Office: Maple Court, Central Park, Reeds Crescent, Watford, Herts, WD24 4QQ
Activities: Other business support service activities n.e.c.
Parent: Hilton Worldwide Manage Limited
Officers: Stuart Beasley [1971] Director/Financial Controller; Richard Geoffrey Beeston [1982] Director/Chartered Accountant; Stephen Patrick Cassidy [1968] Director/Senior Vice President Operations; Michelle Momdjian [1976] Director/Attorney; George Christopher Ogle [1974] Director/Attorney; James Owen Percival [1968] Director/Accountant; Brian McKay Wilson [1962] Director/Attorney

Hilton Worldwide Holding 2 Limited
Incorporated: 12 February 2014
Net Worth: £397,220,800 *Total Assets:* £2,394,284,288
Registered Office: Maple Court, Central Park, Reeds Crescent, Watford, Herts, WD24 4QQ
Activities: Hotels and similar accommodation
Parent: Hilton HHC Limited
Officers: Stuart Beasley [1971] Director/Financial Controller; Richard Geoffrey Beeston [1982] Director/Chartered Accountant; Stephen Patrick Cassidy [1968] Director/Senior Vice President Operations UK & Ireland; Michelle Momdjian [1976] Director/Attorney; George Christopher Ogle [1974] Director/Attorney; James Owen Percival [1968] Director/Accountant; Brian McKay Wilson [1962] Director/Attorney

Hilton Worldwide Holding LLP
Incorporated: 4 April 2014
Net Worth: £2,958,252,800 *Total Assets:* £2,958,253,056
Registered Office: Maple Court, Central Park, Reeds Crescent, Watford, Herts, WD24 4QQ

Hilton Worldwide Manage Limited
Incorporated: 7 December 2010 *Employees:* 32
Net Worth: £1,429,282,432 *Total Assets:* £2,571,142,144
Registered Office: Maple Court, Central Park, Reeds Crescent, Watford, Herts, WD24 4QQ
Activities: Hotels and similar accommodation
Shareholders: Hilton International IP Holding Limited; Hilton International Hotels (UK) Limited
Officers: Stuart Beasley [1971] Director/Financial Controller; Richard Geoffrey Beeston [1982] Director/Chartered Accountant; Stephen Patrick Cassidy [1968] Director/Senior Vice President Operations UK & Ireland; Michelle Momdjian [1976] Director/Attorney; George Christopher Ogle [1974] Director/Attorney; James Owen Percival [1968] Director/Accountant; Brian McKay Wilson [1962] Director/Company Secretary

F.Hinds Limited
Incorporated: 5 January 1918 *Employees:* 722
Net Worth: £28,058,012 *Total Assets:* £44,240,396
Registered Office: 24 Park Road, Uxbridge, Middlesex, UB8 1NH
Activities: Other retail sale of new goods in specialised stores (not commercial art galleries and opticians)
Parent: Hinds Ltd
Officers: Benedetto Mario Colucci [1959] Director/Retail Management; Stephen Barrie Cornwall [1970] Director/Chartered Accountant; Andrew Frank Hinds [1967] Director/Jeweller; David Royden Harcourt Hinds [1959] Director/Jeweller; Jeremy David Hinds [1987] Marketing Director; Neil Alexander Hinds [1960] Director/Chartered Surveyor; Paul Harcourt Hinds [1986] IT Director; Martin Jeffrey Preston [1962] Director/Jeweller

Hinds Ltd
Incorporated: 11 April 2002 *Employees:* 726
Net Worth: £36,342,864 *Total Assets:* £53,229,980
Registered Office: 24 Park Road, Uxbridge, Middlesex, UB8 1NH
Activities: Activities of head offices
Shareholder: Andrew Frank Hinds
Officers: Stephen Barrie Cornwall, Secretary; Andrew Frank Hinds [1967] Director/Retail Jeweller; David Royden Harcourt Hinds [1959] Retail Jeweller (Managing Director); Neil Alexander Hinds [1960] Director/Chartered Surveyor

Hireco (TL) Limited
Incorporated: 6 January 1998 *Employees:* 33
Net Worth: £11,296,738 *Total Assets:* £49,794,180
Registered Office: Unit 2 Colthrop Lane, Thatcham, Berks, RG19 4NN
Activities: Freight transport by road
Officers: Patrick Joseph Carson, Secretary; George Gerard Boyd [1960] Director; Patrick Joseph Carson [1951] Director [Irish]; James Phillip Smith [1975] Director; Derek Whelan [1975] Director/Businessman [Irish]

Historic House Hotels Limited
Incorporated: 30 July 1979 *Employees:* 233
Net Worth: £18,704,148 *Total Assets:* £20,545,322
Registered Office: Hartwell House, Oxford Road, Hartwell, Aylesbury, Bucks, HP17 8NR
Activities: Hotels and similar accommodation
Officers: Neil James Kenyon, Secretary; Richard Broyd [1948] Director; Lionel Antoine Joseph Chatard [1972] Hotel Director [French]; Chris John Feeney [1963] Director/Accountant; Matthew Anthony Chadwick Johnson [1971] Director/Manager; Jacqueline Emily Jordan [1968] Director; Neil James Kenyon [1974] Finance Director; Elgan Lloyd Roberts [1971] Director/Hotel General Manager; Sarah Elizabeth Staniforth [1953] Historic Properties Director; Peter Jules Maria Vermeulen [1975] Director of Finance

Hitachi Capital (UK) PLC
Incorporated: 21 April 1982 *Employees:* 1,238
Net Worth: £590,600,000 *Total Assets:* £5,090,800,128
Registered Office: Hitachi Capital House, Thorpe Road, Staines upon Thames, Surrey, TW18 3HP
Activities: Financial leasing
Parent: Hitachi Capital Corporation
Officers: John Nathaniel McDowall Sims, Secretary; Hiroyuki Fukuro [1958] Director [Japanese]; Robert Douglas Gordon [1961] Director [Australian]; Alan Renatus Frederick Hughes [1951] Director; Gavin Russell Cameron Munnoch [1952] Director; Yoshikazu Ohashi [1962] Director [Japanese]; Anne Whitaker [1958] Director

Hitachi Europe Limited
Incorporated: 13 January 1988 *Employees:* 281
Net Worth: £173,551,008 *Total Assets:* £692,308,992
Registered Office: Whitebrook Park, Lower Cookham Road, Maidenhead, Berks, SL6 8YA
Activities: Other business support service activities n.e.c.
Parent: Hitachi, Ltd.
Officers: Carl William Newton, Secretary; Sir Stephen John Gomersall [1948] Director/Deputy Chairman; Yozo Ito [1965] Director [Japanese]; Naotoshi Nishida [1967] Managing Director [Japanese]; Yoshiyuki Ogura [1957] Director/Chairman [Japanese]; Stephen Keith Pierce [1963] Director/Chief HR Officer

Hitachi Vantara Limited
Incorporated: 3 January 1989 *Employees:* 440
Previous: Hitachi Data Systems Limited
Net Worth: £89,360,000 *Total Assets:* £362,460,000
Registered Office: Sefton Park, Stoke Poges, Bucks, SL2 4HD
Activities: Other information technology service activities
Parent: Hitachi Ltd.
Officers: Nicolas Boin, Secretary; Richard Paul Bradbury [1970] UK and Ireland Managing Director; Richard Gadd [1969] Managing Director; Elena Gifon [1976] Director/Financial Controller [German]

The HMS Trincomalee Trust
Incorporated: 16 January 1992 *Employees:* 14
Net Worth: £21,468,086 *Total Assets:* £21,589,668
Registered Office: NMRN PP66, Stoney Lane, HM Naval Base, Portsmouth, PO1 3NH
Activities: Museums activities
Parent: National Museum of The Royal Navy
Officers: Richard Paul Hatfield [1953] Director; Caroline Anne McDonald [1970] Director/Museum Manager; Richard Timothy Schadla-Hall [1947] Director/Lecturer

The HMS Victory Preservation Company
Incorporated: 3 February 2012
Net Worth: £61,825,244 *Total Assets:* £62,190,632
Registered Office: National Museum of The Royal Navy, Portsmouth Historic Dockyard, HM Naval Base, Portsmouth, PO1 3NH
Activities: Operation of historical sites and buildings and similar visitor attractions
Parent: National Museum of The Royal Navy
Officers: Captain John Rees, Secretary; Michael Cecil Boyce [1943] Director/House of Lords; Mark Frederick Caroe [1961] Director/Venture Capitalist; Charles Julian Cazalet [1947] Director; Jim Higham [1969] Director/Royal Navy; Amjad Mazhar Hussain [1958] Director/Engineer; Tim Laurence [1955] Director; Jamie Graham Matheson [1954] Director/Executive Chairman; Charles Percival Ross Montgomery [1955] Director/Retired; Clive Duncan Thorne [1952] Director/Solicitor; Dr Caroline Ann Williams [1954] Director/Solicitor

Hobbs Brook Limited
Incorporated: 24 March 2004
Net Worth: £28,643,000 *Total Assets:* £28,919,000
Registered Office: 1 Windsor Dials, Windsor, Berks, SL4 1RS
Activities: Other letting and operating of own or leased real estate
Officers: Amy Kelly, Secretary; Kevin Scott Ingram [1962] Director [American]; Thomas Alan Lawson [1956] Director/Insurance Executive [American]; Jonathan Irving Mishara [1961] Director/General Counsel [American]

Richard Hochfeld Limited
Incorporated: 29 June 1936 *Employees:* 50
Net Worth Deficit: £5,472,042 *Total Assets:* £30,856,096
Registered Office: Orchard Place, Comp Road, Borough Green, Sevenoaks, Kent, TN15 8LW
Activities: Retail sale of fruit and vegetables in specialised stores
Officers: Colin Thomas Barber, Company Secretary; Alan Claude Guindi [1961] Director; Christian Sean Guindi [1968] Director; Edward Charles Hickford [1953] Finance Director

Richard Hochfeld Management Limited
Incorporated: 2 August 2004 *Employees:* 68
Net Worth Deficit: £1,208,719 *Total Assets:* £36,207,264
Registered Office: Bidborough Close, Franks Hollow Road, Bidborough Close, Tunbridge Wells, Kent, TN3 0UD
Activities: Financial management
Shareholder: Alan Claude Guindi
Officers: Colin Thomas Barber, Secretary/Director; Colin Thomas Barber [1948] Director; Alan Claude Guindi [1961] Director; Christian Sean Guindi [1968] Director

Hodgson Automotive Limited
Incorporated: 16 November 1998 *Employees:* 438
Net Worth: £26,814,956 *Total Assets:* £76,274,912
Registered Office: Chandlers, Victoria Road, Brighton, BN41 1YH
Activities: Sale of new cars and light motor vehicles
Officers: Darryl Burman, Secretary; Darryl Michael Burman [1958] Director/Lawyer [American]; Darren Guiver [1968] Director; Earl Julius Hesterberg [1953] Director [American]; Daniel James McHenry [1974] Finance Director; John Rickel [1961] Director [American]

Hoechst Marion Roussel Limited
Incorporated: 29 June 1994 *Employees:* 2
Net Worth: £449,006,016 *Total Assets:* £480,816,000
Registered Office: One Onslow Street, Guildford, Surrey, GU1 4YS
Activities: Wholesale of pharmaceutical goods
Parent: Aventis Pharma Holdings Limited
Officers: Francois-Xavier Duhalde [1965] Director/Chief Financial Officer [French]; Hugo Rupert Alexander Fry [1970] Director/UK Country Chair

Hogg Robinson (Travel) Limited
Incorporated: 1 November 1976 *Employees:* 1,100
Net Worth: £72,179,064 *Total Assets:* £131,091,992
Registered Office: Spectrum Point, 279 Farnborough Road, Farnborough, Hants, GU14 7NJ
Activities: Travel agency activities
Parent: Hogg Robinson PLC
Officers: William Francis Brindle [1961] Director; Ian Michael Windsor [1960] Director

Hogg Robinson Group Limited
Incorporated: 13 March 2000 *Employees:* 4,205
Previous: Hogg Robinson Group PLC
Net Worth: £90,900,000 *Total Assets:* £505,300,000
Registered Office: Spectrum Point, 279 Farnborough Road, Farnborough, Hants, GU14 7NJ
Activities: Activities of head offices
Parent: Global Business Travel Holdings Limited
Officers: Nicola Jane Cole, Secretary; Eric J. Bock [1965] Director/Chief Legal Officer [American]; William Francis Brindle [1961] Director; Martine Gerow [1960] Director [French]; Joanna Sutherland MacLeod [1967] Director/Executive Vice President, Global Service Delivery

Hogg Robinson Limited
Incorporated: 6 March 1987 *Employees:* 1,365
Previous: Hogg Robinson PLC
Net Worth: £255,800,000 *Total Assets:* £519,100,000
Registered Office: Spectrum Point, 279 Farnborough Road, Farnborough, Hants, GU14 7NJ
Activities: Activities of head offices
Parent: Farnborough Limited
Officers: William Francis Brindle [1961] Director; Matthew Charles Pancaldi [1969] Director; James George Allsebrook Stevenson [1967] Director; Ian Michael Windsor [1960] Director

Hogg Robinson Money Matters Limited
Incorporated: 28 February 1957
Net Worth: £7,126,737 *Total Assets:* £102,499,792
Registered Office: Spectrum Point, 279 Farnborough Road, Farnborough, Hants, GU14 7NJ
Activities: Activities of head offices
Parent: Hogg Robinson (Travel) Limited
Officers: Aymeric Gibon [1980] Director/Vice President [French]; Sheena Varma [1980] Director/Senior Counsel, EMEA

Holiday Extras Investments Limited
Incorporated: 28 March 2011 *Employees:* 965
Net Worth: £20,369,000 *Total Assets:* £127,729,000
Registered Office: Ashford Road, Newingreen, Hythe, Kent, CT21 4JF
Activities: Other service activities n.e.c.
Officers: Andrew Mark Metson Parker, Secretary; David Thomas Kelly [1963] Director; Jeremy Christopher Pack [1988] Director; Matthew Geoffrey Pack [1976] Director; Andrew Mark Metson Parker [1974] Director; Margaret Frances Rice-Jones [1961] Director; Mark William Smith [1955] Non-Executive Director

Holiday Extras Limited
Incorporated: 21 January 1983 *Employees:* 668
Net Worth: £21,218,000 *Total Assets:* £118,374,000
Registered Office: Ashford Road, Newingreen, Hythe, Kent, CT21 4JF
Activities: Other service activities n.e.c.
Officers: Andrew John Britcliffe [1979] Director; Ian Matthew Copley [1976] Director; Anna Elizabeth Divers [1971] Director; Howard Dove [1970] Director; Sean Arthur Hagger [1983] Commercial Director; Simon Peter Hagger [1974] Director; Adrian Bruce Kemsley [1958] Director; David Conrad Norris [1969] Director; Matthew Geoffrey Pack [1976] Director/Chief Executive Officer; Andrew Mark Metson Parker [1974] Director; Matthew Neil Paxton [1972] Director/Chief Operations Officer

Holly Lodge (Kingswood) Limited
Incorporated: 21 May 1993 *Employees:* 2
Net Worth: £1,040,130 *Total Assets:* £24,475,440
Registered Office: Sterling House, 27 Hatchlands Road, Redhill, Surrey, RH1 6RW
Activities: Recreational vehicle parks, trailer parks and camping grounds
Major Shareholder: John Anthony Sargeant
Officers: John Anthony Sargeant [1945] Director/Mobile Home Park Management

Hollywood Bowl Group PLC
Incorporated: 13 June 2016 *Employees:* 2,044
Net Worth: £94,938,000 *Total Assets:* £153,584,000
Registered Office: Focus 31 West Wing, Cleveland Road, Hemel Hempstead Industrial Estate, Hemel Hempstead, Herts, HP2 7BW
Activities: Other sports activities
Officers: Nicholas Paul Backhouse [1963] Director; Peter Ashley Boddy [1965] Director; Stephen Burns [1976] Director/Chief Executive; Laurence Brian Keen [1976] Finance Director; Ivan Schofield [1967] Director; Claire Tiney [1960] Director

Holophane Europe Limited
Incorporated: 29 March 1965 *Employees:* 103
Net Worth: £4,434,934 *Total Assets:* £21,915,646
Registered Office: Bond Avenue, Bletchley, Milton Keynes, Bucks, MK1 1JG
Activities: Manufacture of electric lighting equipment
Officers: Alasdair Roderick McRury [1956] Managing Director; Richard Kent Reece [1956] Director/Executive Vice President [American]

Holroyd Howe Limited
Incorporated: 17 February 1997 *Employees:* 1,698
Net Worth: £33,229,000 *Total Assets:* £54,516,000
Registered Office: TVP2, 300 Thames Valley Park Drive, Reading, Berks, RG6 1PT
Activities: Other food services
Parent: Westbury Street Limited
Officers: Marc Bradley, Secretary/Director; Marc Bradley [1975] Director; Ronan Brian Harte [1970] Managing Director [Irish]; Nicholas Adrian Howe [1959] Director/Contract Caterer; Alastair Dunbar Storey [1953] Director

Holtzbrinck Investment Limited
Incorporated: 19 June 2014
Net Worth: £58,722,000 *Total Assets:* £154,875,008
Registered Office: Cromwell Place, Hampshire International Business Park, Lime Tree Way, Basingstoke, Hants, RG24 8YJ
Activities: Dormant company
Shareholders: Stefan von Holtzbrinck; Christiane Schoeller
Officers: Gabrielle Williams Hamer, Secretary; Simon Peter Darlington-Cramond [1956] Director; Jens Herbert Schwanewedel [1968] Commercial Director [German]; Jonathan Clifford Treadway [1979] Director, Operational Strategy

Home and Comforts Limited
Incorporated: 22 September 2011
Net Worth: £9,442,000 *Total Assets:* £27,512,000
Registered Office: 2 AC Court, High Street, Thames Ditton, Surrey, KT7 0SR
Activities: Other service activities n.e.c.
Parent: Home and Comforts Holdings Limited
Officers: Alan Albert Horton [1963] Director; Stuart Pace [1962] Director

Home and Legacy Insurance Services Limited
Incorporated: 9 January 1995 *Employees:* 90
Net Worth: £17,090,556 *Total Assets:* £29,334,260
Registered Office: 57 Ladymead, Guildford, Surrey, GU1 1DB
Activities: Activities of insurance agents and brokers
Parent: Allianz Holdings PLC
Officers: Robin Christian Jack-Kee, Secretary; Gary Edward Davess [1963] Director, Speciality; Adrian Garry Ewington [1974] Director/Underwriting and Product Manager; Kathryn Hayley Fryer [1985] Operations Director; Barry O'Neill [1963] Managing Director; Mark Wooldridge [1964] Sales and Marketing Director

Home Grown Hotels Limited
Incorporated: 6 June 2011 *Employees:* 446
Net Worth: £8,782,006 *Total Assets:* £55,176,340
Registered Office: Clayhill, Beechen Lane, Lyndhurst, Hants, SO43 7DD
Activities: Hotels and similar accommodation
Shareholders: James Arthur Ratcliffe; Robin Charles Hutson
Officers: Michael John Rice, Secretary; Peter Harrison Chittick [1957] Director [Canadian]; James William Dawson [1944] Director; David Roger Elton [1960] Director; Brian Robert Foster [1957] Director; Angela Maria Hartnett [1968] Director/Chef Proprietor; Robin Charles Hutson [1957] Director; Vikki Alison Jerram [1985] Director; Thomas Benjamin Ross [1975] Director

Home Retail Group (Finance) LLP
Incorporated: 21 January 2011
Net Worth: £200,362,000 *Total Assets:* £200,362,000
Registered Office: 489-499 Avebury Boulevard, Milton Keynes, Bucks, MK9 2NW

Home Retail Group (UK) Limited
Incorporated: 13 June 2006 *Employees:* 2
Net Worth: £2,005,330,944 *Total Assets:* £2,790,338,048
Registered Office: 489-499 Avebury Boulevard, Milton Keynes, Bucks, MK9 2NW
Activities: Other business support service activities n.e.c.
Parent: Home Retail Group Limited
Officers: Timothy Fallowfield, Secretary; Claire Louise Catlin [1980] Director; John Terence Rogers [1968] Director

Home Retail Group Card Services Limited
Incorporated: 2 June 2000 *Employees:* 654
Net Worth Deficit: £14,264,000 *Total Assets:* £788,092,992
Registered Office: 489-499 Avebury Boulevard, Milton Keynes, Bucks, MK9 2NW
Activities: Credit granting by non-deposit taking finance houses and other specialist consumer credit grantors
Parent: Sainsbury's Bank PLC
Officers: Donald Hamish MacLeod McNaughton, Secretary; Katherine Carlson [1973] Commercial Director; Mark Christopher Hemus [1976] Finance and Credit Risk Director

Home Retail Group Insurance Services Limited
Incorporated: 16 November 2000
Net Worth: £21,000 *Total Assets:* £29,932,000
Registered Office: 489-499 Avebury Boulevard, Milton Keynes, Bucks, MK9 2NW
Activities: Financial intermediation not elsewhere classified
Parent: Sainsbury's Bank PLC
Officers: Donald Hamish MacLeod McNaughton, Secretary; Katherine Carlson [1973] Commercial Director; Mark Christopher Hemus [1976] Finance and Credit Risk Director

Home Retail Group Limited
Incorporated: 30 June 2006
Previous: Home Retail Group PLC
Net Worth: £748,099,968 *Total Assets:* £2,453,499,904
Registered Office: 489-499 Avebury Boulevard, Milton Keynes, Bucks, MK9 2NW
Activities: Activities of head offices
Parent: Sainsbury's Intermediate Holdings Limited
Officers: Timothy Fallowfield, Secretary; Claire Louise Catlin [1980] Director; John Terence Rogers [1968] Director

Homesun Limited
Incorporated: 1 July 2010
Net Worth: £3,439,085 *Total Assets:* £23,434,332
Registered Office: The Green, Easter Park, Benyon Road, Reading, Berks, RG7 2PQ
Activities: Production of electricity
Parent: Aviva Investors Realm Infrastructure No.1 Limited
Officers: Fergus James Helliwell [1981] Director/Fund Manager; Darryl Guy Murphy [1966] Director/Investment Professional; Ian Shervell [1978] Director

Honda Finance Europe PLC
Incorporated: 4 December 1996 *Employees:* 83
Net Worth: £228,224,000 *Total Assets:* £1,122,119,936
Registered Office: Cain Road, Bracknell, Berks, RG12 1HL
Activities: Other credit granting n.e.c.
Parent: Honda Motor Europe Limited
Officers: Ian Howells, Secretary/Finance Manager; Eiji Fujimura [1970] Director [Japanese]; David Hodgetts [1959] Director; Ian Howells [1962] Director; Masamitsu Kobayashi [1959] Director [Japanese]; Hideaki Ueno [1966] Director [Japanese]

Honda Motor Europe Limited
Incorporated: 1 September 1965 *Employees:* 8,938
Net Worth Deficit: £98,811,000 *Total Assets:* £4,639,191,040
Registered Office: Cain Road, Bracknell, Berks, RG12 1HL
Activities: Sale of new cars and light motor vehicles
Parent: Honda Motor Co.Ltd
Officers: Ian Howells, Secretary/Finance Manager; Thomas Gardner [1964] Director; Ian Howells [1962] Director/Chartered Accountant; Kogen Iguchi [1968] Director [Japanese]; Katsushi Inoue [1963] Managing Director [Japanese]; Jun Nishimoto [1962] Managing Director [Japanese]

Honda Trading Europe Limited
Incorporated: 31 January 1990 *Employees:* 84
Net Worth: £35,778,000 *Total Assets:* £123,634,000
Registered Office: Cain Road, Bracknell, Berks, RG12 1HL
Activities: Wholesale of metals and metal ores
Parent: Honda Motor Co. Ltd
Officers: Ian Howells, Secretary/Finance Manager; Kotaro Fujiwara [1970] Director [Japanese]; Yoshiyuki Kurachi [1960] Managing Director [Japanese]; Kazunari Tsuruhigashi [1964] Director [Japanese]

Honey Monster Foods Limited
Incorporated: 13 September 2006 *Employees:* 2
Net Worth: £23,425,000 *Total Assets:* £26,594,000
Registered Office: Benecol Limited, The Mille, 1000 Great West Road, Brentford, Middlesex, TW8 9DW
Activities: Manufacture of breakfast cereals and cereals-based food
Parent: Big Bear Group Limited
Officers: Merja Sisko Lumme [1961] Director/VP Human Resources [Finnish]; Iiro Tapio Wester [1963] Director/Chief Commercial Officer [Finnish]

Honeywell Acquisitions II Limited
Incorporated: 6 January 2006
Net Worth: £737,715,968 *Total Assets:* £1,012,302,016
Registered Office: Honeywell House, Skimped Hill Lane, Bracknell, Berks, RG12 1EB
Activities: Activities of other holding companies n.e.c.
Parent: Novar Europe Limited
Officers: Dagmar Klimentova [1980] Director [Czech]

Honeywell Acquisitions Limited
Incorporated: 22 December 2004
Net Worth: £394,883,008 *Total Assets:* £1,118,036,992
Registered Office: Honeywell House, Skimped Hill Lane, Bracknell, Berks, RG12 1EB
Activities: Activities of other holding companies n.e.c.
Parent: Honeywell Group Holding UK II
Officers: Dagmar Klimentova [1980] Director [Czech]

Honeywell Analytics Limited
Incorporated: 3 June 1946 *Employees:* 225
Net Worth: £32,071,000 *Total Assets:* £244,958,000
Registered Office: Honeywell House, Skimped Hill Lane, Bracknell, Berks, RG12 1EB
Activities: Agents specialised in the sale of other particular products
Parent: Honeywell International Inc.
Officers: Adrian Patrick Fulford [1961] Director/Site Leader; Thomas Christian Gafner [1965] Director/Financial Controller [Swiss]; Hicham Khellafi [1979] Director [French]

Honeywell Avionics Systems Limited
Incorporated: 3 September 1987 *Employees:* 129
Net Worth: £53,131,000 *Total Assets:* £111,527,000
Registered Office: Honeywell House, Skimped Hill Lane, Bracknell, Berks, RG12 1EB
Activities: Other service activities n.e.c.
Parent: Honeywell Limited
Officers: Anthony Richard Vaughan Hutchings [1956] Director; Adrian John Paull [1959] Director

Honeywell Control Systems Limited
Incorporated: 27 November 1926 *Employees:* 1,606
Net Worth: £239,344,992 *Total Assets:* £490,540,992
Registered Office: Honeywell House, Skimped Hill Lane, Bracknell, Berks, RG12 1EB
Activities: Other business support service activities n.e.c.
Parent: Honeywell Limited
Officers: David Juggins [1972] Director; David Andrew Kay [1973] Director; Sarah Rachel Martin [1973] Product Director; James McKenna [1968] Product Director [Irish]; Sharon Treanor [1974] Director; John J Tus [1958] Director [American]

Honeywell Europe Finance Limited
Incorporated: 31 March 2006
Net Worth: £142,331,008 *Total Assets:* £146,272,000
Registered Office: Honeywell House, Skimped Hill Lane, Bracknell, Berks, RG12 1EB
Activities: Banks
Parent: Honeywell International Inc.
Officers: Robert Foldi [1975] Director/General Manager [Hungarian]; Laszlo Petranyi [1963] Director [Hungarian]

Honeywell Group Holding UK
Incorporated: 8 December 1999
Net Worth: £344,206,016 *Total Assets:* £865,548,992
Registered Office: Honeywell House, Skimped Hill Lane, Bracknell, Berks, RG12 1EB
Activities: Activities of other holding companies n.e.c.
Parent: Honeywell International Inc.
Officers: Ashish Kumar Saraf [1979] Director [Indian]

Honeywell Group Holding UK II
Incorporated: 14 December 1999
Net Worth: £878,462,016 *Total Assets:* £1,700,272,000
Registered Office: Honeywell House, Skimped Hill Lane, Bracknell, Berks, RG12 1EB
Activities: Activities of other holding companies n.e.c.
Parent: Garrett Thermal Systems UK Limited
Officers: Dagmar Klimentova [1980] Director [Czech]

Honeywell Group Ltd
Incorporated: 24 July 1997
Net Worth: £1,229,993,984 *Total Assets:* £1,268,519,040
Registered Office: Honeywell House, Skimped Hill Lane, Bracknell, Berks, RG12 1EB
Activities: Activities of other holding companies n.e.c.
Parent: Honeywell Group Holding UK
Officers: David Juggins [1972] Director; David Andrew Kay [1973] Director; Dagmar Klimentova [1980] Director [Czech]; Sharon Treanor [1974] Director

Honeywell Holdings Limited
Incorporated: 8 May 1998
Net Worth: £11,685,000 *Total Assets:* £46,383,000
Registered Office: Honeywell House, Skimped Hill Lane, Bracknell, Berks, RG12 1EB
Activities: Activities of other holding companies n.e.c.
Parent: Honeywell Acquisitions II Limited
Officers: Jonathan Michael Turner [1968] Director/Chartered Surveyor

Honeywell International UK Limited
Incorporated: 11 August 1903
Net Worth: £200,931,008 *Total Assets:* £654,585,024
Registered Office: Honeywell House, Skimped Hill Lane, Bracknell, Berks, RG12 1EB
Activities: Activities of other holding companies n.e.c.
Parent: Honeywell Group Holding UK II
Officers: Marie Astrid Dubois [1961] Director [French]; Dagmar Klimentova [1980] Director [Czech]

Honeywell Limited
Incorporated: 9 November 1936
Net Worth: £65,342,000 *Total Assets:* £168,220,000
Registered Office: Honeywell House, Skimped Hill Lane, Bracknell, Berks, RG12 1EB
Activities: Activities of other holding companies n.e.c.
Parent: Honeywell Holdings Limited
Officers: David Juggins [1972] Director; David Andrew Kay [1973] Director

Honeywell Normalair-Garrett (Holdings) Limited
Incorporated: 15 March 1946 *Employees:* 600
Net Worth: £89,642,000 *Total Assets:* £210,480,000
Registered Office: Honeywell House, Skimped Hill Lane, Bracknell, Berks, RG12 1EB
Activities: Other business support service activities n.e.c.
Parent: Honeywell International UK Limited
Officers: Anthony Richard Vaughan Hutchings [1956] Director; David Mark Orton [1964] Director/Engineer

Honeywell North Atlantic Holdings Limited
Incorporated: 9 November 2006
Net Worth: £550,222,976 *Total Assets:* £600,358,016
Registered Office: Honeywell House, Skimped Hill Lane, Bracknell, Berks, RG12 1EB
Activities: Activities of other holding companies n.e.c.
Parent: Honeywell International Inc.
Officers: Dagmar Klimentova [1980] Director [Czech]; John J Tus [1958] Director [American]

Honeywell Safety Products International Ltd.
Incorporated: 20 November 2013
Net Worth: £535,970,944 *Total Assets:* £961,805,568
Registered Office: Honeywell House, Skimped Hill Lane, Bracknell, Berks, RG12 1EB
Activities: Activities of other holding companies n.e.c.
Parent: Honeywell International Inc.
Officers: Hicham Khellafi [1979] Director [French]; Sofiane Laoussadi [1967] Director [American]; John Daniel Romano Jr [1972] Director [American]; Sharon Treanor [1974] Director

Honeywell Security UK Limited
Incorporated: 12 March 1976 *Employees:* 116
Net Worth: £14,059,000 *Total Assets:* £36,002,000
Registered Office: Honeywell House, Skimped Hill Lane, Bracknell, Berks, RG12 1EB
Activities: Other manufacturing n.e.c.
Parent: Pittway UK Limited
Officers: Frederic Raoul Ann-Marie Haegeman [1975] Director [Belgian]; Piyush Jayantilal Kanji Jutha [1972] Director; Simon Jeremy Michael Kimber [1958] Marketing Director

Honeywell Specialty Wax & Additives Limited
Incorporated: 21 March 1917
Net Worth: £5,908,000 *Total Assets:* £41,700,000
Registered Office: Honeywell House, Skimped Hill Lane, Bracknell, Berks, RG12 1EB
Activities: Activities of other holding companies n.e.c.
Parent: ABI Acquisition 2 Limited
Officers: Glen William Davies [1956] Director; John J Tus [1958] Director [American]

Honeywell UK Limited
Incorporated: 7 June 1935 *Employees:* 165
Net Worth: £174,888,000 *Total Assets:* £337,739,008
Registered Office: Honeywell House, Skimped Hill Lane, Bracknell, Berks, RG12 1EB
Activities: Machining
Parent: Honeywell International UK Limited
Officers: Anthony Richard Vaughan Hutchings [1956] Director; Dagmar Klimentova [1980] Director [Czech]; John J Tus [1958] Director [American]; Melvyn Scott White [1954] Director

Hoover Ferguson Group Holdings Limited
Incorporated: 21 September 2016
Net Worth: £453,878,720 *Total Assets:* £453,896,800
Registered Office: New Kings Court, Tollgate, Chandler's Ford, Eastleigh, Hants, SO53 3LG
Activities: Activities of other holding companies n.e.c.
Parent: HFG Investments Limited
Officers: William Russell Brown [1981] Director/Investor [American]; Cornelius Dupre II [1952] Director/Attorney [American]; Timothy James Probert [1951] Director/Senior Advisor [British/American]; Neil Alan Wizel [1977] Managing Director [American]; Donald Win Young [1973] Director [American]

Hoover Ferguson Group Limited
Incorporated: 20 September 2016 *Employees:* 500
Net Worth: £111,627,120 *Total Assets:* £453,673,824
Registered Office: New Kings Court, Tollgate, Chandler's Ford, Eastleigh, Hants, SO53 3LG
Activities: Activities of other holding companies n.e.c.
Officers: William Russell Brown [1981] Director/Investor [American]; Cornelius Dupre II [1952] Director/Attorney [American]; Timothy James Probert [1951] Director/Senior Advisor [British/American]; Neil Alan Wizel [1977] Managing Director [American]; Donald Win Young [1973] Director [American]

Horder Healthcare
Incorporated: 28 April 1995 *Employees:* 396
Net Worth: £65,250,000 *Total Assets:* £70,395,000
Registered Office: St Johns Road, Crowborough, E Sussex, TN6 1XP
Activities: Hospital activities
Officers: Henry Ian Hatfield, Secretary; Dr Catherine Elisabeth Dorcas Bell [1951] Director; Sarah Elizabeth Brown [1943] Director; Rosemary Cunningham Thomas [1963] Director; Steven Louis Dance [1957] Director; Peter Alan Flamank [1956] Director/Chartered Accountant; Dr Susan Jane Grieve [1954] Director/Solicitor; Amanda Louise Parker [1961] Director; Peter Julius Soer [1965] Director; John William Turner [1962] Director; Richard John Tyler [1963] Director/Chief Executive; Dr David William Yates [1954] Director

Horlicks Limited
Incorporated: 11 December 1925
Net Worth: £79,499,000 *Total Assets:* £79,499,000
Registered Office: 980 Great West Road, Brentford, Middlesex, TW8 9GS
Activities: Other business support service activities n.e.c.
Parent: SmithKline Beecham Limited
Officers: Adam Walker [1967] Director

Hornby Hobbies Limited
Incorporated: 17 October 1986 *Employees:* 139
Net Worth Deficit: £5,296,000 *Total Assets:* £55,248,000
Registered Office: 3rd Floor, The Gateway, Innovation Way, Discovery Park, Sandwich, Kent, CT13 9FF
Activities: Manufacture of other games and toys, n.e.c.
Parent: Hornby PLC
Officers: Kirstie Elaine Gould, Secretary; Lyndon Davies [1960] Director/Chief Executive; Kirstie Elaine Gould [1973] Finance Director

Hornby PLC
Incorporated: 25 February 1981 *Employees:* 163
Net Worth: £30,864,000 *Total Assets:* £35,923,000
Registered Office: 3rd Floor, The Gateway, Innovation Way, Discovery Park, Sandwich, Kent, CT13 9FF
Activities: Manufacture of other games and toys, n.e.c.
Parent: Phoenix Asset Management Partners Limited
Officers: Kirstie Elaine Gould, Secretary; Lyndon Davies [1960] Director/Chief Executive; Martin Peter George [1962] Director; Kirstie Elaine Gould [1973] Finance Director; John Watson Stansfield [1954] Director; James Edward Hully Wilson [1985] Director/Analyst

The Horse Trust
Incorporated: 16 December 1938
Net Worth: £26,224,564 *Total Assets:* £26,617,376
Registered Office: Westcroft Stables, Slad Lane, Lacey Green, Princes Risborough, Bucks, HP27 0PP
Activities: Veterinary activities
Officers: Jeanette Allen, Secretary; Professor Mark Bowen [1973] Director/Veterinary Surgeon; Professor Peter Clegg [1962] Director/Veterinary Surgeon; David Allan Hancock Cook [1946] Director/Retired; Lord Rupert Charles de Mauley [1957] Director/Retired; Bronwen Jones [1963] Director/Solicitor; Christopher James William Marriott [1944] Director/Chartered Surveyor; Professor Bruce Campbell McGorum [1961] Director/Veterinary Surgeon; Rupert Hugh Maxwell Neal [1952] Director/Investment Manager; Professor Julian David Slater [1962] Director/Veterinary Surgeon; Camilla Rose Soames [1960] Director/Farmer

Horsted Estates Limited
Incorporated: 25 November 2013 *Employees:* 282
Net Worth: £52,984,888 *Total Assets:* £57,372,200
Registered Office: East Sussex National, Little Horsted, Uckfield, E Sussex, TN22 5ES
Activities: Activities of other holding companies n.e.c.
Major Shareholder: Michael John Hunt
Officers: Simon Derek Rebbetts, Secretary; Chester John Hunt [1969] Director; Michael John Hunt [1934] Director; Deborah Susan Jenkins [1964] Director

Hospira UK Limited
Incorporated: 18 June 1985 *Employees:* 70
Net Worth: £25,724,000 *Total Assets:* £30,085,000
Registered Office: Horizon, Honey Lane, Hurley, Maidenhead, Berks, SL6 6RJ
Activities: Manufacture of basic pharmaceutical products
Parent: Pfizer Limited
Officers: Ian Eric Franklin [1965] Director/Accountant; Ben John Osborn [1977] Director; Edwin James Pearson [1974] Director/Solicitor

The Hospital Company (Southmead) Holdings Limited
Incorporated: 19 November 2009
Net Worth Deficit: £106,240,000 *Total Assets:* £620,545,984
Registered Office: 8 White Oak Square, London Road, Swanley, Kent, BR8 7AG
Activities: Activities of head offices
Shareholders: Aberdeen Infrastructure Investments (Southmead) Limited; Infrastructure Investments (Health) Limited
Officers: Nicholas Tommy Cole [1978] Investment Director; Andrew Brian Deacon [1980] Portfolio Director, Infrastructure; Mark Christopher Wayment [1958] Director/Investment Banker; Edward Arthur Wilson [1964] Director/Investment Manager

The Hospital Company (Southmead) Limited
Incorporated: 18 November 2009
Net Worth Deficit: £106,240,000 *Total Assets:* £620,545,984
Registered Office: 8 White Oak Square, London Road, Swanley, Kent, BR8 7AG
Activities: Medical nursing home activities
Parent: The Hospital Company (Southmead) Holdings Limited
Officers: Nicholas Tommy Cole [1978] Investment Director; Andrew Brian Deacon [1980] Portfolio Director, Infrastructure; Mark Christopher Wayment [1958] Director/Investment Banker; Edward Arthur Wilson [1964] Director/Investment Manager

Hospitality Holdings Limited
Incorporated: 30 March 2000
Net Worth: £3,117,755,904 *Total Assets:* £10,528,145,408
Registered Office: Compass House, Guildford Street, Chertsey, Surrey, KT16 9BQ
Activities: Activities of head offices
Parent: Compass Group PLC
Officers: Dominic William Blakemore [1969] Director; Alison Rebecca Yapp [1965] Director/Solicitor

Host Europe Group Limited
Incorporated: 30 April 2013 *Employees:* 3
Net Worth: £282,908,000 *Total Assets:* £771,225,024
Registered Office: 5th Floor, The Shipping Building, Old Vinyl Factory, 252-254 Blyth Road, Hayes, Middlesex, UB3 1HA
Activities: Activities of head offices
Parent: Host Europe Investments Limited
Officers: Richard Anthony Winslow [1979] Director; Jonathan Ying Kit Wong [1976] Director

Host Europe Investments Limited
Incorporated: 18 July 2013
Net Worth: £346,612,000 *Total Assets:* £346,960,000
Registered Office: 5th Floor, The Shipping Building, Old Vinyl Factory, 252-254 Blyth Road, Hayes, Middlesex, UB3 1HA
Activities: Dormant company
Parent: Host Europe Finance Co. Limited
Officers: Richard Anthony Winslow [1979] Director; Jonathan Ying Kit Wong [1976] Director

Host Europe Limited
Incorporated: 7 March 2008
Net Worth: £295,087,008 *Total Assets:* £301,600,992
Registered Office: 5th Floor, The Shipping Building, Old Vinyl Factory, 252-254 Blyth Road, Hayes, Middlesex, UB3 1HA
Activities: Activities of head offices
Parent: HEL Bidco Ltd
Officers: Richard Anthony Winslow [1979] Director; Jonathan Ying Kit Wong [1976] Director

Hotchkiss Group Ltd
Incorporated: 26 February 1945 *Employees:* 390
Net Worth: £15,353,000 *Total Assets:* £34,096,000
Registered Office: Hampden Park Industrial Estate, Eastbourne, E Sussex, BN22 9AX
Activities: Plumbing, heat and air-conditioning installation
Shareholders: Giles William Woolley; Michael Edward Ohly
Officers: Andrew Daniel Finch, Secretary; Andrew Daniel Finch [1977] Director; Derrice Patrice Ohly [1954] Director; Michael Edward Ohly [1944] Director; Giles William Woolley [1955] Director

Hotel Inter-Continental London Limited
Incorporated: 4 January 1972
Net Worth: £211,520,992 *Total Assets:* £212,570,000
Registered Office: Broadwater Park, Denham, Bucks, UB9 5HR
Activities: Hotels and similar accommodation
Parent: Six Continents Limited
Officers: Fiona Cuttell, Secretary; Michael Jon Cockcroft [1974] Director/Accountant; Michael Todd Glover [1971] Director/Financial Controller [American]; Nicolette Henfrey [1969] Director; George Turner [1971] Director

Hotel Intercontinental London (Holdings) Limited
Incorporated: 11 December 2007
Net Worth: £506,536,000 *Total Assets:* £508,111,008
Registered Office: Broadwater Park, Denham, Bucks, UB9 5HR
Activities: Other business support service activities n.e.c.
Parent: Six Continents Holdings Limited
Officers: Fiona Cuttell, Secretary; Michael Jon Cockcroft [1974] Director/Accountant; Michael Todd Glover [1971] Director/Financial Controller [American]; Nicolette Henfrey [1969] Director

Hotel Management International (Holdings) Limited
Incorporated: 16 November 2001 *Employees:* 379
Net Worth: £75,446,000 *Total Assets:* £112,061,000
Registered Office: 364 High Street, Harlington, Heathrow, Hayes, Middlesex, UB3 5LF
Activities: Activities of head offices
Major Shareholder: Peter Nicholas Salussolia
Officers: Graeme John Ramsay, Secretary; Graeme John Ramsay [1967] Director/Chartered Accountant; Christina Salussolia [1950] Director/Executive Secretary; Peter Nicholas Salussolia [1968] Director

Hotel Management International Limited
Incorporated: 24 April 1972 *Employees:* 5
Net Worth: £74,755,000 *Total Assets:* £82,119,000
Registered Office: 364 High Street, Harlington, Heathrow, Hayes, Middlesex, UB3 5LF
Activities: Hotels and similar accommodation
Major Shareholder: Peter Nicholas Salussolia
Officers: Graeme John Ramsay, Secretary; Graeme John Ramsay [1967] Director/Chartered Accountant; Alexander Salussolia [1968] Director; Peter Nicholas Salussolia [1968] Director

Hotelplan (U.K. Group) Limited
Incorporated: 26 October 1947 *Employees:* 425
Net Worth: £4,289,000 *Total Assets:* £102,723,000
Registered Office: Mountain House, Station Road, Godalming, Surrey, GU7 1EX
Activities: Activities of head offices
Parent: Hotelplan Holding AG
Officers: Andrew Stewart, Secretary; Markus Glesti [1972] Director [Swiss]; Thomas Stirnimann [1962] Director/Chairman [Swiss]

Hotelplan Limited
Incorporated: 20 March 1939 *Employees:* 199
Net Worth: £20,930,000 *Total Assets:* £69,209,000
Registered Office: Mountain House, Station Road, Godalming, Surrey, GU7 1EX
Activities: Tour operator activities
Parent: Hotelplan (U.K. Group) Limited
Officers: Andrew Stewart, Secretary; Paul Andrew Carter [1965] Director/Chief Executive; Andrew Dominic Stewart [1979] Director/Chartered Accountant

Houserate Limited
Incorporated: 25 August 1995
Net Worth: £1,768,083,968 *Total Assets:* £89,736,880,128
Registered Office: Hanson House, 14 Castle Hill, Maidenhead, Berks, SL6 4JJ
Activities: Activities of other holding companies n.e.c.
Parent: Hanson Limited
Officers: Wendy Fiona Rogers, Secretary; Nicholas Arthur Dawe Benning-Prince [1974] Director/Chartered Accountant; Robert Charles Dowley [1972] Director/Chartered Accountant; Edward Alexander Gretton [1970] Director; Dr Carsten Matthias Wendt [1976] Director [German]

Housing Solutions Capital PLC
Incorporated: 6 July 2012
Net Worth: £50,000 *Total Assets:* £172,371,008
Registered Office: Crown House, 1 Crown Square, Waldeck Reform Road, Maidenhead, Berks, SL6 8BY
Activities: Renting and operating of Housing Association real estate
Officers: Andrew John Stuart Robertson, Secretary; Nigel Roger Cook [1956] Director/Retired; Valerie Claire Kendall [1969] Director/Private Equity Investor; Andrew John Stuart Robertson [1961] Finance Director

Hovis Holdings Limited
Incorporated: 15 January 2014 *Employees:* 3,246
Net Worth: £45,849,000 *Total Assets:* £220,691,008
Registered Office: The Lord Rank Centre, Lincoln Road, High Wycombe, Bucks, HP12 3QS
Activities: Activities of head offices
Shareholder: Premier Foods Group Limited
Officers: Peter Andrew Hill, Secretary; John Paul Danner [1965] Director [American]; Fernando Goni [1973] Director [French]; Nishpank Rameshbabu Kankiwala [1957] Director; Alastair Sholto Neil Murray [1960] Director/Chief Financial Officer

Hovis Limited
Incorporated: 15 January 2014 *Employees:* 2,975
Net Worth: £98,870,000 *Total Assets:* £234,578,000
Registered Office: The Lord Rank Centre, Lincoln Road, High Wycombe, Bucks, HP12 3QS
Activities: Manufacture of bread; manufacture of fresh pastry goods and cakes
Parent: Hovis Holdings Limited
Officers: Peter Andrew Hill, Secretary; Peter Andrew Hill [1980] HR Director; Dr George Idicula [1959] Supply Chain Director; Chad Leembuggen [1972] Director; Lawrence Anthony Watson [1965] Director

How Group Limited
Incorporated: 31 January 1986 *Employees:* 2
Net Worth: £108,822,000 *Total Assets:* £147,767,008
Registered Office: Interserve House, Ruscombe Park, Twyford, Reading, Berks, RG10 9JU
Activities: Activities of other holding companies n.e.c.
Parent: Interserve Group Holdings Limited
Officers: Andrew John McDonald, Secretary; Andrew John McDonald [1974] Director/Company Secretary; Anthony Kenneth Smythe [1965] Director/Accountant

Howard Lloyd & Company,Limited
Incorporated: 12 October 1912
Net Worth: £390,128,000 *Total Assets:* £390,136,000
Registered Office: 103-105 Bath Road, Slough, Berks, SL1 3UH
Activities: Activities of financial services holding companies
Parent: Reckitt Benckiser Holdings (Luxembourg) Limited
Officers: Christine Anne-Marie Logan, Secretary; Richard Mark Greensmith [1973] Group Tax Director; Simon Andrew Neville [1957] Group Treasury Director; Jonathan Timmis [1975] Finance Director

The Howard Partnership Trust
Incorporated: 8 April 2011 *Employees:* 930
Net Worth: £109,256,000 *Total Assets:* £124,044,000
Registered Office: c/o Howard of Effingham School, Lower Road, Effingham, Leatherhead, Surrey, KT24 5JR
Activities: Primary education
Officers: Rhona Julia Barnfield [1953] Director/Executive Head; Paul Conrad Belok [1960] Director/Actuary; Tina Barbara Crombie [1969] Director/Civil Servant; Jane Heather Cunliffe [1979] Director/Civil Servant; Joseph Jerry Liow Yune Loy [1969] Director/Chartered Accountant; Mark Joseph Clarence Swyny [1965] Director/Banker; Miles Howard Templeman [1947] Director; Christopher Williamson [1952] Director/Retired; Ian Stuart Wilson [1951] Director/Education Consultant

J.B.Howard Properties Limited
Incorporated: 24 November 1958 *Employees:* 4
Net Worth: £15,220,095 *Total Assets:* £24,461,964
Registered Office: 43 Preston Street, Brighton, BN1 2HP
Activities: Other letting and operating of own or leased real estate
Officers: Catherine Mary Sobhanpanah, Secretary/Director; David John Howard [1958] Director/Computer Consultant; Catherine Mary Sobhanpanah [1960] Director; Farzin Sobhanpanah [1957] Director

Howarth Homes PLC
Incorporated: 6 July 1988 *Employees:* 45
Net Worth: £6,817,747 *Total Assets:* £40,702,896
Registered Office: Waterside House, 20 Riverside Way, Uxbridge, Middlesex, UB8 2YF
Activities: Development of building projects
Major Shareholder: Adam Peter Howarth
Officers: Adam Peter Howarth, Secretary; Adam Peter Howarth [1963] Director/Property Developer; Brig Eric Howarth [1968] Director

Howitzer Acquisition Limited
Incorporated: 23 January 2006
Net Worth: £23,343,062 *Total Assets:* £60,699,324
Registered Office: Frays Mill Works, Cowley Road, Uxbridge, Middlesex, UB8 2AF
Activities: Activities of other holding companies n.e.c.
Parent: Circor Luxembourg Holdings S.A.R.L
Officers: Peter Graham Crawford Harvey, Secretary; Peter Graham Crawford Harvey [1957] Finance Director; David Mullen [1968] Director/SVP, Finance & Corporate Controller [American]

HP Inc UK Limited
Incorporated: 27 January 2015 *Employees:* 721
Net Worth Deficit: £33,146,000 *Total Assets:* £332,872,000
Registered Office: Cain Road, Amen Corner, Bracknell, Berks, RG12 1HN
Activities: Manufacture of computers and peripheral equipment
Parent: HP Inc UK Holding Limited
Officers: George Walter Brasher [1965] Managing Director [American]; Jo-Anne McDougall [1969] Director

HPC Public Limited Company
Incorporated: 5 March 1959 *Employees:* 207
Net Worth: £9,897,000 *Total Assets:* £23,685,000
Registered Office: 2 Victoria Gardens, Burgess Hill, W Sussex, RH15 9RQ
Activities: Machining
Major Shareholder: Ian Curtis
Officers: Nikki Crossley, Secretary; Ian Curtis [1968] Director/Accountant; James Hunter [1944] Director; Jason ASA Morgan [1969] Director; Ian Henry Ratcliff [1964] Director/Chief Executive; Trevor Gordon Stafford Stott [1949] Director

HPI Holding Limited
Incorporated: 4 December 2008
Net Worth: £212,102,000 *Total Assets:* £722,752,000
Registered Office: The Forum, Station Road, Theale, Reading, Berks, RG7 4RA
Activities: Activities of head offices
Parent: Audatex Holding GmbH
Officers: Tony Aquila [1964] Director/Chairman [American]; Jason Michael Brady [1968] Director/Attorney [American]; Renato Carlo Giger [1960] Director [Swiss]; Frank Johannes Overtoom [1966] Director/Regional CFO [Dutch]

HR Gardens Limited
Incorporated: 12 April 1960
Net Worth: £24,869,000 *Total Assets:* £24,943,000
Registered Office: Havas House, Hermitage Court, Hermitage Lane, Maidstone, Kent, ME16 9NT
Activities: Activities of head offices
Officers: Allan John Ross, Secretary; Rupert Molyneux Grose [1967] Director/Accountant; Allan John Ross [1961] Director/Accountant; Paul Francis Woodhouse [1955] Director/Accountant

HRG Debtco Limited
Incorporated: 31 May 2006
Net Worth: £121,882,448 *Total Assets:* £281,552,192
Registered Office: Spectrum Point, 279 Farnborough Road, Farnborough, Hants, GU14 7NJ
Activities: Other business support service activities n.e.c.
Parent: Hogg Robinson Group PLC
Officers: Aymeric Gibon [1980] Director/Vice President [French]; Sheena Varma [1980] Director/Senior Counsel, EMEA

HRT UK Limited
Incorporated: 6 October 2003 *Employees:* 2
Net Worth: £31,611,000 *Total Assets:* £31,611,000
Registered Office: Osprey House, 63 Station Road, Addlestone, Surrey, KT15 2AR
Activities: Activities of production holding companies
Parent: HRT SAS
Officers: Jonathan Baxter, Secretary; Olivier Vincent Antille [1971] Director [French]; Brian Forster [1953] Director

HSBC Invoice Finance (UK) Limited
Incorporated: 2 May 1963
Net Worth: £177,935,008 *Total Assets:* £4,932,506,112
Registered Office: 21 Farncombe Road, Worthing, W Sussex, BN11 2BW
Activities: Factoring
Parent: HSBC UK Bank PLC
Officers: Molly Ranger, Secretary; Marissa Kristina Adams [1984] Director/Banker [Canadian/Latvian]; Nicholas David Hampton [1969] Director/Banker; Christopher Sean Hawes [1965] Director/Banker; Mary-Anne Jane Moffatt [1980] Director/Banker; Ian John Tandy [1971] Director

HSH Hotels (2017) Limited
Incorporated: 2 March 2017 *Employees:* 269
Net Worth: £14,999,082 *Total Assets:* £47,056,040
Registered Office: Fourteen Acre Barn, Climping Street, Climping, Littlehampton, W Sussex, BN17 5TG
Activities: Other business support service activities n.e.c.
Shareholders: Miranda Anne Carminger; Lars Ivar Pontus Carminger
Officers: Lars Ivar Pontus Carminger, Secretary; Lars Ivar Pontus Carminger [1963] Director/Hotel Manager [Swedish]; Miranda Anne Carminger [1968] Director/Hotel Manager; John Stephen Sixsmith [1957] Director/Financial Controller

HTC Europe Co. Ltd
Incorporated: 9 July 2003 *Employees:* 93
Net Worth: £200,341,728 *Total Assets:* £203,483,888
Registered Office: Salamanca, Wellington Street, Slough, Berks, SL1 1YP
Activities: Other professional, scientific and technical activities n.e.c.
Officers: Gen Keong NG, Secretary; Tao-Pang Peter Shen [1968] Director/Chief Financial Officer [American]; Marcus John Woo [1957] Director [American]

HTEC Limited
Incorporated: 19 March 1980 *Employees:* 247
Net Worth: £15,536,000 *Total Assets:* £21,851,000
Registered Office: George Curl Way, Southampton, SO18 2RX
Activities: Other information technology service activities
Parent: HTEC Group Limited
Officers: Daryl Marc Paton, Secretary; Jeremy Michael James Lewis [1963] Director; Daryl Marc Paton [1964] Director

Huawei Technologies (UK) Co., Ltd.
Incorporated: 28 September 2001 *Employees:* 1,061
Net Worth: £108,853,000 *Total Assets:* £339,543,008
Registered Office: 300 South Oak Way, Green Park, Reading, Berks, RG2 6UF
Activities: Other telecommunications activities
Officers: Yun Chen, Secretary; Andrew Thomas Cahn [1951] Independent Director; Lifang Chen [1971] Director [Chinese]; Houkun Hu [1968] Executive Director [Chinese]; Kang Liu [1979] Director [Chinese]; Edmund John Philip Lord Browne [1948] Director/Chairman; Sir Kenneth Aphunezi Olisa [1951] Independent Director; Wei Zhang [1969] Director [Chinese]

Hudson Energy Supply UK Limited
Incorporated: 11 January 2011 *Employees:* 124
Net Worth: £14,186,000 *Total Assets:* £170,670,000
Registered Office: Third Floor, Elder House, 586-592 Elder Gate, Milton Keynes, Bucks, MK9 1LR
Activities: Trade of electricity
Parent: Hudson Energy Holdings UK Limited
Officers: Claudia Mason, Secretary; James Brown [1963] Director [American]; Patrick McCullough [1972] Director [American]; James Pickren [1966] Director [American]

Huhtamaki (UK) Limited
Incorporated: 17 June 1969 *Employees:* 430
Net Worth: £12,668,000 *Total Assets:* £81,866,000
Registered Office: Rowner Road, Holbrook, Gosport, Hants, PO13 0PR
Activities: Manufacture of other paper and paperboard containers
Parent: Huhtamaki Limited
Officers: Keith James Crossley [1968] Director/General Manager FS - UK Gosport; Karl Johan Mikael Hellstrom [1965] Director/VP Finance Food Service EAO [Finnish]; Tarja Iitti [1959] Director/Group Controller [Finnish]; Eric Pascal Le Lay [1962] Director/EVP Food Service EAO [French]; Sami-Jukka Pauni [1974] Director/Group VP, Legal, and General Counsel [Finnish]

Huhtamaki Finance Limited
Incorporated: 2 March 2012
Net Worth Deficit: £13,976,000 *Total Assets:* £133,624,000
Registered Office: Rowner Road, Gosport, Hants, PO13 0PR
Activities: Activities of other holding companies n.e.c.
Parent: Huhtamaki Finance BV
Officers: Tom Erik Marko Erander [1971] Director/Treasurer [Finnish]; Eric Pascal Le Lay [1962] Director/EVP Food Service EAO [French]; Sami-Jukka Pauni [1974] Director/Group VP, Legal, and General Counsel [Finnish]

Huhtamaki Limited
Incorporated: 13 December 1984
Net Worth: £17,895,000 *Total Assets:* £26,664,000
Registered Office: Rowner Road, Gosport, Hants, PO13 0PR
Activities: Activities of other holding companies n.e.c.
Parent: Huhtamaki Anglo Holding
Officers: Keith James Crossley [1968] Director/General Manager FS - UK Gosport; Tarja Tuulikki Iitti [1959] Director/Group Controller [Finnish]; Sami-Jukka Pauni [1974] Director/Lawyer [Finnish]

Humberside International Airport Limited
Incorporated: 8 October 1987 *Employees:* 141
Net Worth: £19,548,000 *Total Assets:* £25,315,000
Registered Office: Redhill Aerodrome, Kings Mill Lane, Redhill, Surrey, RH1 5JZ
Activities: Scheduled passenger air transport
Parent: Eastern Airways International Limited
Officers: James Lort Howell-Richardson, Secretary; Alan William George Corbett [1957] Director; James Lort Howell-Richardson [1980] Director/Legal Counsel; Richard James Lake [1961] Director; Michael Peter Nicol [1985] Director; Alan Robert Waltham [1972] Director/Leader of The Council

Humiseal Europe Limited
Incorporated: 21 February 1980 *Employees:* 30
Net Worth: £19,411,958 *Total Assets:* £24,029,398
Registered Office: 505 Eskdale Road, Winnersh, Wokingham, Berks, RG41 5TU
Activities: Manufacture of other chemical products n.e.c.
Parent: Concoat Holdings Limited
Officers: Adam Peter Chase [1971] Director/President & CEO [American]; Peter Richards Chase [1947] Director/Executive Chairman [American]; David Greenman [1949] Director

Humphrey Farms Limited
Incorporated: 27 September 2005 *Employees:* 88
Net Worth: £9,048,000 *Total Assets:* £29,519,000
Registered Office: Hazeley Road, Twyford, Winchester, Hants, SO21 1QA
Activities: Activities of head offices
Officers: Peter Francis Ball, Secretary/Chartered Accountant; Sarah Louise Alexandra Andrews [1968] Director; Peter Francis Ball [1957] Director/Chartered Accountant; David Gareth Fison [1952] Director/Civil Engineer; Jonathan Paul Humphrey [1964] Director; Martin Christopher Humphrey [1962] Director

Howard Humphreys & Partners Limited
Incorporated: 1 June 1959
Net Worth: £45,433,888 *Total Assets:* £45,467,092
Registered Office: Hill Park Court, Springfield Drive, Leatherhead, Surrey, KT22 7NL
Activities: Activities of other holding companies n.e.c.
Parent: Kellogg Brown & Root Group Limited
Officers: Martin Nelhams, Secretary; James Arthur Barrett [1965] Director/Accountant; Martin Nelhams [1960] Director/Solicitor

R. Hunt (Agricultural Engineers) Limited
Incorporated: 8 May 1975 *Employees:* 34
Net Worth: £8,109,614 *Total Assets:* £22,229,770
Registered Office: Martins Lane, Chilbolton, Stockbridge, Hants, SO20 6BL
Activities: Repair of machinery
Shareholders: Timothy John Hunt; Faith Hunt
Officers: Susan Barbara Clarke, Secretary; Paul Burnett [1980] Director; Stephen John Cox [1963] Director; James Robert Fisher [1965] Director; Faith Hunt [1935] Director; Timothy Hunt [1964] Director/Agricultural Engineer

Domnick Hunter Group Limited
Incorporated: 14 September 1989
Net Worth: £33,531,000 *Total Assets:* £35,116,000
Registered Office: Parker House, 55 Maylands Avenue, Hemel Hempstead Industrial Estate, Hemel Hempstead, Herts, HP2 4SJ
Activities: Activities of head offices
Parent: Parker Hannifin Manufacturing Limited
Officers: Graham Mark Ellinor, Secretary; Graham Mark Ellinor [1964] Director/Accountant; James Alan David Elsey [1970] HR Director

Huntswood CTC Limited
Incorporated: 11 April 2000 *Employees:* 216
Net Worth: £7,614,631 *Total Assets:* £42,464,440
Registered Office: Abbey Gardens, Abbey Street, Reading, Berks, RG1 3BA
Activities: Management consultancy activities other than financial management
Major Shareholder: David Ellis Brownlow
Officers: Donna Dawn Knight, Secretary; Matthew Bonfield [1978] Director/Chief Executive Officer; David Ellis Brownlow [1963] Founder and Non-Executive Director; Craig Stephen Coffield [1969] Director/Deputy Chairman; Donna Dawn Knight [1982] Director/Chief Financial Officer; Angela Claire Lane [1962] Director/Chairman; Benjamin James Rawson [1987] Director

Hurricane (Whirlwind) Limited
Incorporated: 6 March 2017
Net Worth: £44,774,684 *Total Assets:* £46,050,448
Registered Office: Ground Floor, The Wharf, Abbey Mill Business Park, Lower Eashing, Godalming, Surrey, GU7 2QN
Activities: Extraction of crude petroleum
Parent: Hurricane Energy PLC
Officers: Daniel Joel Jankes, Secretary; Alistair Milburn MacDonald Stobie [1966] Director; Neil Robert Platt [1963] Director; Robert Clive Trice [1961] Director

Hurricane Energy PLC
Incorporated: 29 September 2004 *Employees:* 21
Net Worth: £514,091,136 *Total Assets:* £706,626,752
Registered Office: Ground Floor, The Wharf, Abbey Mill Business Park, Lower Eashing, Godalming, Surrey, GU7 2QN
Activities: Extraction of crude petroleum
Officers: Daniel Jankes, Secretary; Jason Aun Minn Cheng [1972] Director [Australian]; Dr. David Anthony Lawson Jenkins [1938] Director; Roy Thomas Kelly [1960] Director; Steven James McTiernan [1951] Director; Neil Robert Platt [1963] Director; Sandra Nan Demby Shaw [1953] Director [British/American]; Alistair Milburn MacDonald Stobie [1966] Director; Kar Yui Leonard Tao [1980] Director [Australian]; Robert Clive Trice [1961] Director/Geoscientist; John Alexander Van Der Welle [1955] Director

Hurricane GLA Limited
Incorporated: 7 March 2017
Net Worth: £165,186,864 *Total Assets:* £356,287,296
Registered Office: Ground Floor, The Wharf, Abbey Mill Business Park, Lower Eashing, Godalming, Surrey, GU7 2QN
Activities: Extraction of crude petroleum
Parent: Hurricane Holdings Limited
Officers: Daniel Joel Jankes, Secretary; Alistair Milburn MacDonald Stobie [1966] Director; Neil Robert Platt [1963] Director; Robert Clive Trice [1961] Director

Hurricane Holdings Limited
Incorporated: 6 March 2017
Net Worth: £100,015,376 *Total Assets:* £100,015,376
Registered Office: Ground Floor, The Wharf, Abbey Mill Business Park, Lower Eashing, Godalming, Surrey, GU7 2QN
Activities: Extraction of crude petroleum
Parent: Hurricane Energy PLC
Officers: Daniel Joel Jankes, Secretary; Alistair Milburn MacDonald Stobie [1966] Director; Neil Robert Platt [1963] Director; Robert Clive Trice [1961] Director

Hurstlane Limited
Incorporated: 12 July 2000
Net Worth: £20,669,440 *Total Assets:* £33,431,456
Registered Office: Castle House, 69-70 Victoria Street, Englefield Green, Surrey, TW20 0QX
Activities: Renting and operating of Housing Association real estate
Shareholders: Amar Sheikh; Momin Sheikh
Officers: Momin Sheikh, Secretary/Director; Amar Sheikh [1961] Director; Momin Sheikh [1963] Director

Hurstpierpoint College Limited
Incorporated: 28 May 1999 *Employees:* 394
Net Worth: £30,602,000 *Total Assets:* £43,918,000
Registered Office: Hurstpierpoint College, College Lane, Hurstpierpoint, Hassocks, W Sussex, BN6 9JS
Activities: Primary education
Parent: The Woodard Corporation
Officers: Stephen Adrian Holliday, Secretary; Professor Jonathan Peter Bacon [1950] Director/University Professor; Dr Sadhana Brydie [1962] Director/General Practitioner; Jonathan Andrew Chocqueel-Mangan [1969] Director/Market Research Consultant; Lesley Jane Corbett [1954] Director/Education Consultant; Paul Mark Dillon-Robinson [1961] Director of Internal Audit; Robert John Ebdon [1965] Director/Construction Manager; Francesca Margaret Hampton [1970] Finance Director; Anthony Jarvis [1945] Director/Retired; Reverend William Kemp [1967] Director/Priest in Holy Orders; Karen Margaret Mack [1966] Director/Training Consultant; Kevin Stephen Powell [1959] Director/Chartered Accountant; George Anthony Rushton [1953] Director/Retired; Graham John Taysom [1954] Director/Private Investor

Hurtwood House School LLP
Incorporated: 24 September 2008 *Employees:* 151
Net Worth: £26,594,768 *Total Assets:* £32,536,492
Registered Office: Radnor House, Holmbury St Mary, Dorking, Surrey, RH5 6NX
Officers: Cosmo Maxwell Jackson [1967] Member; Kenneth Richard Barry Jackson [1940] Member; Linda Joan Maxwell Jackson [1943] Member

Hutchison 3G UK Holdings Limited
Incorporated: 2 February 2000
Net Worth: £584,892,992 *Total Assets:* £6,136,456,192
Registered Office: Star House, 20 Grenfell Road, Maidenhead, Berks, SL6 1EH
Activities: Activities of other holding companies n.e.c.
Officers: Edith Shih, Secretary; David Richard Dyson [1970] Director/Chief Executive Officer; Kin Ning Canning Fok [1951] Director; Kai Ming Dominic Lai [1953] Director [Canadian]; Tzar Kuoi Victor Li [1964] Director [Chinese]; Neil Douglas McGee [1951] Director [Australian]; Christian Nicolas Roger Salbaing [1950] Director [French]; Edith Shih [1952] Director/Solicitor; Frank John Sixt [1951] Director [Canadian]

Hutchison 3G UK Limited
Incorporated: 29 November 1999 *Employees:* 4,717
Net Worth: £6,602,199,040 *Total Assets:* £7,568,008,192
Registered Office: Star House, 20 Grenfell Road, Maidenhead, Berks, SL6 1EH
Activities: Wireless telecommunications activities
Parent: Hutchinson 3G UK Holdings Limited
Officers: Edith Shih, Secretary; David Richard Dyson [1970] Director/Chief Executive Officer; Robert Martin Finnegan [1962] Managing Director [Irish]; Kin Ning Canning Fok [1951] Director; Kai Ming Dominic Lai [1953] Director [Canadian]; Tzar Kuoi Victor Li [1964] Director [Chinese]; Jonathan Theodore Miller [1971] Director/Chief Financial Officer; Christian Nicolas Roger Salbaing [1950] Director [French]; Edith Shih [1952] Director/Solicitor; Frank John Sixt [1951] Director [Canadian]; Richard Callum Woodward [1972] Director/Chief Financial Officer

Huyck.Wangner UK Limited
Incorporated: 12 July 1999 *Employees:* 6
Net Worth: £150,724,992 *Total Assets:* £155,884,000
Registered Office: Suite 6, 2nd Floor, The Links, Herne Bay, Kent, CT6 7GQ
Activities: Other business support service activities n.e.c.
Parent: Xerium Technologies Limited
Officers: Michael Francis Bly [1966] Director [American]; Harald Weimer [1964] Director [German]

Hy-Ten Group Limited
Incorporated: 25 October 1965 *Employees:* 320
Net Worth: £31,780,204 *Total Assets:* £64,761,272
Registered Office: 12 The Green, Richmond, Surrey, TW9 1PX
Activities: Manufacture of metal structures and parts of structures
Major Shareholder: Adrian Charles Larkins
Officers: Michael Dennis Shattock, Secretary; Adrian Charles Larkins [1967] Director; Michael Dennis Shattock [1951] Director

Hy-Ten Limited
Incorporated: 17 February 1958 *Employees:* 283
Net Worth: £26,252,548 *Total Assets:* £57,861,488
Registered Office: 12 The Green, Richmond, Surrey, TW9 1PX
Activities: Manufacture of metal structures and parts of structures
Parent: Hy-Ten Group Limited
Officers: Michael Dennis Shattock, Secretary; Ian Thomas Dennis Jeffries [1970] Director/Branch Manager Steel Manufacturing; Adrian Charles Larkins [1967] Director; William Macpherson Brooks Mackay [1958] Sales Director; Paul William Nicholls [1957] Director; Michael Dennis Shattock [1951] Director; Richard Keith Webster [1966] Director

Hydac Limited
Incorporated: 8 April 1991 *Employees:* 1,189
Net Worth: £136,536,192 *Total Assets:* £165,738,576
Registered Office: 55 Station Road, Beaconsfield, Bucks, HP9 1QL
Activities: Activities of head offices
Shareholders: Alexander Dieter; Mathias Dieter
Officers: Renate Huber, Secretary [German]; Dr Werner Heinz Dieter [1929] Director [German]; Otmar Peter Schon [1929] Director [German]

Hyperformance Limited
Incorporated: 26 April 1999 *Employees:* 155
Net Worth: £4,949,000 *Total Assets:* £38,561,000
Registered Office: Elmbrook House, 18-19 Station Road, Sunbury on Thames, Surrey, TW16 6SU
Activities: Non-life insurance
Parent: Key Bidco Limited
Officers: Angela Margaret Darling [1959] Compliance Director; Shaun Ian Hooper [1972] Director/Chief Executive; Tim Paul Wills [1972] Finance Director

Hystead Limited
Incorporated: 3 December 2015
Previous: Hystead PLC
Net Worth Deficit: £147,398,000 *Total Assets:* £278,608,736
Registered Office: Doran & Minehane, 3rd Floor, WM Promus, 132-144 High Street, Bromley, Kent, BR1 1EZ
Activities: Management consultancy activities other than financial management
Officers: Wessel Johannes Hamman [1972] Director; Louis Norval [1956] Director [Australian]; Rabia Shihab [1979] Director/Chief Financial Officer [Israeli]; Morne Cornelius Wilken [1971] Director [South African]

Hyster-Yale Group Limited
Incorporated: 12 August 1971
Previous: NACCO Materials Handling Group, Ltd.
Net Worth: £51,190,052 *Total Assets:* £52,241,564
Registered Office: Centennial House, Building 4.5, Frimley Business Park, Frimley, Camberley, Surrey, GU16 7SG
Activities: Manufacture of lifting and handling equipment
Parent: Hyster-Yale Materials Handling, Inc
Officers: Claire Mair, Secretary; Claire Mair [1975] Director of Taxes EMEA; Francis Harry Thomas Sands [1952] Business Executive - Managing Director; Mark Harold Trivett [1969] Finance Director; Roger Toby Stoodley Tyler [1974] Director/Senior Counsel - EMEA

Hyster-Yale UK Limited
Incorporated: 12 August 1991 *Employees:* 996
Previous: NACCO Materials Handling Limited
Net Worth: £63,045,292 *Total Assets:* £197,120,784
Registered Office: Centennial House, Building 4.5, Frimley Business Park, Frimley, Camberley, Surrey, GU16 7SG
Activities: Manufacture of lifting and handling equipment
Parent: Hyster-Yale Group Limited
Officers: Claire Mair, Secretary; Francis Harry Thomas Sands [1952] Business Executive - Managing Director; Mark Harold Trivett [1969] Finance Director; Roger Toby Stoodley Tyler [1974] Director/Solicitor - Associate General Counsel

Hyundai Capital UK Limited
Incorporated: 10 February 2012 *Employees:* 56
Net Worth: £138,486,000 *Total Assets:* £2,166,573,056
Registered Office: London Court, 39 London Road, Reigate, Surrey, RH2 9AQ
Activities: Financial leasing
Parent: Santander Consumer (UK) PLC
Officers: Graham Tony Firmin [1973] Director; Stewart Gavin Grant [1965] Commercial Director; Victor Thomas Hill [1964] Managing Director; Kwanmook Lim [1971] Director [South Korean]; Paul Jonathan Philpott [1966] Director/Automotive Executive

Hyundai Motor UK Limited
Incorporated: 9 May 2005 *Employees:* 217
Net Worth: £66,104,000 *Total Assets:* £566,403,968
Registered Office: 728 London Road, High Wycombe, Bucks, HP11 1HE
Activities: Sale of new cars and light motor vehicles
Officers: Ashley Ward Andrew [1971] Managing Director; Yun Jong Choi [1969] Director [South Korean]; Kyuwan Lim [1976] Director [South Korean]

I C I Finance Limited
Incorporated: 19 October 1895
Net Worth: £852,700,032 *Total Assets:* £2,040,600,064
Registered Office: The Akzonobel Building, Wexham Road, Slough, Berks, SL2 5DS
Activities: Financial intermediation not elsewhere classified
Parent: Ergon Investments UK Limited
Officers: Stephen Bruce Ray [1962] Director/Pensions Accounting Manager; Michael Smalley [1958] Director; David Allan Turner [1971] Director

IAG Cargo Limited
Incorporated: 18 May 2012 *Employees:* 344
Net Worth: £1,805,000 *Total Assets:* £61,458,000
Registered Office: P O Box 99, Carrus Cargo Centre, Sealand Road, London Heathrow Airport, Hounslow, Middlesex, TW6 2JS
Activities: Freight air transport
Parent: International Consolidated Airlines Group S.A.
Officers: Luke Alexander Michael Straver, Secretary; Jose Antonio Barrionuevo Urgel [1972] Director [Spanish]; Robert Boyle [1964] Director; Lynne Louise Embleton [1969] Director/Airline Executive; Lewis Ian Girdwood [1967] Director/Chief Financial Officer; Stephen William Lawrence Gunning [1967] Managing Director; Lynn Fiona McClelland [1968] Director; William David Shepherd [1971] Director/Head of Commercial

IAG GBS Limited
Incorporated: 15 August 2014 *Employees:* 157
Net Worth Deficit: £16,232,000 *Total Assets:* £90,665,000
Registered Office: Waterside, Harmondsworth, West Drayton, Middlesex, UB7 0GB
Activities: Other business support service activities n.e.c.
Parent: International Consolidated Airlines Group SA
Officers: Luke Alexander Michael Straver, Secretary; Sian Louise Davies [1973] Director/Accountant; William John Francis [1962] Director; Stephen William Lawrence Gunning [1967] Director/British Airways PLC - Chief Financial Officer; Marcia Yor Ing Lin [1971] Director

IBM United Kingdom Asset Leasing Limited
Incorporated: 24 January 1975
Net Worth: £76,117,000 *Total Assets:* £367,753,984
Registered Office: P O Box 41, North Harbour, Portsmouth, PO6 3AU
Activities: Renting and leasing of office machinery and equipment (including computers)
Parent: IBM United Kingdom Financial Services Limited
Officers: Hayden James Gunton Reeve, Secretary; Timothy John Martin Clements [1970] Director; Edward Thomas Cook [1975] Director; Joanne Louise Stanton [1972] Director

IBM United Kingdom Financial Services Limited
Incorporated: 24 January 1975 *Employees:* 81
Net Worth: £97,145,000 *Total Assets:* £2,659,856,896
Registered Office: P O Box 41, North Harbour, Portsmouth, PO6 3AU
Activities: Activities of financial services holding companies
Parent: IBM Global Financing UK Company
Officers: Hayden James Gunton Reeve, Secretary; Paul David Brown [1964] Director; Timothy John Martin Clements [1970] Director; Tosca Maria Colangeli [1967] Director [British/Italian]; Edward Thomas Cook [1975] Director; Janine Cook [1964] Director; Jacqueline Anne Davey [1966] Director; Jonathan O'Donnell [1970] Director/IBM Executive; Joanne Louise Stanton [1972] Director

IBM United Kingdom Holdings Limited
Incorporated: 2 July 1912 *Employees:* 3
Net Worth: £1,514,599,936 *Total Assets:* £1,514,599,936
Registered Office: P O Box 41, North Harbour, Portsmouth, PO6 3AU
Activities: Activities of head offices
Parent: IBM North Region Holdings
Officers: Ian Duncan Ferguson, Secretary; Timothy Daren Matthew Eagle [1972] Director/Business Executive; William Anthony Kelleher [1963] Director/IBM Executive; Flavio Sciutti [1961] Director/Finance Executive [Italian]

IBM United Kingdom Limited
Incorporated: 21 November 1962 *Employees:* 12,124
Net Worth: £2,013,299,968 *Total Assets:* £3,942,799,872
Registered Office: P O Box 41, North Harbour, Portsmouth, PO6 3AU
Activities: Manufacture of computers and peripheral equipment
Parent: IBM United Kingdom Holdings Limited
Officers: Ian Duncan Ferguson, Secretary; Timothy Daren Matthew Eagle [1972] Director/Business Executive; William Anthony Kelleher [1963] Director/IBM Executive; Flavio Sciutti [1961] Director/Finance Executive [Italian]

IBRC Asset Finance Limited
Incorporated: 14 August 1995
Net Worth: £28,976,064 *Total Assets:* £29,145,804
Registered Office: Unit 33a Enterprise House, 44-46 Terrace Road, Walton on Thames, Surrey, KT12 2SD
Activities: Other credit granting n.e.c.
Parent: CDB (U.K.) Limited
Officers: James Ednie Brydie [1959] Director/Banker

Ichnaea UK Bidco Limited
Incorporated: 3 June 2016
Net Worth Deficit: £18,526,000 *Total Assets:* £170,022,000
Registered Office: Rath House, 55-65 Uxbridge Road, Slough, Berks, SL1 1SG
Activities: Activities of other holding companies n.e.c.
Officers: Richard Paul Blackburn [1982] Managing Director; William Robert George Macpherson [1963] Director; Nathan Giles Runnicles [1974] Director/Chief Financial Officer

Ichnaea UK Holdings Limited
Incorporated: 23 September 2014
Net Worth Deficit: £13,826,299 *Total Assets:* £133,437,016
Registered Office: Rath House, 55-65 Uxbridge Road, Slough, Berks, SL1 1SG
Activities: Activities of other holding companies n.e.c.
Parent: Ichnaea UK Bidco Limited
Officers: William Robert George Macpherson [1963] Director; Nathan Giles Runnicles [1974] Director/Chief Financial Officer

Ichnaea UK Limited
Incorporated: 30 October 2012
Net Worth Deficit: £55,157,824 *Total Assets:* £76,056,432
Registered Office: Rath House, 55-65 Uxbridge Road, Slough, Berks, SL1 1SG
Activities: Activities of other holding companies n.e.c.
Parent: Ichnaea UK Holdings Limited
Officers: Richard Paul Blackburn [1982] Managing Director; William Robert George Macpherson [1963] Director; Nathan Giles Runnicles [1974] Director/Chief Financial Officer

ICI Chemicals & Polymers Limited
Incorporated: 1 January 1940
Net Worth: £199,000,000 *Total Assets:* £265,000,000
Registered Office: The Akzonobel Building, Wexham Road, Slough, Berks, SL2 5DS
Activities: Buying and selling of own real estate
Parent: Dulux Limited
Officers: Louise Margaret Dinnage [1970] Director; Michael Smalley [1958] Director; David Allan Turner [1971] Director; Stuart Walsh [1964] Director

Icon Clinical Research (U.K.) Limited
Incorporated: 21 September 1990 *Employees:* 560
Net Worth: £61,345,604 *Total Assets:* £72,754,968
Registered Office: Concept House, 6 Stoneycroft Rise, Chandler's Ford, Eastleigh, Hants, SO53 3LD
Activities: Other research and experimental development on natural sciences and engineering
Parent: Icon Public Limited Company
Officers: Erina Fox, Secretary; Michael Gleeson [1978] Director [Irish]; Brendan Harte [1965] Director [Irish]; Dr Quintin Van Wyk [1970] Director

Icopal Limited
Incorporated: 21 February 1990 *Employees:* 136
Net Worth: £9,772,000 *Total Assets:* £26,900,000
Registered Office: BMI House, 2 Pitfield, Kiln Farm, Milton Keynes, Bucks, MK11 3LW
Activities: Production of abrasive products
Parent: BMI Group Holdings UK Limited
Officers: Andrew John Dennis [1965] Managing Director; Klaus Sonne Ravn [1966] Finance Director [Danish]; Dr Johannes Georg Schmidt-Schultes [1966] Director/Chief Financial Officer [German]

Icrossing Europe Limited
Incorporated: 19 December 2006 *Employees:* 127
Net Worth: £15,758,668 *Total Assets:* £22,533,716
Registered Office: Moore House, 13 Black Lion Street, Brighton, BN1 1ND
Activities: Activities of head offices
Officers: Aimee Nisbet, Secretary; Bridgetta Worsley, Secretary; Debi Chirichella [1964] Director [American]; James David Wildman [1966] Director/Chief Executive

ICS Cool Energy Limited
Incorporated: 14 July 2005 *Employees:* 201
Net Worth: £18,706,212 *Total Assets:* £43,085,904
Registered Office: ICS House, Stephenson Road, Calmore Industrial Estate, Totton, Southampton, SO40 3SA
Activities: Agents involved in the sale of machinery, industrial equipment, ships and aircraft
Parent: ICS Group Holdings Limited
Officers: David Hampsey [1970] Director/Accountant; Troy E Kingston [1969] Director/Financial Leader [American]; Simon James West [1967] Director

ICS Group Holdings Limited
Incorporated: 18 July 2005 *Employees:* 278
Net Worth: £26,977,156 *Total Assets:* £54,369,556
Registered Office: ICS House, Stephenson Road, Calmore Industrial Estate, Totton, Southampton, SO40 3SA
Activities: Activities of other holding companies n.e.c.
Parent: Ingersoll-Rand UK Limited
Officers: David Hampsey [1970] Director/Accountant; Troy E Kingston [1969] Director/Financial Leader [American]; Simon James West [1967] Director

ICS Incorporation Limited
Incorporated: 11 June 1999
Net Worth Deficit: £23,939,552 *Total Assets:* £31,552,244
Registered Office: Unit 6 North Radius Park, Faggs Road, Feltham, Middlesex, TW14 0NG
Activities: Other business support service activities n.e.c.
Officers: Bassam Salim Khoury, Secretary/Financial Officer [Lebanese]; Ernie Vibas Cayubit [1983] Director/Accountant [Filipino]; Manu Chennattu Kuriakose [1976] Director/Accountant [Indian]; Charmaine Dela Cerna Encabo [1983] Director/Secretary [Filipino]; Samuel Kutty John [1974] Director/Accountant [Indian]; Bassam Salim Khoury [1963] Director/Financial Officer [Lebanese]

ID Medical Group Limited
Incorporated: 23 August 1999 *Employees:* 543
Net Worth: £4,140,931 *Total Assets:* £27,489,010
Registered Office: ID House, 1 Mill Square, Featherstone Road, Wolverton Mill South, Milton Keynes, Bucks, MK12 5ZD
Activities: Temporary employment agency activities
Parent: ID Medical Group Holdings Limited
Officers: Lynne Alden, Secretary; Gus Haydn Brimson [1974] Director; Ranjit Singh Nandha [1978] Director; David Simbarashe Newton [1981] Director; Deenu Rajesh Patel [1979] Director; Dr Mahomed Hanif Allimahomed Sacoor [1939] Director; Michael Sacoor [1970] Director; Stefan Thygesen [1979] Director

IDE Group Limited
Incorporated: 17 November 2011
Previous: CORETX Limited
Net Worth Deficit: £31,628,356 *Total Assets:* £24,001,432
Registered Office: Napoleon House, Riseley Business Park, Riseley, Reading, Berks, RG7 1NW
Activities: Non-trading company
Parent: IDE Group Holdings PLC
Officers: Andrew George Parker [1969] Director/Chartered Accountant; Charlotte Alexandra Stranner [1979] Director/Chartered Accountant

Idemitsu International (Europe) Limited
Incorporated: 1 May 1987
Previous: Idemitsu International (Europe) Public Limited Company
Net Worth: £12,426,684 *Total Assets:* £24,216,754
Registered Office: c/o Nihonbo, Suite 3, Courtyard House, Mill Lane, Godalming, Surrey, GU7 1EY
Activities: Agents involved in the sale of fuels, ores, metals and industrial chemicals
Parent: Idemitsu Kosan Co., Ltd.
Officers: Koichi Kuroda [1967] Director [Japanese]; Kenji Watanabe [1970] Director [Japanese]

Idox PLC
Incorporated: 26 April 2000 *Employees:* 842
Net Worth: £91,309,000 *Total Assets:* £174,570,000
Registered Office: 2nd Floor, 1310 Waterside, Arlington Business Park, Theale, Reading, Berks, RG7 4SA
Activities: Activities of other holding companies n.e.c.
Officers: Ruth Paterson, Secretary; Robert James Grubb [1980] Director; Richard Graham Quinton Kellett-Clarke [1954] Director/Accountant; David John Meaden [1961] Director; Jeremy Howard Millard [1971] Director/Chartered Accountant; Barbara Jane Moorhouse [1958] Director; Oliver Rupert Andrew Scott [1967] Director; Christopher Michael Renwick Stone [1962] Director

Idox Software Ltd
Incorporated: 27 May 1994 *Employees:* 505
Net Worth: £23,061,466 *Total Assets:* £55,990,396
Registered Office: 2nd Floor, 1310 Waterside, Arlington Business Park, Theale, Reading, Berks, RG7 4SA
Activities: Other information technology service activities
Parent: Idox PLC
Officers: Ruth Paterson, Secretary; Robert James Grubb [1980] Director; David John Meaden [1961] Director; Ian Michael Noble [1956] Director; Ruth Paterson [1984] Director/Solicitor [Irish]

IG Design Group PLC
Incorporated: 22 November 1978 *Employees:* 1,954
Previous: International Greetings PLC
Net Worth: £96,855,000 *Total Assets:* £170,628,000
Registered Office: No 7 Water End Barns, Water End, Eversholt, Beds, MK17 9EA
Activities: Activities of head offices
Officers: Joy Laws, Secretary; Dr Elaine Amanda Bond [1972] Director; Lance Andrew Burn [1964] Director; John Stuart Northcliffe Charlton [1946] Director; Paul Elliot Fineman [1959] Director; Stig Anders Hedlund [1957] Director [Swedish]; Mark Ian Tentori [1963] Finance Director; Giles Kirkley Willits [1966] Finance Director

IG Design Group UK Limited
Incorporated: 8 June 1988 *Employees:* 483
Previous: International Greetings UK Limited
Net Worth: £8,514,000 *Total Assets:* £58,422,000
Registered Office: No 7 Water End Barns, Water End, Eversholt, Beds, MK17 9EA
Activities: Manufacture of other articles of paper and paperboard n.e.c.
Shareholders: IG Design Group PLC; Belgraave Graphics Limited
Officers: Robert Geoffrey Alstead [1967] Finance Director; Lance Andrew Burn [1964] Managing Director; Paul Elliot Fineman [1959] Director; Giles Kirkley Willits [1966] Finance Director

IGE Energy Services (UK) Limited
Incorporated: 26 January 1998 *Employees:* 37
Net Worth: £107,414,000 *Total Assets:* £523,944,000
Registered Office: The Arena, Downshire Way, Bracknell, Berks, RG12 1PU
Activities: Other service activities n.e.c.
Shareholders: IGE USA Holdings; General Electric Company
Officers: Steven Robert Miller [1969] Director/General Manager; Kevin Marc Slaughter [1973] Director/Senior Finance Manager [British/South African]

Igroup 8 Limited
Incorporated: 10 December 1999
Net Worth: £1,434,001,024 *Total Assets:* £3,009,617,920
Registered Office: P O Box 2497, Building 4, Hatters Lane, Watford, Herts, WD18 1YY
Activities: Other business support service activities n.e.c.
Parent: GE Money Home Lending Finance Limited
Officers: Samantha Jones [1981] Director; Jonathan Edward Taylor [1980] Director/Risk and Compliance Leader

IHC Hotel Limited
Incorporated: 29 November 1988
Net Worth: £78,266,000 *Total Assets:* £78,290,000
Registered Office: Broadwater Park, Denham, Bucks, UB9 5HR
Activities: Activities of head offices
Parent: Six Continents Limited
Officers: Fiona Cuttell, Secretary; Michael Jon Cockcroft [1974] Director/Accountant; Michael Todd Glover [1971] Director/Financial Controller [American]; Nicolette Henfrey [1969] Director

IHC May Fair (Holdings) Limited
Incorporated: 29 November 1988
Net Worth Deficit: £30,827,000 *Total Assets:* £392,679,008
Registered Office: Broadwater Park, Denham, Bucks, UB9 5HR
Activities: Activities of head offices
Parent: IHC UK (Holdings) Limited
Officers: Fiona Cuttell, Secretary; Michael Jon Cockcroft [1974] Director/Accountant; Michael Todd Glover [1971] Director/Financial Controller [American]; Nicolette Henfrey [1969] Director

IHC May Fair Hotel Limited
Incorporated: 29 November 1988
Net Worth: £42,473,000 *Total Assets:* £42,486,000
Registered Office: Broadwater Park, Denham, Bucks, UB9 5HR
Activities: Activities of head offices
Parent: Six Continents Limited
Officers: Fiona Littlebury-Cuttell, Secretary; Michael Jon Cockcroft [1974] Director/Accountant; Michael Todd Glover [1971] Director/Financial Controller [American]; Nicolette Henfrey [1969] Director

IHC Overseas (U.K.) Limited
Incorporated: 28 November 1988
Net Worth: £341,419,008 *Total Assets:* £341,574,016
Registered Office: Broadwater Park, Denham, Bucks, UB9 5HR
Activities: Activities of head offices
Parent: Six Continents Limited
Officers: Fiona Cuttell, Secretary; Michael Jon Cockcroft [1974] Director/Accountant; Michael Todd Glover [1971] Director/Financial Controller [American]; Nicolette Henfrey [1969] Director

IHC UK (Holdings) Limited
Incorporated: 28 November 1988
Net Worth: £84,858,000 *Total Assets:* £84,874,000
Registered Office: Broadwater Park, Denham, Bucks, UB9 5HR
Activities: Activities of head offices
Parent: Six Continents Limited
Officers: Fiona Cuttell, Secretary; Michael Jon Cockcroft [1974] Director/Accountant; Michael Todd Glover [1971] Director/Financial Controller [American]; Nicolette Henfrey [1969] Director

IHG Hotels Limited
Incorporated: 24 November 1995
Net Worth: £489,766,016 *Total Assets:* £534,344,992
Registered Office: Broadwater Park, Denham, Bucks, UB9 5HR
Activities: Other business support service activities n.e.c.
Parent: Six Continents Holdings Limited
Officers: Fiona Cuttell, Secretary; Michael Jon Cockcroft [1974] Director/Accountant; Michael Todd Glover [1971] Director/Financial Controller [American]; Nicolette Henfrey [1969] Director; Daisy Eleanor Loveday Caroline Llewellyn [1976] Director; George Turner [1971] Director

IHS Global Investments Limited
Incorporated: 3 February 2016
Net Worth: £980,744,064 *Total Assets:* £980,758,912
Registered Office: 3rd Floor, The Capitol Building, Oldbury, Bracknell, Berks, RG12 8FZ
Activities: Activities of open-ended investment companies
Shareholders: IHS Markit Group Holdings Limited; IHS Markit Ltd
Officers: Christopher Guy McLoughlin [1978] Director; Kathryn Ann Owen [1976] Director/EMEA Controller

IHS Global Limited
Incorporated: 21 January 1964 *Employees:* 1,264
Net Worth: £5,445,899,264 *Total Assets:* £6,688,296,448
Registered Office: 3rd Floor, The Capitol Building, Oldbury, Bracknell, Berks, RG12 8FZ
Activities: Other professional, scientific and technical activities n.e.c.
Parent: IHSM Holdings UK Ltd
Officers: Christopher Guy McLoughlin [1978] Director; Kathryn Ann Owen [1976] Director/EMEA Controller

IHS Group Holdings Limited
Incorporated: 1 December 1981
Net Worth: £5,749,122,048 *Total Assets:* £5,985,950,208
Registered Office: 3rd Floor, The Capitol Building, Oldbury, Bracknell, Berks, RG12 8FZ
Activities: Activities of head offices
Parent: IHS International Holdings Limited
Officers: Christopher Guy McLoughlin [1978] Director; Kathryn Ann Owen [1976] Director/EMEA Controller

IHS International Holdings Limited
Incorporated: 10 July 2008
Net Worth: £4,573,374,976 *Total Assets:* £5,145,225,216
Registered Office: 3rd Floor, The Capitol Building, Oldbury, Bracknell, Berks, RG12 8FZ
Activities: Activities of head offices
Parent: IHS Markit Ltd
Officers: Christopher Guy McLoughlin [1978] Director; Kathryn Ann Owen [1976] Director/EMEA Controller

IHS Markit Global Funding Limited
Incorporated: 3 August 2016
Net Worth: £161,935,200 *Total Assets:* £162,559,296
Registered Office: The Capitol Building, Oldbury, Bracknell, Berks, RG12 8FZ
Activities: Activities of financial services holding companies
Parent: IHS Markit Ltd
Officers: Christopher Guy McLoughlin [1978] Director/MD; Kathryn Ann Owen [1976] Director/EMEA Controller

IHS Markit Global Limited
Incorporated: 18 August 2016
Net Worth: £66,407,840 *Total Assets:* £66,482,440
Registered Office: The Capitol Building, Oldbury, Bracknell, Berks, RG12 8FZ
Activities: Activities of financial services holding companies
Parent: IHS Markit Ltd
Officers: Christopher Guy McLoughlin [1978] Director/MD; Kathryn Ann Owen [1976] Director/EMEA Controller

Ikea Limited
Incorporated: 5 February 1986
Net Worth: £253,328,992 *Total Assets:* £589,835,008
Registered Office: Witan Gate House, 500-600 Witan Gate West, Milton Keynes, Bucks, MK9 1SH
Activities: Retail of furniture, lighting, and similar (not musical instruments or scores) in specialised store
Officers: Javier Quinones Cespedes [1977] Director [Spanish]; Marzanna Deblinska-Hajdas [1969] Director/Business Navigation, Operations & Finance Business [Polish]; Henrik Olshov [1966] Director/Legal Counsel [Swedish]; Sajal Shah [1976] Director; Belen Frau Uriarte [1974] Director [Spanish]

Ikea Properties Investments Limited
Incorporated: 24 February 1995 *Employees:* 19
Net Worth: £681,772,032 *Total Assets:* £1,384,669,056
Registered Office: Witan Gate House, 500-600 Witan Gate West, Milton Keynes, Bucks, MK9 1SH
Activities: Other letting and operating of own or leased real estate
Parent: Ikea Limited
Officers: Javier Quinones Cespedes [1977] Director [Spanish]; Simon Maynard [1959] Director/Deputy Group Property Manager; Richard Rands [1967] Director/Property Manager UK & Ireland; Sajal Shah [1976] Director

ILB Investments Limited
Incorporated: 3 September 2008 *Employees:* 4
Net Worth: £3,520,188 *Total Assets:* £60,520,232
Registered Office: C P House, Otterspool Way, Watford By-Pass, Watford, Herts, WD25 8JJ
Activities: Other letting and operating of own or leased real estate
Shareholders: Iris Gibbor; Lady Lilly Schreier
Officers: Eric Lewis, Secretary; Iris Gibbor [1951] Director; Mark Gibbor [1988] Director/Accountant; Lady Lilly Schreier [1924] Director

ILI Limited
Incorporated: 28 October 2005 *Employees:* 21
Net Worth: £27,663,614 *Total Assets:* £33,845,880
Registered Office: Partis House, Davy Avenue, Knowlhill, Milton Keynes, Bucks, MK5 8HJ
Activities: Other information service activities n.e.c.
Parent: SAI Global CIS UK Limited
Officers: Hean Siew, Secretary; Kim Jenkins [1966] Director [Australian]; Tracy Elaine Roskell [1966] Finance Director

Imagination Technologies Group Limited
Incorporated: 18 April 1994 *Employees:* 1,068
Previous: Imagination Technologies Group PLC
Net Worth: £85,375,000 *Total Assets:* £130,912,000
Registered Office: Imagination House, Home Park Estate, Kings Langley, Herts, WD4 8LZ
Activities: Other information service activities n.e.c.
Parent: CBFI Investment Limited
Officers: Ray Bingham [1945] Director [American]; Ronald Douglas Black [1963] Director [American]; John Kao [1969] Director [Chinese]; Peter Kuo [1971] Director [Chinese]

Imagination Technologies Limited
Incorporated: 1 April 1977 *Employees:* 661
Net Worth: £7,923,000 *Total Assets:* £84,409,000
Registered Office: Imagination House, Home Park Estate, Kings Langley, Herts, WD4 8LZ
Activities: Other information technology service activities
Parent: Imagination Technologies Group PLC
Officers: Ronald Douglas Black [1963] Director [American]

Imagine Cruising Limited
Incorporated: 27 January 2009 *Employees:* 158
Net Worth: £3,040,158 *Total Assets:* £54,304,696
Registered Office: 2nd Floor, Nucleus House, 2 Lower Mortlake Road, Richmond, Surrey, TW9 2JA
Activities: Travel agency activities
Parent: Imagine Enterprises Limited
Officers: Iain Charles Richard Andrew [1965] Director; Robin John Deller [1967] Managing Director; Natalie Ann Maye [1981] Director; Sarah Elizabeth McAllister [1979] Director; Asif Hamza Parkar [1974] Director/Finance Manager; Geoffrey Peter Wood [1957] Director

IMBOLC Limited
Incorporated: 5 July 2016
Net Worth: £20,299,934 *Total Assets:* £20,299,934
Registered Office: Millennium House, 65 Walton Street, Aylesbury, Bucks, HP21 7QG
Activities: Other information technology service activities
Shareholders: Charles Joseph Kennelly; Stuart Richard Bonthrone
Officers: Stuart Richard Bonthrone [1965] Director; Charles Joseph Kennelly [1965] Director

IMCD Holding UK Ltd
Incorporated: 17 August 2005
Net Worth: £17,580,000 *Total Assets:* £22,885,000
Registered Office: 5th Floor, Times House, Throwley Way, Sutton, Surrey, SM1 4AF
Activities: Activities of head offices
Parent: IMCD UK Acquisitions Limited
Officers: Hendrikus Jacobus Jozef Kooijmans, Secretary/Director [Dutch]; Monsieur Olivier Philippe Champault [1967] Managing Director [French]; Paul Christopher Hanbury [1976] Managing Director; Hendrikus Jacobus Jozef Kooijmans [1961] Director [Dutch]

IMCD UK Acquisitions Limited
Incorporated: 10 December 2010
Net Worth: £23,881,000 *Total Assets:* £43,591,000
Registered Office: Times House, Throwley Way, Sutton, Surrey, SM1 4AF
Activities: Activities of head offices
Parent: IMCD N.V.
Officers: Monsieur Olivier Philippe Champault [1967] Managing Director [French]; Paul Christopher Hanbury [1976] Managing Director; Hendrikus Jacobus Jozef Kooijmans [1961] Director/Chief Financial Officer [Dutch]

IMCD UK Limited
Incorporated: 19 September 1988 *Employees:* 134
Net Worth: £55,915,000 *Total Assets:* £93,651,000
Registered Office: Times House, Throwley Way, Sutton, Surrey, SM1 4AF
Activities: Wholesale of chemical products
Parent: IMCD N.V.
Officers: Hans Kooijmans, Secretary; Paul Christopher Hanbury [1976] Managing Director; Hans Kooijmans [1961] Financial Director [Dutch]; Richard John Mell [1968] Finance Director

IMO Car Wash Group Limited
Incorporated: 30 April 2009 *Employees:* 4
Net Worth: £211,848,000 *Total Assets:* £400,265,984
Registered Office: 35-37 Amersham Hill, High Wycombe, Bucks, HP13 6NU
Activities: Activities of head offices
Parent: Rose Midco Ltd
Officers: Jonathan Samuel Booth [1961] Director; Thomas Bruce Mangas [1967] Director/Chief Executive Officer [American]; Nilesh Kundanlal Pandya [1971] Director; Michael Andrew James Smith [1962] Director

Impact Africa Limited
Incorporated: 24 March 2010 *Employees:* 2
Net Worth Deficit: £6,194,732 *Total Assets:* £21,193,022
Registered Office: Elder House, St Georges Business Park, Brooklands Road, Weybridge, Surrey, KT13 0TS
Activities: Extraction of crude petroleum
Parent: Impact Oil & Gas Limited
Officers: Siraj Ahmed, Secretary; Philip Lloyd Birch [1958] Director; Robert Wilde [1964] Finance Director

Impact Multi Academy Trust
Incorporated: 7 March 2011 *Employees:* 389
Previous: Apollo Learning Trust
Net Worth: £35,493,000 *Total Assets:* £38,875,000
Registered Office: Ravens Wood School, Oakley Road, Bromley, Kent, BR2 8HP
Activities: General secondary education
Officers: Joanne Elizabeth Marriott, Secretary; Jeremy Richard Marlow Allen [1966] Director/Computer Programmer; Nicholas Alastair Cross [1968] Director of Education; Lucy Marjorie Jeffreys [1957] Director/Education Consultant; Harendra Madugalle [1980] Director/Accountant; Andrew Michael Naish [1965] Director; Kieran Jude Osborne [1953] Director/Education Consultant; Peter Lewis Ostacchini [1960] Director/Chief Executive Officer, Bank

Impact Oil & Gas Limited
Incorporated: 11 April 2011 *Employees:* 15
Net Worth: £39,841,028 *Total Assets:* £50,431,184
Registered Office: Elder House, St Georges Business Park, Brooklands Road, Weybridge, Surrey, KT13 0TS
Activities: Extraction of crude petroleum
Officers: Siraj Ahmed, Secretary; Siraj Ahmed [1982] Director; Andrew Donald Bartlett [1957] Director; Philip Lloyd Birch [1958] Director; John Anthony Copelyn [1950] Director/Chief Executive Officer HCI [South African]; Michael James Doherty [1949] Director [Irish]; Keith Charles Hill [1959] Director/Businessman [Canadian]; James Robert Nicolella [1968] Director [South African/British]; Charles Richard Theodore Ramsden [1953] Director/Geophysicist [South African]; Robert Wilde [1964] Finance Director

Imperial Car Supermarkets Limited
Incorporated: 12 June 2015 *Employees:* 247
Net Worth: £6,249,000 *Total Assets:* £48,101,000
Registered Office: Imperial House, Second Avenue, Milbrook, Southampton, SO15 0LP
Activities: Sale of used cars and light motor vehicles
Shareholders: Scott John Beazley; Michael John Bell; John Robert Churcher
Officers: Scott John Beazley [1976] Director; Michael John Bell [1970] Director; Jonathan Robert Churcher [1980] Director; Russell Joseph Churcher [1980] Aftersales Director; Michael John Hawkins [1986] Sales Director; Neil Jonathan Smith [1965] Director

Imperial Cars of Swanwick Limited
Incorporated: 13 March 2006 *Employees:* 247
Net Worth: £2,272,000 *Total Assets:* £39,128,000
Registered Office: Imperial House, Second Avenue, Millbrook, Southampton, SO15 0LP
Activities: Sale of used cars and light motor vehicles
Parent: ICVM Holdings Limited
Officers: Scott John Beazley [1976] Director; Michael John Bell [1970] Director; Jonathan Robert Churcher [1980] Director; Russell Joseph Churcher [1980] Aftersales Director; Michael John Hawkins [1986] Sales Director; Neil Jonathan Smith [1965] Director

Imperial Chemical Industries Limited
Incorporated: 7 December 1926 *Employees:* 879
Net Worth: £4,256,000,000 *Total Assets:* £7,784,000,000
Registered Office: The Akzonobel Building, Wexham Road, Slough, Berks, SL2 5DS
Activities: Manufacture of paints, varnishes and similar coatings, mastics and sealants
Parent: Akzo Nobel ICI Holdings
Officers: John Wright Henderson [1966] Director; Wendy MacDonald [1969] Director; Alistair McAuley [1972] Managing Director; Michael Smalley [1958] Director; David Allan Turner [1971] Director

In-Sync Group Limited
Incorporated: 7 September 2011 *Employees:* 87
Previous: OBK Group Limited
Net Worth: £25,212,528 *Total Assets:* £43,021,132
Registered Office: 4 The Millennium Centre, Crosby Way, Farnham, Surrey, GU9 7XX
Activities: Tax consultancy
Shareholders: Malcolm Oliver; Frank Bell; Suzanne Lorraine Bettis
Officers: Frank Bell [1951] Director/Accountant; Malcolm Oliver [1958] Director

INC Research Europe Holdings Limited
Incorporated: 23 September 2010 *Employees:* 2
Net Worth: £90,349,496 *Total Assets:* £109,755,960
Registered Office: Farnborough Business Park, 1 Pinehurst Road, Farnborough, Hants, GU14 7BF
Activities: Other business support service activities n.e.c.
Officers: Robert Alan Parks [1972] Director/Chief Accounting Officer [American]; Thomas Edward Zajkowski [1969] Director [American]

INC Research Holding Limited
Incorporated: 19 May 2009 *Employees:* 3
Net Worth: £48,005,548 *Total Assets:* £52,150,108
Registered Office: Farnborough Business Park, 1 Pinehurst Road, Farnborough, Hants, GU14 7BF
Activities: Other business support service activities n.e.c.
Officers: Robert Alan Parks [1972] Director/Chief Accounting Officer [American]; Thomas Edward Zajkowski [1969] Director/SVP Finance & Treasurer [American]

Incomm Europe Limited
Incorporated: 30 December 2004 *Employees:* 27
Net Worth Deficit: £51,013,876 *Total Assets:* £41,967,016
Registered Office: 1600 Parkway, Solent Business Park, Whiteley, Fareham, Hants, PO15 7AH
Activities: Data processing, hosting and related activities
Shareholder: Merrill Brooks Smith
Officers: Timothy Pope, Secretary; Phillip Craig Graves [1950] Director/Management [American]; Frank Monaco [1974] Director [Canadian]; Simon Osgood [1970] Director; Timothy Pope [1970] Managing Director; Merrill Brooks Smith [1955] Director [American]

Independent Growth Finance Limited
Incorporated: 22 March 2016 *Employees:* 53
Net Worth Deficit: £5,376,109 *Total Assets:* £66,175,492
Registered Office: Kingsgate, High Street, Redhill, Surrey, RH1 1SG
Activities: Activities of head offices
Parent: Spring Ventures Nominees Limited
Officers: Matthew Jonathan Cooper [1966] Director [American]; John Michael Hudson [1968] Director; John Peter Onslow [1958] Director; Nicholas John Price [1964] Finance Director; Peter William Ralph [1979] Director

Independent Inspections Limited
Incorporated: 1 July 1993 *Employees:* 131
Net Worth: £6,125,000 *Total Assets:* £36,191,000
Registered Office: 2 AC Court, High Street, Thames Ditton, Surrey, KT7 0SR
Activities: Other service activities n.e.c.
Parent: Independent Inspections Holdings Limited
Officers: Alan Albert Horton [1963] Director; Stuart Pace [1962] Director

Independent Technology Systems Limited
Incorporated: 28 March 1996 *Employees:* 165
Net Worth: £45,092,000 *Total Assets:* £68,386,000
Registered Office: Wells Court, Albert Drive, Woking, Surrey, GU21 5UB
Activities: Information technology consultancy activities
Parent: Intec Telecom Systems Ltd
Officers: Gregory Lyman Canon, Secretary; Bret Charles Griess [1968] Director/President/CEO [American]; Kenneth Grant Jenkinson [1960] Director/Software Development Manager [Australian]; Suresh Kumar Mani [1981] Accounting Director - APAC [Indian]; Fiona Mary O'Connor [1970] Director/Business Executive [Irish]; Francis Partick O'Sullivan [1967] Director/Business Executive [Irish]; David Neil Schaaf [1969] Director/Senior VP, Business Finance & Treasury [American]; Philip John Vitale [1968] Director/Manager [Australian]

Indivior PLC
Incorporated: 26 September 2014
Net Worth Deficit: £152,919,024 *Total Assets:* £1,087,758,976
Registered Office: 103-105 Bath Road, Slough, Berks, SL1 3UH
Activities: Manufacture of basic pharmaceutical products
Officers: Kathryn Barbara Hudson, Secretary; Mark Wesley Crossley [1969] Director [American]; Dr Yvonne Greenstreet [1962] Director; Tatjana Anni Hilde May [1965] Director; Dr Andrew Thomas McLellan [1948] Director [American]; Lorna Mary Southcombe Parker [1959] Director; Daniel Joseph Phelan [1949] Director [American]; Howard Hao Pien [1957] Director [American]; Christian Stanton Schade [1961] Director [American]; Daniel Tasse [1960] Director [Canadian]; Shaun Thaxter [1967] Director [British/American]; Lizabeth Herbst Zlatkus [1958] Director [American]

Indoor Bowling Acquisitions Limited
Incorporated: 28 November 2014
Net Worth: £5,081,000 *Total Assets:* £49,701,000
Registered Office: Aragon House, Cranfield Technology Park, Cranfield, Bedford, MK43 0EQ
Activities: Activities of head offices
Parent: Indoor Bowling Equity Limited
Officers: Mark Simon Willis, Secretary; Nicolas Andrew Basing [1962] Director; Graham Edwin Blackwell [1969] Director; Dr Duncan Steven Garrood [1958] Director; Mark Simon Willis [1976] Director

Indoor Bowling Equity Limited
Incorporated: 29 May 2015 *Employees:* 2
Net Worth: £39,469,000 *Total Assets:* £84,709,000
Registered Office: Aragon House, Cranfield Technology Park, Cranfield, Bedford, MK43 0EQ
Activities: Activities of head offices
Parent: TEG Holdings Limited
Officers: Mark Willis, Secretary; Nicolas Andrew Basing [1962] Director; Graham Edwin Blackwell [1969] Director; Dr Duncan Steven Garrood [1958] Director; Mark Simon Willis [1976] Director

Industrial and Financial Systems, IFS UK Ltd
Incorporated: 12 November 1996 *Employees:* 262
Net Worth: £13,221,579 *Total Assets:* £57,601,820
Registered Office: Artisan, Hillbottom Road, Sands Industrial Estate, High Wycombe, Bucks, HP12 4HJ
Activities: Business and domestic software development
Officers: Kevin Dennis Fletcher, Secretary; Anders Magnus Lindholm [1979] Director [Swedish]; Mark Soden [1960] Sales Director

INEOS Canada Limited
Incorporated: 7 December 2016
Net Worth: £1,349,780,864 *Total Assets:* £1,360,560,896
Registered Office: Hawkslease, Chapel Lane, Lyndhurst, Hants, SO43 7FG
Activities: Activities of head offices
Parent: INEOS Holdings Limited
Officers: Yasin Stanley Ali, Secretary; Jonathan Frank Ginns [1973] Director; Debra Smeeton [1967] Director

INEOS Capital Limited
Incorporated: 1 October 1999
Net Worth: £40,315,352 *Total Assets:* £40,427,176
Registered Office: Hawkslease, Chapel Lane, Lyndhurst, Hants, SO43 7FG
Activities: Management consultancy activities other than financial management
Major Shareholder: James Arthur Ratcliffe
Officers: Yasin Stanley Ali, Secretary; Jonathan Frank Ginns [1973] Director/Legal Manager

INEOS Chemicals France Holdings Limited
Incorporated: 4 September 2013 *Employees:* 594
Net Worth: £279,931,392 *Total Assets:* £505,849,088
Registered Office: Hawkslease, Chapel Lane, Lyndhurst, Hants, SO43 7FG
Activities: Activities of head offices
Major Shareholder: James Arthur Ratcliffe
Officers: Yasin Stanley Ali, Secretary; Dr Iain Timothy Hogan [1960] Director; Debra Smeeton [1967] Director/Chartered Accountant

INEOS Chemicals Grangemouth Limited
Incorporated: 5 August 2009 *Employees:* 584
Net Worth: £217,464,000 *Total Assets:* £664,244,992
Registered Office: Hawkslease, Chapel Lane, Lyndhurst, Hants, SO43 7FG
Activities: Manufacture of other organic basic chemicals
Parent: INEOS Grangemouth PLC
Officers: Gerard Stephen Hepburn, Secretary; Andrew Ronald Gardner [1967] Director; Gerard Stephen Hepburn [1979] Director/Accountant; John Paul McNally [1960] Director; Gordon David Milne [1969] Director

INEOS Commercial Services UK Limited
Incorporated: 19 November 2010 *Employees:* 93
Net Worth: £269,879,840 *Total Assets:* £625,029,824
Registered Office: Hawkslease, Chapel Lane, Lyndhurst, Hants, SO43 7FG
Activities: Other business support service activities n.e.c.
Parent: INEOS Grangemouth PLC
Officers: Gerard Stephen Hepburn, Secretary; Andrew Ronald Gardner [1967] Director; Gerard Stephen Hepburn [1979] Director/Accountant; John Paul McNally [1960] Director; Gordon David Milne [1969] Director

INEOS Derivatives France Limited
Incorporated: 15 August 2008
Net Worth: £252,618,496 *Total Assets:* £599,658,752
Registered Office: Hawkslease, Chapel Lane, Lyndhurst, Hants, SO43 7FG
Activities: Other engineering activities
Parent: INEOS Chemicals France Holdings Limited
Officers: Yasin Stanley Ali, Secretary; Dr Iain Timothy Hogan [1960] Director; Debra Smeeton [1967] Director/Chartered Accountant

INEOS European Holdings Limited
Incorporated: 10 December 2004
Net Worth: £217,633,168 *Total Assets:* £2,171,935,744
Registered Office: Hawkslease, Chapel Lane, Lyndhurst, Hants, SO43 7FG
Activities: Activities of head offices
Major Shareholder: James Arthur Ratcliffe
Officers: Yasin Stanley Ali, Secretary; Yasin Stanley Ali [1974] Director/Company Secretary; Jonathan Frank Ginns [1973] Director/Legal Manager

INEOS Finance Company 1
Incorporated: 12 December 2013
Net Worth Deficit: £619,544,256 *Total Assets:* £2,742,068,480
Registered Office: Hawkslease, Chapel Lane, Lyndhurst, Hants, SO43 7FG
Activities: Financial management
Parent: INEOS Holdings Limited
Officers: Yasin Ali, Secretary; Debra Smeeton [1967] Director/Chartered Accountant

INEOS Finance Company 2
Incorporated: 12 December 2013
Net Worth: £2,743,992,320 *Total Assets:* £2,743,992,320
Registered Office: Hawkslease, Chapel Lane, Lyndhurst, Hants, SO43 7FG
Activities: Financial management
Parent: INEOS Finance Company 1
Officers: Yasin Ali, Secretary; Debra Smeeton [1967] Director/Chartered Accountant

INEOS Finance Company 3 Limited
Incorporated: 2 December 2014
Net Worth: £6,171,595,776 *Total Assets:* £6,386,802,688
Registered Office: Hawkslease, Chapel Lane, Lyndhurst, Hants, SO43 7FG
Activities: Financial management
Parent: INEOS Oxide Limited
Officers: Yasin Stanley Ali, Secretary; Jonathan Frank Ginns [1973] Director/Legal Manager; Debra Smeeton [1967] Director/Chartered Accountant

INEOS Finance PLC
Incorporated: 23 November 2009
Net Worth: £87,642 *Total Assets:* £2,968,974,592
Registered Office: Hawkslease, Chapel Lane, Lyndhurst, Hants, SO43 7FG
Activities: Financial intermediation not elsewhere classified
Parent: INEOS Holdings Limited
Officers: Yasin Stanley Ali, Secretary; Jonathan Frank Ginns [1973] Director/Legal Manager

INEOS FPS Limited
Incorporated: 8 March 2017 *Employees:* 296
Net Worth Deficit: £6,521,000 *Total Assets:* £324,302,016
Registered Office: Hawkslease, Chapel Lane, Lyndhurst, Hants, SO43 7FG
Activities: Other service activities n.e.c.
Parent: INEOS UK E & P Holdings Limited
Officers: Yasin Stanley Ali, Secretary; Stuart Michael Collings [1967] Director; Andrew Ronald Gardner [1967] Director; Gerard Stephen Hepburn [1979] Director/Accountant; Gordon David Milne [1969] Director

INEOS Grangemouth PLC
Incorporated: 19 September 2013 *Employees:* 677
Net Worth: £482,661,824 *Total Assets:* £899,344,000
Registered Office: Hawkslease, Chapel Lane, Lyndhurst, Hants, SO43 7FG
Activities: Activities of head offices
Parent: INEOS Industries Holdings Limited
Officers: Gerard Stephen Hepburn, Secretary; Andrew Ronald Gardner [1967] Director; Gerard Stephen Hepburn [1979] Director/Accountant; John Paul McNally [1960] Director; Gordon David Milne [1969] Director

INEOS Holdings Limited
Incorporated: 14 May 2001
Net Worth: £1,063,150,528 *Total Assets:* £14,607,802,368
Registered Office: Hawkslease, Chapel Lane, Lyndhurst, Hants, SO43 7FG
Activities: Activities of head offices
Parent: INEOS Holdings (Investments) Limited
Officers: Yasin Stanley Ali, Secretary; Yasin Stanley Ali [1974] Director/Company Secretary; Jonathan Frank Ginns [1973] Director/Legal Manager

INEOS Industries Holdings Limited
Incorporated: 9 July 2009
Net Worth: £789,031,552 *Total Assets:* £2,057,548,160
Registered Office: Hawkslease, Chapel Lane, Lyndhurst, Hants, SO43 7FG
Activities: Activities of head offices
Parent: INEOS Industries Limited
Officers: Yasin Stanley Ali, Secretary; Jonathan Frank Ginns [1973] Director/Legal Manager

INEOS Industries Limited
Incorporated: 10 July 2009 *Employees:* 5,403
Net Worth: £1,450,987,392 *Total Assets:* £7,721,331,712
Registered Office: Hawkslease, Chapel Lane, Lyndhurst, Hants, SO43 7FG
Activities: Activities of head offices
Major Shareholder: James Arthur Ratcliffe
Officers: Yasin Stanley Ali, Secretary; Jonathan Frank Ginns [1973] Director/Legal Manager

INEOS Investment Holdings (Germany) Limited
Incorporated: 11 December 2000
Net Worth Deficit: £113,177,912 *Total Assets:* £788,634,560
Registered Office: Hawkslease, Chapel Lane, Lyndhurst, Hants, SO43 7FG
Activities: Activities of head offices
Parent: INEOS Holdings Limited
Officers: Yasin Stanley Ali, Secretary; Yasin Stanley Ali [1974] Director/Company Secretary; Jonathan Frank Ginns [1973] Director/Legal Manager

INEOS Investments International Limited
Incorporated: 2 March 2000
Net Worth Deficit: £240,027,184 *Total Assets:* £1,063,833,536
Registered Office: Hawkslease, Chapel Lane, Lyndhurst, Hants, SO43 7FG
Activities: Activities of head offices
Parent: INEOS Holdings International Limited
Officers: Yasin Stanley Ali, Secretary; Jonathan Frank Ginns [1973] Director/Legal Manager; Debra Smeeton [1967] Director/Chartered Accountant

INEOS Manufacturing (Hull) Limited
Incorporated: 22 January 2008 *Employees:* 33
Net Worth Deficit: £27,150,000 *Total Assets:* £29,148,000
Registered Office: Hawkslease, Chapel Lane, Lyndhurst, Hants, SO43 7FG
Activities: Manufacture of other organic basic chemicals
Parent: INEOS Oxide Limited
Officers: Yasin Stanley Ali, Secretary; Ghislain Georges Jose Decadt [1955] Director [Belgian]; Jonathan Frank Ginns [1973] Director/Legal Manager; Peter Karel Virginia Huyck [1968] Director/Chief Financial Officer [Belgian]

INEOS Oxide Limited
Incorporated: 6 April 1998 *Employees:* 3
Net Worth: £6,579,635,200 *Total Assets:* £6,927,117,824
Registered Office: Hawkslease, Chapel Lane, Lyndhurst, Hants, SO43 7FG
Activities: Manufacture of other organic basic chemicals
Parent: INEOS Holdings Limited
Officers: Yasin Stanley Ali, Secretary; Jonathan Frank Ginns [1973] Director/Legal Manager; Peter Karel Virginia Huyck [1968] Director/Chief Financial Officer [Belgian]

INEOS Paraform Holdings Limited
Incorporated: 22 November 2004 *Employees:* 136
Net Worth: £3,491,647 *Total Assets:* £24,824,630
Registered Office: Hawkslease House, Chapel Lane, Lyndhurst, Hants, SO43 7FG
Activities: Activities of head offices
Shareholders: INEOS Enterprises Holdings Limited; James Arthur Ratcliffe
Officers: David John Wright Rey, Secretary; Andrew Brown [1981] Director/Chartered Accountant; Anthony White [1961] Director/Accountant

INEOS Sales (UK) Limited
Incorporated: 19 November 2010 *Employees:* 92
Net Worth: £29,811,948 *Total Assets:* £203,429,552
Registered Office: Hawklease, Chapel Lane, Lyndhurst, Hants, SO43 7FG
Activities: Mineral oil refining
Parent: INEOS European Holdings Limited
Officers: Yasin Stanley Ali, Secretary; Luciano Filippi [1975] Director [Italian]; Jonathan Frank Ginns [1973] Director/Legal Manager

INEOS Silicas Holdings Limited
Incorporated: 12 June 2000
Net Worth: £226,116,992 *Total Assets:* £290,558,016
Registered Office: Hawkslease, Chapel Lane, Lyndhurst, Hants, SO43 7FG
Activities: Activities of head offices
Parent: INEOS Investments International Limited
Officers: Yasin Stanley Ali, Secretary; Dr Jill Christine Dolan [1960] Director/Manager; Jonathan Frank Ginns [1973] Director/Legal Manager

INEOS Styrolution Financing Limited
Incorporated: 18 December 2015
Net Worth: £1,094,638,336 *Total Assets:* £1,095,338,112
Registered Office: Hawkslease, Chapel Lane, Lyndhurst, Hants, SO43 7FG
Activities: Financial management
Parent: INEOS Styrolution Holding Limited
Officers: Yasin Stanley Ali, Secretary; Andrew Christopher Currie [1955] Director; Markus Fieseler [1964] Director [German]; Jonathan Frank Ginns [1973] Director; Kevin McQuade [1956] Director [American]

INEOS Styrolution Holding Limited
Incorporated: 18 December 2015 *Employees:* 3,315
Net Worth: £1,711,493,632 *Total Assets:* £3,566,881,792
Registered Office: Hawkslease, Chapel Lane, Lyndhurst, Hants, SO43 7FG
Activities: Activities of head offices
Parent: INEOS Industries Holdings Limited
Officers: Yasin Stanley Ali, Secretary; Andrew Christopher Currie [1955] Director; Markus Fieseler [1964] Director [German]; Jonathan Frank Ginns [1973] Director; Kevin McQuade [1956] Director [American]

INEOS Treasury (UK) Limited
Incorporated: 11 September 2000
Net Worth Deficit: £994,917 *Total Assets:* £187,967,920
Registered Office: Hawkslease, Chapel Lane, Lyndhurst, Hants, SO43 7FG
Activities: Non-trading company
Parent: INEOS Investment Holdings (Germany) Limited
Officers: Yasin Stanley Ali, Secretary; Jonathan Frank Ginns [1973] Director/Legal Manager

INEOS U.K. Finance Company Limited
Incorporated: 6 November 2000
Net Worth: £20,283,100 *Total Assets:* £33,548,200
Registered Office: Hawkslease, Chapel Lane, Lyndhurst, Hants, SO43 7FG
Activities: Financial intermediation not elsewhere classified
Parent: INEOS Oxide Limited
Officers: Yasin Stanley Ali, Secretary; Peter Karel Virginia Huyck [1968] Director/Chief Financial Officer [Belgian]

INEOS U.S. Finance Company Limited
Incorporated: 6 November 2000
Net Worth Deficit: £5,227,207 *Total Assets:* £26,975,174
Registered Office: Hawkslease, Chapel Lane, Lyndhurst, Hants, SO43 7FG
Activities: Financial intermediation not elsewhere classified
Parent: INEOS Oxide Limited
Officers: Yasin Stanley Ali, Secretary; Peter Karel Virginia Huyck [1968] Director/Chief Financial Officer [Belgian]

INEOS Upstream Limited
Incorporated: 8 July 2014
Net Worth Deficit: £38,362,000 *Total Assets:* £99,983,000
Registered Office: Hawkslease, Chapel Lane, Lyndhurst, Hants, SO43 7FG
Activities: Extraction of natural gas
Parent: INEOS Upstream Holdings Limited
Officers: Gemma McLucas, Secretary; Cordelia Pace, Secretary; Anne Mary Tamsin Bowden [1982] Director/Solicitor; David Nicholas Brooks [1966] Director; Tom Pickering [1979] Director; Andrew James Pizzey [1970] Director/Accountant; Geir Tuft [1967] Director [Norwegian]

Inesa UK Limited
Incorporated: 1 December 2015 *Employees:* 2
Net Worth Deficit: £70,827 *Total Assets:* £172,465,488
Registered Office: Feilo Sylvania Europe Ltd, Avis Way, Newhaven, E Sussex, BN9 0ED
Activities: Manufacture of electric lighting equipment
Officers: Panlong Liu [1976] Director; Kui Ouyang [1969] Director [Chinese]

Infinity SDC Limited
Incorporated: 6 October 2005 *Employees:* 30
Net Worth: £44,965,000 *Total Assets:* £185,052,992
Registered Office: Witan Gate House, 500-600 Witan Gate West, Milton Keynes, Bucks, MK9 1SH
Activities: Other business support service activities n.e.c.
Officers: David Mark Ben-Ur [1971] Director/Chief Investment Officer [American]; Clive Martin Dolman [1960] Director/Investor; Simon David Pitcher [1972] Director/Investment Manager; Matthew Cye Sandoval [1966] Director/Financial Management; Stuart Sutton [1968] Director; John Thompson [1961] Financial Director; Stephen Anthony Zimmerman [1949] Director/Investor

Informatica Software Limited
Incorporated: 15 April 1997 *Employees:* 111
Net Worth: £13,530,105 *Total Assets:* £49,263,856
Registered Office: Highlands House, Basingstoke Road, Spencers Wood, Reading, Berks, RG7 1NT
Activities: Other information service activities n.e.c.
Officers: Bradford Charles Lewis [1958] Director/Lawyer [American]; Mark Allen Pellowski [1963] Director/VP Finance [American]

Infotech Trade Services Ltd
Incorporated: 19 September 2013
Net Worth: £3,778 *Total Assets:* £23,333,800
Registered Office: Suite 121, Wey House, 15 Church Street, Weybridge, Surrey, KT13 8NA
Activities: Other business support service activities n.e.c.
Shareholders: Christiana Chioma Ekeh; Leonard Nnamdi Ekeh
Officers: Christiana Chioma Ekeh [1964] Director/Accountant [Nigerian]; Leonard Nnamdi Ekeh [1957] Director/Economist [Nigerian]

Ingersoll-Rand UK Limited
Incorporated: 7 November 1996 *Employees:* 154
Previous: Ingersoll-Rand European Sales Limited
Net Worth: £251,390,000 *Total Assets:* £337,224,000
Registered Office: Harrow House, Bessemer Road, Basingstoke, Hants, RG21 3NB
Activities: Other business support service activities n.e.c.
Parent: Ingersoll-Rand PLC
Officers: Mihaela Cristea, Secretary; Gary Rutherford-Spence [1972] Director/Services Leader, UK, Ireland & Benelux; Stephen Vernon Taylor [1969] Regional Director Sales and Services; Omer Faruk Ucur [1976] Director/District Leader [Turkish]; Marc Anthony Weaver [1975] Director/Financial Controller

John Ingham & Sons Limited
Incorporated: 19 March 1930
Net Worth: £2,344,057 *Total Assets:* £22,497,804
Registered Office: Linton Park, Linton, Maidstone, Kent, ME17 4AN
Activities: Activities of head offices
Parent: Eastern Produce Investments Limited
Officers: Amarpal Takk, Secretary; Graham Harold McLean [1969] Managing Director; Susan Ann Walker [1967] Director

Ingram Micro (UK) Limited
Incorporated: 29 January 1982 *Employees:* 499
Net Worth: £32,090,000 *Total Assets:* £247,646,000
Registered Office: CBXII, 406-432 Midsummer Boulevard, Milton Keynes, Bucks, MK9 2EA
Activities: Wholesale of computers, computer peripheral equipment and software
Parent: Ingram Micro Holdings Ltd
Officers: Karel Everaet, Secretary; Benjamin Gamble, Secretary; Karel Everaet [1965] Director/Lawyer [Belgian]; Kris Emile Paul Mees [1972] Director [Belgian]; Matthew Sanderson [1971] Managing Director

Ingram Micro Holdings Limited
Incorporated: 14 May 1985 *Employees:* 4
Net Worth Deficit: £7,370,000 *Total Assets:* £128,053,000
Registered Office: 2nd Floor, CBX II Building West, 406-432 Midsummer Boulevard, Milton Keynes, Bucks, MK9 2EA
Activities: Activities of head offices
Officers: Karel Everaet, Secretary; Karel Everaet [1965] Director/Lawyer [Belgian]; Kris Emile Paul Mees [1972] Commercial Director [Belgian]; Matthew Sanderson [1971] Managing Director

Inhealth Group Holdings PLC
Incorporated: 29 September 2005 *Employees:* 1,699
Net Worth: £102,538,000 *Total Assets:* £152,156,992
Registered Office: Beechwood Hall, Kingsmead Road, High Wycombe, Bucks, HP11 1JL
Activities: Activities of head offices
Parent: Inhealth UK Holdings Limited
Officers: Alice Sarah Louise Cummings, Secretary; Ivan Harold Bradbury [1946] Director; Richard James Bradford [1963] Director; Sir Arthur David Chessells [1941] Director; Alice Sarah Louise Cummings [1963] Finance Director

Inhealth Group Limited
Incorporated: 18 December 2002 *Employees:* 169
Net Worth: £107,029,000 *Total Assets:* £156,195,008
Registered Office: Beechwood Hall, Kingsmead Road, High Wycombe, Bucks, HP11 1JL
Activities: Activities of head offices
Parent: Inhealth Group Holdings PLC
Officers: Richard James Bradford [1963] Director; Sir Arthur David Chessells [1941] Director; Alice Sarah Louise Cummings [1963] Finance Director

Inhealth Limited
Incorporated: 27 July 2004 *Employees:* 1,080
Net Worth: £54,489,000 *Total Assets:* £145,763,008
Registered Office: Beechwood Hall, Kingsmead Road, High Wycombe, Bucks, HP11 1JL
Activities: General medical practice activities
Parent: Inhealth Group Limited
Officers: Richard James Bradford [1963] Director; Alice Sarah Louise Cummings [1963] Finance Director

Inhealth UK Holdings Limited
Incorporated: 18 August 2009 *Employees:* 1,700
Net Worth: £95,333,000 *Total Assets:* £149,200,992
Registered Office: Beechwood Hall, Kingsmead Road, High Wycombe, Bucks, HP11 1JL
Activities: Activities of head offices
Major Shareholder: Ivan Harold Bradbury
Officers: Ivan Harold Bradbury [1946] Director

Initial Medical Services Limited
Incorporated: 18 March 1996 *Employees:* 168
Net Worth: £10,406,000 *Total Assets:* £21,761,000
Registered Office: Riverbank, Meadows Business Park, Blackwater, Camberley, Surrey, GU17 9AB
Activities: Other business support service activities n.e.c.
Parent: Rentokil Initial 1927 PLC
Officers: Catherine Stead, Secretary; Jeffreys Kristen Hampson [1974] Finance Director; Phillip Paul Wood [1965] Managing Director

Inland Homes PLC
Incorporated: 16 June 2005 *Employees:* 93
Net Worth: £142,400,000 *Total Assets:* £299,600,000
Registered Office: Decimal Place, Chiltern Avenue, Amersham, Bucks, HP6 5FG
Activities: Development of building projects
Officers: Nishith Malde, Secretary; Simon Charles Bennett [1958] Director; Laure Duhot [1961] Director [French]; John Brian Hansen Johnson [1961] Director; Nishith Malde [1958] Director; Terry Rene Roydon [1946] Director; Gary John Skinner [1968] Managing Director; Gary John Skinner [1968] Managing Director; Stephen Desmond Wicks [1951] Director

Inland Limited
Incorporated: 16 June 2005 *Employees:* 87
Net Worth: £20,324,876 *Total Assets:* £169,394,176
Registered Office: Decimal Place, Chiltern Avenue, Amersham, Bucks, HP6 5FG
Activities: Development of building projects
Parent: Inland Homes 2013
Officers: Thomas Cuff [1939] Director/Solicitor; Nishith Malde [1958] Director; Gary John Skinner [1968] Director; Desmond Richard Wicks [1989] Land Director; Stephen Desmond Wicks [1951] Director

Inland Property Limited
Incorporated: 4 March 2015
Net Worth: £25,225,228 *Total Assets:* £45,341,128
Registered Office: Decimal Place, Chiltern Avenue, Amersham, Bucks, HP6 5FG
Activities: Buying and selling of own real estate
Parent: Poole Investments Ltd
Officers: Nishith Malde [1958] Director; Gary John Skinner [1968] Managing Director; Stephen Desmond Wicks [1951] Director

Innisfree Schools (F2C) Limited
Incorporated: 22 March 2013
Net Worth: £35,460,000 *Total Assets:* £73,336,000
Registered Office: 8 White Oak Square, London Road, Swanley, Kent, BR8 7AG
Activities: Activities of other holding companies n.e.c.
Parent: Innisfree Continuation Partners LLP
Officers: Nicholas John Edward Crowther [1960] Investment Director; Burton David [1978] Director

Innisfree Schools (Secondary) Limited
Incorporated: 22 March 2013
Net Worth: £40,924,000 *Total Assets:* £76,075,000
Registered Office: 8 White Oak Square, London Road, Swanley, Kent, BR8 7AG
Activities: Activities of other holding companies n.e.c.
Shareholders: Innisfree Secondary Partners 1 LLP; Innisfree Secondary Partners 2 LLP
Officers: Nicholas John Edward Crowther [1960] Investment Director; Burton David [1978] Director

Innotech Advisers Limited
Incorporated: 23 November 1982 *Employees:* 13
Net Worth: £117,243,408 *Total Assets:* £549,925,120
Registered Office: Q3, The Square, Randalls Way, Leatherhead, Surrey, KT22 7TW
Activities: Financial intermediation not elsewhere classified
Major Shareholder: David John Sainsbury
Officers: Michael David Langford Smith, Secretary; Joseph Christopher Burns [1978] Director; Baron David John Sainsbury of Turville [1940] Director; James Frederick Shea [1964] Director; David Roy Wood [1961] Director

The Innovation Group (EMEA) Limited
Incorporated: 30 July 2001 *Employees:* 137
Net Worth: £28,233,000 *Total Assets:* £48,730,000
Registered Office: Yarmouth House, 1300 Parkway, Solent Business Park, Whiteley, Fareham, Hants, PO15 7AE
Activities: Other information technology service activities
Parent: The Innovation Group Limited
Officers: Magdalena Baugh [1980] Director/FD, Chartered Accountant [Polish]; Alasdair Marnoch [1963] Director; Christopher Timothy Miles Toulson-Clarke [1964] Director/Chief Executive

The Innovation Group Limited
Incorporated: 30 September 1996
Previous: The Innovation Group PLC
Net Worth: £233,063,008 *Total Assets:* £267,650,000
Registered Office: Yarmouth House, 1300 Parkway, Whiteley, Fareham, Hants, PO15 7AE
Activities: Activities of other holding companies n.e.c.
Parent: Axios Bidco Limited
Officers: Timothy Philip Griffiths [1960] Director; Alasdair Marnoch [1963] Director

Inprint Systems Limited
Incorporated: 15 October 1998
Net Worth: £24,737,000 *Total Assets:* £24,744,000
Registered Office: Inprint Systems, Foster Road, Ashford Business Park, Sevington, Ashford, Kent, TN24 0SH
Activities: Other business support service activities n.e.c.
Parent: CCL Industries (UK) Limited
Officers: Marie Gorete Morgan, Secretary [French]; Mark Anthony Beckram [1970] Director; Geoffrey Thomas Martin [1954] Director [American]; Michael John McGarry [1965] Director/General Manager; Glynn Nigel Moyles [1970] Director/General Manager

INS-Sure Holdings Limited
Incorporated: 19 April 2001 *Employees:* 375
Net Worth: £46,814,000 *Total Assets:* £114,317,000
Registered Office: Royal Pavilion, Wellesley Road, Aldershot, Hants, GU11 1PZ
Activities: Other activities auxiliary to insurance and pension funding
Parent: Xpanse Limited
Officers: Gilles Alex Maxime Bonvarlet [1964] Director [French]; David Howard Gittings [1954] Director; Royston Hoggarth [1962] Director; Steve Andre Anthony Jules [1980] Director/Accountant; Daljeet Singh Juttla [1986] Director; Dave John Matcham [1961] Director; Dr Indranil Nath [1969] Director [Indian]; John Barry Taylor [1973] Director/General Manager IT Services; Darren John Temple [1969] Director

INS-Sure Services Limited
Incorporated: 13 December 2000 *Employees:* 286
Net Worth: £4,271,000 *Total Assets:* £191,274,000
Registered Office: Royal Pavilion, Wellesley Road, Aldershot, Hants, GU11 1PZ
Activities: Non-life insurance
Parent: INS-Sure Holdings Limited
Officers: Gilles Alex Maxime Bonvarlet [1964] Director [French]; David Howard Gittings [1954] Director; Royston Hoggarth [1962] Director; Steve Andre Anthony Jules [1980] Director/Accountant; Daljeet Singh Juttla [1986] Director; Dave John Matcham [1961] Director; Dr Indranil Nath [1969] Director [Indian]; John Barry Taylor [1973] Director/General Manager IT Services; Darren John Temple [1969] Director

Inspiral Oldham Holding Company Limited
Incorporated: 29 January 2010
Net Worth Deficit: £8,282,000 *Total Assets:* £78,819,000
Registered Office: 8 White Oak Square, London Road, Swanley, Kent, BR8 7AG
Activities: Activities of head offices
Parent: JLIF Holdings (Regeneration and Social Housing) Limited
Officers: Guy James Cresswell [1966] Director of Housing; Philip Howard Elvy [1967] Finance Director; Vikki Louise Everett [1971] Director/Project Manager; Julian Denzil Sutcliffe [1968] Life Cycle Asset Director

Inspiral Oldham Limited
Incorporated: 4 February 2010
Net Worth Deficit: £8,282,000 *Total Assets:* £78,819,000
Registered Office: 8 White Oak Square, London Road, Swanley, Kent, BR8 7AG
Activities: Other business support service activities n.e.c.
Parent: Inspiral Oldham Holding Company Limited
Officers: Guy James Cresswell [1966] Director of Housing; Philip Howard Elvy [1967] Finance Director; Vikki Louise Everett [1971] Director/Project Manager; Julian Denzil Sutcliffe [1968] Life Cycle Asset Director

Inspiring Learning (Holdings) Limited
Incorporated: 25 July 2007 *Employees:* 898
Net Worth: £1,981,000 *Total Assets:* £53,890,000
Registered Office: 2nd Floor, 1 Jubilee Street, Brighton, BN1 1GE
Activities: Activities of head offices
Parent: Inspiring Learning Services Limited
Officers: Timothy James Gibson [1968] Director [New Zealander]; Charles Robert William McLean [1969] Director

Inspiring Learning Limited
Incorporated: 25 July 2007
Net Worth: £1,695,000 *Total Assets:* £25,036,000
Registered Office: 2nd Floor, 1 Jubilee Street, Brighton, BN1 1GE
Activities: Activities of head offices
Parent: Inspiring Learning (Holdings) Limited
Officers: Timothy James Gibson [1968] Director [New Zealander]; Charles Robert William McLean [1969] Director

Inspiring Learning Services Limited
Incorporated: 5 June 2008
Previous: Inspiring Learning (Bidco) Limited
Net Worth: £28,905,000 *Total Assets:* £32,987,000
Registered Office: 2nd Floor, 1 Jubilee Street, Brighton, BN1 1GE
Activities: Activities of head offices
Parent: Graduation Bidco Limited
Officers: Timothy James Gibson [1968] Director [New Zealander]; Charles Robert William McLean [1969] Director; Anthony Martin Robinson [1962] Director/Chairman

Intec Telecom Systems Limited
Incorporated: 22 February 2000 *Employees:* 5
Net Worth: £76,041,000 *Total Assets:* £76,050,000
Registered Office: Wells Court, Albert Drive, Woking, Surrey, GU21 5UB
Activities: Other telecommunications activities
Parent: CSG Systems UK Limited
Officers: Gregory Lyman Canon, Secretary; Bret Charles Griess [1968] Director/President/CEO [American]; Fiona Mary O'Connor [1970] Director/Business Executive [Irish]; David Neil Schaaf [1969] Director/Senior VP, Business Finance & Treasury [American]

Intelliflo Bidco Limited
Incorporated: 15 July 2013
Net Worth Deficit: £13,294,405 *Total Assets:* £50,401,736
Registered Office: Third Floor, Drapers Court, Kingston Hall Road, Kingston upon Thames, Surrey, KT1 2BQ
Activities: Activities of other holding companies n.e.c.
Parent: Intelliflo Midco Limited
Officers: Robert Rigsby, Secretary; Bryan Patrick Perryman [1979] Director [American]; Hamish John Purdey [1975] Director [Australian/British]

Intelliflo Holdings 2013 Limited
Incorporated: 15 July 2013 *Employees:* 169
Net Worth Deficit: £13,613,391 *Total Assets:* £55,258,876
Registered Office: Third Floor, Drapers Court, Kingston Hall Road, Kingston upon Thames, Surrey, KT1 2BQ
Activities: Activities of other holding companies n.e.c.
Parent: Invesco Holding Company Limited
Officers: Robert Rigsby, Secretary; Akeel Ahmed [1976] Director/Software Consultant; Nick Eatock [1968] IT Director; Bryan Patrick Perryman [1979] Director [American]; Hamish John Purdey [1975] Director [Australian/British]

Intelliflo Intermediate Holdings Limited
Incorporated: 15 July 2013
Net Worth Deficit: £2,731,094 *Total Assets:* £38,501,876
Registered Office: Third Floor, Drapers Court, Kingston Hall Road, Kingston upon Thames, Surrey, KT1 2BQ
Activities: Activities of other holding companies n.e.c.
Parent: Intelliflo Holdings 2013 Ltd
Officers: Robert Rigsby, Secretary; Bryan Patrick Perryman [1979] Director [American]; Hamish John Purdey [1975] Director [Australian/British]

Intelliflo Midco Limited
Incorporated: 15 July 2013 *Employees:* 169
Net Worth Deficit: £8,947,798 *Total Assets:* £55,258,872
Registered Office: Third Floor, Drapers Court, Kingston Hall Road, Kingston upon Thames, Surrey, KT1 2BQ
Activities: Activities of other holding companies n.e.c.
Parent: Intelliflo Intermediate Holdings Limited
Officers: Robert Rigsby, Secretary; Bryan Patrick Perryman [1979] Director [American]; Hamish John Purdey [1975] Director [Australian/British]

Inter Bay Financial II Limited
Incorporated: 13 August 2008
Net Worth: £31,560,000 *Total Assets:* £64,080,000
Registered Office: Reliance House, Sun Pier, Chatham, Kent, ME4 4ET
Activities: Activities of mortgage finance companies
Parent: Interbay Holdings Ltd
Officers: Nickesha Graham-Burrell, Secretary; Clive David Kornitzer [1964] Director; Andrew Parkes [1970] Director/Chief Operating Officer (Subsidiaries); Mark James Parrett [1969] Director; Richard Wilson [1972] Director/Chief Credit Officer

Inter Pipeline Europe Limited
Incorporated: 14 September 2005
Net Worth: £178,818,000 *Total Assets:* £325,313,984
Registered Office: Priory House, 60 Station Road, Redhill, Surrey, RH1 1PE
Activities: Activities of head offices
Officers: Nicholas Charles Coldrey, Secretary; Brent Cameron Heagy [1960] Director/Chartered Accountant [Canadian]; Martyn Joseph Augustine Lyons [1962] Director/Chief Executive; Cory Wade Neufeld [1973] Director/Engineer [Canadian]; Paul William Oseland [1964] Commercial Director

Inter Terminals Immingham Limited
Incorporated: 18 December 1929 *Employees:* 114
Previous: Immingham Storage Company Limited
Net Worth: £40,790,000 *Total Assets:* £65,324,000
Registered Office: Priory House, 60 Station Road, Redhill, Surrey, RH1 1PE
Activities: Operation of warehousing and storage facilities for land transport activities
Parent: Chemicals & Oil Storage Management Limited
Officers: Nicholas Charles Coldrey, Secretary; Peter Brian Channing [1965] Director/Chartered Accountant; Keith Lionel Jackson [1956] Director/Terminal Manager; Martyn Joseph Augustine Lyons [1962] Managing Director

Inter Terminals Limited
Incorporated: 24 June 1999 *Employees:* 50
Previous: Simon Storage Limited
Net Worth: £271,539,008 *Total Assets:* £285,651,008
Registered Office: Priory House, 60 Station Road, Redhill, Surrey, RH1 1PE
Activities: Operation of warehousing and storage facilities for water transport activities
Parent: Inter Pipeline Europe Limited
Officers: Nicholas Charles Coldrey, Secretary; Peter Brian Channing [1965] Director/Chartered Accountant; Martyn Joseph Augustine Lyons [1962] Managing Director; Paul William Oseland [1964] Commercial Director

Inter Terminals Seal Sands Limited
Incorporated: 9 March 1949 *Employees:* 70
Previous: Seal Sands Storage Limited
Net Worth: £25,198,000 *Total Assets:* £43,375,000
Registered Office: Priory House, 60 Station Road, Redhill, Surrey, RH1 1PE
Activities: Operation of warehousing and storage facilities for land transport activities
Parent: Inter Terminals Limited
Officers: Nicholas Charles Coldrey, Secretary; Peter Brian Channing [1965] Director/Chartered Accountant; Keith Lionel Jackson [1956] Operations Director; Martyn Joseph Augustine Lyons [1962] Managing Director

Inter Terminals UK Limited
Incorporated: 20 August 1998 *Employees:* 79
Previous: Nustar Terminals Limited
Net Worth: £33,845,000 *Total Assets:* £76,242,000
Registered Office: Priory House, 60 Station Road, Redhill, Surrey, RH1 1PE
Activities: Operation of warehousing and storage facilities for water transport activities
Parent: Inter Terminals Limited
Officers: Nicholas Charles Coldrey, Secretary; Peter Brian Channing [1965] Director/Chartered Accountant; Martyn Joseph Augustine Lyons [1962] Managing Director; David James McLoughlin [1971] Director/Vice President; Paul William Oseland [1964] Commercial Director

Interbay Funding, Ltd.
Incorporated: 18 October 2005 *Employees:* 35
Net Worth: £30,251,000 *Total Assets:* £48,629,000
Registered Office: Reliance House, Sun Pier, Chatham, Kent, ME4 4ET
Activities: Activities of mortgage finance companies
Parent: Inter Bay Financial II Limited
Officers: Nickesha Graham-Burrell, Secretary; Andrew John Golding [1969] Director; Clive David Kornitzer [1964] Director; Andrew Parkes [1970] Director/Chief Operating Officer (Subsidiaries); Mark James Parrett [1969] Director; Richard Wilson [1972] Director/Chief Credit Officer

Interbay ML, Ltd
Incorporated: 29 December 2006
Net Worth: £29,631,000 *Total Assets:* £972,910,016
Registered Office: Reliance House, Sun Pier, Chatham, Kent, ME4 4ET
Activities: Activities of mortgage finance companies
Parent: Interbay Funding, Ltd.
Officers: Nickesha Graham-Burrell, Secretary; Clive David Kornitzer [1964] Director; Andrew Parkes [1970] Director/Chief Operating Officer (Subsidiaries); Mark James Parrett [1969] Director; Richard Wilson [1972] Director/Chief Credit Officer

Intercontinental (PB) 1
Incorporated: 15 October 2008
Net Worth: £1,865,974,400 *Total Assets:* £1,874,495,616
Registered Office: Broadwater Park, Denham, Bucks, UB9 5HR
Activities: Activities of head offices
Parent: Six Continents Hotels International Limited
Officers: Fiona Cuttell, Secretary; Colin Philip Garwood [1961] Director; Michael Todd Glover [1971] Director/Financial Controller [American]; Nicolette Henfrey [1969] Director

Intercontinental (PB) 3 Limited
Incorporated: 29 June 2009
Net Worth: £1,364,837,632 *Total Assets:* £1,369,897,600
Registered Office: Broadwater Park, Denham, Bucks, UB9 5HR
Activities: Activities of head offices
Parent: Six Continents Hotels International Limited
Officers: Fiona Cuttell, Secretary; Colin Philip Garwood [1961] Director; Michael Todd Glover [1971] Director/Financial Controller [American]; Nicolette Henfrey [1969] Director

Intercontinental Hotels Group PLC
Incorporated: 21 May 2004 *Employees:* 6,658
Net Worth Deficit: £611,415,936 *Total Assets:* £2,262,524,160
Registered Office: Broadwater Park, Denham, Bucks, UB9 5HR
Activities: Hotels and similar accommodation
Officers: George Turner, Secretary; Keith Barr [1970] Director [American]; Anne Busquet [1950] Director [American]; Patrick Jean Pierre Cescau [1948] Director [French]; Ian Dyson [1962] Director; Paul Russell Edgecliffe-Johnson [1972] Director/Certified Chartered Accountant; Jo Nell Harlow [1962] Director [American]; Elie Wajih Maalouf [1964] Director [American]; Malina Ngai Man Lin [1969] Director [Chinese]; Christopher Luke Mayhew [1953] Director; Gillian Clare McDonald [1964] Director; Dale Frederick Morrison [1949] Director [American]

Intercontinental Hotels Group Services Company
Incorporated: 3 December 1956 *Employees:* 568
Net Worth: £99,131,000 *Total Assets:* £127,499,000
Registered Office: Broadwater Park, Denham, Bucks, UB9 5HR
Activities: Other service activities n.e.c.
Parent: IHG Hotels Limited
Officers: Fiona Cuttell, Secretary; Michael Jon Cockcroft [1974] Director; Michael Todd Glover [1971] Director/Financial Controller [American]; Nicolette Henfrey [1969] Director

Intercontinental Hotels Limited
Incorporated: 2 October 2002
Net Worth: £820,241,984 *Total Assets:* £820,990,976
Registered Office: Broadwater Park, Denham, Bucks, UB9 5HR
Activities: Other business support service activities n.e.c.
Parent: Intercontinental Hotels Group PLC
Officers: Fiona Cuttell, Secretary; Paul Russell Edgecliffe-Johnson [1972] Director/Certified Chartered Accountant; Michael Todd Glover [1971] Director/Financial Controller [American]; Nicolette Henfrey [1969] Director; George Turner [1971] Director

Interdist Alliances Limited
Incorporated: 14 February 2008 *Employees:* 46
Net Worth: £1,838,960 *Total Assets:* £23,395,220
Registered Office: 2nd Floor, Nucleus House, 2 Lower Mortlake Road, Richmond, Surrey, TW9 2JA
Activities: Other information technology service activities
Shareholder: Susan Tierney
Officers: Antoine Kareh [1952] Director/Manager [Lebanese]

International Car Wash Group Financing PLC
Incorporated: 9 June 2014 *Employees:* 4
Previous: Boing Group Financing PLC
Net Worth Deficit: £1,535,000 *Total Assets:* £268,332,992
Registered Office: 35-37 Amersham Hill, High Wycombe, Bucks, HP13 6NU
Activities: Other retail sale of new goods in specialised stores (not commercial art galleries and opticians)
Parent: Boing Acquisitions Limited
Officers: Jessica Rowena Shaffrey, Secretary; Thomas Bruce Mangas [1967] Director/Chief Executive Officer [American]; Nilesh Kundanlal Pandya [1971] Director/Chief Financial Officer; Michael Andrew James Smith [1962] Director

International Car Wash Group Ltd.
Incorporated: 9 June 2014 *Employees:* 6
Previous: Boing Topco Limited
Net Worth: £43,285,000 *Total Assets:* £153,356,000
Registered Office: 35-37 Amersham Hill, High Wycombe, Bucks, HP13 6NU
Activities: Other retail sale in non-specialised stores
Parent: Shine Acquisition Co Limited
Officers: Ezra Field [1969] Director/Investment Professional [American]; Matthew Kaelin [1982] Director/Investment Professional [American]; Thomas Bruce Mangas [1967] Director/Chief Executive Officer [American]; Nilesh Kundanlal Pandya [1971] Director; Michael Scott Sharkey [1985] Director/Investment Professional [American]; Michael Andrew James Smith [1962] Director

International Group Limited
Incorporated: 16 September 1977 *Employees:* 303
Net Worth Deficit: £8,593,000 *Total Assets:* £81,943,000
Registered Office: Stoke Park, Park Road, Stoke Poges, Bucks, SL2 4PG
Activities: Activities of head offices
Officers: Hertford Milner King, Secretary; Chester Milner King [1971] Director; Hertford Milner King [1965] Director; Roger Milner King [1936] Director; Witney Milner King [1967] Director

International Marine Transportation Limited
Incorporated: 3 April 1952 *Employees:* 11
Net Worth: £40,897,032 *Total Assets:* £57,075,828
Registered Office: Ermyn House, Ermyn Way, Leatherhead, Surrey, KT22 8UX
Activities: Sea and coastal freight water transport
Parent: Esso UK Limited
Officers: Fiona Harness, Secretary; Jonathan Maxwell Evans [1957] Director/Oil Company Executive; Cory Emil Quarles [1975] Director/Oil Company Executive [American]

International Paint Limited
Incorporated: 18 September 1899 *Employees:* 722
Net Worth: £11,600,000 *Total Assets:* £215,400,000
Registered Office: The Akzonobel Building, Wexham Road, Slough, Berks, SL2 5DS
Activities: Manufacture of paints, varnishes and similar coatings, mastics and sealants
Parent: Akzo Nobel Coatings (BLD) Limited
Officers: Nigel Atkinson [1970] Director/Accountant; James William Morton [1979] Director; David Neil Williams [1966] Director

International Property Finance (Spain) Limited
Incorporated: 5 October 2004
Net Worth: £1,214 *Total Assets:* £22,340,606
Registered Office: Rock Farm, Fort Lane, Reigate Hill, Reigate, Surrey, RH2 9RN
Activities: Activities of financial services holding companies
Parent: Rothschild & Co SCA
Officers: Christopher Lewis Coleman [1968] Director/Banker; Shirley Jane Fleming [1961] Director; Neil David Townson [1960] Director

International Society for Krishna Consciousness Limited
Incorporated: 15 September 1969 *Employees:* 230
Net Worth: £38,726,092 *Total Assets:* £41,681,696
Registered Office: Oak House, 1 Watford Road, Radlett, Herts, WD7 8LA
Activities: Activities of religious organisations
Officers: Grace Olapoju, Secretary; Terry Michael Anderson [1959] Director/Priest; Anthony William Howchin [1956] Director/Priest Branch Manager; George Thomas McMullan [1963] Director/Voluntary Worker; Paul Patrick Murphy [1961] Director/Restaurateur [Irish]; Kamlesh Kumar Maheshwar Patel [1962] Director/Corporate Financial Advisor

Interquest Group (UK) Limited
Incorporated: 5 May 2000 *Employees:* 265
Net Worth: £14,306,818 *Total Assets:* £40,527,684
Registered Office: Castle Chambers, 87a High Street, Berkhamsted, Herts, HP4 2DF
Activities: Other activities of employment placement agencies
Parent: Interquest Group Limited
Officers: Clare Hartnell, Secretary; Gary Peter Ashworth [1960] Director; David Charles Bygrave [1968] Director/Chartered Accountant; Christopher Ernest Eldridge [1973] Director

Interserve Developments No.2 Limited
Incorporated: 8 February 2013
Total Assets: £32,005,000
Registered Office: Interserve House, Ruscombe Park, Twyford, Reading, Berks, RG10 9JU
Activities: Activities of other holding companies n.e.c.
Parent: Interserve Investments Limited
Officers: Stephen Michael Jones [1968] Director/Chartered Accountant

Interserve Engineering Limited
Incorporated: 7 June 1976 *Employees:* 2
Net Worth: £10,882,000 *Total Assets:* £34,379,000
Registered Office: Interserve House, Ruscombe Park, Twyford, Reading, Berks, RG10 9JU
Activities: Activities of other holding companies n.e.c.
Parent: West's Group International Limited
Officers: Andrew John McDonald, Secretary; Andrew John McDonald [1974] Director/Company Secretary; Anthony Kenneth Smythe [1965] Director/Accountant

Interserve Finance (Switzerland) Holdings Limited
Incorporated: 12 November 2013 *Employees:* 3
Net Worth: £204,498,000 *Total Assets:* £205,938,000
Registered Office: Interserve House, Ruscombe Park, Twyford, Reading, Berks, RG10 9JU
Activities: Activities of other holding companies n.e.c.
Parent: Interserve Finance Limited
Officers: Andrew John McDonald, Secretary; Andrew John McDonald [1974] Director/Company Secretary; Anthony Kenneth Smythe [1965] Director/Accountant

Interserve Finance Limited
Incorporated: 5 February 2008 *Employees:* 3
Net Worth Deficit: £22,404,000 *Total Assets:* £1,079,881,984
Registered Office: Interserve House, Ruscombe Park, Twyford, Reading, Berks, RG10 9JU
Activities: Other business support service activities n.e.c.
Parent: Interserve Group Holdings Limited
Officers: Andrew John McDonald, Secretary; Andrew John McDonald [1974] Director/Company Secretary; Anthony Kenneth Smythe [1965] Director/Accountant

Interserve Group Holdings Limited
Incorporated: 17 October 2007 *Employees:* 3
Net Worth Deficit: £2,995,000 *Total Assets:* £905,601,984
Registered Office: Interserve House, Ruscombe Park, Twyford, Reading, Berks, RG10 9JU
Activities: Activities of other holding companies n.e.c.
Parent: Interserve PLC
Officers: Andrew John McDonald, Secretary; Andrew John McDonald [1974] Director/Company Secretary; Debra Jayne White [1962] Director/Chief Executive; Mark Argent Whiteling [1963] Director/Chief Financial Officer

Interserve Investments Limited
Incorporated: 16 August 1902 *Employees:* 61
Net Worth: £130,428,000 *Total Assets:* £170,008,992
Registered Office: Interserve House, Ruscombe Park, Twyford, Reading, Berks, RG10 9JU
Activities: Activities of other holding companies n.e.c.
Parent: Interserve Group Holdings Limited
Officers: Rajan Goyal [1966] Director/Accountant; Stephen Michael Jones [1968] Director/Chartered Accountant; Robert James Marsden [1955] Director/Project Manager; Douglas Iain Sutherland [1965] Director/Civil Engineer

Interserve PFI Holdings 2014 Limited
Incorporated: 13 March 2014 *Employees:* 6
Net Worth Deficit: £7,118,000 *Total Assets:* £73,430,000
Registered Office: Interserve House, Ruscombe Park, Ruscombe, Reading, Berks, RG10 9JU
Activities: Activities of other holding companies n.e.c.
Shareholders: Interserve Investments Limited; PPDI Assetco Limited
Officers: Stephen Michael Jones [1968] Director; John McDonagh [1969] Director/Fund Manager; Alistair Graham Ray [1974] Director/Fund Manager; Douglas Iain Sutherland [1965] Director/Civil Engineer

Interserve PFI Holdings Limited
Incorporated: 9 October 2002 *Employees:* 4
Net Worth: £9,527,000 *Total Assets:* £42,556,000
Registered Office: Interserve House, Ruscombe Park, Twyford, Reading, Berks, RG10 9JU
Activities: Activities of other holding companies n.e.c.
Parent: Interserve PFI Holdings 2014 Limited
Officers: John Stephen Gordon [1962] Director; Stephen Michael Jones [1968] Director/Chartered Accountant; John McDonagh [1969] Director

Interserve PLC
Incorporated: 19 April 1906 *Employees:* 44,711
Net Worth: £47,300,000 *Total Assets:* £1,715,399,936
Registered Office: Interserve House, Ruscombe Park, Twyford, Reading, Berks, RG10 9JU
Activities: Activities of other holding companies n.e.c.
Officers: Andrew John McDonald, Secretary; Glyn Anthony Barker [1953] Director; Gareth Maitland Edwards [1958] Director/Solicitor; Anne Kathleen Fahy [1960] Director/Chief Financial Officer [Irish]; Russell John King [1957] Director; Charles Nicholas Pollard [1958] Director/Civil Engineer; Nicholas Robin Salmon [1952] Director; Debra Jayne White [1962] Director/Chief Executive; Mark Argent Whiteling [1963] Director/Chief Financial Officer

Interserve Service Futures Limited
Incorporated: 9 April 2009
Net Worth Deficit: £1,628,017 *Total Assets:* £60,264,276
Registered Office: Interserve House, Ruscombe Park, Twyford, Reading, Berks, RG10 9JU
Activities: Activities of other holding companies n.e.c.
Parent: Interserve Service Futures Holdings Limited
Officers: Stephen Michael Jones [1968] Director/Chartered Accountant; Ian Fisher Mulholland [1967] Director of Justice; Christopher Mark Victor Peel [1981] Managing Director; Douglas Iain Sutherland [1965] Director/Civil Engineer

Interserve Working Futures Limited
Incorporated: 17 June 1988 *Employees:* 151
Net Worth: £1,565,771 *Total Assets:* £31,849,514
Registered Office: Interserve House, Ruscombe Park, Twyford, Reading, Berks, RG10 9JU
Activities: Other activities of employment placement agencies
Parent: Interserve Service Futures Limited
Officers: Laura Gowens [1980] Finance Director; Stephen Michael Jones [1968] Director/Chartered Accountant; Christopher Mark Victor Peel [1981] Managing Director; Douglas Iain Sutherland [1965] Director/Civil Engineer

Intersurgical Limited
Incorporated: 31 March 1980 *Employees:* 809
Net Worth: £97,648,656 *Total Assets:* £127,195,864
Registered Office: Crane House, Molly Millars Lane, Wokingham, Berks, RG41 2RZ
Activities: Manufacture of medical and dental instruments and supplies
Officers: Stephen Keith Williams, Secretary; Charles Henry Bellm [1985] Commercial Director; Howard Geoffrey Bellm [1956] Managing Director; Stephen Mark Day [1964] Manufacturing Director; Michael Robert Hinton [1976] Technical Director [Canadian]; Kim Jacob [1968] Financial Director; Deborah Ann Williams [1961] Marketing Director; Stephen Keith Williams [1957] Sales Director

Intervet UK Limited
Incorporated: 29 January 1969 *Employees:* 202
Net Worth: £102,744,000 *Total Assets:* £190,439,008
Registered Office: Walton Manor, Walton, Milton Keynes, Bucks, MK7 7AJ
Activities: Other research and experimental development on natural sciences and engineering
Parent: Merck & Co., Inc.
Officers: Ebru Can Temucin [1972] Director [Turkish]; Allen Harberg Jr [1971] Director [American]; Jan Moehlenbrock [1970] Managing Director [German]

Intervet UK Production Limited
Incorporated: 13 May 1996 *Employees:* 192
Net Worth: £61,146,000 *Total Assets:* £118,581,000
Registered Office: Walton Manor, Walton, Milton Keynes, Bucks, MK7 7AJ
Activities: Manufacture of pharmaceutical preparations
Parent: Intervet UK Limited
Officers: Ebru Can Temucin [1972] Director [Turkish]; Allen Harberg Jr [1971] Director [American]; Jan Moehlenbrock [1970] Managing Director [German]

Intex (Radiographic) Limited
Incorporated: 19 March 1965 *Employees:* 2
Net Worth Deficit: £9,943,094 *Total Assets:* £33,150,932
Registered Office: Riding Court House, Riding Court Road, Datchet, Slough, Berks, SL3 9JT
Activities: Information technology consultancy activities
Parent: Blue Minerva Limited
Officers: Michael David Cox [1983] Director; Kevin Peter Dady [1964] Director; Elona Mortimer-Zhika [1979] Director

Into University Partnerships Limited
Incorporated: 13 July 2005 *Employees:* 692
Net Worth: £27,148,000 *Total Assets:* £125,447,000
Registered Office: One Gloucester Place, Brighton, BN1 4AA
Activities: Activities of head offices
Parent: Espalier Ventures Limited
Officers: Andrew Jeremy Colin [1959] Director; Professor Sir David Stephen Eastwood [1959] Director/Vice-Chancellor; John Charles Latham [1969] Director/Executive Chairman; Jeffery Leeds [1956] Director/Corporate Executive [American]; Christopher Mairs [1982] Director/Corporate Executive [Irish]; Steven George Smale [1969] Director; John Buchanan Sykes [1963] Director/Chartered Accountant

Intralot Finance UK Limited
Incorporated: 11 December 2007 *Employees:* 2
Previous: Intralot Finance UK PLC
Net Worth Deficit: £4,683,278 *Total Assets:* £618,260,544
Registered Office: 1st Floor, Sheraton House, Lower Road, Chorleywood, Rickmansworth, Herts, WD3 5LH
Activities: Other business support service activities n.e.c.
Parent: Intralot SA Integrated Lottery Systems and Services
Officers: Antonios Kerastaris [1969] Director/Chief Financial Officer [Greek]; Evangelos Raptis [1969] Director/Treasurer [Greek]; Vasileios Vasdaris [1957] Director/Economist [Greek]

Intrum UK Finance Limited
Incorporated: 12 January 2001 *Employees:* 4
Previous: 1st Credit (Finance) Limited
Net Worth: £60,114,000 *Total Assets:* £112,716,000
Registered Office: The Omnibus Building, Lesbourne Road, Reigate, Surrey, RH2 7JP
Activities: Activities of collection agencies
Parent: Intrum UK Holdings Limited
Officers: Bruce McLaren, Secretary; Anders Eric Engdahl [1974] Director/Chief Investment Officer [Swedish]; Marc Knothe [1968] Managing Director [German]; Bruce McLaren [1966] Director; Edward Brian Nott [1959] Director

Intrum UK Holdings Limited
Incorporated: 19 November 2001 *Employees:* 1
Previous: 1st Credit (Holdings) Limited
Net Worth Deficit: £42,318,000 *Total Assets:* £81,738,000
Registered Office: The Omnibus Building, Lesbourne Road, Reigate, Surrey, RH2 7JP
Activities: Activities of other holding companies n.e.c.
Parent: Intrum UK Acquisitions Limited
Officers: Bruce McLaren, Secretary; Reza Atighi [1973] Investment Director [Dutch]; Marc Knothe [1968] Managing Director [German]; Edward Brian Nott [1959] Director

Inula Holding UK Limited
Incorporated: 18 December 1995
Net Worth: £112,326,000 *Total Assets:* £112,326,000
Registered Office: 165 Bath Road, Slough, Berks, SL1 4AA
Activities: Renting and leasing of cars and light motor vehicles
Officers: Niall Robert Keartland, Secretary; Alfonso Martinez [1961] Director [Spanish]; Patrick Marco Steenvoorden [1972] Finance Director [Dutch]

Invesco Asia Trust PLC
Incorporated: 19 January 1995
Net Worth: £233,252,000 *Total Assets:* £237,240,000
Registered Office: Perpetual Park, Perpetual Park Drive, Henley on Thames, Oxon, RG9 1HH
Activities: Financial intermediation not elsewhere classified
Officers: Owen Richard Jonathan [1952] Director/Solicitor; Thomas Nicholas Ivo Maier [1952] Director/Chief Investment Officer; Fleur Meijs [1971] Director [Dutch]; Neil Alan Hayes Rogan [1960] Director

Invesco Asset Management Limited
Incorporated: 7 March 1969 *Employees:* 15
Net Worth: £205,124,992 *Total Assets:* £235,982,000
Registered Office: Perpetual Park, Perpetual Park Drive, Henley on Thames, Oxon, RG9 1HH
Activities: Fund management activities
Parent: Invesco UK Limited
Officers: Amanda Evans, Secretary; Colin John FitzGenerald [1971] Director [Irish]; Paul Jean Joubert [1965] Director [French]; Nicholas Charles William Mustoe [1961] Director; Graeme John Proudfoot [1964] Director/Solicitor; Andrew R Schlossberg [1974] Director [American]; Alan John Trotter [1968] Finance Director

Invesco Far East Limited
Incorporated: 13 March 1997
Net Worth: £53,202,932 *Total Assets:* £53,202,932
Registered Office: Perpetual Park, Perpetual Park Drive, Henley on Thames, Oxon, RG9 1HH
Activities: Non-trading company
Parent: Invesco Holding Company Limited
Officers: Amanda Evans, Secretary; Graeme John Proudfoot [1964] Director/Solicitor; Jeremy Charles Simpson [1965] Director; Alan John Trotter [1968] Finance Director

Invesco Finance PLC
Incorporated: 31 May 2011
Net Worth: £272,177,440 *Total Assets:* £1,909,806,464
Registered Office: Perpetual Park, Perpetual Park Drive, Henley on Thames, Oxon, RG9 1HH
Activities: Financial intermediation not elsewhere classified
Parent: Invesco Holding Company Limited
Officers: Robert H Rigsby, Secretary; Kevin Michael Carome [1956] Director [American]; Robert Harris Rigsby [1967] Director [American]; Loren Michael Starr [1961] Director [American]

Invesco Fund Managers Limited
Incorporated: 14 February 1967
Net Worth: £432,084,992 *Total Assets:* £689,425,024
Registered Office: Perpetual Park, Perpetual Park Drive, Henley on Thames, Oxon, RG9 1HH
Activities: Financial intermediation not elsewhere classified
Parent: Invesco UK Limited
Officers: Amanda Evans, Secretary; Graeme John Proudfoot [1964] Director/Solicitor; Andrew R Schlossberg [1974] Director [American]; Douglas Sharp [1974] Director [Canadian]; Alan John Trotter [1968] Finance Director

Invesco GT Asset Management Limited
Incorporated: 27 January 1969
Net Worth: £39,083,584 *Total Assets:* £40,548,968
Registered Office: Perpetual Park, Perpetual Park Drive, Henley on Thames, Oxon, RG9 1HH
Activities: Activities of head offices
Parent: Invesco UK Holdings Limited
Officers: Amanda Evans, Secretary; Graeme John Proudfoot [1964] Director/Solicitor; Alan John Trotter [1968] Finance Director

Invesco Holding Company Limited
Incorporated: 19 December 1935
Net Worth: £2,077,207,040 *Total Assets:* £3,377,114,624
Registered Office: Perpetual Park, Perpetual Park Drive, Henley on Thames, Oxon, RG9 1HH
Activities: Financial intermediation not elsewhere classified
Officers: Anne Gerry, Secretary; Kevin M Carome [1956] Director [American]; Robert Harris Rigsby [1967] Director/Company Secretary [American]; Loren Starr [1961] Director [American]

Invesco Income Growth Trust PLC
Incorporated: 22 December 1995
Net Worth: £178,706,000 *Total Assets:* £180,864,000
Registered Office: Perpetual Park, Perpetual Park Drive, Henley on Thames, Oxon, RG9 1HH
Activities: Activities of investment trusts
Officers: Davina Cordelia Curling [1964] Director; Mark William Dampier [1956] Director of Research; Jonathan Charles Silver [1957] Director; Hugh Jolyon Twiss [1949] Director; Roger Benham Walsom [1953] Director/Solicitor; Timothy Hugh Woodhead [1965] Investment Director

Invesco International Holdings Limited
Incorporated: 7 June 1982
Net Worth: £228,054,000 *Total Assets:* £265,755,008
Registered Office: Perpetual Park, Perpetual Park Drive, Henley on Thames, Oxon, RG9 1HH
Activities: Activities of other holding companies n.e.c.
Parent: Invesco UK Limited
Officers: Amanda Evans, Secretary; Graeme John Proudfoot [1964] Director/Solicitor; Alan John Trotter [1968] Finance Director

Invesco Pacific Group Limited
Incorporated: 8 December 1994
Net Worth: £179,041,584 *Total Assets:* £179,208,816
Registered Office: Perpetual Park, Perpetual Park Drive, Henley on Thames, Oxon, RG9 1HH
Activities: Activities of financial services holding companies
Parent: Invesco Holding Company Limited
Officers: Amanda Evans, Secretary; Graeme John Proudfoot [1964] Director/Solicitor; Alan John Trotter [1968] Finance Director

Invesco Pensions Limited
Incorporated: 10 February 1998
Previous: Invesco Perpetual Life Limited
Net Worth: £96,553,000 *Total Assets:* £9,309,619,200
Registered Office: Perpetual Park, Perpetual Park Drive, Henley on Thames, Oxon, RG9 1HH
Activities: Non-life insurance
Parent: Invesco UK Limited
Officers: Amanda Evans, Secretary; Julian Antony Bartlett [1964] Director/Chartered Accountant; Rachel Diane Court [1966] Director; Colin John FitzGenerald [1971] Director [Irish]; Mark Goodale [1955] Director; Graeme John Proudfoot [1964] Director/Solicitor; Alan John Trotter [1968] Director

Invesco Perpetual Select Trust PLC
Incorporated: 25 August 2006
Net Worth: £151,216,000 *Total Assets:* £170,064,000
Registered Office: Perpetual Park, Perpetual Park Drive, Henley on Thames, Oxon, RG9 1HH
Activities: Activities of investment trusts
Officers: Craig McCowan Cleland [1963] Director; Alan Henry Clifton [1946] Director; Patrick Antony Francis Gifford [1945] Director; Graham John Kitchen [1967] Director; Victoria Anne Muir [1971] Director

Invesco Perpetual UK Smaller Companies Investment Trust PLC
Incorporated: 7 May 1987
Net Worth: £178,571,008 *Total Assets:* £181,842,000
Registered Office: Perpetual Park, Perpetual Park Drive, Henley on Thames, Oxon, RG9 1HH
Activities: Financial intermediation not elsewhere classified
Officers: Ian Christopher Simon Barby [1945] Investment Director; Richard John Brooman [1955] Director of Incrementum Limited; Christopher George Alvan Fletcher [1951] Director/Chartered Accountant; Bridget Elisabeth Guerin [1961] Director; Jane Margaret Lewis [1963] Director [British/Australian]

Invesco Software Holdings Limited
Incorporated: 25 June 2013 *Employees:* 195
Net Worth Deficit: £5,034,597 *Total Assets:* £45,828,160
Registered Office: Comino House, Furlong Road, Bourne End, Bucks, SL8 5AQ
Activities: Other information technology service activities
Officers: David Hywel Evans, Secretary; Philip John Brown [1963] Director; Mark Howell [1966] Director [Irish]; Peter David Nagle [1960] Director [Irish]

Invesco UK Holdings Limited
Incorporated: 17 January 1989
Net Worth: £14,611,000 *Total Assets:* £40,707,000
Registered Office: Perpetual Park, Perpetual Park Drive, Henley on Thames, Oxon, RG9 1HH
Activities: Activities of other holding companies n.e.c.
Parent: Invesco Holding Company Limited
Officers: Amanda Evans, Secretary; Graeme John Proudfoot [1964] Director/Solicitor; Alan John Trotter [1968] Finance Director

Invesco UK Limited
Incorporated: 19 December 1994 *Employees:* 878
Net Worth: £1,365,943,040 *Total Assets:* £1,746,840,064
Registered Office: Perpetual Park, Perpetual Park Drive, Henley on Thames, Oxon, RG9 1HH
Activities: Activities of financial services holding companies
Parent: Invesco Ltd
Officers: Clive Bouch [1961] Director; Rachel Diane Court [1966] Director; Judith Elizabeth Eden [1964] Director; Nicholas Charles William Mustoe [1961] Director; Graeme John Proudfoot [1964] Director/Solicitor; Andrew R Schlossberg [1974] Director [American]

Investec Asset Finance PLC
Incorporated: 15 October 1987
Net Worth: £22,145,000 *Total Assets:* £1,644,205,056
Registered Office: Reading International Business Park, Reading, Berks, RG2 6AA
Activities: Financial leasing
Parent: Investec Bank PLC
Officers: Connie Mei Ling Law, Secretary; Michael Richard Francis [1966] Director/Chartered Accountant; Andrew Stuart Hart [1974] Managing Director; Christopher Guy Butt Meyer [1971] Director/Head of Corporate & Institutional Banking [South African]; David Michael Van Der Walt [1964] Director/Banker [South African]; Ian Robert Wohlman [1954] Director/Manager

Investsave Limited
Incorporated: 1 November 1994 *Employees:* 7
Net Worth: £13,562,062 *Total Assets:* £24,400,630
Registered Office: Amelia House, Crescent Road, Worthing, W Sussex, BN11 1QR
Activities: Other letting and operating of own or leased real estate
Shareholders: Omega Estates Southern Limited; Omega Estates Southern Limited
Officers: Roy Geoffrey Michael Pook, Secretary/Director; Deborah Anita Pook [1958] Director/Property Investestor; Roy Geoffrey Michael Pook [1980] Director

Ipreo UK Holdings Ltd
Incorporated: 10 August 2011
Net Worth: £2,571,000 *Total Assets:* £37,693,000
Registered Office: c/o IHS Global Limited, The Capitol Building, Oldbury, Bracknell, Berks, RG12 8FZ
Activities: Other professional, scientific and technical activities n.e.c.
Parent: Ipreo LLC
Officers: Yasmin Hussein, Secretary; Christopher Guy McLoughlin [1978] Director/Deputy General Counsel; Kathryn Ann Owen [1976] Director/VP Accounting

Ipsen Developments Limited
Incorporated: 20 May 1996
Net Worth: £448,500,992 *Total Assets:* £451,131,008
Registered Office: 190 Bath Road, Slough, Berks, SL1 3XE
Activities: Activities of head offices
Parent: Ipsen SA
Officers: Catherine Lamb, Secretary; Isobel Louise Boyne [1969] Director/Accountant; Catherine Lamb [1978] Director/Solicitor

IQVIA Ies European Holdings
Incorporated: 21 November 1996
Previous: Quintiles European Holdings
Net Worth: £31,657,000 *Total Assets:* £31,657,000
Registered Office: 500 Brook Drive, Green Park, Reading, Berks, RG2 6UU
Activities: Activities of other holding companies n.e.c.
Officers: Timothy Peter Sheppard [1971] Director/General Manager; Paul David Simpson [1962] Director; Kevin John Turland [1969] Director/Accountant

IQVIA Ltd.
Incorporated: 15 February 1995 *Employees:* 1,456
Previous: Quintiles Limited
Net Worth: £221,399,008 *Total Assets:* £768,030,016
Registered Office: 500 Brook Drive, Green Park, Reading, Berks, RG2 6UU
Activities: Research and experimental development on biotechnology
Parent: IQVIA RDS Holdings
Officers: Barry Keith Lattimore [1963] Director/Accountant; Kevin John Turland [1969] Director/Accountant

IQVIA RDS Holdings
Incorporated: 2 April 1992
Previous: Quintiles Holdings
Net Worth: £107,818,000 *Total Assets:* £173,538,000
Registered Office: 500 Brook Drive, Green Park, Reading, Berks, RG2 6UU
Activities: Activities of head offices
Parent: Quintiles UK Holdings Limited
Officers: Barry Keith Lattimore [1963] Director/Accountant; Kevin John Turland [1969] Director/Accountant

IQVIA RDS UK Holdings Ltd.
Incorporated: 5 November 2009
Previous: Quintiles UK Holdings Limited
Net Worth: £675,507,968 *Total Assets:* £699,758,016
Registered Office: 500 Brook Drive, Green Park, Reading, Berks, RG2 6UU
Activities: Activities of other holding companies n.e.c.
Officers: Barry Keith Lattimore [1963] Director/Accountant; Kevin John Turland [1969] Director/Accountant

Iris Business Software Limited
Incorporated: 27 August 1986 *Employees:* 2
Net Worth: £35,997,072 *Total Assets:* £132,089,384
Registered Office: Riding Court House, Riding Court Road, Datchet, Berks, SL3 9JT
Activities: Information technology consultancy activities
Parent: Intex (Radiographic) Limited
Officers: Michael David Cox [1983] Director; Kevin Peter Dady [1964] Director; Elona Mortimer-Zhika [1979] Director

Iris Capital Limited
Incorporated: 1 June 2007 *Employees:* 2
Net Worth: £321,851,488 *Total Assets:* £603,346,944
Registered Office: Riding Court House, Riding Court Road, Datchet, Slough, Berks, SL3 9JT
Activities: Other business support service activities n.e.c.
Parent: Software (Holdco 5) Limited
Officers: Michael David Cox [1983] Director; Kevin Peter Dady [1964] Director; Elona Mortimer-Zhika [1979] Director

Iris Group Limited
Incorporated: 2 May 1996 *Employees:* 654
Net Worth: £13,819,774 *Total Assets:* £727,154,688
Registered Office: Riding Court House, Datchet, Berks, SL3 9JT
Activities: Information technology consultancy activities
Parent: Iris Holdings Limited
Officers: Michael David Cox [1983] Director; Kevin Peter Dady [1964] Director; Elona Mortimer-Zhika [1979] Director

Iris Holdings Limited
Incorporated: 11 October 2000 *Employees:* 2
Net Worth: £987,174 *Total Assets:* £212,590,912
Registered Office: Riding Court House, Riding Court Road, Datchet, Slough, Berks, SL3 9JT
Activities: Activities of head offices
Parent: Blue Minerva Limited
Officers: Michael David Cox [1983] Director; Kevin Peter Dady [1964] Director; Elona Mortimer-Zhika [1979] Director

Iris Payroll Software Limited
Incorporated: 24 August 2006
Net Worth: £21,042,864 *Total Assets:* £36,310,344
Registered Office: Riding Court House, Datchet, Berks, SL3 9JT
Activities: Information technology consultancy activities
Parent: Intex (Radiographic) Limited
Officers: Michael David Cox [1983] Director; Kevin Peter Dady [1964] Director; Elona Mortimer-Zhika [1979] Director

Iris Payroll Solutions Limited
Incorporated: 22 November 1984 *Employees:* 2
Net Worth: £19,945,184 *Total Assets:* £40,244,940
Registered Office: Riding Court House, Riding Court Road, Datchet, Slough, Berks, SL3 9JT
Activities: Information technology consultancy activities
Parent: Intex (Radiographic) Limited
Officers: Michael David Cox [1983] Director; Kevin Peter Dady [1964] Director; Elona Mortimer-Zhika [1979] Director

Iris Software Group Limited
Incorporated: 27 June 2007 *Employees:* 1,304
Net Worth Deficit: £83,188,000 *Total Assets:* £489,140,992
Registered Office: Riding Court House, Riding Court Road, Datchet, Slough, Berks, SL3 9JT
Activities: Activities of head offices
Parent: Software (Holdco 2) Limited
Officers: Michael David Cox [1983] Director; Kevin Peter Dady [1964] Director; Elona Mortimer-Zhika [1979] Director

Iris Software Limited
Incorporated: 8 May 1996
Net Worth: £206,061,072 *Total Assets:* £323,285,568
Registered Office: Riding Court House, Riding Court Road, Datchet, Slough, SL3 9JT
Activities: Information technology consultancy activities
Parent: Iris Group Limited
Officers: Michael David Cox [1983] Director; Kevin Peter Dady [1964] Director; Elona Mortimer-Zhika [1979] Director

ISDC Developments (No2) Limited
Incorporated: 12 February 2008
Net Worth Deficit: £23,451,000 *Total Assets:* £89,764,000
Registered Office: Witan Gate House, 500-600 Witan Gate West, Milton Keynes, Bucks, MK9 1SH
Activities: Other business support service activities n.e.c.
Parent: Infinity SDC Limited
Officers: Stuart Sutton [1968] Director; John Thompson [1961] Director

ISG Retail Limited
Incorporated: 9 June 1992 *Employees:* 345
Net Worth: £14,839,000 *Total Assets:* £97,351,000
Registered Office: Boleyn House, St Augustine's Business Park, Whitstable, Kent, CT5 2QJ
Activities: Manufacture of office and shop furniture
Parent: ISG UK Retail Limited
Officers: Nicholas James Heard, Secretary; Paul Martin Cossell [1965] Director; Kevin Patrick Dengate [1962] Contracts Director; David Graham Entwistle [1960] Finance Director; Richard John Hubbard [1968] Director; Mark Stockton [1964] Director/Accountant

Isleworth and Syon School for Boys
Incorporated: 23 February 2012 *Employees:* 115
Net Worth: £17,640,000 *Total Assets:* £20,925,000
Registered Office: Isleworth and Syon School for Boys, Ridgeway Road, Isleworth, Middlesex, TW7 5LJ
Activities: General secondary education
Officers: Premilla George, Secretary; Tamsin Leigh Billimoria [1970] Director/Assistant Headteacher - ICT; Amal Moawad Ahmed Bolbol [1976] Director/Learning Support Assistant; Fergus Euan Ferguson [1960] Director/Headteacher; Dr Roy Gardner [1932] Director/Educational Consultant; Catherine Patrice Gower [1968] Director/University Lecturer in Education; Sophie Hannon [1989] Director/Teacher; Dr Derek Michael Healy [1978] Director/H&S & Environmental Officer & GILO Brunel University; Martin David King [1969] Director/Senior Learning Technologist; Raymond Henry O'Neill [1956] Director/Teacher; Alan John Smith [1948] Director/Local Government Officer; Vanessa Katherine Smith [1947] Director; Dr Emily Jane Tomlinson [1974] Director/Charity Management; Dr Iris Turner [1941] Director/Academic Adviser External Examinations

Isoft Group (UK) Limited
Incorporated: 22 February 1999 *Employees:* 1
Net Worth: £58,174,000 *Total Assets:* £66,950,000
Registered Office: Royal Pavilion, Wellesley Road, Aldershot, Hants, GU11 1PZ
Activities: Information technology consultancy activities
Parent: CSC Computer Sciences International Operations Limited
Officers: Michael Charles Woodfine, Secretary; Andrea Fiumicelli [1960] Director [Italian]; Tina Anne Gough [1962] Director; Maruf Ahmad Majed [1955] Director [American]; Michael Charles Woodfine [1971] Director/Solicitor

ISS Facility Services Limited
Incorporated: 31 October 1966 *Employees:* 24,852
Net Worth: £108,124,000 *Total Assets:* £694,902,016
Registered Office: Velocity, 1 Brooklands Drive, Brooklands, Weybridge, Surrey, KT13 0SL
Activities: Unlicenced restaurants and cafes
Parent: ISS UK Limited
Officers: Matthew Edward Stanley Brabin [1965] Director/Chief Executive Officer; Andrew Owen Chappell [1975] Director/Chief Operating Officer; Philip John Leigh [1967] Director/Chief Operating Officer; Barbara Plucnar Jensen [1971] Director/Chief Financial Officer [Danish]; Robert David Stanley [1976] Director/Chief Operating Officer

ISS Mediclean Limited
Incorporated: 23 August 1982 *Employees:* 15,984
Net Worth: £86,044,000 *Total Assets:* £198,944,992
Registered Office: Velocity, 1 Brooklands Drive, Brooklands, Weybridge, Surrey, KT13 0SL
Activities: Other food services
Parent: ISS UK Ltd
Officers: Michael Barker, Secretary; Michael Barker [1963] Director; Matthew Edward Stanley Brabin [1965] Director/Chief Executive Officer; Philip John Leigh [1967] Director/Chief Operating Officer; Barbara Plucnar Jensen [1971] Director/Chief Financial Officer [Danish]; Wendy Stowell [1966] Commercial Director [New Zealander]

ISS UK Holding Limited
Incorporated: 24 August 2005 *Employees:* 4
Net Worth: £263,684,000 *Total Assets:* £483,235,008
Registered Office: Velocity, 1 Brooklands Drive, Brooklands, Weybridge, Surrey, KT13 0SL
Activities: Activities of head offices
Parent: ISS Global A/S
Officers: Matthew Edward Stanley Brabin [1965] Director/Chief Executive Officer; Barbara Plucnar Jensen [1971] Director/Chief Financial Officer [Danish]; Richard Ian Sykes [1970] Director; Jorn Vestergaard [1968] Director [Danish]

ISS UK Limited
Incorporated: 27 January 1949 *Employees:* 173
Net Worth: £149,790,000 *Total Assets:* £1,033,267,008
Registered Office: Velocity, 1 Brooklands Drive, Brooklands, Weybridge, Surrey, KT13 0SL
Activities: Activities of head offices
Parent: ISS UK Holding Limited
Officers: Matthew Edward Stanley Brabin [1965] Director/Chief Executive Officer; Andrew Owen Chappell [1975] Director/Chief Operating Officer; Stephanie Louise Hamilton [1971] Director/Head People & Culture; Philip John Leigh [1967] Director/Chief Operating Officer; Barbara Plucnar Jensen [1971] Director/Chief Financial Officer [Danish]; Robert David Stanley [1976] Director/Chief Operating Officer

ITAB UK Ltd
Incorporated: 29 July 1997 *Employees:* 193
Previous: ITAB Shop Concept UK Ltd
Net Worth: £13,275,326 *Total Assets:* £27,955,988
Registered Office: ITAB House, Swallowdale Lane, Hemel Hempstead Industrial Estate, Hemel Hempstead, Herts, HP2 7EA
Activities: Manufacture of other fabricated metal products n.e.c.
Parent: ITAB UK Ltd
Officers: Andrew John Tweddle, Secretary; David Anthony Dignam [1977] Director; Roy Timothy French [1965] Director; Mikael Kjell Christer Gustavsson [1964] Director [Swedish]

ITT Industries Limited
Incorporated: 30 July 1964 *Employees:* 68
Net Worth: £30,827,000 *Total Assets:* £63,721,000
Registered Office: Viables Industrial Estate, Jays Close, Basingstoke, Hants, RG22 4BA
Activities: Manufacture of pumps
Parent: ITT Industries Holdings Limited
Officers: Ravi Patel, Secretary; James Buller [1975] International Business Development Director and GM; Jackie Capel [1966] Director/HR Manager; Ravi Patel [1970] Director and Company Secretary; John William Veness [1949] Director/General Manager

ITW Holdings I Limited
Incorporated: 4 November 2015
Net Worth: £2,136,424,192 *Total Assets:* £7,397,315,072
Registered Office: Nexus House, Station Road, Egham, Surrey, TW20 9LB
Activities: Activities of other holding companies n.e.c.
Parent: ITW Holdings Inc.
Officers: Ryan Ronald Dale, Secretary; Giles Matthew Hudson [1972] Director/Chartered Accountant; Stephen James Rowell [1967] Director of International Corporate Finance

ITW Holdings II Limited
Incorporated: 10 December 2015
Net Worth: £4,805,328,896 *Total Assets:* £4,805,328,896
Registered Office: Nexus House, Station Road, Egham, Surrey, TW20 9LB
Activities: Activities of other holding companies n.e.c.
Parent: ITW Holdings I Limited
Officers: Ryan Ronald Dale, Secretary; Giles Matthew Hudson [1972] Director/Chartered Accountant; Stephen James Rowell [1967] Director of International Corporate Finance

ITW Holdings III Limited
Incorporated: 10 December 2015
Net Worth: £7,103,780,352 *Total Assets:* £7,103,780,352
Registered Office: Nexus House, Station Road, Egham, Surrey, TW20 9LB
Activities: Activities of other holding companies n.e.c.
Parent: ITW Holdings VIII Limited
Officers: Ryan Ronald Dale, Secretary; Giles Matthew Hudson [1972] Director/Chartered Accountant; Stephen James Rowell [1967] Director of International Corporate Finance

ITW Holdings IV Limited
Incorporated: 10 December 2015
Net Worth: £2,562,002,432 *Total Assets:* £2,594,297,088
Registered Office: Nexus House, Station Road, Egham, Surrey, TW20 9LB
Activities: Activities of other holding companies n.e.c.
Parent: ITW Holdings I Limited
Officers: Ryan Ronald Dale, Secretary; Giles Matthew Hudson [1972] Director/Chartered Accountant; Stephen James Rowell [1967] Director of International Corporate Finance

ITW Holdings V Limited
Incorporated: 18 December 2015
Net Worth: £1,385,645,312 *Total Assets:* £1,387,344,768
Registered Office: Nexus House, Station Road, Egham, Surrey, TW20 9LB
Activities: Activities of other holding companies n.e.c.
Parent: ITW Holdings II Limited
Officers: Ryan Ronald Dale, Secretary; Giles Matthew Hudson [1972] Director/Chartered Accountant; Stephen James Rowell [1967] Director of International Corporate Finance

ITW Holdings VI Limited
Incorporated: 22 November 2016
Net Worth: £7,397,127,680 *Total Assets:* £7,397,127,680
Registered Office: Nexus House, Station Road, Egham, Surrey, TW20 9LB
Activities: Activities of other holding companies n.e.c.
Shareholders: ITW Holdings III Limited (in Trust for ITW Holdings LP); ITW Holdings III Limited
Officers: Ryan Ronald Dale, Secretary; Giles Matthew Hudson [1972] Director/Chartered Accountant; Stephen James Rowell [1967] Director of International Corporate Finance

ITW Holdings VII Limited
Incorporated: 22 November 2016
Net Worth: £2,399,663,360 *Total Assets:* £2,399,663,360
Registered Office: Nexus House, Station Road, Egham, Surrey, TW20 9LB
Activities: Activities of other holding companies n.e.c.
Parent: ITW (EU) Holdings SARL
Officers: Ryan Ronald Dale, Secretary; Giles Matthew Hudson [1972] Director/Chartered Accountant; Stephen James Rowell [1967] Director of International Corporate Finance

ITW Limited
Incorporated: 6 January 1956 *Employees:* 2,322
Net Worth: £1,521,196,032 *Total Assets:* £2,745,051,904
Registered Office: Nexus House, Station Road, Egham, Surrey, TW20 9LB
Activities: Manufacture of other chemical products n.e.c.
Parent: Berrington UK
Officers: Ryan Ronald Dale, Secretary; Giles Matthew Hudson, Secretary/Chartered Accountant; Giles Matthew Hudson [1972] Director/Chartered Accountant; Stephen James Rowell [1967] Director of International Corporate Finance

IUP 2 LLP
Incorporated: 27 June 2012 *Employees:* 236
Net Worth: £62,391,000 *Total Assets:* £84,851,000
Registered Office: One Gloucester Place, Brighton, BN1 4AA

Ixcellerate Limited
Incorporated: 26 May 2010 *Employees:* 2
Net Worth: £4,414,349 *Total Assets:* £21,431,840
Registered Office: Globe House, Eclipse Park, Sittingbourne Road, Maidstone, Kent, ME14 3EN
Activities: Other business support service activities n.e.c.
Officers: Karen Bach [1970] Director; Andrew Bartley [1963] Director/Investment Manager; Guy Peter de Rohan Willner [1964] Director; Alexis Falcon de Longevialle [1967] Director/Broker [French]; Alexander Pavlovich Levchenko [1973] Director/Sumitomo Corporation GM ICT Business Department [Russian]; Michael Tobin [1964] Director/Entrepreneur; Laurens Van Reijen [1962] Managing Director [Dutch]

IZH Holdings Ltd
Incorporated: 17 March 2015
Net Worth: £28,835,992 *Total Assets:* £30,100,012
Registered Office: Spirit House, 8 High Street, West Molesey, Surrey, KT8 2NA
Activities: Management consultancy activities other than financial management
Officers: Derek Williamson, Secretary; Gilles Christophe Marc Blanchard [1964] Director/Businessman [French]; Afonso Manuel Leao Da Costa Campos [1986] Director [Portuguese]; Imran Ali Khan [1978] Director/Businessman; Zeeshan Ali Khan [1977] Director

J C C Lighting Holdings Limited
Incorporated: 23 October 2013 *Employees:* 427
Net Worth: £5,959,000 *Total Assets:* £88,785,000
Registered Office: Innovation Centre, Southern Cross Trading Estate, Beeding Close, Bognor Regis, W Sussex, PO22 9TS
Activities: Activities of other holding companies n.e.c.
Shareholders: Adrienne Hendler; Patricia Sokolow; Elizabeth Kriegman
Officers: Mark Stephen Baydarian [1954] Director/Executive [American]; Donald Jay Hendler [1945] Director/Executive [American]; Daryoush Larizadeh [1964] Director/Executive [American]

J C C Lighting Products Limited
Incorporated: 11 April 1995 *Employees:* 104
Net Worth: £38,534,256 *Total Assets:* £51,580,672
Registered Office: Innovation Centre, Southern Cross Trading Estate, Beeding Close, Bognor Regis, W Sussex, PO22 9TS
Activities: Manufacture of electric lighting equipment
Parent: Shires Holdings Limited
Officers: Mark Stephen Baydarian [1954] Director/Executive [American]; Donald Jay Hendler [1945] Director/Executive [American]; Daryoush Larizadeh [1964] Director/Executive [American]

J.L.G.Investments Limited
Incorporated: 11 December 1945 *Employees:* 10
Net Worth: £13,552,504 *Total Assets:* £21,596,648
Registered Office: 3 Claridge Court, Lower Kings Road, Berkhamsted, Herts, HP4 2AE
Activities: Other letting and operating of own or leased real estate
Officers: Audrey Godfrey, Secretary; Elaine Rachel Chester [1976] Director/Engineer; Michael Peter Chester [1945] Director/Structural Engineer; Allan Russell Godfrey [1967] Director/Horticulturalist; Audrey Godfrey [1942] Director; Colin Roger Godfrey [1970] Director; John Stephen Godfrey [1953] Director/Chartered Surveyor; Richard Scott Godfrey [1956] Director; Robert Paul Godfrey [1959] Director; Jane Frances Mowat [1950] Director; Walter Stanton [1929] Director/Accountant

J.T.D. Finance Limited
Incorporated: 1 November 2006
Net Worth: £8,441,633 *Total Assets:* £108,458,464
Registered Office: The Bull Courtyard, Bell Street, Henley on Thames, Oxon, RG9 2BA
Activities: Other business support service activities n.e.c.
Parent: J.T. Davies & Sons Holdings Limited
Officers: David Generald Nathan, Secretary; Michael Anthony Trehearne Davies [1953] Director/Chairman; Thomas Anthony Trehearne Davies [1980] Director; David Generald Nathan [1970] Director

J.T.D. Investments Limited
Incorporated: 1 November 2006
Net Worth: £4,425,021 *Total Assets:* £166,517,840
Registered Office: The Bull Courtyard, Bell Street, Henley on Thames, Oxon, RG9 2BA
Activities: Other business support service activities n.e.c.
Parent: J.T.D. Finance Limited
Officers: David Generald Nathan, Secretary; Michael Anthony Trehearne Davies [1953] Director/Chairman; Thomas Anthony Trehearne Davies [1980] Director; David Generald Nathan [1970] Director

Jacobs Douwe Egberts R & D GB Ltd
Incorporated: 22 January 2015 *Employees:* 172
Net Worth: £16,728,000 *Total Assets:* £21,470,000
Registered Office: Horizon, Honey Lane, Hurley, Maidenhead, Berks, SL6 6RJ
Activities: Production of coffee and coffee substitutes
Officers: Sophy Pashley, Secretary; Carolyn Adams [1968] R&D Instant Coffee Category Director; Jean-Pierre Marie Cabri [1971] Director [Belgian]

Jacobs E & C Limited
Incorporated: 18 November 2003
Net Worth: £50,682,000 *Total Assets:* £70,363,000
Registered Office: 1180 Eskdale Road, Winnersh, Wokingham, Berks, RG41 5TU
Activities: Development of building projects
Parent: Jacobs Process Limited
Officers: Tejender Chaudhary, Secretary; Paul Seaton [1964] Director/Business Executive; Jonathan Ross Shattock [1964] Director/Solicitor

Jacobs Engineering UK Limited
Incorporated: 3 August 1990
Previous: Jacobs Industrial Services U.K. Limited
Net Worth Deficit: £3,004,000 *Total Assets:* £23,131,000
Registered Office: 1180 Eskdale Road, Winnersh, Wokingham, Berks, RG41 5TU
Activities: Extraction of crude petroleum
Parent: Jacobs UK Limited
Officers: Tejender Singh Chaudhary, Secretary; Paul Seaton [1964] Director/Business Executive; Jonathan Ross Shattock [1964] Director/Solicitor

Jacobs Field Services Limited
Incorporated: 4 June 1974 *Employees:* 734
Previous: Jacobs LES Limited
Net Worth: £28,859,000 *Total Assets:* £73,293,000
Registered Office: 1180 Eskdale Road, Winnersh, Wokingham, Berks, RG41 5TU
Activities: Machining
Parent: Jacobs UK Limited
Officers: Michael Norris, Secretary; David Ellis [1972] Director/Business Executive; Valerie Roberts [1965] Director/Business Executive [American]; Andrew Scargill [1967] Director/Business Executive; Paul Seaton [1964] Director/Business Executive

Andrew Jacobs LLP
Incorporated: 16 March 2010
Net Worth: £20,578,804 *Total Assets:* £20,581,454
Registered Office: 44 The Pantiles, Tunbridge Wells, Kent, TN2 5TN
Officers: Andrew Jacobs [1959] Member

Jacobs Process Limited
Incorporated: 22 May 1948
Net Worth: £46,171,000 *Total Assets:* £46,337,000
Registered Office: 1180 Eskdale Road, Winnersh, Wokingham, Berks, RG41 5TU
Activities: Other specialised construction activities n.e.c.
Parent: Jacobs UK Limited
Officers: Tejender Singh Chaudhary, Secretary; Paul Seaton [1964] Director/Business Executive; Jonathan Ross Shattock [1964] Director/Solicitor

Jacobs U.K. Limited
Incorporated: 22 March 1991 *Employees:* 6,452
Net Worth: £124,800,000 *Total Assets:* £528,472,992
Registered Office: 1180 Eskdale Road, Winnersh, Wokingham, Berks, RG41 5TU
Activities: Other engineering activities
Parent: Jacobs UK Holdings Limited
Officers: Michael Norris, Secretary; Kevin Christopher Berryman [1959] Director/Business Executive [American]; Joanne Caruso [1960] Director/Business Executive [American]; David Joseph Coultas [1962] Director; David Ellis [1972] Director/Business Executive; Erwin Geene [1970] Director/Financial Controller [Dutch]; Peter Robert Lutwyche [1962] Director/Business Executive; Hugh Donald Morrison [1970] Director/Business Executive; Robert Venkat Pragada [1968] Director/Business Executive [American]; Paul Seaton [1964] Director/Business Executive; Jonathan Ross Shattock [1964] Director/Solicitor

Jacobs UK Holdings Limited
Incorporated: 18 April 2002
Net Worth: £6,433,000 *Total Assets:* £25,014,000
Registered Office: 1180 Eskdale Road, Winnersh, Wokingham, Berks, RG41 5TU
Activities: Activities of head offices
Parent: Jacobs Europe Holdco Limited
Officers: Tejender Singh Chaudhary, Secretary; Kevin Christopher Berryman [1959] Director/Business Executive [American]; David Joseph Coultas [1962] Director/Business Executive; David Ellis [1972] Director/Business Executive; Peter Robert Lutwyche [1962] Director/Business Executive; Paul Seaton [1964] Director/Business Executive; Jonathan Ross Shattock [1964] Director/Solicitor

JAE Europe, Limited
Incorporated: 1 September 1996 *Employees:* 70
Net Worth: £10,266,515 *Total Assets:* £31,950,444
Registered Office: First Floor, Royal Pavilion Tower 3, Wellesley Road, Aldershot, Hants, GU11 1PZ
Activities: Manufacture of telegraph and telephone apparatus and equipment
Parent: Japan Aviation Electronics Industry, Limited
Officers: Wataru Oyamada, Secretary; Kazuo Honda [1960] Director [Japanese]; Masahiro Matsuo [1962] Director [Japanese]; Wataru Oyamada [1959] Managing Director [Japanese]; Hajime Saito [1956] Director (Management) [Japanese]; Koichi Tomizuka [1963] Director [Japanese]

Jain International Foods Limited
Incorporated: 15 October 2009 *Employees:* 11
Previous: SQF 2009 Limited
Net Worth: £8,092,352 *Total Assets:* £49,184,888
Registered Office: 3rd Floor, Rear Right, Regal House, 70 London Road, Twickenham, Middlesex, TW1 3QS
Activities: Manufacture of other food products n.e.c.
Parent: Jain Irrigation Systems Ltd
Officers: Paul David Lawlor, Secretary; James Patrick Arnold [1965] Director; Anil Bhavarlal Jain [1965] Managing Director [Indian]; Atul Bhavarlal Jain [1969] Marketing Director [Indian]; Suvan Kumar Sharma [1972] Director/V.P. Food Products

Jakks Pacific (UK) Ltd
Incorporated: 14 November 2008 *Employees:* 18
Net Worth: £2,591,005 *Total Assets:* £20,872,778
Registered Office: One Arlington Square, Downshire Way, Bracknell, Berks, RG12 1WA
Activities: Wholesale of household goods (other than musical instruments) n.e.c
Parent: Jakks Pacific Inc
Officers: Stephen Berman, Secretary [American]; Stephen Berman [1964] Director/President [American]; John Joseph McGrath [1965] Director/Operations Manager [American]

Nicholas James Care Homes Ltd
Incorporated: 5 December 2001 *Employees:* 327
Net Worth: £15,635,696 *Total Assets:* £33,972,356
Registered Office: 30 Station Road, Orpington, Kent, BR6 0SA
Activities: Residential nursing care facilities
Major Shareholder: Kanagaratnam Rajakanthan
Officers: Kanagaratnam Rajakanthan [1955] Director

The Edward James Foundation Limited
Incorporated: 4 September 2008 *Employees:* 146
Net Worth: £82,604,433,408 *Total Assets:* £90,996,490,240
Registered Office: Estate Office, West Dean Park, Chichester, W Sussex, PO18 0QZ
Activities: Other education n.e.c.
Officers: Martin William Ashley [1952] Director/Architect; Peter MacLeod Benson [1940] Director/Chartered Accountant; Lady Audrey Caroline Egremont [1949] Director/Landscape Designer; Caroline Winifred Griffith [1943] Director/Retired [Australian]; Professor Nigel Graham Llewellyn [1951] Director/Art Historian; Michael John McCart [1948] Director of Development and Policy; Professor Paul Gerard O'Prey [1956] Director/University Vice-Chancellor; Francis John Plowden [1945] Director/Chartered Accountant; Alison Taylor Richmond [1952] Director/Retired Chief Executive; David William Seddon [1946] Director/Retired

A W James Limited
Incorporated: 20 October 1999 *Employees:* 4
Net Worth: £24,795,940 *Total Assets:* £60,900,548
Registered Office: Linford Hall, Church Lane, Little Linford, Milton Keynes, Bucks, MK19 7EB
Activities: Other letting and operating of own or leased real estate
Shareholders: Peter John Wilson; Jane Elizabeth Wilson; Andrew James Wilson
Officers: Sebastian Mark Tubb, Secretary; Paul George Mace [1969] Estates Director; Colin Richard Spring [1952] Director; Sebastian Mark Tubb [1967] Director/Chartered Accountant; Andrew James Wilson [1976] Director; David Andrew Wilson [1947] Director; Jane Elizabeth Wilson [1950] Director; Peter John Wilson [1944] Director

James Villa Holidays Limited
Incorporated: 2 October 1998 *Employees:* 146
Net Worth: £8,657,755 *Total Assets:* £47,470,552
Registered Office: 20/20 Business Park, St Leonards Road, Maidstone, Kent, ME16 0LS
Activities: Tour operator activities
Parent: Vacation Rentals (UK) Ltd
Officers: Henry Bankes, Secretary; Garry Clark Adam [1970] Director; Daniel Ross Butler [1980] Director/Accountant; Geoffrey John Cowley [1961] Director; Henrik Vilhelm Kjellberg [1971] Director/Chief Executive [Swedish]

Jankel Armouring Limited
Incorporated: 3 February 1987 *Employees:* 120
Net Worth: £17,709,924 *Total Assets:* £31,338,052
Registered Office: Belgrave House, 39-43 Monument Hill, Weybridge, Surrey, KT13 8RN
Activities: Defence activities
Parent: The Jankel Group Limited
Officers: Anthony Louis Harry Jankel, Secretary; Daniel Crosby [1981] Business Development Director; Andrew Jankel [1968] Director; Anthony Louis Harry Jankel [1950] Director; Jennifer Anne Jankel [1940] Director; Michael Patrick Mullen [1961] Director/Engineer

The Jankel Group Limited
Incorporated: 22 January 2001 *Employees:* 120
Net Worth: £17,744,046 *Total Assets:* £31,346,048
Registered Office: Belgrave House, 39-43 Monument Hill, Weybridge, Surrey, KT13 8RN
Activities: Activities of head offices
Officers: Anthony Louis Harry Jankel, Secretary; Jonathan Mark Farrow [1965] Director; Andrew Jankel [1968] Sales and Marketing Director; Anthony Louis Harry Jankel [1950] Director; Jennifer Anne Jankel [1940] Director

Janssen-Cilag Limited
Incorporated: 19 October 1971 *Employees:* 939
Net Worth: £266,952,000 *Total Assets:* £415,416,992
Registered Office: 50-100 Holmers Farm Way, High Wycombe, Bucks, HP12 4EG
Activities: Manufacture of pharmaceutical preparations
Parent: Johnson & Johnson
Officers: Liesbeth Aerts [1979] Finance Director [Belgian]; Shelagh Mary Anderson [1960] Regulatory Affairs Director; Rozlyn Cooper [1978] Medical Director; Mark Iain Hicken [1971] Director/Business Executive; Nicholas George Hodges [1972] Director/Vice President, Global Clinical Operations; Clare Sicklen [1971] HR Director

Jardines (U.K.) Limited
Incorporated: 26 June 1984 *Employees:* 170
Net Worth: £19,833,716 *Total Assets:* £35,723,272
Registered Office: Lakeside, Shirwell Crescent, Furzton, Milton Keynes, Bucks, MK4 1GA
Activities: Dispensing chemist in specialised stores
Major Shareholder: Hasmukh Modi
Officers: Prity Modi, Secretary; David John Howton [1954] Director/Estates Manager; Hasmukh Modi [1950] Director/Pharmacist; Prity Modi [1959] Director/Marketing

Jas Forwarding (UK) Limited
Incorporated: 14 June 1984 *Employees:* 115
Net Worth: £22,150,768 *Total Assets:* £32,490,200
Registered Office: Cargo Point, Bedfont Road, Stanwell, Middlesex, TW19 7NZ
Activities: Other transportation support activities
Officers: Noel Rex Broadbent, Secretary; Noel Rex Broadbent [1957] Managing Director; Biagio Bruni [1945] Director [Italian]; Tahira Fumo [1966] Director/Chief Financial Officer [American]; Marco Rebuffi [1961] Director/President and CEO [Italian]

Jato Dynamics Limited
Incorporated: 26 May 1988 *Employees:* 684
Net Worth: £27,845,398 *Total Assets:* £84,783,872
Registered Office: Hunton House, Highbridge Industrial Estate, Oxford Road, Uxbridge, Middlesex, UB8 1LX
Activities: Market research and public opinion polling
Major Shareholder: Jacob Baruch Shafran
Officers: Fiona Lesley Sandford, Secretary; Matthew William Hall [1971] Director/Chartered Accountant; Helene Marie Shafran [1966] Director [American]; Jacob Baruch Shafran [1952] Director

Jawaby Property Investment Limited
Incorporated: 10 February 1982 *Employees:* 4
Net Worth: £51,699,608 *Total Assets:* £66,645,216
Registered Office: Cutlers Farmhouse, Marlow Road, Lane End, High Wycombe, Bucks, HP14 3JW
Activities: Other letting and operating of own or leased real estate
Parent: The Government of National Accord of The State of Libya
Officers: Ahmed Mohamed Ahmida Abdalla [1962] Director/Oil Sector Executive [Libyan]; Naim Khalifa Mohamed Gheriani [1958] Director [Libyan]; Ahmed Ibrahim Hasan [1980] Director/Oil Sector Lawyer/Legal Officer [Libyan]; Abdulfetah Salem Shagan [1954] Director/Oil Sector Executive [Libyan]

Jayar Components Limited
Incorporated: 6 December 1976 *Employees:* 410
Net Worth: £18,397,164 *Total Assets:* £26,519,804
Registered Office: Jayar House, Forstal Road, Aylesford, Kent, ME20 7AF
Activities: Retail trade of motor vehicle parts and accessories
Major Shareholder: John Ratcliffe
Officers: Caroline Jane de Camborne Lucy, Secretary; Caroline Jane de Camborne Lucy [1972] Director/Accountant; John Ratcliffe [1941] Director; Judith Ann Ratcliffe [1948] Director; Nicholas James Ratcliffe [1975] Director/Manager

JBS Global (UK) Limited
Incorporated: 11 September 2001 *Employees:* 24
Net Worth: £28,589,878 *Total Assets:* £54,645,752
Registered Office: 2nd Floor, Building 1, Imperial Place, Maxwell Road, Borehamwood, Herts, WD6 1JN
Activities: Wholesale of meat and meat products
Officers: Ian Geoffrey Kemp, Secretary/Administration Manager; Wesley Mendonca Batista Filho [1991] Director [Brazilian]; Marcus Enda O'Sullivan [1970] Director [Irish]

JCA Charitable Foundation
Incorporated: 10 September 1891 *Employees:* 2
Net Worth: £47,497,000 *Total Assets:* £47,593,000
Registered Office: 39 Church Meadow, Long Ditton, Surbiton, Surrey, KT6 5EP
Activities: Other social work activities without accommodation n.e.c.
Officers: Timothy Robin Martin, Secretary; Yaffa Ben-Amt [1954] Director/Council Member [Israeli]; Jacques Capelluto [1949] Director/Private Investor [Belgian]; William Arthur Lionel Cohen [1961] Director/Lawyer; Geoffrey Sigmund Gestetner [1965] Director; Avner Hermoni [1947] Director [Israeli]; Beatrice Anne Jouan [1957] Director/Consultant [French]; Tal Kvatinsky [1985] Director [Israeli]; Peter Anthony Lawrence [1948] Director; Jacques Martin Paul Marie Tim Philippson [1972] Managing Director Blue Squares Holding [Belgian]; Marc Vellay [1954] Director/Sculptor [French]; Sir Stephen Harry Waley-Cohen [1946] Director; Doron Weiss [1955] Director [Israeli]; Prof Smuel Wolf [1954] Director/Professor [Israeli]

JCB Medway Limited
Incorporated: 13 July 1998 *Employees:* 289
Net Worth: £6,619,674 *Total Assets:* £32,758,146
Registered Office: Bailey Drive, Gillingham Business Park, Gillingham, Kent, ME8 0PZ
Activities: Sale of new cars and light motor vehicles
Major Shareholder: Jonathan Charles Bishoff
Officers: Jonathan Charles Bischoff [1969] Director/Dealer Principal

JCDecaux UK Limited
Incorporated: 19 November 1982 *Employees:* 704
Net Worth: £34,628,000 *Total Assets:* £246,292,000
Registered Office: 991 Great West Road, Brentford, Middlesex, TW8 9DN
Activities: Advertising agencies
Officers: Philip Idris James Thomas, Secretary/Financial Director; Spencer Berwin [1961] Managing Director of Sales; Jean-Francois Decaux [1959] Director/Chief Executive [French]; Philip Stewart Drye [1965] Director; Xavier Dupre [1963] Managing Director [French]; Neil Allan Eddleston [1961] Director; Thibaut Huon de Kermadec [1973] Finance Director [French]; Helena Mary Kavanagh [1959] Director [Irish]; David McEvoy [1961] Director; Alan Sullivan [1973] Director; Philip Idris James Thomas [1958] Financial Director

JCDecaux United Limited
Incorporated: 20 March 1964
Net Worth: £26,768,000 *Total Assets:* £43,353,000
Registered Office: 991 Great West Road, Brentford, Middlesex, TW8 9DN
Activities: Advertising agencies
Officers: Philip Idris James Thomas, Secretary/Financial Director; Thibaut Huon de Kermadec [1973] Finance Director [French]; Helena Mary Kavanagh [1959] Director [Irish]; Philip Idris James Thomas [1958] Financial Director

JCHAC Europe Finco Limited
Incorporated: 30 April 2015
Net Worth: £164,986,816 *Total Assets:* £164,991,344
Registered Office: 9-10 The Briars, Waterberry Drive, Waterlooville, Hants, PO7 7YH
Activities: Activities of head offices
Parent: JCHAC UK Holdco Limited
Officers: Takashi Miki [1960] Director [Japanese]; Gboyega Obafemi [1961] Director

JCHAC India Holdco Limited
Incorporated: 30 April 2015
Net Worth: £24,709,604 *Total Assets:* £189,077,968
Registered Office: 9-10 The Briars, Waterberry Drive, Waterlooville, Hants, PO7 7YH
Activities: Activities of head offices
Parent: JCHAC UK Holdco Limited
Officers: Takashi Miki [1960] Director [Japanese]

JCHAC UK Holdco Limited
Incorporated: 30 April 2015
Net Worth: £331,792,832 *Total Assets:* £331,825,984
Registered Office: 9-10 The Briars, Waterberry Drive, Waterlooville, Hants, PO7 7YH
Activities: Activities of head offices
Parent: Johnson Controls-Hitachi Air Conditioning Holding (UK) Ltd
Officers: Takashi Miki [1960] Director [Japanese]

JDA Software UK Limited
Incorporated: 12 December 1984 *Employees:* 295
Net Worth: £32,547,000 *Total Assets:* £46,949,000
Registered Office: 2nd Floor, Maxis 2, Western Road, Bracknell, Berks, RG12 1RT
Activities: Information technology consultancy activities
Officers: Hebe Smythe Doneski, Secretary; Martin Tanti Felli [1967] Director/Lawyer [American]; Daniel James Maynard [1969] Director/Business Executive [American]

Jeensbannet Investments Limited
Incorporated: 22 April 1964
Net Worth: £18,336,904 *Total Assets:* £27,257,904
Registered Office: 45 Westerham Road, Sevenoaks, Kent, TN13 2QB
Activities: Buying and selling of own real estate
Parent: Armatire Limited
Officers: Christopher James Payne, Secretary; Kevin Ronald Spencer [1965] Director

JEG Acquisition Company Limited
Incorporated: 20 August 2008
Net Worth: £193,434,000 *Total Assets:* £193,891,008
Registered Office: 1180 Eskdale Road, Winnersh, Wokingham, Berks, RG41 5TU
Activities: Activities of head offices
Parent: Jacobs Engineering Group Inc
Officers: Tejender Singh Chaudhary, Secretary; Kevin Christopher Berryman [1959] Director/Business Executive [American]; Terence Hagen [1967] Director/Business Executive [American]; Peter Robert Lutwyche [1962] Director/Business Executive

Jelmac Properties
Incorporated: 11 November 2008
Net Worth: £32,619,098 *Total Assets:* £34,260,152
Registered Office: Jelmac House, 269 High Street, Berkhamsted, Herts, HP4 1AA
Activities: Other letting and operating of own or leased real estate
Shareholder: Elizabeth Jane Burgess
Officers: Frank David George Cattley, Secretary; Claire Elizabeth Rose [1970] Director; Alistair Piers Spooner [1972] Director; Mark Jeremy Spooner [1972] Director

Jembir Estates Limited
Incorporated: 30 January 1945 *Employees:* 8
Net Worth: £13,298,079 *Total Assets:* £20,992,208
Registered Office: 7 Northbrook Industrial Estate, Vincent Avenue, Southampton, SO16 6PB
Activities: Other letting and operating of own or leased real estate
Officers: Janet Mary Hammond, Secretary; Anne Louise Crabtree [1965] Director; Christopher John Hammond [1958] Director; Janet Mary Hammond [1931] Director; John Richmond Paul Hammond [1927] Director/Builder; Richard Paul Hammond [1959] Director; Jane Mary Stringer [1956] Director/Secretary

Jenoptik Traffic Solutions UK Ltd
Incorporated: 30 March 1998 *Employees:* 66
Previous: Vysionics ITS Limited
Net Worth: £20,111,336 *Total Assets:* £25,291,334
Registered Office: 10 Watchmoor Park, Camberley, Surrey, GU15 3YL
Activities: Technical testing and analysis
Parent: Vysionics ITS Holdings Limited
Officers: Kevin Chevis [1960] Director; Geoffrey Alan Collins [1970] Director; Richard Gorringe [1984] Financial Director; Michael Wendlik [1971] Managing Director [German]

Jeppesen U.K. Limited
Incorporated: 15 July 1977 *Employees:* 87
Net Worth: £23,512,640 *Total Assets:* £27,710,200
Registered Office: 6th Floor, Astral Towers, Betts Way, London Road, Crawley, W Sussex, RH10 9UY
Activities: Other service activities n.e.c.
Parent: Boeing United Kingdom Limited
Officers: Simon Howard Jones, Secretary; Sir Michael Anthony Arthur [1950] Director/Businessman; Stephen Mark Dowell [1967] Director; Robert Huntington Kurtz [1965] Director [American]

Jessops (Group) Limited
Incorporated: 1 February 2013 *Employees:* 799
Net Worth Deficit: £1,226,872 *Total Assets:* £27,151,020
Registered Office: Network House, Third Avenue, Globe Park, Marlow, Bucks, SL7 1EY
Activities: Activities of head offices
Shareholders: Peter David Jones; Jessops Holdings Limited
Officers: James Edward Peter Holdgate, Secretary; Peter David Jones [1966] Director; Neil Stewart Old [1971] Director

Jessops Europe Limited
Incorporated: 1 February 2013 *Employees:* 64
Net Worth Deficit: £771,086 *Total Assets:* £21,845,692
Registered Office: Network House, Third Avenue, Globe Park, Marlow, Bucks, SL7 1EY
Activities: Other retail sale of new goods in specialised stores (not commercial art galleries and opticians)
Shareholders: Peter David Jones; Jessops (Group) Limited
Officers: James Edward Peter Holdgate, Secretary; Peter David Jones [1966] Director; Neil Stewart Old [1971] Director

JLW Excellent Homes for Life Holding Company Limited
Incorporated: 1 December 2010
Net Worth Deficit: £6,733,000 *Total Assets:* £67,991,000
Registered Office: 8 White Oak Square, London Road, Swanley, Kent, BR8 7AG
Activities: Activities of head offices
Parent: JLIF Holdings (Regeneration and Social Housing) Limited
Officers: Vikki Louise Everett [1971] Director/Project Manager; Julian Denzil Sutcliffe [1968] Life Cycle Asset Director

JLW Excellent Homes for Life Limited
Incorporated: 3 December 2010
Net Worth Deficit: £6,733,000 *Total Assets:* £67,991,000
Registered Office: 8 White Oak Square, London Road, Swanley, Kent, BR8 7AG
Activities: Other business support service activities n.e.c.
Parent: JLW Excellent Homes for Life Holding Company Limited
Officers: Vikki Louise Everett [1971] Director/Project Manager; Julian Denzil Sutcliffe [1968] Life Cycle Asset Director

Johnson & Johnson Consumer Services EAME Ltd
Incorporated: 17 April 1958 *Employees:* 315
Net Worth: £55,045,292 *Total Assets:* £96,342,808
Registered Office: Foundation Park, Roxborough Way, Maidenhead, Berks, SL6 3UG
Activities: Other professional, scientific and technical activities n.e.c.
Parent: Johnson & Johnson Management Ltd
Officers: Christopher Ronald Thorne, Secretary/Accountant-Director; Andrew Crossley [1968] Finance Director; Christopher Ronald Thorne [1959] Accountant-Director

Johnson & Johnson Finance Limited
Incorporated: 14 November 1973
Net Worth: £25,477,000 *Total Assets:* £93,168,000
Registered Office: Pinewood Campus, Nine Mile Ride, Wokingham, Berks, RG40 3EW
Activities: Renting and leasing of other machinery, equipment and tangible goods n.e.c.
Parent: Johnson & Johnson Management Limited
Officers: Warren Charles Ewart Bowler, Secretary; Warren Charles Ewart Bowler [1968] Director/Financial Controller; Stephen Timothy O'Callaghan [1963] Director/Healthcare

Johnson & Johnson Innovation Limited
Incorporated: 21 August 2000
Net Worth: £29,083,000 *Total Assets:* £36,677,000
Registered Office: 50-100 Holmers Farm Way, High Wycombe, Bucks, HP12 4UL
Activities: Other letting and operating of own or leased real estate
Parent: Johnson & Johnson Management Limited
Officers: Gemma Storey, Secretary; Harpal Kumar [1965] Director/Innovation Centre Leader; Nerida Scott [1969] Senior Director, Transactions; Gert Vandewaerde [1983] Finance Director [Belgian]

Johnson & Johnson Limited
Incorporated: 8 October 1987 *Employees:* 307
Net Worth: £80,768,000 *Total Assets:* £204,111,008
Registered Office: Foundation Park, Roxborough Way, Maidenhead, Berks, SL6 3UG
Activities: Wholesale of perfume and cosmetics
Parent: Johnson & Johnson Management Ltd
Officers: Andrew Crossley [1968] Financial Director; Luc Huys [1967] Managing Director [Belgian]; Christopher Ronald Thorne [1959] Director/Accountant

Johnson & Johnson Management Limited
Incorporated: 2 February 1925
Net Worth: £613,436,992 *Total Assets:* £1,066,600,000
Registered Office: Pinewood Campus, Nine Mile Ride, Wokingham, Berks, RG40 3EW
Activities: Other business support service activities n.e.c.
Parent: Johnson & Johnson
Officers: Christopher Ronald Thorne, Secretary; Warren Charles Ewart Bowler [1968] Finance Director; Gilian Amanda Devonshire [1958] Senior Regional Tax Director EMEA; Christopher Ronald Thorne [1959] Director/Accountant

Johnson & Johnson UK Treasury Company Limited
Incorporated: 10 December 2015
Net Worth: £180,756,688 *Total Assets:* £180,791,296
Registered Office: Pinewood Campus, Nine Mile Ride, Wokingham, Berks, RG40 3EW
Activities: Financial intermediation not elsewhere classified
Parent: Johnson & Johnson Management Limited
Officers: Warren Charles Ewart Bowler, Secretary; Warren Charles Ewart Bowler [1968] Finance Director; Gillian Amanda Devonshire [1958] Senior Regional Tax Director EMEA; Luc Herman Maria Robert Freyne [1968] Director/Vice President, Treasurer [Belgian]; Christopher Ronald Thorne [1959] Accountant-Director

Johnson Controls Air Conditioning (UK) Limited
Incorporated: 30 July 2015
Net Worth: £22,545,456 *Total Assets:* £287,173,056
Registered Office: 9-10 The Briars, Waterberry Drive, Waterlooville, Hants, PO7 7YH
Activities: Activities of head offices
Parent: Johnson Controls-Hitachi Air Conditioning Holding (UK) Ltd
Officers: Mark Ayre [1963] Unity Compliance Director; Enrique Florez Leibar [1967] Director/Vice President & General Manager [Spanish]

Johnson Controls Air Conditioning Investments (UK) Limited
Incorporated: 30 July 2015
Net Worth: £261,487,264 *Total Assets:* £261,494,864
Registered Office: 9-10 The Briars, Waterberry Drive, Waterlooville, Hants, PO7 7YH
Activities: Activities of head offices
Parent: Johnson Controls-Hitachi Air Conditioning Holding (UK) Ltd
Officers: Mark Ayre [1963] Unity Compliance Director; Enrique Florez Leibar [1967] Director/Vice President & General Manager [Spanish]

Johnson Controls Auto India Ltd
Incorporated: 21 December 2012
Net Worth Deficit: £24,581,000 *Total Assets:* £25,117,000
Registered Office: 9-10 The Briars, Waterberry Drive, Waterlooville, Hants, PO7 7YH
Activities: Activities of head offices
Parent: Johnson Controls International PLC
Officers: Mark Ayre [1963] Finance Director; Peter Schieser [1967] Director/Lawyer [German]

Johnson Controls Batteries Limited
Incorporated: 24 June 1970 *Employees:* 13
Net Worth: £15,380,000 *Total Assets:* £32,965,000
Registered Office: 9-10 The Briars, Waterberry Drive, Waterlooville, Hants, PO7 7YH
Activities: Wholesale trade of motor vehicle parts and accessories
Parent: Johnson Controls International PLC
Officers: Ulrich Eich [1966] Director/Bachelor of Business Administration [German]; Brian David Hanna [1976] Director/Bachelor of Business Administration Finance [American]

Johnson Controls Building Efficiency UK Limited
Incorporated: 11 April 2014 *Employees:* 470
Net Worth: £48,871,000 *Total Assets:* £141,308,992
Registered Office: 9-10 The Briars, Waterberry Drive, Waterlooville, Hants, PO7 7YH
Activities: Plumbing, heat and air-conditioning installation
Parent: Johnson Controls International PLC
Officers: Mark Ayre [1963] Director/Global Finance Project Lead; James Paul Earnshaw [1976] Director/Finance; Andrew Ellis [1961] Director; Richard Hilton Jones [1964] Director

Johnson Controls China Holding (UK) Limited
Incorporated: 27 September 2016
Net Worth: £118,089,704 *Total Assets:* £118,094,360
Registered Office: 9-10 The Briars, Waterberry Drive, Waterlooville, Hants, PO7 7YH
Activities: Activities of other holding companies n.e.c.
Parent: Johnson Controls International PLC
Officers: Mark Ayre [1963] Director Finance Transformation; Peter Schieser [1967] Director/Corporate Secretary [German]

Johnson Controls China Investment (UK) Limited
Incorporated: 7 April 2017
Net Worth: £295,670,176 *Total Assets:* £295,674,848
Registered Office: 9-10 The Briars, Waterberry Drive, Waterlooville, Hants, PO7 7YH
Activities: Activities of other holding companies n.e.c.
Parent: Johnson Controls International Public Limited Company
Officers: Mark Ayre [1963] Finance Director; Peter Schieser [1967] Director/Senior Corporate Counsel [German]

Johnson Controls Enterprises Ltd
Incorporated: 24 May 1999
Net Worth Deficit: £488,614,016 *Total Assets:* £380,654,016
Registered Office: 9-10 The Briars, Waterberry Drive, Waterlooville, Hants, PO7 7YH
Activities: Activities of head offices
Parent: Johnson Controls International PLC
Officers: Mark Ayre [1963] Director/Global Finance Project Lead; Peter Schieser [1967] Director/Deputy General Counsel [German]

Johnson Controls Facilities Limited
Incorporated: 9 May 1991
Net Worth: £23,895,000 *Total Assets:* £23,898,000
Registered Office: 9-10 The Briars, Waterberry Drive, Waterlooville, Hants, PO7 7YH
Activities: Activities of head offices
Parent: Johnson Controls International PLC
Officers: Mark Ayre [1963] Director/Global Finance Project Lead; Peter Schieser [1967] Director/Deputy General Counsel [German]

Johnson Controls Holding UK Ltd
Incorporated: 4 March 2015
Net Worth: £132,522,632 *Total Assets:* £288,126,272
Registered Office: 9-10 The Briars, Waterberry Drive, Waterlooville, Hants, PO7 7YH
Activities: Activities of head offices
Parent: Johnson Controls International PLC
Officers: Mark Ayre [1963] Director; Peter Schieser [1967] Director/Lawyer [German]

Johnson Controls International Holdings Ltd
Incorporated: 25 February 2015
Net Worth: £11,312,797 *Total Assets:* £423,506,048
Registered Office: 9-10 The Briars, Waterberry Drive, Waterlooville, Hants, PO7 7YH
Activities: Activities of head offices
Parent: Johnson Controls International PLC
Officers: Mark Ayre [1963] Director; Peter Schieser [1967] Director/Lawyer [German]

Johnson Controls Investments (UK) Limited
Incorporated: 29 December 2000
Net Worth: £328,279,968 *Total Assets:* £463,808,288
Registered Office: 9-10 The Briars, Waterberry Drive, Waterlooville, Hants, PO7 7YH
Activities: Activities of head offices
Parent: Johnson Controls International PLC
Officers: Mark Ayre [1963] Finance Director; Peter Schieser [1967] Director/Deputy General Counsel [German]

Johnson Controls Metal Components Birmingham Limited
Incorporated: 11 December 1997
Net Worth: £125,163,000 *Total Assets:* £231,720,992
Registered Office: 9-10 The Briars, Waterberry Drive, Waterlooville, Hants, PO7 7YH
Activities: Activities of head offices
Parent: Johnson Controls International PLC
Officers: Mark Ayre [1963] Finance Director; Peter Schieser [1967] Director/Lawyer [German]

Johnson Controls Systems Development Limited
Incorporated: 28 November 2013 *Employees:* 20
Net Worth: £33,340,488 *Total Assets:* £35,871,348
Registered Office: 9-10 The Briars, Waterberry Drive, Waterlooville, Hants, PO7 7YH
Activities: Computer facilities management activities
Parent: Johnson Controls International PLC
Officers: Mark Ayre [1963] Finance Director; Peter Schieser [1967] Director/Lawyer [German]

Johnson Controls UAE Holding Ltd.
Incorporated: 10 August 2016 *Employees:* 1
Net Worth: £107,187,640 *Total Assets:* £109,775,080
Registered Office: 9-10 The Briars, Waterberry Drive, Waterlooville, Hants, PO7 7YH
Activities: Activities of head offices
Parent: Johnson Controls International PLC
Officers: Mark Ayre [1963] Finance Director; Peter Schieser [1967] Director [German]

Johnson Controls-Hitachi Air Conditioning Holding (UK) Ltd
Incorporated: 5 March 2015 *Employees:* 1
Net Worth: £701,025,856 *Total Assets:* £701,055,232
Registered Office: 9-10 The Briars, Waterberry Drive, Waterlooville, Hants, PO7 7YH
Activities: Activities of head offices
Shareholders: Johnson Controls International Holdings Ltd; Hitachi Appliances, Inc.
Officers: Franz Wolfgang Cerwinka [1969] Director/General Manager [American]; Shinichi Iizuka [1956] Director [Japanese]; Gboyega Obafemi [1961] Director; Hiroshi Takenaka [1962] Director [Japanese]; Toshiaki Tokunaga [1967] Director [Japanese]

Johnson Wax Limited
Incorporated: 14 November 1921 *Employees:* 344
Net Worth: £51,368,000 *Total Assets:* £114,221,000
Registered Office: Frimley Green, Camberley, Surrey, GU16 7AJ
Activities: Other business support service activities n.e.c.
Officers: John Michael Hayes, Secretary; Luciana Abreu [1973] Director/General Manager [Brazilian]; John Michael Hayes [1958] Finance Director; Thomas Patrick Howard [1967] Director/Tax Counsel [American]

Johnston Sweepers Limited
Incorporated: 11 August 1924 *Employees:* 472
Net Worth: £16,771,000 *Total Assets:* £62,408,000
Registered Office: Curtis Road, Dorking, Surrey, RH4 1XF
Activities: Manufacture of motor vehicles
Parent: Bucher Industries AG
Officers: Nigel Canon Brunning, Secretary; David Francis Bishop [1962] Operations Director; Nigel Canon Brunning [1963] Finance Director; William John MacIntyre Halley [1965] Customer Service Director; Clive Frederick Offley [1962] Engineering Director; Peter Graham Rhodes [1967] Director/Chartered Accountant; Manuela Suter [1974] Director/Chief Financial Officer [Swiss]

P.H Jones Group Limited
Incorporated: 15 January 2008
Net Worth: £28,837,000 *Total Assets:* £35,797,000
Registered Office: Millstream, Maidenhead Road, Windsor, Berks, SL4 5GD
Activities: Activities of head offices
Parent: British Gas New Heating Limited
Officers: Mark Steven Hodges [1965] Director; Ivan Edward Ronald [1972] Director; Dr Rajarshi Roy [1975] Director

JRL Group Holdings Limited
Incorporated: 16 October 2009 *Employees:* 871
Net Worth: £41,824,040 *Total Assets:* £244,142,128
Registered Office: 4 Elstree Way, Borehamwood, Herts, WD6 1RN
Activities: Activities of construction holding companies
Shareholder: Kevin William Keegan
Officers: Ronan Joseph Gleeson, Secretary [Irish]; Ronan Joseph Gleeson [1976] Director [Irish]; Kevin William Keegan [1963] Director [Irish]; John James Reddington [1972] Director [Irish]

JRL Group Limited
Incorporated: 26 March 2008 *Employees:* 871
Net Worth: £39,052,300 *Total Assets:* £229,338,288
Registered Office: 4 Elstree Way, Borehamwood, Herts, WD6 1RN
Activities: Activities of construction holding companies
Parent: JRL Group Holdings Ltd
Officers: Ronan Joseph Gleeson, Secretary [Irish]; Ronan Joseph Gleeson [1976] Director/Chartered Accountant [Irish]; Kevin William Keegan [1963] Director [Irish]; John James Reddington [1972] Director [Irish]

JRL Plant and Logistics Limited
Incorporated: 17 April 2003 *Employees:* 148
Net Worth: £968,887 *Total Assets:* £62,889,348
Registered Office: 4 Elstree Way, Borehamwood, Herts, WD6 1RN
Activities: Renting and leasing of construction and civil engineering machinery and equipment
Parent: JRL Group Ltd
Officers: Ronan Joseph Gleeson, Secretary/Director [Irish]; Ronan Joseph Gleeson [1976] Director [Irish]; Kevin William Keegan [1963] Director/Estimator [Irish]; John James Reddington [1972] Director/Formwork [Irish]

JRL Property Holdings Limited
Incorporated: 24 February 2017 *Employees:* 3
Net Worth: £4,660,324 *Total Assets:* £29,217,624
Registered Office: 4 Elstree Way, Borehamwood, Herts, WD6 1RN
Activities: Activities of other holding companies n.e.c.
Parent: JRL Group Holdings Limited
Officers: Ronan Gleeson, Secretary; Ronan Joseph Gleeson [1976] Director/Chartered Accountant [Irish]; Kevin William Keegan [1963] Director [Irish]; John James Reddington [1972] Director [Irish]

JTI (UK) Management Ltd
Incorporated: 3 November 2006 *Employees:* 4
Net Worth: £1,055,300,992 *Total Assets:* £1,257,982,976
Registered Office: Members Hill, Brooklands Road, Weybridge, Surrey, KT13 0QU
Activities: Activities of head offices
Parent: Japan Tobacco Inc.
Officers: Nicholas Charles David Craig, Secretary; Charles Ashley Cunningham-Reid [1968] Director; Paul Bernard Hennessy [1980] Director [Irish]; Jeroen Rusbach [1977] Director/Accountant [Dutch]; Daniel Sciamma [1970] Director [French]

JTL
Incorporated: 23 March 2000 *Employees:* 295
Net Worth: £36,310,576 *Total Assets:* £41,899,648
Registered Office: Stafford House, 120-122 High Street, Orpington, Kent, BR6 0JS
Activities: Technical and vocational secondary education
Officers: Caroline Anne Turner, Secretary; John Allott [1962] Director/Trades Union Official; Paul Graham Bird [1971] Finance Director; John Alexander Burrows [1954] HR Director; Richard Jeremy Clarke [1972] Director/Trade Union Official; Andrew Colin Eldred [1969] Director/Manager; Christopher Victor Fenton [1962] Director; Bernard McAulay [1951] Director/Trade Union Official; Paul Campbell McNaughton [1958] Managing Director; Geoffrey Russell [1958] Director; Tracey Elaine Shelley [1968] Director/Chief Executive and Company Secretary; William Cameron Spiers [1946] Director/Approved Electrician

Jungheinrich Financial Services Limited
Incorporated: 5 June 2006 *Employees:* 7
Net Worth: £11,223,000 *Total Assets:* £114,947,000
Registered Office: Sherbourne House, Sherbourne Drive, Tilbrook, Milton Keynes, Bucks, MK7 8HX
Activities: Financial leasing
Parent: Jungheinrich UK Holdings Limited
Officers: Christian Hanke [1974] Director/Head of Financial Services [German]; Arne Christian Rosenkranz [1983] Finance Director [German]

Jungheinrich Lift Truck Finance Limited
Incorporated: 5 June 2006
Net Worth: £4,912,000 *Total Assets:* £168,527,008
Registered Office: Sherbourne House, Sherbourne Drive, Tilbrook, Milton Keynes, Bucks, MK7 8HX
Activities: Financial leasing
Parent: Jungheinrich UK Holdings Limited
Officers: Christian Hanke [1974] Director/Head of Financial Services [German]; Arne Christian Rosenkranz [1983] Finance Director [German]

Jungheinrich UK Limited
Incorporated: 10 April 1963 *Employees:* 781
Net Worth: £40,940,000 *Total Assets:* £122,148,000
Registered Office: Sherbourne House, Sherbourne Drive, Tilbrook, Milton Keynes, Bucks, MK7 8HX
Activities: Manufacture of lifting and handling equipment
Parent: Jungheinrich UK Holdings Ltd
Officers: Arne Christian Rosenkranz [1983] Finance Director [German]; Luuk Theodorus Antonius Snijders [1982] Managing Director [Dutch]

Juniper Networks (UK) Limited
Incorporated: 16 September 1999
Net Worth: £64,392,344 *Total Assets:* £151,603,760
Registered Office: Building 1, Aviator Park, Station Road, Addlestone, Surrey, KT15 2PG
Activities: Other information technology service activities
Parent: Juniper Networks, Inc.
Officers: Julie Ann Appelbe [1967] Finance Director; Ketan Kumar Vithalbhai Rambhai Patel [1962] Director; Terrance Floyd Spidell [1968] Director/Chief Accounting Officer [American]

Jupiter Midco 1 Limited
Incorporated: 26 July 2016 *Employees:* 1,808
Net Worth Deficit: £4,505,099 *Total Assets:* £80,529,784
Registered Office: Charta House, 30-38 Church Street, Staines upon Thames, Middlesex, TW18 4EP
Activities: Activities of other holding companies n.e.c.
Parent: Jupiter Topco Limited
Officers: Christopher John Clasper [1981] Director/Investment Professional; Christopher John Wilmot [1973] Director/Investment Professional; Ayal Zylberman [1975] Director [Israeli/French]

Jupiter Midco 2 Limited
Incorporated: 17 June 2016
Net Worth: £624,090 *Total Assets:* £28,821,590
Registered Office: Charta House, 30-38 Church Street, Staines upon Thames, Middlesex, TW18 4EP
Activities: Activities of other holding companies n.e.c.
Parent: Jupiter Midco 1 Limited
Officers: Christopher John Clasper [1981] Director/Investment Professional; Christopher John Wilmot [1973] Director/Investment Professional; Ayal Zylberman [1975] Director [Israeli/French]

Jupiter Topco Limited
Incorporated: 17 June 2016 *Employees:* 1,808
Net Worth Deficit: £4,445,099 *Total Assets:* £77,377,568
Registered Office: Charta House, 30-38 Church Street, Staines upon Thames, Middlesex, TW18 4EP
Activities: Other business support service activities n.e.c.
Officers: Martin Harold Blackburn [1967] Director; Jan Olivier Fillols [1980] Director; Shawn Allister McMorran [1963] Director/Investment Professional [Canadian]; Edward Thomas Richards [1975] Director; Michael Edward Wilkinson [1986] Director; Ayal Zylberman [1975] Director/President, Qualitest Group [Israeli/French]

Just Develop It Limited
Incorporated: 10 January 2008 *Employees:* 125
Net Worth: £70,904,800 *Total Assets:* £109,557,768
Registered Office: Larch House, Parklands Business Park, Denmead, Hants, PO7 6XP
Activities: Other business support service activities n.e.c.
Major Shareholder: Christopher Stephen Phillips
Officers: Nicholas Grahame Baker [1985] Director; Christopher Stephen Phillips [1985] Director

Just Group PLC
Incorporated: 13 June 2013 *Employees:* 1,091
Previous: JRP Group PLC
Net Worth: £1,740,499,968 *Total Assets:* £24,164,900,864
Registered Office: Vale House, Roebuck Close, Bancroft Road, Reigate, Surrey, RH2 7RU
Activities: Activities of head offices
Officers: Simon Andrew O'Hara, Secretary; Paul Bishop [1954] Director; Rodney Malcolm Cook [1957] Director; Ian Donald Cormack [1947] Director; Michael John Deakin [1953] Director; Dr Christopher Shaw Gibson Smith [1945] Director/Chairman; Andrew Stephen Melcher [1949] Director; Keith Nicholson [1949] Director; David Louis Richardson [1972] Director [Irish]; Clare Mary Joan Spottiswoode [1953] Director

Just Retirement (Holdings) Limited
Incorporated: 19 March 2004
Net Worth: £287,596,992 *Total Assets:* £332,139,008
Registered Office: Vale House, Roebuck Close, Bancroft Road, Reigate, Surrey, RH2 7RU
Activities: Activities of head offices
Parent: Just Retirement Group Holdings Limited
Officers: Simon Andrew O'Hara, Secretary; Rodney Malcolm Cook [1957] Director; David Louis Richardson [1972] Director [Irish]

Just Retirement Group Holdings Limited
Incorporated: 10 June 2009
Net Worth: £576,867,968 *Total Assets:* £576,958,976
Registered Office: Vale House, Roebuck Close, Bancroft Road, Reigate, Surrey, RH2 7RU
Activities: Activities of financial services holding companies
Parent: Just Group PLC
Officers: Simon Andrew O'Hara, Secretary; Rodney Malcolm Cook [1957] Director; David Louis Richardson [1972] Director [Irish]

Just Retirement Limited
Incorporated: 16 January 2004
Net Worth: £842,700,032 *Total Assets:* £14,798,900,224
Registered Office: Vale House, Roebuck Close, Bancroft Road, Reigate, Surrey, RH2 7RU
Activities: Other activities auxiliary to insurance and pension funding
Parent: Just Retirement (Holdings) Limited
Officers: Simon Andrew O'Hara, Secretary; Paul Bishop [1954] Director; Rodney Malcolm Cook [1957] Director; Ian Donald Cormack [1947] Director; Michael John Deakin [1953] Director; Dr Christopher Shaw Gibson-Smith [1945] Director/Chairman; Andrew Stephen Melcher [1949] Director; Keith Nicholson [1949] Director; Nicholas Hugh Poyntz-Wright [1963] Director; David Louis Richardson [1972] Director [Irish]; Clare Mary Joan Spottiswoode [1953] Director; Paul James Turner [1971] Director

Just Retirement Management Services Limited
Incorporated: 28 February 2003 *Employees:* 855
Net Worth: £8,564,000 *Total Assets:* £46,142,000
Registered Office: Vale House, Roebuck Close, Bancroft Road, Reigate, Surrey, RH2 7RU
Activities: Other business support service activities n.e.c.
Parent: Just Retirement (Holdings) Limited
Officers: Simon Andrew O'Hara, Secretary; Rodney Malcolm Cook [1957] Director; Paul James Turner [1971] Director

K Capital Investment Ltd
Incorporated: 19 December 2016 *Employees:* 1
Net Worth: £70,469,920 *Total Assets:* £120,054,952
Registered Office: Worting House, Church Lane, Basingstoke, Hants, RG23 8PX
Activities: Other service activities n.e.c.
Major Shareholder: Matteo Pinciroli
Officers: Matteo Pinciroli [1978] Director [Italian]

K2M UK Limited
Incorporated: 2 July 2009 *Employees:* 50
Net Worth: £33,707,376 *Total Assets:* £41,350,028
Registered Office: Ground Floor, 1 Roundwood Avenue, Stockley Park, Uxbridge, Middlesex, UB11 1FG
Activities: Retail sale of medical and orthopaedic goods in specialised stores (not incl. hearing aids) n.e.c.
Parent: K2M Inc
Officers: Luke Russell Miller, Secretary [American]; Eric David Major [1969] Director [American]; Luke Russell Miller [1979] Director [American]

KAC Alarm Company Limited
Incorporated: 27 March 1975 *Employees:* 130
Net Worth: £44,097,000 *Total Assets:* £59,923,000
Registered Office: Honeywell House, Skimped Hill Lane, Bracknell, Berks, RG12 1EB
Activities: Manufacture of other electrical equipment
Parent: Pittway Systems Technology Group Europe Limited
Officers: Piyush Jayantilal Kanji Jutha [1972] Director; Russull John McNamara [1962] Director/Site Leader; Robert O'Hagan [1967] Director

Kallar Investments Limited
Incorporated: 23 July 2003 *Employees:* 2
Net Worth: £7,718,104 *Total Assets:* £21,993,636
Registered Office: 148 The Office, Station Road, Sidcup, Kent, DA15 7AB
Activities: Buying and selling of own real estate
Shareholders: Lakhbinder Kallar; Sukhjeev Kallar
Officers: Sukhjeev Kallar, Secretary; Lakhbinder Kallar [1973] Director/Estate Agent; Sukhjeev Kallar [1981] Director

Kallo Foods Limited
Incorporated: 31 January 1994 *Employees:* 147
Net Worth: £27,288,226 *Total Assets:* £64,671,028
Registered Office: Meadows Business Park, Station Approach, Blackwater, Camberley, Surrey, GU17 9AB
Activities: Agents involved in the sale of food, beverages and tobacco
Parent: Wessanen Great Britain Holdings Limited
Officers: Jason Edward Boxer [1969] Finance Director; Emma Jane Vass [1976] Managing Director

Kamkorp Limited
Incorporated: 2 May 1990 *Employees:* 100
Net Worth Deficit: £33,595,224 *Total Assets:* £25,202,976
Registered Office: Mychett Place, Mytchett Place Road, Mytchett, Surrey, GU16 6DQ
Activities: Activities of head offices
Major Shareholder: Kamal Siddiqi
Officers: Paul Alexander, Secretary/Chartered Accountant; Kamal Siddiqi [1952] Director; Sheban Kamal Siddiqi [1988] Director

Karelia Tobacco Company (UK) Limited
Incorporated: 13 August 2002 *Employees:* 6
Net Worth: £2,006,714 *Total Assets:* £22,936,140
Registered Office: Parkshot House, 5 Kew Road, Richmond, Surrey, TW9 2PR
Activities: Manufacture of tobacco products
Parent: Karelia Tobacco Company Inc
Officers: Andreas George Karelias [1966] Managing Director [Greek]; Efstathios George Karelias [1969] Director/General Manager [Greek]; Anthony Edward Peter Mulcrone [1959] Director

Karium Ltd
Incorporated: 14 August 1990 *Employees:* 61
Previous: Godrej Consumer Products (UK) Limited
Net Worth: £14,725,599 *Total Assets:* £29,025,880
Registered Office: Falcon House, 115-123 Staines Road, Hounslow, Middlesex, TW3 3LL
Activities: Wholesale of perfume and cosmetics
Parent: JZ Consumer Brands Limited
Officers: Benjamin David Hammersley, Secretary; Lee Graham Gelderd [1974] Managing Director; Jock Green-Armytage [1945] Director; Benjamin David Hammersley [1970] Finance Director; Alexander James MacGillivray Langmuir [1985] Director; Richard Reverdy Otley [1974] Director/Chairman [British Virgin Islander]; Miguel Rueda Hernando [1967] Director [Spanish]; Martin Stephen Northcote Wright [1968] Director

Kaye Enterprises Limited
Incorporated: 4 January 1989 *Employees:* 84
Net Worth: £14,224,985 *Total Assets:* £25,524,538
Registered Office: Oakleigh House, High Street, Hartley Wintney, Hook, Hants, RG27 8PE
Activities: Activities of head offices
Officers: Jane Louise Smith, Secretary; Stuart Duncan Bosley [1949] Director; David Wolf Kaye [1954] Director/Company Executive; Joanna Zelma Kaye [1950] Director/Company Executive; Ian Paul Williams [1945] Director/Company Executive; Christopher Murray Cameron Young [1962] Director/Company Executive

Kaysail Limited
Incorporated: 20 October 2004
Net Worth: £85,301,648 *Total Assets:* £130,549,824
Registered Office: 1st Floor, Ash House, Littleton Road, Ashford, Middlesex, TW15 1TZ
Activities: Activities of head offices
Parent: Goodrich Inertial Limited
Officers: Lynn Banis, Secretary; Christian Bruno Jean Idczak [1963] Director/Business Executive [French]; James Terence George Laurence [1964] Director/Accountant; Patricia Catherine Moran [1964] Finance Director [American]; Peter Ross [1964] Finance Director

Kazakh Projects Joint Venture Limited
Incorporated: 25 March 2008
Net Worth: £1,976,460 *Total Assets:* £72,145,216
Registered Office: Fluor Centre, 140 Pinehurst Road, Farnborough, Hants, GU14 7BF
Activities: Other business support service activities n.e.c.
Shareholders: Fluor International Limited; Worley Parsons Europe Ltd
Officers: Werner Dorfling [1970] Director; Michael John Rathge [1965] Director; Trevor Bryan Staples [1967] Director; Keri Elizabeth White [1970] Director

KBC Advanced Technologies Limited
Incorporated: 15 March 1978 *Employees:* 253
Previous: KBC Advanced Technologies PLC
Net Worth: £33,149,000 *Total Assets:* £72,729,000
Registered Office: 42-50 Hersham Road, Hersham, Walton on Thames, Surrey, KT12 1RZ
Activities: Activities of head offices
Officers: James Richard Jordan, Secretary; Andrew John Howell [1968] Board Director; Satoru Kurosu [1960] Director/Company Executive [Japanese]; Matthew Curtis Ray [1966] Director/Financial Executive [American]; Simon Michael Rogers [1964] Director; Masataka Tomonaga [1973] Director/HR Manager [Japanese]

KBC Process Technology Limited
Incorporated: 10 April 1984 *Employees:* 95
Net Worth: £7,501,000 *Total Assets:* £134,964,000
Registered Office: 42-50 Hersham Road, Hersham, Walton on Thames, Surrey, KT12 1RZ
Activities: Other engineering activities
Parent: KBC Advanced Technologies PLC
Officers: James Richard Jordan, Secretary; Mark Patrick Henry Anderson [1959] Director/Chemical Engineer; James Richard Jordan [1965] Director/Accountant; Allan Rudman [1963] Director/Chemical Engineer

KBR (U.K.) Investments Limited
Incorporated: 10 March 2011
Net Worth: £187,851,424 *Total Assets:* £198,719,136
Registered Office: Hill Park Court, Springfield Drive, Leatherhead, Surrey, KT22 7NL
Activities: Activities of other holding companies n.e.c.
Parent: Kellogg Brown & Root Limited
Officers: Susan Meirion Owen, Secretary; James Arthur Barrett [1965] Director/Chartered Accountant; Farhan Mujib [1963] Director [Australian]

KCI Medical Limited
Incorporated: 23 August 1973 *Employees:* 71
Net Worth: £11,279,000 *Total Assets:* £35,710,000
Registered Office: Belmont House, Station Way, Crawley, W Sussex, RH10 1JA
Activities: Activities of head offices
Parent: KCI UK Holdings Limited
Officers: Margo Barry [1970] Director [Irish]; Christiaan Jan Otto Pool [1972] Director [Dutch]; Peter Robert Rhodes [1976] Director/Attorney

KCI UK Holdings Limited
Incorporated: 13 November 1997 *Employees:* 51
Net Worth: £79,122,000 *Total Assets:* £127,373,000
Registered Office: Belmont House, Station Way, Crawley, W Sussex, RH10 1JA
Activities: Activities of head offices
Officers: John Thomas Bibb [1972] Director/Associate General Counsel [American]; Jonathan Robert Lasparini [1980] Director; Christiaan Jan Otto Pool [1972] Director [Dutch]; Peter Robert Rhodes [1976] Director/Attorney

Keadby Wind Farm Limited
Incorporated: 19 March 2009
Net Worth Deficit: £1,300,000 *Total Assets:* £108,400,000
Registered Office: No 1 Forbury Place, 43 Forbury Road, Reading, Berks, RG1 3JH
Activities: Other business support service activities n.e.c.
Parent: SSE Renewables Onshore Windfarm Holdings Limited
Officers: Sally Fairbairn, Secretary; James Isaac Smith [1962] Director/Engineer; Jeremy Williamson [1966] Director

Kebbell Development Limited
Incorporated: 27 July 1959 *Employees:* 52
Net Worth: £52,042,776 *Total Assets:* £70,591,016
Registered Office: Kebbell House, 21 London End, Beaconsfield, Bucks, HP9 2HN
Activities: Construction of domestic buildings
Officers: Simon Jennaway, Secretary; Richard William Barrett [1959] Finance Director; Fiona Shan Alexandra Binney [1959] Director; Andrea Fawell [1965] Sales Director; Nicolas Rowland MacDonald Kebbell [1951] Managing Director; Dudley John Mills [1965] Director/Land Buyer; Michael Mulligan [1962] Director/Building Manager; Denise Hilary Ann Newport [1954] Director

Kebbell Holdings Limited
Incorporated: 15 March 1963 *Employees:* 52
Net Worth: £53,548,984 *Total Assets:* £71,795,368
Registered Office: Kebbell House, 21 London End, Beaconsfield, Bucks, HP9 2HN
Activities: Other letting and operating of own or leased real estate
Officers: Simon Jennaway, Secretary; Meryl Audrey Kebbell [1924] Director; Nicolas Rowland MacDonald Kebbell [1951] Managing Director

Kedleston (Wings Education) Limited
Incorporated: 2 January 2003 *Employees:* 189
Previous: Wings Education Limited
Net Worth: £28,059,390 *Total Assets:* £33,542,588
Registered Office: Office Suite, 1 Ansell Gardens, Holloway Lane, Harmondsworth, West Drayton, Middlesex, UB7 0AE
Activities: General secondary education
Parent: Kedleston Wings Holdco Ltd
Officers: Anthony Robert Hurran, Secretary/Director; Denis Brosnan [1944] Director [Irish]; Paul Brosnan [1975] Director [Irish]; Anthony Robert Hurran [1976] Finance Director

Kedleston Group Limited
Incorporated: 13 August 2012 *Employees:* 472
Previous: Kedleston Education Limited
Net Worth Deficit: £8,163,156 *Total Assets:* £60,707,804
Registered Office: Office Suite, 1 Ansell Gardens, Holloway Lane, Harmondsworth, West Drayton, Middlesex, UB7 0AE
Activities: Activities of head offices
Officers: Denis Brosnan [1944] Director/Businessman [Irish]; Paul Brosnan [1975] Director [Irish]; Lesley Claire Cox [1959] Director; Anthony Robert Hurran [1976] Director/FD; Angela Marion Nightingale [1953] Director; Lee Nigel Reed [1963] Director/Chief Operating Officer; Richard Guy Murray Tassell [1947] Director

Kedleston Schools Limited
Incorporated: 12 April 2006 *Employees:* 472
Net Worth: £13,753,541 *Total Assets:* £51,455,176
Registered Office: Office Suite, 1 Ansell Gardens, Holloway Lane, Harmondsworth, West Drayton, Middlesex, UB7 0AE
Activities: Educational support services
Parent: Kedleston Group Limited
Officers: Anthony Robert Hurran, Finance Director; Denis Brosnan [1944] Director [Irish]; Paul Brosnan [1975] Director [Irish]; Anthony Robert Hurran [1976] Finance Director

Kedleston Wings Holdco Ltd
Incorporated: 4 March 2008
Net Worth: £4,659,965 *Total Assets:* £35,954,744
Registered Office: Office 1, Ansell Gardens, Holloway Lane, Harmondsworth, West Drayton, Middlesex, UB7 0AE
Activities: Activities of other holding companies n.e.c.
Parent: Kedlestson Schools Limited
Officers: Anthony Robert Hurran, Finance Director; Denis Brosnan [1944] Director [Irish]; Paul Brosnan [1975] Director [Irish]; Anthony Robert Hurran [1976] Finance Director

Kellogg Brown & Root (Greenford) Limited
Incorporated: 5 July 1967
Net Worth: £82,622,720 *Total Assets:* £123,680,904
Registered Office: Hill Park Court, Springfield Drive, Leatherhead, Surrey, KT22 7NL
Activities: Other professional, scientific and technical activities n.e.c.
Parent: Kellogg Brown & Root DH Limited
Officers: Gregor Andrej Kosak, Secretary; David Lindsay Gibson [1962] Director/VP Operations; Farhan Mujib [1963] Director [Australian]; Martin Simmonite [1969] Director/Vice President Operations; Richard Francis Sullivan [1971] Director/Chartered Accountant

Kellogg Brown & Root (Services) Limited
Incorporated: 9 July 1975
Net Worth: £36,504,440 *Total Assets:* £36,539,200
Registered Office: Hill Park Court, Springfield Drive, Leatherhead, Surrey, KT22 7NL
Activities: Activities of construction holding companies
Parent: Laurel Financial Services B.V
Officers: Maya Diana Sutorius Feijen, Secretary/Manager Accounting [Dutch]; Maya Diana Sutorius Feijen [1971] Director/Manager Accounting [Dutch]

Kellogg Brown & Root (U.K.) Limited
Incorporated: 21 May 1986 *Employees:* 1,050
Net Worth Deficit: £598,273,024 *Total Assets:* £141,891,008
Registered Office: Hill Park Court, Springfield Drive, Leatherhead, Surrey, KT22 7NL
Activities: Other specialised construction activities n.e.c.
Parent: Kellogg Brown & Root Holdings (U.K.) Limited
Officers: Martin Nelhams, Secretary/Solicitor; James Arthur Barrett [1965] Director/Accountant; Jan Egil Braendeland [1967] Director [Norwegian]; Jalal Jay Ibrahim [1960] Director [American]; James Edward Lewis [1977] QHSE Director; Farhan Mujib [1963] Director [Australian]; Martin Nelhams [1960] Director/Solicitor; Martin Simmonite [1969] Director; Richard Francis Sullivan [1971] Director/Chartered Accountant

Kellogg Brown & Root DH Limited
Incorporated: 28 July 1987
Net Worth: £399,282,432 *Total Assets:* £399,282,432
Registered Office: Hill Park Court, Springfield Drive, Leatherhead, Surrey, KT22 7NL
Activities: Activities of other holding companies n.e.c.
Parent: Kellogg Brown & Root London Limited
Officers: Martin Nelhams, Secretary/Solicitor; James Arthur Barrett [1965] Director/Accountant; Martin Nelhams [1960] Director/Solicitor

Kellogg Brown & Root Group Limited
Incorporated: 27 October 2009
Net Worth Deficit: £253,736,176 *Total Assets:* £366,753,312
Registered Office: Hill Park Court, Springfield Drive, Leatherhead, Surrey, KT22 7NL
Activities: Activities of construction holding companies
Parent: Kellogg Brown & Root Overseas Projects Limited
Officers: Martin Nelhams, Secretary; James Arthur Barrett [1965] Director/Chartered Accountant; Martin Nelhams [1960] Director/Solicitor

Kellogg Brown & Root Holdings (U.K.) Limited
Incorporated: 11 December 1984
Net Worth: £25,794,000 *Total Assets:* £512,745,984
Registered Office: Hill Park Court, Springfield Drive, Leatherhead, Surrey, KT22 7NL
Activities: Activities of construction holding companies
Parent: Kellogg Brown & Root Holdings Limited
Officers: Martin Nelhams, Secretary/Solicitor; James Arthur Barrett [1965] Director/Accountant; Martin Nelhams [1960] Director/Solicitor

Kellogg Brown & Root Holdings Limited
Incorporated: 1 June 1999 *Employees:* 1,335
Net Worth: £966,976,000 *Total Assets:* £1,585,053,056
Registered Office: Hill Park Court, Springfield Drive, Leatherhead, Surrey, KT22 7NL
Activities: Activities of construction holding companies
Parent: Kellogg Brown & Root International Group Limited
Officers: Martin Nelhams, Secretary/Solicitor; James Arthur Barrett [1965] Director/Accountant; Martin Nelhams [1960] Director/Solicitor

Kellogg Brown & Root International Group Holdings LLP
Incorporated: 4 November 2009 *Employees:* 2
Net Worth: £133,496,432 *Total Assets:* £133,496,968
Registered Office: Hill Park Court, Springfield Drive, Leatherhead, Surrey, KT22 7NL

Kellogg Brown & Root International Group Limited
Incorporated: 26 October 2009
Net Worth: £77,243,056 *Total Assets:* £578,924,608
Registered Office: Hill Park Court, Springfield Drive, Leatherhead, Surrey, KT22 7NL
Activities: Activities of construction holding companies
Parent: Kellogg Brown & Root International Group Holdings LLP
Officers: Martin Nelhams, Secretary; James Arthur Barrett [1965] Director/Chartered Accountant; Martin Nelhams [1960] Director/Solicitor

Kellogg Brown & Root Limited
Incorporated: 22 December 1959 *Employees:* 110
Net Worth: £1,342,550,016 *Total Assets:* £1,787,815,936
Registered Office: Hill Park Court, Springfield Drive, Leatherhead, Surrey, KT22 7NL
Activities: Other engineering activities
Parent: Kellogg Brown Root Holdings (U.K.) Limited
Officers: Martin Nelhams, Secretary; James Arthur Barrett [1965] Director/Accountant; Jan Egil Braendeland [1967] Director [Norwegian]; David Lindsay Gibson [1962] Director/Vice President Operations EAME; Jalal Jay Ibrahim [1960] Director [American]; James Edward Lewis [1977] QHSE Director; Farhan Mujib [1963] Director [Australian]; Martin Simmonite [1969] Director; Richard Francis Sullivan [1971] Director/Chartered Accountant

Kellogg Brown & Root London Limited
Incorporated: 16 December 2010
Net Worth: £189,882,800 *Total Assets:* £339,168,064
Registered Office: Hill Park Court, Springfield Drive, Leatherhead, Surrey, KT22 7NL
Activities: Activities of other holding companies n.e.c.
Parent: Kellogg Brown & Root London Holdings Limited
Officers: Susan Meirion Owen, Secretary; James Arthur Barrett [1965] Director/Chartered Accountant; Farhan Mujib [1963] Director [Australian]

Kellogg Brown & Root Overseas Operations Limited
Incorporated: 8 July 1986 *Employees:* 5
Net Worth: £116,061,104 *Total Assets:* £181,719,616
Registered Office: Hill Park Court, Springfield Drive, Leatherhead, Surrey, KT22 7NL
Activities: Other engineering activities
Parent: Kellogg Brown & Root Group Limited
Officers: Susan Meirion Owen, Secretary; Jan Egil Braendeland [1967] Director [Norwegian]; Jalal Jay Ibrahim [1960] Director [American]; Martin Simmonite [1969] Director; Richard Francis Sullivan [1971] Director/Chartered Accountant

Kellogg Brown & Root Overseas Projects Limited
Incorporated: 29 August 1986
Net Worth: £648,128,512 *Total Assets:* £653,177,088
Registered Office: Hill Park Court, Springfield Drive, Leatherhead, Surrey, KT22 7NL
Activities: Other engineering activities
Parent: Kellogg Brown & Root Limited
Officers: Martin Nelhams, Secretary; James Arthur Barrett [1965] Director/Chartered Accountant; Martin Nelhams [1960] Director/Solicitor

Kelly Services (UK) Limited
Incorporated: 23 September 1992 *Employees:* 176
Net Worth Deficit: £811,000 *Total Assets:* £35,458,000
Registered Office: Apple Market House, 17 Union Street, Kingston upon Thames, Surrey, KT1 1RR
Activities: Temporary employment agency activities
Parent: Kelly Services Inc
Officers: Richard Bradley, Secretary; Berendina Maria Bekhuis [1969] Director/VP and Operations Leader [Dutch]; Richard Bradley [1971] Managing Director; George Steven Corona [1958] Director/President and Chief Executive [American]; Olivier Thirot [1961] Director/Business Executive [Swiss]

Keltbray Group (Holdings) Limited
Incorporated: 20 April 1993 *Employees:* 1,393
Net Worth: £34,107,904 *Total Assets:* £177,407,840
Registered Office: St Andrew's House, Portsmouth Road, Esher, Surrey, KT10 9TA
Activities: Construction of other civil engineering projects n.e.c.
Parent: Keltbray Group Ltd
Officers: Peter James Burnside, Secretary; Vincent Corrigan [1961] Director; Paul Francis Deacy [1965] Director; Antony John Douglas [1963] Director; John Patrick Keehan [1955] Director/Accountant; Brendan Martin Kerr [1965] Director [Irish]; John Richard Price [1959] Director/Construction; Philip Reginald Price [1962] Director; Peter Konrad Suchy [1961] Director/Quantity Surveyor

Keltbray Group Limited
Incorporated: 28 October 2015 *Employees:* 1,393
Net Worth: £25,580,930 *Total Assets:* £176,649,984
Registered Office: St Andrews House, Portsmouth Road, Esher, Surrey, KT10 9TA
Activities: Activities of construction holding companies
Major Shareholder: Brendan Martin Kerr
Officers: Peter James Burnside, Secretary; Peter James Burnside [1965] Director/Chartered Accountant; John Patrick Keehan [1955] Director/Chartered Accountant; Brendan Martin Kerr [1965] Director [Irish]

Keltbray Limited
Incorporated: 23 August 1976 *Employees:* 882
Net Worth: £30,592,034 *Total Assets:* £135,913,392
Registered Office: St Andrew's House, Portsmouth Road, Esher, Surrey, KT10 9TA
Activities: Demolition
Parent: Keltbray Group (Holdings) Limited
Officers: Peter James Burnside, Secretary; Peter James Burnside [1965] Director/Chartered Accountant; Paul Francis Deacy [1965] Director; David Anthony Harrison [1982] Director; John Patrick Keehan [1955] Director/Accountant; Brendan Martin Kerr [1965] Director [Irish]; Andrew John McClafferty [1971] Director [Irish]; Holly Price [1979] Director; John Richard Price [1959] Director; Philip Reginald Price [1962] Director; Peter Konrad Suchy [1961] Director/Quantity Surveyor

Keltbray Plant Limited
Incorporated: 3 November 1982 *Employees:* 174
Net Worth: £5,312,376 *Total Assets:* £36,962,956
Registered Office: St Andrew's House, Portsmouth Road, Esher, Surrey, KT10 9TA
Activities: Renting and leasing of construction and civil engineering machinery and equipment
Parent: Keltbray Group (Holdings) Limited
Officers: Peter James Burnside, Secretary; Peter James Burnside [1965] Director/Chartered Accountant; Paul Francis Deacy [1965] Director; Brendan Martin Kerr [1965] Director [Irish]; John Richard Price [1959] Director

Kelvion Limited
Incorporated: 22 August 2000 *Employees:* 234
Previous: GEA Heat Exchangers Limited
Net Worth: £26,818,000 *Total Assets:* £36,426,000
Registered Office: 20 Davis Way, Fareham, Hants, PO14 1AR
Activities: Manufacture of non-domestic cooling and ventilation equipment
Parent: Kelvion Holdings GmbH
Officers: Luke Davies, Secretary; Kevin Apperley [1962] Operations Director; Mark Douglas Knapman [1972] Sale and Engineering Director

Kemble Water Eurobond PLC
Incorporated: 5 October 2006
Net Worth Deficit: £614,600,000 *Total Assets:* £4,233,299,968
Registered Office: Clearwater Court, Vastern Road, Reading, Berks, RG1 8DB
Activities: Other business support service activities n.e.c.
Parent: Kemble Water Holdings Limited
Officers: Sonia Billett, Secretary; David Jonathan Hughes, Secretary; Michael David Bloch-Hansen [1986] Associate Director [Canadian]; Kenton Edward Bradbury [1970] Director/Investment Professional; Stephen Alan John Deeley [1980] Director/Investment Manager; Jerry James Divoky [1966] Director/Portfolio Manager [Canadian]; Alastair Colin Hall [1982] Director/Investment Professional; Guy Lambert [1977] Director/Investment Professional [Dutch]; Emma Lewis [1979] Director/Investment Manager; Patrick Thomas Mulholland [1977] Director [Australian]; Perry Denis Noble [1960] Director/Alternate; Greg Pestrak [1971] Director/Executive Vice President; Christy Nghi Do Truong Pham [1977] Director/Alternate [Canadian]; Fuxin Sheng [1979] Director/Investment Professional [Chinese]; Tianxiao Song [1990] Director/Investment Professional [Chinese]; Giles John Julian Tucker [1960] Director/Principal

Kemble Water Finance Limited
Incorporated: 17 May 2006 *Employees:* 5,426
Net Worth Deficit: £3,449,299,968 *Total Assets:* £18,115,999,744
Registered Office: Clearwater Court, Vastern Road, Reading, Berks, RG1 8DB
Activities: Activities of head offices
Parent: Kemble Water Eurobond PLC
Officers: Sonia Billett, Secretary; David Jonathan Hughes, Secretary; Michael David Bloch-Hansen [1986] Associate Director [Canadian]; Kenton Edward Bradbury [1970] Director/Investment Professional; Stephen Alan John Deeley [1980] Director/Investment Manager; Jerry James Divoky [1966] Director/Portfolio Manager [Canadian]; Alastair Colin Hall [1982] Director/Investment Professional; Guy Lambert [1977] Director/Investment Professional [Dutch]; Emma Lewis [1979] Director/Investment Manager; Patrick Thomas Mulholland [1977] Director [Australian]; Perry Denis Noble [1960] Director/Alternate; Greg Pestrak [1971] Director/Executive Vice President; Christy Nghi Do Truong Pham [1977] Director/Alternate [Canadian]; Fuxin Sheng [1979] Director/Investment Professional [Chinese]; Tianxiao Song [1990] Director/Investment Professional [Chinese]; Giles John Julian Tucker [1960] Director/Principal

Kemble Water Holdings Limited
Incorporated: 17 May 2006 *Employees:* 5,426
Net Worth: £1,463,399,936 *Total Assets:* £17,783,500,800
Registered Office: Clearwater Court, Vastern Road, Reading, Berks, RG1 8DB
Activities: Activities of head offices
Officers: Sonia Billett, Secretary; David Jonathan Hughes, Secretary; Michael David Bloch-Hansen [1986] Associate Director [Canadian]; Kenton Edward Bradbury [1970] Director/Investment Professional; Stephen Alan John Deeley [1980] Director/Investment Manager; Jerry James Divoky [1966] Director/Portfolio Manager [Canadian]; Alastair Colin Hall [1982] Director/Investment Professional; Guy Lambert [1977] Director/Investment Professional [Dutch]; Emma Lewis [1979] Director/Investment Manager; Patrick Thomas Mulholland [1977] Director [Australian]; Perry Denis Noble [1960] Director/Alternate; Greg Pestrak [1971] Director/Executive Vice President; Christy Nghi Do Truong Pham [1977] Director/Alternate [Canadian]; Fuxin Sheng [1979] Director/Investment Professional [Chinese]; Tianxiao Song [1990] Director/Investment Professional [Chinese]; Giles John Julian Tucker [1960] Director/Principal

The Kemnal Academies Trust
Incorporated: 17 August 2010 *Employees:* 3,355
Net Worth: £232,782,000 *Total Assets:* £279,572,992
Registered Office: The Atkins Centre, Kemnal Technology College, Sevenoaks Way, Sidcup, Kent, DA14 5AA
Activities: Other education n.e.c.
Officers: Claire Louise Lee, Secretary; John Peter Atkins [1949] Director/Chief Executive; Gaenor Anne Bagley [1964] Director/Senior Partner; Peter Anthony Baines [1962] Director/Chief Executive; Aruna Anand Mehta [1962] Director/Retired Banker; Dr Karen Louise Roberts [1968] Director/Chief Executive Officer; Elaine Marie Thomas [1971] Global HR Director

Kendallco Limited
Incorporated: 14 August 2014 *Employees:* 5
Net Worth Deficit: £11,876,000 *Total Assets:* £79,369,000
Registered Office: Focus 31 West Wing, Cleveland Road, Hemel Hempstead Industrial Estate, Hemel Hempstead, Herts, HP2 7BW
Activities: Other sports activities
Parent: Kanyeco Limited
Officers: Stephen Burns [1976] Managing Director; Laurence Brian Keen [1976] Finance Director

Kennet School Academies Trust
Incorporated: 25 February 2011 *Employees:* 300
Net Worth: £19,021,000 *Total Assets:* £23,676,000
Registered Office: Kennet School, Stoney Lane, Thatcham, Berks, RG19 4LL
Activities: Primary education
Officers: Reverend Mark David Bennet [1962] Director/Church Minister; Michael Jon de Courcy Cole [1955] Director/Retired; Nicholas John Cornish [1956] Director/Driving Instructor; Dr Elisabeth Mary Crossman [1970] Director/Programme Manager; Rebecca Louise Ebdon [1969] Director/HR Manager; Michelle Harrison [1973] Director/School Business Manager; Matthew Paul Irving [1969] Director/Headteacher; Martin Edward Keogh [1960] Director/Teacher; Nigel Margeson [1968] Director/H&S Manager; Gemma Louise Piper [1983] Director/Teacher

Kensington Mortgage Company Limited
Incorporated: 26 April 1995
Net Worth: £3,527,000 *Total Assets:* £39,478,000
Registered Office: Ascot House, Maidenhead Office Park, Maidenhead, Berks, SL6 3QQ
Activities: Activities of mortgage finance companies
Parent: The Northview Group Limited
Officers: Jayne Doreen Almond [1957] Director; Mark John Arnold [1968] Director/Chief Executive; Rajesh Gupta [1969] Finance Director; Alexander James Maddox [1970] Capital Markets Director, Kensington; Diana Susan Miller [1950] Director; Mark Jeffrey Preston [1960] Director

Kent Auto Panels Limited
Incorporated: 21 June 1960 *Employees:* 188
Net Worth: £10,730,771 *Total Assets:* £23,043,332
Registered Office: Shorncliffe Motor Park, Ross Way, Folkestone, Kent, CT20 3UJ
Activities: Sale of new cars and light motor vehicles
Parent: Tudor Holdings (UK) Limited
Officers: Colin Graham Furneaux, Secretary; Colin Graham Furneaux [1953] Director/Chartered Accountant; Dennis Colin Furneaux [1929] Director; Garry Ian Furneaux [1967] Director; Roland Geoffrey Ambrose Furneaux [1982] Director/Chartered Accountant

Kent Catholic Schools' Partnership
Incorporated: 10 August 2012 *Employees:* 1,480
Net Worth: £56,149,000 *Total Assets:* £74,448,000
Registered Office: Barham Court, Teston, Maidstone, Kent, ME18 5BZ
Activities: Educational support services
Officers: Michelle Boniface, Secretary; Marjeta Brennan [1955] Director [Irish]; Reverend Philip Gilbert [1948] Director/Parish Priest; Julian Anthony Gizzi [1957] Director/Retired (Solicitor); David Adam Lain [1972] Director/Finance Business Partner; Dr Jane Bernadette Overbury [1957] Director/Retired; Michael Francis Powis [1946] Director; Geoffrey Neil Randells [1957] Director/Financial Portfolio Manager; Peter John Ventress [1960] Director/Company CEO; Michael David Walters [1974] Director/Executive Principal; Clive Webster [1962] Director/Chief Executive; Anne Marie Whittle [1963] Director/Headmistress

Kent Education Partnership (Holdings) Limited
Incorporated: 14 June 2005
Net Worth Deficit: £16,503,000 *Total Assets:* £84,467,000
Registered Office: Part First Floor, 1 Grenfell Road, Maidenhead, Berks, SL6 1HN
Activities: Financial intermediation not elsewhere classified
Shareholders: Infrastructure Investments Holdings Limited; BBGI Sicav S.A.
Officers: Emeka Ikechi Ehenulo, Secretary; David Alexander John Foot [1968] Director, Infrastructure; Carlos Abuin Garcia [1985] Director/Investment Executive [Spanish]; Albert Hendrik Naafs [1965] Director [Dutch]; Frank Manfred Schramm [1968] Director [German]

Kent Education Partnership Limited
Incorporated: 14 June 2005
Net Worth Deficit: £16,503,000 *Total Assets:* £84,467,000
Registered Office: Part First Floor, 1 Grenfell Road, Maidenhead, Berks, SL6 1HN
Activities: Financial intermediation not elsewhere classified
Parent: Kent Education Partnership (Holdings) Limited
Officers: Emeka Ikechi Ehenulo, Secretary; David Alexander John Foot [1968] Director, Infrastructure; Carlos Abuin Garcia [1985] Director/Investment Executive [Spanish]; Albert Hendrik Naafs [1965] Director [Dutch]; Frank Manfred Schramm [1968] Director [German]

Kent EHFA Holdco Limited
Incorporated: 10 December 2013 *Employees:* 4
Net Worth Deficit: £11,906,579 *Total Assets:* £48,288,048
Registered Office: Cowley Business Park, Cowley, Uxbridge, Middlesex, UB8 2AL
Activities: Activities of construction holding companies
Parent: PPDI Assetco 2 Limited
Officers: Rory Christie [1958] Director; John Stephen Gordon [1962] Director

Kent EHFA Projectco Limited
Incorporated: 10 December 2013 *Employees:* 2
Net Worth Deficit: £11,906,678 *Total Assets:* £49,430,544
Registered Office: Cowley Business Park, Cowley, Uxbridge, Middlesex, UB8 2AL
Activities: Development of building projects
Parent: Kent EHFA Holdco Limited
Officers: Rory Christie [1958] Director; John Stephen Gordon [1962] Director

Kentstone Properties Limited
Incorporated: 27 November 1862 *Employees:* 5
Net Worth: £25,228,010 *Total Assets:* £40,457,036
Registered Office: Suite 21, Evegate Park Barn, Smeeth, Ashford, Kent, TN25 6SX
Activities: Renting and operating of Housing Association real estate
Officers: Jacqueline Louise Hunter, Secretary; Robert Nigel James Coombe [1960] Director; John Hawkins [1956] Director/Chartered Surveyor; Jacqueline Louise Hunter [1962] Director; Timothy Charles Monckton [1953] Director/Solicitor; John Wilkins [1964] Director/Chartered Surveyor

Kentucky Fried Chicken (Great Britain) Limited
Incorporated: 2 December 1969 *Employees:* 7,507
Net Worth: £434,744,992 *Total Assets:* £722,492,992
Registered Office: Orion Gate, Guildford Road, Woking, Surrey, GU22 7NJ
Activities: Licenced restaurants
Parent: Restaurant Holdings Limited
Officers: Clare Marie Boynton, Secretary; Christopher Alexander Drew [1981] Director/Chief Finance Officer; Christopher Robert Holmes [1981] Development Director; Paula MacKenzie [1977] Business Development Director; Martin Raymond Francis Shuker [1962] Director/General Manager

Kenwood Appliances Limited
Incorporated: 30 May 1989
Net Worth: £90,164,000 *Total Assets:* £90,281,000
Registered Office: 1 Kenwood Business Park, New Lane, Havant, Hants, PO9 2NH
Activities: Activities of head offices
Parent: De Longhi Benelux S.A.
Officers: Alan Cummings, Secretary; Stefano Biella [1963] Director [Italian]; Silvia De'longhi [1984] Director [Italian]; Mark Jonathan Welch [1966] Director

Kenwood International Limited
Incorporated: 16 August 1989
Net Worth: £20,896,000 *Total Assets:* £21,045,000
Registered Office: Unit 1 Kenwood Business Park, New Lane, Havant, Hants, PO9 2NH
Activities: Activities of head offices
Parent: Kenwood Appliances Limited
Officers: Alan Cummings, Secretary; Stefano Biella [1963] Director [Italian]; Silvia De'longhi [1984] Director [Italian]; Mark Jonathan Welch [1966] Director

Kenwood Limited
Incorporated: 22 February 1966 *Employees:* 266
Net Worth: £116,036,000 *Total Assets:* £213,496,000
Registered Office: 1 Kenwood Business Park, New Lane, Havant, Hants, PO9 2NH
Activities: Manufacture of electric domestic appliances
Parent: Kenwood Appliances Limited
Officers: Alan Cummings, Secretary; Stefano Biella [1963] Director [Italian]; Silvia De'longhi [1984] Director [Italian]; Mark Jonathan Welch [1966] Director/Chief Executive Officer

Kerridge Commercial Systems (Bidco) Limited
Incorporated: 12 December 2014
Previous: Florence Bidco Limited
Net Worth: £37,282,000 *Total Assets:* £97,526,000
Registered Office: Unit 2a Herongate, Charnham Park, Hungerford, Berks, RG17 0YU
Activities: Activities of other holding companies n.e.c.
Parent: Kerridge Commercial Systems (Midco) Limited
Officers: Thomas Barnds [1968] Director/Investor [American]; Nigel Bedford [1963] Director/Chartered Accountant; Ian Bendelow [1967] Director; Jason Michael Klein [1973] Director/Investor [American]

Kerridge Commercial Systems (Midco) Limited
Incorporated: 8 January 2015
Previous: Florence Midco Limited
Net Worth: £34,639,000 *Total Assets:* £66,974,000
Registered Office: Unit 2a Herongate, Charnham Park, Hungerford, Berks, RG17 0YU
Activities: Activities of other holding companies n.e.c.
Parent: Kerridge Commercial Systems Group Limited
Officers: Thomas Barnds [1968] Director/Investor [American]; Nigel Bedford [1963] Director/Chartered Accountant; Ian Bendelow [1967] Director; Jason Michael Klein [1973] Director/Investor [American]

Kerridge Commercial Systems Group Limited
Incorporated: 12 December 2014 *Employees:* 529
Previous: Florence Topco Limited
Net Worth: £70,986,000 *Total Assets:* £145,532,000
Registered Office: Unit 2a Herongate, Charnham Park, Hungerford, Berks, RG17 0YU
Activities: Activities of other holding companies n.e.c.
Officers: Thomas Barnds [1968] Director/Investor [American]; Nigel Bedford [1963] Director/Chartered Accountant; Ian Bendelow [1967] Director; Jason Michael Klein [1973] Director/Investor [American]

Kerridge Commercial Systems Limited
Incorporated: 30 November 2009 *Employees:* 199
Net Worth: £15,882,000 *Total Assets:* £31,511,000
Registered Office: Charnham Park, Hungerford, Berks, RG17 0YU
Activities: Business and domestic software development
Parent: Kerridge Commercial Systems (Bidco) Limited
Officers: Nigel Jonathan Bedford [1963] Director; Ian Barrie Bendelow [1967] Director; David Alan Liddle [1958] Director; Des Nangle [1968] Director [Irish]

Kerry Foods Limited
Incorporated: 23 April 1991 *Employees:* 2,969
Net Worth: £62,272,828 *Total Assets:* £538,807,168
Registered Office: Thorpe Lea Manor, Thorpe Lea Road, Egham, Surrey, TW20 8HY
Activities: Production of meat and poultry meat products
Parent: Kerry Holdings (U.K.) Limited
Officers: Ronan Deasy, Secretary; Ronan Deasy [1964] Director/Accountant [Irish]; Trevor James Horan [1972] EMEA Country Compliance Director [Irish]; Marguerite Larkin [1971] Director/Chief Financial Officer [Irish]

Kerry Holdings (U.K.) Limited
Incorporated: 10 September 1982
Net Worth: £231,849,504 *Total Assets:* £382,593,792
Registered Office: Thorpe Lea Manor, Thorpe Lea Road, Egham, Surrey, TW20 8HY
Activities: Activities of head offices
Parent: Kerry Group PLC
Officers: Ronan Deasy, Secretary; Ronan Deasy [1964] Director/Accountant [Irish]; Duncan Everett [1971] Director; Cathal Henry Gunton [1977] Director/Accountant [Irish]; Trevor James Horan [1972] EMEA Country Compliance Director [Irish]; Marguerite Larkin [1971] Director/Chief Financial Officer [Irish]

Kesa Holdings Limited
Incorporated: 7 June 2001
Net Worth: £448,628,288 *Total Assets:* £1,087,058,432
Registered Office: 4th Floor, Reading Bridge House, George Street, Reading, Berks, RG1 8LS
Activities: Non-trading company
Parent: Darty Limited
Officers: Frederique Giavarini [1972] Director [French]; Benoit Andre Francois Jaubert [1969] Director of Retail for France, Swiss and Holland [French]; Jean-Brieuc-Pierre-Marie Le Tinier [1971] Director/Chief Financial Officer and Financial Manager [French]

Kew Green (LRG1) Limited
Incorporated: 20 June 2014 *Employees:* 2
Net Worth: £108,336,608 *Total Assets:* £109,454,512
Registered Office: 1 Towers Place, Eton Street, Richmond, Surrey, TW9 1EG
Activities: Hotels and similar accommodation
Parent: China National Travel Service Group Corporation
Officers: Jamie Andrew Lamb, Secretary; Jamie Andrew Lamb [1972] Director/Chartered Accountant; Alex Edward Pritchard [1976] Director

Kew Green (LRG2) Limited
Incorporated: 3 July 2014
Net Worth: £106,638,624 *Total Assets:* £106,638,624
Registered Office: 1 Towers Place, Eton Street, Richmond, Surrey, TW9 1EG
Activities: Hotels and similar accommodation
Shareholders: China National Travel Service Group Corporation; China National Travel Service Group Corporation
Officers: Jamie Andrew Lamb, Secretary; Jamie Andrew Lamb [1972] Director/Chartered Accountant; Alex Edward Pritchard [1976] Director

Kew Green Group Limited
Incorporated: 7 May 2014 *Employees:* 110
Net Worth: £283,917,568 *Total Assets:* £420,263,904
Registered Office: 1 Towers Place, Eton Street, Richmond, Surrey, TW9 1EG
Activities: Hotels and similar accommodation
Parent: China National Travel Service Group Corporation
Officers: Jamie Andrew Lamb, Secretary; Jamie Andrew Lamb [1972] Director/Chartered Accountant; Alex Edward Pritchard [1976] Director

Kew Green Hotels Limited
Incorporated: 15 May 2000 *Employees:* 2
Net Worth: £292,185,280 *Total Assets:* £297,879,168
Registered Office: 1 Towers Place, Eton Street, Richmond, Surrey, TW9 1EG
Activities: Hotels and similar accommodation
Parent: China National Travel Service Group Corporation
Officers: Jameson Andrew Lamb, Secretary; Jameson Andrew Lamb [1972] Finance Director; Alex Edward Pritchard [1976] Director

Kew Green Intermediate One Limited
Incorporated: 15 May 2014
Net Worth: £86,315,656 *Total Assets:* £87,110,312
Registered Office: 1 Towers Place, Eton Street, Richmond, Surrey, TW9 1EG
Activities: Hotels and similar accommodation
Parent: China National Travel Service Group Corporation
Officers: Jamie Andrew Lamb, Secretary; Jamie Andrew Lamb [1972] Director/Chartered Accountant; Alex Edward Pritchard [1976] Director

Kewsaw Limited
Incorporated: 21 May 2009 *Employees:* 1,077
Net Worth: £9,694,000 *Total Assets:* £48,544,000
Registered Office: 159 Mortlake Road, Kew, Richmond, Surrey, TW9 4AW
Activities: Non-trading company
Major Shareholder: John Graham Robinson
Officers: Charles Spencer James Atterton, Secretary; Charles Spencer James Atterton [1956] Director; Belle Robinson [1964] Director; John Graham Robinson [1947] Director/Chairman

Key Bidco Limited
Incorporated: 2 November 2011
Net Worth: £18,038,000 *Total Assets:* £38,796,000
Registered Office: Elmbrook House, 18-19 Station Road, Sunbury on Thames, Surrey, TW16 6SU
Activities: Non-life insurance
Parent: Key Midco Limited
Officers: James Richard Hastie Cumming [1980] Finance Director; Alan David Maynard [1965] Director

Key Equipment Finance Europe Limited
Incorporated: 1 June 2007 *Employees:* 3
Net Worth: £78,287,928 *Total Assets:* £79,268,224
Registered Office: Arlington Square, Venture House, Downshire Way, Bracknell, Berks, RG12 1WA
Activities: Financial leasing
Parent: Key Equipment Finance International Inc
Officers: John Albert Charles Evans [1964] Director/Businessman; Derek James Hall [1962] Director/Accountant; Adam David Warner [1961] Director/Businessman [American]

Key Midco Limited
Incorporated: 14 December 2011
Net Worth Deficit: £40,731,000 *Total Assets:* £36,345,000
Registered Office: Elmbrook House, 18-19 Station Road, Sunbury on Thames, Surrey, TW16 6SU
Activities: Non-life insurance
Parent: Key Topco Lmited
Officers: James Richard Hastie Cumming [1980] Finance Director; Alan David Maynard [1965] Director

Key Properties Limited
Incorporated: 8 May 1968 *Employees:* 2
Net Worth: £3,046,480 *Total Assets:* £32,403,564
Registered Office: Jubilee House, John Nike Way, Bracknell, Berks, RG12 8TN
Activities: Other letting and operating of own or leased real estate
Officers: Stephen James Hebborn, Secretary; Christopher John Nike [1968] Director; Kathryn Tracy Vickers [1970] Director

Keysight Technologies UK Limited
Incorporated: 20 July 1999 *Employees:* 485
Net Worth: £132,178,000 *Total Assets:* £164,348,992
Registered Office: 610 Wharfedale Road, Winnersh Triangle, Wokingham, Berks, RG41 5TP
Activities: Other business support service activities n.e.c.
Officers: Christopher Michael George Rennie [1963] Director/General Manager Services; Paul Ian Roy [1971] Director/Finance Manager; Christopher Trim [1961] Sales Director

Keystone Holdco Limited
Incorporated: 16 June 2011 *Employees:* 25
Net Worth: £5,748,732 *Total Assets:* £25,853,262
Registered Office: Chart House, 2 Effingham Road, Reigate, Surrey, RH2 7JN
Activities: Activities of financial services holding companies
Shareholder: Anthony Donald John Mowatt
Officers: Christopher James Marden [1953] Director; Anthony Donald John Mowatt [1965] Director of Insurance Company

Keystone Investment Trust PLC
Incorporated: 17 September 1954
Net Worth: £266,146,000 *Total Assets:* £299,432,992
Registered Office: Perpetual Park, Perpetual Park Drive, Henley on Thames, Oxon, RG9 1HH
Activities: Activities of investment trusts
Officers: Griffiths Ian Ashley Armfield [1956] Director/Accountant; Karen Mary Brade [1965] Director [Irish]; Katrina Harriet Hart [1974] Director; William Bruce Kendall [1961] Director/Chief Executive; Egerton John Wood [1958] Director

Kia Motors (UK) Limited
Incorporated: 12 April 2002 *Employees:* 223
Net Worth: £94,641,000 *Total Assets:* £478,931,008
Registered Office: Walton Green, Walton on Thames, Surrey, KT12 1FJ
Activities: Sale of new cars and light motor vehicles
Officers: Paul Jonathan Philpott, Secretary; Woojai Kim [1973] Director [South Korean]; Jin Young Park [1977] Director [South Korean]; Paul Jonathan Philpott [1966] Director

Kidde Finance Limited
Incorporated: 16 August 2000
Net Worth: £25,440,000 *Total Assets:* £157,560,000
Registered Office: 1st Floor, Ash House, Littleton Road, Ashford, Middlesex, TW15 1TZ
Activities: Other business support service activities n.e.c.
Parent: Kidde UK
Officers: Robert Sloss, Secretary; Laura Wilcock, Secretary; Neil Andrew Vincent Gregor MacGregor [1955] Director/Accounting and Controls Manager; Robert John Sloss [1967] Director/Solicitor

Kidde International Limited
Incorporated: 21 December 2000
Net Worth: £1,022,465,024 *Total Assets:* £1,084,392,960
Registered Office: 1st Floor, Ash House, Littleton Road, Ashford, Middlesex, TW15 1TZ
Activities: Activities of head offices
Parent: Goodrich Aftermarket Services Limited
Officers: Robert Sloss, Secretary; Laura Wilcock, Secretary; Neil Andrew Vincent Gregor MacGregor [1955] Director/Accounting and Controls Manager; Robert John Sloss [1967] Director/Solicitor

Kidde Limited
Incorporated: 24 July 2000
Net Worth: £92,981,000 *Total Assets:* £93,275,000
Registered Office: 1st Floor, Ash House, Littleton Road, Ashford, Middlesex, TW15 1TZ
Activities: Activities of head offices
Parent: Goodrich Inertial Limited
Officers: Robert Sloss, Secretary; Laura Wilcock, Secretary; Neil Andrew Vincent Gregor MacGregor [1955] Director/Accounting and Controls Manager; Robert John Sloss [1967] Director/Solicitor

Kidde Products Limited
Incorporated: 19 December 2002 *Employees:* 47
Net Worth: £126,710,000 *Total Assets:* £166,066,000
Registered Office: Stokenchurch House, Oxford Road, Stokenchurch, Bucks, HP14 3SX
Activities: Other manufacturing n.e.c.
Parent: Kidde UK
Officers: Craig Alexander Forbes [1963] Finance Director; Vaclav Mallmanek [1970] Finance Director [Czech]; John Simpson [1963] Director/General Manager

Kidde UK
Incorporated: 22 June 2001
Net Worth: £619,134,016 *Total Assets:* £761,939,968
Registered Office: 1st Floor, Ash House, Littleton Road, Ashford, Middlesex, TW15 1TZ
Activities: Activities of head offices
Parent: Goodrich Aftermarket Services Limited
Officers: Robert Sloss, Secretary; Laura Wilcock, Secretary; Neil Andrew Vincent Gregor MacGregor [1955] Director/Accounting and Controls Manager

Kidsprog Limited
Incorporated: 24 November 1992
Net Worth: £63,200,000 *Total Assets:* £68,727,000
Registered Office: Grant Way, Isleworth, Middlesex, TW7 5QD
Activities: Activities of head offices
Parent: Sky Ventures Limited
Officers: Christopher Jon Taylor, Secretary; Karl Holmes [1973] Director/Finance Professional; Colin Robert Jones [1964] Director; Christopher Jon Taylor [1971] Director/Company Secretary

Killinchy Aerospace Holdings Limited
Incorporated: 5 November 1965 *Employees:* 977
Net Worth: £270,612,992 *Total Assets:* £301,856,000
Registered Office: Aircraft Works, Lower Road, Higher Denham, Uxbridge, Middlesex, UB9 5AJ
Activities: Manufacture of metal structures and parts of structures
Officers: William John Henderson Deeves, Secretary; Amanda Barrington [1975] Director; Charles Merrick Burrell [1981] Director; Daniel David Hess [1979] Director; Andrew James Martin [1973] Director; James William Martin [1942] Director; John Stephen Martin [1942] Director; Robert John Martin [1969] Director/Engineer; Robert Keith Morgan [1975] Director; Ian Steele [1956] Director/Chartered Accountant; Mark Thomas Wearden [1957] Director/Certified Accountant

Kimal Holdings Limited
Incorporated: 17 January 2012 *Employees:* 314
Net Worth: £18,783,000 *Total Assets:* £25,082,000
Registered Office: Kimal, Arundel Road, Uxbridge, Middlesex, UB8 2SA
Activities: Activities of head offices
Shareholder: James Anthony Martin
Officers: Anthony William Wilson, Secretary; Neil Duncan Eaton [1946] Director; Joseph Frederick Fleischhaker [1954] Director [American]; Geoffrey Charles Redmond Morris [1957] Director; Mark Ronald Pettitt [1961] Director; Alan Christopher Press [1953] Director; Andrew George Press [1966] Director; Matthew James Press [1978] Director; Anthony William Wilson [1956] Finance Director

Kimal PLC
Incorporated: 19 November 1964 *Employees:* 273
Net Worth: £15,027,000 *Total Assets:* £20,453,000
Registered Office: Kimal, Arundel Road, Uxbridge, Middlesex, UB8 2SA
Activities: Manufacture of medical and dental instruments and supplies
Parent: Kimal Group PLC
Officers: Anthony William Wilson, Secretary; Damian Paul Donnelly [1976] Business Unit Director; Stephen Cavan Eccles [1968] Operations Director; Claire Louise Nicholson [1983] Sales Director; Mark Ronald Pettitt [1961] Managing Director; Alan Christopher Press [1953] Director; Matthew James Press [1978] Director; Anthony William Wilson [1956] Director

Kimberly - Clark Limited
Incorporated: 28 December 1935 *Employees:* 1,011
Net Worth: £241,779,008 *Total Assets:* £547,524,992
Registered Office: 1 Tower View, Kings Hill, West Malling, Kent, ME19 4HA
Activities: Manufacture of household and sanitary goods and of toilet requisites
Parent: Kimberly-Clark European Services Ltd
Officers: Stuart William Casey, Secretary; Kalbander Singh Dhillon [1964] Director/VP & CFO EMEA; Tristram Otto Wilkinson [1968] Director

Kimberly-Clark Europe Limited
Incorporated: 22 August 2000 *Employees:* 369
Net Worth: £228,382,928 *Total Assets:* £649,741,632
Registered Office: Douglas House, 40 London Road, Reigate, Surrey, RH2 9QP
Activities: Manufacture of household and sanitary goods and of toilet requisites
Parent: Kimberly-Clark European Services Limited
Officers: Thomas Wolfgang Christian Loest, Secretary; Kalbander Singh Dhillon [1964] Director/VP & CFO EMEA; Olena Valentynivna Neznal [1967] Director/President - EMEA [American]; Tristram Otto Wilkinson [1968] Director/Chief Executive

Kimberly-Clark European Services Limited
Incorporated: 14 September 2000 *Employees:* 210
Net Worth: £555,552,000 *Total Assets:* £572,953,024
Registered Office: Douglas House, 40 London Road, Reigate, Surrey, RH2 9QP
Activities: Financial intermediation not elsewhere classified
Parent: Kimberly-Clark Finance Limited
Officers: Stuart William Casey, Secretary; Kalbander Singh Dhillon [1964] Director/VP & CFO EMEA; Olena Valentynivna Neznal [1967] Director/President - EMEA [American]; Tristram Otto Wilkinson [1968] Director/Chief Executive

Kimberly-Clark Finance Limited
Incorporated: 15 March 1951
Net Worth: £935,361,984 *Total Assets:* £938,726,976
Registered Office: 1 Tower View, Kings Hill, West Malling, Kent, ME19 4HA
Activities: Activities of other holding companies n.e.c.
Parent: Kimberly-Clark Holding Limited
Officers: Stuart William Casey, Secretary; Kalbander Singh Dhillon [1964] Director/VP & CFO EMEA; Riccardo Masera [1971] Director/CFO Middle East & Africa, EMEA Finance [Italian]

Kimberly-Clark Holding Limited
Incorporated: 20 November 1985
Net Worth: £390,185,984 *Total Assets:* £1,439,970,944
Registered Office: 1 Tower View, Kings Hill, West Malling, Kent, ME19 4HA
Activities: Other service activities n.e.c.
Parent: Kimberly-Clark Intercontinental Holding Limited
Officers: Stuart William Casey, Secretary; Kalbander Singh Dhillon [1964] Director/VP & CFO EMEA; Riccardo Masera [1971] Director/CFO Middle East & Africa, EMEA Finance [Italian]

Kimberly-Clark Intercontinental Holding Limited
Incorporated: 6 April 2016
Net Worth: £134,222,144 *Total Assets:* £134,222,144
Registered Office: Douglas House, Reigate, Surrey, RH2 9QP
Activities: Manufacture of household and sanitary goods and of toilet requisites
Parent: Kimberly-Clark Puerto Rico Inc
Officers: Stuart William Casey, Secretary; Stuart William Casey [1969] Director/Lawyer; Kalbander Singh Dhillon [1964] Director

Kimberly-Clark International Holding Limited
Incorporated: 21 February 2014
Net Worth: £2,039,592,448 *Total Assets:* £2,039,592,448
Registered Office: 40 London Road, Reigate, Surrey, RH2 9QP
Activities: Manufacture of household and sanitary goods and of toilet requisites
Shareholders: Kimberly-Clark Latin America Investments, Inc; Kimberly-Clark Latin America, Inc
Officers: Stuart William Casey, Secretary; Kalbander Singh Dhillon [1964] Director/VP & CFO EMEA; Riccardo Masera [1971] Director/CFO Middle East & Africa, EMEA Finance [Italian]

Kimberly-Clark U.K. Operations Limited
Incorporated: 29 July 2002
Net Worth: £444,174,080 *Total Assets:* £444,174,080
Registered Office: Douglas House, 40 London Road, Reigate, Surrey, RH2 9QP
Activities: Other business support service activities n.e.c.
Parent: Kimberly-Clark Patriot Holdings Inc
Officers: Stuart William Casey, Secretary; Stuart William Casey [1969] Director/Assistant General Counsel; Kalbander Singh Dhillon [1964] Director/VP & CFO EMEA

KIMS Kent Holdings Limited
Incorporated: 10 December 2015 *Employees:* 315
Net Worth: £15,425,926 *Total Assets:* £48,789,120
Registered Office: KIMS Hospital, Newnham Court Way, Weavering, Maidstone, Kent, ME14 5FT
Activities: Hospital activities
Shareholders: Realta Investments Ireland Limited; Regional Healthcare Limited
Officers: Luca di Rico [1967] Director [Italian]; Georgios Palos [1964] Director/Chartered Surveyor Arbitrator; Gregory Palos [1963] Director/Solicitor

KIMS Property Company Limited
Incorporated: 9 February 2011
Net Worth: £2,092,425 *Total Assets:* £65,092,936
Registered Office: KIMS Hospital, Newnham Court Way, Weavering, Maidstone, Kent, ME14 5FT
Activities: Development of building projects
Parent: KIMS Kent Property Holding Limited
Officers: Luca di Rico [1967] Director/Portfolio Manager [Italian]; Simon Lloyd James [1967] Director/Chief Executive; Georgios Palos [1964] Director/Chartered Surveyor; Gregory Palos [1963] Director/Solicitor; Simon David Rust [1960] Finance Director

Kinedexe UK Limited
Incorporated: 17 July 2014 *Employees:* 7
Net Worth: £19,799,890 *Total Assets:* £20,690,110
Registered Office: 65 Delamere Road, Hayes, Middlesex, UB4 0NN
Activities: Other professional, scientific and technical activities n.e.c.
Major Shareholder: Anil Kumar Sharma
Officers: Jagjeet Kaur Ahluwalia [1962] Director/Manager; Anil Kumar Sharma [1952] Director; Sneh Sharma [1956] Director/Manager

Kinetrol Limited
Incorporated: 10 February 1958 *Employees:* 250
Net Worth: £28,979,696 *Total Assets:* £31,818,934
Registered Office: Trading Estate, Farnham, Surrey, GU9 9NU
Activities: Manufacture of other general-purpose machinery n.e.c.
Shareholder: Caroline Diana Robinson
Officers: John Valentine Nash, Secretary; Michael John Gardner [1943] Director; George Christopher Nash [1989] Director; John Valentine Nash [1955] Director/Engineer; William Nigel Alan Nash [1958] Director/Engineer; Caroline Diana Robinson [1955] Director

W.J.King (Garages) Limited
Incorporated: 14 January 1960 *Employees:* 365
Net Worth: £35,305,592 *Total Assets:* £49,264,216
Registered Office: 70-88 Park View Road, Welling, Kent, DA16 1SF
Activities: Sale of new cars and light motor vehicles
Shareholder: William John King
Officers: Jane Atkins, Secretary; Olivia King [1950] Director/Administrator; William John King [1992] Director/Administrator; William John King [1955] Director/Administrator

Nicholas King Developments PLC
Incorporated: 10 April 2008 *Employees:* 46
Net Worth: £2,597,000 *Total Assets:* £28,041,000
Registered Office: 10 Penn Road, Beaconsfield, Bucks, HP9 2LH
Activities: Construction of domestic buildings
Officers: Nicholas James Philip Bilsland, Secretary; Nicholas James Philip Bilsland [1966] Finance Director; Susan Elizabeth Jacquest [1964] Director; Nicholas Geoffrey King [1951] Director/Chairman; Paul Jeremy Lobatto [1950] Director; Kelly John Speller [1969] Director

King Edward VI School Southampton
Incorporated: 21 June 2001 *Employees:* 322
Net Worth: £33,984,264 *Total Assets:* £38,006,304
Registered Office: King Edward VI School, Wilton Road, Southampton, SO15 5UQ
Activities: Pre-primary education
Officers: Raymond Vincent Maher, Secretary; Dr Yvonne Binge [1940] Director/Doctor; Philip William Brazier [1949] Director; Dr Roger Brade Buchanan [1944] Director/Retired Hospital Doctor; Mark Chaloner [1980] Director/Barrister; Mary Louise Chant [1962] Director/Solicitor; Reverend Jonathan Mark Finch [1986] Director/Clergyman; Brian Edward Gay [1941] Director; Julian John Gray [1971] Director/Chartered Accountant; Penelope Sari Kirk [1957] Director/Retired Headmistress; Sara Jane Mancey [1961] Company HR Director; Janet Charis May [1958] Director/Planning Lawyer; Michael Hardy Mayes [1949] Director/Independent Consultant; John William James Mist [1946] Director/Accountant; Dr Jane Elizabeth Mitchell [1960] Director/Doctor; Alan John Morgan [1958] Director/Accountant; Caryn Gail Musker [1959] Director/Recruitment Consultant; Harriet Victoria Langford Nicholson [1987] Director/Marketing Consultant; Will Anthony Woolley Oscroft [1969] Managing Director; Richard William Page [1959] Director/Headmaster; Benjamin William Richards [1966] Director/Retired; Ian Hugh Rudland [1958] Director/Consultant; Wendy Patricia Swinn [1959] Director/Dentist; Dr Alan Lionel Thomas [1950] Director/Lecturer; Jessica Louise Wadsworth [1970] Director/Police

Kingsbridge Estates Limited
Incorporated: 12 January 2001 *Employees:* 9
Net Worth: £29,548,894 *Total Assets:* £55,506,396
Registered Office: Lincoln House, Chichester Fields Business Park, Tangmere, Chichester, W Sussex, PO20 2FS
Activities: Development of building projects
Major Shareholder: Robert Anthony Langmead
Officers: Lucinda Felicity Sommerville Langmead, Secretary; Christopher John Fry [1974] Director/Chief Executive; Mark James Hooper [1964] Estates Director; Robert Anthony Langmead [1968] Managing Director; Gayna Ruth Sammon [1965] Finance Director

Geo. Kingsbury Holdings Limited
Incorporated: 28 September 1956 *Employees:* 302
Net Worth: £38,828,804 *Total Assets:* £56,679,628
Registered Office: 45 Portsmouth Road, Cobham, Surrey, KT11 1JQ
Activities: Activities of head offices
Shareholders: Christopher Kingsbury; Michael George Kingsbury
Officers: Mark William Kingsbury, Secretary; Christopher Kingsbury [1937] Director; Mark William Kingsbury [1964] Director; Michael George Kingsbury [1934] Director; Peter James Kingsbury [1967] Director; Richard George Kingsbury [1963] Director

Kingston Bidco Limited
Incorporated: 19 November 2013
Net Worth Deficit: £8,108,360 *Total Assets:* £60,137,024
Registered Office: Avantia House, 29 Thames Street, Kingston upon Thames, Surrey, KT1 1PH
Activities: Non-trading company
Parent: Kingston Midco Limited
Officers: Mark Robert Eastham [1972] Director; Shahid Mahmood [1969] Director

Kingston Digital Europe Co LLP
Incorporated: 6 April 2013 *Employees:* 54
Net Worth: £40,691,228 *Total Assets:* £46,547,424
Registered Office: Kingston Court, Brooklands Close, Sunbury on Thames, Middlesex, TW16 7EP

Kingston Grammar School
Incorporated: 22 November 1999 *Employees:* 214
Net Worth: £14,759,000 *Total Assets:* £28,075,000
Registered Office: Kingston Grammar School, London Road, Kingston upon Thames, Surrey, KT2 6PY
Activities: General secondary education
Officers: Lorraine Tanya Adam [1968] Director/Marketing Consultant; Mark Annesley [1956] Director/Chartered Accountant; Catherine Julie Chevallier [1966] Director/HR Manager; Duncan Paul David Combe [1979] Director/Management Consultant; Michael Dohler [1975] Director/University Professor [German]; Andrew David Evans [1979] Director/Accountant; Jatinder Singh Harchowal [1969] Director/Pharmacist; Nima Khandan-Nia [1968] Director/Manager; Frances Claire Le Grys [1964] Director/Lawyer; Robert George O'Dowd [1961] Director/Chief Executive; Diana Rose [1955] Director/Teacher; Kerstin Sonnemann [1966] Director/Architect [German]

Kingston Midco Limited
Incorporated: 19 November 2013
Net Worth: £2,753,331 *Total Assets:* £40,253,276
Registered Office: Avantia House, 29 Thames Street, Kingston upon Thames, Surrey, KT1 1PH
Activities: Non-trading company
Parent: Kingston Topco Limited
Officers: Mark Robert Eastham [1972] Director; Shahid Mahmood [1969] Director

Kingston Technology Europe Co LLP
Incorporated: 8 April 2013 *Employees:* 195
Net Worth: £50,012,828 *Total Assets:* £66,927,244
Registered Office: Kingston Court, Brooklands Close, Sunbury on Thames, Middlesex, TW16 7EP

Kingston Topco Limited
Incorporated: 18 November 2013 *Employees:* 124
Net Worth Deficit: £7,373,254 *Total Assets:* £48,750,108
Registered Office: Avantia House, 29 Thames Street, Kingston upon Thames, Surrey, KT1 1PH
Activities: Non-trading company
Officers: Stephen David Ashton [1963] Director; Mark Robert Eastham [1972] Director; Shahid Mahmood [1969] Director; Paul Dominic Ian McCreadie [1979] Director; David Jonathan Haddon Walker [1965] Director

Kingswood Learning and Leisure Group Limited
Incorporated: 4 December 1997 *Employees:* 687
Net Worth: £22,866,000 *Total Assets:* £64,845,000
Registered Office: 1 Jubilee Street, Brighton, BN1 1GE
Activities: Other education n.e.c.
Parent: Inspiring Learning Limited
Officers: Timothy James Gibson [1968] Director [New Zealander]; Charles Robert William McLean [1969] Director

Kion Financial Services Limited
Incorporated: 16 September 2011 *Employees:* 13
Net Worth: £6,930,796 *Total Assets:* £122,484,896
Registered Office: Kingsclere Road, Basingstoke, Hants, RG21 6XJ
Activities: Financial leasing
Parent: Superlift UK Ltd
Officers: John Richard Canfield [1964] Director/Company Executive

Kirkmore Capital Limited
Incorporated: 9 September 2016
Net Worth: £83,760 *Total Assets:* £26,217,256
Registered Office: Eden House, Reynolds Road, Beaconsfield, Bucks, HP9 2FL
Activities: Other credit granting n.e.c.
Shareholders: Jason Charles Andrew Berger; Peter Ashley Gropper
Officers: Jason Charles Andrew Berger [1969] Director/Surveyor; Peter Ashley Gropper [1967] Director

The Kite Academy Trust
Incorporated: 18 September 2015 *Employees:* 314
Net Worth: £30,784,140 *Total Assets:* £34,758,720
Registered Office: Holly Lodge Primary School, Stratford Road, Ash Vale, Surrey, GU12 5PX
Activities: Primary education
Officers: John Graham Allan [1950] Director/Retired; Debbie Louise Andrews [1971] Director; Lesley Anstey [1960] Director/Consultant; Paula Louise Evans [1955] Director/Senior Education Officer; Karen Deborah Findlay [1974] Director/Management Consultant; Liam Gregory Quinn [1972] IT Director; Aidene Frances Walsh [1967] Commercial Director UCL; Dawn Warwick [1969] Director/Accountant

KLM Cityhopper UK Limited
Incorporated: 7 August 2002 *Employees:* 45
Net Worth Deficit: £57,509,000 *Total Assets:* £38,219,000
Registered Office: Plesman House, Cains Lane, Bedfont, Feltham, Middlesex, TW14 9RL
Activities: Scheduled passenger air transport
Officers: Kirsten Pronk, Secretary; Farah Khan [1979] Director/HR Manager; Warner Arnoud Rootliep [1961] Managing Director [Dutch]; Nigel Hilton Tyson [1962] Director of Finance North Europe

Klober Limited
Incorporated: 4 September 1985 *Employees:* 27
Net Worth: £36,152,576 *Total Assets:* £40,028,992
Registered Office: BMI House, 2 Pitfield, Kiln Farm, Milton Keynes, Bucks, MK11 3LW
Activities: Agents involved in the sale of timber and building materials
Parent: Klober GmbH
Officers: Jason John Bradley [1963] Director/Accountant; Andrew John Dennis [1965] Managing Director; Adrian Gregory Fishley [1960] Director/Sales Manager; Alfons Horn [1970] Managing Director [German]; Klaus Sonne Ravn [1966] Finance Director [Danish]

KN Network Services (Northern Ireland) Limited
Incorporated: 20 August 2003 *Employees:* 151
Net Worth: £3,068,965 *Total Assets:* £25,332,280
Registered Office: KN Network Services (Northern Ireland) Ltd, 221 Dover Road, Slough, Berks, SL1 4RF
Activities: Other specialised construction activities n.e.c.
Shareholders: KN Networks Group Limited; KN Network Services Holdings Ltd
Officers: Donagh Kelly, Secretary; Damien Gallagher [1967] Director [Irish]; Donagh Kelly [1971] Director/General Manager [Irish]; Franck Lavalloir [1969] Director [French]; Eamonn O'Kennedy [1972] Director [Irish]

Knoll UK Investments Unlimited
Incorporated: 23 November 2004 *Employees:* 3
Net Worth: £146,945,552 *Total Assets:* £146,950,176
Registered Office: Abbott House, Vanwall Business Park, Vanwall Road, Maidenhead, Berks, SL6 4XE
Activities: Manufacture of basic pharmaceutical products
Parent: Abbott Laboratories
Officers: Kevan Gogay, Secretary; Neil Harris [1974] Director/General Manager; Georgios Mountrichas [1977] Director/General Manager [Greek]; Brian Yoor [1969] Director/Business Executive [American]

The Knowledge Academy Holdings Limited
Incorporated: 4 July 2013 *Employees:* 258
Net Worth: £13,761,041 *Total Assets:* £26,543,516
Registered Office: Reflex, Cain Road, Bracknell, Berks, RG12 1HL
Activities: Activities of head offices
Shareholders: Barinder Hothi; Dilshad Hothi
Officers: Barinder Hothi [1977] Director; Dilshad Hothi [1976] Director

Koala Bidco Limited
Incorporated: 19 August 2014
Net Worth: £34,667,000 *Total Assets:* £146,696,000
Registered Office: Ascot House, Maidenhead Office Park, Maidenhead, Berks, SL6 3QQ
Activities: Activities of other holding companies n.e.c.
Officers: Syed Qasim Abbas [1976] Managing Director - Banking Professional [Pakistani]; Matthew John Howard-Cairns [1984] Director; Rohan Singhal [1987] Director/Vice President TSSP; Daniel Wanek [1976] Director/Financial Services Industry [American]

Kodak Alaris Holdings Limited
Incorporated: 30 May 2013 *Employees:* 2,207
Net Worth: £115,790,560 *Total Assets:* £361,712,192
Registered Office: Hemel One, Boundary Way, Hemel Hempstead, Herts, HP2 7YU
Activities: Activities of other holding companies n.e.c.
Parent: KPP (No.2) Trustees Limited
Officers: John O'Reilly, Secretary; Mark Robert William Alflatt [1966] Director/Chartered Accountant; Patrick Jean-Marie de Smedt [1955] Director [Belgian]; Mark Wynne Elliott [1949] Director/Retired Information Technology and Services Executive [American]; Marc Jourlait [1967] Director/Chief Executive [French]; Brian Paul Larcombe [1953] Director/Investment Banker; Stephen Paul Webster [1952] Director/Chartered Accountant

Kodak Alaris Limited
Incorporated: 31 May 2013 *Employees:* 158
Net Worth: £29,983,392 *Total Assets:* £95,606,152
Registered Office: Hemel One, Boundary Way, Hemel Hempstead, Herts, HP2 7YU
Activities: Manufacture of photographic and cinematographic equipment
Parent: Kodak Alaris Holdings Limited
Officers: John O'Reilly, Secretary; Mark Robert William Alflatt [1966] Director/Chartered Accountant; Dennis Bruce Olbrich [1960] Director/Business President [American]; Nicoletta Assaro Zongrone [1958] Director [American]

Kodak International Finance Limited
Incorporated: 30 March 1983
Net Worth: £56,501,848 *Total Assets:* £408,733,472
Registered Office: Building 8, Croxley Green Business Park, Hatters Lane, Watford, Herts, WD18 8PX
Activities: Financial intermediation not elsewhere classified
Officers: Helen Veronica Griffiths, Secretary; Evelina Latuta [1973] Director/Financial Controller; William George Love [1956] Director/Finance/Treasurer [American]; Manfred Hubert Stegmaier [1957] Director/EAMER Controller [German]

Kodak Limited
Incorporated: 15 November 1898 *Employees:* 205
Net Worth: £95,900,000 *Total Assets:* £255,500,000
Registered Office: Building 8, Croxley Green Business Park, Hatters Lane, Watford, Herts, WD18 8PX
Activities: Other publishing activities
Officers: Helen Veronica Griffiths, Secretary; Helen Veronica Griffiths [1962] Legal Director; John Gerard O'Grady [1964] Director/General Manager WW Sales, Senior Vice President [Irish]; Susan White [1972] HR Director

Kofax Holdings International Limited
Incorporated: 17 May 1996 *Employees:* 3
Net Worth: £71,983,128 *Total Assets:* £306,429,856
Registered Office: 7 Elmwood, Crockford Lane, Chineham, Basingstoke, Hants, RG24 8WG
Activities: Other information technology service activities
Parent: Kofax London Holdings Limited
Officers: Cort Steven Townsend, Secretary; Christian Jorg Franz Hefner [1968] Director/Corporate Counsel [German]; Martin Gustav Oberholzer [1969] Director/Business Executive [Swiss]; Cort Steven Townsend [1979] Director/Senior VP Finance [American]

Kofax London Holdings Limited
Incorporated: 30 October 1995 *Employees:* 2
Net Worth: £771,002,048 *Total Assets:* £907,213,824
Registered Office: 7 Elmwood, Crockford Lane, Chineham, Basingstoke, Hants, RG24 8WG
Activities: Information technology consultancy activities
Parent: Kofax Parent Limited
Officers: Cort Steven Townsend, Secretary; Samantha Louise Kirby [1970] Tax Director; Cort Steven Townsend [1979] Director/Senior VP Finance [American]

Kofax US Holdings Limited
Incorporated: 5 August 2008
Net Worth: £154,444,528 *Total Assets:* £154,452,960
Registered Office: 7 Elmwood, Crockford Lane, Chineham, Basingstoke, Hants, RG24 8WG
Activities: Other business support service activities n.e.c.
Officers: Cort Steven Townsend, Secretary; Christian Jorg Franz Hefner [1968] Director/Corporate Counsel [German]; Martin Gustav Oberholzer [1969] Director/Business Executive [Swiss]; Cort Steven Townsend [1979] Director/Senior VP Finance [American]

Kohler Uninterruptible Power Limited
Incorporated: 1 August 2008 *Employees:* 95
Net Worth: £28,892,080 *Total Assets:* £35,500,504
Registered Office: Woodgate, Bartley Wood Business Park, Bartley Way, Hook, Hants, RG27 9XA
Activities: Activities of head offices
Parent: Kohler Co
Officers: Thomas Gerard Alder [1960] Director/Chief Financial Officer [American]; Herbert Kohler [1939] Director/Executive [American]

Kone Public Limited Company
Incorporated: 13 June 1978 *Employees:* 1,721
Net Worth: £93,244,000 *Total Assets:* £208,575,008
Registered Office: Global House, Station Place, Fox Lane North, Chertsey, Surrey, KT16 9HW
Activities: Other manufacturing n.e.c.
Parent: Kone Corporation
Officers: Tebogo Brenda Msi, Secretary; Thomas Hinnerskov [1971] Director [Danish]; Tim John Joyce [1965] Managing Director [American]; Gerard Keith Loty [1972] Director [Australian]; Andrew Brian Miles [1981] Finance Director; Andrew James Todd [1972] Director; Patrick Weil [1971] Director; Michael Anthony Williams [1965] Managing Director [Australian]

Kordal Limited
Incorporated: 18 November 2015
Net Worth: £1,455,083 *Total Assets:* £42,047,696
Registered Office: Old Mile House, Kier Park, Ascot, Berks, SL5 7DS
Activities: Other letting and operating of own or leased real estate
Officers: Graham Stephen Coopey [1957] Director/Chartered Accountant; Simon John Hargreaves [1963] Director; Charles Barry Roberts [1940] Director/Investor; Graham Richard John Snell [1954] Director; Linda Christine Snell [1956] Director

KP Snacks Limited
Incorporated: 30 November 2012 *Employees:* 1,604
Net Worth: £207,058,000 *Total Assets:* £571,792,000
Registered Office: Fifth Floor, The Urban Building, 3-9 Albert Street, Slough, SL1 2BE
Activities: Manufacture of other food products n.e.c.
Officers: Giles Alexander Glidden Henderson [1976] Finance Director; Andrew Steven Riddle [1971] Sales Director; Mark Christopher Thorpe [1963] Director

KPJV Limited
Incorporated: 19 November 2010 *Employees:* 12
Net Worth: £4,096,661 *Total Assets:* £54,723,048
Registered Office: Fluor Centre, 140 Pinehurst Road, Farnborough, Hants, GU14 7BF
Activities: Other business support service activities n.e.c.
Officers: James Francis Hooper, Secretary; Alexandra Bekisheva [1983] Director/Vice President Finance and Commerce [Ukrainian]; Alan Stewart Gordon [1964] Regional Director Europe Central Asia; Ashley Graham Rees [1965] General Manager, Director; Aidar Yespayev [1978] Deputy General Director Business Development [Kazakh]

Kraft Foods Investment Holdings UK Limited
Incorporated: 24 March 2011
Net Worth: £7,831,298,048 *Total Assets:* £10,462,016,512
Registered Office: Cadbury House, Sanderson Road, Uxbridge, Middlesex, UB8 1DH
Activities: Activities of head offices
Parent: Vantas International Limited
Officers: Adrian John Paul Arrighi [1978] Tax Director; Michael Brendan Foye [1965] Treasury Director; John Michael Hladusz [1972] Director/Chartered Accountant; Carole Noelle Keene [1966] Director

Kraft Foods UK IP & Production Holdings Limited
Incorporated: 25 March 2011
Net Worth: £1,648,612,992 *Total Assets:* £1,648,612,992
Registered Office: Cadbury House, Sanderson Road, Uxbridge, Middlesex, UB8 1DH
Activities: Activities of head offices
Parent: Kraft Foods Investment Holdings UK Limited
Officers: Adrian John Paul Arrighi [1978] Tax Director; Michael Brendan Foye [1965] Treasury Director; John Michael Hladusz [1972] Director/Chartered Accountant; Carole Noelle Keene [1966] Director

Krispy Kreme Holding UK Ltd
Incorporated: 17 October 2016
Net Worth: £190,151,008 *Total Assets:* £217,436,000
Registered Office: Unit 4 Albany Park, Frimley Road, Camberley, Surrey, GU16 7PQ
Activities: Activities of other holding companies n.e.c.
Officers: Joshua Alan Charlesworth [1974] Director/Chief Financial Officer [Canadian/British]; Niren Chaudhary [1963] Director/President and COO; Richard Cheshire [1968] Director; Timothy James Hennessy [1961] Director/Chief Financial Officer [American]; Margareta Caroline Elisabet Wullrich [1973] Director/Chief Financial Officer [Swedish]

Krispy Kreme U.K. Limited
Incorporated: 11 September 2002 *Employees:* 1,490
Net Worth: £34,580,000 *Total Assets:* £48,113,000
Registered Office: Unit 4 Albany Park, Frimley Road, Camberley, Surrey, GU16 7PQ
Activities: Retail sale of bread, cakes, flour confectionery and sugar confectionery in specialised stores
Parent: Frimley Bidco Limited
Officers: Joshua Alan Charlesworth [1974] Director/Chief Financial Officer [Canadian/British]; Niren Chaudhary [1963] Director/President and COO; Richard Cheshire [1968] Director/Chief Operating Officer; Timothy James Hennessy [1961] Director/Chief Financial Officer [American]; Margareta Caroline Elisabet Wullrich [1973] Director/Chief Financial Officer [Swedish]

Kronos Systems Limited
Incorporated: 6 August 1990 *Employees:* 189
Net Worth: £9,949,367 *Total Assets:* £35,007,464
Registered Office: 2nd Floor, South Wing, The Capitol Building, Oldbury, Bracknell, Berks, RG12 8FZ
Activities: Other service activities n.e.c.
Parent: Kronos Worldwide Limited
Officers: Mark Julien, Secretary; Aron Joel Ain [1957] Director/Chief Executive Officer [American]; John Arthur Butler [1963] Director [American]; Mark Julien [1964] Director/Chief Financial Officer [American]

Kronos Worldwide Limited
Incorporated: 16 April 2012 *Employees:* 726
Net Worth: £121,266,632 *Total Assets:* £235,976,384
Registered Office: 2nd Floor, South Wing, The Capitol Building, Oldbury, Bracknell, Berks, RG12 8FZ
Activities: Information technology consultancy activities
Officers: Mark Julien, Secretary; Aron Joel Ain [1957] Director/Chief Executive Officer [American]; John Arthur Butler [1963] Director [American]; Mark Victor Julien [1962] Director/Chief Financial Officer [American]

Kuehne + Nagel (UK) Limited
Incorporated: 26 November 1979
Net Worth: £24,484,014 *Total Assets:* £132,956,480
Registered Office: 1 Roundwood Avenue, Stockley Park, Uxbridge, Middlesex, UB11 1FG
Activities: Other business support service activities n.e.c.
Parent: Kuehne + Nagel International AG
Officers: Tristan Richard Michael Stokes, Secretary; Martin Arzethauser [1965] Director/Head of Group Tax [Swiss]; Allison Michelle Best [1969] Finance Director; Brian Cox [1969] Director

Kuehne + Nagel Drinkflow Logistics Holdings Limited
Incorporated: 19 April 2006
Net Worth Deficit: £153,000 *Total Assets:* £70,906,000
Registered Office: Kuehne + Nagel House, Sunrise Parkway, Linford Wood, Milton Keynes, Bucks, MK14 6BW
Activities: Activities of head offices
Shareholder: Kuehne + Nagel Limited
Officers: Tristan Richard Michael Stokes, Secretary; Allison Michelle Best [1969] Finance Director; Brian Cox [1969] Managing Director

Kuehne + Nagel Drinkflow Logistics Limited
Incorporated: 19 April 2006 *Employees:* 3
Net Worth: £2,344,000 *Total Assets:* £70,906,000
Registered Office: Kuehne + Nagel House, Sunrise Parkway, Linford Wood, Milton Keynes, Bucks, MK14 6BW
Activities: Operation of warehousing and storage facilities for land transport activities
Parent: Kuehne + Nagel Drinkflow Logistics Holdings Limited
Officers: Tristan Richard Michael Stokes, Secretary; Allison Michelle Best [1969] Finance Director; Brian Cox [1969] Managing Director

Kuehne + Nagel Drinks Logistics Limited
Incorporated: 29 March 2006 *Employees:* 2,399
Net Worth Deficit: £16,226,000 *Total Assets:* £43,669,000
Registered Office: Kuehne + Nagel House, Sunrise Parkway, Linford Wood, Milton Keynes, Bucks, MK14 6BW
Activities: Operation of warehousing and storage facilities for land transport activities
Parent: Kuehne + Nagel Limited
Officers: Tristan Richard Michael Stokes, Secretary; Allison Michelle Best [1969] Finance Director; Brian Cox [1969] Managing Director

Kuehne + Nagel Limited
Incorporated: 11 May 1983 *Employees:* 9,181
Net Worth: £68,401,000 *Total Assets:* £436,123,008
Registered Office: 1 Roundwood Avenue, Stockley Park, Uxbridge, Middlesex, UB11 1FG
Activities: Other transportation support activities
Parent: Kuehne + Nagel (UK) Limited
Officers: Tristan Richard Michael Stokes, Secretary; Allison Michelle Best [1969] Finance Director; Brian Cox [1969] Managing Director; Mark David James Jenkins [1962] Director

Kuwait Petroleum (U.K. Holdings) Limited
Incorporated: 10 October 1986
Net Worth Deficit: £253,876,000 *Total Assets:* £75,475,000
Registered Office: Dukes Court, Duke Street, Woking, Surrey, GU21 5BH
Activities: Wholesale of petroleum and petroleum products
Parent: State of Kuwait
Officers: Peter Coules, Secretary; Azzam Al-Mutawa [1969] Director/VP-International Operations [Kuwaiti]; Naser Mubarak Mohammed Ben-Butain [1973] Director/General Manager [Kuwaiti]; Rutger Jan Christiaan de Kreij [1969] Finance Director [Dutch]

Kuwait Petroleum International Aviation Company (U.K.) Limited
Incorporated: 9 August 1983
Net Worth: £55,424,552 *Total Assets:* £157,263,424
Registered Office: Duke's Court, Duke Street, Woking, Surrey, GU21 5BH
Activities: Wholesale of petroleum and petroleum products
Parent: Kuwait Petroleum (U.K. Holdings) Limited
Officers: Peter Coules, Secretary; Khaled Al-Mushaileh [1963] Director/VP-Strategy & Finance [Kuwaiti]; Talal Alsheetan [1975] Projects Director [Kuwaiti]; Naser Mubarak Mohammed Ben-Butain [1973] Director/General Manager [Kuwaiti]; Peter Coules [1966] Financial Director

Kuwait Petroleum International Aviation Company Limited
Incorporated: 24 August 1983 *Employees:* 54
Net Worth: £7,051,000 *Total Assets:* £55,840,000
Registered Office: 6th Floor, Dukes Court, Duke Street, Woking, Surrey, GU21 5BH
Activities: Wholesale of petroleum and petroleum products
Parent: Kuwait Petroleum (U.K. Holdings) Limited
Officers: Peter Coules, Secretary; Naser Mubarak Mohammed Ben-Butain [1973] Director/General Manager [Kuwaiti]; Patrick Joseph Collins [1958] Director/Planning & Business Development Manager; Peter Coules [1966] Financial Director; Ali Razzaq [1974] Director/Senior Supply Coordinator [Kuwaiti]

Kuwait Petroleum International Limited
Incorporated: 24 June 1983 *Employees:* 168
Net Worth Deficit: £37,569,000 *Total Assets:* £35,566,000
Registered Office: Dukes Court, Duke Street, Woking, Surrey, GU21 5BH
Activities: Activities of head offices
Parent: Kuwait Petroleum (U.K Holdings) Limited
Officers: Peter Coules, Secretary; Azzam Al-Mutawa [1969] Director/VP International Operations [Kuwaiti]; Rutger Jan Christiaan de Kreij [1969] Finance Director [Dutch]

KWay Holdings Limited
Incorporated: 30 November 2000 *Employees:* 1
Net Worth Deficit: £1,611,204 *Total Assets:* £34,809,120
Registered Office: Celcon House, Ightham, Sevenoaks, Kent, TN15 9HZ
Activities: Other business support service activities n.e.c.
Parent: H+H International A/S
Officers: Neil Julian Peter Griffiths, Company Secretary; Neil Julian Peter Griffiths [1970] Director and Company Secretary; Ian LEA Perkins [1965] Finance Director

Kyocera Document Solutions (U.K.) Limited
Incorporated: 28 July 1987 *Employees:* 166
Net Worth: £4,709,633 *Total Assets:* £36,096,192
Registered Office: Eldon Court, 75-77 London Road, Reading, Berks, RG1 5BS
Activities: Manufacture of communication equipment other than telegraph, and telephone apparatus and equipment
Officers: Nicholas John Miller, Secretary; Norihiko Ina [1963] Director/Worldwide President;Kyocera Document Solutions Inc [Japanese]; Hironao Katsukura [1965] Managing Director [Japanese]; Takuya Marubayashi [1967] Director [Japanese]; Rod Anthony Tonna-Barthet [1968] Director/Chief Executive

L-J Bidco Limited
Incorporated: 8 February 2012
Net Worth Deficit: £17,438,000 *Total Assets:* £41,577,000
Registered Office: Braboeuf Manor, St Catherines, Guildford, Surrey, GU3 1HA
Activities: Post-graduate level higher education
Parent: L-J Midco Limited
Officers: Arkady Etingen [1979] Director

L-J Finco Limited
Incorporated: 8 February 2012
Net Worth: £29,452,000 *Total Assets:* £58,988,000
Registered Office: Braboeuf Manor, St Catherines, Guildford, Surrey, GU3 1HA
Activities: Post-graduate level higher education
Parent: Lake International Limited
Officers: Arkady Etingen [1979] Director; Valery Kisilevsky [1984] Director [Canadian]

Labcorp Neon Ltd.
Incorporated: 27 November 2014
Net Worth: £24,302,776 *Total Assets:* £24,357,550
Registered Office: Osprey House, Westacott Way, Maidenhead, Berks, SL6 3QH
Activities: Technical testing and analysis
Parent: Labcorp UK Holdings, Ltd.
Officers: Sandra Dillard Van Der Vaart, Secretary; Floyd Samuel Eberts III [1959] Director/Chief Legal Officer [American]; Glenn Andrew Eisenberg [1961] Director/Chief Financial Officer [American]

Lactalis Nestle Chilled Dairy Company Limited
Incorporated: 16 June 2006 *Employees:* 162
Net Worth: £16,836,000 *Total Assets:* £51,369,000
Registered Office: Red Central, 60 High Street, Redhill, Surrey, RH1 1SH
Activities: Non-specialised wholesale of food, beverages and tobacco
Shareholders: Emmanuel Besnier; Jean-Michel Besnier; Marie Besnier
Officers: Jean-Paul Mouchotte [1963] Director [French]; Michel Peslier [1959] Director/Audit & Legal General Manager [French]; Alan Prior [1969] Managing Director; Anthony Sharpe [1965] Director/Chartered Accountant

Ladham Properties Limited
Incorporated: 28 February 2011 *Employees:* 3
Net Worth: £2,271,318 *Total Assets:* £31,546,912
Registered Office: Hill View House, The Hill, Cranbrook, Kent, TN17 3AD
Activities: Fund management activities
Shareholders: Christopher Guy Johnson; Nicola Jane Johnson
Officers: Stephen Thomas Clews [1967] Director; Christopher Guy Johnson [1964] Director; Nicola Jane Johnson [1971] Director

The Lady Eleanor Holles School
Incorporated: 6 April 2009 *Employees:* 268
Net Worth: £19,280,730 *Total Assets:* £39,625,652
Registered Office: The Bursary, The Lady Eleanor Holles School, Hanworth Road, Hampton, Surrey, TW12 3HF
Activities: Primary education
Officers: Sarah Whitehouse, Secretary; Annabel Emma Blair [1977] Executive Director; David Harold King [1951] Director/Retired; Neil Dewar Lewis [1962] Director/Solicitor; Dr Sophia Jane Aubrey McCormick [1950] Director/Educational Consultant Retired Voluntary Worker; Alison Hamilton Meyric Hughes [1944] Director/University Lecturer; Robert John Milburn [1956] Director/Accountant; Catherine Ann Millis [1971] HR Director; Barbara Anne Parson [1953] Director/Retired; Christopher Stanley Stokes [1949] Director/IP Rights Specialist [Irish]; Catherine Susan Thomas [1965] Director/Management Consultant; Charlotte Victoria Thomas [1983] Director/Architect; Sister Paula Susan Thomas [1956] Director/Headmistress; Wendy Jennifer Wildman [1945] Director/Retired

Lafarge Building Materials Limited
Incorporated: 1 October 1997 *Employees:* 3
Net Worth: £1,359,011,968 *Total Assets:* £2,930,156,032
Registered Office: Park Lodge, London Road, Dorking, Surrey, RH4 1TH
Activities: Management consultancy activities other than financial management
Parent: Financiere Lafarge SAS
Officers: Howard Bruce Moller, Secretary; Simon Gregory Crossley [1973] Director; Laurent Jaques [1976] Director/Holding Management [Swiss]; Howard Bruce Moller [1962] Director/Finance Manager

Lafarge International Holdings Limited
Incorporated: 19 December 1952
Net Worth: £1,924,011,008 *Total Assets:* £1,965,474,048
Registered Office: Park Lodge, London Road, Dorking, Surrey, RH4 1TH
Activities: Activities of head offices
Parent: Lafarge Building Materials Limited
Officers: Howard Bruce Moller, Secretary; General Counsel James Atherton-Ham [1970] Director; Simon Gregory Crossley [1973] Director; David Robert Forder [1965] Director/Manager Financial Reporting and Planning; Laurent Jaques [1976] Director/Holding Management [Swiss]; Howard Bruce Moller [1962] Director/Finance Manager; Markus Leo Unternahrer [1968] Director [Swiss]

Lafarge Minerals Limited
Incorporated: 3 February 1994
Net Worth: £430,800,000 *Total Assets:* £1,065,000,000
Registered Office: Park Lodge, London Road, Dorking, Surrey, RH4 1TH
Activities: Activities of head offices
Parent: Lafarge Building Materials Limited
Officers: Howard Bruce Moller, Secretary; Simon Gregory Crossley [1973] Director; David Robert Forder [1965] Director/Manager Financial Reporting and Planning; Laurent Jaques [1976] Director/Holding Management [Swiss]; Howard Bruce Moller [1962] Director/Finance Manager; Markus Leo Unternahrer [1968] Director [Swiss]

Lafarge Nigeria (UK) Limited
Incorporated: 14 March 2005
Net Worth: £69,032,000 *Total Assets:* £69,032,000
Registered Office: Park Lodge, London Road, Dorking, Surrey, RH4 1TH
Activities: Non-trading company
Parent: Associated International Cement Limited
Officers: Howard Bruce Moller, Secretary; Simon Gregory Crossley [1973] Director; Laurent Jaques [1976] Director/Holding Management [Swiss]; Howard Bruce Moller [1962] Director/Finance Manager

Lafarge UK Holdings Limited
Incorporated: 26 March 1969
Net Worth: £736,979,008 *Total Assets:* £737,894,976
Registered Office: Park Lodge, London Road, Dorking, Surrey, RH4 1TH
Activities: Non-trading company
Parent: Lafarge Building Materials Limited
Officers: Howard Bruce Moller, Secretary; Simon Gregory Crossley [1973] Director; Laurent Jaques [1976] Director/Holding Management [Swiss]; Howard Bruce Moller [1962] Director/Finance Manager

Laing Construction Limited
Incorporated: 29 June 1995
Net Worth: £25,064,000 *Total Assets:* £25,064,000
Registered Office: Bridge Place, Anchor Boulevard, Admirals Park, Crossways, Dartford, Kent, DA2 6SN
Activities: Construction of commercial buildings
Parent: Laing O'Rourke Holdings Limited
Officers: Robert Edward Turner, Secretary; Alexander Stewart McIntyre [1956] Director

John Laing Construction Limited
Incorporated: 21 December 1920
Net Worth: £1,184,000 *Total Assets:* £21,434,000
Registered Office: Bridge Place, Anchor Boulevard, Admirals Park, Crossways, Dartford, Kent, DA2 6SN
Activities: Construction of commercial buildings
Parent: Laing Construction Limited
Officers: Robert Edward Turner, Secretary; Alexander Stewart McIntyre [1956] Director

Laing Limited
Incorporated: 24 September 1998
Net Worth: £43,220,000 *Total Assets:* £43,262,000
Registered Office: Bridge Place, Anchor Boulevard, Admirals Park, Crossways, Dartford, Kent, DA2 6SN
Activities: Construction of commercial buildings
Shareholders: John Laing Construction Limited; R O'Rourke & Son Limited
Officers: Robert Edward Turner, Secretary; Alexander Stewart McIntyre [1956] Director

Laing O'Rourke Construction Limited
Incorporated: 23 October 2001
Net Worth: £58,095,000 *Total Assets:* £513,598,016
Registered Office: Bridge Place, Anchor Boulevard, Admirals Park, Crossways, Dartford, Kent, DA2 6SN
Activities: Construction of commercial buildings
Parent: Laing O'Rourke Holdings Limited
Officers: Robert Edward Turner, Secretary; Liam John Cummins [1970] Director; Alexander Stewart McIntyre [1956] Director; Hubert Desmond O'Rourke [1949] Director/Structural Engineer [Irish]

Laing O'Rourke Holdings Limited
Incorporated: 23 May 2001
Net Worth: £13,141,000 *Total Assets:* £310,592,000
Registered Office: Bridge Place, Anchor Boulevard, Admirals Park, Crossways, Dartford, Kent, DA2 6SN
Activities: Construction of commercial buildings
Parent: Laing O'Rourke PLC
Officers: Robert Edward Turner, Secretary; Alexander Stewart McIntyre [1956] Director

Laing O'Rourke Infrastructure Limited
Incorporated: 23 October 2001
Net Worth: £22,417,000 *Total Assets:* £59,629,000
Registered Office: Bridge Place, Anchor Boulevard, Admirals Park, Crossways, Dartford, Kent, DA2 6SN
Activities: Construction of other civil engineering projects n.e.c.
Parent: Laing O'Rourke Holdings Limited
Officers: Robert Edward Turner, Secretary; Alexander Stewart McIntyre [1956] Director

Laing O'Rourke Manufacturing Limited
Incorporated: 16 October 2008
Previous: Bison Manufacturing Limited
Net Worth: £15,640,000 *Total Assets:* £20,212,000
Registered Office: Bridge Place, Anchor Boulevard, Admirals Park, Crossways, Dartford, Kent, DA2 6SN
Activities: Manufacture of concrete products for construction purposes
Parent: Bison Holdings Limited
Officers: Robert Edward Turner, Secretary; Stephen John Harley [1951] Director; Alexander Stewart McIntyre [1956] Director; Paul William McNerney [1977] Director/Business Unit Leader

Laing O'Rourke PLC.
Incorporated: 23 May 2001 *Employees:* 7,669
Net Worth Deficit: £217,900,000 *Total Assets:* £788,600,000
Registered Office: Bridge Place, Anchor Boulevard, Admirals Park, Crossways, Dartford, Kent, DA2 6SN
Activities: Construction of commercial buildings
Parent: O'Rourke Investments Limited
Officers: Robert Edward Turner, Secretary; Declan James McGeeney [1978] Director/General Manager [Irish]; Alexander Stewart McIntyre [1956] Director; Paul William McNerney [1977] Director/Business Unit Leader; Hugh Desmond O'Rourke [1949] Director/Structural Engineer [Irish]; Raymond Gabriel O'Rourke [1947] Director/Structural Engineer [Irish]

Laing O'Rourke Services Limited
Incorporated: 1 February 2002 *Employees:* 7,640
Net Worth: £859,000 *Total Assets:* £704,140,992
Registered Office: Bridge Place, Anchor Boulevard, Admirals Park, Crossways, Dartford, Kent, DA2 6SN
Activities: Construction of commercial buildings
Parent: Laing O'Rourke Holdings Limited
Officers: Robert Edward Turner, Secretary; Alexander Stewart McIntyre [1956] Director; John Christopher O'Connor [1965] Commercial Director

Lake Bridge International PLC
Incorporated: 30 March 2015
Net Worth: £1,405,864 *Total Assets:* £312,154,112
Registered Office: Belmont House, Station Way, Crawley, W Sussex, RH10 1JA
Activities: Other education n.e.c.
Major Shareholder: Arkady Etingen
Officers: Aaron Arkady Etingen [1979] Director; Valery Kisilevsky [1984] Director/Company Secretary

Lake International Ltd
Incorporated: 30 March 2015
Net Worth Deficit: £25,960,568 *Total Assets:* £180,703,904
Registered Office: Belmont House, Station Way, Crawley, W Sussex, RH10 1JA
Activities: Other education n.e.c.
Parent: Lake Bridge International PLC
Officers: Arkady Etingen [1979] Director

Lakefield Holdings Limited
Incorporated: 6 February 2001 *Employees:* 1,107
Net Worth: £41,358,000 *Total Assets:* £184,108,000
Registered Office: Buckingham House, West Street, Newbury, Berks, RG14 1BD
Activities: Wholesale of other intermediate products
Officers: Alan James McIvor, Secretary; Alan James McIvor [1963] Director/Accountant; Daniel Samann [1980] Director/Student [Canadian]; Dr Ronald Samann [1951] Director [Canadian]

Laleham Health and Beauty Limited
Incorporated: 16 December 1970 *Employees:* 558
Net Worth: £15,054,000 *Total Assets:* £59,888,000
Registered Office: Sycamore Park, Mill Lane, Alton, Hants, GU34 2PR
Activities: Other manufacturing n.e.c.
Parent: Laleham Health & Beauty Solutions Ltd
Officers: Giles Alastair Harrison, Secretary; Conor Francis Costigan [1971] Director [Irish]; Mark Crawley [1960] Technical Director; Louise Cruickshanks [1970] Director/Marketing Guru; Sarah Louise Fernihough [1973] Director; Giles Alastair Harrison [1965] Director; Redmond McEvoy [1964] Director [Irish]; Stephen Clifford O'Connor [1964] Director/Chartered Accountant; Timothy Paul O'Connor [1968] Managing Director; Adrian Mark Williams [1965] Director/Chartered Accountant

W.T. Lamb Holdings Limited
Incorporated: 31 December 1947 *Employees:* 37
Net Worth: £33,725,988 *Total Assets:* £40,614,824
Registered Office: Nyewood Court, Brookers Road, Billingshurst, W Sussex, RH14 9RZ
Activities: Operation of gravel and sand pits; mining of clays and kaolin
Officers: Robert Smith, Secretary; James Robin Cardain Lamb [1966] Director; Jonathan Robert Lamb [1971] Sales Director; Robert Harry Simms Lamb [1948] Director/Brick Manufacturer; Robin Antony Lamb [1938] Director/Brick Merchant; Robert Graham Smith [1966] Director/Chartered Accountant

W Lamb Limited
Incorporated: 20 August 1942 *Employees:* 4
Net Worth: £10,897,947 *Total Assets:* £25,146,604
Registered Office: Painesend Farm, Painesend, Tring, Herts, HP23 6JU
Activities: Operation of warehousing and storage facilities for land transport activities
Parent: W Lamb Holdings Ltd
Officers: Philippa Jane Gill, Secretary; Peter Samuel Vallis [1942] Director

Lambert Pressland Limited
Incorporated: 22 March 1999 *Employees:* 4
Net Worth: £7,318,713 *Total Assets:* £28,628,188
Registered Office: The Shrubbery, 14 Church Street, Whitchurch, Basingstoke, Hants, RG28 7AB
Activities: Buying and selling of own real estate
Shareholders: Paul Ian Hamilton Pressland; Oliver Edward Lambert
Officers: Paul Ian Hamilton Pressland, Secretary/Property Manager; Oliver Edward Lambert [1965] Director/Property Investor; Paul Ian Hamilton Pressland [1963] Director/Property Manager

Lamberts Healthcare Limited
Incorporated: 1 August 2002 *Employees:* 53
Net Worth: £24,337,000 *Total Assets:* £28,585,000
Registered Office: 1 Lamberts Road, Tunbridge Wells, Kent, TN2 3EH
Activities: Other retail sale of food in specialised stores
Parent: Merck Consumer Healthcare Limited
Officers: Anthony Joseph Appleton [1962] Director & General Counsel; Alexander George Buckthorp [1973] Finance Director; Heidrun Gresle [1966] Director/General Manager UK & Ireland [German]; Vijay Indroo Sitlani [1975] Finance Director [Singaporean]; John Geoffrey Todd [1957] Director; Christopher John Young [1974] HR Director

Lamp Group Limited
Incorporated: 23 July 2003 *Employees:* 84
Net Worth: £17,128,000 *Total Assets:* £61,794,000
Registered Office: Chester House, Harlands Road, Haywards Heath, W Sussex, RH16 1LR
Activities: Non-life insurance
Shareholder: Michael John Symons
Officers: Tony Giannetta, Secretary; Peter Richard Abbott [1950] Director; Jaspal Singh Kainth [1976] Finance Director; Michael John Symons [1954] Director

Lampton School Academy Trust
Incorporated: 13 August 2010 *Employees:* 146
Net Worth: £24,262,000 *Total Assets:* £30,033,000
Registered Office: Lampton School, Lampton Avenue, Hounslow, Middlesex, TW3 4EP
Activities: General secondary education
Officers: Rina Sehgal, Secretary; Sharan Bangar [1976] Director/Senior Administrator; Harjinder Singh Chaudry [1969] Director/IT Consultant; Stephen Davis [1974] Director/Headteacher; Elizabeth Ellis [1965] Director/Librarian [American]; Dr Parvinder Singh Garcha [1958] Director/G.P; Glen Grace [1971] Director/Health and Safety Officer; Raghav Gupta-Chaudhary [1987] Director/Chartered Accountant; Birna Helgadottir [1964] Director/Teacher [Icelander]; Edward Jonathan Locke [1953] Director/Landscape Gardener; Ruby Mir [1987] Director; Thomas Peter Samuel [1989] Director/Financial Consultant; Dorina Scott [1955] Director/Headteacher; Gurjit Sisodia [1971] Director; Moira Stuart [1951] Director; Ruth Williams [1970] Director/Teacher; Natasha Woolman [1978] Director

Lancer Property Holdings Limited
Incorporated: 7 February 2006 *Employees:* 14
Net Worth: £30,107,060 *Total Assets:* £33,733,008
Registered Office: c/o Freeths LLP, Routeco Office Park, Davy Avenue, Knowlhill, Milton Keynes, Bucks, MK5 8HJ
Activities: Management of real estate on a fee or contract basis
Parent: ABDJ Holdings Limited
Officers: Duncan Robert Ferguson, Secretary/Chartered Surveyor; Duncan Robert Ferguson [1960] Director/Chartered Surveyor; John Townley Kevill [1962] Director; Andrew John Windle Lax [1949] Director; Byron Howard Pull [1947] Director

Lancing College Limited
Incorporated: 28 May 1999 *Employees:* 373
Net Worth: £13,223,717 *Total Assets:* £31,526,408
Registered Office: Lancing College, Lancing, W Sussex, BN15 0RW
Activities: Pre-primary education
Parent: The Woodard Corporation
Officers: Tanya Louise Jones, Secretary; David Elliott Austin [1952] Director/Retired Teacher; Dr Henry Otto Brunjes [1954] Director/Private Doctor Company Chairman; Baroness Julia Cumberlege [1943] Director; Charles Frederick Dennis [1974] Director/Headhunter; Anne-Marie Edgell [1951] Director/Retired Solicitor; Professor Michael Farthing [1947] Director/Professor of Medicine; Dr Sally Godward [1958] Director/Medical Doctor; Timothy John Pennington Hancock [1955] Director/Finance; Eugenia Lopez Harrop [1973] Director/Headmistress [Spanish]; Justin Beresford Higgo [1968] Director/Barrister; Charlotte Elizabeth Houston [1978] Director/Management Consultant; Henry Clifford Ryder Lawson [1963] Director/Company Chief Executive; Helen O'Sullivan [1975] Director/Marketing Consultant; Martin Richard Slumbers [1960] Director/Chartered Accountant; Richard Harvey Stapleton [1946] Director/Chartered Surveyor

Landlink Estates Limited
Incorporated: 29 March 1993 *Employees:* 7
Net Worth: £13,336,731 *Total Assets:* £29,623,802
Registered Office: Ham Farm, Main Road, Bosham, Chichester, W Sussex, PO18 8EH
Activities: Other service activities n.e.c.
Major Shareholder: David Langmead
Officers: Sandra Ann Langmead, Secretary; Paul Edward Hanson [1963] Property Director; David Winston Langmead [1962] Director; Peter James Scrimshaw [1971] Director/Chief Finance Officer

Landmark Mortgages Limited
Incorporated: 30 October 1996 *Employees:* 16
Previous: Landmark Mortgages PLC
Net Worth: £56,234,000 *Total Assets:* £157,900,000
Registered Office: Admiral House, Harlington Way, Fleet, Hants, GU51 4YA
Activities: Activities of mortgage finance companies
Parent: Landmark Bidco Limited
Officers: Hilary Susanna Young, Secretary; David Robert Clinton [1954] Director; Michiel Jozef Alexander Heijmeijer [1959] Managing Director [Dutch]; Charlotte Marie Insinger [1965] Director/Management and Business Advisory [Dutch]; Lee James Kelly [1970] Director/Chartered Accountant; Hiteshkumar Rameshchandra Patel [1961] Director

Landmark Space Limited
Incorporated: 23 February 2005 *Employees:* 156
Previous: I2 Office Limited
Net Worth: £4,023,000 *Total Assets:* £63,933,000
Registered Office: 4 Tilgate Forest Business Park, Brighton Road, Crawley, W Sussex, RH11 9BP
Activities: Activities of other membership organisations n.e.c.
Parent: OCS Group Limited
Officers: Malcolm Clark, Secretary; James Farnworth [1983] Director [Australian]; John Robert Spencer [1958] Director

Langbourn Properties Limited
Incorporated: 15 February 1990
Net Worth: £70,149,728 *Total Assets:* £72,824,720
Registered Office: 30 Triggs Close, Triggs Lane, Woking, Surrey, GU22 0EJ
Activities: Buying and selling of own real estate
Major Shareholder: Nigel Charles Wiggins
Officers: Ian Robin Campbell, Secretary; Derek Deshborough Brown [1958] Director/Chartered Surveyor; Ian Robin Campbell [1946] Director/Retired; Nigel Anthony Collins [1950] Director/Chartered Surveyor; Nigel Charles Wiggins [1949] Director/Chartered Surveyor

The Langley Academy Trust
Incorporated: 9 February 2005 *Employees:* 311
Net Worth: £37,960,760 *Total Assets:* £43,376,212
Registered Office: The Langley Academy, Langley Road, Slough, SL3 7EF
Activities: Primary education
Officers: Coralyn Ann Selman, Secretary; Emmajane Avery [1974] Director of Learning and Visitor Experience, V&A; Rhodri Bryant [1967] Director/Principal; Martin Christopher Burford [1952] Director/Education Consultant; John Clive Hedger [1942] Director/Chairman of NHS Foundation Trust; William Ian David Lazarus [1953] Director/Chartered Accountant; David Arthur Mallen [1939] Director/Retired; Annabel Suva Nicoll [1970] Director/Chartered Physiotherapist; Dr Oona Mary Stannard [1954] Director/Educationalist

Langley Park Learning Trust
Incorporated: 7 July 2011 *Employees:* 320
Previous: Langley Park Academies
Net Worth: £39,185,000 *Total Assets:* £42,240,000
Registered Office: Langley Park School for Girls, Hawksbrook Lane, South Eden Park Road, Beckenham, Kent, BR3 3BE
Activities: Primary education
Officers: Micon Metcalfe, Secretary; David Laurence Appleton [1947] Director/Retired; John Budden [1971] Director/Headteacher; Andrea Felicity Carr [1964] Director; George Thomas Chalmers [1988] Director; Gareth Scott Fendick [1980] HR Director; Barbara Florence Hart [1949] Director/Retired; Enkanah Soobadoo [1953] Director/Retired; James Edward Weatherill [1983] Director

The Langley Park School for Boys Academy Trust
Incorporated: 7 March 2011 *Employees:* 173
Net Worth: £27,744,000 *Total Assets:* £29,243,000
Registered Office: Langley Park School for Boys, Hawksbrook Lane, Beckenham, Kent, BR3 3BP
Activities: General secondary education
Officers: Vicky Stockwell, Secretary; David Laurence Appleton [1947] Director/Consultant; Leonard Edmund Blomstrand [1947] Director/Education Consultant; Andrea Felicity Carr [1964] Director/Publisher; Wendy Anne Coello [1970] Director/Civil Servant; Alana Dave [1964] Director/Education Officer; Caroline Sarah Davies [1968] Director/School Business Manager; Mario di Clemente [1963] Director/College Principal; Sandra Lauren Dodds [1946] Director/NHS Officer; Lee Terence Game [1990] Director/Teacher; Julia Garvey [1969] Director/Marketing Consultant; Lawrence Richard Gold [1965] Director; Sian Elizabeth Henderson [1964] Director/Civil Servant; Paul Michael Monaghan [1972] Director/Bank Manager; Stephen Ivor James Parsons [1974] Director/Headmaster; Claudette Thomas [1965] Director/People and Operations Manager

Langmead Farms Limited
Incorporated: 26 August 1999 *Employees:* 109
Net Worth: £3,107,092 *Total Assets:* £22,975,116
Registered Office: Langmead Farms Limited, Ham Farm, Main Road, Bosham, Chichester, W Sussex, PO18 8EH
Activities: Growing of cereals (except rice), leguminous crops and oil seeds
Major Shareholder: David Winston Langmead
Officers: David Winston Langmead [1962] Director/Farmer/Market Gardener; Peter James Scrimshaw [1971] Director/Chief Finance Officer

Lantmannen UK Holding Limited
Incorporated: 22 September 2011 *Employees:* 4
Net Worth: £16,105,000 *Total Assets:* £113,233,000
Registered Office: Maidstone Road, Kingston, Milton Keynes, Bucks, MK10 0BD
Activities: Manufacture of bread; manufacture of fresh pastry goods and cakes
Officers: Morten Leth [1967] Finance Director [Danish]; Erik Flemming Nielsen [1951] Director [Danish]; Nils Olov Nyberg [1958] Director [Swedish]; Tim Robinson [1974] Managing Director

Lantmannen Unibake UK Limited
Incorporated: 23 April 1997
Net Worth: £62,073,000 *Total Assets:* £133,280,000
Registered Office: 3 Tanners Yard, London Road, Bagshot, Surrey, GU19 5HD
Activities: Manufacture of bread; manufacture of fresh pastry goods and cakes
Parent: Lantmannen UK Holding Ltd
Officers: Morten Leth [1967] Finance Director [Danish]; Erik Flemming Nielsen [1951] Director [Danish]; Tim Robinson [1974] Managing Director

Lanxess Limited
Incorporated: 26 January 1998 *Employees:* 54
Net Worth: £21,734,000 *Total Assets:* £23,961,000
Registered Office: Unit 1B, The Vo-Tec Centre, Hambridge Lane, Newbury, Berks, RG14 5TN
Activities: Manufacture of dyes and pigments
Parent: Lanxess Deutschland GmbH
Officers: Christopher James Flett, Secretary; Holger Huppeler [1967] Director/Head of Business Line Inorganic Pigments [German]; Jacques Louis Albert Perez [1962] Managing Director [French]

Lapid Developments Limited
Incorporated: 29 January 1971
Net Worth: £21,827,756 *Total Assets:* £24,292,516
Registered Office: 5 Elstree Gate, Elstree Way, Borehamwood, Herts, WD6 1JD
Activities: Renting and operating of Housing Association real estate
Parent: Meekport Limited
Officers: Eldad Aizenberg, Secretary; Eldad Aizenberg [1957] Managing Director; Naomi Braybrooke [1967] Director/Museum Education; Daniel Cigman [1969] Director; Julie Cigman [1954] Director/Advisory Teacher; Dr Ruth Cigman [1951] Director/University Lecturer

Larger London Land Company Limited
Incorporated: 11 January 1906 *Employees:* 6
Net Worth: £24,767,560 *Total Assets:* £27,365,056
Registered Office: The Loft, 1 Navarino Court, High Street, Lymington, Hants, SO41 9AE
Activities: Other service activities n.e.c.
Officers: Jane Elizabeth Fairbairn, Secretary; David Aubrey [1957] Director/Senior Manager; David Alun Cledwyn [1955] Director/Solicitor; Richard Paul Knight [1961] Director/Bank Manager

The Last Mile Company Limited
Incorporated: 11 November 1999
Net Worth Deficit: £310,000 *Total Assets:* £66,203,000
Registered Office: 2 The Deans, Bridge Road, Bagshot, Surrey, GU19 5AT
Activities: Activities of real estate investment trusts
Parent: Big Yellow Group PLC
Officers: Shauna Louise Beavis, Secretary; James Ernest Gibson [1960] Director; Adrian Charles Jonathan Lee [1965] Director; John Richard Trotman [1977] Director/Chartered Accountant; Nicholas John Vetch [1961] Director

James Latham Public Limited Company
Incorporated: 7 April 1900 *Employees:* 385
Net Worth: £89,789,000 *Total Assets:* £131,763,000
Registered Office: Unit 3 Swallow Park, Finway Road, Hemel Hempstead, Herts, HP2 7QU
Activities: Wholesale of wood, construction materials and sanitary equipment
Officers: David Alan Dunmow, Secretary; David Alan Dunmow [1964] Finance Director; Philip Luke Fabian French [1959] Director; Nicholas Charles Latham [1968] Director; Piers Francis Latham [1971] Director; Christopher David Sutton [1958] Director; Andrew George Wright [1964] Director

Lathams Limited
Incorporated: 1 December 1969 *Employees:* 360
Net Worth: £92,158,000 *Total Assets:* £125,868,000
Registered Office: Unit 3 Swallow Park, Finway Road, Hemel Hempstead, Herts, HP2 7QU
Activities: Wholesale of wood, construction materials and sanitary equipment
Parent: James Latham PLC
Officers: David Alan Dunmow, Finance Director; Andrew Carey Duffin [1962] Director; David Alan Dunmow [1964] Finance Director; Stephen Andrew Frommont [1971] Commercial Director; Nicholas Charles Latham [1968] Director; Piers Francis Latham [1971] Director; Christopher David Sutton [1958] Director; Nicholas James Widlinski [1981] Panel Sales Director; Andrew George Wright [1964] Director

Ralph Lauren UK Limited
Incorporated: 17 August 1994
Net Worth: £8,572,470 *Total Assets:* £79,218,344
Registered Office: 46 Clarendon Road, Watford, Herts, WD1 1DR
Activities: Wholesale of clothing and footwear
Parent: RL Retail Services Limited
Officers: Aldo Alex Fleri [1961] Director/Vice President Sales UK; Carmel Ann Pedatella [1974] Director/Business Executive [American]; Robert Patrick Ranftl [1971] Director/Business Executive [American]; Andrew Howard Smith [1971] Director/Business Executive

Lavazza Professional UK Limited
Incorporated: 18 July 2008 *Employees:* 268
Previous: Mars Drinks UK Limited
Net Worth: £43,483,000 *Total Assets:* £77,259,000
Registered Office: Armstrong Road, Basingstoke, Hants, RG24 8NU
Activities: Production of coffee and coffee substitutes
Officers: Hossam Ashraf [1973] Director; Kimberley Anne Bott [1986] Director/Accountant; Amy Michelle Fernandez [1976] Director/Lawyer [American]

Lawrie Group Public Limited Company
Incorporated: 19 April 1978
Net Worth: £39,018,932 *Total Assets:* £88,532,648
Registered Office: Linton Park, Linton, Maidstone, Kent, ME17 4AB
Activities: Activities of head offices
Parent: Camellia PLC
Officers: Amarpal Takk, Secretary; Thomas Kenric Franks [1963] Director; Malcolm Courtney Perkins [1945] Director/Chartered Accountant; Susan Ann Walker [1967] Director

LDFA Limited
Incorporated: 3 March 2016 *Employees:* 1
Net Worth: £264,093 *Total Assets:* £41,633,020
Registered Office: 4th Floor, Reading Bridge House, George Street, Reading, Berks, RG1 8LS
Activities: Security and commodity contracts dealing activities
Major Shareholder: Robert Charles Standing
Officers: Robert Charles Standing [1960] Director/Fund Manager

Lea Redway Limited
Incorporated: 25 March 1943 *Employees:* 502
Net Worth: £40,047,336 *Total Assets:* £47,061,912
Registered Office: 59a Mosslea Road, Whyteleafe, Surrey, CR3 0DS
Activities: Activities of head offices
Shareholder: Nigel Bedggood
Officers: Maria Adaway, Secretary; Maria Adaway [1965] Director/Board Member; Luke Edward Victor Bedggood [1974] Director/Board Member; Margaret Anne Bedggood [1945] Director/Administrator [Australian]; Nigel Edward Lawrence Bedggood [1941] Director/Engineer; Carol Ann Catt [1944] Director/Administrator

Leaderboard Golf Holdings Limited
Incorporated: 31 August 2011 *Employees:* 245
Net Worth: £11,538,871 *Total Assets:* £34,707,660
Registered Office: c/o Dale Hill Hotel and Golf Limited, Ticehurst, Wadhurst, E Sussex, TN5 7DQ
Activities: Other business support service activities n.e.c.
Shareholder: Paul Gibbons
Officers: Barry James Lewis, Secretary; David Alan Douglas Colyer [1966] Director; Jennifer Ann Gibbons [1948] Director; Paul Gibbons [1947] Director; Peter Joseph Gibbons [1987] Director/Group Media and Production Manager

Leaders Lettings Limited
Incorporated: 22 December 2009 *Employees:* 10
Net Worth: £16,201,745 *Total Assets:* £22,161,460
Registered Office: Crowthorne House, Nine Mile Ride, Wokingham, Berks, RG40 3GZ
Activities: Activities of head offices
Shareholders: The Leaders Romans Bidco Limited; Titus Bidco Limited
Officers: Michael Edward John Palmer, Secretary; Antonia Dale Cheong [1987] Director; Richard Andrew Connell [1955] Director; Charles Thomas Messiter Ind [1963] Director; Peter Kavanagh [1962] Managing Director; Matthew James Light [1971] Director/Certified Accountant; Michael Edward John Palmer [1973] Director; Tom Shelford [1980] Director; Paul Stanley Weller [1960] Director

Leaders Limited
Incorporated: 12 January 1983 *Employees:* 1,157
Net Worth: £9,949,440 *Total Assets:* £57,419,616
Registered Office: Crowthorne House, Nine Mile Ride, Wokingham, Berks, RG40 3GZ
Activities: Management of real estate on a fee or contract basis
Parent: Leaders Lettings Trading Limited
Officers: Michael Edward John Palmer, Secretary; Richard John Churchill [1966] Lettings Director; Michael Brian Cook [1983] Director; Peter Kavanagh [1962] Managing Director; Matthew James Light [1971] Director/Certified Accountant; Michael Edward John Palmer [1973] Director; Allison Thompson [1972] Director; Paul Stanley Weller [1960] Director/Chartered Accountant Company

The Leaders Romans Group Limited
Incorporated: 6 January 2016 *Employees:* 2,033
Net Worth Deficit: £148,373,984 *Total Assets:* £166,117,984
Registered Office: Crowthorne House, Nine Mile Ride, Wokingham, Berks, RG40 3GZ
Activities: Activities of head offices
Shareholders: Bowmark Investment Partnership IV Nominees Limited; Ventry Nominees Limited
Officers: Michael Edward John Palmer, Secretary; Antonia Dale Cheong [1987] Director/Investment Manager; Peter Anthony Coles [1967] Director; Richard Andrew Connell [1955] Non-Executive Director Chairman; Michael Brian Cook [1983] Director; Charles Thomas Messiter Ind [1963] Director; Peter Kavanagh [1962] Director; Matthew James Light [1971] Acquisitions Director; Michael Edward John Palmer [1973] Director; Tom Shelford [1980] Director; Paul Stanley Weller [1960] Director

The Leaders Romans Midco 2 Limited
Incorporated: 6 January 2016 *Employees:* 2,033
Net Worth Deficit: £148,283,472 *Total Assets:* £167,336,256
Registered Office: Crowthorne House, Nine Mile Ride, Wokingham, Berks, RG40 3GZ
Activities: Activities of head offices
Parent: Titus Midco Limited
Officers: Michael Edward John Palmer, Secretary; Antonia Dale Cheong [1987] Director/Investment Manager; Peter Anthony Coles [1967] Director; Peter Kavanagh [1962] Director; Michael Edward John Palmer [1973] Director; Tom Shelford [1980] Director; Paul Stanley Weller [1960] Director

The Leaders Romans Midco Limited
Incorporated: 6 January 2016 *Employees:* 6
Net Worth Deficit: £9,947 *Total Assets:* £156,313,616
Registered Office: Crowthorne House, Nine Mile Ride, Wokingham, Berks, RG40 3GZ
Activities: Activities of head offices
Shareholders: The Leaders Romans Group Limited; Property Services Holdings Limited
Officers: Michael Edward John Palmer, Secretary; Antonia Dale Cheong [1987] Director/Investment Manager; Peter Anthony Coles [1967] Director; Peter Kavanagh [1962] Director; Michael Edward John Palmer [1973] Director; Tom Shelford [1980] Director; Paul Stanley Weller [1960] Director

Leaders The Rental Agents Limited
Incorporated: 22 July 2013
Net Worth Deficit: £29,292,168 *Total Assets:* £56,956,028
Registered Office: Crowthorne House, Nine Mile Ride, Wokingham, Berks, RG40 3GZ
Activities: Activities of head offices
Parent: Leaders First in Letting Limited
Officers: Michael Edward John Palmer, Secretary; Antonia Dale Cheong [1987] Director; Peter Kavanagh [1962] Director; Matthew James Light [1971] Director; Michael Edward John Palmer [1973] Director; Tom Shelford [1980] Director; Paul Stanley Weller [1960] Director

The Learning Alliance Academy Trust
Incorporated: 13 July 2011 *Employees:* 202
Net Worth: £28,767,068 *Total Assets:* £34,703,016
Registered Office: Lynch Hill School Primary Academy, Garrard Road, Slough, Berks, SL2 2AN
Activities: Primary education
Officers: Dale Francis Butcher [1955] Director; Gillian Duncan [1955] Director/Executive Headteacher; Denise Fletcher [1964] Director/Company Secretary; Linda Hazell [1947] Director/Retired; Peter Ward [1947] Director/Consultant; Roderick George Watson [1937] Director/Certified Chartered Accountant

Leaseplan UK Limited
Incorporated: 6 November 1978 *Employees:* 543
Net Worth: £249,327,008 *Total Assets:* £2,253,332,992
Registered Office: 165 Bath Road, Slough, Berks, SL1 4AA
Activities: Renting and leasing of cars and light motor vehicles
Parent: Inula Holding UK Limited
Officers: Niall Robert Keartland, Secretary; Alfonso Martinez [1961] Director [Spanish]; Patrick Marco Steenvoorden [1972] Finance Director [Dutch]

Leasys UK Ltd
Incorporated: 11 June 1997 *Employees:* 15
Previous: FCA Fleet Services UK Ltd
Net Worth: £31,565,000 *Total Assets:* £158,987,008
Registered Office: Fiat House, 240 Bath Road, Slough, Berks, SL1 4DX
Activities: Renting and leasing of cars and light motor vehicles
Shareholders: Credit Agricole SA; Fiat Chrysler Automobiles N.V.
Officers: Peter John Farley, Secretary; Sebastiano Fedrigo [1974] Director/Motor Executive [Italian]; Alberto Grippo [1971] Director/Motor Executive [Italian]; Anne Marie Guirchoux [1966] Director [French]; Alexander Paul Hughes [1976] Director; Jonathan Mark Tilney [1965] Director

Leeds Castle Foundation
Incorporated: 30 May 1974 *Employees:* 262
Net Worth: £21,351,000 *Total Assets:* £23,998,000
Registered Office: Leeds Castle, Maidstone, Kent, ME17 1PL
Activities: Operation of historical sites and buildings and similar visitor attractions
Officers: Robin Andrew Richman, Secretary; Lord Mark Thomas Bridges [1954] Director/Solicitor; Niall Forbes Ross Dickson [1953] Director/Charity Chief Executive; Richard George Laing [1954] Director; Jonathan Beale Neame [1964] Director; Laura Cicely Alison Nesfield [1981] Director/Chartered Surveyor; Timothy John Stevens [1940] Director/Retired; Adrian John Tinniswood [1954] Director/Historian; Thomas Charles Kendal Knox Wright [1962] Director

Leeu London Limited
Incorporated: 13 March 2017
Net Worth: £14,132,330 *Total Assets:* £84,405,816
Registered Office: Dixcart House, Addlestone Road, Bourne Business Park, Addlestone, Surrey, KT15 2LE
Activities: Hotels and similar accommodation
Shareholders: Analjit Singh; Neelu Singh
Officers: Analjit Singh [1954] Director [Indian]

Lego Company Limited
Incorporated: 19 July 1941 *Employees:* 687
Net Worth: £38,430,000 *Total Assets:* £160,032,000
Registered Office: Capital Point, 33 Bath Road, Slough, Berks, SL1 3UF
Activities: Wholesale of household goods (other than musical instruments) n.e.c
Major Shareholder: Kjeld Kirk Kristiansen
Officers: Anne Lene Sonnichsen Cumming, Secretary; Julia Goldin [1968] Director/Executive VP, Chief Marketing Officer [American]; Marjorie Lao [1974] Director/Senior Vice President, Corporate Finance [Filipino]; Poul Hartvig Nielsen [1960] Director/General Counsel [Danish]; Victor Eric Saeys [1965] Director/Senior Vice President [Dutch]

Legolas Debt Holdco Limited
Incorporated: 7 March 2017 *Employees:* 4
Net Worth: £3,772,068 *Total Assets:* £114,980,712
Registered Office: Munro House, Portsmouth Road, Cobham, Surrey, KT11 1PP
Activities: Financial intermediation not elsewhere classified
Parent: GCP Bridge Holdings Ltd
Officers: Stephen Campbell Joseph Ellis [1959] Director; Ronan Niall Kierans [1978] Director [Irish]; Nicholas Simon Parker [1969] Director; Rollo Andrew Johnstone Wright [1976] Director

Lehigh UK Limited
Incorporated: 21 November 2000
Net Worth: £13,299,584,000 *Total Assets:* £13,437,815,808
Registered Office: Hanson House, 14 Castle Hill, Maidenhead, Berks, SL6 4JJ
Activities: Activities of other holding companies n.e.c.
Parent: HeidelbergCement UK Holding Limited
Officers: Wendy Fiona Rogers, Secretary; Nicholas Arthur Dawe Benning-Prince [1974] Director/Chartered Accountant; Robert Charles Dowley [1972] Director/Chartered Accountant; Edward Alexander Gretton [1970] Director; Dr Lorenz Nager [1960] Director/CFO Heidelbergcement AG [German]; Dr Carsten Matthias Wendt [1976] Director [German]; Simon Lloyd Willis [1965] Director/Chief Executive, Hanson UK

Leica Geosystems Limited
Incorporated: 31 August 1964 *Employees:* 106
Net Worth: £15,714,000 *Total Assets:* £30,730,000
Registered Office: Hexagon House, Michigan Drive, Tongwell, Milton Keynes, Bucks, MK15 8HT
Activities: Wholesale of mining, construction and civil engineering machinery
Parent: Hexagon AB
Officers: Andrew Paul Young, Secretary; John Edward Fraser [1972] Regional Director

Leigh Academies Trust
Incorporated: 19 January 1989 *Employees:* 1,822
Net Worth: £157,508,992 *Total Assets:* £196,876,000
Registered Office: Strood Academy, Carnation Road, Rochester, Kent, ME2 2SX
Activities: Pre-primary education
Officers: Stephen Avis, Secretary; Anne Barritte [1957] Director/IT Manager; Simon Beamish [1977] Director/Teacher; Graham Charles Clewes [1966] Director/CEO MYT Trust; Michael Edward Costello [1955] Director/Investigative Coach/Trainer; Theresa Barbara Davies [1956] Director/Business Manager; Keith John Ellis [1957] Managing Director; Robert John Findlay [1943] Director/Publisher [Canadian]; Alban Francis Xavier Green [1950] Director/Principal; William James Hogan- O'Neill [1950] Director/Architect [Irish]; Jeremy Alan Kite [1963] Director/Councillor; James Nicholson [1964] Director/Senior Relationship Officer; Professor Martin John Snowden [1964] Director/Pro Vice-Chancellor; Tracey Trusler [1962] Director/Headteacher

Leighton Park Trust
Incorporated: 8 December 1920 *Employees:* 222
Net Worth: £16,554,603 *Total Assets:* £22,935,076
Registered Office: Leighton Park School, Shinfield Road, Reading, Berks, RG2 7ED
Activities: General secondary education
Officers: Keith Richard Eldridge, Secretary; Sally Jayne Bonner [1959] Director/Governor; John Edward Crosfield [1953] Director; Edwina Mary Ellen Dean-Lewis [1963] Director/Governor; Janet Mary Digby [1957] Director/Trustee; Caroline George [1966] Director/School Governor; Philip Griffin [1956] Director/School Governor; David Fleming Hickok [1959] Director/Governor [American]; Simon Nevill Hollands [1967] Director/Governor; Christopher Houston [1962] Director/Governor; David Isherwood [1981] Director/Marketing Manager; Bruce Johnson [1964] Director/Governor; Helen Johnson [1949] Director/Governor; Dr Martin Hugh Lloyd [1944] Director/Governor; Mary Elizabeth Phipps [1947] Director/Governor; Matthew James Winkless [1992] Director/School Governor

Lenham Storage Company Limited
Incorporated: 22 January 1949 *Employees:* 422
Net Worth: £17,332,368 *Total Assets:* £30,010,920
Registered Office: Ashcombe House, 5 The Crescent, Leatherhead, Surrey, KT22 8DY
Activities: Freight transport by road
Shareholders: Dorothy Janet Abrehart; Rodney Frederic Tolhurst
Officers: Anthony Michael Burgess, Secretary; Dorothy Janet Abrehart [1946] Director; Keith Nicholas Abrehart [1972] Managing Director; Anthony Michael Burgess [1963] Financial Director; Andrew Charles Fulcher [1968] Operational Director; Stephen Leslie Phibbs [1951] Director; Christopher Frederick Tolhurst [1973] IT Director; Rodney Frederic Tolhurst [1943] Director

Lenovo Global Technology UK Limited
Incorporated: 7 June 2016 *Employees:* 182
Net Worth: £12,364,084 *Total Assets:* £114,094,632
Registered Office: Redwood 3, Chineham Business Park, Crockford Lane, Chineham, Basingstoke, Hants, RG24 8WQ
Activities: Other information technology service activities
Officers: Colm Brendan Gleeson [1974] Director [Irish]; Christophe Laurent [1973] Director [Belgian]

Lenovo Technology (United Kingdom) Limited
Incorporated: 26 September 2003 *Employees:* 350
Net Worth: £49,186,256 *Total Assets:* £309,658,880
Registered Office: 2nd Floor, Redwood 3, Chineham Park, Crockford Lane, Basingstoke, Hants, RG24 8WQ
Activities: Manufacture of computers and peripheral equipment
Officers: Paula Caldwell, Secretary; Colm Gleeson [1974] Director/Tax Specialist [Irish]; Gareth James Holton [1974] Director/Accountant; Christophe Laurent [1973] Director/Attorney [Belgian]

Lenster Investments Limited
Incorporated: 9 February 1981 *Employees:* 6
Net Worth: £31,819,308 *Total Assets:* £36,915,084
Registered Office: 8th Floor, South Reading Bridge House, George Street, Reading, Berks, RG1 8LS
Activities: Financial intermediation not elsewhere classified
Officers: Clive Brangwin [1942] Director/Retired; Kamurai Moyo [1972] Director/Carriage and Wagon Fitter [Zimbabwean]; Stanley Shava [1982] Director [Zimbabwean]; Kevin James Thomas Walmsley [1959] Director/Chartered Accountant; Roger Walter Williams [1949] Director

Lenta Properties Limited
Incorporated: 4 March 1981 *Employees:* 55
Net Worth: £54,831,952 *Total Assets:* £70,508,912
Registered Office: CP House, Otterspool Way, Watford, Herts, WD25 8HR
Activities: Other letting and operating of own or leased real estate
Parent: Lenta Business Space Limited
Officers: Eric Lewis, Secretary/Solicitor; Paul Andrew Filer [1957] Director/Chartered Accountant; Ian Leslie Gibbor [1950] Director; Iris Gibbor [1951] Director; Mark Gibbor [1988] Director; Geoffrey Grodner [1961] Director/Chartered Accountant; Eric Lewis [1927] Director/Solicitor; Alexei James Schreier [1976] Director; Sarra Gay Temple [1959] Commercial Director

Leo Energy Limited
Incorporated: 12 March 2015 *Employees:* 4
Net Worth: £30,788,094 *Total Assets:* £30,804,952
Registered Office: Loddon Reach, Reading Road, Arborfield, Reading, Berks, RG2 9HU
Activities: Activities of other holding companies n.e.c.
Parent: Draff Lion Limited
Officers: Serkan Bahceci [1972] Director; Francis John Burns [1962] Managing Director; Charles John Gore Hazelwood [1963] Director

Leo Laboratories Limited
Incorporated: 14 June 1960 *Employees:* 141
Net Worth: £11,963,000 *Total Assets:* £95,717,000
Registered Office: Horizon, Honey Lane, Hurley, Maidenhead, Berks, SL6 6RJ
Activities: Wholesale of pharmaceutical goods
Officers: Philip Walker, Secretary; Gitte Pugholm Aabo [1967] Director/President, CEO [Danish]; Anders Kronborg [1964] Director [Danish]

Lesser & Pavey Ltd.
Incorporated: 4 January 1971 *Employees:* 32
Net Worth: £23,670,144 *Total Assets:* £27,842,092
Registered Office: Leonardo House, Fawkes Avenue, Dartford Trade Park, Dartford, Kent, DA1 1JQ
Activities: Wholesale of china and glassware and cleaning materials
Parent: Leonardo Group Limited
Officers: Derek Howard Fieldman [1949] Director; Julian Allemby Hunt [1958] Director/Importer; Ronald Frank Pavey [1948] Director/Importer

Leumi ABL Limited
Incorporated: 13 February 1959 *Employees:* 45
Net Worth: £5,829,000 *Total Assets:* £248,936,992
Registered Office: 126 Dyke Road, Brighton, BN1 3TE
Activities: Credit granting by non-deposit taking finance houses and other specialist consumer credit grantors
Parent: Bank Leumi (UK) PLC
Officers: Glenn Beatham [1961] Director; Alan Kevin Couzins [1965] Operations Director; Dhavarajh Leonard Frank [1970] Director; Paul Grant Self Hird [1959] Director; Gil Karni [1966] Director [Israeli]; Adrian Philip Woodward [1967] Director; Kevin David Yates [1973] Director of Risk & Compliance

Leven Wharf Limited
Incorporated: 1 May 2015
Net Worth Deficit: £77,764 *Total Assets:* £32,341,948
Registered Office: C K R House, 70 East Hill, Dartford, Kent, DA1 1RZ
Activities: Construction of domestic buildings
Shareholders: Giles William Underhill; Permjit Singh Sulh; Grahame Donald Crisp Seaman
Officers: Grahame Donald Crisp Seaman [1946] Director/Property Developer; Permjit Singh Sulh [1968] Director/Property Developer; Giles William Underhill [1964] Director/Property Developer

The Harry Levy Group Limited
Incorporated: 17 December 2015 *Employees:* 251
Net Worth: £13,503,884 *Total Assets:* £29,850,702
Registered Office: Unit 6 Patricia Way, Pysons Road Industrial Estate, Broadstairs, Kent, CT10 2LE
Activities: Activities of head offices
Shareholder: Harold John Levy
Officers: Harold John Levy [1946] Director/Engineer; Mark Levy [1973] Director; Natasha Levy [1974] Director

LexisNexis Risk Solutions UK Limited
Incorporated: 22 October 2010 *Employees:* 326
Net Worth Deficit: £25,428,422 *Total Assets:* £308,595,072
Registered Office: 1st Floor, 80 Moorbridge Road, Maidenhead, Berks, SL6 8BW
Activities: Other information technology service activities
Parent: RELX (UK) Limited
Officers: Keith Alexander Binley [1972] Director; William Sydney Madison [1961] Director [American]; Richard Edward Trainor [1965] Director [American]

LG Electronics U.K. Ltd
Incorporated: 1 July 1987 *Employees:* 229
Net Worth: £52,531,000 *Total Assets:* £319,664,992
Registered Office: Velocity 2, Brooklands Drive, Weybridge, Surrey, KT13 0SL
Activities: Wholesale of electronic and telecommunications equipment and parts
Parent: LG Electronics European Holding B.V.
Officers: Jae Ho Min, Secretary; Byeongseon Ban [1968] Director/CFO - Europe [South Korean]; Bum Seop Lee [1968] Director/President of UK Subsidiary [South Korean]; Jae Ho Min [1975] Director [South Korean]

LGC (Holdings) Limited
Incorporated: 27 December 1995 *Employees:* 10
Net Worth: £557,251,008 *Total Assets:* £1,122,893,056
Registered Office: Queens Road, Teddington, Middlesex, TW11 0LY
Activities: Other business support service activities n.e.c.
Parent: LGC Investments Limited
Officers: Navneet Kaur Ogle, Secretary; Simon Lawrence Parsons [1969] Finance Director; Timothy Michael Robinson [1963] Director

LGC (Teddington) Limited
Incorporated: 13 October 2000 *Employees:* 2
Net Worth Deficit: £8,171,949 *Total Assets:* £28,820,978
Registered Office: Queens Road, Teddington, Middlesex, TW11 0LY
Activities: Non-trading company
Parent: LGC (Holdings) Limited
Officers: Navneet Kaur Ogle, Secretary; Ian David Burrell [1975] Director/Chartered Accountant; Simon Lawrence Parsons [1969] Finance Director

LGC Genomics Limited
Incorporated: 28 June 2011 *Employees:* 116
Net Worth: £67,616,000 *Total Assets:* £85,633,000
Registered Office: LGC, Queens Road, Teddington, Middlesex, TW11 0LY
Activities: Research and experimental development on biotechnology
Parent: KBiosciences Limited
Officers: Navneet Kaur Ogle, Secretary; Ross Frazer Finlay [1971] Director/Chartered Accountant; Simon Lawrence Parsons [1969] Finance Director

LGC Investments Limited
Incorporated: 23 July 2003 *Employees:* 2
Net Worth Deficit: £53,447,000 *Total Assets:* £164,500,992
Registered Office: LGC, Queens Road, Teddington, Middlesex, TW11 0LY
Activities: Other business support service activities n.e.c.
Parent: LGC Group Holdings Limited
Officers: Navneet Kaur Ogle, Secretary; Simon Lawrence Parsons [1969] Finance Director; Timothy Michael Robinson [1963] Director

LGC Limited
Incorporated: 18 November 1994 *Employees:* 1,265
Net Worth: £18,057,000 *Total Assets:* £336,591,008
Registered Office: Queens Road, Teddington, Middlesex, TW11 0LY
Activities: Other professional, scientific and technical activities n.e.c.
Parent: LGC Holdings Limited
Officers: Navneet Kaur Ogle, Secretary; Julian Hugh Braybrook [1963] Director/Scientific Management; Simon Lawrence Parsons [1969] Finance Director; Timothy Michael Robinson [1963] Director

LGC Science Group Holdings Limited
Incorporated: 4 December 2015 *Employees:* 2,626
Net Worth: £494,812,992 *Total Assets:* £1,370,514,944
Registered Office: LGC, Queens Road, Teddington, Middlesex, TW11 0LY
Activities: Activities of head offices
Parent: Elwy 3 Limited
Officers: Navneet Kaur Ogle, Secretary; Dr Derek Harry Craston [1961] Director/Chemist; Mark Simon Danzey [1979] Director, KKR Capital Markets; Brian Kim [1970] Director/Life Science Executive [American]; Euan Ralph Herbert O'Sullivan [1979] Director/Executive; Simon Lawrence Parsons [1969] Director/Chief Financial Officer; Edouard Jean Charles Pillot [1977] Director [French]; Timothy Michael Robinson [1963] Director; Nicolas Henry Roelofs [1958] Director [American]; Kugan Sathiyanandarajah [1986] Director/Principal, Private Equity

LGC Science Group Limited
Incorporated: 22 December 2009 *Employees:* 2
Net Worth: £118,281,000 *Total Assets:* £223,668,992
Registered Office: LGC, Queens Road, Teddington, Middlesex, TW11 0LY
Activities: Activities of head offices
Parent: LGC Science Group Holdings Limited
Officers: Navneet Kaur Ogle, Secretary; Simon Lawrence Parsons [1969] Finance Director; Timothy Michael Robinson [1963] Director

LGC Science Holdings Limited
Incorporated: 4 January 2010 *Employees:* 2
Net Worth: £221,244,992 *Total Assets:* £345,708,992
Registered Office: LGC, Queens Road, Teddington, Middlesex, TW11 0LY
Activities: Other business support service activities n.e.c.
Parent: Teddington 2 Limited
Officers: Navneet Kaur Ogle, Secretary; Simon Lawrence Parsons [1969] Finance Director; Timothy Michael Robinson [1963] Director

LGC Science Investments Limited
Incorporated: 6 November 2009
Net Worth: £154,780,000 *Total Assets:* £787,196,032
Registered Office: LGC, Queens Road, Teddington, Middlesex, TW11 0LY
Activities: Other business support service activities n.e.c.
Parent: LGC Science Holdings Limited
Officers: Navneet Kaur Ogle, Secretary; Simon Lawrence Parsons [1969] Finance Director; Timothy Michael Robinson [1963] Director

LGC Whirlwind Limited
Incorporated: 28 June 2011
Net Worth: £37,773,000 *Total Assets:* £162,715,008
Registered Office: LGC, Queens Road, Teddington, Middlesex, TW11 0LY
Activities: Other business support service activities n.e.c.
Parent: LGC (Holdings) Limited
Officers: Navneet Kaur Ogle, Secretary; Ian David Burrell [1975] Director/Chartered Accountant; Simon Lawrence Parsons [1969] Chief Financial Director

LHR Airports Limited
Incorporated: 13 December 1985 *Employees:* 7
Net Worth: £9,772,999,680 *Total Assets:* £11,187,999,744
Registered Office: The Compass Centre, Nelson Road, Hounslow, Middlesex, TW6 2GW
Activities: Scheduled passenger air transport
Parent: Heathrow Holdco Limited
Officers: Ross Findlay Scott Baker [1974] Director; William Stuart Birrell [1964] Director/Chief Information Officer; Javier Echave Espot [1980] Director [Spanish]; Christopher Charles Garton [1961] Director; Charlotte Emma Tiffany Gilthorpe [1970] Director/Employed Barrister; John William Holland Kaye [1965] Director/Chief Executive Officer; Carol Hui [1956] Director/Lawyer; Andrew Hugh Macmillan [1975] Director; Paula Stannett [1965] HR Director

Liberata UK Limited
Incorporated: 22 December 1975 *Employees:* 1,403
Net Worth: £7,627,000 *Total Assets:* £29,794,000
Registered Office: 5th Floor, Knollys House, 17 Addiscombe Road, Croydon, Surrey, CR0 6SR
Activities: Management consultancy activities other than financial management
Parent: Outsourcing UK Limited
Officers: Timothy John Francis Collins, Secretary; Charles Edward Bruin [1971] Business Director; Masaki Motegi [1978] Director [Japanese]; Yuya Ono [1977] Director/General Manager [Japanese]; Robert David Price [1974] Finance Director; Kazuhiko Suzuki [1969] Director [Japanese]; Allan Leigh Wood [1964] Director

Liberty Leasing Limited
Incorporated: 10 October 2001 *Employees:* 49
Previous: Liberty Leasing PLC
Net Worth: £17,456,568 *Total Assets:* £87,941,120
Registered Office: Liberty House, Brook Avenue, Warsash, Southampton, SO31 9HP
Activities: Other credit granting n.e.c.
Shareholder: Anthony Albert Captain
Officers: Alan William Cooper, Secretary; Anthony Albert Captain [1946] Director; Allan Xenophon Clegg [1972] Director; Alan William Cooper [1980] Finance Director; Daniel James Randall [1983] Property Director; Gregory Lawrence Randall [1947] Director; Laura Jane Roberts [1983] Director/Solicitor; Paul Francis Sheedy [1976] Director; Michael David Wilmot Wilkinson [1948] Director/Chartered Accountant

Liberty Property Trust UK Limited
Incorporated: 24 January 2005 *Employees:* 24
Net Worth: £1,298,996 *Total Assets:* £26,697,092
Registered Office: The Control Tower, 29 Liberty Square, Kings Hill, West Malling, Kent, ME19 4RG
Activities: Development of building projects
Parent: Liberty Property Trust
Officers: Andrew Joseph Blevins [1964] Managing Director; Michael Thomas Hagan [1957] Director/Chief Investment Officer [American]; William Paul Hankowsky [1951] Director/Chairman President & CEO [American]; Jane Victoria Harrison [1973] Director/Accountant; Elizabeth Susan Roche [1973] Finance Director

Lighthouse Healthcare Group Limited
Incorporated: 21 March 2014
Net Worth: £11,832,000 *Total Assets:* £45,142,000
Registered Office: 2 Imperial Place, Maxwell Road, Borehamwood, Herts, WD6 1JN
Activities: Activities of head offices
Parent: Elysium Healthcare Holdings 3 Limited
Officers: Sarah Juliette Livingston, Secretary; Lesley Joy Chamberlain [1963] Director/Group Chief Executive; Dr Quazi Shams Mahfooz Haque [1968] Executive Medical Director; Steven John Woolgar [1955] Director of Policy and Regulation

Lilac Limited
Incorporated: 9 July 2004 *Employees:* 207
Net Worth: £10,331,000 *Total Assets:* £24,119,000
Registered Office: Abbots Leigh Place, Slugwash Lane, Haywards Heath, W Sussex, RH17 7SS
Activities: Machining
Major Shareholder: Ian Curtis
Officers: Ian Curtis, Secretary/Accountant; Ian Curtis [1968] Director/Accountant; Liza Katharine Curtis [1969] Director/Housewife

Eli Lilly and Company Limited
Incorporated: 5 February 1934 *Employees:* 1,513
Net Worth: £645,555,008 *Total Assets:* £1,206,620,032
Registered Office: Lilly House, Priestley Road, Basingstoke, Hants, RG24 9NL
Activities: Manufacture of basic pharmaceutical products
Parent: Eli Lilly Group Limited
Officers: Hamish John Carmichael Bennett, Secretary; Karen Ann Alexander [1967] Director; Hamish John Carmichael Bennett [1974] Director; Ashley Diaz-Granados [1976] Director/General Manager [American]; Dr Susan Renee Forda [1958] Director/VP Global Regulatory Affairs - International; Nicholas Lemen [1974] Finance Director [American]

Eli Lilly Group Limited
Incorporated: 10 September 1979
Net Worth: £55,074,000 *Total Assets:* £108,451,000
Registered Office: Lilly House, Priestley Road, Basingstoke, Hants, RG24 9NL
Activities: Manufacture of basic pharmaceutical products
Parent: Eli Lilly and Company
Officers: Hamish John Carmichael Bennett, Secretary; Hamish John Carmichael Bennett [1974] Director; Ashley Diaz-Granados [1976] Director/General Manager [American]; Nicholas Lemen [1974] Finance Director [American]

Limay Drilling Rigs Limited
Incorporated: 2 April 2014
Net Worth: £12,410,395 *Total Assets:* £82,636,072
Registered Office: New Kings Court, Tollgate, Chandler's Ford, Eastleigh, Hants, SO53 3LG
Activities: Extraction of crude petroleum
Parent: Archer Assets UK Limited
Officers: Kenneth David Dey [1959] Managing Director/Platform Drilling Manager; Espen Joranger [1977] Director/Group Controller [Norwegian]; Adam Mark Alexander Todd [1977] Director/Lawyer [Canadian]

Lime Wood Group Limited
Incorporated: 16 July 1999 *Employees:* 260
Net Worth: £19,278,340 *Total Assets:* £45,776,488
Registered Office: Clayhill, Beechen Lane, Lyndhurst, Hants, SO43 7DD
Activities: Hotels and similar accommodation
Major Shareholder: James Arthur Ratcliffe
Officers: Michael John Rice, Secretary; Brian Robert Foster [1957] Director/Chief Executive Officer; Angela Maria Hartnett [1968] Director/Chef Proprietor; Robin Charles Hutson [1957] Director

Limecay Limited
Incorporated: 25 May 2006 *Employees:* 3
Net Worth: £128,116,000 *Total Assets:* £1,621,892,992
Registered Office: New Kings Court, Tollgate, Chandler's Ford, Eastleigh, Hants, SO53 3LG
Activities: Renting and operating of Housing Association real estate
Officers: Alan William Green [1954] Director/Accountant [Irish]; Timothy John Otway [1964] Director/Accountant; Alan Joseph Sherling [1954] Director/Business Consultant [Irish]

Linde Canada Holdings Limited
Incorporated: 26 November 2010
Net Worth: £423,940,992 *Total Assets:* £514,917,760
Registered Office: The Priestley Centre, 10 Priestley Road, Surrey Research Park, Guildford, Surrey, GU2 7XY
Activities: Activities of head offices
Parent: Linde UK Holdings Limited
Officers: Susan Kathleen Kelly, Secretary; Julian Michael Bland [1967] Director/Head of Accounting; Benjamin Patterson [1962] Director/Solicitor; Sally Ann Williams [1970] Director/Accountant

Linde Creighton Limited
Incorporated: 26 February 1993 *Employees:* 333
Net Worth: £18,836,000 *Total Assets:* £43,411,000
Registered Office: Kingsclere Road, Basingstoke, Hants, RG21 6XJ
Activities: Renting and leasing of other machinery, equipment and tangible goods n.e.c.
Parent: Kion Group AG
Officers: Colin Blebta [1964] Director/Company Executive; Eamonn Parker [1978] Director/Vice President, Sales & Marketing; Massimiliano Sammartano [1972] Director [Italian]; David Roger Woodward [1959] Director/Chartered Accountant

Linde Cryogenics Limited
Incorporated: 31 July 1997
Net Worth: £127,160,136 *Total Assets:* £127,236,976
Registered Office: The Priestley Centre, 10 Priestley Road, The Surrey Research Park, Guildford, Surrey, GU2 7XY
Activities: Activities of head offices
Parent: The BOC Group Limited
Officers: Susan Kathleen Kelly, Secretary; Julian Michael Bland [1967] Director/Head of Accounting; Benjamin Patterson [1962] Director/Solicitor; Sally Ann Williams [1970] Director/Accountant

Linde Holdings Limited
Incorporated: 24 February 1966 *Employees:* 1
Net Worth: £117,676,000 *Total Assets:* £202,627,008
Registered Office: Kingsclere Road, Basingstoke, Hants, RG21 6XJ
Activities: Activities of head offices
Parent: Kion Group AG
Officers: Colin Blebta, Secretary; Andreas Ulf Krinninger [1967] Director [German]

Linde Investments No.1 Limited
Incorporated: 26 November 2013
Net Worth: £3,593,204,224 *Total Assets:* £4,556,568,064
Registered Office: The Priestley Centre, 10 Priestley Road, The Surrey Research Park, Guildford, Surrey, GU2 7XY
Activities: Activities of head offices
Parent: The BOC Group Limited
Officers: Susan Kathleen Kelly, Secretary; Julian Michael Bland [1967] Director/Head of Accounting; Benjamin Patterson [1962] Director/Solicitor; Sally Ann Williams [1970] Director/Accountant

Linde Jewsbury's Limited
Incorporated: 19 February 1993 *Employees:* 125
Net Worth: £13,430,000 *Total Assets:* £26,605,000
Registered Office: Kingsclere Road, Basingstoke, Hants, RG21 6XJ
Activities: Renting and leasing of other machinery, equipment and tangible goods n.e.c.
Parent: Kion Group AG
Officers: Colin Blebta [1964] Director/Company Executive; Andrew David Lawton [1966] Managing Director; Eamonn Parker [1978] Director/Vice President, Sales & Marketing; Massimiliano Sammartano [1972] Director [Italian]

Linde Material Handling (UK) Limited
Incorporated: 17 February 1937 *Employees:* 264
Net Worth: £28,231,000 *Total Assets:* £194,840,992
Registered Office: Kingsclere Road, Basingstoke, Hants, RG21 6XJ
Activities: Wholesale of other machinery and equipment
Parent: Kion Group AG
Officers: Colin Blebta [1964] Director/Company Executive; Andreas Ulf Krinninger [1967] Director [German]; Christophe Paul Bernard Lautray [1962] Director/Company Executive [French]; Eamonn Parker [1978] Director/Vice President, Sales & Marketing; Massimiliano Sammartano [1972] Managing Director [Italian]

Linde North America Holdings Limited
Incorporated: 25 June 2012
Net Worth: £1,147,380,736 *Total Assets:* £3,083,053,568
Registered Office: The Priestley Centre, 10 Priestley Road, The Surrey Research Park, Guildford, Surrey, GU2 7XY
Activities: Activities of head offices
Parent: BOC Holdings
Officers: Susan Kathleen Kelly, Secretary; Julian Michael Bland [1967] Director/Head of Accounting; Christopher James Cossins [1966] Director/Tax Manager; Benjamin Patterson [1962] Director/Solicitor; Sally Ann Williams [1970] Director/Accountant

Linde Severnside Limited
Incorporated: 3 October 1997 *Employees:* 119
Net Worth: £9,053,000 *Total Assets:* £20,420,000
Registered Office: Kingsclere Road, Basingstoke, Hants, RG21 6XJ
Activities: Renting and leasing of other machinery, equipment and tangible goods n.e.c.
Parent: Kion Group AG
Officers: Colin Blebta [1964] Director/Company Executive; Peter Daley [1960] Managing Director; Eamonn Parker [1978] Director/Vice President, Sales & Marketing; Massimiliano Sammartano [1972] Director [Italian]

Linde Sterling Limited
Incorporated: 26 February 1993 *Employees:* 324
Net Worth: £13,017,000 *Total Assets:* £28,998,000
Registered Office: Kingsclere Road, Basingstoke, Hants, RG21 6XJ
Activities: Renting and leasing of other machinery, equipment and tangible goods n.e.c.
Parent: Kion Group AG
Officers: Colin Blebta [1964] Director/Company Executive; Sammartano Massimiliano [1973] Director [Italian]; Eamonn Parker [1978] Director/Vice President, Sales & Marketing; Craig Williamson [1981] Managing Director

Linde UK Holdings Limited
Incorporated: 6 August 2007 *Employees:* 5
Net Worth: £15,181,339,648 *Total Assets:* £17,694,590,976
Registered Office: The Priestley Centre, 10 Priestley Road, The Surrey Research Park, Guildford, Surrey, GU2 7XY
Activities: Activities of head offices
Parent: Linde Public Limited Company
Officers: Susan Kathleen Kelly, Secretary; Julian Michael Bland [1967] Director/Head of Accounting; Benjamin Patterson [1962] Director/Solicitor; Sally Ann Williams [1970] Director/Accountant

Linden (Avery Hill) LLP
Incorporated: 1 August 2016
Net Worth: £579,000 *Total Assets:* £32,658,000
Registered Office: Cowley Business Park, Cowley, Uxbridge, Middlesex, UB8 2AL

Linden (Biddenham) LLP
Incorporated: 24 June 2015
Net Worth: £599,000 *Total Assets:* £23,149,000
Registered Office: Cowley Business Park, Cowley, Uxbridge, Middlesex, UB8 2AL

Linden (Brampton) LLP
Incorporated: 27 July 2016
Net Worth Deficit: £253,000 *Total Assets:* £33,835,000
Registered Office: Cowley Business Park, Cowley, Uxbridge, Middlesex, UB8 2AL

Linden (Enfield) LLP
Incorporated: 11 July 2016
Net Worth Deficit: £1,121,000 *Total Assets:* £39,953,000
Registered Office: Cowley Business Park, Cowley, Uxbridge, Middlesex, UB8 2AL

Linden (Northstowe) LLP
Incorporated: 19 July 2016
Net Worth: £592,000 *Total Assets:* £41,094,000
Registered Office: Cowley Business Park, Cowley, Uxbridge, Middlesex, UB8 2AL

Linden Germany A Limited
Incorporated: 7 November 1994 *Employees:* 3
Net Worth: £187,449,376 *Total Assets:* £221,846,352
Registered Office: 103-105 Bath Road, Slough, Berks, SL1 3UH
Activities: Activities of other holding companies n.e.c.
Parent: Reckitt Benckiser (UK) Limited
Officers: Christine Anne-Marie Logan, Secretary; Arnoud Hensing [1973] Director/Accountant Holdings NL, Finance [Dutch]; Matus Rajnak [1971] Finance Director [Slovak]; Adrian Enno Weis [1969] Finance Director [German]

Linden Germany B Limited
Incorporated: 7 November 1994 *Employees:* 3
Net Worth: £199,076,384 *Total Assets:* £249,152,752
Registered Office: 103-105 Bath Road, Slough, Berks, SL1 3UH
Activities: Activities of other holding companies n.e.c.
Parent: Reckitt Benckiser (UK) Limited
Officers: Christine Anne-Marie Logan, Secretary; Arnoud Hensing [1973] Director/Accountant Holdings NL, Finance [Dutch]; Matus Rajnak [1971] Finance Director [Slovak]; Adrian Enno Weis [1969] Finance Director [German]

Linden Homes (Sherford) LLP
Incorporated: 18 April 2013
Previous: Sherford Developments LLP
Net Worth Deficit: £3,171,000 *Total Assets:* £85,858,000
Registered Office: Cowley Business Park, Cowley, Uxbridge, Middlesex, UB8 2AL

Linden Limited
Incorporated: 16 April 1973 *Employees:* 989
Net Worth: £200,251,008 *Total Assets:* £1,588,732,032
Registered Office: Cowley Business Park, Cowley, Uxbridge, Middlesex, UB8 2AL
Activities: Construction of commercial buildings
Parent: Galliford Try Homes Limited
Officers: Andrew James Duxbury [1975] Director/Accountant; Andrew Richard Hammond [1970] Director; Tom Marshall Nicholson [1965] Director; Stephen John Teagle [1959] Director; Peter Martin Truscott [1962] Director

Linden St Albans LLP
Incorporated: 26 June 2008
Net Worth: £21,091,000 *Total Assets:* £22,389,000
Registered Office: Cowley Business Park, Cowley, Uxbridge, Middlesex, UB8 2AL

Linden Wates (Royston) LLP
Incorporated: 10 May 2017
Net Worth Deficit: £79,000 *Total Assets:* £41,105,000
Registered Office: Cowley Business Park, Cowley, Uxbridge, Middlesex, UB8 2AL

Linden/Downland Graylingwell LLP
Incorporated: 19 December 2007
Net Worth Deficit: £62,867,000 *Total Assets:* £69,750,000
Registered Office: Cowley Business Park, Cowley, Uxbridge, Middlesex, UB8 2AL

Lindt & Sprungli (U.K.) Limited
Incorporated: 20 June 1932 *Employees:* 331
Net Worth: £23,421,000 *Total Assets:* £87,928,000
Registered Office: Top Floor, 4 New Square, Bedfont Lakes, Feltham, Middlesex, TW14 8HA
Activities: Wholesale of sugar and chocolate and sugar confectionery
Parent: Chocoladefabriken Lindt & Sprungli AG
Officers: Alain Germiquet [1971] Director/Group Management Member [Swiss]; Dieter Weisskopf [1955] Director

Link Asset Services (Holdings) Limited
Incorporated: 12 July 2005 *Employees:* 1
Previous: Capita International Financial Services Holdings Limited
Net Worth: £44,999,328 *Total Assets:* £133,232,328
Registered Office: The Registry, 34 Beckenham Road, Beckenham, Kent, BR3 4TU
Activities: Other business support service activities n.e.c.
Parent: Link Market Services (EMEA) Limited
Officers: Jacqueline Millan [1966] Finance Director [Canadian]; Howard Alan Montagu [1970] Director; Anthony Patrick O'Keeffe [1965] Director

Link Market Services Limited
Incorporated: 26 April 1991 *Employees:* 906
Previous: Capita Registrars Limited
Net Worth: £47,041,840 *Total Assets:* £131,760,304
Registered Office: The Registry, 34 Beckenham Road, Beckenham, Kent, BR3 4TU
Activities: Other business support service activities n.e.c.
Parent: Link Market Services (EMEA) Limited
Officers: Justin Ashley Cooper [1969] Managing Director; Nigel Timothy Fish [1967] Finance Director; Michael John Kempe [1970] Director [German]; David John Kilmartin [1968] Director; Graham Philip Renn [1957] Director

Link Market Services Trustees Limited
Incorporated: 7 July 1992 *Employees:* 238
Previous: Capita IRG Trustees Limited
Net Worth: £23,336,708 *Total Assets:* £26,423,796
Registered Office: The Registry, 34 Beckenham Road, Beckenham, Kent, BR3 4TU
Activities: Other service activities n.e.c.
Parent: Link Market Services (EMEA) Limited
Officers: Justin Ashley Cooper [1969] Managing Director; Nigel Timothy Fish [1967] Finance Director; Maureen Hadaway [1957] Director; Michael John Kempe [1970] Director [German]; Nicholas Michael Sharrock [1963] Director; Antony John Stuart [1952] Director

Linton Park Public Limited Company
Incorporated: 27 June 1957 *Employees:* 23
Net Worth: £56,561,352 *Total Assets:* £133,432,264
Registered Office: Linton Park, Linton, Maidstone, Kent, ME17 4AN
Activities: Activities of head offices
Parent: Camellia PLC
Officers: Amarpal Takk, Secretary; Thomas Kenric Franks [1963] Director; Malcolm Courtney Perkins [1945] Director/Chartered Accountant; Susan Ann Walker [1967] Director

Lionel Road Developments Ltd
Incorporated: 24 March 2006
Net Worth: £1,729,939 *Total Assets:* £34,820,496
Registered Office: Griffin Park, Braemar Road, Brentford, Middlesex, TW8 0NT
Activities: Buying and selling of own real estate
Parent: Brentford FC Ltd
Officers: Clifford Crown [1956] Finance Director; Conor Hayes [1954] Director/Corporate Adviser [Irish]

The Little Group Limited
Incorporated: 5 September 1996 *Employees:* 1,218
Net Worth: £85,498,368 *Total Assets:* £147,676,880
Registered Office: 1 Whittle Drive, Eastbourne, E Sussex, BN23 6QH
Activities: Other service activities n.e.c.
Shareholders: Yvette Jane Stafford; Andrew Thomas Little; Jonathan James Little
Officers: Andrew Thomas Little [1960] Director; Jonathan James Little [1965] Managing Director; Yvette Jane Stafford [1961] Director

LKQ Euro Limited
Incorporated: 20 September 2011
Net Worth: £685,838,976 *Total Assets:* £977,774,976
Registered Office: 1 London Street, Reading, Berks, RG1 4QW
Activities: Activities of head offices
Officers: Andrew Hamilton [1974] Operations Director; Joseph Holsten [1952] Director/Chairman [American]; John Quinn [1958] Director/Executive Vice President and Chief Financial Officer [Canadian]; Dominick Paul Zarcone [1958] Director/President and CEO [American]

Local Car and Van Rental Limited
Incorporated: 15 May 2006 *Employees:* 29
Net Worth: £9,520,811 *Total Assets:* £79,721,456
Registered Office: 2 Redman Court, Bell Street, Princes Risborough, Bucks, HP27 0AA
Activities: Sale of new cars and light motor vehicles
Shareholders: John Patrick Ryan; Karen Ryan
Officers: Karen Ryan, Secretary; John Lewis Davies [1949] Director; Guy Jonathan Easton [1956] Director; Shaun Parnaby [1968] Director; Owain Ashley Price [1971] Sales and Marketing Director; John Patrick Ryan [1961] Director

Lockheed Martin Helicopter Company Ltd
Incorporated: 13 October 2015
Net Worth: £196,780,000 *Total Assets:* £202,123,808
Registered Office: Legal Counsel, Building 7000, Langstone Technology Park, Langstone, Hants, PO9 1SW
Activities: Other engineering activities
Parent: Lockheed Martin UK Holdings Limited
Officers: Marian Susan Block, Secretary; Marian Susan Block [1953] Director/Attorney [American]; Jonathan Murray Diamond [1957] Director/Business Executive; Stephen Michael Piper [1956] Director/Attorney [American]

Lockheed Martin UK Ampthill Group Limited
Incorporated: 15 January 2001
Net Worth: £6,045,000 *Total Assets:* £33,037,000
Registered Office: Reddings Wood, Ampthill, Bedford, MK45 2HD
Activities: Activities of head offices
Parent: Lockheed Martin UK Holdings Limited
Officers: David Arms Heywood, Secretary; James Joseph Glaub [1963] Director/Business Executive [American]; Neil Martin Hebron [1962] Director/Engineer; Alan Edward Lines [1958] Managing Director; Peter William David Ruddock [1954] Director/Business Executive; Michael Eric Williamson [1960] Director/Business Executive [American]

Lockheed Martin UK Ampthill Limited
Incorporated: 20 June 1957 *Employees:* 791
Net Worth Deficit: £59,863,000 *Total Assets:* £109,705,000
Registered Office: Reddings Wood, Ampthill, Beds, MK45 2HD
Activities: Manufacture of military fighting vehicles
Parent: Lockheed Martin UK Ampthill Group
Officers: David Arms Heywood, Secretary; James Joseph Glaub [1963] Director/Business Executive [American]; Neil Martin Hebron [1962] Director/Engineer; Alan Edward Lines [1958] Managing Director; Peter William David Ruddock [1954] Director/Business Executive; Michael Eric Williamson [1960] Director/Business Executive [American]

Lockheed Martin UK Holdings Limited
Incorporated: 12 April 1996
Net Worth: £410,401,984 *Total Assets:* £410,401,984
Registered Office: Building 7000, Langstone Technology Park, Langstone, Havant, Hants, PO9 1SW
Activities: Activities of head offices
Parent: Lockheed Martin Corporation
Officers: Chanel Maelia Bradden, Secretary; Jeffrey K. Fasick, Secretary; David Arms Heywood, Secretary; Alan Edward Lines [1958] Director/Business Executive; John Wesley Mollard [1957] Director/Business Executive [American]; Peter William David Ruddock [1954] Director/Business Executive

Lockheed Martin UK Limited
Incorporated: 17 April 1989 *Employees:* 694
Net Worth: £135,230,000 *Total Assets:* £271,347,008
Registered Office: Building 7000, Langstone Technology Park, Langstone, Havant, Hants, PO9 1SW
Activities: Other professional, scientific and technical activities n.e.c.
Parent: Lockheed Martin UK Holdings Limited
Officers: Chanel Maelia Bradden, Secretary; Jonathan Murray Diamond [1957] Director/Business Executive; Paul Nmn Lemmo [1965] Director/Business Executive [American]; Peter William David Ruddock [1954] Director/Business Executive

Lodge Bros. (Funerals) Limited
Incorporated: 1 January 1965 *Employees:* 156
Net Worth: £7,316,040 *Total Assets:* £25,171,020
Registered Office: Ludlow House, Ludlow Road, Feltham, Middlesex, TW13 7JF
Activities: Funeral and related activities
Officers: Michael Lodge, Secretary; Beverley Ann Harris [1960] Director; Andrew John Lodge [1969] Director; Christopher David Lodge [1970] Director; Janet Rachel Lodge [1969] Director; Michael James Lodge [1966] Financial Director; Robert John Lodge [1965] Director

Loesche Energy Systems Limited
Incorporated: 19 January 2006 *Employees:* 32
Net Worth: £5,469,537 *Total Assets:* £23,197,602
Registered Office: Ashurst, Broadlands Business Park, Langhurstwood Road, Horsham, W Sussex, RH12 4QP
Activities: Manufacture of other general-purpose machinery n.e.c.
Major Shareholder: Thomas Loesche
Officers: Daniel Hughes [1980] Finance Director; Ruediger Nikolaus Kleusch [1963] Director/Corporate Finance Manager [German]; Frans-Josef Mors [1956] Director/Mechanical Engineer [German]; Ruediger Zerbe [1965] Director [German]

Logicalis Group Limited
Incorporated: 12 June 2000 *Employees:* 4,394
Net Worth: £209,068,064 *Total Assets:* £970,493,824
Registered Office: 110 Buckingham Avenue, Slough, Berks, SL1 4PF
Activities: Activities of head offices
Parent: Datatec PLC
Officers: Mark Grant, Secretary; Robert Broncho Bailkoski [1975] Director/Accountant; Ivan Philip Dittrich [1972] Director/Chief Financial Officer [South African]; Jens Peter Montanana [1960] Director; Carlos Alberto Moller Pingarilho [1970] Director/Engineer [Brazilian]; Stuart Edward Radcliffe [1965] Director/Chief Financial Officer; Mark Rogers [1958] Finance Director

Logicalis UK Limited
Incorporated: 10 March 1999 *Employees:* 387
Net Worth: £11,306,000 *Total Assets:* £69,739,000
Registered Office: 110 Buckingham Avenue, Slough, Berks, SL1 4PF
Activities: Other telecommunications activities
Parent: Logicalis Group Limited
Officers: Leopoldo Dal Bianco, Secretary; Robert Broncho Bailkoski [1975] Director; Stuart Edward Radcliffe [1965] Finance Director; Ruediger Rath [1966] Director/Head of Europe [German]; Mark Rogers [1958] Finance Director; Robert Ian James Swallow [1958] Managing Director

Logoplaste UK Limited
Incorporated: 1 September 1999 *Employees:* 228
Net Worth: £18,457,846 *Total Assets:* £35,195,872
Registered Office: Suite 7, East Wing, 100 Longwater Avenue, Reading, Berks, RG2 6GP
Activities: Manufacture of plastic packing goods
Parent: Logoplaste UK Parent Limited
Officers: Filipe Mauricio de Botton [1958] Director [Portuguese]; Luis Guedes Da Cruz Almeida [1978] Director [Portuguese]; Stephen John Mancey [1960] Director

Logoplaste UK Parent Limited
Incorporated: 18 March 2016 *Employees:* 1
Net Worth: £95,799,408 *Total Assets:* £169,986,128
Registered Office: Suite 7, East Wing, 100 Longwater Avenue, Reading, Berks, RG2 6GP
Activities: Activities of other holding companies n.e.c.
Officers: Filipe de Botton [1958] Director [Portuguese]; Luis Guedes Da Cruz Almeida [1978] Director [Portuguese]; Stephen John Mancey [1960] Director

London Airports 1992 Limited
Incorporated: 3 August 1992
Net Worth: £996,345,984 *Total Assets:* £1,026,076,032
Registered Office: The Compass Centre, Nelson Road, Hounslow, Middlesex, TW6 2GW
Activities: Activities of head offices
Parent: LHR Airports Limited
Officers: Yuanyuan Ding [1979] Director; Javier Echave Espot [1980] Director [Spanish]; Nicholas Francis Golding [1963] Director

London Arena Investments Limited
Incorporated: 16 November 2012
Net Worth: £59,036,132 *Total Assets:* £59,096,132
Registered Office: World Business Centre, 3 Newall Road, London Heathrow Airport, Hounslow, Middlesex, TW6 2TA
Activities: Activities of other holding companies n.e.c.
Parent: Grove Acquisitions Limited
Officers: Athos George Yiannis, Secretary; Surinder Arora [1958] Director; Carlton Jeffrey Brown [1972] Director/Chartered Accountant; Athos George Yiannis [1963] Director/Chartered Accountant

London Britannia Hotel Limited
Incorporated: 18 December 1962 *Employees:* 235
Net Worth: £76,620,000 *Total Assets:* £86,241,000
Registered Office: Victoria House, Victoria Road, Horley, Surrey, RH6 7AF
Activities: Hotels and similar accommodation
Parent: Millennium Hotels Limited
Officers: Jonathon MacKenzie Grech [1977] Director/Senior VP Group Legal Counsel; Leng Beng Kwek [1941] Director [Singaporean]

London Care Partnership Limited
Incorporated: 9 January 2007 *Employees:* 207
Net Worth: £14,114,941 *Total Assets:* £26,390,636
Registered Office: c/o Elysium Healthcare, 2 Imperial Place, Maxwell Road, Borehamwood, Herts, WD6 1JN
Activities: Other residential care activities n.e.c.
Parent: Careprogress Limited
Officers: Sarah Juliette Livingston, Secretary; Lesley Joy Chamberlain [1963] Director/Group Chief Executive; Dr Quazi Shams Mahfooz Haque [1968] Executive Medical Director; Steven John Woolgar [1955] Director of Policy and Regulation

London General Insurance Company Limited
Incorporated: 22 November 1984 *Employees:* 1
Net Worth: £126,461,000 *Total Assets:* £472,912,000
Registered Office: Twenty Kingston Road, Staines upon Thames, Surrey, TW18 4LG
Activities: Non-life insurance
Parent: TWG Europe Limited
Officers: Natalie Ann Paddock, Secretary; George Derek Wilson Bartlett [1948] Director; Michael John Carter [1981] Director; Colin Martin Kersley [1956] Director; Ricardo Jesus Morales-Gomez [1970] Director [American]; Andrew James Morris [1971] Director/Chief Executive Officer; Claude Kwasi Sarfo-Agyare [1969] Director

London International Group Limited
Incorporated: 15 November 1950
Net Worth: £480,735,008 *Total Assets:* £603,320,000
Registered Office: 103-105 Bath Road, Slough, Berks, SL1 3UH
Activities: Activities of other holding companies n.e.c.
Parent: Sonet Prebbles Limited
Officers: Christine Anne-Marie Logan, Secretary; Richard Mark Greensmith [1973] Group Tax Director; Simon Andrew Neville [1957] Group Treasury Director; Jonathan Timmis [1975] Finance Director

London Irish Holdings Limited
Incorporated: 1 April 1997 *Employees:* 89
Net Worth: £7,340,591 *Total Assets:* £21,320,320
Registered Office: Hazelwood, Hazelwood Drive, Sunbury on Thames, Middlesex, TW16 6QU
Activities: Activities of head offices
Parent: London Irish Consortium (2013) Limited
Officers: Paul Forsyth, Secretary; Mark Laurence Bensted [1958] Director; Michael Rowland Crossan [1956] Director; Brian William Ernest Facer [1970] Director/Chief Executive; Nigel Northridge [1956] Director; Michael O'Hagan [1964] Director [Irish]; Allan Robson [1954] Director; Jonathan Robert Turner [1975] Director [Irish]

London May Fair Hotel Limited
Incorporated: 17 July 2003 *Employees:* 483
Net Worth: £367,048,992 *Total Assets:* £550,019,968
Registered Office: 140 Bath Road, Hayes, Middlesex, UB3 5AW
Activities: Hotels and similar accommodation
Parent: Edwardian Hotel Finance Ltd
Officers: Vijay Wason, Secretary; John Robert Morley [1945] Director/Financial Consultant; Inderneel Singh [1984] Director; Jasminder Singh [1951] Director/Hotelier; Vijay Wason [1948] Director/Company Secretary

London Pharma & Chemicals Holdings Ltd
Incorporated: 18 November 2009 *Employees:* 135
Net Worth: £18,496,670 *Total Assets:* £35,091,484
Registered Office: Unit 10 Delta Court, Manor Way, Borehamwood, Herts, WD6 1FJ
Activities: Activities of head offices
Shareholders: Claire Joanne Sharon Straus; Daniel Reuben Straus
Officers: Claire Joanne Sharon Straus [1969] Director; Daniel Reuben Straus [1972] Director/Business Manager

London Residential Healthcare Limited
Incorporated: 18 February 1997 *Employees:* 796
Net Worth: £43,950,320 *Total Assets:* £78,004,168
Registered Office: 12-14 Langley Avenue, Surbiton, Surrey, KT6 6QL
Activities: Development of building projects
Parent: LRH Care Homes Limited
Officers: Eirik Peter Robson [1958] Director; Arnon Nir Rubinstein [1964] Director

London Square (Fulham) Limited
Incorporated: 27 September 2011
Net Worth: £17,429,564 *Total Assets:* £29,057,560
Registered Office: One York Road, Uxbridge, Middlesex, UB8 1RN
Activities: Development of building projects
Parent: London Square Developments (Ventures) Ltd
Officers: Adam Paul Lawrence, Secretary; Scott Douglas Brown [1968] Director [Australian]; Mark Stewart Evans [1969] Director/Chief Operating Officer; Adam Paul Lawrence [1970] Director

London Square (Holdings) Limited
Incorporated: 16 February 2010
Net Worth: £27,498,476 *Total Assets:* £27,528,478
Registered Office: One York Road, Uxbridge, Middlesex, UB8 1RN
Activities: Development of building projects
Parent: London Square Developments (Ventures) Ltd
Officers: Adam Lawrence, Secretary; Scott Douglas Brown [1968] Director [Australian]; Mark Stewart Evans [1969] Director/Chief Operating Officer; Adam Paul Lawrence [1970] Director

London Square (Putney) Limited
Incorporated: 10 May 2011
Net Worth: £23,652,620 *Total Assets:* £32,865,840
Registered Office: One York Road, Uxbridge, Middlesex, UB8 1RN
Activities: Development of building projects
Parent: London Square Developments Ltd
Officers: Adam Lawrence, Secretary; Scott Douglas Brown [1968] Director [Australian]; Mark Stewart Evans [1969] Director/Chief Operating Officer; Steven Simon Hudson [1970] Commercial Director; Adam Paul Lawrence [1970] Director; Rebecca Susan Littler [1982] Sales and Marketing Director; Andy Maciejewski [1965] Construction Director; Matthew Steven Phillips [1979] Technical Director; Mark Clive Smith [1973] Development and Technical Director

London Square (Streatham) Limited
Incorporated: 18 June 2013
Net Worth: £17,003,000 *Total Assets:* £37,852,000
Registered Office: One York Road, Uxbridge, Middlesex, UB8 1RN
Activities: Development of building projects
Parent: London Square (Investments) Ltd
Officers: Adam Lawrence, Secretary; Scott Douglas Brown [1968] Director [Australian]; Mark Stewart Evans [1969] Director/Chief Operating Officer; Steven Simon Hudson [1970] Commercial Director; Adam Paul Lawrence [1970] Director; Rebecca Susan Littler [1982] Sales and Marketing Director; Andy Maciejewski [1965] Construction Director; Matthew Steven Phillips [1979] Technical Director; Mark Clive Smith [1973] Development and Technical Director

London Square Developments (Holdings) Limited
Incorporated: 20 June 2014 *Employees:* 142
Net Worth Deficit: £59,871,000 *Total Assets:* £496,519,008
Registered Office: One York Road, Uxbridge, Middlesex, UB8 1RN
Activities: Construction of domestic buildings
Parent: LSQ Holdings (Luxembourg) SARL
Officers: William Stephen Benjamin [1964] Director [American]; Scott Douglas Brown [1968] Director [Australian]; Mark Buckland [1960] Director [American]; Stephen Charles Casey [1949] Director; Mark Stewart Evans [1969] Director/Chief Operating Officer; Adam Paul Lawrence [1970] Director; Mark Andrew Pain [1961] Director; Charles Richard Arklay Steel [1975] Director; William Gowanloch Westbrook [1976] Director

London Square Developments (Ventures) Limited
Incorporated: 15 September 2011 *Employees:* 142
Net Worth: £98,451,000 *Total Assets:* £473,415,008
Registered Office: One York Road, Uxbridge, Middlesex, UB8 1RN
Activities: Development of building projects
Parent: London Square Ltd
Officers: Adam Paul Lawrence, Secretary; Scott Douglas Brown [1968] Director [Australian]; Mark Stewart Evans [1969] Director/Chief Operating Officer; Adam Paul Lawrence [1970] Director

London Square Developments Limited
Incorporated: 17 February 2010 *Employees:* 142
Net Worth Deficit: £17,185,000 *Total Assets:* £370,248,000
Registered Office: One York Road, Uxbridge, Middlesex, UB8 1RN
Activities: Development of building projects
Parent: London Square (Holdings) Ltd
Officers: Adam Lawrence, Secretary; Scott Douglas Brown [1968] Director [Australian]; Mark Stewart Evans [1969] Director/Chief Operating Officer; Steven Simon Hudson [1970] Commercial Director; Adam Paul Lawrence [1970] Director; Rebecca Susan Littler [1982] Sales and Marketing Director; Andy Maciejewski [1965] Construction Director; Matthew Steven Phillips [1979] Technical Director; Mark Clive Smith [1973] Development and Technical Director

London Square Limited
Incorporated: 14 September 2011 *Employees:* 142
Net Worth: £157,144,992 *Total Assets:* £460,803,008
Registered Office: One York Road, Uxbridge, Middlesex, UB8 1RN
Activities: Development of building projects
Parent: LSQ Holdco 3 Ltd
Officers: Adam Paul Lawrence, Secretary; Scott Douglas Brown [1968] Director [Australian]; Stephen Charles Casey [1949] Director/Executive; Mark Stewart Evans [1969] Director/Chief Operating Officer; Steven Simon Hudson [1970] Commercial Director; Adam Paul Lawrence [1970] Director; Rebecca Susan Littler [1982] Sales & Marketing Director; Andy Maciejewski [1965] Construction Director; Mark Andrew Pain [1961] Director; Matthew Steven Phillips [1979] Technical Director; Mark Clive Smith [1973] Development Director

London Tara Hotel Limited
Incorporated: 22 March 1971 *Employees:* 308
Net Worth: £64,564,000 *Total Assets:* £75,439,000
Registered Office: Victoria House, Victoria Road, Horley, Surrey, RH6 7AF
Activities: Hotels and similar accommodation
Parent: Copthorne Hotel Holdings Limited
Officers: Jonathon MacKenzie Grech [1977] Director/Senior VP Group Legal Counsel

London Tower Crane Hire & Sales Limited
Incorporated: 25 April 2003 *Employees:* 58
Net Worth: £21,214,614 *Total Assets:* £46,363,016
Registered Office: 4 Elstree Way, Borehamwood, Herts, WD6 1RN
Activities: Renting and leasing of construction and civil engineering machinery and equipment
Parent: JRL Group Ltd
Officers: Ronan Joseph Gleeson, Secretary/Director [Irish]; Ronan Joseph Gleeson [1976] Director [Irish]; Martin Harvey [1972] Director/Operations Manager; Kevin William Keegan [1963] Director/Estimator [Irish]; John James Reddington [1972] Director/Formwork [Irish]

London United Busways Limited
Incorporated: 14 December 1988 *Employees:* 2,556
Net Worth: £47,625,000 *Total Assets:* £75,454,000
Registered Office: Busways House, Wellington Road, Twickenham, Middlesex, TW2 5NX
Activities: Other urban, suburban or metropolitan passenger land transport (not underground, metro or similar)
Parent: RATP DEV UK Ltd
Officers: Catherine Marie-Jeanne Chardon [1970] Transformation Director [French]; Romain Ferriere [1975] Director/Chief Financial Officer [French]; Karen Rose Fuller [1968] HR Director; Howard Charles Goodbourn [1961] Director/Chief Financial Officer; David Andrew Kaye [1962] Director; Kuldeep Singh Nothey [1965] Service Delivery Director; Peter Richardson [1974] Finance Director; Florence Rodet [1969] Director/Secretary General - Public Relations [French]; Fiona Jacqueline Taylor [1962] Managing Director

London Vista Hotel Limited
Incorporated: 9 September 1997 *Employees:* 605
Net Worth: £14,480,000 *Total Assets:* £143,279,008
Registered Office: Corus House, 1 Auckland Park, Milton Keynes, Bucks, MK1 1BU
Activities: Hotels and similar accommodation
Parent: Malayan United Industries
Officers: Khurram Mohmand, Secretary; Andrew Khoo [1972] Director [Australian]; Yet King Loy [1946] Director [Canadian]; Khurram Mohmand [1972] Director/Accountant

Lonepiper Limited
Incorporated: 5 September 2006 *Employees:* 438
Net Worth: £2,290,759 *Total Assets:* £30,743,972
Registered Office: The Pavilion, Botleigh Grange Business Park, Hedge End, Southampton, SO30 2AF
Activities: Other business support service activities n.e.c.
Shareholders: Christopher Osgood Philip Hanbury; Hugo Duncan Thomas Torquil MacKenzie Smith
Officers: Hugo Duncan Thomas Torquil MacKenzie Smith [1972] Director

Longacres Garden Centre Limited
Incorporated: 1 July 2011 *Employees:* 373
Net Worth: £16,576,855 *Total Assets:* £26,421,984
Registered Office: Longacres Nursery, London Road, Bagshot, Surrey, GU19 5JB
Activities: Retail sale of flowers, plants, seeds, fertilizers, pet animals and pet food in specialised stores
Officers: Julie Margaret Erridge [1965] Director; Carol Jane Long [1962] Director; Nigel Peter Long [1968] Director; Peter John Long [1932] Director

Longsand Limited
Incorporated: 22 November 2002
Net Worth: £211,681,248 *Total Assets:* £233,113,728
Registered Office: Cain Road, Amen Corner, Bracknell, Berks, RG12 1HN
Activities: Other information technology service activities
Parent: Micro Focus International PLC
Officers: Ian Cumming Fraser [1961] Director/Chief Human Resources Officer; Christopher John Kennedy [1964] Director/Chief Financial Officer; Stephen Edward Murdoch [1966] Director/Chief Executive Officer; Richard Paul Rodgers [1963] Director/Chief Operating Officer [Irish]

Longview Holding Parent UK Limited
Incorporated: 18 December 2014 *Employees:* 187
Net Worth Deficit: £37,752,428 *Total Assets:* £47,795,592
Registered Office: Nexus House, Station Road, Egham, Surrey, TW20 9LB
Activities: Business and domestic software development
Officers: Nick Kaiser [1976] Director/Private Equity [American]; Grant Bennett Schachter [1964] Director/Private Equity [American]; Michael Edward Wilkinson [1986] Director/Private Equity

Longview Holding UK 2 Limited
Incorporated: 14 April 2014
Net Worth: £18,459,710 *Total Assets:* £25,975,620
Registered Office: Nexus House, Station Road, Egham, Surrey, TW20 9LB
Activities: Business and domestic software development
Parent: Longview Holding UK Limited
Officers: Jerome Jon Dolinsky [1965] Director [American]; Nick Kaiser [1976] Director/Private Equity [American]; Grant Bennett Schachter [1984] Director/Private Equity [American]; Michael Edward Wilkinson [1986] Director/Private Equity

Michael Lonsdale Limited
Incorporated: 28 September 2004 *Employees:* 159
Net Worth: £6,999,101 *Total Assets:* £92,284,232
Registered Office: 1 Langley Quay, Waterside Drive, Langley, Berks, SL3 6EY
Activities: Plumbing, heat and air-conditioning installation
Officers: Michael John Hoodless, Secretary/Building Services Contractor; Kevin Francis Feerick [1959] Director/Mechanical Services Engineer; Panayiotis Hadjioannou [1959] Director/Contracts Manager; Mark Darvil Heath [1971] Director/Engineer; Gary Alfred Herbert [1962] Director/Building Services Contractor; Michael John Hoodless [1958] Director/Building Services Contractor; Anu Kohli [1964] Finance Director

Michael J. Lonsdale Limited
Incorporated: 22 October 1986 *Employees:* 133
Net Worth: £7,046,797 *Total Assets:* £90,222,120
Registered Office: Unit 1 Langley Quay, Waterside Drive, Langley, Berks, SL3 6EY
Activities: Plumbing, heat and air-conditioning installation
Parent: Michael Lonsdale Limited
Officers: Michael John Hoodless, Secretary/Environmental Engineer/Building; Kevin Francis Feerick [1959] Director/Mechanical Services Engineer; Panayiotis Hadjioannou [1959] Director/Contracts Manager; Mark Darvil Heath [1971] Director/Engineering; Gary Alfred Herbert [1962] Director/Building Services Contractor; Michael John Hoodless [1958] Director/Building Services Contractor; Anu Kohli [1964] Finance Director

Lonza Biologics PLC
Incorporated: 25 August 1992 *Employees:* 652
Net Worth: £77,179,000 *Total Assets:* £144,699,008
Registered Office: 228 Bath Road, Slough, Berks, SL1 4DX
Activities: Other service activities n.e.c.
Parent: Lonza Group UK Ltd
Officers: Gerard Kennedy, Secretary; Michael Edward Brown [1959] Director/Operations Manager; Nick Carter [1981] Director/Financial Controller; Edward Garfield [1978] Director/Financial Controller; Ralf Manfred Geier-Cibin [1962] Director/Head of Corporate Controlling [German]

Lord Wandsworth College
Incorporated: 1 August 2011 *Employees:* 189
Net Worth: £31,465,228 *Total Assets:* £50,147,784
Registered Office: Lord Wandsworth College, Long Sutton, Hook, Hants, RG29 1TB
Activities: General secondary education
Officers: Caroline Cazenove [1948] Director; Simon Antony Clements [1959] Director/Crown Prosecutor; Lucinda Jane Fleming [1960] Director; Nicholas Clive Goulding [1948] Director/Chartered Accountant; Daniel Robert Gowan [1951] Director/Solicitor [New Zealander]; Robert James Hannington [1955] Director/Chartered Surveyor; Rachael Jane Henshilwood [1974] Director/Fundraiser; Richard George Janaway [1945] Director/Farmer; Alasdair John Samuel Kennedy [1973] Director/Teacher; Timothy Richard Prideaux [1946] Director/Consultant; Dr Niall Jervis Riddell [1952] Director/Retired Doctor; James Peyton Robinson [1953] Director; Mark Stephen Eagle Scoggins [1957] Director/Solicitor Advocate; David Walter Watts [1949] Director

Lotus Flower Holdings Limited
Incorporated: 4 December 2013 *Employees:* 2,472
Net Worth: £33,848,784 *Total Assets:* £65,505,608
Registered Office: Jetha House, Unit 5 Auriol Drive, Greenford Park, Greenford, Middlesex, UB6 0TP
Activities: Activities of head offices
Major Shareholder: Leena Avnish Malde
Officers: Leena Malde, Secretary; Avnish Amritlal Malde [1965] Director; Leena Avnish Malde [1966] Director

Lotus Leisure Ltd
Incorporated: 1 November 1995 *Employees:* 35
Net Worth: £47,775,764 *Total Assets:* £82,010,008
Registered Office: The Old Stables, Foxhole Lane, Wadhurst, E Sussex, TN5 6NB
Activities: Other reservation service activities n.e.c.
Parent: Lotus Group Limited
Officers: Christine Burrowes, Secretary; Christine Burrowes [1948] Director; Anthony Howard Griffiths [1965] Director/Travel Agent; John Christopher Phelps [1949] Director; George Ross [1952] Director; Pam Spratt [1959] Personnel Director; Peter Anthony Stephens [1950] Director; David Whittaker [1979] Sales Director; Sarah Wilson [1965] Hotel Product Director

Lousada Investments Limited
Incorporated: 16 September 2014 *Employees:* 2
Net Worth: £923,069 *Total Assets:* £31,533,344
Registered Office: Estate Office, Oakley House, The Drive, Church Lane, Oakley, Bedford, MK43 7ST
Activities: Buying and selling of own real estate
Parent: Lousada Investments Holdings Limited
Officers: Sharon Anne Hunt, Secretary; Simon Charles Lousada [1963] Director; Susan Jane Lousada [1960] Director

Lousada PLC
Incorporated: 27 June 1969 *Employees:* 9
Net Worth: £43,058,400 *Total Assets:* £45,876,936
Registered Office: Estate Office, Oakley House, Oakley, Beds, MK43 7ST
Activities: Buying and selling of own real estate
Parent: Lousada Holdings Limited
Officers: Sharon Anne Hunt, Secretary; Simon Charles Lousada [1963] Director; Susan Jane Lousada [1960] Director

Lovering Foods Limited
Incorporated: 7 June 1979 *Employees:* 33
Net Worth: £15,899,000 *Total Assets:* £39,301,000
Registered Office: Red Central, 60 High Street, Redhill, Surrey, RH1 1SH
Activities: Wholesale of other food, including fish, crustaceans and molluscs
Shareholders: John Patrick Sexton; Lovering Group Limited
Officers: Michael Robert Charles Shepherd, Secretary/Director; John Patrick Sexton [1959] Director; Michael Robert Charles Shepherd [1966] Director

LPSO Limited
Incorporated: 21 December 1999 *Employees:* 79
Net Worth: £35,485,000 *Total Assets:* £177,784,000
Registered Office: Royal Pavilion, Wellesley Road, Aldershot, Hants, GU11 1PZ
Activities: Non-life insurance
Parent: INS-Sure Holdings Limited
Officers: Gilles Alex Maxime Bonvarlet [1964] Director [French]; David Howard Gittings [1954] Director; Royston Hoggarth [1962] Director; Steve Andre Anthony Jules [1980] Director/Accountant; Daljeet Singh Juttla [1986] Director; Dave John Matcham [1961] Director; Dr Indranil Nath [1969] Director [Indian]; John Barry Taylor [1973] Director/General Manager IT Services; Darren John Temple [1969] Director

LQAL UK Limited
Incorporated: 14 June 2017
Net Worth: £18,954,204 *Total Assets:* £20,657,178
Registered Office: 2 Victoria Works, 6 Fairway, Orpington, Kent, BR5 1EG
Activities: Hotels and similar accommodation
Officers: Michael Bornitz [1982] Director [American]; Andrew Steven Lazzaro [1971] Director [American]

LR (UK) Limited
Incorporated: 7 February 2007 *Employees:* 3
Net Worth Deficit: £79,546,624 *Total Assets:* £107,567,520
Registered Office: BMI House, 2 Pitfield, Kiln Farm, Milton Keynes, Bucks, MK11 3LW
Activities: Roofing activities
Parent: BMI Group Holdings UK Limited
Officers: Andrew John Dennis [1965] Managing Director; Klaus Sonne Ravn [1966] Finance Director [Danish]; Dr Johannes Georg Schmidt-Schultes [1966] Director/Chief Financial Officer [German]

LRC Products Limited
Incorporated: 14 July 1961
Net Worth: £634,280,000 *Total Assets:* £776,812,032
Registered Office: 103-105 Bath Road, Slough, Berks, SL1 3UH
Activities: Manufacture of basic pharmaceutical products
Parent: London International Group Limited
Officers: Christine Anne-Marie Logan, Secretary; John Dixon [1956] Director/SVP Tax; Charles David Everitt [1973] Director; Harminder Singh Virdi [1978] Finance Director

LRH Care Homes Limited
Incorporated: 24 November 2016 *Employees:* 796
Net Worth: £24,630,758 *Total Assets:* £82,756,456
Registered Office: 12-14 Langley Avenue, Surbiton, Surrey, KT6 6QL
Activities: Other business support service activities n.e.c.
Officers: Eirik Peter Robson [1958] Director/Surveyor; Arnon Nir Rubinstein [1964] Managing Director

LSG/Sky Chefs Europe Holdings Limited
Incorporated: 4 February 1998 *Employees:* 14
Net Worth: £16,558,000 *Total Assets:* £67,589,000
Registered Office: Heathrow Boulevard 2, 284 Bath Road, Sipson, West Drayton, Middlesex, UB7 0DQ
Activities: Event catering activities
Shareholders: LSG South America GmbH; LSG Lufthansa Service Europa/Africa GmbH
Officers: Muhammad Waqas, Secretary; Matteo Bagliani [1966] Managing Director [Italian]

LSI Logic Europe Limited
Incorporated: 5 May 1982
Net Worth: £11,891,436 *Total Assets:* £29,006,364
Registered Office: Fourth Floor, Abbots House, Abbey Street, Reading, Berks, RG1 3BD
Activities: Other professional, scientific and technical activities n.e.c.
Parent: Broadcom Inc.
Officers: Mark David Brazeal, Secretary; Mark David Brazeal [1968] Director [American]; Thomas Harry Krause Jr [1977] Director/Business Executive [American]

LSQ (Crimscott Street) Holdings Limited
Incorporated: 9 March 2017
Net Worth: £2 *Total Assets:* £31,261,704
Registered Office: 1 York Road, Uxbridge, Middlesex, UB8 1RN
Activities: Development of building projects
Parent: London Square (Investments) Limited
Officers: Scott Douglas Brown [1968] Director/Chief Financial Officer [Australian]; Mark Stewart Evans [1969] Director/Chief Operating Officer; Adam Paul Lawrence [1970] Director/Chief Executive Officer

LSQ Holdco 3 Limited
Incorporated: 20 June 2014
Net Worth Deficit: £73,047,000 *Total Assets:* £179,984,000
Registered Office: One York Road, Uxbridge, Middlesex, UB8 1RN
Activities: Construction of domestic buildings
Parent: LSQ Holdco 2 Ltd
Officers: Scott Douglas Brown [1968] Director [Australian]; Mark Stewart Evans [1969] Director/Chief Operating Officer; Adam Paul Lawrence [1970] Director; Charles Richard Arklay Steel [1975] Director; William Gowanloch Westbrook [1976] Director

Lubricants UK Limited
Incorporated: 13 March 1908 *Employees:* 721
Net Worth: £189,942,000 *Total Assets:* £408,201,984
Registered Office: Chertsey Road, Sunbury on Thames, Middlesex, TW16 7BP
Activities: Mineral oil refining
Parent: Burmah Castrol PLC
Officers: Peter James Mather [1960] Director/Oil Company Executive; Andrew Michael Moore [1964] Director/Oil Company Executive; Daniel Chukumah Odogwu [1966] Director/Oil Company Executive; Paul Ian Winton Turner [1963] Director/Oil Company Executive

Lucozade Ribena Suntory Limited
Incorporated: 10 July 2013 *Employees:* 720
Net Worth: £864,452,992 *Total Assets:* £1,394,434,944
Registered Office: 2 Longwalk Road, Stockley Park, Uxbridge, Middlesex, UB11 1BA
Activities: Manufacture of soft drinks; production of mineral waters and other bottled waters
Parent: Suntory Beverage & Food Limited
Officers: Mary Guest, Secretary; Mary Elizabeth Guest [1980] Director and Company Secretary; Peter John Harding [1964] Director/Chief Operating Officer; Toby Peter McKeever [1969] Director; Jaime Antonio Mussons Freixas [1961] Director/Chief Marketing Officer [Spanish]; Carol Robert [1979] Director; Takayuki Sanno [1968] Director [Japanese]; Craig William Shelden [1964] Director/Chief Financial Officer [Australian]; Tetsu Tanaka [1967] Director [Japanese]; Peter James Thomlinson [1967] Director/Chief Financial Officer; Yuji Yamazaki [1957] Director [Japanese]

Ludgate 329 Limited
Incorporated: 12 December 2003 *Employees:* 64
Net Worth Deficit: £9,152,926 *Total Assets:* £36,485,988
Registered Office: Homedics House, Somerhill Business Park, Five Oak Green Road, Tonbridge, Kent, TN11 0GP
Activities: Activities of head offices
Major Shareholder: Alon David Kaufman
Officers: Swarup Banerjee, Secretary; Simon Jonathan Bluring [1956] Managing Director EMEA; Alon D Kaufman [1962] Director/Businessman [American]; Sabyasachi SEN [1962] Director/Chief Financial Officer [American]

Luff Investments Limited
Incorporated: 22 April 1971
Net Worth: £25,787,676 *Total Assets:* £26,994,260
Registered Office: The Granary, Ashridgewood Farm, Warren House Road, Wokingham, Berks, RG40 5RD
Activities: Construction of commercial buildings
Parent: Luff Group Limited
Officers: Ian James Brown-Lee, Secretary; Ian James Brown-Lee [1964] Finance Director; Roy Richard Butterworth [1954] Director/Builder; Gary Peter Luff [1962] Director; June Margaret Luff [1939] Director

Lufthansa Technik Landing Gear Services UK Limited
Incorporated: 3 November 1997 *Employees:* 278
Net Worth Deficit: £5,843,000 *Total Assets:* £25,961,000
Registered Office: Unit 3 Dawley Park, Kestrel Way, Hayes, Middlesex, UB3 1HP
Activities: Repair and maintenance of aircraft and spacecraft
Shareholders: Lufthansa Technik A.G.; Deutsche Lufthansa AG
Officers: Olaf Behn, Secretary; Sandra Ecksten [1973] Director [German]; Robert Gaag [1960] Director [German]; Klaus Wachholz [1968] Director [German]

Lunar 101 Limited
Incorporated: 31 March 2016
Net Worth: £3,381,000 *Total Assets:* £33,739,000
Registered Office: Towergate House, Eclipse Park, Sittingbourne Road, Maidstone, Kent, ME14 3EN
Activities: Activities of other holding companies n.e.c.
Parent: Paymentshield Limited
Officers: Dean Clarke, Secretary; Antonios Erotocritou [1971] Director/Deputy CFO [Cypriot]; David Christopher Ross [1969] Director [Irish]

Lutob Investment Ltd
Incorporated: 28 September 2016
Net Worth: £12,347,593 *Total Assets:* £27,806,644
Registered Office: Knoll House, Knoll Road, Camberley, Surrey, GU15 3SY
Activities: Activities of other holding companies n.e.c.
Major Shareholder: Luca Botter
Officers: Luca Botter [1965] Director [Italian]; Gregory Robert John Davis [1960] Director

Luton Hoo Park Limited
Incorporated: 13 October 1998 *Employees:* 475
Net Worth: £24,553,732 *Total Assets:* £51,297,848
Registered Office: Ashdown Park, Wych Cross, Forest Row, E Sussex, RH18 5JR
Activities: Hotels and similar accommodation
Parent: Elite Hotels (Rotherwick) Ltd
Officers: Ronan Sean Callaghan, Secretary; Graeme Carl Bateman [1961] Managing Director; Ronan Sean Callaghan [1983] Finance Director; Simon Jeremy Willis [1968] Director of Operations

Luxury Travel Acquisitions Limited
Incorporated: 16 December 2014 *Employees:* 6
Net Worth Deficit: £4,787,000 *Total Assets:* £78,649,000
Registered Office: Scott Dunn, Madgwick Lane, Westhampnett, Chichester, W Sussex, PO18 0FB
Activities: Tour operator activities
Parent: Luxury Travel Financing Limited
Officers: Sonia Davies [1977] Director/Chief Operating Officer; Simon Nicholas McMurtrie [1966] Director; Simon John Russell [1971] Director; Robin Wooldridge [1968] Executive Director

Luxury Travel Financing Limited
Incorporated: 16 December 2014
Net Worth Deficit: £20,965,000 *Total Assets:* £53,064,000
Registered Office: Scott Dunn, Madgwick Lane, Westhampnett, Chichester, W Sussex, PO18 0FB
Activities: Tour operator activities
Parent: Luxury Travel Holdings Limited
Officers: Sonia Davies [1977] Director/Chief Operating Officer; Simon Nicholas McMurtrie [1966] Director; Simon John Russell [1971] Director; Robin Wooldridge [1968] Executive Director

The Luxury Travel Group Limited
Incorporated: 26 February 2008 *Employees:* 339
Previous: Scott Dunn Holdings Limited
Net Worth: £17,502,000 *Total Assets:* £48,829,000
Registered Office: Scott Dunn, Madgwick Lane, Westhampnett, Chichester, W Sussex, PO18 0FB
Activities: Activities of head offices
Parent: Luxury Travel Acquisitions Limited
Officers: Sonia Davies [1977] Director/Chief Operating Officer; Oliver Evans [1975] Director; Simon John Russell [1971] Managing Director; Brian Wewege [1976] IT Director [South African]; Robin Wooldridge [1968] Executive Director

Luxury Travel Holdings Limited
Incorporated: 16 December 2014 *Employees:* 339
Net Worth Deficit: £36,746,000 *Total Assets:* £92,718,000
Registered Office: Scott Dunn, Madgwick Lane, Westhampnett, Chichester, W Sussex, PO18 0FB
Activities: Tour operator activities
Officers: Andreas Constantinides [1989] Director/Investment Executive; Sonia Davies [1977] Director/Chief Operating Officer; Andrew Weston Dunn [1963] Director; Philip James Edmans [1983] Investment Director; Simon Nicholas McMurtrie [1966] Director; Robin Wooldridge [1968] Executive Director

Lymington Precision Engineering (LPE) Limited
Incorporated: 1 February 2011
Net Worth: £26,576,000 *Total Assets:* £26,579,000
Registered Office: 59-61 High Street, Rickmansworth, Herts, WD3 1RH
Activities: Manufacture of other fabricated metal products n.e.c.
Parent: Senior UK Limited
Officers: Andrew John Bodenham, Secretary; Martin John Barnes [1966] Director; Andrew John Bodenham [1966] Director; Bindi Jayantilal Jivraj Foyle [1973] Director

L. Lynch (Holdings) Limited
Incorporated: 14 June 1990 *Employees:* 3
Net Worth: £13,180,713 *Total Assets:* £27,694,116
Registered Office: Boundary Way, Hemel Hempstead, Herts, HP2 7YU
Activities: Renting and leasing of construction and civil engineering machinery and equipment
Major Shareholder: Liam Lynch
Officers: Fabian Swampillai, Secretary; Liam Lynch [1954] Managing Director [Irish]; Merrill Liam Lynch [1979] Director; Robert Martin Lynch [1980] Director

L. Lynch (Plant Hire & Haulage) Limited
Incorporated: 2 August 1993 *Employees:* 124
Net Worth: £13,416,444 *Total Assets:* £55,744,604
Registered Office: Boundary Way, Hemel Hempstead, Herts, HP2 7YU
Activities: Renting and leasing of construction and civil engineering machinery and equipment
Major Shareholder: Liam Lynch
Officers: Fabian Swampillai, Secretary; Liam Lynch [1954] Managing Director [Irish]; Merrill Liam Lynch [1979] Director; Robert Martin Lynch [1980] Director

Lyndendown Limited
Incorporated: 19 July 1954 *Employees:* 5
Net Worth: £19,232,304 *Total Assets:* £34,180,372
Registered Office: Pippingford Manor, Millbrook Hill, Nutley, Uckfield, E Sussex, TN22 3HW
Activities: Other letting and operating of own or leased real estate
Major Shareholder: Jacklyn Nicole Martin-Betts
Officers: Thaddeus Mary McErlean, Secretary; Brian Frederick Cradick [1949] Director/Surveyor; Jacklyn Nicole Martin-Betts [1963] Director; Thaddeus Mary McErlean [1946] Director/Accountant

Lyndon Scaffolding PLC
Incorporated: 26 June 1968 *Employees:* 635
Net Worth: £21,534,798 *Total Assets:* £30,829,792
Registered Office: Regent Park, 299 Kingston Road, Leatherhead, Surrey, KT22 7SG
Activities: Scaffold erection
Major Shareholder: Donald Gogel
Officers: Andreas Akhtar, Secretary; Andreas Akhtar [1974] Director [German]; Michael Edward Herke [1964] Director [Irish]; Marcus Paul Leonardus Marie Niederer [1963] Director [Dutch]; Benjamin Stevenson Read [1974] Director

M & C (CB) Limited
Incorporated: 22 September 1999
Net Worth: £338,097,056 *Total Assets:* £339,152,800
Registered Office: Victoria House, Victoria Road, Horley, Surrey, RH6 7AF
Activities: Activities of head offices
Parent: Millennium & Copthorne Hotels PLC
Officers: Jonathon MacKenzie Grech [1977] Director/Senior VP Group Legal Counsel; Clive Anthony Harrington [1967] Director/Senior Vice President Operations

M & C (CD) Limited
Incorporated: 22 September 1999
Net Worth: £338,097,056 *Total Assets:* £339,152,800
Registered Office: Victoria House, Victoria Road, Horley, Surrey, RH6 7AF
Activities: Activities of head offices
Parent: Millennium & Copthorne Hotels PLC
Officers: Jonathon MacKenzie Grech [1977] Director/Senior VP Group Legal Counsel; Clive Anthony Harrington [1967] Director/Senior Vice President Operations

M & C Asia Holdings (UK) Limited
Incorporated: 31 January 2013 *Employees:* 2
Net Worth: £506,616,576 *Total Assets:* £506,616,576
Registered Office: Victoria House, Victoria Road, Horley, Surrey, RH6 7AF
Activities: Activities of head offices
Parent: Millennium & Copthorne Hotels PLC
Officers: Jonathon MacKenzie Grech [1977] Director/Senior VP Group Legal Counsel; Chwee Peng Ong [1965] Director [Malaysian]

M & C Finance (1) Limited
Incorporated: 6 January 2009
Net Worth: £97,524,000 *Total Assets:* £98,009,000
Registered Office: Victoria House, Victoria Road, Horley, Surrey, RH6 7AF
Activities: Financial intermediation not elsewhere classified
Parent: M & C Hotels Holdings Limited
Officers: Jonathon MacKenzie Grech [1977] Director/Senior VP Group Legal Counsel; Clive Anthony Harrington [1967] Director/Senior Vice President Operations

M & C Hotels Holdings Limited
Incorporated: 2 April 2002
Net Worth: £75,126,000 *Total Assets:* £92,073,000
Registered Office: Victoria House, Victoria Road, Horley, Surrey, RH6 7AF
Activities: Activities of other holding companies n.e.c.
Parent: Millennium & Copthorne Hotels PLC
Officers: Jonathon MacKenzie Grech [1977] Director/Senior VP Group Legal Counsel; Clive Anthony Harrington [1967] Director

M & C New York Finance (UK) Limited
Incorporated: 28 May 2014
Net Worth: £230,660,896 *Total Assets:* £431,978,080
Registered Office: Victoria House, Victoria Road, Horley, Surrey, RH6 7AF
Activities: Financial intermediation not elsewhere classified
Shareholders: M & C (CB) Limited; M & C (CD) Limited
Officers: Jonathon MacKenzie Grech [1977] Director/Group General Counsel; Clive Anthony Harrington [1967] Director/SVP Operations - Europe

M & C Singapore Holdings (UK) Limited
Incorporated: 31 January 2013
Net Worth: £1,567,633,920 *Total Assets:* £1,568,007,424
Registered Office: Victoria House, Victoria Road, Horley, Surrey, RH6 7AF
Activities: Activities of head offices
Parent: Millennium & Copthorne Hotels PLC
Officers: Jonathon MacKenzie Grech [1977] Director/Senior VP Group Legal Counsel; Chwee Peng Ong [1965] Director [Malaysian]

M & J Seafood Limited
Incorporated: 7 November 2014
Net Worth Deficit: £32,451,000 *Total Assets:* £25,411,000
Registered Office: Enterprise House, Eureka Business Park, Ashford, Kent, TN25 4AG
Activities: Wholesale of other food, including fish, crustaceans and molluscs
Parent: Fresh Direct Group Limited
Officers: Sarah Whibley, Secretary; Rajesh Vishwanath Tugnait [1969] Director/Chief Executive Officer; Sarah Leanne Whibley [1976] Director/Solicitor

M C Group Limited
Incorporated: 9 July 1986 *Employees:* 374
Net Worth: £27,144,872 *Total Assets:* £151,719,440
Registered Office: Beddow Way, Forstal Road, Aylesford, Maidstone, Kent, ME20 7BT
Activities: Sale of other motor vehicles
Major Shareholder: Simon James Dawson
Officers: Peter David Booth, Secretary; Peter David Booth [1963] Director/Chartered Accountant; Simon James Dawson [1971] Director/Sales Manager; David Kenneth Hutchins [1966] Sales Director

M New Holdings Limited
Incorporated: 14 February 2017 *Employees:* 364
Net Worth: £20,691,348 *Total Assets:* £52,452,424
Registered Office: 7th Floor, Vantage London, Great West Road, Brentford, Middlesex, TW8 9AG
Activities: Activities of other holding companies n.e.c.
Major Shareholder: Jonathan George Mills
Officers: Richard Hutchinson, Secretary; Edmund Lazarus [1968] Director; Jonathan George Mills [1968] Director

M.A.T. Davies Holdings Limited
Incorporated: 5 April 1993 *Employees:* 221
Net Worth: £30,101,000 *Total Assets:* £112,299,000
Registered Office: The Bull Courtyard, Bell Street, Henley on Thames, Oxon, RG9 2BA
Activities: Public houses and bars
Shareholder: Michael Anthony Trehearne Davies
Officers: David Generald Nathan, Secretary; Michael Anthony Trehearne Davies [1953] Director; Thomas Anthony Trehearne Davies [1980] Director; David Generald Nathan [1970] Director

Mabey Engineering (Holdings) Limited
Incorporated: 8 May 1981
Net Worth: £119,504,472 *Total Assets:* £119,507,480
Registered Office: One Valpy, 20 Valpy Street, Reading, Berks, RG1 1AR
Activities: Activities of head offices
Parent: Mabey Holdings Limited
Officers: Juliette Natasha Stacey [1970] Director; Edward Godwin Wilcox [1966] Director/Accountant

Mabey Holdings Limited
Incorporated: 6 March 1985 *Employees:* 808
Net Worth: £154,403,008 *Total Assets:* £219,060,992
Registered Office: One Valpy, 20 Valpy Street, Reading, Berks, RG1 1AR
Activities: Activities of head offices
Parent: Blagrave No 1 Limited
Officers: Joanna Kate Beauchamp, Secretary; Joanna Kate Beauchamp [1974] Director/Lawyer; Rodney John Bennion [1946] Director; Mark Andrew Carey [1967] Director; Richard Baskcomb Haryott [1941] Director; Richard Raeburn [1946] Director; Juliette Natasha Stacey [1970] Director

MacDermid (UK) Limited
Incorporated: 2 September 1998
Net Worth: £99,800,000 *Total Assets:* £120,187,000
Registered Office: Unit 2 Genesis Business Park, Albert Drive, Sheerwater, Woking, Surrey, GU21 5RW
Activities: Activities of head offices
Parent: MacDermid Continental Investments Limited
Officers: John Edward Capps, Secretary; Paul Andrew Bray [1969] Managing Director; John Edward Capps [1964] Director [American]; John Patrick Connolly [1966] Director/Chief Financial Officer [American]

MacDermid Continental Investments Limited
Incorporated: 24 July 2007
Net Worth: £938,035,968 *Total Assets:* £951,390,016
Registered Office: Unit 2 Genesis Business Park, Albert Drive, Sheerwater, Woking, Surrey, GU21 5RW
Activities: Activities of head offices
Parent: MacDermid European Capital Investments I LLC
Officers: John Edward Capps, Secretary; Paul Andrew Bray [1969] Managing Director; John Edward Capps [1964] Director [American]

MacDermid Europe Limited
Incorporated: 1 June 1920
Net Worth: £47,918,000 *Total Assets:* £101,278,000
Registered Office: Unit 2 Genesis Business Park, Albert Drive, Sheerwater, Woking, Surrey, GU21 5RW
Activities: Activities of head offices
Parent: MacDermid (UK) Limited
Officers: John Edward Capps, Secretary; Paul Andrew Bray [1969] Managing Director; John Edward Capps [1964] Director [American]; John Patrick Connolly [1966] Director/Chief Financial Officer [American]

MacDermid G.B. Holdings Limited
Incorporated: 9 June 2005
Net Worth: £53,060,000 *Total Assets:* £54,642,000
Registered Office: Unit 2 Genesis Business Park, Albert Drive, Sheerwater, Woking, Surrey, GU21 5RW
Activities: Activities of head offices
Parent: Platform Specialty Products Corporation
Officers: Petrus Jacobus Thoedurus Maria Van de Louw, Secretary; Denis Braeuer [1977] Director/EMEA Treasurer [Swiss]; Petrus Jacobus Theodurus Maria Van de Louw [1955] Director/Financial Controller [Dutch]

MacDermid Performance Solutions UK Limited
Incorporated: 16 December 1976 *Employees:* 91
Previous: MacDermid Limited
Net Worth: £23,125,000 *Total Assets:* £89,792,000
Registered Office: Unit 2 Genesis Business Park, Albert Drive, Sheerwater, Woking, Surrey, GU21 5RW
Activities: Manufacture of other inorganic basic chemicals
Parent: MacDermid Continental Investments Limited
Officers: Paul Andrew Bray [1969] Sales Director; Terence Joseph Clarke [1957] Research Director; John Patrick Connolly [1966] Director/Chief Financial Officer [American]; Steven Geoffrey Sheffield [1962] Sales Director

MacIntyre Care
Incorporated: 15 December 1966 *Employees:* 2,198
Net Worth: £30,400,000 *Total Assets:* £35,098,000
Registered Office: 602 South Seventh Street, Central Milton Keynes, Bucks, MK9 2JA
Activities: Residential care activities for the elderly and disabled
Officers: Claire Toombs, Secretary; John Robert Lloyd Berriman [1956] Director/Chartered Accountant; Rajdeep Kaur Gahir [1989] Director/Consultant; Adam Farley Goldstein [1978] Director/Chief Operating Officer; Rosemary Diane Hart [1954] Director/Solicitor; Dragana Josifova [1958] Director/Consultant Clinical Geneticist [Macedonian]; Neil Stephen Macmillan [1962] Director/Insurance; Pamela Katharine Meek [1971] Director/Deputy Principal; Ruth Elizabeth Smyth [1976] Director/HR Consultant; Duncan Anthony Strachan [1954] Director/Solicitor; Rachel Mary Taylor [1976] Director/Professional Services Consultant; Nikki Williams-Ellis [1956] Director; Martin Zahra [1959] Director [Maltese]

MacIntyre Hudson LLP
Incorporated: 19 March 2005 *Employees:* 683
Net Worth: £11,142,451 *Total Assets:* £30,524,516
Registered Office: Moorgate House, 201 Silbury Boulevard, Milton Keynes, Bucks, MK9 1LZ
Officers: Atul Kariya [1972] Member; Steven Moore [1963] Member; Rachel Nutt [1975] Member; Rakesh Shaunak [1956] Member; Stephen James Thomas Askew [1954] LLP Member; Michael Jonathan Ball [1975] LLP Member; Christopher Stephen Barlow [1971] LLP Member; Dennis Neil Berry [1976] LLP Member; Tasneem Bharmal [1974] LLP Member; Christopher John Blundell [1962] LLP Member; Jay Boyce [1958] LLP Member; Anthony David Brand [1957] LLP Member; Michael James Brown [1949] LLP Member; John Charles Burwood [1951] LLP Member; Patrick Joseph Byrne [1949] LLP Member; Francis Peter Cheney [1950] LLP Member; Duncan George Cochrane-Dyet [1966] LLP Member; Alison Jayne Conley [1964] LLP Member; Andrew Cameron Cook [1954] LLP Member; David John Coppard [1954] LLP Member; John Edwin Coverdale [1965] LLP Member; Matthew Alexander Coward [1966] LLP Member; Alan Peter Craddock [1964] LLP Member; Georgette Alicia Crisp [1985] LLP Member; Candice Terri-Anne Czeremuszkin [1986] LLP Member; Gavin Clifford Davis [1961] LLP Member; Paul Michael Davis [1960] LLP Member; Christian Stephen Denning [1966] LLP Member; Sarah Jane Dodds [1975] LLP Member; Georgina Marie Eason [1978] LLP Member; Nigel Antony Eastaway [1943] LLP Member; Stephen Kenneth Freeman [1968] LLP Member; David Mark Gallagher [1970] LLP Member; Harminther Singh Gill [1960] LLP Member; Grant Courtney Gleghorn [1956] LLP Member; James Gransby [1979] LLP Member; Marcel Samuel Grech-Marguerat [1950] LLP Member; Christopher Alexander Harris [1963] LLP Member; Alan Peter Herbert [1963] LLP Member; Martin Steve Herron [1968] LLP Member; Alison Clare Horner [1964] LLP Member; Alyson Marina Howard [1962] LLP Member; Rebecca Jane Hughes [1977] LLP Member; Frances Catherine James [1963] LLP Member; Michael John Kay [1969] LLP Member; Robert John Kidson [1956] LLP Member; Patrick George King [1962] LLP Member; James Robert Kipping [1983] LLP Member; Simon Andrew Vivian Knibbs [1980] LLP Member; Howard Keith Lewis [1951] LLP Member; Stuart John Manning [1959] LLP Member; Nigel Campbell May [1965] LLP Member; John Baptist Avelino Mendes [1956] LLP Member; Cara Colleen Miller [1981] LLP Member; Colin George Mills [1954] LLP Member; Mark Ernest James Minus [1963] LLP Member; Jason Michel Mitchell [1964] LLP Member; Justin Stephen Moss [1980] LLP Member; Andrew Jamie Moyser [1982] LLP Member; Robert Anthony Nelson [1963] LLP Member; Elaine Susan Olson-Williams [1962] LLP Member; Yogan Adabhai Patel [1959] LLP Member; Martin David Payne [1952] LLP Member; Gareth David Peters [1981] LLP Member; Stephen John Poleykett [1973] LLP Member; Richard John Powell [1971] LLP Member; David Keith Purser [1954] LLP Member; Martin Ramsey [1968] LLP Member; Brian Neil Richens [1952] LLP Member; Michael Colin John Sanders [1966] LLP Member; Brendan Michael Sharkey [1955] LLP Member; Rajeev Shaunak [1968] LLP Member; Elaine Rosemary Shoesmith [1951] LLP Member; Bianca Kamala Silva [1960] LLP Member; Katharine Jane Simon [1977] LLP Member; Sudhir Singh [1963] LLP Member; Tobias Robert Stephenson [1966] LLP Member; Neil Richard Stern [1981] LLP Member; Christopher Frederick Stratton [1949] LLP Member; Christopher Nigel Sutton [1956] LLP Member; Gregory Luke Taylor [1978] LLP Member; Glen David Thomas [1967] LLP Member; Robert William Trunchion [1956] LLP Member; David James Walker [1977] LLP Member; Jane Walker-Smith [1977] LLP Member; Deborah Weston [1959] LLP Member; Laurence Whitehead [1966] LLP Member; David Wignall [1965] LLP Member; Adam John Young [1969] LLP Member; Graeme Lindsay Young [1956] LLP Member

M.& W.Mack Limited
Incorporated: 2 January 1948 *Employees:* 609
Net Worth: £23,550,000 *Total Assets:* £66,083,000
Registered Office: The Fresh Produce Centre, Transfesa Road, Paddock Wood, Kent, TN12 6UT
Activities: Wholesale of fruit and vegetables
Parent: Fresca Group Limited
Officers: Veronica Warner, Secretary; Ian Alexander Craig [1957] Director; Christopher Peter Mack [1955] Director; Charles Hugh Rees [1957] Managing Director; Brett Geoffrey Sumner [1973] Finance Director; Nigel John Trood [1965] Director

Macmillan Publishers International Limited
Incorporated: 10 October 1986 *Employees:* 573
Previous: Pan Books Publishers Limited
Net Worth: £33,383,000 *Total Assets:* £215,110,000
Registered Office: Cromwell Place, Hampshire International Business Park, Lime Tree Way, Basingstoke, Hants, RG24 8YJ
Activities: Book publishing
Shareholders: Stefan von Holtzbrinck; Holtzbrinck Investment Limited; Christiane Schoeller
Officers: Gabrielle Mary Williams Hamer, Secretary; Lara Marianne Elizabeth Borlenghi [1973] Director/Chartered Accountant; Guy Browning [1965] Director/Distribution Executive; Simon Peter Darlington Cramond [1956] Director; Anthony David Forbes Watson [1954] Director/Publisher; Annie Lapaz [1959] Director/Lawyer; Roger Ian Priddy [1960] Director/Publisher; Andrew Weber [1967] Director/Global Trade Chief Operating Officer [American]

Macro 4 Limited
Incorporated: 20 February 1968 *Employees:* 136
Net Worth: £117,262,000 *Total Assets:* £135,856,992
Registered Office: The Orangery, Turners Hill Road, Worth, Crawley, W Sussex, RH10 4SS
Activities: Business and domestic software development
Officers: Corry Sungsoo Hong, Secretary/Executive [American]; Christine Huikyong Hong [1965] Director/Executive [American]; Corry Sungsoo Hong [1956] Director/Executive [American]

Magal Engineering Limited
Incorporated: 2 April 2002 *Employees:* 14
Net Worth: £20,823,224 *Total Assets:* £32,734,108
Registered Office: 47 Castle Street, Reading, Berks, RG1 7SR
Activities: Manufacture of metal structures and parts of structures
Parent: Arlington Automotive Holdings Limited
Officers: Mark Bernard Franckel [1962] Director; Simon George Greenhalgh [1972] Director; Moshe Gamil Magal [1956] Director

Magma Global Limited
Incorporated: 10 March 2008 *Employees:* 49
Net Worth: £31,267,960 *Total Assets:* £35,912,080
Registered Office: Magma House, Trafalgar Wharf, Hamilton Road, Portsmouth, PO6 4PX
Activities: Other manufacturing n.e.c.
Officers: Michael Andrew Boyd, Secretary; Mark Gunnar Bryant [1962] Investor Director; Martin Court [1961] Director; Barry Allen Glickman [1968] Director [American]; Martin Peter William Jones [1960] Director; Jonas Jonhede [1973] Director [Swedish]; Jens Christian Mathiesen [1956] Director/Private Equity Investor [Danish]; Justin Rounce [1967] Director; Charles Alexander Tavner [1975] Director; Dik Jeffrey Van Steenbergen [1955] Director/General Partner [Canadian]

Maiden Erlegh Trust
Incorporated: 2 March 2011 *Employees:* 449
Net Worth: £53,778,000 *Total Assets:* £60,368,000
Registered Office: Maiden Erlegh School, Silverdale Road, Earley, Reading, Berks, RG6 7HS
Activities: General secondary education
Officers: Jonathon Raymond Peck, Secretary; Lindsey Claire Bowden [1965] Director/Social Worker; Mary Davies [1967] Director/Headmaster; John Fredrick Hobson [1960] HR Director; Nicholas Paul Jones [1960] Director/Retired; Robert John Kenwrick [1955] Director/Retired; Ian May [1962] Director/Head of University Building; Janette Clare Rothwell [1957] Director/Manager; Alastair John Robertson Starnes [1968] Director/Chartered Surveyor

Maintenance Management Limited
Incorporated: 21 August 2001 *Employees:* 98
Net Worth: £1,552,670 *Total Assets:* £32,688,378
Registered Office: Apollo House, 6 Bramley Road, Mount Farm, Milton Keynes, Bucks, MK1 1PT
Activities: Other business support service activities n.e.c.
Parent: Seckloe 280 Limited
Officers: Charles Hawkins, Secretary; Michael Hughes [1964] Director; Colin John Seggie [1973] Director; Alan John Tough [1959] Finance Director

Maisonparc Ltd
Incorporated: 14 April 2016
Net Worth Deficit: £1,595,394 *Total Assets:* £42,652,240
Registered Office: Greenstedes, Marden Paddock, Brockenhurst, Hants, SO42 7SU
Activities: Fund management activities
Shareholders: Allen David Gosman; Margaret Jane Gosman
Officers: Margaret Jane Gosman, Secretary; Allen David Gosman [1940] Director/Professor Emeritus [Canadian]; Margaret Jane Gosman [1941] Director/Retired; Laurence Meakin [1946] Director/Administrator

Majestic Securities Limited
Incorporated: 21 December 2012 *Employees:* 66
Net Worth: £19,716,844 *Total Assets:* £21,535,766
Registered Office: 7-9 Stafford Road, Wallington, Surrey, SM6 9AN
Activities: Activities of head offices
Major Shareholder: Parminder Singh Dosanjh
Officers: Arjan Singh Dosanjh [1987] Director; Parminder Singh Dosanjh [1955] Director; Sarvjeet Kaur Dosanjh [1960] Director/Accounts Manager

Majestic Wine PLC
Incorporated: 28 July 1988 *Employees:* 1,528
Net Worth: £121,761,000 *Total Assets:* £251,967,008
Registered Office: Majestic House, The Belfry, Colonial Way, Watford, Herts, WD24 4WH
Activities: Wholesale of wine, beer, spirits and other alcoholic beverages
Officers: Alex Iapichino, Secretary; Justin James Apthorp [1962] Director/Buyer; James Crawford [1977] Finance Director; Rowan Gormley [1962] Director/Chief Executive Officer [Irish]; Ian Andrew Harding [1964] Director/Company Executive; Brian Gregory Hodder [1952] Director; David Anthony Stead [1958] Director/Auditor

Majestic Wine Warehouses Limited
Incorporated: 30 October 1981 *Employees:* 1,168
Net Worth: £86,652,000 *Total Assets:* £138,679,008
Registered Office: Majestic House, The Belfry, Colonial Way, Watford, Herts, WD24 4WH
Activities: Wholesale of wine, beer, spirits and other alcoholic beverages
Parent: Majestic Wine PLC
Officers: Alex Iapichino, Secretary; James Crawford [1977] Director; Olivia FitzGenerald [1972] Director/Businesswoman; Rowan Gormley [1962] Director/Chief Executive [Irish]; Stuart Christopher Lane [1981] Finance Director; Joshua Benjamin Geoffrey Lincoln-Creese [1984] Managing Director

Makita (UK) Limited
Incorporated: 13 December 1972 *Employees:* 171
Net Worth: £96,723,000 *Total Assets:* £147,726,000
Registered Office: Michigan Drive, Tongwell, Milton Keynes, Bucks, MK15 8JD
Activities: Wholesale of other machinery and equipment
Parent: Makita International Europe Ltd
Officers: Ryuichi Hashizume, Secretary; Yasushi Fukaya [1959] Director/Manager [Japanese]; Kenichi Ohara [1968] Director/Chief Executive [Japanese]; Takashi Omote [1959] Director/General Manager of International Sales HQ [Japanese]; Barry Forbes Smart [1958] Sales and Marketing Director

Makita International Europe Limited
Incorporated: 9 March 1995 *Employees:* 5
Net Worth: £232,355,008 *Total Assets:* £232,562,000
Registered Office: Michigan Drive, Tongwell, Milton Keynes, Bucks, MK15 8JD
Activities: Management consultancy activities other than financial management
Parent: Makita Corporation
Officers: Hiromu Ishikawa, Secretary; Yasushi Fukaya [1959] Director [Japanese]; Takashi Omote [1959] Director [Japanese]

Mallinckrodt Chemical Limited
Incorporated: 11 August 1987
Net Worth: £56,340,488 *Total Assets:* £72,142,376
Registered Office: 3 Lotus Park, The Causeway, Staines upon Thames, Middlesex, TW18 3AG
Activities: Manufacture of other organic basic chemicals
Parent: Mallinckrodt UK Ltd
Officers: Dean Leslie Erdal [1956] Finance Director [American]; Stephanie Dorn Miller [1974] Director/Corporate Secretary [American]; Jason Tilly [1973] Director/Attorney [American]; Stephen Andrew Welch [1977] Director/Senior Staff Liaison to The President and CEO [American]

Mallinckrodt Enterprises UK Limited
Incorporated: 17 June 2014 *Employees:* 3
Net Worth: £181,436,656 *Total Assets:* £181,503,984
Registered Office: 3 Lotus Park, The Causeway, Staines upon Thames, Middlesex, TW18 3AG
Activities: Activities of other holding companies n.e.c.
Parent: Mushi UK Holdings Limited
Officers: Alan Catterson [1961] Director/Financial Controller; Stephanie Dorn Miller [1974] Director/Corporate Secretary [American]; Stephen Andrew Welch [1977] Director/Senior Staff Liaison to The President and CEO [American]

Mallinckrodt Medical Holdings (UK) Limited
Incorporated: 17 January 1992
Net Worth: £20,057,250 *Total Assets:* £20,057,250
Registered Office: 3 Lotus Park, The Causeway, Staines upon Thames, Middlesex, TW18 3AG
Activities: Activities of head offices
Parent: Mallinckrodt Enterprises UK Limited
Officers: Dean Leslie Erdal [1956] Finance Director [American]; Stephen Andrew Welch [1977] Director/Senior Staff Liaison to The President and CEO [American]

Mallinckrodt Pharmaceuticals Limited
Incorporated: 16 September 2015 *Employees:* 11
Net Worth: £4,698,839,040 *Total Assets:* £4,702,202,368
Registered Office: 3 Lotus Park, The Causeway, Staines upon Thames, Middlesex, TW18 3AG
Activities: Management consultancy activities other than financial management
Parent: Mallinckrodt UK Ltd
Officers: Stephanie Dorn Miller, Secretary; Stephanie Dorn Miller [1974] Director/Corporate Secretary [American]; Josh Schafer [1971] Director/Pharmaceutical Executive [American]; Mark Trudeau [1961] Director/President and Chief Executive Officer [American]

Mallinckrodt UK Finance LLP
Incorporated: 22 September 2015
Net Worth: £1,035,037,952 *Total Assets:* £1,142,992,384
Registered Office: 3 Lotus Park, The Causeway, Staines upon Thames, Middlesex, TW18 3AG

Mallinckrodt UK Ltd
Incorporated: 23 June 1986
Net Worth: £4,961,617,408 *Total Assets:* £9,481,590,784
Registered Office: 3 Lotus Park, The Causeway, Staines upon Thames, Middlesex, TW18 3AG
Activities: Non-trading company
Officers: Stephanie Dorn Miller [1974] Director/Corporate Secretary [American]; Stephen Andrew Welch [1977] Director/Senior Staff Liaison to The President and CEO [American]

Malta Topco Limited
Incorporated: 9 December 2016 *Employees:* 200
Net Worth Deficit: £8,192,000 *Total Assets:* £50,732,000
Registered Office: Mill Pool House, Mill Lane, Godalming, Surrey, GU7 1EY
Activities: Data processing, hosting and related activities
Parent: Endless IV (GP) LP
Officers: Simon Goodwin [1977] Director and Company Secretary; Scott William Haddow [1973] Director/Chief Executive; Edward Ransome [1984] Director

Manco South Limited
Incorporated: 11 February 2015 *Employees:* 125
Net Worth: £12,483,158 *Total Assets:* £38,147,944
Registered Office: Redeham Hall, 137 Redehall Road, Burstow, Surrey, RH6 9RJ
Activities: Development of building projects
Shareholders: James Gerard Hickey; Michael Anthony Hickey
Officers: James Gerard Hickey [1962] Director [Irish]; Michael Anthony Hickey [1965] Director [Irish]; Paul David Timlin [1979] Director [Irish]

Manitowoc Crane Group (UK) Limited
Incorporated: 3 September 1984 *Employees:* 40
Net Worth: £20,609,000 *Total Assets:* £29,569,000
Registered Office: Manitowoc House, Network 421, Radclive Road, Gawcott, Buckingham, MK18 4FD
Activities: Agents involved in the sale of machinery, industrial equipment, ships and aircraft
Parent: The Manitowoc Company Inc
Officers: Kim Dandridge [1959] Director; Corinne Nathalie Pouyet [1970] Director [French]

Manitowoc Crane Group (UK) Subco Limited
Incorporated: 28 June 2017
Net Worth: £22,040,852 *Total Assets:* £22,040,852
Registered Office: Manitowoc House, Network 421, Radclive Road, Gawcott, Bucks, MK18 4FD
Activities: Non-trading company
Parent: Manitowoc Crane Group (UK) Limited
Officers: David Antoniuk [1957] Director [American]; Uwe Woywode [1964] Director/Tax Manager [German]

The Manor House Hotel (Castle Combe) Limited
Incorporated: 11 May 1988 *Employees:* 761
Net Worth: £41,253,316 *Total Assets:* £94,559,960
Registered Office: Executive Office, Pennyhill Park Hotel & Spa, Bagshot, Surrey, GU19 5EU
Activities: Hotels and similar accommodation
Officers: Christine Linda Davies, Secretary; Christine Linda Davies [1956] Director/Accountant; Richard Michael Gradon [1959] Director; Nicholas Lawrence Luff [1967] Director; Daniel Leopoldo Enrico Pecorelli [1966] Director/Hotelier; Giuseppe Patrick Pecorelli [1970] Director/Manager; Giuseppe Pecorelli [1939] Director/Hotelier

The Manor Trust
Incorporated: 11 November 2011 *Employees:* 152
Previous: Norbury Manor Business and Enterprise College for Girls
Net Worth: £19,024,000 *Total Assets:* £20,544,000
Registered Office: Norbury Manor Business and Enterprise College, Kensington Avenue, Thornton Heath, Croydon, Surrey, CR7 8BT
Activities: General secondary education
Officers: Roger Charles Lowe, Secretary; Alan Chambers [1989] Director/Business Consultant; Jane Rosemary Chandler [1960] Director/Accountant; Amanda Jane Compton [1961] Director/Headteacher; Clare Cranham [1970] Director/Headmistress; Richard Trevor McIntosh [1953] Director/Retired; Maria Miller [1964] Director/Self Employed; Desmond Leslie Ogg [1947] Director/Retired; Mary Eileen Turner [1942] Director

Manpower Public Limited Company
Incorporated: 9 May 1956 *Employees:* 1
Net Worth: £133,964,000 *Total Assets:* £168,376,000
Registered Office: Capital Court, Windsor Street, Uxbridge, Middlesex, UB8 1AB
Activities: Activities of head offices
Parent: Manpower Holdings Limited
Officers: Damian Paul Whitham, Secretary; Mark Anthony Cahill [1958] Director; Donald Mondano [1971] Director [American]; Damian Paul Whitham [1967] Director

Manpower UK Limited
Incorporated: 15 September 1999 *Employees:* 19,215
Net Worth: £70,881,000 *Total Assets:* £220,271,008
Registered Office: Capital Court, Windsor Street, Uxbridge, Middlesex, UB8 1AB
Activities: Temporary employment agency activities
Parent: Manpower Public Limited Company
Officers: Lee Anthony Paul Graham, Secretary; Christopher Arthur [1966] Director; Mark Anthony Cahill [1958] Director; Mark Joseph Donnelly [1968] Director; James Hick [1968] Director; Damian Paul Whitham [1967] Director

Manzana Bidco Limited
Incorporated: 8 August 2016 *Employees:* 949
Net Worth Deficit: £19,602,000 *Total Assets:* £363,640,000
Registered Office: Nimbus House, Liphook Way, 20/20 Business Park, Maidstone, Kent, ME16 0FZ
Activities: Activities of other holding companies n.e.c.
Parent: Perigee Midco UK Limited
Officers: James Alexander Clark [1979] Finance Director; Jason Patrick Collins [1970] Director; Martin Keith Randall [1959] Director

Mapeley Steps Contractor Limited
Incorporated: 12 October 2000
Net Worth Deficit: £73,247,000 *Total Assets:* £46,538,000
Registered Office: Cambridge House, Clarendon Road, Watford, Herts, WD17 1HP
Activities: Other letting and operating of own or leased real estate
Officers: Michael Anthony Wilson, Secretary; Simon David Ainslie Jones [1970] Director/Chief Financial Officer; Mark Julian Smith [1970] Director; Edward Michael Swales [1979] Director; Michael Anthony Wilson [1956] Director/Solicitor

Mapil Bidco Limited
Incorporated: 23 September 2011 *Employees:* 3
Net Worth: £80,582,000 *Total Assets:* £258,519,008
Registered Office: Suite 310, Third Floor, N E Wing, 1000 Lakeside, Portsmouth, PO6 3EN
Activities: Activities of head offices
Parent: Mapil Midco 2 Limited
Officers: Alexander Ross Clemmow [1974] Director; Michael Robert Davy [1961] Director; Nicholas John Gresham [1971] Director

Mapil Midco 1 Limited
Incorporated: 19 October 2011
Net Worth: £223,932,992 *Total Assets:* £404,497,984
Registered Office: Suite 310, Third Floor, N E Wing, 1000 Lakeside, Portsmouth, PO6 3EN
Activities: Activities of head offices
Parent: Mapil Topco Limited
Officers: Alexander Ross Clemmow [1974] Director; Michael Robert Davy [1961] Director; Nicholas John Gresham [1971] Director

Mapil Midco 2 Limited
Incorporated: 14 November 2011
Net Worth: £211,128,992 *Total Assets:* £341,451,008
Registered Office: Suite 310, Third Floor, N E Wing, 1000 Lakeside, Portsmouth, PO6 3EN
Activities: Activities of head offices
Parent: Mapil Midco 1 Limited
Officers: Alexander Ross Clemmow [1974] Director; Michael Robert Davy [1961] Director; Nicholas John Gresham [1971] Director

Mapil Topco Limited
Incorporated: 28 November 2011 *Employees:* 1,323
Net Worth Deficit: £11,771,000 *Total Assets:* £503,628,000
Registered Office: Suite 310, Third Floor, N E Wing, 1000 Lakeside North Harbour, Portsmouth, PO6 3EN
Activities: Activities of head offices
Parent: Bridgepoint Europe (SGP) Limited
Officers: Alexander Ross Clemmow [1974] Director; Michael Robert Davy [1961] Director; Ian Robert Dugan [1956] Director [Irish]; Martin James Dunn [1971] Director/Investment Banker [Irish]; Nicholas John Gresham [1971] Director; Brian McBride [1955] Director; Christopher William George Watson [1974] Non-Executive Investor Director

Maple Topco Limited
Incorporated: 9 February 2017
Net Worth: £11,728,000 *Total Assets:* £100,901,000
Registered Office: St Lawrence House, Station Approach, Horley, Surrey, RH6 9HJ
Activities: Other business support service activities n.e.c.
Shareholders: Borealis Smart Holdings B.V.; 2349466 Ontario Limited; SSE Maple Limited
Officers: Nicola Anne Shand, Secretary; Charlotte Louise Brunning [1986] Director/Investment Management; Alejandro Lopez Delgado [1977] Director [Spanish]; Ines Grund [1978] Director/Investment Professional [German]; Fraser McGregor Alexander [1963] Director; Barry O'Regan [1977] Director [Irish]; Toby Penrose Parkinson [1981] Director/Solicitor; Charles Thomazi [1963] Managing Director of Infrastructure and Natural Resources [Canadian]

Mapleco1 Ltd
Incorporated: 9 February 2017
Net Worth: £9,978,000 *Total Assets:* £107,351,000
Registered Office: St Lawrence House, Station Approach, Horley, Surrey, RH6 9HJ
Activities: Other business support service activities n.e.c.
Parent: Maple Holdco 1 Limited
Officers: Nicola Anne Shand, Secretary; Charlotte Louise Brunning [1986] Director/Investment Management; Alejandro Lopez Delgado [1977] Director [Spanish]; Fraser McGregor Alexander [1963] Director; Barry O'Regan [1977] Director [Irish]; Toby Penrose Parkinson [1981] Director/Solicitor; Charles Thomazi [1963] Managing Director of Infrastructure and Natural Resources [Canadian]

Marbank Construction Limited
Incorporated: 2 February 1994 *Employees:* 30
Net Worth: £6,480,000 *Total Assets:* £20,111,000
Registered Office: 2 Wintersells Road, Byfleet, West Byfleet, Surrey, KT14 7LF
Activities: Construction of commercial buildings
Major Shareholder: Mark James Edward Woods
Officers: Stephen Andrew Brown, Secretary; Stephen Andrew Brown [1954] Director/Chartered Accountant; Wayne Ian Harris [1975] Construction Director; Glenn Wensley [1968] Project Director; Mark James Edward Woods [1964] Director/Quantity Surveyor

Marchwood Power Limited
Incorporated: 5 June 2001 *Employees:* 44
Net Worth: £126,098,000 *Total Assets:* £314,396,000
Registered Office: Oceanic Way, Marchwood Industrial Park, Marchwood, Southampton, SO40 4BD
Activities: Production of electricity
Shareholders: SSE Generation Limited; Munchener Ruckversicherungs Gesellschaft Aktiengesellschaft
Officers: Paul Andrew James Lomas, Secretary; Robert Abt [1963] Director/Senior Underwriter [German]; Arlene Bowman [1969] Director of Wholesale Finance; Alexander Matthias Bogle [1979] Director [German]; Stefan Michael Holzmair [1985] Director/Investment Manager [German]; Dr Alexander Kristian Poll [1976] Director/Senior Investment Manager [German]; Adrian Marc James Rudd [1971] Director/Chartered Mechanical Engineer; Anthony Thomas [1961] Director

Marco Island Developments Limited
Incorporated: 6 February 2014 *Employees:* 8
Net Worth: £2,234,609 *Total Assets:* £35,785,968
Registered Office: First Floor, Unit 1b St Georges Business Centre, St Georges Square, Portsmouth, PO1 3EY
Activities: Development of building projects
Shareholders: Simon Christopher Brock; Kenneth James Gordon Harvey Ross; Graham Nicholas Hazell
Officers: Simon Christopher Brock [1964] Director

Marina Developments Limited
Incorporated: 2 June 1972 *Employees:* 284
Net Worth: £68,981,000 *Total Assets:* £188,224,992
Registered Office: Outlook House, School Lane, Hamble Point, Hamble, Hants, SO31 4NB
Activities: Development of building projects
Parent: MDL Marinas Group Limited
Officers: Catherine Elinor Fleming, Secretary; Richard Anthony Broadribb [1970] Property Director; Michael James Glanville [1978] Director; James Ross Hiley [1970] Director; The Honourable Edward Richard Iliffe [1968] Director/Chartered Surveyor; Michael Generald Spencer [1947] Director/Barrister, QC, Recorder of Crown Court; David Grey Williams [1951] Director

The Marine Insurance Company Limited
Incorporated: 1 January 1881
Net Worth: £49,704,000 *Total Assets:* £180,386,000
Registered Office: St Marks Court, Chart Way, Horsham, W Sussex, RH12 1XL
Activities: Non-life insurance
Parent: Royal & Sun Alliance Insurance PLC
Officers: Anthony Buckle [1969] Director/Insurance; Scott Egan [1971] Director/Chief Financial Officer; William Rufus Benjamin McDonnell [1973] Director/Group Chief Risk Officer; Nathan Philip Williams [1965] Insurance Director

Mariner International (UK) Limited
Incorporated: 11 September 1992
Previous: First Choice Marine Limited
Net Worth: £84,489,000 *Total Assets:* £85,543,000
Registered Office: Origin One, 108 High Street, Crawley, W Sussex, RH10 1BD
Activities: Activities of head offices
Parent: First Choice Holidays Limited
Officers: Janet Northey, Secretary; Peter Vincent Young Cochran [1959] Director; Simon Barrie Michael Cross [1968] Director; Oliver Rahim Goodarzi [1986] Financial Director

Markerstudy Insurance Services Limited
Incorporated: 29 May 1987 *Employees:* 333
Previous: Zenith Marque Insurance Services Limited
Net Worth: £4,641,000 *Total Assets:* £65,741,000
Registered Office: 45 Westerham Road, Bessels Green, Sevenoaks, Kent, TN13 2QB
Activities: Non-life insurance
Major Shareholder: Kevin Ronald Spencer
Officers: Christopher James Payne, Secretary; Keith John Barber [1974] Director; Christopher Thomas Collings [1955] Director; Gary Humphreys [1965] Director; Kevin Ronald Spencer [1965] Director; Stephen Richard Stone [1964] Director

Marley Plastics Limited
Incorporated: 9 December 1997
Net Worth: £20,066,000 *Total Assets:* £41,500,000
Registered Office: Dickley Lane, Lenham, Maidstone, Kent, ME17 2DE
Activities: Other letting and operating of own or leased real estate
Parent: Aliaxis Holdings UK Limited
Officers: Ian Charles McNair, Secretary; Fabien Gauthier-Lafaye [1975] Director [French]; Stanley Carl James [1962] Director; Ian Charles McNair [1960] Director/Accountant; Warwick Denis Mitton [1969] Director/Accountant; Frankie Bernard Eugene Thielen [1974] Director [Luxembourger]

Marlin Capital Europe Limited
Incorporated: 20 December 2002
Net Worth: £2,927,000 *Total Assets:* £54,163,000
Registered Office: Marlin House, 16-22 Grafton Road, Worthing, W Sussex, BN11 1QP
Activities: Credit granting by non-deposit taking finance houses and other specialist consumer credit grantors
Parent: Marlin Portfolio Holdings Limited
Officers: Charlotte Taggart, Secretary; Craig Anthony Buick [1969] Finance Director [British/Australian]; Peter Charles Richardson [1959] Director; Kenneth John Stannard [1966] Director

Marlin Europe I Limited
Incorporated: 27 September 2006
Net Worth: £11,298,000 *Total Assets:* £43,782,000
Registered Office: Marlin House, 16-22 Grafton Road, Worthing, W Sussex, BN11 1QP
Activities: Other business support service activities n.e.c.
Parent: Marlin Portfolio Holdings Limited
Officers: Charlotte Taggart, Secretary; Craig Anthony Buick [1969] Finance Director [British/Australian]; Peter Charles Richardson [1959] Director; Kenneth John Stannard [1966] Director

Marlin Europe II Limited
Incorporated: 8 March 2007
Net Worth: £13,893,000 *Total Assets:* £56,401,000
Registered Office: Marlin House, 16-22 Grafton Road, Worthing, W Sussex, BN11 1QP
Activities: Other business support service activities n.e.c.
Parent: Marlin Portfolio Holdings Limited
Officers: Charlotte Taggart, Secretary; Craig Anthony Buick [1969] Finance Director [British/Australian]; Peter Charles Richardson [1959] Director; Kenneth John Stannard [1966] Director

Marlin Financial Group Limited
Incorporated: 19 March 2010
Net Worth: £6,017,000 *Total Assets:* £106,453,000
Registered Office: Marlin House, 16-22 Grafton Road, Worthing, W Sussex, BN11 1QP
Activities: Activities of financial services holding companies
Parent: Cabot Credit Management Group Limited
Officers: Charlotte Taggart, Secretary; Craig Anthony Buick [1969] Finance Director [British/Australian]; Peter Charles Richardson [1959] Director; Kenneth John Stannard [1966] Director

Marlin Financial Intermediate II Limited
Incorporated: 3 January 2013
Net Worth: £48,114,000 *Total Assets:* £48,680,000
Registered Office: 16-22 Grafton Road, Worthing, W Sussex, BN11 1QP
Activities: Activities of financial services holding companies
Parent: Marlin Financial Intermediate Limited
Officers: Charlotte Taggart, Secretary; Craig Anthony Buick [1969] Finance Director [British/Australian]; Peter Charles Richardson [1959] Director; Kenneth John Stannard [1966] Director

Marlin Financial Intermediate Limited
Incorporated: 19 March 2010
Net Worth: £29,919,000 *Total Assets:* £37,119,000
Registered Office: Marlin House, 16-22 Grafton Road, Worthing, W Sussex, BN11 1QP
Activities: Other business support service activities n.e.c.
Parent: Marlin Financial Group Limited
Officers: Charlotte Taggart, Secretary; Craig Anthony Buick [1969] Finance Director [British/Australian]; Peter Charles Richardson [1959] Director; Kenneth John Stannard [1966] Director

Marlin Intermediate Holdings PLC
Incorporated: 10 October 2012
Net Worth: £74,908,000 *Total Assets:* £388,655,008
Registered Office: Marlin House, 16-22 Grafton Road, Worthing, W Sussex, BN11 1QP
Activities: Activities of financial services holding companies
Parent: Marlin Intermediate Holdings Limited
Officers: Charlotte Taggart, Secretary; Craig Anthony Buick [1969] Finance Director [British/Australian]; Peter Charles Richardson [1959] Director; Kenneth John Stannard [1966] Director

Marlin Midway Limited
Incorporated: 16 October 2012
Net Worth: £39,916,000 *Total Assets:* £104,075,000
Registered Office: Marlin House, 16-22 Grafton Road, Worthing, W Sussex, BN11 1QP
Activities: Activities of financial services holding companies
Parent: Marlin Intermediate Holdings PLC
Officers: Charlotte Taggart, Secretary; Craig Anthony Buick [1969] Finance Director [British/Australian]; Peter Charles Richardson [1959] Director; Kenneth John Stannard [1966] Director

Marlin Portfolio Holdings Limited
Incorporated: 14 September 2012
Net Worth: £77,172,000 *Total Assets:* £169,674,000
Registered Office: Marlin House, 16-22 Grafton Road, Worthing, W Sussex, BN11 1QP
Activities: Activities of financial services holding companies
Parent: Marlin Senior Holdings Limited
Officers: Charlotte Taggart, Secretary; Craig Anthony Buick [1969] Finance Director [British/Australian]; Peter Charles Richardson [1959] Director; Kenneth John Stannard [1966] Director

Marlin Senior Holdings Limited
Incorporated: 14 September 2012
Net Worth: £77,811,000 *Total Assets:* £130,649,000
Registered Office: Marlin House, 16-22 Grafton Road, Worthing, W Sussex, BN11 1QP
Activities: Activities of financial services holding companies
Officers: Charlotte Taggart, Secretary; Craig Anthony Buick [1969] Finance Director [British/Australian]; Peter Charles Richardson [1959] Director; Kenneth John Stannard [1966] Director

Mars Chocolate UK Holdings Limited
Incorporated: 18 July 2008
Net Worth: £71,160,024 *Total Assets:* £71,160,024
Registered Office: 3D Dundee Road, Slough, Berks, SL1 4LG
Activities: Activities of head offices
Parent: Food Manufacturers
Officers: David James Haines [1969] Director; Ian James Langer [1965] Director; David Arnaud Manzini [1972] Director [French]; Andrew Richard Parton [1968] Director

Mars Food UK Limited
Incorporated: 18 July 2008 *Employees:* 305
Net Worth: £80,536,000 *Total Assets:* £161,460,000
Registered Office: 3D Dundee Road, Slough, Berks, SL1 4LG
Activities: Manufacture of other food products n.e.c.
Parent: Mars Melton UK Holdings Limited
Officers: David James Haines [1969] Director; Ian James Langer [1965] Director; Andrew Richard Parton [1968] Director; Craig Andrew Sargeant [1968] Director [Australian]

Mars Investments
Incorporated: 6 August 2004 *Employees:* 4
Net Worth: £155,104,992 *Total Assets:* £159,407,008
Registered Office: 3D Dundee Road, Slough, Berks, SL1 4LG
Activities: Other business support service activities n.e.c.
Parent: Food Manufacturers
Officers: David James Haines [1969] Director; Ian James Langer [1965] Director; Otis Onyekachi Otih [1957] Director [American]; Andrew Richard Parton [1968] Director

Mars Melton UK Holdings Limited
Incorporated: 18 July 2008
Net Worth: £94,197,000 *Total Assets:* £94,197,000
Registered Office: 3D Dundee Road, Slough, Berks, SL1 4LG
Activities: Activities of head offices
Parent: Mars Slough UK Holdings Limited
Officers: David James Haines [1969] Director; Ian James Langer [1965] Director; Andrew Richard Parton [1968] Director; Deri Llewellyn Watkins [1973] Director

Mars Petcare UK
Incorporated: 18 July 2008 *Employees:* 1,028
Net Worth: £223,702,000 *Total Assets:* £497,560,000
Registered Office: 3D Dundee Road, Slough, Berks, SL1 4LG
Activities: Manufacture of prepared pet foods
Parent: Mars Peterborough UK Holdings Limited
Officers: David James Haines [1969] Director; Ian James Langer [1965] Director; Andrew Richard Parton [1968] Director; Deri Llewellyn Watkins [1973] Director

Mars Petcare UK Holdings Limited
Incorporated: 18 July 2008
Net Worth: £237,400,000 *Total Assets:* £421,537,984
Registered Office: 3D Dundee Road, Slough, Berks, SL1 4LG
Activities: Activities of head offices
Parent: Food Manufacturers
Officers: David James Haines [1969] Director; Ian James Langer [1965] Director; Andrew Richard Parton [1968] Director; Deri Llewellyn Watkins [1973] Director

Mars Slough UK Holdings Limited
Incorporated: 18 July 2008
Net Worth Deficit: £95,000 *Total Assets:* £93,096,000
Registered Office: 3D Dundee Road, Slough, Berks, SL1 4LG
Activities: Activities of head offices
Parent: Mars Petcare UK Holdings Limited
Officers: David James Haines [1969] Director; Ian James Langer [1965] Director; Andrew Richard Parton [1968] Director; Deri Llewellyn Watkins [1973] Director

Mars Wrigley Confectionery UK Limited
Incorporated: 18 July 2008 *Employees:* 1,404
Previous: Mars Chocolate UK Limited
Net Worth: £318,000,992 *Total Assets:* £797,521,984
Registered Office: 3D Dundee Road, Slough, Berks, SL1 4LG
Activities: Manufacture of cocoa and chocolate confectionery
Parent: Mars Chocolate UK Holdings Limited
Officers: David James Haines [1969] Director; Ian James Langer [1965] Director; David Arnaud Manzini [1972] Director [French]; Colin James Wright Moss [1979] Director; Andrew Richard Parton [1968] Director

Marsh Wall Limited
Incorporated: 23 July 2007 *Employees:* 239
Net Worth: £2,449,663 *Total Assets:* £37,376,164
Registered Office: 6 Shield Drive, Brentford, Middlesex, TW8 9EX
Activities: Sale of new cars and light motor vehicles
Shareholder: Wayne Berry
Officers: Deborah Ann Lowles, Secretary; Wayne Robert Berry [1966] Director; Deborah Ann Lowles [1975] Director/Chartered Accountant; John Barry Naylor [1952] Director Corporate Sales

Marshall Amplification PLC
Incorporated: 19 May 1964 *Employees:* 426
Net Worth: £24,074,732 *Total Assets:* £30,101,176
Registered Office: Denbigh Road, Denbigh Industrial Estate, Bletchley, Milton Keynes, Bucks, MK1 1DQ
Activities: Manufacture of other electrical equipment
Officers: Andrew Robert Charles, Secretary; Andrew Robert Charles [1966] Director; Jonathan Martin Ellery [1957] Managing Director; Barry Moon [1955] Director

Martin-Baker Aircraft Company Limited
Incorporated: 3 January 1966 *Employees:* 827
Net Worth: £109,292,000 *Total Assets:* £161,972,992
Registered Office: Lower Road, Higher Denham, Uxbridge, Middlesex, UB9 5AJ
Activities: Manufacture of metal structures and parts of structures
Parent: Killinchy Aerospace Holdings Limited
Officers: William John Henderson Deeves, Secretary; Andrew James Martin [1973] Director; James William Martin [1942] Director; John Stephen Martin [1942] Director; Robert John Martin [1969] Director/Engineer; Robert Keith Morgan [1975] Director

Martin-Brower UK Ltd
Incorporated: 2 December 1981 *Employees:* 2,004
Net Worth: £42,531,000 *Total Assets:* £297,467,008
Registered Office: Third Floor, South Wing, One Park Lane, Hemel Hempstead, Herts, HP2 4YJ
Activities: Freight transport by road
Shareholders: Michael Jude Reyes; Joseph Christopher Reyes
Officers: Cynthia Sysol McCauley [1983] Director/General Counsel [American]; Robert McGonigle [1961] Director/Chief Operating Officer [American]

Marwell Wildlife
Incorporated: 2 March 1978 *Employees:* 228
Net Worth: £20,269,326 *Total Assets:* £22,280,718
Registered Office: Marwell Wildlife, Colden Common, Winchester, Hants, SO21 1JH
Activities: Other research and experimental development on natural sciences and engineering
Officers: Christopher Stuart Cairns, Secretary; Richard Mark Charter [1960] Director/Solicitor; Teresa Frost [1962] HR Director (Retired); Peter Jakob [1962] Director/Marketing Professional; Christopher Edward Langford [1950] Director/Rural Estates Management Consultant; Francis McCaffrey [1960] Director; David Plackett Pape [1957] Director; Nicola Robinson [1972] Director/Veterinarian; David Michael Stalker [1963] Director; Dr Mark Stanley Price [1947] Director/Academic; Dr Miranda Faye Stevenson [1947] Director/Retired; Barry Watson [1954] Director/Chartered Accountant

Mary Rose Trust (The)
Incorporated: 19 February 1979 *Employees:* 59
Net Worth: £33,041,300 *Total Assets:* £33,645,604
Registered Office: 1-10 College Road, HM Naval Base, Portsmouth, PO1 3LX
Activities: Cultural education
Officers: Susan Alison Wright, Secretary; Doctor Robert Howard Bewley [1956] Director/Archaeologist; Helen Bonser-Wilton [1970] Director/Chief Executive; Christopher John Brandon [1950] Director/Architect; Timothy Mark Busby [1962] Director/Consultant; Professor Sir Barrington Windsor Cunliffe [1939] Director/Prof of European Archaeology; Caroline Elisabeth Anne Dudley [1948] Director/Museum Consultant; Professor Van Jonathan Gore [1948] Director/Vice Chancellor; Rupert Christopher Grey [1946] Director/Solicitor; Peter Derek Hudson [1961] Director; Adam Salisbury Humphreys [1946] Director/Chairman; Alan Charles Lovell [1953] Director; Sophia Mary Mason [1966] Director [Canadian]; Dr Janet Elizabeth Owen [1968] Director/Chief Executive; David Errol Prior Palmer [1941] Director/Businessman; Dr David Robert Starkey [1945] Director/Writer and Broadcaster

Marylebone Finco Limited
Incorporated: 5 February 2016
Net Worth: £45,646 *Total Assets:* £61,022,936
Registered Office: Regent House, Allum Gate, Theobald Street, Elstree, Borehamwood, Herts, WD6 4RS
Activities: Other letting and operating of own or leased real estate
Officers: Rishi Ramesh Sachdev [1976] Director; Uday Vyas [1978] Director

Mash Holdings Limited
Incorporated: 27 March 2009 *Employees:* 17,634
Net Worth: £1,098,973,952 *Total Assets:* £3,041,364,992
Registered Office: Grenville Court, Britwell Road, Burnham, Bucks, SL1 8DF
Activities: Other service activities n.e.c.
Major Shareholder: Michael James Wallace Ashley
Officers: Leila Sangar, Secretary

Massey Group Limited
Incorporated: 26 March 1974 *Employees:* 12
Net Worth: £9,439,019 *Total Assets:* £39,990,436
Registered Office: 1 Castle Square, Brighton, BN1 1EG
Activities: Other letting and operating of own or leased real estate
Major Shareholder: Peter Frederick White
Officers: John Mier, Secretary; Rosalind Amy Cann [1976] Director/Property Manager; Nicholas John White [1967] Director; Peter Frederick White [1933] Director

Mast-Jaegermeister UK Limited
Incorporated: 12 August 2013 *Employees:* 72
Net Worth: £11,296,000 *Total Assets:* £28,586,000
Registered Office: 1st Floor, Building 11, Riverside Way, Watchmoor Park, Camberley, Surrey, GU15 3YL
Activities: Wholesale of wine, beer, spirits and other alcoholic beverages
Parent: Mast-Jaegermeister UK Holding Limited
Officers: Brett Hugh Keartland [1975] Finance Director; Guy Edward Lawrence [1965] Director/Chief Executive Officer

Mastek (UK) Ltd.
Incorporated: 15 July 1992 *Employees:* 374
Net Worth: £37,411,768 *Total Assets:* £49,106,184
Registered Office: Pennant House, 2 Napier Court, Napier Road, Reading, Berks, RG1 8BW
Activities: Business and domestic software development
Parent: Mastek Limited
Officers: Sidhartha Agarwal, Secretary; Keith Selwyn Bogg [1948] Director; Prahlad Koti [1968] Director; John Timothy Owen [1965] Director; Rajagopalan Venkataraman [1953] Director

Masternaut Bidco Limited
Incorporated: 15 April 2014
Net Worth Deficit: £65,623,448 *Total Assets:* £66,977,796
Registered Office: 18 Oxford Road, Marlow, Bucks, SL7 2NL
Activities: Business and domestic software development
Parent: Masternaut Luxembourg Holding S.A.R.L.
Officers: Djamel Souici, Secretary; Anthony Clavel [1980] Director [Swiss]; Bruce Roger Evans [1959] Director/Venture Capitalist [American]; Anthony David Johnson [1967] Director; William Patrick McHale [1949] Director/Management Consultant [American]; Dhruv Suryakant Parekh [1984] Director [American]; Han Sikkens [1978] Director [Dutch]

Masternaut Group Holdings Limited
Incorporated: 4 December 2009 *Employees:* 355
Net Worth Deficit: £66,269,984 *Total Assets:* £96,400,536
Registered Office: 18 Oxford Road, Marlow, Bucks, SL7 2NL
Activities: Business and domestic software development
Parent: Masternaut Bidco Limited
Officers: Djamel Souici, Secretary; Anthony David Johnson [1967] Director; Dhruv Suryakant Parekh [1984] Director [American]; Han Sikkens [1978] Director [Dutch]

Masternaut Holdings Limited
Incorporated: 2 January 2001
Net Worth Deficit: £94,152,000 *Total Assets:* £27,153,000
Registered Office: 18 Oxford Road, Marlow, Bucks, SL7 2NL
Activities: Business and domestic software development
Officers: Djamel Souici, Secretary; Anthony David Johnson [1967] Director; Dhruv Suryakant Parekh [1984] Director [American]; Han Sikkens [1978] Director [Dutch]

Masterson Holdings Limited
Incorporated: 29 June 2001 *Employees:* 268
Net Worth: £24,080,776 *Total Assets:* £78,976,696
Registered Office: Atlantic House, 7 Stirling Way, Borehamwood, Herts, WD6 2BT
Activities: Activities of head offices
Shareholder: Michael Masterson
Officers: Michael Masterson, Secretary; Keith Leonard Masterson [1973] Director/Surveyor [Irish]; Margaret Masterson [1976] Director/Accountant [Irish]; Michael Christian Masterson [1980] Director [Irish]; Michael Masterson [1950] Director Construction Company [Irish]; Mona Ann Masterson [1952] Director; Sean Masterson [1977] Director/Construction Manager [Irish]; Nigel Mark Warnes [1955] Construction Director

Matchtech Group (Holdings) Limited
Incorporated: 22 December 2011
Net Worth: £1,379,021 *Total Assets:* £97,148,904
Registered Office: 1450 Parkway, Solent Business Park, Whiteley, Fareham, Hants, PO15 7AF
Activities: Activities of other holding companies n.e.c.
Parent: Gattaca PLC
Officers: Katie Mary Selves, Secretary; Salar Farzad [1965] Director/Chief Financial Officer; Kevin Freeguard [1960] Director; Keith John Lewis [1966] Managing Director

Matchtech Group (UK) Limited
Incorporated: 29 April 2002
Net Worth: £37,300,000 *Total Assets:* £121,491,000
Registered Office: 1450 Parkway, Solent Business Park, Whiteley, Fareham, Hants, PO15 7AF
Activities: Other activities of employment placement agencies
Parent: Matchtech Group (Holdings) Ltd
Officers: Katie Mary Selves, Secretary; Salar Farzad [1965] Director/Chief Financial Officer; Kevin Freeguard [1960] Director; Keith John Lewis [1966] Sales Director; George Douglas Peter Materna [1953] Director; Mark Wilkie [1975] Director; Matthew Wragg [1979] Business Development Director

Matrix SCM Limited
Incorporated: 7 March 1988 *Employees:* 52
Net Worth: £2,865,740 *Total Assets:* £60,740,224
Registered Office: 2nd Floor, Partis House, Knowlhill, Milton Keynes, Bucks, MK5 8HJ
Activities: Other business support service activities n.e.c.
Shareholders: FTR Holdings Limited; FTR Holdings Limited
Officers: Barry Andrew Moseley [1965] Director; Mark Anthony Pepper [1972] Director

Matsim Properties Limited
Incorporated: 26 October 1995 *Employees:* 13
Net Worth: £17,890,522 *Total Assets:* £30,573,182
Registered Office: Maria House, 35 Millers Road, Brighton, BN1 5NP
Activities: Development of building projects
Shareholders: Andrew Lambor; Sarah Lambor
Officers: Sarah Lambor, Secretary; Andrew Lambor [1956] Director; Mathew Lambor [1983] Director; Simon Lambor [1989] Director

Mattel U.K. Limited
Incorporated: 7 January 1980 *Employees:* 131
Net Worth: £15,004,000 *Total Assets:* £119,275,000
Registered Office: Mattel House, Vanwall Business Park, Vanwall Road, Maidenhead, Berks, SL6 4UB
Activities: Wholesale of household goods (other than musical instruments) n.e.c
Parent: Mattel UK Holdings Limited
Officers: Sukhjiwan Kaur Tung, Secretary; Prashant Bapna [1973] Finance Director [Indian]; Michael Brian Hick [1978] Sales Director; Robert John Normile [1959] Director/Executive VP & Chief Legal Officer [American]

Mattel UK Holdings Limited
Incorporated: 14 November 2000
Net Worth Deficit: £6,256,000 *Total Assets:* £62,164,000
Registered Office: Mattel House, Vanwall Business Park, Vanwall Road, Maidenhead, Berks, SL6 4UB
Activities: Non-trading company
Parent: Mattel, Inc.
Officers: Sukhjiwan Kaur Tung, Secretary; Prashant Bapna [1973] Finance Director [Indian]; Michael Brian Hick [1978] Sales Director; Robert John Normile [1959] Director/Executive VP & Chief Legal Officer [American]

Mavenir Global Limited
Incorporated: 5 September 2014
Previous: Xura Global Limited
Net Worth: £143,843,440 *Total Assets:* £147,948,336
Registered Office: Reading International Business Park, Part Spur AG, Basingstoke Street, Reading, Berks, RG2 6DH
Activities: Other telecommunications activities
Parent: Mavenir Private Holdings II Ltd
Officers: Michael Knobloch [1975] Director/Accountant [Israeli]; Roy Shimon Luria [1971] Director/Legal Executive and General Counsel [American]; Robin James Thorn [1975] Director/Chartered Tax Adviser

Mavenir Systems Limited
Incorporated: 3 March 1992 *Employees:* 55
Previous: Acision UK Limited
Net Worth Deficit: £15,965,000 *Total Assets:* £84,625,000
Registered Office: Reading International Business Park, Part Spur AG, Basingstoke Road, Reading, Berks, RG2 6DH
Activities: Information technology consultancy activities
Parent: Mavenir Private Holdings II Ltd
Officers: Roy Shimon Luria, Secretary; Terrence Gerard Hungle [1954] Director [American]; Michael Knobloch [1975] Director/Accountant [Israeli]; Roy Shimon Luria [1971] Director/Legal Executive and General Counsel [American]; Robin James Thorn [1975] Director/Chartered Tax Adviser

Mavenir Systems UK Limited
Incorporated: 7 March 2002 *Employees:* 28
Previous: Mitel Mobility UK Limited
Net Worth Deficit: £6,602,000 *Total Assets:* £39,400,000
Registered Office: Reading International Business Park, Part Spur AG, Basingstoke Street, Reading, Berks, RG2 6DH
Activities: Wireless telecommunications activities
Parent: Mavenir Private Holdings II Ltd
Officers: Terrence Gerard Hungle [1954] Director [American]; Balagopal Gopa Kumar [1965] Director [American]; Roy Shimon Luria [1971] Director [American]; Robin James Thorn [1975] Director/Chartered Tax Adviser

Maxell Europe Limited
Incorporated: 18 March 1980 *Employees:* 85
Net Worth: £23,634,024 *Total Assets:* £41,125,600
Registered Office: Whitebrook Park, Lower Cookham Road, Maidenhead, Berks, SL6 8YA
Activities: Wholesale of electronic and telecommunications equipment and parts
Parent: Maxell Ltd
Officers: Andrew John Camm, Secretary; Andrew John Camm [1964] Director; Masazumi Ishiwata [1968] Managing Director [Japanese]; Hiroyuki Ishiyama [1970] Director [Japanese]; Noritoshi Masuda [1964] Director [Japanese]; Yutaka Okuda [1958] Director [Japanese]

Maxxia (UK) Limited
Incorporated: 24 January 2013
Net Worth: £40,668,120 *Total Assets:* £54,919,792
Registered Office: Corporate House, Jenna Way, Interchange Park, Newport Pagnell, Bucks, MK16 9QB
Activities: Activities of financial services holding companies
Parent: McMillan Shakespeare Limited
Officers: Lisa Joanne Edwards, Secretary; Mark Sutherland Blackburn [1957] Director [Australian]; Geoffrey Robert Kruyt [1968] Director/Business Executive [Australian]; Michael Neil Salisbury [1965] Director [Australian]; Gareth Shaw [1971] Director/Chartered Accountant

Maxxia Finance Limited
Incorporated: 24 January 2013 *Employees:* 4
Net Worth: £26,971,140 *Total Assets:* £89,681,024
Registered Office: Corporate House, Jenna Way, Interchange Park, Newport Pagnell, Bucks, MK16 9QB
Activities: Financial leasing
Parent: McMillan Shakespeare Limited
Officers: Lisa Joanne Edwards, Secretary; Mark Sutherland Blackburn [1957] Director [Australian]; Geoffrey Robert Kruyt [1968] Director/Business Executive [Australian]; Michael Neil Salisbury [1965] Director [Australian]; Gareth Shaw [1971] Director/Chartered Accountant

May & Baker Limited
Incorporated: 7 December 1989 *Employees:* 4
Net Worth: £130,619,000 *Total Assets:* £157,120,992
Registered Office: One Onslow Street, Guildford, Surrey, GU1 4YS
Activities: Manufacture of basic pharmaceutical products
Parent: Sanofi-Aventis UK Holdings Limited
Officers: Francois-Xavier Duhalde [1965] Director/Chief Financial Officer [French]; Hugo Rupert Alexander Fry [1970] Director/UK Country Chair

Robert May's School
Incorporated: 8 December 2011 *Employees:* 160
Net Worth: £19,421,186 *Total Assets:* £20,780,596
Registered Office: Robert May's School, West Street, Odiham, Hook, Hants, RG29 1NA
Activities: General secondary education
Officers: Katie Truesdale, Secretary; Stephen Alec Bentley [1968] Director/RAF Officer; Roger Thomas Buck [1947] Director/Retired; Nicholas George Crowson [1960] Director; Sean Patmore Dillow [1966] Director/Photographer; Edward John Fearon [1985] Director/Teacher; Jane Victoria Jones [1962] Director; Rita Hildegarde Moczulski [1953] Director/Interim & Freelance Consultant; Dr Anthony Kevin Murphy [1957] Director/IT System Architect; Lynne Denise Parker [1967] Director/Learning Support Assistant; Charles Justin Ravenhill [1966] Director/Head of Programme Management; Mark Reader [1969] Director/Marketing; Simon David Reigh [1972] Director/Assistant Principal; Anna Rigby [1960] Director/Management; Nicholas Martin Stevens [1974] Finance Director; Joanna West [1959] Director/Headteacher

Oscar Mayer Limited
Incorporated: 7 January 1976 *Employees:* 3,397
Net Worth: £59,164,164 *Total Assets:* £115,167,984
Registered Office: c/o Aztec Financial Services (UK) Limited, Forum 3, Solent Business Park, Whiteley, Fareham, Hants, PO15 7FH
Activities: Manufacture of prepared meals and dishes
Parent: Ontario Management Limited
Officers: Francois Denis Marie Legrain [1966] Director [French]; Alan John Wotton [1972] Director/Chief Commercial Officer

Mazda Motors UK Limited
Incorporated: 8 May 2001 *Employees:* 136
Net Worth: £7,402,000 *Total Assets:* £106,210,000
Registered Office: Victory Way, Crossways Business Park, Dartford, Kent, DA2 6DT
Activities: Sale of new cars and light motor vehicles
Parent: Mazda Motor Corporation
Officers: Ian Fraser, Secretary; Martijn Ten Brink [1973] Director/Vice President, Sales [Dutch]; Colin Maddocks [1969] Director, Financial Services; Jeremy Andrew Thomson [1966] Managing Director

MB Group Limited
Incorporated: 1 March 1988
Net Worth: £72,987,000 *Total Assets:* £124,661,000
Registered Office: Honeywell House, Skimped Hill Lane, Bracknell, Berks, RG12 1EB
Activities: Activities of other holding companies n.e.c.
Parent: Honeywell International Inc.
Officers: Ashish Kumar Saraf [1979] Director [Indian]

MC Rental Limited
Incorporated: 19 January 1989 *Employees:* 47
Net Worth: £14,669,649 *Total Assets:* £107,021,840
Registered Office: Beddow Way, Forstal Road, Aylesford, Maidstone, Kent, ME20 7BT
Activities: Renting and leasing of trucks and other heavy vehicles
Major Shareholder: Simon James Dawson
Officers: Peter David Booth, Secretary; Mark Sheldon Barton [1963] Director; Peter David Booth [1963] Director/Chartered Accountant; Simon James Dawson [1971] Director/Sales Manager; David Kenneth Hutchins [1966] Director

MC Treasury Limited
Incorporated: 23 October 2007
Net Worth: £763,508,992 *Total Assets:* £1,086,730,624
Registered Office: Maple Court, Central Park, Reeds Crescent, Watford, Herts, WD24 4QQ
Activities: Other business support service activities n.e.c.
Parent: HIC Treasury Limited
Officers: Stuart Beasley [1971] Director/Financial Controller; Richard Geoffrey Beeston [1982] Director/Chartered Accountant; James Owen Percival [1968] Director/Accountant; Brian McKay Wilson [1962] Director/Company Secretary

MC Truck & Bus Limited
Incorporated: 20 January 1976 *Employees:* 327
Net Worth: £7,798,964 *Total Assets:* £34,889,420
Registered Office: Beddow Way, Aylesford, Maidstone, Kent, ME20 7BT
Activities: Sale of other motor vehicles
Major Shareholder: Simon James Dawson
Officers: Peter David Booth, Secretary; Peter David Booth [1963] Director/Chartered Accountant; Nigel Frederick Brooks [1964] Director/Aftermarket Manager; Simon James Dawson [1971] Director/Sales Manager; David Kenneth Hutchins [1966] Director; Steven John Moon [1975] Director

Sir Robert McAlpine (A19) Limited
Incorporated: 8 June 2015
Net Worth: £2,039,591 *Total Assets:* £71,256,816
Registered Office: Eaton Court, Maylands Avenue, Hemel Hempstead Industrial Estate, Hemel Hempstead, Herts, HP2 7TR
Activities: Financial intermediation not elsewhere classified
Parent: Robert McAlpine Road Holdings Limited
Officers: Kevin John Pearson, Secretary; David Honeyman [1967] Director/Financial Controller; Robert John William Wotherspoon [1967] Director/Chartered Accountant

Sir Robert McAlpine (Holdings) Limited
Incorporated: 12 October 1992 *Employees:* 2,203
Net Worth: £78,855,000 *Total Assets:* £880,270,976
Registered Office: Eaton Court, Maylands Avenue, Hemel Hempstead Industrial Estate, Hemel Hempstead, Herts, HP2 7TR
Activities: Activities of head offices
Parent: Newarthill Limited
Officers: John Alistair Dempsey, Secretary; Kevin John Pearson, Secretary; Kevin John Pearson, Secretary; Karen Joy Brookes [1962] Director of People & Infrastructure; Paul Christopher Hamer [1969] Director/Chief Executive; Hector George McAlpine [1980] Director; Robert Edward Thomas William McAlpine [1978] Director; Boyd Atkinson McFee [1958] Director/Civil Engineer; James Leighton More [1976] Director/Chief Financial Officer; Martin Clive Pitt [1964] Director

Sir Robert McAlpine Capital Ventures Limited
Incorporated: 9 February 1995
Net Worth: £81,581,632 *Total Assets:* £182,715,392
Registered Office: Eaton Court, Maylands Avenue, Hemel Hempstead Industrial Estate, Hemel Hempstead, Herts, HP2 7TR
Activities: Financial intermediation not elsewhere classified
Parent: Robert McAlpine Enterprises Limited
Officers: Kevin John Pearson, Secretary; David Honeyman [1967] Director/Financial Controller; Robert John William Wotherspoon [1967] Director/Accountant

Sir Robert McAlpine Enterprises Limited
Incorporated: 14 September 1978
Net Worth: £58,972,000 *Total Assets:* £189,664,992
Registered Office: Eaton Court, Maylands Avenue, Hemel Hempstead, Herts, HP2 7TR
Activities: Activities of other holding companies n.e.c.
Parent: Newarthill Limited
Officers: Elizabeth Carol Beard, Secretary; Kevin John Pearson, Secretary; Adrian Neil Raeburn McAlpine [1944] Director/Property Executive; Sir Andrew William McAlpine [1960] Director/Civil Engineering; Cullum McAlpine [1947] Director/Civil Engineering & Building Contractor; The Hon David Malcolm McAlpine [1946] Director/Civil Engineering & Building Contractor; Douglas James McAlpine [1983] Director/Manager, Demand Side Management, Americas; Gavin Malcolm McAlpine [1966] Director; Hector George McAlpine [1980] Director; Ian Malcolm McAlpine [1942] Director/Building & Civil Engineering Contractor; Kenneth McAlpine [1920] Director/Civil Engineering & Building Construction; Richard Hugh McAlpine [1958] Director; Robert Edward Thomas William McAlpine [1978] Director; Robert John William Wotherspoon [1967] Director/Chartered Accountant

Sir Robert McAlpine Limited
Incorporated: 31 May 1956 *Employees:* 2,118
Net Worth: £43,183,000 *Total Assets:* £833,086,016
Registered Office: Eaton Court, Maylands Avenue, Hemel Hempstead Industrial Estate, Hemel Hempstead, Herts, HP2 7TR
Activities: Construction of commercial buildings
Parent: Robert McAlpine (Holdings) Limited
Officers: John Alistair Dempsey, Secretary; Kevin John Pearson, Secretary; Kevin John Pearson, Secretary; Karen Joy Brookes [1962] Director of People & Infrastructure; Paul Christopher Hamer [1969] Director/Chief Executive; Hector George McAlpine [1980] Director; Robert Edward Thomas William McAlpine [1978] Director; Boyd Atkinson McFee [1958] Director/Civil Engineer; James Leighton More [1976] Director/Chief Financial Officer; Martin Clive Pitt [1964] Director

Sir Robert McAlpine Road Holdings Limited
Incorporated: 23 June 2015
Net Worth Deficit: £641,184 *Total Assets:* £77,887,336
Registered Office: Eaton Court, Maylands Avenue, Hemel Hempstead Industrial Estate, Hemel Hempstead, Herts, HP2 7TR
Activities: Activities of other holding companies n.e.c.
Parent: Robert McAlpine Capital Ventures Limited
Officers: Kevin John Pearson, Secretary; David Honeyman [1967] Director/Financial Controller; Robert John William Wotherspoon [1967] Director/Chartered Accountant

McCormick Europe Limited
Incorporated: 26 October 1995
Net Worth: £297,451,008 *Total Assets:* £309,884,000
Registered Office: Haddenham Business Park, Pegasus Way, Haddenham, Aylesbury, Bucks, HP17 8LB
Activities: Activities of other holding companies n.e.c.
Parent: McCormick & Company Incorporated
Officers: Laird Everett Creighton [1974] Director [American]; Francois Gouby [1960] Director/VP Operations [French]; Christopher Jinks [1961] Director/Vice President Industrial EMEA; Lawrence Erik Kurzius [1958] Director/President EMEA [American]; Malcolm Stuart Swift [1960] Director/President; Melanie Clare Williams [1964] Director/Vice President HR

McCormick International Holdings
Incorporated: 21 January 2000
Net Worth: £293,673,984 *Total Assets:* £394,406,016
Registered Office: Haddenham Business Park, Pegasus Way, Haddenham, Aylesbury, Bucks, HP17 8LB
Activities: Activities of other holding companies n.e.c.
Parent: McCormick Europe Limited
Officers: Laird Everett Creighton [1974] Director [American]; Christopher Jinks [1961] Director; Lawrence Erik Kurzius [1958] Director/President - EMEA [American]; Malcolm Stuart Swift [1960] Director/President

McCormick Kutas Food Service Limited
Incorporated: 5 January 1996 *Employees:* 156
Net Worth: £16,355,737 *Total Assets:* £33,466,626
Registered Office: Haddenham Business Park, Pegasus Way, Haddenham, Aylesbury, Bucks, HP17 8LB
Activities: Activities of other holding companies n.e.c.
Shareholders: McCormick (UK) Limited; Kutas Tarim Urunleri Dis Tic Ve San AS
Officers: Laird Everett Creighton [1974] Director [American]; Francois Gouby [1960] Director/VP Supply Chain Operations [French]; Ilhan Feyzi Gurel [1942] Director/Industrialist [Turkish]; Kazim Ilter Gurel [1964] Director/Industrialist [Turkish/British]; Christopher Jinks [1961] Director/Vice President Industrial EMEA; Mehmet Gurel Kapani [1972] Director/Industrialist [Turkish]

J.P.McDougall & Co.Limited
Incorporated: 18 March 1931 *Employees:* 1,076
Net Worth Deficit: £36,984,000 *Total Assets:* £95,502,000
Registered Office: The Akzonobel Building, Wexham Road, Slough, Berks, SL2 5DS
Activities: Non-specialised wholesale trade
Parent: Dulux Limited
Officers: John Wright Henderson [1966] Director; Wendy MacDonald [1969] Director; Alistair McAuley [1972] Managing Director; Michael Smalley [1958] Director; David Allan Turner [1971] Director

MCF Commercial Limited
Incorporated: 13 June 2007 *Employees:* 3
Net Worth: £1,550,036 *Total Assets:* £48,084,928
Registered Office: Lunar House, Wooburn Green, High Wycombe, Bucks, HP10 0HH
Activities: Activities of head offices
Parent: Comland Group Limited
Officers: Christopher Giles Martin, Secretary/Director; Christopher Robert Ayres [1982] Director; Stuart James Crossley [1944] Director; Christopher Giles Martin [1968] Director

MCG (Holdings) Ltd
Incorporated: 11 September 2009 *Employees:* 374
Net Worth: £27,148,776 *Total Assets:* £151,723,344
Registered Office: MC Truck Depot, Beddow Way, Forstal Road, Aylesford, Kent, ME20 7BT
Activities: Sale of other motor vehicles
Major Shareholder: Simon James Dawson
Officers: Kimberley Dawson [1970] Director; Simon James Dawson [1971] Director

McGraw-Hill Global Education UK Holdco II Limited
Incorporated: 22 February 2013
Net Worth: £181,164,544 *Total Assets:* £201,636,832
Registered Office: McGraw-Hill Education (UK) Limited, Unit 4 Foundation Park, Roxborough Way, Maidenhead, Berks, SL6 3UD
Activities: Activities of other holding companies n.e.c.
Parent: McGraw-Hill Global Education UK Holdco Limited
Officers: Christopher Phillip Knight [1969] Director/Chartered Certified Accountant; David Kraut [1970] Director/Treasurer McGraw Hill Education [American]; David Stafford [1962] Director/Attorney [American]; Ian Edward White [1972] Director/Finance

McGraw-Hill Global Education UK Holdco Limited
Incorporated: 21 February 2013
Net Worth: £89,823,880 *Total Assets:* £216,799,120
Registered Office: McGraw-Hill Education (UK) Limited, Unit 4 Foundation Park, Roxborough Way, Maidenhead, Berks, SL6 3UD
Activities: Activities of other holding companies n.e.c.
Officers: Christopher Phillip Knight [1969] Director/Chartered Certified Accountant; David Kraut [1970] Director/Treasurer McGraw-Hill Education [American]; David Stafford [1962] Director/Attorney [American]; Ian Edward White [1972] Director/Finance

McGrove Developments Limited
Incorporated: 29 May 2014
Net Worth: £8,362,000 *Total Assets:* £214,795,008
Registered Office: Grenville Court, Britwell Road, Burnham, Bucks, SL1 8DF
Activities: Development of building projects
Shareholder: Mash Holdings Limited
Officers: Toby Richard Baines [1962] Director/Chartered Surveyor; Justin Douglas William Barnes [1965] Director; Malcolm Donald Dalgleish [1952] Director/Chartered Surveyor; John Andrew Gatley [1964] Managing Director; Michael Patrick Murray [1989] Director/Property Developer

McKay Securities P L C
Incorporated: 14 October 1946 *Employees:* 19
Net Worth: £306,440,000 *Total Assets:* £467,108,000
Registered Office: 20 Greyfriars Road, Reading, Berks, RG1 1NL
Activities: Other letting and operating of own or leased real estate
Officers: Joanne Sarah McKeown, Secretary; Jonathan Martin Austen [1956] Director/Chartered Accountant; Jeremy Neil Bates [1965] Director/Chartered Surveyor; Thomas Charles Elliott [1975] Director/Chartered Surveyor; Richard Stuart Grainger [1960] Director/Chartered Accountant; Simon Christopher Perkins [1965] Director/Chartered Surveyor; Giles Pollock Salmon [1966] Director/Chartered Accountant; Nicholas Jose Shepherd [1958] Director/Chartered Surveyor

McLaren Applied Technologies Limited
Incorporated: 29 November 1988 *Employees:* 377
Net Worth: £12,831,000 *Total Assets:* £39,447,000
Registered Office: McLaren Technology Centre, Chertsey Road, Woking, Surrey, GU21 4YH
Activities: Manufacture of other parts and accessories for motor vehicles
Parent: McLaren Holdings Limited
Officers: Timothy Nicholas Murnane, Secretary; Paul Anthony Buddin [1980] Director; Jonathan Neale [1962] Director

McLaren Automotive Limited
Incorporated: 2 December 1985 *Employees:* 1,699
Net Worth: £318,817,984 *Total Assets:* £920,251,008
Registered Office: McLaren Technology Centre, Chertsey Road, Woking, Surrey, GU21 4YH
Activities: Manufacture of motor vehicles
Parent: McLaren Holdings Limited
Officers: Ruth Louise Nic Aoidh, Secretary; Paul Anthony Buddin [1980] Director; Michael Robert Flewitt [1962] Director/Chief Executive Officer

McLaren Finance PLC
Incorporated: 21 June 2017
Net Worth Deficit: £245,000 *Total Assets:* £550,508,992
Registered Office: McLaren Technology Centre, Chertsey Road, Woking, Surrey, GU21 4YH
Activities: Other service activities n.e.c.
Parent: McLaren Holdings Limited
Officers: Timothy Nicholas Murnane, Secretary; Zakary Challen Brown [1971] Director [American]; Paul Anthony Buddin [1980] Director; Michael Robert Flewitt [1962] Director; Jonathan Neale [1962] Director

McLaren Group Limited
Incorporated: 11 April 2017 *Employees:* 3,178
Net Worth: £148,535,008 *Total Assets:* £1,340,724,992
Registered Office: McLaren Technology Centre, Chertsey Road, Woking, Surrey, GU21 4YH
Activities: Activities of other holding companies n.e.c.
Parent: The Government of The Kingdom of Bahrain
Officers: Timothy Nicholas Murnane, Secretary; Roberto Aguirre [1955] Director/Businessman Investor [Mexican]; Shaikh Mohammed Bin Isa Bin Mohammed Al Khalifa [1969] Director/Political Advisor [Bahraini]; Rima Al Masri [1977] Director/General Counsel, BMHC [Australian]; Hisham Saleh Ahmed Al Saie [1975] Director [Bahraini]; Mahmood Hashem Ahmed Alkooheji [1958] Director/Bahrain Mumtalakat Holding Company B.S.C CEO [Bahraini]; Lay Hoon Chan [1964] Alternate Director [Singaporean]; Cromwell Lloyd William Griffiths [1971] Director/Advisor [Bahraini]; Michael Mehrdad Latifi [1962] Director/Chairman/CEO [Canadian]; Eng Hock Peter Lim [1953] Director [Singaporean]; Mansour Akram Ojjeh [1952] Director/Businessman [French]

McLaren Racing Limited
Incorporated: 16 September 1980 *Employees:* 706
Net Worth: £73,767,000 *Total Assets:* £160,582,000
Registered Office: McLaren Technology Centre, Chertsey Road, Woking, Surrey, GU21 4YH
Activities: Other sports activities
Parent: McLaren Holdings Limited
Officers: Timothy Nicholas Murnane, Secretary; John Maxwell Allert [1969] Director [Australian]; Zakary Challen Brown [1971] Director [American]; Paul Anthony Buddin [1980] Director; John Philip Cooper [1970] Finance Director; Timothy Nicholas Murnane [1960] Director/Solicitor Head of Legal Affair; Jonathan Neale [1962] Director/Engineer

McLaren Services Limited
Incorporated: 2 December 1985 *Employees:* 237
Previous: McLaren Technology Group Limited
Net Worth Deficit: £1,925,000 *Total Assets:* £273,292,000
Registered Office: McLaren Technology Centre, Chertsey Road, Woking, Surrey, GU21 4YH
Activities: Activities of other holding companies n.e.c.
Parent: McLaren Holdings Limited
Officers: Timothy Nicholas Murnane, Secretary; Paul Anthony Buddin [1980] Director; Jonathan Neale [1962] Director

McNeil Healthcare (UK) Limited
Incorporated: 13 May 1994
Net Worth: £162,355,008 *Total Assets:* £210,890,000
Registered Office: c/o Johnson & Johnson Ltd, Roxborough Way, Maidenhead, Berks, SL6 3UG
Activities: Wholesale of pharmaceutical goods
Parent: McNeil Products Ltd.
Officers: Andrew Crossley [1968] Finance Director; Luc Huys [1967] Managing Director [Belgian]

McNeil Products Limited
Incorporated: 4 March 1994
Net Worth: £61,234,000 *Total Assets:* £61,570,000
Registered Office: c/o Johnson & Johnson Limited, Foundation Park, Roxborough Way, Maidenhead, Berks, SL6 3UG
Activities: Non-trading company
Parent: Johnson & Johnson
Officers: Andrew Crossley [1968] Financial Director; Luc Huys [1967] Managing Director [Belgian]

MCPA Limited
Incorporated: 18 February 2013
Net Worth: £17,797,238 *Total Assets:* £25,347,940
Registered Office: 2 Castle Business Village, Station Road, Hampton, Surrey, TW12 2BX
Activities: Buying and selling of own real estate
Shareholders: Christopher Paul Anthony; Mark Christopher Cherry
Officers: Christopher Paul Anthony [1958] Director/Fund Manager; Mark Christopher Cherry [1962] Director/Property Developer

Alexander McQueen Trading Limited
Incorporated: 14 May 2002 *Employees:* 42
Net Worth Deficit: £5,790,851 *Total Assets:* £23,968,636
Registered Office: 5th Floor, Rear Suite, Oakfield House, 35 Perrymount Road, Haywards Heath, W Sussex, RH16 3BW
Activities: Other business support service activities n.e.c.
Parent: Birdswan Solutions Limited
Officers: Emmanuel Andre Gintzburger [1974] Director/Chief Executive Officer of Alexander McQueen [French]; Eric Sandrin [1964] Director/Group General Counsel [French]; Bryan Dany Van Holderbeke [1975] Director/Chief Financial Officer [French]

MDH (Group) Limited
Incorporated: 20 June 2014 *Employees:* 72
Net Worth: £17,248,000 *Total Assets:* £40,517,000
Registered Office: Bordyke End, East Street, Tonbridge, Kent, TN9 1HA
Activities: Construction of domestic buildings
Parent: Places for People Ventures Operations Limited
Officers: David Cowans [1957] Director; Colin Kenneth Rae [1964] Director; Andrew Winstanley [1978] Finance Director

MDL Development Company Number 2 Limited
Incorporated: 31 October 2005
Net Worth: £130,325,000 *Total Assets:* £131,226,000
Registered Office: Outlook House, School Lane, Hamble Point, Hamble, Hants, SO31 4NB
Activities: Other business support service activities n.e.c.
Parent: MDL Marinas Group Limited
Officers: Catherine Elinor Fleming, Secretary; Richard Anthony Broadribb [1970] Property Director; Michael James Glanville [1978] Director; James Ross Hiley [1970] Director; The Honourable Edward Richard Iliffe [1968] Director/Chartered Surveyor

MDL Developments Limited
Incorporated: 15 April 1981
Net Worth: £7,341,000 *Total Assets:* £24,347,000
Registered Office: Outlook House, School Lane, Hamble Point, Hamble, Hants, SO31 4NB
Activities: Development of building projects
Parent: Lockset Limited
Officers: Catherine Elinor Fleming, Secretary; Richard Anthony Broadribb [1970] Property Director; Michael James Glanville [1978] Director; James Ross Hiley [1970] Director; The Honourable Edward Richard Iliffe [1968] Director/Chartered Surveyor; Kristi Gabrielle Roger [1974] Director/Property Development Manager; David Grey Williams [1951] Director

MDL Marinas Group Limited
Incorporated: 20 September 1985 *Employees:* 300
Net Worth: £114,716,000 *Total Assets:* £209,352,992
Registered Office: Outlook House, School Lane, Hamble Point, Hamble, Hants, SO31 4NB
Activities: Activities of head offices
Parent: Yattendon Group PLC
Officers: Catherine Elinor Fleming, Secretary; Richard Anthony Broadribb [1970] Property Director; Michael James Glanville [1978] Director; James Ross Hiley [1970] Director; The Honourable Edward Richard Iliffe [1968] Director/Chartered Surveyor; David Grey Williams [1951] Director

ME III Limited
Incorporated: 17 May 2010
Net Worth: £22,503,000 *Total Assets:* £129,792,000
Registered Office: Marlin House, 16-22 Grafton Road, Worthing, W Sussex, BN11 1QP
Activities: Other business support service activities n.e.c.
Parent: Black Tip Capital Holdings Limited
Officers: Charlotte Taggart, Secretary; Craig Anthony Buick [1969] Finance Director [British/Australian]; Peter Charles Richardson [1959] Director; Kenneth John Stannard [1966] Director

Meantime Brewing Company Limited
Incorporated: 8 April 1999
Net Worth: £11,617,000 *Total Assets:* £20,091,000
Registered Office: One Forge End, Woking, Surrey, GU21 6DB
Activities: Manufacture of beer
Parent: Asahi Europe Ltd
Officers: James Smith, Secretary; Rohan Cummings [1975] Director/Chief Financial Officer; Hector Gorosabel [1960] Director/MD Western Europe [Canadian]; Alastair Frederick Hook [1963] Managing Director; Yusuke Naritsuka [1972] Director [Japanese]

Mecca Bingo Limited
Incorporated: 10 October 1984 *Employees:* 2,927
Net Worth: £57,783,000 *Total Assets:* £106,409,000
Registered Office: Tor, Saint-Cloud Way, Maidenhead, Berks, SL6 8BN
Activities: Gambling and betting activities
Parent: Rank Group Gaming Division Limited
Officers: Luisa Ann Wright, Secretary; William James Spencer Floydd [1969] Director; Alan Morgan [1977] Director; John Patrick O'Reilly [1960] Director

Medequip Assistive Technology Limited
Incorporated: 11 April 2001 *Employees:* 703
Net Worth: £21,679,000 *Total Assets:* £43,960,000
Registered Office: Unit 2 Summit Centre, Skyport Drive, Harmondsworth, West Drayton, Middlesex, UB7 0LJ
Activities: Retail sale of medical and orthopaedic goods in specialised stores (not incl. hearing aids) n.e.c.
Parent: Siddall Group Limited
Officers: Jonathan Paul Cockroft [1969] Director; Nigel Stewart Paul Cook [1963] Director of Human Resources; Andrew Paul Firth [1964] Operations Director; Michael Frank Greenwood [1965] Director/Chartered Accountant; David Griffiths [1961] Managing Director; James Ibbotson [1977] Director; Adrienne Helen Siddall [1958] Non-Executive Director; Andrew John Siddall [1959] Director/Group Chief Executive; Clive Philip Siddall [1962] Director; Jeremy Charles Siddall [1958] Director; Susan Tracey Siddall [1962] Non-Executive Director; Lyndsey Jane Wainwright [1961] Non-Executive Director; Mike West [1963] Procurement Director

Medequip Group Limited
Incorporated: 21 April 2015 *Employees:* 703
Net Worth: £42,295,000 *Total Assets:* £69,806,000
Registered Office: Unit 2 Summit Centre, Skyport Drive, Harmondsworth, West Drayton, Middlesex, UB7 0LJ
Activities: Retail sale of medical and orthopaedic goods in specialised stores (not incl. hearing aids) n.e.c.
Parent: Medequip Holdings Limited
Officers: Jonathan Paul Cockroft [1969] Director; Nigel Stewart Paul Cook [1963] Director; Andrew Paul Firth [1964] Director; Michael Frank Greenwood [1965] Director/Chartered Accountant; David Griffiths [1961] Director; James Ibbotson [1977] Director; Andrew John Siddall [1959] Director; Clive Philip Siddall [1962] Director; Jeremy Charles Siddall [1958] Director; Mike West [1963] Procurement Director

Medica Group PLC
Incorporated: 22 April 2013 *Employees:* 89
Previous: Medica Group Limited
Net Worth: £24,900,000 *Total Assets:* £42,163,000
Registered Office: Havelock Place, Havelock Road, Hastings, E Sussex, TN34 1BG
Activities: Activities of head offices
Officers: Anthony Leonard Lee, Secretary; Dr Michael Bewick [1956] Director; Dr Stephen Griffith Davies [1956] Director/Doctor of Medicine Radiologist; Gordon Roy Davis [1956] Director; John Michael Graham [1964] Director; Anthony Leonard Lee [1975] Director; Stephen Lee Whittern [1974] Director

Medica Reporting Finance Limited
Incorporated: 22 April 2013 *Employees:* 5
Net Worth: £710,609 *Total Assets:* £31,527,144
Registered Office: Havelock Place, Havelock Road, Hastings, E Sussex, TN34 1BG
Activities: Activities of head offices
Officers: Anthony Leonard Lee, Secretary; Dr Stephen Griffith Davies [1956] Director/Doctor of Medicine Radiologist; John Michael Graham [1964] Director; Anthony Leonard Lee [1975] Director; Kevin Patrick Terrins [1976] Director

Medina Dairy Limited
Incorporated: 7 April 1993 *Employees:* 316
Net Worth Deficit: £4,771,938 *Total Assets:* £22,723,420
Registered Office: Medina House, Shirley Avenue, Windsor, Berks, SL4 5LH
Activities: Wholesale of dairy products, eggs and edible oils and fats
Parent: Medina Holdings Limited
Officers: Sheraz Hussain, Secretary; Mohammed Azam [1965] Director/Dairyman; Sheazad Hussain [1979] Director; Taibraiz Hussain [1979] Director/Operational

Medina Holdings Limited
Incorporated: 3 September 2003 *Employees:* 482
Net Worth: £3,599,062 *Total Assets:* £50,164,084
Registered Office: Medina Dairy House, Vale Road, Windsor, Berks, SL4 5JL
Activities: Activities of head offices
Major Shareholder: Sheazad Hussain
Officers: Mohammed Azam [1965] Director/Shopkeeper and Dairy; Sheazad Hussain [1979] Executive Director; Sheraz Hussain [1976] Director

Medispeed
Incorporated: 11 December 2007
Net Worth: £250,873,632 *Total Assets:* £253,904,288
Registered Office: Surrey Research Park, The Priestley Centre, 10 Priestley Road, Guildford, Surrey, GU2 7XY
Activities: Activities of head offices
Parent: Linde UK Holdings Limited
Officers: Susan Kathleen Kelly, Secretary; Julian Michael Bland [1967] Director/Head of Accounting; Benjamin Patterson [1962] Director/Solicitor; Sally Ann Williams [1970] Director/Accountant

Medivet Group Limited
Incorporated: 16 December 1997 *Employees:* 1,298
Net Worth: £17,021,080 *Total Assets:* £128,100,616
Registered Office: 4 Mowat Industrial Estate, Sandown Road, Watford, Herts, WD24 7UY
Activities: Veterinary activities
Parent: Medivet Partnership LLP
Officers: Arnold Stephen Levy, Secretary/Veterinary Surgeon; Dr Guy Richard Carter [1964] Director/Veterinary Surgeon; Arnold Stephen Levy [1959] Director/Veterinary Surgeon; Kevin Lance Morris [1973] Director; John William Hampden Smithers [1963] Director/Veterinary Surgeon

Medivet Partnership LLP
Incorporated: 20 March 2009 *Employees:* 1,297
Net Worth Deficit: £160,000 *Total Assets:* £72,368,000
Registered Office: 4 Mowat Industrial Estate, Sandown Road, Watford, Herts, WD24 7UY
Officers: David Abratt [1973] Member; Yorram Ariel [1966] Member; Dr Guy Richard Carter [1964] Member; Jan Harold Doedens [1966] Member; Erwin Wilhelm Hohn [1959] Member; Matthew James Holgate [1974] Member; Nitzan Kroter [1969] Member; Jeffrey Stephen Langberg [1958] Member; Richard Mary Leonard [1958] Member; Arnold Stephen Levy [1959] Member; Kevin Lance Morris [1973] Member; Adi Nell [1968] Member; Daniel Preter [1967] Member; Gareth Richardson [1970] Member; John William Hampden Smithers [1963] Member

Medreich PLC
Incorporated: 7 November 1995 *Employees:* 58
Net Worth: £20,507,924 *Total Assets:* £40,756,208
Registered Office: Ibex House, Baker Street, Weybridge, Surrey, KT13 8AH
Activities: Wholesale of pharmaceutical goods
Officers: Ashish Gupta, Secretary; Shinya Katafuchi [1960] Director [Japanese]; John McCullough [1970] Director; Yuji Sasaki [1958] Director [Japanese]; Hiromasa Takizawa [1964] Director [Japanese]

Medtronic Limited
Incorporated: 8 September 1972 *Employees:* 763
Net Worth: £31,142,000 *Total Assets:* £212,692,992
Registered Office: Building 9, Croxley Park, Hatters Lane, Watford, Herts, WD18 8WW
Activities: Manufacture of medical and dental instruments and supplies
Parent: Medtronic Public Limited Company
Officers: Philip John Albert [1965] Director/Vice-President of Corporate Tax [American]; Helen Louise Brown [1975] HR Director; Mark Justin Elsey [1967] Finance Director; Jacqueline Fielding [1964] VP & Regional Director, UK/Ireland

Medway Fundco Limited
Incorporated: 28 July 2004
Net Worth Deficit: £8,613,196 *Total Assets:* £23,485,214
Registered Office: 55 Station Road, Beaconsfield, Bucks, HP9 1QL
Activities: Management of real estate on a fee or contract basis
Parent: Medway Community Estates Limited
Officers: Nigel Raymond Dodds, Secretary; Ross William Driver [1981] Finance Director; David Alexander John Foot [1968] Investment Director, Infrastructure; James Christopher Heath [1975] Director; Balasingham Ravi Kumar [1975] Investment Director; Ashley Brendon George West [1944] Director; Adam Iden Wickings [1962] Director/NHS Chief Operating Officer

Medway Power Limited
Incorporated: 7 September 1990
Net Worth Deficit: £126,800,000 *Total Assets:* £38,600,000
Registered Office: No 1 Forbury Place, 43 Forbury Road, Reading, Berks, RG1 3JH
Activities: Production of electricity
Parent: SSE Generation Limited
Officers: Sally Fairbairn, Secretary; Mark Richard Hayward [1963] Director/Manager; James Isaac Smith [1962] Director/Engineer

Megger Group Limited
Incorporated: 14 February 1991 *Employees:* 1,279
Net Worth: £68,248,400 *Total Assets:* £181,630,432
Registered Office: Archcliffe Road, Dover, Kent, CT17 9EN
Activities: Activities of head offices
Officers: Richard Talbot Aylwin, Secretary; Richard Talbot Aylwin [1968] Director; Andrew John Boughtwood [1958] Director; Dr Andrew Colin Dodds [1964] Director; James Bennett Fairbairn [1968] Director

Melesey Limited
Incorporated: 9 June 2000 *Employees:* 283
Net Worth: £33,488,000 *Total Assets:* £108,172,000
Registered Office: No 1 Park Lane, Hemel Hempstead, Herts, HP2 4YL
Activities: Activities of head offices
Parent: Bourne Leisure Limited
Officers: Jane Elizabeth Bentall [1970] Director/Accountant; Paul Charles Flaum [1970] Director; Iain Stuart Macmillan [1976] Director

The Meller Educational Trust
Incorporated: 12 June 2009 *Employees:* 284
Net Worth: £48,465,204 *Total Assets:* £50,062,852
Registered Office: The Bushey Academy, London Road, Bushey, Herts, WD23 3AA
Activities: General secondary education
Officers: David Robert Hughes, Secretary; Kate Prudence Bearman [1971] Director; Richard Arthur Elms [1947] Director/Chief Executive; Rita Susan Halbright [1961] Director/School Administrator [British/American]; David Robert Hughes [1970] Director of Finance and Operations; Clive Ashley Ross [1949] Director/Chartered Surveyor; Andrew Jonathan Sheach [1963] Director/Solicitor; Gillian Elizabeth Wiscarson [1954] Director/University Lecturer

Melton House Investments Limited
Incorporated: 7 March 2011 *Employees:* 43
Net Worth: £8,949,815 *Total Assets:* £26,362,588
Registered Office: Melton House, 65-67 Clarendon Road, Watford, Herts, WD17 1DS
Activities: Hotels and similar accommodation
Shareholders: Gursharan Singh Chadha; Jasbir Chadha
Officers: Gursharan Singh Chadha [1960] Director; Vivek Singh Chadha [1988] Director

MEMS Power Generation Limited
Incorporated: 16 June 1986 *Employees:* 103
Net Worth: £20,632,080 *Total Assets:* £24,310,780
Registered Office: Eastcourt Works, Beechings Way Industrial Estate, Beechings Way, Gillingham, Kent, ME8 6PS
Activities: Renting and leasing of other machinery, equipment and tangible goods n.e.c.
Major Shareholder: Colin Arthur Jarvis
Officers: Claire Helena Jarvis, Secretary; Mark Ian Diffey [1977] Rental Director; Colin Arthur Jarvis [1946] Director/Chairman; Glen Jarvis [1973] Managing Director; Iain Andrew Maxwell [1978] Commercial Director

Mentmore Limited
Incorporated: 23 November 1935 *Employees:* 2
Net Worth: £130,272,000 *Total Assets:* £376,945,984
Registered Office: c/o Safestore Holdings PLC, Brittanic House, Stirling Way, Borehamwood, Herts, WD6 2BT
Activities: Activities of other holding companies n.e.c.
Parent: Safestore Acquisition Limited
Officers: Andrew Brian Jones [1966] Director/Chartered Accountant; Federico Vecchioli [1966] Director [French]

John Menzies (108) Limited
Incorporated: 10 November 1994
Net Worth: £54,400,000 *Total Assets:* £77,400,000
Registered Office: 2 World Business Centre Heathrow, Newall Road, London Heathrow Airport, Hounslow, Middlesex, TW6 2SF
Activities: Activities of head offices
Parent: Menzies Group Holdings Limited
Officers: John Francis Alexander Geddes, Secretary; John Francis Alexander Geddes [1968] Director/Company Secretary; Giles Robert Bryant Wilson [1973] Director/Accountant

Menzies Aviation (ASIG) Limited
Incorporated: 14 February 1984 *Employees:* 872
Previous: ASIG Limited
Net Worth: £23,200,000 *Total Assets:* £39,800,000
Registered Office: 2 World Business Centre Heathrow, Newall Road, London Heathrow Airport, Hounslow, Middlesex, TW6 2SF
Activities: Scheduled passenger air transport
Parent: ASIG Holdings Limited
Officers: John Francis Alexander Geddes, Secretary; Deon Van Niekerk [1972] Director/Accountant [South African]; Laura Relf [1982] Director/Accountant; Sheena Robertson [1956] Operations Director

Menzies Aviation (UK) Limited
Incorporated: 27 April 2000 *Employees:* 4,396
Net Worth: £5,200,000 *Total Assets:* £39,600,000
Registered Office: 2 World Business Centre Heathrow, Newall Road, London Heathrow Airport, Hounslow, Middlesex, TW6 2SF
Activities: Service activities incidental to air transportation
Parent: Menzies Aviation PLC
Officers: Tristan George Turnbull, Secretary/Solicitor; Deon Van Niekerk [1972] Director [South African]; David Alastair Trollope [1960] Director/Accountant

Menzies Aviation Holdings Limited
Incorporated: 17 August 2000 *Employees:* 68
Net Worth: £6,600,000 *Total Assets:* £151,800,000
Registered Office: 2 World Business Centre Heathrow, Newall Road, London Heathrow Airport, Hounslow, Middlesex, TW6 2SF
Activities: Service activities incidental to air transportation
Parent: Menzies Group Holdings Limited
Officers: John Francis Alexander Geddes, Secretary; Forsyth Rutherford Black [1969] Director; John Francis Alexander Geddes [1968] Director/Company Secretary; David Alastair Trollope [1960] Director/Accountant; Giles Robert Bryant Wilson [1973] Director/Accountant

Menzies Aviation PLC
Incorporated: 23 August 1994 *Employees:* 5
Net Worth: £49,700,000 *Total Assets:* £609,699,968
Registered Office: 2 World Business Centre Heathrow, Newall Road, London Heathrow Airport, Hounslow, Middlesex, TW6 2SF
Activities: Service activities incidental to air transportation
Parent: Menzies Aviation Holdings Limited
Officers: John Francis Alexander Geddes, Secretary; Forsyth Rutherford Black [1969] Director; John Francis Alexander Geddes [1968] Director/Company Secretary; David Alastair Trollope [1960] Director/Accountant; Giles Robert Bryant Wilson [1973] Director/Accountant

John Menzies Finance Limited
Incorporated: 11 June 2007
Net Worth: £60,100,000 *Total Assets:* £80,100,000
Registered Office: 2 World Business Centre Heathrow, Newall Road, London Heathrow Airport, Hounslow, Middlesex, TW6 2SF
Activities: Financial intermediation not elsewhere classified
Parent: John Menzies PLC
Officers: John Francis Alexander Geddes, Secretary; John Francis Alexander Geddes [1968] Director/Company Secretary; Giles Robert Bryant Wilson [1973] Director/Accountant

Menzies Group Holdings Limited
Incorporated: 31 January 1963
Net Worth: £38,900,000 *Total Assets:* £203,200,000
Registered Office: 2 World Business Centre Heathrow, Newall Road, London Heathrow Airport, Hounslow, Middlesex, TW6 2SF
Activities: Non-trading company
Parent: John Menzies PLC
Officers: John Francis Alexander Geddes, Secretary; John Francis Alexander Geddes [1968] Director/Company Secretary; Giles Robert Bryant Wilson [1973] Director/Accountant

Merant Holdings
Incorporated: 18 December 1984
Net Worth: £28,799,000 *Total Assets:* £41,525,000
Registered Office: The Lawn, 22-30 Old Bath Road, Newbury, Berks, RG14 1QN
Activities: Activities of head offices
Parent: Serena Holdings
Officers: Graham Howard Norton, Secretary; Kenneth Robert Jukes [1967] Director/Accountant; Graham Howard Norton [1959] Director; Jane Caroline Grantham Smithard [1954] Director

Mercedes-Benz Cars UK Limited
Incorporated: 1 December 1989 *Employees:* 507
Previous: Mercedes-Benz UK Limited
Net Worth: £235,114,000 *Total Assets:* £1,414,178,048
Registered Office: Mercedes-Benz UK Limited, Delaware Drive, Tongwell, Milton Keynes, Bucks, MK15 8BA
Activities: Sale of new cars and light motor vehicles
Parent: Daimler UK Limited
Officers: Jonathan Philip Reuben Lipman, Secretary; Marcus Werner Breitschwerdt [1961] Director/President & CEO [German]; Harald Henn [1964] Director/Economist [German]; Gary Mark Savage [1961] CEO/Managing Director

Mercedes-Benz Financial Services UK Limited
Incorporated: 21 February 1990 *Employees:* 506
Net Worth: £473,240,992 *Total Assets:* £7,566,894,080
Registered Office: Delaware Drive, Tongwell, Milton Keynes, Bucks, MK15 8BA
Activities: Financial intermediation not elsewhere classified
Parent: Daimler UK Limited
Officers: Jonathan Lipman, Secretary; Brian Evon [1963] Finance Director [Canadian]; Ilka Fuerstenberger [1969] Managing Director Financial Services Industry [German]; Richard Andrew Howard [1965] Director/President & CEO; Christian Peters [1967] Managing Director [German]; Oliver Christian Winkler [1970] Finance Director [Austrian]

Mercedes-Benz Retail Group UK Limited
Incorporated: 10 September 1946 *Employees:* 1,612
Net Worth: £82,581,000 *Total Assets:* £519,217,984
Registered Office: Mercedes-Benz UK Limited, Tongwell, Milton Keynes, Bucks, MK15 8BA
Activities: Sale of new cars and light motor vehicles
Parent: Daimler UK Limited
Officers: Jonathan Philip Reuben Lipman, Secretary; Vittorio Braguglia [1970] Director After Sales and Retail Operations [Swiss]; Marcus Werner Breitschwerdt [1961] Director [German]; Marcell Ruoff [1980] Director/CFO Own Retail Group Europe [German]

Merck Consumer Healthcare Limited
Incorporated: 28 August 1979 *Employees:* 9
Net Worth Deficit: £43,683,000 *Total Assets:* £32,178,000
Registered Office: Bedfont Cross, Stanwell Road, Feltham, Middlesex, TW14 8NX
Activities: Non-trading company
Parent: Merck KGaA
Officers: Anthony Joseph Appleton [1962] Director & General Counsel; Alexander George Buckthorp [1973] Finance Director; Vijay Indroo Sitlani [1975] Finance Director [Singaporean]; Christopher John Young [1974] HR Director

Merck Holding Ltd.
Incorporated: 16 May 2013
Net Worth: £1,130,476,928 *Total Assets:* £1,389,846,400
Registered Office: Bedfont Cross, Stanwell Road, Feltham, Middlesex, TW14 8NX
Activities: Activities of other holding companies n.e.c.
Parent: Merck KGaA
Officers: Peter Biro [1967] Director/US Certified Public Accountant [Dutch]; Victor Mark Jackson [1962] Director/Operations Manager

Merck Serono Limited
Incorporated: 2 October 1970 *Employees:* 173
Net Worth: £20,986,000 *Total Assets:* £60,114,000
Registered Office: Bedfont Cross, Stanwell Road, Feltham, Middlesex, TW14 8NX
Activities: Wholesale of pharmaceutical goods
Parent: Merck KGaA
Officers: Peter Biro [1967] Director/US Certified Public Accountant [Dutch]; Charles William Dring [1962] Director; Mary Elizabeth Henderson [1971] Managing Director [Irish]

Merial Limited
Incorporated: 7 March 1997
Net Worth: £194,750,848 *Total Assets:* £272,727,264
Registered Office: Ellesfield Avenue, Bracknell, Berks, RG12 8YS
Activities: Manufacture of basic pharmaceutical products
Officers: Marshall Burke Barton, Secretary; Christian Orth [1962] Director/Senior Vice President Finance & CFO [Swiss]

Meridian Hospital Company (Holdings) Limited
Incorporated: 7 November 1997
Net Worth: £21,808,000 *Total Assets:* £116,998,000
Registered Office: 8 White Oak Square, London Road, Swanley, Kent, BR8 7AG
Activities: Combined facilities support activities
Shareholders: Innisfree M & G PPP LLP; JLIF (GP) Limited
Officers: Graham Beazley - Long [1960] Investment Managing Director; David John Brooking [1975] Investment Director; Carl Harvey Dix [1966] Operations Director; Julian Denzil Sutcliffe [1968] Life Cycle Asset Director; Sir John Wickerson [1937] Director/Solicitor

Meridian Hospital Company PLC
Incorporated: 7 November 1997
Net Worth: £21,808,000 *Total Assets:* £116,998,000
Registered Office: 8 White Oak Square, London Road, Swanley, Kent, BR8 7AG
Activities: Combined facilities support activities
Parent: Meridian Hospital Company (Holdings) Limited
Officers: Graham Maurice Beazley-Long [1960] Investment Managing Director; David John Brooking [1975] Investment Director; Carl Harvey Dix [1966] Operations Director; Julian Denzil Sutcliffe [1968] Life Cycle Asset Director; Sir John Wickerson [1937] Director/Solicitor

Meridian Residential Developments Limited
Incorporated: 18 December 2012 *Employees:* 5
Net Worth: £23,950,626 *Total Assets:* £34,862,720
Registered Office: World Business Centre, 3 Newall Road, London Heathrow Airport, Hounslow, Middlesex, TW6 2TA
Activities: Buying and selling of own real estate
Parent: Grove Acquisitions Limited
Officers: Surinder Arora [1958] Director; Carlton Jeffrey Brown [1972] Director/Chartered Accountant

Meritas Group Holdings Limited
Incorporated: 27 January 2017 *Employees:* 213
Net Worth Deficit: £2,863,901 *Total Assets:* £41,288,968
Registered Office: Coopers Bridge, Braziers Lane, Winkfield, Bracknell, Berks, RG42 6NS
Activities: Activities of other holding companies n.e.c.
Parent: Inflexion TIC Services Holdings LLP
Officers: Henry Miles Arundel [1987] Director; Robert Bell [1967] Finance Director; Lord Donald Thomas Younger Curry [1944] Director; Nigel John Patrick [1957] Director; Linda Joyce Radnor [1956] Director; Carl Edmund Wormald [1969] Director

Meritas Group Limited
Incorporated: 14 December 2016
Net Worth Deficit: £2,303,910 *Total Assets:* £28,790,814
Registered Office: Coopers Bridge, Braziers Lane, Winkfield, Bracknell, Berks, RG42 6NS
Activities: Activities of other holding companies n.e.c.
Parent: Meritas Group Holdings Limited
Officers: Henry Miles Arundel [1987] Director; Robert Bell [1967] Finance Director; Lord Donald Thomas Younger Curry [1944] Director; Nigel John Patrick [1957] Director; Linda Joyce Radnor [1956] Director; Carl Edmund Wormald [1969] Director

Merkur Casino UK Ltd
Incorporated: 14 August 2012 *Employees:* 1,408
Net Worth: £55,035,000 *Total Assets:* £133,593,000
Registered Office: Seebeck House, 1a Seebeck Place, Knowlhill, Milton Keynes, Bucks, MK5 8FR
Activities: Activities of other holding companies n.e.c.
Officers: Stefan Bruns [1971] Director/Chief Executive Officer [German]; Borris Lungen [1962] Director/Chief Financial Officer [German]; Meik Sellenriek [1968] Director [German]

Mermaid UK Holdco Limited
Incorporated: 7 February 2017
Net Worth: £77,173,872 *Total Assets:* £93,189,656
Registered Office: c/o Tam Enterprises Limited, Stalham Business Centre, Rushenden Road, Queenborough, Kent, ME11 5HE
Activities: Activities of investment trusts
Officers: Diane Mary Miles [1954] Director/Operating Partner [American/British]; Colin Welch [1970] Director/Financial Professional [American]

Merritts Properties Limited
Incorporated: 2 November 1960 *Employees:* 6
Net Worth: £28,839,952 *Total Assets:* £42,388,588
Registered Office: Merritt House, Hill Avenue, Amersham, Bucks, HP6 5BQ
Activities: Other letting and operating of own or leased real estate
Shareholders: Anthony David Holt; Christina Jane Hitchcock; Timothy James Merritt
Officers: Charles Nicholas Morton, Secretary; Christina Jane Hitchcock [1964] Director/Property Manager; Sandra Ann McGrath [1968] Finance Director [Irish]; Timothy James Merritt [1960] Director; Arthur Leonard Robert Morton [1942] Director/Chartered Accountant; Charles Nicholas Morton [1984] Director; David Maurice Norman [1957] Director/Chartered Surveyor

Mersen UK Portslade Limited
Incorporated: 1 April 1966 *Employees:* 22
Net Worth: £10,442,184 *Total Assets:* £29,133,362
Registered Office: Unit 12 Tungsten Building, George Street, Portslade, Brighton, BN41 1RA
Activities: Other manufacturing n.e.c.
Parent: Mersen UK Holdings Ltd
Officers: Ivan Herrero, Secretary; Andrew Freer [1962] Director/General Manager; Luc Themelin [1961] Director/Engineer [French]

Merseyside Energy Recovery Holdings Ltd
Incorporated: 9 March 2012
Previous: SITA Sembcorp UK Holdings Limited
Net Worth Deficit: £62,370,000 *Total Assets:* £323,318,016
Registered Office: Suez House, Grenfell Road, Maidenhead, Berks, SL6 1ES
Activities: Activities of head offices
Shareholders: Suez Recycling and Recovery UK Ltd; Sembcorp Utilitied PTE Limited
Officers: Nauman Ahmad [1970] Director/Business Executive [Pakistani]; Stephen Christopher Hands [1968] Director/SVP Legal; Belinda Faith Knox [1972] Investment Director; Graham Arthur McKenna-Mayes [1968] Director/Chief Operating Officer; Amanda Padfield [1968] Director/Principal PPP Project Manager; Ian Anthony Sexton [1956] Director/Chairman - SCL, SCHL, SNL, SNHL, SSTWL, SSTWHL; Yuji Suzuki [1970] Managing Director [Japanese]

Merseyside Energy Recovery Ltd
Incorporated: 17 April 2012
Previous: SITA Sembcorp UK Limited
Net Worth Deficit: £62,370,000 *Total Assets:* £323,318,016
Registered Office: Suez House, Grenfell Road, Maidenhead, Berks, SL6 1ES
Activities: Collection of non-hazardous waste
Parent: Merseyside Energy Recovery Holdings Ltd
Officers: Nauman Ahmad [1970] Director/Business Executive [Pakistani]; Stephen Christopher Hands [1968] Director/SVP Legal; Belinda Faith Knox [1972] Investment Director; Graham Arthur McKenna-Mayes [1968] Director/Chief Operating Officer; Amanda Padfield [1968] Director/Principal PPP Project Manager; Ian Anthony Sexton [1956] Director/Chairman - SCL, SCHL, SNL, SNHL, SSTWL, SSTWHL; Yuji Suzuki [1970] Managing Director [Japanese]

Mersham Hatch Estate LLP
Incorporated: 19 June 2012 *Employees:* 2
Net Worth: £22,536,488 *Total Assets:* £25,387,036
Registered Office: Quarrington Farmhouse, Quarrington Lane, West Brabourne, Ashford, Kent, TN25 5NG
Officers: Kelly Louise Doreen Knatchbull [1988] Member; The Honourable Michael John Knatchbull [1950] Member

MES Interco
Incorporated: 5 October 1999
Net Worth: £813,910,016 *Total Assets:* £1,299,442,944
Registered Office: P O Box 87, Warwick House, Farnborough Aerospace Centre, Farnborough, Hants, GU14 6YU
Activities: Non-trading company
Parent: BAE Systems (Holdings) Limited
Officers: David Stanley Parkes, Secretary; Ann Louise Holding [1961] Director/Chartered Secretary; David Stanley Parkes [1963] Director/Company Secretary

Meslink Limited
Incorporated: 29 April 1999
Net Worth: £671,702,016 *Total Assets:* £1,159,083,008
Registered Office: P O Box 87, Warwick House, Farnborough Aerospace Centre, Farnborough, Hants, GU14 6YU
Activities: Non-trading company
Parent: MES Interco
Officers: Ann-Louise Holding, Secretary; Ann-Louise Holding [1961] Director/Chartered Secretary; David Stanley Parkes [1963] Director/Company Secretary

MessageLabs Group Limited
Incorporated: 20 August 1999
Net Worth: £39,284,000 *Total Assets:* £39,319,000
Registered Office: Reading International Business Park, Reading, Berks, RG2 6DH
Activities: Other information technology service activities
Parent: Symantec (UK) Holding Limited
Officers: Eunice Jeeyoon Kim [1973] Director/Attorney [American]; Norman Osumi [1964] Director/Certified Public Accountant [American]

MessageLabs Limited
Incorporated: 1 September 1999 *Employees:* 80
Net Worth: £35,732,000 *Total Assets:* £40,946,000
Registered Office: Reading International Business Park, Reading, Berks, RG2 6DH
Activities: Other information technology service activities
Parent: MessageLabs Group Limited
Officers: Eunice Jeeyoon Kim [1973] Director/Attorney [American]

Metropole Hotels (Holdings) Limited
Incorporated: 11 March 1949 *Employees:* 1,194
Net Worth: £125,635,000 *Total Assets:* £512,972,992
Registered Office: Forum 3, Solent Business Park, Parkway, Whiteley, Fareham, Hants, PO15 7FH
Activities: Hotels and similar accommodation
Officers: Charles Richard Power [1964] Director/Consultant; Subbash Chandra Thammanna [1976] Finance Director

Metropolis Group Holdings Limited
Incorporated: 16 April 2013
Net Worth: £26,025,700 *Total Assets:* £50,160,608
Registered Office: 7th Floor, Vantage London, Great West Road, Brentford, Middlesex, TW8 9AG
Activities: Publishing of consumer and business journals and periodicals
Parent: M New Holdings Limited
Officers: Richard Hutchinson, Secretary; Richard Hutchinson [1966] Finance Director; Robert Andrew Marr [1965] Director/Chief Executive Officer

Metropolis International Group Ltd
Incorporated: 7 April 1994 *Employees:* 194
Net Worth: £2,014,080 *Total Assets:* £40,544,320
Registered Office: 7th Floor, Vantage London, Great West Road, Brentford, Middlesex, TW8 9AG
Activities: Publishing of consumer and business journals and periodicals
Parent: Metropolis Group Holdings Ltd
Officers: Richard Hutchinson, Secretary/Accountant; Richard Hutchinson [1966] Finance Director; Robert Andrew Marr [1965] Director/Chief Executive

MF UK FC Limited
Incorporated: 16 April 2012
Net Worth Deficit: £136,339,296 *Total Assets:* £100,144,592
Registered Office: Oracle Parkway, Thames Valley Park, Reading, Berks, RG6 1RA
Activities: Activities of other holding companies n.e.c.
Parent: Oracle Corporation UK Limited
Officers: David James Hudson, Secretary; Simon Thomas Allison [1974] EMEA Senior Tax Director; David James Hudson [1966] Director/Solicitor

MFG Parentco Limited
Incorporated: 18 August 2016
Net Worth: £34,000 *Total Assets:* £40,391,000
Registered Office: Millbank House, 171-185 Ewell Road, Surbiton, Surrey, KT6 6AP
Activities: Activities of head offices
Parent: MFG Midco Limited
Officers: Justin Christopher Bowman [1972] Director; Christopher Denis Stephen Leach [1949] Director; Adrian Paul Lurie [1973] Director; Stewart Pitt [1972] Director; Mark Henry Storey [1961] Director

MFS Portfolio Limited
Incorporated: 10 June 2005
Net Worth: £12,684,000 *Total Assets:* £69,784,000
Registered Office: Marlin House, 16-22 Grafton Road, Worthing, W Sussex, BN11 1QP
Activities: Financial management
Parent: Marlin Portfolio Holdings Limited
Officers: Charlotte Taggart, Secretary; Craig Anthony Buick [1969] Finance Director [British/Australian]; Peter Charles Richardson [1959] Director; Kenneth John Stannard [1966] Director

MGT Teesside Limited
Incorporated: 23 April 2008
Net Worth Deficit: £13,288,000 *Total Assets:* £544,942,976
Registered Office: 8 White Oak Square, London Road, Swanley, Kent, BR8 7AG
Activities: Production of electricity
Parent: Chaptre Holdings Limited
Officers: Matthew James Spencer Booth [1971] Director; Jens Christian Clausen [1948] Director/Consultant [Danish]; Matthew John Edgar [1985] Director/Senior Vice President [Australian]; Kasper Hansen [1978] Director [Danish]; Andrew Horsley Clifford Hartley [1958] Director; David Jensen [1974] Director/Senior Asset Manager [Danish]

MHI Vestas Offshore Wind Blades UK Ltd
Incorporated: 11 August 2014 *Employees:* 323
Net Worth: £16,909,000 *Total Assets:* £29,897,000
Registered Office: West Medina Mills, Stag Lane, Newport, Isle of Wight, PO30 5TR
Activities: Manufacture of engines and turbines, except aircraft, vehicle and cycle engines
Officers: Flemming Obenhausen Andersen [1963] Director/Senior Vice President, Finance [Danish]; Robert Christian Gustaf Borin [1977] Director/Senior Vice President Manufacturing, MVOW [Swedish]; Tatsuichiro Honda [1964] Director [Japanese]

Micheldever Group Limited
Incorporated: 12 December 2005 *Employees:* 5
Net Worth: £13,705,000 *Total Assets:* £89,859,000
Registered Office: Micheldever Station, Winchester, Hants, SO21 3AP
Activities: Activities of head offices
Officers: Jonathan Cowles, Secretary; Jonathan Robert Cowles [1971] Director/Chartered Accountant; Akio Hohana [1966] Director [Japanese]; Isamu Ishida [1955] Director [Japanese]; Yutaka Kuroda [1959] Director [Japanese]; Duncan Stewart Wilkes [1958] Director

Micheldever Tyre Services Limited
Incorporated: 18 May 1984 *Employees:* 1,762
Net Worth: £48,701,000 *Total Assets:* £173,140,000
Registered Office: Micheldever Station, Winchester, Hants, SO21 3AP
Activities: Wholesale trade of motor vehicle parts and accessories
Parent: Micheldever Group Ltd
Officers: Jonathan Cowles, Secretary; Jonathan Robert Cowles [1971] Director/Chartered Accountant; Akio Hohana [1966] Director [Japanese]; Isamu Ishida [1955] Director [Japanese]; Yutaka Kuroda [1959] Director [Japanese]; Duncan Stewart Wilkes [1958] Director

Michelmersh Brick Holdings PLC
Incorporated: 3 November 1997 *Employees:* 373
Net Worth: £59,383,000 *Total Assets:* £96,935,000
Registered Office: Freshfield Lane, Danehill, Haywards Heath, W Sussex, RH17 7HH
Activities: Manufacture of bricks, tiles and construction products, in baked clay
Shareholder: Eric John Spencer Gadsden
Officers: Stephen Huw Perrott Morgan, Secretary; Stephen Gerard Bellamy [1960] Director [New Zealander]; Robert William Carlton Porter [1944] Director; Francis John Hanna [1968] Director; Stephen Huw Perrott Morgan [1960] Director; Peter Nigel Sharp [1968] Director; Martin Russell Warner [1953] Director

Michelmersh Brick UK Limited
Incorporated: 2 August 1990 *Employees:* 293
Net Worth: £8,298,000 *Total Assets:* £34,294,000
Registered Office: Freshfield Lane, Danehill, Haywards Heath, W Sussex, RH17 7HH
Activities: Manufacture of bricks, tiles and construction products, in baked clay
Parent: Michelmersh Brick Holdings PLC
Officers: Stephen Huw Perrott Morgan, Secretary; Francis John Hanna [1968] Director; Peter Nigel Sharp [1968] Director; Martin Russell Warner [1953] Director/Chartered Surveyor

Micro Focus (IP) Ltd
Incorporated: 2 March 2004
Net Worth: £132,065,032 *Total Assets:* £132,065,032
Registered Office: The Lawn, 22-30 Old Bath Road, Newbury, Berks, RG14 1QN
Activities: Other information service activities n.e.c.
Parent: Micro Focus Holdings Unlimited
Officers: Jane Caroline Grantham Smithard, Secretary; Stuart Alexander McGill [1961] Director; Graham Howard Norton [1959] Director

Micro Focus (US) Holdings
Incorporated: 7 January 2010
Net Worth: £1,586,379,008 *Total Assets:* £1,722,185,344
Registered Office: The Lawn, 22-30 Old Bath Road, Newbury, Berks, RG14 1QN
Activities: Other information technology service activities
Parent: Micro Focus Group Limited
Officers: Jane Caroline Grantham Smithard, Secretary; Stuart Alexander McGill [1961] Director/Chief Operating Officer; Graham Howard Norton [1959] Director

Micro Focus CHC Limited
Incorporated: 14 January 2016
Net Worth: £987,397,184 *Total Assets:* £2,416,492,288
Registered Office: The Lawn, 22-30 Old Bath Road, Newbury, Berks, RG14 1QN
Activities: Other information technology service activities
Parent: Micro Focus (US) Holdings
Officers: Jane Caroline Grantham Smithard, Secretary; Robert Mark Ebrey [1974] Director; Darren Michael Fisher [1966] Finance Director

Micro Focus Group Limited
Incorporated: 27 September 2011
Net Worth: £1,294,828,544 *Total Assets:* £4,043,976,448
Registered Office: The Lawn, 22-30 Old Bath Road, Newbury, Berks, RG14 1QN
Activities: Other information technology service activities
Parent: Micro Focus Midco Limited
Officers: Jane Smithard, Secretary; Robert Mark Ebrey [1974] Director; Darren Michael Fisher [1966] Finance Director; Jane Caroline Grantham Smithard [1954] Director/Group General Counsel and Company Secretary

Micro Focus International PLC
Incorporated: 21 May 2004 *Employees:* 4,663
Net Worth: £1,251,385,984 *Total Assets:* £3,605,430,016
Registered Office: The Lawn, Old Bath Road, Newbury, Berks, RG14 1QN
Activities: Other information technology service activities
Officers: Jane Caroline Grantham Smithard, Secretary; Richard Charles Atkins [1952] Director; Amanda Victoria Brown [1968] Group Human Resources Director; Lawton Wehle Fitt [1953] Director [American]; Kevin LooSeniore [1959] Director; Brian David McArthur-Muscroft [1963] Director/Chief Financial Officer; Stephen Edward Murdoch [1966] Director; Darren Roos [1974] Director [South African]; Silke Christina Scheiber [1973] Director [Austrian]; Karen Slatford [1956] Director

Micro Focus IP Development Limited
Incorporated: 23 April 2010 *Employees:* 102
Net Worth: £136,635,104 *Total Assets:* £359,788,928
Registered Office: The Lawn, 22-30 Old Bath Road, Newbury, Berks, RG14 1QN
Activities: Information technology consultancy activities
Parent: Micro Focus (IP) Limited
Officers: Jane Caroline Grantham Smithard, Secretary; Ian Cumming Fraser [1961] Director/Chief Human Resources Officer; Christopher John Kennedy [1964] Director/Chief Financial Officer; Stephen Edward Murdoch [1966] Director/Chief Executive Officer; Richard Paul Rodgers [1963] Director/Chief Operating Officer [Irish]

Micro Focus Limited
Incorporated: 27 June 1980 *Employees:* 320
Net Worth: £38,322,000 *Total Assets:* £79,895,000
Registered Office: The Lawn, 22-30 Old Bath Road, Newbury, Berks, RG14 1QN
Activities: Other information technology service activities
Parent: Micro Focus Holdings Unlimited
Officers: Jane Caroline Grantham Smithard, Secretary; Darren Michael Fisher [1966] Finance Director; Stuart Alexander McGill [1961] Director/Sales Manager; Graham Howard Norton [1959] Director/Accountant; Jane Caroline Grantham Smithard [1954] Director/Group General Counsel and Company Secretary

Micro Focus MHC Limited
Incorporated: 3 December 2015
Net Worth: £812,556,288 *Total Assets:* £812,556,288
Registered Office: The Lawn, 22-30 Old Bath Road, Newbury, Berks, RG14 1QN
Activities: Other information technology service activities
Parent: Micro Focus CHC Limited
Officers: Jane Caroline Grantham Smithard, Secretary; Robert Mark Ebrey [1974] Director; Darren Michael Fisher [1966] Finance Director

Micro Focus Midco Limited
Incorporated: 14 January 2016
Net Worth: £2,345,740,288 *Total Assets:* £2,345,740,288
Registered Office: The Lawn, 22-30 Old Bath Road, Newbury, Berks, RG14 1QN
Activities: Other information technology service activities
Parent: Micro Focus Midco Holdings Limited
Officers: Jane Caroline Grantham Smithard, Secretary; Robert Mark Ebrey [1974] Director; Darren Michael Fisher [1966] Finance Director

Microchip Limited
Incorporated: 6 November 1987 *Employees:* 84
Net Worth: £22,948,888 *Total Assets:* £42,055,428
Registered Office: Microchip House, 720 Wharfedale Road, Winnersh Triangle, Wokingham, Berks, RG41 5TP
Activities: Wholesale of radio, television goods & electrical household appliances (other than records, tapes, CDs)
Parent: Microchip Technology Inc.
Officers: Nawaz Sharif, Secretary/Director; James Eric Bjornholt [1970] Director/Accountant [American]; Gary Paul Marsh [1961] Sales Director; Steve Sanghi [1955] Director/President & C O O [American]

Micromuse Limited
Incorporated: 10 March 1988
Net Worth: £37,272,784 *Total Assets:* £48,949,308
Registered Office: P O Box 41, North Harbour, Portsmouth, PO6 3AU
Activities: Other software publishing
Parent: Micromuse U.K. Holdings Limited
Officers: Alison Mary Catherine Sullivan, Secretary; Ian Duncan Ferguson [1968] Director/Solicitor

Micron Europe Limited
Incorporated: 30 January 1989 *Employees:* 196
Net Worth: £104,081,280 *Total Assets:* £306,213,344
Registered Office: Greenwood House, London Road, Bracknell, Berks, RG12 2AA
Activities: Other manufacturing n.e.c.
Parent: Micron Technology, Inc.
Officers: Donald Edward Whitt Jnr, Secretary; Giles Ballard [1968] Director, Sales Distribution; Graham Paul Kingwell [1974] Director/Senior Manager European Financial Accounting; Patrick Villepreux [1970] Director, Sales [French]; Donald Edward Whitt Jnr [1966] Director/VP, Tax - Micron Technology, Inc [American]

Microsoft Limited
Incorporated: 24 March 1982 *Employees:* 3,046
Net Worth: £196,551,008 *Total Assets:* £997,073,024
Registered Office: Microsoft Campus, Thames Valley Park, Reading, Berks, RG6 1WG
Activities: Information technology consultancy activities
Parent: Microsoft Corporation
Officers: Keith Ranger Dolliver [1963] Director/Attorney [American]; Benjamin Owen Orndorff [1971] Director/Attorney [American]; Cindy Helen Rose [1965] Director/Chief Executive Officer

Microsoft Properties UK Limited
Incorporated: 17 May 1991
Net Worth: £25,127,000 *Total Assets:* £42,548,000
Registered Office: Microsoft Campus, Thames Valley Park, Reading, Berks, RG6 1WG
Activities: Buying and selling of own real estate
Parent: Microsoft Corporation
Officers: Keith Ranger Dolliver [1963] Director/Attorney [American]; Benjamin Owen Orndorff [1971] Director/Attorney [American]; Cindy Helen Rose [1965] Director/Chief Executive Officer

Midgard Ltd
Incorporated: 22 February 2006 *Employees:* 100
Net Worth: £4,822,688 *Total Assets:* £71,057,872
Registered Office: 4 Elstree Way, Borehamwood, Herts, WD6 1RN
Activities: Construction of commercial buildings
Parent: JRL Group Ltd
Officers: Ronan Joseph Gleeson, Secretary/Director [Irish]; Ronan Joseph Gleeson [1976] Director [Irish]; Kevin William Keegan [1963] Director/Estimator [Irish]; John James Reddington [1972] Director/Formwork [Irish]

Midland Quarry Products Limited
Incorporated: 15 March 1996 *Employees:* 157
Net Worth: £121,202,000 *Total Assets:* £150,768,992
Registered Office: Hanson House, 14 Castle Hill, Maidenhead, Berks, SL6 4JJ
Activities: Other mining and quarrying n.e.c.
Parent: Hanson Quarry Products Europe Limited
Officers: Wendy Fiona Rogers, Secretary; David Anthony Bagshaw [1959] Managing Director; Philip Andrew Bradshaw [1963] Operations Director - Aggregates and Asphalt; Gareth Day [1977] Managing Director; Edward Alexander Gretton [1970] Director; Nicholas Lemon [1972] Director/Accountant; Dr Carsten Matthias Wendt [1976] Director [German]; Simon Lloyd Willis [1965] Director/Chief Executive, Hanson UK

Miles 33 Group Limited
Incorporated: 22 November 1993 *Employees:* 94
Net Worth: £46,837,000 *Total Assets:* £52,316,000
Registered Office: Miles House, Easthampstead Road, Bracknell, Berks, RG12 1NJ
Activities: Activities of head offices
Parent: Project Mars Finance Limited
Officers: David Farlow, Secretary/Chartered Accountant; David Farlow [1970] Director/Chartered Accountant; Michael David Moore [1965] Director

Miles 33 Limited
Incorporated: 29 April 1994 *Employees:* 59
Net Worth: £37,695,000 *Total Assets:* £51,152,000
Registered Office: Miles House, Easthampstead Road, Bracknell, Berks, RG12 1NJ
Activities: Business and domestic software development
Officers: David Farlow, Secretary/Chartered Accountant; David Farlow [1970] Director/Chartered Accountant; Peter Charles Meek [1958] Director; Michael David Moore [1965] Director; John Frederick Skarin [1966] Director

Milkwood Care Ltd
Incorporated: 9 March 1999 *Employees:* 315
Net Worth: £9,747,209 *Total Assets:* £22,975,510
Registered Office: Dylan House, 17 Bowen Lane, Petersfield, Hants, GU31 4DR
Activities: Residential nursing care facilities
Shareholders: Robin Anthony Cheesman; Janet Lloyd-Leech
Officers: Robin Anthony Cheesman, Secretary; Robin Anthony Cheesman [1952] Director/Chartered Builder; Janet Lloyd-Leech [1954] Director/Registered Nurse

Millbrook Healthcare Ltd
Incorporated: 12 January 1965 *Employees:* 863
Previous: Millbrook Furnishing Industries Limited
Net Worth: £14,435,000 *Total Assets:* £37,048,000
Registered Office: Nutsey Lane, Calmore Industrial Estate, Totton, Southampton, SO40 3XJ
Activities: Other human health activities
Parent: Millbrook Industries Ltd
Officers: Paul Alexander James Croll, Secretary; Annette Cairns [1970] Operations Director; Phillip John Campling [1974] Director; Colin Croll [1945] Director; Paul Alexander James Croll [1973] Director/Chartered Accountant; David John Lock [1968] Commercial Director; Neil Mecklenburgh [1960] HR Director; Tim Pollard [1963] Director

Millbrook Industries Limited
Incorporated: 26 February 1998 *Employees:* 1,085
Net Worth: £27,440,000 *Total Assets:* £63,308,000
Registered Office: Nutsey Lane, Calmore Industrial Estate, Totton, Southampton, SO40 3XJ
Activities: Activities of head offices
Major Shareholder: Colin Croll
Officers: Paul Alexander James Croll, Secretary; Colin Croll [1945] Director; Mark Edward Croll [1970] Director; Paul Alexander James Croll [1973] Director/Chartered Accountant

Millbrook Proving Ground Limited
Incorporated: 14 March 1988 *Employees:* 527
Net Worth: £25,244,000 *Total Assets:* £63,680,000
Registered Office: Millbrook, Bedford, MK45 2JQ
Activities: Technical testing and analysis
Parent: Spectris Group Holdings Limited
Officers: Alexander Mark Burns [1963] Director/Engineer; Jonathan Andrew Eaton [1959] Director; Martin Owen Hughes [1964] Director; Andrew Edward Bass Nelson [1976] Director/Chief Finance Officer; Eoghan Pol O'Lionaird [1966] Business Group Director

Millennium & Copthorne (Jersey Holdings) Limited
Incorporated: 14 June 2006
Net Worth: £230,239,008 *Total Assets:* £231,444,992
Registered Office: Victoria House, Victoria Road, Horley, Surrey, RH6 7AF
Activities: Activities of head offices
Parent: M & C Singapore Holdings (UK) Limited
Officers: Jonathon MacKenzie Grech [1977] Director/Senior VP Group Legal Counsel; Clive Anthony Harrington [1967] Director/Senior Vice President Operations

Millennium & Copthorne Hotels PLC
Incorporated: 22 December 1994 *Employees:* 11,602
Net Worth: £2,676,000,000 *Total Assets:* £4,714,999,808
Registered Office: Victoria House, Victoria Road, Horley, Surrey, RH6 7AF
Activities: Activities of head offices
Officers: Jonathon Grech, Secretary; Shaukat Aziz [1949] Director [Pakistani]; Daniel Marie Ghislain Desbaillets [1950] Independent Non-Executive Director; Christian Gautier de Charnace [1949] Director [French]; Eik Sheng Kwek [1981] Director/Chief Strategy Officer [Singaporean]; Leng Peck Kwek [1956] Director [Singaporean]; Leng Beng Kwek [1941] Director [Singaporean]; Angus Martin Leitch [1958] Independent Non-Executive Director

Millennium Hotels (West London) Limited
Incorporated: 5 July 2013 *Employees:* 3
Net Worth: £64,420,000 *Total Assets:* £65,847,000
Registered Office: Victoria House, Victoria Road, Horley, Surrey, RH6 7AF
Activities: Activities of head offices
Parent: Millennium Hotels London Limited
Officers: Jonathon MacKenzie Grech [1977] Director/Senior VP Group Legal Counsel; Chwee Peng Ong [1965] Director [Malaysian]

Millennium Hotels Europe Holdings Limited
Incorporated: 14 January 2014 *Employees:* 2
Net Worth: £54,633,216 *Total Assets:* £63,557,728
Registered Office: Victoria House, Victoria Road, Horley, Surrey, RH6 7AF
Activities: Activities of head offices
Parent: Millennium & Copthorne Hotels PLC
Officers: Jonathon MacKenzie Grech [1977] Director/Group General Counsel; Chwee Peng Ong [1965] Director [Malaysian]

Millennium Hotels Limited
Incorporated: 22 December 1995 *Employees:* 2
Net Worth: £87,177,000 *Total Assets:* £87,177,000
Registered Office: Victoria House, Victoria Road, Horley, Surrey, RH6 7AF
Activities: Activities of head offices
Parent: Millennium Hotels London Limited
Officers: Jonathon MacKenzie Grech [1977] Director/Senior VP Group Legal Counsel

Millennium Hotels London Limited
Incorporated: 5 January 1999
Net Worth: £216,816,992 *Total Assets:* £217,300,000
Registered Office: Victoria House, Victoria Road, Horley, Surrey, RH6 7AF
Activities: Activities of head offices
Parent: Millennium & Copthorne Hotels PLC
Officers: Jonathon MacKenzie Grech [1977] Director/Senior VP Group Legal Counsel

Millgate Developments Limited
Incorporated: 10 March 1988 *Employees:* 78
Net Worth: £68,534,000 *Total Assets:* £100,427,000
Registered Office: Millgate House, Ruscombe Lane, Ruscombe, Twyford, Berks, RG10 9JT
Activities: Construction of domestic buildings
Parent: Millgate (UK) Holdings Limited
Officers: Paul Andrew Wills, Secretary; Paul David Beaney [1968] Construction Director; Phillip Victor Lyons [1964] Director/Chief Executive - Housebuilding; Ian Calvert Sutcliffe [1959] Director; Rebecca Jane Worthington [1971] Director/Chartered Accountant

Millipore (U.K.) Limited
Incorporated: 22 December 2000 *Employees:* 175
Net Worth: £122,555,000 *Total Assets:* £129,667,000
Registered Office: Bedfont Cross, Stanwell Road, Feltham, Middlesex, TW14 8NX
Activities: Other research and experimental development on natural sciences and engineering
Shareholders: Sigma Chemical Company Limited; SAFC Biosciences Limited
Officers: Peter Biro [1967] Director/US Certified Public Accountant [Dutch]; Victor Mark Jackson [1962] Director/Operations Manager

Millipore UK Holdings LLP
Incorporated: 26 August 2009
Net Worth: £314,939,008 *Total Assets:* £314,942,016
Registered Office: Bedfont Cross, Stanwell Road, Feltham, Middlesex, TW14 8NX

Millmead Properties Limited
Incorporated: 11 July 1949 *Employees:* 7
Net Worth: £43,757,056 *Total Assets:* £52,219,892
Registered Office: 50 West Street, Chichester, W Sussex, PO19 1RP
Activities: Other letting and operating of own or leased real estate
Officers: Paul Curtecka, Secretary; Christopher Curtecka [1955] Director/Gardening Contractor; Marcia Curtecka [1953] Director/Property Manager; Paul Curtecka [1953] Director/Property Manager

Millwood Designer Homes Limited
Incorporated: 7 April 1992 *Employees:* 72
Net Worth: £13,344,000 *Total Assets:* £39,120,000
Registered Office: Bordyke End, East Street, Tonbridge, Kent, TN9 1HA
Activities: Construction of domestic buildings
Parent: MDH (Group) Limited
Officers: Robert David Sisley, Secretary; Philip Francis Christopher Brown [1962] Sales Director; David Cowans [1957] Director/Chief Executive; Jeffery Elliott [1954] Director/Valuer Land Surveyor; Roy Magro [1957] Director; Robert David Sisley [1970] Director/Chartered Accountant; Nicholas Stonley [1960] Managing Director

The Milton Group Limited
Incorporated: 26 October 1998 *Employees:* 7
Net Worth: £39,045,840 *Total Assets:* £54,775,520
Registered Office: 4 Station Court, Station Approach, Borough Green, Sevenoaks, Kent, TN15 8AD
Activities: Activities of head offices
Major Shareholder: Melanie Johanne Coburn
Officers: David John Slevin, Secretary; Timothy Charles Baker [1976] Director/Chartered Surveyor; David John Slevin [1970] Director/Chartered Accountant; Stuart James Smith [1964] Director/Chartered Surveyor; Graham Richard John Snell [1954] Director; Oliver Justin Sylge [1974] Director/Surveyor

Milton Keynes Academy Trust
Incorporated: 29 March 2007 *Employees:* 166
Net Worth: £22,977,298 *Total Assets:* £27,840,644
Registered Office: The Milton Keynes Academy, Fulwoods Drive, Leadenhall, Milton Keynes, Bucks, MK6 5LA
Activities: General secondary education
Officers: Mark Andrew Blyton, Secretary; Adrian Mark Bowater [1958] Director of Finance; Nicolas John Heslop [1966] Director/Public Affairs Manager; Vic Maher [1952] Director/Consultant; Barry John Neale [1969] Director/Fast Food; Brian Rabe [1966] Director/Company Secretary; Fiona Seddon [1978] Director/Principal; Dr Philip Henry Smith [1946] Director; Diane Taylor [1964] Director/Data Manager Education

Milton Keynes Community Foundation Limited
Incorporated: 30 June 1986 *Employees:* 19
Net Worth: £62,117,640 *Total Assets:* £64,318,392
Registered Office: Acorn House, 381 Midsummer Boulevard, Central Milton Keynes, Bucks, MK9 3HP
Activities: Other social work activities without accommodation n.e.c.
Officers: Carole Diane Baume [1949] Director/Retired; Kate Elizabeth Chadwick [1980] Director/Gallery Manager; Steve Harris [1957] Director/Retired; Jill Eileen Heaton [1962] Director/Solicitor; Shirley Jones [1958] Director/Businesswoman; Folashade Oluyemisi Komolafe [1967] Director; Shaun Lee [1956] Director/Retired; Dr Alice Mary Maynard [1957] Director; Kurshida Mirza [1958] Director/Retired Civil Servant; Lawrence Louis Revill [1956] Director/Town Planner; Keith Silverthorne [1949] Director/Retired

Milton Keynes Development Partnership LLP
Incorporated: 7 December 2012 *Employees:* 10
Net Worth: £30,340,000 *Total Assets:* £65,392,000
Registered Office: Civic Offices, 1 Saxon Gate East, Milton Keynes, Bucks, MK9 3HG
Officers: Peter Marland [1980] Member

Milton Keynes Education Trust
Incorporated: 9 June 2011 *Employees:* 409
Net Worth: £34,562,656 *Total Assets:* £40,484,816
Registered Office: Walton High, Fyfield Barrow, Walnut Tree, Milton Keynes, Bucks, MK7 7WH
Activities: General secondary education
Officers: Sheila Mary Bushnell, Secretary; Lisa Jane Alexander [1966] Director [British/New Zealander]; Michelle Elizabeth Currie [1961] Director/Principal; Jane Trudy Edwards [1966] Director/Headteacher; Kevin John Gowans [1959] Director; Simon Paul Haddy [1979] Managing Director - Construction; Reynold Philip James Lee [1965] HR Director; Dr Ann Generaldine Limb [1953] Non-Executive Director Chairman; Robert John George Rymarz [1949] Director/Retired; Richard Clive Smith [1964] Director/Chartered Accountant

Milton Keynes Parks Trust Limited
Incorporated: 6 July 1990 *Employees:* 58
Net Worth: £109,754,000 *Total Assets:* £145,340,992
Registered Office: Campbell Park Pavillion, 1300 Silbury Boulevard, Campbell Park, Milton Keynes, Bucks, MK9 4AD
Activities: Landscape service activities
Officers: David Richard Foster, Secretary/Chief Executive; Alexander David Chapman [1989] Director/Postgraduate Researcher; Samuel Bennett Crooks [1946] Director/Retired; John Bertram Eaton [1951] Director; Junita Fernandez [1966] Director, Finance & Corporate Operations; Richard John Foreman [1955] Director; Daniel Gilbert [1986] Director/Public Relations; Ian William Jackson [1967] Director/Chartered Surveyor; Andrew David Lawes [1963] Director/Chartered Accountant; Nicholas Geoffrey Lloyd [1971] Director/Solicitor; James Armour Macmillan [1965] Director/Charity Executive; Jennifer McCelvie Marklew [1985] Director/Insight Analyst; Jean Marion Nicholas [1944] Director/Retired Accountant; Richard Pearce [1973] Director/Woodland Officer; Zoe Anne Raven [1962] Director; Ian John Russell [1980] Director/Environment Manager; Clare Meg Stacey [1988] Director/Athlete Liaison Officer; Dr Philip Wheeler [1978] Director/University Lecturer; Gamiel Ahmed Yafai [1962] Director/Management Consultant

Milton Property Investments Limited
Incorporated: 2 April 2001 *Employees:* 4
Net Worth: £30,117,274 *Total Assets:* £41,349,264
Registered Office: 4 Station Court, Station Approach, Borough Green, Sevenoaks, Kent, TN15 8AD
Activities: Buying and selling of own real estate
Major Shareholder: Melanie Johanne Coburn
Officers: David John Slevin, Secretary; Timothy Charles Baker [1976] Director/Chartered Surveyor; David John Slevin [1970] Director/Chartered Accountant; Stuart James Smith [1964] Director/Chartered Surveyor; Oliver Justin Sylge [1974] Director/Surveyor

Minster Care Group Limited
Incorporated: 11 April 2017
Net Worth: £658,786 *Total Assets:* £27,477,660
Registered Office: 238 Station Road, Addlestone, Surrey, KT15 2PS
Activities: Residential care activities for the elderly and disabled
Shareholders: Alka Patel; Mahesh Shivabhai Patel
Officers: John Neal Alflatt, Secretary; John Neal Alflatt [1967] Director/Businessman; Colin William Farebrother [1965] Director/Businessman; Alka Patel [1960] Director/Businesswoman; Mahesh Shivabhai Patel [1953] Director/Businessman

Minster Care Management Limited
Incorporated: 1 December 1998 *Employees:* 1,037
Net Worth Deficit: £1,551,080 *Total Assets:* £60,828,656
Registered Office: 238 Station Road, Addlestone, Surrey, KT15 2PS
Activities: Residential care activities for the elderly and disabled
Parent: Minster Care Group Limited
Officers: John Neal Alflatt, Secretary; Colin William Farebrother [1965] Director; Mahesh Shivabhai Patel [1953] Director

MIQ Logistics EU Limited
Incorporated: 21 January 2004 *Employees:* 346
Net Worth: £12,137,600 *Total Assets:* £23,101,756
Registered Office: Unit 1 Alpha Way, Thorpe Industrial Estate, Egham, Surrey, TW20 8RZ
Activities: Activities of head offices
Officers: Brenda Jean Stasiulis [1966] Director/Accountant [American]; Darren Ross Williams [1966] Director

MIQ Logistics Limited
Incorporated: 15 December 1992 *Employees:* 324
Net Worth: £17,476,296 *Total Assets:* £24,334,236
Registered Office: Unit 1 Alpha Way, Thorpe Industrial Estate, Egham, Surrey, TW20 8RZ
Activities: Other transportation support activities
Parent: MIQ Logistics EU Limited
Officers: Darren Ross Williams, Secretary; Andrew Giles Martin [1962] Managing Director; Brenda Jean Stasiulis [1966] Director/Accountant [American]; Darren Ross Williams [1966] Financial Director

Mission Aviation Fellowship International
Incorporated: 9 January 1996 *Employees:* 552
Net Worth: £49,751,448 *Total Assets:* £55,045,568
Registered Office: Operations Centre, Henwood, Ashford, Kent, TN24 8DH
Activities: Non-scheduled passenger air transport
Officers: Anna Clare Beck, Secretary; Peter Gregory Curtis [1962] Director/Businessman [Australian]; Ndabaethethwa Petrus Mazabani [1958] Director/Pastor [South African]; Stephen Osei-Mensah [1966] Director/Consultant; Leighton Pittendrigh-Smith [1971] Director/Aviation Engineering Manager [Australian]; John Barrington Quin [1940] Director/Consultant; Elizabeth Ann Saunders [1960] HR Director; Carey Hrangchal Vanlalmuana [1968] Director/Manager [Indian]; William Watson [1947] Director/Manager [Canadian]

Mission Foods UK Limited
Incorporated: 23 April 1992 *Employees:* 267
Previous: Gruma Seaham Limited
Net Worth: £20,112,000 *Total Assets:* £31,083,000
Registered Office: Second Floor, Heathrow Boulevard 4, 282 Bath Road, Sipson, West Drayton, Middlesex, UB7 0DQ
Activities: Manufacture of bread; manufacture of fresh pastry goods and cakes
Shareholders: Mayra Adela Gonzalez Moreno; Graciela Silvia Gonzalez Moreno; Juan Antonio de Jesus Gonzalez Moreno
Officers: Amy Lucy Ashman, Secretary; Dannie Lee Burke [1969] Director/Treasurer [American]; Simon Mark Colaco [1975] Procurement Director; Peter Hall Ellis [1965] Managing Director; Rodolfo Maldonado [1953] Director/Chief Executive Officer [American]; Mohamme Saeed [1969] Human Resources Director

Mitac Technology UK Ltd.
Incorporated: 1 August 2014
Net Worth: £48,232,568 *Total Assets:* £48,232,568
Registered Office: Spectrum House, Beehive Ring Road, London Gatwick Airport, Gatwick, W Sussex, RH6 0LG
Activities: Manufacture of computers and peripheral equipment
Parent: Mitac Holdings Corporation
Officers: Jhi-Wu Ho [1952] Director [Chinese]; Chung-Liang Lin [1964] Director [Chinese]; Hsiang-Yun Yang [1960] Director [Chinese]

Mitchellson Formwork & Civil Engineering Limited
Incorporated: 10 November 1986 *Employees:* 90
Net Worth: £11,973,421 *Total Assets:* £40,298,424
Registered Office: Mitchellson House, Horton Trading Estate, Stanwell Road, Horton, Slough, SL3 9PF
Activities: Construction of commercial buildings
Shareholders: Martin Lawrence Masterson; Corneilius Michael Mitchell
Officers: Brendan John Courtney, Secretary; Martin Lawrence Masterson [1954] Director/Construction Engineer [Irish]; Corneilius Michael Mitchell [1952] Director/Carpenter

Mitsubishi Electric Finance Europe PLC
Incorporated: 8 January 1990 *Employees:* 4
Net Worth: £19,754,000 *Total Assets:* £1,049,174,016
Registered Office: Harman House, 1 George Street, Uxbridge, Middlesex, UB8 1QQ
Activities: Financial intermediation not elsewhere classified
Officers: Keiichi Tobinaga, Secretary; Masayuki Nakajima [1968] Director [Japanese]; Masaki Okamoto [1970] Director [Japanese]; Keiichi Tobinaga [1960] Director and Company Secretary [Japanese]

Mitsubishi Heavy Industries Air-Conditioning Europe, Ltd.
Incorporated: 6 February 2013 *Employees:* 32
Net Worth: £63,458,848 *Total Assets:* £104,789,312
Registered Office: 5 The Square, Stockley Park, Uxbridge, Middlesex, UB11 1ET
Activities: Wholesale of other machinery and equipment
Parent: Mitsubishi Heavy Industries, Ltd.
Officers: Henrieta Marcincinova, Secretary; Ryoichi Kariya [1972] Managing Director [Japanese]; Shinichiro Morisaki [1975] Director/Business Executive [Japanese]; Nobuaki Suzuki [1970] Director/Business Executive [Japanese]; Yusuke Tsunashima [1968] Director/Business Executive [Japanese]

Mizen Properties Limited
Incorporated: 15 April 1988 *Employees:* 30
Net Worth: £11,094,804 *Total Assets:* £41,955,016
Registered Office: No 1 Railshead Road, St Margarets, Isleworth, Middlesex, TW7 7EP
Activities: Buying and selling of own real estate
Officers: Barry Bernard Tansey, Secretary/Accountant [Irish]; Alan Joseph Tansey [1972] Director/Economist [Irish]; Bernard Joseph Tansey [1944] Director/Engineer [Irish]

Mizzen Bidco Limited
Incorporated: 25 July 2012
Net Worth: £34,521,000 *Total Assets:* £175,308,992
Registered Office: Ermyn House, Ermyn Way, Leatherhead, Surrey, KT22 8UX
Activities: Fund management activities
Parent: Mizzen Mezzco 2 Limited
Officers: Elizabeth Sarah Annys, Secretary; Andrew Phillip Chapman [1969] Director/Chief Financial Officer; Anthony Santospirito [1984] Director [Australian]; Thomas Woolgrove [1970] Director/Chief Executive Officer

Mizzen Mezzco 2 Limited
Incorporated: 26 September 2012
Net Worth: £158,323,008 *Total Assets:* £165,444,000
Registered Office: Ermyn House, Ermyn Way, Leatherhead, Surrey, KT22 8UX
Activities: Activities of other holding companies n.e.c.
Parent: Mizzen Midco Limited
Officers: Elizabeth Sarah Annys, Secretary; Andrew Phillip Chapman [1969] Director/Chief Financial Officer; Anthony Santospirito [1984] Director [Australian]; Thomas Woolgrove [1970] Director/Chief Executive Officer

Mizzen Mezzco Limited
Incorporated: 14 August 2012 *Employees:* 417
Net Worth Deficit: £59,343,000 *Total Assets:* £1,551,892,992
Registered Office: Ermyn House, Ermyn Way, Leatherhead, Surrey, KT22 8UX
Activities: Activities of other holding companies n.e.c.
Parent: Pomegranate Acquisitions Limited
Officers: Elizabeth Sarah Annys, Secretary; Andrew Phillip Chapman [1969] Director/Chief Financial Officer; Anthony Santospirito [1984] Director [Australian]; Thomas Woolgrove [1970] Director/Chief Executive Officer

Mizzen Midco Limited
Incorporated: 14 April 2014
Net Worth: £218,204,992 *Total Assets:* £232,080,992
Registered Office: Ermyn House, Ermyn Way, Leatherhead, Surrey, KT22 8UX
Activities: Fund management activities
Parent: Mizzen Mezzco Limited
Officers: Elizabeth Sarah Annys, Secretary; Andrew Phillip Chapman [1969] Director/Chief Financial Officer; Anthony Santospirito [1984] Director [Australian]; Thomas Woolgrove [1970] Director/Chief Executive Officer

MJ UK Holdings Limited
Incorporated: 30 March 2017
Net Worth: £3,585,628,160 *Total Assets:* £12,750,233,600
Registered Office: 103-105 Bath Road, Slough, Berks, SL1 3UH
Activities: Other service activities n.e.c.
Parent: Reckitt Benckiser (Health) Holdings Limited
Officers: Christine Anne-Marie Logan, Secretary; John Dixon [1956] Director/SVP Tax; Richard Mark Greensmith [1973] Group Tax Director; Simon Andrew Neville [1957] Group Treasury Director; Jonathan Timmis [1975] Director/SVP Corporate Controller

MJN International Holdings (UK), Ltd.
Incorporated: 16 May 2017
Net Worth: £1,054,898,432 *Total Assets:* £1,054,898,432
Registered Office: 103-105 Bath Road, Slough, Berks, SL1 3UH
Activities: Other business support service activities n.e.c.
Officers: Christine Anne-Marie Logan, Secretary; John Dixon [1956] Director/SVP Tax; Simon Andrew Neville [1957] Group Treasury Director; Jonathan Timmis [1975] Director/SVP Corporate Controller

MK International Limited
Incorporated: 2 January 1991
Net Worth: £212,571,008 *Total Assets:* £216,360,000
Registered Office: Reading International Business Park, Basingstoke Road, Reading, Berks, RG2 6DA
Activities: Other telecommunications activities
Parent: Verizon UK Limited
Officers: Clare Brenda Aikenhead [1965] Director Accounting; Francesco Cesare de Maio [1968] Strategic Planning Director [Italian]

MMA Holdings UK PLC
Incorporated: 12 July 1999
Net Worth: £272,616,000 *Total Assets:* £350,336,000
Registered Office: Norman Place, Reading, Berks, RG1 8DA
Activities: Life insurance
Officers: Annabel Felicity Wilson, Secretary; Francois Xavier Michel Josse [1972] Insurance Director [French]; Bertrand Lefebvre [1963] Director Controlling & Reporting [French]; Pierre Albert Jean Michel [1968] Director [French]; Gilles Normand [1968] Director [French]; Dominique Salvy [1957] Director [French]; Steven Whittaker [1958] Director

MMO2 Limited
Incorporated: 30 March 2001
Previous: MMO2 PLC
Net Worth: £260,287,008 *Total Assets:* £260,700,000
Registered Office: 260 Bath Road, Slough, Berks, SL1 4DX
Activities: Other telecommunications activities
Parent: Telefonica Europe PLC
Officers: Patricia Cobian [1975] Director [Spanish]; Mark Evans [1969] Director/Accountant

MNA Finance Limited
Incorporated: 12 October 2016
Net Worth Deficit: £24,579,000 *Total Assets:* £366,308,992
Registered Office: Quadrant, 55-57 High Street, Windsor, Berks, SL4 1LP
Activities: Activities of other holding companies n.e.c.
Parent: Morgan Advanced Materials PLC
Officers: Stephanie Helen Mackie, Secretary; Claire Rose Collins [1974] Director/Accountant; Stacey Ann Kent [1985] Director/Treasury Manager; Stephanie Helen Mackie [1968] Director/Company Secretary

Moat Homes Finance PLC
Incorporated: 17 August 2011
Net Worth: £50,000 *Total Assets:* £153,255,008
Registered Office: Mariner House, Galleon Boulevard, Dartford, Kent, DA2 6QE
Activities: Activities of other holding companies n.e.c.
Shareholder: Moat Homes Limited
Officers: Gregory Robert Taylor, Secretary; Hazel Anne Sharp [1961] Director/Accountant; Gregory Robert Taylor [1959] Executive Director - Finance

Mobil Trading and Supply Limited
Incorporated: 18 December 1958 *Employees:* 4
Net Worth: £13,878,135 *Total Assets:* £24,515,328
Registered Office: Ermyn House, Ermyn Way, Leatherhead, Surrey, KT22 8UX
Activities: Agents involved in the sale of fuels, ores, metals and industrial chemicals
Parent: Esso UK Limited
Officers: Fiona Harness, Secretary; Per-Erik Aasum [1964] Director/Oil Company Executive [Norwegian]; Robert Michael Cooper [1961] Director/Oil Company Executive; Alex Volkov [1972] Director/Oil Company Executive [American]

Mobile Broadband Network Limited
Incorporated: 19 September 2007 *Employees:* 107
Net Worth: £30,100,000 *Total Assets:* £389,560,000
Registered Office: Sixth Floor, Thames Tower, Station Road, Reading, Berks, RG1 1LX
Activities: Other telecommunications activities
Shareholders: EE Limited; Hutchinson 3G UK Limited
Officers: Edith Shih, Secretary; Thomas Lesley Bennett [1970] Director Network Services & Devices; Patrick Binchy [1966] Director [Irish]; Patrick Edward Coxen [1964] Managing Director; Simon Leslie Elliot Frumkin [1970] Director/Chartered Accountant; Stephen Daniel Lerner [1966] Director/General Counsel [Canadian]; Louise May Parker [1974] Procurement Director; Darren Purkis [1972] Director; Matthew William Redding [1975] Director/Solicitor; Nigel Rowe [1963] Director/CTO Acting; John Howard Watson [1963] Director/CEO - BT Technology Service and Operations

Modern Schools (Barnsley) Limited
Incorporated: 14 October 2004
Net Worth Deficit: £4,717,000 *Total Assets:* £29,249,000
Registered Office: 8 White Oak Square, London Road, Swanley, Kent, BR8 7AG
Activities: Construction of commercial buildings
Parent: Modern Schools (Barnsley) Holdings Limited
Officers: Benjamin Christopher Jacob Dean [1979] Director/Portfolio Manager; Alastair James Watson [1974] Investment Director

Modern Schools (Exeter) Limited
Incorporated: 18 February 2004
Net Worth Deficit: £10,123,000 *Total Assets:* £60,781,000
Registered Office: 8 White Oak Square, London Road, Swanley, Kent, BR8 7AG
Activities: Development of building projects
Parent: Modern Schools (Exeter) Holdings Limited
Officers: Benjamin Christopher Jacob Dean [1979] Director/Investment Manager; Richard Keith Sheehan [1975] Investment Director

Mondays (Topco) Limited
Incorporated: 9 December 2014 *Employees:* 3,261
Net Worth Deficit: £45,565,000 *Total Assets:* £228,910,000
Registered Office: Wey House, Farnham Road, Guildford, Surrey, GU1 4YD
Activities: Licenced restaurants
Parent: Electra Private Equity PLC
Officers: Karen Martha Forrester [1959] Director; Stuart Alan Greener [1962] Director; Gavin Maxwell Manson [1966] Director/Chartered Accountant; Stephen Louis Welker [1983] Director/Partner [American]

Mondelez UK Biscuit Financing Limited
Incorporated: 11 November 2013
Net Worth: £2,820,495,616 *Total Assets:* £2,820,495,616
Registered Office: Uxbridge Business Park, Sanderson Road, Uxbridge, Middlesex, UB8 1DH
Activities: Activities of head offices
Parent: Mondelez UK Limited
Officers: Adrian John Paul Arrighi [1978] Tax Director; Michael Brendan Foye [1965] Treasury Director; John Michael Hladusz [1972] Director/Chartered Accountant; Carole Noelle Keene [1966] Director

Mondelez UK Finance Company Limited
Incorporated: 26 April 2016
Net Worth: £4,029,776 *Total Assets:* £329,451,520
Registered Office: Cadbury House, Uxbridge Business Park, Sanderson Road, Uxbridge, Middlesex, UB8 1DH
Activities: Activities of head offices
Parent: Kraft Foods Investment Holdings UK Limited
Officers: Adrian John Paul Arrighi [1978] Tax Director; Michael Brendan Foye [1965] Treasury Director; John Michael Hladusz [1972] Director/Chartered Accountant; Carole Noelle Keene [1966] Director

Mondelez UK Holdings & Services Limited
Incorporated: 6 May 1897 *Employees:* 185
Net Worth: £4,284,000,000 *Total Assets:* £4,785,999,872
Registered Office: Cadbury House, Sanderson Road, Uxbridge, Middlesex, UB8 1DH
Activities: Manufacture of cocoa and chocolate confectionery
Parent: Cadbury Limited
Officers: Adrian John Paul Arrighi [1978] Tax Director; Simon Ashbell [1985] Director/Finance Manager; Michael Brendan Foye [1965] Treasury Director; John Michael Hladusz [1972] Director/Chartered Accountant; Darren Redhead [1964] Director; Jason Bryan Vickery [1968] Director/Accountant

Mondelez UK Limited
Incorporated: 6 February 1925 *Employees:* 585
Net Worth: £2,479,772,928 *Total Assets:* £2,928,550,912
Registered Office: Uxbridge Business Park, Sanderson Road, Uxbridge, Middlesex, UB8 1DH
Activities: Other business support service activities n.e.c.
Parent: Mondelez International, Inc
Officers: Jonathan Briscoe [1984] Sales Director; Claire Parkes [1974] Category Development & Market Activation Director; Mark Henry Stananought [1971] Customer Development Director; Louise Anne Stigant [1967] Managing Director

Mondi Finance PLC
Incorporated: 25 August 2006
Net Worth: £367,182,048 *Total Assets:* £2,212,484,352
Registered Office: 1st Floor, Building 1, Aviator Park, Station Road, Addlestone, Surrey, KT15 2PG
Activities: Credit granting by non-deposit taking finance houses and other specialist consumer credit grantors
Parent: Mondi Investments Limited
Officers: Jennifer Louise Hampshire, Secretary; Jennifer Louise Hampshire [1983] Director/Chartered Secretary; Andrew Charles Wallis King [1969] Director/Chief Financial Officer [South African]; Maureen Angela McHugh [1960] Director/Group Head of Tax; James Campbell Paterson [1964] Director/Treasurer

Mondi Investments Limited
Incorporated: 23 January 2004
Net Worth: £3,313,024,256 *Total Assets:* £3,314,483,712
Registered Office: 1st Floor, Building 1, Aviator Park, Station Road, Addlestone, Surrey, KT15 2PG
Activities: Activities of head offices
Parent: Mondi PLC
Officers: Jennifer Louise Hampshire, Secretary; Jennifer Louise Hampshire [1983] Director/Chartered Secretary; Andrew Charles Wallis King [1969] Director/Chief Financial Officer [South African]; James Campbell Paterson [1964] Director/Treasurer; Paul Wessels [1962] Director/Group Head of Reward [South African]

Mondi PLC
Incorporated: 11 April 2007 *Employees:* 26,300
Net Worth: £3,288,762,880 *Total Assets:* £6,383,600,640
Registered Office: 1st Floor, Building 1, Aviator Park, Station Road, Addlestone, Surrey, KT15 2PG
Activities: Activities of head offices
Officers: Jennifer Louise Hampshire, Secretary; Tanya Dianne Fratto [1960] Director [American]; Stephen Clive Harris [1958] Director/CEO, Bodycote PLC; Andrew Charles Wallis King [1969] Director/Chief Financial Officer [South African]; Peter Josef Oswald [1962] Director/CEO Europe & International Div [Austrian]; Tshamano Mohau Frederik Phaswana [1944] Director [South African]; Dominique Jacqueline Nicole Reiniche [1955] Director [French]; David Michael Williams [1946] Director; Stephen Gareth Young [1955] Director

Moneybarn No.1 Limited
Incorporated: 26 July 2002
Net Worth: £18,163,000 *Total Assets:* £384,886,016
Registered Office: The New Barn, Bedford Road, Petersfield, Hants, GU32 3LJ
Activities: Financial leasing
Parent: Moneybarn Group Limited
Officers: David George Whincup, Secretary; Shamus Hodgson [1971] Director; Malcolm John Le May [1958] Director; Laoiseach Sean O'Loingsigh [1971] Finance Director [Irish]; Simon George Thomas [1964] Director/Chief Finance Officer

Monier (China) Holdings Limited
Incorporated: 31 December 1976
Net Worth: £22,673,000 *Total Assets:* £23,212,000
Registered Office: BMI House, 2 Pitfield, Kiln Farm, Milton Keynes, Bucks, MK11 3LW
Activities: Activities of head offices
Parent: Braas Monier Building Group Holding SA
Officers: Jason John Bradley, Secretary; Thomas Joseph Anderson [1956] Director/Chief Operating Officer [American]; Jason John Bradley [1963] Director/Accountant; Dr Johannes Georg Schmidt-Schultes [1966] Director/Chief Financial Officer [German]

Monier (UK) Holdings Limited
Incorporated: 7 March 1996 *Employees:* 3
Net Worth: £77,004,000 *Total Assets:* £152,170,000
Registered Office: BMI House, 2 Pitfield, Kiln Farm, Milton Keynes, Bucks, MK11 3LW
Activities: Activities of head offices
Officers: Jason John Bradley [1963] Director/Accountant; Andrew John Dennis [1965] Managing Director; Alfons Horn [1970] Managing Director [German]; Klaus Sonne Ravn [1966] Finance Director [Danish]

Monier Redland Limited
Incorporated: 2 April 1946 *Employees:* 480
Net Worth: £65,581,000 *Total Assets:* £79,748,000
Registered Office: BMI House, 2 Pitfield, Kiln Farm, Milton Keynes, Bucks, MK11 3LW
Activities: Manufacture of concrete products for construction purposes
Parent: Braas Monier Building Group Holding SA
Officers: Graham Roy Barlow [1981] HR Director; Jason John Bradley [1963] Director/Accountant; Andrew John Dennis [1965] Sales Director; Alfons Horn [1970] Managing Director [German]; Klaus Sonne Ravn [1966] Finance Director [Danish]

Monster Energy Europe Limited
Incorporated: 9 October 2007 *Employees:* 389
Net Worth: £31,493,468 *Total Assets:* £53,013,208
Registered Office: Unit 51 Metropolitan Park, Bristol Road, Greenford, Middlesex, UB6 8UP
Activities: Manufacture of soft drinks; production of mineral waters and other bottled waters
Officers: Neil Shirley, Secretary; Guy Philip Carling [1977] Director; Rodney Cyril Sacks [1949] Director [American]; Hilton Schlosberg [1952] Director; Neil Shirley [1962] Director/VP Finance

Montgomery Property Group Limited
Incorporated: 3 December 1996 *Employees:* 22
Net Worth: £21,241,972 *Total Assets:* £43,807,376
Registered Office: Chappell House, The Green, Datchet, Berks, SL3 9EH
Activities: Other letting and operating of own or leased real estate
Officers: Jeremy James Oldroyd, Secretary/Accountant; Anthony George McClellan [1941] Director; Jeremy James Oldroyd [1968] Director/Accountant; David Bruce Reed [1967] Director/Surveyor

Montgomery Property Investments Limited
Incorporated: 24 October 1994
Net Worth: £15,818,235 *Total Assets:* £37,592,876
Registered Office: Chappell House, The Green, Datchet, Berks, SL3 9EH
Activities: Other letting and operating of own or leased real estate
Officers: George Quintin Scott, Secretary; Jeremy James Oldroyd [1968] Director/Accountant; David Bruce Reed [1967] Director/Surveyor

Mood Media Limited
Incorporated: 30 November 1956 *Employees:* 67
Net Worth: £13,840,000 *Total Assets:* £24,609,000
Registered Office: West House, 46 High Street, Orpington, Kent, BR6 0JQ
Activities: Reproduction of sound recording
Parent: Mood Media UK Holdings Limited
Officers: Caroline Sarah Trenter, Secretary; Mick Bennett [1965] Managing Director; Kenneth H Eissing [1970] Director/President in Store Media [American]; Caroline Trenter [1977] Finance Director

Moog Reading Limited
Incorporated: 1 July 1957 *Employees:* 99
Previous: Moog Components Group Limited
Net Worth: £16,920,854 *Total Assets:* £32,379,382
Registered Office: 30 Suttons Park Avenue, Suttons Business Park, Reading, Berks, RG6 1AW
Activities: Manufacture of other electronic and electric wires and cables
Parent: Moog Controls Ltd
Officers: Terry Martin, Secretary; Steven John Curtis [1976] Director/General Manager; James Russell Muscatello [1957] Director/Vice President Moog Power & Data [American]; David John Norman [1954] Director

Moorepay Limited
Incorporated: 10 November 1966 *Employees:* 199
Net Worth: £17,472,000 *Total Assets:* £23,245,000
Registered Office: Peoplebuilding 2, Peoplebuilding Estate, Maylands Avenue, Hemel Hempstead Industrial Estate, Hemel Hempstead, Herts, HP2 4NW
Activities: Data processing, hosting and related activities
Parent: Moorepay Group Limited
Officers: Elizabeth Leppard, Secretary; John Richard Martin Petter [1970] Director; Nicholas Paul Wain [1972] Director

Moove Lubricants Limited
Incorporated: 19 November 1986 *Employees:* 162
Previous: Comma Oil & Chemicals Limited
Net Worth: £25,383,000 *Total Assets:* £99,059,000
Registered Office: Moove, Dering Way, Gravesend, Kent, DA12 2QX
Activities: Other treatment of petroleum products (excluding petrochemicals manufacture)
Parent: Cosan Lubes Investments Limited
Officers: Gary Michael Sands, Secretary/Accountant; Filipe Affonso Ferreira [1965] Director [Brazilian]; Marcos Marinho Lutz [1969] Director [Brazilian]; Rubens Ometto Silveira Mello [1950] Director [Brazilian]

Moretons Investments Limited
Incorporated: 13 December 2012
Net Worth: £10,578,798 *Total Assets:* £25,986,796
Registered Office: The Old Casino, 28 Fourth Avenue, Hove, E Sussex, BN3 2PJ
Activities: Buying and selling of own real estate
Major Shareholder: Michael Anthony Richard Blencowe
Officers: Michael Blencowe [1983] Director/Property Investor

Morgan Advanced Materials PLC
Incorporated: 11 April 1934 *Employees:* 8,720
Net Worth: £195,200,000 *Total Assets:* £929,699,968
Registered Office: Quadrant, 55-57 High Street, Windsor, Berks, SL4 1LP
Activities: Activities of head offices
Officers: Stephanie Helen Mackie, Secretary; Elizabeth Jane Aikman [1965] Director/Accountant; Helen Patricia Bunch [1965] Managing Director; Douglas Caster [1953] Director; Laurence Blanche Lucette Eleonore Mulliez [1966] Director [French/British]; Peter Raby [1967] Director; Peter Andrew Turner [1970] Director

Morgan Europe Holding Limited
Incorporated: 18 September 1990
Net Worth: £17,080,000 *Total Assets:* £59,364,000
Registered Office: Quadrant, 55-57 High Street, Windsor, Berks, SL4 1LP
Activities: Activities of other holding companies n.e.c.
Parent: Morgan Advanced Materials PLC
Officers: Stephanie Helen Mackie, Secretary; Paul Andrew Boulton [1968] Director/Solicitor; Claire Rose Collins [1974] Director/Accountant; Stephanie Helen Mackie [1968] Director/Company Secretary

Morgan Finance Management Limited
Incorporated: 12 October 2016
Net Worth: £178,091,008 *Total Assets:* £180,232,992
Registered Office: Quadrant, 55-57 High Street, Windsor, Berks, SL4 1LP
Activities: Activities of head offices
Parent: MNA Finance Limited
Officers: Stephanie Helen Mackie, Secretary; Claire Rose Collins [1974] Director/Accountant; Stacey Ann Kent [1985] Director/Treasury Manager; Stephanie Helen Mackie [1968] Director/Company Secretary

Morgan Holdings Limited
Incorporated: 8 November 1985
Net Worth: £131,916,000 *Total Assets:* £131,916,000
Registered Office: Quadrant, 55-57 High Street, Windsor, Berks, SL4 1LP
Activities: Activities of head offices
Parent: Morgan Advanced Materials PLC
Officers: Stephanie Helen Mackie, Secretary; Paul Andrew Boulton [1968] Director; Claire Rose Collins [1974] Director/Accountant; Stephanie Helen Mackie [1968] Director/Company Secretary

Morgan North America Holding Limited
Incorporated: 25 November 2013
Net Worth: £78,711,000 *Total Assets:* £133,511,000
Registered Office: Quadrant, 55-57 High Street, Windsor, Berks, SL4 1LP
Activities: Activities of head offices
Parent: Morgan International Holding Limited
Officers: Stephanie Helen Mackie, Secretary; Paul Andrew Boulton [1968] Director/Solicitor; Claire Rose Collins [1974] Director/Accountant; Stephanie Helen Mackie [1968] Director/Company Secretary

A.J. Morrisroe & Sons Limited
Incorporated: 1 March 1977 *Employees:* 83
Net Worth: £27,699,638 *Total Assets:* £83,417,040
Registered Office: Unit 4 Oaks Court, Warwick Road, Borehamwood, Herts, WD6 1GS
Activities: Construction of commercial buildings
Major Shareholder: Brian Quinlan Morrisroe
Officers: Brian Quinlan Morrisroe, Secretary; Daniel James Bannister [1976] Health & Safety Director; Michael Ioannou [1968] Commercial Director; Gerard Olaivar Marapao [1961] Director/Accountant; Brian Quinlan Morrisroe [1955] Managing Director

Morrisroe Group Limited
Incorporated: 14 November 2006 *Employees:* 208
Net Worth: £43,130,848 *Total Assets:* £108,799,408
Registered Office: Unit 4 Oaks Court, Warwick Road, Borehamwood, Herts, WD6 1GS
Activities: Other professional, scientific and technical activities n.e.c.
Major Shareholder: Brian Quinlan Morrisroe
Officers: Gerard Olaivar Marapao, Secretary/Chartered Accountant; Daniel James Bannister [1976] Health & Safety Director; Michael Ioannou [1968] Commercial Director; Gerard Olaivar Marapao [1961] Director/Certified Chartered Accountant; Brian Quinlan Morrisroe [1955] Managing Director

Mortar Investments International Limited
Incorporated: 23 November 1992
Net Worth: £2,987,148,032 *Total Assets:* £3,025,893,120
Registered Office: The Akzonobel Building, Wexham Road, Slough, Berks, SL2 5DS
Activities: Activities of head offices
Parent: Ergon Investments UK Limited
Officers: Stephen Bruce Ray [1962] Director/Pensions Accounting Manager; Michael Smalley [1958] Director; David Allan Turner [1971] Director

Moss Electrical Holdings Limited
Incorporated: 26 March 2003 *Employees:* 95
Net Worth: £9,272,191 *Total Assets:* £20,248,884
Registered Office: Maxmor House, Sandpit Road, Dartford, Kent, DA1 5BU
Activities: Financial leasing
Major Shareholder: Robert Jospeh Moss
Officers: Andrew Porter, Secretary; Lindsay Claire Goubel [1971] Operations Director; Christopher John Homer [1959] Commercial Director; Robert Joseph Moss [1953] Director; Andrew Porter [1963] Finance Director

Mothercare Group Limited (The)
Incorporated: 21 July 1927
Net Worth Deficit: £13,809,000 *Total Assets:* £70,013,000
Registered Office: Cherry Tree Road, Watford, Herts, WD24 6SH
Activities: Activities of head offices
Parent: Mothercare PLC
Officers: Lynne Samantha Medini, Secretary; Taimoor Anwar [1980] Director/Chartered Accountant [Pakistani]; Kirsty Rowena Homer [1974] HR Director

Mothercare PLC.
Incorporated: 26 September 1985 *Employees:* 4,737
Net Worth: £4,600,000 *Total Assets:* £276,700,000
Registered Office: Cherry Tree Road, Watford, Herts, WD24 6SH
Activities: Other retail sale of new goods in specialised stores (not commercial art galleries and opticians)
Officers: Lynne Samantha Medini, Secretary; William Glyn Lawrence Hughes [1976] Director/Chief Financial Officer; Gillian Dawn Celia Kent [1963] Director; Mark Newton-Jones [1967] Director; Nicholas Barry Edward Wharton [1966] Director; Clive Peter Whiley [1960] Director/Executive Chairman

Mothercare UK Limited
Incorporated: 8 May 1954 *Employees:* 2,604
Net Worth Deficit: £183,600,000 *Total Assets:* £231,000,000
Registered Office: Cherry Tree Road, Watford, Herts, WD24 6SH
Activities: Other retail sale of new goods in specialised stores (not commercial art galleries and opticians)
Parent: Mothercare (Holdings) Limited
Officers: Lynne Samantha Medini, Secretary; Kirsty Rowena Homer [1974] HR Director; William Glyn Lawrence Hughes [1976] Director/Chief Financial Officer; Mark Newton-Jones [1967] Director; Kevin Jonathan Rusling [1977] Managing Director, International

Motor Insurers' Bureau
Incorporated: 14 June 1946 *Employees:* 519
Total Assets: £2,400,355,072
Registered Office: Linford Wood House, 6-12 Capital Drive, Linford Wood, Milton Keynes, Bucks, MK14 6XT
Activities: Other business support service activities n.e.c.
Officers: Wendy Budd, Secretary; Dr Jacob Abboud [1960] Director/Chief Information Officer; Simon Paul Baker [1960] Director/Insurance Manager; Timothy Bishop [1966] Director/Chief Risk Officer; Rhodri Prys Charles [1975] Director/Insurance Executive; Adam James Clarke [1972] Underwriting Director; Dominic John Clayden [1966] Director of Claims; Michael Paul Crane [1968] Managing Director; Karl Helgesen [1972] Director/Chief Claims Officer, UK & International; Steven Maddock [1968] Managing Director; Gareth David McChesney [1969] Director Underwriting & Pricing

Motoring & Leisure Services Limited
Incorporated: 28 April 1993 *Employees:* 233
Net Worth: £13,242,077 *Total Assets:* £38,537,088
Registered Office: Britannia House, 21 Station Street, Brighton, BN1 4DE
Activities: Activities of other membership organisations n.e.c.
Parent: The Civil Service Motoring Association Ltd
Officers: Colin John Slinn, Secretary; Carl Fillery [1966] Director/Group Chief Executive; Colin John Slinn [1967] Director/Chartered Accountant

Motorline (Kent) Limited
Incorporated: 15 September 2003 *Employees:* 213
Net Worth: £961,945 *Total Assets:* £23,309,046
Registered Office: Motorline House, Shalloak Road, Broad Oak, Canterbury, Kent, CT2 0PR
Activities: Sale of new cars and light motor vehicles
Parent: Motorline Holdings Limited
Officers: Glen Richard Obee, Secretary; Paul Alex Betts [1954] Director/Chartered Accountant; Gary Myles Obee [1961] Director/Motor Dealer; Glen Richard Obee [1963] Director/Motor Dealer; Thomas Giles Obee [1968] Director/Motor Dealer

Motorline Holdings Limited
Incorporated: 13 June 2005 *Employees:* 1,219
Net Worth: £20,482,644 *Total Assets:* £174,670,896
Registered Office: Motorline House, Shalloak Road, Broad Oak, Canterbury, Kent, CT2 0PR
Activities: Other business support service activities n.e.c.
Shareholders: Gary Myles Obee; Glen Richard Obee; Thomas Giles Obee
Officers: Glen Richard Obee, Secretary/Motor Dealer; Paul Alex Betts [1954] Director/Chartered Accountant; Gary Myles Obee [1961] Director/Motor Dealer; Glen Richard Obee [1963] Director/Motor Dealer; Thomas Giles Obee [1968] Director/Motor Dealer

Motorline Limited
Incorporated: 17 September 1984 *Employees:* 450
Net Worth: £15,132,279 *Total Assets:* £38,117,216
Registered Office: Motorline House, Shalloak Road, Broad Oak, Canterbury, Kent, CT2 0PR
Activities: Other business support service activities n.e.c.
Parent: Motorline Holdings Limited
Officers: Glen Richard Obee, Secretary; Paul Alex Betts [1954] Director/Chartered Accountant; Gary Myles Obee [1961] Director/Dealer Principal; Glen Richard Obee [1963] Director/Dealer Principal; Thomas Giles Obee [1968] Director/Dealer Principal

Motorola Mobility UK Ltd
Incorporated: 22 July 2009 *Employees:* 8
Net Worth: £12,976,000 *Total Assets:* £23,442,000
Registered Office: Redwood, Chineham Business Park, Crockford Lane, Basingstoke, Hants, RG24 8WQ
Activities: Manufacture of electronic components
Officers: Saurabh Agrawal [1971] Finance Director [Indian]; Ashley James Cooper [1978] Director/Chartered Accountant

Motorsport Vision Limited
Incorporated: 8 October 1997 *Employees:* 640
Net Worth: £14,988,437 *Total Assets:* £30,917,884
Registered Office: Motorsport Vision Centre, Brands Hatch, Fawkham, Longfield, Kent, DA3 8NG
Activities: Operation of sports facilities
Parent: MSV Group Limited
Officers: Philip Graham Hopkins, Secretary; Dr Jonathan Charles Palmer [1956] Director

Motorway Services Limited
Incorporated: 14 September 1959 *Employees:* 678
Net Worth: £89,656,000 *Total Assets:* £112,291,000
Registered Office: 2 Vantage Court, Tickford Street, Newport Pagnell, Bucks, MK16 9EZ
Activities: Retail sale in non-specialised stores with food, beverages or tobacco predominating
Parent: Welcome Break Limited
Officers: Joseph James Barrett [1966] Director [Irish]; Timothy Edward Lightfoot [1974] Director/Group Financial Controller

Mott MacDonald Group Limited
Incorporated: 30 April 1973 *Employees:* 14,730
Net Worth: £124,305,000 *Total Assets:* £712,019,968
Registered Office: Mott MacDonald House, 8-10 Sydenham Road, Croydon, Surrey, CR0 2EE
Activities: Other engineering activities
Officers: Paul Edward Ferguson, Secretary; Nicholas Mauro Denichilo [1952] Executive Director [American]; Ian Martin Richard Galbraith [1963] Director; Michael David Haigh [1960] Director/Chartered Engineer; James Huw Keir Harris [1968] Director/Civil Engineer; Keith John Howells [1953] Director/Engineer; Guy William Ingledew Leonard [1955] Director/Chartered Quantity Surveyors; Edwin George Roud [1963] Finance Director

Mott MacDonald International Limited
Incorporated: 15 October 1986
Net Worth: £26,927,146 *Total Assets:* £80,366,896
Registered Office: Mott MacDonald House, 8-10 Sydenham Road, Croydon, Surrey, CR0 2EE
Activities: Other engineering activities
Parent: Mott MacDonald Group Limited
Officers: Diana Zivko, Secretary; Ian Martin Richard Galbraith [1963] Director; Michael David Haigh [1960] Director/Chartered Engineer; James Huw Keir Harris [1968] Director; Keith John Howells [1953] Director/Engineer; Guy William Ingledew Leonard [1955] Director/Chartered Quantity Surveyors; Edwin George Roud [1963] Finance Director

Mott MacDonald Limited
Incorporated: 11 February 1976 *Employees:* 6,619
Net Worth: £337,348,000 *Total Assets:* £732,182,016
Registered Office: Mott MacDonald House, 8-10 Sydenham Road, Croydon, Surrey, CR0 2EE
Activities: Other engineering activities
Parent: Mott MacDonald Group Limited
Officers: Diana Zivko, Secretary; Ian Martin Richard Galbraith [1963] Director/Engineer; Michael David Haigh [1960] Director/Chartered Engineer; James Huw Keir Harris [1968] Director/Civil Engineer; Keith John Howells [1953] Director/Engineer; Guy William Ingledew Leonard [1955] Chief Executive Director; Edwin George Roud [1963] Finance Director

Motus Group (UK) Limited
Incorporated: 23 March 1960 *Employees:* 1,157
Previous: Imperial Commercials Ltd
Net Worth: £23,186,000 *Total Assets:* £105,122,000
Registered Office: Ground Floor, Oakingham House, West Wing, London Road, Loudwater, High Wycombe, Bucks, HP11 1JU
Activities: Sale of other motor vehicles
Parent: Motus Holdings (UK) Ltd
Officers: Andrew Barrie Welch, Finance Director; Osman Suluman Arbee [1959] Director [South African]; Matthew Derek Lawrenson [1970] Divisional Executive Director; Philip Bernard Michaux [1960] Director [South African]; Andrew Barrie Welch [1965] Finance Director

Motus Holdings (UK) Limited
Incorporated: 12 September 2005
Previous: IH Mobility Holdings (UK) Limited
Net Worth: £20,692,748 *Total Assets:* £42,667,856
Registered Office: Ground Floor, Oakingham House, West Wing, London Road, Loudwater, High Wycombe, Bucks, HP11 1JU
Activities: Activities of head offices
Officers: Andrew Barrie Welch, Secretary/Director; Osman Suluman Arbee [1959] Director [South African]; Philip Bernard Michaux [1960] Director [South African]; Andrew Barrie Welch [1965] Director

The Mountbatten School
Incorporated: 10 March 2011 *Employees:* 287
Net Worth: £26,909,020 *Total Assets:* £29,701,510
Registered Office: The Mountbatten School, Whitenap Lane, Romsey, Hants, SO51 5SY
Activities: General secondary education
Officers: Terese Swain, Secretary; Tushar Bijur [1961] Director/Marine Surveyor; Mark Lester Edgerley [1952] Director/Business Support Manager; Charlotte Fisher-Barkhuizen [1979] Director/Teacher; Sean Richard Flood [1962] Director/IT Consultant; Christopher John Goodrich [1977] Director of IT; Andrew Gunn [1966] Director/Banker; Jill Hall [1945] Director/Retired; Robert Legrice [1956] Director/Retired Bank Manager; Margaret Heather McIlroy [1956] Director/Headteacher; Michael John Murphy [1967] Director/Strategic Project Manager NHS; Cheryl Jayne Parish [1964] Director/Volunteer; Gavin William Rumsey [1982] Director/Teacher; Karl Staples [1974] Director/University Lecturer; Amanda Jane Stevens [1973] HR Director; Reverend Jane Elspeth Christine Thompson [1958] Director/Teacher; Paul Urben [1961] Director/Retail Investment Delivery

Mova Property Limited
Incorporated: 5 December 2016
Net Worth: £10,913,467 *Total Assets:* £32,178,886
Registered Office: c/o Mole Valley District Council, Pippbrook, Dorking, Surrey, RH4 1SJ
Activities: Buying and selling of own real estate
Parent: Mova Holdings Limited
Officers: Karen Brimacombe [1968] Director/Local Government Officer; Nicholas Ian Gray [1961] Director/Local Government Officer; Jonathan Straw [1951] Director/Chartered Town Planner

Movianto UK Limited
Incorporated: 11 February 1976 *Employees:* 670
Net Worth Deficit: £510,000 *Total Assets:* £92,244,000
Registered Office: 1 Progress Park, Elstow, Bedford, MK42 9XE
Activities: Wholesale of pharmaceutical goods
Parent: Healthcare Services Group Limited
Officers: Kamaljit Singh Hunjan [1967] Director/Senior VP Movianto; Julia M. Munzinger [1968] Director/Accountant [American]; Nicholas Joseph Pace [1970] Director [American]; David John Tinsley [1977] Director

MSK Holdings Limited
Incorporated: 12 April 2006 *Employees:* 154
Net Worth: £25,194,872 *Total Assets:* £33,842,548
Registered Office: Numeric House, 98 Station Road, Sidcup, Kent, DA15 7BY
Activities: Activities of other holding companies n.e.c.
Shareholders: David John Guildford; Anthony Richard Stone
Officers: Maureen Elizabeth Stone, Secretary; Mark Doughty [1964] Director; David John Guildford [1952] Director; Anthony Richard Stone [1950] Director; Richard Mark Stone [1977] Director

MSV Group Limited
Incorporated: 25 November 2003 *Employees:* 734
Net Worth: £23,351,000 *Total Assets:* £43,991,000
Registered Office: Motorsport Vision Centre, Brands Hatch Circuit, Fawkham, Longfield, Kent, DA3 8NG
Activities: Operation of sports facilities
Major Shareholder: Jonathan Charles Palmer
Officers: Philip Graham Hopkins, Secretary; Sir Peter James Ogden [1947] Director; Dr Jonathan Charles Palmer [1956] Director

MTI Technology Group Limited
Incorporated: 9 December 2016 *Employees:* 3
Net Worth: £4,955,538 *Total Assets:* £22,870,972
Registered Office: Mill Pool House, Mill Lane, Godalming, Surrey, GU7 1EY
Activities: Data processing, hosting and related activities
Shareholders: Malta Topco Limited; Malta Topco Limited
Officers: Keith Clark [1953] Director [Canadian]; Ben Cranham [1975] Director; Angelo di Ventura [1968] Director; Simon Goodwin [1977] Director; Scott William Haddow [1973] Director; Pieter Knook [1958] Director [Dutch]; Edward Ransome [1984] Director; Aidan Robson [1978] Director

MTS Cleansing Services Limited
Incorporated: 11 August 1986 *Employees:* 426
Previous: M.T.S. Cleansing Services Limited
Net Worth: £9,916,086 *Total Assets:* £26,693,916
Registered Office: Stanley House, Anthonys Way, Medway City Estate, Rochester, Kent, ME2 4NF
Activities: Sewerage
Shareholders: Brian Stanley Crust; Keith Albert Crust
Officers: Antony Keith Crust, Secretary/Managing Director; Sian Marie Cropper [1969] Contracts Director; Allen Charles Crust [1971] Director/General Manager; Antony Keith Crust [1968] Managing Director; Brian Alexander Crust [1965] Compliance Director; Brian Stanley Crust [1946] Executive Director; Keith Albert Crust [1947] Director/Chairman; Spencer John Crust [1975] Operations Director; Terry Stanley Crust [1968] HR Director; Scott Leonard Diamond [1984] Fleet Compliance Director; Stephen Patrick Gilson [1968] Sales Director; Christopher Rodney Henderson [1966] Director; Richard Spencer-Tanner [1970] Finance Director

MTS Systems Limited
Incorporated: 17 October 1979 *Employees:* 28
Net Worth: £5,683,809 *Total Assets:* £32,938,512
Registered Office: 40 Alan Turing Road, Surrey Research Park, Guildford, Surrey, GU2 7YF
Activities: Installation of industrial machinery and equipment
Officers: Marcus Piepenschneider, Secretary; Patrick Edouard Joseph Dhommee [1968] Director/Business Executive [French]; Brian Thomas Ross [1976] Director/Corporate Controller [American]; Martin Nicholas Smaller [1963] Director/Business Executive

MTWOM B Limited
Incorporated: 10 August 2011
Net Worth: £29,000 *Total Assets:* £49,793,000
Registered Office: Horizon, Honey Lane, Hurley, Maidenhead, Berks, SL6 6RJ
Activities: Wireless telecommunications activities
Parent: MTWOM 1 Limited
Officers: Richard Miller [1964] Finance Director; Oliver Robert Stewart Tucker [1962] Director

Murex Biotech Limited
Incorporated: 12 December 1991 *Employees:* 7
Net Worth: £41,989,000 *Total Assets:* £42,680,000
Registered Office: Abbott House, Vanwall Business Park, Vanwall Road, Maidenhead, Berks, SL6 4XE
Activities: Other manufacturing n.e.c.
Parent: Abbott Laboratories Ltd
Officers: Kevan Gogay, Secretary; Neil Harris [1974] Director/General Manager; Georgios Mountrichas [1977] Director/General Manager [Greek]; Brian Yoor [1969] Director/Business Executive [American]

Mushi UK Holdings Limited
Incorporated: 17 June 2014 *Employees:* 3
Net Worth: £181,436,656 *Total Assets:* £181,503,984
Registered Office: 3 Lotus Park, The Causeway, Staines upon Thames, Middlesex, TW18 3AG
Activities: Activities of other holding companies n.e.c.
Parent: Mallinckrodt ARD Holdings Limited
Officers: Alan Catterson [1961] Director/Financial Controller; Stephanie Dorn Miller [1974] Director/Corporate Secretary [American]; Stephen Andrew Welch [1977] Director/Senior Staff Liaison to The President and CEO [American]

Mustard Global Limited
Incorporated: 8 October 2015
Net Worth: £147,797,872 *Total Assets:* £147,909,088
Registered Office: St John's Place, Easton Street, High Wycombe, Bucks, HP11 1NL
Activities: Activities of other holding companies n.e.c.
Parent: Mustard Holdings Limited
Officers: Judith Bean, Secretary; Lisa Agar-Rea [1968] Director; Peter Wynne Davies [1949] Director; Stuart Antony Grant [1975] Director; Kara Eugenie Groves [1969] Director; Elizabeth Claire Houghton [1964] Director; Benjamin Joseph Lewis [1967] Director; Bernard Lewis [1926] Director; Clive Robert Lewis [1956] Director

Mutual Services (Portsmouth) Limited
Incorporated: 14 August 2006 *Employees:* 61
Net Worth: £60,999,208 *Total Assets:* £61,233,104
Registered Office: 1000 Lakeside, Western Road, North Harbour, Portsmouth, PO6 3FE
Activities: Funeral and related activities
Officers: Silena Jane Dominy, Secretary; Gareth Lewis [1960] Director/Loss Prevention and Security Manager; Mark Alexander Ralf [1956] Director/Retired; Dr Elizabeth Rogers [1957] Director/Retired; Mark Stephen Smith [1959] Director/Chief Executive; Amber Vincent-Prior [1949] Director/Parish Clerk and Sexton; Gregory Wilkins [1973] Finance Director

MVV Environment Ridham Limited
Incorporated: 12 January 2012 *Employees:* 33
Net Worth: £25,004,716 *Total Assets:* £117,564,096
Registered Office: Ridham Dock Biomass Facility, Lord Nelson Road, Iwade, Sittingbourne, Kent, ME9 8FQ
Activities: Production of electricity
Parent: MVV Energie AG
Officers: Paul Michael Carey [1957] Managing Director; Michael Andrew Turner [1967] Managing Director; Uwe Zickert [1969] Director/Engineer [German]

MYA Property Limited
Incorporated: 4 December 2006 *Employees:* 19
Net Worth: £29,078,720 *Total Assets:* £70,069,704
Registered Office: 142 Lodge Road, Southampton, SO14 6QR
Activities: Development of building projects
Major Shareholder: Massoud Yeganegy
Officers: Peter James Cousins [1953] Director/Accountant; Natascha Manley [1967] Director; Dr Roxanne Robinson [1984] Director; Babak Yeganegy [1987] Director; Deborah Anne Yeganegy [1968] Director; Laleh Yeganegy [1980] Director/Designer; Massoud Yeganegy [1955] Director

Naga UK Bidco Limited
Incorporated: 27 June 2013
Net Worth: £235,443,008 *Total Assets:* £364,713,984
Registered Office: Dagger Lane, Elstree, Herts, WD6 3BX
Activities: Other human health activities
Parent: Naga UK Topco Limited
Officers: Kieu Hoang [1944] Director [American]; Kevin Lane [1961] Director/President [American]; Xu Wu [1967] Director/Businessman [Chinese]

Naga UK Topco Limited
Incorporated: 27 June 2013 *Employees:* 2,893
Net Worth: £157,711,008 *Total Assets:* £409,176,992
Registered Office: Dagger Lane, Elstree, Herts, WD6 3BX
Activities: Other human health activities
Parent: Tiancheng International Investment Limited
Officers: Kieu Hoang [1944] Director [American]; Lars Holmqvist [1959] Director/Senior Advisor [Swedish]; Kevin Patrick Lane [1961] Director/Consultant [American]; Xu Wu [1967] Director/Manager [Hong Kong]; Tan Yang [1972] Director/Business Executive [Chinese]

Nampak Holdings (UK) Limited
Incorporated: 19 September 1994
Net Worth: £200,582,960 *Total Assets:* £333,298,176
Registered Office: Interchange Park, Jenna Way, Newport Pagnell, Bucks, MK16 9QJ
Activities: Activities of head offices
Parent: Nampak International Limited
Officers: Andre Marinus de Ruyter [1968] Director [Dutch]; Glenn Ramsay Fullerton [1967] Director/Chartered Accountant [South African]; Luke Domonic Mark Haggett [1981] Director; Arnold Mitterer [1964] Director [Austrian]; David John Tocher [1961] Director

Nampak Plastics Europe Limited
Incorporated: 2 November 1945 *Employees:* 488
Net Worth: £19,878,000 *Total Assets:* £59,979,000
Registered Office: Jenna Way, Interchange Park, Newport Pagnell, Bucks, MK16 9QJ
Activities: Manufacture of plastic packing goods
Parent: Nampak Holdings UK Limited
Officers: Andre Marinus de Ruyter [1968] Director [Dutch]; Glenn Ramsay Fullerton [1967] Director/Chartered Accountant [South African]; Luke Domonic Mark Haggett [1981] Director; Arnold Mitterer [1964] Director [Austrian]

Napsbury Limited
Incorporated: 29 June 2016 *Employees:* 241
Net Worth: £33,477,728 *Total Assets:* £82,074,680
Registered Office: Ridgeworth House, Liverpool Gardens, Worthing, W Sussex, BN11 1RS
Activities: Activities of other holding companies n.e.c.
Parent: Radlett Limited
Officers: Zoe Rachel Cadiz, Secretary; William Francis Chisholm [1969] Managing Director [American]; Sunit Shankar Mukherjee [1977] Director/Principal [Indian]

Nastor Investments Limited
Incorporated: 10 July 2009
Net Worth: £58,098,000 *Total Assets:* £58,098,000
Registered Office: Charles River Laboratories, Manston Road, Margate, Kent, CT9 4LT
Activities: Manufacture of other chemical products n.e.c.
Parent: Celsis Group Limited
Officers: Sarah Margaret Price, Secretary; Foster Timmons Jordan [1967] Director/Corporate Senior Vice President [American]; Dr John Gary Montana [1963] Director/Scientist; David Ross Smith [1965] Director/Corporate Senior Vice President

Natco Foods Limited
Incorporated: 28 November 1963 *Employees:* 156
Net Worth: £6,388,966 *Total Assets:* £21,791,392
Registered Office: Unit 2 Swan Business Park, Osier Way, Buckingham, MK18 1TB
Activities: Non-specialised wholesale of food, beverages and tobacco
Parent: T Choithram & Sons (London) Ltd
Officers: Ramesh Pohumal Thanwani, Secretary; Lekhraj Thakurdas Pagarani [1954] Director/Merchant; Luke Pagarani [1983] Director/Merchant; Ramchand Dharamdas Rajwani [1930] Director/Merchant [Indian]; Ramesh Pohumal Thanwani [1946] Director/Merchant [Indian]

National Adhesives Holding Ltd.
Incorporated: 3 March 2008
Net Worth: £39,505,000 *Total Assets:* £39,540,000
Registered Office: National Adhesives Holding Ltd, Wood Lane End, Hemel Hempstead, Herts, HP2 4RQ
Activities: Other manufacturing n.e.c.
Parent: Henkel AG & Co. KGaA
Officers: Sutinder Bhandal, Secretary; Peter David Budden [1963] Director/Accountant; Csaba Pal Szendrei [1967] Business Director [Hungarian]

National Film and Television School (The)
Incorporated: 11 June 1970 *Employees:* 107
Net Worth: £25,658,344 *Total Assets:* £37,639,464
Registered Office: Beaconsfield Film Studios, Station Road, Beaconsfield, Bucks, HP9 1LG
Activities: Technical and vocational secondary education
Officers: Trevor Hall, Secretary; Riffat Ahmed [1985] Film Director and Visual Artist; Professor Geoffrey Joel Crossick [1946] Director/Retired University Vice-Chancellor; Neil Andrew Forster [1970] Finance Director; Patrick Fuller [1966] Director; Caroline Daniela Kavan Woodford Hollick [1975] Director/Head of Drama at Channel 4; Oliver Richard Hyatt [1979] Director, Chair of Animation; Timothy Kyte [1968] Director/IT Support; Ian Lewis Lewis [1962] Group Director, Sky Cinema; Stephen David Louis [1966] Director/Venture Capitalist; Andrew Imre Flint MacDonald [1966] Director/Producer; Patrick Anthony McKenna [1956] Director/CEO Ingenious Media; Steven William Mertz [1957] Director/Lawyer [American]; Susan Nicola Moffat [1960] Producer & Board Director; Siobhan Margaret Reddy [1979] Studio Director [Irish/Australian]; Raja Adil Rehman [1974] Director/Actor, Writer, Broadcaster; Laurent David Henri Samama [1971] Director - Strategic Relations [French]; Balraj Samra [1966] Commercial Director BBC

The National Fostering Agency (Scotland) Limited
Incorporated: 14 June 2005 *Employees:* 20
Net Worth: £1,279,000 *Total Assets:* £32,132,000
Registered Office: Frays Court, 71 Cowley Road, Uxbridge, Middlesex, UB8 2AE
Activities: Other social work activities without accommodation n.e.c.
Parent: NFAG Limited
Officers: Helen Elizabeth Lecky, Secretary; Antony Vincent Holt [1959] Director/Chartered Accountant; Isabella Mary Hutchison [1956] Managing Director; Jean-Luc Emmanuel Janet [1970] Director [French]; David Jon Leatherbarrow [1969] Director/Group Chief Executive Officer

The National Fostering Agency Limited
Incorporated: 17 November 1995 *Employees:* 224
Net Worth: £27,798,000 *Total Assets:* £54,551,000
Registered Office: Frays Court, 71 Cowley Road, Uxbridge, Middlesex, UB8 2AE
Activities: Other social work activities without accommodation n.e.c.
Parent: NFAG Limited
Officers: Helen Elizabeth Lecky, Secretary; Antony Vincent Holt [1959] Director/Chartered Accountant; Isabella Mary Hutchison [1956] Managing Director; Jean-Luc Emmanuel Janet [1970] Director [French]; David Jon Leatherbarrow [1969] Director/Group Chief Executive Officer

National Foundation for Educational Research in England and Wales (The)
Incorporated: 15 March 1967 *Employees:* 246
Net Worth: £8,047,000 *Total Assets:* £35,798,000
Registered Office: The Mere, Upton Park, Slough, Berks, SL1 2DQ
Activities: Other education n.e.c.
Officers: Richard Henry Struan Birkett, Secretary; Ian Roger Bauckham [1962] Director/Headteacher; Jennifer Anne Fiona Capstick [1959] Director/Management Consultant; Joan Lorna Cocking [1941] Director; Professor Michael Donald Day [1954] Director/Retired; Susan Frances Douglas [1970] Director/Chief Executive; Hemlata Meghani Ghantiwala [1961] Director/Solicitor; Nicholas Piers Huxley Hillman [1972] Director; Neil Hollister [1971] Director; Melvyn Keen [1955] Director/Chartered Accountant; Samuel Hugh John MacDonald [1971] Director/Solicitor; David Madoc-Jones [1960] Director/Corporate Adviser; Conor Francis Ryan [1963] Director of Research and Communications [Irish]

National House-Building Council
Incorporated: 17 November 1936 *Employees:* 1,252
Net Worth: £462,449,984 *Total Assets:* £1,674,989,952
Registered Office: NHBC House, Davy Avenue, Knowlhill, Milton Keynes, Bucks, MK5 8FP
Activities: Non-life insurance
Officers: Anne Carol Durkin, Secretary; Paul Bishop [1954] Director; Ian Adam Craston [1966] Investment Director; Katherine Davies [1956] Director/Chief Executive; Paul John Hosking [1967] Director/Chief Financial Officer; Isabel Frances Hudson [1959] Director; Neil Jefferson [1971] Director; Jean Craig Park [1954] Director/Chief Risk Officer; Sir Alistair Muir Russell [1949] Director; Stephen Stone [1954] Director/Architect; Steven Archibald Wood [1960] Director/Chief Executive

The National Museum of The Royal Navy
Incorporated: 16 September 2008 *Employees:* 387
Net Worth: £179,427,616 *Total Assets:* £184,765,936
Registered Office: National Museum of The Royal Navy, HM Naval Base, Portsmouth, PO1 3NH
Activities: Operation of historical sites and buildings and similar visitor attractions
Officers: Sir Jonathon Band [1950] Director; Michael James Bedingfield [1961] Sales and Marketing Director; Professor John Scott Davidson [1954] Director/University Vice-Chancellor; Mike Gambazzi [1947] Director/Retired; Helen Margaret Jackson [1958] Director/Consultant; Adrian James Johns [1951] Director/Retired; Councillor Donna Jones [1977] Director/Politician; Major General Jeffrey Sinclair Mason [1959] Director/Clerk to Worshipful Company of Butchers; Mary Rachel Montagu-Scott [1964] Director; Tim Schadla-Hall [1947] Director; Professor Sara Michel Selwood [1953] Director/Consultant; Robert Patrick Stevens [1948] Director/Consultant; Gavin Whitter [1970] Director/Chartered Accountant; Dr Caroline Ann Williams [1954] Director; Charles Martin Wilson [1935] Director/Retired

NATS (En Route) Public Limited Company
Incorporated: 21 December 2000 *Employees:* 3,237
Net Worth: £662,899,968 *Total Assets:* £1,652,800,000
Registered Office: 4000 Parkway, Whiteley, Fareham, Hants, PO15 7FL
Activities: Scheduled passenger air transport
Officers: Richard Paul Churchill-Coleman, Secretary; Maria Antoniou [1965] Director/Senior Vice President Human Resources; Harry John Bush [1953] Director; Michael Campbell [1957] Director; Nigel Terence Chell Fotherby [1958] Finance Director; Dr Paul Golby [1951] Director/Chairman; Richard John Keys [1951] Director; Kathryn Maria Leahy [1973] Director; Hugh McConnellogue [1970] Director/Head of Network Operations [Irish]; Iain Walter McNicoll [1953] Director; Gavin Bruce Merchant [1969] Director; Martin John Rolfe [1972] Managing Director; Louise Anne Street [1974] Director/Head of Planning and Business Development

NATS (Services) Limited
Incorporated: 21 December 2000 *Employees:* 951
Net Worth: £210,000,000 *Total Assets:* £270,900,000
Registered Office: 4000 Parkway, Whiteley, Fareham, Hants, PO15 7FL
Activities: Scheduled passenger air transport
Officers: Richard Paul Churchill-Coleman, Secretary; Guy Anthony Adams [1968] Commercial Director; Nigel Terence Chell Fotherby [1958] Finance Director; Martin John Rolfe [1972] Director

NATS Holdings Limited
Incorporated: 10 January 2001 *Employees:* 4,310
Net Worth: £880,800,000 *Total Assets:* £1,901,400,064
Registered Office: 4000 Parkway, Whiteley, Fareham, Hants, PO15 7FL
Activities: Scheduled passenger air transport
Officers: Richard Paul Churchill-Coleman, Secretary; Maria Antoniou [1965] Director/Senior Vice President - Human Resources; Harry John Bush [1953] Director/Consultant; Michael Campbell [1957] Director; Nigel Terence Chell Fotherby [1958] Finance Director; Dr Paul Golby [1951] Director/Chairman; Richard John Keys [1951] Director; Kathryn Maria Leahy [1973] Director; Hugh McConnellogue [1970] Director/Head of Network Operations [Irish]; Iain Walter McNicoll [1953] Director; Gavin Bruce Merchant [1969] Director; Martin John Rolfe [1972] Managing Director; Louise Anne Street [1974] Director/Head of Planning and Business Development

NATS Limited
Incorporated: 31 January 1996 *Employees:* 4,221
Net Worth: £255,900,000 *Total Assets:* £320,100,000
Registered Office: 4000 Parkway, Whiteley, Fareham, Hants, PO15 7FL
Activities: Scheduled passenger air transport
Officers: Richard Paul Churchill-Coleman, Secretary; Nigel Terence Chell Fotherby [1958] Director/Chartered Accountant; Martin John Rolfe [1972] Managing Director

Natural Sante Limited
Incorporated: 13 March 2013
Net Worth Deficit: £2,117,347 *Total Assets:* £41,377,484
Registered Office: Unit E, Ashford Business Park, Foster Road, Sevington, Ashford, Kent, TN24 0SH
Activities: Activities of head offices
Parent: NDG Group SA
Officers: Marcos David Pozo Caballero [1973] Business Development Director [Spanish]

Nature Delivered Limited
Incorporated: 17 October 2007 *Employees:* 250
Net Worth: £45,124,320 *Total Assets:* £56,597,200
Registered Office: Palm Court, 4 Heron Square, Richmond, Surrey, TW9 1EW
Activities: Other food services
Parent: ND4A Limited
Officers: Anthony Fletcher [1981] Director; Andrew Gibbs [1978] Director/Accountant

Natures Way Foods Europe Limited
Incorporated: 23 November 2009 *Employees:* 1,171
Net Worth: £31,933,198 *Total Assets:* £64,314,088
Registered Office: Park Farm, Chichester Road, Selsey, W Sussex, PO20 9HP
Activities: Activities of production holding companies
Shareholders: Robert Langmead; David Winston Langmead
Officers: David Winston Langmead [1962] Director; Lucinda Felicity Sommerville Langmead [1971] Director; Robert Anthony Langmead [1968] Director; Sandra Ann Langmead [1962] Director

Natures Way Foods Limited
Incorporated: 9 February 1994 *Employees:* 1,170
Net Worth: £31,878,164 *Total Assets:* £73,873,112
Registered Office: Park Farm, Chichester Road, Selsey, W Sussex, PO20 9HP
Activities: Other processing and preserving of fruit and vegetables
Officers: Anita Marie Barker [1962] Director; Stewart Charles Gilliland [1957] Non-Executive Director/Business Consultant; Benjamin David Rowe Jones [1967] Finance Director; David Winston Langmead [1962] Director/Farmer Market Gardener; Robert Anthony Langmead [1968] Director/Property Manager; Richard Parr [1969] Operations Director; Colin David Smith [1970] Director/Chief Executive Officer; David Gay Williams [1946] Director

Navitas Life Sciences Holdings Limited
Incorporated: 29 November 2010
Previous: Take Global Ltd
Net Worth: £15,689,571 *Total Assets:* £32,995,410
Registered Office: Pure Offices, Office 50, One Port Way, Port Solent, Portsmouth, PO6 4TY
Activities: Activities of other holding companies n.e.c.
Parent: Take Solutions Global Holdings PTE Limited
Officers: Shobana Srinivasan [1970] Director/Accountant [Indian]; Varaha Narasimha Sastri Viswanadha [1970] Director/Accountant [Indian]

Navy,Army and Air Force Institutes,(The)
Incorporated: 9 December 1920 *Employees:* 567
Net Worth: £20,485,000 *Total Assets:* £24,351,000
Registered Office: Naafi Building 1-150, Room 103, Murrays Lane (PP19B), HM Naval Base, Portsmouth, PO1 3NH
Activities: Retail sale in non-specialised stores with food, beverages or tobacco predominating
Officers: Steven Marshall, Secretary; Reginald James Scott Curtis [1963] Director/Chief Executive; Steven David Marshall [1974] Operations Director; Sir Ian Maurice Gray Prosser [1943] Director; Alan Frank Smith [1946] Director; Sir Charles Redmond Watt [1950] Director

NBS Trade and Investment Limited
Incorporated: 9 April 2013
Net Worth: £751,199 *Total Assets:* £1,501,340,416
Registered Office: Aquis House, 27-37 Station Road, Hayes, Middlesex, UB3 4DX
Activities: Non-specialised wholesale trade
Officers: Muhammad Abdulwahab Dastagir [1970] Director [American]

NCL Holdings Limited
Incorporated: 17 July 2000
Net Worth: £55,848,544 *Total Assets:* £56,203,348
Registered Office: Power Solutions House, Presley Way, Crown Hill, Milton Keynes, Bucks, MK8 0ES
Activities: Activities of head offices
Officers: Jane Ridley, Secretary; Tatsuo Bizen [1961] Director [Japanese]; Norio Nakajima [1961] Director [Japanese]

NCMT Holdings Limited
Incorporated: 10 July 2007 *Employees:* 114
Net Worth: £7,130,000 *Total Assets:* £33,940,000
Registered Office: Unit 1 Ferry Works, Summer Road, Thames Ditton, Surrey, KT7 0QJ
Activities: Activities of head offices
Officers: David Burley, Secretary; David Burley [1959] Director/CD; Laurence Howard Ireland [1961] Director/CD; Adrian Joseph Maughan [1956] Director/CD; Michael Roland Terry [1955] Director/CD

NCMT Limited
Incorporated: 6 March 1964 *Employees:* 114
Net Worth: £9,364,000 *Total Assets:* £35,459,000
Registered Office: Unit 1 Ferry Works, Summer Road, Thames Ditton, Surrey, KT7 0QJ
Activities: Agents involved in the sale of machinery, industrial equipment, ships and aircraft
Officers: David Burley, Secretary; David Burley [1959] Director; Laurence Howard Ireland [1961] Director; Adrian Joseph Maughan [1956] Director; Michael Roland Terry [1955] Director

ND1T Limited
Incorporated: 9 October 2012 *Employees:* 386
Net Worth Deficit: £44,311,156 *Total Assets:* £80,257,536
Registered Office: Palm Court, 4 Heron Square, Richmond, Surrey, TW9 1EW
Activities: Activities of other holding companies n.e.c.
Officers: Andrew David Gibbs, Secretary; Mr Graham James Bosher [1981] Director; Christopher Paul Britton [1957] Director; Fernando Chueca [1971] Director [Spanish]; Dr. Robert James Campbell Easton [1963] Director; Anthony Fletcher [1981] Director; Charlotte Lucy Elizabeth Lawrence [1984] Director; Alexander Ian Macpherson [1964] Director

ND2F Limited
Incorporated: 9 October 2012
Net Worth Deficit: £30,627,408 *Total Assets:* £77,814,816
Registered Office: Palm Court, 4 Heron Square, Richmond, Surrey, TW9 1EW
Activities: Activities of other holding companies n.e.c.
Parent: ND1T Limited
Officers: Anthony Fletcher [1981] Director; Andrew Gibbs [1978] Director

ND3M Limited
Incorporated: 9 October 2012
Net Worth: £2,612,103 *Total Assets:* £77,729,696
Registered Office: Palm Court, 4 Heron Square, Richmond, Surrey, TW9 1EW
Activities: Activities of other holding companies n.e.c.
Parent: ND2F Limited
Officers: Anthony Fletcher [1981] Director; Andrew Gibbs [1978] Director

Necessity Supplies Limited
Incorporated: 15 April 1986 *Employees:* 21
Net Worth: £18,206,732 *Total Assets:* £23,210,598
Registered Office: Unit 4-5 Northolt Trading Estate, Belvue Road, Northolt, Middlesex, UB5 5QS
Activities: Wholesale of pharmaceutical goods
Officers: Vandana Wadhar, Secretary; Bharat Himatlal Mehta [1952] Director; Ketan Himatlal Mehta [1958] Director/Pharmacist

Needspace? Limited
Incorporated: 28 April 2005 *Employees:* 9
Net Worth: £12,409,716 *Total Assets:* £50,340,344
Registered Office: Wates House, Station Approach, Leatherhead, Surrey, KT22 7SW
Activities: Other letting and operating of own or leased real estate
Parent: Wates Group Limited
Officers: David Owen Allen [1972] Director/Chief Financial Officer; David Alexander Bowen [1967] Finance Director; Richard Maurice Trimming [1954] Director/Chartered Surveyor; Philip Michael Wainwright [1965] Director/Chief Financial Officer; Charles William Randag Wates [1976] Director

Neilcott Construction Limited
Incorporated: 14 December 1973 *Employees:* 159
Net Worth: £9,357,819 *Total Assets:* £57,488,768
Registered Office: Excel House, Cray Avenue, Orpington, Kent, BR5 3ST
Activities: Development of building projects
Parent: Neilcott Construction Services Ltd
Officers: Malcolm Charles Elster, Secretary; Malcolm Charles Elster [1957] Director; Joseph Gissane [1956] Director [Irish]; Neil Eric Harrison [1960] Director; Robert Weatherston [1967] Divisional Construction Director

Neilson Active Holidays (Holdings) Limited
Incorporated: 15 July 2013 *Employees:* 749
Net Worth Deficit: £3,052,000 *Total Assets:* £35,042,000
Registered Office: Locksview, Brighton Marina, Brighton, BN2 5HA
Activities: Activities of other holding companies n.e.c.
Parent: Project Tennessee Bidco Limited
Officers: David Michael Taylor, Secretary; Richard William Bowden-Doyle [1960] Director; Richard Kevin Mills [1972] Finance Director; David Michael Taylor [1970] Director; Phillip Tyler [1960] Director

Neilson Active Holidays Limited
Incorporated: 1 November 1994 *Employees:* 503
Net Worth: £6,270,000 *Total Assets:* £28,216,000
Registered Office: Locksview, Brighton Marina, Brighton, BN2 5HA
Activities: Tour operator activities
Parent: Neilson Active Holidays (Holdings) Limited
Officers: David Michael Taylor, Secretary; Richard William Bowden Doyle [1960] Director; Richard Kevin Mills [1972] Finance Director; Richard Stuart Mills [1973] Director; David Michael Taylor [1970] Director; Phillip Tyler [1960] Director/Tour Operator

NEOS Networks Limited
Incorporated: 2 December 1997 *Employees:* 98
Net Worth: £55,100,000 *Total Assets:* £98,100,000
Registered Office: No 1 Forbury Place, 43 Forbury Road, Reading, Berks, RG1 3JH
Activities: Other telecommunications activities
Parent: SSE Telecommunications Limited
Officers: Laura Kate Tudor, Secretary; David Eddy [1963] Director; Colin Douglas Sempill [1970] Director

NEP UK Film I Limited
Incorporated: 16 November 2016 *Employees:* 365
Net Worth: £25,293,000 *Total Assets:* £60,956,000
Registered Office: Unit E2, Sussex Manor Business Park, Gatwick Road, Crawley, W Sussex, RH10 9NH
Activities: Activities of other holding companies n.e.c.
Officers: David Mark Leadbetter, Secretary; David Andrew Crump [1961] Managing Director; Generald Delon [1970] Director [American]; Stephen Anthony Jenkins [1970] Director; Simon Anthony Mort [1974] Finance Director; Mark Andrew Wilson [1975] Finance Director

NEP UK Film II Limited
Incorporated: 17 November 2016
Net Worth: £26,135,000 *Total Assets:* £123,991,000
Registered Office: Unit E2, Sussex Manor Business Park, Gatwick Road, Crawley, W Sussex, RH10 9NH
Activities: Activities of other holding companies n.e.c.
Parent: NEP UK Film I Limited
Officers: David Mark Leadbetter, Secretary; David Andrew Crump [1961] Managing Director; Generald Delon [1970] Director [American]; Stephen Anthony Jenkins [1970] Director; Simon Anthony Mort [1974] Finance Director; Mark Andrew Wilson [1975] Finance Director

NEP Visions Limited
Incorporated: 14 December 2004 *Employees:* 151
Net Worth: £15,400,398 *Total Assets:* £63,179,220
Registered Office: Gemini House, Downmill Road, Bracknell, Berks, RG12 1QS
Activities: Television programming and broadcasting activities
Parent: NEP UK Film II Limited
Officers: David Leadbetter, Secretary; Generald Delon [1970] Director/Chief Financial Officer, NEP LLC [American]; Stephen Anthony Jenkins [1970] Managing Director, NEP UK; Simon Moorhead [1973] Director; Simon Anthony Mort [1974] Finance Director

Nespresso UK Ltd
Incorporated: 10 July 1919 *Employees:* 625
Net Worth: £6,646,000 *Total Assets:* £52,598,000
Registered Office: 1 City Place, Gatwick, W Sussex, RH6 0PA
Activities: Retail sale of electrical household appliances in specialised stores
Parent: Nestle UK Ltd.
Officers: Guillaume Chesneau [1974] Director/MD Nespresso UK & ROI [French/Australian]; David Steven McDaniel [1968] Finance Director

Nesstra Services (UK) Limited
Incorporated: 15 November 1982 *Employees:* 21
Net Worth: £8,037,638 *Total Assets:* £53,372,868
Registered Office: 22-23 Progress Business Centre, Whittle Parkway, Slough, Berks, SL1 6DQ
Activities: Wholesale of chemical products
Major Shareholder: Alwan Hitti
Officers: Generald Oliver, Secretary; Alwan Hitti [1965] Director [French]; Mireille Hitti [1972] Director/Industrialist [French]; Bert Lichtenheldt [1957] Director [German]

Nestec York Ltd.
Incorporated: 20 April 1988 *Employees:* 166
Net Worth: £13,457,000 *Total Assets:* £27,667,000
Registered Office: 1 City Place, Gatwick, W Sussex, RH6 0PA
Activities: Other research and experimental development on natural sciences and engineering
Officers: Stefano Agostini [1964] Director [Italian]; David Anthony Hix [1966] Director of Supply Chain UK & Ireland; David Steven McDaniel [1968] Finance Director; Aristides Protonotarios [1965] Group Technical & Production Director [Greek/British]; Jaswinder Scott de Martinville [1968] Director/Global Head of Confectionery, R & D

Nestle Holdings (U.K.) PLC
Incorporated: 17 December 1948
Net Worth: £1,739,709,952 *Total Assets:* £3,106,449,920
Registered Office: 1 City Place, Gatwick, W Sussex, RH6 0PA
Activities: Activities of other holding companies n.e.c.
Officers: Mark Nicholas Maurice-Jones, Secretary; Stefano Agostini [1964] Director [Italian]; David Anthony Hix [1966] Director of Supply Chain UK & Ireland; David Steven McDaniel [1968] Finance Director

Nestle Purina Petcare (U.K.) Limited
Incorporated: 30 April 1912 *Employees:* 1,194
Net Worth: £62,544,000 *Total Assets:* £201,740,000
Registered Office: 1 City Place, Gatwick, W Sussex, RH6 0PA
Activities: Manufacture of prepared pet foods
Parent: Nestle UK Ltd.
Officers: Matthew John Chandler [1979] Finance Director; Calum Fionn MacRae [1967] Director/Business Executive Officer, Nestle Purina UK; David Steven McDaniel [1968] Finance Director

Nestle UK Ltd.
Incorporated: 3 March 1897 *Employees:* 5,017
Net Worth: £1,369,181,056 *Total Assets:* £3,759,622,912
Registered Office: 1 City Place, Gatwick, W Sussex, RH6 0PA
Activities: Butter and cheese production
Parent: Nestle Holdings (U.K.) PLC
Officers: Stefano Agostini [1964] Director [Italian]; David Anthony Hix [1966] Director of Supply Chain UK & Ireland; David Steven McDaniel [1968] Finance Director; Mark Timothy McKenzie [1969] Director; Neil Lloyd Stephens [1968] Managing Director - Beverage Division, NUK

Nestle Waters UK Limited
Incorporated: 12 January 1989 *Employees:* 262
Net Worth: £6,706,000 *Total Assets:* £72,126,000
Registered Office: 1 City Place, Gatwick, W Sussex, RH6 0PA
Activities: Manufacture of soft drinks; production of mineral waters and other bottled waters
Parent: Nestle UK Ltd.
Officers: Michel Beneventi [1971] Managing Director Nestle Waters UK [Swiss]; Charles David Hardy Roberts [1974] Director/Factory Manager; Richard James Shaw [1974] Director/Management Accountant

Net Pay (EUR) Limited
Incorporated: 29 December 2004 *Employees:* 2
Net Worth: £54,959 *Total Assets:* £35,109,772
Registered Office: 5 Elstree Gate, Elstree Way, Borehamwood, Herts, WD6 1JD
Activities: Information technology consultancy activities
Major Shareholder: Alon Elbaz
Officers: Alon Elbaz [1971] Director/Computer Consultant [Israeli]

NetApp UK Ltd
Incorporated: 6 December 1994 *Employees:* 325
Net Worth: £5,544,023 *Total Assets:* £69,980,512
Registered Office: Rivermead, Oxford Road, Uxbridge, Middlesex, UB9 4BF
Activities: Wholesale of computers, computer peripheral equipment and software
Parent: NetApp, Inc.
Officers: Stephen Peter Faulkner [1973] Director/International Field Operations Finance

Netcall PLC
Incorporated: 1 May 1984 *Employees:* 217
Net Worth: £21,704,000 *Total Assets:* £44,958,000
Registered Office: 1st Floor, Building 2, People Building Estate, Maylands Avenue, Hemel Hempstead Industrial Estate, Hemel Hempstead, Herts, HP2 4NW
Activities: Activities of head offices
Officers: Michael Charles Greensmith, Secretary; Henrik Peter Bang [1958] Director [Danish]; Michael Edward Wilson Jackson [1950] Director; Michael Patrick Neville [1954] Director; James Andrew Ormondroyd [1972] Director

Network Aviation Group Ltd
Incorporated: 21 December 2012 *Employees:* 168
Net Worth: £2,172,260 *Total Assets:* £29,602,844
Registered Office: First Floor, Unit A2 Windsor Place, Faraday Road, Manor Royal, Crawley, W Sussex, RH10 9TF
Activities: Activities of head offices
Parent: Equiom (Guernsey) Limited as Trustee for Network Aviation Group Limited Employee Ownership Trust
Officers: Andrew Michael Ballard, Secretary; Andrew Michael Ballard [1983] Director; John Gilfeather [1970] Director; Patricia Heilbrink [1959] Director [Dutch]; Malcolm James Higginson [1969] Director; Andrew Jeremy King [1953] Director; Andrew Graham Leslie [1952] Director; Andrew Keith Walters [1963] Director

Networkers International (UK) Limited
Incorporated: 28 February 2000 *Employees:* 149
Previous: Networkers International (UK) PLC
Net Worth: £10,756,000 *Total Assets:* £40,041,000
Registered Office: 1450 Parkway Solent Business Park, Whiteley, Fareham, Hants, PO15 7AF
Activities: Temporary employment agency activities
Parent: Networkers International Ltd
Officers: Katie Mary Selves, Secretary; Salar Farzad [1965] Director/Chief Financial Officer; Keith John Lewis [1966] Managing Director

Networkers International Limited
Incorporated: 14 March 2000 *Employees:* 2
Previous: Networkers International PLC
Net Worth: £17,554,000 *Total Assets:* £22,432,000
Registered Office: 1450 Parkway Solent Business Park, Whiteley, Fareham, Hants, PO15 7AF
Activities: Temporary employment agency activities
Parent: Gattaca PLC
Officers: Katie Mary Selves, Secretary; Salar Farzad [1965] Director/Chief Financial Officer; Keith John Lewis [1966] Managing Director

Neusentis Limited
Incorporated: 2 October 1997
Net Worth: £5,815,000 *Total Assets:* £155,036,992
Registered Office: Ramsgate Road, Sandwich, Kent, CT13 9NJ
Activities: Other business support service activities n.e.c.
Parent: Pfizer Limited
Officers: Jacqueline Ann Mount, Secretary; Ian Eric Franklin [1965] Director; Hendrikus Hermannus Nordkamp [1969] UK Managing Director, Pfizer [Dutch]; Edwin James Pearson [1974] Director/Solicitor; Colin Malcolm Seller [1963] Director

New Blue Chip Limited
Incorporated: 15 July 2016 *Employees:* 242
Net Worth: £10,734,000 *Total Assets:* £75,807,000
Registered Office: Unit 1 Franklin Court, Stannard Way, Priory Business Park, Bedford, MK44 3JZ
Activities: Other software publishing
Officers: Andrew Rounding, Secretary; Lee John Bailey [1976] Director; Eddy Conway [1960] Director; Brian Meredith [1950] Director; Sadie Vanessa Nesbitt [1967] Director; Andrew James Rounding [1972] Director; Tim Stringer [1976] Director; Derek Waterman [1972] Director

New Era Cap Company Limited
Incorporated: 25 November 2002 *Employees:* 165
Net Worth: £14,190,970 *Total Assets:* £26,233,362
Registered Office: 1st Floor, CBX II East, Midsummer Boulevard, Milton Keynes, Bucks, MK9 2EA
Activities: Wholesale of clothing and footwear
Major Shareholder: Christopher Koch
Officers: Alan Jones, Secretary; Paul Gils [1960] Director [Belgian]; Alan Jones [1960] Director/Chartered Accountant; Christopher Koch [1960] Director [American]; Kevin Robert Wilson [1964] Director [Canadian]

New Terex Holdings UK Limited
Incorporated: 26 August 1994 *Employees:* 2
Net Worth: £117,543,000 *Total Assets:* £296,780,000
Registered Office: The Pinnacle, 170 Midsummer Boulevard, Milton Keynes, Bucks, MK9 1FE
Activities: Activities of other holding companies n.e.c.
Parent: Terex Corporation
Officers: Eric I Cohen, Secretary/Lawyer [American]; Eric I Cohen [1958] Director/Lawyer [American]; Brian Henry [1958] Director/Executive; John Daniel Sheehan [1960] Director/Chief Financial Officer [American]

New Topco 1 Limited
Incorporated: 27 April 2016 *Employees:* 105
Net Worth: £20,502,592 *Total Assets:* £25,749,740
Registered Office: Claygate Building, Pattenden Lane, Marden, Tonbridge, Kent, TN12 9QJ
Activities: Other business support service activities n.e.c.
Shareholders: Andrew Martin Streek; Melvyn Barry Streek
Officers: Andrew Martin Streek [1962] Director; Melvyn Barry Streek [1960] Director

The New Victoria Hospital Limited
Incorporated: 11 August 2006 *Employees:* 260
Net Worth Deficit: £29,835,000 *Total Assets:* £24,828,000
Registered Office: The New Victoria Hospital, 184 Coombe Lane West, Kingston upon Thames, Surrey, KT2 7EG
Activities: Hospital activities
Officers: Graham Arthur Ridgeway Ball [1950] Director; Mark James Curtis [1959] Director/Consultant Surgeon; John Alan Hamblin [1949] Director/Chartered Accountant; Catriona Ann MacKay [1963] Director/Executive Coach; Martin Anthony Matthews [1950] Director

Newarthill Limited
Incorporated: 21 April 1972 *Employees:* 2,209
Net Worth: £71,938,000 *Total Assets:* £781,009,984
Registered Office: Eaton Court, Maylands Avenue, Hemel Hempstead Industrial Estate, Hemel Hempstead, Herts, HP2 7TR
Activities: Activities of head offices
Parent: R H McAlpine, A W McAlpine, G M McAlpine, R E T McAlpine and Others as Trustees of The McAlpine Partnership Trust
Officers: John Alistair Dempsey, Secretary; Kevin John Pearson, Secretary; David Stannard Jenkins [1947] Director; Donald Crawford Joyce [1973] Director; Sir Andrew William McAlpine [1960] Director/Civil Engineering & Building Contractor; Cullum McAlpine [1947] Director/Civil Engineering and Building; The Hon David Malcolm McAlpine [1946] Director/Civil Engineering and Building; Robert John William Wotherspoon [1967] Director/Chartered Accountant

Newbury & Thatcham Hospital Building Trust
Incorporated: 15 August 1997
Net Worth: £7,581,711 *Total Assets:* £21,267,470
Registered Office: 2nd Floor, Aquis House, 49-51 Blagrave Street, Reading, Berks, RG1 1PL
Activities: Other human health activities
Officers: Keith Endersby, Secretary; Susan Ethel Bishop [1945] Director/Retired Matron; Doctor Keith Endersby [1949] Director/Medical Practitioner; Sylvia Galbraith [1942] Director/Retired Veterinary Practice Manager; Victoria Anne Hopgood [1963] Director/Solicitor; Shane David Prater [1974] Director/Chartered Surveyor; Dr Robert Geoffrey Tayton [1947] Director/Retired Medical Practitioner; Paul Townsend [1960] Relationship Director - Banking

Newbury Investments (UK) Limited
Incorporated: 21 August 1990 *Employees:* 1,722
Net Worth: £163,212,992 *Total Assets:* £285,363,008
Registered Office: Votec House, Hambridge Lane, Newbury, Berks, RG14 5TN
Activities: Activities of head offices
Officers: Leo Yu, Secretary; Richard Whiting Colburn [1943] Director [American]; Carol Colburn Hogel [1944] Director [American]; Nigel John Palmer [1956] Director/Chairman; Steven Westbrook [1956] Director/Chief Executive

Newbury Racecourse PLC
Incorporated: 26 April 1904 *Employees:* 89
Net Worth: £48,552,000 *Total Assets:* £66,164,000
Registered Office: The Racecourse, Newbury, Berks, RG14 7NZ
Activities: Operation of sports facilities
Officers: Claire Emma Spencer, Secretary; Dominic James Burke [1958] Director; Bryan Robert Hardy Burrough [1960] Director; John Dodds [1945] Director; Henry Malcolm Herbert [1959] Director [American]; Lady Madeleine Astrid Lloyd Webber [1962] Director; James Christopher McGrath [1955] Director/Broadcaster; Nils Wilhelm Erik Penser [1942] Director [Swedish]; Claire Emma Spencer [1978] Director/Chartered Accountant; Brian Trevor Stewart-Brown [1945] Director/Retired; Julian Mark Thick [1970] Director; Matthew Longstreth Thompson [1964] Director

Newcourt Residential (Wadhurst) Limited
Incorporated: 24 April 2015
Net Worth: £2,277,355 *Total Assets:* £25,080,012
Registered Office: First Floor, Front Suite, The Grange, 26 Market Square, Westerham, Kent, TN16 1HB
Activities: Development of building projects
Parent: Newcourt Residential Holdings Limited
Officers: Anouar Elkhadraoui [1978] Director; Aziz Elkhadraoui [1982] Finance Director; Khalid Elkhadraoui [1980] Director; John Phillips McMonigall [1943] Director

Newhall Projects Limited
Incorporated: 12 July 1995
Net Worth Deficit: £9,082,593 *Total Assets:* £27,813,504
Registered Office: Churchill House, Church Hill, Harbledown, Canterbury, Kent, CT2 9AB
Activities: Other service activities n.e.c.
Officers: Dr Jon Andreas Moen, Secretary/Director; Freda Elizabeth Bayne [1953] Director; Dr Jon Andreas Moen [1947] Director; Philip Andrew Soper [1954] Director

Newhospitals (St Helens and Knowsley) Finance PLC
Incorporated: 2 November 2005
Net Worth: £50,000 *Total Assets:* £355,201,984
Registered Office: 8 White Oak Square, London Road, Swanley, Kent, BR8 7AG
Activities: Financial intermediation not elsewhere classified
Parent: Newhospitals (St Helens and Knowsley) Holdings Limited
Officers: David John Brooking [1967] Investment Director; Nicholas John Edward Crowther [1960] Director/Chartered Accountant; Michael Davis [1946] Director

Newhospitals (St Helens and Knowsley) Holdings Limited
Incorporated: 26 October 2005
Net Worth Deficit: £36,655,000 *Total Assets:* £327,828,992
Registered Office: 8 White Oak Square, London Road, Swanley, Kent, BR8 7AG
Activities: Activities of head offices
Shareholders: Innisfree Secondary Partners 1 LLP; Innisfree Secondary Partners 2 LLP
Officers: David John Brooking [1967] Investment Director; Nicholas John Edward Crowther [1960] Director/Chartered Accountant

Newhospitals (St Helens and Knowsley) Limited
Incorporated: 26 October 2005
Net Worth Deficit: £36,705,000 *Total Assets:* £327,828,992
Registered Office: 8 White Oak Square, London Road, Swanley, Kent, BR8 7AG
Activities: Hospital activities
Parent: Newhospitals (St Helens and Knowsley) Holdings Limited
Officers: David John Brooking [1967] Investment Director; Nicholas John Edward Crowther [1960] Director

Newincco 1222 Limited
Incorporated: 4 February 2013
Net Worth: £29,213,034 *Total Assets:* £29,213,034
Registered Office: One Gloucester Place, Brighton, BN1 4AA
Activities: Activities of head offices
Major Shareholder: Andrew Jeremy Colin
Officers: Timothy Slater [1972] Director/Accountant

Newincco 1270 Limited
Incorporated: 13 November 2013 *Employees:* 4
Net Worth: £61,679,296 *Total Assets:* £123,700,328
Registered Office: 3rd Floor, Premier House, Elstree Way, Borehamwood, Herts, WD6 1JH
Activities: Other business support service activities n.e.c.
Parent: Galene Bidco Limited
Officers: Emily Henrietta Gestetner [1967] Director; Harry Leon Landy [1978] Director; Stephen Bryan Wasserman [1984] Director; Danny Stephen Waters [1984] Director

Newlands Girls' School
Incorporated: 13 July 2015 *Employees:* 171
Net Worth: £25,119,062 *Total Assets:* £27,103,622
Registered Office: Newlands Girls' School, Farm Road, Maidenhead, Berks, SL6 5JB
Activities: General secondary education
Officers: Lesley Elizabeth Allaway [1969] Director/Teacher; Stephen Bridge [1950] Director; Huw David Buckle [1960] Director/Assistant Headteacher; Shelley Joanne Carroll [1967] Director/Accounts Manager; Dr Louise Virginia Victoria Ceska [1958] Director/Headteacher; Sofia Gondal [1970] Director/Lecturer; Dr Clare Frances Jones [1970] Director/Management Consultant; Bartholomew George de La Fosse Leach [1973] Director/Solicitor; Tahir Mahmood [1970] Director/Accountant; Paul David Manby [1968] Director/Deputy Head; Patrick Alastair McMaster [1972] Director/Senior Learning and Development Partner; Caroline Louise Mulvihill [1974] Director/Head of Sales; Karnail Singh Pannu [1938] Director/Retired Teacher; Richard George Preece [1949] Director/Retired; Farah Naaz Sheikh [1971] Director/Chartered Architect; Lisa Suzanne Swanson [1967] Director/Management Consultant; Clare Louise Vincent [1971] Director/Businesswoman; Hannah Faith Wheeler [1969] Director/Police Officer

Newmafruit Farms Limited
Incorporated: 23 November 1951 *Employees:* 333
Net Worth: £24,381,812 *Total Assets:* £27,622,816
Registered Office: Howfield Farm, Howfield Lane, Chartham, Canterbury, Kent, CT4 7HQ
Activities: Growing of vegetables and melons, roots and tubers
Shareholders: Melvyn Leigh Newman; Jacqueline Hornick
Officers: John Richard Clark [1964] Director; Katie Helena Newman [1988] Director; Melvyn Leigh Newman [1948] Director/Fruit & Vegetable Merchant; Tania Gail Newman [1989] Director; Paul Charles Nicholls [1964] Director

Newmarket Promotions Limited
Incorporated: 22 March 1983 *Employees:* 236
Net Worth: £11,712,941 *Total Assets:* £28,809,550
Registered Office: Cantium House, Railway Approach, Wallington, Surrey, SM6 0BP
Activities: Tour operator activities
Shareholders: Toni Paul Frei; Jeremy Charles Griffin
Officers: Simon Charles Hibbs, Secretary/Director; Toni Paul Frei [1956] Director; Jeremy Charles Griffin [1954] Director; Simon Charles Hibbs [1956] Director; Alan James McWalter [1953] Director; Marc Thomas Raymond Vincent [1969] Finance Director

Newschools (Merton) Limited
Incorporated: 27 June 2002
Net Worth: £1,985,000 *Total Assets:* £39,979,000
Registered Office: 8 White Oak Square, London Road, Swanley, Kent, BR8 7AG
Activities: Combined facilities support activities
Parent: Newschools (Merton) Holdings Limited
Officers: Sheila Jamieson Clark [1973] Director; Benjamin Christopher Jacob Dean [1979] Director/Investment Manager

Newship Group Limited
Incorporated: 3 August 1978 *Employees:* 601
Net Worth: £37,125,000 *Total Assets:* £109,240,000
Registered Office: Fernside Place, 179 Queens Road, Weybridge, Surrey, KT13 0AH
Activities: Activities of head offices
Major Shareholder: John Watson Newman
Officers: Andrew St Clair Harrison, Secretary/Accountant; Jeremy David Clarkson [1961] Director; Sarah Elizabeth Leach [1975] Director; John Watson Newman [1945] Director/Accountant; Lesley Jean Newman [1948] Director; Richard John Newman [1979] Director/Accountant; Amanda Jane Parker [1974] Director/Accounts Executive

Newship Limited
Incorporated: 31 January 2001 *Employees:* 599
Net Worth: £45,223,000 *Total Assets:* £111,119,000
Registered Office: Fernside Place, 179 Queens Road, Weybridge, Surrey, KT13 0AH
Activities: Activities of head offices
Parent: Newship Group Limited
Officers: Andrew Paul Bale, Secretary/Director; Andrew Paul Bale [1957] Director; Jeremy David Clarkson [1961] Director/Accountant; Stephen Edwin John Compson [1954] Director; John Watson Newman [1945] Director/Chartered Accountant; Richard John Newman [1979] Director/Accountant; David Anthony Thornton [1971] Finance Director

Newsquest Capital Limited
Incorporated: 31 July 1995
Previous: Newsquest Capital PLC
Net Worth Deficit: £94,232,000 *Total Assets:* £219,000,000
Registered Office: Loudwater Mill, Station Road, High Wycombe, Bucks, HP10 9TY
Activities: Activities of head offices
Parent: Newsquest Limited
Officers: Neil Edward Carpenter, Secretary; Barbara Wartelle Wall, Secretary; Simon Alton Westrop, Secretary; Robert John Dickey [1957] Director [American]; Alison Kaye Engel [1970] Director [American]; Henry Kennedy Faure Walker [1972] Director; Paul Anthony Hunter [1964] Financial Director; Barbara Wartelle Wall [1956] Director/Solicitor [American]

Newsquest Media Group Limited
Incorporated: 9 November 1982 *Employees:* 1,891
Net Worth: £102,287,000 *Total Assets:* £262,886,000
Registered Office: Loudwater Mill, Station Road, High Wycombe, Bucks, HP10 9TY
Activities: Publishing of newspapers
Parent: Newsquest Capital Limited
Officers: Neil Edward Carpenter, Secretary; Barbara Wartelle Wall, Secretary; Simon Alton Westrop, Secretary; Robert John Dickey [1957] Director [American]; Alison Kaye Engel [1970] Director [American]; Henry Kennedy Faure Walker [1972] Director; Paul Anthony Hunter [1964] Financial Director; Barbara Wartelle Wall [1956] Director/Solicitor [American]

NewVoiceMedia Limited
Incorporated: 23 July 1998 *Employees:* 388
Net Worth Deficit: £5,081,920 *Total Assets:* £26,424,108
Registered Office: NewVoiceMedia House, Jays Close, Basingstoke, Hants, RG22 4BS
Activities: Other telecommunications activities
Officers: Randy Rutherford, Secretary; David Todd Pearson [1965] Director/Chief Financial Officer [American]; Randy Rutherford [1973] Director/Attorney [American]; Guy Edward Sochovsky [1976] Director/Business Executive

Nexen Petroleum U.K. Holdings Limited
Incorporated: 14 October 2004
Net Worth: £314,124,288 *Total Assets:* £315,630,880
Registered Office: Prospect House, 97 Oxford Road, Uxbridge, Middlesex, UB8 1LU
Activities: Other business support service activities n.e.c.
Parent: CNOOC UK Limited
Officers: Jamie David Doyle, Secretary; Jamie David Doyle [1975] Director; Ray Christopher John Riddoch [1961] Managing Director; Brent Christian Tilford [1978] Finance Director

Next Generation Data Infrastructure 1 Limited
Incorporated: 21 April 2016 *Employees:* 49
Net Worth: £1,732,000 *Total Assets:* £150,591,008
Registered Office: 2 Old Bath Road, Newbury, Berks, RG14 1QL
Activities: Other information technology service activities
Parent: Infravia Invest S.A.
Officers: Robert Edwards, Secretary; Bruno Richard Leonce Candes [1972] Director/Investment [French]; Olivier Laroche [1977] Director/Asset Manager, Infravia Capital Partners [French]; William McHenry [1953] Director; Nicholas James Razey [1962] Director; Simon Taylor [1966] Director; Athanasios Zoulovitz [1980] Director/Investment [Greek]

Next Generation Data Infrastructure 2 Limited
Incorporated: 21 April 2016
Net Worth: £8,749,000 *Total Assets:* £76,170,000
Registered Office: 2 Old Bath Road, Newbury, Berks, RG14 1QL
Activities: Other information technology service activities
Parent: Next Generation Data Infrastructure 1 Limited
Officers: Robert Edwards, Secretary; Olivier Laroche [1977] Director/Asset Manager, Infravia Capital Partners [French]; Nicholas James Razey [1962] Director; Simon Taylor [1966] Director

Next Generation Data Ltd
Incorporated: 1 March 2007 *Employees:* 49
Net Worth: £18,566,000 *Total Assets:* £95,246,000
Registered Office: 2 Old Bath Road, Newbury, Berks, RG14 1QL
Activities: Other information technology service activities
Parent: Next Generation Data Infrastructure 2 Limited
Officers: Robert Kenneth Edwards, Secretary; Robert Kenneth Edwards [1955] Director; Justin Marcus Jenkins [1975] Director; Nicholas James Razey [1962] Director; Simon Taylor [1966] Director

Nextonline Limited
Incorporated: 13 April 2000
Net Worth: £21,201,784 *Total Assets:* £24,053,180
Registered Office: Compass House, Guildford Street, Chertsey, Surrey, KT16 9BQ
Activities: Non-trading company
Parent: Compass Overseas Holdings No.2 Limited
Officers: Sarah Jane Sergeant [1973] Director/Accountant

Nextpharma UK Topco Limited
Incorporated: 16 June 2017 *Employees:* 1,031
Net Worth: £12,295,082 *Total Assets:* £202,245,184
Registered Office: 1 Tannery House, Tannery Lane, Send, Woking, Surrey, GU23 7EF
Activities: Activities of other holding companies n.e.c.
Officers: Peter Arend William Burema [1958] Director [Dutch]; Christopher John Campbell [1973] Director/Partner; Othmane Khelladi [1986] Investment Director [French]; Jason Rodrigues [1982] Managing Director

NFAG Limited
Incorporated: 6 November 2006
Net Worth: £5,803,000 *Total Assets:* £60,975,000
Registered Office: Frays Court, 71 Cowley Road, Uxbridge, Middlesex, UB8 2AE
Activities: Other social work activities without accommodation n.e.c.
Parent: NFAH Limited
Officers: Helen Elizabeth Lecky, Secretary; Antony Vincent Holt [1959] Director/Chartered Accountant; Isabella Mary Hutchison [1956] Managing Director; Jean-Luc Emmanuel Janet [1970] Director/Chief Financial Officer [French]; David Jon Leatherbarrow [1969] Director/Group Chief Executive Officer

NHS Professionals Limited
Incorporated: 23 September 2008 *Employees:* 17,036
Net Worth: £55,940,000 *Total Assets:* £162,048,992
Registered Office: Breakspear Park, Breakspear Way, Hemel Hempstead, Herts, HP2 4TZ
Activities: Temporary employment agency activities
Parent: Secretary of State for Health
Officers: Colin McCready, Secretary; Oliver Guy Blackaby [1962] Director/Consultant; Anne Challinor [1954] Director; Stephen John Collier [1957] Director; John Flook [1949] Director; Nicholas George Kirkbride [1959] Director/Chief Executive Officer; Colin McCready [1975] Director/Chief Financial Officer; Anne O'Brien [1968] Director of Clinical Governance; Elizabeth Jane Robb [1953] Director/Healthcare Consultant

NHS Shared Business Services Limited
Incorporated: 8 November 2004 *Employees:* 811
Net Worth: £39,046,000 *Total Assets:* £59,393,000
Registered Office: Three Cherry Trees Lane, Hemel Hempstead, Herts, HP2 7AH
Activities: Information technology consultancy activities
Shareholders: Sopra Steria Limited; Secretary of State for Dept of Health
Officers: Peter Atherton Cashmore, Secretary; Davinder Singh Ahluwalia [1952] Director; David Albert Edmonds [1944] Director; Professor Justin Allan Spaven Jewitt [1954] Director; Benjamin Michael Patrick Masterson [1964] Director/Senior Civil Servant; Marcus James Thorman [1972] Director/Accountant; John Powell Torrie [1954] Director

Nibgreen
Incorporated: 3 April 2017
Net Worth: £430,365 *Total Assets:* £22,979,872
Registered Office: Suite 100, Regus-Atterbury Lakes, Fairbourne Drive, Atterbury, Milton Keynes, Bucks, MK10 9RG
Activities: Security dealing on own account
Shareholders: Andrew Robinson; Julie Elizabeth Robinson
Officers: Andrew Robinson [1968] Director; Julie Elizabeth Robinson [1972] Director

Nice Systems UK Finance Limited
Incorporated: 14 December 2010
Net Worth: £217,213,056 *Total Assets:* £218,074,064
Registered Office: Tollbar House, Tollbar Way, Hedge End, Southampton, SO30 2ZP
Activities: Other business support service activities n.e.c.
Parent: Nice Limited
Officers: Dan Meir Rhodes, Secretary; Dan Meir Rhodes [1966] Director/Solicitor; Hagit Hana Ynon [1971] Director/Accountant [Israeli]

Nice Systems UK Limited
Incorporated: 14 July 1997 *Employees:* 220
Net Worth: £38,044,312 *Total Assets:* £114,989,504
Registered Office: Tollbar House, Tollbar Way, Hedge End, Southampton, SO30 2ZP
Activities: Information technology consultancy activities
Parent: Nice Systems Limited
Officers: Dan Meir Rhodes, Secretary; Barak Eilam [1975] Director/Chief Executive Officer [Israeli]; Mary Beth Gaspich [1965] Director/Chief Financial Officer [American]; John Edward O'Hara [1958] Director/Regional CEO; Dan Meir Rhodes [1966] Director/Solicitor

Nice Systems US Finance Limited
Incorporated: 14 December 2010 *Employees:* 2
Net Worth: £94,682,208 *Total Assets:* £319,611,296
Registered Office: Tollbar House, Tollbar Way, Hedge End, Southampton, SO30 2ZP
Activities: Other business support service activities n.e.c.
Parent: Nice Limited
Officers: Dan Meir Rhodes, Secretary; Dan Meir Rhodes [1966] Director/Solicitor; Hagit Hana Ynon [1971] Director/Accountant [Israeli]

Anthony Nicholas (UK) Limited
Incorporated: 5 July 2007
Net Worth: £16,890,974 *Total Assets:* £58,186,260
Registered Office: 3rd Floor, Premier House, Elstree Way, Borehamwood, Herts, WD6 1JH
Activities: Activities of head offices
Officers: Noel Coyle [1962] Director [Irish]; Mark Naughton-Rumbo [1960] Director; Tony Obernik [1943] Director [Irish]

E.H. Nicholls Holdings Limited
Incorporated: 17 January 2000 *Employees:* 163
Net Worth: £35,095,280 *Total Assets:* £47,994,392
Registered Office: Nicholls Transport, Sittingbourne Logistics Park, Swale Way, Sittingbourne, Kent, ME10 2FF
Activities: Development of building projects
Shareholders: Ernest Henry Nicholls; Maureen Winifred Nicholls; Paul Nicholls; Cripps Trust Corporation Limited
Officers: Darren James Sherlock, Finance Director; Ernest Henry Nicholls [1938] Director; Paul Nicholls [1959] Director; Darren James Sherlock [1972] Finance Director

Niftylift Limited
Incorporated: 21 June 1976 *Employees:* 481
Net Worth: £42,972,000 *Total Assets:* £72,273,000
Registered Office: Niftylift Limited, Chalkdell Drive, Shenley Wood, Milton Keynes, Bucks, MK5 6GF
Activities: Manufacture of other special-purpose machinery n.e.c.
Major Shareholder: Frank Roger Bowden
Officers: Simon Mark Beadle, Secretary; Simon Mark Beadle [1963] Finance Director; Steven Douglas Beckwith [1968] Operations Director; Frank Roger Bowden [1947] Director and Engineer; John Phillip Keely [1960] Managing Director; Steven Alan Redding [1969] Development Director

Nike Land Securities Limited
Incorporated: 5 February 1976 *Employees:* 585
Net Worth: £11,924,294 *Total Assets:* £36,287,336
Registered Office: Jubilee House, John Nike Way, Bracknell, Berks, RG12 8TN
Activities: Activities of head offices
Officers: Carl Fredrik Larsson, Secretary; Steve James Hebborn [1968] Director/Consultant; Christopher John Nike [1968] Director; Suzanne Nike [1941] Director; Kathryn Tracy Vickers [1970] Director

Nikon UK Limited
Incorporated: 17 September 1979 *Employees:* 124
Net Worth: £19,801,028 *Total Assets:* £36,741,208
Registered Office: Nikon House, 380 Richmond Road, Kingston upon Thames, Surrey, KT2 5PR
Activities: Wholesale of household goods (other than musical instruments) n.e.c
Parent: Nikon Holdings Europe B.V.
Officers: Toru Iwaoka [1958] Director [Japanese]; Takaharu Sasaoka [1971] Director/President Nikon Instruments Europe BV [Japanese]; John Kevin Walshe [1965] Director

Nikon X-Tek Systems Limited
Incorporated: 23 January 1986 *Employees:* 111
Previous: X-Tek Systems Limited
Net Worth Deficit: £1,654,000 *Total Assets:* £32,208,000
Registered Office: Tring Business Centre, Icknield Way, Tring, Herts, HP23 4JX
Activities: Manufacture of electronic industrial process control equipment
Parent: Nikon Metrology UK Limited
Officers: Koenraad Van Der Elst, Secretary; Tadashi Nakayama [1961] Director/Business Manager [Japanese]; Satoru Nishiura [1965] Director [Japanese]; Jeffry Ward Walker [1956] Director [American]

Nilvip Holdings Limited
Incorporated: 23 February 2000 *Employees:* 73
Net Worth: £12,076,647 *Total Assets:* £23,335,044
Registered Office: 10-12 King Street, Reading, Berks, RG1 2HE
Activities: Activities of head offices
Shareholder: Nilesh Nautamlal Patel
Officers: Nilesh Nautamlal Patel, Secretary; Bhupesh Bhagwandas Patel [1964] Director [Indian]; Nilesh Nautamlal Patel [1965] Managing Director; Surendra Vrajlal Patel [1952] Director [Indian]; Vipul Nautamlal Patel [1969] Director

Nippon Express (U.K.) Limited
Incorporated: 11 December 1980 *Employees:* 288
Net Worth: £8,518,215 *Total Assets:* £30,495,964
Registered Office: Heathrow 360, 2 Millington Road, Hayes, Middlesex, UB3 4AZ
Activities: Other transportation support activities
Officers: Toshinori Sakai [1961] Director [Japanese]

NIS Acquisitions Limited
Incorporated: 3 December 2007
Net Worth: £329,867,008 *Total Assets:* £687,932,032
Registered Office: Peoplebuilding 2, Peoplebuilding Estate, Maylands Avenue, Hemel Hempstead Industrial Estate, Hemel Hempstead, Herts, HP2 4NW
Activities: Activities of head offices
Parent: Northgate Information Solutions Limited
Officers: Malcolm Robert Bennett, Secretary; Steven James Chalker [1974] Chief Financial Director; Andrew Phillip Monshaw [1962] Director [American]

NIS Receivables No. 2 Limited
Incorporated: 3 December 2007
Net Worth: £49,100,000 *Total Assets:* £49,100,000
Registered Office: Peoplebuilding 2, Peoplebuilding Estate, Maylands Avenue, Hemel Hempstead Industrial Estate, Hemel Hempstead, Herts, HP2 4NW
Activities: Other business support service activities n.e.c.
Parent: Northgate Information Solutions Holdings Limited
Officers: Malcolm Robert Bennett, Secretary; Steven James Chalker [1974] Chief Financial Director; Andrew Phillip Monshaw [1962] Director [American]

NIS Receivables No.1 Limited
Incorporated: 26 March 2008
Net Worth: £75,000,000 *Total Assets:* £75,000,000
Registered Office: Peoplebuilding 2, Peoplebuilding Estate, Maylands Avenue, Hemel Hempstead Industrial Estate, Hemel Hempstead, Herts, HP2 4NW
Activities: Activities of head offices
Parent: Northgate Information Solutions Holdings Limited
Officers: Malcolm Robert Bennett, Secretary; Steven James Chalker [1974] Chief Financial Director; Andrew Phillip Monshaw [1962] Director [American]

Nissan Motor (GB) Limited
Incorporated: 21 June 1990 *Employees:* 196
Net Worth: £183,110,000 *Total Assets:* £767,649,024
Registered Office: The Rivers Office Park, Denham Way, Maple Cross, Rickmansworth, Herts, WD3 9YS
Activities: Sale of new cars and light motor vehicles
Parent: Nissan Holdings (UK) Limited
Officers: Steven Neil Tiffin, Secretary; Laurent Franck Christian David [1971] Director/Senior Vice President - Administration and Finance [French]; Gareth John Main [1967] Director/General Manager; Kenneth Alexander Ramirez [1968] Director [American]; Alan David Tennant [1954] Director

NMRN Operations
Incorporated: 4 February 2016 *Employees:* 374
Net Worth: £18,140,288 *Total Assets:* £22,942,300
Registered Office: National Museum of The Royal Navy, HM Naval Base, Portsmouth, PO1 3NH
Activities: Operation of historical sites and buildings and similar visitor attractions
Parent: National Museum of The Royal Navy
Officers: Michael James Bedingfield [1961] Director/Retired; Jane Elizabeth Bonnar Dean [1955] Director; Richard Paul Hatfield [1953] Director/Retired; Carol Louise Marlow [1961] Director; Professor Dominic Tweddle [1954] Director General NMRN

No.7 Limited
Incorporated: 10 May 2001
Net Worth: £14,365,641 *Total Assets:* £49,497,208
Registered Office: 38-42 Brunswick Street West, Hove, E Sussex, BN3 1EL
Activities: Management of real estate on a fee or contract basis
Parent: BIMM Limited
Officers: Adam Peter Carswell, Secretary; Adam Peter Carswell [1968] Director/Chartered Accountant; Vaseema Hamilton [1960] Director/College Principal; David Jones-Owen [1980] Director

Noble Energy (Oilex) Limited
Incorporated: 20 March 1964 *Employees:* 3
Net Worth Deficit: £4,176,407 *Total Assets:* £25,766,688
Registered Office: Oceana House, 39-49 Commercial Road, Southampton, SO15 1GA
Activities: Extraction of crude petroleum
Parent: Noble Energy Capital Limited
Officers: Dustin Anthony Hatley [1966] Director/Executive [American]; Amy Elizabeth Jolley [1968] Director/Tax Attorney [American]

Nomad Foods BondCo PLC
Incorporated: 19 June 2014
Previous: Iglo Foods BondCo PLC
Net Worth: £2,765,430 *Total Assets:* £621,933,056
Registered Office: 1 New Square, Bedfont Lakes Business Park, Feltham, Middlesex, TW14 8HA
Activities: Other business support service activities n.e.c.
Parent: Nomad Foods Europe Midco Limited
Officers: Johanna Maria Van Kruijsbergen, Secretary; Stefan Descheemaeker [1960] Director [Belgian]; Johanna Maria Van Kruijsbergen [1961] Director/General Counsel [Dutch]; Samy Rene Zekhout [1962] Director/Chief Financial Officer [French]

Nomad Foods Europe Finco Limited
Incorporated: 18 July 2006
Previous: Iglo Foods Finco Limited
Net Worth: £15,984,400 *Total Assets:* £1,585,529,856
Registered Office: 1 New Square, Bedfont Lakes Business Park, Feltham, Middlesex, TW14 8HA
Activities: Non-trading company
Parent: Nomad Foods Europe Holdco Limited
Officers: Johanna Maria Van Kruijsbergen, Secretary; Stefan Descheemaeker [1960] Director [Belgian]; Johanna Maria Van Kruijsbergen [1961] Director/General Counsel [Dutch]; Samy Rene Zekhout [1962] Director/Chief Financial Officer [French]

Nomad Foods Europe Holdco Limited
Incorporated: 18 July 2006
Previous: Iglo Foods Holdco Limited
Net Worth: £126,698,944 *Total Assets:* £1,348,299,264
Registered Office: 1 New Square, Bedfont Lakes Business Park, Feltham, Middlesex, TW14 8HA
Activities: Non-trading company
Parent: Nomad Foods Europe Holdings Limited
Officers: Johanna Maria Van Kruijsbergen, Secretary; Stefan Descheemaeker [1960] Director [Belgian]; Johanna Maria Van Kruijsbergen [1961] Director/General Counsel [Dutch]; Samy Rene Zekhout [1962] Director/Chief Financial Officer [French]

Nomad Foods Europe Holdings Limited
Incorporated: 18 July 2006
Previous: Iglo Foods Holdings Limited
Net Worth: £394,835,936 *Total Assets:* £394,835,936
Registered Office: 1 New Square, Bedfont Lakes Business Park, Feltham, Middlesex, TW14 8HA
Activities: Other business support service activities n.e.c.
Shareholders: Nomad Foods Limited; Nomad Foods Limited
Officers: Johanna Maria Van Kruijsbergen, Secretary; Stefan Descheemaeker [1960] Director [Belgian]; Johanna Maria Van Kruijsbergen [1961] Director/General Counsel [Dutch]; Samy Rene Zekhout [1962] Director/Chief Financial Officer [French]

Nomad Foods Europe Limited
Incorporated: 18 July 2006 *Employees:* 196
Previous: Iglo Foods Group Limited
Net Worth: £504,436,960 *Total Assets:* £2,627,912,960
Registered Office: 1 New Square, Bedfont Lakes Business Park, Feltham, Middlesex, TW14 8HA
Activities: Manufacture of other food products n.e.c.
Parent: Nomad Foods Europe Midco Limited
Officers: Johanna Maria Van Kruijsbergen, Secretary; Stefan Descheemaeker [1960] Director [Belgian]; Jason Musk [1971] Director; Sarah Pollard [1974] Finance Director; Johanna Maria Van Kruijsbergen [1961] Director/General Counsel [Dutch]; Samy Rene Zekhout [1962] Director/Chief Financial Officer [French]

Nomad Foods Europe Midco Limited
Incorporated: 18 July 2006
Previous: Iglo Foods Midco Limited
Net Worth: £742,139,136 *Total Assets:* £2,808,313,600
Registered Office: 1 New Square, Bedfont Lakes Business Park, Feltham, Middlesex, TW14 8HA
Activities: Non-trading company
Parent: Nomad Foods Europe Finco Limited
Officers: Johanna Maria Van Kruijsbergen, Secretary; Stefan Descheemaeker [1960] Director [Belgian]; Jason Musk [1971] Director; Johanna Maria Van Kruijsbergen [1961] Director/General Counsel [Dutch]; Samy Rene Zekhout [1962] Director/Chief Financial Officer [French]

Noon Products Limited
Incorporated: 17 September 1987 *Employees:* 1,927
Net Worth: £58,443,284 *Total Assets:* £224,222,848
Registered Office: Thorpe Lea Manor, Thorpe Lea Road, Egham, Surrey, TW20 8HY
Activities: Other processing and preserving of fruit and vegetables
Parent: Noon Group Limited
Officers: Ronan Deasy, Secretary; Ronan Deasy [1964] Director/Accountant [Irish]; Trevor James Horan [1972] EMEA Country Compliance Director [Irish]; Marguerite Larkin [1971] Director/Chief Financial Officer [Irish]

Norbain Holdings Limited
Incorporated: 16 May 2007 *Employees:* 234
Previous: Norbain SD Limited
Net Worth: £25,344,000 *Total Assets:* £58,005,000
Registered Office: Votec House, Hambridge Lane, Newbury, Berks, RG14 5TN
Activities: Non-specialised wholesale trade
Parent: Newbury Investments (UK) Ltd
Officers: Leo Yu, Secretary; Nigel John Palmer [1956] Director/Chairman; Steven Westbrook [1956] Director/Chief Executive; Leo Yu [1984] Director

Norebo Europe Limited
Incorporated: 22 November 2007 *Employees:* 18
Previous: Ocean Trawlers Europe Limited
Net Worth: £43,610,392 *Total Assets:* £99,121,456
Registered Office: 80 Moorbridge Road, Maidenhead, Berks, SL6 8BW
Activities: Marine fishing
Major Shareholder: Vitaly Orlov
Officers: Sturlaugur Haraldsson [1973] Managing Director [Icelander]; Laurie Macmillan [1968] Finance Director

Norma UK Limited
Incorporated: 19 May 1981 *Employees:* 284
Net Worth: £30,924,708 *Total Assets:* £41,667,864
Registered Office: Weber Road, Greenham Business Park, Greenham, Thatcham, Newbury, Berks, RG19 6HW
Activities: Other business support service activities n.e.c.
Parent: DNL UK Ltd
Officers: Thomas Kraus [1967] Director [German]; Richard David Smith [1968] Director

Northamber PLC
Incorporated: 3 June 1980 *Employees:* 85
Net Worth: £17,520,000 *Total Assets:* £24,484,000
Registered Office: Namber House, 23 Davis Road, Chessington, Surrey, KT9 1HS
Activities: Wholesale of computers, computer peripheral equipment and software
Major Shareholder: David Michael Phillips
Officers: Sivapragasam Yoganathan, Secretary; John Phelim Henry [1962] Director; David Michael Phillips [1945] Director/Company Chairman; Geoffrey Paul Walters [1952] Director

Northgate Information Solutions Holdings Limited
Incorporated: 5 November 1992 *Employees:* 139
Net Worth Deficit: £141,783,008 *Total Assets:* £965,958,016
Registered Office: Peoplebuilding 2, Peoplebuilding Estate, Maylands Avenue, Hemel Hempstead Industrial Estate, Hemel Hempstead, Herts, HP2 4NW
Activities: Activities of head offices
Parent: NIS Acquisitions Limited
Officers: Malcolm Robert Bennett, Secretary; Steven James Chalker [1974] Chief Financial Director; Andrew Phillip Monshaw [1962] Director [American]

Northgate Information Solutions Limited
Incorporated: 3 December 2007 *Employees:* 6,693
Net Worth: £164,100,000 *Total Assets:* £295,300,000
Registered Office: Peoplebuilding 2, Peoplebuilding Estate, Maylands Avenue, Hemel Hempstead Industrial Estate, Hemel Hempstead, Herts, HP2 4NW
Activities: Other business support service activities n.e.c.
Parent: Northgate UK Holdings 4 Limited
Officers: Malcolm Robert Bennett, Secretary; Steven James Chalker [1974] Chief Financial Director; Andrew Phillip Monshaw [1962] Director [American]

Northgate Public Services (UK) Limited
Incorporated: 17 December 1969 *Employees:* 1,228
Previous: Northgate Information Solutions UK Limited
Net Worth: £163,456,000 *Total Assets:* £431,332,000
Registered Office: Peoplebuilding 2, Peoplebuilding Estate, Maylands Avenue, Hemel Hempstead Industrial Estate, Hemel Hempstead, Herts, HP2 4NW
Activities: Manufacture of computers and peripheral equipment
Parent: NPS (Holdings) Limited
Officers: Stephen James Callaghan [1960] Director; Tomonori Hira [1968] Director [Japanese]; Alan George O'Reilly [1961] Director [Irish]

Northgate Public Services Limited
Incorporated: 3 December 2014 *Employees:* 2
Net Worth Deficit: £38,500,000 *Total Assets:* £126,600,000
Registered Office: Peoplebuilding 2, Peoplebuilding Estate, Maylands Avenue, Hemel Hempstead Industrial Estate, Hemel Hempstead, Herts, HP2 4NW
Activities: Other information technology service activities
Officers: Stephen James Callaghan [1960] Director; Alan George O'Reilly [1961] Director [Irish]

Northgate UK Holdings 1 Limited
Incorporated: 3 February 2016
Net Worth Deficit: £40,000,000 *Total Assets:* £232,000,000
Registered Office: Peoplebuilding 2, Peoplebuilding Estate, Maylands Avenue, Hemel Hempstead Industrial Estate, Hemel Hempstead, Herts, HP2 4NW
Activities: Other business support service activities n.e.c.
Officers: Malcolm Robert Bennett, Secretary; Michael John Magee [1991] Director/Investment Professional [Irish]; Andrew Phillip Monshaw [1962] Director [American]; Emilie Railhac [1979] Director/Investment Professional [French]; James Reynolds [1975] Director/Investment Professional [French]; Michael Christopher Small [1973] Director/Partner

Northgate UK Holdings 2 Limited
Incorporated: 3 February 2016
Net Worth: £232,900,000 *Total Assets:* £232,900,000
Registered Office: Peoplebuilding 2, Peoplebuilding Estate, Maylands Avenue, Hemel Hempstead Industrial Estate, Hemel Hempstead, Herts, HP2 4NW
Activities: Other business support service activities n.e.c.
Parent: Northgate UK Holdings 1 Limited
Officers: Malcolm Robert Bennett, Secretary; Michael John Magee [1991] Director/Investment Professional [Irish]; Andrew Phillip Monshaw [1962] Director [American]; Emilie Railhac [1979] Director/Investment Professional [French]; James Reynolds [1975] Director/Investment Professional [French]; Michael Christopher Small [1973] Director/Partner

Northgate UK Holdings 3 Limited
Incorporated: 3 February 2016
Net Worth: £232,000,000 *Total Assets:* £232,000,000
Registered Office: Peoplebuilding 2, Peoplebuilding Estate, Maylands Avenue, Hemel Hempstead Industrial Estate, Hemel Hempstead, Herts, HP2 4NW
Activities: Other business support service activities n.e.c.
Parent: Northgate UK Holdings 2 Limited
Officers: Malcolm Robert Bennett, Secretary; Michael John Magee [1991] Director/Investment Professional [Irish]; Andrew Phillip Monshaw [1962] Director [American]; Emilie Railhac [1979] Director/Investment Professional [French]; James Reynolds [1975] Director/Investment Professional [French]; Michael Christopher Small [1973] Director/Partner

Northgate UK Holdings 4 Limited
Incorporated: 3 February 2016
Net Worth: £168,200,000 *Total Assets:* £790,800,000
Registered Office: Peoplebuilding 2, Peoplebuilding Estate, Maylands Avenue, Hemel Hempstead Industrial Estate, Hemel Hempstead, Herts, HP2 4NW
Activities: Other business support service activities n.e.c.
Parent: Northgate UK Holdings 3 Limited
Officers: Malcolm Robert Bennett, Secretary; Michael John Magee [1991] Director/Investment Professional [Irish]; Andrew Phillip Monshaw [1962] Director [American]; Emilie Railhac [1979] Director/Investment Professional [French]; James Reynolds [1975] Director/Investment Professional [French]; Michael Christopher Small [1973] Director/Partner

Northumberland Energy Recovery Holdings Ltd
Incorporated: 22 September 2006
Previous: SITA Northumberland Holdings Limited
Net Worth: £1,750,000 *Total Assets:* £110,215,000
Registered Office: Suez House, Grenfell Road, Maidenhead, Berks, SL6 1ES
Activities: Activities of head offices
Shareholders: PPDI Assetco 2 Limited; Equitix Concessions 3 Limited; Suez Recycling and Recovery UK Ltd
Officers: Florent Thierry Antoine Duval [1976] Director/Chief Finance Officer [French]; Gregor Scott Jackson [1974] Director/Fund Manager; Graham Arthur McKenna-Mayes [1968] Director/Public Sector Commercial Manager; Barry Paul Millsom [1974] Director; Adrian Neil Peacock [1975] Investment Director; Ian Anthony Sexton [1956] Director/Chairman; Nathan John Wakefield [1974] Director; Philip Arthur Would [1971] Director/Asset Management

Northumberland Energy Recovery Ltd
Incorporated: 13 September 2006
Previous: SITA Northumberland Limited
Net Worth: £1,750,000 *Total Assets:* £110,215,000
Registered Office: Suez House, Grenfell Road, Maidenhead, Berks, SL6 1ES
Activities: Collection of non-hazardous waste
Parent: Northumberland Energy Recovery Holdings Ltd
Officers: Florent Thierry Antoine Duval [1976] Director/Chief Finance Officer [French]; Gregor Scott Jackson [1974] Director/Fund Manager; Graham Arthur McKenna-Mayes [1968] Director/Public Sector Commercial Manager; Barry Paul Millsom [1974] Director; Adrian Neil Peacock [1975] Investment Director; Ian Anthony Sexton [1956] Director/Chairman; Nathan John Wakefield [1974] Director; Philip Arthur Would [1971] Director/Asset Management

Northumberland Waste Management Limited
Incorporated: 7 June 1991 *Employees:* 11
Net Worth: £30,551,000 *Total Assets:* £35,024,000
Registered Office: Suez House, Grenfell Road, Maidenhead, Berks, SL6 1ES
Activities: Collection of non-hazardous waste
Parent: Suez Recycling and Recovery North East Ltd
Officers: Joan Knight, Secretary; Florent Thierry Antoine Duval [1976] Director/Chief Finance Officer [French]

The Northview Group Limited
Incorporated: 26 April 1995 *Employees:* 593
Previous: Kensington Group Limited
Net Worth: £58,019,000 *Total Assets:* £97,998,000
Registered Office: Ascot House, Maidenhead Office Park, Maidenhead, Berks, SL6 3QQ
Activities: Activities of financial services holding companies
Parent: Koala Bidco Limited
Officers: Syed Qasim Abbas [1976] Director [Pakistani]; Jayne Doreen Almond [1957] Director; Mark John Arnold [1968] Director/Chief Executive; Rajesh Gupta [1969] Director; Matthew John Howard-Cairns [1984] Director; Alexdander James Maddox [1970] Capital Markets Director; Amir Sharifi Mehr [1970] Director [American]; Diana Susan Miller [1950] Director; Anthony Michael Muscolino [1971] Director [American]; Mark Jeffrey Preston [1960] Director; Rohan Singhal [1987] Director

Novar (Stelrad) Limited
Incorporated: 1 March 1988
Net Worth: £226,738,000 *Total Assets:* £226,738,000
Registered Office: Honeywell House, Skimped Hill Lane, Bracknell, Berks, RG12 1EB
Activities: Other service activities n.e.c.
Parent: Rallip Aluminium Limited
Officers: Ashish Kumar Saraf [1979] Director [Indian]

Novar ED & S Limited
Incorporated: 17 April 1923 *Employees:* 320
Net Worth: £113,451,000 *Total Assets:* £246,922,000
Registered Office: Honeywell House, Skimped Hill Lane, Bracknell, Berks, RG12 1EB
Activities: Manufacture of electric domestic appliances
Parent: Novar Electrical Holdings Limited
Officers: Neil Eric Garland [1976] Director; Madeleine Orbell-Thompson [1976] Director/Chartered Accountant; Ian Snadden [1966] Director/Vice President; John J Tus [1958] Director [American]

Novar Electrical Holdings Limited
Incorporated: 16 December 1965
Net Worth: £90,075,000 *Total Assets:* £90,798,000
Registered Office: Honeywell House, Skimped Hill Lane, Bracknell, Berks, RG12 1EB
Activities: Activities of head offices
Parent: Novar Holdings Limited
Officers: Jonathan Michael Turner [1968] Director/Chartered Surveyor; John J Tus [1958] Director [American]

Novar Europe Limited
Incorporated: 14 November 1955 *Employees:* 2
Net Worth: £472,609,984 *Total Assets:* £750,708,992
Registered Office: Honeywell House, Skimped Hill Lane, Bracknell, Berks, RG12 1EB
Activities: Activities of other holding companies n.e.c.
Parent: Novar Limited
Officers: Jonathan Michael Turner [1968] Director/Chartered Surveyor; John J Tus [1958] Director [American]

Novar International Limited
Incorporated: 11 August 1994
Net Worth: £47,010,000 *Total Assets:* £47,010,000
Registered Office: Honeywell House, Skimped Hill Lane, Bracknell, Berks, RG12 1EB
Activities: Other service activities n.e.c.
Parent: Novar Europe Limited
Officers: Michele Elaine Hudson [1966] Director; Allan Richards [1962] Director

Novar Limited
Incorporated: 25 May 1988
Net Worth: £813,216,000 *Total Assets:* £1,890,841,984
Registered Office: Honeywell House, Skimped Hill Lane, Bracknell, Berks, RG12 1EB
Activities: Activities of head offices
Parent: Honeywell Acquisitions Limited
Officers: Jonathan Michael Turner [1968] Director/Chartered Surveyor; John J Tus [1958] Director [American]

Novar Systems Limited
Incorporated: 1 April 1932 *Employees:* 274
Net Worth: £117,534,000 *Total Assets:* £178,494,000
Registered Office: Honeywell House, Skimped Hill Lane, Bracknell, Berks, RG12 1EB
Activities: Other business support service activities n.e.c.
Parent: Novar Electrical Holdings Limited
Officers: David Juggins [1972] Director; Piyush Jayantilal Kanji Jutha [1972] Director; David Andrew Kay [1973] Director; John J Tus [1958] Director [American]

Novartis Grimsby Limited
Incorporated: 11 September 1920 *Employees:* 381
Net Worth: £281,785,984 *Total Assets:* £348,511,008
Registered Office: Frimley Business Park, Frimley, Camberley, Surrey, GU16 7SR
Activities: Manufacture of dyes and pigments
Parent: Novartis UK Limited
Officers: Rebecca Ann Weston, Secretary; Haseeb Ahmad [1976] Director/CPO Head UK & Ireland; Cynthia Helena Chiaramitara [1976] Managing Director [Brazilian]; Jeremiah Carmel Collins [1965] Director/Head of Chemical Operations and NIPBI [Irish]; Oriane Fanny Lacaze [1979] Director/Country Chief Financial Officer [French]

Novartis Pharmaceuticals UK Limited
Incorporated: 8 December 1911 *Employees:* 821
Net Worth: £72,936,000 *Total Assets:* £303,975,008
Registered Office: Frimley Business Park, Frimley, Camberley, Surrey, GU16 7SR
Activities: Manufacture of basic pharmaceutical products
Parent: Novartis UK Limited
Officers: Rebecca Ann Weston, Secretary; Haseeb Ahmad [1976] Director/CPO Head UK & Ireland; Oriane Fanny Lacaze [1979] Director/Country Chief Financial Officer [French]; Dr Anna Mari Scheiffele [1974] Director/General Manager, Oncology UK & Ireland [Finnish]; Marie-France Tschudin [1971] Director/Head Novartis Pharma Region Europe [Swiss]

Novartis UK Limited
Incorporated: 24 August 1945
Net Worth: £141,000,000 *Total Assets:* £347,400,000
Registered Office: Frimley Business Park, Frimley, Camberley, Surrey, GU16 7SR
Activities: Activities of head offices
Parent: Novartis AG
Officers: Rebecca Ann Weston, Secretary; Haseeb Ahmad [1976] Director/CPO Head UK & Ireland; Felix Hermann Eichhorn [1961] Director/Head International Treasury [Swiss]; Oriane Fanny Lacaze [1979] Director/Country Chief Financial Officer [French]

Novell UK Software Limited
Incorporated: 20 November 2014
Net Worth: £185,382,128 *Total Assets:* £185,444,000
Registered Office: The Lawn, 22-30 Old Bath Road, Newbury, Berks, RG14 1QN
Activities: Other information technology service activities
Parent: Micro Focus MHC Limited
Officers: Jane Caroline Grantham Smithard, Secretary; Darren Mark Curtis [1974] Director/Corporate Counsel; Graham Howard Norton [1959] Director/Accountant

Novo Nordisk Limited
Incorporated: 18 June 1973 *Employees:* 367
Net Worth: £23,704,000 *Total Assets:* £106,459,000
Registered Office: 3 City Place, Beehive Ring Road, Gatwick, W Sussex, RH6 0PA
Activities: Wholesale of pharmaceutical goods
Parent: Novo Nordisk Holding Limited
Officers: Matthew O'Flynn, Secretary; Nicholas James Bailey [1973] Finance Director; Tomas Haagen [1966] Director [Danish]; Matt Joseph Regan [1971] Director/General Manager [Irish]; Pinder Sahota [1961] Director/General Manager and CVP UK

NPL Management Limited
Incorporated: 10 June 1994 *Employees:* 769
Net Worth: £84,963,000 *Total Assets:* £128,708,000
Registered Office: National Physical Laboratory, Hampton Road, Teddington, Middlesex, TW11 0LW
Activities: Other service activities n.e.c.
Parent: Secretary of State for Business, Energy and Industrial Strategy
Officers: Andrew John Armstrong, Secretary; Dr David Grant [1947] Director; Penelope Jane Holt [1972] Director/Chief Financial Officer; Dr Paul John Arton Howarth [1970] Managing Director; Dr Stephanie Hurst [1961] Director/Senior Civil Servant; Professor Gaoqing Max Lu [1963] Director/Vice-Chancellor [Australian]; Professor Sir James Rufus McDonald [1957] Director/University Principal; Nigel John Perry [1957] Director/Chief Executive; Martyn Russell Sene [1957] Director; Brigid Ann Sutcliffe [1959] Director; Doctor Peter Anthony Thompson [1967] Director/Chief Executive Officer

NPS (Holdings) Limited
Incorporated: 5 November 2014
Net Worth: £315,700,000 *Total Assets:* £346,600,000
Registered Office: Peoplebuilding 2, Peoplebuilding Estate, Maylands Avenue, Hemel Hempstead Industrial Estate, Hemel Hempstead, Herts, HP2 4NW
Activities: Other information technology service activities
Parent: Argon NPS Limited
Officers: Stephen James Callaghan [1960] Director; Alan George O'Reilly [1961] Director [Irish]

NPS (UK2) Limited
Incorporated: 7 March 2008
Previous: Northgate Public Sector Holdings Limited
Net Worth: £61,786,000 *Total Assets:* £61,786,000
Registered Office: Peoplebuilding 2, Peoplebuilding Estate, Maylands Avenue, Hemel Hempstead Industrial Estate, Hemel Hempstead, Herts, HP2 4NW
Activities: Information technology consultancy activities
Parent: Northgate Public Services (UK) Limited
Officers: Stephen James Callaghan [1960] Director

NPS (UK4) Limited
Incorporated: 22 July 1987
Previous: Northgate Land and Property Solutions Limited
Net Worth: £36,500,000 *Total Assets:* £36,500,000
Registered Office: Peoplebuilding 2, Peoplebuilding Estate, Maylands Avenue, Hemel Hempstead Industrial Estate, Hemel Hempstead, Herts, HP2 4NW
Activities: Information technology consultancy activities
Parent: MVM Holdings Limited
Officers: Stephen James Callaghan [1960] Director

NPS (UK5) Limited
Incorporated: 14 January 1998
Previous: Northgate Public Sector Limited
Net Worth: £49,887,000 *Total Assets:* £49,887,000
Registered Office: Peoplebuilding 2, Peoplebuilding Estate, Maylands Avenue, Hemel Hempstead Industrial Estate, Hemel Hempstead, Herts, HP2 4NW
Activities: Other information technology service activities
Parent: NPS (UK2) Limited
Officers: Stephen James Callaghan [1960] Director

NSK Bearings Europe Limited
Incorporated: 4 April 1974 *Employees:* 833
Net Worth: £11,772,096 *Total Assets:* £160,969,344
Registered Office: Belmont Place, Belmont Road, Maidenhead, Berks, SL6 6TB
Activities: Manufacture of bearings, gears, gearing and driving elements
Parent: NSK Europe Ltd
Officers: Timothy Parker, Secretary; Timothy Constantine [1958] Director; Yasuhiro Kamio [1959] Director [Japanese]; Issei Murata [1959] Director [Japanese]; Shigeyuki Suzuki [1959] Director [Japanese]

NSK Europe Limited
Incorporated: 22 February 1988 *Employees:* 4,055
Net Worth: £292,254,048 *Total Assets:* £612,325,184
Registered Office: Belmont Place, Belmont Road, Maidenhead, Berks, SL6 6TB
Activities: Activities of head offices
Parent: NSK Ltd
Officers: Timothy Parker, Secretary; Adrian Browne [1961] Director; Timothy Constantine [1958] Director/Chief Financial Officer; Masatada Fumoto [1961] Director [Japanese]; Issei Murata [1959] Director [Japanese]; Toshihiro Uchiyama [1958] Director [Japanese]

NSK UK Limited
Incorporated: 29 January 1988 *Employees:* 28
Net Worth: £37,611,368 *Total Assets:* £86,559,160
Registered Office: Belmont Place, Belmont Road, Maidenhead, Berks, SL6 6TB
Activities: Non-specialised wholesale trade
Parent: NSK Europe Ltd
Officers: Timothy Parker, Secretary; Timothy Constantine [1958] Director; Issei Murata [1959] Director [Japanese]

NSL (Holdings) Limited
Incorporated: 17 March 2014 *Employees:* 108
Net Worth: £17,830,518 *Total Assets:* £23,043,112
Registered Office: Unit 4-5 Northolt Trading Estate, Belvue Road, Northolt, Middlesex, UB5 5QS
Activities: Wholesale of pharmaceutical goods
Shareholder: Ketan Himatlal Mehta
Officers: Ketan Mehta, Secretary; Bharat Himatlal Mehta [1952] Director; Ketan Himatlal Mehta [1958] Director

NSSLGlobal Limited
Incorporated: 18 November 1999 *Employees:* 174
Net Worth: £21,948,000 *Total Assets:* £43,698,000
Registered Office: 6 Wells Place, Gatton Park Business Centre, Redhill, Surrey, RH1 3DR
Activities: Satellite telecommunications activities
Parent: Arendals Fossekompani ASA
Officers: Sara Jayne Gordon, Secretary; Torkil Sigurd Mogstad [1958] Director [Norwegian]; Arild Nysaether [1971] Director/Financial Analyst [Norwegian]; Sally Anne Ray [1969] Managing Director

NTL (B) Limited
Incorporated: 30 July 1992
Net Worth: £2,084,632,960 *Total Assets:* £2,226,475,008
Registered Office: Media House, Bartley Wood Business Park, Hook, Hants, RG27 9UP
Activities: Other business support service activities n.e.c.
Parent: NTL (CWC) Limited
Officers: Gillian Elizabeth James, Secretary; Robert Dominic Dunn [1966] Director/Chief Financial Officer; Mine Ozkan Hifzi [1966] Director/Solicitor

NTL (CWC) Limited
Incorporated: 3 December 1996
Net Worth Deficit: £748,945,024 *Total Assets:* £1,388,226,048
Registered Office: Media House, Bartley Wood Business Park, Hook, Hants, RG27 9UP
Activities: Other business support service activities n.e.c.
Parent: NTL Rectangle Limited
Officers: Gillian Elizabeth James, Secretary; Robert Dominic Dunn [1966] Director/Chief Financial Officer; Mine Ozkan Hifzi [1966] Director/Solicitor

NTL Cablecomms Cheshire
Incorporated: 4 May 1989
Net Worth: £143,106,000 *Total Assets:* £155,074,000
Registered Office: Media House, Bartley Wood Business Park, Hook, Hants, RG27 9UP
Activities: Other telecommunications activities
Parent: NTL Cablecomms Holdings No 1 Limited
Officers: Gillian Elizabeth James, Secretary; Robert Dominic Dunn [1966] Director/Chief Financial Officer; Mine Ozkan Hifzi [1966] Director/Solicitor

NTL Cablecomms East Lancashire
Incorporated: 24 March 1987
Net Worth: £56,675,000 *Total Assets:* £80,380,000
Registered Office: Media House, Bartley Wood Business Park, Hook, Hants, RG27 9UP
Activities: Other telecommunications activities
Parent: NTL Cablecomms Holdings No 1 Limited
Officers: Gillian Elizabeth James, Secretary; Robert Dominic Dunn [1966] Director/Chief Financial Officer; Mine Ozkan Hifzi [1966] Director/Solicitor

NTL Cablecomms Greater Manchester
Incorporated: 25 July 1989
Net Worth Deficit: £175,354,000 *Total Assets:* £60,159,000
Registered Office: Media House, Bartley Wood Business Park, Hook, Hants, RG27 9UP
Activities: Other telecommunications activities
Parent: NTL Manchester Cablevision Holding Company
Officers: Gillian Elizabeth James, Secretary; Robert Dominic Dunn [1966] Director/Chief Financial Officer; Mine Ozkan Hifzi [1966] Director/Solicitor

NTL Cablecomms Group Limited
Incorporated: 16 February 1995
Net Worth: £389,001,984 *Total Assets:* £389,001,984
Registered Office: Media House, Bartley Wood Business Park, Hook, Hants, RG27 9UP
Activities: Activities of head offices
Parent: NTL (CWC) Limited
Officers: Gillian Elizabeth James, Secretary; Robert Dominic Dunn [1966] Director/Chief Financial Officer; Mine Ozkan Hifzi [1966] Director/Solicitor

NTL Cablecomms Holdings No.1 Limited
Incorporated: 9 February 1999
Net Worth: £613,403,008 *Total Assets:* £1,166,099,968
Registered Office: Media House, Bartley Wood Business Park, Hook, Hants, RG27 9UP
Activities: Activities of other holding companies n.e.c.
Parent: Virgin Media Limited
Officers: Gillian Elizabeth James, Secretary; Robert Dominic Dunn [1966] Director/Chief Financial Officer; Mine Ozkan Hifzi [1966] Director/Solicitor

NTL Cablecomms Surrey
Incorporated: 16 August 1990
Net Worth Deficit: £152,507,008 *Total Assets:* £67,074,000
Registered Office: Media House, Bartley Wood Business Park, Hook, Hants, RG27 9UP
Activities: Other telecommunications activities
Parent: NTL Cablecomms Holdings No 2 Limited
Officers: Gillian Elizabeth James, Secretary; Robert Dominic Dunn [1966] Director/Chief Financial Officer; Mine Ozkan Hifzi [1966] Director/Solicitor

NTL Cambridge Limited
Incorporated: 14 August 1987
Net Worth: £336,004,000 *Total Assets:* £627,492,992
Registered Office: Media House, Bartley Wood Business Park, Hook, Hants, RG27 9UP
Activities: Other telecommunications activities
Parent: Virgin Media Limited
Officers: Gillian Elizabeth James, Secretary; Robert Dominic Dunn [1966] Director/Chief Financial Officer; Mine Ozkan Hifzi [1966] Director/Solicitor

NTL Communications Services Limited
Incorporated: 16 July 1997
Net Worth: £437,088,992 *Total Assets:* £437,619,008
Registered Office: Media House, Bartley Wood Business Park, Hook, Hants, RG27 9UP
Activities: Other business support service activities n.e.c.
Parent: Virgin Media Investment Holdings Limited
Officers: Gillian Elizabeth James, Secretary; Robert Dominic Dunn [1966] Director/Chief Financial Officer; Mine Ozkan Hifzi [1966] Director/Solicitor

NTL Glasgow Holdings Limited
Incorporated: 28 February 2001
Net Worth: £350,199,008 *Total Assets:* £350,199,008
Registered Office: Media House, Bartley Wood Business Park, Hook, Hants, RG27 9UP
Activities: Dormant company
Shareholders: Virgin Media Operations Limited; Virgin Media Communications Limited
Officers: Gillian Elizabeth James, Secretary; Robert Dominic Dunn [1966] Director/Chief Financial Officer; Mine Ozkan Hifzi [1966] Director/Solicitor

NTL Kirklees
Incorporated: 24 April 1990
Net Worth: £33,882,000 *Total Assets:* £34,230,000
Registered Office: Media House, Bartley Wood Business Park, Hook, Hants, RG27 9UP
Activities: Other telecommunications activities
Parent: NTL Kirklees Holdings Limited
Officers: Gillian Elizabeth James, Secretary; Robert Dominic Dunn [1966] Director/Chief Financial Officer; Mine Ozkan Hifzi [1966] Director/Solicitor

NTL Kirklees Holdings Limited
Incorporated: 28 February 2001
Net Worth: £107,295,000 *Total Assets:* £107,295,000
Registered Office: Media House, Bartley Wood Business Park, Hook, Hants, RG27 9UP
Activities: Dormant company
Shareholders: Virgin Media Operations Limited; Virgin Media Communications Limited
Officers: Gillian Elizabeth James, Secretary; Robert Dominic Dunn [1966] Director/Chief Financial Officer; Mine Ozkan Hifzi [1966] Director/Solicitor

NTL Manchester Cablevision Holding Company
Incorporated: 27 December 1989
Net Worth: £165,360,000 *Total Assets:* £185,863,008
Registered Office: Media House, Bartley Wood Business Park, Hook, Hants, RG27 9UP
Activities: Activities of other holding companies n.e.c.
Parent: NTL Cablecomms Holdings No 1 Limited
Officers: Gillian Elizabeth James, Secretary; Robert Dominic Dunn [1966] Director/Chief Financial Officer; Mine Ozkan Hifzi [1966] Director/Solicitor

NTL Midlands Limited
Incorporated: 9 March 1989
Net Worth: £284,795,008 *Total Assets:* £360,168,992
Registered Office: Media House, Bartley Wood Business Park, Hook, Hants, RG27 9UP
Activities: Other telecommunications activities
Parent: Diamond Cable Communications Limited
Officers: Gillian Elizabeth James, Secretary; Robert Dominic Dunn [1966] Director/Chief Financial Officer; Mine Ozkan Hifzi [1966] Director/Solicitor

NTL Rectangle Limited
Incorporated: 27 November 2001
Net Worth: £1,524,016,000 *Total Assets:* £2,827,026,944
Registered Office: Media House, Bartley Wood Business Park, Hook, Hants, RG27 9UP
Activities: Other business support service activities n.e.c.
Parent: Virgin Media Senior Investments Limited
Officers: Gillian Elizabeth James, Secretary; Robert Dominic Dunn [1966] Director/Chief Financial Officer; Mine Ozkan Hifzi [1966] Director/Solicitor

NTL Victoria Limited
Incorporated: 23 January 2006
Net Worth Deficit: £61,566,000 *Total Assets:* £180,482,000
Registered Office: Media House, Bartley Wood Business Park, Hook, Hants, RG27 9UP
Activities: Other business support service activities n.e.c.
Parent: Virgin Media Senior Investments Limited
Officers: Gillian Elizabeth James, Secretary; Robert Dominic Dunn [1966] Director/Chief Financial Officer; Mine Ozkan Hifzi [1966] Director/Solicitor

NTL Wirral Telephone and Cable TV Company
Incorporated: 14 June 1990
Net Worth Deficit: £54,529,000 *Total Assets:* £40,243,000
Registered Office: Media House, Bartley Wood Business Park, Hook, Hants, RG27 9UP
Activities: Other telecommunications activities
Parent: NTL Cablecomms East Lancashire
Officers: Gillian Elizabeth James, Secretary; Robert Dominic Dunn [1966] Director/Chief Financial Officer; Mine Ozkan Hifzi [1966] Director/Solicitor

NTT Security (UK) Limited
Incorporated: 14 July 1997 *Employees:* 270
Previous: NTT Com Security (UK) Limited
Net Worth Deficit: £7,698,541 *Total Assets:* £25,090,184
Registered Office: Theale House, Brunel Road, Theale, Berks, RG7 4AQ
Activities: Other information technology service activities
Parent: Nocitra Limited
Officers: Frank Brandenburg [1962] Managing Director [German]; Clive Lewis [1956] Director

The Nuance Group (UK) Limited
Incorporated: 29 August 1973 *Employees:* 259
Net Worth: £10,762,000 *Total Assets:* £22,405,000
Registered Office: 4 New Square, Bedfont Lakes, Feltham, Middlesex, TW14 8HA
Activities: Other retail sale in non-specialised stores
Officers: Paul Henry Donaldson, Secretary/Financial Controller; Christopher David Bouttle [1968] Director; Frederick Robert Creighton [1958] Director; Benjamin Harmstorf [1976] Director/Chief Financial Officer [German]

Nucleus Financial Group PLC
Incorporated: 29 July 2005 *Employees:* 180
Net Worth: £16,182,000 *Total Assets:* £28,785,000
Registered Office: Elder House, St Georges Business Park, 207 Brooklands Road, Weybridge, Surrey, KT13 0TS
Activities: Financial intermediation not elsewhere classified
Officers: Nicola Megaw, Secretary; Tracy Dunley-Owen [1972] Director; David Ritchie Ferguson [1969] Director; Stuart James Geard [1974] Director/Chartered Accountant [South African]; Jeremy Paul Gibson [1973] Director/Chartered Accountant; Margaret Grace Hassall [1961] Director; John Anthony Levin [1963] Director; Jonathan Charles Polin [1959] Director/Chief Executive Officer, Sanlam UK; James Anthony Angus Samuels [1950] Director

Nuffield Health
Incorporated: 14 January 1957 *Employees:* 16,198
Net Worth: £64,100,000 *Total Assets:* £737,299,968
Registered Office: Epsom Gateway, Ashley Avenue, Epsom, Surrey, KT18 5AL
Activities: Other human health activities
Officers: Toby Newman, Secretary; Martin Warwick Bryant [1952] Director; Fiona Elizabeth Driscoll [1958] Director; Patrick Adam Fernesley Figgis [1957] Director; Russell Stephen Mons Hardy [1960] Director; David William Lister [1958] Director/Chief Information Officer; Dr Natalie-Jane Anne MacDonald [1962] Director/Chief Executive; Stephen Maslin [1957] Director/Chartered Accountant; Philip Guy McCracken [1948] Director; Nilesh Sachdev [1958] Director

Nuffield Health Pension Trustees Limited
Incorporated: 12 February 2016
Net Worth: £5,087,696 *Total Assets:* £76,287,696
Registered Office: Epsom Gateway, Ashley Avenue, Epsom, Surrey, KT18 5AL
Activities: Other business support service activities n.e.c.
Parent: Nuffield Health
Officers: Toby Newman, Secretary; Alan Davies [1950] Director/Retired Pharmacist; Michael Haffenden [1960] Director/Hospital Doctor; John Edward Jones [1947] Director/Retired; David McNair [1963] Director/Hospital Doctor; Colin Roderick Miller [1955] Director/Accountant; Jose Perez [1949] Director/Retired [Spanish]

Numatic International Limited
Incorporated: 9 September 1963 *Employees:* 1,008
Net Worth: £85,300,000 *Total Assets:* £114,768,000
Registered Office: Knoll House, Knoll Road, Camberley, Surrey, GU15 3SY
Activities: Manufacture of electric domestic appliances
Major Shareholder: Christopher Robert Duncan
Officers: Stephen Brian Whitlock, Secretary/Accountant; Ann Rosemary Duncan [1938] Director; Christopher Robert Duncan [1939] Managing Director; Simon Joseph Scott Lawson [1967] Managing Director; Stephen Brian Whitlock [1963] Financial Director

Nuneham Estate Limited
Incorporated: 20 December 2016 *Employees:* 2
Net Worth Deficit: £91,311 *Total Assets:* £26,720,908
Registered Office: Elvendon Priory, Reading Road, Goring, Reading, Berks, RG8 0LJ
Activities: Other letting and operating of own or leased real estate
Officers: Lucinda Grace Shaw, Secretary; Lucinda Grace Shaw [1980] Director/Chartered Surveyor

Nurse Plus and Carer Plus (UK) Limited
Incorporated: 19 July 2005 *Employees:* 226
Net Worth: £28,891,172 *Total Assets:* £32,708,020
Registered Office: Unit 2 Eurogate Business Park, Ashford, Kent, TN24 8XW
Activities: Temporary employment agency activities
Parent: Friars 662 Ltd
Officers: Pamela Anne Bruce [1967] Operations Director; Joshua Arthur Stanley Collins [1972] Director; Janice Anne Drain [1956] Director

Nutfield Holdings Limited
Incorporated: 17 February 2005 *Employees:* 33
Net Worth: £12,536,000 *Total Assets:* £36,018,000
Registered Office: Red Central, 60 High Street, Redhill, Surrey, RH1 1SH
Activities: Wholesale of other food, including fish, crustaceans and molluscs
Major Shareholder: John Patrick Sexton
Officers: Michael Robert Charles Shepherd, Secretary/Director; John Patrick Sexton [1959] Director; Michael Robert Charles Shepherd [1966] Director

Nutrix Capital Limited
Incorporated: 26 May 2016 *Employees:* 307
Net Worth Deficit: £3,286,464 *Total Assets:* £29,850,992
Registered Office: North Cottage, Langton Road, Langton Green, Tunbridge Wells, Kent, TN3 0BB
Activities: Activities of head offices
Parent: Vespa Capital II LLP
Officers: Julie-Anne Afrin, Secretary; Ruth Emma Busby [1967] Director; David Forbes [1983] Director; Graham Alan Hawthorn [1970] Director; Matthew William Lyons [1971] Director/Fund Manager; Christopher Richard Phillips [1960] Managing Director; Judith Inez Phillips [1962] Recruitment Director

Nuvias Group Limited
Incorporated: 11 September 2015 *Employees:* 497
Net Worth: £33,203,000 *Total Assets:* £191,974,000
Registered Office: Unit 1 Genesis Business Park, Albert Drive, Woking, Surrey, GU21 5RW
Activities: Other business support service activities n.e.c.
Parent: Ingleby (1981) Limited
Officers: Paul Andrew Eccleston [1961] Director; Julian Hodge [1970] Director/Chief Financial Officer; Steven Paul Rigby [1972] Director

nVent International (UK) Ltd
Incorporated: 25 August 2015
Previous: Pentair International (UK) Ltd
Net Worth: £749,903,168 *Total Assets:* £749,903,168
Registered Office: 8th Floor, The Mille, 1000 Great West Road, Brentford, Middlesex, TW8 9DW
Activities: Financial management
Parent: nVent Electric PLC
Officers: Neil Stuart Mackintosh [1959] Director of Tax; Marek Tapsik [1974] Director/Associate General Counsel [Czech]; Roman Zubinski [1980] Director/Europe Controller [French]

O & M-Movianto UK Holdings Ltd.
Incorporated: 14 August 2012 *Employees:* 27
Net Worth: £36,373,000 *Total Assets:* £136,410,000
Registered Office: 1 Progress Park, Elstow, Bedford, MK42 9XE
Activities: Activities of head offices
Officers: Kamaljit Singh Hunjan [1967] Director/Senior VP Movianto; Julia M. Munzinger [1968] Director/Accountant [American]; Barbara O'Neill [1969] Director/Lawyer [American]; Nicholas Joseph Pace [1970] Director [American]

O'Halloran & O'Brien Limited
Incorporated: 11 April 1972 *Employees:* 75
Net Worth: £61,027,696 *Total Assets:* £113,127,728
Registered Office: O'Brien House, 197-199 Garth Road, Morden, Surrey, SM4 4NE
Activities: Other specialised construction activities n.e.c.
Shareholder: OHOB Group Ltd
Officers: Colin David Southey, Secretary; Brian Hector Bonnyman [1958] Director/Group MD; Steve John Burke [1973] Director/Civil Engineer [Irish]; Martin Walter Alfred Francis [1959] Health & Safety Director; Leslie John Gosling [1959] Director/Contracts Manager; Thomas Jason O'Brien [1976] Director/Company Manager; Thomas Francis O'Brien [1947] Director/Builder [Irish]; Stephen John Richards [1972] Director/Surveyor; Colin David Southey [1959] Director

O'Rourke Investments Holdings (UK) Limited
Incorporated: 14 June 2004
Net Worth: £307,433,984 *Total Assets:* £400,808,000
Registered Office: Bridge Place, Anchor Boulevard, Admirals Park, Crossways, Dartford, Kent, DA2 6SN
Activities: Activities of head offices
Major Shareholder: James Fairweather Edmondson
Officers: Robert Edward Turner, Secretary; Barry Dye [1958] Director/Quantity Surveyor; Gerard Loftus [1960] Director; Declan James McGeeney [1978] Director/General Manager [Irish]; Alexander Stewart McIntyre [1956] Director; Paul William McNerney [1977] Director/Business Unit Leader; John Christopher O'Connor [1965] Commercial Director; Hubert Desmond O'Rourke [1949] Director/Building Contractor [Irish]; Raymond Gabriel O'Rourke [1947] Director/Structural Engineer [Irish]

O.C.S. Group Limited
Incorporated: 11 February 1977 *Employees:* 82,623
Net Worth: £84,487,000 *Total Assets:* £451,606,016
Registered Office: 4 Tilgate Forest Business Park, Brighton Road, Crawley, W Sussex, RH11 9BP
Activities: Activities of head offices
Officers: Malcolm Clark, Secretary; Wendy Jacqueline Barnes [1957] Director; John Bernard Coghlan [1958] Director [Irish]; Ian Alexander Hemming [1963] Director; John Hunter [1966] Director; Peter Slator [1960] Director; Christopher Berkeley Stephens [1948] Director; Louise Stewart [1960] Director

O.S.T.C. Limited
Incorporated: 30 September 2004 *Employees:* 459
Net Worth: £13,181,628 *Total Assets:* £52,668,920
Registered Office: 2nd Floor, Imperial House, 21-25 North Street, Bromley, Kent, BR1 1SD
Activities: Activities auxiliary to financial intermediation n.e.c.
Officers: Justina Naik, Secretary; Jonathan Dean Aucamp [1968] Director; Robert James Brophy [1968] Director; Dr Ian Paul Firla [1970] Director [Polish]; Lee Antony Hodgkinson [1972] Director/Chief Executive; Danny Langley [1972] Director; Michael Peter Saunter [1969] Director; Michael Jose Shirley [1975] Managing Director; Mark Adam Slade [1969] Director/Futures Trader

O2 (Europe) Limited
Incorporated: 5 July 2001
Net Worth: £4,263,360,512 *Total Assets:* £6,179,268,096
Registered Office: 260 Bath Road, Slough, Berks, SL1 4DX
Activities: Other telecommunications activities
Parent: Telefonica S A
Officers: Mark David Hardman [1975] Director; Robert John Harwood [1960] Director; Enrique Medina Malo [1972] Director/Lawyer [Spanish]

O2 Cedar Limited
Incorporated: 26 February 2003
Net Worth: £96,001,392 *Total Assets:* £96,001,392
Registered Office: 260 Bath Road, Slough, Berks, SL1 4DX
Activities: Other telecommunications activities
Parent: O2 Holdings Limited
Officers: Mark David Hardman [1975] Director; Robert John Harwood [1960] Director

O2 Holdings Limited
Incorporated: 23 April 1991
Net Worth: £4,281,999,872 *Total Assets:* £8,264,999,936
Registered Office: 260 Bath Road, Slough, Berks, SL1 4DX
Activities: Other telecommunications activities
Parent: Telefonica Europe PLC
Officers: Patricia Cobian [1975] Director [Spanish]; Mark Evans [1969] Director/Accountant

O2 International Holdings Limited
Incorporated: 5 July 2001
Net Worth: £45,546,000 *Total Assets:* £45,546,000
Registered Office: 260 Bath Road, Slough, Berks, SL1 4DX
Activities: Other telecommunications activities
Parent: O2 (Europe) Limited
Officers: Mark David Hardman [1975] Director; Robert John Harwood [1960] Director; Enrique Medina Malo [1972] Director/Lawyer [Spanish]

O2 Networks Limited
Incorporated: 23 April 1991
Net Worth: £397,521,984 *Total Assets:* £403,140,992
Registered Office: 260 Bath Road, Slough, Berks, SL1 4DX
Activities: Other telecommunications activities
Parent: O2 Holdings Limited
Officers: Mark David Hardman [1975] Director; Robert John Harwood [1960] Director

O2 Unify Limited
Incorporated: 21 March 2012 *Employees:* 7
Net Worth: £4,850,000 *Total Assets:* £25,054,000
Registered Office: 260 Bath Road, Slough, Berks, SL1 4DX
Activities: Information technology consultancy activities
Parent: Telefonica UK Limited
Officers: Patricia Cobian [1975] Director [Spanish]; Mark Evans [1969] Director/Accountant

Oairo Alliance Limited
Incorporated: 12 December 2016 *Employees:* 2
Net Worth: £20,000,100 *Total Assets:* £20,000,100
Registered Office: Unit M, Bourne End Business Park, Cores End Road, Bourne End, Bucks, SL8 5AS
Activities: Other construction installation
Major Shareholder: Bryan Andrew Saxby
Officers: Katie Mullane [1978] Director; Bryan Andrew Saxby [1971] Director; Mark Stenning [1980] Global Project Director

Oakfield (Foods) Limited
Incorporated: 24 February 1987 *Employees:* 52
Net Worth: £23,582,060 *Total Assets:* £44,994,880
Registered Office: 1st Floor, 3 Elstree Gate, Elstree Way, Borehamwood, Herts, WD6 1JD
Activities: Production of meat and poultry meat products
Officers: David Lee Burr, Secretary; David Lee Burr [1971] Finance Director; Mark David Glass [1967] Sales Director; Thomas Matthew Greaney [1988] Director; Daniel Ian Hargreaves [1981] Technical Director; Harvey Philip Ingram [1947] Director/Solicitor; Alison Levy [1959] Director; Miles Ivor Levy [1956] Sales Director; Darren John Short [1966] Director

Oakview Estates Limited
Incorporated: 2 November 1999 *Employees:* 179
Net Worth: £19,231,000 *Total Assets:* £22,275,000
Registered Office: Nepicar House, London Road, Wrotham Heath, Sevenoaks, Kent, TN15 7RS
Activities: Residential nursing care facilities
Parent: Cygnet Health Care Limited
Officers: Anthony Coleman, Secretary; Generald Thomas Corbett [1963] Director/Finance [American]; Mark George Ground [1970] Director; Clynton John Hall [1977] Finance Director; Laurence Harrod [1956] Director/Finance [American]; Michael James McQuaid [1958] Director; Antonio Romero [1971] Director [Spanish]

Ocean Overseas Holdings Limited
Incorporated: 29 November 1957
Net Worth: £273,966,016 *Total Assets:* £273,966,016
Registered Office: Ocean House, The Ring, Bracknell, Berks, RG12 1AN
Activities: Activities of head offices
Parent: Exel Limited
Officers: Steven Fink [1975] Director/Solicitor; Thorsten Kuhl [1974] Director [German]; Michael James Trimm [1968] Director/Accountant

Ocean Partners Holdings Limited
Incorporated: 6 July 2004 *Employees:* 109
Net Worth: £71,759,456 *Total Assets:* £775,645,184
Registered Office: The Pearce Building, West Street, Maidenhead, Berks, SL6 1RL
Activities: Wholesale of metals and metal ores
Officers: John Patrick Foley, Secretary; Stephen John Ball [1966] Director/Trader; Jeffrey Howitt Beck [1958] Director/Trader [American]; Sinisa Bogicevic [1965] Director [Serbian]; Devin Burnett [1977] Director/Trader [American]; William Walter Cimowsky [1957] Director/Trader [Canadian]; Brent Raymond Omland [1979] Director/Chief Financial Officer [Canadian]; Alan Herbert Paterson [1961] Director/Trader [American]; Siva Jothie Pillay [1963] Director/Chief Financial Officer; Adrianus Andreas Everdina Maria Van Halder [1952] Director/Trader [Dutch]

Ocean Partners UK Limited
Incorporated: 6 July 2004 *Employees:* 39
Net Worth: £32,401,568 *Total Assets:* £602,769,920
Registered Office: The Pearce Building, West Street, Maidenhead, Berks, SL6 1RL
Activities: Wholesale of metals and metal ores
Officers: Neil Poulter, Secretary; Sandeep Mittal [1972] Director/Administration Manager; Richard John North [1964] Director/Accountant; Siva Jothie Pillay [1963] Director; Neil Poulter [1968] Director; Samuel Laurie Wooldridge [1979] Director/Treasurer

Oceanic Finance Limited
Incorporated: 6 March 2014 *Employees:* 2
Net Worth: £51,509,680 *Total Assets:* £54,238,528
Registered Office: Oceanic House, Cracknore Hard, Marchwood, Southampton, SO40 4ZD
Activities: Activities of other holding companies n.e.c.
Shareholders: Philip John Hutchinson; Lawrence Edward Smith
Officers: Harry John Hutchinson, Secretary; Philip John Hutchinson [1949] Director; Lawrence Edward Smith [1956] Director

Ocobase Limited
Incorporated: 14 December 1978 *Employees:* 2
Net Worth: £106,970,032 *Total Assets:* £111,565,152
Registered Office: 198 Lower Addiscombe Road, Croydon, Surrey, CR0 7AB
Activities: Buying and selling of own real estate
Shareholders: Paul David Upward; Simon Leslie Upward
Officers: Simon Leslie Upward, Secretary; Paul David Upward [1962] Director; Simon Leslie Upward [1961] Director

OCS Group International Limited
Incorporated: 8 July 1994
Net Worth: £1,024,000 *Total Assets:* £101,186,000
Registered Office: 4 Tilgate Forest Business Park, Brighton Road, Crawley, W Sussex, RH11 9BP
Activities: Activities of head offices
Parent: OCS Group Limited
Officers: Malcolm Clark, Secretary; Malcolm Clark [1958] Director; John Hunter [1966] Director; Ratiwan Lees [1957] Director; Peter Slator [1960] Director

OCS Group UK Limited
Incorporated: 15 May 1995 *Employees:* 24,493
Net Worth: £41,453,000 *Total Assets:* £152,020,000
Registered Office: 4 Tilgate Forest Business Park, Brighton Road, Crawley, W Sussex, RH11 9BP
Activities: Combined facilities support activities
Parent: OCS Group Limited
Officers: Jacqueline Ann Lewis, Secretary; James Darnton [1965] Director; Ian Thomas Goodliffe [1962] Director; Robert John Taylor [1957] Director

Octagon Developments Limited
Incorporated: 18 December 1979 *Employees:* 61
Net Worth: £37,877,000 *Total Assets:* £44,604,000
Registered Office: Weir House, Hurst Road, East Molesey, Surrey, KT8 9AY
Activities: Construction of commercial buildings
Parent: Octagon Group Limited
Officers: Timothy David Robert Banks, Secretary/Director; Timothy David Robert Banks [1967] Director; Robert John Birch [1961] Director; David John James [1943] Director; Angus Jason McQuhae [1966] Director; Jonathan Valentine Pope [1955] Regional Director; Colin Tutt [1956] Director; Roger Stanley Wyatt [1937] Director

Octagon Group Holdings Limited
Incorporated: 11 July 2007 *Employees:* 61
Net Worth: £7,558,000 *Total Assets:* £40,730,000
Registered Office: Weir House, Hurst Road, East Molesey, Surrey, KT8 9AY
Activities: Activities of head offices
Officers: Timothy David Robert Banks, Secretary/Director; Timothy David Robert Banks [1967] Director; David John James [1943] Director; Angus Jason McQuhae [1966] Director; Colin Tutt [1956] Director; Roger Stanley Wyatt [1937] Director

Octagon Group Limited
Incorporated: 7 June 2001
Net Worth: £20,855,000 *Total Assets:* £47,297,000
Registered Office: Weir House, Hurst Road, East Molesey, Surrey, KT8 9AY
Activities: Activities of head offices
Parent: Octagon Group Holdings Limited
Officers: Timothy David Robert Banks, Secretary/Director; Timothy David Robert Banks [1967] Director; David John James [1943] Director; Angus Jason McQuhae [1966] Director; Colin Tutt [1956] Director

Odyssey Trust for Education
Incorporated: 11 November 2011 *Employees:* 185
Previous: Townley Grammar School
Net Worth: £23,206,000 *Total Assets:* £25,015,000
Registered Office: Townley Grammer School, Townley Road, Bexleyheath, Kent, DA6 7AB
Activities: General secondary education
Officers: Kal Joshi, Secretary; Steven Thomas Darsey [1958] Director/Group Chairman; Desmond Deehan [1967] Director/Headteacher; Professor Stephen Mark Vernon Hailes [1965] Director/Lecturer; Emily Elizabeth Larson [1990] Director of International Positive Education [American]; Daniel Southon Morrow [1978] Director/CEO of Multi Academy Trust; John Paterson [1951] Director/Environmental Health Officer; Yunita Ramgoolam [1973] Director/Accountant; Aamer Mirza Mohammed Safdar [1971] Director/Pharmacist

The Offer Group Ltd
Incorporated: 5 September 1986 *Employees:* 4
Net Worth: £19,492,774 *Total Assets:* £24,458,782
Registered Office: Burgoine House, 8 Lower Teddington Road, Hampton Wick, Surrey, KT1 4ER
Activities: Other letting and operating of own or leased real estate
Officers: Daye Offer, Secretary; Daye Offer [1933] Director; Lucy Elizabeth Offer [1961] Director/Home Economist; Timothy Henry Miles Offer [1959] Director/Chartered Surveyor

Officeteam Group Limited
Incorporated: 4 March 2004 *Employees:* 886
Net Worth: £21,184,000 *Total Assets:* £70,184,000
Registered Office: Unit 4, 500 Purley Way, Croydon, Surrey, CR0 4NZ
Activities: Activities of head offices
Major Shareholder: Jonathan Paul Moulton
Officers: Philippa Anne Maynard, Secretary; Nicholas Robin Hodges [1959] Director; Andrew Graham Mobbs [1978] Finance Director; Robert James Moore [1970] Director

Officeteam Limited
Incorporated: 6 April 2004 *Employees:* 844
Net Worth Deficit: £3,430,000 *Total Assets:* £104,854,000
Registered Office: c/o Oyezstraker, Unit 4, 500 Purley Way, Croydon, Surrey, CR0 4NZ
Activities: Non-specialised wholesale trade
Major Shareholder: Jonathan Paul Moulton
Officers: Philippa Anne Maynard, Secretary; David John Harvell [1966] Director; Nicholas Robin Hodges [1959] Director; Andrew Graham Mobbs [1978] Director; Robert James Moore [1970] Director

Offshore Containers Holdings Limited
Incorporated: 8 February 2008
Net Worth: £3,248,164 *Total Assets:* £85,758,864
Registered Office: 298 Sandycombe Road, Kew, Richmond, Surrey, TW9 3NG
Activities: Support activities for petroleum and natural gas mining
Parent: OCHL (Globe) Limited
Officers: John Miller Heiton [1976] Director

OGF Bidco Limited
Incorporated: 18 January 2016
Net Worth: £2,373,291 *Total Assets:* £32,987,248
Registered Office: Wavendon Tower, Ortensia Drive, Wavendon, Milton Keynes, Bucks, MK17 8LX
Activities: Activities of head offices
Parent: OGF Midco Limited
Officers: Jo August [1971] Director; Jonathan David Clark [1977] Director; Venetia Cooper [1974] Director/Chartered Accountant

Oil Spill Response (Capping) Limited
Incorporated: 29 February 2012 *Employees:* 36
Total Assets: £424,874,656
Registered Office: Oil Spill Response Limited, Lower William Street, Southampton, SO14 5QE
Activities: Other professional, scientific and technical activities n.e.c.
Parent: Oil Spill Response Limited
Officers: Matthew Clements [1977] Director; Robert Martin Limb [1957] Director; Anthony Richard Prest [1956] Director/Chartered Accountant

Oil Spill Response Limited
Incorporated: 13 April 1984 *Employees:* 263
Net Worth: £58,887,000 *Total Assets:* £512,464,000
Registered Office: Oil Spill Response Limited, Lower William Street, Southampton, SO14 5QE
Activities: Other business support service activities n.e.c.
Officers: Denis John Dowling, Secretary; Gordon George Reid Ballard [1959] Executive Director IOGP; Yong Sai Chung [1965] Director/Head of Health and Safety [Malaysian]; Michel Jean Marcel Contie [1947] Director/Vice-Chairman IOGP [French]; Joel Conwell [1974] Director/Oil Industry Executive [American]; Eric Jacques Daflon [1959] Director/VP Drilling and Sub-Sea [French]; Gregory de Marco [1962] Director/EP&R Operations Support Manager [American]; Joshua Shane Dubach [1979] Director/EHS Advisor Emergency Preparedness & Response [American]; Brian Robert Horsburgh [1963] Director/Manager; Robert Martin Limb [1957] Director/Chief Executive Officer; Roderick Guy Mason [1964] Director/Chief Financial Officer; Mahmood Merza [1962] Director/Mechanical Engineer [Bahraini]; Declan O'Driscoll [1954] Technical Director [Irish]; Anthony Richard Prest [1956] Director/Chartered Accountant; Astrid Sorensen [1964] Director/Senior Vice President Joint Operations Support [Norwegian]

Oki Europe Limited
Incorporated: 7 December 1987 *Employees:* 530
Net Worth: £14,551,730 *Total Assets:* £128,627,400
Registered Office: Blays House, Wick Road, Englefield Green, Egham, Surrey, TW20 0HJ
Activities: Wholesale of computers, computer peripheral equipment and software
Parent: Oki Data Corporation
Officers: Rakesh Ramniklal Rabheru, Secretary; Takaaki Hagiwara [1967] Director [Japanese]; Hiroshi Ito [1955] Director [Japanese]; Kazuo Kawahara [1967] Director [Japanese]; Akira Ogasawara [1963] Director [Japanese]; Shigeru Ogasawara [1966] Director [Japanese]; Tsukasa Takasawa [1964] Director [Japanese]

Old ML Limited
Incorporated: 11 April 2000 *Employees:* 1,259
Previous: Markerstudy Limited
Net Worth: £1,762,912 *Total Assets:* £325,898,144
Registered Office: Markerstudy House, 45 Westerham Road, Bessels Green, Sevenoaks, Kent, TN13 2QB
Activities: Non-life insurance
Major Shareholder: Kevin Ronald Spencer
Officers: Christopher James Payne, Secretary; Keith John Barber [1974] Director; Christopher Thomas Collings [1955] Director; Gary Humphreys [1965] Director/Insurance; Kevin Ronald Spencer [1965] Director

Old Mutual Wealth Business Services Limited
Incorporated: 11 August 1981 *Employees:* 1,861
Net Worth: £56,140,000 *Total Assets:* £159,424,000
Registered Office: Old Mutual House, Portland Terrace, Southampton, SO14 7EJ
Activities: Other business support service activities n.e.c.
Parent: Quilter PLC
Officers: Duncan John Lane Eardley [1967] Director/Solicitor; Paul Jonathan Hucknall [1971] Human Resources Director; Mark Oscar Satchel [1969] Director/Chartered Accountant [British/South African]

Old Mutual Wealth Holdings Limited
Incorporated: 5 January 1982
Net Worth: £1,514,646,016 *Total Assets:* £1,792,427,008
Registered Office: Old Mutual House, Portland Terrace, Southampton, SO14 7EJ
Activities: Activities of head offices
Parent: Quilter PLC
Officers: Duncan John Lane Eardley [1967] Director/Solicitor; Lynzi Harrison [1974] Director/Head of Operational Assurance; Mark Oscar Satchel [1969] Director/Chartered Accountant [British/South African]; Andrew Stephen Tuddenham [1978] Director/Actuary

Old Mutual Wealth Life & Pensions Limited
Incorporated: 20 February 2001
Net Worth: £120,922,000 *Total Assets:* £25,837,291,520
Registered Office: Old Mutual House, Portland Terrace, Southampton, SO14 7EJ
Activities: Life insurance
Parent: Old Mutual Wealth UK Holding Limited
Officers: John Easton Gill [1964] Director; Scott Kilgour Goodsir [1965] Managing Director; Steven David Levin [1975] Director/Actuary [German]; George McGrimmon Reid [1965] Director; David John Still [1967] Director; Simon Vincent Wood [1967] Director/Chief Financial Officer

Old Mutual Wealth Life Assurance Limited
Incorporated: 19 April 1978
Net Worth: £297,000,000 *Total Assets:* £15,659,899,904
Registered Office: Old Mutual House, Portland Terrace, Southampton, SO14 7EJ
Activities: Life insurance
Parent: Old Mutual Wealth UK Holding Limited
Officers: John Easton Gill [1964] Director; Scott Kilgour Goodsir [1965] Managing Director; Steven David Levin [1975] Director/Actuary [German]; George McGrimmon Reid [1965] Director; David John Still [1967] Director; Simon Vincent Wood [1967] Director/Chief Financial Officer

Old Mutual Wealth Limited
Incorporated: 22 November 1982
Net Worth: £114,141,000 *Total Assets:* £132,054,000
Registered Office: Old Mutual House, Portland Terrace, Southampton, SO14 7EJ
Activities: Other business support service activities n.e.c.
Parent: Old Mutual Wealth Holdings Limited
Officers: John Easton Gill [1964] Director; Scott Kilgour Goodsir [1965] Managing Director; Steven David Levin [1975] Director/Actuary [German]; George McGrimmon Reid [1965] Director; David John Still [1967] Director; Simon Vincent Wood [1967] Director/Chief Financial Officer

Old Mutual Wealth UK Holding Limited
Incorporated: 12 September 1983
Net Worth: £235,758,000 *Total Assets:* £945,518,976
Registered Office: Old Mutual House, Portland Terrace, Southampton, SO14 7EJ
Activities: Activities of head offices
Parent: Old Mutual Wealth Holdings Limited
Officers: Paul Andrew Dark [1971] Director/Head of Finance Operations; Duncan John Lane Eardley [1967] Director/Solicitor

Old Thorns Golf Hotel and Country Estate (Holdings) Limited
Incorporated: 18 December 2006 *Employees:* 286
Net Worth: £1,860,787 *Total Assets:* £42,793,096
Registered Office: Old Thorns Golf Hotel and Country Estate, Longmoor Road, Liphook, Hants, GU30 7PE
Activities: Hotels and similar accommodation
Officers: Yew-Kiat Phang [1968] Director [Singaporean]; Zhenxin Zhang [1971] Director [Chinese]

Old Thorns Golf Hotel and Country Estate Limited
Incorporated: 28 December 1983 *Employees:* 286
Net Worth: £8,545,001 *Total Assets:* £42,910,688
Registered Office: Longmoor Road, Liphook, Hants, GU30 7PE
Activities: Hotels and similar accommodation
Parent: Old Thorns Golf Hotel & Country Estate (Holdings) Ltd
Officers: Cathal Paul Lynch [1979] Managing Director [Irish]; Yew-Kiat Phang [1968] Director [Singaporean]; Zhenxin Zhang [1971] Director [Chinese]

Old Thorns Luxury Apartments Limited
Incorporated: 28 June 2016
Net Worth Deficit: £1,920,226 *Total Assets:* £21,905,572
Registered Office: Old Thorns Golf Hotel and Country Estate, Longmoor Road, Liphook, Hants, GU30 7PE
Activities: Hotels and similar accommodation
Major Shareholder: Jun Kai Soh
Officers: Yew-Kiat Phang [1968] Director [Singaporean]; Kai Jun Soh [1983] Director [Singaporean]

Oldercare (Haslemere) Limited
Incorporated: 19 July 1996 *Employees:* 279
Net Worth: £16,943,464 *Total Assets:* £25,825,426
Registered Office: Rosemary Park Nursing Home, Marley Lane, Marley Common, Haslemere, Surrey, GU27 3PX
Activities: Other human health activities
Shareholder: Roger John Frederick White
Officers: Lloyd Julian Ellis, Secretary; Lloyd Julian Ellis [1983] Director/Business Manager [South African]; Joanne Mary Randall [1965] Director/Registered General Nurse; Roger John Frederick White [1944] Director/Quantity Surveyor

Olive Business Solutions Limited
Incorporated: 27 January 2003 *Employees:* 125
Net Worth Deficit: £3,524,451 *Total Assets:* £21,160,996
Registered Office: Olive House, Mercury Park, Wooburn Green, High Wycombe, Bucks, HP10 0HH
Activities: Other telecommunications activities
Parent: Olive Communications Solutions Limited
Officers: Martin Dieter Flick [1967] Managing Director; Roger Patrick Flynn [1962] Director/Chief Executive; Mark Geraghty [1975] Sales Director [Australian]

OMC Investments Limited
Incorporated: 13 October 1970 *Employees:* 11
Net Worth: £74,306,936 *Total Assets:* £75,202,016
Registered Office: Springfield House, Springfield Road, Horsham, W Sussex, RH12 2RG
Activities: Other business support service activities n.e.c.
Parent: Omarca Investment Holdings Limited
Officers: Jonathan Charles Glyn Evans [1972] Director; Brian Arthur Groves [1933] Managing Director; Dawn Pamela Rose [1956] Director

Omega (After Alpha) Limited
Incorporated: 13 November 1985 *Employees:* 80
Net Worth: £17,539,232 *Total Assets:* £24,258,556
Registered Office: c/o Alliotts, Friary Court, 13-21 High Street, Guildford, Surrey, GU1 3DL
Activities: Other letting and operating of own or leased real estate
Shareholders: Richard David Ernest Hopes; George Trevor Carney; Michael Greets
Officers: Andrew John Cox [1958] Director; Stuart Roderick Jenkin [1957] Director

Omex Agricultural Holdings Ltd.
Incorporated: 9 July 1973 *Employees:* 73
Net Worth: £33,649,592 *Total Assets:* £57,546,420
Registered Office: Kingsbury House, 6 Sheet Street, Windsor, Berks, SL4 1BG
Activities: Manufacture of fertilizers and nitrogen compounds
Officers: David O'Donnell, Secretary; David O'Donnell [1958] Director/Chartered Accountant; Maximilian Olof Winkler [1985] Commercial Director; Olof Joachim Winkler Von Stiernhielm [1949] Director [German]

On Semiconductor Limited
Incorporated: 7 May 1999 *Employees:* 11
Net Worth: £86,173,040 *Total Assets:* £161,569,296
Registered Office: 2nd & 4th Floor, Greenwood House, London Road, Bracknell, Berks, RG12 2AA
Activities: Non-specialised wholesale trade
Parent: ON Semiconductor Corporation
Officers: Yolande Ursula Louisa Isidora de Busschop, Secretary/Vice President; Yolande Ursula Louisa Isidora de Busschop [1959] Director/General Counsel Europe [Belgian]; Sophie Marie Francoise Penent [1967] Director/EMEA Corporate Controller [French]

One GE Healthcare UK
Incorporated: 21 December 2010
Net Worth: £52,154,000 *Total Assets:* £54,736,000
Registered Office: Pollards Wood, Nightingales Lane, Chalfont St Giles, Bucks, HP8 4SP
Activities: Activities of head offices
Parent: GE UK Group
Officers: Katherine Ann Jones [1976] Director/Financial Controller; Adrian Ashwin Narayan [1973] Director/Accountant

Onecom Group Limited
Incorporated: 26 June 2012 *Employees:* 439
Net Worth: £22,153,500 *Total Assets:* £73,876,784
Registered Office: Onecom House, 4400 Parkway, Whiteley, Fareham, Hants, PO15 7FJ
Activities: Other service activities n.e.c.
Shareholders: Darren Michael Ridge; Maria Victoria Tonia Ridge
Officers: Lawrence Mark Furlong, Secretary; Aaron Maurice Brown [1982] Director; Stephen Martin Burton Hunter [1950] Director/Chairman; Darren Michael Ridge [1962] Director; Maria Victoria Tonia Ridge [1963] Director

Onecom Limited
Incorporated: 11 July 2000 *Employees:* 356
Net Worth: £27,424,684 *Total Assets:* £71,520,112
Registered Office: Onecom House, 4400 Parkway, Whiteley, Fareham, Hants, PO15 7FJ
Activities: Other telecommunications activities
Parent: Onecom Group Limited
Officers: Aaron Maurice Brown [1982] Director; Darren Michael Ridge [1962] Director

Onesavings Bank PLC
Incorporated: 13 July 2010 *Employees:* 813
Net Worth: £578,800,000 *Total Assets:* £8,589,100,032
Registered Office: Reliance House, Sun Pier, Chatham, Kent, ME4 4ET
Activities: Banks
Officers: Jason Stanley Elphick, Secretary; John Graham Allatt [1948] Director; Eric Edward Anstee [1951] Director/Chartered Accountant; Rodney Jympson Duke [1950] Director; Andrew John Golding [1969] Director; Margaret Grace Hassall [1961] Independent Non-Executive Director/Consultant; Sarah Ann Hedger [1965] Director; Mary Jane McNamara [1960] Director; April Carolyn Talintyre [1965] Finance Director; David Avery Weymouth [1955] Director

Onix Investments UK Ltd
Incorporated: 25 August 2017
Net Worth: £379,004,064 *Total Assets:* £795,908,160
Registered Office: 2nd Floor, Building 1, Imperial Place, Maxwell Road, Borehamwood, Herts, WD6 1JN
Activities: Activities of financial services holding companies
Parent: Pilgrim's Pride Corporation
Officers: Jose Jardim [1975] Director; Fabio Sandri [1971] Director/Chief Financial Officer [Brazilian]

Onkar International Limited
Incorporated: 5 March 1980 *Employees:* 40
Net Worth: £88,944,200 *Total Assets:* £140,223,632
Registered Office: 19 South Road, Southall, Middlesex, UB1 1SU
Activities: Development of building projects
Officers: Donna Bahia, Secretary; Donna Bahia [1974] Director; Kuljinder Singh Bahia [1972] Director

Ontex Retail UK Limited
Incorporated: 12 February 1982 *Employees:* 18
Net Worth: £16,203,679 *Total Assets:* £35,052,964
Registered Office: 1st Floor, Unit 5 Grovelands Business Park, Boundary Way, Hemel Hempstead, Herts, HP2 7TE
Activities: Wholesale of pharmaceutical goods
Parent: Ontex Group NV
Officers: Thierry Navarre [1967] Director/Chief Operating Officer [French]; Steven Paul Jules Vandenbogaerde [1970] Finance Director [Belgian]

Onyx Information Technology Holdings Limited
Incorporated: 1 August 2011
Net Worth Deficit: £8,384,422 *Total Assets:* £36,589,256
Registered Office: Blue Square House, Priors Way, Maidenhead, Berks, SL6 2HP
Activities: Other information technology service activities
Parent: Pulsant Bidco Limited
Officers: Bradley Petzer, Secretary; Bradley Mark Petzer [1973] Director; Niclas Sanfridsson [1970] Director [Swedish]

Opal (Silvertown) LLP
Incorporated: 8 December 2014
Net Worth Deficit: £1,754,000 *Total Assets:* £80,879,000
Registered Office: Cowley Business Park, Cowley, Uxbridge, Middlesex, UB8 2AL

Opal Ventures Limited
Incorporated: 22 June 2010 *Employees:* 44
Net Worth: £16,830,562 *Total Assets:* £30,214,660
Registered Office: Studio F2/B, Witan Studios, 319 Upper Fourth Street, Milton Keynes, Bucks, MK9 1EH
Activities: Management consultancy activities other than financial management
Shareholders: Alice Jane English; Alan Henry English
Officers: Kanagaratnam Jeyakanthan, Secretary; Alan Henry English [1942] Director; Peter William Grose [1958] Director/Chartered Accountant

Open Text UK Limited
Incorporated: 18 January 1996 *Employees:* 428
Net Worth: £7,519,538 *Total Assets:* £122,314,392
Registered Office: 420 Thames Valley Park Drive, Reading, Berks, RG6 1PT
Activities: Business and domestic software development
Parent: Open Text Corporation
Officers: Gordon Allan Davies [1962] Director/Chief Legal Officer and Corporate Development [Canadian]; Oliver Jon Gallienne [1973] Director/SVP, Worldwide Professional Services; Madhu Ranganathan [1964] Director/EVP & Chief Financial Officer [American]; Christian Waida [1966] Director/General Counsel [German]

Optasense Limited
Incorporated: 19 February 2008 *Employees:* 64
Net Worth: £1,391,000 *Total Assets:* £21,964,000
Registered Office: Cody Technology Park, Ively Road, Farnborough, Hants, GU14 0LX
Activities: Other professional, scientific and technical activities n.e.c.
Parent: Optasense Holdings Limited
Officers: Jon Messent, Secretary; James Pollard [1966] Director/Chief Executive Officer; Kathryn Margaret Robinson [1954] Finance Director; Thomas Neville Walton Salkeld [1962] Director

Optegra International Limited
Incorporated: 21 June 2016 *Employees:* 16
Net Worth: £50,644,584 *Total Assets:* £53,722,528
Registered Office: Oakhill House, 130 Tonbridge Road, Hildenborough, Kent, TN11 9DZ
Activities: Other human health activities
Officers: John Bernard Behrendt [1961] Director/Business Consultant; Dr Peter Jan Elvire Byloos [1968] Director/Chief Executive Officer [Belgian]; Cyrus David Jilla [1969] Director/Company President; Roger Duncan Kibble-White [1968] Finance Director; Karen Dawn MacKay [1965] Director/Chief Financial Officer; Jane Maria Birgitta Stymne Goransson [1957] Board Director and Strategic Industrial Advisor [Swedish]

Optegra UK Limited
Incorporated: 14 June 2006 *Employees:* 211
Net Worth: £17,369,826 *Total Assets:* £27,385,258
Registered Office: Oakhill House, 130 Tonbridge Road, Hildenborough, Kent, TN11 9DZ
Activities: Hospital activities
Parent: Optegra International Limited
Officers: Karen Dawn MacKay [1965] Director; John Fraser Milne McKie [1968] Director/Solicitor; Rory Christopher Passmore [1971] Director

Optionis Group Limited
Incorporated: 2 September 2014 *Employees:* 136
Previous: Arkarius Group Limited
Net Worth Deficit: £26,814,368 *Total Assets:* £25,394,012
Registered Office: KD Tower, Cotterells, Hemel Hempstead, Herts, HP1 1FW
Activities: Activities of head offices
Parent: Optionis Limited
Officers: Ifti Ahmed [1966] Director; Kevin John Budge [1961] Director/Chief Financial Officer; Heather Hayden [1967] Director; Derek Andrew Kelly [1972] Director; Jeremy Steven Newman [1959] Director/Chartered Accountant

Optionis Limited
Incorporated: 2 September 2014 *Employees:* 7,426
Previous: Optionis Holdco Limited
Net Worth Deficit: £66,315,780 *Total Assets:* £148,430,544
Registered Office: KD Tower, Cotterells, Hemel Hempstead, Herts, HP1 1FW
Activities: Activities of other holding companies n.e.c.
Shareholders: Management Opportunities Limited; Sovereign Capital Partners LLP
Officers: Kevin John Budge [1961] Director/Chief Financial Officer; Derek Andrew Kelly [1972] Director; Jeremy Steven Newman [1959] Director/Chartered Accountant

Optiva Solutions (UK) Limited
Incorporated: 19 November 2008 *Employees:* 31
Previous: Redknee Solutions (UK) Limited
Net Worth: £7,635,236 *Total Assets:* £34,161,892
Registered Office: 450 Brook Drive, Green Park, Reading, Berks, RG2 6UU
Activities: Wireless telecommunications activities
Parent: Optiva Canada Inc.
Officers: John Michael Abolt [1986] Director [American]; Anindyaraj Basu [1968] Director/Finance Executive [Canadian]; Sudhanshu Sinha [1982] Director [Indian]

Optivo Finance PLC
Incorporated: 2 February 2012
Previous: AmicusHorizon Finance PLC
Net Worth: £100,000 *Total Assets:* £302,900,000
Registered Office: Grosvenor House, 125 High Street, Croydon, Surrey, CR0 9XP
Activities: Financial intermediation not elsewhere classified
Officers: Josephine Kay Robinson, Secretary; David Phillimore Clifford [1952] Director; Paul Denniston Hackett [1966] Director/Chief Executive; Thomas James Paul [1984] Director of Treasury & Commercial; Sarah Anne Smith [1966] Finance and Resources Director

Optoma Europe Ltd
Incorporated: 7 July 1997 *Employees:* 98
Net Worth: £14,382,000 *Total Assets:* £52,228,000
Registered Office: 1 Bourne End Mills, Hemel Hempstead, Herts, HP1 2UJ
Activities: Wholesale of computers, computer peripheral equipment and software
Parent: Optoma Corporation
Officers: Peter Fosh, Secretary; Wei Yi Chang [1953] Director/Merchant [Taiwanese]; Shih Yuan Chen [1961] Director/Merchant [Taiwanese]; Thierry Michel Marius Millet [1963] Managing Director [French]; Hsiu-Hui Wu [1962] Director [Chinese]

Optum Solutions UK Holdings Limited
Incorporated: 16 September 2009
Net Worth Deficit: £6,446,187 *Total Assets:* £43,473,144
Registered Office: Thames House, Mere Park, Dedmere Road, Marlow, Bucks, SL7 1PB
Activities: Activities of head offices
Parent: UnitedHealth Group Inc
Officers: Brigid Spicola, Secretary; Neil David Anderson [1973] Director; Nathan Phillip Sonstegard [1975] Director/Executive [American]

Optum UK Solutions Group Limited
Incorporated: 11 January 2007
Net Worth: £52,936,104 *Total Assets:* £54,957,288
Registered Office: Thames House, Mere Park, Dedmere Road, Marlow, Bucks, SL7 1PB
Activities: Activities of other holding companies n.e.c.
Parent: Optum Solutions UK Holdings Limited
Officers: Brigid Spicola, Secretary; Neil David Anderson [1973] Director; David Bruce Orbuch [1961] Director/Executive [American]; Nathan Phillip Sonstegard [1975] Director/Executive [American]

Oracle Corporation UK Holdings Limited
Incorporated: 22 February 2005
Net Worth Deficit: £99,296,000 *Total Assets:* £313,872,992
Registered Office: Oracle Parkway, Thames Valley Park, Reading, Berks, RG6 1RA
Activities: Other information technology service activities
Parent: Oracle Corporation
Officers: David James Hudson, Secretary; Simon Thomas Allison [1974] Tax Director; David James Hudson [1966] Director/Solicitor; Glenn Sharpe [1976] Director/Financial Controller [Irish]

Oracle Corporation UK Limited
Incorporated: 12 January 1984 *Employees:* 4,622
Net Worth Deficit: £63,318,000 *Total Assets:* £1,001,036,992
Registered Office: Oracle Parkway, Thames Valley Park, Reading, Berks, RG6 1RA
Activities: Business and domestic software development
Parent: Oracle Corporation UK Holdings Limited
Officers: David James Hudson, Secretary; Simon Thomas Allison [1974] EMEA Senior Tax Director; David James Hudson [1966] Director/Solicitor; Glenn Sharpe [1976] Director/Financial Controller [Irish]

Orange Business Holdings UK Limited
Incorporated: 28 April 1995 *Employees:* 474
Net Worth Deficit: £7,755,000 *Total Assets:* £77,253,000
Registered Office: Betjeman Place, 217 Bath Road, Slough, Berks, SL1 4AA
Activities: Other business support service activities n.e.c.
Parent: Orange S.A.
Officers: Tarsem Dhillon, Secretary; Ibiyemi Solanke, Secretary; Lorenzo Romano [1968] Managing Director UK and Ireland; Kristiaan Van Den Eynde [1960] Director [Belgian]

Orange Business UK Limited
Incorporated: 8 August 1991 *Employees:* 3
Net Worth: £16,604,309 *Total Assets:* £26,168,826
Registered Office: Betjeman Place, 217 Bath Road, Slough, Berks, SL1 4AA
Activities: Other business support service activities n.e.c.
Parent: Orange S.A.
Officers: Tarsem Dhillon, Secretary; Ibiyemi Solanke, Secretary; Lorenzo Romano [1968] Managing Director UK and Ireland; Kristiaan Van Den Eynde [1960] Director [Belgian]

The Oratory Schools Association
Incorporated: 16 September 1931 *Employees:* 251
Net Worth: £13,630,491 *Total Assets:* £24,704,566
Registered Office: c/o The Oratory School, Woodcote, Reading, Berks, RG8 0PJ
Activities: Pre-primary education
Officers: Martin William Halsall, Secretary; Martin John Berkeley [1967] Director; Barney Francis Hassan Bettesworth [1944] Director/Chartered Surveyor; Mary Anne Cochrane [1945] Director; Margaret Ellen Edwards [1953] Director/Art Specialist; Professor Peter William Evans [1946] Director/Professor; Francis Joseph Fitzherbert-Brockholes [1951] Director/Lawyer; Michael Henry Roche Hasslacher [1939] Director/Retired; Dr Christina Bernadette Therese Hill Williams [1952] Director/Magistrate; Jonathan Richard Barnard Hobbs [1971] Director; Charles James Sehmer [1941] Director/Chartered Accountant/Financial; Daniel Seward [1974] Director/Priest; Matthew Stilwell [1956] Director/Businessman; Colonel Craig Robertson Sutherland [1967] Director/General Manager; Nicholas John Tanner [1946] Director/General Manager

The Ordnance Building Limited
Incorporated: 15 December 2016
Net Worth Deficit: £3,056,455 *Total Assets:* £43,701,624
Registered Office: Manderley, Lower South Park, South Godstone, Surrey, RH9 8LF
Activities: Development of building projects
Major Shareholder: Lucy Mason
Officers: Max Barth [1968] Director/Investment Advisor [Swiss]; Reto Gall [1979] Director/Accountant [Swiss]; Lucy Mason [1987] Director; Ravina Kaur Sond [1988] Director

Organised Computer Systems Limited
Incorporated: 28 November 1990 *Employees:* 6
Net Worth: £12,019,485 *Total Assets:* £27,522,672
Registered Office: East House, Newpound Common, Wisborough Green, W Sussex, RH14 0AZ
Activities: Information technology consultancy activities
Parent: The Organised Group Limited
Officers: Mathias Michael Giesemann [1978] Director [German]; Martin Hugo Hess [1959] Director; Thomas Paul Erich Volk [1958] Director [German]

The Organised Group Limited
Incorporated: 30 January 1998 *Employees:* 215
Net Worth: £13,666,595 *Total Assets:* £33,676,676
Registered Office: East House, Newpound, Wisborough Green, Billingshurst, W Sussex, RH14 0AZ
Activities: Activities of head offices
Parent: Cancom UK Ltd
Officers: Mathias Michael Giesemann [1978] Director [German]; Martin Hugo Hess [1959] Director; Thomas Paul Erich Volk [1958] Director [German]

The Original Bowling Company Limited
Incorporated: 25 June 2004 *Employees:* 1,802
Net Worth: £58,337,000 *Total Assets:* £100,523,000
Registered Office: Focus 31, West Wing, Cleveland Road, Hemel Hempstead Industrial Estate, Hemel Hempstead, Herts, HP2 7BW
Activities: Other sports activities
Parent: Kendallco Limited
Officers: Stephen Burns [1976] Director; Melanie Dickinson [1974] Talent Director; Mathew Hart [1969] Director; Laurence Brian Keen [1976] Finance Director

Orleans Park School
Incorporated: 2 August 2012 *Employees:* 138
Net Worth: £29,629,432 *Total Assets:* £31,701,936
Registered Office: Orleans Park School, Richmond Road, Twickenham, Middlesex, TW1 3BB
Activities: General secondary education
Officers: Kelly Louise Wallis, Secretary; Elaine Margaret Ball [1966] Director/Headteacher; Jennifer Kim Baskerville [1984] Director/Corporate Responsibility Senior Manager; Julian Bell [1962] Director/Teacher; Jeanette Best [1962] Director; Adam Andrew Dunlop [1964] Director/Editor; Adam Steuart Gladstone [1973] Director/Teacher; Sarah Kate MacKenzie [1966] Director/Homemaker; Laurence Norman Mann [1960] Director/Solicitor; Karen Jane Miller [1971] Director/Partner in a Wholesaler; Stuart Nevill [1970] Director/Charity CEO; Katie O'Connor [1979] Director/Head of Mathematics; Elizabeth Pawsey [1967] Director/Executive Coach & Facilitator; John Martin Riglin [1962] Director/Manager; Anthony Charles Shoebridge [1948] Director/Retired; Eleanor Catherine Stewart [1970] University Programme Director; Sir David Whitlock Tanner [1947] Performance Director (British Rowing)

Orthofix Limited
Incorporated: 14 September 1993 *Employees:* 29
Net Worth: £273,112,000 *Total Assets:* £291,487,008
Registered Office: 6 Waltham Park, Waltham Road, White Waltham, Maidenhead, Berks, SL6 3TN
Activities: Non-specialised wholesale trade
Parent: Orthofix Medical Inc.
Officers: Michael John Barry, Secretary; Joseph Brent Alldredge [1974] Director [American]; Michael John Barry [1971] Sales and Marketing Director; Stacy Leann Kohn [1969] Director/Business Executive [American]; Bradley Robert Mason [1953] Director/President and CEO [American]; Douglas Clinton Rice [1965] Director/Chief Financial Officer [American]

Orthopaedic Research UK
Incorporated: 6 October 2005 *Employees:* 5
Net Worth: £25,502,792 *Total Assets:* £28,451,824
Registered Office: c/o Brayne Williams & Barnard Limited, Rosemount House, Rosemount Avenue, West Byfleet, Surrey, KT14 6LB
Activities: Other business support service activities n.e.c.
Officers: Anthony John Edge [1944] Director/Orthopaedic Surgeon; Peter Evans Harrison [1962] Managing Director; Patrick Latham [1945] Director/Chartered Accountant; David Simeon Martin [1949] Director; Robert Ross Vallings [1943] Director/Solicitor

Osborne Group Holdings Ltd
Incorporated: 9 November 2017 *Employees:* 915
Net Worth: £17,379,000 *Total Assets:* £116,717,000
Registered Office: Fonteyn House, 47-49 London Road, Reigate, Surrey, RH2 9PY
Activities: Activities of other holding companies n.e.c.
Shareholder: Rosewood Group Holdings Ltd
Officers: Stuart Hammond [1972] Director; Alison Louise Littley [1962] Director; Andrew Simon Charles Osborne [1967] Director/Chartered Accountant; Andrew Philip Steele [1964] Director; Michael John Strong [1947] Director/Chartered Surveyor

Geoffrey Osborne Limited
Incorporated: 7 March 1966 *Employees:* 914
Net Worth: £15,975,000 *Total Assets:* £112,879,000
Registered Office: Fonteyn House, 47-49 London Road, Reigate, Surrey, RH2 9PY
Activities: Construction of commercial buildings
Parent: Osborne Group Holdings Ltd
Officers: Dr. John Rennie Chadwick [1964] Director/Chartered Civil Engineer; John David Craig [1959] Managing Director, Construction; John Vincent Dowsett [1973] Managing Director; Stuart Hammond [1972] Director; Richard Martyn King [1961] Director/Chartered Marketer & Chartered Engineer; Andrew Simon Charles Osborne [1967] Director/Accountant; Andrew Philip Steele [1964] Director; Mark David Taylor [1965] Chartered Surveyor and Director; Sarah Catherine Taylor [1960] Group People Director

OTC Direct Limited
Incorporated: 27 October 1995
Net Worth: £59,200,000 *Total Assets:* £111,000,000
Registered Office: 43 Cox Lane, Chessington, Surrey, KT9 1SN
Activities: Wholesale of pharmaceutical goods
Parent: Alliance Boots Holdings Limited
Officers: Lucie Charlotte Massart, Secretary; Alexandro Depau [1970] Director [American]; Pablo Cortes Rivas [1972] Director [Spanish]

Otsuka Pharmaceutical Europe Ltd.
Incorporated: 28 October 1997 *Employees:* 125
Net Worth: £164,761,120 *Total Assets:* £262,469,072
Registered Office: Gallions, Wexham Springs, Framewood Road, Wexham, Slough, SL3 6PJ
Activities: Activities of head offices
Parent: Otsuka Holdings Co., Ltd.
Officers: Klaus Dieter Rudolf Julicher [1939] Director [German]; Hiroaki Ono [1966] Director/Vice President Clinical R&D [Japanese]; Dr Taku Seriu [1962] Executive Director, Otsuka Pharmaceutical Co. Ltd [Japanese]; Susumu Tamai [1955] Japan Vice President and Executive Director [Japanese]; Ole Vahlgren [1963] Director [Danish]

OTV Birwelco Limited
Incorporated: 1 September 1989
Net Worth: £2,408,000 *Total Assets:* £48,530,000
Registered Office: Windsor Court, Kingsmead Business Park, High Wycombe, Bucks, HP11 1JU
Activities: Activities of other holding companies n.e.c.
Parent: Veolia UK Ltd
Officers: Ian Thomas Heggie, Secretary; Philip Andrew Chattle [1958] Director; Martyn Paul Fisher [1961] Director; Sunil Kumar Lakhenpaul [1961] Director/Accountant

Ousedale School
Incorporated: 25 May 2011 *Employees:* 203
Net Worth: £29,748,180 *Total Assets:* £33,919,824
Registered Office: Ousedale School, Newport Pagnell Campus, The Grove, Newport Pagnell, Bucks, MK16 0BJ
Activities: General secondary education
Officers: Imogen Mary Allen [1964] Director/Home Maker; David Beaney [1971] Director/Certified Chartered Accountant; Vicki Beynon [1977] Director/Senior Manager; Susan Margaret Carbert [1961] Director/Headteacher; Paul Robert Collins [1950] Director; Susan Rita Garner [1969] Managing Director, Training Company; Dr Yolande Frances Elizabeth Herbath [1966] Director/Solicitor; Clair Ann King [1972] Director/Solicitor; Andrew Peter Lawson [1974] Director/Head of Finance; Hazel Leighfield [1965] Director/Service Delivery Manager; Faye McClenahan [1974] Managing Director; Andrew Charles Millburn [1953] Director/Retired Civil Servant; David Trevor Malcolm Moulson [1950] Director/Programme Manager; Urvashi Parashar [1974] Director/Civil Servant/Economist; Jennifer Ann Frances Parker [1958] Director/Risk and Control Manager; Karen Spriddle [1981] Director/Head of S&V Finance; John James Stevenson [1960] Director/Workshop Manager; Claire Tierney [1980] Director/6th Form Study Centre Co-ordinator

Oval (2284) Limited
Incorporated: 5 November 2014
Net Worth: £746,588 *Total Assets:* £20,198,324
Registered Office: 5a Franscati Way, Maidenhead, Berks, SL6 4UY
Activities: Financial intermediation not elsewhere classified
Shareholders: Graeme Simpson; Debbie Simpson
Officers: Graeme Simpson [1960] Director

Overseas Air Travel Limited
Incorporated: 22 November 1995 *Employees:* 5
Net Worth: £3,237,000 *Total Assets:* £121,246,000
Registered Office: P O Box 365, Waterside, Harmondsworth, Middlesex, UB7 0GB
Activities: Travel agency activities
Parent: British Airways Holidays Limited
Officers: Katie Louise Bishop, Secretary; Claire Marie Elizabeth Bentley [1968] Director/Airline Executive; Andrew Peter David Brem [1968] Director [Swiss]; Henry James Adam Daniels [1969] Director; Colm Leo Lacy [1970] Director/Airline Executive [Irish]; Sarah Elizabeth Mussenden [1965] Director; Jack Robert Smith [1977] Director

Overton Grange School
Incorporated: 9 May 2011 *Employees:* 138
Net Worth: £22,666,000 *Total Assets:* £26,386,000
Registered Office: Overton Grange School, Stanley Road, Sutton, Surrey, SM2 6TQ
Activities: General secondary education
Officers: Karen Brown, Secretary; Charlotte Susan Auger [1974] Director/Teacher; Aaron Michael Banham [1972] Director; Generald Bennett [1959] Director/Teacher; Shelene Louise Brown [1981] Director/Teacher; Simon David Michael Doubell [1963] Director/IT Analyst; Peter Michael Duus [1973] Director/Teacher [Danish]; James Christopher Eales [1989] Director/NHS Manager; Stephen Gillmore [1964] Director; Brenda Pauline Morley [1943] Director; David John Nicholls [1965] Director/Driving Instructor; Karthik Sankaran [1975] Director/Associate Manager [Indian]; Mohan Shekar [1981] Director/Chief Advisor; Keith Benjamin Stride [1964] Director/Headteacher (Acting); Marion Helen Williams [1953] Director

Overture Bidco Limited
Incorporated: 14 October 2016
Net Worth: £83,261,000 *Total Assets:* £129,579,000
Registered Office: Mandeville House, 62 The Broadway, Amersham, Bucks, HP7 0HJ
Activities: Non-trading company
Parent: Overture Midco II lmited
Officers: Steven William James Kent [1962] Director; Richard James Riegel [1963] Director [American]; Jacqueline Susan Veness [1960] Director

Overture Midco II Limited
Incorporated: 14 October 2016
Net Worth: £82,830,000 *Total Assets:* £82,830,000
Registered Office: Mandeville House, 62 The Broadway, Amersham, Bucks, HP7 0HJ
Activities: Non-trading company
Parent: Overture Midco Limited
Officers: Richard James Riegel [1963] Director [American]; Jacqueline Susan Veness [1960] Director

Overture Midco Limited
Incorporated: 14 October 2016 *Employees:* 2
Net Worth: £82,830,000 *Total Assets:* £82,830,000
Registered Office: Mandeville House, 62 The Broadway, Amersham, Bucks, HP7 0HJ
Activities: Non-trading company
Parent: Overture Topco Limited
Officers: Richard James Riegel [1963] Director [American]; Jacqueline Susan Veness [1960] Director

Overture Topco Limited
Incorporated: 14 October 2016 *Employees:* 357
Net Worth Deficit: £16,823,000 *Total Assets:* £122,598,000
Registered Office: Mandeville House, 62 The Broadway, Amersham, Bucks, HP7 0HJ
Activities: Non-trading company
Parent: Vitruvian Partners LLP
Officers: Steven William James Kent [1962] Director/Chairman; Richard James Riegel [1963] Director [American]; Karen Jane Roy [1966] Director; Jacqueline Susan Veness [1960] Director

Oxford Aviation Academy (Oxford) Limited
Incorporated: 12 June 2007 *Employees:* 104
Net Worth: £18,521,000 *Total Assets:* £35,762,000
Registered Office: CAE Training & Services UK Ltd, Fleming Way, Crawley, W Sussex, RH10 9UH
Activities: Other education n.e.c.
Officers: William Richard Balicki, Secretary; Hasnain Mohsin [1978] Director of Finance; Onno Rijsdijk [1965] Director [Dutch]; Johannes Hendrick Van Engelen [1967] Director [Dutch]

Oxford International Education 1 Limited
Incorporated: 31 January 2014 *Employees:* 759
Net Worth Deficit: £32,022,784 *Total Assets:* £63,895,920
Registered Office: New Kings Court, Tollgate, Chandler's Ford, Eastleigh, Hants, SO53 3LG
Activities: Activities of other holding companies n.e.c.
Shareholder: Ventry Nominees Limited
Officers: Lil Gabriela Bremermann-Richard [1979] Group Commercial Director; David Charles Brown [1962] Director; Robert St George Darell [1966] Director; Michael Kevin Peter Grassby [1961] Director/Managing Partner - Fund Management; Tom Shelford [1980] Director; Christopher John Spanoudakis [1965] Director; Vishal Verma [1978] Finance Director

Oxford International Education 2 Limited
Incorporated: 31 January 2014
Net Worth Deficit: £5,403,782 *Total Assets:* £36,600,000
Registered Office: New Kings Court, Tollgate, Chandler's Ford, Eastleigh, Hants, SO53 3LG
Activities: Activities of other holding companies n.e.c.
Parent: Oxford International Education 1 Limited
Officers: Lil Gabriela Bremermann-Richard [1979] Group Commercial Director; David Charles Brown [1962] Director; Robert St George Darell [1966] Director; Michael Kevin Peter Grassby [1961] Director/Managing Partner - Fund Management; Tom Shelford [1980] Director; Christopher John Spanoudakis [1965] Director/Corporate Financier; Vishal Verma [1978] Finance Director

Oxford International Education 3 Limited
Incorporated: 31 January 2014
Net Worth Deficit: £4,894,167 *Total Assets:* £58,002,268
Registered Office: New Kings Court, Tollgate, Chandler's Ford, Eastleigh, Hants, SO53 3LG
Activities: Activities of other holding companies n.e.c.
Parent: Oxford International Education 2 Limited
Officers: Lil Gabriela Bremermann-Richard [1979] Group Commercial Director; David Charles Brown [1962] Director; Robert St George Darell [1966] Director; Michael Kevin Peter Grassby [1961] Director/Managing Partner - Fund Management; Tom Shelford [1980] Director; Christopher John Spanoudakis [1965] Director/Corporate Financier; Vishal Verma [1978] Finance Director

Oyezstraker Group Limited
Incorporated: 4 April 1996
Net Worth: £601,000 *Total Assets:* £51,260,000
Registered Office: Unit 4, 500 Purley Way, Croydon, Surrey, CR0 4NZ
Activities: Activities of head offices
Major Shareholder: Jonathan Paul Moulton
Officers: Philippa Anne Maynard, Secretary; Andrew Graham Mobbs [1978] Finance Director

P & O European Ferries (Irish Sea) Limited
Incorporated: 5 September 1936 *Employees:* 217
Net Worth Deficit: £72,740,000 *Total Assets:* £73,217,000
Registered Office: Channel House, Channel View Road, Dover, Kent, CT17 9TJ
Activities: Sea and coastal passenger water transport
Officers: Susan Frances Kitchin, Secretary; Christopher Bryan Bailey [1962] Ship Support Services Director; Janette Susan Bell [1964] Commercial Director; Lesley Anne Cotton [1965] HR Director; Peter Douglas Generald Hebblethwaite [1971] Overnight Ropax Director; Karl Howarth [1964] Director/Chief Financial Officer

P & O Ferries Division Holdings Limited
Incorporated: 29 December 2006 *Employees:* 3,764
Net Worth: £474,643,008 *Total Assets:* £1,023,758,976
Registered Office: Channel House, Channel View Road, Dover, Kent, CT17 9TJ
Activities: Sea and coastal passenger water transport
Officers: Susan Frances Kitchin, Secretary; Janette Susan Bell [1964] Director; Karl Howarth [1964] Director; Ronald Sibongiseni Ntuli [1970] Director/Chief Executive Officer [South African]; Junaid Rahimullah [1968] Director [Emirati]; Saadi Abdul Rahim Hassan Al Rais [1951] Group Managing Director [Emirati]

P & O Ferries Holdings Limited
Incorporated: 29 December 2006 *Employees:* 1,678
Net Worth Deficit: £184,088,000 *Total Assets:* £765,254,976
Registered Office: Channel House, Channel View Road, Dover, Kent, CT17 9TJ
Activities: Sea and coastal passenger water transport
Officers: Susan Frances Kitchin, Secretary; Christopher Bryan Bailey [1962] Director; Janette Susan Bell [1964] Commercial Director; Lesley Anne Cotton [1965] HR Director; Peter Douglas Generald Hebblethwaite [1971] Overnight Ropax Director; Karl Howarth [1964] Director; David Stretch [1968] Director; Tom Wechsler [1974] Director

P & O Ferries Limited
Incorporated: 2 March 1929 *Employees:* 909
Net Worth: £143,776,992 *Total Assets:* £449,163,008
Registered Office: Channel House, Channel View Road, Dover, CT17 9TJ
Activities: Sea and coastal passenger water transport
Officers: Susan Frances Kitchin, Secretary; Christopher Bryan Bailey [1962] Director; Janette Susan Bell [1964] Commercial Director; Lesley Anne Cotton [1965] HR Director; Karl Howarth [1964] Director/Chief Financial Officer

P & O Ferries Pride of Hull Limited
Incorporated: 1 August 1958
Net Worth: £6,279,000 *Total Assets:* £51,845,000
Registered Office: Channel House, Channel View Road, Dover, Kent, CT17 9TJ
Activities: Operation of warehousing and storage facilities for water transport activities
Officers: Susan Frances Kitchin, Secretary; Christopher Bryan Bailey [1962] Ship Support Services Director; Janette Susan Bell [1964] Director; Karl Howarth [1964] Director/Chief Financial Officer

P & O North Sea Ferries Limited
Incorporated: 15 June 1964 *Employees:* 162
Net Worth: £4,351,000 *Total Assets:* £211,534,000
Registered Office: Channel House, Channel View Road, Dover, Kent, CT17 9TJ
Activities: Sea and coastal passenger water transport
Officers: Susan Frances Kitchin, Secretary/Solicitor; Christopher Bryan Bailey [1962] Ship Support Services Director; Janette Susan Bell [1964] Commercial Director; Lesley Anne Cotton [1965] HR Director; Karl Howarth [1964] Director/Chief Financial Officer

P & O Short Sea Ferries Limited
Incorporated: 9 December 1996 *Employees:* 911
Net Worth: £248,028,992 *Total Assets:* £536,428,992
Registered Office: Channel House, Channel View Road, Dover, CT17 9TJ
Activities: Sea and coastal passenger water transport
Officers: Susan Frances Kitchin, Secretary/Solicitor; Christopher Bryan Bailey [1962] Director; Janette Susan Bell [1964] Commercial Director; Lesley Anne Cotton [1965] H R Director; Karl Howarth [1964] Director/Chief Financial Officer; David Stretch [1968] Director

Andrew Page 1917 Limited
Incorporated: 30 September 2016 *Employees:* 2,272
Net Worth Deficit: £8,385,000 *Total Assets:* £85,414,000
Registered Office: 1 London Street, Reading, Berks, RG1 4PN
Activities: Wholesale trade of motor vehicle parts and accessories
Parent: Euro Car Parts Limited
Officers: Andrew Hamilton [1974] Operations Director; Paula Andrea Huesca de Crean [1975] Director; Annick Jourdenais [1969] Director [Canadian]; John Quinn [1957] Director/Executive Vice President [Canadian]

Michael Page Holdings Limited
Incorporated: 8 June 1984 *Employees:* 141
Net Worth: £14,283,000 *Total Assets:* £948,027,008
Registered Office: Page House, 1 Dashwood Lang Road, Bourne Business Park, Addlestone, Surrey, KT15 2QW
Activities: Other activities of employment placement agencies
Parent: Michael Page Recruitment Group Limited
Officers: Kaye Maguire, Secretary; Kaye Elizabeth Maguire [1977] Director/General Counsel and Company Secretary; Kelvin John Stagg [1971] Director/Accountant; Jeremy Paul Tatham [1969] Director/Accountant

Michael Page International Recruitment Limited
Incorporated: 27 December 2000 *Employees:* 1,274
Net Worth: £833,841,024 *Total Assets:* £1,333,287,936
Registered Office: Page House, 1 Dashwood Lang Road, Bourne Business Park, Addlestone, Surrey, KT15 2QW
Activities: Other activities of employment placement agencies
Parent: Pagegroup PLC
Officers: Kaye Maguire, Secretary; Kaye Elizabeth Maguire [1977] Director/General Counsel and Company Secretary; Kelvin John Stagg [1971] Director/Accountant; Jeremy Paul Tatham [1969] Director/Accountant

Michael Page International Southern Europe Limited
Incorporated: 14 December 2000 *Employees:* 5
Net Worth: £1,248,000 *Total Assets:* £106,235,000
Registered Office: Page House, 1 Dashwood Lang Road, The Bourne Business Park, Addlestone, Surrey, KT15 2QW
Activities: Activities of head offices
Parent: Pagegroup PLC
Officers: Kaye Maguire, Secretary; Geoffroy Marie Humbert de Beaucorps [1974] Finance Director [French]; Patrick Pierre Hollard [1968] Director [French]; Kaye Elizabeth Maguire [1977] Director/General Counsel and Company Secretary; Kelvin John Stagg [1971] Director/Accountant; Jeremy Paul Tatham [1969] Director/Accountant

Pagegroup PLC
Incorporated: 30 January 1997 *Employees:* 6,549
Previous: Michael Page International PLC
Net Worth: £270,056,992 *Total Assets:* £499,812,000
Registered Office: Page House, 1 Dashwood Lang Road, The Bourne Business Park, Addlestone, Surrey, KT15 2QW
Activities: Activities of head offices
Officers: Kaye Elizabeth Maguire, Secretary; Simon Boddie [1960] Finance Director; Patrick Jean-Marie de Smedt [1955] Director [Belgian]; Michelle Miriam Healy [1968] Director/HR Professional [Irish]; Stephen John Ingham [1962] Executive Director; David Soutar Lowden [1957] Director; Sylvia Metayer [1960] Director [French]; Angela Charlotte Seymour-Jackson [1966] Director; Kelvin John Stagg [1971] Director/Management Accountant

Pall Europe Limited
Incorporated: 1 April 2010 *Employees:* 782
Net Worth: £52,452,000 *Total Assets:* £113,301,000
Registered Office: 5 Harbourgate Business Park, Southampton Road, Portsmouth, PO6 4BQ
Activities: Manufacture of other general-purpose machinery n.e.c.
Parent: Pall Manufacturing UK Limited
Officers: Christina Ellen Munslow, Secretary; Deen William Harman [1964] Manufacturing Director; Antony Paul Mason [1966] Managing Director; Christina Ellen Munslow [1959] Director/Solicitor

Pall European Holdings Limited
Incorporated: 17 December 2013
Net Worth: £70,089,824 *Total Assets:* £156,093,536
Registered Office: 5 Harbourgate Business Park, Southampton Road, Portsmouth, PO6 4BQ
Activities: Activities of head offices
Parent: Danaher Corporation
Officers: Antony Paul Mason [1966] Director/Accountant; Christina Ellen Munslow [1959] Legal Director; Adam Luke Tursi [1976] Tax Director [American]

Pall Manufacturing UK Limited
Incorporated: 26 July 1963 *Employees:* 1,088
Net Worth: £112,958,000 *Total Assets:* £134,012,000
Registered Office: 5 Harbourgate Business Park, Southampton Road, Portsmouth, PO6 4BQ
Activities: Manufacture of other general-purpose machinery n.e.c.
Parent: Launchchange Operations Limited
Officers: Christina Ellen Munslow, Secretary; Deen William Harman [1964] Manufacturing Director; Antony Paul Mason [1966] Managing Director; Christina Ellen Munslow [1959] Director/Solicitor

Pall Technology UK Limited
Incorporated: 17 December 2013
Net Worth: £33,044,576 *Total Assets:* £36,075,900
Registered Office: 5 Harbourgate Business Park, Southampton Road, Portsmouth, PO6 4BQ
Activities: Research and experimental development on biotechnology
Parent: Danaher Corporation
Officers: Antony Paul Mason [1966] Director/Accountant; Christina Ellen Munslow [1959] Legal Director; Adam Luke Tursi [1976] Tax Director [American]

Pallant House Gallery
Incorporated: 16 February 2004 *Employees:* 38
Net Worth: £35,103,512 *Total Assets:* £35,225,600
Registered Office: 8-9 North Pallant, Chichester, W Sussex, PO19 1TJ
Activities: Museums activities
Officers: Elizabeth Jane Davis, Secretary; John David Sebastian Booth [1958] Director/Co Chairman; Ruth Susan Butler [1968] Director/Architect; Adrian Spencer Clark [1957] Director/Solicitor; Elizabeth Jane Davis [1956] Director/Solicitor; Pamela Margaret Dignum [1940] Director/Councillor; Zachary Roger Leonard [1963] Managing Director [American]; Charles David Zelenka Martin [1961] Director/Solicitor; Harold Roger Wallis Mavity [1943] Director/Writer; Andrea Rose [1950] Former Director of Visual Arts British Council; Jacqueline Russell [1963] Director; Andrew Guy Tyrie [1957] Director/Chair, Competition and Markets Authority; Jane Weeks [1947] Director/Consultant for Heritage Sector

Palmier Ltd
Incorporated: 13 April 2016
Net Worth Deficit: £713,778 *Total Assets:* £29,273,812
Registered Office: Greenstedes, Marden Paddock, Brockenhurst, Hants, SO42 7SU
Activities: Fund management activities
Officers: Margaret Jane Gosman, Secretary; Allen David Gosman [1940] Director/Professor Emeritus [Canadian]; Margaret Jane Gosman [1941] Director/Retired; Laurence Meakin [1946] Director/Administrator

Panalpina World Transport Limited
Incorporated: 15 November 1939 *Employees:* 356
Net Worth Deficit: £815,000 *Total Assets:* £47,638,000
Registered Office: Panalpina House, Great South West Road, Feltham, Middlesex, TW14 8NU
Activities: Operation of warehousing and storage facilities for water transport activities
Parent: Panalpina World Transport (Holding) Ltd.
Officers: Caterina Rossi Herdman, Secretary; Christopher David Cooper [1968] Director/Freight Forwarder; Caterina Rossi Herdman [1954] Director/Human Resources [Italian]; Frank Simmen [1965] Director/Accountant [Swiss]; Rachel Wilton [1974] Director/Country Head of Marketing and Sales UK and Ireland

Panalux Limited
Incorporated: 10 April 2001 *Employees:* 198
Net Worth: £22,570,000 *Total Assets:* £37,341,000
Registered Office: 47 Castle Street, Reading, Berks, RG1 7SR
Activities: Renting and leasing of media entertainment equipment
Parent: AFM Group Limited
Officers: Jeffrey Thomas Allen [1953] Managing Director; Jasminder Singh Kalsey [1974] Finance Director; Kimberly Ann Snyder [1962] Director [American]

Panavision Europe Limited
Incorporated: 17 August 1990 *Employees:* 713
Net Worth Deficit: £7,115,000 *Total Assets:* £108,122,000
Registered Office: Corporate Office, Metropolitan Centre, Bristol Road, Greenford, Middlesex, UB6 8GU
Activities: Renting and leasing of media entertainment equipment
Shareholder: Stephen Andrew Feinberg
Officers: Jeffrey Thomas Allen [1953] Director; Mark Vincent Furssedonn [1965] Group Operations Director; Jasminder Singh Kalsey [1974] Director; Kimberly Ann Snyder [1962] Director [American]

PandoraExpress 2 Limited
Incorporated: 6 March 2003
Net Worth: £3,444,000 *Total Assets:* £248,162,000
Registered Office: Hunton House, Highbridge Estate, Oxford Road, Uxbridge, Middlesex, UB8 1LX
Activities: Licenced restaurants
Parent: PandoraExpress 1 Limited
Officers: Andrew David Pellington, Secretary; Andrew David Pellington [1964] Director; Jinlong Wang [1957] Director [American]

PandoraExpress 3 Limited
Incorporated: 6 March 2003
Net Worth Deficit: £1,815,000 *Total Assets:* £244,707,008
Registered Office: Hunton House, Highbridge Estate, Oxford Road, Uxbridge, Middlesex, UB8 1LX
Activities: Licenced restaurants
Parent: PandoraExpress 2 Limited
Officers: Andrew David Pellington, Secretary; Andrew David Pellington [1964] Director; Jinlong Wang [1957] Director [American]

PandoraExpress 4 Limited
Incorporated: 6 March 2003 *Employees:* 2
Net Worth: £239,012,000 *Total Assets:* £246,580,000
Registered Office: Hunton House, Highbridge Estate, Oxford Road, Uxbridge, Middlesex, UB8 1LX
Activities: Licenced restaurants
Parent: PandoraExpress 3 Limited
Officers: Andrew David Pellington, Secretary; Andrew David Pellington [1964] Director; Jinlong Wang [1957] Director [American]

PandoraExpress 7 Limited
Incorporated: 11 December 2003 *Employees:* 2
Net Worth: £54,686,000 *Total Assets:* £83,505,000
Registered Office: Hunton House, Highbridge Industrial Estate, Oxford Road, Uxbridge, Middlesex, UB8 1LX
Activities: Non-trading company
Parent: PizzaExpress Operations Limited
Officers: Andrew David Pellington, Secretary; Andrew David Pellington [1964] Director; Jinlong Wang [1957] Director [American]

Pandrol Finance Limited
Incorporated: 30 July 1999 *Employees:* 2
Net Worth: £104,517,000 *Total Assets:* £110,940,000
Registered Office: Osprey House, 63 Station Road, Addlestone, Surrey, KT15 2AR
Activities: Activities of production holding companies
Parent: Pandrol Group Limited
Officers: Jonathan Baxter, Secretary; Olivier Vincent Antille [1971] Director [French]; Brian Forster [1953] Director

Pandrol Group Limited
Incorporated: 30 July 1999 *Employees:* 2
Net Worth: £79,568,000 *Total Assets:* £85,962,000
Registered Office: Osprey House, 63 Station Road, Addlestone, Surrey, KT15 2AR
Activities: Activities of production holding companies
Parent: Pandrol Holdings Limited
Officers: Jonathan Baxter, Secretary; Olivier Vincent Antille [1971] Director [French]; Brian Forster [1953] Director

Pandrol Holdings Limited
Incorporated: 15 September 1999
Net Worth: £84,916,000 *Total Assets:* £85,686,000
Registered Office: Osprey House, 63 Station Road, Addlestone, Surrey, KT15 2AR
Activities: Activities of production holding companies
Parent: HRT UK Limited
Officers: Jonathan Baxter, Secretary; Olivier Vincent Antille [1971] Director [French]; Brian Forster [1953] Director

Pandrol International Limited
Incorporated: 14 September 1945 *Employees:* 2
Net Worth: £2,645,000 *Total Assets:* £126,180,000
Registered Office: Osprey House, 63 Station Road, Addlestone, Weybridge, Surrey, KT15 2AR
Activities: Activities of production holding companies
Parent: Pandrol Finance Limited
Officers: Jonathan Baxter, Secretary; Olivier Vincent Antille [1971] Director [French]; Brian Forster [1953] Director

Pandrol Limited
Incorporated: 4 July 1953 *Employees:* 229
Net Worth: £20,706,000 *Total Assets:* £54,439,000
Registered Office: Osprey House, 63 Station Road, Addlestone, Weybridge, Surrey, KT15 2AR
Activities: Manufacture of other fabricated metal products n.e.c.
Parent: Pandrol International Limited
Officers: Jonathan Baxter, Secretary; Olivier Vincent Antille [1971] Director [French]; Stephen John Cox [1961] Director; Brian Forster [1953] Director; Wayne Martin Peacock [1958] Director; Guy Henri Jean Paul Talbourdet [1965] Managing Director [French]

Pangbourne Developments Limited
Incorporated: 21 December 2011
Net Worth: £2,933,000 *Total Assets:* £20,678,000
Registered Office: Gate House, Turnpike Road, High Wycombe, Bucks, HP12 3NR
Activities: Buying and selling of own real estate
Parent: Taylor Wimpey UK Limited
Officers: Katherine Elizabeth Hindmarsh, Secretary; Ingrid Ruth Osborne [1977] Director; Richard Buchanan Smith [1973] Associate Development Director

Panini UK Limited
Incorporated: 3 September 1976 *Employees:* 35
Net Worth: £29,566,988 *Total Assets:* £73,684,416
Registered Office: Brockbourne House, 77 Mount Ephraim, Tunbridge Wells, Kent, TN4 8AR
Activities: Other publishing activities
Major Shareholder: Aldo Hugo Sallustro
Officers: John Peter Harris [1960] Director; Michael Thomas Riddell [1956] Director; Aldo Hugo Sallustro [1945] Director [Italian]

Papa John's (GB) Limited
Incorporated: 20 December 1990 *Employees:* 105
Net Worth: £26,182,000 *Total Assets:* £37,525,000
Registered Office: Papa John's UK & European Campus, 11 Northfield Drive, Northfield, Milton Keynes, Bucks, MK15 0DQ
Activities: Retail sale in non-specialised stores with food, beverages or tobacco predominating
Officers: Joseph Hale Smith [1963] Director/Global Franchisee Sales [American]; Jack Harold Swaysland [1964] Managing Director; Elizabeth Williams [1975] Managing Director

Paradigm (UK) Holding Limited
Incorporated: 20 June 2012 *Employees:* 3
Net Worth: £8,753,018 *Total Assets:* £23,453,904
Registered Office: 3rd Floor, Building C, Dukes Court, Duke Street, Woking, Surrey, GU21 5BH
Activities: Combined office administrative service activities
Parent: Paradigm B.V.
Officers: Ryan Michael Hamlin [1980] Director [American]; Arnaud Laurent [1977] Director/VP Global Accounting [French]; Cherieke Suzette Zunder [1971] Director/Corporate Secretary [Dutch]

Paradigm Commercial PLC
Incorporated: 13 January 1993
Net Worth: £25,791,000 *Total Assets:* £26,445,000
Registered Office: 1 Glory Park Avenue, Wooburn Green, High Wycombe, Bucks, HP10 0DF
Activities: Development of building projects
Parent: Paradigm Homes Charitable Housing Association Limited
Officers: Richard Archer [1973] Director/Chief Risk Advisor; Julian Charles Corbett Ashby [1947] Director; Matthew Roy Bailes [1970] Director/Chief Executive Officer; Mathew George Bishop [1978] Managing Director; Patricia Elizabeth Brandum [1955] Director/Consultant; John William Cross [1953] Director/Consultant; Eva Cullen [1966] Director/Head of Customer Fulfillment Operations [Irish]; Philippa Simone Lowe [1961] Director; Janet Ogundele [1967] HR Director; Peter Anthony Quinn [1957] Director; Philip Ernest Shepley [1973] Director/Chief Operating Officer; John Nicol Simpson [1947] Director

Paragon Treasury PLC
Incorporated: 30 October 2014
Net Worth: £13,000 *Total Assets:* £224,140,000
Registered Office: Case House, 85-89 High Street, Walton on Thames, Surrey, KT12 1DZ
Activities: Financial intermediation not elsewhere classified
Parent: Paragon Asra Housing Ltd
Officers: Marion Hall, Secretary; Stephen David Amos [1957] Director/Retired Banker; David Edgar Hunter [1955] Director; Curtis Mark Juman [1968] Finance Director

Parallel Learning Trust
Incorporated: 11 July 2013 *Employees:* 293
Net Worth: £11,721,000 *Total Assets:* £23,066,000
Registered Office: Suite 1, Baker House, Horsley Road, Bromley, Kent, BR1 3LB
Activities: Primary education
Officers: Richard Francis Pugh, Secretary; Mark Peter Jordan [1977] Director/Chief Executive Officer; Michael Martell [1952] Director/Education Consultant; Ross Alexander Neal [1956] Director/Youth Engagement Manager; Rosemary Newlove [1952] Director/Retired Headteacher; Richard Francis Pugh [1975] Director/Solicitor; Andrea Smith [1969] Director/Parenting Support Worker; Bhaavin Wallia [1993] Director/Management Consultant

Parametric Holdings (UK) Limited
Incorporated: 25 February 1999
Net Worth: £7,148,664 *Total Assets:* £67,224,880
Registered Office: Abbey House, 282 Farnborough Road, Farnborough, Hants, GU14 7NA
Activities: Activities of head offices
Parent: PTC Inc.
Officers: Charles Christopher William Dunn, Secretary; Stephen Generald Bouchard [1968] Director [American]; Charles Christopher William Dunn [1965] Director/Solicitor; Marina Alexandra Stavrinides [1971] Director/Solicitor

Paratus AMC Limited
Incorporated: 6 January 1998 *Employees:* 196
Net Worth: £100,900,000 *Total Assets:* £1,259,399,936
Registered Office: 5 Arlington Square, Downshire Way, Bracknell, Berks, RG12 1WA
Activities: Financial intermediation not elsewhere classified
Parent: Sterling Holdings LP
Officers: Nicola Townsend, Secretary; John Philip de Blocq Van Kuffeler [1949] Director [Dutch]; Nicholas Paul Fegan [1974] Director; Hans Geberbauer [1971] Director [German]; Anthony John Keeble [1970] Finance Director; Christopher Carl Linkas [1969] Director [American]; Dominic Maher [1969] Director/Chief Operating Officer

Parexel International Holding UK Limited
Incorporated: 3 June 2008
Net Worth: £93,048,000 *Total Assets:* £145,184,992
Registered Office: Hart House, Priestley Road, Basingstoke, Hants, RG24 9PU
Activities: Research and experimental development on social sciences and humanities
Parent: Parexel International Corporation Ltd.
Officers: Michael Francis Crowley III, Secretary; Michael Francis Crowley III [1969] Director/Business Executive [American]; Duncan Jamie MacDonald [1968] Director/Chief Executive Officer [British/American]

Parexel International Limited
Incorporated: 29 November 1988 *Employees:* 866
Net Worth: £57,884,000 *Total Assets:* £135,332,992
Registered Office: Hart House, Priestley Road, Basingstoke, Hants, RG24 9PU
Activities: Other research and experimental development on natural sciences and engineering
Parent: Parexel International Holding UK Limited
Officers: Michael Francis Crowley III, Secretary; Michael Francis Crowley III [1969] Director/Business Executive [American]; Duncan Jamie MacDonald [1968] Director/Chief Executive Officer [British/American]

Park Avenue Estates Limited
Incorporated: 11 December 1996 *Employees:* 5
Net Worth: £32,612,928 *Total Assets:* £70,582,160
Registered Office: 99 Western Road, Hove, E Sussex, BN3 1FA
Activities: Other letting and operating of own or leased real estate
Officers: Ghanim Hamza, Secretary/Director; Farzin Sobhanpanah, Secretary/Director; Ann Celina Hamza [1961] Director/Businesswoman; Ghanim Hamza [1957] Director; Catherine Mary Sobhanpanah [1960] Director/Businesswoman; Farzin Sobhanpanah [1957] Director

The Park Federation Academy Trust
Incorporated: 17 July 2012 *Employees:* 798
Net Worth: £56,272,000 *Total Assets:* £67,274,000
Registered Office: Botwell Common Road, Hayes, Middlesex, UB3 1JA
Activities: Primary education
Officers: Elaine Armstrong, Secretary; Jasjit Sohal, Secretary; Simon Neil Carter [1964] Director/Government Servant; Afsheen Chowdhry [1980] Director/Solicitor; Ranisha Dhamu [1973] Director/Corporate Information Governance Officer; Peter John Dollimore [1956] Director/Retired; Anoop Kumar Ghai [1958] Director/Banker; Muralee Nair [1965] Director/Banker; Dr Adel Ben Mohamed Rouz [1965] Director/Business/HR [Tunisian]; Nicola Jane Tranter [1968] Director/Deputy Headteacher; Dr Martin John Young [1960] Director/Executive Headteacher

Park Garage Group PLC
Incorporated: 16 January 1998 *Employees:* 17
Net Worth: £20,167,968 *Total Assets:* £46,549,408
Registered Office: 1-3 Station Approach, Hayes, Bromley, Kent, BR2 7EQ
Activities: Retail sale in non-specialised stores with food, beverages or tobacco predominating
Shareholder: Sunil Tandon
Officers: Balraj Tandon, Secretary; Balraj Tandon [1959] Director/Businessman; Sunil Tandon [1962] Director/Businessman

Park Holidays UK Limited
Incorporated: 19 October 1989 *Employees:* 1,016
Net Worth: £348,848,000 *Total Assets:* £786,558,976
Registered Office: Glovers House, Glovers End, Bexhill on Sea, E Sussex, TN39 5ES
Activities: Holiday centres and villages
Parent: CP Equity Co Ltd
Officers: Alasdair Bell Loch, Secretary/Chartered Accountant; Anthony Norman Clish [1961] Director; Alasdair Bell Loch [1963] Director/Chartered Accountant; Jeffrey Alan Sills [1963] Director; Richard Lewis Ullman [1973] Director

Park Lane Limited
Incorporated: 22 June 1981 *Employees:* 229
Net Worth: £16,140,000 *Total Assets:* £99,669,000
Registered Office: Summit One, Summit Avenue, Farnborough, Hants, GU14 0FB
Activities: Sale of new cars and light motor vehicles
Parent: BMW (UK) Limited
Officers: William Edwin Johnson, Secretary; Christopher John Learmonth [1977] Director; Richard Gavin Price [1967] Director

John Parker & Son Limited
Incorporated: 31 March 1960 *Employees:* 492
Net Worth: £12,254,000 *Total Assets:* £91,812,000
Registered Office: Main Building, Vauxhall Road, Canterbury, Kent, CT1 1HD
Activities: Manufacture of metal structures and parts of structures
Major Shareholder: Peter Guy Parker
Officers: Lisa Sarah Canning, Secretary; Dylan Christopher Alexander [1983] Director; David Guy Cox [1961] Director; Michelle Parker [1963] Director [Irish]; Peter Guy Parker [1960] Director; Sharon Mary Parker [1960] Director

Parker Hannifin (GB) Limited
Incorporated: 17 December 1946
Net Worth: £8,709,000 *Total Assets:* £266,548,992
Registered Office: Parker House, 55 Maylands Avenue, Hemel Hempstead Industrial Estate, Hemel Hempstead, Herts, HP2 4SJ
Activities: Management of real estate on a fee or contract basis
Parent: Alenco (Holdings) Limited
Officers: Graham Mark Ellinor, Secretary; Graham Mark Ellinor [1964] Director/Accountant; James Alan David Elsey [1970] HR Director

Parker Hannifin (Holdings) Limited
Incorporated: 10 February 2000
Net Worth: £22,233,000 *Total Assets:* £22,234,000
Registered Office: Parker House, Maylands Avenue, Hemel Hempstead Industrial Estate, Hemel Hempstead, Herts, HP2 4SJ
Activities: Activities of head offices
Parent: Parker Hannifin Corporation
Officers: Graham Mark Ellinor, Secretary; Graham Mark Ellinor [1964] Director/Accountant; James Alan David Elsey [1970] HR Director

Parker Hannifin 2007 LLP
Incorporated: 23 April 2007
Net Worth: £268,478,016 *Total Assets:* £268,478,016
Registered Office: Parker House, 55 Maylands Avenue, Hemel Hempstead Industrial Estate, Hemel Hempstead, Herts, HP2 4SJ

Parker Hannifin Limited
Incorporated: 7 April 2011 *Employees:* 367
Net Worth: £52,595,000 *Total Assets:* £143,076,000
Registered Office: Parker House, 55 Maylands Avenue, Hemel Hempstead Industrial Estate, Hemel Hempstead, Herts, HP2 4SJ
Activities: Manufacture of fluid power equipment
Parent: Parker Hannifin Corporation
Officers: Graham Mark Ellinor, Secretary; Jane Brogan [1973] Director/Customer Service Manager; Martin Peter Eldridge [1969] Director/General Manager; Graham Mark Ellinor [1964] Director; James Alan David Elsey [1970] HR Director; William Ellard Sheedy [1973] Director/Mechanical Engineer [Irish]

Parker Hannifin Manufacturing (UK) Limited
Incorporated: 3 February 1998 *Employees:* 219
Net Worth: £49,493,000 *Total Assets:* £61,215,000
Registered Office: Parker House, 55 Maylands Avenue, Hemel Hempstead Industrial Estate, Hemel Hempstead, Herts, HP2 4SJ
Activities: Manufacture of fluid power equipment
Parent: Parker Hannifin Industries Limited
Officers: Graham Mark Ellinor, Secretary; Graham Mark Ellinor [1964] Director/Accountant; James Alan David Elsey [1970] HR Director; Harvey Preston [1965] Director/General Manager

Parker Hannifin Manufacturing Limited
Incorporated: 20 June 2003 *Employees:* 1,494
Net Worth: £203,582,000 *Total Assets:* £512,844,000
Registered Office: Parker House, 55 Maylands Avenue, Hemel Hempstead Industrial Estate, Hemel Hempstead, Herts, HP2 4SJ
Activities: Manufacture of fluid power equipment
Parent: Parker Hannifin (GB) Limited
Officers: Graham Mark Ellinor, Secretary; Graham Eric Bielinski-Bradbury [1960] Director/General Manager; Graham Mark Ellinor [1964] Director/Accountant; James Alan David Elsey [1970] HR Director; Kris Robert Holmes [1977] Director/General Manager; Harvey Preston [1965] Director/General Manager; Andrew Spivey [1971] Director/General Manager; Mark Zanna [1975] Director/Group Quality Manager MSGE

Parkside Capital Limited
Incorporated: 1 November 1999 *Employees:* 6
Net Worth: £52,811,752 *Total Assets:* £53,131,352
Registered Office: Mill House, Overbridge Square, Hambridge Lane, Newbury, Berks, RG14 5UX
Activities: Activities of head offices
Shareholders: Ales Ortuzar; Iban Ortuzar; Luz Ortuzar
Officers: Gaizka Andere Ortuzar [1936] Director; Iban Ortuzar [1970] Director/Investment Manager; Richard John Stobart Prosser [1960] Director/Accountant; Generald Stewart Warwick [1958] Director/Accountant; Lorna Zimny [1971] Director/Accountant

Parkview Treasury Services (UK) Limited
Incorporated: 22 October 2007
Net Worth: £241,660,000 *Total Assets:* £1,834,680,960
Registered Office: 1st Floor, Ash House, Littleton Road, Ashford, Middlesex, TW15 1TZ
Activities: Activities of head offices
Parent: United Technologies Holdings Limited
Officers: Lynn Banis, Secretary; Christian Bruno Jean Idczak [1963] Director/Business Executive [French]; James Terence George Laurence [1964] Financial Director; Patricia Catherine Moran [1964] Finance Director [American]; Peter Ross [1964] Finance Director; Louise Kay Thompson [1983] Director/Chartered Management Accountant

Parthenon Entertainment Limited
Incorporated: 19 February 2002 *Employees:* 63
Net Worth: £9,545,000 *Total Assets:* £95,502,000
Registered Office: Grant Way, Isleworth, Middlesex, TW7 5QD
Activities: Television programme distribution activities
Parent: Parthenon Media Group Limited
Officers: Christopher Jon Taylor, Secretary; Karl Holmes [1973] Director/Finance Professional; Colin Robert Jones [1964] Director; Christopher Jon Taylor [1971] Director/Company Secretary

Partnerships in Children's Services Limited
Incorporated: 23 July 2012 *Employees:* 311
Net Worth Deficit: £599,936 *Total Assets:* £22,451,042
Registered Office: Wavendon Tower, Ortensia Drive, Wavendon, Milton Keynes, Bucks, MK17 8LX
Activities: Activities of head offices
Parent: Nutrius UK Bidco Limited
Officers: Jo August [1971] Director; Jonathan David Clark [1977] Director; Venetia Cooper [1974] Director/Chief Financial Officer

Partridge of Hampshire Holdings Limited
Incorporated: 29 March 2017 *Employees:* 143
Net Worth: £4,014,400 *Total Assets:* £44,750,732
Registered Office: Arcadia House, Maritime Walk, Ocean Village, Southampton, SO14 3TL
Activities: Activities of other holding companies n.e.c.
Major Shareholder: Toby Benjamin Raymond Partridge
Officers: Graham Woodrow, Secretary; Toby Benjamin Raymond Partridge [1968] Director; Steven Soper [1951] Director

Partridge of Hampshire Limited
Incorporated: 29 November 2012 *Employees:* 139
Net Worth: £1,624,928 *Total Assets:* £40,427,520
Registered Office: Arcadia House, Maritime Walk, Ocean Village, Southampton, SO14 3TL
Activities: Sale of new cars and light motor vehicles
Major Shareholder: Toby Partridge
Officers: Toby Partridge, Secretary; Toby Benjamin Raymond Partridge [1968] Director; Steven Soper [1951] Director

Patek Philippe Salon Limited
Incorporated: 25 October 2005 *Employees:* 24
Net Worth: £27,598,504 *Total Assets:* £35,443,052
Registered Office: 55 Station Road, Beaconsfield, Bucks, HP9 1QL
Activities: Other business support service activities n.e.c.
Parent: Rhone Products (UK) Limited
Officers: Andrew Mark Hearn, Secretary; Andrew Mark Hearn [1959] Director; Claude Peny [1951] Director [Belgian]

Pathways Care Group Limited
Incorporated: 24 July 1997 *Employees:* 523
Net Worth Deficit: £2,074,000 *Total Assets:* £34,873,000
Registered Office: Minton Place, Victoria Street, Windsor, Berks, SL4 1EG
Activities: Residential care activities for learning difficulties, mental health and substance abuse
Parent: Salutem LD Bidco Limited
Officers: John Steven Godden [1965] Director; Kenneth James Gribben Hillen [1956] Director; Paul Raymond Lawes [1973] Director/Chief Finance Officer

Patrolmake Limited
Incorporated: 29 February 1996 *Employees:* 2
Net Worth: £13,164,908 *Total Assets:* £38,229,480
Registered Office: Corus House, 1 Auckland Park, Milton Keynes, Bucks, MK1 1BU
Activities: Hotels and similar accommodation
Parent: Corus Hotels Limited
Officers: Khurram Mohmand, Secretary; Andrew Khoo [1972] Director [Australian]; Yet King Loy [1946] Director [Canadian]; Khurram Mohmand [1972] Director/Accountant

Paultons Park Limited
Incorporated: 19 June 1986 *Employees:* 530
Net Worth: £16,389,620 *Total Assets:* £21,573,410
Registered Office: Paultons Park, Ower, Romsey, Hants, SO51 6AL
Activities: Other amusement and recreation activities n.e.c.
Parent: Heronswood Holdings Ltd.
Officers: Sara Jane Mancey, Secretary; Stephen John Lorton [1960] Director; James William Mancey [1992] Operations Director; Richard William Mancey [1960] Director/Leisure Park Proprietor; Sara Jane Mancey [1961] Director/Leisure Park Proprietor

Paydens Group Holdings Limited
Incorporated: 24 March 2010 *Employees:* 1,887
Net Worth: £44,702,960 *Total Assets:* £125,737,032
Registered Office: Parkwood, Sutton Road, Maidstone, Kent, ME15 9NE
Activities: Dispensing chemist in specialised stores
Major Shareholder: Dennis Charles Pay
Officers: John Patrick McConville [1959] Director; Alexander George Pay [1984] Managing Director; Dennis Charles Pay [1942] Director/Pharmacist; Rosemary Elizabeth Ann Pay [1949] Director

Paydens Holdings Limited
Incorporated: 24 March 2010 *Employees:* 1,556
Net Worth: £41,350,832 *Total Assets:* £128,977,896
Registered Office: Parkwood, Sutton Road, Maidstone, Kent, ME15 9NE
Activities: Dispensing chemist in specialised stores
Parent: Paydens Group Holdings Limited
Officers: John Patrick McConville [1959] Director; Alexander George Pay [1984] Managing Director; Dennis Charles Pay [1942] Director/Pharmacist

Paydens Limited
Incorporated: 26 November 1956 *Employees:* 1,556
Net Worth: £71,280,720 *Total Assets:* £148,709,936
Registered Office: Parkwood, Sutton Road, Maidstone, Kent, ME15 9NE
Activities: Dispensing chemist in specialised stores
Parent: Paydens Holdings Limited
Officers: John Patrick McConville [1959] Director/Pharmacist; Alexander George Pay [1984] Managing Director; Dennis Charles Pay [1942] Director

Paymaster (1836) Limited
Incorporated: 13 September 1996 *Employees:* 789
Net Worth: £68,100,000 *Total Assets:* £114,300,000
Registered Office: Sutherland House, Russell Way, Crawley, W Sussex, RH10 1UH
Activities: Other business support service activities n.e.c.
Parent: Equiniti Services Limited
Officers: Ceri Joanne Charles Young, Secretary; Anthony James Dear [1977] Finance Director; Guy Richard Wakeley [1970] Director; Duncan Stuart Watson [1970] Director

Paymentshield Services Limited
Incorporated: 8 April 2016
Net Worth: £6,697,197 *Total Assets:* £34,345,000
Registered Office: Towergate House, Eclipse Park, Sittingbourne Road, Maidstone, Kent, ME14 3EN
Activities: Other business support service activities n.e.c.
Parent: Lunar 101 Limited
Officers: Dean Clarke, Secretary; Antonios Erotocritou [1971] Director/Deputy CFO [Cypriot]; David Christopher Ross [1969] Director [Irish]

PB Bidco Limited
Incorporated: 1 July 2013
Net Worth: £34,403,000 *Total Assets:* £115,077,000
Registered Office: Two Bridges, Guildford Street, Chertsey, Surrey, KT16 9AU
Activities: Business and domestic software development
Officers: Jason Phillip Conley [1975] Finance Director [American]; Robert Christopher Crisci [1975] Finance Director [American]; Robin Tarquinn Morris-Weston [1970] Director; John Kenneth Stipancich [1968] Director/Vice President, General Counsel and Secretary [American]

PB Holdco Limited
Incorporated: 5 July 2013
Net Worth: £41,625,000 *Total Assets:* £114,291,000
Registered Office: Two Bridges, Guildford Street, Chertsey, Surrey, KT19 9AU
Activities: Business and domestic software development
Officers: Jason Phillip Conley [1975] Finance Director [American]; Robert Christopher Crisci [1975] Finance Director [American]; Robin Tarquinn Morris-Weston [1970] Director; John Kenneth Stipancich [1968] Director/Vice President, General Counsel and Secretary [American]

PB Midco Limited
Incorporated: 1 July 2013 *Employees:* 4
Net Worth: £105,528,000 *Total Assets:* £114,290,000
Registered Office: Two Bridges, Guildford Street, Chertsey, Surrey, KT16 9AU
Activities: Business and domestic software development
Officers: Jason Phillip Conley [1975] Finance Director [American]; Robert Christopher Crisci [1975] Finance Director [American]; Robin Tarquinn Morris-Weston [1970] Director; John Kenneth Stipancich [1968] Director/Vice President, General Counsel and Secretary [American]

PB Topco Limited
Incorporated: 1 July 2013 *Employees:* 4
Net Worth: £128,494,000 *Total Assets:* £131,370,000
Registered Office: Two Bridges, Guildford Street, Chertsey, Surrey, KT16 9AU
Activities: Business and domestic software development
Officers: Jason Phillip Conley [1975] Finance Director [American]; Robert Christopher Crisci [1975] Finance Director [American]; Robin Tarquinn Morris-Weston [1970] Director; John Kenneth Stipancich [1968] Director/Vice President, General Counsel and Secretary [American]

PCL Bidco Limited
Incorporated: 29 October 2012
Net Worth Deficit: £50,806,000 *Total Assets:* £109,900,000
Registered Office: Grove House, Guildford Road, Leatherhead, Surrey, KT22 9DF
Activities: Activities of head offices
Parent: PCL Holdco Limited
Officers: Christopher Michael Higgs, Secretary; Christopher Michael Higgs [1956] Finance Director; Uwe Nickel [1958] Director/Chief Executive Officer [German]; Duncan Paul Stonehouse [1970] Operations Director

PCL Holdco Limited
Incorporated: 29 October 2012
Net Worth: £68,861,000 *Total Assets:* £68,861,000
Registered Office: Grove House, Guildford Road, Leatherhead, Surrey, KT22 9DF
Activities: Activities of head offices
Parent: HCS Group GmbH
Officers: Christopher Michael Higgs, Secretary; Christopher Michael Higgs [1956] Finance Director; Uwe Nickel [1958] Director/Chief Executive Officer [German]; Duncan Paul Stonehouse [1970] Operations Director

PCL Transport 24/7 Limited
Incorporated: 11 February 2009 *Employees:* 976
Net Worth: £3,369,000 *Total Assets:* £22,939,000
Registered Office: 814 Leigh Road, Slough, SL1 4BD
Activities: Freight transport by road
Parent: Bid Corporation Limited
Officers: Stephen David Bender, Secretary; Grant Leslie Cox [1967] Director [South African]; Paul Anthony Winter [1964] Director

PDC Brands UK Limited
Incorporated: 22 March 2016 *Employees:* 96
Net Worth: £3,490,904 *Total Assets:* £48,029,652
Registered Office: Ventura House, Bullsbrook Road, Hayes, Middlesex, UB4 0UJ
Activities: Other service activities n.e.c.
Officers: James Rogers [1966] Director/Chief Operating Officer [American]; James Stammer [1974] Director/President & Chief Executive Officer, PDC Brands [American]; Mark Alexander Wood [1973] Director

PEAC (UK) Limited
Incorporated: 7 August 1995 *Employees:* 48
Previous: CIT Vendor Finance (UK) Limited
Net Worth: £110,273,000 *Total Assets:* £367,700,000
Registered Office: Inspired, Easthampstead Road, Bracknell, Berks, RG12 1YQ
Activities: Financial leasing
Parent: PEAC Holdings (UK) Limited
Officers: Phillip Venner, Secretary; Jonathan Ashley [1966] Managing Director [American]; Stephen Charlton [1958] Director/Accountant; John Edward Phillipou [1972] Director; Justin Staadecker [1968] Managing Director

PEAC Holdings (UK) Limited
Incorporated: 15 September 2015
Net Worth Deficit: £10,264,000 *Total Assets:* £110,077,000
Registered Office: Inspired, Easthampstead Road, Bracknell, Berks, RG12 1YQ
Activities: Activities of financial services holding companies
Officers: Philip Jonathan Venner, Secretary; Jonathan Ashley [1966] Managing Director [American]; Justin Staadecker [1968] Managing Director

Pearl River Delta Investments Limited
Incorporated: 20 December 2002
Net Worth: £98,322,296 *Total Assets:* £98,754,248
Registered Office: Chertsey Road, Sunbury on Thames, Middlesex, TW16 7BP
Activities: Activities of head offices
Parent: BP Global Investments Limited
Officers: David William Knipe [1974] Director/Oil Company Executive

The Pegasus Academy Trust
Incorporated: 24 February 2011 *Employees:* 332
Net Worth: £31,267,000 *Total Assets:* £35,930,000
Registered Office: Whitehorse Manor School, Brigstock Road, Thornton Heath, Surrey, CR7 7JN
Activities: Primary education
Officers: Josephine Mary Ridge, Secretary; Shelley Davies [1972] Director/Educationalist; Fiona Fearon [1980] Director/HR Consultant; Gary Griffin [1959] Director/Retired School Teacher; Richard Henry Hill [1948] Director; Sylvia Ann McNamara [1953] Director/Education Consultant; Ian Patterson [1956] Director/Retired; Nina Pogossova [1981] Managing Director; Matthew Jolyon Roberts [1965] Director/Headteacher; Lynne Diane Sampson [1964] Director/Headteacher; Kevin Paul Smith [1959] Director/Fire Officer

Pegasus Life Limited
Incorporated: 19 September 2012 *Employees:* 107
Net Worth: £44,323,000 *Total Assets:* £447,932,000
Registered Office: Unit 3 Royal Court, Church Green Close, Kings Worthy, Winchester, Hants, SO23 7TW
Activities: Buying and selling of own real estate
Parent: Oaktree Capital Group, LLC
Officers: Marc Dafydd Evans, Secretary; Christopher Paul Compton-Goddard [1963] Director; Antonin Demargerie [1975] Director/Chief Executive [French]; Mark Davies Dickinson [1968] Director; Alison Endemano [1970] Director; Stefano Mazzoli [1980] Director/Investment Manager [Italian]; Dion Joseph Petri [1968] Director; Aletheia Zoe Powell [1977] Director; David Simpson [1955] Director; Ian Calvert Sutcliffe [1959] Director; Ian Jens Trinder [1973] Director; James Peter Van Steenkiste [1978] Director/Investment Manager [American/British]

Pegasuslife Development Limited
Incorporated: 4 December 2014 *Employees:* 5
Net Worth Deficit: £11,080,000 *Total Assets:* £364,956,992
Registered Office: Royal Court, Church Green Close, Kings Worthy, Winchester, Hants, SO23 7TW
Activities: Buying and selling of own real estate
Parent: PegasusLife Holdings Limited
Officers: Marc Dafydd Evans, Secretary; Antonin Demargerie [1975] Director/Chief Executive [French]; Michael John Gill [1964] Director; Dion Joseph Petri [1968] Director; Ian Jens Trinder [1973] Director

Pegasystems Limited
Incorporated: 1 January 1994 *Employees:* 294
Net Worth: £23,395,224 *Total Assets:* £151,736,368
Registered Office: 3rd Floor, 23 Forbury Road, Reading, Berks, RG1 3JH
Activities: Information technology consultancy activities
Officers: Janet Anne Mesrobian, Secretary; Efstathios Kouninis [1961] Director/Vice President [American]; Douglas Kra [1962] Director [American]; Janet Mesrobian [1963] Director/Lawyer [American]; David Wells [1965] Managing Director

Pelham Capital Real Estate Limited
Incorporated: 26 August 2016 *Employees:* 9
Net Worth: £9,363,866 *Total Assets:* £30,717,572
Registered Office: Hillside House, 19-28 Allcroft Road, Reading, Berks, RG1 5DJ
Activities: Other letting and operating of own or leased real estate
Major Shareholder: Ross James Turner
Officers: Hamant Lad, Secretary; Lloyd Jonathan Turner [1973] Director/Real Estate Management; Ross James Turner [1977] Director/Fund Manager

Pennyhill Park Limited
Incorporated: 29 July 1982 *Employees:* 322
Net Worth: £23,714,998 *Total Assets:* £45,962,144
Registered Office: Executive Office, Pennyhill Park Hotel & Spa, Bagshot, Surrey, GU19 5EU
Activities: Hotels and similar accommodation
Parent: The Manor House Hotel (Castle Combe) Ltd
Officers: Christine Linda Davies, Secretary; Daniel Leopoldo Enrico Pecorelli [1966] Director/Hotelier; Penelope Pecorelli [1941] Director; Julian Tomlin [1965] Operations Director

The Penspen Group Limited
Incorporated: 27 May 1970
Net Worth: £5,002,000 *Total Assets:* £67,325,000
Registered Office: 3 Water Lane, Richmond, Surrey, TW9 1TJ
Activities: Activities of head offices
Parent: Dar Al-Handasah (UK) Limited
Officers: Susan Jane McDonald, Secretary; Dany Aoun [1970] Director [Lebanese]; Gillian Anne Empringham [1974] Director/HR; Peter Bernard O'Sullivan [1969] Director/Chief Executive [Irish]; Talal Shair [1967] Director/Executive [Jordanian]

Penspen Limited
Incorporated: 23 May 1957 *Employees:* 249
Net Worth: £4,332,000 *Total Assets:* £63,387,000
Registered Office: 3 Water Lane, Richmond, Surrey, TW9 1TJ
Activities: Engineering related scientific and technical consulting activities
Parent: The Penspen Group Limited
Officers: Susan Jane McDonald, Secretary; Neale Carter [1968] Director/Business Development; Nigel St John Thomas Curson [1961] Director/Engineer; Gillian Anne Empringham [1974] HR Director; Peter Bernard O'Sullivan [1969] Director/Chief Executive [Irish]; Timothy Webber [1964] Finance Director

Pentagon Freight Services PLC
Incorporated: 6 March 1974 *Employees:* 126
Net Worth: £29,182,128 *Total Assets:* £39,823,044
Registered Office: Pentagon House, Unit 1.02 Crayfields Industrial Estate, Main Road, Orpington, Kent, BR5 3HP
Activities: Other transportation support activities
Parent: Pentagon Holdings Limited
Officers: Kim Lesley Ochiltree, Secretary; Kim Lesley Ochiltree [1969] Finance Director; Ashley Paul Taylor [1972] Director [Australian]

Pentagon Holdings Limited
Incorporated: 30 October 2000 *Employees:* 728
Net Worth: £44,689,576 *Total Assets:* £85,540,848
Registered Office: Unit 1.02, Crayfield Industrial Estate, Main Road, Orpington, Kent, BR5 3HP
Activities: Activities of other holding companies n.e.c.
Officers: Clare Madeleine Smith [1938] Director; Ashley Paul Taylor [1972] Director [Australian]

Pentair UK Holdings Limited
Incorporated: 10 January 2014
Net Worth: £133,198,552 *Total Assets:* £133,198,552
Registered Office: Regal House, 70 London Road, Twickenham, Middlesex, TW1 3QS
Activities: Activities of head offices
Parent: Pentair PLC
Officers: Grant William O'Grady [1970] Director [Australian]; Andrew Gary Smyth [1976] Director/Tax Planning; Henning Wolfgang Wistorf [1982] Director [German]

Pentland Homes (Holdings) Limited
Incorporated: 6 September 2007 *Employees:* 44
Net Worth: £21,920,932 *Total Assets:* £42,882,248
Registered Office: The Estate Office, Canterbury Road, Etchinghill, Folkestone, Kent, CT18 8FA
Activities: Development of building projects
Shareholders: Peter Nettlam Tory; James Nettlam Tory
Officers: Steven Robert Coates, Secretary; Steven Robert Coates [1957] Finance Director; James Nettlam Tory [1973] Director; Peter Nettlam Tory [1939] Director

Pentland Homes Limited
Incorporated: 18 November 1971 *Employees:* 44
Net Worth: £21,720,086 *Total Assets:* £42,573,540
Registered Office: The Estate Office, Canterbury Road, Etchinghill, Folkestone, Kent, CT18 8FA
Activities: Construction of domestic buildings
Officers: Steven Robert Coates, Secretary; Timothy Michael Giles Barton [1960] Director; David Johnathan Callister [1973] Director/Golf Professional; Steven Robert Coates [1957] Finance Director; Daren Blake Eagle [1973] Build Director; Ian James Hardman [1961] Director; Martin John Hart [1959] Director/Residential Developer; Anthony Robert Martin [1946] Director/Farmer; Julia Ellen Price [1950] Sales Marketing Director; James Nettlam Tory [1973] Director; Peter Nettlam Tory [1939] Director

People Against Dirty Holdings Limited
Incorporated: 17 November 2015 *Employees:* 406
Net Worth: £117,970,552 *Total Assets:* £232,747,920
Registered Office: The Ministry of Clean, 1 Eton Street, Richmond, Surrey, TW9 1AG
Activities: Activities of production holding companies
Officers: Brian Patrick Tippett, Secretary; Timothy Earl Bailey [1962] Director/Executive VP [American]; Audrey Sue Ditter [1962] Director/Senior Vice President [American]

Perbury (Developments) Limited
Incorporated: 23 August 1962 *Employees:* 5
Net Worth: £3,834,824 *Total Assets:* £20,030,540
Registered Office: 3 West Links, Tollgate, Chandler's Ford, Eastleigh, Hants, SO53 3TG
Activities: Construction of domestic buildings
Parent: Perbury Limited
Officers: Ian Reginald Permain, Secretary; Nicholas John Chase [1949] Director/Chartered Accountant; Michael O'Brien [1966] Director; Barry John Permain [1949] Director/Builder; Ian Reginald Permain [1952] Director/Builder

Perceptive Eclinical Limited
Incorporated: 17 October 1996 *Employees:* 167
Net Worth: £36,137,000 *Total Assets:* £102,702,000
Registered Office: Hart House, Priestley Road, Basingstoke, Hants, RG24 9PU
Activities: Data processing, hosting and related activities
Parent: Clinphone Limited
Officers: Michael Francis Crowley III, Secretary; Michael Francis Crowley III [1969] Director/Business Executive [American]; Duncan Jamie MacDonald [1968] Director/Chief Executive Officer [British/American]

Perceptive Informatics UK Limited
Incorporated: 27 November 1998 *Employees:* 45
Net Worth Deficit: £7,241,000 *Total Assets:* £33,534,000
Registered Office: Hart House, Priestley Road, Basingstoke, Hants, RG24 9PU
Activities: Information technology consultancy activities
Parent: Perceptive Eclinical Limited
Officers: Michael Francis Crowley III, Secretary; Michael Francis Crowley III [1969] Director/Business Executive [American]; Duncan Jamie MacDonald [1968] Director/Chief Executive Officer [British/American]

Perform Group Financing PLC
Incorporated: 17 July 2015
Net Worth Deficit: £406,000 *Total Assets:* £205,448,000
Registered Office: Hanover House, Plane Tree Crescent, Feltham, Middlesex, TW13 7BZ
Activities: Other professional, scientific and technical activities n.e.c.
Parent: Perform Sports Media Limited
Officers: Benedict Luke Barlow, Secretary; Stuart Joel Epstein [1963] Director [American]; Paul Oszkar David Morton [1979] Director

Perform Group Limited
Incorporated: 25 July 2007 *Employees:* 2,445
Previous: Perform Group PLC
Net Worth Deficit: £232,350,000 *Total Assets:* £892,328,000
Registered Office: Hanover House, Plane Tree Crescent, Feltham, Middlesex, TW13 7BZ
Activities: Other professional, scientific and technical activities n.e.c.
Parent: AI Perform Holdings LLP
Officers: Lincoln Eduardo Benet [1963] Director [American]; Simon Cristofer Denyer [1974] Director; Stuart Joel Epstein [1963] Director [American]; John Mark Gleasure [1970] Director; Herman Siegfried Jorg Mohaupt [1966] Director/Investment Executive [German]; Kiyoshi Nakamura [1959] Director/Businessman [Japanese]; John Skipper [1955] Director/Executive Chairman [American]; Paul Ashton Walker [1957] Director

Perform Investment Limited
Incorporated: 8 July 2015
Net Worth Deficit: £343,655,008 *Total Assets:* £464,953,984
Registered Office: Hanover House, Plane Tree Crescent, Feltham, Middlesex, TW13 7BZ
Activities: Other professional, scientific and technical activities n.e.c.
Parent: Perform Media Channels Ltd
Officers: Paul Oszkar David Morton [1979] Director; James David Rushton [1978] Director

Perform Media Channels Ltd
Incorporated: 6 December 2005
Net Worth Deficit: £34,189,000 *Total Assets:* £369,636,992
Registered Office: Hanover House, Plane Tree Crescent, Feltham, Middlesex, TW13 7BZ
Activities: Other professional, scientific and technical activities n.e.c.
Parent: Perform Media Services Ltd
Officers: Simon Cristofer Denyer [1974] Director/Sports Marketing; Paul Oszkar David Morton [1979] Director

Perform Media Sales Ltd
Incorporated: 23 June 2004
Net Worth Deficit: £19,947,000 *Total Assets:* £114,639,000
Registered Office: Sussex House, Plane Tree Crescent, Feltham, Middlesex, TW13 7HE
Activities: Media representation services
Parent: Perform Media Services Ltd
Officers: Simon Cristofer Denyer [1974] Director/Sports Marketing; Paul Oszkar David Morton [1979] Director

Perform Media Services Ltd
Incorporated: 29 August 1997 *Employees:* 947
Net Worth: £25,153,000 *Total Assets:* £360,615,008
Registered Office: Hanover House, Plane Tree Crescent, Feltham, Middlesex, TW13 7BZ
Activities: Other professional, scientific and technical activities n.e.c.
Parent: Perform Sports Media Limited
Officers: Simon Cristofer Denyer [1974] Director/Sports Marketing; Paul Oszkar David Morton [1979] Director

Perform Sporting News Limited
Incorporated: 1 March 2013
Net Worth Deficit: £14,342,510 *Total Assets:* £36,441,864
Registered Office: Sussex House, Plane Tree Crescent, Feltham, Middlesex, TW13 7HE
Activities: Other professional, scientific and technical activities n.e.c.
Parent: Perform Media Channels Ltd
Officers: David Baddeley [1983] Financial Director; Juan Carlos Delgado Vesga [1978] Managing Director [Colombian]; Simon Cristofer Denyer [1974] Director

Perform Sports Media Limited
Incorporated: 17 July 2015
Net Worth: £348,784,000 *Total Assets:* £595,744,000
Registered Office: Hanover House, Plane Tree Crescent, Feltham, Middlesex, TW13 7BZ
Activities: Other professional, scientific and technical activities n.e.c.
Parent: Perform Group Limited
Officers: Paul Oszkar David Morton [1979] Director

Perkinelmer (UK) Holdings Limited
Incorporated: 23 April 1999
Net Worth: £20,844,000 *Total Assets:* £82,093,000
Registered Office: Chalfont Road, Seer Green, Beaconsfield, Bucks, HP9 2FX
Activities: Activities of head offices
Officers: Andrew John Crook, Secretary; Andrew John Crook [1959] Director/Manager; John Leo Healy [1960] Director/Associate General Counsel [American]

Perkinelmer LAS (UK) Limited
Incorporated: 30 April 1999 *Employees:* 151
Net Worth: £18,978,000 *Total Assets:* £26,261,000
Registered Office: Chalfont Road, Seer Green, Beaconsfield, Bucks, HP9 2FX
Activities: Other professional, scientific and technical activities n.e.c.
Officers: Andrew John Crook, Secretary; Andrew John Crook [1959] Director/Manager; John Leo Healy [1960] Director/Associate General Counsel [American]

Perkinelmer Life Sciences International Holdings
Incorporated: 16 April 2002
Net Worth: £4,085,000 *Total Assets:* £72,018,000
Registered Office: Chalfont Road, Seer Green, Beaconsfield, Bucks, HP9 2FX
Activities: Activities of other holding companies n.e.c.
Officers: Andrew John Crook, Secretary; Andrew John Crook [1959] Director/Manager; John Leo Healy [1960] Director/Associate General Counsel [American]

Perkinelmer Limited
Incorporated: 23 April 1999 *Employees:* 162
Net Worth: £54,425,000 *Total Assets:* £60,081,000
Registered Office: Chalfont Road, Seer Green, Beaconsfield, Bucks, HP9 2FX
Activities: Other manufacturing n.e.c.
Officers: Andrew John Crook, Secretary; Andrew John Crook [1959] Director/Manager; John Leo Healy [1960] Director/Associate General Counsel [American]

Perpetual Income and Growth Investment Trust PLC
Incorporated: 2 February 1996
Net Worth: £923,929,024 *Total Assets:* £1,056,697,024
Registered Office: Perpetual Park, Perpetual Park Drive, Henley on Thames, Oxon, RG9 1HH
Activities: Activities of investment trusts
Officers: Michael Warren Balfour [1960] Director; Vivian Paul Bazalgette [1951] Director/Retired Investment Manager; Victoria Susan Cochrane [1956] Director; Alan James Giles [1954] Director; Richard George Laing [1954] Director; Robert John Yerbury [1946] Director

Perpetual Limited
Incorporated: 12 March 1973
Net Worth: £24,154,508 *Total Assets:* £29,713,284
Registered Office: Perpetual Park, Perpetual Park Drive, Henley on Thames, Oxon, RG9 1HH
Activities: Activities of other holding companies n.e.c.
Parent: Invesco UK Holdings Limited
Officers: Amanda Evans, Secretary; Graeme John Proudfoot [1964] Director/Solicitor; Alan John Trotter [1968] Finance Director

Personal Group Holdings PLC
Incorporated: 7 May 1996 *Employees:* 215
Net Worth: £33,756,000 *Total Assets:* £49,568,000
Registered Office: John Ormond House, 899 Silbury Boulevard, Milton Keynes, Bucks, MK9 3XL
Activities: Activities of head offices
Officers: Sarah Anne Mace, Secretary; Michael Ian Dugdale [1962] Director/Chief Financial Officer; Robert Michael Head [1958] Director; Andrew George Lothian [1971] Director/Sales Manager; Deborah Karen Rees-Frost [1966] Director; Kenneth William Rooney [1950] Director; Mark William Scanlon [1968] Director [Irish]; Mark Winlow [1962] Director

Personal Group Limited
Incorporated: 30 January 2015
Net Worth: £22,375,000 *Total Assets:* £22,585,000
Registered Office: John Ormond House, 899 Silbury Boulevard, Milton Keynes, Bucks, MK9 3XL
Activities: Activities of head offices
Parent: Personal Group Holdings PLC
Officers: Sarah Anne Mace, Secretary; Michael Ian Dugdale [1962] Director/Chief Financial Officer; Robert Michael Head [1958] Director; Andrew George Lothian [1971] Director/Sales Manager; Deborah Karen Rees-Frost [1966] Director; Kenneth William Rooney [1950] Director; Mark William Scanlon [1968] Director [Irish]; Mark Winlow [1962] Director

Pet Plan Limited
Incorporated: 22 October 1976
Net Worth: £96,948,000 *Total Assets:* £97,120,000
Registered Office: 57 Ladymead, Guildford, Surrey, GU1 1DB
Activities: Non-life insurance
Parent: Allianz Insurance PLC
Officers: Robin Christian Jack-Kee, Secretary; Gary Edward Davess [1963] Director, Speciality; Jonathan Mark Dye [1966] Director/Chief Executive; Simon Cavendish McGinn [1970] Director/General Manager Commercial & Personal

Petco Trading (UK) Limited
Incorporated: 11 September 2008 *Employees:* 15
Net Worth: £32,146,588 *Total Assets:* £205,126,992
Registered Office: 1 Blake Mews, Richmond upon Thames, Surrey, TW9 3GA
Activities: Other business support service activities n.e.c.
Officers: Alan Michael Jones, Secretary; Ahmad Hakimi Bin Muhammad Radzi [1973] Director/Head of Finance & Accounts [Malaysian]; Shamsul Bahari Salleh [1966] Director [Malaysian]; Emry Mohd Tamrin [1970] Director [Malaysian]

Peter Press Limited
Incorporated: 25 August 1971 *Employees:* 203
Net Worth: £13,913,000 *Total Assets:* £24,468,000
Registered Office: 1st Floor, Chilworth Point, Chilworth Road, Southampton, SO16 7JQ
Activities: Management consultancy activities other than financial management
Major Shareholder: Peter Granville Fowler
Officers: Peter Granville Fowler [1938] Director; Rory James Fowler [1971] Director

Peter Waddell Holdco Limited
Incorporated: 15 September 2016 *Employees:* 222
Net Worth: £61,169,344 *Total Assets:* £95,383,856
Registered Office: The Showroom, Lakeside Services, Sturry Road, Canterbury, Kent, CT1 1DS
Activities: Activities of head offices
Major Shareholder: Peter Jackson Waddell
Officers: Peter Jackson Waddell [1966] Director

Peterborough (Progress Health) Holdings Limited
Incorporated: 15 January 2007
Net Worth Deficit: £57,614,000 *Total Assets:* £415,440,992
Registered Office: 8 White Oak Square, London Road, Swanley, Kent, BR8 7AG
Activities: Activities of construction holding companies
Shareholders: JLIF Holdings (Peterborough Hospital) Limited; Peterborough Hospital Investments Limited
Officers: Andrew Brian Deacon [1980] Portfolio Director; Carl Harvey Dix [1966] Operations Director; Julian Denzil Sutcliffe [1968] Life Cycle Asset Director; Mark Christopher Wayment [1958] Director

Peterborough (Progress Health) Nominee Limited
Incorporated: 15 January 2007
Total Assets: £27,749,000
Registered Office: 8 White Oak Square, London Road, Swanley, Kent, BR8 7AG
Activities: Activities of construction holding companies
Parent: Peterborough (Progress Health) Holdings Limited
Officers: Andrew Brian Deacon [1980] Portfolio Director; Carl Harvey Dix [1966] Operations Director; Julian Denzil Sutcliffe [1968] Life Cycle Asset Director; Mark Christopher Wayment [1958] Director

Peterborough (Progress Health) PLC
Incorporated: 16 January 2007
Net Worth Deficit: £57,614,000 *Total Assets:* £415,440,992
Registered Office: 8 White Oak Square, London Road, Swanley, Kent, BR8 7AG
Activities: Development of building projects
Parent: Peterborough (Progress Health) Holdings Limited
Officers: Andrew Brian Deacon [1980] Portfolio Director; Carl Harvey Dix [1966] Operations Director; Anthony Robert Faulkner [1973] Director; Julian Denzil Sutcliffe [1968] Life Cycle Asset Director; Mark Christopher Wayment [1958] Director

The Petersham Hotel Limited
Incorporated: 19 November 1987 *Employees:* 320
Net Worth: £14,470,878 *Total Assets:* £28,215,508
Registered Office: Nightingale Lane, Richmond, Surrey, TW10 6UZ
Activities: Hotels and similar accommodation
Officers: Greville Richard Hugh Dare, Secretary/Hotel Ownership; Greville Richard Hugh Dare [1963] Director/Hotelier; Luana Carol Luchterhand [1961] Director/Interior Designer

Petrofac Engineering Limited
Incorporated: 30 May 1991 *Employees:* 2
Net Worth: £34,019,000 *Total Assets:* £37,749,000
Registered Office: Brook House, 88-100 Chertsey Road, Woking, Surrey, GU21 5BJ
Activities: Other business support service activities n.e.c.
Parent: Petrofac UK Holdings Limited
Officers: Mohammed Usman Darr [1968] Director; Robert Stephen McKnight [1964] Director; Diane Stephen [1969] Director

Petroleum Geo-Services (UK) Limited
Incorporated: 23 November 1993
Net Worth: £96,148,000 *Total Assets:* £130,185,000
Registered Office: 4 The Heights, Brooklands, Weybridge, Surrey, KT13 0NY
Activities: Support activities for petroleum and natural gas mining
Parent: Petroleum Geo-Services ASA
Officers: Gottfred Langseth [1966] Director [Norwegian]; Rune Olav Pedersen [1970] Director [Norwegian]; Christin Steen Nilsen [1953] Director/VP Chief Accountant [Norwegian]

PFC Property Ltd
Incorporated: 15 August 2017 *Employees:* 3
Net Worth: £5,508,977 *Total Assets:* £103,663,744
Registered Office: 8 Packhorse Road, Gerrards Cross, Bucks, SL9 7QE
Activities: Other letting and operating of own or leased real estate
Shareholders: Prowting 1968 Trustee One Limited; Prowting 1968 Trustee Two Limited; Prowting 1987 Trustee One Limited; Prowting 1987 Trustee Two Limited
Officers: Barry Peter Amos-Yeo [1980] Director; Sonya Lorraine Richards [1969] Director/Accountant; Wendy Jane Trott [1966] Director

Pfizer Consumer Healthcare Limited
Incorporated: 6 November 1913
Net Worth: £221,754,000 *Total Assets:* £256,190,000
Registered Office: Pfizer, Ramsgate Road, Sandwich, Kent, CT13 9NJ
Activities: Wholesale of pharmaceutical goods
Parent: Pfizer Inc
Officers: Jacqueline Ann Mount, Secretary; Mark Wayne Davidson [1968] Director [Cypriot]; Ian Eric Franklin [1965] Director; Denise Jean Harnett [1964] Director; Jacqueline Ann Mount [1963] Director; Hendrikus Hermannus Nordkamp [1969] UK Managing Director, Pfizer [Dutch]; Edwin James Pearson [1974] Director/Solicitor; Paul Rose [1963] Director [Australian]

Pfizer Limited
Incorporated: 27 November 1953 *Employees:* 2,557
Net Worth: £777,881,984 *Total Assets:* £1,879,758,976
Registered Office: Pfizer Limited, Ramsgate Road, Sandwich, Kent, CT13 9NJ
Activities: Wholesale of pharmaceutical goods
Parent: Pfizer Inc
Officers: Jacqueline Ann Mount, Secretary; Ian Eric Franklin [1965] Director; Denise Jean Harnett [1964] Director; Hendrikus Hermannus Nordkamp [1969] UK Managing Director, Pfizer [Dutch]; Ben Osborn [1977] Director; Edwin James Pearson [1974] Director/Solicitor; Dr Berkeley Simon Phillips [1969] Director; Paul Rose [1963] Director [Australian]; Colin Malcolm Seller [1963] Director; Doctor Julian Keith Thompson [1960] Director/Doctor

PFU (EMEA) Limited
Incorporated: 7 August 1981 *Employees:* 107
Previous: PFU Imaging Solutions Europe Limited
Net Worth: £34,858,572 *Total Assets:* £63,459,240
Registered Office: Hayes Park Central, Hayes End Road, Hayes, Middlesex, UB4 8FE
Activities: Wholesale of computers, computer peripheral equipment and software
Parent: Fujitsu Limited
Officers: Akihisa Kamata [1963] Director/Corporate Senior Vice President, PFU Limited [Japanese]; Hiroaki Kashiwagi [1964] Director/General Manager, PFU (EMEA) Limited [Japanese]; Toru Maki [1959] Director/President and CEO, PFU (EMEA) Limited [Japanese]; Yasunori Miyauchi [1965] Director/Corporate Senior Vice President, PFU Limited [Japanese]; Michael Paul Nelson [1961] Director/Vice President; Shigeaki Suzuki [1962] Director/CFO, PFU (EMEA) Limited [Japanese]

PGA European Tour
Incorporated: 29 November 1984 *Employees:* 266
Net Worth: £129,507,400 *Total Assets:* £246,515,536
Registered Office: European Tour Building, Wentworth Drive, Virginia Water, Surrey, GU25 4LX
Activities: Other sports activities
Officers: Susan Gordon, Secretary; Countess Jutta Grevinde Af Rosenborg [1958] Director [Danish]; Martha Ellen Brass [1963] Director; Sir Damon Marcus Buffini [1962] Director; Paul Eales [1963] Director/Professional Golfer; Christopher Lars Henrik Hanell [1973] Director/Professional Golfer [Swedish]; David Jones [1947] Director/Professional Golfer [Irish]; Robert William Lee [1961] Director Broadcaster; Paul Noel McGinley [1966] Director [Irish]; Mark Adrian Roe [1963] Director/Professional Golfer; David John Russell [1954] Director/Professional Golfer; Ove Sellberg [1959] Director/Professional Golfer [Swedish]; James Stephen Spence [1963] Director/Professional Golfer; David Gay Williams [1946] Director/Chairman

PGS Exploration (UK) Limited
Incorporated: 3 March 1994 *Employees:* 201
Net Worth: £62,412,024 *Total Assets:* £94,821,744
Registered Office: 4 The Heights, Brooklands, Weybridge, Surrey, KT13 0NY
Activities: Support activities for petroleum and natural gas mining
Parent: Petroleum Geo-Services (UK) Limited
Officers: Gottfred Langseth [1966] Director [Norwegian]; Olav Rune Pedersen [1970] Director [Norwegian]; Christin Steen Nilsen [1953] Director/VP Chief Accountant [Norwegian]

Pharmacia Limited
Incorporated: 8 April 1952
Net Worth: £614,150,976 *Total Assets:* £963,942,016
Registered Office: c/o Pfizer Limited, Ramsgate Road, Sandwich, Kent, CT13 9NJ
Activities: Activities of head offices
Parent: Pfizer Inc
Officers: Ian Eric Franklin [1965] Director; Denise Jean Harnett [1964] Director; Jacqueline Ann Mount [1963] Director; Hendrikus Hermannus Nordkamp [1969] Commercial Director [Dutch]; Edwin James Pearson [1974] Director/Solicitor; Parry Rao [1966] Director; Colin Malcolm Seller [1963] Director

PHF Investments Limited
Incorporated: 12 December 2008
Net Worth: £3,544,716 *Total Assets:* £43,045,832
Registered Office: Foundation House, 42-48 London Road, Reigate, Surrey, RH2 9QQ
Activities: Other letting and operating of own or leased real estate
Officers: Peter John Gorringe Lee, Secretary; Sir Peter Robert Harrison [1937] Director/Entrepreneur; Peter John Gorringe Lee [1965] Director/Solicitor

PHH 1 Limited
Incorporated: 2 November 2012 *Employees:* 8,038
Net Worth: £22,300,000 *Total Assets:* £87,468,000
Registered Office: Building 1, Imperial Place, Elstree Way, Borehamwood, Herts, WD6 1JN
Activities: Licenced restaurants
Parent: HWS 3 Limited
Officers: Maria Rachael Watkins, Secretary; Jens Tjeerd Hofma [1966] Managing Director [Dutch]; Andrew Mark Platt [1967] Director/Accountant

Philips Electronics UK Limited
Incorporated: 19 December 1947 *Employees:* 1,424
Net Worth: £235,000,000 *Total Assets:* £427,000,000
Registered Office: Philips Centre, Guildford Business Park, Guildford, Surrey, GU2 8XG
Activities: Manufacture of other plastic products
Parent: Philips UK Limited
Officers: Louise Helen Best, Secretary; Louise Helen Best [1981] Director/Head of Legal; Jonathan Coles [1975] HR Director; Neil Anthony Mesher [1966] Managing Director; Graham Tranter [1960] Director/Head of Finance

Philips U.K. Limited
Incorporated: 1 July 1985 *Employees:* 2
Net Worth: £977,500,032 *Total Assets:* £977,500,032
Registered Office: Philips Centre, Guildford Business Park, Guildford, Surrey, GU2 8XG
Activities: Activities of head offices
Parent: Koninklijke Philips N.V.
Officers: Louise Helen Best, Secretary; Neil Anthony Mesher [1966] Managing Director; Graham Tranter [1960] Director/Head of Finance

Phivco UK II Limited
Incorporated: 25 June 2009
Net Worth: £229,423,008 *Total Assets:* £287,228,992
Registered Office: 980 Great West Road, Brentford, Middlesex, TW8 9GS
Activities: Other business support service activities n.e.c.
Parent: ViiV Healthcare Limited
Officers: Jill Dawn Anderson [1964] Director; Karen Marion Grainger [1978] Director/Pharmaceutical Regulatory Executive [Irish]; Deborah Jayne Waterhouse [1967] Director

Phoenix Software Limited
Incorporated: 15 October 1990 *Employees:* 163
Net Worth: £7,374,000 *Total Assets:* £32,899,000
Registered Office: Bytes House, Randalls Way, Leatherhead, Surrey, KT22 7TW
Activities: Wholesale of computers, computer peripheral equipment and software
Parent: Blenheim Group Limited
Officers: Paul David Emms [1967] Director; Clare Lucy Metcalfe [1968] Director; Samantha Jayne Mudd [1969] Director; Neil Robert Murphy [1964] Director; Keith Alan Richardson [1959] Director; Robert Eben Venter [1960] Director [South African]

Photo - Me International P L C
Incorporated: 14 September 1962 *Employees:* 1,371
Net Worth: £143,256,992 *Total Assets:* £238,908,992
Registered Office: Unit 3b Blenheim Road, Epsom, Surrey, KT19 9AP
Activities: Other service activities n.e.c.
Officers: Delmo Rinaldo Vincenzo Primo Mansi, Secretary; Yitzhak Apeloig [1959] Director/Manager and Investor [Israeli]; Francoise Rose Georgette Coutaz-Replan [1957] Finance Director [French]; Serge Paul Crasnianski [1942] Director [French]; Jean Marcel Denis [1938] Director/Chartered Accountant [French]; John Henry James Lewis [1940] Director; Eric Armand Mergui [1955] Director/Chief Operating Officer [French]; Emmanuel John Olympitis [1948] Director

Photo-Me Limited
Incorporated: 15 August 2016 *Employees:* 7
Net Worth: £26,564,876 *Total Assets:* £73,950,312
Registered Office: Unit 3b Blenheim Road, Epsom, Surrey, KT19 9AP
Activities: Other business support service activities n.e.c.
Parent: Photo-Me International PLC
Officers: Delmo Rinaldo Vincenzo Primo Mansi, Secretary; Serge Paul Crasnianski [1942] Director [French]

Pic Fyfield Limited
Incorporated: 29 April 1884 *Employees:* 2
Net Worth: £202,850,000 *Total Assets:* £298,352,000
Registered Office: Matrix House, Basing View, Basingstoke, Hants, RG21 4DZ
Activities: Activities of head offices
Parent: Genus Investments Limited
Officers: Cara Crichton, Secretary; Karim Bitar [1965] Director [American]; Denis Mary Noonan [1966] Director/Accountant [Irish]; Stephen David Wilson [1959] Finance Director

Picturehouse Cinemas Limited
Incorporated: 28 October 1988 *Employees:* 689
Net Worth: £5,283,227 *Total Assets:* £38,594,624
Registered Office: 8th Floor, Vantage London, Great West Road, Brentford, Middlesex, TW8 9AG
Activities: Motion picture projection activities
Parent: Cineworld Holdings Limited
Officers: Fiona Smith, Secretary; Clare Louise Binns [1954] Director; Israel Greidinger [1961] Director/Cinema Proprietor [Israeli]; Mr Moshe Joseph Greidinger [1952] Director/Cinema Proprietor [Israeli]; Roei Kaufman [1985] Director/Accountant

PIG Improvement Company UK Limited
Incorporated: 26 February 1962 *Employees:* 28
Net Worth: £31,363,000 *Total Assets:* £42,245,000
Registered Office: Matrix House, Basing View, Basingstoke, Hants, RG21 4DZ
Activities: Raising of swine and pigs
Parent: PIC Fyfield Limited
Officers: Cara Crichton, Secretary; Karim Bitar [1965] Director [American]; Jurgen Ewald Kramer [1967] Director of PIC Europe [German/American]; Denis Mary Noonan [1966] Director/Group Head of Tax & Treasury [Irish]; Stephen David Wilson [1959] Finance Director

The Piggott Church of England School
Incorporated: 24 June 2011 *Employees:* 208
Net Worth: £19,159,452 *Total Assets:* £21,781,780
Registered Office: Twyford Road, Wargrave, Reading, Berks, RG10 8DS
Activities: Primary education
Officers: Rebecca Jane Marr, Secretary; Jack Rollo Andrews [1986] Director/Teacher; James Andrew Bell [1977] Director/Bursar; The Reverend John Richard Millward Cook [1961] Director/Clerk in Holy Orders; Mark Neale Cowieson [1975] Director/Project Manager; Joanne Michelle Cowley [1973] Director/Advice Worker; Helen Rosemary Craig [1962] Director/Housewife; Derren Gray [1970] Director/Headteacher; Gary James Hughes [1964] Director/Businessman; Joanne Marie Humphrey [1970] Director/Teacher; Marianne Newman [1975] Director/Teacher; John Matthew Gregory Perowne [1983] Director/Finance; Ian George Stephen Pogue [1971] Director/Chartered Accountant; Andrew Russell Shapland [1969] Finance Director; Doctor Alison Silby [1974] Director/University Lecturer; Michael Richard Edward Simpson [1964] Director; Alison Smyly [1973] Director/Teacher; Richard Malcolm Charles Thiele [1960] Director; Lucy Walton [1967] Director/Teaching Assistant; Christopher Timothy West [1979] Director/Youth Minister

Pilgrims Hospices in East Kent
Incorporated: 14 March 1986 *Employees:* 284
Net Worth: £23,481,000 *Total Assets:* £24,661,000
Registered Office: 56 London Road, Canterbury, Kent, CT2 8JA
Activities: Other human health activities
Officers: Helen Clare Julia Bennett, Secretary; Stephanie Bates [1960] Director; Jennifer Ruth Billings [1957] Director/Academic; Philip John Bradshaw [1949] Director; Grahame Henry Connor [1951] Director/Retired [Irish]; Richard James Davis [1947] Director/Chartered Accountant; Hereward Donald McKaig Harrison [1943] Director/Retired; Margo Shewan Laing [1961] Director; Simon Harvey Perks [1961] Director/NHS Manager; Elizabeth Jean Sharp [1957] Director/Doctor/Surgeon; Terry John Smith [1939] Director/Retired; Anthony Michael Arnold Turnbull [1935] Director/Retired; Karen Frances Warden [1957] Director/Business Consultant; Paul Stuart Williamson [1972] Managing Director; Dr Ruth Edna Mary Wilson [1948] Director/Doctor of Medicine

Pinewood Finco PLC
Incorporated: 8 November 2017
Net Worth: £99,000 *Total Assets:* £250,472,000
Registered Office: Pinewood Studios, Pinewood Road, Iver, Bucks, SL0 0NH
Activities: Other business support service activities n.e.c.
Parent: Pinewood Group Limited
Officers: Bridget Sheldon-Hill, Secretary; Paul William Martin Golding [1965] Director/Partner; Chris John Naisby [1972] Finance Director; Luis Moner Parra [1981] Director/Principal [Spanish]

Pinewood Group Limited
Incorporated: 7 December 1999 *Employees:* 290
Previous: Pinewood Group PLC
Net Worth: £148,983,008 *Total Assets:* £448,764,000
Registered Office: Pinewood Studios, Pinewood Road, Iver, Bucks, SL0 0NH
Activities: Motion picture production activities
Parent: Picture Holdco Limited
Officers: Bridget Sheldon-Hill, Secretary; Paul William Martin Golding [1965] Director; Luis Moner Parra [1981] Director/Principal [Spanish]; Chris John Naisby [1972] Financial Director; Nathan Nissim Shike [1981] Director [American]; Andrew Mark Smith [1962] Director; Alison Claire Trewartha [1981] Director [British/Australian]

Pinewood MBS Lighting Limited
Incorporated: 12 September 2014 *Employees:* 48
Net Worth: £2,275,294 *Total Assets:* £27,935,808
Registered Office: Pinewood Studios, Pinewood Road, Iver Heath, Bucks, SL0 0NH
Activities: Renting and leasing of media entertainment equipment
Parent: PMBS Holding Limited
Officers: Jonathan Bard [1977] Director/Private Equity Investor [American]; Paul William Martin Golding [1965] Director/Partner; Richard Joseph Nelson [1956] Director/President [American]; Darren Christopher Smith [1974] Director

Pinewood PSB Limited
Incorporated: 3 July 2007
Net Worth: £3,138,000 *Total Assets:* £82,596,000
Registered Office: Pinewood Studios, Pinewood Road, Iver Heath, Bucks, SL0 0NH
Activities: Other letting and operating of own or leased real estate
Parent: Pinewood Group Limited
Officers: Bridget Sheldon-Hill, Secretary; Paul William Martin Golding [1965] Director/Partner; Luis Moner Parra [1981] Director/Principal [Spanish]; Chris John Naisby [1972] Director; James Howard Rider [1978] Commercial Director; Andrew Mark Smith [1962] Director

Pinewood Studios Limited
Incorporated: 18 January 1945 *Employees:* 185
Net Worth: £36,561,000 *Total Assets:* £131,588,000
Registered Office: Pinewood Studios, Pinewood Road, Iver, Bucks, SL0 0NH
Activities: Motion picture production activities
Parent: Pinewood-Shepperton Studios Limited
Officers: Bridget Sheldon-Hill, Secretary; Paul William Martin Golding [1965] Director/Partner; Luis Moner Parra [1981] Director/Principal [Spanish]; Chris John Naisby [1972] Director; James Howard Rider [1978] Commercial Director; Andrew Mark Smith [1962] Group Director Corporate Affairs

Pinewood-Shepperton Studios Limited
Incorporated: 1 November 1994
Net Worth: £32,706,000 *Total Assets:* £325,759,008
Registered Office: c/o Pinewood Studios, Pinewood Road, Iver Heath, Bucks, SL0 0NH
Activities: Motion picture, video and television programme post-production activities
Parent: Pinewood Group Limited
Officers: Bridget Sheldon-Hill, Secretary; Paul William Martin Golding [1965] Director/Partner; Luis Moner Parra [1981] Director/Principal [Spanish]; Chris John Naisby [1972] Director

Pinnacle Insurance PLC
Incorporated: 14 April 1971
Net Worth: £158,516,992 *Total Assets:* £332,326,016
Registered Office: Pinnacle House, A1 Barnet Way, Borehamwood, Herts, WD6 2XX
Activities: Life insurance
Parent: Cardif Pinnacle Insurance Holdings PLC
Officers: Matthew Justin Lorimer, Secretary; Gerard Binet [1953] Development and Strategy Director [French]; Peter John Box [1952] Director; Stanislas Louis Paul Francois Chevalt [1961] Director/Exco Member - Co - BNPPC [French]; Marie Haderer [1979] Director/Actuary [French]; Matthew Justin Lorimer [1967] Director/Solicitor; Nicholas Dutfield Rochez [1954] Director; Andrew Miles Wigg [1972] Director

Pinnacle Schools (Fife) Limited
Incorporated: 24 October 2000
Net Worth: £3,569,000 *Total Assets:* £32,899,000
Registered Office: 8 White Oak Square, London Road, Swanley, Kent, BR8 7AG
Activities: Other business support service activities n.e.c.
Parent: Pinnacle Schools (Fife) Holdings Limited
Officers: John Stephen Gordon [1962] Director; Matthew Templeton [1973] Director

Pinnacle Schools (Gateshead) Limited
Incorporated: 20 April 2005
Net Worth Deficit: £5,836,056 *Total Assets:* £48,456,844
Registered Office: Eaton Court, Maylands Avenue, Hemel Hempstead Industrial Estate, Hemel Hempstead, Herts, HP2 7TR
Activities: Other business support service activities n.e.c.
Parent: Pinnacle Schools (Gateshead) Holdings Limited
Officers: Kevin John Pearson, Secretary; David Honeyman [1967] Director/Financial Controller

Pioneer Concrete Holdings Limited
Incorporated: 22 November 1962
Net Worth: £116,431,000 *Total Assets:* £126,924,000
Registered Office: Hanson House, 14 Castle Hill, Maidenhead, Berks, SL6 4JJ
Activities: Activities of other holding companies n.e.c.
Parent: Houserate Limited
Officers: Wendy Fiona Rogers, Secretary; Nicholas Arthur Dawe Benning-Prince [1974] Director/Chartered Accountant; Robert Charles Dowley [1972] Director/Chartered Accountant; Edward Alexander Gretton [1970] Director; Dr Carsten Matthias Wendt [1976] Director [German]

Pioneer Educational Trust
Incorporated: 7 December 2010 *Employees:* 253
Previous: Upton Court Educational Trust
Net Worth: £36,909,000 *Total Assets:* £42,896,000
Registered Office: Upton Court Grammar School, Lascelles Road, Slough, SL3 7PR
Activities: Primary education
Officers: Sarah Isobelle Sarll, Secretary; Vinay Dhir [1977] Director/Trustee; Russell Ford [1968] Director; Maria Mercedes Hernandez Estrada [1966] Co-opted Director [Spanish]; Mark Jervis [1970] Director; Nigel Miller [1971] Director; Edward Jonathan Neighbour [1971] Director/Joint CEO; Mark Andrew Roper [1964] Director/Management Consultant; Danny Sohal [1986] Director/School Business Manager; Antonia Spinks [1976] Director/Joint CEO

Pioneer International Group Holdings Limited
Incorporated: 28 February 1994
Net Worth: £885,331,008 *Total Assets:* £887,662,976
Registered Office: Hanson House, 14 Castle Hill, Maidenhead, Berks, SL6 4JJ
Activities: Activities of other holding companies n.e.c.
Parent: Houserate Limited
Officers: Wendy Fiona Rogers, Secretary; Nicholas Arthur Dawe Benning-Prince [1974] Director/Chartered Accountant; Robert Charles Dowley [1972] Director/Chartered Accountant; Edward Alexander Gretton [1970] Director; Dr Carsten Matthias Wendt [1976] Director [German]

Piramal Critical Care Limited
Incorporated: 22 June 2004 *Employees:* 16
Previous: Piramal Life Sciences (UK) Limited
Net Worth: £18,122,694 *Total Assets:* £276,387,680
Registered Office: Ground Floor, Suite 4, Heathrow Boulevard East Wing, 280 Bath Road, West Drayton, Middlesex, UB7 0DQ
Activities: Manufacture of basic pharmaceutical products
Officers: Kaushik Upadhyay, Secretary; Peter Daniel Deyoung [1978] Director/Chief Executive Officer of Piramal Critical Care B [American]; William John Hargan [1958] Director/VP Sales and Marketing; Kaushik Upadhyay [1980] Director [Indian]

The Pirbright Institute
Incorporated: 7 January 1956 *Employees:* 322
Net Worth: £279,086,016 *Total Assets:* £289,688,000
Registered Office: Pirbright Laboratory, Ash Road, Pirbright, Woking, Surrey, GU24 0NF
Activities: Other research and experimental development on natural sciences and engineering
Officers: Keith Simpson, Secretary; Ian Black [1952] Director, Arch Management Consultants Ltd; Jonathan Roger Elliot Coles [1955] Director/Partner, Brunswick Group LLP; Professor Vince Emery [1960] Director/Professor; Roger Louth [1951] Finance Director; Dr Vanessa Linda Mayatt [1954] Director/Consultant; Dr Sandy Blackadder Primrose [1944] Director/Senior Partner; Sir Bertie Ross [1950] Director/Consultant; Professor David John Rowlands [1940] Director/University Professor; Professor John Robert Stephenson [1948] Director/University Professor

Pittway Systems Technology Group Europe Limited
Incorporated: 22 April 1988 *Employees:* 29
Net Worth: £30,247,000 *Total Assets:* £31,514,000
Registered Office: Honeywell House, Skimped Hill Lane, Bracknell, Berks, RG12 1EB
Activities: Other business support service activities n.e.c.
Parent: Pittway UK Limited
Officers: Piyush Jayantilal Kanji Jutha [1972] Director; Jurgen Amelie Alois Van Goethem [1966] Director [Belgian]

Pizza Hut (U.K.) Limited
Incorporated: 21 September 1972 *Employees:* 8,033
Net Worth: £53,007,000 *Total Assets:* £97,308,000
Registered Office: Building 1, Imperial Place, Elstree Way, Borehamwood, Herts, WD6 1JN
Activities: Licenced restaurants
Parent: PHH 2 Limited
Officers: Maria Rachael Watkins, Secretary; Kathryn Elizabeth Austin [1976] HR Director; Jens Tjeerd Hofma [1966] Director [Dutch]; Susan Marshall [1973] Chief Director for Operations; Andrew Mark Platt [1967] Director/Accountant; Michael William Edward Spencer [1969] Director of Operations - Dine-In

PizzaExpress (Restaurants) Limited
Incorporated: 31 March 1993 *Employees:* 10,646
Net Worth: £714,636,992 *Total Assets:* £983,900,032
Registered Office: Hunton House, Highbridge Estate, Oxford Road, Uxbridge, Middlesex, UB8 1LX
Activities: Licenced restaurants
Parent: PizzaExpress Limited
Officers: Andrew David Pellington, Secretary; Nicola Zoe Bowley [1971] Director; David Roger Murphy [1974] Director; Andrew David Pellington [1964] Director; Jinlong Wang [1957] Director [American]

PizzaExpress (Wholesale) Limited
Incorporated: 28 April 1993 *Employees:* 17
Net Worth: £22,347,000 *Total Assets:* £82,605,000
Registered Office: Hunton House, Highbridge Estate, Oxford Road, Uxbridge, Middlesex, UB8 1LX
Activities: Licenced restaurants
Parent: PizzaExpress Limited
Officers: Andrew David Pellington, Secretary; Andrew David Pellington [1964] Director; Jinlong Wang [1957] Director [American]

PizzaExpress Financing 1 PLC
Incorporated: 4 July 2014 *Employees:* 14,510
Net Worth Deficit: £57,921,000 *Total Assets:* £1,233,755,008
Registered Office: Hunton House, Highbridge Estate, Oxford Road, Uxbridge, Middlesex, UB8 1LX
Activities: Non-trading company
Parent: PizzaExpress Group Holdings Limited
Officers: Andrew David Pellington, Secretary; Andrew David Pellington [1964] Director; Xiaoxin Shao [1981] Director [Chinese]; Jinlong Wang [1957] Director [American]; Bing Yuan [1968] Director [Chinese]

PizzaExpress Financing 2 PLC
Incorporated: 7 July 2014
Net Worth Deficit: £5,454,000 *Total Assets:* £1,280,556,032
Registered Office: Hunton House, Highbridge Estate, Oxford Road, Uxbridge, Middlesex, UB8 1LX
Activities: Non-trading company
Parent: PizzaExpress Financing 1 PLC
Officers: Andrew David Pellington, Secretary; Andrew David Pellington [1964] Director; Xiaoxin Shao [1981] Director [Chinese]; Jinlong Wang [1957] Director [American]; Bing Yuan [1968] Director [Chinese]

PizzaExpress Group Holdings Limited
Incorporated: 3 July 2014 *Employees:* 14,510
Net Worth Deficit: £57,921,000 *Total Assets:* £1,233,755,008
Registered Office: Hunton House, Highbridge Estate, Oxford Road, Uxbridge, Middlesex, UB8 1LX
Activities: Non-trading company
Officers: Andrew David Pellington, Secretary; Jianzhong Gong [1962] Director/Banker [Chinese]; Ma Mingju [1961] Director/VP of Jin Jiang International (Holdings) Co., Ltd [Chinese]; Andrew David Pellington [1964] Director; Xiaoxin Shao [1981] Director [Chinese]; Jinlong Wang [1957] Director [American]; Bing Yuan [1968] Director [Chinese]

PizzaExpress Group Limited
Incorporated: 14 July 2014 *Employees:* 228
Net Worth Deficit: £212,971,008 *Total Assets:* £1,113,291,008
Registered Office: Hunton House, Highbridge Estate, Oxford Road, Uxbridge, Middlesex, UB8 1LX
Activities: Activities of head offices
Parent: PizzaExpress Financing 2 PLC
Officers: Andrew David Pellington, Secretary; Andrew David Pellington [1964] Director; Xiaoxin Shao [1981] Director [Chinese]; Jinlong Wang [1957] Director [American]; Bing Yuan [1968] Director [Chinese]

PizzaExpress International Holdings Limited
Incorporated: 25 March 2015 *Employees:* 2
Net Worth Deficit: £10,510,000 *Total Assets:* £65,241,000
Registered Office: Hunton House, Highbridge Estate, Oxford Road, Uxbridge, Middlesex, UB8 1LX
Activities: Activities of other holding companies n.e.c.
Parent: PizzaExpress Group Limited
Officers: Andrew David Pellington, Secretary; Andrew David Pellington [1964] Director; Jinlong Wang [1957] Director [American]

PizzaExpress Limited
Incorporated: 11 December 1978 *Employees:* 4
Net Worth: £106,198,000 *Total Assets:* £824,732,032
Registered Office: Hunton House, Highbridge Estate, Oxford Road, Uxbridge, Middlesex, UB8 1LX
Activities: Licenced restaurants
Parent: PizzaExpress Operations Limited
Officers: Andrew David Pellington, Secretary; Nicola Zoe Bowley [1971] Director; David Roger Murphy [1974] Director; Andrew David Pellington [1964] Director; Jinlong Wang [1957] Director [American]

PizzaExpress Merchandising Limited
Incorporated: 29 November 1996
Net Worth: £106,751,000 *Total Assets:* £118,259,000
Registered Office: Hunton House, Highbridge Estate, Oxford Road, Uxbridge, Middlesex, UB8 1LX
Activities: Licenced restaurants
Parent: PizzaExpress Limited
Officers: Andrew David Pellington, Secretary; Andrew David Pellington [1964] Director; Jinlong Wang [1957] Director [American]

PizzaExpress Operations Limited
Incorporated: 18 July 2003
Net Worth Deficit: £272,502,016 *Total Assets:* £1,203,827,968
Registered Office: Hunton House, Highbridge Industrial Estate, Oxford Road, Uxbridge, Middlesex, UB8 1LX
Activities: Financial management
Parent: PizzaExpress Group Limited
Officers: Andrew David Pellington, Secretary; Nicola Zoe Bowley [1971] Director; Andrew David Pellington [1964] Director; Jinlong Wang [1957] Director [American]

PJ Care Group Limited
Incorporated: 1 June 2016 *Employees:* 451
Net Worth: £7,322,901 *Total Assets:* £24,134,532
Registered Office: 153 Sherwood Drive, Bletchley, Milton Keynes, Bucks, MK3 6RT
Activities: Other residential care activities n.e.c.
Major Shareholder: Janice Flawn
Officers: Janice Evelyn Flawn [1947] Director; Neil Russell [1969] Director

PJ Care Limited
Incorporated: 29 February 2000 *Employees:* 451
Net Worth: £11,434,948 *Total Assets:* £26,641,616
Registered Office: 153 Sherwood Drive, Bletchley, Milton Keynes, Bucks, MK3 6RT
Activities: Other residential care activities n.e.c.
Parent: P J Care Holdings Limited
Officers: Mark Peter Butler [1957] Director; Janice Evelyn Flawn [1947] Director/Registered Nurse; Allan David Perry [1968] Director of Clinical Services; Neil Russell [1969] Director

PKA WLWF Holding (UK) Limited
Incorporated: 19 June 2017
Net Worth: £119,903,000 *Total Assets:* £242,544,000
Registered Office: 8 White Oak Square, London Road, Swanley, Kent, BR8 7AG
Activities: Activities of other holding companies n.e.c.
Officers: James Edward Burbidge [1975] Director/Chartered Accountant; Mark Alan Cade [1972] Director/Chartered Engineer; Domenico Tripodi [1984] Director [Italian]

Pladis Foods Limited
Incorporated: 4 November 2014 *Employees:* 8,093
Net Worth: £936,300,032 *Total Assets:* £5,041,800,192
Registered Office: United Biscuits, Hayes Park, Hayes End Road, Hayes, Middlesex, UB4 8EE
Activities: Activities of head offices
Major Shareholder: Murat Ulker
Officers: Mark Oldham, Secretary; Richard Handscombe [1954] Director/Accountant; Simon Edward Munir [1964] Director/Fund Manager; Murat Ulker [1959] Director/Chairman [Turkish]

Platinum Acquisition Limited
Incorporated: 22 August 2016 *Employees:* 3
Net Worth: £70,676,224 *Total Assets:* £149,896,496
Registered Office: Catalyst House, 720 Centennial Court, Centennial Park, Elstree, Herts, WD6 3SY
Activities: Other business support service activities n.e.c.
Parent: Platinum Midco Limited
Officers: Thomas Christopher Barnds [1968] Director [American]; Maurice Andre Hernandez [1981] Director [American]; Jason Michael Klein [1973] Director [American]

Platinum Midco 2 Limited
Incorporated: 1 September 2016 *Employees:* 3
Net Worth: £90,332,704 *Total Assets:* £90,332,704
Registered Office: Catalyst House, 720 Centennial Court, Centennial Park, Elstree, Herts, WD6 3SY
Activities: Other business support service activities n.e.c.
Parent: Platinum Topco Limited
Officers: Thomas Christopher Barnds [1968] Director [American]; Maurice Andre Hernandez [1981] Director [American]; Jason Michael Klein [1973] Director [American]

Platinum Midco Limited
Incorporated: 22 August 2016 *Employees:* 3
Net Worth: £90,332,704 *Total Assets:* £90,332,704
Registered Office: Catalyst House, 720 Centennial Court, Centennial Park, Elstree, Herts, WD6 3SY
Activities: Other business support service activities n.e.c.
Parent: Platinum Midco 2 Limited
Officers: Thomas Christopher Barnds [1968] Director [American]; Maurice Andre Hernandez [1981] Director [American]; Jason Michael Klein [1973] Director [American]

Platinum Newco II Limited
Incorporated: 1 August 2016 *Employees:* 1
Net Worth: £119,901,816 *Total Assets:* £125,000,000
Registered Office: Catalyst House, 720 Centennial Court, Centennial Park, Elstree, Herts, WD6 3SY
Activities: Activities of other holding companies n.e.c.
Parent: Platinum Newco III Limited
Officers: James Brown [1971] Director; Jon Stratford [1970] Director

Platinum Topco Limited
Incorporated: 22 August 2016 *Employees:* 176
Net Worth Deficit: £50,161,772 *Total Assets:* £171,971,168
Registered Office: Catalyst House, 720 Centennial Court, Centennial Park, Elstree, Herts, WD6 3SY
Activities: Other business support service activities n.e.c.
Officers: Thomas Christopher Barnds [1968] Director [American]; James Brown [1971] Director; Maurice Andre Hernandez [1981] Director [American]; Jason Michael Klein [1973] Director [American]; Rachel Spasser [1967] Director/Operating Principal [American]

Plaza on Hyde Park Limited
Incorporated: 3 October 1997 *Employees:* 114
Net Worth: £55,433,648 *Total Assets:* £141,871,712
Registered Office: Corus House, 1 Auckland Park, Milton Keynes, Bucks, MK1 1BU
Activities: Hotels and similar accommodation
Parent: Corus Hotels Limited
Officers: Khurram Mohmand, Secretary; Andrew Khoo [1972] Director [Australian]; Yet King Loy [1946] Director [Canadian]; Khurram Mohmand [1972] Director/Accountant

Plexus Holdings PLC
Incorporated: 24 February 1997 *Employees:* 54
Net Worth: £40,916,000 *Total Assets:* £46,154,000
Registered Office: Elder House, St Georges Business Park, 207 Brooklands Road, Weybridge, Surrey, KT13 0TS
Activities: Activities of head offices
Officers: Kerin Williams, Secretary; Craig Francis Bryce Hendrie [1973] Director; Charles Jones [1959] Director [American]; Kunming Liu [1977] Director [Chinese]; Graham Paul Stevens [1958] Director; Jerome Jeffrey Thrall [1949] Director [American]; Bernard Herman Van Bilderbeek [1948] Executive Director [Dutch]

PMP Recruitment Limited
Incorporated: 24 December 1997 *Employees:* 22,537
Net Worth: £9,126,477 *Total Assets:* £138,570,784
Registered Office: Chevron House, Long Lane, Hillingdon, Uxbridge, Middlesex, UB10 9PF
Activities: Temporary employment agency activities
Parent: Cordant People Limited
Officers: Alan Connor, Secretary/Director; Chris Martin Kenneally [1960] Director; Jack Rainer Ullmann [1928] Director; Phillip Lionel Ullmann [1964] Director/Group Managing

PNC Financial Services UK Ltd
Incorporated: 10 August 2010 *Employees:* 57
Net Worth: £275,626,560 *Total Assets:* £1,246,605,440
Registered Office: PNC House, 34-36 Perrymount Road, Haywards Heath, W Sussex, RH16 3DN
Activities: Credit granting by non-deposit taking finance houses and other specialist consumer credit grantors
Parent: The PNC Financial Services Group, Inc.
Officers: Paul John Beveridge [1959] Director/Banker; William a Kosis [1956] Director [American]; James B. Yahner [1956] Director [American]

Police Care UK
Incorporated: 1 March 2013 *Employees:* 7
Previous: The Police Dependants' Trust Limited
Net Worth: £33,471,324 *Total Assets:* £33,646,736
Registered Office: Nova Scotia House, 70 Goldsworth Road, Woking, Surrey, GU21 6LQ
Activities: Other social work activities without accommodation n.e.c.
Officers: Simon Bray [1959] Director; Christopher Greany [1964] Director/Retired; Paul Griffiths [1971] Director/Trustee; Bernard Higgins [1967] Director/Chief Constable; Mark Lindsay [1967] Director/Chairman; Andrea Elizabeth MacDonald [1968] Director/Inspector; Neil Fraser Massey [1953] Director/President of The RPOAS; Tamian Packham [1966] Director/Police Inspector; Stuart Edward Purdy [1962] Director/Trustee

The Police Rehabilitation Centre
Incorporated: 14 March 2012 *Employees:* 139
Net Worth: £33,642,056 *Total Assets:* £34,054,292
Registered Office: Flint House, Reading Road, Goring on Thames, Oxon, RG8 0LL
Activities: Other business support service activities n.e.c.
Officers: Jenny Abbott [1952] Director/Retired; Stephen Bozward [1971] Director/Police Officer; Simon Bray [1959] Director; Ollie Cochran [1982] Director/Police Officer; Clive Robert Field [1985] Director/NHA Accountant; David Neil Flint [1953] Director/Retired; Graham Gilbert [1961] Director/Police Officer; Dr Rhys William Hamilton [1951] Director/Retired GP; Kenneth James Marsh [1966] Director; Daniel Murphy [1972] Director/Police Officer

Polycom (United Kingdom) Ltd.
Incorporated: 4 March 1999 *Employees:* 200
Net Worth: £9,049,199 *Total Assets:* £21,985,260
Registered Office: Building 4, Foundation Park, Roxborough Way, Maidenhead, Berks, SL6 3UD
Activities: Other business support service activities n.e.c.
Parent: Plantronics, Inc.
Officers: Bartus de Vries, Secretary; Bartus de Vries [1972] Finance Director [Dutch]; Mary Therese Huser [1963] Director/Business Executive [American]; William James Pflugh [1958] Director/Business Executive [American]; Pamela Jean Strayer [1968] Director/Business Executive [American]

Porcelanosa U.K. Limited
Incorporated: 5 September 1995 *Employees:* 456
Net Worth: £110,485,000 *Total Assets:* £134,772,000
Registered Office: Units 1-6 Otterspool Way, Bushey, Watford, Herts, WD25 8HL
Activities: Leasing of intellectual property and similar products, except copyright works
Shareholder: Asuncion Manzanet
Officers: Deep Shah, Secretary; Manuel Colonques [1942] Director [Spanish]

Porsche Cars Great Britain Limited
Incorporated: 8 October 1965 *Employees:* 116
Net Worth: £69,527,000 *Total Assets:* £220,220,992
Registered Office: Bath Road, Calcot, Reading, Berks, RG31 7SE
Activities: Sale of new cars and light motor vehicles
Parent: Volkswagen AG
Officers: Bernard John Moloney, Secretary; Frank Angelkoetter [1964] Director/Business Executive [German]; Dr Oliver Blume [1968] Director/Business Executive [German]; Marcus Peter Eckermann [1968] Director/Business Executive [German]; Lutz Meschke [1966] Director/Chief Financial Officer [German]; Doctor Michael Piech [1942] Director [Austrian]; Dr Wolfgang Porsche [1943] Director [Austrian]; Barbara Vollert [1963] Director/Chemical Engineer [German]; Detlev Von Platen [1964] Director/Business Executive [German]

Porsche Financial Services Great Britain Limited
Incorporated: 1 February 1999 *Employees:* 1
Net Worth: £45,172,828 *Total Assets:* £47,314,604
Registered Office: Bath Road, Calcot, Reading, Berks, RG31 7SE
Activities: Financial leasing
Parent: Volkswagen AG
Officers: Bernard John Moloney, Secretary; Frank Angelkoetter [1964] Director/Business Executive [German]; Jorg Michael Pape [1966] Director/Business Executive [German]; Konrad Riedl [1961] Director [German]

Porsche Retail Group Limited
Incorporated: 11 March 1927 *Employees:* 284
Net Worth: £17,851,000 *Total Assets:* £48,279,000
Registered Office: Bath Road, Calcot, Reading, Berks, RG31 7SE
Activities: Sale of new cars and light motor vehicles
Parent: Porsche Cars Great Britain Limited
Officers: Bernard John Moloney, Secretary; Frank Angelkoetter [1964] Director/Business Executive [German]; Marcus Peter Eckermann [1968] Director/Business Executive [German]; Adrian Smith [1964] Managing Director

Portals Group Limited
Incorporated: 26 February 1920
Net Worth: £34,999,000 *Total Assets:* £36,036,000
Registered Office: De La Rue House, Jays Close Viables, Basingstoke, Hants, RG22 4BS
Activities: Activities of other holding companies n.e.c.
Parent: De La Rue Investments Limited
Officers: Jean-Francois Hermans, Secretary; Edward Hugh Davidson Peppiatt [1967] Director/Lawyer; Lesley Sharon Roche [1967] Director/Accountant - Group Financial Controller

Portchester Equity Limited
Incorporated: 4 January 2010 *Employees:* 1,056
Net Worth: £52,521,000 *Total Assets:* £140,914,000
Registered Office: 20 Jewry Street, Winchester, Hants, SO23 8RZ
Activities: Activities of head offices
Major Shareholder: Mark Edward Thistlethwayte
Officers: Paul Lambert, Secretary; David Christopher Harbord [1961] Director/Accountant; Paul Lambert [1974] Director/Accountant; Mark Edward Thistlethwayte [1964] Director; Robin Thistlethwayte [1935] Director

Porter and Haylett Limited
Incorporated: 3 November 1958 *Employees:* 67
Net Worth: £41,391,000 *Total Assets:* £68,469,000
Registered Office: Origin One, 108 High Street, Crawley, W Sussex, RH10 1BD
Activities: Building of pleasure and sporting boats
Parent: Crown Blue Line Limited
Officers: Janet Northey, Secretary; Cheryl Frances Brown [1969] Director; Trevor Fahy [1979] Director/Accountant

Porthaven Finance Limited
Incorporated: 21 June 2011
Net Worth Deficit: £25,627,352 *Total Assets:* £25,910,068
Registered Office: 1 High Street, Windsor, Berks, SL4 1LD
Activities: Activities of head offices
Parent: Porthaven Group Holdings Ltd
Officers: Sean Kime, Secretary; Lance Herbert [1965] Operations Director; Sean Thomas Kime [1967] Director; Clive Russell Snellgrove [1978] Finance Director; John Storey [1968] Director

Porthaven Management Limited
Incorporated: 4 July 2011 *Employees:* 22
Net Worth Deficit: £17,317,314 *Total Assets:* £41,589,348
Registered Office: 1 High Street, Windsor, Berks, SL4 1LD
Activities: Activities of head offices
Parent: Porthaven Finance Limited
Officers: Sean Kime, Secretary; Lance Herbert [1965] Operations Director; Sean Thomas Kime [1967] Director; Clive Russell Snellgrove [1978] Finance Director; John Storey [1968] Director

Porthaven Properties Limited
Incorporated: 4 July 2011
Net Worth: £89,538,216 *Total Assets:* £211,394,768
Registered Office: 1 High Street, Windsor, Berks, SL4 1LD
Activities: Development of building projects
Parent: Porthaven Management Limited
Officers: Sean Kime, Secretary; Lance Herbert [1965] Operations Director; Sean Thomas Kime [1967] Director; Clive Russell Snellgrove [1978] Finance Director; John Storey [1968] Director

Porthaven Properties No 2 Limited
Incorporated: 3 August 2012
Net Worth: £62,313,792 *Total Assets:* £174,895,712
Registered Office: 1 High Street, Windsor, Berks, SL4 1LD
Activities: Residential nursing care facilities
Parent: Porthaven Management Limited
Officers: Sean Thomas Kime, Secretary; Lance Herbert [1965] Operations Director; Sean Thomas Kime [1967] Director; Clive Russell Snellgrove [1978] Finance Director; John Storey [1968] Director

Portrait Software Limited
Incorporated: 22 April 1997
Net Worth: £21,307,000 *Total Assets:* £21,307,000
Registered Office: The Smith Centre, Fairmile, Henley on Thames, Oxon, RG9 6AB
Activities: Business and domestic software development
Parent: Pitney Bowes Inc
Officers: Gerard Willsher, Secretary; Simon John Alderson [1977] Director/Vice President, EMEA; Gerard Richard Willsher [1967] Director/Solicitor

Portsmouth Aviation Holdings Limited
Incorporated: 5 January 1950 *Employees:* 209
Net Worth: £29,926,276 *Total Assets:* £39,500,888
Registered Office: The Airport, Portsmouth, PO3 5PF
Activities: Manufacture of other fabricated metal products n.e.c.
Shareholders: Simon Peter Escott; Dominic Paul Escott
Officers: Andrew John Hall, Secretary; Simon Peter Escott [1966] Managing Director; William Charles Frederick Turner [1937] Director/Chairman; Christopher Webb [1961] Technical Director

Portsmouth Diocesan Board of Finance (The)
Incorporated: 9 December 1927 *Employees:* 31
Net Worth: £69,872,800 *Total Assets:* £74,232,064
Registered Office: 1st Floor, Peninsular House, Wharf Road, Portsmouth, PO2 8HB
Activities: Activities of religious organisations
Officers: Victoria James, Secretary; The Revd Canon Paul Richard Armstead [1963] Director/Clerk in Holy Orders; The Revd Marcus Bagg [1975] Director/Clerk in Holy Orders; David Hugh Bennison [1945] Director/Retired Senior Civil Servant; Paul Martin Chamberlain [1974] Director/Clerk in Holy Orders; Norman Chapman [1941] Director/Retired; The Venerable Gavin Andrew Collins [1966] Director/Clerk in Holy Orders; Mary Anne Crittenden [1943] Director/Retired; Elizabeth Davidson [1993] Director/Youth and Outreach Co-ordinator; Lucy Clare Docherty [1955] Director/Consultant; The Reverend Michael Ian Duff [1963] Director/Clerk in Holy Orders; Mark Simon Emerton [1961] Director/Judge; Stuart Kenneth Forster [1949] Director/Civil Servant; The Right Reverend Christopher Richard James Foster [1953] Director/Clerk in Holy Orders; Joanne Woolway Grenfell [1972] Director/Clerk in Holy Orders; John Gwynn [1956] Director/Nurseryman; The Reverend William Piers Maximilian Hughes [1976] Director/Clerk in Holy Orders; The Revd James Hunt [1966] Director/Clerk in Holy Orders; Irene Anne James [1953] Director/Retired; Adrian Jordan [1968] Director/Dentist; Canon Hugh Laurence Mason [1941] Director/Lecturer; Eugene Organ [1971] Director/Equipment Management Engineer; The Reverend Ian Snares [1968] Director/Clerk in Holy Orders; Canon Hilary Olive Mary Spurgeon [1944] Director/Assistant Bank Manager; Deborah Sutton [1957] Director/Dietitian; Canon Robert Charles White [1961] Director/Clergyman

The Portsmouth Grammar School
Incorporated: 9 July 1997 *Employees:* 363
Net Worth: £21,917,000 *Total Assets:* £33,812,544
Registered Office: High Street, Portsmouth, PO1 2LN
Activities: Primary education
Officers: Donald James Kent, Secretary; Kathy Lee Carol Bishop [1965] Director/Chartered Accountant; Fiona Jane Boulton [1964] Director/Headmistress; Walter Jen Bang Cha [1959] Director/Solicitor; Michael Robert Coffin [1959] Director/Chartered Accountant; Sally Gingell [1968] Director/Local Authority; Dr Martin Christopher Grossel [1948] Director/Retired Academic; Neil Degge Latham [1955] Director/Armed Forces; Peter Norman Lodder [1958] Director/Barrister; Edmund James Newey [1971] Director/Minister of Religion; Jonathan Clive Nicholls [1957] Director/Chairman; Philip Parkinson [1952] Director/Architect; Dr Sally Ross [1962] Director/Doctor; Margaret Scott [1955] Director/NHS Trust Chairman; Anne Stanford [1963] Director/Press and Public Relations Manager

Portsmouth Surgical Holdings Limited
Incorporated: 18 September 2008 *Employees:* 55
Net Worth: £25,962,344 *Total Assets:* £29,631,684
Registered Office: 44 New Lane, Havant, Hants, PO9 2NF
Activities: Non-trading company
Major Shareholder: Guy Schofield
Officers: Guy Schofield, Secretary; Guy Schofield [1964] Director

Portsmouth Water Limited
Incorporated: 31 August 1990 *Employees:* 261
Net Worth: £78,215,000 *Total Assets:* £244,846,000
Registered Office: P O Box No 8, West Street, Havant, Hants, PO9 1LG
Activities: Water collection, treatment and supply
Parent: Ancala Fornia Limited
Officers: Christopher Neil Hardyman, Secretary; Heather Virginia Benjamin [1958] Director; Michael Robert Coffin [1959] Director; Martin Johnson [1973] Director; Mike Kirk [1960] Director; Helen Mary Grace Orton [1969] Director; David William Owens [1952] Director; Colin Robert Taylor [1961] Director

The Potanin Foundation
Incorporated: 21 July 2005
Net Worth: £102,533,064 *Total Assets:* £102,669,944
Registered Office: 25 Kings Hill Avenue, Kings Hill, West Malling, Kent, ME19 4TA
Activities: Financial intermediation not elsewhere classified
Officers: Sir John Menzies Low [1953] Director

Pourshins Limited
Incorporated: 27 July 1981 *Employees:* 64
Net Worth: £8,670,000 *Total Assets:* £31,332,000
Registered Office: Ash House, Littleton Road, Ashford, Middlesex, TW15 1TZ
Activities: Operation of warehousing and storage facilities for water transport activities
Officers: Willem Hendrik Human, Secretary; Stephen Philip Corr [1960] Managing Director; Thomas William Fountain [1969] Director/Chief Financial Officer; Willem Hendrik Human [1982] Finance Director [British/South African]

Powerscreen International Limited
Incorporated: 7 August 1970
Net Worth: £51,771,000 *Total Assets:* £77,711,000
Registered Office: The Pinnacle, 170 Midsummer Boulevard, Milton Keynes, Bucks, MK9 1FE
Activities: Activities of other holding companies n.e.c.
Parent: New Terex Holdings UK Limited
Officers: Eric I Cohen, Secretary [American]; Eric I Cohen [1958] Director/Lawyer [American]; John Daniel Sheehan [1960] Director/Chief Financial Officer [American]

PPP Capital Limited
Incorporated: 2 February 2016 *Employees:* 6
Net Worth: £20,761,856 *Total Assets:* £35,069,812
Registered Office: 9 Bridle Close, Kingston upon Thames, Surrey, KT1 2JW
Activities: Other letting and operating of own or leased real estate
Shareholders: Chandrakant Babubhai Patel; Pratima Chandrakant Patel; Sanjeev Charles Patel; Rajeev Charles Patel
Officers: Kenneth Bradley, Secretary; Chandrakant Babubhai Patel [1939] Director; Pratima Chandrakant Patel [1941] Director; Dr Rajeev Charles Patel [1972] Director; Sanjeev Charles Patel [1974] Director

PRA Group (UK) Limited
Incorporated: 9 August 2001 *Employees:* 300
Net Worth: £24,391,000 *Total Assets:* £492,511,008
Registered Office: Wells House, 15-17 Elmfield Road, Bromley, Kent, BR1 1LT
Activities: Financial intermediation not elsewhere classified
Parent: PRA Group Inc
Officers: Steven Edward Daws [1969] Director; Richard Owen James [1967] Managing Director; Per Martin Sjolund [1972] Director [Swedish]

Praesepe Holdings Limited
Incorporated: 3 November 2011 *Employees:* 58
Net Worth: £38,586,000 *Total Assets:* £110,447,000
Registered Office: Seebeck House, 1a Seebeck Place, Knowlhill, Milton Keynes, Bucks, MK5 8FR
Activities: Activities of other holding companies n.e.c.
Parent: Merkur Casino UK Limited
Officers: Stefan Bruns [1971] Director/Chief Executive Officer [German]; Borris Lungen [1962] Director/Chief Financial Officer [German]

Prater Limited
Incorporated: 6 March 1987 *Employees:* 388
Net Worth: £18,813,832 *Total Assets:* £50,723,148
Registered Office: Perrywood Business Park, Honeycrock Lane, Salfords, Surrey, RH1 5JQ
Activities: Construction of commercial buildings
Parent: Rayfix Limited
Officers: David Bowie Whillans, Secretary; Stephen James Foster [1970] Operations Director; Gavin Dixon Hamblett [1972] Pre Construction Director; Andrew John Newman [1966] Business Development Director; Christopher Roberts [1975] Commercial Director; Kevin Michael Smith [1979] Sales Director; Richard David Unwin [1967] Director/CEO Lindner Group; David Bowie Whillians [1958] Finance Director; Stuart James Whiting [1978] Technical Director

Prax Petroleum Limited
Incorporated: 20 November 2002
Net Worth: £16,705,960 *Total Assets:* £188,040,848
Registered Office: Prax House, Horizon Business Village, 1 Brooklands Road, Weybridge, Surrey, KT13 0TJ
Activities: Wholesale of petroleum and petroleum products
Officers: Arani Soosaipillai, Secretary; Don Camillo Emilio Borneo [1957] Director/Oil Trader; Winston Sanjeevkumar Soosaipillai [1973] Director

Premier Asset Management Group PLC
Incorporated: 9 July 2007 *Employees:* 107
Previous: Premier Asset Management Group Ltd
Net Worth: £45,268,000 *Total Assets:* £106,012,000
Registered Office: Eastgate Court, High Street, Guildford, Surrey, GU1 3DE
Activities: Financial intermediation not elsewhere classified
Officers: Neil Macpherson, Secretary/Director; Robert Charles Lumsden Colthorpe [1963] Director; Neil Macpherson [1960] Director; Michael Patrick O'Shea [1962] Director; William Longden Smith [1959] Director; Michael Andrew Vogel [1959] Director; Luke Anton Wiseman [1967] Director

Premier Asset Management Holdings Ltd.
Incorporated: 9 July 2007
Net Worth: £38,354,000 *Total Assets:* £60,348,000
Registered Office: Eastgate Court, High Street, Guildford, Surrey, GU1 3DE
Activities: Financial intermediation not elsewhere classified
Parent: Premier Asset Management Midco Limited
Officers: Neil Macpherson, Secretary/Director; Neil Macpherson [1960] Director; Michael Patrick O'Shea [1962] Director

Premier Asset Management Limited
Incorporated: 20 September 1995 *Employees:* 107
Net Worth: £15,938,000 *Total Assets:* £36,079,000
Registered Office: Eastgate Court, High Street, Guildford, Surrey, GU1 3DE
Activities: Activities of financial services holding companies
Parent: Premier Asset Management Holdings Ltd
Officers: Neil Macpherson, Secretary; Neil Macpherson [1960] Director/Chartered Accountant; Michael Patrick O'Shea [1962] Investment Director

Premier Asset Management Midco Ltd.
Incorporated: 9 July 2007
Net Worth: £33,278,000 *Total Assets:* £41,920,000
Registered Office: Eastgate Court, High Street, Guildford, Surrey, GU1 3DE
Activities: Financial intermediation not elsewhere classified
Parent: Premier Asset Management Group PLC
Officers: Neil Macpherson, Secretary/Director; Neil Macpherson [1960] Director; Michael Patrick O'Shea [1962] Director

Premier Fleet Management and Contract Hire Limited
Incorporated: 12 December 2006 *Employees:* 114
Net Worth: £317,008 *Total Assets:* £47,869,992
Registered Office: Venson House, 1 AC Court, High Street, Thames Ditton, Surrey, KT7 0SR
Activities: Activities of other holding companies n.e.c.
Major Shareholder: Dermot Fachtna Desmond
Officers: John Gerard Bateson [1963] Director [Irish]; Mark William Gerard [1965] Finance Director; Samantha Jane Roff [1968] Director; Simon John Staton [1973] Sales Director

Premier Fruit & Nut Limited
Incorporated: 24 October 1986
Net Worth: £42,394,444 *Total Assets:* £45,135,876
Registered Office: Premier House, 56-59 Leslie Park Road, Croydon, Surrey, CR0 6TP
Activities: Wholesale of fruit and vegetables
Shareholders: Narendra Hirji Shah; Minaxi Narendra Shah
Officers: Minaxi Narendra Shah, Secretary; Minaxi Narendra Shah [1952] Director; Narendra Hirji Shah [1950] Director; Rajeev Narendra Shah [1981] Director/Trader

Premier Global Infrastructure Trust PLC
Incorporated: 12 September 2003
Previous: Premier Energy and Water Trust PLC
Net Worth: £29,859,000 *Total Assets:* £56,489,000
Registered Office: Eastgate Court, High Street, Guildford, Surrey, GU1 3DE
Activities: Activities of investment trusts
Officers: Victoria Anne Muir [1971] Director; Gillian Nott [1945] Director; Katarzynia Maria Robinski [1962] Director

Premier Lotteries Capital UK Limited
Incorporated: 17 March 2010 *Employees:* 963
Net Worth Deficit: £137,000,000 *Total Assets:* £815,200,000
Registered Office: Tolpits Lane, Watford, Herts, WD18 9RN
Activities: Activities of head offices
Parent: Premier Lotteries Investments UK Limited
Officers: John Edward Michael Dillon, Secretary; John Edward Michael Dillon [1963] Legal Director and Company Secretary; Ilya Kachko [1979] Director/Portfolio Manager [Canadian]; Andrew Jonathan Mark Taylor [1961] Director/Private Equity Investor

Premier Lotteries UK Limited
Incorporated: 17 March 2010 *Employees:* 963
Net Worth Deficit: £19,800,000 *Total Assets:* £814,899,968
Registered Office: Tolpits Lane, Watford, Herts, WD18 9RN
Activities: Non-trading company
Parent: Premier Lotteries Capital UK Limited
Officers: John Edward Michael Dillon, Secretary; John Edward Michael Dillon [1963] Legal Director and Company Secretary; Ilya Kachko [1979] Director/Portfolio Manager [Canadian]; Andrew Jonathan Mark Taylor [1961] Director/Private Equity Investor

Premier Marinas Holdings Limited
Incorporated: 1 August 2005 *Employees:* 166
Net Worth: £171,026,000 *Total Assets:* £183,960,992
Registered Office: Head Office, Swanwick Marina, Swanwick, Southampton, SO31 1ZL
Activities: Activities of head offices
Parent: Gower Place Investments Limited
Officers: Carolyn Kloet, Secretary; Peter Hamilton Bradshaw [1964] Director/Chartered Accountant; Mark Sydney Clare [1957] Director; Timothy James Livett [1962] Director/Chief Financial Officer; Lisha Nagin Patel [1980] Director/Investments; Peter John Pereira Gray [1963] Managing Director Investments

Premier Marinas Limited
Incorporated: 6 October 1994 *Employees:* 62
Net Worth: £133,094,000 *Total Assets:* £137,364,000
Registered Office: Swanwick Marina, Swanwick, Southampton, SO31 1ZL
Activities: Other specialised construction activities n.e.c.
Parent: Premier Marinas Holdings Limited
Officers: Peter Hamilton Bradshaw [1964] Managing Director; John Mischa Cervenka [1968] Director; Geoffrey Andrew Collins [1968] Director/Accountant

Premier Medical Holdings Limited
Incorporated: 8 January 2016 *Employees:* 300
Net Worth: £16,199,540 *Total Assets:* £45,809,084
Registered Office: 4th Floor, Park Gate, 161-163 Preston Road, Brighton, BN1 6AF
Activities: Activities of other holding companies n.e.c.
Major Shareholder: Henry Otto Brunjes
Officers: Timothy John Mellor Aspinall [1956] Director/Solicitor; Dr Henry Otto Brunjes [1954] Director/Company Chairman; Dr Robert Colin Goodall [1955] Director/Doctor; Barry Gray [1975] Director; John Douglas Warner [1951] Director/Chartered Accountant

Premier Portfolio Managers Limited
Incorporated: 1 December 1975 *Employees:* 107
Net Worth: £16,220,000 *Total Assets:* £65,943,000
Registered Office: Eastgate Court, High Street, Guildford, Surrey, GU1 3DE
Activities: Financial intermediation not elsewhere classified
Parent: Premier Asset Management Limited
Officers: Neil Macpherson, Secretary; Rosamond Borer [1963] Director/Chief Risk Officer; Gregor Alexander Craig [1974] Director/Head of Legal & Compliance; Michael John Hammond [1965] Sales Director; Neil Macpherson [1960] Director/Chartered Accountant; Michael Patrick O'Shea [1962] Investment Director; Ian West [1971] Director; Simon Guy Wilson [1964] Marketing Director

Premier Research Group Limited
Incorporated: 19 February 2003 *Employees:* 117
Net Worth Deficit: £4,333,000 *Total Assets:* £31,621,000
Registered Office: 1st Floor, Rubra 2, Mulberry Business Park, Fishponds Road, Wokingham, Berks, RG41 2GY
Activities: Technical testing and analysis
Parent: PRGCO Limited
Officers: Anthony Charles Nicholson [1969] Director/Chief Financial Officer; Ludo Jan-Anna Reynders [1953] Director [Belgian]

Premier Research International Us Limited
Incorporated: 30 May 2008
Net Worth: £38,451,000 *Total Assets:* £38,697,000
Registered Office: 1st Floor, Rubra 2, Mulberry Business Park, Fishponds Road, Wokingham, Berks, RG41 2GY
Activities: Other research and experimental development on natural sciences and engineering
Officers: Anthony Charles Nicholson [1969] Director/Chief Financial Officer; Ludo Jan-Anna Reynders [1953] Director/Company CEO [Belgian]

Premier Rugby Limited
Incorporated: 31 August 1995 *Employees:* 30
Net Worth: £30,650 *Total Assets:* £24,510,050
Registered Office: Regal House, 70 London Road, Twickenham, Middlesex, TW1 3QS
Activities: Activities of sport clubs
Officers: Adrian Alli, Secretary; Christopher Arthur Booy [1952] Director; Bruce Timothy Craig [1962] Director; Michael Rowland Crossan [1956] Director/President; Nicholas John Eastwood [1959] Director/Chief Executive; Ismail Walid Kurdi [1968] Director; David John Morgan [1957] Director; Simon Sebastian Orange [1967] Director/Chairman; Anthony George Edward Rowe [1948] Director/Chairman; Martin George St Quinton [1957] Director; Peter William Gregory Tom [1940] Director; Mitesh Velani [1982] Director; John White [1951] Director/Chairman; Jason Whittingham [1971] Director/Financier

Premiere Employment Group Limited
Incorporated: 13 November 2003 *Employees:* 3,446
Net Worth: £5,923,020 *Total Assets:* £20,152,888
Registered Office: Chevron House, 346 Long Lane, Hillingdon, Middlesex, UB10 9PF
Activities: Temporary employment agency activities
Parent: Cordant People Limited
Officers: Alan Connor, Secretary; Chris Martin Kenneally [1960] Director; Jack Rainer Ullmann [1928] Director; Phillip Lionel Ullmann [1964] Director

Premium Credit Limited
Incorporated: 29 April 1986 *Employees:* 417
Net Worth: £182,362,000 *Total Assets:* £1,533,364,992
Registered Office: Ermyn House, Ermyn Way, Leatherhead, Surrey, KT22 8UX
Activities: Credit granting by non-deposit taking finance houses and other specialist consumer credit grantors
Parent: Vendcrown Limited
Officers: Elizabeth Sarah Annys, Secretary; Christopher Stephen Burke [1960] Director; Peter Anthony Colin Catterall [1968] Director; Andrew Phillip Chapman [1969] Director/Chief Financial Officer; Maxim Devin Crewe [1980] Director; Colin Denis Keogh [1953] Director/Chairman; John Reeve [1944] Director; Anthony Santospirito [1984] Director [Australian]; Thomas Woolgrove [1970] Director/Chief Executive Officer; David Thomas McAree Young [1961] Director

Preziosa Cruise Limited
Incorporated: 6 December 2016
Net Worth: £21,322,380 *Total Assets:* £386,967,136
Registered Office: 5 Roundwood Avenue, Stockley Park, Uxbridge, Middlesex, UB11 1AF
Activities: Sea and coastal passenger water transport
Shareholders: Gianluigi Aponte; Rafaela Aponte-Diamant
Officers: Domenico Ferrara, Secretary; Jonathan Francis Campbell [1971] Director/Chartered Accountant; Emilio La Scala [1960] Director [Italian]; Pierfrancesco Vago [1961] Director [Italian]

Pricketts Limited
Incorporated: 22 November 1945 *Employees:* 6
Net Worth: £36,536,624 *Total Assets:* £38,022,408
Registered Office: 225 London Road, Staines upon Thames, Middlesex, TW18 4HR
Activities: Buying and selling of own real estate
Officers: Judith Margaret Prickett, Secretary; Jennifer Eileen Cross [1955] Director; Christopher Charles Prickett [1949] Director; Judith Margaret Prickett [1953] Director

Prime Care Solutions (Kingston) Holdings Limited
Incorporated: 22 December 2003
Net Worth Deficit: £11,429,000 *Total Assets:* £38,657,000
Registered Office: 8 White Oak Square, London Road, Swanley, Kent, BR8 7AG
Activities: Activities of head offices
Shareholders: Palio (No 3) Limited; Dolphin One Limited
Officers: Carl Harvey Dix [1966] Operations Director; Paul Allyn Edwards [1976] Director/Tax Adviser; Gary William Mills [1956] Director/Project Manager

Prime Care Solutions (Kingston) Limited
Incorporated: 11 June 2003
Net Worth Deficit: £11,429,000 *Total Assets:* £38,657,000
Registered Office: 8 White Oak Square, London Road, Swanley, Kent, BR8 7AG
Activities: Construction of commercial buildings
Parent: Prime Care Solutions (Kingston) Holdings Limited
Officers: Carl Harvey Dix [1966] Operations Director; Paul Allyn Edwards [1976] Director/Tax Adviser; Gary William Mills [1956] Director/Project Manager

The Principal Edinburgh George Street Limited
Incorporated: 15 April 2005 *Employees:* 270
Previous: Troy Management Services (George) Limited
Net Worth: £12,946,000 *Total Assets:* £21,181,000
Registered Office: Broadwater Park, Denham, Uxbridge, Middlesex, UB9 5HR
Activities: Hotels and similar accommodation
Parent: IHC May Fair Hotel Limited
Officers: Catherine Elizabeth Lindsay, Secretary; Michael Todd Glover [1971] Director/Financial Controller [American]; Nicolette Henfrey [1969] Director; Geoffrey Howard Lee [1955] Director [Australian]; Daisy Eleanor Loveday Caroline Llewellyn [1976] Director; David James Taylor [1976] Director; Matthew Woollard [1985] Director

The Principal London Limited
Incorporated: 26 November 2003 *Employees:* 34
Previous: Troy Management Services (Russell) Limited
Net Worth: £6,548,000 *Total Assets:* £63,768,000
Registered Office: Broadwater Park, North Orbital Road, Denham, Uxbridge, Middlesex, UB9 5HR
Activities: Hotels and similar accommodation
Parent: IHC May Fair Hotel Limited
Officers: Catherine Elizabeth Lindsay, Secretary; Michael Todd Glover [1971] Director/Financial Controller [American]; Nicolette Henfrey [1969] Director; Geoffrey Howard Lee [1955] Director [Australian]; Daisy Eleanor Loveday Caroline Llewellyn [1976] Director; David James Taylor [1976] Director; Matthew Woollard [1985] Director

The Principal Manchester Limited
Incorporated: 26 November 2003 *Employees:* 347
Previous: Troy Management Services (Manchester Palace) Limited
Net Worth Deficit: £4,980,000 *Total Assets:* £35,954,000
Registered Office: Broadwater Park, North Orbital Road, Denham, Uxbridge, Middlesex, UB9 5HR
Activities: Hotels and similar accommodation
Parent: IHC May Fair Hotel Limited
Officers: Catherine Elizabeth Lindsay, Secretary; Michael Todd Glover [1971] Director/Financial Controller [American]; Nicolette Henfrey [1969] Director; Geoffrey Howard Lee [1955] Director [Australian]; Daisy Eleanor Loveday Caroline Llewellyn [1976] Director; David James Taylor [1976] Director; Matthew Woollard [1985] Director

Prinhold Limited
Incorporated: 1 August 2011 *Employees:* 1
Net Worth: £3,164,371 *Total Assets:* £23,869,468
Registered Office: c/o Hillier Hopkins LLP, Radius House, 51 Clarendon Road, Watford, Herts, WD17 1HP
Activities: Other letting and operating of own or leased real estate
Major Shareholder: Jonathan Russell Beck
Officers: Jonathan Russell Beck [1967] Director/Investor

Prior's Court Foundation
Incorporated: 12 June 1998 *Employees:* 437
Net Worth: £18,537,372 *Total Assets:* £27,385,808
Registered Office: Prior's Court School, Priors Court Road, Hermitage, Thatcham, Berks, RG18 9NU
Activities: Other education n.e.c.
Officers: Neil John Atherton, Secretary; Christoper Robert Barrett [1948] Director; Alison Margaret Bateson [1959] Director; Kenneth Alisdair Bisset [1957] Director/Accountant; Gordon Arthur Bull [1955] Director/Trustee; John Charles Byrne [1951] Director/Trustee; Susan Duncan [1955] Director; Claire Benita Miller [1962] Director/Trustee; Christopher John Morley [1957] Director; Clive Douglas Nickolds [1946] Director/Retired; Thomas James Buchan Scott [1962] Director/Lawyer; Margaret Jean Shirman [1950] Director; William Hubert Powlett Smith [1950] Director/Trustee; Dr Catherine Tissot Demidoff [1959] Director/Lecturer

Giles W. Pritchard-Gordon & Co. Limited
Incorporated: 26 September 1973 *Employees:* 115
Net Worth: £60,668,644 *Total Assets:* £90,024,160
Registered Office: Slaugham Park, Slaugham, W Sussex, RH17 6AH
Activities: Activities of head offices
Shareholders: Alice Clare Wingfield Digby; Emily Kate Aird; Lucy Clementine Keane; Eliza Mary Stoop; Veronica Pritchard-Gordon; Nicholas Henry Dudley Ryder
Officers: Mark Talbot Lewis, Secretary; Emily Kate Aird [1979] Director; Rory Charles MacGregor Aird [1968] Director; Lucy Clementine Keane [1983] Director; Veronica Pritchard-Gordon [1947] Director; Nicholas Henry Dudley Ryder [1960] Director; Eliza Mary Stoop [1986] Director; Alice Clare Wingfield Digby [1974] Director

Pritchard-Gordon Tankers Limited
Incorporated: 5 March 1992 *Employees:* 88
Net Worth: £59,769,344 *Total Assets:* £87,383,320
Registered Office: Slaugham Park, Slaugham, W Sussex, RH17 6AH
Activities: Sea and coastal freight water transport
Parent: Giles W Pritchard-Gordon (Shipowning) Ltd
Officers: Mark Talbot Lewis, Secretary; Emily Kate Aird [1979] Director; Rory Charles MacGregor Aird [1968] Director; Ian Fraser Campbell [1952] Director; Henry Oliver Keane [1982] Director; Lucy Clementine Keane [1983] Director; Eliza Mary Stoop [1986] Director; Alice Clare Wingfield Digby [1974] Director

L.E. Pritchitt & Company Limited
Incorporated: 18 May 1983 *Employees:* 223
Net Worth: £3,959,000 *Total Assets:* £24,888,000
Registered Office: 2nd Floor, Kingfisher House, 21-23 Elmfield Road, Bromley, Kent, BR1 1LT
Activities: Liquid milk and cream production
Officers: Tom Griffin, Secretary; Dermot Farrell [1966] Director/Manager [Irish]; Thomas Anthony Griffin [1978] Director [Irish]; Peter Sheridan [1962] Director/Financial Controller [Irish]

ProAV Holdings Limited
Incorporated: 26 February 2014 *Employees:* 323
Net Worth: £498,325 *Total Assets:* £25,243,768
Registered Office: ProAV House, Omega Way, Egham, Surrey, TW20 8RD
Activities: Wholesale of other intermediate products
Major Shareholder: Richard Brookes
Officers: LEA Brookes [1966] Director; Richard James Brookes [1964] Managing Director; Francesca Hazell [1969] Director

Procter & Gamble (Health & Beauty Care) Limited
Incorporated: 6 June 1947
Net Worth: £325,384,000 *Total Assets:* £411,360,000
Registered Office: The Heights, Brooklands, Weybridge, Surrey, KT13 0XP
Activities: Non-trading company
Parent: Procter & Gamble UK Group Holdings Limited
Officers: Anthony Joseph Appleton, Secretary; Anthony Joseph Appleton [1962] Director/Solicitor; Gianluca Branda [1970] Director/Product Supply Leader [Italian]; Alexander George Buckthorp [1973] Finance Director; Aimee Karen Goldsmith [1973] Associate Director, Communications P&G Northern Europe; Rebecca Jane Goodall [1976] Customer Accounts Director; Daisy Victoria Gray [1980] Sales Director; Ian Douglas Morley [1966] Group Sales Director; Aileen Louise Nathan [1981] Commercial Operations Associate Director; Vijay Indroo Sitlani [1975] Finance Director [Singaporean]; Christopher John Young [1974] HR Director

Procter & Gamble (L & CP) Limited
Incorporated: 5 December 1996
Net Worth: £112,389,000 *Total Assets:* £125,951,000
Registered Office: The Heights, Brooklands, Weybridge, Surrey, KT13 0XP
Activities: Other service activities n.e.c.
Parent: Procter & Gamble UK Group Holdings Limited
Officers: Anthony Joseph Appleton, Secretary; Anthony Joseph Appleton [1962] Director/Solicitor; Gianluca Branda [1970] Director/Product Supply Leader [Italian]; Alexander George Buckthorp [1973] Finance Director; Aimee Karen Goldsmith [1973] Associate Director, Communications P&G Northern Europe; Rebecca Jane Goodall [1976] Customer Accounts Director; Daisy Victoria Gray [1980] Sales Director; Ian Douglas Morley [1966] Group Sales Director; Aileen Louise Nathan [1981] Commercial Operations Associate Director; Vijay Indroo Sitlani [1975] Finance Director [Singaporean]; Christopher John Young [1974] HR Director

Procter & Gamble Finance (UK) Limited
Incorporated: 30 April 2004
Net Worth: £1,474,711,936 *Total Assets:* £1,474,711,936
Registered Office: The Heights, Brooklands, Weybridge, Surrey, KT13 0XP
Activities: Non-trading company
Parent: Procter & Gamble Investment Company (UK) Limited
Officers: Anthony Joseph Appleton, Secretary; Anthony Joseph Appleton [1962] Director/Solicitor; Alexander George Buckthorp [1973] Finance Director; Vijay Indroo Sitlani [1975] Finance Director [Singaporean]

Procter & Gamble Holdings (UK) Limited
Incorporated: 30 April 2004
Net Worth: £1,450,305,536 *Total Assets:* £1,450,305,536
Registered Office: The Heights, Brooklands, Weybridge, Surrey, KT13 0XP
Activities: Activities of head offices
Officers: Anthony Joseph Appleton, Secretary; Anthony Joseph Appleton [1962] Director/Solicitor; Alexander George Buckthorp [1973] Finance Director; Vijay Indroo Sitlani [1975] Finance Director [Singaporean]

Procter & Gamble Investment Company (UK) Limited
Incorporated: 30 April 2004
Net Worth: £1,430,648,704 *Total Assets:* £1,430,648,704
Registered Office: The Heights, Brooklands, Weybridge, Surrey, KT13 0XP
Activities: Non-trading company
Parent: Procter & Gamble Holdings (UK) Limited
Officers: Anthony Joseph Appleton, Secretary; Anthony Joseph Appleton [1962] Director/Solicitor; Alexander George Buckthorp [1973] Finance Director; Vijay Indroo Sitlani [1975] Finance Director [Singaporean]

Procter & Gamble Limited
Incorporated: 1 March 1905
Net Worth: £307,371,008 *Total Assets:* £307,380,992
Registered Office: The Heights, Brooklands, Weybridge, Surrey, KT13 0XP
Activities: Non-trading company
Officers: Anthony Joseph Appleton, Secretary; Anthony Joseph Appleton [1962] Director/Solicitor; Alexander George Buckthorp [1973] Finance Director; Vijay Indroo Sitlani [1975] Finance Director [Singaporean]

Procter & Gamble Overseas Limited
Incorporated: 30 April 2004
Net Worth: £1,509,418,752 *Total Assets:* £1,509,418,752
Registered Office: The Heights, Brooklands, Weybridge, Surrey, KT13 0XP
Activities: Non-trading company
Parent: Procter & Gamble Finance (UK) Limited
Officers: Anthony Joseph Appleton, Secretary; Anthony Joseph Appleton [1962] Director/Solicitor; Alexander George Buckthorp [1973] Finance Director; Vijay Indroo Sitlani [1975] Finance Director [Singaporean]

Procter & Gamble Product Supply (U.K.) Limited
Incorporated: 27 June 1995 *Employees:* 839
Net Worth: £290,435,008 *Total Assets:* £432,592,992
Registered Office: The Heights, Brooklands, Weybridge, Surrey, KT13 0XP
Activities: Manufacture of soap and detergents
Parent: Procter & Gamble (Health & Beauty Care) Limited
Officers: Anthony Joseph Appleton, Secretary; Anthony Joseph Appleton [1962] Director/Solicitor; Gianluca Branda [1970] Director/Product Supply Leader [Italian]; Alexander George Buckthorp [1973] Finance Director; Adina Pascu [1971] Director/Plant Manager [Romanian]; Vijay Indroo Sitlani [1975] Finance Director [Singaporean]; Gary Kenneth Wightman [1971] Director/Plant Manager; Christopher John Young [1974] HR Director

Procter & Gamble Technical Centres Limited
Incorporated: 20 November 1996 *Employees:* 1,029
Net Worth: £110,775,000 *Total Assets:* £234,520,000
Registered Office: The Heights, Brooklands, Weybridge, Surrey, KT13 0XP
Activities: Other professional, scientific and technical activities n.e.c.
Parent: Procter & Gamble (Health & Beauty Care) Limited
Officers: Anthony Joseph Appleton, Secretary; Anthony Joseph Appleton [1962] Director/Solicitor; Alexander George Buckthorp [1973] Finance Director; Claire Elaine Long [1969] Finance Director; Vasiliki Poulopoulou [1965] R&D Associate Director [Greek/British]; Scott Anthony Rodrigue [1963] Research Director [American]; Vijay Indroo Sitlani [1975] Finance Director [Singaporean]; Christopher John Young [1974] HR Director

Procter & Gamble UK Group Holdings Limited
Incorporated: 9 March 1994 *Employees:* 4
Previous: Procter & Gamble UK Holdings Limited
Net Worth: £251,771,008 *Total Assets:* £251,772,000
Registered Office: The Heights, Brooklands, Weybridge, Surrey, KT13 0XP
Activities: Operation of warehousing and storage facilities for land transport activities
Parent: Procter & Gamble Limited
Officers: Anthony Joseph Appleton, Secretary; Anthony Joseph Appleton [1962] Director/Solicitor; Alexander George Buckthorp [1973] Finance Director; Vijay Indroo Sitlani [1975] Finance Director [Singaporean]

Procter & Gamble UK Parent Company Limited
Incorporated: 7 April 2011 *Employees:* 3
Net Worth: £1,013,041,408 *Total Assets:* £1,013,041,408
Registered Office: The Heights, Brooklands, Weybridge, Surrey, KT13 0XP
Activities: Non-trading company
Officers: Anthony Joseph Appleton, Secretary; Anthony Joseph Appleton [1962] Director/Solicitor; Alexander George Buckthorp [1973] Finance Director; Vijay Indroo Sitlani [1975] Finance Director [Singaporean]

Progress Software Limited
Incorporated: 14 April 1988 *Employees:* 44
Net Worth: £7,510,000 *Total Assets:* £37,678,000
Registered Office: Highfield Court, Tollgate, Chandler's Ford, Eastleigh, Hants, SO53 3TY
Activities: Business and domestic software development
Officers: Stephen Howard Faberman, Secretary; Stephen Howard Faberman [1969] Director/General Counsel [American]; Brian Flanagan [1961] Director, Treasury [American]

Project Farm Bidco Limited
Incorporated: 24 September 2015 *Employees:* 11
Net Worth Deficit: £2,206,079 *Total Assets:* £37,061,456
Registered Office: Kynetec, Weston Court, Weston, Newbury, Berks, RG20 8JE
Activities: Activities of other holding companies n.e.c.
Parent: Project Farm Bidco 2016 Limited
Officers: Stephen Robert Hearn [1970] Director; Peter Stanley McDowell [1971] Director/Chief Financial Officer; Nicholas William Rosenberg [1991] Director/Finance; Stephen Burford Warshaw [1948] Director; Mark Llewellyn Williams [1978] Director

Project Farm Topco Limited
Incorporated: 24 September 2015 *Employees:* 262
Net Worth Deficit: £6,703,919 *Total Assets:* £40,158,924
Registered Office: Kynetec, Weston Court, Weston, Newbury, Berks, RG20 8JE
Activities: Activities of other holding companies n.e.c.
Officers: Stephen Robert Hearn [1970] Director/Chief Executive Officer; Peter Stanley McDowell [1971] Director/Chief Financial Officer; Nicholas William Rosenberg [1991] Director/Finance; Stephen Burford Warshaw [1948] Director; Mark Llewellyn Williams [1978] Director

Project Tristar Limited
Incorporated: 22 November 2007
Net Worth Deficit: £574,000 *Total Assets:* £24,763,000
Registered Office: Unit 1 Horton Road, West Drayton, Middlesex, UB7 8BQ
Activities: Other passenger land transport
Parent: Addison Lee Group Limited
Officers: Lee Gage, Secretary; Andrew Kenneth Boland [1969] Director/Chief Executive Officer; Simon Gordon [1970] Director

Project Ventures Rail Investments I Limited
Incorporated: 8 October 2012
Net Worth: £50,068,000 *Total Assets:* £50,100,000
Registered Office: Faraday House, Sir William Siemens Square, Frimley, Camberley, Surrey, GU16 8QD
Activities: Activities of other holding companies n.e.c.
Parent: Siemens Aktiengesellschaft
Officers: Simone Eufemia Agatha Davina, Secretary; Richard Anthony Hargraves [1964] Director; Petra Regge [1973] Director/Investment Manager (Portfolio) [German]; Basil Justin Bromley Wetters [1967] Director

Promon-Logicalis Latin America Limited
Incorporated: 18 February 2002 *Employees:* 1,485
Net Worth: £103,555,000 *Total Assets:* £411,554,528
Registered Office: 110 Buckingham Avenue, Slough, Berks, SL1 4PF
Activities: Other information technology service activities
Officers: Mark Grant, Secretary; Robert Broncho Bailkoski [1975] Director/Accountant; Jens Peter Montanana [1960] Director; Carlos Alberto Moller Pingarilho [1970] Director/Engineer [Brazilian]; Stuart Edward Radcliffe [1965] Director/Chief Financial Officer; Mark Rogers [1958] Finance Director; Luiz Fernando Telles Rudge [1956] Director/Administrator [Brazilian]; Marcio Nieblas Zapater [1980] Executive Director [Brazilian]

Propane Company Limited (The)
Incorporated: 5 April 1933 *Employees:* 8
Net Worth: £36,017,936 *Total Assets:* £43,813,068
Registered Office: Frenchay, Appledore Road, Tenterden, Kent, TN30 7DJ
Activities: Manufacture of other food products n.e.c.
Parent: Propane Holdings Limited
Officers: Andrew Le Pla, Secretary; James Francis Corrin [1962] Director/Legal/Financial; The Hon. Francesca Nicola Sternberg [1962] Director; Jessica Rk Sternberg [1990] Director/Graduate; The Honourable Rosanne Monica Michelle Sternberg [1960] Director

Prospect Healthcare (Hairmyres) Group Limited
Incorporated: 7 April 2003
Net Worth Deficit: £9,561,000 *Total Assets:* £84,352,000
Registered Office: 8 White Oak Square, London Road, Swanley, Kent, BR8 7AG
Activities: Activities of head offices
Officers: David John Brooking [1967] Investment Director; Christopher James [1968] Investment Director; Jeffrey Michael Thornton [1953] Director/Consultant

Prospect Healthcare (Hairmyres) Limited
Incorporated: 11 February 1998
Net Worth Deficit: £9,056,000 *Total Assets:* £84,789,000
Registered Office: 8 White Oak Square, London Road, Swanley, Kent, BR8 7AG
Activities: Hospital activities
Officers: David John Brooking [1967] Investment Director; Christopher James [1968] Investment Director; Jeffrey Michael Thornton [1953] Director/Consultant

Prospect Healthcare (Hinchingbrooke) Limited
Incorporated: 24 July 2003
Net Worth Deficit: £67,000 *Total Assets:* £23,405,000
Registered Office: 8 White Oak Square, London Road, Swanley, Kent, BR8 7AG
Activities: Combined facilities support activities
Parent: Prospect Healthcare (Hinchingbrooke) Holdings Limited
Officers: Ross William Driver [1981] Director; Julian Mark Rudd-Jones [1955] Director/Property Developer; Mark Christopher Wayment [1958] Investment Director Infrastructure

Prospect Healthcare (Reading) Limited
Incorporated: 19 July 1999
Net Worth: £2,890,000 *Total Assets:* £29,903,000
Registered Office: 8 White Oak Square, London Road, Swanley, Kent, BR8 7AG
Activities: Combined facilities support activities
Parent: Prospect Healthcare (Reading) Holdings Limited
Officers: David John Brooking [1967] Investment Director; Sabrina Sidhu [1979] Director

Prospect School, Reading
Incorporated: 7 June 2011 *Employees:* 197
Net Worth: £17,025,184 *Total Assets:* £20,911,444
Registered Office: Cockney Hill, Tilehurst, Reading, Berks, RG30 4EX
Activities: General secondary education
Officers: Helen Louise Willingale, Secretary; Lisa Maria Akister [1964] Director/Personal Assistant; Paul Barker [1953] Director/Project Manager; Marjorie Florence Caballero [1952] Director/Legal Executive; Philip Antony Davies [1962] Director/Headteacher; Ann Margaret Giubertoni [1954] Director; Helen Muriel Hathaway [1947] Director [Irish]; Alexa Sian Holt [1976] Director/Teacher; Joanne Lannon [1977] Director/Legal Assistant/Completions Clerk; Callum Purvis [1965] Director/Full Time Carer; Paul Reilly [1965] Director/Managing Partner; Margaret Mary Sampson [1951] Director/Retired; Carol Janet Thomas [1973] Director/HR Manager

Prospects Group 2011 Limited
Incorporated: 18 July 2011 *Employees:* 1,219
Net Worth Deficit: £32,012,000 *Total Assets:* £37,933,000
Registered Office: Shaw Trust House, 19 Elmfield Road, Bromley, Kent, BR1 1LT
Activities: Activities of head offices
Parent: The Shaw Trust Limited
Officers: Nicholas Oliver Carey, Secretary; Paul Michael Baldwin [1965] Director; James Nicholas Bell [1966] Director; Victoria Blakeman [1968] Director; Brenda Patricia Cabras [1955] Director; Nicholas Oliver Charles Carey [1986] Director; Peter David Holmes [1953] Director; Vanessa Helen Miner [1962] Director; Jacqueline Maria Oughton [1964] Director; David George Phipps [1970] Director/Chief Finance Officer; Alison Ruth Williams [1965] Director

Prospects Services
Incorporated: 30 March 1995 *Employees:* 1,154
Net Worth Deficit: £31,112,000 *Total Assets:* £37,111,000
Registered Office: Shaw Trust House, 19 Elmfield Road, Bromley, Kent, BR1 1LT
Activities: Educational support services
Parent: Prospects Services Midco Limited
Officers: Catherine Joanne Trevorrow, Secretary; Paul Michael Baldwin [1965] Director; James Nicholas Bell [1966] Director; Victoria Blakeman [1968] Director; Brenda Patricia Cabras [1955] Director; Nicholas Oliver Charles Carey [1986] Director; Peter David Holmes [1953] Director; Vanessa Helen Miner [1962] Director; Jacqueline Maria Oughton [1964] Director; David George Phipps [1970] Finance Director; Alison Ruth Williams [1965] Director

The Protection Specialist Limited
Incorporated: 22 July 2009 *Employees:* 325
Net Worth: £29,913,292 *Total Assets:* £40,166,728
Registered Office: Fair Trade House, 3 Whittle Avenue, Fareham, Hants, PO15 5SH
Activities: Activities auxiliary to financial intermediation n.e.c.
Major Shareholder: Mark Jonathan Lance
Officers: Elaine Knapp, Secretary; Carlina Lindsay Lance [1979] Director; Mark Jonathan Lance [1975] Managing Director; Kelly Ann Sichel [1976] Director; Peter Robert Sichel [1975] Director

Proudreed Limited
Incorporated: 19 August 1981 *Employees:* 17
Net Worth: £208,246,000 *Total Assets:* £599,505,024
Registered Office: 16 Carlton Crescent, Southampton, SO15 2ES
Activities: Buying and selling of own real estate
Shareholders: Jeffrey Colin Smith; Caspar MacDonald-Hall
Officers: Rachel Louise Edwards, Secretary; James Andrew Fife, Secretary/Surveyor; Caspar MacDonald-Hall [1950] Director; Jeffrey Colin Smith [1945] Director

Proudreed Real Estate Limited
Incorporated: 8 June 2005
Net Worth: £40,778,000 *Total Assets:* £102,313,000
Registered Office: 16 Carlton Crescent, Southampton, SO15 2ES
Activities: Buying and selling of own real estate
Parent: Proudreed Limited
Officers: Rachel Louise Edwards, Secretary; Nicholas John Burgess [1955] Director/Chartered Surveyor; James Andrew Fife [1966] Director/Chartered Surveyor; Caspar MacDonald-Hall [1950] Director; Jeffrey Colin Smith [1945] Director

Prowting Investments PLC
Incorporated: 6 August 1987 *Employees:* 12
Net Worth: £23,034,152 *Total Assets:* £39,889,556
Registered Office: 8 Packhorse Road, Gerrards Cross, Bucks, SL9 7QE
Activities: Development of building projects
Officers: Sonya Lorraine Richards, Secretary; Barry Peter Amos-Yeo [1980] Director; Kevin Richard Amos-Yeo [1982] Director; Elizabeth Anne Prowting [1939] Director; Wendy Jane Trott [1966] Director

Prysmian Cables & Systems Limited
Incorporated: 18 July 1969 *Employees:* 1,094
Net Worth: £134,280,000 *Total Assets:* £396,783,008
Registered Office: Chickenhall Lane, Eastleigh, Hants, SO50 6YU
Activities: Manufacture of other electronic and electric wires and cables
Parent: Prysmian UK Group Limited
Officers: Colin Anthony Briggs, Secretary; Luca Caserta [1973] Director [Italian]; Marcello Maria Giuseppe Ambrogio Del Brenna [1969] Director/Executive [Italian]; Fabio Ignazio Romeo [1955] Director/Business Executive [Italian]

Prysmian Powerlink Services Limited
Incorporated: 2 June 2011
Net Worth: £43,909,400 *Total Assets:* £84,558,600
Registered Office: Prysmian, Chickenhall Lane, Eastleigh, Hants, SO50 6YU
Activities: Other specialised construction activities n.e.c.
Parent: Prysmian UK Group Limited
Officers: Colin Anthony Briggs, Secretary; Mirko Beretta [1974] Director [Italian]; Luca Caserta [1973] Director [Italian]; Marcello Maria Giuseppe Ambrogio Del Brenna [1969] Director/Executive [Italian]; Hakan Ozmen [1970] Director/Executive [American]

Prysmian UK Group Limited
Incorporated: 2 April 2012
Net Worth: £166,408,000 *Total Assets:* £298,881,984
Registered Office: Chickenhall Lane, Eastleigh, Hants, SO50 6YU
Activities: Activities of head offices
Parent: Prysmian S.P.A.
Officers: Colin Anthony Briggs, Secretary; Luca Caserta [1973] Director [Italian]; Marcello Maria Giuseppe Ambrogio Del Brenna [1969] Director/Executive [Italian]; Giovanni Giorgio Angelo Arturo Maria Zancan [1963] Director/Executive [Italian]

PSA Finance UK Limited
Incorporated: 16 September 1971 *Employees:* 268
Previous: PSA Wholesale Limited
Net Worth: £308,080,000 *Total Assets:* £3,208,998,912
Registered Office: 61 London Road, Redhill, Surrey, RH1 1QA
Activities: Sale of new cars and light motor vehicles
Shareholders: Santander Consumer (UK) PLC; Banque PSA Finance SA
Officers: Kathleen Fiona Conroy, Secretary; Arnaud Du Teilhet de Lamothe [1966] Director/Deputy CEO [Swiss/French]; Magalie Marie-France Durreche [1978] Director/Chief Financial Officer [French]; Adam Roy Goldhagen [1964] Director; Victor Thomas Hill [1964] Chartered Director; Bruno Montalvo Wilmot [1962] Director-Banking [Spanish]; Bruno Perrin [1967] Director [French]

PSI - Pay Ltd
Incorporated: 8 August 2006 *Employees:* 11
Net Worth: £5,181,458 *Total Assets:* £50,119,196
Registered Office: Afon Building, Worthing Road, Horsham, W Sussex, RH12 1TL
Activities: Financial intermediation not elsewhere classified
Officers: Anthony Richard Davis, Secretary; Jonathan Amrani [1979] Director/Business Executive; Philip James Davies [1951] Director; Anthony Richard Davis [1953] Director/Chartered Accountant; Craig James [1970] Director/Compliance Consultant

PSN Holdco Limited
Incorporated: 9 March 2015
Net Worth Deficit: £869,000 *Total Assets:* £27,428,000
Registered Office: Hanover House, Plane Tree Crescent, Feltham, Middlesex, TW13 7BZ
Activities: Non-trading company
Parent: Perform Sports Media Limited
Officers: Paul Oszkar David Morton [1979] Director

PT UK Holding Limited
Incorporated: 13 July 2016
Net Worth: £22,704,360 *Total Assets:* £23,870,848
Registered Office: Forum 3, Solent Business Park Parkway, Whiteley, Fareham, Hants, PO15 7FH
Activities: Activities of other holding companies n.e.c.
Shareholders: Thomas Broe-Anderson; Peter Olof Moller
Officers: David Terence Bridger [1984] Associate Director; Paul David Harrison [1976] Managing Director

PTP Software Limited
Incorporated: 1 March 1996
Net Worth: £29,389,884 *Total Assets:* £52,246,808
Registered Office: Riding Court House, Riding Court Road, Datchet, Berks, SL3 9JT
Activities: Information technology consultancy activities
Parent: Iris Group Limited
Officers: Michael David Cox [1983] Director; Kevin Peter Dady [1964] Director; Elona Mortimer-Zikha [1979] Director

Pulsant Acquisitions Limited
Incorporated: 26 February 2014 *Employees:* 7
Net Worth: £134,278,816 *Total Assets:* £215,129,360
Registered Office: Blue Square House, Priors Way, Maidenhead, Berks, SL6 2HP
Activities: Other information technology service activities
Parent: Pulsant Parent Limited
Officers: Robert Davies [1971] Director; Pieter Knook [1958] Director [Dutch]; Bradley Mark Petzer [1973] Director; Niclas Sanfridsson [1970] Director [Swedish]; David S Scott [1978] Director [American]; Marion Stewart [1966] Director

Pulsant Bidco Limited
Incorporated: 11 March 2010
Net Worth Deficit: £41,675,064 *Total Assets:* £149,950,752
Registered Office: Blue Square House, Priors Way, Maidenhead, Berks, SL6 2HP
Activities: Other information technology service activities
Parent: Pulsant Midco 2 Limited
Officers: Bradley Mark Petzer [1973] Director; Niclas Sanfridsson [1970] Director [Swedish]

Pulsant Group Holdings Limited
Incorporated: 6 June 2014 *Employees:* 384
Net Worth: £24,014,000 *Total Assets:* £250,235,008
Registered Office: Blue Square House, Priors Way, Maidenhead, Berks, SL6 2HP
Activities: Activities of other holding companies n.e.c.
Officers: Martin Francis Brennan [1980] Director/Venture Capitalist; J. Taylor Crandall [1954] Director [American]; William J Pade [1951] Director [American]; David S Scott [1978] Director [American]

Pulsant Group Limited
Incorporated: 6 June 2014
Net Worth Deficit: £46,170,000 *Total Assets:* £145,164,000
Registered Office: Blue Square House, Priors Way, Maidenhead, Berks, SL6 2HP
Activities: Other business support service activities n.e.c.
Parent: Pulsant Group Holdings Limited
Officers: Martin Francis Brennan [1980] Director; J. Taylor Crandall [1954] Director [American]; Robert Davies [1971] Director; Pieter Cornelis Knook [1958] Director [Dutch]; William J Pade [1951] Director [American]; Bradley Mark Petzer [1973] Director; Niclas Sanfridsson [1970] Director [Swedish]; David S Scott [1978] Director [American]; Marion Stewart [1966] Director; Michael Tobin [1964] Director

Pulsant Midco 1 Limited
Incorporated: 8 October 2010
Net Worth: £5,431,523 *Total Assets:* £118,125,360
Registered Office: Blue Square House, Priors Way, Maidenhead, Berks, SL6 2HP
Activities: Other business support service activities n.e.c.
Parent: Pulsant Topco Limited
Officers: Bradley Mark Petzer [1973] Director; Niclas Sanfridsson [1970] Director [Swedish]

Pulsant Midco 2 Limited
Incorporated: 8 October 2010
Net Worth: £1,905,240 *Total Assets:* £118,125,360
Registered Office: Blue Square House, Priors Way, Maidenhead, Berks, SL6 2HP
Activities: Other business support service activities n.e.c.
Parent: Pulsant Midco 1 Limited
Officers: Bradley Mark Petzer [1973] Director; Niclas Sanfridsson [1970] Director [Swedish]

Pulsant Parent Limited
Incorporated: 6 June 2014 *Employees:* 391
Net Worth: £69,055,000 *Total Assets:* £236,727,008
Registered Office: Blue Square House, Priors Way, Maidenhead, Berks, SL6 2HP
Activities: Other business support service activities n.e.c.
Parent: Pulsant Group Limited
Officers: Bradley Mark Petzer [1973] Director; Niclas Sanfridsson [1970] Director [Swedish]; David S Scott [1978] Director [American]

Pulsant Topco Limited
Incorporated: 11 October 2010
Net Worth: £10,397,924 *Total Assets:* £53,450,548
Registered Office: Blue Square House, Priors Way, Maidenhead, Berks, SL6 2HP
Activities: Other professional, scientific and technical activities n.e.c.
Parent: Pulsant Acquisitions Limited
Officers: Robert Davies [1971] Director/Consultant; Bradley Mark Petzer [1973] Director; Niclas Sanfridsson [1970] Director [Swedish]

Pura Foods Limited
Incorporated: 28 August 1987 *Employees:* 174
Net Worth: £62,272,000 *Total Assets:* £110,393,752
Registered Office: ADM International Offices, Church Manorway, Erith, Kent, DA8 1DL
Activities: Manufacture of oils and fats
Shareholders: ADM Pura Limited; Archer Daniels Midland (UK) Limited
Officers: Douwe Alserda [1968] Director/Financial Controller [Dutch]; Marcus Degen [1966] Director/General Manager [Dutch]; Lance Thomas Rogers [1973] Director/Financial Controller

Purecircle (UK) Limited
Incorporated: 23 August 2011 *Employees:* 14
Net Worth Deficit: £6,606,775 *Total Assets:* £25,042,014
Registered Office: Unit 140 Wharfedale Road, Winnersh Triangle, Wokingham, Berks, RG41 5RB
Activities: Non-specialised wholesale of food, beverages and tobacco
Shareholder: Purecircle Limited
Officers: Suzanna Collette Bancroft [1964] Director/Vice President; Magomet Malsagov [1974] Director [Russian]; Rakesh Ranjan Sinha [1968] Director/Chief Financial Officer

Purelake Investments Limited
Incorporated: 1 April 1998
Net Worth: £34,220,308 *Total Assets:* £85,338,672
Registered Office: Purelake House, Plaistow Lane, Bromley, Kent, BR1 4DS
Activities: Other letting and operating of own or leased real estate
Parent: Purelake Properties Ltd
Officers: Sara Ann White, Secretary; Generald Anthony Dowd [1962] Finance Director; Barry John White [1962] Director/Property Developer; Sara Ann White [1965] Director/Company Secretary

Purelake New Homes Limited
Incorporated: 9 March 1992 *Employees:* 49
Net Worth: £38,515,208 *Total Assets:* £44,710,352
Registered Office: Purelake House, Plaistow Lane, Bromley, Kent, BR1 4DS
Activities: Construction of other civil engineering projects n.e.c.
Parent: Purelake Properties Ltd
Officers: Sara Ann White, Secretary; Noel Robert Convert [1971] Construction Director; Generald Anthony Dowd [1962] Finance Director; Tracey Ann Wheelan [1978] Sales Director; Barry John White [1962] Director/Property Developer; Sara Ann White [1965] Director/Secretary

Purelake Properties Limited
Incorporated: 10 July 1991 *Employees:* 49
Net Worth: £59,287,748 *Total Assets:* £109,685,592
Registered Office: Purelake House, Plaistow Lane, Bromley, Kent, BR1 4DS
Activities: Other letting and operating of own or leased real estate
Shareholders: Barry John White; Sara Ann White
Officers: Sara Ann White, Secretary; Barry John White [1962] Director/Property Developer; Sara Ann White [1965] Director/Secretary

Pureprint Group Limited
Incorporated: 28 April 1980 *Employees:* 305
Net Worth: £871,755 *Total Assets:* £24,576,468
Registered Office: Beacon House, Brambleside, Bellbrook Park, Uckfield, E Sussex, TN22 1PL
Activities: Printing n.e.c.
Parent: East Sussex Press Limited
Officers: Ian Brown, Secretary; Ian Brown [1955] Finance Director; Mark William Handford [1965] Director; Richard Osborne [1962] Managing Director; Richard William Owers [1956] Business Development Director; Bridget Mary Tucker [1967] Group Financial Director

Puzzler Media Group Limited
Incorporated: 25 February 2002
Net Worth: £593,797 *Total Assets:* £32,481,222
Registered Office: Stonecroft, 69 Station Road, Redhill, Surrey, RH1 1EY
Activities: Activities of head offices
Parent: Puzzler Media Holdings Limited
Officers: Irene Douglas, Secretary; Robert Paul Daly [1957] Director/Chartered Accountant; Neil Douglas Flockhart [1963] Managing Director; Ellis Alan Nicholas Watson [1967] Managing Director

Puzzler Media Holdings Limited
Incorporated: 24 November 2005
Net Worth: £35,514,032 *Total Assets:* £72,380,280
Registered Office: Stonecroft, 69 Station Road, Redhill, Surrey, RH1 1EY
Activities: Activities of head offices
Parent: John Leng and Company Limited
Officers: Irene Douglas, Secretary; Robert Paul Daly [1957] Director/Chartered Accountant; Neil Douglas Flockhart [1963] Sales Director; Andrew Francis Thomson [1942] Director/Publisher; Christopher Harold William Thomson [1950] Director/Publisher; David Howard Eric Thomson [1973] Director/Chief Operating Officer; Ellis Alan Nicholas Watson [1967] Managing Director

Puzzler Media Limited
Incorporated: 28 September 1973 *Employees:* 54
Net Worth: £63,809,304 *Total Assets:* £76,868,808
Registered Office: Stonecroft, 69 Station Road, Redhill, Surrey, RH1 1EY
Activities: Publishing of consumer and business journals and periodicals
Parent: Puzzler Media Group Limited
Officers: Irene Douglas, Secretary; Robert Paul Daly [1957] Director/Head of Group Finance; Neil Douglas Flockhart [1963] Managing Director; Andrew Francis Thomson [1942] Director/Publisher; Christopher Harold William Thomson [1950] Director/Publisher; David Howard Eric Thomson [1973] Director/Chief Operating Officer; Ellis Alan Nicholas Watson [1967] Managing Director

Pye Properties Limited
Incorporated: 1 December 2005
Net Worth: £27,377,248 *Total Assets:* £46,900,996
Registered Office: 3-4 Faulknor Square, Charnham Street, Hungerford, Berks, RG17 0EP
Activities: Buying and selling of own real estate
Officers: George Gordon Nottage Palmer, Secretary; Jennifer Ellen Kidston [1980] Director/Housewife; George Gordon Nottage Palmer [1985] Director/Chartered Accountant; Colin Christopher Tett [1946] Director; Henry George MacRae Tett [1982] Director/Event Rider; Victoria Roselle Tett [1955] Director

Pyramid Schools (Sheffield) Limited
Incorporated: 17 February 2000
Net Worth Deficit: £1,623,000 *Total Assets:* £33,368,000
Registered Office: 8 White Oak Square, London Road, Swanley, Kent, BR8 7AG
Activities: Other business support service activities n.e.c.
Parent: Sheffield Schools Services Holdings Limited
Officers: David John Brooking [1967] Investment Director; Alastair James Watson [1974] Investment Director

Pyxis Investment Strategies LLP
Incorporated: 7 October 2004
Net Worth: £185,232,480 *Total Assets:* £188,715,376
Registered Office: 4th Floor, Reading Bridge House, George Street, Reading, Berks, RG1 8LS
Officers: Carlo de Benedetti [1934] Member

Q Squared Solutions Holdings Limited
Incorporated: 12 June 2015
Net Worth: £237,563,008 *Total Assets:* £243,836,000
Registered Office: 500 Brook Drive, Green Park, Reading, Berks, RG2 6UU
Activities: Other human health activities
Shareholders: Quest Diagnostics Subsidiary Holdings Ltd; IQVIA Ltd.
Officers: Santiago Estrada, Secretary; Helen Fovargue, Secretary; Ronald Earl Bruehlman [1960] Director/Senior Advisor to the CEO [American]; Randy Lee Funk [1960] Executive Director Joint Ventures [American]; Mark James Guinan [1962] Director/Executive Vice President & Chief Financial Officer [American]; Rene Lorenz [1959] Director/Senior VP Chief Business Office [American]; Wendy Stewart [1972] Director/Project Management; Cynthia Verst [1965] Director/Pharmacist [American]

Q Squared Solutions Limited
Incorporated: 12 June 2015 *Employees:* 745
Net Worth: £46,050,000 *Total Assets:* £183,684,000
Registered Office: 500 Brook Drive, Green Park, Reading, Berks, RG2 6UU
Activities: Other professional, scientific and technical activities n.e.c.
Parent: Q Squared Solutions Holdings Limited
Officers: Tony Brown [1963] Director/Executive; Kevin John Turland [1969] Director

QA Limited
Incorporated: 14 August 1989 *Employees:* 1,154
Net Worth: £139,368,496 *Total Assets:* £217,856,032
Registered Office: Rath House, 55-65 Uxbridge Road, Slough, Berks, SL1 1SG
Activities: Other education n.e.c.
Parent: Seckloe 208 Limited
Officers: Nathan Giles Runnicles, Secretary; Lisa Catherine Harrington [1972] Managing Director - QA Learning [Irish]; William Robert George Macpherson [1963] Director; Stuart Martin [1974] Sales Director; Nathan Giles Runnicles [1974] Director/Chief Financial Officer

QA-IQ Group Limited
Incorporated: 2 April 2004
Net Worth: £5,540,877 *Total Assets:* £207,454,352
Registered Office: Rath House, 55-65 Uxbridge Road, Slough, Berks, SL1 1SG
Activities: Activities of head offices
Parent: QA-IQ Investments Limited
Officers: Nathan Giles Runnicles, Secretary; William Robert George Macpherson [1963] Director; Nathan Giles Runnicles [1974] Director/Chief Financial Officer

QA-IQ Investments Limited
Incorporated: 23 May 2007
Net Worth Deficit: £45,609,000 *Total Assets:* £79,243,000
Registered Office: Rath House, 55-65 Uxbridge Road, Slough, Berks, SL1 1SG
Activities: Activities of head offices
Parent: QA-IQ Holdings Limited
Officers: Nathan Giles Runnicles, Secretary; Richard Paul Blackburn [1982] Managing Director; William Robert George Macpherson [1963] Director; Nathan Giles Runnicles [1974] Director/Chief Financial Officer

QED (Clacton) Limited
Incorporated: 14 May 2003
Net Worth: £2,552,000 *Total Assets:* £30,126,000
Registered Office: 8 White Oak Square, London Road, Swanley, Kent, BR8 7AG
Activities: Combined facilities support activities
Parent: QED (Clacton) Holdings Limited
Officers: David John Brooking [1967] Investment Director; Benjamin Christopher Jacob Dean [1979] Director/Investment Manager

QED (Leeds) Limited
Incorporated: 19 December 2003
Net Worth: £1,317,000 *Total Assets:* £28,176,000
Registered Office: 8 White Oak Square, London Road, Swanley, Kent, BR8 7AG
Activities: Combined facilities support activities
Parent: QED (Leeds) Holdings Limited
Officers: Benjamin Christopher Jacob Dean [1979] Director/Investment Manager; Alastair James Watson [1974] Investment Director

QH Estates Ltd
Incorporated: 22 February 2011
Net Worth: £11,582,685 *Total Assets:* £22,161,596
Registered Office: 2 Peterwood Way, Croydon, Surrey, CR0 4UQ
Activities: Other letting and operating of own or leased real estate
Major Shareholder: Naliniben Kiritkumar Patel
Officers: Ameet Patel, Secretary; Kirit Chimanbhai Patel Junior [1980] Director; Heena Patel [1963] Finance Director; Rupa Patel [1981] Director; Jayanti Chimanbhai Patel Junior [1984] Director

Qinetiq Group Holdings Limited
Incorporated: 23 February 2010
Net Worth: £424,500,000 *Total Assets:* £424,500,000
Registered Office: Cody Technology Park, Ively Road, Farnborough, Hants, GU14 0LX
Activities: Activities of head offices
Parent: Qinetiq Group PLC
Officers: Jon Messent, Secretary; Dr Malcolm Andrew Coffin [1968] Director/Accountant; Jon Messent [1964] Director/Company Secretary; Stephen Webster [1958] Director

Qinetiq Group PLC
Incorporated: 11 November 2002 *Employees:* 6,065
Net Worth: £744,099,968 *Total Assets:* £1,198,000,000
Registered Office: Cody Technology Park, Ively Road, Farnborough, Hants, GU14 0LX
Activities: Activities of head offices
Officers: Jon Messent, Secretary; Lynn Brubaker [1957] Director [American]; Sir James Michael Burnell-Nugent [1949] Director; Mark Wynne Elliott [1949] Director [American]; John Michael Harper [1945] Director; Ian Mason [1962] Director; Paul Colbeck Murray [1961] Director; Susan Jane Searle [1963] Director; David Miles Smith [1961] Director; Stephen John Wadey [1969] Director

Qinetiq Holdings Limited
Incorporated: 6 February 2001 *Employees:* 6
Net Worth: £8,500,000 *Total Assets:* £260,900,000
Registered Office: Cody Technology Park, Ively Road, Farnborough, Hants, GU14 0LX
Activities: Other business support service activities n.e.c.
Parent: Qinetiq Group Holdings Limited
Officers: Jon Messent, Secretary; Dr Malcolm Andrew Coffin [1968] Director/Accountant; Jon Messent [1964] Director/Company Secretary; Stephen Webster [1958] Director

Qinetiq Limited
Incorporated: 25 June 1999 *Employees:* 4,961
Net Worth: £807,699,968 *Total Assets:* £1,258,800,000
Registered Office: Cody Technology Park, Ively Road, Farnborough, Hants, GU14 0LX
Activities: Engineering related scientific and technical consulting activities
Parent: Qinetiq Holdings Limited
Officers: Jon Messent, Secretary; Dr Malcolm Andrew Coffin [1968] Director/Accountant; Jon Messent [1964] Director/Company Secretary; Stephen Webster [1958] Director

Qinetiq Overseas Holdings Limited
Incorporated: 15 May 2002
Net Worth: £77,732,000 *Total Assets:* £90,387,000
Registered Office: Cody Technology Park, Ively Road, Farnborough, Hants, GU14 0LX
Activities: Activities of head offices
Parent: Qinetiq Holdings Limited
Officers: Jon Messent, Secretary; Dr Malcolm Andrew Coffin [1968] Director/Accountant; Jon Messent [1964] Director/Company Secretary; Stephen Webster [1958] Director

QlikTech UK Limited
Incorporated: 21 November 2004 *Employees:* 230
Net Worth: £18,844,000 *Total Assets:* £75,926,000
Registered Office: 1020 Eskdale Road, IQ Winnersh, Wokingham, Berks, RG41 5TS
Activities: Other information technology service activities
Officers: Marcus Aaron Gordon, Secretary; Deborah Marie Cleary Lofton [1968] Director/Attorney [American]

QSC 1208 Limited
Incorporated: 4 December 2006
Net Worth: £5,520,317 *Total Assets:* £56,909,872
Registered Office: Two Bridges, Guildford Street, Chertsey, Surrey, KT16 9AU
Activities: Business and domestic software development
Parent: PB Bidco Limited
Officers: Jason Phillip Conley [1975] Finance Director [American]; Robert Christopher Crisci [1975] Finance Director [American]; Robin Tarquinn Morris-Weston [1970] Director; John Kenneth Stipancich [1968] Director/Vice President, General Counsel and Secretary [American]

QSC 1209 Limited
Incorporated: 4 December 2006 *Employees:* 4
Net Worth: £78,974,000 *Total Assets:* £79,262,000
Registered Office: Two Bridges, Guildford Street, Chertsey, Surrey, KT16 9AU
Activities: Business and domestic software development
Parent: QSC 1208 Limited
Officers: Jason Phillip Conley [1975] Finance Director [American]; Robert Christopher Crisci [1975] Finance Director [American]; Robin Tarquinn Morris-Weston [1970] Director; John Kenneth Stipancich [1968] Director/Vice President, General Counsel and Secretary [American]

Quaker Holdings (UK) Limited
Incorporated: 17 December 2001 *Employees:* 3
Net Worth: £50,918,500 *Total Assets:* £119,866,592
Registered Office: 450 South Oak Way, Green Park, Reading, Berks, RG2 6UW
Activities: Other business support service activities n.e.c.
Parent: Pepsico, Inc
Officers: Holly King, Secretary; Joanne Kerry Averiss [1963] Director/VP Law; Victoria Elizabeth Evans [1970] Director/Solicitor; Claire Ellen Stone [1969] Finance Director

Quality Spirits International Limited
Incorporated: 3 March 1986 *Employees:* 12
Net Worth: £112,124,000 *Total Assets:* £116,992,000
Registered Office: Independence House, 84 Lower Mortlake Road, Richmond, Surrey, TW9 2HS
Activities: Wholesale of wine, beer, spirits and other alcoholic beverages
Parent: William Grant & Sons Enterprises Limited
Officers: Karen Louise Forbes, Secretary; Alexander John Davies [1982] Director/Head of Finance & Business Development; John Michael Harvey [1956] Managing Director; Ewan John Henderson [1968] Director; Michael Lamont [1960] Director

Quantel Group Limited
Incorporated: 23 September 1982
Net Worth: £36,284,000 *Total Assets:* £39,590,000
Registered Office: Turnpike Road, Newbury, Berks, RG14 2NX
Activities: Activities of head offices
Parent: Quantel Holdings (2010) Limited
Officers: Brian Edward Anderson [1974] Attorney - General Director [American]; Alec Thomas Lappe [1981] Director/VP Tax [American]; Anne La Belle Malyszko [1980] Director/VP of Corporate Finance [American]

Quantel Holdings (2010) Limited
Incorporated: 31 May 2000
Net Worth Deficit: £37,340,000 *Total Assets:* £74,137,000
Registered Office: 31 Turnpike Road, Newbury, Berks, RG14 2NE
Activities: Activities of head offices
Parent: Belden, Inc.
Officers: Brian Edward Anderson [1974] Director/Attorney - General Counsel [American]; Alec Thomas Lappe [1981] Director/VP Tax [American]; Anne La Belle Malyszko [1980] Director/VP of Corporate Finance [American]

Quantel Limited
Incorporated: 21 August 1973 *Employees:* 118
Net Worth Deficit: £40,261,000 *Total Assets:* £35,309,000
Registered Office: Turnpike Road, Newbury, Berks, RG14 2NX
Activities: Wholesale of computers, computer peripheral equipment and software
Parent: Quantel Group Limited
Officers: Brian Edward Anderson [1974] Director/Attorney - General Counsel [American]; Alec Thomas Lappe [1981] Director/VP Tax [American]; Anne La Belle Malyszko [1980] Director/VP of Corporate Finance [American]

Quantum Funding Limited
Incorporated: 7 April 2005
Net Worth: £3,092,000 *Total Assets:* £69,678,000
Registered Office: Reading International Business Park, Reading, Berks, RG2 6AA
Activities: Financial leasing
Parent: Investec Bank PLC
Officers: Connie Mei Ling Law, Secretary; James Stephen Collins [1985] Director/Head of Finance; Michael Richard Francis [1966] Director/Chartered Accountant; Andrew Stuart Hart [1974] Managing Director

Quayside Homes Holdings Limited
Incorporated: 5 July 2001
Net Worth: £24,958,776 *Total Assets:* £30,958,776
Registered Office: Hardys Yard, London Road, Riverhead, Sevenoaks, Kent, TN13 2DN
Activities: Activities of head offices
Parent: Ramac Holdings (Trading) Limited
Officers: James David Charles Hambling, Secretary; James David Charles Hambling [1978] Director; Michael McGuirk [1942] Director [Irish]

Quayside Homes Limited
Incorporated: 29 May 2003 *Employees:* 3
Net Worth Deficit: £1,658,118 *Total Assets:* £22,026,744
Registered Office: Hardy's Yard, London Road, Riverhead, Sevenoaks, Kent, TN13 2DN
Activities: Construction of domestic buildings
Parent: Quayside Homes Holdings Ltd
Officers: James David Charles Hambling, Secretary; James David Charles Hambling [1978] Director/Accountancy; Richard William Ashley Lawrence [1976] Director; Michael McGuirk [1942] Director [Irish]

Queens' School (Bushey)
Incorporated: 27 May 2011 *Employees:* 175
Net Worth: £39,479,916 *Total Assets:* £41,587,780
Registered Office: Queens' School, Aldenham Road, Bushey, Herts, WD23 2LX
Activities: General secondary education
Officers: Tracy Anne Jenner, Secretary; Catherine Agnihotri [1965] Director/Support Worker (SEND); Lyndsey Rebecca Billinge [1984] Director/Teacher; Keith Burberry Cook [1963] Director/Accountant; Susan Mary Gorton [1960] Director/Examinations Officer; Gillian Sarah Kate Gray [1966] Director/Librarian; David Charles Hall [1944] Director/Retired; Sian Elizabeth Ann Henry [1969] Director/Social Work; Stephen Robert Jakeman [1956] Director/Accountant; Sunil Jobanputra [1989] Director/Civil Servant; Jonathan Morrell [1973] Director/Headteacher; Jayesh Jayantilal Patel [1982] Director/Train Operator; Rakesh Patel [1972] Director/Bank Manager; Julie Raybould [1967] Director/Recruitment Consultant; Clare Jean Rose [1975] Director/Service Delivery Manager; Carole Watson [1952] Director/Retired

R & M Electrical Group Limited
Incorporated: 5 February 1988 *Employees:* 205
Net Worth: £7,393,288 *Total Assets:* £25,978,636
Registered Office: Units 1 & 2, 362a Spring Road, Sholing, Southampton, SO19 2PB
Activities: Wholesale of radio, television goods & electrical household appliances (other than records, tapes, CDs)
Parent: R & M Electrical Holdings Limited
Officers: William Kingston Crook, Secretary; Andrew Leslie Baggott [1964] Director; Andrew Mark Chandler [1964] Director; Timothy Coomer [1965] Director/Chartered Accountant; William Kingston Crook [1970] Director; Brian Andrew Robinson [1956] Director; David Alan Robinson [1983] UK Sales Director; Richard John Sherin [1967] Director

Rackspace Limited
Incorporated: 20 December 1999 *Employees:* 1,046
Net Worth: £59,453,228 *Total Assets:* £236,999,472
Registered Office: Unit 8 Millington Road, Hayes, Middlesex, UB3 4AZ
Activities: Data processing, hosting and related activities
Officers: Christopher Rosas, Secretary; Darren George Norfolk [1977] Managing Director; Christopher Rosas [1977] Director/VP Global Tax [American]; Reinhard Waldinger [1976] Director [Swiss]

Rackspace UK Leasing Limited
Incorporated: 3 September 2015
Net Worth: £47,380,000 *Total Assets:* £66,431,580
Registered Office: Unit 8 Millington Road, Hayes, Middlesex, UB3 4AZ
Activities: Renting and leasing of office machinery and equipment (including computers)
Parent: Rackspace Hosting, Inc.
Officers: Darren George Norfolk [1977] Managing Director; Christopher Rosas [1977] Director/VP of Global Tax [American]; Reinhard Waldinger [1976] Director [Swiss]

Radian Capital PLC
Incorporated: 22 December 2011
Net Worth: £50,000 *Total Assets:* £228,728,992
Registered Office: Collins House, Bishopstoke Road, Eastleigh, Hants, SO50 6AD
Activities: Financial intermediation not elsewhere classified
Parent: Radian Group Limited
Officers: Malcolm Stuart Rule, Secretary; Beverley Anne Costain [1967] Director of Finance; Peter James Evans [1966] Director of Technical Services; John Gary Orr [1972] Director/Chief Executive of Radian Group

Radian Group Limited
Incorporated: 17 December 1997 *Employees:* 749
Net Worth: £626,214,016 *Total Assets:* £1,578,747,008
Registered Office: Collins House, Bishopstoke Road, Eastleigh, Hants, SO50 6AD
Activities: Renting and operating of Housing Association real estate
Officers: Malcolm Stuart Rule, Secretary; Jane Dorothy Alderman [1962] Director/Property/Housing Consultant; Carol Ann Bode [1957] Director; Mandy Dawn Clarke [1965] Director; Jonathan Martin Stuart Hurst [1960] Director/Portfolio NED; John Gary Orr [1972] Director/Chief Executive of Radian Group; Simon John Porter [1957] Director/Chartered Accountant; Richard Stephen Williams [1966] Director

Radiosite Limited
Incorporated: 16 September 2004
Net Worth: £20,438,122 *Total Assets:* £23,128,140
Registered Office: 2 River Court, Albert Drive, Woking, Surrey, GU21 5RP
Activities: Wireless telecommunications activities
Parent: Shere Midco Limited
Officers: Peter Charles Collins [1956] Director; Mary Annabel Gatehouse [1973] Director/Lawyer; Alexandre Mestre Molins [1964] Director/Manager [Spanish]; Alexander James Woodward [1963] Director/Chartered Accountant

Radlett Limited
Incorporated: 29 June 2016 *Employees:* 241
Net Worth: £30,501,418 *Total Assets:* £82,074,680
Registered Office: Ridgeworth House, Liverpool Gardens, Worthing, W Sussex, BN11 1RS
Activities: Activities of other holding companies n.e.c.
Officers: Zoe Rachel Cadiz, Secretary; William Francis Chisholm [1969] Managing Director [American]; Dominic Joseph Gallello [1955] Director [American]; Stephen Edward Henkenmeier [1969] Director [American]; Rachit Joshi [1989] Director/Senior Associate [American]; Sunit Shankar Mukherjee [1977] Director/Principal [Indian]; Michael Pehl [1961] Director/Partner [American]; Roderick Smyth [1975] Director/Group Chief Product & Strategy Officer [Irish]

Radnor House School (Holdings) Limited
Incorporated: 5 August 2010 *Employees:* 182
Net Worth: £30,950,608 *Total Assets:* £54,664,096
Registered Office: Pope's Villa, Cross Deep, Twickenham, Middlesex, TW1 4QG
Activities: General secondary education
Shareholders: David Paton; Josephine Claire Paton; Albion Venture Capital Trust PLC; Albion Development VCT PLC; Crown Place VCT PLC; Albion Technology & General VCT PLC; Albion Enterprise VCT PLC; David Paton; Josephine Claire Paton; Albion Ventures LLP
Officers: Eleanor Rose Allen [1981] Director/Education Consultant; Dr Colin Diggory [1954] Director; Emil Slavchev Gigov [1970] Director/Banker [British/Bulgarian]; Barry Robert Martin [1950] Non-Executive Director; Neil Moulding [1970] Finance Director; David Paton [1977] Director

Radnor House School (Property) Limited
Incorporated: 6 August 2010
Net Worth: £24,153,904 *Total Assets:* £36,183,008
Registered Office: Popes Villa, Cross Deep, Twickenham, Middlesex, TW1 4QG
Activities: General secondary education
Parent: Radnor House School (Holdings) Limited
Officers: Neil Moulding [1970] Finance Director; David Paton [1977] Director

Raisio UK Limited
Incorporated: 19 January 2010 *Employees:* 2
Net Worth: £44,273,000 *Total Assets:* £58,564,000
Registered Office: Benecol Limited, The Mille, 1000 Great West Road, Brentford, Middlesex, TW8 9DW
Activities: Activities of head offices
Parent: Raisio Oyj
Officers: Merja Sisko Lumme [1961] Director/VP Human Resources [Finnish]; Iiro Tapio Wester [1963] Director/Chief Commercial Officer [Finnish]

RAK Petroleum PLC
Incorporated: 17 June 2013
Net Worth: £504,105,472 *Total Assets:* £1,310,131,840
Registered Office: Elder House, St Georges Business Park, Brooklands Road, Weybridge, Surrey, KT13 0TS
Activities: Activities of other holding companies n.e.c.
Officers: Kevin Toner, Secretary; Sultan Abdulla Ahmad Majid Al Ghurair [1980] Director/Chief Executive Officer [Emirati]; Bjorn Kenneth Dale [1974] Managing Director DNO ASA [Norwegian]; Amirali Handjani [1977] Director/Business Executive [American]; Ahmed Jamal Jawa [1956] Director/Businessman [Saudi Arabian]; Bijan Mossavar-Rahmani [1952] Director/Business Executive [American]

RAL Limited
Incorporated: 16 August 1985 *Employees:* 1,026
Net Worth: £22,067,596 *Total Assets:* £36,601,640
Registered Office: Birch House, Woodlands Business Park, Linford Wood, Milton Keynes, Bucks, MK14 6EW
Activities: Gambling and betting activities
Parent: Talarius Limited
Officers: Neil Paramore, Secretary; Tom Allison [1963] Director; Paul David Hyman [1969] Director; Zane Cedomir Mersich [1972] Director; Neil Paramore [1962] Director

Ramac Holdings (Trading) Limited
Incorporated: 5 July 2001 *Employees:* 136
Net Worth: £66,590,000 *Total Assets:* £80,006,272
Registered Office: Hardys Yard, London Road, Riverhead, Sevenoaks, Kent, TN13 2DN
Activities: Development of building projects
Major Shareholder: Michael McGuirk
Officers: James David Charles Hambling, Secretary; James David Charles Hambling [1978] Director; Richard William Ashley Lawrence [1976] Director; Michael McGuirk [1942] Director [Irish]; Adam Taylor [1969] Director/Chartered Accountant

Ramac Holdings Limited
Incorporated: 30 December 1968 *Employees:* 3
Net Worth: £24,694,480 *Total Assets:* £40,258,468
Registered Office: Hardy's Yard, London Road, Riverhead, Kent, TN13 2DN
Activities: Other letting and operating of own or leased real estate
Parent: Ramac Group Ltd
Officers: James David Charles Hambling, Secretary; James David Charles Hambling [1978] Director/Ramac Group Limited; Richard William Ashley Lawrence [1976] Director; Michael McGuirk [1942] Director/Building Contractor [Irish]

Rambler Metals and Mining PLC
Incorporated: 14 April 2004 *Employees:* 185
Net Worth: £46,771,196 *Total Assets:* £70,515,392
Registered Office: Salatin House, 19 Cedar Road, Sutton, Surrey, SM2 5DA
Activities: Other mining and quarrying n.e.c.
Major Shareholder: Bradford Alan Mills
Officers: Peter Mercer, Secretary; Terrell Iver Ackerman [1953] Director/Consultant [American]; Eason Cong Chen [1981] Director/Corporate Controller [Canadian]; Belinda Labatte [1974] Director/Mining [American]; Bradford Alan Mills [1954] Director/Mining Executive [American]; Glenn Robert Poulter [1964] Director/Consultant; Mark Vandyke Sander [1955] Director/Mining Executive [American]; Norman Patrick Williams [1974] Director/Chief Executive [Canadian]

Sir William Ramsay School Academy Trust
Incorporated: 7 July 2011 *Employees:* 134
Net Worth: £18,672,470 *Total Assets:* £21,760,852
Registered Office: Sir William Ramsay School, Rose Avenue, Hazlemere, High Wycombe, Bucks, HP15 7UB
Activities: General secondary education
Officers: Elizabeth Walker, Secretary; Clifford William Brown [1952] Director/Charity Worker; Stuart Carter [1976] Director/Business Analyst; Nigel Cole [1953] Director/Accountant; Paul Fleming [1966] Director/Marketing Manager; Kim Brian Frost [1960] University Secretary & Director of Human Resources; Kieran Hughes [1969] Director/Teacher; Julie Irwin [1963] Director, Student Success, Bucks New University; Christine McLintock [1966] Director/Headteacher; Mark Meardon [1973] Director/Minister of Religion (Church of England); Professor Bryan Mogford [1940] Director/Retired; Matt Spooner [1988] Director/Businessman

Ranbaxy (U.K.) Limited
Incorporated: 21 November 1994 *Employees:* 19
Net Worth: £15,061,894 *Total Assets:* £28,360,372
Registered Office: 5th Floor, Hyde Park Hayes 3, 11 Millington Road, Hayes, Middlesex, UB3 4AZ
Activities: Wholesale of pharmaceutical goods
Officers: Hellen de Kloet [1965] Director/Business Executive [Dutch]; Prashant Savla [1974] Director [Dutch]; Neeraj Sharma [1972] Director [Indian]

Ranbaxy Holdings (UK) Limited
Incorporated: 23 May 1995 *Employees:* 2
Net Worth: £32,087,286 *Total Assets:* £32,096,450
Registered Office: 5th Floor, Hyde Park Hayes 3, 11 Millington Road, Hayes, Middlesex, UB3 4AZ
Activities: Financial intermediation not elsewhere classified
Officers: Prashant Lakhamshi Savla [1974] Finance Director [Indian]; Neeraj Sharma [1972] Director [Indian]

Rank Digital Holdings Limited
Incorporated: 3 March 2017
Net Worth: £45,574,000 *Total Assets:* £90,059,000
Registered Office: Tor, Saint-Cloud Way, Maidenhead, Berks, SL6 8BN
Activities: Activities of head offices
Parent: Rank Leisure Holdings Limited
Officers: Luisa Ann Wright, Secretary; William James Spencer Floydd [1969] Director; John Patrick O'Reilly [1960] Director

Rank Group Finance PLC
Incorporated: 26 March 1985
Net Worth: £181,202,000 *Total Assets:* £379,888,000
Registered Office: Tor, Saint-Cloud Way, Maidenhead, Berks, SL6 8BN
Activities: Financial leasing
Parent: The Rank Group PLC
Officers: Luisa Ann Wright, Secretary; William James Spencer Floydd [1969] Director; John Patrick O'Reilly [1960] Director

Rank Group Gaming Division Limited
Incorporated: 18 June 1996 *Employees:* 259
Net Worth: £118,828,000 *Total Assets:* £136,159,008
Registered Office: Tor, Saint-Cloud Way, Maidenhead, Berks, SL6 8BN
Activities: Activities of head offices
Parent: Rank Leisure Holdings Limited
Officers: Luisa Ann Wright, Secretary; William James Spencer Floydd [1969] Director; John Patrick O'Reilly [1960] Director

The Rank Group PLC
Incorporated: 22 December 1995
Net Worth: £396,500,000 *Total Assets:* £720,300,032
Registered Office: Tor, Saint-Cloud Way, Maidenhead, Berks, SL6 8BN
Activities: Activities of head offices
Officers: Luisa Ann Wright, Secretary; Christopher Bell [1957] Director; Michael Ian Burke [1956] Director; Steven Derek Esom [1960] Director; Susan Mary Hooper [1960] Director; Alan Morgan [1977] Director; John Patrick O'Reilly [1960] Director; Hong Cheong Tang [1955] Director [Malaysian]; Alexander Vincent Thursby [1960] Director

Rank Hovis Milling Limited
Incorporated: 12 December 2014 *Employees:* 271
Net Worth: £15,317,000 *Total Assets:* £52,255,000
Registered Office: The Lord Rank Centre, Lincoln Road, High Wycombe, Bucks, HP12 3QS
Activities: Grain milling
Parent: Hovis Limited
Officers: Peter Andrew Hill, Secretary; Peter Andrew Hill [1980] HR Director; Dr George Idicula [1959] Supply Chain Director; Terence Strain [1960] Director; Lawrence Anthony Watson [1965] Director

Rank Leisure Holdings Limited
Incorporated: 15 August 1984 *Employees:* 106
Net Worth: £819,561,024 *Total Assets:* £841,622,976
Registered Office: Tor, Saint-Cloud Way, Maidenhead, Berks, SL6 8BN
Activities: Activities of head offices
Parent: Rank Nemo (Twenty-Five) Limited
Officers: Luisa Ann Wright, Secretary; William James Spencer Floydd [1969] Director; John Patrick O'Reilly [1960] Director

Rank Nemo (Twenty-Five) Limited
Incorporated: 29 August 2002
Net Worth: £950,800,000 *Total Assets:* £950,800,000
Registered Office: Tor, Saint-Cloud Way, Maidenhead, Berks, SL6 8BN
Activities: Non-trading company
Parent: The Rank Group PLC
Officers: Luisa Ann Wright, Secretary; William James Spencer Floydd [1969] Director; John Patrick O'Reilly [1960] Director

The Joseph Rank Trust
Incorporated: 20 June 2002
Net Worth: £71,634,000 *Total Assets:* £74,443,000
Registered Office: Worth Corner, Turners Hill Road, Crawley, W Sussex, RH10 7SL
Activities: Activities auxiliary to financial intermediation n.e.c.
Officers: Dr John Harnden Higgs, Secretary; David Stanbury Cruise [1935] Director/Retired Methodist Minister; Rev Darren Holland [1969] Director/Minister of Religion; Reverend Carole Holmes [1968] Director/Minister of Religion; John Dudley Irvine [1949] Director/Minister of Religion; Joseph Piers Jennings [1975] Director/Advisor; Elizabeth Gay Moon [1950] Director/Solicitor; Colin Rowland Hopwood Rank [1948] Director; James Benjamin Rank [1974] Director/Marketing Manager; James Anthony Reddall [1926] Director/Retired; Susan Voase Warner [1949] Director/Charity Consultant

Rapport Housing and Care
Incorporated: 13 June 1967 *Employees:* 410
Previous: The Abbeyfield Kent Society
Net Worth: £11,357,974 *Total Assets:* £33,806,760
Registered Office: Station Road, Cuxton, Rochester, Kent, ME2 1AB
Activities: Other human health activities
Officers: Danielle Bride [1972] Director/Manager, Early Help & Preventative Services, KCC [Australian]; Robin Graham Caven [1961] Director; Cathy Elaine Deplessis [1962] Director/Housing Consultant; Michele Low [1947] Director/Retired; Charles Kenneth Zachary Miles [1949] Director/CEO, Recruitment Organisation; Tony Harry Searles [1951] Director, Hammond & Searles Co Ltd; Stephen Sumner Tomlinson [1945] Director/Solicitor; John Stuart Townend [1943] Director/Retired Estate Agent

RATP DEV UK Ltd
Incorporated: 11 June 2010 *Employees:* 40
Net Worth: £60,347,000 *Total Assets:* £195,572,992
Registered Office: Busways House, Wellington Road, Twickenham, Middlesex, TW2 5NX
Activities: Other service activities incidental to land transportation, n.e.c.
Officers: Laurence Batlle [1971] Director [French]; Romain Ferriere [1975] Director/Chief Financial Officer [French]; Howard Charles Goodbourn [1961] Director/Chief Financial Officer

Raymarine UK Limited
Incorporated: 31 October 2002 *Employees:* 173
Net Worth: £77,613,000 *Total Assets:* £81,630,000
Registered Office: Marine House, Cartwright Drive, Fareham, Hants, PO15 5RJ
Activities: Manufacture of electronic measuring, testing etc. equipment, not for industrial process control
Parent: RIHL Limited
Officers: Heather Fiona Christiansen [1971] Director/Manager and Secretary [American]; Todd Michael Duchene [1963] Director/General Counsel and Secretary [American]; Gregoire Pierre Georges Outters [1971] Director/General Manager [French]

Rayner Intraocular Lenses Limited
Incorporated: 25 November 1958 *Employees:* 212
Net Worth: £14,465,000 *Total Assets:* £49,124,000
Registered Office: 10 Dominion Way, Worthing, W Sussex, BN14 8AQ
Activities: Manufacture of medical and dental instruments and supplies
Parent: Rayner Surgical Group Limited
Officers: Cepta Kelly, Secretary; Darren Michael Millington [1976] Director/Chief Financial Officer

Rayner Surgical Group Limited
Incorporated: 28 September 1910 *Employees:* 248
Net Worth: £33,829,000 *Total Assets:* £57,308,000
Registered Office: 10 Dominion Way, Worthing, W Sussex, BN14 8AQ
Activities: Activities of head offices
Shareholder: Phoenix Equity Partners 2016 LLP
Officers: Cepta Kelly, Secretary [Irish]; Justin David Christian Barnes [1966] Investor/Director; Timothy James Clover [1966] Director; Cary Edward Dawes [1967] Sales Director; Niels Harald de Coninck Smith [1956] Director; Kevin Jennings Keck [1974] Director/Investment Manager [British/American]; Cepta Kelly [1954] Director/Lawyer [Irish]; Darren Michael Millington [1976] Director/Chief Financial Officer

RB (China Trading) Limited
Incorporated: 22 December 2015 *Employees:* 5
Net Worth: £87,405,000 *Total Assets:* £96,318,000
Registered Office: 103-105 Bath Road, Slough, SL1 3UH
Activities: Wholesale of pharmaceutical goods
Parent: Reckitt Benckiser PLC
Officers: Christine Anne-Marie Logan, Secretary; John Dixon [1956] Director/SVP Tax; Adrian Nevil Hennah [1957] Director/Chief Financial Officer; Jonathan Timmis [1975] Director/SVP Corporate Controller; Lu Youming [1971] Director [Hong Kong]

RB Holdings (Nottingham) Limited
Incorporated: 5 February 2002
Net Worth: £1,828,050,048 *Total Assets:* £1,840,948,992
Registered Office: 103-105 Bath Road, Slough, Berks, SL1 3UH
Activities: Activities of other holding companies n.e.c.
Parent: Reckitt Benckiser Healthcare (UK) Limited
Officers: Christine Anne-Marie Logan, Secretary; Richard Mark Greensmith [1973] Group Tax Director; Jonathan Timmis [1975] Finance Director

RB Hotels Limited
Incorporated: 26 October 2011 *Employees:* 176
Net Worth Deficit: £387,964 *Total Assets:* £42,454,992
Registered Office: The Ageas Bowl, Botley Road, West End, Southampton, SO30 3XH
Activities: Hotels and similar accommodation
Shareholder: Roderick Bransgrove
Officers: Michael William Lashmar, Secretary; Roderick Granville Bransgrove [1950] Director; David Andrew Guile [1964] Director; Michael William Lashmar [1977] Finance Director; David Mann [1964] Director

RB Lease Company Ltd
Incorporated: 31 May 1894
Net Worth: £2,097,815 *Total Assets:* £33,154,304
Registered Office: The Ageas Bowl, Botley Road, West End, Southampton, SO30 3XH
Activities: Other letting and operating of own or leased real estate
Major Shareholder: Roderick Bransgrove
Officers: Michael William Lashmar, Secretary; Roderick Granville Bransgrove [1950] Director/Chairman; Michael William Lashmar [1977] Finance Director; David Mann [1964] Finance Director

RB Luxembourg (2016) Limited
Incorporated: 22 November 2016 *Employees:* 3
Net Worth: £985,732,992 *Total Assets:* £985,870,976
Registered Office: 103-105 Bath Road, Slough, Berks, SL1 3UH
Activities: Financial intermediation not elsewhere classified
Parent: RB Luxembourg Holdings (TFFC) Limited
Officers: Christine Anne-Marie Logan, Secretary; John Dixon [1956] Director/SVP Tax; Simon Andrew Neville [1957] Group Treasury Director; Jonathan Timmis [1975] Director/SVP Corporate Controller

RB Luxembourg Holdings (TFFC) Limited
Incorporated: 27 March 2014
Previous: The French's Food Finance Company Limited
Net Worth: £643,283,008 *Total Assets:* £651,155,008
Registered Office: 103-105 Bath Road, Slough, Berks, SL1 3UH
Activities: Manufacture of condiments and seasonings
Parent: Reckitt Benckiser Holdings (TFFC) Limited
Officers: Christine Anne-Marie Logan, Secretary; Richard Mark Greensmith [1973] Group Tax Director; Jonathan Timmis [1975] Finance Director

RB Mexico Investments Limited
Incorporated: 22 April 2016
Net Worth: £108,184,080 *Total Assets:* £108,184,080
Registered Office: 103-105 Bath Road, Slough, SL1 3UH
Activities: Activities of financial services holding companies
Parent: Reckitt Benckiser Investments Limited
Officers: Christine Anne-Marie Logan, Secretary; Richard Mark Greensmith [1973] Group Tax Director; Jonathan Timmis [1975] Finance Director

RB Reigate (UK) Limited
Incorporated: 20 March 2006
Net Worth: £466,996,000 *Total Assets:* £467,292,000
Registered Office: 103-105 Bath Road, Slough, Berks, SL1 3UH
Activities: Activities of financial services holding companies
Parent: Reckitt Benckiser Finance (2005) Limited
Officers: Christine Anne-Marie Logan, Secretary; Richard Mark Greensmith [1973] Group Tax Director; Jonathan Timmis [1975] Finance Director

RB Sport & Leisure Holdings PLC
Incorporated: 6 February 2002 *Employees:* 269
Net Worth: £5,970,763 *Total Assets:* £73,947,648
Registered Office: The Ageas Bowl, Botley Road, West End, Southampton, SO30 3XH
Activities: Operation of sports facilities
Major Shareholder: Roderick Bransgrove
Officers: Michael William Lashmar, Secretary; Roderick Granville Bransgrove [1950] Director; Feroze Issa Ismail Janmohamed [1946] Director; Michael William Lashmar [1977] Finance Director; David Mann [1964] Director/Chief Executive; Anthony Edward Middle [1970] Director; Stuart James Robertson [1968] Director; Barry Smith [1956] Director; Anthony Neville Williams [1956] Director

RB UK Commercial Limited
Incorporated: 20 November 2013 *Employees:* 408
Net Worth Deficit: £134,646,000 *Total Assets:* £689,331,008
Registered Office: 103-105 Bath Road, Slough, Berks, SL1 3UH
Activities: Wholesale of pharmaceutical goods
Parent: Reckitt Benckiser PLC
Officers: Christine Anne-Marie Logan, Secretary; John Dixon [1956] Director/SVP Tax; Ariadna Granena Aracil [1974] Director/Lawyer [Spanish]; Bart Meermans [1972] Director/RD UK, Ireland, Turkey, Health [Belgian]; Harminder Singh Virdi [1978] Finance Director

RBMR Topco Limited
Incorporated: 21 January 2016
Net Worth: £20,405,850 *Total Assets:* £39,638,328
Registered Office: A1 Omega Enterprise Park, Electron Way, Chandler's Ford, Eastleigh, Hants, SO53 4SE
Activities: Activities of other holding companies n.e.c.
Parent: Binder Bidco Limited
Officers: Edward James Timothy Brett [1967] Director/Investment Manager; Stephen Charles Clasby [1965] Director; Donald William Coates [1960] Director; James Alan Cunningham [1964] Director/Investment Manager; Wayne Roberts [1972] Director/Accountant [New Zealander]

RCI Financial Services Limited
Incorporated: 15 January 1997 *Employees:* 268
Net Worth: £304,297,984 *Total Assets:* £5,533,118,976
Registered Office: Rivers Office Park, Denham Way, Maple Cross, Rickmansworth, Herts, WD3 9YS
Activities: Credit granting by non-deposit taking finance houses and other specialist consumer credit grantors
Parent: RCI Banque SA
Officers: Sukhraj Jouhal, Secretary; Jean-Louis Labauge [1968] Managing Director [French]; Peter McEvoy [1978] Finance Director [Irish]; Enrico Rossini [1970] Director [Italian]

RCL (UK) Ltd.
Incorporated: 11 June 2002 *Employees:* 87
Net Worth: £9,037,450 *Total Assets:* £107,839,368
Registered Office: 3 The Heights, Brooklands, Weybridge, Surrey, KT13 0NY
Activities: Sea and coastal passenger water transport
Officers: Ruth Generaldine Marshall, Secretary; Ruth Generaldine Marshall [1964] Director/Solicitor; Gavin Stuart Smith [1966] Director/Senior Vice President [Australian]

RCL Cruises Ltd
Incorporated: 6 September 2010 *Employees:* 529
Net Worth: £403,416,640 *Total Assets:* £945,661,312
Registered Office: 3 The Heights, Brooklands, Weybridge, Surrey, KT13 0NY
Activities: Sea and coastal passenger water transport
Officers: Ruth Marshall, Secretary; Captain Manolis Kasselas [1965] Director/AVP Marine Operations [Greek]; Stuart Leven [1968] Director/Vice President EMEA; Ruth Generaldine Marshall [1964] Director/Solicitor; Gavin Stuart Smith [1966] Director/Senior Vice President [Australian]

Reach Holdings Limited
Incorporated: 30 May 2007 *Employees:* 1
Net Worth: £21,326,000 *Total Assets:* £36,387,000
Registered Office: Ground Floor, Block A, Dukes Court, Duke Street, Woking, Surrey, GU21 5BH
Activities: Activities of head offices
Parent: Acosta RH Limited
Officers: Charlene Emma Friend, Secretary; Charlene Emma Friend [1984] Director/Accountant; Todd Johnson [1965] Director [American]; Justine Maxwell [1978] Director/Chartered Accountant

The Reading Football Club Limited
Incorporated: 11 August 1897 *Employees:* 457
Net Worth Deficit: £29,499,786 *Total Assets:* £50,809,012
Registered Office: Madejski Stadium, Junction 11 M4, Reading, Berks, RG2 0FL
Activities: Other sports activities
Parent: Renhe Sports Management Ltd
Officers: Bryan Stabler, Secretary; Xiu Li Dai [1963] Director; Yongge Dai [1968] Director [Chinese]; Nigel Howe [1958] Director/Chief Executive; Narin Niruttinanon [1976] Director [Thai]

Reading Transport Limited
Incorporated: 27 March 1986 *Employees:* 586
Net Worth Deficit: £1,919,000 *Total Assets:* £42,945,000
Registered Office: Great Knollys Street, Reading, Berks, RG1 7HH
Activities: Other urban, suburban or metropolitan passenger land transport (not underground, metro or similar)
Parent: Reading Borough Council
Officers: Anthony Kenneth Pettitt, Secretary; Mark Andrew Adams [1969] Director/Bus Driver; Caroline Dorothy Anscombe [1960] Human Resources Director; Francis Connolly [1942] Director; Keith Anthony Moffatt [1954] Director; Anthony Kenneth Pettitt [1952] Director of Resources; Jane Elizabeth Stanford-Beale [1964] Director/Member of a Local Authority; David Christopher Sutton [1950] Director/Librarian; Trish Thomas [1957] Director/Local Government Officer; Michael Anthony Townend [1958] Director/Marketing; Robert Edward Williams [1982] Director/Chief Executive; Paul Woodward [1961] Director/Careers Advisor

Readypower Rail Services Finance Limited
Incorporated: 24 November 2016
Net Worth: £2,040,406 *Total Assets:* £33,509,584
Registered Office: Unit 620 Wharfedale Road, Winnersh, Wokingham, Berks, RG41 5TP
Activities: Other service activities incidental to land transportation, n.e.c.
Parent: Brunel Topco Limited
Officers: Alistair Paul Armstrong [1978] Director/Investment Manager; William Gerard Devanney [1965] Director; Anthony Hepburn [1962] Director; Russell George Jack [1969] Director; Anthony William Rieger [1945] Director

Readypower Rail Services Group Holdings Limited
Incorporated: 24 November 2016 *Employees:* 251
Net Worth: £5,710,808 *Total Assets:* £64,078,876
Registered Office: Unit 620 Wharfedale Road, Winnersh, Wokingham, Berks, RG41 5TP
Activities: Other service activities incidental to land transportation, n.e.c.
Parent: Primary Capital IV (Nominees) Limited
Officers: Alistair Paul Armstrong [1978] Director/Investment Manager; William Gerard Devanney [1965] Director; Anthony Hepburn [1962] Director; Russell George Jack [1969] Director; Anthony William Rieger [1945] Director

Readypower Rail Services Group Limited
Incorporated: 24 November 2016 *Employees:* 6
Net Worth: £22,330,096 *Total Assets:* £70,379,944
Registered Office: Unit 620 Wharfedale Road, Winnersh, Wokingham, Berks, RG41 5TP
Activities: Other service activities incidental to land transportation, n.e.c.
Parent: Brunel Midco Limited
Officers: Alistair Paul Armstrong [1978] Director/Investment Manager; William Gerard Devanney [1965] Director; Anthony Hepburn [1962] Director; Russell George Jack [1969] Director; Anthony William Rieger [1945] Director

Readypower Rail Services Limited
Incorporated: 28 January 1992 *Employees:* 206
Previous: Readypower Engineering Limited
Net Worth: £13,999,865 *Total Assets:* £33,216,620
Registered Office: Unit 620 Wharfedale Road, Winnersh, Wokingham, Berks, RG41 5TP
Activities: Renting and leasing of construction and civil engineering machinery and equipment
Parent: Readypower Rail Services Group Limited
Officers: William Gerard Devanney [1965] Director; Anthony Hepburn [1962] Director; Russell George Jack [1969] Director

Rebound Technology Group Holdings Limited
Incorporated: 6 June 2003 *Employees:* 295
Net Worth: £4,261,963 *Total Assets:* £32,978,704
Registered Office: Rivergate House, Newbury Business Park, Newbury, Berks, RG14 2PZ
Activities: Wholesale of electronic and telecommunications equipment and parts
Shareholder: Simon Lee Thake
Officers: Cecilia Taylor, Secretary; Gavin Bell [1966] Director; Peter Laugharne Griffith-Jones [1954] Director; David Mark Letori [1968] Director; Stephen John Madley [1960] Group Sales Director; Simon Lee Thake [1965] Director

Rebus Group Limited
Incorporated: 3 October 1995
Net Worth: £53,963,000 *Total Assets:* £53,963,000
Registered Office: Peoplebuilding 2, Peoplebuilding Estate, Maylands Avenue, Hemel Hempstead Industrial Estate, Hemel Hempstead, Herts, HP2 4NW
Activities: Activities of other holding companies n.e.c.
Parent: Rebus HR Holdings Limited
Officers: Malcolm Robert Bennett, Secretary; Steven James Chalker [1974] Chief Financial Director; Andrew Phillip Monshaw [1962] Director [American]

Rebus Holdings Limited
Incorporated: 19 October 1994
Net Worth: £48,950,000 *Total Assets:* £53,017,000
Registered Office: Peoplebuilding 2, Peoplebuilding Estate, Maylands Avenue, Hemel Hempstead Industrial Estate, Hemel Hempstead, Herts, HP2 4NW
Activities: Other professional, scientific and technical activities n.e.c.
Parent: Rebus Group Limited
Officers: Malcolm Robert Bennett, Secretary; Steven James Chalker [1974] Chief Financial Director; Andrew Phillip Monshaw [1962] Director [American]

Reckitt & Colman (Overseas) Limited
Incorporated: 4 November 1957 *Employees:* 3
Net Worth: £296,887,008 *Total Assets:* £322,519,008
Registered Office: 103-105 Bath Road, Slough, Berks, SL1 3UH
Activities: Leasing of intellectual property and similar products, except copyright works
Parent: Reckitt Benckiser PLC
Officers: Christine Anne-Marie Logan, Secretary; Richard Mark Greensmith [1973] Group Tax Director; Adrian Nevil Hennah [1957] Director/Chief Financial Officer; Jonathan Timmis [1975] Director/SVP Corporate Controller

Reckitt & Colman (UK) Limited
Incorporated: 20 June 1938
Net Worth: £2,573,633,024 *Total Assets:* £2,600,382,976
Registered Office: 103-105 Bath Road, Slough, Berks, SL1 3UH
Activities: Activities of financial services holding companies
Parent: Suffolk Finance Company Limited
Officers: Christine Anne-Marie Logan, Secretary; Richard Mark Greensmith [1973] Group Tax Director; Jonathan Timmis [1975] Finance Director

Reckitt & Colman Holdings Limited
Incorporated: 8 October 1998
Net Worth: £23,339,307,008 *Total Assets:* £26,165,360,640
Registered Office: 103-105 Bath Road, Slough, Berks, SL1 3UH
Activities: Activities of financial services holding companies
Parent: Reckitt Colman Chiswick (OTC) Limited
Officers: Christine Anne-Marie Logan, Secretary; Richard Mark Greensmith [1973] Group Tax Director; Simon Andrew Neville [1957] Group Treasury Director; Jonathan Timmis [1975] Director/SVP Corporate Controller

Reckitt & Sons Limited
Incorporated: 18 February 1956
Net Worth: £5,355,529,216 *Total Assets:* £5,362,917,888
Registered Office: 103-105 Bath Road, Slough, Berks, SL1 3UH
Activities: Activities of financial services holding companies
Parent: Reckitt & Colman Holdings Limited
Officers: Christine Anne-Marie Logan, Secretary; Richard Mark Greensmith [1973] Group Tax Director; Simon Andrew Neville [1957] Group Treasury Director; Jonathan Timmis [1975] Director/SVP Corporate Controller

Reckitt Benckiser (Brands) Limited
Incorporated: 28 August 2012 *Employees:* 810
Net Worth: £717,003,008 *Total Assets:* £887,260,992
Registered Office: 103-105 Bath Road, Slough, Berks, SL1 3UH
Activities: Other professional, scientific and technical activities n.e.c.
Parent: Reckitt Benckiser PLC
Officers: Christine Anne-Marie Logan, Secretary; Karen Cawdell [1971] Director; John Dixon [1956] Director/SVP Tax; Simon Andrew Neville [1957] Group Treasury Director; Jonathan Timmis [1975] Director/SVP Corporate Controller

Reckitt Benckiser (Grosvenor) Holdings Limited
Incorporated: 6 February 2006
Net Worth: £4,152,615,936 *Total Assets:* £5,141,645,824
Registered Office: 103-105 Bath Road, Slough, SL1 3UH
Activities: Activities of other holding companies n.e.c.
Parent: Green,Young & Company Limited
Officers: Christine Anne-Marie Logan, Secretary; Richard Mark Greensmith [1973] Group Tax Director; Simon Andrew Neville [1957] Group Treasury Director; Jonathan Timmis [1975] Director/SVP Corporate Controller

Reckitt Benckiser (RUMEA) Limited
Incorporated: 19 April 2013 *Employees:* 52
Net Worth Deficit: £63,899,000 *Total Assets:* £127,924,000
Registered Office: 103-105 Bath Road, Slough, Berks, SL1 3UH
Activities: Activities of head offices
Parent: Reckitt Benckiser PLC
Officers: Christine Anne-Marie Logan, Secretary; John Dixon [1956] Director/SVP Tax; Adrian Nevil Hennah [1957] Director/Chief Financial Officer; Jonathan Timmis [1975] Director/SVP Corporate Controller

Reckitt Benckiser (UK) Limited
Incorporated: 28 April 2000 *Employees:* 332
Net Worth: £2,188,468,992 *Total Assets:* £2,247,467,008
Registered Office: 103-105 Bath Road, Slough, Berks, SL1 3UH
Activities: Manufacture of household and sanitary goods and of toilet requisites
Parent: Reckitt & Colman Holdings Limited
Officers: Christine Anne-Marie Logan, Secretary; Rohit Chandarana [1981] Finance Director; Jaime Cruz [1950] Site Director, Manufacturing [Portuguese]; John Dixon [1956] Director/SVP Tax

Reckitt Benckiser (USA) Limited
Incorporated: 21 July 2005
Net Worth: £643,161,984 *Total Assets:* £3,289,890,048
Registered Office: 103-105 Bath Road, Slough, Berks, SL1 3UH
Activities: Activities of financial services holding companies
Parent: Reckitt Benckiser Investments Limited
Officers: Christine Anne-Marie Logan, Secretary; Richard Mark Greensmith [1973] Group Tax Director; Jonathan Timmis [1975] Finance Director

Reckitt Benckiser Asia Pacific Limited
Incorporated: 20 July 2004 *Employees:* 2
Net Worth: £34,452,000 *Total Assets:* £80,899,000
Registered Office: 103-105 Bath Road, Slough, Berks, SL1 3UH
Activities: Wholesale of pharmaceutical goods
Parent: Reckitt Benckiser PLC
Officers: Christine Anne-Marie Logan, Secretary; Richard Mark Greensmith [1973] Group Tax Director; Jonathan Timmis [1975] Finance Director

Reckitt Benckiser Corporate Services Limited
Incorporated: 5 July 2000
Net Worth: £2,345,629,952 *Total Assets:* £2,469,594,880
Registered Office: 103-105 Bath Road, Slough, Berks, SL1 3UH
Activities: Management consultancy activities other than financial management
Parent: Reckitt & Colman Holdings Limited
Officers: Christine Anne-Marie Logan, Secretary; John Dixon [1956] Director/SVP Tax; Gurveen Singh [1957] Director/Chief Human Resources Officer [Indian]; Jonathan Timmis [1975] Director/SVP Corporate Controller

Reckitt Benckiser Finance (2005) Limited
Incorporated: 27 June 2005
Net Worth: £377,241,984 *Total Assets:* £379,395,008
Registered Office: 103-105 Bath Road, Slough, Berks, SL1 3UH
Activities: Activities of financial services holding companies
Parent: Reckitt Benckiser Investments Limited
Officers: Christine Anne-Marie Logan, Secretary; Richard Mark Greensmith [1973] Group Tax Director; Simon Andrew Neville [1957] Group Treasury Director; Jonathan Timmis [1975] Finance Director

Reckitt Benckiser Finance (2010) Limited
Incorporated: 21 October 2010
Net Worth: £3,476,825,088 *Total Assets:* £4,880,451,072
Registered Office: 103-105 Bath Road, Slough, Berks, SL1 3UH
Activities: Activities of financial services holding companies
Parent: Reckitt Benckiser (Hygiene Home) Holdings Limited
Officers: Christine Anne-Marie Logan, Secretary; Richard Mark Greensmith [1973] Group Tax Director; Simon Andrew Neville [1957] Group Treasury Director; Jonathan Timmis [1975] Director/SVP Corporate Controller

Reckitt Benckiser Finance Company Limited
Incorporated: 30 April 2003
Net Worth: £179,087,008 *Total Assets:* £179,144,000
Registered Office: 103-105 Bath Road, Slough, Berks, SL1 3UH
Activities: Activities of financial services holding companies
Parent: Reckitt Benckiser Investments Limited
Officers: Christine Anne-Marie Logan, Secretary; Richard Mark Greensmith [1973] Group Tax Director; Jonathan Timmis [1975] Finance Director

Reckitt Benckiser Group PLC
Incorporated: 6 June 2007
Net Worth: £13,532,999,680 *Total Assets:* £37,013,000,192
Registered Office: 103-105 Bath Road, Slough, Berks, SL1 3UH
Activities: Activities of head offices
Officers: Rupert Bondy, Secretary; Andrew Robert John Bonfield [1962] Director; Nicandro Durante [1956] Director [Brazilian/Italian]; Mary Elaine Harris [1966] Director; Adrian Nevil Hennah [1957] Director; Rakesh Kapoor [1958] Director/Chief Executive Officer; Dr Mehmood Khan [1958] Director [American/British]; Dr Pamela Josephine Kirby [1953] Director; Christopher Alan Sinclair [1950] Director [American]; Elane Stock [1964] Director [American]

Reckitt Benckiser Healthcare (Central & Eastern Europe) Limited
Incorporated: 9 May 1997
Net Worth: £197,412,000 *Total Assets:* £197,468,992
Registered Office: 103-105 Bath Road, Slough, Berks, SL1 3UH
Activities: Non-trading company
Parent: Reckitt Benckiser Treasury (2007) Limited
Officers: Christine Anne-Marie Logan, Secretary; Richard Mark Greensmith [1973] Group Tax Director; Jonathan Timmis [1975] Finance Director

Reckitt Benckiser Healthcare (CIS) Limited
Incorporated: 28 May 1997
Net Worth: £643,354,176 *Total Assets:* £643,354,176
Registered Office: 103-105 Bath Road, Slough, Berks, SL1 3UH
Activities: Financial management
Parent: Reckitt Benckiser Treasury (2007) Limited
Officers: Christine Anne-Marie Logan, Secretary; Richard Mark Greensmith [1973] Group Tax Director; Jonathan Timmis [1975] Finance Director

Reckitt Benckiser Healthcare (UK) Limited
Incorporated: 22 December 1931 *Employees:* 631
Net Worth: £1,163,757,952 *Total Assets:* £3,929,607,936
Registered Office: 103-105 Bath Road, Slough, Berks, SL1 3UH
Activities: Manufacture of household and sanitary goods and of toilet requisites
Parent: Reckitt Benckiser (Grosvenor) Holdings Limited
Officers: Christine Anne-Marie Logan, Secretary; John Dixon [1956] Director/SVP Tax; Ariadna Granena Aracil [1974] Director/Lawyer [Spanish]; Simon Andrew Neville [1957] Group Treasury Director; Harminder Singh Virdi [1978] Finance Director

Reckitt Benckiser Healthcare International Limited
Incorporated: 20 August 1992 *Employees:* 742
Net Worth: £249,376,000 *Total Assets:* £301,283,008
Registered Office: 103-105 Bath Road, Slough, Berks, SL1 3UH
Activities: Manufacture of household and sanitary goods and of toilet requisites
Parent: RB Holdings (Nottingham) Limited
Officers: Christine Anne-Marie Logan, Secretary; John Dixon [1956] Director/SVP Tax; Harminder Singh Virdi [1978] Finance Director

Reckitt Benckiser Holdings (Luxembourg) Limited
Incorporated: 19 November 2004
Net Worth: £2,731,431,936 *Total Assets:* £4,508,191,232
Registered Office: 103-105 Bath Road, Slough, Berks, SL1 3UH
Activities: Activities of other holding companies n.e.c.
Parent: Reckitt Benckiser Investments Limited
Officers: Christine Anne-Marie Logan, Secretary; Richard Mark Greensmith [1973] Group Tax Director; Adrian Nevil Hennah [1957] Director/Chief Financial Officer; Jonathan Timmis [1975] Director/SVP Corporate Controller

Reckitt Benckiser Holdings (Overseas) Limited
Incorporated: 13 December 2002
Net Worth: £504,400,000 *Total Assets:* £504,535,008
Registered Office: 103-105 Bath Road, Slough, Berks, SL1 3UH
Activities: Activities of financial services holding companies
Parent: Reckitt & Colman Holdings Limited
Officers: Christine Anne-Marie Logan, Secretary; Richard Mark Greensmith [1973] Group Tax Director; Simon Andrew Neville [1957] Group Treasury Director; Jonathan Timmis [1975] Director/SVP Corporate Controller

Reckitt Benckiser Holdings (TFFC) Limited
Incorporated: 13 September 2013
Previous: The R.T. French's Food Group Limited
Net Worth: £896,728,000 *Total Assets:* £902,689,024
Registered Office: 103-105 Bath Road, Slough, Berks, SL1 3UH
Activities: Activities of other holding companies n.e.c.
Parent: Reckitt Benckiser Investments Limited
Officers: Christine Anne-Marie Logan, Secretary; Richard Mark Greensmith [1973] Group Tax Director; Simon Andrew Neville [1957] Group Treasury Director; Jonathan Timmis [1975] Director/SVP Corporate Controller

Reckitt Benckiser Holdings (USA) Limited
Incorporated: 22 September 2003
Net Worth: £1,923,801,984 *Total Assets:* £2,186,580,992
Registered Office: 103-105 Bath Road, Slough, Berks, SL1 3UH
Activities: Activities of other holding companies n.e.c.
Parent: Reckitt Benckiser (USA) Limited
Officers: Christine Anne-Marie Logan, Secretary; Richard Mark Greensmith [1973] Group Tax Director; Simon Andrew Neville [1957] Group Treasury Director; Jonathan Timmis [1975] Director/SVP Corporate Controller

Reckitt Benckiser Investments Limited
Incorporated: 4 July 2003
Net Worth: £21,908,492,288 *Total Assets:* £49,974,116,352
Registered Office: 103-105 Bath Road, Slough, SL1 3UH
Activities: Activities of financial services holding companies
Parent: Reckitt Benckiser PLC
Officers: Christine Anne-Marie Logan, Secretary; Richard Mark Greensmith [1973] Group Tax Director; Simon Andrew Neville [1957] Group Treasury Director; Jonathan Timmis [1975] Director/SVP Corporate Controller

Reckitt Benckiser Luxembourg (2010) Limited
Incorporated: 22 July 2010
Net Worth: £876,841,984 *Total Assets:* £880,072,000
Registered Office: 103-105 Bath Road, Slough, Berks, SL1 3UH
Activities: Activities of financial services holding companies
Parent: Reckitt & Colman Holdings Limited
Officers: Christine Anne-Marie Logan, Secretary; John Dixon [1956] Director/SVP Tax; Richard Mark Greensmith [1973] Group Tax Director; Simon Andrew Neville [1957] Group Treasury Director; Jonathan Timmis [1975] Finance Director

Reckitt Benckiser Luxembourg (No. 1) Limited
Incorporated: 7 December 2005
Net Worth: £24,142,000 *Total Assets:* £24,171,000
Registered Office: 103-105 Bath Road, Slough, Berks, SL1 3UH
Activities: Activities of financial services holding companies
Parent: Reckitt & Colman Holdings Limited
Officers: Christine Anne-Marie Logan, Secretary; Richard Mark Greensmith [1973] Group Tax Director; Jonathan Timmis [1975] Finance Director

Reckitt Benckiser Luxembourg (No.2) Limited
Incorporated: 7 December 2005
Net Worth: £7,133,564,928 *Total Assets:* £7,142,112,256
Registered Office: 103-105 Bath Road, Slough, Berks, SL1 3UH
Activities: Activities of financial services holding companies
Parent: Reckitt & Colman Holdings Limited
Officers: Christine Anne-Marie Logan, Secretary; Richard Mark Greensmith [1973] Group Tax Director; Jonathan Timmis [1975] Finance Director

Reckitt Benckiser Luxembourg (No.3) Limited
Incorporated: 7 December 2005
Net Worth: £3,679,023,104 *Total Assets:* £3,680,079,872
Registered Office: 103-105 Bath Road, Slough, Berks, SL1 3UH
Activities: Activities of financial services holding companies
Parent: Reckitt Benckiser Holdings (USA) Limited
Officers: Christine Anne-Marie Logan, Secretary; Richard Mark Greensmith [1973] Group Tax Director; Simon Andrew Neville [1957] Group Treasury Director; Jonathan Timmis [1975] Director/SVP Corporate Controller

Reckitt Benckiser Luxembourg (No.4) Limited
Incorporated: 7 December 2005
Net Worth: £5,986,002,944 *Total Assets:* £5,987,720,192
Registered Office: 103-105 Bath Road, Slough, Berks, SL1 3UH
Activities: Activities of financial services holding companies
Parent: Reckitt Benckiser Holdings (USA) Limited
Officers: Christine Anne-Marie Logan, Secretary; Richard Mark Greensmith [1973] Group Tax Director; Simon Andrew Neville [1957] Group Treasury Director; Jonathan Timmis [1975] Director/SVP Corporate Controller

Reckitt Benckiser PLC
Incorporated: 23 December 1953
Net Worth: £32,200,146,944 *Total Assets:* £49,818,198,016
Registered Office: 103-105 Bath Road, Slough, Berks, SL1 3UH
Activities: Activities of other holding companies n.e.c.
Parent: Reckitt Benckiser Group PLC
Officers: Christine Anne-Marie Logan, Secretary; John Dixon [1956] Director/SVP Tax; Adrian Nevil Hennah [1957] Director/Chief Financial Officer; Simon Andrew Neville [1957] Group Treasury Director; Jonathan Timmis [1975] Director/SVP Corporate Controller

Reckitt Benckiser Service Bureau Limited
Incorporated: 28 July 1998
Net Worth: £656,068,992 *Total Assets:* £664,321,984
Registered Office: 103-105 Bath Road, Slough, Berks, SL1 3UH
Activities: Non-trading company
Parent: Reckitt Benckiser PLC
Officers: Christine Anne-Marie Logan, Secretary; Richard Mark Greensmith [1973] Group Tax Director; Jonathan Timmis [1975] Finance Director

Reckitt Benckiser Treasury (2007) Limited
Incorporated: 10 September 2007
Net Worth: £1,777,129,984 *Total Assets:* £2,421,181,952
Registered Office: 103-105 Bath Road, Slough, Berks, SL1 3UH
Activities: Activities of financial services holding companies
Parent: Reckitt Benckiser (USA) Limited
Officers: Christine Anne-Marie Logan, Secretary; Richard Mark Greensmith [1973] Group Tax Director; Simon Andrew Neville [1957] Group Treasury Director; Jonathan Timmis [1975] Director/SVP Corporate Controller

Reckitt Benckiser Treasury Services PLC
Incorporated: 9 October 2006 *Employees:* 10
Net Worth: £4,854,561,792 *Total Assets:* £46,614,740,992
Registered Office: 103-105 Bath Road, Slough, Berks, SL1 3UH
Activities: Activities of financial services holding companies
Parent: Reckitt Benckiser PLC
Officers: Christine Anne-Marie Logan, Secretary; John Dixon [1956] Director/SVP Tax; Adrian Nevil Hennah [1957] Director/Chief Financial Officer; Simon Andrew Neville [1957] Group Treasury Director; Jonathan Timmis [1975] Director/SVP Corporate Controller

Reckitt Benckiser USA Finance (No.1) Limited
Incorporated: 17 September 2003
Net Worth: £656,140,032 *Total Assets:* £656,515,968
Registered Office: 103-105 Bath Road, Slough, Berks, SL1 3UH
Activities: Activities of financial services holding companies
Parent: Reckitt Benckiser Investments Limited
Officers: Christine Anne-Marie Logan, Secretary; Richard Mark Greensmith [1973] Group Tax Director; Jonathan Timmis [1975] Finance Director

Reckitt Benckiser USA Finance (No.2) Limited
Incorporated: 17 September 2003
Net Worth: £330,294,016 *Total Assets:* £330,468,000
Registered Office: 103-105 Bath Road, Slough, Berks, SL1 3UH
Activities: Activities of financial services holding companies
Parent: Reckitt Benckiser Investments Limited
Officers: Christine Anne-Marie Logan, Secretary; Richard Mark Greensmith [1973] Group Tax Director; Jonathan Timmis [1975] Finance Director

Reckitt Benckiser USA Finance (No.3) Limited
Incorporated: 17 September 2003
Net Worth: £149,316,992 *Total Assets:* £149,368,000
Registered Office: 103-105 Bath Road, Slough, Berks, SL1 3UH
Activities: Activities of financial services holding companies
Parent: Reckitt Benckiser Investments Limited
Officers: Christine Anne-Marie Logan, Secretary; Richard Mark Greensmith [1973] Group Tax Director; Jonathan Timmis [1975] Finance Director

Reckitt Colman Chiswick (OTC) Limited
Incorporated: 4 November 1957
Net Worth: £3,203,173,888 *Total Assets:* £4,301,777,920
Registered Office: 103-105 Bath Road, Slough, Berks, SL1 3UH
Activities: Activities of financial services holding companies
Parent: Reckitt Benckiser Investments Limited
Officers: Christine Anne-Marie Logan, Secretary; Richard Mark Greensmith [1973] Group Tax Director; Simon Andrew Neville [1957] Group Treasury Director; Jonathan Timmis [1975] Finance Director

Record Currency Management Limited
Incorporated: 30 March 1983
Net Worth: £19,847,000 *Total Assets:* £22,723,000
Registered Office: Morgan House, Madeira Walk, Windsor, Berks, SL4 1EP
Activities: Fund management activities
Parent: Record PLC
Officers: Joanne Manning, Secretary; Steven Peter Cullen [1968] Finance Director; Timothy Peter Warren Edwards [1956] Director; Rosemary Hilary [1955] Director; Leslie Francoise Meier [1955] Director; Bob F Noyen [1962] Director [Dutch]; Neil Peter Record [1953] Director; Rosina Jane Tufnell [1964] Director; David Alistair James Wood-Collins [1972] Director

Record PLC
Incorporated: 1 July 1985 *Employees:* 81
Net Worth: £26,551,000 *Total Assets:* £32,076,000
Registered Office: Morgan House, Madeira Walk, Windsor, Berks, SL4 1EP
Activities: Activities of financial services holding companies
Officers: Joanne Manning, Secretary; Steven Peter Cullen [1968] Finance Director; Timothy Peter Warren Edwards [1956] Director; Rosemary Hilary [1955] Director; Leslie Francoise Meier [1955] Director; Bob F Noyen [1962] Director [Dutch]; Neil Peter Record [1953] Director; Rosina Jane Tufnell [1964] Director; David Alistair James Wood-Collins [1972] Director

Rectory Homes Limited
Incorporated: 18 January 1991 *Employees:* 48
Net Worth: £12,603,720 *Total Assets:* £35,903,320
Registered Office: Rectory House, Thame Road, Haddenham, Aylesbury, Bucks, HP17 8DA
Activities: Construction of domestic buildings
Major Shareholder: Simon Peter Vickers
Officers: Jayne Caroline Blake, Secretary; Robert Davidson [1972] Finance Director; David Ullathorne [1958] Director/Deputy Chief Executive; Sarah Vickers [1961] Director; Simon Peter Vickers [1958] Managing Director

Red Bull Racing Limited
Incorporated: 1 November 1995 *Employees:* 58
Net Worth: £4,959,000 *Total Assets:* £37,651,000
Registered Office: Building 2, Bradbourne Drive, Tilbrook, Milton Keynes, Bucks, MK7 8AT
Activities: Other sports activities
Parent: Red Bull Technology Limited
Officers: Christian Horner [1973] Director/Team Principal; Dr Helmut Marko [1943] Director/Hotelier [Austrian]; Dietrich Mateschitz [1944] Director Soft Drinks Manufacturer [Austrian]

Red Bull Technology Limited
Incorporated: 11 August 2004 *Employees:* 793
Net Worth: £33,425,000 *Total Assets:* £143,099,008
Registered Office: Building 1, Bradbourne Drive, Tilbrook, Milton Keynes, Bucks, MK7 8BJ
Activities: Other manufacturing n.e.c.
Shareholder: Dietrich Mateschitz
Officers: Christian Horner [1973] Director - Motor Racing; Alistair David Rew [1963] Finance Director

Red Circle Security Services Limited
Incorporated: 24 December 1985 *Employees:* 3
Net Worth: £18,267,732 *Total Assets:* £25,980,226
Registered Office: 792 Wickham Road, Croydon, Surrey, CR0 8EA
Activities: Other letting and operating of own or leased real estate
Shareholders: Veena Bahl; Bashir Ahmed Rana
Officers: Veena Bahl, Secretary; Bashir Ahmed Rana [1940] Director

Red Funnel Limited
Incorporated: 16 June 2017 *Employees:* 485
Net Worth: £140,035,008 *Total Assets:* £383,686,016
Registered Office: 12 Bugle Street, Southampton, SO14 2JY
Activities: Non-trading company
Officers: Michael Francis Campbell [1956] Director/Deputy Chief Investment Officer [Canadian]; Mary Chang [1970] Director [Canadian]; Frances Charlotte Collins [1977] Director/Chief Executive Officer; Stephen Donald Dowd [1964] Director [Canadian]; Kevin Alan George [1956] Director/Chief Executive; George Christopher Gray [1944] Director; Charles John Gore Hazelwood [1963] Director/Chartered Accountant; Claire Elizabeth Bradley Locke [1960] Director; Elizabeth Anne MacArtney [1962] Director; Michelle Perry [1967] Director; Ceri Richards [1958] Director; Patrick Michael Seely [1960] Director; Edward Arthur Wilson [1965] Director/Investment Manager; Paul Richard Winter [1963] Director/Chief Finance Officer

Red Tree (2004) LLP
Incorporated: 2 November 2004
Net Worth: £21,267,900 *Total Assets:* £21,403,640
Registered Office: c/o Rickaby & Co, 4 Claridge Court, Lower Kings Road, Berkhamsted, Herts, HP4 2AF
Officers: James Koe [1961] Member

J. Reddington Ltd
Incorporated: 23 July 1996 *Employees:* 123
Net Worth: £32,858,140 *Total Assets:* £85,098,440
Registered Office: 4 Elstree Way, Borehamwood, Herts, WD6 1RN
Activities: Construction of commercial buildings
Parent: JRL Group Ltd
Officers: Ronan Joseph Gleeson, Secretary/Director [Irish]; Ronan Joseph Gleeson [1976] Director [Irish]; Kevin William Keegan [1963] Director/Estimator [Irish]; John James Reddington [1972] Director/Formwork [Irish]

Redring Xpelair Group Ltd
Incorporated: 14 October 1935 *Employees:* 221
Net Worth: £11,823,000 *Total Assets:* £25,661,000
Registered Office: Millbrook House, Grange Drive, Hedge End, Southampton, SO30 2DF
Activities: Manufacture of electric domestic appliances
Parent: Applied Energy Products Ltd
Officers: Michael Maher, Secretary; Donal Francis Flynn [1973] Director/Chartered Accountant [Irish]; Michael Maher [1964] Director/Accountant [Irish]; Fergal John Naughton [1975] Director [Irish]; Martin Lawrence Naughton [1939] Director Engineer [Irish]; Major Singh [1968] Director/Accountant

Redsky IT Holdings Limited
Incorporated: 27 November 1998
Net Worth: £21,569,000 *Total Assets:* £32,542,000
Registered Office: Breakspear Park, Breakspear Way, Hemel Hempstead, Herts, HP2 4TZ
Activities: Other business support service activities n.e.c.
Parent: Explorer Holdings UK Limited
Officers: James Douglas McFarlane [1950] Director [Canadian]

Redwing Holdings 2 Limited
Incorporated: 21 May 2007
Net Worth: £135,921,184 *Total Assets:* £144,091,856
Registered Office: 3M Centre, Cain Road, Bracknell, Berks, RG12 8HT
Activities: Activities of head offices
Parent: Capital Safety Row Limited
Officers: Ian Richard Brown, Secretary; David James Ashley [1968] Director/General Counsel; Simla Semerciyan [1973] Director/Finance Manager [Turkish]

The Alec Reed Academy
Incorporated: 22 May 2002 *Employees:* 210
Net Worth: £36,593,000 *Total Assets:* £40,347,000
Registered Office: Bengarth Road, Northolt, Middlesex, UB5 5LQ
Activities: Pre-primary education
Officers: Marghanita Helen Muris, Secretary; Baba Abu [1966] Director/Banker; Sofina Bhatti [1982] Director/Teacher; Heather Flint [1951] Director/Education Consultant; Claudia Lashmore-Bennett [1980] Director/Teacher; Dee Martin [1962] Director/Campus Operation Manager; Allison Janice Moise-Dixon [1976] Director/Principal & CEO; Dee Morrison [1969] Director/Legal PA; Mike Phillips [1961] Managing Director; Emma Price [1990] Director/Programme Lead, Teach First; Louise Prince [1969] Director/Rights Executive; Tamana Sayed [1979] Director/Registered Nurse; Richard Antony Taylor [1969] Divisional Director Recruitment

Reed Business Information Limited
Incorporated: 27 September 1918 *Employees:* 1,514
Net Worth: £678,201,984 *Total Assets:* £946,572,992
Registered Office: Quadrant House, The Quadrant, Sutton, Surrey, SM2 5AS
Activities: Other information technology service activities
Parent: Reed Business Information (Holdings) Limited
Officers: Mark Vickers Kelsey [1960] Director; Jamie Andrew O'Sullivan [1971] Director/Chief Finance Officer

William Reed Business Media Ltd
Incorporated: 24 December 1993 *Employees:* 332
Net Worth: £5,958,000 *Total Assets:* £29,530,000
Registered Office: Broadfield Park, Crawley, W Sussex, RH11 9RT
Activities: Publishing of directories and mailing lists
Parent: William Reed Holdings Limited
Officers: Robert William Proctor, Secretary; Richard Alexander Woolley Oscroft [1972] Director/Chief Financial Officer; Charles Christian Thomas Reed [1959] Director

Reed Exhibitions Limited
Incorporated: 21 December 1960 *Employees:* 475
Net Worth: £32,753,048 *Total Assets:* £236,997,920
Registered Office: Gateway House, 28 The Quadrant, Richmond, Surrey, TW9 1DN
Activities: Activities of exhibition and fair organisers
Parent: RELX (UK)
Officers: Jacqueline Mary Poole, Secretary/Company Lawyer; Kumsal Bayazit Besson [1974] Director [Turkish]; Alexander David Stuart Bowden [1967] Director/Accountant; Darren Geoffrey Johnson [1966] Director; Richard John Norman Mortimore [1960] Director/Chief Executive; Michele Ruth Tiley-Hill [1972] Director

William Reed Group Ltd
Incorporated: 1 March 2017 *Employees:* 381
Net Worth: £5,016,000 *Total Assets:* £29,375,000
Registered Office: Broadfield Park, Crawley, W Sussex, RH11 9RT
Activities: Activities of head offices
Shareholders: Laurence Cecil Reed; Nicholas William Reed; Andrew Laurence Reed; Charles Christian Thomas Reed
Officers: Robert William Proctor, Secretary; Mark Jeremy Varnham Allin [1961] Director/Consultant; Richard Alexander Woolley Oscroft [1972] Director/Chief Financial Officer; Andrew Laurence Reed [1962] Director; Charles Christian Thomas Reed [1959] Managing Director; Nicholas William Reed [1958] Director; Holly Elizabeth Widdowson [1987] Director

William Reed Holdings Limited
Incorporated: 1 October 1927 *Employees:* 3
Net Worth: £36,027,000 *Total Assets:* £46,802,000
Registered Office: Broadfield Park, Crawley, W Sussex, RH11 9RT
Activities: Activities of head offices
Shareholders: William Reed Group Ltd; William Reed Group Ltd
Officers: Robert William Proctor, Secretary; Richard Alexander Woolley Oscroft [1972] Director/Chief Financial Officer; Andrew Laurence Reed [1962] Director; Charles Christian Thomas Reed [1959] Director

REG Holdings Limited
Incorporated: 19 November 1992 *Employees:* 19
Net Worth: £14,238,530 *Total Assets:* £23,815,574
Registered Office: 2nd Floor, Edgeborough House, Upper Edgeborough Road, Guildford, Surrey, GU1 2BJ
Activities: Activities of head offices
Parent: REG Power Management Limited
Officers: Zoe Catherine Crockford, Secretary; Stephen Booth [1959] Development Director; Ian Kenneth Collins [1959] Director; David Edward Crockford [1972] Director/Accountant; Matthew Richard Partridge [1971] Director; Simon Thomas Wannop [1979] Commercial Director; Andrew Nicholas Whalley [1964] Director

The Regard ACH Holdco Limited
Incorporated: 2 August 2016
Net Worth: £21,416,000 *Total Assets:* £22,046,000
Registered Office: Unit 6 & 7 Princeton Mews, 167-169 London Road, Kingston upon Thames, Surrey, KT2 6PT
Activities: Other business support service activities n.e.c.
Parent: Galaxy Group Bidco Limited
Officers: Nicola Hopkins, Secretary; Nicola Rosemary Lucy Hopkins [1968] Director/Chartered Accountant

The Regard Partnership Limited
Incorporated: 31 January 1996 *Employees:* 1,561
Net Worth: £66,339,000 *Total Assets:* £89,982,000
Registered Office: Unit 6 Princeton Mews, 167-169 London Road, Kingston upon Thames, Surrey, KT2 6PT
Activities: Residential care activities for learning difficulties, mental health and substance abuse
Parent: Ruby Topco Limited
Officers: Nicola Hopkins, Secretary; Nicola Rosemary Lucy Hopkins [1968] Director/Chartered Accountant; Peter Kinsey [1964] Director

Regenter B3 Holdco Limited
Incorporated: 6 February 2002
Net Worth Deficit: £5,005,000 *Total Assets:* £57,194,000
Registered Office: 8 White Oak Square, London Road, Swanley, Kent, BR8 7AG
Activities: Activities of head offices
Parent: Palio (No 5) Limited
Officers: Carl Harvey Dix [1966] Operations Director; Edward Mountney [1985] Director/Investment Professional

Regenter B3 Limited
Incorporated: 6 February 2002
Net Worth Deficit: £5,005,000 *Total Assets:* £57,194,000
Registered Office: 8 White Oak Square, London Road, Swanley, Kent, BR8 7AG
Activities: Other business support service activities n.e.c.
Parent: Regenter B3 Holdco Limited
Officers: Carl Harvey Dix [1966] Operations Director; Edward Mountney [1985] Director/Investment Professional

Regenter Myatts Field North Holding Company Limited
Incorporated: 7 January 2011
Net Worth Deficit: £5,025,000 *Total Assets:* £78,731,000
Registered Office: 8 White Oak Square, London Road, Swanley, Kent, BR8 7AG
Activities: Activities of head offices
Parent: JLIF Holdings (Lambeth Social Housing) Limited
Officers: David Richard Bradbury [1969] Asset Director; Vikki Louise Everett [1971] Director/Project Manager

Regenter Myatts Field North Limited
Incorporated: 11 January 2011
Net Worth Deficit: £5,025,000 *Total Assets:* £78,731,000
Registered Office: 8 White Oak Square, London Road, Swanley, Kent, BR8 7AG
Activities: Other business support service activities n.e.c.
Parent: Regenter Myatts Field North Holding Company Limited
Officers: David Richard Bradbury [1969] Asset Director; Vikki Louise Everett [1971] Director/Project Manager

Regentrealm Limited
Incorporated: 29 November 1999
Net Worth: £8,800,000 *Total Assets:* £439,400,000
Registered Office: Hayes Park, Hayes End Road, Hayes, Middlesex, UB4 8EE
Activities: Non-trading company
Parent: United Biscuits Bidco Limited
Officers: Mark Oldham, Secretary/Barrister; Helen Josephine McCarthy [1966] Director; Mark Oldham [1959] Director

Regulus Bidco Limited
Incorporated: 3 March 2015
Net Worth: £9,964,489 *Total Assets:* £48,721,544
Registered Office: Financial Research Centre, Haddenham Business Park, Pegasus Way, Haddenham, Aylesbury, Bucks, HP17 8LJ
Activities: Activities of financial services holding companies
Parent: Regulus Midco Limited
Officers: Remko Peter Bijtjes [1971] Director [Dutch]; Syed Zahid Hussain Bilgrami [1971] Director; Alastair Colin Gillies Brown [1974] Director; Christopher John Loraine Samuel [1958] Director; Philip Simon Shapiro [1975] Director

Regulus Midco Limited
Incorporated: 3 March 2015 *Employees:* 125
Net Worth Deficit: £6,192,681 *Total Assets:* £26,996,276
Registered Office: Financial Research Centre, Haddenham Business Park, Pegasus Way, Haddenham, Aylesbury, Bucks, HP17 8LJ
Activities: Activities of other holding companies n.e.c.
Parent: Regulus Topco Limited
Officers: Remko Peter Bijtjes [1971] Director [Dutch]; Syed Zahid Hussain Bilgrami [1971] Director; Alastair Colin Gillies Brown [1974] Director

Regulus Topco Limited
Incorporated: 3 March 2015 *Employees:* 125
Net Worth Deficit: £6,065,684 *Total Assets:* £27,001,328
Registered Office: Financial Research Centre, Haddenham Business Park, Pegasus Way, Haddenham, Aylesbury, Bucks, HP17 8LJ
Activities: Activities of other holding companies n.e.c.
Officers: Remko Peter Bijtjes [1971] Director [Dutch]; Syed Zahid Hussain Bilgrami [1971] Director; Alastair Colin Gillies Brown [1974] Director; Christopher John Loraine Samuel [1958] Director; Philip Simon Shapiro [1975] Director

Reigate Grammar School
Incorporated: 22 March 2000 *Employees:* 320
Net Worth: £18,540,026 *Total Assets:* £41,145,264
Registered Office: Reigate Grammar School, Reigate Road, Reigate, Surrey, RH2 0QS
Activities: Primary education
Officers: Stephen Peter Douty, Secretary; Marc Robert Benton [1972] Director/Investment Banker; Mary Kathryn Braughler-Edmunds [1967] Director/Business Consultant; Colin Morris Cobain [1956] Director/Management Consultant; David Garth Cole [1975] Director/Headmaster; Brian Vernon Day [1951] Director/Architect; James William Dean [1957] Director/Chartered Accountant; Christopher Mark Dixon [1973] Director/Solicitor; Mark Elsey [1960] Director/Solicitor; Luke Herbert [1964] Director/Consultant Retinal Surgeon; Maxine Julie Hulme [1967] Director/Consultant & Speaker; Roger Charles Newstead [1938] Director/Retired; Mark Joseph O'Dwyer [1967] Director/Chartered Accountant; Lisa Page [1977] Director/Business Development/Service Management; Sarah Louise Sayce [1950] Director/University Professor; Nicholas Henry Weber [1972] Director [French]

John Reilly (Civil Engineering) Limited
Incorporated: 10 February 1986 *Employees:* 282
Net Worth: £12,514,720 *Total Assets:* £36,394,180
Registered Office: Highfield Court, Tollgate, Chandler's Ford, Eastleigh, Hants, SO53 3TY
Activities: Construction of commercial buildings
Parent: Reilly JDM Holdings Limited
Officers: David Patrick Reilly, Secretary; James Stuart Austin [1969] Director/Engineer; Stephen Batterson [1966] Director; David Hutchinson [1971] Director; Robert Norman Jones [1967] Director; Yip Lieu [1973] Director; Graham O'Neill [1964] Director; Candice Jayne Reilly [1968] Director/Administrator; David Patrick Reilly [1959] Director/Civil Engineer [Irish]; Michael Joseph Reilly [1960] Director/Civil Engineer [Irish]; Theresa Margaret Reilly [1961] Director/Administrator; David Spruce [1965] Director; Lee Williams [1973] Director

Reilly JDM Holdings Limited
Incorporated: 28 August 2014 *Employees:* 288
Net Worth: £8,782,383 *Total Assets:* £34,004,840
Registered Office: Highfield Court, Tollgate, Chandler's Ford, Eastleigh, Hants, SO53 3TY
Activities: Activities of other holding companies n.e.c.
Parent: Barley House Trustee Limited
Officers: John Reilly, Secretary; James Stuart Austin [1969] Director/Engineer; Robert Norman Jones [1967] Director; Yip Lieu [1973] Director; David Patrick Reilly [1959] Director/Civil Engineer [Irish]; John Reilly [1957] Director/Civil Engineer [Irish]; Michael Joseph Reilly [1960] Director/Civil Engineer [Irish]; Lee Williams [1973] Director

Reliance Communications (U.K.) Limited
Incorporated: 13 December 2002 *Employees:* 1
Net Worth: £31,973,284 *Total Assets:* £37,609,052
Registered Office: Sovereign Court, 635 Sipson Road, Sipson, West Drayton, Middlesex, UB7 0JE
Activities: Wired telecommunications activities
Shareholder: Anil Dhirubhai Ambani
Officers: Andrew Peter Goldie, Secretary; Andrew Peter Goldie [1960] Director/Service

Reliance Vanco Group Limited
Incorporated: 9 April 1992
Net Worth: £56,389,056 *Total Assets:* £129,491,488
Registered Office: Sovereign Court, 635 Sipson Road, Sipson, West Drayton, Middlesex, UB7 0JE
Activities: Activities of head offices
Major Shareholder: Anil Dhirajlal Ambani
Officers: Andrew Peter Goldie [1960] Director

Relta Limited
Incorporated: 15 May 2002 *Employees:* 2
Net Worth: £19,636,688 *Total Assets:* £21,222,828
Registered Office: Estate Office, Oakley House, Oakley, Beds, MK43 7ST
Activities: Buying and selling of own real estate
Shareholders: Iain Catleugh Hutchinson; Lousada Investments Limited
Officers: Sharon Anne Hunt, Secretary; Iain Catleugh Hutchinson [1965] Director; Simon Charles Lousada [1963] Director

Remy Cointreau UK Limited
Incorporated: 4 July 2012 *Employees:* 2
Net Worth: £58,708,336 *Total Assets:* £86,171,200
Registered Office: Mazars LLP, The Pinnacle, 160 Midsummer Boulevard, Milton Keynes, Bucks, MK9 1FF
Activities: Non-trading company
Parent: Remy Cointreau S.A.
Officers: Madame Valerie Marie Anne Chapoulaud-Floquet [1962] Managing Director [French]; Luca Calogero Pietro Marotta [1965] Director/Chief Financial Officer [Italian]

Remy's Limited
Incorporated: 13 January 1984 *Employees:* 20
Net Worth: £14,364,887 *Total Assets:* £24,588,120
Registered Office: Unit 6 ZK Park, 23 Commerce Way, Croydon, Surrey, CR0 4ZS
Activities: Buying and selling of own real estate
Officers: Arvindkumar Devji Shah, Secretary; Arvindkumar Devji Shah [1946] Director/Clothing Merchant; Mansukhlal Devji Shah [1941] Director/Clothing Merchant; Sailesh Devji Shah [1958] Director/Clothing Merchant; Suresh Devji Shah [1949] Director/Clothing Merchant

Renaissance Retirement Limited
Incorporated: 7 October 1996 *Employees:* 31
Net Worth: £3,902,961 *Total Assets:* £56,394,280
Registered Office: Unit 3 Royal Court, Church Green Close, Kings Worthy, Winchester, Hants, SO23 7TW
Activities: Development of building projects
Parent: PegasusLife Renaissance Holdings Limited
Officers: Dion Joseph Petri [1968] Director; Ian Jens Trinder [1973] Director

Renand Properties Limited
Incorporated: 9 October 1997
Net Worth: £12,443,212 *Total Assets:* £20,191,398
Registered Office: 44 The Pantiles, Tunbridge Wells, Kent, TN2 5TN
Activities: Development of building projects
Parent: Renand (Cyprus) Limited
Officers: George Panayiotou [1961] Director

Renatus Property Management Limited
Incorporated: 29 November 2011 *Employees:* 9
Net Worth Deficit: £3,819 *Total Assets:* £37,320,448
Registered Office: Suite 2, West Hill House, West Hill, Epsom, Surrey, KT19 8JD
Activities: Other letting and operating of own or leased real estate
Parent: Street Family Group of Companies (Holdings) Limited
Officers: Andrew Mark Munday, Secretary; Patricia Jane French [1951] Director; Rivkah Hazel McCullough [1980] Director/Commercial Portfolio Executive; Andrew Mark Munday [1969] Director/Property Manager

Renault U.K. Limited
Incorporated: 19 December 1904 *Employees:* 230
Net Worth: £26,936,000 *Total Assets:* £300,583,008
Registered Office: The Rivers Office Park, Denham Way, Maple Cross, Rickmansworth, Herts, WD3 9YS
Activities: Sale of new cars and light motor vehicles
Parent: Renault Group UK Limited
Officers: James Alexander Blendis, Secretary; El-Hassan Aitsaid [1964] Finance Director [Belgian]; Mark Alexander Crockett [1967] Director, Services and Quality; Lucy Kate Jones [1976] HR Director; Jean-Louis Labauge [1968] Managing Director [French]; Timothy Peter Mariott [1969] Aftersales Director; Nicholas Roy Tame [1965] Sales Director; Vincent Noel Tourette [1969] Managing Director [French]; Adam Vance Thomas Wood [1983] Marketing Director

Renesas Electronics Europe Limited
Incorporated: 11 November 2002 *Employees:* 93
Net Worth: £90,236,160 *Total Assets:* £93,864,256
Registered Office: Dukes Meadow, Millboard Road, Bourne End, Bucks, SL8 5FH
Activities: Wholesale of electronic and telecommunications equipment and parts
Parent: Renesas Electronics Corporation
Officers: Graham Leslie Smith, Secretary; Michael Georg Hannawald [1962] Director [German]; Hisanori Kawahara [1965] Director/Vice President Accounting and Control Division [Japanese]; Douglas William Pigott [1964] Director/Global Vice President [American]; Bettina Scholz [1971] Director/General Counsel [German]

Renewable Energy Systems Holdings Limited
Incorporated: 26 September 2003 *Employees:* 1,683
Net Worth: £296,894,016 *Total Assets:* £620,592,000
Registered Office: Beaufort Court, Egg Farm Lane, off Station Road, Kings Langley, Herts, WD4 8LR
Activities: Activities of head offices
Shareholders: Douglas James McAlpine; Richard Hugh McAlpine; Andrew William McAlpine; Gavin Malcolm McAlpine; Robert Edward Thomas William McAlpine; Hector George McAlpine
Officers: Dominic James Hearth, Secretary; Ivor Douglas Catto [1966] Director/Deputy CEO; Donald Crawford Joyce [1973] Director/Chief Financial Officer; Chris Michael Marsh [1963] Director; Douglas James McAlpine [1983] Director; Dr Gavin Malcolm McAlpine [1976] Director; Marco Perona [1967] Director [French]; Graham Matthew Reid [1962] Director/Chief Executive Officer, Americas; Rachel Ruffle [1967] Managing Director, UK & Ireland

Renewable Energy Systems Limited
Incorporated: 8 October 1981 *Employees:* 357
Net Worth: £193,522,000 *Total Assets:* £336,766,016
Registered Office: Beaufort Court, Egg Farm Lane, Station Road, Kings Langley, Herts, WD4 8LR
Activities: Construction of commercial buildings
Parent: Renewable Energy Systems Holdings Limited
Officers: Dominic James Hearth, Secretary; Ivor Douglas Catto [1966] Director/Deputy CEO; Dominic James Hearth [1966] Director/General Counsel; Steven William Hughes [1972] Generation & Asset Management Director; Donald Crawford Joyce [1973] Director/Chief Financial Officer; Chris Michael Marsh [1963] Director; Rachel Ruffle [1967] Projects Director, Western Europe and Deputy MD; Richard Paul Russell [1981] Finance Director

Renewi Cumbria Limited
Incorporated: 23 January 2009
Previous: Shanks Cumbria Limited
Net Worth Deficit: £11,947,000 *Total Assets:* £66,065,000
Registered Office: Dunedin House, Auckland Park, Mount Farm, Milton Keynes, Bucks, MK1 1BU
Activities: Other service activities n.e.c.
Parent: Renewi Cumbria Holdings Limited
Officers: Philip Bernard Griffin-Smith, Secretary; Alistair Daniel Brookes [1976] Director; Mark Alfred Cowan [1970] Director; Mark Andrew Rawling [1979] Director/Financial Controller

Renewi European Holdings Limited
Incorporated: 22 July 2014
Previous: Shanks European Holdings Limited
Net Worth: £561,234,880 *Total Assets:* £567,320,000
Registered Office: Dunedin House, Auckland Park, Mount Farm, Milton Keynes, Bucks, MK1 1BU
Activities: Other service activities n.e.c.
Parent: Renewi Holdings Limited
Officers: Philip Bernard Griffin-Smith, Secretary; Peter George Dilnot [1969] Director; Toby Richard Woolrych [1966] Director/Accountant

Renewi Financial Management Limited
Incorporated: 16 February 2005
Previous: Shanks Financial Management Limited
Net Worth: £154,336,000 *Total Assets:* £154,980,992
Registered Office: Dunedin House, Auckland Park, Mount Farm, Milton Keynes, Bucks, MK1 1BU
Activities: Non-trading company
Parent: Renewi European Holdings Limited
Officers: Philip Bernard Griffin-Smith, Secretary; Peter George Dilnot [1969] Director; Toby Richard Woolrych [1966] Director

Renewi Holdings Limited
Incorporated: 30 November 1999
Previous: Shanks Holdings Limited
Net Worth: £213,676,000 *Total Assets:* £497,993,984
Registered Office: Dunedin House, Auckland Park, Mount Farm, Milton Keynes, Bucks, MK1 1BU
Activities: Other service activities n.e.c.
Parent: Renewi PLC
Officers: Philip Bernard Griffin-Smith, Secretary; Peter George Dilnot [1969] Director; Toby Richard Woolrych [1966] Director

Renewi UK Services Limited
Incorporated: 8 June 1989 *Employees:* 654
Previous: Shanks Waste Management Limited
Net Worth Deficit: £95,630,000 *Total Assets:* £63,642,000
Registered Office: Dunedin House, Auckland Park, Milton Keynes, Bucks, MK1 1BU
Activities: Collection of non-hazardous waste
Parent: Renewi PLC
Officers: Philip Bernard Griffin-Smith, Secretary; Neil Rowland Miles [1970] Director; James Austin Priestley [1963] Managing Director; Toby Richard Woolrych [1966] Director

Renhe Sports Management Co Limited
Incorporated: 28 November 2016 *Employees:* 457
Net Worth Deficit: £1,341,772 *Total Assets:* £91,875,864
Registered Office: Madejski Stadium, Junction 11, M4, Reading, Berks, RG2 0FL
Activities: Activities of head offices
Major Shareholder: Yongge Dai
Officers: Bryan Stabler, Secretary; Xiu Li Dai [1963] Director; Yongge Dai [1968] Director [Hong Kong]

Renoir Bidco Limited
Incorporated: 18 March 2011
Net Worth: £10,540,000 *Total Assets:* £47,338,000
Registered Office: Daler-Rowney House, Peacock Lane, Southern Industrial Area, Bracknell, Berks, RG12 8SS
Activities: Activities of head offices
Parent: Renoir Midco Limited
Officers: Stefano de Rosa, Secretary; Massimo Candela [1965] Director [Italian]; Stefano de Rosa [1968] Finance Director [Italian]; Dominique Willy Michel Ghislain Paradis [1966] Director [Belgian]

Rentokil Initial (1896) Limited
Incorporated: 26 October 1896
Net Worth: £1,180,867,968 *Total Assets:* £2,180,212,992
Registered Office: Riverbank, Meadows Business Park, Blackwater, Camberley, Surrey, GU17 9AB
Activities: Activities of households as employers of domestic personnel
Parent: Rentokil Initial 1927 PLC
Officers: Catherine Stead, Secretary; Daragh Patrick Feltrim Fagan [1969] Director/Lawyer; Jonathan Ellis Hauck [1973] Director/Accountant

Rentokil Initial (1993) Limited
Incorporated: 15 October 1993
Net Worth: £188,100,000 *Total Assets:* £712,499,968
Registered Office: Riverbank, Meadows Business Park, Blackwater, Camberley, Surrey, GU17 9AB
Activities: Activities of head offices
Parent: Rentokil Initial (1896) Limited
Officers: Catherine Stead, Secretary; Daragh Patrick Feltrim Fagan [1969] Director/Solicitor; Jonathan Ellis Hauck [1973] Director/Accountant

Rentokil Initial 1927 PLC
Incorporated: 1 October 1927 *Employees:* 334
Net Worth: £2,184,900,096 *Total Assets:* £5,959,199,744
Registered Office: Riverbank, Meadows Business Park, Blackwater, Camberley, Surrey, GU17 9AB
Activities: Other business support service activities n.e.c.
Parent: Rentokil Initial Holdings Limited
Officers: Catherine Stead, Secretary; Daragh Patrick Feltrim Fagan [1969] Director/Solicitor; Jonathan Ellis Hauck [1973] Director/Accountant; Jeremy Charles Douglas Townsend [1964] Director

Rentokil Initial Americas Limited
Incorporated: 27 April 2011
Net Worth: £35,879,000 *Total Assets:* £36,043,000
Registered Office: Riverbank, Meadows Business Park, Blackwater, Camberley, Surrey, GU17 9AB
Activities: Other business support service activities n.e.c.
Parent: Rentokil Initial 1927 PLC
Officers: Catherine Stead, Secretary; Daragh Patrick Feltrim Fagan [1969] Director/Solicitor; Christopher Brian Terrence Filby [1961] Director; Jonathan Ellis Hauck [1973] Director/Accountant

Rentokil Initial Finance Limited
Incorporated: 12 March 2004
Net Worth: £100,583,544 *Total Assets:* £100,583,544
Registered Office: Riverbank, Meadows Business Park, Blackwater, Camberley, Surrey, GU17 9AB
Activities: Other business support service activities n.e.c.
Parent: Rentokil Initial 1927 PLC
Officers: Catherine Stead, Secretary; Daragh Patrick Feltrim Fagan [1969] Director/Solicitor; Christopher Brian Terrence Filby [1961] Director; Jonathan Ellis Hauck [1973] Director/Accountant

Rentokil Initial Holdings Limited
Incorporated: 19 December 1994
Net Worth: £313,800,000 *Total Assets:* £3,124,499,968
Registered Office: Riverbank, Meadows Business Park, Blackwater, Camberley, Surrey, GU17 9AB
Activities: Non-trading company
Parent: Rentokil Initial PLC
Officers: Catherine Stead, Secretary; Daragh Patrick Feltrim Fagan [1969] Director/Solicitor; Jonathan Ellis Hauck [1973] Director/Accountant

Rentokil Initial Investments South Africa
Incorporated: 25 April 1951
Net Worth: £58,522,032 *Total Assets:* £58,533,316
Registered Office: Riverbank, Meadows Business Park, Blackwater, Camberley, Surrey, GU17 9AB
Activities: Activities of head offices
Parent: Stratton House Leasing Limited
Officers: Daragh Patrick Feltrim Fagan, Secretary; Antoinette Campbell [1972] Finance Director [South African]; Nombeko Langeni [1958] Director [South African]; Nkosinathi Sidney Solomon [1969] Managing Director [South African]

Rentokil Initial PLC
Incorporated: 15 March 2005 *Employees:* 36,036
Net Worth: £933,699,968 *Total Assets:* £3,107,699,968
Registered Office: Riverbank, Meadows Business Park, Blackwater, Camberley, Surrey, GU17 9AB
Activities: Other business support service activities n.e.c.
Officers: Daragh Patrick Feltrim Fagan, Secretary; Richard Burrows [1946] Director [Irish]; Sir Crispin Davis [1949] Director; Dr John David Gibson McAdam [1948] Director; John Mark Pettigrew [1968] Director; Andrew Mark Ransom [1963] Director; Angela Charlotte Seymour-Jackson [1966] Director; Richard Leslie Solomons [1961] Director; Julie Helen Southern [1959] Director/Accountant; Jeremy Charles Douglas Townsend [1964] Director; Dr Linda Yueh [1971] Director/Economist

Rentokil Initial UK Ltd
Incorporated: 23 May 1935 *Employees:* 2,583
Net Worth: £142,124,000 *Total Assets:* £389,139,008
Registered Office: Riverbank, Meadows Business Park, Blackwater, Camberley, Surrey, GU17 9AB
Activities: Other business support service activities n.e.c.
Parent: Rentokil Initial (1896) Limited
Officers: Catherine Stead, Secretary; Daragh Patrick Feltrim Fagan [1969] Director/Solicitor; Jeffreys Kristen Hampson [1974] Finance Director; Phillip Paul Wood [1965] Managing Director

Rentokil Limited
Incorporated: 10 December 1926
Previous: BET Finance Limited
Net Worth: £2,290,642,944 *Total Assets:* £2,290,642,944
Registered Office: Riverbank, Meadows Business Park, Blackwater, Camberley, Surrey, GU17 9AB
Activities: Other business support service activities n.e.c.
Parent: Rentokil Overseas Holdings Limited
Officers: Catherine Stead, Secretary; Daragh Patrick Feltrim Fagan [1969] Director/Solicitor; Jonathan Ellis Hauck [1973] Director/Accountant

Rentokil Overseas Holdings Limited
Incorporated: 10 June 1959
Net Worth: £1,240,717,056 *Total Assets:* £1,240,717,056
Registered Office: Riverbank, Meadows Business Park, Blackwater, Camberley, Surrey, GU17 9AB
Activities: Non-trading company
Parent: Rentokil Initial UK Limited
Officers: Catherine Stead, Secretary; Daragh Patrick Feltrim Fagan [1969] Director/Solicitor; Jonathan Ellis Hauck [1973] Director/Accountant

RES UK & Ireland Limited
Incorporated: 26 September 2003
Net Worth: £54,556,000 *Total Assets:* £78,506,000
Registered Office: Beaufort Court, Egg Farm Lane, off Station Road, Kings Langley, Herts, WD4 8LR
Activities: Other business support service activities n.e.c.
Parent: Renewable Energy Systems Limited
Officers: Dominic James Hearth, Secretary; Jasbir Singh Bains [1966] Director/Commercial Manager; Steven William Hughes [1972] Generation & Asset Management Director; Rachel Ruffle [1967] Projects Director, Western Europe and Deputy MD; Richard Paul Russell [1981] Finance Director

Resource Recovery Solutions (Derbyshire) Limited
Incorporated: 3 March 2009
Net Worth Deficit: £18,973,000 *Total Assets:* £177,975,008
Registered Office: Dunedin House, Auckland Park, Mount Farm, Milton Keynes, Bucks, MK1 1BU
Activities: Collection of non-hazardous waste
Parent: Resource Recovery Solutions (Derbyshire) Holdings Limited
Officers: Philip Bernard Griffin-Smith, Secretary; Nicholas John Bliss [1959] Director/Solicitor, Consultant; Alistair Daniel Brookes [1976] Director; Rajan Goyal [1966] Director/Accountant; Neil Rowland Miles [1970] Director; Andrew John Sutton [1956] Director

Restaurant Holdings Limited
Incorporated: 9 March 2006
Net Worth: £591,238,976 *Total Assets:* £1,111,698,944
Registered Office: Orion Gate, Guildford Road, Woking, Surrey, GU22 7NJ
Activities: Activities of other holding companies n.e.c.
Parent: Yum! Brands, Inc.
Officers: Timothy Michael Colborn, Secretary; Clare Marie Boynton [1978] Director/Accountant; Timothy Michael Colborn [1957] Director/International Tax Manager; Christopher Alexander Drew [1981] Director/Chief Finance Officer; Paula MacKenzie [1977] Business Development Director

Restore PLC
Incorporated: 2 July 2004 *Employees:* 1,893
Net Worth: £155,900,000 *Total Assets:* £300,000,000
Registered Office: The Databank, Unit 5 Redhill Distribution Centre, Salbrook Road, Redhill, Surrey, RH1 5DY
Activities: Other business support service activities n.e.c.
Officers: Sarah Lesley Waudby, Secretary; Sharon Baylay [1968] Director; Adam Thomas Councell [1978] Director; Stephen James Davidson [1955] Director; Susan Jane Davy [1969] Director; Charles Antony Lawrence Skinner [1960] Director; Martin George Towers [1952] Director; James Christie Falconer Wilde [1953] Director

Resurgam Holdings Limited
Incorporated: 18 March 1997 *Employees:* 2
Net Worth: £26,119,582 *Total Assets:* £26,494,532
Registered Office: 99 London Street, Reading, Berks, RG1 4QA
Activities: Other letting and operating of own or leased real estate
Shareholder: Robert Henry Hunt-Grubbe
Officers: Julia Susan Hunt-Grubbe, Secretary; Julia Susan Hunt-Grubbe [1946] Director; Robert Henry Hunt-Grubbe [1938] Director/Chartered Electrical Engineer

Retirement Villages Group Limited
Incorporated: 18 January 2005 *Employees:* 633
Net Worth: £132,932,000 *Total Assets:* £160,166,000
Registered Office: 1st Floor, Brunswick House, Regent Park, 297-299 Kingston Road, Leatherhead, Surrey, KT22 7LU
Activities: Activities of head offices
Shareholder: Harvitour Limited
Officers: Sally Irene Rees, Secretary; Sarah Denise Burgess [1971] Director; William Edwin John Crawford [1970] Director; Neil Donaldson [1966] Director/Accountant; Christina Elizabeth Edwards [1943] Director; Emmanuel Lefebvre [1974] Director/Fund Management [French]; Andrew George Esmond Ovey [1971] Director/Investment Manager; Oscar Russell [1987] Director

Retirement Villages Limited
Incorporated: 29 June 1999 *Employees:* 3
Net Worth: £21,071,008 *Total Assets:* £65,107,568
Registered Office: 1st Floor, Brunswick House, Regent Park, 297-299 Kingston Road, Leatherhead, Surrey, KT22 7LU
Activities: Other business support service activities n.e.c.
Parent: Retirement Villages Group Limited
Officers: Sally Irene Rees, Secretary; William Edwin John Crawford [1970] Director/Development; Neil Donaldson [1966] Director/Accountant; Andrew George Esmond Ovey [1971] Director/Investment Banker

RFC Prop Co Limited
Incorporated: 18 November 2014
Net Worth: £14,990,000 *Total Assets:* £20,640,716
Registered Office: Madejski Stadium, Junction 11 M4, Reading, Berks, RG2 0FL
Activities: Buying and selling of own real estate
Officers: John Roddison, Secretary; Praphant Asava-Aree [1956] Director/Advisor [Thai]; Nigel Howe [1958] Director/Chief Executive; Pairoj Piempongsant [1955] Director [Thai]; Taweesuk Srisumrid [1971] Director [Thai]; Sumrith Thanakarnjanasuth [1962] Director [Thai]

RGCM Limited
Incorporated: 5 March 1990 *Employees:* 142
Net Worth: £7,004,731 *Total Assets:* £47,456,760
Registered Office: 4 Abbey Wood Road, Kings Hill, West Malling, Kent, ME19 4AB
Activities: Construction of commercial buildings
Officers: Michael Anthony Steel, Secretary; John Raymond Casey [1965] Director/Construction Manager; John Henry Chadwick [1942] Director/Structural Engineer; David Brian Dixon [1973] Director; John Anthony Kallend [1965] Director/Project Manager; Michael Daniel Mullarkey [1969] Director/Chartered Quantity Surveyor; Jonathan Charles David Noble [1962] Director/Quantity Surveyor; Trevor Puttick [1964] Director; Stephen Warren Roe [1965] Director/Construction Manager; Michael Anthony Steel [1947] Director/Structural Engineer

Rhodia Holdings Limited
Incorporated: 22 November 1995
Net Worth: £249,571,008 *Total Assets:* £501,308,992
Registered Office: 34 Clarendon Road, Watford, Herts, WD17 1JJ
Activities: Activities of head offices
Officers: Alison Murphy, Secretary; Alexis Michel Brouhns [1955] Director/Manager [Belgian]; Melvin John Dawes [1967] Director/Solicitor; Nathan Mills [1977] Director/Engineer [American]; Alison Murphy [1965] Director/Financial Controller

Rhodia International Holdings Limited
Incorporated: 27 July 1898
Net Worth: £55,610,000 *Total Assets:* £55,991,000
Registered Office: 34 Clarendon Road, Watford, Herts, WD17 1JJ
Activities: Activities of head offices
Parent: Rhodia Holdings Limited
Officers: Alison Murphy, Secretary; Melvin John Dawes [1967] Director/Solicitor; Tom Dutton [1964] Director/Health, Safety & Environment Manager; Alison Murphy [1965] Director/Financial Controller

Rhodia Limited
Incorporated: 6 May 1926
Net Worth: £150,058,000 *Total Assets:* £211,896,000
Registered Office: 34 Clarendon Road, Watford, Herts, WD17 1JJ
Activities: Manufacture of other inorganic basic chemicals
Parent: Rhodia Holdings Limited
Officers: Alison Murphy, Secretary; Tom Dutton [1964] Director/Health, Safety & Environment Manager; John Stuart Moorhouse [1951] Director/Chemical Engineer; Alison Murphy [1965] Director/Financial Controller

Rhombi Holdings Limited
Incorporated: 22 June 2011 *Employees:* 5
Net Worth: £78,694,320 *Total Assets:* £528,601,536
Registered Office: Aviation House, The Lodge, Harmondsworth Lane, West Drayton, Middlesex, UB7 0LQ
Activities: Activities of head offices
Parent: Teledyne Technologies Incorporated
Officers: Nicholas James Wargent, Secretary; Stephen F. Blackwood [1962] Director/Corporate Treasurer [American]; Susan Lee Main [1958] Director/Senior Vice President and Chief Financial Officer [American]; Edwin Roks [1964] Director/Corporate President [Dutch]; Nicholas James Wargent [1973] Director/Solicitor

Rhone Products (UK) Limited
Incorporated: 10 May 1946 *Employees:* 74
Net Worth: £48,693,332 *Total Assets:* £77,570,408
Registered Office: 55 Station Road, Beaconsfield, Bucks, HP9 1QL
Activities: Wholesale of household goods (other than musical instruments) n.e.c
Major Shareholder: Thierry Henri Stern
Officers: Andrew Mark Hearn, Secretary; Andrew Mark Hearn [1959] Director/Manager; Claude Peny [1951] Director [Belgian]; Thierry Henri Stern [1970] Director [Swiss]

Rhone-Poulenc Rorer Limited
Incorporated: 13 February 1986
Net Worth: £114,355,000 *Total Assets:* £114,358,000
Registered Office: One Onslow Street, Guildford, Surrey, GU1 4YS
Activities: Activities of other holding companies n.e.c.
Parent: Hoechst Marion Roussel Limited
Officers: Francois-Xavier Duhalde [1965] Director/Chief Financial Officer [French]; Hugo Rupert Alexander Fry [1970] Director/UK Country Chair

RHP Finance PLC
Incorporated: 27 November 2014
Net Worth: £13,000 *Total Assets:* £138,651,008
Registered Office: 8 Waldegrave Road, Teddington, Middlesex, TW11 8GT
Activities: Financial intermediation not elsewhere classified
Officers: Corinna Jayne Bishopp, Secretary; Corinna Jayne Bishopp [1973] Finance Director; David Done [1962] Director/Chief Executive; John Edward Newbury [1949] Director; Stephen Geoffrey Michael Speak [1963] Director/Councillor

Ricardo Investments Limited
Incorporated: 4 May 1988 *Employees:* 5
Previous: Ricardo Consulting Engineers Limited
Net Worth: £480,790,016 *Total Assets:* £533,633,984
Registered Office: Shoreham Technical Centre, Shoreham by Sea, W Sussex, BN43 5FG
Activities: Activities of head offices
Parent: Ricardo PLC
Officers: Mark William Garrett [1962] Product Group Director; Ian Jeffrey Gibson [1960] Finance Director; Patricia Mary Ryan [1964] Director/General Counsel; David John Shemmans [1966] Director

Ricardo PLC
Incorporated: 30 June 1927 *Employees:* 2,896
Net Worth: £176,100,000 *Total Assets:* £339,700,000
Registered Office: Shoreham Technical Centre, Shoreham by Sea, W Sussex, BN43 5FG
Activities: Activities of head offices
Officers: Patricia Mary Ryan, Secretary; Laurie Bowen [1961] Director [American]; Mark William Garrett [1962] Director; Ian Jeffrey Gibson [1960] Director; Peter Gilchrist [1952] Director; Sir Terence Keith Morgan [1948] Director; Eva Christina Malin Persson [1968] Director [Swedish]; David John Shemmans [1966] Director/Chief Executive Officer; William Spencer [1959] Director

Ricardo UK Limited
Incorporated: 6 May 1993 *Employees:* 1,056
Net Worth: £133,406,000 *Total Assets:* £201,140,992
Registered Office: Shoreham Technical Centre, Old Shoreham Road, Shoreham-by-Sea, W Sussex, BN43 5FG
Activities: Engineering related scientific and technical consulting activities
Parent: Ricardo Investments Limited
Officers: Kerry Joanne Norwood Steer, Secretary; Mark Stephen Barge [1961] Motorsport Director; Markus Doerr [1965] Managing Director [German]; Mark William Garrett [1962] Product Group Director; Ian Jeffrey Gibson [1960] Finance Director; James Alan Mills [1973] Finance Director; David John Shemmans [1966] Director

Ricardo-AEA Limited
Incorporated: 26 September 2012 *Employees:* 467
Net Worth: £25,434,000 *Total Assets:* £36,639,000
Registered Office: Shoreham Technical Centre, Old Shoreham Road, Shoreham-by-Sea, W Sussex, BN43 5FG
Activities: Information technology consultancy activities
Shareholders: Ricardo Investments Limited; Ricardo PLC
Officers: Patricia Ryan, Secretary; Timothy John Curtis [1966] Director; Mark William Garrett [1962] Director; Ian Jeffrey Gibson [1960] Finance Director; Ian Fraser Rogerson [1962] Director/Accountant; David John Shemmans [1966] Director

The Richmond West Schools Trust
Incorporated: 23 March 2016 *Employees:* 225
Net Worth: £32,253,784 *Total Assets:* £36,118,740
Registered Office: Twickenham School, Percy Road, Twickenham, Middlesex, TW2 6JW
Activities: General secondary education
Officers: Adele Suzanne Kimber [1961] Director/Editor; Claire Little [1967] Group HR Director; Annmarie Loughlin [1968] Director/Certified Accountant; Joanne Merritt [1966] Director; Philippa Jane Nunn [1965] Director/Headteacher; Charis Laura Jane Penfold [1963] Director/Teacher; Siobhan Peters [1970] Director/Chief Financial Officer; Neil Philip Smith [1981] Director/Head of Strategic & Business Development; Angela Mary Thomas [1957] Director [Irish]; Brian Winstanley [1964] Director/Programme Manager

Richstone Properties Limited
Incorporated: 2 May 2014
Net Worth: £23,092,330 *Total Assets:* £46,332,496
Registered Office: Gladstone House, 77-79 High Street, Egham, Surrey, TW20 9HY
Activities: Other letting and operating of own or leased real estate
Shareholders: David Graham Peter Rich-Jones; Laura Elizabeth Rich-Jones
Officers: David Graham Peter Rich-Jones [1961] Director [British/Canadian]; Laura Elizabeth Rich-Jones [1966] Director

Rico Logistics Ltd
Incorporated: 4 November 1993 *Employees:* 1,198
Net Worth: £26,096,000 *Total Assets:* £66,564,000
Registered Office: Unit 4 Kennet House, Langley Quay, Waterside Drive, Slough, Berks, SL3 6EY
Activities: Operation of warehousing and storage facilities for air transport activities
Parent: TVS Logistics Investment UK Limited
Officers: Paul John Roberts, Secretary; Dinesh Ramachandran [1965] Managing Director [Indian]; Paul John Roberts [1968] Director/Accountant; Ravichandran Sargunaraj [1955] Director [Indian]; Sanjive Sharma [1965] Managing Director

Ridge Hill Trading Limited
Incorporated: 16 March 2016
Previous: Ridge Hill Investments Limited
Net Worth: £1,357,698 *Total Assets:* £21,589,348
Registered Office: Ashcombe Court, Woolsack Way, Godalming, Surrey, GU7 1LQ
Activities: Activities of other holding companies n.e.c.
Shareholders: Simon Christopher Duncan Hosking; Jonathan Robert Lunau Olsen
Officers: Simon Christopher Duncan Hosking [1964] Director; Spencer Tremaine Lock [1967] Director; Jonathan Robert Olsen [1962] Director

Riemser Pharma UK Limited
Incorporated: 5 November 2015 *Employees:* 4
Net Worth: £3,986,064 *Total Assets:* £22,431,392
Registered Office: The Courtyard Barns, Choke Lane, Maidenhead, Berks, SL6 6PT
Activities: Other business support service activities n.e.c.
Parent: Riemser Pharma GmbH
Officers: Rene Just [1967] Director [Danish]; Dr Mohammed Choudhary Shafiq [1964] Director/Manager; Konstantin Von Alvensleben [1957] Director/Manager [German]

RIF Holdings Limited
Incorporated: 24 February 2016
Net Worth Deficit: £7,200 *Total Assets:* £165,064,064
Registered Office: Mountbatten House, Grosvenor Square, Southampton, SO15 2JU
Activities: Other business support service activities n.e.c.
Parent: Rockfire Investment Finance PLC
Officers: Liam James Kavanagh [1977] Director/Investment Manager; Andrew Paul Williams [1964] Director/Chartered Accountant

Rightmove Group Limited
Incorporated: 16 May 2000 *Employees:* 477
Net Worth: £45,322,000 *Total Assets:* £101,245,000
Registered Office: 2 Caldecotte Lake Business Park, Caldecotte Lake Drive, Caldecotte, Milton Keynes, Bucks, MK7 8LE
Activities: Other information technology service activities
Parent: Rightmove PLC
Officers: Sandra Judith Odell, Secretary; Peter Brooks-Johnson [1972] Director; Robyn Perriss [1973] Finance Director

Rightmove PLC
Incorporated: 14 November 2007 *Employees:* 479
Net Worth: £17,183,000 *Total Assets:* £71,813,000
Registered Office: 2 Caldecotte Lake Business Park, Caldecotte Lake Drive, Caldecotte, Milton Keynes, Bucks, MK7 8LE
Activities: Other information technology service activities
Officers: Sandra Judith Odell, Secretary; Peter Brooks Johnson [1972] Director; Jacqueline de Rojas CBE [1962] Director; Andrew Robert Findlay [1969] Finance Director; Scott Edward Forbes [1957] Director [American/British]; Rakhi Parekh [1974] Director [American]; Robyn Perriss [1973] Finance Director; Lorna Mona Tilbian [1957] Director; Peter Wodehouse Williams [1953] Director

RIHL Limited
Incorporated: 29 December 2011 *Employees:* 3
Net Worth: £90,090,000 *Total Assets:* £90,090,000
Registered Office: Marine House, Cartwright Drive, Fareham, Hants, PO15 5RJ
Activities: Activities of head offices
Parent: FLIR Systems Inc
Officers: Heather Fiona Christiansen [1971] Director/Manager and Secretary [American]; Todd Michael Duchene [1963] Director/General Counsel and Secretary [American]; Gregoire Pierre Georges Outters [1971] Director/General Manager [French]

Ringmerit Limited
Incorporated: 5 September 2000 *Employees:* 8
Net Worth: £181,548,000 *Total Assets:* £1,093,650,048
Registered Office: 24 Park Road South, Havant, Hants, PO9 1HB
Activities: Activities of head offices
Shareholders: Caspar MacDonald-Hall; Ringworth Holdings BV; Ringview Holdings BV
Officers: Christopher Winsley Tranter, Secretary; Anthony Michael Chandris [1987] Director; John Demetrius Chandris [1950] Director; Christophe Gaston Yves Le Corre [1968] Director [French]; Caspar MacDonald-Hall [1950] Director; Sebastian Sam MacDonald-Hall [1982] Director; Anthony Tomazos [1968] Director; Christopher Winsley Tranter [1957] Director

Ringway Infrastructure Services Limited
Incorporated: 16 October 1992 *Employees:* 1,510
Net Worth: £14,034,156 *Total Assets:* £91,745,000
Registered Office: Albion House, Springfield Road, Horsham, W Sussex, RH12 2RW
Activities: Construction of roads and motorways
Parent: Eurovia UK Limited
Officers: Susan Mary Lysionek, Secretary; Christophe Gaetan Louis Ferrer [1983] Financial Director [French]; Robert Innes Gillespie [1963] Director; Nick Goddard [1963] Director/Civil Engineer; John Nicholson [1963] Director; Michael Irving Notman [1962] Director/Civil Engineer; Clive William Rillstone [1964] Regional Director; David Rowley [1954] Regional Director; Philippe George Skegg [1981] Director; John Mark Sunderland [1968] Director/Civil Engineer; Scott Alexander Wardrop [1966] Director

Ringway Jacobs Limited
Incorporated: 28 September 2005 *Employees:* 1,289
Net Worth: £11,847,778 *Total Assets:* £84,995,408
Registered Office: Albion House, Springfield Road, Horsham, W Sussex, RH12 2RW
Activities: Construction of roads and motorways
Shareholders: Eurovia UK Limited; Jacobs One Limited
Officers: Susan Mary Lysionek, Secretary; David Joseph Coultas [1962] Director/Civil Engineer; Mark John Davies [1968] Director/Civil Engineer; Christophe Gaetan Louis Ferrer [1983] Financial Director [French]; John McGrath [1970] Finance Director [Irish]; Hugh Donald Morrison [1970] Director/Business Executive; Michael O'Neill [1962] Director/Engineer; Philippe George Skegg [1981] Director; Scott Alexander Wardrop [1966] Director

Riposte Limited
Incorporated: 18 July 2003 *Employees:* 2
Net Worth: £273,600,992 *Total Assets:* £275,720,992
Registered Office: Hunton House, Highbridge Industrial Estate, Oxford Road, Uxbridge, Middlesex, UB8 1LX
Activities: Financial management
Parent: PandoraExpress 7 Limited
Officers: Andrew David Pellington, Secretary; Andrew David Pellington [1964] Director; Jinlong Wang [1957] Director [American]

Riverdale Developments Limited
Incorporated: 20 April 2004 *Employees:* 16
Net Worth: £7,438,065 *Total Assets:* £37,863,328
Registered Office: O'Brien House, 197-199 Garth Road, Morden, Surrey, SM4 4NE
Activities: Development of building projects
Parent: OHOB Group Ltd
Officers: Colin David Southey, Secretary; Brian Hector Bonnyman [1958] Director/Group MD; Richard John Matthews [1960] Managing Director; Thomas Francis O'Brien [1947] Director/Builder [Irish]; Louise Patricia O'Brien Smith [1979] Director; Colin David Southey [1959] Director

Riverstone Corporate Capital Limited
Incorporated: 23 October 1998
Net Worth: £45,000 *Total Assets:* £94,180,000
Registered Office: Park Gate, 161-163 Preston Road, Brighton, BN1 6AU
Activities: Other activities auxiliary to insurance and pension funding
Parent: Riverstone Holdings Limited
Officers: Sarah Louise Garrod, Secretary; Fraser Henry, Secretary; Nicholas Craig Bentley [1960] Managing Director; Lorna Ann Hemsley [1967] Director/Accountant; Luke Robert Tanzer [1965] Insurance Director [British/Australian]

Riverstone Holdings Limited
Incorporated: 24 April 1992
Net Worth: £507,632,000 *Total Assets:* £538,518,976
Registered Office: Park Gate, 161-163 Preston Road, Brighton, BN1 6AU
Activities: Activities of head offices
Officers: Sarah Louise Garrod, Secretary; Fraser Henry, Secretary; Nicholas Craig Bentley [1960] Managing Director; Lorna Ann Hemsley [1967] Director/Accountant; Luke Robert Tanzer [1965] Insurance Director [British/Australian]

Riverstone Insurance (UK) Limited
Incorporated: 19 April 1974
Net Worth: £273,551,520 *Total Assets:* £564,441,920
Registered Office: Park Gate, 161-163 Preston Road, Brighton, BN1 6AU
Activities: Non-life insurance
Parent: Riverstone Holdings Limited
Officers: Sarah Louise Garrod, Secretary; Fraser Henry, Secretary; Mark Julian Bannister [1970] Operations Director; Nicholas Craig Bentley [1960] Managing Director; Lorna Ann Hemsley [1967] Director/Accountant; Adrian John Edward Masterson [1947] Director/Consultant [Irish]; Tom Riddell [1952] Director [Australian/British]; Kalpana Shah [1969] Director/Actuary; Luke Robert Tanzer [1965] Director/Insurance Executive [British/Australian]

Riverstone Insurance Limited
Incorporated: 11 November 1992
Net Worth: £258,115,008 *Total Assets:* £532,907,008
Registered Office: Park Gate, 161-163 Preston Road, Brighton, BN1 6AU
Activities: Non-life insurance
Parent: Riverstone Holdings Limited
Officers: Sarah Louise Garrod, Secretary; Fraser Henry, Secretary; Mark Julian Bannister [1970] Operations Director; Nicholas Craig Bentley [1960] Managing Director; Lorna Ann Hemsley [1967] Director/Accountant; Luke Robert Tanzer [1965] Director/Insurance Executive [British/Australian]

Riverstone Management Limited
Incorporated: 12 July 1976 *Employees:* 139
Net Worth: £872,000 *Total Assets:* £41,604,000
Registered Office: Park Gate, 161-163 Preston Road, Brighton, BN1 6AU
Activities: Financial intermediation not elsewhere classified
Parent: Riverstone Holdings Limited
Officers: Sarah Louise Garrod, Secretary; Fraser Henry, Secretary; Mark Julian Bannister [1970] Operations Director; Nicholas Craig Bentley [1960] Managing Director; Lorna Ann Hemsley [1967] Director/Accountant; Fraser Henry [1966] Director/General Counsel and Company Secretary; Stephen Charles Roberts [1965] Director/Chartered Accountant; Luke Robert Tanzer [1965] Director/Insurance Executive [British/Australian]; Antony Charles Tilley [1965] Reinsurance Director

RL Retail Services Limited
Incorporated: 23 December 1999 *Employees:* 1,748
Net Worth: £15,512,272 *Total Assets:* £27,429,290
Registered Office: 46 Clarendon Road, Watford, Herts, WD17 1HE
Activities: Other business support service activities n.e.c.
Parent: Ralph Lauren Corporation
Officers: Aldo Alex Fleri [1961] Director/Vice President Sales UK; Carmel Ann Pedatella [1974] Director/Business Executive [American]; Robert Patrick Ranftl [1971] Director/Business Executive [American]; Andrew Howard Smith [1971] Director/Business Executive

RMAC Securities No. 1 PLC
Incorporated: 14 October 2005
Net Worth: £13,507,000 *Total Assets:* £1,693,400,064
Registered Office: 5 Arlington Square, Downshire Way, Bracknell, Berks, RG12 1WA
Activities: Financial intermediation not elsewhere classified
Parent: RMAC Securities Holdings Limited
Officers: Nicola Townsend, Secretary; Paivi Helena Whitaker [1963] Director [Finnish]

RMET
Incorporated: 1 June 2011 *Employees:* 266
Previous: Rainham Mark Grammar School
Net Worth: £25,850,000 *Total Assets:* £29,340,000
Registered Office: Rainham Mark Grammar School, Pump Lane, Gillingham, Kent, ME8 7AJ
Activities: General secondary education
Officers: Michele Ann Brighton, Secretary; Alison Jane Bovis [1972] Director/Accountant; Simon James Decker [1959] Director/Headteacher; Nigel John Goodall [1957] Director/Production Engineer; Elaine Jackson [1956] Director/Manager; Cheryl Anne Lane [1972] Director/Finance Business Partner; Rita Lawrence [1969] Director/Head of Organisational Development; Terence James Whittaker [1961] Director/Chief Executive Officer

RMIS (RTW) Limited
Incorporated: 15 February 1951 *Employees:* 93
Previous: Reliance Mutual Insurance Society Limited
Total Assets: £1,841,937,024
Registered Office: Utmost House, 6 Vale Avenue, Tunbridge Wells, Kent, TN1 1RG
Activities: Life insurance
Officers: Christopher Mark Utting, Secretary; Edward Ian Gardner [1959] Director/Chartered Accountant; Ian Graham Maidens [1964] Director; Stephen Shone [1957] Director; Andrew Paul Thompson [1962] Director

RMS Holdco Limited
Incorporated: 2 February 2017 *Employees:* 264
Net Worth Deficit: £84,000 *Total Assets:* £127,123,000
Registered Office: Matrix House, North Fourth Street, Milton Keynes, Bucks, MK9 1NJ
Activities: Activities of other holding companies n.e.c.
Officers: Muzammal Ashraf [1986] Director/Investment Manager [Pakistani]; James Michael Aviles [1960] Director/Business Owner/Investor [American]; Paul Generald Bentham [1960] Director; Christopher Phelan Marshall [1968] Director/Investment Manager [American]; Kevin Patrick O'Keefe [1973] Director/Chief Executive Officer [American]

J.& H.Robinson (Iford Farms) Limited
Incorporated: 9 October 1941 *Employees:* 14
Net Worth: £26,847,754 *Total Assets:* £42,295,364
Registered Office: Sutton House, Iford, Lewes, E Sussex, BN7 3EU
Activities: Mixed farming
Shareholder: John Henry Robinson
Officers: Generaldine Ann Robinson, Secretary; Generaldine Ann Robinson [1946] Director/Company Secretary; John Henry Robinson [1946] Director/Farmer; May Evelyn Robinson [1984] Director/Sole Trader; Sheila Mary Robinson [1924] Director; Wendy Jane Robinson [1972] Event Director; Benjamin David Taylor [1976] Director/Farm Manager

Robinson Webster (Holdings) Limited
Incorporated: 4 September 1972 *Employees:* 1,067
Net Worth: £9,573,000 *Total Assets:* £48,406,000
Registered Office: 159 Mortlake Road, Richmond, Surrey, TW9 4AW
Activities: Retail sale of clothing in specialised stores
Shareholders: Best Dressed Group Limited; Robinson Property Company Limited
Officers: Rebecca Sheila Paul, Secretary; Belle Robinson [1964] Director; Kieron Bartholemew Traynor [1960] Director

Robinsons (Finance) No.2 Limited
Incorporated: 23 September 2010
Net Worth: £295,417,984 *Total Assets:* £295,481,984
Registered Office: Breakspear Park, Breakspear Way, Hemel Hempstead, Herts, HP2 4TZ
Activities: Manufacture of soft drinks; production of mineral waters and other bottled waters
Officers: Judith Moore, Secretary; Mathew James Dunn [1974] Director/Chief Financial Officer; Peter Simon Litherland [1964] Director/Chief Executive; Alexandra Clare Thomas [1974] Director/General Counsel and Company Secretary

Robinsons Soft Drinks Limited
Incorporated: 4 November 1994
Net Worth: £205,435,008 *Total Assets:* £371,625,984
Registered Office: Breakspear Park, Breakspear Way, Hemel Hempstead, Herts, HP2 4TZ
Activities: Manufacture of soft drinks; production of mineral waters and other bottled waters
Parent: Britvic Soft Drinks Limited
Officers: Judith Moore, Secretary; Mathew James Dunn [1974] Director/Chief Financial Officer; Peter Simon Litherland [1964] Director/Chief Executive; Alexandra Clare Thomas [1974] Director/General Counsel and Company Secretary

ROC Transformation (Corporate) Limited
Incorporated: 14 September 2017 *Employees:* 87
Net Worth Deficit: £1,059,062,976 *Total Assets:* £39,823,577,088
Registered Office: Wharf House, Wharf Street, Newbury, Berks, RG14 5AP
Activities: Wired telecommunications activities
Parent: ROC Transformation (Group) Limited
Officers: Matthew Nicholas Franklin [1970] Director; Duncan Charles Gooding [1971] Director; Paul James Hart [1966] Director/Chief Finance Officer; Steve Shirley [1963] Director

ROC Transformation (Holdings) Limited
Incorporated: 14 September 2017 *Employees:* 89
Net Worth: £10,640,505 *Total Assets:* £39,766,988
Registered Office: Wharf House, Wharf Street, Newbury, Berks, RG14 5AP
Activities: Wired telecommunications activities
Shareholder: BGF Investments LP
Officers: Trevor Andrew Rolls, Secretary; James McLelland Austin [1969] Director/Equity Investor; Matthew Nicholas Franklin [1970] Director; Duncan Charles Gooding [1971] Director; Paul James Hart [1966] Director/Chief Finance Officer; Trevor Andrew Rolls [1972] Director/Chairman; Steve Shirley [1963] Director

Rocco Homes Limited
Incorporated: 29 August 2007
Net Worth: £17,659,332 *Total Assets:* £44,745,772
Registered Office: 2nd Floor, 45-47 High Street, Cobham, Surrey, KT11 3DP
Activities: Other business support service activities n.e.c.
Shareholders: Georgina Clarke; Rupert Clarke
Officers: Georgina Clarke, Secretary; Georgina Clarke [1968] Director; Rupert Clarke [1969] Director/Property Developer

Roche Diagnostics Limited
Incorporated: 14 September 1956 *Employees:* 508
Net Worth: £75,485,000 *Total Assets:* £208,670,000
Registered Office: Roche House, Charles Avenue, Burgess Hill, W Sussex, RH15 9RY
Activities: Other professional, scientific and technical activities n.e.c.
Parent: Roche Holding (UK) Limited
Officers: Oren Reich, Secretary; Richard William Erwin [1967] Director/General Manager; Oren Reich [1976] Director/Solicitor; Geoffrey John Twist [1971] Managing Director

Rochester Diocesan Society and Board of Finance (The)
Incorporated: 14 June 1915 *Employees:* 47
Net Worth: £68,513,000 *Total Assets:* £83,379,000
Registered Office: Diocesan Office, St Nicholas Church, Boley Hill, Rochester, Kent, ME1 1SL
Activities: Other social work activities without accommodation n.e.c.
Officers: Geoffrey Richard Marsh, Secretary; Judith Jane Armitt [1953] Director/Retired; The Rev Mark Barker [1962] Director/Minister of Religion; Dr Jeffrey Vincent Blyth [1961] Director/Education and Mental Health Consultant; Christine Mary Bostock [1950] Director/Retired; Julie Elizabeth Bowen [1964] Director/Minister of Religion; Simon David Burton-Jones [1962] Director/Archdeacon; The Ven Julie Anne Conalty [1963] Director/Minister of Religion; The Rev Alyson Elizabeth Davie [1958] Director/Minister of Religion; David Roy Fitzpatrick [1954] Director/Retired Shipping Clerk; Philip Colin French [1960] Director/IT Executive; Christopher Huish Gallico [1945] Director/Retired; Philip John Hesketh [1964] Director/Dean of Rochester; The Right Reverend James Henry Langstaff [1956] Director/Minister of Religion; Generald Michael O'Brien [1948] Director; Sarah Penelope Poole [1952] Director/Retired; Alan Keith Strachan [1955] Director/Maritime Historian; The Rev Dylan Lawrence Turner [1972] Director/Minister of Religion; The Ven Andrew David Wooding Jones [1961] Director/Minister of Religion; Dr Paul Wright [1954] Director/Archdeacon

Rockley Sands (Estates) Limited
Incorporated: 17 January 1956 *Employees:* 239
Net Worth: £6,050,000 *Total Assets:* £25,649,000
Registered Office: 1 Park Lane, Hemel Hempstead, Herts, HP2 4YL
Activities: Recreational vehicle parks, trailer parks and camping grounds
Parent: Bourne Leisure Group Limited
Officers: Jane Elizabeth Bentall [1970] Director/Accountant; Paul Charles Flaum [1970] Director; Iain Stuart Macmillan [1976] Director

Rockwell Automation Limited
Incorporated: 23 February 1966 *Employees:* 688
Net Worth: £79,940,000 *Total Assets:* £111,699,000
Registered Office: Pitfield, Kiln Farm, Milton Keynes, Bucks, MK11 3DR
Activities: Manufacture of electronic industrial process control equipment
Parent: Rockwell Automation, Inc
Officers: Mark Christopher Bottomley [1976] Director; Kawal Maharaj [1967] Director/EMEA Regional Controller [Dutch]; William Joseph Quinn [1955] Director/Chartered Engineer; Alan Kenneth Suttle [1948] Director/Electrical Engineer

Rockwell Collins UK Limited
Incorporated: 7 January 1955 *Employees:* 304
Net Worth: £19,586,000 *Total Assets:* £58,850,000
Registered Office: 730 Wharfedale Road, Winnersh, Wokingham, Berks, RG41 5TP
Activities: Wholesale of electronic and telecommunications equipment and parts
Parent: Rockwell Collins, Inc.
Officers: Helen Poppy Barton, Secretary; Claude Alber [1962] VP & Managing Director EUMEA [French]; Christopher Hazeel [1958] Director, Strategy; Paul John Hickox [1976] Director/Head, Airport Systems Sales & Account Management; Dean Jordan [1976] Finance Director; Colin Roy Mahoney [1965] Director/Senior VP, International & Service Solutions; Sarah Helen Minett [1969] Managing Director; Leann Ridgeway [1964] Director/VP & GM, Simulation Training & Solutions [American]

Rockwell Commercial Holdings Limited
Incorporated: 24 September 2009
Net Worth: £24,048,000 *Total Assets:* £24,071,000
Registered Office: Pitfield, Kiln Farm, Milton Keynes, Bucks, MK11 3DR
Activities: Activities of head offices
Parent: Rockwell European Holdings Limited
Officers: Kawal Maharaj [1967] Director/EMEA Regional Controller [Dutch]

Rockwell European Holdings Limited
Incorporated: 28 May 1980
Net Worth: £40,098,000 *Total Assets:* £40,651,000
Registered Office: Pitfield, Kiln Farm, Milton Keynes, Bucks, MK11 3DR
Activities: Other business support service activities n.e.c.
Parent: Rockwell Automation, Inc
Officers: Erik Julien Jozef Casselman [1967] Director/General Counsel EMEA Region [Belgian]; Kawal Maharaj [1967] Director/EMEA Regional Controller [Dutch]

Roffey Homes Limited
Incorporated: 2 May 1960 *Employees:* 6
Net Worth: £14,508,005 *Total Assets:* £27,778,732
Registered Office: Amelia House, Crescent Road, Worthing, W Sussex, BN11 1QR
Activities: Development of building projects
Major Shareholder: Ian Reginald Cheal
Officers: Jane Cheal, Secretary; Benjamin James Cheal [1971] Director; Ian Reginald Cheal [1943] Director/Builder; Jane Cheal [1947] Director; Jonathan Ian Cheal [1969] Director; Matthew John Cheal [1975] Director

Rohde & Schwarz U.K. Limited
Incorporated: 23 October 1954 *Employees:* 62
Net Worth: £7,008,625 *Total Assets:* £23,586,832
Registered Office: Ancells Business Park, Fleet, Hants, GU51 2UZ
Activities: Wholesale of electronic and telecommunications equipment and parts
Parent: Rusint AG
Officers: George Campbell Morrow, Secretary; Jorg Fries [1972] Director/Engineer [German]; Hartmut Jaschke [1967] Sales Director [German]; Frank Mackel [1963] Director [German]; Jens Patrick Poetschke [1966] Financial Director [German]

Rohm Electronics Europe Limited
Incorporated: 18 October 2000
Net Worth: £48,843,000 *Total Assets:* £48,865,000
Registered Office: 41 Caldecotte Lake Drive, Caldecotte Lake Business Park, Milton Keynes, Bucks, MK7 8LF
Activities: Activities of head offices
Parent: Rohm Co. Ltd
Officers: Robert Christian Andre [1961] Director [French]; Kunio Uehara [1960] Director/General Manager of Accounting & Finance Division [Japanese]; Shinichi Yoshimi [1966] Director/General Manager of Human Resources Division [Japanese]

Roke Manor Research Limited
Incorporated: 6 August 1932 *Employees:* 379
Net Worth: £23,809,000 *Total Assets:* £29,575,000
Registered Office: Roke Manor, Old Salisbury Lane, Romsey, Hants, SO51 0ZN
Activities: Information technology consultancy activities
Parent: Chemring Group PLC
Officers: Sarah Louise Ellard, Secretary; David Edward Aston Cole [1970] Director; Ian Charles Cooper [1969] Director; Sarah Louise Ellard [1970] Group Legal Director; Andrew Gregory Lewis [1971] Director; Michael Ord [1967] Director

Rolls-Royce Motor Cars Limited
Incorporated: 5 March 1998 *Employees:* 1,277
Net Worth: £119,758,000 *Total Assets:* £322,323,008
Registered Office: Summit One, Summit Avenue, Farnborough, Hants, GU14 0FB
Activities: Manufacture of motor vehicles
Parent: BMW (UK) Holdings Limited
Officers: William Edwin Johnson, Secretary; Juergen Brzank [1973] Director/Chief Finance Officer [German]; Lord Charles Henry March [1955] Director; Torsten Gerd Mueller-Oetvoes [1960] Director/CEO of Rolls-Royce Motor Cars Limited [German]; Sir Ralph Robins [1932] Director; Peter Schwarzenbauer [1959] Director [German]

Rolta UK Limited
Incorporated: 28 May 2002 *Employees:* 16
Net Worth Deficit: £37,504,776 *Total Assets:* £21,473,340
Registered Office: 100 Longwater Avenue, Green Park, Reading, Berks, RG2 6GP
Activities: Other information technology service activities
Officers: Reida Elwannas [1972] Director [American]; Kamal Krishan Singh [1949] Director/Corporate Executive [Indian]

Romans 2 Limited
Incorporated: 16 August 2013
Net Worth Deficit: £14,404,952 *Total Assets:* £45,899,672
Registered Office: Crowthorne House, Nine Mile Ride, Wokingham, Berks, RG40 3GZ
Activities: Activities of head offices
Parent: Romans 1 Limited
Officers: Antonia Dale Cheong [1987] Director/Investment Manager; Peter Anthony Coles [1967] Group Managing Director; Peter Kavanagh [1962] Director; Michael Edward John Palmer [1973] Finance Director; Tom Shelford [1980] Director

Romans 3 Limited
Incorporated: 16 August 2013 *Employees:* 5
Net Worth Deficit: £13,187,776 *Total Assets:* £61,690,316
Registered Office: Crowthorne House, Nine Mile Ride, Wokingham, Berks, RG40 3GZ
Activities: Activities of head offices
Parent: Romans 2 Limited
Officers: Antonia Dale Cheong [1987] Director/Investment Manager; Peter Anthony Coles [1967] Group Managing Director; Peter Kavanagh [1962] Director; Michael Edward John Palmer [1973] Finance Director; Tom Shelford [1980] Director

The Romans Group (UK) Limited
Incorporated: 7 September 1987 *Employees:* 519
Net Worth: £21,775,948 *Total Assets:* £49,610,972
Registered Office: Crowthorne House, Nine Mile Ride, Wokingham, Berks, RG40 3GZ
Activities: Real estate agencies
Parent: Romans 3 Limited
Officers: Michael Edward John Palmer, Secretary; Antonia Dale Cheong [1987] Director/Investment Manager; Peter Anthony Coles [1967] Director/Estate Agent; Michael Brian Cook [1983] Managing Director, Lettings; Peter Fuller [1965] Director/Estate Agent; Peter Kavanagh [1962] Managing Director; Michael Edward John Palmer [1973] Finance Director; Tom Shelford [1980] Director

The Romsey School
Incorporated: 7 July 2011 *Employees:* 233
Net Worth: £42,368,116 *Total Assets:* £44,674,568
Registered Office: The Romsey School, Greatbridge Road, Romsey, Hants, SO51 8ZB
Activities: General secondary education
Officers: Pamela Carol Leech, Secretary; Nicolette Adens [1974] Director/Businesswoman; James Nicholas Bastow [1941] Director; John Bennett [1957] Director; Sheila June Caine [1944] Director; Ian Clapton [1976] Director/Curriculum Leader-Geography; Councillor Mark Geoffrey Cooper [1948] Director; Cara Cox [1977] Director/Accountant; Jonathan de Sausmarez [1960] Director/Headteacher Education; Nicola Kate French [1972] Director/Ecological Planning Consultant; Matthew Christopher Gilks [1971] Director/Solicitor; Gary David Hiscock [1973] Director; Judith Emma Houghton [1962] Director/IT Controls Advisor; Malcolm Albert Kaill [1950] Director/Higher Education Manager; Dr Elizabeth Ann Lee [1957] Director/Teacher; Colm McKavanagh [1961] Director/Headteacher; Keith Normington [1975] Director/Computer Consultant; Peter Michael O'Hara [1972] Director/Businessman; Sarah Lesley Weare [1964] Director/Accountancy

Roos Energy Limited
Incorporated: 17 May 2011
Net Worth Deficit: £2,740,000 *Total Assets:* £33,296,000
Registered Office: Beaufort Court, Egg Farm Lane, Kings Langley, Herts, WD4 8LR
Activities: Production of electricity
Parent: Trafalgar Wind Holdings Limited
Officers: Dominic James Hearth, Secretary; Steven William Hughes [1972] Generation & Asset Management Director; Fraser Stephen Merry [1968] Director/Chartered Surveyor; Mitesh Raj Patel [1982] Director/Group Financial Controller

Rose Holdco Limited
Incorporated: 30 April 2009 *Employees:* 28
Net Worth: £189,862,000 *Total Assets:* £273,116,992
Registered Office: 35-37 Amersham Hill, High Wycombe, Bucks, HP13 6NU
Activities: Activities of head offices
Parent: Boing Acquisitions Ltd
Officers: Jonathan Samuel Booth [1961] Director; Thomas Bruce Mangas [1967] Director/Chief Executive Officer [American]; Nilesh Kundanlal Pandya [1971] Director; Michael Andrew James Smith [1962] Director

Rose Midco Limited
Incorporated: 30 April 2009 *Employees:* 4
Net Worth: £155,838,000 *Total Assets:* £383,684,992
Registered Office: 35-37 Amersham Hill, High Wycombe, Bucks, HP13 6NU
Activities: Activities of head offices
Parent: Rose Holdco Ltd
Officers: Jonathan Samuel Booth [1961] Director; Thomas Bruce Mangas [1967] Director/Chief Executive Officer [American]; Nilesh Kundanlal Pandya [1971] Director; Michael Andrew James Smith [1962] Director

The Rosedale Hewens Academy Trust
Incorporated: 27 June 2011 *Employees:* 235
Net Worth: £86,428,000 *Total Assets:* £88,925,000
Registered Office: Wood End Green Road, Hayes, Middlesex, UB3 2SE
Activities: Pre-primary education
Officers: Susan Galloway, Secretary; Marie Diane Ashley [1964] Director/Service Manager; Anthony Laurence Cohen [1957] Director/Electrical Engineer; Norman Leslie Deas [1946] Director/Catering Consultant; Sarah Morgan Driscoll [1979] Director/Chief Operating Officer; Stewart John Michie Duguid [1967] Director/ICT Manager; Jane Mary Ellis [1959] Director/Executive Headteacher; Heidi Paula Faure [1975] Director/Executive Principal; Clive Ian Neathey [1955] Director/Executive Principal; Ian O'Connor [1979] Director/Principal; Devard Darien Russell-Jones [1984] Director/Service Manager [Jamaican]

The Rothschild Foundation
Incorporated: 18 August 2010 *Employees:* 238
Net Worth: £654,974,912 *Total Assets:* £673,321,664
Registered Office: Windmill Hill, Silk Street, Waddesdon, Aylesbury, Bucks, HP18 0JZ
Activities: Activities of extraterritorial organisations and bodies
Officers: The Honourable Janet Francis de Botton [1952] Director; Emily Magda Freeman-Attwood [1967] Director/Farmer; Francesco Jonathan Goedhuis [1982] Director/Principal; Lord David John Ogilvy [1958] Director/Landowner/Musician; The Hon Hannah Mary Rothschild [1962] Director/Film Producer; Lord Nathaniel Charles Jacob Rothschild [1936] Director; Peter John Charles Troughton [1948] Director

Routeco Limited
Incorporated: 15 July 1976 *Employees:* 256
Net Worth: £16,211,000 *Total Assets:* £39,037,000
Registered Office: Davy Avenue, Knowlhill, Milton Keynes, Bucks, MK5 8HJ
Activities: Wholesale of other machinery and equipment
Officers: Sean Thomas Evans, Secretary; David Amps [1975] Director; Sean Thomas Evans [1968] Finance Director; Ian Stewart [1960] Director

Royal & Sun Alliance Insurance PLC
Incorporated: 19 June 1907 *Employees:* 5,754
Net Worth: £7,942,000,128 *Total Assets:* £24,476,000,256
Registered Office: St Marks Court, Chart Way, Horsham, W Sussex, RH12 1XL
Activities: Non-life insurance
Parent: Royal Insurance Holdings Limited
Officers: Anthony Buckle [1969] Director/Insurance; Scott Egan [1971] Director/Chief Financial Officer; William Rufus Benjamin McDonnell [1973] Director/Group Chief Risk Officer; Nathan Philip Williams [1965] Insurance Director

Royal & Sun Alliance Reinsurance Limited
Incorporated: 31 October 1908
Net Worth: £89,417,000 *Total Assets:* £544,027,008
Registered Office: St Mark's Court, Chart Way, Horsham, W Sussex, RH12 1XL
Activities: Non-life insurance
Parent: Royal & Sun Alliance Insurance PLC
Officers: Anthony Buckle [1969] Director/Insurance; Scott Egan [1971] Director/Chief Financial Officer; William Rufus Benjamin McDonnell [1973] Director/Group Chief Risk Officer; Nathan Philip Williams [1965] Insurance Director

The Royal Air Force Central Fund
Incorporated: 4 June 2013 *Employees:* 11
Net Worth: £41,842,520 *Total Assets:* £44,561,656
Registered Office: Hurricane Building, HQ Air Command, Wycombe Road, RAF High Wycombe, High Wycombe, Bucks, HP14 4UE
Activities: Defence activities
Officers: Nicola Graske, Secretary; Sally Bridgeland [1964] Director/Actuary; Jonathan Crossley [1968] Director/RAF Warrant Officer; Alison Farmery [1962] Director/Media Consultant; John Charles Michaelson [1953] Director/Venture Capital [American]; Dr Eamonn Mark Molloy [1971] Director/Professor; Michael Wigston [1968] Director/RAF Officer; Mark Williams [1959] Director/RAF Reserve

Royal British Legion Industries Ltd.
Incorporated: 2 September 1919 *Employees:* 400
Net Worth: £22,844,000 *Total Assets:* £27,579,000
Registered Office: Hall Road, Aylesford, Maidstone, Kent, ME20 7NL
Activities: Manufacture of other products of wood; manufacture of articles of cork, straw and plaiting materials
Officers: Philip Edwin Defraine, Secretary; Nadra Khanum Ahmed [1958] Director/Chairman; Kathryn Cearns [1964] Director/Chartered Accountant; Desmond Crampton [1953] Director [South African]; Arthur Blair Gulland [1951] Director/Solicitor; Brigadier Harold Hamilton Tony Kerr [1941] Director/Retired; Stephen William Kingsman [1952] Non-Executive Director Chairman; Frank Martin [1952] Director; Sarah Elizabeth Louise Mason [1982] Director/Chartered Surveyor; David Wyndham Montgomery [1951] Director; Alistair Fraser Watson [1950] Director/Retired

Royal British Legion Poppy Factory Limited (The)
Incorporated: 11 March 1925 *Employees:* 66
Net Worth: £25,792,162 *Total Assets:* £29,247,398
Registered Office: 20 Petersham Road, Richmond, Surrey, TW10 6UR
Activities: Other manufacturing n.e.c.
Officers: William Robert Kay, Secretary; Michael Francis Bustard [1946] Director/Part Time Training Consultant; Clifford Roderick Stanton Dare [1967] Director/Chartered Surveyor; Peter Richard Gill [1955] Director/Retired; Dr Sridevi Kalidindi [1971] Director/Doctor; Alistair James Kett [1971] Director/Management Consultant; Steven Colin Monger-Godfrey [1952] Director/Chartered Surveyor; Andrew Richard Dawren Sharpe [1960] Director/Army Officer; Simon Anthony Taylor [1962] Director/Chartered Surveyor; Andrew John Truscott [1973] Director/Investment Banker; Andrew Ian Fergusson Wishart [1964] Director; Julius Peregrine Harold Shepherd Wolff-Ingham [1963] Director/Charity Executive

Royal Insurance Holdings Limited
Incorporated: 16 February 1988
Previous: Royal Insurance Holdings PLC
Net Worth: £2,224,999,936 *Total Assets:* £4,096,000,000
Registered Office: St Mark's Court, Chart Way, Horsham, W Sussex, RH12 1XL
Activities: Activities of financial services holding companies
Parent: RSA Insurance Group PLC
Officers: Ian Adam Craston [1966] Director; Simon de Baat [1980] Director/Actuary; Charlotte Dawn Alethea Heiss [1979] Director/Solicitor; Rupert Taylor Rea [1978] Director/Chartered Accountant

Royal International Insurance Holdings Limited
Incorporated: 26 August 1910
Net Worth: £4,444,700,160 *Total Assets:* £4,481,500,160
Registered Office: St Mark's Court, Chart Way, Horsham, W Sussex, RH12 1XL
Activities: Activities of financial services holding companies
Parent: Royal & Sun Alliance Insurance PLC
Officers: Ian Adam Craston [1966] Director; Simon de Baat [1980] Director/Actuary; Martin David Postles [1959] Director/Group Manager, International Legacy Businesses

The Royal Navy and Royal Marines Charity
Incorporated: 10 January 2007 *Employees:* 51
Net Worth: £96,384,576 *Total Assets:* £101,062,496
Registered Office: Building 37, HMS Excellent, Whale Island, Hants, PO2 8ER
Activities: Educational support services
Officers: Michael Burningham, Secretary; Roderic Aidan Birkett [1961] Director/Consultant; Harriet Mary Delbridge [1988] Director/Naval Officer; Mark Peter Louden Dowie [1961] Director/Investment & Commercial Banking MD; Andrew Charles Jameson [1964] Director/Lawyer; Mark Lewthwaite [1956] Director/Retired; Gary Kenneth Nicolson WO1 [1968] Director/Royal Navy; James Miles Benjamin Parkin [1974] Director/HM Forces; Annette Mary Picton [1950] Director/Retired; James David Crichton Pitt [1966] Director/Asset Management; Jennifer Rowe [1955] Director/Senior Civil Servant; William John Stocks [1949] Director/Retired; Michael John Tanner [1969] Director/Military Officer; William Gennydd Thomas [1959] Director; Jamie Webb [1973] Director/Charity Fundraising

Royale Park Home Estates Limited
Incorporated: 5 February 2001 *Employees:* 22
Previous: Starglade Park Developments Limited
Net Worth: £11,303,041 *Total Assets:* £26,897,790
Registered Office: Royale House, Southwick Road, North Boarhunt, Fareham, Hants, PO17 6JN
Activities: Other letting and operating of own or leased real estate
Parent: Royale Parks Limited
Officers: Robert Lee Jack Bull [1977] Director; Robert Bull [1948] Director; Stephen Gary Meredith [1961] Sales Director; Jason Mark Williams [1985] Director

Royale Parks Limited
Incorporated: 27 November 2014
Net Worth: £5,006,893 *Total Assets:* £30,513,246
Registered Office: Royale House, Southwick Road, North Boarhunt, Fareham, Hants, PO17 6JN
Activities: Other holiday and other collective accommodation
Shareholders: Robert Lee Jack Bull; Robert Bull
Officers: Robert Lee Jack Bull [1977] Director; Robert Bull [1948] Director; Stephen Gary Meredith [1961] Sales Director; Jason Mark Williams [1985] Director

Royalton Group Holdings Limited
Incorporated: 28 April 2014 *Employees:* 17
Net Worth: £783,056 *Total Assets:* £25,218,560
Registered Office: 3000 Cathedral Hill, Guildford, Surrey, GU2 7YB
Activities: Activities of other holding companies n.e.c.
Shareholders: Royalton Ventures Limited; Kenneth Richard Parker
Officers: Jeremy David Maxfield [1963] Director; Kenneth Richard Parker [1971] Director

Royalton RS Limited
Incorporated: 8 July 2015
Net Worth Deficit: £7,654 *Total Assets:* £24,254,922
Registered Office: 3000 Cathedral Hill, Guildford, Surrey, GU2 7YB
Activities: Buying and selling of own real estate
Parent: Royalton Limited
Officers: Jeremy David Maxfield [1963] Director; Kenneth Richard Parker [1971] Director

RPR (US) Limited
Incorporated: 24 May 1996 *Employees:* 2
Net Worth: £258,583,008 *Total Assets:* £258,583,008
Registered Office: One Onslow Street, Guildford, Surrey, GU1 4YS
Activities: Activities of other holding companies n.e.c.
Parent: Sanofi
Officers: Francois-Xavier Duhalde [1965] Director/Chief Financial Officer [French]; Hugo Rupert Alexander Fry [1970] Director/UK Country Chair

RS Furbs Limited
Incorporated: 13 April 2003 *Employees:* 1
Net Worth: £14,401,463 *Total Assets:* £21,404,464
Registered Office: 4th Floor, Reading Bridge House, George Street, Reading, Berks, RG1 8LS
Activities: Other business support service activities n.e.c.
Major Shareholder: Robert Charles Standing
Officers: Robert Charles Standing [1960] Director/Fund Manager

RSA Accident Repairs Limited
Incorporated: 3 September 1962 *Employees:* 73
Net Worth: £20,893,000 *Total Assets:* £23,996,000
Registered Office: St Mark's Court, Chart Way, Horsham, W Sussex, RH12 1XL
Activities: Sale of new cars and light motor vehicles
Parent: Royal Insurance Holdings Limited
Officers: Jonathan Cope [1979] Director/Lawyer; Julian Heath [1970] Director, UK Motor and Injury Claims

RSA Finance
Incorporated: 30 March 2009
Net Worth: £2,499,521,024 *Total Assets:* £2,506,701,056
Registered Office: St Mark's Court, Chart Way, Horsham, W Sussex, RH12 1XL
Activities: Non-trading company
Parent: Royal & Sun Alliance Insurance PLC
Officers: Ian Adam Craston [1966] Director; Simon de Baat [1980] Director/Actuary; Rupert Taylor Rea [1978] Director/Chartered Accountant

Rubicon Drinks Limited
Incorporated: 14 September 1981
Net Worth: £80,284,000 *Total Assets:* £82,823,000
Registered Office: Crossley Drive, Magna Park, Milton Keynes, Bucks, MK17 8FL
Activities: Manufacture of soft drinks; production of mineral waters and other bottled waters
Parent: A.G. Barr P.L.C.
Officers: Julie Anne Barr, Secretary; Stuart Lorimer [1966] Finance Director; Roger Alexander White [1965] Director

Ruby Topco Limited
Incorporated: 12 June 2014
Net Worth Deficit: £419,000 *Total Assets:* £145,100,000
Registered Office: Unit 6 & 7 Princeton Mews, 167-169 London Road, Kingston upon Thames, Surrey, KT2 6PT
Activities: Residential care activities for learning difficulties, mental health and substance abuse
Parent: The Regard (Group) Bidco Limited
Officers: Nicola Hopkins, Secretary; Nicola Rosemary Lucy Hopkins [1968] Director/Chartered Accountant

Ruddy Joinery Limited
Incorporated: 13 February 1978 *Employees:* 170
Net Worth: £18,865,300 *Total Assets:* £36,239,128
Registered Office: Enterprise Way, Flitwick, Beds, MK45 5BS
Activities: Other construction installation
Major Shareholder: Patrick Joseph Ruddy
Officers: Michael McGilloway [1963] Director/Commercial Manager [Irish]; Alan Joseph Ruddy [1974] Director/Surveyor; Eileen Catherine Ruddy [1939] Director/Secretary [Irish]; Lee Myles Ruddy [1976] Director/Chartered Management Accountant; Patrick Joseph Ruddy [1938] Director [Irish]

Runecorp Limited
Incorporated: 12 November 1999
Net Worth: £444,852,992 *Total Assets:* £571,641,024
Registered Office: Hayes Park, Hayes End Road, Hayes, Middlesex, UB4 8EE
Activities: Non-trading company
Parent: Solvecorp Limited
Officers: Mark Oldham, Secretary/Barrister; Helen Josephine McCarthy [1966] Director; Mark Oldham [1959] Director

Runnymede Investments Limited
Incorporated: 5 May 1994 *Employees:* 4
Net Worth: £26,498,192 *Total Assets:* £34,758,336
Registered Office: 182 Brooklands Road, Weybridge, Surrey, KT13 0RJ
Activities: Other letting and operating of own or leased real estate
Major Shareholder: Andrew Stuart Beaumont
Officers: Kirsty Michelle Hunt, Secretary; Andrew Stuart Beaumont [1949] Director; Martin Arthur Brown [1946] Director

Runtime Collective Limited
Incorporated: 21 December 1999 *Employees:* 355
Net Worth: £12,564,080 *Total Assets:* £33,625,744
Registered Office: 1st Floor, Sovereign House, Church Street, Brighton, BN1 1UJ
Activities: Information technology consultancy activities
Officers: Dylan Marvin, Secretary; Omri Benayoun [1976] Director/Partner in an Investment Firm [French]; Samuel Woodworth Brooks [1978] Director/Venture Capital Investor [American]; Jo Ann Corkran [1955] Director/Venture Fund General Partner [American]; Carles Ferrer Roqueta [1970] Director/Venture Capital General Partner [Spanish]; Dean Nelson [1959] Director/Private Equity Partner [American]; Giles John Palmer [1968] Director/Accountant

Rush Hair Group Limited
Incorporated: 4 October 2016 *Employees:* 940
Net Worth Deficit: £1,234,000 *Total Assets:* £25,265,000
Registered Office: 23 George Street, Croydon, Surrey, CR0 1LA
Activities: Other retail sale not in stores, stalls or markets
Major Shareholder: Andrew Panayiotis Phouli
Officers: Stelios Andrew [1964] Director; Gerard Gould [1966] Director/Investor; Stephen Richard Knight [1962] Director; Andreas Panayiotis Phouli [1967] Director; Alastair James Weinel [1965] Director

Russell & Bromley Limited
Incorporated: 3 November 1952 *Employees:* 948
Net Worth: £73,445,424 *Total Assets:* £86,099,560
Registered Office: 24-34 Farwig Lane, Bromley, Kent, BR1 3RB
Activities: Retail sale of footwear in specialised stores
Shareholder: Roger John Bromley
Officers: Philip Wright, Secretary; Andrew Michael James Bromley [1968] Director; Roger John Bromley [1943] Director; Sebastian Michael Alan Bromley [1986] Director/Business Executive; Stuart Peter William Bromley [1971] Director

Russell Finex Limited
Incorporated: 29 November 1934 *Employees:* 340
Net Worth: £21,434,680 *Total Assets:* £38,615,720
Registered Office: Browells Lane, Feltham, Middlesex, TW13 7EW
Activities: Manufacture of machinery for food, beverage and tobacco processing
Parent: Russell-Hurst Trustees Ltd
Officers: Lisa Jane Harris, Secretary; Kenneth John Armour [1966] Finance Director; Martin William Chipperfield [1960] Sales & Marketing Director; Stanley John Keyworth [1943] Director/Consultant; Robert Joseph O'Connell [1971] Sales & Marketing Director USA & India; Resham Singh [1956] Managing Director; Ian Charles Wardlaw [1968] Manufacturing Director

Russell School Trust
Incorporated: 15 March 1974 *Employees:* 215
Net Worth: £14,303,798 *Total Assets:* £27,174,608
Registered Office: Royal Russell School, Coombe Lane, Croydon, Surrey, CR9 5BX
Activities: Pre-primary education
Officers: Jane Victoria Burton [1965] Director; Nicholas Cobill [1976] Director/Barrister; Dr Agnelo Teles Fernandes [1960] Director; Lisa Jane Jessup [1970] Director/General Manager Support Services; Simon Henry Kolesar [1948] Director/Chartered Surveyor; James Douglas Lacey [1975] Director/Partner, Planning Consultancy; Andrew Gideon Lorie [1967] Director/Barrister; Anne Martin [1959] Director/Lawyer; Rohit Mathur [1978] Director/Banker; Andrew John Merriman [1966] Finance Director; Sir Philip Drury Moor [1959] Director/QC; James Richard Penny [1965] Director/Banker; Jane Ellen Ann Stevens [1957] Director/Headmistress

RWF Health and Community Developers (Tranche 1) Limited
Incorporated: 17 February 2004
Net Worth Deficit: £7,780,078 *Total Assets:* £22,827,822
Registered Office: 55 Station Road, Beaconsfield, Bucks, HP9 1QL
Activities: Other letting and operating of own or leased real estate
Parent: RWF Health and Community Developers Limited
Officers: Nigel Raymond Dodds, Secretary; Jamie Andrews [1970] Director; Ross William Driver [1981] Finance Director; David Alexander John Foot [1968] Investment Director, Infrastructure; James Christopher Heath [1975] Director

RWS (Overseas) Limited
Incorporated: 15 June 1971
Net Worth: £102,881,152 *Total Assets:* £337,112,352
Registered Office: Europa House, Chiltern Park, Chiltern Hill, Chalfont St Peter, Bucks, SL9 9FG
Activities: Activities of other holding companies n.e.c.
Parent: RWS Group Limited
Officers: Desmond Kenneth Glass, Secretary; Andrew Stephen Brode [1940] Director; Desmond Kenneth Neil Glass [1969] Director [Irish]; Richard James Thompson [1962] Financial Director

RWS Group Limited
Incorporated: 17 July 1981 *Employees:* 50
Net Worth: £101,162,328 *Total Assets:* £330,401,344
Registered Office: Europa House, Chiltern Park, Chiltern Hill, Chalfont St Peter, Bucks, SL9 9FG
Activities: Activities of head offices
Parent: RWS Holdings PLC
Officers: Desmond Kenneth Glass, Secretary; Andrew Stephen Brode [1940] Director; Stuart Carter [1974] Director; Caroline Harriet Chenique [1960] European Sales Director; Desmond Kenneth Neil Glass [1969] Director [Irish]; Alistair Stuart Hargreaves [1975] IT Director; David Leech [1961] HR Director; Neil Thomas Simpkin [1970] Director; Charles Edward Sitch [1969] Director; Richard James Thompson [1962] Financial Director; Catherine Elizabeth Walsh [1970] Finance Director

RWS Holdings PLC
Incorporated: 16 December 1994 *Employees:* 896
Net Worth: £158,884,992 *Total Assets:* £231,544,000
Registered Office: Europa House, Chiltern Park, Chiltern Hill, Chalfont St Peter, Bucks, SL9 9FG
Activities: Activities of other holding companies n.e.c.
Shareholder: Andrew Stephen Brode
Officers: Desmond Kenneth Glass, Secretary; Lara Boro [1967] Director; Andrew Stephen Brode [1940] Director; Desmond Kenneth Neil Glass [1969] Director and Company Secretary [Irish]; Tomas Kratochvil [1966] Director [Czech]; Elisabeth Ann Lucas [1956] Director; David Everard Shrimpton [1943] Director; Richard James Thompson [1962] Financial Director

RWS Translations Limited
Incorporated: 6 November 1972 *Employees:* 319
Net Worth: £55,226,008 *Total Assets:* £72,210,096
Registered Office: Europa House, Chiltern Park, Chiltern Hill, Chalfont St Peter, Bucks, SL9 9FG
Activities: Translation and interpretation activities
Parent: RWS Group Limited
Officers: Desmond Kenneth Glass, Secretary; Andrew Stephen Brode [1940] Director; Stuart Carter [1974] Director; Erica Gatland [1971] IP Director; Desmond Kenneth Neil Glass [1969] Director [Irish]; Neil Thomas Simpkin [1970] Director; Charles Edward Sitch [1969] Director; Richard James Thompson [1962] Financial Director

RWS UK Holding Co Limited
Incorporated: 5 October 2015
Net Worth: £106,645,528 *Total Assets:* £152,845,552
Registered Office: Europa House, Chiltern Park, Chiltern Hill, Chalfont St Peter, Bucks, SL9 9FG
Activities: Translation and interpretation activities
Parent: RWS Overseas Limited
Officers: Desmond Kenneth Glass, Secretary; Andrew Stephen Brode [1940] Director; Desmond Kenneth Neil Glass [1969] Director [Irish]; Richard James Thompson [1962] Financial Director

Rydon Construction Limited
Incorporated: 29 December 1976
Net Worth: £21,708,534 *Total Assets:* £84,980,216
Registered Office: Rydon House, Station Road, Forest Row, E Sussex, RH18 5DW
Activities: Development of building projects
Parent: Rydon Group Limited
Officers: Alan Penrhyn-Lowe, Secretary; Robert Bond [1956] Construction Director; Mark Day [1960] Finance Director; Timothy Edwards [1964] Commercial Director; Mark Mitchener [1965] Construction Director; Simon Moore [1958] Director/Manager; Alan Penrhyn-Lowe [1963] Finance Director; Tom Wilding Rigby [1976] Development Director; Mark Unsworth [1968] Director

Rydon Group Limited
Incorporated: 3 September 1981 *Employees:* 750
Net Worth: £59,064,000 *Total Assets:* £159,254,000
Registered Office: Rydon House, Station Road, Forest Row, E Sussex, RH18 5DW
Activities: Activities of head offices
Parent: Rydon Holdings Limited
Officers: Mark Day, Secretary; Warwick James Barnes [1968] Managing Director; Robert Bond [1956] Construction Director; Stephen Maurice Collinson [1958] Director; Mark Day [1960] Finance Director; Lisa Claire Fitzsimons [1965] Director; Andrew Paul Goldman [1962] Director; Jeffrey David Henton [1961] Director; Aileen Agnes Ivanec [1964] Director/Lawyer; Mark Mitchener [1965] Director; Nicholas Charles Standen [1961] Director

Rydon Holdings Limited
Incorporated: 7 September 2005 *Employees:* 750
Net Worth: £26,721,000 *Total Assets:* £128,395,000
Registered Office: Rydon House, Station Road, Forest Row, E Sussex, RH18 5DW
Activities: Activities of head offices
Parent: Rydon Group Holdings Limited
Officers: Mark Day, Secretary; Robert Bond [1956] Director; Nicholas Charles Standen [1961] Director

Rydon Homes Limited
Incorporated: 21 May 2003
Net Worth: £9,927,558 *Total Assets:* £25,341,240
Registered Office: Rydon House, Station Road, Forest Row, E Sussex, RH18 5DW
Activities: Development of building projects
Parent: Rydon Group Limited
Officers: Anne Joan Hall, Secretary; Warwick James Barnes [1968] Managing Director; Robert Bond [1956] Director; Mark Day [1960] Finance Director; Anne Joan Hall [1969] Finance Director; Paul Ronald Mepham [1969] Design & Planning Director; Kevin Willcox [1957] Director

Rydon Maintenance Limited
Incorporated: 14 July 1982
Net Worth: £26,682,080 *Total Assets:* £44,077,060
Registered Office: Rydon House, Station Road, Forest Row, E Sussex, RH18 5DW
Activities: Combined facilities support activities
Parent: Rydon Group Limited
Officers: Alan Penrhyn-Lowe, Secretary; Barrie Charles Beckett [1959] Director/Contracts Manager; Stephen William Blake [1965] Director; Robert Bond [1956] Director; Mark Day [1960] Director; Jeffrey David Henton [1961] Director; Robert Benjamin Irvine [1964] Director; Alan Penrhyn-Lowe [1963] Finance Director; Laurence Rudman [1955] Director

Rye Academy Trust
Incorporated: 13 August 2012 *Employees:* 183
Net Worth: £17,667,868 *Total Assets:* £20,069,100
Registered Office: Rye College, The Grove, Rye, E Sussex, TN31 7NQ
Activities: General secondary education
Officers: Howard Spencer Brown [1962] Director/Executive Coach; Andrew Galloway Ferguson [1959] Director/Lead Executive; Stephen Michael Ward [1957] Director/Management Consultant

S & B Herba Foods Limited
Incorporated: 4 July 1919 *Employees:* 101
Net Worth: £60,955,000 *Total Assets:* £79,704,000
Registered Office: 2nd Floor, North Block, Central Court, 1b Knoll Rise, Orpington, Kent, BR6 0JA
Activities: Grain milling
Officers: Peter John Cattaneo, Secretary; Antonio Hernandez Callejas [1955] Director [Spanish]; Felix Hernandez Callejas [1958] Director [Spanish]; Peter John Cattaneo [1949] Director; Robert Leslie Holben [1946] Director; Rafael Angel Lopez Relimpio [1971] Director [Spanish]

S A Designer Parfums Limited
Incorporated: 11 April 2001 *Employees:* 58
Net Worth: £9,479,150 *Total Assets:* £38,092,696
Registered Office: Amertrans Park, Bushey Mill Lane, Watford, Herts, WD24 7JG
Activities: Wholesale of perfume and cosmetics
Parent: Shaneel Enterprises Ltd
Officers: Hitesh Bhogilal Mehta, Secretary; Dilesh Bhogilal Mehta [1960] Director; Hitesh Bhogilal Mehta [1956] Director

S A Printing Group Limited
Incorporated: 25 July 2013 *Employees:* 158
Net Worth: £3,642,000 *Total Assets:* £24,165,000
Registered Office: 1st Floor, Chilworth Point, Chilworth Road, Southampton, SO16 7JQ
Activities: Activities of production holding companies
Major Shareholder: Peter Granville Fowler
Officers: Peter Granville Fowler [1938] Director; Rory James Fowler [1971] Managing Director

S D C (Holdings) Limited
Incorporated: 26 September 1983 *Employees:* 376
Net Worth: £10,437,292 *Total Assets:* £66,188,496
Registered Office: Limegrove House, Caxton Road, Elms Farm Industrial Estate, Bedford, MK41 0QQ
Activities: Activities of construction holding companies
Parent: The SDC EBT Limited
Officers: Andrew Ronald Mitchell, Secretary; Martin Alan Lowndes [1950] Director/Accountant; Craig William Millar [1968] Director/Mechanical Engineer; Francis Peter Shiner [1959] Director/Quantity Surveyor; Gary Lloyd Wykes [1963] Director/Quantity Surveyor

S.D.C. Builders Limited
Incorporated: 26 March 1976 *Employees:* 369
Net Worth: £8,153,387 *Total Assets:* £54,579,932
Registered Office: Lime Grove House, Caxton Road, Bedford, MK41 0QQ
Activities: Construction of commercial buildings
Parent: SDC (Holdings) Limited
Officers: Andrew Ronald Mitchell, Secretary; Adam Ratliffe Knaggs [1977] Director/Construction Engineer; Martin Alan Lowndes [1950] Director/Accountant; Craig William Millar [1968] Director/Building Services; Francis Peter Shiner [1959] Director/Quantity Surveyor; Gary Lloyd Wykes [1963] Director/Quantity Surveyor

S.H.B. Hire Limited
Incorporated: 29 September 1978 *Employees:* 734
Net Worth: £58,877,072 *Total Assets:* £276,442,112
Registered Office: 18 Premier Way, Abbey Park Industrial Estate, Romsey, Hants, SO51 9DQ
Activities: Renting and leasing of cars and light motor vehicles
Parent: PJS One Limited
Officers: Sharon Grantham-Davis, Secretary; Richard Llewelyn Evans [1970] Customer Services Director; Nicola Jane Simpson [1970] Commercial Director; Michael George Street [1948] Director; Paul John Street [1973] Director/Sales & Hire Manager

S.S.S.Gears Limited
Incorporated: 1 June 1950 *Employees:* 43
Net Worth: £81,394,520 *Total Assets:* £93,697,616
Registered Office: Park Road, Sunbury on Thames, Middlesex, TW16 5BL
Activities: Other engineering activities
Parent: Synchro Clutch Company Ltd
Officers: James Michael George Neeves, Secretary/Sales Engineer; Paul Stuart Bizzill [1973] Director of Engineering; Morgan Leland Hendry [1950] Director/Engineer [American]; James Michael George Neeves [1962] Director/Sales Engineer

Saab Seaeye Limited
Incorporated: 23 May 1986 *Employees:* 147
Net Worth: £18,693,176 *Total Assets:* £21,932,248
Registered Office: 20 Brunel Way, Segensworth East, Fareham, Hants, PO15 5SD
Activities: Manufacture of other electrical equipment
Parent: Saab Seaeye Holdings Limited
Officers: Seumas Kilpatrick, Secretary; Matthew David Bates [1968] Director and Company Secretary; Timothy Broom [1965] Director; Anders Mathias Gustafsson [1986] Director/Business Controller [Swedish]; Bert Ake Johansson [1958] Sales Director Defence [Swedish]; Jon Mortimer Robertson [1974] Managing Director; Anne-Marie Vosu [1964] Director [Swedish]

SAB Australia Beverage Holdings LLP
Incorporated: 21 October 2011
Previous: Sabmiller Australia Beverage Holdings LLP
Net Worth: £1,468,490,880 *Total Assets:* £1,468,508,544
Registered Office: Ab InBev House, Church Street West, Woking, Surrey, GU21 6HT

Saba Infra Holdings UK Limited
Incorporated: 31 October 1991
Previous: Indigo Infra Holdings UK Limited
Net Worth: £14,647,520 *Total Assets:* £28,750,320
Registered Office: Oak House, Reeds Crescent, Watford, Herts, WD24 4PH
Activities: Activities of head offices
Parent: Saba Group UK Limited
Officers: Gary Charles Pickard, Secretary; Phillip David Herring [1970] Managing Director; Josep Oriol Carreras [1961] Director [Spanish]; Gary Charles Pickard [1965] Finance Director

Sabre Global Technologies Limited
Incorporated: 2 February 1995 *Employees:* 154
Previous: Sabre Europe Management Services Limited
Net Worth: £19,891,016 *Total Assets:* £108,301,144
Registered Office: 1 Church Road, Richmond, Surrey, TW9 2QE
Activities: Activities of head offices
Parent: Sabre International B.V.
Officers: Gina Nouri, Secretary; Roshan Mendis [1972] Director/Senior Vice President [Sri Lankan]; Laurence Woodhouse [1981] Director/Vice President

Sabre Insurance Company Limited
Incorporated: 19 May 1989 *Employees:* 153
Net Worth: £79,050,000 *Total Assets:* £447,563,008
Registered Office: Sabre House, 150 South Street, Dorking, Surrey, RH4 2YY
Activities: Non-life insurance
Parent: Binomial Group Limited
Officers: Anneka Samantha Kingan, Secretary; Angus Ball [1963] Director; Catherine Elizabeth Barton [1974] Director; Geoffrey Richard Carter [1969] Insurance Director; Ian Edward Clark [1960] Director; Keith John Morris [1953] Director; James Thomas Ockenden [1980] Director/Actuary; Andrew David Pomfret [1960] Director; Rebecca Ann Shelley [1965] Director; Patrick Joseph Robert Snowball [1950] Director; Trevor Neil Webb [1965] Director; Adam Richard Westwood [1983] Director/Chartered Accountant

Sabre Insurance Group PLC
Incorporated: 21 September 2017 *Employees:* 153
Net Worth: £231,992,992 *Total Assets:* £605,953,024
Registered Office: Sabre House, 150 South Street, Dorking, Surrey, RH4 2YY
Activities: Activities of financial services holding companies
Officers: Anneka Samantha Kingan, Secretary; Catherine Elizabeth Barton [1974] Director; Geoffrey Richard Carter [1969] Director/Chief Executive Officer; Ian Edward Clark [1960] Independent Non-Executive Director; Andrew David Pomfret [1960] Director; Rebecca Ann Shelley [1965] Director; Patrick Joseph Robert Snowball [1950] Director/Chairman; Adam Richard Westwood [1983] Director/Chief Financial Officer

Sabre Retail Fashion Limited
Incorporated: 23 January 2012 *Employees:* 817
Net Worth: £28,590,000 *Total Assets:* £50,532,000
Registered Office: St John's Place, Easton Street, High Wycombe, Bucks, HP11 1NL
Activities: Retail sale of clothing in specialised stores
Parent: Mustard Global Limited
Officers: Judith Anne Bean, Secretary; Lisa Agar-Rea [1968] Brand Director; Peter Wynne Davies [1949] Director; Stuart Antony Grant [1975] Director/Chief Operating Officer; Kara Eugenie Groves [1969] Director; Elizabeth Claire Houghton [1964] Director/Chief Executive

Sabroe Limited
Incorporated: 29 March 1984
Net Worth: £799,345,984 *Total Assets:* £799,350,976
Registered Office: 9-10 The Briars, Waterberry Drive, Waterlooville, Hants, PO7 7YH
Activities: Activities of head offices
Parent: Johnson Controls International PLC
Officers: Mark Ayre [1963] Director/Global Finance Project Lead; Peter Schieser [1967] Company Secretary/Director [German]

Safe Haven London
Incorporated: 11 January 2005 *Employees:* 2
Net Worth: £29,279,716 *Total Assets:* £53,576,304
Registered Office: GO5, Thorncroft Manor, Thorncroft Drive, Leatherhead, Surrey, KT22 8JB
Activities: Other letting and operating of own or leased real estate
Officers: Edward John Chesterman [1966] Director; Nicholas Francis Markham [1968] Director/Chief Operating Officer

Safenet UK Limited
Incorporated: 17 May 1988 *Employees:* 124
Net Worth: £3,237,000 *Total Assets:* £23,215,000
Registered Office: 3 Meadows Business Park, Station Approach, Blackwater, Camberley, Surrey, GU17 9AB
Activities: Other information technology service activities
Parent: Safenet Technologies B.V.
Officers: Gary Alfred Clark [1954] Sales Director; Valerie Lyon [1965] Finance Director

Safestore Acquisition Limited
Incorporated: 16 July 2003 *Employees:* 2
Net Worth: £251,432,992 *Total Assets:* £576,177,024
Registered Office: Brittanic House, Stirling Way, Borehamwood, Herts, WD6 2BT
Activities: Activities of head offices
Parent: Safestore Group Limited
Officers: Andrew Brian Jones [1966] Director/Chartered Accountant; Federico Vecchioli [1966] Director [French]

Safestore Group Limited
Incorporated: 16 July 2003 *Employees:* 2
Net Worth: £8,886,000 *Total Assets:* £543,182,976
Registered Office: Brittanic House, Stirling Way, Borehamwood, Herts, WD6 2BT
Activities: Activities of head offices
Parent: Safestore Investments Limited
Officers: Andrew Brian Jones [1966] Director/Chartered Accountant; Federico Vecchioli [1966] Director [French]

Safestore Holdings PLC
Incorporated: 8 April 2003 *Employees:* 584
Net Worth: £637,699,968 *Total Assets:* £1,156,600,064
Registered Office: Brittanic House, Stirling Way, Borehamwood, Herts, WD6 2BT
Activities: Activities of head offices
Officers: Helen Mary Bramall, Secretary; Claire Balmforth [1967] Director; Andrew Brian Jones [1966] Director/Chartered Accountant; Joanne Louise Kenrick [1966] Director; Ian Stephen Krieger [1952] Director; Alan Stuart Lewis [1952] Director/Investment Banker; William Alder Oliver [1956] Director; Federico Vecchioli [1966] Director [French]

Safestore Investments Limited
Incorporated: 23 November 2006 *Employees:* 2
Net Worth: £1,256,000 *Total Assets:* £150,000,000
Registered Office: Brittanic House, Stirling Way, Borehamwood, Herts, WD6 2BT
Activities: Activities of other holding companies n.e.c.
Parent: Safestore Holdings PLC
Officers: Andrew Brian Jones [1966] Director/Chartered Accountant; Federico Vecchioli [1966] Director [French]

Safestore Limited
Incorporated: 19 July 2005 *Employees:* 453
Net Worth: £156,804,992 *Total Assets:* £447,948,000
Registered Office: Brittanic House, Stirling Way, Borehamwood, Herts, WD6 2BT
Activities: Other letting and operating of own or leased real estate
Parent: Safestore Acquisition Limited
Officers: Andrew Brian Jones [1966] Director/Chartered Accountant; David Roy Penniston [1958] Property Director; Federico Vecchioli [1966] Director [French]

Safestore Properties Limited
Incorporated: 15 January 1996 *Employees:* 3
Net Worth: £126,238,000 *Total Assets:* £223,668,992
Registered Office: Brittanic House, Stirling Way, Borehamwood, Herts, WD6 2BT
Activities: Other letting and operating of own or leased real estate
Parent: Mentmore Limited
Officers: Andrew Brian Jones [1966] Director/Chartered Accountant; David Roy Penniston [1958] Property Director; Federico Vecchioli [1966] Director [French]

Safety-Kleen Europe Limited
Incorporated: 15 December 1998 *Employees:* 2
Net Worth: £33,205,000 *Total Assets:* £66,915,000
Registered Office: Profile West, 950 Great West Road, Brentford, Middlesex, TW8 9ES
Activities: Activities of head offices
Parent: WP SK Limited
Officers: Andrew Gregory Firth, Secretary; Andrew Patrick Griffith [1968] Director; Philippe Robert Francis Mauguy [1960] Director [French]

Safety-Kleen U.K. Limited
Incorporated: 8 November 1974 *Employees:* 551
Net Worth: £151,648,992 *Total Assets:* £164,420,000
Registered Office: Profile West, 950 Great West Road, Brentford, Middlesex, TW8 9ES
Activities: Repair of other equipment
Officers: Andrew Gregory Firth, Secretary; Mark Stephen Cawley [1971] Director; Andrew Patrick Griffith [1968] Director; Philippe Robert Francis Mauguy [1960] Director [French]

Safety-Kleen UK (Europe) Limited
Incorporated: 25 November 1998 *Employees:* 2
Net Worth: £22,381,000 *Total Assets:* £84,911,000
Registered Office: Profile West, 950 Great West Road, Brentford, Middlesex, TW8 9ES
Activities: Activities of head offices
Parent: Safety-Kleen Europe Limited
Officers: Andrew Gregory Firth, Secretary; Andrew Patrick Griffith [1968] Director; Philippe Robert Francis Mauguy [1960] Director [French]

Safetykleen Group Services Limited
Incorporated: 26 March 2008 *Employees:* 44
Net Worth Deficit: £259,104,000 *Total Assets:* £710,739,008
Registered Office: Profile West, 950 Great West Road, Brentford, Middlesex, TW8 9ES
Activities: Activities of head offices
Parent: WP Midco 3 Limited
Officers: Andrew Gregory Firth, Secretary; Andrew Gregory Firth [1964] Director/Chartered Accountant; Andrew Patrick Griffith [1968] Director; Philippe Robert Francis Mauguy [1960] Director [French]

Safran Helicopter Engines UK Limited
Incorporated: 29 November 1973 *Employees:* 169
Previous: Turbomeca UK Limited
Net Worth: £18,933,788 *Total Assets:* £53,722,556
Registered Office: Concorde Way, Segensworth, North Fareham, Hants, PO15 5RL
Activities: Manufacture of air and spacecraft and related machinery
Parent: Safran UK Ltd
Officers: Rafael Carino Almeida de Carvalho, Secretary; Rafael Carino Almeida de Carvalho [1980] Financial Director [Brazilian]; Nicholas Julian Christopher Earl [1970] Director; Olivier Le Merrer [1960] Director [French]

Saftdwin Limited
Incorporated: 8 June 1979 *Employees:* 273
Net Worth: £10,166,373 *Total Assets:* £24,902,216
Registered Office: London Road, Hatch, Basingstoke, Hants, RG24 7NZ
Activities: Sale of new cars and light motor vehicles
Major Shareholder: Brian Michael Graham Martin
Officers: John Stephen Miles, Secretary; Terence John Handley [1958] Director/Manager; Juliet Rebecca Lock [1967] Director/Manager; Brian Michael Graham Martin [1939] Director/Garage Proprietor; Sarah Louise Martin [1965] Director/Manager; John Stephen Miles [1963] Director/Financial Controller

Saga Cruises IV Limited
Incorporated: 5 October 2010
Net Worth Deficit: £2,610,000 *Total Assets:* £36,016,000
Registered Office: Enbrook Park, Sandgate, Folkestone, Kent, CT20 3SE
Activities: Sea and coastal freight water transport
Parent: Saga Cruises Limited
Officers: Victoria Haynes, Secretary; Stephen Adrian Jenkins [1967] Director; Peter Robin Shaw [1963] Director

Saga Cruises Limited
Incorporated: 24 October 1996 *Employees:* 56
Previous: Acromas Shipping Limited
Net Worth: £48,202,000 *Total Assets:* £101,972,000
Registered Office: Enbrook Park, Sandgate, Folkestone, Kent, CT20 3SE
Activities: Sea and coastal passenger water transport
Parent: ST & H Limited
Officers: Victoria Haynes, Secretary; Thomas Allan [1943] Director/International Maritime Consultant; Lance Henry Lowe Bachelor [1964] Director/Group Chief Executive; Stephen Adrian Jenkins [1967] Director; James Quin [1969] Director; Peter Robin Shaw [1963] Director

Saga Group Limited
Incorporated: 6 October 1959 *Employees:* 494
Net Worth: £954,331,008 *Total Assets:* £1,377,177,984
Registered Office: Enbrook Park, Sandgate, Folkestone, Kent, CT20 3SE
Activities: Activities of head offices
Parent: Saga Leisure Limited
Officers: Victoria Haynes, Secretary; Lance Henry Lowe Bachelor [1964] Director/Group Chief Executive; David Moore [1981] Director; James Quin [1969] Director

Saga Mid Co Limited
Incorporated: 5 December 2013
Net Worth: £772,264,000 *Total Assets:* £2,102,734,976
Registered Office: Enbrook Park, Sandgate, Folkestone, Kent, CT20 3SE
Activities: Dormant company
Parent: Saga PLC
Officers: Victoria Haynes, Secretary; Lance Henry Lowe Bachelor [1964] Director/Group Chief Executive; David Moore [1981] Director; James Quin [1969] Director

Saga Personal Finance Limited
Incorporated: 17 February 1995 *Employees:* 27
Previous: Acromas Financial Services Limited
Net Worth: £29,375,000 *Total Assets:* £30,046,000
Registered Office: Enbrook Park, Sandgate, Folkestone, Kent, CT20 3SE
Activities: Financial intermediation not elsewhere classified
Parent: Saga Group Limited
Officers: Victoria Haynes, Secretary; Lance Henry Lowe Bachelor [1964] Director/Group Chief Executive; Jeff Bromage [1973] Director; Gary Duggan [1961] Director; Clifton Adrian Melvin [1954] Director/Actuary; James Quin [1969] Director

Saga PLC
Incorporated: 5 December 2013 *Employees:* 5,329
Net Worth: £1,223,500,032 *Total Assets:* £2,643,800,064
Registered Office: Enbrook Park, Sandgate, Folkestone, Kent, CT20 3SE
Activities: Activities of head offices
Officers: Victoria Haynes, Secretary; Lance Henry Lowe Bachelor [1964] Director/Group Chief Executive; Eva Kristina Eisenschimmel [1962] Director [British/Austrian]; Julie Hopes [1968] Director; Raymond King [1953] Director; Orna Gabrielle Ni-Chionna [1956] Director [Irish]; Patrick O'Sullivan [1949] Director [Irish]; James Quin [1969] Director; Gareth Williams [1953] Non-Executive Director

Saga Services Limited
Incorporated: 15 August 1962 *Employees:* 1,766
Net Worth: £232,214,000 *Total Assets:* £430,273,984
Registered Office: Enbrook Park, Sandgate, Folkestone, Kent, CT20 3SE
Activities: Activities of insurance agents and brokers
Parent: Saga Group Limited
Officers: Victoria Haynes, Secretary; Lance Henry Lowe Bachelor [1964] Director/Group Chief Executive; Gary Duggan [1961] Director; John Edwards [1955] Director; Julie Hopes [1968] Director; Clifton Adrian Melvin [1954] Director/Actuary; James Quin [1969] Director

SAI Global CIS UK Limited
Incorporated: 3 November 2010 *Employees:* 3
Net Worth Deficit: £3,761,697 *Total Assets:* £26,484,280
Registered Office: Partis House, Davy Avenue, Knowlhill, Milton Keynes, Bucks, MK5 8HJ
Activities: Activities of head offices
Officers: Hean Siew, Secretary; Kim Jenkins [1966] Commercial Director [Australian]; Tracy Elaine Roskell [1966] Finance Director

Sailtown Limited
Incorporated: 21 October 2004
Net Worth: £908,083,584 *Total Assets:* £908,083,584
Registered Office: Hanson House, 14 Castle Hill, Maidenhead, Berks, SL6 4JJ
Activities: Activities of head offices
Parent: Shapedirect Limited
Officers: Wendy Fiona Rogers, Secretary; Nicholas Arthur Dawe Benning-Prince [1974] Director/Chartered Accountant; Robert Charles Dowley [1972] Director/Chartered Accountant; Edward Alexander Gretton [1970] Director; Dr Carsten Matthias Wendt [1976] Director [German]

Saipem Limited
Incorporated: 18 March 2010 *Employees:* 596
Net Worth: £146,761,664 *Total Assets:* £251,528,448
Registered Office: Saipem House, 12-42 Wood Street, Kingston upon Thames, Surrey, KT1 1TG
Activities: Other construction installation
Officers: Lisa Cooper, Secretary; Paolo Formica [1967] Managing Director [Italian]; Massimiliano Guerra [1967] Director [Italian]; Dominique Jean Seng [1957] Director/Chairman [French]

Salaft Properties Limited
Incorporated: 15 May 1959 *Employees:* 5
Net Worth: £57,556,992 *Total Assets:* £79,544,768
Registered Office: Aissela, 46 High Street, Esher, Surrey, KT10 9QY
Activities: Development of building projects
Shareholders: Russell Gavin Baum; Lincoln Fraser Small
Officers: Lincoln Fraser Small, Secretary; Abigail Sarah Baum [1970] Director/PA; Russell Gavin Baum [1970] Director/Accountant; Suzanne Ferreira [1976] Director; Lincoln Fraser Small [1944] Director

Salisbury Holdings Limited
Incorporated: 11 March 2014 *Employees:* 407
Net Worth: £11,356,000 *Total Assets:* £22,835,000
Registered Office: Cambridge House, 47 Clarendon Road, Watford, Herts, WD17 1HP
Activities: Combined facilities support activities
Officers: Michael Anthony Wilson, Secretary; Simon David Ainslie Jones [1970] Director/Chief Financial Officer; Mark Julian Smith [1970] Director; Edward Michael Swales [1979] Director; Michael Anthony Wilson [1956] Director/Solicitor

Salisbury Workplace Services Limited
Incorporated: 6 March 2012 *Employees:* 137
Previous: Salisbury FM Limited
Net Worth: £10,552,000 *Total Assets:* £21,566,000
Registered Office: Cambridge House, Clarendon Road, Watford, Herts, WD17 1HP
Activities: Combined facilities support activities
Parent: Salisbury Holdings Limited
Officers: Michael Anthony Wilson, Secretary; Simon David Ainslie Jones [1970] Director/Chief Financial Officer; Mark Julian Smith [1970] Director; Edward Michael Swales [1979] Director; Michael Anthony Wilson [1956] Director/Solicitor

Sally Salon Services Limited
Incorporated: 7 July 1972 *Employees:* 1,712
Net Worth: £41,906,000 *Total Assets:* £88,778,000
Registered Office: Inspired, Ground Floor, Easthampstead Road, Bracknell, Berks, RG12 1YQ
Activities: Other retail sale of new goods in specialised stores (not commercial art galleries and opticians)
Parent: Sally UK Holdings Limited
Officers: Nina Azemoudeh, Secretary; Olivier Badezet [1969] Managing Director (Senior VP) [French]; Warren Peter Scarr [1966] Managing Director; Heidi Van Ocken [1968] Director [Belgian]

Sally UK Holdings Limited
Incorporated: 5 June 2006
Net Worth: £235,390,336 *Total Assets:* £334,478,560
Registered Office: Ground Floor, Inspired, Easthampstead Road, Bracknell, Berks, RG12 1YQ
Activities: Activities of other holding companies n.e.c.
Parent: Sally Beauty Holdings, Inc
Officers: Nina Azemoudeh, Secretary; Olivier Badezet [1969] Managing Director (Senior VP) [French]; Warren Peter Scarr [1966] Managing Director; Heidi Van Ocken [1968] Director [Belgian]

The Salterns Academy Trust
Incorporated: 4 March 2014 *Employees:* 254
Net Worth: £22,287,656 *Total Assets:* £26,521,170
Registered Office: Admiral Lord Nelson School, Dundas Lane, Portsmouth, PO3 5XT
Activities: General secondary education
Officers: Amanda Barrett [1971] Director/Academy Regional Officer; Claire Copeland [1979] Director/Headteacher; Andrew Martin Cree [1965] Director/Royal Navy; Felicia Jane Beatrix Drummond [1962] Director; Nysrene Hardingham [1967] Director/Headteacher; Paul Hayes [1956] Director/Pro Vice Chancellor; Steven Labedz [1957] Director/Executive Headteacher; Tania Louise Osborne [1965] Director/Civil Servant; Maria Louise Phillips [1968] Director/Business Manager

Salutem LD Bidco Limited
Incorporated: 23 February 2017 *Employees:* 948
Net Worth Deficit: £6,668,000 *Total Assets:* £54,990,000
Registered Office: Minton Place, Victoria Street, Windsor, Berks, SL4 1EG
Activities: Residential care activities for learning difficulties, mental health and substance abuse
Parent: Salutem LD Topco Limited
Officers: John Steven Godden [1965] Director; Kenneth James Gribben Hillen [1956] Director; Paul Raymond Lawes [1973] Director/Chief Finance Officer; Ian Bertrand Morle [1951] Director

Samsung C & T U.K. Limited
Incorporated: 24 June 1975 *Employees:* 14
Net Worth: £9,280,000 *Total Assets:* £27,098,000
Registered Office: 5th Floor, Profile West, 950 Great West Road, Brentford, Middlesex, TW8 9ES
Activities: Non-specialised wholesale trade
Officers: DOO Yul Lee [1976] Director [South Korean]; Hyun Suk Lee [1973] Director

Samsung Electronics (UK) Limited
Incorporated: 28 July 1995 *Employees:* 1,129
Net Worth: £361,736,000 *Total Assets:* £1,121,426,048
Registered Office: Samsung House, 1000 Hillswood Drive, Chertsey, Surrey, KT16 0PS
Activities: Manufacture of consumer electronics
Parent: Samsung Electronics Co. Limited
Officers: Sung Wuk Kang, Secretary; Sung Wuk Kang [1971] Director [South Korean]; Taekwan Kim [1965] Director/European CFO [South Korean]

Samsung SDS Europe Limited
Incorporated: 30 March 2000 *Employees:* 286
Net Worth: £80,362,000 *Total Assets:* £100,519,000
Registered Office: 1st Floor, No 5 The Heights, Brooklands, Weybridge, Surrey, KT13 0NY
Activities: Data processing, hosting and related activities
Officers: Jong Cheel Im, Secretary; Jongcheel Im [1968] Managing Director [South Korean]; Dong Kyu Kim [1982] Director [South Korean]

Samsung Semiconductor Europe Limited
Incorporated: 3 March 1997
Net Worth: £61,102,300 *Total Assets:* £61,102,300
Registered Office: 1st Floor, No 5 The Heights, Brooklands, Weybridge, Surrey, KT13 0NY
Activities: Manufacture of other electrical equipment
Officers: Dermot John Ryan [1962] Director/Company President [Irish]

Sanden International (Europe) Limited
Incorporated: 25 June 1979 *Employees:* 223
Net Worth: £72,561,760 *Total Assets:* £389,180,896
Registered Office: Rosewood, Crockford Lane, Chineham Park, Chineham, Basingstoke, Hants, RG24 8UT
Activities: Wholesale trade of motor vehicle parts and accessories
Parent: Sanden Holdings Corporation
Officers: Douglas Alexander Black, Secretary; Douglas Alexander Black [1959] Director/Accountant; Olivier Campy [1971] Director/COO - Environmental Solutions [French]; Tsuguo Ito [1956] Director [Japanese]; Norio Kamikura [1960] Director [Japanese]; Edwin Koller [1954] Director [German]; Junya Takahashi [1969] Director/Business Executive [Japanese]; Maria Wuensch-Guaraldi [1967] Managing Director & COO - Automotive Division [German]

Thomas Sanderson Limited
Incorporated: 2 January 2003 *Employees:* 309
Net Worth: £21,560,000 *Total Assets:* £28,285,000
Registered Office: 7 Waterberry Drive, Waterlooville, Hants, PO7 7UW
Activities: Other manufacturing n.e.c.
Parent: Hunter Douglas (UK) Limited
Officers: Adrianus Kuiper [1960] Director [Dutch]; John Risman [1965] Director; Andrew Richard Thomas [1972] Director

Sandown Surrey and Hampshire Limited
Incorporated: 6 February 1995 *Employees:* 201
Net Worth: £8,712,000 *Total Assets:* £56,138,000
Registered Office: Edison Road, Houndmills, Basingstoke, Hants, RG21 6YH
Activities: Sale of new cars and light motor vehicles
Parent: Selenac Holdings Limited
Officers: Gareth Robert Copling, Secretary; Gareth Robert Copling [1967] Director; Gavin Alan McAllister [1981] Director

Sandoz Limited
Incorporated: 24 February 1981 *Employees:* 119
Net Worth: £10,852,000 *Total Assets:* £47,303,000
Registered Office: Frimley Business Park, Frimley, Camberley, Surrey, GU16 7SR
Activities: Manufacture of basic pharmaceutical products
Shareholder: Novartis AG
Officers: Rebecca Ann Weston, Secretary; Haseeb Ahmad [1976] Director/CPO Head; Francesco Balestrieri [1969] Director/Head Sandoz Region Europe [Italian]; Timothy Charles de Gavre [1974] Director; Oriane Fanny Lacaze [1979] Director/Country Chief Financial Officer [French]

Sands Heritage Ltd
Incorporated: 19 June 2014 *Employees:* 209
Net Worth: £22,474,064 *Total Assets:* £24,397,516
Registered Office: 49 Marine Terrace, Margate, Kent, CT9 1XJ
Activities: Activities of amusement parks and theme parks
Officers: Aidan Whiteman de Brunner [1972] Director; Anastasia Giannakou [1972] Director [Greek]; Andrew Trowbridge [1971] Director

Sangers (Maidstone) Limited
Incorporated: 16 October 1979 *Employees:* 161
Net Worth: £23,646,672 *Total Assets:* £29,492,576
Registered Office: Parkwood, Sutton Road, Maidstone, Kent, ME15 9NE
Activities: Wholesale of pharmaceutical goods
Parent: Paydens Limited
Officers: John Patrick McConville [1959] Director; Alexander George Pay [1984] Managing Director; Dennis Charles Pay [1942] Director

Sanlam Private Investments (UK) Holdings Ltd
Incorporated: 10 January 2008 *Employees:* 11
Net Worth: £24,238,000 *Total Assets:* £31,809,000
Registered Office: 16 South Park, Sevenoaks, Kent, TN13 1AN
Activities: Activities of head offices
Parent: Sanlam UK Limited
Officers: Jeremy Paul Gibson, Secretary; Jeremy Paul Gibson [1973] Finance Director; David John Mason [1971] Director/Group Chief Operating Officer; Jonathan Charles Polin [1959] Director/Chief Executive Officer; John David White [1966] Director/CEO Wealth Management

Sanlam Private Investments (UK) Ltd
Incorporated: 29 July 1986
Net Worth: £14,550,000 *Total Assets:* £22,966,000
Registered Office: 16 South Park, Sevenoaks, Kent, TN13 1AN
Activities: Fund management activities
Parent: Sanlam Private Investments (UK) Holdings Limited
Officers: Jeremy Paul Gibson, Secretary; Jeremy Paul Gibson [1973] Director/Group Chief Financial Officer; David John Mason [1971] Director/Group COO; Jonathan Charles Polin [1959] Director/Chief Executive Officer; John David White [1966] Director/CEO Wealth Management

Sanofi Pasteur Holding Limited
Incorporated: 19 October 1993
Net Worth: £183,342,000 *Total Assets:* £188,395,008
Registered Office: One Onslow Street, Guildford, Surrey, GU1 4YS
Activities: Activities of other holding companies n.e.c.
Parent: Sanofi
Officers: Francois-Xavier Duhalde [1965] Director/Chief Financial Officer [French]; Hugo Rupert Alexander Fry [1970] Director/UK Country Chair

Sanofi-Aventis UK Holdings Limited
Incorporated: 24 May 1996
Net Worth: £285,796,992 *Total Assets:* £2,259,814,912
Registered Office: One Onslow Street, Guildford, Surrey, GU1 4YS
Activities: Activities of other holding companies n.e.c.
Shareholders: Sanofi-Synthelabo UK Limited; Aventis Pharma Holdings Limited
Officers: Francois-Xavier Duhalde [1965] Director/Chief Financial Officer [French]; Hugo Rupert Alexander Fry [1970] Director/UK Country Chair

Sanofi-Synthelabo UK Limited
Incorporated: 16 May 1961 *Employees:* 1
Net Worth: £204,998,000 *Total Assets:* £204,998,000
Registered Office: One Onslow Street, Guildford, Surrey, GU1 4YS
Activities: Activities of other holding companies n.e.c.
Parent: Sanofi
Officers: Francois-Xavier Duhalde [1965] Director/Chief Financial Officer [French]; Hugo Rupert Alexander Fry [1970] Director/UK Country Chair

Santander Consumer (UK) PLC
Incorporated: 27 April 1988 *Employees:* 558
Net Worth: £536,832,000 *Total Assets:* £7,537,210,880
Registered Office: Santander House, 86 Station Road, Redhill, Surrey, RH1 1SR
Activities: Financial leasing
Parent: Santander UK PLC
Officers: Javier Anton San Pablo [1968] Director/Economist [Spanish]; Reza Attar-Zadeh [1972] Director; Adam Roy Goldhagen [1964] Director; Victor Thomas Hill [1964] Director; Bruno Montalvo Wilmot [1962] Director [Spanish]; Diane Elisabeth Roberts [1959] Director/Chartered Accountant; Mark Elliott Staveley [1963] Director

SAP (UK) Limited
Incorporated: 31 July 1987 *Employees:* 1,567
Net Worth Deficit: £24,664,000 *Total Assets:* £431,924,000
Registered Office: Clockhouse Place, Bedfont Road, Feltham, Middlesex, TW14 8HD
Activities: Other software publishing
Parent: SAP SE
Officers: Jens Claus Amail [1967] Managing Director [German]; Yu-Ho Cheung [1970] Director/General Counsel; Peter David [1965] Director/Financial Officer [German]; Renaud Valery Heyd [1972] Director/Chief Financial Officer [French]

SAS Holdings Limited
Incorporated: 7 February 1983 *Employees:* 789
Net Worth: £58,154,000 *Total Assets:* £82,320,000
Registered Office: 28 Sutton Park Avenue, Earley, Reading, Berks, RG6 1AZ
Activities: Manufacture of metal structures and parts of structures
Officers: Brigid Sarah Matthews, Secretary; Roderick Craig Altman [1962] Director; Hew Edward Ogilvy Balfour [1952] Director; Alyn Huw Gammon [1970] Director/Accountant; Edward Anthony McElhinney [1943] Director/Ceiling & Lighting Consultant [Irish]; Siobhan Johanna McElhinney [1973] Director; Gary McRae [1960] Director; Phillip John Smith [1977] Sales & Marketing Director

SAS International Limited
Incorporated: 18 July 1994 *Employees:* 759
Net Worth: £51,864,000 *Total Assets:* £80,366,000
Registered Office: 28 Sutton Park Avenue, Reading, Berks, RG6 1AZ
Activities: Manufacture of other fabricated metal products n.e.c.
Parent: SAS Holdings Ltd
Officers: Brigid Sarah Matthews, Secretary; Roderick Craig Altman [1962] Director; Elizabeth Ann Fisher [1959] General Manager Director; Alyn Huw Gammon [1970] Director; Rikky Charles Lenney [1957] Construction Director; Tracy Mason [1971] HR Director; Christopher Powell [1963] Operations Director; Phillip John Smith [1977] Sales Director; Richard Lyndon White [1962] Director/Designer

SAS Software Limited
Incorporated: 8 June 1977 *Employees:* 664
Net Worth: £8,621,672 *Total Assets:* £128,887,496
Registered Office: Wittington House, Henley Road, Medmenham, Marlow, Bucks, SL7 2EB
Activities: Business and domestic software development
Officers: James Allan Elliott, Secretary; Donald Ray Parker [1959] Director/Business Executive [American]

Sauvello Limited
Incorporated: 4 November 2016 *Employees:* 2
Net Worth Deficit: £265,829 *Total Assets:* £27,625,672
Registered Office: Rosebank, Claremont Park Road, Esher, Surrey, KT10 9LT
Activities: Activities of open-ended investment companies
Shareholders: Ross William Snape; Lisa Search
Officers: Lisa Snape [1965] Director; Ross William Snape [1964] Director

Saxon Weald Capital PLC
Incorporated: 30 April 2012
Net Worth: £50,000 *Total Assets:* £224,572,000
Registered Office: Saxon Weald House, 38-42 Worthing Road, Horsham, W Sussex, RH12 1DT
Activities: Other credit granting n.e.c.
Parent: Saxon Weald Homes Limited
Officers: Norman Edwin Hill, Secretary; Steven Dennis [1963] Director/Chief Executive; Norman Edwin Hill [1961] Finance Director; Simon Ross Turpitt [1949] Director/Consultant; Stephanie Jane White [1963] Director/Business Consultant

Saywell International Limited
Incorporated: 6 March 1957 *Employees:* 71
Net Worth: £20,882,728 *Total Assets:* £53,995,216
Registered Office: Aviation Centre, Downlands Business Park, Lyons Way, Worthing, W Sussex, BN14 9LA
Activities: Service activities incidental to air transportation
Major Shareholder: Peter Leonard Saywell
Officers: Heather Anne Edmonds, Secretary; Margaret Ellen Saywell [1948] Director; Peter Leonard Saywell [1945] Managing Director; Sunil Sutaria [1968] Director; Russell Tudor [1973] Director

SC Johnson Ltd
Incorporated: 22 February 2001 *Employees:* 43
Net Worth: £53,980,000 *Total Assets:* £76,456,000
Registered Office: Frimley Green, Camberley, Surrey, GU16 7AJ
Activities: Manufacture of cleaning and polishing preparations
Parent: Johnson Wax Limited
Officers: John Michael Hayes, Secretary; Luciana Abreu [1973] Director/General Manager [Brazilian]; John Michael Hayes [1958] Finance Director; Thomas Patrick Howard [1967] Director/Tax Counsel [American]

SC Leisure Group Limited
Incorporated: 11 May 1960
Net Worth: £166,655,008 *Total Assets:* £168,168,992
Registered Office: Broadwater Park, Denham, Bucks, UB9 5HR
Activities: Other service activities n.e.c.
Parent: Six Continents Investments Limited
Officers: Fiona Cuttell, Secretary; Michael Jon Cockcroft [1974] Director/Accountant; Michael Todd Glover [1971] Director/Financial Controller [American]; Nicolette Henfrey [1969] Director

SC Osney Lane Limited
Incorporated: 4 September 2014 *Employees:* 1
Net Worth: £9,204,886 *Total Assets:* £55,449,400
Registered Office: Kintyre House, 70 High Street, Fareham, Hants, PO16 7BB
Activities: Development of building projects
Parent: Student Castle Limited
Officers: Sam Dance, Secretary; Richard Ainsworth [1966] Director; Charles Edward Cade [1969] Director; Sam Dance [1981] Director; Jacqueline Rebecca Hawthorn [1964] Director

SC Walmgate Limited
Incorporated: 26 April 2012
Net Worth: £29,795,288 *Total Assets:* £91,441,480
Registered Office: 70 High Street, Fareham, Hants, PO16 7BB
Activities: Construction of domestic buildings
Parent: Student Castle Developments Limited
Officers: Sam Dance, Secretary; Richard Ainsworth [1966] Director; Charles Edward Cade [1969] Director; Sam Dance [1981] Director; Jacqueline Rebecca Hawthorn [1964] Director

Scancem Recovery Limited
Incorporated: 18 May 1998
Net Worth: £17,036,000 *Total Assets:* £31,595,000
Registered Office: Hanson House, 14 Castle Hill, Maidenhead, Berks, SL6 4JJ
Activities: Activities of other holding companies n.e.c.
Parent: Scancem Energy and Recovery Limited
Officers: Wendy Fiona Rogers, Secretary; Nicholas Arthur Dawe Benning-Prince [1974] Director/Chartered Accountant; Robert Charles Dowley [1972] Director/Chartered Accountant; Edward Alexander Gretton [1970] Director; Dr Carsten Matthias Wendt [1976] Director [German]

Scandinavian Tobacco Group United Kingdom Limited
Incorporated: 25 July 1913 *Employees:* 31
Net Worth: £19,238,708 *Total Assets:* £25,105,782
Registered Office: 1st Floor, West Wing, Davidson House, Forbury Square, Reading, Berks, RG1 3EU
Activities: Wholesale of tobacco products
Parent: Scandinavian Tobacco Group A/S
Officers: Morten Ostergard Guldager [1969] Director/Senior Vice President Global Financial Processes [Danish]; Jurjan Wybe Klep [1971] Director/Senior Vice President Machine Made Cigars [Dutch]; Alastair Hamilton Williams [1970] Country Director UK

Scania (Great Britain) Limited
Incorporated: 14 December 1964 *Employees:* 1,687
Net Worth: £48,784,000 *Total Assets:* £692,945,984
Registered Office: Delaware Drive, Tongwell, Milton Keynes, Bucks, MK15 8HB
Activities: Sale of other motor vehicles
Parent: Volkswagen Aktiengesellschaft
Officers: Richard Kevin Gray, Secretary; Urban Birger Erdtman [1945] Director [Swedish]; Martin Hay [1965] Managing Director; Roger McCarthy [1951] Director; Carl Johan Martin Stahlberg [1964] Director [Swedish]; Per Anders Williamsson [1969] Director [Swedish]

Scape Opportunities Dublin Limited
Incorporated: 22 October 2015
Net Worth Deficit: £599,205 *Total Assets:* £20,804,240
Registered Office: Munro House, Portsmouth Road, Cobham, Surrey, KT11 1PP
Activities: Other business support service activities n.e.c.
Shareholder: Nigel Duncan Taee
Officers: Ronan Niall Kierans [1978] Director [Irish]; Nigel Duncan Taee [1961] Director; Thomas Ward [1978] Director

SCCI Group Limited
Incorporated: 7 February 2007 *Employees:* 429
Net Worth: £2,629,264 *Total Assets:* £30,145,584
Registered Office: The Pavilion, Botleigh Grange Business Park, Hedge End, Southampton, SO30 2AF
Activities: Other professional, scientific and technical activities n.e.c.
Parent: Lonepiper Limited
Officers: Paul William Dellow [1974] Finance Director; David Jason Fogelman [1970] Director; Louise Jane Hutchings [1972] HR Director; Hugo Duncan Thomas Torquil MacKenzie Smith [1972] Director; Robert Charles Wickings [1965] Director/Engineer

Scentrics Information Security Technologies Limited
Incorporated: 19 March 2008 *Employees:* 4
Net Worth: £405,525,984 *Total Assets:* £505,965,952
Registered Office: 238 Station Road, Addlestone, Surrey, KT15 2PS
Activities: Information technology consultancy activities
Officers: Guruparan Chandrasekaran [1967] Director/Business Executive; Jerome Jehan Mohamed [1975] Director/Consultant; Phillip John Price [1952] Director/Business Executive; David Edward Svendsen [1948] Director [Australian]

Henry Schein UK Finance Limited
Incorporated: 25 June 1998
Net Worth: £21,607,340 *Total Assets:* £78,904,512
Registered Office: Medcare House, Centurion Close, Gillingham Business Park, Gillingham, Kent, ME8 0SB
Activities: Activities of other holding companies n.e.c.
Officers: Paul David Brownridge, Secretary; Patrick Thompson Allen [1966] Managing Director; Adrian Spencer Martin [1969] Director; Robert Nathan Minowitz [1958] Director [American]; Helen Louise Redding [1975] Director/Chief Financial Officer; Graham Barry Stanley [1968] Director

The Schelwood Trust
Incorporated: 6 January 2012 *Employees:* 200
Previous: Herschel Grammar School
Net Worth: £51,581,464 *Total Assets:* £54,801,880
Registered Office: Herschel Grammar School, Northampton Avenue, Slough, Berks, SL1 3BW
Activities: General secondary education
Officers: Judith Vucic, Secretary; Wendy Susan Barnett [1962] Director/Self Employed; Kathleen Mary Higgins [1962] Director/Headteacher; Krishnakanth Iyer [1979] Director/Certified Chartered Accountant; Jonathan McNaughton Reekie [1940] Director/Retired; Robert Sinclair Robertson [1951] Director; Joanne Rockall [1967] Director/Headteacher; Paul Edmund Rowley [1946] Director/Consultant; Salima Begum Shariff [1975] Director/Human Resources

Schenker Limited
Incorporated: 16 November 1943 *Employees:* 624
Net Worth: £12,137,000 *Total Assets:* £68,653,000
Registered Office: Schenker House, Unit 3 LHR Portal, Scylla Road, London Heathrow Airport, Hounslow, Middlesex, TW6 3FE
Activities: Freight transport by road
Parent: DB (UK) Investments Ltd
Officers: Declan Joseph Byrne, Secretary; Declan Joseph Byrne [1967] Finance Director [Irish]; Doug John Coull [1956] Air Product Director UK & Ireland; Steve Cuddeford [1965] Director; Julie Heard [1969] Sales Director UK & Ireland; Ray Hennessy [1961] Director/Chief Executive Officer [Irish]; Adrian Mark Jennings [1970] Ocean Product Director UK & Ireland; Deborah Jane Mansfield [1971] HR Director

Schindler Ltd.
Incorporated: 21 June 1960 *Employees:* 734
Net Worth: £27,782,000 *Total Assets:* £92,323,000
Registered Office: 205 Brooklands Road, Weybridge, Surrey, KT13 0BG
Activities: Manufacture of other special-purpose machinery n.e.c.
Officers: Frederik Jacobus Van Rensburg Wepener, Secretary; Aldo Braccetti [1961] Managing Director [Italian]; Frederik Jacobus Van Rensburg Wepener [1975] Director/Chief Financial Officer

Schlumberger Cambridge Research Limited
Incorporated: 12 June 1958 *Employees:* 128
Net Worth: £13,232,000 *Total Assets:* £31,375,000
Registered Office: Schlumberger House, Buckingham Gate, Gatwick Airport, W Sussex, RH6 0NZ
Activities: Other business support service activities n.e.c.
Shareholders: Schlumberger Oilfield UK PLC; Schlumberger Oilfield UK PLC
Officers: Simon Smoker, Secretary; David Marsh [1962] Director/Chartered Accountant; Simon Smoker [1962] Director/Accountant; Gokturk Tunc [1976] Director/Well Construction Platform Manager [American]

Schlumberger Oilfield UK PLC
Incorporated: 9 February 2001 *Employees:* 2,149
Net Worth: £1,398,146,048 *Total Assets:* £3,935,472,128
Registered Office: Schlumberger House, Buckingham Gate, Gatwick Airport, W Sussex, RH6 0NZ
Activities: Activities of head offices
Parent: Schlumberger Public Limited Company
Officers: Simon Smoker, Secretary; Gwenola Jacqueline Stephanie Boyault [1972] Director/Geologist [French]; Patrice Hellouin de Cenival [1961] Director/SIS Segment Controller [French]; Gillian Gordon [1957] Director/HR Manager UK; Manuel Alejandro Guedez [1977] Director/Finance Controller [Italian]; David Marsh [1962] Director/Chartered Accountant; Brian Laurence McBeath [1970] Regional HSE Director; Catherine McCandless [1971] Director/Center Manager; Simon Smoker [1962] Director/Accountant

Schlumberger Public Limited Company
Incorporated: 30 September 1977 *Employees:* 6
Net Worth: £1,731,524,992 *Total Assets:* £1,876,827,008
Registered Office: Schlumberger House, Buckingham Gate, Gatwick Airport, W Sussex, RH6 0NZ
Activities: Activities of head offices
Parent: Schlumberger UK Limited
Officers: Simon Smoker, Secretary; Gillian Gordon [1957] Director/HR Manager UK; David Marsh [1962] Director/Chartered Accountant; Simon Smoker [1962] Director/Accountant

Schlumberger UK Limited
Incorporated: 13 September 2010
Net Worth: £1,237,894,016 *Total Assets:* £1,978,862,976
Registered Office: Schlumberger House, Buckingham Gate, Gatwick Airport, W Sussex, RH6 0NZ
Activities: Activities of head offices
Parent: Schlumberger Limited
Officers: Simon Smoker, Secretary; Gillian Gordon [1957] Director/HR Manager UK; David Marsh [1962] Director/Chartered Accountant; Simon Smoker [1962] Director/Accountant

Scholl Limited
Incorporated: 20 May 1985
Net Worth: £118,437,000 *Total Assets:* £322,296,992
Registered Office: 103-105 Bath Road, Slough, Berks, SL1 3UH
Activities: Activities of other holding companies n.e.c.
Parent: London International Group Limited
Officers: Christine Anne-Marie Logan, Secretary; Richard Mark Greensmith [1973] Group Tax Director; Simon Andrew Neville [1957] Group Treasury Director; Jonathan Timmis [1975] Finance Director

Schoolsworks Academy Trust
Incorporated: 23 February 2012 *Employees:* 398
Net Worth: £33,398,000 *Total Assets:* £37,177,000
Registered Office: 23 Connaught Road, Littlehampton, W Sussex, BN17 6ER
Activities: Primary education
Officers: Frances Louise Pope, Secretary; Stuart Collins [1974] Director/Transport Provision Manager; Adam Hackett [1950] Director/Retired; Susan Hawthorn [1956] Director; Dr Paul Mervyn Jones [1963] Director/Headteacher; Norman Hunter Rose [1949] Director/Managing Partner; Christopher Mark Seaton [1962] Director/Company Secretary; Stella Turner [1959] Director/Retired; Nicholas Jesse White [1963] Director/Headteacher; Catherine Elizabeth Williams [1959] Director/Headteacher

Schueco UK Limited
Incorporated: 19 October 2009 *Employees:* 142
Net Worth: £28,952,000 *Total Assets:* £36,897,000
Registered Office: Whitehall Avenue, Kingston, Milton Keynes, Bucks, MK10 0AL
Activities: Wholesale of other machinery and equipment
Officers: David Dees, Secretary; Andreas Engelhardt [1960] Director [German]; Thomas Stefan Humpf [1965] Director [German]; Herr Philipp Caspar Alfred Hubertus Neuhaus [1965] Director [German]; Michael John Simpson Lane [1968] Managing Director

Schweppes Limited
Incorporated: 6 November 1958
Net Worth: £389,079,008 *Total Assets:* £389,079,008
Registered Office: Cadbury House, Sanderson Road, Uxbridge, Middlesex, UB8 1DH
Activities: Activities of head offices
Parent: Mondelez International, Inc
Officers: Adrian John Paul Arrighi [1978] Tax Director; Michael Brendan Foye [1965] Treasury Director; John Michael Hladusz [1972] Director/Chartered Accountant; Carole Noelle Keene [1966] Director

Science, Engineering and Manufacturing Technologies Alliance
Incorporated: 5 December 1988
Net Worth: £29,402,000 *Total Assets:* £35,358,000
Registered Office: Unit 2 The Orient Centre, Greycaine Road, Watford, Herts, WD24 7GP
Activities: Technical and vocational secondary education
Officers: Andrew Stephen McLachrie, Secretary; Paul Adrian Birt [1961] HR Director; Karen Boswell [1963] Managing Director; Michael James Evans [1963] Managing Director; Dame Judith Elizabeth Hackitt [1954] Director/Chair; Selma Hunter [1964] Director; Jose Luis Martins Dos Santos Lopes [1964] Director/Manager Product Development; Indro Mario Mukerjee [1960] Director/Chief Executive Officer; Sharron Alexandra Pamplin [1969] Director/HR; Sarah Louise Sandle [1969] Director/VP Strategy; Mark Ian Tarry [1971] Director/Accountant; Ian Waddell [1965] Director/National Officer of Unite

SCIH Branston 3
Incorporated: 9 August 2002
Net Worth: £1,545,063,040 *Total Assets:* £1,545,536,000
Registered Office: Broadwater Park, Denham, Bucks, UB9 5HR
Activities: Activities of head offices
Shareholder: Six Continents Limited
Officers: Fiona Jane Littlebury-Cuttell, Secretary; Michael Jon Cockcroft [1974] Director/Accountant; Michael Todd Glover [1971] Director/Financial Controller [American]; Nicolette Henfrey [1969] Director

SCJ EurAFNE Ltd
Incorporated: 22 February 2001 *Employees:* 295
Net Worth: £62,720,000 *Total Assets:* £66,510,000
Registered Office: Frimley Green, Camberley, Surrey, GU16 7AJ
Activities: Other business support service activities n.e.c.
Parent: Johnson Wax Limited
Officers: John Michael Hayes, Secretary; Luciana Abreu [1973] Director/General Manager [Brazilian]; John Michael Hayes [1958] Finance Director; Thomas Patrick Howard [1967] Director/Tax Counsel [American]

SCJ UK Finco Ltd
Incorporated: 12 February 2015 *Employees:* 754
Net Worth: £212,403,008 *Total Assets:* £960,801,024
Registered Office: Frimley Green, Camberley, Surrey, GU16 7AJ
Activities: Other business support service activities n.e.c.
Officers: Audrey Sue Ditter [1962] Director/Corporate Finance Officer [American]; Thomas Patrick Howard [1967] Director/Lawyer [American]

Scotia Gas Networks Limited
Incorporated: 10 November 2003 *Employees:* 3,821
Net Worth: £696,400,000 *Total Assets:* £7,328,300,032
Registered Office: St Lawrence House, Station Approach, Horley, Surrey, RH6 9HJ
Activities: Activities of head offices
Shareholder: SSE PLC
Officers: Nicola Anne Shand, Secretary; Fraser McGregor Alexander [1963] Director/Chartered Accountant; Charlotte Louise Brunning [1986] Director/Investment Management; Natalie Michaela Flageul [1975] Director/Head of Metering; Ines Grund [1978] Director/Investment Professional [German]; Guy Lambert [1977] Director/Investments, Head of Utilities [Dutch]; Alejandro Lopez Delgado [1977] Director [Spanish]; Robert McDonald [1971] Director of Regulation; John James McManus [1959] Director/Investment Manager [Canadian]; Mariana Popa [1984] Director/Senior Investment Manager [Romanian]; Andrew Jonathan Mark Taylor [1961] Director/Investor; Charles Thomazi [1963] Managing Director of Infrastructure and Natural Resources [Canadian]

Scott Dunn Limited
Incorporated: 21 May 1986 *Employees:* 267
Net Worth: £17,948,000 *Total Assets:* £43,091,000
Registered Office: Scott Dunn, Madgwick Lane, Westhampnett, Chichester, W Sussex, PO18 0FB
Activities: Tour operator activities
Parent: The Luxury Travel Group Limited
Officers: Sonia Davies [1977] Director/Chief Operating Officer; Oliver Evans [1975] Director; Simon John Russell [1971] Managing Director; Robin Wooldridge [1968] Executive Director

Scott Health & Safety Limited
Incorporated: 28 June 1946 *Employees:* 344
Net Worth: £27,966,000 *Total Assets:* £48,938,000
Registered Office: 3M Centre, Cain Road, Bracknell, Berks, RG12 8HT
Activities: Other manufacturing n.e.c.
Parent: 3M United Kingdom Public Limited Company
Officers: Ian Richard Brown, Secretary; David James Ashley [1968] Director/General Counsel; Mohammad Irfan Malik [1965] Director [Pakistani]; Simla Semerciyan [1973] Director/Finance Manager [Turkish]; Jason Michael Thompstone [1976] Director/Accountant

Scottish Borders Education Partnership (Holdings) Limited
Incorporated: 25 May 2006
Net Worth: £202,000 *Total Assets:* £80,360,000
Registered Office: Part First Floor, 1 Grenfell Road, Maidenhead, Berks, SL6 1HN
Activities: Financial intermediation not elsewhere classified
Parent: BBGI Sicav S.A.
Officers: Emeka Ikechi Ehenulo, Secretary; Albert Hendrik Naafs [1965] Director [Dutch]; Frank Manfred Schramm [1968] Director [German]

Scottish Borders Education Partnership Limited
Incorporated: 25 May 2006
Net Worth: £202,000 *Total Assets:* £80,360,000
Registered Office: Part First Floor, 1 Grenfell Road, Maidenhead, Berks, SL6 1HN
Activities: Financial intermediation not elsewhere classified
Parent: Scottish Borders Education Partnership (Holdings) Limited
Officers: Emeka Ikechi Ehenulo, Secretary; Albert Hendrik Naafs [1965] Director [Dutch]; Frank Manfred Schramm [1968] Director [German]

SD Worx UK Limited
Incorporated: 8 September 1995 *Employees:* 570
Previous: Ceridian UK Limited
Net Worth: £23,217,000 *Total Assets:* £36,830,000
Registered Office: 100 Longwater Avenue, Greenpark, Reading, Berks, RG2 6GP
Activities: Other business support service activities n.e.c.
Parent: Informatie Verwerkende Diensten NV
Officers: Leon Roger Daniel, Secretary; Leon Roger Daniel [1964] Director/Head of Legal; Melissa Goddard [1968] Director/Chief Product Officer; Fabienne Lallemand [1967] Director/Chief Legal Officer [Belgian]; Brenda May Morris [1964] Managing Director

SDH Bidco Limited
Incorporated: 1 February 2012
Net Worth Deficit: £17,201,652 *Total Assets:* £25,114,396
Registered Office: Securedata House, Hermitage Court, Hermitage Lane, Maidstone, Kent, ME16 9NT
Activities: Other information technology service activities
Parent: SDH Holdco Limited
Officers: Ian Christopher Brown [1964] Director; Etienne Greeff [1966] Director; Matthew Charles Tomlinson [1973] Director; Christian Patrick Lorenzo Winning [1965] Finance Director

SDH Holdco Limited
Incorporated: 1 February 2012 *Employees:* 205
Net Worth Deficit: £15,378,210 *Total Assets:* £40,905,444
Registered Office: Securedata House, Hermitage Court, Hermitage Lane, Maidstone, Kent, ME16 9NT
Activities: Other information technology service activities
Parent: Orange S.A.
Officers: Helene Auriol Potier [1962] Director [French]; Ian Christopher Brown [1964] Director; Matthieu Cordier [1975] Director [French]; Fabrice de Windt [1975] Director [Belgian]; Hugues Foulon [1968] Director and Chairman of SDH Holdco Limited [French]; Michel Van Den Berghe [1960] Director [French]

SDL PLC
Incorporated: 6 January 1992 *Employees:* 3,647
Net Worth: £189,100,000 *Total Assets:* £283,600,000
Registered Office: New Globe House, Vanwall Business Park, Vanwall Road, Maidenhead, Berks, SL6 4UB
Activities: Business and domestic software development
Officers: Pamela Pickering, Secretary; David Hugh Clayton [1957] Strategy Director; Glenn Collinson [1963] Director; Amanda Jane Gradden [1968] Director; Adolfo Hernandez [1970] Director; Christopher John Humphrey [1957] Director; Alan James McWalter [1953] Director; Xenia Walters [1970] Director

SDL Tridion Limited
Incorporated: 11 November 1999 *Employees:* 3
Net Worth: £10,620,479 *Total Assets:* £34,494,056
Registered Office: New Globe House, Vanwall Business Park, Vanwall Road, Maidenhead, Berks, SL6 4UB
Activities: Business and domestic software development
Parent: SDL Holdings BV
Officers: Christopher Coker [1968] Director/Chartered Accountant

Sea Cloud 1 Limited
Incorporated: 7 April 2016 *Employees:* 112
Net Worth: £9,353,129 *Total Assets:* £22,157,740
Registered Office: Elder House, St Georges Business Park, Brooklands Road, Weybridge, Surrey, KT13 0TS
Activities: Activities of head offices
Major Shareholder: Andrea Susan Greystoke
Officers: John David Clarke [1953] Director/Solicitor; Andrea Susan Greystoke [1946] Director [American/British]; David William Morse [1960] Director/Education Consultant; Sheila Patricia Redrupp [1959] Director/Chartered Accountant; Abigail Melinda Fawn Snell [1978] Director

Sea Corner Group Limited
Incorporated: 20 November 1970 *Employees:* 4
Net Worth: £7,653,759 *Total Assets:* £27,253,186
Registered Office: 20 New Street, Lymington, Hants, SO41 9BQ
Activities: Activities of other holding companies n.e.c.
Major Shareholder: Edwin Rufus Walpole Eyre
Officers: Edwin Rufus Walpole Eyre [1926] Director; Giles Eric Pemberton [1952] Director/Solicitor

Seagreen Wind Energy Limited
Incorporated: 8 April 2009
Net Worth Deficit: £1,292,000 *Total Assets:* £37,613,000
Registered Office: No 1 Forbury Place, 43 Forbury Road, Reading, Berks, RG1 3JH
Activities: Production of electricity
Shareholder: SSE Renewables Developments (UK) Limited
Officers: Suzanne Borrowman, Secretary; Paul Generald Cooley [1971] Director/Engineer [Irish]; Finlay Alexander McCutcheon [1977] Director

Sealion Shipping Limited
Incorporated: 2 January 1974 *Employees:* 30
Net Worth: £2,956,375 *Total Assets:* £21,199,110
Registered Office: Gostrey House, Union Road, Farnham, Surrey, GU9 7PT
Activities: Other transportation support activities
Major Shareholder: Grigorios Kallimanopoulos
Officers: Kenneth Michael Thomas, Secretary; Jonathan Charles Golding [1952] Commercial Director; Stephen Robert Marshall [1954] Director/Fleet Manager; Christopher Moncur [1979] Chartering Director; Captain Philip John Wood [1944] Director/Chartered Ship Broker

Search Consultancy Acquisition Limited
Incorporated: 13 April 2017 *Employees:* 3
Net Worth Deficit: £176,000 *Total Assets:* £22,515,000
Registered Office: 117-119 High Street, Crawley, W Sussex, RH10 1DD
Activities: Human resources provision and management of human resources functions
Parent: Search Consultancy Midco Limited
Officers: Deborah Jane Caswell [1965] Director; Grahame Charles Harold Caswell [1956] Director; Stuart John MacFarlane Dick [1974] Director/Accountant; Katherine Wai Ming Ho [1983] Investment Director; Patrick Henricus Lambertus Kalverboer [1972] Director [Dutch]

Search Consultancy Group Limited
Incorporated: 19 January 2000 *Employees:* 3
Net Worth: £2,390,000 *Total Assets:* £23,594,000
Registered Office: 117-119 High Street, Crawley, W Sussex, RH10 1DD
Activities: Activities of head offices
Parent: Search Consultancy Acquisition Limited
Officers: Deborah Jane Caswell [1965] Director; Grahame Charles Harold Caswell [1956] Director; Stuart John MacFarlane Dick [1974] Finance Director

Search Consultancy Topco Limited
Incorporated: 13 April 2017 *Employees:* 637
Net Worth: £12,467,000 *Total Assets:* £51,752,000
Registered Office: 117-119 High Street, Crawley, W Sussex, RH10 1DD
Activities: Human resources provision and management of human resources functions
Officers: Mark Bailey [1975] Director; Deborah Jane Caswell [1965] Director; Grahame Charles Harold Caswell [1956] Director; Stuart John MacFarlane Dick [1974] Director/Accountant; Katherine Wai Ming Ho [1983] Investment Director; Patrick Henricus Lambertus Kalverboer [1972] Director [Dutch]

Secom PLC
Incorporated: 26 February 1991 *Employees:* 778
Net Worth: £30,498,000 *Total Assets:* £43,885,000
Registered Office: Secom House, 52 Godstone Road, Kenley, Surrey, CR8 5JF
Activities: Security systems service activities
Officers: Neil Fanthome-Hodgson, Secretary; Alan Blake [1965] Director; Neil Fanthome-Hodgson [1965] Director; Sadahiro Sato [1960] Director [Japanese]; Minoru Takezawa [1963] Director [Japanese]; Paul Arnold Weaver [1969] Director

Secure Meters (UK) Limited
Incorporated: 27 November 1987 *Employees:* 1,725
Net Worth: £72,450,800 *Total Assets:* £260,913,168
Registered Office: Secure House, Moorside Road, Winchester, Hants, SO23 7RX
Activities: Other business support service activities n.e.c.
Officers: Kaushak Patel [1966] Director/Business Development; Ananya Singhal [1984] Director [Indian]

Secureworks Europe Limited
Incorporated: 16 April 2015 *Employees:* 219
Net Worth: £16,430,000 *Total Assets:* £33,757,000
Registered Office: Dell House, The Boulevard, Cain Road, Bracknell, Berks, RG12 1LF
Activities: Other information technology service activities
Parent: Dell Technologies Inc.
Officers: Janet Merritt Bawcom [1964] Director/Lawyer [American]; George Barry Hanna [1966] Director [American]; Jeffrey Longoria [1960] Director [American]; John Canright Nelson [1981] Director, Legal Counsel [American]

Security Monitoring Centres Limited
Incorporated: 4 September 1936 *Employees:* 1
Net Worth: £21,526,000 *Total Assets:* £42,449,000
Registered Office: Littleton Road, Ashford, Middlesex, TW15 1TZ
Activities: Private security activities
Parent: Chubb Group Security Limited
Officers: Laura Wilcock, Secretary; Craig Alexander Forbes [1963] Finance Director; Colin Walters [1965] Director/General Manager

Sedgemoor Limited
Incorporated: 11 May 1934
Net Worth: £38,258,000 *Total Assets:* £46,707,000
Registered Office: 2 Chancellor Court, Occam Road, Surrey Research Park, Guildford, Surrey, GU2 7AH
Activities: Activities of head offices
Parent: ACAL Electronics Holdings Limited
Officers: Joanna Alwen Harkus Madge, Secretary; Simon Mark Gibbins [1966] Director/Chartered Accountant; Nicholas John Jefferies [1966] Director

Sega Europe Limited
Incorporated: 4 October 1982 *Employees:* 154
Net Worth: £15,846,000 *Total Assets:* £60,303,000
Registered Office: 27 Great West Road, Brentford, Middlesex, TW8 9BW
Activities: Other service activities n.e.c.
Parent: Sega Sammy Holdings Inc
Officers: Nicola Ormrod, Secretary; Gary Robert Dale [1961] Director/Chief Operating Officer; Kenji Matsubara [1962] Director [Japanese]; Tatsuyuki Miyazaki [1967] Director/Chief Executive Officer [Japanese]; David Jonathon Ward [1965] Director/Chief Financial Officer

Sega Publishing Europe Limited
Incorporated: 13 September 2005 *Employees:* 61
Net Worth Deficit: £50,000 *Total Assets:* £39,371,000
Registered Office: 27 Great West Road, Brentford, Middlesex, TW8 9BW
Activities: Publishing of computer games
Parent: Sega Sammy Holdings Inc
Officers: Nicola Ormrod, Secretary; Gary Robert Dale [1961] Director/Chief Operating Officer; Kenji Matsubara [1962] Director [Japanese]; Tatsuyuki Miyazaki [1967] Director/Chief Executive Officer [Japanese]; David Jonathon Ward [1965] Director/Chief Financial Officer

Seiko U.K. Limited
Incorporated: 29 November 1971 *Employees:* 301
Net Worth: £35,887,000 *Total Assets:* £55,748,000
Registered Office: SC House, Vanwall Business Park, Maidenhead, Berks, SL6 4UW
Activities: Wholesale of watches and jewellery
Shareholder: Seiko Holdings Corporation
Officers: David Simon Edwards [1968] Managing Director; Shinya Fukui [1971] Finance Director [Japanese]; Atsushi Kaneko [1957] Chairman and Managing Director, Europe [Japanese]; Yoshikatsu Kawada [1962] Director [Japanese]; Philip Wolkind [1969] Sales Director; Taku Yoneyama [1962] Director [Japanese]

Sekisui Diagnostics (UK) Limited
Incorporated: 1 December 2010 *Employees:* 119
Net Worth: £61,871,244 *Total Assets:* £65,660,568
Registered Office: Sekisui Diagnostics (UK) Ltd, Liphook Way, Allington, Maidstone, Kent, ME16 0LQ
Activities: Manufacture of medical and dental instruments and supplies
Officers: Robert Timothy Schruender [1966] Director/President of Sekisui Diagnostics LLC [American]; Dr William Albert Stockburn [1959] Director; Eiichi Takahashi [1963] Director/Plant Manager [Japanese]

Select Plant Hire Company Limited
Incorporated: 20 December 1985
Net Worth: £183,522,000 *Total Assets:* £259,896,992
Registered Office: Bridge Place, Anchor Boulevard, Admirals Park, Crossways, Dartford, Kent, DA2 6SN
Activities: Other specialised construction activities n.e.c.
Parent: R O'Rourke & Son Limited
Officers: Robert Edward Turner, Secretary; Matthew Clement Hugh Gill [1971] Director/Group Financial Controller; Stephen John Harley [1951] Director; Alexander Stewart McIntyre [1956] Director; Paul William McNerney [1977] Director/Business Unit Leader; Hubert Desmond O'Rourke [1949] Director/Structural Engineer [Irish]

Selecta Refreshments Limited
Incorporated: 16 July 1919 *Employees:* 560
Previous: Selecta UK Limited
Net Worth: £57,000 *Total Assets:* £32,032,000
Registered Office: 1st Floor, Spinnaker House, Lime Tree Way, Hampshire International Business Park, Chineham, Basingstoke, Hants, RG24 8GG
Activities: Other retail sale not in stores, stalls or markets
Parent: Selecta UK Holding Limited
Officers: Daniel Henry Abrahams [1973] Director; Jan Marck Vrijlandt [1965] Managing Director [Dutch]

Selits Limited
Incorporated: 26 June 1953 *Employees:* 2
Net Worth: £21,764,746 *Total Assets:* £35,990,508
Registered Office: 8 Roedean Crescent, Brighton, BN2 5RH
Activities: Buying and selling of own real estate
Parent: Selits Holdings Limited
Officers: Nicholas Charles Bradbeer [1958] Director/Chartered Surveyor; Robert Deverell Stiles [1947] Director/Chartered Surveyor

Selwood Group Limited
Incorporated: 27 April 1994
Net Worth: £11,735,000 *Total Assets:* £41,918,000
Registered Office: Bournemouth Road, Chandler's Ford, Eastleigh, Hants, SO53 3ZL
Activities: Other specialised construction activities n.e.c.
Parent: Selwood Holdings Limited
Officers: Nigel Mark Apps [1969] Director; Carole Denise Bright [1960] Director; Richard James Bright [1987] Director; Richard Allan Brown [1967] Director; Lisa Marie Carter [1985] Director; Christopher Mark Garrett [1969] Financial Director

Selwood Holdings Limited
Incorporated: 1 November 2007 *Employees:* 492
Net Worth: £46,507,000 *Total Assets:* £95,950,000
Registered Office: 32-36 Bournemouth Road, Chandler's Ford, Eastleigh, Hants, SO53 3ZL
Activities: Activities of construction holding companies
Parent: Workdry International Limited
Officers: Nigel Mark Apps [1969] Director; Richard James Bright [1987] Director; Richard Allan Brown [1967] Director; Christopher Mark Garrett [1969] Director

Selwood Ltd
Incorporated: 19 April 1951 *Employees:* 492
Net Worth: £68,899,000 *Total Assets:* £98,014,000
Registered Office: Bournemouth Road, Chandler's Ford, Eastleigh, Southampton, SO53 3ZL
Activities: Other specialised construction activities n.e.c.
Parent: Selwood Group Limited
Officers: Nigel Mark Apps [1969] Director; Richard James Bright [1987] Director; Richard Allan Brown [1967] Director; Christopher Mark Garrett [1969] Financial Director

SEM Limited
Incorporated: 17 October 1914 *Employees:* 205
Net Worth: £26,317,848 *Total Assets:* £36,391,328
Registered Office: One Hundred House, Brunel Way, Dartford, Kent, DA1 5TH
Activities: Manufacture of electric motors, generators and transformers
Parent: Westec Holding Company Limited
Officers: Michael Alexander Laming, Company Secretary; Fiona Blyth [1967] Joint Managing Director; Michael Alexander Laming [1953] Director; Thomas Peter Walther [1963] Joint Managing Director [German]

Senior Engineering Investments Limited
Incorporated: 17 September 1968
Net Worth: £669,816,000 *Total Assets:* £1,019,582,976
Registered Office: 59-61 High Street, Rickmansworth, Herts, WD3 1RH
Activities: Activities of head offices
Parent: Senior PLC
Officers: Andrew John Bodenham, Secretary; Andrew John Bodenham [1966] Director and Company Secretary; Bindi Jayantilal Jivraj Foyle [1973] Director; David Hamilton Squires [1963] Director

Senior Finance Four Limited
Incorporated: 12 June 2009
Net Worth: £43,373,000 *Total Assets:* £183,024,992
Registered Office: 59-61 High Street, Rickmansworth, Herts, WD3 1RH
Activities: Activities of head offices
Parent: Senior Engineering Investments Limited
Officers: Andrew John Bodenham, Secretary; Andrew John Bodenham [1966] Director; Bindi Jayantilal Jivraj Foyle [1973] Director

Senior Finance Six Limited
Incorporated: 16 November 2011
Net Worth: £86,993,320 *Total Assets:* £130,925,520
Registered Office: 59-61 High Street, Rickmansworth, Herts, WD3 1RH
Activities: Activities of head offices
Parent: Senior Engineering Investments Limited
Officers: Andrew John Bodenham, Secretary; Andrew John Bodenham [1966] Director; Bindi Jayantilal Jivraj Foyle [1973] Director

Senior Five Limited
Incorporated: 13 September 2011
Net Worth: £283,276,704 *Total Assets:* £570,557,504
Registered Office: 59-61 High Street, Rickmansworth, Herts, WD3 1RH
Activities: Activities of head offices
Parent: Senior US Holdings Inc.
Officers: Andrew John Bodenham, Secretary; Andrew John Bodenham [1966] Director and Company Secretary; Bindi Jayantilal Jivraj Foyle [1973] Director

Senior PLC
Incorporated: 18 December 1933 *Employees:* 7,658
Net Worth: £531,600,000 *Total Assets:* £950,800,000
Registered Office: 59-61 High Street, Rickmansworth, Herts, WD3 1RH
Activities: Activities of head offices
Officers: Andrew John Bodenham, Secretary; Dr Celia Frances Baxter [1958] Director; Susan Brennan [1962] Director [American]; Bindi Jayantilal Jivraj Foyle [1973] Director; Giles Frances Bertram Kerr [1959] Director; Ian Graham King [1956] Director; Rajiv Sharma [1966] Director [Singaporean]; David Hamilton Squires [1963] Director; Mark Edward Vernon [1953] Director [American]

Senior UK Limited
Incorporated: 3 July 1985 *Employees:* 1,299
Net Worth: £66,473,000 *Total Assets:* £149,584,000
Registered Office: 59-61 High Street, Rickmansworth, Herts, WD3 1RH
Activities: Manufacture of other special-purpose machinery n.e.c.
Parent: Senior Engineering Investments Limited
Officers: Andrew John Bodenham, Company Secretary; Andrew John Bodenham [1966] Director and Company Secretary; Bindi Jayantilal Jivraj Foyle [1973] Director; Michael Sheppard [1959] Director/President-APD [American]; David Hamilton Squires [1963] Director

Sensient Flavors Limited
Incorporated: 29 August 1980 *Employees:* 222
Net Worth: £4,328,703 *Total Assets:* £63,280,836
Registered Office: Bilton Road, Bletchley, Milton Keynes, Bucks, MK1 1HP
Activities: Other processing and preserving of fruit and vegetables
Parent: Sensient Holdings UK
Officers: Michael Francois de Meyer [1959] Director/General Manager; Jeffrey Thomas Makal [1963] Director [American]

Sensient Holdings UK
Incorporated: 20 July 1977
Net Worth: £30,338,972 *Total Assets:* £43,981,096
Registered Office: Bilton Road, Bletchley, Milton Keynes, Bucks, MK1 1HP
Activities: Other processing and preserving of fruit and vegetables
Parent: Sensient Technologies Corporation
Officers: Bradley Michael Conners [1977] Director/Senior Attorney [American]; Leroy Clark Watson [1973] Director of Taxation

Sentinel Health Care Limited
Incorporated: 4 November 1992 *Employees:* 212
Net Worth: £13,889,254 *Total Assets:* £25,525,984
Registered Office: Fritham House, Fritham, Lyndhurst, Hants, SO43 7HH
Activities: Hotels and similar accommodation
Shareholders: Colin Malcolm Brumpton; Russell Geoffrey Donnelly
Officers: Russell Geoffrey Donnelly, Secretary/Director; Colin Malcolm Brumpton [1949] Director/Treasury Trading Manager; Aelred Lance Donnelly [1956] Director; Russell Geoffrey Donnelly [1953] Director

Seqirus Holdings UK Limited
Incorporated: 29 May 2015
Net Worth: £634,094,336 *Total Assets:* £634,094,336
Registered Office: Point, 29 Market Street, Maidenhead, Berks, SL6 8AA
Activities: Activities of head offices
Officers: John Andrew Goodman Levy, Secretary; Martin Thomas Quinn, Secretary; John Andrew Goodman Levy [1959] Director/Business Executive [Australian]; Kian Meng Lim [1973] Director/Business Executive [Australian]

Seqirus Limited
Incorporated: 29 May 2015
Net Worth: £620,031,552 *Total Assets:* £731,576,512
Registered Office: Point, 29 Market Street, Maidenhead, Berks, SL6 8AA
Activities: Activities of head offices
Parent: Seqirus Holdings UK Limited
Officers: John Andrew Goodman Levy, Secretary; Martin Thomas Quinn, Secretary; John Andrew Goodman Levy [1959] Director/Business Executive [Australian]; Kian Meng Lim [1973] Director/Business Executive [Australian]

Seqirus UK Limited
Incorporated: 29 May 2015 *Employees:* 53
Net Worth: £129,614,872 *Total Assets:* £249,937,088
Registered Office: Point, 29 Market Street, Maidenhead, Berks, SL6 8AA
Activities: Activities of head offices
Parent: Seqirus Limited
Officers: John Andrew Goodman Levy, Secretary; Martin Thomas Quinn, Secretary; John Andrew Goodman Levy [1959] Director/Business Executive [Australian]; Kian Meng Lim [1973] Director/Business Executive [Australian]

Seqirus Vaccines Holdings Limited
Incorporated: 26 February 2003
Previous: Novartis Vaccines Holdings Limited
Net Worth: £124,281,000 *Total Assets:* £143,595,008
Registered Office: Point, 29 Market Street, Maidenhead, Berks, SL6 8AA
Activities: Activities of head offices
Parent: Seqirus Limited
Officers: John Andrew Goodman Levy, Secretary; Martin Thomas Quinn, Secretary; John Andrew Goodman Levy [1959] Director/Business Executive [Australian]; Kian Meng Lim [1973] Director/Business Executive [Australian]; Dr Laura Elizabeth O'Brien [1968] Director/Business Executive

Seqirus Vaccines Limited
Incorporated: 11 April 2000 *Employees:* 475
Previous: Novartis Vaccines and Diagnostics Limited
Net Worth: £196,200,000 *Total Assets:* £263,800,000
Registered Office: Point, 29 Market Street, Maidenhead, Berks, SL6 8AA
Activities: Manufacture of basic pharmaceutical products
Parent: Seqirus Vaccines Holdings Limited
Officers: John Andrew Goodman Levy, Secretary; Martin Thomas Quinn, Secretary; John Andrew Goodman Levy [1959] Director/Business Executive [Australian]; Kian Meng Lim [1973] Director/Business Executive [Australian]; Stephen Michael Marlow [1971] Director/Business Executive; Dr Laura Elizabeth O'Brien [1968] Director/Business Executive

Serco Group PLC
Incorporated: 21 August 1986 *Employees:* 42,764
Net Worth: £305,900,000 *Total Assets:* £1,512,800,000
Registered Office: Serco House, 16 Bartley Wood Business Park, Bartley Way, Hook, Hants, RG27 9UY
Activities: Activities of head offices
Officers: David Charles Eveleigh, Secretary; Kirsty Bashforth [1970] Director; Eric Martin Born [1970] Director [Swiss]; Angus George Cockburn [1963] Director/Chief Financial Officer; Ian Ramsey Safwat El-Mokadem [1968] Director; Sir Roy Alan Gardner [1945] Director/Chairman; Janis Rachel Lomax [1945] Director/Economist; Lynne Peacock [1953] Director; John Frederick Rishton [1958] Director; The Right Honourable Rupert Christopher Soames [1959] Director/Chief Executive Officer

Serco Holdings Limited
Incorporated: 11 April 2000
Net Worth: £1,246,958,976 *Total Assets:* £1,446,995,968
Registered Office: Serco House, 16 Bartley Wood Business Park, Bartley Way, Hook, Hants, RG27 9UY
Activities: Activities of head offices
Parent: Serco Group PLC
Officers: Nigel Crossley [1963] Director/Financial Controller; Stuart John Haydon [1958] Director/Company Secretary

Serco Limited
Incorporated: 10 September 1929 *Employees:* 22
Net Worth: £171,800,000 *Total Assets:* £814,600,000
Registered Office: Serco House, 16 Bartley Wood Business Park, Bartley Way, Hook, Hants, RG27 9UY
Activities: Activities of head offices
Parent: Serco Holdings Limited
Officers: Kevin David Craven [1961] Director/CEO UK Central Government Division; Nigel Crossley [1963] Director/Financial Controller

Serco-IAL Limited
Incorporated: 9 January 1947 *Employees:* 375
Net Worth: £67,759,000 *Total Assets:* £78,222,000
Registered Office: Serco House, 16 Bartley Wood Business Park, Bartley Way, Hook, Hants, RG27 9UY
Activities: Other service activities n.e.c.
Parent: Serco Holdings Limited
Officers: Scott Michael Ashby [1962] Director/Chief Financial Officer; Peter James Mohring [1959] Managing Director [New Zealander]

Serena Holdings
Incorporated: 23 July 2004
Net Worth: £28,031,784 *Total Assets:* £39,090,080
Registered Office: The Lawn, 22-30 Old Bath Road, Newbury, Berks, RG14 1QN
Activities: Other information technology service activities
Parent: Micro Focus Integration Limited
Officers: Graham Howard Norton, Secretary; Kenneth Robert Jukes [1967] Director/Businessman; Graham Howard Norton [1959] Director; Jane Caroline Grantham Smithard [1954] Director

Serena Software Europe Limited
Incorporated: 12 August 1976 *Employees:* 70
Net Worth: £10,072,000 *Total Assets:* £42,992,000
Registered Office: The Lawn, 22-30 Old Bath Road, Newbury, Berks, RG14 1QN
Activities: Other information technology service activities
Parent: Merant Holdings
Officers: Graham Howard Norton, Secretary; Kenneth Robert Jukes [1967] Director/Accountant; Graham Howard Norton [1959] Director; Jane Caroline Grantham Smithard [1954] Director

Sericol Ink Limited
Incorporated: 10 December 2002
Net Worth: £42,169,000 *Total Assets:* £46,495,000
Registered Office: Patricia Way, Pysons Road Industrial Estate, Broadstairs, Kent, CT10 2LE
Activities: Other manufacturing n.e.c.
Parent: Fujifilm Holdings Corporation
Officers: Neil Llewellyn Denham, Secretary; Aiichiro Hiruma [1959] Director [Japanese]; Martin Wilhelm Schoeppler [1955] Director/Chief Executive Officer [American/German]; Tatsuo Suzuki [1964] Director/General Manager [Japanese]; Ian David Wilkinson [1964] Director/Chief Operating Officer

Serocor Holdings Limited
Incorporated: 21 May 2007 *Employees:* 147
Net Worth: £3,242,000 *Total Assets:* £21,570,000
Registered Office: Langstone Technology Park, Langstone Road, Havant, Hants, PO9 1SA
Activities: Activities of head offices
Major Shareholder: Paul Andrew Huntingdon
Officers: Mark David Gawthorne, Finance Director; Simon Jonathan Ainslie Church [1957] Director; Mark David Gawthorne [1969] Finance Director; Michael John Gawthorne [1976] Director/Recruitment Consultant; Paul Andrew Huntingdon [1969] Director/Recruitment Consultant; David John Wilson [1962] Director

Services Sound and Vision Corporation (The)
Incorporated: 29 March 1946 *Employees:* 211
Net Worth: £34,501,000 *Total Assets:* £41,036,000
Registered Office: Chalfont Grove, Narcot Lane, Gerrards Cross, Bucks, SL9 8TN
Activities: Radio broadcasting
Officers: David James Cochran Hamilton, Secretary; Mark David Browning [1972] Managing Director; Helen Louise Depree [1976] Director/Solicitor; Antony John Hales [1948] Director; Deborah Jane Loudon [1955] Director/Recruitment Consultant; Howard Stephen Perlin [1946] Director/Chartered Accountant; Anthony John Rix [1956] Director; Graham David Brice Robinson [1944] Director/Government Service; Ian Richard Tolfts [1964] Managing Director; Major General Christopher Colin Wilson [1953] Director/Army Officer

Services Support (Gravesend) Holdings Limited
Incorporated: 20 January 2000
Net Worth: £4,293,000 *Total Assets:* £39,864,000
Registered Office: 8 White Oak Square, London Road, Swanley, Kent, BR8 7AG
Activities: Activities of head offices
Shareholders: Palio (No.1) Limited; Amalie PFI (UK) Limited
Officers: David Richard Bradbury [1969] Asset Director; James Christopher Heath [1975] Director; Elena Giorgiana Wegener [1975] Director/Investment Executive

Services Support (Gravesend) Limited
Incorporated: 20 January 2000
Net Worth: £4,293,000 *Total Assets:* £39,864,000
Registered Office: 8 White Oak Square, London Road, Swanley, Kent, BR8 7AG
Activities: Other business support service activities n.e.c.
Parent: Services Support (Gravesend) Holdings Limited
Officers: David Richard Bradbury [1969] Asset Director; James Christopher Heath [1975] Director; Elena Giorgiana Wegener [1975] Director/Investment Executive

Services Support (Manchester) Holdings Limited
Incorporated: 24 August 2001
Net Worth Deficit: £12,344,000 *Total Assets:* £83,626,000
Registered Office: 8 White Oak Square, London Road, Swanley, Kent, BR8 7AG
Activities: Activities of head offices
Shareholders: Palio (No 1) Limited; Amalie PFI (UK) Limited
Officers: James Christopher Heath [1975] Director; Clement David Baptiste Leverd [1986] Director/Investment Executive [French]; Neil Woodburn [1979] Director/Chartered Building Surveyor

Services Support (Manchester) Limited
Incorporated: 24 August 2001
Net Worth Deficit: £12,344,000 *Total Assets:* £83,626,000
Registered Office: 8 White Oak Square, London Road, Swanley, Kent, BR8 7AG
Activities: Other business support service activities n.e.c.
Parent: Services Support (Manchester) Holdings Limited
Officers: James Christopher Heath [1975] Director; Clement David Baptiste Leverd [1986] Director/Investment Executive [French]; Neil Woodburn [1979] Director/Chartered Building Surveyor

Services Support (SEL) Holdings Limited
Incorporated: 20 January 2000
Net Worth Deficit: £4,790,000 *Total Assets:* £77,453,000
Registered Office: 8 White Oak Square, London Road, Swanley, Kent, BR8 7AG
Activities: Activities of head offices
Shareholders: JLIF Holdings (Justice and Emergency Services) Limited; Amalie PFI (UK) Limited
Officers: Farid Barekati [1984] Director/Chartered Accountant; David Richard Bradbury [1969] Director/Senior Investment Manager; James Christopher Heath [1975] Director; Elena Giorgiana Wegener [1975] Director/Investment Executive

Services Support (SEL) Limited
Incorporated: 7 December 1998
Net Worth Deficit: £4,790,000 *Total Assets:* £77,453,000
Registered Office: 8 White Oak Square, London Road, Swanley, Kent, BR8 7AG
Activities: Other business support service activities n.e.c.
Parent: Services Support (SEL) Holdings Limited
Officers: Farid Barekati [1984] Director/Chartered Accountant; David Richard Bradbury [1969] Director/Senior Investment Manager; James Christopher Heath [1975] Director; Elena Giorgiana Wegener [1975] Director/Investment Executive

Servier IP UK Limited
Incorporated: 3 February 2006
Previous: Servier UK IP Limited
Net Worth: £182,211,152 *Total Assets:* £189,847,904
Registered Office: Sefton House, Sefton Park, Bells Hill, Stoke Poges, Slough, Berks, SL2 4JS
Activities: Wholesale of pharmaceutical goods
Officers: Charles Michael Brooks, Secretary; Claude Philippe Bertrand [1962] General Director of R&D [French]; Patricia Lafaix-Houser [1957] Director/Executive Assistant [French]

Servomex Group Limited
Incorporated: 29 September 1987 *Employees:* 202
Net Worth: £37,922,000 *Total Assets:* £45,937,000
Registered Office: Servomex Group Limited, Jarvis Brook, Crowborough, E Sussex, TN6 3FB
Activities: Manufacture of electronic industrial process control equipment
Parent: Spectris Group Holdings Ltd
Officers: Victoria Anne Louise Hammond [1973] Human Resources Director; Catherine Sian Haynes [1969] Finance Director; Trevor Martin Sands [1965] Director

SES (Engineering Services) Limited
Incorporated: 19 April 1961 *Employees:* 903
Previous: Shepherd Engineering Services Limited
Net Worth Deficit: £3,321,000 *Total Assets:* £62,982,000
Registered Office: Wates House, Station Approach, Leatherhead, Surrey, KT22 7SW
Activities: Construction of commercial buildings
Parent: Wates Construction Limited
Officers: Philip Michael Wainwright, Secretary; David Owen Allen [1972] Director/Chief Financial Officer; Paul Chandler [1964] Managing Director; Simon James Potter [1963] Group Commercial Director; Paul Campbell Rowan [1964] Group HR Director; Philip Michael Wainwright [1965] Director/Chief Financial Officer

Sesame Bankhall Group Limited
Incorporated: 1 June 1998
Net Worth: £18,643,000 *Total Assets:* £62,323,000
Registered Office: Pixham End, Dorking, Surrey, RH4 1QA
Activities: Activities of head offices
Parent: Friends Life Distribution Limited
Officers: Clare Binmore [1973] Director; John Cowan [1947] Director; Nick Criticos [1958] Director; Diana Susan Miller [1950] Director

Sesame Limited
Incorporated: 11 August 1993
Net Worth: £7,418,000 *Total Assets:* £69,173,000
Registered Office: Pixham End, Dorking, Surrey, RH4 1QA
Activities: Other business support service activities n.e.c.
Parent: Sesame Bankhall Group Limited
Officers: Clare Binmore [1973] Director; John Cowan [1947] Director; Nick Criticos [1958] Director; Diana Susan Miller [1950] Director

Sesame Services Limited
Incorporated: 24 January 1989 *Employees:* 273
Net Worth: £13,088,000 *Total Assets:* £24,636,000
Registered Office: Pixham End, Dorking, Surrey, RH4 1QA
Activities: Other business support service activities n.e.c.
Parent: Sesame Bankhall Group Limited
Officers: John Cowan [1947] Director; James Michael Kelly [1956] Director/Accountant; Lisa Winnard [1972] HR Director

SESW Holding Company Limited.
Incorporated: 31 January 2001
Net Worth: £16,410,476 *Total Assets:* £29,278,068
Registered Office: 66-74 London Road, Redhill, Surrey, RH1 1LJ
Activities: Activities of production holding companies
Parent: East Surrey Holdings Limited
Officers: Anthony John David Ferrar [1957] Director; Paul Kerr [1973] Finance and Regulation Director; Daniel Jonathan Wynne [1970] Director

Setfirst Limited
Incorporated: 3 January 1989
Net Worth: £15,873,934,336 *Total Assets:* £35,656,830,976
Registered Office: 980 Great West Road, Brentford, Middlesex, TW8 9GS
Activities: Activities of head offices
Parent: GlaxoSmithKline Finance PLC
Officers: Simon Paul Dingemans [1963] Director; Adam Walker [1967] Director

Sevenoaks School
Incorporated: 23 September 2003 *Employees:* 422
Net Worth: £29,897,000 *Total Assets:* £48,017,000
Registered Office: Sevenoaks School, High Street, Sevenoaks, Kent, TN13 1HU
Activities: General secondary education
Officers: Gail Tracey Jones, Secretary; Alison Cheryl Beckett [1960] Director/Consultant; Roger Simon Melliship Best [1955] Director/Solicitor; Adam Babington Boulton [1959] Director/TV Journalist; Sian Elizabeth Carr [1959] Director/Headteacher; Lord Alastair Colin Leckie Colgrain [1951] Director/HR; John Graham Davies [1956] Director/Solicitor; Ian Doherty [1952] Director; Sarah Jane Dunnett [1957] Director/Chairman Hospital; Eliza Jane Ecclestone [1973] Director/Estate Manager; Christopher Paul Gill [1957] Director/Merchant Banker; Professor Susan Diana Iversen [1940] Director/Retired; James Frederick Justin London [1964] Director/Solicitor; Mark Simon Merson [1968] Director; David Michael Phillips [1956] Director/Chartered Accountant; Dr Andrew Timms [1978] Director/Bursar; Professor David Ian Wilson [1965] Director/University Lecturer; Anita Pratap Shirke Yuravlivker [1981] Director

Sevita (UK) Limited
Incorporated: 20 May 2008
Net Worth: £24,309,000 *Total Assets:* £38,614,000
Registered Office: Compass House, Guildford Street, Chertsey, Surrey, KT16 9BQ
Activities: Other business support service activities n.e.c.
Parent: Compass Overseas Holdings No.2 Limited
Officers: Sarah Jane Sergeant [1973] Director/Accountant

SF Funding Limited
Incorporated: 18 June 2014 *Employees:* 1
Net Worth Deficit: £39,481,000 *Total Assets:* £334,044,992
Registered Office: Prospect Place, Moorside Road, Winchester, Hants, SO23 7RX
Activities: Buying and selling of own real estate
Parent: E & J SF Limited
Officers: James Edward Tuttiett [1963] Director

SF Ground Rents Limited
Incorporated: 19 June 2014 *Employees:* 1
Net Worth Deficit: £8,428,470 *Total Assets:* £57,922,540
Registered Office: Prospect Place, Moorside Road, Winchester, Hants, SO23 7RX
Activities: Buying and selling of own real estate
Parent: SF Funding Limited
Officers: James Edward Tuttiett [1963] Director

SG Equipment Finance (December) Limited
Incorporated: 19 November 1980
Net Worth: £4,080,969 *Total Assets:* £22,868,920
Registered Office: Parkshot House, Kew Road, Richmond, Surrey, TW9 2PR
Activities: Financial leasing
Parent: Societe Generale Equipment Finance Limited
Officers: Timothy Edward Goodship, Secretary; Stephen John Bowden [1964] Director/Senior Account Manager; Timothy Edward Goodship [1979] Director/Certified Chartered Accountant; Dominic Lawson Hughes [1972] Director/Financier; David Robert George Yates-Mercer [1964] Director/Accountant

SGB Infrastructure Middle East Limited
Incorporated: 15 August 2007
Previous: Harsco Infrastructure Middle East Limited
Net Worth: £67,126,000 *Total Assets:* £67,144,000
Registered Office: Regent Park, 299 Kingston Road, Leatherhead, Surrey, KT22 7SG
Activities: Activities of head offices
Major Shareholder: Donald Gogel
Officers: Andreas Akhtar [1974] Director/Lawyer [German]; Christopher McGalpine [1972] Director/Accountant

SGL No.1 Limited
Incorporated: 17 December 2007
Net Worth: £6,754,000 *Total Assets:* £944,232,000
Registered Office: 3 Guildford Business Park, Guildford, Surrey, GU2 8XG
Activities: Non-life insurance
Parent: Shelbourne Group Limited
Officers: Siobhan Mary Hextall, Secretary; James Robert Francis Lee [1962] Director; Brendan Richard Anthony Merriman [1958] Director

SGN Commercial Services Limited
Incorporated: 17 October 2006
Net Worth: £8,015,000 *Total Assets:* £156,082,000
Registered Office: St Lawrence House, Station Approach, Horley, Surrey, RH6 9HJ
Activities: Other business support service activities n.e.c.
Parent: Scotia Gas Networks Limited
Officers: Nicola Anne Shand, Secretary; Fraser McGregor Alexander [1963] Director/Chartered Accountant; Charlotte Louise Brunning [1986] Director/Investment Management; Natalie Michaela Flageul [1975] Director/Head of Metering; Ines Grund [1978] Director/Investment Professional [German]; Guy Lambert [1977] Director/Investments, Head of Utilities [Dutch]; Alejandro Lopez Delgado [1977] Director [Spanish]; Robert McDonald [1971] Director of Regulation; John James McManus [1959] Director/Investment Manager [Canadian]; Mariana Popa [1984] Director/Senior Investment Manager [Romanian]; Andrew Jonathan Mark Taylor [1961] Director/Investor; Charles Thomazi [1963] Managing Director of Infrastructure and Natural Resources [Canadian]

Shadowgrade Developments Limited
Incorporated: 19 February 1988 *Employees:* 28
Net Worth: £9,376,252 *Total Assets:* £20,069,988
Registered Office: Wraysbury Hall, Ferry Lane, Staines upon Thames, Middlesex, TW19 6HG
Activities: Hotels and similar accommodation
Major Shareholder: David Winn
Officers: Colin Higgins, Secretary; Joanna Cross [1980] Director; Scott Hamilton [1953] Managing Director; Colin Higgins [1965] Director/Accountant

Shanly Homes Limited
Incorporated: 4 January 1993 *Employees:* 173
Net Worth: £183,379,440 *Total Assets:* £213,357,648
Registered Office: Sorbon, Aylesbury End, Beaconsfield, Bucks, HP9 1LW
Activities: Development of building projects
Parent: Sorbon Homes Limited
Officers: Nicholas Mark Trott, Secretary; Tamra Michelle Booth [1974] Director; Robin Nicholas Dorran [1957] Director; Michael James Shanly [1945] Director; Nicholas Mark Trott [1964] Director/Chartered Accountant

Shapedirect Limited
Incorporated: 5 September 1997
Net Worth: £6,270,283,776 *Total Assets:* £6,791,440,896
Registered Office: Hanson House, 14 Castle Hill, Maidenhead, Berks, SL6 4JJ
Activities: Activities of other holding companies n.e.c.
Parent: Hanson International Holdings Limited
Officers: Wendy Fiona Rogers, Secretary; Nicholas Arthur Dawe Benning-Prince [1974] Director/Chartered Accountant; Robert Charles Dowley [1972] Director/Chartered Accountant; Edward Alexander Gretton [1970] Director; Dr Carsten Matthias Wendt [1976] Director [German]

The Share Centre Limited
Incorporated: 22 January 1990 *Employees:* 207
Net Worth: £12,077,000 *Total Assets:* £38,213,000
Registered Office: Oxford House, Oxford Road, Aylesbury, Bucks, HP21 8SZ
Activities: Security and commodity contracts dealing activities
Parent: Share PLC
Officers: Giles Pemberton, Secretary; Michael David Birkett [1972] Finance Director; Francesca Eva Ecsery [1963] Director/Businesswoman; Gavin David Redvers Oldham [1949] Director/Member of Stock Exchange; Linda Elizabeth Roberts [1962] Director; John Victor Sargeant [1970] Director; Richard Adam Stollery [1962] Director; Richard William Stone [1973] Finance Director; Gareth Vaughan Thomas [1957] Director; Richard Ian Tolkien [1955] Director/Businessman

Share PLC
Incorporated: 8 September 1994 *Employees:* 207
Net Worth: £18,189,000 *Total Assets:* £45,286,000
Registered Office: Oxford House, Oxford Road, Aylesbury, Bucks, HP21 8SZ
Activities: Activities of head offices
Major Shareholder: Gavin David Redvers Oldham
Officers: Giles Pemberton, Secretary; Michael David Birkett [1972] Finance Director; Francesca Eva Ecsery [1963] Director; Gavin David Redvers Oldham [1949] Director/Member of Stock Exchange; Richard William Stone [1973] Finance Director; Gareth Vaughan Thomas [1957] Director; Richard Ian Tolkien [1955] Director/Businessman

Shared Services Connected Ltd
Incorporated: 25 March 2013 *Employees:* 1,466
Net Worth: £39,491,000 *Total Assets:* £150,602,000
Registered Office: Three Cherry Trees Lane, Hemel Hempstead, Herts, HP2 7AH
Activities: Other business support service activities n.e.c.
Parent: Sopra Steria Limited
Officers: Peter Atherton Cashmore, Secretary; Davinder Singh Ahluwalia [1952] Director; Peter Atherton Cashmore [1962] Director/Solicitor [New Zealander]; Peter Atherton Cashmore [1962] Director/Solicitor [New Zealander]; Michael Brian Driver [1961] Director/Chief Financial Officer; Maria Greene [1967] Director/Accountant; John Nairn MacGregor Neilson [1961] Human Resources Director; Mark David Thomson [1962] Director; John Powell Torrie [1954] Director

Sharnbrook Academy Federation
Incorporated: 20 January 2011 *Employees:* 523
Net Worth: £52,199,536 *Total Assets:* £58,341,944
Registered Office: Sharnbrook Upper School, Odell Road, Sharnbrook, Bedford, MK44 1JL
Activities: Other education n.e.c.
Officers: Tracy Bannister, Secretary; Jonathan Abbott [1971] Director/Retired; Alexander Kristian Ginns [1981] Director; Sean Hanson [1964] Director/Chief Executive, Local Partnerships LLP [Irish]; Alison Clare Horner [1964] Director/Partner at MHA MacIntyre Hudson; Tanja Kuveljic [1969] Director; Stelios Mores [1964] Director; Jeremy Francis Reynolds [1963] Director/Management Consultant; Marie-Chantal Thomas [1964] Director/Solicitor

Sharp Electronics (Europe) Limited
Incorporated: 8 May 2012 *Employees:* 208
Net Worth: £73,973,384 *Total Assets:* £202,510,208
Registered Office: 4 Furzeground Way, Stockley Park, Uxbridge, Middlesex, UB11 1EZ
Activities: Other manufacturing n.e.c.
Parent: Sharp Corporation
Officers: Gosia Grant-Lipinska, Secretary; Jun Ashida [1966] Director [Japanese]; Seitaro Nomura [1976] Director [Japanese]

Sharp International Finance (U.K.) PLC
Incorporated: 2 May 1990 *Employees:* 3
Net Worth: £33,154,948 *Total Assets:* £116,652,608
Registered Office: 4 Furzeground Way, Stockley Park, Uxbridge, Middlesex, UB11 1EZ
Activities: Financial intermediation not elsewhere classified
Officers: Tatsuaki Watanabe, Secretary; Satoshi Sakakibara [1958] Director/Businessman [Japanese]; Tatsuaki Watanabe [1965] Director/Businessman [Japanese]

Shearwater Geoservices Limited
Incorporated: 20 December 2010 *Employees:* 56
Previous: Dolphin Geophysical Limited
Net Worth: £7,218,445 *Total Assets:* £26,130,916
Registered Office: Brockbourne House, 77 Mount Ephraim, Tunbridge Wells, Kent, TN4 8GN
Activities: Other business support service activities n.e.c.
Shareholders: Einar Johan Rasmussen; Rannfrid Rasmussen
Officers: Andreas Hveding Aubert [1980] Director [Norwegian]; Simon William Telfer [1979] Director

Shepherd Neame Limited
Incorporated: 9 November 1914 *Employees:* 1,569
Net Worth: £201,052,000 *Total Assets:* £334,227,008
Registered Office: 17 Court Street, Faversham, Kent, ME13 7AX
Activities: Manufacture of beer
Officers: Robin Neil Duncan, Secretary; George Harold Abbott Barnes [1954] Director; William John Brett [1965] Director; Nigel James Bunting [1967] Retail Director; Jonathan Beale Neame [1964] Director; Richard John Oldfield [1955] Director; Mark John Rider [1976] Finance Director; Hilary Susan Riva [1957] Director; Miles Howard Templeman [1947] Director/Consultant

Shepperton Studios Limited
Incorporated: 6 October 1994 *Employees:* 78
Net Worth: £10,657,000 *Total Assets:* £82,082,000
Registered Office: c/o Pinewood Studios, Pinewood Road, Iver Heath, Bucks, SL0 0NH
Activities: Motion picture, video and television programme post-production activities
Parent: Pinewood-Shepperton Studios Limited
Officers: Bridget Sheldon-Hill, Secretary; Paul William Martin Golding [1965] Director/Partner; Luis Moner Parra [1981] Director/Principal [Spanish]; Chris John Naisby [1972] Director; James Howard Rider [1978] Commercial Director; Neville Shulman [1939] Director/Chartered Accountant; Andrew Mark Smith [1962] Group Director Corporate Affairs

Shilton Bidco Limited
Incorporated: 28 April 2017 *Employees:* 3
Net Worth: £106,638,000 *Total Assets:* £1,029,436,992
Registered Office: Profile West, 950 Great West Road, Brentford, Middlesex, TW8 9ES
Activities: Non-trading company
Parent: Shilton Holdco Limited
Officers: Andrew Gregory Firth [1964] Director; Andrew Patrick Griffith [1968] Director; Philippe Robert Francis Mauguy [1960] Director [French]

Shilton Holdco Limited
Incorporated: 28 April 2017
Net Worth: £211,656,992 *Total Assets:* £439,038,016
Registered Office: Profile West, 950 Great West Road, Brentford, Middlesex, TW8 9ES
Activities: Non-trading company
Officers: Andrew Gregory Firth [1964] Director; Andrew Patrick Griffith [1968] Director; Philippe Robert Francis Mauguy [1960] Director [French]

Shimtech Industries Group Limited
Incorporated: 17 December 2014 *Employees:* 457
Previous: Auctus Scorpion Topco Limited
Net Worth: £48,860,720 *Total Assets:* £194,229,792
Registered Office: 7 A/B, Millington Road, Hayes, Middlesex, UB3 4AZ
Activities: Activities of head offices
Officers: Andrew David Caffyn [1964] Director/Business Executive; Alastair Scott Fanning [1967] Director/Business Executive; John Frederik Hartz [1973] Director/Investment Professional [Danish]; Prince Valerio Camillo Francesco Massimo [1973] Director/Business Executive; Catherine Allingham Richards [1973] Director/Investment Professional; Lord Edward Albert Charles Spencer-Churchill [1974] Director/Business Executive; Brian Williams [1957] Director [American]

Shimtech Industries Holdco Limited
Incorporated: 17 December 2014
Previous: Auctus Scorpion Holdco Limited
Net Worth: £3,163,000 *Total Assets:* £108,458,000
Registered Office: 7 A/B, Millington Road, Hayes, Middlesex, UB3 4AZ
Activities: Activities of head offices
Parent: Auctus Scorpion Midco Limited
Officers: Heath Denis Batwell [1983] Director/Accountant [Irish]; Andrew David Caffyn [1964] Director/Business Executive; Alastair Scott Fanning [1967] Director/Business Executive; John Frederik Hartz [1963] Director/Investment Professional [Danish]; Prince Valerio Camillo Francesco Massimo [1973] Director/Business Executive; Catherine Allingham Richards [1973] Director/Investment Professional; Lord Edward Albert Charles Spencer-Churchill [1974] Director/Business Executive; Brian Williams [1957] Director [American]

Shimtech Industries Holdco2 Limited
Incorporated: 17 December 2014 *Employees:* 1
Previous: Auctus Industries Limited
Net Worth Deficit: £17,760,000 *Total Assets:* £248,446,000
Registered Office: 7 A/B, Millington Road, Hayes, Middlesex, UB3 4AZ
Activities: Activities of head offices
Parent: Auctus Scorpion Holdco Limited
Officers: Heath Denis Batwell [1983] Director/Accountant [Irish]; Andrew David Caffyn [1964] Director/Business Executive; Alastair Scott Fanning [1967] Director/Business Executive; John Frederik Hartz [1963] Director/Investment Professional [Danish]; Prince Valerio Camillo Francesco Massimo [1973] Director/Business Executive; Catherine Allingham Richards [1973] Director/Investment Professional; Lord Edward Albert Charles Spencer-Churchill [1974] Director/Business Executive; Brian Williams [1957] Director [American]

Shimtech Industries Limited
Incorporated: 4 February 2011 *Employees:* 4
Net Worth Deficit: £21,796,152 *Total Assets:* £74,196,240
Registered Office: 7A/B Millington Road, Hayes, Middlesex, UB3 4AZ
Activities: Activities of head offices
Parent: Shimtech Industries Holdco2 Limited
Officers: Heath Denis Batwell [1983] Director/Accountant [Irish]; Alastair Scott Fanning [1967] Director/Accountant; Christopher Eric Smith [1971] Director

Shires Holdings Limited
Incorporated: 23 November 2007 *Employees:* 3
Net Worth: £7,321,000 *Total Assets:* £78,567,000
Registered Office: Innovation Centre, Southern Cross Trading Estate, Beeding Close, Bognor Regis, W Sussex, PO22 9TS
Activities: Manufacture of electric lighting equipment
Parent: JCC Lighting Holdings Limited
Officers: Mark Stephen Baydarian [1954] Director/Executive [American]; Donald Jay Hendler [1945] Director/Executive [American]; Daryoush Larizadeh [1964] Director/Executive [American]

SHL Group Limited
Incorporated: 5 September 1977 *Employees:* 469
Net Worth: £54,856,000 *Total Assets:* £73,779,000
Registered Office: The Pavilion, 1 Atwell Place, Thames Ditton, Surrey, KT7 0NE
Activities: Activities of head offices
Parent: SHL International Management Limited
Officers: Andrew James Bradshaw [1971] Director/General Manager; Michael Edmondson [1976] Director/Head of Finance; Andrew William Myers [1964] Director/Chief Financial Officer; David Edward Ryell [1971] Director/Head of Financial Controller

SHOO 802AA Limited
Incorporated: 26 April 2017 *Employees:* 102
Net Worth: £535,000 *Total Assets:* £20,611,000
Registered Office: Burleighfield House, London Road, Loudwater, Bucks, HP10 9RF
Activities: Public relations and communications activities
Officers: Robert John Jozef Apollo [1985] Director; Christian Lewis Bruning [1969] Director; Matthew Robert James Gorham [1976] Director; Dennis Simon O'Brien [1975] Director; Janet Elizabeth Steele [1964] Director; Timothy Hugh Southcombe Trotter [1959] Director/Chairman

Shoosmiths LLP
Incorporated: 4 May 2012 *Employees:* 1,337
Net Worth: £39,742,000 *Total Assets:* £82,722,000
Registered Office: Witan Gate House, 500-600 Witan Gate West, Milton Keynes, Bucks, MK9 1SH
Officers: Simon Andrew Boss [1964] Member; Melanie Chell [1975] Member; Stephen Mark Dawson [1977] Member; Peter Howarth Duff [1968] Member; Alastair Jonathan Taylor Peet [1974] Member; James Marlin Taylor [1972] Member; Sean Brian Wright [1966] Member; David Andrew Adams [1973] LLP Member; Bhavesh Amlani [1973] LLP Member; Craig Simon Armstrong [1975] LLP Member; Charles William Arrand [1969] LLP Member; Edell Mary Asquez [1976] LLP Member; Gary Dean Assim [1961] LLP Member; Richard Stephen Atha [1964] LLP Member; Melissa Kate Barker [1976] LLP Member; Philip Tudor Barnes [1975] LLP Member; Simon Timothy Barnes [1974] LLP Member; Steven Paul Barnett [1970] LLP Member; Paul James Peter Bachelor [1982] LLP Member; Richard Nicholas Bellamy [1974] LLP Member; Stephen Eric Belshaw [1961] LLP Member; Alexandra Elizabeth Bishop [1973] LLP Member; Angela Dawn Bowman [1971] LLP Member; Andrew John Brennan [1978] LLP Member; Anthony Crispin Bridges Webb [1962] LLP Member; Simon Matthew Briggs [1969] LLP Member; John Peter Buckley [1979] LLP Member; Helen Burgess [1980] LLP Member; Sean Robert Nicholas Patrick Burke [1962] LLP Member; Suzanne Ruth Burrell [1976] LLP Member; Jason Byrne [1979] LLP Member; Paul Bernard Carney [1965] LLP Member; Anna Lowri Cartledge [1980] LLP Member; Ruth Margaret Zanre Clare [1976] LLP Member; John Robert Cleaveley [1968] LLP Member; Stuart Alexander Clubb [1978] LLP Member; Alan Corcoran [1968] LLP Member; Hamish Richard Corner [1976] LLP Member; Gillian Elizabeth Crotty [1983] LLP Member; Philip Andrew Crowe [1980] LLP Member; Suman Dally [1969] LLP Member; Rosemary Donoghue [1957] LLP Member; Stephen Paul Dougherty [1961] LLP Member; Adam Draper [1976] LLP Member; Charlotte Dunn [1972] LLP Member; Mark Joseph Elder [1972] LLP Member; Angus Kenneth David Evers [1972] LLP Member; David Robert Farnell [1968] LLP Member; Vaqas Farooq [1977] LLP Member; Judy Anne Fawcett [1968] LLP Member; Kate Louise Featherstone [1977] LLP Member; Richard Thomas Follis [1956] LLP Member; James Alan Foster [1981] LLP Member; Andrew Joseph Foyle [1977] LLP Member; Heather Maxine Freeman [1966] LLP Member; Ellis Gardner-Browne [1972] LLP Member; Patrick Alan Garner [1973] LLP Member; Lisa Callen Gibbs [1971] LLP Member; Paul James Gidman [1974] LLP Member; Alison Mary Gilson [1978] LLP Member; Philip Edward Goldsborough [1969] LLP Member; Deborah Gordon Brown [1964] LLP Member; Thomas David Hall [1981] LLP Member; Daniel Edward Hargreaves [1979] LLP Member; Aaron Michael Harlow [1982] LLP Member; Laura Jayne Harper [1973] LLP Member; David Ian Harrison [1980] LLP Member; Kellie Hatton [1978] LLP Member; Adele Julie Hayfield [1982] LLP Member; Tracey Hemingway [1966] LLP Member; Kirsten Joanne Hewson [1971] LLP Member; Neil Hobden [1960] LLP Member; Catherine Elizabeth Hood [1974] LLP Member; William Ian Howard [1956] LLP Member; Charles Matthew Howarth [1968] LLP Member; Sara Mary Hunt [1973] LLP Member; Nicholas Patrick Iliff [1966] LLP Member; David Antony Jackson [1975] LLP Member; Jason Ronald Jackson [1969] LLP Member; Timothy David Jackson-Smith [1969] LLP Member; Alexander Francis Jones [1966] LLP Member; Kathryn Louise Jump [1972] LLP Member; James Laurence Keates [1970] LLP Member; Daniel John Kennedy [1978] LLP Member; Matthew William James Kenwood [1973] LLP Member; Alexander William Christopher Thompson Kirkhope [1979] LLP Member; James Klein [1970] LLP Member; Paul Russell Knight [1962] LLP Member; Stuart Owen Lawrenson [1973] LLP Member; Lynette Ann Lewis [1969] LLP Member; Stuart Little [1968] LLP Member; Katherine Livingston [1969] LLP Member; Matthew Jason Lonergan [1969] LLP Member; Roderick Gray MacPhail [1957] LLP Member; Sherif Malak [1980] LLP Member; Waine Gerard Mannix [1966] LLP Member; Melissa Mary Maple [1976] LLP Member; Rebecca Margaret Mauleverer [1975] LLP Member; Joseph Mazzucca [1973] LLP Member; Elizabeth Ann McArdle [1973] LLP Member

Shoppertrak Limited
Incorporated: 16 October 1987 *Employees:* 58
Previous: Footfall Limited
Net Worth Deficit: £5,792,000 *Total Assets:* £23,559,000
Registered Office: Security House, The Summit, Hanworth Road, Sunbury on Thames, Middlesex, TW16 5DB
Activities: Other service activities n.e.c.
Parent: Tyco Holdings (UK) Limited
Officers: Mark Ayre [1963] Finance Director; Nicholas Dominic Pompa [1963] Director

Shorefield Holidays Limited
Incorporated: 15 July 1958 *Employees:* 252
Net Worth: £56,570,192 *Total Assets:* £80,820,976
Registered Office: Shorefield Country Park, Shorefield Road, Milford on Sea, Lymington, Hants, SO41 0LH
Activities: Holiday centres and villages
Officers: Sara Bertin, Secretary; Sara Bertin [1951] Director/Accountant; Andrew James Bowden [1975] Director/IT Professional; Paula Jane Curtis [1964] Director/Company Accountant; Lesley Lawrence [1953] Director/Park Operator; Susan Morley [1955] Director/Park Operator; Ann Pollock [1960] Director/Park Operator; Simon Pollock [1956] Director/Park Operator

Shukco 327 Ltd
Incorporated: 25 November 1996 *Employees:* 1
Previous: SITA Waste Services Limited
Net Worth Deficit: £2,400,000 *Total Assets:* £42,015,000
Registered Office: Suez House, Grenfell Road, Maidenhead, Berks, SL6 1ES
Activities: Activities of other holding companies n.e.c.
Parent: Shukco Ltd
Officers: Joan Knight, Secretary; Florent Thierry Antoine Duval [1976] Director/Chief Finance Officer [French]

Shukco Ltd
Incorporated: 27 November 1984
Previous: SITA Waste Limited
Net Worth: £60,371,000 *Total Assets:* £60,371,000
Registered Office: Suez House, Grenfell Road, Maidenhead, Berks, SL6 1ES
Activities: Activities of head offices
Parent: Group Fabricom Limited
Officers: Joan Knight, Secretary; Florent Thierry Antoine Duval [1976] Director/Chief Finance Officer [French]

Shurgard UK Limited
Incorporated: 11 April 2003 *Employees:* 77
Net Worth: £166,884,784 *Total Assets:* £194,987,392
Registered Office: 2 AC Court, High Street, Thames Ditton, Surrey, KT7 0SR
Activities: Operation of warehousing and storage facilities for land transport activities
Parent: Shurgard Holding Luxembourg SARL
Officers: Marc Pierre Francois Oursin [1962] Director [French]

Siemens Financial Services Holdings Limited
Incorporated: 12 January 2001
Net Worth: £118,007,000 *Total Assets:* £118,007,000
Registered Office: Sefton Park, Bells Hill, Stoke Poges, Bucks, SL2 4JS
Activities: Activities of financial services holding companies
Parent: Siemens Holdings PLC
Officers: Ralph Thomas Britton, Secretary; Julian Martin Hobbs [1967] Director; Martin Klein [1966] Director [German]; James Erik Murnieks [1977] Director/Chartered Accountant

Siemens Financial Services Limited
Incorporated: 1 January 1960 *Employees:* 246
Net Worth: £205,928,992 *Total Assets:* £1,578,504,960
Registered Office: Sefton Park, Bells Hill, Stoke Poges, Bucks, SL2 4JS
Activities: Financial leasing
Officers: Ralph Thomas Britton, Secretary; Richard Anthony Hargraves [1964] Director; Julian Martin Hobbs [1967] Director; Martin Klein [1966] Director [German]; James Erik Murnieks [1977] Director/Chartered Accountant

Siemens Gamesa Renewable Energy Limited
Incorporated: 27 June 2016 *Employees:* 2,107
Net Worth Deficit: £2,026,000 *Total Assets:* £435,076,992
Registered Office: Faraday House, Sir William Siemens Square, Frimley, Camberley, Surrey, GU16 8QD
Activities: Construction of utility projects for electricity and telecommunications
Parent: Siemens Gamesa Renewable Energy S.A.
Officers: Martin James Heath, Secretary; Ross Keyzer-Dean [1976] Finance Director; William Clark MacFarlane [1964] Managing Director; Grant Walker [1964] Director

Siemens Healthcare Diagnostics Ltd
Incorporated: 27 April 1995
Net Worth: £32,210,000 *Total Assets:* £55,420,000
Registered Office: Faraday House, Sir William Siemens Square, Frimley, Camberley, Surrey, GU16 8QD
Activities: Manufacture of other chemical products n.e.c.
Parent: Siemens Healthineers Aktiengesellschaft
Officers: Mahan Athwal, Secretary; Russell Adam Challis [1980] Director/Accountant; Marlen Suller [1978] Director/Country Business Lead for Siemens Healthcare [German]

Siemens Healthcare Diagnostics Manufacturing Ltd
Incorporated: 22 May 1985 *Employees:* 251
Net Worth: £23,379,000 *Total Assets:* £36,215,000
Registered Office: Faraday House, Sir William Siemens Square, Frimley, Camberley, Surrey, GU16 8QD
Activities: Manufacture of medical and dental instruments and supplies
Parent: Siemens Healthineers Aktiengesellschaft
Officers: Mahan Athwal, Secretary; Alastair Burns [1976] Managing Director; Kwai So [1970] Director/Accountant

Siemens Healthcare Diagnostics Products Ltd
Incorporated: 2 April 1986 *Employees:* 379
Net Worth: £41,970,000 *Total Assets:* £48,849,000
Registered Office: Faraday House, Sir William Siemens Square, Frimley, Camberley, Surrey, GU16 8QD
Activities: Manufacture of other chemical products n.e.c.
Parent: Siemens Healthineers Aktiengesellschaft
Officers: Mahan Athwal, Secretary; Martin William Gray [1973] Finance Director; Fraser Campbell Logue [1953] Vice President Operations/Managing Director

Siemens Holdings PLC
Incorporated: 30 January 1990
Net Worth: £1,034,356,992 *Total Assets:* £1,918,364,032
Registered Office: Faraday House, Sir William Siemens Square, Frimley, Camberley, Surrey, GU16 8QD
Activities: Activities of head offices
Parent: Siemens Aktiengesellschaft
Officers: Simone Eufemia Agatha Davina, Secretary; Simone Eufemia Agatha Davina [1972] Director/Lawyer/General Counsel [Dutch]; Professor Juergen Wolfgang Maier [1964] Director/Chief Executive [Austrian]; Axel Meier [1963] Director [German]; Angela Noon [1973] Director/Chief Financial Officer

Siemens Industrial Turbomachinery Limited
Incorporated: 10 April 2003 *Employees:* 1,474
Net Worth: £484,523,008 *Total Assets:* £649,585,984
Registered Office: Faraday House, Sir William Siemens Square, Frimley, Camberley, Surrey, GU16 8QD
Activities: Manufacture of engines and turbines, except aircraft, vehicle and cycle engines
Parent: Siemens Aktiengesellschaft
Officers: Simone Eufemia Agatha Davina, Secretary; Neil Alan Corner [1967] Managing Director; John George Stephen Hunt [1964] Director/Chief Financial Officer; Mark Andrew Speed [1971] Director

Siemens Industry Software Computational Dynamics Limited
Incorporated: 19 October 1987 *Employees:* 158
Previous: Computational Dynamics Limited
Net Worth: £56,998,000 *Total Assets:* £86,061,000
Registered Office: Faraday House, Sir William Siemens Square, Frimley, Camberley, Surrey, GU16 8QD
Activities: Other information technology service activities
Parent: Siemens Aktiengesellschaft
Officers: Simone Eufemia Agatha Davina, Secretary; Darren Lee MacAskill [1975] Director; Benjamin Miles Sheath [1971] VP and Managing Director

Siemens Industry Software Limited
Incorporated: 1 December 1997 *Employees:* 493
Net Worth: £61,824,000 *Total Assets:* £83,811,000
Registered Office: Faraday House, Sir William Siemens Square, Frimley, Camberley, Surrey, GU16 8QD
Activities: Information technology consultancy activities
Parent: Siemens Aktiengesellschaft
Officers: Sarah Brufal-De-Melgarejo, Secretary; Brian Aubrey Holliday [1969] Chartered Engineer/Division Director; Darren Lee MacAskill [1975] Director; Benjamin Miles Sheath [1971] VP and Managing Director

Siemens Mobility Limited
Incorporated: 7 November 1881 *Employees:* 1,559
Previous: Siemens Rail Automation Holdings Limited
Net Worth: £182,048,992 *Total Assets:* £354,891,008
Registered Office: Faraday House, Sir William Siemens Square, Frimley, Camberley, Surrey, GU16 8QD
Activities: Manufacture of other transport equipment n.e.c.
Parent: Siemens Aktiengesellschaft
Officers: Nicola Diane Jordan, Secretary; Professor Juergen Wolfgang Maier [1964] Director/Chief Executive [Austrian]; Sandra Julie Owen [1960] Finance Director; Gordon Lawrence Wakeford [1962] Managing Director

Siemens Pension Funding Limited
Incorporated: 18 September 2012 *Employees:* 2
Net Worth: £421,929,728 *Total Assets:* £427,636,928
Registered Office: Faraday House, Sir William Siemens Square, Frimley, Camberley, Surrey, GU16 8QD
Activities: Pension funding
Parent: Siemens Holdings PLC
Officers: Simone Eufemia Agatha Davina, Secretary; Dr Benedikt Sipple [1985] Director/Senior Referent Corporate Pension A&C [German]; John Hamilton Smith [1961] Director/Head of Pensions Siemens PLC & Cluster North West [Irish]

Siemens Public Limited Company
Incorporated: 25 June 1962 *Employees:* 5,720
Net Worth: £1,257,347,968 *Total Assets:* £2,339,685,888
Registered Office: Faraday House, Sir William Siemens Square, Frimley, Camberley, Surrey, GU16 8QD
Activities: Manufacture of electronic components
Parent: Siemens Holdings PLC
Officers: Simone Eufemia Agatha Davina, Secretary; Simone Eufemia Agatha Davina [1972] Director/Lawyer/General Counsel [Dutch]; Professor Juergen Wolfgang Maier [1964] Director/Chief Executive [Austrian]; Angela Noon [1973] Director/Chief Financial Officer

Siemens Transmission and Distribution Limited
Incorporated: 3 July 1959 *Employees:* 387
Net Worth: £65,154,000 *Total Assets:* £189,503,008
Registered Office: Faraday House, Sir William Siemens Square, Frimley, Camberley, Surrey, GU16 8QD
Activities: Manufacture of electricity distribution and control apparatus
Parent: VA Tech (UK) Limited
Officers: Simone Eufemia Agatha Davina, Secretary; Carl Ennis [1968] Managing Director; Alistair James Gemmell [1961] Director/Accountant

Signature Senior Lifestyle Finance Limited
Incorporated: 30 November 2005 *Employees:* 3
Net Worth: £45,574,424 *Total Assets:* £63,823,416
Registered Office: Grosvenor House, Horseshoe Crescent, Beaconsfield, Bucks, HP9 1LJ
Activities: Other letting and operating of own or leased real estate
Parent: Signature Senior Lifestyle Holdings Limited
Officers: Tom James Ball, Secretary; Tom James Ball [1983] Finance Director; Frank Cerrone [1959] Director/Senior Vice President, General Counsel & Secretary [Canadian]; James Hardy [1959] Director/Chief Investment Officer & CFO [Canadian]; Thomas Bruce Newell [1957] Director [American]; Aidan Gerard Roche [1966] Director [Irish]

Signet Direct Diamond Sourcing Limited
Incorporated: 12 April 2011
Net Worth: £79,225,376 *Total Assets:* £86,724,216
Registered Office: Imperial Place, 3 Maxwell Road, Borehamwood, Herts, WD6 1JN
Activities: Other business support service activities n.e.c.
Parent: Signet Holdings Limited
Officers: Benjamin Harris [1983] Director/Attorney; Rory O'Donnell [1977] Director/Financial Controller [American]; Michele Santana [1970] Director/Chief Financial Officer [American]

Signet Group Limited
Incorporated: 27 January 1950 *Employees:* 1
Net Worth: £631,923,072 *Total Assets:* £1,798,029,184
Registered Office: Imperial Place, 3 Maxwell Road, Borehamwood, Herts, WD6 1JN
Activities: Activities of head offices
Parent: Signet Jewelers Limited
Officers: Benjamin Harris, Secretary; Marianne Kelly [1974] Director/Head of Finance; Raina Margaret Miles [1962] Director/Chartered Accountant; Michele Santana [1970] Director/Chief Financial Officer [American]

Signet Holdings Limited
Incorporated: 13 May 1999
Net Worth: £1,155,329,152 *Total Assets:* £1,202,115,712
Registered Office: Imperial Place, 3 Maxwell Road, Borehamwood, Herts, WD6 1JN
Activities: Non-trading company
Parent: Signet Group Limited
Officers: Benjamin Harris, Secretary; Marianne Kelly [1974] Director/Head of Finance; Raina Margaret Miles [1962] Director/Chartered Accountant; Michele Santana [1970] Director/Chief Financial Officer [American]

Signet Trading Limited
Incorporated: 12 May 1999 *Employees:* 3,255
Net Worth: £290,904,000 *Total Assets:* £369,443,008
Registered Office: Imperial Place, 3 Maxwell Road, Borehamwood, Herts, WD6 1JN
Activities: Other business support service activities n.e.c.
Parent: Signet Holdings Limited
Officers: Benjamin Harris, Secretary; Shaun David Carney [1966] Finance Director; Benjamin Harris [1983] Director/Attorney

Signet UK Finance PLC
Incorporated: 17 April 2014
Net Worth: £4,957,018 *Total Assets:* £306,881,696
Registered Office: Imperial Place, 3 Maxwell Road, Borehamwood, Herts, WD6 1JN
Activities: Other business support service activities n.e.c.
Parent: Signet Group Limited
Officers: Benjamin Harris, Secretary; Marianne Kelly [1974] Director/Head of Finance; Raina Margaret Miles [1962] Director/Chartered Accountant; Michele Santana [1970] Director/Chief Financial Officer [American]

Silicon Storage Technology Ltd
Incorporated: 28 April 2017 *Employees:* 2
Net Worth: £183,246,448 *Total Assets:* £184,910,112
Registered Office: 720 Wharfedale Road, Winnersh Triangle, Wokingham, Berks, RG41 5TP
Activities: Engineering design activities for industrial process and production
Parent: Microchip Technology Ireland Ltd
Officers: James Eric Bjornholt [1970] Director/Chief Financial Officer [American]; William Nicholas Edwards [1974] Finance Director; Mohammed Nawaz Sharif [1970] Director/VP European Finance and IR

Silver Acquisition Co Limited
Incorporated: 19 December 2014
Net Worth Deficit: £97,260,832 *Total Assets:* £271,498,624
Registered Office: Innovation House, 70 Norden Road, Maidenhead, Berks, SL6 4AY
Activities: Research and experimental development on biotechnology
Parent: Biogen Inc.
Officers: Steven John Green [1977] Finance Director; Trevor Anthony Mill [1971] Director/Vice President

Sime Darby London Limited
Incorporated: 27 July 1972 *Employees:* 1
Net Worth: £22,124,000 *Total Assets:* £24,157,000
Registered Office: Thomas Eggar House, Friary Lane, Chichester, W Sussex, PO19 1UF
Activities: Activities of head offices
Officers: Kamarul Ariffin Abdul Samad [1969] Director/Head of Corporate Services [Malaysian]; Wan Norjihan Binti Wan Ismail [1965] Director/Head, Treasury and Credit Management [Malaysian]; Zahari Bin Salleh [1966] Director [Malaysian]

Sinclair Gardens Investments (Kensington) Limited
Incorporated: 21 August 1963 *Employees:* 8
Net Worth: £131,510,128 *Total Assets:* £227,857,984
Registered Office: Regis House, Regis Business Centre, Durban Road, Bognor Regis, W Sussex, PO22 9QT
Activities: Development of building projects
Officers: Karen Wainwright, Secretary; Gregory Reginald Cutler [1967] Director

Sinclair Knight Merz (Europe) Limited
Incorporated: 15 May 1997 *Employees:* 290
Net Worth: £13,037,000 *Total Assets:* £44,633,000
Registered Office: 1180 Eskdale Road, Winnersh, Wokingham, Berks, RG41 5TU
Activities: Other engineering activities
Parent: Jacobs Engineering Group Inc
Officers: Tejender Singh Chaudhary, Secretary; Erwin Geene [1970] Director/Financial Controller [Dutch]; Jonathan Ross Shattock [1964] Director/Solicitor

Sirhowy Enterprise Way (Holdings) Limited
Incorporated: 6 October 2003
Net Worth Deficit: £3,398,000 *Total Assets:* £39,123,000
Registered Office: 8 White Oak Square, London Road, Swanley, Kent, BR8 7AG
Activities: Activities of head offices
Parent: JLIF (GP) Limited
Officers: Carl Harvey Dix [1966] Operations Director; Johannes Petrus Heemelaar [1956] Director [Dutch]

Sirhowy Enterprise Way Limited
Incorporated: 3 October 2003
Net Worth Deficit: £3,398,000 *Total Assets:* £39,123,000
Registered Office: 8 White Oak Square, London Road, Swanley, Kent, BR8 7AG
Activities: Construction of commercial buildings
Parent: Sirhowy Enterprise Way (Holdings) Limited
Officers: Carl Harvey Dix [1966] Operations Director; Johannes Petrus Heemelaar [1956] Director [Dutch]

Sirigen II Limited
Incorporated: 4 September 2012
Net Worth: £41,063,492 *Total Assets:* £41,425,020
Registered Office: 1030 Eskdale Road, Winnersh Triangle, Wokingham, Berks, RG41 5TS
Activities: Activities of other holding companies n.e.c.
Officers: Michael John Fairbourn [1959] Director/Vice President, General Manager; Edward Daniel Hopkin [1973] Director/International Counsel; John Konrad Neat [1967] Finance Director

SITA Advanced Travel Solutions Limited
Incorporated: 29 September 1978 *Employees:* 91
Net Worth Deficit: £9,716,148 *Total Assets:* £28,013,746
Registered Office: Royal Pavilion, Wellesley Road, Aldershot, Hants, GU11 1PZ
Activities: Other telecommunications activities
Parent: SITA N.V.
Officers: Alain Brodeur, Secretary; Aileen Teresa Mary McEntee, Secretary; Nicolas Emmanuel Husson [1969] Director/Chief Financial Officer [French]; Nicolas Emmanuel Husson [1969] Director/Chief Financial Officer [French]; Jeremy Colin Springall [1968] Director/Senior Vice President

SITA Information Networking Computing UK Limited
Incorporated: 16 May 2000 *Employees:* 396
Net Worth Deficit: £90,415,984 *Total Assets:* £89,077,264
Registered Office: c/o Sita Legal, 1 London Gate, 252-254 Blyth Road, Hayes, Middlesex, UB3 1BW
Activities: Other information service activities n.e.c.
Parent: SITA N.V.
Officers: Alain Brodeur, Secretary; Aileen Teresa Mary McEntee, Secretary; Nicolas Emmanuel Husson [1969] Director/Chief Financial Officer [French]; Barbara Marguerite Ploux Dalibard [1958] Director/Chief Executive Officer [French]; Jeremy Colin Springall [1968] Director/Senior Vice President

Siva Holdings Limited
Incorporated: 24 July 1979 *Employees:* 225
Net Worth: £15,281,042 *Total Assets:* £45,913,316
Registered Office: Spitfire House, Hazel Road, Woolston, Southampton, SO19 7GB
Activities: Manufacture of plastic packing goods
Shareholders: Tej Pal Kaur Mehta; Gurjinder Singh Mehta
Officers: Preet Pal Babna Kaur Athwal, Secretary; Tej Pal Mehta, Secretary; Preet Pal Babna Kaur Athwal [1973] Financial Director; Gurjinder Singh Mehta [1941] Director/Chairman; Tej Pal Kaur Mehta [1953] Managing Director; Vijinder Singh Mehta [1975] Marketing Director; Vrind Pal Mehta [1972] Commercial Director

Siva Plastics Limited
Incorporated: 31 July 1989 *Employees:* 225
Net Worth: £12,987,735 *Total Assets:* £39,980,168
Registered Office: Spitfire House, Hazel Road, Woolston, Southampton, SO19 7GB
Activities: Manufacture of plastic packing goods
Parent: Siva Holdings Limited
Officers: Hannah Mehta, Secretary; Adrian Francis Glen [1961] Technical Director; Hannah Mehta [1977] Director

Six Continents Holdings Limited
Incorporated: 12 June 1996
Net Worth: £1,027,502,976 *Total Assets:* £1,028,201,984
Registered Office: Broadwater Park, Denham, Bucks, UB9 5HR
Activities: Activities of head offices
Shareholders: Six Continents Limited; Asia Pacific Holdings Limited
Officers: Fiona Cuttell, Secretary; Paul Russell Edgecliffe-Johnson [1972] Director/Accountant; Michael Todd Glover [1971] Director/Financial Controller [American]; Nicolette Henfrey [1969] Director

Six Continents Hotels International Limited
Incorporated: 26 April 1962
Net Worth: £5,885,918,208 *Total Assets:* £5,887,932,928
Registered Office: Broadwater Park, Denham, Bucks, UB9 5HR
Activities: Activities of head offices
Parent: Six Continents Limited
Officers: Fiona Jane Littlebury-Cuttell, Secretary; Colin Philip Garwood [1961] Director; Michael Todd Glover [1971] Director/Financial Controller [American]; Nicolette Henfrey [1969] Director; George Turner [1971] Director/Company Secretary

Six Continents Investments Limited
Incorporated: 1 June 1961
Net Worth: £271,105,984 *Total Assets:* £271,191,008
Registered Office: Broadwater Park, Denham, Bucks, UB9 5HR
Activities: Other business support service activities n.e.c.
Parent: Six Continents Limited
Officers: Fiona Jane Littlebury-Cuttell, Secretary; Michael Jon Cockcroft [1974] Director/Accountant; Michael Todd Glover [1971] Director/Financial Controller [American]; Nicolette Henfrey [1969] Director

Six Continents Limited
Incorporated: 17 August 1967 *Employees:* 192
Net Worth: £2,916,999,936 *Total Assets:* £10,364,999,680
Registered Office: Broadwater Park, Denham, Bucks, UB9 5HR
Activities: Other business support service activities n.e.c.
Parent: Intercontinental Hotels Limited
Officers: Fiona Cuttell, Secretary; Paul Russell Edgecliffe-Johnson [1972] Director/Certified Chartered Accountant; Michael Todd Glover [1971] Director/Financial Controller [American]; Nicolette Henfrey [1969] Director; George Turner [1971] Director

Six Continents Overseas Holdings Limited
Incorporated: 7 November 1991
Net Worth: £2,179,664,896 *Total Assets:* £2,185,080,064
Registered Office: Broadwater Park, Denham, Bucks, UB9 5HR
Activities: Other business support service activities n.e.c.
Parent: Six Continents Limited
Officers: Fiona Cuttell, Secretary; Michael Jon Cockcroft [1974] Director/Accountant; Michael Todd Glover [1971] Director/Financial Controller [American]; Nicolette Henfrey [1969] Director; George Turner [1971] Director

Six Continents Restaurants Limited
Incorporated: 13 June 1962
Net Worth: £61,081,000 *Total Assets:* £61,100,000
Registered Office: Broadwater Park, Denham, Bucks, UB9 5HR
Activities: Other business support service activities n.e.c.
Parent: Six Continents Limited
Officers: Fiona Jane Littlebury-Cuttell, Secretary; Michael Jon Cockcroft [1974] Director/Accountant; Michael Todd Glover [1971] Director/Financial Controller [American]; Nicolette Henfrey [1969] Director

Sixt Rent A Car Limited
Incorporated: 18 August 1947 *Employees:* 378
Previous: Sixt Kenning Limited
Net Worth: £36,395,000 *Total Assets:* £105,307,000
Registered Office: Sixt House, 5 Langley Quay, Waterside Drive, Langley, Slough, SL3 6EY
Activities: Renting and leasing of cars and light motor vehicles
Parent: United Kenning Rental Group Limited
Officers: Per Ingo Voegerl, Secretary; Ian Walter Lawrence [1959] Group Managing Director; Tim Vetters [1984] Operations Director [German]; Per Ingo Voegerl [1973] Managing Director UK [German]

SK Hynix UK Limited
Incorporated: 5 July 1995 *Employees:* 12
Net Worth: £10,931,376 *Total Assets:* £216,451,216
Registered Office: Unit 4 Horizon Business Village, 1 Brooklands Road, Weybridge, Surrey, KT13 0TJ
Activities: Wholesale of computers, computer peripheral equipment and software
Parent: SK Hynix Inc.
Officers: Jae Kwon Hwang, Secretary; Jae Kwon Hwang [1980] Director/General Manager [South Korean]; Ho Sang Lee [1966] Managing Director [South Korean]; Dong Hui Son [1970] Director/General Manager [South Korean]

Skanska Cementation International Limited
Incorporated: 26 July 1948
Net Worth: £20,569,000 *Total Assets:* £33,210,000
Registered Office: Maple Cross House, Denham Way, Maple Cross, Rickmansworth, Herts, WD3 9SW
Activities: Construction of commercial buildings
Parent: Skanska Construction Holdings UK Limited
Officers: Steven Leven, Secretary; Mark Lawson Galloway [1955] Director/Solicitor; Culdip Kelly Kaur Gangotra [1970] Director/Accountant

Skanska Construction Holdings UK Limited
Incorporated: 30 October 2000
Net Worth: £2,960,000 *Total Assets:* £314,691,008
Registered Office: Maple Cross House, Denham Way, Maple Cross, Rickmansworth, Herts, WD3 9SW
Activities: Activities of head offices
Parent: Skanska AB
Officers: Mark Lawson Galloway, Secretary; Gregor Lawrence Craig [1963] Managing Director; Culdip Kelly Kaur Gangotra [1970] Director/Accountant

Skanska Construction UK Limited
Incorporated: 19 July 1923 *Employees:* 5,125
Net Worth: £250,718,000 *Total Assets:* £774,459,008
Registered Office: Maple Cross House, Denham Way, Maple Cross, Rickmansworth, Herts, WD3 9SW
Activities: Construction of commercial buildings
Parent: Skanska UK PLC
Officers: Steven Leven, Secretary; Gregor Lawrence Craig [1963] Managing Director; Katrina Mary Dowding [1970] Director; Thomas Peter Faulkner [1974] Director; Culdip Kelly Kaur Gangotra [1970] Director/Accountant; Martin George Neeson [1968] Director/Manager

Skanska Infrastructure Development UK Limited
Incorporated: 21 February 1995 *Employees:* 39
Net Worth Deficit: £50,734,000 *Total Assets:* £22,338,000
Registered Office: Maple Cross House, Denham Way, Maple Cross, Rickmansworth, Herts, WD3 9SW
Activities: Development of building projects
Parent: Skanska AB
Officers: Steven Leven, Secretary; Paul Alan Bannister [1959] Director; Simon Richard Thorpe Beauchamp [1973] Commercial Director

Skanska Infrastructure Investment UK Limited
Incorporated: 23 December 2002
Net Worth: £71,613,000 *Total Assets:* £91,503,000
Registered Office: Maple Cross House, Denham Way, Maple Cross, Rickmansworth, Herts, WD3 9SW
Activities: Other business support service activities n.e.c.
Parent: Skanska AB
Officers: Steven Leven, Secretary; Paul Alan Bannister [1959] Director; Simon Richard Thorpe Beauchamp [1973] Commercial Director

Skanska J.V. Projects Ltd
Incorporated: 18 December 1998 *Employees:* 30
Net Worth: £46,048,000 *Total Assets:* £97,344,000
Registered Office: Maple Cross House, Denham Way, Maple Cross, Rickmansworth, Herts, WD3 9SW
Activities: Other business support service activities n.e.c.
Parent: Skanska Construction UK Limited
Officers: Steven Leven, Secretary; Katrina Mary Dowding [1970] Director; Thomas Peter Faulkner [1974] Director; Culdip Kelly Kaur Gangotra [1970] Director/Accountant

Skanska Major Projects Limited
Incorporated: 9 November 1970 *Employees:* 8
Net Worth: £13,079,000 *Total Assets:* £22,816,000
Registered Office: Maple Cross House, Denham Way, Maple Cross, Rickmansworth, Herts, WD3 9SW
Activities: Other specialised construction activities n.e.c.
Parent: Skanska Construction UK Limited
Officers: Steven Leven, Secretary; Katrina Mary Dowding [1970] Director; Culdip Kelly Kaur Gangotra [1970] Director/Accountant

Skanska Rashleigh Weatherfoil Limited
Incorporated: 26 March 1964 *Employees:* 1,074
Net Worth: £66,226,000 *Total Assets:* £202,738,000
Registered Office: Maple Cross House, Denham Way, Maple Cross, Rickmansworth, Herts, WD3 9SW
Activities: Electrical installation
Parent: Skanska Construction UK Limited
Officers: Steven Leven, Secretary; Katrina Mary Dowding [1970] Director; Adam Michael McDonald [1983] Director

Skanska TAM Limited
Incorporated: 1 March 2013
Net Worth: £42,658,000 *Total Assets:* £87,536,000
Registered Office: Maple Cross House, Denham Way, Maple Cross, Rickmansworth, Herts, WD3 9SW
Activities: Development of building projects
Parent: Skanska Construction Services Trustee Limited
Officers: Nigel John Pitchers, Secretary; Harvey James Francis [1965] Director; Philippa Jane Smith [1958] Director; David Ian Wills [1962] Director

Skanska UK PLC
Incorporated: 16 December 1963 *Employees:* 5,741
Net Worth: £261,776,000 *Total Assets:* £891,872,000
Registered Office: Maple Cross House, Denham Way, Maple Cross, Rickmansworth, Herts, WD3 9SW
Activities: Construction of commercial buildings
Parent: Skanska Construction Holdings UK Limited
Officers: Mark Lawson Galloway, Secretary; Gregor Lawrence Craig [1963] Managing Director; Katrina Mary Dowding [1970] Director; Thomas Peter Faulkner [1974] Director; Harvey James Francis [1965] Director; Mark Lawson Galloway [1955] Director/Solicitor; Culdip Kelly Kaur Gangotra [1970] Director/Accountant; Martin George Neeson [1968] Director/Manager

Ski Bound Limited
Incorporated: 21 December 1984 *Employees:* 94
Net Worth: £9,640,000 *Total Assets:* £23,616,000
Registered Office: Origin One, 108 High Street, Crawley, W Sussex, RH10 1BD
Activities: Other service activities n.e.c.
Parent: First Choice Holidays Limited
Officers: Janet Northey, Secretary; Brendan Derek Lee Jones [1965] Managing Director; Bryn Glyndwr Robinson [1960] Director; Neil Kenneth Rust [1964] Director/Accountant

Skillbond Limited
Incorporated: 27 December 1973 *Employees:* 6
Net Worth: £60,961,136 *Total Assets:* £65,711,776
Registered Office: Herschel House, 58 Herschel Street, Slough, Berks, SL1 1PG
Activities: Other letting and operating of own or leased real estate
Shareholders: Nicholas Gregory Sargent; Wendy Ann Sargent
Officers: Wendy Ann Sargent, Secretary; Nicholas Gregory Sargent [1942] Director; Wendy Ann Sargent [1945] Director

Skillcrown Holdings Limited
Incorporated: 29 October 2013 *Employees:* 39
Net Worth: £8,138,446 *Total Assets:* £37,200,196
Registered Office: Terrance House, 151 Hastings Road, Bromley, Kent, BR2 8NQ
Activities: Development of building projects
Parent: Skillcrown Holdings (2018) Limited
Officers: Yalpiray Osman, Secretary; Angela Anne Osman [1952] Director/Secretary [Irish]; Arif Salik Osman [1980] Director/Builder; Yalpiray Osman [1951] Director/Builder; Steven Taylor [1962] Director/Solicitor

Skills for Life Trust
Incorporated: 27 February 2012 *Employees:* 248
Previous: Skills for Life Trust Ltd
Net Worth: £20,887,032 *Total Assets:* £25,064,252
Registered Office: 157 Walderslade Road, Walderslade, Chatham, Kent, ME5 0LP
Activities: General secondary education
Officers: Ann Theresa Bracknell [1951] Director/Retired Headteacher & Consultant; Ihator Brown [1979] Managing Director; David English [1971] Director; James Fouracre [1986] Director/Banking; Kim Johnson [1955] Director/Education Advisor; Nicolette King [1947] Director; Thomas James Maddison [1963] Director/HR Consultant; Andrew John Reese [1957] Director/Headteacher; William Joseph Mark Wilkins [1959] Director; Darren James Winter [1968] Director/Engineering Leader

Sky Comedy Limited
Incorporated: 13 July 1995
Previous: BSkyB Comedy Limited
Net Worth: £34,004,000 *Total Assets:* £35,250,000
Registered Office: Grant Way, Isleworth, Middlesex, TW7 5QD
Activities: Non-trading company
Parent: Sky Ventures Limited
Officers: Christopher Jon Taylor, Secretary; Karl Holmes [1973] Director/Finance Professional; Colin Robert Jones [1964] Director; Christopher Jon Taylor [1971] Director/Company Secretary

Sky CP Limited
Incorporated: 27 March 2015 *Employees:* 1,170
Net Worth: £1,575,000,064 *Total Assets:* £1,830,000,000
Registered Office: Grant Way, Isleworth, Middlesex, TW7 5QD
Activities: Television programme production activities
Parent: Sky UK Limited
Officers: Christopher Jon Taylor, Secretary; Robin John Crossley [1958] Director/Technology Consultant; Karl Holmes [1973] Director/Finance Professional; Didier Lebrat [1960] Director/Chief Technology Officer [French]; Colin Smith [1973] Director/CFO, UK & Ireland; Alun David Webber [1966] Managing Director

Sky Finance Europe Limited
Incorporated: 18 February 2015
Total Assets: £727,587,968
Registered Office: Grant Way, Isleworth, Middlesex, TW7 5QD
Activities: Other business support service activities n.e.c.
Parent: Sky PLC
Officers: Christopher Jon Taylor, Secretary; Karl Holmes [1973] Director/Finance Professional; Colin Robert Jones [1964] Director; Christopher Jon Taylor [1971] Director/Company Secretary

Sky Group Finance PLC
Incorporated: 28 September 2005 *Employees:* 2
Previous: BSkyB Finance UK PLC
Net Worth: £451,200,992 *Total Assets:* £1,193,028,992
Registered Office: Grant Way, Isleworth, Middlesex, TW7 5QD
Activities: Other business support service activities n.e.c.
Parent: Sky Limited
Officers: Christopher Jon Taylor, Secretary; Tanya Claire Richards [1971] Director/Group Financial Controller; Colin Smith [1973] Director/CFO, UK & Ireland; Christopher Jon Taylor [1971] Director/Company Secretary

Sky Home Communications Limited
Incorporated: 18 October 2004 *Employees:* 3
Net Worth: £30,687,000 *Total Assets:* £34,752,000
Registered Office: Grant Way, Isleworth, Middlesex, TW7 5QD
Activities: Wired telecommunications activities
Parent: Sky UK Limited
Officers: Christopher Jon Taylor, Secretary; Karl Holmes [1973] Director/Finance Professional; Colin Robert Jones [1964] Director; Christopher Jon Taylor [1971] Director/Company Secretary

Sky In-Home Service Limited
Incorporated: 24 October 1986 *Employees:* 3,325
Net Worth: £298,203,008 *Total Assets:* £689,548,032
Registered Office: Grant Way, Isleworth, Middlesex, TW7 5QD
Activities: Television programme production activities
Parent: Sky UK Limited
Officers: Christopher Jon Taylor, Secretary; Denise Elizabeth Catherine Allan [1966] Director Customer Service; Colin Smith [1973] Director/CFO, UK & Ireland; Andrew Christopher Stylianou [1966] Director/Chartered Accountant; Christopher Jon Taylor [1971] Director/Company Secretary

Sky International Operations Limited
Incorporated: 2 May 2012
Net Worth: £2,932,312,832 *Total Assets:* £8,306,297,344
Registered Office: Grant Way, Isleworth, Middlesex, TW7 5QD
Activities: Activities of head offices
Parent: Sky UK Limited
Officers: Christopher Jon Taylor, Secretary; Karl Holmes [1973] Director/Finance Professional; Colin Robert Jones [1964] Director; Christopher Jon Taylor [1971] Director/Company Secretary

Sky IQ Limited
Incorporated: 6 May 2010
Net Worth: £15,606,000 *Total Assets:* £24,724,000
Registered Office: Grant Way, Isleworth, Middlesex, TW7 5QD
Activities: Data processing, hosting and related activities
Parent: Sky Ventures Limited
Officers: Christopher Jon Taylor, Secretary; Karl Holmes [1973] Director/Finance Professional; Colin Robert Jones [1964] Director; Christopher Jon Taylor [1971] Director/Company Secretary

Sky Limited
Incorporated: 25 April 1988 *Employees:* 28,927
Previous: Sky PLC
Net Worth: £4,016,000,000 *Total Assets:* £18,001,999,872
Registered Office: Grant Way, Isleworth, Middlesex, TW7 5QD
Activities: Activities of head offices
Parent: Comcast Bidco Limited
Officers: Christopher Jon Taylor, Secretary; Arthur R Block [1955] Director/General Counsel [American]; Michael J Cavanagh [1966] Director/Senior Executive Vice President & CFO [American]; David L Cohen [1955] Director/Senior Executive VP & Chief Diversity Officer [American]

Sky Operational Finance Limited
Incorporated: 10 March 1994
Previous: BSkyB Finance Limited
Net Worth: £168,471,008 *Total Assets:* £9,861,266,432
Registered Office: Grant Way, Isleworth, Middlesex, TW7 5QD
Activities: Financial intermediation not elsewhere classified
Parent: Sky Limited
Officers: Christopher Jon Taylor, Secretary; Karl Holmes [1973] Director/Finance Professional; Colin Robert Jones [1964] Director; Christopher Jon Taylor [1971] Director/Company Secretary

Sky SNI Limited
Incorporated: 22 March 2013
Net Worth: £44,752,000 *Total Assets:* £47,161,000
Registered Office: Grant Way, Isleworth, Middlesex, TW7 5QD
Activities: Other information service activities n.e.c.
Parent: Sky UK Limited
Officers: Christopher Jon Taylor, Secretary; Colin Robert Jones [1964] Director; Christopher Jon Taylor [1971] Director/Company Secretary

Sky Subscribers Services Limited
Incorporated: 27 January 1989 *Employees:* 8,604
Net Worth: £616,659,008 *Total Assets:* £858,601,024
Registered Office: Grant Way, Isleworth, Middlesex, TW7 5QD
Activities: Other service activities n.e.c.
Parent: Sky UK Limited
Officers: Christopher Jon Taylor, Secretary; Denise Elizabeth Catherine Allan [1966] Director Customer Service; Colin Smith [1973] Director/CFO, UK & Ireland; Andrew Christopher Stylianou [1966] Director/Chartered Accountant; Christopher Jon Taylor [1971] Director/Company Secretary

Sky Telecommunications Services Limited
Incorporated: 21 December 1993
Previous: BSkyB Telecommunications Services Limited
Net Worth: £1,259,000,064 *Total Assets:* £1,444,999,936
Registered Office: Grant Way, Isleworth, Middlesex, TW7 5QD
Activities: Other business support service activities n.e.c.
Parent: Sky UK Limited
Officers: Christopher Jon Taylor, Secretary; Colin Smith [1973] Director/CFO, UK & Ireland; Andrew Christopher Stylianou [1966] Director/Chartered Accountant; Christopher Jon Taylor [1971] Director/Company Secretary

Sky Television Limited
Incorporated: 24 September 1980
Net Worth: £84,776,000 *Total Assets:* £1,006,201,024
Registered Office: Grant Way, Isleworth, Middlesex, TW7 5QD
Activities: Activities of head offices
Parent: Sky PLC
Officers: Christopher Jon Taylor, Secretary; Karl Holmes [1973] Director/Finance Professional; Colin Robert Jones [1964] Director; Christopher Jon Taylor [1971] Director/Company Secretary

Sky UK Limited
Incorporated: 10 March 1994 *Employees:* 6,038
Previous: British Sky Broadcasting Limited
Net Worth: £1,123,000,064 *Total Assets:* £18,364,999,680
Registered Office: Grant Way, Isleworth, Middlesex, TW7 5QD
Activities: Television programme production activities
Parent: Sky PLC
Officers: Christopher Jon Taylor, Secretary; Colin Smith [1973] Finance Director; Andrew Christopher Stylianou [1966] Director/Chartered Accountant; Christopher Jon Taylor [1971] Director/Company Secretary; Stephen John Van Rooyen [1973] Director/Chief Executive Officer, UK & Ireland

Sky Ventures Limited
Incorporated: 17 August 1995
Net Worth: £383,636,992 *Total Assets:* £647,968,000
Registered Office: Grant Way, Isleworth, Middlesex, TW7 5QD
Activities: Activities of head offices
Parent: Sky UK Limited
Officers: Christopher Jon Taylor, Secretary; Karl Holmes [1973] Director/Finance Professional; Colin Robert Jones [1964] Director; Christopher Jon Taylor [1971] Director/Company Secretary

SLF of Canada UK Limited
Incorporated: 23 September 2008
Net Worth: £412,160,992 *Total Assets:* £412,174,016
Registered Office: Matrix House, Basing View, Basingstoke, Hants, RG21 4DZ
Activities: Other activities auxiliary to insurance and pension funding
Parent: Sun Life Assurance Company of Canada
Officers: Fleur Margaret Hobbs, Secretary; Katherine Angela Garner [1968] Director/Chief Executive; Neville Dean Kent [1960] Director/Chief Operating Officer; Frances Clare MacLachlan [1970] Director/UK Group Financial Controller

Sloggett Group Limited
Incorporated: 12 October 1988 *Employees:* 6
Net Worth: £28,511,648 *Total Assets:* £41,359,968
Registered Office: 1 Mount Mews, High Street, Hampton, Surrey, TW12 2SH
Activities: Activities of head offices
Officers: Gerard Raymond Sloggett, Secretary; Christopher Anthony Grady [1960] Director/Chartered Surveyor; Samuel Jennings [1971] Director/Chartered Surveyor; Angus Mervyn Sloggett [1969] Director/Building Manager; Dudley Harold Sloggett [1936] Director; Gerard Raymond Sloggett [1940] Director; Ian Charles Sloggett [1970] Director/Sales Executive

The Slough and East Berkshire C of E Multi Academy Trust
Incorporated: 29 July 2011 *Employees:* 181
Net Worth: £30,893,022 *Total Assets:* £34,066,424
Registered Office: Slough & Eton C of E Business & Enterprise College, Ragstone Road, Slough, SL1 2PU
Activities: Primary education
Officers: Angela Browne, Secretary; Revd Andrew Allen [1955] Director/Local Rector; Thomas James Marshall Arbuthnott [1974] Director of Outreach & Partnership; Robin Derick Crofts [1950] Director/Consultant; Frederick Royden Evans [1939] Director; Rebecca Elizabeth Ivers [1964] People Director - Expansion; Jonathan McNaughton Reekie [1940] Director; James Robert Beech Scragg [1977] Director/Eton College Housemaster; Christopher Spencer [1957] Corporate Director :People

Slough Heat & Power Limited
Incorporated: 9 April 1921 *Employees:* 46
Net Worth: £25,800,000 *Total Assets:* £65,200,000
Registered Office: No 1 Forbury Place, 43 Forbury Road, Reading, Berks, RG1 3JH
Activities: Production of electricity
Parent: SSE Generation Limited
Officers: Brian Dominic Sharma, Secretary; Mark Richard Hayward [1963] Director/Manager; John Mullen [1972] Director

SLR Consulting Limited
Incorporated: 19 November 1999 *Employees:* 400
Net Worth: £37,028,220 *Total Assets:* £45,580,956
Registered Office: 7 Wornal Park, Menmarsh Road, Worminghall, Aylesbury, Bucks, HP18 9PH
Activities: Environmental consulting activities
Parent: SLR Holdings Limited
Officers: John Martin Green, Secretary; Dr Alan Jonathan Edwards [1967] Director/Environmental Consultant; John Martin Green [1957] Company Secretary/Director; Peter Robert MacKellar [1965] Director; Neil Christopher Penhall [1964] Director

SLR Management Limited
Incorporated: 18 March 2008 *Employees:* 1,184
Net Worth: £40,782,592 *Total Assets:* £101,139,400
Registered Office: 7 Wornal Park, Menmarsh Road, Worminghall, Aylesbury, Bucks, HP18 9PH
Activities: Environmental consulting activities
Shareholder: 3i Group PLC
Officers: John Martin Green, Secretary; Peter Robert MacKellar [1965] Director; Neil Christopher Penhall [1964] Director; Kevin Grant Rattue [1959] Director

SLS Holding Company Limited
Incorporated: 1 September 2009
Net Worth Deficit: £15,738,000 *Total Assets:* £91,498,000
Registered Office: 8 White Oak Square, London Road, Swanley, Kent, BR8 7AG
Activities: Activities of head offices
Shareholders: JLIF Holdings (Street Lighting) Limited; Skanska TAM Limited
Officers: Paul Alan Bannister [1959] Director/Accountant; David Richard Bradbury [1969] Director/Senior Investment Manager; Jennifer Kathryn Fegan [1973] Director/Lawyer; Katherine Mary Rae [1980] Director/Legal Advisor; Paul Sydney Shadbolt [1957] Asset Management Director; Keerthana Sivanathan [1988] Director/Senior Management Accountant

Smartspace Software PLC
Incorporated: 13 January 2005 *Employees:* 349
Previous: RedstoneConnect PLC
Net Worth: £22,402,000 *Total Assets:* £36,344,000
Registered Office: Room 104, Grenville Court, Britwell Road, Burnham, Slough, SL1 8DF
Activities: Other business support service activities n.e.c.
Officers: Kristian Stuart Shaw, Secretary; Francis Beechinor-Collins [1964] Director [Irish]; Diana Dyer Bartlett [1962] Finance Director; Bruce Anthony Morrison [1961] Director/Chartered Accountant; Guy Christopher Van Zwanenberg [1954] Director

SMC Pneumatics (U.K.) Limited
Incorporated: 14 February 1978 *Employees:* 369
Net Worth: £84,509,056 *Total Assets:* £100,994,928
Registered Office: Vincent Avenue, Crownhill, Milton Keynes, Bucks, MK8 0AN
Activities: Other manufacturing n.e.c.
Parent: SMC Corporation
Officers: Lewis John Williams, Secretary; Kevin Patrick O'Carroll [1960] Director; Yoshiyuki Takada [1926] Director/President [Japanese]; Ikuji Usui [1943] Director [Japanese]

Smith Bradbeer & Company Limited
Incorporated: 30 June 1892 *Employees:* 217
Net Worth: £13,709,989 *Total Assets:* £28,469,072
Registered Office: 14 Bell Street, Romsey, Hants, SO51 8ZE
Activities: Other retail sale in non-specialised stores
Shareholder: Peter Lloyd Davies
Officers: Gregory John Davies, Secretary; Anthony Edward Davies [1937] Director/Manager; Gregory John Davies [1968] Retail Director; Justyn Anthony Davies [1978] Director; Peter Lloyd Davies [1939] Director/Manager; Rupert Gwilym Davies [1977] Director; Sarah Mary Robinson [1975] Director

Smith International (North Sea) Limited
Incorporated: 23 August 1990 *Employees:* 90
Net Worth: £38,674,000 *Total Assets:* £51,043,000
Registered Office: Schlumberger House, Buckingham Gate, Gatwick Airport, W Sussex, RH6 0NZ
Activities: Support activities for petroleum and natural gas mining
Shareholders: Schlumberger Oilfield UK PLC; Schlumberger Oilfield UK PLC
Officers: Simon Smoker, Secretary; Gwenola Jacqueline Stephanie Boyault [1972] Director/Geologist [French]; Manuel Alejandro Guedez [1977] Director/Finance Controller [Italian]; Brian Laurence McBeath [1970] Regional HSE Director

Smith Kline & French Laboratories Limited
Incorporated: 21 April 1897
Net Worth: £464,864,000 *Total Assets:* £464,873,984
Registered Office: 980 Great West Road, Brentford, Middlesex, TW8 9GS
Activities: Manufacture of basic pharmaceutical products
Parent: SmithKline Beecham Limited
Officers: Simon Paul Dingemans [1963] Director

SmithKline Beecham (H) Limited
Incorporated: 18 December 1996
Net Worth: £69,482,000 *Total Assets:* £69,504,000
Registered Office: 980 Great West Road, Brentford, Middlesex, TW8 9GS
Activities: Activities of head offices
Parent: Wellcome Limited
Officers: Adam Walker [1967] Director

SmithKline Beecham (Investments) Limited
Incorporated: 21 June 1935
Net Worth: £471,728,992 *Total Assets:* £495,331,008
Registered Office: 980 Great West Road, Brentford, Middlesex, TW8 9GS
Activities: Financial intermediation not elsewhere classified
Shareholders: Setfirst Limited; SmithKline Beecham Limited
Officers: Adam Walker [1967] Director

SmithKline Beecham Limited
Incorporated: 24 January 1989 *Employees:* 1,333
Net Worth: £1,310,000,000 *Total Assets:* £2,496,000,000
Registered Office: 980 Great West Road, Brentford, Middlesex, TW8 9GS
Activities: Manufacture of soft drinks; production of mineral waters and other bottled waters
Parent: GlaxoSmithKline Finance PLC
Officers: Victoria Anne Whyte, Secretary; Simon Paul Dingemans [1963] Director

SmithKline Beecham Overseas Limited
Incorporated: 29 October 1990
Net Worth: £40,316,000 *Total Assets:* £56,486,000
Registered Office: 980 Great West Road, Brentford, Middlesex, TW8 9GS
Activities: Activities of head offices
Parent: SmithKline Beecham Limited
Officers: Simon Paul Dingemans [1963] Director

SmithKline Beecham Research Limited
Incorporated: 21 March 1928 *Employees:* 107
Net Worth: £15,345,000 *Total Assets:* £25,847,000
Registered Office: 980 Great West Road, Brentford, Middlesex, TW8 9GS
Activities: Activities of head offices
Parent: GlaxoSmithKline Consumer Healthcare Holdings Limited
Officers: Richard Green [1974] Director; Richard Philip Tattershall [1982] Director/Accountant

Smiths Detection-Watford Limited
Incorporated: 14 April 1950 *Employees:* 234
Net Worth Deficit: £21,115,000 *Total Assets:* £48,547,000
Registered Office: Century House, Maylands Avenue, Hemel Hempstead Industrial Estate, Hemel Hempstead, Herts, HP2 7DE
Activities: Manufacture of electronic measuring, testing etc. equipment, not for industrial process control
Parent: Smiths Detection Group Limited
Officers: Liam Peter King [1985] Director; Richard Edward Thompson [1969] Commercial Director

Smiths Industries Industrial Group Limited
Incorporated: 31 October 1968 *Employees:* 49
Net Worth: £65,134,000 *Total Assets:* £68,211,000
Registered Office: Unit 130 Centennial Park, Elstree, Herts, WD6 3TJ
Activities: Other service activities n.e.c.
Parent: Smiths Interconnect Group Limited
Officers: Eric Lakin, Secretary; Paul Harris [1957] Director/President Smiths Connectors; Giuseppe Lancella [1961] Managing Director [Italian]

Smiths Interconnect Group Limited
Incorporated: 9 July 2008 *Employees:* 6
Net Worth: £269,216,992 *Total Assets:* £474,943,008
Registered Office: Unit 130 Centennial Park, Elstree, Herts, WD6 3TJ
Activities: Activities of head offices
Parent: Smiths Group International Holdings Limited
Officers: Eric Lakin, Secretary; Karen Maria Bomba [1964] Director/President [American]; Eric Daniel Lakin [1970] Director/Vice President, Finance; Simon James Price [1974] Director

Smiths Medical Group Limited
Incorporated: 25 May 2004 *Employees:* 4
Net Worth: £1,086,723,968 *Total Assets:* £1,690,849,024
Registered Office: 1500 Eureka Park, Lower Pemberton, Ashford, Kent, TN25 4BF
Activities: Activities of head offices
Parent: Smiths Group International Holdings Limited
Officers: Joanne Ede, Secretary; Nigel John Bark [1961] Director/Vice President Sales, EMEA; Louis Philip Jones [1964] Finance Director; Gregory Paul Peter McGrath [1975] Director/Vice President, Operations [Irish]

Smiths Medical International Limited
Incorporated: 16 August 1940 *Employees:* 561
Net Worth: £285,124,992 *Total Assets:* £332,592,000
Registered Office: 1500 Eureka Park, Lower Pemberton, Ashford, Kent, TN25 4BF
Activities: Manufacture of other plastic products
Shareholders: Smiths Medical Group Limited; John Crane Group Limited
Officers: Joanne Ede, Secretary; Nigel John Bark [1961] Director/Vice President Sales, EMEA; Louis Philip Jones [1964] Finance Director; Gregory Paul Peter McGrath [1975] Director/Vice President, Operations [Irish]

SMR Automotive Mirror Parts and Holdings UK Limited
Incorporated: 26 May 2000 *Employees:* 4
Net Worth: £117,847,472 *Total Assets:* £154,942,096
Registered Office: Castle Trading Estate, East Street, Portchester, Hants, PO16 9SD
Activities: Manufacture of other transport equipment n.e.c.
Officers: Angela Bernadette Whiting, Secretary; Andreas Heuser [1966] Corporate Director [German]; Laksh Vaaman Sehgal [1982] Director [Australian]; Vivek Chaand Sehgal [1956] Director [Australian]; Cezary Zawadzinski [1970] Director/Chief Operating Officer [American]

SMR Automotive Mirrors UK Limited
Incorporated: 11 January 2000 *Employees:* 499
Net Worth: £4,419,102 *Total Assets:* £33,245,724
Registered Office: Castle Trading Estate, East Street, Portchester, Hants, PO16 9SD
Activities: Manufacture of other transport equipment n.e.c.
Officers: Angela Bernadette Whiting, Secretary; Mario Enrique Flores Camacho [1972] Director/Executive Vice President [Mexican]; Andreas Heuser [1966] Corporate Director [German]; Laksh Vaaman Sehgal [1982] Director [Australian]; Cezary Zawadzinski [1970] Director/Chief Operating Officer [American]

SNA Solutions UK Limited
Incorporated: 12 July 2007
Net Worth: £92,064,808 *Total Assets:* £92,079,976
Registered Office: Imperium, Imperial Way, Reading, Berks, RG2 0TD
Activities: Activities of head offices
Parent: Snap-On Investment Limited
Officers: Richard Thomas Miller, Secretary; Steven K Bartels [1963] Director/Assistant Treasurer [American]

Snap-On Business Solutions Limited
Incorporated: 30 November 1978 *Employees:* 106
Net Worth: £78,113,800 *Total Assets:* £90,818,536
Registered Office: Imperium, Imperial Way, Reading, Berks, RG2 0TD
Activities: Other information technology service activities
Parent: SNA Solutions UK Limited
Officers: Gordon Stanford Garrett, Secretary/Accountant; Generald Heinz [1960] Director/Attorney [American]; David Ian Stott [1969] Director; Paul Richard Wyeth [1967] Finance Director

SNC-Lavalin (GB) Holdings Limited
Incorporated: 7 April 2017
Net Worth: £913,605,888 *Total Assets:* £2,316,271,872
Registered Office: Woodcote Grove, Ashley Road, Epsom, Surrey, KT18 5BW
Activities: Activities of head offices
Officers: Arden Furlotte, Secretary; Louise Mary McAllister, Secretary; Elliot Michael Nobelen, Secretary; Mark Stephen Anderson [1965] Finance Director; Simon Glenister Cole [1965] Director/Accountant

SNC-Lavalin (GB) Limited
Incorporated: 6 May 2014
Net Worth: £2,242,508,800 *Total Assets:* £2,262,006,272
Registered Office: Woodcote Grove, Ashley Road, Epsom, Surrey, KT18 5BW
Activities: Activities of head offices
Officers: Louise Mary McAllister, Secretary; Elliot Michael Nobelen, Secretary; Mark Stephen Anderson [1965] Finance Director; Simon Glenister Cole [1965] Director/Accountant; James Richard Compston [1965] Director/SVP - Customer Relationships & Business; Richard Thomas Glandon George [1955] Director/MD

SNC-Lavalin Co. Ltd.
Incorporated: 13 November 2013
Net Worth: £23,589,672 *Total Assets:* £23,647,700
Registered Office: Woodcote Grove, Ashley Road, Epsom, Surrey, KT18 5BW
Activities: Other professional, scientific and technical activities n.e.c.
Officers: Louise Mary McAllister, Secretary; Elliot Michael Nobelen, Secretary; Simon Glenister Cole [1965] Director/Accountant; James Richard Compston [1965] Director/SVP Customer Relationships & Business Development; Richard Thomas Glandon George [1955] Director/MD

Snell Corporation Limited
Incorporated: 14 May 2008
Net Worth: £32,925,000 *Total Assets:* £51,167,000
Registered Office: 31 Turnpike Road, Newbury, Berks, RG14 2NX
Activities: Activities of other holding companies n.e.c.
Parent: Quantel Holdings (2010) Limited
Officers: Brian Edward Anderson [1974] Director/Attorney - General Counsel [American]; Alec Thomas Lappe [1981] Director/VP Tax [American]; Anne La Belle Malyszko [1980] Director/VP of Corporate Finance [American]

Snowcentres Limited
Incorporated: 1 August 2007 *Employees:* 232
Net Worth: £13,607,000 *Total Assets:* £23,279,000
Registered Office: The Snow Centre, St Albans Hill, Hemel Hempstead, Herts, HP3 9NH
Activities: Operation of sports facilities
Officers: David Ian Brown [1967] Managing Director; Richard John Cook [1972] Director; Thomas Woodstock Harris [1963] Director

Snows Business Holdings Limited
Incorporated: 22 December 1980 *Employees:* 766
Net Worth: £12,258,870 *Total Assets:* £102,906,976
Registered Office: Snows House, Second Avenue, Millbrook, Southampton, SO15 0BT
Activities: Activities of head offices
Officers: Alexandre Richard Domone [1982] Director; Shawn James Gates [1965] Director; Philip Carol Maddison [1946] Director; Neil Robert McCue [1972] Director; Evelyn Snow [1964] Director; Joyce Snow [1937] Director; Stephen Paul Snow [1964] Director; Mark Anthony Trapani [1955] Director

Snows Motor Group Limited
Incorporated: 22 June 1977 *Employees:* 693
Net Worth: £1,494,485 *Total Assets:* £68,783,856
Registered Office: Snows House, Second Avenue, Millbrook, Southampton, SO15 0BT
Activities: Sale of new cars and light motor vehicles
Parent: Snows Business Holdings Limited
Officers: Alexandre Richard Domone [1982] Director; Shawn James Gates [1965] Director; Philip Carol Maddison [1946] Director; Neil Robert McCue [1972] Director; Stephen Paul Snow [1964] Director; Mark Anthony Trapani [1955] Director

Societe Generale Equipment Finance Limited
Incorporated: 7 July 1998 *Employees:* 96
Net Worth: £48,127,000 *Total Assets:* £977,971,968
Registered Office: Parkshot House, 5 Kew Road, Richmond, Surrey, TW9 2PR
Activities: Financial leasing
Parent: Societe Generale SA
Officers: Timothy Edward Goodship, Secretary; Stephen John Bowden [1964] Director/Senior Account Manager; Timothy Edward Goodship [1979] Director/Certified Chartered Accountant; Dominic Lawson Hughes [1972] Director/Financier; David Robert George Yates-Mercer [1964] Director/Accountant

Sodexo Motivation Solutions U.K. Limited
Incorporated: 23 January 1992 *Employees:* 320
Net Worth: £21,951,000 *Total Assets:* £123,465,000
Registered Office: Avalon House, Breckland, Linford Wood, Milton Keynes, Bucks, MK14 6LD
Activities: Other professional, scientific and technical activities n.e.c.
Officers: Jean Armand Istasse [1972] Director [Belgian]; Nicolas Jean Baudouin Morel [1973] Director/CFO (Group BRS) [French]; Burcin Ressamoglu [1969] Director/Chief Executive Officer [Turkish]; Aurelien Marie Pascal Dominique Sonet [1975] Director [French]

Softbox (Bidco) Limited
Incorporated: 20 June 2014 *Employees:* 3
Net Worth: £262,602 *Total Assets:* £35,043,948
Registered Office: Units 1-2 Ridgeway, Drakes Drive, Long Crendon, Aylesbury, Bucks, HP18 9BF
Activities: Activities of head offices
Parent: Softbox (Midco) Limited
Officers: Richard William Jones [1961] Director; Edwin Francis Tattam [1961] Director/Consultant; Richard Alexander Everingham Wallace [1966] Financial Director

Softbox (Topco) Limited
Incorporated: 20 June 2014 *Employees:* 188
Net Worth Deficit: £7,477,199 *Total Assets:* £76,984,640
Registered Office: Units 1-2 Ridgeway, Drakes Drive, Long Crendon, Aylesbury, Bucks, HP18 9BF
Activities: Activities of head offices
Officers: Adam Dolder [1973] Director/Investment Manager [American]; Bernhard Hampl [1949] Director/Consultant [American]; Jeffrey Jay [1958] Director [American]; Richard William Jones [1961] Director; Wayne Langlois [1952] Director/Global Vice-President [American]; Martin Leblanc [1966] Director/President and Chief Executive Officer [Canadian]; Noah Rhodes [1981] Director/Investor [American]; Edwin Francis Tattam [1961] Director/Consultant

Softcat PLC
Incorporated: 7 October 1987 *Employees:* 1,128
Previous: Softcat Limited
Net Worth: £100,816,000 *Total Assets:* £294,235,008
Registered Office: Solar House, Fieldhouse Lane, Marlow, Bucks, SL7 1LW
Activities: Other information technology service activities
Officers: Luke Thomas, Secretary; Graham Charlton [1977] Director/Chief Finance Officer; Lee Dale Ginsberg [1957] Director; Martin John Hellawell [1965] Managing Director; Vinodka Murria [1962] Director; Peter John Ventress [1960] Director; Graeme Alistair Watt [1961] Director

Software (Holdco 4) Limited
Incorporated: 17 November 2011
Net Worth: £61,213,632 *Total Assets:* £687,751,296
Registered Office: Riding Court House, Riding Court Road, Datchet, Slough, Berks, SL3 9JT
Activities: Activities of head offices
Parent: Iris Software Group Limited
Officers: Michael David Cox [1983] Director; Kevin Peter Dady [1964] Director; Elona Mortimer-Zhika [1979] Director

Software (Holdco2) Limited
Incorporated: 27 June 2007 *Employees:* 1,304
Net Worth Deficit: £181,740,992 *Total Assets:* £684,937,984
Registered Office: Riding Court House, Riding Court Road, Datchet, Slough, Berks, SL3 9JT
Activities: Activities of head offices
Parent: Perennial Bidco A Guernsey
Officers: Michael David Cox [1983] Director; Kevin Peter Dady [1964] Director; Elona Mortimer-Zhika [1979] Director

Software of Excellence UK Holdings Limited
Incorporated: 12 May 2008 *Employees:* 2
Net Worth: £16,278,319 *Total Assets:* £30,106,948
Registered Office: Medcare, South Bailey Drive, Gillingham Business Park, Gillingham, Kent, ME8 0PZ
Activities: Other information technology service activities
Parent: Henry Schein Inc
Officers: James Robert Ludlow, Secretary; Robert Nathan Minowitz [1958] Director [American]; Brian William Weatherly [1967] Director [New Zealander]

Software of Excellence United Kingdom Limited
Incorporated: 21 June 1994 *Employees:* 185
Net Worth: £20,505,732 *Total Assets:* £29,869,568
Registered Office: Medcare, South Bailey Drive, Gillingham Business Park, Gillingham, Kent, ME8 0PZ
Activities: Information technology consultancy activities
Parent: Henry Schein One LLC
Officers: James Robert Ludlow, Secretary; Michael Saul Ettinger [1961] Director/Senior VP of Legal [American]; James Robert Ludlow [1978] Director; Robert Nathan Minowitz [1958] Director/Business Executive [American]; Graham Barry Stanley [1968] Director/Business Executive; Brian William Weatherly [1967] Director [New Zealander]

Softwareone UK Limited
Incorporated: 25 June 2008 *Employees:* 141
Net Worth: £3,700,108 *Total Assets:* £55,639,360
Registered Office: 1 Parkshot, Richmond, Surrey, TW9 2RD
Activities: Information technology consultancy activities
Parent: SoftwareOne AG
Officers: Andrew Martin, Secretary; Dr Hans Grueter [1959] Director [Swiss]; Pascal Rene Hungerbuehler [1985] Director/Head of Legal [Swiss]; Andrew Martin [1972] Finance Director; Satpaul Virdi [1970] Managing Director

Sogea Holdings (UK) Limited
Incorporated: 6 May 1997
Net Worth: £166,660,992 *Total Assets:* £186,660,992
Registered Office: Astral House, Imperial Way, Watford, Herts, WD24 4WW
Activities: Activities of head offices
Parent: Vinci Construction SAS
Officers: Bruno Michel Dupety [1956] Director/Engineer [French]; Yann Paul Grolimund [1959] Director/Chief Financial Officer [French]

Soka Gakkai International - UK
Incorporated: 28 April 2004 *Employees:* 39
Net Worth: £48,206,808 *Total Assets:* £48,387,364
Registered Office: Taplow Court, Cliveden Road, Taplow, Maidenhead, Berks, SL6 0ER
Activities: Activities of religious organisations
Officers: Toni-Ann Hirayama, Secretary; Stephanie Jane Ball [1949] Director/Project Manager; Kazuo Fujii [1947] Vice General Director [Japanese]; Robert Philip Harrap [1965] General Director; Fiona Jane Harrow [1967] Director/Civil Servant; Graham Holman [1966] Director/Solicitor; Jennie Yolande Elizabeth Peters-Smith [1968] Director/Account Manager (Banking); Robert Anthony Samuels [1950] Director/Executive Advisor; Susan Thornton [1945] Director/Retired; Paul Stephen Williams [1958] Director/Chief Executive of a Charity; Sachiyo Wilson [1951] Director/Housewife [Japanese]

Solarsoft Acquisition Limited
Incorporated: 18 February 2008
Net Worth: £49,071,940 *Total Assets:* £67,079,472
Registered Office: c/o Epicor Software UK Limited, No 1 The Arena, Downshire Way, Bracknell, Berks, RG12 1PU
Activities: Activities of other holding companies n.e.c.
Officers: Dawn Murray, Secretary; Richard John Clark [1964] Director/Accountant; Timothy Bernard Harrington [1955] Director/Finance VP [Irish]; John David Ireland [1962] Director/Attorney [American]

Solvay Solutions UK Limited
Incorporated: 15 July 1892 *Employees:* 283
Net Worth Deficit: £536,819,008 *Total Assets:* £207,010,000
Registered Office: 34 Clarendon Road, Watford, Herts, WD17 1JJ
Activities: Manufacture of other chemical products n.e.c.
Parent: Rhodia Holdings Limited
Officers: Alison Murphy, Secretary; Tom Dutton [1964] Director/Health, Safety & Environment Manager; Michael Neil Holland [1971] Market Director HPC EMEA; Nathan Mills [1977] Director/Engineer [American]; Alison Murphy [1965] Director/Financial Controller

Solvecorp Limited
Incorporated: 12 November 1999
Net Worth Deficit: £281,971,008 *Total Assets:* £464,835,008
Registered Office: Hayes Park, Hayes End Road, Hayes, Middlesex, UB4 8EE
Activities: Non-trading company
Parent: Deluxestar Limited
Officers: Mark Oldham, Secretary/Barrister; Helen Josephine McCarthy [1966] Director; Mark Oldham [1959] Director

Solventis Ltd.
Incorporated: 7 May 1997 *Employees:* 32
Net Worth: £25,380,040 *Total Assets:* £76,020,016
Registered Office: Compton House, The Guildway, Old Portsmouth Road, Guildford, Surrey, GU3 1LR
Activities: Wholesale of chemical products
Officers: Lisa Lubbock, Secretary; David John Brimacombe [1958] Director/Management Consultant; Adrian John Hancock [1964] Director/Accountant; Nicholas Peter Johnson [1959] Director; David Warwick Andrew Lubbock [1959] Director/Chemical Trader; Lisa Lubbock [1958] Director/Secretary; John Piers Tregarthen Marmion [1959] Director/Management Consultant

Somerhill Charitable Trust Limited
Incorporated: 29 December 1988 *Employees:* 125
Net Worth: £19,321,500 *Total Assets:* £22,766,304
Registered Office: The Schools at Somerhill, Somerhill, Tonbridge, Kent, TN11 0NJ
Activities: Primary education
Officers: Michael Stephen Scragg, Secretary/School Bursar; Peter Charles Braggins [1945] Director/Retired Headteacher Consultant; Peter Robert Brooks [1953] Director/Retired; Peter Murray Goodyer [1973] Director/Education; Jeremy Coleridge Hills [1942] Director/Chartered Accountant; Diane Margaret Huntingford [1946] Director/Retired; Mark Anthony Jiskoot [1959] Director/Manager; Michael Anthony Norrie [1951] Director/Chartered Accountant; Helen Patricia Tebay [1969] Director/Teacher; Philip Thomas [1943] Director/Chartered Accountant; Robert Edward Verrell [1955] Director/Chartered Surveyor; David Robert Walsh [1946] Director/Retired; Charles John Warner [1950] Director/Solicitor; David Andrew Hester Wells [1951] Director/Retired

Somerset Equipment Finance (UK) Ltd
Incorporated: 15 December 2011 *Employees:* 5
Net Worth Deficit: £1,454,524 *Total Assets:* £22,412,556
Registered Office: The Pinnacle, 170 Midsummer Boulevard, Milton Keynes, Bucks, MK9 1FE
Activities: Renting and leasing of other machinery, equipment and tangible goods n.e.c.
Officers: Evan M Bokor [1962] Director/Chief Executive Officer [American]; Mark Fiorentino [1958] Director/Executive VP [American]; Adam Simon [1971] Director/Executive VP - Sales [American]

Sonardyne Group Limited
Incorporated: 4 December 1985 *Employees:* 275
Net Worth: £89,659,216 *Total Assets:* £96,389,896
Registered Office: Ocean House, Blackbushe Business Park, Saxony Way, Yateley, Hants, GU46 6GD
Activities: Manufacture of electronic measuring, testing etc. equipment, not for industrial process control
Shareholders: Charles John Partridge; Betsan Felicity Partridge
Officers: Charles John Partridge, Secretary; Betsan Felicity Partridge [1941] Director; Charles John Partridge [1939] Director

Sonardyne International Limited
Incorporated: 21 February 1977 *Employees:* 232
Net Worth: £43,268,852 *Total Assets:* £49,461,796
Registered Office: Ocean House, Blackbushe Business Park, Saxony Way, Yateley, Hants, GU46 6GD
Activities: Manufacture of electronic measuring, testing etc. equipment, not for industrial process control
Parent: Sonardyne Group Limited
Officers: Dr Graham Brown [1971] Director; Martin Davey [1958] Director; Dr Darryl Newborough [1975] Director/Chartered Engineer; Betsan Felicity Partridge [1941] Director; Charles John Partridge [1939] Director; Simon Charles Partridge [1970] Director; John Edward Ramsden [1963] Director; Dr Ralph Frank Rayner [1954] Director

Sondex Limited
Incorporated: 10 September 2002
Net Worth: £203,868,000 *Total Assets:* £203,868,000
Registered Office: Building X107, Range Road, Cody Technology Park, Farnborough, Hants, GU14 0FG
Activities: Activities of head offices
Officers: Michael Vinod Garib [1969] Director/Accountant; Amer Khayyat [1978] Director/General Manager [Lebanese]

Sondex Wireline Limited
Incorporated: 24 July 1998 *Employees:* 141
Net Worth: £88,772,000 *Total Assets:* £94,505,000
Registered Office: Building X107, Range Road, Cody Technology Park, Farnborough, Hants, GU14 0FG
Activities: Support activities for petroleum and natural gas mining
Parent: Sondex Limited
Officers: Michael Vinod Garib [1969] Director/Accountant; Amer Khayyat [1978] Director/General Manager [Lebanese]

Sonepar UK Limited
Incorporated: 4 September 2014 *Employees:* 5
Net Worth: £103,598,000 *Total Assets:* £137,339,008
Registered Office: Davy Avenue, Knowlhill, Milton Keynes, Bucks, MK5 8HJ
Activities: Activities of other holding companies n.e.c.
Parent: Otra NV
Officers: Marco Brunetti [1966] Director [Italian]; Eric Gerard Therese Joseph Coisne [1959] Director [French]; David George Gabriel [1958] Director [American]; Louise Garcia de Sola [1989] Director [French]; Andros Neocleous [1964] Director/Finance Executive [Cypriot]

Sonet Investments Limited
Incorporated: 20 January 1995
Net Worth Deficit: £15,127,000 *Total Assets:* £216,330,000
Registered Office: 103-105 Bath Road, Slough, Berks, SL1 3UH
Activities: Activities of financial services holding companies
Parent: SSL International PLC
Officers: Christine Anne-Marie Logan, Secretary; Richard Mark Greensmith [1973] Group Tax Director; Jonathan Timmis [1975] Finance Director

Sonet Scholl Overseas Investments Limited
Incorporated: 20 November 1998
Net Worth: £331,776,000 *Total Assets:* £331,776,000
Registered Office: 103-105 Bath Road, Slough, Berks, SL1 3UH
Activities: Activities of other holding companies n.e.c.
Parent: Scholl Limited
Officers: Christine Anne-Marie Logan, Secretary; Richard Mark Greensmith [1973] Group Tax Director; Adrian Nevil Hennah [1957] Director/Chief Financial Officer; Jonathan Timmis [1975] Director/SVP Corporate Controller

Sony Europe Limited
Incorporated: 14 September 1989 *Employees:* 2,730
Net Worth Deficit: £604,445,248 *Total Assets:* £1,102,010,112
Registered Office: c/o Legal Department, The Heights, Brooklands, Weybridge, Surrey, KT13 0XW
Activities: Manufacture of consumer electronics
Parent: Sony Overseas Holding B.V.
Officers: Katherine Bromley, Secretary; Shigeru Kumekawa [1963] Director/President [Japanese]; Masaki Kurebayashi [1967] Director [Japanese]; Ricky Londema [1964] Director/Business Executive [Dutch]

Sony Global Treasury Services PLC
Incorporated: 30 November 2000
Net Worth: £742,964,544 *Total Assets:* £14,148,797,440
Registered Office: Sony Europe Limited, The Heights, Brooklands, Weybridge, Surrey, KT13 0XW
Activities: Other business support service activities n.e.c.
Parent: Sony Overseas Holding BV
Officers: Jane Helen Lawrence, Secretary; Jiro Aikawa [1963] Managing Director [Japanese]; Hiroyuki Ishiguro [1968] Director/General Manager [Japanese]; Masaki Kurebayashi [1967] Director [Japanese]; Atsuko Murakami [1958] Director/Business Executive [Japanese]

Sopheon PLC
Incorporated: 27 June 1996 *Employees:* 125
Net Worth: £14,009,189 *Total Assets:* £27,403,028
Registered Office: Dorna House, Guildford Road, West End, Woking, Surrey, GU24 9PW
Activities: Other information technology service activities
Officers: Arif Karimjee, Secretary; Arif Karimjee [1967] Director; Barry Keith Mence [1952] Director; Daniel Metzger [1953] Director/Consultant [American]; Andrew Lloyd Michuda [1954] Director [American]; Stuart Andrew Silcock [1947] Director/Chartered Accountant

Sopra Steria Holdings Limited
Incorporated: 7 August 2001
Previous: Steria Holdings Limited
Net Worth: £185,052,000 *Total Assets:* £567,552,000
Registered Office: Three Cherry Trees Lane, Hemel Hempstead, Herts, HP2 7AH
Activities: Other business support service activities n.e.c.
Parent: Sopra Steria Group SA
Officers: Peter Cashmore, Secretary; Davinder Singh Ahluwalia [1952] Director; Kathleen Mary Clark-Bracco [1967] Commercial Director [American]; John Powell Torrie [1954] Director

Sopra Steria Limited
Incorporated: 26 September 2000 *Employees:* 3,444
Previous: Steria Limited
Net Worth: £211,415,008 *Total Assets:* £646,472,000
Registered Office: Three Cherry Trees Lane, Hemel Hempstead, Herts, HP2 7AH
Activities: Information technology consultancy activities
Parent: Sopra Steria Services Limited
Officers: Peter Cashmore, Secretary; Davinder Singh Ahluwalia [1952] Director; Kathleen Mary Clark-Bracco [1967] Commercial Director [American]; Pierre-Yves Commanay [1965] Director [French]; John Joseph Moran [1961] Director Corporate Finance; John Powell Torrie [1954] Director

Sopra Steria Recruitment Limited
Incorporated: 18 July 1979 *Employees:* 38
Previous: Steria Recruitment Limited
Net Worth: £4,927,000 *Total Assets:* £21,681,000
Registered Office: Three Cherry Trees Lane, Hemel Hempstead, Herts, HP2 7AH
Activities: Temporary employment agency activities
Parent: Sopra Steria Limited
Officers: Peter Atherton Cashmore, Secretary; Davinder Singh Ahluwalia [1952] Director; Peter Atherton Cashmore [1962] Director/Solicitor [New Zealander]; Peter James Holliday [1955] Managing Director

Sopra Steria Services Limited
Incorporated: 13 April 1992
Previous: Steria Services Limited
Net Worth: £193,912,000 *Total Assets:* £286,088,000
Registered Office: Three Cherry Trees Lane, Hemel Hempstead, Herts, HP2 7AH
Activities: Other information technology service activities
Parent: Sopra Steria Holdings Ltd
Officers: Peter Cashmore, Secretary; Davinder Singh Ahluwalia [1952] Director; Kathleen Mary Clark-Bracco [1967] Commercial Director [American]; Pierre-Yves Commanay [1965] Director [French]; John Joseph Moran [1961] Director Corporate Finance; John Powell Torrie [1954] Director

Sopress Investments Limited
Incorporated: 5 January 1970
Net Worth: £20,604,000 *Total Assets:* £21,077,000
Registered Office: Loudwater Mill, Station Road, High Wycombe, Bucks, HP10 9TY
Activities: Renting and operating of Housing Association real estate
Officers: Neil Edward Carpenter, Secretary; Simon Alton Westrop, Secretary; Henry Kennedy Faure Walker [1972] Director; Paul Anthony Hunter [1964] Finance Director

Sorbon Estates Limited
Incorporated: 10 August 1973 *Employees:* 37
Net Worth: £72,743,072 *Total Assets:* £175,584,336
Registered Office: Sorbon, Aylesbury End, Beaconsfield, Bucks, HP9 1LW
Activities: Development of building projects
Parent: Sorbon Investments Limited
Officers: Nicholas Mark Trott, Secretary; Tamra Michelle Booth [1974] Director; Michael James Shanly [1945] Director; Nicholas Mark Trott [1964] Director/Accountant

Sorbon Finance Limited
Incorporated: 11 September 2015 *Employees:* 2
Net Worth: £101,864,008 *Total Assets:* £101,949,224
Registered Office: Sorbon, Aylesbury End, Beaconsfield, Bucks, HP9 1LW
Activities: Other credit granting n.e.c.
Parent: Sorbon Homes Limited
Officers: Michael James Shanly [1945] Director; Nicholas Mark Trott [1964] Director/Accountant

Sorbon Homes Limited
Incorporated: 8 October 1998 *Employees:* 178
Net Worth: £281,009,152 *Total Assets:* £362,632,832
Registered Office: Sorbon, Aylesbury End, Beaconsfield, Bucks, HP9 1LW
Activities: Development of building projects
Major Shareholder: Michael James Shanly
Officers: Nicholas Mark Trott, Secretary; Tamra Michelle Booth [1974] Director; Timothy James Potter [1950] Director; Michael James Shanly [1945] Director; Nicholas Mark Trott [1964] Director/Accountant; Donald Anthony Tucker [1954] Director

Sorbon Investments Limited
Incorporated: 8 October 1998 *Employees:* 39
Net Worth: £112,409,920 *Total Assets:* £287,305,344
Registered Office: Sorbon, Aylesbury End, Beaconsfield, Bucks, HP9 1LW
Activities: Development of building projects
Major Shareholder: Michael James Shanly
Officers: Nicholas Mark Trott, Secretary; Tamra Michelle Booth [1974] Director; Timothy James Potter [1950] Director; Michael James Shanly [1945] Director; Nicholas Mark Trott [1964] Director/Accountant; Donald Anthony Tucker [1954] Director/Accountant

Sound Energy PLC
Incorporated: 27 January 2005 *Employees:* 41
Previous: Sound Oil PLC
Net Worth: £172,492,992 *Total Assets:* £202,152,000
Registered Office: 1st Floor, 4 Pembroke Road, Sevenoaks, Kent, TN13 1XR
Activities: Extraction of crude petroleum
Officers: David Clarkson [1952] Director; Marco Fumagalli [1970] Director [Italian]; Richard Thomas Liddell [1947] Director; Brian Christopher Mitchener [1957] Director; James Parsons [1972] Director; John Joseph Traynor [1964] Director

Sourcecode UK Limited
Incorporated: 23 July 2003 *Employees:* 41
Net Worth Deficit: £7,021,702 *Total Assets:* £34,420,536
Registered Office: Number 1 The Heights, Brooklands, Weybridge, Surrey, KT13 0NY
Activities: Other information technology service activities
Officers: Shelley Hall, Secretary; John Ederer [1969] Director [American]; Loyd Evan Ellis [1955] Director [American]

South Darenth Farms and Cold Store Company Limited
Incorporated: 27 May 1960 *Employees:* 11
Net Worth: £15,853,690 *Total Assets:* £24,169,964
Registered Office: St Margarets Farm, St Margarets Road, South Darenth, Dartford, Kent, DA4 9LB
Activities: Growing of cereals (except rice), leguminous crops and oil seeds
Parent: Favourquick Ltd
Officers: Alison Eleanor Hawkins, Secretary; Alison Eleanor Hawkins [1958] Director; Derek George Hawkins [1955] Director; Lisa Jane Alexandra Hawkins [1969] Director; Yvonne Suzette Maria Hawkins Houiller [1962] Director; Sharon Claretta Angela Kirby [1957] Director; Fiona Kathryn Louise Taylor [1964] Director/CD/Research Scientist

South Downs Capital Limited
Incorporated: 17 September 2001 *Employees:* 261
Net Worth: £35,977,000 *Total Assets:* £202,456,992
Registered Office: Brockhampton Springs, West Street, Havant, Hants, PO9 1LG
Activities: Non-trading company
Parent: Ancala Fornia Limited
Officers: Christopher Neil Hardyman, Secretary; Helen Mary Grace Orton [1969] Director; David William Owens [1952] Director; Colin Robert Taylor [1961] Director

South Downs Limited
Incorporated: 13 July 2001
Net Worth: £17,896,000 *Total Assets:* £77,171,000
Registered Office: Brockhampton Springs, West Street, Havant, Hants, PO9 1LG
Activities: Water collection, treatment and supply
Parent: Ancala Fornia Limited
Officers: Christopher Neil Hardyman, Secretary; Helen Mary Grace Orton [1969] Director; Colin Robert Taylor [1961] Director

South Downs Real Estate Limited
Incorporated: 10 February 2005
Net Worth: £12,089,356 *Total Assets:* £62,515,272
Registered Office: Nyetimber Vineyard, Gay Street, West Chiltington, W Sussex, RH20 2HH
Activities: Growing of pome fruits and stone fruits
Parent: Nyetimber Wines Limited
Officers: Robert Andrew MacDonald Watson, Secretary; Eric Niels Heerema [1960] Director [Dutch]

South East Surrey Schools Education Trust
Incorporated: 15 November 2016 *Employees:* 388
Net Worth: £56,054,000 *Total Assets:* £61,745,000
Registered Office: The Ashcombe School, Ashcombe Road, Dorking, Surrey, RH4 1LY
Activities: Primary education
Officers: Paula Stace, Secretary; David Blow [1954] Director/Headteacher; Peter Hugh Butterworth [1957] Director/Charity Community Fundraising Officer; Raymond Derek Elgy [1960] Director/Chartered Aeronautical Engineer; Philip Lawrence May [1957] Director/Self Employed; Terence McDonald [1958] Director/Licensing Consultant; Ben Mearns [1975] Director/Doctor; Katherine Jane Milliken [1973] Director/Solicitor; Timothy Leo Oliver Poole [1947] Director/Retired; Ian Stuart Wilson [1951] Director/Education Consultant; Deborah Zambardino [1960] Director/Chartered Accountant

South East Water (Holdings) Limited
Incorporated: 20 May 2003
Net Worth: £95,175,000 *Total Assets:* £367,340,000
Registered Office: South East Water Limited, Rocfort Road, Snodland, Kent, ME6 5AH
Activities: Non-trading company
Officers: Nicolas Alexandre Desire Truillet, Secretary; Stephen Francis Jordan [1980] Director/Portfolio Manager; Oliver Jan Schubert [1972] Executive Director [Austrian]

South East Water Limited
Incorporated: 4 February 1992 *Employees:* 975
Net Worth: £458,638,016 *Total Assets:* £1,808,726,016
Registered Office: South East Water Limited, Rocfort Road, Snodland, Kent, ME6 5AH
Activities: Water collection, treatment and supply
Shareholder: South East Water (Holdings) Limited
Officers: Nicolas Alexandre Desire Truillet, Secretary; John Anthony Barnes [1954] Independent Non-Executive Director; Paul Butler [1961] Director; Andrew Robert Farmer [1969] Finance Director; Christopher Francis Girling [1954] Director; David Hinton [1967] Director; Celia Pronto Hussey [1973] Director/Chief Customer & Digital Officer; Stephen Francis Jordan [1980] Director/Portfolio Manager; Nicholas Robin Salmon [1952] Director; Marissa Ann Szczepaniak [1980] Director

Southall Travel Limited
Incorporated: 6 December 1984 *Employees:* 38
Net Worth: £44,537,160 *Total Assets:* £92,942,480
Registered Office: 19 South Road, Southall, Middlesex, UB1 1SU
Activities: Travel agency activities
Officers: Donna Bahia, Secretary; Donna Bahia [1974] Director; Kuljinder Singh Bahia [1972] Director; Jaymin Dhirajlal Borkhatria [1965] Director

Southampton Football Club Limited
Incorporated: 12 July 1897 *Employees:* 340
Net Worth: £66,245,000 *Total Assets:* £184,922,000
Registered Office: St Mary's Stadium, Britannia Road, Southampton, SO14 5FP
Activities: Operation of sports facilities
Parent: St Mary's Football Group Limited
Officers: Tim Greenwell, Secretary; Ralph Krueger [1959] Director/Chairman [German]; Martin Semmens [1972] Director; Toby Andrew Murray Steele [1976] Director/Chartered Accountant; David Thomas [1969] Director

Southampton International Airport Limited
Incorporated: 12 October 1989 *Employees:* 184
Net Worth: £112,029,000 *Total Assets:* £137,055,008
Registered Office: Southampton Airport, Wide Lane, Southampton, SO18 2NL
Activities: Scheduled passenger air transport
Parent: Airport Holdings NDH1 Limited
Officers: Ignacio Aitor Garcia Bilbao [1970] Director/Financier [Spanish]; John Kevin Bruen [1972] Director [Irish]; Neil Trevor Garwood [1979] Managing Director; Simon Boyd Geere [1968] Director/Banker; Derek Rodger Provan [1966] Director/Chief Executive Officer; Gonzalo Velasco Zabalza [1979] Director [Spanish]

Southampton Isle of Wight and South of England Royal Mail Steam Packet Company Limited
Incorporated: 10 September 1861 *Employees:* 485
Net Worth: £44,750,000 *Total Assets:* £75,901,000
Registered Office: 12 Bugle Street, Southampton, SO14 2JY
Activities: Sea and coastal passenger water transport
Parent: Falcon Acquisitions Limited
Officers: Michael Francis Campbell [1956] Director [Canadian]; Frances Charlotte Collins [1977] Director/Chief Executive Officer; Kevin Alan George [1956] Director/Chief Executive; Charles John Gore Hazelwood [1963] Director; Lee Richard Hudson [1980] Director; Deborah Louise Reed [1975] Director; James Mark Slawson [1958] Director; Edward Arthur Wilson [1965] Director; Paul Richard Winter [1963] Director/Accountant

Southampton Row Trust Limited
Incorporated: 22 December 1999
Net Worth: £67,567,000 *Total Assets:* £67,766,000
Registered Office: 25 Kings Hill Avenue, Kings Hill, West Malling, Kent, ME19 4TA
Activities: Financial intermediation not elsewhere classified
Officers: Kate Louise Mayor, Secretary; Andrew Michael Morley Dixon [1959] Finance Director; Theodore Richard Hart [1964] Director [American]; Sir John Menzies Low [1953] Director; David Charles Stead [1965] Executive Director

Southern Co-operative Funerals Limited
Incorporated: 9 September 1943
Net Worth: £658,763 *Total Assets:* £57,423,404
Registered Office: 1000 Lakeside, Western Road, North Harbour, Portsmouth, PO6 3FE
Activities: Funeral and related activities
Officers: Silena Jane Dominy, Secretary; Gareth Lewis [1960] Director/Loss Prevention and Security Manager; Mark Alexander Ralf [1956] Director/Retired; Dr Elizabeth Georgina Rogers [1957] Director/Retired; Mark Stephen Smith [1959] Director/Chief Executive; Amber Vincent-Prior [1949] Director/Parish Clerk and Sexton; Gregory Wilkins [1973] Finance Director

Southern Co-operative Properties Limited
Incorporated: 15 January 2004
Net Worth: £7,252,406 *Total Assets:* £50,647,000
Registered Office: 1000 Lakeside, Western Road, North Harbour, Portsmouth, PO6 3FE
Activities: Other letting and operating of own or leased real estate
Officers: Silena Jane Dominy, Secretary; Gareth Lewis [1960] Director/Loss Prevention and Security Manager; Mark Alexander Ralf [1956] Director/Retired; Dr Elizabeth Georgina Rogers [1957] Director/Retired; Mark Stephen Smith [1959] Director/Chief Executive Officer; Amber Vincent-Prior [1949] Director/Parish Clerk and Sexton; Gregory Wilkins [1973] Finance Director

Southern Communications Group Limited
Incorporated: 9 March 2016 *Employees:* 234
Net Worth Deficit: £16,120,342 *Total Assets:* £85,502,248
Registered Office: Glebe Farm, Down Street, Dummer, Hants, RG25 2AD
Activities: Other telecommunications activities
Shareholders: Paul James Bradford; Livingbridge 5 LP
Officers: Paul James Bradford [1968] Director; Matthew Caffrey [1974] Director; David Carruth Goldie [1963] Director; Simon Hollingsworth [1983] Investment Director [Irish]; Mathew Owen Kirk [1970] Director; Alex James Moody [1968] Director; David Charles Phillips [1968] Director; James Neil Wilson [1966] Director

Southern Communications Investments Limited
Incorporated: 9 March 2016 *Employees:* 8
Net Worth Deficit: £12,526,837 *Total Assets:* £77,560,800
Registered Office: Glebe Farm, Down Street, Dummer, Hants, RG25 2AD
Activities: Other telecommunications activities
Parent: Southern Communications Group Limited
Officers: Paul James Bradford [1968] Director; Matthew Caffrey [1974] Director; David Carruth Goldie [1963] Director; Simon Hollingsworth [1983] Investment Director [Irish]; Mathew Owen Kirk [1970] Director; Alex James Moody [1968] Director; David Charles Phillips [1968] Director; James Neil Wilson [1966] Director

Southern Electric Gas Limited
Incorporated: 20 May 1992
Net Worth: £264,900,000 *Total Assets:* £823,200,000
Registered Office: No 1 Forbury Place, 43 Forbury Road, Reading, Berks, RG1 3JH
Activities: Distribution of gaseous fuels through mains
Parent: SSE Energy Services Group Limited
Officers: Peter Grant Lawns, Secretary; Stephen Alexander Forbes [1970] Director; Anthony Edward Keeling [1972] Director

Southern Electric Power Distribution PLC
Incorporated: 23 October 2000 *Employees:* 2,366
Net Worth: £950,400,000 *Total Assets:* £3,194,299,904
Registered Office: No 1 Forbury Place, 43 Forbury Road, Reading, Berks, RG1 3JH
Activities: Distribution of electricity
Parent: Scottish and Southern Energy Power Distribution Limited
Officers: Mark McLaughlin, Secretary; Fraser McGregor Alexander [1963] Director/Chartered Accountant; Alistair John Borthwick [1979] Director/Chartered Accountant; Dale Neil Cargill [1965] Director; Stuart John Hogarth [1963] Operations Director; Katherine Helen Marshall [1970] Director; Robert McDonald [1971] Managing Director, Regulation and Strategy; Rachel McEwen [1972] Director; Colin Clarke Nicol [1960] Director/Engineer; David Rutherford [1963] Director; Gary Clachan Steel [1952] Director

Southern Gas Networks PLC
Incorporated: 30 June 2004 *Employees:* 632
Net Worth: £896,600,000 *Total Assets:* £4,954,399,744
Registered Office: St Lawrence House, Station Approach, Horley, Surrey, RH6 9HJ
Activities: Distribution of gaseous fuels through mains
Parent: SGN Midco Limited
Officers: Nicola Anne Shand, Secretary; Fraser McGregor Alexander [1963] Director/Chartered Accountant; Charlotte Louise Brunning [1986] Director/Investment Management; Natalie Michaela Flageul [1975] Director/Head of Metering; Ines Grund [1978] Director/Investment Professional [German]; Paul Robert Jeffrey [1955] Director/Retired Investment Banker; Guy Lambert [1977] Director/Investments, Head of Utilities [Dutch]; Alejandro Lopez Delgado [1977] Director [Spanish]; Robert McDonald [1971] Director of Regulation; John James McManus [1959] Director/Investment Manager [Canadian]; Mariana Popa [1984] Director/Senior Investment Manager [Romanian]; Laura Sandys [1964] Director/Consultant; Andrew Jonathan Mark Taylor [1961] Director/Investor; Charles Thomazi [1963] Managing Director of Infrastructure and Natural Resources [Canadian]

The Southern Motor Group Limited
Incorporated: 2 May 1967 *Employees:* 91
Net Worth: £4,112,904 *Total Assets:* £21,786,532
Registered Office: 22 Lansdowne Road, Croydon, Surrey, CR0 2BD
Activities: Retail trade of motor vehicle parts and accessories
Officers: Stephen Paul Price, Secretary; Peter John Price [1966] Director/Sales Manager; Stephen Paul Price [1964] Director/Accountant

Southern Water (NR) Holdings Limited
Incorporated: 21 May 2003
Total Assets: £176,100,000
Registered Office: Southern House, Yeoman Road, Worthing, W Sussex, BN13 3NX
Activities: Non-trading company
Parent: Southern Water Investments Limited
Officers: Joanne Statton, Secretary; Ian James McAulay [1965] Director; Joanne Statton [1969] Director/Solicitor

Southern Water Capital Limited
Incorporated: 4 December 2002
Net Worth: £63,900,000 *Total Assets:* £233,700,000
Registered Office: Southern House, Yeoman Road, Worthing, W Sussex, BN13 3NX
Activities: Other business support service activities n.e.c.
Parent: Greensands Finance Limited
Officers: Joanne Statton, Secretary; Andrew Emerson Gilbert [1970] Director [American]; Brian Michael Goodwin [1969] Director/Investment Adviser [American]; Bronte Louise Somes [1972] Director/Infrastructure Investment Executive

Southern Water Investments Limited
Incorporated: 28 January 2003
Net Worth: £47,300,000 *Total Assets:* £49,700,000
Registered Office: Southern House, Yeoman Road, Worthing, W Sussex, BN13 3NX
Activities: Activities of head offices
Parent: Southern Water Capital Limited
Officers: Joanne Statton, Secretary; Ian James McAulay [1965] Director; Joanne Statton [1969] Director/Solicitor

Southern Water Limited
Incorporated: 1 April 1989
Net Worth: £1,140,300,032 *Total Assets:* £1,201,699,968
Registered Office: Southern House, Yeoman Road, Worthing, W Sussex, BN13 3NX
Activities: Non-trading company
Parent: Southern Water (NR) Limited
Officers: Joanne Statton, Secretary; Ian James McAulay [1965] Director; Joanne Statton [1969] Director/Solicitor

Southern Water Services Group Limited
Incorporated: 15 February 2002
Net Worth: £5,100,000 *Total Assets:* £828,700,032
Registered Office: Southern House, Yeoman Road, Worthing, W Sussex, BN13 3NX
Activities: Non-trading company
Parent: Southern Water Investments Limited
Officers: Joanne Statton, Secretary; Ian James McAulay [1965] Director; Joanne Statton [1969] Director/Solicitor

Southern Water Services Limited
Incorporated: 1 April 1989 *Employees:* 2,289
Net Worth: £1,062,800,000 *Total Assets:* £7,258,299,904
Registered Office: Southern House, Yeoman Road, Worthing, W Sussex, BN13 3NX
Activities: Water collection, treatment and supply
Parent: SWS Holdings Limited
Officers: Richard Denley John Manning, Secretary; Wendy Jacqueline Barnes [1957] Director; Sebastianus Antonius Theodorus Boelen [1961] Director [Dutch]; Rosemary Jane Cecilia Boot [1962] Director/Strategy Adviser; Gillian Lesley Guy [1955] Director; Ian James McAulay [1965] Director; Michael Colin Putnam [1960] Director; Michael Paul Sheffield [1961] Director/Civil Engineer; Sara Sulaiman [1977] Director/Investment Principal [Omani]; William Tame [1954] Director/Chartered Accountant

Southwater Property Promotion Limited
Incorporated: 20 November 2014
Net Worth: £30,262,630 *Total Assets:* £31,320,696
Registered Office: The Estate Office, Dorton Road, Chilton, Aylesbury, Bucks, HP18 9LR
Activities: Development of building projects
Officers: Sir Henry Egerton Aubrey-Fletcher [1945] Director; Peter Robert Michael Bond [1935] Director/Solicitor

Southwick Solar Farm Limited
Incorporated: 27 February 2013
Previous: Primrose Solar 7 Limited
Net Worth Deficit: £507,522 *Total Assets:* £42,722,420
Registered Office: 2nd Floor, 2 City Place, Beehive Ring Road, Gatwick, W Sussex, RH6 0PA
Activities: Production of electricity
Parent: Mikado Solar Projects (1) Limited
Officers: Helen Ruth Down [1979] Director/Solicitor; Luke James Brandon Roberts [1976] Director, Portfolio; Neil Anthony Wood [1980] Director/Accountant

Sovereign Advances Limited
Incorporated: 9 June 2009
Net Worth: £13,000 *Total Assets:* £175,556,992
Registered Office: Woodlands, 90 Bartholomew Street, Newbury, Berks, RG14 5EE
Activities: Credit granting by non-deposit taking finance houses and other specialist consumer credit grantors
Parent: Sovereign Housing Association Limited
Officers: Claire Marie McKenna, Secretary; Heather Bowman [1962] Housing Director; Barry Nethercott [1954] Director/Chief Financial Officer; Mark Wyatt Washer [1961] Director/Chief Executive

Sovereign Housing Capital PLC
Incorporated: 17 August 2009
Net Worth: £50,000 *Total Assets:* £429,559,008
Registered Office: Woodlands, 90 Bartholomew Street, Newbury, Berks, RG14 5EE
Activities: Financial intermediation not elsewhere classified
Parent: Sovereign Advances Limited
Officers: Claire Marie McKenna, Secretary; Lee Frederick Bambridge [1963] Finance Director; Heather Bowman [1962] Housing Director; Barry Nethercott [1954] Director/Chief Financial Officer; Mark Wyatt Washer [1961] Director/Chief Executive

Sowmac Investments Limited
Incorporated: 22 March 1965 *Employees:* 8
Net Worth: £20,082,536 *Total Assets:* £28,576,408
Registered Office: Pheasant Copse, Bere Court Road, Pangbourne, Berks, RG8 8JU
Activities: Other letting and operating of own or leased real estate
Shareholders: Hilary Jane Rollason; Elizabeth Rawes
Officers: Amelia Sint Jago, Secretary; Elizabeth Rawes [1948] Director; George Rollason [1981] Director; Hilary Jane Rollason [1951] Director

Spaces Personal Storage Limited
Incorporated: 12 February 1998 *Employees:* 3
Net Worth: £53,262,000 *Total Assets:* £53,262,000
Registered Office: c/o Safestore Holdings Limited, Brittanic House, Stirling Way, Borehamwood, Herts, WD6 2BT
Activities: Other letting and operating of own or leased real estate
Parent: Safestore Acquisition Limited
Officers: Andrew Brian Jones [1966] Director/Chartered Accountant; David Roy Penniston [1958] Property Director; Federico Vecchioli [1966] Director [French]

Sparshatts Holdings Limited
Incorporated: 1 May 1981 *Employees:* 215
Net Worth: £11,502,065 *Total Assets:* £49,030,188
Registered Office: Unit 10 Eurolink Industrial Estate, Castle Road, Sittingbourne, Kent, ME10 3RN
Activities: Sale of new cars and light motor vehicles
Parent: Belfry Trucks Limited
Officers: Peter Martin Davies [1959] Director/Accountant; Paul Anthony Rooney [1964] Director/Sales Manager; Stephen John Rooney [1958] Director/General Manager

Sparshatts of Kent Limited
Incorporated: 10 January 1975 *Employees:* 214
Net Worth: £6,431,271 *Total Assets:* £44,086,932
Registered Office: Unit 10 Eurolink Industrial Estate, Castle Road, Sittingbourne, Kent, ME10 3RN
Activities: Sale of new cars and light motor vehicles
Parent: Sparshatts Holdings Limited
Officers: Peter Martin Davies [1959] Director/Accountant; Paul Anthony Rooney [1964] Director/Sales Manager; Stephen John Rooney [1958] Director/General Manager; Gary James Wilson [1978] Group Operations Director

J.W. Spear & Sons Limited
Incorporated: 31 December 1930
Net Worth: £21,129,000 *Total Assets:* £21,794,000
Registered Office: Mattel House, Vanwall Business Park, Vanwall Road, Maidenhead, Berks, SL6 4UB
Activities: Non-trading company
Parent: Mattel, Inc.
Officers: Sukhjiwan Kaur Tung, Secretary; Prashant Bapna [1973] Finance Director [Indian]; Michael Brian Hick [1978] Sales Director; Robert John Normile [1959] Director/Executive VP & Chief Legal Officer [American]

Specialist Holidays (Travel) Limited
Incorporated: 15 December 1947 *Employees:* 221
Net Worth: £7,364,000 *Total Assets:* £31,027,000
Registered Office: Origin One, 108 High Street, Crawley, W Sussex, RH10 1BD
Activities: Travel agency activities
Parent: Travelopia Holdings Limited
Officers: Janet Northey, Secretary; Sally Ann Cowdry [1968] Director; Samuel Allan McCloskey [1985] Director/Accountant

Specialized (UK) Ltd
Incorporated: 1 March 1989 *Employees:* 46
Net Worth: £17,434,538 *Total Assets:* £20,316,866
Registered Office: 65 Woodbridge Road, Guildford, Surrey, GU1 4RD
Activities: Non-specialised wholesale trade
Parent: Specialized Bicycle Components Inc
Officers: Eric Brian Edgecumbe [1964] Director/President and Chief Product Officer [American]; Simon Homer [1974] Director; Edward Alan Mitchell [1975] Director [American]

Specsavers Optical Superstores Limited
Incorporated: 9 May 1983 *Employees:* 1,981
Net Worth: £78,058,000 *Total Assets:* £197,983,008
Registered Office: Forum 6, Parkway, Solent Business Park, Whiteley, Fareham, Hants, PO15 7PA
Activities: Development of building projects
Shareholders: Douglas John David Perkins; Mary Lesley Perkins
Officers: Paul Brian Bott [1978] Director; Paul Bryan Fussey [1966] Director/Chief Financial Officer; Srechko Kontelj [1961] Group Legal Director [Australian]; John Paul Marshall [1971] Director of Hearcare; Douglas John David Perkins [1943] Director/Consultant; John Douglas Perkins [1972] Managing Director; Mary Lesley Perkins [1944] Director/Wholesale Merchandising; Adrian Geoffrey Thompson [1972] Director [Irish]

Specsavers UK Holdings Limited
Incorporated: 27 June 2017 *Employees:* 20,734
Net Worth Deficit: £4,290,000 *Total Assets:* £249,955,008
Registered Office: Forum 6, Parkway, Solent Business Park, Whiteley, Fareham, Hants, PO15 7PA
Activities: Activities of other holding companies n.e.c.
Shareholders: Mary Lesley Perkins; Douglas John David Perkins
Officers: Stephen David Moore, Secretary; Thomas Michael Buller [1977] Director of GRP Finance & Senior Accounts Officer; John Paul Marshall [1971] Director of Hearcare; Stephen David Moore [1974] Legal Director - UK & ROI; John Douglas Perkins [1972] Managing Director

Spectris Group Holdings Limited
Incorporated: 27 March 1973
Net Worth: £1,131,335,040 *Total Assets:* £1,745,929,984
Registered Office: Heritage House, Church Road, Egham, Surrey, TW20 9QD
Activities: Activities of head offices
Parent: Spectris PLC
Officers: Rebecca Louise Dunn, Secretary; Eoghan Pol O'Lionaird [1966] Director [Irish]; Clive Graeme Watson [1958] Director

Spectris PLC
Incorporated: 4 June 1986 *Employees:* 8,713
Net Worth: £1,204,099,968 *Total Assets:* £1,798,899,968
Registered Office: Heritage House, Church Road, Egham, Surrey, TW20 9QD
Activities: Activities of head offices
Officers: Mark Janos Serfozo, Secretary; Karim Bitar [1965] Director [American]; Andrew James Heath [1964] Director; Russell John King [1957] Director; Ulf Quellmann [1965] Director/Treasurer [German]; William Claire Seeger Jr [1951] Director [American]; Clive Graeme Watson [1958] Finance Director; Kjersti Wiklund [1962] Director [Norwegian]; Mark David Williamson [1957] Director; Martha Brown Wyrsch [1958] Director/President [American]

Spectris UK Holdings Limited
Incorporated: 30 May 2002
Net Worth: £114,803,000 *Total Assets:* £146,976,992
Registered Office: Heritage House, Church Road, Egham, Surrey, TW20 9QD
Activities: Activities of head offices
Parent: Spectris Group Holdings Limited
Officers: Rebecca Louise Dunn, Secretary; Anthony William Dumpleton [1969] Director/Accountant; Clive Graeme Watson [1958] Director

Spectris US Holdings Limited
Incorporated: 30 May 2002
Net Worth: £284,519,008 *Total Assets:* £455,179,008
Registered Office: Heritage House, Church Road, Egham, Surrey, TW20 9QD
Activities: Activities of head offices
Parent: Spectris Group Holdings Limited
Officers: Rebecca Louise Dunn, Secretary; Anthony William Dumpleton [1969] Director/Accountant; Clive Graeme Watson [1958] Director

Spectrum Franchising Limited
Incorporated: 11 May 1987 *Employees:* 52
Net Worth: £24,667,000 *Total Assets:* £27,182,000
Registered Office: Velocity, 1 Brooklands Drive, Brooklands, Weybridge, Surrey, KT13 0SL
Activities: Other cleaning services
Parent: Spectrum Holdings Limited
Officers: Matthew Edward Stanley Brabin [1965] Director/Chief Executive Officer; Kenneth Ian Mackintosh [1962] Director; Stephen Graham Mitchell [1964] Managing Director; Barbara Plucnar Jensen [1971] Director/Chief Financial Officer [Danish]

Speyside Renewable Energy Finance PLC
Incorporated: 19 June 2014
Net Worth: £64,000 *Total Assets:* £46,536,000
Registered Office: 8 White Oak Square, London Road, Swanley, Kent, BR8 7AG
Activities: Production of electricity
Parent: Speyside Renewable Energy Partnership Hold Co Limited
Officers: Maxwell Francis Aitken [1977] Director; David Richard Bradbury [1969] Asset Director; Benjamin Matthew Cashin [1972] Director; Paul John Ireland [1979] Director; David Adam Whitehurst [1971] Director/Investment Professional

SPI Lasers PLC
Incorporated: 25 August 2005
Net Worth: £27,829,000 *Total Assets:* £27,936,000
Registered Office: 3 Wellington Park, Tollbar Way, Hedge End, Southampton, SO30 2QU
Activities: Other business support service activities n.e.c.
Officers: Dr Malcolm Paul Varnham, Secretary; Dr Lutz Aschke [1970] Director [German]; Dr Mark Greenwood [1965] Director/Company Executive; Dr Christian Karl Joseph Schmitz [1959] Director/Engineer [German]

SPI Lasers UK Limited
Incorporated: 11 December 1996 *Employees:* 291
Net Worth: £43,882,000 *Total Assets:* £64,137,000
Registered Office: 3 Wellington Park, Tollbar Way, Hedge End, Southampton, SO30 2QU
Activities: Manufacture of optical precision instruments
Parent: SPI Lasers PLC
Officers: Dr Malcolm Paul Varnham, Secretary; Dr Mark Greenwood [1965] Director/Company Executive; Graham Parsons [1968] HR Director; Thomas Reinauer [1970] Financial Director [German]; Dr Malcolm Paul Varnham [1959] Director/Engineer

Spicers Limited
Incorporated: 16 December 1946 *Employees:* 419
Net Worth: £37,327,000 *Total Assets:* £95,105,000
Registered Office: c/o The Spicers-Officeteam Group Limited, Unit 4, 500 Purley Way, Croydon, Surrey, CR0 4NZ
Activities: Wholesale of office furniture
Major Shareholder: Jonathan Paul Moulton
Officers: Philippa Anne Maynard, Secretary; Edwin Richard Ford [1967] Director; Richard Ashley Jones [1965] Director; Andrew Graham Mobbs [1978] Director

The Spicers-Officeteam Group Limited
Incorporated: 5 June 2014 *Employees:* 1,352
Net Worth Deficit: £30,774,000 *Total Assets:* £153,911,008
Registered Office: Unit 4, 500 Purley Way, Croydon, Surrey, CR0 4NZ
Activities: Activities of head offices
Major Shareholder: Jonathan Paul Moulton
Officers: Philippa Anne Maynard, Secretary; Robert Alexander Asplin [1979] Director; Edwin Richard Ford [1967] Director; Richard Ashley Jones [1965] Director; Andrew Graham Mobbs [1978] Director; Octavia Kate Morley [1968] Director

Spincrest Limited
Incorporated: 17 December 1979 *Employees:* 9
Net Worth: £39,274,536 *Total Assets:* £57,678,024
Registered Office: Greenhills Estate Office, Greenhills Estate, Tilford Road, Tilford, Farnham, Surrey, GU10 2DZ
Activities: Development of building projects
Parent: Trevellyan Developments Ltd
Officers: Lance John Philip Trevellyan, Secretary; Alexandra Hilary Trevellyan [1959] Director; Lance John Philip Trevellyan [1953] Director; Lewis Derek Trevellyan [1988] Director/Management

Spire Automotive Limited
Incorporated: 11 May 2006 *Employees:* 766
Net Worth: £8,476,357 *Total Assets:* £91,670,752
Registered Office: Chandlers, Victoria Road, Portslade, Brighton, BN41 1YH
Activities: Sale of new cars and light motor vehicles
Officers: Darryl Burman, Secretary; Darryl Michael Burman [1958] Director/General Counsel [American]; Darren Guiver [1968] Director; Earl Julius Hesterberg [1953] Director [American]; Daniel James McHenry [1974] Finance Director; John Rickel [1961] Director [American]

Spirent Communications PLC
Incorporated: 16 July 1949 *Employees:* 1,505
Net Worth: £266,139,360 *Total Assets:* £389,905,824
Registered Office: Northwood Park, Gatwick Road, Crawley, W Sussex, RH10 9XN
Activities: Other telecommunications activities
Officers: Angus Edward Iveson, Secretary; Paula Bell [1967] Director; Gary Bruce Bullard [1957] Director; Eric George Hutchinson [1955] Director/Accountant; Wendy Meng Weng Koh [1969] Director/Business Executive [Singaporean]; Edgar Masri [1958] Director [American]; Jonathan Charles Silver [1957] Director; William Gennydd Thomas [1959] Director

Spirent Holdings Limited
Incorporated: 17 October 1997
Net Worth: £28,315,000 *Total Assets:* £28,315,000
Registered Office: Northwood Park, Gatwick Road, Crawley, W Sussex, RH10 9XN
Activities: Dormant company
Parent: Spirent Communications PLC
Officers: Angus Edward Iveson, Secretary; Paula Bell [1967] Director; Eric George Hutchinson [1955] Director/Accountant

Spirent Investment Limited
Incorporated: 28 November 2000
Net Worth: £254,236,528 *Total Assets:* £254,237,296
Registered Office: Northwood Park, Gatwick Road, Crawley, W Sussex, RH10 9XN
Activities: Non-trading company
Parent: Spirent Communications PLC
Officers: Angus Edward Iveson, Secretary; Paula Bell [1967] Director; Eric George Hutchinson [1955] Director/Accountant

Spirit Energy North Sea Limited
Incorporated: 19 November 2002
Previous: Centrica North Sea Limited
Net Worth: £70,212,000 *Total Assets:* £956,955,008
Registered Office: 1st Floor, 20 Kingston Road, Staines upon Thames, Middlesex, TW18 4LG
Activities: Extraction of crude petroleum
Parent: Centrica Newco 123 Limited
Officers: Nicola MacLeod, Secretary; Generald Martin Harrison [1954] Director; Andrew Daryl Le Poidevin [1958] Director; Nicola Jane MacLeod [1974] Director/General Counsel; Neil James McCulloch [1970] Director/EVP Technical and Operated Production

Spirit Energy Production UK Limited
Incorporated: 18 October 1995 *Employees:* 263
Previous: Hydrocarbon Resources Limited
Net Worth: £924,329,984 *Total Assets:* £1,535,412,992
Registered Office: 1st Floor, 20 Kingston Road, Staines upon Thames, Middlesex, TW18 4LG
Activities: Extraction of crude petroleum
Shareholders: GB Gas Holdings Limited; Centrica Newco 123 Limited
Officers: Nicola MacLeod, Secretary; Generald Martin Harrison [1954] Director; Andrew Daryl Le Poidevin [1958] Director; Nicola Jane MacLeod [1974] Director/General Counsel; Neil James McCulloch [1970] Director/EVP Technical and Operated Production

Spirit Energy Resources Limited
Incorporated: 21 September 1993
Previous: Spirit Norway Limited
Net Worth Deficit: £597,174,976 *Total Assets:* £488,572,992
Registered Office: 1st Floor, 20 Kingston Road, Staines upon Thames, Middlesex, TW18 4LG
Activities: Extraction of crude petroleum
Parent: Spirit Energy Limited
Officers: Nicola MacLeod, Secretary; Generald Martin Harrison [1954] Director; Andrew Daryl Le Poidevin [1958] Director; Nicola Jane MacLeod [1974] Director/General Counsel; Neil James McCulloch [1970] Director/EVP Technical and Operated Production

Spirit Energy Southern North Sea Limited
Incorporated: 8 March 2006 *Employees:* 1
Previous: Bayerngas Europe Limited
Net Worth: £208,274,464 *Total Assets:* £300,243,456
Registered Office: 1st Floor, 20 Kingston Road, Staines upon Thames, Middlesex, TW18 4LG
Activities: Support activities for petroleum and natural gas mining
Parent: Spirit Europe Ltd
Officers: Nicola MacLeod, Secretary; Generald Martin Harrison [1954] Director; Andrew Daryl Le Poidevin [1958] Director; Nicola Jane MacLeod [1974] Director/General Counsel; Neil James McCulloch [1970] Director/EVP Technical and Operated Production

Spirit Europe Limited
Incorporated: 30 March 2004 *Employees:* 11
Previous: Spirit Europe Ltd
Net Worth: £221,987,536 *Total Assets:* £271,979,104
Registered Office: 1st Floor, 20 Kingston Road, Staines upon Thames, Middlesex, TW18 4LG
Activities: Other mining and quarrying n.e.c.
Parent: Spirit Energy Limited
Officers: Nicola MacLeod, Secretary; Generald Martin Harrison [1954] Director; Nicola Jane MacLeod [1974] Director/General Counsel; Neil James McCulloch [1970] Director/EVP Technical and Operated Production

Spirit Norway Limited
Incorporated: 17 March 2006 *Employees:* 119
Previous: Centrica Norway Limited
Net Worth: £340,781,088 *Total Assets:* £1,857,423,872
Registered Office: 1st Floor, 20 Kingston Road, Staines upon Thames, Middlesex, TW18 4LG
Activities: Activities of head offices
Parent: Spirit Energy Limited
Officers: Andrew Daryl Le Poidevin [1958] Director; Nicola Jane MacLeod [1974] Director/General Counsel; Dag Halvard Omre [1958] Regional Director [Norwegian]

Spirit Resources (Armada) Limited
Incorporated: 16 March 2001
Previous: Spirit Energy Resources (Armada) Limited
Net Worth: £37,379,000 *Total Assets:* £50,855,000
Registered Office: 1st Floor, 20 Kingston Road, Staines upon Thames, Middlesex, TW18 4LG
Activities: Extraction of crude petroleum
Parent: Centrica Newco 123 Limited
Officers: Nicola MacLeod, Secretary; Generald Martin Harrison [1954] Director; Nicola Jane MacLeod [1974] Director/General Counsel; Neil James McCulloch [1970] Director/EVP Technical and Operated Production

Sports Information Services (Holdings) Limited
Incorporated: 16 August 1985 *Employees:* 459
Previous: Satellite Information Services (Holdings) Limited
Net Worth: £81,100,000 *Total Assets:* £142,440,000
Registered Office: 2 Whitehall Avenue, Kingston, Milton Keynes, Bucks, MK10 0AX
Activities: Television programming and broadcasting activities
Officers: Richard Jonathan Ames [1970] Director; Trevor Kenneth Beaumont [1950] Director; Mark Russel Chambers [1972] Director/Retail COO; Fred Done [1943] Director; Sally Deborah Flanagan [1962] Director; Michael James Ford [1980] Director; John Michael Barry Gibson [1951] Director/Chairman; Duncan Edward Johnson [1970] Director; Paul James Kirszanek [1977] Director; Melvin Anthony Lawson [1958] Director; Christopher Harwood Bernard Mills [1952] Director/Investment Banker; Joseph Matthias Scanlon [1951] Managing Director

Sports Information Services Limited
Incorporated: 28 June 2001 *Employees:* 357
Previous: Satellite Information Services Limited
Net Worth: £77,600,000 *Total Assets:* £146,928,992
Registered Office: Unit 1-2 Whitehall Avenue, Kingston, Milton Keynes, Bucks, MK10 0AX
Activities: Television programming and broadcasting activities
Parent: Sports Information Services (Holdings) Limited
Officers: Richard Jonathan Ames [1970] Director; Nigel Stocks [1970] Director/Chief Financial Officer

Spritestore Limited
Incorporated: 28 April 1997 *Employees:* 142
Net Worth: £7,020,528 *Total Assets:* £47,458,560
Registered Office: 4 Abbey Wood Road, Kings Hill, West Malling, Kent, ME19 4AB
Activities: Construction of commercial buildings
Shareholder: John Henry Chadwick
Officers: Michael Anthony Steel, Secretary/Director; John Henry Chadwick [1942] Director/Structural Engineer; Jonathan Charles David Noble [1962] Director/Quantity Surveyor; Michael Anthony Steel [1947] Director/Structural Engineer

SPX Flow Technology Crawley Limited
Incorporated: 20 November 1900 *Employees:* 50
Net Worth: £12,885,000 *Total Assets:* £21,873,000
Registered Office: Building A, Compass House, Manor Royal, Crawley, W Sussex, RH10 9PY
Activities: Manufacture of machinery for food, beverage and tobacco processing
Parent: SPX Flow Technology London Limited
Officers: Jaime Manson Easley [1977] Director/Corporate Controller [American]; Stephen Tsoris [1957] Director [American]

SQIB Limited
Incorporated: 14 May 2013 *Employees:* 198
Net Worth: £2,351,201 *Total Assets:* £178,522,848
Registered Office: 45 Westerham Road, Sevenoaks, Kent, TN13 2QB
Activities: Activities of head offices
Parent: Armatire Limited
Officers: Christopher James Payne, Secretary; Keith John Barber [1974] Director; Gary Humphreys [1965] Director; Kevin Ronald Spencer [1965] Director

D.J.Squire & Co.,Limited
Incorporated: 8 July 1936 *Employees:* 821
Net Worth: £33,790,000 *Total Assets:* £49,522,000
Registered Office: Sixth Cross Road, Twickenham, Middlesex, TW2 5PA
Activities: Retail sale of flowers, plants, seeds, fertilizers, pet animals and pet food in specialised stores
Shareholder: Colin Squire
Officers: Mark Alastair Wilson, Secretary; Martin Nicholas Breddy [1961] Director; Janet Deirdre Elaine Cody [1932] Director/Administrator; Darran Oakley [1966] Director; Adrian Humphrey Austen Osborn [1944] Director; Colin Stuart Squire [1936] Director/Horticulturalist; Sarah Catherine Elaine Squire [1965] Director; Mark Alastair Wilson [1962] Finance Director

SRM (Redcar & Cleveland) Limited
Incorporated: 5 December 2007
Net Worth Deficit: £7,462,474 *Total Assets:* £40,153,800
Registered Office: Eaton Court, Maylands Avenue, Hemel Hempstead Industrial Estate, Hemel Hempstead, Herts, HP2 7TR
Activities: Medical nursing home activities
Parent: SRM (Redcar & Cleveland) Holdings Limited
Officers: Kevin John Pearson, Secretary; David Honeyman [1967] Director/Financial Controller

SSCP Spring Midco 2 Limited
Incorporated: 28 March 2015 *Employees:* 2
Net Worth Deficit: £955,000 *Total Assets:* £148,200,992
Registered Office: Frays Court, 71 Cowley Road, Uxbridge, Middlesex, UB8 2AE
Activities: Other professional, scientific and technical activities n.e.c.
Parent: SSCP Spring Midco 1 Limited
Officers: Helen Elizabeth Lecky, Secretary; Jean-Luc Emmanuel Janet [1970] Director/Chief Financial Officer [French]; David Jon Leatherbarrow [1969] Director/Group Chief Executive Officer

SSCP Spring Topco Limited
Incorporated: 3 October 2014 *Employees:* 1,717
Net Worth Deficit: £69,611,000 *Total Assets:* £450,452,992
Registered Office: Frays Court, 71 Cowley Road, Uxbridge, Middlesex, UB8 2AE
Activities: Activities of head offices
Officers: Helen Elizabeth Lecky, Secretary; Iain James Anderson [1955] Director/Chief Executive; Enrico Biale [1977] Director [Italian]; Jonathan Lister Heathcote [1961] Director; Benjamin Hopper [1985] Director/Investment Executive; Jean-Luc Emmanuel Janet [1970] Director/Chief Financial Officer [French]; David Jon Leatherbarrow [1969] Director/Group Chief Executive Officer; Douglas John Quinn [1955] Director/Chairman

SSE Contracting Limited
Incorporated: 14 November 1988
Net Worth: £166,200,000 *Total Assets:* £274,200,000
Registered Office: No 1 Forbury Place, 43 Forbury Road, Reading, Berks, RG1 3JH
Activities: Electrical installation
Parent: SSE Contracting Group Limited
Officers: Brian Dominic Sharma, Secretary; Scott Keelor Anderson [1970] Director/Accountant; Stuart Paul Chaston [1968] Managing Director; Andrew David O'Connor [1965] Director; Rajeev Kumar Sinha [1968] Director; Thomas Wood [1983] Director

SSE Energy Supply Limited
Incorporated: 22 April 1999 *Employees:* 1,546
Net Worth: £400,800,000 *Total Assets:* £5,415,799,808
Registered Office: No 1 Forbury Place, 43 Forbury Road, Reading, Berks, RG1 3JH
Activities: Other business support service activities n.e.c.
Parent: SSE PLC
Officers: Peter Grant Lawns, Secretary; Finlay Alexander McCutcheon [1977] Director; Iwan Rees Morgan [1961] Director

SSE EPM Limited
Incorporated: 17 February 2015 *Employees:* 148
Net Worth: £50,200,000 *Total Assets:* £1,608,700,032
Registered Office: No 1 Forbury Place, 43 Forbury Road, Reading, Berks, RG1 3JH
Activities: Trade of electricity
Parent: SSE PLC
Officers: Sally Fairbairn, Secretary; Pauline Lynsey Babb [1974] Director; David Arthur Fernie [1965] Director; Calum Milne Kennedy [1964] Director; Mandy MacKay [1976] Director

SSE Generation Limited
Incorporated: 31 October 1988 *Employees:* 701
Net Worth: £1,551,500,032 *Total Assets:* £4,567,900,160
Registered Office: No 1 Forbury Place, 43 Forbury Road, Reading, Berks, RG1 3JH
Activities: Production of electricity
Parent: SSE PLC
Officers: Sally Fairbairn, Secretary; John Anthony Downes [1970] Director of Engineering,Generation; Mark Richard Hayward [1963] Director/Manager; James Isaac Smith [1962] Director/Engineer; Jeremy Williamson [1966] Director

SSE Hornsea Limited
Incorporated: 24 June 2002 *Employees:* 88
Net Worth Deficit: £222,800,000 *Total Assets:* £82,300,000
Registered Office: No 1 Forbury Place, 43 Forbury Road, Reading, Berks, RG1 3JH
Activities: Distribution of gaseous fuels through mains
Parent: SSE PLC
Officers: Yvonne Louise Taylor-Robertson, Secretary; Alastair Iain Cleland [1965] Director/Business Manager; James Isaac Smith [1962] Director/Engineer

SSE Production Services Limited
Incorporated: 8 May 1990 *Employees:* 54
Net Worth: £30,500,000 *Total Assets:* £32,600,000
Registered Office: No 1 Forbury Place, 43 Forbury Road, Reading, Berks, RG1 3JH
Activities: Production of electricity
Parent: SSE PLC
Officers: Sally Fairbairn, Secretary; Mark Richard Hayward [1963] Director/Manager

SSE Renewables Walney (UK) Limited
Incorporated: 24 February 2011
Net Worth: £149,300,000 *Total Assets:* £354,000,000
Registered Office: No 1 Forbury Place, 43 Forbury Road, Reading, Berks, RG1 3JH
Activities: Distribution of electricity
Parent: SSE Renewables Offshore Windfarm Holdings Limited
Officers: Sally Fairbairn, Secretary; James Isaac Smith [1962] Director/Engineer

SSE Seabank Investments Limited
Incorporated: 22 July 1991
Net Worth: £23,000,000 *Total Assets:* £26,400,000
Registered Office: No 1 Forbury Place, 43 Forbury Road, Reading, Berks, RG1 3JH
Activities: Production of electricity
Parent: SSE Generation Limited
Officers: Sally Fairbairn, Secretary; John Anthony Downes [1970] Director of Engineering,Generation; Alexander Hughes Honeyman [1960] Director/Head of Project Development; Iwan Rees Morgan [1961] Director

SSE Services PLC
Incorporated: 1 April 1989 *Employees:* 6,380
Net Worth Deficit: £295,800,000 *Total Assets:* £1,278,000,000
Registered Office: No 1 Forbury Place, 43 Forbury Road, Reading, Berks, RG1 3JH
Activities: Other business support service activities n.e.c.
Parent: SSE PLC
Officers: Peter Grant Lawns, Secretary; Fraser McGregor Alexander [1963] Director/Chartered Accountant; John William Stewart [1970] Director of Human Resources

SSG Logistic Solutions Limited
Incorporated: 9 December 2002 *Employees:* 60
Net Worth: £14,886,000 *Total Assets:* £71,774,000
Registered Office: Granville House, Gatton Park Business Centre, Wells Place, Redhill, Surrey, RH1 3AS
Activities: Freight transport by road
Parent: The Compleat Food Group Limited
Officers: David Jonathan Kimber, Secretary; Steven James Higginson [1960] Director; Mark John Lane [1970] Director; Damian Johnson Shaw [1971] Commercial Director

SSL Group (UK) Limited
Incorporated: 9 January 2015 *Employees:* 1,309
Net Worth: £12,390,701 *Total Assets:* £78,824,912
Registered Office: Grosvenor House, Horseshoe Crescent, Beaconsfield, Bucks, HP9 1LJ
Activities: Other letting and operating of own or leased real estate
Officers: Tom James Ball [1983] Director; Frank Cerrone [1959] Director/Senior Vice President, General Counsel & Secretary [Canadian]; James Hardy [1959] Director/Chief Investment Officer & CFO [Canadian]; Thomas Bruce Newell [1957] Director [American]; Wayne Paul Pryce [1974] Director; Aidan Gerard Roche [1966] Director [Irish]

SSL International PLC
Incorporated: 20 July 1944
Net Worth: £116,460,000 *Total Assets:* £806,897,984
Registered Office: 103-105 Bath Road, Slough, Berks, SL1 3UH
Activities: Activities of financial services holding companies
Parent: Reckitt Benckiser PLC
Officers: Christine Anne-Marie Logan, Secretary; Richard Mark Greensmith [1973] Group Tax Director; Adrian Nevil Hennah [1957] Director/Chief Financial Officer; Jonathan Timmis [1975] Director/SVP Corporate Controller

ST & H Group Limited
Incorporated: 5 April 1962
Previous: Acromas Travel Limited
Net Worth: £46,685,000 *Total Assets:* £46,685,000
Registered Office: Enbrook Park, Sandgate, Folkestone, Kent, CT20 3SE
Activities: Other service activities n.e.c.
Parent: Saga Group Limited
Officers: Victoria Haynes, Secretary; Stephen Adrian Jenkins [1967] Director; Peter Robin Shaw [1963] Director

ST & H Limited
Incorporated: 6 October 1987 *Employees:* 1,216
Previous: Acromas Holidays Limited
Net Worth: £93,694,000 *Total Assets:* £299,948,000
Registered Office: Enbrook Park, Sandgate, Folkestone, Kent, CT20 3SE
Activities: Other service activities n.e.c.
Parent: ST & H Group Limited
Officers: Victoria Haynes, Secretary; Lance Henry Lowe Bachelor [1964] Director/Group Chief Executive; Richard William Bowden-Doyle [1960] Director; Stephen Adrian Jenkins [1967] Director; James Quin [1969] Director; Peter Robin Shaw [1963] Director

St Barnabas Hospices (Sussex) Ltd
Incorporated: 5 April 1968 *Employees:* 336
Net Worth: £46,125,000 *Total Assets:* £47,057,000
Registered Office: St Barnabas House, Titnore Lane, Goring-by-Sea, Worthing, W Sussex, BN12 6NZ
Activities: Specialists medical practice activities
Officers: Max Caunhye, Secretary; Neil Blanchard [1969] Director/Chief Executive; Jill Carnie [1957] Director/Retired; Maureen Chowen [1953] Director/Personal Assistant; Anthony Clark [1947] Director/Retired; Patrick Neil Gatley [1946] Director/Management Consultant; Martin Richard Godsmark [1952] Director/Retired; Derwyn Howard Jones [1960] Marketing Director; Mark Milling [1971] Director/School Bursar; Tony Moss [1946] Director/Retired; Stuart Palma [1988] Director/Physiotherapist; David Brian Pegler [1968] Director/Chartered Wealth Manager; Michael Rymer [1946] Medical Director; Ruth Taylor [1953] Director/Nurse; Patricia Woolgar [1957] Director/Solicitor

St Bartholomew's School
Incorporated: 28 July 2011 *Employees:* 228
Net Worth: £32,366,608 *Total Assets:* £35,965,372
Registered Office: St Bartholomew's School, Andover Road, Newbury, Berks, RG14 6JP
Activities: General secondary education
Officers: Catherine Colston [1965] Director; Richard Deal [1955] Director/Chartered Surveyor; Stephen Mark Foyle [1958] Director; Catherine Laura Elizabeth Lefever [1966] HR Director; Julia Ann Mortimore [1962] Director/Headteacher; Gary Arthur Norman [1957] Director/Retired; Ian James Peddie [1953] Director/Civil Engineer; Patricia Elaine Ray [1960] Director/Fitness Instructor; Karen Marie Sadler [1964] Director; Dr Gareth Scourfield [1970] Director/Programme Manager; Campbell Jonathan Holdich Smith [1970] Director/Chartered Accountant; Bruce Steiner [1950] Director/Retired; Jonathan Nicholas Hudson Taylor [1954] Director

St Bede's School Trust Sussex
Incorporated: 1 September 1978 *Employees:* 509
Net Worth: £22,600,000 *Total Assets:* £39,939,000
Registered Office: Bede's Senior School, Upper Dicker, Hailsham, E Sussex, BN27 3QH
Activities: Pre-primary education
Officers: Dr Jonathan Ross Northway, Secretary; John Warwick Burbidge [1958] Director/Retired; Andrew Stuart Reginald Corbett [1952] Director; Dr Matthew Crummack [1970] Director/Chief Executive; Christopher John Doidge [1947] Director/Retired Teacher; Sarah Elizabeth Jelly [1954] Director/Family Law Consultant; Dermot Michael Keegan [1957] Senior Managing Director; Katharine Eleanor Lees-Jones [1956] Director/JP; Professor Andrew William Lloyd [1965] Director/Dean - College of Life, Health & Physical Sciences; Mark Scanlan McFadden [1959] Director/Chartered Surveyor; Nicholas Andrew Mercer [1957] Commercial Director; Catherine Mary Nash [1958] Director/Educational Consultant; Xavier Charles Andre Van Hove [1975] Director/Fund Manager [Swiss]; Generaldine Patricia Watkins [1956] Director/Property Manager; Jenifer Rosemary Woodhouse [1949] Director/Retired; Chris Paul Yates [1962] Director

St Edward Homes Limited
Incorporated: 26 June 2006
Net Worth: £5,343,000 *Total Assets:* £28,772,000
Registered Office: Berkeley House, 19 Portsmouth Road, Cobham, Surrey, KT11 1JG
Activities: Construction of commercial buildings
Shareholders: The Berkeley Group PLC; The Prudential Assurance Company Limited
Officers: Jared Stephen Philip Cranney, Secretary; Trevor John Hankin [1959] Director; David Geoffrey Morris [1967] Director/Chartered Surveyor; Robert Charles Grenville Perrins [1965] Director; Anthony William Pidgley [1947] Director; Tom Edward Pocock [1983] Director; Frances Luisa Ruocco [1985] Director

St George Blackfriars Limited
Incorporated: 4 March 2005
Net Worth: £206,874,432 *Total Assets:* £514,294,368
Registered Office: Berkeley House, 19 Portsmouth Road, Cobham, Surrey, KT11 1JG
Activities: Construction of domestic buildings
Parent: St George South London Limited
Officers: Jared Stephen Philip Cranney, Secretary; Benjamin James Marks, Secretary; Marcus Giles Blake [1971] Director; Piers Martin Clanford [1970] Director; Mark Richard Elgar [1974] Director; Paul Roger Kimber [1977] Director; Benjamin James Marks [1977] Director; James Paul Nicolson [1980] Director [Finnish]; Edward Villiers Noble [1979] Director; Robert Charles Grenville Perrins [1965] Director; Anthony William Pidgley [1947] Director; Richard James Stearn [1968] Director

St George PLC
Incorporated: 11 March 1991 *Employees:* 466
Net Worth: £639,779,968 *Total Assets:* £1,104,471,040
Registered Office: Berkeley House, 19 Portsmouth Road, Cobham, Surrey, KT11 1JG
Activities: Activities of head offices
Shareholders: The Berkeley Group PLC; The Berkeley Group PLC
Officers: Jared Stephen Philip Cranney, Secretary; Benjamin James Marks, Secretary; Piers Martin Clanford [1970] Director; Benjamin James Marks [1977] Director; Robert Charles Grenville Perrins [1965] Director; Anthony William Pidgley [1947] Director; Richard James Stearn [1968] Director; David Gregory Tillotson [1964] Director

St George's Weybridge
Incorporated: 11 February 1993 *Employees:* 574
Net Worth: £38,261,220 *Total Assets:* £49,638,200
Registered Office: St George's College, Weybridge Road, Addlestone, Surrey, KT15 2QS
Activities: Pre-primary education
Officers: Gregory Cole, Secretary; David Joseph Alfred Anderson [1943] Retired Managing Director; Sarah Helen Conrad [1969] Director/Headteacher; Diane Lesley Ewart [1961] Director/Investment Banker; Caroline Louise Gordon [1956] Director/Retired Medical Academic; Jason Matthew Hood [1970] Director; Christopher Trevor Peter Jansen [1970] Managing Director; Timothy Joseph Kirkham [1965] Sales Director; John Michael Lewin [1960] Director/Banker; Prof Ann Helen Muggeridge [1962] Director/Professor; Father William MacKenzie Muir [1945] Director/RC Priest; Denis Nowlan [1954] Director/Senior Manager; Karen Lacovara Patterson [1969] Director/Counsellor [American/British]; Charles Stanley William Prescott [1952] Director/Financial Analyst; Catherine Shevlin [1976] Director/Accountant; Simon Patrick Willis [1963] Director

St James Group Limited
Incorporated: 24 April 1996 *Employees:* 312
Net Worth: £590,302,016 *Total Assets:* £744,556,992
Registered Office: Berkeley House, 19 Portsmouth Road, Cobham, Surrey, KT11 1JG
Activities: Development of building projects
Parent: The Berkeley Group PLC
Officers: Jared Stephen Philip Cranney, Secretary; Alison Jane Dowsett [1966] Director; Sean Ellis [1968] Director; Paul Ivan Hopkins [1961] Director; Peter Kemkers [1971] Director; Robert Charles Grenville Perrins [1965] Director; Anthony William Pidgley [1947] Director; Richard James Stearn [1968] Director; Clive Nicholas Walter [1969] Director

St James Holdings Limited
Incorporated: 21 May 2007
Net Worth Deficit: £2,422,000 *Total Assets:* £279,559,008
Registered Office: Grenville Court, Britwell Road, Burnham, Bucks, SL1 8DF
Activities: Other business support service activities n.e.c.

St James Homes (Grosvenor Dock) Limited
Incorporated: 8 December 2000
Net Worth: £3,145,316 *Total Assets:* £23,036,194
Registered Office: Berkeley House, 19 Portsmouth Road, Cobham, Surrey, KT11 1JG
Activities: Development of building projects
Parent: St James Group Limited
Officers: Jared Stephen Philip Cranney, Secretary; Sean Ellis [1968] Director; Paul Ivan Hopkins [1961] Director; Peter Kemkers [1971] Director; Robert Charles Grenville Perrins [1965] Director; Anthony William Pidgley [1947] Director; Richard James Stearn [1968] Director; Clive Nicholas Walter [1969] Director

St Mary's Football Group Limited
Incorporated: 3 July 2009 *Employees:* 380
Net Worth: £79,080,000 *Total Assets:* £216,800,000
Registered Office: St Marys Stadium, Britannia Road, Southampton, SO14 5FP
Activities: Activities of head offices
Parent: Lander Sports (UK) International Investment Co., Ltd
Officers: Tim Greenwell, Secretary; Ralph Krueger [1959] Director/Chairman [German]; Martin Semmens [1972] Director

St Mary's School Ascot
Incorporated: 29 August 1984 *Employees:* 252
Net Worth: £27,598,000 *Total Assets:* £34,791,000
Registered Office: St Marys School Ascot, St Marys Road, Ascot, Berks, SL5 9JF
Activities: General secondary education
Officers: Giles Kentigern Brand, Secretary; Announshka Ayton [1966] Director/Jewellery Designer; Clare Elizabeth Vivienne Colacicchi [1958] Director/Solicitor; Joanna Elizabeth Ebner [1967] Director/Headmistress; Patrick Spencer Gaynor [1954] Director/Solicitor; Edward Francis Horswell [1956] Director/Art Dealer; The Hon Martin John Hunt [1962] Director/Fund Manager; Peter Joseph McKenna [1969] Director/Insurance [American]; Gordon James Moore [1966] Director/Investment; Professor Richard John Parish [1948] Director/University Teacher; Dermot Anthony Power [1952] Director/School Chaplain; Sister Anne Mary Robinson [1944] Director/Retired Teacher; Generald Vincent Bodenham Thompson [1951] Director/Corporate Finance Advisor; Clementine Mary Vaughan [1981] Investment Director

St Mary's Training Ground Limited
Incorporated: 3 July 2009
Net Worth: £1,376,796 *Total Assets:* £30,587,804
Registered Office: St Marys Stadium, Britannia Road, Southampton, SO14 5FP
Activities: Buying and selling of own real estate
Parent: St Mary's Football Group Limited
Officers: Tim Greenwell, Secretary; Toby Andrew Murray Steele [1976] Director/Chartered Accountant; David Thomas [1969] Director

St Mary's University, Twickenham
Incorporated: 25 October 2006 *Employees:* 738
Net Worth: £101,973,000 *Total Assets:* £130,741,000
Registered Office: Waldegrave Road, Strawberry Hill, Twickenham, Middlesex, TW1 4SX
Activities: First-degree level higher education
Officers: Andrew Murray Browning, Secretary; Professor Edward David Joseph Acton [1949] Director/Higher Education Consultant; Professor Francis Martin Campbell [1970] Director/Vice-Chancellor; Jeffery William Cottle [1964] Director/Lawyer [American/British]; Noreen Doyle [1949] Director [Irish]; Richard Damian Finn [1963] Director/Priest; David Anthony Hartnett [1951] Director/Independent Taxation Advisor; Natalie Mary-Jean Hobkirk [1997] Director; Claire McDonnell [1971] Director; Professor Anne Moran [1950] Director; Charles Philip Richard Moth [1958] Director/Bishop of The Armed Forces; June Patricia Mulroy [1949] Director/Chartered Accountant; Kristen Pilbrow [1975] Director/International Student Experience Manager; Professor Anthony Towey [1959] Director

St William Homes LLP
Incorporated: 7 November 2014
Net Worth: £129,159,000 *Total Assets:* £269,284,000
Registered Office: Berkeley House, 19 Portsmouth Road, Cobham, Surrey, KT11 1JG

St. Catherine's School, Bramley
Incorporated: 10 July 1998 *Employees:* 238
Net Worth: £30,973,732 *Total Assets:* £41,666,404
Registered Office: St Catherine's School, Station Road, Bramley, Guildford, Surrey, GU5 0DF
Activities: Primary education
Officers: Diane Elizabeth Haeffele, Secretary; Albert Domingo Reloj Alonzo [1956] Director/Retired; John Adam Peter Blauth [1953] Managing Director; Michael Francis Bustard [1946] Director/Retired; Professor Finbarr Edward Cotter [1953] Director/Consultant Haematologist; Penelope Jane Crouch [1957] Director/Lawyer; Karen Belinda Maria Farrell [1959] Director [Norwegian]; Clare Slade Johnstone [1950] Director/Consultant Physician; Dr Michael John Jordan [1949] Director/Consultant Anaesthetist; Brigadier Matthew Peter Lowe [1962] Director/Army Officer; Peter James Martin [1947] Director/Retired Finance Executive; Dr Janet Filmer McGowan [1952] Director/Medical Practitioner; Andrew John Pianca [1951] Director/Retired; Susan Elizabeth Shipway [1954] Director; Jonathan Charles Morley Tippett [1956] Director/Chartered Accountant; Denis Brian Ulyet [1952] Director/Retired

St. Margaret's School Bushey
Incorporated: 20 May 1996 *Employees:* 173
Net Worth: £21,346,244 *Total Assets:* £23,384,684
Registered Office: St Margaret's School, Merry Hill Road, Bushey, Herts, WD23 1DT
Activities: Primary education
Officers: Dr Kenneth Victor Young, Secretary/Bursar; Justin Alford [1970] Director/Lawyer; David Clout [1941] Director/Retired; Brian Thomas Coulshed [1950] Director/Retired Headmaster; Judith Elizabeth Fenn [1966] Director/Business Executive; Rev William John Morris Gibbs [1971] Director/Clerk in Holy Orders; Ellen Hill [1952] Director/Retired; Rachel Floretta Hodgson [1969] Director/Marketing Consultant; Malcolm Spooner [1955] Director/Head of Markets

St. Nicholas Court Farms Limited
Incorporated: 15 January 2008 *Employees:* 18
Net Worth: £52,548,912 *Total Assets:* £79,154,632
Registered Office: St Nicholas Court, Court Road, St Nicholas at Wade, Birchington, Kent, CT7 0NJ
Activities: Growing of cereals (except rice), leguminous crops and oil seeds
Shareholders: James Bedford Pace; Alexandra Ruth Pace
Officers: Alexandra Ruth Pace, Secretary; Alexandra Ruth Pace [1969] Director/Farmer; James Bedford Pace [1970] Director Surveyor

St. Patrick's International College Limited
Incorporated: 21 January 1999 *Employees:* 741
Net Worth: £52,586,504 *Total Assets:* £92,561,656
Registered Office: Belmont House, Station Way, Crawley, W Sussex, RH10 1JA
Activities: Other education n.e.c.
Parent: UK Academic Holdings Ltd
Officers: Professor Maurits Van Rooijen [1956] Director/Principal [Dutch]

St.Swithuns School (Winchester)
Incorporated: 8 July 1910 *Employees:* 296
Net Worth: £29,968,316 *Total Assets:* £39,225,996
Registered Office: St Swithun's School, Alresford Road, Winchester, Hants, SO21 1HA
Activities: Primary education
Officers: Professor Robert Adam [1948] Director/Architect; Thomas James Bremridge [1944] Director National Charity Chief Executive; Emma Jane Katharine Clancey [1981] Director/Solicitor; Julia Christine Eager [1960] Director/Headmistress; Doctor Timothy Roderick Hands [1956] Director/Headmaster; Professor Natalie Jane Lee [1951] Director/Professor of Tax Law; Andrew John Ward Lilley [1962] Director/Solicitor; Alison Jane McGhee [1962] Director/Legal Partner; Doctor Heather Dawn Mycock [1957] Director/Doctor; The Very Reverend Catherine Ogle [1961] Director/Dean of Winchester; Sarah Jane Parrish [1963] Director/Senior Technical Executive; Anna-Louise Peters [1979] Finance Director; Frances Robinson [1964] Director/Company Secretary; Margaret Florence Rudland [1945] Director/Headmistress (Retired); Jonathan Brian Cameron Russell [1960] Director/Chairman; Claire Nicola Thorne [1971] Director/University Lecturer; John Richard Tyson [1970] Director/Chief Executive

Stackhouse Poland Bidco Limited
Incorporated: 27 October 2014 *Employees:* 4
Net Worth: £11,523,000 *Total Assets:* £75,007,000
Registered Office: Blenheim House, 1-2 Bridge Street, Guildford, Surrey, GU1 4RY
Activities: Non-life insurance
Parent: Stackhouse Poland Midco Limited
Officers: Iain Jamieson, Secretary; James Ion Daniel Agnew [1968] Director; Jeremy Michael George Cary [1960] Director; Iain Alexander Jamieson [1966] Director; Timothy David Johnson [1967] Director

Stackhouse Poland Group Limited
Incorporated: 11 November 2014 *Employees:* 344
Net Worth Deficit: £18,457,000 *Total Assets:* £128,186,000
Registered Office: Blenheim House, 1-2 Bridge Street, Guildford, Surrey, GU1 4RY
Activities: Activities of insurance agents and brokers
Shareholder: Synova Capital General Partner 4 Ltd
Officers: Iain Jamieson, Secretary; James Ion Daniel Agnew [1968] Director; Alexander Charles Spencer Bowden [1974] Director; Jeremy Michael George Cary [1960] Director; Timothy David Johnson [1967] Director; David Jeremy Menton [1977] Director [Irish]

Stackhouse Poland Holdings Ltd
Incorporated: 4 September 2001 *Employees:* 4
Net Worth: £6,015,000 *Total Assets:* £77,162,000
Registered Office: Blenheim House, 1-2 Bridge Street, Guildford, Surrey, GU1 4RY
Activities: Activities of insurance agents and brokers
Parent: Stackhouse Poland Bidco Limited
Officers: Iain Jamieson, Secretary; James Ion Daniel Agnew [1968] Director/Insurance Broker; Jeremy Michael George Cary [1960] Director/Insurance Broker; Iain Alexander Jamieson [1966] Director; Timothy David Johnson [1967] Director

Stackhouse Poland Limited
Incorporated: 18 March 1974 *Employees:* 198
Net Worth: £14,819,000 *Total Assets:* £37,922,000
Registered Office: Blenheim House, 1-2 Bridge Street, Guildford, Surrey, GU1 4RY
Activities: Activities of insurance agents and brokers
Parent: Stackhouse Poland Holdings Limited
Officers: Iain Jamieson, Secretary; James Ion Daniel Agnew [1968] Director/Insurance Broker; Jeremy Michael George Cary [1960] Director/Insurance Broker; Iain Alexander Jamieson [1966] Director/Chief Operating Officer; Timothy David Johnson [1967] Director/Chief Executive Officer

Stackhouse Poland Midco Limited
Incorporated: 27 October 2014 *Employees:* 4
Net Worth Deficit: £4,935,000 *Total Assets:* £38,579,000
Registered Office: Blenheim House, 1-2 Bridge Street, Guildford, Surrey, GU1 4RY
Activities: Non-life insurance
Parent: Stackhouse Poland Group Limited
Officers: Iain Jamieson, Secretary; James Ion Daniel Agnew [1968] Director; Jeremy Michael George Cary [1960] Director; Iain Alexander Jamieson [1966] Director; Timothy David Johnson [1967] Director

Stada UK Holdings Ltd.
Incorporated: 5 August 2013 *Employees:* 1
Net Worth: £444,660,640 *Total Assets:* £861,665,920
Registered Office: 200 Longwater Avenue, Reading, Berks, RG2 6GP
Activities: Wholesale of pharmaceutical goods
Parent: Stada Arzneimittel Aktiengesellschaft
Officers: Edwin Charles Blythe [1968] Finance Director; Frank Seiler [1968] Director/Vice President Corporate Treasury [German]

Stadium MK Group Limited
Incorporated: 29 June 2007 *Employees:* 629
Previous: Inter MK Group Limited
Net Worth: £78,208,960 *Total Assets:* £113,836,768
Registered Office: Stadium MK, Stadium Way, Milton Keynes, Bucks, MK1 1ST
Activities: Activities of head offices
Major Shareholder: Peter John Winkelman
Officers: Anthony Neil Richens, Secretary; Mark Turner [1968] Director; Peter John Winkelman [1957] Director; Bernadette Winkleman [1958] Director

Standard Commercial Tobacco Company (UK) Limited
Incorporated: 26 January 1979
Net Worth: £38,129,972 *Total Assets:* £38,134,232
Registered Office: Building A, Riverside Way, Camberley, Surrey, GU15 3YL
Activities: Manufacture of tobacco products
Parent: Alliance One International AG
Officers: Amanda Kaberle, Secretary; Joan Teresa Goulden [1955] Director; Paul Thornton [1974] Director/Manager UK Office; Simon Mark Usher [1974] IT Director

Stanley Black & Decker UK Limited
Incorporated: 28 October 2009 *Employees:* 371
Net Worth: £11,466,000 *Total Assets:* £155,943,008
Registered Office: 210 Bath Road, Slough, Berks, SL1 3YD
Activities: Other professional, scientific and technical activities n.e.c.
Officers: Erica Lynn Brennan [1974] Director/Chief Financial Officer [Canadian]; Mark Richard Smiley [1977] Director/General Manager UK & ROI

Stanley Electric (U.K.) Company Limited
Incorporated: 14 September 2000 *Employees:* 19
Net Worth: £15,983,111 *Total Assets:* £21,499,160
Registered Office: Suite 3c, Part 3rd Floor, The Columbia Centre, Station Road, Bracknell, Berks, RG12 1LP
Activities: Other retail sale of new goods in specialised stores (not commercial art galleries and opticians)
Parent: Stanley Electric Co., Ltd.
Officers: Iain Evans, Secretary; Iain Evans [1963] Director/Engineer; Naomichi Saito [1961] Managing Director [Japanese]

Stanley Electric Holding Europe Co., Limited
Incorporated: 31 July 2006 *Employees:* 1
Net Worth: £25,038,120 *Total Assets:* £25,063,614
Registered Office: Suite 3c, Part 3rd Floor, The Columbia Centre, Station Road, Bracknell, Berks, RG12 1LP
Activities: Other business support service activities n.e.c.
Parent: Stanley Electric Co., Ltd
Officers: Katsutoshi Iino [1961] Director [Japanese]; Takanori Kitano [1956] Director/President [Japanese]; Keisuke Ueda [1962] Director [Japanese]

Stanmore Contractors Limited
Incorporated: 9 October 1992 *Employees:* 241
Net Worth: £23,930,244 *Total Assets:* £44,200,124
Registered Office: Stanmore House, Gyproc Park, Church Manorway, Erith, Kent, DA8 1DE
Activities: Plastering
Major Shareholder: Rajbir Singh Manak
Officers: Tanya Maria Barrett, Secretary; Rajbir Singh Manak, Secretary [Indian]; Rajbir Singh Manak [1966] Managing Director [Indian]; Surinder Singh Manak [1969] Director

Stansted Park Foundation
Incorporated: 22 September 2003 *Employees:* 19
Net Worth: £39,481,880 *Total Assets:* £39,718,180
Registered Office: Stansted House, Stansted Park, Rowlands Castle, Hants, PO9 6DX
Activities: Other business support service activities n.e.c.
Officers: James Edwin Tilney Cooper, Secretary; Roger Max Davies [1942] Director; Claire Louise Fitzalan Howard [1960] Director; James Royston Kenroy [1932] Director/Retired; Clive Douglas Nickolds [1946] Director; Yanni Petsopoulos [1949] Director/Publisher [Greek]; Myles Fitzhugh Longfield Ponsonby [1941] Director/Banker; Richard Guy Murray Tassell [1947] Director

Stantec Europe Limited
Incorporated: 31 October 1989 *Employees:* 1,701
Previous: MWH Europe Limited
Net Worth: £26,719,000 *Total Assets:* £138,834,000
Registered Office: Buckingham Court, Kingsmead Business Park, London Road, High Wycombe, Bucks, HP11 1JU
Activities: Activities of head offices
Parent: Stantec Holding B.V.
Officers: Victoria Hall Sturt, Secretary; Victoria Jayne Hall-Sturt [1973] Director/Lawyer; Catherine Margaret Schefer [1968] Managing Director; David Anthony Smith [1963] Director/Chief Strategy Officer; Andrew Charles Wilson [1971] Director/Vice President of Financial Services [American]

Stantec Treatment Group Limited
Incorporated: 14 January 2003
Previous: MWH Constructors Limited
Net Worth: £15,617,000 *Total Assets:* £27,792,000
Registered Office: Buckingham Court, Kingsmead Business Park, London Road, High Wycombe, Bucks, HP11 1JU
Activities: Construction of water projects
Parent: Stantec Constructors Holding B.V.
Officers: Victoria Hall-Sturt, Secretary; Paul Jeremy David Alpern [1964] Director/Solicitor [Canadian]; Victoria Jayne Hall-Sturt [1973] Director/Managing Counsel; Catherine Margaret Schefer [1968] Director/Executive Vice President

Stantec UK Limited
Incorporated: 22 October 1974 *Employees:* 1,064
Previous: MWH UK Limited
Net Worth: £33,542,000 *Total Assets:* £91,520,000
Registered Office: Buckingham Court, Kingsmead Business Park, London Road, High Wycombe, Bucks, HP11 1JU
Activities: Other engineering activities
Parent: Stantec Europe Limited
Officers: Victoria Hall Sturt, Secretary; Victoria Jayne Hall-Sturt [1973] Director/Lawyer; Ian Andrew Noble [1957] Director/Civil Engineer; Catherine Margaret Schefer [1968] UK Managing Director; David Anthony Smith [1963] Director/Chief Strategy Officer

Staples UK Limited
Incorporated: 29 August 1990 *Employees:* 361
Previous: Corporate Express Limited
Net Worth: £13,101,000 *Total Assets:* £38,789,000
Registered Office: Hampden Court, Kingsmead Business Park, Frederick Place, High Wycombe, Bucks, HP11 1JU
Activities: Non-specialised wholesale trade
Parent: Corporate Express (Holdings) Limited
Officers: Steven Mayes, Secretary; Lisa Cole [1976] Human Resources Director; Michael Celina Herman Henckaers [1983] Director [Belgian]; Steven Paul Mayes [1982] Director/Head of FP&A

F.C. Stark Limited
Incorporated: 20 May 1936 *Employees:* 12
Net Worth: £38,788,268 *Total Assets:* £86,386,232
Registered Office: Gay Dawn Offices, Pennis Lane, Fawkham, Longfield, Kent, DA3 8LZ
Activities: Development of building projects
Officers: Stephen John Billings, Secretary; Andrew John Billings [1964] Director/Manager; Clive John Billings [1955] Director/Manager; Ronald John Billings [1960] Director; Stephen John Billings [1961] Director

State Oil Limited
Incorporated: 22 November 2000 *Employees:* 114
Net Worth: £25,545,760 *Total Assets:* £286,220,000
Registered Office: Prax House, Horizon Business Village, 1 Brooklands Road, Weybridge, Surrey, KT13 0TJ
Activities: Extraction of crude petroleum
Officers: Arani Soosaipillai, Secretary; Don Camillo Emilio Borneo [1957] Director/Oil Trader; Winston Sanjeevkumar Soosaipillai [1973] Director/Accountant

Staten Investments Limited
Incorporated: 15 March 2006
Net Worth Deficit: £22,464 *Total Assets:* £22,459,124
Registered Office: Formacompany & Co Ltd, 11 Church Road, Great Bookham, Leatherhead, Surrey, KT23 3PB
Activities: Other information technology service activities
Major Shareholder: Gennady Kotlyarov
Officers: Gennadiy Konstantinovich Kotlyarov [1936] Director/Businessman [Russian]

Stats UK Holdco Limited
Incorporated: 10 April 2015 *Employees:* 2
Net Worth: £43,975,316 *Total Assets:* £43,975,316
Registered Office: Prospect House, 58 Queens Road, Reading, Berks, RG1 4RP
Activities: Other information service activities n.e.c.
Officers: Jill Diana Hansen [1978] Director [American]; Carl Eugene Mergele [1962] Director [American]; Andrew Douglas Tate [1984] Director/Finance [American]

Steamer Properties Limited
Incorporated: 27 March 2000 *Employees:* 469
Net Worth: £10,014,294 *Total Assets:* £28,001,416
Registered Office: Steamer Trading Ltd, The Malthouse, Daveys Lane, Lewes, E Sussex, BN7 2BF
Activities: Activities of head offices
Major Shareholder: Ben Sebastian Phillips
Officers: Ben Sebastian Phillips [1968] Director

Stearn Electric Company Limited
Incorporated: 18 October 1924 *Employees:* 387
Net Worth: £78,153,000 *Total Assets:* £116,069,000
Registered Office: Votec House, Hambridge Lane, Newbury, Berks, RG14 5TN
Activities: Wholesale of radio, television goods & electrical household appliances (other than records, tapes, CDs)
Parent: Newbury Investments (UK) Ltd
Officers: Leo Yu, Secretary; Nigel John Palmer [1956] Director/Chairman; Steven Westbrook [1956] Director/Chief Executive; Leo Yu [1984] Director

Steelstock UK Limited
Incorporated: 7 July 1997 *Employees:* 126
Net Worth: £8,015,242 *Total Assets:* £20,816,836
Registered Office: The Mill House, Anstey Mill Lane, Alton, Hants, GU34 2YA
Activities: Activities of head offices
Shareholders: Ian Harding; Jennifer Ann Harding
Officers: Jennifer Ann Harding, Secretary; Ian Harding [1955] Director; Douglas Gibb Lawrie [1966] Director; Thomas Stannage Wilson [1957] Director; Jason Alan Wood [1975] Director/Operations Manager

Stena Line (UK) Limited
Incorporated: 21 December 1989
Net Worth: £106,700,000 *Total Assets:* £169,800,000
Registered Office: Suite 4, First Floor, Pluto House, Station Road, Ashford, Kent, TN23 1PP
Activities: Activities of head offices
Major Shareholder: Dan Sten Olsson
Officers: Leslie David Stracey, Secretary; Anna Marica Derenstrand [1967] Finance Director [Swedish]; Ian James Hampton [1981] Director/Chief People & Communication Officer; Ulf Niklas Martensson [1971] Director/Chief Executive [Swedish]; Hans Erik Noren [1957] Director [Swedish]; Leslie David Stracey [1955] Director/Accountant

Stena Line Irish Sea Ferries Limited
Incorporated: 30 April 1930 *Employees:* 583
Net Worth: £55,059,000 *Total Assets:* £72,438,000
Registered Office: Suite 4, First Floor, Pluto House, Station Road, Ashford, Kent, TN23 1PP
Activities: Sea and coastal passenger water transport
Parent: Stena Line (UK) Ltd
Officers: Leslie David Stracey, Secretary; Anna Marica Derenstrand [1967] Finance Director [Swedish]; Ian James Hampton [1981] Director/Chief People & Communications Officer; Ulf Niklas Martensson [1971] Director/Chief Executive [Swedish]; Hans Erik Noren [1957] Director [Swedish]; Leslie David Stracey [1955] Director/Company Secretary

Stena Line Limited
Incorporated: 28 November 1978 *Employees:* 2
Net Worth: £61,500,000 *Total Assets:* £137,000,000
Registered Office: Suite 4, First Floor, Pluto House, Station Road, Ashford, Kent, TN23 1PP
Activities: Sea and coastal passenger water transport
Parent: Stena Line (UK) Ltd
Officers: Leslie David Stracey, Secretary; Anna Marica Denrenstrand [1967] Finance Director [Swedish]; Ian James Hampton [1981] Director/Chief People & Communications Officer; Ulf Niklas Martensson [1971] Director/Chief Executive [Swedish]; Hans Erik Noren [1957] Director [Swedish]; Leslie David Stracey [1955] Director/Accountant

Stena Line Ports Limited
Incorporated: 26 October 1981
Net Worth: £202,702,000 *Total Assets:* £246,896,000
Registered Office: Suite 4, First Floor, Pluto House, Station Road, Ashford, Kent, TN23 1PP
Activities: Sea and coastal passenger water transport
Parent: Stena Line (UK) Ltd
Officers: Leslie David Stracey, Secretary; Anna Marica Derenstrand [1967] Finance Director [Swedish]; Ian James Hampton [1981] Director/Chief People & Communication Officer; Ulf Niklas Martensson [1971] Director/Chief Executive [Swedish]; Hans Erik Noren [1957] Director [Swedish]; Leslie David Stracey [1955] Director/Accountant

Step Academy Trust
Incorporated: 21 April 2011 *Employees:* 673
Previous: The Step Academy Trust
Net Worth: £86,502,000 *Total Assets:* £93,763,000
Registered Office: Gonville Road, Thornton Heath, Surrey, CR7 6DL
Activities: Primary education
Officers: Kirstie Martin, Secretary; Alan Michael Armstrong [1947] Director/Retired; Dr Katherine Sarah Chhatwal [1976] Director/Chief Programme Officer; Isabelle Dennigan [1968] Director/Banking Professional [French]; Mark Ducker OBE [1965] Director/Chief Executive Officer; Ross Gardner [1972] Director/Global Delivery & Business Engagement Lead; Navdeep Sanghara [1981] Director/Executive Headteacher, Inspire Partnership

M R Stephenson Limited
Incorporated: 17 December 2002 *Employees:* 16
Net Worth: £12,020,864 *Total Assets:* £29,563,524
Registered Office: Provender Mill, Mill Bay Lane, Horsham, W Sussex, RH12 1SS
Activities: Activities of head offices
Major Shareholder: Martin Richard Stephenson
Officers: Stephen David James Hemsley [1963] Director; Tobias Jonathan Hemsley [1970] Managing Director; Elaine Sheil [1971] Financial Director; Martin Richard Stephenson [1959] Director

Steria UK Corporate Limited
Incorporated: 27 January 1971
Net Worth: £181,152,000 *Total Assets:* £222,722,000
Registered Office: Three Cherry Trees Lane, Hemel Hempstead, Herts, HP2 7AH
Activities: Information technology consultancy activities
Parent: Sopra Steria Group SA
Officers: Peter Cashmore, Secretary; Davinder Singh Ahluwalia [1952] Director; John Joseph Moran [1961] Director, Corporate Finance; John Powell Torrie [1954] Director

Steris CH Limited
Incorporated: 28 January 2003 *Employees:* 3
Net Worth: £10,103,608 *Total Assets:* £34,842,332
Registered Office: Bridgwater House, Jays Close, Viables, Basingstoke, Hants, RG22 4AX
Activities: Activities of other holding companies n.e.c.
Parent: Steris UK Holding Limited
Officers: Ronald Snyder, Secretary; Julia Kipnis [1977] Director/Corporate Counsel [American]; Ronald E Snyder [1948] Director/Associate and Group General Counsel [American]; Michael Joseph Tokich [1968] Director/Chief Financial Officer [American]

Steris UK Holding Limited
Incorporated: 20 January 2014
Net Worth: £71,740,160 *Total Assets:* £72,182,376
Registered Office: Bridgwater House, Jays Close, Viables, Basingstoke, Hants, RG22 4AX
Activities: Activities of other holding companies n.e.c.
Parent: Steris PLC
Officers: Ronald Snyder, Secretary; Julia Kipnis [1977] Director/Corporate Counsel [American]; Ronald E Snyder [1948] Director/Associate and Group General Counsel [American]; Michael Joseph Tokich [1968] Director/Chief Financial Officer [American]

STI Enterprises Limited
Incorporated: 27 April 2011 *Employees:* 881
Previous: STI Enterprises PLC
Net Worth Deficit: £399,000 *Total Assets:* £42,614,000
Registered Office: Surface Technology International, Osborn Way, Hook, Hants, RG27 9HX
Activities: Defence activities
Parent: Integrated Micro-Electronics, Inc
Officers: Craig Stuart Petrie, Secretary; Gilles George Lucien Bernard [1957] Director [French]; Simon Andre Best [1959] Director; Craig Stuart Petrie [1970] Director/Chief Financial Officer; Josef Pfister [1954] Director [German]; Ignacio Suarez de Puga [1962] Director [Spanish]; Arthur Ramos Tan [1959] Director [American]

Stiefel Consumer Healthcare (UK) Limited
Incorporated: 2 February 2015
Net Worth: £156,755,008 *Total Assets:* £226,192,000
Registered Office: 980 Great West Road, Brentford, Middlesex, TW8 9GS
Activities: Activities of other holding companies n.e.c.
Parent: GlaxoSmithKline Consumer Healthcare Holdings Limited
Officers: Richard Green [1974] Director; Tobias Hestler [1972] Director [German/Swiss]

Andreas Stihl Limited
Incorporated: 30 June 1978 *Employees:* 123
Net Worth: £20,841,868 *Total Assets:* £38,716,048
Registered Office: Stihl House, Stanhope Road, Camberley, Surrey, GU15 3YT
Activities: Wholesale of other machinery and equipment
Parent: Stihl Holding AG & Co.KG
Officers: Nicholas Jason Burroughs, Secretary; Karl Dieter Angler [1956] Director/Executive Board Member [Canadian]; Nicholas Jason Burroughs [1970] Director/Chartered Accountant; Robert Lochhead Lennie [1954] Managing Director; Norbert Johannes Pick [1957] Director/Executive Board Member [German]

Stock Finance (Koruna) Limited
Incorporated: 10 October 2013
Net Worth: £28,622,324 *Total Assets:* £28,645,654
Registered Office: Solar House, Mercury Park, Wooburn Green, Bucks, HP10 0HH
Activities: Financial intermediation not elsewhere classified
Parent: Stock Spirits (UK) Limited
Officers: Sally Kenward, Secretary; Raj Paul Singh Bal [1967] Director/Chief Financial Officer; Steven Colin Weatherley [1968] Director/Lawyer

Stock Spirits (UK) Limited
Incorporated: 20 June 2007 *Employees:* 15
Net Worth: £197,630,000 *Total Assets:* £216,776,992
Registered Office: Solar House, Mercury Park, Wooburn Green, Bucks, HP10 0HH
Activities: Activities of other holding companies n.e.c.
Parent: Stock Spirits Group PLC
Officers: Sally Kenward, Secretary; Raj Paul Singh Bal [1967] Director/Chief Financial Officer; Steven Colin Weatherley [1968] Director/Lawyer

Stock Spirits Group PLC
Incorporated: 12 September 2013 *Employees:* 1,003
Net Worth: £307,561,408 *Total Assets:* £548,683,712
Registered Office: Solar House, Mercury Park, Wooburn Green, Bucks, HP10 0HH
Activities: Activities of head offices
Officers: Sally Kenward, Secretary; Helen Catherine Allum [1965] Director; Raj Paul Singh Bal [1967] Director/Chief Financial Officer; Diego Bevilacqua [1953] Director; Tomasz Wojciech Blawat [1966] Director [Polish]; Michael Guy Butterworth [1961] Director; David Ossian Maloney [1955] Director; John Ross Nicolson [1953] Director; Miroslaw Stachowicz [1962] Director/Chief Executive Officer [Polish]

Stockford Limited
Incorporated: 30 December 1981 *Employees:* 527
Net Worth: £37,460,000 *Total Assets:* £95,469,000
Registered Office: Buckingham House, West Street, Newbury, Berks, RG14 1BE
Activities: Activities of other holding companies n.e.c.
Shareholders: Paul James Michael; Peter Colin Michael
Officers: Malcolm Vincent Morris, Secretary; Paul James Michael [1965] Director; Sir Peter Colin Michael [1938] Director

Stoke Park Limited
Incorporated: 17 July 1992 *Employees:* 254
Net Worth: £28,213,000 *Total Assets:* £70,058,000
Registered Office: Stoke Park Club, Park Road, Stoke Poges, Bucks, SL2 4PG
Activities: Hotels and similar accommodation
Officers: Hertford Milner King, Secretary; Chester Milner King [1971] Director; Hertford Milner King [1965] Director; Roger Milner King [1936] Director; Witney Milner King [1967] Director

Stonefield Estates, Limited
Incorporated: 10 February 1936 *Employees:* 6
Net Worth: £47,691,096 *Total Assets:* £50,552,612
Registered Office: Shorehill Farm, Shorehill Lane, Knatts Valley, Sevenoaks, Kent, TN15 6XL
Activities: Other letting and operating of own or leased real estate
Officers: Howard George Cloke, Secretary; Howard George Cloke [1961] Director/Chartered Surveyor; Claire Tracey Daniels [1971] Director/IT; Clive Jonathan Daniels [1944] Director/Economist; Adele Freda Entwistle [1929] Director

Stoneham Park Developments LLP
Incorporated: 6 July 2017
Net Worth: £1,000 *Total Assets:* £20,646,572
Registered Office: Artillery House, Fort Fareham Industrial Site, Newgate Lane, Fareham, Hants, PO14 1AH

Store Property Holdings Limited
Incorporated: 5 June 1979 *Employees:* 14
Net Worth: £159,091,856 *Total Assets:* £281,789,408
Registered Office: Farr House, 4 New Park Road, Chichester, W Sussex, PO19 7XA
Activities: Activities of head offices
Officers: Gary Neil Hawkins, Secretary; Gary Neil Hawkins [1971] Director/Chartered Accountant; Paul Michael Albert Rowland [1969] Construction Director; Jacqueline Jennifer Wickens [1946] Director; Roger Foster Wickens [1944] Director; Sarah Foster Wickens [1970] Property Surveyor & Director

Store Property Investments Limited
Incorporated: 23 May 1955 *Employees:* 8
Net Worth: £151,593,616 *Total Assets:* £265,173,728
Registered Office: Farr House, 4 New Park Road, Chichester, W Sussex, PO19 7XA
Activities: Buying and selling of own real estate
Parent: Store Property Holdings Limited
Officers: Gary Neil Hawkins, Secretary; Gary Neil Hawkins [1971] Director/Chartered Accountant; Ross Daniel Moyler [1976] Director/Chartered Surveyor; Paul Michael Albert Rowland [1969] Construction Director; Jacqueline Jennifer Wickens [1946] Director; Roger Foster Wickens [1944] Director; Sarah Foster Wickens [1970] Property Surveyor & Director; Tim John Wilmer [1974] Director/Chartered Surveyor

Storeshield Limited
Incorporated: 28 June 1973
Net Worth: £242,592,992 *Total Assets:* £243,415,008
Registered Office: The Priestley Centre, 10 Priestley Road, The Surrey Research Park, Guildford, Surrey, GU2 7XY
Activities: Activities of head offices
Parent: The BOC Group Limited
Officers: Susan Kathleen Kelly, Secretary; Julian Michael Bland [1967] Director/Head of Accounting; Benjamin Patterson [1962] Director/Solicitor; Sally Ann Williams [1970] Director/Accountant

Storm UK Holdco Limited
Incorporated: 14 September 2016 *Employees:* 106
Net Worth: £140,155,008 *Total Assets:* £251,430,000
Registered Office: St Annes House, Oxford Square, Oxford Street, Newbury, Berks, RG14 1JQ
Activities: Activities of other holding companies n.e.c.
Officers: Carol Martha Browner [1955] Director/Consultant [American]; Mairi Clare Bull [1972] Director/HR & Operations Manager; Richard James Campione [1963] Director/Chairman [American]; Matthew Levine [1975] Director/Finance [American]; Colby Travis Manwaring [1972] Director/President [American]; Geoffrey D. Roberts [1960] Director/Chartered Engineer [American]; Karen Roter Davis [1972] Director/Technology Executive [American]

Storrington Equityco Limited
Incorporated: 23 April 2014 *Employees:* 464
Net Worth: £23,618,000 *Total Assets:* £45,589,000
Registered Office: Unit 1 Water Lane Industrial Estate, Storrington, W Sussex, RH20 3EA
Activities: Activities of head offices
Officers: Michael Colin Begg [1959] Director/Engineer; Dr James Cumming Ramage [1951] Director/Physicist; Prof Stephen Williamson [1948] Director

Storrington Industries Limited
Incorporated: 8 February 2005 *Employees:* 3
Net Worth: £15,857,000 *Total Assets:* £23,087,000
Registered Office: Unit 1 Water Lane Industrial Estate, Storrington, W Sussex, RH20 3EA
Activities: Activities of head offices
Parent: Storrington Equityco Limited
Officers: Dr Michael Colin Begg, Secretary/Engineer; Dr Michael Colin Begg [1959] Director/Engineer; Dr James Cumming Ramage [1951] Director/Physicist; Prof Stephen Williamson [1948] Director/University Administration

The Stowe House Preservation Trust
Incorporated: 30 June 1997 *Employees:* 3
Net Worth: £21,536,264 *Total Assets:* £21,734,460
Registered Office: Stowe House, Stowe, Buckingham, MK18 5EH
Activities: Operation of historical sites and buildings and similar visitor attractions
Officers: Mark Anthony Jackson Stops, Secretary; John Richard Charles Arkwright [1950] Director/Chartered Surveyor; Richard Broyd [1948] Director/Hotelier; Julie Christine Brunskill [1958] Director/Retired; Juliet Ursula Colman [1967] Director/Architect; Simon Charles Creedy Smith [1959] Director/Chartered Accountant; Andrew William Mildmay Fane [1949] Director/Chartered Accountant; Jeffrey Philip Haworth [1944] Director/Architect; Mark Anthony Jackson-Stops [1950] Director/Surveyor; Robert Charles Morley [1942] Director/Retired; Jeremy Gibson Dixon Musson [1965] Director/Writer; Duncan William Angus Stirling [1963] Director/Marketing Executive; Annabel Chaundy Westman [1953] Director/Textile Historian

Stowe School,Limited
Incorporated: 20 January 1923 *Employees:* 500
Net Worth: £43,479,320 *Total Assets:* £54,321,720
Registered Office: Stowe School, Stowe, Buckingham, MK18 5EH
Activities: General secondary education
Officers: Michael Beauchamp Mansel Porter, Secretary; Reverend Peter Michael Ackroyd [1960] Director/Clergyman; Jonathan Michael Arundell Bewes [1965] Director/Investment Banker; Julie Christine Brunskill [1958] Chartered Surveyor/Group Property Director; Sir James Michael Burnell Nugent [1949] Director; Geoffrey David Granville Carr [1959] Director; David Watson Cheyne [1948] Director/Solicitor; Juliet Ursula Colman [1967] Director/Architect; Simon Charles Creedy Smith [1959] Director/Accountant; Elizabeth Joy de Burgh Sidley [1951] Director/Retired Chartered Surveyor; John Philip Cardain Frost [1966] Director/Chartered Surveyor; Professor Guy Manning Goodwin [1947] Director/Professor of Psychiatry; Joanne Elizabeth Hastie-Smith [1960] Director/Vicar's Wife; Andrea Karen Johnson [1960] Director/Headmistress; Robert Anthony Lankester [1958] Director/Headmaster; Catriona Helen Lloyd [1967] Director/Solicitor; Elizabeth Mary Kirby Phillips [1940] Director/Education Consultant; Vanessa Jane Stanley [1966] Director/Teacher; Lady Jennifer Avril Kinmond Stringer [1952] Director/Doctor (Retired); Christopher John Tate [1953] Director

Strand Court Properties Limited
Incorporated: 22 February 1946
Net Worth: £22,533,000 *Total Assets:* £25,068,000
Registered Office: 889 Greenford Road, Greenford, Middlesex, UB6 0HE
Activities: Other letting and operating of own or leased real estate
Parent: Thorntons Limited
Officers: Tim John Shirley, Secretary; David Stuart Murby [1965] Director/Accountant; Tim John Shirley [1979] Director/Solicitor

Stratton House Leasing Limited
Incorporated: 19 February 1986
Net Worth: £161,000 *Total Assets:* £104,199,000
Registered Office: Riverbank, Meadows Business Park, Blackwater, Camberley, Surrey, GU17 9AB
Activities: Activities of head offices
Parent: Rentokil Limited
Officers: Catherine Stead, Secretary; Daragh Patrick Feltrim Fagan [1969] Director/Solicitor; Catherine Jane Stead [1978] Director/Company Secretary

John Street & Company (Surrey) Limited
Incorporated: 10 September 1949 *Employees:* 3
Net Worth: £1,348,773 *Total Assets:* £43,769,624
Registered Office: Suite 2, West Hill House, West Hill, Epsom, Surrey, KT19 8JD
Activities: Other letting and operating of own or leased real estate
Parent: Street Family Group of Companies (Holdings) Limited
Officers: Andrew Mark Munday, Secretary; Patricia Jane French [1951] Director; Rivkah Hazel McCullough [1980] Director/Commercial Portfolio Executive; Andrew Mark Munday [1969] Director/Property Manager; Jonathan Justin Selig Symons [1949] Director

Street Family Group of Companies (Holdings) Limited
Incorporated: 16 October 2012 *Employees:* 3
Net Worth: £63,992,172 *Total Assets:* £65,420,112
Registered Office: Suite 2, West Hill House, West Hill, Epsom, Surrey, KT19 8JD
Activities: Non-trading company
Parent: Rothschild & Co
Officers: Andrew Mark Munday, Secretary; Patricia Jane French [1951] Director; Joanna Hudaly [1955] Director/Counsellor; Rivkah Hazel McCullough [1980] Director/Commercial Portfolio Executive; Andrew Mark Munday [1969] Director/Property Manager

Street Property (Holdings) Limited
Incorporated: 17 October 2012 *Employees:* 2
Net Worth: £9,572,812 *Total Assets:* £44,051,604
Registered Office: Suite 2, West Hill House, West Hill, Epsom, Surrey, KT19 8JD
Activities: Other letting and operating of own or leased real estate
Parent: Street Family Group of Companies (Holdings) Limited
Officers: Andrew Mark Munday, Secretary; Patricia Jane French [1951] Director; Rivkah Hazel McCullough [1980] Director/Commercial Portfolio Executive; Andrew Mark Munday [1969] Director/Property Manager

Henry Streeter (Sand & Ballast) Limited
Incorporated: 19 January 1955 *Employees:* 2
Net Worth: £22,701,684 *Total Assets:* £24,456,736
Registered Office: 2 Station Road West, Oxted, Surrey, RH8 9EP
Activities: Operation of gravel and sand pits; mining of clays and kaolin
Parent: Henry Streeter Limited
Officers: Josephine Mary Green, Secretary; Rodney John Cruse [1945] Director; Toby James Green Cruse [1985] Director; Josephine Mary Green Aka Cruse [1944] Director

Strides Pharma Global (UK) Ltd
Incorporated: 29 July 2015 *Employees:* 2
Net Worth: £16,483,671 *Total Assets:* £20,348,244
Registered Office: Unit 4 Metro Centre, Tolpits Lane, Watford, Herts, WD18 9SS
Activities: Wholesale of pharmaceutical goods
Parent: Strides Arcolab International Limited
Officers: Vikesh Kumar [1984] Director/Service [Indian]; Krishnan Tirucherai Parthasarathy [1971] Director [Indian]; Mohana Kumar Pillai [1956] Director [Indian]

Strollmoor Limited
Incorporated: 7 August 1972 *Employees:* 37
Net Worth: £22,976,248 *Total Assets:* £48,476,724
Registered Office: E3 The Premier Centre, Premier Way, Abbey Park, Romsey, Hants, SO51 9DG
Activities: Buying and selling of own real estate
Major Shareholder: Priscilla Graham
Officers: Michael Chee Keong See, Secretary; Priscilla Sarah Graham [1946] Director

Strongdraw Limited
Incorporated: 2 July 1965
Net Worth: £74,018,000 *Total Assets:* £74,018,000
Registered Office: Avis Budget House, Park Road, Bracknell, Berks, RG12 2EW
Activities: Activities of head offices
Parent: Avis Europe Holdings Ltd
Officers: Inderpal Lall, Secretary; Paul Leslie Ford [1970] Director/Chartered Accountant; Paul Edward Rollason [1979] Director/Accountant

Stryker UK Limited
Incorporated: 12 November 1998 *Employees:* 486
Net Worth: £59,508,000 *Total Assets:* £78,394,000
Registered Office: Stryker House, Hambridge Road, Newbury, Berks, RG14 5AW
Activities: Other human health activities
Parent: Stryker Corporation
Officers: Peter Ewart Bradley [1961] Director/Business Executive; Robert Andrew Nathan Mills [1977] Director/Business Executive

Student Castle Limited
Incorporated: 8 January 2010 *Employees:* 18
Net Worth: £135,361,280 *Total Assets:* £137,570,592
Registered Office: Kintyre House, 70 High Street, Fareham, Hants, PO16 7BB
Activities: Development of building projects
Officers: Sam Dance, Secretary; Charles Edward Cade [1969] Director; Sam Dance [1981] Director; Jacqueline Rebecca Hawthorn [1964] Director; Peter Morton [1953] Director; Roger Taylor [1964] Director

Study Group Holdings UK Limited
Incorporated: 26 July 2006
Net Worth: £14,938,895 *Total Assets:* £113,022,976
Registered Office: Brighton Study Centre, 1 Billinton Way, Brighton, BN1 4LF
Activities: General secondary education
Parent: EDU UK Management Services Limited
Officers: Gordon Anthony Bull, Secretary; Gordon Anthony Bull [1975] Director/Solicitor; James Henry Pitman [1961] Managing Director

Study Group UK Limited
Incorporated: 29 September 1995 *Employees:* 360
Net Worth: £14,169,000 *Total Assets:* £131,459,000
Registered Office: Brighton Study Centre, 1 Billinton Way, Brighton, BN1 4LF
Activities: General secondary education
Parent: Study Group Holdings UK Limited
Officers: Gordon Anthony Bull, Secretary; Gordon Anthony Bull [1975] Director/Solicitor; Michael John Everett [1966] Director/Chief Operating Officer; Emma Voirrey Lancaster [1969] Director; James Henry Pitman [1961] Managing Director

Subsea 7 Crewing Limited
Incorporated: 21 August 1973
Net Worth: £15,510,612 *Total Assets:* £63,792,680
Registered Office: 40 Brighton Road, Sutton, Surrey, SM2 5BN
Activities: Other service activities n.e.c.
Parent: Subsea 7 Senior Holdings (UK) Limited
Officers: Lorna Helen Peace, Secretary; Simon David Ellis [1975] Group Legal Director - Commercial; John Alexander Gordon [1967] Finance Director; Neil McDonald [1961] Director/Vice President - Offshore Resources

Subsea 7 Engineering Limited
Incorporated: 18 April 2006
Net Worth: £23,708,000 *Total Assets:* £72,891,000
Registered Office: 40 Brighton Road, Sutton, Surrey, SM2 5BN
Activities: Other business support service activities n.e.c.
Parent: Subsea 7 Limited
Officers: Lorna Helen Peace, Secretary; James Richard Haylock [1974] Director/Senior Counsel; Paul Thomas Rosier [1960] Director/Chartered Engineer; David Robert Williams [1971] Director/Vice President - AFGOM

Subsea 7 Interim UK Holdings Limited
Incorporated: 24 August 2011
Net Worth: £2,575,193,856 *Total Assets:* £2,577,399,296
Registered Office: 40 Brighton Road, Sutton, Surrey, SM2 5BN
Activities: Activities of other holding companies n.e.c.
Parent: Subsea 7 International Holdings (UK) Limited
Officers: Alexandre Armand Bringer [1975] Director/VP & Group Controller [French]; Nathalie Veronique Jacqueline Ghislaine Louys [1963] Director/General Counsel [Belgian]; Douglas James Young [1964] Director/Group Financial Controller

Subsea 7 International Contracting Limited
Incorporated: 23 June 1995
Net Worth: £135,740,112 *Total Assets:* £247,003,392
Registered Office: 40 Brighton Road, Sutton, Surrey, SM2 5BN
Activities: Other specialised construction activities n.e.c.
Parent: Subsea 7 Senior Holdings (UK) Limited
Officers: Lorna Helen Peace, Secretary; Simon David Ellis [1975] Legal Director; John Alexander Gordon [1967] Finance Director; Marcelo Lopes Xavier [1980] Director/Vice President [Brazilian]; Neil McDonald [1961] Director/Vice President - Offshore Resources

Subsea 7 Investments (UK) Limited
Incorporated: 2 September 2014
Net Worth: £1,144,120,576 *Total Assets:* £1,149,899,776
Registered Office: 40 Brighton Road, Sutton, Surrey, SM2 5BN
Activities: Other business support service activities n.e.c.
Parent: Subsea 7 Interim UK Holdings Limited
Officers: Lorna Helen Peace, Secretary; Alexandre Armand Bringer [1975] Director/VP & Group Controller [French]; Mark Austin Hodgkinson [1961] Director/Head of Treasury [Australian]; Jihane Karim [1983] Finance Director [French]; Nathalie Veronique Jacqueline Ghislaine Louys [1963] Director/General Counsel [Belgian]; Douglas James Young [1964] Director

Subsea 7 Limited
Incorporated: 5 November 2001
Net Worth: £884,398,976 *Total Assets:* £1,134,483,968
Registered Office: 40 Brighton Road, Sutton, Surrey, SM2 5BN
Activities: Support activities for petroleum and natural gas mining
Parent: Subsea 7 Interim UK Holdings Limited
Officers: Lorna Helen Peace, Secretary; Simon David Ellis [1975] UK Legal Director; John Alexander Gordon [1967] Director/Finance Manager; David Lowther [1966] Director/Vice President - Middle East; Graham Christopher Sharland [1961] Director/VP - Life of Field/Itech; Philip John Simons [1966] Director/VP Canada, Med & Russia; Colin Strachan [1965] Finance Director; Jonathan Richard Tame [1965] Director/Vice President - UK & Canada; Stephen George Wisely [1962] Director/EVP Northern Hemisphere and Life of Field

Subsea 7 Offshore Resources (UK) Limited
Incorporated: 5 September 2011
Net Worth: £2,456,738,560 *Total Assets:* £2,468,395,520
Registered Office: 40 Brighton Road, Sutton, Surrey, SM2 5BN
Activities: Support activities for petroleum and natural gas mining
Parent: Subsea 7 Senior Holdings (UK) Limited
Officers: Simon David Ellis [1975] Group Legal Director - Commercial; John Alexander Gordon [1967] Finance Director; Neil McDonald [1961] Director/Vice President - Offshore Resources

Subsea 7 Senior Holdings (UK) Limited
Incorporated: 24 August 2011
Net Worth: £1,719,828,480 *Total Assets:* £4,240,687,360
Registered Office: 40 Brighton Road, Sutton, Surrey, SM2 5BN
Activities: Activities of other holding companies n.e.c.
Parent: Subsea 7 International Holdings (UK) Limited
Officers: Alexandre Armand Bringer [1975] Director/VP & Group Controller [French]; Nathalie Veronique Jacqueline Ghislaine Louys [1963] Director/General Counsel [Belgian]; Douglas James Young [1964] Director/Group Financial Controller

Subsea 7 Treasury (UK) Limited
Incorporated: 17 March 1970
Net Worth: £938,905,472 *Total Assets:* £5,851,809,280
Registered Office: 40 Brighton Road, Sutton, Surrey, SM2 5BN
Activities: Other business support service activities n.e.c.
Parent: Subsea 7 International Holdings (UK) Limited
Officers: Lorna Helen Peace, Secretary; Alexandre Armand Bringer [1975] Director/VP & Group Controller [French]; Mark Austin Hodgkinson [1961] Director/Head of Treasury [Australian]; Nathalie Veronique Jacqueline Ghislaine Louys [1963] Director/General Counsel [Belgian]; Ricardo Horacio Rosa [1956] Director/Chief Financial Officer

Suez Advanced Solutions Holding UK Limited
Incorporated: 23 March 2010 *Employees:* 3
Previous: Aqualogy Solutions and Technologies Limited
Net Worth: £47,537,000 *Total Assets:* £49,707,000
Registered Office: Suez House, Grenfell Road, Maidenhead, Berks, SL6 1ES
Activities: Other business support service activities n.e.c.
Parent: Ondeo Industrial Solutions UK Limited
Officers: Joan Knight, Secretary; Xavier Lazennec [1965] Director/Europe ES Manager [French]; Julien Joseph Rojo [1981] Director/Vice President [French]; Matthew Joseph Stephenson [1974] Director

Suez Advanced Solutions UK Limited
Incorporated: 25 January 2006 *Employees:* 143
Previous: Aqualogy Environment Limited
Net Worth: £3,903,000 *Total Assets:* £40,718,000
Registered Office: Suez House, Grenfell Road, Maidenhead, Berks, SL6 1ES
Activities: Water collection, treatment and supply
Parent: Suez Advanced Solutions Holding UK Limited
Officers: Joan Knight, Secretary; Xavier Lazennec [1965] Director/Europe ES Manager [French]; Julien Joseph Rojo [1981] Director/Vice President [French]; Matthew Joseph Stephenson [1974] Director

Suez Recycling and Recovery Holdings UK Ltd
Incorporated: 3 December 1997 *Employees:* 5,067
Previous: SITA Holdings UK Limited
Net Worth: £362,718,016 *Total Assets:* £1,050,508,032
Registered Office: Suez House, Grenfell Road, Maidenhead, Berks, SL6 1ES
Activities: Activities of head offices
Parent: Suez UK Group Holdings Ltd
Officers: Mark Hedley Thompson, Secretary/Head of Legal and Company Secretary; Jean-Marc Marc Boursier [1967] Director/Group Senior Executive Vice President [French]; Florent Thierry Antoine Duval [1976] Director/Chief Finance Officer [French]; David Courtenay Palmer-Jones [1963] Director/Chief Executive Officer

Suez Recycling and Recovery Kirklees Ltd
Incorporated: 22 January 1998 *Employees:* 122
Previous: SITA (Kirklees) Limited
Net Worth: £1,055,000 *Total Assets:* £62,060,000
Registered Office: Suez House, Grenfell Road, Maidenhead, Berks, SL6 1ES
Activities: Collection of non-hazardous waste
Parent: Shukco 327 Ltd
Officers: Mark Hedley Thompson, Secretary/Head of Legal and Company Secretary; Councillor Naheed Arshad-Mather [1958] Director/Councillor; Florent Thierry Antoine Duval [1976] Director/Chief Finance Officer [French]; Marek Robert Gordon [1953] Director; Gary Mayson [1969] Director/General Manager; David Courtenay Palmer-Jones [1963] Director/Chief Executive Officer; John James Scanlon [1969] Operations Director; Councillor Michael Richard Watson [1967] Director/Councillor; John Wilkinson [1974] Director/General Manager

Suez Recycling and Recovery Lancashire Ltd
Incorporated: 28 August 1991 *Employees:* 206
Previous: SITA (Lancashire) Limited
Net Worth: £59,311,000 *Total Assets:* £75,249,000
Registered Office: Suez House, Grenfell Road, Maidenhead, Berks, SL6 1ES
Activities: Collection of non-hazardous waste
Parent: Group Fabricom Limited
Officers: Mark Hedley Thompson, Secretary/Head of Legal and Company Secretary; Florent Thierry Antoine Duval [1976] Director/Chief Finance Officer [French]; David Courtenay Palmer-Jones [1963] Director/Chief Executive Officer; John James Scanlon [1969] Director

Suez Recycling and Recovery North East Ltd
Incorporated: 23 December 1988 *Employees:* 140
Previous: SITA North East Limited
Net Worth Deficit: £2,580,000 *Total Assets:* £26,868,000
Registered Office: Suez House, Grenfell Road, Maidenhead, Berks, SL6 1ES
Activities: Treatment and disposal of non-hazardous waste
Parent: Suez Recycling and Recovery Holdings UK Ltd
Officers: Mark Hedley Thompson, Secretary/Head of Legal and Company Secretary; Florent Thierry Antoine Duval [1976] Director/Chief Finance Officer [French]; David Courtenay Palmer-Jones [1963] Director/Chief Executive Officer

Suez Recycling and Recovery Packington Ltd
Incorporated: 17 May 1979 *Employees:* 12
Previous: Shukco 346 Ltd
Net Worth: £61,356,000 *Total Assets:* £62,237,000
Registered Office: Suez House, Grenfell Road, Maidenhead, Berks, SL6 1ES
Activities: Treatment and disposal of non-hazardous waste
Parent: Suez Recycling and Recovery Holdings UK Ltd
Officers: Joan Knight, Secretary; Florent Thierry Antoine Duval [1976] Director/Chief Finance Officer [French]

Suez Recycling and Recovery South East Ltd
Incorporated: 31 December 1934 *Employees:* 171
Previous: Shukco 347 Ltd
Net Worth Deficit: £50,514,000 *Total Assets:* £32,036,000
Registered Office: Suez House, Grenfell Road, Maidenhead, Berks, SL6 1ES
Activities: Treatment and disposal of non-hazardous waste
Parent: Shukco 340 Ltd
Officers: Joan Knight, Assistant Company Secretary; Florent Thierry Antoine Duval [1976] Director/Chief Finance Officer [French]; David Courtenay Palmer-Jones [1963] Director/Chief Executive Officer

Suez Recycling and Recovery South Gloucestershire Ltd
Incorporated: 3 April 2000 *Employees:* 262
Previous: Suez Recycling and Recovery South Gloucestershre Ltd
Net Worth: £29,066,000 *Total Assets:* £30,445,000
Registered Office: Suez House, Grenfell Road, Maidenhead, Berks, SL6 1ES
Activities: Collection of non-hazardous waste
Parent: Shukco 340 Ltd
Officers: Mark Hedley Thompson, Secretary/Head of Legal and Company Secretary; Florent Thierry Antoine Duval [1976] Director/Chief Finance Officer [French]; David Courtenay Palmer-Jones [1963] Director/Chief Executive Officer

Suez Recycling and Recovery Suffolk Ltd
Incorporated: 16 August 2010
Previous: SITA Suffolk Limited
Net Worth: £4,044,000 *Total Assets:* £176,440,992
Registered Office: Suez House, Grenfell Road, Maidenhead, Berks, SL6 1ES
Activities: Collection of non-hazardous waste
Parent: Suez Recycling and Recovery UK Ltd
Officers: Joan Knight, Secretary; Selcuk Vahyi Birler [1968] Director/Head of Financial Modelling; Florent Thierry Antoine Duval [1976] Director/Chief Finance Officer [French]; Graham Arthur McKenna-Mayes [1968] Director/Chief Operating Officer; David Courtenay Palmer-Jones [1963] Director/Chief Executive Officer; John James Scanlon [1969] Director/Chief Operating Officer

Suez Recycling and Recovery Surrey Ltd
Incorporated: 11 April 1996 *Employees:* 191
Previous: SITA Surrey Limited
Net Worth: £11,931,000 *Total Assets:* £154,164,000
Registered Office: Suez House, Grenfell Road, Maidenhead, Berks, SL6 1ES
Activities: Collection of non-hazardous waste
Parent: Suez Recycling and Recovery UK Ltd
Officers: Mark Hedley Thompson, Secretary/Head of Legal and Company Secretary; Florent Thierry Antoine Duval [1976] Director/Chief Finance Officer [French]; David Courtenay Palmer-Jones [1963] Director/Chief Executive Officer; John James Scanlon [1969] Director

Suez Recycling and Recovery Tees Valley Ltd
Incorporated: 9 December 1991 *Employees:* 152
Previous: SITA Tees Valley Limited
Net Worth: £51,990,000 *Total Assets:* £69,767,000
Registered Office: Suez House, Grenfell Road, Maidenhead, Berks, SL6 1ES
Activities: Treatment and disposal of non-hazardous waste
Parent: Suez Recycling and Recovery North East Ltd
Officers: Mark Hedley Thompson, Secretary/Head of Legal and Company Secretary; Florent Thierry Antoine Duval [1976] Director/Chief Finance Officer [French]; Marek Robert Gordon [1953] Director; Councillor Marjorie Anne James [1958] Director/Councillor; James Michael Kay [1952] Director; Gary Mayson [1969] Director/Project Manager; Tim Otley [1973] Director/Head of Energy Solutions; David Courtenay Palmer-Jones [1963] Director/Chief Executive Officer; John James Scanlon [1969] Director/Chief Operating Officer

Suez Recycling and Recovery UK Group Holdings Ltd
Incorporated: 18 December 2006 *Employees:* 2
Previous: SITA UK Group Holdings Limited
Net Worth: £333,224,000 *Total Assets:* £508,148,992
Registered Office: Suez House, Grenfell Road, Maidenhead, Berks, SL6 1ES
Activities: Activities of head offices
Parent: Suez UK Group Holdings Ltd
Officers: Mark Hedley Thompson, Secretary/Head of Legal and Company Secretary; Florent Thierry Antoine Duval [1976] Director/Chief Finance Officer [French]; David Courtenay Palmer-Jones [1963] Director/Chief Executive Officer

Suez Recycling and Recovery UK Ltd
Incorporated: 30 August 1988 *Employees:* 3,057
Previous: SITA UK Limited
Net Worth: £133,277,000 *Total Assets:* £346,992,000
Registered Office: Suez House, Grenfell Road, Maidenhead, Berks, SL6 1ES
Activities: Collection of non-hazardous waste
Parent: Suez Recycling and Recovery Holdings UK Ltd
Officers: Mark Hedley Thompson, Secretary/Head of Legal and Company Secretary; Florent Thierry Antoine Duval [1976] Director/Chief Finance Officer [French]; David Courtenay Palmer-Jones [1963] Director/Chief Executive Officer; John James Scanlon [1969] Director/Chief Operating Officer

Suez UK Environment Ltd
Incorporated: 13 June 1978 *Employees:* 9
Previous: SITA Environment Limited
Net Worth: £50,397,000 *Total Assets:* £67,233,000
Registered Office: Suez House, Grenfell Road, Maidenhead, Berks, SL6 1ES
Activities: Treatment and disposal of non-hazardous waste
Parent: Suez Recycling and Recovery Holdings UK Ltd
Officers: Mark Hedley Thompson, Secretary/Head of Legal and Company Secretary; Florent Thierry Antoine Duval [1976] Director/Chief Finance Officer [French]

Suez UK Group Holdings Ltd
Incorporated: 3 June 1988
Previous: Suez Environment UK Limited
Net Worth: £541,497,024 *Total Assets:* £592,094,016
Registered Office: Suez House, Grenfell Road, Maidenhead, Berks, SL6 1ES
Activities: Activities of head offices
Parent: Suez Groupe S.A.S.
Officers: Mark Hedley Thompson, Secretary/Head of Legal & Company Secretary; Florent Thierry Antoine Duval [1976] Director/Chief Finance Officer [French]; Eric Taupin [1961] Director [French]

Suffolk Finance Company Limited
Incorporated: 12 March 1927
Net Worth: £1,586,120,960 *Total Assets:* £1,889,229,952
Registered Office: 103-105 Bath Road, Slough, Berks, SL1 3UH
Activities: Activities of financial services holding companies
Parent: Reckitt & Colman Holdings Limited
Officers: Christine Anne-Marie Logan, Secretary; Richard Mark Greensmith [1973] Group Tax Director; Jonathan Timmis [1975] Finance Director

Sugarich Limited
Incorporated: 11 August 2009 *Employees:* 187
Net Worth: £11,128,040 *Total Assets:* £33,083,772
Registered Office: Unit 8 Minster Court, Tuscam Way, Camberley, Surrey, GU15 3YY
Activities: Activities of other holding companies n.e.c.
Shareholder: Andrew Charles Newton
Officers: Christopher John Houghton, Secretary; Paul Richard Bright [1976] Director/Accountant; Darrel Evans [1944] Director; Paul Anthony Featherstone [1965] Director; Nicholas Alexander Keogh [1979] Commercial Director; John Stephen Knight [1957] Director; Andrew Charles Newton [1969] Director

Sumika Polymer Compounds (Europe) Ltd
Incorporated: 22 March 1991 *Employees:* 130
Net Worth: £21,962,000 *Total Assets:* £55,065,000
Registered Office: 28 New Lane, Havant, Hants, PO9 2NQ
Activities: Activities of head offices
Parent: Sumitomo Chemical Company Ltd
Officers: Paul Victor Claydon, Secretary; Shinya Goda [1972] Director [Japanese]; Takeo Kitayama [1965] Managing Director [Japanese]; Kenji Manabe [1960] Director [Japanese]; Masutaka Onishi [1967] Director [Japanese]; Hironori Sakai [1954] Director [Japanese]; Ludovic Sebastien Dominique Seynave [1974] Director/President [French]; Yasushi Yoshizawa [1973] Director [Japanese]

Sumika Polymer Compounds (UK) Ltd
Incorporated: 22 March 1991 *Employees:* 69
Net Worth: £12,535,000 *Total Assets:* £33,891,000
Registered Office: 28 New Lane, Havant, Hants, PO9 2NQ
Activities: Manufacture of other plastic products
Parent: Sumitomo Chemical Company, Ltd
Officers: Paul Victor Claydon, Secretary; Paul Victor Claydon [1965] Director; Pascal Grippon [1963] Director [French]; Kenji Manabe [1960] Director [Japanese]; Hironori Sakai [1954] Director [Japanese]; Manfred Schmidt [1965] Managing Director [German]; Ludovic Sebastien Dominique Seynave [1974] Director/President [French]

Sumitomo Electric Europe Limited
Incorporated: 29 February 1996 *Employees:* 46
Net Worth: £7,014,000 *Total Assets:* £43,287,000
Registered Office: Unit 220 Centennial Avenue, Centennial Park, Elstree Hill South, Elstree, Borehamwood, Herts, WD6 3SL
Activities: Wholesale of electronic and telecommunications equipment and parts
Parent: Sumitomo Electric Industries Limited
Officers: Koji Kimura, Secretary; Koji Kimura [1969] Director [Japanese]; Eizo Mitani [1961] Director/General Manager - Electron Devices [Japanese]; Yasuyuki Shibata [1964] Director [Japanese]; Masakazu Watanabe [1961] Managing Director [Japanese]

Summerleaze Limited
Incorporated: 12 July 1983 *Employees:* 115
Net Worth: £53,218,044 *Total Assets:* £66,876,152
Registered Office: 7 Summerleaze Road, Maidenhead, Berks, SL6 8SP
Activities: Silviculture and other forestry activities
Shareholders: Peter Herbert Prior; Jeremy Paul Malkinson
Officers: Jeremy Paul Malkinson, Secretary; Michael Andrew Lowe [1963] Director; Jeremy Paul Malkinson [1959] Finance Director; Bruno George Prior [1966] Director; Peter Herbert Prior [1943] Managing Director

Ann Summers Ltd.
Incorporated: 10 December 1971 *Employees:* 1,242
Net Worth: £48,093,220 *Total Assets:* £82,357,000
Registered Office: Gold Group House, Godstone Road, Whyteleafe, Surrey, CR3 0GG
Activities: Retail sale of clothing in specialised stores
Major Shareholder: David Gold
Officers: John Edward Boyle [1963] Director/Chief Operating Officer; Jacqueline Gold [1960] Director/Chief Executive; Vanessa Gold [1967] Managing Director

Sun Alliance and London Insurance Limited
Incorporated: 6 October 1959
Previous: Sun Alliance and London Insurance PLC
Net Worth: £646,249,024 *Total Assets:* £1,322,238,976
Registered Office: St Mark's Court, Chart Way, Horsham, W Sussex, RH12 1XL
Activities: Activities of financial services holding companies
Parent: Royal & Sun Alliance Insurance PLC
Officers: Charlotte Dawn Alethea Heiss [1979] Director/Solicitor; Jennifer Ann Margetts [1958] Regulatory Compliance Director; Jane Carmel Poole [1980] Director/Group Financial Controller

Sun Alliance Insurance Overseas Limited
Incorporated: 12 March 1906
Net Worth: £400,500,000 *Total Assets:* £523,000,000
Registered Office: St Mark's Court, Chart Way, Horsham, W Sussex, RH12 1XL
Activities: Activities of financial services holding companies
Parent: Royal & Sun Alliance Insurance PLC
Officers: Ian Adam Craston [1966] Director; Martin David Postles [1959] Director/Group Manager, International Legacy Businesses; Rupert Taylor Rea [1978] Director/Chartered Accountant

Sun Hotel Limited
Incorporated: 4 March 2004 *Employees:* 38
Net Worth: £6,065,292 *Total Assets:* £21,087,584
Registered Office: Unit 7 & 8c Kingston House Estate, Portsmouth Road, Long Ditton, Surbiton, Surrey, KT6 5QG
Activities: Hotels and similar accommodation
Major Shareholder: Sampathkumar Mallaya
Officers: Komathy Sampathkumar [1959] Director/Company Secretary; Mallaya Sampathkumar [1958] Director

Sun Insurance Office Limited
Incorporated: 15 June 1926
Net Worth: £86,700,000 *Total Assets:* £89,500,000
Registered Office: St Mark's Court, Chart Way, Horsham, W Sussex, RH12 1XL
Activities: Non-life insurance
Parent: Sun Alliance Insurance Overseas Limited
Officers: Tracy Diane Noble [1973] Director/Chartered Accountant; Jane Carmel Poole [1980] Director/Group Financial Controller; Martin David Postles [1959] Director/Group Manager, International Legacy Businesses

Sun Life Assurance Company of Canada (U.K.) Limited
Incorporated: 28 July 1969
Net Worth: £444,287,008 *Total Assets:* £15,375,290,368
Registered Office: Matrix House, Basing View, Basingstoke, Hants, RG21 4DZ
Activities: Other activities auxiliary to insurance and pension funding
Parent: SLF of Canada UK Limited
Officers: Margaret Fleur Hobbs, Secretary; Eric Edward Anstee [1951] Director; Andrew Seaton Birrell [1969] Director [South African]; Katherine Angela Garner [1968] Director/Chief Finance Officer; James Harry Sutcliffe [1956] Director

Sun Life Financial of Canada (U.K.) Overseas Investments Limited
Incorporated: 16 March 2000
Net Worth: £152,324,000 *Total Assets:* £152,328,992
Registered Office: Matrix House, Basing View, Basingstoke, Hants, RG21 4DZ
Activities: Other activities auxiliary to insurance and pension funding
Parent: Sun Life Assurance Company of Canada
Officers: Fleur Margaret Hobbs, Secretary; Katherine Angela Garner [1968] Director/Chief Executive; Frances Clare MacLachlan [1970] Director/Chief Financial Officer; Julian Charles Reynolds [1968] Director/Chief Actuary

Sun Mark Limited
Incorporated: 16 January 1995 *Employees:* 77
Net Worth: £38,094,772 *Total Assets:* £73,485,520
Registered Office: Sun House, 428 Long Drive, Greenford, Middlesex, UB6 8UH
Activities: Agents involved in the sale of food, beverages and tobacco
Shareholders: Raminder Singh Ranger; Renu Ranger
Officers: Renu Ranger, Secretary; Harmeet Singh Ahuja [1972] Director; Raminder Singh Ranger [1948] Director

Sun Valley Foods Limited
Incorporated: 19 December 1960 *Employees:* 2,225
Net Worth: £6,344,000 *Total Assets:* £177,972,000
Registered Office: Velocity V1, Brooklands Drive, Weybridge, Surrey, KT13 0SL
Activities: Raising of poultry
Parent: Cargill PLC
Officers: Dena Michelle L O'Bue, Secretary; Peter Michael Allan [1968] Director/General Manager; Christopher John Shooter [1957] Director/BU FP&A Lead; Federico Urquidi Negron [1965] Director/UK & Ireland Controller [Spanish]

Sungard Availability Services (DR) Limited
Incorporated: 22 November 1994
Net Worth: £33,489,000 *Total Assets:* £54,004,000
Registered Office: Unit B, Heathrow Corporate Park, Green Lane, Hounslow, Middlesex, TW4 6ER
Activities: Activities of head offices
Parent: Guardian IT
Officers: Susan Diane Lynch [1961] Director/Chief Financial Officer [American]; Michael John Threlfall [1961] Director/Senior Vice President - Global Consulting

Sungard Availability Services (UK) Limited
Incorporated: 4 April 1989
Net Worth: £21,577,000 *Total Assets:* £137,739,008
Registered Office: Unit B, Heathrow Corporate Park, Green Lane, Hounslow, Middlesex, TW4 6ER
Activities: Other information technology service activities
Parent: Sungard Availability Services (Holdings) Europe, Inc.
Officers: Susan Diane Lynch [1961] Director/Chief Financial Officer [American]; Michael John Threlfall [1961] Director/Senior Vice President - Global Consulting

Sunlight Clinical Solutions Limited
Incorporated: 16 September 2004
Net Worth: £25,005,224 *Total Assets:* £28,688,580
Registered Office: Intec 3, Wade Road, Basingstoke, Hants, RG24 8NE
Activities: Dormant company
Parent: Berendsen UK Limited
Officers: Mark Leslie Franklin [1969] Director/Workwear Representative; Mark South [1963] Director

Sunny Bidco Limited
Incorporated: 3 August 2016 *Employees:* 103
Net Worth Deficit: £21,973,488 *Total Assets:* £107,374,400
Registered Office: Salamander Quay, West Park Lane, Harefield, Middlesex, UB9 6NZ
Activities: Activities of financial services holding companies
Parent: Sunny Midco Limited
Officers: Simon James Banks [1967] Director; Edward Heale [1973] Director; Philip Hollett [1961] Director; Thomas William Elliott Leigh [1971] Director

Sunny Midco Limited
Incorporated: 3 August 2016
Net Worth: £27 *Total Assets:* £67,133,896
Registered Office: Salamander Quay, West Park Lane, Harefield, Middlesex, UB9 6NZ
Activities: Activities of financial services holding companies
Parent: Sunny Topco Limited
Officers: Simon James Banks [1967] Director; Edward Heale [1973] Director; Philip Hollett [1961] Director; Thomas William Elliott Leigh [1971] Director

Sunny Topco Limited
Incorporated: 3 August 2016 *Employees:* 103
Net Worth Deficit: £22,143,228 *Total Assets:* £107,375,296
Registered Office: Salamander Quay, West Park Lane, Harefield, Uxbridge, Middlesex, UB9 6NZ
Activities: Activities of financial services holding companies
Officers: Simon James Banks [1967] Director; Paraag Dave [1975] Director/Investment Manager; Edward Heale [1973] Director; Philip Hollett [1961] Director; Kassir Huassin Kayani [1971] Director; Thomas William Elliott Leigh [1971] Director; Simon David Pitcher [1972] Director/Chartered Accountant; Mateusz Michal Szeszkowski [1972] Director/Investor [Canadian]

Sunrise UK Holdco Limited
Incorporated: 7 August 2014
Net Worth: £3,339,000 *Total Assets:* £31,534,000
Registered Office: Sunrise House, Post Office Lane, Beaconsfield, Bucks, HP9 1FN
Activities: Medical nursing home activities
Officers: Antony Nigel Brister [1972] Director; Dr Natalie-Jane MacDonald [1962] Director; Marcus Edwin Roder [1952] Director/Corporate Controller [American]; Wendy Catherine Sekel [1977] Director/VP Tax [American]

Sunsail Worldwide Sailing Limited
Incorporated: 13 August 1982 *Employees:* 98
Net Worth: £26,168,000 *Total Assets:* £72,913,000
Registered Office: Origin One, 108 High Street, Crawley, W Sussex, RH10 1BD
Activities: Renting and leasing of passenger water transport equipment
Parent: Mariner International (UK) Limited
Officers: Janet Northey, Secretary; Franck Bauguil [1965] Director [French/American]; Peter Vincent Young Cochran [1959] Director; Simon Barrie Michael Cross [1968] Director; Oliver Rahim Goodarzi [1986] Financial Director

Sunspot Tours Limited
Incorporated: 31 December 1979 *Employees:* 91
Net Worth: £10,050,856 *Total Assets:* £37,841,624
Registered Office: St John's House, Suffolk Way, Sevenoaks, Kent, TN13 1YL
Activities: Travel agency activities
Major Shareholder: Martin Timothy Bugeja
Officers: Irina Ropotan, Secretary; Martin Timothy Bugeja [1957] Director/Chairman; Thomas Paul Bugeja [1984] Director; Sarah Butcher [1975] Marketing Director; Emma Lyttleton [1985] Director; Peter Joseph Deane McNally [1933] Director/Retired; Irina Ropotan [1975] Director/Chief Financial Officer [British/Romanian]; Generaldine Stimson [1966] Managing Director [French]; Peter Sultana [1958] Director [Maltese]

Suntory UK Holdings Limited
Incorporated: 10 August 2016
Net Worth: £2,240,600,320 *Total Assets:* £2,312,583,424
Registered Office: 2 Longwalk Road, Stockley Park, Uxbridge, Middlesex, UB11 1BA
Activities: Activities of production holding companies
Officers: Akira Haraguchi [1959] Director/Executive Officer [Japanese]; Shinichiro Hizuka [1955] Senior Managing Director [Japanese]

Superdrug Stores PLC
Incorporated: 28 May 1964 *Employees:* 6,644
Net Worth: £254,990,000 *Total Assets:* £753,222,016
Registered Office: 51 Sydenham Road, Croydon, Surrey, CR0 2EU
Activities: Dispensing chemist in specialised stores
Parent: A.S. Watson (Health & Beauty UK) Limited
Officers: Edith Shih, Secretary; Richard Alexander Fleming [1971] Finance Director; Dr Alan John Heaton [1962] Director; Dominic Kai Ming Lai [1953] Director [Canadian]; Peter William MacNab [1957] Director

Superlift UK Limited
Incorporated: 18 December 2006
Net Worth: £53,276,072 *Total Assets:* £314,275,200
Registered Office: Kingsclere Road, Basingstoke, Hants, RG21 6XJ
Activities: Activities of head offices
Parent: Kion Group AG
Officers: Colin Blebta, Secretary; Colin Blebta [1964] Director; Johannes Karl Borsche [1965] Director/Head of Corporate Finance for Kion Group AG [German]

Surface Technology International Limited
Incorporated: 2 September 1988 *Employees:* 388
Net Worth: £2,139,000 *Total Assets:* £38,027,000
Registered Office: Osborn Way, Hook, Hants, RG27 9HX
Activities: Manufacture of telegraph and telephone apparatus and equipment
Parent: STI Enterprises Limited
Officers: Craig Stuart Petrie, Secretary; Anthony John Best [1960] Director; Simon Andre Best [1959] Director/Consultant; Nicholas John Davey [1972] Director; Christopher William Lyon [1963] Operations Director; Craig Stuart Petrie [1970] Director/Chief Financial Officer; Arthur Ramos Tan [1959] Director [American]

Surface Treatments Limited
Incorporated: 4 December 1963
Net Worth: £18,681,000 *Total Assets:* £78,754,000
Registered Office: Unit 2 Genesis Business Park, Albert Drive, Sheerwater, Woking, Surrey, GU21 5RW
Activities: Activities of head offices
Parent: MacDermid Europe Limited
Officers: John Edward Capps, Secretary; Paul Andrew Bray [1969] Sales Director; John Edward Capps [1964] Director [American]; Terence Joseph Clarke [1957] Director

Surfcontrol Limited
Incorporated: 4 June 1981
Net Worth: £41,408,796 *Total Assets:* £49,694,708
Registered Office: 420 Thames Valley Park Drive, Reading, Berks, RG6 1PT
Activities: Non-trading company
Parent: Websense SC Holdings Limited
Officers: Lisa Susan Burns [1971] Director [Irish]; Matthew Thomas Santangelo [1978] Director [American]; Nuala Takovac [1975] Technical Support Director [Irish]

Surrey Blue Limited
Incorporated: 30 April 2010 *Employees:* 25
Net Worth: £7,720,521 *Total Assets:* £38,712,928
Registered Office: Allen House, 1 Westmead Road, Sutton, Surrey, SM1 4LA
Activities: Other business support service activities n.e.c.
Major Shareholder: Justin Douglas William Barnes
Officers: Justin Douglas William Barnes [1965] Director

Surrey Lighting Services Limited
Incorporated: 2 September 2009
Net Worth Deficit: £15,738,000 *Total Assets:* £91,498,000
Registered Office: 8 White Oak Square, London Road, Swanley, Kent, BR8 7AG
Activities: Other business support service activities n.e.c.
Parent: SLS Holding Company Limited
Officers: Paul Alan Bannister [1959] Director/Accountant; David Richard Bradbury [1969] Director/Senior Investment Manager; Jennifer Kathryn Fegan [1973] Director/Lawyer; Katherine Mary Rae [1980] Director/Legal Advisor; Paul Sydney Shadbolt [1957] Asset Management Director; Keerthana Sivanathan [1988] Director/Senior Management Accountant

Surrey Satellite Technology Limited
Incorporated: 23 May 1985 *Employees:* 448
Net Worth Deficit: £19,720,000 *Total Assets:* £92,824,000
Registered Office: Tycho House, 20 Stephenson Road, Surrey Research Park, Guildford, Surrey, GU2 7YE
Activities: Manufacture of electronic components
Parent: Airbus Space and Defence Limted
Officers: Caroline Peace, Secretary; Nicolas Chamussy [1967] Director [French]; Luis Miguel Cardoso Do Amaral Gomes [1971] Director [Portuguese]; Bruno Le Stradic [1958] Director [French]; Abdel-Ilah Marrakchi [1959] Director/Finance [French]; Sarah Parker [1963] Director/Accountant; Colin Paynter [1958] Managing Director of Astrium Limited; Sir Martin Nicholas Sweeting [1951] Director; Lord David Lindsay Willetts [1956] Director; Lee James Wilson [1981] Finance Director

Sussex Learning Trust
Incorporated: 14 July 2011 *Employees:* 223
Previous: Warden Park Academy Trust
Net Worth: £31,842,000 *Total Assets:* £34,353,000
Registered Office: Warden Park, Broad Street, Cuckfield, Haywards Heath, W Sussex, RH17 5DP
Activities: General secondary education
Officers: Jennifer Anne Howard, Secretary; Jonathan Christopher Ash-Edwards [1987] Director/District Councillor; Peter Bradbury [1950] Director/Retired; Michael Jon Caidan [1967] Director - Global Banking Relationships; Esther Mary Gunter [1978] Director of Recruitment; Hamish Robert Mason Hill [1981] Director/Clinical Psychologist [Australian]; Claire Homer [1964] Director; Joelle Mary Packham [1969] Director/University Relations and Communications Manager; Jennifer Mary Pearman [1971] Director/Head of Client Services; Roger Frederick Tapping [1955] Director/Teacher and Reporting Inspector; Philip Andrew Todd [1977] Director/Chartered Building Services; Simon Watt [1967] Director of Organisational Development

Sutton and East Surrey Water PLC
Incorporated: 11 December 1989 *Employees:* 291
Net Worth: £86,025,000 *Total Assets:* £358,622,016
Registered Office: 66-74 London Road, Redhill, Surrey, RH1 1LJ
Activities: Water collection, treatment and supply
Parent: SESW Holding Company Limited
Officers: Anthony John David Ferrar [1957] Director; Paul Kerr [1973] Finance and Regulations Director; Seiji Kitajima [1969] Director [Japanese]; Murray Legg [1957] Senior Non-Executive Director; Ryuichi Nishida [1965] Managing Director [Japanese]; Jeremy David Pelczer [1957] Director; David John Shemmans [1966] Director/Chief Executive Officer; Jonathan Mark Woods [1968] Director/General Manager

Suzuki GB PLC
Incorporated: 23 July 1963 *Employees:* 162
Net Worth: £50,296,000 *Total Assets:* £220,314,000
Registered Office: Steinbeck Crescent, Snelshall West, Milton Keynes, Bucks, MK4 4AE
Activities: Sale of new cars and light motor vehicles
Parent: Suzuki Motor Corporation
Officers: Junita Fernandez, Secretary; Nobuo Suyama [1958] Director [Japanese]; Takanori Suzuki [1957] Director [Japanese]

R.Swain & Sons Limited
Incorporated: 26 December 1941
Net Worth: £11,494,612 *Total Assets:* £36,858,296
Registered Office: Vulcan House, Medway Freight Centre, Strood, Rochester, Kent, ME2 2BD
Activities: Freight transport by road
Major Shareholder: Robert John Swain
Officers: Matthew Deer [1975] Managing Director; Stuart James Rigby [1963] Director; Matthew George Swain [1976] Director; Robert John Swain [1947] Director; Matthew Ian Sweet [1974] Director; James Henry Wyatt [1980] Director

Swale Academies Trust
Incorporated: 12 August 2010 *Employees:* 1,298
Net Worth: £77,856,120 *Total Assets:* £92,538,136
Registered Office: Ashdown House, Johnson Road, Sittingbourne, Kent, ME10 1JS
Activities: Primary education
Officers: Christopher Duckling [1948] Director/Engineering Consultant; Paul Andrew Goodson [1963] Director/Private Equity Investor; Philip Robert Jarvis [1966] Director; Dorothy Irene Victoria Jessel [1958] Director/Self Employed; Simon James Penney [1973] Director/Lead Consultant; Grahame William George Ward [1953] Director/Certified Chartered Accountant; Jonathan Whitcombe [1967] Director/Trust Principal

Swan Group
Incorporated: 23 August 1988
Net Worth: £43,690,000 *Total Assets:* £43,723,000
Registered Office: Rocfort Road, Snodland, Kent, ME6 5AH
Activities: Activities of head offices
Parent: HDF (UK) Holding Limited
Officers: Nicolas Truillet, Secretary; Stephen Francis Jordan [1980] Director/Portfolio Manager; Oliver Jan Schubert [1972] Executive Director [Austrian]

Swan Mill (Holdings) Limited
Incorporated: 19 June 1930 *Employees:* 266
Net Worth: £36,570,000 *Total Assets:* £44,979,000
Registered Office: Swan Mill, Goldsel Road, Swanley, Kent, BR8 8EU
Activities: Activities of head offices
Shareholders: Stephen Richard Lewin; John William Williams; Richard Alexander Jennings
Officers: James Bryan [1962] Manufacturing Director; David Charles Byk [1967] Managing Director; Graham Rogers [1968] Finance Director; Tom Aiden Worton [1965] Welsh Operations Director

Swan Mill Paper Company Limited
Incorporated: 14 September 1983 *Employees:* 175
Net Worth: £31,525,000 *Total Assets:* £37,843,000
Registered Office: Swan Mill, Goldsel Road, Swanley, Kent, BR8 8EU
Activities: Manufacture of other articles of paper and paperboard n.e.c.
Parent: Swan Mill (Holdings) Limited
Officers: James Bryan [1962] Manufacturing Director; David Charles Byk [1967] Managing Director; Graham Rogers [1968] Finance Director; Tom Aiden Worton [1965] Director Wales

Swindon Pressings Limited
Incorporated: 14 March 2000 *Employees:* 688
Net Worth: £49,024,000 *Total Assets:* £90,676,000
Registered Office: Summit One, Summit Avenue, Farnborough, Hants, GU14 0FB
Activities: Manufacture of bodies (coachwork) for motor vehicles (except caravans)
Parent: BMW (UK) Holdings Limited
Officers: William Edwin Johnson, Secretary; Frank Juergen Bachmann [1961] Director [Swiss]; Jeremy Patrick Stoyle [1971] Finance Director

Swiss Post Solutions Ltd
Incorporated: 10 July 2002 *Employees:* 1,555
Net Worth: £11,434,000 *Total Assets:* £39,237,000
Registered Office: Parkshot House, 5 Kew Road, Richmond, Surrey, TW9 2PR
Activities: Other business support service activities n.e.c.
Parent: Die Schweizerische Post
Officers: Adam Cater, Secretary/Accountant; Gary Harrold [1972] Director; Jorg Vollmer [1967] Director [German]

SWM UK Wind One Limited
Incorporated: 22 December 2009 *Employees:* 1
Net Worth: £503,380,992 *Total Assets:* £555,629,632
Registered Office: Suite 8, Pantiles Chambers, 85 High Street, Tunbridge Wells, Kent, TN1 1XP
Activities: Production of electricity
Parent: Landeshauptstadt Munchen
Officers: Agnieszka Cieplinska [1972] Director/Project Manager [Polish/German]; Generald Martin Harrison [1954] Director; Christian Moldan [1974] Director/Project Manager [German]; Elaine Lynne Pavis [1968] Director/Chartered Accountant

Sword Soft Limited
Incorporated: 22 February 2007
Net Worth: £49,338,144 *Total Assets:* £49,414,896
Registered Office: 1000 Great West Road, Brentford, Middlesex, TW8 9DW
Activities: Other information technology service activities
Officers: Frederic Goosse [1969] Director [Belgian]; Jacques Francois Mottard [1952] Director [French]

SWS Group Holdings Limited
Incorporated: 19 November 2001
Net Worth: £46,300,000 *Total Assets:* £46,300,000
Registered Office: Southern House, Yeoman Road, Worthing, W Sussex, BN13 3NX
Activities: Non-trading company
Parent: Southern Water Services Group Limited
Officers: Joanne Statton, Secretary; Ian James McAulay [1965] Director; Joanne Statton [1969] Director/Solicitor

SWS Holdings Limited
Incorporated: 19 November 2001
Net Worth: £46,300,000 *Total Assets:* £46,300,000
Registered Office: Southern House, Yeoman Road, Worthing, W Sussex, BN13 3NX
Activities: Non-trading company
Parent: SWS Group Holdings Limited
Officers: Joanne Statton, Secretary; Ian James McAulay [1965] Director; Joanne Statton [1969] Director/Solicitor

Symantec (UK) Holding Limited
Incorporated: 15 September 2008
Net Worth: £1,390,112,000 *Total Assets:* £1,390,139,136
Registered Office: Reading International Business Park, Reading, Berks, RG2 6DH
Activities: Other information technology service activities
Parent: Symantec Corporation
Officers: Gerard Simon Chan Weng Yew [1961] Director/VP, EMEA [Malaysian]; Norman Osumi [1964] Director/Certified Public Accountant [American]

Symantec Security (UK) Limited
Incorporated: 17 March 2015 *Employees:* 311
Net Worth: £16,949,000 *Total Assets:* £60,658,000
Registered Office: Reading International Business Park, Reading, Berks, RG2 6DH
Activities: Other business support service activities n.e.c.
Parent: MessageLabs Limited
Officers: Donald Anthony Blach [1963] Director/Business Executive [American]; Eunice Jeeyoon Kim [1973] Director/Attorney [American]

Symmetry Logistics Holdings Limited
Incorporated: 28 June 2013 *Employees:* 604
Net Worth: £676,569 *Total Assets:* £51,057,244
Registered Office: Littlebrook DC1, Shield Road, Dartford, Kent, DA1 5UR
Activities: Activities of head offices
Officers: Robert William Gilbert Ross, Secretary; Andrew Neville Baxter [1975] Director; Robert William Gilbert Ross [1982] Finance Director

Symrise Holding Limited
Incorporated: 13 September 2002
Net Worth: £32,947,256 *Total Assets:* £53,461,332
Registered Office: Fieldhouse Lane, Marlow, Bucks, SL7 1TB
Activities: Manufacture of condiments and seasonings
Officers: Nicholas Russell [1965] Director; Markus Sattler [1967] Director [German]; Heinrich Friedrich Ludwig Schaper [1956] Director/President Flavour Division [German]

Symrise Limited
Incorporated: 13 January 1966 *Employees:* 107
Net Worth: £23,468,000 *Total Assets:* £31,371,000
Registered Office: Fieldhouse Lane, Marlow, Bucks, SL7 1TB
Activities: Manufacture of condiments and seasonings
Officers: Nicholas Russell [1965] Director; Markus Sattler [1967] Director/Lawyer [German]; Heinrich Friedrich Ludwig Schaper [1956] Director/President Flavour Division [German]

Synamedia Limited
Incorporated: 18 July 1995
Previous: NDS Limited
Net Worth: £165,757,840 *Total Assets:* £369,984,768
Registered Office: One London Road, Staines upon Thames, Middlesex, TW18 4EX
Activities: Other information technology service activities
Parent: Triton UK Bidco Limited
Officers: Ismat Levin [1967] Director; Charles Richard Kenneth Medlock [1960] Director; Yves Padrines [1976] Director [French]

Synaptic Trust
Incorporated: 1 April 2011 *Employees:* 315
Net Worth: £33,559,000 *Total Assets:* £38,895,000
Registered Office: West Thornton Primary Academy, Rosecourt Road, Croydon, Surrey, CR0 3BS
Activities: Primary education
Officers: Julie Anne Newman, Secretary; Keith Kirby [1961] Director/PR and Communications; Remi Ladega [1964] Director/Company Secretary; Anthony Stuart Roberts [1964] Director/Executive Headteacher; Keith Harold Robinson [1947] Director/Retired; Roger White [1949] Director/Retired; Muyideen Olufemi Oluwole Yusoof [1972] Director/Recruitment Manager

Synbra UK Limited
Incorporated: 1 May 1996
Net Worth: £27,531,770 *Total Assets:* £40,757,260
Registered Office: Infinity House, Anderson Way, Belvedere, Kent, DA17 6BG
Activities: Other business support service activities n.e.c.
Parent: Jablite Holdings Ltd
Officers: Matthew David Groom, Secretary; Wayne Robert Brown [1961] Manufacturing Director; Richard Peter Simon Lee [1968] Director

Synchro Clutch Company Limited
Incorporated: 24 July 1979 *Employees:* 77
Net Worth: £88,795,216 *Total Assets:* £96,960,448
Registered Office: Synchro House, Park Road, Sunbury on Thames, Middlesex, TW16 5BL
Activities: Activities of head offices
Officers: Paul Stuart Bizzill, Secretary; Paul Stuart Bizzill [1973] Director of Engineering; Morgan Leland Hendry [1950] Director [American]; James Michael George Neeves [1962] Managing Director

Syneos Health Clinical Development Services Limited
Incorporated: 18 January 1988 *Employees:* 65
Previous: INC Research Clinical Development Services Limited
Net Worth: £65,529,116 *Total Assets:* £66,266,880
Registered Office: Farnborough Business Park, 1 Pinehurst Road, Farnborough, Hants, GU14 7BF
Activities: Other research and experimental development on natural sciences and engineering
Officers: Kirstin Maura MacKenzie Connell [1967] HR Director; Alistair John MacDonald [1970] Director/Chief Executive Officer; Nyla Natalie Donna Maria Singh [1963] Finance Director

Syneos Health Holdings UK Limited
Incorporated: 3 November 2016 *Employees:* 4
Previous: Inventiv Health Holdings UK Limited
Net Worth: £839,593,216 *Total Assets:* £1,840,349,952
Registered Office: Farnborough Business Park, 1 Pinehurst Road, Farnborough, Hants, GU14 7BF
Activities: Activities of head offices
Parent: INC Research II Limited Partnership
Officers: Robert Alan Parks [1972] Director/Chief Accounting Officer [American]; Thomas Edward Zajkowski [1969] Director/SVP Finance [American]

Syneos Health International Holdings Limited
Incorporated: 19 October 1992 *Employees:* 2
Previous: INC Research International Holdings Limited
Net Worth: £33,096,268 *Total Assets:* £36,101,752
Registered Office: Farnborough Business Park, 1 Pinehurst Road, Farnborough, Hants, GU14 7BF
Activities: Activities of head offices
Officers: Robert Alan Parks [1972] Director/Chief Accounting Officer [American]; Thomas Edward Zajkowski [1969] Director [American]

Syneos Health International Limited
Incorporated: 7 December 2015 *Employees:* 2
Previous: INC Research International Limited
Net Worth: £407,201,248 *Total Assets:* £419,843,520
Registered Office: Farnborough Business Park, 1 Pinehurst Road, Farnborough, Hants, GU14 7BF
Activities: Other business support service activities n.e.c.
Officers: Alistair John MacDonald [1970] Director/CEO/President; Thomas Edward Zajkowski [1969] Director [American]

Syneos Health IVH UK Limited
Incorporated: 24 November 1983 *Employees:* 479
Previous: Inventiv Health Clinical UK Ltd
Net Worth: £219,123,712 *Total Assets:* £287,761,664
Registered Office: Farnborough Business Park, 1 Pinehurst Road, Farnborough, Hants, GU14 7BF
Activities: Other human health activities
Parent: Syneos Health Holdings UK Limited
Officers: Nyla Natalie Donna Maria Singh [1963] Director; Ruth Wessendorff [1967] Associate Director, Project Finance

Syneos Health UK Limited
Incorporated: 30 April 2002 *Employees:* 766
Previous: INC Research UK Limited
Net Worth: £98,104,224 *Total Assets:* £278,504,672
Registered Office: Farnborough Business Park, 1 Pinehurst Road, Farnborough, Hants, GU14 7BF
Activities: Other business support service activities n.e.c.
Officers: Kirstin Maura MacKenzie Connell [1967] Executive Director, Human Resources; Alistair John MacDonald [1970] Director/Chief Executive Officer; Nyla Natalie Donna Maria Singh [1963] Senior Director, Accounting Operations

Syngenta Holdings Limited
Incorporated: 13 April 2000
Net Worth: £1,086,376,576 *Total Assets:* £1,777,755,136
Registered Office: Syngenta, Jealott's Hill International Research Centre, Bracknell, Berks, RG42 6EY
Activities: Activities of head offices
Parent: Syngenta AG
Officers: Matthew David Bayliss, Secretary; Dr Alistair David Conn [1965] Director/Site Manager; Kirsten Elizabeth Elce [1970] Director/Accountant [Canadian]; Andrew David Johnson [1964] Director/Finance Manager

Syngenta Limited
Incorporated: 29 April 1992 *Employees:* 1,612
Net Worth: £311,000,000 *Total Assets:* £640,000,000
Registered Office: Syngenta, Jealott's Hill International Research Centre, Bracknell, Berks, RG42 6EY
Activities: Activities of head offices
Parent: Syngenta Holdings Limited
Officers: Matthew David Bayliss, Secretary; Dr Pascal Bugnon [1966] Director/Head Global AI Manufacturer [Swiss]; Dr Alistair David Conn [1965] Director/Site Manager; James Dominic Halliwell [1963] Director/Accountant; Andrew David Johnson [1964] Director/Finance Manager; Dr Fraser John Lewis [1961] Director/Environmental Services Manager

Synventive Acquisition UK Limited
Incorporated: 3 March 2005
Previous: 05381782 Limited
Net Worth Deficit: £20,389,376 *Total Assets:* £95,638,120
Registered Office: The Pinnacle, 160 Midsummer Boulevard, Milton Keynes, Bucks, MK9 1FF
Activities: Non-trading company
Parent: Barnes Group Inc
Officers: Michael Vincent Kennedy [1961] Director [American]; Douglas William McNeilly [1964] Director/Accountant; Klaus Peter Peya [1984] Director/Controller [German]

Synventive Acquisition Unlimited
Incorporated: 26 July 2005
Net Worth: £78,956,808 *Total Assets:* £79,989,104
Registered Office: The Pinnacle, 160 Midsummer Boulevard, Milton Keynes, Bucks, MK9 1FF
Activities: Manufacture of other plastic products
Parent: Barnes Group Inc
Officers: Michael Vincent Kennedy [1961] Director/Vice President of Tax [American]; Douglas William McNeilly [1964] Director/Accountant; Klaus Peter Peya [1984] Director/Controller [German]

Synventive Holding Limited
Incorporated: 16 July 2003
Net Worth Deficit: £1,464,957 *Total Assets:* £33,511,908
Registered Office: The Pinnacle, 160 Midsummer Boulevard, Milton Keynes, Bucks, MK9 1FF
Activities: Other manufacturing n.e.c.
Officers: Michael Vincent Kennedy [1961] Director/Vice President of Tax [American]; Douglas William McNeilly [1964] Director/Accountant; Klaus-Peter Peya [1984] Director/Controller [German]; Jason Todd Ulery [1975] Finance Director [American]

Sysmex UK Limited
Incorporated: 5 April 1991 *Employees:* 147
Net Worth: £23,082,572 *Total Assets:* £37,554,648
Registered Office: Sysmex House, Garamonde Drive, Wymbush, Milton Keynes, Bucks, MK8 8DF
Activities: Hospital activities
Officers: Robert Victor Kaukis, Secretary; Seido Biwa [1972] Managing Director [Japanese]; Keith Lawrence Howes [1959] Managing Director; Nigel Pattinson [1963] Director of Sales & Marketing; Matthias Volkel [1967] Director/Senior Executive Officer EMEA [German]

Systagenix Wound Management, Limited
Incorporated: 27 August 2008 *Employees:* 42
Net Worth: £34,725,000 *Total Assets:* £128,827,000
Registered Office: 2 City Place, Beehive Ring Road, Gatwick Airport, W Sussex, RH6 0PA
Activities: Other business support service activities n.e.c.
Parent: Systagenix Wound Management B.V.
Officers: John Elwood [1969] Director/Vice President, Manufacturing [Irish]; Simon James Peter Gilderson [1970] Director/VP European Indirect Channel & Commercial Operations; Jonathan Robert Lasparini [1980] Director/Vice President, Finance; Christiaan Jan Otto Pool [1972] Director [Dutch]; Peter Robert Rhodes [1976] Director/Solicitor; Ramesh Subrahmanian [1961] Director [American]

System C Healthcare Limited
Incorporated: 21 September 1983 *Employees:* 304
Net Worth: £5,620,921 *Total Assets:* £48,630,304
Registered Office: The Maidstone Studios, Vinters Business Park, New Cut Road, Maidstone, Kent, ME14 5NZ
Activities: Other information technology service activities
Officers: Jane Marie Conner, Secretary; Markus Simon Bolton [1957] Director; Dr Ian Sean Denley [1964] Director; Quinlan Don-Lee Fang [1982] Director/Private Equity [American]; Jr. Haines [1967] Director/Private Equity Investor [American]

T G Products Limited
Incorporated: 17 December 1992 *Employees:* 19
Net Worth: £20,500,000 *Total Assets:* £74,453,000
Registered Office: Littleton Road, Ashford, Middlesex, TW15 1TZ
Activities: Other manufacturing n.e.c.
Parent: Chubb Group Security Limited
Officers: Robert John Sloss, Secretary/Solicitor; Anthony Brennan [1966] Finance Director [Irish]; Craig Alexander Forbes [1963] Finance Director

T S S Group PLC
Incorporated: 24 December 1992 *Employees:* 105
Net Worth: £11,327,136 *Total Assets:* £24,804,046
Registered Office: Thames Motor Group, North Farm Industrial Estate, Longfield Road, Tunbridge Wells, Kent, TN2 3EY
Activities: Activities of head offices
Major Shareholder: Vipen Khanna
Officers: Kandasamy Jeyavarathan, Secretary; Peter William Featherstone [1948] Director; Anna Elizabeth Khanna [1949] Director [Swiss]; Kevin Paul Khanna [1979] Director; Natasha Nancy Khanna [1977] Director; Vipen Khanna [1946] Director/Chairman and MD

T-Mobile Holdings Limited
Incorporated: 6 September 1999
Net Worth: £3,339,553,536 *Total Assets:* £3,339,591,936
Registered Office: Futura House, Bradbourne Drive, Tilbrook, Milton Keynes, Bucks, MK7 8AZ
Activities: Activities of head offices
Parent: CTA Holding GmbH
Officers: Jeevan D'Silva, Secretary; Jeremy Stuart Boorman [1972] Director; Jeevan D'Silva [1962] Director; Claire Sandra Hilton [1958] Director; Dr Uli Kuehbacher [1961] Director [German]

T.J.D. Trade Limited
Incorporated: 10 January 2003 *Employees:* 5
Net Worth Deficit: £235,333 *Total Assets:* £21,399,280
Registered Office: TJD Trade Ltd, Manton Lane, Manton Industrial Estate, Bedford, MK41 7TL
Activities: Development of building projects
Major Shareholder: Johanna Kesmin Marks
Officers: Johanna Kesmin Marks [1962] Director

T.R. Fastenings Limited
Incorporated: 23 March 1973 *Employees:* 391
Net Worth: £14,510,000 *Total Assets:* £35,298,000
Registered Office: Trifast House, Bellbrook Park, Uckfield, E Sussex, TN22 1QW
Activities: Manufacture of fasteners and screw machine products
Parent: Trifast PLC
Officers: Lyndsey Case, Secretary; Mark Belton [1969] Director; Geoffrey Paul Budd [1957] Director; Colin John Coddington [1968] IT Director; David Fisk [1971] Managing Director; Clare Foster [1974] Director; Anna-Maria Stella Johnson [1963] Finance Director; Stephen Adam Meiklem [1967] Purchasing and Operations Director; Glenda Christina Roberts [1950] Director; Helen Jane Toole [1965] HR Director

T.S.L. Finance Limited
Incorporated: 30 August 2000 *Employees:* 14
Net Worth: £1,031,533 *Total Assets:* £35,641,412
Registered Office: Unit 8 West London Industrial Park, Iver Lane, Uxbridge, Middlesex, UB8 2JG
Activities: Sale of used cars and light motor vehicles
Major Shareholder: Fil Levi Gray
Officers: Fil Levi Gray [1958] Director

TAG Aviation (UK) Limited
Incorporated: 30 September 1998 *Employees:* 206
Net Worth: £1,065,501 *Total Assets:* £37,214,180
Registered Office: Business Aviation Centre, Farnborough Airport, Farnborough, Hants, GU14 6XA
Activities: Non-scheduled passenger air transport
Shareholders: Mansour Akram Ojjeh; Abdulaziz Ojjeh; Jacques Charles Rosset
Officers: Ronald Hedges, Secretary; Daniel Olivier Christe [1966] Director [Swiss]; Sydney Gillibrand [1934] Director/Business Executive; Carlos Enrique Gomez [1960] Director [Spanish]; Ronald Hedges [1930] Director/Businessman; Roger McMullin [1942] Director/Business Executive [American]

TAG Farnborough (Holdings) Limited
Incorporated: 19 January 1998 *Employees:* 376
Net Worth: £113,042,960 *Total Assets:* £166,773,168
Registered Office: Business Aviation Centre, Farnborough Airport, Farnborough, Hants, GU14 6XA
Activities: Activities of head offices
Shareholders: Mansour Akram Ojjeh; Jacques Charles Rosset; Abdulaziz Ojjeh
Officers: Ronald Hedges, Secretary; Mohamed Isa Mohamed Isa Al Khalifa [1969] Director/Advisor [Bahraini]; Russ Van Vleck Bradley [1941] Director/Lawyer [Swiss/American]; Sydney Gillibrand [1934] Director/Business Executive; Roger McMullin [1942] Director/Business Executive [American]; Abdulaziz Ojjeh [1954] Director/Businessman [French]; Mansour Akram Ojjeh [1952] Director/Businessman [French]; Jacques Charles Rosset [1942] Managing Director [Swiss]; Andru Bramantya Subowo [1970] Director/Businessman [Indonesian]; Steven Hao Ran Young [1963] Director/Businessman [American]

TAG Farnborough Airport Limited
Incorporated: 23 October 1997 *Employees:* 143
Net Worth: £92,151,280 *Total Assets:* £142,810,128
Registered Office: Business Aviation Centre, Farnborough Airport, Farnborough, Hants, GU14 6XA
Activities: Service activities incidental to air transportation
Parent: TAG Farnborough (Holdings) Limited
Officers: Ronald Hedges, Secretary; Mohamed Isa Mohamed Isa Al Khalifa [1969] Director/Advisor [Bahraini]; Russ Van Vleck Bradley [1941] Director/Lawyer [Swiss/American]; Sydney Gillibrand [1934] Director/Business Executive; Roger McMullin [1942] Director/Business Executive [American]; Abdulaziz Ojjeh [1954] Director/Businessman [French]; Mansour Akram Ojjeh [1952] Director/Businessman [French]; Jacques Charles Rosset [1942] Managing Director [Swiss]; Andru Bramantya Subowo [1970] Director/Businessman [Indonesian]; Steven Hao Ran Young [1963] Director/Businessman [American]

Tailwind Mistral Ltd
Incorporated: 11 June 2002 *Employees:* 5
Previous: EOG Resources United Kingdom Limited
Net Worth: £92,405,792 *Total Assets:* £190,924,192
Registered Office: Andrews House, College Road, Guildford, Surrey, GU1 4QB
Activities: Extraction of crude petroleum
Parent: EOGI International Company
Officers: Dr Stephen Cross Edwards [1968] Managing Director; Dr David Peter Freeman [1968] Director/Chief Operating Officer; Jacques Joseph Tohme [1983] Director/Chief Financial Officer [American]; Tomasz Zbigniew Harding Ujejski [1956] Director/Chairman [Canadian]

Takeda UK Limited
Incorporated: 25 April 1997 *Employees:* 192
Net Worth: £33,735,072 *Total Assets:* £91,023,712
Registered Office: Building 3, Glory Park Avenue, Wooburn Green, High Wycombe, Bucks, HP10 0DF
Activities: Wholesale of pharmaceutical goods
Parent: Takeda Pharmaceuticals International AG
Officers: Jon Neal [1971] Director/General Manager; Andrius Varanavicius [1979] Director/Chief Financial Officer EuCAN [Lithuanian]; William Charles Walker [1953] Director/Business Operations Manager

Talacrest 2000 A.D. Limited
Incorporated: 19 October 1999 *Employees:* 4
Net Worth: £18,873,764 *Total Assets:* £21,567,384
Registered Office: Fides House, 10 Chertsey Road, Woking, Surrey, GU21 5AB
Activities: Sale of used cars and light motor vehicles
Major Shareholder: John Alexander Collins
Officers: John Alexander Collins [1952] Director

Talkmobile Limited
Incorporated: 6 February 2001
Previous: Talk Mobile Limited
Net Worth: £102,488,000 *Total Assets:* £114,482,000
Registered Office: Vodafone House, The Connection, Newbury, Berks, RG14 2FN
Activities: Other telecommunications activities
Parent: Vodafone Limited
Officers: David Nigel Evans [1966] Director; Diane Josephine McIntyre [1973] Director; Glafkos Persianis [1967] Director [Cypriot]; Philip James Roberson [1969] Director

Tallentire Energy Limited
Incorporated: 17 January 2012
Net Worth Deficit: £4,980,000 *Total Assets:* £20,532,000
Registered Office: Beaufort Court, Egg Farm Lane, Kings Langley, Herts, WD4 8LR
Activities: Production of electricity
Parent: Trafalgar Wind Holdings Limited
Officers: Dominic James Hearth, Secretary; Steven William Hughes [1972] Generation & Asset Management Director; Fraser Stephen Merry [1968] Director/Chartered Surveyor; Mitesh Raj Patel [1982] Director/Group Financial Controller

Tamar Energy Limited
Incorporated: 13 July 2011 *Employees:* 75
Net Worth: £22,962,000 *Total Assets:* £46,351,000
Registered Office: c/o Biogen, Milton Parc, Milton Ernest, Bedford, MK44 1YU
Activities: Construction of utility projects for electricity and telecommunications
Parent: Ancala Bioenergy Limited
Officers: Adam Feneley [1980] Managing Director; Cathryn Lister [1982] Compliance Director; Simon Musther [1958] Commercial Director; Graeme Kenneth Charles Vincent [1965] Operations Director

Tamar Energy Operating Company (One) Limited
Incorporated: 17 June 2014
Net Worth Deficit: £23,563,000 *Total Assets:* £23,734,000
Registered Office: c/o Biogen, Milton Parc, Milton Ernest, Bedford, MK44 1YU
Activities: Activities of production holding companies
Parent: Tamar Energy (Hermes Holdings) Limited
Officers: Adam Feneley [1980] Managing Director; Stuart Peter Greenfield [1962] Director/Financial Controller; Cathryn Lister [1982] Compliance Director; Simon Musther [1958] Commercial Director; Graeme Kenneth Charles Vincent [1965] Operations Director

Tandridge Learning Trust
Incorporated: 10 October 2012 *Employees:* 354
Previous: Warlingham School
Net Worth: £32,195,000 *Total Assets:* £37,693,000
Registered Office: Tandridge Learning Trust, Tithepit, Shaw Lane, Warlingham, Surrey, CR6 9YB
Activities: Primary education
Officers: Paula Chowdhury, Secretary; Richard Calverley Baker [1963] Finance Director; Steven Burn [1961] Director/Finance and Marketing; Alex Ghattas [1971] Director/Finance Manager; David Humphrey Prothero [1946] Director/Education; Karen Jayne Quinton [1959] Director

Tangmere Airfield Nurseries Ltd
Incorporated: 31 May 1988 *Employees:* 147
Net Worth: £28,036,416 *Total Assets:* £33,911,460
Registered Office: The Old Airfield, City Fields Way, Tangmere, Chichester, W Sussex, PO20 2FT
Activities: Growing of vegetables and melons, roots and tubers
Officers: Robert Searle, Secretary; Dick Johannes Houweling [1974] Director/Grower [Dutch]; Dirk Houweling [1949] Director/Grower [Dutch]

Tanita International Ltd.
Incorporated: 9 September 1997 *Employees:* 27
Net Worth: £41,427,496 *Total Assets:* £43,626,796
Registered Office: 5th Floor, Hyde Park Hayes 3, 11 Millington Road, Hayes, Middlesex, UB3 4AZ
Activities: Wholesale of other machinery and equipment
Officers: Shinsuke Nakagawa, Secretary; Isamu Kobayashi [1961] Director [Japanese]; Senri Tanida [1972] Director/President of Tanita Corporation [Japanese]; Shunji Tanida [1971] Director [Japanese]

Tanjong Public Limited Company
Incorporated: 2 January 1926
Net Worth: £187,762,768 *Total Assets:* £444,819,264
Registered Office: Elder House, St Georges Business Park, 207 Brooklands Road, Weybridge, Surrey, KT13 0TS
Activities: Activities of head offices
Officers: Wai Ping Goh, Secretary; Ashwin Kumar Das [1976] Director/General Manager of Usaha Tegas Sdn Bhd [Malaysian]; Mazita Binti Mokty [1972] Director/General Counsel of Usaha Tegas Sdn Bhd [Malaysian]; Rohan Rajan Rajasooria [1972] Director/Group Treasurer of Usaha Tegas Sdn Bhd [Malaysian]

Target Media Limited
Incorporated: 15 August 2005 *Employees:* 40
Net Worth: £15,123,000 *Total Assets:* £29,422,000
Registered Office: Havas House, Hermitage Court, Hermitage Lane, Maidstone, Kent, ME16 9NT
Activities: Advertising agencies
Parent: Cooler King Limited
Officers: Allan John Ross, Secretary; Alan Ralston Adamson [1966] Director/Chief Financial Officer; Richard Dennis-Jones [1977] Trading Director; Louise Mary Gaynor [1970] Director [Australian]; Darren Todhunter [1968] Director/Accountant; Susan Joan Wickerson [1948] Director; Robert Frank Wilkerson [1961] Director

TASIS The American School in England
Incorporated: 15 December 1981 *Employees:* 239
Net Worth: £3,160,710 *Total Assets:* £20,860,680
Registered Office: Coldharbour Lane, Thorpe, Surrey, TW20 8TE
Activities: Pre-primary education
Officers: David Riley, Secretary; Fernando Gonzalez [1948] Administrative Director [American]; Chawki Karam [1985] Director/Banker; David Harold King [1951] Director/Chartered Accountant; Fiona Elisabeth Stafford Loveridge [1962] Director; Laurence Eric McKell [1964] Director/Teacher; Teresa Ferguson McLaughlin [1964] Director/Homemaker [American]; John Stuurman Wyper [1950] Managing Director Hines Europe [American]

TASIS UK Limited
Incorporated: 30 October 1981 *Employees:* 239
Net Worth: £3,160,710 *Total Assets:* £20,860,670
Registered Office: Coldharbour Lane, Thorpe, Surrey, TW20 8TE
Activities: Pre-primary education
Officers: David Riley, Secretary; Lynn Fleming Aeschlimann [1945] Director/Company Administrator [American]; William Thomas Fleming [1943] Director [American]; Fernando Gonzalez [1948] Director [American]

Tasmar Limited
Incorporated: 28 September 2004 *Employees:* 188
Net Worth: £24,522,588 *Total Assets:* £33,117,756
Registered Office: 55 Station Road, Beaconsfield, Bucks, HP9 1QL
Activities: Activities of head offices
Major Shareholder: Sylvester Christopher Patrick McDonagh
Officers: Paul Martin McDonagh, Secretary; Paul Martin McDonagh [1971] Managing Director; Sylvester Christopher Patrick McDonagh [1947] Director/Consultant [Irish]

Tata Global Beverages Capital Limited
Incorporated: 12 September 2006
Net Worth: £89,858,000 *Total Assets:* £162,334,000
Registered Office: 325 Oldfield Lane North, Greenford, Middlesex, UB6 0AZ
Activities: Activities of other holding companies n.e.c.
Parent: Tata Global Beverages Limited
Officers: Miles Thomas Bailey, Secretary; Miles Thomas Bailey [1974] Director/General Counsel & Company Secretary; John Jacob [1962] Director/Vice President-Group Finance [Indian]; Krishna Kumar Lakshmanan [1958] Director [Indian]; Ajoy Kumar Misra [1957] Director [Indian]; Shirish Amratlal Shah [1959] Director/Chartered Accountant; Manesh Thakrar [1961] Director

Tata Global Beverages GB Limited
Incorporated: 9 February 1995 *Employees:* 359
Net Worth: £202,342,000 *Total Assets:* £241,331,008
Registered Office: 325 Oldfield Lane North, Greenford, Middlesex, UB6 0AZ
Activities: Non-specialised wholesale of food, beverages and tobacco
Parent: Tata Global Beverages Holdings Limited
Officers: Miles Thomas Bailey, Secretary; Adil Ahmad [1962] Director/Service, Global CMO [Indian]; John Mark Edward Burdett [1967] Director/Chartered Engineer; Krishna Kumar Lakshmanan [1958] Director [Indian]; Manesh Thakrar [1961] Director

Tata Global Beverages Group Limited
Incorporated: 3 September 1999 *Employees:* 624
Net Worth: £506,776,992 *Total Assets:* £683,667,008
Registered Office: 325 Oldfield Lane North, Greenford, Middlesex, UB6 0AZ
Activities: Other credit granting n.e.c.
Shareholder: Tata Global Beverages Capital Limited
Officers: Miles Thomas Bailey, Secretary; Adil Ahmad [1962] Director/Service, Global CMO [Indian]; John Mark Edward Burdett [1967] Director/Chartered Engineer; Krishna Kumar Lakshmanan [1958] Director [Indian]; Ajoy Kumar Misra [1957] Director [Indian]; Shirish Amratlal Shah [1959] Director/Chartered Accountant; Manesh Thakrar [1961] Director/Chief Financial Officer - EMEA

Tata Global Beverages Holdings Limited
Incorporated: 18 October 1996
Net Worth: £174,531,008 *Total Assets:* £189,515,008
Registered Office: 325 Oldfield Lane North, Greenford, Middlesex, UB6 0AZ
Activities: Activities of other holding companies n.e.c.
Parent: Tata Global Beverages Group Limited
Officers: Miles Thomas Bailey, Secretary; Miles Thomas Bailey [1974] Director/General Counsel & Company Secretary; John Jacob [1962] Director/Vice President-Group Finance [Indian]; Krishna Kumar Lakshmanan [1958] Finance Director [Indian]; Manesh Thakrar [1961] Director

Tata Global Beverages Investments Limited
Incorporated: 12 September 2006 *Employees:* 5
Net Worth: £365,472,992 *Total Assets:* £371,004,000
Registered Office: 325 Oldfield Lane North, Greenford, Middlesex, UB6 0AZ
Activities: Activities of other holding companies n.e.c.
Parent: Tata Global Beverages Group Limited
Officers: Miles Thomas Bailey, Secretary; Krishna Kumar Lakshmanan [1958] Director [Indian]; Ajoy Kumar Misra [1957] Director [Indian]; Shirish Amratlal Shah [1959] Director/Chartered Accountant; Manesh Thakrar [1961] Director/Chief Financial Officer - EMEA

Tata Global Beverages Overseas Holdings Limited
Incorporated: 3 February 1995
Net Worth Deficit: £44,601,000 *Total Assets:* £51,138,000
Registered Office: 325 Oldfield Lane North, Greenford, Middlesex, UB6 0AZ
Activities: Activities of other holding companies n.e.c.
Parent: Tata Global Beverages Holdings Limited
Officers: Miles Thomas Bailey, Secretary; John Jacob [1962] Director/Vice President-Group Finance [Indian]; Krishna Kumar Lakshmanan [1958] Director [Indian]; Ajoy Kumar Misra [1957] Director [Indian]; Manesh Thakrar [1961] Director

Tata Global Beverages Services Limited
Incorporated: 9 January 1995 *Employees:* 53
Net Worth: £345,663,008 *Total Assets:* £529,515,008
Registered Office: 325 Oldfield Lane North, Greenford, Middlesex, UB6 0AZ
Activities: Activities of head offices
Parent: Tata Global Beverages Holdings Limited
Officers: Miles Thomas Bailey, Secretary; Krishna Kumar Lakshmanan [1958] Director [Indian]; Ajoy Kumar Misra [1957] Director [Indian]; Manesh Thakrar [1961] Director

Tate Bros. Limited
Incorporated: 8 January 1953 *Employees:* 202
Net Worth: £26,534,196 *Total Assets:* £32,126,454
Registered Office: Tates Adminstration Offices, Paradise Park, Avis Road, Newhaven, E Sussex, BN9 0DH
Activities: Other letting and operating of own or leased real estate
Officers: David Stephen Patterson, Secretary; Trevor Ian Meadows [1960] Director/Garage Manager; Jonathan David Tate [1960] Director/Horticulturist; Molly Jean Tate [1929] Director/Secretary

Tates of Sussex Limited
Incorporated: 20 October 2017 *Employees:* 333
Net Worth: £41,183,928 *Total Assets:* £50,424,912
Registered Office: Paradise Park, Avis Road, Newhaven, E Sussex, BN9 0DH
Activities: Activities of other holding companies n.e.c.
Major Shareholder: Jonathan David Tate
Officers: David Stephen Patterson, Secretary; Darren Paul Clift [1985] Director; Trevor Ian Meadows [1960] Director; Jonathan David Tate [1960] Director

Tato Holdings Limited
Incorporated: 2 October 1996 *Employees:* 1,409
Net Worth: £439,823,392 *Total Assets:* £495,609,632
Registered Office: Bramling House, Bramling, Canterbury, Kent, CT3 1NB
Activities: Activities of other holding companies n.e.c.
Shareholders: Jeremy William Cowley; Simon John Cowley; 3i PLC
Officers: Simon Pearson, Secretary; Kelvin James Dally [1956] Director [American]; Giuseppe de Lucia [1964] Director [Italian]; Peter Hahn [1965] Business Director [German]; David Alain Hewitt [1960] Director/Accountant; Thomas Muller [1963] Business Director [German]; Joan Antoni Pujante Mitjavila [1967] Director [Spanish]; Hans Jurgen Schmidt [1952] Director/Chemical Engineer [German]

The Taunton Linac Company Limited
Incorporated: 16 March 2005
Net Worth Deficit: £6,899,000 *Total Assets:* £27,053,000
Registered Office: 8 White Oak Square, London Road, Swanley, Kent, BR8 7AG
Activities: Combined facilities support activities
Parent: The Taunton Linac (Holdings) Company Limited
Officers: Benjamin Christopher Jacob Dean [1979] Director/Investment Manager; Richard Keith Sheehan [1975] Investment Director

Tavistock Investments PLC
Incorporated: 8 March 2004 *Employees:* 133
Net Worth: £18,690,000 *Total Assets:* £26,071,000
Registered Office: 1 Bracknell Beeches, Old Bracknell Lane, Bracknell, Berks, RG12 7BW
Activities: Activities of head offices
Officers: Oliver Charles Hewardine Cooke, Secretary; Oliver Charles Hewardine Cooke [1954] Director; Brian Kenneth Raven [1956] Director/Chief Executive; Roderic Henry Patrick Rennison [1955] Director

Tax Systems Holdings Limited
Incorporated: 6 June 2017
Net Worth: £73,252,864 *Total Assets:* £76,449,880
Registered Office: Ground Floor, Magna House, 18-32 London Road, Staines upon Thames, Middlesex, TW18 4BP
Activities: Activities of other holding companies n.e.c.
Parent: Tax Systems PLC
Officers: Kevin Paul Goggin [1962] Finance Director; Gavin Anthony Peter Lyons [1977] Director

Tax Systems PLC
Incorporated: 17 December 2003 *Employees:* 82
Previous: Eco City Vehicles PLC
Net Worth: £47,279,000 *Total Assets:* £88,376,000
Registered Office: Ground Floor, Magna House, 18-32 London Road, Staines upon Thames, Middlesex, TW18 4BP
Activities: Activities of distribution holding companies
Shareholder: MXC Capital Limited
Officers: Kevin Goggin, Secretary; Linda Janice Beal [1961] Director; Clive Nathan Carver [1961] Director; Paul David Gibson [1964] Director/Business Development; Kevin Paul Goggin [1962] Finance Director; Gavin Anthony Peter Lyons [1977] Director

Taylor Made Golf Limited
Incorporated: 31 May 1979 *Employees:* 160
Net Worth: £974,000 *Total Assets:* £46,902,000
Registered Office: TaylorMade Court, Jays Close, Viables Business Park, Basingstoke, Hants, RG22 4BS
Activities: Non-specialised wholesale trade
Parent: 19th Holdings (UK) Limited
Officers: Charlotte Jessica Durman, Secretary; David Abeles [1971] Director [American]; Jeffrey Barker [1976] Finance Director [Canadian]; David Silvers [1971] Managing Director

Taylor Wimpey 2007 Limited
Incorporated: 6 December 2007
Net Worth: £118,685,000 *Total Assets:* £118,685,000
Registered Office: Gate House, Turnpike Road, High Wycombe, Bucks, HP12 3NR
Activities: Other business support service activities n.e.c.
Parent: Taylor Wimpey PLC
Officers: Michael Andrew Lonnon, Secretary; Stephen Roy Impey [1957] Director/Group Treasurer; James John Jordan [1961] Director/Chartered Secretary

Taylor Wimpey Developments Limited
Incorporated: 1 December 1959 *Employees:* 8
Net Worth: £1,938,701,952 *Total Assets:* £2,906,313,984
Registered Office: Gate House, Turnpike Road, High Wycombe, Bucks, HP12 3NR
Activities: Development of building projects
Parent: Taylor Wimpey Holdings Limited
Officers: Michael Andrew Lonnon, Secretary; Jennifer Daly [1970] Director; Nigel Holland [1960] Managing Director; James John Jordan [1961] Director/Company Secretary

Taylor Wimpey Holdings Limited
Incorporated: 6 December 1945
Net Worth: £671,195,008 *Total Assets:* £1,941,644,032
Registered Office: Gate House, Turnpike Road, High Wycombe, Bucks, HP12 3NR
Activities: Development of building projects
Parent: Taylor Wimpey PLC
Officers: Katherine Elizabeth Hindmarsh, Secretary; Christopher Carney [1974] Director; Jennifer Daly [1970] Director; James John Jordan [1961] Director/Company Secretary

Taylor Wimpey PLC
Incorporated: 1 February 1935 *Employees:* 4,995
Net Worth: £3,137,299,968 *Total Assets:* £4,966,099,968
Registered Office: Gate House, Turnpike Road, High Wycombe, Bucks, HP12 3NR
Activities: Activities of head offices
Officers: James John Jordan, Secretary; Dame Katharine Mary Barker [1957] Director; Kevin Stanley Beeston [1962] Director; Gwyneth Victoria Burr [1963] Director; Christopher Carney [1974] Director; Jennifer Daly [1970] Director; James John Jordan [1961] Director/Company Secretary; Angela Ann Knight [1950] Director; Peter Timothy Redfern [1970] Director; Humphrey Stewart Morgan Singer [1965] Director

Taylor Wimpey Property Company Limited
Incorporated: 3 June 1964
Net Worth: £33,185,000 *Total Assets:* £119,677,000
Registered Office: Gate House, Turnpike Road, High Wycombe, Bucks, HP12 3NR
Activities: Development of building projects
Parent: Taylor Wimpey PLC
Officers: Michael Andrew Lonnon, Secretary; Colin Richard Clapham [1945] Director/Company Secretary; Alex David Green [1981] Director

Taylor Wimpey SH Capital Limited
Incorporated: 24 January 2013
Net Worth: £12,061,000 *Total Assets:* £116,364,000
Registered Office: Gate House, Turnpike Road, High Wycombe, Bucks, HP12 3NR
Activities: Management of real estate on a fee or contract basis
Parent: Taylor Wimpey UK Limited
Officers: Katherine Elizabeth Hindmarsh, Secretary; Stephen Roy Impey [1957] Director; Barbara Inskip [1968] Director; Michael Andrew Lonnon [1957] Director/Company Secretary

Taylor Wimpey UK Limited
Incorporated: 6 October 1978 *Employees:* 4,893
Net Worth: £2,093,880,960 *Total Assets:* £4,373,367,808
Registered Office: Gate House, Turnpike Road, High Wycombe, Bucks, HP12 3NR
Activities: Development of building projects
Parent: Taylor Wimpey Developments Limited
Officers: James John Jordan, Secretary; Katherine Anne Billson-Ross [1968] Director; Lee Michael Bishop [1965] Director; Christopher Carney [1974] Director; Jennifer Daly [1970] Director; Nigel Holland [1960] Director; James John Jordan [1961] Director/Company Secretary; Daniel Hugh McGowan [1969] Director; Ingrid Ruth Osborne [1977] Director; Peter Timothy Redfern [1970] Director

Taylor Woodrow Construction
Incorporated: 19 June 1996 *Employees:* 154
Net Worth: £84,972,000 *Total Assets:* £132,612,000
Registered Office: Astral House, Imperial Way, Watford, Herts, WD24 4WW
Activities: Development of building projects
Parent: Vinci Construction UK Limited
Officers: Bruno Michel Dupety [1956] Director/Engineer [French]; Julian Paul Gatward [1966] Director/Civil Engineer; Anthony Kennedy Raikes [1964] Director/Chartered Civil Engineer

TBC Bank Group PLC
Incorporated: 26 February 2016 *Employees:* 6,993
Net Worth: £724,201,920 *Total Assets:* £5,045,101,056
Registered Office: Elder House, St Georges Business Park, 207 Brooklands Road, Weybridge, Surrey, KT13 0TS
Activities: Activities of financial services holding companies
Officers: Vakhtang Butskhrikidze [1970] Director [Georgian]; Maria Luisa Cicognani [1964] Director [Italian]; Nikoloz Enukidze [1970] Director; Nicholas Dominic Haag [1958] Director; Badri Japaridze [1960] Director [Georgian]; Tsira Kemularia [1977] Director; Mamuka Khazaradze [1966] Director [Georgian]; Eric Jeyarajan Rajendra [1958] Director [American]; Giorgi Shagidze [1975] Director [Georgian]

TBE (Southern) Limited
Incorporated: 8 June 1983
Net Worth: £32,340,068 *Total Assets:* £38,875,668
Registered Office: 2nd Floor, The Atrium, 31 Church Road, Ashford, Middlesex, TW15 2UD
Activities: Other letting and operating of own or leased real estate
Parent: JWL Property Finance Limited
Officers: Marie Annick Avis, Secretary; Adrian Eyre Lloyd [1979] Director; Britta Adrienne Lloyd [1945] Director/Psychotherapist [Swiss]; Jeremy William Lloyd [1942] Director/Banker; Bryan Kevin Meehan [1968] Director/Entrepreneur [Irish]; Antonia Gillian Silcock [1985] Director; Colin Laird Walker-Robson [1952] Director/Chartered Accountant

TBG (1) 2009 Limited
Incorporated: 14 October 2009
Net Worth: £507,999,008 *Total Assets:* £507,999,008
Registered Office: Berkeley House, 19 Portsmouth Road, Cobham, Surrey, KT11 1JG
Activities: Development of building projects
Parent: The Berkeley Group PLC
Officers: Jared Stephen Philip Cranney, Secretary; David Martin Lowry [1981] Director; Robert Charles Grenville Perrins [1965] Director; Anthony William Pidgley [1947] Director; Richard James Stearn [1968] Director

TBG (3) 2009 Limited
Incorporated: 14 October 2009
Net Worth: £555,097,984 *Total Assets:* £1,382,528,000
Registered Office: Berkeley House, 19 Portsmouth Road, Cobham, Surrey, KT11 1JG
Activities: Development of building projects
Parent: The Berkeley Group PLC
Officers: Jared Stephen Philip Cranney, Secretary; David Martin Lowry [1981] Director; Robert Charles Grenville Perrins [1965] Director; Anthony William Pidgley [1947] Director; Richard James Stearn [1968] Director

TBG (4) Limited
Incorporated: 5 October 2010
Net Worth: £525,227,008 *Total Assets:* £525,227,008
Registered Office: Berkeley House, 19 Portsmouth Road, Cobham, Surrey, KT11 1JG
Activities: Other business support service activities n.e.c.
Shareholders: TBG (1) 2009 Limited; The Berkeley Group PLC
Officers: Jared Stephen Philip Cranney, Secretary; David Martin Lowry [1981] Director; Robert Charles Grenville Perrins [1965] Director; Anthony William Pidgley [1947] Director; Richard James Stearn [1968] Director

TCFG Holdings Limited
Incorporated: 15 December 2010 *Employees:* 11
Net Worth: £8,410,000 *Total Assets:* £179,362,000
Registered Office: Granville House, Gatton Park Business Centre, Wells Place, Redhill, Surrey, RH1 3AS
Activities: Activities of other holding companies n.e.c.
Parent: Helsinki Bidco Ltd
Officers: David Jonathan Kimber, Secretary; Steven James Higginson [1960] Director; Mark John Lane [1970] Director; Damian Johnson Shaw [1971] Director

Tchibo Coffee International Limited
Incorporated: 23 May 1963 *Employees:* 149
Net Worth: £24,446,268 *Total Assets:* £28,856,822
Registered Office: Tchibo House, 7-8 Blenheim Road, Epsom, Surrey, KT19 9BE
Activities: Non-specialised wholesale of food, beverages and tobacco
Officers: Kate Asamoa, Secretary; Kate Elizabeth Jane Asamoa [1976] Finance Director; Paul Chadderton [1963] Managing Director

TCR UK Limited
Incorporated: 5 October 2001 *Employees:* 218
Net Worth: £6,047,381 *Total Assets:* £46,323,968
Registered Office: Dixcart House, Addlestone Road, Bourne Business Park, Addlestone, Surrey, KT15 2LE
Activities: Renting and leasing of freight air transport equipment
Parent: Envol Investments Limited
Officers: Patrice de Hemptinne, Secretary; Tom Joeri W Bellekens [1978] Director/Chief Operating Officer [Belgian]; Benoit Biebuyck [1972] Director/Chief Finance Officer [Belgian]; Jan de Leeuw [1974] Managing Director [Belgian]; Kristof Philips [1980] Director/General Manager [Belgian]

TD United Kingdom Acquisition Limited
Incorporated: 28 November 2002
Net Worth: £1,973,910,656 *Total Assets:* £3,072,709,376
Registered Office: Redwood 2, Crockford Lane, Chineham Business Park, Chineham, Basingstoke, Hants, RG24 8WQ
Activities: Activities of head offices
Parent: Tech Data UK Finance Limited
Officers: Philip James Auld, Secretary; Samy Amsellem [1960] Director [French]; Charles Dannewitz [1955] Director [American]; Svitlana Murray [1984] Finance Director [American]; Howard Tuffnail [1964] Finance Director [Canadian]; Scott Walker [1973] Director [American]

Tearfund
Incorporated: 13 November 1970 *Employees:* 878
Net Worth: £32,632,000 *Total Assets:* £37,725,000
Registered Office: 100 Church Road, Teddington, Middlesex, TW11 8QE
Activities: Other social work activities without accommodation n.e.c.
Officers: Mary Ann Drew, Secretary; Stephanie Clare Biden [1980] Director/Solicitor; William Ian Curtis [1953] Director/International Development Consultant; John Davidson [1959] Director/Solicitor; Stephanie Jane Heald [1963] Director/Publisher, Editor & Writer; Sally Ann Jones-Evans [1966] Director; Anna Elisabeth Laszlo [1969] Director; Philip Duncan Loney [1964] Director; Rev Mark Melluish [1959] Director/Vicar; Reverend Harold Creeth Miller [1950] Director/Bishop of Down and Dromore; Jillian Mills [1958] Director/Consultant; Rosemary Winifred Nuamah Williams [1974] Director/Self Employed; Anthony Dangasuk Poggo [1964] Director/Bishop [South Sudanese]; Craig Rowland [1956] Director; John Shaw [1951] Director

Tech 21 UK Limited
Incorporated: 20 November 2005 *Employees:* 81
Net Worth: £19,051,154 *Total Assets:* £64,286,460
Registered Office: Syds Quay, Eel Pie Island, Twickenham, Middlesex, TW1 3DY
Activities: Other manufacturing n.e.c.
Major Shareholder: Jason Lloyd Roberts
Officers: Peter Vernon Charles Cass, Secretary; Peter Vernon Charles Cass [1955] Director/Accountant; Jason Lloyd Roberts [1969] Director

Tech Data as UK Limited
Incorporated: 23 November 1995 *Employees:* 278
Previous: Avnet Technology Solutions Limited
Net Worth: £30,934,000 *Total Assets:* £243,294,000
Registered Office: The Capitol Building, Oldbury, Bracknell, Berks, RG12 8FZ
Activities: Other information technology service activities
Parent: Tenva TS Holdings Limited
Officers: Wayne Hanewicz [1969] Director/Company Secretary [American]; Miriam Anne Murphy [1969] Director [Irish]; Howard James Tuffnail [1964] Finance Director [Canadian]

Tech Data Holding Limited
Incorporated: 7 February 2017
Net Worth: £1,680,162,304 *Total Assets:* £1,680,162,304
Registered Office: Redwood 2, Crockford Lane, Chineham Business Park, Chineham, Basingstoke, Hants, RG24 8WQ
Activities: Activities of other holding companies n.e.c.
Parent: Tech Data Corporation
Officers: Philip James Auld, Secretary; Samy Amsellem [1960] Director [French]; Charles Dannewitz [1955] Director [American]; Svitlana Murray [1984] Finance Director [American]; Howard Tuffnail [1964] Finance Director [Canadian]; Scott William Walker [1973] Director [American]

Tech Data Limited
Incorporated: 14 January 1983 *Employees:* 944
Net Worth: £217,446,000 *Total Assets:* £1,047,009,024
Registered Office: Redwood 2, Crockford Lane, Chineham Business Park, Chineham, Basingstoke, Hants, RG24 8WQ
Activities: Wholesale of computers, computer peripheral equipment and software
Parent: TD Uited Kingdom Acquisition Limited
Officers: Philip James Auld, Secretary; Samy Amsellem [1960] Director/Chartered Accountant [French]; Andrew Gass [1964] Director; Howard Tuffnail [1964] Finance Director [Canadian]; David Watts [1970] Director

Tech Data UK Finance Limited
Incorporated: 7 December 2016
Net Worth: £847,344,448 *Total Assets:* £1,983,862,272
Registered Office: Redwood 2, Crockford Lane, Chineham Business Park, Chineham, Basingstoke, Hants, RG24 8WQ
Activities: Activities of other holding companies n.e.c.
Parent: Tech Data Corporation
Officers: Philip James Auld, Secretary; Samy Amsellem [1960] Director [French]; Charles Dannewitz [1955] Director [American]; Svitlana Murray [1984] Finance Director [American]; Howard Tuffnail [1964] Finance Director [Canadian]; Scott William Walker [1973] Director [American]

Tech Data UK Finance Partner Limited
Incorporated: 8 February 2017
Net Worth: £588,056,768 *Total Assets:* £588,056,768
Registered Office: Redwood 2, Crockford Lane, Chineham Business Park, Chineham, Basingstoke, Hants, RG24 8WQ
Activities: Activities of other holding companies n.e.c.
Officers: Philip James Auld, Secretary; Samy Amsellem [1960] Director [French]; Charles Dannewitz [1955] Director [American]; Svitlana Murray [1984] Finance Director [American]; Howard Tuffnail [1964] Finance Director [Canadian]; Scott William Walker [1973] Director [American]

Tech Data UK Resources Limited
Incorporated: 5 December 2016
Net Worth: £107,353,416 *Total Assets:* £206,429,984
Registered Office: Redwood 2, Crockford Lane, Chineham Business Park, Chineham, Basingstoke, Hants, RG24 8WQ
Activities: Activities of other holding companies n.e.c.
Parent: TD United Kingdom Acquisition Limited
Officers: Philip James Auld, Secretary; Samy Amsellem [1960] Director [French]; Charles Dannewitz [1955] Director [American]; Svitlana Murray [1984] Finance Director [American]; Howard Tuffnail [1964] Finance Director [Canadian]; Scott William Walker [1973] Director [American]

Techaid Facilities Limited
Incorporated: 7 August 1973 *Employees:* 56
Net Worth: £12,539,529 *Total Assets:* £29,912,552
Registered Office: Loudwater House, London Road, Loudwater, High Wycombe, Bucks, HP10 9TL
Activities: Development of building projects
Shareholders: Martin John Francis Gardener; Julie Dawn Sinton
Officers: Martin John Francis Gardener [1964] Director/Estate Manager; Robin Francis Gardener [1996] Director

Technetix Group Limited
Incorporated: 3 December 2004 *Employees:* 184
Net Worth: £24,626,000 *Total Assets:* £64,900,000
Registered Office: Innovation House, Technetix Business Park, Muddleswood Road, Albourne, Hassocks, W Sussex, BN6 9EB
Activities: Activities of head offices
Major Shareholder: Paul Antony Broadhurst
Officers: Emma Louise Hamilton, Secretary; Dirk Jan Ariesen [1963] Director/Chief Technology Officer [Dutch]; Paul Antony Broadhurst [1960] Director; John Henry Brougham [1951] Director; Dr Colin Buechner [1968] Managing Director Access Network [German]; Andrew John Kellett [1968] Director/Chief Financial Officer; Duncan James McIntyre [1959] Director

Technetix Limited
Incorporated: 26 March 1990 *Employees:* 71
Net Worth: £3,221,000 *Total Assets:* £43,462,000
Registered Office: Innovation House, Technetix Business Park, Muddleswood Road, Albourne, Hassocks, W Sussex, BN6 9EB
Activities: Manufacture of electronic components
Parent: Technetix Group Limited
Officers: Emma Louise Hamilton, Secretary; Paul Antony Broadhurst [1960] Director; Andrew John Kellett [1968] Director/Chief Financial Officer

Technical Staffing Resources Limited
Incorporated: 14 January 2011 *Employees:* 5
Net Worth: £556,124 *Total Assets:* £66,808,688
Registered Office: Hill Park Court, Springfield Drive, Leatherhead, Surrey, KT22 7NL
Activities: Other activities of employment placement agencies
Parent: Kellogg Brown & Root International Group Holdings LLP
Officers: Susan Meirion Owen, Secretary; David Lindsay Gibson [1962] Director/Vice President Operations-EMEA; Jalal Jay Ibrahim [1960] Director [American]; Martin Nelhams [1960] Director

TechnoGym U.K. Limited
Incorporated: 22 January 1993 *Employees:* 109
Net Worth: £6,006,985 *Total Assets:* £39,574,148
Registered Office: Two The Boulevard, Cain Road, Bracknell, Berks, RG12 1WP
Activities: Other business support service activities n.e.c.
Officers: Michelle Kenny, Secretary; Andrea Alghisi [1968] Director [Italian]; Stephen George Barton [1969] Director; Kenrick Briffa [1964] Director/Business Manager [Italian]; Adrian Mark Drew [1962] Finance Director; Davide Pasqualini [1976] Director [Italian]; Stefano Zanelli [1965] Director/Business Executive [Italian]

Techtronic Industries (UK) Ltd
Incorporated: 8 March 1990 *Employees:* 170
Net Worth Deficit: £2,915,816 *Total Assets:* £85,589,400
Registered Office: 3 Globeside Business Park, Fieldhouse Lane, Marlow, Bucks, SL7 1HZ
Activities: Wholesale of other machinery and equipment
Parent: A & M Industries SARL
Officers: Kwok-Hung Peter Chau [1967] Finance Director; Amelia Rosa Mirone [1971] Director/Vice President Commercial Finance [Portuguese/British]

Teddington 2 Limited
Incorporated: 22 December 2009 *Employees:* 2
Net Worth: £223,000,992 *Total Assets:* £350,064,000
Registered Office: LGC, Queens Road, Teddington, Middlesex, TW11 0LY
Activities: Other business support service activities n.e.c.
Parent: LGC Science Group Limited
Officers: Navneet Kaur Ogle, Secretary; Simon Lawrence Parsons [1969] Finance Director; Timothy Michael Robinson [1963] Director

Teddington School
Incorporated: 4 July 2012 *Employees:* 141
Net Worth: £42,265,624 *Total Assets:* £44,062,220
Registered Office: Teddington School, Broom Road, Teddington, Middlesex, TW11 9PJ
Activities: General secondary education
Officers: Andrea Louise Arbiter, Secretary; Carl Ainley [1969] Director/Chartered Civil Engineer & Project Manager; Catherine Balfour-Roberts [1971] Director/Senior Lecturer; Anne Davison [1969] Director/Head of Finance; Daryl Greenwood [1959] Director/Marketing Manager; Juliet Claire Hartridge [1970] Director/Gardener; Trevor Alexander Huggins [1958] Director/Journalist; Andrew Oliva-Hauxwell [1973] Director/Charity Executive; Sarah Tate [1963] Director/Teacher; Katie Wade [1973] Finance Director; Marie Wylde [1983] Director/Accountant

TEG Holdings Limited
Incorporated: 22 February 2017
Net Worth: £38,635,000 *Total Assets:* £154,504,000
Registered Office: Aragon House, University Way, Cranfield Technology Park, Cranfield, Bedford, MK43 0EQ
Activities: Other amusement and recreation activities n.e.c.
Officers: Mark Simon Willis, Secretary; Nicolas Andrew Basing [1962] Director; Graham Edwin Blackwell [1969] Director; Dr Duncan Steven Garrood [1958] Director; Mark Simon Willis [1976] Director

Tektronix U.K.Limited
Incorporated: 22 November 1952 *Employees:* 47
Net Worth: £7,701,000 *Total Assets:* £27,947,000
Registered Office: Capitol Building, Oldbury, Bracknell, Berks, RG12 8FZ
Activities: Manufacture of electronic measuring, testing etc. equipment, not for industrial process control
Parent: TGA Industries Ltd
Officers: Trevor Sinkinson [1971] Director/VP Finance EMEA & ANZ; Philip Wray [1978] Director/Financial Controller; Sally Wright [1976] Marketing Director

Teledyne Limited
Incorporated: 19 October 1999 *Employees:* 540
Net Worth: £98,531,000 *Total Assets:* £139,464,992
Registered Office: Aviation House, The Lodge, Harmondsworth Lane, West Drayton, Middlesex, UB7 0LQ
Activities: Manufacture of electronic components
Parent: Rhombi Holdings Limited
Officers: Nicholas James Wargent, Secretary; Susan Lee Main [1958] Director/Senior Vice President and Chief Financial Officer [American]; Robert Mehrabian [1941] Director/Corporate Executive [American]; Ian Michael Skiggs [1967] Director/General Manager; Nicholas James Wargent [1973] Director/Solicitor

Telefonica Digital Limited
Incorporated: 16 December 2011 *Employees:* 135
Net Worth: £89,957,000 *Total Assets:* £128,938,000
Registered Office: 260 Bath Road, Slough, Berks, SL1 4DX
Activities: Video distribution activities
Parent: Telefonica S A
Officers: Michael Alan Duncan [1962] Director; Antonio Marti Ciruelos [1962] Director/Accountant [Spanish]

Telefonica Europe PLC
Incorporated: 10 December 2004
Net Worth: £9,724,999,680 *Total Assets:* £9,905,000,448
Registered Office: 260 Bath Road, Slough, Berks, SL1 4DX
Activities: Other telecommunications activities
Parent: Telefonica S A
Officers: Robert John Harwood, Secretary; Patricia Cobian [1975] Director [Spanish]; Mark Evans [1969] Director/Accountant

Telefonica Germany Holdings Limited
Incorporated: 5 September 2012
Net Worth: £6,441,826,304 *Total Assets:* £9,999,205,376
Registered Office: 260 Bath Road, Slough, Berks, SL1 4DX
Activities: Other telecommunications activities
Parent: O2 (Europe) Limited
Officers: Mark David Hardman [1975] Director; Robert John Harwood [1960] Director/Chartered Secretary; Enrique Medina Malo [1972] Director/Lawyer [Spanish]

Telefonica UK Limited
Incorporated: 28 July 1983 *Employees:* 5,885
Net Worth: £1,700,999,936 *Total Assets:* £5,821,000,192
Registered Office: 260 Bath Road, Slough, Berks, SL1 4DX
Activities: Wireless telecommunications activities
Parent: O2 Holdings Limited
Officers: Patricia Cobian [1975] Director [Spanish]; Mark Evans [1969] Director/Accountant

Telegenic Limited
Incorporated: 18 March 1981 *Employees:* 106
Net Worth: £12,076,206 *Total Assets:* £23,560,308
Registered Office: 8 The Merlin Centre, Lancaster Road, High Wycombe, Bucks, HP12 3QL
Activities: Television programme production activities
Parent: Telegenic Holdings Limited
Officers: Peter Andrew Bates, Secretary/Director; Peter Andrew Bates [1963] Director of Production; Peter John Bowen [1968] Director/Head of Cameras; Eamonn Cornelius Curtin [1975] Commercial Director; Clive Harold Eggs [1963] Finance Director; Terence Peter James [1958] Director of Operations; Sean Patrick Mulhern [1972] Director of Engineering; David John Rowley [1971] Director/Head of Sound

Teletrac Navman (UK) Ltd
Incorporated: 2 September 1988 *Employees:* 234
Previous: Trafficmaster Limited
Net Worth: £29,977,000 *Total Assets:* £58,012,000
Registered Office: First Floor, K1, Kents Hill Business Park, Milton Keynes, Bucks, MK7 6BZ
Activities: Other professional, scientific and technical activities n.e.c.
Parent: TGA Industries Ltd
Officers: Radomir Lalovic, Secretary; Radomir Lalovic [1960] Director/Accountant; Richard George Lilwall [1977] Managing Director; Mark David Schwarz [1965] Commercial Director

Telewest Communications (London South) Limited
Incorporated: 7 February 1983
Net Worth: £7,400,000 *Total Assets:* £146,903,008
Registered Office: Media House, Bartley Wood Business Park, Hook, Hants, RG27 9UP
Activities: Other telecommunications activities
Shareholders: Theseus No.1 Limited; Theseus No.2 Limited
Officers: Gillian Elizabeth James, Secretary; Robert Dominic Dunn [1966] Director/Chief Financial Officer; Mine Ozkan Hifzi [1966] Director/Solicitor

Telewest Communications (Midlands and North West) Limited
Incorporated: 25 February 1993
Net Worth: £191,124,000 *Total Assets:* £737,171,008
Registered Office: Media House, Bartley Wood Business Park, Hook, Hants, RG27 9UP
Activities: Other telecommunications activities
Parent: Telewest Limited
Officers: Gillian Elizabeth James, Secretary; Robert Dominic Dunn [1966] Director/Chief Financial Officer; Mine Ozkan Hifzi [1966] Director/Solicitor

Telewest Communications Holdings Limited
Incorporated: 24 October 1994
Net Worth: £1,960,663,040 *Total Assets:* £1,969,148,032
Registered Office: Media House, Bartley Wood Business Park, Hook, Hants, RG27 9UP
Activities: Dormant company
Parent: Telewest Communications Networks Limited
Officers: Gillian Elizabeth James, Secretary; Robert Dominic Dunn [1966] Director/Chief Financial Officer; Mine Ozkan Hifzi [1966] Director/Solicitor

Telewest Communications Networks Limited
Incorporated: 21 June 1995
Net Worth: £3,997,338,880 *Total Assets:* £3,997,603,072
Registered Office: Media House, Bartley Wood Business Park, Hook, Hants, RG27 9UP
Activities: Other business support service activities n.e.c.
Parent: General Cable Limited
Officers: Gillian Elizabeth James, Secretary; Robert Dominic Dunn [1966] Director/Chief Financial Officer; Mine Ozkan Hifzi [1966] Director/Solicitor

Telewest Limited
Incorporated: 12 December 1996
Net Worth: £2,852,891,904 *Total Assets:* £3,798,996,992
Registered Office: Media House, Bartley Wood Business Park, Hook, Hants, RG27 9UP
Activities: Other business support service activities n.e.c.
Parent: Telewest Communications Networks Limited
Officers: Gillian Elizabeth James, Secretary; Robert Dominic Dunn [1966] Director/Chief Financial Officer; Mine Ozkan Hifzi [1966] Director/Solicitor

Ten Entertainment Group PLC
Incorporated: 15 March 2017 *Employees:* 1,134
Net Worth: £53,193,000 *Total Assets:* £72,000,000
Registered Office: Aragon House, University Way, Cranfield Technology Park, Cranfield, Bedford, MK43 0EQ
Activities: Other amusement and recreation activities n.e.c.
Parent: Harwood Capital Nominees Limited
Officers: Mark Willis, Secretary; Nicolas Andrew Basing [1962] Director; Graham Blackwell [1969] Director; Dr Duncan Steven Garrood [1958] Director/Chief Executive; Christopher Harwood Bernard Mills [1952] Director; Julie Mary Sneddon [1964] Director; David James Wild [1955] Director; Mark Simon Willis [1976] Director

Teneo Group Limited
Incorporated: 22 October 2004 *Employees:* 79
Net Worth: £669,980 *Total Assets:* £28,246,322
Registered Office: Units 20-21 Theale Lakes Business Park, Moulden Way, Sulhamstead, Reading, Berks, RG7 4GB
Activities: Activities of head offices
Major Shareholder: Piers Martin Jude Carey
Officers: Piers Martin Jude Carey, Secretary; Piers Martin Jude Carey [1969] Director; James Simon Hall [1970] Operations Director; Marc James Sollars [1972] Pre Sales Director

Tengo (Holdings) Limited
Incorporated: 29 January 2014 *Employees:* 345
Net Worth: £222,405 *Total Assets:* £38,451,932
Registered Office: Salisbury House, Weyside Park, Catteshall Lane, Godalming, Surrey, GU7 1XE
Activities: Activities of head offices
Officers: Ajay Patel, Secretary; Simon Christopher Mason [1976] Director; Ajay Patel [1964] Director; Andrew Ross [1977] Director; Scott Scott [1974] Director; Matthew Tod [1964] Director; Sarah Walden [1974] Director; William Valerian Wellesley [1966] Director; James Christopher Michael Woolley [1977] Director

Tenpin Limited
Incorporated: 6 June 2003 *Employees:* 1,126
Net Worth: £52,936,000 *Total Assets:* £75,270,000
Registered Office: Aragon House, Cranfield Technology Park, Cranfield, Bedford, MK43 0EQ
Activities: Other amusement and recreation activities n.e.c.
Parent: TEG Holdings Limited
Officers: George Jason Sheppard, Secretary; Nicholas Andrew Basing [1962] Director; Graham Edwin Blackwell [1969] Commercial Director; Dr Duncan Steven Garrood [1958] Director; George Jason Sheppard [1981] Director/Chartered Accountant; Mark Willis [1976] Director

Tensator Group Limited
Incorporated: 24 December 2001 *Employees:* 6
Net Worth: £10,026,000 *Total Assets:* £24,480,000
Registered Office: Unit 7 Danbury Court, Linford Wood, Milton Keynes, Bucks, MK14 6TS
Activities: Activities of head offices
Parent: Tensator Holdings Ltd
Officers: Alan Robert McPherson [1973] Director

Tensator Holdings Ltd
Incorporated: 11 July 2008 *Employees:* 165
Net Worth: £18,020,000 *Total Assets:* £38,924,000
Registered Office: Unit 7 Danbury Court, Linford Wood, Milton Keynes, Bucks, MK14 6TS
Activities: Activities of other holding companies n.e.c.
Parent: Prudential Financial Inc
Officers: Michael Philip Berry [1955] Director/Investment Manager; Marie Louise Fioramonti [1961] Managing Director [American]; Alan Robert McPherson [1973] Director; Stephen Rushworth Smith [1953] Director

Tensator Limited
Incorporated: 3 August 2000 *Employees:* 69
Net Worth: £26,957,000 *Total Assets:* £41,491,000
Registered Office: Unit 7 Danbury Court, Linford Wood, Milton Keynes, Bucks, MK14 6TS
Activities: Manufacture of other fabricated metal products n.e.c.
Parent: Tensator Group Limited
Officers: Alan Robert McPherson [1973] Director

Tenterden Schools Trust
Incorporated: 10 August 2011 *Employees:* 341
Previous: Homewood School & Sixth Form Centre
Net Worth: £31,371,084 *Total Assets:* £35,766,656
Registered Office: Homewood School & Sixth Form Centre, Ashford Road, Tenterden, Kent, TN30 6LT
Activities: General secondary education
Officers: Karen Douglas, Secretary; Lindsay John Hammond [1957] Director/Vicar; Vanessa Diane Hardy [1955] Director/Financial Advisor; Peter Michael Hill [1939] Director/County Councillor; Ian Herbert Kirkland [1950] Director/Retired; Sally Jane Lees [1957] Director/Principal of a Secondary School; Susan Moon [1948] Director/Retired; Nicola Jane Paterson [1970] Deputy Director of Education-Diocese of Canterbury; Dr Katherine Lucy Smith [1968] Director/Senior Lecturer; Neil Vincer [1958] Director/Environment, Health & Safety; Joanna Elizabeth Vos [1974] Director/Community Warden

Tenva TS Holdings Limited
Incorporated: 31 March 1998
Net Worth: £11,996,000 *Total Assets:* £91,926,000
Registered Office: The Capitol Building, Oldbury, Bracknell, Berks, RG12 8FZ
Activities: Activities of head offices
Parent: Tenva Holdings LLC
Officers: Miriam Anne Murphy [1969] Director/Senior VP, Advanced Solutions Europe, Value Added [Irish]; Howard James Tuffnail [1964] Finance Director [Canadian]

Teoco UK Limited
Incorporated: 12 November 2013
Net Worth Deficit: £23,983,700 *Total Assets:* £28,921,400
Registered Office: c/o Aircom International Ltd, Pascal Place, Randalls Way, Leatherhead, Surrey, KT22 7TW
Activities: Other telecommunications activities
Major Shareholder: Atul Jain
Officers: Philip Merritt Giuntini [1946] Director [American]; Atul Jain [1960] Director/CEO - Chairman [American]

Terex Cranes UK Limited
Incorporated: 13 September 1991 *Employees:* 29
Net Worth: £27,695,000 *Total Assets:* £31,691,000
Registered Office: 14 Hikers Way, Crendon Industrial Park, Long Crendon, Bucks, HP18 9RW
Activities: Agents involved in the sale of machinery, industrial equipment, ships and aircraft
Parent: Terex Corporation
Officers: Eric I Cohen, Secretary/Lawyer [American]; Eric I Cohen [1958] Director/Lawyer [American]; Stoyan Filipov [1968] Director/President [American]; John Daniel Sheehan [1960] Director/Chief Financial Officer [American]; Carsten Von Der Geest [1974] Director [Dutch]

Terex Pegson Limited
Incorporated: 13 August 1931 *Employees:* 85
Net Worth: £6,083,000 *Total Assets:* £27,317,000
Registered Office: The Pinnacle, 170 Midsummer Boulevard, Milton Keynes, Bucks, MK9 1FE
Activities: Manufacture of pumps
Parent: Pegson Group Limited
Officers: Eric I Cohen, Secretary/Lawyer [American]; Eric I Cohen [1958] Director/Lawyer [American]; John Daniel Sheehan [1960] Director/Chief Financial Officer [American]

Terrassen Holdings Limited
Incorporated: 14 February 1978
Net Worth: £128,559,000 *Total Assets:* £128,616,000
Registered Office: Quadrant, 55-57 High Street, Windsor, Berks, SL4 1LP
Activities: Activities of head offices
Parent: Morgan Holdings Limited
Officers: Stephanie Helen Mackie, Secretary; Paul Andrew Boulton [1968] Director/Solicitor; Claire Rose Collins [1974] Director/Accountant; Stephanie Helen Mackie [1968] Director/Company Secretary

Terrestrial Developments Ltd
Incorporated: 13 October 2014
Net Worth: £25,492,818 *Total Assets:* £39,288,088
Registered Office: 35 Ruddlesway, Windsor, Berks, SL4 5SF
Activities: Other service activities n.e.c.
Major Shareholder: Darbara Singh Dhanoa
Officers: Darbara Singh Dhanoa [1961] Director

Tesco Underwriting Limited
Incorporated: 20 July 2009
Net Worth: £182,000,000 *Total Assets:* £1,061,100,032
Registered Office: Ageas House, Hampshire Corporate Park, Templars Way, Eastleigh, Hants, SO53 3YA
Activities: Non-life insurance
Shareholders: Ageas (UK) Limited; Tesco Personal Finance PLC
Officers: Rosemary Anne Smith, Secretary; Colin James Anthony [1974] Director; Karl Robert Douglas Bedlow [1967] Director; Robin Challand [1969] Director; Adam James Clarke [1972] Director; Margot Cronin [1963] Director [Irish]; Stephen Grainge [1962] Director; Declan Joseph Hourican [1976] Director [Irish]; Simon Christopher John Machell [1963] Director; Caroline Frances Ramsay [1962] Director; Mark Winlow [1962] Director

Tesla Engineering Limited
Incorporated: 4 February 1993 *Employees:* 461
Net Worth: £17,884,000 *Total Assets:* £48,323,000
Registered Office: Water Lane Industrial Estate, Storrington, W Sussex, RH20 3EA
Activities: Manufacture of other special-purpose machinery n.e.c.
Officers: Dr Michael Colin Begg, Secretary/Engineering Manager; Stephen Andrew Bates [1965] Operations Director; Dr Michael Colin Begg [1959] Director/Businessman; David Paul Cracknell [1966] Director/Accountant; Benjamin David Leigh [1973] Director/Manager; Dr James Cumming Ramage [1951] Director; Marc Henry Van Leusen [1965] Operations Director [Dutch]

Tesla Limited
Incorporated: 19 May 1995 *Employees:* 2
Net Worth: £23,846,000 *Total Assets:* £23,846,000
Registered Office: Unit 1 Water Lane Industrial Estate, Storrington, W Sussex, RH20 3EA
Activities: Activities of production holding companies
Officers: Dr Michael Colin Begg, Secretary; Dr Michael Colin Begg [1959] Director/Businessman; Dr James Cumming Ramage [1951] Director

Tesla Motors Limited
Incorporated: 28 February 2002 *Employees:* 432
Net Worth: £17,905,932 *Total Assets:* £314,548,416
Registered Office: 197 Horton Road, West Drayton, Middlesex, UB7 8JD
Activities: Manufacture of motor vehicles
Parent: Tesla, Inc.
Officers: Marc Jesus Cerda [1966] Director/Business Executive [American]; Vaibhav Taneja [1978] Director/Business Executive [American]; Stephan William Werkman [1973] Director/Business Executive [Dutch]

TF1 Limited
Incorporated: 11 July 2016
Net Worth: £4,086,000 *Total Assets:* £121,257,000
Registered Office: Headway House, Crosby Way, Farnham, Surrey, GU9 7XG
Activities: Activities of other holding companies n.e.c.
Parent: BCA Trading Limited
Officers: Martin Richard Letza, Secretary; David Francis Harris [1971] Director; Timothy Giles Lampert [1970] Director

TFX Group Limited
Incorporated: 24 December 1993 *Employees:* 43
Net Worth: £10,514,000 *Total Assets:* £23,063,000
Registered Office: Grosvenor House, Horseshoe Crescent, Beaconsfield, Bucks, HP9 1LJ
Activities: Other manufacturing n.e.c.
Parent: Teleflex Incorporated
Officers: Gerard Daniel McCaffrey, Secretary; Jean-Luc Albert Dianda [1963] Director/Executive [French]; Matthew James [1971] Director/General Manager; Gerard Daniel McCaffrey [1954] Director [Irish]

TGS Geophysical Company (UK) Limited
Incorporated: 6 March 2006
Net Worth Deficit: £14,329,054 *Total Assets:* £43,833,228
Registered Office: 1 The Crescent, Surbiton, Surrey, KT6 4BN
Activities: Support activities for petroleum and natural gas mining
Parent: TGS-Nopec Geophysical Company ASA
Officers: Paul William Bradbury [1978] Director/Business Executive; Erik Finnstrom [1957] Director/Business Executive [American]; Tanya Flor Herwanger [1973] Director/Businesswoman [Belizean]

TH UK & Ireland Limited
Incorporated: 29 July 2016 *Employees:* 113
Net Worth: £24,321,048 *Total Assets:* £29,562,736
Registered Office: Fortune House, Crabtree Office Village, Eversley Way, Egham, Surrey, TW20 8RY
Activities: Unlicenced restaurants and cafes
Officers: Gurprit Dhaliwal [1982] Director; Jaipal Singh Dhillon [1990] Director; Kevin John Hydes [1978] Director/Chief Financial and Commercial Officer; Surinderjit Singh Kandola [1965] Director; Alexandre Grein de Macedo [1977] Director/President, Tim Hortons [American]; Lucas Lopes Muniz [1986] Director/President, Tim Hortons International [Canadian]

Thakeham Homes Limited
Incorporated: 9 June 2010 *Employees:* 67
Net Worth: £903,859 *Total Assets:* £60,685,088
Registered Office: Thakeham House, Summers Place, Stane Street, Billingshurst, W Sussex, RH14 9GN
Activities: Development of building projects
Shareholders: Paul Anthony Rooney; Robert Paul Boughton
Officers: Christopher Andrew Coxon, Secretary; Robert Paul Boughton [1973] Group Managing Director; Meyrick Cox [1964] Independent Non-Executive Director; Mark Jeremy Featherstone [1969] Independent Non-Executive Director; Stuart Nigel Fullwood [1969] Business Development Director; John Andrew Gaffney [1963] Group Production Director; Christopher Paul Heney [1966] Group Projects Director; Barbara Rosemary Henwood [1957] Director; Colin John Rogers [1956] Group Financial Director; Julian Anthony Rooney [1978] Group Operations Director; Paul Anthony Rooney [1947] Director; Peter James Youll [1969] Group Commercial Director

Thales Electronics Limited
Incorporated: 30 June 1951
Net Worth: £325,000,000 *Total Assets:* £325,000,000
Registered Office: 350 Longwater Avenue, Green Park, Reading, Berks, RG2 6GF
Activities: Activities of other holding companies n.e.c.
Parent: Thales Holdings UK PLC
Officers: Michael William Peter Seabrook, Secretary; Ewen Angus McCrorie [1958] Finance Director; Michael William Peter Seabrook [1966] Director/Accountant Chartered

Thales Ground Transportation Systems UK Limited
Incorporated: 4 May 2006 *Employees:* 496
Net Worth Deficit: £10,234,000 *Total Assets:* £51,224,000
Registered Office: 350 Longwater Avenue, Green Park, Reading, Berks, RG2 6GF
Activities: Other service activities incidental to land transportation, n.e.c.
Parent: Thales Transport and Security Limited
Officers: Michael William Peter Seabrook, Secretary; Andrew Richard Bell [1974] Director; Mark Stephen Garrity [1963] Director; James Neal Brindley Jackson [1982] Director; Shaun Kevin Jones [1966] Director; Paul Maynard [1969] Director

Thales Holdings UK PLC
Incorporated: 7 March 2000
Net Worth: £1,130,336,000 *Total Assets:* £1,888,355,968
Registered Office: 350 Longwater Avenue, Green Park, Reading, Berks, RG2 6GF
Activities: Activities of other holding companies n.e.c.
Parent: Thales SA
Officers: Michael William Peter Seabrook, Secretary; Victor Manuel Chavez [1963] Director; Ewen Angus McCrorie [1958] Finance Director; Denis Vincent Bernard Marie Plantier [1962] Director [French]; Suzanne Jayne Stratton [1972] Director

Thales Properties Limited
Incorporated: 28 December 1973 *Employees:* 13
Net Worth: £31,047,000 *Total Assets:* £102,333,000
Registered Office: 350 Longwater Avenue, Green Park, Reading, Berks, RG2 6GF
Activities: Other letting and operating of own or leased real estate
Parent: Thales UK Limited
Officers: Michael William Peter Seabrook, Secretary; Stephen Graham Davies [1965] Director; Christopher William Hindle [1968] Director; Robert Frank Lucas [1967] Director; Suzanne Jayne Stratton [1972] Director

Thales Training & Simulation (Ace) Limited
Incorporated: 17 February 1995 *Employees:* 32
Net Worth: £27,192,000 *Total Assets:* £37,320,000
Registered Office: 350 Longwater Avenue, Green Park, Reading, Berks, RG2 6GF
Activities: Manufacture of electronic components
Parent: Thales Training & Simulation (Ace Holdings) Limited
Officers: Michael William Peter Seabrook, Secretary; Paul Andrew Jayne [1964] Finance Director; Stephen Francis McCann [1968] Managing Director; Jeremy Harold Standen [1957] Director

Thales Transport and Security Limited
Incorporated: 24 November 1995 *Employees:* 541
Net Worth Deficit: £44,082,000 *Total Assets:* £111,779,000
Registered Office: 350 Longwater Avenue, Green Park, Reading, Berks, RG2 6GF
Activities: Activities of head offices
Parent: Thales UK Limited
Officers: Michael William Peter Seabrook, Secretary; Andrew Richard Bell [1974] Director; Mark Stephen Garrity [1963] Director; James Neal Brindley Jackson [1982] Director; Shaun Kevin Jones [1966] Director; Paul Maynard [1969] Director

Thales UK Limited
Incorporated: 6 January 1966 *Employees:* 5,173
Net Worth: £214,434,000 *Total Assets:* £1,930,288,000
Registered Office: 350 Longwater Avenue, Green Park, Reading, Berks, RG2 6GF
Activities: Manufacture of electronic components
Parent: Thales Holdings UK PLC
Officers: Michael William Peter Seabrook, Secretary; Edwin Awang [1962] Director/Company Executive; Robert Nathaniel Baxter [1961] Director; Alexander David Beatty [1959] Director; Stuart Michael Boulton [1963] Director; Victor Manuel Chavez [1963] Director; Paul Gosling [1962] Director; Shaun Kevin Jones [1966] Director; Stephen Francis McCann [1968] Managing Director; Ewen Angus McCrorie [1958] Finance Director; Philip Martin Naybour [1960] Director; Denis Vincent Bernard Marie Plantier [1962] Director [French]; Suzanne Jayne Stratton [1972] Director; Ian Michael Waite [1962] Director; Lynne Watson [1967] Director; William Alvin Wilby [1958] Director; Gareth Williams [1976] Director

Thames Hospice
Incorporated: 20 December 2004 *Employees:* 232
Net Worth: £20,996,000 *Total Assets:* £21,862,000
Registered Office: Pine Lodge, Hatch Lane, Windsor, Berks, SL4 3RW
Activities: Medical nursing home activities
Officers: Ruth Bartholomew, Secretary; Christopher Grant Aitken [1951] Director/Trustee; Jacinta Mary Ashworth [1971] Director/Researcher; Kenneth Francis Coppock [1949] Director/Trustee; Jonathan Jones [1952] Director/Orthopaedic Surgeon; Andy Francis Yuk Ho Ka [1976] Director/Accountant; Dr Judith Kinder [1945] Director/Doctor; Craig David Linton [1978] Fundraising Director; Bruce Montgomery [1956] Director/Retired Consultant Urologist; Stephen John Moore [1969] Director/Trustee; Margaret Patricia Neal [1949] Director/Retired; Lesley Rudd [1947] Director/Retired Nurse

Thames Properties Ltd.
Incorporated: 2 December 1988
Net Worth: £46,987,732 *Total Assets:* £53,337,912
Registered Office: 6 Forge Lane, Petersham Road, Richmond, Surrey, TW10 7BF
Activities: Buying and selling of own real estate
Shareholders: Barbara Anderman; Margaret Ann Fruchter; Tessa Frances Goldstein
Officers: Margaret Ann Fruchter, Secretary/College Lecturer; Barbara Anderman [1948] Director/Professor; Margaret Ann Fruchter [1945] Director; Simon Maurice Fruchter [1976] Director/Property Developer; Tessa Frances Goldstein [1954] Director

Thames Water (Kemble) Finance PLC
Incorporated: 4 February 2011
Net Worth: £105,000 *Total Assets:* £590,460,032
Registered Office: Clearwater Court, Vastern Road, Reading, Berks, RG1 8DB
Activities: Other business support service activities n.e.c.
Parent: Kemble Water Finance Limited
Officers: Sonia Billett, Secretary; David Jonathan Hughes, Secretary; Tom Bolton [1980] Director/Head of Corporate Finance; Tonia Lewis [1974] Director/Group Financial Controller; Stephen Wheeler [1969] Director/Deputy Group Treasurer

Thames Water Investments Limited
Incorporated: 10 December 1990
Net Worth: £19,592,884 *Total Assets:* £20,643,620
Registered Office: Clearwater Court, Vastern Road, Reading, Berks, RG1 8DB
Activities: Development of building projects
Parent: Thames Water Limited
Officers: Sonia Billett, Secretary; David Jonathan Hughes, Secretary; David Jonathan Hughes [1967] Director/Company Secretary; Tonia Lewis [1974] Director/Group Financial Controller

Thames Water Limited
Incorporated: 1 April 1989
Net Worth: £2,175,099,904 *Total Assets:* £2,712,900,096
Registered Office: Clearwater Court, Vastern Road, Reading, Berks, RG1 8DB
Activities: Water collection, treatment and supply
Parent: Kemble Water Finance Limited
Officers: Sonia Billett, Secretary; David Jonathan Hughes, Secretary; Michael David Bloch-Hansen [1986] Associate Director [Canadian]; Kenton Edward Bradbury [1970] Director/Investment Professional; Stephen Alan John Deeley [1980] Director/Investment Manager; Jerry James Divoky [1966] Director/Portfolio Manager [Canadian]; Alastair Colin Hall [1982] Director/Investment Professional; Guy Lambert [1977] Director/Investment Professional [Dutch]; Emma Lewis [1979] Director/Investment Manager; Patrick Thomas Mulholland [1977] Director [Australian]; Perry Denis Noble [1960] Director/Alternate; Greg Pestrak [1971] Director/Executive Vice President; Christy Nghi Do Truong Pham [1977] Director/Alternate [Canadian]; Fuxin Sheng [1979] Director/Investment Professional [Chinese]; Tianxiao Song [1990] Director/Investment Professional [Chinese]; Giles John Julian Tucker [1960] Director/Principal

Thames Water Products Limited
Incorporated: 28 April 1988
Net Worth Deficit: £22,025,000 *Total Assets:* £22,153,000
Registered Office: Clearwater Court, Vastern Road, Reading, Berks, RG1 8DB
Activities: Manufacture of plastics and rubber machinery
Parent: Thames Water Limited
Officers: Sonia Billett, Secretary; David Jonathan Hughes [1967] Director/Company Secretary

Thames Water Utilities Finance PLC
Incorporated: 12 July 1989
Previous: Thames Water Utilities Finance Limited
Net Worth Deficit: £175,700,000 *Total Assets:* £2,981,100,032
Registered Office: Clearwater Court, Vastern Road, Reading, Berks, RG1 8DB
Activities: Financial intermediation not elsewhere classified
Parent: Thames Water Utilities Limited
Officers: Sonia Billett, Secretary; David Jonathan Hughes, Secretary; Mark Christopher Bamford [1975] Director/Group Financial Controller; Tom Bolton [1980] Director/Head of Corporate Finance; Stephen Wheeler [1969] Director/Deputy Group Treasurer

Thames Water Utilities Holdings Limited
Incorporated: 30 March 2007
Net Worth Deficit: £109,100,000 *Total Assets:* £4,369,299,968
Registered Office: Clearwater Court, Vastern Road, Reading, Berks, RG1 8DB
Activities: Activities of other holding companies n.e.c.
Parent: Thames Water Limited
Officers: Sonia Billett, Secretary; David Jonathan Hughes, Secretary; Michael David Bloch-Hansen [1986] Associate Director [Canadian]; Kenton Edward Bradbury [1970] Director/Investment Professional; Stephen Alan John Deeley [1980] Director/Investment Manager; Jerry James Divoky [1966] Director/Portfolio Manager [Canadian]; Alastair Colin Hall [1982] Director/Investment Professional; Guy Lambert [1977] Director/Investment Professional [Dutch]; Emma Lewis [1979] Director/Investment Manager; Patrick Thomas Mulholland [1977] Director [Australian]; Perry Denis Noble [1960] Director/Alternate; Greg Pestrak [1971] Director/Executive Vice President; Christy Nghi Do Truong Pham [1977] Director/Alternate [Canadian]; Fuxin Sheng [1979] Director/Investment Professional [Chinese]; Tianxiao Song [1990] Director/Investment Professional [Chinese]; Giles John Julian Tucker [1960] Director/Principal

Thames Water Utilities Limited
Incorporated: 1 April 1989 *Employees:* 5,421
Net Worth: £3,147,399,936 *Total Assets:* £18,003,200,000
Registered Office: Clearwater Court, Vastern Road, Reading, Berks, RG1 8DB
Activities: Water collection, treatment and supply
Parent: Thames Water Utilities Holdings Limited
Officers: Sonia Billett, Secretary; David Jonathan Hughes, Secretary; Lorraine Ingrid Baldry [1949] Director; Kenton Edward Bradbury [1970] Director/Investment Professional; Alistair Buchanan [1961] Director/Chartered Accountant; Christopher Richard Deacon [1947] Director/Independent Consultant; Nicholas Robert Fincham [1970] Director; Nicholas Charles Edward Land [1948] Director and Advisor; Catherine Susan Lynn [1964] Director/Aviation Advisor - Sole Trader; Ian Marchant [1961] Director/Chairman; John Victor Morea [1964] Director/Chief Executive Officer; Ian Phares Pearson [1959] Director; Gregory Pestrak [1971] Director/Executive Vice President; Brandon James Rennet [1972] Director/Chief Financial Officer; Edward Charles Richards [1965] Director; Stephen James Robertson [1958] Director/Chief Executive Officer; Jill Belinda Shedden [1965] HR Director; David Gogo Waboso [1956] Director/Chartered Engineer

Thanet Earth Holdings Limited
Incorporated: 19 September 2007 *Employees:* 169
Previous: Thanet Growers Eight Limited
Net Worth: £3,530,000 *Total Assets:* £25,128,000
Registered Office: The Packhouse, Barrow Man Road, Birchington, Kent, CT7 0AX
Activities: Wholesale of fruit and vegetables
Shareholder: Thanet Earth Investments Limited
Officers: Mark Huckstep, Secretary; Ian Alexander Craig [1957] Director; Arjan Johan de Gier [1969] Director/Grower [Dutch]; Wilhelmus Johannes Maria Grootscholten [1949] Director/Grower [Dutch]; Mark Huckstep [1973] Director/Accountant; Desmond Anthony Kingsley [1964] Director; Henricus Jozef Gerardus Marie Lambriex [1958] Director [Dutch]; Christopher Peter Mack [1955] Director

Thanet Earth Limited
Incorporated: 19 March 2007 *Employees:* 169
Previous: Thanet Earth Marketing Limited
Net Worth: £3,316,000 *Total Assets:* £25,242,000
Registered Office: The Packhouse, Barrow Man Road, Birchington, Kent, CT7 0AX
Activities: Wholesale of fruit and vegetables
Parent: Thanet Earth Holdings Limited
Officers: Mark Huckstep, Secretary; Ian Alexander Craig [1957] Director; Arjan Johan de Gier [1969] Director/Grower [Dutch]; Wilhelmus Johannes Maria Grootscholten [1949] Director/Grower [Dutch]; Mark Huckstep [1973] Director/Accountant; Desmond Anthony Kingsley [1964] Director; Henricus Jozef Gerardus Marie Lambriex [1958] Director [Dutch]; Christopher Peter Mack [1955] Director

Therakos (UK), Ltd
Incorporated: 9 October 2012 *Employees:* 23
Net Worth: £6,315,817 *Total Assets:* £26,275,732
Registered Office: 3 The Causeway, Lotus Park, Staines upon Thames, Middlesex, TW18 3AG
Activities: Activities of other holding companies n.e.c.
Parent: Mallinckrodt PLC
Officers: Paul Robert Coiante [1969] Director [American]; Thomas Joseph Englese [1974] Director [American]; Alasdair John Fenlon [1966] Director [Irish]; Christopher Hirt [1968] VP and Managing Director [German]; Gary James McCutcheon [1959] Finance Director

Theseus No. 1 Limited
Incorporated: 18 November 1994
Net Worth Deficit: £327,822,016 *Total Assets:* £339,864,000
Registered Office: Media House, Bartley Wood Business Park, Hook, Hants, RG27 9UP
Activities: Other business support service activities n.e.c.
Parent: Telewest Communications Cable Limited
Officers: Gillian Elizabeth James, Secretary; Robert Dominic Dunn [1966] Director/Chief Financial Officer; Mine Ozkan Hifzi [1966] Director/Solicitor

Theseus No. 2 Limited
Incorporated: 18 November 1994
Net Worth Deficit: £328,020,000 *Total Assets:* £339,665,984
Registered Office: Media House, Bartley Wood Business Park, Hook, Hants, RG27 9UP
Activities: Other business support service activities n.e.c.
Parent: Telewest Communications Cable Limited
Officers: Gillian Elizabeth James, Secretary; Robert Dominic Dunn [1966] Director/Chief Financial Officer; Mine Ozkan Hifzi [1966] Director/Solicitor

Thesis Unit Trust Management Limited
Incorporated: 6 February 1998
Net Worth: £11,084,049 *Total Assets:* £48,684,904
Registered Office: Exchange Building, St Johns Street, Chichester, W Sussex, PO19 1UP
Activities: Fund management activities
Parent: Thesis Asset Management Limited
Officers: Stephen Ronald Mugford [1966] Director/Accountant; Daniel Konrad Mytnik [1971] Director/Managing Partner of Ventiga Capital Partners LLP [Swedish]; Sarah Noone [1968] Client Services Director; Nicola Claire Palios [1967] Director/Self-Employed Management Consultant; Vincent Robert Smith [1958] Director/Private Equity Investor; David William Tyerman [1965] Director/Investment Manager

Think One Limited
Incorporated: 11 January 2013 *Employees:* 387
Net Worth: £8,493,903 *Total Assets:* £85,175,616
Registered Office: Chandlers BMW, Victoria Road, Portslade, Brighton, BN41 1YH
Activities: Sale of new cars and light motor vehicles
Officers: Darryl Michael Burman [1958] Director/Lawyer/VP and General Counsel [American]; Darren Guiver [1968] Director; Earl Julius Hesterberg [1953] Director [American]; Daniel James McHenry [1974] Finance Director; John Rickel [1961] Director [American]

The Thinking Schools Academy Trust
Incorporated: 27 August 2010 *Employees:* 944
Net Worth: £76,638,000 *Total Assets:* £91,073,000
Registered Office: The Thinking Schools Academy Trust, Park Crescent, Chatham, Kent, ME4 6NR
Activities: General secondary education
Officers: Lee Philip Miller, Secretary; Michael Robin Bailey [1945] Director/Retired; Annette Beard [1956] Director/Education Advisor; Stuart Rae Gardner [1974] Director/Headmaster; Peter Victor Martin [1954] Director/Business Consultant; Derek Morrison [1954] Director/Maintenance Manager; Gerard Newman [1958] Director/Auditor; Linda Randall [1950] Director/Consultant; Lee Malcolm Trimby [1969] Director/Financial Adviser

Thomas Homes Limited
Incorporated: 25 February 2003 *Employees:* 27
Net Worth: £30,507,872 *Total Assets:* £41,321,548
Registered Office: Arlington House, Curridge, Thatcham, Berks, RG18 9EF
Activities: Development of building projects
Shareholders: Christopher Anthony Shaw Brotherton; Tracey Ann Brotherton
Officers: James Simon Thomas, Secretary/Accountant; Christopher Anthony Shaw Brotherton [1965] Director/Surveyor; David Paul Skeet [1961] Director/Manager; Hugh Morton Thomas [1943] Director/Surveyor; James Simon Thomas [1974] Director/Accountant

Thompsons (UK) Holdings Limited
Incorporated: 3 August 2015 *Employees:* 235
Net Worth: £12,201,453 *Total Assets:* £22,517,220
Registered Office: Rutland Works, Vulcan Way, New Addington, Croydon, Surrey, CR9 0DE
Activities: Activities of head offices
Major Shareholder: Margaret Elizabeth Burton
Officers: Trevor David Russell, Secretary; Margaret Elizabeth Burton [1949] Director; Scott Leigh Burton [1974] Director; Simon Karl Shields [1973] Director; Patrick Allen Thomas [1946] Director [Irish]

Thorn Security Limited
Incorporated: 28 June 1962 *Employees:* 232
Net Worth: £32,056,000 *Total Assets:* £61,857,000
Registered Office: Security House, The Summit, Hanworth Road, Sunbury on Thames, Middlesex, TW16 5DB
Activities: Other manufacturing n.e.c.
Parent: Thorn Security Group Limited
Officers: Mark Ayre [1963] Finance Director; Moosa Farook Meah [1965] Director

Thorney Lane LLP
Incorporated: 16 July 2008
Net Worth: £31,351,044 *Total Assets:* £45,342,036
Registered Office: Thorney Business Park, Thorney Lane North, Iver, Bucks, SL0 9HF

Thornton Park (London) Limited
Incorporated: 13 October 2015
Previous: Parkside Clapham Limited
Net Worth Deficit: £411 *Total Assets:* £44,908,752
Registered Office: 30-34 North Street, Hailsham, E Sussex, BN27 1DW
Activities: Development of building projects
Parent: Parkside Clapham Holdings Limited
Officers: Rakan Abdulaziz Alfadl [1980] Director; Marcus John Williams [1981] Director; Roger David Williams [1943] Director

Thornton Properties Limited
Incorporated: 5 February 2009
Net Worth: £19,619,058 *Total Assets:* £25,253,648
Registered Office: 2-4 Ash Lane, Rustington, Littlehampton, W Sussex, BN16 3BZ
Activities: Other letting and operating of own or leased real estate
Major Shareholder: Michael John Holland
Officers: Michael John Holland [1947] Director

Thorntons Limited
Incorporated: 13 May 1921 *Employees:* 2,962
Previous: Thorntons PLC
Net Worth Deficit: £47,468,000 *Total Assets:* £125,707,000
Registered Office: 889 Greenford Road, Greenford, Middlesex, UB6 0HE
Activities: Manufacture of cocoa and chocolate confectionery
Parent: Ferholding UK Ltd
Officers: Tim John Shirley, Secretary; Salvatore Castelli [1971] Finance Director [Italian]; Pieraldo Oldano [1965] Managing Director [Italian]; Marco Pescarolo [1957] Director/Global Treasurer [Italian]

Three Rivers Property Investments Limited
Incorporated: 2 October 1984
Net Worth: £50,024,096 *Total Assets:* £51,317,440
Registered Office: Hawridge Place, Hawridge Common, Hawridge, Chesham, Bucks, HP5 2ZD
Activities: Other letting and operating of own or leased real estate
Parent: Church Cottage Investments Ltd
Officers: Carys Gadsden, Secretary; Carys Gadsden [1950] Director; Eric John Spencer Gadsden [1944] Director

Thrive Homes Finance PLC
Incorporated: 19 February 2014
Net Worth: £50,000 *Total Assets:* £135,878,000
Registered Office: Westside, London Road, Hemel Hempstead, Herts, HP3 9TD
Activities: Security dealing on own account
Officers: Shaun McLean, Secretary; Elspeth MacKenzie [1959] Director/Chief Executive; Shaun McLean [1970] Director and Company Secretary; Graham Leslie Olive [1965] Director/Deputy Chief Executive

Thursdays (Holdings) Limited
Incorporated: 4 November 1985
Previous: T.G.I. Friday Limited
Net Worth: £32,577,000 *Total Assets:* £42,550,000
Registered Office: Wey House, Farnham Road, Guildford, Surrey, GU1 4YD
Activities: Non-trading company
Parent: Wednesdays (Bidco) Limited
Officers: Karen Martha Forrester [1959] Director; Stuart Alan Greener [1962] Director

Thursdays (UK) Limited
Incorporated: 20 December 2006 *Employees:* 3,256
Previous: T.G.I. Friday's UK Limited
Net Worth: £98,866,000 *Total Assets:* £128,667,000
Registered Office: Wey House, Farnham Road, Guildford, Surrey, GU1 4YD
Activities: Licenced restaurants
Parent: Thursdays (Holdings) Limited
Officers: Karen Martha Forrester [1959] Managing Director; Stuart Alan Greener [1962] Director

TIG Acquisition Holdings
Incorporated: 16 October 2006
Net Worth: £85,517,904 *Total Assets:* £85,517,904
Registered Office: 1300 Parkway, Whiteley, Fareham, Hants, PO15 7AE
Activities: Activities of other holding companies n.e.c.
Parent: The Innovation Group Limited
Officers: Alasdair Marnoch [1963] Director

Tiger Group Limited
Incorporated: 5 April 2013
Previous: Caledonia Lion Limited
Net Worth: £2,089,000 *Total Assets:* £171,698,000
Registered Office: Glovers House, Glovers End, Bexhill on Sea, E Sussex, TN39 5ES
Activities: Activities of head offices
Parent: Tiger Bidco Ltd
Officers: Anthony Norman Clish [1961] Director; Alasdair Bell Loch [1963] Director/Chartered Accountant; Jeffrey Alan Sills [1963] Director; Richard Lewis Ullman [1973] Director

Tiger Midco 1 Limited
Incorporated: 26 August 2015
Net Worth Deficit: £76,133,000 *Total Assets:* £358,198,016
Registered Office: Yarmouth House, 1300 Parkway, Solent Business Park, Whiteley, Fareham, Hants, PO15 7AE
Activities: Activities of other holding companies n.e.c.
Parent: Tiger Topco Limited
Officers: Timothy Philip Griffiths [1960] Director/Chief Executive; Alasdair Marnoch [1963] Director; Gregory Mark Wood [1953] Director

Tiger Midco 2 Limited
Incorporated: 26 August 2015
Net Worth: £417,625,984 *Total Assets:* £417,625,984
Registered Office: Yarmouth House, 1300 Parkway, Solent Business Park, Whiteley, Fareham, Hants, PO15 7AE
Activities: Activities of other holding companies n.e.c.
Parent: Tiger Midco 1 Limited
Officers: Timothy Philip Griffiths [1960] Director; Alasdair Marnoch [1963] Director; Gregory Mark Wood [1953] Director

Tiger Topco 1 Limited
Incorporated: 28 November 2016 *Employees:* 1,017
Net Worth: £10,635,000 *Total Assets:* £541,753,024
Registered Office: Glovers House, Glovers End, Bexhill on Sea, E Sussex, TN39 5ES
Activities: Activities of other holding companies n.e.c.
Parent: Tiger VI Investments SARL
Officers: Anthony Norman Clish [1961] Director; Bernard Julien Coady [1979] Investment Director; Adrian John Fawcett [1968] Director; Gareth James Knight [1978] Director/Investment Banker; Alasdair Bell Loch [1963] Director; Simon James Edward Roddis [1968] Director; Jeffrey Alan Sills [1963] Director; Richard Lewis Ullman [1973] Director

Tiger Topco Limited
Incorporated: 26 August 2015 *Employees:* 3,419
Net Worth Deficit: £378,776,000 *Total Assets:* £590,934,976
Registered Office: Yarmouth House, 1300 Parkway, Solent Business Park, Whiteley, Fareham, Hants, PO15 7AE
Activities: Activities of other holding companies n.e.c.
Officers: Zeina Jalal Bain [1977] Director/Investment Professional; Andrew Richard Burgess [1964] Director/Investment Professional; Timothy Philip Griffiths [1960] Director; Alasdair Marnoch [1963] Director; Shaun Mercer [1980] Director/Investment Professional; Gregory Mark Wood [1953] Director

Tigers Logistics Group Limited
Incorporated: 11 June 2003
Net Worth: £18,707,230 *Total Assets:* £22,401,420
Registered Office: Unit 3b, Gatwick Metro Centre, Balcombe Road, Horley, Surrey, RH6 9GA
Activities: Activities of head offices
Officers: Clinton Smith [1969] Director; Man Yi Tam [1963] Human Resources Director [Chinese]

TIGI International Limited
Incorporated: 30 July 1996 *Employees:* 147
Net Worth Deficit: £5,702,556 *Total Assets:* £33,217,912
Registered Office: Unilever House, Springfield Drive, Leatherhead, Surrey, KT22 7GR
Activities: Hairdressing and other beauty treatment
Parent: TIGI Holdings Limited
Officers: James Oliver Earley, Secretary; Richard Clive Hazell, Secretary; Mark Bleathman [1969] Director/TIGI Global GM; Philip James Cheadle [1977] Director/General Manager TIGI Western Europe; Bijal Vikram Sheth [1970] Finance Director

Tilhill Forestry Limited
Incorporated: 27 August 1996 *Employees:* 187
Net Worth: £8,784,000 *Total Assets:* £33,755,000
Registered Office: Coffin Mew, 1000 Lakeside, North Harbour, Portsmouth, PO6 3EN
Activities: Silviculture and other forestry activities
Parent: BSW Timber Limited
Officers: Alan Graham Milne, Secretary; Gavin Paul Adkins [1970] Director; Iggy Dunn [1965] Director [Sri Lankan]; Anthony Malcolm Hackney [1958] Director; Timothy John Liddon [1957] Director; George Murray McRobbie [1954] Director/Chartered Forester; Alan Graham Milne [1982] Director/Accountant; Harry Christopher George Stevens [1968] Director; Peter Robert Amadeus Whitfield [1956] Director/Forestry

Tillotson Commercial Motors Limited
Incorporated: 17 May 1929
Net Worth Deficit: £18,650,000 *Total Assets:* £114,266,000
Registered Office: Hanson House, 14 Castle Hill, Maidenhead, Berks, SL6 4JJ
Activities: Activities of other holding companies n.e.c.
Parent: Hanson International Holdings Limited
Officers: Wendy Fiona Rogers, Secretary; Nicholas Arthur Dawe Benning-Prince [1974] Director/Chartered Accountant; Robert Charles Dowley [1972] Director/Chartered Accountant; Edward Alexander Gretton [1970] Director; Dr Carsten Matthias Wendt [1976] Director [German]

Tim Bidco 1 Limited
Incorporated: 7 February 2017
Net Worth: £31,305,000 *Total Assets:* £230,316,992
Registered Office: Origin One, 108 High Street, Crawley, W Sussex, RH10 1BD
Activities: Other service activities n.e.c.
Parent: Tim Holdco Limited
Officers: Dominic Antonio Binefa [1983] Director/Chartered Accountant; Andrew John Duncan [1962] Director/Chief Executive Officer; Simon Martin [1959] Director/Treasurer; Joerg Metzner [1985] Director/Investor [German]; Edouard Jean Charles Pillot [1977] Director/Investor [French]

Tim Holdco Limited
Incorporated: 7 February 2017
Net Worth: £229,468,992 *Total Assets:* £229,859,008
Registered Office: Origin One, 108 High Street, Crawley, W Sussex, RH10 1BD
Activities: Other service activities n.e.c.
Parent: Tim Midco Limited
Officers: Dominic Antonio Binefa [1983] Director/Chartered Accountant; Mattia Caprioli [1974] Director [Italian]; Andrew John Duncan [1962] Director/Chief Executive Officer; Joerg Metzner [1985] Director/Investor [German]; Edouard Jean Charles Pillot [1977] Director/Investor [French]

TIM Intermediateco Limited
Incorporated: 7 February 2017 *Employees:* 3,463
Net Worth: £234,500,000 *Total Assets:* £747,200,000
Registered Office: Origin One, 108 High Street, Crawley, W Sussex, RH10 1BD
Activities: Other service activities n.e.c.
Officers: Joerg Metzner [1985] Director/Investor [German]; Edouard Jean Charles Pillot [1977] Director/Investor [French]

Tim Midco Limited
Incorporated: 7 February 2017
Net Worth: £227,807,008 *Total Assets:* £227,807,008
Registered Office: Origin One, 108 High Street, Crawley, W Sussex, RH10 1BD
Activities: Other service activities n.e.c.
Parent: TIM Intermediateco Limited
Officers: Joerg Metzner [1985] Director/Investor [German]; Edouard Jean Charles Pillot [1977] Director/Investor [French]

Tindle Newspapers Limited
Incorporated: 31 March 1964 *Employees:* 28
Net Worth: £30,253,684 *Total Assets:* £34,429,744
Registered Office: Old Court House, Union Road, Farnham, Surrey, GU9 7PT
Activities: Activities of other holding companies n.e.c.
Major Shareholder: Raymond Stanley Tindle
Officers: Alastair James Manson, Secretary; Lady Beryl Julia Tindle, Secretary/Director; Danny Cammiade [1960] Director; Wendy Diane Craig [1944] Director/Vice Chairman; Lady Beryl Julia Tindle [1927] Director; Owen Charles Tindle [1956] Director/Chairman; Sir Raymond Stanley Tindle [1926] Director/Newspaper Proprietor

Tindle Press Holdings Limited
Incorporated: 10 November 2003 *Employees:* 575
Net Worth: £32,753,154 *Total Assets:* £37,237,612
Registered Office: The Old Court House, Union Road, Farnham, Surrey, GU9 7PT
Activities: Activities of other holding companies n.e.c.
Major Shareholder: Raymond Stanley Tindle
Officers: Alastair James Manson, Secretary; Lady Beryl Julia Tindle [1927] Director; Owen Charles Tindle [1956] Director/Chairman; Sir Raymond Stanley Tindle [1926] Director/Newspaper Proprietor

TJX Europe Buying Limited
Incorporated: 24 January 2011
Net Worth: £268,000 *Total Assets:* £55,088,000
Registered Office: 50 Clarendon Road, Watford, Herts, WD17 1TX
Activities: Other business support service activities n.e.c.
Parent: TJX UK
Officers: Alicia Colarte Kelly, Secretary; David Lawrence Averill [1967] SVP Corporate Tax Director [American]; John Joseph Klinger [1964] Director/SVP, Corporate Controller [American]; Mary Blier Reynolds [1955] Director/SVP Treasurer [American]

TJX Europe Limited
Incorporated: 18 August 1995
Net Worth: £207,720,992 *Total Assets:* £643,612,992
Registered Office: 50 Clarendon Road, Watford, Herts, WD17 1TX
Activities: Other retail sale of new goods in specialised stores (not commercial art galleries and opticians)
Parent: The TJX Companies, Inc.
Officers: Susan Beaumont, Secretary; Alicia Colarte Kelly, Secretary; Lisa Schwartz, Secretary; David Lawrence Averill [1967] SVP, Corporate Tax Director [American]; John Joseph Klinger [1964] Director/SVP, Corporate Controller [American]; Mary Blier Reynolds [1955] Director/SVP Treasurer [American]

TJX Germany Ltd.
Incorporated: 25 July 2013
Net Worth: £36,442,000 *Total Assets:* £36,500,000
Registered Office: 50 Clarendon Road, Watford, Herts, WD17 1TX
Activities: Activities of other holding companies n.e.c.
Parent: TJX Europe Limited
Officers: Susan Beaumont, Secretary; Alicia Colarte Kelly, Secretary; Lisa Schwartz, Secretary; David Lawrence Averill [1967] SVP, Corporate Tax Director [American]; John Joseph Klinger [1964] Director/SVP, Corporate Controller [American]; Mary Blier Reynolds [1955] Director/SVP, Treasurer [American]

TJX UK
Incorporated: 18 August 1995 *Employees:* 20,177
Net Worth: £645,600,000 *Total Assets:* £1,234,300,032
Registered Office: 50 Clarendon Road, Watford, Herts, WD17 1TX
Activities: Other retail sale of new goods in specialised stores (not commercial art galleries and opticians)
Parent: TJX Europe Limited
Officers: Susan Beaumont, Secretary; Alicia Colarte Kelly, Secretary; Lisa Schwartz, Secretary; David Lawrence Averill [1967] SVP Corporate Tax Director [American]; John Joseph Klinger [1964] Director/SVP, Corporate Controller [American]; Mary Blier Reynolds [1955] Director/SVP Treasurer [American]

TLC (Southern) Limited
Incorporated: 13 March 1990 *Employees:* 283
Net Worth: £23,548,820 *Total Assets:* £33,350,280
Registered Office: The TLC Building, Newton Road, Crawley, W Sussex, RH10 9TS
Activities: Wholesale of other intermediate products
Shareholders: Terence John Carr; Nigel Greenwood; Peter Charles West
Officers: Nigel Greenwood, Secretary; Terence John Carr [1951] Director; Nigel Greenwood [1957] Director; Robert Donald Gregor MacGregor [1962] Director/Electrical Wholesaler; Peter Charles West [1955] Director

Tokyo Electron Europe Limited
Incorporated: 27 April 1994 *Employees:* 338
Net Worth: £210,675,648 *Total Assets:* £644,873,792
Registered Office: Pioneer Building, Crawley Business Quarter, Fleming Way, Crawley, W Sussex, RH10 9QL
Activities: Installation of industrial machinery and equipment
Parent: Tokyo Electron Limited
Officers: Christopher Rayner Kelly, Secretary; David Copland Brough [1960] Managing Director; Toshiki Kawai [1963] Director [Japanese]; Tatsuya Nagakubo [1963] Director [Japanese]; Takeshi Okubo [1963] Director [Japanese]; Tetsuo Tsuneishi [1952] Director [Japanese]

Toll Investments (NA) Ltd
Incorporated: 25 March 2010
Net Worth: £77,613,328 *Total Assets:* £77,613,328
Registered Office: Australis House, Unit 2 Heron Way, Feltham, Middlesex, TW14 0AR
Activities: Activities of head offices
Parent: Japan Post Holdings Co. Ltd
Officers: Bruce James Chaplin [1976] Director [South African]; Mark Steven Kurzeja [1957] Director

Tombstone Limited
Incorporated: 21 December 1982
Net Worth: £49,861,532 *Total Assets:* £49,950,428
Registered Office: Hamilton House, 14 The Drive, Hove, E Sussex, BN3 3JA
Activities: Other letting and operating of own or leased real estate
Officers: Caroline Williams, Secretary; Alexander Sethi Hamilton [1988] Director/Financier; Britannia Eugenie Hamilton [1990] Director; Maximilian Rhett Hamilton [1985] Director/Financier; Richmond Louis Hamilton [1991] Director

Tonbridge School
Incorporated: 4 June 2003 *Employees:* 656
Net Worth: £25,358,278 *Total Assets:* £44,337,820
Registered Office: Tonbridge School, High Street, Tonbridge, Kent, TN9 1JP
Activities: General secondary education
Officers: Anthony Charles Moore, Secretary/Bursar; Timothy Michael Attenborough [1967] Director/Investment Banker; Desmond Philip Devitt [1950] Director/School Registrar; Matthew Frederick Dobbs [1959] Director/Fund Manager; Robert James Elliott [1952] Director/Solicitor; Professor Helena Frances Gaunt [1965] Director/College Principal; Sally-Anne Huang [1971] Director/Headteacher; Andrew Henry Mayer [1948] Director/Surveyor; Josephine Isabel Naismith [1957] Director; Gavin Mark Rochussen [1959] Director/Chief Executive; Dr Michael Stephen Spurr [1953] Education Director; Dr George Edward Taggart [1967] Director/General Practitioner; James William Graham Thompson [1979] Managing Director; Katharine Mary Wheadon [1965] Director/Underwriter; Graham Peter White [1955] Director; Earl Simon Frederick Woolton [1958] Director/Merchant Banker

Tonroe Group Limited
Incorporated: 23 July 2002 *Employees:* 98
Net Worth: £5,550,056 *Total Assets:* £38,496,136
Registered Office: Chalfont Park House, Chalfont Park, Gerrards Cross, Bucks, SL9 0DZ
Activities: Activities of head offices
Shareholders: Michael Aidan McDonnell; Jacqueline Wild
Officers: Jacqueline Wild, Secretary/Director; Michael Aidan McDonnell [1974] Director; Jacqueline Wild [1967] Director

Topps Europe Limited
Incorporated: 23 December 1991 *Employees:* 55
Net Worth Deficit: £16,543,446 *Total Assets:* £21,238,248
Registered Office: 18 Vincent Avenue, Crownhill Business Centre, Milton Keynes, Bucks, MK8 0AW
Activities: Printing n.e.c.
Parent: Topps Europe Holdings Limited
Officers: Stephen Hancock, Secretary; Michael Neil Brandstaedter [1970] Director/Chief Executive [American]; David Leiner [1983] Director/Global General Manager [American]

Toshiba Global Commerce Solutions (U.K.) Limited
Incorporated: 24 July 2012 *Employees:* 73
Net Worth Deficit: £11,942,470 *Total Assets:* £26,720,284
Registered Office: Abbey Cloisters, Abbey Green, Chertsey, Surrey, KT16 8RB
Activities: Other information technology service activities
Parent: TGCS Holdings Corporation
Officers: Valerie Anne Jacqueline Amand [1965] Director/Office Worker (Finance Operating Officer) [Belgian]; Toshiharu Higuchi [1969] Director/Office Worker [Japanese]; Adam Nicholas Sheppard [1961] Director/President & CEO Toshiba TEC Retail Operations

Toshiba Information Systems (UK) Limited
Incorporated: 19 October 1967 *Employees:* 11
Net Worth: £29,776,600 *Total Assets:* £37,230,544
Registered Office: Consort House, 1 Princes Road, Weybridge, Surrey, KT13 9TU
Activities: Wholesale of computers, computer peripheral equipment and software
Parent: Toshiba Corporation, Japan
Officers: Patrick Emmanuel Whelan, Secretary/Head of Legal Services [Irish]; Thomas Peter Cunliffe [1973] Director/Chief Operating Officer & Chief Financial Officer; Masato Kaneko [1970] Director [Japanese]; Hitoshi Otsuka [1958] Managing Director [Japanese]; Patrick Emmanuel Whelan [1971] Legal Director & Company Secretary [Irish]

Toshiba of Europe Limited
Incorporated: 13 November 1997 *Employees:* 51
Net Worth: £14,561,434 *Total Assets:* £318,844,928
Registered Office: 3 Furzeground Way, Stockley Park, Uxbridge, Middlesex, UB11 1EZ
Activities: Other business support service activities n.e.c.
Parent: Toshiba Corporation
Officers: Masato Kaneko [1970] Director [Japanese]; Hitoshi Otsuka [1958] Director [Japanese]; Takuya Tsukuda [1963] Director [Japanese]

Toshiba Tec U.K. Imaging Systems Limited
Incorporated: 13 December 2000 *Employees:* 286
Net Worth: £24,373,000 *Total Assets:* £43,535,000
Registered Office: Abbey Cloisters, Abbey Green, Chertsey, Surrey, KT16 8RB
Activities: Manufacture of other electrical equipment
Parent: Toshiba TEC Corporation
Officers: Martin Andrew Langridge, Secretary/Accountant; Martin Andrew Langridge [1963] Director/Chartered Accountant; Tatsuya Ogawa [1979] Deputy Managing Director [Japanese]; Adam Nicholas Sheppard [1961] Director; Toshiyasu Takahashi [1963] Director [Japanese]; Masayuki Takesue [1981] Director [Japanese]

Total Aircraft Product Support (Holdings) Limited
Incorporated: 9 May 2005 *Employees:* 69
Net Worth: £37,237,636 *Total Assets:* £86,094,720
Registered Office: Westley House, Fleming Way, Crawley, W Sussex, RH10 9GA
Activities: Service activities incidental to air transportation
Shareholders: Neil Anthony Westley; Mark Peter Westley
Officers: Jacqueline Westley, Secretary; Kevin Goodall [1956] Director; Gene Whitford Mashlan [1944] Director/Aviation Consultant [New Zealander]; Anthony Maurice Westley [1946] Managing Director; Mark Peter Westley [1975] Director; Neil Anthony Westley [1970] Director; Robert John Wilson [1942] Director/Chartered Accountant

Toucan Gen Co Limited
Incorporated: 16 November 2016
Net Worth: £185,603 *Total Assets:* £75,889,176
Registered Office: Mountbatten House, Grosvenor Square, Southampton, SO15 2JU
Activities: Activities of other holding companies n.e.c.
Parent: Toucan Energy Holdings Limited
Officers: Liam James Kavanagh [1977] Director/Investment Manager; Andrew Paul Williams [1964] Director/Chartered Accountant

Toucan Solar Assets 1 Holdco Limited
Incorporated: 16 May 2016
Net Worth Deficit: £4,226,537 *Total Assets:* £55,142,260
Registered Office: Mountbatten House, Grosvenor Square, Southampton, SO15 2JU
Activities: Activities of other holding companies n.e.c.
Parent: Toucan Solar Assets 1 Topco Limited
Officers: Andrew Paul Williams, Secretary; Liam James Kavanagh [1977] Director/Investment Manager; Andrew Paul Williams [1964] Director/Chartered Accountant

Toucan Solar Assets 2 Holdco Limited
Incorporated: 15 September 2016
Net Worth Deficit: £4,461,968 *Total Assets:* £70,416,288
Registered Office: Mountbatten House, Grosvenor Square, Southampton, SO15 2JU
Activities: Activities of other holding companies n.e.c.
Parent: Toucan Solar Assets 2 Topco Limited
Officers: Andrew Paul Williams, Secretary; Liam James Kavanagh [1977] Director/Investment Manager; Andrew Paul Williams [1964] Director/Chartered Accountant

The Tower, One St George Wharf Limited
Incorporated: 6 August 2002
Net Worth: £67,077,000 *Total Assets:* £201,730,000
Registered Office: Berkeley House, 19 Portsmouth Road, Cobham, Surrey, KT11 1JG
Activities: Construction of commercial buildings
Parent: The Berkeley Group PLC
Officers: Jared Stephen Philip Cranney, Secretary; Piers Martin Clanford [1970] Director; Mark Richard Elgar [1974] Director; Benjamin James Marks [1977] Director; Ian Antony Pearcey [1969] Director; Robert Charles Grenville Perrins [1965] Director; Anthony William Pidgley [1947] Director; Richard James Stearn [1968] Director

Towergate Insurance Limited
Incorporated: 22 December 2010 *Employees:* 470
Net Worth: £637,505,024 *Total Assets:* £1,327,869,056
Registered Office: Tower Gate House, Eclipse Park Sittingbourne Road, Maidstone, Kent, ME14 3EN
Activities: Activities of financial services holding companies
Parent: Ardonagh Finco PLC
Officers: Dean Clarke, Secretary; Clive Bouch [1961] Director; Matthieu Yann Arnaud Boulanger [1975] Director/Investment Manager; Patrick Noel Butler [1960] Director [Irish]; Diane Cougill [1963] Director/Chief Finance Officer; Aurelio Cusaro [1985] Director; Christine Elaine Dandridge [1956] Director; Vahe Alex Dombalagian [1973] Director/Private Equity [American]; Scot French [1970] Director [American]; Feilim Mackle [1967] Director [Irish]; Matthew William Raino [1978] Director [American]; David Christopher Ross [1969] Director [Irish]; John Ivan Tiner [1957] Director

Towergate Risk Solutions Limited
Incorporated: 28 March 2007
Net Worth: £36,288,220 *Total Assets:* £37,428,432
Registered Office: Towergate House, Eclipse Park, Sittingbourne Road, Maidstone, Kent, ME14 3EN
Activities: Non-life insurance
Parent: Towergate Insurance Limited
Officers: Dean Clarke, Secretary; Antonios Erotocritou [1971] Director/Deputy CFO [Cypriot]; David Christopher Ross [1969] Director [Irish]

Towergate Underwriting Group Limited
Incorporated: 31 July 2000 *Employees:* 2,547
Net Worth: £295,665,984 *Total Assets:* £494,864,992
Registered Office: Towergate House, Eclipse Park, Sittingbourne Road, Maidstone, Kent, ME14 3EN
Activities: Non-life insurance
Parent: Towergate Insurance Limited
Officers: Dean Clarke, Secretary; Antonios Erotocritou [1971] Director/Deputy CFO [Cypriot]; David Christopher Ross [1969] Director [Irish]

Towers Perrin Europe Limited
Incorporated: 15 October 2002
Net Worth: £131,741,000 *Total Assets:* £133,222,000
Registered Office: Watson House, London Road, Reigate, Surrey, RH2 9PQ
Activities: Activities of head offices
Parent: Towers Perrin UK Holdings Limited
Officers: Steven James Alcock [1979] Director

Towers Perrin UK Holdings Limited
Incorporated: 15 October 2002
Net Worth: £22,535,000 *Total Assets:* £23,994,000
Registered Office: Watson House, London Road, Reigate, Surrey, RH2 9PQ
Activities: Activities of head offices
Parent: Willis Group Limited
Officers: Steven James Alcock [1979] Director

Towers Watson Global 2 Limited
Incorporated: 22 March 2013
Net Worth: £403,237,184 *Total Assets:* £840,491,712
Registered Office: Watson House, London Road, Reigate, Surrey, RH2 9PQ
Activities: Activities of head offices
Parent: Willis Group Limited
Officers: Steven James Alcock [1979] Director

Towers Watson Global 3 Limited
Incorporated: 5 June 2013
Net Worth Deficit: £38,417,792 *Total Assets:* £394,667,456
Registered Office: Watson House, London Road, Reigate, Surrey, RH2 9PQ
Activities: Activities of head offices
Shareholders: Willis Group Limited; Towers Watson Global 2 Limited
Officers: Steven James Alcock [1979] Director

Towers Watson Limited
Incorporated: 1 March 2005 *Employees:* 3,040
Net Worth: £487,233,984 *Total Assets:* £770,336,000
Registered Office: Watson House, London Road, Reigate, Surrey, RH2 9PQ
Activities: Other professional, scientific and technical activities n.e.c.
Parent: Watson Wyatt (UK) Acquisitions 2 Limited
Officers: Marco Boschetti [1967] Director [Italian/British]; Edward James Francis [1971] Director; Tammy Marie Richardson [1967] Director/UK P&C Leader; Ingmar Rinck [1973] Director [Dutch]

Towers Watson Software Limited
Incorporated: 14 February 1997 *Employees:* 145
Net Worth: £61,447,696 *Total Assets:* £151,673,472
Registered Office: Watson House, London Road, Reigate, Surrey, RH2 9PQ
Activities: Other software publishing
Parent: Towers Watson Global 2 Limited
Officers: Joanna Maria Field, Secretary; John Duncan Anderson [1968] Director/Global Leader, Insurance Technology; Mark Simon Beardall [1967] Director/Chief Information Officer; Chad Patrick Daugherty [1970] Operations and Technology Managing Director [American/British]; Andrew Richard Lingard [1964] Director, Insurance Technology

Towers Watson UK Limited
Incorporated: 14 April 2009
Net Worth: £45,863,000 *Total Assets:* £45,887,000
Registered Office: Watson House, London Road, Reigate, Surrey, RH2 9PQ
Activities: Non-trading company
Parent: Towers Watson Limited
Officers: Steven James Alcock [1979] Director

Towry Finance Company Limited
Incorporated: 24 February 2006
Net Worth: £5,779,000 *Total Assets:* £214,524,992
Registered Office: The Observatory, Western Road, Bracknell, Berks, RG12 1TL
Activities: Activities of head offices
Parent: Towry Security Company Limited
Officers: Rehana Hasan, Secretary; Andrew Martin Baddeley [1964] Director; Donald William Sherret Reid [1959] Director/Chief Operating Officer; Christopher Woodhouse [1961] Director/Chief Executive Officer

Towry Group Limited
Incorporated: 18 December 2009
Net Worth: £59,740,000 *Total Assets:* £70,007,000
Registered Office: The Observatory, Western Road, Bracknell, Berks, RG12 1TL
Activities: Activities of head offices
Parent: TL JerseyCo Finance Limited
Officers: Rehana Hasan, Secretary; Andrew Martin Baddeley [1964] Director; Donald William Sherret Reid [1959] Director/Chief Operating Officer; Christopher Woodhouse [1961] Director/Chief Executive Officer

Towry Holdings Limited
Incorporated: 21 May 2003
Net Worth: £21,005,000 *Total Assets:* £22,134,000
Registered Office: The Observatory, Western Road, Bracknell, Berks, RG12 1TL
Activities: Activities of financial services holding companies
Parent: Towry Group Limited
Officers: Rehana Hasan, Secretary; Andrew Martin Baddeley [1964] Director; Lee John Dooley [1966] Director/Chief Commercial Officer; Alan William Edwards [1964] Director/Head of Investment Management: England; Paul Martin Fraser Frame [1972] Director/Head of Investment Management: Scotland; Donald William Sherret Reid [1959] Director/Chief Operating Officer; Christopher Woodhouse [1961] Director/Chief Executive Officer

Toyota (G.B.) PLC
Incorporated: 28 September 1967 *Employees:* 272
Net Worth: £14,392,000 *Total Assets:* £721,769,024
Registered Office: Great Burgh, Burgh Heath, Epsom, Surrey, KT18 5UX
Activities: Sale of new cars and light motor vehicles
Parent: Toyota Motor Corporation
Officers: Darren Paul Morris, Secretary; Matthew Peter Harrison [1968] Director/Chairman; Akito Takami [1967] Director [Japanese]; Paul Michael Van Der Burgh [1964] Director

Toyota Financial Services (UK) PLC
Incorporated: 26 September 1988 *Employees:* 405
Net Worth: £576,649,984 *Total Assets:* £6,119,365,120
Registered Office: Great Burgh, Burgh Heath, Epsom, Surrey, KT18 5UZ
Activities: Other credit granting n.e.c.
Parent: Toyota Financial Services Corporation
Officers: Rupert Charles Wentworth-Jessop, Secretary; Douglas Frank Gillies [1959] Managing Director; Yoshiyuki Hiramine [1973] Director [Japanese]; Ivo Josko Ljubica [1967] Director/Chief Executive Officer [Croatian]; Christian Ties Ruben [1967] Director/Chief Financial Officer [German]; Paul Michael Van Der Burgh [1964] Managing Director

Toyota Material Handling UK Limited
Incorporated: 2 August 1961 *Employees:* 874
Net Worth: £23,967,000 *Total Assets:* £340,287,008
Registered Office: 706 Stirling Road, Trading Estate, Slough, Berks, SL1 4SY
Activities: Agents involved in the sale of machinery, industrial equipment, ships and aircraft
Parent: Toyota Material Handling Europe AB
Officers: Liam Generald Spencer, Secretary; Nicholas James Duckworth [1965] Director; Matthias Fischer [1961] Director/President & CEO [German]; Liam Generald Spencer [1968] Director [Irish]

TP Group PLC
Incorporated: 29 January 1996 *Employees:* 201
Previous: Corac Group PLC
Net Worth: £40,118,000 *Total Assets:* £54,024,000
Registered Office: A2-1064 Cody Technology Park, Old Ively Road, Farnborough, Hants, GU14 0LX
Activities: Activities of head offices
Officers: Claire Louise Macpherson, Secretary; Philip Cartmell [1951] Director; Philip John Holland [1970] Director; Andrew Charles McCree [1957] Director; Derren Mark Stroud [1970] Director/Chief Financial Officer; Jeremy Carlisle Warner Allen [1955] Director

TP-Link UK Limited
Incorporated: 26 March 2010 *Employees:* 314
Net Worth: £2,311,000 *Total Assets:* £187,512,992
Registered Office: Units 2 & 3 Riverview, Cardiff Road, Reading, Berks, RG1 8EW
Activities: Other information technology service activities
Shareholders: Jianjun Zhao; Jiaxing Zhao
Officers: Chunlei Liu, Secretary; Jianjun Zhao [1968] Director [Chinese]

TRAD Hire & Sales Limited
Incorporated: 12 January 1998 *Employees:* 99
Net Worth: £33,305,510 *Total Assets:* £92,950,464
Registered Office: 1 Elmfield Park, Bromley, Kent, BR1 1LU
Activities: Other specialised construction activities n.e.c.
Major Shareholder: Mohamed Altrad
Officers: James Arthur Fassenfelt, Secretary; Dr Mohed Altrad [1948] Director [French]; James Arthur Fassenfelt [1975] Finance Director; Madame Isabelle Marie Andree Montfort Epouse Garcia [1966] Director [French]; Louis Marie Maurice Roger Huetz [1970] Director [French]; Desmond Anthony Moore [1956] Managing Director; Raymond Kennedy Neilson [1966] Director; John Paterson [1964] Director

TRAD Scaffolding Co.Limited
Incorporated: 17 November 1971 *Employees:* 304
Net Worth: £16,203,635 *Total Assets:* £22,854,960
Registered Office: 1 Elmfield Park, Bromley, Kent, BR1 1LU
Activities: Other specialised construction activities n.e.c.
Parent: TRAD Group Limited
Officers: James Arthur Fassenfelt, Secretary; Dr Mohed Altrad [1948] Director [French]; Gary Mark Checketts [1968] Divisional Director; James Arthur Fassenfelt [1975] Finance Director; Madame Isabelle Marie Andree Montfort Epouse Garcia [1966] Director [French]; Neil Stephen Garner [1963] Director; Rosalind Anne Howe [1970] Human Resources Director; Louis Marie Maurice Roger Huetz [1970] Director [French]; Steve Laurence Kearney [1961] Director/Safety, Health and Environment Manager; Peter McShane [1972] Director; Desmond Anthony Moore [1956] Director; Raymond Kennedy Neilson [1966] Director

Trade Sale Ltd
Incorporated: 10 November 1997 *Employees:* 4
Net Worth: £14,548,128 *Total Assets:* £62,124,796
Registered Office: Unit 8 West London Industrial Park, Iver Lane, Uxbridge, Middlesex, UB8 2JG
Activities: Sale of used cars and light motor vehicles
Major Shareholder: Fil Levi Gray
Officers: Fil Levi Gray [1958] Director

Tradebe Environmental Services Limited
Incorporated: 9 November 1999 *Employees:* 746
Net Worth: £10,652,000 *Total Assets:* £217,479,008
Registered Office: Atlas House, Third Avenue, Globe Park, Marlow, Bucks, SL7 1EY
Activities: Activities of other holding companies n.e.c.
Officers: Jordi Creixell, Secretary; Victor Creixell de Villalonga [1982] Director [Spanish]; Robin Randall [1958] Director

Tradebe Fawley Limited
Incorporated: 4 February 1993
Net Worth: £30,398,000 *Total Assets:* £36,464,000
Registered Office: Atlas House, Third Avenue, Globe Park, Marlow, Bucks, SL7 1EY
Activities: Treatment and disposal of hazardous waste
Parent: Tradebe Fawley Midco Limited
Officers: Jordi Creixell Sureda, Secretary; Victor Creixell de Villalonga [1982] Director [Spanish]; Robin Randall [1958] Director

Tradebe Management Limited
Incorporated: 12 February 2002
Net Worth Deficit: £33,900,000 *Total Assets:* £183,418,000
Registered Office: Atlas House, Third Avenue, Globe Park, Marlow, Bucks, SL7 1EY
Activities: Treatment and disposal of hazardous waste
Parent: Tradebe Environmental Services Limited
Officers: Jordi Creixell, Secretary; Victor Creixell de Villalonga [1982] Director [Spanish]; Robin Randall [1958] Director

Tradebe Solvent Recycling Limited
Incorporated: 8 December 1999
Net Worth: £21,159,000 *Total Assets:* £28,998,000
Registered Office: Atlas House, Third Avenue, Globe Park, Marlow, Bucks, SL7 1EY
Activities: Treatment and disposal of hazardous waste
Parent: Tradebe Environmental Services Limited
Officers: Jordi Creixell Sureda, Secretary; Victor Creixell de Villalonga [1982] Director [Spanish]; Robin Randall [1958] Director

Tradeteam Limited
Incorporated: 11 July 1995 *Employees:* 1,518
Net Worth: £28,996,000 *Total Assets:* £108,880,000
Registered Office: Ocean House, The Ring, Bracknell, Berks, RG12 1AN
Activities: Non-specialised wholesale of food, beverages and tobacco
Parent: Exel Holdings Limited
Officers: Lindsay Elizabeth Bridges [1969] Director [Irish]; Ian David Clough [1967] Director; Louise Miller [1968] Director/Accountant; Gavin John Murdoch [1967] Director

Trafalgar Entertainment Group Limited
Incorporated: 4 October 2016 *Employees:* 74
Net Worth: £18,999,000 *Total Assets:* £32,341,000
Registered Office: Ashcombe Court, Woolsack Way, Godalming, Surrey, GU7 1LQ
Activities: Activities of other holding companies n.e.c.
Officers: Helen Johnstone Enright, Secretary; Brian Gerard Egan [1985] Director [American]; Sir Howard Hugh Panter [1949] Director; Stephen Smith [1954] Director [American]; Rosemary Anne Squire [1956] Director; Alexander Thomson [1972] Director

Trafalgar Insurance Public Limited Company
Incorporated: 23 December 1907
Net Worth: £39,044,000 *Total Assets:* £46,897,000
Registered Office: 57 Ladymead, Guildford, Surrey, GU1 1DB
Activities: Non-life insurance
Parent: Allianz Insurance PLC
Officers: Robin Christian Jack-Kee, Secretary; Jonathan Mark Dye [1966] Director/Chief Executive; Simon Cavendish McGinn [1970] Director/General Manager Commercial & Personal

Trafficinvest Limited
Incorporated: 6 May 2016 *Employees:* 39
Net Worth: £13,781,325 *Total Assets:* £28,090,748
Registered Office: 1 Parkshot, Richmond, Surrey, TW9 2RD
Activities: Activities of other holding companies n.e.c.
Officers: Erik Langaker [1963] Director/Investment Professional [Norwegian]; Anders Christian Wilhelmsen [1987] Director/Investment Professional [Norwegian]; Oscar Alexander Garmann Wilhelmsen [1991] Director/Student [Norwegian]

Tranche 5 Limited
Incorporated: 8 November 2013
Net Worth Deficit: £1,715,169 *Total Assets:* £73,683,544
Registered Office: 2nd Floor, Edgeborough House, Upper Edgeborough Road, Guildford, Surrey, GU1 2BJ
Activities: Activities of head offices
Parent: Blackrock Renewables UK Limited
Officers: Achal Prakash Bhuwania [1979] Director; Peter George Raftery [1968] Director/Engineer; Jonathan Charles Smith [1980] Director; Stephane Christophe Tetot [1981] Director/Corporate Financier [French]

Trans Global Freight Management Limited
Incorporated: 11 August 1976 *Employees:* 187
Net Worth: £4,284,668 *Total Assets:* £37,289,880
Registered Office: Woodlands, 79 High Street, Greenhithe, Kent, DA9 9RD
Activities: Other transportation support activities
Parent: Trans Global Limited
Officers: Dilsher SEN, Secretary; Lee Andrew Bolsover [1966] Director/Freight Forwarder; David Carpentier [1972] Director/Information Technology Management [French]; Prasad Santosh Chogle [1972] Director/Freight Forwarder; Stephen Knight [1960] Director/Shipping Agent; Simon David Rawlinson [1967] Director/Freight Forwarder; Barry John Ruck [1959] Director; Dilsher SEN [1968] Director/Company Solicitor

Trans Global Limited
Incorporated: 31 December 1963 *Employees:* 231
Net Worth: £4,642,000 *Total Assets:* £37,490,000
Registered Office: Woodlands, 79 High Street, Greenhithe, Kent, DA9 9RD
Activities: Activities of head offices
Shareholder: Dunstan Trust Nominee Ltd
Officers: Dilsher SEN, Secretary/Lawyer; Subir Ranjan Dasgupta [1945] Director [Singaporean]; Kevin Leon Jones [1952] Director; Padam Kumar Khaitan [1953] Director/Advocate [Indian]; Stephen Knight [1960] Director; Barry John Ruck [1959] Director/Accountant; Suvamoy Saha [1958] Director [Indian]; Dilsher SEN [1968] Director

Trans Ocean Bulk Logistics Limited
Incorporated: 31 October 2006 *Employees:* 42
Net Worth: £54,796,544 *Total Assets:* £133,872,640
Registered Office: Trans Ocean House, Tollbar Way, Hedge End, Southampton, SO30 2UH
Activities: Other transportation support activities
Officers: Kevin William Fry, Secretary; Kevin William Fry [1967] Finance Director; Gavin Herman [1967] Director

Transaction Services Group Limited
Incorporated: 8 September 2015 *Employees:* 595
Net Worth: £134,594,032 *Total Assets:* £350,052,128
Registered Office: Rockwood House, Perrymount Road, Haywards Heath, W Sussex, RH16 3TW
Activities: Activities of other holding companies n.e.c.
Shareholders: Murray John Bolton; Robyn Jo-Anne Bolton
Officers: Guy Kent Bolton [1974] Director; Murray John Bolton [1948] Director [New Zealander]; James Thomas Farrell [1964] Director [American]; Brian Ford Fearnow [1977] Director [American]; Steven John Holmes [1979] Director [New Zealander]; Lawrence Ronald Margrain [1952] Director [New Zealander]; Craig Marshall [1958] Director [New Zealander]; Clyde Laurence Thomas [1952] Director [American]; Paul Francis Walsh [1949] Director [American]

Transeur Properties Limited
Incorporated: 25 February 2002
Net Worth: £9,388,332 *Total Assets:* £26,975,800
Registered Office: Overseas House, 66-68 High Road, Bushey Heath, Herts, WD23 1GG
Activities: Renting and operating of Housing Association real estate
Major Shareholder: Philip Nandwani
Officers: Philip Nandwani, Secretary; Gobind Hemandas Nandwani [1931] Director/Marketing Manager; Philip Nandwani [1963] Director/General Manager

Transform Housing & Support
Incorporated: 13 June 1972 *Employees:* 143
Previous: Surrey Community Development Trust
Net Worth: £20,369,000 *Total Assets:* £45,192,000
Registered Office: Bradmere House, Brook Way, Leatherhead, Surrey, KT22 7NA
Activities: Other accommodation
Officers: Ratna Sukumaran, Secretary; Mark Edward Austen [1949] Director; Jane Bolton [1957] Director; Christopher James Deacon [1954] Director/Management Consultant; Sally Ann Dubery [1964] Director/Charity Chief Executive; Lee Harris [1962] Director; Nickie Johnson [1984] Director; Robert William Mills [1969] Director; Christopher John Relleen [1948] Director; David John Turner [1936] Director

Transform Schools (Bassetlaw) Limited
Incorporated: 3 February 2005
Net Worth Deficit: £12,648,000 *Total Assets:* £84,582,000
Registered Office: 8 White Oak Square, London Road, Swanley, Kent, BR8 7AG
Activities: Other business support service activities n.e.c.
Parent: Transform Schools (Bassetlaw) Holdings Limited
Officers: Todd Malcolm Anderson [1980] Director/Accountant [New Zealander]; Christopher James [1968] Investment Director; Richard Keith Sheehan [1975] Investment Director

Transform Schools (Birmingham) Holdings Limited
Incorporated: 12 September 2005
Net Worth Deficit: £20,047,000 *Total Assets:* £80,415,000
Registered Office: 8 White Oak Square, London Road, Swanley, Kent, BR8 7AG
Activities: Activities of construction holding companies
Parent: Innisfree Schools (Secondary) Limited
Officers: Gaynor Birley-Smith [1966] Investment Director; Richard Keith Sheehan [1975] Investment Director

Transform Schools (Birmingham) Limited
Incorporated: 12 September 2005
Net Worth Deficit: £20,047,000 *Total Assets:* £80,415,000
Registered Office: 8 White Oak Square, London Road, Swanley, Kent, BR8 7AG
Activities: Development of building projects
Parent: Transform Schools (Birmingham) Holdings Limited
Officers: Gaynor Birley-Smith [1966] Investment Director; Richard Keith Sheehan [1975] Investment Director

Transform Schools (Knowsley) Holdings Limited
Incorporated: 29 May 2007
Net Worth Deficit: £39,047,000 *Total Assets:* £186,576,992
Registered Office: 8 White Oak Square, London Road, Swanley, Kent, BR8 7AG
Activities: Activities of other holding companies n.e.c.
Parent: PPDI Assetco Limited
Officers: Stephen Gordon [1962] Director; Roger Thompson [1954] Director

Transform Schools (Knowsley) Limited
Incorporated: 29 May 2007
Net Worth Deficit: £39,047,000 *Total Assets:* £186,576,992
Registered Office: 8 White Oak Square, London Road, Swanley, Kent, BR8 7AG
Activities: Other business support service activities n.e.c.
Parent: Transform Schools (Knowsley) Holdings Limited
Officers: Stephen Gordon [1962] Director; Roger Thompson [1954] Director

Transform Schools (North Lanarkshire) Funding PLC
Incorporated: 9 February 2005
Net Worth: £50,000 *Total Assets:* £175,468,992
Registered Office: 8 White Oak Square, London Road, Swanley, Kent, BR8 7AG
Activities: Financial intermediation not elsewhere classified
Parent: Transform Schools (North Lanarkshire) Holdings Limited
Officers: David John Brooking [1967] Investment Director; Robert Alistair Martin Gillespie [1990] Director/Financial Controller; Christopher James [1968] Investment Director; Kirsty O'Brien [1982] Director/Operations Manager

Transform Schools (North Lanarkshire) Holdings Limited
Incorporated: 16 February 2005
Net Worth: £8,004,000 *Total Assets:* £185,952,992
Registered Office: 8 White Oak Square, London Road, Swanley, Kent, BR8 7AG
Activities: Activities of head offices
Shareholders: Equitix Education 2 Limited; Innisfree Secondary Partners 2 LLP
Officers: David John Brooking [1967] Investment Director; Robert Alistair Martin Gillespie [1990] Director/Financial Controller; Christopher James [1968] Investment Director; Kirsty O'Brien [1982] Director/Operations Manager

Transform Schools (North Lanarkshire) Limited
Incorporated: 9 February 2005
Net Worth: £7,954,000 *Total Assets:* £185,952,992
Registered Office: 8 White Oak Square, London Road, Swanley, Kent, BR8 7AG
Activities: Other building completion and finishing
Parent: Transform Schools (North Lanarkshire) Holdings Limited
Officers: David John Brooking [1967] Investment Director; Robert Alistair Martin Gillespie [1990] Director/Financial Controller; Christopher James [1968] Investment Director; Kirsty O'Brien [1982] Director/Operations Manager

Transform Schools (Rotherham) Limited
Incorporated: 25 March 2003
Net Worth: £1,710,000 *Total Assets:* £95,697,000
Registered Office: 8 White Oak Square, London Road, Swanley, Kent, BR8 7AG
Activities: Other business support service activities n.e.c.
Parent: Transform Schools (Rotherham) Holdings Limited
Officers: Todd Malcolm Anderson [1980] Director/Accountant [New Zealander]; Christopher James [1968] Investment Director; Richard Keith Sheehan [1975] Investment Director

Transform Schools (Stoke) Holdings Limited
Incorporated: 22 September 2000
Net Worth Deficit: £2,416,000 *Total Assets:* £36,008,000
Registered Office: 8 White Oak Square, London Road, Swanley, Kent, BR8 7AG
Activities: Activities of construction holding companies
Parent: Innisfree Schools (F2C) Limited
Officers: David John Brooking [1975] Investment Director; Richard Keith Sheehan [1975] Investment Director

Transform Schools (Stoke) Limited
Incorporated: 22 September 2000
Net Worth Deficit: £2,416,000 *Total Assets:* £36,008,000
Registered Office: 8 White Oak Square, London Road, Swanley, Kent, BR8 7AG
Activities: Development of building projects
Parent: Transform Schools (Stoke) Holdings Limited
Officers: David John Brooking [1975] Investment Director; Richard Keith Sheehan [1975] Investment Director

Transport Research Foundation
Incorporated: 19 January 1995 *Employees:* 314
Net Worth Deficit: £5,548,000 *Total Assets:* £26,137,000
Registered Office: Crowthorne House, Nine Mile Ride, Wokingham, Berks, RG40 3GA
Activities: Other research and experimental development on natural sciences and engineering
Officers: Peter Millard, Secretary; Pauline Mason [1967] Employee Appointed Director; Stephen Parker [1953] Director; Charles James Rice [1953] Director/Logistics Production; Peter Van Campen [1961] Director [Canadian]; Robert Wallis [1964] Director; Craig Beresford Wilson [1964] Director

Transserv UK Limited
Incorporated: 30 October 2013
Net Worth: £13,142,693 *Total Assets:* £43,903,200
Registered Office: Rockwood House, Perrymount Road, Haywards Heath, W Sussex, RH16 3TW
Activities: Financial intermediation not elsewhere classified
Parent: TSG Holdings (UK) Limited
Officers: Roger Justin Bracken [1965] Director/General Manager; Steven John Holmes [1979] Director [New Zealander]

Trant Engineering Limited
Incorporated: 30 July 1963 *Employees:* 517
Net Worth: £8,671,000 *Total Assets:* £38,926,000
Registered Office: Rushington House, Rushington, Southampton, SO40 9LT
Activities: Construction of utility projects for electricity and telecommunications
Parent: Trant Holding Company Ltd
Officers: Timothy John Bullen [1967] Director/Mechanical & Electrical; Brendan Michael Dowd [1974] Director/Chartered Engineer [Irish]; James Alastair Henderson [1976] Director/Chartered Engineer; Sean Michael Jordan [1965] Director/Civil Engineer; Colin John Monaghan [1974] Director [Irish]; Alistair Graeme Parker [1969] Director/Civil Engineer; Gerry Somers [1960] Director/Civil Engineer [Irish]; Mark William Swallow [1963] Director/Quantity Surveyor; Patrick Murray Trant [1953] Director; Philip Francis Trant [1981] Director/Civil Engineer [Irish]; Simon Trant [1966] Director/Civil Engineer

Trant Holding Company Limited
Incorporated: 19 December 2013 *Employees:* 548
Net Worth: £17,590,000 *Total Assets:* £51,177,000
Registered Office: Rushington House, Rushington, Southampton, SO40 9LT
Activities: Activities of head offices
Officers: Gerry Somers [1960] Director/Civil Engineer [Irish]; Patrick Murray Trant [1953] Director; Philip Francis Trant [1981] Director/Engineer [Irish]; Simon Trant [1966] Director; Timothy Trant [1954] Director

Trapoc Limited
Incorporated: 12 June 2007
Net Worth: £68,680,000 *Total Assets:* £73,593,000
Registered Office: Acrey Fields, Woburn Road, Wootton, Beds, MK43 9EJ
Activities: Buying and selling of own real estate
Parent: TRPC Limited
Officers: Aaron Jayson Adair [1969] Director/Chief Executive Officer [American]; Jonathan David Canning [1972] Director/General Counsel; Gregory Depasquale [1968] Director/SVP, General Counsel and Secretary of Copart, Inc [American]; William Easley Franklin [1956] Director/Chief Financial Officer [American]; Nigel James Paget [1966] Managing Director; Simon Sheldon-Wilson [1969] Director; Paul Anthony Styer [1956] Director/General Counsel [American]

Travel Republic Holdings Ltd.
Incorporated: 20 June 2007
Net Worth: £26,314,000 *Total Assets:* £69,617,000
Registered Office: Clarendon House, 147 London Road, Kingston upon Thames, Surrey, KT2 6NH
Activities: Other business support service activities n.e.c.
Parent: Travel Technology Investments Limited
Officers: Iain Charles Richard Andrew [1965] Director; Asif Hamza Parkar [1974] Director/Finance Manager

Travel Republic Ltd
Incorporated: 1 August 2003 *Employees:* 352
Net Worth: £17,588,000 *Total Assets:* £118,592,000
Registered Office: Clarendon House, 147 London Road, Kingston upon Thames, Surrey, KT2 6NH
Activities: Travel agency activities
Parent: Dnata Travel Holdings UK Limited
Officers: Iain Charles Richard Andrew [1965] Director; John Constantine Bevan [1965] Director; Joshua Wilfrid Gubbay [1969] Director; Asif Hamza Parkar [1974] Director/Finance Manager; Frank Fouad Rejwan [1970] Director

Travel Technology Investments Limited
Incorporated: 16 June 2010
Net Worth: £23,877,000 *Total Assets:* £81,911,000
Registered Office: Clarendon House, 147 London Road, Kingston upon Thames, Surrey, KT2 6NH
Activities: Activities of head offices
Parent: Dnata World Travel Limited
Officers: Iain Charles Richard Andrew [1965] Director; Asif Hamza Parkar [1974] Director/Finance Manager

Travel Up Group PLC
Incorporated: 31 August 2014 *Employees:* 74
Net Worth: £3,827,088 *Total Assets:* £34,515,496
Registered Office: Unit 1 Zodiac House, Calleva Park, Aldermaston, Reading, Berks, RG7 8HN
Activities: Activities of other holding companies n.e.c.
Major Shareholder: Ali Shah
Officers: Ali Shah, Secretary; William Alexander O' Neill [1955] Director; Ali Shah [1977] Managing Director

Travel Up Limited
Incorporated: 6 May 2004 *Employees:* 74
Net Worth: £4,369,462 *Total Assets:* £35,034,504
Registered Office: Unit 1 Zodiac House, Calleva Park, Aldermaston, Reading, Berks, RG7 8HN
Activities: Travel agency activities
Major Shareholder: Ali Shah
Officers: Ayesha Shah, Company Secretary; Ali Shah [1977] Managing Director

Travelopia Holdings Limited
Incorporated: 13 September 2006 *Employees:* 36
Previous: TUI Travel SAS Holdings Limited
Net Worth: £209,405,248 *Total Assets:* £315,241,472
Registered Office: Origin One, 108 High Street, Crawley, W Sussex, RH10 1BD
Activities: Travel agency activities
Parent: Tim Bidco 1 Limited
Officers: Janet Northey, Secretary; Dominic Antonio Binefa [1983] Director/Chartered Accountant; Michael Edward Blakemore [1971] IT Director; Andrew John Duncan [1962] Director/Chief Executive Officer; Christine Franks [1972] Director/Chartered Accountant

Travelport (UK) Services Limited
Incorporated: 10 September 2004
Net Worth: £53,953,740 *Total Assets:* £76,916,552
Registered Office: Axis One, Axis Park, 10 Hurricane Way, Langley, Berks, SL3 8AG
Activities: Other business support service activities n.e.c.
Parent: Travelport Worldwide Limited
Officers: Helen Wenman, Secretary; Rochelle Jennifer Boas [1973] Director/Attorney [American]; Timothy James Hampton [1957] Director

Travelport Finance Limited
Incorporated: 7 July 2010
Net Worth: £66,655,928 *Total Assets:* £307,008,992
Registered Office: Axis One, Axis Park, 10 Hurricane Way, Langley, Berks, SL3 8AG
Activities: Other business support service activities n.e.c.
Parent: Travelport Group Investments Limited
Officers: Helen Wenman, Secretary; Rochelle Jennifer Boas [1973] Director/Attorney [American]; Timothy James Hampton [1957] Director; Peter Brian Russell [1968] Director

Travelport Global Limited
Incorporated: 28 May 2014
Net Worth: £301,520,640 *Total Assets:* £2,526,378,240
Registered Office: Axis One, Axis Park, 10 Hurricane Way, Langley, Berks, SL3 8AG
Activities: Activities of other holding companies n.e.c.
Parent: Travelport Group Investments Limited
Officers: Helen Wenman, Secretary; Timothy James Hampton [1957] Director; Peter Brian Russell [1968] Director

Travelport Group Investments Limited
Incorporated: 30 March 2015
Net Worth: £71,484,560 *Total Assets:* £1,307,796,480
Registered Office: Axis One, Axis Park, 10 Hurricane Way, Langley, Berks, SL3 8AG
Activities: Activities of other holding companies n.e.c.
Parent: Travelport Worldwide Limited
Officers: Helen Wenman, Secretary; Rochelle Jennifer Boas [1973] Director/Attorney [American]; Timothy James Hampton [1957] Director/Head of Tax; Peter Brian Russell [1968] Director

Travelport Holdings (UK) Limited
Incorporated: 29 November 2012
Net Worth: £33,219,964 *Total Assets:* £37,226,724
Registered Office: Axis One, Axis Park, 10 Hurricane Way, Langley, Berks, SL3 8AG
Activities: Activities of other holding companies n.e.c.
Parent: Travelport Worldwide Limited
Officers: Helen Wenman, Secretary; Rochelle Jennifer Boas [1973] Director/Attorney [American]; Timothy James Hampton [1957] Director; Peter Brian Russell [1968] Director

Travelport International Limited
Incorporated: 15 April 1976 *Employees:* 658
Net Worth: £78,667,000 *Total Assets:* £144,884,000
Registered Office: Axis One, Axis Park, 10 Hurricane Way, Langley, Berks, SL3 8AG
Activities: Other reservation service activities n.e.c.
Parent: Travelport Global Limited
Officers: Helen Wenman, Secretary; Jason Robert Clarke [1969] President and Managing Director Europe & Brazil; Timothy James Hampton [1957] Director

Travelport International Operations Limited
Incorporated: 11 August 2015
Net Worth: £516,407,264 *Total Assets:* £894,539,392
Registered Office: Axis One, Axis Park, 10 Hurricane Way, Langley, Berks, SL3 8AG
Activities: Activities of other holding companies n.e.c.
Parent: Travelport International Management Limited
Officers: Helen Wenman, Secretary; Rochelle Jennifer Boas [1973] Director/Attorney [American]; Jason Robert Clarke [1969] Managing Director; Timothy James Hampton [1957] Director

Travelport Operations Limited
Incorporated: 29 May 2014
Net Worth: £2,436,069,376 *Total Assets:* £2,469,649,408
Registered Office: Axis One, Axis Park, 10 Hurricane Way, Langley, Berks, SL3 8AG
Activities: Activities of other holding companies n.e.c.
Parent: Travelport Global Limited
Officers: Helen Wenman, Secretary; Timothy James Hampton [1957] Director; Peter Brian Russell [1968] Director

Travelport Travel Commerce Platform Limited
Incorporated: 3 June 2014
Net Worth: £230,407,696 *Total Assets:* £1,721,926,528
Registered Office: Axis One, Axis Park, 10 Hurricane Way, Langley, Berks, SL3 8AG
Activities: Activities of other holding companies n.e.c.
Parent: Travelport Group Investments Limited
Officers: Helen Wenman, Secretary; Timothy James Hampton [1957] Director; Peter Brian Russell [1968] Director

Treasury Wine Estates EMEA Limited
Incorporated: 26 September 1986 *Employees:* 113
Net Worth: £110,482,000 *Total Assets:* £205,760,000
Registered Office: Regal House, 70 London Road, Twickenham, Middlesex, TW1 3QS
Activities: Manufacture of wine from grape
Officers: Michelle Elizabeth Brampton [1972] Finance Director; Richard John Renwick [1969] Director/Chief Financial Officer Europe

Treasury Wine Estates UK Brands Limited
Incorporated: 25 February 2011
Net Worth: £92,093,024 *Total Assets:* £92,878,672
Registered Office: 9th Floor, Regal House, 70 London Road, Twickenham, Middlesex, TW1 3QS
Activities: Manufacture of wine from grape
Parent: FBL Holdings Limited
Officers: Michelle Elizabeth Brampton [1972] Finance Director; Richard John Renwick [1969] Director/Chief Financial Officer Europe

Trek Bicycle Corporation Limited
Incorporated: 6 March 1989 *Employees:* 85
Net Worth: £13,877,319 *Total Assets:* £25,287,584
Registered Office: 9 Sherbourne Drive, Tilbrook, Milton Keynes, Bucks, MK7 8HX
Activities: Retail sale of sports goods, fishing gear, camping goods, boats and bicycles
Parent: Trek Bicycle Corporation
Officers: Jennifer Lee Naeger, Secretary; Chad Robert Brown [1978] Director/Finance [American]; John Burke [1962] Director/President [American]; Jennifer Lee Naeger [1978] Director [American]

Trek Investco Limited
Incorporated: 12 May 1999
Net Worth: £8,482,265 *Total Assets:* £21,376,324
Registered Office: Origin One, 108 High Street, Crawley, W Sussex, RH10 1BD
Activities: Other business support service activities n.e.c.
Parent: Travelopia Holdings Limited
Officers: Martin James Froggatt [1969] Director; Richard William Isaacs [1975] Director/Accountant

Trellis Acquisitions Limited
Incorporated: 20 December 2011
Net Worth Deficit: £165,554,000 *Total Assets:* £610,833,984
Registered Office: Wyevale Garden Centres, Syon Park, London Road, Brentford, Middlesex, TW8 8JF
Activities: Activities of other holding companies n.e.c.
Parent: Trellis Investments Limited
Officers: Laura Harradine-Greene, Secretary; Charlotte Broadbent [1990] Director; Alexander Rupert Gavin [1954] Director; Anthony Generald Jones [1973] Director; Justin Matthew King [1961] Director

Trellis Finance Limited
Incorporated: 9 February 2012 *Employees:* 6,290
Net Worth: £71,927,000 *Total Assets:* £422,680,000
Registered Office: Wyevale Garden Centres, Syon Park, London Road, Brentford, Middlesex, TW8 8JF
Activities: Activities of other holding companies n.e.c.
Parent: Trellis Holdco Limited
Officers: Laura Harradine-Greene, Secretary; Charlotte Broadbent [1990] Director; Anthony Generald Jones [1973] Director; Justin Matthew King [1961] Director

Trellis Holdco Limited
Incorporated: 9 February 2012
Net Worth Deficit: £97,384,000 *Total Assets:* £189,350,000
Registered Office: Wyevale Garden Centres, Syon Park, London Road, Brentford, Middlesex, TW8 8JF
Activities: Activities of other holding companies n.e.c.
Parent: Wyevale Garden Centres Capital Limited
Officers: Laura Harradine-Greene, Secretary; Charlotte Broadbent [1990] Director; Anthony Generald Jones [1973] Director; Justin Matthew King [1961] Director

Trellis Investments Limited
Incorporated: 9 February 2012 *Employees:* 6,290
Net Worth: £120,332,000 *Total Assets:* £422,860,992
Registered Office: Wyevale Garden Centres, Syon Park, London Road, Brentford, Middlesex, TW8 8JF
Activities: Activities of other holding companies n.e.c.
Parent: Trellis Finance Limited
Officers: Laura Harradine-Greene, Secretary; Charlotte Broadbent [1990] Director; Anthony Generald Jones [1973] Director; Justin Matthew King [1961] Director

Treloar Trust
Incorporated: 20 June 2002 *Employees:* 597
Net Worth: £28,133,000 *Total Assets:* £40,499,000
Registered Office: Treloar Trust, Powell Drive, Holybourne, Alton, Hants, GU34 4GL
Activities: Primary education
Officers: Anthony John Reid, Secretary; Alexander Claud Stuart Allan [1951] Director/Civil Servant; James Graham Dingwall Bateson [1961] Director/Solicitor; Michael John Chadwick [1953] Director/Retired; Jane Lesley Cooke [1948] Director; Rhys Calvin Iley [1971] Director; Alistair Angus Mackintosh [1963] Director/Investment Manager; David Victor Matthews [1961] Director/Company Executive; Brian McNamara [1966] Director/Chief Executive Officer [American]; Christine Ann Slaymaker [1958] Director/Retired

Trenchard Aviation Group Limited
Incorporated: 13 October 2015
Net Worth: £1 *Total Assets:* £38,609,824
Registered Office: Unit 2a, Gatwick Gate, Charlwood Road, Lowfield Heath, Crawley, W Sussex, RH11 0TG
Activities: Service activities incidental to air transportation
Parent: Trenchard Aviation Holdings 1 Limited
Officers: Bryan Harvey Bodek [1953] Director; Steven Lindsay Cloran [1964] Director; Mark Carl Faulkner [1962] Director

Trenchard Aviation Holdings 1 Limited
Incorporated: 12 October 2015
Net Worth Deficit: £983,591 *Total Assets:* £39,133,680
Registered Office: Unit 2a, Gatwick Gate, Charlwood Road, Lowfield Heath, Crawley, W Sussex, RH11 0TG
Activities: Service activities incidental to air transportation
Parent: Trenchard Aviation Holdings Limited
Officers: Bryan Bodek [1954] Director; Steven Lindsay Cloran [1964] Director; Mark Carl Faulkner [1962] Director

Trenchard Aviation Holdings Limited
Incorporated: 7 October 2015 *Employees:* 364
Net Worth Deficit: £20,291,300 *Total Assets:* £34,763,996
Registered Office: Unit 2a, Gatwick Gate, Charlwood Road, Lowfield Heath, Crawley, W Sussex, RH11 0TG
Activities: Service activities incidental to air transportation
Shareholder: Steven Lindsay Cloran
Officers: Bryan Harvey Bodek [1953] Director; Steven Lindsay Cloran [1964] Director; Mark Carl Faulkner [1961] Director

Trenchard Aviation Limited
Incorporated: 14 October 2015 *Employees:* 20
Net Worth Deficit: £5,912,746 *Total Assets:* £50,345,828
Registered Office: Unit 2a, Gatwick Gate, Charlwood Road, Lowfield Heath, Crawley, W Sussex, RH11 0TG
Activities: Service activities incidental to air transportation
Parent: Trenchard Aviation Group Limited
Officers: Bryan Harvey Bodek [1953] Director; Lee James Butterfield [1974] Director; Steven Lindsay Cloran [1964] Director; Mark Carl Faulkner [1962] Director; Neil Andrew Watkins [1965] Director

Trend Control Systems Limited
Incorporated: 16 September 1982 *Employees:* 309
Net Worth: £35,772,000 *Total Assets:* £169,760,000
Registered Office: Honeywell House, Skimped Hill Lane, Bracknell, Berks, RG12 1EB
Activities: Manufacture of electronic components
Parent: Novar Limited
Officers: Madeleine Orbell-Thompson [1976] Director/Chartered Accountant; Andrew Justin Paddock [1965] Director

Trescal Limited
Incorporated: 9 June 2008 *Employees:* 467
Net Worth: £970,462 *Total Assets:* £23,153,244
Registered Office: Saxony Way, Blackbushe Business Park, Yateley, Hants, GU46 6GT
Activities: Other professional, scientific and technical activities n.e.c.
Officers: Guillaume Philippe Bruno Caroit [1973] Director/General Secretary [French]; Olivier Marc Philippe Delrieu [1965] Director [French]; James Andrew Evans [1964] Director/General Manager; Jean-Philippe Gelbert Maury [1960] Director [French]; Robin Barry Hastie [1964] Director/Trescal UK General Manager

Trevellyan Developments Limited
Incorporated: 20 February 1980 *Employees:* 118
Net Worth: £63,626,824 *Total Assets:* £117,325,632
Registered Office: Estate Management Office, Greenhills Estate, Tilford Road, Tilford, Surrey, GU10 2DZ
Activities: Development of building projects
Major Shareholder: Lance John Philip Trevellyan
Officers: Lance John Philip Trevellyan, Secretary; Alexandra Hilary Trevellyan [1959] Director; Lance John Philip Trevellyan [1953] Director; Lewis Derek Trevellyan [1988] Director/Management

Tricomm Housing (Portsmouth) Limited
Incorporated: 18 May 2005
Net Worth Deficit: £8,737,449 *Total Assets:* £51,347,824
Registered Office: 8 White Oak Square, London Road, Swanley, Kent, BR8 7AG
Activities: Development of building projects
Parent: Tricomm Housing (Portsmouth) Holdings Limited
Officers: Neeti Mukundrai Anand [1984] Director; Stewart Chalmers Grant [1951] Director; Adam George Waddington [1974] Investment Director

Trident Acquisition Limited
Incorporated: 29 October 2014
Net Worth: £217,573 *Total Assets:* £96,172,688
Registered Office: Highfield Court, Tollgate, Chandler's Ford, Eastleigh, Hants, SO53 3TY
Activities: Dormant company
Officers: Stephen Howard Faberman [1969] Director [American]; Brian Flanagan [1961] Director [American]

Tridonic UK Limited
Incorporated: 13 September 1966 *Employees:* 211
Net Worth: £16,748,000 *Total Assets:* £31,482,000
Registered Office: 7 Lindenwood, Chineham Business Park, Crockford Lane, Chineham, Basingstoke, Hants, RG24 8LB
Activities: Manufacture of electric lighting equipment
Parent: Tridonic Holding GmbH
Officers: Simon Steele, Secretary; Alexander Jankovsky [1974] Director/Chief Operating Officer [Austrian]; Joerg Kessler [1964] Director/SVP Global Sales and Marketing [German]; Richard Charles Strode [1964] Director

Trifast Overseas Holdings Limited
Incorporated: 1 December 1994
Net Worth: £26,319,000 *Total Assets:* £54,421,000
Registered Office: Trifast House, Bellbrook Park, Uckfield, E Sussex, TN22 1QW
Activities: Non-trading company
Parent: Trifast PLC
Officers: Lyndsey Case, Secretary; Mark Belton [1969] Director; Clare Foster [1974] Director

Trifast PLC
Incorporated: 6 June 1985 *Employees:* 1,216
Net Worth: £110,289,000 *Total Assets:* £188,656,000
Registered Office: Trifast House, Bellbrook Park, Uckfield, E Sussex, TN22 1QW
Activities: Non-trading company
Officers: Lyndsey Case, Secretary; Mark Belton [1969] Director/Company Secretary; Malcolm McDonald Diamond [1948] Director; Clare Foster [1974] Director; Scott MacMeekin [1958] Director [Singaporean]; Glenda Christina Roberts [1950] Director; Jonathan Paul David Shearman [1970] Director; Neil William Warner [1953] Senior Independent Non-Executive Director

Tristmire Limited
Incorporated: 7 February 1995
Net Worth: £15,295,904 *Total Assets:* £28,489,294
Registered Office: Unit 7 Horizon Business Village, 1 Brooklands Road, Weybridge, Surrey, KT13 0TJ
Activities: Development of building projects
Officers: Sandra Joanne Brownlie, Secretary; Lauren Atkins [1976] Director/Manager; Malcolm Paul Atkins [1952] Director/Property Developer

Tritoria UK Ltd
Incorporated: 23 February 2016
Net Worth: £60,047,560 *Total Assets:* £60,103,044
Registered Office: 9 Greyfriars Road, Reading, Berks, RG1 1NU
Activities: Activities of other holding companies n.e.c.
Shareholders: Jan Lindstad; Oivind Lindstad
Officers: Jan Lindstad [1961] Director [Norwegian]; John Samuel Savage [1977] Director/Engineer; Louis Peter Van AS [1984] Director/General Manager

Triumph Aerospace Operations UK, Ltd.
Incorporated: 27 October 1961
Previous: Truimph Aerospace Operations UK, Ltd.
Net Worth Deficit: £53,184,360 *Total Assets:* £117,256,144
Registered Office: 21 Invincible Road, Farnborough, Hants, GU14 7QU
Activities: Manufacture of air and spacecraft and related machinery
Parent: Triumph Group Inc.
Officers: Jennifer Helen Allen [1972] Director/Senior Vice President, General Counsel & Secretary [American]; Daniel Joseph Crowley [1963] Director/President and CEO of Triumph Group Inc [American]; Frank Dubey [1963] Director/EVP, Integrated Systems [French]; Peter Andrew Fowler [1967] Director; James Francis McCabe Jr [1963] Director [American]; Peter Karl Allen Wick [1969] Director/Executive Vice President, Precision Components [British/American]

TRL Limited
Incorporated: 29 December 1995 *Employees:* 312
Net Worth Deficit: £5,264,000 *Total Assets:* £26,507,000
Registered Office: Crowthorne House, Nine Mile Ride, Wokingham, Berks, RG40 3GA
Activities: Other research and experimental development on natural sciences and engineering
Parent: Transport Research Foundation
Officers: Peter Millard, Secretary; Peter Van Campen [1961] Director [Canadian]; Robert Wallis [1964] Director/Chief Executive

Trochair Limited
Incorporated: 10 March 1930
Net Worth: £2,365,000 *Total Assets:* £26,068,000
Registered Office: 5 Queensway, Croydon, Surrey, CR9 4DL
Activities: Other letting and operating of own or leased real estate
Officers: Paul Stuart Gaff, Secretary; Alberto Fasanotti [1974] Finance Director [Italian]; Martin Hamilton [1953] Company Secretary/Solicitor/Director; Steven Antony Wright [1980] Director/Accountant

Tropicana United Kingdom Limited
Incorporated: 23 January 1991 *Employees:* 3
Net Worth: £5,535,000 *Total Assets:* £50,739,000
Registered Office: 450 South Oak Way, Green Park, Reading, Berks, RG2 6UW
Activities: Retail sale of beverages in specialised stores
Parent: Pepsico, Inc.
Officers: Holly King, Secretary; Joanne Kerry Averiss [1963] Director/VP Law; Andrew John MacLeod [1962] Director/Solicitor; Claire Ellen Stone [1969] Finance Director

Try Homes Limited
Incorporated: 1 May 1991
Net Worth: £27,414,000 *Total Assets:* £27,716,000
Registered Office: Cowley Business Park, Cowley, Uxbridge, Middlesex, UB8 2AL
Activities: Construction of commercial buildings
Parent: Linden Holdings Limited
Officers: Kevin Allan Corbett [1960] Director/Solicitor; Andrew James Duxbury [1975] Director/Accountant

TSG Holdings (UK) Limited
Incorporated: 10 September 2015
Net Worth: £132,434,640 *Total Assets:* £166,970,592
Registered Office: Rockwood House, Perrymount Road, Haywards Heath, W Sussex, RH16 3TW
Activities: Activities of other holding companies n.e.c.
Parent: Transaction Services Group Limited
Officers: Roger Justin Bracken [1965] Director/Chief Executive Officer; Steven John Holmes [1979] Director [New Zealander]

TSL Limited
Incorporated: 23 July 2002 *Employees:* 98
Previous: TSL Projects Limited
Net Worth: £4,700,472 *Total Assets:* £33,886,424
Registered Office: Chalfont Park House, Chalfont Park, Gerrards Cross, Bucks, SL9 0DZ
Activities: Engineering design activities for industrial process and production
Parent: Tonroe Group Limited
Officers: Jacqueline Wild, Secretary/Director; Michael Aidan McDonnell [1974] Director; Jacqueline Wild [1967] Director

TT Electronics Group Holdings Limited
Incorporated: 4 April 1935
Previous: A.B. Electronic Products Group Limited
Net Worth: £104,779,000 *Total Assets:* £222,830,000
Registered Office: Fourth Floor, St Andrews House, West Street, Woking, Surrey, GU21 6EB
Activities: Activities of head offices
Parent: TT Electronics PLC
Officers: Lynton David Boardman, Secretary; Lynton David Boardman [1967] Director/Solicitor; Mark Hoad [1970] Director; Christopher Adrian Jewell [1964] Director; Timothy Hal Roberts [1970] Director

TT Electronics IoT Solutions Limited
Incorporated: 14 January 1929 *Employees:* 648
Previous: Stadium Group Limited
Net Worth: £22,453,000 *Total Assets:* £57,442,000
Registered Office: Fourth Floor, St Andrews House, West Street, Woking, Surrey, GU21 6EB
Activities: Manufacture of other electrical equipment
Parent: TT Electronics PLC
Officers: Lynton David Boardman, Secretary; Rohit Jain [1980] Director/Group Finance Executive; Stewart Mark Partridge [1970] Director/VP Procurement; Charles St John Stewart Peppiatt [1970] Director

TT Electronics PLC
Incorporated: 16 January 1906 *Employees:* 4,137
Net Worth: £266,800,000 *Total Assets:* £364,600,000
Registered Office: Fourth Floor, St Andrews House, West Street, Woking, Surrey, GU21 6EB
Activities: Activities of head offices
Officers: Lynton David Boardman, Secretary; Michael John Baunton [1951] Director; Jack Byron Boyer [1959] Director; Neil Andrew Patrick Carson [1957] Director; Mark Hoad [1970] Director; Mr Stephen Anthony King [1960] Director; John Richard Tyson [1970] Director; Alison Jane Wood [1963] Director

TTG Investments Limited
Incorporated: 24 February 1984
Net Worth: £10,610,000 *Total Assets:* £155,038,000
Registered Office: Fourth Floor, St Andrews House, West Street, Woking, Surrey, GU21 6EB
Activities: Other business support service activities n.e.c.
Parent: TT Electronics PLC
Officers: Lynton David Boardman, Secretary; Lynton David Boardman [1967] Director/Solicitor; Mark Hoad [1970] Director; Timothy Hal Roberts [1970] Director

TTNG Investments Limited
Incorporated: 26 November 2015 *Employees:* 90
Net Worth: £4,215,723 *Total Assets:* £49,877,500
Registered Office: 2 Crown Square, Woking, Surrey, GU21 6HR
Activities: Activities of other holding companies n.e.c.
Major Shareholder: Gary Innes Lewis
Officers: Lisa Kerrie Henning [1979] Director; Gary Innes Lewis [1970] Managing Director Travel Industry; Sl Jake Morris [1982] Director; Vim Vithaldas [1967] Director

Tubifoam Limited
Incorporated: 29 April 1960
Net Worth: £222,775,008 *Total Assets:* £222,840,992
Registered Office: 103-105 Bath Road, Slough, Berks, SL1 3UH
Activities: Other manufacturing n.e.c.
Parent: SSL Products Limited
Officers: Christine Anne-Marie Logan, Secretary; Richard Mark Greensmith [1973] Group Tax Director; Jonathan Timmis [1975] Finance Director

Tudor Holdings (UK) Limited
Incorporated: 11 December 2013 *Employees:* 215
Net Worth: £12,213,937 *Total Assets:* £31,437,104
Registered Office: 71 New Dover Road, Canterbury, Kent, CT1 3DZ
Activities: Activities of other holding companies n.e.c.
Shareholders: Colin Graham Furneaux; Garry Ian Furneaux
Officers: Colin Graham Furneaux, Secretary; Colin Graham Furneaux [1953] Director/Chartered Accountant; Dennis Colin Furneaux [1929] Director/Motor Engineer; Garry Ian Furneaux [1967] Director/Motor Engineer; Roland Geoffrey Ambrose Furneaux [1982] Director/Chartered Accountant

Tuesdays (Midco) Limited
Incorporated: 9 December 2014 *Employees:* 4
Net Worth Deficit: £38,091,000 *Total Assets:* £141,940,000
Registered Office: Wey House, Farnham Road, Guildford, Surrey, GU1 4YD
Activities: Licenced restaurants
Parent: Mondays (Topco) Limited
Officers: Karen Martha Forrester [1959] Director; Stuart Alan Greener [1962] Director; Gavin Maxwell Manson [1966] Director/Chartered Accountant

Tuskerdirect Limited
Incorporated: 25 October 1999 *Employees:* 171
Net Worth: £26,149,160 *Total Assets:* £185,849,040
Registered Office: Building 4, Hatters Lane, Croxley Green Business Park, Watford, Herts, WD18 8YF
Activities: Renting and leasing of cars and light motor vehicles
Parent: Hamsard 3353 Limited
Officers: Laura Catherine Elizabeth Alexander [1979] Director/Chief Financial Officer; Clive Andrew Whistler Baker [1974] Director [British/South African]; Simon English [1960] Director; Paul Gilshan [1975] Director

TUV SUD (UK) Limited
Incorporated: 15 July 1996
Net Worth: £25,965,000 *Total Assets:* £35,398,000
Registered Office: Octagon House, Concorde Way, Segensworth North, Fareham, Hants, PO15 5RL
Activities: Non-trading company
Officers: William John McKnight, Secretary; Brian Sergio Austin [1960] Director/Chief Executive; Peter Maurice Crystal [1948] Director/Solicitor; William John McKnight [1962] Director/Chartered Accountant; Christoph Schipper [1966] Director [German]

TVH Fizzy Holdings Limited
Incorporated: 21 March 2012
Net Worth Deficit: £1,923,000 *Total Assets:* £26,628,000
Registered Office: Premier House, 52 London Road, Twickenham, Middlesex, TW1 3RP
Activities: Other letting and operating of own or leased real estate
Officers: Patricia Etter, Secretary; Guy John Burnett [1969] Group Development Director; Ian Roderick Johnson [1965] Finance Director; Nicholas John Lloyd [1967] Director/Head of Keyworker Rented Housing; Kush Rawal [1982] Commercial Director

TW Metals Limited
Incorporated: 28 August 1969 *Employees:* 196
Net Worth: £45,544,000 *Total Assets:* £68,520,000
Registered Office: Majestic Road, Nursling Estate, Nursling, Southampton, SO16 0AF
Activities: Wholesale of metals and metal ores
Shareholder: Henry Craft O'Neal
Officers: Christopher John Lewis, Secretary; Michael Arthur Rowland, Secretary; Henry Craft O'Neal [1961] Director/Chairman [American]; Kirk Elwood Moore [1962] Director [American]; Gail Lisa Thomas [1962] Managing Director

TWE Finance (UK) Limited
Incorporated: 31 January 2011
Net Worth: £3,446,432 *Total Assets:* £60,580,812
Registered Office: 9th Floor, Regal House, London Road, Twickenham, Middlesex, TW1 3QS
Activities: Manufacture of wine from grape
Parent: Treasury Wine Estates EMEA Limited
Officers: Michelle Elizabeth Brampton [1972] Finance Director; Richard John Renwick [1969] Director/Chief Financial Officer Europe

TWG Europe Limited
Incorporated: 27 May 2009 *Employees:* 345
Net Worth: £126,431,000 *Total Assets:* £519,175,008
Registered Office: Twenty Kingston Road, Staines upon Thames, Surrey, TW18 4LG
Activities: Activities of financial services holding companies
Parent: Assurant, Inc.
Officers: Natalie Ann Paddock, Secretary; George Derek Wilson Bartlett [1948] Director; Michael John Carter [1981] Director; Colin Martin Kersley [1956] Director; Ricardo Jesus Morales-Gomez [1970] Director [American]; Andrew James Morris [1971] Director/Chief Executive; Claude Kwasi Sarfo-Agyare [1969] Director

TWG Services Limited
Incorporated: 6 February 1985 *Employees:* 344
Net Worth: £1,556,000 *Total Assets:* £73,476,000
Registered Office: Twenty Kingston Road, Staines upon Thames, Surrey, TW18 4LG
Activities: Activities of insurance agents and brokers
Parent: TWG Europe Limited
Officers: Natalie Ann Paddock, Secretary; George Derek Wilson Bartlett [1948] Director; Michael John Carter [1981] Director; Colin Martin Kersley [1956] Director; Ricardo Jesus Morales-Gomez [1970] Director [American]; Andrew James Morris [1971] Director/Chief Executive Officer; Claude Kwasi Sarfo-Agyare [1969] Director

Twickenham Experience Ltd
Incorporated: 13 April 2000 *Employees:* 18
Net Worth: £40,696,000 *Total Assets:* £53,160,000
Registered Office: Rugby House, Twickenham Stadium, 200 Whitton Road, Twickenham, Middlesex, TW2 7BA
Activities: Event catering activities
Shareholders: Compass Services (UK) Limited; Rugby Football Union
Officers: Angus Roch Bujalski, Secretary; Robert Thomas Johnson Briers [1951] Director/Retired; Susan Margaret Day [1972] Director/Chief Financial Officer; Michael Andrew Jones [1982] Finance Director; Simon Edwin Massie-Taylor [1980] Director/Chief Commercial Officer; Helen Alison Weir [1962] Independent Director

Ty Danjuma Family Office Limited
Incorporated: 15 June 2009 *Employees:* 9
Net Worth: £72,400,000 *Total Assets:* £91,351,000
Registered Office: 1st Floor, Two Furlongs, Esher, Surrey, KT10 9AA
Activities: Activities auxiliary to financial intermediation n.e.c.
Major Shareholder: Theophilus Yakubu Danjuma
Officers: Gloria Amina Atta [1971] Executive Director [Nigerian]; Daniel Pontoppidan Broby [1964] Director; Theophilus Yakubu Danjuma [1938] Director/Retired [Nigerian]; Simon Miles Foster [1968] Director/Chief Executive Officer; Hannatu Kizeya Gentles [1975] Director/Chief Operating Officer; Dipankar Shewaram [1973] Director/Asset Management Banking & Finance

TY Properties (UK) Limited
Incorporated: 12 February 2010 *Employees:* 4
Net Worth: £38,902,000 *Total Assets:* £49,173,000
Registered Office: 1st Floor, Two Furlongs, Esher, Surrey, KT10 9AA
Activities: Buying and selling of own real estate
Parent: Ty Danjuma Family Office Limited
Officers: Theophilus Danjuma [1985] Director [Nigerian]; Simon Miles Foster [1968] Director/Accountant; Hannatu Kizeya Gentles [1975] Director/Family Officer

Tyco Building Services Products (UK) Limited
Incorporated: 15 November 1990 *Employees:* 74
Net Worth Deficit: £2,770,000 *Total Assets:* £35,127,000
Registered Office: Security House, The Summit, Hanworth Road, Sunbury on Thames, Middlesex, TW16 5DB
Activities: Non-specialised wholesale trade
Parent: Johnson Controls International PLC
Officers: Mark Ayre [1963] Finance Director; Laurens Swennenhuis [1965] Managing Director [Dutch]

Tyco Fire Products Manufacturing Limited
Incorporated: 16 August 1984 *Employees:* 175
Net Worth: £68,420,000 *Total Assets:* £84,488,000
Registered Office: Security House, The Summit, Hanworth Road, Sunbury on Thames, Middlesex, TW16 5DB
Activities: Non-specialised wholesale trade
Parent: Tyco European Metal Framing Limited
Officers: Joseph Paul Harvey-Nimmo [1978] Manufacturing Operations Director; Mark James MacMichael [1966] Director; Damien Morris [1960] Director

Tyrolese (751) Limited
Incorporated: 14 December 2012 *Employees:* 159
Net Worth: £5,455,091 *Total Assets:* £45,411,928
Registered Office: Excel House, Cray Avenue, Orpington, Kent, BR5 3ST
Activities: Activities of head offices
Major Shareholder: Malcolm Charles Elster
Officers: Malcolm Charles Elster [1957] Director

U K Land Ltd.
Incorporated: 8 April 1991 *Employees:* 10
Net Worth: £48,891,168 *Total Assets:* £61,847,744
Registered Office: 3-4 Faulknor Square, Charnham Street, Hungerford, Berks, RG17 0EP
Activities: Buying and selling of own real estate
Officers: George Gordon Nottage Palmer, Secretary; Simon Andrew Camamile [1955] Director/Chartered Surveyor; James Richard Grace [1957] Director/Consultant; Jennifer Ellen Kidston [1980] Director; Rupert George Martyn Spice [1979] Director; Christopher Colin Tett [1946] Director; Henry George MacRae Tett [1982] Director/Racehorse Trainer; Victoria Roselle Tett [1955] Director

UB Overseas Limited
Incorporated: 13 May 1980
Net Worth: £1,216,610,048 *Total Assets:* £1,367,154,048
Registered Office: Hayes Park, Hayes End Road, Hayes, Middlesex, UB4 8EE
Activities: Activities of head offices
Parent: United Biscuits (Holdings) Limited
Officers: Mark Oldham, Secretary/Director; Helen Josephine McCarthy [1966] Director; Mark Oldham [1959] Director

Ubisoft Limited
Incorporated: 28 July 1989 *Employees:* 41
Net Worth: £15,561,000 *Total Assets:* £37,321,000
Registered Office: 3rd Floor, Ranger House, Walnut Tree Close, Guildford, Surrey, GU1 4UL
Activities: Publishing of computer games
Parent: Ubisoft Entertainment
Officers: Yves Marie Remy Guillemot [1960] Director [French]

UCB (Investments) Limited
Incorporated: 4 April 1973
Net Worth: £986,990,976 *Total Assets:* £987,009,984
Registered Office: 208 Bath Road, Slough, Berks, SL1 3WE
Activities: Activities of head offices
Officers: Mark Glyn Hardy, Secretary; Dan Coombes [1975] Area Head, British & Irish Isles (Managing Director); Mark Glyn Hardy [1953] Director/Solicitor; Yogesh Khatri [1965] Director/Head of Finance and Administration

UCB Pharma Limited
Incorporated: 24 November 1925 *Employees:* 193
Net Worth: £88,308,000 *Total Assets:* £141,030,000
Registered Office: 208 Bath Road, Slough, Berks, SL1 3WE
Activities: Manufacture of basic pharmaceutical products
Parent: Celltech Group Limited
Officers: Mark Glyn Hardy, Secretary; Willy Constant Cnops [1961] Director/Head of EMEA Operations [Belgian]; Dan Coombes [1975] Area Head, British & Irish Isles (Managing Director); Mark Glyn Hardy [1953] Director/Solicitor; Yogesh Khatri [1965] Director/Head of Finance and Administration; Steven Craig Price [1969] Director, Financial Control UK & Ireland

UCC Coffee UK Limited
Incorporated: 28 August 1987 *Employees:* 515
Net Worth: £35,989,268 *Total Assets:* £66,925,424
Registered Office: 2 Bradbourne Drive, Tilbrook, Milton Keynes, Bucks, MK7 8AT
Activities: Non-specialised wholesale trade
Parent: UCC Europe Ltd
Officers: Anthony Jessup, Secretary; Patrick David Cooke [1947] Director; Anthony Jessup [1977] Director; Elaine Swift [1967] Director; Marcus Richard Swift [1970] Director; Laura Turrell [1976] Director; Seisuke Ueshima [1973] Director [Japanese]

UK Acquisitions No. 6 Limited
Incorporated: 15 September 2014 *Employees:* 6,268
Net Worth: £394,376,000 *Total Assets:* £892,033,984
Registered Office: Nepicar House, London Road, Wrotham Heath, Sevenoaks, Kent, TN15 7RS
Activities: Hospital activities
Parent: Universal Health Services Inc.
Officers: Steve Filton, Secretary; Steve Filton [1957] Director/Finance [American]; Mark George Ground [1970] Director; Laurence Harrod [1956] Director/Finance [American]; Dr Antonio Romero [1971] Director [Spanish]; Robert Zurad [1958] Director/Treasurer [American]

UK Assistance Accident Repair Centres Limited
Incorporated: 13 December 1990
Net Worth: £50,241,000 *Total Assets:* £80,181,000
Registered Office: Churchill Court, Westmoreland Road, Bromley, Kent, BR1 1DP
Activities: Maintenance and repair of motor vehicles
Parent: Direct Line Insurance Group PLC
Officers: Roger Cheston Clifton, Secretary; Cormac Bradley [1973] Director [Irish]; Jessie Burrows [1968] Director; Stuart Robert Forrester [1970] Director of Legal Services and Claims; Steven Maddock [1968] Director/Bank Official; Paul Nightingale [1964] Director; Helen Clare O'Murchu [1967] Director

UK Broadband Limited
Incorporated: 27 March 2003
Net Worth: £35,234,284 *Total Assets:* £52,781,064
Registered Office: Star House, 20 Grenfell Road, Maidenhead, Berks, SL6 1EH
Activities: Wireless telecommunications activities
Parent: Hutchison 3G UK Limited
Officers: Edith Shih, Secretary; Graham Curtis Baxter [1966] Director/Chief Operating Officer; David Richard Dyson [1970] Director/Chief Executive Officer; Darren Martin Purkis [1972] Director/Chief Financial Officer; Christian Nicolas Roger Salbaing [1950] Director [French]; Frank John Sixt [1951] Director [Canadian]; Richard Callum Woodward [1972] Director/Chief Financial Officer

UK Cables Limited
Incorporated: 29 June 1993 *Employees:* 78
Net Worth: £9,342,000 *Total Assets:* £25,421,000
Registered Office: Votec House, Hambridge Lane, Newbury, Berks, RG14 5TN
Activities: Non-specialised wholesale trade
Parent: Newbury Investments (UK) Ltd
Officers: Leo Yu, Secretary; Nigel John Palmer [1956] Director/Chairman; Steven Westbrook [1956] Director/Chief Executive; Leo Yu [1984] Director

UK Electric Limited
Incorporated: 21 August 1992 *Employees:* 260
Net Worth: £29,159,000 *Total Assets:* £53,052,000
Registered Office: Votec House, Hambridge Lane, Newbury, Berks, RG14 5TN
Activities: Non-specialised wholesale trade
Parent: Newbury Investments (UK) Ltd
Officers: Leo Yu, Secretary; Nigel John Palmer [1956] Director/Chairman; Steven Westbrook [1956] Director/Chief Executive; Leo Yu [1984] Director

UK Highways A55 (Holdings) Limited
Incorporated: 20 July 1998
Net Worth: £22,878,000 *Total Assets:* £92,167,000
Registered Office: 8 White Oak Square, London Road, Swanley, Kent, BR8 7AG
Activities: Activities of other holding companies n.e.c.
Parent: JLIF (Holdings) A55 Limited
Officers: David Richard Bradbury [1969] Director/Senior Investment Manager; Johannes Petrus Heemelaar [1956] Director [Dutch]

UK Highways A55 Limited
Incorporated: 20 July 1998
Net Worth: £22,881,000 *Total Assets:* £92,167,000
Registered Office: 8 White Oak Square, London Road, Swanley, Kent, BR8 7AG
Activities: Construction of roads and motorways
Parent: UK Highways A55 (Holdings) Limited
Officers: David Richard Bradbury [1969] Director/Senior Investment Manager; Johannes Petrus Heemelaar [1956] Director [Dutch]

UK Highways M40 (Holdings) Limited
Incorporated: 16 June 1994
Net Worth: £1,491,000 *Total Assets:* £105,969,000
Registered Office: 8 White Oak Square, London Road, Swanley, Kent, BR8 7AG
Activities: Other business support service activities n.e.c.
Shareholders: Palio (No. 7) Limited; Semperian Subholdings M40 Limited
Officers: David Richard Bradbury [1969] Director/Senior Investment Manager; Ian Richard Gethin [1971] Director/Investment Banker; Johannes Petrus Heemelaar [1956] Director [Dutch]; Neil Rae [1971] Director

UK Highways M40 Limited
Incorporated: 12 April 1995
Net Worth: £1,326,000 *Total Assets:* £105,964,000
Registered Office: 8 White Oak Square, London Road, Swanley, Kent, BR8 7AG
Activities: Other business support service activities n.e.c.
Officers: David Richard Bradbury [1969] Director/Senior Investment Manager; Ian Richard Gethin [1971] Director/Investment Banker; Johannes Petrus Heemelaar [1956] Director [Dutch]; Neil Rae [1971] Director

UK Mail Group Limited
Incorporated: 16 March 1993
Previous: UK Mail Group PLC
Net Worth: £24,509,000 *Total Assets:* £24,509,000
Registered Office: 120 Buckingham Avenue, Slough, SL1 4LZ
Activities: Activities of head offices
Parent: Deutsche Post AG
Officers: Peter Stanley Fuller [1964] Director/Chief Executive; Peter Michael Krohn [1957] Finance Director [Danish]; Scott Laird [1982] Director/Vice President - Operations; Albert Christopher Mangham [1964] Director

UK Software Holdings Limited
Incorporated: 2 October 2006
Net Worth: £49,300,000 *Total Assets:* £49,512,000
Registered Office: Epicor Software UK Limited, No 1 The Arena, Downshire Way, Bracknell, Berks, RG12 1PU
Activities: Activities of other holding companies n.e.c.
Officers: Dawn Murray, Secretary; Richard John Clark [1964] Director/Accountant; Timothy Bernard Harrington [1955] Director/Finance VP [Irish]; John David Ireland [1962] Director/Attorney [American]

UK Waste Management Limited
Incorporated: 12 April 1978
Net Worth: £151,243,008 *Total Assets:* £198,639,008
Registered Office: Coronation Road, Cressex, High Wycombe, Bucks, HP12 3TZ
Activities: Collection of non-hazardous waste
Parent: UK Waste Management Holdings Limited
Officers: Richard Neil Pike [1969] Director/Chief Financial Officer; Michael Robert Mason Topham [1972] Director/Chief Executive Officer

Ultima Business Solutions Ltd.
Incorporated: 12 July 1990 *Employees:* 391
Net Worth: £5,644,953 *Total Assets:* £32,987,508
Registered Office: Gainsborough House, Manor Farm Road, Reading, Berks, RG2 0NA
Activities: Other information technology service activities
Major Shareholder: Max Seddon McNeill
Officers: Jennifer Hall, Secretary/Finance Manager; Peter Scott MacDonald Dodds [1963] Director; Jennifer Hall [1970] Finance Director; Max Seddon McNeill [1962] Director/Chairman; Robin John Shuff [1950] Services Director

Ultra Electronics Holdings PLC
Incorporated: 25 June 1993 *Employees:* 4,172
Net Worth: £512,172,000 *Total Assets:* £1,083,816,960
Registered Office: 417 Bridport Road, Greenford, Middlesex, UB6 8UA
Activities: Activities of head offices
Officers: Brenda Louise Ruppel, Secretary; Martin Tilston Broadhurst [1953] Director; Douglas Caster [1953] Director/Chairman; Geeta Gopalan [1964] Director; John Raymond Hirst [1952] Director; Victoria Mary Hull [1962] Director; Simon Charles Conrad Pryce [1961] Director; William Anthony Rice [1952] Director; Amitabh Sharma [1967] Finance Director; Sir Robert Walmsley [1941] Director

Ultra Electronics Limited
Incorporated: 25 June 1993 *Employees:* 1,878
Net Worth: £144,234,000 *Total Assets:* £447,919,008
Registered Office: 417 Bridport Road, Greenford, Middlesex, UB6 8UA
Activities: Other manufacturing n.e.c.
Parent: Ultra Electronics Holdings PLC
Officers: Anant Prakash, Secretary; Michael Baptist [1965] Divisional Managing Director; Simon Charles Conrad Pryce [1961] Director; Carlos Ricardo Santiago [1955] Director [American]; Amitabh Sharma [1967] Finance Director; Graeme David Stacey [1965] Director

Ultra-Centrifuge Nederland Limited
Incorporated: 12 August 1993
Net Worth: £89,494,352 *Total Assets:* £89,521,248
Registered Office: Urenco Court, Sefton Park, Bells Hill, Stoke Poges, Bucks, SL2 4JS
Activities: Activities of other holding companies n.e.c.
Parent: Ultra-Centrifuge Nederland N.V.
Officers: Sarah Newby, Secretary; Antonius Everhardus Maria Broenink [1957] Director [Dutch]

UMV Global Foods Company Ltd.
Incorporated: 30 October 2014
Net Worth: £1,028,400,000 *Total Assets:* £2,077,799,936
Registered Office: United Biscuits, Hayes Park, Hayes End Road, Hayes, Middlesex, UB4 8EE
Activities: Activities of head offices
Parent: UMV Global Foods Holding Company Limited
Officers: Baris Oner, Secretary; Richard Handscombe [1954] Director/Accountant; Simon Edward Munir [1964] Director/Fund Manager; Murat Ulker [1959] Director/Chairman [Turkish]

UMV Global Foods Holding Company Ltd.
Incorporated: 30 October 2014 *Employees:* 8,093
Net Worth: £1,106,400,000 *Total Assets:* £2,754,500,096
Registered Office: United Biscuits, Hayes Park, Hayes End Road, Hayes, Middlesex, UB4 8EE
Activities: Activities of head offices
Parent: Pladis Foods Limited
Officers: Mark Oldham, Secretary; Richard Handscombe [1954] Director/Accountant; Simon Edward Munir [1964] Director/Fund Manager; Murat Ulker [1959] Director/Chairman [Turkish]

Unilever UK Limited
Incorporated: 9 December 1937 *Employees:* 2,976
Net Worth: £1,239,565,952 *Total Assets:* £1,671,614,976
Registered Office: Unilever House, Springfield Drive, Leatherhead, Surrey, KT22 7GR
Activities: Manufacture of ice cream
Parent: Unilever UK Group Limited
Officers: James Oliver Earley, Secretary; Richard Clive Hazell, Secretary; Hazel Karen Detsiny [1972] Managing Director FMCG; Paul William Fenwick [1970] Director/Accountant; Placid Oriol Jover Goma [1981] Director/VP HR UK & Ireland [Spanish]; Sebastian John Munden [1968] Director/EVP & GM Unilever UK & Ireland; Jonathan David Strachan [1964] Director/Manager; Marc John Woodward [1974] Director/VP Customer Development

Unipath Limited
Incorporated: 14 August 1946 *Employees:* 82
Net Worth: £20,609,000 *Total Assets:* £41,001,000
Registered Office: Clearblue Innovation Centre, Priory Business Park, Stannard Way, Bedford, MK44 3UP
Activities: Other business support service activities n.e.c.
Parent: Alere UK Holdings Limited
Officers: David Bond [1971] Director/Accountant; Trevor Fellows [1969] Director/Chartered Accountant

Unit4 Business Software Limited
Incorporated: 8 July 1983 *Employees:* 322
Net Worth: £38,298,000 *Total Assets:* £84,972,000
Registered Office: Suite 201, 100 Longwater Avenue, Green Park, Reading, Berks, RG2 6GP
Activities: Information technology consultancy activities
Parent: Unit4 UK Software Holdings Limited
Officers: Jacques Andre Martin Bruins Slot [1966] Director/Lawyer [Dutch]; Paul Cross [1964] Finance Director; Derren Nisbet [1970] Managing Director; Stephan Sieber [1975] EVP Strategy & Operations Director [Swiss]

United Biscuits (UK) Limited
Incorporated: 25 May 1990 *Employees:* 4,514
Net Worth: £1,566,000,000 *Total Assets:* £3,558,799,872
Registered Office: Hayes Park, Hayes End Road, Hayes, Middlesex, UB4 8EE
Activities: Manufacture of rusks and biscuits; manufacture of preserved pastry goods and cakes
Parent: McVitie & Price Limited
Officers: Mark Oldham, Secretary/Director; Ahmed Salman Amin [1959] Director [American]; Nicholas Robert Bunker [1964] Managing Director; Richard Handscombe [1954] Director; Helen Marie Pitcher [1958] Director; Mustafa Tercan [1974] Director/Chief Financial Officer [Turkish]; Ali Ulker [1969] Director [Turkish]; Murat Ulker [1959] Director/Chairman [Turkish]; Jim Nafez Zaza [1957] Director/Executive Vice Chairman-Chief Operating Officer [American]

United Biscuits Bidco Limited
Incorporated: 5 October 2006
Net Worth: £220,300,000 *Total Assets:* £2,108,099,968
Registered Office: Hayes Park, Hayes End Road, Hayes, Middlesex, UB4 8EE
Activities: Activities of head offices
Parent: United Biscuits Holdco 2 Limited
Officers: Mark Oldham, Secretary/Director; Helen Josephine McCarthy [1966] Director; Huseyin Avni Metinkale [1963] Director [Turkish]

United Biscuits BondCo Limited
Incorporated: 5 October 2006
Net Worth Deficit: £395,300,000 *Total Assets:* £331,800,000
Registered Office: Hayes Park, Hayes End Road, Hayes, Middlesex, UB4 8EE
Activities: Activities of head offices
Parent: United Biscuits Topco Limited
Officers: Mark Oldham, Secretary/Director; Helen Josephine McCarthy [1966] Director; Huseyin Avni Metinkale [1963] Director [Turkish]

United Biscuits Holdco 2 Limited
Incorporated: 5 October 2006
Net Worth: £219,000,000 *Total Assets:* £1,658,300,032
Registered Office: Hayes Park, Hayes End Road, Hayes, Middlesex, UB4 8EE
Activities: Activities of head offices
Parent: United Biscuits Holdco Limited
Officers: Mark Oldham, Secretary/Director; Helen Josephine McCarthy [1966] Director; Mark Oldham [1959] Company Secretary/Director; Murat Ulker [1959] Director/Chairman [Turkish]

United Biscuits Holdco Limited
Incorporated: 5 October 2006
Net Worth Deficit: £294,200,000 *Total Assets:* £1,439,299,968
Registered Office: Hayes Park, Hayes End Road, Hayes, Middlesex, UB4 8EE
Activities: Activities of head offices
Parent: United Biscuits VLNCo Limited
Officers: Mark Oldham, Secretary/Director; Helen Josephine McCarthy [1966] Director; Huseyin Avni Metinkale [1963] Director [Turkish]

United Biscuits Vlnco Limited
Incorporated: 5 October 2006
Net Worth: £600,000,000 *Total Assets:* £600,000,000
Registered Office: Hayes Park, Hayes End Road, Hayes, Middlesex, UB4 8EE
Activities: Activities of head offices
Parent: United Biscuits BondCo Limited
Officers: Mark Oldham, Secretary/Director; Helen Josephine McCarthy [1966] Director; Huseyin Avni Metinkale [1963] Director [Turkish]

United Healthcare (South Buckinghamshire) Group Limited
Incorporated: 4 June 2001
Net Worth: £8,085,000 *Total Assets:* £55,167,000
Registered Office: 8 White Oak Square, London Road, Swanley, Kent, BR8 7AG
Activities: Combined facilities support activities
Parent: Innisfree Nominees Limited
Officers: Ellen Charlotte Le Breton Schroder [1957] Director; Richard Keith Sheehan [1975] Investment Director; Alastair James Watson [1974] Investment Director

United Healthcare (South Buckinghamshire) Holdings Limited
Incorporated: 27 February 1997
Net Worth: £123,000 *Total Assets:* £24,603,000
Registered Office: 8 White Oak Square, London Road, Swanley, Kent, BR8 7AG
Activities: Combined facilities support activities
Parent: United Healthcare (South Buckinghamshire) Group Limited
Officers: Ellen Charlotte Le Breton Schroder [1957] Director; Richard Keith Sheehan [1975] Investment Director; Alastair James Watson [1974] Investment Director

United Healthcare (South Buckinghamshire) Limited
Incorporated: 28 August 1997
Net Worth: £3,631,000 *Total Assets:* £45,954,000
Registered Office: 8 White Oak Square, London Road, Swanley, Kent, BR8 7AG
Activities: Combined facilities support activities
Parent: United Healthcare (South Buckinghamshire) Holdings Limited
Officers: Ellen Charlotte Le Breton Schroder [1957] Director; Richard Keith Sheehan [1975] Investment Director; Alastair James Watson [1974] Investment Director

United Helicopters Limited
Incorporated: 22 July 1955 *Employees:* 2
Net Worth: £83,223,072 *Total Assets:* £104,754,048
Registered Office: Redhill Aerodrome, Kings Mill Lane, Redhill, Surrey, RH1 5JZ
Activities: Non-scheduled passenger air transport
Parent: Bristow Helicopter Group Limited
Officers: James Lort Howell-Richardson, Secretary; Alan William George Corbett [1957] Director; James Lort Howell-Richardson [1980] Director/Legal Counsel

United Kenning Rental Group Limited
Incorporated: 24 June 1994
Net Worth: £35,054,000 *Total Assets:* £49,009,000
Registered Office: Sixt House, 5 Waterside Drive, Langley, Slough, SL3 6EY
Activities: Renting and leasing of cars and light motor vehicles
Parent: Sixt SE
Officers: Ian Lawrence, Secretary; Ian Walter Lawrence [1959] Director; Per Ingo Voegerl [1973] Director [German]

United Living (North) Holdings Limited
Incorporated: 30 June 2005 *Employees:* 4
Previous: DTB Holdings Limited
Net Worth: £26,000 *Total Assets:* £42,618,000
Registered Office: Media House, Azalea Drive, Swanley, Kent, BR8 8HU
Activities: Activities of head offices
Parent: United Living (North) Group Limited
Officers: Ian George Burnett [1959] Director; Stuart Wilson Laird [1953] Director; David Masters [1971] Finance Director; Timothy Nicholas Wood [1965] Director

United Living (North) Limited
Incorporated: 10 March 1955 *Employees:* 183
Previous: Bullock Construction Limited
Net Worth: £13,789,000 *Total Assets:* £35,102,000
Registered Office: Media House, Azalea Drive, Swanley, Kent, BR8 8HU
Activities: Development of building projects
Parent: United Living (North) Holdings Limited
Officers: Ian George Burnett [1959] Director/Chief Executive; Steve Denis Carden [1958] Director; Charles Neil Dunn [1962] Director; Joanne Jamieson [1975] Director; Stuart Wilson Laird [1953] Director; David Masters [1971] Finance Director; Daren Moseley [1970] Director; Anne Catherine Newman [1960] People Services Director

United Living (South) Group Limited
Incorporated: 9 February 2010
Previous: UHG Holdings Limited
Net Worth: £2,086,000 *Total Assets:* £55,203,000
Registered Office: Media House, Azalea Drive, Swanley, Kent, BR8 8HU
Activities: Activities of head offices
Parent: United Living Group Limited
Officers: Ian George Burnett [1959] Director; Stuart Wilson Laird [1953] Director; David Masters [1971] Finance Director; Timothy Nicholas Wood [1965] Commercial Director

United Living (South) Limited
Incorporated: 28 August 1964 *Employees:* 325
Previous: United House Limited
Net Worth: £41,196,000 *Total Assets:* £114,285,000
Registered Office: Media House, Azalea Drive, Swanley, Kent, BR8 8HU
Activities: Development of building projects
Parent: ULS Living Limited
Officers: Ian George Burnett [1959] Director; Steve Denis Carden [1958] Director; Joanne Jamieson [1975] Director; Stuart Wilson Laird [1953] Director; David Masters [1971] Finance Director; Daren Moseley [1970] Director; Anne Catherine Newman [1960] People Services Director

United Living Group Limited
Incorporated: 22 August 2014 *Employees:* 520
Net Worth: £13,828,000 *Total Assets:* £132,833,000
Registered Office: Media House, Azalea Drive, Swanley, Kent, BR8 8HU
Activities: Activities of head offices
Officers: Ian George Burnett [1959] Director; Charles Neil Dunn [1962] Director; Christopher Richard Hurley [1974] Director; Stuart Wilson Laird [1953] Director; David Masters [1971] Director/Chartered Accountant; Christopher John Thomas [1955] Director; Martyn John Vitty [1975] Director; Timothy Nicholas Wood [1965] Director

United Reformed Church (Wessex) Trust Limited (The)
Incorporated: 14 April 1981 *Employees:* 9
Net Worth: £43,041,072 *Total Assets:* £44,573,088
Registered Office: 120 Alma Road, Southampton, SO14 6UW
Activities: Activities of religious organisations
Officers: Stuart MacLean, Secretary; Reverend Nigel John William Appleton [1946] Director/Business Consultant; Susan Anne Brown [1950] Director/Training Supervisor; Margaret Rose Carrick Smith [1950] Director/Housewife; Reverend Clare Downing [1958] Director/Minister of Religion; Raymond Michael Dunnett [1947] Director/Retired; Andrew Naysmith Gibb [1942] Director/Retired; Michael Stewart Liddle [1949] Director/Management Consultant; Colin Forbes MacBean [1949] Director/Retired; Reverend Julian James Macro [1942] Director/Minister of Religion; Revd Dr Romilly Wakefield Micklem [1960] Director/Minister of Religion; Dr David Richard Page [1944] Director/Retired; Peter Malcolm Pay [1946] Director/Management Consultant; Generald Prosser [1940] Director/Retired; Peter James Stevenson [1945] Director/Financial Consultant; Reverend Anthea Josey Wickens [1955] Director/Minister

United Technologies Finance (U.K.) Limited
Incorporated: 5 October 1922
Net Worth: £237,822,000 *Total Assets:* £237,822,000
Registered Office: 1st Floor, Ash House, Littleton Road, Ashford, Middlesex, TW15 1TZ
Activities: Non-trading company
Parent: Parkview Treasury Services (UK) Limited
Officers: Lynn Banis, Secretary; Christian Bruno Jean Idczak [1963] Director/Business Executive [French]; James Terence George Laurence [1964] Financial Director; Patricia Catherine Moran [1964] Director [American]; Michael Patrick Ryan [1969] Director/Businessman [American]

United Technologies Holdings Limited
Incorporated: 18 December 1963
Net Worth: £326,270,016 *Total Assets:* £768,590,016
Registered Office: 1st Floor, Ash House, Littleton Road, Ashford, Middlesex, TW15 1TZ
Activities: Activities of head offices
Parent: Goodrich Aftermarket Services Limited
Officers: Lynn Banis, Secretary; Christian Bruno Jean Idczak [1963] Director/Business Executive [French]; James Terence George Laurence [1964] Financial Director; Patricia Catherine Moran [1964] Finance Director [American]; Louise Kay Thompson [1983] Director/Chartered Management Accountant

Unity Schools Trust
Incorporated: 4 July 2011 *Employees:* 252
Previous: The Magna Carta School
Net Worth: £31,003,000 *Total Assets:* £35,321,000
Registered Office: The Magna Carta School, Thorpe Road, Staines upon Thames, Surrey, TW18 3HJ
Activities: General secondary education
Officers: Elizabeth Simmons, Secretary; Jennifer Anne Febry [1964] Director/Accountant; Paul Allen Green [1963] Director/Civil Servant; Christopher Paul Howorth [1965] Director/University Lecturer; Robin Michael Kent [1964] Director/Retired; Jessica McMichael [1966] Director/Teacher; Suresh Pillai [1969] Director/Banker; David Benjamin Wales [1975] Director/Management Consultant

Universal Meats (UK) Limited
Incorporated: 20 December 1989
Net Worth: £13,845,000 *Total Assets:* £26,120,000
Registered Office: 130 Eureka Park, Upper Pemberton, Kennington, Boughton Aluph, Kent, TN25 4AZ
Activities: Wholesale of meat and meat products
Parent: BRF Invicta Limited
Officers: Daniel Paulo Hamada [1983] Director [Brazilian]; Colin James Norton [1968] Director; Rubens Fernandes Pereira [1972] Director [Brazilian]

Universal Salvage Limited
Incorporated: 4 December 1979
Net Worth: £123,877,000 *Total Assets:* £138,166,000
Registered Office: Acrey Fields, Woburn Road, Wootton, Beds, MK43 9EJ
Activities: Sale of used cars and light motor vehicles
Parent: Copart Europe Limited
Officers: Aaron Jayson Adair [1969] Director/Chief Executive Officer [American]; Jonathan David Canning [1972] Director/General Counsel; Gregory Depasquale [1968] Director/SVP, General Counsel and Secretary of Copart, Inc [American]; William Easley Franklin [1956] Director/Senior VP & Chief Financial [American]; Nigel James Paget [1966] Managing Director; Simon Sheldon-Wilson [1969] Director; Paul Anthony Styer [1956] Director/General Counsel [American]

Universe Group PLC
Incorporated: 21 August 1991 *Employees:* 249
Net Worth: £23,161,000 *Total Assets:* £29,281,000
Registered Office: George Curl Way, Southampton, SO18 2RX
Activities: Activities of head offices
Officers: Daryl Marc Paton, Secretary; Andrew Robert Blazye [1958] Director; Malcolm David Coster [1944] Director; Jeremy Michael James Lewis [1963] Director; Daryl Marc Paton [1964] Director

University of Brighton Academies Trust
Incorporated: 10 March 2010 *Employees:* 1,505
Previous: Hastings Academies Trust
Net Worth: £99,315,000 *Total Assets:* £107,894,000
Registered Office: Multi Academy Trust Office, Room A304 Checkland Building, University of Brighton, Falmer, Brighton, BN1 9PH
Activities: Pre-primary education
Officers: Samantha Louise Coates, Secretary; Arthur Tyrer Copple [1954] Director/Financial Consultant; Jill Elizabeth Gray [1946] Director; Lorraine Harrison [1957] Director/Principal Lecturer; Christopher Desmond Kirkness [1954] Director/Leadership Consultant; Professor Chris John Pole [1959] Director/Deputy Vice-Chancellor; Dr John Smith [1969] Director/Head of School and Interim Chief Executive; Janey Walker [1958] Managing Director; Mark Brian Whitby [1964] Director/Education Consultant; Andrew Vernon Wilson [1965] Director/Solicitor

The University of Chichester
Incorporated: 22 April 2003 *Employees:* 650
Net Worth: £74,854,000 *Total Assets:* £107,533,000
Registered Office: Bishop Otter Campus, College Lane, Chichester, W Sussex, PO19 6PE
Activities: First-degree level higher education
Officers: Sophie Louise Egleton, Secretary; Stephen John Xavier Baysted [1969] Director/University Lecturer; Andrew James Carpenter [1972] Director/Business Systems Specialist; Jill Cook [1959] Director/Writer; Nicola Catherine Curtis [1955] Director; Christopher Joseph Dicks [1953] Director; Jill Elizabeth Gray [1946] Director/Retired; Jack Greenwood [1996] Director/Students' Union President; Terence Hancock [1958] Director; The Reverend Rachel Hawes [1954] Director/Associate Rector; Professor Michael Andrew Lauder [1968] University Director of Institute of Sport; Professor Jane Longmore [1954] Director/Vice-Chancellor; Richard Martin [1947] Director/Company Chairman; Nicola Victoria Nageon de Lestang [1957] Director/Lecturer; Dr Arthur Naylor [1949] Director/Retired; Robin Glenn Smith [1948] Director/Management Accountant; The Right Reverend Mark Crispin Rake Sowerby [1963] Director/Bishop of Horsham; Marilyn Elaine Surgeon [1955] Director/Principal of Further Education College

University of Chichester (Multi) Academy Trust
Incorporated: 3 July 2013 *Employees:* 711
Net Worth: £59,066,000 *Total Assets:* £65,304,000
Registered Office: Bishop Otter Campus, College Lane, Chichester, W Sussex, PO19 6PE
Activities: Educational support services
Officers: Helen Clare Turner, Secretary; Jill Cook [1959] Director/Writer; Michael Steele Keith Grant [1947] Director/Retired; Charles Henry Gregson [1947] Director/Chairman; Deamonn Hewett-Dale [1966] Director/Headteacher; Colin Martin James [1958] Director/Management Consultant; Rosemary Helena Jones [1958] Director/Strategic Development Manager; Professor Jane Longmore [1954] Director/Vice Chancellor; James Nicholas Martin [1969] Director/Head of Partnership, University of Chichester; Dr Sharon Lydia Menghini [1958] Director; David Keith Myers [1950] Director/Semi Retired Business Consultant; Graham Olway [1963] Director/Strategic Development Commissioning Manager; Susan Margaret Samson [1951] Director/C.E.O of University of Chichester Academy Trust; Alan Taylor-Bennett [1957] Director/Retired

The University of Kent Academies Trust
Incorporated: 10 March 2010 *Employees:* 242
Previous: Brompton Academy
Net Worth: £28,991,000 *Total Assets:* £35,228,000
Registered Office: Brompton Academy, Marlborough Road, Gillingham, Kent, ME7 5HT
Activities: General secondary education
Officers: Katrina Allen, Secretary; Margaret Baker Moss [1969] Director/School Librarian; Richard Mark Ebanks [1964] Director/Dental Surgeon; Nigel Paul Ingram [1950] Director/Retired; Professor Daniel Robert Lloyd [1973] Director/Academic; Oliver David Martin [1979] Director/Senior Manager; David Roydon Nightingale [1948] Director/Senior Deputy Vice-Chancellor; Neil Paul Oliver [1961] Assistant Director of Finance; Richard Henry Patey [1965] Director; Dr Georgina Randsley de Moura [1977] Director/Academic [British/Portuguese]; Robert Lloyd Ryan [1965] Director/Vicar; Jennifer Anne Wyatt [1965] Director/Head of Partnership Development

The University of Law Limited
Incorporated: 2 February 2012 *Employees:* 578
Net Worth: £42,900,000 *Total Assets:* £136,400,000
Registered Office: Braboeuf Manor, St Catherines, Guildford, Surrey, GU3 1HA
Activities: Post-graduate level higher education
Parent: COL Newco Limited
Officers: Carolyn Jane Aitchison [1963] Director; Lord David Blunkett [1947] Director/Professor of Politics; Elisabetta Ceragioli [1973] Director/Deputy Chief Executive Officer [Italian]; Arkady Etingen [1979] Director; Lord Anthony Stephen Grabiner [1945] Director/Barrister; John Christopher Headley [1961] Director/Accountant; Valery Kisilevsky [1984] Director [Canadian]; Alfred Cosier Morris [1941] Director/Higher Education Consultant; Carol Andrea Nollent [1962] Director/University Provost

The University of Southampton Science Park Limited
Incorporated: 10 February 1983 *Employees:* 13
Net Worth: £25,640,696 *Total Assets:* £41,792,820
Registered Office: 2 Venture Road, University of Southampton, Science Park, Southampton, SO16 7NP
Activities: Other letting and operating of own or leased real estate
Parent: University of Southampton
Officers: Jane Marguerite Holt, Secretary; Stephen Ian Lee Barber [1960] Director; Peter Ronald Birkett [1960] Director; Dr Robin Arthur Chave [1967] Operations Director; Ian Derek Dunn [1962] Director/Chief Operating Officer, University of Southampton; Jonathan Peter Kamm [1950] Director/Town Planner; Kevin Peter Monaghan [1957] Director; Philip Ronald Sharpe [1949] Director/Business Development; Professor Simon Mark Spearing [1964] Director/Academic; Irene Spencer [1954] Director/Surveyor; Mary Anne Louise White [1972] Director/Accountant

University of Winchester
Incorporated: 17 October 2006 *Employees:* 775
Net Worth: £145,738,000 *Total Assets:* £202,306,000
Registered Office: Sparkford Road, Winchester, Hants, SO22 4NR
Activities: First-degree level higher education
Officers: Nigel Garnett Trethewy, Secretary; Talivaldis Janis Rainis Ringolds Atvars [1994] Director/Student Union President; Dr Lesley Jane Black [1974] Director/University Employee; Mark Byford [1958] Director/Retired; Professor Joy Carter [1955] Director/Vice Chancellor; Margaret Chin-Wolf [1953] Director/Retired Portfolio Manager; David Cook [1952] Director/Retired; Professor Louise Hill Curth [1958] Director/Lecturer; The Right Reverend Timothy John Dakin [1958] Director/Bishop of Church of England; Mary Bernadette Edwards [1959] Director/Retired; Professor Christopher John Gaskell [1948] Director/Retired; Winifred Anne Charlotte Harris [1947] Director/Retired Civil Servant; Jane Frances Mary Jessop [1952] Director/Volunteer; Peter Frank Lidgitt [1953] Director/Company Manager; Alan Charles Lovell [1953] Director/Retired; Thomas Andrew Lowe [1991] Director/Manager; Professor David Neil Marriott [1960] Director/Deputy Vice-Chancellor; Peter Martin North [1949] Director/Self Employed Consultant; Emma Rachel Page [1952] Director/Retired; Andrew Ronald Robinson [1974] Director; Professor Elizabeth Bridget Stuart [1963] Director/Deputy Vice Chancellor; Professor Nigel Tubbs [1961] Director/University Professor; David Grant Williams [1961] Director/Bishop of Basingstoke

Unum European Holding Company Limited
Incorporated: 22 January 1990 *Employees:* 766
Net Worth: £102,203,000 *Total Assets:* £114,407,000
Registered Office: Milton Court, Dorking, Surrey, RH4 3LZ
Activities: Activities of financial services holding companies
Shareholder: Unum Group
Officers: Steven John Leverett, Secretary; Cheryl Campbell Black [1958] Director; Jonathan Paul Fletcher [1972] Director; Samantha Jane Hoe-Richardson [1971] Director; Malcolm Graham McCaig [1955] Director; Richard Paul McKenney [1968] Director/Chief Executive Officer UNUM Group [American]; Clifton Adrian Melvin [1954] Director; Peadar Gerard Owen O'Donnell [1966] Director/Chief Financial Officer [Irish]

Unum Limited
Incorporated: 3 July 1970
Net Worth: £554,288,000 *Total Assets:* £2,928,732,928
Registered Office: Milton Court, Dorking, Surrey, RH4 3LZ
Activities: Life insurance
Shareholders: Unum European Holding Company Limited; UnumProvident Finance Company Limited
Officers: Steven John Leverett, Secretary; Cheryl Campbell Black [1958] Director; Jonathan Paul Fletcher [1972] Director; Samantha Jane Hoe-Richardson [1971] Director; Malcolm Graham McCaig [1955] Director; Richard Paul McKenney [1968] Director/Chief Executive Officer UNUM Group [American]; Clifton Adrian Melvin [1954] Director; Peadar Gerard Owen O'Donnell [1966] Director/Chief Executive Officer [Irish]

UnumProvident Finance Company Limited
Incorporated: 10 February 2003
Previous: UnumProvident Finance Company PLC
Net Worth: £457,671,008 *Total Assets:* £457,712,992
Registered Office: Milton Court, Dorking, Surrey, RH4 3LZ
Activities: Financial intermediation not elsewhere classified
Parent: Unum Group
Officers: Steven John Leverett, Secretary; Jonathan Paul Fletcher [1972] Director; John Francis McGarry [1958] Director/CFO UNUM Group [American]; Peadar Gerard Owen O'Donnell [1966] Director/Chief Financial Officer [Irish]

UOP International Holdings Limited
Incorporated: 26 February 2004
Net Worth: £172,096,992 *Total Assets:* £224,458,000
Registered Office: Liongate, Ladymead, Guildford, Surrey, GU1 1AT
Activities: Activities of other holding companies n.e.c.
Parent: Honeywell International Inc.
Officers: Glen William Davies [1956] Director; David Allen Gledhill [1965] Director; Nigel John Davison Orchard [1954] Director

UOP Limited
Incorporated: 9 July 1953 *Employees:* 182
Net Worth: £301,542,016 *Total Assets:* £379,372,992
Registered Office: Liongate, Ladymead, Guildford, Surrey, GU1 1AT
Activities: Manufacture of other inorganic basic chemicals
Parent: Honeywell International Inc.
Officers: Glen William Davies [1956] Director; David Allen Gledhill [1965] Director; Nigel John Davison Orchard [1954] Director; John Pitkin [1951] Director; Gordon Davies Walker Jr [1975] Finance Director [American]; John Grantly Woodcock [1956] Director

Upham Group Limited
Incorporated: 7 November 2011 *Employees:* 243
Previous: Upham Group PLC
Net Worth: £14,453,000 *Total Assets:* £31,542,000
Registered Office: The Old Bakehouse, Course Road, Ascot, Berks, SL5 7HL
Activities: Licenced restaurants
Officers: Hugh Jackson, Secretary; David Butcher [1970] Director; Robert Edward Harris [1975] Finance Director; Hugh Jackson [1962] Director/Accountant; John Moore McMillan [1960] Director; Christopher Michael Generald Phillips [1961] Director

Upperton Holdings Limited
Incorporated: 9 September 1999
Net Worth: £4,224,677 *Total Assets:* £117,124,000
Registered Office: Hill Ash Farm, West Harting, Petersfield, Hants, GU31 5NY
Activities: Other activities auxiliary to insurance and pension funding
Major Shareholder: Nigel John Hanbury
Officers: Nicholas David Lewis, Secretary; Elizabeth Evelyn Huger Hanbury [1990] Director/Student; George Snowden Hanbury [1989] Director/Member of Lloyd's Partnership; Nigel John Hanbury [1957] Director/Lloyds Agent

UPS (UK Holding) Limited
Incorporated: 10 November 2003
Net Worth: £149,615,408 *Total Assets:* £239,067,920
Registered Office: UPS House, Forest Road, Feltham, Middlesex, TW13 7DY
Activities: Activities of head offices
Parent: United Parcel Service, Inc.
Officers: Elisabel Rodriguez Marquez, Secretary; Louis Anthony Rivieccio Jr [1965] Director [American]; Elisabel Rodriguez Marquez [1980] Finance Director [Spanish]; Peter Raoul Stewardson [1964] Director/Legal Attorney; Mark Simon Vale [1965] Director

UPS (UK) Limited
Incorporated: 2 October 1984 *Employees:* 21
Net Worth: £588,991,488 *Total Assets:* £2,179,633,664
Registered Office: UPS House, Forest Road, Feltham, Middlesex, TW13 7DY
Activities: Activities of head offices
Parent: United Parcel Service, Inc.
Officers: Peter Raoul Stewardson, Secretary; Ronald Woo-Sung Chang [1965] Director/Corporate Finance, President [American]; Tim Regis Helsen [1979] Director/Manager [Belgian]; Elisabel Rodriguez Marquez [1980] Finance Director [Spanish]; Peter Raoul Stewardson [1964] Director/Legal Attorney

UPS Global Treasury PLC
Incorporated: 6 March 1985 *Employees:* 21
Net Worth: £80,841,776 *Total Assets:* £2,141,116,800
Registered Office: UPS House, Forest Road, Feltham, Middlesex, TW13 7DY
Activities: Financial intermediation not elsewhere classified
Parent: UPS (UK) Limited
Officers: Peter Raoul Stewardson, Secretary; Ronald Woo-Sung Chang [1965] Director/Corporate Finance, President [American]; Parvinder Singh Gill [1973] Treasury Director; Tim Regis Helsen [1979] Director/Manager [Belgian]; Jennifer Leigh Powers [1970] Director/Treasury Manager [American]; Peter Raoul Stewardson [1964] Director/Legal Attorney

UPS Limited
Incorporated: 24 July 1985 *Employees:* 8,145
Net Worth: £262,695,008 *Total Assets:* £664,441,984
Registered Office: UPS House, Forest Road, Feltham, Middlesex, TW13 7DY
Activities: Unlicensed carriers
Parent: UPS (UK Holding) Limited
Officers: Elisabel Rodriguez Marquez, Secretary; Louis Anthony Rivieccio Jr [1965] Director [American]; Elisabel Rodriguez Marquez [1980] Finance Director [Spanish]; Peter Raoul Stewardson [1964] Director/Legal Attorney; Mark Simon Vale [1965] Director

UPS SCS (UK) Limited
Incorporated: 12 May 1994 *Employees:* 578
Net Worth: £19,598,000 *Total Assets:* £44,975,000
Registered Office: Unit 1 Blackthorne Road, Poyle, Berks, SL3 0DA
Activities: Operation of warehousing and storage facilities for land transport activities
Parent: United Parcel Service, Inc.
Officers: Elisabel Rodriguez Marquez, Secretary; Elisabel Rodriguez Marquez [1980] Finance Director [Spanish]; Peter Raoul Stewardson [1964] Director/Legal Attorney; Mark Simon Vale [1965] Director

Uranit UK Limited
Incorporated: 12 August 1993
Net Worth: £94,122,024 *Total Assets:* £94,147,704
Registered Office: Urenco Court, Sefton Park, Bells Hill, Stoke Poges, Bucks, SL2 4JS
Activities: Activities of other holding companies n.e.c.
Parent: Uranit GmbH
Officers: Sarah Newby, Secretary; Dr Thomas Beermann [1971] Director [German]; Thorsten Lott [1969] Director [German]

Urbis Schreder Ltd
Incorporated: 12 February 1973 *Employees:* 87
Net Worth: £17,752,304 *Total Assets:* £29,056,368
Registered Office: Sapphire House, Lime Tree Way, Hampshire International Business Park, Chineham, Basingstoke, Hants, RG24 8GG
Activities: Manufacture of electric lighting equipment
Parent: Schreder SA
Officers: Martin Tootill, Secretary; Natasha Suzanne Jean Andre Marie Seghers [1968] Director/Company Lawyer [Belgian]; Coline Elisabeth Muriel Simmons [1985] Director/Business Development Consultant [Belgian]; Maria Antonia Velez Vestia [1965] Zone Director South Western Europe [Portuguese]

Urenco Enrichment Company Limited
Incorporated: 13 March 2003 *Employees:* 32
Net Worth: £205,722,032 *Total Assets:* £312,150,784
Registered Office: Urenco Court, Sefton Park, Bells Hill, Stoke Poges, Bucks, SL2 4JS
Activities: Activities of head offices
Parent: Urenco Limited
Officers: Sarah Newby, Secretary; Thomas Michael Haeberle [1956] Director [German]; Dominic John Kieran [1974] Director

Urenco Limited
Incorporated: 31 August 1971 *Employees:* 1,544
Net Worth: £1,598,860,672 *Total Assets:* £5,607,186,432
Registered Office: Urenco Court, Sefton Park, Bells Hill, Stoke Poges, Bucks, SL2 4JS
Activities: Activities of head offices
Shareholders: Enrichment Investments Limited; Uranit UK Limited; Ultra-Centrifuge Nederland Limited
Officers: Sarah Newby, Secretary; Alan Bevan [1967] Director; Doctor Stephen Robert Billingham [1958] Director; Thomas Michael Haeberle [1956] Director [German]; Jacob Melchior Kroon [1957] Director [Dutch]; Maria Henrica Maes [1956] Director [Dutch]; Christopher John Justin Manson [1960] Director; Richard Henry Charles Nourse [1964] Director/Civil Servant; Ralf Ter Haar [1965] Director [Dutch]; Dr Frank Weigand [1966] Director [German]

USF International Limited
Incorporated: 23 December 2015 *Employees:* 1,194
Net Worth: £33,061,328 *Total Assets:* £106,498,208
Registered Office: The Old Courtyard, 11 Lower Cookham Road, Maidenhead, Berks, SL6 8JN
Activities: Other business support service activities n.e.c.
Parent: Gores Capital Partners III, LP
Officers: Peter Rankin Sandringham, Secretary; Andrew Joseph Greenlee [1967] Director/Business Executive [American]; James Christopher Gregory [1966] Director/Business Executive [American]; Kevin Edward Lupton [1970] Director/Business Executive [American]

Utilita Energy Limited
Incorporated: 29 July 2003 *Employees:* 747
Net Worth: £32,525,000 *Total Assets:* £155,603,008
Registered Office: Hutwood Court, Bournemouth Road, Chandler's Ford, Eastleigh, Hants, SO53 3QB
Activities: Distribution of electricity
Parent: Utilita Group Limited
Officers: Michael David Edwin Smith, Secretary; William Nicholas Bullen [1961] Director; Michael David Edwin Smith [1959] Director/Chartered Accountant

Utilita Group Limited
Incorporated: 28 July 2003 *Employees:* 1,597
Net Worth: £32,906,000 *Total Assets:* £180,798,000
Registered Office: Hutwood Court, Bournemouth Road, Chandler's Ford, Eastleigh, Hants, SO53 3QB
Activities: Activities of other holding companies n.e.c.
Major Shareholder: William Nicholas Bullen
Officers: Michael David Edwin Smith, Secretary; William Nicholas Bullen [1961] Director; Derek Arthur Lickorish Mbe [1951] Director; Michael David Edwin Smith [1959] Director/Chartered Accountant

Uxbridge High School Academy Trust
Incorporated: 5 May 2011 *Employees:* 136
Net Worth: £22,468,504 *Total Assets:* £24,446,592
Registered Office: Uxbridge High School Academy Trust, The Greenway, Uxbridge, Middlesex, UB8 2PR
Activities: General secondary education
Officers: Norwena Thomas, Secretary; David Andrew Aldridge [1978] Director of Research; Ben Beadle [1981] Director of Customer Relations; Jessica Timandra Beishon [1964] Director/Medical Communications Manager; Jennifer Bull [1988] Director/Local Government Officer; Rajiv Harry Deo Cahannac [1987] Director/Senior Internal Auditor; Nigel Brian Clemens [1963] Director/Principal; Samuel Frederick Michael Head [1994] Director/Teacher; Avril Ann James [1965] Director/Office Manager; Ada Jarvis-Kanayo [1964] Director/Teacher; Nigel McGreeghan [1965] Director/Prison Officer; Ian Fergus Moules [1965] Director/Civil Servant; Susan Elaine O'Sullivan [1942] Director/Project Manager; Minesh Parmar [1964] Director/Independent Financial Advisor; Peter Neil Waine [1954] Director

V.B. Investments Limited
Incorporated: 2 July 2003
Net Worth Deficit: £6,584,000 *Total Assets:* £31,251,000
Registered Office: Astral House, Imperial Way, Watford, Herts, WD24 4WW
Activities: Financial management
Parent: Vinci Pensions Limited
Officers: Christopher Carl Brennan [1969] Director/Accountant; Ian David Hudson [1964] Director/Chartered Accountant

V1 Limited
Incorporated: 15 November 1989 *Employees:* 50
Net Worth: £17,754,000 *Total Assets:* £32,158,000
Registered Office: Ditton Park, Riding Court Road, Datchet, Berks, SL3 9LL
Activities: Business and domestic software development
Parent: Advanced Business Software and Solutions Limited
Officers: Natalie Amanda Shaw, Secretary; Andrew William Hicks [1975] Director/Chief Financial Officer; Gordon James Wilson [1960] Director

VA Tech (UK) Limited
Incorporated: 12 May 1998
Net Worth: £55,951,000 *Total Assets:* £121,481,000
Registered Office: Faraday House, Sir William Siemens Square, Frimley, Camberley, Surrey, GU16 8QD
Activities: Manufacture of electricity distribution and control apparatus
Parent: Siemens Holdings PLC
Officers: Simone Eufemia Agatha Davina, Secretary; Carl Ennis [1968] Managing Director; Alistair James Gemmell [1961] Director/Accountant

Vale of Aylesbury Housing Trust Limited
Incorporated: 28 April 2005 *Employees:* 248
Net Worth: £153,399,008 *Total Assets:* £310,596,000
Registered Office: Fairfax House, 69 Buckingham Street, Aylesbury, Bucks, HP20 2NJ
Activities: Renting and operating of Housing Association real estate
Officers: Linda Foster, Secretary; John Roland Balshaw [1944] Director/Consultant; Julian Blundell-Thompson [1974] Director/Copywriter; Stephen Michael Bright [1949] Director; Olivia Jane Clymer [1966] Director/Chief Executive Officer; David George Keeling [1954] Director/Housing Consultant; Steven Michael Lambert [1970] Director/District Councillor; Angela Ria Joyce Macpherson [1959] Director; Barbara Ann Richardson [1967] Managing Director; Stephen Edward Spencer Stringer [1957] Director; Kelly Webster [1975] Director

Valley Invicta Academies Trust
Incorporated: 10 March 2011 *Employees:* 513
Net Worth: £50,737,000 *Total Assets:* £59,020,000
Registered Office: Invicta Grammar School, Huntsman Lane, Maidstone, Kent, ME14 5DS
Activities: Primary education
Officers: Albert Victor Ashdown [1961] Director/Headteacher and Joint CEO; Duncan George Cochrane-Dyet [1966] Director/Chartered Accountant; Catherine Louise Daw [1973] Director/Solicitor; Julie Alison Derrick [1961] Director/Headteacher and Joint CEO; Matthew Gregory Fletcher [1967] Director/Project/Business Consultant; Anthony James Moore [1957] Director/Retired; Dr John Pedder Moss [1957] Director/Dean of Education; Sheila Margaret Potipher [1950] Director/Retired; Brendan Roodt [1971] Director/Lawyer [South African]; Dr Nicholas Borman Ware [1952] Director/Consultant

Valour Bidco Limited
Incorporated: 22 October 2014
Net Worth Deficit: £13,212,172 *Total Assets:* £58,793,560
Registered Office: Unit 2 Eurogate Business Park, Ashford, Kent, TN24 8XW
Activities: Temporary employment agency activities
Parent: Valour Midco II Ltd
Officers: Pamela Anne Bruce [1967] Director; Joshua Arthur Stanley Collins [1972] Director; Janice Anne Drain [1956] Director

Valour Holdco Limited
Incorporated: 22 October 2014 *Employees:* 226
Net Worth Deficit: £13,970,681 *Total Assets:* £51,776,156
Registered Office: Unit 2 Eurogate Business Park, Ashford, Kent, TN24 8XW
Activities: Temporary employment agency activities
Officers: Heath Robert Blake [1967] Director; Pamela Anne Bruce [1967] Director; Joshua Arthur Stanley Collins [1972] Director; Janice Anne Drain [1956] Director; Reece Michael Hayden [1998] Director; Sir Gerrard Jude Robinson [1948] Director/Chairman; Stewart James Rogers [1953] Director

Valour Midco I Limited
Incorporated: 22 October 2014
Net Worth Deficit: £899,511 *Total Assets:* £34,694,064
Registered Office: Unit 2 Eurogate Business Park, Ashford, Kent, TN24 8XW
Activities: Temporary employment agency activities
Parent: Valour Holdco Ltd
Officers: Sarah Charles, Secretary; Pamela Anne Bruce [1967] Director; Joshua Arthur Stanley Collins [1972] Director; Janice Anne Drain [1956] Director

Valour Midco II Limited
Incorporated: 22 October 2014
Net Worth: £5,668 *Total Assets:* £34,694,064
Registered Office: Unit 2 Eurogate Business Park, Ashford, Kent, TN24 8XW
Activities: Temporary employment agency activities
Parent: Valour Midco I Ltd
Officers: Pamela Anne Bruce [1967] Director; Joshua Arthur Stanley Collins [1972] Director; Janice Anne Drain [1956] Director

Van Oord UK Limited
Incorporated: 2 April 1984 *Employees:* 61
Net Worth: £17,188,440 *Total Assets:* £36,153,704
Registered Office: Bankside House, Henfield Road, Small Dole, Henfield, W Sussex, BN5 9XQ
Activities: Construction of other civil engineering projects n.e.c.
Parent: Van Oord Dredging and Marine Contractors BV
Officers: Mark Simeon Goddard, Secretary; Jurjan Pieter Cornelis Blokland [1974] Managing Director [Dutch]; Govert Van Oord [1970] Director/Civil Engineer [Dutch]

Vanderbilt Development Finance Ltd
Incorporated: 5 July 2013
Net Worth: £17,213,000 *Total Assets:* £50,253,000
Registered Office: Apollo House, Mercury Park, Wooburn Green, High Wycombe, Bucks, HP10 0HH
Activities: Construction of domestic buildings
Parent: Vanderbilt Holdings Limited
Officers: Daniel Kevin Stern, Secretary; Chris Chiles [1969] Director

Vanderbilt Homes Limited
Incorporated: 9 January 2004 *Employees:* 59
Net Worth Deficit: £4,390,000 *Total Assets:* £70,113,000
Registered Office: Apollo House, Mercury Park, Wooburn Green, Bucks, HP10 0HH
Activities: Development of building projects
Parent: Vanderbilt Development Finance Ltd
Officers: Daniel Kevin Stern, Secretary; Christopher Chiles [1969] Director

Vanderbilt Hotels Limited
Incorporated: 8 April 1993 *Employees:* 128
Net Worth: £14,917,000 *Total Assets:* £38,533,000
Registered Office: 140 Bath Road, Hayes, Middlesex, UB3 5AW
Activities: Hotels and similar accommodation
Parent: Edwardian Group Limited
Officers: Vijay Wason, Secretary; John Robert Morley [1945] Director/Financial Consultant; Jasminder Singh [1951] Director/Hotelier

Vanderbilt Thames Valley Limited
Incorporated: 5 July 2013
Previous: Vanderbilt Beaconsfield Ltd
Net Worth Deficit: £7,583,000 *Total Assets:* £66,667,000
Registered Office: Apollo House, Mercury Park, Wooburn Green, High Wycombe, Bucks, HP10 0HH
Activities: Construction of domestic buildings
Parent: Vanderbilt Homes Limited
Officers: Daniel Kevin Stern, Secretary; Christopher Chiles [1969] Director

Vanderbilt Topco Ltd
Incorporated: 12 May 2014 *Employees:* 60
Net Worth Deficit: £55,787,000 *Total Assets:* £69,853,000
Registered Office: Apollo House, Mercury Park, Wooburn Green, High Wycombe, Bucks, HP10 0HH
Activities: Construction of domestic buildings
Officers: Daniel Kevin Stern, Secretary; Lord Edward Albert Charles Spencer-Churchill [1974] Director

Vanguard Holdings Limited
Incorporated: 31 July 1964 *Employees:* 17
Net Worth: £31,352,484 *Total Assets:* £35,381,472
Registered Office: The Vanguard Business Centre, Alperton Lane, off Western Avenue, Greenford, Middlesex, UB6 8AA
Activities: Activities of head offices
Shareholder: Edward McKim Lyell McCullagh
Officers: Denise McCullagh, Secretary; Charlotte Alison McCullagh [1984] Marketing Director; Edward McKim Lyell McCullagh [1935] Director; William Alistair McCullagh [1985] Logistics and IT Director

Vanguard Learning Trust
Incorporated: 4 October 2011 *Employees:* 217
Previous: Vyners Learning Trust
Net Worth: £17,313,000 *Total Assets:* £20,323,000
Registered Office: Vyners School, Warren Road, Ickenham, Uxbridge, Middlesex, UB10 8AB
Activities: Pre-primary education
Officers: Janet Anne Beater, Secretary; Peter Wynne Davies [1949] Director; William Henry Gardner [1945] Director/Retired Teacher; Mark Hague [1958] Director/Accountant; Edward Francis Lavery [1960] Director; Dr Martina Anne Bernadette Lecky [1971] Director/Headteacher; Pamela Nash [1968] Director/ICT Account Manager; Pauline Anne Nixon [1952] Director; Andrew Jeremy Sykes [1963] Director/IT Programme Manager; David Peter Trood [1971] Director/Solicitor; Colin Peter Tucker [1973] Director/Headteacher

Vantas International Limited
Incorporated: 13 January 1977
Net Worth: £9,365,630,976 *Total Assets:* £9,697,094,656
Registered Office: Cadbury House, Sanderson Road, Uxbridge, Middlesex, UB8 1DH
Activities: Activities of head offices
Parent: Mondelez UK Holdings & Services Limited
Officers: Adrian John Paul Arrighi [1978] Tax Director; Michael Brendan Foye [1965] Treasury Director; John Michael Hladusz [1972] Director/Chartered Accountant; Carole Noelle Keene [1966] Director

Varian Medical Systems UK Limited
Incorporated: 10 December 1955 *Employees:* 220
Net Worth: £77,115,624 *Total Assets:* £124,600,352
Registered Office: Oncology House, Gatwick Road, Crawley, W Sussex, RH10 9RG
Activities: Manufacture of irradiation, electromedical and electrotherapeutic equipment
Parent: Varian Medical Systems UK Holdings Limited
Officers: Nicholas John Moritz, Secretary; Patrick Jonathan Joda [1958] Director [American]; John Wei Ching Kuo [1963] Director/Attorney [American]; Nicholas John Moritz [1963] Director/Accountant; Per Magnus Persson [1965] Director/Regulatory Manager [Swedish]

Vectis Property Co. Limited
Incorporated: 16 September 1952
Net Worth: £12,257,975 *Total Assets:* £44,387,352
Registered Office: Christopher Wren House, West Street, Reigate, Surrey, RH2 9BT
Activities: Buying and selling of own real estate
Major Shareholder: Christopher Neville Rayner
Officers: Christopher Neville Rayner, Secretary; Charles John Pearson Battersby [1953] Director; Gianluca Giangolini [1973] Director/Real Estate Finance Consultant; Richard John Groom [1942] Director/Management Consultant; Christopher Neville Rayner [1964] Director

Vector Aerospace International Limited
Incorporated: 19 October 2007 *Employees:* 691
Net Worth: £39,584,000 *Total Assets:* £130,261,000
Registered Office: Fleetlands, Fareham Road, Gosport, Hants, PO13 0AA
Activities: Repair and maintenance of aircraft and spacecraft
Officers: Gary Scott Carruthers [1980] Finance Director; Brent Jeffrey Fawkes [1969] Director/VP Finance [Canadian]; Simon Griffith Jones [1969] Commercial Director; Michael Robert Scott [1967] Director [Canadian]

Veeam Software UK Limited
Incorporated: 14 October 2008 *Employees:* 59
Net Worth: £7,899,199 *Total Assets:* £62,334,832
Registered Office: 1st Floor, West Wing, Davidson House, Forbury Square, Reading, Berks, RG1 3EU
Activities: Other software publishing
Parent: VS International Holdings Limited
Officers: William Howard Largent [1955] Director [American]

Veetee Foods Limited
Incorporated: 21 September 2005 *Employees:* 72
Net Worth: £10,104,243 *Total Assets:* £27,535,366
Registered Office: Veetee House, Sir Thomas Longley Road, Medway City Estate, Rochester, Kent, ME2 4DU
Activities: Manufacture of prepared meals and dishes
Major Shareholder: Manmohan Chander Varma
Officers: Shashi Prakash Surana, Secretary; Vikas Magoon [1969] Director/Company Executive; Shashi Prakash Surana [1965] Director/Company Executive; Manmohan Chander Varma [1949] Director; Rajiv Varma [1985] Director

Veetee Rice Limited
Incorporated: 10 April 1986 *Employees:* 156
Net Worth: £23,772,428 *Total Assets:* £64,440,648
Registered Office: Veetee House, Neptune Close, Medway City Estate, Rochester, Kent, ME2 4LT
Activities: Grain milling
Officers: Shashi Prakash Surana, Secretary; Vikas Magoon [1969] Director/Company Executive; Shashi Prakash Surana [1965] Director/Company Executive; Manmohan Chander Varma [1949] Director; Rajiv Varma [1985] Director

Vendcrown Limited
Incorporated: 5 June 1996
Net Worth: £50,669,000 *Total Assets:* £58,671,000
Registered Office: Ermyn House, Ermyn Way, Leatherhead, Surrey, KT22 8UX
Activities: Other business support service activities n.e.c.
Parent: Mizzen Bidco Limited
Officers: Elizabeth Sarah Annys, Secretary; Andrew Phillip Chapman [1969] Director/Chief Financial Officer; Anthony Santospirito [1984] Director [Australian]; Thomas Woolgrove [1970] Director/Chief Executive Officer

Venn Partners LLP
Incorporated: 30 July 2009 *Employees:* 19
Net Worth: £2,827,804 *Total Assets:* £27,595,680
Registered Office: 4th Floor, Reading Bridge House, George Street, Reading, Berks, RG1 8LS
Officers: Gary Paul McKenzie-Smith [1973] Member; Luke Oliver Joseph Venables [1973] Member; Peter Antony Bowden [1966] LLP Member; Kawai Chung [1978] LLP Member; Jonathan Charles Llewellyn Clayton [1972] LLP Member; David Alan Cuin-Wood [1973] LLP Member; Beatrice Dupont de Rivaltz [1976] LLP Member; Richard Neville Green [1975] LLP Member; Paul House [1968] LLP Member; Olivier Mette [1978] LLP Member

Venson Automotive Solutions Limited
Incorporated: 13 May 1992 *Employees:* 80
Net Worth: £13,348,766 *Total Assets:* £50,620,388
Registered Office: Venson House, 1 AC Court, High Street, Thames Ditton, Surrey, KT7 0SR
Activities: Sale of new cars and light motor vehicles
Parent: Premier Fleet Management and Contract Hire Limited
Officers: John Gerard Bateson, Secretary/Director [Irish]; John Gerard Bateson [1963] Director [Irish]; Mark William Gerard [1965] Finance Director; Brian Michael O'Sullivan [1963] Director [Irish]; Samantha Jane Roff [1968] Director; Simon John Staton [1973] Director

Vent-Axia Group Limited
Incorporated: 20 March 1973 *Employees:* 360
Net Worth: £17,021,000 *Total Assets:* £34,130,000
Registered Office: Vent-Axia, Fleming Way, Crawley, W Sussex, RH10 9YX
Activities: Manufacture of other electrical equipment
Parent: Volution Ventilation Group Limited
Officers: Michael Anscombe, Secretary; Ian Dew [1959] Director/Chartered Accountant; Ronnie George [1969] Director

Venture Life Group PLC
Incorporated: 12 December 2005 *Employees:* 99
Net Worth: £14,185,000 *Total Assets:* £31,309,000
Registered Office: Venture House, Arlington Square, Downshire Way, Bracknell, Berks, RG12 1WA
Activities: Activities of other holding companies n.e.c.
Officers: Giuseppe Gioffre, Secretary; Lodivico Gianluca Braguti [1960] Manufacturing Director [Italian]; Peter Edward Bream [1966] Finance Director; Sharon Mary Collins [1974] Director; Carl Douglas Dempsey [1961] Director/Self Employed; Dr Lynn Drummond [1959] Director; Jeremy Anthony Philip Randall [1964] Director/Management Consultant

Verifone (U.K.) Limited
Incorporated: 15 March 1988 *Employees:* 174
Net Worth: £10,336,000 *Total Assets:* £32,080,000
Registered Office: 3 Roundwood Avenue, Stockley Park, Uxbridge, Middlesex, UB11 1AF
Activities: Other information technology service activities
Officers: Vikram Kalidindi Varma, Secretary; Marc Evan Rothman [1964] Director [American]; Vikram Kalidindi Varma [1978] Director/Attorney [American]

Verint Systems UK Limited
Incorporated: 18 April 1991 *Employees:* 440
Net Worth: £30,895,000 *Total Assets:* £91,495,000
Registered Office: 241 Brooklands Road, Weybridge, Surrey, KT13 0RH
Activities: Information technology consultancy activities
Parent: Verint WS Holdings Limited
Officers: Peter Demian Fante [1967] Director/General Counsel [American]; Nicola Guiseppe Nonini [1961] Director; Douglas Edward Robinson [1956] Director/Chief Financial Officer [American]

Verint Technology UK Limited
Incorporated: 7 October 2011 *Employees:* 3
Net Worth: £245,266,640 *Total Assets:* £333,026,240
Registered Office: 241 Brooklands Road, Weybridge, Surrey, KT13 0RH
Activities: Other information technology service activities
Parent: Verint Systems Inc
Officers: Peter Demian Fante [1967] Director/General Counsel [American]; David Peter Outram [1962] Director; Douglas Edward Robinson [1956] Director/Chief Financial Officer [American]

Verint WS Holdings Limited
Incorporated: 22 April 2003 *Employees:* 4
Net Worth: £211,632,000 *Total Assets:* £257,842,000
Registered Office: 241 Brooklands Road, Weybridge, Surrey, KT13 0RH
Activities: Business and domestic software development
Parent: Verint Technology UK Limited
Officers: Peter Demian Fante [1967] Director/General Counsel [American]; Nicola Guiseppe Nonini [1961] Director; David Peter Outram [1962] Director; Douglas Edward Robinson [1956] Director/Chief Financial Officer [American]

Veritas Technologies (UK) Limited
Incorporated: 18 January 1991 *Employees:* 505
Previous: Symantec (UK) Limited
Net Worth: £22,132,000 *Total Assets:* £40,190,000
Registered Office: 350 Brook Drive, Green Park, Reading, Berks, RG2 6UH
Activities: Information technology consultancy activities
Parent: Veritas UK Holding Limited
Officers: Tatiana Bayeva [1981] Director/Attorney [Belarusian]; Paul Bolger [1963] Director/Solicitor

Veritas UK Holding Limited
Incorporated: 9 December 2015
Net Worth: £17,724,560 *Total Assets:* £36,946,128
Registered Office: 350 Brook Drive, Green Park, Reading, Berks, RG2 6UH
Activities: Activities of head offices
Officers: Tatiana Bayeva [1981] Director/Attorney [Belarusian]; Paul Bolger [1963] Director/Solicitor

Verizon Connect UK Limited
Incorporated: 21 October 2004 *Employees:* 70
Previous: Fleetmatics (UK) Limited
Net Worth: £21,010,722 *Total Assets:* £37,205,376
Registered Office: Reading International Business Park, Basingstoke Road, Reading, Berks, RG2 6DA
Activities: Other business support service activities n.e.c.
Officers: Clare Brenda Aitkenhead [1965] Accounting Director; Peter Mitchell [1973] Director [Irish]; John Paul Molamphy [1972] Director/Vice President Software Engineering [Irish]

Verizon European Holdings Limited
Incorporated: 18 July 2002
Net Worth: £1,098,746,496 *Total Assets:* £2,187,184,640
Registered Office: Reading International Business Park, Basingstoke Road, Reading, Berks, RG2 6DA
Activities: Other telecommunications activities
Parent: Verizon Business International Holdings B.V.
Officers: Clare Brenda Aitkenhead [1965] Director Accounting; Francesco Cesare de Maio [1968] Strategic Planning Director [Italian]

Verizon International Limited
Incorporated: 14 January 2003
Net Worth Deficit: £26,049,640 *Total Assets:* £114,782,008
Registered Office: Reading International Business Park, Basingstoke Road, Reading, Berks, RG2 6DA
Activities: Other information technology service activities
Parent: Verizon Communications Inc.
Officers: Clare Brenda Aitkenhead [1965] Accounting Director; Francesco Cesare de Maio [1968] Strategic Planning Director [Italian]

Verizon UK Financing Limited
Incorporated: 19 August 2016
Net Worth: £4,147,980,544 *Total Assets:* £7,794,118,144
Registered Office: Reading International Business Park, Basingstoke Road, Reading, Berks, RG2 6DA
Activities: Other service activities n.e.c.
Parent: Verizon UK Holding Limited
Officers: Clare Brenda Aitkenhead [1965] Director/Accountant; Francesco Cesare de Maio [1968] Director/Accountant [Italian]; Johan Coenraad Schoeman [1964] Director/Accountant

Verizon UK Holding Limited
Incorporated: 19 August 2016
Net Worth: £5,294,593,024 *Total Assets:* £8,376,727,552
Registered Office: Reading International Business Park, Basingstoke Road, Reading, Berks, RG2 6DA
Activities: Other service activities n.e.c.
Parent: Verizon Communication Inc.
Officers: Clare Brenda Aitkenhead [1965] Director/Accountant; Francesco Cesare de Maio [1968] Director/Accountant [Italian]; Johan Coenraad Schoeman [1964] Director/Accountant

Verizon UK Limited
Incorporated: 23 December 1992 *Employees:* 1,194
Net Worth: £718,088,000 *Total Assets:* £899,713,024
Registered Office: Reading International Business Park, Basingstoke Road, Reading, Berks, RG2 6DA
Activities: Wired telecommunications activities
Parent: Verizon European Holdings Limited
Officers: Clare Brenda Aitkenhead [1965] Director Accounting; Francesco Cesare de Maio [1968] Strategic Planning Director [Italian]

The Vernon Educational Trust Limited
Incorporated: 18 December 1974 *Employees:* 161
Net Worth: £32,141,448 *Total Assets:* £40,220,160
Registered Office: Danes Hill School, Leatherhead Road, Oxshott, Leatherhead, Surrey, KT22 0JG
Activities: Primary education
Officers: Richard Quinn, Secretary; Dr Adrian Fairbank [1961] Director/Medical Doctor; Ian Michael Hunt [1960] Director/Chief Executive Officer; Alexandra Mary Selina Hutchinson [1971] Director/Headmistress; Timothy William Jones [1957] Director/Solicitor; Anthony John Lunn [1964] Director; Robert George Mansfield [1950] Director/Chief Executive; John Andrew McLaren [1963] Communications Director; Andrew Hugh Monro [1950] Director/Educational Consultant; Doctor Heather Frances Patel [1959] Director/General Medical Practitioner; Mark Anthony Smith [1962] Director/Educational Consultant; Dr Marc Van Grondelle [1970] Director/Partner Professional Services Firm

Vernon Wholesale Investments Company Limited
Incorporated: 29 January 1992
Net Worth: £155,014,000 *Total Assets:* £159,151,008
Registered Office: 61 London Road, Redhill, Surrey, RH1 1QA
Activities: Activities of other holding companies n.e.c.
Parent: Economydrive Cars Limited
Officers: Kathleen Fiona Conroy, Secretary; Cruciano Infosino [1964] Managing Director [Belgian]; Nigel John Willetts [1972] Director/Chartered Accountant

Vertiv Infrastructure Ltd
Incorporated: 18 August 1967 *Employees:* 539
Previous: Emerson Network Power Limited
Net Worth: £3,982,000 *Total Assets:* £52,474,000
Registered Office: Tor, Saint-Cloud Way, Maidenhead, Berks, SL6 8BN
Activities: Manufacture of other electrical equipment
Parent: Chloride Group Limited
Officers: Anthony Moss, Secretary; Giordano Albertazzi [1966] Sales Director [Italian]; Michael Anthony O'Keeffe [1964] Managing Director; Eamon John Rowan [1959] Director/Vice President Finance [Irish]

Verus Petroleum (UKCS) Limited
Incorporated: 10 December 1991 *Employees:* 17
Previous: Verus Petroleum (UKCS) Limited Limited
Net Worth Deficit: £89,780,000 *Total Assets:* £290,048,992
Registered Office: Harbour Court, Compass Road, North Harbour, Portsmouth, PO6 4ST
Activities: Extraction of crude petroleum
Parent: Verus Petroleum UK Limited
Officers: Andrew Graham McIntosh, Secretary; John Miller Baillie [1963] Director; Peter Findlay Campbell [1958] Director [Australian]; Colin Christie [1966] Finance Director; Alan Thomas Curran [1960] Director/Chief Executive

Vestas Technology UK Limited
Incorporated: 23 December 1993 *Employees:* 134
Net Worth Deficit: £3,097,000 *Total Assets:* £36,010,000
Registered Office: Monks Brook, St Cross Business Park, Newport, Isle of Wight, PO30 5WZ
Activities: Information technology consultancy activities
Parent: Vestas Wind Systems A/S
Officers: Steen Moller [1965] Director/Finance [Danish]; John George Rimmer [1964] Managing Director; Anders Jakob Vedel [1957] Director [Danish]

Vestel UK Limited
Incorporated: 20 May 2003 *Employees:* 71
Net Worth: £8,309,675 *Total Assets:* £140,486,176
Registered Office: Vestel House, 1 Waterside Drive, Langley, Berks, SL3 6EZ
Activities: Wholesale of electronic and telecommunications equipment and parts
Officers: Enis Turan Erdogan [1955] Director and Chairman [Turkish]; Bekir Cem Koksal [1967] Director [Turkish]; Omer Yungul [1955] Director [Turkish]

Vestey Foods Limited
Incorporated: 16 November 1994
Previous: Vestey Foods Group Limited
Net Worth: £22,165,000 *Total Assets:* £22,644,000
Registered Office: 29 Ullswater Crescent, Coulsdon, Surrey, CR5 2HR
Activities: Activities of head offices
Parent: Vestey Holdings Limited
Officers: Neil Thornton, Secretary; Colin George Copland [1954] Director; Neil Thornton [1968] Director; George Moubray William Vestey [1964] Director

Vestey Foods UK Limited
Incorporated: 12 April 2000 *Employees:* 243
Net Worth: £15,999,000 *Total Assets:* £53,420,000
Registered Office: 29 Ullswater Crescent, Coulsdon, Surrey, CR5 2HR
Activities: Wholesale of meat and meat products
Parent: Vestey Foods UK (Holdings) Limited
Officers: Neil Thornton, Secretary; Colin George Copland [1954] Finance Director; Matthew William Flood [1983] Director/Chief Executive Officer; Kenneth Hermansen [1968] Director; George Moubray William Vestey [1964] Director; Neal Wakeham [1970] Director/Accountant

Vestey Group Limited
Incorporated: 24 July 2002
Net Worth: £88,246,000 *Total Assets:* £95,996,000
Registered Office: 29 Ullswater Crescent, Coulsdon, Surrey, CR5 2HR
Activities: Activities of head offices
Parent: Western United Investment Company Limited
Officers: Neil Thornton, Secretary; George Moubray William Vestey [1964] Director/Retail Butchery; Lord Samuel George Armstrong Vestey [1941] Director/Merchant; Honourable William Guy Vestey [1983] Director; Robin John Henry Vesty [1968] Director

Vestey Holdings Limited
Incorporated: 28 May 1900 *Employees:* 940
Net Worth: £74,299,000 *Total Assets:* £168,658,000
Registered Office: 29 Ullswater Crescent, Coulsdon, Surrey, CR5 2HR
Activities: Activities of head offices
Parent: Vestey Group Limited
Officers: Neil Thornton, Secretary; Colin George Copland [1954] Director; James Alexander Scott [1940] Director/Chartered Accountant; George Moubray William Vestey [1964] Director/Retail Butchery; Robin John Henry Vestey [1968] Director

VFS Legal Limited
Incorporated: 11 July 2011
Net Worth: £878,919 *Total Assets:* £26,235,670
Registered Office: Kingfisher House, 21-23 Elmfield Road, Bromley, Kent, BR1 1LT
Activities: Other business support service activities n.e.c.
Parent: Vertical Financial Services Limited
Officers: Alan Irving [1944] Director; Norman John Kenvyn [1957] Director; Robert Andrew Norman [1956] Director; Kathryn Thomson [1978] Director/Lawyer

Viavi Solutions UK Limited
Incorporated: 9 September 1966 *Employees:* 174
Previous: JDSU UK Limited
Net Worth Deficit: £46,195,000 *Total Assets:* £33,317,000
Registered Office: Astor House, Newbury Business Park, London Road, Newbury, Berks, RG14 2PZ
Activities: Wired telecommunications activities
Parent: Viavi Solutions Inc.
Officers: Michael Todd Taylor, Secretary; Amar Mandanna Maletira [1969] Director/Chief Financial Officer [American]; Payam Maveddat [1962] Director/VP and GM [American]; Kevin Christopher Siebert [1968] Director/General Counsel [American]; Michael Todd Taylor [1973] EMEA Legal Director

The Victoria Foundation
Incorporated: 11 September 1985 *Employees:* 261
Net Worth Deficit: £4,511,000 *Total Assets:* £25,976,000
Registered Office: St Davids House, 15 Worple Way, Richmond, Surrey, TW10 6DG
Activities: Hospital activities
Officers: Graham Arthur Ridgeway Ball, Secretary/Director; Graham Arthur Ridgeway Ball [1950] Director; Anthony Ralph Cooke [1948] Director; John Alan Hamblin [1949] Director/Chartered Accountant; Henry Peter Hope [1942] Director/Retired Veterinary Surgeon; Christopher Peter Lyons [1951] Director; Martin Anthony Matthews [1950] Director

Victorygame Limited
Incorporated: 10 February 1983 *Employees:* 3
Net Worth: £10,347,781 *Total Assets:* £36,794,544
Registered Office: 7 The Triangle Centre, Uxbridge Road, Southall, Middlesex, UB1 3ED
Activities: Development of building projects
Officers: Valveer Kaur Pandher, Secretary; Jaswinder Singh Pandher [1977] Director; Surjit Singh Pandher [1954] Director; Tersham Singh Pandher [1975] Director; Valveer Kaur Pandher [1956] Director

ViiV Healthcare Finance 2 Limited
Incorporated: 28 October 2015
Net Worth: £849,372,096 *Total Assets:* £861,767,552
Registered Office: 980 Great West Road, Brentford, Middlesex, TW8 9GS
Activities: Financial intermediation not elsewhere classified
Parent: ViiV Healthcare Limited
Officers: Joceyln Brown [1974] Director/Head of HR; Rebecca Elizabeth Hall [1982] Director, Financial Controller; Timothy Andrew Tordoff [1964] Director/Senior Vice President VIIV Healthcare Europe

ViiV Healthcare Finance Limited
Incorporated: 11 January 2016
Net Worth: £202,044,000 *Total Assets:* £2,271,303,936
Registered Office: 980 Great West Road, Brentford, Middlesex, TW8 9GS
Activities: Financial intermediation not elsewhere classified
Parent: ViiV Healthcare UK (No.3) Limited
Officers: Jill Dawn Anderson [1964] Director; Karen Marion Grainger [1978] Director/Pharmaceutical Regulatory Executive [Irish]; Deborah Jayne Waterhouse [1967] Director

ViiV Healthcare Limited
Incorporated: 14 April 2009
Net Worth: £1,488,999,936 *Total Assets:* £7,080,999,936
Registered Office: 980 Great West Road, Brentford, Middlesex, TW8 9GS
Activities: Activities of head offices
Parent: GlaxoSmithKline Mercury Limited
Officers: Agnieszka Moskal Gallagher, Secretary; Douglas Ernest Giordano [1962] Director [American]; Dr John Apeler Keller [1964] Director/President and CEO Shionogi Inc [American]; John Joseph Lepore [1966] Director [American]; Dr Sabine Luik [1969] Director/Chief Medical Officer [German]; Alexander Roderick MacKenzie [1959] Director/Head of Pharmatherapeutics R & D; Luke Victor Miels [1974] Director/President, Global Pharmaceuticals [Australian]; David Simon Redfern [1966] Director/Chief Strategy Officer; Regis Jean-Pierre Simard [1965] Director/Head of Supply Chain [French]; Deborah Jayne Waterhouse [1967] Director; Dr Pauline Margaret Williams [1967] Director

ViiV Healthcare Overseas Limited
Incorporated: 23 September 2009
Net Worth: £131,093,000 *Total Assets:* £131,581,000
Registered Office: 980 Great West Road, Brentford, Middlesex, TW8 9GS
Activities: Wholesale of pharmaceutical goods
Parent: ViiV Healthcare Limited
Officers: Jill Dawn Anderson [1964] Director; Karen Marion Grainger [1978] Director/Pharmaceutical Regulatory Executive [Irish]; Deborah Jayne Waterhouse [1967] Director

ViiV Healthcare Trading Services UK Limited
Incorporated: 5 August 2009
Net Worth: £52,910,000 *Total Assets:* £3,306,328,064
Registered Office: 980 Great West Road, Brentford, Middlesex, TW8 9GS
Activities: Wholesale of pharmaceutical goods
Parent: ViiV Healthcare Limited
Officers: Jill Dawn Anderson [1964] Director; Karen Marion Grainger [1978] Director/Pharmaceutical Regulatory Executive [Irish]; Deborah Jayne Waterhouse [1967] Director

ViiV Healthcare UK (No.3) Limited
Incorporated: 26 October 2012
Net Worth: £3,944,185,088 *Total Assets:* £4,336,324,096
Registered Office: 980 Great West Road, Brentford, Middlesex, TW8 9GS
Activities: Activities of other holding companies n.e.c.
Shareholders: ViiV Healthcare UK Limited; ViiV Healthcare Limited
Officers: Jill Dawn Anderson [1964] Director; Karen Grainger Marion [1978] Director/Pharmaceutical Regulatory Executive [Irish]; Deborah Jayne Waterhouse [1967] Director

ViiV Healthcare UK (No.4) Limited
Incorporated: 18 December 2015
Net Worth: £210,515,008 *Total Assets:* £256,428,992
Registered Office: 980 Great West Road, Brentford, Middlesex, TW8 9GS
Activities: Other professional, scientific and technical activities n.e.c.
Parent: ViiV Healthcare Limited
Officers: Jill Dawn Anderson [1964] Director; Karen Marion Grainger [1978] Director/Pharmaceutical Regulatory Executive [Irish]; Deborah Jayne Waterhouse [1967] Director

ViiV Healthcare UK (No.5) Limited
Incorporated: 18 January 2016
Net Worth: £13,046,000 *Total Assets:* £77,537,000
Registered Office: 980 Great West Road, Brentford, Middlesex, TW8 9GS
Activities: Other professional, scientific and technical activities n.e.c.
Parent: ViiV Healthcare Limited
Officers: Jill Dawn Anderson [1964] Director; Karen Marion Grainger [1978] Director/Pharmaceutical Regulatory Executive [Irish]; Deborah Jayne Waterhouse [1967] Director

ViiV Healthcare UK Limited
Incorporated: 13 August 2009 *Employees:* 175
Net Worth: £4,456,565,248 *Total Assets:* £7,015,779,840
Registered Office: 980 Great West Road, Brentford, Middlesex, TW8 9GS
Activities: Wholesale of pharmaceutical goods
Parent: ViiV Healthcare Limited
Officers: Jill Dawn Anderson [1964] Director; Karen Marion Grainger [1978] Director/Pharmaceutical Regulatory Executive [Irish]; Deborah Jayne Waterhouse [1967] Director

Vinci Construction UK Limited
Incorporated: 13 September 1988 *Employees:* 3,298
Net Worth: £120,806,000 *Total Assets:* £546,112,000
Registered Office: Astral House, Imperial Way, Watford, Herts, WD24 4WW
Activities: Construction of commercial buildings
Parent: Vinci PLC
Officers: Jean-Pierre Bonnet, Secretary; Christopher Carl Brennan [1969] Director/Accountant; Bruno Michel Dupety [1956] Director/Engineer [French]; Julian Paul Gatward [1966] Director/Civil Engineer; Christopher Michael Hamer [1959] Director/Civil Engineer; Anthony Kennedy Raikes [1964] Director/Chartered Civil Engineer

Vinci PLC
Incorporated: 5 October 1962 *Employees:* 3,482
Net Worth: £80,003,000 *Total Assets:* £556,436,992
Registered Office: Astral House, Imperial Way, Watford, Herts, WD24 4WW
Activities: Activities of head offices
Parent: Sogea Holdings (UK) Limited
Officers: Ruth Elizabeth Tilbrook, Secretary; Bruno Michel Dupety [1956] Director/Engineer [French]; Richard Michel Rene Francioli [1959] Director/Company Chairman [French]; Yann Paul Grolimund [1959] Director [French]

Vinci UK Developments Limited
Incorporated: 13 January 1960 *Employees:* 5
Previous: Vinci Investments Limited
Net Worth: £14,502,000 *Total Assets:* £58,511,000
Registered Office: Astral House, Imperial Way, Watford, Herts, WD24 4WW
Activities: Activities of head offices
Parent: Vinci Construction UK Limited
Officers: Bruno Michel Dupety [1956] Director/Engineer [French]; Graham Lambert [1969] Director

Vines Limited
Incorporated: 19 September 1984 *Employees:* 337
Net Worth: £12,106,585 *Total Assets:* £50,147,448
Registered Office: Vines House, Slyfield Green, Guildford, Surrey, GU1 1RD
Activities: Sale of new cars and light motor vehicles
Parent: Guildford Portfolios Limited
Officers: Sean Patrick Kelly, Secretary; Sean Patrick Kelly [1968] Director; Brendan Gael Moynahan [1948] Director/Consultant [American]; Lesley Shelly [1948] Director/Executive [American]

Vink UK Limited
Incorporated: 25 July 1975 *Employees:* 436
Previous: Vink UK PLC
Net Worth: £23,877,000 *Total Assets:* £46,216,000
Registered Office: Holmes House, 24-30 Baker Street, Weybridge, Surrey, KT13 8AU
Activities: Wholesale of wood, construction materials and sanitary equipment
Parent: Vink Holdings Limited
Officers: Robin Michael Howard, Finance Director; Anthony Michael Bird [1965] Finance Director; Keith Whiting Colburn [1948] Director [American]; Roger David Goddard [1953] Director/Chartered Accountant; Robin Michael Howard [1961] Finance Director; Douglas Talbot McNair [1947] Director; David Whittow Williams [1957] Director/General Manager; William Sones Woof [1951] Director/Solicitor

Virgin Atlantic Airways Limited
Incorporated: 26 November 1981 *Employees:* 7,331
Net Worth: £47,800,000 *Total Assets:* £1,653,299,968
Registered Office: Company Secretariat, The VHQ, Fleming Way, Crawley, W Sussex, RH10 9DF
Activities: Scheduled passenger air transport
Parent: Virgin Travel Group Limited
Officers: Ian Mario Joseph de Sousa, Secretary; Mark Michael Charles Anderson [1966] Director; Edward Herman Bastian [1957] Director [American]; Sir Richard Charles Nicholas Branson [1950] Director; Glen William Hauenstein [1960] Director [American]; Dwight Lamar James [1973] Director [American]; Dwight Lamar James [1973] Director [American]; Cornelis Johan Albert Koster [1971] Director [Dutch]; Thomas MacKay [1975] Director; Gordon Douglas McCallum [1960] Director; Peter Michael Russell Norris [1955] Director/Self Employed; Shai Joseph Weiss [1968] Director; Ian Philip Woods [1974] Director

Virgin Atlantic International Limited
Incorporated: 13 April 2015
Net Worth: £2,742,000 *Total Assets:* £454,659,008
Registered Office: Company Secretariat, The VHQ, Fleming Way, Crawley, W Sussex, RH10 9DF
Activities: Scheduled passenger air transport
Parent: VAA Holdings UK Limited
Officers: Ian Mario Joseph de Sousa, Secretary; Mark Michael Charles Anderson [1966] Director; Edward Herman Bastian [1957] Director [American]; Sir Richard Charles Nicholas Branson [1950] Director; Glen William Hauenstein [1960] Director [American]; Dwight Lamar James [1973] Director [American]; Cornelis Johan Albert Koster [1971] Director [Dutch]; Thomas MacKay [1975] Director; Gordon Douglas McCallum [1960] Director; Peter Michael Russell Norris [1955] Director/Self Employed; Shai Joseph Weiss [1968] Director; Ian Philip Woods [1974] Director

Virgin Atlantic Limited
Incorporated: 29 January 2014 *Employees:* 8,303
Net Worth Deficit: £25,000,000 *Total Assets:* £1,723,800,064
Registered Office: Company Secretariat, The VHQ, Fleming Way, Crawley, W Sussex, RH10 9DF
Activities: Activities of head offices
Shareholders: Richard Charles Nicholas Branson; Delta Air Lines Inc.
Officers: Ian Mario Joseph de Sousa, Secretary; Mark Michael Charles Anderson [1966] Director; Edward Herman Bastian [1957] Director [American]; Sir Richard Charles Nicholas Branson [1950] Director; Glen William Hauenstein [1960] Director [American]; Dwight Lamar James [1973] Director [American]; Cornelis Johan Albert Koster [1971] Director [Dutch]; Thomas MacKay [1975] Director; Gordon Douglas McCallum [1960] Director; Peter Michael Russell Norris [1955] Director/Self Employed; Shai Joseph Weiss [1968] Group Legal Director; Ian Philip Woods [1974] Director

Virgin Atlantic Two Limited
Incorporated: 24 April 1998 *Employees:* 8,303
Net Worth Deficit: £24,400,000 *Total Assets:* £1,724,800,000
Registered Office: Company Secretariat, The VHQ, Fleming Way, Crawley, W Sussex, RH10 9DF
Activities: Activities of head offices
Parent: Virgin Atlantic Limited
Officers: Ian Mario Joseph de Sousa, Secretary; Mark Michael Charles Anderson [1966] Director; Edward Herman Bastian [1957] Director [American]; Sir Richard Charles Nicholas Branson [1950] Director; Glen William Hauenstein [1960] Director [American]; Dwight Lamar James [1973] Director [American]; Cornelis Johan Albert Koster [1971] Director [Dutch]; Thomas MacKay [1975] Director; Gordon Douglas McCallum [1960] Director; Peter Michael Russell Norris [1955] Director/Self Employed; Shai Joseph Weiss [1968] Director; Ian Philip Woods [1974] Director

Virgin Holidays Limited
Incorporated: 21 December 1984 *Employees:* 972
Net Worth: £53,937,000 *Total Assets:* £272,508,000
Registered Office: Company Secretariat, The VHQ, Fleming Way, Crawley, W Sussex, RH10 9DF
Activities: Tour operator activities
Parent: Virgin Travel Group Limited
Officers: Ian Mario Joseph de Sousa, Secretary; Mark Michael Charles Anderson [1966] Director; Edward Herman Bastian [1957] Director [American]; Sir Richard Charles Nicholas Branson [1950] Director; Glen William Hauenstein [1960] Director [American]; Dwight Lamar James [1973] Director [American]; Cornelis Johan Albert Koster [1971] Director [Dutch]; Thomas MacKay [1975] Director; Gordon Douglas McCallum [1960] Director; Peter Michael Russell Norris [1955] Director/Self Employed; Shai Joseph Weiss [1968] Director; Ian Philip Woods [1974] Director

Virgin Media Business Limited
Incorporated: 24 January 1984
Net Worth: £307,360,000 *Total Assets:* £308,745,984
Registered Office: Media House, Bartley Wood Business Park, Hook, Hants, RG27 9UP
Activities: Other business support service activities n.e.c.
Parent: Virgin Media Operations Limited
Officers: Gillian Elizabeth James, Secretary; Robert Dominic Dunn [1966] Director/Chief Financial Officer; Mine Ozkan Hifzi [1966] Director/Solicitor; Peter John Anthony Kelly [1963] Managing Director; Thomas Mockridge [1955] Director/Chief Executive Officer [New Zealander]

Virgin Media Communications Limited
Incorporated: 4 March 1998
Net Worth: £11,976,165,376 *Total Assets:* £12,160,775,168
Registered Office: Media House, Bartley Wood Business Park, Hook, Hants, RG27 9UP
Activities: Other business support service activities n.e.c.
Parent: Liberty Global Europe 2 Limited
Officers: Gillian Elizabeth James, Secretary; Robert Dominic Dunn [1966] Director/Chief Financial Officer; Mine Ozkan Hifzi [1966] Director/Solicitor; Thomas Mockridge [1955] Director/Chief Executive Officer [New Zealander]

Virgin Media Finance PLC
Incorporated: 3 March 2004 *Employees:* 14,061
Net Worth: £1,098,599,936 *Total Assets:* £16,046,799,872
Registered Office: Media House, Bartley Wood Business Park, Hook, Hants, RG27 9UP
Activities: Other business support service activities n.e.c.
Parent: Virgin Media Communications Limited
Officers: Gillian Elizabeth James, Secretary; Robert Dominic Dunn [1966] Director/Chief Financial Officer; Michael Thomas Fries [1963] Director/CEO, Liberty Global PLC [American]; Mine Ozkan Hifzi [1966] Director/Solicitor; Thomas Mockridge [1955] Director/Chief Executive Officer [New Zealander]

Virgin Media Finco Limited
Incorporated: 25 April 2012
Net Worth: £555,633,984 *Total Assets:* £10,793,962,496
Registered Office: Media House, Bartley Wood Business Park, Hook, Hants, RG27 9UP
Activities: Other business support service activities n.e.c.
Parent: Virgin Media Investment Holdings Limited
Officers: Gillian Elizabeth James, Secretary; Robert Dominic Dunn [1966] Director/Chief Financial Officer; Mine Ozkan Hifzi [1966] Director/Solicitor

Virgin Media Investment Holdings Limited
Incorporated: 15 March 1996
Net Worth: £322,190,016 *Total Assets:* £11,721,251,840
Registered Office: Media House, Bartley Wood Business Park, Hook, Hants, RG27 9UP
Activities: Activities of other holding companies n.e.c.
Parent: Virgin Media Finance PLC
Officers: Gillian Elizabeth James, Secretary; Robert Dominic Dunn [1966] Director/Chief Financial Officer; Mine Ozkan Hifzi [1966] Director/Solicitor; Thomas Mockridge [1955] Director/Chief Executive Officer [New Zealander]

Virgin Media Investments Limited
Incorporated: 18 December 2009
Net Worth: £6,021,791,744 *Total Assets:* £6,021,791,744
Registered Office: Media House, Bartley Wood Business Park, Hook, Hants, RG27 9UP
Activities: Other business support service activities n.e.c.
Parent: Virgin Media Investment Holdings Limited
Officers: Gillian Elizabeth James, Secretary; Robert Dominic Dunn [1966] Director/Chief Financial Officer; Mine Ozkan Hifzi [1966] Director/Solicitor

Virgin Media Limited
Incorporated: 13 March 1991 *Employees:* 13,084
Net Worth: £6,514,803,200 *Total Assets:* £17,811,765,248
Registered Office: Media House, Bartley Wood Business Park, Hook, Hants, RG27 9UP
Activities: Other telecommunications activities
Parent: Virgin Media Operations Limited
Officers: Gillian Elizabeth James, Secretary; Robert Dominic Dunn [1966] Director/Chief Financial Officer; Mine Ozkan Hifzi [1966] Director/Solicitor; Thomas Mockridge [1955] Director/Chief Executive Officer [New Zealander]; Lutz Markus Schuler [1968] Director/Chief Operating Officer [German]

Virgin Media Mobile Finance Limited
Incorporated: 27 May 2014
Net Worth: £30,483,000 *Total Assets:* £227,052,000
Registered Office: Media House, Bartley Wood Business Park, Hook, Hants, RG27 9UP
Activities: Other business support service activities n.e.c.
Parent: Liberty Global Europe 2 Limited
Officers: Gillian Elizabeth James, Secretary; Robert Dominic Dunn [1966] Director/Chief Financial Officer; Duncan Higgins [1978] Executive Director, Commercial

Virgin Media Payments Ltd
Incorporated: 11 December 2006
Net Worth: £34,173,000 *Total Assets:* £34,173,000
Registered Office: Media House, Bartley Wood Business Park, Hook, Hants, RG27 9UP
Activities: Other business support service activities n.e.c.
Parent: Virgin Media Limited
Officers: Gillian Elizabeth James, Secretary; Robert Dominic Dunn [1966] Director/Chief Financial Officer; Maxwell Kendrew Handforth [1971] Director of Shared Services; Mine Ozkan Hifzi [1966] Director/Solicitor; Thomas Mockridge [1955] Director/Chief Executive Officer [New Zealander]

Virgin Media Secured Finance PLC
Incorporated: 18 December 2009
Net Worth: £100,731,000 *Total Assets:* £5,158,961,152
Registered Office: Media House, Bartley Wood Business Park, Hook, Hants, RG27 9UP
Activities: Other business support service activities n.e.c.
Parent: Virgin Media Investment Holdings Limited
Officers: Gillian Elizabeth James, Secretary; Robert Dominic Dunn [1966] Director/Chief Financial Officer; Mine Ozkan Hifzi [1966] Director/Solicitor

Virgin Media Senior Investments Limited
Incorporated: 7 September 2016
Net Worth: £6,231,620,096 *Total Assets:* £6,231,620,096
Registered Office: Media House, Bartley Wood Business Park, Bartley Way, Hook, Hants, RG27 9UP
Activities: Activities of head offices
Parent: Virgin Media Investments Limited
Officers: Gillian Elizabeth James, Secretary; Robert Dominic Dunn [1966] Director/Chief Financial Officer; Mine Ozkan Hifzi [1966] Director/Solicitor

Virgin Media SFA Finance Limited
Incorporated: 3 March 2010
Net Worth: £204,882,000 *Total Assets:* £3,649,946,112
Registered Office: Media House, Bartley Wood Business Park, Hook, Hants, RG27 9UP
Activities: Other business support service activities n.e.c.
Parent: Virgin Media Investment Holdings Limited
Officers: Gillian Elizabeth James, Secretary; Robert Dominic Dunn [1966] Director/Chief Financial Officer; Mine Ozkan Hifzi [1966] Director/Solicitor

Virgin Media Wholesale Limited
Incorporated: 21 June 1990
Net Worth: £589,937,024 *Total Assets:* £3,200,429,056
Registered Office: Media House, Bartley Wood Business Park, Hook, Hants, RG27 9UP
Activities: Other business support service activities n.e.c.
Parent: Virgin Media Operations Limited
Officers: Gillian Elizabeth James, Secretary; Robert Dominic Dunn [1966] Director/Chief Financial Officer; Mine Ozkan Hifzi [1966] Director/Solicitor; Thomas Mockridge [1955] Director/Chief Executive Officer [New Zealander]

Virgin Mobile Telecoms Limited
Incorporated: 29 January 1999
Net Worth: £475,223,008 *Total Assets:* £686,273,024
Registered Office: Media House, Bartley Wood Business Park, Hook, Hants, RG27 9UP
Activities: Other telecommunications activities
Parent: Virgin Media Operations Limited
Officers: Gillian Elizabeth James, Secretary; Robert Dominic Dunn [1966] Director/Chief Financial Officer; Mine Ozkan Hifzi [1966] Director/Solicitor; Thomas Mockridge [1955] Director/Chief Executive Officer [New Zealander]

Virgin Travel Group Limited
Incorporated: 5 July 1988
Net Worth: £16,714,000 *Total Assets:* £176,088,992
Registered Office: Company Secretariat, The VHQ, Fleming Way, Crawley, W Sussex, RH10 9DF
Activities: Activities of head offices
Parent: Virgin Atlantic Two Limited
Officers: Ian Mario Joseph de Sousa, Secretary; Mark Michael Charles Anderson [1966] Director; Edward Herman Bastian [1957] Director [American]; Sir Richard Charles Nicholas Branson [1950] Director; Glen William Hauenstein [1960] Director [American]; Dwight Lamar James [1973] Director [American]; Cornelis Johan Albert Koster [1971] Director [Dutch]; Thomas MacKay [1975] Director; Gordon Douglas McCallum [1960] Director; Peter Michael Russell Norris [1955] Director/Self Employed; Shai Joseph Weiss [1968] Director; Ian Philip Woods [1974] Director

Viridor Resource Management Limited
Incorporated: 13 October 1998 *Employees:* 26
Net Worth: £11,896,000 *Total Assets:* £31,902,000
Registered Office: First Floor Offices, Riverside House, Sir Thomas Longley Road, Medway City Estate, Rochester, Kent, ME2 4FN
Activities: Recovery of sorted materials
Parent: Viridor Waste Management Limited
Officers: Scott Edward Massie, Secretary; Simon Anthony Follett Pugsley, Secretary; Karen Senior, Secretary; Phillip Charles Piddington [1956] Director; Elliot Arthur James Rees [1974] Director/Accountant; Keith Trower [1954] Director [Irish]

Vision Engineering Limited
Incorporated: 26 February 1958 *Employees:* 163
Net Worth: £28,181,272 *Total Assets:* £38,766,024
Registered Office: The Freeman Building, Galileo Drive, Send, Woking, Surrey, GU23 7ER
Activities: Manufacture of optical precision instruments
Shareholders: Janet Paula Curtis; Mark Edward Curtis; Joyce Marie Freeman
Officers: Jacqueline Arnold [1960] Finance Director; Janet Paula Curtis [1957] Director; Mark Edward Curtis [1959] Managing Director; Joyce Marie Freeman [1929] Director; Stephen Arthur Mead [1958] Manufacturing Director; Graham Peter Francis Mercer [1959] Design & Development Director

Visiontrend Limited
Incorporated: 7 December 2005
Net Worth: £92,615,656 *Total Assets:* £114,855,480
Registered Office: 24 Park Road South, Havant, Hants, PO9 1HB
Activities: Other service activities n.e.c.
Shareholders: James Leslie Shaw; Robert Anthony Green; Caspar MacDonald-Hall
Officers: Sandra Margaret MacDonald Hall, Secretary; Caspar MacDonald-Hall [1950] Director

Visual Impact (UK) Limited
Incorporated: 7 April 1987 *Employees:* 125
Net Worth: £20,098,052 *Total Assets:* £29,229,290
Registered Office: Unit 3 Teddington Business Park, Station Road, Teddington, Middlesex, TW11 9BQ
Activities: Television programme production activities
Major Shareholder: Neil Jonathan Quincey
Officers: Graham Hawkins [1967] Director; Paresh Jani [1966] Director/Accountant; Tim Sparrock [1968] Sales Director

Vitec Group Holdings Limited
Incorporated: 5 July 1999
Net Worth: £82,590,000 *Total Assets:* £162,190,000
Registered Office: Bridge House, Heron Square, Richmond, Surrey, TW9 1EN
Activities: Activities of head offices
Parent: The Vitec Group PLC
Officers: Jonathan Mark Bolton, Secretary; Jonathan Mark Bolton [1966] Director/Company Secretary; Martin Jon Green [1968] Director/Head of Business Development; Katharina Helen Marie Kearney-Croft [1974] Finance Director

The Vitec Group PLC.
Incorporated: 30 January 1928 *Employees:* 1,675
Net Worth: £135,600,000 *Total Assets:* £289,700,000
Registered Office: Bridge House, Heron Square, Richmond, Surrey, TW9 1EN
Activities: Activities of head offices
Officers: Jonathan Mark Bolton, Secretary; Stephen Clive Bird [1960] Director/Chief Executive; Martin Jon Green [1968] Director/Business Development; Christopher John Humphrey [1957] Director/Accountant; Katharina Helen Marie Kearney-Croft [1974] Finance Director; John McDonough [1951] Director; Ian Philip McHoul [1960] Director; Duncan John Penny [1963] Director/Chief Executive; Caroline Agnes Morgan Thomson [1954] Director; John Richard Tyson [1970] Director

Vitec Investments Limited
Incorporated: 19 August 1998
Net Worth: £131,802,000 *Total Assets:* £260,059,008
Registered Office: Bridge House, Heron Square, Richmond, Surrey, TW9 1EN
Activities: Activities of head offices
Parent: Vitec Group Holdings Limited
Officers: Jonathan Mark Bolton, Secretary; Jonathan Mark Bolton [1966] Director/Company Secretary; Martin Jon Green [1968] Director/Head of Business Development; Katharina Helen Marie Kearney-Croft [1974] Finance Director

Vitec Production Solutions Limited
Incorporated: 11 July 1983 *Employees:* 180
Previous: Vitec Videocom Limited
Net Worth: £129,394,000 *Total Assets:* £164,204,000
Registered Office: Bridge House, Heron Square, Richmond, Surrey, TW9 1EN
Activities: Machining
Parent: The Vitec Group PLC
Officers: Jonathan Mark Bolton, Secretary; Jonathan Mark Bolton [1966] Director/Company Secretary; Martin Jon Green [1968] Director/Head of Business Development; Dr Alan Charles Hollis [1964] Managing Director; Katharina Helen Marie Kearney-Croft [1974] Finance Director; Andrew John Kelly [1977] Director/Chartered Accountant; Richard Graham Satchell [1980] Director

Viva Eyewear UK Limited
Incorporated: 23 May 1995
Net Worth: £28,518,000 *Total Assets:* £29,155,000
Registered Office: 107 Main Street, Greenham Business Park, Greenham, Thatcham, Berks, RG19 6HN
Activities: Manufacture of other wearing apparel and accessories n.e.c.
Officers: James Alexander Bernard Gotch, Secretary; Massimo Stefanello [1961] Director [Italian]; Giovanni Zoppas [1958] Director [Italian]

Vivid Imaginations Limited
Incorporated: 13 October 1992 *Employees:* 67
Net Worth: £58,833,000 *Total Assets:* £107,855,000
Registered Office: Ashbourne House, The Guildway, Old Portsmouth Road, Guildford, Surrey, GU3 1LS
Activities: Manufacture of other games and toys, n.e.c.
Parent: Vivid Toy Group Limited
Officers: Richard John Brooks, Secretary; Richard John Brooks [1966] Director; Adar Golad [1952] Director/Chairman [Israeli]; Jochanan Golad [1984] Director [Dutch]

Vivid Topco Ltd
Incorporated: 8 March 2017 *Employees:* 118
Net Worth Deficit: £4,304,000 *Total Assets:* £42,276,000
Registered Office: Ashbourne House, The Guildway, Old Portsmouth Road, Guildford, Surrey, GU3 1LS
Activities: Activities of other holding companies n.e.c.
Parent: Guk Holding Limited
Officers: Jochanan Golad [1984] Director [Dutch]

VM Transfers (No 5) Limited
Incorporated: 10 March 1993
Previous: General Cable Holdings Limited
Net Worth: £185,422,000 *Total Assets:* £185,422,000
Registered Office: Media House, Bartley Wood Business Park, Hook, Hants, RG27 9UP
Activities: Activities of other holding companies n.e.c.
Parent: Telewest Limited
Officers: Gillian Elizabeth James, Secretary; Robert Dominic Dunn [1966] Director/Chief Financial Officer; Mine Ozkan Hifzi [1966] Director/Solicitor

VMFH Limited
Incorporated: 15 December 2014
Net Worth: £2,880,235,008 *Total Assets:* £2,880,235,008
Registered Office: Media House, Bartley Wood Business Park, Hook, Hants, RG27 9UP
Activities: Other business support service activities n.e.c.
Parent: Virgin Media Finance PLC
Officers: Gillian Elizabeth James, Secretary; Robert Dominic Dunn [1966] Director/Chief Financial Officer; Mine Ozkan Hifzi [1966] Director/Solicitor

Voda Limited
Incorporated: 12 September 1984
Net Worth: £6,620,428,800 *Total Assets:* £6,620,496,896
Registered Office: Vodafone House, The Connection, Newbury, Berks, RG14 2FN
Activities: Activities of head offices
Parent: Vodafone International Operations Limited
Officers: Dr Malcolm Finn [1975] Director; Jonathan Paul Mitchell [1981] Director; Andrew Thurston Raggett [1972] Director

Vodafone (New Zealand) Hedging Limited
Incorporated: 12 February 2001
Net Worth: £449,255,296 *Total Assets:* £453,859,808
Registered Office: Vodafone House, The Connection, Newbury, Berks, RG14 2FN
Activities: Banks
Parent: Vodafone International Operations Limited
Officers: Dr Malcolm Finn [1975] Director; Jonathan Paul Mitchell [1981] Director; Andrew Thurston Raggett [1972] Director

Vodafone 2.
Incorporated: 4 October 2000
Net Worth: £106,668,007,424 *Total Assets:* £258,799,370,240
Registered Office: Vodafone House, The Connection, Newbury, Berks, RG14 2FN
Activities: Other service activities n.e.c.
Parent: Vodaphone Limited
Officers: Dr Malcolm Finn [1975] Director; Jonathan Paul Mitchell [1981] Director; Andrew Thurston Raggett [1972] Director

Vodafone 5 Limited
Incorporated: 3 September 2008
Net Worth: £10,753,825,792 *Total Assets:* £15,891,663,872
Registered Office: Vodafone House, The Connection, Newbury, Berks, RG14 2FN
Activities: Other business support service activities n.e.c.
Parent: Vodafone Americas 4
Officers: Dr Malcolm Finn [1975] Director; Jonathan Paul Mitchell [1981] Director; Andrew Thurston Raggett [1972] Director

Vodafone 6 UK
Incorporated: 10 December 2013
Net Worth: £31,894,018,048 *Total Assets:* £31,920,627,712
Registered Office: Vodafone House, The Connection, Newbury, Berks, RG14 2FN
Activities: Other business support service activities n.e.c.
Shareholders: Vodafone Finance UK Limited; Vodafone Holdings Luxembourg Limited
Officers: Simon Bailey [1978] Director; Dr Malcolm Finn [1975] Director; Jonathan Paul Mitchell [1981] Director; Andrew Thurston Raggett [1972] Director

Vodafone Americas 4
Incorporated: 3 October 2007
Net Worth: £113,643,585,536 *Total Assets:* £113,643,651,072
Registered Office: Vodafone House, The Connection, Newbury, Berks, RG14 2FN
Activities: Other telecommunications activities
Shareholders: Vodafone Finance UK Limited; Vodafone Holdings Luxembourg Limited
Officers: Dr Malcolm Finn [1975] Director; Jonathan Paul Mitchell [1981] Director; Andrew Thurston Raggett [1972] Director

Vodafone Benelux Limited
Incorporated: 18 April 2001
Net Worth: £86,941,097,984 *Total Assets:* £117,624,102,912
Registered Office: Vodafone House, The Connection, Newbury, Berks, RG14 2FN
Activities: Activities of head offices
Parent: Vodafone Holdings Luxembourg Limited
Officers: Dr Malcolm Finn [1975] Director; Jonathan Paul Mitchell [1981] Director; Andrew Thurston Raggett [1972] Director

Vodafone Cellular Limited
Incorporated: 20 January 1967
Net Worth: £1,527,368,576 *Total Assets:* £2,859,026,688
Registered Office: Vodafone House, The Connection, Newbury, Berks, RG14 2FN
Activities: Activities of head offices
Parent: Vodafone Group PLC
Officers: Dr Malcolm Finn [1975] Director; Jonathan Paul Mitchell [1981] Director; Andrew Thurston Raggett [1972] Director

Vodafone Enterprise U.K.
Incorporated: 28 January 1981
Previous: Cable & Wireless U.K
Net Worth: £608,182,976 *Total Assets:* £613,563,008
Registered Office: Vodafone House, The Connection, Newbury, Berks, RG14 2FN
Activities: Other telecommunications activities
Shareholders: Cable & Wireless Waterside Holdings Limited; Cable and Wireless Nominee Limited
Officers: Alan Mark Milton [1978] Director; Helen Ruth Watson [1972] Director/Solicitor

Vodafone Euro Hedging Limited
Incorporated: 17 March 2000
Net Worth: £52,906,643,456 *Total Assets:* £52,929,667,072
Registered Office: Vodafone House, The Connection, Newbury, Berks, RG14 2FN
Activities: Financial intermediation not elsewhere classified
Parent: Vodafone Benelux Limited
Officers: Dr Malcolm Finn [1975] Director; Jonathan Paul Mitchell [1981] Director; Andrew Thurston Raggett [1972] Director

Vodafone Euro Hedging Two
Incorporated: 14 August 2000
Net Worth Deficit: £28,058,673,152 *Total Assets:* £416,108,576
Registered Office: Vodafone House, The Connection, Newbury, Berks, RG14 2FN
Activities: Activities of head offices
Parent: Vodafone Worldwide Holdings Limited
Officers: Dr Malcolm Finn [1975] Director; Jonathan Paul Mitchell [1981] Director; Andrew Thurston Raggett [1972] Director

Vodafone Europe UK
Incorporated: 27 April 2006
Net Worth: £2,704,178,432 *Total Assets:* £2,704,178,432
Registered Office: Vodafone House, The Connection, Newbury, Berks, RG14 2FN
Activities: Other telecommunications activities
Parent: Vodafone Consolidated Holdings Limited
Officers: Dr Malcolm Finn [1975] Director; Jonathan Paul Mitchell [1981] Director; Andrew Thurston Raggett [1972] Director

Vodafone European Investments
Incorporated: 31 March 2000
Net Worth: £48,103,342,080 *Total Assets:* £62,744,809,472
Registered Office: Vodafone House, The Connection, Newbury, Berks, RG14 2FN
Activities: Other business support service activities n.e.c.
Parent: Vodafone Group PLC
Officers: Dr Malcolm Finn [1975] Director; Jonathan Paul Mitchell [1981] Director; Andrew Thurston Raggett [1972] Director

Vodafone Finance Limited
Incorporated: 14 March 1995
Net Worth: £1,472,621,440 *Total Assets:* £47,205,191,680
Registered Office: Vodafone House, The Connection, Newbury, Berks, RG14 2FN
Activities: Banks
Parent: Vodafone Group PLC
Officers: Simon Bailey [1978] Director; Dr Malcolm Finn [1975] Director; Jonathan Paul Mitchell [1981] Director; Andrew Thurston Raggett [1972] Director

Vodafone Finance Sweden
Incorporated: 9 June 1987
Net Worth: £17,986,588,672 *Total Assets:* £17,986,588,672
Registered Office: Vodafone House, The Connection, Newbury, Berks, RG14 2FN
Activities: Non-trading company
Parent: Vodafone Consolidated Holdings Limited
Officers: Dr Malcolm Finn [1975] Director; Jonathan Paul Mitchell [1981] Director; Andrew Thurston Raggett [1972] Director

Vodafone Finance UK Limited
Incorporated: 4 February 2000
Net Worth: £83,368,878,080 *Total Assets:* £86,096,789,504
Registered Office: Vodafone House, The Connection, Newbury, Berks, RG14 2FN
Activities: Financial intermediation not elsewhere classified
Parent: Vodafone Benelux Limited
Officers: Dr Malcolm Finn [1975] Director; Jonathan Paul Mitchell [1981] Director; Andrew Thurston Raggett [1972] Director

Vodafone Financial Operations
Incorporated: 13 June 2000
Net Worth: £531,379,232 *Total Assets:* £539,256,640
Registered Office: Vodafone House, The Connection, Newbury, Berks, RG14 2FN
Activities: Other telecommunications activities
Parent: Vodafone International Operations Limited
Officers: Dr Malcolm Finn [1975] Director; Jonathan Paul Mitchell [1981] Director; Andrew Thurston Raggett [1972] Director

Vodafone Global Content Services Limited
Incorporated: 5 September 2000
Net Worth Deficit: £374,245,440 *Total Assets:* £65,571,856
Registered Office: Vodafone House, The Connection, Newbury, Berks, RG14 2FN
Activities: Management consultancy activities other than financial management
Parent: Vizzavi Limited
Officers: Dr Malcolm Finn [1975] Director; Jonathan Paul Mitchell [1981] Director; Andrew Thurston Raggett [1972] Director

Vodafone Global Enterprise Limited
Incorporated: 16 August 1993 *Employees:* 1,043
Net Worth: £295,932,832 *Total Assets:* £441,131,488
Registered Office: Vodafone House, The Connection, Newbury, Berks, RG14 2FN
Activities: Other telecommunications activities
Parent: Vodafone International Operations Limited
Officers: Gary Adey [1971] Director; Erik Brenneis [1970] Director [German]; Alan Royston Kinch [1978] Director; Kerry Phillip [1967] Director/Solicitor; Justin Shields [1973] Director; Neil Colin Smith [1969] Director

Vodafone Group Public Limited Company
Incorporated: 17 July 1984 *Employees:* 106,135
Net Worth: £67,640,000,512 *Total Assets:* £145,610,997,760
Registered Office: Vodafone House, The Connection, Newbury, Berks, RG14 2FN
Activities: Other telecommunications activities
Officers: Rosemary Elisabeth Scudamore Martin, Secretary; Sanjiv Ahuja [1956] Director [American]; Sir Crispin Davis [1949] Director; Margherita Della Valle [1965] Director [Italian/British]; Michel Roger Demare [1956] Director [Belgian/Swiss]; Dame Clara Hedwig Frances Furse [1957] Director; Valerie Frances Gooding [1950] Director; Renee James [1964] Director [American]; Samuel Esson Jonah [1949] Director [Ghanaian]; Gerhard Johannes Kleisterlee [1946] Director [Dutch]; Maria Amparo Moraleda Martinez [1964] Director [Spanish]; David Thomas Nish [1960] Director; Nicholas Jonathan Read [1964] Director

Vodafone Group Services Limited
Incorporated: 7 July 1999 *Employees:* 3,410
Net Worth: £613,232,896 *Total Assets:* £1,385,153,280
Registered Office: Vodafone House, The Connection, Newbury, Berks, RG14 2FN
Activities: Other telecommunications activities
Parent: Vodafone International Operations Limited
Officers: Peter Becker-Pennrich [1974] Director [German]; John Connors [1963] Director of Tax; Jacqueline Conway [1964] Director/Solicitor; Alberto Ripepi [1960] Director [Italian]; Gianluca Ventura [1967] Director [Italian]

Vodafone Holdings Luxembourg Limited
Incorporated: 18 April 2001
Net Worth: £171,057,643,520 *Total Assets:* £177,893,588,992
Registered Office: Vodafone House, The Connection, Newbury, Berks, RG14 2FN
Activities: Other business support service activities n.e.c.
Parent: Vodafone 2.
Officers: Dr Malcolm Finn [1975] Director; Jonathan Paul Mitchell [1981] Director; Andrew Thurston Raggett [1972] Director

Vodafone Intermediate Enterprises Limited
Incorporated: 1 November 1999
Net Worth: £98,479,210,496 *Total Assets:* £127,809,896,448
Registered Office: Vodafone House, The Connection, Newbury, Berks, RG14 2FN
Activities: Activities of head offices
Shareholders: Vodafone International Holdings Limited; Vodafone Worldwide Holdings Limited
Officers: Dr Malcolm Finn [1975] Director; Jonathan Paul Mitchell [1981] Director; Andrew Thurston Raggett [1972] Director

Vodafone International Holdings Limited
Incorporated: 9 March 1993
Net Worth: £78,659,330,048 *Total Assets:* £78,708,416,512
Registered Office: Vodafone House, The Connection, Newbury, Berks, RG14 2FN
Activities: Activities of head offices
Parent: Vodafone International Operations Limited
Officers: Dr Malcolm Finn [1975] Director; Jonathan Paul Mitchell [1981] Director; Andrew Thurston Raggett [1972] Director

Vodafone International Operations Limited
Incorporated: 9 March 1993
Net Worth: £34,587,602,944 *Total Assets:* £142,090,059,776
Registered Office: Vodafone House, The Connection, Newbury, Berks, RG14 2FN
Activities: Activities of head offices
Parent: Vodafone European Investments
Officers: Dr Malcolm Finn [1975] Director; Jonathan Paul Mitchell [1981] Director; Andrew Thurston Raggett [1972] Director

Vodafone Investment UK
Incorporated: 27 April 2006
Net Worth: £3,570,189,824 *Total Assets:* £3,570,189,824
Registered Office: Vodafone House, The Connection, Newbury, Berks, RG14 2FN
Activities: Other telecommunications activities
Parent: Vodafone Consolidated Holdings Limited
Officers: Dr Malcolm Finn [1975] Director; Jonathan Paul Mitchell [1981] Director; Andrew Thurston Raggett [1972] Director

Vodafone Investments Limited
Incorporated: 27 November 1980
Net Worth Deficit: £326,370,336 *Total Assets:* £2,096,534,656
Registered Office: Vodafone House, The Connection, Newbury, Berks, RG14 2FN
Activities: Other telecommunications activities
Parent: Vodafone Group PLC
Officers: Dr Malcolm Finn [1975] Director; Jonathan Paul Mitchell [1981] Director; Andrew Thurston Raggett [1972] Director

Vodafone Limited
Incorporated: 7 January 1980 *Employees:* 4,699
Net Worth: £6,246,000,128 *Total Assets:* £10,822,800,384
Registered Office: Vodafone House, The Connection, Newbury, Berks, RG14 2FN
Activities: Installation of industrial machinery and equipment
Parent: Vodafone Mobile Network Limited
Officers: Helen Lamprell, Secretary; Nicholas Simon Jeffery [1968] Director; Helen Lamprell [1972] Director; Emanuele Tournon [1960] Director [Italian]

Vodafone Marketing UK
Incorporated: 25 March 2009
Net Worth: £24,650,704,896 *Total Assets:* £24,650,733,568
Registered Office: Vodafone House, The Connection, Newbury, Berks, RG14 2FN
Activities: Other telecommunications activities
Shareholders: Vodafone Finance UK Limited; Vodafone Holdings Luxembourg Limited
Officers: Dr Malcolm Finn [1975] Director; Jonathan Paul Mitchell [1981] Director; Andrew Thurston Raggett [1972] Director

Vodafone Mobile Communications Limited
Incorporated: 8 March 2000
Net Worth: £4,438,352,384 *Total Assets:* £4,438,440,448
Registered Office: Vodafone House, The Connection, Newbury, Berks, RG14 2FN
Activities: Activities of head offices
Parent: Vodafone International Operations Limited
Officers: Dr Malcolm Finn [1975] Director; Jonathan Paul Mitchell [1981] Director; Andrew Thurston Raggett [1972] Director

Vodafone Mobile Enterprises Limited
Incorporated: 31 March 2000
Net Worth: £11,002,535,936 *Total Assets:* £18,664,331,264
Registered Office: Vodafone House, The Connection, Newbury, Berks, RG14 2FN
Activities: Activities of head offices
Parent: Vodafone 5 Limited
Officers: Dr Malcolm Finn [1975] Director; Jonathan Paul Mitchell [1981] Director; Andrew Thurston Raggett [1972] Director

Vodafone Mobile Network Limited
Incorporated: 31 March 2000
Net Worth: £16,495,235,072 *Total Assets:* £16,567,668,736
Registered Office: Vodafone House, The Connection, Newbury, Berks, RG14 2FN
Activities: Activities of head offices
Parent: Vodafone Mobile Enterprises Limited
Officers: Dr Malcolm Finn [1975] Director; Jonathan Paul Mitchell [1981] Director; Andrew Thurston Raggett [1972] Director

Vodafone Oceania Limited
Incorporated: 14 April 2000
Net Worth: £1,371,168,000 *Total Assets:* £1,372,180,096
Registered Office: Vodafone House, The Connection, Newbury, Berks, RG14 2FN
Activities: Other business support service activities n.e.c.
Parent: Vodafone Consolidated Holdings Limited
Officers: Dr Malcolm Finn [1975] Director; Jonathan Paul Mitchell [1981] Director; Andrew Thurston Raggett [1972] Director

Vodafone Overseas Finance Limited
Incorporated: 2 March 2001
Net Worth: £2,123,751,808 *Total Assets:* £4,182,124,800
Registered Office: Vodafone House, The Connection, Newbury, Berks, RG14 2FN
Activities: Banks
Parent: Vodafone Finance Limited
Officers: Simon Bailey [1978] Director; Dr Malcolm Finn [1975] Director; Jonathan Paul Mitchell [1981] Director; Andrew Thurston Raggett [1972] Director

Vodafone Overseas Holdings Limited
Incorporated: 15 April 1993
Net Worth: £5,348,871,168 *Total Assets:* £5,756,371,456
Registered Office: Vodafone House, The Connection, Newbury, Berks, RG14 2FN
Activities: Non-trading company
Parent: Vodafone International Operations Limited
Officers: Dr Malcolm Finn [1975] Director; Jonathan Paul Mitchell [1981] Director; Andrew Thurston Raggett [1972] Director

Vodafone Panafon UK
Incorporated: 27 July 2007
Net Worth: £28,383,660 *Total Assets:* £28,383,658
Registered Office: Vodafone House, The Connection, Newbury, Berks, RG14 2FN
Activities: Activities of other holding companies n.e.c.
Parent: Vodafone Consolidated Holdings Limited
Officers: Dr Malcolm Finn [1975] Director; Jonathan Paul Mitchell [1981] Director; Andrew Thurston Raggett [1972] Director

Vodafone Property Investments Limited
Incorporated: 4 January 2000
Net Worth: £13,413,000 *Total Assets:* £136,118,000
Registered Office: Vodafone House, The Connection, Newbury, Berks, RG14 2FN
Activities: Buying and selling of own real estate
Parent: Vodafone UK Limited
Officers: Diane Josephine McIntyre [1973] Director; Adam Martin Parsons [1977] Director; Emanuele Tournon [1960] Director [Italian]

Vodafone Sales & Services Limited
Incorporated: 11 March 2009 *Employees:* 83
Net Worth: £1,079,061,888 *Total Assets:* £1,225,272,320
Registered Office: Vodafone House, The Connection, Newbury, Berks, RG14 2FN
Activities: Other telecommunications activities
Parent: Vodafone International Operations Limited
Officers: Phillip Paul Kesha Patel [1971] Director [New Zealander]; Sara Martins de Oliveira [1974] Director [Portuguese]; Diego Massidda [1965] Director [Italian]; Stefano Parisse [1967] Strategy & New Business Director [Italian]; Christian Sommer [1967] Director [German]; Martin David Spink [1974] Finance Director

Vodafone UK Limited
Incorporated: 7 March 1988
Net Worth: £4,596,311,040 *Total Assets:* £5,884,290,048
Registered Office: Vodafone House, The Connection, Newbury, Berks, RG14 2FN
Activities: Activities of head offices
Parent: Vodafone Group PLC
Officers: Nicholas Simon Jeffery [1968] Director; Helen Lamprell [1972] Director; Emanuele Tournon [1960] Director [Italian]

Vodafone Worldwide Holdings Limited
Incorporated: 18 December 1996
Net Worth: £26,069,698,560 *Total Assets:* £43,352,322,048
Registered Office: Vodafone House, The Connection, Newbury, Berks, RG14 2FN
Activities: Activities of head offices
Parent: Vodafone International Operations Limited
Officers: Dr Malcolm Finn [1975] Director; Jonathan Paul Mitchell [1981] Director; Andrew Thurston Raggett [1972] Director

Vodafone Yen Finance Limited
Incorporated: 13 February 2002
Net Worth: £5,450,684,928 *Total Assets:* £5,450,707,968
Registered Office: Vodafone House, The Connection, Newbury, Berks, RG14 2FN
Activities: Financial intermediation not elsewhere classified
Parent: Vodafone Benelux Limited
Officers: Dr Malcolm Finn [1975] Director; Jonathan Paul Mitchell [1981] Director; Andrew Thurston Raggett [1972] Director

Vodaphone Limited
Incorporated: 18 April 1989
Net Worth: £59,568,795,648 *Total Assets:* £120,346,157,056
Registered Office: Vodafone House, The Connection, Newbury, Berks, RG14 2FN
Activities: Activities of head offices
Parent: Vodafone Intermediate Enterprises Limited
Officers: Dr Malcolm Finn [1975] Director; Jonathan Paul Mitchell [1981] Director; Andrew Thurston Raggett [1972] Director

Vodata Limited
Incorporated: 15 May 1990
Net Worth: £74,748,583,936 *Total Assets:* £82,321,711,104
Registered Office: Vodafone House, The Connection, Newbury, Berks, RG14 2FN
Activities: Activities of head offices
Parent: Vodafone Intermediate Enterprises Limited
Officers: Dr Malcolm Finn [1975] Director; Jonathan Paul Mitchell [1981] Director; Andrew Thurston Raggett [1972] Director

Volex PLC
Incorporated: 19 September 1919 *Employees:* 6,466
Net Worth: £36,625,332 *Total Assets:* £117,791,552
Registered Office: Holbrook House, 34-38 Hill Rise, Richmond, Surrey, TW10 6UA
Activities: Manufacture of electronic components
Officers: Daren John Morris, Secretary; Adrian Chamberlain [1957] Director; Dean Roderick Moore [1957] Director; Daren John Morris [1970] Director; Nathaniel Rothschild [1971] Director [Canadian]

Volga-Dnepr UK Ltd.
Incorporated: 3 August 1999 *Employees:* 45
Net Worth: £93,069,952 *Total Assets:* £105,627,016
Registered Office: 3 Roundwood Avenue, Stockley Park, Uxbridge, Middlesex, UB11 1AF
Activities: Freight air transport
Major Shareholder: Alexey Ivanovich Isaykin
Officers: Elena Lebedeva, Secretary; Alexey Isaykin [1952] Director/Businessman [Cypriot]

Volkswagen Financial Services (UK) Limited
Incorporated: 12 July 1993 *Employees:* 929
Net Worth: £1,245,260,032 *Total Assets:* £14,847,398,912
Registered Office: Brunswick Court, Yeomans Drive, Blakelands, Milton Keynes, Bucks, MK14 5LR
Activities: Financial intermediation not elsewhere classified
Parent: Volkswagen Aktiengesellschaft
Officers: Harald Hesske [1962] Director [German]; Jens Legenbauer [1965] Director [German]; Dr Michael Eberhard Reinhart [1963] Director [German]; Michael John Todd [1966] Director/Chief Executive; Albertus Antonius Maria Van Den Bergh [1961] Director [Dutch]; Patrick Ortwin Welter [1969] Director [German]

Volkswagen Group United Kingdom Limited
Incorporated: 1 January 1953 *Employees:* 1,028
Net Worth: £719,299,968 *Total Assets:* £3,532,100,096
Registered Office: Yeomans Drive, Blakelands, Milton Keynes, Bucks, MK14 5AN
Activities: Sale of new cars and light motor vehicles
Parent: Volkswagen Aktiengesellschaft
Officers: James Trainor, Secretary; Christian Dahlheim [1968] Director/Chairman [German]; Ulf Konrad Dierkesmann [1975] Director/Head of Sales Europe West/South [German]; Lukas Folc [1978] Finance Director [Czech]; Jaroslav Hercog [1973] Director [Slovak]; Manfred Kantner [1966] Director Sales Europe [Austrian]; Fintan Roger Knight [1971] Director/Audi Vice President Sales - Europe; Michael Alexander Obrowski [1969] Director [German]; Alexander James Campbell Smith [1974] Managing Director; Dr. Jan Utermarck [1967] Executive Director Sales Europe [German]

Volt Europe Limited
Incorporated: 14 July 1983 *Employees:* 88
Net Worth: £2,463,704 *Total Assets:* £25,277,672
Registered Office: Volt House, 3 Chapel Road, Redhill, Surrey, RH1 1QD
Activities: Temporary employment agency activities
Parent: Volt Europe Holdings Limited
Officers: Dawn Maureen Mary Ford, Secretary; Dawn Maureen Mary Ford [1977] Director/Solicitor; Richard Henry Herring [1957] Director

Voluntary Service Overseas
Incorporated: 18 September 1961 *Employees:* 730
Net Worth: £22,137,000 *Total Assets:* £47,489,000
Registered Office: 100 London Road, Kingston upon Thames, Surrey, KT2 6QJ
Activities: Other education n.e.c.
Officers: Jennifer Margaret Owen, Secretary; Charles Paul Abani [1960] Director/International Development Practitioner [Nigerian/British]; Gustaaf Teunis Franciscus Eskens [1949] Director/Company Chair [Dutch]; Hardeep Jhutty [1982] Director; Dr Noerine Kaleeba [1951] Director/HIV & Aids Campaigner (Retired) [Ugandan]; Christopher James Merry [1961] Director/Chief Executive; Stephen Meredith Pidgeon [1947] Director/Fundraising Consultant; Amanda Rowlatt [1962] Director/Economist; Biranchi Naryan Upadhyaya [1964] Director/Development Expert [Indian]; James Samuel Younger [1951] Director

Volution Group PLC
Incorporated: 15 May 2014 *Employees:* 1,617
Net Worth: £165,212,992 *Total Assets:* £326,948,992
Registered Office: Fleming Way, Crawley, W Sussex, RH10 9YX
Activities: Other manufacturing n.e.c.
Officers: Michael John Anscombe, Secretary; Ian Dew [1959] Director/Chief Financial Officer; Ronnie George [1969] Director/Chief Executive Officer; Peter John Hill [1952] Director; Paul Robert Hollingworth [1960] Director; Amanda Mellor [1964] Director; Anthony John Reading [1943] Director; Claire Tiney [1960] Director

Volution Holdings Limited
Incorporated: 22 October 2002 *Employees:* 4
Net Worth: £17,878,000 *Total Assets:* £21,703,000
Registered Office: c/o Volution Group PLC, Fleming Way, Crawley, W Sussex, RH10 9YX
Activities: Manufacture of other electrical equipment
Parent: Volution Group PLC
Officers: Ian Dew [1959] Director/Chartered Accountant; Ronnie George [1969] Director

Volution Ventilation Group Limited
Incorporated: 22 October 2002 *Employees:* 4
Net Worth: £148,752,000 *Total Assets:* £200,487,008
Registered Office: c/o Volution Group PLC, Fleming Way, Crawley, W Sussex, RH10 9YX
Activities: Manufacture of other electrical equipment
Parent: Volution Holdings Limited
Officers: Ian Dew [1959] Director/Chartered Accountant; Ronnie George [1969] Director

Volvo Car UK Limited
Incorporated: 27 July 1988 *Employees:* 116
Net Worth: £15,467,000 *Total Assets:* £339,385,984
Registered Office: Scandinavia House, Norreys Drive, Maidenhead, Berks, SL6 4FL
Activities: Sale of new cars and light motor vehicles
Major Shareholder: Li Shufu
Officers: Michael David Evans, Secretary; Per Anders Ansgar [1963] Director/Group Controller [Swedish]; Alf Soren Edlund [1955] Finance Director [Swedish]; Hans Erik Oscarsson [1965] Director/CFO & Senior Vice President, Volvo Car Group [Swedish]; Jonathan Michael Wakefield [1966] Managing Director

Vostochnaya Technica UK Limited
Incorporated: 30 July 2004 *Employees:* 3
Net Worth: £73,418,760 *Total Assets:* £114,761,320
Registered Office: First Floor, Aurora Vanwall Business Park, Vanwall Road, Maidenhead, Berks, SL6 4UB
Activities: Renting and leasing of trucks and other heavy vehicles
Parent: Barloworld Equipment UK Limited
Officers: Anton Globus [1979] Finance Director [South African]; Gavin Arthur Knight [1964] General Director [South African]; Trevor Quinton McGeer [1964] Director [South African]; Dominic Malentsha Sewela [1965] Director/Chief Executive Officer [South African]; Donald Gert Wilson [1957] Finance Director [South African]

VS Alliance Limited
Incorporated: 10 August 2012
Net Worth: £103,472,256 *Total Assets:* £103,512,560
Registered Office: Dixcart House, Addlestone Road, Bourne Business Park, Addlestone, Surrey, KT15 2LE
Activities: Activities of other holding companies n.e.c.
Major Shareholder: Victor Shkulev
Officers: Laurence Binge [1959] Director/Accountant; Simon Peter Barry Horne [1963] Director/Chief Financial Officer Hearst; Peter Anthony Robertson [1980] Director/Lawyer; Victor Shkulev [1958] Director/CEO of Media Group [Russian]

VS International Holdings Limited
Incorporated: 2 November 2016 *Employees:* 2,766
Net Worth: £69,226,488 *Total Assets:* £690,030,784
Registered Office: 1st Floor, West Davidson House, Forbury Square, Reading, Berks, RG1 3EU
Activities: Other software publishing
Parent: Veeam Software International UK Limited
Officers: William Howard Largent [1955] Director/Chief Executive Officer [American]

VWS (UK) Ltd
Incorporated: 14 May 1937 *Employees:* 433
Net Worth: £29,956,000 *Total Assets:* £76,190,000
Registered Office: Windsor Court, Kingsmead Business Park, High Wycombe, Bucks, HP11 1JU
Activities: Water collection, treatment and supply
Parent: OTV Birwelco Ltd
Officers: Ian Thomas Heggie, Secretary; Philip Andrew Chattle [1958] HR Director; Mark Dyson [1961] Director; Beverley Michelle Eagle [1958] HR Director; Martyn Paul Fisher [1961] Director; Ian Thomas Heggie [1968] Financial Director; Nora Ikene [1969] Director; Sunil Kumar Lakhenpaul [1961] Director/Accountant; Annabel Marie Odile Dolores Mouquet [1980] Finance Director [French]

W.N. Developments Limited
Incorporated: 20 February 1987
Net Worth: £28,460,100 *Total Assets:* £36,522,976
Registered Office: 13 College Road, Bedford, MK42 9PL
Activities: Development of building projects
Shareholder: Seamus Neville
Officers: Therese Kelly, Secretary; Michelle Nolan, Secretary/Office Administrator [Irish]; Edmond William Daly [1963] Director/Surveyor [Irish]; Therese Kelly [1982] Director [Irish]; Brendan Neville [1960] Director [Irish]; Eoin Neville [1985] Director/Site Manager [Irish]; Seamus Neville [1952] Director [Irish]; William Neville [1980] Director [Irish]

The W1 London Limited
Incorporated: 23 May 2014 *Employees:* 3
Previous: Royalton 35MHS Limited
Net Worth: £124,463 *Total Assets:* £160,808,032
Registered Office: The Observatory, Castlefield Road, Reigate, Surrey, RH2 0SG
Activities: Development of building projects
Officers: Adam James Bulmer [1983] Director/Solicitor; Nicholas John Edwards [1973] Director; Peter John Wood [1946] Director

Wadlow Energy Holdings Limited
Incorporated: 23 June 2011
Net Worth: £1,000 *Total Assets:* £23,460,000
Registered Office: Beaufort Court, Egg Farm Lane, Kings Langley, Herts, WD4 8LR
Activities: Activities of head offices
Parent: DIF Infra 4 UK Limited
Officers: Dominic James Hearth, Secretary; David Lau [1981] Director/Originator [German]; Helen Mary Murphy [1981] Director/Asset Manager [Irish]

Wadlow Energy Limited
Incorporated: 30 November 2010
Net Worth Deficit: £12,638,000 *Total Assets:* £47,619,000
Registered Office: Beaufort Court, Egg Farm Lane, Kings Langley, Herts, WD4 8LR
Activities: Other specialised construction activities n.e.c.
Parent: Wadlow Energy Holdings Limited
Officers: Dominic James Hearth, Secretary; David Lau [1981] Director/Originator [German]; Helen Mary Murphy [1981] Director/Asset Manager [Irish]

Waingels Academies Trust
Incorporated: 2 June 2015 *Employees:* 150
Net Worth: £30,579,952 *Total Assets:* £32,906,436
Registered Office: Waingels Road, Woodley, Reading, Berks, RG5 4RF
Activities: General secondary education
Officers: Gareth Morgan Hayes [1963] Director/Engineer; Michael Marsden [1967] Director/Engineer; Caroline Norris [1962] Director/Headteacher; David McLean Reilly [1958] Director/Civil Servant; David Simon Whittall [1960] Director/IT Programme Manager

Wakefield Waste Holdings Limited
Incorporated: 22 December 2015
Net Worth Deficit: £12,444,000 *Total Assets:* £112,236,000
Registered Office: Dunedin House, Auckland Park, Mount Farm, Bletchley, Milton Keynes, Bucks, MK1 1BU
Activities: Non-trading company
Shareholders: Equitix Infrastructure 4 Limited; Renewi PFI Investments Limited
Officers: Philip Bernard Griffin-Smith, Secretary; Alistair Daniel Brookes [1976] Director/Accountant; Andrew Keith Harmer [1964] Investment Director; Richard Daniel Knight [1974] Director; Adam Nathaniel Richford [1976] Director; William Spurr [1964] Contract Director; Nathan John Wakefield [1974] Director

Wakefield Waste PFI Limited
Incorporated: 28 August 2012
Net Worth Deficit: £12,444,000 *Total Assets:* £112,236,000
Registered Office: Dunedin House, Auckland Park, Mount Farm, Milton Keynes, Bucks, MK1 1BU
Activities: Other service activities n.e.c.
Parent: Wakefield Waste PFI Holdings Limited
Officers: Philip Bernard Griffin-Smith, Secretary; Alistair Daniel Brookes [1976] Director; Andrew Keith Harmer [1964] Investment Director; Richard Daniel Knight [1974] Director; Adam Nathaniel Richford [1976] Director; William Spurr [1964] Director; Nathan John Wakefield [1974] Director

Walbrook Investments Limited
Incorporated: 15 October 1996
Net Worth: £6,757,295 *Total Assets:* £20,875,936
Registered Office: Unit 3 Stalham Business Park, Rushenden Road, Queenborough, Kent, ME11 5HE
Activities: Other letting and operating of own or leased real estate
Major Shareholder: Thomas Donald Allsworth
Officers: Clive Andrew Morris, Secretary; Thomas Donald Allsworth [1965] Director; Clive Andrew Morris [1970] Director

The Waldegrave Trust
Incorporated: 4 July 2012 *Employees:* 154
Net Worth: £22,315,844 *Total Assets:* £24,606,262
Registered Office: Waldegrave School, Fifth Cross Road, Twickenham, Middlesex, TW2 5LH
Activities: General secondary education
Officers: Alexandra Clare Warburton, Secretary; Karen Janette Oliver [1969] Director/Home; Frances Joy Perrow [1964] Director/Communications Consultant; Tracy Victoria Royle [1970] Director/Employee at Microsoft; Andrew Michael Tanner [1968] Director/IT Consultant; Elizabeth Tongue [1973] Director/Headteacher; Michael Barry Wilkinson [1957] Director/Employee at BP

Walgreens Boots Alliance Services Limited
Incorporated: 11 November 2009 *Employees:* 299
Previous: Alliance Boots Management Services Limited
Net Worth: £40,490,000 *Total Assets:* £82,593,000
Registered Office: 2 The Heights, Brooklands, Weybridge, Surrey, KT13 0NY
Activities: Other business support service activities n.e.c.
Parent: Alliance Boots Holdings Limited
Officers: Frank Standish, Secretary; Claude Louis Bahoshy [1973] Director; Martin Christopher Delve [1967] Director/Accountant; Mark Francis Muller [1964] Director; Frank Standish [1963] Director [Irish]

James Walker & Co. Limited
Incorporated: 16 October 1989 *Employees:* 416
Net Worth: £22,143,000 *Total Assets:* £27,391,000
Registered Office: Lion House, Oriental Road, Woking, Surrey, GU22 8AP
Activities: Manufacture of other rubber products
Parent: James Walker Group Limited
Officers: Anthony Balko [1964] Director; Ian Howard Bell [1962] Director; Mark Brook [1971] Director; Peter Hall [1963] Finance Director; Diederik Neeb [1965] Director [Dutch]; Peter George Needham [1959] Director; Geoffrey Teasdale [1961] Commercial Director

Walker Greenbank PLC.
Incorporated: 3 May 1899 *Employees:* 686
Net Worth: £61,612,000 *Total Assets:* £99,653,000
Registered Office: Chalfont House, Oxford Road, Denham, Bucks, UB9 4DX
Activities: Activities of head offices
Officers: Caroline Geary, Secretary; Michael David Gant [1969] Director; Christopher Charles Bevan Rogers [1960] Director; Terry George Stannard [1950] Director/Consultant; Vijaykumar Champaklal Thakrar [1961] Director; Dame Ila Dianne Thompson [1950] Director

James Walker Group Limited
Incorporated: 2 September 1921 *Employees:* 1,991
Net Worth: £98,692,000 *Total Assets:* £136,724,992
Registered Office: Lion House, Oriental Road, Woking, Surrey, GU22 8AP
Activities: Activities of head offices
Officers: Andrew Donald Douglas Cook [1939] Director; Naomi Jane Coxwell [1963] Director; David Bernard Murray Jackson [1972] Director; Diederik Neeb [1965] Director [Dutch]; Peter George Needham [1959] Director/Chairman; William Murray Black Steele [1948] Director

Walker Logistics (Holdings) Ltd
Incorporated: 12 January 2005 *Employees:* 75
Net Worth: £2,995,729 *Total Assets:* £20,948,136
Registered Office: 337 Bath Road, Slough, Berks, SL1 5PR
Activities: Activities of head offices
Major Shareholder: Philip Nigel Walker
Officers: Amanda Jane Hall, Secretary; Philip Nigel Walker [1957] Director; William Joseph Robert Walker [1987] Director

Walkers Snack Foods Limited
Incorporated: 9 January 1989 *Employees:* 2,879
Net Worth: £170,076,992 *Total Assets:* £467,982,016
Registered Office: 450 South Oak Way, Green Park, Reading, Berks, RG2 6UW
Activities: Other business support service activities n.e.c.
Parent: Pepsico Holdings
Officers: Holly King, Secretary; Joanne Kerry Averiss [1963] Director/VP Law; Ian Lindsay Ellington [1967] Director/General Manager; Victoria Elizabeth Evans [1970] Director/Solicitor; Angus MacDonald [1972] Director/Vice President Sales; Andrew John MacLeod [1962] Director/Vice President; Claire Ellen Stone [1969] Finance Director

Walkers Snacks (Distribution) Limited
Incorporated: 13 May 1998 *Employees:* 615
Net Worth: £24,851,000 *Total Assets:* £80,737,000
Registered Office: 450 South Oak Way, Green Park, Reading, Berks, RG2 6UW
Activities: Other business support service activities n.e.c.
Parent: Pepsico Holdings
Officers: Holly King, Secretary; Joanne Kerry Averiss [1963] Director/VP Law; Ian Lindsay Ellington [1967] Director/General Manager; Victoria Elizabeth Evans [1970] Director/Solicitor; Angus MacDonald [1972] Director/Vice President Sales; Andrew John MacLeod [1962] Director/Vice President; Claire Ellen Stone [1969] Finance Director

Walkers Snacks Limited
Incorporated: 2 December 1997 *Employees:* 390
Net Worth: £147,730,000 *Total Assets:* £304,375,008
Registered Office: 450 South Oak Way, Green Park, Reading, Berks, RG2 6UW
Activities: Other business support service activities n.e.c.
Parent: Pepsico Holdings
Officers: Holly King, Secretary; Joanne Kerry Averiss [1963] Director/VP Law; Ian Lindsay Ellington [1967] Director/General Manager; Victoria Elizabeth Evans [1970] Director/Solicitor; Angus MacDonald [1972] Director/Vice President Sales; Andrew John MacLeod [1962] Director/Vice President; Claire Ellen Stone [1969] Finance Director

Walnut Investments Limited
Incorporated: 12 September 2003 *Employees:* 2
Net Worth: £21,532,900 *Total Assets:* £29,585,306
Registered Office: Globe House, Eclipse Park, Sittingbourne Road, Maidstone, Kent, ME14 3EN
Activities: Activities of open-ended investment companies
Shareholders: Christopher Michael Brake; Paul Reginald Brake; Francis Robert Brake; Penelope Ann Lang; Michelle Louise Leveridge; Michael John Trigg; Philip Riches Wilson
Officers: Paul Reginald Brake, Secretary/Director; Paul Reginald Brake [1947] Director; Philip Riches Wilson [1955] Director

Walon Limited
Incorporated: 6 November 1978 *Employees:* 764
Net Worth: £22,338,000 *Total Assets:* £81,161,000
Registered Office: Headway House, Crosby Way, Farnham, Surrey, GU9 7XG
Activities: Freight transport by road
Parent: BCA Automotive Limited
Officers: Martin Richard Letza, Secretary; Nigel Gregory Glenn [1972] Managing Director; Timothy Giles Lampert [1970] Director; Nicholas John Trowell [1976] Finance Director

The Walsall Hospital Company (Holdings) Limited
Incorporated: 10 July 2007
Net Worth Deficit: £8,427,000 *Total Assets:* £164,771,008
Registered Office: 8 White Oak Square, London Road, Swanley, Kent, BR8 7AG
Activities: Activities of head offices
Shareholders: BIIF Hold Co III Limited; Innisfree Secondary Partners 2 LLP
Officers: Bryan Michael Acutt [1979] Director/Investment Manager; Gaynor Birley-Smith [1966] Investment Director; David John Brooking [1967] Investment Director; John Ivor Cavill [1972] Director; Benjamin Christopher Jacob Dean [1979] Director/Investment Manager

The Walsall Hospital Company PLC
Incorporated: 31 August 2007
Net Worth Deficit: £8,427,000 *Total Assets:* £164,771,008
Registered Office: 8 White Oak Square, London Road, Swanley, Kent, BR8 7AG
Activities: Combined facilities support activities
Parent: The Walsall Hospital Company (Holdings) Limited
Officers: Bryan Michael Acutt [1979] Director/Investment Manager; Gaynor Birley-Smith [1966] Investment Director; David John Brooking [1967] Investment Director; John Ivor Cavill [1972] Director; Benjamin Christopher Jacob Dean [1979] Director/Investment Manager; Michael Edward Fry [1958] Director

A J Walter Aviation Limited
Incorporated: 21 July 1961 *Employees:* 499
Net Worth: £66,948,620 *Total Assets:* £192,894,608
Registered Office: The Headquarters, Maydwell Avenue, Slinfold, Horsham, W Sussex, RH13 0AS
Activities: Service activities incidental to air transportation
Officers: Henry Joseph Lorrimore Preston, Secretary; Andrew Sylvain Bernhardt [1960] Director; Christopher Hammond Broadhead [1955] Director/Banker; Randeep Grewal [1965] Director [Italian]; Christopher Angus Drake Whiteside [1968] Director; John Calum Wolstenholme [1973] Director/Sales & Commercial

Walthamstow Hall
Incorporated: 29 August 1996 *Employees:* 121
Net Worth: £19,190,368 *Total Assets:* £22,273,568
Registered Office: Walthamstow Hall Bursars Office, Holly Bush Lane, Sevenoaks, Kent, TN13 3UL
Activities: Pre-primary education
Officers: Patrick Andrew Horner, Secretary; Jayne Briony Adams [1975] Director/Solicitor; Andrew Martin Baddeley [1964] Director/Chartered Accountant; Alun Grant Evans [1955] Director/Stockbroker; Roger Nicholas Evernden [1946] Director/Musician & Education Consultant; Peter Andrew Gloyne [1956] Director/Banker; Simon Craig Heather [1977] Director/Youth Minister; Dr Nigel Wolfe Jepps [1955] Director/Scientist; Janet Joynes [1953] Director/Retired; Dr Jane Clare Higginson Kevis [1956] Director/Consultant Clinical Psychologist; Thomas Graham Lacey [1957] Director/Retired; Jonathan Wayne Lewis [1967] Finance Director; Sarah Alison Lewis-Davies [1960] Director/Teacher; Professor Alastair Tom Parslow Pearce [1953] Director/Educationalist; Belinda Rattray [1961] Director

Warborough Investments Limited
Incorporated: 30 March 1962 *Employees:* 2
Net Worth: £58,755,496 *Total Assets:* £61,271,024
Registered Office: 198 Lower Addiscombe Road, Croydon, Surrey, CR0 7AB
Activities: Other letting and operating of own or leased real estate
Parent: Ocobase Limited
Officers: Simon Leslie Upward, Secretary; Paul David Upward [1962] Director; Simon Leslie Upward [1961] Director

Waremoss Limited
Incorporated: 3 July 1979 *Employees:* 716
Net Worth: £26,758,504 *Total Assets:* £45,366,268
Registered Office: 6 Bolton Close, Bellbrook Industrial Park, Uckfield, E Sussex, TN22 1PH
Activities: Dispensing chemist in specialised stores
Officers: Anna Piyoosh Chotai, Secretary; Bipin Kamarshi Chotai [1947] Director/Pharmacist; Piyoosh Kamarshibhai Chotai [1950] Director/Accountant

Warrant Investments PLC
Incorporated: 22 March 1994 *Employees:* 5
Net Worth: £19,620,204 *Total Assets:* £42,415,112
Registered Office: One Wellstones, Watford, Herts, WD17 2AE
Activities: Other business support service activities n.e.c.
Shareholder: Jeremy Laurence Stevens
Officers: Jeremy Laurence Stevens, Secretary; Anthony Ian Fine [1938] Director/Chartered Surveyor; Jeremy Laurence Stevens [1959] Director/Surveyor

Wartsila UK Limited
Incorporated: 16 March 1971 *Employees:* 418
Net Worth: £11,846,000 *Total Assets:* £56,391,000
Registered Office: 4 Marples Way, Havant, Hants, PO9 1NX
Activities: Repair and maintenance of ships and boats
Officers: Jayne Louise Proctor, Secretary; Tamara de Gruijter [1972] Director [Dutch]; John Richard Henshaw [1964] Director; Timo Ensio Koponen [1969] Director [Finnish]; Christopher David Rowlands [1972] Director; David Joseph Szymanski [1976] Director [French]

Wartsila Voyage Holding Limited
Incorporated: 15 September 2016 *Employees:* 962
Previous: Transas Limited
Net Worth: £23,447,968 *Total Assets:* £92,429,616
Registered Office: Building 2000, Lakeside North Harbour, Western Road, Portsmouth, PO6 3FP
Activities: Activities of other holding companies n.e.c.
Officers: Thomas Barr, Secretary; Johannes Arjen Marco Jan Berends [1968] Director/Vice President Finance and Business Control Marine [Dutch]; Matti Juhani Hupli [1966] Director/Engineer [Finnish]; Joonas Makkonen [1975] Director/Vice President Voyage Solutions [Finnish]; Andrey Sitkov [1974] Operations Director [Russian]

Wasp Management Software Limited
Incorporated: 18 August 2011
Net Worth: £50,720,000 *Total Assets:* £51,981,000
Registered Office: c/o Workforce Software Ltd, Precedent Drive, Rooksley, Milton Keynes, Bucks, MK13 8PP
Activities: Other information technology service activities
Parent: Whistler Acquisitions Limited
Officers: Tammy Jones, Secretary; Denise Broady [1974] Director [American]; Robert Feller [1968] Director/CFO/Treasurer [American]; Mike Morini [1962] Director [American]

Watchstone Group PLC
Incorporated: 22 August 2005 *Employees:* 709
Previous: Quindell PLC
Net Worth: £65,127,000 *Total Assets:* £97,914,000
Registered Office: Highfield Court, Tollgate, Chandler's Ford, Eastleigh, Hants, SO53 3TY
Activities: Activities of head offices
Officers: Stefan Leon Borson, Secretary; Stefan Leon Borson [1975] Director/Solicitor; Lord Michael Howard [1941] Director; Richard Sidney Rose [1956] Director; Mark Pritchard Williams [1965] Director; David Thomas McAree Young [1961] Director

Water Process Limited
Incorporated: 2 September 2002 *Employees:* 64
Net Worth: £27,823,000 *Total Assets:* £42,276,000
Registered Office: 106 Hawley Lane, Farnborough, Hants, GU14 8JE
Activities: Manufacture of other special-purpose machinery n.e.c.
Parent: Xylem Water Solutions UK Holdings Ltd
Officers: Nicola Anne Tancred, Secretary; Andrew Michael George Lager [1971] Director/Business Development Manager; Pushpendra Tomar [1974] Director/Site Manager

Waterlogic Finance Limited
Incorporated: 2 December 2015
Net Worth Deficit: £5,061,679 *Total Assets:* £155,011,568
Registered Office: 1 Grenfell Road, Maidenhead, Berks, SL6 1HN
Activities: Combined office administrative service activities
Parent: Waterlogic Holdings Limited
Officers: Jill Lee Young, Secretary; Jeremy Ben David [1963] Director; Huw William Howell Jenkins [1965] Director

Waterlogic Group Holdings Limited
Incorporated: 5 November 2014 *Employees:* 1,868
Net Worth Deficit: £45,477,896 *Total Assets:* £490,826,240
Registered Office: 1 Grenfell Road, Maidenhead, Berks, SL6 1HN
Activities: Combined office administrative service activities
Officers: Jill Lee-Young, Secretary; Jeremy Ben David [1963] Director; Huw William Howell Jenkins [1965] Director; Mark Taylor [1970] Commercial Director

Waterlogic Holdings Limited
Incorporated: 5 November 2014 *Employees:* 1,868
Net Worth Deficit: £51,345,184 *Total Assets:* £490,823,968
Registered Office: 1 Grenfell Road, Maidenhead, Berks, SL6 1HN
Activities: Combined office administrative service activities
Parent: Waterlogic Group Holdings Limited
Officers: Jill Lee Young, Secretary; Jeremy Ben David [1963] Director; John Dundon [1951] Director; Huw William Howell Jenkins [1965] Director; Mark Taylor [1970] Commercial Director

Waters Limited
Incorporated: 24 March 1994 *Employees:* 156
Net Worth: £8,637,000 *Total Assets:* £36,251,000
Registered Office: 610 Centennial Park, Centennial Avenue, Elstree, Herts, WD6 3TJ
Activities: Manufacture of electronic measuring, testing etc. equipment, not for industrial process control
Parent: Micromass Limited
Officers: James Hallam [1973] Director/General Manager, Northern Europe; Michael Cornelius Harrington [1960] Director [Irish]; Gary Joseph Murphy [1960] Director [American]; Columbanus Patrick O'Mahony [1964] Director [Irish]

Wates Construction Limited
Incorporated: 15 January 1986 *Employees:* 3,683
Net Worth: £101,108,000 *Total Assets:* £591,993,024
Registered Office: Wates House, Station Approach, Leatherhead, Surrey, KT22 7SW
Activities: Construction of commercial buildings
Parent: Wates Group Limited
Officers: Philip Michael Wainwright, Secretary; David Owen Allen [1972] Director/Chief Financial Officer; Stephen James Beechey [1968] Group Strategy Director; Helen Patricia Bunch [1965] Group Strategic Director; Paul Chandler [1964] Director/Construction Group MD; David Keir Ewart Morgan [1974] Managing Director; Simon James Potter [1963] Group Commercial Director; Paul Campbell Rowan [1964] Group HR Director; Philip Michael Wainwright [1965] Director/Chief Financial Officer

Wates Developments Limited
Incorporated: 30 August 1947 *Employees:* 30
Net Worth: £46,175,000 *Total Assets:* £95,624,000
Registered Office: Wates House, Station Approach, Leatherhead, Surrey, KT22 7SW
Activities: Development of building projects
Parent: Wates Group Limited
Officers: David Owen Allen [1972] Director/Chief Financial Officer; David Alexander Bowen [1967] Finance Director; David Michael Brocklebank [1970] Director; Martin Geoffrey Leach [1965] Operations Director; Timothy Andrew de Burgh Wates [1966] Director

Wates Group Limited
Incorporated: 14 June 1984 *Employees:* 3,972
Net Worth: £119,415,000 *Total Assets:* £702,764,032
Registered Office: Wates House, Station Approach, Leatherhead, Surrey, KT22 7SW
Activities: Activities of construction holding companies
Shareholders: Annabelle Louisa Mary Elliott; Andrew Eugene Paul Wates; Annette Beatrice Therese Wates; Paul Christopher Ronald Wates
Officers: Philip Michael Wainwright, Secretary; David Owen Allen [1972] Director/Chief Financial Officer; David Martin Barclay [1954] Director; Paul Chandler [1964] Director/Construction Group MD; Deena Elizabeth Mattar [1965] Director; Jeremy Henry Moore Newsum [1955] Director/Chartered Surveyor; Jonathan Mark Oatley [1968] Director/Chief Executive; Philip Michael Wainwright [1965] Director/Chief Financial Officer; Andrew Eugene Paul Wates [1969] Managing Director; Charles William Randag Wates [1976] Managing Director; James Garwood Michael Wates [1960] Director; Jonathan Giles MacArtney Wates [1967] Director; Timothy Andrew de Burgh Wates [1966] Director

Wates Group Services Limited
Incorporated: 1 June 1938 *Employees:* 250
Net Worth Deficit: £30,531,000 *Total Assets:* £48,559,000
Registered Office: Wates House, Station Approach, Leatherhead, Surrey, KT22 7SW
Activities: Other business support service activities n.e.c.
Parent: Wates Group Limited
Officers: Philip Michael Wainwright, Secretary; David Owen Allen [1972] Director/Chief Financial Officer; Simon James Potter [1963] Group Commercial Director; Paul Campbell Rowan [1964] Group HR Director; Philip Michael Wainwright [1965] Director/Chief Financial Officer; Timothy Andrew de Burgh Wates [1966] Managing Director

Wates Living Space (Maintenance) Limited
Incorporated: 26 October 1973 *Employees:* 852
Net Worth: £20,481,000 *Total Assets:* £60,934,000
Registered Office: Wates House, Station Approach, Leatherhead, Surrey, KT22 7SW
Activities: Other service activities n.e.c.
Parent: Wates Constructon Limited
Officers: Philip Michael Wainwright, Secretary; David Owen Allen [1972] Director/Chief Financial Officer; Helen Patricia Bunch [1965] Managing Director; David Keir Ewart Morgan [1974] Business Unit Managing Director; Simon James Potter [1963] Group Commercial Director; Paul Campbell Rowan [1964] Group HR Director; Philip Michael Wainwright [1965] Director/Chief Financial Officer

Watford Association Football Club Limited (The)
Incorporated: 22 July 1909 *Employees:* 254
Net Worth: £2,859,090 *Total Assets:* £168,852,896
Registered Office: Vicarage Road Stadium, Vicarage Road, Watford, Herts, WD18 0ER
Activities: Other sports activities
Parent: Hornets Investment Limited
Officers: Peter James Wastall, Secretary; Scott Ian Duxbury [1972] Director; David Bernard Fransen [1951] Director; Professor Stuart Read Timperley [1943] Director

Watson Wyatt (UK) Acquisitions 1 Limited
Incorporated: 1 March 2005
Net Worth: £175,344,640 *Total Assets:* £528,770,624
Registered Office: Watson House, London Road, Reigate, Surrey, RH2 9PQ
Activities: Activities of head offices
Parent: Towers Watson Global 3 Limited
Officers: Steven James Alcock [1979] Director

Watson Wyatt (UK) Acquisitions 2 Limited
Incorporated: 1 March 2005
Net Worth: £571,729,024 *Total Assets:* £590,958,976
Registered Office: Watson House, London Road, Reigate, Surrey, RH2 9PQ
Activities: Non-trading company
Parent: Watson Wyatt (UK) Acquisitions 1 Limited
Officers: Steven James Alcock [1979] Director

Watson Wyatt European Investment Holdings Limited
Incorporated: 11 July 2005
Net Worth: £25,487,048 *Total Assets:* £25,851,184
Registered Office: Watson House, London Road, Reigate, Surrey, RH2 9PQ
Activities: Activities of head offices
Parent: Watson Wyatt Holdings Limited
Officers: Steven James Alcock [1979] Director

Watson Wyatt European Region Limited
Incorporated: 23 July 2002
Net Worth: £42,237,204 *Total Assets:* £42,237,204
Registered Office: Watson House, London Road, Reigate, Surrey, RH2 9PQ
Activities: Activities of head offices
Parent: Watson Wyatt Holdings (Europe) Limited
Officers: Joanna Maria Field, Secretary; Stuart John Edwards [1974] Director; Paul Geoffrey Morris [1964] Director; Tina Ann Rhodes [1964] Director/Lawyer

Watson Wyatt Holdings (Europe) Limited
Incorporated: 24 August 1994
Net Worth: £8,339,238 *Total Assets:* £43,446,796
Registered Office: Watson House, London Road, Reigate, Surrey, RH2 9PQ
Activities: Activities of head offices
Parent: Watson Wyatt Holdings Limited
Officers: Joanna Maria Field, Secretary; Stuart Edwards [1964] Director; Paul Geoffrey Morris [1964] Director; Tina Ann Rhodes [1964] Director/Lawyer

Watson Wyatt Holdings Limited
Incorporated: 24 September 1957
Net Worth: £12,660,261 *Total Assets:* £24,110,628
Registered Office: Watson House, London Road, Reigate, Surrey, RH2 9PQ
Activities: Non-trading company
Parent: Towers Watson Limited
Officers: Steven James Alcock [1979] Director

Watts Gallery
Incorporated: 8 March 2007 *Employees:* 60
Net Worth: £40,199,208 *Total Assets:* £40,436,452
Registered Office: Down Lane, Compton, Guildford, Surrey, GU3 1DQ
Activities: Museums activities
Officers: Thea Elspeth Gwatkin Adair [1947] Director/Partner, Adair Consultants; Martin Lawrence Beisly [1960] Director/Fine Art Consultant; Matthew Philip Bowcock [1956] Charity Director; James Brice [1946] Director [American]; Alistair John Burtenshaw [1969] Charity Director; Robert Dickins [1950] Director/Professor; Isabel Marcelle Cristina Goldsmith [1954] Director/Hotelier; Robert Stewart Napier [1947] Director/Chief Executive; Maryanne Victoria Stevens [1947] Director/Independent Art Historian and Curator; Emma Katharine Verey [1953] Director

WCR Group Limited
Incorporated: 13 June 2008 *Employees:* 3
Net Worth: £263,207 *Total Assets:* £21,838,092
Registered Office: Aspen House, 13 Highpoint Business Village, Henwood, Ashford, Kent, TN24 8DH
Activities: Activities of other holding companies n.e.c.
Major Shareholder: William Jon Record
Officers: Kevin David Saunby, Secretary; Anthony Record [1939] Director/Chartered Accountant; Dr Charles Anthony Record [1964] Director/Doctor; William Jon Record [1966] Director

WD-40 Company Limited
Incorporated: 26 September 1983 *Employees:* 200
Net Worth: £109,085,000 *Total Assets:* £126,676,000
Registered Office: Brick Close, Kiln Farm, Milton Keynes, Bucks, MK11 3LJ
Activities: Manufacture of other chemical products n.e.c.
Parent: WD-40 Holdings Limited
Officers: William Brian Noble [1958] Managing Director [Australian]; Garry Owen Ridge [1956] Director [Australian]

WDFG UK Holdings Limited
Incorporated: 28 February 1996 *Employees:* 14
Net Worth: £166,526,000 *Total Assets:* £429,328,000
Registered Office: Bedfont Lakes, 4 New Square, Feltham, Middlesex, TW14 8HA
Activities: Retail sale of beverages in specialised stores
Officers: Christopher David Bouttle [1968] Director; Frederick Robert Creighton [1958] Director; Benjamin Harmstorf [1976] Director [German]; Eugenio Miguel Andrades Yunta [1986] Director [Spanish]

WDFG UK Limited
Incorporated: 11 November 1993 *Employees:* 3,698
Net Worth: £150,624,000 *Total Assets:* £340,180,000
Registered Office: 4 New Square, Bedfont Lakes, Feltham, Middlesex, TW14 8HA
Activities: Retail sale of beverages in specialised stores
Parent: WDFG UK Holdings Limited
Officers: Christopher David Bouttle [1968] Director; Frederick Robert Creighton [1958] Director; Benjamin Harmstorf [1976] Director [German]; Eugenio Miguel Andrades Yunta [1968] Director [Spanish]

We Buy Any Car Limited
Incorporated: 2 March 2006 *Employees:* 537
Net Worth: £25,943,000 *Total Assets:* £55,664,000
Registered Office: Headway House, Crosby Way, Farnham, Surrey, GU9 7XG
Activities: Sale of used cars and light motor vehicles
Parent: Pennine Metals B Limited
Officers: Martin Richard Letza, Secretary; Timothy Giles Lampert [1970] Director; Paul MacMahon [1984] Director; Darren Thomas McKee [1971] Director; Noel Francis William McKee [1969] Director; Avril Palmer-Baunack [1964] Director

Weald of Kent Grammar School Academy Trust
Incorporated: 25 November 2010 *Employees:* 164
Net Worth: £35,896,444 *Total Assets:* £37,756,752
Registered Office: Weald of Kent Grammar School, Tudeley Lane, Tonbridge, Kent, TN9 2JP
Activities: General secondary education
Officers: Melanie Lisa Mercer, Secretary; Elizabeth Jane Bone [1979] Director/Headteacher; Jeremy Dahdi [1974] Commercial/Financial Director; Timothy Norman French [1952] Director/Quantity Surveyor; Gerard Annecelto Garcia [1962] Director; Richard Michael Lloyd [1967] Director/Insurance Broker; Carmai Pestell [1985] Director/University Administration Manager; Antonia Rubin [1977] Director/Freelance Legal Editor, Writer and Tutor; Julia Wilson [1974] Director/Education

Wealmoor Limited
Incorporated: 6 March 1973 *Employees:* 940
Net Worth: £25,666,690 *Total Assets:* £55,834,576
Registered Office: Unit 5 Jetha House, Auriol Drive, Greenford Park, Greenford, Middlesex, UB6 0TP
Activities: Post-harvest crop activities
Officers: Leena Avnish Malde, Secretary; Vilasgauri Ratilal Dhanani [1937] Director; Avnish Amritlal Malde [1965] Director; Leena Avnish Malde [1966] Director

Websense SC Holdings Limited
Incorporated: 3 April 2007
Net Worth: £45,146,056 *Total Assets:* £46,323,700
Registered Office: 420 Thames Valley Park Drive, Reading, Berks, RG6 1PT
Activities: Other information technology service activities
Parent: Raytheon Company
Officers: Lisa Susan Burns [1971] Director [Irish]; Matthew Thomas Santangelo [1978] Director [American]; Nuala Takovac [1975] Technical Support Director [Irish]

Websense SC Operations Limited
Incorporated: 3 April 2007
Net Worth Deficit: £4,393,928 *Total Assets:* £29,237,138
Registered Office: 420 Thames Valley Park Drive, Reading, Berks, RG6 1PT
Activities: Other information technology service activities
Parent: Raytheon Company
Officers: Lisa Susan Burns [1971] Director [Irish]; Matthew Thomas Santangelo [1978] Director [American]; Nuala Takovac [1975] Technical Support Director [Irish]

W K Webster & Co Ltd
Incorporated: 24 February 1972 *Employees:* 191
Net Worth: £8,404,073 *Total Assets:* £37,320,556
Registered Office: Webster House, 207 Longlands Road, Sidcup, Kent, DA15 7JH
Activities: Other business support service activities n.e.c.
Shareholders: Anthony Steven Smith; Gregg Victor Newman; Christopher John Osman
Officers: Ann Castle, Secretary; Timothy Ross Champkins [1979] Director/Chartered Accountant; Gregg Victor Newman [1961] Director/Claims Agent; Christopher John Osman [1959] Director/Marine Claims Adjuster; Anthony Steven Smith [1979] Director/Claims Agent

Wedge Property Company Limited (The)
Incorporated: 2 April 1951 *Employees:* 6
Net Worth: £22,286,672 *Total Assets:* £28,819,740
Registered Office: 123a Station Road East, Oxted, Surrey, RH8 0QE
Activities: Other letting and operating of own or leased real estate
Parent: Wedge Property (Holdings) Ltd
Officers: Simon John Biggart, Secretary; Simon John Biggart [1964] Solicitor & Director; Susan Elizabeth Biggart [1964] Director; Lise Charlotte Edwards [1966] Director; Nicholas Hedley Stockbridge [1950] Director

Wednesdays (Bidco) Limited
Incorporated: 9 December 2014 *Employees:* 5
Net Worth Deficit: £28,112,000 *Total Assets:* £222,330,000
Registered Office: Wey House, Farnham Road, Guildford, Surrey, GU1 4YD
Activities: Licenced restaurants
Parent: Tuesdays (Midco) Limited
Officers: Karen Martha Forrester [1959] Director; Stuart Alan Greener [1962] Director; Gavin Maxwell Manson [1966] Director/Chartered Accountant

Weight Watchers UK Holdings Ltd
Incorporated: 27 September 1999
Net Worth: £140,502,192 *Total Assets:* £150,088,176
Registered Office: Millennium House, Ludlow Road, Maidenhead, Berks, SL6 2SL
Activities: Activities of head offices
Parent: Weight Watchers International Inc.
Officers: Nicholas Hotchkin [1965] Director/Management [American]; Corinne Pollier [1964] Director/General Manager [French]

Andrew Weir & Company Limited
Incorporated: 4 September 1945 *Employees:* 27
Net Worth: £20,162,000 *Total Assets:* £30,743,000
Registered Office: Bridgeways House, Four Acres, Oving, Aylesbury, Bucks, HP22 4FJ
Activities: Activities of head offices
Officers: Iain Donald MacRitchie [1964] Director; Nicholas John Cordeaux Walters [1958] Director; Andrew Peter Weir [1966] Director/Doctor

WEL Solar Park 2 Limited
Incorporated: 5 November 2013 *Employees:* 3
Net Worth Deficit: £6,283,440 *Total Assets:* £30,179,792
Registered Office: 2nd Floor, 2 City Place, Beehive Ring Road, Gatwick, W Sussex, RH6 0PA
Activities: Other business support service activities n.e.c.
Parent: Bluefield SIF Investments Limited
Officers: Helen Ruth Down [1979] Director/Solicitor; Luke James Brandon Roberts [1976] Director, Portfolio; Neil Anthony Wood [1980] Director/Accountant

Welborne Energy LLP
Incorporated: 24 March 2014
Net Worth Deficit: £2,392,584 *Total Assets:* £40,948,368
Registered Office: 2nd Floor, 2 City Place, Beehive Ring Road, Gatwick, W Sussex, RH6 0PA
Officers: John Robin Thistlethwayte [1935] Member; Mark Edward Thistlethwayte [1964] Member

Welcome Break Group Limited
Incorporated: 18 January 1996 *Employees:* 1,492
Net Worth: £20,947,000 *Total Assets:* £701,206,016
Registered Office: 2 Vantage Court, Tickford Street, Newport Pagnell, Bucks, MK16 9EZ
Activities: Retail sale in non-specialised stores with food, beverages or tobacco predominating
Parent: Welcome Break Holdings 1 Limited
Officers: Joseph James Barrett [1966] Director [Irish]; John Diviney [1979] Director/Chief Executive Officer [Irish]; Niall Dolan [1973] Director/Financial Controller [Irish]; Charles John Gore Hazelwood [1963] Director/Accountant; Surinder Singh Toor [1972] Director/Accountant

Welcome Break Holdings (1) Limited
Incorporated: 31 October 2000 *Employees:* 4,811
Net Worth Deficit: £83,611,000 *Total Assets:* £321,244,992
Registered Office: 2 Vantage Court, Tickford Street, Newport Pagnell, Bucks, MK16 9EZ
Activities: Activities of other holding companies n.e.c.
Parent: Welcome Break Holdings 2 Limited
Officers: Joseph James Barrett [1966] Director [Irish]; John Diviney [1979] Director/Chief Executive Officer [Irish]; Niall Dolan [1973] Director/Financial Controller [Irish]; Charles John Gore Hazelwood [1963] Director/Accountant; Surinder Singh Toor [1972] Director/Accountant

Welcome Break Holdings Limited
Incorporated: 11 December 1996 *Employees:* 4,951
Net Worth Deficit: £192,022,000 *Total Assets:* £342,236,992
Registered Office: 2 Vantage Court, Tickford Street, Newport Pagnell, Bucks, MK16 9EZ
Activities: Activities of other holding companies n.e.c.
Parent: Appia Europe Limited
Officers: Joseph James Barrett [1966] Director [Irish]; John Diviney [1979] Director/Chief Executive Officer [Irish]; Niall Dolan [1973] Director/Financial Controller [Irish]; Charles John Gore Hazelwood [1963] Director/Accountant; Surinder Singh Toor [1972] Director/Accountant

Welcome Break Limited
Incorporated: 30 June 1983 *Employees:* 2,531
Net Worth: £219,879,008 *Total Assets:* £423,462,016
Registered Office: 2 Vantage Court, Tickford Street, Newport Pagnell, Bucks, MK16 9EZ
Activities: Retail sale in non-specialised stores with food, beverages or tobacco predominating
Parent: Welcome Break Group Limited
Officers: Joseph James Barrett [1966] Director [Irish]; John Diviney [1979] Director/Chief Executive Officer [Irish]; Niall Dolan [1973] Director/Financial Controller [Irish]; Charles John Gore Hazelwood [1963] Director/Accountant; Surinder Singh Toor [1972] Director/Accountant

Welcome Break No. 1 Limited
Incorporated: 14 December 2012
Net Worth: £332,108,992 *Total Assets:* £466,100,000
Registered Office: 2 Vantage Court, Tickford Street, Newport Pagnell, Bucks, MK16 9EZ
Activities: Activities of other holding companies n.e.c.
Parent: Welcome Break No. 2 Limited
Officers: Joseph James Barrett [1966] Director [Irish]; John Diviney [1979] Director/Chief Executive Officer [Irish]; Niall Dolan [1973] Director/Financial Controller [Irish]; Charles John Gore Hazelwood [1963] Director/Accountant; Surinder Singh Toor [1972] Director/Accountant

Welcome Break No. 2 Limited
Incorporated: 14 December 2012
Net Worth: £339,100,992 *Total Assets:* £339,100,992
Registered Office: 2 Vantage Court, Tickford Street, Newport Pagnell, Bucks, MK16 9EZ
Activities: Activities of other holding companies n.e.c.
Parent: Welcome Break Holdings Limited
Officers: Joseph James Barrett [1966] Director [Irish]; John Diviney [1979] Director/Chief Executive Officer [Irish]; Niall Dolan [1973] Director/Financial Controller [Irish]; Charles John Gore Hazelwood [1963] Director/Accountant; Surinder Singh Toor [1972] Director/Accountant

Wellcome Foundation Limited (The)
Incorporated: 1 January 1924
Net Worth: £293,239,008 *Total Assets:* £457,700,992
Registered Office: 980 Great West Road, Brentford, Middlesex, TW8 9GS
Activities: Activities of head offices
Parent: Wellcome Limited
Officers: Victoria Anne Whyte, Secretary; Simon Paul Dingemans [1963] Director

Wellcome Limited
Incorporated: 6 November 1985
Net Worth: £1,804,000,000 *Total Assets:* £1,843,000,064
Registered Office: 980 Great West Road, Brentford, Middlesex, TW8 9GS
Activities: Activities of head offices
Parent: GlaxoSmithKline Finance PLC
Officers: Victoria Anne Whyte, Secretary; Simon Paul Dingemans [1963] Director

Charles Wells Brewery Limited
Incorporated: 24 February 2006 *Employees:* 204
Previous: Wells & Young's Brewing Company Limited
Net Worth: £7,753,000 *Total Assets:* £65,067,000
Registered Office: The Brewery, Havelock Street, Bedford, MK40 4LU
Activities: Manufacture of beer
Parent: Charles Wells Limited
Officers: Anthony Robert Fryer [1973] Finance Director; William Andrew Justin Phillimore [1962] Director; Paul Richard Wells [1958] Director

Charles Wells,Limited
Incorporated: 7 January 1910 *Employees:* 365
Net Worth: £75,246,000 *Total Assets:* £141,250,000
Registered Office: Eagle Brewery, Havelock Street, Bedford, MK40 4LU
Activities: Manufacture of beer
Officers: Anthony Robert Fryer [1973] Finance Director; Robert Lewis Ivell [1952] Director; William Andrew Justin Phillimore [1962] Director/Chief Executive; Paul Stephen Rawlinson [1959] Director; Geoffrey Charles Vaughan Wells [1970] Director/Lawyer [Canadian]; Paul Richard Wells [1958] Director; Peter John Wells [1970] Director

Michael Wenman Limited
Incorporated: 19 February 1979 *Employees:* 3
Net Worth: £25,150,904 *Total Assets:* £30,052,412
Registered Office: Amelia House, Crescent Road, Worthing, W Sussex, BN11 1QR
Activities: Development of building projects
Major Shareholder: Michael Wenman
Officers: Michael Levi Wenman, Secretary; Michael Wenman [1954] Director/Vehicle Dealer

Wescot Acquisitions Limited
Incorporated: 25 May 2005
Net Worth Deficit: £23,087,000 *Total Assets:* £81,687,000
Registered Office: 1 Kings Hill Avenue, Kings Hill, West Malling, Kent, ME19 4UA
Activities: Activities of financial services holding companies
Parent: Cabot Financial Debt Recovery Services Limited
Officers: Craig Anthony Buick [1969] Finance Director [British/Australian]; Jonathan Andrew Graham [1969] Director; Paul Jenkins [1969] Director; John Richard Sharman [1970] Managing Director; Kenneth John Stannard [1966] Director/Chief Executive

Wescot Topco Limited
Incorporated: 25 May 2005 *Employees:* 811
Net Worth Deficit: £16,594,000 *Total Assets:* £41,748,000
Registered Office: 1 Kings Hill Avenue, Kings Hill, West Malling, Kent, ME19 4UA
Activities: Activities of financial services holding companies
Parent: Cabot Financial Debt Recovery Services Limited
Officers: Craig Anthony Buick [1969] Finance Director [British/Australian]; Jonathan Andrew Graham [1969] Director; Paul Jenkins [1969] Director; John Richard Sharman [1970] Managing Director [Australian]; Kenneth John Stannard [1966] Director/Chief Executive

Wessanen Great Britain Holdings Limited
Incorporated: 10 January 2003
Net Worth: £8,236,000 *Total Assets:* £30,207,000
Registered Office: 2 Riverview Meadows Business Park, Station Approach, Blackwater, Camberley, Surrey, GU17 9AB
Activities: Activities of head offices
Officers: Jason Edward Boxer [1969] Finance Director; Ronald Johannes Josephus Bernardus Merckx [1967] Director [Dutch]; Emma Jane Vass [1976] Managing Director

Wessex Children's Hospice Trust
Incorporated: 15 April 1991 *Employees:* 188
Net Worth: £25,012,638 *Total Assets:* £25,720,740
Registered Office: Naomi House, Stockbridge Road, Sutton Scotney, Winchester, Hants, SO21 3JE
Activities: Other human health activities
Officers: Claire Emma Imhofe, Secretary; Nicholas Allen [1958] Director/Project Manager; Julian Frederick Charles Cracknell [1971] Managing Director; Samantha Jane Curd [1970] Director/Chief Financial Officer; David Charles Holmes [1967] Director/Chief Executive; Dr Michael George Miller [1954] Director/Paediatric Care Consultant; Stevo Radjen [1962] Director/Digital Marketing; Faith Lesley Ramsay [1971] Director/Consultant; Professor Alison Richardson [1962] Director/Clinical Professor; Shaun Paul Capps Southern [1970] Director/Actuary; Julian Walker [1956] Director/Chartered Surveyor; Elizabeth Margaret Wallace [1958] Director/HR Professional

Wessex Petroleum Limited
Incorporated: 17 September 1971 *Employees:* 137
Net Worth: £16,366,935 *Total Assets:* £39,265,928
Registered Office: Suite 1, Second Floor, Grosvenor House, Grosvenor Square, Southampton, SO15 2BE
Activities: Freight transport by road
Parent: Stanbridge Group Limited
Officers: Lee Andrew Tybinkowski, Secretary; Filipe Affonso Ferreira [1965] Director [Brazilian]; Marcos Marinho Lutz [1969] Director [Brazilian]; Rubens Ometto Silveira Mello [1950] Director [Brazilian]

West London Energy Recovery Holdings Ltd
Incorporated: 26 June 2013
Previous: SITA West London Holdings Limited
Net Worth Deficit: £20,672,000 *Total Assets:* £237,766,000
Registered Office: Suez House, Grenfell Road, Maidenhead, Berks, SL6 1ES
Activities: Activities of other holding companies n.e.c.
Shareholders: I-Environment Investments Limited; PIP Infrastructure Investments (No 5) Limited; Suez Recycling and Recovery UK Ltd
Officers: Nicholas Tommy Cole [1978] Investment Director; Florent Thierry Antoine Duval [1976] Director/Chief Finance Officer [French]; Rahul Dipinkumar Kadiwar [1984] Director/Head of Business Development; Belinda Faith Knox [1972] Investment Director; Graham Arthur McKenna-Mayes [1968] Director/Chief Operating Officer; Ian Anthony Sexton [1956] Director/Chairman; Yuji Suzuki [1970] Managing Director [Japanese]; Edward Arthur Wilson [1965] Director/Investment Manager

West London Energy Recovery Ltd
Incorporated: 27 June 2013
Previous: SITA West London Limited
Net Worth Deficit: £20,672,000 *Total Assets:* £237,766,000
Registered Office: Suez House, Grenfell Road, Maidenhead, Berks, SL6 1ES
Activities: Non-trading company
Parent: West London Energy Recovery Holdings Ltd
Officers: Nicholas Tommy Cole [1978] Investment Director; Florent Thierry Antoine Duval [1976] Director/Chief Finance Officer [French]; Rahul Dipinkumar Kadiwar [1984] Director/Head of Business Development; Belinda Faith Knox [1972] Investment Director; Graham Arthur McKenna-Mayes [1968] Director/Chief Operating Officer; Ian Anthony Sexton [1956] Director/Chairman; Yuji Suzuki [1970] Managing Director [Japanese]; Edward Arthur Wilson [1965] Director/Investment Manager

West London YMCA
Incorporated: 2 September 1996 *Employees:* 144
Net Worth: £7,179,414 *Total Assets:* £28,731,302
Registered Office: St James House, 9-15 St James Road, Surbiton, Surrey, KT6 4QH
Activities: Other accommodation
Officers: Gwynne Myfanwy Price Jarvis, Secretary; Generald Chifamba [1992] Director; Howard Peter Dawson [1970] Housing Director; Louise Hedges [1981] Director/Civil Servant; Andrew John Palmer [1956] Director/Charity Chief Executive; Helen Posner [1981] Director/Principal Investment; Albin Andrew Stadtmiller [1966] Director/Charity Manager Fundraiser [American/British]; Edward Louis Samuel Weiss [1932] Director/Retired; Kenneth John Youngman [1956] Finance Director

West Raynham Solar Limited
Incorporated: 7 June 2013 *Employees:* 3
Previous: Good Energy West Raynham Solar Park (030) Limited
Net Worth Deficit: £6,122,207 *Total Assets:* £44,512,368
Registered Office: 2nd Floor, 2 City Place, Beehive Ring Road, Gatwick, W Sussex, RH6 0PA
Activities: Production of electricity
Parent: Bluefield SIF Investments Limited
Officers: Helen Ruth Down [1979] Director/Solicitor; Luke James Brandon Roberts [1976] Director, Portfolio; Neil Anthony Wood [1980] Director/Accountant

West's Group International Limited
Incorporated: 4 June 1894
Net Worth: £4,745,000 *Total Assets:* £29,904,000
Registered Office: Interserve House, Ruscombe Park, Twyford, Reading, Berks, RG10 9JU
Activities: Activities of other holding companies n.e.c.
Parent: Bandt Limited
Officers: Andrew John McDonald, Secretary; Andrew John McDonald [1974] Director/Company Secretary; Anthony Kenneth Smythe [1965] Director/Accountant

Westbury Street Holdings Limited
Incorporated: 9 February 2011
Net Worth: £197,679,008 *Total Assets:* £304,436,000
Registered Office: TVP2, 300 Thames Valley Park Drive, Reading, Berks, RG6 1PT
Activities: Activities of other holding companies n.e.c.
Parent: WSH Hospitality Limited
Officers: Marc Bradley, Secretary; Marc Bradley [1975] Director; Alastair Dunbar Storey [1953] Director

Westbury Street Limited
Incorporated: 9 November 2007
Net Worth: £192,610,000 *Total Assets:* £320,564,000
Registered Office: TVP2, 300 Thames Valley Park Drive, Reading, Berks, RG6 1PT
Activities: Activities of other holding companies n.e.c.
Parent: Westbury Street Holdings Limited
Officers: Marc Bradley, Secretary; Marc Bradley [1975] Director; Alastair Dunbar Storey [1953] Director

Westcoast (Holdings) Limited
Incorporated: 25 April 1997 *Employees:* 1,301
Net Worth: £68,236,000 *Total Assets:* £517,742,016
Registered Office: Arrowhead Park, Arrowhead Road, Theale, Reading, Berks, RG7 4AH
Activities: Activities of head offices
Major Shareholder: Amin Hemani
Officers: Christine Bachelor, Secretary; Duncan Gavin Forsyth [1965] Director; Amin Hemani [1946] Director; Leon Hemani [1971] Director; Sunil Jayantilal Madhani [1966] Director

Westcoast Limited
Incorporated: 16 May 1984 *Employees:* 612
Net Worth: £68,891,000 *Total Assets:* £443,567,008
Registered Office: Arrowhead Park, Arrowhead Road, Theale, Reading, Berks, RG7 4AH
Activities: Non-specialised wholesale trade
Parent: Westcoast (Holdings) Ltd
Officers: Emily Elizabeth Garvey, Secretary; Duncan Gavin Forsyth [1965] Finance Director; Paul Jackson Hamilton [1975] Director; Paul Harman [1972] Director; Karl James Harris [1971] Director; Amin Hemani [1946] Director; Alan Hunt [1957] Sales Director; Sunil Jayantilal Madhani [1966] Director; Andrew Peter Newberry [1963] Director; Carl Jason Oxley [1967] Retail Director; Alex Tatham [1965] Sales Director

Westec Holding Company Limited
Incorporated: 4 November 1999 *Employees:* 254
Net Worth: £35,662,964 *Total Assets:* £45,861,412
Registered Office: 200 London Road, Burgess Hill, W Sussex, RH15 9RD
Activities: Activities of head offices
Officers: Michael Alexander Laming, Secretary/Commercial Manager; Dr Hubert Alfred Ermer [1967] Director [German]; Michael Alexander Laming [1953] Director

Western United Investment Company Limited
Incorporated: 26 August 1918 *Employees:* 944
Net Worth: £80,600,000 *Total Assets:* £188,700,000
Registered Office: 29 Ullswater Crescent, Coulsdon, Surrey, CR5 2HR
Activities: Activities of head offices
Shareholders: Carl Hermann Konrad Friedlaender; Russell Clark; Michael John Seymour Eades
Officers: Neil Thornton, Secretary; George Moubray William Vestey [1964] Director/Retail Butchery; Robin John Henry Vestey [1968] Director/Agricultural Consultant; Lord Samuel George Armstrong Vestey [1941] Director/Merchant; Honourable William Guy Vestey [1983] Director

Western Wines Holdings Limited
Incorporated: 15 July 2002
Net Worth: £114,755,000 *Total Assets:* £114,755,000
Registered Office: Thomas Hardy House, 2 Heath Road, Weybridge, Surrey, KT13 8TB
Activities: Non-trading company
Parent: Accolade Wines Europe No. 2 Limited
Officers: Anthony Graham Wood, Secretary; Adrian Francis McKeon [1963] Regional Managing Director, UKIR; Andrew Peter Smith [1974] Director/Accountant; Anthony Graham Wood [1975] Director/Financial Controller [Australian]

Westerngeco Limited
Incorporated: 19 September 1978 *Employees:* 253
Net Worth: £138,562,000 *Total Assets:* £172,503,008
Registered Office: Schlumberger House, Buckingham Gate, Gatwick Airport, W Sussex, RH6 0NZ
Activities: Support activities for petroleum and natural gas mining
Parent: Schlumberger Oilfield UK PLC
Officers: Simon Smoker, Secretary; Mohamed Achmaoui [1973] Director/Controller, Treasury & Tax [French]; Julie Margaret Branston [1976] Director/Region Manager; Philip George Davey [1967] Director/EAF & Eastern Hemisphere Multiclient Manager

Westfalia Fruit International Limited
Incorporated: 14 September 1993 *Employees:* 5
Net Worth: £51,825,912 *Total Assets:* £80,812,896
Registered Office: 42 Kings Hill Avenue, Kings Hill, West Malling, Kent, ME19 4AJ
Activities: Activities of other holding companies n.e.c.
Officers: Chantelle Grobler, Secretary; Rian Johannes Du Toit [1971] Director [South African]; Claus Burkhard Lippert [1963] Director [German]

Westgate Properties Limited
Incorporated: 26 September 1927
Net Worth: £2,903,000 *Total Assets:* £28,806,000
Registered Office: St Mark's Court, Chart Way, Horsham, W Sussex, RH12 1XL
Activities: Development of building projects
Parent: Royal & Sun Alliance Insurance PLC
Officers: Ian Adam Craston [1966] Director; Paul Mackman [1973] Director/Tax Accountant

Westmoreland Developments Limited
Incorporated: 24 July 2001
Net Worth: £15,678,865 *Total Assets:* £40,961,376
Registered Office: The White House, 2 Meadrow, Godalming, Surrey, GU7 3HN
Activities: Buying and selling of own real estate
Major Shareholder: Toby Richard Baines
Officers: Philip Andrew Waddell, Secretary/Director; Toby Richard Baines [1962] Director/Chartered Surveyor; Andrew James Rennie [1966] Director/Chartered Surveyor; Daemon Leonard Sheehan [1968] Director; Philip Andrew Waddell [1954] Director

J D Wetherspoon PLC
Incorporated: 25 March 1983 *Employees:* 38,384
Net Worth: £286,561,984 *Total Assets:* £1,476,313,984
Registered Office: Wetherspoon House, Reeds Crescent, Watford, Herts, WD24 4QL
Activities: Public houses and bars
Officers: Nigel Connor, Secretary; Sir Richard Gervase Beckett [1944] Director; Susan Alina Cacioppo [1966] Personnel & Legal Director; John David Hutson [1965] Director/Chief Executive Officer; Timothy Randall Martin [1955] Non-Executive Director Chairman; Elizabeth McMeikan [1962] Director; Harry Michael Charles Morley [1965] Director; Debra Van Gene [1954] Director/Executive Research Consultant; Benjamin Newton Whitley [1978] Finance Director

Weydon Multi Academy Trust
Incorporated: 4 March 2011 *Employees:* 383
Previous: Weydon School
Net Worth: £56,649,116 *Total Assets:* £64,445,260
Registered Office: Weydon School, Weydon Lane, Farnham, Surrey, GU9 8UG
Activities: General secondary education
Officers: Elaine Felton, Secretary; Peter Graham Brinsden [1949] Director/Retired; Julie Fisher [1968] Director/Consultant; Charlotte Elizabeth Hurst [1968] Director/Consultant; Christopher Hyland [1960] Director/Accountant; Ralph Johnson [1961] Director/Accountant; Mark Rosling [1959] Director; Robert Edward Williams [1973] Director; John Winter [1961] Director/Headteacher

Whatman International Limited
Incorporated: 1 January 1910
Net Worth: £270,891,008 *Total Assets:* £274,862,016
Registered Office: Whatman House, St Leonards Road, Allington, Maidstone, Kent, ME16 0LS
Activities: Manufacture of paper and paperboard
Parent: Whatman Limited
Officers: Andrew Lawrence Lester, Secretary; Maria de Los Angeles Khoury Gonzalo [1970] Director/Financial Management [American]; Kevin Michael O'Neill [1968] Director/Accountant

Whatman Limited
Incorporated: 23 June 1959
Net Worth: £304,140,992 *Total Assets:* £305,492,992
Registered Office: Whatman House, St Leonards Road, Allington, Maidstone, Kent, ME16 0LS
Activities: Activities of head offices
Parent: GE Healthcare UK Limited
Officers: Judit Kalman, Secretary; Maria de Los Angeles Khoury Gonzalo [1970] Director/Financial Management [American]; Kevin Michael O'Neill [1968] Director/Accountant

Whistl Group Holdings Limited
Incorporated: 16 September 2015 *Employees:* 1,704
Net Worth: £15,921,000 *Total Assets:* £120,346,000
Registered Office: Meridian House, Fieldhouse Lane, Marlow, Bucks, SL7 1TB
Activities: Licensed carriers
Shareholder: Nicholas Mark Wells
Officers: John Evans, Secretary; James Brett Greenbury [1961] Director; Manoj Kumar Parmar [1966] Finance Director; Nigel Graham Polglass [1961] Director; Nicholas Mark Wells [1959] Director

Whistl Group Limited
Incorporated: 12 March 1974
Previous: PostNL UK Limited
Net Worth: £22,376,000 *Total Assets:* £28,609,000
Registered Office: Meridian House, Fieldhouse Lane, Marlow, Bucks, SL7 1TB
Activities: Combined office administrative service activities
Parent: Whistl NN1 Limited
Officers: John Evans, Secretary; Manoj Kumar Parmar [1966] Finance Director; Nigel Graham Polglass [1961] Director; Nicholas Mark Wells [1959] Director

Whistl Limited
Incorporated: 30 July 2001
Previous: Whistl NN1 Limited
Net Worth: £10,995,000 *Total Assets:* £28,680,000
Registered Office: Meridian House, Fieldhouse Lane, Marlow, Bucks, SL7 1TB
Activities: Combined office administrative service activities
Parent: Whistl Group Holdings Limited
Officers: John Evans, Secretary; Manoj Kumar Parmar [1966] Finance Director; Nigel Graham Polglass [1961] Director; Nicholas Mark Wells [1959] Director

Whistl UK Limited
Incorporated: 15 April 2002 *Employees:* 1,597
Net Worth: £25,103,000 *Total Assets:* £141,404,000
Registered Office: Meridian House, Fieldhouse Lane, Marlow, Bucks, SL7 1TB
Activities: Licensed carriers
Parent: PostNL UK Limited
Officers: John Evans, Secretary; Manoj Kumar Parmar [1966] Finance Director; Nigel Graham Polglass [1961] Director; Nicholas Mark Wells [1959] Director

Whistler Acquisitions Limited
Incorporated: 26 April 2016 *Employees:* 142
Net Worth: £13,355,000 *Total Assets:* £47,073,000
Registered Office: c/o Workforce Software Ltd, Precedent Drive, Rooksley, Milton Keynes, Bucks, MK13 8PP
Activities: Other information technology service activities
Parent: Workforce Software LLC
Officers: Tammy Jones, Secretary; Denise Broady [1974] Director [American]; Robert Feller [1968] Director [American]; Mike Morini [1962] Director [American]

White Horse Caravan Company Limited
Incorporated: 15 January 1981 *Employees:* 358
Net Worth: £26,459,322 *Total Assets:* £36,647,516
Registered Office: Douglas Bunn House, Warners Lane, Selsey, W Sussex, PO20 9EL
Activities: Recreational vehicle parks, trailer parks and camping grounds
Shareholders: Neil Winston Benson OBE FCA; Frank Nicholas Fraser Haddock; Jacqueline Margaret Haddock
Officers: John Benedict Philip Bunn, Secretary; Chloe Margaret Alice Breen [1980] Director; Charles Henry Douglas Bunn [1987] Director; Edward Henry Douglas Bunn [1961] Director; Elizabeth Susan Patricia Bunn [1963] Director; John Benedict Philip Bunn [1966] Director; Daisy Henrietta Diana Honeybunn [1983] Director

White Rock Land LLP
Incorporated: 23 August 2013
Net Worth: £2,392,000 *Total Assets:* £48,318,000
Registered Office: Cowley Business Park, Cowley, Uxbridge, Middlesex, UB8 2AL

Whitehill & Bordon Development Company Phase 1A Ltd
Incorporated: 28 March 2017
Net Worth Deficit: £573,000 *Total Assets:* £20,580,000
Registered Office: Gate House, Turnpike Road, High Wycombe, Bucks, HP12 3NR
Activities: Development of building projects
Parent: Bordon Developments Holdings Limited
Officers: Michael Andrew Lonnon, Secretary; Ian Michael Amdur [1963] Director; Lee Michael Bishop [1965] Director; James Edward Child [1966] Director; David Hill [1964] Managing Director; Raymond Anthony Peacock [1966] Director; Nicholas John Prior-Davis [1978] Director; Gary Silver [1970] Director/Physician; Paul Anthony Silver [1972] Director

The Whiteley Homes Trust
Incorporated: 10 November 2003 *Employees:* 148
Net Worth: £48,317,912 *Total Assets:* £57,607,644
Registered Office: Octagon Road, Whiteley Village, Walton on Thames, Surrey, KT12 4EH
Activities: Other accommodation
Officers: Dr Beverly Ann Castleton [1948] Director/Consultant Physician; Roger Myles Formby [1938] Director/Solicitor; Keith John Hiscock [1958] Director/Stockbroker/Investment Banker; Michael Alan Pomery [1944] Director/Consulting Actuary; Michael George Sadler [1947] Director/Retired; Jason Shaw [1973] Director/Chartered Accountant; Jackie Stevens [1963] Director/NHS Executive; Duncan Alan Mordue Straughen [1954] Director; Michael Frederick Arthur Tolley [1947] Director/Semi-Retired Consultant Surveyor; Aileen Woollhead [1959] Director

Wiggle Limited
Incorporated: 3 December 1991 *Employees:* 564
Net Worth Deficit: £8,378,000 *Total Assets:* £231,918,000
Registered Office: Suite 310, Third Floor, N E Wing, 1000 Lakeside, Portsmouth, PO6 3EN
Activities: Retail sale of sports goods, fishing gear, camping goods, boats and bicycles
Parent: Ensco 503 Limited
Officers: Alexander Ross Clemmow [1974] Director; Michael Robert Davy [1961] Director; Nicholas John Gresham [1971] Director

Wightlink Limited
Incorporated: 23 June 1972 *Employees:* 249
Net Worth: £120,580,000 *Total Assets:* £171,871,008
Registered Office: Gunwharf Terminal, Gunwharf Road, Portsmouth, PO1 2LA
Activities: Sea and coastal freight water transport
Parent: Arca Shipping Limited
Officers: Jonathan Mark Pascoe, Secretary; Robert John Gregor [1969] Director/Managing Partner Investment Adviser [Australian]; Holt William John Hanna [1977] Director/Vice President Investment Adviser; Steven Lowry [1972] Director/Partner Investment Advisor; Jonathan Mark Pascoe [1967] Director/Chartered Accountant; Richard Douglas Sammons [1956] Director/Chartered Accountant

WIH UK Limited
Incorporated: 21 April 2016
Net Worth: £2,882,777,856 *Total Assets:* £2,882,777,856
Registered Office: Pemberton House, Bakers Road, Uxbridge, Middlesex, UB8 1EZ
Activities: Activities of other holding companies n.e.c.
Parent: Coca-Cola European Partners PLC
Officers: Paul Van Reesch, Secretary; Frank Govaerts [1961] Director [Belgian]; Joyce Marie King-Lavinder [1959] Director [American]; Paul Van Reesch [1976] Director; Edward Owen Walker [1967] Director

Wildern Academy Trust
Incorporated: 7 March 2011 *Employees:* 322
Previous: Wildern School
Net Worth: £23,783,912 *Total Assets:* £26,464,192
Registered Office: Wildern School, Wildern Lane, Hedge End, Southampton, SO30 4EJ
Activities: General secondary education
Officers: Anthony Palmer Jardine [1957] Director/Civil Servant; Glenda Ann Lane [1955] Director/Local Government Officer; Marie-Louise Louise Litton [1964] Director/Headteacher; Stephen Paul Lucas [1980] Director/Mortgage Advisor; Matthew Phelps [1979] Director/Vice Principal Commercial; Ruth Elizabeth Saw [1966] Director/Programme Manager; Karen Mallalue Wigley [1963] Director/Occupational Therapist

John Wiley & Sons Limited
Incorporated: 3 November 1959 *Employees:* 1,004
Net Worth: £11,432,000 *Total Assets:* £377,636,992
Registered Office: The Atrium, Southern Gate, Chichester, W Sussex, PO19 8SQ
Activities: Book publishing
Parent: Wiley Europe Ltd
Officers: Caroline Jane McPhee, Secretary; Ursula Leonie D'Arcy [1970] Financial Director [Irish]; Rosamund Claire Johnson [1961] Director; Philip Jeffrey Mac Kisray [1960] Director; John Anthony Kritzmacher [1960] Director [American]

John Wiley & Sons UK LLP
Incorporated: 29 March 2011
Net Worth: £1,657,449,984 *Total Assets:* £1,657,449,984
Registered Office: The Atrium, Southern Gate, Chichester, W Sussex, PO19 8SQ

Wiley Europe Investment Holdings Limited
Incorporated: 17 August 2001
Net Worth: £464,888,992 *Total Assets:* £698,851,968
Registered Office: The Atrium, Southern Gate, Chichester, W Sussex, PO19 8SQ
Activities: Activities of head offices
Parent: John Wiley & Sons UK 2 LLP
Officers: Caroline Jane McPhee, Secretary; Ursula D'Arcy [1970] Financial Director [Irish]; Rosamund Claire Johnson [1961] Director; Philip Jeffrey Mac Kisray [1960] Director; John Anthony Kritzmacher [1960] Director [American]

Wiley Europe Limited
Incorporated: 17 October 1988
Net Worth: £645,918,976 *Total Assets:* £803,859,008
Registered Office: The Atrium, Southern Gate, Chichester, W Sussex, PO19 8SQ
Activities: Activities of head offices
Parent: Wiley UK
Officers: Caroline Jane McPhee, Secretary; Ursula D'Arcy [1970] Financial Director [Irish]; Rosamund Claire Johnson [1961] Director; Philip Jeffrey Mac Kisray [1960] Director; John Anthony Kritzmacher [1960] Director [American]

Wiley Heyden Limited
Incorporated: 11 February 1982
Net Worth: £80,292,000 *Total Assets:* £92,049,000
Registered Office: The Atrium, Southern Gate, Chichester, W Sussex, PO19 8SQ
Activities: Book publishing
Parent: Wiley Europe Ltd
Officers: Caroline Jane McPhee, Secretary; Ursula D'Arcy [1970] Financial Director [Irish]; Rosamund Claire Johnson [1961] Director; Philip Jeffrey Mac Kisray [1960] Director; John Anthony Kritzmacher [1960] Director [American]

J Wiley Limited
Incorporated: 14 October 2013
Net Worth: £320,128,000 *Total Assets:* £320,128,000
Registered Office: The Atrium, Southern Gate, Chichester, W Sussex, PO19 8SQ
Activities: Activities of head offices
Parent: John Wiley & Sons Ltd
Officers: Caroline Jane McPhee, Secretary; Ursula Leonie D'Arcy [1970] Director [Irish]; Rosamund Claire Johnson [1961] Director; Philip Jeffrey Mac Kisray [1960] Director; John Anthony Kritzmacher [1960] Director [American]

Wilhelmsen Lines Car Carriers Ltd.
Incorporated: 23 February 2004 *Employees:* 8
Net Worth: £232,521,776 *Total Assets:* £452,423,040
Registered Office: 3rd Floor, Friary House, Briton Street, Southampton, SO14 3JL
Activities: Sea and coastal freight water transport
Officers: Ole Kristian Baervahr [1966] Director/Head of Ship Owning & Planning [Norwegian]; Paul Jeffrey Reeves [1976] Managing Director WWL UK; Sarah Jane Walsh [1975] Managing Director

Wilkinson Sword Limited
Incorporated: 8 July 1889 *Employees:* 84
Net Worth: £49,581,000 *Total Assets:* £73,601,000
Registered Office: Sword House, Totteridge Road, High Wycombe, Bucks, HP13 6DG
Activities: Non-specialised wholesale trade
Parent: Edgewell Personal Care Holdings UK Limited
Officers: David Paul Hatfield [1960] Director/Executive Officer [American]; Colin Anthony Hutchison [1958] Director/Chief Operating Officer; Rod Ryan Little [1969] Director/Chief Financial Officer [American]

Wilky Group Limited (The)
Incorporated: 23 November 1971 *Employees:* 27
Net Worth: £32,731,212 *Total Assets:* £40,837,968
Registered Office: Parallel House, 32 London Road, Guildford, Surrey, GU1 2AB
Activities: Activities of head offices
Shareholders: Julian Carl Munday; Susan May Martin; Sandra Denise Young; Malcolm Roderick Young; Thomas Eggar Trust Corporation
Officers: Julian Carl Munday, Finance Director; Laura Jane Caudery [1980] Director/Marketing Executive; Colin Ronald Moore [1950] Director; Julian Carl Munday [1964] Finance Director; Malcolm Roderick Young [1948] Director; Sandra Denise Young [1950] Director

William Willett Learning Trust
Incorporated: 7 February 2011 *Employees:* 182
Net Worth: £37,125,000 *Total Assets:* £39,579,000
Registered Office: Coopers School, Hawkwood Lane, Chislehurst, Kent, BR7 5PS
Activities: General secondary education
Officers: Robert Carling, Secretary; Andrew Downes [1950] Director/Consultant Engineer; Shirley Puxty [1959] Director/School Principal; Claire Agnes Singleton [1956] Director/Solicitor; Lorraine Anne Stuart [1955] Director/Local Government Officer

Williams Trade Supplies Holdings Limited
Incorporated: 18 March 2015 *Employees:* 238
Net Worth: £7,400,224 *Total Assets:* £28,389,528
Registered Office: Unit 13 Standard Way, Fareham, Hants, PO16 8XB
Activities: Activities of other holding companies n.e.c.
Shareholders: Rachel Anne Moore; Ramon Stafford; Michael Terence Williams
Officers: Michael Alan Mann, Secretary; Ann Williams, Secretary; Rachel Anne Moore [1970] Director; Ramon Stafford [1962] Director; Michael Terence Williams [1948] Director

Williams Trade Supplies Limited
Incorporated: 19 November 1984 *Employees:* 238
Net Worth: £16,802,296 *Total Assets:* £33,458,266
Registered Office: Unit 13 Standard Way, Fareham Industrial Park, Fareham, Hants, PO16 8XB
Activities: Wholesale of hardware, plumbing and heating equipment and supplies
Parent: Williams Trade Supplies Holdings Limited
Officers: Rachel Anne Moore [1970] Director; Ramon Stafford [1962] Director/Plumbers Merchant; Michael Terence Williams [1948] Director

The Williamson Trust
Incorporated: 18 March 2011 *Employees:* 359
Net Worth: £39,420,500 *Total Assets:* £49,124,800
Registered Office: Sir Joseph Williamson's Mathematical School, Maidstone Road, Rochester, Kent, ME1 3EL
Activities: Primary education
Officers: Richard John Carter [1965] Director/Solicitor; Michael Edward Costello [1955] Director/Police Advisor; Graham Paul Cottle [1967] Director/IT Consultant; Naushabah Parveen Khan [1986] Associate Director; Lawrence John McVeigh [1946] Director; Richard McDonald Robinson [1954] Director

Willoughby (880) Limited
Incorporated: 6 March 2015 *Employees:* 627
Net Worth Deficit: £1,673,000 *Total Assets:* £120,908,000
Registered Office: IMEX, Embassy House, 575-559 Maxted Road, Hemel Hempstead Industrial Estate, Hemel Hempstead, Herts, HP2 7DX
Activities: Management consultancy activities other than financial management
Officers: Carl Anthony Castledine [1969] Director; Gary Padbury Fletcher [1965] Director; Greg Lashley [1964] Director; Neill Timothy Ryder [1976] Director; Michael Edward Smith [1947] Director; Richard Peter Whitwell [1964] Director

The Willow Learning Trust
Incorporated: 16 May 2011 *Employees:* 257
Previous: Glenthorne High School
Net Worth: £45,442,000 *Total Assets:* £50,639,000
Registered Office: Glenthorne High School, Sutton Common Road, Sutton, Surrey, SM3 9PS
Activities: General secondary education
Officers: Dr Kerry Guest, Secretary; Dayo Balogun [1974] Director/Marketing Consultant; Simon Brown [1956] Director/Retired; Stephan Cook [1960] Director/Headteacher; Nigel Edward Griffiths [1947] Director/Retired; Marilyn Antoinette Holness [1959] Director/Head of Department; Stephen John Hume [1961] Director/Headteacher; Tom Magill [1969] Director/Social Care Manager; Isabelle Paget [1948] Director/Retired; Grant Alan Stonell [1974] Director/Financial Controller; Stephen Waring [1945] Director; Janet Elizabeth Flett Wright [1952] Director/Retired

Arnold Wills and Company Limited
Incorporated: 20 August 1946 *Employees:* 215
Net Worth: £21,543,572 *Total Assets:* £23,868,674
Registered Office: Aston House, York Road, Maidenhead, Berks, SL6 1SF
Activities: Manufacture of luggage, handbags and the like, saddlery and harness
Shareholders: Robert Hugo Weyl Wills; Belinda Katie Kew
Officers: Carol Mary Wills, Secretary; Belinda Katie Kew [1981] Director/Office Manager; Philippa Jane Weyl Wills [1982] Director/Administrator; Robert Hugo Weyl Wills [1949] Director/Leather Goods Manufacturer

Wilson Connolly Holdings Limited
Incorporated: 28 December 1964
Net Worth: £138,352,992 *Total Assets:* £173,555,008
Registered Office: Gate House, Turnpike Road, High Wycombe, Bucks, HP12 3NR
Activities: Activities of head offices
Parent: Taylor Wimpey PLC
Officers: Michael Andrew Lonnon, Secretary; Colin Richard Clapham [1945] Director/Company Secretary; Michael Andrew Lonnon [1957] Director/Company Secretary

Wilson Connolly Limited
Incorporated: 2 January 1930
Net Worth: £2,712,000 *Total Assets:* £23,140,000
Registered Office: Gate House, Turnpike Road, High Wycombe, Bucks, HP12 3NR
Activities: Development of building projects
Parent: Wilson Connolly Holdings Limited
Officers: Michael Andrew Lonnon, Secretary; Colin Richard Clapham [1945] Director/Company Secretary; Sarah Judith Thornley [1985] Director

Wilsons Automobiles and Coachworks Limited
Incorporated: 3 February 1933 *Employees:* 223
Net Worth: £25,710,900 *Total Assets:* £47,490,304
Registered Office: Nonsuch Business Park, Kiln Lane, Epsom, Surrey, KT17 1DH
Activities: Sale of new cars and light motor vehicles
Shareholders: Teresa Wilson; Ian Anthony Wilson
Officers: Teresa Wilson, Secretary; John Patrick Butler [1970] Director; Maria Fenwick [1966] Director/Manager; Wojciech Gumienny [1983] Director [Polish]; Gina Storr [1959] Projects Director; David Michael Wheatcroft [1973] Sales Director; Ian Anthony Wilson [1940] Director/Chairman; Teresa Wilson [1940] Sales Director; Toni Wilson [1961] Sales Director

Wilton House Limited
Incorporated: 10 March 1986 *Employees:* 158
Net Worth: £17,809,914 *Total Assets:* £29,044,988
Registered Office: Wilton House Limited, 171 Adeyfield Road, Hemel Hempstead, Herts, HP2 5JU
Activities: Residential nursing care facilities
Major Shareholder: Nittianund Reekhaye
Officers: Vishwanand Singh Ramoutar [1968] Director/Nurse

Wilton Park Developments Limited
Incorporated: 7 May 2014 *Employees:* 3
Net Worth: £2,942,768 *Total Assets:* £41,221,760
Registered Office: Decimal Place, Chiltern Avenue, Amersham, Bucks, HP6 5FG
Activities: Buying and selling of own real estate
Parent: Bucks Developments Ltd
Officers: Nishith Malde, Secretary; Nishith Malde [1958] Director; Stephen Desmond Wicks [1951] Director

Wimpey Dormant Investments Limited
Incorporated: 31 July 1959
Net Worth: £31,245,000 *Total Assets:* £651,478,976
Registered Office: Gate House, Turnpike Road, High Wycombe, Bucks, HP12 3NR
Activities: Non-trading company
Parent: Wimpey Group Services Limited
Officers: Katherine Elizabeth Hindmarsh, Secretary; James John Jordan [1961] Director/Company Secretary; Michael Andrew Lonnon [1957] Director/Company Secretary

George Wimpey Limited
Incorporated: 3 November 1978
Net Worth: £1,073,544,000 *Total Assets:* £2,676,461,056
Registered Office: Gate House, Turnpike Road, High Wycombe, Bucks, HP12 3NR
Activities: Activities of head offices
Parent: Taylor Wimpey PLC
Officers: James John Jordan, Secretary/Solicitor/Company Secretary; Christopher Carney [1974] Director; James John Jordan [1961] Director/Company Secretary; Peter Timothy Redfern [1970] Director/Group Chief Executive

Wimpey Overseas Holdings Limited
Incorporated: 27 February 2001
Net Worth: £714,009,984 *Total Assets:* £719,470,976
Registered Office: Gate House, Turnpike Road, High Wycombe, Bucks, HP12 3NR
Activities: Activities of head offices
Parent: George Wimpey Limited
Officers: Michael Andrew Lonnon, Secretary; Alex David Green [1981] Director; Stephen Roy Impey [1957] Director; James John Jordan [1961] Director/Company Secretary

Winchester Diocesan Board of Finance (The)
Incorporated: 8 December 1915 *Employees:* 42
Net Worth: £133,929,000 *Total Assets:* £140,656,000
Registered Office: The Diocesan Office, Old Alresford Place, Alresford, Hants, SO24 9DH
Activities: Activities of religious organisations
Officers: Andrew Ronald Robinson, Secretary; Alastair James Lamont Barron [1957] Director/Head of Group Security; Esther Louise Clift [1967] Director/Business Professional; Alison Jane Coulter [1964] Director of a Consultancy Business; The Right Reverend Timothy John Dakin [1958] Director/Bishop of Winchester; Richard Harlow [1963] Director/Rector; Reverend Andrew Mark Micklefield [1971] Director/Vicar; Ian Nigel Newman [1955] Director/Undertaker; Charles Stewart [1955] Director/Vicar; Mark Stephen Ward [1962] Director/Head of Fundraising

Winchester Holdings Limited
Incorporated: 16 December 2015 *Employees:* 454
Net Worth: £21,812,696 *Total Assets:* £37,813,092
Registered Office: 17-19 Station Road West, Oxted, Surrey, RH8 9EE
Activities: Activities of head offices
Shareholder: Thomas James Ferris
Officers: Edward William Ferris [1980] Director; Thomas James Ferris [1981] Director

Wind Farm Holdings Limited
Incorporated: 26 September 2003
Previous: RES Wind Farm Holdings Limited
Net Worth: £9,735,000 *Total Assets:* £39,600,000
Registered Office: Beaufort Court, Egg Farm Lane, off Ststion Road, Kings Langley, Herts, WD4 8LR
Activities: Activities of head offices
Parent: The Renewables Infrastructure Group (UK) Investments Limited
Officers: Dominic James Hearth, Secretary; Caroline Elizabeth Gilpin [1977] Director/PPA Origination Manager; Steven William Hughes [1972] Generation & Asset Management Director; Mitesh Raj Patel [1982] Director/Group Financial Controller

Windmill Organics Limited
Incorporated: 28 April 1998 *Employees:* 90
Net Worth: £36,343,552 *Total Assets:* £44,271,744
Registered Office: 34a Clifton Road, Kingston upon Thames, Surrey, KT2 6PH
Activities: Wholesale of other food, including fish, crustaceans and molluscs
Shareholders: Noel McDonald; Donata Berger
Officers: Donata Berger, Secretary; Noel McDonald [1947] Director [Irish]

Windsor Learning Partnership
Incorporated: 27 January 2015 *Employees:* 293
Net Worth: £43,861,940 *Total Assets:* £48,872,824
Registered Office: c/o Windsor Girls' School, Imperial Road, Windsor, Berks, SL4 3RT
Activities: General secondary education
Officers: Paul David Cash [1965] Director; Katherine Ann Chevis [1968] Director of Training Company; Anthony Richard Evans [1963] Director, Communications Consultant; Gillian Clare Labrum [1968] Director/Headteacher; Ammer Masood [1971] Director/General Manager; David Isaac Oliver [1958] Director/Management Consultant; Andrew Robert Wardlow [1963] Director

Windsor Television Limited
Incorporated: 11 August 1983
Net Worth Deficit: £180,652,992 *Total Assets:* £211,638,000
Registered Office: Media House, Bartley Wood Business Park, Hook, Hants, RG27 9UP
Activities: Other telecommunications activities
Parent: General Cable Limited
Officers: Gillian Elizabeth James, Secretary; Robert Dominic Dunn [1966] Director/Chief Financial Officer; Mine Ozkan Hifzi [1966] Director/Solicitor

Wintel Petrochemicals Limited
Incorporated: 26 May 2005 *Employees:* 5
Net Worth: £15,435,215 *Total Assets:* £42,683,424
Registered Office: 14 St Johns Road, Woking, Surrey, GU21 7SE
Activities: Agents involved in the sale of fuels, ores, metals and industrial chemicals
Officers: Richard Mew, Secretary; Stephen Derek Burgess [1982] Director [Irish]; Richard Netherton Mew [1964] Director/Company Secretary

Winterbotham,Darby & Co.Limited
Incorporated: 2 October 1962
Net Worth: £24,409,000 *Total Assets:* £158,110,000
Registered Office: Granville House, 9 Wells Place, Merstham, Redhill, Surrey, RH1 3AS
Activities: Wholesale of meat and meat products
Parent: The Compleat Food Group Limited
Officers: David Jonathan Kimber, Secretary; Steven James Higginson [1960] Managing Director; Mark John Lane [1970] Director; Damian Johnson Shaw [1971] Director

Winterhalter Ltd
Incorporated: 22 October 1970 *Employees:* 138
Net Worth: £6,201,795 *Total Assets:* £25,037,508
Registered Office: Winterhalter House, Roebuck Way, Knowlhill, Milton Keynes, Bucks, MK5 8WH
Activities: Repair of other equipment
Officers: David John Parsons, Secretary; Peter John Alsworth [1962] Director; Andrew Keith Blake [1957] Director; Viktor Faller [1964] Director [German]; Peter Huber [1957] Director [German]; Stephen Kinkead [1970] Director; Kieran Raymond Lynch [1960] Director [Irish]; David John Parsons [1961] Finance Director; Glenn Ernest Roberts [1960] Sales Director; David Smithson [1949] Director; Jurgen Winterhalter [1944] Director/Engineer [German]; Ralph Winterhalter [1978] Director [German]

Wipac Limited
Incorporated: 14 July 1969 *Employees:* 318
Net Worth: £20,100,048 *Total Assets:* £45,089,432
Registered Office: London Road, Buckingham, MK18 1BH
Activities: Manufacture of other parts and accessories for motor vehicles
Parent: Carclo PLC
Officers: Richard John Ottaway, Secretary; David Robert William Benton [1971] Director; Philip Dobbie [1966] Director/Chartered Engineer; Michael Terence Greenrod [1976] Director/Design; Christopher John Malley [1967] Director; Mark Andrew Ross [1965] Director/Accountant; Neil Sibley [1968] Sales Director

Wireless Logic Limited
Incorporated: 19 November 1999 *Employees:* 61
Net Worth: £46,554,000 *Total Assets:* £63,225,000
Registered Office: Horizon, Honey Lane, Hurley, Maidenhead, Berks, SL6 6RJ
Activities: Wireless telecommunications activities
Parent: Wireless Logic Group Limited
Officers: Richard Miller [1964] Finance Director; Oliver Robert Stewart Tucker [1962] Managing Director

Wisdom Properties Limited
Incorporated: 4 December 2002 *Employees:* 167
Net Worth: £12,567,573 *Total Assets:* £23,045,208
Registered Office: Broomham Hall, Rye Road, Guestling, Hastings, Kent, TN35 4LT
Activities: Other letting and operating of own or leased real estate
Major Shareholder: Giles Harvey Sutton
Officers: Giles Harvey Sutton [1967] Marketing Director

The Wisley Golf Club PLC
Incorporated: 28 September 1987 *Employees:* 102
Net Worth: £20,225,786 *Total Assets:* £24,183,180
Registered Office: The Wisley Golf Club PLC, Ripley, Woking, Surrey, GU23 6QU
Activities: Activities of sport clubs
Officers: Richard Goodley, Secretary; Simon Christopher Bunce [1963] Director/Retired; Vincent Chandler [1956] Director/Consultant; Philip Peter Clinton Gregory [1955] Director; Peter Bruce Hockless [1955] Director/Retired; Charles Max Lesser [1959] Director; Anthony Tregerthen Morgan [1956] Director/Retired; Brendan Robert Nelson [1949] Director; John Richard Notman-Watt [1963] Director/Business Consultant; Nicholas Edward Wenman [1956] Director

WJH Holdings Limited
Incorporated: 18 January 2016 *Employees:* 869
Net Worth: £62,337,956 *Total Assets:* £198,068,720
Registered Office: 1 Liverpool Gardens, Worthing, W Sussex, BN11 1TF
Activities: Activities of other holding companies n.e.c.
Shareholders: James Matthew Sawer; Amanda Jill Perrett; Guy Harwood
Officers: Lucinda Jane Crowley [1980] Director; Archie Guy Harwood [1990] Director; Gaye Michelle Harwood [1972] Director; Guy Harwood [1939] Director; Tessa Rose Harwood [1994] Director; Amanda Jill Perrett [1969] Director

WL One Bidco Limited
Incorporated: 30 January 2015
Net Worth Deficit: £70,211,000 *Total Assets:* £179,403,008
Registered Office: Horizon, Honey Lane, Hurley, Berks, SL6 6RJ
Activities: Activities of financial services holding companies
Parent: WL One Midco 2 Limited
Officers: Richard Miller [1964] Director/Chief Financial Officer; Oliver Robert Stewart Tucker [1962] Director/Chief Executive Officer

WL One Holdco Limited
Incorporated: 30 January 2015 *Employees:* 132
Net Worth Deficit: £45,001,000 *Total Assets:* £224,458,000
Registered Office: Horizon, Honey Lane, Hurley, Berks, SL6 6RJ
Activities: Activities of financial services holding companies
Parent: WL One Holding Limited
Officers: Richard Miller [1964] Finance Director; Oliver Robert Stewart Tucker [1962] Director

WL One Midco 1 Limited
Incorporated: 30 January 2015
Net Worth: £912,000 *Total Assets:* £143,346,000
Registered Office: Horizon, Honey Lane, Hurley, Berks, SL6 6RJ
Activities: Activities of financial services holding companies
Parent: WL One Holdco Limited
Officers: Richard Miller [1964] Director/Chief Financial Officer; Oliver Robert Stewart Tucker [1962] Director/Chief Executive Officer

WL One Midco 2 Limited
Incorporated: 30 January 2015
Net Worth: £904,000 *Total Assets:* £143,188,000
Registered Office: Horizon, Honey Lane, Hurley, Berks, SL6 6RJ
Activities: Activities of financial services holding companies
Parent: WL One Midco 1 Limited
Officers: Richard Miller [1964] Director/Chief Financial Officer; Oliver Robert Stewart Tucker [1962] Director/Chief Executive Officer

WLHC Projectco Limited
Incorporated: 22 October 2009
Net Worth Deficit: £21,195 *Total Assets:* £37,067,272
Registered Office: 8 White Oak Square, London Road, Swanley, Kent, BR8 7AG
Activities: Library activities
Parent: WLHC Holdco Limited
Officers: Neeti Mukundrai Anand [1984] Director; Adam George Waddington [1974] Director

WNDirect Limited
Incorporated: 14 July 2011 *Employees:* 83
Net Worth: £6,007,965 *Total Assets:* £21,585,420
Registered Office: 2 AC Court, High Street, Thames Ditton, Surrey, KT7 0SR
Activities: Other transportation support activities
Parent: DPDgroup UK Ltd
Officers: Robert Anthony Betts, Secretary; Simon Batt [1977] Director; Gwenael Clement [1981] Director [French]; Francois Copigneaux [1963] Director [French]

Woburn Enterprises Limited
Incorporated: 12 November 1969
Net Worth: £21,235,352 *Total Assets:* £21,520,904
Registered Office: The Bedford Office, Woburn, Beds, MK17 9PQ
Activities: Other retail sale not in stores, stalls or markets
Shareholders: James Fitzroy Dean; Charles William Cayzer; Edmond Conolly Mahony; Paul Vere Lindon
Officers: Kevin Leslie Shurrock, Secretary; The Hon Charles William Cayzer [1957] Director; Timothy Francis How [1950] Director/Company Chairman; Paul Vere Lindon [1962] Director/Chartered Surveyor; Louise Rona Russell [1962] Director; Andrew Ian Henry Russell Fifteenth Duke of Bedford [1962] Director

Woldingham School
Incorporated: 2 July 2008 *Employees:* 211
Net Worth: £20,665,518 *Total Assets:* £27,910,932
Registered Office: Woldingham School, Marden Park, Woldingham, Caterham, Surrey, CR3 7YA
Activities: General secondary education
Officers: Simon David William Hopkins, Secretary; Ian Edward Baker [1961] Director/Chartered Accountant; Ciara Mary Brown [1962] Director/Communications Consultant [Irish]; Simon Dempster Collins [1959] Director/Headmaster; Nicholas Paul Le Cuirot Crapp [1963] Managing Director; William Crothers [1960] Director/Civil Servant; Heather Gail Hanbury [1960] Director/Headmistress; Alexandra Sara Christine Maule [1965] Director; Robert Henry Parkinson [1956] Director/Recruitment Consultant; Martin Louis Redman [1955] Director; Christopher Scattergood [1969] Director; Tim Woffenden [1953] Director/Teacher; James Nicholas Wright [1971] Director/Chartered Accountant

Wolseley Group Holdings Limited
Incorporated: 17 November 2005
Net Worth: £3,707,194,880 *Total Assets:* £7,776,714,240
Registered Office: 1020 Eskdale Road, Winnersh Triangle, Wokingham, Berks, RG41 5TS
Activities: Activities of head offices
Parent: Wolseley Limited
Officers: Katherine Mary McCormick, Secretary; Mark John Fearon [1970] Director of Corporate Communications and Investor; Paul Simon Fox [1978] Director; Julia Amanda Mattison [1982] Director/Accountant; Michael Andrew Powell [1967] Director; Philip Andrew Scott [1978] Director/Group Treasurer

Wolseley Limited
Incorporated: 9 October 1889 *Employees:* 4
Net Worth: £1,912,903,424 *Total Assets:* £8,133,097,984
Registered Office: 1020 Eskdale Road, Winnersh Triangle, Wokingham, Berks, RG41 5TS
Activities: Activities of head offices
Parent: Ferguson PLC
Officers: Katherine Mary McCormick, Secretary; Mark John Fearon [1970] Director of Corporate Communications and Investor; Paul Simon Fox [1978] Director; Julia Amanda Mattison [1982] Director/Accountant; Michael Andrew Powell [1967] Director; Philip Andrew Scott [1978] Director/Group Treasurer

Wolseley Overseas Limited
Incorporated: 24 September 1964
Net Worth: £8,078,825,472 *Total Assets:* £8,078,825,472
Registered Office: 1020 Eskdale Road, Winnersh Triangle, Wokingham, Berks, RG41 5TS
Activities: Activities of head offices
Parent: Wolseley Group Holdings Limited
Officers: Katherine Mary McCormick, Secretary; Mark John Fearon [1970] Director of Corporate Communications and Investor; Paul Simon Fox [1978] Director; Julia Amanda Mattison [1982] Director/Accountant; Michael Andrew Powell [1967] Director; Philip Andrew Scott [1978] Director/Group Treasurer

Wolters Kluwer (UK) Limited
Incorporated: 9 March 1948 *Employees:* 257
Net Worth: £31,772,484 *Total Assets:* £97,016,512
Registered Office: 145 London Road, Kingston upon Thames, Surrey, KT2 6SR
Activities: Other software publishing
Parent: Wolters Kluwer Holdings (UK) PLC
Officers: John Goudie, Secretary; Samantha Joanne Bond [1972] Finance Director; Claire Louise Carter [1973] Managing Director; John Goudie [1965] Director/Chartered Accountant

Wolters Kluwer Health (Medical Research) Limited
Incorporated: 7 December 1983 *Employees:* 113
Net Worth: £7,211,000 *Total Assets:* £24,669,000
Registered Office: Croner House, 145 London Road, Kingston upon Thames, Surrey, KT2 6SR
Activities: Other publishing activities
Parent: Wolters Kluwer Health (Europe) Limited
Officers: John Goudie, Secretary; Roy Mulder [1971] Director/VP Finance [Dutch]; Philip Warren [1953] Finance Director; Gareth Robert Williams [1971] Director

Wolters Kluwer Holdings (UK) PLC
Incorporated: 8 September 1977
Net Worth Deficit: £28,851,976 *Total Assets:* £146,081,552
Registered Office: 145 London Road, Kingston upon Thames, Surrey, KT2 6SR
Activities: Activities of other holding companies n.e.c.
Parent: Wolters Kluwer International Holding BV
Officers: John Goudie, Secretary; Samantha Joanne Bond [1972] Finance Director; Claire Louise Carter [1973] Managing Director

Wood Group Industrial Services Limited
Incorporated: 22 June 2004 *Employees:* 2,001
Net Worth: £39,458,000 *Total Assets:* £80,461,000
Registered Office: Compass Point, 79-87 Kingston Road, Staines upon Thames, Middlesex, TW18 1DT
Activities: Other specialised construction activities n.e.c.
Parent: Wood Group Engineering & Operations Support Limited
Officers: Iain Angus Jones, Secretary; Derek Byrne [1972] Director/President - Industrial Services [Irish]; Richard Manson Duff [1958] Director; Andrew James Findlay [1974] Director/Financial Controller; Alan James Johnstone [1963] Director; Stephen James Nicol [1975] Director/Chief Financial Officer; Craig Shanaghey [1971] Director/SVP Industrial Services

Wood Group Kenny Limited
Incorporated: 7 November 1978 *Employees:* 30
Net Worth: £20,270,000 *Total Assets:* £22,648,000
Registered Office: Compass Point, 79-87 Kingston Road, Staines upon Thames, Middlesex, TW18 1DT
Activities: Construction of other civil engineering projects n.e.c.
Parent: Wood Group Kenny Corporate Limited
Officers: Iain Angus Jones, Secretary; Grant Rae Angus [1970] Director; Alan Rae Fotheringham [1966] Director; Robert Alexander MacDonald [1968] Director

Wood Hall Land & Properties Limited
Incorporated: 20 July 2012
Net Worth: £4,574,605 *Total Assets:* £28,376,944
Registered Office: Wood Hall Farm Office, Woodhall Lane, Shenley, Herts, WD7 9AA
Activities: Activities of head offices
Major Shareholder: Andrew Lynton Cohen
Officers: Iain Williamson, Secretary; Andrew Lynton Cohen [1953] Director

Woodcote Estates Limited
Incorporated: 31 March 2003
Net Worth: £18,661,508 *Total Assets:* £45,316,128
Registered Office: Crown House Mews, Chequers Lane, Walton on the Hill, Tadworth, Surrey, KT20 7ST
Activities: Other letting and operating of own or leased real estate
Major Shareholder: Martin James Morris
Officers: David Mark Pay, Secretary; Martin James Morris [1963] Director

Woodgavil Limited
Incorporated: 16 July 2009
Net Worth: £19,324,168 *Total Assets:* £24,964,550
Registered Office: Crown House Mews, Chequers Lane, Walton on the Hill, Tadworth, Surrey, KT20 7ST
Activities: Other letting and operating of own or leased real estate
Parent: Woodgavil Properties Ltd
Officers: David Mark Pay, Secretary; Martin James Morris [1963] Director

Woodgavil Properties Limited
Incorporated: 23 December 1954
Net Worth: £27,082,972 *Total Assets:* £29,440,504
Registered Office: Crown House Mews, Chequers Lane, Walton on the Hill, Tadworth, Surrey, KT20 7ST
Activities: Other letting and operating of own or leased real estate
Shareholders: Martin James Morris; Paul Edward Morris
Officers: Martin James Morris [1963] Director; Paul Edward Morris [1954] Director

The Woodland Academy Trust
Incorporated: 5 July 2011 *Employees:* 222
Net Worth: £19,845,000 *Total Assets:* £22,939,000
Registered Office: Northumberland Heath Primary School, Wheelock Close, Byron Drive, Erith, Kent, DA8 1JE
Activities: Primary education
Officers: Dr Deborah Joan Absalom [1955] Director/Retired; Chika Chukwujekwu [1974] Director/Forensic Accountant; Heather Rosanne Daley [1963] Director/HR Professional; Kamaldeen Giwa [1978] Director/Chartered Surveyor; Rebecca Johnson [1985] Director/Learning & Events Manager; Daniel Morrow [1978] Director/Executive Principal/CEO [Irish]; Neil Howard Riddington [1965] Director/Insurance Clerical; Jim Rouncefield [1951] Director/Retired

Wootton Academy Trust
Incorporated: 15 August 2011 *Employees:* 133
Net Worth: £34,535,824 *Total Assets:* £36,341,524
Registered Office: Wootton Upper School, Hall End Road, Wootton, Bedford, MK43 9HT
Activities: General secondary education
Officers: Jonathan Kimber Billington [1964] Director; David Clare [1959] Director/Electrical Engineer; Michael George Gleeson [1961] Director/Teacher; Peter Laurence Walby Haddon [1955] Director/Retired; Michael James Ridley [1967] Director/Department of Education; Ian Sibbald [1969] Director of Finance; Timothy Humphreys Williams [1953] Director/HR Consultant

Workdry International Limited
Incorporated: 19 August 2014 *Employees:* 492
Net Worth: £3,077,000 *Total Assets:* £135,715,008
Registered Office: 32-36 Bournemouth Road, Chandler's Ford, Eastleigh, Hants, SO53 3ZL
Activities: Other specialised construction activities n.e.c.
Shareholders: Carole Denise Bright; Richard James Bright
Officers: Nigel Mark Apps [1969] Director; Carole Denise Bright [1960] Director; Richard James Bright [1987] Director; Richard Allan Brown [1967] Director; Christopher Mark Garrett [1969] Director

World Duty Free Limited
Incorporated: 30 July 1997
Net Worth: £21,245,000 *Total Assets:* £21,408,000
Registered Office: The Compass Centre, Nelson Road, Hounslow, Middlesex, TW6 2GW
Activities: Other retail sale of new goods in specialised stores (not commercial art galleries and opticians)
Parent: LHR Airports Limited
Officers: Christopher John Annetts [1972] Director; Ross Findlay Scott Baker [1974] Director

World Mission Agency - Winners Chapel International
Incorporated: 19 August 2009 *Employees:* 40
Net Worth: £21,502,440 *Total Assets:* £24,500,488
Registered Office: 1 Churchill Close, Green Street, Green Road, Dartford, Kent, DA1 1QE
Activities: Activities of religious organisations
Officers: Dr. Olumuyiwa John Olumoroti, Secretary; Alakoro Syrenius Abaya [1956] Director/Administration; Adebayo Arowolo [1972] Director/Accountant; Abosede Olufunke Obanobi [1964] Director/Accountant; Mamiroro Christine Ogunkanmi [1965] Director/Chartered Architect/Project Manager; Olumuyiwa Olufote [1980] Director/Certified Chartered Accountant; Dr. Olumuyiwa John Olumoroti [1968] Director/Medical Doctor

World Vision UK
Incorporated: 3 November 1982 *Employees:* 301
Net Worth: £21,710,000 *Total Assets:* £30,207,000
Registered Office: World Vision House, Opal Drive, Fox Milne, Milton Keynes, Bucks, MK15 0ZR
Activities: Other social work activities without accommodation n.e.c.
Officers: Paul Jack James Hewitt Wratten, Secretary; Serena Marie Brown [1974] Director/Corporate Citizenship; Simon Shelford Burne [1954] Director/Fundraising and Marketing Specialist; Jennifer Mary Collins [1948] Executive Director; Linda Emery [1960] Talent & Diversity Director; Marcus James Frost [1969] Director/Partnership Leader Marketing & Resource Development; Richard Philip Izard [1963] Director/Consultant; Marcus William George Manuel [1962] Director/Senior Research Associate; John Douglas MacLean Millican [1964] Director/Chief Executive; Mark Richard Parsons [1977] Director/Banking; David Gareth Richards [1960] Director/Church Minister; Julian Clive Vaughan Thomas [1959] Director/Marketing Consultant

Worldwide Flight Services Limited
Incorporated: 2 December 1999 *Employees:* 459
Net Worth: £13,058,354 *Total Assets:* £37,583,808
Registered Office: Building 552, Shoreham Road East, London Heathrow Airport, Hounslow, Middlesex, TW6 3UA
Activities: Operation of warehousing and storage facilities for air transport activities
Officers: Steven Greenhalgh [1974] Finance Director; Francois Jean Pierre Mirallie [1962] Director/Group CFO [French]; Patrick Ian Roberts [1950] Managing Director

WorleyParsons Europe Limited
Incorporated: 5 December 2001 *Employees:* 505
Net Worth: £317,726,016 *Total Assets:* £401,252,992
Registered Office: 27 Great West Road, Brentford, Middlesex, TW8 9BW
Activities: Architectural activities
Officers: Victor Jibuike, Secretary; John Robert Creasy [1970] Director/Finance Manager; Werner Dorfling [1970] Director; Alan Stewart Gordon [1964] Director; Thomas Francis Honan [1962] Director/Chief Financial Officer [Australian]; Andrew Wood [1959] Director [Australian]

WorleyParsons UK Finance Sub Limited
Incorporated: 21 February 2008
Net Worth: £333,431,008 *Total Assets:* £426,903,008
Registered Office: 27 Great West Road, Brentford, Middlesex, TW8 9BW
Activities: Financial management
Parent: WorleyParsons Europe Limited
Officers: Victor Jibuike, Secretary; Alan Stewart Gordon [1964] Managing Director; Thomas Francis Honan [1962] Director/Chief Financial Officer [Australian]; Andrew Wood [1959] Director [Australian]

WorleyParsons UK Finance Sub No. 2 Ltd
Incorporated: 8 December 2016
Net Worth: £328,763,520 *Total Assets:* £330,134,528
Registered Office: 27 Great West Road, Brentford, Middlesex, TW8 9BW
Activities: Financial management
Parent: WorleyParsons UK Finance Sub Limited
Officers: Victor Jibuike, Secretary; Alan Stewart Gordon [1964] Director; Thomas Francis Honan [1962] Director/Chief Financial Officer [Australian]; Andrew Peter Wood [1959] Director/Chief Executive Officer [Australian]

Worth Abbey
Incorporated: 2 July 2002 *Employees:* 240
Net Worth: £21,396,328 *Total Assets:* £33,568,976
Registered Office: Worth Abbey, Paddockhurst Road, Turners Hill, Crawley, W Sussex, RH10 4SB
Activities: Activities of religious organisations
Officers: Rev Patrick Vincent Fludder, Secretary; Reverend John Mark Barrett [1957] Director/Clerk in Holy Orders; Rev Anthony Brockman [1962] Director/Monk; Patrick Vincent Fludder [1951] Director/Clerk in Holy Orders; Richard Luke Jolly [1953] Director/Clerk in Holy Orders; Rev Martin Edward McGee [1950] Director/Clerk in Holy Orders; Christopher Aidan Murray [1948] Director/Clerk in Holy Orders

Worthing Homes Limited
Incorporated: 26 February 1998 *Employees:* 95
Net Worth: £75,593,000 *Total Assets:* £204,392,992
Registered Office: Davison House, North Street, Worthing, W Sussex, BN11 1ER
Activities: Renting and operating of Housing Association real estate
Officers: Julian Reginald Pitcher, Secretary; Amy Louise Dewey [1978] Director/HR Manager; Colin Goodwin [1960] Director/Board Member; Jennifer Graham [1957] Director; Louise Murphy [1984] Director/Councillor; Nigel Robin Perryman [1958] Director; Helen Laura Rice [1975] Director; Celia Anne Rowe [1957] Director/Support Worker; Christopher David Simpson [1968] Managing Director; Paul George Smith [1956] Managing Director; Stephen William John Wills [1945] Director/Retired

Wozair Limited
Incorporated: 23 March 1995 *Employees:* 198
Net Worth: £19,604,730 *Total Assets:* £32,712,796
Registered Office: 32 Grosvenor Road, Gillingham Business Park, Gillingham, Kent, ME8 0SA
Activities: Manufacture of non-domestic cooling and ventilation equipment
Officers: Simon John Collins, Company Secretary; Paul Marcel Azzopardi [1958] Director; Sheila Devi Azzopardi [1968] Director [Singaporean]; Christopher Richard Cherrington [1978] Sales Director; Hazel Anntoinette Collins [1959] Director; Simon John Collins [1955] Director/Company Secretary; Philip Richard Pendrill [1974] Technical Director

WP Midco1 Limited
Incorporated: 26 March 2008 *Employees:* 2
Net Worth Deficit: £467,728,000 *Total Assets:* £280,068,992
Registered Office: Profile West, 950 Great West Road, Brentford, Middlesex, TW8 9ES
Activities: Activities of head offices
Parent: WP Safetykleen Limited
Officers: Andrew Gregory Firth, Secretary; Andrew Patrick Griffith [1968] Director; Philippe Robert Francis Mauguy [1960] Director [French]

WP Midco2 Limited
Incorporated: 26 March 2008
Net Worth: £267,900,000 *Total Assets:* £267,900,000
Registered Office: Profile West, 950 Great West Road, Brentford, Middlesex, TW8 9ES
Activities: Activities of head offices
Parent: WP Midco 1 Limited
Officers: Andrew Gregory Firth, Secretary; Andrew Patrick Griffith [1968] Director; Philippe Robert Francis Mauguy [1960] Director [French]

WP Midco3 Limited
Incorporated: 26 March 2008 *Employees:* 2
Net Worth: £391,524,992 *Total Assets:* £752,249,984
Registered Office: Profile West, 950 Great West Road, Brentford, Middlesex, TW8 9ES
Activities: Activities of head offices
Parent: WP Midco 2 Limited
Officers: Andrew Gregory Firth, Secretary; Andrew Patrick Griffith [1968] Director; Philippe Robert Francis Mauguy [1960] Director [French]

WP Safety-Kleen Limited
Incorporated: 26 March 2008
Net Worth: £303,664,000 *Total Assets:* £310,040,000
Registered Office: Profile West, 950 Great West Road, Brentford, Middlesex, TW8 9ES
Activities: Activities of head offices
Officers: Andrew Gregory Firth, Secretary; Andrew Patrick Griffith [1968] Director; Philippe Robert Francis Mauguy [1960] Director [French]

WP SK Holdings Limited
Incorporated: 21 May 2004
Net Worth: £46,000,000 *Total Assets:* £46,000,000
Registered Office: Profile West, 950 Great West Road, Brentford, Middlesex, TW8 9ES
Activities: Activities of head offices
Parent: Safetykleen Group Services Limited
Officers: Andrew Gregory Firth, Secretary; Andrew Patrick Griffith [1968] Director; Philippe Robert Francis Mauguy [1960] Director [French]

WP SK Limited
Incorporated: 21 May 2004 *Employees:* 2
Net Worth: £112,267,000 *Total Assets:* £224,239,008
Registered Office: Profile West, 950 Great West Road, Brentford, Middlesex, TW8 9ES
Activities: Activities of head offices
Parent: WP SK Midco Limited
Officers: Andrew Gregory Firth, Secretary; Andrew Patrick Griffith [1968] Director; Philippe Robert Francis Mauguy [1960] Director [French]

WP SK Midco Limited
Incorporated: 8 March 2005 *Employees:* 2
Net Worth Deficit: £101,056,000 *Total Assets:* £176,288,992
Registered Office: Profile West, 950 Great West Road, Brentford, Middlesex, TW8 9ES
Activities: Activities of head offices
Parent: WP SK Holdings Limited
Officers: Andrew Gregory Firth, Secretary; Andrew Patrick Griffith [1968] Director; Philippe Robert Francis Mauguy [1960] Director [French]

Wryde Croft Wind Farm Limited
Incorporated: 27 September 2004
Net Worth Deficit: £6,705,000 *Total Assets:* £42,107,000
Registered Office: Beaufort Court, Egg Farm Lane, off Station Road, Kings Langley, Herts, WD4 8LR
Activities: Production of electricity
Parent: Notos Energy Limited
Officers: Dominic James Hearth, Secretary; Peter Edward Dias [1981] Director; Christopher Peter Gaydon [1978] Director [Hungarian]; Paul Stephen Latham [1956] Director; Thomas James Rosser [1985] Director

WSH Events Limited
Incorporated: 1 July 2014 *Employees:* 813
Net Worth Deficit: £4,600,000 *Total Assets:* £26,454,000
Registered Office: TVP2, 300 Thames Valley Park Drive, Reading, Berks, RG6 1PT
Activities: Activities of other holding companies n.e.c.
Parent: WSH International Investments Limited
Officers: Marc Bradley, Secretary; Marc Bradley [1975] Director; Alastair Dunbar Storey [1953] Director

WSH Hospitality Limited
Incorporated: 25 October 2013 *Employees:* 2
Net Worth: £233,508,992 *Total Assets:* £620,857,024
Registered Office: TVP2, 300 Thames Valley Park Drive, Reading, Berks, RG6 1PT
Activities: Activities of other holding companies n.e.c.
Parent: WSH UK & Ireland Limited
Officers: Marc Bradley, Secretary; Marc Bradley [1975] Director; Alastair Dunbar Storey [1953] Director

WSH International Investments Limited
Incorporated: 24 October 2013
Net Worth: £61,951,000 *Total Assets:* £393,848,992
Registered Office: TVP2, 300 Thames Valley Park Drive, Reading, Berks, RG6 1PT
Activities: Activities of other holding companies n.e.c.
Parent: WSH Investments Limited
Officers: Marc Bradley, Secretary; Marc Bradley [1975] Director; Alastair Dunbar Storey [1953] Director

WSH Investments Limited
Incorporated: 21 November 2016 *Employees:* 16,270
Net Worth Deficit: £36,677,000 *Total Assets:* £468,308,000
Registered Office: TVP2, 300 Thames Valley Park Drive, Reading, Berks, RG6 1PT
Activities: Dormant company
Major Shareholder: Alastair Dunbar Storey
Officers: Marc Bradley, Secretary; Marc Bradley [1975] Director; Alastair Dunbar Storey [1953] Director; Michael Anthony Street [1947] Director; Sean Williams [1964] Director/Chartered Accountant/Corporate Finance Adviser

WSH UK & Ireland Limited
Incorporated: 24 October 2013 *Employees:* 15,192
Net Worth: £165,971,008 *Total Assets:* £489,639,008
Registered Office: TVP2, 300 Thames Valley Park Drive, Reading, Berks, RG6 1PT
Activities: Activities of other holding companies n.e.c.
Parent: WSH International Investments Ltd
Officers: Marc Bradley, Secretary; John David Bennett [1963] Director; Marc Bradley [1975] Director; Simon Paul Esner [1962] Director; Nicholas Adrian Howe [1959] Director; Christopher Noel Mahony [1966] Director [Irish]; Andrew David Milner [1974] Procurement and Supply Chain Director; Maria Janette Stanford [1962] People and Talent Director; Alastair Dunbar Storey [1953] Director; Michael Anthony Street [1947] Director; Benedict Warner [1964] Director; Sean Williams [1964] Director/Chartered Accountant/Corporate Finance Adviser

Wurth UK Limited
Incorporated: 26 July 1973 *Employees:* 569
Net Worth: £4,037,000 *Total Assets:* £21,901,000
Registered Office: 1 Centurion Way, Erith, Kent, DA18 4AF
Activities: Wholesale trade of motor vehicle parts and accessories
Parent: Wurth Holding UK Limited
Officers: Andrew Richard Dagnall, Secretary; Andrew Richard Dagnall [1963] Finance Director; Ivor Laurence Morgan Jones [1974] Director/Operations Manager; Jason Murphy [1969] Managing Director

WW GBR Limited
Incorporated: 11 March 1976 *Employees:* 1,279
Previous: Weight Watchers (U.K.) Limited
Net Worth: £104,877,000 *Total Assets:* £145,891,008
Registered Office: Millennium House, Ludlow Road, Maidenhead, Berks, SL6 2SL
Activities: Other human health activities
Parent: Weight Watchers Holdings Limited
Officers: Nicholas Hotchkin [1965] Director/Chief Financial Officer [American]; Corinne Pollier [1964] Director/President International [French]

Ww.co.uk Online Limited
Incorporated: 17 January 2002 *Employees:* 12
Previous: Weightwatchers.co.uk Limited
Net Worth: £21,582,000 *Total Assets:* £24,441,000
Registered Office: Millennium House, Ludlow Road, Maidenhead, Berks, SL6 2SL
Activities: Other information technology service activities
Parent: Weightwatchers.Com, Inc.
Officers: Nicholas Hotchkin [1965] Director/Management [American]; Corinne Pollier [1964] Director/General Manager [French]

WWF-UK
Incorporated: 16 June 2000 *Employees:* 314
Net Worth: £63,660,000 *Total Assets:* £69,625,000
Registered Office: The Living Planet Centre, Rufford House, Brewery Road, Woking, Surrey, GU21 4LL
Activities: Other publishing activities
Officers: Andrew John Napier, Secretary; Sir Andrew Thomas Cahn [1951] Director/Chairman; Jane Catherine Cotton [1959] HR Director; Sir Michael Dixon [1956] Chief Executive/Director; Catherine Thea Dugmore [1967] Director; Andrew James Green [1955] Director/Chairman; Abdelilah Kasem [1967] Director/Management Consultant [Dutch]; Dame Georgina Mary Mace [1953] Director/University Professor; Professor Eleanor Jane Milner-Gulland [1967] Director/Tasso Leventis Professor of Biodiversity; Steve John Morris [1974] Director/Consultant; Justin Rupert John Hainult Mundy [1960] Director; Professor Malcolm Colin Press [1958] Director/Pro-Vice-Chancellor, University; Christopher Mark Richardson [1956] Director/Accountant

Wy (Nutfield Priory) Limited
Incorporated: 30 July 1999 *Employees:* 101
Net Worth: £23,277,476 *Total Assets:* £24,383,960
Registered Office: The Old Library, The Drive, Sevenoaks, Kent, TN13 3AB
Activities: Hotels and similar accommodation
Parent: Hand Picked Hotels Limited
Officers: Kenneth Arkley [1954] Commercial Director; Stewart John Fairs [1966] Finance Director; Peter Smith Fullerton [1943] Director/Lawyer/Consultant

Wyatt Company Holdings Limited (The)
Incorporated: 16 June 1967
Net Worth: £154,474,000 *Total Assets:* £160,240,992
Registered Office: Watson House, London Road, Reigate, Surrey, RH2 9PQ
Activities: Activities of head offices
Parent: Watson Wyatt (UK) Acquisitions 1 Limited
Officers: Steven James Alcock [1979] Director

Wyboston Lakes Limited
Incorporated: 16 July 1973 *Employees:* 409
Net Worth: £35,141,404 *Total Assets:* £40,988,432
Registered Office: Wyboston Lakes Hotel, Great North Road, Wyboston, Beds, MK44 3AL
Activities: Development of building projects
Shareholders: Steve Richard Hutchinson; Jill Chapman
Officers: Julie Ireland, Secretary; David Howard Barford [1943] Director/Surveyor; Jill Chapman [1958] Director; Chelsey Rae Hutchinson [1986] Director; Steve Richard Hutchinson [1955] Director; Julie Ireland [1971] Director/Chartered Certified Accountant; Mark Charles Jones [1955] Director; Stephen Jones [1976] Managing Director; Craig Alfred Warner [1969] IT Director

Wycombe High School Academies Trust
Incorporated: 8 April 2011 *Employees:* 249
Net Worth: £30,976,376 *Total Assets:* £35,518,004
Registered Office: Marlow Road, High Wycombe, Bucks, HP11 1TB
Activities: General secondary education
Officers: Dr David John Palmer, Secretary; Sharon Nadine Cromie [1965] Director/Headteacher; Michael Dollin [1942] Director/Retired; Richard Ivor Lloyd Jones [1940] Director/Retired; Stephen Thomas Jordan [1953] Director; James Gerard O'Hagan [1954] Technical Director; Malcolm Douglas Peckham [1946] Director/Retired

John Wyeth & Brother Limited
Incorporated: 20 May 1914 *Employees:* 272
Net Worth: £338,726,016 *Total Assets:* £393,776,992
Registered Office: Pfizer, Ramsgate Road, Sandwich, Kent, CT13 9NJ
Activities: Manufacture of basic pharmaceutical products
Parent: Pfizer Limited
Officers: Jacqueline Ann Mount, Secretary; Sukhdave Singh Aujla [1975] Director/Site Leader; Ian Eric Franklin [1965] Director; Denise Jean Harnett [1964] Director; Jacqueline Ann Mount [1963] Director; Hendrikus Hermannus Nordkamp [1969] UK Managing Director, Pfizer [Dutch]; Edwin James Pearson [1974] Director/Solicitor; Colin Malcolm Seller [1963] Director

Wyevale Acquisitions Borrower Limited
Incorporated: 15 August 2007
Net Worth Deficit: £3,137,000 *Total Assets:* £134,244,992
Registered Office: Wyevale Garden Centres, Syon Park, London Road, Brentford, Middlesex, TW8 8JF
Activities: Buying and selling of own real estate
Parent: Wyevale Garden Centres Holdings Limited
Officers: Laura Harradine-Greene, Secretary; Anthony Generald Jones [1973] Director; Richard MacLachlan [1976] Director

Wyevale Garden Centres Acquisitions Limited
Incorporated: 21 May 2013
Net Worth: £3,139,000 *Total Assets:* £66,081,000
Registered Office: Wyevale Garden Centres, Syon Park, London Road, Brentford, Middlesex, TW8 8JF
Activities: Activities of other holding companies n.e.c.
Parent: Wyevale Garden Centres Limited
Officers: Laura Harradine-Greene, Secretary; Anthony Generald Jones [1973] Director; Richard MacLachlan [1976] Director

Wyevale Garden Centres Capital Limited
Incorporated: 9 February 2012 *Employees:* 6,290
Net Worth: £82,242,000 *Total Assets:* £422,868,000
Registered Office: Wyevale Garden Centres, Syon Park, London Road, Brentford, Middlesex, TW8 8JF
Activities: Activities of other holding companies n.e.c.
Major Shareholder: Guy Hands
Officers: Laura Harradine-Greene, Secretary; Charlotte Broadbent [1990] Director; David Browne [1979] Director [American]

Wyevale Garden Centres G & L Limited
Incorporated: 10 November 1997
Net Worth: £21,153,000 *Total Assets:* £66,015,000
Registered Office: Wyevale Garden Centres, Syon Park, London Road, Brentford, Middlesex, TW8 8JF
Activities: Other retail sale of new goods in specialised stores (not commercial art galleries and opticians)
Parent: EHGT Limited
Officers: Laura Harradine-Greene, Secretary; Anthony Generald Jones [1973] Director; Richard MacLachlan [1976] Director

Wyevale Garden Centres Holdings Limited
Incorporated: 18 December 1985
Net Worth: £299,280,000 *Total Assets:* £455,476,992
Registered Office: Wyevale Garden Centres, Syon Park, London Road, Brentford, Middlesex, TW8 8JF
Activities: Activities of head offices
Parent: Garden Centre Holdings Limited
Officers: Laura Harradine-Greene, Secretary; Anthony Generald Jones [1973] Director; Richard MacLachlan [1976] Director

Wyevale Garden Centres Limited
Incorporated: 15 June 1960
Net Worth: £11,174,000 *Total Assets:* £528,996,000
Registered Office: Wyevale Garden Centres, Syon Park, London Road, Brentford, Middlesex, TW8 8JF
Activities: Retail sale of flowers, plants, seeds, fertilizers, pet animals and pet food in specialised stores
Parent: Wyevale Garden Centres Holdings Limited
Officers: Laura Harradine-Greene, Secretary; Anthony Generald Jones [1973] Director; Richard MacLachlan [1976] Director

X P PLC
Incorporated: 20 September 1988 *Employees:* 96
Net Worth: £5,631,000 *Total Assets:* £25,207,000
Registered Office: 16 Horseshoe Park, Pangbourne, Berks, RG8 7JW
Activities: Manufacture of other electrical equipment
Parent: XP Power PLC
Officers: Jonathan Simon Rhodes, Secretary; Gary Robin Bocock [1963] Product Director; Stephen Mark Elliot [1971] Director/Salesman; Paul Martin Garner [1968] Key Accounts Director; Steven William Head [1970] Regional Sales Director; Anne MacDonald Honeyman [1969] Director/Accountant; Duncan John Penny [1963] Director/Chartered Accountant

Xafinity Consulting (Reading) Limited
Incorporated: 9 November 2012 *Employees:* 4
Net Worth Deficit: £4,569,000 *Total Assets:* £243,382,000
Registered Office: Phoenix House, 1 Station Hill, Reading, Berks, RG1 1NB
Activities: Activities of financial services holding companies
Parent: Xafinity (Reading) Limited
Officers: Michael Robert Arthur Ainslie [1961] Director/Chief Financial Officer; Jonathan Samuel Bernstein [1968] Director/Actuary; Benjamin Oliver Bramhall [1977] Director/Actuary; Paul Gareth Cuff [1976] Director/Actuary

Xafinity Consulting Limited
Incorporated: 15 January 1990 *Employees:* 367
Net Worth: £22,798,000 *Total Assets:* £40,452,000
Registered Office: Phoenix House, 1 Station Hill, Reading, Berks, RG1 1NB
Activities: Management consultancy activities other than financial management
Parent: Xafinity Consulting (Reading) Limited
Officers: Michael Robert Arthur Ainslie [1961] Director/Chief Financial Officer; Jonathan Samuel Bernstein [1968] Director/Actuary; Benjamin Oliver Bramhall [1977] Director/Actuary; Paul Gareth Cuff [1976] Director/Actuary

Xchanging Global Insurance Solutions Limited
Incorporated: 23 May 1952 *Employees:* 490
Net Worth Deficit: £83,077,000 *Total Assets:* £63,728,000
Registered Office: Royal Pavilion, Wellesley Road, Aldershot, Hants, GU11 1PZ
Activities: Information technology consultancy activities
Parent: Xchanging Global Insurance Systems Limited
Officers: Tina Anne Gough [1962] Director; Maruf Ahmad Majed [1955] Director [American]; Michael Charles Woodfine [1971] Director/Solicitor

Xchanging Holdco No.3 Limited
Incorporated: 11 March 2004
Net Worth: £55,398,000 *Total Assets:* £55,539,000
Registered Office: Royal Pavilion, Wellesley Road, Aldershot, Hants, GU11 1PZ
Activities: Activities of head offices
Parent: Xchanging Holdings Limited
Officers: Tina Anne Gough [1962] Director; Maruf Ahmad Majed [1955] Director [American]; Claus Ludwig Schunemann [1959] Director [German]; Michael Charles Woodfine [1971] Director/Solicitor

Xchanging Holdings Limited
Incorporated: 31 October 2006
Net Worth: £132,451,000 *Total Assets:* £475,608,000
Registered Office: Royal Pavilion, Wellesley Road, Aldershot, Hants, GU11 1PZ
Activities: Activities of head offices
Parent: Xchanging Limited
Officers: Tina Anne Gough [1962] Director; Maruf Ahmad Majed [1955] Director [American]; Michael Charles Woodfine [1971] Director/Solicitor

Xchanging Limited
Incorporated: 16 May 2006
Previous: Xchanging PLC
Net Worth: £271,040,992 *Total Assets:* £339,188,000
Registered Office: Royal Pavilion, Wellesley Road, Aldershot, Hants, GU11 1PZ
Activities: Other information technology service activities
Parent: CSC Computer Sciences International Operations Limited
Officers: Tina Anne Gough [1962] Director; Maruf Ahmad Majed [1955] Director [American]; Michael Charles Woodfine [1971] Director/Solicitor

Xchanging UK Limited
Incorporated: 17 August 1998 *Employees:* 65
Net Worth: £71,438,000 *Total Assets:* £585,593,024
Registered Office: Royal Pavilion, Wellesley Road, Aldershot, Hants, GU11 1PZ
Activities: Management consultancy activities other than financial management
Parent: Xchanging Holdings Limited
Officers: Tina Anne Gough [1962] Director; Maruf Ahmad Majed [1955] Director [American]; Michael Charles Woodfine [1971] Director/Solicitor

Xchanging US Funding Limited
Incorporated: 28 November 2011
Net Worth: £32,845,254 *Total Assets:* £33,180,498
Registered Office: Royal Pavilion, Wellesley Road, Aldershot, Hants, GU11 1PZ
Activities: Management consultancy activities other than financial management
Parent: Xchanging UK Limited
Officers: Tina Anne Gough [1962] Director; Maruf Ahmad Majed [1955] Director [American]; Michael Charles Woodfine [1971] Director/Solicitor

Xeretec Group Limited
Incorporated: 4 July 2016 *Employees:* 198
Net Worth: £1,349,910 *Total Assets:* £27,142,838
Registered Office: Ashridge House, Oaklands Park, Wokingham, Berks, RG41 2FD
Activities: Activities of head offices
Shareholders: Steven John Hawkins; Steven John Hawkins
Officers: Alyn Gruffydd Jenkins, Secretary; Steven John Hawkins [1974] Director; Alyn Gruffydd Jenkins [1954] Director

Xerox (UK) Limited
Incorporated: 16 August 1937 *Employees:* 1,594
Net Worth: £390,800,000 *Total Assets:* £667,699,968
Registered Office: Riverview, Oxford Road, Uxbridge, Middlesex, UB8 1HS
Activities: Wholesale of other office machinery and equipment
Parent: Xerox Capital (Europe) Limited
Officers: Richard Stuart Pitceathly, Secretary; David Brian Dyas [1963] Director/President, UK & Ireland, Eurasia, India, MEA; Julie Hesselgrove Ward [1963] Director/Senior Vice President; Rodney Noonoo [1962] Director/CFO, UK & Ireland, Eurasia, India, MEA [American]; Richard Stuart Pitceathly [1965] Director/Lawyer

Xerox Capital (Europe) Limited
Incorporated: 20 June 1995
Net Worth: £512,366,016 *Total Assets:* £807,499,008
Registered Office: Riverview, Oxford Road, Uxbridge, Middlesex, UB8 1HS
Activities: Financial intermediation not elsewhere classified
Parent: Xerox Limited
Officers: Richard Pitceathly, Secretary; Anthony William Arthurton [1972] Director/Accountant; Daniel Marc Benoit [1967] Director/International Operations CFO [French]; Stuart William Kirk [1960] Director EMEA Treasury Operations [Irish]

Xerox Finance Limited
Incorporated: 16 August 1937 *Employees:* 27
Net Worth: £123,226,000 *Total Assets:* £309,790,016
Registered Office: Riverview, Oxford Road, Uxbridge, Middlesex, UB8 1HS
Activities: Renting and leasing of office machinery and equipment (including computers)
Parent: Xerox (UK) Limited
Officers: Richard Pitceathly, Secretary; Martin Boyle [1976] Director/General Manager; Rodney Noonoo [1962] Director/CFO, UK & Ireland, Eurasia, India, MEA [American]

Xerox Limited
Incorporated: 19 December 1956
Net Worth: £2,796,000,000 *Total Assets:* £3,376,000,000
Registered Office: Riverview, Oxford Road, Uxbridge, Middlesex, UB8 1HS
Activities: Wholesale of other office machinery and equipment
Parent: Xerox Overseas Holdings Limited
Officers: Richard Pitceathly, Secretary; Daniel Marc Benoit [1967] Director/International Operations CFO [French]; Lisa Marie Oliver [1966] HR Director; Richard Stuart Pitceathly [1965] Director/Lawyer; Herve Tessler [1963] Director/President, International Operations [French]

Xerox Overseas Holdings Limited
Incorporated: 7 November 1996
Net Worth: £4,630,000,128 *Total Assets:* £7,706,999,808
Registered Office: Riverview, Oxford Road, Uxbridge, Middlesex, UB8 1HS
Activities: Activities of head offices
Parent: Xerox UK Holdings Limited
Officers: Richard Pitceathly, Secretary; Anthony William Arthurton [1972] Director/Accountant; Daniel Marc Benoit [1967] Director/International Operations CFO [French]; Lisa Marie Oliver [1966] HR Director

Xerox UK Holdings Limited
Incorporated: 14 April 1998
Net Worth: £4,295,000,064 *Total Assets:* £4,295,000,064
Registered Office: Riverview, Oxford Road, Uxbridge, Middlesex, UB8 1HS
Activities: Activities of other holding companies n.e.c.
Parent: Xerox Investments Europe BV
Officers: Richard Pitceathly, Secretary; Anthony William Arthurton [1972] Director/Accountant; Daniel Marc Benoit [1967] Director/International Operations CFO [French]; Lisa Marie Oliver [1966] HR Director

XP Power PLC
Incorporated: 6 January 2000
Net Worth: £27,357,000 *Total Assets:* £27,426,000
Registered Office: 16 Horseshoe Park, Pangbourne, Reading, Berks, RG8 7JW
Activities: Manufacture of other electrical equipment
Parent: XP Power Limited
Officers: Jonathan Simon Rhodes, Secretary; Anne MacDonald Honeyman [1969] Director/Chartered Accountant; Michael R Laver [1962] Director [American]; Duncan John Penny [1963] Director/Chartered Accountant

Xpanse Limited
Incorporated: 20 February 2001
Net Worth: £40,214,000 *Total Assets:* £53,329,000
Registered Office: Royal Pavilion, Wellesley Road, Aldershot, Hants, GU11 1PZ
Activities: Activities of head offices
Parent: Xchanging Holdings Limited
Officers: Tina Anne Gough [1962] Director; Maruf Ahmad Majed [1955] Director [American]; Michael Charles Woodfine [1971] Director/Solicitor

XPS Pensions Group PLC
Incorporated: 2 November 2012
Previous: Xafinity PLC
Net Worth: £192,679,008 *Total Assets:* £198,036,992
Registered Office: Phoenix House, 1 Station Hill, Reading, Berks, RG1 1NB
Activities: Activities of other holding companies n.e.c.
Parent: CBPE Capital LLP
Officers: Zoe Adlam, Secretary; Michael Robert Arthur Ainslie [1961] Director/Chief Financial Officer; Alan Robert Bannatyne [1970] Director; John Paul Batting [1958] Director; Jonathan Samuel Bernstein [1968] Director/Actuary; Benjamin Oliver Bramhall [1977] Director/Actuary; Tom Cross Brown [1947] Director; Paul Gareth Cuff [1976] Director/Actuary; Jonathan Dominic Punter [1957] Director; Margaret Locke Snowdon [1955] Director

Xtrac Limited
Incorporated: 15 June 1984 *Employees:* 294
Net Worth: £49,677,000 *Total Assets:* £55,453,000
Registered Office: Gables Way, Kennet Park, Thatcham, Berks, RG19 4ZA
Activities: Manufacture of bearings, gears, gearing and driving elements
Parent: Xtrac Group Limited
Officers: Peter Digby, Secretary; Peter Digby [1958] Managing Director; Martin Anthony Halley [1965] Director/Chartered Engineer; Clifford Arthur Hawkins [1962] Design Director; Stephen John Roger Lane [1966] Director/Chartered Accountant; Adrian Paul Moore [1966] Director/Engineer

Xtrac Transmissions (Holdings) Limited
Incorporated: 12 December 2014 *Employees:* 306
Net Worth: £58,859,000 *Total Assets:* £75,838,000
Registered Office: Gables Way, Thatcham, Berks, RG19 4ZA
Activities: Manufacture of other parts and accessories for motor vehicles
Parent: Viola Bidco Limited
Officers: Stephen John Roger Lane, Secretary; Peter Digby [1958] Managing Director; Clifford Arthur Hawkins [1962] Design Director; Stephen John Roger Lane [1966] Director/Chartered Accountant; Adrian Paul Moore [1966] Director/Engineer

Xtralis (UK) Limited
Incorporated: 19 May 1989 *Employees:* 33
Net Worth: £6,474,000 *Total Assets:* £56,254,000
Registered Office: Honeywell House, Skimped Hill Lane, Bracknell, Berks, RG12 1EB
Activities: Wholesale of other machinery and equipment
Parent: Xtralis Holdings UK Limited
Officers: Piyush Jayantilal Kanji Jutha [1972] Director; Martin Norris [1969] Director; Ashish Kumar Saraf [1979] Director [Indian]

Xylem Water Holdings Limited
Incorporated: 3 May 2011
Net Worth Deficit: £68,075,000 *Total Assets:* £59,614,000
Registered Office: 106 Hawley Lane, Farnborough, Hants, GU14 8JE
Activities: Activities of head offices
Shareholders: Xylem Industries S.A.R.L.; Xylem Inc.
Officers: Nicola Anne Tancred, Secretary; Claire Jane Rhodes [1972] Director/Accountant; Barbara Ann West [1955] Director/UK Benefits Manager

Xylem Water Solutions UK Holdings Limited
Incorporated: 19 June 2002
Net Worth: £64,624,000 *Total Assets:* £78,650,000
Registered Office: 106 Hawley Lane, Farnborough, Hants, GU14 8JE
Activities: Activities of head offices
Parent: Xylem Water Holdings Ltd
Officers: Nicola Anne Tancred, Secretary; Claire Jane Rhodes [1972] Director/Accountant; Barbara Ann West [1955] Director/UK Benefits Manager

Yacht Havens Group Limited
Incorporated: 28 July 1988 *Employees:* 190
Net Worth: £45,881,712 *Total Assets:* £68,203,976
Registered Office: King's Saltern Road, Lymington, Hants, SO41 3QD
Activities: Activities of head offices
Officers: Dirk Hems Kalis, Secretary; Nigel Harry Case [1943] Director; Thomas Harry Case [1966] Director/Fish Merchant; Carolyn Ross Elder [1961] Director; Helen Jean Grew [1965] Finance Director; Dirk Hems Kalis [1943] Director; Dylan Illingworth Richard Kalis [1972] Director/Marina Operator

Yacht Havens Limited
Incorporated: 4 May 1962 *Employees:* 17
Net Worth: £2,908,354 *Total Assets:* £47,021,132
Registered Office: Kings Saltern Road, Lymington, Hants, SO41 3QD
Activities: Activities of head offices
Parent: Yacht Havens Group Limited
Officers: Dirk Hems Kalis, Secretary; Nigel Harry Case [1943] Director; Carolyn Ross Elder [1961] Marina Manager/Director; Benjamin Matthew Jones Fox [1979] Group IT Director; Helen Jean Grew [1965] Finance Director; Dirk Hems Kalis [1943] Director; Dylan Illingworth Richard Kalis [1972] Director/Marina Operator; Rupert David Neville Wagstaff [1973] Director

Yanfeng UK Automotive Interior Systems Co., Ltd
Incorporated: 16 July 2014 *Employees:* 6
Net Worth: £683,015,424 *Total Assets:* £718,915,136
Registered Office: Highfield Court, Tollgate, Chandler's Ford, Eastleigh, Hants, SO53 3TY
Activities: Activities of head offices
Parent: Yanfeng Global Automotive Interior Systems Co., Ltd.
Officers: Michael Eric Kleinheksel [1965] Director [American]; Steve Meszaros [1963] Director [Canadian]; Yiru Su [1969] Director [Chinese]; Xinhua Yuan [1965] Director [Chinese]

Yattendon Estates Limited
Incorporated: 9 June 1955 *Employees:* 34
Net Worth: £70,677,000 *Total Assets:* £101,130,000
Registered Office: The Estate Office, Yattendon, Berks, RG18 0UY
Activities: Mixed farming
Parent: Yattendon Group PLC
Officers: Catherine Elinor Fleming, Secretary; Anthony Oscar Colburn [1954] Director/Farmer; The Honourable Edward Richard Iliffe [1968] Director/Chartered Surveyor; John David Iliffe [1947] Director/Engineer; The Right Honourable Robert Peter Richard Iliffe [1944] Director/Publisher; Stephen Paul Sadler [1966] Finance Director; David James Slack [1968] Director/Chartered Surveyor

Yattendon Group PLC
Incorporated: 18 May 1934 *Employees:* 371
Net Worth: £272,188,992 *Total Assets:* £457,383,008
Registered Office: Barn Close, Yattendon, Newbury, Berks, RG18 0UX
Activities: Activities of other holding companies n.e.c.
Parent: R P R Iliffe, E R Iliffe, F Austin
Officers: Catherine Elinor Fleming, Secretary; Francois Alexandre Austin [1966] Director; The Honourable Edward Richard Iliffe [1968] Director/Chartered Surveyor; The Right Honourable Robert Peter Richard Iliffe [1944] Director/Publisher; Stephen Paul Sadler [1966] Finance Director; Michael Generald Spencer [1947] Director/Barrister

Yavneh College Academy Trust
Incorporated: 23 May 2011 *Employees:* 131
Previous: Yavneh College
Net Worth: £30,547,060 *Total Assets:* £31,446,916
Registered Office: Hillside Avenue, Borehamwood, Herts, WD6 1HL
Activities: General secondary education
Officers: Hayley Ann Fraser, Secretary; Daniel Iain Album [1963] Director/Fund Manager; Mark Elliot Frazer [1985] Director/PR; Richard Michael Gilbert [1969] Director/Solicitor; Rolanda Gail Hyams [1955] Director/Chartered Accountant; Roz Levin [1950] Director/Retired; Spencer Lewis [1967] Director/Headteacher; Doreen Morris [1946] Director/Academic Standards Manager; Susan Neale [1952] Director/Retired; Susan Annette Nyman [1956] Director/Chartered Accountant; Daniel Paul Summerfield [1969] Director/Investment Manager

Yazaki Europe Limited
Incorporated: 14 April 1980 *Employees:* 2,162
Net Worth: £358,226,112 *Total Assets:* £1,034,148,224
Registered Office: 1 Zodiac, Boundary Way, Hemel Hempstead, Herts, HP2 7SJ
Activities: Wholesale trade of motor vehicle parts and accessories
Officers: Bo Inge Andersson [1955] Director/President [Swedish/American]; Hiroshi Ichikawa [1956] Director/Executive of Business Firm [Japanese]; Masahiro Kanda [1955] Director/Managing Executive Officer [Japanese]; Junichi Kitami [1959] Director [Japanese]; Naoki Sugie [1958] Director/Executive of Business Firm [Japanese]; Munenori Yamada [1958] Director/Managing Executive Officer [Japanese]; Ryosuke Yazaki [1981] Director/Executive Officer [Japanese]

Yehudi Menuhin School Limited (The)
Incorporated: 3 September 1964 *Employees:* 39
Net Worth: £22,650,024 *Total Assets:* £23,135,464
Registered Office: Millfield, Cobham Road, Stoke D'Abernon, Cobham, Surrey, KT11 3QQ
Activities: General secondary education
Officers: Shelley Thurman Twitchin, Secretary; Dominic Benthall [1976] Director/Barrister; Lord Norman Roy Blackwell [1952] Director/Bank Chairman; Jonathan Deakin [1983] Director/Consultant; John Ellis Everett [1947] Director/Consultant; Andrew Malcolm Hunter Johnston [1953] Director; Anna Jane Rebecca Joseph [1964] Managing Director; Oscar Max Lewisohn [1938] Director [Danish]; Stuart Walter Mitchell [1964] Director/Fund Manager; Richard Francis Maxwell Morris [1944] Director/Chief Executive; John Clovis Pagella [1943] Director/Chartered Surveyor; Alice Mary Phillips [1960] Director/Headteacher; Anthea Vanessa Richards [1947] Director; Geoffrey William Richards [1948] Director/Lawyer; Veronica Judith Colleton Wadley [1952] Director; Jonathan Peter Willcocks [1953] Director/Musician

Yell Limited
Incorporated: 25 April 2001 *Employees:* 276
Previous: Hibu (UK) Limited
Net Worth Deficit: £95,360,000 *Total Assets:* £290,008,992
Registered Office: 3 Forbury Place, Forbury Road, Reading, Berks, RG1 3YL
Activities: Publishing of directories and mailing lists
Parent: YH Limited
Officers: Christian Henry Wells, Secretary; Richard John Hanscott [1961] Director; David William Henry Sharman [1963] Director; Oliver Edward James Wilson [1972] Finance Director

YH Limited
Incorporated: 4 April 2001
Net Worth: £215,184,000 *Total Assets:* £672,841,024
Registered Office: 3 Forbury Place, Forbury Road, Reading, Berks, RG1 3YL
Activities: Advertising agencies
Parent: Owl Finance Limited
Officers: Christian Henry Wells, Secretary; Richard John Hanscott [1961] Director; David William Henry Sharman [1963] Director; Oliver Edward James Wilson [1972] Finance Director

Yoplait UK Limited
Incorporated: 2 April 1991 *Employees:* 17
Net Worth: £59,594,000 *Total Assets:* £83,861,000
Registered Office: Floor 5, Harman House, 1 George Street, Uxbridge, Middlesex, UB8 1QQ
Activities: Non-specialised wholesale of food, beverages and tobacco
Parent: General Mills, Inc.
Officers: Jana Marie-Rose Gaffaney [1980] Legal Director [American]; Anne-Laure Jacquemart [1969] Finance Director [French]; Benjamin John Pearman [1972] Managing Director

York Cee Holdings Limited
Incorporated: 14 June 1996
Net Worth: £38,984,000 *Total Assets:* £38,987,000
Registered Office: 9-10 The Briars, Waterberry Drive, Waterlooville, Hants, PO7 7YH
Activities: Activities of head offices
Parent: York International (Holdings) Ltd
Officers: Mark Ayre [1963] Director/Global Finance Project Lead; Peter Schieser [1967] Director [German]

York Engineered Systems Limited
Incorporated: 16 July 1945
Net Worth: £22,591,072 *Total Assets:* £50,356,000
Registered Office: 9-10 The Briars, Waterberry Drive, Waterlooville, Hants, PO7 7YH
Activities: Activities of head offices
Parent: Johnson Controls Investments (UK) Limited
Officers: Mark Ayre [1963] Finance Director; Peter Schieser [1967] Director/Deputy General Counsel [German]

York International (Holdings) Limited
Incorporated: 16 November 1994
Net Worth: £16,180,000 *Total Assets:* £24,669,000
Registered Office: 9-10 The Briars, Waterberry Drive, Waterlooville, Hants, PO7 7YH
Activities: Activities of head offices
Parent: Johnson Controls International PLC
Officers: Mark Ayre [1963] Finance Director; Peter Schieser [1967] Director [German]

York International Investments
Incorporated: 11 March 1994
Net Worth: £22,359,000 *Total Assets:* £22,362,000
Registered Office: 9-10 The Briars, Waterberry Drive, Waterlooville, Hants, PO7 7YH
Activities: Activities of head offices
Parent: York International (Holdings) Limited
Officers: Mark Ayre [1963] Director/Global Finance Project Lead; Peter Schieser [1967] Finance Director [German]

Yorkshire Transformations Limited
Incorporated: 18 May 2003
Net Worth Deficit: £7,361,000 *Total Assets:* £32,537,000
Registered Office: 8 White Oak Square, London Road, Swanley, Kent, BR8 7AG
Activities: Construction of commercial buildings
Parent: Yorkshire Transformations Holdings Limited
Officers: Neeti Mukundrai Anand [1984] Director; David Bolton [1968] Director; Stewart Chalmers Grant [1951] Director; Guy Christopher Millichamp [1964] Director; Angela Louise Roshier [1975] Director/Finance; Martin Timothy Smith [1967] Director/Banker; Christopher Thomas Solley [1970] Director/Investment Manager

H Young (Operations) Limited
Incorporated: 30 October 1961 *Employees:* 656
Net Worth: £65,471,000 *Total Assets:* £132,413,000
Registered Office: Buckingham House, West Street, Newbury, Berks, RG14 1BD
Activities: Wholesale of other intermediate products
Officers: Alan James McIvor, Secretary; Alan James McIvor [1963] Director/Accountant; Dr Ronald Samann [1951] Director [Canadian]

H Young Holdings Public Limited Company
Incorporated: 7 January 1924 *Employees:* 1,107
Net Worth: £86,121,000 *Total Assets:* £184,108,000
Registered Office: Buckingham House, West Street, Newbury, Berks, RG14 1BD
Activities: Wholesale of other intermediate products
Officers: Alan James McIvor, Secretary; Alan James McIvor [1963] Director/Accountant; Daniel Samann [1980] Director/Student [Canadian]; Dr Ronald Samann [1951] Director [Canadian]

Yourcash Europe Limited
Incorporated: 24 January 2013
Net Worth: £28,305,000 *Total Assets:* £28,639,000
Registered Office: Willow House, Woodland Business Park, Linford Wood, Milton Keynes, Bucks, MK14 6EU
Activities: Activities of financial services holding companies
Officers: Nikos Fountas [1963] Director/EVP & CEO EMEA [Greek]; Daniel James Entwistle Marland [1982] Director/Solicitor; Andrea Valacsay [1974] Finance Director [Hungarian]; Ricky Lee Weller [1957] Director [American]

Yourcash Limited
Incorporated: 5 January 2000 *Employees:* 98
Net Worth: £7,154,000 *Total Assets:* £56,644,000
Registered Office: Willow House, Breckland, Linford Wood, Milton Keynes, Bucks, MK14 6EU
Activities: Financial intermediation not elsewhere classified
Officers: Nikos Fountas [1963] Director/EVP & CEO EMEA [Greek]; Daniel James Entwistle Marland [1982] Director/Solicitor; Andrea Valacsay [1974] Finance Director [Hungarian]; Ricky Lee Weller [1957] Director [American]

Yourcash Solutions Limited
Incorporated: 24 January 2013
Net Worth Deficit: £13,959,000 *Total Assets:* £23,115,000
Registered Office: Willow House, Woodland Business Park, Linford Wood, Milton Keynes, Bucks, MK14 6EU
Activities: Activities of financial services holding companies
Officers: Daniel James Entwistle Marland, Secretary; Nikos Fountas [1963] Director/EVP & CEO EMEA [Greek]; Daniel James Entwistle Marland [1982] Director/Solicitor; Andrea Valacsay [1974] Finance Director [Hungarian]; Ricky Lee Weller [1957] Director [American]

Yourway Transport Limited
Incorporated: 16 January 2004 *Employees:* 16
Net Worth: £3,117,514 *Total Assets:* £23,926,840
Registered Office: 2 Pulborough Way, Hounslow, Middlesex, TW4 6DE
Activities: Unlicensed carriers
Major Shareholder: Gulamali Jaffer
Officers: Maliha Jaffer, Secretary; Gulamali Jaffer [1975] Director/President [American]

Yum! Franchise II LLP
Incorporated: 5 December 2003
Net Worth: £44,652,676 *Total Assets:* £45,353,404
Registered Office: Orion Gate, Guildford Road, Woking, Surrey, GU22 7NJ

Yum! Restaurant Holdings
Incorporated: 10 June 1997
Net Worth: £56,452,000 *Total Assets:* £56,545,000
Registered Office: Orion Gate, Guildford Road, Woking, Surrey, GU22 7NJ
Activities: Activities of other holding companies n.e.c.
Parent: YRH Holdco Limited
Officers: Timothy Michael Colborn, Secretary; Clare Marie Boynton [1978] Director/Accountant; Timothy Michael Colborn [1957] Director/International Tax Manager; Christopher Alexander Drew [1981] Director/Chief Finance Officer; Paula MacKenzie [1977] Business Development Director

Zanlia Limited
Incorporated: 29 December 1999 *Employees:* 1
Net Worth: £40,960,784 *Total Assets:* £43,096,324
Registered Office: East Sussex National, Uckfield, E Sussex, TN22 5ES
Activities: Other business support service activities n.e.c.
Parent: Horsted Estates Limited
Officers: Simon Derek Rebbetts, Secretary; Chester John Hunt [1969] Director; Deborah Susan Jenkins [1964] Director

Zebra Diamond Holdings Limited
Incorporated: 11 June 2012
Net Worth: £523,301,952 *Total Assets:* £989,404,224
Registered Office: Dukes Meadow, Millboard Road, Bourne End, Bucks, SL8 5XF
Activities: Business and domestic software development
Officers: Michael Kim [1973] Director [American]; Stephen Michael Piercey [1964] Finance Director; John Paul Ragland [1960] Director [American]; Michael Hugo Terzich [1961] Director [American]

Zebra Technologies Europe Limited
Incorporated: 15 December 1993 *Employees:* 495
Net Worth: £94,708,896 *Total Assets:* £935,570,560
Registered Office: Dukes Meadow, Millboard Road, Bourne End, Bucks, SL8 5XF
Activities: Business and domestic software development
Parent: Zebra Diamond Holdings Limited
Officers: Richard Edward Hudson [1967] Director; Colleen Maura O'Sullivan [1967] Director [American]; Stephen Michael Piercey [1964] Director/Accountant

Zellis UK Limited
Incorporated: 25 September 1981 *Employees:* 1,065
Previous: NorthgateArinso UK Limited
Net Worth: £24,510,000 *Total Assets:* £198,071,008
Registered Office: Peoplebuilding 2, Peoplebuilding Estate, Maylands Avenue, Hemel Hempstead Industrial Estate, Hemel Hempstead, Herts, HP2 4NW
Activities: Other software publishing
Parent: Colour Bidco Limited
Officers: Elizabeth Leppard, Secretary; John Richard Martin Petter [1970] Director; Nicholas Paul Wain [1972] Director

Zeltiq Limited
Incorporated: 9 August 2011 *Employees:* 44
Net Worth Deficit: £1,255,332 *Total Assets:* £34,529,580
Registered Office: 1st Floor, Marlow International, The Parkway, Marlow, Bucks, SL7 1YL
Activities: Manufacture of pharmaceutical preparations
Parent: Allergan PLC
Officers: Patricia Haran, Secretary; Judith Tomkins, Secretary; Glen Curran [1973] Director [Australian]; Nick Hudson [1975] Director; Duncan James Reeves [1978] Director

Zene Finance Limited
Incorporated: 27 March 2002
Net Worth: £3,586,449 *Total Assets:* £20,308,716
Registered Office: Oak Green House, 250-256 High Street, Dorking, Surrey, RH4 1QT
Activities: Financial intermediation not elsewhere classified
Parent: Grafton Group (UK) PLC
Officers: Brian O'Hara [1967] Director/Accountant [Irish]; Charles Anthony Rinn [1960] Director/Accountant [Irish]; Jonathon Paul Sowton [1962] Director

Zenimax Europe Limited
Incorporated: 3 August 2007 *Employees:* 106
Net Worth: £159,248,144 *Total Assets:* £215,146,592
Registered Office: 1st Floor, West Wing, Davidson House, Forbury Square, Reading, Berks, RG1 3EU
Activities: Other software publishing
Officers: John Griffin Lesher, Secretary; James Lawrence Leder [1961] Director [Canadian/American]; Cindy Lehmann Tallent [1957] Director [American]

Zennor CNS Limited
Incorporated: 2 August 2006
Previous: First Oil and Gas Limited
Net Worth: £93,254,496 *Total Assets:* £132,967,536
Registered Office: First Floor, Hays House, Milmead, Guildford, Surrey, GU2 4HJ
Activities: Extraction of crude petroleum
Parent: Zennor Petroleum Limited
Officers: David Robert Beaghan [1966] Director; William Graham Cooper [1957] Director; Roderick Ian Selwyn Crawford [1960] Director; James Martin Richard Henry [1958] Director; Martin James Rowe [1970] Director

Zennor Pathway Limited
Incorporated: 13 April 2007
Previous: MPX Pathway Limited
Net Worth Deficit: £2,875,000 *Total Assets:* £47,456,000
Registered Office: First Floor, Hays House, Millmead, Guildford, Surrey, GU2 4HJ
Activities: Extraction of crude petroleum
Parent: Zennor CNS Limited
Officers: David Robert Beaghan [1966] Director/Drilling Engineer; William Graham Cooper [1957] Commercial Director; Roderick Ian Selwyn Crawford [1960] Director/Geophysicist; James Martin Richard Henry [1958] Director/Accountant; Martin James Rowe [1970] Director/Engineer

Zennor Petroleum Limited
Incorporated: 18 December 2013 *Employees:* 16
Net Worth: £137,191,392 *Total Assets:* £193,829,936
Registered Office: First Floor, Hays House, Millmead, Guildford, Surrey, GU2 4HJ
Activities: Extraction of crude petroleum
Officers: Jason Aun Minn Cheng [1972] Director/Managing Partner [Australian]; Roderick Ian Selwyn Crawford [1960] Director/Geophysicist; James Martin Richard Henry [1958] Director/Accountant; Anthony Philip Jackson [1959] Director/Fund Manager; Dr Alan John Parsley [1943] Director/Geologist; Martin James Rowe [1970] Director/Engineer; Kumar Tushar [1978] Director/Investment Manager [Indian]

Zest Living Limited
Incorporated: 1 October 1982 *Employees:* 3
Net Worth: £3,765,521 *Total Assets:* £20,862,288
Registered Office: 4 Elstree Gate, Elstree Way, Borehamwood, Herts, WD6 1JD
Activities: Other letting and operating of own or leased real estate
Officers: Ronan Patrick Murphy, Secretary; Daniel Gerard Durkan [1964] Director [Irish]; Ronan Patrick Murphy [1969] Director/Chartered Accountant [Irish]

ZG Lighting (UK) Limited
Incorporated: 8 September 1993 *Employees:* 245
Previous: Zumtobel Lighting Limited
Net Worth: £5,388,000 *Total Assets:* £45,073,000
Registered Office: Chiltern Park, Chiltern Hill, Chalfont St Peter, Bucks, SL9 9FG
Activities: Other service activities n.e.c.
Parent: Zumtobel Group AG
Officers: Christopher Colin Whitehead, Secretary; Matthew James Boucher [1972] Managing Director; Claire Therese Thomson [1970] Director/Chartered Accountant

Zion Care Limited
Incorporated: 5 August 2005
Net Worth: £11,387,363 *Total Assets:* £22,973,620
Registered Office: 23 Marsham Way, Gerrards Cross, Bucks, SL9 8AB
Activities: Residential nursing care facilities
Major Shareholder: Timothy Kayode Ogunleye
Officers: Omobonuola Ibidunni Ogunleye, Secretary; Omobonuola Ibidunni Ogunleye [1964] Director/Certified Chartered Accountant; Timothy Kayode Ogunleye [1962] Director

Zionstone Limited
Incorporated: 16 November 1982 *Employees:* 10
Net Worth: £15,589,543 *Total Assets:* £42,309,000
Registered Office: Unit 7 Horizon Business Village, 1 Brooklands Road, Weybridge, Surrey, KT13 0TJ
Activities: Buying and selling of own real estate
Officers: Sandra Joanne Brownlie, Secretary; Lauren Atkins [1976] Director/Manager; Malcolm Paul Atkins [1952] Director

Zipcar International Finance Company Limited
Incorporated: 8 January 2016
Net Worth Deficit: £301,066 *Total Assets:* £35,139,432
Registered Office: Avis Budget House, Park Road, Bracknell, Berks, RG12 2EW
Activities: Activities of other holding companies n.e.c.
Parent: Zipcar, Inc.
Officers: Inderpal Lall, Secretary; Paul Leslie Ford [1970] Finance Director; Paul Edward Rollason [1979] Finance Director

Zodiac Europe Limited
Incorporated: 13 January 2003 *Employees:* 4
Net Worth: £55,062,000 *Total Assets:* £57,647,000
Registered Office: Avis Budget House, Park Road, Bracknell, Berks, RG12 2EW
Activities: Activities of head offices
Parent: Avis Europe Holdings Ltd
Officers: Inderpal Lall, Secretary; Paul Leslie Ford [1970] Director/Chartered Accountant; Paul Andrew Briant Mitchell [1963] Director; Paul Edward Rollason [1979] Director/Accountant

Zoom Gas Pipelines Limited
Incorporated: 11 April 2006 *Employees:* 74
Net Worth Deficit: £76,977,000 *Total Assets:* £376,759,008
Registered Office: First Floor, Bluebird House, Mole Business Park, Randalls Road, Leatherhead, Surrey, KT22 7BA
Activities: Activities of other holding companies n.e.c.
Parent: Zoom Infrastructure Limited
Officers: Thomas William Butler [1959] Director [Irish]; Anna Louise Dellis [1973] Director; Nicholas Horler [1959] Director/Chairman; Paul Miles [1971] Director/Chief Financial Officer; Kevin O'Connor [1976] Director/Chief Executive Officer; Sebastian Schwengber [1979] Director/Investment Professional [German]; Bernardo de SA Braamcamp Sobral Sottomayor [1973] Director [Portuguese]

Zoom Holding Limited
Incorporated: 11 April 2006 *Employees:* 74
Net Worth Deficit: £159,046,000 *Total Assets:* £375,684,992
Registered Office: First Floor, Bluebird House, Mole Business Park, Randalls Road, Leatherhead, Surrey, KT22 7BA
Activities: Activities of other holding companies n.e.c.
Parent: 3i MIA Holdings Limited
Officers: Thomas William Butler [1959] Director [Irish]; Anna Louise Dellis [1973] Director; Nicholas Horler [1959] Director/Chairman; Paul Miles [1971] Director/Chief Financial Officer; Kevin O'Connor [1976] Director/Chief Executive Officer; Sebastian Schwengber [1979] Director/Investment Professional [German]; Bernardo de SA Braamcamp Sobral Sottomayor [1973] Director [Portuguese]

Zoom Infrastructure Limited
Incorporated: 11 April 2006 *Employees:* 74
Net Worth Deficit: £175,252,000 *Total Assets:* £375,833,984
Registered Office: First Floor, Bluebird House, Mole Business Park, Leatherhead, Surrey, KT22 7BA
Activities: Activities of other holding companies n.e.c.
Parent: Zoom Holding Limited
Officers: Thomas William Butler [1959] Director [Irish]; Anna Louise Dellis [1973] Director; Nicholas Horler [1959] Director/Chairman; Paul Miles [1971] Director/Chief Financial Officer; Kevin O'Connor [1976] Director/Chief Executive Officer; Sebastian Schwengber [1979] Director/Investment Professional [German]; Bernardo de SA Braamcamp Sobral Sottomayor [1973] Director [Portuguese]

Zotefoams PLC
Incorporated: 14 May 1992 *Employees:* 360
Net Worth: £59,090,000 *Total Assets:* £100,264,000
Registered Office: 675 Mitcham Road, Croydon, Surrey, CR9 3AL
Activities: Manufacture of other plastic products
Officers: Alex Charles Small, Secretary; Angela Claire Bromfield [1962] Director; Jonathan Douglas Carling [1965] Director; Stephen Paul Good [1961] Director; Gary Christopher McGrath [1967] Director/Chartered Accountant; Douglas Grant Robertson [1953] Director; David Burns Stirling [1966] Director/Accountant

Zurich Holdings (UK) Limited
Incorporated: 18 October 1988
Net Worth: £5,291,000 *Total Assets:* £36,410,000
Registered Office: The Zurich Centre, 3000 Parkway, Whiteley, Fareham, Hants, PO15 7JZ
Activities: Activities of other holding companies n.e.c.
Parent: Zurich Insurance Group AG
Officers: Timothy James Grant [1964] Director; Helen Alison Pickford [1971] Director

Zurich Management Services Limited
Incorporated: 19 August 1992
Net Worth: £31,729,678 *Total Assets:* £77,650,216
Registered Office: The Zurich Centre, 3000 Parkway, Whiteley, Fareham, Hants, PO15 7JZ
Activities: Other business support service activities n.e.c.
Parent: Zurich Holdings (UK) Limited
Officers: Vinicio Cellerini [1964] Director [Swiss]; Timothy James Grant [1964] Director; John Patrick Hartigan [1965] Director; Kumudeshan Surendrakumar [1972] Director

Zurich UK General Services Limited
Incorporated: 16 September 1999 *Employees:* 3,462
Net Worth Deficit: £601,547,072 *Total Assets:* £584,336,704
Registered Office: The Zurich Centre, 3000 Parkway, Whiteley, Fareham, Hants, PO15 7JZ
Activities: Other business support service activities n.e.c.
Parent: Zurich Holdings (UK) Limited
Officers: Stephen Michael Collinson [1972] Director; John Herbert Keppel [1970] Director [New Zealander]; Helen Alison Pickford [1971] Director

Standard Industrial Classification

01110 Growing of cereals (except rice), leguminous crops and oil seeds
Barfoot Farms Limited
Blackmoor Estate Limited
Chilton Home Farms Ltd
Exagris Limited
Langmead Farms Limited
South Darenth Farms and Cold Store Co
St. Nicholas Court Farms Ltd

01130 Growing of vegetables and melons, roots and tubers
Barfoot Farms Limited
Glinwell PLC
Newmafruit Farms Limited
Tangmere Airfield Nurseries Ltd

01160 Growing of fibre crops
Cargill Cotton Limited

01190 Growing of other non-perennial crops
Hall Hunter Partnership (Farming)

01240 Growing of pome fruits and stone fruits
Blackmoor Estate Limited
Newmafruit Farms Limited
South Downs Real Estate Ltd

01250 Growing of other tree and bush fruits and nuts
Blackmoor Estate Limited

01410 Raising of dairy cattle
Chilton Home Farms Ltd

01420 Raising of other cattle and buffaloes
Chilton Home Farms Ltd

01430 Raising of horses and other equines
Fishdance Limited

01460 Raising of swine and pigs
PIG Improvement Company UK Ltd

01470 Raising of poultry
Sun Valley Foods Limited

01500 Mixed farming
Chilton Home Farms Ltd
Davison & Co. (Barford) Ltd
Goodwood Estate Co Ltd
J.& H.Robinson (Iford Farms) Ltd
Yattendon Estates Limited

01610 Support activities for crop production
Bartholomews Agri Food Limited

01629 Support activities for animal production (other than farm animal boarding)
EWOS Limited
Genus PLC

01630 Post-harvest crop activities
Blackmoor Estate Limited
Wealmoor Limited

02100 Silviculture and other forestry activities
Summerleaze Limited
Tilhill Forestry Limited
Yattendon Estates Limited

02200 Logging
Tilhill Forestry Limited

02400 Support services to forestry
Euroforest Limited
Tilhill Forestry Limited

03110 Marine fishing
Norebo Europe Limited

06100 Extraction of crude petroleum [44]
Amoco (Fiddich) Limited
Aria Petroleum (UK) Ltd.
BP Amoco Exploration (Faroes) Ltd
BP Exploration (Algeria) Ltd
BP Exploration (Alpha) Limited
BP Exploration (Angola) Ltd
BP Exploration (Azerbaijan) Ltd
BP Exploration (Caspian Sea) Ltd
BP Exploration (Delta) Limited
BP Exploration (Epsilon) Ltd
BP Exploration (Shah Deniz) Ltd
BP Exploration Beta Limited
BP Exploration Indonesia Ltd
BP Exploration Libya Limited
BP Exploration North Africa Ltd
BP Exploration Operating Co Ltd
CNOOC Ettrick U.K. Limited
CNOOC Petroleum Europe Limited
Egdon Resources PLC
Egdon Resources U.K. Limited
Esso Exploration and Production UK
Esso Petroleum Co Ltd
Esso UK Limited
ExxonMobil International Ltd
Hurricane (Whirlwind) Limited
Hurricane Energy PLC
Hurricane GLA Limited
Hurricane Holdings Limited
Impact Africa Limited
Impact Oil & Gas Limited
Jacobs Engineering UK Limited
Limay Drilling Rigs Limited
Noble Energy (Oilex) Limited
Sound Energy PLC
Spirit Energy North Sea Ltd
Spirit Energy Production UK Ltd
Spirit Energy Resources Ltd
Spirit Resources (Armada) Ltd
State Oil Limited
Tailwind Mistral Ltd
Verus Petroleum (UKCS) Limited
Zennor CNS Limited
Zennor Pathway Limited
Zennor Petroleum Limited

06200 Extraction of natural gas [13]
Egdon Resources PLC
Egdon Resources U.K. Limited
Hurricane (Whirlwind) Limited
Hurricane Energy PLC
Hurricane GLA Limited
Hurricane Holdings Limited
INEOS Upstream Limited
Impact Oil & Gas Limited
Noble Energy (Oilex) Limited
Sound Energy PLC
Tailwind Mistral Ltd
Zennor Pathway Limited
Zennor Petroleum Limited

08110 Quarrying of ornamental and building stone, limestone, gypsum, chalk and slate
Hanson Quarry Products Europe Ltd

08120 Operation of gravel and sand pits; mining of clays and kaolin
Raymond Brown Minerals & Recycling Ltd
J Clubb Limited
W.T. Lamb Holdings Limited
Henry Streeter (Sand & Ballast) Ltd
Summerleaze Limited

08990 Other mining and quarrying n.e.c.
Hanson Aggregates Marine Ltd
Hanson Marine Limited
Hanson Quarry Products Europe Ltd
Midland Quarry Products Ltd
Rambler Metals and Mining PLC
Spirit Europe Limited

09100 Support activities for petroleum and natural gas mining [30]
BP (Abu Dhabi) Limited
BP Exploration China Limited
BP Gas Marketing Limited
BP Senegal Investments Limited
Bowland Resources (No.2) Ltd
Bowland Resources Limited
Centrica LNG Co Ltd
Centrica LNG UK Limited
Deep Sea Atlantic (UK) Ltd
Deep Sea Stavanger (UK) Ltd
Dolphin Drilling Operations Ltd
Egdon Resources PLC
Egdon Resources U.K. Limited
Expro Eurasia Limited
Expro North Sea Limited
Galileo Global Technologies Ltd
Galileo Holdco 1 Limited
Galileo Holdco 2 Limited
Impact Oil & Gas Limited
Jacobs Engineering UK Limited
Offshore Containers Holdings Ltd
PGS Exploration (UK) Limited
Petroleum Geo-Services (UK) Ltd
Smith International (North Sea) Ltd
Sondex Wireline Limited
Spirit Energy Southern North Sea Ltd
Subsea 7 Limited
Subsea 7 Offshore Resources (UK) Ltd
TGS Geophysical Company (UK) Ltd
Westerngeco Limited

10130 Production of meat and poultry meat products

Atlantic Foods Limited
Kerry Foods Limited
Oakfield (Foods) Limited
Sun Valley Foods Limited

10390 Other processing and preserving of fruit and vegetables

Archer Daniels Midland Erith Ltd
Ardo UK Limited
Del Monte Europe Limited
Natures Way Foods Limited
Noon Products Limited
Sensient Flavors Limited
Sensient Holdings UK

10410 Manufacture of oils and fats

Archer Daniels Midland Erith Ltd
Pura Foods Limited

10420 Manufacture of margarine and similar edible fats

Dairy Crest Group PLC
Dairy Crest Limited
Pura Foods Limited

10511 Liquid milk and cream production

Dairy Crest France Holdings 2 Ltd
Dairy Crest Group PLC
Dairy Crest Limited
L.E. Pritchitt & Co Ltd

10512 Butter and cheese production

Dairy Crest Limited
Nestle UK Ltd.

10519 Manufacture of other milk products

Dairy Crest Limited

10520 Manufacture of ice cream

L.E. Pritchitt & Co Ltd
Unilever UK Limited

10611 Grain milling

ADM Milling Limited
Rank Hovis Milling Limited
S & B Herba Foods Limited
Veetee Rice Limited

10612 Manufacture of breakfast cereals and cereals-based food

Honey Monster Foods Limited

10710 Manufacture of bread; manufacture of fresh pastry goods and cakes

Bonne Bouche Catering Limited
Brioche Pasquier U.K. Limited
Gruma Europe Limited
Hovis Limited
Lantmannen UK Holding Limited
Lantmannen Unibake UK Limited
Mission Foods UK Limited

10720 Manufacture of rusks and biscuits; manufacture of preserved pastry goods and cakes

Brioche Pasquier U.K. Limited
United Biscuits (UK) Limited

10821 Manufacture of cocoa and chocolate confectionery

Ferrero UK Limited
Mars Wrigley Confectionery UK Ltd
Mondelez UK Holdings & Services Ltd
Nestle UK Ltd.
Thorntons Limited

10832 Production of coffee and coffee substitutes

Jacobs Douwe Egberts R & D GB Ltd
Lavazza Professional UK Ltd

10840 Manufacture of condiments and seasonings

RB Luxembourg Holdings (TFFC) Ltd
Symrise Holding Limited
Symrise Limited

10850 Manufacture of prepared meals and dishes

Oscar Mayer Limited
Veetee Foods Limited

10890 Manufacture of other food products n.e.c. [16]

Adelie Foods Limited
Allos Holdings Limited
Aunt Bessie's Limited
Benecol Limited
Birds Eye Limited
Cook Trading Limited
Creative Foods Europe Limited
Ella's Kitchen (Brands) Ltd
Gruma Europe Limited
Jain International Foods Ltd
KP Snacks Limited
Mars Food UK Limited
Nestle UK Ltd.
Nomad Foods Europe Limited
Propane Co Ltd
RB Luxembourg Holdings (TFFC) Ltd

10910 Manufacture of prepared feeds for farm animals

Factory Services UK Limited

10920 Manufacture of prepared pet foods

Mars Petcare UK
Nestle Purina Petcare (U.K.) Ltd

11010 Distilling, rectifying and blending of spirits

Beam Suntory UK Limited
John Dewar and Sons Limited

11020 Manufacture of wine from grape

Accolade Wines Limited
Cellarmaster Wines Holdings (UK) Ltd
FBL Holdings Limited
TWE Finance (UK) Limited
Treasury Wine Estates EMEA Ltd
Treasury Wine Estates UK Brands Ltd

11050 Manufacture of beer

Harvey & Son (Lewes) Limited
Meantime Brewing Co Ltd
Shepherd Neame Limited
Charles Wells Brewery Limited
Charles Wells,Limited

11070 Manufacture of soft drinks; production of mineral waters and other bottled waters [16]

Britannia Soft Drinks Limited
Britvic EMEA Limited
Britvic International Investments
Britvic Overseas Limited
Britvic PLC
Britvic Soft Drinks Limited
Coca-Cola European Partners GB Ltd
Coca-Cola European Partners PLC
Eden Springs UK Limited
Lucozade Ribena Suntory Ltd
Monster Energy Europe Limited
Nestle Waters UK Limited
Robinsons (Finance) No.2 Ltd
Robinsons Soft Drinks Limited
Rubicon Drinks Limited
SmithKline Beecham Limited

12000 Manufacture of tobacco products

Gallaher Limited
Karelia Tobacco Company (UK) Ltd
Standard Commercial Tobacco Company (UK)

14190 Manufacture of other wearing apparel and accessories n.e.c.

Viva Eyewear UK Limited

14310 Manufacture of knitted and crocheted hosiery

Covidien UK Limited

15120 Manufacture of luggage, handbags and the like, saddlery and harness

Arnold Wills and Co Ltd

16100 Sawmilling and planing of wood

David Cover and Son Limited

16210 Manufacture of veneer sheets and wood-based panels

Egger (UK) Limited

16290 Manufacture of other products of wood; manufacture of articles of cork, straw and plaiting materials

Royal British Legion Industries Ltd.

17120 Manufacture of paper and paperboard

Whatman International Limited

17219 Manufacture of other paper and paperboard containers

Huhtamaki (UK) Limited

17220 Manufacture of household and sanitary goods and of toilet requisites

Kimberly - Clark Limited
Kimberly-Clark Europe Limited
Kimberly-Clark Intercontinental Holding
Kimberly-Clark International Holding
Reckitt Benckiser (UK) Limited
Reckitt Benckiser Healthcare (UK)
Reckitt Benckiser Healthcare International

17230 Manufacture of paper stationery

Acco UK Limited

17290 Manufacture of other articles of paper and paperboard n.e.c.

Avery Dennison U.K. Limited
IG Design Group UK Limited
Kimberly - Clark Limited
Swan Mill Paper Co Ltd

18129 Printing n.e.c.

De La Rue International Limited.
De La Rue PLC
East Sussex Press Limited
Pureprint Group Limited
Topps Europe Limited

18201 Reproduction of sound recording

Mood Media Limited

19201 Mineral oil refining

BP Oil UK Limited
BP Turkey Refining Limited
ExxonMobil Marine Limited
INEOS Sales (UK) Limited
Lubricants UK Limited

19209 Other treatment of petroleum products (excluding petrochemicals manufacture)

Moove Lubricants Limited

20110 Manufacture of industrial gases

Air Products (BR) Limited
Air Products PLC
BOC Limited

20120 Manufacture of dyes and pigments

Lanxess Limited
Novartis Grimsby Limited

20130 Manufacture of other inorganic basic chemicals

BP Aromatics Limited
BP Chemicals Limited
Lanxess Limited
MacDermid Performance Solutions UK
Novartis Grimsby Limited
Rhodia Limited
UOP Limited

20140 Manufacture of other organic basic chemicals

Evonik Chemicals Limited
ExxonMobil Chemical Limited
INEOS Chemicals Grangemouth Ltd
INEOS Manufacturing (Hull) Ltd
INEOS Oxide Limited
Mallinckrodt Chemical Limited

20150 Manufacture of fertilizers and nitrogen compounds

Andigestion Limited
Omex Agricultural Holdings Ltd.

20160 Manufacture of plastics in primary forms

Advanced Elastomer Systems Ltd
Campact Limited
INEOS Chemicals Grangemouth Ltd
Novartis Grimsby Limited

20301 Manufacture of paints, varnishes and similar coatings, mastics and sealants

3M United Kingdom PLC
Akzo Nobel Packaging Coatings Ltd
Akzo Nobel Powder Coatings Ltd
Imperial Chemical Industries Ltd
International Paint Limited

20411 Manufacture of soap and detergents

Evonik Goldschmidt UK Limited
Procter & Gamble Product Supply (U.K.)
Unilever UK Limited

20412 Manufacture of cleaning and polishing preparations

SC Johnson Ltd

20420 Manufacture of perfumes and toilet preparations

Coty Manufacturing UK Limited
Liz Earle Beauty Co. Limited
Firmenich UK Limited
Gillette U.K. Limited

20510 Manufacture of explosives

Chemring Countermeasures Ltd

20520 Manufacture of glues

Beardow and Adams (Adhesives) Ltd

20590 Manufacture of other chemical products n.e.c. [16]

Alpha Assembly Solutions UK Ltd
Apatech Limited
Celsis Group Limited
Celsis International Limited
GCP Applied Technologies (UK) Ltd
Haltermann Carless UK Limited
Henkel Limited
Humiseal Europe Limited
INEOS Oxide Limited
ITW Limited
Moove Lubricants Limited
Nastor Investments Limited
Siemens Healthcare Diagnostics Ltd
Siemens Healthcare Diagnostics Products
Solvay Solutions UK Limited
WD-40 Co Ltd

21100 Manufacture of basic pharmaceutical products [36]

Aesica BC Limited
Aesica M1 Limited
Aesica M2 Limited
Aesica Pharmaceuticals Limited
Aesica Queenborough Limited
Bespak Europe Limited
Boehringer Ingelheim Animal Health UK
Boehringer Ingelheim Limited
Bristol-Myers Squibb Pharmaceuticals
Chemidex Pharma Limited
Church & Dwight UK Limited
Colorcon Limited
Crescent Pharma Limited
D.D.D. Limited
Eco Animal Health Ltd.
Ennogen Healthcare Ltd
Fresenius Kabi Oncology PLC
GE Healthcare Limited
GE Healthcare UK Limited
Hospira UK Limited
Indivior PLC
Knoll UK Investments Unlimited
LRC Products Limited
Eli Lilly Group Limited
Eli Lilly and Co Ltd
May & Baker Limited
Merial Limited
Novartis Grimsby Limited
Novartis Pharmaceuticals UK Ltd
Piramal Critical Care Limited
Sandoz Limited
Seqirus Vaccines Limited
Smith Kline & French Laboratories
SmithKline Beecham Limited
UCB Pharma Limited
John Wyeth & Brother Limited

21200 Manufacture of pharmaceutical preparations [15]

Allergy Therapeutics (UK) Ltd
Allergy Therapeutics PLC
Chemidex Pharma Limited
Crescent Pharma Limited
Fisons Limited
Fresenius Kabi Oncology PLC
Glaxo Operations UK Limited
GlaxoSmithKline Consumer Healthcare (UK) Trading
Hospira UK Limited
Intervet UK Production Limited
Janssen-Cilag Limited
May & Baker Limited
Merial Limited
Seqirus Vaccines Limited
Zeltiq Limited

22190 Manufacture of other rubber products

James Walker & Co. Limited

22220 Manufacture of plastic packing goods

Essentra Packaging & Security Ltd
Huhtamaki (UK) Limited
Logoplaste UK Limited
Nampak Plastics Europe Limited
Siva Holdings Limited
Siva Plastics Limited

22230 Manufacture of builders ware of plastic

Cordek Limited

22290 Manufacture of other plastic products [15]

DHM Plastics Limited
Essentra Components Limited
Essentra Packaging & Security Ltd
Essentra Packaging Limited
Floplast Limited
Glynwed Pipe Systems Limited
John Guest Limited
HellermannTyton Group PLC
HellermannTyton Limited
ITW Limited
Philips Electronics UK Limited
Smiths Medical International Ltd
Sumika Polymer Compounds (UK) Ltd
Synventive Acquisition Unlimited
Zotefoams PLC

23320 Manufacture of bricks, tiles and construction products, in baked clay

Michelmersh Brick Holdings PLC
Michelmersh Brick UK Limited

23510 Manufacture of cement

Castle Cement Limited
Civil and Marine Limited

23610 Manufacture of concrete products for construction purposes

Castacrete Limited
H+H UK Limited
Laing O'Rourke Manufacturing Ltd
Monier Redland Limited

23630 Manufacture of ready-mixed concrete

J Clubb Limited
Hanson Quarry Products Europe Ltd

23640 Manufacture of mortars

CPI Mortars (North) Limited
CPI Mortars Limited

23690 Manufacture of other articles of concrete, plaster and cement

Hanson Packed Products Limited

23910 Production of abrasive products

3M United Kingdom PLC
Icopal Limited

23990 Manufacture of other non-metallic mineral products n.e.c.

Armstrong World Industries Ltd
Day Group Limited

24410 Precious metals production

Britannia Refined Metals Ltd

24430 Lead, zinc and tin production

Britannia Refined Metals Ltd

25110 Manufacture of metal structures and parts of structures

Hy-Ten Group Limited
Hy-Ten Limited
Killinchy Aerospace Holdings Ltd
Magal Engineering Limited
Martin-Baker Aircraft Co Ltd
John Parker & Son Limited
SAS Holdings Limited

25400 Manufacture of weapons and ammunition

BAE Systems Global Combat Systems Munitions
Chemring Countermeasures Ltd
FNH UK Limited

25620 Machining

John Crane UK Limited
Eaton Limited
Flexibox International Limited
HPC PLC
Honeywell UK Limited
Jacobs Field Services Limited
Lilac Limited
Smith International (North Sea) Ltd
Vitec Production Solutions Ltd

25940 Manufacture of fasteners and screw machine products

HellermannTyton Limited
T.R. Fastenings Limited

25990 Manufacture of other fabricated metal products n.e.c.

APG Cash Drawer UK, Ltd
Bolzoni Capital UK Limited
ITAB UK Ltd
Lymington Precision Engineering (LPE)
Pandrol Limited
Portsmouth Aviation Holdings Ltd
SAS International Limited
Tensator Limited

26110 Manufacture of electronic components [15]

AVX Limited
Albright International Limited
Amphenol Limited
Axis Electronics Limited
Gemalto UK Limited
ITW Limited
Motorola Mobility UK Ltd
Siemens PLC
Surrey Satellite Technology Ltd
Technetix Limited
Teledyne Limited
Thales Training & Simulation (Ace)
Thales UK Limited
Trend Control Systems Limited
Volex PLC

26200 Manufacture of computers and peripheral equipment

Centerprise Intl Holdings Ltd
HP Inc UK Limited
IBM United Kingdom Limited
Lenovo Technology (United Kingdom)
Mitac Technology UK Ltd.
Northgate Public Services (UK) Ltd

26301 Manufacture of telegraph and telephone apparatus and equipment

JAE Europe, Limited
Surface Technology International Ltd
Teledyne Limited

26309 Manufacture of communication equipment other than telegraph, and telephone apparatus and equipment

Kyocera Document Solutions (U.K.)
Thales UK Limited

26400 Manufacture of consumer electronics

B & W Group Ltd
Focusrite Audio Engineering Ltd
Samsung Electronics (UK) Ltd
Sony Europe Limited
Technetix Limited

26511 Manufacture of electronic measuring, testing etc. equipment, not for industrial process control [11]

Celsis Group Limited
Celsis International Limited
Nastor Investments Limited
Raymarine UK Limited
Siemens Healthcare Diagnostics Ltd
Smiths Detection-Watford Ltd
Sonardyne Group Limited
Sonardyne International Ltd
Sondex Wireline Limited
Tektronix U.K.Limited
Waters Limited

26512 Manufacture of electronic industrial process control equipment

Nikon X-Tek Systems Limited
Rockwell Automation Limited
Servomex Group Limited
Siemens PLC

26513 Manufacture of non-electronic measuring, testing etc. equipment, not for industrial process control

Elster Metering Limited
Elster Water Metering Limited

26600 Manufacture of irradiation, electromedical and electrotherapeutic equipment

Canon Medical Systems Limited
Varian Medical Systems UK Ltd

26701 Manufacture of optical precision instruments

Flir Systems Limited
Nikon X-Tek Systems Limited
SPI Lasers UK Limited
Vision Engineering Limited

26702 Manufacture of photographic and cinematographic equipment

Kodak Alaris Limited
Sony Europe Limited

27110 Manufacture of electric motors, generators and transformers
Elu Power Tools Ltd
Nikon X-Tek Systems Limited
SEM Limited
Siemens PLC

27120 Manufacture of electricity distribution and control apparatus
Automated Technology Group Ltd
Chemigraphic Limited
Electrium Sales Limited
Siemens PLC
Siemens Transmission and Distribution
VA Tech (UK) Limited

27320 Manufacture of other electronic and electric wires and cables
Moog Reading Limited
Prysmian Cables & Systems Ltd

27330 Manufacture of wiring devices
Electrium Sales Limited

27400 Manufacture of electric lighting equipment
Feilo Sylvania Europe Limited
Holophane Europe Limited
Inesa UK Limited
J C C Lighting Products Ltd
Shires Holdings Limited
Tridonic UK Limited
Urbis Schreder Ltd

27510 Manufacture of electric domestic appliances
B & W Group Ltd
Beko PLC
Black & Decker
GDC Group Limited
Kenwood Limited
Novar ED & S Limited
Numatic International Limited
Redring Xpelair Group Ltd

27900 Manufacture of other electrical equipment [27]
Apollo Fire Detectors Limited
Axis Electronics Limited
Canon Europe Limited
Canon Holdings (UK) Limited
Cubic Transportation Systems Ltd
Dewhurst PLC
Diebold Nixdorf (UK) Limited
Digico UK Limited
Dynniq UK Ltd
Eaton Electric Limited
Focusrite PLC
Hanover Displays Limited
Harman International Industries Ltd
KAC Alarm Co Ltd
Marshall Amplification PLC
Novar ED & S Limited
Saab Seaeye Limited
Samsung Semiconductor Europe Ltd
TT Electronics IoT Solutions Ltd
Toshiba Tec U.K. Imaging Systems Ltd
Vent-Axia Group Limited
Vertiv Infrastructure Ltd
Volex PLC
Volution Holdings Limited
Volution Ventilation Group Ltd
X P PLC
XP Power PLC

28110 Manufacture of engines and turbines, except aircraft, vehicle and cycle engines
Allen Diesels Limited
MHI Vestas Offshore Wind Blades UK Ltd
Siemens Industrial Turbomachinery

28120 Manufacture of fluid power equipment
Parker Hannifin Limited
Parker Hannifin Manufacturing (UK)
Parker Hannifin Manufacturing Ltd

28131 Manufacture of pumps
Eaton Limited
Edwards High Vacuum International
Edwards Limited
ITT Industries Limited
Terex Pegson Limited

28132 Manufacture of compressors
Galileo Global Technologies Ltd

28140 Manufacture of taps and valves
Aqualisa Products Limited

28150 Manufacture of bearings, gears, gearing and driving elements
HPC PLC
NSK Bearings Europe Limited
Xtrac Limited

28220 Manufacture of lifting and handling equipment
Hyster-Yale Group Limited
Hyster-Yale UK Limited
Jungheinrich UK Limited

28230 Manufacture of office machinery and equipment (except computers and peripheral equipment)
Acco UK Limited

28240 Manufacture of power-driven hand tools
Black & Decker International

28250 Manufacture of non-domestic cooling and ventilation equipment
J & E Hall Limited
Kelvion Limited
Wozair Limited

28290 Manufacture of other general-purpose machinery n.e.c.
Alfa Laval Limited
Harsco Rail Limited
Kinetrol Limited
Loesche Energy Systems Limited
Pall Europe Limited
Pall Manufacturing UK Limited

28921 Manufacture of machinery for mining
Terex Pegson Limited

28930 Manufacture of machinery for food, beverage and tobacco processing
Garbuio Limited
Russell Finex Limited
SPX Flow Technology Crawley Ltd

28960 Manufacture of plastics and rubber machinery
Glory Global Solutions Ltd
Thames Water Products Limited

28990 Manufacture of other special-purpose machinery n.e.c. [17]
Altair (UK) Ltd
Doosan Babcock Limited
Doosan Power Systems Overseas Investments
G.E.W. (EC) Limited
Glory Global Solutions (Holdings)
Glory Global Solutions (International)
Glory Global Solutions (Midco) Ltd
Glory Global Solutions (Topco) Ltd
Harvey Water Softeners Limited
Niftylift Limited
Nikon X-Tek Systems Limited
Pall Manufacturing UK Limited
Russell Finex Limited
Schindler Ltd.
Senior UK Limited
Tesla Engineering Limited
Water Process Limited

29100 Manufacture of motor vehicles
BAE Systems Global Combat Systems
BMW (UK) Manufacturing Limited
Johnston Sweepers Limited
McLaren Automotive Limited
Rolls-Royce Motor Cars Limited
Tesla Motors Limited

29201 Manufacture of bodies (coachwork) for motor vehicles (except caravans)
Fasttrax Limited
Swindon Pressings Limited

29310 Manufacture of electrical and electronic equipment for motor vehicles and their engines
Centrica Business Solutions UK Ltd
Harman Automotive UK Limited
VA Tech (UK) Limited

29320 Manufacture of other parts and accessories for motor vehicles
CT Automotive Group Limited
McLaren Applied Technologies Ltd
Wipac Limited
Xtrac Transmissions (Holdings) Ltd

30110 Building of ships and floating structures
BAE Systems Marine Limited
BAE Systems Surface Ships Ltd

30120 Building of pleasure and sporting boats
Porter and Haylett Limited

30300 Manufacture of air and spacecraft and related machinery
BAE Systems (Operations) Ltd
Safran Helicopter Engines UK Ltd
Surrey Satellite Technology Ltd
Triumph Aerospace Operations UK, Ltd.

30400 Manufacture of military fighting vehicles
Lockheed Martin UK Ampthill Ltd

30990 Manufacture of other transport equipment n.e.c.
SMR Automotive Mirror Parts and Holdings UK
SMR Automotive Mirrors UK Ltd
Siemens Mobility Limited

31010 Manufacture of office and shop furniture
ISG Retail Limited

31020 Manufacture of kitchen furniture
Crown Products (Kent) Limited
Dennis & Robinson Limited
E.L.Head Limited

31090 Manufacture of other furniture
Crown Products (Kent) Limited

32120 Manufacture of jewellery and related articles
Citizen Watch United Kingdom, Ltd

32300 Manufacture of sports goods
Amer Sports UK Limited
Grays of Cambridge (International)

32409 Manufacture of other games and toys, n.e.c.
Hornby Hobbies Limited
Hornby PLC
Vivid Imaginations Limited

32500 Manufacture of medical and dental instruments and supplies [18]
Becton Dickinson Infusion Therapy UK
Becton, Dickinson U.K. Limited
Carefusion U.K. 305 Limited
Carefusion U.K. 306 Limited
Carestream Health UK, Limited
Consort Medical PLC
CooperVision Limited
CooperVision Manufacturing Ltd
Elekta Limited
Femcare Limited
Gluco RX Limited
Intersurgical Limited
Kimal PLC
Medtronic Limited
Rayner Intraocular Lenses Ltd
Sekisui Diagnostics (UK) Ltd
Siemens Healthcare Diagnostics Manufacturing
Siemens Healthcare Diagnostics Products

32990 Other manufacturing n.e.c. [55]
3M United Kingdom PLC
AWE PLC
Afton Chemical Limited
Aspen Pumps Limited
Attewell Limited
Avery Dennison U.K. Limited
Biocompatibles UK Limited
Biomerieux UK Limited
Chas.A.Blatchford & Sons,Limited
Britax Excelsior Limited
CSL (Dualcom) Limited
Capital Safety Group (Northern Europe)
City Technology Limited
Dage Precision Industries Ltd
Daler-Rowney Limited
Danfoss Limited
Essentra Packaging & Security Ltd
Fibercore Limited
Formaplex Limited
Fujifilm Sericol Overseas Holdings
Fujifilm Speciality Ink Systems Ltd
Gillette U.K. Limited
Givaudan UK Limited
Gurit (UK) Limited
Gurit Material Systems (UK) Ltd
Harris Defence Limited
Honeywell Security UK Limited
ITW Limited
Kidde Products Limited
Kone PLC
Laleham Health and Beauty Ltd
Magma Global Limited
Mersen UK Portslade Limited
Micron Europe Limited
Murex Biotech Limited
National Adhesives Holding Ltd.
Pall Manufacturing UK Limited
Perkinelmer Limited
Red Bull Technology Limited
Royal British Legion Industries Ltd.
Royal British Legion Poppy Factory
SMC Pneumatics (U.K.) Limited
Thomas Sanderson Limited
Scott Health & Safety Limited
Sericol Ink Limited
Sharp Electronics (Europe) Ltd
Synventive Holding Limited
T G Products Limited
TFX Group Limited
Tech 21 UK Limited
Thorn Security Limited
Tubifoam Limited
Ultra Electronics Limited
Volution Group PLC
James Walker & Co. Limited

33120 Repair of machinery
Dresser-Rand (U.K.) Limited
Greenshields JCB Limited
R. Hunt (Agricultural Engineers)

33140 Repair of electrical equipment
Centrica Business Solutions UK Ltd
VA Tech (UK) Limited

33150 Repair and maintenance of ships and boats
Berthon Boat Co Ltd
Wartsila UK Limited

33160 Repair and maintenance of aircraft and spacecraft
British Airways Maintenance Cardiff
Gama Aviation (Engineering) Ltd
Lufthansa Technik Landing Gear Services UK
Safran Helicopter Engines UK Ltd
Vector Aerospace International Ltd

33170 Repair and maintenance of other transport equipment n.e.c.
Gemini Rail Services UK Ltd
Harsco Rail Limited

33190 Repair of other equipment
CTDI Repair Services Limited
Elliott TurboMachinery Limited
HPC PLC
J & E Hall Limited
MHI Vestas Offshore Wind Blades UK Ltd
Safety-Kleen U.K. Limited
Winterhalter Ltd

33200 Installation of industrial machinery and equipment [10]
Beck & Pollitzer Engineering Ltd
GE Energy (UK) Limited
Global Invacom Limited
Greenshields JCB Limited
Heidelberg Graphic Equipment Ltd
MTS Systems Limited
Philips Electronics UK Limited
Safety-Kleen U.K. Limited
Tokyo Electron Europe Limited
Vodafone Limited

35110 Production of electricity [41]
Amber Solar Parks (Holdings) Ltd
Amber Solar Parks Limited
Andigestion Limited
Atlantica Yield PLC
BL Wind Limited
Biogen (UK) Limited
Bradenstoke Solar Park Limited
Centrica Brigg Limited
Centrica Distributed Generation Ltd
Centrica KPS Limited
Centrica PB Limited
Centrica PLC
Dreachmhor Wind Farm Limited
EDL (UK) LFG Generation Ltd
Energy Developments (UK) Ltd
Exagris Limited
Ferrybridge MFE Limited
Glenchamber Wind Energy Ltd
Grange Renewable Energy Ltd
Greater Gabbard Offshore Winds Ltd
Gym Offshore One Limited
Gym Offshore Three Limited
Gym Offshore Two Limited
Hall Farm Wind Farm Ltd
Homesun Limited
MGT Teesside Limited
MVV Environment Ridham Limited
Marchwood Power Limited
Medway Power Limited
Roos Energy Limited
SSE Generation Limited
SSE Production Services Ltd
SSE Seabank Investments Ltd

SWM UK Wind One Limited
Seagreen Wind Energy Limited
Slough Heat & Power Limited
Southwick Solar Farm Limited
Speyside Renewable Energy Finance PLC
Tallentire Energy Limited
West Raynham Solar Limited
Wryde Croft Wind Farm Limited

35120 Transmission of electricity

Atlantica Yield PLC
Gym Offshore One Limited
Gym Offshore Three Limited
SWM UK Wind One Limited
Siemens Transmission and Distribution

35130 Distribution of electricity

British Gas Trading Limited
Centrica PLC
ESP Electricity Limited
SSE Production Services Ltd
SSE Renewables Walney (UK) Ltd
Siemens Transmission and Distribution
Southern Electric Power Distribution PLC
Utilita Energy Limited

35140 Trade of electricity

British Gas Energy Procurement Ltd
Centrica Energy Marketing Ltd
Corona Energy Retail 4 Limited
Dual Energy Direct Limited
Green Network UK PLC
Hudson Energy Supply UK Ltd
SSE EPM Limited
Utilita Energy Limited

35210 Manufacture of gas

Centrica PLC

35220 Distribution of gaseous fuels through mains

British Gas Trading Limited
Centrica PLC
Corona Energy Retail 4 Limited
SSE Hornsea Limited
Southern Electric Gas Limited
Southern Gas Networks PLC

35230 Trade of gas through mains

Andigestion Limited
British Gas Energy Procurement Ltd
Centrica Energy Marketing Ltd
Corona Energy Retail 1 Limited
Utilita Energy Limited

35300 Steam and air conditioning supply

Daikin Airconditioning UK Ltd

36000 Water collection, treatment and supply [11]

Biwater International Limited
Canal & River Trust
Portsmouth Water Limited
South Downs Limited
South East Water Limited
Southern Water Services Ltd
Suez Advanced Solutions UK Ltd
Sutton and East Surrey Water PLC
Thames Water Limited
Thames Water Utilities Limited
VWS (UK) Ltd

37000 Sewerage

Biwater International Limited
MTS Cleansing Services Limited
Southern Water Services Ltd
Suez Advanced Solutions UK Ltd

38110 Collection of non-hazardous waste [21]

Biffa Corporate Holdings Ltd
Biffa Environmental Municipal Services
Biffa GS UK Holdings Limited
Biffa Holdings Limited
Biffa Municipal Limited
Biffa Waste Management Limited
Biffa Waste Services Limited
Cornwall Energy Recovery Ltd
Merseyside Energy Recovery Ltd
Northumberland Energy Recovery Ltd
Northumberland Waste Management Ltd
Renewi UK Services Limited
Resource Recovery Solutions (Derbyshire)
Safety-Kleen U.K. Limited
Suez Recycling and Recovery Kirklees Ltd
Suez Recycling and Recovery Lancashire
Suez Recycling and Recovery South Gloucestershire
Suez Recycling and Recovery Suffolk Ltd
Suez Recycling and Recovery Surrey Ltd
Suez Recycling and Recovery UK Ltd
UK Waste Management Limited

38120 Collection of hazardous waste [10]

Biffa Corporate Holdings Ltd
Biffa Environmental Municipal Services
Biffa Holdings Limited
Biffa Waste Services Limited
Safety-Kleen U.K. Limited
Suez Recycling and Recovery South Gloucestershire
Suez Recycling and Recovery Suffolk Ltd
Suez Recycling and Recovery Surrey Ltd
Suez Recycling and Recovery UK Ltd
UK Waste Management Limited

38210 Treatment and disposal of non-hazardous waste [24]

Andigestion Limited
Biffa Corporate Holdings Ltd
Biffa GS UK Holdings Limited
Biffa Holdings Limited
Biffa Waste Management Limited
Biffa Waste Services Limited
Biogen (UK) Limited
Cornwall Energy Recovery Ltd
Countrystyle Group Limited
Countrystyle Recycling Limited
MTS Cleansing Services Limited
Merseyside Energy Recovery Ltd
Northumberland Energy Recovery Ltd
Northumberland Waste Management Ltd
Suez Recycling and Recovery Kirklees Ltd
Suez Recycling and Recovery North East
Suez Recycling and Recovery Packington
Suez Recycling and Recovery South East
Suez Recycling and Recovery South Gloucestershire
Suez Recycling and Recovery Suffolk Ltd
Suez Recycling and Recovery Surrey Ltd
Suez Recycling and Recovery Tees Valley
Suez UK Environment Ltd
UK Waste Management Limited

38220 Treatment and disposal of hazardous waste [11]

Biffa Corporate Holdings Ltd
Biffa Holdings Limited
Biffa Waste Services Limited
Erith Contractors Limited
Suez Recycling and Recovery South Gloucestershire
Suez Recycling and Recovery Suffolk Ltd
Suez Recycling and Recovery Surrey Ltd
Tradebe Fawley Limited
Tradebe Management Limited
Tradebe Solvent Recycling Ltd
UK Waste Management Limited

38320 Recovery of sorted materials

Biffa Environmental Municipal Services
Day Group Limited
Merseyside Energy Recovery Ltd
Renewi UK Services Limited
Viridor Resource Management Ltd

39000 Remediation activities and other waste management services

Erith Contractors Limited
MTS Cleansing Services Limited
Suez Recycling and Recovery Tees Valley
Summerleaze Limited

41100 Development of building projects [136]

A A Homes and Housing (Exchange Court)
Ability Developments Limited
Ability Hotels (Luton Inn) Ltd
Archaylen Property Limited
Avon Capital Estates (Australia) Ltd
Baron Homes Corporation Ltd
Berkeley Homes (Southall) Ltd
Birmingham Schools Partnership Ltd
Bostall Estates Limited
Bourne Holidays Limited
Bowsprit Property Development Ltd
Bugler Developments Limited
Bugler Group Limited
CNM Estates (Tolworth Tower MB) Ltd
CNM Estates (Tolworth Tower MBP) Ltd
CNM Estates (Tolworth Tower SBP) Ltd
CNM Estates Holdings Limited
Canal & River Trading CIC
Cheshunt Lakeside Developments Ltd
Collins 2017 Limited
Commercial Freeholds & Investments Ltd
Cooper Estates Limited
Core Property Developments Ltd
Cranbury Investment Co Ltd
Crest Nicholson Operations Ltd
Cross Stone Properties Limited
Cross Stone Securities Limited
DP Group Developments Limited
DP Realty Limited
Derby Healthcare PLC
Dolphin Head Group Holdings PLC
Dominvs Project Company 9 Ltd
Dominvs Project Co Ltd
Doncaster School Solutions Ltd
Durkan Estates Limited
Durkan Holdings Limited
Durkan Limited

East Sussex Energy Infrastructure and Development
Fawley Waterside Limited
Fynecast Limited
GFZ Properties Limited
Galliford Try Services Limited
Gravesend and District Real Estate Co
Grove Developments Limited
Harding Holdings U.K. Limited
Hargreaves Properties Limited
Howarth Homes PLC
Inland Homes PLC
Inland Limited
Jacobs E & C Limited
KIMS Property Co Ltd
Kent EHFA Projectco Limited
Kingsbridge Estates Limited
LSQ (Crimscott Street) Holdings Ltd
W.T. Lamb Holdings Limited
Liberty Property Trust UK Ltd
London Residential Healthcare Ltd
London Square (Fulham) Limited
London Square (Holdings) Ltd
London Square (Putney) Limited
London Square (Streatham) Ltd
London Square Developments (Ventures)
London Square Developments Ltd
London Square Limited
MDL Developments Limited
MYA Property Limited
Manco South Limited
Marco Island Developments Ltd
Marina Developments Limited
Matsim Properties Limited
McGrove Developments Limited
Modern Schools (Exeter) Ltd
Neilcott Construction Limited
Newcourt Residential (Wadhurst) Ltd
E.H. Nicholls Holdings Ltd
Onkar International Limited
Ordnance Building Limited
Paradigm Commercial PLC
Pentland Homes (Holdings) Ltd
Peterborough (Progress Health) PLC
Porthaven Properties Limited
Prowting Investments PLC
Ramac Holdings (Trading) Ltd
Renaissance Retirement Limited
Renand Properties Limited
Riverdale Developments Limited
Roffey Homes Limited
Rydon Construction Limited
Rydon Homes Limited
SC Osney Lane Limited
Salaft Properties Limited
Shanly Homes Limited
Sinclair Gardens Investments (Kensington)
Skanska Infrastructure Development UK
Skanska TAM Limited
Skillcrown Holdings Limited
Sorbon Estates Limited
Sorbon Homes Limited
Sorbon Investments Limited
Southwater Property Promotion Ltd
Specsavers Optical Superstores Ltd
Spincrest Limited
St James Group Limited
St James Homes (Grosvenor Dock) Ltd
F.C. Stark Limited
Student Castle Limited
T.J.D. Trade Limited
TBG (1) 2009 Limited
TBG (3) 2009 Limited
Taylor Wimpey Developments Ltd
Taylor Wimpey Holdings Limited
Taylor Wimpey Property Co Ltd
Taylor Wimpey UK Limited
Taylor Woodrow Construction
Techaid Facilities Limited
Thakeham Homes Limited
Thames Water Investments Ltd
Thomas Homes Limited
Thornton Park (London) Limited
Transform Schools (Birmingham) Ltd
Transform Schools (Stoke) Ltd
Trevellyan Developments Ltd
Tricomm Housing (Portsmouth) Ltd
Tristmire Limited
United Living (North) Limited
United Living (South) Limited
Vanderbilt Homes Limited
Victorygame Limited
W.N. Developments Limited
W1 London Limited
Wates Developments Limited
Michael Wenman Limited
Westgate Properties Limited
Whitehill & Bordon Development Company Phase 1A
Wilson Connolly Limited
Wyboston Lakes Limited

41201 Construction of commercial buildings [80]

AHL Holdings (Manchester) Ltd
Alder Hey (Special Purpose Vehicle)
Amey Highways Lighting (Manchester)
Aura (Newcastle) Project Co Ltd
Autolink Concessionaires (M6) PLC
BAM Construct UK Limited
BAM Construction Limited
Blenheim House Construction Ltd
Boskalis Subsea Limited
Buckingham Group Contracting Ltd
Bynorth Limited
Cementation Skanska Limited
Changeregard Limited
Collaborative Services Support NE
Cross Stone Securities Limited
Crown House Technologies Ltd
Defence Support (St Athan) Ltd
Education Support (Enfield 2) Holdings
Education Support (Enfield 2) Ltd
Education Support (Newham) Holdings
Education Support (Newham) Ltd
Education Support (Swindon) Ltd
Explore Manufacturing Limited
T A Fisher & Sons Limited
Forth Health Holdings Limited
Forth Health Limited
GT NEPS (Holdings) Limited
GT NEPS Limited
Galliford Try Building Limited
Galliford Try Homes Limited
Galliford Try PLC
Galliford Try Partnerships Ltd
Hambridge Limited
Healthcare Support (Newcastle) Holdings
Healthcare Support (Newcastle) Ltd
Healthcare Support (North Staffs)
Henry Construction Projects Ltd
ISG Retail Limited
KIMS Property Co Ltd
LSQ (Crimscott Street) Holdings Ltd
Laing Construction Limited
John Laing Construction Ltd
Laing Limited
Laing O'Rourke Construction Ltd
Laing O'Rourke Holdings Ltd
Laing O'Rourke PLC.
Laing O'Rourke Services Ltd
Linden Limited
London Square (Streatham) Ltd
Luff Investments Limited
Marbank Construction Limited
Sir Robert McAlpine Limited
Midgard Ltd
Mitchellson Formwork & Civil Engineering
Modern Schools (Barnsley) Ltd
A.J. Morrisroe & Sons Limited
Octagon Developments Limited
Geoffrey Osborne Limited
Prater Limited
Prime Care Solutions (Kingston) Ltd
RGCM Limited
J. Reddington Ltd
John Reilly (Civil Engineering) Ltd
Renewable Energy Systems Ltd
S.D.C. Builders Limited
SES (Engineering Services) Ltd
Sirhowy Enterprise Way Limited
Skanska Cementation International
Skanska Construction UK Ltd
Skanska UK PLC
Spritestore Limited
St Edward Homes Limited
Tower, One St George Wharf Ltd
Transform Schools (Birmingham) Ltd
Transform Schools (Stoke) Ltd
Try Homes Limited
United Living (South) Limited
Vinci Construction UK Limited
Wates Construction Limited
Yorkshire Transformations Ltd

41202 Construction of domestic buildings [46]

Antler Homes PLC
BH (City Forum) Limited
Bargate Homes Limited
Bewley Group Limited
Bewley Homes PLC
W.E.Black Limited
Buxted Construction Limited
CALA 1 Limited
CALA Group (Holdings) Limited
Cross Stone Securities Limited
Croudace Homes Group Limited
Croudace Homes Limited
Evolution (Woking) Limited
Fairfax Acquisitions Limited
T A Fisher & Sons Limited
Kebbell Development Limited
Nicholas King Developments PLC
LSQ (Crimscott Street) Holdings Ltd
LSQ Holdco 3 Limited
Leven Wharf Limited
London Square (Fulham) Limited
London Square (Holdings) Ltd
London Square (Putney) Limited
London Square (Streatham) Ltd
London Square Developments (Holdings)
London Square Developments (Ventures)
London Square Developments Ltd
London Square Limited
MDH (Group) Limited

Marbank Construction Limited
Midgard Ltd
Millgate Developments Limited
Millwood Designer Homes Ltd
Pentland Homes Limited
Perbury (Developments) Limited
Quayside Homes Limited
Rectory Homes Limited
J. Reddington Ltd
SC Walmgate Limited
St George Blackfriars Limited
T.J.D. Trade Limited
United Living (North) Limited
United Living (South) Limited
Vanderbilt Development Finance Ltd
Vanderbilt Thames Valley Ltd
Vanderbilt Topco Ltd

42110 Construction of roads and motorways [21]

Autolink Concessionaires (A19) Ltd
Autolink Concessionaires (M6) PLC
Autolink Holdings (M6) Ltd
BAM Nuttall Limited
Buckingham Group Contracting Ltd
Colas Limited
Conway Aecom Limited
F M Conway Limited
Costain Building & Civil Engineering
Costain Engineering & Construction
Costain Group PLC
Costain Limited
Countyroute (A130) PLC.
Countyroute Limited
Ensign Highways Limited
Eurovia Infrastructure Limited
Eurovia UK Limited
Geoffrey Osborne Limited
Ringway Infrastructure Services Ltd
Ringway Jacobs Limited
UK Highways A55 Limited

42120 Construction of railways and underground railways

BAM Nuttall Limited
Buckingham Group Contracting Ltd

42130 Construction of bridges and tunnels

BAM Nuttall Limited
Costain Building & Civil Engineering
Costain Engineering & Construction
Costain Limited

42220 Construction of utility projects for electricity and telecommunications

Siemens Gamesa Renewable Energy Ltd
Tamar Energy Limited
Trant Engineering Limited

42910 Construction of water projects

Black & Veatch Limited
Clancy Docwra Limited
Costain Building & Civil Engineering
Costain Engineering & Construction
Costain Limited
Stantec Treatment Group Ltd
Trant Engineering Limited

42990 Construction of other civil engineering projects n.e.c. [16]

BAM Nuttall Limited
Buckingham Group Contracting Ltd
Costain Building & Civil Engineering
Costain Engineering & Construction
Costain Limited
Costain Oil, Gas & Process Ltd
Keltbray Group (Holdings) Ltd
Laing O'Rourke Infrastructure Ltd
Purelake New Homes Limited
Taylor Woodrow Construction
Transform Schools (Birmingham) Ltd
Transform Schools (Stoke) Ltd
Trant Engineering Limited
Van Oord UK Limited
Vinci Construction UK Limited
Wood Group Kenny Limited

43110 Demolition

Brown and Mason Limited
Erith Contractors Limited
Keltbray Group (Holdings) Ltd
Keltbray Limited

43120 Site preparation

Erith Contractors Limited

43130 Test drilling and boring

BP Exploration Angola (Kwanza Benguela)

43210 Electrical installation

British Gas New Heating Ltd
British Gas Social Housing Ltd
C.L.C. Contractors Limited
Centrica Business Solutions UK Ltd
ESSCI Limited
ESSCI Technical Services Ltd
Emcor Group (UK) PLC
SSE Contracting Limited
Skanska Rashleigh Weatherfoil Ltd

43220 Plumbing, heat and air-conditioning installation

British Gas New Heating Ltd
British Gas Social Housing Ltd
ESSCI Limited
ESSCI Technical Services Ltd
Emcor Group (UK) PLC
Hotchkiss Group Ltd
Johnson Controls Building Efficiency UK
Michael Lonsdale Limited
Michael J. Lonsdale Limited

43290 Other construction installation

C.L.C. Contractors Limited
Oairo Alliance Limited
Geoffrey Osborne Limited
Ruddy Joinery Limited
Saipem Limited

43310 Plastering

Stanmore Contractors Limited

43320 Joinery installation

Beck Interiors Limited
Ruddy Joinery Limited

43330 Floor and wall covering

Faithdean PLC

43341 Painting

C.L.C. Contractors Limited

43390 Other building completion and finishing

C.L.C. Contractors Limited
Faithdean PLC
Halamar (Chancery Lane) Ltd
Ruddy Joinery Limited
Transform Schools (North Lanarkshire)

43910 Roofing activities

LR (UK) Limited

43991 Scaffold erection

Lyndon Scaffolding PLC

43999 Other specialised construction activities n.e.c. [36]

Alandale Logistics Limited
Anesco Limited
Ansa UK Limited
Area Sq. Limited
Beck Interiors Limited
Beck MBI Limited
Boral (UK) Limited
Boskalis Subsea Limited
Boskalis Westminster (Holdings) Ltd
Boskalis Westminster Limited
Brisko Scaffolding Limited
Collins Construction Ltd
Faithdean PLC
Claude Fenton (Holdings) Ltd
Fluor Limited
Foundation Developments Ltd
Foundocean Group Limited
Martin Grant (Holdings) Ltd
Martin Grant Homes Limited
Jacobs Process Limited
KN Network Services (Northern Ireland)
Kellogg Brown & Root (U.K.) Ltd
O'Halloran & O'Brien Limited
Premier Marinas Limited
Prysmian Powerlink Services Ltd
SES (Engineering Services) Ltd
Select Plant Hire Co Ltd
Selwood Group Limited
Selwood Ltd
Skanska Major Projects Limited
Subsea 7 International Contracting
TRAD Hire & Sales Limited
TRAD Scaffolding Co.Limited
Wadlow Energy Limited
Wood Group Industrial Services Ltd
Workdry International Limited

45111 Sale of new cars and light motor vehicles [55]

Aprite (GB) Limited
BMW (UK) Limited
F.G. Barnes & Sons Limited
Barons Automotive Limited
Barons Autostar Limited
Barretts of Canterbury Limited
Beadles Group Limited
Beadles Sidcup Limited
Caffyns PLC
Dinnages Garages Limited
Drift Bridge Garage Limited
Eden Automotive Limited
Fiat Chrysler Automobiles UK Ltd
Harwoods Limited
Haynes Brothers,Limited
Hendy Group Limited
Hodgson Automotive Limited
Honda Motor Europe Limited
Hyundai Motor UK Limited
JCB Medway Limited
Kent Auto Panels Limited
Kia Motors (UK) Limited
W.J.King (Garages) Limited
Local Car and Van Rental Ltd
Marsh Wall Limited
Mazda Motors UK Limited
McLaren Automotive Limited
Mercedes-Benz Cars UK Limited
Mercedes-Benz Retail Group UK Ltd
Motorline (Kent) Limited
Nissan Motor (GB) Limited
PSA Finance UK Limited
Park Lane Limited
John Parker & Son Limited
Partridge of Hampshire Limited
Porsche Cars Great Britain Ltd
Porsche Retail Group Limited
RSA Accident Repairs Limited
Renault U.K. Limited
Rolls-Royce Motor Cars Limited
Saftdwin Limited
Sandown Surrey and Hampshire Ltd
Snows Motor Group Limited
Sparshatts Holdings Limited
Sparshatts of Kent Limited
Spire Automotive Limited
Suzuki GB PLC
Tesla Motors Limited
Think One Limited
Toyota (G.B.) PLC
Venson Automotive Solutions Ltd
Vines Limited
Volkswagen Group United Kingdom Ltd
Volvo Car UK Limited
Wilsons Automobiles and Coachworks

45112 Sale of used cars and light motor vehicles [31]

Aprite (GB) Limited
Bapchild Motoring World (Kent) Ltd
F.G. Barnes & Sons Limited
Barons Autostar Limited
Barretts of Canterbury Limited
Copart UK Limited
Dinnages Garages Limited
Drift Bridge Garage Limited
Eagle Racing Limited
Fiat Chrysler Automobiles UK Ltd
D Hales Limited
Hendy Group Limited
Honda Motor Europe Limited
Imperial Car Supermarkets Ltd
Imperial Cars of Swanwick Ltd
JCB Medway Limited
Local Car and Van Rental Ltd
Marsh Wall Limited
Mercedes-Benz Retail Group UK Ltd
Motorline (Kent) Limited
PSA Finance UK Limited
John Parker & Son Limited
Sandown Surrey and Hampshire Ltd
Spire Automotive Limited
T.S.L. Finance Limited
Talacrest 2000 A.D. Limited
Trade Sale Ltd
Universal Salvage Limited
We Buy Any Car Limited
Michael Wenman Limited
Wilsons Automobiles and Coachworks

45190 Sale of other motor vehicles [13]

F.G. Barnes & Sons Limited
CPRT (Europe) Limited
Caffyns PLC
Channel Commercials PLC
Copart UK Limited
D Hales Limited
Heathrow Truck Centre Limited
M C Group Limited
MC Truck & Bus Limited
MCG (Holdings) Ltd
Motus Group (UK) Limited
Scania (Great Britain) Limited
Universal Salvage Limited

45200 Maintenance and repair of motor vehicles [29]

Aprite (GB) Limited
BCA Fleet Solutions Limited
BCA Vehicle Services Limited
F.G. Barnes & Sons Limited
Barons Autostar Limited
Barretts of Canterbury Limited
Belron UK Limited
Caffyns PLC
Dinnages Garages Limited
Fasttrax Limited
Harwoods Limited
Heathrow Truck Centre Limited
Hendy Group Limited
Hyundai Motor UK Limited
JCB Medway Limited
M C Group Limited
MC Truck & Bus Limited
MCG (Holdings) Ltd
Marsh Wall Limited
Mercedes-Benz Retail Group UK Ltd
Motus Group (UK) Limited
Park Lane Limited
RSA Accident Repairs Limited
Sandown Surrey and Hampshire Ltd
Snows Motor Group Limited
Spire Automotive Limited
Tesla Motors Limited
UK Assistance Accident Repair Centres
Venson Automotive Solutions Ltd

45310 Wholesale trade of motor vehicle parts and accessories [20]

Aprite (GB) Limited
Bharat Forge International Ltd
Ferdinand Bilstein UK Limited
Chinatool UK Limited
Continental Tyre Group Ltd.
Fiat Chrysler Automobiles UK Ltd
Hendy Group Limited
Honda Motor Europe Limited
Hyundai Motor UK Limited
Johnson Controls Batteries Ltd
Mazda Motors UK Limited
Micheldever Tyre Services Ltd
Andrew Page 1917 Limited
Park Lane Limited
RSA Accident Repairs Limited
Sanden International (Europe) Ltd
Snows Motor Group Limited
Tesla Motors Limited
Wurth UK Limited
Yazaki Europe Limited

45320 Retail trade of motor vehicle parts and accessories [14]

Barons Autostar Limited
Barretts of Canterbury Limited
Caffyns PLC
Dinnages Garages Limited
Jayar Components Limited
M C Group Limited
MC Truck & Bus Limited
MCG (Holdings) Ltd
Marsh Wall Limited
Micheldever Tyre Services Ltd
Motus Group (UK) Limited
Sandown Surrey and Hampshire Ltd
Southern Motor Group Limited
Spire Automotive Limited

45400 Sale, maintenance and repair of motorcycles and related parts and accessories

Bike Alert PLC
Honda Motor Europe Limited
Park Lane Limited

46110 Agents selling agricultural raw materials, livestock, textile raw materials and semi-finished goods

Agricultural Central Trading Ltd

46120 Agents involved in the sale of fuels, ores, metals and industrial chemicals

Agricultural Central Trading Ltd
Idemitsu International (Europe) Ltd
Mobil Trading and Supply Ltd
Wintel Petrochemicals Limited

46130 Agents involved in the sale of timber and building materials

David Cover and Son Limited
Elliott Brothers (Builders Merchants)
Elliott Brothers Limited
Grant & Stone Limited
Klober Limited

46140 Agents involved in the sale of machinery, industrial equipment, ships and aircraft

All Metal Services Limited
Citizen Machinery UK Ltd
R. Hunt (Agricultural Engineers)
ICS Cool Energy Limited
Manitowoc Crane Group (UK) Ltd
NCMT Limited
Terex Cranes UK Limited
Tokyo Electron Europe Limited
Toyota Material Handling UK Ltd

46150 Agents involved in the sale of furniture, household goods, hardware and ironmongery

FKA Brands Limited

46170 Agents involved in the sale of food, beverages and tobacco

Cellarmaster Wines Holdings (UK) Ltd
General Mills UK Limited
Hatch, Mansfield Agencies Ltd
Kallo Foods Limited
Sun Mark Limited

46180 Agents specialised in the sale of other particular products

Biogen Idec Limited
Forum Health Products Ltd.
Forum Products Holdings Ltd
John Guest Speedfit Limited
Honeywell Analytics Limited

46210 Wholesale of grain, unmanufactured tobacco, seeds and animal feeds

ADM Arkady Limited
Archer Daniels Midland (UK) Ltd

46220 Wholesale of flowers and plants

Hillier Nurseries Limited

46310 Wholesale of fruit and vegetables [16]

A.G. Thames Holdings Limited
Barfoots of Botley Limited
Berry Gardens Limited
Chingford Fruit Limited
Compagnie Fruitiere UK Limited
Del Monte (UK) Limited
Del Monte Foods International Ltd
Fresh Direct (UK) Limited
Fyffes Group Limited
A Gomez Limited
Greencell Limited
M.& W.Mack Limited
Newmafruit Farms Limited
Premier Fruit & Nut Limited
Thanet Earth Holdings Limited
Thanet Earth Limited

46320 Wholesale of meat and meat products

JBS Global (UK) Limited
Universal Meats (UK) Limited
Vestey Foods UK Limited
Winterbotham,Darby & Co.Limited

46330 Wholesale of dairy products, eggs and edible oils and fats

ADM Trading (UK) Limited
Bel UK Limited
Fridays Limited
Medina Dairy Limited

46342 Wholesale of wine, beer, spirits and other alcoholic beverages [15]

Asahi UK Ltd
Bacardi-Martini Limited
W.H. Brakspear & Sons Limited
John Dewar and Sons Limited
John E.Fells & Sons Limited
William Grant & Sons Brands Ltd
William Grant & Sons UK Ltd
Majestic Wine PLC
Majestic Wine Warehouses Ltd
Mast-Jaegermeister UK Limited
Quality Spirits International Ltd
Shepherd Neame Limited
South Downs Real Estate Ltd
Charles Wells Brewery Limited
Charles Wells,Limited

46350 Wholesale of tobacco products

British American Tobacco UK Ltd
Scandinavian Tobacco Group United Kingdom

46360 Wholesale of sugar and chocolate and sugar confectionery

ADM Trading (UK) Limited
Empire Bespoke Foods Limited
Lindt & Sprungli (U.K.) Ltd

46370 Wholesale of coffee, tea, cocoa and spices

Falcon Coffees Limited

46380 Wholesale of other food, including fish, crustaceans and molluscs

Bel UK Limited
Empire Bespoke Foods Limited
Lovering Foods Limited
M & J Seafood Limited
Nutfield Holdings Limited
Windmill Organics Limited

46390 Non-specialised wholesale of food, beverages and tobacco [22]

ADM Trading (UK) Limited
BFS Group Limited
Bel UK Limited
Bidcorp (UK) Limited
Bidcorp Foodservice (Europe) Ltd
Brake Bros Foodservice Limited
Brake Bros Limited
Britannia Soft Drinks Limited
Britvic EMEA Limited
Britvic International Investments
Britvic Soft Drinks Limited
Continental Trade and Commodity Services
Delice de France Limited
Euro Food Brands Limited
Lactalis Nestle Chilled Dairy Co Ltd
Natco Foods Limited
Purecircle (UK) Limited
Robinsons Soft Drinks Limited
Tata Global Beverages GB Ltd
Tchibo Coffee International Ltd
Tradeteam Limited
Yoplait UK Limited

46420 Wholesale of clothing and footwear

Ralph Lauren UK Limited
New Era Cap Co Ltd

46431 Wholesale of audio tapes, records, CDs and video tapes and the equipment on which these are played

B & W Group Ltd
Bose Limited
Sony Europe Limited

46439 Wholesale of radio, television goods & electrical household appliances (other than records, tapes, CDs)

BSH Home Appliances Limited
Conair Group Limited
Deta Electrical Co Ltd
Fisher & Paykel Appliances Ltd
Fujifilm UK Limited
Microchip Limited
Philips Electronics UK Limited
R & M Electrical Group Limited
Stearn Electric Co Ltd

46440 Wholesale of china and glassware and cleaning materials

Lesser & Pavey Ltd.

46450 Wholesale of perfume and cosmetics [10]

Body Shop International Ltd
Capital (Hair and Beauty) Ltd
Colgate-Palmolive (U.K.) Ltd
Dermalogica (UK) Limited
Gojo Industries - Europe Ltd
Kenneth Green Associates Ltd
HFC Prestige Products Limited
Johnson & Johnson Limited
Karium Ltd
S A Designer Parfums Limited

46460 Wholesale of pharmaceutical goods [54]

AbbVie Ltd
Abbott Healthcare Products Ltd
Abbott Laboratories Limited
Allergan Limited
Alliance Healthcare (Distribution)
Aspire Pharma Holdings Limited
Astellas Pharma Europe Ltd.
Astellas Pharma Ltd.
Aventis Pharma Limited
Bayer PLC
Bristol Laboratories Limited
Britannia Pharmaceuticals Ltd
CSL Behring Holdings Limited
CSL Behring UK Limited
Celgene Limited
Chemidex Generics Limited
Colgate-Palmolive (U.K.) Ltd
CooperVision Lens Care Limited
Crescent Pharma Limited
EUSA Pharma (UK) Limited
Eco Animal Health Group PLC
Ennogen Healthcare Ltd
Glaxo Wellcome UK Limited
GlaxoSmithKline Caribbean Ltd
GlaxoSmithKline Consumer Trading Services
GlaxoSmithKline Export Limited
GlaxoSmithKline UK Limited
Hoechst Marion Roussel Limited
Hospira UK Limited
Leo Laboratories Limited
McNeil Healthcare (UK) Limited
Medreich PLC
Merck Serono Limited
Movianto UK Limited
NSL (Holdings) Limited
Necessity Supplies Limited
Novo Nordisk Limited
OTC Direct Limited
Ontex Retail UK Limited
Pfizer Consumer Healthcare Ltd
Pfizer Limited
Piramal Critical Care Limited
RB (China Trading) Limited
RB UK Commercial Limited
Ranbaxy (U.K.) Limited
Reckitt Benckiser Asia Pacific Ltd
Sangers (Maidstone) Limited
Servier IP UK Limited
Stada UK Holdings Ltd.
Strides Pharma Global (UK) Ltd
Takeda UK Limited
ViiV Healthcare Overseas Ltd
ViiV Healthcare Trading Services UK
ViiV Healthcare UK Limited

46470 Wholesale of furniture, carpets and lighting equipment

R & M Electrical Group Limited

46480 Wholesale of watches and jewellery

Fossil (UK) Limited
Seiko U.K. Limited

46499 Wholesale of household goods (other than musical instruments) n.e.c [10]

ARRI (GB) Limited
Bic U.K. Limited
Colgate-Palmolive (U.K.) Ltd
Groupe SEB UK Limited
Jakks Pacific (UK) Ltd
Lego Co Ltd
Mattel U.K. Limited
Nikon UK Limited
RB UK Commercial Limited
Rhone Products (UK) Limited

46510 Wholesale of computers, computer peripheral equipment and software [16]

Acer U.K. Limited
Dell Emerging Markets (EMEA) Ltd
Epson (U.K.) Limited
Exclusive Networks Limited
Ingram Micro (UK) Limited
NetApp UK Ltd
Northamber PLC
Oki Europe Limited
Optoma Europe Ltd
PFU (EMEA) Limited
Phoenix Software Limited
Quantel Limited
SK Hynix UK Limited
Sony Europe Limited
Tech Data Limited
Toshiba Information Systems (UK) Ltd

46520 Wholesale of electronic and telecommunications equipment and parts [19]

Click Entertainment Limited
Future Electronics Limited
Garmin (Europe) Limited
Hanwha Techwin Europe Limited
Ingram Micro (UK) Limited
LG Electronics U.K. Ltd
Maxell Europe Limited
R & M Electrical Group Limited
Rebound Technology Group Holdings
Renesas Electronics Europe Ltd
Rockwell Collins UK Limited
Rohde & Schwarz U.K. Limited
Samsung Electronics (UK) Ltd
Sharp Electronics (Europe) Ltd
Sumitomo Electric Europe Ltd
Technetix Limited
Toshiba Information Systems (UK) Ltd
Tridonic UK Limited
Vestel UK Limited

46620 Wholesale of machine tools

Draper Tools Limited

46630 Wholesale of mining, construction and civil engineering machinery

Leica Geosystems Limited

46650 Wholesale of office furniture

Spicers Limited

46660 Wholesale of other office machinery and equipment

Spicers Limited
Xerox (UK) Limited
Xerox Limited

46690 Wholesale of other machinery and equipment [18]

3D Systems Europe Limited
Crown Lift Trucks Limited
Fujifilm UK Limited
J & E Hall Limited
ICS Cool Energy Limited
Leica Geosystems Limited
Linde Material Handling (UK) Ltd
Makita (UK) Limited
Mitsubishi Heavy Industries Air-Conditioning Europe, Ltd.
Routeco Limited
Sanden International (Europe) Ltd
Schueco UK Limited
Andreas Stihl Limited
Tanita International Ltd.
Tchibo Coffee International Ltd
Techtronic Industries (UK) Ltd
Winterhalter Ltd
Xtralis (UK) Limited

46711 Wholesale of petroleum and petroleum products

Harvest Energy Limited
Kuwait Petroleum (U.K. Holdings) Ltd
Kuwait Petroleum International Aviation Company (U.K.)
Kuwait Petroleum International Aviation Co
Prax Petroleum Limited

46719 Wholesale of other fuels and related products [11]

Air BP Limited
BNK (UK) Limited
BP International Limited
BP Marine Limited
BP Middle East Limited
BP Oil International Limited
BP Oil Vietnam Limited
Centrica Energy Limited
Corona Gas Management Limited
ExxonMobil Gas Marketing Europe Ltd
Idemitsu International (Europe) Ltd

46720 Wholesale of metals and metal ores

Euro Alloys Limited
Honda Trading Europe Limited
Ocean Partners Holdings Ltd
Ocean Partners UK Limited
TW Metals Limited

46730 Wholesale of wood, construction materials and sanitary equipment

Castacrete Limited
David Cover and Son Limited
Day Group Limited
Decco Limited
James Latham PLC
Lathams Limited
Vink UK Limited
Wurth UK Limited

46740 Wholesale of hardware, plumbing and heating equipment and supplies

Bathroom Brands Holdings UK Ltd
Crosswater Limited
Williams Trade Supplies Ltd
Wurth UK Limited

46750 Wholesale of chemical products

Chemetall Limited
Evonik Goldschmidt UK Limited
GCP RIW Holdings Limited
Gantrade Europe Limited
IMCD UK Limited
Nesstra Services (UK) Limited
Solventis Ltd.

46760 Wholesale of other intermediate products [13]

Batt Cables PLC
Cargill PLC
Denmaur Independent Papers Ltd
Elliott Baxter & Co Ltd
Fujifilm UK Limited
Gould International UK Limited
Gould Publication Papers UK Ltd
Honda Trading Europe Limited
Lakefield Holdings Limited
ProAV Holdings Limited
TLC (Southern) Limited
H Young (Operations) Limited
H Young Holdings PLC

46900 Non-specialised wholesale trade [40]

Amscan International Limited
Anixter Limited
Aquilant Limited
Balton CP Limited
Bandai Namco Holdings UK Ltd
Bard Limited
Beckman Coulter United Kingdom Ltd
Bio-Rad Laboratories Limited
Blue Sky Intermodal (UK) Ltd.
Bosch Automotive Service Solutions Ltd
Bullitt Mobile Limited
CooperVision Manufacturing Ltd
Costco UK Holdings Limited
Costco Wholesale UK Limited
Curtis Holt Limited
European Laminate Glass Ltd
European Toughened Glass (UK) Ltd
GE Medical Systems Limited
GVS Prepaid Limited
Gardners Books Limited
J.P.McDougall & Co.Limited
NBS Trade and Investment Ltd
NSK UK Limited
Norbain Holdings Limited
Officeteam Limited
On Semiconductor Limited
Orthofix Limited
R & M Electrical Group Limited
Samsung C & T U.K. Limited
Specialized (UK) Ltd
Staples UK Limited
Taylor Made Golf Limited
Tchibo Coffee International Ltd
Tyco Building Services Products (UK)
Tyco Fire Products Manufacturing Ltd
UCC Coffee UK Limited
UK Cables Limited
UK Electric Limited
Westcoast Limited
Wilkinson Sword Limited

47110 Retail sale in non-specialised stores with food, beverages or tobacco predominating

Elbrook (Cash & Carry) Limited
George Hammond PLC
Motorway Services Limited
Navy,Army and Air Force Institutes,(The)
Papa John's (GB) Limited
Park Garage Group PLC
Welcome Break Group Limited
Welcome Break Limited

47190 Other retail sale in non-specialised stores

Argos Limited
Avtrade Limited
B & Q PLC
Boing Acquisitions Limited
Boing Midco Limited
W.J.Daniel & Co Ltd
International Car Wash Group Ltd.
Nuance Group (UK) Limited
Smith Bradbeer & Co Ltd

47210 Retail sale of fruit and vegetables in specialised stores

Richard Hochfeld Limited

47220 Retail sale of meat and meat products in specialised stores

Creative Foods Europe Limited

47240 Retail sale of bread, cakes, flour confectionery and sugar confectionery in specialised stores

Brioche Pasquier U.K. Limited
Frimley Topco Limited
Krispy Kreme U.K. Limited

47250 Retail sale of beverages in specialised stores

South Downs Real Estate Ltd
Tropicana United Kingdom Ltd
WDFG UK Holdings Limited
WDFG UK Limited

47260 Retail sale of tobacco products in specialised stores

WDFG UK Holdings Limited
WDFG UK Limited

47290 Other retail sale of food in specialised stores

Cook Trading Limited
Lamberts Healthcare Limited

47300 Retail sale of automotive fuel in specialised stores

Brobot Petroleum Limited
George Hammond PLC
Motorway Services Limited
Welcome Break Group Limited
Welcome Break Limited

47410 Retail sale of computers, peripheral units and software in specialised stores

Phoenix Software Limited

47430 Retail sale of audio and video equipment in specialised stores

Brighthouse Group Limited
Brighthouse Holdings Limited

47540 Retail sale of electrical household appliances in specialised stores

Argos Limited
Brighthouse Group Limited
Brighthouse Holdings Limited
Brighthouse Limited
Caversham Finance Limited
Caversham Trading Limited
Game Retail Limited
Nespresso UK Ltd

47599 Retail of furniture, lighting, and similar (not musical instruments or scores) in specialised store

Argos Limited
B & Q PLC
Brighthouse Limited
Caversham Finance Limited
Caversham Trading Limited
Dreams Limited
Furniture Village Limited
Ikea Limited

47610 Retail sale of books in specialised stores

Gruffalo Bidco Limited
Gruffalo Midco Limited
Gruffalo Topco Limited

47640 Retail sale of sports goods, fishing gear, camping goods, boats and bicycles

Trek Bicycle Corporation Ltd
Wiggle Limited

47650 Retail sale of games and toys in specialised stores

Alex Brands Rocket Holdings Ltd
Entertainer (Amersham) Limited

47710 Retail sale of clothing in specialised stores

ChildrenSalon Limited
Fat Face Limited
Gucci Limited
Ralph Lauren UK Limited
Robinson Webster (Holdings) Ltd
Sabre Retail Fashion Limited
Ann Summers Ltd.
Trek Bicycle Corporation Ltd

47721 Retail sale of footwear in specialised stores

Gucci Limited
Russell & Bromley Limited
Sabre Retail Fashion Limited

47722 Retail sale of leather goods in specialised stores

Sabre Retail Fashion Limited

47730 Dispensing chemist in specialised stores [12]

ABC Drug Stores Limited
AMG Healthcare Limited
Avicenna Holdings Ltd
Canterbury Pharmacies Holdings Ltd
Canterbury Pharmacies Limited
Day Lewis PLC
Jardines (U.K.) Limited
Paydens Group Holdings Limited
Paydens Holdings Limited
Paydens Limited
Superdrug Stores PLC
Waremoss Limited

47749 Retail sale of medical and orthopaedic goods in specialised stores (not incl. hearing aids) n.e.c.

Aquilant Limited
K2M UK Limited
Medequip Assistive Technology Ltd
Medequip Group Limited

47750 Retail sale of cosmetic and toilet articles in specialised stores

Body Shop International Ltd
Coty UK & I Ltd
Liz Earle Beauty Co. Limited
HFC Prestige Products Limited
Superdrug Stores PLC
WDFG UK Holdings Limited
WDFG UK Limited

47760 Retail sale of flowers, plants, seeds, fertilizers, pet animals and pet food in specialised stores

Castacrete Limited
Hillier Nurseries Limited
Longacres Garden Centre Ltd
D.J.Squire & Co.,Limited
Wyevale Garden Centres Limited

47770 Retail sale of watches and jewellery in specialised stores

Fossil (UK) Limited

47782 Retail sale by opticians

Specsavers Optical Superstores Ltd

47789 Other retail sale of new goods in specialised stores (not commercial art galleries and opticians) [16]

B & Q PLC
Blue Diamond UK Limited
Castacrete Limited
Early Learning Centre Limited
T & E Ferris Limited
F.Hinds Limited
International Car Wash Group Financing
Jessops Europe Limited
Mothercare PLC.
Mothercare UK Limited
Sally Salon Services Limited
Stanley Electric (U.K.) Co Ltd
TJX Europe Limited
TJX UK
World Duty Free Limited
Wyevale Garden Centres G & L Ltd

47890 Retail sale via stalls and markets of other goods

Book People Limited

47910 Retail sale via mail order houses or via Internet [10]

B & Q PLC
B & W Group Ltd
Book People Limited
Buyagift PLC
Direct Wines Limited
Esher Mail Order Limited
Ikea Limited
Mothercare UK Limited
Robinson Webster (Holdings) Ltd
Sabre Retail Fashion Limited

47990 Other retail sale not in stores, stalls or markets

Beko PLC
Book People Limited
Rush Hair Group Limited
Selecta Refreshments Limited
WDFG UK Holdings Limited
Woburn Enterprises Limited

49100 Passenger rail transport, interurban

Heathrow Express Operating Co Ltd

49319 Other urban, suburban or metropolitan passenger land transport (not underground, metro or similar)

First Hampshire & Dorset Ltd
London United Busways Limited
Reading Transport Limited

49390 Other passenger land transport

Channel Tunnel Group Limited
Project Tristar Limited

49410 Freight transport by road [21]

A.G. Thames Holdings Limited
DHL Supply Chain Limited
Davison & Co. (Barford) Ltd
Day Group Limited
Europa Road Limited
Exel Overseas Limited
Exel UK Limited
Alan Firmin Limited
Geodis FF United Kingdom Ltd.
Gist Limited
Hireco (TL) Limited
Lenham Storage Co Ltd
Martin-Brower UK Ltd
Movianto UK Limited
PCL Transport 24/7 Limited
SSG Logistic Solutions Limited
Schenker Limited
R.Swain & Sons Limited
Tradeteam Limited
Walon Limited
Wessex Petroleum Limited

49500 Transport via pipeline

BP Gas Marketing Limited
E.S. Pipelines Limited

50100 Sea and coastal passenger water transport [14]

P & O European Ferries (Irish Sea)
P & O Ferries Division Holdings Ltd
P & O Ferries Holdings Limited
P & O Ferries Limited
P & O North Sea Ferries Ltd
P & O Short Sea Ferries Ltd
Preziosa Cruise Limited
RCL (UK) Ltd.
RCL Cruises Ltd
Saga Cruises Limited
Southampton Isle of Wight and South of England Royal Mail Steam Packet Co
Stena Line Irish Sea Ferries Ltd
Stena Line Limited
Stena Line Ports Limited

50200 Sea and coastal freight water transport [13]

Africa Express Line Limited
BP Shipping Limited
Carisbrooke Shipping Holdings Ltd
Carnival PLC
Four Coal Shipping Limited
Geodis FF United Kingdom Ltd.
International Marine Transportation
Pritchard-Gordon Tankers Ltd
Saga Cruises IV Limited
Schenker Limited
Southampton Isle of Wight and South of England Royal Mail Steam Packet Co
Wightlink Limited
Wilhelmsen Lines Car Carriers Ltd.

51101 Scheduled passenger air transport [17]

ASIG Holdings Limited
BA Cityflyer Limited
British Airways Holidays Ltd
British Airways PLC
Eastern Airways (UK) Limited
Heathrow Airport Limited
Humberside International Airport Ltd
KLM Cityhopper UK Limited
LHR Airports Limited
Menzies Aviation (ASIG) Ltd
NATS (En Route) PLC
NATS (Services) Limited
NATS Holdings Limited
NATS Limited
Southampton International Airport
Virgin Atlantic Airways Ltd
Virgin Atlantic International Ltd

51102 Non-scheduled passenger air transport [16]

Air Charter Service Group Ltd
Air Partner PLC
Bristow Aviation Holdings Ltd
Bristow Helicopter Group Ltd
Bristow Helicopters (International)
Bristow Helicopters Limited
British Airways PLC
Chapman Freeborn Airchartering Ltd
DHL Air Limited
DHL Aviation (UK) Limited
Gama Aviation (UK) Limited
Gama Aviation PLC
Humberside International Airport Ltd

Mission Aviation Fellowship International
TAG Aviation (UK) Limited
United Helicopters Limited

51210 Freight air transport

Air Charter Service Group Ltd
Chapman Freeborn Airchartering Ltd
Chapman Freeborn International Ltd
Geodis FF United Kingdom Ltd.
IAG Cargo Limited
Schenker Limited
Volga-Dnepr UK Ltd.

52101 Operation of warehousing and storage facilities for water transport activities

Inter Terminals Limited
Inter Terminals UK Limited
P & O Ferries Pride of Hull Ltd
Panalpina World Transport Ltd
Pourshins Limited

52102 Operation of warehousing and storage facilities for air transport activities

Aerotron Limited
Dnata Limited
Humberside International Airport Ltd
Panalpina World Transport Ltd
Rico Logistics Ltd
Worldwide Flight Services Ltd

52103 Operation of warehousing and storage facilities for land transport activities [18]

Associated Cold Stores & Transport
Europa Road Limited
Exel UK Limited
Hasbro U.K. Limited
Humberside International Airport Ltd
Inter Terminals Immingham Ltd
Inter Terminals Limited
Inter Terminals Seal Sands Ltd
Kuehne + Nagel Drinkflow Logistics
Kuehne + Nagel Drinks Logistics Ltd
W Lamb Limited
Martin-Brower UK Ltd
Procter & Gamble UK Group Holdings
Rico Logistics Ltd
Shurgard UK Limited
Tradeteam Limited
UPS SCS (UK) Limited
Wealmoor Limited

52219 Other service activities incidental to land transportation, n.e.c.

Channel Tunnel Group Limited
Cubic Transportation Systems Ltd
RATP DEV UK Ltd
Readypower Rail Services Finance Ltd
Readypower Rail Services Group Holdings
Readypower Rail Services Group Ltd
Thales Ground Transportation Systems UK

52220 Service activities incidental to water transportation

Canal & River Trust
George Hammond PLC

52230 Service activities incidental to air transportation [18]

Aerotron Limited
Boeing UK Training and Flight Services
Bristow Technical Services Ltd
British Airways Holidays Ltd
British Airways PLC
Dnata Limited
H+S Aviation Limited
Menzies Aviation (UK) Limited
Menzies Aviation Holdings Ltd
Menzies Aviation PLC
Saywell International Limited
TAG Farnborough Airport Ltd
Total Aircraft Product Support (Holdings)
Trenchard Aviation Group Ltd
Trenchard Aviation Holdings 1 Ltd
Trenchard Aviation Holdings Ltd
Trenchard Aviation Limited
A J Walter Aviation Limited

52241 Cargo handling for water transport activities

Panalpina World Transport Ltd

52242 Cargo handling for air transport activities

British Airways PLC
DHL Air Limited
DHL Aviation (UK) Limited
Dnata Limited
IAG Cargo Limited
Panalpina World Transport Ltd
UPS SCS (UK) Limited

52290 Other transportation support activities [27]

3663 Transport Limited
A.N.A. Aviation Group Holdings Ltd
Agility Logistics Limited
Air Partner PLC
Allport Cargo Services Limited
Aquila Air Traffic Management Services
BCA Fleet Solutions Limited
Bollore Logistics UK Ltd
CAE STS Limited
CAE Training & Services UK Ltd
CHEP Pallecon Solutions Ltd
DHL Global Forwarding (UK) Ltd
Expeditors International (UK) Ltd
Gatwick Airport Limited
Geodis FF United Kingdom Ltd.
Jas Forwarding (UK) Limited
Kuehne + Nagel Limited
MIQ Logistics Limited
Nippon Express (U.K.) Limited
Pentagon Freight Services PLC
Schenker Limited
Sealion Shipping Limited
Thales Ground Transportation Systems UK
Trans Global Freight Management Ltd
Trans Ocean Bulk Logistics Ltd
UPS SCS (UK) Limited
WNDirect Limited

53201 Licensed carriers

DHL Parcel UK Limited
DX Network Services Limited
Whistl Group Holdings Limited
Whistl UK Limited

53202 Unlicensed carriers

Citysprint (UK) Limited
DHL Parcel UK Limited
Deltec International Courier Ltd
UPS Limited
Yourway Transport Limited

55100 Hotels and similar accommodation [84]

Ability Hotels (Cambridge) Ltd
Ability Hotels (Dunblane) Ltd
Ability Hotels (Liverpool) Ltd
Ability Hotels (Luton Inn) Ltd
Ability Hotels (Syon Park) Ltd
Adda Hotels
R. J. and D. E. Billings Ltd
Bloc Gatwick Limited
Bloc Hotel Group Limited
CDL Hotels (Chelsea) Limited
CDL Hotels (U.K.) Limited
CP Regents Park Two Limited
CTS Metropark Limited
City Hotel (London) Limited
Corus Hotels Limited
Delaquest Limited
Edwardian Bloomsbury Street Ltd
Edwardian Canary Wharf Hotel Ltd
Edwardian Exclusive Hotels Ltd
Edwardian Free Trade Hall Ltd
Edwardian Grafton Hotel Ltd
Edwardian Hampshire Hotels Ltd
Edwardian International Hotels Ltd
Edwardian Ltd
Edwardian Mercer Street Ltd
Edwardian Pastoria Hotels Ltd
Elite Hotels (Rotherwick) Ltd
Flamepro Limited
GHH Holdings Limited
Grand Central Hotel Glasgow Ltd
Greenclose Holdings Limited
Grove HR Limited
Hand Picked Hotels Limited
Heathrow Edwardian Hotel Ltd
Heythrop Park Limited
Hilton International Hotels (UK) Ltd
Hilton International IP Holding 2
Hilton International IP Holding Ltd
Hilton UK Hotels Limited
Hilton UK Manage Limited
Hilton Worldwide Holding 2 Ltd
Hilton Worldwide Manage Ltd
Historic House Hotels Limited
Home Grown Hotels Limited
Hotel Inter-Continental London Ltd
Hotel Management International Ltd
Intercontinental Hotels Group PLC
Kew Green (LRG1) Limited
Kew Green (LRG2) Limited
Kew Green Group Limited
Kew Green Hotels Limited
Kew Green Intermediate One Ltd
LQAL UK Limited
Leeu London Limited
Lime Wood Group Limited
London Britannia Hotel Limited
London May Fair Hotel Limited
London Tara Hotel Limited
London Vista Hotel Limited
Luton Hoo Park Limited
Manor House Hotel (Castle Combe) Ltd
Melton House Investments Ltd

Metropole Hotels (Holdings) Ltd
Motorway Services Limited
Old Thorns Golf Hotel and Country Estate (Holdings)
Old Thorns Golf Hotel and Country Estate
Old Thorns Luxury Apartments Ltd
Patrolmake Limited
Pennyhill Park Limited
Petersham Hotel Limited
Plaza on Hyde Park Limited
Principal Edinburgh George Street
Principal London Limited
Principal Manchester Limited
RB Hotels Limited
Sentinel Health Care Limited
Shadowgrade Developments Ltd
Shepherd Neame Limited
Stoke Park Limited
Sun Hotel Limited
Vanderbilt Hotels Limited
Welcome Break Group Limited
Welcome Break Limited
Wy (Nutfield Priory) Limited

55201 Holiday centres and villages

Away Resorts Limited
Sandy Balls Estate Limited
Park Holidays UK Limited
Shorefield Holidays Limited

55209 Other holiday and other collective accommodation

Haulfryn Group Limited
Royale Parks Limited

55300 Recreational vehicle parks, trailer parks and camping grounds

Bourne Leisure (Hopton) Ltd
Bourne Leisure Group Limited
Bourne Leisure Holdings Ltd
Bourne Leisure Limited
Butlins Skyline Limited
Haven Leisure Limited
Holly Lodge (Kingswood) Ltd
Rockley Sands (Estates) Ltd
White Horse Caravan Co Ltd

55900 Other accommodation

Ben-Motor and Allied Trades Benevolent Fund
Brighton & Hove Seaside Community Homes
Shadowgrade Developments Ltd
Transform Housing & Support
West London YMCA
Whiteley Homes Trust

56101 Licenced restaurants [25]

Benugo Limited
Blanc Brasseries Limited
Bookcash Trading Limited
Brasserie Bar Co Limited
CH & Co Catering Limited
Domino's Pizza Group PLC
Haulfryn Group Limited
Historic House Hotels Limited
Home Grown Hotels Limited
Kentucky Fried Chicken (Great Britain)
Mondays (Topco) Limited
PHH 1 Limited
PandoraExpress 2 Limited
PandoraExpress 3 Limited
PandoraExpress 4 Limited
Pizza Hut (U.K.) Limited
PizzaExpress (Restaurants) Ltd
PizzaExpress (Wholesale) Ltd
PizzaExpress Limited
PizzaExpress Merchandising Ltd
T.J.D. Trade Limited
Thursdays (UK) Limited
Tuesdays (Midco) Limited
Upham Group Limited
Wednesdays (Bidco) Limited

56102 Unlicenced restaurants and cafes

Benugo Limited
P A Crocker Limited
ISS Facility Services Limited
Motorway Services Limited
Navy,Army and Air Force Institutes,(The)
Pizza Hut (U.K.) Limited
TH UK & Ireland Limited
Welcome Break Group Limited
Welcome Break Limited

56103 Take-away food shops and mobile food stands

Benugo Limited
Hala Limited

56210 Event catering activities

CH & Co Catering Limited
Compass Group Holdings PLC
Compass Group Procurement Ltd
Gate Gourmet London Limited
Heythrop Park Limited
LSG/Sky Chefs Europe Holdings Ltd
Twickenham Experience Ltd

56290 Other food services [11]

Ali UK Limited
Aramark Limited
Baxterstorey Limited
CH & Co Catering Limited
Cater Link Limited
DPSK Limited
Holroyd Howe Limited
ISS Mediclean Limited
Kentucky Fried Chicken (Great Britain)
Nature Delivered Limited
Pourshins Limited

56301 Licenced clubs

Deltic Group Limited

56302 Public houses and bars

J.T.Davies & Sons Limited
Harvey & Son (Lewes) Limited
Heartstone Inns Limited
M.A.T. Davies Holdings Limited
Shepherd Neame Limited
Upham Group Limited
Charles Wells,Limited
J D Wetherspoon PLC

58110 Book publishing

Church Communities UK
Paula Hawkins Limited
Macmillan Publishers International
John Wiley & Sons Limited
Wiley Heyden Limited

58120 Publishing of directories and mailing lists

William Reed Business Media Ltd
Yell Limited

58130 Publishing of newspapers

Newsquest Media Group Limited

58142 Publishing of consumer and business journals and periodicals [11]

Autosport Media UK Ltd
Blackwell Science Limited
East Sussex Press Limited
Haymarket Media Group Ltd.
Macmillan Publishers International
Metropolis Group Holdings Ltd
Metropolis International Group Ltd
Puzzler Media Limited
William Reed Business Media Ltd
John Wiley & Sons Limited
Wiley Heyden Limited

58190 Other publishing activities [11]

Carte Blanche Greetings Ltd
EMAP Publishing Limited
Simon Elvin Limited
GL Assessment Limited
GL Education Group Limited
Hibu Group Limited
Kodak Limited
Panini UK Limited
WWF-UK
Wolters Kluwer Health (Medical Research)
Yell Limited

58210 Publishing of computer games

Puzzler Media Limited
Sega Publishing Europe Limited
Ubisoft Limited

58290 Other software publishing [13]

Amtech Group Limited
Blue Chip Customer Engineering Ltd
Electronic Arts Limited
Filemaker International
Micromuse Limited
New Blue Chip Limited
SAP (UK) Limited
Towers Watson Software Limited
VS International Holdings Ltd
Veeam Software UK Limited
Wolters Kluwer (UK) Limited
Zellis UK Limited
Zenimax Europe Limited

59111 Motion picture production activities

Baltray No. 1 Limited
Creative Video Productions Ltd
Pinewood Group Limited
Pinewood Studios Limited

59113 Television programme production activities

ATP Media Operations Limited
Arqiva Limited
BBC Studioworks Limited
CTV Outside Broadcasts Limited
Sky CP Limited
Sky In-Home Service Limited
Sky UK Limited
Telegenic Limited
Visual Impact (UK) Limited

59120 Motion picture, video and television programme post-production activities

Pinewood-Shepperton Studios Ltd
Shepperton Studios Limited

59131 Motion picture distribution activities

Cine-UK Limited
Cineworld Cinemas Limited

59132 Video distribution activities

Telefonica Digital Limited

59133 Television programme distribution activities

ATP Media Operations Limited
Parthenon Entertainment Ltd

59140 Motion picture projection activities

Picturehouse Cinemas Limited

60100 Radio broadcasting

Services Sound and Vision Corporation

60200 Television programming and broadcasting activities

ATP Media Operations Limited
BBC Studioworks Limited
Gearhouse Broadcast Limited
NEP Visions Limited
Services Sound and Vision Corporation
Sports Information Services (Holdings)
Sports Information Services Ltd

61100 Wired telecommunications activities

ROC Transformation (Corporate) Ltd
ROC Transformation (Holdings) Ltd
Reliance Communications (U.K.) Ltd
Sky Home Communications Ltd
Verizon UK Limited
Viavi Solutions UK Limited

61200 Wireless telecommunications activities [18]

Aeromobile Communications Ltd
Airspan Communications Limited
Blackberry UK Limited
Ericsson (Holdings) Limited
Ericsson Limited
Harris Defence Limited
Hutchison 3G UK Limited
MTWOM B Limited
Mavenir Systems UK Limited
Optiva Solutions (UK) Limited
Radiosite Limited
Reliance Communications (U.K.) Ltd
Sky Home Communications Ltd
Telefonica Digital Limited
Telefonica UK Limited
UK Broadband Limited
Viavi Solutions UK Limited
Wireless Logic Limited

61300 Satellite telecommunications activities

NSSLGlobal Limited
Telefonica Digital Limited

61900 Other telecommunications activities [77]

Apollo Submarine Cable System Ltd
Arqiva Limited
Arqiva No 2 Limited
Arqiva Smart Metering Limited
Arqiva Telecoms Investment Ltd
Arrow Business Communications Group
Arrow Business Communications Holdings
Avaya UK
Cable & Wireless Global Holding Ltd
Cable & Wireless Worldwide Ltd
Cleartone Group Limited
Cloud Networks Limited
Cornerstone Telecommunications Infrastructure
Cyxtera Technology UK Limited
Data Select Limited
Diamond Cable Communications Ltd
Eckoh PLC
Ericsson Television Limited
Giffgaff Limited
Huawei Technologies (UK) Co., Ltd.
Intec Telecom Systems Limited
Logicalis UK Limited
MK International Limited
MMO2 Limited
Mavenir Global Limited
Mobile Broadband Network Ltd
NEOS Networks Limited
NTL Cablecomms Cheshire
NTL Cablecomms East Lancashire
NTL Cablecomms Greater Manchester
NTL Cablecomms Surrey
NTL Cambridge Limited
NTL Kirklees
NTL Midlands Limited
NTL Wirral Telephone and Cable TV Company
NewVoiceMedia Limited
O2 (Europe) Limited
O2 Cedar Limited
O2 Holdings Limited
O2 International Holdings Ltd
O2 Networks Limited
Olive Business Solutions Ltd
Onecom Limited
ROC Transformation (Corporate) Ltd
ROC Transformation (Holdings) Ltd
SITA Advanced Travel Solutions Ltd
Samsung Electronics (UK) Ltd
Sky Home Communications Ltd
Sky UK Limited
Southern Communications Group Ltd
Southern Communications Investments
Spirent Communications PLC
Talkmobile Limited
Telefonica Digital Limited
Telefonica Europe PLC
Telefonica Germany Holdings Ltd
Telefonica UK Limited
Telewest Communications (London South)
Telewest Communications (Midlands and North West)
Teoco UK Limited
Verizon European Holdings Ltd
Viavi Solutions UK Limited
Virgin Media Limited
Virgin Mobile Telecoms Limited
Vodafone Americas 4
Vodafone Enterprise U.K.
Vodafone Europe UK
Vodafone Financial Operations
Vodafone Global Enterprise Ltd
Vodafone Group PLC
Vodafone Group Services Ltd
Vodafone Investment UK
Vodafone Investments Limited
Vodafone Limited
Vodafone Marketing UK
Vodafone Sales & Services Ltd
Windsor Television Limited

62011 Ready-made interactive leisure and entertainment software development

Activision Blizzard UK Ltd
Creative Assembly Limited
Global Draw Limited
Hawk-Eye Innovations Limited

62012 Business and domestic software development [42]

ACI Global Limited
Autodesk Limited
Citrix R & D Limited
Citrix Systems UK Limited
Clinisys Group Limited
Clinisys Solutions Limited
Construction Industry Solutions Ltd
ESRI (UK) Limited
Exela Technologies Limited
Flexera Software Limited
Frontier Software PLC
Grass Valley Limited
Hawk-Eye Innovations Limited
Industrial and Financial Systems, IFS UK
Kerridge Commercial Systems Ltd
Longview Holding Parent UK Ltd
Longview Holding UK 2 Limited
Macro 4 Limited
Mastek (UK) Ltd.
Masternaut Bidco Limited
Masternaut Group Holdings Ltd
Masternaut Holdings Limited
Miles 33 Limited
Open Text UK Limited
Oracle Corporation UK Limited
PB Bidco Limited
PB Holdco Limited
PB Midco Limited
PB Topco Limited
Phoenix Software Limited
Portrait Software Limited
Progress Software Limited
QSC 1208 Limited
QSC 1209 Limited
SAS Software Limited
SDL PLC
SDL Tridion Limited
V1 Limited
Verint WS Holdings Limited
Wolters Kluwer (UK) Limited
Zebra Diamond Holdings Limited
Zebra Technologies Europe Ltd

62020 Information technology consultancy activities [87]

ACI Worldwide (EMEA) Limited
Advanced Business Software and Solutions
Advanced Health and Care Ltd
Advanced Legal Solutions Ltd
Allocate Bidco Limited
Allocate Holdco Limited
Allocate Midco Limited
Allocate Software Limited
Allocate Topco Limited
Amphora Acquisitions Limited
Aptos Solutions UK Limited
Arinso People Services Limited
Aspentech Ltd.
Axon Solutions Limited
BAE Systems Applied Intelligence (International)
BAE Systems Applied Intelligence Ltd
BMC Software Limited
Bytes Technology Group Limited
CSC Computer Sciences Limited
Capgemini UK PLC
CeleritiFinTech Limited
Clinphone Development Limited
Commvault Systems Limited
Computer Associates UK Limited
Construction Industry Solutions Ltd
DST Process Solutions Limited
Dell Corporation Limited
EMC Consulting (UK) Limited
EMC Europe Limited
ESRI (UK) Limited
Ellucian Global Limited
Ensono Limited
Entserv UK Limited
Epicor Software (UK) Limited
Flexera Software Limited
Gemalto UK Limited
HCL Great Britain Limited
Hawk-Eye Innovations Limited
Help/Systems International Ltd
Independent Technology Systems Ltd
Intec Telecom Systems Limited
Intex (Radiographic) Limited
Iris Business Software Limited
Iris Group Limited
Iris Payroll Software Limited
Iris Payroll Solutions Limited
Iris Software Limited
Isoft Group (UK) Limited
JDA Software UK Limited
Kerridge Commercial Systems Ltd
Kofax London Holdings Limited
Kronos Worldwide Limited
Longview Holding Parent UK Ltd
Longview Holding UK 2 Limited
Mavenir Global Limited
Mavenir Systems Limited
Mavenir Systems UK Limited
Micro Focus IP Development Ltd
Microsoft Limited
NHS Shared Business Services Ltd
NPS (UK2) Limited
NPS (UK4) Limited
Net Pay (EUR) Limited
Nice Systems UK Limited
O2 Unify Limited
Open Text UK Limited
Oracle Corporation UK Limited
Organised Computer Systems Ltd
PTP Software Limited
Pegasystems Limited
Perceptive Informatics UK Ltd
Ricardo-AEA Limited
Roke Manor Research Limited
Runtime Collective Limited
SAP (UK) Limited
SAS Software Limited
Scentrics Information Security Technologies
Siemens Industry Software Ltd
Software of Excellence United Kingdom
Softwareone UK Limited
Sopra Steria Limited
Steria UK Corporate Limited
Unit4 Business Software Ltd
Verint Systems UK Limited
Veritas Technologies (UK) Ltd
Vestas Technology UK Limited
Xchanging Global Insurance Solutions

62030 Computer facilities management activities [14]

Allegis Global Solutions Ltd
Allegis Group (UK) Holdings II Ltd
Allegis Group (UK) Holdings Ltd
Allegis Group Limited
Amphora Acquisitions Limited
Construction Industry Solutions Ltd
Ellucian Global Limited
Ensono Limited
Johnson Controls Systems Development
Kerridge Commercial Systems Ltd
Longview Holding Parent UK Ltd
NetApp UK Ltd
Oracle Corporation UK Limited
Organised Computer Systems Ltd

62090 Other information technology service activities [138]

Advanced 365 Limited
Agfa Healthcare UK Limited
Alliance Healthcare (IT Services)
Amphora Acquisitions Limited
Annodata Limited
Apogee Corporation Limited
Argon NPS Limited
Arinso People Services Limited
Arinso UK Limited
Arqiva Limited
Aspentech Ltd.
Audatex (UK) Limited
Aurasma Limited
Automatic Data Processing Ltd
Autonomy Systems Limited
Axial Systems Ltd.
Bell Microsystems Limited
Boston Limited
Bytes Software Services Ltd
CAE Technology Services Ltd
CDK Global (UK) Limited
CDK Global Holdings (UK) Ltd
CSB Holdings Limited
CSC Computer Sciences International
CSC Computer Sciences Limited
Citrix R & D Limited
Citrix Systems UK Limited
Clearswift Holding Limited
Clearswift Limited
Cogeco Peer 1 (UK) Ltd.
Computer Software Group Ltd
Construction Industry Solutions Ltd
D4T4 Solutions PLC
DST Process Solutions Limited
Diebold Nixdorf (UK) Limited
Dimension Data Network Services Ltd
Dynatrace Limited
EMC Computer Systems (U.K.) Ltd
Ellucian Global Limited
Endace Europe Limited
Enghouse Holdings (UK) Limited
Ensono Limited
Entco Situla Holding Ltd
Enterprise Services Information Security UK
Experis Group Limited
Explorer Holdings UK Limited
F5 Networks Limited
GD UK Holdings, Ltd
GXS Limited
Genesys Telecommunications Laboratories - Europe
HTEC Limited
Hewlett - Packard Limited
Hewlett-Packard CDS Limited
Hitachi Vantara Limited
IMBOLC Limited
Idox Software Ltd
Imagination Technologies Ltd
Innovation Group (EMEA) Ltd
Interdist Alliances Limited
Invesco Software Holdings Ltd
Iris Payroll Solutions Limited
Isoft Group (UK) Limited
Juniper Networks (UK) Limited
Kofax Holdings International Ltd
Lenovo Global Technology UK Ltd
LexisNexis Risk Solutions UK Ltd
Longsand Limited
Longview Holding Parent UK Ltd
Longview Holding UK 2 Limited
MessageLabs Group Limited
MessageLabs Limited
Micro Focus (US) Holdings
Micro Focus CHC Limited
Micro Focus Group Limited
Micro Focus International PLC
Micro Focus Limited
Micro Focus MHC Limited
Micro Focus Midco Limited
NPS (Holdings) Limited
NPS (UK5) Limited
NTT Security (UK) Limited
NetApp UK Ltd
Next Generation Data Infrastructure 1
Next Generation Data Infrastructure 2
Next Generation Data Ltd
Northgate Public Services Ltd
Novell UK Software Limited
O2 Unify Limited
Onyx Information Technology Holdings
Open Text UK Limited
Oracle Corporation UK Holdings Ltd
Organised Computer Systems Ltd
Phoenix Software Limited
Promon-Logicalis Latin America Ltd
Pulsant Acquisitions Limited
Pulsant Bidco Limited
QlikTech UK Limited
Reed Business Information Ltd
Rightmove Group Limited
Rightmove PLC
Rolta UK Limited
SDH Bidco Limited
SDH Holdco Limited
Safenet UK Limited

Scentrics Information Security Technologies
Secureworks Europe Limited
Serena Holdings
Serena Software Europe Limited
Siemens Industry Software Computational Dynamics
Snap-On Business Solutions Ltd
Softcat PLC
Software of Excellence UK Holdings
Sopheon PLC
Sopra Steria Services Limited
Sourcecode UK Limited
Staten Investments Limited
Sungard Availability Services (UK)
Sword Soft Limited
Symantec (UK) Holding Limited
Synamedia Limited
System C Healthcare Limited
TP-Link UK Limited
Tech Data as UK Limited
Toshiba Global Commerce Solutions (U.K.)
Ultima Business Solutions Ltd.
Unit4 Business Software Ltd
Verifone (U.K.) Limited
Verint Systems UK Limited
Verint Technology UK Limited
Verint WS Holdings Limited
Verizon International Limited
Wasp Management Software Ltd
Websense SC Holdings Limited
Websense SC Operations Limited
Whistler Acquisitions Limited
Ww.co.uk Online Limited
Xchanging Limited
Xerox (UK) Limited

63110 Data processing, hosting and related activities [25]

123-Reg Limited
Amphora Acquisitions Limited
Bottomline Technologies Ltd
Chatham Street Technologies Ltd
Clinphone Limited
Ensono Limited
Flexera Software Limited
Gartner U.K. Limited
Gyron Internet Limited
HCL Great Britain Limited
Heart Internet Limited
Incomm Europe Limited
MTI Technology Group Limited
Malta Topco Limited
Moorepay Limited
Oracle Corporation UK Limited
Perceptive Eclinical Limited
Rackspace Limited
Ricardo-AEA Limited
Roke Manor Research Limited
Rolta UK Limited
Samsung SDS Europe Limited
Sky IQ Limited
Snap-On Business Solutions Ltd
Zellis UK Limited

63120 Web portals

Rightmove Group Limited
Rightmove PLC

63990 Other information service activities n.e.c. [14]

Arris Solutions UK Ltd.
CEB Global Limited
Emperor 2 Limited
Emperor 3 Limited
ILI Limited
Imagination Technologies Group Ltd
Informatica Software Limited
MTI Technology Group Limited
Malta Topco Limited
Micro Focus (IP) Ltd
SITA Advanced Travel Solutions Ltd
SITA Information Networking Computing UK
Sky SNI Limited
Stats UK Holdco Limited

64191 Banks [12]

CAF Bank Limited
Cape Claims Services Limited
Counties Home Loan Management Ltd
First Rate Exchange Services Holdings
First Rate Exchange Services Ltd
Guernsey Home Loans Limited
Healthcare Support (North Staffs) Finance
Honeywell Europe Finance Ltd
Onesavings Bank PLC
Vodafone (New Zealand) Hedging Ltd
Vodafone Finance Limited
Vodafone Overseas Finance Ltd

64201 Activities of agricultural holding companies

Borelli Tea Holdings Limited
Crop Demetra Limited

64202 Activities of production holding companies [27]

ADM Pura Limited
Aliaxis Holdings UK Limited
Amber Solar Parks (Holdings) Ltd
Aqualisa Holdings (International)
Aqualisa Holdings Limited
B & W Acquisition Ltd
Beardow Adams Holdings Ltd
Bowers & Wilkins Holding Ltd
Braeforge Investment Limited
Fujifilm Ink Solutions Limited
GDC Holding Limited
John Guest Holdings Limited
John Guest International Ltd
HRT UK Limited
Jain International Foods Ltd
Mitac Technology UK Ltd.
Natures Way Foods Europe Ltd
Pandrol Finance Limited
Pandrol Group Limited
Pandrol Holdings Limited
Pandrol International Limited
People Against Dirty Holdings Ltd
S A Printing Group Limited
SESW Holding Co Ltd.
Suntory UK Holdings Limited
Tamar Energy Operating Company (One)
Tesla Limited

64203 Activities of construction holding companies [30]

ABL Capital Investments Ltd
BAM Construct UK Limited
BAM Group (UK) Limited
Birchwood Omnia Limited
Brookworth Group Limited
Civil and Marine (Holdings) Ltd
Clancy Group PLC
Coinford Holdings Limited
Country Estates Holdings Ltd
Deneep Limited
Hanson Limited
Hanson Quarry Products Europe Ltd
P.C. Harrington Holdings Ltd
JRL Group Holdings Limited
JRL Group Limited
Kellogg Brown & Root (Services) Ltd
Kellogg Brown & Root Group Ltd
Kellogg Brown & Root Holdings (U.K.)
Kellogg Brown & Root Holdings Ltd
Kellogg Brown & Root International Group
Keltbray Group Limited
Kent EHFA Holdco Limited
Kone PLC
Peterborough (Progress Health) Holdings
Peterborough (Progress Health) Nominee
S D C (Holdings) Limited
Selwood Holdings Limited
Transform Schools (Birmingham) Holdings
Transform Schools (Stoke) Holdings
Wates Group Limited

64204 Activities of distribution holding companies [10]

B & W Acquisition Ltd
BRF Invicta Limited
Bowers & Wilkins Holding Ltd
Braeforge Investment Limited
Citysprint (UK) Bidco Limited
Citysprint (UK) Holdings Ltd
Citysprint (UK) Midco Limited
Courier and Passenger Transport Holdings
Tax Systems PLC
ViiV Healthcare Overseas Ltd

64205 Activities of financial services holding companies [101]

Abbott (UK) Finance Limited
Ageas (UK) Limited
Aldermore Group PLC
Ardonagh Finco PLC
Argos Business Solutions Ltd
Ashcourt Holdings Limited
Ashcourt Rowan Limited
Blue Auto Finance Limited
Blue Auto Holdings Limited
Bottomline Technologies Europe Ltd
CDB (U.K.) Limited
Cabot Credit Management Ltd
Cabot Financial Debt Recovery Services
Cabot Financial Limited
Carat UK Midco Limited
Coats Group Finance Co Ltd
Coventry and Rugby Hospital Company (Holdings)
Economydrive Cars Limited
Equiniti Financial Services Ltd
Everyday Lending Limited
Franklin UK Bidco Limited
Franklin UK Midco Limited

Friends Life FPG Limited
Friends Life FPL Limited
Friends Life Holdings PLC
Geo Specialty Group Holdings Ltd
Glasgow Square Limited
Globe Insurance Co Ltd
H & T Group PLC
Hamsard 3414 Limited
Harwood Wealth Management Group PLC
Howard Lloyd & Co Ltd
IBM United Kingdom Financial Services
IHS Markit Global Funding Ltd
IHS Markit Global Limited
International Property Finance (Spain)
Invesco Pacific Group Limited
Invesco UK Limited
Just Retirement Group Holdings Ltd
Keystone Holdco Limited
Marlin Financial Group Limited
Marlin Financial Intermediate II Ltd
Marlin Intermediate Holdings PLC
Marlin Midway Limited
Marlin Portfolio Holdings Ltd
Marlin Senior Holdings Limited
Maxxia (UK) Limited
Northview Group Limited
Onix Investments UK Ltd
PEAC Holdings (UK) Limited
Premier Asset Management Ltd
RB Mexico Investments Limited
RB Reigate (UK) Limited
Reckitt & Colman (UK) Limited
Reckitt & Colman Holdings Ltd
Reckitt & Sons Limited
Reckitt Benckiser (USA) Ltd
Reckitt Benckiser Finance (2005) Ltd
Reckitt Benckiser Finance (2010) Ltd
Reckitt Benckiser Finance Co Ltd
Reckitt Benckiser Holdings (Overseas)
Reckitt Benckiser Investments Ltd
Reckitt Benckiser Luxembourg (2010)
Reckitt Benckiser Luxembourg (No. 1)
Reckitt Benckiser Luxembourg (No.2)
Reckitt Benckiser Luxembourg (No.3)
Reckitt Benckiser Luxembourg (No.4)
Reckitt Benckiser Treasury (2007)
Reckitt Benckiser Treasury Services PLC
Reckitt Benckiser USA Finance (No.1)
Reckitt Benckiser USA Finance (No.2)
Reckitt Benckiser USA Finance (No.3)
Reckitt Colman Chiswick (OTC) Ltd
Record PLC
Regulus Bidco Limited
Royal Insurance Holdings Ltd
Royal International Insurance Holdings
SSL International PLC
Sabre Insurance Group PLC
Siemens Financial Services Holdings
Sonet Investments Limited
Suffolk Finance Co Ltd
Sun Alliance Insurance Overseas Ltd
Sun Alliance and London Insurance
Sunny Bidco Limited
Sunny Midco Limited
Sunny Topco Limited
TBC Bank Group PLC
TWG Europe Limited
Towergate Insurance Limited
Towry Holdings Limited
Unum European Holding Co Ltd
WL One Bidco Limited
WL One Holdco Limited
WL One Midco 1 Limited
WL One Midco 2 Limited
Wescot Acquisitions Limited
Wescot Topco Limited
Xafinity Consulting (Reading) Ltd
Yourcash Europe Limited
Yourcash Solutions Limited

64209 Activities of other holding companies n.e.c. [527]

3M Asia Pacific UK Holding Ltd
3M Products Limited
3M UK Holdings Limited
3T Bros Limited
8x8 UK Investments Limited
A6 Audio Bidco Limited
AA PLC
AB InBev Harmony Limited
ANSYS UK Limited
ARRK Product Development Group Ltd
ATP Media Holdings Limited
AbbVie Investments Limited
Abbott (UK) Holdings Limited
Abbott Asia Holdings Limited
Abbott Asia Investments Ltd
Abbott Capital India Limited
Abbott Equity Holdings Unlimited
Ability Hotels (Cambridge) Ltd
Ability Hotels (Dunblane) Ltd
Ability Hotels (III) Finance Ltd
Ability Hotels (III) Group Ltd
Ability Hotels (III) UK Ltd
Ability Hotels (IV) Finance Ltd
Ability Hotels (Luton) Limited
Adare International Holdings Ltd
Adelie Foods Group Limited
Aibel Finance Limited
Aibel Group Limited
Air Bidco Limited
Albain Bidco UK Limited
Altair Filter Technology Ltd
Alvis Limited
Anno 2017 Joint Holding (UK) Ltd
Apogee Group Limited
Appia Europe Limited
Appleby Group Limited
April Bidco Limited
April Midco Limited
April Topco Limited
Arora Hotels Limited
Ascension Healthcare PLC
Asteral Holdings Limited
Audio UK 2 Limited
Audio UK 3 Limited
Audiotonix Group Limited
Audley Group Limited
Augustus 1 Limited
Augustus 2 Limited
Autodesk UK Holdings Limited
Aventis Pharma Holdings Ltd
Axiom Education (Edinburgh) Holdings
Axiom Education (Perth & Kinross) Holdings
Axios Bidco Limited
B & P Acquisitionco Limited
B & P Holdings II Limited
B & P Midco Limited
BAE Systems (Holdings) Limited
BAE Systems (MEH) Limited
BAE Systems Land Systems (Finance)
BAE Systems Marine (Holdings) Ltd
BAE Systems Surface Ships (Holdings)
BFIM Limited
BL Bottling Holdings UK Ltd
BP Mauritania Investments Ltd
Bandt Holdings Limited
Bathroom Brands Group Limited
Bathroom Brands Limited
Beam Suntory UK Holdings Ltd
Beazer Limited
Beck & Pollitzer Holdings Ltd
Berendsen Limited
Bidvest Group (UK) Limited
Bidvest Services Group (UK) Ltd
Biffa PLC
Binder Holdco Limited
Bio Energy (UK) Limited
Blackstown Holdings Limited
Bottling Holdings Europe Ltd
Brambles Holdings Unlimited
Brambles Investment Ltd.
Brambles U.K. Limited
CAS Aspirations Properties Ltd
CCEP Holdings UK Limited
CEB Global Holdings Limited
CHB P H R Limited
CPL Bidco Limited
CPL Topco Limited
CSC Computer Sciences International Holdings
CSC Computer Sciences International Operations
CSC Computer Sciences International Services
CSC Computer Sciences UK Holdings
Cash Processing Solutions Ltd
Castle Cement Limited
Cauta Capital Limited
Central Nottinghamshire Hospitals (Holdings)
Centrica Lake Limited
Chemigraphic Mid-Co Limited
Chromium Acquisitions Limited
Cineworld Group PLC
Cirrus Logic UK International Holding Co
Citrix Global Holdings UK Ltd
Civil and Marine Limited
Club Company (Group) Limited
Coast2coast Technologies Ltd
Cognita BondCo Parent Limited
Cognita Financing PLC
Cognita Funding 1 Limited
Cognita Holdings Limited
Cognita International Holdings Ltd
Cognita Limited
Cognita Midco Limited
Cognita UK Brazil Holdings Ltd
Cognita UK Holdings Limited
Colorcon European Holdings (No.5)
Compatriot Holdings Limited
Connacht SPV 1 Limited
Connacht SPV 2 Limited
Connacht SPV 3 Limited
Console Midco Limited
CooperSurgical Holdings Ltd
Copart Europe Limited
Coty Brands Group Limited
Cramlington Renewable Energy Developments Hold Co
Crescent Pharmaceuticals Ltd
Cross Stone Properties Limited
Croudace Investment Group Ltd
Croudace Trading Group Limited
Cucina French Holdings Limited
DLR (No.1) Limited
DLR (No.2) Limited

DX (VCP) Limited
De La Rue Holdings Limited
De La Rue Investments Limited
Deltic Group Holdings Limited
Detica Group Limited
Dimension Data Holdings PLC
Donamount Limited
Dreams Topco Limited
Drew Marine UK Holdings Ltd
Dynamic Procurement Holdings Ltd
EDL Holdings (UK) Limited
ESPUG Finance Limited
East Surrey Holdings Limited
Edge UK Holdings Limited
Edwardian Exclusive Ltd
Edwardian Finance Ltd
Edwardian Group Limited
Edwardian Hotel Finance Ltd
Edwardian Hotel Investments Ltd
Edwardian Investments Ltd
Edwardian New Finance Limited
Ellenbrook Holdings Limited
Endeavour SCH Holdings Limited
Environments for Learning Sandwell PFI Holdco One
Equiniti Services Limited
FMP Global Bidco Limited
FMP Global Holdings Limited
FRC Star Group Bidco Limited
FRC Star Group Holdings Ltd
FTR Holdings Ltd
Fast Holdings Limited
Fasttrax Holdings Limited
Ferholding UK Ltd
Firebolt RB Holdings Limited
Flexera Software Holdings Ltd
Flight Centre Travel Group (European Holdings)
Fourfront Holdings Limited
GCH Corporation Limited
GH Equity UK Limited
GR Bottling Holdings UK Ltd
Galaxy Group Bidco Limited
Game Digital Holdings Limited
Garrett Thermal Systems UK Ltd
Gate Gourmet Holdings U.K. Ltd
Gattaca PLC
General Cable Programming Ltd
Genesis Specialist Care UK Ltd
Genesis Specialist Care UK No 2 Ltd
Geting Capital Limited
GlaxoSmithKline Consumer Healthcare (Overseas)
GlaxoSmithKline Consumer Healthcare (UK) IP
GlaxoSmithKline Intellectual Property (No.2)
GlaxoSmithKline Intellectual Property Development
GlaxoSmithKline Intellectual Property Holdings
GlaxoSmithKline Intellectual Property
Graduation Holdco Limited
Graduation Midco Limited
Graduation Topco Limited
Granitte Investments (UK) Ltd
Green Flag Holdings Limited
Grouse Bidco Limited
Grouse Midco Limited
Grouse Topco Limited
Gym Group Midco1 Limited
Gym Group Midco2 Limited
Gym Group PLC
HFG Finance Limited
HFG Investments Limited
HH Global Group Limited
HH Global Limited
Hanson (ER - No 5) Limited
Hanson (SH) Limited
Hanson Aggregates Marine Ltd
Hanson Building Materials Ltd
Hanson Finance (2003) Limited
Hanson Finance Limited
Hanson Holdings (1) Limited
Hanson Holdings Limited
Hanson Marine Limited
Hanson Overseas Holdings Ltd
Hanson Packed Products Limited
Hanson Quarry Products Ventures Ltd
Hanson Retail Limited
Hargreaves Property Holdings Ltd
Harlequin FC Holdings Limited
HeidelbergCement Canada Holding Ltd
HeidelbergCement UK Holding II Ltd
HeidelbergCement UK Holding Ltd
Hephaestus II Limited
Heronswood Holdings Limited
Honeywell Acquisitions II Ltd
Honeywell Acquisitions Limited
Honeywell Group Holding UK
Honeywell Group Holding UK II
Honeywell Group Ltd
Honeywell Holdings Limited
Honeywell International UK Ltd
Honeywell Limited
Honeywell North Atlantic Holdings
Honeywell Safety Products International Ltd.
Honeywell Specialty Wax & Additives
Hoover Ferguson Group Holdings Ltd
Hoover Ferguson Group Limited
Horsted Estates Limited
Houserate Limited
How Group Limited
Howitzer Acquisition Limited
Huhtamaki Finance Limited
Huhtamaki Limited
Howard Humphreys & Partners Ltd
Hutchison 3G UK Holdings Ltd
ICS Group Holdings Limited
IQVIA Ies European Holdings
IQVIA RDS UK Holdings Ltd.
ITW Holdings I Limited
ITW Holdings II Limited
ITW Holdings III Limited
ITW Holdings IV Limited
ITW Holdings V Limited
ITW Holdings VI Limited
ITW Holdings VII Limited
Ichnaea UK Bidco Limited
Ichnaea UK Holdings Limited
Ichnaea UK Limited
Idox PLC
Incomm Europe Limited
Innisfree Schools (F2C) Ltd
Innisfree Schools (Secondary) Ltd
Innovation Group Limited
Intelliflo Bidco Limited
Intelliflo Holdings 2013 Ltd
Intelliflo Intermediate Holdings Ltd
Intelliflo Midco Limited
Interserve Developments No.2 Ltd
Interserve Engineering Limited
Interserve Finance (Switzerland) Holdings
Interserve Group Holdings Ltd
Interserve Investments Limited
Interserve PFI Holdings 2014 Ltd
Interserve PFI Holdings Ltd
Interserve PLC
Interserve Service Futures Ltd
Intrum UK Holdings Limited
Invesco International Holdings Ltd
Invesco UK Holdings Limited
J C C Lighting Holdings Ltd
JRL Property Holdings Limited
Johnson Controls China Holding (UK)
Johnson Controls China Investment (UK)
Jupiter Midco 1 Limited
Jupiter Midco 2 Limited
KBR (U.K.) Investments Limited
Kedleston Wings Holdco Ltd
Kellogg Brown & Root DH Ltd
Kellogg Brown & Root Group Ltd
Kellogg Brown & Root Holdings (U.K.)
Kellogg Brown & Root Holdings Ltd
Kellogg Brown & Root International Group
Kellogg Brown & Root London Ltd
Kentucky Fried Chicken (Great Britain)
Kerridge Commercial Systems (Bidco)
Kerridge Commercial Systems (Midco)
Kerridge Commercial Systems Group
Kimberly-Clark Finance Limited
Koala Bidco Limited
Kodak Alaris Holdings Limited
Krispy Kreme Holding UK Ltd
Lehigh UK Limited
Leo Energy Limited
Linden Germany A Limited
Linden Germany B Limited
Logoplaste UK Parent Limited
London Arena Investments Ltd
London International Group Ltd
Lunar 101 Limited
Lutob Investment Ltd
M & C Hotels Holdings Limited
M New Holdings Limited
MB Group Limited
MF UK FC Limited
MNA Finance Limited
MSK Holdings Limited
Mallinckrodt Enterprises UK Ltd
Manzana Bidco Limited
Matchtech Group (Holdings) Ltd
Sir Robert McAlpine Enterprises Ltd
Sir Robert McAlpine Road Holdings
McCormick Europe Limited
McCormick International Holdings
McCormick Kutas Food Service Ltd
McGraw-Hill Global Education UK Holdco II
McGraw-Hill Global Education UK Holdco
McLaren Group Limited
McLaren Services Limited
Mentmore Limited
Merck Holding Ltd.
Meritas Group Holdings Limited
Meritas Group Limited
Merkur Casino UK Ltd
Mizzen Mezzco 2 Limited
Mizzen Mezzco Limited
Moat Homes Finance PLC
Mondays (Topco) Limited
Morgan Europe Holding Limited
Mushi UK Holdings Limited
Mustard Global Limited
ND1T Limited
ND2F Limited
ND3M Limited
NEP UK Film I Limited

NEP UK Film II Limited
NTL Cablecomms Holdings No.1 Ltd
NTL Manchester Cablevision Holding Company
Napsbury Limited
Navitas Life Sciences Holdings Ltd
Neilson Active Holidays (Holdings)
Nestle Holdings (U.K.) PLC
New Terex Holdings UK Limited
Nextpharma UK Topco Limited
Novar Europe Limited
OTV Birwelco Limited
Oceanic Finance Limited
Onix Investments UK Ltd
Optionis Limited
Optum UK Solutions Group Ltd
Oracle Corporation UK Holdings Ltd
Osborne Group Holdings Ltd
Oxford International Education 1 Ltd
Oxford International Education 2 Ltd
Oxford International Education 3 Ltd
PKA WLWF Holding (UK) Limited
PT UK Holding Limited
Partridge of Hampshire Holdings Ltd
Pentagon Holdings Limited
Perkinelmer Life Sciences International Holdings
Perpetual Limited
Pioneer Concrete Holdings Ltd
Pioneer International Group Holdings
PizzaExpress International Holdings
Platinum Newco II Limited
Portals Group Limited
Powerscreen International Ltd
Praesepe Holdings Limited
Premier Fleet Management and Contract Hire
Premier Medical Holdings Ltd
Project Farm Bidco Limited
Project Farm Topco Limited
Project Ventures Rail Investments I
Pulsant Group Holdings Limited
RAK Petroleum PLC
RB Holdings (Nottingham) Ltd
RBMR Topco Limited
RMS Holdco Limited
RPR (US) Limited
RWS (Overseas) Limited
RWS Holdings PLC
Radlett Limited
Rebus Group Limited
Reckitt Benckiser (Grosvenor) Holdings
Reckitt Benckiser Holdings (Luxembourg)
Reckitt Benckiser Holdings (TFFC)
Reckitt Benckiser Holdings (USA) Ltd
Reckitt Benckiser PLC
Regulus Midco Limited
Regulus Topco Limited
Reilly JDM Holdings Limited
Restaurant Holdings Limited
Rhone-Poulenc Rorer Limited
Ridge Hill Trading Limited
Royalton Group Holdings Ltd
Safestore Investments Limited
Sally UK Holdings Limited
Sanofi Pasteur Holding Limited
Sanofi-Aventis UK Holdings Ltd
Sanofi-Synthelabo UK Limited
Scancem Recovery Limited
Henry Schein UK Finance Ltd
Scholl Limited
Sea Corner Group Limited
Shapedirect Limited
Shukco 327 Ltd
Sirigen II Limited
Snell Corporation Limited
Solarsoft Acquisition Limited
Sonepar UK Limited
Sonet Scholl Overseas Investments
Specsavers UK Holdings Limited
Steris CH Limited
Steris UK Holding Limited
Stiefel Consumer Healthcare (UK) Ltd
Stock Spirits (UK) Limited
Stockford Limited
Storm UK Holdco Limited
Subsea 7 Interim UK Holdings Ltd
Subsea 7 Senior Holdings (UK) Ltd
Suez Recycling and Recovery North East
Sugarich Limited
TCFG Holdings Limited
TF1 Limited
TIG Acquisition Holdings
TJX Germany Ltd.
TSG Holdings (UK) Limited
TTNG Investments Limited
Tata Global Beverages Capital Ltd
Tata Global Beverages Holdings Ltd
Tata Global Beverages Investments
Tata Global Beverages Overseas Holdings
Tates of Sussex Limited
Tato Holdings Limited
Tax Systems Holdings Limited
Tech Data Holding Limited
Tech Data UK Finance Limited
Tech Data UK Finance Partner Ltd
Tech Data UK Resources Limited
Tensator Holdings Ltd
Thales Electronics Limited
Thales Holdings UK PLC
Thames Water Utilities Holdings Ltd
Therakos (UK), Ltd
Tiger Midco 1 Limited
Tiger Midco 2 Limited
Tiger Topco 1 Limited
Tiger Topco Limited
Tillotson Commercial Motors Ltd
Tindle Newspapers Limited
Tindle Press Holdings Limited
Toucan Gen Co Limited
Toucan Solar Assets 1 Holdco Ltd
Toucan Solar Assets 2 Holdco Ltd
Tradebe Environmental Services Ltd
Trafalgar Entertainment Group Ltd
Trafficinvest Limited
Transaction Services Group Ltd
Transform Schools (Birmingham) Holdings
Transform Schools (Knowsley) Holdings
Transform Schools (Stoke) Holdings
Travel Up Group PLC
Travelport Global Limited
Travelport Group Investments Ltd
Travelport Holdings (UK) Ltd
Travelport International Operations
Travelport Operations Limited
Travelport Travel Commerce Platform
Trellis Acquisitions Limited
Trellis Finance Limited
Trellis Holdco Limited
Trellis Investments Limited
Tritoria UK Ltd
Tudor Holdings (UK) Limited
Tuesdays (Midco) Limited
UK Highways A55 (Holdings) Ltd
UK Software Holdings Limited
UOP International Holdings Ltd
Ultra-Centrifuge Nederland Ltd
Uranit UK Limited
Utilita Group Limited
VM Transfers (No 5) Limited
VS Alliance Limited
Venture Life Group PLC
Verint Technology UK Limited
Verint WS Holdings Limited
Vernon Wholesale Investments Co Ltd
ViiV Healthcare UK (No.3) Ltd
Virgin Media Investment Holdings Ltd
Vivid Topco Ltd
Vodafone Panafon UK
WCR Group Limited
WIH UK Limited
WJH Holdings Limited
WSH Events Limited
WSH Hospitality Limited
WSH International Investments Ltd
WSH UK & Ireland Limited
Wartsila Voyage Holding Ltd
Wednesdays (Bidco) Limited
Welcome Break Holdings (1) Ltd
Welcome Break Holdings Limited
Welcome Break No. 1 Limited
Welcome Break No. 2 Limited
West London Energy Recovery Holdings Ltd
West's Group International Ltd
Westbury Street Holdings Ltd
Westbury Street Limited
Westfalia Fruit International Ltd
Williams Trade Supplies Holdings Ltd
Wolters Kluwer Holdings (UK) PLC
Wyevale Garden Centres Acquisitions
Wyevale Garden Centres Capital Ltd
XPS Pensions Group PLC
Xerox UK Holdings Limited
Yattendon Group PLC
Yum! Restaurant Holdings
Zipcar International Finance Co Ltd
Zoom Gas Pipelines Limited
Zoom Holding Limited
Zoom Infrastructure Limited
Zurich Holdings (UK) Limited

64301 Activities of investment trusts [11]

Fidelity Asian Values PLC
Fidelity China Special Situations PLC
Fidelity European Values PLC
Fidelity Japan Trust PLC
Fidelity Special Values PLC
Invesco Income Growth Trust PLC
Invesco Perpetual Select Trust PLC
Keystone Investment Trust PLC
Mermaid UK Holdco Limited
Perpetual Income and Growth Investment Trust
Premier Global Infrastructure Trust PLC

64303 Activities of venture and development capital companies

Anglo Suisse Investments Ltd
B & P Buyco Limited
B & P Midco 1 Limited
B & P Midco 2 Limited
Beck & Pollitzer Limited
Cauta Capital Limited
Flexibon Limited

64304 Activities of open-ended investment companies

Grigg Investments Limited
IHS Global Investments Limited
Sauvello Limited
Walnut Investments Limited

64306 Activities of real estate investment trusts

.Big Yellow Self Storage Co Ltd
Last Mile Co Ltd

64910 Financial leasing [44]

Alphabet (GB) Limited
BNP Paribas Lease Group PLC
BNP Paribas Leasing Solutions Ltd
BP Car Fleet Limited
Brighthouse Group Limited
Brighthouse Holdings Limited
Brighthouse Limited
British Airways 777 Leasing Ltd
CF Corporate Finance Limited
CHG-Meridian Computer Leasing UK Ltd
CHG-Meridian UK Limited
Caversham Finance Limited
Claas Financial Services Ltd
Cross London Trains Finance Co Ltd
Cross London Trains Holdco 2 Ltd
Cross London Trains Holdco Ltd
Cross London Trains Limited
De Lage Landen Leasing Limited
Deutsche Leasing (UK) Limited
FCA Automotive Services UK Ltd
FCA Dealer Services UK Ltd
Fortis Lease UK Ltd
Grafton UK Leasing Co Ltd
Grenke Leasing Limited
Hitachi Capital (UK) PLC
Hyundai Capital UK Limited
Investec Asset Finance PLC
Jungheinrich Financial Services Ltd
Jungheinrich Lift Truck Finance Ltd
Key Equipment Finance Europe Ltd
Kion Financial Services Ltd
Maxxia Finance Limited
Moneybarn No.1 Limited
Moss Electrical Holdings Ltd
PEAC (UK) Limited
PSA Finance UK Limited
Porsche Financial Services Great Britain
Quantum Funding Limited
Rank Group Finance PLC
SG Equipment Finance (December) Ltd
Santander Consumer (UK) PLC
Siemens Financial Services Ltd
Societe Generale Equipment Finance
Venson Automotive Solutions Ltd

64921 Credit granting by non-deposit taking finance houses and other specialist consumer credit grantors [22]

Alphabet (GB) Limited
BMW Financial Services (GB) Ltd
Bamboo Topco Limited
Car Finance Company (2007) Ltd
Counties Home Loan Management Ltd
Croudace Finance Limited
FCA Automotive Services UK Ltd
Hitachi Capital (UK) PLC
Home Retail Group Card Services Ltd
Hyundai Capital UK Limited
Leumi ABL Limited
Marlin Capital Europe Limited
Mondi Finance PLC
Moneybarn No.1 Limited
PEAC (UK) Limited
PNC Financial Services UK Ltd
PSA Finance UK Limited
Porsche Financial Services Great Britain
Premium Credit Limited
RCI Financial Services Limited
Santander Consumer (UK) PLC
Sovereign Advances Limited

64922 Activities of mortgage finance companies

Capital Home Loans Limited
Counties Home Loan Management Ltd
Inter Bay Financial II Limited
Interbay Funding, Ltd.
Interbay ML, Ltd
Kensington Mortgage Co Ltd
Landmark Mortgages Limited

64929 Other credit granting n.e.c. [15]

BCA Vehicle Finance Limited
Capital Hospitals (Issuer) PLC
FCA Automotive Services UK Ltd
FCA Dealer Services UK Ltd
Flight Centre Robin Limited
Honda Finance Europe PLC
IBM United Kingdom Financial Services
IBRC Asset Finance Limited
Kirkmore Capital Limited
Liberty Leasing Limited
Prowting Investments PLC
Saxon Weald Capital PLC
Sorbon Finance Limited
Tata Global Beverages Group Ltd
Toyota Financial Services (UK) PLC

64991 Security dealing on own account

BPHA Finance PLC
Nibgreen
Thrive Homes Finance PLC

64992 Factoring

Advantedge Commercial Finance Ltd
BNP Paribas Commercial Finance Ltd
Calverton Finance Limited
FCA Automotive Services UK Ltd
FCA Dealer Services UK Ltd
HSBC Invoice Finance (UK) Ltd
Hitachi Capital (UK) PLC
IBM United Kingdom Financial Services

64999 Financial intermediation not elsewhere classified [143]

AA Financial Services Limited
ACM Group Limited
ADT Finance Limited
AGCO Finance Limited
Acenden Limited
Agria Pet Insurance Limited
Akzo Nobel Finance Limited
Akzo Nobel ICI Holdings
Allianz Equity Investments Ltd
Asset Advantage Group Limited
Asset Advantage Limited
B & C E Financial Services Ltd
B & CE Holdings Limited
BP Australia Swaps Management Ltd
BP Capital Markets P.L.C.
BP Finance P.L.C
Bedford Education Partnership Holdings
Bedford Education Partnership Ltd
Blue Light Partnership (ASP) Holdings
Blue Light Partnership (ASP) Ltd
Brambles Finance PLC
Brooklime Limited
Business Lending Residential Funding
CHMC Limited
Cabot Financial (Europe) Ltd
Cabot Financial (UK) Limited
Cabot Financial Holdings Group Ltd
Capital Home Loans Limited
Cargill Financial Markets Ltd
Cargill Global Funding PLC
Cargill Investments
Cargill UK Finance Limited
Chaptre Finance PLC
Chaptre Investments Limited
Charity Bank Limited
Clackmannanshire Schools Education Partnership (Holdings)
Clackmannanshire Schools Education Partnership
Colgate-Palmolive Finance (UK) PLC
Consort Medical Finance 2010 Ltd
Consort Medical Finance Ltd
Counties Home Loan Management Ltd
Countrywide Principal Services Ltd
Crown Agents Bank Limited
Direct Wines Finance Limited
E & J Capital Partners Limited
Esure Services Limited
European Investments (Cornwall) Holdings
Evergreen Finance Limited
FIL Pensions Management
Fire Support (SSFR) Holdings Ltd
Fire Support (SSFR) Limited
First Rate Exchange Services Holdings
First Rate Exchange Services Ltd
Foreign Currency Direct PLC
GE Money Home Finance Limited
GVS Prepaid Limited
Givaudan Holdings UK Limited
GlaxoSmithKline Capital PLC
GlaxoSmithKline Consumer Healthcare Finance
GlaxoSmithKline Consumer Healthcare Finance No. 2
GlaxoSmithKline Finance PLC
GlaxoSmithKline IHC Limited
Glaxochem (UK) Unlimited
Gloucester Healthcare Partnership
The Edward Gostling Foundation
Grand Union Group Funding PLC
Harvey & Thompson Limited
Hastoe Capital PLC
Healthcare Providers (Gloucester)
Healthcare Support (Newcastle) Finance
HiFX Europe Limited
Highway Management (Scotland) Holding
Highway Management (Scotland) Ltd
Highway Management M80 Investment
Home Retail Group Insurance Services
I C I Finance Limited
INEOS Finance PLC
INEOS U.K. Finance Co Ltd
INEOS U.S. Finance Co Ltd
Innotech Advisers Limited

Invesco Asia Trust PLC
Invesco Finance PLC
Invesco Fund Managers Limited
Invesco Holding Co Ltd
Invesco Perpetual UK Smaller Companies Investment Trust
Johnson & Johnson UK Treasury Co Ltd
Kent Education Partnership (Holdings)
Kent Education Partnership Ltd
Kimberly-Clark European Services Ltd
Kodak International Finance Ltd
Legolas Debt Holdco Limited
Lenster Investments Limited
M & C Finance (1) Limited
M & C New York Finance (UK) Ltd
Sir Robert McAlpine (A19) Ltd
Sir Robert McAlpine Capital Ventures
John Menzies Finance Limited
Mercedes-Benz Financial Services UK
Mitsubishi Electric Finance Europe PLC
Mondi Finance PLC
Newhospitals (St Helens and Knowsley) Finance
Nucleus Financial Group PLC
Optivo Finance PLC
Oval (2284) Limited
PRA Group (UK) Limited
PSI - Pay Ltd
Paragon Treasury PLC
Paratus AMC Limited
Porsche Financial Services Great Britain
Potanin Foundation
Premier Asset Management Group PLC
Premier Asset Management Holdings Ltd.
Premier Asset Management Midco Ltd.
Premier Portfolio Managers Ltd
RB Luxembourg (2016) Limited
RHP Finance PLC
RMAC Securities No. 1 PLC
Radian Capital PLC
Ranbaxy Holdings (UK) Limited
Riverstone Management Limited
Saga Personal Finance Limited
Scottish Borders Education Partnership (Holdings)
Scottish Borders Education Partnership
Sharp International Finance (U.K.) PLC
Sky Operational Finance Ltd
SmithKline Beecham (Investments) Ltd
Southampton Row Trust Limited
Sovereign Housing Capital PLC
Stock Finance (Koruna) Limited
Thames Water Utilities Finance PLC
Transform Schools (North Lanarkshire) Funding
Transserv UK Limited
UPS Global Treasury PLC
UnumProvident Finance Co Ltd
ViiV Healthcare Finance 2 Ltd
ViiV Healthcare Finance Ltd
Vodafone Euro Hedging Limited
Vodafone Finance UK Limited
Vodafone Yen Finance Limited
Volkswagen Financial Services (UK)
Xerox Capital (Europe) Limited
Yourcash Limited
Zene Finance Limited

65110 Life insurance [12]

B & C E Insurance Limited
Cardif Pinnacle Insurance Holdings PLC
Covea Life Limited
Equitable Life Assurance Society,(The)
FIL Life Insurance Limited
Forester Life Limited
MMA Holdings UK PLC
Old Mutual Wealth Life & Pensions
Old Mutual Wealth Life Assurance Ltd
Pinnacle Insurance PLC
RMIS (RTW) Limited
Unum Limited

65120 Non-life insurance [47]

AA Underwriting Limited
Ageas Insurance Limited
Allianz Insurance PLC
B.I.B. Underwriters Limited
BDML Connect Limited
British Gas Insurance Limited
CCV Risk Solutions Limited
Catalina Worthing Insurance Ltd
Churchill Insurance Co Ltd
Community Reinsurance Corporation
Complete Cover Group Limited
Covea Insurance PLC
Cullum Capital Ventures Ltd
DL Insurance Services Limited
Esure Insurance Limited
F.M. Insurance Co Ltd
First Title Insurance PLC
Geo Underwriting Services Ltd
Hyperformance Limited
INS-Sure Services Limited
Invesco Pensions Limited
Key Bidco Limited
Key Midco Limited
LPSO Limited
Lamp Group Limited
London General Insurance Co Ltd
MMA Holdings UK PLC
Marine Insurance Co Ltd
Markerstudy Insurance Services Ltd
National House-Building Council
Old ML Limited
Pet Plan Limited
Pinnacle Insurance PLC
Riverstone Insurance (UK) Ltd
Riverstone Insurance Limited
Royal & Sun Alliance Insurance PLC
Royal & Sun Alliance Reinsurance Ltd
SGL No.1 Limited
Sabre Insurance Co Ltd
Stackhouse Poland Bidco Ltd
Stackhouse Poland Midco Ltd
Sun Insurance Office Limited
Tesco Underwriting Limited
Towergate Risk Solutions Ltd
Towergate Underwriting Group Ltd
Trafalgar Insurance PLC
Unum Limited

65201 Life reinsurance

B & C E Insurance Limited

65202 Non-life reinsurance

B.I.B. Underwriters Limited
CCV Risk Solutions Limited
Community Reinsurance Corporation
Cullum Capital Ventures Ltd
First Title Insurance PLC
Geo Underwriting Services Ltd
Towergate Risk Solutions Ltd
Towergate Underwriting Group Ltd

65300 Pension funding

B & C E Insurance Limited
BP Pension Trustees Limited
Siemens Pension Funding Ltd

66110 Administration of financial markets

Nucleus Financial Group PLC

66120 Security and commodity contracts dealing activities

ACM Group Limited
Aliunde Limited
Arcus Investment Limited
FIL Investment Services (UK) Ltd
FIL Investments International
LDFA Limited
Share Centre Limited

66190 Activities auxiliary to financial intermediation n.e.c. [12]

ACP Europe Limited
Acenden Limited
Cargill Financial Services Europe
Family Capital Limited
Financial Administration Services
Lamp Group Limited
Nucleus Financial Group PLC
O.S.T.C. Limited
Onix Investments UK Ltd
Protection Specialist Limited
The Joseph Rank Trust
Ty Danjuma Family Office Ltd

66220 Activities of insurance agents and brokers [15]

Ageas Retail Limited
Automobile Association Insurance Services
Cullum Capital Ventures Ltd
First Central Insurance Management
Hastings (Holdings) Limited
Hastings Insurance Services Ltd
Home and Legacy Insurance Services
Markerstudy Insurance Services Ltd
Saga Services Limited
Stackhouse Poland Group Ltd
Stackhouse Poland Holdings Ltd
Stackhouse Poland Limited
TWG Services Limited
Towergate Risk Solutions Ltd
Towergate Underwriting Group Ltd

66290 Other activities auxiliary to insurance and pension funding [10]

Covea Insurance Services Ltd
Wilfred T Fry Limited
INS-Sure Holdings Limited
Just Retirement Limited
Riverstone Corporate Capital Ltd
SLF of Canada UK Limited
Sun Life Assurance Company of Canada (U.K.)
Sun Life Financial of Canada (U.K.)
Overseas Investments
TWG Services Limited
Upperton Holdings Limited

66300 Fund management activities [15]

Arjun Infrastructure Partners II Ltd
Beamish Investments Limited
Grangette Ltd
Hill of The Hermitage Limited
Invesco Asset Management Ltd
Invesco Fund Managers Limited
Invesco UK Limited
Ladham Properties Limited
Maisonparc Ltd
Mizzen Bidco Limited
Mizzen Midco Limited
Palmier Ltd
Record Currency Management Ltd
Sanlam Private Investments (UK) Ltd
Thesis Unit Trust Management Ltd

68100 Buying and selling of own real estate [112]

ACG Rented Properties PLC
AGP Holdings (1) Limited
AKA London Limited
Adeptus Limited
Admiral House Property Trading Ltd
Ambec Limited
Audley Court Limited
Avamore Limited
B & Q Properties Limited
BAM Properties Limited
BP Properties Limited
R. J. and D. E. Billings Ltd
Bishops U.K. Limited
W.E.Black Limited
Blue Lizard Consulting Limited
Bovis Homes Group PLC
Bovis Homes Limited
British and Foreign Wharf Co Ltd
CSSC Properties Limited
Campmoss Property Co Ltd
Canadian & Arcadia Limited
Capital Investment and Finance Ltd
Cardiff Property PLC
Cleanland Limited
Combined Counties Properties Ltd
Richard Cook Limited
Cooper Estates Limited
County & District Properties Ltd
Cross Stone Properties Limited
DST Global Solutions (Realty) Ltd
Dolphin Head Group Holdings PLC
Dolphin Head Group Limited
E & J Ground Rents No 15 Ltd
Eagle Estates Limited
East Malling Trust
Elite Homes (North West) Ltd
Ellis & Sons Amalgamated Properties
Esure Property Limited
T A Fisher Developments Ltd
G & O Securities Limited
Geneva Investment Group Ltd
Glen House Estates Limited
Goulden Properties Limited
Gravesend and District Real Estate Co
Hambridge Limited
Handsale Limited
ICI Chemicals & Polymers Ltd
Inland Property Limited
Jeensbannet Investments Ltd
Kallar Investments Limited
Kingsbridge Estates Limited
Ladham Properties Limited
Lambert Pressland Limited
Langbourn Properties Limited
Lionel Road Developments Ltd
London Square (Fulham) Limited
London Square (Holdings) Ltd
London Square (Putney) Limited
London Square Developments (Ventures)
London Square Developments Ltd
London Square Limited
Lousada Investments Limited
Lousada PLC
Luff Investments Limited
MCPA Limited
MYA Property Limited
Marco Island Developments Ltd
Melton House Investments Ltd
Meridian Residential Developments
Microsoft Properties UK Ltd
Milton Property Investments Ltd
Mizen Properties Limited
Moretons Investments Limited
Mova Property Limited
Ocobase Limited
Pangbourne Developments Ltd
Paradigm Commercial PLC
Pegasus Life Limited
Pegasuslife Development Ltd
Pricketts Limited
Proudreed Limited
Proudreed Real Estate Limited
Pye Properties Limited
Quayside Homes Limited
RFC Prop Co Limited
Relta Limited
Remy's Limited
Renand Properties Limited
Royalton RS Limited
SF Funding Limited
SF Ground Rents Limited
Selits Limited
Sorbon Estates Limited
Sorbon Investments Limited
Spincrest Limited
St Mary's Training Ground Ltd
F.C. Stark Limited
Store Property Investments Ltd
Strollmoor Limited
TY Properties (UK) Limited
Thames Properties Ltd.
Trapoc Limited
Tristmire Limited
U K Land Ltd.
Vectis Property Co. Limited
Victorygame Limited
Vodafone Property Investments Ltd
Westgate Properties Limited
Westmoreland Developments Ltd
Wilton Park Developments Ltd
Wyevale Acquisitions Borrower Ltd
Zionstone Limited

68201 Renting and operating of Housing Association real estate [13]

Ability Housing Association
Brymore Investments Limited
A.A.Fisher (Properties) Ltd
Housing Solutions Capital PLC
Hurstlane Limited
Kentstone Properties Limited
Lapid Developments Limited
Limecay Limited
Radian Group Limited
Sopress Investments Limited
Transeur Properties Limited
Vale of Aylesbury Housing Trust Ltd
Worthing Homes Limited

68202 Letting and operating of conference and exhibition centres

East Malling Trust

68209 Other letting and operating of own or leased real estate [201]

A A Homes and Housing Ltd
AGB Properties (Woking) Ltd
Ability Developments Limited
Ability Hotels (Liverpool Plaza) Ltd
Ability Hotels (Manchester) Ltd
Acre 1176 Limited
Adams Morey Holdings Limited
Alphalarch Limited
Ambec Limited
Apperly Estates Limited
Archaylen Property Limited
Atkins Properties Limited
Atlantis Holdings Limited
Avtrade Leasing Limited
BAE Systems (Property Investments)
BPDM Group Ltd
Baldwin House Limited
Baron Homes Corporation Ltd
Basinghall Estate Co Ltd
Ben-Motor and Allied Trades Benevolent Fund
Big Yellow (Battersea) Limited
Big Yellow Self Storage Company A
Big Yellow Self Storage Company M
Bostall Estates Limited
Burt Boulton Holdings Limited
W.H. Brakspear & Sons Limited
Bridgwater Bros.Holdings Ltd
British Agricultural Services Ltd
British and Foreign Wharf Co Ltd
W & R Buxton Holdings Limited
Cablefile Limited
Camden Motors (Holdings) Ltd
Camden Ventures Limited
Campmoss Property Co Ltd
Canadian & Arcadia Limited
Cardiff Property PLC
Castle Marinas Limited
Chartwell Properties Limited
Chatham Historic Dockyard Trust
T Clark & Son Limited
Coldunell Limited
Richard Cook Limited
Cooper Estates Limited
Robert Cort Properties Ltd
Costco Limited
County Catering & Leisure Ltd
County Catering & Leisure Properties
Cross Stone Properties Limited
Cross Stone Securities Limited
Crown Golf Property Limited
Crown Golf St Mellion Limited
Cuffe Holdings Limited
Currie Motors Limited
DST Global Solutions (Realty) Ltd
Davison & Co. (Barford) Ltd
Dunmoore (West London) Limited
Eagle Estates Limited
East Malling Trust
Endeavour Holdings Limited

George Farmiloe & Sons Ltd
Alan Firmin Limited
T A Fisher & Sons Limited
T A Fisher (Holdings) Limited
T A Fisher Developments Ltd
Fleetwood Developments Limited
Forextra Developments Limited
Fynecast Limited
G & O Securities Limited
Gardeners' Royal Benevolent Society
George House Developments Ltd
Gerald Palmer Eling Trust Company
Glen House Estates Limited
Goodman Property Investments (Hove)
Goulden Properties Limited
Greenham Trust Ltd
Greensands Limited
Greenstone Oxford Limited
Grove Court Properties (Beaconsfield)
Haig Housing Trust
Hambridge Limited
Handsale Limited
Harding Holdings U.K. Limited
Hargreaves Properties Limited
Harlequin Estates (Twickenham) Ltd
Harvestore Systems (Holdings) Ltd
Harwood Properties Limited
Healthcare Facilities Management Services
Hobbs Brook Limited
J.B.Howard Properties Limited
ILB Investments Limited
Ikea Properties Investments Ltd
Investsave Limited
J.L.G.Investments Limited
A W James Limited
Jawaby Property Investment Ltd
Jelmac Properties
Jembir Estates Limited
Johnson & Johnson Innovation Ltd
Kallar Investments Limited
Kebbell Holdings Limited
Key Properties Limited
Kingsbridge Estates Limited
Kordal Limited
Ladham Properties Limited
W.T. Lamb Holdings Limited
Lambert Pressland Limited
Lenta Properties Limited
Luff Investments Limited
Lyndendown Limited
MYA Property Limited
Mapeley Steps Contractor Ltd
Marley Plastics Limited
Marylebone Finco Limited
Massey Group Limited
Matsim Properties Limited
McKay Securities P L C
Merritts Properties Limited
Millmead Properties Limited
Montgomery Property Group Ltd
Montgomery Property Investments Ltd
Mova Property Limited
Needspace? Limited
Nuneham Estate Limited
Ocobase Limited
Offer Group Ltd
Omega (After Alpha) Limited
Onkar International Limited
PFC Property Ltd
PHF Investments Limited
PPP Capital Limited
Pangbourne Developments Ltd
Park Avenue Estates Limited
Pegasus Life Limited
Pegasuslife Development Ltd
Pelham Capital Real Estate Ltd
Pinewood PSB Limited
Porthaven Properties Limited
Pricketts Limited
Prinhold Limited
Proudreed Limited
Proudreed Real Estate Limited
Prowting Investments PLC
Purelake Investments Limited
Purelake Properties Limited
QH Estates Ltd
RB Lease Co Ltd
RWF Health and Community Developers (Tranche 1)
Ramac Holdings Limited
Red Circle Security Services Ltd
Renand Properties Limited
Renatus Property Management Ltd
Resurgam Holdings Limited
Richstone Properties Limited
Royal British Legion Poppy Factory
Royale Park Home Estates Ltd
Runnymede Investments Limited
SSL Group (UK) Limited
Safe Haven London
Safestore Limited
Safestore Properties Limited
Sea Corner Group Limited
Selits Limited
Shadowgrade Developments Ltd
Signature Senior Lifestyle Finance
Skillbond Limited
Sorbon Estates Limited
Sorbon Homes Limited
Sorbon Investments Limited
Southern Co-operative Properties Ltd
Sowmac Investments Limited
Spaces Personal Storage Ltd
Stonefield Estates, Limited
Store Property Investments Ltd
Strand Court Properties Ltd
John Street & Company (Surrey) Ltd
Street Property (Holdings) Ltd
Summerleaze Limited
TBE (Southern) Limited
TVH Fizzy Holdings Limited
Tate Bros. Limited
Techaid Facilities Limited
Thales Properties Limited
Thornton Properties Limited
Three Rivers Property Investments
Tombstone Limited
Tristmire Limited
Trochair Limited
University of Southampton Science Park
Vectis Property Co. Limited
Victorygame Limited
Walbrook Investments Limited
Warborough Investments Limited
Wedge Property Co Ltd
Michael Wenman Limited
Westmoreland Developments Ltd
Wisdom Properties Limited
Woodcote Estates Limited
Woodgavil Limited
Woodgavil Properties Limited
Yattendon Estates Limited
Zest Living Limited

68310 Real estate agencies

Romans Group (UK) Limited

68320 Management of real estate on a fee or contract basis [26]

AS & Sons Ltd
Axiom Education (Edinburgh) Ltd
Axiom Education (Perth & Kinross)
BAE Systems Properties Limited
Brookton 2000 Limited
Chartwell Properties Limited
Comland Commercial Limited
E & J Capital Partners Limited
Exemplar Properties Limited
Henley Camland Ebbsfleet 801H Ltd
Kingsbridge Estates Limited
Lancer Property Holdings Ltd
Leaders Limited
Liberty Property Trust UK Ltd
MYA Property Limited
Mapeley Steps Contractor Ltd
Medway Fundco Limited
Modern Schools (Exeter) Ltd
No.7 Limited
Ocobase Limited
Parker Hannifin (GB) Limited
Romans Group (UK) Limited
South Downs Real Estate Ltd
Specsavers Optical Superstores Ltd
John Street & Company (Surrey) Ltd
Taylor Wimpey SH Capital Ltd

69109 Activities of patent and copyright agents; other legal activities n.e.c.

AA Brand Management Limited

69203 Tax consultancy

Bluecastle Enterprises Limited
In-Sync Group Limited

70100 Activities of head offices [1226]

3D European Holdings Limited
A.C. Lighting (Holdings) Ltd
AA Acquisition Co Limited
AA Corporation Limited
AA Intermediate Co Limited
AA Mid Co Limited
AA Senior Co Limited
ABHL Digital Limited
ACAL Electronics Holdings Ltd
ACI Worldwide (EMEA) Limited
ADI Finance 1 Limited
ADI Finance 2 Limited
ADT (UK) Limited
ADT Group Limited
AE Consolidation Limited
AERL Holding Limited
AGF Holdings (UK) Limited
AHL Holdings (Manchester) Ltd
AVMI Group Limited
Abaris Holdings Limited
Abriand Limited
Acco Brands Europe Limited
Acco Europe Limited
Acco-Rexel Group Services Ltd
Accolade Wines Holdings Europe Ltd
Acquisition U.K. Limited
Adelie Foods Bidco Limited
Advanced Computer Software Group Ltd
Advanced Lighting Technologies Europe

Afton Chemical UK Holdings Ltd
Air Products Group Limited
Akaal Group PLC
Akzo Nobel Coatings (BLD) Ltd
Akzo Nobel Decorative Coatings Ltd
Akzo Nobel Holdings Limited
Akzo Nobel Limited
Akzo Nobel UK Ltd
Alder Hey Holdco 1 Limited
Alder Hey Holdco 2 Limited
Alder Hey Holdco 3 Limited
Alent Investments Limited
Alent Limited
Alere UK Holdings Limited
Alere as Holdings Limited
Alfa Laval Holdings Limited
Ian Allan Group Limited
M.J. Allen Holdings Limited
Allergan Holdco UK Limited
Allergan Holdings Limited
Allianz Holdings PLC
Allport Group Limited
Altonwood Holdings Limited
Aluminium Services (UK) Ltd
Amersham Biosciences
Amsric Holdings Limited
Amtech Group Limited
Antler New Homes Limited
Apogee Group Limited
Arca Shipping Limited
Archer Assets UK Limited
Archer Daniels Midland (UK) Ltd
Argos Holdings Limited
Arkarius Bidco Limited
Armadillo Storage Holding Co Ltd
Arora Management Services Ltd
Arora T5 Holdings Limited
Arqiva Broadcast Finance PLC
Arqiva Broadcast Intermediate Ltd
Arqiva Broadcast Parent Ltd
Arqiva Financing No 1 Limited
Arqiva Financing No 2 Limited
Arqiva Financing No 3 PLC
Arqiva Financing PLC
Arqiva Group Holdings Limited
Arqiva Group Intermediate Ltd
Arqiva Group Limited
Arqiva Group Parent Limited
Arqiva Holdings Limited
Arqiva PP Financing PLC
Arqiva Senior Finance Limited
Arqiva UK Broadcast Holdings Ltd
Aryzta UK Holdings I Limited
Asahi Breweries Europe Ltd
Asahi Europe Ltd
Associated Fisheries Limited
Associated International Cement Ltd
Aston Carter Group Limited
Atkins Holdings Limited
WS Atkins Limited
Atlas Copco UK Holdings Ltd
Aura (Newcastle) Project Company Phase 2
Aura Holdings (Newcastle) Ltd
Avalon Cellars Two Limited
Avesco Holdings Limited
Avis Budget EMEA Limited
Avis Europe Holdings Limited
Avis Europe Investment Holdings Ltd
Avis Europe Investments Ltd
Avis Europe Overseas Limited
Avis Finance Company (No.2) Ltd
Avis Investment Services Ltd

Axon Group Limited
Azlan Group Limited
Azlan Limited
B & M Care Group Limited
B O C Holdings
BA and AA Holdings Limited
BAE Systems (Overseas Holdings) Ltd
BAM Construct UK Limited
BBGI (NI) Limited
BBGI Holding Limited
BCA Central Limited
BCA Europe Limited
BCA Group Europe Limited
BCA Holdings Limited
BCA Marketplace PLC
BCA Osprey I Limited
BCA Osprey II Limited
BCA Remarketing Group Limited
BCA Trading Limited
BE Aerospace (UK) Europe Holdings
BE Aerospace Thermal and Power Management Holdings (UK)
BECAP Spicers (UK) Limited
BI Worldwide Holdings Limited
BMW (UK) Holdings Limited
BOC Gases Limited
BOC Group Limited
BOC Helex
BOC Investment Holdings Ltd
BOC Investments No.1 Limited
BOC Investments No.5
BOC Korea Holdings Limited
BOC Netherlands Holdings Ltd
BP Africa Limited
BP Alternative Energy Investments
BP America Limited
BP Asia Pacific Holdings Ltd
BP Biofuels Brazil Investments Ltd
BP Chemicals (Korea) Limited
BP Chemicals East China Investments
BP Chemicals Investments Ltd
BP Corporate Holdings Limited
BP Exploration Operating Co Ltd
BP Global Investments Limited
BP Greece Limited
BP Holdings Canada Limited
BP Holdings North America Ltd
BP International Limited
BP Investments Asia Limited
BP Pipelines (BTC) Limited
BP Pipelines (SCP) Limited
BP Pipelines Tap Limited
BP Russian Investments Limited
BP Technology Ventures Limited
BTC Pipeline Holding Co Ltd
BVG Group Limited
Bacardi U.K. Limited
Bandhart
Bandhart Overseas
Bard Holdings Limited
Barloworld Holdings Limited
Barloworld UK Limited
Barrow Hepburn Group Limited
Barrow Hepburn International Ltd
Bartholomews (Holdings) Ltd
Beck MBI Limited
Bedfordia Group Limited
Belron International Limited
Benson & Hedges Limited
Berkeley Group Holdings PLC
Berkeley Group PLC
Berkeley Homes PLC

Bespak Holdings Limited
Bidvest Freight UK Limited
Bidvest Outsourced Services Ltd
Biffa Group Holdings (UK) Ltd
Biffa Group Limited
Big Yellow Group PLC
Biogen (UK) Limited
Birchwood Garages Limited
Biwater Holdings Limited
Biwater Overseas Limited
Black & Decker Europe
Black & Decker Finance
Black & Decker International Finance Holdings (UK)
Black Tip Capital Holdings Ltd
Blue Light Partnership (ASP) Newco
Blue Lizard Consulting Limited
Blue Minerva Limited
Boeing UK Training and Flight Services Holding
Bordure Limited
Robert Bosch UK Holdings Ltd
Bottling Great Britain Limited
Bourne Leisure Group Limited
Bourne Leisure Holdings Ltd
Bourne Leisure Limited
Brake Bros Holding I Limited
Brambles Enterprises Limited
Brambles Holdings (UK) Limited
Brasserie Bar Co Limited
Bridge Leisure Bidco Limited
Bridge Leisure Finco Limited
Bridge Leisure Midco Limited
Bridge Leisure Topco Limited
Bridgwater Bros.Holdings Ltd
Brighton & Hove Albion Holdings Ltd
Bristol-Myers Squibb Holdings 2002
Britair Holdings Limited
Britannia Holdings (UK) Ltd
Britannia Security Group Ltd
Britax Childcare Group Limited
Britax Childcare Holdings Ltd
Britax Group Limited
British Agricultural Services Ltd
British Airways Associated Companies
British Car Auction Group Ltd
British Fittings Group Limited
British and Foreign Wharf Co Ltd
Britvic International Investments
Britvic PLC
Broadway Malyan Holdings Ltd
Brymore Holdings Limited
Burhill Group Limited
Burroughs Wellcome International Ltd
By Chelmer (Holdings) Limited
Bycentral Holdings Limited
Bynorth (Holdings) Limited
Bywest (Holdings) Limited
CAS Healthcare Properties Ltd
CC 1 (2011) Limited
CC 2 (2011) Limited
CC 4 (2011) Limited
CDK U.K. Limited
CG EU NSC Limited
CGS Holdings Ltd.
CH & Co Catering Group (Holdings)
CH & Co Catering Group Limited
CHB P H R Limited
CHG Overseas Ltd
CLC Group Limited
CP Holdings Limited
CSL Communications Group Ltd

CSL UK Holdings Limited
CSM Motor Group Limited
CSPH Limited
Cable & Wireless Europe Holdings Ltd
Cable & Wireless UK Holdings Ltd
Cabot Credit Management Group Ltd
Cadbury Limited
Cadbury Schweppes Finance Ltd
Cadbury Schweppes Overseas Ltd
Cadbury South Africa (Holdings)
Camellia PLC
Cape Intermediate Holdings Ltd
Capital Safety Acquisitions Ltd
Capital Safety Global Holdings Ltd
Capital Safety Limited
Capital Safety Row Limited
Cardif Pinnacle Insurance Holdings PLC
Care Management Group (Acquisition)
Carewatch Bidco Limited
Carewatch Holdings Limited
Carnival PLC
Carte Blanche Group Limited
Castle Bidco PLC
Castrol Limited
Cathay Investments 2 Limited
Cathay Investments Limited
Ceesail Limited
Cellnex UK Midco Limited
Celltech Group Limited
Centrica (Lincs) Wind Farm Ltd
Centrica Holdings Limited
Centrica Renewable Energy Ltd
Centrica Services Limited
Chandlers Garage Holdings Ltd
Channel Commercials Kent Ltd
Chemring Group PLC
Chemring North America Unlimited
Chiltern International Holdings Ltd
Chromium Assets Limited
Chubb Fire & Security Limited
Chubb Group (International) Ltd
Chubb Group Limited
Chubb Group Properties Limited
Chubb Group Security Limited
Chubb International Holdings Ltd
Chubb Limited
Cilva Holdings Limited
Cineworld Cinemas Holdings Ltd
Cineworld Holdings Limited
City Link (Cardiff) Limited
I.P. Clarke & Co. Limited
Cleansing Service Group Ltd
Clinimed (Holdings) Limited
Club Company Acquisitions (Holdings)
Cluff Oil Limited
Coats Group PLC
Coats Industrial Thread Ltd
Coats Limited
Coca-Cola European Partners Holdings
Great Britain
Coca-Cola European Partners Services
Europe
Cohort PLC
Andrew Colin Investments Ltd
Collaborative Services Support (NE)
Holdings
Collard Group Limited
Colorado Bidco Limited
Colorado Holdco Limited
Colorado Midco Limited
Colorado Newco Limited
Colt Group Limited
Colt Investments Limited
Comland Commercial Limited
Comland Group Limited
Compass Group Finance No. 3 Ltd
Compass Group Finance No.2 Ltd
Compass Group Holdings PLC
Compass Group PLC
Compass Overseas Holdings Ltd
Compass Overseas Holdings No.2 Ltd
Computer Associates Holding Ltd
Consolidated Timber Holdings Group
Consolidated Timber Holdings Ltd
Consort Healthcare (Blackburn) Holdings
Consort Medical PLC
Constantine Group Limited
Contact Technologies UK Ltd
Contemplation Holdings Limited
Continental U.K. Group Holdings Ltd
Richard Cook Limited
Copthorne Hotel Holdings Ltd
Copthorne Hotels Limited
Cornwall Energy Recovery Holdings Ltd
Corona Energy Limited
Cosan Lubes Investments Ltd
Costain Alcaidesa Limited
Costain Civil Engineering Ltd
Costain Group PLC
Covea Insurance Services Ltd
John Crane Group Limited
Crawley Down Holdings Ltd
Creative Technology Group Ltd
Crest Nicholson Holdings PLC
Crest Nicholson PLC
Cromwell Holdings Limited
Croydon and Lewisham Lighting Services
(Holdings)
Crystalate Electronics Limited
Cucina Acquisition (UK) Ltd
Cucina Finance (UK) Limited
Cucina Fresh Finance Limited
Cucina Fresh Investments Ltd
Cucina Lux Investments Limited
Cyberfort Bidco Limited
Cyberfort Group Limited
D & B Europe Limited
D-R Holdings (UK) Ltd
D.E Holding UK Limited
DDD Investments Limited
DHL Exel Supply Chain Limited
DPG Holdings Limited
DS (Holdings) 2 Limited
DS (Holdings) 3 Limited
DSTI Holdings Limited
DX (Group) PLC
DX Holdings Limited
DX Services Limited
Daimler UK Limited
Darty Limited
Datatec PLC
J.T. Davies & Sons Holdings Ltd
Dawsongroup PLC
De Lage Landen Limited
Defaqto Group Limited
Defence Support (St Athan) Holdings
Delta Limited
Descram Holdings Limited
Devine Holdings Limited
Dimension Data (UK) Investments Ltd
Direct Line Group Limited
Direct Line Insurance Group PLC
Direct Wines International Ltd
Discoverie Group PLC
Discoverie Management Services Ltd
Discoverie Nordic Holdings Ltd
Dnata Aviation Services Ltd
Dnata World Travel Limited
Doctors Chambers Group Limited
Dolphin Head Group Limited
Doncaster School Solutions (Holdings)
Dormole Limited
Draper Tool Group Limited
Druid Group Limited
Dulux Limited
Dun & Bradstreet Investments Ltd
Dwellcourt Limited
E.F.B. Group Limited
EDU UK Intermediate Limited
EDU UK Management Services Ltd
EDU UK Topco Limited
EHGT Limited
ESNT Holdings (No.1) Limited
ESNT Holdings (No.2) Limited
ESP Utilities Group Limited
EWDB Limited
Eastbury Park (Holdings) Ltd
Echostar UK Holdings Limited
Edif Group Finance Limited
Edif Group Management Limited
Education Support (Enfield 2) Holdings
Education Support (Newham) Holdings
Education Support (Newham) Ltd
Education Support (Swindon) Holdings
Effem Holdings Limited
Elekta Holdings Limited
Elite Hotels (Rotherwick) Ltd
Elster Metering Holdings Ltd
Elster Solutions Limited
Elster Water Metering Holdings Ltd
Simon Elvin Holdings Limited
S Elvin Limited
Elysium Healthcare (Lighthouse) Ltd
Emerald Bidco Limited
Emerald Midco 1 Limited
Emerald Midco 2 Limited
Emerald Topco Limited
Empresaria Group PLC
Enstar Acquisitions Limited
Enterprise Rent-a-Car European Holdings
Enterprise Rent-a-Car UK Holdings
Equiniti Group PLC
Equiniti Holdings Limited
Ercol (Holdings) Limited
Ergon Investments International Ltd
Ergon Investments UK Limited
Erith Holdings Limited
Esselte Holdings Limited
Essentra Filter Products International
Essentra International Limited
Essentra PLC
Esure Group PLC
Esure Holdings Limited
Europa Worldwide Group Limited
M.P.Evans & Co Limited
Everyday Loans Holdings Ltd
Evolving Systems Holdings Ltd
Evonik Speciality Organics Ltd
Evonik UK Holdings Limited
Exel Holdings Limited
Exel Investments Limited
Exel Limited
Expanded Limited
Experis Group Limited
Exploration Service Co Ltd
Exploration and Production Services

(Holdings)
Expro Benelux Limited
Expro Holdings UK 3 Limited
Expro Holdings UK 4 Limited
Expro International Group Ltd
FBG Holdings (UK) Limited
FGP Topco Limited
FT Finance Limited
FT North America Limited
Faber Prest Limited
Famous Brands UK Limited
Farnborough Finance (2007) Ltd
Farnborough Limited
Fat Face Holdings Limited
Fatface Group Borrowings Ltd
Fatface Group Limited
Fatface Group Parent Limited
Feltham Group Limited
Femcare Group Limited
Ferring Laboratories Limited
Fevore Limited
Fifthgrange Limited
Finance Ireland Limited
First Technology Limited
First Technology Overseas Ltd
Folkestone Harbour Holdings Ltd
Food Manufacturers (G.B. Company)
Foray 989 Limited
Foreman Homes Group Limited
Forester Holdings (Europe) Ltd
Formaplex Group Limited
Forth Health Holdings Limited
Foss Holdings Limited
Alexander Fraser Holdings Ltd
Fresca Group Limited
Fresh Direct Group Limited
Furniture Village Group Ltd
Furniture Village Holdings Ltd
Future Electronics Management Services
GB Gas Holdings Limited
GE Bio-Sciences Investments Ltd
GE Money Home Lending Holdings Ltd
GEA Group Holdings (UK) Ltd
GGI Holdings Limited
GMK Limited
GPG (UK) Holdings Limited
GS Acquisitions Limited
Galaxy Acquisition Co 1 Ltd
Galaxy Acquisition Co 2 Ltd
Galaxy Holdco 1 Ltd
Galaxy Holdco 2 Ltd
Gallaher Group Limited
Gallaher Overseas (Holdings) Ltd
Gallaher Overseas Limited
Galliford Try Construction & Investments Holdings
Galliford Try PLC
Game Digital PLC
Gap Partnership Bidco Limited
Gap Partnership Group Limited
Genus Investments Limited
Gibb Holdings Ltd
Glasgow Learning Quarter (Holdings)
Glaxo Group Limited
GlaxoSmithKline Consumer Healthcare Holdings
GlaxoSmithKline Holdings (One) Ltd
GlaxoSmithKline Holdings Ltd
GlaxoSmithKline Investment Holdings
GlaxoSmithKline Mercury Ltd
GlaxoSmithKline PLC
GlaxoSmithKline Services Unlimited
Glendola Leisure (Holdings) Ltd
Global Invacom Holdings Ltd
Glynwed Overseas Holdings Ltd
Gold Group International Ltd
Goodwood Estate Co Ltd
Goshawk Insurance Holdings Ltd
Gould International UK Limited
Graduation Bidco Limited
Grafise Holdings Limited
Grafton Group (UK) PLC
Gravity Media Group Holdings Ltd
Greeneden UK Acquisition Co Ltd
Greensands (UK) Limited
Greensands Europe Limited
Greensands Investments Limited
Greensands Junior Finance Ltd
Greensands Senior Finance Ltd
Group 1 Automotive UK Limited
Group Fabricom Limited
Grove Court Properties (Holdings)
Guangdong Investments Limited
Guildford Portfolios Limited
Gym Group Operations Limited
H & D Support Services (Holdings)
H.E. Group Ltd
H.I.G. Europe - Fibercore Bidco Ltd
HCL EAS Ltd
HCL Technologies UK Limited
HEL Bidco Ltd
HPI Holding Limited
HR Gardens Limited
Halma Euro Trading Limited
Halma Financing Limited
Halma International Limited
Halma Investment Holdings Ltd
Halma Overseas Funding Limited
Halma PLC
Hampden Holdings Limited
Hanson America Holdings (1) Ltd
Hanson America Holdings (4) Ltd
Hanson Finance (2003) Limited
Hanson Finance Limited
Hanson Holdings Limited
Hanson Overseas Holdings Ltd
Harsco (UK) Group Limited
Harsco Infrastructure Group Ltd
Harsco Investment Limited
Harsco Leatherhead Limited
Harsco Metals 385 Limited
Harsco Metals Group Limited
Harsco Metals Holdings Limited
Harsco Mole Valley Limited
Hartford Care Group Limited
Harvest Midco Limited
Hastings Group Holdings PLC
Hastings Water (UK) Limited
Havas Canada Holdings Limited
Havas Holdings Limited
Havas Shared Services Limited
Havas UK Limited
Havenhill Limited
Haymarket Group Limited
Healthcare Support (Newcastle) Holdings
Healthcare Support (North Staffs) Holdings
Heathrow (AH) Limited
Heathrow (DSH) Limited
Heathrow (SP) Limited
Heathrow Airport Holdings Ltd
Heathrow Enterprises Limited
Heathrow Finance PLC
Heathrow Holdco Limited
HeidelbergCement Euro I Ltd
HeidelbergCement Euro II Ltd
HeidelbergCement Euro III Ltd
HeidelbergCement UK Holding II Ltd
HeidelbergCement UK Holding Ltd
HellermannTyton Holdings Ltd
Hendy Automotive Limited
Hendy Holdings Limited
Hewlett-Packard (Bracknell) Holdings
Hewlett-Packard Cain Holdings Ltd
Hewlett-Packard Holdings Ltd
Hexagon Positioning Intelligence Ltd
Hilbre Holdings Limited
Hilton HHC Limited
Hinds Ltd
Hogg Robinson Group Limited
Hogg Robinson Limited
Hogg Robinson Money Matters Ltd
Home Retail Group Limited
Hospital Company (Southmead) Holdings
Hospitality Holdings Limited
Host Europe Group Limited
Host Europe Limited
Hotel Management International (Holdings)
Hotelplan (U.K. Group) Limited
Hovis Holdings Limited
Humphrey Farms Limited
Domnick Hunter Group Limited
Hydac Limited
IBM United Kingdom Holdings Ltd
IG Design Group PLC
IHC Hotel Limited
IHC May Fair (Holdings) Ltd
IHC May Fair Hotel Limited
IHC Overseas (U.K.) Limited
IHC UK (Holdings) Limited
IHS Group Holdings Limited
IHS International Holdings Ltd
IMCD Holding UK Ltd
IMCD UK Acquisitions Limited
IMO Car Wash Group Limited
INEOS Canada Limited
INEOS Chemicals France Holdings Ltd
INEOS European Holdings Ltd
INEOS Grangemouth PLC
INEOS Holdings Limited
INEOS Industries Holdings Ltd
INEOS Industries Limited
INEOS Investment Holdings (Germany)
INEOS Investments International Ltd
INEOS Paraform Holdings Ltd
INEOS Silicas Holdings Limited
INEOS Styrolution Holding Ltd
INS-Sure Holdings Limited
IQVIA RDS Holdings
ISS UK Holding Limited
ISS UK Limited
Icrossing Europe Limited
Independent Growth Finance Ltd
Indoor Bowling Acquisitions Ltd
Indoor Bowling Equity Limited
John Ingham & Sons Limited
Ingram Micro Holdings Limited
Inhealth Group Holdings PLC
Inhealth Group Limited
Inhealth UK Holdings Limited
Inspiral Oldham Holding Co Ltd
Inspiring Learning (Holdings) Ltd
Inspiring Learning Limited
Inspiring Learning Services Ltd
Inter Pipeline Europe Limited
Intercontinental (PB) 1
Intercontinental (PB) 3 Ltd

Intercontinental Hotels Group PLC
International Group Limited
International Paint Limited
Intex (Radiographic) Limited
Into University Partnerships Ltd
Invesco Asset Management Ltd
Invesco GT Asset Management Ltd
Ipsen Developments Limited
Iris Holdings Limited
Iris Software Group Limited
JCHAC Europe Finco Limited
JCHAC India Holdco Limited
JCHAC UK Holdco Limited
JEG Acquisition Co Ltd
JLW Excellent Homes for Life Holding Co
JTI (UK) Management Ltd
Jacobs UK Holdings Limited
A W James Limited
Jankel Group Limited
Jessops (Group) Limited
Johnson Controls Air Conditioning (UK)
Johnson Controls Air Conditioning Investments (UK)
Johnson Controls Auto India Ltd
Johnson Controls Enterprises Ltd
Johnson Controls Facilities Ltd
Johnson Controls Holding UK Ltd
Johnson Controls International Holdings
Johnson Controls Investments (UK)
Johnson Controls Metal Components Birmingham
Johnson Controls UAE Holding Ltd.
Johnson Controls-Hitachi Air Conditioning Holding (UK)
P.H Jones Group Limited
Just Group PLC
Just Retirement (Holdings) Ltd
KBC Advanced Technologies Ltd
KCI Medical Limited
KCI UK Holdings Limited
Kamkorp Limited
Kaye Enterprises Limited
Kaysail Limited
Kebbell Holdings Limited
Kedleston Group Limited
Kemble Water Finance Limited
Kemble Water Holdings Limited
Kentucky Fried Chicken (Great Britain)
Kenwood Appliances Limited
Kenwood International Limited
Kerry Holdings (U.K.) Limited
Kidde International Limited
Kidde Limited
Kidde UK
Kidsprog Limited
Kimal Holdings Limited
Geo. Kingsbury Holdings Ltd
Knowledge Academy Holdings Ltd
Kohler Uninterruptible Power Ltd
Kraft Foods Investment Holdings UK
Kraft Foods UK IP & Production Holdings
Kuehne + Nagel Drinkflow Logistics Holdings
Kuwait Petroleum International Ltd
LGC Science Group Holdings Ltd
LGC Science Group Limited
LKQ Euro Limited
Lafarge International Holdings Ltd
Lafarge Minerals Limited
W.T. Lamb Holdings Limited
Lapid Developments Limited
Lawrie Group PLC
Lea Redway Limited

Leaders Lettings Limited
Leaders Romans Group Limited
Leaders Romans Midco 2 Limited
Leaders Romans Midco Limited
Leaders The Rental Agents Ltd
The Harry Levy Group Limited
Lighthouse Healthcare Group Ltd
Linde Canada Holdings Limited
Linde Cryogenics Limited
Linde Holdings Limited
Linde Investments No.1 Limited
Linde North America Holdings Ltd
Linde UK Holdings Limited
Linton Park PLC
Lockheed Martin UK Ampthill Group
Lockheed Martin UK Holdings Ltd
Logicalis Group Limited
London Airports 1992 Limited
London Irish Holdings Limited
London Pharma & Chemicals Holdings Ltd
Lotus Flower Holdings Limited
Ludgate 329 Limited
Luxury Travel Group Limited
M & C (CB) Limited
M & C (CD) Limited
M & C Asia Holdings (UK) Ltd
M & C Singapore Holdings (UK) Ltd
MCF Commercial Limited
MDL Marinas Group Limited
MFG Parentco Limited
MIQ Logistics EU Limited
Mabey Engineering (Holdings) Ltd
Mabey Holdings Limited
MacDermid (UK) Limited
MacDermid Continental Investments
MacDermid Europe Limited
MacDermid G.B. Holdings Ltd
Majestic Securities Limited
Mallinckrodt Medical Holdings (UK)
Manpower PLC
Mapil Bidco Limited
Mapil Midco 1 Limited
Mapil Midco 2 Limited
Mapil Topco Limited
Mariner International (UK) Ltd
Marley Plastics Limited
Mars Chocolate UK Holdings Ltd
Mars Melton UK Holdings Ltd
Mars Petcare UK Holdings Ltd
Mars Slough UK Holdings Ltd
Masterson Holdings Limited
Sir Robert McAlpine (Holdings) Ltd
Medica Group PLC
Medica Reporting Finance Ltd
Medina Holdings Limited
Medispeed
Megger Group Limited
Melesey Limited
John Menzies (108) Limited
Merant Holdings
Merseyside Energy Recovery Holdings Ltd
Micheldever Group Limited
Miles 33 Group Limited
Millbrook Industries Limited
Millennium & Copthorne (Jersey Holdings)
Millennium & Copthorne Hotels PLC
Millennium Hotels (West London) Ltd
Millennium Hotels Europe Holdings
Millennium Hotels Limited
Millennium Hotels London Ltd
Milton Group Limited
Mondelez UK Biscuit Financing Ltd

Mondelez UK Finance Co Ltd
Mondelez UK Holdings & Services Ltd
Mondi Finance PLC
Mondi Investments Limited
Mondi PLC
Monier (China) Holdings Ltd
Monier (UK) Holdings Limited
Morgan Advanced Materials PLC
Morgan Finance Management Ltd
Morgan Holdings Limited
Morgan North America Holding Ltd
Mortar Investments International Ltd
Mothercare Group Limited
Motus Holdings (UK) Limited
NCL Holdings Limited
NCMT Holdings Limited
NIS Acquisitions Limited
NIS Receivables No.1 Limited
NSK Europe Limited
NTL Cablecomms Group Limited
Nampak Holdings (UK) Limited
Natural Sante Limited
Netcall PLC
Network Aviation Group Ltd
Newarthill Limited
Newbury Investments (UK) Ltd
Newhospitals (St Helens and Knowsley) Holdings
Newincco 1222 Limited
Newship Group Limited
Newship Limited
Newsquest Capital Limited
Anthony Nicholas (UK) Limited
E.H. Nicholls Holdings Ltd
Nike Land Securities Limited
Nilvip Holdings Limited
Northgate Information Solutions Holdings
Northumberland Energy Recovery Holdings
Novar Electrical Holdings Ltd
Novar Limited
Novartis UK Limited
Nutrix Capital Limited
O & M-Movianto UK Holdings Ltd.
O'Rourke Investments Holdings (UK)
O.C.S. Group Limited
OCS Group International Ltd
OGF Bidco Limited
Ocean Overseas Holdings Ltd
Ocobase Limited
Octagon Group Holdings Limited
Octagon Group Limited
Officeteam Group Limited
Oki Europe Limited
Old Mutual Wealth Holdings Ltd
Old Mutual Wealth UK Holding Ltd
One GE Healthcare UK
Optionis Group Limited
Optum Solutions UK Holdings Ltd
Optum UK Solutions Group Ltd
Organised Group Limited
Otsuka Pharmaceutical Europe Ltd.
Oyezstraker Group Limited
PCL Bidco Limited
PCL Holdco Limited
Michael Page International Southern Europe
Pagegroup PLC
Pall European Holdings Limited
Parametric Holdings (UK) Ltd
Parker Hannifin (Holdings) Ltd
Parkside Capital Limited
Parkview Treasury Services (UK) Ltd
Partnerships in Children's Services

Pearl River Delta Investments Ltd
Penspen Group Limited
Pentair UK Holdings Limited
PerkinElmer (UK) Holdings Ltd
Personal Group Holdings PLC
Personal Group Limited
Peter Waddell Holdco Limited
Petroleum Geo-Services (UK) Ltd
Pharmacia Limited
Philips Electronics UK Limited
Philips U.K. Limited
Pic Fyfield Limited
PizzaExpress Group Limited
Pladis Foods Limited
Plexus Holdings PLC
Portchester Equity Limited
Porthaven Finance Limited
Porthaven Management Limited
Premier Lotteries Capital UK Ltd
Premier Marinas Holdings Ltd
Prime Care Solutions (Kingston) Holdings
Giles W. Pritchard-Gordon & Co. Ltd
Procter & Gamble Holdings (UK) Ltd
Prospect Healthcare (Hairmyres) Group
Prospects Group 2011 Limited
Proudreed Limited
Prysmian UK Group Limited
Puzzler Media Group Limited
Puzzler Media Holdings Limited
QA-IQ Group Limited
QA-IQ Investments Limited
Qinetiq Group Holdings Limited
Qinetiq Group PLC
Qinetiq Overseas Holdings Ltd
Quantel Group Limited
Quantel Holdings (2010) Ltd
Quayside Homes Holdings Ltd
REG Holdings Limited
RIHL Limited
RWS Group Limited
Raisio UK Limited
Rank Digital Holdings Limited
Rank Group Gaming Division Ltd
Rank Group PLC
Rank Leisure Holdings Limited
Rayner Surgical Group Limited
Reach Holdings Limited
Reckitt Benckiser (RUMEA) Ltd
Reckitt Benckiser Group PLC
Redwing Holdings 2 Limited
William Reed Group Ltd
William Reed Holdings Limited
Regenter B3 Holdco Limited
Regenter Myatts Field North Holding Co
Reliance Vanco Group Limited
Renewable Energy Systems Holdings
Renhe Sports Management Co Ltd
Renoir Bidco Limited
Rentokil Initial (1993) Ltd
Rentokil Initial Investments South Africa
Retirement Villages Group Ltd
Rhodia Holdings Limited
Rhodia International Holdings Ltd
Rhombi Holdings Limited
Ricardo Investments Limited
Ricardo PLC
Ringmerit Limited
Riverstone Holdings Limited
Rockwell Commercial Holdings Ltd
Rohm Electronics Europe Ltd
Romans 2 Limited
Romans 3 Limited

Rose Holdco Limited
Rose Midco Limited
Rydon Group Limited
Rydon Holdings Limited
SAI Global CIS UK Limited
SCIH Branston 3
SGB Infrastructure Middle East Ltd
SHL Group Limited
SLS Holding Co Ltd
SNA Solutions UK Limited
SNC-Lavalin (GB) Holdings Ltd
SNC-Lavalin (GB) Limited
SQIB Limited
SSCP Spring Topco Limited
SSE Seabank Investments Ltd
Saba Infra Holdings UK Limited
Sabre Global Technologies Ltd
Sabroe Limited
Safestore Acquisition Limited
Safestore Group Limited
Safestore Holdings PLC
Safety-Kleen Europe Limited
Safety-Kleen UK (Europe) Ltd
Safetykleen Group Services Ltd
Saga Group Limited
Saga PLC
Sailtown Limited
Sanlam Private Investments (UK) Holdings
Schlumberger Oilfield UK PLC
Schlumberger PLC
Schlumberger UK Limited
Schweppes Limited
Scotia Gas Networks Limited
Sea Cloud 1 Limited
Search Consultancy Group Ltd
Sedgemoor Limited
Senior Engineering Investments Ltd
Senior Finance Four Limited
Senior Finance Six Limited
Senior Five Limited
Senior PLC
Seqirus Holdings UK Limited
Seqirus Limited
Seqirus UK Limited
Seqirus Vaccines Holdings Ltd
Serco Group PLC
Serco Holdings Limited
Serco Limited
Serocor Holdings Limited
Services Support (Gravesend) Holdings
Services Support (Manchester) Holdings
Services Support (SEL) Holdings Ltd
Sesame Bankhall Group Limited
Setfirst Limited
Share PLC
Shimtech Industries Group Ltd
Shimtech Industries Holdco Ltd
Shimtech Industries Holdco2 Ltd
Shimtech Industries Limited
Shukco Ltd
Siemens Holdings PLC
Siemens Industrial Turbomachinery
Signet Group Limited
Sime Darby London Limited
Sirhowy Enterprise Way (Holdings)
Six Continents Holdings Ltd
Six Continents Hotels International
Skanska Construction Holdings UK Ltd
Sky International Operations Ltd
Sky Limited
Sky Television Limited
Sky Ventures Limited

Sloggett Group Limited
SmithKline Beecham (H) Limited
SmithKline Beecham Overseas Ltd
SmithKline Beecham Research Ltd
Smiths Interconnect Group Ltd
Smiths Medical Group Limited
Snows Business Holdings Ltd
Softbox (Bidco) Limited
Softbox (Topco) Limited
Software (Holdco 4) Limited
Software (Holdco2) Limited
Sogea Holdings (UK) Limited
Sondex Limited
Southern Water Investments Ltd
Spectris Group Holdings Ltd
Spectris PLC
Spectris UK Holdings Limited
Spectris US Holdings Limited
Spicers-Officeteam Group Ltd
Spirent Communications PLC
Spirit Norway Limited
St George PLC
St Mary's Football Group Ltd
Stadium MK Group Limited
Stantec Europe Limited
Steamer Properties Limited
Steelstock UK Limited
Stena Line (UK) Limited
M R Stephenson Limited
Stock Spirits Group PLC
Store Property Holdings Ltd
Storeshield Limited
Storrington Equityco Limited
Storrington Industries Limited
Stratton House Leasing Limited
Strongdraw Limited
Suez Recycling and Recovery Holdings UK
Suez Recycling and Recovery UK Group Holdings
Suez UK Group Holdings Ltd
Sumika Polymer Compounds (Europe) Ltd
Sungard Availability Services (DR)
Superlift UK Limited
Surface Treatments Limited
Swan Group
Swan Mill (Holdings) Limited
Symmetry Logistics Holdings Ltd
Synchro Clutch Co Ltd
Syneos Health Holdings UK Ltd
Syneos Health International Holdings
Syngenta Holdings Limited
Syngenta Limited
T S S Group PLC
T-Mobile Holdings Limited
TAG Farnborough (Holdings) Ltd
TD United Kingdom Acquisition Ltd
TFX Group Limited
TP Group PLC
TT Electronics Group Holdings Ltd
TT Electronics PLC
Tanjong PLC
Tasmar Limited
Tata Global Beverages Group Ltd
Tata Global Beverages Investments
Tata Global Beverages Overseas Holdings
Tata Global Beverages Services Ltd
Tavistock Investments PLC
Taylor Wimpey PLC
Technetix Group Limited
Teneo Group Limited
Tengo (Holdings) Limited
Tensator Group Limited

Tenva TS Holdings Limited
Terrassen Holdings Limited
Thales Transport and Security Ltd
Thompsons (UK) Holdings Ltd
Tiger Group Limited
Tigers Logistics Group Limited
Toll Investments (NA) Ltd
Tonroe Group Limited
Towers Perrin Europe Limited
Towers Perrin UK Holdings Ltd
Towers Watson Global 2 Limited
Towers Watson Global 3 Limited
Towry Finance Co Ltd
Towry Group Limited
Tranche 5 Limited
Trans Global Limited
Transform Schools (North Lanarkshire) Holdings
Trant Holding Co Ltd
Travel Technology Investments Ltd
Trevellyan Developments Ltd
Tyrolese (751) Limited
UB Overseas Limited
UCB (Investments) Limited
UK Mail Group Limited
UMV Global Foods Co Ltd.
UMV Global Foods Holding Co Ltd.
UPS (UK Holding) Limited
UPS (UK) Limited
Ultra Electronics Holdings PLC
United Biscuits Bidco Limited
United Biscuits BondCo Limited
United Biscuits Holdco 2 Ltd
United Biscuits Holdco Limited
United Biscuits Vlnco Limited
United Living (North) Holdings Ltd
United Living (South) Group Ltd
United Living Group Limited
United Technologies Holdings Ltd
Universe Group PLC
Urenco Enrichment Co Ltd
Urenco Limited
Van Oord UK Limited
Vanguard Holdings Limited
Vantas International Limited
Veritas UK Holding Limited
Vestey Foods Limited
Vestey Group Limited
Vestey Holdings Limited
ViiV Healthcare Limited
ViiV Healthcare UK Limited
Vinci PLC
Vinci UK Developments Limited
Virgin Atlantic Limited
Virgin Atlantic Two Limited
Virgin Media Senior Investments Ltd
Virgin Travel Group Limited
Vitec Group Holdings Limited
Vitec Group PLC.
Vitec Investments Limited
Voda Limited
Vodafone Benelux Limited
Vodafone Cellular Limited
Vodafone Euro Hedging Two
Vodafone Group PLC
Vodafone Intermediate Enterprises
Vodafone International Holdings Ltd
Vodafone International Operations
Vodafone Investments Limited
Vodafone Mobile Communications Ltd
Vodafone Mobile Enterprises Ltd
Vodafone Mobile Network Ltd
Vodafone UK Limited
Vodafone Worldwide Holdings Ltd
Vodaphone Limited
Vodata Limited
WP Midco1 Limited
WP Midco2 Limited
WP Midco3 Limited
WP SK Holdings Limited
WP SK Limited
WP SK Midco Limited
WP Safety-Kleen Limited
Wadlow Energy Holdings Limited
Walker Greenbank PLC.
James Walker Group Limited
Walker Logistics (Holdings) Ltd
Walsall Hospital Company (Holdings)
Watchstone Group PLC
Watson Wyatt (UK) Acquisitions 1 Ltd
Watson Wyatt European Investment Holdings
Watson Wyatt European Region Ltd
Watson Wyatt Holdings (Europe) Ltd
Weight Watchers UK Holdings Ltd
Andrew Weir & Co Ltd
Wellcome Foundation Limited
Wellcome Limited
Wessanen Great Britain Holdings Ltd
Westcoast (Holdings) Limited
Westec Holding Co Ltd
Western United Investment Co Ltd
Whatman Limited
Wiley Europe Investment Holdings Ltd
Wiley Europe Limited
J Wiley Limited
Wilky Group Limited
Wilson Connolly Holdings Ltd
George Wimpey Limited
Wimpey Overseas Holdings Ltd
Winchester Holdings Limited
Wind Farm Holdings Limited
Wolseley Group Holdings Ltd
Wolseley Limited
Wolseley Overseas Limited
Wood Hall Land & Properties Ltd
Wyatt Company Holdings Limited
Wyevale Garden Centres Holdings Ltd
Xchanging Holdco No.3 Limited
Xchanging Holdings Limited
Xeretec Group Limited
Xerox Overseas Holdings Ltd
Xpanse Limited
Xylem Water Holdings Limited
Xylem Water Solutions UK Holdings
Yacht Havens Group Limited
Yacht Havens Limited
Yanfeng UK Automotive Interior Systems Co.,
York Cee Holdings Limited
York Engineered Systems Ltd
York International (Holdings) Ltd
York International Investments
Zodiac Europe Limited
Zotefoams PLC

70210 Public relations and communications activities

Future Electronics Management Services
SHOO 802AA Limited

70221 Financial management [24]

Binder Bidco Limited
CPRT European Investments Ltd
CSC Computer Sciences EMEA Finance
Capital Professional Limited
Chaucer Management Services Ltd
Erac UK Finance Limited
Future Electronics Management Services
GlaxoSmithKline Holdings (Ireland)
Hexagon Corporate Management Ltd
Hexagon Manufacturing Intelligence Management
Richard Hochfeld Management Ltd
INEOS Finance Company 1
INEOS Finance Company 2
INEOS Finance Company 3 Ltd
INEOS Styrolution Financing Ltd
MFS Portfolio Limited
PizzaExpress Operations Ltd
Reckitt Benckiser Healthcare (CIS)
Riposte Limited
Thrive Homes Finance PLC
V.B. Investments Limited
WorleyParsons UK Finance Sub Ltd
WorleyParsons UK Finance Sub No. 2 Ltd
nVent International (UK) Ltd

70229 Management consultancy activities other than financial management [39]

AON Consulting Limited
Arora Management Services Ltd
Atkins Limited
BMT Group Limited
Belron Finance Issuer Limited
Belron Finance Limited
Belron Lending UK Limited
CEB Holdings UK 1 Limited
CEB Holdings UK 2 Limited
Console Bidco Limited
Court Cavendish Limited
Dai Europe Ltd
EUSA Pharma Holdco 1 (UK) Ltd
EUSA Pharma Holdco 2 (UK) Ltd
Eden Automotive Investments Ltd
Faithful+Gould Limited
Future Electronics Management Services
Huntswood CTC Limited
Hystead Limited
INEOS Capital Limited
IZH Holdings Ltd
International Group Limited
Lafarge Building Materials Ltd
Liberata UK Limited
Logoplaste UK Limited
Makita International Europe Ltd
Mallinckrodt Pharmaceuticals Ltd
Opal Ventures Limited
Optum Solutions UK Holdings Ltd
Peter Press Limited
Reckitt Benckiser Corporate Services
SDL Tridion Limited
Serco Limited
Tata Global Beverages Services Ltd
Vodafone Global Content Services Ltd
Willoughby (880) Limited
Xafinity Consulting Limited
Xchanging UK Limited
Xchanging US Funding Limited

71111 Architectural activities

WorleyParsons Europe Limited

71112 Urban planning and landscape architectural activities

Atkins Limited
Southwater Property Promotion Ltd

71121 Engineering design activities for industrial process and production

Black & Veatch Limited
Jacobs E & C Limited
Silicon Storage Technology Ltd
Suez Advanced Solutions UK Ltd
TSL Limited
WorleyParsons Europe Limited

71122 Engineering related scientific and technical consulting activities

Black & Veatch Limited
Edif Group Limited
Penspen Limited
Qinetiq Limited
Ricardo PLC
Ricardo UK Limited
WorleyParsons Europe Limited

71129 Other engineering activities [26]

Allianz Engineering Inspection Services
Atkins Limited
BMT Group Limited
Beck & Pollitzer Engineering Ltd
Boustead International Heaters Ltd
Broadway Malyan Holdings Ltd
Costain Group PLC
Costain Integrated Services Ltd
Richard Costain Limited
Cubic Transportation Systems Ltd
Gemalto UK Limited
INEOS Derivatives France Ltd
Jacobs U.K. Limited
KBC Process Technology Limited
Kellogg Brown & Root Limited
Kellogg Brown & Root Overseas Operations
Kellogg Brown & Root Overseas Projects
Lockheed Martin Helicopter Co Ltd
Mott MacDonald Group Limited
Mott MacDonald International Ltd
Mott MacDonald Limited
S.S.S.Gears Limited
Sinclair Knight Merz (Europe) Ltd
Stantec UK Limited
Thales UK Limited
Tokyo Electron Europe Limited

71200 Technical testing and analysis

Genus Breeding Limited
Jenoptik Traffic Solutions UK Ltd
Labcorp Neon Ltd.
Millbrook Proving Ground Ltd
Premier Research Group Limited
Qinetiq Limited
Ricardo-AEA Limited
Southern Water Services Ltd

72110 Research and experimental development on biotechnology [10]

Charles River U.K. Limited
Convergence Pharmaceuticals Holdings
Convergence Pharmaceuticals Ltd
Creabilis Holdings Limited
EUSA Pharma (UK) Limited
Exagon Industries Limited
IQVIA Ltd.
LGC Genomics Limited
Pall Technology UK Limited
Silver Acquisition Co Limited

72190 Other research and experimental development on natural sciences and engineering [39]

Acambis Research Limited
Afton Chemical Limited
BMT Group Limited
BRE Trust
Beko PLC
Bespak Europe Limited
Biocompatibles UK Limited
Building Research Establishment Ltd
Celgene Europe Limited
Celsis Group Limited
Celsis International Limited
Ceres Power Intermediate Holdings
Covance Clinical and Periapproval Services
Domantis Limited
East Malling Trust
Galvani Bioelectronics Limited
GlaxoSmithKline Research & Development
Icon Clinical Research (U.K.) Ltd
Intervet UK Limited
Marwell Wildlife
Millipore (U.K.) Limited
Nastor Investments Limited
Nestec York Ltd.
Otsuka Pharmaceutical Europe Ltd.
Parexel International Limited
Pfizer Limited
Pirbright Institute
Premier Research International Us
Qinetiq Limited
Roke Manor Research Limited
Serco Limited
Smith International (North Sea) Ltd
SmithKline Beecham Limited
Surrey Satellite Technology Ltd
Syneos Health Clinical Development Services
TGS Geophysical Company (UK) Ltd
TRL Limited
Transport Research Foundation
Vestas Technology UK Limited

72200 Research and experimental development on social sciences and humanities

Parexel International Holding UK Ltd

73110 Advertising agencies

Affiperf Limited
JCDecaux UK Limited
JCDecaux United Limited
Target Media Limited
YH Limited

73120 Media representation services

Perform Media Sales Ltd

73200 Market research and public opinion polling

Jato Dynamics Limited

74100 Specialised design activities

Biogen (UK) Limited
Cadence Design Systems Limited
Jacobs E & C Limited

74300 Translation and interpretation activities

RWS Translations Limited
RWS UK Holding Co Limited
SDL PLC
SDL Tridion Limited

74901 Environmental consulting activities

AECOM Infrastructure & Environment UK
Black & Veatch Limited
Costain Integrated Services Ltd
Ricardo-AEA Limited
SLR Consulting Limited
SLR Management Limited
Sinclair Knight Merz (Europe) Ltd
WWF-UK

74902 Quantity surveying activities

Costain Integrated Services Ltd
Faithful+Gould Limited

74909 Other professional, scientific and technical activities n.e.c. [58]

AVM Impact Ltd
Alligent Biopharm Consulting (Europe)
Althea UK and Ireland Limited
Amazon Spring Waters Investment Ltd
Black & Decker Finance
Black & Decker International Finance (UK)
Borrow Foundation
Brand Reputation Compliance Ltd
CGG Services (UK) Limited
Chiltern International Limited
Chloride Group Limited
Chloride Supplies Limited
Cidron Healthcare - It 3 Ltd
E & J Capital Partners Limited
Ergomed PLC
Five Arrows Limited
Grigny (UK) Limited
HTC Europe Co. Ltd
Harris Defence Limited
IHS Global Limited
Ipreo UK Holdings Ltd
Johnson & Johnson Consumer Services EAME
Johnson & Johnson Innovation Ltd
Kellogg Brown & Root (Greenford) Ltd
Kinedexe UK Limited
LGC Limited
LSI Logic Europe Limited
Lockheed Martin UK Limited
Morrisroe Group Limited
Oil Spill Response (Capping) Ltd
Optasense Limited
Perform Group Financing PLC
Perform Group Limited
Perform Investment Limited
Perform Media Channels Ltd
Perform Media Services Ltd
Perform Sporting News Limited
Perform Sports Media Limited
Perkinelmer LAS (UK) Limited
Procter & Gamble Technical Centres
Pulsant Topco Limited
Q Squared Solutions Limited
Rebus Holdings Limited
Reckitt Benckiser (Brands) Ltd
Roche Diagnostics Limited
SCCI Group Limited

SNC-Lavalin Co Ltd
SSCP Spring Midco 2 Limited
Sodexo Motivation Solutions U.K. Ltd
Stanley Black & Decker UK Ltd
TRL Limited
Teletrac Navman (UK) Ltd
Towers Watson Limited
Trescal Limited
ViiV Healthcare UK (No.3) Ltd
ViiV Healthcare UK (No.4) Ltd
ViiV Healthcare UK (No.5) Ltd
ViiV Healthcare UK Limited

74990 Non-trading company [186]

103-105 Bath Road Limited
ADA PD UK Limited
ADT South Africa Holding Ltd
Accolade Wines Europe No. 2 Ltd
Acheson Industries (Europe) Ltd
Akzo Nobel Finance (2) Limited
Alenco (Holdings) Limited
Alent Finance Limited
Alent New Finance (UK) Limited
Alere UK Holdings Limited
Alestra Limited
Anixter International Limited
Ardonagh Finco PLC
Aspen Marketing Group Limited
Atlantic 2/3 UK Holdings Ltd
B & M Care Group Limited
BPS Offshore Services Limited
Beckman Holdings Limited
Berendsen Finance (DKK) Ltd
Berendsen Finance (Euro 2) Ltd
Berendsen Finance (Euro) Ltd
Berendsen Finance Limited
Berkeley (SQP) Limited
Berkeley Homes (PCL) Limited
Berkeley Seventy-Six Limited
By Chelmer PLC
CHG Overseas Investments Ltd
Cargill Holdings
Cargill Investments Holdings Ltd
Cargill UK Holdings Limited
Cerestar UK Ltd
Charity for St Joseph's Missionary Society (Generalate)
Charles River Laboratories Holdings
Comland Holdings Limited
Compass Group Finance No.4 Ltd
Compass Group North America Investments
Compass Group North America Investments No.2
Compass Hotels Chertsey
Continental Investment Limited
Crest Nicholson Developments (Chertsey)
Cullum Family Trust
D & B Group Holdings (UK)
Dairy Crest (Services) Limited
Dawsongroup UK Limited
Derrin Brothers Properties Ltd
Direct Wines Holdings Limited
Dunlop International Group Ltd
ELWA Holdings Limited
ESNT Filter Products Limited
ESNT International Limited
Eastern Quarry Limited
Eaton Holding Limited
Edgewell Personal Care Holdings UK Ltd.
Edgewell Personal Care Investments UK Ltd.
Edgewell Personal Care UK Ltd
Effem Holdings Limited
Elysium Healthcare Holdings 2 Ltd
Elysium Healthcare Holdings 3 Ltd
Elysium Healthcare LC Limited
Endon Europe Power 1 Limited
Endon Europe Power 3 Limited
Endon Europe Power 6 Limited
Ensco 1212 Limited
Ensco 1214 Limited
Envision Pharma Bidco Limited
Envision Pharma Finco Limited
Envision Pharma Group Limited
Envision Pharma Holdco Limited
Envision Pharma Midco Limited
Essentra Services Limited
Esure Holdings Limited
Exel Logistics Property Ltd
Falcon Acquisitions Limited
Ferring Asset Management Ltd
First Technology (2002) Ltd
Fitesa Limited
Food Manufacturers (G.B. Company)
Geos Group Limited
Global Consortium Limited
Godrej UK Limited
Goodrich Inertial Limited
Grafise Holdings Limited
Green,Young & Co Ltd
Gym Renewables Limited
HIC Racing (Chiswick) Limited
HIC Treasury Limited
Hamilton Palace Limited
Hamol Limited
Heathrow Airport Fuel Co Ltd
IDE Group Limited
INEOS Treasury (UK) Limited
Invesco Far East Limited
Kesa Holdings Limited
Kewsaw Limited
Kingston Bidco Limited
Kingston Midco Limited
Kingston Topco Limited
LGC (Teddington) Limited
Lafarge Nigeria (UK) Limited
Lafarge UK Holdings Limited
MES Interco
MMO2 Limited
Mallinckrodt UK Ltd
Manitowoc Crane Group (UK) Subco Ltd
Mattel UK Holdings Limited
McNeil Products Limited
Menzies Group Holdings Limited
Merck Consumer Healthcare Ltd
Meslink Limited
Nextonline Limited
Nomad Foods Europe Finco Ltd
Nomad Foods Europe Holdco Ltd
Nomad Foods Europe Midco Ltd
O2 (Europe) Limited
O2 Cedar Limited
O2 Holdings Limited
O2 International Holdings Ltd
O2 Networks Limited
Overture Bidco Limited
Overture Midco II Limited
Overture Midco Limited
Overture Topco Limited
PSN Holdco Limited
PandoraExpress 7 Limited
PizzaExpress Financing 1 PLC
PizzaExpress Financing 2 PLC
PizzaExpress Group Holdings Ltd
Portals Group Limited
Portsmouth Surgical Holdings Ltd
Premier Lotteries UK Limited
Procter & Gamble (Health & Beauty Care)
Procter & Gamble Finance (UK) Ltd
Procter & Gamble Investment Company (UK)
Procter & Gamble Limited
Procter & Gamble Overseas Ltd
Procter & Gamble UK Parent Co Ltd
RSA Finance
Rank Nemo (Twenty-Five) Ltd
Reckitt Benckiser Finance (2010) Ltd
Reckitt Benckiser Healthcare (Central & Eastern Europe)
Reckitt Benckiser Service Bureau Ltd
Red Funnel Limited
Regentrealm Limited
Remy Cointreau UK Limited
Renewi Financial Management Ltd
Rentokil Initial Holdings Ltd
Rentokil Overseas Holdings Ltd
Runecorp Limited
SWS Group Holdings Limited
SWS Holdings Limited
Shilton Bidco Limited
Shilton Holdco Limited
Shukco 327 Ltd
Signet Holdings Limited
Sky Comedy Limited
Solvecorp Limited
South Downs Capital Limited
South East Water (Holdings) Ltd
Southern Water (NR) Holdings Ltd
Southern Water Limited
Southern Water Services Group Ltd
J.W. Spear & Sons Limited
Spirent Investment Limited
Street Family Group of Companies (Holdings)
Sun Alliance and London Insurance
Surfcontrol Limited
Synventive Acquisition UK Ltd
TUV SUD (UK) Limited
Telefonica Europe PLC
Telefonica Germany Holdings Ltd
Thursdays (Holdings) Limited
Towergate Insurance Limited
Towers Watson UK Limited
Trifast Overseas Holdings Ltd
Trifast PLC
United Technologies Finance (U.K.)
Vodafone Finance Sweden
Vodafone Overseas Holdings Ltd
Wakefield Waste Holdings Ltd
Watson Wyatt (UK) Acquisitions 2 Ltd
Watson Wyatt Holdings Limited
West London Energy Recovery Ltd
Western Wines Holdings Limited
Wimpey Dormant Investments Ltd
XPS Pensions Group PLC
Xafinity Consulting (Reading) Ltd

75000 Veterinary activities

Boehringer Ingelheim Animal Health UK
Horse Trust
Intervet UK Limited
Intervet UK Production Limited
Medivet Group Limited

77110 Renting and leasing of cars and light motor vehicles [20]

Apex Car Rental PLC

Burnt Tree Group Limited
Buy 2 Let Cars Ltd
Cargobull Finance Limited
Dawsongroup Vans Limited
Enterprise Rent-a-Car UK Holdings
Enterprise Rent-a-Car UK Ltd
Erac UK Finance Limited
Hamsard 3352 Limited
Hamsard 3353 Limited
Hertz (U.K.) Limited
Inula Holding UK Limited
Leaseplan UK Limited
Leasys UK Ltd
Local Car and Van Rental Ltd
Moneybarn No.1 Limited
S.H.B. Hire Limited
Sixt Rent A Car Limited
Tuskerdirect Limited
United Kenning Rental Group Ltd

77120 Renting and leasing of trucks and other heavy vehicles [11]

BNP Paribas Rental Solutions Ltd
Barloworld Equipment UK Ltd
Burnt Tree Group Limited
Cargobull Finance Limited
Dawsongroup Truck and Trailer Ltd
M C Group Limited
MC Rental Limited
MCG (Holdings) Ltd
E.H. Nicholls Holdings Ltd
S.H.B. Hire Limited
Vostochnaya Technica UK Ltd

77291 Renting and leasing of media entertainment equipment

Creative Technology Limited
Panalux Limited
Panavision Europe Limited
Pinewood MBS Lighting Limited

77299 Renting and leasing of other personal and household goods

Berendsen UK Limited

77310 Renting and leasing of agricultural machinery and equipment

R. Hunt (Agricultural Engineers)

77320 Renting and leasing of construction and civil engineering machinery and equipment [11]

Clive Barford Limited
Clancy Plant Limited
Facelift (GB) Limited
H.E. Group Ltd
JRL Plant and Logistics Ltd
Keltbray Plant Limited
London Tower Crane Hire & Sales Ltd
L. Lynch (Holdings) Limited
L. Lynch (Plant Hire & Haulage) Ltd
Readypower Rail Services Ltd
Selwood Holdings Limited

77330 Renting and leasing of office machinery and equipment (including computers)

Econocom Limited
IBM United Kingdom Asset Leasing Ltd
Rackspace UK Leasing Limited
Xerox (UK) Limited
Xerox Finance Limited

77341 Renting and leasing of passenger water transport equipment

Sunsail Worldwide Sailing Ltd

77342 Renting and leasing of freight water transport equipment

Blue Sky Intermodal (UK) Ltd.

77351 Renting and leasing of air passenger transport equipment

Bristow Aircraft Leasing Ltd
Bristow Southeast Asia Limited
British Midland Airways Ltd
Caledonian Helicopters Limited
Lufthansa Technik Landing Gear Services UK

77352 Renting and leasing of freight air transport equipment

TCR UK Limited

77390 Renting and leasing of other machinery, equipment and tangible goods n.e.c. [18]

Althea (Leicester 2) Limited
Chep UK Limited
Dawsongroup Bus and Coach Ltd
Dawsongroup Material Handling Ltd
Dawsongroup Temperature Control Solutions
Expro Resources Limited
IBM United Kingdom Asset Leasing Ltd
Johnson & Johnson Finance Ltd
KCI Medical Limited
Linde Creighton Limited
Linde Jewsbury's Limited
Linde Severnside Limited
Linde Sterling Limited
MEMS Power Generation Limited
PEAC (UK) Limited
Pinewood MBS Lighting Limited
Sanden International (Europe) Ltd
Somerset Equipment Finance (UK) Ltd

77400 Leasing of intellectual property and similar products, except copyright works

IBM United Kingdom Asset Leasing Ltd
Porcelanosa U.K. Limited
Reckitt & Colman (Overseas) Ltd

78109 Other activities of employment placement agencies [12]

Allegis Global Solutions Ltd
Allegis Group (UK) Holdings II Ltd
Allegis Group (UK) Holdings Ltd
Allegis Group Limited
Aston Carter International Ltd
Interquest Group (UK) Limited
Interserve Working Futures Ltd
Matchtech Group (UK) Limited
Michael Page Holdings Limited
Michael Page International Recruitment
Royal British Legion Poppy Factory
Technical Staffing Resources Ltd

78200 Temporary employment agency activities [23]

A24 Group Limited
Allegis Global Solutions Ltd
Allegis Group (UK) Holdings II Ltd
Allegis Group (UK) Holdings Ltd
Allegis Group Limited
Aston Carter International Ltd
Cordant People Limited
ID Medical Group Limited
Kelly Services (UK) Limited
Manpower UK Limited
Matchtech Group (UK) Limited
NHS Professionals Limited
Networkers International (UK) Ltd
Networkers International Ltd
Nurse Plus and Carer Plus (UK) Ltd
PMP Recruitment Limited
Premiere Employment Group Ltd
Sopra Steria Recruitment Ltd
Valour Bidco Limited
Valour Holdco Limited
Valour Midco I Limited
Valour Midco II Limited
Volt Europe Limited

78300 Human resources provision and management of human resources functions

Allegis Global Solutions Ltd
Allegis Group (UK) Holdings II Ltd
Allegis Group (UK) Holdings Ltd
Allegis Group Limited
Aston Carter International Ltd
Celltech R & D Limited
Guild Resources Limited
Search Consultancy Acquisition Ltd
Search Consultancy Topco Ltd

79110 Travel agency activities [19]

Australian Pacific Touring (U.K.)
BI Worldwide Limited
Exodus Travels Limited
Flight Centre (UK) Limited
Flight Centre (UK) Wholesale Ltd
Hayes & Jarvis (Travel) Ltd
Hogg Robinson (Travel) Limited
Imagine Cruising Limited
Onkar International Limited
Overseas Air Travel Limited
RCL Cruises Ltd
Southall Travel Limited
Specialist Holidays (Travel) Ltd
Sunsail Worldwide Sailing Ltd
Sunspot Tours Limited
Travel Republic Ltd
Travel Up Group PLC
Travel Up Limited
Travelopia Holdings Limited

79120 Tour operator activities [11]

Der Touristik UK Limited
Hotelplan Limited
James Villa Holidays Limited
Luxury Travel Acquisitions Ltd
Luxury Travel Financing Ltd
Luxury Travel Holdings Limited
Neilson Active Holidays Ltd
Newmarket Promotions Limited
Scott Dunn Limited
Sunspot Tours Limited
Virgin Holidays Limited

79901 Activities of tourist guides
Sunspot Tours Limited

79909 Other reservation service activities n.e.c.
Lotus Leisure Ltd
Sunspot Tours Limited
Travelport International Ltd

80100 Private security activities
G4S Cash Centres (UK) Limited
G4S Cash Solutions (UK) Ltd
G4S Secure Solutions (UK) Ltd
G4S Security Services (UK) Ltd
ISS Facility Services Limited
Security Monitoring Centres Ltd

80200 Security systems service activities
Chubb Fire & Security Limited
Secom PLC

81100 Combined facilities support activities [28]
Academy Services (Waltham Forest)
Affinity (Reading) Limited
Capital Hospitals (Holdings) Ltd.
Capital Hospitals Ltd.
Coventry and Rugby Hospital Company PLC
Derby Healthcare (Holdings) Ltd
Emcor Group (UK) PLC
H & D Support Services Limited
ISS Facility Services Limited
ISS Mediclean Limited
Johnson Controls Building Efficiency UK
Mapeley Steps Contractor Ltd
Meridian Hospital Company (Holdings)
Meridian Hospital Company PLC
Newschools (Merton) Limited
OCS Group UK Limited
Prospect Healthcare (Hinchingbrooke)
Prospect Healthcare (Reading) Ltd
QED (Clacton) Limited
QED (Leeds) Limited
Rydon Maintenance Limited
Salisbury Holdings Limited
Salisbury Workplace Services Ltd
Taunton Linac Co Ltd
United Healthcare (South Buckinghamshire) Group
United Healthcare (South Buckinghamshire) Holdings
United Healthcare (South Buckinghamshire)
Walsall Hospital Company PLC

81210 General cleaning of buildings
Cordant Cleaning Limited
ISS Facility Services Limited
OCS Group UK Limited

81222 Specialised cleaning services
Suez Advanced Solutions UK Ltd

81229 Other building and industrial cleaning activities
OCS Group UK Limited

81299 Other cleaning services
Spectrum Franchising Limited

81300 Landscape service activities
Milton Keynes Parks Trust Ltd

82110 Combined office administrative service activities
Compleat Food Group Limited
G & O Securities Limited
Paradigm (UK) Holding Limited
Waterlogic Finance Limited
Waterlogic Group Holdings Ltd
Waterlogic Holdings Limited
Whistl Group Limited
Whistl Limited

82190 Photocopying, document preparation and other specialised office support activities
Kodak Alaris Limited

82200 Activities of call centres
Argos Limited

82301 Activities of exhibition and fair organisers
Reed Exhibitions Limited

82302 Activities of conference organisers
BI Worldwide Limited

82911 Activities of collection agencies
G & O Securities Limited
Intrum UK Finance Limited

82990 Other business support service activities n.e.c. [519]
1948 Group Limited
55VS No 2 Limited
AB InBev International Brands Ltd
ACAL BFI Central Procurement UK Ltd
APCOA Parking (UK) Limited
APCOA Parking Holdings (UK) Ltd
AVM Impact Ltd
Abertis Motorways UK Limited
Accesso Technology Group PLC
Acquaspen Limited
Affinion International Limited
Affinion International Travel Ltd
Airinmar Limited
Aitch Care Homes (London) Ltd
Akari Therapeutics, PLC
Alcon Eye Care UK Limited
Alestra Group Holdings Limited
Alexion Pharma UK Limited
Alimera Sciences Limited
Alliance BMP Limited
Allianz (UK) Limited
Allianz Management Services Ltd
Allianz Properties Limited
Almus Pharmaceuticals Limited
Anesco Acquisitionco Limited
Anesco Bidco 1 Limited
Annes Gate Property PLC
Aramark Investments Limited
Aramark Japan Holdings Limited
Archer Assets UK Limited
Arinso People Services Limited
Arlacross Limited
Arlaform Limited
Armatire Limited
Arqiva No 2 Limited
Arqiva No 3 Limited
Arqiva Services Limited
Arun Estate Agencies Limited
Asia Pacific Holdings Limited
Atkins ATK Investments Limited
Atkins International Holdings Ltd
W.S. Atkins International Ltd
Atkins Investments UK Limited
Atkins Limited
Atlas Copco Limited
Aura Finance Limited
Automobile Association Developments
Autumnpaper Limited
Avios Group (AGL) Limited
Avis Budget Services Limited
Avis Finance Co Ltd
Aviva Administration Limited
Aviva Management Services UK Ltd
Avtrade Holdings Limited
Axis Group Integrated Services Ltd
B O C Holdings
BAE Systems (Dynamics) Limited
BAE Systems (Funding Two) Ltd
BAE Systems Enterprises Ltd
BAM Construct UK Limited
BAP Pharma Group Limited
BCMV Limited
BI Worldwide Limited
BIMM Topco Limited
BOC Gases Limited
BOC Group Limited
BOC Helex
BOC Investment Holdings Ltd
BOC Investments No.1 Limited
BOC Investments No.5
BOC Korea Holdings Limited
BOC Netherlands Holdings Ltd
BP Gas Marketing Limited
BP Investment Management Ltd
BP Subsea Well Response Ltd
Bandai Namco Amusement Europe Ltd
Becton Dickinson Infusion Therapy Holdings UK
Beecham Group P L C
Belron UK Limited
Berkeley Two Hundred and Three Ltd
Bio Products Laboratory Ltd
Biocompatibles International Ltd
Bluefield SIF Investments Ltd
Brentwick Limited
Bristol-Myers Squibb Business Services
Britannic Trading Limited
British Car Auctions Limited
British Gas Finance Limited
British Gas New Heating Ltd
British and Foreign Wharf Co Ltd
Broadway Malyan Employee Ownership Trustees
Brown and Mason Holdings Ltd
Bullitt Group Limited
Burnfield Limited
By Design (UK) Limited
CNOOC UK Limited
CSG Systems UK Limited
Cable & Wireless Global Telecommunication Services
Cabot Financial (Marlin) Ltd
Canon (UK) Limited
Canterbury Diocesan Board of Finance
Carscreugh Renewable Energy Park Ltd
Central G H Trust

Centrica Beta Holdings Limited
Centrica Energy Limited
Centrica Finance (Canada) Ltd
Centrica Finance (US) Limited
Centrica Gamma Holdings Ltd
Centrica Overseas Holdings Ltd
Challenger Multi Academy Trust
Chiltern International Limited
Chrysalis (Stanhope) Limited
Cineworld Estates Limited
Civil Service Benevolent Fund
Coats Finance Co. Limited
Colgate Holdings
Colgate-Palmolive (U.K.) Ltd
Compressor Products Holdings Ltd
Consort Healthcare (Blackburn) Funding
Consort Healthcare (Blackburn) Holdings
Consort Healthcare (Blackburn) Ltd
Constantine Wind Energy Ltd
Continua Limited
CooperVision (UK) Holdings Ltd
Cosan Lubes Investments Ltd
Costa Express Limited
Crane Payment Innovations International
Creative Technology Limited
Crown Agents Bank Limited
Croydon and Lewisham Lighting Services
DF Group Limited
DG Partners Services Limited
DHL Distribution Holdings (UK) Ltd
DHL GBS (UK) Limited
DHL Services Limited
DHL UK Foundation
Dairy Crest France Holdings 1 Ltd
Dairy Crest UK Limited
Danu Holding Limited
Danu II Holdings Limited
Data Solutions 2016 Limited
De La Rue Finance Limited
De La Rue Holdings Limited
Dealcyber Limited
Defence Investments Limited
Driveline Limited
Dun & Bradstreet Finance Ltd
Dun & Bradstreet Limited
Dynama Solutions Ltd
ENRA Group Limited
ESP Connections Limited
ESRI Holdings Limited
Eastern Leasing Co Ltd
Education Support (Enfield 2) Holdings
Education Support (Enfield 2) Ltd
Egger (UK) Holdings Limited
Ellenbrook Developments PLC
Elwy 2 Limited
Elwy 3 Limited
Emery Oleochemicals UK Limited
Environments for Learning Sandwell PFI One
Equiniti Limited
Eskaylab Limited
Essentra Finance Limited
Esure Finance Limited
Esure Services Limited
European Glass Group Limited
European Investments (Cornwall) Ltd
M.P. Evans Group PLC
Everyday Loans Limited
ExxonMobil Chemical Investment Co Ltd
ExxonMobil Finance Co Ltd
ExxonMobil Financial Investment Co Ltd
ExxonMobil Holding Co Ltd
ExxonMobil Investment Co Ltd
ExxonMobil UK Limited
FCA Dealer Services UK Ltd
FWPJV Limited
Faithful+Gould Limited
Ferguson Group Services Ltd
First Rate Exchange Services Holdings
First Rate Exchange Services Ltd
Fluor International Limited
Fogarty Group Limited
Francotyp-Postalia Limited
GBF Capital Limited
GCP Asset Finance 1 Limited
GCP Biomass 1 Ltd
GCP Biomass 4 Limited
GCP Cardale PFI Ltd
GCP Green Energy 1 Limited
GCP Onshore Wind 3 Limited
GCP Programme Funding 1 Ltd
GCP Rooftop Solar 4 Limited
GCP Rooftop Solar 5 Ltd
GCP Rooftop Solar 6 PLC
GCP Rooftop Solar Finance PLC
GCP Social Housing 1 Limited
GE Money Servicing Limited
GL Assessment Limited
GVS Prepaid Limited
Garreg Lwyd Energy Limited
Gazelli Art House Limited
Gemalto UK Limited
Gilead Sciences Europe Ltd.
Ginger Bidco Limited
Ginger Midco Limited
Ginger Topco Limited
Glasgow Learning Quarter Ltd
GlaxoSmithKline Intellectual Property Management
GlaxoSmithKline International Ltd
GlaxoSmithKline Investment Services
Green Hill Energy Limited
Greenshields JCB Holdings Ltd
Gym Renewables One Limited
H+H UK Holdings Limited
HDF (UK) Holdings Limited
HRG Debtco Limited
HSH Hotels (2017) Limited
Harsco Rail Limited
Hasbro U.K. Limited
Hawk Incentives Holdings Ltd
Hawk Incentives Limited
Haymarket UK2 Limited
Health Management Limited
Healthcare Support (North Staffs) Finance
Heathrow Airport Limited
Helsinki Bidco Limited
Helsinki Midco Limited
Helsinki Topco Limited
Hertz Holdings III UK Limited
Hill of Towie Limited
Hilton Finance (UK) Limited
Hilton Worldwide FS Treasury Ltd
Hitachi Europe Limited
Home Retail Group (UK) Limited
Honeywell Control Systems Ltd
Honeywell Normalair-Garrett (Holdings)
Horlicks Limited
Hotel Intercontinental London (Holdings)
Huyck.Wangner UK Limited
IAG GBS Limited
ICS Incorporation Limited
IHG Hotels Limited
INC Research Europe Holdings Ltd
INC Research Holding Limited
INEOS Commercial Services UK Ltd
ISDC Developments (No2) Ltd
Idemitsu International (Europe) Ltd
Igroup 8 Limited
Infinity SDC Limited
Infotech Trade Services Ltd
Ingersoll-Rand UK Limited
Initial Medical Services Ltd
Inprint Systems Limited
Inspiral Oldham Limited
Intercontinental Hotels Ltd
Interserve Finance Limited
Intralot Finance UK Limited
Invesco Asset Management Ltd
Invesco GT Asset Management Ltd
Iris Capital Limited
Ixcellerate Limited
J.T.D. Finance Limited
J.T.D. Investments Limited
JLW Excellent Homes for Life Ltd
Jacobs Process Limited
Jacobs U.K. Limited
Jakks Pacific (UK) Ltd
Johnson & Johnson Management Ltd
Johnson Wax Limited
Jupiter Topco Limited
Just Develop It Limited
Just Retirement Management Services
KN Network Services (Northern Ireland)
KPJV Limited
KWay Holdings Limited
Kazakh Projects Joint Venture Ltd
Keadby Wind Farm Limited
Kemble Water Eurobond PLC
Keysight Technologies UK Ltd
Kidde Finance Limited
Kimberly-Clark U.K. Operations Ltd
Kofax US Holdings Limited
Kuehne + Nagel (UK) Limited
LGC (Holdings) Limited
LGC Investments Limited
LGC Science Holdings Limited
LGC Science Investments Ltd
LGC Whirlwind Limited
LRH Care Homes Limited
Leaderboard Golf Holdings Ltd
Liberata UK Limited
Linde Canada Holdings Limited
Linde Cryogenics Limited
Linde Investments No.1 Limited
Linde North America Holdings Ltd
Linde UK Holdings Limited
Link Asset Services (Holdings) Ltd
Link Market Services Limited
Logoplaste UK Limited
Lonepiper Limited
MC Treasury Limited
MDL Development Company Number 2 Ltd
ME III Limited
MJN International Holdings (UK), Ltd.
MTS Systems Limited
Maintenance Management Limited
Maple Topco Limited
Mapleco1 Ltd
Marlin Europe I Limited
Marlin Europe II Limited
Marlin Financial Intermediate Ltd
Mars Investments
Masterson Holdings Limited
Matrix SCM Limited
Alexander McQueen Trading Ltd
Medispeed

Mondelez UK Limited
Motor Insurers' Bureau
Motorline Holdings Limited
Motorline Limited
NIS Receivables No. 2 Limited
NTL (B) Limited
NTL (CWC) Limited
NTL Communications Services Ltd
NTL Rectangle Limited
NTL Victoria Limited
Netcall PLC
Neusentis Limited
New Topco 1 Limited
Newincco 1270 Limited
Nexen Petroleum U.K. Holdings Ltd
Nice Systems UK Finance Ltd
Nice Systems US Finance Ltd
Nomad Foods BondCo PLC
Nomad Foods Europe Finco Ltd
Nomad Foods Europe Holdco Ltd
Nomad Foods Europe Holdings Ltd
Nomad Foods Europe Midco Ltd
Norma UK Limited
Northgate Information Solutions Ltd
Northgate UK Holdings 1 Ltd
Northgate UK Holdings 2 Ltd
Northgate UK Holdings 3 Ltd
Northgate UK Holdings 4 Ltd
Novar Systems Limited
Nuffield Health Pension Trustees Ltd
Nuvias Group Limited
OCS Group UK Limited
OMC Investments Limited
Oil Spill Response Limited
Old Mutual Wealth Business Services
Old Mutual Wealth Limited
Orange Business Holdings UK Ltd
Orange Business UK Limited
Orthopaedic Research UK
Patek Philippe Salon Limited
Paymaster (1836) Limited
Paymentshield Services Limited
Petco Trading (UK) Limited
Petrofac Engineering Limited
Pharmacia Limited
Phivco UK II Limited
Photo-Me Limited
Pinewood Finco PLC
Pinnacle Schools (Fife) Ltd
Pinnacle Schools (Gateshead) Ltd
Pittway Systems Technology Group Europe
Platinum Acquisition Limited
Platinum Midco 2 Limited
Platinum Midco Limited
Platinum Topco Limited
Police Rehabilitation Centre
Polycom (United Kingdom) Ltd.
Procter & Gamble Technical Centres
Pulsant Group Limited
Pulsant Midco 1 Limited
Pulsant Midco 2 Limited
Pulsant Parent Limited
Pyramid Schools (Sheffield) Ltd
Qinetiq Holdings Limited
Quaker Holdings (UK) Limited
RES UK & Ireland Limited
RIF Holdings Limited
RL Retail Services Limited
RS Furbs Limited
Redsky IT Holdings Limited
Regard ACH Holdco Limited
Regenter B3 Limited
Regenter Myatts Field North Ltd
Rentokil Initial 1927 PLC
Rentokil Initial Americas Ltd
Rentokil Initial Finance Ltd
Rentokil Initial PLC
Rentokil Initial UK Ltd
Rentokil Limited
Restore PLC
Retirement Villages Limited
Riemser Pharma UK Limited
Rocco Homes Limited
Rockwell European Holdings Ltd
Rush Hair Group Limited
S A Designer Parfums Limited
SCIH Branston 3
SCJ EurAFNE Ltd
SCJ UK Finco Ltd
SD Worx UK Limited
SGN Commercial Services Ltd
SPI Lasers PLC
SSE Energy Supply Limited
SSE Services PLC
Samsung Electronics (UK) Ltd
Scape Opportunities Dublin Ltd
Schlumberger Cambridge Research Ltd
Secure Meters (UK) Limited
Seqirus UK Limited
Services Support (Gravesend) Ltd
Services Support (Manchester) Ltd
Services Support (SEL) Limited
Sesame Limited
Sesame Services Limited
Sevita (UK) Limited
Shared Services Connected Ltd
Shearwater Geoservices Limited
Signet Direct Diamond Sourcing Ltd
Signet Trading Limited
Signet UK Finance PLC
Six Continents Investments Ltd
Six Continents Limited
Six Continents Overseas Holdings Ltd
Six Continents Restaurants Ltd
Skanska Infrastructure Investment UK
Skanska J.V. Projects Ltd
Sky Finance Europe Limited
Sky Group Finance PLC
Sky Telecommunications Services Ltd
Sky UK Limited
Smartspace Software PLC
Sony Global Treasury Services PLC
Sopra Steria Holdings Limited
Southern Water Capital Limited
St James Holdings Limited
Stanley Electric Holding Europe Co.,
Stansted Park Foundation
Storeshield Limited
Subsea 7 Engineering Limited
Subsea 7 Investments (UK) Ltd
Subsea 7 Treasury (UK) Limited
Suez Advanced Solutions Holding UK
Surrey Blue Limited
Surrey Lighting Services Ltd
Swiss Post Solutions Ltd
Symantec Security (UK) Limited
Synbra UK Limited
Syneos Health International Ltd
Syneos Health UK Limited
Systagenix Wound Management, Ltd
TBG (4) Limited
TJX Europe Buying Limited
TTG Investments Limited
TWG Services Limited
Taylor Wimpey 2007 Limited
TechnoGym U.K. Limited
Teddington 2 Limited
Telewest Communications Networks Ltd
Telewest Limited
Thames Water (Kemble) Finance PLC
Theseus No. 1 Limited
Theseus No. 2 Limited
Toshiba of Europe Limited
Transform Schools (Bassetlaw) Ltd
Transform Schools (Knowsley) Ltd
Transform Schools (North Lanarkshire) Holdings
Transform Schools (Rotherham) Ltd
Travel Republic Holdings Ltd.
Travelport (UK) Services Ltd
Travelport Finance Limited
Travelport International Ltd
Trek Investco Limited
UK Highways M40 (Holdings) Ltd
UK Highways M40 Limited
UOP Limited
USF International Limited
Unipath Limited
VFS Legal Limited
VMFH Limited
Vendcrown Limited
Verizon Connect UK Limited
ViiV Healthcare UK Limited
Virgin Media Business Limited
Virgin Media Communications Ltd
Virgin Media Finance PLC
Virgin Media Finco Limited
Virgin Media Investments Ltd
Virgin Media Mobile Finance Ltd
Virgin Media Payments Ltd
Virgin Media SFA Finance Ltd
Virgin Media Secured Finance PLC
Virgin Media Wholesale Limited
Vodafone 5 Limited
Vodafone 6 UK
Vodafone European Investments
Vodafone Holdings Luxembourg Ltd
Vodafone Marketing UK
Vodafone Oceania Limited
WEL Solar Park 2 Limited
Walgreens Boots Alliance Services
Walkers Snack Foods Limited
Walkers Snacks (Distribution) Ltd
Walkers Snacks Limited
Warrant Investments PLC
Wates Group Services Limited
W K Webster & Co Ltd
Western United Investment Co Ltd
Wyboston Lakes Limited
Zanlia Limited
Zurich Management Services Ltd
Zurich UK General Services Ltd

84110 General public administration activities

Achieving for Children CIC
Liberata UK Limited
NHS Professionals Limited
Royal British Legion Industries Ltd.
Serco Limited

84220 Defence activities [17]

AWE Management Limited
Aquila Air Traffic Management Services
BAE Systems (Defence Systems) Ltd

BAE Systems (Land and Sea Systems)
BAE Systems (Military Air) Overseas
BAE Systems (Oman) Limited
BAE Systems (Operations) Ltd
BAE Systems Electronics Ltd
BMT Group Limited
Chemring Technology Solutions Ltd
Eastbury Park Limited
Harris Defence Limited
Jankel Armouring Limited
Rockwell Collins UK Limited
Royal Air Force Central Fund
STI Enterprises Limited
Thales UK Limited

84250 Fire service activities

Chubb Fire & Security Limited
Chubb Fire Limited

85100 Pre-primary education [27]

Bellevue Education International Ltd
Berkhamsted Schools Group
Brighton College
CFBT Schools Trust
Caterham School Limited
Childbase Partnership Limited
Claremont Fan Court Foundation Ltd
Cognita Schools Limited
Dover Federation for The Arts
Eastbourne College (Incorporated)
Future Schools Trust
Grandir UK Limited
Hampton School
King Edward VI School Southampton
Lancing College Limited
Leigh Academies Trust
Oratory Schools Association
The Alec Reed Academy
Rosedale Hewens Academy Trust
Russell School Trust
St Bede's School Trust Sussex
St George's Weybridge
TASIS The American School in England
TASIS UK Limited
University of Brighton Academies Trust
Vanguard Learning Trust
Walthamstow Hall

85200 Primary education [64]

1509 Group
Ardingly College Limited
Bellevue Education International Ltd
Berkhamsted Schools Group
Bourne Education Trust
Brighton College
CFBT Schools Trust
Caterham School Limited
Children's Trust
Claremont Fan Court Foundation Ltd
Cognita Schools Limited
Cranleigh School
Dover Federation for The Arts
Eastbourne College (Incorporated)
Future Schools Trust
GFM Education
GLF Schools
Guildford Education Partnership
Hampton School
Howard Partnership Trust
Hurstpierpoint College Limited
Kennet School Academies Trust
King Edward VI School Southampton
Kite Academy Trust
Lady Eleanor Holles School
Lancing College Limited
Langley Academy Trust
Langley Park Learning Trust
Learning Alliance Academy Trust
Leigh Academies Trust
Oratory Schools Association
Parallel Learning Trust
Park Federation Academy Trust
Pegasus Academy Trust
Piggott Church of England School
Pioneer Educational Trust
Portsmouth Grammar School
The Alec Reed Academy
Reigate Grammar School
Rosedale Hewens Academy Trust
Russell School Trust
Schoolsworks Academy Trust
Slough and East Berkshire C of E Multi Academy Trust
Somerhill Charitable Trust Ltd
South East Surrey Schools Education Trust
St Bede's School Trust Sussex
St George's Weybridge
St. Catherine's School, Bramley
St. Margaret's School Bushey
St.Swithuns School (Winchester)
Step Academy Trust
Swale Academies Trust
Synaptic Trust
TASIS The American School in England
TASIS UK Limited
Tandridge Learning Trust
Treloar Trust
University of Brighton Academies Trust
Valley Invicta Academies Trust
Vanguard Learning Trust
Vernon Educational Trust Ltd
Walthamstow Hall
Williamson Trust
Woodland Academy Trust

85310 General secondary education [164]

1509 Group
5 Dimensions Trust
ACS International Schools Ltd
Abbey School, Reading
Ardingly College Limited
Attwood Academies
Baylis Court Trust
Beacon Community College Academy Trust
Beaconsfield High School
Bedales School
Bellerbys Educational Services Ltd
Benenden School (Kent) Limited
Berkhamsted Schools Group
Bishopshalt School
Blackfen School for Girls
Bohunt Education Trust
Bourne Education Trust
Brentford School for Girls
Brighton College
Brook Learning Trust
Bullers Wood Multi Academy Trust
CFBT Schools Trust
Cams Hill School
Carshalton Boys Sports College
Caterham School Limited
Charters School
Chatham & Clarendon Grammar School
Children's Trust
Chislehurst and Sidcup Grammar School
Chobham School Academy (Stratford)
Christ's Hospital
Claremont Fan Court Foundation Ltd
Coastal Academies Trust
Cognita Schools Limited
Collegiate Trust
Collingwood College
Coombe Academy Trust
Cowplain School
Cox Green School
Cranleigh School
DYRMS - An Academy with Military Traditions
Charles Darwin Academy Trust
Denbigh Alliance
Dover Federation for The Arts
Downe House School
Durrington Multi Academy Trust
Eastbourne College (Incorporated)
Education Development Trust
Education for The 21st Century
Elmwey Learning Trust
Epsom College
Erith School
Every Child, Every Day Academy Trust
Fort Pitt Thomas Aveling Academies
Fulston Manor Academies Trust
Furze Platt Senior School
Future Schools Trust
GFM Education
GLF Schools
Girls' Education Co Ltd
Girls' Learning Trust
Greenshaw Learning Trust
Guildford Education Partnership
Hampton School
Harefield Academy Trust
Hazeley Academy
Hazelwick School
Herne Bay High School
Hertswood Academy
Howard Partnership Trust
Hurstpierpoint College Limited
Impact Multi Academy Trust
Isleworth and Syon School for Boys
Kedleston (Wings Education) Ltd
Kennet School Academies Trust
King Edward VI School Southampton
Kingston Grammar School
Lady Eleanor Holles School
Lampton School Academy Trust
Lancing College Limited
Langley Academy Trust
Langley Park Learning Trust
Langley Park School for Boys Academy Trust
Learning Alliance Academy Trust
Leigh Academies Trust
Leighton Park Trust
Lord Wandsworth College
Maiden Erlegh Trust
Manor Trust
Robert May's School
Meller Educational Trust
Milton Keynes Academy Trust
Milton Keynes Education Trust
Mountbatten School
Newlands Girls' School
Odyssey Trust for Education
Oratory Schools Association
Orleans Park School
Ousedale School

Overton Grange School
Parallel Learning Trust
Piggott Church of England School
Pioneer Educational Trust
Portsmouth Grammar School
Prospect School, Reading
Queens' School (Bushey)
RMET
Radnor House School (Holdings) Ltd
Radnor House School (Property) Ltd
Sir William Ramsay School Academy Trust
The Alec Reed Academy
Reigate Grammar School
Richmond West Schools Trust
Romsey School
Rosedale Hewens Academy Trust
Russell School Trust
Rye Academy Trust
Salterns Academy Trust
Schelwood Trust
Sevenoaks School
Skills for Life Trust
Slough and East Berkshire C of E Multi Academy Trust
South East Surrey Schools Education Trust
St Bartholomew's School
St Bede's School Trust Sussex
St George's Weybridge
St Mary's School Ascot
St. Catherine's School, Bramley
St. Margaret's School Bushey
St.Swithuns School (Winchester)
Stowe School,Limited
Study Group Holdings UK Ltd
Study Group UK Limited
Sussex Learning Trust
Swale Academies Trust
TASIS The American School in England
TASIS UK Limited
Tandridge Learning Trust
Teddington School
Tenterden Schools Trust
Thinking Schools Academy Trust
Tonbridge School
Treloar Trust
Unity Schools Trust
University of Brighton Academies Trust
University of Kent Academies Trust
Uxbridge High School Academy Trust
Valley Invicta Academies Trust
Vanguard Learning Trust
Waingels Academies Trust
Waldegrave Trust
Walthamstow Hall
Weald of Kent Grammar School Academy Trust
Weydon Multi Academy Trust
Wildern Academy Trust
William Willett Learning Trust
Williamson Trust
Willow Learning Trust
Windsor Learning Partnership
Woldingham School
Wootton Academy Trust
Wycombe High School Academies Trust
Yavneh College Academy Trust
Yehudi Menuhin School Limited

85320 Technical and vocational secondary education

Crossknowledge Group Limited
Dover Federation for The Arts
JTL
Marwell Wildlife
National Film and Television School
Science, Engineering and Manufacturing Technologies Alliance

85410 Post-secondary non-tertiary education

Brighton College
Interserve Working Futures Ltd
Valley Invicta Academies Trust
Willow Learning Trust

85421 First-degree level higher education

BIMM 1 Limited
BIMM Holdings Limited
BIMM Limited
Canterbury Christ Church University
GL Assessment Limited
St Mary's University, Twickenham
University of Chichester
University of Winchester

85422 Post-graduate level higher education

COL Newco Limited
Canterbury Christ Church University
L-J Bidco Limited
L-J Finco Limited
Services Sound and Vision Corporation
St Mary's University, Twickenham
University of Chichester
University of Law Limited
University of Winchester

85520 Cultural education

Mary Rose Trust

85530 Driving school activities

Automobile Association Developments

85590 Other education n.e.c. [23]

Ardingly College Limited
Aurora Academies Trust
CAE (UK) PLC
Columbus Bidco Limited
Columbus Midco Limited
Columbus Topco Limited
Dolphin Two Limited
Fast Training Services Limited
Harris Federation
The Edward James Foundation Ltd
Kemnal Academies Trust
Kingswood Learning and Leisure Group
Lake Bridge International PLC
Lake International Ltd
Milton Keynes Education Trust
National Foundation for Educational Research in England and Wales
Oxford Aviation Academy (Oxford) Ltd
Prior's Court Foundation
QA Limited
Sharnbrook Academy Federation
St. Patrick's International College
Voluntary Service Overseas
WWF-UK

85600 Educational support services [18]

Achieving for Children CIC
Bellevue Education Group Ltd
Education Development Trust
Environments for Learning Sandwell PFI One
Espalier Finance Limited
Espalier Ventures Limited
GLF Schools
Gordon Foundation
Gus UK Management Limited
Kedleston Schools Limited
Kent Catholic Schools' Partnership
Oxford International Education 1 Ltd
Oxford International Education 2 Ltd
Oxford International Education 3 Ltd
Prospects Group 2011 Limited
Prospects Services
Royal Navy and Royal Marines Charity
University of Chichester (Multi) Academy Trust

86101 Hospital activities [29]

CAS St Paul's Limited
Central Nottinghamshire Hospitals PLC
Consort Healthcare (Mid Yorkshire) Funding
Consort Healthcare (Mid Yorkshire) Holdings
Consort Healthcare (Mid Yorkshire)
Cygnet 2002 Limited
Cygnet Aspirations Developments Ltd
Cygnet Behavioural Health Ltd
Cygnet Health Care Limited
Cygnet Health UK Limited
Cygnet Inter-Holdings Limited
Cygnet Propco Limited
Cygnet Surrey Limited
Elysium Healthcare No. 2 Ltd
Elysium Healthcare Property 2 Ltd
Endeavour SCH PLC
Genesis Cancer Care UK Limited
Genesis Specialist Care Holding UK
Glenside Care Group Limited
Horder Healthcare
ISS Mediclean Limited
KIMS Kent Holdings Limited
New Victoria Hospital Limited
Newhospitals (St Helens and Knowsley)
Optegra UK Limited
Prospect Healthcare (Hairmyres) Ltd
Sysmex UK Limited
UK Acquisitions No. 6 Limited
Victoria Foundation

86102 Medical nursing home activities

Forth Health Limited
Hospital Company (Southmead) Ltd
SRM (Redcar & Cleveland) Ltd
Sentinel Health Care Limited
Sunrise UK Holdco Limited
Thames Hospice

86210 General medical practice activities

Ascenti Health Limited
Inhealth Limited

86220 Specialists medical practice activities

Combat Stress
St Barnabas Hospices (Sussex) Ltd

86900 Other human health activities [38]

Active Assistance Finance Ltd
Agfa Healthcare UK Limited
Aquilant Limited
BAP Pharma Limited
Bio Products Laboratory Holdings Ltd
CBI International Parent Ltd
CBI UK Topco Limited
CSC Life Sciences Limited
Carefusion U.K. 235 Limited
Centre for Health and Disability Assessments
Cochlear Europe Limited
Cygnet NW Limited
Doctorlink Limited
Doctors Chambers (UK) Limited
Elysium Healthcare (Ultimate Care)
Elysium Healthcare No. 3 Ltd
Elysium Healthcare No. 4 Ltd
Epilepsy Society
Falck UK Limited
Galvani Bioelectronics Limited
Gracewell Healthcare Limited
Handsale Limited
Medtronic Limited
Millbrook Healthcare Ltd
Naga UK Bidco Limited
Naga UK Topco Limited
Newbury & Thatcham Hospital Building Trust
Nuffield Health
Oldercare (Haslemere) Limited
Optegra International Limited
Pilgrims Hospices in East Kent
Q Squared Solutions Holdings Ltd
Rapport Housing and Care
Stryker UK Limited
Syneos Health IVH UK Limited
Voluntary Service Overseas
WW GBR Limited
Wessex Children's Hospice Trust

87100 Residential nursing care facilities [13]

Colleycare Limited
Custodes Midco Limited
Danshell Healthcare Limited
Epilepsy Society
Glenside Care Group Limited
Graham Care (YB) Limited
Nicholas James Care Homes Ltd
Milkwood Care Ltd
Oakview Estates Limited
Porthaven Properties No 2 Ltd
Whiteley Homes Trust
Wilton House Limited
Zion Care Limited

87200 Residential care activities for learning difficulties, mental health and substance abuse [16]

CMG Holdco Limited
Care Management Group Limited
Choice Care Group 2 Limited
Choice Care Group 3 Limited
Choice Care Group Holdings Ltd
Choice Holdings Limited
Choice Support
Cygnet Learning Disabilities Ltd
Cygnet Learning Disabilities Midlands
Danshell Healthcare Limited
Milkwood Care Ltd
Oakview Estates Limited
Pathways Care Group Limited
Regard Partnership Limited
Ruby Topco Limited
Salutem LD Bidco Limited

87300 Residential care activities for the elderly and disabled [18]

Aitch Care Homes Holdco Ltd
Avante Care and Support Ltd
Ben-Motor and Allied Trades Benevolent Fund
Brendoncare Foundation
Careprogress Limited
Children's Trust
Community Homes of Intensive Care and Education
Danshell Healthcare Limited
Disabilities Trust
Glenside Care Group Limited
MacIntyre Care
Milkwood Care Ltd
Minster Care Group Limited
Minster Care Management Ltd
Oakview Estates Limited
Royal British Legion Industries Ltd.
Treloar Trust
Whiteley Homes Trust

87900 Other residential care activities n.e.c.

Children's Trust
London Care Partnership Ltd
Omega (After Alpha) Limited
PJ Care Group Limited
PJ Care Limited
Treloar Trust

88100 Social work activities without accommodation for the elderly and disabled

Avante Care and Support Ltd
Brendoncare Foundation
Carewatch Care Services Ltd
Disabilities Trust

88910 Child day-care activities

Action for Children
West London YMCA

88990 Other social work activities without accommodation n.e.c. [24]

Achieving for Children CIC
Avante Care and Support Ltd
Belton Associates (Group Holdings)
Belton Associates Holdings Ltd
Belton Associates Limited
Ben-Motor and Allied Trades Benevolent Fund
British Kidney Patient Association
Change, Grow, Live
Childcare Corporation Limited
DHL UK Foundation
Gardeners' Royal Benevolent Society
Greenham Trust Ltd
JCA Charitable Foundation
Milton Keynes Community Foundation
NFAG Limited
National Fostering Agency (Scotland)
National Fostering Agency Ltd
Paradigm Commercial PLC
Police Care UK
Rochester Diocesan Society and Board of Finance
Royal Navy and Royal Marines Charity
Tearfund
West London YMCA
World Vision UK

90010 Performing arts

Chichester Festival Theatre
Glyndebourne Productions Ltd
Yehudi Menuhin School Limited

90020 Support activities to performing arts

Chichester Festival Theatre
Trafalgar Entertainment Group Ltd

90030 Artistic creation

Chichester Festival Theatre

90040 Operation of arts facilities

ATG London Limited
Ambassador Entertainment Group Ltd
Ambassador Theatre Group (Venues)
Ambassador Theatre Group Ltd
Ambassador Theatre Group Overseas Holdings
Chichester Festival Theatre

91011 Library activities

Services Sound and Vision Corporation
WLHC Projectco Limited

91020 Museums activities

Canal & River Trading CIC
Canal & River Trust
HMS Trincomalee Trust
Mary Rose Trust
Pallant House Gallery
Watts Gallery

91030 Operation of historical sites and buildings and similar visitor attractions

Canal & River Trust
HMS Victory Preservation Company
Leeds Castle Foundation
Mary Rose Trust
NMRN Operations
National Museum of The Royal Navy
Stowe House Preservation Trust

91040 Botanical and zoological gardens and nature reserves activities

Gardeners' Royal Benevolent Society
Marwell Wildlife

92000 Gambling and betting activities

Barcrest Group Limited
Camelot Business Solutions Ltd
Camelot Global Lottery Solutions Ltd
Camelot UK Lotteries Limited
Cashino Gaming Limited
Grosvenor Casinos (GC) Limited
Grosvenor Casinos Limited
Mecca Bingo Limited
RAL Limited

93110 Operation of sports facilities [15]
Ascot Authority (Holdings) Ltd
Ascot Racecourse Limited
Bohunt Education Trust
Burhill Golf and Leisure Ltd
Burhill Group Limited
Community Stadium Limited
Fulham Stadium Limited
MSV Group Limited
Motorsport Vision Limited
Newbury Racecourse PLC
RB Sport & Leisure Holdings PLC
Snowcentres Limited
Southampton Football Club Ltd
St. Margaret's School Bushey
Stoke Park Limited

93120 Activities of sport clubs
Brentford FC Limited
Fulham Football Club Limited
Fulham Football Leisure Ltd
Premier Rugby Limited
Wisley Golf Club PLC

93130 Fitness facilities
Gym Limited

93191 Activities of racehorse owners
Fishdance Limited

93199 Other sports activities [13]
Cougar Holdco London Limited
Crown Golf Group Limited
Crown Golf Operations Limited
Hollywood Bowl Group PLC
Kendallco Limited
McLaren Racing Limited
Motorsport Vision Limited
Old Thorns Golf Hotel and Country Estate
Original Bowling Co Ltd
PGA European Tour
Reading Football Club Limited
Red Bull Racing Limited
Watford Association Football Club

93210 Activities of amusement parks and theme parks
Sands Heritage Ltd

93290 Other amusement and recreation activities n.e.c. [11]
Activision Blizzard UK Ltd
Arqiva Limited
Brighton I-360 Limited
Georgica Limited
Hollywood Bowl Group PLC
Navy,Army and Air Force Institutes,(The)
Paultons Park Limited
Royal Navy and Royal Marines Charity
TEG Holdings Limited
Ten Entertainment Group PLC
Tenpin Limited

94110 Activities of business and employers membership organisations
Electrical Contractors Association

94910 Activities of religious organisations [11]
Charity for St Joseph's Missionary Society (Generalate)
Chichester Diocesan Fund and Board of Finance (Incorporated)
Church Communities UK
Guildford Diocesan Board of Finance
International Society for Krishna Consciousness
Portsmouth Diocesan Board of Finance
Soka Gakkai International - UK
United Reformed Church (Wessex) Trust
Winchester Diocesan Board of Finance
World Mission Agency - Winners Chapel International
Worth Abbey

94990 Activities of other membership organisations n.e.c.
Automobile Association Developments
Caravan Club Limited
Civil Service Motoring Association,Limited
Foundation and Friends of The Royal Botanic Gardens, Kew
Landmark Space Limited
Motoring & Leisure Services Ltd
Premier Rugby Limited
WWF-UK

95110 Repair of computers and peripheral equipment
HCL Great Britain Limited

96010 Washing and (dry-)cleaning of textile and fur products
Berendsen UK Limited
Clean Linen Services Limited
Clean Viking Acquisition Co Ltd
Clean Viking Bidco Limited
Clean Viking Holdings Limited

96020 Hairdressing and other beauty treatment
TIGI International Limited

96030 Funeral and related activities
Golden Leaves Limited
Lodge Bros. (Funerals) Limited
Mutual Services (Portsmouth) Ltd
Southern Co-operative Funerals Ltd

96090 Other service activities n.e.c. [110]
3SE (Barnsley, Doncaster & Rotherham)
ADT Fire and Security PLC
Air Menzies International Ltd
Alder Hey (Special Purpose Vehicle)
Anduff Car Wash Limited
Aquilant Limited
Avis Budget UK Limited
BE Aerospace Global Holdings Ltd
BE Aerospace International Holdings
Beam Global Finance UK Limited
Bellman Property Group Limited
Blackwell Publishing (Holdings) Ltd
Blackwell Science (Overseas Holdings)
Brand Energy & Infrastructure Services UK, Ltd.
British Gas Services Limited
Bycentral Limited
Bynorth Limited
Bywest Limited
CML Reporting Limited
Caligor Opco UK, Ltd
Canal & River Trading CIC
Change, Grow, Live
Cleansing Service Group Ltd
Clearwater Technology Bidco Ltd
Clearwater Technology Holdco Ltd
Convatec Group PLC
Cordant Group PLC
Cordant Security Limited
Crown Blue Line Limited
DHL International (UK) Limited
De La Rue International Limited.
De La Rue PLC
Dyno-Rod Limited
ELWA Limited
Emac Limited
Fire Fighters Charity
GE Medical Systems Limited
Guide Dogs for the Blind Association
Guildford Diocesan Board of Finance
H. K. S. Holdings Limited
H.K.S. Motors Limited
HCP Packaging UK Limited
Heathrow Hydrant Operating Co Ltd
Hemel Snowcentre Limited
Hertz Europe Limited
Holiday Extras Investments Ltd
Holiday Extras Limited
Home and Comforts Limited
Honeywell Avionics Systems Ltd
Honeywell Control Systems Ltd
IGE Energy Services (UK) Ltd
INEOS FPS Limited
Independent Inspections Ltd
Intercontinental Hotels Group Services Company
Jeppesen U.K. Limited
K Capital Investment Ltd
Kimberly-Clark Holding Limited
Kronos Systems Limited
Landlink Estates Limited
Larger London Land Co Ltd
Link Market Services Trustees Ltd
Little Group Limited
London Residential Healthcare Ltd
Lonza Biologics PLC
MJ UK Holdings Limited
Manitowoc Crane Group (UK) Ltd
Mash Holdings Limited
McLaren Finance PLC
NPL Management Limited
Newbury & Thatcham Hospital Building Trust
Newhall Projects Limited
Novar (Stelrad) Limited
Novar International Limited
Old Mutual Wealth Limited
Onecom Group Limited
PDC Brands UK Limited
Photo - Me International P L C
Procter & Gamble (L & CP) Ltd
Renewi Cumbria Limited
Renewi European Holdings Ltd
Renewi Holdings Limited
Renewi UK Services Limited
Rentokil Initial 1927 PLC
Rentokil Initial PLC
SC Leisure Group Limited
ST & H Group Limited

ST & H Limited
Sega Europe Limited
Serco-IAL Limited
Shoppertrak Limited
Ski Bound Limited
Sky Subscribers Services Ltd
Smiths Industries Industrial Group
Subsea 7 Crewing Limited
TIM Intermediateco Limited
Teledyne Limited
Terrestrial Developments Ltd
Tim Bidco 1 Limited
Tim Holdco Limited
Tim Midco Limited
Verizon UK Financing Limited
Verizon UK Holding Limited
Visiontrend Limited
Vodafone 2.
Voluntary Service Overseas
Wakefield Waste PFI Limited
Wates Living Space (Maintenance) Ltd
Westerngeco Limited
Winchester Diocesan Board of Finance
ZG Lighting (UK) Limited

97000 Activities of households as employers of domestic personnel

Rentokil Initial (1896) Ltd

98000 Residents property management

Ash Properties Limited
Martin Grant Homes Limited
Trevellyan Developments Ltd

99000 Activities of extraterritorial organisations and bodies

Biogen Holdings Limited
Rothschild Foundation

99999 Dormant company [22]

Barfoot Holdings Limited
Broadcast Relay Service (Overseas)
Chubb Group (International) Ltd
Citysprint (UK) Group Limited
Console Lowco Limited
Digico Global Limited
Essentra Filter Products Ltd
Exclaimer Group (Holdings) Ltd
Exclaimer Group Limited
Filtrona Limited
General Cable Limited
Heiton Holdings UK Limited
Holtzbrinck Investment Limited
Host Europe Investments Ltd
NTL Glasgow Holdings Limited
NTL Kirklees Holdings Limited
Saga Mid Co Limited
Spirent Holdings Limited
Sunlight Clinical Solutions Ltd
Telewest Communications Holdings Ltd
Trident Acquisition Limited
WSH Investments Limited

Printed in 8pt Nimbus Sans L

Designed by URW++ Design and Development GmbH

Dellam Publishing Limited

2 Heath Drive, Sutton, Surrey, SM2 5RP

Fax: 020 8770 7478 email: enquiries@dellam.com

SAN: 0177881 EAN/GLN: 5030670177882

www.ingramcontent.com/pod-product-compliance
Lightning Source LLC
LaVergne TN
LVHW082004200926
848481LV00010B/2803